Harrap's
Super-Mini
FRENCH
and
ENGLISH
Dictionary

Michael Janes

National Textbook Company
4255 West Touhy Avenue
Lincolnwood, Illinois 60646-1975 U.S.A.

French Consultant
Fabrice Antoine

English Consultants
Hazel Curties
Stuart Fortey

First published in Great Britain 1988
by HARRAP Ltd
19-23 Ludgate Hill, London EC4M 7PD

© Harrap Limited 1988

Dépôt légal pour cette édition: avril 1988

Printed in Great Britain by
Richard Clay Ltd, Bungay, Suffolk

Contents/Table des matières

TRADEMARKS

MARQUES DÉPOSÉES

iii

Preface

This dictionary is an entirely new publication designed to provide an up-to-date, practical and concise work of reference giving translations of the most useful French and English vocabulary.

The aim has been to achieve a work of great clarity of equal value to French and to English speakers, whether students, tourists, businessmen or -women or general readers, and to produce a text offering the maximum amount of guidance in pinpointing and understanding translations. Equal importance has been given to the presentation of French and English. Different translations of the same word or phrase are clearly labelled by means of bracketed context indicators and/or style and field labels. A single translation of a word is also often labelled as an additional aid to the user (e.g. **hedgehog** *n* (*animal*) hérisson *m*; **ungainly** *a* (*clumsy*) gauche; **béotien**, **-ienne** *nmf* (*inculte*) philistine). The user is helped by having indicators and labels in French in the French section and in English in the English section of the dictionary.

Style and field labels follow bracketed indicators (e.g. **grid** *n* . . . (*system*) *El* réseau *m*; **bidule** *nm* (*chose*) *Fam* thingummy). In the event of more than one translation within a grammatical category being qualified by the same style or field label, the label may then precede (see **calé, liquidizer, trucker**).

The user will find in the text important abbreviations, useful geographical information such as names of countries, and wide coverage of American words and usage. The vocabulary treated includes French and English colloquialisms and slang, and important technical jargon. Comparatives and superlatives of English adjectives are also indicated.

In order to save space, derived words are usually included within the entry of a headword. All such words are highlighted by means of a lozenge. Derivatives may be written in full or abbreviated, as is usually the case for important derived forms (such as English **-ly** or French **-ment**).

An oblique stroke in bold is used to mark the stem of a headword at which point the derived ending is added. A bold dash stands for a headword or the portion of a headword to the left of the oblique stroke (e.g. **awkward** *a* . . . ◆—**ly** *adv* . . . ◆—**ness** *n* . . . ; **boulevers/er** *vt* . . . ◆—**ant** *a* . . . ◆—**ement** *nm*).

An oblique stroke within an entry is another space-saving device. It is used to separate non equivalent alternative parts of a phrase or expression matched exactly in French and English (e.g. **les basses/hautes classes** the lower/upper classes is to be understood as: **les basses classes** the lower classes and **les hautes classes** the upper classes; **to give s.o./sth a push** pousser qn/qch as: **to give s.o. a push** pousser qn and **to give sth a push** pousser qch).

A further typographical device, a filled square, may be used to introduce a string of English phrasal verbs (see **come, take**).

In common with other Harrap dictionaries, when a headword appears in an example in the same form, it is represented by its initial letter. This applies whether the headword starts a new line (e.g. **advance** *n* **in a. of s.o.** avant qn) or appears within an entry, either in full form (e.g. ◆**arterial** *a* **a. road** route *f* principale), or in abbreviated form (e.g. (where ◆—**ed** stands for **advanced**) ◆**ed** *a* **a. in years** âgé).

The pronunciation of both English and French is shown using the latest symbols of the International Phonetic Alphabet. Pronunciation is given for headwords at the start of an entry, and, as an additional help to the user, for a word within an entry where the correct pronunciation is difficult to derive from the form of the word (e.g. ◆**aristocratie** [-asi]; ◆**aoûtien, -ienne** [ausjɛ̃, -jɛn]; ◆**rabid** [ˈræbid]; ◆**prayer** [preər]).

Stress in English is indicated for headwords and for derived words in which stress differs from that of a headword (e.g. **civilize** [ˈsɪvɪlaɪz] and ◆**civili'zation**). American English pronunciation is listed wherever it is considered to differ substantially from that of British English (e.g. **aristocrat** [ˈærɪstəkræt, *Am* əˈrɪstəkræt], **quinine** [ˈkwɪniːn, *Am* ˈkwaɪnaɪn]). American spelling is also given if considered sufficiently different (e.g. **tire** and **tyre, plow** and **plough**).

An original feature of this dictionary is its semantic approach to the order and arrangement of entries. An approach whereby the meaning of words is allowed to influence the structure of entries is felt to be of particular benefit to the user in his or her understanding of language.

Important semantic categories have been indicated by bold Arabic numerals within an entry (see **bolt**, **tail**, **général**) or have been entered as separate headwords (see **bug¹** and **bug²**, **draw¹** and **draw²**, **start¹** and **start²**). Note that grammatical categories, apart from the first, have been marked by a dash.

Words are entered under the headword from which they are considered to derive (e.g. **approfondi**, abbreviated as ◆—i follows **approfondir**; ◆**astronomer** and ◆**astro′nomical** follow **astronomy**). Present and past participles (used adjectively) are felt to be closely associated in meaning and form with the infinitive from which they derive. They are entered, usually in abbreviated form, within an entry immediately after the infinitive, any other derivatives there may be following in alphabetical order (e.g. **exalt/er** *vt* . . . ◆—**ant** *a* . . . ◆—**é** *a* . . . ◆**exaltation** *nf*; **accommodat/e** *vt* . . . ◆—**ing** *a* . . . ◆**accommo′dation** *n*; **expir/e** *vi* . . . ◆—**ed** *a* . . . ◆**expi′ration** *n* . . . ◆**expiry** *n*).

Derived words and compounds are felt to be semantically distinct and are, wherever possible, grouped together alphabetically and listed separately from each other (e.g. **base** *n*. . . ◆—**less** *a* . . . ◆**baseball** *n* . . . ◆**baseboard** *n*; **bouton** *nm* . . . ◆**b.-d'or** *nm* . . . ◆**b.-pression** *nm* . . . ◆**boutonner** *vt* . . . ◆**boutonneux**, **-euse** *a* . . . ◆**boutonnière** *nf*). Compounds may be listed in the place within an entry where they are felt best to belong by virtue of meaning.

The author wishes to express his gratitude to Monsieur F. Antoine, Mrs H. Curties and Mr S. Fortey for their advice and help, to Mrs R. Hillmore for her assistance with proofreading, and to Mr J.-L. Barbanneau for his support and encouragement.

M. Janes
London, 1988

Préface

Ce dictionnaire entièrement nouveau a pour ambition d'être un ouvrage de référence moderne, pratique et compact, offrant les traductions des termes les plus courants du français comme de l'anglais.

Il veut être un ouvrage qui, par sa grande clarté, soit utile autant au francophone qu'à l'anglophone, pour les études, le tourisme, les affaires aussi bien que pour l'usage courant: il tente de fournir le plus d'indications possible pour aider l'utilisateur à cerner et à comprendre les traductions proposées. On a accordé la même importance à la présentation du français qu'à celle de l'anglais. Les différentes traductions d'un même mot ou d'une même expression sont clairement définies à l'aide d'indications de contexte entre parenthèses et/ou de symboles indiquant le niveau de langue et le domaine d'utilisation. Lorsqu'un mot est accompagné d'une seule traduction, celle-ci est également souvent précédée d'une indication destinée à fournir à l'utilisateur une aide supplémentaire (par exemple **hedgehog** *n* (*animal*) hérisson *m*; **ungainly** *a* (*clumsy*) gauche; **béotien, -ienne** *nmf* (*inculte*) philistine). L'accès à cet ouvrage est facilité par l'utilisation d'indications en français dans la partie français-anglais et en anglais dans la partie anglais-français.

Les indications de niveau de langue et de domaine d'utilisation viennent à la suite de celles entre parenthèses (par exemple **grid** *n* . . . (*system*) El réseau *m*; **bidule** *nm* (*chose*) *Fam* thingummy). Lorsque plusieurs traductions dans la même catégorie grammaticale sont définies par la même indication, celle-ci peut alors venir en tête (voir **calé**, **liquidizer**, **trucker**).

L'utilisateur trouvera dans cet ouvrage des abréviations importantes, de précieux éléments de géographie tels que des noms de pays, ainsi qu'une large sélection d'américanismes. Le lexique retenu comprend des mots et des expressions familiers et argotiques, tant en français qu'en anglais, ainsi que des termes techniques courants. De plus, les comparatifs et superlatifs des adjectifs anglais sont donnés.

Par souci de concision, les mots dérivés sont généralement donnés dans le corps des articles. Tous ces mots sont repérés par un losange. Les dérivés sont donnés soit sous leur forme complète, soit en abrégé, ce qui est généralement le cas pour les formes dérivées courantes (telles que celles en **-ly** en anglais ou en **-ment** en français).

On utilise une barre oblique pour indiquer le radical d'une entrée à la suite duquel la terminaison d'un dérivé sera ajoutée. Un tiret en gras remplace le mot d'entrée ou la partie de ce mot qui précède la barre oblique (par exemple **awkward** a . . . ◆**ly** adv . . . ◆**ness** n . . . ; **boule:vers/er** vt . . . ◆**ant** a . . . ◆**ement** nm).

Toujours par souci de concision, une barre oblique est utilisée dans un article pour éviter la répétition d'un même élément de phrase (par exemple **les basses/hautes classes** the lower/upper classes se lira: **les basses** the lower classes et **les hautes classes** the upper classes; **to give s.o./sth a push** pousser qn/qch se lira: **to give s.o. a push** pousser qn et **to give sth a push** pousser qch).

Enfin, un carré plein peut être utilisé pour introduire une série de verbes à particule en anglais (voir **come**, **take**).

Comme il est d'usage dans les autres dictionnaires Harrap, lorsqu'un mot d'entrée est repris sous la même forme dans un exemple, il est remplacé par sa première lettre. Cela est le cas aussi bien lorsque le mot est au début d'un article (par exemple **advance** n in a. **of s.o.** avant qn) ou apparaît dans un article, sous la forme complète (par exemple ◆**arterial** a a. road route f principale) ou en abrégé (◆**ed** remplaçant **advanced**) ◆**ed** a a. in years âgé).

La prononciation de l'anglais comme du français est fournie; elle utilise la notation la plus moderne de l'Alphabet Phonétique International. La phonétique est donnée pour les mots d'entrée au début de l'article et, pour aider l'utilisateur, pour tout mot dans un article dont il pourrait être difficile de déduire la prononciation à partir de l'orthographe (par exemple ◆**aristocratie** [-asi]; ◆**aoûtien, -ienne** [ausjɛ̃, -jɛn]; ◆**rabid** ['ræbid]; ◆**prayer** [preər]).

En anglais, l'accent tonique est indiqué pour les mots d'entrée et pour les dérivés chaque fois que l'accentuation diffère de celle de l'entrée (par exemple **civilize** et ◆**civili'zation**). Les prononciations américaines sont indiquées chaque fois qu'elles diffèrent de façon substantielle de celles de l'anglais britannique (par exemple **aristocrat** ['ærɪstəkræt, Am ə'rɪstəkræt], **quinine** ['kwiniːn, Am 'kwainain]). On indique également l'orthographe américaine lorsqu'elle est suffisamment différente de celle de l'anglais britannique (par exemple **tire** et **tyre**, **plow** et **plough**).

Une des caractéristiques originales de ce dictionnaire est son approche sémantique du classement et de l'organisation des articles. On a considéré que cette approche, où le sens des mots détermine leur part l'organisation des articles, serait d'un grand secours à l'utilisateur en ce qui concerne sa compréhension de la langue.

Les catégories sémantiques importantes sont indiquées dans un article par des chiffres arabes en gras (voir **bolt**, **tail**, **général**) ou sont présentées comme des mots distincts (voir **bug**[1] et **bug**[2], **draw**[1] et **draw**[2], **start**[1] et **start**[2]). Les catégories grammaticales autres que la première traitée sont indiquées par un tiret.

Les mots apparaissent sous les mots d'entrée dont ils sont dérivés (par exemple **approfondi**, abrégé en ◆**-i** suit **approfond/ir**; **astronomer** et ◆**astro'nomical** suivent **astronomy**). Les participes présents et passés (utilisés comme adjectifs) sont considérés comme étant étroitement associés par le sens et par la forme à l'infinitif dont ils sont dérivés. Ils sont placés dans l'article, généralement en abrégé, immédiatement après l'infinitif; tous les autres dérivés éventuels apparaissent ensuite par ordre alphabétique (par exemple **exalt/er** vt . . . ◆**ant** a . . . ◆**é** a . . . ◆**exaltation** nf; **accommodat/e** vt . . . ◆**ing** a . . . ◆**accommo'dation** n; **expir/e** vi . . . ◆**ed** a . . . ◆**expi'ration** n . . . ◆**expiry** n).

Les mots dérivés et les mots composés sont considérés comme étant distincts, du point de vue du sens, et sont, chaque fois que possible, regroupés séparément (par exemple **base** n . . . ◆**less** a . . . ◆**ness** n . . . ◆**baseball** n; ◆**baseboard** n; **bouton** nm . . . ◆**b.-d'or** nm . . . ◆**b.-pression** nm . . . ◆**boutonner** vt . . . ◆**boutonneux, -euse** a . . . ◆**boutonnière** nf). Les composés se trouvent placés dans les articles là où leur sens a semblé devoir les appeler.

L'auteur tient à exprimer sa gratitude à Monsieur F. Antoine, à Mrs H. Curties et à Mr S. Fortey pour leurs conseils et leur collaboration, à Mrs R. Hillmore qui a bien voulu nous aider à relire les épreuves, et à Monsieur J.-L. Barbanneau pour son soutien et ses encouragements.

M. Janes
Londres, 1988

Grammar notes

In French, the feminine of an adjective is formed as a rule by adding **e** to the masculine form (e.g. grand, grande; carré, carrée; chevalin, chevaline). If the masculine already ends in **e**, the feminine is the same as the masculine (e.g. utile). Irregular feminine forms of adjectives (e.g. généreux, généreuse; léger, légère; doux, douce) are given in the French-English side of the dictionary. In the English-French side, French adjectives are shown in the masculine form only. Irregular feminines of adjectives are listed in the following way: généreux, -euse; léger, -ère; doux, douce.

To form the plural of a French noun or adjective **s** is usually added to the singular (e.g. arbre, arbres; taxi, taxis; petit, petits). The plural form of a noun ending in **s**, **x** or **z** (e.g. pois, croix, nez) is the same as that of the singular. Plurals of nouns and adjectives which do not follow these general rules are listed in the French section, including the plurals of French compounds where the formation of the plural involves a change other than the addition of final **s** (e.g. arc-en-ciel, arcs-en-ciel). Those nouns and adjectives where **x** or **aux** is added in the plural are shown in the following way: cerveau, -x; général, -aux.

In English also, **s** is added to form the plural of a noun (e.g. cat, cats; taxi, taxis) but a noun ending in **ch**, **s**, **sh**, **x** or **z** forms its plural by the addition of **es** (e.g. glass, glasses; match, matches). (Note that when **ch** is pronounced [k], the plural is in **s**, e.g. monarch, monarchs.) When a noun ends in **y** preceded by a consonant, **y** is changed to **ies** to form the plural (e.g. army, armies). Irregular English plurals are given in the English-French side, including the plurals of English compounds where the formation of the plural involves a change other than the addition of final **s** (e.g. brother-in-law, brothers-in-law).

English nouns may be used as adjectives. When a French adjective is translated in this way, this use is made clear by the addition of a hyphen following the noun translation (e.g. farm- as a translation of **agricole**).

Most French verbs have regular conjugations though some display spelling anomalies (see French verb conjugations on p (i)). In the French section an asterisk is used to mark an irregular verb, and refers the user to the table of irregular verbs on p (ii).

Most English verbs form their past tense and past participle by adding **ed** to the infinitive (e.g. look, looked) or **d** to an infinitive already ending in **e** (e.g. love, loved). When a verb ends in **y** preceded by a consonant **y** becomes **ied** (e.g. satisfy, satisfied). To form the third person singular of a verb in the present tense **s** is added to the infinitive (e.g. know, knows) but an infinitive in **ch**, **s**, **sh**, **x** or **z** forms its third person singular by the addition of **es** (e.g. dash, dashes). When an infinitive ends in **y** preceded by a consonant, **y** is changed to **ies** to form the third person singular (e.g. satisfy, satisfies).

The English present participle is formed by the addition of **ing** to the infinitive (e.g. look, looking) but final **e** is omitted when an infinitive ends in **e** (e.g. love, loving). When the infinitive ends in a single consonant preceded by a vowel (e.g. tug), the final consonant is usually doubled in the past tense, past and present participles (e.g. tug, tugged, tugging).

Irregular English verb conjugations are given in the English headword list, and a summary of the most important irregular verbs may also be found on p (vii). The doubling of consonants in English verbs is indicated in the text. The latter is shown in the following way: **tug** . . . *vt* (**-gg-**).

Notes sur la grammaire

En français, le féminin d'un adjectif se forme en général en ajoutant **e** au masculin (par exemple grand, grande; carré, carrée; chevalin, chevaline). Lorsque le masculin se termine déjà par **e**, le féminin est identique (par exemple utile). Les féminins d'adjectifs qui ne se conforment pas à ces règles (par exemple généreux, généreuse; léger, légère; doux, douce) sont donnés dans la partie français-anglais où ils sont notés comme suit: généreux, -euse; léger, -ère; doux, douce. Dans la partie anglais-français, on ne donne que la forme masculine des adjectifs.

On forme en général le pluriel d'un nom ou d'un adjectif français en ajoutant **s** au singulier (par exemple arbre, arbres; taxi, taxis; petit, petits). Le pluriel d'un nom se terminant par **s**, **x** ou **z** (par exemple pois, croix, nez) est identique au singulier. Les pluriels des noms et adjectifs qui font exception à ces règles générales sont signalés dans la partie français-anglais, de même que les pluriels des mots composés anglais dont le passage au pluriel appelle une modification autre que le simple ajout d'un **s** final (par exemple arc-en-ciel, arcs-en-ciel). Les noms et adjectifs dont le pluriel se forme à l'aide d'un **x** ou de **aux** sont notés comme suit: cerveau, -x; général, -aux.

De la même façon, en anglais, on forme le pluriel des noms en ajoutant **s** (par exemple cat, cats; taxi, taxis) mais on ajoutera **es** aux noms qui se terminent par **ch**, **s**, **sh**, **x** ou **z** (par exemple glass, glasses; match, matches). (Noter cependant que lorsque **ch** se prononce [k], le pluriel est en **s**, comme dans monarch, monarchs.) Lorsqu'un nom se termine par un **y** précédé d'une consonne, ce **y** devient **ies** au pluriel (par exemple army, armies). Les pluriels irréguliers de l'anglais sont signalés dans la partie anglais-français, de même que les pluriels des mots composés anglais dont le passage au pluriel entraîne une modification autre que le simple ajout d'un **s** final (par exemple brother-in-law, brothers-in-law).

Les noms anglais peuvent s'utiliser comme adjectifs. Lorsqu'un adjectif français est traduit par un nom, cela est signalé par l'ajout d'un trait d'union à la suite de ce nom (par exemple farm- comme traduction de **agricole**).

La plupart des verbes français ont des conjugaisons régulières; cependant, certains subissent des variations orthographiques (voir: Conjugaisons des verbes français à la page (i)) Dans la partie français-anglais, un astérisque signale un verbe irrégulier et renvoie à la table des verbes irréguliers donnée en page (ii).

En anglais, le passé et le participe passé des verbes se forment dans la plupart des cas en ajoutant **ed** à l'infinitif (par exemple look, looked) ou seulement **d** lorsque l'infinitif se termine par un **e** (par exemple love, loved). Lorsqu'un verbe se termine par un **y** précédé d'une consonne, ce **y** devient **ied** (par exemple satisfy, satisfied). La troisième personne du singulier d'un verbe au présent se forme en ajoutant **s** à l'infinitif (par exemple know, knows), mais on ajoutera **es** aux infinitifs qui se terminent par **ch**, **s**, **sh**, **x** ou **z** (par exemple dash, dashes). Enfin, lorsqu'un verbe se termine par un **y** précédé d'une consonne, ce **y** devient **ies** à la troisième personne du singulier (par exemple satisfy, satisfies).

Le participe présent en anglais se forme en ajoutant la désinence **ing** à l'infinitif (par exemple look, looking); lorsqu'un infinitif comporte un **e** final, celui-ci disparaît (par exemple love, loving). Lorsque l'infinitif se termine par une seule consonne précédée d'une voyelle (par exemple tug), la consonne finale est le plus souvent doublée au passé et aux participes passé et présent (par exemple tug, tugged, tugging).

Les formes des verbes irréguliers anglais sont données dans la partie anglais-français et une liste récapitulative des verbes irréguliers usuels figure en page (vii). Le doublement des consonnes dans les verbes irréguliers anglais est signalé dans le corps de l'ouvrage; il est noté comme suit: **tug** . . . *vt* (**–gg–**).

Abbreviations   Abréviations

adjective	*a*	adjectif
abbreviation	*abbr, abrév*	abréviation
adverb	*adv*	adverbe
agriculture	*Agr*	agriculture
American	*Am*	américain
anatomy	*Anat*	anatomie
architecture	*Archit*	architecture
slang	*Arg*	argot
article	*art*	article
cars, motoring	*Aut*	automobile
auxiliary	*aux*	auxiliaire
aviation, aircraft	*Av*	aviation
biology	*Biol*	biologie
botany	*Bot*	botanique
British	*Br*	britannique
Canadian	*Can*	canadien
carpentry	*Carp*	menuiserie
chemistry	*Ch*	chimie
cinema	*Cin*	cinéma
commerce	*Com*	commerce
conjunction	*conj*	conjonction
cookery	*Culin*	cuisine
definite	*def, déf*	défini
demonstrative	*dem, dém*	démonstratif
economics	*Econ, Écon*	économie
electricity	*El, Él*	électricité
et cetera	*etc*	et cetera
feminine	*f*	féminin
familiar	*Fam*	familier
football	*Fb*	football
figurative	*Fig*	figuré
finance	*Fin*	finance
feminine plural	*fpl*	féminin pluriel
French	*Fr*	français
geography	*Geog, Géog*	géographie
geology	*Geol, Géol*	géologie
geometry	*Geom, Géom*	géométrie
grammar	*Gram*	grammaire
history	*Hist*	histoire
humorous	*Hum*	humoristique
indefinite	*indef, indéf*	indéfini
indicative	*indic*	indicatif
infinitive	*inf*	infinitif
interjection	*int*	interjection
invariable	*inv*	invariable
ironic	*Iron*	ironique
journalism	*Journ*	journalisme
legal, law	*Jur*	juridique
linguistics	*Ling*	linguistique
literary	*Lit, Litt*	littéraire
literature	*Liter, Littér*	littérature

masculine	*m*	masculin
mathematics	*Math*	mathématique
medicine	*Med, Méd*	médecine
carpentry	*Menuis*	menuiserie
meteorology	*Met, Mét*	météorologie
military	*Mil*	militaire
masculine plural	*mpl*	masculin pluriel
music	*Mus*	musique
noun	*n*	nom
nautical	*Nau*	nautique
noun feminine	*nf*	nom féminin
noun masculine	*nm*	nom masculin
noun masculine and feminine	*nmf*	nom masculin et féminin
pejorative	*Pej, Péj*	péjoratif
philosophy	*Phil*	philosophie
photography	*Phot*	photographie
physics	*Phys*	physique
plural	*pl*	pluriel
politics	*Pol*	politique
possessive	*poss*	possessif
past participle	*pp*	participe passé
prefix	*pref, préf*	préfixe
preposition	*prep, prép*	préposition
present participle	*pres p*	participe présent
present tense	*pres t*	temps présent
pronoun	*pron*	pronom
psychology	*Psy*	psychologie
past tense	*pt*	prétérit
	qch	quelque chose
	qn	quelqu'un
registered trademark	®	marque déposée
radio	*Rad*	radio
railway, *Am* railroad	*Rail*	chemin de fer
relative	*rel*	relatif
religion	*Rel*	religion
school	*Sch, Scol*	école
singular	*sing*	singulier
slang	*Sl*	argot
someone	*s.o.*	
sport	*Sp*	sport
something	*sth*	
subjunctive	*sub*	subjonctif
technical	*Tech*	technique
telephone	*Tel, Tél*	téléphone
textiles	*Tex*	industrie textile
theatre	*Th*	théâtre
television	*TV*	télévision
typography, printing	*Typ*	typographie
university	*Univ*	université
United States	*US*	États-Unis
auxiliary verb	*v aux*	verbe auxiliaire
intransitive verb	*vi*	verbe intransitif
impersonal verb	*v imp*	verbe impersonnel
pronominal verb	*vpr*	verbe pronominal
transitive verb	*vt*	verbe transitif
transitive and intransitive verb	*vti*	verbe transitif et intransitif

Pronunciation of French

TABLE OF PHONETIC SYMBOLS

Vowels

[i]	vite, cygne		[y]	cru, sûr
[e]	été, donner		[ø]	feu, meule
[ɛ]	elle, mais		[œ]	œuf, jeune
[a]	chat, fameux		[ə]	le, refaire
[ɑ]	pas, âgé		[ɛ̃]	vin, plein, faim
[ɔ]	donne, fort		[ɑ̃]	enfant, temps
[o]	dos, chaud, peau		[ɔ̃]	mon, nombre
[u]	tout, cour		[œ̃]	lundi, humble

Consonants

[p]	pain, absolu		[z]	cousin, zéro
[b]	beau, abbé		[ʃ]	chose, schéma
[t]	table, nette		[ʒ]	gilet, jeter
[d]	donner, sud		[l]	lait, facile
[k]	camp, képi		[r]	rare, rhume
[g]	garde, second		[m]	mon, flamme
[f]	feu, phrase		[n]	né, canne
[v]	voir, wagon		[ɲ]	campagne
[s]	sou, cire		[ŋ]	jogging
			[']	hanche (*i.e. no liaison or elision*)

Semi-consonants

[j]	piano, voyage
[w]	ouest, noir
[ɥ]	muet, lui

Prononciation de l'anglais

TABLEAU DES SIGNES PHONÉTIQUES

Voyelles et diphtongues

[iː]	bee, police		[ɒ]	lot, what
[ɪə]	beer, real		[ɔː]	all, saw
[ɪ]	bit, added		[ɔɪ]	boil, toy
[e]	bet, said		[əʊ]	iow, soap
[eɪ]	date, nail		[ʊ]	put, wool
[eə]	bear, air		[uː]	shoe, too
[æ]	bat, plan		[uə]	poor, sure
[aɪ]	fly, life		[ʌ]	cut, some
[ɑː]	art, ask		[ɜː]	burn, learn
[aʊ]	fowl, house		[ə]	china, annoy
			[(ə)]	relation

Consonnes

[p]	pat, top		[ð]	that, breathe
[b]	but, tab		[h]	hat, rehearse
[t]	tap, patter		[l]	lad, all
[d]	dab, sadder		[r]	red, barring
[k]	cat, kite		[r]	better, here (*représente un r*
[g]	go, rogue			*final qui se prononce en*
[f]	fat, phrase			*liaison devant une voyelle,*
[v]	veal, rave			*par exemple 'here is' [hɪərɪz])*
[s]	sat, ace		[m]	mat, hammer
[z]	zero, houses		[n]	no, banner
[ʃ]	dish, pressure		[ŋ]	singing, link
[ʒ]	pleasure		[j]	yet, onion
[tʃ]	charm, rich		[w]	wall, quite
[dʒ]	judge, rage		[']	*marque l'accent tonique;*
[θ]	thatch, breath			*précède la syllabe accentuée*

A

A, a [ɑ] *nm* A, a.

a [a] *voir* **avoir**.

à [a] *prép* (à + le = **au** [o], à + les = **aux** [o]) **1** (*direction: lieu*) to; (*temps*) till, to; **aller à Paris** to go to Paris; **de 3 à 4 h** from 3 till *ou* to 4 (o'clock). **2** (*position: lieu*) at, in; (*surface*) on; (*temps*) at; **être au bureau/à la ferme/au jardin/à Paris** to be at *ou* in the office/on *ou* at the farm/in the garden/in Paris; **à la maison** at home; **à l'horizon** on the horizon; **à 8 h** at 8 (o'clock); **à mon arrivée** on (my) arrival; **à lundi!** see you (on) Monday! **3** (*description*) **l'homme à la barbe** the man with the beard; **verre à liqueur** liqueur glass. **4** (*attribution*) **donner qch à qn** to give sth to s.o., give s.o. sth. **5** (*devant inf*) **apprendre à lire** to learn to read; **travail à faire** work to do; **maison à vendre** house for sale; **prêt à partir** ready to leave. **6** (*appartenance*) **c'est (son livre) à lui** it's his (book); **c'est à vous de** (*décider, protester etc*) it's up to you to; (*lire, jouer etc*) it's your turn to. **7** (*prix*) for; **pain à 2F** loaf for 2F. **8** (*poids*) by; **vendre au kilo** to sell by the kilo. **9** (*moyen, manière*) **à bicyclette** by bicycle; **à la main** by hand; **à pied** on foot; **au crayon** with a pencil, in pencil; **au galop** at a gallop; **à la française** in the French style *ou* way; **deux à deux** two by two. **10** (*appel*) **au voleur!** (stop) thief!

abaiss/er [abese] *vt* to lower; **a. qn** to humiliate s.o.; — **s'a.** *vpr* (*barrière*) to lower; (*température*) to drop; **s'a. à faire** to stoop to doing. **◆—ement** [-esmɑ̃] *nm* (*chute*) drop.

abandon [abɑ̃dɔ̃] *nm* abandonment; surrender; desertion; *Sp* withdrawal; (*naturel*) abandon; (*confiance*) lack of restraint; **à l'a.** in a neglected state. **◆abandonner** *vt* (*renoncer à*) to give up, abandon; (*droit*) to surrender; (*quitter*) to desert, abandon; — *vi* to give up; *Sp* to withdraw; — **s'a.** *vpr* (*se détendre*) to let oneself go; (*se confier*) to open up; **s'a. à** to give oneself up to, abandon oneself to.

abasourdir [abazurdir] *vt* to stun, astound.

abat-jour [abaʒur] *nm inv* lampshade.

abats [aba] *nmpl* offal; (*de volaille*) giblets.

abattant [abatɑ̃] *nm* leaf, flap.

abattis [abati] *nmpl* giblets.

abatt/re* [abatr] *vt* (*mur*) to knock down; (*arbre*) to cut down, fell; (*animal etc*) to slaughter; (*avion*) to shoot down; (*déprimer*) to demoralize; (*épuiser*) to exhaust; — **s'a.** *vpr* (*tomber*) to collapse; (*oiseau*) to swoop down; (*pluie*) to pour down. **◆—u** *a* (*triste*) dejected, demoralized; (*faible*) at a low ebb. **◆—age** *nm* felling; slaughter(ing). **◆—ement** *nm* (*faiblesse*) exhaustion; (*désespoir*) dejection. **◆abattoir** *nm* slaughterhouse.

abbaye [abei] *nf* abbey.

abbé [abe] *nm* (*chef d'abbaye*) abbot; (*prêtre*) priest. **◆abbesse** *nf* abbess.

abcès [apsɛ] *nm* abscess.

abdiquer [abdike] *vti* to abdicate. **◆abdication** *nf* abdication.

abdomen [abdɔmɛn] *nm* abdomen. **◆abdominal, -aux** *a* abdominal.

abeille [abɛj] *nf* bee.

aberrant [aberɑ̃] *a* (*idée etc*) ludicrous, absurd. **◆aberration** *nf* (*égarement*) aberration; (*idée*) ludicrous idea; **dire des aberrations** to talk sheer nonsense.

abhorrer [abɔre] *vt* to abhor, loathe.

abîme [abim] *nm* abyss, chasm, gulf.

abîmer [abime] *vt* to spoil, damage; — **s'a.** *vpr* to get spoilt; **s'a. dans ses pensées** *Litt* to lose oneself in one's thoughts.

abject [abʒɛkt] *a* abject, despicable.

abjurer [abʒyre] *vti* to abjure.

ablation [ablasjɔ̃] *nf* (*d'organe*) removal.

ablutions [ablysjɔ̃] *nfpl* ablutions.

abnégation [abnegasjɔ̃] *nf* self-sacrifice, abnegation.

abois (aux) [ozabwa] *adv* at bay.

abolir [abɔlir] *vt* to abolish. **◆abolition** *nf* abolition.

abominable [abɔminabl] *a* abominable, obnoxious. **◆abomination** *nf* abomination.

abondant [abɔ̃dɑ̃] *a* abundant, plentiful. **◆abondamment** *adv* abundantly. **◆abondance** *nf* abundance (**de** of); **en a.** in abundance; **années d'a.** years of plenty. **◆abonder** *vi* to abound (**en** in).

abonné, -ée [abɔne] *nmf* (*à un journal, au téléphone*) subscriber; *Rail Sp Th* season ticket holder; (*du gaz etc*) consumer.

◆**abonnement** *nm* subscription; (*carte d'*)a. season ticket. ◆**s'abonner** *vpr* to subscribe (à to); to buy a season ticket.

abord [abɔr] **1** *nm* (*accès*) **d'un a. facile** easy to approach. **2** *nm* (*vue*) **au premier a.** at first sight. **3** *nmpl* (*environs*) surroundings; **aux abords de** around, nearby. ◆**abordable** *a* (*personne*) approachable; (*prix, marchandises*) affordable.

abord (d') [dabɔr] *adv* (*avant tout*) first; (*au début*) at first.

aborder [abɔrde] *vi* to land; − *vt* (*personne*) to approach, accost; (*lieu*) to approach, reach; (*problème*) to tackle, approach; (*attaquer*) Nau to board; (*heurter*) Nau to run foul of. ◆**abordage** *nm* (*assaut*) Nau boarding; (*accident*) Nau collision.

aborigène [abɔriʒɛn] *a* & *nm* aboriginal.

about/ir [abutir] *vi* to succeed; **a. à** to end at, lead to, end up in; **n'a. à rien** to come to nothing. ◆**−issants** *nmpl voir* **tenants.** ◆**−issement** *nm* (*résultat*) outcome; (*succès*) success.

aboyer [abwaje] *vi* to bark. ◆**aboiement** *nm* bark; *pl* barking.

abrasif, -ive [abrazif, -iv] *a* & *nm* abrasive.

abrég/er [abreʒe] *vt* (*récit*) to shorten, abridge; (*mot*) to abbreviate. ◆**−é** *nm* summary; **en a.** (*phrase*) in shortened form; (*mot*) in abbreviated form.

abreuver [abrœve] *vt* (*cheval*) to water; − **s'a.** *vpr* to drink. ◆**abreuvoir** *nm* (*récipient*) drinking trough; (*lieu*) watering place.

abréviation [abrevjasjɔ̃] *nf* abbreviation.

abri [abri] *nm* shelter; **à l'a. de** (*vent*) sheltered from; (*besoin*) safe from; **sans a.** homeless. ◆**abriter** *vt* (*protéger*) to shelter; (*loger*) to house; − **s'a.** *vpr* to (take) shelter.

abricot [abriko] *nm* apricot. ◆**abricotier** *nm* apricot tree.

abroger [abrɔʒe] *vt* to abrogate.

abrupt [abrypt] *a* (*versant*) sheer; (*sentier*) steep, abrupt; (*personne*) abrupt.

abrut/ir [abrytir] *vt* (*alcool*) to stupefy (*s.o.*); (*propagande*) to brutalize (*s.o.*); (*travail*) to leave (*s.o.*) dazed, wear (*s.o.*) out. ◆**−i, -ie** *nmf* idiot; − *a* idiotic.

absence [apsɑ̃s] *nf* absence. ◆**absent, -e** *a* (*personne*) absent, away; (*chose*) missing; **air a.** faraway look; − *nmf* absentee. ◆**absentéisme** *nm* absenteeism. ◆**s'absenter** *vpr* to go away.

abside [apsid] *nf* (*d'une église*) apse.

absolu [apsɔly] *a* & *nm* absolute. ◆**−ment** *adv* absolutely.

absolution [apsɔlysjɔ̃] *nf* absolution.

absorb/er [apsɔrbe] *vt* to absorb. ◆**−ant** *a* absorbent; **travail a.** absorbing job. ◆**absorption** *nf* absorption.

absoudre* [apsudr] *vt* to absolve.

absten/ir* (s') [sapstənir] *vpr* to abstain; **s'a. de** to refrain *ou* abstain from. ◆**abstention** *nf* abstention.

abstinence [apstinɑ̃s] *nf* abstinence.

abstraire* [apstrɛr] *vt* to abstract. ◆**abstrait** *a* & *nm* abstract. ◆**abstraction** *nf* abstraction; **faire a. de** to disregard, leave aside.

absurde [apsyrd] *a* & *nm* absurd. ◆**absurdité** *nf* absurdity; **dire des absurdités** to talk nonsense.

abus [aby] *nm* abuse, misuse; over-indulgence; (*injustice*) abuse. ◆**abuser 1** *vi* to go too far; **a. de** (*situation, personne*) to take unfair advantage of; (*autorité*) to abuse, misuse; (*friandises*) to over-indulge in. **2 s'a.** *vpr* to be mistaken.

abusi/f, -ive [abyzif, -iv] *a* excessive; **emploi a.** Ling improper use, misuse. ◆**−vement** *adv* Ling improperly.

acabit [akabi] *nm* **de cet a.** Péj of that ilk *ou* sort.

acacia [akasja] *nm* (*arbre*) acacia.

académie [akademi] *nf* academy; Univ = (regional) education authority. ◆**académicien, -ienne** *nmf* academician. ◆**académique** *a* academic.

acajou [akaʒu] *nm* mahogany; **cheveux a.** auburn hair.

acariâtre [akarjɑtr] *a* cantankerous.

accabl/er [akable] *vt* to overwhelm, overcome; **a. d'injures** to heap insults upon; **accablé de dettes** (over)burdened with debt. ◆**−ement** *nm* dejection.

accalmie [akalmi] *nf* lull.

accaparer [akapare] *vt* to monopolize; (*personne*) Fam to take up all the time of.

accéder [aksede] *vi* **a.** à (*lieu*) to have access to, reach; (*pouvoir, trône, demande*) to accede to.

accélérer [akselere] *vi* Aut to accelerate; − *vt* (*travaux etc*) to speed up; (*allure, pas*) to quicken, speed up; − **s'a.** *vpr* to speed up. ◆**accélérateur** *nm* Aut accelerator. ◆**accélération** *nf* acceleration; speeding up.

accent [aksɑ̃] *nm* accent; (*sur une syllabe*) stress; **mettre l'a. sur** to stress. ◆**accentuation** *nf* accentuation. ◆**accentuer** *vt* to emphasize, accentuate, stress; − **s'a.** *vpr* to become more pronounced.

accepter [aksɛpte] *vt* to accept; **a. de faire**

to agree to do. ◆**acceptable** a acceptable. ◆**acceptation** nf acceptance.

acception [aksepsjɔ̃] nf sense, meaning.

accès [akse] nm access (à to); (de folie, colère, toux) fit; (de fièvre) attack, bout; pl (routes) approaches. ◆**accessible** a accessible; (personne) approachable. ◆**accession** nf accession (à to); (à un traité) adherence; à. à la propriété home ownership.

accessoire [akseswar] a secondary; — nmpl Th props; (de voiture etc) accessories; **accessoires de toilette** toilet requisites.

accident [aksidɑ̃] nm accident; a. d'avion/de train plane/train crash; par a. by accident, by chance. ◆**accidenté, -ée** a (terrain) uneven; (région) hilly; (voiture) damaged (in an accident); — nmf accident victim, casualty. ◆**accidentel, -elle** a accidental. ◆**accidentellement** adv accidentally, unintentionally.

acclamer [aklame] vt to cheer, acclaim. ◆**acclamations** nfpl cheers, acclamations.

acclimater [aklimate] vt, — **s'a.** vpr to acclimatize, Am acclimate. ◆**acclimatation** nf acclimatization, Am acclimation.

accointances [akwɛ̃tɑ̃s] nfpl Péj contacts.

accolade [akɔlad] nf (embrassade) embrace; Typ brace, bracket.

accoler [akɔle] vt to place (side by side) (à against).

accommod/er [akɔmɔde] vt to adapt; Culin to prepare; **s'a. à** to adapt (oneself) to; **s'a. de** to make the best of. ◆—**ant** a accommodating, easy to please. ◆—**ement** nm arrangement, compromise.

accompagner [akɔ̃paɲe] vt (personne) to accompany, go ou come with, escort; (chose) & Mus to accompany; **s'a. de** to be accompanied by, go with. ◆**accompagnateur, -trice** nmf Mus accompanist; (d'un groupe) guide. ◆**accompagnement** nm Mus accompaniment.

accompl/ir [akɔ̃plir] vt to carry out, fulfil, accomplish. ◆—**i** a accomplished. ◆—**issement** nm fulfilment.

accord [akɔr] nm agreement; (harmonie) harmony; Mus chord; **être d'a.** to agree, be in agreement (**avec** with); **d'a.!** all right! ◆**accorder** vt (donner) to grant; Mus to tune; Gram to make agree; — **s'a.** vpr to agree; (s'entendre) to get along.

accordéon [akɔrdeɔ̃] nm accordion; **en a.** (chaussette etc) wrinkled.

accoster [akɔste] vt to accost; Nau to come alongside; — vi Nau to berth.

accotement [akɔtmɑ̃] nm roadside, verge.

accouch/er [akuʃe] vi to give birth (**de** to); — vt (enfant) to deliver. ◆—**ement** nm delivery. ◆—**eur** nm (médecin) a. obstetrician.

accouder (s') [sakude] vpr s'a. à ou sur to lean on (with one's elbows). ◆**accoudoir** nm armrest.

accoupl/er [akuple] vt to couple; — **s'a.** vpr (animaux) to mate (**à** with). ◆—**ement** nm coupling; mating.

accourir* [akurir] vi to come running, run over.

accoutrement [akutrəmɑ̃] nm Péj garb, dress.

accoutumer [akutyme] vt to accustom; — **s'a.** vpr to get accustomed (**à** to); **comme à l'accoutumée** as usual. ◆**accoutumance** nf familiarization (à with); Méd addiction.

accréditer [akredite] vt (ambassadeur) to accredit; (rumeur) to lend credence to.

accroc [akro] nm (déchirure) tear; (difficulté) hitch, snag.

accroch/er [akrɔʃe] vt (déchirer) to catch; (fixer) to hook; (suspendre) to hang up (on a hook); (heurter) to hit, knock; — vi (affiche etc) to grab one's attention; — **s'a.** vpr (ne pas céder) to persevere; (se disputer) Fam to clash; **s'a. à** (se cramponner etc) to cling to; (s'écorcher) to catch oneself on. ◆—**age** nm Aut knock, slight hit; (friction) Fam clash. ◆—**eur, -euse** a (personne) tenacious; (affiche etc) eyecatching, catchy.

accroître* [akrwatr] vt to increase; — **s'a.** vpr to increase, grow. ◆**accroissement** nm increase; growth.

accroup/ir (s') [sakrupir] vpr to squat ou crouch (down). ◆—**i** a squatting, crouching.

accueil [akœj] nm reception, welcome. ◆**accueill/ir*** vt to receive, welcome, greet. ◆—**ant** a welcoming.

acculer [akyle] vt **a. qn à qch** to drive s.o. to ou against sth.

accumuler [akymyle] vt, — **s'a.** vpr to pile up, accumulate. ◆**accumulateur** nm accumulator, battery. ◆**accumulation** nf accumulation.

accus/er [akyze] vt (dénoncer) to accuse; (rendre responsable) to blame (**de** for); (révéler) to show; (faire ressortir) to bring out; **a. réception** to acknowledge receipt (**de** of); **a. le coup** to stagger under the blow. ◆—**é, -ée 1** nmf accused; (cour d'assises) defendant. **2** a prominent. ◆**accusateur, -trice** a (regard) accusing;

(*document*) incriminating; — *nmf* accuser.
◆**accusation** *nf* accusation; *Jur* charge.
acerbe [asɛrb] *a* bitter, caustic.
acéré [asere] *a* sharp.
acétate [asetat] *nm* acetate. ◆**acétique** *a* acetic.
achalandé [aʃalɑ̃de] *a* **bien a.** (*magasin*) well-stocked.
acharn/er (s') [aʃarne] *vpr* **s'a. sur** (*attaquer*) to set upon, lay into; **s'a. contre** (*poursuivre*) to pursue (relentlessly); **s'a. à faire** to struggle to do, try desperately to do. ◆**-é, -ée** *a* relentless; — *nmf* (*du jeu etc*) fanatic. ◆**-ement** *nm* relentlessness.
achat [aʃa] *nm* purchase; *pl* shopping.
acheminer [aʃmine] *vt* to dispatch; — **s'a.** *vpr* to proceed (**vers** towards).
achet/er [aʃte] *vti* to buy, purchase; **a. à qn** (*vendeur*) to buy from s.o.; (*pour qn*) to buy for s.o. ◆**-eur, -euse** *nmf* buyer, purchaser; (*dans un magasin*) shopper.
achever [aʃve] *vt* to finish (off); **a. de faire qch** (*personne*) to finish doing sth; **a. qn** (*tuer*) to finish s.o. off; — **s'a.** *vpr* to end, finish. ◆**achèvement** *nm* completion.
achoppement [aʃɔpmɑ̃] *nm* **pierre d'a.** stumbling block.
acide [asid] *a* acid, sour; — *nm* acid. ◆**acidité** *nf* acidity.
acier [asje] *nm* steel. ◆**aciérie** *nf* steelworks.
acné [akne] *nf* acne.
acolyte [akɔlit] *nm Péj* confederate, associate.
acompte [akɔ̃t] *nm* part payment, deposit.
à-côté [akote] *nm* (*d'une question*) side issue; *pl* (*gains*) little extras.
à-coup [aku] *nm* jerk, jolt; **sans à-coups** smoothly; **par à-coups** in fits and starts.
acoustique [akustik] *a* acoustic; — *nf* acoustics.
acquérir* [akerir] *vt* to acquire, gain; (*par achat*) to purchase; **s'a. une réputation/etc** to win a reputation/*etc*; **être acquis à** (*idée, parti*) to be a supporter of. ◆**acquéreur** *nm* purchaser. ◆**acquis** *nm* experience. ◆**acquisition** *nf* acquisition; purchase.
acquiesc/er [akjese] *vi* to acquiesce (**à** to). ◆**-ement** *nm* acquiescence.
acquit [aki] *nm* receipt; **'pour a.'** 'paid'; **par a. de conscience** for conscience sake. ◆**acquitt/er** *vt* (*dette*) to clear, pay; (*accusé*) to acquit; **s'a. de** (*devoir, promesse*) to discharge; **s'a. envers qn** to repay s.o. ◆**-ement** *nm* payment; acquittal; discharge.
âcre [ɑkr] *a* bitter, acrid, pungent.

acrobate [akrɔbat] *nmf* acrobat. ◆**acrobatie(s)** *nf(pl)* acrobatics. ◆**acrobatique** *a* acrobatic.
acrylique [akrilik] *a* & *nm* acrylic.
acte [akt] *nm* act, deed; *Th* act; **un a. d'un** act of; **a. de naissance** birth certificate; **prendre a. de** to take note of.
acteur, -trice [aktœr, -tris] *nmf* actor, actress.
actif, -ive [aktif, -iv] *a* active; — *nm Fin* assets; **à son a.** to one's credit; (*vols, meurtres*) *Hum* to one's name.
action [aksjɔ̃] *nf* action; *Fin* share. ◆**actionnaire** *nmf* shareholder. ◆**actionner** *vt* to set in motion, activate, actuate.
activer [aktive] *vt* to speed up; (*feu*) to boost; — **s'a.** *vpr* to bustle about; (*se dépêcher*) *Fam* to get a move on.
activiste [aktivist] *nmf* activist.
activité [aktivite] *nf* activity; **en a.** (*personne*) fully active; (*volcan*) active.
actuaire [aktyɛr] *nmf* actuary.
actualité [aktyalite] *nf* (*d'un problème*) topicality; (*évènements*) current events; *pl* TV *Cin* news; **d'a.** topical.
actuel, -elle [aktyɛl] *a* (*présent*) present; (*contemporain*) topical. ◆**actuellement** *adv* at present, at the present time.
acuité [akyite] *nf* (*de douleur*) acuteness; (*de vision*) keenness.
acupuncture [akypɔ̃ktyr] *nf* acupuncture. ◆**acupuncteur, -trice** *nmf* acupuncturist.
adage [adaʒ] *nm* (*maxime*) adage.
adapter [adapte] *vt* to adapt; (*ajuster*) to fit (**à** to); **s'a. à** (*s'habituer*) to adapt to; (*tuyau etc*) to fit. ◆**adaptable** *a* adaptable. ◆**adaptateur, -trice** *nmf* adapter. ◆**adaptation** *nf* adaptation.
additif [aditif] *nm* additive.
addition [adisjɔ̃] *nf* addition; (*au restaurant*) bill, *Am* check. ◆**additionnel, -elle** *a* additional. ◆**additionner** *vt* to add up; (*nombres*) to add up.
adepte [adɛpt] *nmf* follower.
adéquat [adekwa] *a* appropriate.
adhérer [adere] *vi* **a. à** (*coller*) to adhere ou stick to; (*s'inscrire*) to join; (*pneu*) to grip. ◆**adhérence** *nf* (*de pneu*) grip. ◆**adhérent, -ente** *nmf* member.
adhésif, -ive [adezif, -iv] *a* & *nm* adhesive. ◆**adhésion** *nf* membership; (*accord*) support.
adieu [adjø] *int* & *nm* farewell, goodbye.
adipeux, -euse [adipø, -øz] *a* (*tissu*) fatty; (*visage*) fat.

adjacent [adʒasɑ̃] *a* (*contigu*) & *Géom* adjacent.

adjectif [adʒɛktif] *nm* adjective.

adjoindre* [adʒwɛ̃dr] *vt* (*associer*) to appoint (*s.o.*) as an assistant (**à** to); (*ajouter*) to add; **s'a. qn** to appoint s.o. **◆adjoint, -ointe** *nmf* & *a* assistant; **a. au maire** deputy mayor.

adjudant [adʒydɑ̃] *nm* warrant officer.

adjuger [adʒyʒe] *vt* (*accorder*) to award; **s'a. qch** *Fam* to grab sth for oneself.

adjurer [adʒyre] *vt* to beseech, entreat.

admettre* [admɛtr] *vt* (*laisser entrer, accueillir, reconnaître*) to admit; (*autoriser, tolérer*) to allow; (*supposer*) to admit, grant; (*candidat*) to pass; **être admis à** (*examen*) to have passed.

administrer [administre] *vt* (*gérer, donner*) to administer. **◆administrateur, -trice** *nmf* administrator. **◆administratif, -ive** *a* administrative. **◆administration** *nf* administration; **l'A.** (*service public*) government service, the Civil Service.

admirer [admire] *vt* to admire. **◆admirable** *a* admirable. **◆admirateur, -trice** *nmf* admirer. **◆admiratif, -ive** *a* admiring. **◆admiration** *nf* admiration.

admissible [admisibl] *a* acceptable, admissible; (*après un concours*) eligible (**à** for). **◆admission** *nf* admission.

adolescent, -ente [adolesɑ̃, -ɑ̃t] *nmf* adolescent, teenager; — *a* teenage. **◆adolescence** *nf* adolescence.

adonner (s') [sadone] *vpr* **s'a. à** (*boisson*) to take to; (*étude*) to devote oneself to.

adopter [adopte] *vt* to adopt. **◆adoptif, -ive** *a* (*fils, patrie*) adopted. **◆adoption** *nf* adoption; **suisse d'a.** Swiss by adoption.

adorer [adore] *vt* (*personne* & *Rel*) to worship, adore; (*chose*) *Fam* to adore, love; **a. faire** to adore *ou* love doing. **◆adorable** *a* adorable. **◆adoration** *nf* adoration, worship.

adosser [adose] *vt* **a. qch à** to lean sth back against; **s'a. à** to lean back against.

adouc/ir [adusir] *vt* (*voix, traits etc*) to soften; (*boisson*) to sweeten; (*chagrin*) to mitigate, ease; — **s'a.** *vpr* (*temps*) to turn milder; (*caractère*) to mellow. **◆—issement** *nm* **a. de la température** milder weather.

adrénaline [adrenalin] *nf* adrenalin(e).

adresse [adrɛs] *nf* **1** (*domicile*) address. **2** (*habileté*) skill. **◆adresser** *vt* (*lettre*) to send; (*compliment, remarque etc*) to address; (*coup*) to direct, aim; (*personne*) to direct (**à** to); **a. la parole à** to speak to;

s'a. à to speak to; (*aller trouver*) to go and see; (*bureau*) to enquire at; (*être destiné à*) to be aimed at.

Adriatique [adriatik] *nf* **l'A.** the Adriatic.

adroit [adrwa] *a* skilful, clever.

adulation [adylasjɔ̃] *nf* adulation.

adulte [adylt] *a* & *nmf* adult, grown-up.

adultère [adyltɛr] *a* adulterous; — *nm* adultery.

advenir [advənir] *v imp* to occur; **a. de** (*devenir*) to become of; **advienne que pourra** come what may.

adverbe [advɛrb] *nm* adverb. **◆adverbial, -aux** *a* adverbial.

adversaire [advɛrsɛr] *nmf* opponent, adversary. **◆adverse** *a* opposing.

adversité [advɛrsite] *nf* adversity.

aérer [aere] *vt* (*chambre*) to air (out), ventilate; (*lit*) to air (out); — **s'a.** *vpr* *Fam* to get some air. **◆aéré** *a* airy. **◆aération** *nf* ventilation. **◆aérien, -ienne** *a* (*ligne, attaque etc*) air-; (*photo*) aerial; (*câble*) overhead; (*léger*) airy.

aérobic [aerɔbik] *nf* aerobics.

aéro-club [aerɔklœb] *nm* flying club. **◆aérodrome** *nm* aerodrome. **◆aérodynamique** *a* streamlined, aerodynamic. **◆aérogare** *nf* air terminal. **◆aéroglisseur** *nm* hovercraft. **◆aérogramme** *nm* air letter. **◆aéromodélisme** *nm* model aircraft building and flying. **◆aéronautique** *nf* aeronautics. **◆aéronavale** *nf* = *Br* Fleet Air Arm, = *Am* Naval Air Force. **◆aéroport** *nm* airport. **◆aéroporté** *a* airborne. **◆aérosol** *nm* aerosol.

affable [afabl] *a* affable.

affaiblir [afeblir] *vt*, — **s'a.** *vpr* to weaken.

affaire [afɛr] *nf* (*question*) matter, affair; (*marché*) deal; (*firme*) concern, business; (*scandale*) affair; (*procès*) *Jur* case; *pl Com* business; (*d'intérêt public, personnel*) affairs; (*effets*) belongings, things; **avoir a. à** to have to deal with; **c'est mon a.** that's my business *ou* affair *ou* concern; **faire une bonne a.** to get a good deal, get a bargain; **ça fera l'a.** that will do nicely; **toute une a.** (*histoire*) quite a business.

affair/er (s') [safere] *vpr* to busy oneself, run *ou* bustle about. **◆—é** *a* busy. **◆affairiste** *nm* (political) racketeer.

affaiss/er (s') [safese] *vpr* (*personne*) to collapse; (*plancher*) to cave in, give way; (*sol*) to subside, sink. **◆—ement** [afesmɑ̃] *nm* (*du sol*) subsidence.

affaler (s') [safale] *vpr* to flop down, collapse.

affamé [afame] a starving; **a. de** Fig hungry for.

affect/er [afɛkte] vt (destiner) to earmark, assign; (nommer à un poste) to post; (feindre, émouvoir) to affect. ◆**—é** a (manières, personne) affected. ◆**affectation** nf assignment; posting; (simulation) affectation.

affectif, -ive [afɛktif, -iv] a emotional.

affection [afɛksjɔ̃] nf (attachement) affection; (maladie) ailment. ◆**affectionn/er** vt to be fond of. ◆**—é** a loving. ◆**affectueux, -euse** a affectionate.

affermir [afɛrmir] vt (autorité) to strengthen; (muscles) to tone up; (voix) to steady.

affiche [afiʃ] nf poster; Th bill. ◆**affich/er** vt (affiche etc) to post ou stick up; Th to bill; (sentiment) Péj to display; **a. qn** Péj to parade s.o., flaunt s.o. ◆**—age** nm (bill-)posting; **panneau d'a.** hoarding, Am billboard.

affilée (d') [dafile] adv (à la suite) in a row, at a stretch.

affiler [afile] vt to sharpen.

affilier (s') [safilje] vpr **s'a. à** to join, become affiliated to. ◆**affiliation** nf affiliation.

affiner [afine] vt to refine.

affinité [afinite] nf affinity.

affirmatif, -ive [afirmatif, -iv] a (ton) assertive, positive; (proposition) affirmative; **il a été a.** he was quite positive; **— nf répondre par l'affirmative** to reply in the affirmative.

affirmer [afirme] vt to assert; (proclamer solennellement) to affirm. ◆**affirmation** nf assertion.

affleurer [aflœre] vi to appear on the surface.

affliger [afliʒe] vt to distress; **affligé de** stricken ou afflicted with.

affluence [aflyɑ̃s] nf crowd; **heures d'a.** rush hours.

affluent [aflyɑ̃] nm tributary.

affluer [aflye] vi (sang) to flow, rush; (gens) to flock. ◆**afflux** nm (flow; (arrivée) influx.

affol/er [afole] vt to drive out of one's mind; (effrayer) to terrify; **— s'a.** vpr to panic. ◆**—ement** nm panic.

affranch/ir [afrɑ̃ʃir] vt (timbrer) to stamp; (émanciper) to free. ◆**—issement** nm tarifs d'a. postage.

affréter [afrete] vt (avion) to charter; (navire) to freight.

affreux, -euse [afrø, -øz] a hideous, dreadful, ghastly. ◆**affreusement** adv dreadfully.

affriolant [afrijɔlɑ̃] a enticing.

affront [afrɔ̃] nm insult, affront; **faire un a. à** to insult.

affront/er [afrɔ̃te] vt to confront, face; (mauvais temps, difficultés etc) to brave. ◆**—ement** nm confrontation.

affubler [afyble] vt Péj to dress, rig out (**de** in).

affût [afy] nm **à l'a. de** Fig on the look-out for.

affûter [afyte] vt (outil) to sharpen, grind.

Afghanistan [afganistɑ̃] nm Afghanistan.

afin [afɛ̃] prép **a. de** (+ inf) in order to; **— conj a. que** (+ sub) so that.

Afrique [afrik] nf Africa. ◆**africain, -aine** a & nmf African.

agac/er [agase] vt (personne) to irritate, annoy. ◆**—ement** nm irritation.

âge [ɑʒ] nm age; **quel â. as-tu?** how old are you?; **avant l'â.** before one's time; **d'un certain â.** middle-aged; **l'â. adulte** adulthood; **la force de l'â.** the prime of life; **le moyen â.** the Middle Ages. ◆**âgé** a elderly; **â. de six ans** six years old; **un enfant â. de six ans** a six-year-old child.

agence [aʒɑ̃s] nf agency; (succursale) branch office; **a. immobilière** estate agent's office, Am real estate office.

agenc/er [aʒɑ̃se] vt to arrange; **bien agencé** (maison etc) well laid-out; (phrase) well put-together. ◆**—ement** nm (de maison etc) lay-out.

agenda [aʒɛ̃da] nm diary, Am datebook.

agenouiller (s') [saʒnuje] vpr to kneel (down); **être agenouillé** to be kneeling (down).

agent [aʒɑ̃] nm agent; **a. (de police)** policeman; **a. de change** stockbroker; **a. immobilier** estate agent, Am real estate agent.

aggloméré [aglɔmere] nm & a (bois) chipboard, fibreboard.

agglomérer (s') [saglɔmere] vpr (s'entasser) to conglomerate. ◆**agglomération** nf conglomeration; (habitations) built-up area; (ville) town.

aggraver [agrave] vt to worsen, aggravate; **— s'a.** vpr to worsen. ◆**aggravation** nf worsening.

agile [aʒil] a agile, nimble. ◆**agilité** nf agility, nimbleness.

agir [aʒir] **1** vi to act; **a. auprès de** to intercede with. **2 s'agir** v imp **il s'agit d'argent**/etc it's a question ou matter of money/etc, it concerns money/etc; **de quoi s'agit-il?** what is it?, what's it about?; **il s'agit de se dépêcher**/etc we have to hurry/*etc.* ◆**agissant** *a* active, effective. ◆**agissements** *nmpl Péj* dealings.

agit/er [aʒite] *vt* (*remuer*) to stir; (*secouer*) to shake; (*brandir*) to wave; (*troubler*) to agitate; (*discuter*) to debate; — **s'a.** *vpr* (*enfant*) to fidget; (*peuple*) to stir. ◆—**é** *a* (*mer*) rough; (*malade*) restless, agitated; (*enfant*) fidgety, restless. ◆**agitateur, -trice** *nmf* (*political*) agitator. ◆**agitation** *nf* (*de la mer*) roughness; (*d'un malade etc*) restlessness; (*nervosité*) agitation; (*de la rue*) bustle; *Pol* unrest.

agneau, -x [aɲo] *nm* lamb.

agonie [agɔni] *nf* death throes; **être à l'a.** to be suffering the pangs of death. ◆**agoniser** *vi* to be dying.

agrafe [agraf] *nf* hook; (*pour papiers*) staple. ◆**agrafer** *vt* to fasten, hook, do up; (*papiers*) to staple. ◆**agrafeuse** *nf* stapler.

agrand/ir [agrɑ̃dir] *vt* to enlarge; (*grossir*) to magnify; — **s'a.** *vpr* to expand, grow. ◆—**issement** *nm* (*de ville*) expansion; (*de maison*) extension; (*de photo*) enlargement.

agréable [agreabl] *a* pleasant, agreeable, nice. ◆—**ment** [-əmɑ̃] *adv* pleasantly.

agré/er [agree] *vt* to accept; **veuillez a. mes salutations distinguées** (*dans une lettre*) yours faithfully. ◆—**é** *a* (*fournisseur, centre*) approved.

agrégation [agregasjɔ̃] *nf* competitive examination for recruitment of *lycée* teachers. ◆**agrégé, -ée** *nmf* teacher who has passed the *agrégation*.

agrément [agremɑ̃] *nm* (*attrait*) charm; (*accord*) assent; **voyage d'a.** pleasure trip. ◆**agrémenter** *vt* to embellish; **a. un récit d'anecdotes** to pepper a story with anecdotes.

agrès [agre] *nmpl Nau* tackle, rigging; (*de gymnastique*) apparatus.

agresser [agrese] *vt* to attack. ◆**agresseur** *nm* attacker; (*dans la rue*) mugger; (*dans un conflit*) aggressor. ◆**agressif, -ive** *a* aggressive. ◆**agression** *nf* (*d'un État*) aggression; (*d'un individu*) attack. ◆**agressivité** *nf* aggressiveness.

agricole [agrikɔl] *a* (*peuple*) agricultural, farming; (*ouvrier, machine*) farm-.

agriculteur [agrikyltœr] *nm* farmer. ◆**agriculture** *nf* agriculture, farming.

agripper [agripe] *vt* to clutch, grip; **s'a. à** to cling to, clutch, grip.

agronomie [agrɔnɔmi] *nf* agronomics.

agrumes [agrym] *nmpl* citrus fruit(s).

aguerri [ageri] *a* seasoned, hardened.

aguets (aux) [ozage] *adv* on the look-out.

aguich/er [agiʃe] *vt* to tease, excite. ◆—**ant** *a* enticing.

ah! [a] *int* ah!, oh!

ahur/ir [ayrir] *vt* to astound, bewilder. ◆—**i, -ie** *nmf* idiot.

ai [e] *voir* **avoir**.

aide [ed] *nf* help, assistance, aid; — *nmf* (*personne*) assistant; **à l'a. de** with the help ou aid of. ◆**a.-électricien** *nm* electrician's mate. ◆**a.-familiale** *nf* home help. ◆**a.-mémoire** *nm inv Scol* handbook (*of facts etc*).

aider [ede] *vt* to help, assist, aid (**à faire** to do); **s'a. de** to make use of.

aïe! [aj] *int* ouch!, ow!

aïeul, -e [ajœl] *nmf* grandfather, grandmother.

aïeux [ajø] *nmpl* forefathers, forebears.

aigle [egl] *nmf* eagle. ◆**aiglon** *nm* eaglet.

aiglefin [eglafɛ̃] *nm* haddock.

aigre [egr] *a* (*acide*) sour; (*voix, vent, parole*) sharp, cutting. ◆**a.-doux, -douce** *a* bitter-sweet. ◆**aigreur** *nf* sourness; (*de ton*) sharpness; **a. d'estomac** heartburn. ◆**aigrette** [egret] *nf* (*de plumes*) tuft.

aigr/ir (s') [segrir] *vpr* (*vin*) to turn sour; (*caractère*) to sour. ◆—**i** [egri] *a* (*personne*) embittered, bitter.

aigu, -uë [egy] *a* (*crise etc*) acute; (*dents*) sharp, pointed; (*voix*) shrill.

aiguille [egɥij] *nf* (*à coudre, de pin*) needle; (*de montre*) hand; (*de balance*) pointer; **a.** (**rocheuse**) peak.

aiguill/er [egɥije] *vt* (*train*) to shunt, *Am* switch; *Fig* to steer, direct. ◆—**age** *nm* (*appareil*) *Rail* points, *Am* switches. ◆—**eur** *nm Rail* switchman, *Am* switchman; **a. du ciel** air traffic controller. ◆**aiguillon** *nm* (*dard*) sting; (*stimulant*) spur. ◆**aiguillonner** *vt* to spur (on), goad.

aiguiser [eg(ɥ)ize] *vt* (*affiler*) to sharpen; (*appétit*) to whet.

ail [aj] *nm* garlic.

aile [el] *nf* wing; (*de moulin à vent*) sail; *Aut* wing, *Am* fender; **battre de l'a.** to be in a bad way; **d'un coup d'a.** (*avion*) in continuous flight. ◆**ailé** *a* winged. ◆**aileron** *nm* (*de requin*) fin; (*d'avion*) aileron; (*d'oiseau*) pinion. ◆**ailier** [elje] *nm Fb* wing(er).

ailleurs [ajœr] *adv* somewhere else, elsewhere; **partout a.** everywhere else; **d'a.** (*du reste*) besides, anyway; **par a.** (*en outre*) moreover; (*autrement*) otherwise.

ailloli [ajɔli] *nm* garlic mayonnaise.

aimable [emabl] *a* (*complaisant*) kind;

(*sympathique*) likeable, amiable; (*agréable*) pleasant. ◆**—ment** [-əmɑ̃] *adv* kindly.

aimant [emɑ̃] **1** *nm* magnet. **2** *a* loving. ◆**aimanter** *vt* to magnetize.

aimer [eme] *vt* (*chérir*) to love; **a. (bien)** (*apprécier*) to like, be fond of; **a. faire** to like doing *ou* to do; **a. mieux** to prefer; **ils s'aiment** they're in love.

aine [en] *nf* groin.

aîné, -e [ene] *a* (*de deux frères etc*) elder, older; (*de plus de deux*) eldest, oldest; — *nmf* (*enfant*) elder *ou* older (child); eldest *ou* oldest (child); **c'est mon a.** he's my senior.

ainsi [ɛ̃si] *adv* (*comme ça*) (in) this *ou* that way, thus; (*alors*) so; **a. que** as well as; **et a. de suite** and so on; **pour a. dire** so to speak.

air [ɛr] *nm* **1** air; **en plein a.** in the open (air), outdoors; **ficher** *ou* **flanquer en l'a.** *Fam* (*jeter*) to chuck away; (*gâcher*) to mess up, upset; **en l'a.** (*jeter*) (up) in the air; (*paroles, menaces*) empty; (*projets*) uncertain, (up) in the air; **dans l'a.** (*grippe, idées*) about, around. **2** (*expression*) look, appearance; **avoir l'a.** to look, seem; **avoir l'a. de** to look like; **a. de famille** family likeness. **3** (*mélodie*) tune; **a. d'opéra** aria.

aire [ɛr] *nf* (*de stationnement etc*) & *Math* area; (*d'oiseau*) eyrie; **a. de lancement** launching site.

airelle [ɛrɛl] *nf* bilberry, *Am* blueberry.

aisance [ɛzɑ̃s] *nf* (*facilité*) ease; (*prospérité*) easy circumstances, affluence.

aise [ɛz] *nf* **à l'a.** (*dans un vêtement etc*) comfortable; (*dans une situation*) at ease; (*fortuné*) comfortably off; **aimer ses aises** to like one's comforts; **mal à l'a.** uncomfortable, ill at ease. ◆**aisé** [eze] *a* (*fortuné*) comfortably off; (*naturel*) free and easy; (*facile*) easy. ◆**aisément** *adv* easily.

aisselle [ɛsɛl] *nf* armpit.

ait [ɛ] *voir* **avoir**.

ajonc(s) [aʒɔ̃] *nm(pl)* gorse, furze.

ajouré [aʒure] *a* (*dentelle etc*) openwork.

ajourn/er [aʒurne] *vt* to postpone, adjourn. ◆**—ement** *nm* postponement, adjournment.

ajout [aʒu] *nm* addition. ◆**ajouter** *vti* to add (à to); **s'a.** à to add to.

ajust/er [aʒyste] *vt* (*pièce, salaires*) to adjust; (*coiffure*) to arrange; (*coup*) to aim; **a. à** (*adapter*) to fit to. ◆**—é** (*serré*) close-fitting. ◆**—ement** *nm* adjustment. ◆**—eur** *nm* (*ouvrier*) fitter.

alaise [alɛz] *nf* (*waterproof*) undersheet.

alambic [alɑ̃bik] *nm* still.

alambiqué [alɑ̃bike] *a* convoluted, over-subtle.

alanguir [alɑ̃gir] *vt* to make languid.

alarme [alarm] *nf* (*signal, inquiétude*) alarm; **jeter l'a.** to cause alarm; ◆**alarmer** *vt* to alarm; **s'a. de** to become alarmed at.

Albanie [albani] *nf* Albania. ◆**albanais, -aise** *a* & *nmf* Albanian.

albâtre [albɑtr] *nm* alabaster.

albatros [albatros] *nm* albatross.

albinos [albinos] *nmf* & *a inv* albino.

album [albɔm] *nm* (*de timbres etc*) album; (*de dessins*) sketchbook.

alcali [alkali] *nm* alkali. ◆**alcalin** *a* alkaline.

alchimie [alʃimi] *nf* alchemy.

alcool [alkɔl] *nm* alcohol; (*spiritueux*) spirits; **a. à brûler** methylated spirit(s); **lampe à a.** spirit lamp. ◆**alcoolique** *a* & *nmf* alcoholic. ◆**alcoolisé** *a* (*boisson*) alcoholic. ◆**alcoolisme** *nm* alcoholism. ◆**alcootest®** *nm* breath test; (*appareil*) breathalyzer.

alcôve [alkov] *nf* alcove.

aléas [alea] *nmpl* hazards, risks. ◆**aléatoire** *a* chancy, uncertain; (*sélection*) random.

alentour [alɑ̃tur] *adv* round about, around; **d'a.** surrounding; — *nmpl* surroundings, vicinity; **aux alentours de** in the vicinity of.

alerte [alɛrt] **1** *a* (*leste*) agile, spry; (*éveillé*) alert. **2** *nf* alarm; **en état d'a.** on the alert; **a. aérienne** air-raid warning. ◆**alerter** *vt* to warn, alert.

alezan, -ane [alzɑ̃ -an] *a* & *nmf* (*cheval*) chestnut.

algarade [algarad] *nf* (*dispute*) altercation.

algèbre [alʒɛbr] *nf* algebra. ◆**algébrique** *a* algebraic.

Alger [alʒe] *nm ou f* Algiers.

Algérie [alʒeri] *nf* Algeria. ◆**algérien, -ienne** *a* & *nmf* Algerian.

algue [alg] *nf*(*pl*) seaweed.

alias [aljɑs] *adv* alias.

alibi [alibi] *nm* alibi.

alién/er [aljene] *vt* to alienate; **s'a.** qn to alienate s.o. ◆**—é, -ée** *nmf* insane person; *Péj* lunatic. ◆**aliénation** *nf* alienation; *Méd* derangement.

align/er [aliɲe] *vt* to align, line up; **les à** *Arg* to fork out, pay up; — **s'a.** *vpr* (*personnes*) to fall into line, line up; *Pol* to align oneself (**sur** with). ◆**—ement** *nm* alignment.

aliment [alimɑ̃] *nm* food. ◆**alimentaire** *a* (*industrie, produit etc*) food-. ◆**alimentation** *nf* feeding; supply(ing); (*régime*) diet, nutrition; (*nourriture*) food; **magasin d'a.** grocer's, grocery store. ◆**alimenter** *vt* (*nourrir*) to feed; (*fournir*) to supply (**en** with); (*débat, feu*) to fuel.

alinéa [alinea] *nm* paragraph.

alité [alite] *a* bedridden.

allaiter [alete] *vti* to (breast)feed.

allant [alɑ̃] *nm* drive, energy, zest.

allécher [aleʃe] *vt* to tempt, entice.

allée [ale] *nf* path, walk, lane; (*de cinéma*) aisle; **allées et venues** comings and goings, running about.

allégation [alegasjɔ̃] *nf* allegation.

alléger [aleʒe] *vt* to alleviate, lighten.

allégorie [alegɔri] *nf* allegory.

allègre [alegr] *a* gay, lively, cheerful. ◆**allégresse** *nf* gladness, rejoicing.

alléguer [alege] *vt* (*excuse etc*) to put forward.

alléluia [aleluja] *nm* hallelujah.

Allemagne [almaɲ] *nf* Germany. ◆**allemand, -ande** *a* & *nmf* German; – *nm* (*langue*) German.

aller* [ale] **1** *vi* (*aux* **être**) to go; (*montre etc*) to work, go; **a. à** (*convenir à*) to suit; **a. avec** (*vêtement*) to go with, match; **a. bien/mieux** (*personne*) to be well/better; **il va savoir/venir/*etc*** he'll know/come/*etc*, he's going to know/come/*etc*; **il va partir** he's about to leave, he's going to leave; **va voir!** go and see!; **comment vas-tu?, (comment) ça va?** how are you?; **ça va!** all right!, fine!; **ça va (comme ça)?** that's enough!; **allez-y** go on, go ahead; **j'y vais** I'm coming; **allons (donc)!** come on!, come off it!; **allez! au lit!** come on *ou* go on to bed!; **ça va de soi** that's obvious; – **s'en aller** *vpr* to go away; (*tache*) to come out. **2** *nm* outward journey; **a. (simple)** single (ticket), *Am* one-way (ticket); **a. (et) retour** return (ticket), *Am* round-trip (ticket).

allergie [alerʒi] *nf* allergy. ◆**allergique** *a* allergic (**à** to).

alliage [aljaʒ] *nm* alloy.

alliance [aljɑ̃s] *nf* (*anneau*) wedding ring; *Pol* alliance; *Rel* covenant; (*mariage*) marriage.

alli/er [alje] *vt* (*associer*) to combine (**à** with); (*pays*) to ally (**à** with); – **s'a.** *vpr* (*couleurs*) to combine; (*pays*) to become allied (**à** with, to); **s'a. à** (*famille*) to ally oneself with. ◆**-é, -ée** *nmf* ally.

alligator [aligatɔr] *nm* alligator.

allô! [alo] *int Tél* hullo!, hello!, hello!

allocation [alɔkasjɔ̃] *nf* (*somme*) allowance; **a. (de) chômage** unemployment benefit. ◆**allocataire** *nmf* claimant.

allocution [alɔkysjɔ̃] *nf* (short) speech, address.

allong/er [alɔ̃ʒe] *vt* (*bras*) to stretch out; (*jupe*) to lengthen; (*sauce*) to thin; – *vi* (*jours*) to get longer; – **s'a.** *vpr* to stretch out. ◆**-é** *a* (*oblong*) elongated.

allouer [alwe] *vt* to allocate.

allum/er [alyme] *vt* (*feu, pipe etc*) to light; (*électricité*) to turn *ou* switch on; (*désir, colère*) Fig to kindle; – **s'a.** *vpr* to light up; (*feu, guerre*) to flare up. ◆**-age** *nm* lighting; *Aut* ignition. ◆**allume-gaz** *nm inv* gas lighter. ◆**allumeuse** *nf* (*femme*) teaser.

allumette [alymɛt] *nf* match.

allure [alyr] *nf* (*vitesse*) pace; (*de véhicule*) speed; (*démarche*) gait, walk; (*maintien*) bearing; (*air*) look; *pl* (*conduite*) ways.

allusion [alyzjɔ̃] *nf* allusion; (*voilée*) hint; **faire a. à** to refer *ou* allude to; to hint at.

almanach [almana] *nm* almanac.

aloi [alwa] *nm* **de bon a.** genuine, worthy.

alors [alɔr] *adv* (*en ce temps-là*) then; (*en ce cas-là*) so, then; **a. que** (*lorsque*) when; (*tandis que*) whereas.

alouette [alwɛt] *nf* (sky)lark.

alourd/ir [alurdir] *vt* to weigh down; – **s'a.** *vpr* to become heavy *ou* heavier. ◆**-i** *a* heavy.

aloyau [alwajo] *nm* sirloin.

alpaga [alpaga] *nm* (*tissu*) alpaca.

alpage [alpaʒ] *nm* mountain pasture. ◆**Alpes** *nfpl* **les A.** the Alps. ◆**alpestre** *a*, ◆**alpin** *a* alpine. ◆**alpinisme** *nm* mountaineering. ◆**alpiniste** *nmf* mountaineer.

alphabet [alfabɛ] *nm* alphabet. ◆**alphabétique** *a* alphabetic(al). ◆**alphabétiser** *vt* to teach to read and write.

altercation [alterkasjɔ̃] *nf* altercation.

altér/er [altere] *vt* (*denrée, santé*) to impair, spoil; (*voix, vérité*) to distort; (*monnaie, texte*) to falsify; (*donner soif à*) to make thirsty; – **s'a.** *vpr* (*santé, relations*) to deteriorate. ◆**-ation** *nf* deterioration, change (**de** in); (*de visage*) distortion.

alternatif, -ive [alternatif, -iv] *a* alternating. ◆**alternative** *nf* alternative; *pl* alternate periods. ◆**alternativement** *adv* alternately.

altern/er [alterne] *vti* to alternate. ◆**-é** *a* alternate. ◆**alternance** *nf* alternation.

altesse [altɛs] *nf* (*titre*) Highness.

altier, -ière [altje, -jɛr] *a* haughty.

altitude [altityd] *nf* altitude, height.

alto [alto] *nm* (*instrument*) viola.

aluminium [alyminjɔm] *nm* aluminium, *Am*

aluminum; **papier a.**, *Fam* **papier alu** tin foil.

alunir [alynir] *vi* to land on the moon.

alvéole [alveɔl] *nf* (*de ruche*) cell; (*dentaire*) socket. ◆**alvéolé** *a* honeycombed.

amabilité [amabilite] *nf* kindness; **faire des amabilités à** to show kindness to.

amadouer [amadwe] *vt* to coax, persuade.

amaigr/ir [amegrir] *vt* to make thin(ner). ◆**—i** *a* thin(ner). ◆**—issant** *a* (*régime*) slimming.

amalgame [amalgam] *nm* amalgam, mixture. ◆**amalgamer** *vt*, **— s'a.** *vpr* to blend, mix, amalgamate.

amande [amɑ̃d] *nf* almond.

amant [amɑ̃] *nm* lover.

amarre [amar] *nf* (mooring) rope, hawser; *pl* moorings. ◆**amarrer** *vt* to moor; *Fig* to tie down, make fast.

amas [amɑ] *nm* heap, pile. ◆**amasser** *vt* to pile up; (*richesse, preuves*) to amass, gather; **— s'a.** *vpr* to pile up; (*gens*) to gather.

amateur [amatœr] *nm* (*d'art etc*) lover; *Sp* amateur; (*acheteur*) *Fam* taker; **d'a.** (*talent*) amateur; (*travail*) *Péj* amateurish; **une équipe a.** an amateur team. ◆**amateurisme** *nm Sp* amateurism; *Péj* amateurishness.

amazone [amazon] *nf* horsewoman; **monter en a.** to ride sidesaddle.

ambages (sans) [sɑ̃zɑ̃baʒ] *adv* to the point, in plain language.

ambassade [ɑ̃basad] *nf* embassy. ◆**ambassadeur, -drice** *nmf* ambassador.

ambiance [ɑ̃bjɑ̃s] *nf* atmosphere. ◆**ambiant** *a* surrounding.

ambigu, -guë [ɑ̃bigy] *a* ambiguous. ◆**ambiguïté** [-gɥite] *nf* ambiguity.

ambitieux, -euse [ɑ̃bisjø, -øz] *a* ambitious. ◆**ambition** *nf* ambition. ◆**ambitionner** *vt* to aspire to; **il ambitionne de** his ambition is to.

ambre [ɑ̃br] *nm* (*jaune*) amber; (*gris*) ambergris.

ambulance [ɑ̃bylɑ̃s] *nf* ambulance. ◆**ambulancier, -ière** *nmf* ambulance driver.

ambulant [ɑ̃bylɑ̃] *a* itinerant, travelling.

âme [ɑm] *nf* soul; **â. qui vive** a living soul; **état d'â.** state of mind; **â. sœur** soul mate; **â. damnée** evil genius, henchman; **avoir charge d'âmes** to be responsible for human life.

améliorer [ameljɔre] *vt*, **— s'a.** *vpr* to improve. ◆**amélioration** *nf* improvement.

amen [amɛn] *adv* amen.

aménag/er [amenaʒe] *vt* (*arranger, installer*) to fit up, fit out (**en** as); (*bateau*) to fit out; (*transformer*) to convert (**en** into); (*construire*) to set up; (*ajuster*) to adjust. ◆**—ement** *nm* fitting up; fitting out; conversion; setting up; adjustment.

amende [amɑ̃d] *nf* fine; **frapper d'une a.** to impose a fine on; **faire a. honorable** to make an apology.

amender [amɑ̃de] *vt Pol* to amend; (*terre*) to improve; **— s'a.** *vpr* to mend *ou* improve one's ways.

amener [amne] *vt* to bring; (*causer*) to bring about; **— s'a.** *vpr Fam* to come along, turn up.

amenuiser (s') [samənɥize] *vpr* to grow smaller, dwindle.

amer, -ère [amɛr] *a* bitter. ◆**amèrement** *adv* bitterly.

Amérique [amerik] *nf* America; **A. du Nord/du Sud** North/South America. ◆**américain, -aine** *a* & *nmf* American.

amerrir [amerir] *vi* to make a sea landing; (*cabine spatiale*) to splash down.

amertume [amertym] *nf* bitterness.

améthyste [ametist] *nf* amethyst.

ameublement [amœbləmɑ̃] *nm* furniture.

ameuter [amøte] *vt* (*soulever*) to stir up; (*attrouper*) to gather, muster; (*voisins*) to bring out; **— s'a.** *vpr* to gather, muster.

ami, -e [ami] *nmf* friend; (*des livres, de la nature etc*) lover (**de** of); **petit a.** boyfriend; **petite amie** girlfriend; **— a** friendly.

amiable (à l') [alamjɑbl] *a* amicable; **— adv** amicably.

amiante [amjɑ̃t] *nm* asbestos.

amical, -aux [amikal, -o] *a* friendly. ◆**—ement** *adv* in a friendly manner.

amicale [amikal] *nf* association.

amidon [amidɔ̃] *nm* starch. ◆**amidonner** *vt* to starch.

amincir [amɛ̃sir] *vt* to make thin(ner); **— vi** (*personne*) to slim; **— s'a.** *vpr* to become thinner.

amiral, -aux [amiral, -o] *nm* admiral. ◆**amirauté** *nf* admiralty.

amitié [amitje] *nf* friendship; (*amabilité*) kindness; *pl* kind regrds; **prendre en a.** to take a liking to.

ammoniac [amɔnjak] *nm* (*gaz*) ammonia. ◆**ammoniaque** *nf* (*liquide*) ammonia.

amnésie [amnezi] *nf* amnesia.

amnistie [amnisti] *nf* amnesty.

amocher [amɔʃe] *vt Arg* to mess up, bash.

amoindrir [amwɛ̃drir] vt, — s'a. vpr to decrease, diminish.

amoll/ir [amɔlir] vt to soften; (affaiblir) to weaken. ◆—issant a enervating.

amonceler [amɔ̃sle] vt, — s'a. vpr to pile up. ◆amoncellement nm heap, pile.

amont (en) [ɑ̃namɔ̃] adv upstream.

amoral, -aux [amɔral, -o] a amoral.

amorce [amɔrs] nf (début) start; Pêche bait; (détonateur) fuse, detonator; (de pistolet d'enfant) cap. ◆amorcer vt to start; (hameçon) to bait; (pompe) to prime; — s'a. vpr to start.

amorphe [amɔrf] a listless, apathetic.

amort/ir [amɔrtir] vt (coup) to cushion, absorb; (bruit) to deaden; (dette) to pay off; il a vite amorti sa voiture his car has been made to pay for itself quickly. ◆—issement nm Fin redemption. ◆—isseur nm shock absorber.

amour [amur] nm love; (liaison) romance, love; (Cupidon) Cupid; pour l'a. de for the sake of; mon a. my darling, my love. ◆a.-propre nm self-respect, self-esteem. ◆s'amouracher vpr Péj to become infatuated (de with). ◆amoureux, -euse nm lover; — a amorous, loving; a. de (personne) in love with; (gloire) Fig enamoured of.

amovible [amɔvibl] a removable, detachable.

ampère [ɑ̃pɛr] nm Él amp(ere).

amphi [ɑ̃fi] nm Univ Fam lecture hall.

amphibie [ɑ̃fibi] a amphibious; — nm amphibian.

amphithéâtre [ɑ̃fiteatr] nm Hist amphitheatre; Univ lecture hall.

ample [ɑ̃pl] a (vêtement) ample, roomy; (provision) full; (vues) broad. ◆amplement adv amply, fully; a. suffisant ample. ◆ampleur nf (de robe) fullness; (importance, étendue) scale, extent; prendre de l'a. to grow.

amplifier [ɑ̃plifje] vt (accroître) to develop; (exagérer) to magnify; (son, courant) to amplify; — s'a. vpr to increase. ◆amplificateur nm amplifier. ◆amplification nf (extension) scale.

amplitude [ɑ̃plityd] nf Fig magnitude.

ampoule [ɑ̃pul] nf (électrique) (light) bulb; (aux pieds etc) blister; (de médicament) phial.

ampoulé [ɑ̃pule] a turgid.

amputer [ɑ̃pyte] vt 1 (membre) to amputate; a. qn de la jambe to amputate s.o.'s leg. 2 (texte) to curtail, cut (de by).

◆amputation nf amputation; curtailment.

amuse-gueule [amyzgœl] nm inv cocktail snack, appetizer.

amus/er [amyze] vt (divertir) to amuse, entertain; (occuper) to divert the attention of; — s'a. vpr to enjoy oneself, have fun; (en chemin) to dawdle, loiter; s'a. avec to play with; s'a. à faire to amuse oneself doing. ◆—ant a amusing. ◆—ement nm amusement; (jeu) game. ◆amusette nf frivolous pursuit.

amygdale [amidal] nf tonsil.

an [ɑ̃] nm year; il a dix ans he's ten (years old); par a. per annum, per year; bon a., mal a. putting the good years and the bad together; Nouvel A. New Year.

anachronisme [anakrɔnism] nm anachronism.

anagramme [anagram] nf anagram.

analogie [analɔʒi] nf analogy. ◆analogue a similar; — nm analogue.

analphabète [analfabɛt] a & nmf illiterate. ◆analphabétisme nm illiteracy.

analyse [analiz] nf analysis; a. grammaticale parsing. ◆analyser vt to analyse; (phrase) to parse. ◆analytique a analytic(al).

ananas [anana(s)] nm pineapple.

anarchie [anarʃi] nf anarchy. ◆anarchique a anarchic. ◆anarchiste nmf anarchist; — a anarchistic.

anathème [anatɛm] nm Rel anathema.

anatomie [anatɔmi] nf anatomy. ◆anatomique a anatomical.

ancestral, -aux [ɑ̃sɛstral, -o] a ancestral.

ancêtre [ɑ̃sɛtr] nm ancestor.

anche [ɑ̃ʃ] nf Mus reed.

anchois [ɑ̃ʃwa] nm anchovy.

ancien, -ienne [ɑ̃sjɛ̃, -jɛn] a (vieux) old; (meuble) antique; (qui n'est plus) former, ex-, old; (antique) ancient; (dans une fonction) senior; a. élève old boy, Am alumnus; a. combattant ex-serviceman, Am veteran; — nmf (par l'âge) elder; (dans une fonction) senior; les anciens (auteurs, peuples) the ancients. ◆anciennement adv formerly. ◆ancienneté nf age; (dans une fonction) seniority.

ancre [ɑ̃kr] nf anchor; jeter l'a. to (cast) anchor; lever l'a. to weigh anchor. ◆ancrer vt Nau to anchor; (idée) Fig to root, fix; ancré dans rooted in.

andouille [ɑ̃duj] nf sausage (made from chitterlings); espèce d'a.! Fam (you) nitwit!

âne [ɑn] nm (animal) donkey, ass; (personne) Péj ass; bonnet d'â. dunce's cap; **dos d'â.** (*d'une route*) hump; **pont en dos d'â.** humpback bridge.

anéant/ir [aneãtir] *vt* to annihilate, wipe out, destroy; **— s'a.** *vpr* to vanish. **◆—i** *a* (*épuisé*) exhausted; (*stupéfait*) dismayed; (*accablé*) overwhelmed. **◆—issement** *nm* annihilation; (*abattement*) dejection.

anecdote [anɛkdɔt] *nf* anecdote. **◆anecdotique** *a* anecdotal.

anémie [anemi] *nf* an(a)emia. **◆anémique** *a* an(a)emic. **◆s'anémier** *vpr* to become an(a)emic.

anémone [anemɔn] *nf* anemone.

ânerie [ɑnri] *nf* stupidity; (*action etc*) stupid thing. **◆ânesse** *nf* she-ass.

anesthésie [anɛstezi] *nf* an(a)esthesia; **a. générale/locale** general/local an(a)es-thetic. **◆anesthésier** *vt* to an(a)esthetize. **◆anesthésique** *nm* an(a)esthetic.

anfractuosité [ɑ̃fraktɥozite] *nf* crevice, cleft.

ange [ɑ̃ʒ] *nm* angel; **aux anges** in seventh heaven. **◆angélique** *a* angelic.

angélus [ɑ̃ʒelys] *nm* Rel angelus.

angine [ɑ̃ʒin] *nf* sore throat; **a. de poitrine** angina (pectoris).

anglais, -aise [ɑ̃glɛ, -ɛz] *a* English; **—** *nmf* Englishman, Englishwoman; **—** *nm* (*langue*) English; **filer à l'anglaise** to take French leave.

angle [ɑ̃gl] *nm* (*point de vue*) & Géom angle; (*coin*) corner.

Angleterre [ɑ̃glətɛr] *nf* England.

anglican, -ane [ɑ̃glikɑ̃, -an] *a* & *nmf* Anglican.

anglicisme [ɑ̃glisism] *nm* Anglicism. **◆angliciste** *nmf* English specialist.

anglo- [ɑ̃glo] *préf* Anglo-. **◆anglo-normand** *a* Anglo-Norman; **îles a.-normandes** Channel Islands. **◆anglophile** *a* & *nmf* anglophile. **◆anglophone** *a* English-speaking; **—** *nmf* English speaker. **◆anglo-saxon, -onne** *a* & *nmf* Anglo-Saxon.

angoisse [ɑ̃gwas] *nf* anguish. **◆angoissant** *a* distressing. **◆angoissé** *a* (*personne*) in anguish; (*geste, cri*) anguished.

angora [ɑ̃gɔra] *nm* (*laine*) angora.

anguille [ɑ̃gij] *nf* eel.

angulaire [ɑ̃gylɛr] *a* **pierre a.** cornerstone. **◆anguleux, -euse** *a* (*visage*) angular.

anicroche [anikrɔʃ] *nf* hitch, snag.

animal, -aux [animal, -o] *nm* animal; (*personne*) Péj brute, animal; **—** *a* animal. **◆animer** [anime] *vt* (*inspirer*) to animate; (*encourager*) to spur on; (*débat, groupe*) to

lead; (*soirée*) to enliven; (*regard*) to light up, brighten up; (*mécanisme*) to actuate, drive; **à la course** Sp to set the pace; **animé de** (*sentiment*) prompted by; **— s'a.** *vpr* (*rue etc*) to come to life; (*yeux*) to light up, brighten up. **◆animé** *a* (*rue*) lively; (*conversation*) animated, lively; (*doué de vie*) animate. **◆animateur, -trice** *nmf* TV compere, Am master of ceremonies, emcee; (*de club*) leader, organizer; (*d'entreprise*) driving force, spirit. **◆animation** *nf* (*des rues*) activity; (*de réunion*) liveliness; (*de visage*) brightness; Cin animation.

animosité [animozite] *nf* animosity.

anis [ani(s)] *nm* (*boisson, parfum*) aniseed. **◆anisette** *nf* (*liqueur*) anisette.

ankylose [ɑ̃kiloz] *nf* stiffening. **◆s'ankylos/er** *vpr* to stiffen up. **◆—é** *a* stiff.

annales [anal] *nfpl* annals.

anneau, -x [ano] *nm* ring; (*de chaîne*) link.

année [ane] *nf* year; **bonne a.!** Happy New Year!

annexe [anɛks] *nf* (*bâtiment*) annex(e); **—** *a* (*pièces*) appended; **bâtiment a.** annex(e). **◆annexer** *vt* (*pays*) to annex; (*document*) to append. **◆annexion** *nf* annexation.

annihiler [aniile] *vt* to destroy, annihilate.

anniversaire [aniversɛr] *nm* (*d'événement*) anniversary; (*de naissance*) birthday; **—** *a* anniversary.

annonce [anɔ̃s] *nf* (*avis*) announcement; (*publicitaire*) advertisement; (*indice*) sign; **petites annonces** classified advertisements, small ads. **◆annoncer** *vt* (*signaler*) to announce, report; (*être l'indice de*) to indicate; (*vente*) to advertise; **a. le printemps** to herald spring; **s'a. pluvieux/difficile/**etc to look like being rainy/difficult/etc. **◆annonceur** *nm* advertiser; Rad TV announcer.

annonciation [anɔ̃sjasjɔ̃] *nf* Annunciation.

annoter [anɔte] *vt* to annotate. **◆annotation** *nf* annotation.

annuaire [anɥɛr] *nm* yearbook; (*téléphonique*) directory, phone book.

annuel, -elle [anɥɛl] *a* annual, yearly. **◆annuellement** *adv* annually. **◆annuité** *nf* annual instalment.

annulaire [anylɛr] *nm* ring or third finger.

annuler [anyle] *vt* (*visite etc*) to cancel; (*mariage*) to annul; (*jugement*) to quash; **— s'a.** *vpr* to cancel each other out. **◆annulation** *nf* cancellation; annulment; quashing.

anoblir [anɔblir] *vt* to ennoble.

anodin [anɔdɛ̃] a harmless; (remède) ineffectual.

anomalie [anɔmali] nf (irrégularité) anomaly; (difformité) abnormality.

ânonner [anɔne] vt (en hésitant) to stumble through; (d'une voix monotone) to drone out.

anonymat [anɔnima] nm anonymity; garder l'a. to remain anonymous. ◆**anonyme** a & nmf anonymous (person).

anorak [anɔrak] nm anorak.

anorexie [anɔreksi] nf anorexia.

anormal, -aux [anɔrmal, -o] a abnormal; (enfant) educationally subnormal.

anse [ãs] nf (de tasse etc) handle; (baie) cove.

antagonisme [ãtagɔnism] nm antagonism. ◆**antagoniste** a antagonistic; – nmf antagonist.

antan (d') [dãtã] a Litt of yesteryear.

antarctique [ãtarktik] a antarctic; – nm l'A. the Antarctic, Antarctica.

antécédent [ãtesedã] nm Gram antecedent; pl past history, antecedents.

antenne [ãten] nf TV Rad aerial, Am antenna; (station) station; (d'insecte) antenna, feeler; **a. chirurgicale** surgical outpost; Aut emergency unit; **sur ou à l'a.** on the air.

antérieur [ãterjœr] a (précédent) former, previous, earlier; (placé devant) front; **membre a.** forelimb; **a. à** prior to. ◆**antérieurement** adv previously. ◆**antériorité** nf precedence.

anthologie [ãtɔlɔʒi] nf anthology.

anthropologie [ãtrɔpɔlɔʒi] nf anthropology.

anthropophage [ãtrɔpɔfaʒ] nm cannibal. ◆**anthropophagie** nf cannibalism.

antiaérien, -ienne [ãtiaerjɛ̃, -jɛn] a (canon) antiaircraft; (abri) air-raid.

antiatomique [ãtiatɔmik] a **abri a.** fallout shelter.

antibiotique [ãtibjɔtik] a & nm antibiotic.

antibrouillard [ãtibrujar] a & nm (phare) **a.** fog lamp.

anticancéreux, -euse [ãtikãserø, -øz] a **centre a.** cancer hospital.

antichambre [ãtiʃãbr] nf antechamber, anteroom.

antichoc [ãtiʃɔk] a inv shockproof.

anticip/er [ãtisipe] vti **a. (sur)** to anticipate. ◆**-é** a (retraite etc) early; (paiement) advance; **avec mes remerciements anticipés** thanking you in advance. ◆**anticipation** nf anticipation; **par a.** in advance; **d'a.** (roman etc) science-fiction.

anticlérical, -aux [ãtiklerikal, -o] a anticlerical.

anticonformiste [ãtikɔ̃fɔrmist] a & nmf nonconformist.

anticonstitutionnel, -elle [ãtikɔ̃stitysjɔnɛl] a unconstitutional.

anticorps [ãtikɔr] nm antibody.

anticyclone [ãtisiklon] nm anticyclone.

antidater [ãtidate] vt to backdate, antedate.

antidémocratique [ãtidemɔkratik] a undemocratic.

antidérapant [ãtiderapã] a non-skid.

antidote [ãtidɔt] nm antidote.

antigel [ãtiʒɛl] nm antifreeze.

Antilles [ãtij] nfpl **les A.** the West Indies. ◆**antillais, -aise** a & nmf West Indian.

antilope [ãtilɔp] nf antelope.

antimite [ãtimit] a mothproof; – nm mothproofing agent.

antiparasite [ãtiparazit] a **dispositif a.** Rad suppressor.

antipathie [ãtipati] nf antipathy. ◆**antipathique** a disagreeable.

antipodes [ãtipɔd] nmpl **aux a.** (partir) to the antipodes; **aux a. de** at the opposite end of the world from; Fig poles apart from.

antique [ãtik] a ancient. ◆**antiquaire** nmf antique dealer. ◆**antiquité** nf (temps, ancienneté) antiquity; (objet ancien) antique; pl (monuments etc) antiquities.

antirabique [ãtirabik] a (anti-)rabies.

antisémite [ãtisemit] a anti-Semitic. ◆**antisémitisme** nm anti-Semitism.

antiseptique [ãtisɛptik] a & nm antiseptic.

antisudoral, -aux [ãtisydɔral, -o] nm antiperspirant.

antithèse [ãtitɛz] nf antithesis.

antivol [ãtivɔl] nm anti-theft lock ou device.

antonyme [ãtɔnim] nm antonym.

antre [ãtr] nm (de lion etc) den.

anus [anys] nm anus.

Anvers [ãver(s)] nm ou f Antwerp.

anxiété [ãksjete] nf anxiety. ◆**anxieux, -euse** a anxious; – nmf worrier.

août [u(t)] nm August. ◆**aoûtien, -ienne** [ausjɛ̃, -jɛn] nmf August holidaymaker ou Am vacationer.

apais/er [apeze] vt (personne) to appease, calm; (scrupules, faim) to appease; (douleur) to allay; – **s'a.** (personne) to calm down. ◆**-ant** a soothing. ◆**-ements** nmpl reassurances.

apanage [apanaʒ] nm privilege, monopoly (de of).

aparté [aparte] nm Th aside; (dans une réunion) private exchange; **en a.** in private.

apartheid [aparted] nm apartheid.

apathie [apati] *nf* apathy. ◆**apathique** *a* apathetic, listless.

apatride [apatrid] *nmf* stateless person.

apercevoir* [apɛrsavwar] *vt* to see, perceive; (*brièvement*) to catch a glimpse of; **s'a. de** to notice, realize. ◆**aperçu** *nm* overall view, general outline; (*intuition*) insight.

apéritif [aperitif] *nm* aperitif. ◆**apéro** *nm Fam* aperitif.

apesanteur [apəzɑ̃tœr] *nf* weightlessness.

à-peu-près [apøprɛ] *nm inv* vague approximation.

apeuré [apœre] *a* frightened, scared.

aphone [afɔn] *a* voiceless.

aphorisme [afɔrism] *nm* aphorism.

aphrodisiaque [afrɔdizjak] *a* & *nm* aphrodisiac.

aphte [aft] *nm* mouth ulcer. ◆**aphteuse** *af* fièvre a. foot-and-mouth disease.

apiculture [apikyltyr] *nf* bee keeping.

apit/oyer [apitwaje] *vt* to move (to pity); **s'a. sur** to pity. ◆**—oiement** *nm* pity, commiseration.

aplanir [aplanir] *vt* (*terrain*) to level; (*difficulté*) to iron out, smooth out.

aplat/ir [aplatir] *vt* to flatten (out); — **s'a.** *vpr* (*s'étendre*) to lie flat; (*s'humilier*) to grovel; (*tomber*) *Fam* to fall flat on one's face; **s'a. contre** to flatten oneself against. ◆**—i** *a* flat. ◆**—issement** *nm* (*état*) flatness.

aplomb [aplɔ̃] *nm* self-possession, self-assurance; *Péj* impudence; **d'a.** (*équilibré*) well-balanced; (*sur ses jambes*) steady; (*bien portant*) in good shape; **tomber d'a.** (*soleil*) to beat down.

apocalypse [apɔkalips] *nf* apocalypse; **d'a.** (*vision etc*) apocalyptic. ◆**apocalyptique** *a* apocalyptic.

apogée [apɔʒe] *nm* apogee; *Fig* peak, apogee.

apolitique [apɔlitik] *a* apolitical.

Apollon [apɔlɔ̃] *nm* Apollo.

apologie [apɔlɔʒi] *nf* defence, vindication. ◆**apologiste** *nmf* apologist.

apoplexie [apɔplɛksi] *nf* apoplexy. ◆**apoplectique** *a* apoplectic.

apostolat [apɔstɔla] *nm* (*prosélytisme*) proselytism; (*mission*) *Fig* calling. ◆**apostolique** *a* apostolic.

apostrophe [apɔstrɔf] *nf* **1** (*signe*) apostrophe. **2** (*interpellation*) sharp *ou* rude remark. ◆**apostropher** *vt* to shout at.

apothéose [apɔteoz] *nf* final triumph, apotheosis.

apôtre [apotr] *nm* apostle.

apparaître* [aparɛtr] *vi* (*se montrer, sembler*) to appear.

apparat [apara] *nm* pomp; **d'a.** (*tenue etc*) ceremonial, formal.

appareil [aparɛj] *nm* (*instrument etc*) apparatus; (*électrique*) appliance; *Anat* system; *Tél* telephone; (*avion*) aircraft; (*législatif etc*) *Pol* machinery; **a. (photo)** camera; **a. (auditif)** hearing aid; **a. (dentier)** brace; **qui est à l'a.?** *Tél* who's speaking?

appareiller [apareje] **1** *vi Nau* to get under way. **2** *vt* (*assortir*) to match (up).

apparence [aparɑ̃s] *nf* appearance; (*vestige*) semblance; **en a.** outwardly; **sous l'a. de** under the guise of; **sauver les apparences** to keep up appearances. ◆**apparemment** [-amɑ̃] *adv* apparently. ◆**apparent** *a* apparent; (*ostensible*) conspicuous.

apparent/er (s') [saparɑ̃te] *vpr* (*ressembler*) to be similar *ou* akin (à to). ◆**—é** *a* (*allié*) related; (*semblable*) similar.

appariteur [aparitœr] *nm Univ* porter.

apparition [aparisjɔ̃] *nf* appearance; (*spectre*) apparition.

appartement [apartəmɑ̃] *nm* flat, *Am* apartment.

appartenir* [apartənir] **1** *vi* to belong (à to); **il vous appartient de** it's your responsibility to. **2 s'a.** *vpr* to be one's own master. ◆**appartenance** *nf* membership (à of).

appât [apa] *nm* (*amorce*) bait; (*attrait*) lure. ◆**appâter** *vt* (*attirer*) to lure.

appauvrir [apovrir] *vt* to impoverish; — **s'a.** *vpr* to become impoverished *ou* poorer.

appel [apel] *nm* (*cri, attrait etc*) call; (*demande pressante*) & *Jur* appeal; *Mil* call-up; **faire l'a.** *Scol* to take the register; *Mil* to have a roll call; **faire a. à** to appeal to, call upon; (*requérir*) to call for.

appel/er [aple] *vt* (*personne, nom etc*) to call; (*en criant*) to call out to; *Mil* to call up; (*nécessiter*) to call for; **a. à l'aide** to call for help; **en a. à** to appeal to; **il est appelé à** (*de hautes fonctions*) he is marked out for; (*témoigner etc*) he is called upon to; — **s'a.** *vpr* to be called; **il s'appelle Paul** his name is Paul. ◆**—é** *nm Mil* conscript. ◆**appellation** *nf* (*nom*) term; **a. contrôlée** *trade name guaranteeing quality of wine.*

appendice [apɛ̃dis] *nm* appendix; (*d'animal*) appendage. ◆**appendicite** *nf* appendicitis.

appentis [apɑ̃ti] *nm* (*bâtiment*) lean-to.

appesantir (s') [sapazɑ̃tir] *vpr* to become heavier; **s'a. sur** (*sujet*) to dwell upon.

appétit [apeti] *nm* appetite (**de** for); **mettre**

qn en a. to whet s.o.'s appetite; **bon a.!** enjoy your meal! ◆**appétissant** a appetizing.

applaud/ir [aplodir] vti to applaud, clap; **a. à** (approuver) to applaud. ◆**—issements** nmpl applause.

applique [aplik] nf wall lamp.

appliqu/er [aplike] vt to apply (à to); (surnom, baiser, gifle) to give; (loi, décision) to put into effect; **s'a. à** (un travail) to apply oneself to; (concerner) to apply to; **s'a. à faire** to take pains to do. ◆**—é** a (travailleur) painstaking; (sciences) applied. ◆**applicable** a applicable. ◆**application** nf application.

appoint [apwɛ̃] nm contribution; **faire l'a.** to give the correct money ou change.

appointements [apwɛ̃tmã] nmpl salary.

appointement [apõtmã] nm landing stage.

apport [apɔr] nm contribution.

apporter [apɔrte] vt to bring.

apposer [apoze] vt Jur to affix. ◆**apposition** nf Gram apposition.

apprécier [apresje] vt (évaluer) to appraise; (aimer, percevoir) to appreciate. ◆**appréciable** a appreciable. ◆**appréciation** nf appraisal; appreciation.

appréhender [apreɑ̃de] vt (craindre) to fear; (arrêter) to apprehend. ◆**appréhension** nf apprehension.

apprendre* [aprɑ̃dr] vti (étudier) to learn; (événement, fait) to hear of, learn of; (nouvelle) to hear; **a. à faire** to learn to do; **a. qch à qn** (enseigner) to teach s.o. sth; (informer) to tell s.o. sth; **a. à qn à faire** to teach s.o. to do; **a. que** to learn that; (être informé) to hear that.

apprenti, -ie [aprɑ̃ti] nmf apprentice; (débutant) novice. ◆**apprentissage** nm apprenticeship; **faire l'a. de** Fig to learn the experience of.

apprêt/er [aprete] vt, **— s'a.** vpr to prepare. ◆**—é** a Fig affected.

apprivois/er [aprivwaze] vt to tame; **— s'a.** vpr to become tame. ◆**—é** a tame.

approbation [aprɔbasjɔ̃] nf approval. ◆**approbateur, -trice** a approving.

approche [aprɔʃ] nf approach. ◆**approch/er** vt (chaise etc) to bring up, draw up (de to, close to); (personne) to approach, come close to; — vi to approach, come close to; — vi to approach; **a. de, s'a. de** to approach, come close(r) ou near(er) to. ◆**—ant** a similar. ◆**—é** a approximate. ◆**—able** a approachable.

approfond/ir [aprɔfɔ̃dir] vt (trou etc) to deepen; (question) to go into thoroughly;

(mystère) to plumb the depths of. ◆**—i** a thorough. ◆**—issement** nm deepening; (examen) thorough examination.

approprié [aprɔprije] a appropriate.

approprier (s') [saprɔprije] vpr **s'a.** qch to appropriate sth.

approuver [apruve] vt (autoriser) to approve; (apprécier) to approve of.

approvisionn/er [aprɔvizjɔne] vt (ville etc) to supply (with provisions); (magasin) to stock; **— s'a.** vpr to stock up (de with), get one's supplies (de of). ◆**—ements** nmpl stocks, supplies.

approximat/if, -ive [aprɔksimatif, -iv] a approximate. ◆**—ivement** adv approximately. ◆**approximation** nf approximation.

appui [apɥi] nm support; (pour coude etc) rest; (de fenêtre) sill; **à hauteur d'a.** breast-high. ◆**appuie-tête** nm inv headrest. ◆**appuyer** vt (soutenir) to support; (accentuer) to stress; **a. qch sur** (poser) to lean ou rest sth on; (presser) to press sth on; — vi **a. sur** to rest on; (bouton etc) to press (on); (mot, élément etc) to stress; **s'a. sur** to lean on, rest on; (compter) to rely on; (se baser) to base oneself on.

âpre [ɑpr] a harsh, rough; **a. au gain** grasping.

après [aprɛ] prép (temps) after; (espace) beyond; **a. un an** after a year; **a. le pont** beyond the bridge; **a. coup** after the event; **a. avoir mangé** after eating; **a. qu'il t'a vu** after he saw you; **d'a.** (selon) according to, from; — adv after(wards); **l'année d'a.** the following year; **et a.?** and then what?

après-demain [apredmɛ̃] adv the day after tomorrow. ◆**a.-guerre** nm post-war period; **d'a.-guerre** post-war. ◆**a.-midi** nm ou f inv afternoon. ◆**a.-shampooing** nm (hair) conditioner. ◆**a.-ski** nm ankle boot, snow boot.

a priori [aprijɔri] adv at the very outset, without going into the matter; — nm inv assumption.

à-propos [apropo] nm timeliness, aptness.

apte [apt] a suited (à to), capable (à of). ◆**aptitude** nf aptitude, capacity (à, pour for).

aquarelle [akwarɛl] nf watercolour, aquarelle.

aquarium [akwarjɔm] nm aquarium.

aquatique [akwatik] a aquatic.

aqueduc [akdyk] nm aqueduct.

aquilin [akilɛ̃] a aquiline.

arabe [arab] a & nmf Arab; — a & nm (langue) Arabic; **chiffres arabes** Arabic

numerals; **désert a.** Arabian desert.
◆**Arabie** nf Arabia; **A. Séoudite** Saudi Arabia.

arabesque [arabɛsk] nf arabesque.

arable [arabl] a arable.

arachide [araʃid] nf peanut, groundnut.

araignée [arɛɲe] nf spider.

arbalète [arbalɛt] nf crossbow.

arbitraire [arbitrɛr] a arbitrary.

arbitre [arbitr] nm Jur arbitrator; (maître absolu) arbiter; Fb referee; Tennis umpire; **libre a.** free will. ◆**arbitr/er** vt to arbitrate; to referee; to umpire. ◆**—age** nm arbitration; refereeing; umpiring.

arborer [arbɔre] vt (insigne, vêtement) to sport, display.

arbre [arbr] nm tree; Aut shaft, axle. ◆**arbrisseau, -x** nm shrub. ◆**arbuste** nm (small) shrub, bush.

arc [ark] nm (arme) bow; (voûte) arch; Math arc; **tir à l'a.** archery. ◆**arcade** nf arch(way); pl arcade.

arc-boutant [arkbutã] nm (pl arcs-boutants) flying buttress. ◆**s'arc-bouter** vpr **s'a.** à ou contre to brace oneself against.

arceau, -x [arso] nm (de voûte) arch.

arc-en-ciel [arkãsjɛl] nm (pl arcs-en-ciel) rainbow.

archaïque [arkaik] a archaic.

archange [arkãʒ] nm archangel.

arche [arʃ] nf (voûte) arch; **l'a. de Noé** Noah's ark.

archéologie [arkeɔlɔʒi] nf arch(a)eology. ◆**archéologue** nmf arch(a)eologist.

archer [arʃe] nm archer, bowman.

archet [arʃɛ] nm Mus bow.

archétype [arketip] nm archetype.

archevêque [arʃəvɛk] nm archbishop.

archicomble [arʃikɔbl] a jam-packed.

archipel [arʃipɛl] nm archipelago.

archiplein [arʃiplɛ̃] a chock-full, chock-a-block.

architecte [arʃitɛkt] nm architect. ◆**architecture** nf architecture.

archives [arʃiv] nfpl archives, records. ◆**archiviste** nmf archivist.

arctique [arktik] a arctic; – nm **l'A.** the Arctic.

ardent [ardã] a (chaud) burning, scorching; (actif, passionné) ardent, fervent; (empressé) eager. ◆**ardemment** [-amã] adv eagerly, fervently. ◆**ardeur** nf heat; (énergie) ardour, fervour.

ardoise [ardwaz] nf slate.

ardu [ardy] a arduous, difficult.

are [ar] nm (mesure) 100 square metres.

arène [arɛn] nf Hist arena; (pour taureaux) bullring; pl Hist amphitheatre; bullring.

arête [arɛt] nf (de poisson) bone; (de cube etc) & Géog ridge.

argent [arʒã] nm (métal) silver; (monnaie) money; **a. comptant** cash. ◆**argenté** a (plaqué) silver-plated; (couleur) silvery. ◆**argenterie** nf silverware.

Argentine [arʒãtin] nf Argentina. ◆**argentin, -ine** a & nmf Argentinian.

argile [arʒil] nf clay. ◆**argileux, -euse** a clayey.

argot [argo] nm slang. ◆**argotique** a (terme) slang.

arguer [argɥe] vi **a. de qch** to put forward sth as an argument; **a. que** (protester) to protest that. ◆**argumentation** nf argumentation, arguments. ◆**argumenter** vi to argue.

argument [argymã] nm argument.

argus [argys] nm guide to secondhand cars.

argutie [argysi] nf specious argument, quibble.

aride [arid] a arid, barren.

aristocrate [aristokrat] nmf aristocrat. ◆**aristocratie** [-asi] nf aristocracy. ◆**aristocratique** a aristocratic.

arithmétique [aritmetik] nf arithmetic; – a arithmetical.

arlequin [arləkɛ̃] nm harlequin.

armateur [armatœr] nm shipowner.

armature [armatyr] nf (charpente) framework; (de lunettes, tente) frame.

arme [arm] nf arm, weapon; **a. à feu** firearm; **carrière des armes** military career. ◆**arm/er** vt (personne etc) to arm (de with); (fusil) to cock; (appareil photo) to wind on; (navire) to equip; (béton) to reinforce; – **s'a.** vpr to arm oneself (de with). ◆**—ement(s)** nm(pl) arms.

armée [arme] nf army; **a. active/de métier** regular/professional army; **a. de l'air** air force.

armistice [armistis] nm armistice.

armoire [armwar] nf cupboard, Am closet; (penderie) wardrobe, Am closet; **a. à pharmacie** medicine cabinet.

armoiries [armwari] nfpl (coat of) arms.

armure [armyr] nf armour.

armurier [armyrje] nm gunsmith.

arôme [arom] nm aroma. ◆**aromate** nm spice. ◆**aromatique** a aromatic.

arpent/er [arpãte] vt (terrain) to survey; (trottoir etc) to pace up and down. ◆**—eur** nm (land) surveyor.

arqué [arke] a arched, curved; (jambes) bandy.

arrache-pied (d') [daraʃpje] *adv* unceasingly, relentlessly.

arrach/er [araʃe] *vt* (*clou, dent etc*) to pull out; (*cheveux, page*) to tear out, pull out; (*plante*) to pull up; (*masque*) to tear off, pull off; **a. qch à qn** to snatch sth from s.o.; (*aveu, argent*) to force sth out of s.o.; **a. un bras à qn** (*obus etc*) to blow s.o.'s arm off; **a. qn de son lit** to drag s.o. out of bed. ◆**—age** *nm* (*de plante*) pulling up.

arraisonner [arezɔne] *vt* (*navire*) to board and examine.

arrang/er [arɑ̃ʒe] *vt* (*chambre, visite etc*) to arrange, fix up; (*voiture, texte*) to put right; (*différend*) to settle; **a. qn** (*maltraiter*) *Fam* to fix s.o.; **ça m'arrange** that suits me (fine); **— s'a.** *vpr* (*se réparer*) to be put right; (*se mettre d'accord*) to come to an agreement *ou* arrangement; (*finir bien*) to turn out fine; **s'a. pour faire** to arrange to do, manage to do. ◆**—eant** *a* accommodating. ◆**—ement** *nm* arrangement.

arrestation [arestasjɔ̃] *nf* arrest.

arrêt [are] *nm* (*halte, endroit*) stop; (*action*) stopping; pause; *Méd* arrest; *Jur* decree; **temps d'a.** pause; **à l'a.** stationary; **a. de travail** (*grève*) stoppage; (*congé*) sick leave; **sans a.** constantly, non-stop.

arrêté [arete] *nm* order, decision.

arrêt/er [arete] *vt* to stop; (*appréhender*) to arrest; (*regard, jour*) to fix; (*plan*) to draw up; **— vi** to stop; **il n'arrête pas de critiquer/***etc* he doesn't stop criticizing/*etc*, he's always criticizing/*etc*; **— s'a.** *vpr* to stop; **s'a. de faire** to stop doing. ◆**—é** *a* (*projet*) fixed; (*volonté*) firm.

arrhes [ar] *nfpl Fin* deposit.

arrière [arjer] *adv* **en a.** (*marcher*) backwards; (*rester*) behind; (*regarder*) back; **en a. de qn/qch** behind s.o./sth; **— nm & a inv** rear, back; **— nm Fb** (full) back; **faire marche a.** to reverse, back.

arrière-boutique [arjerbutik] *nm* back room (*of a shop*). ◆**a.-garde** *nf* rearguard. ◆**a.-goût** *nm* aftertaste. ◆**a.-grand-mère** *nf* great-grand-mother. ◆**a.-grand-père** *nm* (*pl* **arrière-grands-pères**) great-grand-father. ◆**a.-pays** *nm* hinterland. ◆**a.-pensée** *nf* ulterior motive. ◆**a.-plan** *nm* background. ◆**a.-saison** *nf* end of season, (late) autumn. ◆**a.-train** *nm* hindquarters.

arriéré [arjere] **1** *a* (*enfant*) (mentally) retarded; (*idée*) backward. **2** *nm* (*dette*) arrears.

arrimer [arime] *vt* (*fixer*) to rope down, secure.

arriv/er [arive] *vi* (*aux être*) (*venir*) to arrive, come; (*réussir*) to succeed; (*survenir*) to happen; **a. à** (*atteindre*) to reach; **a. à faire** to manage to do, succeed in doing; **a. à qn** to happen to s.o.; **il m'arrive d'oublier/***etc* I happen (sometimes) to forget/*etc*, I (sometimes) forget/*etc*; **en a. à faire** to get to the point of doing. ◆**—ant, -ante** *nmf* new arrival. ◆**—ée** *nf* arrival; *Sp* (winning) post. ◆**—age** *nm* consignment. ◆**arriviste** *nmf Péj* social climber, self-seeker.

arrogant [arɔgɑ̃] *a* arrogant. ◆**arrogance** *nf* arrogance.

arroger (s') [aroʒe] *vpr* (*droit etc*) to assume (falsely).

arrond/ir [arɔ̃dir] *vt* to make round; (*somme, chiffre*) to round off. ◆**—i** *a* rounded.

arrondissement [arɔ̃dismɑ̃] *nm* (*d'une ville*) district.

arros/er [aroze] *vt* (*terre*) to water; (*repas*) to wash down; (*succès*) to drink to. ◆**—age** *nm* watering; *Fam* booze-up, celebration. ◆**arrosoir** *nm* watering can.

arsenal, -aux [arsənal, -o] *nm Nau* dockyard; *Mil* arsenal.

arsenic [arsənik] *nm* arsenic.

art [ar] *nm* art; **film/critique d'a.** art film/critic; **arts ménagers** domestic science.

artère [arter] *nf* *Anat* artery; *Aut* main road. ◆**artériel, -elle** *a* arterial.

artichaut [artiʃo] *nm* artichoke.

article [artikl] *nm* (*de presse, de commerce*) & *Gram* article; (*dans un contrat, catalogue*) item; **a. de fond** feature (article); **articles de toilette/de voyage** toilet/travel requisites; **à l'a. de la mort** at death's door.

articuler [artikyle] *vt* (*mot etc*) to articulate; **— s'a.** *vpr Anat* to articulate; *Fig* to connect. ◆**articulation** *nf Ling* articulation; *Anat* joint; **a. du doigt** knuckle.

artifice [artifis] *nm* trick, contrivance; **feu d'a.** (*spectacle*) fireworks, firework display.

artificiel, -elle [artifisjel] *a* artificial. ◆**artificiellement** *adv* artificially.

artillerie [artijri] *nf* artillery. ◆**artilleur** *nm* gunner.

artisan [artizɑ̃] *nm* craftsman, artisan. ◆**artisanal, -aux** *a* (*métier*) craftsman's. ◆**artisanat** *nm* (*métier*) craftsman's trade; (*classe*) artisan class.

artiste [artist] *nmf* artist; *Th Mus Cin* performer, artist. ◆**artistique** *a* artistic.

as [as] *nm* (*carte, champion*) ace; **a. du volant** crack driver.

ascendant [asɑ̃dɑ̃] *a* ascending, upward; – *nm* ascendancy, power; *pl* ancestors. ◆**ascendance** *nf* ancestry.

ascenseur [asɑ̃sœr] *nm* lift, *Am* elevator.

ascension [asɑ̃sjɔ̃] *nf* ascent; **l'A.** Ascension Day.

ascète [asɛt] *nmf* ascetic. ◆**ascétique** *a* ascetic. ◆**ascétisme** *nm* asceticism.

Asie [azi] *nf* Asia. ◆**Asiate** *nmf* Asian. ◆**asiatique** *a* & *nmf* Asian, Asiatic.

asile [azil] *nm* (*abri*) refuge, shelter; (*pour vieillards*) home; *Pol* asylum; **a. (d'aliénés)** *Péj* (lunatic) asylum; **a. de paix** haven of peace.

aspect [aspɛ] *nm* (*vue*) sight; (*air*) appearance; (*perspective*) & *Gram* aspect.

asperge [aspɛrʒ] *nf* asparagus.

asperger [aspɛrʒe] *vt* to spray, sprinkle (**de** with).

aspérité [asperite] *nf* rugged edge, bump.

asphalte [asfalt] *nm* asphalt.

asphyxie [asfiksi] *nf* suffocation. ◆**asphyxier** *vt* to suffocate, asphyxiate.

aspic [aspik] *nm* (*vipère*) asp.

aspirant [aspirɑ̃] *nm* (*candidat*) candidate.

aspirateur [aspiratœr] *nm* vacuum cleaner, hoover®; **passer (à) l'a.** to vacuum, hoover.

aspir/er [aspire] *vt* (*respirer*) to breathe in, inhale; (*liquide*) to suck up; **a. à** to aspire to. ◆**–é** *a Ling* aspirate(d). ◆**aspiration** *nf* inhaling; suction; (*ambition*) aspiration.

aspirine [aspirin] *nf* aspirin.

assagir (s') [sasaʒir] *vpr* to sober (down), settle down.

assaill/ir [asajir] *vt* to assault, attack; **a. de** (*questions etc*) to assail with. ◆**–ant** *nm* assailant, attacker.

assainir [asenir] *vt* (*purifier*) to clean up; *Fin* to stabilize.

assaisonn/er [asɛzɔne] *vt* to season. ◆**–ement** *nm* seasoning.

assassin [asasɛ̃] *nm* murderer; assassin. ◆**assassinat** *nm* murder; assassination. ◆**assassiner** *vt* to murder; (*homme politique etc*) to assassinate.

assaut [aso] *nm* assault, onslaught; **prendre d'a.** to (take by) storm.

assécher [asefe] *vt* to drain.

assemblée [asɑ̃ble] *nf* (*personnes réunies*) gathering; (*réunion*) meeting; *Pol Jur* assembly; (*de fidèles*) *Rel* congregation.

assembl/er [asɑ̃ble] *vt* to assemble, put together; **– s'a.** *vpr* to assemble, gather. ◆**–age** *nm* (*montage*) assembly; (*réunion d'objets*) collection.

asséner [asene] *vt* (*coup*) to deal, strike.

assentiment [asɑ̃timɑ̃] *nm* assent, consent.

asseoir* [aswar] *vt* (*personne*) to sit (down), seat (**sur** on); (*fondations*) to lay; (*autorité, réputation*) to establish; **a. sur** (*théorie etc*) to base on; **– s'a.** *vpr* to sit (down).

assermenté [asɛrmɑ̃te] *a* sworn.

assertion [asɛrsjɔ̃] *nf* assertion.

asserv/ir [asɛrvir] *vt* to enslave. ◆**–issement** *nm* enslavement.

assez [ase] *adv* enough; **a. de pain/de gens** enough bread/people; **j'en ai a.** I've had enough; **a. grand/intelligent/***etc* (*suffisamment*) big/clever/*etc* enough (**pour** to); **a. fatigué/***etc* (*plutôt*) rather *ou* quite tired/*etc*.

assidu [asidy] *a* (*appliqué*) assiduous, diligent; **a. auprès de** attentive to. ◆**assiduité** *nf* assiduousness, diligence; (*empressement*) attentiveness. ◆**assidûment** *adv* assiduously.

assiég/er [asjeʒe] *vt* (*ville*) to besiege; (*guichet*) to mob, crowd round; (*importuner*) to pester, harry; **assiégé de** (*demandes*) besieged with; (*maux*) beset by. ◆**–eant, -eante** *nmf* besieger.

assiette [asjɛt] *nf* **1** (*récipient*) plate; **a. anglaise** *Culin* (assorted) cold meats, *Am* cold cuts. **2** (*à cheval*) seat; **il n'est pas dans son a.** he's feeling out of sorts.

assigner [asiɲe] *vt* (*attribuer*) to assign; *Jur* to summon, subpoena. ◆**assignation** *nf Jur* subpoena, summons.

assimiler [asimile] *vt* to assimilate; **– s'a.** *vpr* (*immigrants*) to assimilate, become assimilated (**à** with). ◆**assimilation** *nf* assimilation.

assis [asi] *a* sitting (down), seated; (*caractère*) settled; (*situation*) stable, secure.

assise [asiz] *nf* (*base*) *Fig* foundation; *pl* assizes; *Pol* congress; **cour d'assises** court of assizes.

assistance [asistɑ̃s] *nf* **1** (*assemblée*) audience; (*nombre de personnes présentes*) turn-out. **2** (*aide*) assistance; **l'A. (publique)** the child care service; **enfant de l'A.** child in care. ◆**assist/er** **1** *vt* (*aider*) to assist, help. **2** *vi* **a. à** (*réunion, cours etc*) to attend, be present at; (*accident*) to witness. ◆**–ant, -ante** *nmf* assistant; – *nmpl* (*spectateurs*) members of the audience; (*témoins*) those present; **assistante sociale** social worker; **assistante maternelle** mother's help.

associ/er [asɔsje] *vt* to associate (**à** with); **a. qn à** (*ses travaux, profits*) to involve s.o. in; **s'a.** (*collaborer*) to associate with, become associated with; (*aux vues ou au chagrin de qn*) to share; (*s'harmoniser*) to combine with. ◆—é, -ée *nmf* partner, associate; — *a* associate. ◆**association** *nf* association; *(amitié, alliance)* partnership, association.

assoiffé [aswafe] *a* thirsty (de).

assombrir [asɔ̃brir] *vt (obscurcir)* to darken; *(attrister)* to cast a cloud over, fill with gloom; — **s'a.** *vpr* to darken; to cloud over.

assomm/er [asɔme] *vt (animal)* to stun, brain; *(personne)* to knock unconscious; *(ennuyer)* to bore stiff. ◆—**ant** *a* tiresome, boring.

assomption [asɔ̃psjɔ̃] *nf* Rel Assumption.

assort/ir [asɔrtir] *vt*, — **s'a.** *vpr* to match. ◆—**i** *a* bien a. *(magasin)* well-stocked; — **apl** *(objets semblables)* matching; *(fromages etc variés)* assorted; **époux bien assortis** well-matched couple. ◆—**iment** *nm* assortment.

assoup/ir [asupir] *vt (personne)* to make drowsy; *(douleur, sentiment etc)* Fig to dull; — **s'a.** *vpr* to doze off; Fig to subside. ◆—**i** *a (personne)* drowsy. ◆—**issement** *nm* drowsiness.

assoupl/ir [asuplir] *vt (étoffe, muscles)* to make supple; *(corps)* to limber up; *(caractère)* to soften; *(règles)* to ease, relax. ◆—**issement** *nm* exercices d'a. limbering up exercises.

assourd/ir [asurdir] *vt (personne)* to deafen; *(son)* to muffle. ◆—**issant** *a* deafening.

assouvir [asuvir] *vt* to appease, satisfy.

assujet/ir [asyʒetir] *vt (soumettre)* to subject (à to); *(peuple)* to subjugate; *(fixer)* to secure; **s'a.** *à* to subject oneself to, submit to. ◆—**issant** *a (travail)* constraining. ◆—**issement** *nm* subjection; *(contrainte)* constraint.

assumer [asyme] *vt (tâche, rôle)* to assume, take on; *(emploi)* to take up, assume; *(remplir)* to fill, hold.

assurance [asyrɑ̃s] *nf (aplomb)* (self-)assurance; *(promesse)* assurance; *(contrat)* insurance; **a. au tiers/tous risques** third-party/comprehensive insurance; **assurances sociales** = national insurance, *Am* = social security.

assur/er [asyre] *vt (rendre sûr)* to ensure, *Am* insure; *(par un contrat)* to insure; *(travail etc)* to carry out; *(fixer)* to secure; **a. à qn que** to assure s.o. that; **a. qn de qch, a. qch à qn** to assure s.o. of sth; — **s'a.** *vpr (se procurer)* to ensure, secure; *(par un contrat)* to insure oneself, get insured **(contre** against); **s'a. que/de** to make sure that/of. ◆—**é, -ée** *a (succès)* assured, certain; *(pas)* firm, secure; *(air)*

(self-)assured, (self-)confident; — *nmf* policyholder, insured person. ◆—**ément** *adv* certainly, assuredly. ◆**assureur** *nm* insurer.

astérisque [asterisk] *nm* asterisk.

asthme [asm] *nm* asthma. ◆**asthmatique** *a & nmf* asthmatic.

asticot [astiko] *nm* maggot, worm.

astiquer [astike] *vt* to polish.

astre [astr] *nm* star.

astreindre* [astrɛ̃dr] *vt* a. à *(discipline)* to compel to accept; **a. à faire** to compel to do. ◆**astreignant** *a* exacting ◆**astreinte** *nf* constraint.

astrologie [astrɔlɔʒi] *nf* astrology. ◆**astrologue** *nm* astrologer.

astronaute [astronot] *nmf* astronaut. ◆**astronautique** *nf* space travel.

astronomie [astronɔmi] *nf* astronomy. ◆**astronome** *nm* astronomer. ◆**astronomique** *a* astronomical.

astuce [astys] *nf (pour faire qch)* knack, trick; *(invention)* gadget; *(plaisanterie)* clever joke, wisecrack; *(finesse)* astuteness; **les astuces du métier** the tricks of the trade. ◆**astucieux, -euse** *a* clever, astute.

atelier [atəlje] *nm (d'ouvrier)* workshop; *(de peintre)* studio.

atermoyer [atɛrmwaje] *vi* to procrastinate.

athée [ate] *a* atheistic; — *nmf* atheist. ◆**athéisme** *nm* atheism.

Athènes [atɛn] *nm ou f* Athens.

athlète [atlɛt] *nmf* athlete. ◆**athlétique** *a* athletic. ◆**athlétisme** *nm* athletics.

atlantique [atlɑ̃tik] *a* Atlantic; — *nm* l'A. the Atlantic.

atlas [atlɑs] *nm* atlas.

atmosphère [atmɔsfɛr] *nf* atmosphere. ◆**atmosphérique** *a* atmospheric.

atome [atom] *nm* atom. ◆**atomique** [atɔmik] *a* atomic; **bombe a.** atom *ou* atomic bomb.

atomis/er [atɔmize] *vt (liquide)* to spray; *(région)* to destroy *(by atomic weapons)*. ◆—**eur** *nm* spray.

atone [atɔn] *a (personne)* lifeless; *(regard)* vacant.

atours [atur] *nmpl Hum* finery.

atout [atu] *nm* trump (card); *(avantage)* Fig trump card, asset; **l'a. est cœur** hearts are trumps.

âtre [ɑtr] *nm (foyer)* hearth.

atroce [atrɔs] *a* atrocious; *(crime)* heinous, atrocious. ◆**atrocité** *nf* atrociousness; *pl (actes)* atrocities.

atrophie [atrɔfi] *nf* atrophy. ◆**atrophié** *a* atrophied.

attabl/er (s') [satable] *vpr* to sit down at the table. **◆—é** *a* (seated) at the table.

attache [ataʃ] *nf* (*objet*) attachment, fastening; *pl* (*liens*) links.

attach/er [ataʃe] *vt* (*lier*) to tie (up), attach (à to); (*boucler, fixer*) to fasten; **s'a. du prix/un sens à qch** to attach great value/a meaning to sth; **cette obligation m'attache à lui** this obligation binds me to him; **s'a. à** (*adhérer*) to stick to; (*se lier*) to become attached to; (*se consacrer*) to apply oneself to. **◆—ant** *a* (*enfant etc*) engaging, appealing. **◆—é, -ée** *nmf* (*personne*) *Pol Mil* attaché. **◆—ement** *nm* attachment, affection.

attaque [atak] *nf* attack; **a. aérienne** air raid; **d'a.** in tip-top shape, on top form. **◆attaqu/er** *vt,* **s'a.** à to attack; (*difficulté, sujet*) to tackle; — *vi* to attack. **◆—ant, -ante** *nmf* attacker.

attard/er (s') [atarde] *vpr* (*chez qn*) to linger (on), stay on; (*en chemin*) to loiter, dawdle; **s'a. sur** *ou* à (*détails etc*) to linger over; **s'a. derrière qn** to lag behind s.o. **◆—é** *a* (*enfant etc*) backward; (*passant*) late.

atteindre* [atɛ̃dr] *vt* (*parvenir à*) to reach; (*idéal*) to attain; (*blesser*) to hit, wound; (*toucher*) to affect; (*offenser*) to hurt, wound; **être atteint de** (*maladie*) to be suffering from.

atteinte [atɛ̃t] *nf* attack; **porter a. à** to attack, undermine; **a. à** (*honneur*) slur on; **hors d'a.** (*objet, personne*) out of reach; (*réputation*) unassailable.

attel/er [atle] *vt* (*bêtes*) to harness, hitch up; (*remorque*) to couple; **s'a. à** (*travail etc*) to apply oneself to. **◆—age** *nm* harnessing; coupling; (*bêtes*) team.

attenant [atnɑ̃] *a* **a. (à)** adjoining.

attend/re [atɑ̃dr] *vt* to wait for, await; (*escompter*) to expect (de of, from); **elle attend un bébé** she's expecting a baby; — *vi* to wait; **s'a. à** to expect; **a. d'être informé** to wait to be informed; **a. que qn vienne** to wait for s.o. to come, wait until s.o. comes; **faire a. qn** to keep s.o. waiting; **se faire a.** (*réponse, personne etc*) to be a long time coming; **attends voir** *Fam* let me see; **en attendant** meanwhile; **en attendant que** (+ *sub*) until. **◆—u** *a* (*avec joie*) eagerly-awaited; (*prévu*) expected; − *prép* considering; **a. que** considering that.

compassionate. **◆—issant** *a* moving. **◆—issement** *nm* compassion.

attentat [atɑ̃ta] *nm* attempt (*on s.o.'s life*), murder attempt; *Fig* crime, outrage (à against); **a. (à la bombe)** (*bomb*) attack. **◆attenter** *vi* **a. à** (*la vie de qn*) to make an attempt on; *Fig* to attack.

attente [atɑ̃t] *nf* (*temps*) wait(ing); (*espérance*) expectation(s); **une a. prolongée** a long wait; **être dans l'a.** de to be waiting for; **salle d'a.** waiting room.

attentif, -ive [atɑ̃tif, -iv] *a* (*personne*) attentive; (*travail, examen*) careful; **a. à** (*plaire etc*) anxious to; (*ses devoirs etc*) mindful of. **◆attentivement** *adv* attentively.

attention [atɑ̃sjɔ̃] *nf* attention; *pl* (*égards*) consideration; **faire** *ou* **prêter a. à** (*écouter, remarquer*) to pay attention to; **faire a. à/que** (*prendre garde*) to be careful of/that; **a.!** look out!, be careful!; **a. à la voiture!** mind *ou* watch the car! **◆attentionné** *a* considerate.

atténu/er [atenɥe] *vt* to attenuate, mitigate; − **s'a.** *vpr* to subside. **◆—antes** *afpl* **circonstances a.** extenuating circumstances.

atterrer [atere] *vt* to dismay.

atterr/ir [aterir] *vi Av* to land. **◆—issage** *nm Av* landing; **a. forcé** crash *ou* emergency landing.

attester [atɛste] *vt* to testify to; **a. que** to testify that. **◆attestation** *nf* (*document*) declaration, certificate.

attifer [atife] *vt Fam Péj* to dress up, rig out.

attirail [atiraj] *nm* (*équipement*) *Fam* gear.

attir/er [atire] *vt* (*faire venir*) to attract, draw; (*plaire à*) to attract; (*attention*) to draw (sur on); **a. qch à qn** (*causer*) to bring s.o. sth; (*gloire etc*) to win *ou* earn s.o. sth; **a. dans** (*coin, guet-apens*) to draw into; − **s'a.** *vpr* (*ennuis etc*) to bring upon oneself; (*sympathie de qn*) to win; **s'a. sur soi** (*colère de qn*) to bring down upon oneself. **◆—ant** *a* attractive **◆attirance** *nf* attraction.

attiser [atize] *vt* (*feu*) to poke; (*sentiment*) *Fig* to rouse.

attitré [atitre] *a* (*représentant*) appointed; (*marchand*) regular.

attitude [atityd] *nf* attitude; (*maintien*) bearing.

attraction [atraksjɔ̃] *nf* attraction.

attrait [atrɛ] *nm* attraction.

attrape [atrap] *nf* trick. **◆a.-nigaud** *nm* con, trick.

attraper [atrape] *vt* (*ballon, maladie, voleur, train etc*) to catch; (*accent, contravention etc*) to pick up; **se laisser a.** (*duper*) to get taken in *ou* tricked; **se faire a.** (*gronder*) *Fam* to get a telling off. **◆attrapade** *nf* (*gronderie* *Fam* telling off.

attrayant [atrεjɑ̃] *a* attractive.

attribuer [atribɥe] *vt* (*donner*) to assign, allot (à to); (*imputer, reconnaître*) to attribute, ascribe to; (*décerner*) to grant, award (à to). **◆attribuable** *a* attributable. **◆attribution** *nf* assignment; attribution; (*de prix*) awarding; *pl* (*compétence*) powers.

attrister [atriste] *vt* to sadden.

attroup/er [atrupe] *vt*, **— s'a.** *vpr* to gather. **◆—ement** *nm* gathering, (disorderly) crowd.

au [o] *voir* à.

aubaine [obɛn] *nf* (*bonne*) **a.** stroke of good luck, godsend.

aube [ob] *nf* dawn; **dès l'a.** at the crack of dawn.

aubépine [obepin] *nf* hawthorn.

auberge [obεrʒ] *nf* inn; **a. de jeunesse** youth hostel. **◆aubergiste** *nmf* innkeeper.

aubergine [obεrʒin] *nf* aubergine, eggplant.

aucun, -une [okœ̃, -yn] *a* no, not any; **il n'a a. talent** he has no talent, he doesn't have any talent; **a. professeur n'est venu** no teacher has come; — *pron* none, not any; **il n'en a a.** he has none (at all), he doesn't have any (at all); **plus qu'a.** more than any(one); **d'aucuns** some (people). **◆aucunement** *adv* not at all.

audace [odas] *nf* (*courage*) daring, boldness; (*impudence*) audacity; *pl* daring innovations. **◆audacieux, -euse** *a* daring, bold.

au-dedans, au-dehors, au-delà *voir* **dedans** *etc*.

au-dessous [odsu] *adv* (*en bas*) (down) below, underneath; (*moins*) below, under; (*à l'étage inférieur*) downstairs; — *prép* **au-d. de** (*arbre etc*) below, under, beneath; (*âge, prix*) under; (*température*) below; **au-d. de sa tâche** not up to *ou* unequal to one's task.

au-dessus [odsy] *adv* above; over; on top; (*à l'étage supérieur*) upstairs; — *prép* **au-d. de** above; (*âge, température, prix*) over; (*posé sur*) on top of.

au-devant de [odvɑ̃də] *prép* **aller au-d. de** (*personne*) to go to meet; (*danger*) to court; (*désirs de qn*) to anticipate.

audible [odibl] *a* audible.

audience [odjɑ̃s] *nf* *Jur* hearing; (*entretien*) audience.

audio [odjo] *a inv* (*cassette etc*) audio.

◆audiophone *nm* hearing aid.
◆audio-visuel, -elle *a* audio-visual.

auditeur, -trice [oditœr, -tris] *nmf* *Rad* listener; **les auditeurs** the audience; **a.** *libre* *Univ* auditor, student allowed to attend classes but not to sit examinations. **◆auditif, -ive** *a* (*nerf*) auditory. **◆audition** *nf* (*ouïe*) hearing; (*séance d'essai*) *Th* audition; (*séance musicale*) recital. **◆auditionner** *vti* to audition. **◆auditoire** *nm* audience. **◆auditorium** *nm* *Rad* recording studio (*for recitals*).

auge [oʒ] *nf* (feeding) trough.

augmenter [ogmɑ̃te] *vt* to increase (**de** by); (*salaire, prix, impôt*) to raise, increase; **a. qn** to give s.o. a rise *ou* *Am* raise; — *vi* to increase (**de** by); (*prix, population*) to rise, go up. **◆augmentation** *nf* increase (**de** in, of); **a. de salaire** (pay) rise, *Am* raise; **a. de prix** price rise *ou* increase.

augure [ogyr] *nm* (*présage*) omen; (*devin*) oracle; **être de bon/mauvais a.** to be a good/bad omen. **◆augurer** *vt* to augur, predict.

auguste [ogyst] *a* august.

aujourd'hui [oʒurdɥi] *adv* today; (*actuellement*) nowadays, today; **a. en quinze** two weeks today.

aumône [omon] *nf* alms.

aumônier [omonje] *nm* chaplain.

auparavant [oparavɑ̃] *adv* (*avant*) before(hand); (*d'abord*) first.

auprès de [opre] *prép* (*assis, situé etc*) by, close to, next to; (*en comparaison de*) compared to; **agir a. de** (*ministre etc*) to use one's influence with; **accès a. de qn** access to s.o.

auquel [okεl] *voir* **lequel**.

aura, aurait [ora, ore] *voir* **avoir**.

auréole [oreol] *nf* (*de saint etc*) halo; (*trace*) ring.

auriculaire [orikyler] *nm* **l'a.** the little finger.

aurore [oror] *nf* dawn, daybreak.

ausculter [oskylte] *vt* (*malade*) to examine (*with a stethoscope*); (*cœur*) to listen to. **◆auscultation** *nf* *Méd* auscultation.

auspices [ospis] *nmpl* **sous les a. de** under the auspices of.

aussi [osi] *adv* **1** (*comparaison*) as; **a. sage que** as wise as. **2** (*également*) too, also, as well; **moi a.** so do, can, am *etc* I; (*plus*) **a. bien que** as well as. **3** (*tellement*) so; **un repas a. délicieux** so delicious a meal, such a delicious meal. **4** *conj* (*donc*) therefore.

aussitôt [osito] *adv* immediately, at once; **a. que** as soon as; **a. levé, il partit** as soon as he was up, he left; **a. dit, a. fait** no sooner said than done.

austère [ɔstɛr] *a* austere. ◆**austérité** *nf* austerity.

austral, *mpl* **-als** [ɔstral] *a* southern.

Australie [ɔstrali] *nf* Australia. ◆**australien, -ienne** *a* & *nmf* Australian.

autant [otɑ̃] *adv* **1 a. de ... que** (*quantité*) as much . . . as; (*nombre*) as many . . . as; **il a a. d'argent/de pommes que vous** he has as much money/as many apples as you. **2 a. de** (*tant de*) so much; (*nombre*) so many; **je n'ai jamais vu a. d'argent/de pommes** I've never seen so much money/so many apples; **pourquoi manges-tu a.?** why are you eating so much? **3 a. que** (*souffrir, lire etc*) as much as; **il lit a. que vous/que possible** he reads as much as you/as possible; **il n'a jamais souffert a.** he's never suffered as *ou* so much; **a. que je sache** as far as I know; **d'a. (plus) que** all the more (so) since; **d'a. moins que** even less since; **a. avouer/etc** we, you *etc* might as well confess/*etc*; **en faire/dire a.** to do/say the same; **j'aimerais a. aller au cinéma** I'd just as soon go to the cinema.

autel [otel] *nm* altar.

auteur [otœr] *nm* (*de livre*) author, writer; (*de chanson*) composer; (*de procédé*) originator; (*de crime*) perpetrator; (*d'accident*) cause; **droit d'a.** copyright; **droits d'a.** royalties.

authenticité [otɑ̃tisite] *nf* authenticity. ◆**authentifier** *vt* to authenticate. ◆**authentique** *a* genuine, authentic.

autiste [otist] *a*, **autistique** *a* autistic.

auto [oto] *nf* car; **autos tamponneuses** bumper cars, dodgems.

auto- [oto] *préf* self-.

autobiographie [otobjografi] *nf* autobiography.

autobus [otobys] *nm* bus.

autocar [otokar] *nm* coach, bus.

autochtone [otɔktɔn] *a & nmf* native.

autocollant [otokɔlɑ̃] *nm* sticker.

autocrate [otokrat] *nm* autocrat. ◆**autocratique** *a* autocratic.

autocuiseur [otokɥizœr] *nm* pressure cooker.

autodéfense [otodefɑ̃s] *nf* self-defence.

autodestruction [otodestryksjɔ̃] *nf* self-destruction.

autodidacte [otodidakt] *a & nmf* self-taught (person).

autodrome [otodrom] *nm* motor-racing track.

auto-école [otoekɔl] *nf* driving school, school of motoring.

autographe [otograf] *nm* autograph.

automate [otɔmat] *nm* automaton. ◆**automation** *nf* automation. ◆**automatisation** *nf* automation. ◆**automatiser** *vt* to automate.

automatique [otɔmatik] *a* automatic; – *nm* **l'a. Tél** direct dialling. ◆**—ment** *adv* automatically.

automne [otɔn] *nm* autumn, *Am* fall. ◆**automnal, -aux** *a* autumnal.

automobile [otɔmɔbil] *nf & a* (motor)car, *Am* automobile; **l'a.** *Sp* motoring; **Salon de l'a.** Motor Show; **canot a.** motor boat. ◆**automobiliste** *nmf* motorist.

autonome [otonɔm] *a* (*région etc*) autonomous, self-governing; (*personne*) *Fig* independent. ◆**autonomie** *nf* autonomy.

autopsie [otɔpsi] *nf* autopsy, post-mortem.

autoradio [otoradjo] *nm* car radio.

autorail [otoraj] *nm* railcar.

autoris/er [otorize] *vt* (*habiliter*) to authorize (**à faire** to do); (*permettre*) to permit (**à faire** to do). ◆**—é** *a* (*qualifié*) authoritative. ◆**autorisation** *nf* authorization; permission.

autorité [otorite] *nf* authority. ◆**autoritaire** *a* authoritarian; (*homme, ton*) authoritative.

autoroute [otorut] *nf* motorway, *Am* highway, freeway.

auto-stop [otostɔp] *nm* hitchhiking; **faire de l'a.** to hitchhike. ◆**autostoppeur, -euse** *nmf* hitchhiker.

autour [otur] *adv* around; – *prép* **a. de** around.

autre [otr] *a & pron* other; **un a. livre** another book; **un a.** another (one); **d'autres** others; **as-tu d'autres questions?** have you any other *ou* further questions? **qn/personne/rien d'a.** s.o./no one/nothing else; **a. chose/part** sth/somewhere else; **qui/quoi d'a.?** who/what else? **l'un l'a., les uns les autres** each other; **l'un et l'a.** both (of them); **l'un ou l'a.** either (of them); **ni l'un ni l'a.** neither (of them); **les uns . . . les autres** some . . . others; **nous/vous autres Anglais** we/you English; **d'un moment à l'a.** any moment (now); **. . . et d'autres . . .** and so on. ◆**autrement** *adv* (*différemment*) differently; (*sinon*) otherwise; (*plus*) far more (**que** than); **pas a. satisfait/*etc*** not particularly satisfied/*etc*.

autrefois [otrəfwa] *adv* in the past, in days gone by.

Autriche [otriʃ] nf Austria. ◆**autrichien, -ienne** a & nmf Austrian.

autruche [otryʃ] nf ostrich.

autrui [otrɥi] pron others, other people.

auvent [ovɑ̃] nm awning, canopy.

aux [o] voir **à**.

auxiliaire [oksiljɛr] a auxiliary; – nm Gram auxiliary; – nmf (aide) helper, auxiliary.

auxquels, -elles [okɛl] voir **lequel**.

avachir (s') [savaʃir] vpr (soulier, personne) to become flabby ou limp.

avait [avɛ] voir **avoir**.

aval (en) [ɑ̃naval] adv downstream (de from).

avalanche [avalɑ̃ʃ] nf avalanche; Fig flood, avalanche.

avaler [avale] vt to swallow; (livre) to devour; (mots) to mumble; – vi to swallow.

avance [avɑ̃s] nf (marche, acompte) advance; (de coureur, chercheur etc) lead; pl (galantes) advances; **à l'a., d'a., par a.** in advance; **en a.** (arriver, partir) early; (avant l'horaire prévu) ahead (of time); (dans son développement) ahead, in advance; (montre etc) fast; **en a. sur** (qn, son époque etc) ahead of, in advance of; **avoir une heure d'a.** (train etc) to be an hour early.

avanc/er [avɑ̃se] vt (thèse, argent) to advance; (date) to bring forward; (main, chaise) to move forward; (travail) to speed up; – vi to advance, move forward; (montre) to be fast; (faire saillie) to jut out (sur over); **en âge** to be getting on (in years); – **s'a.** vpr to advance, move forward; (faire saillie) to jut out. ◆**-é a** advanced; (saison) well advanced. ◆**-ée** nf projection, overhang. ◆**-ement** nm advancement.

avanie [avani] nf affront, insult.

avant [avɑ̃] prép before; **a. de voir** before seeing; **a. qu'il (ne) parte** before he leaves; **a. huit jours** within a week; **a. tout** above all; **a. toute chose** first and foremost; **a. peu** before long; – adv before; **en a.** (mouvement) forward; (en tête) ahead; **en a. de** in front of; **bien a. dans** (creuser etc) very deep(ly) into; **la nuit d'a.** the night before; – nm & a inv front; – nm (joueur) Sp forward.

avantage [avɑ̃taʒ] nm advantage; (bénéfice) Fin benefit; **tu as a. à le faire** it's worth your while to do it; **tirer a. de** to benefit from. ◆**avantager** vt (favoriser) to favour; (faire valoir) to show off to advantage. ◆**avantageux, -euse** a worthwhile, attractive; (flatteur) flattering; Péj conceited; **a. pour qn** advantageous to s.o.

avant-bras [avɑ̃bra] nm inv forearm. ◆**a.-centre** nm Sp centre-forward. ◆**a.-coureur** am a. coureur de (signe) heralding. ◆**a.-dernier, -ière** a & nmf last but one. ◆**a.-garde** nf Mil advance guard; (idée, film etc) **d'a.-garde** (idée, film etc) avant-garde. ◆**a.-goût** nm foretaste. ◆**a.-guerre** nm ou f pre-war period; **d'a.-guerre** pre-war. ◆**a.-hier** [avɑ̃tjɛr] adv the day before yesterday. ◆**a.-poste** nm outpost. ◆**a.-première** nf preview. ◆**a.-propos** nm inv foreword. ◆**a.-veille** nf **l'a.-veille (de)** two days before.

avare [avar] a miserly; **a. de** (compliments etc) sparing of; – nmf miser. ◆**avarice** nf avarice.

avarie(s) [avari] nf(pl) damage. ◆**avarié** a (aliment) spoiled, rotting.

avatar [avatar] nm Péj Fam misadventure.

avec [avɛk] prép with; (envers) to(wards); **et a. ça?** (dans un magasin) Fam anything else?; – adv **il est venu a.** (son chapeau etc) Fam he came with it.

avenant [avnɑ̃] a pleasing, attractive; **à l'a.** in keeping (de with).

avènement [avɛnmɑ̃] nm **l'a. de** the coming ou advent of; (roi) the accession of.

avenir [avnir] nm future; **d'a.** (personne, métier) with future prospects; **à l'a.** (désormais) in future.

aventure [avɑ̃tyr] nf adventure; (en amour) affair; **à l'a.** (marcher etc) aimlessly; **dire la bonne a. à qn** to tell s.o.'s fortune. ◆**aventur/er** vt to risk; (remarque) to venture; (réputation) to risk; – **s'a.** vpr to venture (sur on to, à faire to do). ◆**-é a** risky. ◆**aventureux, -euse** a (personne, vie) adventurous; (risqué) risky. ◆**aventurier, -ière** nmf Péj adventurer.

avenue [avny] nf avenue.

avér/er (s') [savere] vpr (juste etc) to prove (to be); **il s'avère que** it turns out that. ◆**-é a** established.

averse [avɛrs] nf shower, downpour.

aversion [avɛrsjɔ̃] nf aversion (pour to).

avert/ir [avɛrtir] vt (mettre en garde, menacer) to warn; (informer) to notify, inform. ◆**-i a** informed. ◆**-issement** nm warning; notification; (dans un livre) foreword. ◆**-isseur** nm Aut horn; **a. d'incendie** fire alarm.

aveu, -x [avø] nm confession; **de l'a. de** by the admission of.

aveugle [avœgl] a blind; – nmf blind man, blind woman; **les aveugles** the blind. ◆**aveuglément** [-emɑ̃] adv blindly.

◆**aveugl/er** [avœgle] vt to blind. ◆**—ement** [-əmɑ̃] nm (égarement) blindness.

aveuglette (à l') [alavœglɛt] adv blindly; **chercher qch à l'a.** to grope for sth.

aviateur, -trice [avjatœr, -tris] nmf airman, airwoman. ◆**aviation** nf (industrie, science) aviation; (armée de l'air) air force; (avions) aircraft; **l'a.** Sp flying; **d'a.** (terrain, base) air-.

avide [avid] a (rapace) greedy (de for); **a. d'apprendre/etc** (désireux) eager to learn/etc. ◆**—ment** adv greedily. ◆**avidité** nf greed.

avilir [avilir] vt to degrade, debase.

avion [avjɔ̃] nm aircraft, (aero)plane, Am airplane; **a. à réaction** jet; **a. de ligne** airliner; **par a.** (lettre) airmail; **en a., par a.** (voyager) by plane, by air; **aller en a.** to fly.

aviron [avirɔ̃] nm oar; **faire de l'a.** to row, practise rowing.

avis [avi] nm opinion; Pol Jur judgement; (communiqué) notice; (conseil) & Fin advice; **à mon a.** in my opinion, to my mind; **changer d'a.** to change one's mind.

avis/er [avize] vt to advise, inform; (voir) to notice; **s'a. de qch** to realize sth suddenly; **s'a. de faire** to venture to do. ◆**—é** a prudent, wise; **bien/mal a.** well-/ill-advised.

aviver [avive] vt (couleur) to bring out; (douleur) to sharpen.

avocat, -ate [avoka, -at] 1 nmf barrister, counsel, Am attorney, counselor; (d'une cause) Fig advocate. 2 nm (fruit) avocado (pear).

avoine [avwan] nf oats; **farine d'a.** oatmeal.

avoir* [avwar] 1 v aux to have; **je l'ai vu** I've seen him. 2 vt (posséder) to have; (obtenir) to get; (tromper) Fam to take for a ride; **il a** he has, he's got; **qu'est-ce que tu as?** what's the matter with you?, what's wrong with you?; **j'ai à lui parler** I have to speak

to her; **il n'a qu'à essayer** he only has to try; **a. faim/chaud/etc** to be ou feel hungry/hot/etc; **a. cinq ans/etc** to be five (years old)/etc; **en a. pour longtemps** to be busy for quite a while; **j'en ai pour dix minutes** this will take me ten minutes; (ne bougez pas) I'll be with you in ten minutes; **en a. pour son argent** to get ou have one's money's worth; **en a. après** ou **contre** to have a grudge against. 3 v imp **il y a** there is, pl there are; **il y a six ans** six years ago; **il n'y a pas de quoi!** don't mention it!; **qu'est-ce qu'il y a?** what's the matter?, what's wrong? 4 nm assets, property; (d'un compte) Fin credit.

avoisin/er [avwazine] vt to border on. ◆**—ant** a neighbouring, nearby.

avort/er [avorte] vi (projet etc) Fig to miscarry, fail; (se faire) a. (femme) to have ou get an abortion. ◆**—ement** nm abortion; Fig failure. ◆**avorton** nm Péj runt, puny shrimp.

avou/er [avwe] vt to confess, admit (que that); **s'a. vaincu** to admit defeat; — vi (coupable) to confess. ◆**—é** a (ennemi, but) avowed; — nm solicitor, Am attorney.

avril [avril] nm April; **un poisson d'a.** (farce) an April fool joke.

axe [aks] nm Math axis; (essieu) axle; (d'une politique) broad direction; **grands axes** (routes) main roads. ◆**axer** vt to centre; **il est axé sur** his mind is drawn towards.

axiome [aksjom] nm axiom.

ayant [ɛjɑ̃] voir avoir.

azalée [azale] nf (plante) azalea.

azimuts [azimyt] nmpl **dans tous les a.** Fam all over the place, here there and everywhere; **tous a.** (guerre, publicité etc) all-out.

azote [azɔt] nm nitrogen.

azur [azyr] nm azure, (sky) blue; **la Côte d'A.** the (French) Riviera.

azyme [azim] a (pain) unleavened.

B

B, b [be] nm B, b.

babeurre [babœr] nm buttermilk.

babill/er [babije] vi to prattle, babble. ◆**—age** nm prattle, babble.

babines [babin] nfpl (lèvres) chops, chaps.

babiole [babjɔl] nf (objet) knick-knack; (futilité) trifle.

bâbord [babɔr] nm Nau Av port (side).

babouin [babwɛ̃] nm baboon.

baby-foot [babifut] nm inv table ou miniature football.

bac [bak] nm 1 (bateau) ferry(boat). 2 (cuve) tank; **b. à glace** ice tray; **b. à laver** washtub. 3 abrév = **baccalauréat**.

baccalauréat [bakalɔrea] nm school leaving certificate.

bâche [baʃ] *nf* (*toile*) tarpaulin. ◆**bâcher** *vt* to cover over (*with a tarpaulin*).

bachelier, -ière [baʃəlje, -jɛr] *nmf* holder of the *baccalauréat*.

bachot [baʃo] *nm abrév* = **baccalauréat**. ◆**bachoter** *vi* to cram (*for an exam*).

bacille [basil] *nm* bacillus, germ.

bâcler [bɑkle] *vt* (*travail*) to dash off carelessly, botch (up).

bactéries [bakteri] *nfpl* bacteria. ◆**bactériologique** *a* bacteriological; **la guerre b.** germ warfare.

badaud, -aude [bado, -od] *nmf* (inquisitive) onlooker, bystander.

baderne [badɛrn] *nf* **vieille b.** *Péj* old fogey, old fuddy-duddy.

badigeon [badiʒɔ̃] *nm* whitewash. ◆**badigeonner** *vt* (*mur*) to whitewash, distemper; (*écorchure*) *Méd* to paint, coat.

badin [badɛ̃] *a* (*peu sérieux*) light-hearted, playful. ◆**badin/er** *vi* to jest, joke; **b. avec** (*prendre à la légère*) to trifle with. ◆**-age** *nm* banter, jesting.

badine [badin] *nf* cane, switch.

bafouer [bafwe] *vt* to mock *ou* scoff at.

bafouiller [bafuje] *vti* to stammer, splutter.

bâfrer [bɑfre] *vi Fam* to stuff oneself (with food).

bagage [bagaʒ] *nm* (*valise etc*) piece of luggage *ou* baggage; (*connaissances*) *Fig* (fund of) knowledge; *pl* (*ensemble des valises*) luggage, baggage. ◆**bagagiste** *nm* baggage handler.

bagarre [bagar] *nf* brawl. ◆**bagarrer** *vi Fam* to struggle, fight; — **se b.** *vpr* to fight, brawl; (*se disputer*) to fight, quarrel.

bagatelle [bagatɛl] *nf* trifle, mere bagatelle; **la b. de** *Iron* the trifling sum of.

bagne [baɲ] *nm* convict prison; **c'est le b. ici** *Fig* this place is a real hell hole *ou* workhouse. ◆**bagnard** *nm* convict.

bagnole [baɲɔl] *nf Fam* car; **vieille b.** *Fam* old banger.

bagou(t) [bagu] *nm Fam* glibness; **avoir du b.** to have the gift of the gab.

bague [bag] *nf* (*anneau*) ring; (*de cigare*) band. ◆**bagué** *a* (*doigt*) ringed.

baguenauder [bagnode] *vi*, — **se b.** *vpr* to loaf around, saunter.

baguette [bagɛt] *nf* (*canne*) stick; (*de chef d'orchestre*) baton; (*pain*) (long thin) loaf, stick of bread; *pl* (*de tambour*) drumsticks; (*pour manger*) chopsticks; **b.** (**magique**) (magic) wand; **mener à la b.** to rule with an iron hand.

bah! [bɑ] *int* really!, bah!

bahut [bay] *nm* (*meuble*) chest, cabinet; (*lycée*) *Fam* school.

baie [bɛ] *nf* **1** *Géog* bay. **2** *Bot* berry. **3** (*fenêtre*) picture window.

baignade [bɛɲad] *nf* (*bain*) bathe, bathing; (*endroit*) bathing place. ◆**baign/er** *vt* (*immerger*) to bathe; (*enfant*) to bath, *Am* bathe; **b. les rivages** (*mer*) to wash the shores; **baigné de** (*sueur, lumière*) bathed in; (*sang*) soaked in; — *vi* **b. dans** (*tremper*) to soak in; (*être imprégné de*) to be steeped in; — **se b.** *vpr* to go swimming *ou* bathing; (*dans une baignoire*) to have *ou* take a bath. ◆**-eur, -euse 1** *nmf* bather. **2** *nm* (*poupée*) baby doll. ◆**baignoire** *nf* bath (tub).

bail, pl baux [baj, bo] *nm* lease. ◆**bailleur** *nm Jur* lessor; **b. de fonds** financial backer.

bâill/er [bɑje] *vi* to yawn; (*chemise etc*) to gape; (*porte*) to stand ajar. ◆**-ement** *nm* yawn; gaping.

bâillon [bɑjɔ̃] *nm* gag. ◆**bâillonner** *vt* (*victime, presse etc*) to gag.

bain [bɛ̃] *nm* bath; (*de mer*) swim, bathe; **salle de bain(s)** bathroom; **être dans le b.** (*au courant*) *Fam* to have got into the swing of things; **petit/grand b.** (*piscine*) shallow/deep end; **b. de bouche** mouthwash. ◆**b.-marie** *nm* (*pl* **bains-marie**) *Culin* double boiler.

baïonnette [bajonɛt] *nf* bayonet.

baiser [beze] **1** *vt* **b. au front/sur la joue** to kiss on the forehead/cheek; — *nm* kiss; **bons baisers** (*dans une lettre*) (with) love. **2** *vt* (*duper*) *Fam* to con.

baisse [bɛs] *nf* fall, drop (**de** in); **en b.** (*température*) falling.

baisser [bese] *vt* (*voix, prix etc*) to lower, drop; (*tête*) to bend; (*radio, chauffage*) to turn down; — *vi* (*prix, niveau etc*) to drop, go down; (*soleil*) to go down, sink; (*marée*) to decline; (*santé, popularité*) to decline; — **se b.** *vpr* to bend down, stoop.

bajoues [baʒu] *nfpl* (*d'animal, de personne*) chops.

bal, pl bals [bal] *nm* (*réunion de grand apparat*) ball; (*populaire*) dance; (*lieu*) dance hall.

balade [balad] *nf Fam* walk; (*en auto*) drive; (*excursion*) tour. ◆**balader** *vt* (*enfant etc*) to take for a walk *ou* drive; (*objet*) to trail around; — **se b.** (*à pied*) (to go for a) walk; (*excursionner*) to tour (around); **se b.** (*en voiture*) to go for a drive. ◆**baladeur** *nm* Walkman®. ◆**baladeuse** *nf* inspection lamp.

balafre [balafr] *nf* (*blessure*) gash, slash;

(cicatrice) scar. ◆**balafrer** vt to gash, slash; to scar.

balai [balɛ] nm broom; **b. mécanique** carpet sweeper; **manche à b.** broomstick; Av joystick. ◆**b.-brosse** nm (pl **balais-brosses**) garden brush ou broom (for scrubbing paving stones).

balance [balɑ̃s] nf (instrument) (pair of) scales; (équilibre) Pol Fin balance; **la B.** (signe) Libra; **mettre en b.** to balance, weigh up.

balanc/er [balɑ̃se] vt (bras) to swing; (hanches, tête, branches) to sway; (lancer) Fam to chuck; (se débarrasser de) Fam to chuck out; **b. un compte** Fin to balance an account; — **se b.** vpr (personne) to swing (from side to side); (arbre, bateau etc) to sway; **je m'en balance!** I couldn't care less! ◆**-é à bien b.** (phrase) well-balanced; (personne) Fam well-built. ◆**-ement** nm swinging; swaying. ◆**balancier** nm (d'horloge) pendulum; (de montre) balance wheel. ◆**balançoire** nf (escarpolette) swing; (bascule) seesaw.

balayer [baleje] vt (chambre, rue) to sweep (out ou up); (enlever, chasser) to sweep away; **le vent balayait la plaine** the wind swept the plain. ◆**balayette** [balejɛt] nf (hand) brush; (balai) short-handled broom. ◆**balayeur, -euse** [balejœr, -øz] nmf roadsweeper.

balbutier [balbysje] vti to stammer.

balcon [balkɔ̃] nm balcony; Th Cin dress circle.

baldaquin [baldakɛ̃] nm (de lit etc) canopy.

baleine [balɛn] nf (animal) whale; (fanon) whalebone; (de parapluie) rib. ◆**baleinier** nm (navire) whaler. ◆**baleinière** nf whaleboat.

balise [baliz] nf Nau beacon; Av (ground) light; (route) to signpost. ◆**balis/er** vt to mark with beacons ou lights; (route) to signpost. ◆**-age** nm Nau beacons; Av lighting; Aut signposting.

balistique [balistik] a ballistic.

balivernes [balivɛrn] nfpl balderdash, nonsense.

ballade [balad] nf (légende) ballad; (poème court) &·Mus ballade.

ballant [balɑ̃] a (bras, jambes) dangling.

ballast [balast] nm ballast.

balle [bal] nf (de tennis, golf etc) ball; (projectile) bullet; (paquet) bale; pl (francs) Fam francs; **se renvoyer la b.** to pass the buck (to each other).

ballet [balɛ] nm ballet. ◆**ballerine** [balrin] nf ballerina.

ballon [balɔ̃] nm (jouet d'enfant) & Av balloon; (sport) ball; **b. de football** football; **lancer un b. d'essai** Fig to put out a feeler. ◆**ballonné** a (ventre) bloated, swollen. ◆**ballot** nm (paquet) bundle; (imbécile) Fam idiot.

ballottage [balɔtaʒ] nm (scrutin) second ballot (no candidate having achieved the required number of votes).

ballotter [balɔte] vti to shake (about); **ballotté entre** (sentiments contraires) torn between.

balnéaire [balneɛr] a **station b.** seaside resort.

balourd, -ourde [balur, -urd] nmf (clumsy) oaf. ◆**balourdise** nf clumsiness, oafishness; (gaffe) blunder.

Baltique [baltik] nf **la B.** the Baltic.

balustrade [balystrad] nf (hand)rail, railing(s).

bambin [bɑ̃bɛ̃] nm tiny tot, toddler.

bambou [bɑ̃bu] nm bamboo.

ban [bɑ̃] nm (de tambour) roll; (applaudissements) round of applause; pl (de mariage) banns; **mettre qn au b. de** to cast s.o. out from, outlaw s.o. from; **un b. pour...** three cheers for ....

banal, mpl -als [banal] a (fait, accident etc) commonplace, banal; (idée, propos) banal, trite. ◆**banalisé** a (voiture de police) unmarked. ◆**banalité** nf banality; (propos) banalities.

banane [banan] nf banana.

banc [bɑ̃] nm (siège, établi) bench; (de poissons) shoal; **b. d'église** pew; **b. d'essai** Fig testing ground; **b. de sable** sandbank; **b. des accusés** Jur dock.

bancaire [bɑ̃kɛr] a (opération) banking-; (chèque) bank-.

bancal, mpl -als [bɑ̃kal] a (personne) bandy, bow-legged; (meuble) wobbly; (idée) shaky.

bande [bɑ̃d] nf **1** (de terrain, papier etc) strip; (de film) reel; (de journal) wrapper; (rayure) stripe; (de fréquences) Rad band; (pansement) bandage; (sur la chaussée) line; **b.** (magnétique) tape; **b. vidéo** videotape; **b. sonore** sound track; **b. dessinée** comic strip, strip cartoon; **par la b.** indirectly. **2** (groupe) gang, troop, band; (de chiens) pack; (d'oiseaux) flock; **on a fait b. à part** we split into our own groups; **b. d'idiots!** you load of idiots! ◆**bandeau, -x** nm (sur les yeux) blindfold; (pour la tête) headband; (pansement) head bandage. ◆**band/er** vt (blessure etc) to bandage; (yeux) to blindfold; (arc) to bend; (muscle) to tense. ◆**—age** nm (pansement) bandage.

banderole [bãdrɔl] nf (sur mât) pennant, streamer; (sur montants) banner.

bandit [bãdi] nm robber, bandit; (enfant) Fam rascal. ◆**banditisme** nm crime.

bandoulière [bãduljɛr] nf shoulder strap; en b. slung across the shoulder.

banjo [bã(d)ʒo] nm Mus banjo.

banlieue [bãljø] nf suburbs, outskirts; la grande b. the outer suburbs; de b. (magasin etc) suburban; (train) commuter-. ◆**banlieusard, -arde** nmf (habitant) suburbanite; (voyageur) commuter.

banne [ban] nf (de magasin) awning.

bannière [banjɛr] nf banner.

bann/ir [banir] vt (exiler) to banish; (supprimer) to ban, outlaw. ◆**—issement** nm banishment.

banque [bãk] nf bank; (activité) banking.

banqueroute [bãkrut] nf (fraudulent) bankruptcy.

banquet [bãkɛ] nm banquet.

banquette [bãkɛt] nf (bench) seat.

banquier [bãkje] nm banker.

banquise [bãkiz] nf ice floe ou field.

baptême [batɛm] nm christening, baptism; b. du feu baptism of fire; b. de l'air first flight. ◆**baptiser** (enfant) to christen, baptize; (appeler) Fig to christen; (basin).

baquet [bakɛ] nm tub, basin.

bar [bar] nm 1 (lieu, comptoir, meuble) bar. 2 (poisson marin) bass.

baragouin [baragwẽ] nm gibberish, gabble. ◆**baragouiner** vt (langue) to gabble (a few words of); — vi to gabble away.

baraque [barak] nf hut, shack; (maison) Fam house, place; Péj hovel; (de forain) stall. ◆**—ment** nm (makeshift) huts.

baratin [baratẽ] nm Fam sweet talk; Com patter. ◆**baratiner** vt to chat up; Am sweet-talk.

barbare [barbar] a (manières, crime) barbaric; (peuple, invasions) barbarian; — nmf barbarian. ◆**barbarie** nf (cruauté) barbarity. ◆**barbarisme** nm Gram barbarism.

barbe [barb] nf beard; une b. de trois jours three days' growth of beard; se faire la b. to shave; à la b. de under the nose(s) of; rire dans sa b. to laugh up one's sleeve; la b.! enough! quelle b.! what a drag!; b. à papa candyfloss, Am cotton candy.

barbecue [barbəkju] nm barbecue.

barbelé [barbəle] a barbed; — nmpl barbed wire.

barb/er [barbe] vt Fam to bore (stiff); — se

b. vpr to be ou get bored (stiff). ◆**—ant** a Fam boring.

barbiche [barbiʃ] nf goatee (beard).

barbiturique [barbityrik] nm barbiturate.

barbot/er [barbɔte] 1 vi (s'agiter) to splash about, paddle. 2 vt (voler) Fam to filch. ◆**—euse** nf (de bébé) rompers.

barbouill/er [barbuje] vt (salir) to smear; (peindre) to daub; (gribouiller) to scribble; avoir l'estomac barbouillé Fam to feel queasy. ◆**—age** nm smear; daub; scribble.

barbu [barby] a bearded.

barda [barda] nm Fam gear; (de soldat) kit.

bardé [barde] a b. de (décorations etc) covered with.

barder [barde] v imp ça va b.! Fam there'll be fireworks!

barème [barɛm] nm (des tarifs) table; (des salaires) scale; (livre de comptes) ready reckoner.

baril [bari(l)] nm barrel; b. de poudre powder keg.

bariolé [barjɔle] a brightly-coloured.

barman pl **-men** ou **-mans** [barman, -mɛn] nm barman, Am bartender.

baromètre [barɔmɛtr] nm barometer.

baron, -onne [barɔ̃, -ɔn] nm baron; — nf baroness.

baroque [barɔk] 1 a (idée etc) bizarre, weird. 2 a & nm Archit Mus etc baroque.

baroud [barud] nm b. d'honneur Arg gallant last fight.

barque [bark] nf (small) boat.

barre [bar] nf bar; (trait) line, stroke; Nau helm; b. de soustraction minus sign; b. fixe Sp horizontal bar. ◆**barreau, -x** nm (de fenêtre etc) & Jur bar; (d'échelle) rung.

barr/er [bare] 1 vt (route etc) to block (off), close (off); (porte) to bar; (chèque) to cross; (phrase) to cross out; Nau to steer; b. la route à qn, b. qn to bar s.o.'s way; 'rue barrée' 'road closed'. 2 se b. vpr Arg to hop it, make off. ◆**—age** nm (sur une route) roadblock; (barrière) barrier; (ouvrage hydraulique) dam; (de petite rivière) weir; le b. d'une rue the closing of a street; tir de b. barrage fire; b. d'agents cordon of police. ◆**—eur** nm Sp Nau cox.

barrette [barɛt] nf (pince) (hair)slide, Am barrette.

barricade [barikad] nf barricade. ◆**barricader** vt to barricade; — se b. vpr to barricade oneself.

barrière [barjɛr] nf (porte) gate; (clôture) fence; (obstacle, mur) barrier.

barrique [barik] nf (large) barrel.

baryton [baritɔ̃] nm baritone.

bas¹, basse [bɑ, bɑs] a (table, prix etc) low; (âme, action) base, mean; (partie de ville etc) lower; (origine) lowly; **au b. mot** at the very least; **enfant en b. âge** young child; **avoir la vue basse** to be short-sighted; **le b. peuple** Péj the lower orders; **coup b.** Boxe blow below the belt; – adv low; (parler) in a whisper, softly; **mettre b.** (animal) to give birth; **mettre b. les armes** to lay down one's arms; **jeter b.** to overthrow; **plus b.** further ou lower down; **en b.** down (below); (par l'escalier) downstairs, down below; **en ou au b. de** at the foot ou bottom of; **de haut en b.** from top to bottom; **sauter à b. du lit** jump out of bed; **à b. les dictateurs/etc!** down with dictators/etc!; – nm (de côte, page etc) bottom, foot; **du b.** (tiroir, étagère) bottom.

bas² [bɑ] nm (chaussette) stocking; **b. de laine** Fig nest egg.

basané [bazane] a (visage etc) tanned.

bas-bleu [bablø] nm Péj bluestocking.

bas-côté [bakote] nm (de route) roadside, shoulder.

bascule [baskyl] nf (jeu de) b. (game of) seesaw; (balance à) b. weighing machine; **cheval/fauteuil à b.** rocking horse/chair. ◆**basculer** vti (personne) to topple over; (benne) to tip up.

base [bɑz] nf base; (principe fondamental) basis, foundation; **de b.** (salaire etc) basic; **produit à b. de lait** milk-based product; **militant de b.** rank-and-file militant. ◆**baser** vt to base; **se b. sur** to base oneself on.

bas-fond [bafɔ̃] nm (eau) shallows; (terrain) low ground; pl (population) Péj dregs.

basilic [bazilik] nm Bot Culin basil.

basilique [bazilik] nf basilica.

basket(-ball) [basket(bol)] nm basketball.

basque [bask] 1 a & nmf Basque. 2 nfpl (pans de veste) skirts.

basse [bɑs] 1 voir bas¹. 2 nf Mus bass.

basse-cour [baskur] nf (pl basses-cours) farmyard.

bassement [basmɑ̃] adv basely, meanly. ◆**bassesse** nf baseness, meanness; (action) base ou mean act.

bassin [basɛ̃] nm (pièce d'eau) pond; (piscine) pool; (cuvette) bowl, basin; (rade) dock; Anat pelvis; Géog basin; **b. houiller** coalfield. ◆**bassine** nf bowl.

basson [basɔ̃] nm (instrument) bassoon; (musicien) bassoonist.

bastingage [bastɛ̃gaʒ] nm Nau bulwarks, rail.

bastion [bastjɔ̃] nm bastion.

bastringue [bastrɛ̃g] nm (bal) Fam popular dance hall; (tapage) Arg shindig, din; (attirail) Arg paraphernalia.

bas-ventre [bavɑ̃tr] nm lower abdomen.

bat [ba] voir battre.

bât [ba] nm packsaddle.

bataclan [bataklɑ̃] nm Fam paraphernalia; **et tout le b.** Fam and the whole caboodle.

bataille [batɑj] nf battle; Cartes beggar-my-neighbour. ◆**bataill/er** vi to fight, battle. ◆**-eur, -euse** nmf fighter; – a belligerent. ◆**bataillon** nm battalion.

bâtard, -arde [batar, -ard] a & nmf bastard; **chien b.** mongrel; **œuvre bâtarde** hybrid work.

bateau, -x [bato] nm boat; (grand) ship. ◆**b.-citerne** nm (pl bateaux-citernes) tanker. ◆**b.-mouche** nm (pl bateaux-mouches) (sur la Seine) pleasure boat.

batifoler [batifole] vi Hum to fool ou lark about.

bâtiment [batimɑ̃] nm (édifice) building; (navire) vessel; **le b.,** l'industrie du b. the building trade; **ouvrier du b.** building worker. ◆**bât/ir** vt (construire) to build; (coudre) to baste, tack; **terrain à b.** building site. ◆**–i** a bien b. well-built; – nm Menuis frame, support. ◆**bâtisse** nf Péj building. ◆**bâtisseur, -euse** nmf builder (de of).

bâton [batɔ̃] nm (canne) stick; (de maréchal, d'agent) baton; **b. de rouge** lipstick; **donner des coups de b. à qn** to beat s.o. (with a stick); **parler à bâtons rompus** to ramble from one subject to another; **mettre des bâtons dans les roues à qn** to put obstacles in s.o.'s way.

batterie [batri] nf Mil Aut battery; **la b.** Mus the drums; **b. de cuisine** set of kitchen utensils.

batt/re* [batr] 1 vt (frapper, vaincre) to beat; (blé) to thresh; (cartes) to shuffle; (pays, chemins) to scour; (à coups redoublés) to batter, pound; **b. la mesure** to beat time; **b. à mort** to batter ou beat to death; **b. pavillon** to fly a flag; – vi to beat; (porte) to bang; **b. des mains** to clap (one's hands); **b. des paupières** to blink; **b. des ailes** (oiseau) to flap its wings; **le vent fait b. la porte** the wind bangs the door. **2 se b.** vpr to fight. ◆**–ant 1** a (pluie) driving; (porte) swing-. **2** nm (de cloche) tongue; (vantail de porte etc) flap; **porte à deux battants** double door. **3** nm (personne) fighter. ◆**–u** a **chemin ou sentier b.** beaten track. ◆**–age** nm (du blé) threshing; (publicité) Fam publicity, hype, ballyhoo. ◆**—ement** *nm* (*de cœur, de tambour*) beat; (*délai*) interval; **battements de cœur** palpitations. ◆**—eur** *nm* (*musicien*) percussionist; **b. à œufs** egg beater.

baudet [bodε] *nm* donkey.

baume [bom] *nm* (*résine*) & *Fig* balm.

baux [bo] *voir* **bail.**

bavard, -arde [bavar, -ard] *a* (*loquace*) talkative; (*cancanier*) gossipy; — *nmf* chatterbox; gossip. ◆**bavard/er** *vi* to chat, chatter; (*papoter*) to gossip; (*divulguer*) to blab. ◆**—age** *nm* chatting, chatter(ing); gossip(ing).

bave [bav] *nf* dribble, slobber; foam; (*de limace*) slime. ◆**baver** *vi* to dribble, slobber; (*chien enragé*) to foam; (*encre*) to smudge; **en b.** *Fam* to have a rough time of it. ◆**bavette** *nf* bib. ◆**baveux, -euse** *a* (*bouche*) slobbery; (*omelette*) runny. ◆**bavoir** *nm* bib. ◆**bavure** *nf* smudge; (*erreur*) blunder; **sans b.** perfect(ly), flawless(ly).

bazar [bazar] *nm* (*magasin, marché*) bazaar; (*désordre*) mess, clutter; (*attirail*) *Fam* stuff, gear. ◆**bazarder** *vt Fam* to sell off, get rid of.

bazooka [bazuka] *nm* bazooka.

béant [beɑ̃] *a* (*plaie*) gaping; (*gouffre*) yawning.

béat [bea] *a Péj* smug; (*heureux*) *Hum* blissful. ◆**béatitude** *nf Hum* bliss.

beau (*or* **bel** *before vowel or mute* h), **belle**, *pl* **beaux, belles** [bo, bεl] *a* (*femme, fleur etc*) beautiful, attractive; (*homme*) handsome, good-looking; (*voyage, temps etc*) fine, lovely; **au b. milieu** right in the middle; **j'ai b. crier/essayer/etc** it's no use (my) shouting/trying/etc; **un b. morceau** a good *or* sizeable bit; **de plus belle** (*recommencer etc*) worse than ever; **bel et bien** really; — *nm* **le b.** the beautiful; **faire le b.** (*chien*) to sit up and beg; **le plus b. de l'histoire** the best part of the story; — *nf* (*femme*) beauty; *Sp* deciding game.

beaucoup [boku] *adv* (*lire etc*) a lot, a great deal; **aimer b.** to like very much; **s'intéresser b. à** to be very interested in; **b. de** (*livres etc*) many, a lot *ou* a great deal of; (*courage etc*) a lot *ou* a great deal of, much; **pas b. d'argent/etc** not much money/etc; **j'en ai b.** (*quantité*) I have much, (*nombre*) I have many; **b. plus/moins** much more/less; **b. plus/moins de** (*nombre*) many more/fewer; (*quantité*) much more/less; **b. trop** much too much; much too many; **de b.** by far; **b. sont ...** many are ...

beau-fils [bofis] *nm* (*pl* **beaux-fils**) (*d'un*

précédent mariage) stepson; (*gendre*) son-in-law. ◆**b.-frère** *nm* (*pl* **beaux-frères**) brother-in-law. ◆**b.-père** *nm* (*pl* **beaux-pères**) father-in-law; (*parâtre*) stepfather.

beauté [bote] *nf* beauty; **institut** *ou* **salon de b.** beauty parlour; **en b.** (*gagner etc*) magnificently; **être en b.** to look one's very best; **de toute b.** beautiful.

beaux-arts [bozar] *nmpl* fine arts. ◆**b.-parents** *nmpl* parents-in-law.

bébé [bebe] *nm* baby; **b.-lion/etc** (*pl* **bébés-lions/etc**) baby lion/etc.

bébête [bebεt] *a Fam* silly.

bec [bεk] *nm* (*d'oiseau*) beak, bill; (*de cruche*) lip, spout; (*de plume*) nib; (*bouche*) *Fam* mouth; *Mus* mouthpiece; **coup de b.** peck; **b. de gaz** gas lamp; **clouer le b. à qn** *Fam* to shut s.o. up; **tomber sur un b.** *Fam* to come up against a serious snag. ◆**b.-de-cane** (*pl* **becs-de-cane**) door handle.

bécane [bekan] *nf Fam* bike.

bécarre [bekar] *nm Mus* natural.

bécasse [bekas] *nf* (*oiseau*) woodcock; (*personne*) *Fam* simpleton.

bêche [bεʃ] *nf* spade. ◆**bêcher** *vt* **1** (*cultiver*) to dig. **2** *Fig* to criticize; (*snober*) to snub. ◆**bêcheur, -euse** *nmf* snob.

bécot [beko] *nm Fam* kiss. ◆**bécoter** *vt,* — **se b.** *vpr Fam* to kiss.

becquée [beke] *nf* beakful; **donner la b. à** (*oiseau, enfant*) to feed. ◆**becqueter** *vt* (*picorer*) to peck (at); (*manger*) *Fam* to eat.

bedaine [bədεn] *nf Fam* paunch, potbelly.

bedeau, -x [bado] *nm* beadle, verger.

bedon [bad] *nm Fam* paunch. ◆**bedonnant** *a* paunchy, potbellied.

bée [be] *a* **bouche b.** open-mouthed.

beffroi [befrwa] *nm* belfry.

bégayer [begeje] *vi* to stutter, stammer. ◆**bègue** [bεg] *nmf* stutterer, stammerer; — *a* **être b.** to stutter, stammer.

bégueule [begœl] *a* prudish; — *nf* prude.

béguin [begɛ̃] *nm* **avoir le b. pour qn** *Fam* to have taken a fancy to s.o.

beige [bεʒ] *a & nm* beige.

beignet [bεɲε] *nm Culin* fritter.

bel [bεl] *voir* **beau.**

bêler [bele] *vi* to bleat.

belette [bəlεt] *nf* weasel.

Belgique [bεlʒik] *nf* Belgium. ◆**belge** *a & nmf* Belgian.

bélier [belje] *nm* (*animal, machine*) ram; **le B.** (*signe*) Aries.

belle [bεl] *voir* **beau.**

belle-fille [bεlfij] *nf* (*pl* **belles-filles**) (*d'un* *précédent mariage*) stepdaughter; (*bru*) daughter-in-law. ◆**b.-mère** *nf* (*pl* **belles-mères**) mother-in-law; (*marâtre*) stepmother. ◆**b.-sœur** *nf* (*pl* **belles-sœurs**) sister-in-law.

belligérant [beliʒerɑ̃] *a* & *nm* belligerent.

belliqueux, -euse [belikø, -øz] *a* warlike; *Fig* aggressive.

belvédère [bɛlvedɛr] *nm* (*sur une route*) viewpoint.

bémol [bemɔl] *nm Mus* flat.

bénédiction [benediksjɔ̃] *nf* blessing, benediction.

bénéfice [benefis] *nm* (*gain*) profit; (*avantage*) benefit; **b.** (**ecclésiastique**) living, benefice. ◆**bénéficiaire** *nmf* beneficiary; – *a* (*marge, solde*) profit. ◆**bénéficier** *vi* **b. de** to benefit from, have the benefit of. ◆**bénéfique** *a* beneficial.

Bénélux [benelyks] *nm* Benelux.

benêt [bənɛ] *nm* simpleton; – *am* simple-minded.

bénévole [benevɔl] *a* voluntary, unpaid.

bénin, -igne [benɛ̃, -iɲ] *a* (*tumeur, critique*) benign; (*accident*) minor.

bénir [benir] *vt* to bless; (*exalter, remercier*) to give thanks to. ◆**bénit** *a* (*pain*) consecrated; **eau bénite** holy water. ◆**bénitier** [-itje] *nm* (holy-water) stoup.

benjamin, -ine [bɛ̃ʒamɛ̃, -in] *nmf* youngest child; *Sp* young junior.

benne [bɛn] *nf* (*de grue*) scoop; (*à charbon*) tub, skip; (*de téléphérique*) cable car; **camion à b. basculante** dump truck; **b. à ordures** skip.

béotien, -ienne [beɔsjɛ̃, -jɛn] *nmf* (*inculte*) philistine.

béquille [bekij] *nf* (*canne*) crutch; (*de moto*) stand.

bercail [berkaj] *nm* (*famille etc*) *Hum* fold.

berceau, -x [bɛrso] *nm* cradle.

berc/er [bɛrse] *vt* (*balancer*) to rock; (*apaiser*) to lull; (*leurrer*) to delude (**de** with); **se b. d'illusions** to delude oneself. ◆**—euse** *nf* lullaby.

béret [berɛ] *nm* beret.

berge [bɛrʒ] *nf* (*rivage*) (raised) bank.

berger, -ère [bɛrʒe, -ɛr] **1** *nm* shepherd; **chien (de) b.** sheepdog; – *nf* shepherdess. **2** *nm* **b. allemand** Alsatian (dog), *Am* German shepherd. ◆**bergerie** *nf* sheepfold.

berline [bɛrlin] *nf Aut* (four-door) saloon, *Am* sedan.

berlingot [bɛrlɛ̃go] *nm* (*bonbon aux fruits*) boiled sweet; (*à la menthe*) mint; (*emballage*) (milk) carton.

berlue [bɛrly] *nf* **avoir la b.** to be seeing things.

berne (en) [ɛ̃bɛrn] *adv* at half-mast.

berner [bɛrne] *vt* to fool, hoodwink.

besogne [bəzɔɲ] *nf* work, job, task. ◆**besogneux, -euse** *a* needy.

besoin [bəzwɛ̃] *nm* need; **avoir b. de** to need; **au b.** if necessary, if need(s) be; **dans le b.** in need, needy.

bestial, -aux [bɛstjal, -o] *a* bestial, brutish. ◆**bestiaux** *nmpl* livestock; (*bovins*) cattle. ◆**bestiole** *nf* (*insecte*) creepy-crawly, bug.

bétail [betaj] *nm* livestock; (*bovins*) cattle.

bête[1] [bɛt] *nf* animal; (*bestiole*) bug, creature; **b. de somme** beast of burden; **b. à bon dieu** ladybird, *Am* ladybug; **b. noire** pet hate, pet peeve; **chercher la petite b.** (*critiquer*) to pick holes.

bête[2] [bɛt] *a* silly, stupid. ◆**bêtement** *adv* stupidly; **tout b.** quite simply. ◆**bêtise** [betiz] *nf* silliness, stupidity; (*action, parole*) silly ou stupid thing; (*bagatelle*) mere trifle.

béton [betɔ̃] *nm* concrete; **en b.** concrete-; **b. armé** reinforced concrete. ◆**bétonnière** *nf*, ◆**bétonneuse** *nf* cement ou concrete mixer.

betterave [bɛtrav] *nf Culin* beetroot, *Am* beet; **b. sucrière** ou **à sucre** sugar beet.

beugler [bøgle] *vi* (*taureau*) to bellow; (*vache*) to moo; (*radio*) to blare (out).

beurre [bœr] *nm* butter; **b. d'anchois** anchovy paste. ◆**beurrer** *vt* to butter. ◆**beurrier** *nm* butter dish.

beuverie [bøvri] *nf* drinking session, booze-up.

bévue [bevy] *nf* blunder, mistake.

biais [bjɛ] *nm* (*moyen détourné*) device, expedient; (*aspect*) angle; **regarder de b.** to look at sidelong; **traverser en b.** to cross at an angle. ◆**biaiser** [bjeze] *vi* to prevaricate, hedge.

bibelot [biblo] *nm* curio, trinket.

biberon [bibrɔ̃] *nm* (feeding) bottle.

bible [bibl] *nf* bible; **la B.** the Bible. ◆**biblique** *a* biblical.

bibliobus [biblijobys] *nm* mobile library.

bibliographie [biblijɔgrafi] *nf* bibliography.

bibliothèque [biblijɔtɛk] *nf* library; (*meuble*) bookcase; (*à la gare*) bookstall. ◆**bibliothécaire** *nmf* librarian.

bic® [bik] *nm* ballpoint, biro®.

bicarbonate [bikarbɔnat] *nm* bicarbonate.

bicentenaire [bisɑ̃tnɛr] *nm* bicentenary, bicentennial.

biceps [bisɛps] *nm Anat* biceps.

biche [biʃ] *nf* doe, hind; **ma b.** *Fig* my pet.

bichonner [biʃɔne] vt to doll up.

bicoque [bikɔk] nf Péj shack, hovel.

bicyclette [bisiklɛt] nf bicycle, cycle; **la b.** Sp cycling; **aller à b.** to cycle.

bide [bid] nm (ventre) Fam belly; **faire un b.** Arg to flop.

bidet [bide] nm (cuvette) bidet.

bidon [bidɔ̃] **1** nm (d'essence) can; (pour boissons) canteen; (ventre) Fam belly. **2** nm **du b.** Fam rubbish, bluff; – a inv (simulé) Fam fake, phoney. **◆se bidonner** vpr Fam to have a (daily) good laugh.

bidonville [bidɔ̃vil] nf shantytown.

bidule [bidyl] nm (chose) Fam thingummy, whatsit.

bielle [bjɛl] nf Aut connecting rod.

bien [bjɛ̃] adv well; **il joue b.** he plays well; **je vais b.** I'm fine ou well; **b. fatigué/ souvent/etc** (très) very tired/often/etc; **merci b.!** thanks very much!; **b.! fine!, right!; b. du courage/etc** a lot of courage/etc; **b. des fois/des gens/etc** lots of ou many times/people/etc; **je l'ai b. dit** (intensif) I did say so; **c'est b. compris?** is that quite understood?; **c'est b. toi?** is it really you?; **tu as b. fait** you did right; **c'est b. fait (pour lui)** it serves him right; – a inv (convenable) all right, fine; (agréable) nice, fine; (compétent, bon) good, fine; (à l'aise) comfortable, fine; (beau) attractive; (en forme) well; (moralement) nice; **une fille b.** a nice ou respectable girl; – nm (avantage) good; (capital) possession; **ça te fera du b.** it will do you good; **le b. et le mal** good and evil; **biens de consommation** consumer goods. **◆b.-aimé, -ée** a & nmf beloved. **◆b.-être** nm wellbeing. **◆b.-fondé** nm validity, soundness.

bienfaisance [bjɛ̃fəzɑ̃s] nf benevolence, charity; **de b.** (société etc) benevolent, charitable. **◆bienfaisant** a beneficial.

bienfait [bjɛ̃fɛ] nm (générosité) favour; Pl benefits, blessings. **◆bienfaiteur, -trice** nmf benefactor, benefactress.

bienheureux, -euse [bjɛ̃nœrø, -øz] a blessed, blissful.

biennal, -aux [bjenal, -o] a biennial.

bien que [bjɛ̃k(ə)] conj although.

bienséant [bjɛ̃seɑ̃] a proper. **◆bienséance** nf propriety.

bientôt [bjɛ̃to] adv soon; **à b.!** see you soon!; **il est b. dix heures/etc** it's nearly ten o'clock/etc.

bienveillant [bjɛ̃vɛjɑ̃] a kindly. **◆bienveillance** nf kindliness.

bienvenu, -ue [bjɛ̃vny] a welcome; – nmf

soyez le b.! welcome!; – nf welcome; **souhaiter la bienvenue à** to welcome.

bière [bjɛr] nf **1** (boisson) beer; **b. pression** draught beer. **2** (cercueil) coffin.

biffer [bife] vt to cross ou strike out.

bifteck [biftɛk] nm steak; **gagner son b.** Fam to earn one's (daily) bread.

bifurquer [bifyrke] vi to branch off, fork. **◆bifurcation** nf fork, junction.

bigame [bigam] a bigamous; – nmf bigamist. **◆bigamie** nf bigamy.

bigarré [bigare] a (bariolé) mottled; (hétéroclite) motley, mixed.

bigler [bigle] vi (loucher) Fam to squint; – vti **b. (sur)** (lorgner) Fam to leer at. **◆bigleux, -euse** a Fam cock-eyed.

bigorneau, -x [bigɔrno] nm (coquillage) winkle.

bigot, -ote [bigo, -ɔt] nmf Péj religious bigot; – a over-devout, fanatical.

bigoudi [bigudi] nm (hair)curler ou roller.

bigrement [bigrəmɑ̃] adv Fam awfully.

bijou, -x [biʒu] nm jewel; (ouvrage élégant) Fig gem. **◆bijouterie** nf (commerce) jeweller's shop; (bijoux) jewellery. **◆bijoutier, -ière** nmf jeweller.

bikini [bikini] nm bikini.

bilan [bilɑ̃] nm Fin balance sheet; (résultat) outcome; (d'un accident) (casualty) toll; **b. de santé** checkup; **faire le b.** to make an assessment (**de** of).

bilboquet [bilbɔkɛ] nm cup-and-ball (game).

bile [bil] nf bile; **se faire de la b.** Fam to worry, fret. **◆bilieux, -euse** a bilious.

bilingue [bilɛ̃g] a bilingual.

billard [bijar] nm (jeu) billiards; (table) billiard table; Méd Fam operating table; **c'est du b.** Fam it's a cinch.

bille [bij] nf (d'un enfant) marble; (de billard) billiard ball; **stylo à b.** ballpoint pen, biro®.

billet [bije] nm ticket; **b. (de banque)** (bank)note, Am bill; **b. simple** single ticket, Am one-way ticket; **b. (d')aller et retour** return ticket, Am round trip ticket; **b. doux** love letter.

billion [biljɔ̃] nm billion, Am trillion.

billot [bijo] nm (de bois) block.

bimensuel, -elle [bimɑ̃sɥɛl] a bimonthly, fortnightly.

bimoteur [bimɔtœr] a twin-engined.

binaire [binɛr] a binary.

biner [bine] vt to hoe. **◆binette** nf hoe; (visage) Arg mug, face.

biochimie [bjɔʃimi] nf biochemistry.

biodégradable [bjɔdegradabl] *a* biodégradable.

biographie [bjɔgrafi] *nf* biography. ◆**biographe** *nmf* biographer.

biologie [bjɔlɔʒi] *nf* biology. ◆**biologique** *a* biological.

bip-bip [bipbip] *nm* bleeper.

bipède [biped] *nm* biped.

bique [bik] *nf Fam* nanny-goat.

Birmanie [birmani] *nf* Burma. ◆**birman, -ane** *a & nm* Burmese.

bis¹ [bis] *adv* (*cri*) *Th* encore; *Mus* repeat; **4 bis** (*numéro*) 4A; – *nm Th* encore.

bis², **bise** [bi, biz] *a* greyish-brown.

bisbille [bisbij] *nf* squabble; **en b. avec** *Fam* at loggerheads with.

biscornu [biskɔrny] *a* (*objet*) distorted, misshapen; (*idée*) cranky.

biscotte [biskɔt] *nf* (*pain*) Melba toast; (*biscuit*) rusk, *Am* zwieback.

biscuit [biskɥi] *nm* (*salé*) biscuit, *Am* cracker; (*sucré*) biscuit, *Am* cookie; **b. de Savoie** sponge (cake). ◆**biscuiterie** *nf* biscuit factory.

bise [biz] *nf* **1** (*vent*) north wind. **2** (*baiser*) *Fam* kiss.

biseau, -x [bizo] *nm* bevel.

bison [bizɔ̃] *nm* bison, (American) buffalo.

bisou [bizu] *nm Fam* kiss.

bisser [bise] *vt* (*musicien, acteur*) to encore.

bissextile [bisɛkstil] *af* **année b.** leap year.

bistouri [bisturi] *nm* scalpel, lancet.

bistre [bistr] *a inv* bistre, dark-brown.

bistro(t) [bistro] *nm* bar, café.

bitume [bitym] *nm* (*revêtement*) asphalt.

bivouac [bivwak] *nm Mil* bivouac.

bizarre [bizar] *a* peculiar, odd, bizarre. ◆**-ment** *adv* oddly. ◆**bizarrerie** *nf* peculiarity.

blabla(bla) [blabla(bla)] *nm* claptrap, bunkum.

blafard [blafar] *a* pale, pallid.

blague [blag] *nf* **1** (*à tabac*) pouch. **2** (*plaisanterie, farce*) *Fam* joke; *pl* (*absurdités*) *Fam* nonsense; **sans b.!** you're joking! ◆**blagu/er** *vi* to be joking; – *vt* to tease. ◆**-eur, -euse** *nmf* joker.

blair [blɛr] *nm* (*nez*) *Arg* snout, conk. ◆**blairer** *vt Arg* to stomach.

blaireau, -x [blɛro] *nm* **1** (*animal*) badger. **2** (*brosse*) (shaving) brush.

blâme [blɑm] *nm* (*réprimande*) rebuke; (*reproche*) blame. ◆**blâmable** *a* blameworthy. ◆**blâmer** *vt* to rebuke; to blame.

blanc, blanche [blɑ̃, blɑ̃ʃ] **1** *a* white; (*page etc*) blank; **nuit blanche** sleepless night; **voix blanche** expressionless voice; – *nmf* (*personne*) white (man *ou* woman); – *nm* (*couleur*) white; (*de poulet*) white meat, breast; (*espace, interligne*) blank; **b. (d'œuf)** (egg) white; **le b.** (*linge*) whites; **magasin de b.** linen shop; **laisser en b.** to leave blank; **chèque en b.** blank cheque; **cartouche à b.** blank (cartridge); **saigner à b.** to bleed white. **2** *nf Mus* minim, *Am* half-note. ◆**blanchâtre** *a* whitish. ◆**blancheur** *nf* whiteness.

blanchir [blɑ̃ʃir] *vt* to whiten; (*draps*) to launder; (*mur*) to whitewash; *Culin* to blanch; (*argent*) *Fig* to launder; **b. qn** (*disculper*) to clear s.o.; – *vi* to turn white, whiten. ◆**blanchissage** *nm* laundering. ◆**blanchisserie** *nf* (*lieu*) laundry. ◆**blanchisseur, -euse** *nmf* laundryman, laundrywoman.

blanquette [blɑ̃kɛt] *nf* **b. de veau** veal stew in white sauce.

blasé [blaze] *a* blasé.

blason [blazɔ̃] *nm* (*écu*) coat of arms; (*science*) heraldry.

blasphème [blasfɛm] *nf* blasphemy. ◆**blasphématoire** *a* (*propos*) blasphemous. ◆**blasphémer** *vti* to blaspheme.

blatte [blat] *nf* cockroach.

blazer [blazœr] *nm* blazer.

blé [ble] *nm* wheat; (*argent*) *Arg* bread.

bled [blɛd] *nm Péj Fam* (dump of a) village.

blême [blɛm] *a* sickly pale, wan; **b. de colère** livid with anger.

bless/er [blese] *vt* to injure, hurt; (*avec un couteau, une balle etc*) to wound; (*offenser*) to hurt, offend, wound; **se b. le** *ou* **au bras/etc** to hurt one's arm/*etc*. ◆**-ant** [blɛsɑ̃] *a* (*parole, personne*) hurtful. ◆**-é, -ée** *nmf* casualty, injured *ou* wounded person. ◆**blessure** *nf* injury; wound.

blet, blette [blɛ, blɛt] *a* (*fruit*) overripe.

bleu [blø] *a* blue; **b. de colère** blue in the face; **steak b.** *Culin* very rare steak; – *nm* (*couleur*) blue; (*contusion*) bruise; (*vêtement*) overalls; (*conscrit*) raw recruit; **bleus de travail** overalls. ◆**bleuir** *vti* to turn blue.

bleuet [bløɛ] *nm* cornflower.

blind/er [blɛ̃de] *vt Mil* to armour(-plate). ◆**-é, -ée** *a* (*train etc*) *Mil* armoured; **porte blindée** reinforced steel door; – *nm Mil* armoured vehicle.

bloc [blɔk] *nm* block; (*de pierre*) lump, block; (*de papier*) pad; (*masse compacte*) unit; *Pol* bloc; **en b.** all together; **à b.** (*serrer etc*) tight, hard; **travailler à b.** *Fam* to work flat out. ◆**b.-notes** *nm* (*pl* **blocs-notes**) writing pad.

blocage [blɔkaʒ] *nm* (*des roues*) locking; *Psy* mental block; **b. des prix** price freeze.

blocus [blɔkys] *nm* blockade.

blond, -onde [blɔ̃, -ɔ̃d] *a* (*air*)(*haired*), blond; — *nm* fair-haired man; (*couleur*) blond; — *nf* fair-haired woman, blonde; (**bière**) **blonde** lager, pale ou light ale. ◆**blondeur** *nf* fairness, blondness.

bloquer [blɔke] *vt* (*obstruer*) to block; (*coincer*) to jam; (*grouper*) to group together; (*ville*) to block; (*freins*) to slam ou jam on; (*roue*) to lock; (*salaires, prix*) to freeze; **bloqué par la neige/la glace** snowbound/icebound; — **se b.** *vpr* to stick, jam; (*roue*) to lock.

blottir (se) [səblɔtir] *vpr* (*dans un coin etc*) to crouch; (*dans son lit*) to snuggle down; **se b. contre** to huddle ou snuggle up to.

blouse [bluz] *nf* (*tablier*) overall, smock; (*corsage*) blouse. ◆**blouson** *nm* (*waist-length*) jacket.

blue-jean [bludʒin] *nm* jeans, denims.

bluff [blœf] *nm* bluff. ◆**bluffer** *vti* to bluff.

boa [bɔa] *nm* (*serpent, tour de cou*) boa.

bobard [bɔbar] *nm Fam* fib, yarn, tall story.

bobine [bɔbin] *nf* (*de fil, film etc*) reel, spool; (*pour machine à coudre*) bobbin, spool; *El* coil.

bobo [bobo] *nm* (*langage enfantin*) pain; **j'ai b., ça fait b.** it hurts.

bocage [bɔkaʒ] *nm* copse.

bocal, -aux [bɔkal, -o] *nm* glass jar; (*à poissons*) bowl.

bock [bɔk] *nm* (*récipient*) beer glass; (*contenu*) glass of beer.

bœuf, *pl* **-fs** [bœf, bø] *nm* (*animal*) ox (*pl* oxen), bullock; (*viande*) beef.

bohème [bɔɛm] *a & nmf* bohemian. ◆**bohémien, -ienne** *a & nmf* gipsy.

boire* [bwar] *vt* to drink; (*absorber*) to soak up; (*paroles*) *Fig* to take ou drink in; **b. un coup** to have a drink; **offrir à b. à qn** to offer s.o. a drink; **b. à petits coups** to sip; — *vi* to drink.

bois¹ [bwa] *voir* **boire**.

bois² [bwa] *nm* (*matière, forêt*) wood; (*de construction*) timber; (*gravure*) woodcut; *pl* (*de cerf*) antlers; *Mus* woodwind instruments; **en ou de b.** wooden; **b. de chauffage** firewood; **b. de lit** bedstead. ◆**boisé** *a* wooded. ◆**boiserie(s)** *nf*(*pl*) panelling.

boisson [bwasɔ̃] *nf* drink, beverage.

boit [bwa] *voir* **boire**.

boîte [bwat] *nf* box; (*de conserve*) tin, *Am* can; (*lieu de travail*) *Fam* firm; **b. de nuit** nightclub; **mettre qn en b.** *Fam* to pull s.o.'s leg. ◆**boîtier** *nm* (*de montre etc*) case.

boiter [bwate] *vi* (*personne*) to limp. ◆**boiteux, -euse** *a* lame; (*meuble*) wobbly; (*projet etc*) *Fig* shaky.

bol [bɔl] *nm* (*récipient*) bowl; **prendre un b. d'air** to get a breath of fresh air; **avoir du b.** *Fam* to be lucky.

bolide [bɔlid] *nm* (*véhicule*) racing car.

Bolivie [bɔlivi] *nf* Bolivia. ◆**bolivien, -ienne** *a & nmf* Bolivian.

bombard/er [bɔ̃barde] *vt* (*ville etc*) to bomb; (*avec des obus*) to shell; **b.** *Fam* (*nommer*) to pitchfork s.o. (**à un poste** into a job); **b. de** (*questions*) to bombard with; (*objets*) to pelt with. ◆**-ement** *nm* bombing; shelling. ◆**bombardier** *nm* (*avion*) bomber.

bombe [bɔ̃b] *nf* (*projectile*) bomb; (*atomiseur*) spray; **tomber comme une b.** *Fig* to be a bombshell, be quite unexpected; **faire la b.** *Fam* to have a binge.

bomb/er [bɔ̃be] **1** *vi* (*gonfler*) to bulge; — *vt* **b. la poitrine** to throw out one's chest. **2** *vi* (*véhicule etc*) *Fam* to bomb ou belt along. ◆**-é** *a* (*verre etc*) rounded; (*route*) cambered.

bon¹, **bonne** [bɔ̃, bɔn] *a* **1** (*satisfaisant etc*) good. **2** (*charitable*) kind, good. **3** (*agréable*) nice, good; **il fait b.** it's nice ou good to rest; **b. anniversaire!** happy birthday! **4** (*qui convient*) right; **c'est le b. clou** it's the right nail. **5** (*approprié, apte*) fit; **b. à manger** fit to eat; **b. pour le service** fit for service; **ce n'est à b. à rien** it's useless; **comme b. te semble** as you think ou best; **c'est b. à savoir** it's worth knowing. **6** (*prudent*) wise, good; **croire b. de** to think it wise ou good to. **7** (*compétent*) good; **b. en français** good at French. **8** (*valable*) good; **ce billet est encore b.** this ticket's still good. **9** (*intensif*) **un b. moment** a good while. **10 à quoi b.?** what's the use ou point ou good?; **pour de b.** in earnest; **tenir b.** to stand firm; **ah b.?** is that so? **11 un du b.** some good; **les bons** the good.

bon² [bɔ̃] *nm* (*billet*) coupon, voucher; (*titre*) *Fin* bond; (*formulaire*) slip.

bonasse [bɔnas] *a* feeble, soft.

bonbon [bɔ̃bɔ̃] *nm* sweet, *Am* candy. ◆**bonbonnière** *nf* sweet box, *Am* candy box.

bonbonne [bɔ̃bɔn] *nf* (*récipient*) demijohn.

bond [bɔ̃] *nm* leap, bound; (*de balle*) bounce; **faire faux b. à qn** to stand s.o. up, let s.o. down (*by not turning up*). ◆**bondir** *vi* to leap, bound.

bonde [bɔ̃d] *nf* (*bouchon*) plug; (*trou*) plughole.

bondé [bõde] a packed, crammed.

bonheur [bɔnœr] nm (chance) good luck, good fortune; (félicité) happiness; **par b.** luckily; **au petit b.** haphazardly.

bonhomie [bɔnɔmi] nf good-heartedness.

bonhomme, pl **bonshommes** [bɔnɔm, bõzɔm] **1** nm fellow, guy; **b. de neige** snowman; **aller son petit b. de chemin** to go on in one's own sweet way. **2** a inv good-hearted.

boniment(s) [bɔnimã] nm(pl) (bobard) claptrap; (baratin) patter.

bonjour [bõʒur] nm & int good morning; (après-midi) good afternoon; **donner le b. à, dire b. à** to say hello to.

bonne² [bɔn] nf (domestique) maid; **b. d'enfants** nanny.

bonnement [bɔnmã] adv **tout b.** simply.

bonnet [bɔne] nm cap; (de femme, d'enfant) bonnet; (de soutien-gorge) cup; **gros b.** Fam bigshot, bigwig. **◆bonneterie** nf hosiery.

bonsoir [bõswar] nm & int (en rencontrant qn) good evening; (en quittant qn) goodbye; (au coucher) good night.

bonté [bõte] nf kindness, goodness.

bonus [bɔnys] nm no claims bonus.

bonze [bõz] nm Péj Fam bigwig.

boom [bum] nm Écon boom.

bord [bɔr] nm (rebord) edge; (rive) bank; (de vêtement) border; (de chapeau) brim; (de verre) rim, brim, edge; **au b. de la mer/route** at ou by the seaside/roadside; **b. du trottoir** kerb, Am curb; **au b. de** (précipice) on the brink of; **au b. des larmes** on the verge of tears; **à bord (de)** Nau Av on board; **jeter par-dessus b.** to throw overboard. **◆border** vt (vêtement) to border, edge; (lit, personne) to tuck in; **b. la rue/etc** (maisons, arbres etc) to line the street/etc. **◆bordure** nf border; **en b. de** bordering on.

bordeaux [bɔrdo] a inv maroon.

bordée [bɔrde] nf (salve) Nau broadside; (d'injures) Fig torrent, volley.

bordel [bɔrdɛl] nm **1** Fam brothel. **2** (désordre) Fam mess.

bordereau, -x [bɔrdəro] nm (relevé) docket, statement; (formulaire) note.

borgne [bɔrɲ] a (personne) one-eyed, blind in one eye; (hôtel etc) Fig shady.

borne [bɔrn] nf (pierre) boundary mark; Él terminal; pl (limites) Fig bounds; **b. kilométrique** = milestone; **dépasser ou franchir les bornes** to go too far. **◆born/er** vt (limiter) to confine; **se b. à** to confine oneself to. **◆-é** a (personne) narrow-minded; (intelligence) narrow, limited.

bosquet [bɔske] nm grove, thicket, copse.

bosse [bos] nf (grosseur dorsale) hump; (enflure) bump, lump; (de terrain) hump; **avoir la b. de** Fam to have a flair for; **rouler sa b.** Fam to knock about the world. **◆bossu, -ue** a hunchbacked; dos b. hunchback; – nmf (personne) hunchback.

bosseler [bosle] vt (orfèvrerie) to emboss; (déformer) to dent.

bosser [bose] vi Fam to work (hard).

bot [bo] am **pied b.** club foot.

botanique [bɔtanik] a botanical; – nf botany.

botte [bot] nf (chaussure) boot; (faisceau) bunch, bundle. **◆botter** vt (ballon etc) Fam to boot. **◆bottier** nm bootmaker. **◆bottillon** nm, **◆bottine** nf (ankle) boot.

Bottin® [bɔtɛ̃] nm telephone book.

bouc [buk] nm billy goat; (barbe) goatee; **b. émissaire** scapegoat.

boucan [bukã] nm Fam din, row, racket.

bouche [buʃ] nf mouth; **faire la petite ou fine b.** Péj to turn up one's nose; **une fine b.** a gourmet; **b. de métro** métro entrance; **b. d'égout** drain opening, manhole; **b. d'incendie** fire hydrant; **le b.-à-b.** the kiss of life. **◆bouchée** nf mouthful.

bouch/er¹ [buʃe] **1** vt (évier, nez etc) to block (up), stop up; (bouteille) to close, cork; (vue, rue etc) to block; **se b. le nez** to hold one's nose. **◆-é** a (vin) bottled; (temps) overcast; (personne) Fig stupid, dense. **◆bouche-trou** nm stopgap. **◆bouchon** nm stopper, top; (de liège) cork; (de tube, bidon) cap, top; Pêche float; (embouteillage) Fig traffic jam.

boucher² [buʃe] nm butcher. **◆boucherie** nf butcher's (shop); (carnage) butchery.

boucle [bukl] nf **1** (de ceinture) buckle; (de fleuve etc) & Av loop; (de ruban) bow; **b. d'oreille** earring. **2** b. (de cheveux) curl. **◆boucl/er 1** vt to fasten, buckle; (travail etc) to finish off; (enfermer, fermer) Fam to lock up; (budget) to balance; (circuit) to lap; (encercler) to surround, cordon off; **la boucle** Av to loop the loop; **la b.** Fam to shut up. **2** vt (cheveux) to curl; – vi to be curly. **◆-é** a (cheveux) curly.

bouclier [buklije] nm shield.

bouddhiste [budist] a & nmf Buddhist.

bouder [bude] vi to sulk; – vt (personne, plaisirs etc) to steer clear of. **◆bouderie** nf sulkiness. **◆boudeur, -euse** a sulky, moody.

boudin [budɛ̃] nm black pudding, Am blood pudding.

boue [bu] nf mud. **◆boueux, -euse 1** a

muddy. **2** *nm* dustman, *Am* garbage collector.

bouée [bwe] *nf* buoy; **b. de sauvetage** lifebuoy.

bouffe [buf] *nf Fam* food, grub, nosh.

bouffée [bufe] *nf* (*de fumée*) puff; (*de parfum*) whiff; (*d'orgueil*) fit; **b. de chaleur** *Méd* hot flush. ◆**bouff/er 1** *vi* to puff out. **2** *vti* (*manger*) *Fam* to eat. ◆—**ant** *a* (*manche*) puff(ed). ◆**bouffi** *a* puffy, bloated.

bouffon, -onne [bufɔ̃, -ɔn] *a* farcical; — *nm* buffoon. ◆**bouffonneries** *nfpl* antics, buffoonery.

bouge [buʒ] *nm* (*bar*) dive; (*taudis*) hovel.

bougeotte [buʒɔt] *nf* **avoir la b.** *Fam* to have the fidgets.

boug/er [buʒe] *vi* to move; (*agir*) to stir; (*rétrécir*) to shrink; — *vt* to move; — **se b.** *vpr Fam* to move.

bougie [buʒi] *nf* candle; *Aut* spark(ing) plug. ◆**bougeoir** *nm* candlestick.

bougon, -onne [bugɔ̃, -ɔn] *a* grumpy; — *nmf* grumbler, grouch. ◆**bougonner** *vi Fam* to grumble, grouch.

bougre [bugr] *nm* fellow, bloke; (*enfant*) *Péj* (little) devil. ◆**bougrement** *adv Arg* damned.

bouillabaisse [bujabes] *nf* fish soup.

bouillie [buji] *nf* porridge; **en b.** in a mush, mushy.

bouill/ir* [bujir] *vi* to boil; **b. à gros bouillons** to bubble, boil hard; **faire b. qch** to boil sth. ◆—**ant** *a* boiling; **b. de colère**/*etc* seething with anger/*etc*. ◆**bouilloire** *nf* kettle. ◆**bouillon** *nm* (*eau*) broth, stock; (*bulle*) bubble. ◆**bouillonner** *vi* to bubble. ◆**bouillotte** *nf* hot water bottle.

boulanger, -ère [bulɑ̃ʒe, -ɛr] *nmf* baker. ◆**boulangerie** *nf* baker's (shop).

boule [bul] *nf* (*sphère*) ball; *pl* (*jeu*) bowls; **b. de neige** snowball; **faire b. de neige** to snowball; **perdre la b.** *Fam* to go out of one's mind; **se mettre en b.** (*chat etc*) to curl up into a ball; **boules Quiès®** earplugs. ◆**boulet** *nm* (*de forçat*) ball and chain; **b. de canon** cannonball. ◆**boulette** *nf* (*de papier*) pellet; (*de viande*) meatball; (*gaffe*) *Fam* blunder.

bouleau, -x [bulo] *nm* (silver) birch.

bouledogue [buldɔg] *nm* bulldog.

boulevard [bulvar] *nm* boulevard.

boulevers/er [bulverse] *vt* (*déranger*) to turn upside down; (*émouvoir*) to upset deeply, distress; (*vie de qn, pays*) to disrupt. ◆—**ant** *a* upsetting, distressing. ◆—**ement** *nm* upheaval.

boulon [bulɔ̃] *nm* bolt.

boulot, -otte [bulo, -ɔt] **1** *a* dumpy. **2** *nm* (*travail*) *Fam* work.

boum [bum] **1** *int & nm* bang. **2** *nf* (*surprise-partie*) *Fam* party.

bouquet [buke] *nm* (*de fleurs*) bunch, bouquet; (*d'arbres*) clump; (*de vin*) bouquet; (*crevette*) prawn; **c'est le b.!** that's the last straw!

bouquin [bukɛ̃] *nm Fam* book. ◆**bouquiner** *vti Fam* to read. ◆**bouquiniste** *nmf* second-hand bookseller.

bourbeux, -euse [burbø, -øz] *a* muddy. ◆**bourbier** *nm* (*lieu, situation*) quagmire, morass.

bourde [burd] *nf* blunder, bloomer.

bourdon [burdɔ̃] *nm* (*insecte*) bumblebee. ◆**bourdonn/er** *vi* to buzz, hum. ◆—**ement** *nm* buzzing, humming.

bourg [bur] *nm* (small) market town. ◆**bourgade** *nf* (large) village.

bourgeois, -oise [burʒwa, -waz] *a & nmf* middle-class (person); *Péj* bourgeois. ◆**bourgeoisie** *nf* middle class, bourgeoisie.

bourgeon [burʒɔ̃] *nm* bud. ◆**bourgeonner** *vi* to bud; (*nez*) *Fam* to be pimply.

bourgmestre [burgmɛstr] *nm* (*en Belgique, Suisse*) burgomaster.

bourgogne [burgɔɲ] *nm* (*vin*) Burgundy.

bourlinguer [burlɛ̃ge] *vi* (*voyager*) *Fam* to knock about.

bourrade [burad] *nf* (*du coude*) poke.

bourrasque [burask] *nf* squall.

bourratif, -ive [buratif, -iv] *a* (*aliment*) *Fam* filling, stodgy.

bourreau, -x [buro] *nm* executioner; **b. d'enfants** child batterer; **b. de travail** workaholic.

bourrelet [burlɛ] *nm* weather strip; **b. de graisse** roll of fat, spare tyre.

bourr/er [bure] **1** *vt* to stuff, cram (full) (**de** with); (*pipe, coussin*) to fill; **b. de coups** to thrash; **b. le crâne à qn** to brainwash s.o. **2** **se b.** *vpr* (*s'enivrer*) *Fam* to get plastered. ◆—**age** *nm* **b. de crâne** brainwashing.

bourrique [burik] *nf* ass.

bourru [bury] *a* surly, rough.

bourse [burs] *nf* (*sac*) purse; *Scol Univ* grant, scholarship; **la B.** the Stock Exchange; **sans b. délier** without spending a penny. ◆**boursier, -ière 1** *a* Stock Exchange-. **2** *nmf Scol Univ* grant holder, scholar.

boursouflé [bursufle] *a* (*visage etc*) puffy; (*style*) *Fig* inflated.

bousculer [buskyle] *vt* (*heurter, pousser*) to

jostle; (*presser*) to rush, push; **b. qch** (*renverser*) to knock sth over; **b. les habitudes**/*etc* to turn one's habits/*etc* upside down. ◆**bousculade** *nf* rush, jostling.

bouse [buz] *nf* **b. de vache** cow dung.

bousiller [buzije] *vt Fam* to mess up, wreck.

boussole [busɔl] *nf* compass.

bout [bu] *nm* end; (*de langue, canne, doigt*) tip; (*de papier, pain, ficelle*) bit; **un b. de temps/chemin** a little while/way; **au b. d'un moment** after a moment; **à b.** exhausted; **à b. de souffle** out of breath; **à b. de bras** at arm's length; **venir à b. de** (*travail*) to get through; (*adversaire*) to get the better of; **à tout b. de champ** at every turn, every minute; **à b. portant** point-blank.

boutade [butad] *nf* (*plaisanterie*) quip, witticism.

boute-en-train [butɑ̃trɛ̃] *nm inv* (*personne*) live wire.

bouteille [butej] *nf* bottle; (*de gaz*) cylinder.

bouteur [butœr] *nm* bulldozer.

boutique [butik] *nf* shop; (*d'un grand couturier*) boutique. ◆**boutiquier, -ière** *nmf Péj* shopkeeper.

boutoir [butwar] *nm* **coup de b.** staggering blow.

bouton [butɔ̃] *nm* (*bourgeon*) bud; (*pustule*) pimple, spot; (*de vêtement*) button; (*poussoir*) (push-)button; (*de porte, de télévision*) knob; **b. de manchette** cuff link. ◆**b.-d'or** *nm* (*pl* **boutons-d'or**) buttercup. ◆**b.-pression** *nm* (*pl* **boutons-pression**) press-stud, *Am* snap. ◆**boutonner** *vt,* — **se b.** *vpr* to button (up). ◆**boutonneux, -euse** *a* pimply, spotty. ◆**boutonnière** *nf* buttonhole.

bouture [butyr] *nf* (*plante*) cutting.

bouvreuil [buvrœj] *nm* (*oiseau*) bullfinch.

bovin [bɔvɛ̃] *a* bovine; — *nmpl* cattle.

bowling [boliŋ] *nm* (tenpin) bowling; (*lieu*) bowling alley.

box, *pl* **boxes** [bɔks, bɔks] *nm* (*d'écurie*) (loose) box; (*de dortoir*) cubicle; *Jur* dock; *Aut* lockup *ou* individual garage.

boxe [bɔks] *nf* boxing. ◆**boxer** *vi Sp* to box; — *vt Fam* to whack, punch. ◆**boxeur** *nm* boxer.

boyau, -x [bwajo] *nm Anat* gut; (*corde*) catgut; (*de bicyclette*) (racing) tyre *ou Am* tire.

boycott/er [bɔjkɔte] *vt* to boycott. ◆—**age** *nm* boycott.

BP [bepe] *abrév* (*boîte postale*) PO Box.

bracelet [braslɛ] *nm* bracelet, bangle; (*de montre*) strap.

braconner [brakɔne] *vi* to poach. ◆**braconnier** *nm* poacher.

brader [brade] *vt* to sell off cheaply. ◆**braderie** *nf* open-air (clearance) sale.

braguette [bragɛt] *nf* (*de pantalon*) fly, flies.

braille [braj] *nm* Braille.

brailler [braje] *vti* to bawl. ◆**braillard** *a* bawling.

braire* [brɛr] *vi* (*âne*) to bray.

braise(s) [brɛz] *nf(pl)* embers, live coals. ◆**braiser** [breze] *vt Culin* to braise.

brancard [brɑ̃kar] *nm* (*civière*) stretcher; (*de charrette*) shaft. ◆**brancardier** *nm* stretcher-bearer.

branche [brɑ̃ʃ] *nf* (*d'un arbre, d'une science etc*) branch; (*de compas*) leg; (*de lunettes*) side piece. ◆**branchages** *nmpl* (cut *ou* fallen) branches.

branch/er [brɑ̃ʃe] *vt El* to plug in; (*installer*) to connect. ◆—**é** *a* (*informé*) *Fam* with it. ◆—**ement** *nm El* connection.

brandir [brɑ̃dir] *vt* to brandish, flourish.

brandon [brɑ̃dɔ̃] *nm* (*paille, bois*) firebrand.

branle [brɑ̃l] *nm* impetus; **mettre en b.** to set in motion. ◆**b.-bas** *nm inv* turmoil. ◆**branl/er** *vi* to be shaky, shake. ◆—**ant** *a* shaky.

braqu/er [brake] **1** *vt* (*arme etc*) to point, aim; (*yeux*) to fix; **b. qn contre qn** to set *ou* turn s.o. against s.o. **2** *vti Aut* to steer, turn. ◆—**age** *nm Aut* steering; **rayon de b.** turning circle.

bras [bra] *nm* arm; **en b. de chemise** in one's shirtsleeves; **b. dessus b. dessous** arm in arm; **sur les b.** *Fig* on one's hands; **son b. droit** *Fig* his right-hand man; **à b. ouverts** with open arms; **à tour de b.** with all one's might; **faire le b. d'honneur** *Fam* to make an obscene gesture; **à b.-le-corps** round the waist. ◆**brassard** *nm* armband. ◆**brassée** *nf* armful. ◆**brassière** *nf* (*de bébé*) vest, *Am* undershirt.

brasier [brazje] *nm* inferno, blaze.

brasse [bras] *nf* (*nage*) breaststroke; (*mesure*) fathom; **b. papillon** butterfly stroke.

brasser [brase] *vt* to mix; (*bière*) to brew. ◆**brassage** *nm* mixture; brewing. ◆**brasserie** *nf* (*usine*) brewery; (*café*) brasserie. ◆**brasseur** *nm* **b. d'affaires** *Péj* big businessman.

bravache [bravaʃ] *nm* braggart.

bravade [bravad] *nf* **par b.** out of bravado.

brave [brav] *a & nm* (*hardi*) brave (man); (*honnête*) good (man). ◆**bravement** *adv* bravely. ◆**braver** *vt* to defy; (*danger*) to brave. ◆**bravoure** *nf* bravery.

bravo [bravo] *int* well done, bravo, good show; — *nm* cheer.

break [brɛk] *nm* estate car, *Am* station wagon.

brebis [brəbi] *nf* ewe; **b. galeuse** black sheep.

brèche [brɛʃ] *nf* breach, gap; **battre en b.** (*attaquer*) to attack (mercilessly).

bredouille [brəduj] *a* **rentrer b.** to come back empty-handed.

bredouiller [brəduje] *vti* to mumble.

bref, brève [brɛf, brɛv] *a* brief, short; — *adv* (**enfin**) **b.** in a word.

breloque [brələk] *nf* charm, trinket.

Brésil [brezil] *nm* Brazil. ◆**brésilien, -ienne** *a* & *nmf* Brazilian.

Bretagne [brətaɲ] *nf* Brittany. ◆**breton, -onne** *a* & *nmf* Breton.

bretelle [brətɛl] *nf* strap; (*voie de raccordement*) *Aut* access road; *pl* (*pour pantalon*) braces, *Am* suspenders.

breuvage [brœvaʒ] *nm* drink, brew.

brève [brɛv] *voir* **bref.**

brevet [brəvɛ] *nm* diploma; **b. (d'invention)** patent. ◆**brevet/er** *vt* to patent. ◆**-é** *a* (*technicien*) qualified.

bréviaire [brevjɛr] *nm* breviary.

bribes [brib] *nfpl* scraps, bits.

bric-à-brac [brikabrak] *nm inv* bric-à-brac, jumble, junk.

brick [brik] *nm* (*de lait, jus d'orange etc*) carton.

bricole [brikɔl] *nf* (*objet, futilité*) trifle. ◆**bricol/er** *vi* to do odd jobs; — *vt* (*réparer*) to patch up; (*fabriquer*) to put together. ◆**-age** *nm* (*petits travaux*) odd jobs; (*passe-temps*) do-it-yourself; **salon/rayon du b.** do-it-yourself exhibition/department. ◆**-eur, -euse** *nmf* handyman, handywoman.

bride [brid] *nf* (*de cheval*) bridle; **à b. abattue** at full gallop. ◆**brider** *vt* (*cheval*) to bridle; (*personne, désir*) to curb; *Culin* to truss; **avoir les yeux bridés** to have slit eyes.

bridge [bridʒ] *nm* (*jeu*) bridge.

brièvement [brijɛvmɑ̃] *adv* briefly. ◆**brièveté** *nf* brevity.

brigade [brigad] *nf* (*de gendarmerie*) squad; *Mil* brigade; **b. des mœurs** vice squad. ◆**brigadier** *nm* police sergeant; *Mil* corporal.

brigand [brigɑ̃] *nm* robber; (*enfant*) rascal.

briguer [brige] *vt* to covet; (*faveurs, suffrages*) to court.

brillant [brijɑ̃] *a* (*luisant*) shining; (*astiqué*) shiny; (*couleur*) bright; (*magnifique*) *Fig* brilliant; — *nm* shine; brightness; *Fig* bril-

liance; (*diamant*) diamond. ◆**brillamment** *adv* brilliantly.

briller [brije] *vi* to shine; **faire b.** (*meuble*) to polish (up).

brimer [brime] *vt* to bully. ◆**brimade** *nm Scol* bullying, ragging, *Am* hazing; *Fig* vexation.

brin [brɛ̃] *nm* (*d'herbe*) blade; (*de corde, fil*) strand; (*de muguet*) spray; **un b. de** *Fig* a bit of.

brindille [brɛ̃dij] *nf* twig.

bringue [brɛ̃g] *nf* **faire la b.** *Fam* to have a binge.

bringuebaler [brɛ̃gbale] *vi* to wobble about.

brio [brijo] *nm* (*virtuosité*) brilliance.

brioche [brijɔʃ] *nf* **1** brioche (*light sweet bun*). **2** (*ventre*) *Fam* paunch.

brique [brik] *nf* brick. ◆**briquette** *nf* (*aggloméré*) breezeblock.

briquer [brike] *vt* to polish (up).

briquet [brikɛ] *nm* (*cigarette*) lighter.

brise [briz] *nf* breeze.

bris/er [brize] *vt* to break; (*en morceaux*) to smash, break; (*espoir, carrière*) to shatter; (*fatiguer*) to exhaust; **— se b.** *vpr* to break. ◆**—ants** *nmpl* reefs. ◆**brise-lames** *nm inv* breakwater.

britannique [britanik] *a* British; — *nmf* Briton; **les Britanniques** the British.

broc [bro] *nm* pitcher, jug.

brocanteur, -euse [brɔkɑ̃tœr, -øz] *nmf* secondhand dealer (*in furniture etc*).

broche [brɔʃ] *nf Culin* spit; (*bijou*) brooch; *Méd* pin. ◆**brochette** *nf* (*tige*) skewer; (*plat*) kebab.

broché [brɔʃe] *a* **livre b.** paperback.

brochet [brɔʃɛ] *nm* (*poisson*) pike.

brochure [brɔʃyr] *nf* brochure, booklet, pamphlet.

broder [brɔde] *vt* to embroider (**de** with). ◆**broderie** *nf* embroidery.

broncher [brɔ̃ʃe] *vi* (*bouger*) to budge; (*reculer*) to flinch; (*regimber*) to balk.

bronches [brɔ̃ʃ] *nfpl* bronchial tubes. ◆**bronchite** *nf* bronchitis.

bronze [brɔ̃z] *nm* bronze.

bronz/er [brɔ̃ze] *vt* to tan; — *vi*, **— se b.** *vpr* to get (sun)tanned; **se (faire) b.** to sunbathe. ◆**-age** *nm* (sun)tan, sunburn.

brosse [brɔs] *nf* brush; **b. à dents** toothbrush; **cheveux en b.** crew cut. ◆**brosser** *vt* to brush; **b. un tableau de** to give an outline of; **se b. les dents/les cheveux** to brush one's teeth/one's hair.

brouette [bruɛt] *nf* wheelbarrow.

brouhaha [bruaa] *nm* hubbub.

brouillard [brujar] nm fog; **il fait du b.** it's foggy.

brouille [bruj] nf disagreement, quarrel. ◆**brouiller 1** vt (papiers, idées etc) to mix up; (vue) to blur; (œufs) to scramble; Rad to jam; **— se b.** vpr (idées) to be ou get confused; (temps) to cloud over; (vue) to blur. **2** vt (amis) to cause a split between; **— se b.** vpr to fall out (avec with). ◆**brouillon, -onne 1** a confused. **2** nm rough draft.

broussailles [brusaj] nfpl brushwood.

brousse [brus] nf **la b.** the bush.

brouter [brute] vti to graze.

broyer [brwaje] vt to grind; (doigt, bras) to crush; **b. du noir** to be (down) in the dumps.

bru [bry] nf daughter-in-law.

brugnon [bryɲɔ̃] nm (fruit) nectarine.

bruine [brɥin] nf drizzle. ◆**bruiner** v imp to drizzle.

bruissement [brɥismɑ̃] nm (de feuilles) rustle, rustling.

bruit [brɥi] nm noise, sound; (nouvelle) rumour; **faire du b.** to be noisy, make a noise. ◆**bruitage** nm Cin sound effects.

brûle-pourpoint (à) [abrylpurpwɛ̃] adv point-blank.

brûl/er [bryle] vt to burn; (consommer) to use up, burn; (signal, station) to go through (without stopping); **b. un feu (rouge)** to jump ou go through the lights; **ce désir le brûlait** this desire consumed him; **— vi** to burn; **b. (d'envie) de faire** to be burning to do; **ça brûle** (temps) it's baking ou scorching; **— se b.** vpr to burn oneself. ◆**—ant** a (objet, soleil) burning (hot); (sujet) Fig red-hot. ◆**—é 1** nm **odeur de b.** smell of burning. **2** a **cerveau b.**, **tête brûlée** hothead. ◆**brûlure** nf burn; **brûlures d'estomac** heartburn.

brume [brym] nf mist, haze. ◆**brumeux, -euse** a misty, hazy; (obscur) Fig hazy.

brun, brune [brœ̃, bryn] a brown; (cheveux) dark, brown; (personne) dark-haired; **—** nm (couleur) brown; **—** nmf dark-haired person. ◆**brunette** nf brunette. ◆**brunir** vt (peau) to tan; **—** vi to turn brown; (cheveux) to go darker.

brushing [brœʃiŋ] nm blow-dry.

brusque [brysk] a (manière etc) abrupt, blunt; (subit) sudden, abrupt. ◆**brusquement** adv suddenly, abruptly. ◆**brusquer** vt to rush. ◆**brusquerie** nf abruptness, bluntness.

brut [bryt] a (pétrole) crude; (diamant) rough; (sucre) unrefined; (soie) raw; (poids) & Fin gross.

brutal, -aux [brytal, -o] a (violent) savage, brutal; (franchise, réponse) crude, blunt; (fait) stark. ◆**brutaliser** vt to ill-treat. ◆**brutalité** nf (violence, acte) brutality. ◆**brute** nf brute.

Bruxelles [brysɛl] nm ou f Brussels.

bruyant [brɥijɑ̃] a noisy. ◆**bruyamment** adv noisily.

bruyère [brɥijɛr] nf (plante) heather; (terrain) heath.

bu [by] voir **boire**.

buanderie [bɥɑ̃dri] nf (lieu) laundry.

bûche [byʃ] nf log; **ramasser une b.** Fam to come a cropper, Am take a spill. ◆**bûcher 1** nm (local) woodshed; (supplice) stake. **2** vt (étudier) Fam to slog away at. ◆**bûcheron** nm woodcutter, lumberjack.

budget [bydʒɛ] nm budget. ◆**budgétaire** a budgetary; (année) financial.

buée [bɥe] nf condensation, mist.

buffet [byfɛ] nm (armoire) sideboard; (table, restaurant, repas) buffet.

buffle [byfl] nm buffalo.

buis [bɥi] nm (arbre) box; (bois) boxwood.

buisson [bɥisɔ̃] nm bush.

buissonnière [bɥisɔnjɛr] af **faire l'école b.** to play truant ou Am hookey.

bulbe [bylb] nm bulb. ◆**bulbeux, -euse** a bulbous.

Bulgarie [bylgari] nf Bulgaria. ◆**bulgare** a & nmf Bulgarian.

bulldozer [byldozɛr] nm bulldozer.

bulle [byl] nf **1** bubble; (de bande dessinée) balloon. **2** (décret du pape) bull.

bulletin [byltɛ̃] nm (communiqué, revue) bulletin; (de la météo) & Scol report; (de bagages) ticket, Am check; **b. de paie** pay slip; **b. de vote** ballot paper.

buraliste [byralist] nmf (à la poste) clerk; (au tabac) tobacconist.

bureau, -x [byro] nm **1** (table) desk. **2** (lieu) office; (comité) board; **b. de change** bureau de change; **b. de location** Th Cin box office; **b. de tabac** tobacconist's (shop). ◆**bureaucrate** nmf bureaucrat. ◆**bureaucratie** [-asi] nf bureaucracy. ◆**bureautique** nf office automation.

burette [byrɛt] nf oilcan; Culin cruet.

burlesque [byrlɛsk] a (idée etc) ludicrous; (genre) burlesque.

bus¹ [bys] nm Fam bus.

bus² [by] voir **boire**.

busqué [byske] a (nez) hooked.

buste [byst] nm (torse, sculpture) bust. ◆**bustier** nm long-line bra(ssiere).

but¹ [by(t)] nm (dessein, objectif) aim, goal;

(cible) target; *Fb* goal; **de b. en blanc** point-blank; **aller droit au b.** to go straight to the point; **j'ai pour b. de ...** my aim is to ....

but² [by] *voir* **boire**.

butane [bytan] *nm (gaz)* butane.

but/er [byte] **1** *vi* **b. contre** to stumble over; *(difficulté) Fig* to come up against. **2 se b.** *vpr (s'entêter)* to get obstinate. **◆—é** *a* obstinate.

butin [bytɛ̃] *nm* loot, booty.

butiner [bytine] *vi (abeille)* to gather nectar.

butoir [bytwar] *nm Rail* buffer; *(de porte)* stop(per).

butor [bytɔr] *nm Péj* lout, oaf, boor.

butte [byt] *nf* hillock, mound; **en b. à** *(calomnie etc)* exposed to.

buvable [byvabl] *a* drinkable. **◆buveur, -euse** *nmf* drinker.

buvard [byvar] *a & nm (papier)* b. blotting paper.

buvette [byvɛt] *nf* refreshment bar.

C

C, c [se] *nm* C, c

c *abrév* centime.

c' [s] *voir* **ce¹**.

ça [sa] *pron dém (abrév de* **cela)** *(pour désigner)* that; *(plus près)* this; *(sujet indéfini)* it, that; **ça m'amuse que ...** it amuses me that...; **où/quand/ comment/** *etc* **ça?** where?/when?/how?/ *etc;* **ça va (bien)?** how's it going?; **ça va!** fine!, OK!; **ça alors!** *(surprise, indignation)* well I never!, how about that!; **c'est ça** that's right; **et avec ça?** *(dans un magasin)* anything else?

çà [sa] *adv* **çà et là** here and there.

caban [kabɑ̃] *nm (veste)* reefer.

cabane [kaban] *nf* hut, cabin; *(à outils)* shed; *(à lapins)* hutch.

cabaret [kabarɛ] *nm* night club, cabaret.

cabas [kabɑ] *nm* shopping bag.

cabillaud [kabijo] *nm* (fresh) cod.

cabine [kabin] *nf Nau Av* cabin; *Tél* phone booth, phone box; *(de camion)* cab; *(d'ascenseur)* car, cage; **c. (de bain)** beach hut; *(à la piscine)* cubicle; **c. (de pilotage)** cockpit; *(d'un grand avion)* flight deck; **c. d'essayage** fitting room; **c. d'aiguillage** signal box.

cabinet [kabinɛ] *nm (local) Méd* surgery, *Am* office; *(d'avocat)* office, chambers; *(clientèle de médecin ou d'avocat)* practice; *Pol* cabinet; *pl (toilettes)* toilet; **c. de toilette** bathroom, toilet; **c. de travail** study.

câble [kɑbl] *nm* cable; *(cordage)* rope; **la télévision par c.** cable television; **le c.** *TV* cable. **◆câbler** *vt (message)* to cable; **être câblé** *TV* to have cable.

caboche [kabɔʃ] *nf (tête) Fam* nut, noddle.

cabosser [kabose] *vt* to dent.

caboteur [kabotœr] *nm (bateau)* coaster.

cabotin, -ine [kabotɛ̃, -in] *nmf Th* ham actor, ham actress; *Fig* play-actor. **◆cabotinage** *nm* histrionics, play-acting.

cabrer (se) [səkabre] *vpr (cheval)* to rear (up); *(personne)* to rebel.

cabri [kabri] *nm (chevreau)* kid.

cabrioles [kabriɔl] *nfpl* **faire des c.** *(sauts)* to cavort, caper.

cabriolet [kabriɔlɛ] *nm Aut* convertible.

cacah(o)uète [kakawɛt] *nf* peanut.

cacao [kakao] *nm (boisson)* cocoa.

cacatoès [kakatɔɛs] *nm* cockatoo.

cachalot [kaʃalo] *nm* sperm whale.

cache-cache [kaʃkaʃ] *nm inv* hide-and-seek. **◆c.-col** *nm inv,* **◆c.-nez** *nm inv* scarf, muffler. **◆c.-sexe** *nm inv* G-string.

cachemire [kaʃmir] *nm (tissu)* cashmere.

cacher [kaʃe] *vt* to hide, conceal *(à* from); **je ne cache pas que ...** I don't hide the fact that ...; **c. la lumière à qn** to stand in s.o.'s light; **— se c.** *vpr* to hide. **◆cachette** *nf* hiding place; **en c.** in secret; **en c. de qn** without s.o. knowing.

cachet [kaʃɛ] *nm (sceau)* seal; *(de la poste)* postmark; *(comprimé)* tablet; *(d'acteur etc)* fee; *Fig* distinctive character. **◆cacheter** *vt* to seal.

cachot [kaʃo] *nm* dungeon.

cachotteries [kaʃɔtri] *nfpl* secretiveness; *(petits secrets)* little mysteries. **◆cachottier, -ière** *a & nmf* secretive (person).

cacophonie [kakɔfɔni] *nf* cacophony.

cactus [kaktys] *nm* cactus.

cadastre [kadastr] *nm (registre)* land register.

cadavre [kadɑvr] *nm* corpse. **◆cadavéri-**

que *a* (*teint etc*) cadaverous; **rigidité** c. rigor mortis.

caddie® [kadi] *nm* supermarket trolly *ou* *Am* cart.

cadeau, -x [kado] *nm* present, gift.

cadenas [kadna] *nm* padlock. ◆**cadenasser** *vt* to padlock.

cadence [kadɑ̃s] *nf* rhythm; *Mus* cadence; (*taux, vitesse*) rate; **en c.** in time. ◆**cadencé** *a* rhythmical.

cadet, -ette [kadɛ, -ɛt] *a* (*de deux frères etc*) younger; (*de plus de deux*) youngest; — *nmf* (*enfant*) younger (child); youngest (child); *Sp* junior; **c'est mon c.** he's my junior.

cadran [kadrɑ̃] *nm* (*de téléphone etc*) dial; (*de montre*) face; **c. solaire** sundial; **faire le tour du c.** to sleep round the clock.

cadre [kadr] *nm* 1 (*de photo, vélo etc*) frame; (*décor*) setting; (*sur un imprimé*) box; **dans le c. de** (*limites, contexte*) within the framework *ou* scope of, as part of. 2 (*chef*) *Com* executive, manager; *pl* (*personnel*) *Mil* officers; *Com* management, managers.

cadr/er [kadre] *vi* to tally (**avec** with); — *vt* (*image*) *Cin Phot* to centre. ◆**—eur** *nm* cameraman.

caduc, -uque [kadyk] *a* (*usage*) obsolete; *Bot* deciduous; *Jur* null and void.

cafard [kafar, -ard] 1 *nmf* (*espion*) sneak. 2 *nm* (*insecte*) cockroach; **avoir le c.** to be in the dumps; **ça me donne le c.** it depresses me. ◆**cafardeux, -euse** *a* (*personne*) in the dumps; (*qui donne le cafard*) depressing.

café [kafe] *nm* coffee; (*bar*) café; **c. au lait, c. crème** white coffee, coffee with milk; **c. noir, c. nature** black coffee; **tasse de c.** cup of black coffee. ◆**caféine** *nf* caffeine. ◆**cafétéria** *nf* cafeteria. ◆**cafetier** *nm* café owner. ◆**cafetière** *nf* percolator, coffeepot.

cafouiller [kafuje] *vi Fam* to make a mess (of things). ◆**cafouillage** *nm Fam* mess, muddle, snafu.

cage [kaʒ] *nf* cage; (*d'escalier*) well; (*d'ascenseur*) shaft; **c. des buts** *Fb* goal (area).

cageot [kaʒo] *nm* crate.

cagibi [kaʒibi] *nm* (*storage*) room, cubbyhole.

cagneux, -euse [kaɲø, -øz] *a* knock-kneed.

cagnotte [kaɲɔt] *nf* (*tirelire*) kitty.

cagoule [kagul] *nf* (*de bandit, pénitent*) hood.

cahier [kaje] *nm* (*carnet*) (note)book; *Scol* exercise book.

cahin-caha [kaɛ̃kaa] *adv* **aller c.-caha** to jog along (with ups and downs).

cahot [kao] *nm* jolt, bump. ◆**cahot/er** *vt* to jolt, bump; — *vi* (*véhicule*) to jolt along. ◆**—ant** *a,* ◆**cahoteux, -euse** *a* bumpy.

caïd [kaid] *nm Fam* big shot, leader.

caille [kaj] *nf* (*oiseau*) quail.

cailler [kaje] *vti,* — **se c.** *vpr* (*sang*) to clot, congeal; (*lait*) to curdle; **faire c.** (*lait*) to curdle; **ça caille** *Fam* it's freezing cold. ◆**caillot** *nm* (*blood*) clot.

caillou, -x [kaju] *nm* stone; (*galet*) pebble. ◆**caillouté** *a* gravelled. ◆**caillouteux, -euse** *a* stony.

caisse [kɛs] *nf* (*boîte*) case, box; (*cageot*) crate; (*guichet*) cash desk, pay desk; (*de supermarché*) checkout; (*fonds*) fund; (*bureau*) (paying-in) office; *Mus* drum; *Aut* body; **c. (enregistreuse)** cash register, till; **c. d'épargne** savings bank; **de c.** (*livre, recettes*) cash-. ◆**caissier, -ière** *nmf* cashier; (*de supermarché*) checkout assistant.

caisson [kɛsɔ̃] *nm* (*de plongeur*) & *Mil* caisson.

cajoler [kaʒɔle] *vt* (*câliner*) to pamper, pet, cosset. ◆**cajolerie(s)** *nf(pl)* pampering.

cajou [kaʒu] *nm* (*noix*) cashew.

cake [kɛk] *nm* fruit cake.

calamité [kalamite] *nf* calamity.

calandre [kalɑ̃dr] *nf Aut* radiator grille.

calcaire [kalkɛr] *a* (*terrain*) chalky; (*eau*) hard; — *nm Géol* limestone.

calciné [kalsine] *a* charred, burnt to a cinder.

calcium [kalsjɔm] *nm* calcium.

calcul [kalkyl] *nm* 1 calculation; (*estimation*) calculation, reckoning; (*discipline*) arithmetic; (*différentiel*) calculus. 2 *Méd* stone. ◆**calcul/er** *vt* (*compter*) to calculate, reckon; (*évaluer, combiner*) to calculate. ◆**—é** *a* (*risque etc*) calculated. ◆**calculateur** *nm* calculator, computer. ◆**calculatrice** *nf* (*ordinateur*) calculator.

cale [kal] *nf* 1 (*pour maintenir*) wedge. 2 *Nau* hold; **c. sèche** dry dock.

calé [kale] *a Fam* (*instruit*) clever (**en qch** at sth); (*difficile*) tough.

caleçon [kalsɔ̃] *nm* underpants; **c. de bain** bathing trunks.

calembour [kalɑ̃bur] *nm* pun.

calendrier [kalɑ̃drije] *nm* (*mois et jours*) calendar; (*programme*) timetable.

cale-pied [kalpje] *nm* (*de bicyclette*) toe-clip.

calepin [kalpɛ̃] *nm* (*pocket*) notebook.

caler [kale] 1 *vt* (*meuble etc*) to wedge (up); (*appuyer*) to prop (up). 2 *vt* (*moteur*) to stall; — *vi* to stall; (*abandonner*) *Fam* give up.

calfeutrer [kalføtre] *vt* (*avec du bourrelet*) to draughtproof; **se c.** (**chez soi**) to shut oneself away, hole up.

calibre [kalibr] *nm* (*diamètre*) calibre; (*d'œuf*) grade; **de ce c.** (*bêtise etc*) of this degree. ◆**calibrer** *vt* (*œufs*) to grade.

calice [kalis] *nm* (*vase*) *Rel* chalice.

calicot [kaliko] *nm* (*tissu*) calico.

califourchon (à) [akalifurʃɔ̃] *adv* astride; **se mettre à c. sur** to straddle.

câlin [kalɛ̃] *a* endearing, cuddly. ◆**câliner** *vt* (*cajoler*) to make a fuss of; (*caresser*) to cuddle. ◆**câlineries** *nfpl* endearing ways.

calleux, -euse [kalø, -øz] *a* callous, horny.

calligraphie [kaligrafi] *nf* calligraphy.

calme [kalm] *a* calm; (*flegmatique*) calm, cool; (*journée etc*) quiet, calm; — *nm* calm(ness); **du c.!** keep quiet!; (*pas de panique*) keep calm!; **dans le c.** (*travailler, étudier*) in peace and quiet. ◆**calm/er** *vt* (*douleur*) to soothe; (*inquiétude*) to calm; (*ardeur*) to damp(en); **c. qn** to calm s.o. (down); — **se c.** *vpr* to calm down. ◆**—ant** *nm* sedative; **sous calmants** under sedation.

calomnie [kalɔmni] *nf* slander; (*par écrit*) libel. ◆**calomnier** *vt* to slander; to libel. ◆**calomnieux, -euse** *a* slanderous; libellous.

calorie [kalɔri] *nf* calorie.

calorifère [kalɔrifɛr] *nm* stove.

calorifuge [kalɔrifyʒ] *a* (heat-)insulating. ◆**calorifuger** *vt* to lag.

calot [kalo] *nm* *Mil* forage cap.

calotte [kalɔt] *nf* *Rel* skull cap; (*gifle*) *Fam* slap; **c. glaciaire** icecap.

calque [kalk] *nm* (*dessin*) tracing; (*imitation*) (exact *ou* carbon) copy; (**papier-**)**c.** tracing paper. ◆**calquer** *vt* to trace; to copy; **c. sur** to model on.

calumet [kalyme] *nm* **c. de la paix** peace pipe.

calvaire [kalvɛr] *nm* *Rel* calvary; *Fig* agony.

calvitie [kalvisi] *nf* baldness.

camarade [kamarad] *nmf* friend, chum; *Pol* comrade; **c. de jeu** playmate; **c. d'atelier** workmate. ◆**camaraderie** *nf* friendship, companionship.

cambouis [kɑ̃bwi] *nm* grease, (engine) oil.

cambrer [kɑ̃bre] *vt* to arch; **c. les reins** *ou* **le buste** to throw out one's chest; — **se c.** *vpr* to throw back one's shoulders. ◆**cambrure** *nf* (*du pied*) arch, instep.

cambriol/er [kɑ̃brijɔle] *vt* to burgle, *Am* burglarize. ◆**—age** *nm* burglary. ◆**—eur, -euse** *nm* burglar.

came [kam] *nf* *Tech* cam; **arbre à cames** camshaft.

camée [kame] *nm* (*pierre*) cameo.

caméléon [kameleɔ̃] *nm* (*reptile*) chameleon.

camélia [kamelja] *nm* *Bot* camellia.

camelot [kamlo] *nm* street hawker. ◆**camelote** *nf* cheap goods, junk.

camembert [kamɑ̃bɛr] *nm* Camembert (cheese).

camer (se) [səkame] *vpr Fam* to get high (on drugs).

caméra [kamera] *nf* (TV *ou* film) camera. ◆**cameraman** *nm* (*pl* **-mans** *ou* **-men**) cameraman.

camion [kamjɔ̃] *nm* lorry, *Am* truck. ◆**c.-benne** *nm* (*pl* **camions-bennes**) dustcart, *Am* garbage truck. ◆**c.-citerne** *nm* (*pl* **camions-citernes**) tanker, *Am* tank truck. ◆**camionnage** *nm* (road) haulage, *Am* trucking. ◆**camionnette** *nf* van. ◆**camionneur** *nm* (*entrepreneur*) haulage contractor, *Am* trucker; (*conducteur*) lorry *ou Am* truck driver.

camisole [kamizɔl] *nf* **c. de force** straitjacket.

camomille [kamɔmij] *nf* *Bot* camomile; (*tisane*) camomile tea.

camoufl/er [kamufle] *vt* to camouflage. ◆**—age** *nm* camouflage.

camp [kɑ̃] *nm* camp; **feu de c.** campfire; **lit de c.** camp bed; **c. de concentration** concentration camp; **dans mon c.** (*jeu*) on my side; **ficher** *ou* **foutre le c.** *Arg* to clear off. ◆**camp/er** *vi* to camp; — *vt* (*personnage*) to portray (boldly); (*chapeau etc*) to plant boldly; — **se c.** *vpr* to plant oneself (boldly) (**devant** in front of). ◆**—ement** *nm* encampment, camp. ◆**—eur, -euse** *nmf* camper. ◆**camping** *nm* camping; (*terrain*) camp(ing) site. ◆**camping-car** *nm* camper.

campagne [kɑ̃paɲ] *nf* **1** country(side); **à la c.** in the country. **2** (*électorale, militaire etc*) campaign. ◆**campagnard, -arde** *a* country; — *nm* countryman; — *nf* countrywoman.

campanile [kɑ̃panil] *nm* belltower.

camphre [kɑ̃fr] *nm* camphor.

campus [kɑ̃pys] *nm* *Univ* campus.

camus [kamy] *a* (*personne*) snub-nosed; **nez c.** snub nose.

Canada [kanada] *nm* Canada. ◆**canadien, -ienne** *a* & *nmf* Canadian; — *nf* fur-lined jacket.

canaille [kanɑj] *nf* rogue, scoundrel; — *a* vulgar, cheap.

canal, -aux [kanal, -o] *nm* (*artificiel*) canal; (*bras de mer*) & *TV* channel; (*conduite*) & *Anat* duct; **par le c. de** via, through. ◆**canalisation** *nf* (*de gaz etc*) mains. ◆**canaliser** *vt* (*rivière etc*) to canalize; (*diriger*) *Fig* to channel.

canapé [kanape] *nm* **1** (*siège*) sofa, couch, settee. **2** (*tranche de pain*) canapé.

canard [kanar] *nm* **1** duck; (*mâle*) drake. **2** *Mus* false note. **3** (*journal*) *Péj* rag. ◆**canarder** *vt* (*faire feu sur*) to fire at *ou* on.

canari [kanari] *nm* canary.

cancans [kãkã] *nmpl* (*malicious*) gossip. ◆**cancaner** *vi* to gossip. ◆**cancanier, -ière** *a* gossipy.

cancer [kãser] *nm* cancer; **le C.** (*signe*) Cancer. ◆**cancéreux, -euse** *a* cancerous; – *nmf* cancer patient. ◆**cancérigène** *a* carcinogenic. ◆**cancérologue** *nmf* cancer specialist.

cancre [kãkr] *nm* *Scol Péj* dunce.

cancrelat [kãkrəla] *nm* cockroach.

candélabre [kãdelabr] *nm* candelabra.

candeur [kãdœr] *nf* innocence, artlessness. ◆**candide** *a* artless, innocent.

candidat, -ate [kãdida, -at] *nmf* candidate; (*à un poste*) applicant, candidate; **être** *ou* **se porter c.** to apply for. ◆**candidature** *nf* application; *Pol* candidacy; **poser sa c.** to apply (**à** for).

cane [kan] *nf* (*female*) duck. ◆**caneton** *nm* duckling.

canette [kanɛt] *nf* **1** (*de bière*) (small) bottle. **2** (*bobine*) spool.

canevas [kanva] *nm* (*toile*) canvas; (*ébauche*) framework, outline.

caniche [kaniʃ] *nm* poodle.

canicule [kanikyl] *nf* scorching heat; (*période*) dog days.

canif [kanif] *nm* penknife.

canine [kanin] *a* **1** (*espèce, race*) canine; **exposition c.** dog show. **2** *nf* (*dent*) canine.

caniveau, -x [kanivo] *nm* gutter (*in street*).

canne [kan] *nf* (*walking*) stick; (*à sucre, de bambou*) cane; (*de roseau*) reed; **c. à pêche** fishing rod.

cannelle [kanɛl] *nf* *Bot Culin* cinnamon.

cannelure [kanlyr] *nf* groove; *Archit* flute.

cannette [kanɛt] *nf* = **canette**.

cannibale [kanibal] *nmf* & *a* cannibal. ◆**cannibalisme** *nm* cannibalism.

canoë [kanɔe] *nm* canoe; *Sp* canoeing. ◆**canoéiste** *nmf* canoeist.

canon [kanɔ̃] *nm* **1** (big) gun; *Hist* cannon; (*de fusil etc*) barrel; **c. lisse** smooth bore; **chair à c.** cannon fodder. **2** (*règle*) canon.

◆**canoniser** *vt* to canonize. ◆**canonnade** *nf* gunfire. ◆**canonnier** *nm* gunner.

cañon [kanɔ̃] *nm* canyon.

canot [kano] *nm* boat; **c. de sauvetage** lifeboat; **c. pneumatique** rubber dinghy. ◆**canot/er** *vi* to boat, go boating. ◆**–age** *nm* boating.

cantaloup [kãtalu] *nm* (*melon*) cantaloup(e).

cantate [kãtat] *nf* *Mus* cantata.

cantatrice [kãtatris] *nf* opera singer.

cantine [kãtin] *nf* **1** (*réfectoire*) canteen; **manger à la c.** *Scol* to have school dinners. **2** (*coffre*) tin trunk.

cantique [kãtik] *nm* hymn.

canton [kãtɔ̃] *nm* (*en France*) district (*division of arrondissement*); (*en Suisse*) canton. ◆**cantonal, -aux** *a* divisional; cantonal.

cantonade (à la) [alakãtɔnad] *adv* (*parler etc*) to all and sundry, to everyone in general.

cantonn/er [kãtɔne] *vt* *Mil* to billet; (*confiner*) to confine; – *vi* *Mil* to be billeted; **— se c.** *vpr* to confine oneself (**dans**) to. ◆**–ement** *nm* (*lieu*) billet, quarters.

cantonnier [kãtɔnje] *nm* road mender.

canular [kanylar] *nm* practical joke, hoax.

canyon [kanjɔ̃] *nm* canyon.

caoutchouc [kautʃu] *nm* rubber; (*élastique*) rubber band; *pl* (*chaussures*) galoshes; **en c.** (*balle etc*) rubber-; **c. mousse** foam. ◆**caoutchouter** *vt* to rubberize. ◆**caoutchouteux, -euse** *a* rubbery.

CAP [seape] *nm abrév* (*certificat d'aptitude professionnelle*) technical and vocational diploma.

cap [kap] *nm* *Géog* cape, headland; *Nau* course; **mettre le c. sur** to steer a course for; **franchir** *ou* **doubler le c. de** (*difficulté*) to get over the worst of; **franchir** *ou* **doubler le c. de la trentaine**/*etc* to turn thirty/*etc*.

capable [kapabl] *a* capable, able; **c. de faire** able to do, capable of doing. ◆**capacité** *nf* ability, capacity; (*contenance*) capacity.

cape [kap] *nf* (*grande*) cloak.

CAPES [kapɛs] *nm abrév* (*certificat d'aptitude professionnelle à l'enseignement secondaire*) teaching diploma.

capillaire [kapilɛr] *a* (*huile, lotion*) hair-.

capitaine [kapiten] *nm* captain.

capital, -ale, -aux [kapital, -o] *a* **1** major, fundamental, capital; (*peine*) capital; (*péché*) deadly. **2** *a* (*lettre, ville*) capital. **3** *nm* & *nmpl* *Fin* capital. ◆**capitaliser** *vt* (*accumuler*) to build up; – *vi* to save up. ◆**capitalisme** *nm* capitalism. ◆**capitaliste** a & nmf capital-ist.

capiteux, -euse [kapitø, -øz] a (vin, parfum) heady.

capitonn/er [kapitɔne] vt to pad, upholster. ◆**—age** nm (garniture) padding, upholstery.

capituler [kapityle] vi to surrender, capitulate. ◆**capitulation** nf surrender, capitulation.

caporal, -aux [kapɔral, -o] nm corporal.

capot [kapo] nm Aut bonnet, Am hood.

capote [kapɔt] nf Aut hood, Am (convertible) top; Mil greatcoat; **c. (anglaise)** (préservatif) Fam condom. ◆**capoter** vi Aut Av to overturn.

câpre [kɑpr] nf Bot Culin caper.

caprice [kapris] nm (passing) whim, caprice. ◆**capricieux, -euse** a capricious.

Capricorne [kaprikɔrn] nm le C. (signe) Capricorn.

capsule [kapsyl] nf (spatiale) & Méd etc capsule; (de bouteille, pistolet d'enfant) cap. ◆**capter** [kapte] vt (faveur etc) to win; (attention) to capture, win; (eau) to draw off; Rad to pick up.

captif, -ive [kaptif, -iv] a & nmf captive. ◆**captiver** vt to captivate, fascinate. ◆**captivité** nf captivity.

capture [kaptyr] nf capture; catch. ◆**capturer** vt (criminel, navire) to capture; (animal) to catch, capture.

capuche [kapyʃ] nf hood. ◆**capuchon** nm hood; (de moine) cowl; (pèlerine) hooded (rain)coat; (de stylo) cap, top.

capucine [kapysin] nf (plante) nasturtium.

caquet [kake] nm (bavardage) cackle. ◆**caquet/er** vi (poule, personne) to cackle. ◆**—age** nm cackle.

car [kar] 1 conj because, for. 2 nm coach, bus, Am bus; **c. de police** police van.

carabine [karabin] nf rifle, carbine; **c. à air comprimé** airgun.

carabiné [karabine] a Fam violent; (punition, amende) very stiff.

caracoler [karakɔle] vi to prance, caper.

caractère [karaktɛr] nm 1 (lettre) Typ character; **en petits caractères** in small print; **caractères d'imprimerie** block capitals ou letters; **caractères gras** bold type ou characters. 2 (tempérament, nature) character, nature; (attribut) characteristic; **aucun c. de gravité** no serious element; **son ou his ou her uneven temper; avoir bon c.** to be good-natured. ◆**caractériel, -ielle** a (trait, troubles) character-; – a & nmf

disturbed (child). ◆**caractériser** vt to characterize; **se c. par** to be characterized by. ◆**caractéristique** a & nf characteristic.

carafe [karaf] nf decanter, carafe.

carambol/er [karãbɔle] vt Aut to smash into. ◆**—age** nm pileup, multiple smash-up.

caramel [karamɛl] nm caramel; (bonbon dur) toffee.

carapace [karapas] nf (de tortue etc) & Fig shell.

carat [kara] nm carat.

caravane [karavan] nf (dans le désert) caravan; Aut caravan, Am trailer; **c. publicitaire** publicity convoy. ◆**caravaning** n, ◆**caravanage** n caravanning.

carbone [karbɔn] nm carbon; (papier) c. carbon (paper). ◆**carboniser** vt to burn (to ashes), char; (substance) Ch to carbonize; **être mort carbonisé** to be burned to death.

carburant [karbyrã] nm Aut fuel. ◆**carburateur** nm carburettor, Am carburetor.

carcan [karkã] nm Hist iron collar; (contrainte) Fig yoke.

carcasse [karkas] nf Anat carcass; (d'immeuble etc) frame, shell.

cardiaque [kardjak] a (trouble etc) heart-; **crise c.** heart attack; **arrêt c.** cardiac arrest; – nmf heart patient.

cardinal, -aux [kardinal, -o] 1 a (nombre, point) cardinal. 2 nm Rel cardinal.

Carême [karɛm] nm Lent.

carence [karãs] nf inadequacy, incompetence; Méd deficiency.

carène [karɛn] nf Nau hull. ◆**caréné** a Aut Av streamlined.

caresse [karɛs] nf caress. ◆**caress/er** [karese] vt (animal, enfant etc) to stroke, pat, fondle; (femme, homme) to caress; (espoir) to cherish. ◆**—ant** a endearing, loving.

cargaison [kargɛzɔ̃] nf cargo, freight. ◆**cargo** nm freighter, cargo boat.

caricature [karikatyr] nf caricature. ◆**caricatural, -aux** a ludicrous; **portrait c.** portrait in caricature. ◆**caricaturer** vt to caricature.

carie [kari] nf **la c. (dentaire)** tooth decay; **une c.** a cavity. ◆**carié** a (dent) decayed, bad.

carillon [karijɔ̃] nm (cloches) chimes, peal; (horloge) chiming clock. ◆**carillonner** vi to chime, peal.

carlingue [karlɛ̃g] nf (fuselage) Av cabin.

carnage [karnaʒ] nm carnage.
carnassier, -ière [karnasje, -jɛr] a carnivorous; — nm carnivore.
carnaval, pl **-als** [karnaval] nm carnival.
carné [karne] a (régime) meat-.
carnet [karnɛ] nm notebook; (de timbres, chèques, adresses etc) book; **c. de notes** school report; **c. de route** logbook; **c. de vol** Av logbook.
carnivore [karnivɔr] a carnivorous; — nm carnivore.
carotte [karɔt] nf carrot.
carotter [karɔte] vt Arg to wangle, cadge (à qn from s.o.).
carpe [karp] nf carp.
carpette [karpɛt] nf rug.
carquois [karkwa] nm (étui) quiver.
carré [kare] a square; (en affaires) plain-dealing; — nm square; (de jardin) patch; Nau messroom; **c. de soie** (square) silk scarf.
carreau, -x [karo] nm (vitre) (window) pane; (pavé) tile; (sol) tiled floor; Cartes diamonds; **à carreaux** (nappe etc) check(ed); **se tenir à c.** to watch one's step; **rester sur le c.** to be left for dead; (candidat) Fig to be left out in the cold. ◆**carrel/er** vt to tile. ◆**-age** nm (sol) tiled floor; (action) tiling.
carrefour [karfur] nm crossroads.
carrelet [karlɛ] nm (poisson) plaice, Am flounder.
carrément [karemã] adv (dire etc) straight out, bluntly; (complètement) downright, well and truly.
carrer (se) [səkare] vpr to settle down firmly.
carrière [karjɛr] nf 1 (terrain) quarry. 2 (métier) career.
carrosse [karɔs] nm Hist (horse-drawn) carriage. ◆**carrossable** a suitable for vehicles. ◆**carrosserie** nf Aut body(work).
carrousel [karuzɛl] nm (tourbillon) Fig whirl, merry-go-round.
carrure [karyr] nf breadth of shoulders, build; Fig calibre.
cartable [kartabl] nm Scol satchel.
carte [kart] nf card; (de lecteur) ticket; Géog map; Nau Mét chart; Culin menu; pl (jeu) cards; **c. (postale)** (post)card; **c. à jouer** playing card; **c. de crédit** credit card; **c. des vins** wine list; **c. grise** Aut vehicle registration; **c. blanche** Fig free hand.
cartel [kartɛl] nm Écon Pol cartel.
carter [kartɛr] nm (de moteur) Aut crankcase; (de bicyclette) chain guard.

cartilage [kartilaʒ] nm cartilage.
carton [kartɔ̃] nm cardboard; (boîte) cardboard box, carton; (à dessin) portfolio; **en c.-pâte** (faux) Péj pasteboard; **faire un c. sur** Fam to take a potshot at. ◆**cartonn/er** vt (livre) to case; **livre cartonné** hardback. ◆**-age** nm (emballage) cardboard package.
cartouche [kartuʃ] nf cartridge; (de cigarettes) carton; Phot cassette. ◆**cartouchière** nf (ceinture) cartridge belt.
cas [kɑ] nm case; **en tout c.** in any case ou event; **en aucun c.** on no account; **en c. de besoin** if need(s) be; **en c. d'accident** in the event of an accident; **en c. d'urgence** in (case of) an emergency; **faire c. de/peu de c. de** to set great/little store by; **au c. où elle tomberait** if she should fall; **pour le c. où il pleuvrait** in case it rains.
casanier, -ière [kazanje, -jɛr] a & nmf home-loving (person); (pantouflard) Péj stay-at-home (person).
casaque [kazak] nf (de jockey) shirt, blouse.
cascade [kaskad] nf 1 waterfall; (série) spate; **en c.** in succession. 2 Cin stunt. ◆**cascadeur, -euse** nmf Cin stunt man, stunt woman.
case [kaz] nf 1 pigeonhole; (de tiroir) compartment; (d'échiquier etc) square; (de formulaire) box. 2 (hutte) hut, cabin.
caser [kaze] vt Fam (ranger) to park, place; **c. qn** (dans un logement ou un travail) to find a place for s.o.; (marier) to marry s.o. off; — **se c.** vpr to settle down.
caserne [kazɛrn] nf Mil barracks; **c. de pompiers** fire station.
casier [kazje] nm pigeonhole, compartment; (meuble à tiroirs) filing cabinet; (fermant à clef, à consigne automatique) locker; **c. à bouteilles/à disques** bottle/record rack; **c. judiciaire** criminal record.
casino [kazino] nm casino.
casque [kask] nm helmet; (pour cheveux) (hair) dryer; (à écouteurs) headphones; **les Casques bleus** the UN peace-keeping force. ◆**casqué** a helmeted, wearing a helmet.
casquer [kaske] vi Fam to pay up, cough up.
casquette [kaskɛt] nf (coiffure) cap.
cassation [kasasjɔ̃] nf Cour de c. supreme court of appeal.
casse¹ [kas] nf 1 (action) breakage; (objets) breakages; (grabuge) Fam trouble; **mettre à la c.** to scrap; **vendre à la c.** to sell for

scrap. **2** *Typ* case; **bas/haut de c.** lower/upper case.

casse² [kɑs] *nm* (*cambriolage*) *Arg* break-in.

casse-cou [kasku] *nmf inv* (*personne*) *Fam* daredevil. ◆**c.-gueule** *nm inv* snack. ◆**c.-croûte** *nm inv* snack. — *a (annuler*) perilous. ◆**c.-noisettes** *nm inv,* ◆**c.-noix** *nm inv* nut-cracker(s). ◆**c.-pieds** *nmf inv* (*personne*) *Fam* pain in the neck. ◆**c.-tête** *nm inv* **1** (*massue*) club. **2** (*problème*) headache; (*jeu*) puzzle, brain teaser.

cass/er [kɑse] *vt* to break; (*noix*) to crack; (*annuler*) *Jur* to annul; (*dégrader*) *Mil* to cashier; — *vi,* — **se c.** *vpr* to break; **il me casse la tête** *Fam* he's giving me a headache; **elle me casse les pieds** *Fam* she's getting on my nerves; **se c. la tête** *Fam* to rack one's brains; **se c. la figure à qn** *Fam* to smash s.o.'s face in; **se c. la figure** (*tomber*) *Fam* to come a cropper, *Am* take a spill; **ça ne casse rien** *Fam* it's nothing special; **ça vaut 50F à tout c.** *Fam* it's worth 50F at the very most; **il ne s'est pas cassé** *Iron Fam* he didn't bother himself *ou* exhaust himself. ◆—**ant** *a* (*fragile*) brittle; (*brusque*) imperious; (*fatigant*) *Fam* exhausting. ◆—**eur** *nm Aut* breaker, scrap merchant; (*manifestant*) demonstrator who damages property.

casserole [kasrɔl] *nf* (sauce)pan.

cassette [kasɛt] *nf* (*pour magnétophone ou magnétoscope*) cassette; **sur c.** (*film*) on video; **faire une c. de** (*film*) to make a video of.

cassis 1 [kasis] *nm Bot* blackcurrant; (*boisson*) blackcurrant liqueur. **2** [kasi] *nm Aut* dip (across road).

cassoulet [kasule] *nm* stew (*of meat and beans*).

cassure [kɑsyr] *nf* (*fissure, rupture*) break; *Géol* fault.

castagnettes [kastaɲɛt] *nfpl* castanets.

caste [kast] *nf* caste; **esprit de c.** class consciousness.

castor [kastɔr] *nm* beaver.

castrer [kastre] *vt* to castrate. ◆**castration** *nf* castration.

cataclysme [kataklism] *nm* cataclysm.

catacombes [katakɔ̃b] *nfpl* catacombs.

catalogue [katalɔg] *nm* catalogue. ◆**cataloguer** *vt* (*livres etc*) to catalogue; **c. qn** *Péj* to categorize s.o.

catalyseur [katalizœr] *nm Ch & Fig* catalyst.

cataphote® [katafɔt] *nm Aut* reflector.

cataplasme [kataplasm] *nm Méd* poultice.

catapulte [katapylt] *nf Hist Av* catapult. ◆**catapulter** *vt* to catapult.

cataracte [katarakt] *nf* **1** *Méd* cataract. **2** (*cascade*) falls, cataract.

catastrophe [katastrɔf] *nf* disaster, catastrophe; **atterrir en c.** to make an emergency landing. ◆**catastrophique** *a* disastrous, catastrophic.

catch [katʃ] *nm* (all-in) wrestling. ◆**catcheur, -euse** *nmf* wrestler.

catéchisme [kateʃism] *nm Rel* catechism.

catégorie [kategɔri] *nf* category. ◆**catégorique** *a* categorical.

cathédrale [katedral] *nf* cathedral.

catholicisme [katɔlisism] *nm* Catholicism. ◆**catholique** *a & nmf* Catholic; **pas (très) c.** (*affaire, personne*) *Fig* shady, doubtful.

catimini (en) [ɑ̃katimini] *adv* on the sly.

cauchemar [koʃmar] *nm* nightmare.

cause [koz] *nf Jur* case; **à c. de** because of, on account of; **et pour c.!** for a very good reason!; **pour c. de** on account of; **en connaissance de c.** in full knowledge of the facts; **mettre en c.** (*la bonne foi de qn etc*) to (call into) question; (*personne*) to implicate; **en c.** involved, in question.

caus/er [koze] **1** *vt* (*provoquer*) to cause. **2** *vi* (*bavarder*) to chat (**de** about); (*discourir*) to talk; (*jaser*) to blab. ◆—**ant** *a Fam* chatty, talkative. ◆**causerie** *nf* talk. ◆**causette** *nf* **faire la c.** *Fam* to have a little chat.

caustique [kostik] *a* (*substance, esprit*) caustic.

cauteleux, -euse [kotlø, -øz] *a* wily, sly.

cautériser [koterize] *vt Méd* to cauterize.

caution [kosjɔ̃] *nf* surety; (*pour libérer qn*) *Jur* bail; **sous c.** on bail; **sujet à c.** (*nouvelle etc*) very doubtful. ◆**cautionn/er** *vt* (*approuver*) to sanction. ◆—**ement** *nm* (*garantie*) surety.

cavalcade [kavalkad] *nf Fam* stampede; (*défilé*) cavalcade. ◆**cavale** *nf* **en c.** *Arg* on the run. ◆**cavaler** *vi Fam* to run, rush.

cavalerie [kavalri] *nf Mil* cavalry; (*de cirque*) horses. ◆**cavalier, -ière 1** *nmf* rider; — *nm Mil* trooper, cavalryman; *Échecs* knight; — *af* **allée cavalière** bridle path. **2** *nmf* (*pour danser*) partner, escort. **3** *a* (*insolent*) offhand.

cave [kav] **1** *nf* cellar, vault. **2** *a* sunken, hollow. ◆**caveau, -x** *nm* (*sépulture*) (burial) vault.

caverne [kavɛrn] *nf* cave, cavern; **homme**

des **cavernes** caveman. ◆**caverneux, -euse** a (voix, rire) hollow, deep-sounding.

caviar [kavjar] nm caviar(e).

cavité [kavite] nf cavity.

CCP [sesepe] nm abrév (Compte chèque postal) PO Giro account, Am Post Office checking account.

ce¹ [s(ə)] (c' before e and ê) pron dém **1** it, that; **c'est toi/bon/demain**/etc it's ou that's you/good/tomorrow/etc; **c'est mon médecin** he's my doctor; **ce sont eux qui ...** they are the ones who ...; **c'est à elle de jouer** it's her turn to play; **est-ce que tu viens?** are you coming?; **sur ce** at this point, thereupon. **2 ce que, ce qui** what; **je sais ce qui est bon/ce que tu veux** I know what is good/what you want; **ce que c'est beau!** how beautiful it is!

ce², **cette**, pl **ces** [s(ə), sɛt, se] (ce becomes cet before a vowel or mute h) a dém this, that, pl these, those; (+ -ci) this, pl these; (+ -là) that, pl those; **ce man** ou **cet homme** this ou that man; **cet homme-ci** this man; **cet homme-là** that man.

ceci [səsi] pron dém this; **écoutez bien c.** listen to this.

cécité [sesite] nf blindness.

céder [sede] vt to give up (à to); Jur to transfer; **c. le pas à** to give way ou precedence to; – vi (personne) to give way, give in, yield (à to); (branche, chaise etc) to give way.

cédille [sedij] nf Gram cedilla.

cèdre [sɛdr] nm (arbre, bois) cedar.

CEE [seøø] nf abrév (Communauté économique européenne) EEC.

ceindre [sɛdr] vt (épée) Lit to gird on.

ceinture [sɛtyr] nf belt; (de robe de chambre) cord; (taille) Anat waist; (de remparts) Hist girdle; **petite/grande c.** Rail inner/outer circle; **c. de sécurité** Aut Av seatbelt; **c. de sauvetage** lifebelt. ◆**ceinturer** vt to seize round the waist; Rugby to tackle; (ville) to girdle, surround.

cela [s(ə)la] pron dém (pour désigner) that; (sujet indéfini) it, that; **c. m'attriste que ...** it saddens me that ...; **quand/comment**/etc **c.?** when?/how?/etc; **c'est c.** that is so.

célèbre [selɛbr] a famous. ◆**célébrité** nf fame; (personne) celebrity.

célébrer [selebre] vt to celebrate. ◆**célébration** nf celebration (de of).

céleri [sɛlri] nm (en branches) celery.

céleste [selɛst] a celestial, heavenly.

célibat [seliba] nm celibacy. ◆**célibataire** a (non marié) single, unmarried; (chaste) celibate; – nm bachelor; – nf unmarried woman, spinster.

celle voir **celui**.

cellier [selje] nm storeroom (for wine etc).

cellophane® [selɔfan] nf cellophane®.

cellule [selyl] nf cell. ◆**cellulaire** a (tissu etc) Biol cell-; **voiture c.** prison van.

celluloïd [selyloid] nm celluloid.

cellulose [selyloz] nf cellulose.

celtique ou **celte** [sɛltik, sɛlt] a Celtic.

celui, **celle**, pl **ceux**, **celles** [səlųi, sɛl, sø, sɛl] pron dém **1** the one, pl those, the ones; **c. de Jean** John's (one); **ceux de Jean** John's (ones), those of John. **2** (+ -ci) this one, pl these (ones); (dont on vient de parler) the latter; (+ -là) that one, pl those (ones); the former; **ceux-ci sont gros** these (ones) are big.

cendre [sɑdr] nf ash. ◆**cendré** a ash(-coloured), ashen. ◆**cendrée** nf Sp cinder track.

Cendrillon [sɑdrijɔ] nm Cinderella.

censé [sɑse] a supposed; **il n'est pas c. le savoir** he's not supposed to know.

censeur [sɑsœr] nm Scol assistant headmaster, vice-principal. ◆**censure** nf la c. (examen) censorship; (comité, service) the censor; **motion de c.** Pol censure motion. ◆**censurer** vt (film etc) to censor; (critiquer) & Pol to censure.

cent [sɑ] ([sɑt] pl [sɑz] before vowel and mute h except un and onze) a & nm hundred; **c. pages** a ou one hundred pages; **deux cents pages** two hundred pages; **deux c. trois pages** two hundred and three pages; **cinq pour c.** five per cent. ◆**centaine** nf une c. a hundred (or so); **des centaines de** hundreds of. ◆**centenaire** a & nmf centenarian; – nm (anniversaire) centenary. ◆**centième** a & nmf hundredth; **un c.** a hundredth. ◆**centigrade** a centigrade. ◆**centime** nm centime. ◆**centimètre** nm centimetre; (ruban) tape measure.

central, -aux [sɑtral, -o] **1** a central; **pouvoir c.** (power of) central government. **2** nm **c.** (téléphonique) (telephone) exchange. ◆**centrale** nf (usine) power station. ◆**centraliser** vt o centralize. ◆**centre** nm centre; **c. commercial** shopping centre. ◆**c.-ville** nm inv city ou town centre. ◆**centrer** vt to centre. ◆**centrifuge** a centrifugal. ◆**centrifugeuse** nf liquidizer, juice extractor.

centuple [sɑtypl] nm hundredfold; **au c.** a hundredfold. ◆**centupler** vti to increase a hundredfold.

cep [sɛp] *nm* vine stock. ◆**cépage** *nm* vine (plant).

cependant [səpɑ̃dɑ̃] *conj* however, yet.

céramique [seramik] *nf* (*art*) ceramics; (*matière*) ceramic; **de** *ou* **en c.** ceramic.

cerceau, -x [sɛrso] *nm* hoop.

cercle [sɛrkl] *nm* (*forme, groupe, étendue*) circle; **c. vicieux** vicious circle.

cercueil [sɛrkœj] *nm* coffin.

céréale [sereal] *nf* cereal.

cérébral, -aux [serebral, -o] *a* cerebral.

cérémonie [seremɔni] *nf* ceremony; **de c.** (*tenue etc*) ceremonial; **sans c.** (*inviter, manger*) informally; **faire des cérémonies** *Fam* to make a lot of fuss. ◆**cérémonial,** *pl* **-als** *nm* ceremonial. ◆**cérémonieux, -euse** *a* ceremonious.

cerf [sɛr] *nm* deer; (*mâle*) stag. ◆**cerf-volant** *nm* (*pl* **cerfs-volants**) (*jouet*) kite.

cerise [s(ə)riz] *nf* cherry. ◆**cerisier** *nm* cherry tree.

cerne [sɛrn] *nm* (*cercle, marque*) ring. ◆**cerner** *vt* to surround; (*problème*) to define; **les yeux cernés** with rings under one's eyes.

certain [sɛrtɛ̃] **1** *a* (*sûr*) certain, sure; **il est ou c'est c. que tu réussiras** you're certain *ou* sure to succeed; **je suis c. de réussir** I'm certain *ou* sure I'll succeed; **être c. de qch** to be certain *ou* sure of sth. **2** *a* (*imprécis, difficile à fixer*) certain; *pl* certain, some; **un c. temps** a certain (amount of) time; **— *pron* c.** some (people), certain people; (*choses*) some. ◆**certainement** *adv* certainly. ◆**certes** *adv* indeed.

certificat [sɛrtifika] *nm* certificate. ◆**certifi/er** *vt* to certify; **je vous certifie que** I assure you that. ◆**-é** *a* (*professeur*) qualified.

certitude [sɛrtityd] *nf* certainty; **avoir la c.** que to be certain that.

cerveau, -x [sɛrvo] *nm* (*organe*) brain; (*intelligence*) mind, brain(s); **rhume de c.** head cold; **fuite des cerveaux** brain drain.

cervelas [sɛrvəla] *nm* saveloy.

cervelle [sɛrvɛl] *nf* (*substance*) brain; *Culin* brains; **tête sans c.** scatterbrain.

ces *voir* **ce** [2].

CES [seəɛs] *nm abrév* (*collège d'enseignement secondaire*) comprehensive school, *Am* high school.

césarienne [sezarjɛn] *nf* *Méd* Caesarean (section).

cessation [sɛsasjɔ̃] *nf* (*arrêt, fin*) suspension.

cesse [sɛs] *nf* **sans c.** incessantly; **elle n'a** (pas) **eu de c. que je fasse . . .** she had no rest until I did . . .

cesser [sese] *vti* to stop; **faire c.** to put a stop *ou* halt to; **il ne cesse** (**pas**) **de parler** he doesn't stop talking. ◆**cessez-le-feu** *nm inv* ceasefire.

cession [sɛsjɔ̃] *nf* *Jur* transfer.

c'est-à-dire [setadir] *conj* that is (to say), in other words.

cet, cette *voir* **ce** [2].

ceux *voir* **celui**.

chacal, *pl* **-als** [ʃakal] *nm* jackal.

chacun, -une [ʃakœ̃, -yn] *pron* each (one), every one; (*tout le monde*) everyone.

chagrin [ʃagrɛ̃] **1** *nm* sorrow, grief; **avoir du c.** to be very upset. **2** *a* *Lit* doleful. ◆**chagriner** *vt* to upset, distress.

chahut [ʃay] *nm* racket, noisy disturbance. ◆**chahut/er** *vi* to create a racket *ou* a noisy disturbance; **— *vt*** (*professeur*) to be rowdy with, play up. ◆**-eur, -euse** *nmf* rowdy.

chai [ʃɛ] *nm* wine and spirits storehouse.

chaîne [ʃɛn] *nf* chain; *TV* channel, network; *Géog* chain; range; *Nau* cable; *Tex* warp; (*pl* **liens**) *Fig* shackles, chains; **c. de montage** assembly line; **travail à la c.** production-line work; **c. haute fidélité, c. hi-fi** hi-fi system; **c. de magasins** chain of shops *ou* *Am* stores; **collision en c.** *Aut* multiple collision; **réaction en c.** chain reaction. ◆**chaînette** *nf* (*small*) chain. ◆**chaînon** *nm* (*anneau, lien*) link.

chair [ʃɛr] *nf* flesh; (*couleur*) **c.** flesh-coloured; **en c. et en os** in the flesh; **la c. de poule** goose pimples, gooseflesh; **bien en c.** plump; **c. à saucisses** sausage meat.

chaire [ʃɛr] *nf* *Univ* chair; *Rel* pulpit.

chaise [ʃɛz] *nf* chair, seat; **c. longue** (*siège pliant*) deckchair; **c. d'enfant, c. haute** high-chair.

chaland [ʃalɑ̃] *nm* barge, lighter.

châle [ʃal] *nm* shawl.

chalet [ʃalɛ] *nm* chalet.

chaleur [ʃalœr] *nf* heat; (*douce*) warmth; (*d'un accueil, d'une voix etc*) warmth; (*des convictions*) ardour; (*d'une discussion*) heat. ◆**chaleureux, -euse** *a* warm.

challenge [ʃalɑ̃ʒ] *nm* *Sp* contest.

chaloupe [ʃalup] *nf* launch, long boat.

chalumeau, -x [ʃalymo] *nm* blowlamp, *Am* blowtorch; *Mus* pipe.

chalut [ʃaly] *nm* trawl net, drag net. ◆**chalutier** *nm* (*bateau*) trawler.

chamailler (se) [səʃamaje] *vpr* to squabble, bicker. ◆**chamailleries** *nfpl* squabbling, bickering.

chamarré [ʃamare] a (robe etc) richly coloured; **c. de** (décorations etc) Péj bedecked with.

chambard [ʃābar] nm Fam (tapage) rumpus, row. ◆**chambarder** vt Fam to turn upside down; **il a tout chambardé dans** he's turned everything upside down in.

chambouler [ʃābule] vt Fam to make topsy-turvy, turn upside down.

chambre [ʃābr] nf (bed)room; Pol Jur Tech Anat chamber; **c. à coucher** bedroom; (mobilier) bedroom suite; **c. à air** (de pneu) inner tube; **c. des Communes** Pol House of Commons; **c. d'ami** guest ou spare room; **c. forte** strongroom; **c. noire** Phot darkroom; **garder la c.** to stay indoors. ◆**chambrée** nf Mil barrack room. ◆**chambrer** vt (vin) to bring to room temperature.

chameau, -x [ʃamo] nm camel.

chamois [ʃamwa] **1** nm (animal) chamois; **peau de c.** chamois (leather), shammy. **2** a inv buff(-coloured).

champ [ʃā] nm field; (domaine) Fig scope, range; **c. de bataille** battlefield; **c. de courses** racecourse, racetrack; **c. de foire** fairground; **c. de tir** (terrain) rifle range; **laisser le c. libre à qn** to leave the field open for s.o. ◆**champêtre** a rustic, rural.

champagne [ʃāpaɲ] nm champagne; **c. brut** extra-dry champagne.

champignon [ʃāpiɲ3] nm **1** Bot mushroom; **c. vénéneux** toadstool, poisonous mushroom; **c. atomique** mushroom cloud. **2** Aut Fam accelerator pedal.

champion [ʃāpj3] nm champion. ◆**championnat** nm championship.

chance [ʃās] nf luck; (probabilité de réussir, occasion) chance; **avoir de la c.** to be lucky; **tenter ou courir sa c.** to try one's luck; **c'est une c. que...** it's a stroke of luck that ...; **mes chances de succès** my chances of success. ◆**chanceux, -euse** a lucky.

chancel/er [ʃāsle] vi to stagger, totter; (courage) Fig to falter. ◆**-ant** a (pas, santé) faltering, shaky.

chancelier [ʃāsəlje] nm chancellor. ◆**chancellerie** nf chancellery.

chancre [ʃākr] nm Méd & Fig canker.

chandail [ʃādaj] nm (thick) sweater, jersey.

chandelier [ʃādəlje] nm candlestick.

chandelle [ʃādɛl] nf candle; **voir trente-six chandelles** Fig to see stars; **en c.** Av Sp straight into the air.

change [ʃāʒ] nm Fin exchange; **le contrôle des changes** exchange control; **donner le c. à qn** to deceive s.o. ◆**chang/er** vt (modifier, remplacer, échanger) to change; **qn**

en to change s.o. into; **ça la changera de ne pas travailler** it'll be a change for her not to be working; – vi to change; **c. de voiture/d'adresse/etc** to change one's car/address/etc; **c. de train/de place** to change trains/places; **c. de vitesse/de cap** to change gear/course; **c. de sujet** to change the subject; – **se c.** vpr to change (one's clothes). ◆**-eant** a (temps) changeable; (humeur) fickle; (couleurs) changing. ◆**-ement** nm change; **aimer le c.** to like change. ◆**-eur** nm moneychanger; **c. de monnaie** change machine.

chanoine [ʃanwan] nm (personne) Rel canon.

chanson [ʃās3] nf song. ◆**chant** nm singing; (chanson) song; (hymne) chant; **c. de Noël** Christmas carol. ◆**chant/er** vi to sing; (oiseau) to chant; (coq) to crow; **si ça te chante** Fam if you feel like it; **faire c. qn** to blackmail s.o.; – vt to sing; (glorifier) to sing of; (dire) Fam to say. ◆**-ant** a (air, voix) melodious. ◆**-age** nm blackmail. ◆**-eur, -euse** nm singer.

chantier [ʃātje] nm (building) site; (entrepôt) builder's yard; (naval) shipyard; **mettre un travail en c.** to get a task under way.

chantonner [ʃātɔne] vti to hum.

chantre [ʃātr] nm Rel cantor.

chanvre [ʃāvr] nm hemp; **c. indien** (plante) cannabis.

chaos [kao] nm chaos. ◆**chaotique** a chaotic.

chaparder [ʃaparde] vt Fam to filch, pinch (à from).

chapeau, -x [ʃapo] nm hat; (de champignon, roue) cap; **c.!** well done!; **donner un coup de c.** (pour saluer etc) to raise one's hat; **c. mou** trilby, Am fedora. ◆**chapelier** nm hatter.

chapelet [ʃaplɛ] nm rosary; **dire son c.** to tell one's beads; **un c. de** (saucisses, injures etc) a string of.

chapelle [ʃapɛl] nf chapel; **c. ardente** chapel of rest.

chaperon [ʃapr3] nm chaperon(e). ◆**chaperonner** vt to chaperon(e).

chapiteau, -x [ʃapito] nm (de cirque) big top; (pour expositions etc) marquee, tent; (de colonne) Archit capital.

chapitre [ʃapitr] nm chapter; **sur le c. de** on the subject of. ◆**chapitrer** vt to scold, lecture.

chaque [ʃak] a each, every.

char [ʃar] nm Hist chariot; (de carnaval)

float; *Can Fam* car; **c. à bœufs** oxcart; **c. (d'assaut)** *Mil* tank.

charabia [ʃarabja] *nm Fam* gibberish.

charade [ʃarad] *nf* (*énigme*) riddle; (*mimée*) charade.

charbon [ʃarbɔ̃] *nm* coal; (*fusain*) charcoal; **c. de bois** charcoal; **sur des charbons ardents** like a cat on hot bricks. ◆**charbonnages** *nmpl* coalmines, collieries. ◆**charbonnier, -ière** *a* coal-; – *nm* coal merchant.

charcuter [ʃarkyte] *vt* (*opérer*) *Fam Péj* to cut up (badly).

charcuterie [ʃarkytri] *nf* pork butcher's shop; (*aliment*) cooked (pork) meats. ◆**charcutier, -ière** *nmf* pork butcher.

chardon [ʃardɔ̃] *nm Bot* thistle.

chardonneret [ʃardɔnrɛ] *nm* (*oiseau*) goldfinch.

charge [ʃarʒ] *nf* (*poids*) load; (*fardeau*) burden; *Jur Él Mil* charge; (*fonction*) office; *pl Fin* financial obligations, (*dépenses*) expenses; (*de locataire*) (maintenance) charges; **charges sociales** national insurance contributions, *Am* Social Security contributions; **à c.** (*enfant, parent*) dependent; **être à c. à qn** to be a burden to s.o.; **à la c. de qn** (*frais*) payable by s.o.; **prendre en c.** to take charge of, take responsibility for.

charg/er [ʃarʒe] *vt* to load; *Él Mil* to charge; (*passager*) *Fam* to pick up; **se c. de** (*enfant, tâche etc*) to take charge of; **c. qn de** (*impôts etc*) to burden s.o. with; (*paquets etc*) to load s.o. with; (*tâche etc*) to entrust s.o. with; **c. qn de faire** to instruct s.o. to do. ◆**-é, -ée** *a* (*personne, véhicule, arme etc*) loaded; (*journée etc*) heavy, busy; (*langue*) coated; **c. de** (*arbre, navire etc*) laden with; – *nmf* **c. de cours** *Univ* (temporary) lecturer. ◆**-ement** *nm* (*action*) loading; (*objet*) load. ◆**-eur** *nm* (*de piles*) charger.

chariot [ʃarjo] *nm* (*à bagages etc*) trolley, *Am* cart; (*de ferme*) waggon; (*de machine à écrire*) carriage.

charité [ʃarite] *nf* (*vertu, secours*) charity; (*acte*) act of charity; **faire la c.** to give to charity; **faire la c. à** (*mendiant*) to give to. ◆**charitable** *a* charitable.

charivari [ʃarivari] *nm Fam* hubbub, hullabaloo.

charlatan [ʃarlatɑ̃] *nm* charlatan, quack.

charme [ʃarm] *nm* 1 charm; (*magie*) spell. 2 (*arbre*) hornbeam. ◆**charm/er** *vt* to charm; **je suis charmé de vous voir** I'm delighted to see you. ◆**-ant** *a* charming.

◆**-eur, -euse** *nmf* charmer; – *a* engaging.

charnel, -elle [ʃarnɛl] *a* carnal.

charnier [ʃarnje] *nm* mass grave.

charnière [ʃarnjɛr] *nf* hinge; *Fig* meeting point (**de** between).

charnu [ʃarny] *a* fleshy.

charogne [ʃarɔɲ] *nf* carrion.

charpente [ʃarpɑ̃t] *nf* frame(work); (*de personne*) build. ◆**charpenté** *a* **bien c.** solidly built. ◆**charpenterie** *nf* carpentry. ◆**charpentier** *nm* carpenter.

charpie [ʃarpi] *nf* **mettre en c.** (*déchirer*) & *Fig* to tear to shreds.

charrette [ʃarɛt] *nf* cart. ◆**charretier** *nm* carter. ◆**charrier 1** *vt* (*transporter*) to cart; (*rivière*) to carry along, wash down (*sand etc*). **2** *vti* (*taquiner*) *Fam* to tease.

charrue [ʃary] *nf* plough, *Am* plow.

charte [ʃart] *nf Pol* charter.

charter [ʃartɛr] *nm Av* charter (flight).

chas [ʃa] *nm* eye (*of a needle*).

chasse [ʃas] *nf* **1** hunting, hunt; (*poursuite*) chase; *Av* fighter forces; **de c.** (*pilote, avion*) fighter-; **c. sous-marine** underwater (harpoon) fishing; **c. à courre** hunting; **tableau de c.** (*animaux abattus*) bag; **faire la c. à** to hunt down, hunt for; **donner la c. à** to give chase to; **c. à l'homme** manhunt. **2 c. d'eau** toilet flush; **tirer la c.** to flush the toilet.

châsse [ʃas] *nf* shrine.

chassé-croisé [ʃasekrwaze] *nm* (*pl* **chassés-croisés**) *Fig* confused coming(s) and going(s).

chass/er [ʃase] *vt* (*animal*) to hunt; (*papillon*) to chase; (*faire partir*) to drive out ou off; (*employé*) to dismiss; (*mouche*) to brush away; (*odeur*) to get rid of; – *vi* to hunt; *Aut* to skid. ◆**-eur, -euse** *nmf* hunter; – *nm* (*domestique*) pageboy, bellboy; *Av* fighter; **à pied** infantryman. ◆**chasse-neige** *nm inv* snowplough, *Am* snowplow.

châssis [ʃasi] *nm* frame; *Aut* chassis.

chaste [ʃast] *a* chaste, pure. ◆**chasteté** *nf* chastity.

chat, chatte [ʃa, ʃat] *nmf* cat; **un c. dans la gorge** a frog in one's throat; **d'autres chats à fouetter** other fish to fry; **pas un c.** not a soul; **ma (petite) chatte** *Fam* my darling; **c. perché** (*jeu*) tag.

châtaigne [ʃatɛɲ] *nf* chestnut. ◆**châtaignier** *nm* chestnut tree. ◆**châtain** *a inv* (chestnut) brown.

château, -x [ʃato] *nm* (*forteresse*) castle; (*palais*) palace, stately home; **c. fort** fortified castle; **châteaux en Espagne** *Fig* castles in the air; **c. d'eau** water tower; **c. de cartes** house of cards. ◆**châtelain, -aine** *nmf* lord of the manor, lady of the manor.

châtier [ʃatje] *vt Litt* to chastise, castigate; *(style)* to refine.

châtiment [ʃatimɑ̃] *nm* punishment.

chaton [ʃatɔ̃] *nm* **1** *(chat)* kitten. **2** *(de bague)* setting, mounting. **3** *Bot* catkin.

chatouill/er [ʃatuje] *vt (pour faire rire)* to tickle; *(exciter, plaire à) Fig* to titillate. ◆**—ement** *nm* tickle; *(action)* tickling. ◆**chatouilleux, -euse** *a* ticklish; *(irritable)* touchy.

chatoyer [ʃatwaje] *vi* to glitter, sparkle.

châtrer [ʃɑtre] *vt* to castrate.

chatte [ʃat] *voir* **chat.**

chatteries [ʃatri] *nfpl* cuddles; *(friandises)* delicacies.

chatterton [ʃatɛrtɔn] *nm* adhesive insulating tape.

chaud [ʃo] *a* hot; *(doux)* warm; *(fervent) Fig* warm; **pleurer à chaudes larmes** to cry bitterly; — *nm* heat; warmth; **avoir c.** to be hot; **to be warm**; **il fait c.** it's hot; it's warm; **être au c.** to be in the warm(th); **ça ne me fait ni c. ni froid** it leaves me indifferent. ◆**chaudement** *adv* warmly; *(avec passion)* hotly.

chaudière [ʃodjɛr] *nf* boiler.

chaudron [ʃodrɔ̃] *nm* cauldron.

chauffard [ʃofar] *nm* road hog, reckless driver.

chauff/er [ʃofe] *vt* to heat up, warm up; *(métal etc) Tech* to heat; — *vi* to heat up, warm up; *Aut* to overheat; **ça va c.** *Fam* things are going to hot up; — **se c.** *vpr* to warm oneself up. ◆**—ant** *a (couverture)* electric; *(plaque)* hot-; *(surface)* heating. ◆**—age** *nm* heating. ◆**—eur** *nm* **1** *(de chaudière)* stoker. **2** *Aut* driver; *(employé, domestique)* chauffeur. ◆**chauffe-bain** *nm,* ◆**chauffe-eau** *nm inv* water heater. ◆**chauffe-plats** *nm inv* hotplate.

chaume [ʃom] *nm (tiges coupées)* stubble, straw; *(pour toiture)* thatch; **toit de c.** thatched roof. ◆**chaumière** *nf* thatched cottage.

chaussée [ʃose] *nf* road(way).

chausser [ʃose] *vt (chaussures)* to put on; *(fournir)* to supply in footwear; **c. qn** to put shoes on (to) s.o.; **c. du 40** to take a size 40 shoe; **ce soulier te chausse bien** this shoe fits (you) well; — **se c.** *vpr* to put on one's shoes. ◆**chausse-pied** *nm* shoehorn. ◆**chausson** [ʃosɔ̃] *nm* slipper; *(de danse)* shoe; **c. (aux pommes)** apple turnover. ◆**chaus-**

sure *nf* shoe; *pl* shoes, footwear; **chaussures à semelles compensées** platform shoes.

chaussette [ʃosɛt] *nf* sock.

chauve [ʃov] *a & nmf* bald (person).

chauve-souris [ʃovsuri] *nf (pl* **chauves-souris)** *(animal)* bat.

chauvin, -ine [ʃovɛ̃, -in] *a & nmf* chauvinist.

chaux [ʃo] *nf* lime; **blanc de c.** whitewash.

chavirer [ʃavire] *vti Nau* to capsize.

chef [ʃɛf] *nm* **1** **de son propre c.** on one's own authority. **2** leader, head; *(de tribu)* chief; *Culin* chef; **en c.** *(commandant, rédacteur)* in chief; **c'est un c.!** *(personne remarquable)* he's an ace!; **c. d'atelier** *(shop)* foreman; **c. de bande** ringleader, gang leader; **c. d'entreprise** company head; **c. d'équipe** foreman; **c. d'État** head of state; **c. d'état-major** chief of staff; **c. de famille** head of the family; **c. de file** leader; **c. de gare** stationmaster; **c. d'orchestre** conductor. ◆**chef-lieu** *nm (pl* **chefs-lieux)** chief town *(of a département).*

chef-d'œuvre [ʃɛdœvr] *nm (pl* **chefs-d'œuvre)** masterpiece.

chemin [ʃ(ə)mɛ̃] *nm* way, road, path; *(trajet, direction)* way; **beaucoup de c. à faire** a long way to go; **dix minutes de c.** ten minutes' walk; **se mettre en c.** to start out, set out; **faire du c.** to come a long way; *(idée)* to make considerable headway; **c. faisant** on the way; **à mi-c.** half-way. **2 c. de fer** railway, *Am* railroad. ◆**chemin/er** *vi* to proceed; *(péniblement)* to trudge (along) on foot; *(évoluer) Fig* to progress. ◆**—ement** *nm Fig* progress. ◆**cheminot** *nm railway ou Am* railroad employee.

cheminée [ʃ(ə)mine] *nf (sur le toit)* chimney; *(de navire)* funnel; *(âtre)* fireplace; *(encadrement)* mantelpiece.

chemise [ʃ(ə)miz] *nf* shirt; *(couverture cartonnée)* folder; **c. de nuit** nightdress. ◆**chemiserie** *nf* men's shirt (and underwear) shop. ◆**chemisette** *nf* short-sleeved shirt. ◆**chemisier** *nm (vêtement)* blouse.

chenal, -aux [ʃənal, -o] *nm* channel.

chenapan [ʃ(ə)napɑ̃] *nm Hum* rogue, scoundrel.

chêne [ʃɛn] *nm (arbre, bois)* oak.

chenet [ʃ(ə)nɛ] *nm* firedog, andiron.

chenil [ʃ(ə)ni(l)] *nm* kennels.

chenille [ʃ(ə)nij] *nf* caterpillar; *(de char) Mil* caterpillar track.

cheptel [ʃɛptɛl] *nm* livestock.

chèque [ʃɛk] *nm* cheque, *Am* check; **c. de voyage** traveller's cheque, *Am* traveler's check. ◆**c.-repas** *nm* (*pl* **chèques-repas**) luncheon voucher. ◆**chéquier** *nm* cheque book, *Am* checkbook.

cher, chère [ʃɛr] **1** *a* (*aimé*) dear (à to); − *nmf* **mon c.** my dear fellow; **ma chère** my dear (woman). **2** *a* (*coûteux*) dear, expensive; (*quartier, hôtel etc*) expensive; **la vie chère** the high cost of living; **payer c.** (*objet*) to pay a lot for; (*erreur etc*) *Fig* to pay dearly for. ◆**chèrement** *adv* dearly.

cherch/er [ʃɛrʃe] *vt* to look for, search for; (*du secours, la paix etc*) to seek; (*dans un dictionnaire*) to look up; **c. ses mots** to fumble for one's words; **aller c.** to (go and) fetch *ou* get; **c. à faire** to attempt to do; **tu l'as bien cherché!** it's your own fault!, you asked for it! ◆**—eur, -euse** *nmf* research worker; **c. d'or** gold-digger.

chér/ir [ʃerir] *vt* to cherish. ◆**—i, -ie** *a* dearly loved, beloved; − *nmf* darling.

chérot [ʃero] *am Fam* pricey.

cherté [ʃɛrte] *nf* high cost, expensiveness.

chétif, -ive [ʃetif, -iv] *a* puny; (*dérisoire*) wretched.

cheval, -aux [ʃ(ə)val, -o] *nm* horse; **c. (vapeur)** *Aut* horsepower; **à c.** on horseback; **faire du c.** to go horse riding; **à c. sur** straddling; **à c. sur les principes** a stickler for principle; **monter sur ses grands chevaux** to get excited; **c. à bascule** rocking horse; **c. d'arçons** *Sp* vaulting horse; **c. de bataille** (*dada*) hobbyhorse; **chevaux de bois** (*manège*) merry-go-round. ◆**chevaleresque** *a* chivalrous.

chevalier [ʃ(ə)valje] *nm* knight. ◆**chevalin** *a* equine; (*boucherie*) horse-.

chevalet [ʃ(ə)valɛ] *nm* easel; *Menuis* trestle.

chevalière [ʃ(ə)valjɛr] *nf* signet ring.

chevauchée [ʃ(ə)voʃe] *nf* (horse) ride.

chevaucher [ʃ(ə)voʃe] *vt* to straddle; − *vi*, − **se c.** *vpr* to overlap.

chevet [ʃ(ə)vɛ] *nm* bedhead; **table/livre de c.** bedside table/book; **au c. de** at the bedside of.

cheveu, -x [ʃ(ə)vø] *nm* **un c.** a hair; **les cheveux** hair; **couper les cheveux en quatre** *Fig* to split hairs; **tiré par les cheveux** (*argument*) far-fetched. ◆**chevelu** *a* hairy. ◆**chevelure** *nf* (head of) hair.

cheville [ʃ(ə)vij] *nf Anat* ankle; *Menuis* peg, pin; (*pour vis*) (wall)plug; **c. ouvrière** *Aut* & *Fig* linchpin; **en c. avec** *Fam* in cahoots with. ◆**cheviller** *vt Menuis* to pin, peg.

chèvre [ʃɛvr] *nf* goat; (*femelle*) nanny-goat. ◆**chevreau, -x** *nm* kid.

chèvrefeuille [ʃɛvrœfœj] *nm* honeysuckle.

chevreuil [ʃəvrœj] *nm* roe deer; *Culin* venison.

chevron [ʃəvrɔ̃] *nm* (*poutre*) rafter; *Mil* stripe, chevron; **à chevrons** (*tissu, veste etc*) herringbone.

chevronné [ʃəvrɔne] *a* seasoned, experienced.

chevroter [ʃəvrɔte] *vi* to quaver, tremble.

chez [ʃe] *prép* **c. qn** at s.o.'s house, flat *etc*; **il est c. Jean/c. l'épicier** he's at John's (place)/at the grocer's; **il va c. Jean/c. l'épicier** he's going to John's (place)/to the grocer's; **c. moi, c. nous** at home; **je vais c. moi** I'm going home; **c. les Suisses/les jeunes** among the Swiss/the young; **c. Camus** in Camus; **c. l'homme** in man; **une habitude c. elle** a habit with her; **c. Mme Dupont** (*adresse*) care of *ou* c/o Mme Dupont. ◆**c.-soi** *nm inv* **un c.-soi** a home (of one's own).

chialer [ʃjale] *vi* (*pleurer*) *Fam* to cry.

chic [ʃik] **1** *a inv* stylish, smart; (*gentil*) *Fam* decent, nice; − *int* **c. (alors)!** great!; − *nm* style, elegance. **2** **avoir le c. pour faire** to have the knack of doing.

chicane [ʃikan] **1** *nf* (*querelle*) quibble. **2** *nfpl* (*obstacles*) zigzag barriers. ◆**chicaner** *vt* to quibble with (*s.o.*); − *vi* to quibble.

chiche [ʃiʃ] **1** *a* mean, niggardly; **c. de** sparing of. **2** *int* (*défi*) *Fam* I bet you I do, can *etc*; **c. que je parte sans lui** I bet I leave without him.

chichis [ʃiʃi] *nmpl* **faire des c.** to make a lot of fuss.

chicorée [ʃikore] *nf* (*à café*) chicory; (*pour salade*) endive.

chien [ʃjɛ̃] *nm* dog; **c. d'arrêt** pointer, retriever; **un mal de c.** a hell of a job; **temps de c.** filthy weather; **vie de c.** *Fig* dog's life; **entre c. et loup** at dusk, in the gloaming. ◆**c.-loup** *nm* (*pl* **chiens-loups**) wolfhound. ◆**chienne** *nf* dog, bitch.

chiendent [ʃjɛ̃dɑ̃] *nm Bot* couch grass.

chiffon [ʃifɔ̃] *nm* rag; **c. (à poussière)** duster. ◆**chiffonner** *vt* to crumple; (*ennuyer*) *Fig* to bother, distress. ◆**chiffonnier** *nm* ragman.

chiffre [ʃifr] *nm* figure, number; (*romain, arabe*) numeral; (*code*) cipher; **c. d'affaires** *Fin* turnover. ◆**chiffrer** *vt* (*montant*) to assess, work out; (*message*) to cipher, code; − *vi* to mount up; **se c. à** to amount to, work out at.

chignon [ʃiɲɔ̃] *nm* bun, chignon.

Chili [ʃili] *nm* Chile. ◆**chilien, -ienne** *a* & *nmf* Chilean.

chimère [ʃimɛr] *nf* fantasy, (wild) dream. ◆**chimérique** *a* fanciful.

chimie [ʃimi] *nf* chemistry. ◆**chimique** *a* chemical. ◆**chimiste** *nmf* (research) chemist.

chimpanzé [ʃɛ̃pɑ̃ze] *nm* chimpanzee.

Chine [ʃin] *nf* China. ◆**chinois, -oise** *a* & *nmf* Chinese; – *nm* (*langue*) Chinese. ◆**chinoiser** *vi* to quibble. ◆**chinoiserie** *nf* (*objet*) Chinese curio; *pl* (*bizarreries*) *Fig* weird complications.

chiner [ʃine] *vi* (*brocanteur etc*) to hunt for bargains.

chiot [ʃjo] *nm* pup(py).

chiper [ʃipe] *vt Fam* to swipe, pinch (à from).

chipie [ʃipi] *nf* **vieille c.** (*femme*) *Péj* old crab.

chipoter [ʃipote] *vi* **1** (*manger*) to nibble. **2** (*chicaner*) to quibble.

chips [ʃips] *nmpl* (potato) crisps, *Am* chips.

chiquenaude [ʃiknod] *nf* flick (of the finger).

chiromancie [kirɔmɑ̃si] *nf* palmistry.

chirurgie [ʃiryrʒi] *nf* surgery. ◆**chirurgical, -aux** *a* surgical. ◆**chirurgien** *nm* surgeon.

chlore [klɔr] *nm* chlorine. ◆**chloroforme** *nm* chloroform. ◆**chlorure** *nm* chloride.

choc [ʃɔk] *nm* (*heurt*) impact, shock; (*émotion*) & *Méd* shock; (*collision*) crash; (*des opinions, entre manifestants etc*) clash.

chocolat [ʃɔkɔla] *nm* chocolate; **c. à croquer** plain *ou Am* bittersweet chocolate; **c. au lait** milk chocolate; **c. glacé** choc-ice; – *a inv* chocolate(-coloured). ◆**chocolaté** *a* chocolate-flavoured.

chœur [kœr] *nm* (*chanteurs, nef*) *Rel* choir; (*composition musicale*) & *Fig* chorus; **en c.** (all) together, in chorus.

choir [ʃwar] *vi* **laisser c. qn** *Fam* to turn one's back on s.o.

choisir [ʃwazir] *vt* to choose, pick, select. ◆**–i** *a* (*œuvres*) selected; (*terme, langage*) well-chosen; (*public*) select. ◆**choix** *nm* choice; (*assortiment*) selection; **morceau de c.** choice piece; **au c. du client** according to choice.

choléra [kɔlera] *nm* cholera.

cholestérol [kɔlɛsterɔl] *nm* cholesterol.

chôm/er [ʃome] *vi* (*ouvrier etc*) to be unemployed; **jour chômé** (*public*) holiday. ◆**–age** *nm* unemployment; **en** *ou* **au c.** unemployed; **mettre en c. technique** to lay off, dismiss.

chope [ʃɔp] *nf* beer mug, tankard; (*contenu*) pint.

choqu/er [ʃɔke] *vt* to offend, shock; (*verres*) to clink; (*commotionner*) to shake up. ◆**–ant** *a* shocking, offensive.

choral, -als [kɔral] *a* choral. ◆**chorale** *nf* choral society. ◆**choriste** *nmf* chorister.

chorégraphe [kɔregraf] *nmf* choreographer. ◆**chorégraphie** *nf* choreography.

chose [ʃoz] *nf* thing; **état de choses** state of affairs; **par la force des choses** through force of circumstance; **dis-lui bien des choses de ma part** remember me to him *ou* her; **ce monsieur C.** that Mr What's-his-name; **se sentir tout c.** *Fam* (*décontenancé*) to feel all funny; (*malade*) to feel out of sorts.

chou, -x [ʃu] *nm* cabbage; **choux de Bruxelles** Brussels sprouts; **mon c.!** my pet!; **c. à la crème** cream puff. ◆**c.-fleur** *nm* (*pl* choux-fleurs) cauliflower.

choucas [ʃuka] *nm* jackdaw.

chouchou, -oute [ʃuʃu, -ut] *nmf* (*favori*) *Fam* pet, darling. ◆**chouchouter** *vt* to pamper.

choucroute [ʃukrut] *nf* sauerkraut.

chouette [ʃwɛt] **1** *nf* (*oiseau*) owl. **2** *a* (*chic*) *Fam* super, great.

choyer [ʃwaje] *vt* to pet, pamper.

chrétien, -ienne [kretjɛ̃, -jɛn] *a* & *nmf* Christian. ◆**chrétienté** *nf* Christendom. ◆**Christ** [krist] *nm* Christ. ◆**christianisme** *nm* Christianity.

chrome [krom] *nm* chromium, chrome. ◆**chromé** *a* chromium-plated.

chromosome [krɔmozom] *nm* chromosome.

chronique [krɔnik] **1** *a* (*malade, chômage etc*) chronic. **2** *nf* (*annales*) chronicle; *Journ* report, news; (*rubrique*) column. ◆**chroniqueur** *nm* chronicler; *Journ* reporter, columnist.

chronologie [krɔnɔlɔʒi] *nf* chronology. ◆**chronologique** *a* chronological.

chronomètre [krɔnɔmɛtr] *nm* stopwatch. ◆**chronométr/er** *vt Sp* to time. ◆**–eur** *nm Sp* timekeeper.

chrysanthème [krizɑ̃tɛm] *nm* chrysanthemum.

chuchot/er [ʃyʃote] *vti* to whisper. ◆**–ement** *nm* whisper(ing). ◆**chuchoteries** *nfpl Fam* whispering.

chuinter [ʃwɛ̃te] *vi* (*vapeur*) to hiss.

chut! [ʃyt] *int* sh!, hush!

chute [ʃyt] *nf* fall; (*défaite*) (down)fall; **c. d'eau** waterfall; **c. de neige** snowfall; **c. de pluie** rainfall; **c. des cheveux** hair loss. ◆**chuter** *vi Fam* to fall.

Chypre [ʃipr] *nf* Cyprus. ◆**chypriote** *a* & *nmf* Cypriot.

ci [si] **1** *adv* par-ci par-là here and there. **2** *pron dém* comme ci comme ça so so. **3** *voir* ce², celui.

ci-après [siaprε] *adv* below, hereafter. ◆**ci-contre** *adv* opposite. ◆**ci-dessous** *adv* below. ◆**ci-dessus** *adv* above. ◆**ci-gît** *adv* here lies (*on gravestones*). ◆**ci-inclus** *a*, ◆**ci-joint** *a* (*inv before n*) (*dans une lettre*) enclosed (herewith).

cible [sibl] *nf* target.

ciboulette [sibulεt] *nf* Culin chives.

cicatrice [sikatris] *nf* scar. ◆**cicatriser** *vt*, — **se c.** *vpr* to heal up (*leaving a scar*).

cidre [sidr] *nm* cider.

Cie *abrév* (*compagnie*) Co.

ciel [sjεl] *nm* **1** (*pl* ciels) sky; à c. ouvert (*piscine etc*) open-air; **c. de lit** canopy. **2** (*pl* cieux [sjø]) *Rel* heaven; **juste c.!** good heavens!; **sous d'autres cieux** *Hum* in other climes.

cierge [sjεrʒ] *nm Rel* candle.

cigale [sigal] *nf* (*insecte*) cicada.

cigare [sigar] *nm* cigar. ◆**cigarette** *nf* cigarette.

cigogne [sigɔɲ] *nf* stork.

cil [sil] *nm* (eye)lash.

cime [sim] *nf* **1** (*d'un arbre*) top; (*d'une montagne*) & *Fig* peak.

ciment [simā] *nm* cement. ◆**cimenter** *vt* to cement.

cimetière [simtjεr] *nm* cemetery, graveyard; **c. de voitures** scrapyard, breaker's yard, *Am* auto graveyard.

ciné [sine] *nm Fam* cinema. ◆**c.-club** *nm* film society. ◆**cinéaste** *nmf* film maker. ◆**cinéphile** *nmf* film buff.

cinéma [sinema] *nm* cinema; **faire du c.** to make films. ◆**cinémascope** *nm* cinemascope. ◆**cinémathèque** *nf* film library; (*salle*) film theatre. ◆**cinématographique** *a* cinema-.

cinglé [sεgle] *a Fam* crazy.

cingl/er [sεgle] *vt* to lash. ◆**—ant** *a* (*vent, remarque*) cutting, biting.

cinoche [sinɔʃ] *nm Fam* cinema.

cinq [sεk] *nm* five; *a* ([sε] *before consonant*) five. ◆**cinquième** *a* & *nmf* fifth; **un c.** a fifth.

cinquante [sεkāt] *a* & *nm* fifty. ◆**cinquantaine** *nf* about fifty. ◆**cinquantenaire** *a* & *nmf* fifty-year-old (person); — *nm* fiftieth anniversary. ◆**cinquantième** *a* & *nmf* fiftieth.

cintre [sεtr] *nm* coathanger; *Archit* arch.
◆**cintré** *a* arched; (*veste etc*) tailored, slim-fitting.

cirage [siraʒ] *nm* (shoe) polish.

circoncis [sirkɔsi] *a* circumcised. ◆**circoncision** *nf* circumcision.

circonférence [sirkɔ̃ferās] *nf* circumference.

circonflexe [sirkɔ̃flεks] *a Gram* circumflex.

circonlocution [sirkɔ̃lɔkysjɔ̃] *nf* circumlocution.

circonscrire [sirkɔ̃skrir] *vt* to circumscribe.
◆**circonscription** *nf* division; **c. (électorale)** constituency.

circonspect, -ecte [sirkɔ̃spε(kt), -εkt] *a* cautious, circumspect. ◆**circonspection** *nf* caution.

circonstance [sirkɔ̃stās] *nf* circumstance; **pour/en la c.** for/on this occasion; **de c.** (*habit, parole etc*) appropriate. ◆**circonstancié** *a* detailed. ◆**circonstanciel, -ielle** *a Gram* adverbial.

circonvenir [sirkɔ̃vnir] *vt* to circumvent.

circuit [sirkɥi] *nm Sp Él Fin* circuit; (*périple*) tour, trip; (*détour*) roundabout way; *pl Él* circuitry, circuits.

circulaire [sirkyler] *a* circular; — *nf* (*lettre*) circular. ◆**circulation** *nf* circulation; *Aut* traffic. ◆**circuler** *vi* to circulate; (*véhicule, train*) to move, travel; (*passant*) to walk about; (*rumeur*) to go round, circulate; **faire c.** to circulate; (*piétons etc*) to move on; **circulez!** keep moving!

cire [sir] *nf* wax; (*pour meubles*) polish, wax. ◆**cir/er** *vt* to polish, wax. ◆**—é** *nm* (*vêtement*) oilskin(s). ◆**—eur** *nm* bootblack. ◆**—euse** *nf* (*appareil*) floor polisher. ◆**cireux, -euse** *a* waxy.

cirque [sirk] *nm Th Hist* circus.

cirrhose [siroz] *nf Méd* cirrhosis.

cisaille(s) [sizaj] *nf(pl)* shears. ◆**ciseau, -x** [sizo] *nm* chisel; *pl* scissors. ◆**ciseler** *vt* to chisel.

citadelle [sitadεl] *nf* citadel.

cité [site] *nf* city; (*ouvrière*) housing estate (*for workers*), *Am* housing project or development; **c. universitaire** (students') halls of residence. ◆**citadin, -ine** *nmf* city dweller; — *a* city-, urban.

citer [site] *vt* to quote; *Jur* to summon; *Mil* to mention, cite. ◆**citation** *nf* quotation; *Jur* summons; *Mil* mention, citation.

citerne [sitεrn] *nf* (*réservoir*) tank.

cithare [sitar] *nf* zither.

citoyen, -enne [sitwajε̃, -εn] *nmf* citizen. ◆**citoyenneté** *nf* citizenship.

citron [sitrɔ̃] *nm* lemon; **c. pressé** (fresh)

lemon juice. ◆**citronnade** *nf* lemon drink, (still) lemonade.

citrouille [sitruj] *nf* pumpkin.

civet [sivɛ] *nm* stew; **c. de lièvre** jugged hare.

civière [sivjɛr] *nf* stretcher.

civil [sivil] **1** *a* (*droits, guerre, mariage etc*) civil; (*non militaire*) civilian; (*courtois*) civil; **année civile** calendar year. **2** *nm* civilian; **dans le c.** in civilian life; **en c.** (*policier*) in plain clothes; (*soldat*) in civilian clothes. ◆**civilité** *nf* civility.

civiliser [sivilize] *vt* to civilize; — **se c.** *vpr* to become civilized. ◆**civilisation** *nf* civilization.

civique [sivik] *a* civic; **instruction c.** *Scol* civics. ◆**civisme** *nm* civic sense.

clair [klɛr] *a* (*distinct, limpide, évident*) clear; (*éclairé*) light; (*pâle*) light(-coloured); (*sauce, chevelure*) thin; **bleu/vert c.** light blue/green; **il fait c.** it's light *ou* bright; — *adv* (*voir*) clearly; — *nm* **c. de lune** moonlight; **le plus c. de** the major *ou* greater part of; **tirer au c.** (*question etc*) to clear up. ◆—**ement** *adv* clearly. ◆**claire-voie** *nf* à **c.-voie** (*barrière*) lattice-; (*caisse*) openwork; (*porte*) louvre(d).

clairière [klɛrjɛr] *nf* clearing, glade.

clairon [klɛrɔ̃] *nm* bugle; (*soldat*) bugler. ◆**claironner** *vt* (*annoncer*) to trumpet forth.

clairsemé [klɛrsəme] *a* sparse.

clairvoyant [klɛrvwajɑ̃] *a* (*perspicace*) clear-sighted. ◆**clairvoyance** *nf* clear-sightedness.

clam/er [klame] *vt* to cry out. ◆—**eur** *nf* clamour, outcry.

clan [klɑ̃] *nm* clan, clique, set.

clandestin [klɑ̃dɛstɛ̃] *a* secret, clandestine; (*journal, mouvement*) underground; **passager c.** stowaway.

clapet [klapɛ] *nm* *Tech* valve; (*bouche*) *Arg* trap.

clapier [klapje] *nm* (*rabbit*) hutch.

clapot/er [klapɔte] *vi* (*vagues*) to lap. ◆—**ement** *nm*, ◆**clapotis** *nm* lap(ping).

claque [klak] *nf* smack, slap. ◆**claquer** *vt* (*porte*) to slam, bang; (*gifler*) to smack, slap; (*fouet*) to crack; (*fatiguer*) *Fam* to tire out; (*dépenser*) *Arg* to blow; **se c. un muscle** to tear a muscle; **faire c.** (*doigts*) to snap; (*langue*) to click; (*fouet*) to crack; — *vi* (*porte*) to slam, bang; (*drapeau*) to flap; (*coup de revolver*) to ring out; (*mourir*) *Fam* to die; (*tomber en panne*) *Fam* to break down; — **des mains** to clap one's hands; **elle claque des dents** her teeth are chattering.

claquemurer (se) [səklakmyre] *vpr* to shut oneself up, hole up.

claquettes [klakɛt] *nfpl* tap dancing.

clarifier [klarifje] *vt* to clarify. ◆**clarification** *nf* clarification.

clarinette [klarinɛt] *nf* clarinet.

clarté [klarte] *nf* light, brightness; (*précision*) clarity, clearness.

classe [klɑs] *nf* class; **aller en c.** to go to school; **c. ouvrière/moyenne** working/middle class; **avoir de la c.** to have class.

class/er [klɑse] *vt* to classify, class; (*papiers*) to file; (*candidats*) to grade; (*affaire*) to close; **se c. parmi** to rank *ou* be classed among; **se c. premier** to come first. ◆—**ement** *nm* classification; filing; grading; (*rang*) place; *Sp* placing. ◆—**eur** *nm* (*meuble*) filing cabinet; (*portefeuille*) (loose leaf) file. ◆**classification** *nf* classification. ◆**classifier** *vt* to classify.

classique [klasik] *a* classical; (*typique*) classic; — *nm* (*œuvre, auteur*) classic. ◆**classicisme** *nm* classicism.

clause [kloz] *nf* clause.

claustrophobie [klostrɔfɔbi] *nf* claustrophobia. ◆**claustrophobe** *a* claustrophobic.

clavecin [klavsɛ̃] *nm* *Mus* harpsichord.

clavicule [klavikyl] *nf* collarbone.

clavier [klavje] *nm* keyboard.

clé, clef [kle] *nf* key; (*outil*) spanner, wrench; *Mus* clef; **fermer à c.** to lock; **sous c.** under lock and key; **c. de contact** ignition key; **c. de voûte** keystone; **poste/industrie c.** key post/industry; **clés en main** (*acheter une maison etc*) ready to move in; **prix clés en main** (*voiture*) on the road price.

clément [klemɑ̃] *a* (*temps*) mild, clement; (*juge*) lenient, clement. ◆**clémence** *nf* mildness; leniency; clemency.

clémentine [klemɑ̃tin] *nf* clementine.

clerc [klɛr] *nm* *Rel* cleric; (*de notaire*) clerk. ◆**clergé** *nm* clergy. ◆**clérical, -aux** *a* *Rel* clerical.

cliché [kliʃe] *nm* *Phot* negative; *Typ* plate; (*idée*) cliché.

client, -ente [klijɑ̃, -ɑ̃t] *nmf* (*de magasin etc*) customer; (*d'un avocat etc*) client; (*d'un médecin*) patient; (*d'hôtel*) guest. ◆**clientèle** *nf* customers, clientele; (*d'un avocat*) practice, clientele; (*d'un médecin*) practice, patients; **accorder sa c. à** to give one's custom to.

cligner [kliɲe] *vi* **c. des yeux** (*ouvrir et fermer*) to blink; (*fermer à demi*) to screw up one's eyes; **c. de l'œil** to wink.

◆**clignot/er** vi to blink; (*lumière*) to flicker; *Aut* to flash; (*étoile*) to twinkle. ◆**—ant** nm Aut indicator, Am directional signal.

climat [klima] nm Mét & Fig climate. ◆**climatique** a climatic. ◆**climatisation** nf air-conditioning. ◆**climatiser** vt to air-condition.

clin d'œil [klɛ̃dœj] nm wink; **en un c. d'œil** in the twinkling of an eye.

clinique [klinik] a clinical; — nf (*hôpital*) (private) clinic.

clinquant [klɛ̃kɑ̃] a tawdry.

clique [klik] nf Péj clique; Mus Mil (drum and bugle) band.

cliqueter [klikte] vi to clink. ◆**cliquetis** nm click(ing).

clivage [klivaʒ] nm split, division (de in).

cloaque [klɔak] nm cesspool.

clochard, -arde [klɔʃar, -ard] nmf tramp, vagrant.

cloche [klɔʃ] nf 1 bell; **c. à fromage** cheese cover. 2 (*personne*) Fam idiot, oaf. ◆**clocher** 1 nm bell tower; (*en pointe*) steeple; **de c.** Fig parochial; **esprit de c.** parochialism. 2 vi to be wrong ou amiss. ◆**clochette** nf (small) bell.

cloche-pied (à) [aklɔʃpje] adv **sauter à c.-pied** to hop on one foot.

cloison [klwazɔ̃] nf partition; Fig barrier. ◆**cloisonner** vt to partition; (*activités etc*) Fig to compartmentalize.

cloître [klwatr] nm cloister. ◆**se cloîtrer** vpr to shut oneself away, cloister oneself.

clopin-clopant [klɔpɛ̃klɔpɑ̃] adv **aller c.-clopant** to hobble.

cloque [klɔk] nf blister.

clore [klɔr] vt (*débat, lettre*) to close. ◆**clos** a (*incident, lettre*) closed; (*espace*) enclosed; — nm (*enclosed*) field.

clôture [klotyr] nf (*barrière*) enclosure, fence; (*fermeture*) closing. ◆**clôturer** vt to enclose; (*compte, séance etc*) to close.

clou [klu] nm nail; (*furoncle*) boil; **le c.** (*du spectacle*) Fam the star attraction; **les clous** (*passage*) pedestrian crossing; **des clous!** Fam nothing at all! ◆**clouer** vt to nail; **cloué au lit** confined to (one's) bed; **cloué sur place** nailed to the spot; **le bec à qn** Fam to shut s.o. up. ◆**clouté** a (*chaussures*) hobnailed; (*ceinture, pneus*) studded; **passage c.** pedestrian crossing, Am crosswalk.

clown [klun] nm clown.

club [klœb] nm (*association*) club.

cm abrév (*centimètre*) cm.

co- [kɔ] préf co-.

coaguler [kɔagyle] vti, — **se c.** vpr to coagulate.

coaliser (se) [sakɔalize] vpr to form a coalition, join forces. ◆**coalition** nf coalition.

coasser [kɔase] vi (*grenouille*) to croak.

cobaye [kɔbaj] nm (*animal*) & Fig guinea pig.

cobra [kɔbra] nm (*serpent*) cobra.

coca [kɔka] nm (Coca-Cola®) coke.

cocagne [kɔkaɲ] nf **pays de c.** dreamland, land of plenty.

cocaïne [kɔkain] nf cocain.

cocarde [kɔkard] nf rosette, cockade; Av roundel. ◆**cocardier, -ière** a Péj flag-waving.

cocasse [kɔkas] a droll, comical. ◆**cocasserie** nf drollery.

coccinelle [kɔksinɛl] nf ladybird, Am ladybug.

cocher¹ [kɔʃe] vt to tick (off), Am to check (off).

cocher² [kɔʃe] nm coachman. ◆**cochère** af **porte c.** main gateway.

cochon, -onne [kɔʃɔ̃, -ɔn] 1 nm pig; (*mâle*) hog; **c. d'Inde** guinea pig. 2 nmf (*personne sale*) (dirty) pig; (*salaud*) swine; — a (*histoire, film*) dirty, filthy. ◆**cochonnerie(s)** nf(pl) (*obscénité(s)*) filth; (*pacotille*) Fam rubbish.

cocktail [kɔktɛl] nm (*boisson*) cocktail; (*réunion*) cocktail party.

coco [kɔko] nm **noix de c.** coconut. ◆**cocotier** nm coconut palm.

cocon [kɔkɔ̃] nm cocoon.

cocorico [kɔkɔriko] int & nm cock-a-doodle-doo; **faire c.** (*crier victoire*) Fam to give three cheers for France, wave the flag.

cocotte [kɔkɔt] nf (*marmite*) casserole; **c. minute®** pressure cooker.

cocu [kɔky] nm Fam cuckold.

code [kɔd] nm code; **codes, phares c.** Aut dipped headlights, Am low beams; **C. de la route** Highway Code. ◆**coder** vt to code. ◆**codifier** vt to codify.

coefficient [kɔefisjɑ̃] nm Math coefficient; (*d'erreur, de sécurité*) Fig margin.

coéquipier, -ière [kɔekipje, -jɛr] nmf team mate.

cœur [kœr] nm heart; Cartes hearts; **au c. de** (*ville, hiver etc*) in the heart of; **par c.** by heart; **ça me (soulève le c.** that turns my stomach; **à c. ouvert** (*opération*) open-heart; (*parler*) freely; **avoir mal au c.** to feel sick; **avoir le c. gros ou serré** to have a heavy heart; **ça me tient à c.** that's close to my heart; **avoir bon c.** to be kind-hearted; **de bon c.** (*offrir*) with a good heart, willingly; (*rire*) heartily; **si le c. vous en dit** if you so desire.

coexister [kɔɛgziste] *vi* to coexist. ◆**coexistence** *nf* coexistence.

coffre [kɔfr] *nm* chest; (*de banque*) safe; (*de voiture*) boot, *Am* trunk; (*d'autocar*) luggage *ou Am* baggage compartment. ◆**c.-fort** *nm* (*pl* coffres-forts) safe. ◆**coffret** *nm* casket, box.

cogiter [kɔʒite] *vi Iron* to cogitate.

cognac [kɔɲak] *nm* cognac.

cogner [kɔɲe] *vti* to knock; (*tabasser*) to beat s.o. up; **se c. la tête/etc** to knock one's head/etc.

cohabiter [kɔabite] *vi* to live together. ◆**cohabitation** *nf* living together; *Pol Fam* power sharing.

cohérent [kɔerɑ̃] *a* coherent. ◆**cohérence** *nf* coherence. ◆**cohésion** *nf* cohesion, cohesiveness.

cohorte [kɔɔrt] *nf* (*groupe*) troop, band, cohort.

cohue [kɔy] *nf* crowd, mob.

coiffe [kwaf] *nf* headdress.

coiff/er [kwafe] *vt* (*chapeau*) to put on, wear; (*surmonter*) *Fig* to cap; (*être à la tête de*) to head; **c. qn** to do s.o.'s hair; **c. qn d'un chapeau** to put a hat on s.o.; **— se c.** *vpr* to do one's hair; **se c. d'un chapeau** to put on a hat. ◆**—eur, -euse**[1] *nmf* (*pour hommes*) barber, hairdresser; (*pour dames*) hairdresser. ◆**—euse**[2] *nf* dressing table. ◆**coiffure** *nf* headgear, hat; (*arrangement*) hairstyle; (*métier*) hairdressing.

coin [kwɛ̃] *nm* (*angle*) corner; (*endroit*) spot; (*de terre, de ciel*) patch; (*cale*) wedge; **du c.** (*magasin etc*) local; **dans le c.** in the (local) area; **au c. du feu** by the fireside; **petit c.** *Fam* loo, *Am* john.

coinc/er [kwɛ̃se] *vt* (*mécanisme, tiroir*) to jam; (*caler*) to wedge; **c. qn** *Fam* to catch s.o., corner s.o.; **— se c.** *vpr* (*mécanisme etc*) to get jammed *ou* stuck. ◆**—é a** (*tiroir etc*) stuck, jammed; (*personne*) *Fam* stuck.

coïncider [kɔɛ̃side] *vi* to coincide. ◆**coïncidence** *nf* coincidence.

coin-coin [kwɛ̃kwɛ̃] *nm inv* (*de canard*) quack.

coing [kwɛ̃] *nm* (*fruit*) quince.

coke [kɔk] *nm* (*combustible*) coke.

col [kɔl] *nm* (*de chemise*) collar; (*de bouteille*) & *Anat* neck; *Géog* pass; **c. roulé** polo neck, *Am* turtleneck.

colère [kɔlɛr] *nf* anger; **une c.** (*accès*) a fit of anger; **en c.** angry (**contre** with); **se mettre**

en c. to lose one's temper. ◆**coléreux, -euse** *a*, ◆**colérique** *a* quick-tempered.

colibri [kɔlibri] *nm* hummingbird.

colifichet [kɔlifiʃɛ] *nm* trinket.

colimaçon (en) [ɑ̃kɔlimasɔ̃] *adv* **escalier en c.** spiral staircase.

colin [kɔlɛ̃] *nm* (*poisson*) hake.

colique [kɔlik] *nf* diarrh(o)ea; (*douleur*) stomach pain, colic.

colis [kɔli] *nm* parcel, package.

collaborer [kɔlabɔre] *vi* collaborate (**avec** with, **à** on); **c. à** (*journal*) to contribute to. ◆**collaborateur, -trice** *nmf* collaborator; contributor. ◆**collaboration** *nf* collaboration; contribution.

collage [kɔlaʒ] *nm* (*œuvre*) collage.

collant [kɔlɑ̃] **1** *a* (*papier*) sticky; (*vêtement*) skin-tight; **être c.** (*importun*) *Fam* to be a pest. **2** *nm* (pair of) tights; (*de danse*) leotard.

collation [kɔlasjɔ̃] *nf* (*repas*) light meal.

colle [kɔl] *nf* (*transparente*) glue; (*blanche*) paste; (*question*) *Fam* poser, teaser; (*interrogation*) *Scol Arg* oral; (*retenue*) *Scol Arg* detention.

collecte [kɔlɛkt] *nf* (*quête*) collection. ◆**collect/er** *vt* to collect. ◆**—eur** *nm* collector; (*égout*) **c.** main sewer.

collectif, -ive [kɔlɛktif, -iv] *a* collective; (*hystérie, démission*) mass-; **billet c.** group ticket. ◆**collectivement** *adv* collectively. ◆**collectivisme** *nm* collectivism. ◆**collectivité** *nf* community, collectivity.

collection [kɔlɛksjɔ̃] *nf* collection. ◆**collectionn/er** *vt* (*timbres etc*) to collect. ◆**—eur, -euse** *nmf* collector.

collègue [kɔlɛg] *nmf* colleague.

coller [kɔle] *vt* (*timbre etc*) to stick; (*à la colle transparente*) to glue; (*à la colle blanche*) to paste; (*affiche*) to stick up; (*papier peint*) to hang; (*mettre*) *Fam* to stick, shove; **c. contre** (*nez, oreille etc*) to press against; **c. qn** (*embarrasser*) *Fam* to stump s.o., catch s.o. out; (*consigner*) *Scol* to keep s.o. in; **être collé à** (*examen*) *Fam* to fail, flunk; **se c. contre** to cling (close) to; **se c. qn/qch** *Fam* to get stuck with s.o./sth.; **—** *vi* to stick, cling; **c. à** (*s'adapter*) to fit, correspond to; **ça colle!** *Fam* everything's just fine! ◆**colleur, -euse** *nmf* **c. d'affiches** billsticker.

collet [kɔlɛ] *nm* (*lacet*) snare; **prendre qn au c.** to grab s.o. by the scruff of the neck; **elle**

est/ils sont c. monté she is/they are prim and proper *ou* straight-laced.

collier [kɔlje] *nm* (*bijou*) necklace; (*de chien, cheval*) & *Tech* collar.

colline [kɔlin] *nf* hill.

collision [kɔlizjɔ̃] *nf* (*de véhicules*) collision; (*bagarre, conflit*) clash; **entrer en c. avec** to collide with.

colloque [kɔlɔk] *nm* symposium.

collusion [kɔlyzjɔ̃] *nf* collusion.

colmater [kɔlmate] *vt* (*fuite, fente*) to seal; (*trou*) to fill in; (*brèche Mil*) to close, seal.

colombe [kɔlɔ̃b] *nf* dove.

colon [kɔlɔ̃] *nm* settler, colonist; (*enfant*) *child taking part in a holiday camp.* ◆**colonial, -aux** *a* colonial. ◆**colonie** *nf* colony; **c. de vacances** (children's) holiday camp *ou Am* vacation camp.

coloniser [kɔlɔnize] *vt Pol* to colonize; (*peupler*) to settle. ◆**colonisateur, -trice** *a* colonizing; – *nmf* colonizer. ◆**colonisation** *nf* colonization.

côlon [kolɔ̃] *nm Anat* colon.

colonel [kɔlɔnɛl] *nm* colonel.

colonne [kɔlɔn] *nf* column; **c. vertébrale** spine. ◆**colonnade** *nf* colonnade.

color/er [kɔlɔre] *vt* to colour. ◆**–ant** *a* & *nm* colouring. ◆**–é** *a* (*verre etc*) coloured; (*teint*) ruddy; (*style, foule*) colourful. ◆**coloration** *nf* colouring, colour. ◆**coloriage** *nm* colouring; (*dessin*) coloured drawing. ◆**colorier** *vt* (*dessin etc*) to colour (in). ◆**coloris** *nm* (*effet*) colouring; (*nuance*) shade.

colosse [kɔlɔs] *nm* giant, colossus. ◆**colossal, -aux** *a* colossal, gigantic.

colporter [kɔlpɔrte] *vt* to peddle, hawk.

coltiner [kɔltine] *vt* (*objet lourd*) *Fam* to lug, haul; – **se c.** *vpr* (*tâche pénible*) *Fam* to take on, tackle.

coma [kɔma] *nm* coma; **dans le c.** in a coma.

combat [kɔ̃ba] *nm* fight; *Mil* combat. ◆**combatif, -ive** *a* (*personne*) eager to fight; (*instinct, esprit*) fighting. ◆**combat/re*** *vt* to fight; (*maladie, inflation etc*) to combat, fight; – *vi* to fight. ◆**–ant** *nm Mil* combattant; (*bagarreur*) *Fam* brawler; – *a* (*unité*) fighting.

combien [kɔ̃bjɛ̃] **1** *adv* (*quantité*) how much; (*nombre*) how many; **c. de** (*temps, argent etc*) how much; (*gens, livres etc*) how many. **2** *adv* (*à quel point*) how; **tu verras c. il est bête** you'll see how silly he is. **3** *adv* (*distance*) **c. y a-t-il d'ici à ...?** how far is it to...? **4** *nm inv* **le c. sommes-nous?** (*date*) *Fam* what date is it?; **tous les c.?** (*fréquence*) *Fam* how often?

combine [kɔ̃bin] *nf* (*truc, astuce*) *Fam* trick.

combin/er [kɔ̃bine] *vt* (*disposer*) to combine; (*calculer*) to devise, plan (out). ◆**–é** *nm* (*de téléphone*) receiver. ◆**combinaison** *nf* **1** combination; (*manœuvre*) scheme. **2** (*vêtement de femme*) slip; (*de mécanicien*) boiler suit, *Am* overalls; (*de pilote*) flying suit; **c. de ski** ski suit.

comble [kɔ̃bl] **1** *nm* **le c. de** (*la joie etc*) the height of; **pour c.** (*de malheur*) to crown *ou* cap it all; **c'est un ou le c.!** that's the limit! **2** *nmpl* (*mansarde*) attic, loft; **sous les combles** beneath the roof, in the loft *ou* attic. **3** *a* (*bondé*) packed, full.

combler [kɔ̃ble] *vt* (*trou, lacune etc*) to fill; (*retard, perte*) to make good; (*vœu*) to fulfil; **c. qn de** (*cadeaux etc*) to lavish on s.o.; (*joie*) to fill s.o. with; **je suis comblé** I'm completely satisfied; **vous me comblez!** you're too good to me!

combustible [kɔ̃bystibl] *nm* fuel; – *a* combustible. ◆**combustion** *nf* combustion.

comédie [kɔmedi] *nf* comedy; (*complication*) *Fam* fuss, palaver; **c. musicale** musical; **jouer la c.** *Fig* to put on an act, play-act; **c'est de la c.** (*c'est faux*) it's a sham. ◆**comédien** *nm Th* & *Fig* actor. ◆**comédienne** *nf Th* & *Fig* actress.

comestible [kɔmɛstibl] *a* edible; – *nmpl* foods.

comète [kɔmɛt] *nf* comet.

comique [kɔmik] *a* (*style etc*) *Th* comic; (*amusant*) *Fig* comical, funny; (*auteur*) **c.** comedy writer; – *nm* (*acteur*) comic (actor); **le c.** (*genre*) comedy; *Fig* the comical side (**de** of).

comité [kɔmite] *nm* committee; **c. de gestion** board (of management); **en petit c.** in a small group.

commande [kɔmɑ̃d] **1** *nf* (*achat*) order; **sur c.** to order. **2** *nfpl* **les commandes** *Av Tech* the controls; **tenir les commandes** (*diriger*) *Fig* to have control.

command/er [kɔmɑ̃de] **1** *vt* (*diriger, exiger, dominer*) to command; (*faire fonctionner*) to control; – *vi* **c. à** (*ses passions etc*) to have control over; **c. à qn de faire** to command s.o. to do. **2** *vt* (*acheter*) to order. ◆**–ant** *nm Nau* captain; (*grade*) *Mil* major; (*grade*) *Av* squadron leader; **c. de bord** *Av* captain. ◆**–ement** *nm* (*autorité*) command; *Rel* commandment. ◆**commando** *nm* commando.

commanditaire [kɔmɑ̃ditɛr] *nm Com* sleeping *ou* limited partner, *Am* silent partner.

comme [kɔm] **1** *adv* & *conj* as, like; **un peu**

c. a bit like; **c. moi** like me; **c. cela** like that; **blanc c. neige** (as) white as snow; **c. si** as if; **c. pour faire** as if to do; **c. par hasard** as if by chance; **joli c. tout** *Fam* ever so pretty; **c. ami** as a friend; **c. quoi** *(disant que)* to the effect that; *(ce qui prouve que)* so, which goes to show that; **qu'as-tu c. diplômes?** what do you have in the way of certificates? **2** *adv (exclamatif)* **regarde c. il pleut!** look how it's raining!; **c. c'est petit!** isn't it small! **3** *conj (temps)* as; **c. elle entrait** (just) as she was coming in.

commémorer [kɔmemɔre] *vt* to commemorate. ◆**commémoratif, -ive** *a* commemorative. ◆**commémoration** *nf* commemoration.

commenc/er [kɔmɑ̃se] *vti* to begin, start (**à faire** to do, doing; **par** with; **par faire** by doing; **pour c.** to begin with). ◆**—ement** *nm* beginning, start.

comment [kɔmɑ̃] *adv* how; **c. le sais-tu?** how do you know?; **et c.!** and how!; **c.?** *(répétition, surprise)* what?; **c.!** *(indignation)* what!; **c. est-il?** what is he like?; **c. faire?** what's to be done?; **c. t'appelles-tu?** what's your name?; **c. allez-vous?** how are you?

commentaire [kɔmɑ̃tɛr] *nm (explications)* commentary; *(remarque)* comment. ◆**commentateur, -trice** *nmf* commentator. ◆**commenter** *vt* to comment (up)on.

commérage(s) [kɔmeraʒ] *nm(pl)* gossip.

commerce [kɔmɛrs] *nm* trade, commerce; *(magasin)* shop, business; **de c.** *(voyageur, maison, tribunal)* commercial; *(navire)* trading; **chambre de c.** chamber of commerce; **faire du c.** to trade; **dans le c.** *(objet)* (on sale) in the shops. ◆**commercer** *vi* to trade. ◆**commerçant, -ante** *nmf* shopkeeper. **c. en gros** wholesale dealer; – *a (nation)* trading, mercantile; *(rue, quartier)* shopping-; *(personne)* business-minded. ◆**commercial, -aux** *a* commercial, business-. ◆**commercialiser** *vt* to market.

commère [kɔmɛr] *nf (femme)* gossip.

commettre* [kɔmɛtr] *vt (délit etc)* to commit; *(erreur)* to make.

commis [kɔmi] *nm (de magasin)* assistant, *Am* clerk; *(de bureau)* clerk, *Am* clerical worker.

commissaire [kɔmisɛr] *nm Sp* steward; **c. (de police)** police superintendent *ou Am* chief; **c. aux comptes** auditor; **c. du bord** *Nau* purser. ◆**c.-priseur** *nm (pl commissaires-priseurs)* auctioneer. ◆**commis-**

sariat *nm* **c. (de police)** (central) police station.

commission [kɔmisjɔ̃] *nf (course)* errand; *(message)* message; *(réunion)* commission, committee; *(pourcentage) Com* commission (**sur** on); **faire les commissions** to do the shopping. ◆**commissionnaire** *nm* messenger; *(d'hôtel)* commissionaire; *Com* agent.

commod/e [kɔmɔd] **1** *a (pratique)* handy; *(simple)* easy; **il n'est pas c.** *(pas aimable)* he's unpleasant; *(difficile)* he's a tough one. **2** *nf* chest of drawers, *Am* dresser. ◆**—ément** *adv* comfortably. ◆**commodité** *nf* convenience.

commotion [kɔmosjɔ̃] *nf* shock; **c. (cérébrale)** concussion. ◆**commotionner** *vt* to shake up.

commuer [kɔmɥe] *vt (peine) Jur* to commute (**en** to).

commun [kɔmœ̃] **1** *a (collectif, comparable, habituel)* common; *(frais, cuisine etc)* shared; *(action, démarche etc)* joint; **ami c.** mutual friend; **peu c.** uncommon; **en c.** in common; **transports en c.** public transport; **avoir** *ou* **mettre en c.** to share; **vivre en c.** to live together; **il n'a rien de c. avec** he has nothing in common with. **2** *nm* **le c. des mortels** ordinary mortals. ◆**—ément** [kɔmynemɑ̃] *adv* commonly.

communauté [kɔmynote] *nf* community. ◆**communautaire** *a* community-.

commune [kɔmyn] *nf (municipalité française)* commune; **les Communes** *Br Pol* the Commons. ◆**communal, -aux** *a* communal, local, municipal.

communi/er [kɔmynje] *vi* to receive Holy Communion, communicate. ◆**—ant, -ante** *nmf Rel* communicant. ◆**communion** *nf* communion; *Rel* (Holy) Communion.

communiqu/er [kɔmynike] *vt* to communicate, pass on; *(mouvement)* to impart, communicate; **se c. à** *(feu, rire)* to spread to; – *vi (personne, pièces etc)* to communicate. ◆**—é** *nm (avis) Pol* communiqué; *(publicitaire)* message; **c. de presse** press release. ◆**communicatif, -ive** *a* communicative; *(contagieux)* infectious. ◆**communication** *nf* communication; **c. (téléphonique)** (telephone) call; **mauvaise c.** *Tél* bad line.

communisme [kɔmynism] *nm* communism. ◆**communiste** *a & nmf* communist.

communs [kɔmœ̃] *nmpl (bâtiments)* outbuildings.

commutateur [kɔmytatœr] nm (bouton) Él switch.

compact [kɔ̃pakt] a dense; (mécanisme, disque, véhicule) compact.

compagne [kɔ̃paɲ] nf (camarade) friend; (épouse, maîtresse) companion. ◆**compagnie** nf (présence, société) & Com Mil company; **tenir c. à qn** to keep s.o. company. ◆**compagnon** nm companion; (ouvrier) workman; **c. de route** travelling companion, fellow traveller; **c. de jeu/de travail** playmate/workmate.

comparaître* [kɔ̃paʀɛtʀ] vi Jur to appear (in court) (**devant** before).

compar/er [kɔ̃paʀe] vt to compare; **— se c.** vpr to be compared (**à** to). ◆**—é** a (science etc) comparative. ◆**—able** a comparable. ◆**comparaison** nf comparison; Littér simile. ◆**comparatif, -ive** a (méthode etc) comparative; **— nm** Gram comparative.

comparse [kɔ̃paʀs] nmf Jur minor accomplice, stooge.

compartiment [kɔ̃paʀtimɑ̃] nm compartment. ◆**compartimenter** vt to compartmentalize, divide up.

comparution [kɔ̃paʀysjɔ̃] nf Jur appearance (in court).

compas [kɔ̃pa] nm 1 (pour mesurer etc) (pair of) compasses, Am compass. 2 (boussole) Nau compass.

compassé [kɔ̃pase] a (affecté) starchy, stiff.

compassion [kɔ̃pasjɔ̃] nf compassion.

compatible [kɔ̃patibl] a compatible. ◆**compatibilité** nf compatibility.

compat/ir [kɔ̃patir] vi to sympathize; **c. à** (la douleur etc de qn) to share in. ◆**—issant** a sympathetic.

compatriote [kɔ̃patrijɔt] nmf compatriot.

compenser [kɔ̃pɑ̃se] vt to make up for, compensate for; **— vi** to compensate. ◆**compensation** nf compensation; **en c. de** in compensation for.

compère [kɔ̃pɛr] nm accomplice.

compétent [kɔ̃petɑ̃] a competent. ◆**compétence** nf competence.

compétition [kɔ̃petisjɔ̃] nf competition; (épreuve) Sp event; **de c.** (esprit, sport) competitive. ◆**compétitif, -ive** a competitive. ◆**compétitivité** nf competitiveness.

compiler [kɔ̃pile] vt (documents) to compile.

complainte [kɔ̃plɛ̃t] nf (chanson) lament.

complaire (se) [səkɔ̃plɛr] vpr **se c. dans qch/à faire** to delight in sth/in doing.

complaisant [kɔ̃plɛzɑ̃] a kind, obliging; (indulgent) self-indulgent, complacent. ◆**complaisance** nf kindness, obligingness; self-indulgence, complacency.

complément [kɔ̃plemɑ̃] nm complement; **le c.** (le reste) the rest; **un c. d'information** additional information. ◆**complémentaire** a complementary; (détails) additional.

complet, -ète [kɔ̃plɛ, -ɛt] **1** a complete; (train, hôtel, examen etc) full; (aliment) whole; **au (grand) c.** in full strength. **2** nm (costume) suit. ◆**complètement** adv completely. ◆**compléter** vt to complete; (ajouter à) to complement; (somme) to make up; **— se c.** vpr (caractères) to complement each other.

complexe [kɔ̃plɛks] **1** a complex. **2** nm (sentiment, construction) complex. ◆**complexé** a Fam hung up, inhibited. ◆**complexité** nf complexity.

complication [kɔ̃plikasjɔ̃] nf complication; (complexité) complexity.

complice [kɔ̃plis] nm accomplice; **— a** (regard) knowing; (silence, attitude) conniving; **c. de** Jur a party to. ◆**complicité** nf complicity.

compliment [kɔ̃plimɑ̃] nm compliment; pl (éloges) compliments; (félicitations) congratulations. ◆**complimenter** vt to compliment (**sur, pour** on).

compliqu/er [kɔ̃plike] vt to complicate; **— se c.** vpr (situation) to get complicated. ◆**—é** a complicated; (mécanisme etc) intricate; complicated; (histoire, problème etc) involved, complicated.

complot [kɔ̃plo] nm plot, conspiracy. ◆**comploter** vti to plot (**de faire** to do).

comport/er [kɔ̃pɔrte] **1** vt (impliquer) to involve, contain; (comprendre en soi, présenter) to contain, comprise, have. **2 se c.** vpr to behave; (joueur, voiture) to perform. ◆**—ement** nm behaviour; (de joueur etc) performance.

compos/er [kɔ̃poze] vt (former, constituer) to compose, make up; (musique, visage) to compose; (numéro) Tél to dial; (texte) Typ to set (up); **se c. de, être composé de** to be composed of; **— vi** Scol to take an examination; **c. avec** to come to terms with. ◆**—ant** nm (chimique, électronique) component. ◆**—ante** nf (d'une idée etc) component. ◆**—é** a & nm compound. ◆**compositeur, -trice** nmf Mus composer; Typ typesetter. ◆**composition** nf (action) composing, making up; Typ typesetting; Mus Littér Ch composition; Scol test, class exam; **c. française** Scol French essay ou composition.

composter [kɔ̃pɔste] vt (billet) to cancel, punch.

compote [kɔ̃pɔt] nf stewed fruit; **c. de pommes** stewed apples, apple sauce. ◆**compotier** nm fruit dish.

compréhensible [kɔ̃preɑ̃sibl] a understandable, comprehensible. ◆**compréhensif, -ive** a (personne) understanding. ◆**compréhension** nf understanding, comprehension.

comprendre* [kɔ̃prɑ̃dr] vt to understand, comprehend; (comporter) to include, comprise; **je n'y comprends rien** I don't understand anything about it; **ça se comprend** that's understandable. ◆**compris** a (inclus) included (dans in); **frais c.** including expenses; **tout c.** (all) inclusive; **y c.** including; **c. entre** (situated) between; (c'est) **c.!** it's agreed!

compresse [kɔ̃prɛs] nf Méd compress.

compresseur [kɔ̃prɛsœr] a **rouleau c.** steam roller.

comprim/er [kɔ̃prime] vt to compress; (colère etc) to repress; (dépenses) to reduce. ◆**—é** nm Méd tablet. ◆**compression** nf compression; (du personnel etc) reduction.

compromettre* [kɔ̃prɔmɛtr] vt to compromise. ◆**compromis** nm compromise. ◆**compromission** nf compromising action, compromise.

comptable [kɔ̃tabl] a (règles etc) book-keeping-; — nmf book-keeper; (expert) accountant. ◆**comptabilité** nf (comptes) accounts; (science) book-keeping, accountancy; (service) accounts department.

comptant [kɔ̃tɑ̃] a **argent c.** (hard) cash; — adv **payer c.** to pay (in) cash; (au) **c.** (acheter, vendre) for cash.

compte [kɔ̃t] nm (comptabilité) account; (calcul) count; (nombre) (right) number; **avoir un c. en banque** to have a bank(ing) account; **c. chèque** cheque account, Am checking account; **tenir c. de** to take into account; **c. tenu de** considering; **entrer en ligne de c.** to be taken into account; **se rendre c. de** to realize; **rendre c. de** (exposer) to report on; (justifier) to account for; (de livre, film) review; **demander des comptes à** to call to account; **faire le c. de** to count; **à son c.** (travailler) for oneself; (s'installer) on one's own; **pour le c. de** on behalf of; **pour mon c.** for my part; **sur le c. de qn** about s.o.; **en fin de c.** all things considered; **à bon c.** (acheter) cheap(ly); **s'en tirer à bon c.** to get off lightly; **avoir un c. à régler avec qn** to have a score to settle with s.o.; **c. à rebours** countdown. ◆**c.-gouttes** nm inv Méd dropper; **au c.-gouttes** very sparingly. ◆**c.-tours** nm inv Aut rev counter.

compt/er [kɔ̃te] vt (calculer) to count; (prévoir) to reckon, allow; (considérer) to consider; (payer) to pay; **c. faire** to expect to do; (avoir l'intention de) to intend to do; **c. qch à qn** (facturer) to charge s.o. for sth; **il compte deux ans de service** he has two years' service; **ses jours sont comptés** his ou her days are numbered; — vi (calculer, avoir de l'importance) to count; **c. sur** to rely on; **c. avec** to reckon with; **c. parmi** to be (numbered) among. ◆**—eur** nm Él meter; **c. de vitesse** Aut speedometer; **c.** (kilométrique) milometer, clock; **c. Geiger** Geiger counter.

comptoir [kɔ̃twar] nm 1 (de magasin) counter; (de café) bar; (de bureau) (reception) desk. 2 Com branch, agency.

compulser [kɔ̃pylse] vt to examine.

comte [kɔ̃t] nm (noble) count; Br earl. ◆**comté** nm county. ◆**comtesse** nf countess.

con, conne [kɔ̃, kɔn] a (idiot) Fam stupid; — nmf Fam stupid fool.

concave [kɔ̃kav] a concave.

concéder [kɔ̃sede] vt to concede, grant (à to, que that).

concentr/er [kɔ̃sɑ̃tre] vt to concentrate; (attention etc) to focus, concentrate; — **se c.** vpr (réfléchir) to concentrate. ◆**—é** a (solution) concentrated; (lait) condensed; (attentif) in a state of concentration; — nm Ch concentrate; **c. de tomates** tomato purée. ◆**concentration** nf concentration.

concentrique [kɔ̃sɑ̃trik] a concentric.

concept [kɔ̃sɛpt] nm concept. ◆**conception** nf (idée) & Méd conception.

concern/er [kɔ̃sɛrne] vt to concern; **en ce qui me concerne** as far as I'm concerned. ◆**—ant** prép concerning.

concert [kɔ̃sɛr] nm Mus concert; (de louanges) chorus; **de c.** (agir) together, in concert.

concert/er [kɔ̃sɛrte] vt to arrange, devise (in agreement); — **se c.** vpr to consult together. ◆**—é** a (plan) concerted. ◆**concertation** nf (dialogue) dialogue.

concession [kɔ̃sesjɔ̃] nf concession (à to); (terrain) plot of land). ◆**concessionnaire** nmf Com (authorized) dealer, agent.

concev/oir* [kɔ̃səvwar] 1 vt (imaginer, éprouver, engendrer) to conceive; (comprendre) to understand; **ainsi conçu** (dépêche etc) worded as follows. 2 vi (femme) to conceive. ◆**—able** a conceivable.

concierge [kɔ̃sjɛrʒ] *nmf* caretaker, *Am* janitor.

concile [kɔ̃sil] *nm Rel* council.

concili/er [kɔ̃silje] *vt* (*choses*) to reconcile; **se c. l'amitié/***etc* de qn to win (over) s.o.'s friendship/*etc*. ◆**—ant** *a* conciliatory. ◆**conciliateur, -trice** *nmf* conciliator. ◆**conciliation** *nf* conciliation.

concis [kɔ̃si] *a* concise, terse. ◆**concision** *nf* concision.

concitoyen, -enne [kɔ̃sitwajɛ̃, -ɛn] *nmf* fellow citizen.

conclu/re* [kɔ̃klyr] *vt* (*terminer, régler*) to conclude; **c. que** (*déduire*) to conclude that; **– vi** (*orateur etc*) to conclude; **c. à** to conclude in favour of. ◆**—ant** *a* conclusive. ◆**conclusion** *nf* conclusion.

concombre [kɔ̃kɔ̃br] *nm* cucumber.

concorde [kɔ̃kɔrd] *nf* concord, harmony. ◆**concord/er** *vi* (*faits etc*) to agree; (*caractères*) to match; **c. avec** to match. ◆**—ant** *a* in agreement. ◆**concordance** *nf* agreement; (*de situations, résultats*) similarity; **c. des temps** *Gram* sequence of tenses.

concourir* [kɔ̃kurir] *vi* (*candidat*) to compete (**pour** for); (*directions*) to converge; **c. à** (*un but*) to contribute to. ◆**concours** *nm Scol Univ* competitive examination; (*jeu*) competition; (*aide*) assistance; (*de circonstances*) combination; **c. hippique** horse show.

concret, -ète [kɔ̃krɛ, -ɛt] *a* concrete. ◆**concrétiser** *vt* to give concrete form to; **– se c.** *vpr* to materialize.

conçu [kɔ̃sy] *voir* **concevoir**; **– a c. pour faire** designed to do; **bien c.** (*maison etc*) well-designed.

concubine [kɔ̃kybin] *nf* (*maîtresse*) concubine. ◆**concubinage** *nm* cohabitation; **en c.** as husband and wife.

concurrent, -ente [kɔ̃kyrɑ̃, -ɑ̃t] *nmf* competitor; *Scol Univ* candidate. ◆**concurrence** *nf* competition; **faire c. à** to compete with; **jusqu'à c. de** up to the amount of. ◆**concurrencer** *vt* to compete with. ◆**concurrentiel, -ielle** *a* (*prix etc*) competitive.

condamn/er [kɔ̃dane] *vt* to condemn; *Jur* to sentence (**à** to); (*porte*) to block up, bar; (*pièce*) to keep locked; **c. à une amende** to fine. ◆**—é, -ée** *nmf Jur* condemned man, condemned woman; **être c.** (*malade*) to be doomed, be a hopeless case. ◆**condamnation** *nf Jur* sentence; (*censure*) condemnation.

condenser [kɔ̃dɑ̃se] *vt*, **– se c.** *vpr* to condense. ◆**condensateur** *nm* *Él* condenser. ◆**condensation** *nf* condensation.

condescendre [kɔ̃dɛsɑ̃dr] *vi* to condescend (**à** to). ◆**condescendance** *nf* condescension.

condiment [kɔ̃dimɑ̃] *nm* condiment.

condisciple [kɔ̃disipl] *nm Scol* classmate, schoolfellow; *Univ* fellow student.

condition [kɔ̃disjɔ̃] *nf* (*état, stipulation, rang*) condition; *pl* (*clauses, tarifs*) *Com* terms; **à c. de faire**, **c. que l'on fasse** providing ou provided (that) one does; **mettre en c.** (*endoctriner*) to condition; **sans c.** (*se rendre*) unconditionally. ◆**conditionnel, -elle** *a* conditional. ◆**conditionn/er** *vt* 1 (*influencer*) to condition. 2 (*article*) *Com* to package. ◆**—é** *a* (*réflexe*) conditioned; **à air c.** (*pièce etc*) air-conditioned. ◆**—ement** *nm* conditioning; packaging.

condoléances [kɔ̃dɔleɑ̃s] *nfpl* condolences.

conducteur, -trice [kɔ̃dyktœr, -tris] 1 *nmf Aut Rail* driver. 2 *a* & *nm* (*corps*) *Él* conductor; (*fil*) *Él* lead (wire).

conduire* [kɔ̃dɥir] 1 *vt* to lead; *Aut* to drive; (*affaire etc*) & *Él* to conduct; (*eau*) to carry; **c. qn à** (*accompagner*) to take s.o. to. 2 **se c.** *vpr* to behave. ◆**conduit** *nm* duct. ◆**conduite** *nf* conduct, behaviour; *Aut* driving (**de** of); (*d'entreprise etc*) conduct; (*d'eau, de gaz*) main; **c. à gauche** (*volant*) left-hand drive; **faire un bout de c. à qn** to go with s.o. part of the way; **sous la c. de** under the guidance of.

cône [kon] *nm* cone.

confection [kɔ̃fɛksjɔ̃] *nf* making (**de** of); **vêtements de c.** ready-made clothes; **magasin de c.** ready-made clothing shop. ◆**confectionner** *vt* (*gâteau, robe*) to make.

confédération [kɔ̃federasjɔ̃] *nf* confederation. ◆**confédéré** *a* confederate.

conférence [kɔ̃ferɑ̃s] *nf* conference; (*exposé*) lecture. ◆**conférencier, -ière** *nmf* lecturer. ◆**conférer** *vt* (*attribuer, donner*) to confer (**à** on).

confess/er [kɔ̃fese] *vt* to confess; **– se c.** *vpr Rel* to confess (**à** to). ◆**—eur** *nm* (*prêtre*) confessor. ◆**confession** *nf* confession. ◆**confessionnal, -aux** *nm Rel* confessional. ◆**confessionnel, -elle** *a* (*école*) *Rel* denominational.

confettis [kɔ̃feti] *nmpl* confetti.

confiance [kɔ̃fjɑ̃s] *nf* trust, confidence; **faire c. à qn, avoir c. en qn** to trust s.o.; **c. en soi** (self-)confidence; **poste/abus de c.** position/breach of trust; **homme de c.** reliable man; **en toute c.** (*acheter*) quite confidently; **poser la question de c.** *Pol* to ask for a vote of confidence. ◆**confiant** *a* trusting; (*sûr de soi*) confident; **être c. en ou dans** to have confidence in.

confidence [kɔ̃fidɑ̃s] *nf* (*secret*) confidence; **en c.** in confidence; **il m'a fait une c.** he confided in me. ◆**confident** *nm* confidant. ◆**confidente** *nf* confidante. ◆**confidentiel, -ielle** *a* confidential.

confier [kɔ̃fje] *vt* **c. à qn** (*enfant, objet*) to give s.o. to look after, entrust s.o. with; **c. un secret/etc à qn** to confide a secret/etc to s.o.; — **se c.** *vpr* to confide (**à qn** in s.o.).

configuration [kɔ̃figyrasjɔ̃] *nf* configuration.

confin/er [kɔ̃fine] *vt* to confine; — *vi* **c. à** to border on; — **se c.** *vpr* to confine oneself (**dans** to). ◆**-é** *a* (*atmosphère*) stuffy.

confins [kɔ̃fɛ̃] *nmpl* confines.

confire [kɔ̃fir] *vt* (*cornichon*) to pickle; (*fruit*) to preserve.

confirmer [kɔ̃firme] *vt* to confirm (**que** that); **c. qn dans sa résolution** to confirm s.o.'s resolve. ◆**confirmation** *nf* confirmation.

confiserie [kɔ̃fizri] *nf* (*magasin*) sweet shop, *Am* candy store; *pl* (*produits*) confectionery, sweets, *Am* candy. ◆**confiseur, -euse** *nmf* confectioner.

confisquer [kɔ̃fiske] *vt* to confiscate (**à qn** from s.o.). ◆**confiscation** *nf* confiscation.

confit [kɔ̃fi] *a* **fruits confits** crystallized *ou* candied fruit. ◆**confiture** *nf* jam, preserves.

conflit [kɔ̃fli] *nm* conflict. ◆**conflictuel, -elle** *a* *Psy* conflict-provoking.

confluent [kɔ̃flyɑ̃] *nm* (*jonction*) confluence.

confondre [kɔ̃fɔ̃dr] *vt* (*choses, personnes*) to confuse, mix up; (*consterner, étonner*) to confound; (*amalgamer*) to fuse; **c. avec** to mistake for; — **se c.** *vpr* (*s'unir*) to merge; **se c. en excuses** to be very apologetic.

conforme [kɔ̃fɔrm] *a* **c. à** in accordance with; **c. (à l'original)** (*copie*) true (to the original); — **se c.** *vpr* to conform (**à** to). ◆**conform/er** *vt* to model, adapt; — **se c.** *vpr* to conform (**à** to). ◆**-ément** *adv* **c. à** in accordance with. ◆**conformisme** *nm* conformity, conformism. ◆**conformiste** *a* & *nmf* conformist. ◆**conformité** *nf* conformity.

confort [kɔ̃fɔr] *nm* comfort. ◆**confortable** *a* comfortable.

confrère [kɔ̃frɛr] *nm* colleague. ◆**confrérie** *nf Rel* brotherhood.

confronter [kɔ̃frɔ̃te] *vt Jur etc* to confront

(**avec** with); (*textes*) to collate; **confronté à** confronted with. ◆**confrontation** *nf* confrontation; collation.

confus [kɔ̃fy] *a* (*esprit, situation, bruit*) confused; (*idée, style*) confused, jumbled, hazy; (*gêné*) embarrassed; **je suis c.!** (*désolé*) I'm terribly sorry!; (*comblé de bienfaits*) I'm overwhelmed! ◆**confusément** *adv* indistinctly, vaguely. ◆**confusion** *nf* confusion; (*gêne, honte*) embarrassment.

congé [kɔ̃ʒe] *nm* leave (of absence); (*avis pour locataire*) notice (to quit); (*pour salarié*) notice (of dismissal); (*vacances*) holiday, *Am* vacation; **c. de maladie** sick leave; **congés payés** holidays with pay, paid holidays; **donner son c. à** (*employé, locataire*) to give notice to; **prendre c. de** to take leave of. ◆**congédier** *vt* (*domestique etc*) to dismiss.

congeler [kɔ̃ʒle] *vt* to freeze. ◆**congélateur** *nm* freezer, deep-freeze. ◆**congélation** *nf* freezing.

congénère [kɔ̃ʒenɛr] *nmf* fellow creature. ◆**congénital, -aux** *a* congenital.

congère [kɔ̃ʒɛr] *nf* snowdrift.

congestion [kɔ̃ʒɛstjɔ̃] *nf* congestion; **c. cérébrale** *Méd* stroke. ◆**congestionn/er** *vt* to congest. ◆**-é** *a* (*visage*) flushed.

Congo [kɔ̃go] *nm* Congo. ◆**congolais, -aise** *a* & *nmf* Congolese.

congratuler [kɔ̃gratyle] *vt Iron* to congratulate.

congrégation [kɔ̃gregasjɔ̃] *nf* (*de prêtres etc*) congregation.

congrès [kɔ̃grɛ] *nm* congress. ◆**congressiste** *nmf* delegate (**to** *a congress*).

conifère [kɔnifɛr] *nm* conifer.

conique [kɔnik] *a* conic(al), cone-shaped.

conjecture [kɔ̃ʒɛktyr] *nf* conjecture. ◆**conjectural, -aux** *a* conjectural. ◆**conjecturer** *vt* to conjecture, surmise.

conjoint [kɔ̃ʒwɛ̃] **1** *a* (*problèmes, action etc*) joint. **2** *nm* spouse; *pl* husband and wife. ◆**conjointement** *adv* jointly.

conjonction [kɔ̃ʒɔ̃ksjɔ̃] *nf Gram* conjunction.

conjoncture [kɔ̃ʒɔ̃ktyr] *nf* circumstances; *Écon* economic situation. ◆**conjoncturel, -elle** *a* (*prévisions etc*) economic.

conjugal, -aux [kɔ̃ʒygal, -o] *a* conjugal.

conjuguer [kɔ̃ʒyge] *vt* (*verbe*) to conjugate; (*efforts*) to combine; — **se c.** *vpr* (*verbe*) to be conjugated. ◆**conjugaison** *nf Gram* conjugation.

conjur/er [kɔ̃ʒyre] *vt* (*danger*) to avert; (*mauvais sort*) to ward off; **c. qn** (*implorer*)

to entreat s.o. (**de faire** to do). ◆**-é, -ée**
nmf conspirator. ◆**conjuration** *nf*
(*complot*) conspiracy.

connaissance [kɔnɛsɑ̃s] *nf* knowledge;
(*personne*) acquaintance; *pl* (*science*)
knowledge (**en of**); **faire la c. de qn, faire la
c.** avec **qn** to make s.o.'s acquaintance, meet
s.o.; (*ami, époux etc*) to get to know s.o.; **à
ma c.** as far as I know; **avoir c. de** to be
aware of; **perdre c.** to lose consciousness,
faint; **sans c.** unconscious. ◆**connaisseur** *nm* connoisseur.

connaître* [kɔnɛtr] *vt* to know; (*rencontrer*)
to meet; (*un succès etc*) to have; (*un
malheur etc*) to experience; **faire c.** to make
known; **— se c.** *vpr* (*amis etc*) to get to
know each other; **nous nous connaissions
déjà** we've met before; **s'y c. à** ou **en qch** to
know (all) about sth; **il ne se connaît plus**
he's losing his cool.

connecter [kɔnɛkte] *vt* Él to connect.
◆**connexe** *a* (*matières*) allied. ◆**con-
nexion** *nf* Él connection.

connerie [kɔnri] *nf Fam* (*bêtise*) stupidity;
(*action*) stupid thing; *pl* (*paroles*) stupid
nonsense.

connivence [kɔnivɑ̃s] *nf* connivance.

connotation [kɔnɔtasjɔ̃] *nf* connotation.

connu *voir* **connaître**; **— a** (*célèbre*)
well-known.

conquérir* [kɔkerir] *vt* (*pays, marché etc*)
to conquer. ◆**-ant, -ante** *nmf* conqueror.
◆**conquête** *nf* conquest; **faire la c. de**
(*pays, marché etc*) to conquer.

consacrer [kɔsakre] *vt* (*temps, vie etc*) to
devote (**à** to); (*église etc*) Rel to consecrate;
(*coutume etc*) to establish, sanction, consecrate; **se c. à** to devote oneself to.

conscience [kɔsjɑ̃s] *nf* 1 (*psychologique*)
consciousness; **la c. de qch** the awareness
ou consciousness of sth; **c. de soi** self-
awareness; **avoir/prendre c. de** to
be/become aware ou conscious of; **perdre
c.** to lose consciousness. 2 (*morale*)
conscience; **avoir mauvaise c.** to have a
guilty conscience; **c. professionnelle**
conscientiousness. ◆**consciemment**
[kɔsjamɑ̃] *adv* consciously. ◆**con-
scienieux, -euse** *a* conscientious.
◆**conscient** *a* conscious; **c. de** aware ou
conscious of.

conscrit [kɔskri] *nm Mil* conscript. ◆**conscription** *nf* conscription.

consécration [kɔsekrasjɔ̃] *nf Rel* consecration; (*confirmation*) sanction, consecration.

consécuti/f, -ive [kɔsekytif, -iv] *a* consecu-

tive; **c. à** following upon. ◆**-vement** *adv*
consecutively.

conseil [kɔsɛj] *nm* 1 **un c.** a piece of advice,
some advice; **des conseils** advice;
(**expert-**)**c.** consultant. 2 (*assemblée*) council, committee; **c. d'administration** board of
directors; **C. des ministres** *Pol* Cabinet;
(*réunion*) Cabinet meeting. ◆**conseiller** [1]
vt (*guider, recommander*) to advise; **c. qch à
qn** to recommend sth to s.o.; **c. à qn de faire**
to advise s.o. to do. ◆**conseiller** [2], **-ère**
nmf (*expert*) consultant; (*d'un conseil*)
councillor.

consent/ir* [kɔsɑ̃tir] *vi* **c. à** to consent to;
— vt to grant (**à** to). ◆**-ement** *nm*
consent.

conséquence [kɔsekɑ̃s] *nf* consequence;
(*conclusion*) conclusion; **en c.** accordingly;
sans c. (*importance*) of no importance.
◆**conséquent** *a* logical; (*important*) *Fam*
important; **par c.** consequently.

conservatoire [kɔsɛrvatwar] *nm* academy,
school (*of music, drama*).

conserve [kɔsɛrv] *nf* **conserves** tinned ou
canned food; **de** ou **en c.** tinned, canned;
mettre en c. to tin, can.

conserv/er [kɔsɛrve] *vt* (*ne pas perdre*) to
retain, keep; (*fruits, vie, tradition etc*) to
preserve; **— se c.** *vpr* (*aliment*) to keep.
◆**-é à bien c.** (*vieillard*) well-preserved.
◆**conservateur, -trice** 1 *a* & *nmf Pol*
Conservative. 2 *nm* (*de musée*) curator; (*de
bibliothèque*) (chief) librarian. 3 *nm*
(*produit*) Culin preservative. ◆**conservation** *nf* preservation; **instinct de c.** survival
instinct. ◆**conservatisme** *nm* conservatism.

considér/er [kɔsidere] *vt* to consider (**que**
that); **c. qn** (*faire cas de*) to respect s.o.; **c.
comme** to consider to be, regard as; **tout
bien considéré** all things considered.
◆**-able** *a* considerable. ◆**considération** *nf* (*motif, examen*) consideration;
(*respect*) regard, esteem; *pl* (*remarques*)
observations; **prendre en c.** to take into
consideration.

consigne [kɔsiɲ] *nf* (*instruction*) orders;
Rail left-luggage office, *Am* baggage checkroom; *Scol* detention; *Mil* confinement to
barracks; (*somme*) deposit; **c. automatique**
Rail luggage lockers, *Am* baggage lockers.
◆**consignation** *nf* (*somme*) deposit.
◆**consigner** *vt* (*écrire*) to record;
(*bouteille etc*) to charge a deposit on;
(*bagages*) to deposit in the left-luggage
office, *Am* to check; (*élève*) Scol to keep in;

(soldat) Mil to confine (to barracks); *(salle)* to seal off, close.

consistant [kɔ̃sistɑ̃] *a (sauce, bouillie)* thick; *(argument, repas)* solid. **◆consistance** *nf (de liquide)* consistency; **sans c.** *(rumeur)* unfounded; *(esprit)* irresolute.

consister [kɔ̃siste] *vi* **c. en/dans** to consist of/in; **c. à faire** to consist in doing.

consistoire [kɔ̃sistwar] *nm Rel* council.

console [kɔ̃sɔl] *nf Tech Él* console.

consoler [kɔ̃sɔle] *vt* to console, comfort (de for); **se c. de** *(la mort de qn etc)* to get over. **◆consolation** *nf* consolation, comfort.

consolider [kɔ̃sɔlide] *vt* to strengthen, consolidate. **◆consolidation** *nf* strengthening, consolidation.

consomm/er [kɔ̃sɔme] *vt (aliment, carburant etc)* to consume; *(crime, œuvre)* Litt to accomplish; — *vi (au café)* to drink; **c. beaucoup/peu** *(véhicule)* to be heavy/light on petrol *ou Am* gas. **◆—é1** *a (achevé)* consummate. **2** *nm* clear meat soup, consommé. **◆consommateur, -trice** *nmf Com* consumer; *(au café)* customer. **◆consommation** *nf* consumption; drink; **biens/société de c.** consumer goods/society.

consonance [kɔ̃sɔnɑ̃s] *nf Mus* consonance; *pl (sons)* sounds.

consonne [kɔ̃sɔn] *nf* consonant.

consortium [kɔ̃sɔrsjɔm] *nm Com* consortium.

consorts [kɔ̃sɔr] *nmpl* **et c.** *Péj* and people of that ilk.

conspirer [kɔ̃spire] *vi* **1** to conspire, plot *(contre* against). **2 c. à faire** *(concourir)* to conspire to do. **◆conspirateur, -trice** *nmf* conspirator. **◆conspiration** *nf* conspiracy.

conspuer [kɔ̃spɥe] *vt (orateur etc)* to boo.

constant, -ante [kɔ̃stɑ̃, -ɑ̃t] *a* constant; — *nf Math* constant. **◆constamment** *adv* constantly. **◆constance** *nf* constancy.

constat [kɔ̃sta] *nm* (official) report; **dresser un c. d'échec** to acknowledge one's failure.

constater [kɔ̃state] *vt* to note, observe *(que* that); *(vérifier)* to establish; *(enregistrer)* to record; **je ne fais que c.** I'm merely stating a fact. **◆constatation** *nf (remarque)* observation.

constellation [kɔ̃stelasjɔ̃] *nf* constellation. **◆constellé** *a* **c. de** *(étoiles, joyaux)* studded with.

consterner [kɔ̃stɛrne] *vt* to distress, dismay. **◆consternation** *nf* distress, (profound) dismay.

constip/er [kɔ̃stipe] *vt* to constipate. **◆—é**

a constipated; *(gêné)* Fam embarrassed, stiff. **◆constipation** *nf* constipation.

constitu/er [kɔ̃stitɥe] *vt (composer)* to make up, constitute; *(être, représenter)* to constitute; *(organiser)* to form; *(instituer)* Jur to appoint; **constitué de** made up of; **se c. prisonnier** to give oneself up. **◆—ant** *a (éléments)* component, constituent; *(assemblée)* Pol constituent. **◆constitutif, -ive** *a* constituent. **◆constitution** *nf (santé)* & Pol constitution; *(fondation)* formation *(de* of); *(composition)* composition. **◆constitutionnel, -elle** *a* constitutional.

constructeur [kɔ̃stryktœr] *nm* builder; *(fabricant)* maker *(de* of). **◆constructif, -ive** *a* constructive. **◆construction** *nf (de pont etc)* building, construction *(de* of); *(édifice)* building, structure; *(de théorie etc)* & Gram construction; **de c.** *(matériaux, jeu)* building-.

construire* [kɔ̃strɥir] *vt (maison, route etc)* to build, construct; *(phrase, théorie etc)* to construct.

consul [kɔ̃syl] *nm* consul. **◆consulaire** *a* consular. **◆consulat** *nm* consulate.

consulter [kɔ̃sylte] **1** *vt* to consult; — **se c.** *vpr* to consult (each other), confer. **2** *vi (médecin)* to hold surgery, Am hold office hours. **◆consultatif, -ive** *a* consultative, advisory. **◆consultation** *nf* consultation; **cabinet de c.** Méd surgery, Am office; **heures de c.** Méd surgery hours, Am office hours.

consumer [kɔ̃syme] *vt (détruire, miner)* to consume.

contact [kɔ̃takt] *nm* contact; *(toucher)* touch; Aut ignition; **être en c. avec** to be in touch *ou* contact with; **prendre c.** to get in touch *(avec* with); **entrer en c. avec** to come into contact with; **prise de c.** first meeting; **mettre/couper le c.** Aut to switch on/off the ignition. **◆contacter** *vt* to contact.

contagieux, -euse [kɔ̃taʒjø, -øz] *a (maladie, rire)* contagious, infectious; **c'est c.** it's catching *ou* contagious. **◆contagion** *nf Méd* contagion, infection; *(de rire etc)* contagiousness.

contaminer [kɔ̃tamine] *vt* to contaminate. **◆contamination** *nf* contamination.

conte [kɔ̃t] *nm* tale; **c. de fée** fairy tale.

contempler [kɔ̃tɑ̃ple] *vt* to contemplate, gaze at. **◆contemplatif, -ive** *a* contemplative. **◆contemplation** *nf* contemplation.

contemporain, -aine [kɔ̃tɑ̃pɔrɛ̃, -ɛn] *a* & *nmf* contemporary.

contenance [kɔ̃tnɑ̃s] *nf* **1** (*contenu*) capacity. **2** (*allure*) bearing; **perdre c.** to lose one's composure.

conten/ir* [kɔ̃tnir] *vt* (*renfermer*) to contain; (*avoir comme capacité*) to hold; (*contrôler*) to hold back, contain; **— se c.** *vpr* to contain oneself. **◆—ant** *nm* container. **◆—eur** *nm* (freight) container.

content [kɔ̃tɑ̃] **1** *a* pleased, happy, glad (**de** faire *to do*); **c. de qn/qch** pleased *ou* happy with s.o./sth; **c. de soi** self-satisfied; **non c. d'avoir fait** not content with having done. **2** *nm* **avoir son c.** to have had one's fill (**de** *of*). **◆content/er** *vt* to satisfy, please; **se c.** **de** to be content with, content oneself with. **◆—ement** *nm* contentment, satisfaction.

contentieux [kɔ̃tɑ̃sjø] *nm* (*affaires*) matters in dispute; (*service*) legal *ou* claims department.

contenu [kɔ̃tny] *nm* (*de récipient*) contents; (*de texte, film etc*) content.

cont/er [kɔ̃te] *vt* (*histoire etc*) to tell, relate. **◆—eur, -euse** *nmf* storyteller.

conteste (sans) [sɑ̃kɔ̃test] *adv* indisputably.

contest/er [kɔ̃teste] **1** *vt* (*fait ou droit*) to dispute, contest. **— se c.** *vi* (*étudiants etc*) to protest; **— vt** to protest against. **◆—é a** (*théorie etc*) controversial. **◆—able** *a* debatable. **◆contestataire** *a* étudiant/ouvrier **c.** student/worker protester; **— nmf** protester. **◆contestation** *nf* (*discussion*) dispute; **faire de la c.** to protest (against the establishment).

contexte [kɔ̃tekst] *nm* context.

contigu, -uë [kɔ̃tigy] *a* **c. (à)** (*maisons etc*) adjoining. **◆contiguïté** *nf* close proximity.

continent [kɔ̃tinɑ̃] *nm* continent; (*opposé à une île*) mainland. **◆continental, -aux** *a* continental.

contingent [kɔ̃tɛ̃ʒɑ̃] **1** *a* (*accidentel*) contingent. **2** *nm* Mil contingent; (*part, quota*) quota. **◆contingences** *nfpl* contingencies.

continu [kɔ̃tiny] *a* continuous. **◆continuel, -elle** *a* continual, unceasing. **◆continuellement** *adv* continually.

continu/er [kɔ̃tinye] *vt* to continue, carry on (**à** *ou* **de** faire *doing*); (*prolonger*) to continue; **— vi** to continue, go on. **◆continuation** *nf* continuation; **bonne c.!** *Fam* I hope the rest of it goes well, keep up the good work! **◆continuité** *nf* continuity.

contondant [kɔ̃tɔ̃dɑ̃] *a* **instrument c.** *Jur* blunt instrument.

contorsion [kɔ̃tɔrsjɔ̃] *nf* contortion. **◆se**

contorsionner *vpr* to contort oneself. **◆contorsionniste** *nmf* contortionist.

contour [kɔ̃tur] *nm* outline, contour; *pl* (*de route, rivière*) twists, bends. **◆contourn/er** *vt* (*colline etc*) to go round, skirt; (*difficulté, loi*) to get round. **◆—é a** (*style*) convoluted, tortuous.

contraception [kɔ̃trasepsjɔ̃] *nf* contraception. **◆contraceptif, -ive** *a* & *nm* contraceptive.

contract/er [kɔ̃trakte] *vt* (*muscle, habitude, dette etc*) to contract; **— se c.** *vpr* (*cœur etc*) to contract. **◆—é a** (*inquiet*) tense. **◆contraction** *nf* contraction.

contractuel, -elle [kɔ̃traktɥel] **1** *nmf* traffic warden; **— nf** Am meter maid. **2** *a* contractual.

contradicteur [kɔ̃tradiktœr] *nm* contradictor. **◆contradiction** *nf* contradiction. **◆contradictoire** *a* (*propos etc*) contradictory; (*rapports, théories*) conflicting; **débat c.** debate.

contraindre* [kɔ̃trɛ̃dr] *vt* to compel, force (**à** faire *to do*); **— se c.** *vpr* to compel *ou* force oneself; (*se gêner*) to restrain oneself. **◆contraignant** *a* constraining, restricting. **◆contraint** *a* (*air etc*) forced, constrained. **◆contrainte** *nf* compulsion, constraint; (*gêne*) constraint, restraint.

contraire [kɔ̃trer] *a* opposite; (*défavorable*) contrary; **c. à** contrary to; **— nm** opposite; **(bien) au c.** on the contrary. **—ment** *adv* **c. à** contrary to.

contrari/er [kɔ̃trarje] *vt* (*projet, action*) to thwart; (*personne*) to annoy. **◆—ant** *a* (*action etc*) annoying; (*personne*) difficult, perverse. **◆contrariété** *nf* annoyance.

contraste [kɔ̃trast] *nm* contrast. **◆contraster** *vi* to contrast (**avec** with); **faire c.** (*mettre en contraste*) to contrast.

contrat [kɔ̃tra] *nm* contract.

contravention [kɔ̃travɑ̃sjɔ̃] *nf* (*amende*) Aut fine; (*pour stationnement interdit*) (parking) ticket; **en c.** contravening the law; **en c. à** in contravention of.

contre [kɔ̃tr] **1** *prép* & *adv* against; (*en échange de*) (in exchange) for; **échanger c.** to exchange for; **fâché c.** angry with; **s'abriter c.** to shelter from; **il va s'appuyer c.** he's going to lean against it; **six voix c. deux** six votes to two; **Nîmes c. Arras** *Sp* Nîmes versus Arras; **un médicament c.** (*toux, grippe etc*) a medicine for; **par c.** on the other hand; **tout c.** close to *ou* by. **2** *nm* (*riposte*) *Sp* counter.

contre- [kɔ̃tr] *préf* counter-.

contre-attaque [kɔ̃tratak] *nf* counterattack. ◆**contre-attaquer** *vt* to counterattack.

contrebalancer [kɔ̃trəbalɑ̃se] *vt* to counterbalance.

contrebande [kɔ̃trəbɑ̃d] *nf* (*fraude*) smuggling, contraband; (*marchandise*) contraband; **de c.** (*tabac etc*) contraband, smuggled; **faire de la c.** to smuggle; **passer qch en c.** to smuggle sth. ◆**contrebandier, -ière** *nmf* smuggler.

contrebas (en) [ɑ̃kɔ̃trəba] *adv* & *prép* **en c. (de)** down below.

contrebasse [kɔ̃trəbas] *nf* Mus doublebass.

contrecarrer [kɔ̃trəkare] *vt* to thwart, frustrate.

contrecœur (à) [akɔ̃trəkœr] *adv* reluctantly.

contrecoup [kɔ̃trəku] *nm* (indirect) effect *ou* consequence; **par c.** as an indirect consequence.

contre-courant (à) [akɔ̃trəkurɑ̃] *adv* against the current.

contredanse [kɔ̃trədɑ̃s] *nf* (*amende*) Aut Fam ticket.

contredire* [kɔ̃trədir] *vt* to contradict; — **se c.** *vpr* to contradict oneself.

contrée [kɔ̃tre] *nf* region, land.

contre-espionnage [kɔ̃trespjɔnaʒ] *nm* counterespionage.

contrefaçon [kɔ̃trəfasɔ̃] *nf* counterfeiting, forgery; (*objet imité*) counterfeit, forgery. ◆**contrefaire** *vt* (*parodier*) to mimic; (*déguiser*) to disguise; (*monnaie etc*) to counterfeit, forge.

contreforts [kɔ̃trəfɔr] *nmpl* Géog foothills.

contre-indiqué [kɔ̃trɛ̃dike] *a* (*médicament*) dangerous, not recommended.

contre-jour (à) [akɔ̃trəʒur] *adv* against the (sun)light.

contremaître [kɔ̃trəmɛtr] *nm* foreman.

contre-offensive [kɔ̃trɔfɑ̃siv] *nf* counteroffensive.

contrepartie [kɔ̃trəparti] *nf* compensation; **en c.** in exchange.

contre-performance [kɔ̃trəperfɔrmɑ̃s] *nf* Sp bad performance.

contre-pied [kɔ̃trəpje] *nm* **le c.-pied d'une opinion/attitude** the (exact) opposite view/attitude; **à c.-pied** Sp on the wrong foot.

contre-plaqué [kɔ̃trəplake] *nm* plywood.

contrepoids [kɔ̃trəpwa] *nm* Tech & Fig counterbalance; **faire c. (à)** to counterbalance.

contrepoint [kɔ̃trəpwɛ̃] *nm* Mus counterpoint.

contrer [kɔ̃tre] *vt* (*personne, attaque*) to counter.

contre-révolution [kɔ̃trərevɔlysjɔ̃] *nf* counter-revolution.

contresens [kɔ̃trəsɑ̃s] *nm* misinterpretation; (*en traduisant*) mistranslation; (*non-sens*) absurdity; **à c.** the wrong way.

contresigner [kɔ̃trəsiɲe] *vt* to countersign.

contretemps [kɔ̃trətɑ̃] *nm* hitch, mishap; **à c.** (*arriver etc*) at the wrong moment.

contre-torpilleur [kɔ̃trətɔrpijœr] *nm* (*navire*) destroyer, torpedo boat.

contrevenir [kɔ̃trəvnir] *vi* **c. à** (*loi etc*) to contravene.

contre-vérité [kɔ̃trəverite] *nf* untruth.

contribu/er [kɔ̃tribɥe] *vi* to contribute (**à** to). ◆**—able** *nmf* taxpayer. ◆**contribution** *nf* contribution; (*impôt*) tax; *pl* (*administration*) tax office; **mettre qn à c.** to use s.o.'s services.

contrit [kɔ̃tri] *a* (*air etc*) contrite. ◆**contrition** *nf* contrition.

contrôle [kɔ̃trol] *nm* (*vérification*) inspection, check(ing) (**de** of); (*des prix, de la qualité*) control; (*maîtrise*) control; (*sur bijou*) hallmark; **un c.** (*examen*) a check (**sur** on); **le c. de soi(-même)** self-control; **le c. des naissances** birth control; **un c. d'identité** an identity check. ◆**contrôl/er** *vt* (*examiner*) to inspect, check; (*maîtriser, surveiller*) to control; — **se c.** *vpr* (*se maîtriser*) to control oneself. ◆**—eur, -euse** *nmf* (*de train*) (ticket) inspector; (*au quai*) ticket collector; (*de bus*) conductor, conductress.

contrordre [kɔ̃trɔrdr] *nm* change of orders.

controverse [kɔ̃trɔvɛrs] *nf* controversy. ◆**controversé** *a* controversial.

contumace (par) [parkɔ̃tymas] *adv* Jur in one's absence, in absentia.

contusion [kɔ̃tyzjɔ̃] *nf* bruise. ◆**contusionner** *vt* to bruise.

convainc/re* [kɔ̃vɛ̃kr] *vt* to convince (**de** of); (*accusé*) to prove guilty (**de** of); **c. qn de faire** to persuade s.o. to do. ◆**—ant** *a* convincing. ◆**—u** *a* (*certain*) convinced (**de** of).

convalescent, -ente [kɔ̃valesɑ̃, -ɑ̃t] *nmf* convalescent; — *a* **être c.** to convalesce. ◆**convalescence** *nf* convalescence; **être en c.** to convalesce; **maison de c.** convalescent home.

conven/ir [kɔ̃vnir] *vi* **c. à** (*être approprié à*) to be suitable for; (*plaire à, aller à*) to suit; **ça convient** (*date etc*) that's suitable; **c. de** (*lieu etc*) to agree upon; (*erreur*) to admit; **c. que** to admit that; **il convient de** it's advisable to; (selon les usages) it is proper ou fitting to. ◆—u a (prix etc) agreed. ◆—able a (approprié, acceptable) suitable; (correct) decent, proper. ◆—ablement adv suitably; decently. ◆convenance nf convenances (usages) convention(s), proprieties; à sa c. to one's satisfaction ou taste.

convention [kɔ̃vɑ̃sjɔ̃] nf (accord) agreement, convention; (règle) & Am Pol convention; c. collective collective bargaining; de c. (sentiment etc) conventional. ◆conventionné a (prix, tarif) regulated (by voluntary agreement); médecin c. = National Health Service doctor (bound by agreement with the State). ◆conventionnel, -elle a conventional.

convergent [kɔ̃vɛrʒɑ̃] a converging, convergent. ◆convergence nf convergence. ◆converger vi to converge.

converser [kɔ̃vɛrse] vi to converse. ◆conversation nf conversation.

conversion [kɔ̃vɛrsjɔ̃] nf conversion. ◆convert/ir vt to convert (à to, en into); — se c. vpr to be converted, convert. ◆—i, -ie nmf convert. ◆convertible a convertible; — nm (canapé) c. bed settee.

convexe [kɔ̃vɛks] a convex.

conviction [kɔ̃viksjɔ̃] nf (certitude, croyance) conviction; pièce à c. Jur exhibit.

convier [kɔ̃vje] vt to invite (à une soirée/etc to a party/etc, à faire to do).

convive [kɔ̃viv] nmf guest (at table).

convoi [kɔ̃vwa] nm (véhicules, personnes etc) convoy; Rail train; c. (funèbre) funeral procession. ◆convoy/er vt to escort. ◆—eur nm Nau escort ship; c. de fonds security guard.

convoiter [kɔ̃vwate] vt to desire, envy, covet. ◆convoitise nf desire, envy.

convoquer [kɔ̃vɔke] vt (candidats, membres etc) to summon ou invite (to attend); (assemblée) to convene, summon; c. à to summon ou invite to. ◆convocation nf (action) summoning; convening; (ordre) summons (to attend); (lettre) (written) notice (to attend).

convulser [kɔ̃vylse] vt to convulse. ◆convulsif, -ive a convulsive. ◆convulsion nf convulsion.

coopérer [kɔɔpere] vi to co-operate (à in, avec with). ◆coopératif, -ive a co-operative; — nf co-operative (society). ◆coopération nf co-operation.

coopter [kɔɔpte] vt to co-opt.

coordonn/er [kɔɔrdɔne] vt to co-ordinate. ◆—ées nfpl Math co-ordinates; (adresse,

téléphone) Fam particulars, details. ◆coordination nf co-ordination.

copain [kɔpɛ̃] nm Fam (camarade) pal; (petit ami) boyfriend; être c. avec to be pals with.

copeau, -x [kɔpo] nm (de bois) shaving.

copie [kɔpi] nf copy; (devoir, examen) Scol paper. ◆copier vti to copy; Scol to copy, crib (sur from). ◆copieur, -euse nmf (élève etc) copycat, copier.

copieux, -euse [kɔpjø, -øz] a copious, plentiful.

copilote [kɔpilɔt] nm co-pilot.

copine [kɔpin] nf Fam (camarade) pal; (petite amie) girlfriend; être c. avec to be pals with.

copropriété [kɔprɔprijete] nf joint ownership; (immeuble en) c. block of flats in joint ownership, Am condominium.

copulation [kɔpylasjɔ̃] nf copulation.

coq [kɔk] nm cock, rooster; c. au vin coq au vin (chicken cooked in wine); passer du c. à l'âne to jump from one subject to another.

coque [kɔk] nf 1 (de noix) shell; (mollusque) cockle; œuf à la c. boiled egg. 2 Nau hull.

coquelicot [kɔkliko] nm poppy.

coqueluche [kɔklyʃ] nf Méd whooping-cough; la c. de Fig the darling of.

coquet, -ette [kɔkɛ, -ɛt] a (chic) smart; (joli) pretty; (provocant) coquettish, flirtatious; (somme) Fam tidy; — nf coquette, flirt. ◆coquetterie nf (élégance) smartness; (goût de la toilette) dress sense; (galanterie) coquetry.

coquetier [kɔktje] nm egg cup.

coquille [kɔkij] nf shell; Typ misprint; c. Saint-Jacques scallop. ◆coquillage nm (mollusque) shellfish; (coquille) shell.

coquin, -ine [kɔkɛ̃, -in] nm rascal; — a mischievous, rascally; (histoire etc) naughty.

cor [kɔr] nm Mus horn; c. (au pied) corn; réclamer ou demander à c. et à cri to clamour for.

corail, -aux [kɔraj, -o] nm coral.

Coran [kɔrɑ̃] nm le C. the Koran.

corbeau, -x [kɔrbo] nm crow; (grand) c. raven.

corbeille [kɔrbɛj] nf basket; c. à papier waste paper basket.

corbillard [kɔrbijar] nm hearse.

corde [kɔrd] nf rope; (plus mince) (fine) cord; (de raquette, violon etc) string; c. (raide) (d'acrobate) tightrope; instrument à cordes Mus string(ed) instrument; c. à linge (washing ou clothes) line; c. à sauter skipping rope, Am jump rope; usé jusqu'à la c. threadbare; **cordes vocales** vocal cords; **prendre un virage à la c.** *Aut* to hug a bend; **pas dans mes cordes** *Fam* not my line. ◆**cordage** *nm Nau* rope. ◆**cordée** *nf* roped (climbing) party. ◆**cordelette** *nf* (fine) cord. ◆**corder** *vt* (*raquette*) to string. ◆**cordon** *nm* (*de tablier, sac etc*) string; (*de soulier*) lace; (*de rideau*) cord, rope; (*d'agents de police*) cordon; (*décoration*) ribbon, sash; (*ombilical*) *Anat* cord. ◆**c.-bleu** *nm* (*pl* **cordons-bleus**) cordon bleu (cook), first-class cook.

cordial, -aux [kɔrdjal, -o] *a* cordial, warm; – *nm Méd* cordial. ◆**cordialité** *nf* cordiality.

cordonnier [kɔrdɔnje] *nm* shoe repairer, cobbler. ◆**cordonnerie** *nf* shoe repairer's shop.

Corée [kɔre] *nf* Korea. ◆**coréen, -enne** *a* & *nmf* Korean.

coriace [kɔrjas] *a* (*aliment, personne*) tough.

corne [kɔrn] *nf* (*de chèvre etc*) horn; (*de cerf*) antler; (*matière, instrument*) horn; (*angle, pli*) corner.

cornée [kɔrne] *nf Anat* cornea.

corneille [kɔrnɛj] *nf* crow.

cornemuse [kɔrnəmyz] *nf* bagpipes.

corner [kɔrne] **1** *vt* (*page*) to turn down the corner of, dog-ear. **2** *vi* (*véhicule*) to sound its horn. **3** [kɔrner] *nm Fb* corner.

cornet [kɔrnɛ] *nm* **1**·**c.** (**à pistons**) *Mus* cornet. **2** (*de glace*) cornet, cone; **c.** (**de papier**) (paper) cone.

corniaud [kɔrnjo] *nm* (*chien*) mongrel; (*imbécile*) *Fam* drip, twit.

corniche [kɔrniʃ] *nf Archit* cornice; (*route*) cliff road.

cornichon [kɔrniʃɔ̃] *nm* (*concombre*) gherkin; (*niais*) *Fam* clot, twit.

cornu [kɔrny] *a* (*diable etc*) horned.

corollaire [kɔrɔlɛr] *nm* corollary.

corporation [kɔrpɔrasjɔ̃] *nf* trade association, professional body.

corps [kɔr] *nm Anat Ch Fig etc* body; *Mil Pol* corps; **c. électoral** electorate; **c. enseignant** teaching profession; **c. d'armée** army corps; **garde du c.** bodyguard; **un c. de bâtiment** a main building; **c. et âme** body and soul; **lutter c. à c.** to fight hand-to-hand; **à son c. défendant** under protest; **prendre c.** (*projet*) to take shape; **donner c. à** (*rumeur, idée*) to give substance to; **faire c. avec** to form a part of, belong with; **perdu c. et biens** *Nau* lost with all hands; **esprit de c.** corporate spirit. ◆**corporel, -elle** *a* bodily; (*châtiment*) corporal.

corpulent [kɔrpylɑ̃] *a* stout, corpulent. ◆**corpulence** *nf* stoutness, corpulence.

corpus [kɔrpys] *nm Ling* corpus.

correct [kɔrɛkt] *a* (*exact*) correct; (*bienséant, honnête*) proper, correct; (*passable*) adequate. ◆**—ement** *adv* correctly; properly; adequately. ◆**correcteur, -trice 1** *a* (*verres*) corrective. **2** *nmf Scol* examiner; *Typ* proofreader. ◆**correctif, -ive** *a* & *nm* corrective.

correction [kɔrɛksjɔ̃] *nf* (*rectification etc*) correction; (*punition*) thrashing; (*exactitude, bienséance*) correctness; **la c. de** (*devoirs, examen*) the marking of; **c. d'épreuves** *Typ* proofreading. ◆**correctionnel, -elle** *a* **tribunal c.,** – *nf* magistrates' court, *Am* police court.

corrélation [kɔrelasjɔ̃] *nf* correlation.

correspond/re [kɔrɛspɔ̃dr] **1** *vi* (*s'accorder*) to correspond (**à** to, with); (*chambres etc*) to communicate; **c. avec** *Rail* to connect with; **– se c.** *vpr* (*idées etc*) to correspond; (*chambres etc*) to communicate. **2** *vi* (*écrire*) to correspond (**avec** with). ◆**—ant, -ante** *a* corresponding; – *nmf* correspondent; (*d'un élève, d'un adolescent*) pen friend; *Tél* caller. ◆**correspondance** *nf* correspondence; (*de train, d'autocar*) connection, *Am* transfer.

corrida [kɔrida] *nf* bullfight.

corridor [kɔridɔr] *nm* corridor.

corrig/er [kɔriʒe] *vt* (*texte, injustice etc*) to correct; (*épreuve*) *Typ* to read; (*devoir*) *Scol* to mark, correct; (*châtier*) to beat, punish; **c. qn de** (*défaut*) to cure s.o. of; **se c. de** to cure oneself of. ◆**—é** *nm Scol* model (answer), correct version, key.

corroborer [kɔrɔbɔre] *vt* to corroborate.

corroder [kɔrɔde] *vt* to corrode. ◆**corrosif, -ive** *a* corrosive. ◆**corrosion** *nf* corrosion.

corromp/re [kɔrɔ̃pr] *vt* to corrupt; (*soudoyer*) to bribe; (*aliment, eau*) to taint. ◆**—u** *a* corrupt; (*altéré*) tainted. ◆**corruption** *nf* (*dépravation*) corruption; (*de juge etc*) bribery.

corsage [kɔrsaʒ] *nm* (*chemisier*) blouse; (*de robe*) bodice.

corsaire [kɔrsɛr] *nm* (*marin*) *Hist* privateer.

Corse [kɔrs] *nf* Corsica. ◆**corse** *a* & *nmf* Corsican.

cors/er [kɔrse] *vt* (*récit, action*) to heighten; **l'affaire se corse** things are hotting up. ◆**—é** *a* (*vin*) full-bodied; (*café*) strong; (*sauce, histoire*) spicy; (*problème*) tough; (*addition de restaurant*) steep.

corset [kɔrse] *nm* corset.

cortège [kɔrtɛʒ] *nm* (*défilé*) procession; (*suite*) retinue; **c. officiel** (*automobiles*) motorcade.

corvée [kɔrve] *nf* chore, drudgery; *Mil* fatigue (duty).

cosaque [kɔzak] *nm* Cossack.

cosmopolite [kɔsmɔpɔlit] *a* cosmopolitan.

cosmos [kɔsmɔs] *nm* (*univers*) cosmos; (*espace*) outer space. ◆**cosmique** *a* cosmic. ◆**cosmonaute** *nmf* cosmonaut.

cosse [kɔs] *nf* (*de pois etc*) pod.

cossu [kɔsy] *a* (*personne*) well-to-do; (*maison etc*) opulent.

costaud [kɔsto] *a Fam* brawny, beefy; — *nm Fam* strong man.

costume [kɔstym] *nm* (*pièces d'habillement*) costume, dress; (*complet*) suit. ◆**costum/er** *vt* **c. qn** to dress s.o. up (**en** as). ◆**-é** *a* **bal c.** fancy-dress ball.

cote [kɔt] *nf* **1** (*marque de classement*) mark, letter, number; (*tableau des valeurs*) (official) listing; (*des valeurs boursières*) quotation; (*évaluation, popularité*) rating; (*de cheval*) odds (**de** on); **c. d'alerte** danger level.

côte [kot] *nf* **1** *Anat* rib; (*de mouton*) chop; (*de veau*) cutlet; **à côtes** (*étoffe*) ribbed; **à c.** side by side; **se tenir les côtes** to split one's sides (laughing). **2** (*montée*) hill; (*versant*) hillside. **3** (*littoral*) coast.

côté [kote] *nm* side; (*direction*) way; **de l'autre c.** on the other side (**de** of); (*direction*) the other way; **de ce c.** (*passer*) this way; **du c. de** (*vers, près de*) towards; **de c.** (*se jeter, mettre de l'argent etc*) to one side; (*regarder*) sideways, to one side; **à c.** close by, nearby; (*pièce*) in the other room; (*maison*) next door; **la maison (d')à c.** the house next door; **à c. de** next to, beside; (*comparaison*) compared to; **à c.** (*balle*) to fall wide (**de** of); **venir de tous côtés** to come from all directions; **d'un c.** on the one hand; **de mon c.** for my part; **à mes côtés** by my side; **laisser de c.** (*travail*) to neglect; (**du**) **c. argent**/*etc Fam* as regards money/*etc*, moneywise/*etc*; **le bon c.** (*d'une affaire*) the bright side (**de** of).

coteau, -x [kɔto] *nm* (small) hill; (*versant*) hillside.

côtelé [kotle] *a* (*étoffe*) ribbed; **velours c.** cord(uroy).

côtelette [kotlɛt] *nf* (*d'agneau, de porc*) chop; (*de veau*) cutlet.

cot/er [kɔte] *vt* (*valeur boursière*) to quote. ◆**-é** *a* **bien c.** highly rated.

coterie [kɔtri] *nf Péj* set, clique.

côtier, -ière [kotje, -jɛr] *a* coastal; (*pêche*) inshore.

cotiser [kɔtize] *vi* to contribute (**à** to, **pour** towards); (*à un club*) to subscribe (to); — **se c.** *vpr* to club together (**pour acheter** to buy). ◆**cotisation** *nf* (*de club*) dues, subscription; (*de pension etc*) contribution(s).

coton [kɔtɔ̃] *nm* cotton; **c. (hydrophile)** cottonwool, *Am* (absorbent) cotton. ◆**cotonnade** *nf* cotton (fabric). ◆**cotonnier, -ière** *a* (*industrie*) cotton-.

côtoyer [kotwaje] *vt* (*route, rivière*) to run along, skirt; (*la misère, la folie etc*) *Fig* to be ou come close to; **c. qn** (*fréquenter*) to rub shoulders with s.o.

cotte [kɔt] *nf* (*de travail*) overalls.

cou [ku] *nm* neck; **sauter au c. de qn** to throw one's arms around s.o.; **jusqu'au c.** *Fig* up to one's eyes ou ears.

couche [kuʃ] *nf* **1** (*épaisseur*) layer; (*de peinture*) coat; *Géol* stratum; **couches sociales** social strata. **2** (*linge de bébé*) nappy, *Am* diaper. **3 faire une fausse c.** *Méd* to have a miscarriage; **les couches** *Méd* confinement.

couch/er [kuʃe] *vt* to put to bed; (*héberger*) to put up; (*allonger*) to lay (down ou out); (*blé*) to flatten; **c. (par écrit)** to put down (in writing); **c. qn en joue** to aim at s.o.; — *vi* to sleep (**avec** with); — **se c.** *vpr* to go to bed; (*s'allonger*) to lie flat ou down; (*soleil*) to set, go down; (*soleil*) bedtime; **c. de soleil** sunset. ◆**-ant** *a* (*soleil*) setting; — *nm* (*aspect*) sunset; **le c.** (*ouest*) west. ◆**-é** *a* **être c.** to be in bed; (*étendu*) to be lying (down). ◆**-age** *nm* sleeping (situation); (*matériel*) bedding; **sac de c.** sleeping bag. ◆**couchette** *nf Rail* sleeping berth, couchette; *Nau* bunk.

couci-couça [kusikusa] *adv Fam* so-so.

coucou [kuku] *nm* (*oiseau*) cuckoo; (*pendule*) cuckoo clock; *Bot* cowslip.

coude [kud] *nm* elbow; (*de chemin, rivière*) bend; **se serrer** ou **se tenir les coudes** to help one another, stick together; **c. à c.** side by side; **coup de c.** poke ou dig (with one's elbow), nudge; **pousser du c.** to nudge. ◆**coudoyer** *vt* to rub shoulders with.

cou-de-pied [kudpje] *nm* (*pl* **cous-de-pied**) instep.

coudre* [kudr] *vti* to sew.

couenne [kwan] *nf* (pork) crackling.

couette [kwɛt] *nf* (*édredon*) duvet, continental quilt.

couffin [kufɛ̃] *nm* (*de bébé*) Moses basket, *Am* bassinet.

couic! [kwik] *int* eek!, squeak! ◆**couiner** *vi Fam* to squeal; (*pleurer*) to whine.

couillon [kujɔ̃] *nm* (*idiot*) *Arg* drip, cretin.

coul/er¹ [kule] *vi* (*eau etc*) to flow; (*robinet, nez, sueur*) to run; (*fuir*) to leak; **c. de source** *Fig* to follow naturally; **faire c. le sang** (*métal, statue*) to cause bloodshed; – *vt* (*métal, statue*) to cast; (*vie*) *Fig* to pass, lead; (*glisser*) to slip; **se c. dans** (*passer*) to slip into; **se la c. douce** to have things easy. ◆**—ant** – *ée* *a* (*style*) flowing; (*caractère*) easygoing. ◆**—ée** *nf* (*de métal*) flow; **c. de lave** lava flow. ◆**—age** *nm* (*de métal, statue*) casting; (*gaspillage*) *Fam* wastage.

couler² [kule] *vi* (*bateau, nageur*) to sink; **c. à pic** to sink to the bottom; – *vt* to sink; (*discréditer*) *Fig* to discredit.

couleur [kulœr] *nf* colour; (*colorant*) paint; *Cartes* suit; *pl* (*teint, carnation*) colour; **c. chair** flesh-coloured; **de c.** (*homme, habit etc*) coloured; **en couleurs** (*photo, télévision*) colour-; **téléviseur c.** colour TV set; **haut en c.** colourful; **sous c. de** faire while pretending to do.

couleuvre [kulœvr] *nf* (grass) snake.

coulisse [kulis] *nf* 1 (*de porte*) runner; **à c.** (*porte/etc*) sliding. 2 **dans les coulisses** *Th* in the wings, backstage; **dans la c.** (*caché*) *Fig* behind the scenes. ◆**coulissant** *a* (*porte/etc*) sliding.

couloir [kulwar] *nm* corridor; (*de circulation*) & *Sp* lane; (*dans un bus*) gangway.

coup [ku] *nm* blow, knock; (*léger*) tap, touch; (*choc moral*) blow; (*de fusil etc*) shot; (*de crayon, d'horloge*) & *Sp* stroke; (*aux échecs etc*) move; (*fois*) *Fam* time; **donner des coups à** to hit; **c. de brosse** brush(-up); **c. de chiffon** wipe (with a rag); **c. de sonnette** ring (on a bell); **c. de dents** bite; **c. de chance** stroke of luck; **c. d'État** coup; **c. dur** *Fam* nasty blow; **sale c.** dirty trick; **mauvais c.** piece of mischief; **c. franc** *Fb* free kick; **tenter le c.** *Fam* to have a go *ou* try; **réussir son c.** to bring it off; **faire les quatre cents coups** to get into all kinds of mischief; **tenir le c.** to hold out; **avoir/attraper le c.** to have/get the knack; **sous le c. de** (*émotion etc*) under the influence of; **il est dans le c.** *Fam* he's in the know; **après c.** after the event, afterwards; **sur le c. de midi** on the stroke of twelve; **sur le c.** (*alors*) at the time; **tué sur le c.** killed outright; **à c. sûr** for sure; **sur c.** (*à la suite*) one after the other, in quick succession; **tout à c., tout d'un c.** suddenly; **à tout c.** at every go; **d'un seul c.** in one go; **du premier c.** *Fam* (at the) first go; **du c.**

suddenly; (*de ce fait*) as a result; **pour le c.** this time. ◆**c.-de-poing** *nm* (*pl* coups-de-poing) **c.-de-poing** (*américain*) knuckle-duster.

coupable [kupabl] *a* guilty (**de** of); (*plaisir, désir*) sinful; **déclarer c.** *Jur* to convict; – *nmf* guilty person, culprit.

coupe [kup] *nf* 1 *Sp* cup; (*à fruits*) dish; (*à boire*) goblet, glass. 2 (*de vêtement etc*) cut; *Géom* section; **c. de cheveux** haircut. ◆**coup/er** *vt* to cut; (*arbre*) to cut down; (*vivres etc*) & *Tél* to cut off; (*courant etc*) to switch off; (*voyage*) to break (off); (*faim, souffle etc*) to take away; (*vin*) to water down; (*morceler*) to cut up; (*croiser*) to cut across; **c. la parole à** to cut short; – *vi* to cut; **c. à** (*corvée*) *Fam* to get out of; **ne coupez pas!** *Tél* hold the line!; – **se c.** (*routes*) to intersect; (*se trahir*) to give oneself away; **se c. au doigt** to cut one's finger. ◆**—ant** *a* sharp; – *nm* (cutting) edge. ◆**—é** *nm* *Aut* coupé.

coupe-circuit [kupsirkɥi] *nm inv* *Él* cutout, circuit breaker. ◆**c.-file** *nm inv* (*carte*) official pass. ◆**c.-gorge** *nm inv* cut-throat alley. ◆**c.-ongles** *nm inv* (finger nail) clippers. ◆**c.-papier** *nm inv* paper knife.

couperet [kupre] *nm* (meat) chopper; (*de guillotine*) blade.

couperosé [kuproze] *a* (*visage*) blotchy.

couple [kupl] *nm* pair, couple. ◆**coupler** *vt* to couple, connect.

couplet [kuple] *nm* verse.

coupole [kupɔl] *nf* dome.

coupon [kupɔ̃] *nm* (*tissu*) remnant, oddment; (*pour la confection d'un vêtement*) length; (*ticket, titre*) coupon; **c. réponse** reply coupon.

coupure [kupyr] *nf* cut; (*de journal*) cutting, *Am* clipping; (*billet*) banknote.

cour [kur] *nf* 1 court(yard); (*de gare*) forecourt; **c. (de récréation)** *Scol* playground. 2 (*de roi*) & *Jur* court. 3 (*de femme, d'homme*) courtship; **faire la c. à qn** to court s.o., woo s.o.

courage [kuraʒ] *nm* courage; (*zèle*) spirit; **perdre c.** to lose heart *ou* courage; **s'armer de c.** to pluck up courage; **bon c.!** keep your chin up! ◆**courageux, -euse** *a* courageous; (*énergique*) spirited.

couramment [kuramɑ̃] *adv* (*parler*) fluently; (*souvent*) frequently.

courant [kurɑ̃] 1 *a* (*fréquent*) common; (*compte, année, langage*) current; (*eau*) running; (*modèle, taille*) standard; (*affaires*) routine; **le dix/etc c.** *Com* the tenth/etc inst(ant). 2 *nm* (*de l'eau, élec-*

trique) current; **c. d'air** draught; **coupure de c.** power cut; **dans le c. de** (*mois etc*) during the course of; **être/mettre au c.** to know/tell (**de** about); **au c.** (*à jour*) up to date.

courbature [kurbatyr] *nf* (muscular) ache. ◆**courbaturé** *a* aching (all over).

courbe [kurb] *a* curved; — *nf* curve. ◆**courber** *vti* to bend; — **se c.** *vpr* to bend (over).

courge [kurʒ] *nf* marrow, *Am* squash. ◆**courgette** *nf* courgette, *Am* zucchini.

cour/ir* [kurir] *vi* to run; (*se hâter*) to rush; (*à bicyclette, en auto*) to race; **en courant** (*vite*) in a rush; **le bruit court que . . .** there's a rumour going around that . . . ; **faire c.** (*nouvelle*) to spread; **il court encore** (*voleur*) he's still at large; — *vt* (*risque*) to run; (*épreuve sportive*) to run (in); (*danger*) to face, court; (*rues, monde*) to roam; (*magasins, cafés*) to go round; (*filles*) to run after. ◆**—eur** *nm Sp etc* runner; (*cycliste*) cyclist; *Aut* racing driver; (*galant*) *Péj* womanizer.

couronne [kurɔn] *nf* (*de roi, dent*) crown; (*funéraire*) wreath. ◆**couronn/er** *vt* to crown; (*auteur, ouvrage*) to award a prize to. ◆**—é** *a* (*tête*) crowned; (*ouvrage*) prize-. ◆**—ement** *nm* (*sacre*) coronation; *Fig* crowning achievement.

courrier [kurje] *nm* post, mail; (*transport*) postal *ou* mail service; (*article*) *Journ* column; **par retour du c.** by return of post, *Am* by return mail.

courroie [kurwa] *nf* (*attache*) strap; (*de transmission*) *Tech* belt.

courroux [kuru] *nm Litt* wrath.

cours [kur] *nm* **1** (*de maladie, rivière, astre, pensées etc*) course; (*cote*) rate, price; **c. d'eau** river, stream; **suivre son c.** (*déroulement*) to follow its course; **avoir c.** (*monnaie*) to be legal tender; (*théorie*) to be current; **en c.** (*travail*) in progress; (*année*) current; (*affaires*) outstanding; **en c. de route** on the way; **au c. de** during; **donner libre c. à** to give free rein to. **2** (*leçon*) class; (*série de leçons*) course; (*conférence*) lecture; (*établissement*) school; (*manuel*) textbook; **c. magistral** lecture. **3** (*allée*) avenue.

course [kurs] *nf* **1** (*action*) run(ning); (*épreuve de vitesse*) *Sp* & *Fig* race; (*trajet*) journey, run; (*excursion*) hike; (*de projectile etc*) path, flight; (*pl* (*de chevaux*) races; **il n'est plus dans la c.** *Fig* he's out of touch; **cheval de c.** racehorse; **voiture de c.** racing car. **2** (*commission*) errand; *pl* (*achats*)

shopping; **faire une c.** to run an errand; **faire les courses** to do the shopping.

coursier, -ière [kursje, -jɛr] *nmf* messenger.

court [kur] **1** *a* short; **c'est un peu c.** *Fam* that's not very much; — *adv* short; **couper c. à** (*entretien*) to cut short; **tout c.** quite simply; **à c. de** (*argent etc*) short of; **pris de c.** caught unawares. **2** *nm* Tennis court. ◆**c.-bouillon** *nm* (*pl* courts-bouillons) court-bouillon (*spiced water for cooking fish*). ◆**c.-circuit** *nm* (*pl* courts-circuits) *Él* short circuit. ◆**c.-circuiter** *vt* to short-circuit.

courtier, -ière [kurtje, -jɛr] *nmf* broker. ◆**courtage** *nm* brokerage.

courtisan [kurtizɑ̃] *nm Hist* courtier. ◆**courtisane** *nf Hist* courtesan. ◆**courtiser** *vt* to court.

courtois [kurtwa] *a* courteous. ◆**courtoisie** *nf* courtesy.

couru [kury] *a* (*spectacle, lieu*) popular; **c'est c.** (*d'avance*) *Fam* it's a sure thing.

couscous [kuskus] *nm Culin* couscous.

cousin, -ine [kuzɛ̃, -in] **1** *nmf* cousin. **2** *nm* (*insecte*) gnat, midge.

coussin [kusɛ̃] *nm* cushion.

cousu [kuzy] *a* sewn; **c. main** handsewn.

coût [ku] *nm* cost. ◆**coût/er** *vt* to cost; **ça coûte combien?** how much is it?, how much does it cost?; **ça lui en coûte de faire** it pains him *ou* her to do; **coûte que coûte** at all costs; **c. les yeux de la tête** to cost the earth. ◆**—ant** *a* **à prix c.** cost price. ◆**coûteux, -euse** *a* costly, expensive.

couteau, -x [kuto] *nm* knife; **coup de c.** stab; **à couteaux tirés** at daggers drawn (**avec** with); **visage en lame de c.** hatchet face; **retourner le c. dans la plaie** *Fig* to rub it in.

coutume [kutym] *nf* custom; **avoir c. de faire** to be accustomed to doing; **comme de c.** as usual; **plus que de c.** more than is customary. ◆**coutumier, -ière** *a* customary.

couture [kutyr] *nf* sewing, needlework; (*métier*) dressmaking; (*raccord*) seam; **maison de c.** fashion house. ◆**couturier** *nm* fashion designer. ◆**couturière** *nf* dressmaker.

couvent [kuvɑ̃] *nm* (*pour religieuses*) convent; (*pour moines*) monastery; (*pensionnat*) convent school.

couv/er [kuve] *vt* (*œufs*) to sit on, hatch; (*projet*) *Fig* to hatch; (*rhume etc*) to be getting; **c. qn** to pamper s.o.; **c. des yeux** (*convoiter*) to look at enviously; — *vi* (*poule*) to brood; (*mal*) to be brewing;

(*feu*) to smoulder. ◆—ée *nf* (*petits*) brood; (*œufs*) clutch. ◆**couveuse** *nf* (*pour nouveaux-nés, œufs*) incubator.

couvercle [kuvɛrkl] *nm* lid, cover.

couvert [kuvɛr] **1** *nm* (*cuiller, fourchette, couteau*) (set of) cutlery; (*au restaurant*) cover charge; **mettre le c.** to lay the table; **table de cinq couverts** table set for five. **2** *nm* **sous** (**le**) **c. de** (*apparence*) under cover of; **se mettre à c.** to take cover. **3** *a* covered (**de** with, in); (*ciel*) overcast. ◆**couverture** *nf* (*de lit*) blanket, cover; (*de livre etc*) & *Fin Mil* cover; (*de toit*) roofing; **c. chauffante** electric blanket; **c. de voyage** travelling rug.

couvre-chef [kuvrəʃɛf] *nm Hum* headgear. ◆**c.-feu** *nm* (*pl* -**x**) curfew. ◆**c.-lit** *nm* bedspread. ◆**c.-pied** *nm* quilt.

couvr/ir* [kuvrir] *vt* to cover (**de** with); (*voix*) to drown; **— se c.** *vpr* (*se vêtir*) to cover up, wrap up; (*se coiffer*) to cover one's head; (*ciel*) to cloud over. ◆—**eur** *nm* roofer.

cow-boy [kɔbɔj] *nm* cowboy.

crabe [krab] *nm* crab.

crac! [krak] *int* (*rupture*) snap!; (*choc*) bang!, smash!

crach/er [kraʃe] *vi* to spit; (*stylo*) to splutter; (*radio*) to crackle; *— vt* to spit (out); **c. sur qch** (*dédaigner*) *Fam* to turn one's nose up at sth. ◆—**é** *a* **c'est son portrait tout c.** *Fam* that's the spitting image of him *ou* her. ◆**crachat** *nm* spit, spittle.

crachin [kraʃɛ̃] *nm* (fine) drizzle.

crack [krak] *nm Fam* ace, wizard, real champ.

craie [krɛ] *nf* chalk.

craindre* [krɛ̃dr] *vt* (*personne, mort, douleur etc*) to be afraid of, fear, dread; (*chaleur etc*) to be sensitive to; **c. de faire** to be afraid of doing, dread doing; **je crains qu'elle ne vienne** I'm afraid *ou* I fear *ou* I dread (that) she might come; **c. pour qch** to fear for sth; **ne craignez rien** have no fear. ◆**crainte** *nf* fear, dread; **de c. de faire** for fear of doing; **de c. que** (+ *sub*) for fear that. ◆**craintif, -ive** *a* timid.

cramoisi [kramwazi] *a* crimson.

crampe [krɑ̃p] *nf Méd* cramp.

crampon [krɑ̃pɔ̃] **1** *nm* (*personne*) *Fam* leech, hanger-on. **2** *nmpl* (*de chaussures*) studs.

cramponner (se) [səkrɑ̃pɔne] *vpr* **se c. à** to hold on to, cling to.

cran [krɑ̃] *nm* **1** (*entaille*) notch; (*de ceinture*) hole; **c. d'arrêt** catch; **couteau à c. d'arrêt** flick-knife, *Am* switchblade; **2** (*de* *feu*) to smoulder. **3** (*audace*) *Fam* pluck, guts. **4** **à c.** (*excédé*) *Fam* on edge.

sûreté safety catch. **2** (*de cheveux*) wave.

crâne [krɑn] *nm* skull; (*tête*) *Fam* head. ◆**crânienne** *af* **boîte c.** cranium, brain pan.

crâner [krɑne] *vi Péj* to show off, swagger.

crapaud [krapo] *nm* toad.

crapule [krapyl] *nf* villain, (filthy) scoundrel. ◆**crapuleux, -euse** *a* vile, sordid.

craqueler [krakle] *vt*, **— se c.** *vpr* to crack.

craqu/er [krake] *vi* (*branche*) to snap; (*chaussure*) to creak; (*bois sec*) to crack; (*sous la dent*) to crunch; (*se déchirer*) to split, rip; (*projet, entreprise etc*) to come apart at the seams, crumble; (*personne*) to break down, reach breaking point; *— vt* (**faire**) **c.** (*allumette*) to strike. ◆—**ement** *nm* snapping *ou* creaking *ou* cracking (sound).

crasse [kras] **1** *a* (*ignorance*) crass. **2** *nf* filth. ◆**crasseux, -euse** *a* filthy.

cratère [kratɛr] *nm* crater.

cravache [kravaʃ] *nf* horsewhip, riding crop.

cravate [kravat] *nf* (*autour du cou*) tie. ◆**cravaté** *a* wearing a tie.

crawl [krol] *nm* (*nage*) crawl. ◆**crawlé** *a* **dos c.** backstroke.

crayeux, -euse [krɛjø, -øz] *a* chalky.

crayon [krɛjɔ̃] *nm* (*en bois*) pencil; (*de* *couleur*) crayon; **c. à bille** ballpoint (pen). ◆**crayonner** *vt* to pencil.

créance [kreɑ̃s] *nf* **1** *Fin Jur* claim (*for* *money*). **2** **lettres de c.** *Pol* credentials. ◆**créancier, -ière** *nmf* creditor.

créateur, -trice [kreatœr, -tris] *nmf* creator; *— a* creative; **esprit c.** creativeness. ◆**créatif, -ive** *a* creative. ◆**création** *nf* creation. ◆**créativité** *nf* creativity. ◆**créature** *nf* (*être*) creature.

crécelle [kresɛl] *nf* (*de supporter*) rattle.

crèche [krɛʃ] *nf* (*de Noël*) *Rel* crib, manger; *Scol* day nursery, crèche. ◆**crécher** *vi* (*loger*) *Arg* to bed down, hang out.

crédible [kredibl] *a* credible. ◆**crédibilité** *nf* credibility.

crédit [kredi] *nm* (*influence*) & *Fin* credit; *pl* (*sommes*) funds; **à c.** (*acheter*) on credit, on hire purchase; **faire c.** *Fin* to give credit (**à** to). ◆**créditer** *vt Fin* to credit (**de** with). ◆**créditeur, -euse** *a* (*solde, compte*) credit-; **son compte est c.** his account is in credit, he is in credit.

credo [kredo] *nm* creed.

crédule [kredyl] *a* credulous. ◆**crédulité** *nf* credulity.

créer [kree] vt to create.

crémaillère [kremajɛr] nf **pendre la c.** to have a house-warming (party).

crématoire [krematwar] a **four c.** crematorium. ◆**crémation** nf cremation.

crème [krɛm] nf cream; (dessert) cream dessert; **café c.** white coffee, coffee with cream ou milk; **c. Chantilly** whipped cream; **c. glacée** ice cream; **c. à raser** shaving cream; **c. anglaise** custard; – a inv cream(-coloured); – nm (café) white coffee. ◆**crémerie** nf (magasin) dairy (shop). ◆**crémeux, -euse** a creamy. ◆**crémier, -ière** nmf dairyman, dairywoman.

créneau, -x [kreno] nm Hist crenellation; (trou) Fig slot, gap; Écon market opportunity, niche; **faire un c.** Aut to park between two vehicles.

créole [kreɔl] nmf Creole; – nm Ling Creole.

crêpe [krɛp] 1 nf Culin pancake. 2 nm (tissu) crepe; (caoutchouc) crepe (rubber). ◆**crêperie** nf pancake bar.

crépi [krepi] a & nm roughcast.

crépit/er [krepite] vi to crackle. ◆**—ement** nm crackling (sound).

crépu [krepy] a (cheveux, personne) frizzy.

crépuscule [krepyskyl] nm twilight, dusk. ◆**crépusculaire** a (lueur etc) twilight-, dusk-.

crescendo [kreʃɛndo] adv & nm inv crescendo.

cresson [krɛsɔ̃] nm (water) cress.

crête [krɛt] nf (d'oiseau, de vague, de montagne) crest; **c. de coq** cockscomb.

Crète [krɛt] nf Crete.

crétin, -ine [kretɛ̃, -in] nmf cretin; – a cretinous.

creus/er [krøze] 1 vt (terre, sol) to dig (a hole ou holes in); (trou, puits) to dig; (évider) to hollow (out); (idée) Fig to go deeply into; **c. l'estomac** to whet the appetite. 2 **se c.** vpr (joues etc) to become hollow; (abîme) Fig to form; **se c. la tête** ou **la cervelle** to rack one's brains. ◆**—é** a **c. de rides** (visage) furrowed with wrinkles.

creuset [krøze] nm (récipient) crucible; (lieu) Fig melting pot.

creux, -euse [krø, -øz] a (tube, joues, paroles etc) hollow; (estomac) empty; (sans activité) slack; **assiette creuse** soup plate; – nm hollow; (de l'estomac) pit; (moment) slack period; **c. des reins** small of the back.

crevaison [krəvɛzɔ̃] nf puncture.

crevasse [krəvas] nf crevice, crack; (de glacier) crevasse; pl (aux mains) chaps.

◆**crevasser** vt, – **se c.** vpr to crack; (peau) to chap.

crève [krɛv] nf (rhume) Fam bad cold.

crev/er [krəve] vi (bulle etc) to burst; (pneu) to puncture, burst; (mourir) Fam to die, drop dead; **c. d'orgueil** to be bursting with pride; **c. de rire** Fam to split one's sides; **c. d'ennui/de froid** Fam to be bored/to freeze to death; **c. de faim** Fam to be starving; – vt to burst; (œil) to put ou knock out; **c. qn** Fam to wear ou knock s.o. out; **ça (vous) crève les yeux** Fam it's staring you in the face; **c. le cœur** to be heartbreaking. ◆**—ant** a (fatigant) Fam exhausting; (drôle) Arg hilarious, killing. ◆**—é** a (fatigué) Fam worn ou knocked out; (mort) Fam dead. ◆**crève-cœur** nm inv heartbreak.

crevette [krəvɛt] nf (grise) shrimp; (rose) prawn.

cri [kri] nm (de joie, surprise) cry, shout; (de peur) scream; (de douleur, d'alarme) cry; (appel) call, cry; **c. de guerre** war cry; **un chapeau/etc dernier c.** the latest hat/etc. ◆**criard** a (enfant) bawling; (son) screeching; (couleur) gaudy, showy.

criant [krijɑ̃] a (injustice etc) glaring.

crible [kribl] nm sieve, riddle. ◆**cribler** vt to sift; **criblé de** (balles, dettes etc) riddled with.

cric [krik] nm (instrument) Aut jack.

cricket [kriket] nm Sp cricket.

crier [krije] vi to shout (out), cry (out); (de peur) to scream; (oiseau) to chirp; (grincer) to creak, squeak; **c. au scandale/etc** to proclaim sth to be a scandal/etc; **c. après qn** Fam to shout at s.o.; – vt (injure, ordre) to shout (out); (son innocence etc) to proclaim; **c. vengeance** to cry out for vengeance. ◆**crieur, -euse** nmf **c. de journaux** newspaper seller.

crime [krim] nm crime; (assassinat) murder. ◆**criminalité** nf crime (in general), criminal practice. ◆**criminel, -elle** a criminal; – nmf criminal; (assassin) murderer.

crin [krɛ̃] nm horsehair; **c. végétal** vegetable fibre; **à tous crins** (pacifiste etc) out-and-out. ◆**crinière** nf mane.

crique [krik] nf creek, cove.

criquet [krike] nm locust.

crise [kriz] nf crisis; (accès) attack; (de colère etc) fit; (pénurie) shortage; **c. de conscience** (moral) dilemma.

crisp/er [krispe] vt (muscle) to tense; (visage) to make tense; (poing) to clench; **c. qn** Fam to aggravate s.o.; **se c. sur** (main) to grip tightly. ◆**—ant** a aggravating. ◆**—é**

a (*personne*) tense. ◆**crispation** *nf* (*agacement*) aggravation.

crisser [krise] *vi* (*pneu, roue*) to screech; (*neige*) to crunch.

cristal, -aux [kristal, -o] *nm* crystal; *pl* (*objets*) crystal(ware); (*pour nettoyer*) washing soda. ◆**cristallin** *a* (*eau, son*) crystal-clear. ◆**cristalliser** *vti*, **— se c.** *vpr* to crystallize.

critère [kriter] *nm* criterion.

critérium [kriterjɔm] *nm* (*épreuve*) Sp eliminating heat.

critique [kritik] *a* critical; **—** *nf* (*reproche*) criticism; (*analyse de film, livre etc*) review; (*de texte*) critique; **faire la c. de** (*film etc*) to review; **affronter la c.** to confront the critics; **—** *nm* critic. ◆**critiquer** *vt* to criticize. ◆**—able** *a* open to criticism.

croasser [krɔase] *vi* (*corbeau*) to caw.

croc [kro] *nm* (*crochet*) hook; (*dent*) fang. ◆**c.-en-jambe** (*pl* **crocs-en-jambe**) = **croche-pied.**

croche [krɔʃ] *nf* Mus quaver, *Am* eighth (note).

croche-pied [krɔʃpje] *nm* **faire un c.-pied à qn** to trip s.o. up.

crochet [krɔʃɛ] *nm* (*pour accrocher*) & Boxe hook; (*aiguille*) crochet hook; (*travail*) crochet; (*clef*) picklock; *Typ* (*square*) bracket; **faire qch au c.** to crochet sth; **faire un c.** (*route*) to make a sudden turn; (*personne*) to make a detour *ou* side trip; (*pour éviter*) to swerve; **vivre aux crochets de qn** *Fam* to sponge off *ou* on s.o. ◆**crocheter** *vt* (*serrure*) to pick. ◆**crochu** *a* (*nez*) hooked.

crocodile [krɔkɔdil] *nm* crocodile.

crocus [krɔkys] *nm* Bot crocus.

croire* [krwar] *vt* to believe; (*estimer*) to think, believe (**que** that); **j'ai cru la voir** I thought I saw her; **je crois que oui** I think *ou* believe so; **je n'en crois pas mes yeux** I can't believe my eyes; **à l'en c.** according to him; **il se croit malin/quelque chose** he thinks he's smart/quite something; **—** *vi* to believe (**à, en** in).

croisé[1] [krwaze] *nm* Hist crusader. ◆**croisade** *nf* crusade.

crois/er [krwaze] *vt* to cross; (*bras*) to fold, cross; **c. qn** to pass *ou* meet s.o.; **—** *vi* (*veston*) to fold over; *Nau* to cruise; **— se c.** *vpr* (*voitures etc*) to pass *ou* meet each other; (*routes*) to cross, intersect; (*lettres*) to cross in the post. ◆**—é[2], -ée** *a* (*bras*) folded, crossed; (*veston*) double-breasted; **mots croisés** crossword; **tirs croisés** crossfire; **race croisée** crossbreed; **—** *nf* (*fenêtre*)

casement; **croisée des chemins** crossroads. ◆**—ement** *nm* (*action*) crossing; (*de routes*) crossroads, intersection; (*de véhicules*) passing. ◆**c.-eur** *nm* (*navire de guerre*) cruiser. ◆**croisière** *nf* cruise; **vitesse de c.** Nau Av & Fig cruising speed.

croître* [krwatr] *vi* (*plante etc*) to grow; (*augmenter*) to grow, increase; (*lune*) to wax. ◆**croissant 1** *a* (*nombre etc*) growing. **2** *nm* crescent; (*pâtisserie*) croissant. ◆**croissance** *nf* growth.

croix [krwa] *nf* cross.

croque-mitaine [krɔkmiten] *nm* bogeyman. ◆**c.-monsieur** *nm inv* toasted cheese and ham sandwich. ◆**c.-mort** *nm* Fam undertaker's assistant.

croqu/er [krɔke] **1** *vt* (*manger*) to crunch; **—** *vi* (*fruit etc*) to be crunchy, crunch. **2** *vt* (*peindre*) to sketch; **joli à c.** pretty as a picture. ◆**—ant** *a* (*biscuit etc*) crunchy. ◆**croquette** *nf* Culin croquette.

croquet [krɔkɛ] *nm* Sp croquet.

croquis [krɔki] *nm* sketch.

crosse [krɔs] *nf* (*d'évêque*) crook; (*de fusil*) butt; (*de hockey*) stick.

crotte [krɔt] *nf* (*de lapin etc*) mess, droppings. ◆**crottin** (*horse*) dung.

crotté [krɔte] *a* (*bottes etc*) muddy.

croul/er [krule] *vi* (*édifice, projet etc*) to crumble, collapse; **c. sous une charge** (*porteur etc*) to totter beneath a burden; **faire c.** (*immeuble etc*) to bring down. ◆**—ant** *a* (*mur etc*) tottering; **—** *nm* (*vieux*) *Fam* old-timer.

croupe [krup] *nf* (*de cheval*) rump; **monter en c.** (*à cheval*) to ride pillion. ◆**croupion** *nm* (*de poulet*) parson's nose.

croupier [krupje] *nm* (*au casino*) croupier.

croupir [krupir] *vi* (*eau*) to stagnate, become foul; **c. dans** (*le vice etc*) to wallow in; **eau croupie** stagnant water.

croustill/er [krustije] *vi* to be crusty; to be crunchy. ◆**—ant** *a* (*pain*) crusty; (*biscuit*) crunchy; (*histoire*) Fig spicy, juicy.

croûte [krut] *nf* (*de pain etc*) crust; (*de fromage*) rind; (*de plaie*) scab; **casser la c.** *Fam* to have a snack; **gagner sa c.** *Fam* to earn one's bread and butter. ◆**croûton** *nm* crust (*at end of loaf*); *pl* (*avec soupe*) croûtons.

croyable [krwajabl] *a* credible, believable. ◆**croyance** *nf* belief (**à, en** in). ◆**croyant, -ante** *a* **être c.** to be a believer; **—** *nmf* believer.

[seers] *nmpl abrév* (*Compagnies républicaines de sécurité*) French state security police, riot police.

cru¹ [kry] *voir* **croire**.

cru² [kry] 1 *a* (*aliment etc*) raw; (*lumière*) glaring; (*propos*) crude; **monter à c.** to ride bareback. 2 *nm* (*vignoble*) vineyard; **un grand c.** (*vin*) a vintage wine; **vin du c.** local wine.

cruauté [kryote] *nf* cruelty (**envers** to).

cruche [kryʃ] *nf* pitcher, jug.

crucial, -aux [krysjal, -o] *a* crucial.

crucifier [krysifje] *vt* to crucify. ◆**crucifix** [krysifi] *nm* crucifix. ◆**crucifixion** *nf* crucifixion.

crudité [krydite] *nf* (*grossièreté*) crudeness; *pl Culin* assorted raw vegetables.

crue [kry] *nf* (*de cours d'eau*) swelling, flood; **en c.** in spate.

cruel, -elle [kryel] *a* cruel (**envers, avec** to).

crûment [krymɑ̃] *adv* crudely.

crustacés [krystase] *nmpl* shellfish, crustaceans.

crypte [kript] *nf* crypt.

Cuba [kyba] *nm* Cuba. ◆**cubain, -aine** *a* & *nmf* Cuban.

cube [kyb] *nm* cube; *pl* (*jeu*) building blocks; – *a* (*mètre etc*) cubic. ◆**cubique** *a* cubic.

cueillir* [kœjir] *vt* to gather, pick; (*baiser*) to snatch; (*voleur*) *Fam* to pick up, run in. ◆**cueillette** *nf* gathering, picking; (*fruits cueillis*) harvest.

cuiller, cuillère [kɥijer] *nf* spoon; **petite c.,** **c. à café** teaspoon; **c. à soupe** table spoon. ◆**cuillerée** *nf* spoonful.

cuir [kɥir] *nm* leather; (*peau épaisse d'un animal vivant*) hide; **c. chevelu** scalp.

cuirasse [kɥiras] *nf Hist* breastplate. ◆**se cuirass/er** *vpr* to steel oneself (**contre** against). ◆**—é** *nm* battleship.

cuire* [kɥir] *vt* to cook; (*à l'eau*) to boil; (*porcelaine*) to bake, fire; **c. (au four)** to bake; (*viande*) to roast; – *vi* to cook; to boil; to bake; to roast; (*soleil*) to bake, boil; **faire c.** to cook. ◆**cuisant** *a* (*affront, blessure etc*) stinging. ◆**cuisson** *nm* cooking; (*de porcelaine*) baking, firing.

cuisine [kɥizin] *nf* (*pièce*) kitchen; (*art*) cooking, cuisine, cookery; (*aliments*) cooking; (*intrigues*) *Péj* scheming; **faire la c.** to cook, do the cooking; **livre de c.** cook(ery) book; **haute c.** high-class cooking. ◆**cuisiner** *vti* to cook; (*interroger*) *Fam* to grill s.o. ◆**cuisinier, -ière** *nmf* cook; – *nf* (*appareil*) cooker, stove, *Am* range.

cuisse [kɥis] *nf* thigh; (*de poulet, mouton*) leg.

cuit [kɥi] 1 *voir* **cuire**; – *a* cooked; **bien c.**

well done *ou* cooked. 2 *a* (*pris*) *Fam* done for.

cuite [kɥit] *nf* **prendre une c.** *Fam* to get plastered *ou* drunk.

cuivre [kɥivr] *nm* (*rouge*) copper; (*jaune*) brass; *pl* (*ustensiles*) & *Mus* brass. ◆**cuivré** *a* copper-coloured, coppery.

cul [ky] *nm* (*derrière*) *Fam* backside; (*de bouteille etc*) bottom. ◆**c.-de-jatte** *nm* (*pl* **culs-de-jatte**) legless cripple. ◆**c.-de-sac** *nm* (*pl* **culs-de-sac**) dead end, cul-de-sac.

culasse [kylas] *nf Aut* cylinder head; (*d'une arme à feu*) breech.

culbute [kylbyt] *nf* (*cabriole*) sommersault; (*chute*) (backward) tumble; **faire une c.** to sommersault; to tumble. ◆**culbuter** *vi* to tumble over (backwards); – *vt* (*personne, chaise*) to knock over.

culinaire [kyliner] *a* (*art*) culinary; (*recette*) cooking.

culmin/er [kylmine] *vi* (*montagne*) to reach its highest point, peak (à at); (*colère*) *Fig* to reach a peak. ◆**—ant** *a* **point c.** (*de réussite, montagne etc*) peak.

culot [kylo] *nm* **1** (*aplomb*) *Fam* nerve, cheek. **2** (*d'ampoule, de lampe etc*) base. ◆**culotté** *a* **être c.** *Fam* to have plenty of nerve *ou* cheek.

culotte [kylot] *nf Sp* (pair of) shorts; (*de femme*) (pair of) knickers *ou Am* panties; **culottes (courtes)** (*de jeune garçon*) short trousers *ou Am* pants; **c. de cheval** riding breeches.

culpabilité [kylpabilite] *nf* guilt.

culte [kylt] *nm* (*hommage*) *Rel* worship, cult; (*pratique*) *Rel* religion; (*service protestant*) service; (*admiration*) *Fig* cult.

cultiv/er [kyltive] *vt* (*terre*) to farm, cultivate; (*plantes*) to grow, cultivate; (*goût, relations etc*) to cultivate; **— se c.** *vpr* to cultivate one's mind. ◆**—é** *a* (*esprit, personne*) cultured, cultivated. ◆**cultivateur, -trice** *nmf* farmer. ◆**culture** *nf* (*action*) farming, cultivation; (*agriculture*) farming; (*horticulture*) growing, cultivation; (*éducation, civilisation*) culture; *pl* (*terres*) fields (under cultivation); (*plantes*) crops; **c. générale** general knowledge. ◆**culturel, -elle** *a* cultural.

cumin [kymɛ̃] *nm Bot Culin* caraway.

cumul [kymyl] *nm* **c. de fonctions** plurality of offices. ◆**cumulatif, -ive** *a* cumulative. ◆**cumuler** *vt* **c. deux fonctions** to hold two offices at the same time).

cupide [kypid] *a* avaricious. ◆**cupidité** *nf* avarice, cupidity.

Cupidon [kypidɔ̃] *nm* Cupid.

cure [kyr] *nf* 1 (course of) treatment, cure. 2 (*fonction*) office of a parish priest; (*résidence*) presbytery. ◆**curable** *a* curable. ◆**curatif, -ive** *a* curative. ◆**curé** *nm* (parish) priest.

curer [kyre] *vt* to clean out; **se c. le nez/les dents** to pick one's nose/teeth. ◆**cure-dent** *nm* toothpick. ◆**cure-ongles** *nm inv* nail cleaner. ◆**cure-pipe** *nm* pipe cleaner.

curieux, -euse [kyrjø, -øz] *a* (*bizarre*) curious; (*indiscret*) inquisitive, curious (**de** about); **c. de savoir** curious to know; – *nmf* inquisitive *ou* curious person; (*badaud*) onlooker. ◆**curieusement** *adv* curiously. ◆**curiosité** *nf* (*de personne, forme etc*) curiosity; (*chose*) curiosity; (*spectacle*) unusual sight.

curriculum (vitæ) [kyrikylɔm(vite)] *nm inv* curriculum (vitae), *Am* résumé.

curseur [kyrsœr] *nm* (*d'un ordinateur*) cursor.

cutané [kytane] *a* (*affection etc*) skin-. ◆**cuti-(réaction)** *nf* skin test.

cuve [kyv] *nf* vat; (*réservoir*) & *Phot* tank. ◆**cuvée** *nf* (*récolte de vin*) vintage.

◆**cuver** *vt* **c. son vin** *Fam* to sleep it off. ◆**cuvette** *nf* (*récipient*) & *Géog* basin, bowl; (*des cabinets*) pan, bowl.

cyanure [sjanyr] *nm* cyanide.

cybernétique [sibɛrnetik] *nf* cybernetics.

cycle [sikl] *nm* 1 (*série, révolution*) cycle. 2 (*bicyclette*) cycle. ◆**cyclable** *a* (*piste*) cycle-. ◆**cyclique** *a* cyclic(al). ◆**cyclisme** *nm Sp* cycling. ◆**cycliste** *nmf* cyclist; – *a* (*course*) cycle-; (*champion*) cycling; **coureur c.** racing cyclist. ◆**cyclomoteur** *nm* moped.

cyclone [siklon] *nm* cyclone.

cygne [siɲ] *nm* swan; **chant du c.** *Fig* swan song.

cylindre [silɛ̃dr] *nm* cylinder; (*de rouleau compresseur*) roller. ◆**cylindrée** *nf Aut* (engine) capacity. ◆**cylindrique** *a* cylindrical.

cymbale [sɛ̃bal] *nf* cymbal.

cynique [sinik] *a* cynical; – *nmf* cynic. ◆**cynisme** *nm* cynicism.

cyprès [siprɛ] *nm* (*arbre*) cypress.

cypriote [siprijɔt] *a* & *nmf* Cypriot.

cytise [sitiz] *nf Bot* laburnum.

D

D, d [de] *nm* D, d.

d' [d] *voir* **de**[1,2].

d'abord [dabɔr] *adv* (*en premier lieu*) first; (*au début*) at first.

dactylo [daktilo] *nf* (*personne*) typist; (*action*) typing. ◆**dactylographie** *nf* typing. ◆**dactylographier** *vt* to type.

dada [dada] *nm* (*manie*) hobby horse, pet subject.

dadais [dadɛ] *nm* (**grand**) **d.** big oaf.

dahlia [dalja] *nm* dahlia.

daigner [deɲe] *vt* **d. faire** to condescend *ou* deign to do.

daim [dɛ̃] *nm* fallow deer; (*mâle*) buck; (*cuir*) suede.

dais [dɛ] *nm* (*de lit, feuillage etc*) canopy.

dalle [dal] *nf* paving stone; (*funèbre*) (flat) gravestone. ◆**dallage** *nm* (*action, surface*) paving. ◆**dallé** *a* (*pièce, cour etc*) paved.

daltonien, -ienne [daltɔnjɛ̃, -jɛn] *a* & *n* colour-blind (person). ◆**daltonisme** *nm* colour blindness.

dame [dam] *nf* 1 lady; (*mariée*) married lady. 2 *Échecs Cartes* queen; (*au jeu de dames*) king; (**jeu de**) **dames** draughts, *Am*

checkers. ◆**damer** *vt* (*au jeu de dames*) to crown; **d. le pion à qn** to outsmart s.o. ◆**damier** *nm* draughtboard, *Am* checkerboard.

damner [dane] *vt* to damn; **faire d.** *Fam* to torment, drive mad; **— se d.** *vpr* to be damned. ◆**damnation** *nf* damnation.

dancing [dɑ̃siŋ] *nm* dance hall.

dandiner (se) [sədɑ̃dine] *vpr* to waddle.

dandy [dɑ̃di] *nm* dandy.

Danemark [danmark] *nm* Denmark. ◆**danois, -oise** *a* Danish; – *nmf* Dane; – *nm* (*langue*) Danish.

danger [dɑ̃ʒe] *nm* danger; **en d.** in danger *ou* jeopardy; **mettre en d.** to endanger, jeopardize; **en cas de d.** in an emergency; **en d. de mort** in peril of death; **'d. de mort'** (*panneau*) 'danger'; **sans d.** (*se promener etc*) safely; **être sans d.** to be safe; **pas de d.!** *Fam* no way!, no fear! ◆**dangereux, -euse** *a* dangerous (**pour** to). ◆**dangereusement** *adv* dangerously.

dans [dɑ̃] *prép* in; (*changement de lieu*) into; (*à l'intérieur de*) inside, within; **entrer d.** to go in(to); **d. Paris** in Paris, within Paris;

d. un rayon de within (a radius of); **boire/prendre/etc d.** to drink/take/etc from *ou* out of; **marcher d. les rues** (*à travers*) to walk through *ou* about the streets; **d. ces circonstances** under *ou* in these circumstances; **d. deux jours/etc** (*temps futur*) in two days/etc, in two days'/etc time; **d. les dix francs/etc** (*quantité*) about ten francs/etc.

danse [dɑ̃s] *nf* dance; (*art*) dancing. ◆**dans/er** *vti* to dance; **faire d. l'anse du panier** (*domestique*) to fiddle on the shopping money. ◆**-eur, -euse** *nmf* dancer; **en danseuse** (*cycliste*) standing on the pedals.

dard [dar] *nm* (*d'abeille etc*) sting; (*de serpent*) tongue. ◆**darder** *vt Litt* (*flèche*) to shoot; (*regard*) to flash, dart; **le soleil dardait ses rayons** the sun cast down its burning rays.

dare-dare [dardar] *adv Fam* at *ou* on the double.

date [dat] *nf* date; **de vieille d.** (*amitié etc*) (of) long-standing; **faire d.** (*événement*) to mark an important date, be epoch-making; **en d. du ...** dated the ...; **d. limite** deadline. ◆**datation** *nf* dating. ◆**dater** *vt* (*lettre etc*) to date; — *vi* (*être dépassé*) to date, be dated; **d. de** to date back to, date from; **à d. de** as from. ◆**dateur** *nm* (*de montre*) date indicator; — *a & nm* (*tampon*) d. date stamp.

datte [dat] *nf* (*fruit*) date. ◆**dattier** *nm* date palm.

daube [dob] *nf* **bœuf en d.** braised beef stew.

dauphin [dofɛ̃] *nm* (*mammifère marin*) dolphin.

davantage [davɑ̃taʒ] *adv* (*quantité*) more; (*temps*) longer; **d. de temps/etc** more time/etc; **d. que** more than; longer than.

de¹ [d(ə)] (**d'** before a vowel or mute h; **de + le = du, de + les = des**) *prép* **1** (*complément d'un nom*) of; **les rayons du soleil** the rays of the sun, the sun's rays; **la ville de Paris** the town of Paris; **le livre de Paul** Paul's book; **un pont de fer** an iron bridge; **le train de Londres** the London train; **une augmentation/diminution de** an increase/decrease in. **2** (*complément d'un adjectif*) **digne de** worthy of; **heureux de partir** happy to leave; **content de qch** pleased with sth. **3** (*complément d'un verbe*) **parler de** to speak of *ou* about; **se souvenir de** to remember; **décider de faire** to decide to do; **traiter de lâche** to call a coward. **4** (*provenance: lieu & temps*) from; **venir/dater de** to come/date from; **mes**

amis du village my friends from the village, my village friends; **le train de Londres** the train from London. **5** (*agent*) **accompagné de** accompanied by. **6** (*moyen*) **armé de** armed with; **se nourrir de** to live on. **7** (*manière*) **d'une voix douce** in *ou* with a gentle voice. **8** (*cause*) **puni de** punished for; **mourir de faim** to die of hunger. **9** (*temps*) **travailler de nuit** to work by night; **six heures du matin** six o'clock in the morning. **10** (*mesure*) **avoir six mètres de haut**, **être haut de six mètres** to be six metres high; **retarder de deux heures** to delay by two hours; **homme de trente ans** thirty-year-old man; **gagner cent francs de l'heure** to earn one hundred francs an hour.

de² [d(ə)] *art partitif* some; **elle boit du vin** she drinks (some) wine; **il ne boit pas de vin** (*négation*) he doesn't drink (any) wine; **des fleurs** (some) flowers; **de jolies fleurs** (some) pretty flowers; **d'agréables soirées** (some) pleasant evenings; **il y en a six de tués** (*avec un nombre*) there are six killed.

dé [de] *nm* (*à jouer*) dice; (*à coudre*) thimble; **les dés** the dice; (*jeu*) dice; **les dés sont jetés** *Fig* the die is cast; **couper en dés** *Culin* to dice.

déambuler [deɑ̃byle] *vi* to stroll, saunter.

débâcle [debakl] *nf Mil* rout; (*ruine*) *Fig* downfall; (*des glaces*) *Géog* breaking up.

déball/er [debale] *vt* to unpack; (*étaler*) to display. ◆**-age** *nm* unpacking; display.

débandade [debɑ̃dad] *nf* (*mad*) rush, stampede; *Mil* rout; **à la d.** in confusion; **tout va à la d.** everything's going to rack and ruin.

débaptiser [debatize] *vt* (*rue*) to rename.

débarbouiller [debarbuje] *vt* **d. qn** to wash s.o.'s face; **se d.** to wash one's face.

débarcadère [debarkader] *nm* landing stage, quay.

débardeur [debardœr] *nm* **1** (*docker*) stevedore. **2** (*vêtement*) slipover, *Am* (*sweater*) vest.

débarqu/er [debarke] *vt* (*passagers*) to land; (*marchandises*) to unload; **d. qn** (*congédier*) *Fam* to sack s.o.; — *vi* (*passagers*) to disembark, land; (*train*) *Fam* not to be quite with it; **d. chez qn** *Fam* to turn up suddenly at s.o.'s place. ◆**-ement** *nm* landing; unloading; *Mil* landing.

débarras [debara] *nm* lumber room, *Am* storeroom; **bon d.!** *Fam* good riddance! ◆**débarrasser** *vt* (*voie, table etc*) to clear (*de* of); **d. qn de** (*ennemi, soucis etc*) to rid s.o. of; (*manteau etc*) to relieve s.o. of; **se d. de** to get rid of, rid oneself of.

débat [deba] *nm* discussion, debate; *pl Pol Jur* proceedings. ◆**débattre*** *vt* to discuss, debate; — **se d.** *vpr* to struggle ou fight (to get free), put up a fight.

débauche [deboʃ] *nf* debauchery; **une d. de** *Fig* a wealth ou profusion of. ◆**débauch/er** *vt* **d. qn** (*détourner*) to entice s.o. away from his work; (*licencier*) to dismiss s.o., lay s.o. off. ◆**-é, -ée** *a* (*libertin*) debauched, profligate; — *nmf* debauchee, profligate.

débile [debil] *a* (*esprit, enfant etc*) weak, feeble; (*personne*) *Fam Péj* idiotic; — *nmf Péj Fam* idiot, moron. ◆**débilité** *nf* debility, weakness; *pl* (*niaiseries*) *Fam* sheer nonsense. ◆**débiliter** *vt* to debilitate, weaken.

débiner [debine] **1** *vt* (*décrier*) *Fam* to run down. **2 se d.** *vpr* (*s'enfuir*) *Arg* to hop it, bolt.

débit [debi] *nm* **1** (*vente*) turnover, sales; (*de fleuve*) (rate of) flow; (*d'un orateur*) delivery; **d. de tabac** tobacconist's shop, tobacco store; **d. de boissons** bar, café. **2** (*compte*) *Fin* debit. ◆**débiter** *vt* **1** (*découper*) to cut up, slice up (**en** into); (*vendre*) to sell; (*fournir*) to yield; (*dire*) *Péj* to utter, spout. **2** *Fin* to debit. ◆**débiteur, -trice** *nmf* debtor; — *a* (*solde, compte*) debit-; **son compte est d.** his account is in debit, is in debit.

déblais [deblɛ] *nmpl* (*terre*) earth; (*décombres*) rubble. ◆**déblayer** *vt* (*terrain, décombres*) to clear.

débloquer [debloke] **1** *vt* (*machine*) to unjam; (*crédits, freins, compte*) to release; (*prix*) to decontrol. **2** *vi* (*divaguer*) *Fam* to talk through one's hat, talk nonsense.

déboires [debwar] *nmpl* disappointments, setbacks.

déboît/er [debwate] **1** *vt* (*tuyau*) to disconnect; (*os*) *Méd* to dislocate. **2** *vi* *Aut* to pull out, change lanes. ◆**-ement** *nm Méd* dislocation.

débonnaire [deboner] *a* good-natured, easy-going.

débord/er [deborde] *vi* (*fleuve, liquide*) to overflow; (*en bouillant*) to boil over; **d. de** (*vie, joie etc*) *Fig* to be overflowing ou bubbling over with; **l'eau déborde du vase** the water is running over the top of the vase ou is overflowing the vase; — *vt* (*dépasser*) to go ou extend beyond; (*faire saillie*) to stick out from; *Mil Sp* to outflank; **débordé de travail/de visites** snowed under with work/visits.

◆**-ement** *nm* overflowing; (*de joie, activité*) outburst.

débouch/er [debuʃe] **1** *vt* (*bouteille*) to open, uncork; (*lavabo, tuyau*) to clear, unblock. **2** *vi* (*surgir*) to emerge, come out (**de** from); **d. sur** (*rue*) to lead out onto, lead into; *Fig* to lead up to. ◆**-é** *nm* (*carrière* & *Géog* opening; (*de rue*) exit; (*marché*) *Com* outlet.

débouler [debule] *vi* (*arriver*) *Fam* to burst in, turn up.

déboulonner [debulone] *vt* to unbolt; **d. qn** *Fam* (*renvoyer*) to sack ou fire s.o.; (*discréditer*) to bring s.o. down.

débours [debur] *nmpl* expenses. ◆**débourser** *vt* to pay out.

debout [d(ə)bu] *adv* standing (up); **mettre d.** (*planche etc*) to stand up, put upright; **se mettre d.** to stand ou get up; **se tenir** ou **rester d.** (*personne*) to stand (up), remain standing (up); **rester d.** (*édifice etc*) to remain standing; **être d.** (*levé*) to be up (and about); **d.!** get up!; **ça ne tient pas d.** (*théorie etc*) that doesn't hold water ou make sense.

déboutonner [debutone] *vt* to unbutton, undo; — **se d.** *vpr* (*personne*) to undo one's buttons.

débraillé [debraje] *a* (*tenue etc*) slovenly, sloppy; — *nm* slovenliness, sloppiness.

débrancher [debrɑ̃ʃe] *vt* *El* to unplug, disconnect.

débrayer [debreje] *vi* **1** *Aut* to declutch, release the clutch. **2** (*se mettre en grève*) to stop work. ◆**débrayage** (*grève*) strike, walk-out.

débridé [debride] *a* (*effréné*) unbridled.

débris [debri] *nmpl* fragments, scraps; (*restes*) remains; (*détritus*) rubbish, debris.

débrouiller [debruje] **1** *vt* (*écheveau etc*) to unravel, disentangle; (*affaire*) to sort out. **2 se d.** *vpr* to manage, get by, make out; **se d. pour faire** to manage (somehow) to do. ◆**débrouillard** *a* smart, resourceful. ◆**débrouillardise** *nf* smartness, resourcefulness.

débroussailler [debrusaje] *vt* (*chemin*) to clear (of brushwood); (*problème*) *Fig* to clarify.

débusquer [debyske] *vt* (*gibier, personne*) to drive out, dislodge.

début [deby] *nm* start, beginning; **au d.** at the beginning; **faire ses débuts** (*sur la scène etc*) to make one's debut. ◆**début/er** *vi* to start, begin; (*dans une carrière*) to start out in life; (*sur la scène etc*) to make one's debut. ◆—ant, -ante *nmf* beginner; — *a* novice.

déca [deka] *nm Fam* decaffeinated coffee.

deçà (en) [ɑ̃d(ə)sa] *adv* (on) this side; — *prép* en d. de (on) this side of; (*succès, prix etc*) *Fig* short of.

décacheter [dekaʃte] *vt* (*lettre etc*) to open, unseal.

décade [dekad] *nf* (*dix jours*) period of ten days; (*décennie*) decade.

décadent [dekadɑ̃] *a* decadent. ◆**décadence** *nf* decay, decadence.

décaféiné [dekafeine] *a* decaffeinated.

décalaminer [dekalamine] *vt* (*moteur*) *Aut* to decoke, decarbonize.

décalcomanie [dekalkɔmani] *nf* (*image*) transfer, *Am* decal.

décal/er [dekale] *vt* 1 (*avancer*) to shift; (*départ, repas*) to shift (the time of). 2 (*ôter les cales de*) to unwedge. ◆—**age** *nm* (*écart*) gap, discrepancy; **d. horaire** time difference.

décalque [dekalk] *nm* tracing. ◆**décalquer** [dekalke] *vt* (*dessin*) to trace.

décamper [dekɑ̃pe] *vi* to make off, clear off.

décanter [dekɑ̃te] *vt* (*liquide*) to settle, clarify; **d. ses idées** to clarify one's ideas; — **se d.** *vpr* (*idées, situation*) to become clearer, settle.

décap/er [dekape] *vt* (*métal*) to clean, scrape down; (*surface peinte*) to strip. ◆—**ant** *nm* cleaning agent; (*pour enlever la peinture*) paint stripper. ◆—**eur** *nm* **d. thermique** hot-air paint stripper.

décapiter [dekapite] *vt* to decapitate, behead.

décapotable [dekapɔtabl] *a* (*voiture*) convertible.

décapsul/er [dekapsyle] *vt* **d. une bouteille** to take the cap ou top off a bottle. ◆—**eur** *nm* bottle-opener.

décarcasser (se) [sədekarkase] *vpr Fam* to flog oneself to death (**pour faire** doing).

décathlon [dekatlɔ̃] *nm Sp* decathlon.

décati [dekati] *a* worn out, decrepit.

décavé [dekave] *a Fam* ruined.

décéd/er [desede] *vi* to die. ◆—é *a* deceased.

déceler [desle] *vt* (*trouver*) to detect, uncover; (*révéler*) to reveal.

décembre [desɑ̃br] *nm* December.

décennie [deseni] *nf* decade.

décent [desɑ̃] *a* (*bienséance, acceptable*) decent. ◆**décemment** [-amɑ̃] *adv* decently. ◆**décence** *nf* decency.

décentraliser [desɑ̃tralize] *vt* to decentral-

ize. ◆**décentralisation** *nf* decentralization.

déception [desɛpsjɔ̃] *nf* disappointment. ◆**décevoir°** *vt* to disappoint. ◆**décevant** *a* disappointing.

décerner [deserne] *vt* (*prix etc*) to award; (*mandat d'arrêt etc*) *Jur* to issue.

décès [desɛ] *nm* death.

déchaîn/er [deʃene] *vt* (*colère, violence*) to unleash, let loose; **d. l'enthousiasme/les rires** to set off wild enthusiasm/a storm of laughter; — **se d.** *vpr* (*tempête, rires*) to break out; (*foule*) to run amok ou riot; (*colère, personne*) to explode. ◆—é *a* (*foule, flots*) wild, raging. ◆—**ement** [-ɛnmɑ̃] *nm* (*de rires, de haine etc*) outburst; (*de violence*) outbreak, eruption; **le d. de la tempête** the raging of the storm.

déchanter [deʃɑ̃te] *vi Fam* to become disillusioned; (*changer de ton*) to change one's tune.

décharge [deʃarʒ] *nf Jur* discharge; **d. (publique)** (*rubbish*) dump ou tip, *Am* (*garbage*) dump; **d. (électrique)** (electrical) discharge, shock; **recevoir une d.** (**électrique**) to get a shock; **à la d. de qn** in s.o.'s defence. ◆**décharg/er** *vt* to unload; (*batterie*) *El* to discharge; (*accusé*) *Jur* to discharge, exonerate; (*arme*) to fire, let off; **d. qn de** (*travail etc*) to relieve s.o. of; **d. sur qn** (*son arme*) to fire at s.o.; (*sa colère*) to vent on s.o.; — **se d.** *vpr* (*batterie*) to go flat; **se d. sur qn du soin de faire qch** to unload onto s.o. the job of doing sth. ◆—**ement** *nm* unloading.

décharné [deʃarne] *a* skinny, bony.

déchausser [deʃose] *vt* **d. qn** to take s.o.'s shoes off; **se d.** to take one's shoes off; (*dent*) to get loose.

dèche [dɛʃ] *nf* **être dans la d.** *Arg* to be flat broke.

déchéance [deʃeɑ̃s] *nf* (*déclin*) decline, decay, degradation.

déchet [deʃɛ] *nm* **déchets** (*résidus*) scraps, waste; **il y a du d.** there's some waste ou wastage.

déchiffrer [deʃifre] *vt* (*message*) to decipher; (*mauvaise écriture*) to make out, decipher.

déchiquet/er [deʃikte] *vt* to tear to shreds, cut to bits. ◆—é *a* (*drapeau etc*) (all) in shreds; (*côte*) jagged.

déchir/er [deʃire] *vt* to tear (up), rip (up); (*vêtement*) to tear, rip; (*ouvrir*) to tear ou rip open; (*pays, groupe*) to tear apart; **d. l'air** (*bruit*) to rend the air; **ce bruit me déchire les oreilles** this noise is ear-splitting; — **se d.** *vpr* (*robe etc*) to tear, rip. ◆**—ant** a (navrant) heart-breaking; (aigu) ear-splitting. ◆**—ement** nm (souffrance) heartbreak; pl (divisions) Pol deep rifts. ◆**déchirure** nf tear, rip; **d. musculaire** torn muscle.

déchoir [defwar] vi to lose prestige. ◆**déchu** a (ange) fallen; **être d. de** (ses droits etc) to have forfeited.

décibel [desibel] nm decibel.

décid/er [deside] vt (envoi, opération) to decide on; **d. que** to decide that; **d. qn à faire** to persuade s.o. to do; — vi **d. de** (destin de qn) to decide; (voyage etc) to decide on; **d. de faire** to decide to do; — **se d.** vpr (question) to be decided; **se d. à faire** to make up one's mind to do; **se d. pour qch** to decide on sth ou in favour of sth. ◆**—é** a (air, ton) determined, decided; (net, pas douteux) decided; **c'est d.** it's settled; **être d. à faire** to be decided about doing ou determined to do. ◆**—ément** adv undoubtedly.

décilitre [desilitr] nm decilitre.

décimal, -aux [desimal, -o] a decimal. ◆**décimale** nf decimal.

décimer [desime] vt to decimate.

décimètre [desimetr] nm decimetre; **double d.** ruler.

décisif, -ive [desizif, -iv] a decisive, crucial; (moment) crucial. ◆**décision** nf decision; (fermeté) determination.

déclamer [deklame] vt to declaim; Péj to spout. ◆**déclamatoire** a Péj bombastic.

déclarer [deklare] vt to declare (que that); (décès, vol etc) to notify; **d. coupable** to convict, find guilty; **d. la guerre** to declare war (à on); — **se d.** vpr (s'expliquer) to declare one's views; (incendie, maladie) to break out; **se d. contre** to come out against. ◆**déclaration** nf declaration; (de décès etc) notification; (commentaire) statement, comment; **d. de revenus** tax return.

déclasser [deklase] vt (livres etc) to put out of order; (hôtel etc) to downgrade; **d. qn** Sp to relegate s.o. (in the placing).

déclench/er [deklɑ̃ʃe] vt (mécanisme) to set ou trigger off, release; (attaque) to launch; (provoquer) to trigger off, spark off; **d. le travail** Méd to induce labour; — **se d.** vpr (sonnerie) to go off; (attaque, grève) to start. ◆**—ement** nm (d'un appareil) release.

déclic [deklik] nm (mécanisme) catch, trigger; (bruit) click.

déclin [deklɛ̃] nm decline; (du jour) close; (de la lune) wane. ◆**décliner 1** vt (refuser) to decline. **2** vt (réciter) to state. **3** vi (forces etc) to decline, wane; (jour) to draw to a close.

déclivité [deklivite] nf slope.

décocher [dekɔʃe] vt (flèche) to shoot, fire; (coup) to let fly, aim; (regard) to flash.

décoder [dekɔde] vt (message) to decode.

décoiffer [dekwafe] vt **d. qn** to mess up s.o.'s hair.

décoincer [dekwɛ̃se] vt (engrenage) to unjam.

décoll/er [dekɔle] **1** vi (avion etc) to take off; **elle ne décolle pas d'ici** Fam she won't leave ou budge. **2** vt (timbre etc) to unstick; — **se d.** vpr to come unstuck. ◆**—age** nm Av takeoff.

décolleté [dekɔlte] a (robe) low-cut; — nm (de robe) low neckline; (de femme) bare neck and shoulders.

décoloniser [dekɔlɔnize] vt to decolonize. ◆**décolonisation** nf decolonization.

décolor/er [dekɔlɔre] vt to discolour, fade; (cheveux) to bleach. ◆**—ant** nm bleach. ◆**décoloration** nf discolo(u)ration; bleaching.

décombres [dekɔ̃br] nmpl ruins, rubble, debris.

décommander [dekɔmɑ̃de] vt (marchandises, invitation) to cancel; (invités) to put off; — **se d.** vpr to cancel (one's appointment).

décomposer [dekɔ̃poze] vt to decompose; (visage) to distort; — **se d.** vpr (pourrir) to decompose; (visage) to become distorted. ◆**décomposition** nf decomposition.

décompresser [dekɔ̃prese] vi Psy Fam to unwind.

décompression [dekɔ̃presjɔ̃] nf decompression.

décompte [dekɔ̃t] nm deduction; (détail) breakdown. ◆**décompter** vt to deduct.

déconcerter [dekɔ̃sɛrte] vt to disconcert.

déconfit [dekɔ̃fi] a downcast. ◆**déconfiture** nf (state of) collapse ou defeat; (faillite) Fam financial ruin.

décongeler [dekɔ̃ʒle] vt (aliment) to thaw, defrost.

décongestionner [dekɔ̃ʒɛstjɔne] vt (rue) & Méd to relieve congestion in.

déconnecter [dekɔnɛkte] vt Él & Fig to disconnect.

déconner [dekɔne] vi (divaguer) Fam to talk nonsense.

déconseiller [dekɔ̃seje] vt **d. qch à qn** to advise s.o. against sth; **d. à qn de faire** to advise s.o. against doing; **c'est déconseillé** it is inadvisable.

déconsidérer [dekɔ̃sidere] vt to discredit.

décontaminer [dekɔ̃tamine] vt to decontaminate.

décontenancer [dekɔ̃tnɑse] vt to disconcert; **— se d.** vpr to lose one's composure, become flustered.

décontracter [dekɔ̃trakte] vt, **— se d.** vpr to relax. ◆**décontraction** nf relaxation.

déconvenue [dekɔ̃vny] nf disappointment.

décor [dekɔr] nm Th scenery, decor; Cin set; (paysage) scenery; (d'intérieur) decoration; (cadre, ambiance) setting; **entrer dans le d.** (véhicule) Fam to run off the road.

décorer [dekɔre] vt (maison, soldat etc) to decorate (de with). ◆**décorateur, -trice** nmf (interior) decorator; Th stage designer; Cin set designer. ◆**décoratif, -ive** a decorative. ◆**décoration** nf decoration.

décortiquer [dekɔrtike] vt (graine) to husk; (homard etc) to shell; (texte) Fam to take to pieces, dissect.

découcher [dekuʃe] vi to stay out all night.

découdre [dekudr] vt to unstitch; **— vi en d.** Fam to fight it out; **— se d.** vpr to come unstitched.

découler [dekule] vi **d. de** to follow from.

découp/er [dekupe] vt (poulet etc) to carve; (article etc) Journ to cut out; **se d. sur** to stand out against. ◆**—é** a (côte) jagged. ◆**—age** nm (carving; cutting out; (image) cut-out. ◆**découpure** nf (contour) jagged outline; (morceau) piece cut out, cut-out.

découplé [dekuple] a **bien d.** (personne) well-built, strapping.

décourag/er [dekuraʒe] vt (dissuader) to discourage (de from); (démoraliser) to dishearten, discourage; **— se d.** vpr to get discouraged ou disheartened. ◆**—ement** nm discouragement.

décousu [dekuzy] a (propos, idées) disconnected.

découvrir* [dekuvrir] vt (trésor, terre etc) to discover; (secret, vérité etc) to find out, discover; (casserole etc) to take the lid off; (dévoiler) to disclose (à to); (dénuder) to uncover, expose; (voir) to perceive; **d. que** to discover ou find out that; **— se d.** vpr (se dénuder) to uncover oneself; (enlever son chapeau) to take one's hat off; (ciel) to clear up). ◆**découvert 1** a (terrain) open; (tête etc) bare; **à d.** exposed, unprotected; **agir à d.** to act openly. **2** nm (d'un compte) Fin overdraft. ◆**découverte** nf discovery; **partir** ou **aller à la d. de** to go in search of.

décrasser [dekrase] vt (éduquer) to take the rough edges off.

décrépit [dekrepi] a (vieillard) decrepit.

décrépitude nf (des institutions etc) decay.

décret [dekre] nm decree. ◆**décréter** vt to order, decree.

décrier [dekrije] vt to run down, disparage.

décrire* [dekrir] vt to describe.

décroch/er [dekrɔʃe] **1** vt (détacher) to unhook; (tableau) to take down; (obtenir) Fam to get, land; **d. (le téléphone)** to pick up the phone. **2** vi Fam (abandonner) to give up; (perdre le fil) to be unable to follow, lose track. ◆**—é** a (téléphone) off the hook.

décroître* [dekrwatr] vi (mortalité etc) to decrease, decline; (eaux) to subside; (jours) to draw in. ◆**décroissance** nf decrease, decline (de in, of).

décrotter [dekrɔte] vt (chaussures) to clean ou scrape (the mud off). ◆**décrottoir** nm shoe scraper.

décrypter [dekripte] vt (message) to decipher, decode.

déçu [desy] voir **décevoir**; **— a** disappointed.

déculotter (se) [sadekylɔte] vpr to take off one's trousers ou Am pants. ◆**déculottée** nf Fam thrashing.

décupler [dekyple] vti to increase tenfold.

dédaigner [dedɛɲe] vt (personne, richesse etc) to scorn, despise; (repas) to turn up one's nose at; (offre) to spurn; (ne pas tenir compte de) to disregard. ◆**dédaigneux, -euse** a scornful, disdainful (de of). ◆**dédain** nm scorn, disdain (pour, de for).

dédale [dedal] nm maze, labyrinth.

dedans [d(ə)dɑ̃] adv inside; **de d.** from (the) inside, from within; **en d.** on the inside; **au-d. (de), au d. (de)** inside; **au-d. ou au d. de lui-même** inwardly; **tomber d.** (trou) to fall in (it); **donner d.** (être dupé) Fam to fall in; **mettre d.** Fam (en prison) to put inside; (tromper) to take in; **je me suis fait rentrer d.** (accident de voiture) Fam someone went ou crashed into me; **— nm le d.** the inside.

dédicace [dedikas] nf dedication, inscription. ◆**dédicacer** vt (livre etc) to dedicate, inscribe (à to).

dédier [dedje] vt to dedicate.

dédire (se) [sadedir] vpr to go back on one's word; **se d. de** (promesse etc) to go back on. ◆**dédit** nm (somme) Com forfeit, penalty.

dédommag/er [dedɔmaʒe] vt to compensate (de for). ◆**—ement** nm compensation.

dédouaner [dedwane] vt (marchandises) to clear through customs; **d. qn** to restore s.o.'s prestige.

dédoubl/er [deduble] vt (classe etc) to split into two; **d. un train** to run an extra train; **— se d.** vpr to be in two places at once. **◆—ement** nm **d. de la personnalité** Psy split personality.

déduire* [deduir] vt (retirer) to deduct (de from); (conclure) to deduce (de from). **◆déductible** a (frais) deductible, allowable. **◆déduction** nf (raisonnement) & Com deduction.

déesse [dees] nf goddess.

défaill/ir* [defajir] vi (s'évanouir) to faint; (forces) to fail, flag; **sans d.** without finishing. **◆—ant** a (personne) faint; (témoin) Jur defaulting. **◆défaillance** nf (évanouissement) fainting fit; (faiblesse) weakness; (panne) fault; **une d. de mémoire** a lapse of memory.

défaire* [defer] vt (nœud etc) to undo, untie; (bagages) to unpack; (installation) to take down; (coiffure) to mess up; **d. qn** de to rid s.o. of; **— se d.** vpr (nœud etc) to come undone ou untied; **se d. de** to get rid of. **◆défait** a (lit) unmade; (visage) drawn; (armée) defeated. **◆défaite** nf defeat. **◆défaitisme** nm defeatism.

défalquer [defalke] vt (frais etc) to deduct (de from).

défaut [defo] nm (faiblesse) fault, shortcoming, failing, defect; (de diamant etc) flaw; (désavantage) drawback; (contumace) Jur default; **le d. de la cuirasse** the chink in the armour; **faire d.** to be lacking; **le temps me fait d.** I lack time; **à d. de** for want of; **en d.** at fault; **prendre qn en d.** to catch s.o. out; **ou, à d....** or, failing that ....

défaveur [defavœr] nf disfavour. **◆défavorable** a unfavourable (à to). **◆défavoriser** vt to a disadvantage, be unfair to.

défection [defeksjɔ̃] nf defection, desertion; **faire d.** to desert; (ne pas venir) to fail to turn up.

défectueux, -euse [defektɥø, -øz] a faulty, defective. **◆défectuosité** nf defectiveness; (défaut) defect (de in).

défendre [defɑ̃dr] 1 vt (protéger) to defend; **— se d.** vpr to defend oneself; **se d. de** (pluie etc) to protect oneself from; **se d. de faire** (s'empêcher de) to refrain from doing; **je me défends (bien)** Fam I can hold my own. 2 vt **d. à qn de faire** (interdire) to forbid s.o. to do, not allow s.o. to do; **d. qch à qn** to forbid s.o. sth. **◆défendable** a defensible.

défense [defɑ̃s] nf 1 (protection) defence, Am defense; (des faibles) protector, defender. **◆défensif, -ive** a defensive; **— nf sur la défensive** on the defensive.

déférent [deferɑ̃] a deferential. **◆déférence** nf deference.

déférer [defere] 1 vt (coupable) Jur to refer (à to). 2 vi **d. à l'avis de qn** to defer to s.o.'s opinion.

déferler [deferle] vi (vagues) to break; (haine etc) to erupt; **d. dans** ou **sur** (foule) to surge ou sweep into.

défi [defi] nm challenge; **lancer un d. à qn** to challenge s.o.; **mettre qn au d. de faire** to defy ou dare s.o. to do.

déficient [defisjɑ̃] a Méd deficient. **◆déficience** nf Méd deficiency.

déficit [defisit] nm deficit. **◆déficitaire** a (budget etc) in deficit; (récolte etc) Fig short, insufficient.

défier¹ [defje] vt (provoquer) to challenge (à to); (braver) to defy; **d. qn de faire** to defy ou challenge s.o. to do.

défier² (se) [sədefje] vpr **se d. de** Litt to distrust. **◆défiance** nf distrust (de of). **◆défiant** a distrustful (à l'égard de of).

défigur/er [defigyre] vt (visage) to disfigure; (vérité etc) to distort. **◆—ement** nm disfigurement; distortion.

défil/er [defile] vi (manifestants) to march (devant past); Mil to march ou file past; (paysage, jours) to pass by; (visiteurs) to keep coming and going, stream in and out; (images) Cin to flash by (on the screen); **— se d.** vpr Fam (s'éloigner) to sneak off; (éviter d'agir) to cop out. **◆—é** nm 1 (cortège) procession; (de manifestants) march; Mil parade, march past; (de visiteurs) stream, succession. 2 Géog gorge, pass.

défin/ir [definir] vt to define. **◆—i** a (article) Gram definite. **◆définition** nf definition; (de mots croisés) clue.

définitif, -ive [definitif, -iv] a final, definitive; **— nf en définitive** in the final analysis, finally. **◆définitivement** adv (partir) permanently, for good; (exclure) definitively.

déflagration [deflagrasjɔ̃] nf explosion.

déflation [deflasjɔ̃] nf Écon deflation.

déflorer [deflore] vt (idée, sujet) to spoil the freshness of.

défonc/er [defɔ̃se] vt 1 (porte, mur etc) to smash in ou down; (trottoir, route etc) to dig up, break up. **2 se d.** vpr (drogué) Fam to get high (à on). ◆—é a 1 (*route*) full of potholes, bumpy. 2 (*drogué*) high.

déform/er [deforme] *vt* (*objet*) to put ou knock out of shape; (*doigt*, *main*) to deform; (*faits*, *image etc*) to distort; (*goût*) to corrupt; — **se d.** *vpr* to lose its shape. ◆—é a (*objet*) misshapen; (*corps etc*) deformed, misshapen; **chaussée déformée** uneven road surface. ◆**déformation** *nf* distortion; corruption; (*de membre*) deformity; **c'est de la d. professionnelle** it's an occupational hazard, it's a case of being conditioned by one's job.

défouler (se) [sədefule] *vpr* *Fam* to let off steam.

défraîchir (se) [sədefreʃir] *vpr* (*étoffe etc*) to lose its freshness, become faded.

défrayer [defreje] *vt* **d. qn** to pay ou defray s.o.'s expenses; **d. la chronique** to be the talk of the town.

défricher [defriʃe] *vt* (*terrain*) to clear (for cultivation); (*sujet etc*) Fig to open up.

défriser [defrize] *vt* (*cheveux*) to straighten; **d. qn** (*contrarier*) Fam to ruffle ou annoy s.o.

défroisser [defrwase] *vt* (*papier*) to smooth out.

défroqué [defrɔke] a (*prêtre*) defrocked.

dégainer [degene] *vti* (*arme*) to draw.

dégarn/ir [degarnir] *vt* to clear, empty; (*arbre*, *compte*) to strip; — **se d.** *vpr* (*crâne*) to go bald; (*salle*) to clear, empty. ◆—**i** a

(*salle*) empty, bare; (*tête*) balding; **front d.** receding hairline.

dégâts [dega] *nmpl* damage; **limiter les d.** Fig to prevent matters getting worse.

dégel [deʒɛl] *nm* thaw. ◆**dégeler** *vt* to thaw (out); (*crédits*) to unfreeze; — *vi* to thaw (out); — *v imp* to thaw; — **se d.** *vpr* (*personne*, *situation*) to thaw (out).

dégénér/er [deʒenere] *vi* to degenerate (**en** into). ◆—é, —ée a & *nmf* degenerate. ◆**dégénérescence** *nf* degeneration.

dégingandé [deʒɛ̃gɑ̃de] a gangling, lanky.

dégivrer [deʒivre] *vt* Aut Av to de-ice; (*réfrigérateur*) to defrost.

déglingu/er (se) [sədeglɛ̃ge] *vpr* Fam to fall to bits. ◆—é a falling to bits, in bits.

dégobiller [degɔbije] *vt* Fam to spew up.

dégonfl/er [degɔ̃fle] *vt* (*pneu etc*) to deflate, let down; — **se d.** *vpr* (*flancher*) Fam to chicken out, get cold feet. ◆—é, —ée a (*pneu*) flat; (*lâche*) Fam chicken, yellow; — *nmf* Fam yellow belly.

dégorger [degɔrʒe] *vi* (*se déverser*) to discharge (**dans** into); **faire d.** (*escargots*) Culin to cover with salt.

dégot(t)er [degɔte] *vt* Fam to find, turn up.

dégouliner [deguline] *vi* to trickle, drip, run.

dégourd/ir [degurdir] *vt* (*doigts etc*) to take the numbness out of; **d. qn** Fig to smarten ou wise s.o. up, sharpen s.o.'s wits; — **se d.** *vpr* to smarten up, wise up; **se d. les jambes** to stretch one's legs. ◆—**i** a (*malin*) smart, sharp.

dégoût [degu] *nm* disgust; **le d. de** (*la vie*, *les gens etc*) disgust for; **avoir un ou du d. pour qch** to have a (strong) dislike ou distaste for sth. ◆**dégoût/er** *vt* to disgust; **d. qn de qch** to put s.o. off sth; **se d. de** to take a (strong) dislike to, become disgusted with. ◆—**ant** a disgusting. ◆—é a disgusted; **être d. de** to be sick of ou disgusted with ou by ou at; **elle est partie dégoûtée** she left in disgust; **il n'est pas d.** (*difficile*) he's not too fussy; **faire le d.** to be fussy.

dégrad/er [degrade] 1 *vt* (*avilir*) to degrade; (*mur etc*) to deface, damage; — **se d.** *vpr* (*s'avilir*) to degrade oneself; (*édifice*, *situation*) to deteriorate. 2 *vt* (*couleur*) to shade off. ◆—**ant** a degrading. ◆—é *nm* (*de couleur*) shading off, gradation. ◆**dégradation** *nf* (*de drogué etc*) & Ch degradation; (*de situation*) deterioration; *pl* (*dégâts*) damage.

dégrafer [degrafe] *vt* (*vêtement*) to unfasten, unhook.

dégager/er [degaʒe] *vt* (*lieu*, *table*) to clear (**de** of); (*objet en gage*) to redeem; (*odeur*) to give off; (*chaleur*) to give out; (*responsabilité*) to disclaim; (*idée*, *conclusion*) to bring out; **d. qn de** (*promesse*) to release s.o. from; (*décombres*) to free s.o. from, pull s.o. out of; **cette robe dégage la taille** this dress leaves the waist free and easy; — *vi* Fb to clear the ball (down the pitch); **d.!** clear the way!; — **se d.** *vpr* (*rue*, *ciel*) to clear; **se d. de** (*personne*) to release oneself from (*promise*); to get free from, free oneself from (*rubble*); **se d. de** (*odeur*) to issue ou emanate from; (*vérité*, *impression*) to emerge from. ◆—é a (*ciel*) clear; (*ton*, *allure*) easy-going, casual; (*vue*) open. ◆—**ement** *nm* 1 (*action*) clearing; redemption; (*d'odeur*) emanation; (*de chaleur*) emission; release; freeing; Fb clearance, kick; **itinéraire de d.** Aut relief road. 2 (*espace libre*) clearing; (*de maison*) passage.

dégraisser [degrese] *vt* 1 (*bœuf*) to take the

fat off; (*bouillon*) to skim. **2** (*entreprise*) *Fam* to slim down, trim down the size of (*by laying off workers*).

degré [dəgre] *nm* **1** degree; **enseignement du premier/second d.** primary/secondary education; **au plus haut d.** (*avare etc*) extremely. **2** (*gradin*) *Litt* step.

dégrever [degrəve] *vt* (*contribuable*) to reduce the tax burden on.

dégriffé [degrife] *a* **vêtement d.** unlabelled designer garment.

dégringoler [degrɛ̃gɔle] *vi* to tumble (down); **faire d. qch** to topple sth over; — *vt* (*escalier*) to rush down. ◆**dégringolade** *nf* tumble.

dégriser [degrize] *vt* **d. qn** to sober s.o. (up).

dégrossir [degrosir] *vt* (*travail*) to rough out; **d. qn** to refine s.o.

déguerpir [degɛrpir] *vi* to clear off *ou* out.

dégueulasse [degœlas] *a* *Fam* lousy, disgusting.

dégueuler [degœle] *vi* (*vomir*) *Arg* to puke.

déguis/er [degize] *vt* (*pour tromper*) to disguise; (*costumer*) to dress s.o. up as, disguise s.o. as; — **se d.** *vpr* to dress oneself up, disguise oneself (**en** as). ◆**—ement** *nm* disguise; (*de bal costumé etc*) fancy dress.

déguster [degyste] **1** *vt* (*goûter*) to taste, sample; (*apprécier*) to relish. **2** *vi* (*subir des coups*) *Fam* to cop it, get a good hiding. ◆**dégustation** *nf* tasting, sampling.

déhancher (se) [sədeɑ̃ʃe] *vpr* (*femme etc*) to sway *ou* wiggle one's hips; (*boiteux*) to walk lop-sided.

dehors [dəɔr] *adv* out(side); (*à l'air*) outdoors, outside; **en d.** on the outside; **en d. de** outside; (*excepté*) apart from; **en d. de la ville/fenêtre** out of town/the window; **au-d. (de), au d. (de)** outside; **déjeuner/jeter/etc d.** to lunch/throw/etc out; — *nm* (*extérieur*) outside; *pl* (*aspect*) outward appearance.

déjà [deʒa] *adv* already; **est-il d. parti?** has he left yet *ou* already?; **elle l'a d. vu** she's seen it before, she's already seen it; **c'est d. pas mal** that's not bad at all; **quand partez-vous, d.?** when are you leaving, again?

déjeuner [deʒœne] *vi* (*à midi*) to (have) lunch; (*le matin*) to (have) breakfast; — *nm* lunch; **petit d.** breakfast.

déjouer [deʒwe] *vt* (*intrigue etc*) to thwart, foil.

déjuger (se) [sədeʒyʒe] *vpr* to go back on one's opinion *ou* decision.

delà [d(ə)la] *adv* **au-d. (de), au d. (de), par-d.,**

par d. beyond; **au-d. du pont/etc** beyond *ou* past the bridge/etc; — *nm* **l'au-d.** the (world) beyond.

délabr/er (se) [sədelabre] *vpr* to become dilapidated, fall into disrepair; (*santé*) to become impaired. ◆**—ement** *nm* dilapidation, disrepair; impaired state.

délacer [delase] *vt* (*chaussures*) to undo.

délai [dele] *nm* time limit; (*répit, sursis*) extra time, extension; **dans un d. de dix jours** within ten days; **sans d.** without delay; **à bref d.** at short notice; **dans les plus brefs délais** as soon as possible; **dernier d.** final date.

délaisser [delese] *vt* to forsake, desert, abandon; (*négliger*) to neglect.

délass/er [delase] *vt,* — **se d.** *vpr* to relax. ◆**—ement** *nm* relaxation, diversion.

délateur, -trice [delatœr, -tris] *nmf* informer.

délavé [delave] *a* (*tissu, jean*) faded; (*ciel*) watery; (*terre*) waterlogged.

délayer [deleje] *vt* (*mélanger*) to mix (with liquid); (*discours, texte*) *Fig* to pad out, drag out.

delco [dɛlko] *nm* *Aut* distributor.

délect/er (se) [sədelɛkte] *vpr* **se d. de qch** *ou* **à faire** to (take) delight in sth/in doing. ◆**—able** *a* delectable. ◆**délectation** *nf* delight.

délégu/er [delege] *vt* to delegate (**à** to). ◆**-é, -ée** *nmf* delegate. ◆**délégation** *nf* delegation.

délest/er [delɛste] *vt* *Él* to cut the power from; **d. qn de** (*voler à qn*) *Fam* to relieve s.o. of. ◆**—age** *nm* *Aut* relief; **itinéraire de d.** alternative route (*to relieve congestion*).

délibér/er [delibere] *vi* (*réfléchir*) to deliberate (**sur** upon); (*se consulter*) to confer, deliberate (**de** about). ◆**-é** *a* (*résolu*) determined; (*intentionnel*) deliberate; **de propos d.** deliberately. ◆**—ément** *adv* (*à dessein*) deliberately. ◆**délibération** *nf* deliberation.

délicat [delika] *a* (*santé, travail etc*) delicate; (*question*) tricky, delicate; (*geste*) tactful; (*conscience*) scrupulous; (*exigeant*) particular. ◆**délicatement** *adv* delicately; tactfully. ◆**délicatesse** *nf* delicacy; tact(fulness); scrupulousness.

délice [delis] *nm* delight; — *nfpl* delights. ◆**délicieux, -euse** *a* (*mets, fruit etc*) delicious; (*endroit, parfum etc*) delightful.

délié [delje] **1** *a* (*esprit*) sharp; (*doigts*) nimble; (*mince*) slender. **2** *nm* (*d'une lettre*) (thin) upstroke.

délier [delje] *vt* to untie, undo; (*langue*) *Fig*

to loosen; **d. qn de** to release s.o. from; — **se d.** *vpr* (*paquet etc*) to come undone *ou* untied.

délimiter [delimite] *vt* to mark off, delimit; (*définir*) to define. ◆**délimitation** *nf* demarcation, delimitation; definition.

délinquant, -ante [delɛkɑ̃, -ɑ̃t] *a* & *nmf* delinquent. ◆**délinquance** *nf* delinquency.

délire [delir] *nm* Méd delirium; (*exaltation*) Fig frenzy. ◆**délirer** *vi* Méd to be delirious; (*dire n'importe quoi*) Fig to rave; **d. de** (*joie etc*) to be wild with. ◆**—ant** *a* (*malade*) delirious; (*joie*) frenzied; wild; (*déraisonnable*) utterly absurd.

délit [deli] *nm* offence, misdemeanour.

délivrer [delivre] *vt* **1** (*prisonnier*) to release, deliver; (*ville*) to deliver; **d. qn de** (*souci etc*) to rid s.o. of. **2** (*billet, diplôme etc*) to issue. ◆**délivrance** *nf* release; deliverance; issue; (*soulagement*) relief.

déloger [deloʒe] *vi* to move out; — *vt* to force *ou* drive out; Mil to dislodge.

déloyal, -aux [delwajal, -o] *a* disloyal; (*concurrence*) unfair. ◆**déloyauté** *nf* disloyalty; unfairness; (*action*) disloyal act.

delta [dɛlta] *nm* (*de fleuve*) delta.

deltaplane® [dɛltaplan] *nm* (*engin*) hang-glider; **faire du d.** to practise hang-gliding.

déluge [delyʒ] *nm* flood; (*de pluie*) downpour; (*de compliments, coups*) shower.

déluré [delyre] *a* (*malin*) smart, sharp; (*fille*) Péj brazen.

démagogie [demagɔʒi] *nf* demagogy. ◆**démagogue** *nmf* demagogue.

demain [d(ə)mɛ̃] *adv* tomorrow; **à d.!** see you tomorrow!; **ce n'est pas d. la veille** Fam that won't happen for a while yet.

demande [d(ə)mɑ̃d] *nf* request; (*d'emploi*) application; (*de renseignements*) inquiry; Écon demand; (*question*) question; **d. (en mariage)** proposal (of marriage); **demandes d'emploi** Journ situations wanted. ◆**demander** *vt* to ask for; (*emploi*) to apply for; (*autorisation*) to request, ask for; (*charité*) to beg for; (*prix*) to charge; (*nécessiter, exiger*) to require; **d. un nom/le chemin/l'heure** to ask a name/the way/the time; **d. qch à qn** to ask s.o. for sth; **d. à qn de faire** to ask s.o. to do; **d. si/où** to ask *ou* inquire whether/where; **on te demande!** you're wanted!; **ça demande du temps/une heure** it takes time/an hour; **d. en mariage** to propose (marriage) to; — **se d.** *vpr* to wonder, ask oneself (**pourquoi** why, **si** if).

démanger [demɑ̃ʒe] *vti* to itch; **son bras le**

ou **lui démange** his arm itches; **ça me démange de ...** Fig I'm itching to ... . ◆**démangeaison** *nf* itch; **avoir des démangeaisons** to be itching; **j'ai une d. au bras** my arm's itching.

démanteler [demɑ̃tle] *vt* (*bâtiment*) to demolish; (*organisation etc*) to break up.

démantibuler [demɑ̃tibyle] *vt* (*meuble etc*) Fam to pull to pieces.

démaquill/er (se) [sədemakije] *vpr* to take off one's make-up. ◆**—ant** *nm* make-up remover.

démarcation [demarkasjɔ̃] *nf* demarcation.

démarche [demarʃ] *nf* walk, step, gait; (*de pensée*) process; **faire des démarches** to take the necessary steps (**pour faire** to do).

démarcheur, -euse [demarʃœr, -øz] *nmf* Pol canvasser; Com door-to-door salesman *ou* saleswoman.

démarquer [demarke] *vt* (*prix*) to mark down; **se d. de** Fig to dissociate oneself from.

démarr/er [demare] *vi* (*moteur*) Aut to start (up); (*partir*) Aut to move *ou* drive off; (*entreprise etc*) Fig to get off the ground; — *vt* (*commencer*) Fam to start. ◆**—age** *nm* Aut start; **d. en côte** hill start. ◆**—eur** *nm* Aut starter.

démasquer [demaske] *vt* to unmask.

démêl/er [demele] *vt* to disentangle; (*discerner*) to fathom. ◆**—é** *nm* (*dispute*) squabble; *pl* (*ennuis*) trouble (**avec** with).

démembrer [demɑ̃bre] *vt* (*pays etc*) to dismember.

déménag/er [demenaʒe] *vi* to move (out), move house; — *vt* (*meubles*) to (re)move. ◆**—ement** *nm* move, moving (house); (*de meubles*) removal, moving (**de** of); **voiture de d.** removal van, Am moving van. ◆**—eur** *nm* removal man, Am (furniture) mover.

démener (se) [sədemne] *vpr* to fling oneself about; **se d. pour faire** to spare no effort to do.

dément, -ente [demɑ̃, -ɑ̃t] *a* insane; (*génial*) Iron fantastic; — *nmf* lunatic. ◆**démence** *nf* insanity. ◆**démentiel, -ielle** *a* insane.

dément/ir [demɑ̃tir] *vt* (*infirmer*) to belie; (*nouvelle, faits etc*) to deny; **d. qn** to give the lie to s.o. ◆**—i** *nm* denial.

démerder (se) [sədemɛrde] *vpr* (*se débrouiller*) Arg to manage (by oneself).

démesure [demezyr] *nf* excess. ◆**démesuré** *a* excessive, inordinate.

démettre [demɛtr] *vt* **1** (*os*) to dislocate; **se d. le pied** to dislocate one's foot. **2 d. qn de**

to dismiss s.o. from; **se d. de ses fonctions** to resign one's office.

demeurant (au) [ədəmœrɑ̃] *adv* for all that, after all.

demeure [dəmœr] *nf* **1** dwelling (place), residence. **2 mettre qn en d. de faire** to summon *ou* instruct s.o. to do. **◆demeurer** *vi* **1** *(aux être)* *(rester)* to remain; **en d. là** *(affaire etc)* to rest there. **2** *(aux avoir)* *(habiter)* to live, reside. **◆—é a** *Fam* (mentally) retarded.

demi [d(ə)mi] *a* half; **d.-journée** half-day; **une heure et demie** an hour and a half; *(horloge)* half past one; *– adv* (à) **d. plein** half-full; **à d. nu** half-naked; **ouvrir à d.** to open halfway; **faire les choses à d.** to do things by halves; *– nmf (moitié)* half; *– nm (verre)* (half-pint) glass of beer; *Fb* half-back; *– nf (à l'horloge)* half-hour. **◆demi-cercle** [d(ə)miserkl] *nm* semicircle. **◆d.-douzaine** *nf* **une d.-douzaine (de)** a half-dozen, half a dozen. **◆d.-finale** *nf Sp* semifinal. **◆d.-frère** *nm* stepbrother. **◆d.-heure** *nf* **une d.-heure a** half-hour, half an hour. **◆d.-mesure** *nf* half-measure. **◆d.-mot** *nm* **tu comprendras à d.-mot** you'll understand without my having to spell it out. **◆d.-pension** *nf* half-board. **◆d.-pensionnaire** *nmf* day boarder, *Am* day student. **◆d.-saison** *nf* **de d.-saison** *(vêtement)* between seasons. **◆d.-sel** *a inv (beurre)* slightly salted; *(fromage)* **d.-sel** cream cheese. **◆d.-sœur** *nf* stepsister. **◆d.-tarif** *nm & a inv (billet)* (à) **d.-tarif** half-price. **◆d.-tour** *nm* about turn, *Am* about face; *Aut* U-turn; **faire d.-tour** to turn back.

démission [demisjɔ̃] *nf* resignation. **◆démissionnaire** *a (ministre etc)* outgoing. **◆démissionner** *vi* to resign.

démobiliser [demɔbilize] *vt* to demobilize. **◆démobilisation** *nf* demobilization.

démocrate [demɔkrat] *nmf* democrat; *– a* democratic. **◆démocratie** [-asi] *nf* democracy. **◆démocratique** *a* democratic.

démod/er (se) [sədemɔde] *vpr* to go out of fashion. **◆—é a** old-fashioned.

démographie [demɔgrafi] *nf* demography.

demoiselle [d(ə)mwazεl] *nf (célibataire)* spinster, single woman; *(jeune fille)* young lady; **d. d'honneur** *(à un mariage)* bridesmaid; *(de reine)* maid of honour.

démolir [demɔlir] *vt (maison, jouet etc)* to demolish; *(projet etc)* to shatter; **d. qn** *(battre, discréditer) Fam* to tear s.o. to

pieces. **◆démolition** *nf* demolition; **en d.** being demolished.

démon [demɔ̃] *nm* demon; **petit d.** *(enfant)* little devil. **◆démoniaque** *a* devilish, fiendish.

démonstrateur, -trice [demɔ̃stratœr, -tris] *nmf (dans un magasin etc)* demonstrator. **◆démonstratif, -ive** *a* demonstrative. **◆démonstration** *nf* demonstration; **d. de force** show of force.

démonter [demɔ̃te] *vt (assemblage)* to dismantle, take apart; *(installation)* to take down; *(personne) Fig* to disconcert s.o.; **une mer démontée** a stormy sea; *— se d.* *vpr* to come apart; *(installation)* to come down; *(personne)* to be put out *ou* disconcerted.

démontrer [demɔ̃tre] *vt* to demonstrate, show.

démoraliser [demɔralize] *vt* to demoralize; *— se d.* *vpr* to become demoralized. **◆démoralisation** *nf* demoralization.

démordre [demɔrdr] *vi* **il ne démordra pas de** *(son opinion etc)* he won't budge from.

démouler [demule] *vt (gâteau)* to turn out *(from its mould)*.

démunir [demynir] *vt* **d. qn de** to deprive s.o. of; **se d. de** to part with.

démystifier [demistifje] *vt (public etc)* to disabuse; *(idée etc)* to debunk.

dénationaliser [denasjɔnalize] *vt* to denationalize.

dénatur/er [denatyre] *vt (propos, faits etc)* to misrepresent, distort. **◆—é a** *(goût, père etc)* unnatural.

dénégation [denegasjɔ̃] *nf* denial.

déneiger [deneʒe] *vt* to clear of snow.

dénicher [denife] *vt (trouver)* to dig up, turn up; *(ennemi, fugitif)* to hunt out, flush out.

dénier [denje] *vt* to deny; *(responsabilité)* to disclaim, deny; **d. qch à qn** to deny s.o. sth.

dénigr/er [denigre] *vt* to denigrate, disparage. **◆—ement** *nm* denigration, disparagement.

dénivellation [denivelasjɔ̃] *nf* unevenness; *(pente)* gradient; *pl (accidents)* bumps.

dénombrer [denɔ̃bre] *vt* to count, number.

dénomm/er [denɔme] *vt* to name. **◆—é, -ée** *nmf* **un d. Dupont** a man named Dupont. **◆dénomination** *nf* designation, name.

dénonc/er [denɔ̃se] *vt (injustice etc)* to denounce (à to); **d. qn** to inform on s.o., denounce s.o. (à to); *Scol* to tell on s.o. (à to); *— se d.* *vpr* to give oneself up (à to). **◆dénonciateur, -trice** *nmf* informer. **◆dénonciation** *nf* denunciation.

dénoter [denɔte] vt to denote.

dénouer [denwe] vt (nœud, corde) to undo, untie; (cheveux) to undo, (situation, intrigue) to unravel; (problème, crise) to clear up; — **se d.** vpr (nœud) to come undone ou untied; (cheveux) to come undone. ◆**dénouement** nm outcome, ending; Th dénouement.

dénoyauter [denwajote] vt (prune etc) to stone, Am to pit.

denrée [dɑ̃re] nf food(stuff); **denrées alimentaires** foodstuffs.

dense [dɑ̃s] a dense. ◆**densité** nf density.

dent [dɑ̃] nf tooth; (de roue) cog; (de fourche) prong; (de timbre-poste) perforation; **d. de sagesse** wisdom tooth; **rien à se mettre sous la d.** nothing to eat; **manger à belles dents/du bout des dents** to eat whole-heartedly/half-heartedly; **faire ses dents** (enfant) to be teething; **coup de d.** bite; **sur les dents** (surmené) exhausted; (énervé) on edge; **avoir une d. contre qn** to have it in for s.o. ◆**dentaire** a dental. ◆**dentée** af **roue d.** cogwheel. ◆**dentier** nm denture(s), (set of) false teeth. ◆**dentifrice** nm toothpaste. ◆**dentiste** nmf dentist; **chirurgien d.** dental surgeon. ◆**dentition** nf (dents) (set of) teeth.

dentelé [dɑ̃tle] a (côte) jagged; (feuille) serrated. ◆**denteure** nf jagged outline ou edge.

dentelle [dɑ̃tɛl] nf lace.

dénud/er [denyde] vt to (lay) bare. ◆**-é** a bare.

dénué [denye] a **d. de** devoid of, without.

dénuement [denymɑ̃] nm destitution; **dans le d.** poverty-stricken.

déodorant [deɔdɔrɑ̃] nm deodorant.

dépann/er [depane] vt (mécanisme) to get going (again), repair; **d. qn** Fam to help s.o. out. ◆**-age** nm (emergency) repair; **voiture/service de d.** breakdown vehicle/ service. ◆**-eur** nm repairman; Aut breakdown mechanic. ◆**-euse** nf (voiture) Aut breakdown lorry, Am wrecker, tow truck.

dépareillé [depareje] a (chaussure etc) odd, not matching; (collection) incomplete.

déparer [depare] vt to mar, spoil.

départ [depar] nm departure; (début) start, beginning; Sp start; **point/ligne de d.** starting point/post; **au d.** at the outset, at the start; **au d. de Paris/etc** (excursion etc) departing from Paris/etc.

départager [departaʒe] vt (concurrents) to decide between; **d. les votes** to give the casting vote.

département [departəmɑ̃] nm department.

◆**départemental, -aux** a departmental; **route départementale** secondary road.

départir (se) [sədepartir] vpr **se d. de** (attitude) to depart from, abandon.

dépass/er [depase] vt (durée, attente etc) to go beyond, exceed; (endroit) to go past, go beyond; (véhicule, bicyclette etc) to overtake, pass; (pouvoir) to go beyond, overstep; **d. qn** (en hauteur) to be taller than s.o.; (surclasser) to be ahead of s.o.; **ça me dépasse** Fig that's (quite) beyond me; — vi (jupon, clou etc) to stick out, show. ◆**-é a** (démodé) outdated; (incapable) unable to cope. ◆**-ement** nm Aut overtaking, passing.

dépays/er [depeize] vt to disorientate, Am disorient. ◆**-ement** nm disorientation; (changement) change of scenery.

dépecer [depase] vt (animal) to cut up, carve up.

dépêche [depeʃ] nf telegram; (diplomatique) dispatch; — **se d.** vpr to hurry (up).

dépeigner [depeɲe] vt **d. qn** to make s.o.'s hair untidy. ◆**-é a être d.** to have untidy hair; **sortir d.** to go out with untidy hair.

dépeindre* [depɛ̃dr] vt to depict, describe.

dépenaillé [depənaje] a in tatters ou rags.

dépend/re [depɑ̃dr] 1 vi to depend (on); **d.** **de** (appartenir à) to belong to; (être soumis à) to be dependent on; **ça dépend de toi** that depends on you, that's up to you. 2 vt (décrocher) to take down. ◆**-ant** a dependent (**de** on). ◆**dépendance** 1 nf dependence; **sous la d. de qn** under s.o.'s domination. 2 nfpl (bâtiments) outbuildings.

dépens [depɑ̃] nmpl Jur costs; **aux d. de** at the expense of; **apprendre à ses d.** to learn to one's cost.

dépense [depɑ̃s] nf (action) spending; (frais) expense, expenditure; (d'électricité etc) consumption; (physique) exertion. ◆**dépenser** vt (argent) to spend; (électricité etc) to use; (forces) to exert; (énergie) to expend; — **se d.** vpr to exert oneself. ◆**dépensier, -ière** a wasteful, extravagant.

déperdition [deperdisjɔ̃] nf (de chaleur etc) loss.

dépér/ir [deperir] vi (personne) to waste away; (plante) to wither; (santé etc) to decline. ◆**-issement** nm (baisse) decline.

dépêtrer [depetre] vt to extricate; — **se d.** vpr to extricate oneself (**de** from).

dépeupl/er [depœple] vt to depopulate. ◆**-ement** nm depopulation.

dépilatoire [depilatwar] *nm* hair-remover.

dépist/er [depiste] *vt* (*criminel etc*) to track down; (*maladie, fraude*) to detect. ◆**—age** *nm* Méd detection.

dépit [depi] *nm* resentment, chagrin; **en d. de** in spite of. ◆**dépiter** *vt* to vex, chagrin; **— se d.** *vpr* to feel resentment ou chagrin.

déplac/er [deplase] *vt* to shift, move; (*fonctionnaire*) to transfer; **— se d.** *vpr* to move (about); (*voyager*) to get about, travel (about). ◆**—é** *a* (*mal à propos*) out of place; **personne déplacée** (*réfugié*) displaced person. ◆**—ement** *nm* (*voyage*) (business ou professional) trip; (*d'ouragan, de troupes*) movement; **les déplacements** (*voyages*) travel(ling); **frais de d.** travelling expenses.

déplaire* [depler] *vi* **d. à qn** to displease s.o.; **cet aliment lui déplaît** he ou she dislikes this food; **n'en déplaise à Iron** with all due respect to; **—** *v imp* **il me déplaît de faire** I dislike doing, it displeases me to do; **— se d.** *vpr* to dislike it. ◆**déplaisant** *a* unpleasant, displeasing. ◆**déplaisir** *nm* displeasure.

dépli/er [deplije] *vt* to open out, unfold. ◆**—ant** *nm* (*prospectus*) leaflet.

déplor/er [deplore] *vt* (*regretter*) to deplore; (*la mort de qn*) to mourn (over), lament (over); **d. qn** to mourn (for) s.o.; **d. que** (+ *sub*) to deplore the fact that, regret that. ◆**—able** *a* deplorable, lamentable.

déployer [deplwaje] *vt* (*ailes*) to spread; (*journal, carte etc*) to unfold, spread (out); (*objets, courage etc*) to display; (*troupes*) to deploy; **— se d.** *vpr* (*drapeau*) to unfurl. ◆**déploiement** *nm* (*démonstration*) display; Mil deployment.

dépoli [depoli] *a* **verre d.** frosted glass.

déport/er [deporte] *vt* **1** (*exiler*) Hist to deport (to a penal colony); (*dans un camp de concentration*) Hist to send to a concentration camp, deport. **2** (*dévier*) to veer ou carry (off course). ◆**—é, -ée** *nmf* deportee; (concentration camp) inmate. ◆**déportation** *nf* deportation; internment (in a concentration camp).

dépos/er [depoze] *vt* (*poser*) to put down; (*laisser*) to leave; (*argent, lie*) to deposit; (*plainte*) to lodge; (*armes*) to lay down; (*gerbe*) to lay; (*ordures*) to dump; (*marque de fabrique*) to register; (*projet de loi*) to introduce; (*souverain*) to depose; **d. qn** Aut to drop s.o. off; (*laisser*) to leave; **d. son bilan** Fin to go into liquidation, file for bankruptcy; **—** *vi* Jur to testify; (*liquide*) to leave a deposit; **— se d.** *vpr* (*poussière, lie*) to

settle. ◆**dépositaire** *nmf* Fin agent; (*de secret*) custodian. ◆**déposition** *nf* Jur statement; (*de souverain*) deposing.

déposséder [deposede] *vt* to deprive, dispossess (**de** of).

dépôt [depo] *nm* (*d'ordures etc*) dumping, (*lieu*) dump; (*de gerbe*) laying; (*d'autobus, de trains*) depot; (*entrepôt*) warehouse; (*argent*) deposit; (*de vin*) deposit, sediment; **d. (calcaire)** (*de chaudière etc*) deposit; **laisser qch à qn en d.** to give s.o. sth for safekeeping ou in trust.

dépotoir [depotwar] *nm* rubbish dump, Am garbage dump.

dépouille [depuj] *nf* hide, skin; (*de serpent*) slough; *pl* (*butin*) spoils; **d. (mortelle)** mortal remains. ◆**dépouill/er** *vt* (*animal*) to skin, flay; (*analyser*) to go through, analyse; **d.** (*dégarnir*) to strip of; (*déposséder*) to deprive of; **se d. de** to rid ou divest oneself of, cast off; **d. un scrutin** to count votes. ◆**—é** *a* (*arbre*) bare; (*style*) austere, spare; **d.** be bereft of. ◆**—ement** *nm* (*de document etc*) analysis; (*privation*) deprivation; (*sobriété*) austerity; **d. du scrutin** counting of the votes.

dépourvu [depurvy] *a* **d.** devoid of; **prendre qn au d.** to catch s.o. unawares ou off his guard.

dépraver [deprave] *vt* to deprave. ◆**dépravation** *nf* depravity.

dépréci/er [depresje] *vt* (*dénigrer*) to disparage; (*monnaie, immeuble etc*) to depreciate; **— se d.** *vpr* (*baisser*) to depreciate, lose (its) value. ◆**dépréciation** *nf* depreciation.

déprédations [depredasjɔ̃] *nfpl* damage, ravages.

dépression [depresjɔ̃] *nf* depression; **zone de d.** trough of low pressure; **d. nerveuse** nervous breakdown; **d. économique** slump. ◆**dépressif, -ive** *a* depressive. ◆**déprime** *nf* la **d.** (*dépression*) Fam the blues. ◆**déprim/er** *vt* to depress. ◆**—é** *a* depressed.

depuis [dəpɥi] *prép* since; **d. lundi** since Monday; **d. qu'elle est partie** since she left; **j'habite ici d. un mois** I've been living here for a month; **d. quand êtes-vous là?** how long have you been here?; **d. peu/longtemps** for a short/long time; **d. Paris jusqu'à Londres** from Paris to London; **—** *adv* since; (*ensuite*) ever since.

députation [depytasjɔ̃] *nf* (*groupe*) deputation, delegation; **candidat à la d.** parliamentary candidate. ◆**député** *nm* delegate, deputy; (*au parlement*) deputy, = *Br* MP, = *Am* congressman, congresswoman.

déracin/er [derasine] *vt* (*personne, arbre etc*) to uproot; (*préjugés etc*) to eradicate, root out. ◆**—ement** *nm* uprooting; eradication.

déraill/er [deraje] *vi* **1** (*train*) to jump the rails, be derailed; **faire d.** to derail. **2** (*divaguer*) *Fam* to drivel, talk through one's hat. ◆**—ement** *nm* (*de train*) derailment. ◆**—eur** *nm* (*de bicyclette*) dérailleur (gear change).

déraisonnable [derɛzɔnabl] *a* unreasonable. ◆**déraisonner** *vi* to talk nonsense.

dérang/er [derɑ̃ʒe] *vt* (*affaires*) to disturb, upset; (*estomac*) to upset; (*projets*) to mess up, upset; (*vêtements*) to mess up; (*cerveau, esprit*) to derange; **d. qn** to disturb *ou* bother *ou* trouble s.o.; **je viendrai si ça ne te dérange pas** I'll come if that doesn't put you out *ou* if that's not imposing; **ça vous dérange si je fume?** do you mind if I smoke?; **— se d.** *vpr* to put oneself to a lot of trouble (**pour faire** to do), (*se déplacer*) to move; **ne te dérange pas!** don't trouble yourself!, don't bother! ◆**—ement** *nm* (*gêne*) bother, inconvenience; (*désordre*) disorder; **en d.** (*téléphone etc*) out of order.

dérap/er [derape] *vi* to skid. ◆**—age** *nm* skid; (*des prix, de l'inflation*) *Fig* loss of control (**de** over).

dératé [derate] *nm* **courir comme un d.** to run like mad.

dérégl/er [deregle] *vt* (*mécanisme*) to put out of order; (*estomac, habitudes*) to upset; (*esprit*) to unsettle; **— se d.** *vpr* (*montre, appareil*) to go wrong. ◆**—é** *a* out of order; (*vie, mœurs*) dissolute, wild; (*imagination*) wild. ◆**dérèglement** *nm* (*de mécanisme*) breakdown; (*d'esprit*) disorder; (*d'estomac*) upset.

dérider [deride] *vt*, **— se d.** *vpr* to cheer up.

dérision [derizjɔ̃] *nf* derision, mockery; **tourner en d.** to mock, deride; **par d.** derisively; **de d.** derisive. ◆**dérisoire** *a* ridiculous, derisory, derisive.

dérive [deriv] *nf* *Nau* drift; **partir à la d.** (*navire*) to drift out to sea; **aller à la d.** (*navire*) to go adrift; (*entreprise etc*) *Fig* to drift (towards ruin). ◆**dériv/er** *vi* *Nau Av* to drift; **d.** (**de** (*venir*) to derive from, be derived from; **— vt** (*cours d'eau*) to divert; *Ling* to derive (**de** from). ◆**—é** *nm* *Ling Ch* derivative; (*produit*) by-product. ◆**dérivatif** *nm* distraction (**à** from). ◆**dérivation** *nf* (*de cours d'eau*) diversion; *Ling* derivation; (*déviation routière*) bypass.

dermatologie [dɛrmatɔlɔʒi] *nf* dermatology.

dernier -ière [dɛrnje, -jɛr] *a* last; (*nouvelles, mode*) latest; (*étage*) top; (*degré*) highest; (*qualité*) lowest; **le d. rang** the back *ou* last row; **ces derniers mois** these past few months, these last *ou* final months; **de la dernière importance** of (the) utmost importance; **en d.** last; **— nmf** last (person *ou* one); **ce d.** (*de deux*) the latter; (*de plusieurs*) the last-mentioned; **être le d. de la classe** to be (at) the bottom of the class; **le d. des derniers** the lowest of the low; **le d. de mes soucis** the least of my worries. ◆**d.-né**, ◆**dernière-née** *nmf* youngest (child). ◆**dernièrement** *adv* recently.

dérob/er [derɔbe] *vt* (*voler*) to steal (**à** from); (*cacher*) to hide (**à** from); **— se d.** *vpr* to get out of one's obligations; (*s'éloigner*) to slip away; (*éviter de répondre*) to dodge the issue; **se d. à** (*obligations*) to shirk, avoid; (*regards*) to hide from; **ses jambes se sont dérobées sous lui** his legs gave way beneath him. ◆**—é** *a* (*porte etc*) hidden, secret; **à la dérobée** *adv* on the sly, stealthily. ◆**dérobade** *nf* dodge, evasion.

déroger [derɔʒe] *vi* **d. à une règle/***etc* to depart from a rule/*etc*. ◆**dérogation** *nf* exemption, (special) dispensation.

dérouiller [deruje] *vt* **d. qn** (*battre*) *Arg* to thrash *ou* thump s.o.; **se d. les jambes** *Fam* to stretch one's legs.

déroul/er [derule] *vt* (*carte etc*) to unroll; (*film*) to unwind; **— se d.** *vpr* (*événement*) to take place, pass off; (*paysage, souvenirs*) to unfold; (*récit*) to develop. ◆**—ement** *nm* (*d'une action*) unfolding, development; (*cours*) course;

dérouter [derute] *vt* (*avion, navire*) to divert, reroute; (*candidat etc*) to baffle; (*poursuivant*) to throw off the scent.

derrick [derik] *nm* derrick.

derrière [dɛrjɛr] *prép & adv* behind; **d. moi** behind me, *Am* in back of me; **assis d.** (*dans une voiture*) sitting in the back; **de d.** (*roue*) back, rear; (*pattes*) hind; **par d.** (*attaquer*) from behind, from the rear; **— nm** (*de maison etc*) back, rear; (*fesses*) behind, bottom.

des [de] *voir* **de** [1,2], **le**.

dès [dɛ] *prép* from; **d. cette époque** (as) from that time, from that time on; **d. le début** (right) from the start; **d. son enfance** since *ou* from (his *ou* her) childhood; **d. le**

sixième siècle as early as *ou* as far back as the sixth century; **d. l'aube** at (the crack of) dawn; **d. qu'elle viendra** as soon as she comes.

désabusé [dezabyze] *a* disenchanted, disillusioned.

désaccord [dezakɔr] *nm* disagreement. ◆**désaccordé** *a Mus* out of tune.

désaccoutumer (se) [sədezakutyme] *vpr* **se d. de** to lose the habit of.

désaffecté [dezafɛkte] *a* (*école etc*) disused.

désaffection [dezafɛksjɔ̃] *nf* loss of affection, disaffection (**pour** for).

désagréable [dezagreabl] *a* unpleasant, disagreeable. ◆**—ment** [-əmɑ̃] *adv* unpleasantly.

désagréger [dezagreʒe] *vt*, **— se d.** *vpr* to disintegrate, break up. ◆**désagrégation** *nf* disintegration.

désagrément [dezagremɑ̃] *nm* annoyance, trouble.

désaltér/er [dezaltere] *vt* **d. qn** to quench s.o.'s thirst; **se d.** to quench one's thirst. ◆**—ant** *a* thirst-quenching.

désamorcer [dezamɔrse] *vt* (*obus, situation*) to defuse.

désappointer [dezapwɛ̃te] *vt* to disappoint.

désapprouver [dezapruve] *vt* to disapprove of; **—** *vi* to disapprove. ◆**désapprobateur, -trice** *a* disapproving. ◆**désapprobation** *nf* disapproval.

désarçonner [dezarsɔne] *vt* (*jockey*) to throw, unseat; (*déconcerter*) *Fig* to nonpluss, throw.

désarm/er [dezarme] *vt* (*émouvoir*) & *Mil* to disarm; **—** *vi Mil* to disarm; (*céder*) to let up. ◆**—ant** *a* (*charme etc*) disarming. ◆**—é** *a* (*sans défense*) unarmed; *Fig* helpless. ◆**—ement** *nm* (*de nation*) disarmament.

désarroi [dezarwa] *nm* (*angoisse*) distress.

désarticuler [dezartikyle] *vt* (*membre*) to dislocate.

désastre [dezastr] *nm* disaster. ◆**désastreux, -euse** *a* disastrous.

désavantage [dezavɑ̃taʒ] *nm* disadvantage, handicap; (*inconvénient*) drawback, disadvantage. ◆**désavantager** *vt* to put at a disadvantage, handicap. ◆**désavantageux, -euse** *a* disadvantageous.

désaveu, -x [dezavø] *nm* repudiation. ◆**désavouer** *vt* (*livre, personne etc*) to disown, repudiate.

désaxé, -ée [dezakse] *a* & *nmf* unbalanced (person).

desceller [desele] *vt* (*pierre etc*) to loosen; **— se d.** *vpr* to come loose.

descend/re [desɑ̃dr] *vi* (*aux être*) to come *ou* go down, descend (**de** from); (*d'un train etc*) to get off *ou* out, alight (**de** from); (*d'un arbre*) to climb down (**de** from); (*nuit, thermomètre*) to fall; (*marée*) to go out; **d. à** (*une bassesse*) to stoop to; **d. à l'hôtel** to put up at a hotel; **d. de** (*être issu de*) to be descended from; **d. de cheval** to dismount; **d. en courant/flânant/etc** to run/stroll/*etc* down; **—** *vt* (*aux avoir*) (*escalier*) to come *ou* go down, descend; (*objets*) to bring *ou* take down; (*avion*) to bring *ou* shoot down; **d. qn** (*tuer*) *Fam* to bump s.o. off. ◆**—ant, -ante 1** *a* descending; (*marée*) outgoing. **2** *nmf* (*personne*) descendant. ◆**descendance** *nf* (*enfants*) descendants; (*origine*) descent.

descente [desɑ̃t] *nf* (*action*) descent; (*irruption*) raid (**dans** upon); (*en parachute*) drop; (*pente*) slope; **la d. des bagages** bringing *ou* taking down the luggage; **il fut accueilli à sa d. d'avion** he was met as he got off the plane; **d. à skis** downhill run; **d. de lit** (*tapis*) bedside rug.

descriptif, -ive [dɛskriptif, -iv] *a* descriptive. ◆**description** *nf* description.

déségrégation [desegregasjɔ̃] *nf* desegregation.

désemparé [dezɑ̃pare] *a* distraught, at a loss; (*navire*) crippled.

désemplir [dezɑ̃plir] *vi* **ce magasin/etc ne désemplit pas** this shop/*etc* is always crowded.

désenchant/er [dezɑ̃ʃɑ̃te] *vt* to disenchant. ◆**—ement** *nm* disenchantment.

désencombrer [dezɑ̃kɔ̃bre] *vt* (*passage etc*) to clear.

désenfler [dezɑ̃fle] *vi* to go down, become less swollen.

déséquilibre [dezekilibr] *nm* (*inégalité*) imbalance; (*mental*) unbalance; **en d.** (*meuble etc*) unsteady. ◆**déséquilibrer** *vt* to throw off balance; (*esprit, personne*) *Fig* to unbalance.

désert [dezɛr] *a* deserted; **île déserte** desert island; **—** *nm* desert, wilderness. ◆**désertique** *a* (*région etc*) desert-.

déserter [dezɛrte] *vti* to desert. ◆**déserteur** *nm Mil* deserter. ◆**désertion** *nf* desertion.

désespér/er [dezɛspere] *vi* to despair (**de** of); **—** *vt* to drive to despair; **— se d.** *vpr* to (be in) despair. ◆**—ant** *a* (*enfant etc*) that drives one to despair, hopeless. ◆**—é, -ée** *a* (*personne*) in despair, despairing; (*cas, situation*) desperate, hopeless; (*efforts, cris*) desperate; **—** *nmf* (*suicidé*) person driven to despair *ou* desperation. ◆—ément *adv* desperately. ◆**désespoir** *nm* despair; **au d.** in despair; **en d. de cause** in desperation, as a (desperate) last resort.

déshabiller [dezabije] *vt* to undress, strip; — **se d.** *vpr* to get undressed, undress.

déshabituer [dezabitɥe] *vt* **d. qn de** to break s.o. of the habit of.

désherb/er [dezerbe] *vti* to weed. ◆—ant *nm* weed killer.

déshérit/er [dezerite] *vt* to disinherit. ◆—é *a* (*pauvre*) underprivileged; (*laid*) ill-favoured.

déshonneur [dezɔnœr] *nm* dishonour, disgrace. ◆**déshonor/er** *vt* to disgrace, dishonour. ◆—ant *a* dishonourable.

déshydrater [dezidrate] *vt* to dehydrate; — **se d.** *vpr* to become dehydrated.

désigner [dezine] *vt* (*montrer*) to point to, point out; (*élire*) to appoint, designate; (*signifier*) to indicate, designate; **ses qualités le désignent pour** his qualities mark him out for. ◆**désignation** *nf* designation.

désillusion [dezilyzjɔ̃] *nf* disillusion(ment). ◆**désillusionner** *vt* to disillusion.

désincarné [dezɛ̃karne] *a* (*esprit*) disembodied.

désinence [dezinɑ̃s] *nf* Gram ending.

désinfect/er [dezɛ̃fɛkte] *vt* to disinfect. ◆—ant *nm* & *a* disinfectant. ◆**désinfection** *nf* disinfection.

désinformation [dezɛ̃fɔrmasjɔ̃] *nf* Pol misinformation.

désintégrer (se) [sədezɛ̃tegre] *vpr* to disintegrate. ◆**désintégration** *nf* disintegration.

désintéress/er (se) [sədezɛ̃terese] *vpr* **se d. de** to lose interest in, take no further interest in. ◆—é *a* (*altruiste*) disinterested. ◆—ement [-ɛsmɑ̃] *nm* (*altruisme*) disinterestedness. ◆**désintérêt** *nm* lack of interest.

désintoxiquer [dezɛ̃tɔksike] *vt* (*alcoolique, drogué*) to cure.

désinvolte [dezɛ̃vɔlt] *a* (*dégagé*) easy-going, casual; (*insolent*) offhand, casual. ◆**désinvolture** *nf* casualness; offhandedness.

désir [dezir] *nm* desire, wish. ◆**désirable** *a* desirable. ◆**désirer** *vt* to want, desire; (*convoiter*) to desire; **je désire venir** I would like to come, I wish *ou* want to come; **je désire que tu viennes** I want you to come; **ça laisse à d.** it leaves something *ou* a lot to be desired. ◆**désireux, -euse** *a* **d. de faire** anxious *ou* eager to do, desirous of doing.

désist/er (se) [sədeziste] *vpr* (*candidat etc*) to withdraw. ◆—ement *nm* withdrawal.

désobé/ir [dezɔbeir] *vi* to disobey; **d. à qn** to disobey s.o. ◆—issant *a* disobedient. ◆**désobéissance** *nf* disobedience (à to).

désobligeant [dezɔbliʒɑ̃] *a* disagreeable, unkind.

désodorisant [dezɔdɔrizɑ̃] *nm* air freshener.

désœuvré [dezœvre] *a* idle, unoccupied. ◆**désœuvrement** *nm* idleness.

désol/er [dezɔle] *vt* to distress, upset (very much); — **se d.** *vpr* to be distressed *ou* upset (**de** at). ◆—ant *a* distressing, upsetting. ◆—é *a* (*région*) desolate; (*affligé*) distressed; **être d.** (*navré*) to be sorry (**que** (+ *sub*) that, **de faire** to do). ◆**désolation** *nf* (*peine*) distress, grief.

désolidariser (se) [sədesɔlidarize] *vpr* to dissociate oneself (**de** from).

désopilant [dezɔpilɑ̃] *a* hilarious, screamingly funny.

désordre [dezɔrdr] *nm* (*de papiers, affaires, idées*) mess, muddle, disorder; (*de cheveux, pièce*) untidiness; Méd disorder; *pl* (*émeutes*) disorder, unrest; **en d.** untidy, messy. ◆**désordonné** *a* (*personne, chambre*) untidy, messy.

désorganiser [dezɔrganize] *vt* to disorganize. ◆**désorganisation** *nf* disorganization.

désorienter [dezɔrjɑ̃te] *vt* **d. qn** to disorientate *ou Am* disorient s.o., make s.o. lose his bearings; (*déconcerter*) to bewilder s.o. ◆**désorientation** *nf* disorientation.

désormais [dezɔrmɛ] *adv* from now on, in future, henceforth.

désosser [dezose] *vt* (*viande*) to bone.

despote [dɛspɔt] *nm* despot. ◆**despotique** *a* despotic. ◆**despotisme** *nm* despotism.

desquels, desquelles [dekɛl] *voir* lequel.

dessaisir (se) [sədesezir] *vpr* **se d. de qch** to part with sth, relinquish sth.

dessaler [desale] *vt* (*poisson etc*) to remove the salt from (by smoking).

dessécher [desefe] *vt* (*végétation*) to dry up, wither; (*gorge, bouche*) to dry, parch; (*fruits*) to desiccate, dry; (*cœur*) to harden; — **se d.** *vpr* (*plante*) to wither, dry up; (*peau*) to dry (up), get dry; (*maigrir*) to waste away.

dessein [desɛ̃] *nm* aim, design; **dans le d. de faire** with the aim of doing; **à d.** intentionally.

desserrer [desere] *vt* (*ceinture etc*) to loosen, slacken; (*poing*) to open, unclench;

(*frein*) to release; **il n'a pas desserré les dents** he didn't open his mouth; **— se d.** *vpr* to come loose.

dessert [desɛr] *nm* dessert, sweet.

desserte [desɛrt] *nf* **assurer la d. de** (*village etc*) to provide a (bus *ou* train) service to. ◆**desservir** *vt* **1** (*table*) to clear (away). **2 d. qn** to harm s.o., do s.o. a disservice. **3 l'autobus/etc dessert ce village** the bus/*etc* provides a service to *ou* stops at this village; **ce quartier est bien desservi** this district is well served by public transport.

dessin [desɛ̃] *nm* drawing; (*rapide*) sketch; (*motif*) design, pattern; (*contour*) outline; **d. animé** *Cin* cartoon; **d. humoristique** *Journ* cartoon; **école de d.** art school; **planche à d.** drawing board. ◆**dessinateur, -trice** *nmf* drawer; sketcher; **d. humoristique** cartoonist; **d. de modes** dress designer; **d. industriel** draughtsman, *Am* draftsman. ◆**dessiner** *vt* to draw; (*rapidement*) to sketch; (*meuble, robe etc*) to design; (*indiquer*) to outline, trace; **(bien) la taille** (*vêtement*) to show off the figure; **— se d.** *vpr* (*colline etc*) to stand out, be outlined; (*projet*) to take shape.

dessoûler [desule] *vti* Fam to sober up.

dessous [d(ə)su] *adv* under(neath), beneath, below; **en d.** (*sous*) under(neath); (*agir*) *Fig* in an underhand way; **vêtement de d.** undergarment; **drap de d.** bottom sheet; **— nm** underneath; *pl* (*vêtements*) underclothes; **d. de table** backhander, bribe; **les gens du d.** the people downstairs *ou* below; **avoir le d.** to be defeated, get the worst of it. ◆**d.-de-plat** *nm inv* table mat.

dessus [d(ə)sy] *adv* (*marcher, écrire*) on it; (*monter*) on top (of it), on it; (*lancer, passer*) over it; **de d. la table** off *ou* from the table; **vêtement de d.** outer garment; **drap de d.** top sheet; **par-d.** (*sauter etc*) over (it); **par-d. tout** above all; **— nm** top; (*de chaussure*) upper; **avoir le d.** to have the upper hand, get the best of it; **les gens du d.** the people upstairs *ou* above. ◆**d.-de-lit** *nm inv* bedspread.

déstabiliser [destabilize] *vt* to destabilize.

destin [destɛ̃] *nm* fate, destiny. ◆**destinée** *nf* fate, destiny (*of an individual*).

destiner [destine] *vt* **d. qch à qn** to intend *ou* mean sth for s.o.; **d. qn à** (*carrière, fonction*) to intend *ou* destine s.o. for; **se d. à** (*carrière etc*) to intend *ou* mean to take up; **destiné à mourir/etc** (*condamné*) destined *ou* fated to die/*etc*. ◆**destinataire** *nmf* addressee. ◆**destination** *nf* (*usage*)

purpose; (*lieu*) destination; **à d. de** (*train etc*) (going) to, (bound) for.

destituer [destitɥe] *vt* (*fonctionnaire etc*) to dismiss (from office). ◆**destitution** *nf* dismissal.

destructeur, -trice [destryktœr, -tris] *a* destructive; **— nmf** (*personne*) destroyer. ◆**destructif, -ive** *a* destructive. ◆**destruction** *nf* destruction.

désuet, -ète [desɥɛ, -ɛt] *a* antiquated, obsolete.

désunir [dezynir] *vt* (*famille etc*) to divide, disunite. ◆**désunion** *nf* disunity, dissension.

détacher [detaʃe] *vt* (*ceinture, vêtement*) to undo; (*nœud*) to untie, undo; (*personne, mains*) to untie; (*ôter*) to take off, detach; (*mots*) to pronounce clearly; **d. qn** (*libérer*) to let s.o. loose; (*affecter*) to transfer s.o. (on assignment) (**à** to); **d. les yeux de qn/qch** to take one's eyes off s.o./sth; **— se d.** *vpr* (*chien, prisonnier*) to break loose; (*se dénouer*) to come undone; **se d.** (**de qch**) (*fragment*) to come off (sth); **se d. de** (*amis*) to break away from, grow apart from; **se d.** (**sur**) (*ressortir*) to stand out (against). ◆**—é** *a* (*nœud*) loose, undone. ◆**—ement** *nm* **1** (*indifférence*) detachment. **2** (*de fonctionnaire*) (temporary) transfer; *Mil* detachment.

détacher² [detaʃe] *vt* (*linge etc*) to remove the spots *ou* stains from. ◆**—ant** *nm* stain remover.

détail [detaj] *nm* **1** detail; **en d.** in detail; **le d. de** (*dépenses etc*) a detailing *ou* breakdown of. **2 de d.** (*magasin, prix*) retail; **vendre au d.** to sell retail; (*par petites quantités*) to sell separately; **faire le d.** to retail to the public. ◆**détailler** *vt* **1** (*vendre*) to sell in small quantities *ou* separately; (*au détail*) to (sell) retail. **2** (*énumérer*) to detail. ◆**—ant, -ante** *nmf* retailer. ◆**—é** *a* (*récit etc*) detailed.

détaler [detale] *vi* Fam to run off, make tracks.

détartrer [detartre] *vt* (*chaudière, dents etc*) to scale.

détaxer [detakse] *vt* (*denrée etc*) to reduce the tax on; (*supprimer*) to take the tax off; **produit détaxé** duty-free article.

détecter [detɛkte] *vt* to detect. ◆**détecteur** *nm* (*appareil*) detector. ◆**détection** *nf* detection.

détective [detɛktiv] *nm* **d.** (*privé*) (private) detective.

déteindre* [detɛ̃dr] *vi* (*couleur ou étoffe au lavage*) to run; (*au soleil*) to fade; **ton**

tablier bleu a déteint sur ma chemise the blue of your apron has come off on(to) my shirt; **d. sur qn** (*influencer*) to leave one's mark on s.o.

dételer [detle] *vt* (*chevaux*) to unhitch, unharness.

détend/re [detɑ̃dr] *vt* (*arc etc*) to slacken, relax; (*situation, atmosphère*) to ease; **d. qn** to relax s.o.; — **se d.** *vpr* to slacken, get slack; to ease; (*se reposer*) to relax; (*rapports*) to become less strained. ◆**—u** *a* (*visage, atmosphère*) relaxed; (*ressort, câble*) slack. ◆**détente** *nf* **1** (*d'arc*) slackening; (*de relations*) easing of tension, *Pol* détente; (*repos*) relaxation; (*saut*) leap, spring. **2** (*gâchette*) trigger.

déten/ir* [detnir] *vt* to hold; (*secret, objet volé*) to be in possession of; (*prisonnier*) to hold, detain. ◆**—u, -ue** *nmf* prisoner. ◆**détenteur, -trice** *nmf* (*de record etc*) holder. ◆**détention** *nf* (*d'armes*) possession; (*captivité*) detention; **d. préventive** *Jur* custody.

détergent [detɛrʒɑ̃] *nm* detergent.

détériorer [deterjɔre] *vt* (*abîmer*) to damage; — **se d.** *vpr* (*empirer*) to deteriorate. ◆**détérioration** *nf* damage (de to); (*d'une situation etc*) deterioration (**de** in).

détermin/er [detɛrmine] *vt* (*préciser*) to determine; (*causer*) to bring about; **d. qn à faire** to induce s.o. to do, make s.o. do; **se d. à faire** to resolve *ou* determine to do. ◆**—ant** *a* (*motif*) determining, deciding; (*rôle*) decisive. ◆**—é** *a* (*précis*) specific; (*résolu*) determined. ◆**détermination** *nf* (*fermeté*) determination; (*résolution*) resolve.

déterrer [detɛre] *vt* to dig up, unearth.

détest/er [detɛste] *vt* to hate, detest; **d. faire** to hate doing *ou* to do, detest doing. ◆**—able** *a* awful, foul.

détonateur [detɔnatœr] *nm* detonator. ◆**détonation** *nf* explosion, blast.

détonner [detɔne] *vi* (*contraster*) to jar, to be out of place.

détour [detur] *nm* (*de route etc*) bend, curve; (*crochet*) detour; **sans d.** (*parler*) without beating about the bush; **faire des détours** (*route*) to wind.

détourn/er [deturne] *vt* (*fleuve, convoi etc*) to divert; (*tête*) to turn (away); (*coups*) to ward off; (*conversation, sens*) to change; (*fonds*) to embezzle, misappropriate; (*avion*) to hijack; **d. qn de** (*son devoir, ses amis*) to take *ou* turn s.o. away from; (*sa route*) to lead s.o. away from; (*projet*) to talk s.o. out of; **d. les yeux** to look away,

avert one's eyes; — **se d.** *vpr* to turn aside *ou* away; **se d. de** (*chemin*) to wander *ou* stray from. ◆**—é** *a* (*chemin, moyen*) roundabout, indirect. ◆**—ement** *nm* (*de cours d'eau*) diversion; **d.** (*d'avion*) hijack(ing); **d.** (*de fonds*) embezzlement.

détraqu/er [detrake] *vt* (*mécanisme*) to break, put out of order; — **se d.** *vpr* (*machine*) to go wrong; **se d. l'estomac** to upset one's stomach; **se d. la santé** to ruin one's health. ◆**—é, -ée** *a* out of order; (*cerveau*) deranged; — *nmf* crazy *ou* deranged person.

détremper [detrɑ̃pe] *vt* to soak, saturate.

détresse [detrɛs] *nf* distress; **en d.** (*navire, âme*) in distress; **dans la d.** (*misère*) in (great) distress.

détriment de (au) [odetrimɑ̃də] *prép* to the detriment of.

détritus [detrtys] *nmpl* refuse, rubbish.

détroit [detrwa] *nm* *Géog* strait(s), sound.

détromper [detrɔ̃pe] *vt* to undeceive s.o., put s.o. right; **détrompez-vous!** don't you believe it!

détrôner [detrone] *vt* (*souverain*) to dethrone; (*supplanter*) to supersede, oust.

détrousser [detruse] *vt* (*voyageur etc*) to rob.

détruire* [detrɥir] *vt* (*ravager, tuer*) to destroy; (*projet, santé*) to ruin, wreck, destroy.

dette [dɛt] *nf* debt; **faire des dettes** to run *ou* get into debt; **avoir des dettes** to be in debt.

deuil [dœj] *nm* (*affliction, vêtements*) mourning; (*mort de qn*) bereavement; **porter le d.,** être en **d.** to be in mourning.

deux [dø] *a & nm* two; **d. fois** twice, two times; **tous (les) d.** both; **en moins de d.** *Fam* in no time. ◆**d.-pièces** *nm inv* (*vêtement*) two-piece; (*appartement*) two-roomed flat *ou* Am apartment. ◆**d.-points** *nm inv* *Gram* colon. ◆**d.-roues** *nm inv* two-wheeled vehicle. ◆**d.-temps** *nm inv* two-stroke (engine).

deuxième [døzjɛm] *a & nmf* second. ◆**—ment** *adv* secondly.

dévaler [devale] *vt* (*escalier etc*) to hurtle *ou* race *ou* rush down; — *vi* (*tomber*) to tumble down, come tumbling down.

dévaliser [devalize] *vt* (*détrousser*) to clean out, strip, rob (of everything).

dévaloriser [devalɔrize] **1** *vt*, — **se d.** *vpr* (*monnaie*) to depreciate. **2** *vt* (*humilier etc*) to devalue, disparage. ◆**dévalorisation** *nf* (*de monnaie*) depreciation.

dévaluer [devalɥe] *vt* (*monnaie*) & *Fig* to devalue. ◆**dévaluation** *nf* devaluation.

devancer [d(ə)vɑ̃se] *vt* to get *ou* be ahead of; (*question etc*) to anticipate, forestall; (*surpasser*) to outstrip; **tu m'as devancé** (*action*) you did it before me; (*lieu*) you got there before me. ◆**devancier, -ière** *nmf* predecessor.

devant [d(ə)vɑ̃] *prép & adv* in front (of); **d.** (**l'hôtel***/etc*) in front (of the hotel*/etc*); **marcher d.** (**qn**) to walk in front (of s.o.) *ou* ahead (of s.o.); **passer d.** (**l'église***/etc*) to go past (the church*/etc*); **assis d.** (*dans une voiture*) sitting in the front; **l'avenir est d. toi** the future is ahead of you; **loin d.** a long way ahead *ou* in front; **d. le danger** (*confronté à*) in the face of danger; **d. mes yeux/la loi** before my eyes/the law; – *nm* front; **de d.** (*roue, porte*) front; **patte de d.** foreleg; **par d.** from *ou* at the front; **prendre les devants** (*action*) to take the initiative. ◆**devanture** *nf* (*vitrine*) shop window; (*façade*) shop front.

dévaster [devaste] *vt* (*ruiner*) to devastate. ◆**dévastation** *nf* devastation.

déveine [devɛn] *nf Fam* tough *ou* bad luck.

développ/er [devlɔpe] *vt* to develop; *Phot* to develop, process; – **se d.** *vpr* to develop. ◆**-ement** *nm* development; *Phot* developing, processing; **les pays en voie de d.** the developing countries.

devenir* [dəvnir] *vi* (*aux* **être**) to become; (*vieux, difficile etc*) to get, grow, become; (*rouge, bleu etc*) to turn, go, become; **d. un papillon/un homme***/etc* to grow into a butterfly *ou* a man*/etc*; **qu'est-il devenu?** what's become of him *ou* it?, where's he *ou* it got to?; **qu'est-ce que tu deviens?** *Fam* how are you doing?

dévergond/er (se) [sədevɛrgɔ̃de] *vpr* to fall into dissolute ways. ◆**-é** *a* dissolute, licentious.

déverser [devɛrse] *vt* (*liquide, rancune*) to pour out; (*bombes, ordures*) to dump; – **se d.** *vpr* (*liquide*) to empty, pour out (**dans** into).

dévêtir [devetir] *vt,* – **se d.** *vpr Litt* to undress.

dévier [devje] *vt* (*circulation, conversation*) to divert; (*coup, rayons*) to deflect; – *vi* (*de ses principes etc*) to deviate (**de** from); (*de sa route*) to veer (off course). ◆**déviation** *nf* deflection; deviation; (*chemin*) bypass; (*itinéraire provisoire*) diversion.

deviner [d(ə)vine] *vt* to guess (**que** that); (*avenir*) to predict; **d. (le jeu de) qn** to see through s.o. ◆**devinette** *nf* riddle.

devis [d(ə)vi] *nm* estimate (*of cost of work to be done*).

dévisager [devizaʒe] *vt* **d. qn** to stare at s.o.

devise [dəviz] *nf* (*légende*) motto; *pl* (*monnaie*) (foreign) currency.

dévisser [devise] *vt* to unscrew, undo; – **se d.** *vpr* (*bouchon etc*) to come undone.

dévoiler [devwale] *vt* (*révéler*) to disclose; (*statue*) to unveil; – **se d.** *vpr* (*mystère*) to come to light.

devoir* [1] [d(ə)vwar] *v aux* **1** (*nécessité*) **je dois refuser** I must refuse, I have (got) to refuse; **j'ai dû refuser** I had to refuse. **2** (*forte probabilité*) **il doit être tard** it must be late; **elle a dû oublier** she must have forgotten; **il ne doit pas être bête** he can't be stupid. **3** (*obligation*) **tu dois l'aider** you should help her, you ought to help her; **il aurait dû venir** he should have come, he ought to have come; **vous devriez rester** you should stay, you ought to stay. **4** (*supposition*) **elle doit venir** she should be coming, she's supposed to be coming, she's due to come; **le train devait arriver à midi** the train was due (to arrive) at noon; **je devais le voir** I was (due) to see him.

devoir* [2] [d(ə)vwar] *vt* **1** to owe; **d. qch à qn** to owe s.o. sth, owe sth to s.o.; **l'argent qui m'est dû** the money due to *ou* owing to me, the money owed (to) me; **se d. à** to have to devote oneself to; **comme il se doit** as is proper. **2** *nm* duty; *Scol* exercise; **devoir(s)** (*travail à faire à la maison*) *Scol* homework; **présenter ses devoirs à qn** to pay one's respects to s.o.

dévolu [devɔly] **1** *a* **d. à qn** (*pouvoirs, tâche*) vested in s.o., allotted to s.o. **2** *nm* **jeter son d. sur** to set one's heart on.

dévor/er [devɔre] *vt* (*manger*) to gobble up, devour; (*incendie*) to ravage, devour; (*tourmenter, lire*) to devour. ◆**-ant** *a* (*faim*) ravenous; (*passion*) devouring.

dévot, -ote [devo, -ɔt] *a & nmf* devout *ou* pious (person). ◆**dévotion** *nf* devotion.

dévou/er (se) [sədevwe] *vpr* (*à une tâche*) to dedicate oneself, devote oneself (**à** to); **se d.** (**pour qn**) (*se sacrifier*) to sacrifice oneself for s.o. ◆**-é** *a* (*ami, femme etc*) devoted (**à qn** to s.o.); (*domestique, soldat etc*) dedicated. ◆**-ement** [-umɑ̃] *nm* devotion, dedication; (*de héros*) devotion to duty.

dévoyé, -ée [devwaje] *a & nmf* delinquent.

dextérité [dɛksterite] *nf* dexterity, skill.

diabète [djabɛt] *nm Méd* diabetes. ◆**diabétique** *a & nmf* diabetic.

diable [djɑbl] *nm* devil; **d.!** heavens!; **où/pourquoi/que d.?** where/why/what the devil?; **un bruit/vent***/etc* **du d.** the devil of a noise/wind/*etc*; **à la d.** anyhow; **habiter au d.** to live miles from anywhere. ◆**diablerie** *nf* devilment, mischief. ◆**diablesse** *nf* **c'est une d.** *Fam* she's a devil. ◆**diablotin** *nm* (*enfant*) little devil. ◆**diabolique** *a* diabolical, devilish.

diabolo [djabɔlo] *nm* (*boisson*) lemonade *ou Am* lemon soda flavoured with syrup.

diacre [djakr] *nm Rel* deacon.

diadème [djadɛm] *nm* diadem.

diagnostic [djagnɔstik] *nm* diagnosis. ◆**diagnostiquer** *vt* to diagnose.

diagonal, -aux [djagɔnal, -o] *a* diagonal. ◆**diagonale** *nf* diagonal (line); **en d.** diagonally.

diagramme [djagram] *nm* (*schéma*) diagram; (*courbe*) graph.

dialecte [djalɛkt] *nm* dialect.

dialogue [djalɔg] *nm* conversation; *Pol Cin Th Littér* dialogue. ◆**dialoguer** *vi* to have a conversation *ou* dialogue.

dialyse [djaliz] *nf Méd* dialysis.

diamant [djamɑ̃] *nm* diamond.

diamètre [djamɛtr] *nm* diameter. ◆**diamétralement** *adv* **d. opposés** (*avis etc*) diametrically opposed, poles apart.

diapason [djapazɔ̃] *nm Mus* tuning fork; **être/se mettre au d.** de *Fig* to be/get in tune with.

diaphragme [djafragm] *nm* diaphragm.

diapositive, *Fam* **diapo** [djapozitiv, djapo] *nf* (colour) slide, transparency.

diarrhée [djare] *nf* diarrh(o)ea.

diatribe [djatrib] *nf* diatribe.

dictateur [diktatœr] *nm* dictator. ◆**dictatorial, -aux** *a* dictatorial. ◆**dictature** *nf* dictatorship.

dict/er [dikte] *vt* to dictate (à to). ◆**—ée** *nf* dictation. ◆**dictaphone®** *nm* dictaphone®.

diction [diksjɔ̃] *nf* diction, elocution.

dictionnaire [diksjɔnɛr] *nm* dictionary.

dicton [diktɔ̃] *nm* saying, adage, dictum.

didactique [didaktik] *a* didactic.

dièse [djɛz] *a & nm Mus* sharp.

diesel [djezɛl] *a & nm* (*moteur*) **d.** diesel (engine).

diète [djɛt] *nf* (*jeûne*) starvation diet; **à la d.** on a starvation diet. ◆**diététicien, -ienne** *nmf* dietician. ◆**diététique** *nf* dietetics; — *a* (*magasin etc*) health-; **aliment** *ou* **produit d.** health food.

dieu, -x [djø] *nm* god; **D.** God; **D. merci!** thank God!, thank goodness!

diffamer [difame] *vt* (*en paroles*) to slander; (*par écrit*) to libel. ◆**diffamation** *nf* defamation; (*en paroles*) slander; (*par écrit*)

libel; **campagne de d.** smear campaign. ◆**diffamatoire** *a* slanderous; libellous.

différent [diferɑ̃] *a* different; *pl* (*divers*) different, various; **d. de** different from *ou* to, unlike. ◆**différemment** [-amɑ̃] *adv* differently (de from, to). ◆**différence** *nf* difference (**de** in); **à la d. de** unlike; **faire la d. entre** to make a distinction between.

différencier [diferɑ̃sje] *vt* to differentiate (**de** from); — **se d.** *vpr* to differ (**de** from).

différend [diferɑ̃] *nm* difference (of opinion).

différentiel, -ielle [diferɑ̃sjɛl] *a* differential.

différ/er [difere] **1** *vi* to differ (**de** from). **2** *vt* (*remettre*) to postpone, defer. ◆**—é** *nm* **en d.** (*émission*) (pre)recorded.

difficile [difisil] *a* difficult; (*exigeant*) fussy, particular, hard *ou* difficult to please; **c'est d. à faire** it's hard *ou* difficult to do; **il (nous) est d. de faire** ça it's hard *ou* difficult (for us) to do that. ◆**—ment** *adv* with difficulty; **d. lisible** not easily read. ◆**difficulté** *nf* difficulty (à **faire** in doing); **en d.** in a difficult situation.

difforme [difɔrm] *a* deformed, misshapen. ◆**difformité** *nf* deformity.

diffus [dify] *a* (*lumière, style*) diffuse.

diffuser [difyze] *vt* (*émission, nouvelle etc*) to broadcast; (*lumière, chaleur*) *Phys* to diffuse; (*livre*) to distribute. ◆**diffusion** *nf* broadcasting; (*de connaissances*) & *Phys* diffusion; (*de livre*) distribution.

digérer [diʒere] *vt* to digest; (*endurer*) *Fam* to stomach; — *vi* to digest. ◆**digeste** *a*, ◆**digestible** *a* digestible. ◆**digestif, -ive** *a* digestive; — *nm* after-dinner liqueur. ◆**digestion** *nf* digestion.

digitale [diʒital] *af* **empreinte d.** fingerprint.

digne [diɲ] *a* (*fier*) dignified; (*honnête*) worthy; **d. de qn** worthy of s.o.; **d. d'admiration/etc** worthy of *ou* deserving of admiration/*etc*; **d. de foi** reliable. ◆**dignement** *adv* with dignity. ◆**dignitaire** *nm* dignitary. ◆**dignité** *nf* dignity.

digression [digresjɔ̃] *nf* digression.

digue [dig] *nf* dyke, dike.

dilapider [dilapide] *vt* to squander, waste.

dilater [dilate] *vt*, — **se d.** *vpr* to dilate, expand. ◆**dilatation** *nf* dilation, expansion.

dilatoire [dilatwar] *a* **manœuvre** *ou* **moyen d.** delaying tactic.

dilemme [dilɛm] *nm* dilemma.

dilettante [diletɑ̃t] *nmf Péj* dabbler, amateur.

diligent [diliʒɑ̃] *a* (*prompt*) speedy and effi-

cient; (*soin*) diligent. ◆**diligence** *nf* **1**
(*célérité*) speedy efficiency; **faire d.** to make
haste. **2** (*véhicule*) *Hist* stagecoach.
diluer [dilɥe] *vt* to dilute. ◆**dilution** *nf*
dilution.
diluvienne [dilyvjεn] *af* **pluie d.** torrential
rain.
dimanche [dimɑ̃ʃ] *nm* Sunday.
dimension [dimɑ̃sjɔ̃] *nf* dimension; **à deux
dimensions** two-dimensional.
diminuer [diminɥe] *vt* to reduce, decrease;
(*frais*) to cut down (on), reduce; (*mérite,
forces*) to diminish, lessen, reduce; **d. qn**
(*rabaisser*) to diminish s.o., lessen s.o.; − *vi*
(*réserves, nombre*) to decrease, diminish;
(*jours*) to get shorter, draw in; (*prix*)
to drop, decrease. ◆**diminutif, -ive** *a* &
nm *Gram* diminutive; − *nm* (*prénom*)
nickname. ◆**diminution** *nf* reduction,
decrease (**de** in).
dinde [dε̃d] *nf* turkey (hen), *Culin* turkey.
◆**dindon** *nm* turkey (cock).
dîner [dine] *vi* to have dinner, dine; (*au
Canada, en Belgique etc*) to (have) lunch; −
nm dinner; lunch; (*soirée*) dinner party.
◆**dînette** *nf* (*jouet*) doll's dinner service;
(*jeu*) doll's dinner party. ◆**dîneur, -euse**
nmf diner.
dingue [dε̃g] *a* *Fam* nuts, screwy, crazy; −
nmf *Fam* nutcase.
dinosaure [dinozɔr] *nm* dinosaur.
diocèse [djɔsεz] *nm* *Rel* diocese.
diphtérie [difteri] *nf* diphtheria.
diphtongue [diftɔ̃g] *nf* *Ling* diphthong.
diplomate [diplɔmat] *nm* *Pol* diplomat; −
nmf (*négociateur*) diplomatist; − *a* (*habile,
plein de tact*) diplomatic. ◆**diplomatie**
[-asi] *nf* (*tact*) & *Pol* diplomacy; (*carrière*)
diplomatic service. ◆**diplomatique** *a* *Pol*
diplomatic.
diplôme [diplom] *nm* certificate, diploma;
Univ degree. ◆**diplômé, -ée** *a* & *nmf*
qualified (person); **être d. (de)** *Univ* to be a
graduate (of).
dire* [dir] *vt* (*mot, avis etc*) to say; (*vérité,
secret, heure etc*) to tell; (*penser*) to think
(**de** of, about); **d. des bêtises** to talk
nonsense; **elle dit que tu mens** she says
(that) you're lying; **d. qch à qn** to tell s.o.
sth, say sth to s.o.; **d. à qn que** to tell s.o.
that, say to s.o. that; **d. à qn de faire** to tell
s.o. to do; **dit-il** he said; **dit-on** they say; **d.
que oui/non** to say yes/no; **d. du mal/du
bien de** to speak ill/well of; **on dirait un
château** it looks like a castle; **on dirait du
Mozart** it sounds like Mozart; **on dirait du
cabillaud** it tastes like cod; **on dirait que il**

would seem that; **ça ne me dit rien** (*envie*) I
don't feel like *ou* fancy that; (*souvenir*) it
doesn't ring a bell; **ça vous dit de rester?** do
you feel like staying?; **dites donc!** I say!; **ça
va sans d.** that goes without saying; **autrement dit** in other words; **c'est beaucoup d.**
that's going too far; **à l'heure dite** at the
agreed time; **à vrai d.** to tell the truth; **il se
dit malade/etc** he says he's ill/*etc*; **ça ne se
dit pas** that's not said; − *nm* **au d. de**
according to; **les dires de** (*déclarations*) the
statements of.
direct [dirεkt] *a* direct; (*chemin*) straight,
direct; (*manière*) straightforward, direct;
train d. through train, non-stop train; − *nm*
en d. (*émission*) live; **un d. du gauche** *Boxe*
a straight left. ◆**-ement** *adv* directly;
(*immédiatement*) straight (away), directly.
directeur, -trice [dirεktœr, -tris] *nmf* director; (*d'entreprise*) manager(ess), director;
(*de journal*) editor; *Scol* headmaster, headmistress; − *a* (*principe*) guiding; **idées** *ou*
lignes directrices guidelines.
direction [dirεksjɔ̃] *nf* **1** (*de société*) running, management; (*de club*) leadership,
running; (*d'études*) supervision; (*mécanisme*) *Aut* steering; **avoir la d. de** to be in
charge of; **sous la d. de** (*orchestre*)
conducted by; **la d.** (*équipe dirigeante*) the
management; **une d.** (*fonction*) *Com* a
directorship; *Scol* a headmastership; *Journ*
an editorship. **2** (*sens*) direction; **en d. de**
(*train*) (going) to, for.
directive [dirεktiv] *nf* directive, instruction.
dirig/er [diriʒe] *vt* (*société*) to run, manage,
direct; (*débat, cheval*) to lead; (*véhicule*) to
steer; (*orchestre*) to conduct; (*études*) to
supervise, direct; (*conscience*) to guide;
(*orienter*) to turn (**vers** towards); (*arme,
lumière*) to point, direct (**vers** towards); **se
d. vers** (*lieu, objet*) to make one's way
towards, head *ou* make for; (*dans une
carrière*) to turn towards. ◆**—eant** *a*
(*classe*) ruling; − *nm* (*de pays, club*) leader;
(*d'entreprise*) manager. ◆**—é** *a* (*économie*)
planned. ◆**—eable** *a* & *nm* (*ballon*) *Av*
airship. ◆**dirigisme** *nm* *Écon* state
control.
dis [di] *voir* **dire.**
discern/er [disεrne] *vt* (*voir*) to make out,
discern; (*différencier*) to distinguish.
◆**—ement** *nm* discernment, discrimination.
disciple [disipl] *nm* disciple, follower.
discipline [disiplin] *nf* (*règle, matière*) discipline. ◆**disciplinaire** *a* disciplinary.
◆**disciplin/er** *vt* (*contrôler, éduquer*) to

discipline; — **se d.** *vpr* to discipline oneself. ◆—é a well-disciplined.

disco [disko] *nf Fam* disco; **aller en d.** to go to a disco.

discontinu [diskɔtiny] *a* (*ligne*) discontinuous; (*bruit etc*) intermittent. ◆**discontinuer** *vi* **sans d.** without stopping.

disconvenir [diskɔvnir] *vi* **je n'en disconviens pas** I don't deny it.

discorde [diskɔrd] *nf* discord. ◆**discordance** *nf* (*de caractères*) clash, conflict; (*de son*) discord. ◆**discordant** *a* (*son*) discordant; (*témoignages*) conflicting; (*couleurs*) clashing.

discothèque [diskɔtɛk] *nf* record library; (*club*) discotheque.

discours [diskur] *nm* speech; (*écrit littéraire*) discourse. ◆**discourir** *vi* *Péj* to speechify, ramble on.

discourtois [diskurtwa] *a* discourteous.

discrédit [diskredi] *nm* disrepute, discredit. ◆**discréditer** *vt* to discredit, bring into disrepute; — **se d.** *vpr* (*personne*) to become discredited.

discret, -ète [diskre, -ɛt] *a* (*personne, manière etc*) discreet; (*vêtement*) simple. ◆**discrètement** *adv* discreetly; (*s'habiller*) simply. ◆**discrétion** *nf* discretion; **vin/etc à d.** as much wine/etc as one wants. ◆**discrétionnaire** *a* discretionary.

discrimination [diskriminasjɔ] *nf* (*ségrégation*) discrimination. ◆**discriminatoire** *a* discriminatory.

disculper [diskylpe] *vt* to exonerate (**de** from).

discussion [diskysjɔ] *nf* discussion; (*conversation*) talk; (*querelle*) argument; **pas de d.!** no argument! ◆**discut/er** *vt* to discuss; (*familièrement*) to talk over; (*contester*) to question; **ça peut se d.,** **ça se discute** that's arguable; — *vi* (*parler*) to talk (**de** about, **avec** with); (*répliquer*) to argue; **d. de ou sur qch** to discuss sth. ◆**—é** *a* (*auteur*) much discussed *ou* debated; (*théorie, question*) disputed, controversial. ◆**—able** *a* arguable, debatable.

disette [dizet] *nf* food shortage.

diseuse [dizœz] *nf* **d. de bonne aventure** fortune-teller.

disgrâce [disgras] *nf* disgrace, disfavour. ◆**disgracier** *vt* to disgrace.

disgracieux, -euse [disgrasjø, -øz] *a* ungainly.

disjoindre [disʒwɛdr] *vt* (*questions*) to treat separately. ◆**disjoint** *a* (*questions*) unconnected, separate. ◆**disjoncteur** *nm* *Él* circuit breaker.

disloquer [dislɔke] *vt* (*membre*) to dislocate; (*meuble, machine*) to break; — **se d.** *vpr* (*cortège*) to break up; (*meuble etc*) to fall apart; **se d. le bras** to dislocate one's arm. ◆**dislocation** *nf* (*de membre*) dislocation.

dispar/aître [disparɛtr] *vi* to disappear; (*être porté manquant*) to be missing; (*mourir*) to die; **d. en mer** to be lost at sea; **faire d.** to remove, get rid of. ◆**—u, -ue** *a* (*soldat etc*) missing, lost; — *nmf* (*absent*) missing person; (*mort*) departed; **être porté d.** to be reported missing. ◆**disparition** *nf* disappearance; (*mort*) death.

disparate [disparat] *a* ill-assorted.

disparité [disparite] *nf* disparity (**entre, de** between).

dispendieux, -euse [dispɑdjø, -øz] *a* expensive, costly.

dispensaire [dispɑser] *nm* community health centre.

dispense [dispɑs] *nf* exemption; **d. d'âge** waiving of the age limit. ◆**dispenser** *vt* (*soins, bienfaits etc*) to dispense; **d. qn de** (*obligation*) to exempt *ou* excuse s.o. from; **je vous dispense de** (*vos réflexions etc*) I can dispense with; **se d. de faire** to spare oneself the bother of doing.

disperser [disperse] *vt* to disperse, scatter; (*efforts*) to dissipate; — **se d.** *vpr* (*foule*) to disperse; **elle se disperse trop** she tries to do too many things at once. ◆**dispersion** *nf* (*d'une armée etc*) dispersal, dispersion.

disponible [dispɔnibl] *a* available; (*place*) spare, available; (*esprit*) alert. ◆**disponibilité** *nf* availability; *pl Fin* available funds.

dispos [dispo] *a* fit, in fine fettle; **frais et d.** refreshed.

dispos/er [dispoze] *vt* to arrange; (*troupes*) *Mil* to dispose; **d. qn à** (*la bonne humeur etc*) to dispose *ou* incline s.o. towards; **se d. à faire** to prepare to do; — *vi* **d. de qch** to have sth at one's disposal; (*utiliser*) to make use of sth; **d. de qn** *Péj* to take advantage of s.o., abuse s.o. ◆**—é** *a* **bien/mal d.** in a good/bad mood; **bien d. envers** well-disposed towards; **d. à faire** prepared *ou* disposed to do. ◆**disposition** *nf* arrangement; (*de troupes*) disposition; (*de maison, page*) layout; (*humeur*) frame of mind; (*tendance*) tendency, (pre)disposition (à to); (*clause*) *Jur* provision; *pl* (*aptitudes*) aptitude, ability (**pour** for); **à la d. de qn** at s.o.'s disposal; **prendre ses** *ou* **des dispositions** (*préparatifs*) to make arrangements, prepare; (*pour l'avenir*) to make provision; **dans de bonnes disposi-tions à l'égard de** well-disposed towards.

dispositif [dispozitif] *nm* (*mécanisme*) device; **de d. de défense** *Mil* defence system; **d. antiparasite** *El* suppressor.

disproportion [disproporsjɔ̃] *nf* disproportion. ◆**disproportionné** *a* disproportionate.

dispute [dispyt] *nf* quarrel. ◆**disputer** *vt* (*match*) to play; (*terrain, droit etc*) to contest, dispute; (*rallye*) to compete in; **d. qch à qn** (*prix, première place etc*) to fight with s.o. for *ou* over sth, contend with s.o. for sth; **d. qn** (*gronder*) *Fam* to tell s.o. off; **— se d.** *vpr* to quarrel (**avec** with); (*match*) to take place; **se d. qch** to fight over sth.

disqualifier [diskalifje] *vt Sp* to disqualify; **— se d.** *vpr Fig* to become discredited. ◆**disqualification** *nf Sp* disqualification.

disque [disk] *nm Mus* record; *Sp* discus; (*cercle*) disc, *Am* disk; (*pour ordinateur*) disk. ◆**disquaire** *nmf* record dealer. ◆**disquette** *nf* (*pour ordinateur*) floppy disk.

dissection [disɛksjɔ̃] *nf* dissection.

dissemblable [disɑ̃blabl] *a* dissimilar (**à** to).

disséminer [disemine] *vt* (*graines, mines etc*) to scatter; (*idées*) *Fig* to disseminate. ◆**dissémination** *nf* scattering; (*d'idées*) *Fig* dissemination.

dissension [disɑ̃sjɔ̃] *nf* dissension.

disséquer [diseke] *vt* to dissect.

disserter [disɛrte] *vi* **d. sur** to comment upon, discuss. ◆**dissertation** *nf Scol* essay.

dissident, -ente [disidɑ̃, -ɑ̃t] *a & nmf* dissident. ◆**dissidence** *nf* dissidence.

dissimul/er [disimyle] *vt* (*cacher*) to conceal, hide (**à** from); **— vi** (*feindre*) to pretend; **— se d.** *vpr* to hide, conceal oneself. ◆**—é** *a* (*enfant*) *Péj* secretive. ◆**dissimulation** *nf* concealment; (*duplicité*) deceit.

dissip/er [disipe] *vt* (*brouillard, craintes*) to dispel; (*fortune*) to squander, dissipate; **d. qn** to lead s.o. astray, distract s.o.; **— se d.** *vpr* (*brume*) to clear, lift; (*craintes*) to disappear; (*élève*) to misbehave. ◆**—é** *a* (*élève*) unruly; (*vie*) dissipated. ◆**dissipation** *nf* (*de brouillard*) clearing; (*indiscipline*) misbehaviour; (*débauche*) *Litt* dissipation.

dissocier [disosje] *vt* to dissociate (**de** from).

dissolu [disoly] *a* (*vie etc*) dissolute.

dissoudre* [disudr] *vt*, **— se d.** *vpr* to dissolve. ◆**dissolution** *nf* dissolution. ◆**dissolvant** *a & nm* solvent; (*pour vernis à ongles*) nail polish remover.

dissuader [disɥade] *vt* to dissuade, deter (**de qch** from sth, **de faire** from doing). ◆**dissuasif, -ive** *a* (*effet*) deterrent; **être d.** *Fig* to be a deterrent. ◆**dissuasion** *nf* dissuasion; **force de d.** *Mil* deterrent.

distant [distɑ̃] *a* distant; (*personne*) aloof, distant; **d. de dix kilomètres** (*éloigné*) ten kilometres away; (*à intervalles*) ten kilometres apart. ◆**distance** *nf* distance; **à deux mètres de d.** two metres apart; **à d.** at *ou* from a distance; **garder ses distances** to keep one's distance. ◆**distancer** *vt* to leave behind, outstrip.

distendre [distɑ̃dr] *vt*, **— se d.** *vpr* to distend.

distiller [distile] *vt* to distil. ◆**distillation** *nf* distillation. ◆**distillerie** *nf* (*lieu*) distillery.

distinct, -incte [distɛ̃, -ɛ̃kt] *a* (*différent*) distinct, separate (**de** from); (*net*) clear, distinct. ◆**distinctement** *adv* distinctly, clearly. ◆**distinctif, -ive** *a* distinctive. ◆**distinction** *nf* (*différence, raffinement*) distinction.

distingu/er [distɛ̃ge] *vt* (*différencier*) to distinguish; (*voir*) to make out; (*choisir*) to single out; **d. le blé de l'orge** to tell wheat from barley, distinguish between wheat and barley; **— se d.** *vpr* (*s'illustrer*) to distinguish oneself; **se d. de** (*différer*) to be distinguishable from; **se d. par** (*sa gaieté, beauté etc*) to be conspicuous for. ◆**—é** *a* (*bien élevé, éminent*) distinguished; **sentiments distingués** (*formule épistolaire*) *Com* yours faithfully.

distorsion [distorsjɔ̃] *nf* (*du corps, d'une image etc*) distortion.

distraction [distraksjɔ̃] *nf* amusement, distraction; (*étourderie*) (fit of) absent-mindedness. ◆**distraire*** *vt* (*divertir*) to entertain, amuse; **d. qn** (**de**) (*détourner*) to distract s.o. (from); **— se d.** *vpr* to amuse oneself, enjoy oneself. ◆**distrait** *a* absent-minded. ◆**distraitement** *adv* absent-mindedly. ◆**distrayant** *a* entertaining.

distribuer [distribɥe] *vt* (*répartir*) to distribute; (*donner*) to give *ou* hand out, distribute; (*courrier*) to deliver; (*eau*) to supply; (*cartes*) to deal; **bien distribué** (*appartement*) well-arranged. ◆**distributeur** *nm Aut Cin* distributor; **d.** (**automatique**) vending machine; **d. de billets** *Rail* ticket machine; (*de billets de banque*) cash dispenser *ou* machine. ◆**distribution** *nf* distribution; (*du courrier*) delivery; (*de l'eau*) supply; (*acteurs*) *Th Cin* cast; **d. des prix** prize giving.

district [distrikt] *nm* district.

dit [di] *voir* **dire**; — *a* (*convenu*) agreed; (*surnommé*) called.

dites [dit] *voir* **dire.**

divaguer [divage] *vi* (*dérailler*) to rave, talk drivel. ◆**divagations** *nfpl* ravings.

divan [divɑ̃] *nm* divan, couch.

divergent [divɛrʒɑ̃] *a* diverging, divergent. ◆**divergence** *nf* divergence. ◆**diverger** *vi* to diverge (**de** from).

divers, -erses [divɛr, -ɛrs] *apl* (*distincts*) varied, diverse; **d. groupes** (*plusieurs*) various *ou* sundry groups. ◆**diversement** *adv* in various ways. ◆**diversifier** *vt* to diversify; **— se d.** *vpr Écon* to diversify. ◆**diversité** *nf* diversity.

diversion [divɛrsjɔ̃] *nf* diversion.

divert/ir [divɛrtir] *vt* to amuse, entertain; **— se d.** *vpr* to enjoy oneself, amuse oneself. ◆**—issement** *nm* amusement, entertainment.

dividende [dividɑ̃d] *nm Math Fin* dividend.

divin [divɛ̃] *a* divine. ◆**divinité** *nf* divinity.

diviser [divize] *vt,* **— se d.** *vpr* to divide (**en** into). ◆**divisible** *a* divisible. ◆**division** *nf* division.

divorce [divɔrs] *nm* divorce. ◆**divorc/er** *vi* to get *ou* be divorced, divorce; **d. d'avec qn** to divorce s.o. ◆**—é, -ée** *a* divorced (**d'avec** from); — *nmf* divorcee.

divulguer [divylge] *vt* to divulge. ◆**divulgation** *nf* divulgence.

dix [dis] ([di] *before consonant,* [diz] *before vowel*) *a & nm* ten. ◆**dixième** [dizjɛm] *a & nmf* tenth; **un d.** a tenth. ◆**dix-huit** [dizɥit] *a & nm* eighteen. ◆**dix-huitième** *a & nmf* eighteenth. ◆**dix-neuf** [diznœf] *a & nm* nineteen. ◆**dix-neuvième** *a & nmf* nineteenth. ◆**dix-sept** [disset] *a & nm* seventeen. ◆**dix-septième** *a & nmf* seventeenth.

dizaine [dizɛn] *nf* about ten.

docile [dɔsil] *a* submissive, docile. ◆**docilité** *nf* submissiveness, docility.

dock [dɔk] *nm Nau* dock. ◆**docker** [dɔkɛr] *nm* docker.

docteur [dɔktœr] *nm Méd Univ* doctor (**ès, en** of). ◆**doctorat** *nm* doctorate; = PhD (**ès, en** in).

doctrine [dɔktrin] *nf* doctrine. ◆**doctrinaire** *a & nm Péj* doctrinaire.

document [dɔkymɑ̃] *nm* document. ◆**documentaire** *a* documentary; — *nm*

(*film*) documentary. ◆**documentaliste** *nmf* information officer.

document/er [dɔkymɑ̃te] *vt* (*informer*) to document; **— se d.** *vpr* to collect material *ou* information. ◆**—é** (**bien** *ou* **très**) **d.** (*personne*) well-informed. ◆**documentation** *nf* (*documents*) documentation, *Com* literature; (*renseignements*) information.

dodeliner [dɔdline] *vi* **d. de la tête** to nod (one's head).

dodo [dɔdo] *nm* (*langage enfantin*) **faire d.** to sleep; **aller au d.** to go to bye-byes.

dodu [dɔdy] *a* chubby, plump.

dogme [dɔgm] *nm* dogma. ◆**dogmatique** *a* dogmatic. ◆**dogmatisme** *nm* dogmatism.

dogue [dɔg] *nm* (*chien*) mastiff.

doigt [dwa] *nm* finger; **d. de pied** toe; **à deux doigts de** within an ace of; **montrer du d.** to point (to); **savoir sur le bout du d.** to have at one's finger tips. ◆**doigté** *nm Mus* fingering, touch; (*savoir-faire*) tact, expertise. ◆**doigtier** *nm* fingerstall.

dois, doit [dwa] *voir* **devoir** [1,2].

doléances [dɔleɑ̃s] *nfpl* (*plaintes*) grievances.

dollar [dɔlar] *nm* dollar.

domaine [dɔmɛn] *nm* (*terres*) estate, domain; (*sphère*) province, domain.

dôme [dom] *nm* dome.

domestique [dɔmɛstik] *a* (*animal*) domestic(ated); (*de la famille*) family-, domestic; (*ménager*) domestic, household; — *nmf* servant. ◆**domestiquer** *vt* to domesticate.

domicile [dɔmisil] *nm* home; *Jur* abode; **travailler à d.** to work at home; **livrer à d.** (*pain etc*) to deliver (to the house). ◆**domicilié** *a* resident (**à, chez** at).

domin/er [dɔmine] *vt* to dominate; (*situation, sentiment*) to master, dominate; (*être supérieur à*) to surpass, outclass; (*tour, rocher*) to tower above, dominate; (*valley, building etc*); — *vi* (*être le plus fort*) to be dominant, dominate; (*être le plus important*) to predominate; **— se d.** *vpr* to control oneself. ◆**—ant** *a* dominant. ◆**—ante** *nf* dominant feature; *Mus* dominant. ◆**dominateur, -trice** *a* domineering. ◆**domination** *nf* domination.

dominicain, -aine [dɔminikɛ̃, -ɛn] *a & nmf Rel* Dominican.

dominical, -aux [dɔminikal, -o] *a* (*repos*) Sunday-.

domino [dɔmino] *nm* domino; *pl* (*jeu*) dominoes.

dommage [dɔmaʒ] *nm* **1** (**c'est**) **d.!** it's a

pity *ou* a shame! **(que** that); **quel d.!** what a pity *ou* a shame! **2** *(tort)* prejudice, harm; *pl (dégâts)* damage; **dommages-intérêts** *Jur* damages.

dompt/er [dɔ̃te] *vt (animal)* to tame; *(passions, rebelles)* to subdue. **◆—eur, -euse** *nmf (de lions)* lion tamer.

don [dɔ̃] *nm (cadeau, aptitude)* gift; *(aumône)* donation; **le d. du sang**/*etc* (the giving of blood/*etc*); **faire d. de** to give; **avoir le d. de** *(le chic pour)* to have the knack of. **◆donateur, -trice** *nmf* *Jur* donor. **◆donation** *nf* *Jur* donation.

donc [dɔ̃(k)] *conj* so, then; *(par conséquent)* so, therefore; **asseyez-vous d.!** *(intensif)* will you sit down!, sit down then!; **qui/quoi d.?** who?/what?; **allons d.!** come on!

donjon [dɔ̃ʒɔ̃] *nm (de château)* keep.

donne [dɔn] *nf* Cartes deal.

donner [dɔne] *vt* to give; *(récolte, résultat)* to produce; *(sa place)* to give up; *(pièce, film)* to put on; *(cartes)* to deal; **d. un coup à** to hit, give a blow to; **d. le bonjour à qn** to say hello to s.o.; **d. à réparer** to take (in) to be repaired; **d. raison à qn** to say s.o. is right; **ça donne soif/faim** it makes you thirsty/hungry; **je lui donne trente ans** I'd say *ou* guess he *ou* she was thirty; **ça n'a rien donné** *(efforts)* it hasn't got us anywhere; **c'est donné** *Fam* it's dirt cheap; **étant donné** *(la situation etc)* considering, in view of; **étant donné que** seeing (that), considering (that); **à un moment donné** at some stage; — *vi* **d. sur** *(fenêtre)* to look out onto, overlook; *(porte)* to open onto; **d. dans** *(piège)* to fall into; **d. de la tête contre** to hit one's head against; — **se d.** *vpr* *(se consacrer)* to devote oneself (à to); **se d. du mal** to go to a lot of trouble **(pour faire** to do); **s'en d. à cœur joie** to have a whale of a time, enjoy oneself to the full. **◆données** *nfpl (information)* data; *(de problème)* (known) facts; *(d'un roman)* basic elements. **◆donneur, -euse** *nmf* giver; *(de sang, d'organe)* donor; Cartes dealer.

dont [dɔ̃] *pron rel* (= **de qui, duquel, de quoi** *etc*) *(personne)* of whom; *(chose)* of which; *(appartenance: personne)* whose of whom; *(appartenance: personne)* whose, of which, whose; **une mère d. le fils est malade** a mother whose son is ill; **la fille d. il est fier** the daughter he is proud of *ou* of whom he is proud; **les outils d. j'ai besoin** the tools I need; **la façon d. elle joue** the way (in which) she plays; **voici ce d. il s'agit** here's what it's about.

doper [dɔpe] *vt (cheval, sportif)* to dope; —

se d. *vpr* to dope oneself. **◆doping** *nm (action)* doping; *(substance)* dope.

dorénavant [dɔʀenavɑ̃] *adv* henceforth.

dor/er [dɔʀe] *vt (objet)* to gild; **d. la pilule** *Fig* to sugar the pill; **se (faire) d.** au soleil to bask in the sun; — *vi* Culin to brown. **◆—é** *a (objet)* gilt; *(couleur)* golden; — *nm (couche)* gilt. **◆dorure** *nf* gilding.

dorloter [dɔʀlɔte] *vt* to pamper, coddle.

dormir* [dɔʀmir] *vi* to sleep; *(être endormi)* to be asleep; *(argent)* to lie idle; **histoire à d. debout** tall story, cock-and-bull story; **eau dormante** stagnant water. **◆dortoir** *nm* dormitory.

dos [do] *nm* back; *(de nez)* bridge; *(de livre)* spine; **voir qn de d.** to have a back view of s.o.; **à d. de chameau** (riding) on a camel; **'voir au d.'** *(verso)* 'see over'; **j'en ai plein le d.** *Fam* I'm sick of it; **mettre qch sur le d. de qn** *(accusation)* to pin sth on s.o. **◆dossard** *nm* *Sp* number *(fixed on back).* **◆dossier** *nm* 1 *(de siège)* back. 2 *(papiers, compte rendu)* file, dossier; *(classeur)* folder, file.

dose [doz] *nf* dose; *(quantité administrée)* dosage. **◆dos/er** *vt (remède)* to measure out the dose of; *(équilibrer)* to strike the correct balance between. **◆—age** *nm (de remède)* measuring out *(of dose)*; *(équilibre)* balance; **faire le d. de** = **doser.** **◆—eur** *nm* **bouchon d.** measuring cap.

dot [dɔt] *nf* dowry.

doter [dɔte] *vt (hôpital etc)* to endow; **d. de** *(matériel)* to equip with; *(qualité)* Fig to endow with, **◆dotation** *nf* endowment; equipping.

douane [dwan] *nf* customs. **◆douanier, -ière** *nm* customs officer; — *a (union etc)* customs-.

double [dublə] *a* double; *(rôle, avantage etc)* twofold, double; — *adv* double; — *nm (de personne)* double; *(copie)* copy, duplicate; *(de timbre)* swap, duplicate; **le d. (de)** *(quantité)* twice as much (as). **◆doublage** *nm (de film)* dubbing. **◆doublement** *adv* doubly; — *nm* doubling. **◆doubler** 1 *vt (augmenter)* to double; *(vêtement)* to line; *(film)* to dub; *(acteur)* to stand in for; *(classe)* Scol to repeat; *(cap)* Nau to round; **se d.** to be coupled with; — *vi (augmenter)* to double. 2 *vti* Aut to overtake, pass. **◆doublure** *nf (étoffe)* lining; Th under-study; Cin stand-in.

douce [dus] *voir* **doux.** **◆doucement** *adv (délicatement)* gently; *(à voix basse)* softly; *(sans bruit)* quietly; *(lentement)* slowly; *(sans à-coups)* smoothly; *(assez bien)* Fam so-so. ◆**douceur** nf (de miel etc) sweetness; (de personne, pente etc) gentleness; (de peau etc) softness; (de temps) mildness; pl (sucreries) sweets, Am candies; **en d.** (démarrer etc) smoothly.

douche [duʃ] nf shower. ◆**doucher** vt **d. qn** to give s.o. a shower; — **se d.** vpr to take ou have a shower.

doué [dwe] a gifted, talented (**en** at); (intelligent) clever; **d. de** gifted with; **il est d. pour** he has a gift ou talent for.

douille [duj] nf (d'ampoule) Él socket; (de cartouche) case.

douillet, -ette [duje, -ɛt] a (lit etc) soft, cosy, snug; **il est d.** (délicat) Péj he's soft.

douleur [dulœr] nf (mal) pain; (chagrin) sorrow, grief. ◆**douloureux, -euse** a (maladie, membre, décision, perte etc) painful.

doute [dut] nm doubt; pl (méfiance) doubts, misgivings; **sans d.** no doubt, probably; **sans aucun d.** without (any ou a) doubt; **mettre en d.** to cast doubt on; **dans le d.** uncertain, doubtful; **ça ne fait pas de d.** there is no doubt about it. ◆**douter** vi to doubt; **d. de qch/qn** to doubt sth/s.o.; **d. que** (+ sub) to doubt whether ou that; **se d. de qch** to suspect sth; **je m'en doute** I suspect so, I would think so. ◆**douteux, -euse** a doubtful; (louche, médiocre) dubious; **il est d. que** (+ sub) it's doubtful whether ou that.

douve(s) [duv] nf(pl) (de château) moat.

Douvres [duvr] nm ou f Dover.

doux, douce [du, dus] a (miel, son etc) sweet; (personne, pente etc) gentle; (peau, lumière, drogue etc) soft; (émotion, souvenir etc) pleasant; (temps, climat) mild; **en douce** on the quiet.

douze [duz] a & nm twelve. ◆**douzaine** nf (douze) dozen; (environ) about twelve; **une d. d'œufs**/etc a dozen eggs/etc. ◆**douzième** a & nmf twelfth; **un d.** a twelfth.

doyen, -enne [dwajɛ̃, -ɛn] nmf Rel Univ dean; **d.** (d'âge) oldest person.

draconien, -ienne [drakɔnjɛ̃, -jɛn] a (mesures) drastic.

dragée [draʒe] nf sugared almond; **tenir la d. haute à qn** (tenir tête à qn) to stand up to s.o.

dragon [dragɔ̃] nm (animal) dragon; Mil Hist dragoon.

drague [drag] nf (appareil) dredge; (filet) drag net. ◆**draguer** vt **1** (rivière etc) to dredge. **2** Arg (racoler) to try and pick up;

(faire du baratin à) to chat up, Am smooth-talk.

drainer [drene] vt to drain.

drame [dram] nm drama; (catastrophe) tragedy. ◆**dramatique** a dramatic; **critique d.** drama critic; **auteur d.** playwright, dramatist; **film d.** drama. ◆**dramatiser** vt (exagérer) to dramatize. ◆**dramaturge** nm dramatist.

drap [dra] nm (de lit) sheet; (tissu) cloth; **dans de beaux draps** Fig in a fine mess.

drapeau, -x [drapo] nm flag; **être sous les drapeaux** Mil to be in the services.

draper [drape] vt to drape (with). ◆**draperie** nf (étoffe) drapery.

dresser [drese] vt **1** (échelle, statue) to put up, erect; (piège) to lay, set; (oreille) to prick up; (liste) to draw up, make out; — **se d.** vpr (personne) to stand up; (statue, montagne) to rise up, stand; **se d. contre** (abus) to stand up against. **2** vt (animal) to train; (personne) Péj to drill, teach. ◆**dressage** nm training. ◆**dresseur, -euse** nmf trainer.

dribbler [drible] vti Fb to dribble.

drogue [drɔg] nf (médicament) Péj drug; **une d.** (stupéfiant) a drug; **la d.** drugs, dope. ◆**drogu/er** vt (victime) to drug; (malade) to dose up; — **se d.** vpr to take drugs, be on drugs; (malade) to dose oneself up. ◆**-é, -ée** nmf drug addict.

droguerie [drɔgri] nf hardware shop ou Am store. ◆**droguiste** nmf owner of a droguerie.

droit [drwa] nm (privilège) right; (d'inscription) fee(s), due; pl (de douane) duty; **le d.** (science juridique) law; **avoir d. à** to be entitled to; **avoir le d. de faire** to be entitled to do, have the right to do; **à bon d.** rightly; **d. d'entrée** entrance fee.

droit² [drwa] a (ligne, route etc) straight; (personne, mur etc) upright, straight; (angle) right; (veston) single-breasted; (honnête) Fig upright; — adv straight; **tout d.** straight ou right ahead. ◆**droite¹** nf (ligne) straight line.

droit³ [drwa] a (côté, bras etc) right; — nm (coup) Boxe right. ◆**droite²** nf **la d.** (côté) the right (side); Pol the right (wing); **à d.** (tourner) (to the) right; (rouler, se tenir) on the right(-hand) side; (fenêtre etc) right-hand; (politique, candidat) right-wing; **à d. de** on ou to the right of; **à d. et à gauche** (voyager etc) here, there and everywhere. ◆**droitier, -ière** a & nmf right-handed (person). ◆**droiture** nf uprightness.

drôle [drol] *a* funny; **d. d'air/de type** funny look/fellow. ◆**—ment** *adv* funnily; (*extrêmement*) *Fam* dreadfully.

dromadaire [drɔmadɛr] *nm* dromedary.

dru [dry] *a* (*herbe etc*) thick, dense; – *adv* **tomber d.** (*pluie*) to pour down heavily; **pousser d.** to grow thick(ly).

du [dy] = **de** + **le**.

dû, due [dy] *a* **d. à** (*accident etc*) due to; – *nm* due; (*argent*) dues.

dualité [dɥalite] *nf* duality.

dubitatif, -ive [dybitatif, -iv] *a* (*regard etc*) dubious.

duc [dyk] *nm* duke. ◆**duché** *nm* duchy. ◆**duchesse** *nf* duchess.

duel [dɥɛl] *nm* duel.

dûment [dymã] *adv* duly.

dune [dyn] *nf* (*sand*) dune.

duo [dɥo] *nm Mus* duet; (*couple*) *Hum* duo.

dupe [dyp] *nf* dupe, fool; – *a* **d. de** duped by, fooled by. ◆**duper** *vt* to fool, dupe.

duplex [dypleks] *nm* split-level flat, *Am* duplex; (**émission en**) **d.** *Tél* link-up.

duplicata [dyplikata] *nm inv* duplicate.

duplicateur [dyplikatœr] *nm* (*machine*) duplicator.

duplicité [dyplisite] *nf* duplicity, deceit.

dur [dyr] *a* (*substance*) hard; (*difficulté*) hard, tough; (*viande*) tough; (*hiver, leçon, ton*) harsh; (*personne*) hard, harsh; (*brosse, carton*) stiff; (*œuf*) hard-boiled; **d. d'oreille** hard of hearing; – *adv* (*travailler*) hard; – *nm Fam* tough guy. ◆**durement** *adv* harshly. ◆**dureté** *nf* hardness; harshness; toughness.

durant [dyrã] *prép* during.

durc/ir [dyrsir] *vti*, – **se d.** *vpr* to harden. ◆**—issement** *nm* hardening.

durée [dyre] *nf* (*de film, événement etc*) length; (*période*) duration; (*de pile*) *El* life; **de longue d.** (*disque*) long-playing. ◆**dur/er** *vi* to last; **ça dure depuis . . .** it's been going on for . . . . ◆**—able** *a* durable, lasting.

durillon [dyrijɔ̃] *nm* callus.

duvet [dyvɛ] *nm* **1** (*d'oiseau, de visage*) down. **2** (*sac*) sleeping bag. ◆**duveté** *a*, ◆**duveteux, -euse** *a* downy.

dynamique [dinamik] *a* dynamic; – *nf* (*force*) *Fig* dynamic force, thrust. ◆**dynamisme** *nm* dynamism.

dynamite [dinamit] *nf* dynamite. ◆**dyna-miter** *vt* to dynamite.

dynamo [dinamo] *nf* dynamo.

dynastie [dinasti] *nf* dynasty.

dysenterie [disɑ̃tri] *nf Méd* dysentery.

dyslexique [disleksik] *a* & *nmf* dyslexic.

E

E, e [ə, ø] *nm* E, e.

eau, -x [o] *nf* water; **il est tombé beaucoup d'e.** a lot of rain fell; **e. douce** (*non salée*) fresh water; (*du robinet*) soft water; **e. salée** salt water; **e. de Cologne** eau de Cologne; **e. de toilette** toilet water; **grandes eaux** (*d'un parc*) ornamental fountains; **tomber à l'e.** (*projet*) to fall through; **ça lui fait venir l'e. à la bouche** it makes his *ou* her mouth water; **tout en e.** sweating; **prendre l'e.** (*chaussure*) to take water, leak. ◆**e.-de-vie** *nf* (*pl* **eaux-de-vie**) brandy. ◆**e.-forte** *nf* (*pl* **eaux-fortes**) (*gravure*) etching.

ébah/ir [ebair] *vt* to astound, dumbfound, amaze. ◆**—issement** *nm* amazement.

ébattre (s') [sebatr] *vpr* to frolic, frisk about. ◆**ébats** *nmpl* frolics.

ébauche [eboʃ] *nf* (*esquisse*) (rough) outline, (rough) sketch; (*début*) beginnings. ◆**ébaucher** *vt* (*projet, tableau, œuvre*) to sketch out, outline; **e. un sourire** to give a faint smile; – **s'é.** *vpr* to take shape.

ébène [ebɛn] *nf* (*bois*) ebony.

ébéniste [ebenist] *nm* cabinet-maker. ◆**ébénisterie** *nf* cabinet-making.

éberlué [eberlɥe] *a Fam* dumbfounded.

éblou/ir [ebluir] *vt* to dazzle. ◆**—isse-ment** *nm* (*aveuglement*) dazzling, dazzle; (*émerveillement*) feeling of wonder; (*malaise*) fit of dizziness.

éboueur [ebwœr] *nm* dustman, *Am* garbage collector.

ébouillanter [ebujãte] *vt* to scald; – **s'é.** *vpr* to scald oneself.

éboul/er (s') [sebule] *vpr* (*falaise etc*) to crumble; (*terre, roches*) to fall. ◆**—ement** *nm* landslide. ◆**éboulis** *nm* (mass of) fallen debris.

ébouriffant [eburifã] *a Fam* astounding.

ébouriffer [eburife] *vt* (*cheveux*) to dishevel, ruffle, tousle.

ébranl/er [ebrɑle] vt (mur, confiance etc) to shake; (santé) to weaken, affect; (personne) to shake, shatter; — **s'é.** vpr (train, cortège etc) to move off. ◆—**ement** nm (secousse) shaking, shock; (nerveux) shock.

ébrécher [ebreʃe] vt (assiette) to chip; (lame) to nick. ◆**ébréchure** nf chip; nick.

ébriété [ebrijete] nf drunkenness.

ébrouer (s') [sebrue] vpr (cheval) to snort; (personne) to shake oneself (about).

ébruiter [ebrɥite] vt (nouvelle etc) to make known, divulge.

ébullition [ebylisjɔ̃] nf boiling; **être en é.** (eau) to be boiling; (ville) Fig to be in turmoil.

écaille [ekaj] nf 1 (de poisson) scale; (de tortue, d'huître) shell; (résine synthétique) tortoise-shell. 2 (de peinture) flake. ◆**écailler 1** (poisson) to scale; (huître) to shell. 2 **s'é.** vpr (peinture) to flake (off), peel.

écarlate [ekarlat] a & nf scarlet.

écarquiller [ekarkije] vt **é. les yeux** to open one's eyes wide.

écart [ekar] nm (intervalle) gap, distance; (mouvement, embardée) swerve; (différence) difference (de in, entre between); **écarts de** (conduite, langage etc) lapses in; **le grand é.** (de gymnaste) the splits; **à l'é.** out of the way; **tenir qn à l'é.** Fig to keep s.o. out of things; **à l'é. de** away from, clear of. ◆**écart/er** vt (objets) to move away from each other, move apart; (jambes) to spread, open; (rideaux) to draw (aside), open; (crainte, idée) to brush aside, dismiss; (carte) to discard; **é. qch de qch** to move sth away from sth; **é. qn de** (éloigner) to keep s.o. away from; (exclure) to keep s.o. out of; — **s'é.** vpr (s'éloigner) to move away (de from); (se séparer) to move aside (de from); **s'é. de** (sujet, bonne route) to stray ou deviate from. ◆—**é** a (endroit) remote; **les jambes écartées** with legs (wide) apart. ◆—**ement** nm (espace) gap, distance (de between).

écartelé [ekartəle] a **é. entre** (tiraillé) torn between.

ecchymose [ekimoz] nf bruise.

ecclésiastique [eklezjastik] a ecclesiastical; — nm ecclesiastic, clergyman.

écervelé, -ée [esɛrvəle] a scatterbrained; — nmf scatterbrain.

échafaud [eʃafo] nm (pour exécution) scaffold.

échafaudage [eʃafodaʒ] nm (construction) scaffold(ing); (tas) heap; (système) Fig fabric. ◆**échafauder** vi to put up scaf-

folding ou a scaffold; — vt (projet etc) to put together, think up.

échalas [eʃala] nm **grand é.** tall skinny person.

échalote [eʃalɔt] nf Bot Culin shallot, scallion.

échancré [eʃɑ̃kre] a (encolure) V-shaped, scooped. ◆**échancrure** nf (de robe) opening.

échange [eʃɑ̃ʒ] nm exchange; **en é.** in exchange (**de** for). ◆**échanger** vt to exchange (**contre** for). ◆**échangeur** nm (intersection) Aut interchange.

échantillon [eʃɑ̃tijɔ̃] nm sample. ◆**échantillonnage** nm (collection) range (of samples).

échappatoire [eʃapatwar] nf evasion, way out.

échapp/er [eʃape] vi **é. à qn** to escape from s.o.; **é. à la mort/un danger/etc** to escape death/a danger/etc; **ce nom m'échappe** that name escapes me; **ça lui a échappé** (des mains) it slipped out of his ou her hands; **laisser é.** (cri) to let out; (objet, occasion) to let slip; **l'é. belle** to have a close shave; **ça m'a échappé** (je n'ai pas compris) I didn't catch it; — **s'é.** vpr (s'enfuir) to escape (**de** from); (s'éclipser) to slip away; Sp to break away; (gaz, eau) to escape, come out. ◆—**é, -ée** nmf runaway. ◆—**ée** nf Sp breakaway; (vue) vista. ◆—**ement** nm **tuyau d'é.** Aut exhaust pipe; **pot d'é.** Aut silencer, Am muffler.

écharde [eʃard] nf (de bois) splinter.

écharpe [eʃarp] nf scarf; (de maire) sash; **en é.** (bras) in a sling; **prendre en é.** Aut to hit sideways.

écharper [eʃarpe] vt **é. qn** to cut to bits.

échasse [eʃas] nf (bâton) stilt. ◆**échassier** nm wading bird.

échauder [eʃode] vt **être échaudé, se faire é.** (déçu) Fam to be taught a lesson.

échauffer [eʃofe] vt (moteur) to overheat; (esprit) to excite; — **s'é.** vpr (discussion) & Sp to warm up.

échauffourée [eʃofure] nf (bagarre) clash, brawl, skirmish.

échéance [eʃeɑ̃s] nf Com date (due), expiry ou Am expiration date; (paiement) payment (due); (obligation) commitment; **à brève/longue é.** (projet, emprunt) short-/long-term.

échéant (le cas) [ləkazeʃeɑ̃] adv if the occasion should arise, possibly.

échec [eʃɛk] nm 1 (insuccès) failure; **faire é. à** (inflation etc) to hold in check. 2 **les**

échecs (*jeu*) chess; **en é.** in check; **é.!** check!; **é. et mat!** checkmate!

échelle [eʃɛl] *nf* 1 (*marches*) ladder; **faire la courte é. à qn** to give s.o. a leg up. 2 (*mesure, dimension*) scale; **à l'é. nationale** on a national scale. ◆**échelon** *nm* (*d'échelle*) rung; (*de fonctionnaire*) grade; (*dans une organisation*) echelon; **à l'é. régional/national** on a regional/national level. ◆**échelonner** *vt* (*paiements*) to spread out, space out; — **s'é.** *vpr* to be spread out.

écheveau, -x [eʃvo] *nm* (*de laine*) skein; Fig muddle, tangle.

échevelé [eʃəvle] *a* (*ébouriffé*) dishevelled; (*course, danse etc*) Fig wild.

échine [eʃin] *nf* Anat backbone, spine.

échiner (s') [seʃine] *vpr* (*s'évertuer*) Fam to knock oneself out (**à faire** doing).

échiquier [eʃikje] *nm* (*tableau*) chessboard.

écho [eko] *nm* (*d'un son*) echo; (*réponse*) response; *pl* Journ gossip (items), local news; **avoir des échos de** to hear some news about; **se faire l'é. de** (*opinions etc*) to echo. ◆**échotier, -ière** *nmf* Journ gossip columnist.

échographie [ekografi] *nf* (ultrasound) scan; **passer une é.** (*femme enceinte*) to have a scan.

échoir* [eʃwar] *vi* (*terme*) to expire; **é. à qn** (*part*) to fall to s.o.

échouer [eʃwe] 1 *vi* to fail; **é. à** (*examen*) to fail. 2 *vi*, — **s'é.** *vpr* (*navire*) to run aground.

éclabousser [eklabuse] *vt* to splash, spatter (**de** with); (*salir*) Fig to tarnish the image of. ◆**éclaboussure** *nf* splash, spatter.

éclair [eklɛr] 1 *nm* (*lumière*) flash; **un é.** Mét a flash of lightning. 2 *nm* (*gâteau*) éclair. 3 *a inv* (*visite, raid*) lightning.

éclairc/ir [eklɛrsir] *vt* (*couleur etc*) to lighten, make lighter; (*sauce*) to thin out; (*question, mystère*) to clear up, clarify; — **s'é.** *vpr* (*ciel*) to clear (up); (*idées*) to become clear(er); (*devenir moins dense*) to thin out; **s'é. la voix** to clear one's throat. ◆—**ie** *nf* (*dans le ciel*) clear patch; (*durée*) sunny spell. ◆—**issement** *nm* (*explication*) clarification.

éclair/er [eklɛre] *vt* (*pièce etc*) to light (up); (*situation*) Fig to throw light on; **é. qn** (*avec une lampe etc*) to give s.o. some light; (*informer*) Fig to enlighten s.o.; — *vi* (*lampe*) to give light; — **s'é.** *vpr* (*visage*) to light up, brighten up; (*question, situation*) Fig to become clear(er); **s'é. à la bougie** to use candlelight. ◆—**é** *a* (*averti*) enlightened; **bien/mal é.** (*illuminé*) well/badly lit.

◆—**age** *nm* (*de pièce etc*) light(ing); (*point de vue*) Fig light.

éclaireur, -euse [eklɛrœr, -øz] *nm* Mil scout; — *nmf* (boy) scout, (girl) guide.

éclat [ekla] *nm* 1 (*de la lumière*) brightness; (*de phare*) Aut glare; (*du feu*) blaze; (*splendeur*) brilliance, radiance; (*de la jeunesse*) bloom; (*de diamant*) glitter, sparkle. 2 (*fragment de verre ou de bois*) splinter; (*de rire, colère*) (out)burst; **é. d'obus** shrapnel; **éclats de voix** noisy outbursts, shouts. ◆**éclat/er** *vi* (*pneu, obus etc*) to burst; (*pétard, bombe*) to go off, explode; (*verre*) to shatter, break into pieces; (*guerre, incendie*) to break out; (*orage, scandale*) to break; (*parti*) to break up; **é. de rire** to burst out laughing; **é. en sanglots** to burst into tears. ◆—**ant** *a* (*lumière, couleur, succès*) brilliant; (*bruit*) thunderous; (*vérité*) blinding; (*beauté*) radiant. ◆—**ement** *nm* (*de pneu etc*) bursting; (*de bombe etc*) explosion; (*de parti*) break-up.

éclectique [eklɛktik] *a* eclectic.

éclipse [eklips] *nf* (*du soleil*) & Fig eclipse. ◆**éclipser** *vt* to eclipse; — **s'é.** *vpr* (*soleil*) to be eclipsed; (*partir*) Fam to slip away.

éclopé, -ée [eklɔpe] *a* & *nmf* limping *ou* lame (person).

éclore [eklɔr] *vi* (*œuf*) to hatch; (*fleur*) to open (out), blossom. ◆**éclosion** *nf* hatching; opening, blossoming.

écluse [eklyz] *nf* Nau lock.

écœur/er [ekœre] *vt* (*aliment etc*) to make (s.o.) feel sick; (*au moral*) to sicken, nauseate. ◆—**ement** *nm* (*répugnance*) nausea, disgust.

école [ekɔl] *nf* school; (*militaire*) academy; **aller à l'é.** to go to school; **é. de danse/dessin** dancing/art school; **faire é.** to gain a following; **les grandes écoles** *university establishments giving high-level professional training;* **é. normale** teachers' training college. ◆**écolier, -ière** *nmf* schoolboy, schoolgirl.

écologie [ekɔlɔʒi] *nf* ecology. ◆**écologique** *a* ecological. ◆**écologiste** *nmf* Pol environmentalist.

éconduire [ekɔ̃dɥir] *vt* (*repousser*) to reject.

économe [ekɔnɔm] 1 *a* thrifty, economical. 2 *nmf* (*de collège etc*) bursar, steward. ◆**économie** *nf* (*activité économique, vertu*) economy; *pl* (*pécule*) savings; **une é. de** (*gain*) a saving of; **faire une é. de temps** to save time; **faire des économies** to save (up); **é. politique** economics. ◆**économique** *a* 1 (*doctrine etc*) economic; **science é.** economics. 2 (*bon marché,* *avantageux*) economical. ◆**économiquement** *adv* economically. ◆**économiser** *vt* (*forces, argent, énergie etc*) to save; – *vi* to economize (**sur** on). ◆**économiste** *nmf* economist.

écoper [ekɔpe] **1** *vt* (*bateau*) to bail out, bale out. **2** *vi Fam* to cop it; **é. (de)** (*punition*) to cop, get.

écorce [ekɔrs] *nf* (*d'arbre*) bark; (*de fruit*) peel, skin; **l'é. terrestre** the earth's crust.

écorcher [ekɔrʃe] *vt* (*animal*) to skin, flay; (*érafler*) to graze; (*client*) *Fam* to fleece; (*langue étrangère*) *Fam* to murder; **é. les oreilles** to grate on one's ears; – **s'é.** *vpr* to graze oneself. ◆**écorchure** *nf* graze.

Écosse [ekɔs] *nf* Scotland. ◆**écossais, -aise** *a* Scottish; (*tissu*) tartan; (*whisky*) Scotch; – *nmf* Scot.

écosser [ekɔse] *vt* (*pois*) to shell.

écot [eko] *nm* (*quote-part*) share.

écoul/er [ekule] **1** *vt* (*se débarrasser de*) to dispose of; (*produits*) *Com* to sell (off), clear. **2 s'é.** *vpr* (*eau*) to flow out, run out; (*temps*) to pass, elapse; (*foule*) to disperse. ◆**—é** *a* (*années etc*) past. ◆**—ement** *nm* **1** (*de liquide, véhicules*) flow; (*de temps*) passage. **2** (*débit*) *Com* sale, selling.

écourter [ekurte] *vt* (*séjour, discours etc*) to cut short; (*texte, tige etc*) to shorten.

écoute [ekut] *nf* listening; **à l'é.** *Rad* tuned in, listening in (**de** to); **être aux écoutes** (*attentif*) to keep one's ears open (**de** for). ◆**écout/er** *vt* to listen to; (*radio*) to listen (**in**) to; – *vi* to listen; (*aux portes etc*) to eavesdrop, listen; **si je m'écoutais** if I did what I wanted. ◆**—eur** *nm* (*de téléphone*) earpiece; *pl* (*casque*) headphones, earphones.

écrabouiller [ekrabuje] *vt Fam* to crush to a pulp.

écran [ekrɑ̃] *nm* screen; **le petit é.** television.

écras/er [ekraze] *vt* (*broyer*) to crush; (*fruit, insecte*) to squash, crush; (*cigarette*) to put out; (*tuer*) *Aut* to run over; (*vaincre*) to beat (hollow), crush; (*dominer*) to outstrip; **écrasé de** (*travail, douleur*) overwhelmed with; **se faire é.** *Aut* to get run over; – **s'é.** *vpr* (*avion, voiture*) to crash (**contre** into); **s'é. dans** (*foule*) to crush ou squash into. ◆**—ant** *a* (*victoire, nombre, chaleur*) overwhelming. ◆**—é** *a* (*nez*) snub. ◆**—ement** *nm* crushing.

écrémer [ekreme] *vt* (*lait*) to skim, cream; (*collection etc*) *Fig* to cream off the best from.

écrevisse [ekrəvis] *nf* (*crustacé*) crayfish.

écrier (s') [ekrije] *vpr* to cry out, exclaim (**que** that).

écrin [ekrɛ̃] *nm* (jewel) case.

écrire* [ekrir] *vt* to write; (*noter*) to write (down); (*orthographier*) to spell; **é. à la machine** to type; – *vi* to write; – **s'é.** *vpr* (*mot*) to be spelt. ◆**écrit** *nm* written document, paper; (*examen*) *Scol* written paper; *pl* (*œuvres*) writings; **par é.** in writing. ◆**écriteau, -x** *nm* notice, sign. ◆**écriture** *nf* (*système*) writing; (*personnelle*) (hand)writing; *pl Com* accounts; **l'É. Rel** the Scripture(s). ◆**écrivain** *nm* author, writer.

écrou [ekru] *nm Tech* nut.

écrouer [ekrue] *vt* to imprison.

écroul/er (s') [ekrule] *vpr* (*édifice, projet etc*) to collapse; (*blessé etc*) to slump down, collapse. ◆**—ement** *nm* collapse.

écru [ekry] *a* **toile é.** unbleached linen; **soie é.** raw silk.

écueil [ekœj] *nm* (*rocher*) reef; (*obstacle*) *Fig* pitfall.

écuelle [ekɥɛl] *nf* (*bol*) bowl.

éculé [ekyle] *a* (*chaussure*) worn out at the heel; *Fig* hackneyed.

écume [ekym] *nf* (*de mer, bave d'animal etc*) foam; *Culin* scum. ◆**écumer** *vt Culin* to skim; (*piller*) to plunder; – *vi* to foam (**de** rage with anger). ◆**écumoire** *nf Culin* skimmer.

écureuil [ekyrœj] *nm* squirrel.

écurie [ekyri] *nf* stable.

écusson [ekysɔ̃] *nm* (*emblème d'étoffe*) badge.

écuyer, -ère [ekɥije, -ɛr] *nmf* (*cavalier*) (horse) rider, equestrian.

eczéma [egzema] *nm Méd* eczema.

édenté [edɑ̃te] *a* toothless.

édicter [edikte] *vt* to enact, decree.

édifice [edifis] *nm* building, edifice; (*ensemble organisé*) *Fig* edifice. ◆**édification** *nf* construction; edification; enlightenment. ◆**édifier** *vt* (*bâtiment*) to construct, erect; (*théorie*) to construct; **é. qn** (*moralement*) to edify s.o.; (*détromper*) *Iron* to enlighten s.o.

Édimbourg [edɛ̃bur] *nm ou f* Edinburgh.

édit [edi] *nm Hist* edict.

éditer [edite] *vt* (*publier*) to publish; (*annoter*) to edit. ◆**éditeur, -trice** *nmf* publisher; editor. ◆**édition** *nf* (*livre, journal*) edition; (*diffusion, métier*) publishing. ◆**éditorial, -aux** *nm* (*article*) editorial.

édredon [edrədɔ̃] *nm* eiderdown.

éducation [edykasjɔ̃] *nf* (*enseignement*) education; (*façon d'élever*) upbringing, education; **avoir de l'é.** to have good manners, be well-bred. ◆**éducateur, -trice** *nmf* educator. ◆**éducatif, -ive** *a* educational. ◆**éduquer** *vt* (*à l'école*) to educate (*s.o.*); (*à la maison*) to bring (*s.o.*) up, educate (*s.o.*) (**à faire** to do); (*esprit*) to educate, train.

effac/er [efase] *vt* (*gommer*) to rub out, erase; (*en lavant*) to wash out; (*avec un chiffon*) to wipe away; (*souvenir*) Fig to blot out, erase; — **s'e.** *vpr* (*souvenir, couleur etc*) to fade; (*se placer en retrait*) to step ou draw aside. ◆**—é** *a* (*modeste*) self-effacing. ◆**—ement** *nm* (*modestie*) self-effacement.

effar/er [efare] *vt* to scare, alarm. ◆**—ement** *nm* alarm.

effaroucher [efaruʃe] *vt* to scare away, frighten away.

effectif, -ive [efektif, -iv] **1** *a* (*réel*) effective, real. **2** *nm* (*nombre*) (total) strength; (*de classe*) Scol size, total number; *pl* (*employés*) & Mil manpower. ◆**effectivement** *adv* (*en effet*) actually, effectively, indeed.

effectuer [efektɥe] *vt* (*expérience etc*) to carry out; (*paiement, trajet etc*) to make.

efféminé [efemine] *a* effeminate.

effervescent [efervesɑ̃] *a* (*mélange, jeunesse*) effervescent. ◆**effervescence** *nf* (*exaltation*) excitement, effervescence; (*de liquide*) effervescence.

effet [efɛ] *nm* **1** (*résultat*) effect; (*impression*) impression, effect (**sur** on); **faire de l'e.** (*remède etc*) to be effective; **rester sans e.** to have no effect; **à cet e.** to this end, for this purpose; **en e.** indeed, in fact; **il me fait l'e. d'être fatigué** he seems to me to be tired; **sous l'e. de la colère** (*agir*) in anger, out of anger. **2 e. de commerce** bill, draft.

effets [efɛ] *nmpl* (*vêtements*) clothes, things.

efficace [efikas] *a* (*mesure etc*) effective; (*personne*) efficient. ◆**efficacité** *nf* effectiveness; efficiency.

effigie [efiʒi] *nf* effigy.

effilé [efile] *a* tapering, slender.

effilocher (s') [sefiloʃe] *vpr* to fray.

efflanqué [eflɑ̃ke] *a* emaciated.

effleurer [eflœre] *vt* (*frôler*) to skim, touch lightly; (*égratigner*) to graze; (*question*) Fig to touch on; **e. qn** (*pensée etc*) to cross s.o.'s mind.

effondr/er (s') [sefɔ̃dre] *vpr* (*projet, édifice, personne*) to collapse; (*toit*) to cave in, collapse. ◆**—ement** *nm* collapse; Com slump; (*abattement*) dejection.

efforcer (s') [seforse] *vpr* **s'e. de faire** to try (hard) ou endeavour ou strive to do.

effort [efor] *nm* effort; **sans e.** (*réussir etc*) effortlessly; (*réussite etc*) effortless.

effraction [efraksjɔ̃] *nf* **pénétrer par e.** (*cambrioleur*) to break in; **vol avec e.** housebreaking.

effranger (s') [sefrɑ̃ʒe] *vpr* to fray.

effray/er [efreje] *vt* to frighten, scare; — **s'e.** *vpr* to be frightened ou scared. ◆**—ant** *a* frightening, scary.

effréné [efrene] *a* unrestrained, wild.

effriter [efrite] *vt*, — **s'e.** *vpr* to crumble (away).

effroi [efrwa] *nm* (*frayeur*) dread. ◆**effroyable** *a* dreadful, appalling. ◆**effroyablement** *adv* dreadfully.

effronté [efrɔ̃te] *a* (*enfant etc*) cheeky, brazen; (*mensonge*) shameless. ◆**effronterie** *nf* effrontery.

effusion [efyzjɔ̃] *nf* **1 e. de sang** bloodshed. **2** (*manifestation*) effusion; **avec e.** effusively.

égailler (s') [segaje] *vpr* to disperse.

égal, -ale, -aux [egal, -o] *a* equal (**à** to); (*uniforme, régulier*) even; **ça m'est é.** I don't care, it's all the same to me; — *nmf* (*personne*) equal; **traiter qn d'é. à é.** to treat s.o. as an equal; **sans é.** without match. ◆**—ement** *adv* (*au même degré*) equally; (*aussi*) also, as well. ◆**égaler** *vt* to equal, match (**en** in); (*en quantité*) Math to equal. ◆**égalisation** *nf* Sp equalization; levelling. ◆**égaliser** *vt* to equalize; (*terrain*) to level; — *vi* Sp to equalize. ◆**égalitaire** *a* egalitarian. ◆**égalité** *nf* equality; (*régularité*) evenness; **à é.** (**de score**) Sp equal (on points); **signe d'é.** Math equals sign.

égard [egar] *nm* **à l'é. de** (*concernant*) with respect ou regard to; (*envers*) towards; **avoir des égards pour** to have respect ou consideration for; **à cet é.** in this respect; **à certains égards** in some respects.

égarer [egare] *vt* (*objet*) to mislay; **é. qn** (*dérouter*) to mislead s.o.; (*aveugler, troubler*) to lead s.o. astray, misguide s.o.; — **s'é.** *vpr* to lose one's way, get lost; (*objet*) to get mislaid, go astray; (*esprit*) to wander.

égayer [egeje] *vt* (*pièce*) to brighten up; **é. qn** (*réconforter, amuser*) to cheer s.o. up; — **s'é.** *vpr* (*par la moquerie*) to be amused.

égide [eʒid] *nf* **sous l'é. de** under the aegis of.

églantier [eglɑ̃tje] *nm* (*arbre*) wild rose. ◆**églantine** *nf* (*fleur*) wild rose.

église [egliz] *nf* church.

égocentrique [egɔsɑ̃trik] *a* egocentric.

égoïne [egɔin] *nf* (scie) é. hand saw.

égoïsme [egɔism] *nm* selfishness, egoism. ◆**égoïste** *a* selfish, egoistic(al); — *nmf* egoist.

égorger [egɔrʒe] *vt* to cut ou slit the throat of.

égosiller (s') [segɔzije] *vpr* to scream one's head off, bawl out.

égotisme [egɔtism] *nm* egotism.

égout [egu] *nm* sewer; **eaux d'é.** sewage.

égoutter [egute] *vt* (vaisselle) to drain; (légumes) to strain, drain; — *vi*, — **s'é.** *vpr* to drain; to strain; (linge) to drip. ◆**égouttoir** *nm* (panier) (dish) drainer.

égratigner [egratiɲe] *vt* to scratch. ◆**égratignure** *nf* scratch.

égrener [egrəne] *vt* (raisins) to pick off; (épis) to shell; (grains) Rel to count one's beads.

Égypte [eʒipt] *nf* Egypt. ◆**égyptien, -ienne** [-sjɛ̃, -sjɛn] *a* & *nmf* Egyptian.

eh! [e] *int* hey!; **eh bien!** well!

éhonté [eɔ̃te] *a* shameless; **mensonge é.** barefaced lie.

éjecter [eʒɛkte] *vt* to eject. ◆**éjectable** *a* **siège é.** *Av* ejector seat. ◆**éjection** *nf* ejection.

élaborer [elabɔre] *vt* (système etc) to elaborate. ◆**élaboration** *nf* elaboration.

élaguer [elage] *vt* (arbre, texte etc) to prune.

élan [elɑ̃] *nm* **1** (vitesse) momentum, impetus; (impulsion) impulse; (fougue) fervour, spirit; **prendre son é.** *Sp* to take a run (up); **d'un seul é.** in one bound. **2** (animal) elk.

élancé [elɑ̃se] *a* (mince) slender.

élancer [elɑ̃se] *vi* (dent etc) to give shooting pains. **2 s'é.** *vpr* (bondir) to leap ou rush (forward); **s'é. vers le ciel** (tour) to soar up (high) into the sky. ◆**—é** *a* (personne, taille etc) slender. ◆**—ement** *nm* shooting pain.

élargir [elarʒir] **1** *vt* (chemin) to widen; (esprit, débat) to broaden; — **s'é.** *vpr* (sentier etc) to widen out. **2** *vt* (prisonnier) to free.

élastique [elastik] *a* (objet, caractère) elastic; (règlement, notion) flexible, supple; — *nm* (tissu) elastic; (lien) elastic ou rubber band. ◆**élasticité** *nf* elasticity.

élection [elɛksjɔ̃] *nf* election; **é. partielle** by-election. ◆**électeur, -trice** *nmf* voter, elector. ◆**électoral, -aux** *a* (campagne, réunion) election-; **collège é.** electoral college. ◆**électorat** *nm* (électeurs) electorate, voters.

électricien [elɛktrisjɛ̃] *nm* electrician. ◆**électricité** *nf* electricity; **coupure d'é.**

power cut. ◆**électrifier** *vt* Rail to electrify.

◆**électrique** *a* (pendule, décharge) electric; (courant, fil) electric(al); (phénomène, effet) Fig electric. ◆**électriser** *vt* (animer) Fig to electrify. ◆**électrocuter** *vt* to electrocute.

électrode [elɛktrɔd] *nf* Él electrode.

électrogène [elɛktrɔʒɛn] *a* **groupe é.** Él generator.

électroménager [elɛktrɔmenaʒe] *am* **appareil é.** household electrical appliance.

électron [elɛktrɔ̃] *nm* electron. ◆**électronicien, -ienne** *nmf* electronics engineer. ◆**électronique** *a* electronic; (microscope) electron-; — *nf* electronics.

électrophone [elɛktrɔfɔn] *nm* record player.

élégant [elegɑ̃] *a* (style, mobilier, solution etc) elegant; (bien habillé) smart, elegant. ◆**élégamment** *adv* elegantly; smartly. ◆**élégance** *nf* elegance.

élégie [eleʒi] *nf* elegy.

élément [elemɑ̃] *nm* (composante, personne) & Ch element; (de meuble) unit; (d'ensemble) Math member; *pl* (notions) rudiments, elements; **dans son é.** (milieu) in one's element. ◆**élémentaire** *a* elementary.

éléphant [elefɑ̃] *nm* elephant. ◆**éléphantesque** *a* (énorme) Fam elephantine.

élévateur [elevatœr] *am* **chariot é.** forklift truck.

élévation [elevasjɔ̃] *nf* raising; Géom elevation; **é. de** (hausse) rise in.

élève [elɛv] *nmf* Scol pupil.

élev/er [elve] *vt* (prix, objection, voix etc) to raise; (enfant) to bring up, raise; (animal) to breed, rear; (âme) to uplift, raise; — **s'é.** *vpr* (prix, montagne, ton, avion etc) to rise; **s'é. à** (prix etc) to amount to; **s'é. contre** to rise up against. ◆**—é** *a* (haut) high; (noble) noble; **bien/mal é.** well-/bad-mannered. ◆**—age** *nm* (de bovins) cattle rearing; **é. de** the breeding ou rearing of. ◆**—eur, -euse** *nmf* breeder.

élider [elide] *vt* Ling to elide.

éligible [eliʒibl] *a* Pol eligible (à for).

élimé [elime] *a* (tissu) threadbare, worn thin.

éliminer [elimine] *vt* to eliminate. ◆**élimination** *nf* elimination. ◆**éliminatoire** *a* & *nf* (épreuve) é. Sp heat, qualifying round.

élire* [elir] *vt* Pol to elect (à to).

élision [elizjɔ̃] *nf* Ling elision.

élite [elit] *nf* elite (de of); **d'é.** (chef, sujet etc) top-notch.

elle [ɛl] *pron* **1** (sujet) she; (chose, animal) it;

pl they; **e. est** she is; it is; **elles sont** they are. **2** (*complément*) her; (*chose, animal*) it; *pl* them; **pour e.** for her; **pour elles** for them; **plus grande qu'e./qu'elles** taller than her/them. ◆**e.-même** *pron* herself; (*chose, animal*) itself; *pl* themselves.

ellipse [elips] *nf Géom* ellipse. ◆**elliptique** *a* elliptical.

élocution [elɔkysjɔ̃] *nf* diction; **défaut d'é.** speech defect.

éloge [elɔʒ] *nm* praise; (*panégyrique*) eulogy; **faire l'é. de** to praise. ◆**élogieux, -euse** *a* laudatory.

éloign/er [elwaɲe] *vt* (*chose, personne*) to move ou take away (**de** from); (*clients*) to keep away; (*crainte, idée*) to get rid of, banish; (*date*) to put off; **é. qn de** (*sujet, but*) to take s.o. away from; — **s'é.** *vpr* (*partir*) to move ou go away (**de** from); (*dans le passé*) to become (more) remote; **s'é. de** (*sujet, but*) to get away from. ◆**-é** *a* far-off, remote, distant; (*parent*) distant; **é. de** (*village, maison etc*) far (away) from; (*très différent*) far remoyed from. ◆**-ement** *nm* remoteness, distance; (*absence*) separation (**de** from); **avec l'é.** (*avec le recul*) with time.

élongation [elɔ̃gasjɔ̃] *nf Méd* pulled muscle.

éloquent [elɔkɑ̃] *a* eloquent. ◆**éloquence** *nf* eloquence.

élu, -ue [ely] *voir* **élire;** — *nmf Pol* elected member ou representative; **les élus** *Rel* the chosen, the elect.

élucider [elyside] *vt* to elucidate. ◆**élucidation** *nf* elucidation.

éluder [elyde] *vt* to elude, evade.

émacié [emasje] *a* emaciated.

émail, -aux [emaj, -o] *nm* enamel; **en é.** enamel-. ◆**émailler** *vt* to enamel.

émaillé [emaje] *a* **é. de fautes**/*etc* (*texte*) peppered with errors/*etc*.

émanciper [emɑ̃sipe] *vt* (*femmes*) to emancipate; — **s'é.** *vpr* to become emancipated. ◆**émancipation** *nf* emancipation.

émaner [emane] *vi* to emanate. ◆**émanation** *nf* emanation; **une é. de** *Fig* a product of.

emball/er [ɑ̃bale] **1** *vt* (*dans une caisse etc*) to pack; (*dans du papier*) to wrap (up). **2** *vt* (*moteur*) to race; **e. qn** (*passionner*) *Fam* to enthuse with, thrill s.o.; — **s'é.** *vpr* (*personne*) *Fam* to get carried away; (*cheval*) to bolt; (*moteur*) to race. ◆**-é** *a Fam* enthusiastic. ◆**-age** *nm* (*action*) ⸸ packing; wrapping; (*caisse*) packaging; (*papier*) wrapping (paper). ◆**-ement** *nm Fam* (sudden) enthusiasm.

embarcadère [ɑ̃barkader] *nm* landing place, quay.

embarcation [ɑ̃barkasjɔ̃] *nf* (small) boat.

embardée [ɑ̃barde] *nf Aut* (sudden) swerve; **faire une e.** to swerve.

embargo [ɑ̃bargo] *nm* embargo.

embarqu/er [ɑ̃barke] *vt* (*passagers*) to embark, take on board; (*marchandises*) to load (up); (*voler*) *Fam* to walk off with; (*prisonnier*) *Fam* to cart off; **e. qn dans** (*affaire*) *Fam* to involve s.o. in, launch s.o. into; — *vi*, — **s'e.** *vpr* to embark, (go on) board; **s'e. dans** (*aventure etc*) *Fam* to embark on. ◆**-ement** *nm* (*de passagers*) boarding.

embarras [ɑ̃bara] *nm* (*malaise, gêne*) embarrassment; (*difficulté*) difficulty, trouble; (*obstacle*) obstacle; **dans l'e.** in difficulty; **faire des e.** (*chichis*) to make a fuss. ◆**embarrass/er** *vt* (*obstruer*) to clutter, encumber; **e. qn** in s.o.'s way; (*déconcerter*) to embarrass s.o., bother s.o.; **s'e. de** to burden oneself with; (*se soucier*) to bother oneself about. ◆**-ant** *a* (*paquet*) cumbersome; (*question*) embarrassing.

embauche [ɑ̃boʃ] *nf* (*action*) hiring; (*travail*) work. ◆**embaucher** *vt* (*ouvrier*) to hire, take on.

embaumer [ɑ̃bome] **1** *vt* (*cadavre*) to embalm. **2** *vt* (*parfumer*) to give a sweet smell to; — *vi* to smell sweet.

embell/ir [ɑ̃belir] *vt* (*texte, vérité*) to embellish; **e. qn** to make s.o. attractive. ◆**-issement** *nm* (*de ville etc*) improvement, embellishment.

embêt/er [ɑ̃bete] *vt Fam* (*contrarier, taquiner*) to annoy, bother; (*raser*) to bore; — **s'e.** *vpr Fam* to get bored. ◆**-ant** *a Fam* annoying; boring. ◆**-ement** [-ɛtmɑ̃] *nm Fam* un e. (some) trouble ou bother; **des embêtements** trouble(s), bother.

emblée (d') [dɑ̃ble] *adv* right away.

emblème [ɑ̃blɛm] *nm* emblem.

embobiner [ɑ̃bobine] *vt* (*tromper*) *Fam* to hoodwink.

emboît/er [ɑ̃bwate] *vt*, — **s'e.** *vpr* (*pièces*) to fit into each other, fit together; **e. le pas à qn** to follow in s.o.'s heels; (*imiter*) *Fig* to follow in s.o.'s footsteps.

embonpoint [ɑ̃bɔ̃pwɛ̃] *nm* plumpness.

embouchure [ɑ̃buʃyr] *nf* (*de cours d'eau*) mouth; *Mus* mouthpiece.

embourber (s') [sɑ̃burbe] *vpr* (*véhicule*) & *Fig* to get bogged down.

embourgeoiser (s') [sɑ̃burʒwaze] *vpr* to become middle-class.

embout [ãbu] nm (de canne) tip, end piece; (de seringue) nozzle.

embouteill/er [ãbuteje] vt Aut to jam, congest. **◆-age** nm traffic jam.

emboutir [ãbutir] vt (voiture) to bash ou crash into; (métal) to stamp, emboss.

embranch/er (s') [sãbrãʃe] vpr (voie) to branch off. **◆-ement** nm (de voie) junction, fork; (de règne animal) branch.

embras/er [ãbraze] vt to set ablaze; — **s'e.** vpr (prendre feu) to flare up. **◆-ement** nm (troubles) flare-up.

embrasser [ãbrase] vt (adopter, contenir) to embrace; e. qn to kiss s.o.; (serrer) to embrace ou hug s.o.; — **s'e.** vpr to kiss (each other). **◆embrassade** nf embrace, hug.

embrasure [ãbrazyr] nf (de fenêtre, porte) opening.

embray/er [ãbreje] vi to let in ou engage the clutch. **◆-age** nm (mécanisme, pédale) Aut clutch.

embrigader [ãbrigade] vt to recruit.

embrocher [ãbrɔʃe] vt Culin & Fig to skewer.

embrouiller [ãbruje] vt (fils) to tangle (up); (papiers etc) to muddle (up), mix up; e. qn to confuse s.o., get s.o. muddled; — **s'e.** vpr to get confused ou muddled (dans in, with). **◆embrouillamini** nm Fam muddle, mixup. **◆embrouillement** nm confusion, muddle.

embroussaillé [ãbrusaje] a (barbe, chemin) bushy.

embruns [ãbrœ̃] nmpl (sea) spray.

embryon [ãbrijɔ̃] nm embryo. **◆embryonnaire** a Méd & Fig embryonic.

embûches [ãbyʃ] nfpl (difficultés) traps, pitfalls.

embuer [ãbɥe] vt (vitre, yeux) to mist up.

embusquer (s') [sãbyske] vpr to lie in ambush. **◆embuscade** nf ambush.

éméché [emeʃe] a (ivre) Fam tipsy.

émeraude [emrod] nf emerald.

émerger [emerʒe] vi to emerge (de from).

émeri [emri] nm toile (d')é. emery cloth.

émerveill/er [emerveje] vt to amaze; — **s'é.** vpr to marvel, be filled with wonder (de at). **◆-ement** nm wonder, amazement.

émett/re* [emetr] vt (lumière, son etc) to give out, emit; Rad to transmit, broadcast; (cri) to utter; (opinion, vœu) to express; (timbre-poste, monnaie) to issue; (chèque) to draw; (emprunt) Com to float. **◆-eur** nm (poste) é. Rad transmitter.

émeute [emøt] nf riot. **◆émeutier, -ière** nmf rioter.

émietter [emjete] vt, — **s'é.** vpr (pain etc) to crumble.

émigr/er [emigre] vi (personne) to emigrate. **◆-ant, -ante** nmf emigrant. **◆-é, -ée** nmf exile, émigré. **◆émigration** nf emigration.

éminent [eminã] a eminent. **◆éminemment** [-amã] adv eminently. **◆éminence** nf 1 (colline) hillock. 2 son É. Rel his Eminence.

émissaire [emiser] nm emissary.

émission [emisjɔ̃] nf (programme) TV Rad broadcast; (action) emission (de of); (de programme) TV Rad transmission; (de timbre-poste, monnaie) issue.

emmagasiner [ãmagazine] vt to store (up).

emmanchure [ãmãʃyr] nf (de vêtement) arm hole.

emmêler [ãmele] vt to tangle (up).

emménag/er [ãmenaʒe] vi (dans un logement) to move in; e. dans to move into. **◆-ement** nm moving in.

emmener [ãmne] vt to take (à to); (prisonnier) to take away; e. qn faire une promenade to take s.o. for a walk.

emmerd/er [ãmerde] vt Arg to annoy, bug; (raser) to bore stiff; — **s'e.** vpr Arg to get bored stiff. **◆-ement** nm Arg bother, trouble. **◆-eur, -euse** nmf (personne) Arg pain in the neck.

emmitoufler (s') [sãmitufle] vpr to wrap (oneself) up.

emmurer [ãmyre] vt (personne) to wall in.

émoi [emwa] nm excitement; en é. agog, excited.

émoluments [emɔlymã] nmpl remuneration.

émotion [emosjɔ̃] nf (trouble) excitement; (sentiment) emotion; une é. (peur) a scare. **◆émotif, -ive** a emotional. **◆émotionné** a Fam upset.

émouss/er [emuse] vt (pointe) to blunt; (sentiment) to dull. **◆-é** a (pointe) blunt; (sentiment) dulled.

émouv/oir* [emuvwar] vt (affecter) to move, touch; — **s'é.** vpr to be moved ou touched. **◆-ant** a moving, touching.

empailler [ãpaje] vt (animal) to stuff.

empaler (s') [sãpale] vpr to impale oneself.

empaqueter [ãpakte] vt to pack(age).

emparer (s') [sãpare] vpr s'e. de to seize, take hold of.

empât/er (s') [sãpate] vpr to fill out, get fat(ter). **◆-é** a fleshy, fat.

empêch/er [ãpeʃe] vt to prevent, stop; e. qn de faire to prevent ou stop s.o. (from) doing; n'empêche qu'elle a raison Fam all the same she's right; **n'empêche!** *Fam* all the same!; **elle ne peut pas s'e. de rire** she can't help laughing. ◆**—ement** [-ɛʃmɑ̃] *nm* difficulty, hitch; **avoir un e.** to be unavoidably detained.

empereur [ɑ̃prœr] *nm* emperor.

empeser [ɑ̃pəze] *vt* to starch.

empester [ɑ̃pɛste] *vt* (*pièce*) to make stink, stink out; (*tabac etc*) to stink of; **e. qn** to stink s.o. out; — *vi* to stink.

empêtrer (s') [sɑ̃petre] *vpr* to get entangled (**dans** in).

emphase [ɑ̃faz] *nf* pomposity. ◆**emphatique** *a* pompous.

empiéter [ɑ̃pjete] *vi* **e. sur** to encroach upon. ◆**empiétement** *nm* encroachment.

empiffrer (s') [sɑ̃pifre] *vpr Fam* to gorge *ou* stuff oneself (**de** with).

empil/er [ɑ̃pile] *vt*, **— s'e.** *vpr* to pile up (**sur** on); **s'e. dans** (*personnes*) to pile into (*building, car etc*). ◆**—ement** *nm* (*tas*) pile.

empire [ɑ̃pir] *nm* (*territoires*) empire; (*autorité*) hold, influence; **sous l'e. de** (*peur etc*) in the grip of.

empirer [ɑ̃pire] *vi* to worsen, get worse.

empirique [ɑ̃pirik] *a* empirical. ◆**empirisme** *nm* empiricism.

emplacement [ɑ̃plasmɑ̃] *nm* site, location; (*de stationnement*) place.

emplâtre [ɑ̃plɑtr] *nm* (*onguent*) *Méd* plaster.

emplette [ɑ̃plɛt] *nf* purchase; *pl* shopping.

emplir [ɑ̃plir] *vt*, **— s'e.** *vpr* to fill (**de** with).

emploi [ɑ̃plwa] *nm* **1** (*usage*) use; **e. du temps** timetable; **mode d'e.** directions (for use). **2** (*travail*) job, position, employment; **l'e.** (*travail*) *Écon Pol* employment; **sans e.** unemployed. ◆**employ/er** *vt* (*utiliser*) to use; **e. qn** (*occuper*) to employ s.o.; **— s'e.** *vpr* (*expression etc*) to be used; **s'e. à faire** to devote oneself to doing. ◆**—é, -ée** *nmf* employee; (*de bureau, banque*) clerk, employee; **e. des postes**/*etc* postal/*etc* worker; **e. de magasin** shop assistant, *Am* sales clerk. ◆**employeur, -euse** *nmf* employer.

empocher [ɑ̃pɔʃe] *vt* (*argent*) to pocket.

empoigner [ɑ̃pwaɲe] *vt* (*saisir*) to grab, grasp; **— s'e.** *vpr* to come to blows, fight. ◆**empoignade** *nf* (*querelle*) fight.

empoisonn/er [ɑ̃pwazɔne] *vt* (*personne, aliment, atmosphère*) to poison; (*empester*) to stink out; (*gâter, altérer*) to trouble, bedevil; **e. qn** (*embêter*) *Fam* to get on s.o.'s nerves; **— s'e.** *vpr* (*par accident*) to be poisoned; (*volontairement*) to poison oneself. ◆**—ant** *a* (*embêtant*) *Fam* irritating.

◆**—ement** *nm* poisoning; (*ennui*) *Fam* problem, trouble.

emport/er [ɑ̃pɔrte] *vt* (*prendre*) to take (away) (**avec soi** with one); (*enlever*) to take away; (*prix, trophée*) to carry off; (*décision*) to carry; (*entraîner*) to carry along *ou* away; (*par le vent*) to blow off *ou* away; (*par les vagues*) to sweep away; (*par la maladie*) to carry off; **l'e. sur qn** to get the upper hand over s.o.; **se laisser e.** *Fig* to get carried away (**par** by); **— s'e.** *vpr* to lose one's temper (**contre** with). ◆**—é** *a* (*caractère*) hot-tempered. ◆**—ement** *nm* anger; *pl* fits of anger.

empoté [ɑ̃pɔte] *a Fam* clumsy.

empourprer (s') [sɑ̃purpre] *vpr* to turn crimson.

empreint [ɑ̃prɛ̃] *a* **e. de** stamped with, heavy with.

empreinte [ɑ̃prɛ̃t] *nf* (*marque*) & *Fig* mark, stamp; **e. digitale** fingerprint; **e. des pas** footprint.

empress/er (s') [sɑ̃prese] *vpr* **s'e. de faire** to hasten to do; **s'e. auprès de qn** to busy oneself with s.o., be attentive to s.o.; **s'e. autour de qn** to rush around s.o. ◆**—é** *a* eager, attentive; **e. à faire** eager to do. ◆**—ement** [-ɛsmɑ̃] *nm* (*hâte*) eagerness; (*auprès de qn*) attentiveness.

emprise [ɑ̃priz] *nf* ascendancy, hold (**sur** over).

emprisonn/er [ɑ̃prizɔne] *vt Jur* to imprison; (*enfermer*) *Fig* to confine. ◆**—ement** *nm* imprisonment.

emprunt [ɑ̃prœ̃] *nm* (*argent*) *Com* loan; (*mot*) *Ling* borrowed word; **un e. à** *Ling* a borrowing from; **l'e. de qch** the borrowing of sth; **d'e.** borrowed; **nom d'e.** assumed name. ◆**emprunt/er** *vt* (*obtenir*) to borrow (**à qn** from s.o.); (*route etc*) to use; (*nom*) to assume; **e. à** (*tirer de*) to derive *ou* borrow from. ◆**—é** *a* (*gêné*) ill-at-ease.

empuantir [ɑ̃pɥɑ̃tir] *vt* to make stink, stink out.

ému [emy] *voir* **émouvoir**; **—** *a* (*attendri*) moved; (*apeuré*) nervous; (*attristé*) upset; **une voix émue** a voice charged with emotion.

émulation [emylasjɔ̃] *nf* emulation.

émule [emyl] *nmf* imitator, follower.

en[1] [ɑ̃] *prép* **1** (*lieu*) in; (*direction*) to; **être en ville/en France** to be in town/in France; **aller en ville/en France** to go (in)to town/to France. **2** (*temps*) in; **en été** in summer; **en février** in February; **d'heure en heure** from hour to hour. **3** (*moyen, état etc*) by; in; at; on; **en avion** by plane; **en groupe**

in a group; **en mer** at sea; **en guerre** at war; **en fleur** in flower; **en congé** on leave; **en vain** in vain. **4** (*matière*) in; **en bois** wooden, in wood; **chemise en nylon** nylon shirt; **c'est en or** it's (made of) gold. **5** (*comme*) **en cadeau** as a present; **en ami** as a friend. **6** (+ *participe présent*) **en mangeant/chantant/**etc while eating/singing/etc; **en apprenant que . . .** on hearing that . . . ; **en souriant** smiling, with a smile; **en ne disant rien** by saying nothing; **sortir en courant** to run out. **7** (*transformation*) into; **traduire en** to translate into.

en² [ɑ̃] *pron & adv* **1** (= *de là*) from there; **j'en viens** I've just come from there. **2** (= *de ça, lui, eux etc*) **il en est content** he's pleased with it *ou* him *ou* them; **j'en parle** to talk about it; **en mourir** to die *ou* from it; **elle m'en frappa** she struck me with it. **3** (*partitif*) some; **j'en ai** I have some; **en veux-tu?** do you want some *ou* any?; **je t'en supplie** I beg you (to).

encadr/er [ɑ̃kadre] *vt* (*tableau*) to frame; (*entourer d'un trait*) to box in; (*troupes, étudiants*) to supervise, train; (*prisonnier, accusé*) to flank. ◆**—ement** *nm* (*action*) framing; supervision; (*de porte, photo*) frame; (*décor*) setting; (*personnel*) training and supervisory staff.

encaissé [ɑ̃kese] *a* (*vallée*) deep.

encaisser [ɑ̃kese] *vt* (*argent, loyer etc*) to collect; (*effet, chèque* Com) to cash; (*coup* Fam) to take; **je ne peux pas l'e.** Fam I can't stand him *ou* her. ◆**encaissement** *nm* (*de loyer etc*) collection; (*de chèque*) cashing.

encapuchonné [ɑ̃kapyʃɔne] *a* hooded.

encart [ɑ̃kar] *nm* (*feuille*) insert. ◆**encarter** *vt* to insert.

en-cas [ɑ̃kɑ] *nm inv* (*repas*) snack.

encastrer [ɑ̃kastre] *vt* to build in (**dans** to), embed (**dans** into).

encaustique [ɑ̃kostik] *nf* (wax) polish. ◆**encaustiquer** *vt* to wax, polish.

enceinte [ɑ̃sɛ̃t] **1** *af* (*femme*) pregnant; **e. de six mois/**etc six months/etc pregnant. **2** *nf* (*muraille*) (surrounding) wall; (*espace*) enclosure; **e. acoustique** (loud)speakers.

encens [ɑ̃sɑ̃] *nm* incense. ◆**encensoir** *nm* Rel censer.

encercler [ɑ̃serkle] *vt* to surround, encircle.

enchaîner [ɑ̃ʃene] *vt* (*animal*) to chain (up); (*prisonnier*) to put in chains, chain (up); (*assembler*) to link (up), connect; — *vi* (*continuer à parler*) to continue; — **s'e.** *vpr* (*idées etc*) to be linked (up). ◆**enchaînement** *nm* (*succession*) chain, series; (*liaison*) link(ing) (**de** between, of).

enchant/er [ɑ̃ʃɑ̃te] *vt* (*ravir*) to delight, enchant; (*ensorceler*) to bewitch, enchant. ◆**—é** *a* (*ravi*) delighted (**de** with, **que** (+ *sub*)); **e. de faire votre connaissance!** pleased to meet you! ◆**—ement** *nm* delight; enchantment; **comme par e.** as if by magic. ◆**—eur** a delightful, enchanting; — *nm* (*sorcier*) magician.

enchâsser [ɑ̃ʃɑse] *vt* (*diamant*) to set, embed.

enchère [ɑ̃ʃɛr] *nf* (*offre*) bid; **vente aux enchères** auction; **mettre aux enchères** to (put up for) auction. ◆**enchér/ir** *vi* **e. sur qn** to outbid s.o. ◆**—isseur** *nm* bidder.

enchevêtrer [ɑ̃ʃvetre] *vt* to (en)tangle; — **s'e.** *vpr* to get entangled (**dans** in). ◆**enchevêtrement** *nm* tangle, entanglement.

enclave [ɑ̃klav] *nf* enclave. ◆**enclaver** *vt* to enclose (completely).

enclencher [ɑ̃klɑ̃ʃe] *vt* Tech to engage.

enclin [ɑ̃klɛ̃] *am* **e.** à inclined *ou* prone to.

enclore [ɑ̃klɔr] *vt* (*terrain*) to enclose. ◆**enclos** *nm* (*terrain, clôture*) enclosure.

enclume [ɑ̃klym] *nf* anvil.

encoche [ɑ̃kɔʃ] *nf* notch, nick (**à** in).

encoignure [ɑ̃kwaɲyr] *nf* corner.

encoller [ɑ̃kɔle] *vt* to paste.

encolure [ɑ̃kɔlyr] *nf* (*de cheval, vêtement*) neck; (*tour du cou*) collar (size).

encombre (sans) [sɑ̃zɑ̃kɔ̃br] *adv* without a hitch.

encombr/er [ɑ̃kɔ̃bre] *vt* (*couloir, pièce etc*) to clutter up (**de** with); (*rue*) to congest, clog (**de** with); **e. qn** to hamper s.o.; **s'e. de** to burden *ou* saddle oneself with. ◆**—ant** *a* (*paquet*) bulky, cumbersome; (*présence*) awkward. ◆**—é** *a* (*profession, marché*) overcrowded, saturated. ◆**—ement** *nm* (*embarras*) clutter; Aut traffic jam; (*volume*) bulk(iness).

encontre de (à l') [alɑ̃kɔ̃trədə] *adv* against; (*contrairement à*) contrary to.

encore [ɑ̃kɔr] *adv* **1** (*toujours*) still; **tu es e. là?** are you still here? **2** (*avec négation*) yet; **pas e.** not yet; **ne pars pas e.** don't go yet; **je ne suis pas e. prêt** I'm not ready yet, I'm still not ready. **3** (*de nouveau*) again; **essaie e.** try again. **4** (*de plus*) **e. un café** another coffee, one more coffee; **e. une fois** (once) again, once more; **e. un** another (one), one more; **e. du pain** (some) more bread; **que veut-il e.?** what else *ou* more does he want?; **e. quelque chose** something else; **qui/quoi e.?** who/what else?; **chante e.** sing some more. **5** (*avec comparatif*) even, still; **e. mieux** even better, better still. **6** (*aussi*) also. **7 si e.** (*si seulement*) if only; **et e.!** (*à peine*) if that!, only just! **8 e. que** (+ *sub*) although.

encourag/er [ãkuraʒe] *vt* to encourage (à faire *ou* to do). ◆—**eant** *a* encouraging. ◆—**ement** *nm* encouragement.

encourir* [ãkurir] *vt* (*amende etc*) to incur.

encrasser [ãkrase] *vt* to clog up (with dirt).

encre [ãkr] *nf* ink; **e. de Chine** Indian ink; **e. sympathique** invisible ink. ◆**encrier** *nm* inkwell, inkpot.

encroûter (s') [sãkrute] *vpr Péj* to get set in one's ways; **s'e. dans** (*habitude*) to get stuck in.

encyclique [ãsiklik] *nf Rel* encyclical.

encyclopédie [ãsiklɔpedi] *nf* encyclop(a)edia. ◆**encyclopédique** *a* encyclop(a)edic.

endémique [ãdemik] *a* endemic.

endetter [ãdete] *vt* **e. qn** to get s.o. into debt; — **s'e.** *vpr* to get into debt. ◆**endettement** *nm* (*dettes*) debts.

endeuiller [ãdœje] *vt* to plunge into mourning.

endiablé [ãdjable] *a* (*rythme etc*) frantic, wild.

endiguer [ãdige] *vt* (*fleuve*) to dam (up); (*réprimer*) Fig to stem.

endimanché [ãdimãʃe] *a* in one's Sunday best.

endive [ãdiv] *nf* chicory, endive.

endoctrin/er [ãdɔktrine] *vt* to indoctrinate. ◆—**ement** *nm* indoctrination.

endolori [ãdɔlɔri] *a* painful, aching.

endommager [ãdɔmaʒe] *vt* to damage.

endorm/ir* [ãdɔrmir] *vt* (*enfant, patient*) to put to sleep; (*ennuyer*) to send to sleep; (*soupçons etc*) to lull; (*douleur*) to deaden; — **s'e.** *vpr* to fall asleep, go to sleep. ◆—**i** *a* asleep, sleeping; (*indolent*) Fam sluggish.

endosser [ãdose] *vt* (*vêtement*) to put on, don; (*responsabilité*) to assume; (*chèque*) to endorse.

endroit [ãdrwa] *nm* **1** place, spot; (*de film, livre*) part, place. **2** (*de tissu*) right side; à l'e. (*vêtement*) right side out, the right way round.

endur/ir [ãdyrir] *vt* to harden; **s'e. à** (*personne*) to become hardened to (*pain etc*). ◆—**i** *a* hardened; (*célibataire*) confirmed. ◆—**issement** *nm* hardening.

endurer [ãdyre] *vt* to endure, bear.

énergie [enɛrʒi] *nf* energy; **avec é.** (*protester etc*) forcefully. ◆**énergétique** *a* (*ressources etc*) energy-. ◆**énergique** *a* (*dynamique*) energetic; (*remède*) powerful; (*mesure, ton*) forceful. ◆**énergiquement** *adv* (*protester etc*) energetically.

énergumène [enɛrgymɛn] *nmf Péj* rowdy character.

énerv/er [enɛrve] *vt* **é. qn** (*irriter*) to get on s.o.'s nerves; (*rendre énervé*) to make s.o. nervous; — **s'é.** *vpr* to get worked up. ◆—**é** *a* on edge, irritated. ◆—**ement** *nm* irritation, nervousness.

enfant [ãfã] *nmf* child (*pl* children); **e. en bas âge** infant; **un e. de** (*originaire*) a native of; **attendre un e.** to expect a baby *ou* a child; **e. trouvé** foundling; **e. de chœur** Rel altar boy; **e. prodige** child prodigy; **e. prodigue** prodigal son; **bon e.** (*caractère*) good natured. ◆**enfance** *nf* childhood; **première e.** infancy, early childhood; **dans son e.** (*science etc*) in its infancy. ◆**enfanter** *vt* to give birth to; — *vi* to give birth. ◆**enfantillage** *nm* childishness. ◆**enfantin** *a* (*voix, joie*) childlike; (*langage, jeu*) children's; (*puéril*) childish; (*simple*) easy.

enfer [ãfer] *nm* hell; **d'e.** (*vision, bruit*) infernal; **feu d'e.** roaring fire; **à un train d'e.** at breakneck speed.

enferm/er [ãferme] *vt* (*personne etc*) to shut up, lock up; (*objet précieux*) to lock up, shut away; (*jardin*) to enclose; **s'e. dans** (*chambre etc*) to shut *ou* lock oneself (up) in; (*attitude etc*) Fig to maintain stubbornly.

enferrer (s') [sãfere] *vpr* **s'e. dans** to get caught up in.

enfiévré [ãfjevre] *a* (*surexcité*) feverish.

enfiler [ãfile] *vt* (*aiguille*) to thread; (*perles etc*) to string; (*vêtement*) Fam to slip on, pull on; (*rue, couloir*) to take; **s'e. dans** (*rue etc*) to take. ◆**enfilade** *nf* (*série*) row, string.

enfin [ãfɛ̃] *adv* (à la fin) finally, at last; (*en dernier lieu*) lastly; (*en somme*) in a word; (*conclusion résignée*) well; **e. bref** (*en somme*) Fam in a word; (il est grand, **e. pas trop petit** he's tall – well, not too short anyhow; **mais e.** but; (mais) **e.!** for heaven's sake!

enflamm/er [ãflame] *vt* to set fire to, ignite; (*allumette*) to light; (*irriter*) Méd to inflame; (*imagination, colère*) to excite, inflame; — **s'e.** *vpr* to catch fire, ignite; **s'e. de colère** to flare up. ◆—**é** *a* (*discours*) fiery.

enfler [ɑ̃fle] vt to swell; (voix) to raise; − vi Méd to swell (up). ◆**enflure** nf swelling.

enfonc/er [ɑ̃fɔ̃se] vt (clou etc) to knock in, drive in; (chapeau) to push ou force down; (porte, voiture) to smash in; e. dans (couteau, mains etc) to plunge into; − vi, − **s'e.** vpr (s'enliser) to sink (dans into); **s'e. dans** (pénétrer) to plunge into, disappear (deep) into. ◆−é a (yeux) sunken.

enfouir [ɑ̃fwir] vt to bury.

enfourcher [ɑ̃furʃe] vt (cheval etc) to mount, bestride.

enfourner [ɑ̃furne] vt to put in the oven.

enfreindre* [ɑ̃frɛ̃dr] vt to infringe.

enfuir* (s') [sɑ̃fɥir] vpr to run away ou off, flee (de from).

enfumer [ɑ̃fyme] vt (pièce) to fill with smoke; (personne) to smoke out.

engag/er [ɑ̃gaʒe] vt (bijou etc) to pawn; (parole) to pledge; (discussion, combat) to start; (clef etc) to insert (dans into); (capitaux) to tie up, invest; e. la bataille avec to join battle with; e. qn (lier) to bind s.o., commit s.o.; (embaucher) to hire s.o., engage s.o.; e. qn dans (affaire etc) to involve s.o. in; e. qn à faire (exhorter) to urge s.o. to do; − s'e. vpr (s'inscrire) Mil to enlist; Sp to enter; (au service d'une cause) to commit oneself; (action) to start; **s'e. à faire** to commit oneself to doing, undertake to do; **s'e. dans** (voie) to enter; (affaire etc) to get involved in. ◆−eant a engaging, inviting. ◆−é a (écrivain etc) committed. ◆−ement nm (promesse) commitment; (commencement) start; (de recrues) Mil enlistment; (inscription) Sp entry; (combat) Mil engagement; **prendre l'e. de** to undertake to.

engelure [ɑ̃ʒlyr] nf chilblain.

engendrer [ɑ̃ʒɑ̃dre] vt (procréer) to beget; (causer) to generate, engender.

engin [ɑ̃ʒɛ̃] nm machine, device; (projectile) missile; e. explosif explosive device.

englober [ɑ̃glɔbe] vt to include, embrace.

engloutir [ɑ̃glutir] vt (avaler) to wolf (down), gobble (up); (faire sombrer ou disparaître) to engulf.

engorger [ɑ̃gɔrʒe] vt to block up, clog.

engouement [ɑ̃gumɑ̃] nm craze.

engouffrer [ɑ̃gufre] vt (avaler) to wolf (down); (fortune) to consume; **s'e. dans** to sweep ou rush into.

engourd/ir [ɑ̃gurdir] vt (membre) to numb; (esprit) to dull; − s'e. vpr to go numb; to become dull. ◆−issement nm numbness; dullness.

engrais [ɑ̃grɛ] nm (naturel) manure; (chimique) fertilizer.

engraisser [ɑ̃grese] vt (animal) to fatten (up); − vi, − **s'e.** vpr to get fat, put on weight.

engrenage [ɑ̃grənaʒ] nm Tech gears; Fig mesh, chain, web.

engueuler [ɑ̃gœle] vt e. qn Fam to swear at s.o., give s.o. hell. ◆**engueulade** nf Fam (réprimande) dressing-down, severe talking-to; (dispute) slanging match, row.

enhardir [ɑ̃ardir] vt to make bolder; **s'e. à faire** to make bold to do.

énième [ɛnjɛm] a Fam umpteenth, nth.

énigme [enigm] nf enigma, riddle. ◆**énigmatique** a enigmatic.

enivrer [ɑ̃nivre] vt (soûler, troubler) to intoxicate; − **s'e.** vpr to get drunk (de on).

enjamber [ɑ̃ʒɑ̃be] vt to step over; (pont etc) to span (river etc). ◆**enjambée** nf stride.

enjeu, -x [ɑ̃ʒø] nm (mise) stake(s).

enjoindre [ɑ̃ʒwɛ̃dr] vt e. à qn de faire Litt to order s.o. to do.

enjôler [ɑ̃ʒole] vt to wheedle, coax.

enjoliv/er [ɑ̃ʒɔlive] vt to embellish. ◆−eur nm Aut hubcap.

enjoué [ɑ̃ʒwe] a playful. ◆**enjouement** nm playfulness.

enlacer [ɑ̃lase] vt to entwine; (serrer dans ses bras) to clasp.

enlaidir [ɑ̃ledir] vt to make ugly; − vi to grow ugly.

enlev/er [ɑ̃lve] vt to take away ou off, remove (à qn from s.o.); (ordures) to collect; (vêtement) to take off, remove; (tache) to take out, lift, remove; (enfant etc) to kidnap, abduct; − **s'e.** vpr (tache) to come out; (vernis) to come off. ◆−é a (scène, danse etc) well-rendered. ◆**enlèvement** nm kidnapping, abduction; (d'un objet) removal; (des ordures) collection.

enliser (s') [sɑ̃lize] vpr (véhicule) & Fig to get bogged down (dans in).

enneigé [ɑ̃neʒe] a snow-covered. ◆**enneigement** nm snow coverage; **bulletin d'e.** snow report.

ennemi, -ie [ɛnmi] nmf enemy; − a (personne) hostile (de to); (pays etc) enemy-.

ennui [ɑ̃nɥi] nm boredom; (mélancolie) weariness; **un e.** (tracas) (some) trouble ou bother; **des ennuis** trouble(s), bother; **l'e., c'est que...** the annoying thing is that...

ennuy/er [ɑ̃nɥije] vt (agacer) to annoy, bother; (préoccuper) to bother; (fatiguer) to bore; − **s'e.** vpr to get bored. ◆−é *a* (*air*) bored; **je suis e.** that annoys *ou* bothers me. ◆**ennuyeux, -euse** *a* (*fastidieux*) boring; (*contrariant*) annoying.

énonc/er [enɔse] *vt* to state, express. ◆**—é** *nm* (*de texte*) wording, terms; (*phrase*) Ling utterance.

enorgueillir [ɑ̃nɔrgœjir] *vt* to make proud; **s'e. de** to pride oneself on.

énorme [enɔrm] *a* enormous, huge, tremendous. ◆**énormément** *adv* enormously, tremendously; **e. de** an enormous *ou* tremendous amount of. ◆**énormité** *nf* (*dimension*) enormity; (*faute*) (enormous) blunder.

enquérir (s') [sɑ̃kerir] *vpr* **s'e. de** to inquire about.

enquête [ɑ̃kɛt] *nf* (*de police etc*) investigation; (*judiciaire, administrative*) inquiry; (*sondage*) survey. ◆**enquêter** *vi* (*police etc*) to investigate; **e. sur** (*crime*) to investigate. ◆**enquêteur, -euse** *nmf* investigator.

enquiquiner [ɑ̃kikine] *vt* Fam to annoy, bug.

enraciner (s') [sɑ̃rasine] *vpr* to take root; **enraciné dans** (*personne, souvenir*) rooted in; **bien enraciné** (*préjugé etc*) deep-rooted.

enrag/er [ɑ̃raʒe] *vi* **e. de faire** to be furious about doing; **faire e. qn** to get on s.o.'s nerves. ◆**—eant** *a* infuriating. ◆**—é** *a* (*chien*) rabid, mad; (*joueur etc*) Fam fanatical (**de** about); **rendre/devenir e.** (*furieux*) to make/become furious.

enrayer [ɑ̃reje] *vt* (*maladie etc*) to check; — **s'e.** *vpr* (*fusil*) to jam.

enregistr/er [ɑ̃rʒistre] *vt* **1** (*inscrire*) to record; (*sur registre*) to register; (*constater*) to note, register; (*faire*) **e.** (*bagages*) to register, *Am* check. **2** (*musique, émission etc*) to record. ◆**—ement** *nm* (*des bagages*) registration, *Am* checking; (*d'un acte*) registration; (*sur bande etc*) recording. ◆**—eur, -euse** *a* (*appareil*) recording-; **caisse enregistreuse** cash register.

enrhumer [ɑ̃ryme] *vt* **e. qn** to give s.o. a cold; **être enrhumé** to have a cold; — **s'e.** *vpr* to catch a cold.

enrich/ir [ɑ̃riʃir] *vt* to enrich (**de** with); — **s'e.** *vpr* (*personne*) to get rich. ◆**—issement** *nm* enrichment.

enrober [ɑ̃rɔbe] *vt* to coat (**de** in); **enrobé de chocolat** chocolate-coated.

enrôl/er [ɑ̃role] *vt*, — **s'e.** *vpr* to enlist. ◆**—ement** *nm* enlistment.

enrou/er (s') [sɑ̃rwe] *vpr* to get hoarse. ◆**—é** *a* hoarse. ◆**—ement** [ɑ̃rumɑ̃] *nm* hoarseness.

enrouler [ɑ̃rule] *vt* (*fil etc*) to wind; (*tapis, cordage*) to roll up; **s'e. dans** (*couvertures*) to roll *ou* wrap oneself up in; **s'e. sur** *ou* **autour de qch** to wind round sth.

ensabler [ɑ̃sable] *vt*, — **s'e.** *vpr* (*port*) to silt up.

ensanglanté [ɑ̃sɑ̃glɑ̃te] *a* bloodstained.

enseigne [ɑ̃sɛɲ] **1** *nf* (*de magasin etc*) sign; **e. lumineuse** neon sign; **logés à la même e.** Fig in the same boat. **2** *nm* **e. de vaisseau** *Am* ensign.

enseign/er [ɑ̃seɲe] *vt* to teach; **e. qch à qn** to teach s.o. sth; — *vi* to teach. ◆**—ant, -ante** [-ɲɑ̃, -ɑ̃t] *a* (*corps*) teaching-; — *nmf* teacher. ◆**—ement** [-ɲmɑ̃] *nm* education; (*action, métier*) teaching.

ensemble [ɑ̃sɑ̃bl] **1** *adv* together. **2** *nm* (*d'objets*) group, set; Math set; Mus ensemble; (*mobilier*) suite; (*vêtement féminin*) outfit; (*harmonie*) unity; **l'e. du personnel** (*totalité*) the whole (*ou* all) of the staff; **l'e. des enseignants** all (*ou* the whole) of the teachers; **dans l'e.** on the whole; **d'e.** (*vue etc*) general; **grand e.** (*quartier*) housing complex *ou Am* development; (*ville*) = new town, = *Am* planned community. ◆**ensemblier** *nm* (interior) decorator.

ensemencer [ɑ̃səmɑ̃se] *vt* (*terre*) to sow.

ensevelir [ɑ̃səvlir] *vt* to bury.

ensoleillé [ɑ̃sɔleje] *a* (*endroit, journée*) sunny.

ensommeillé [ɑ̃sɔmeje] *a* sleepy.

ensorcel/er [ɑ̃sɔrsəle] *vt* (*envoûter, séduire*) to bewitch. ◆**—ellement** *nm* (*séduction*) spell.

ensuite [ɑ̃sɥit] *adv* (*puis*) next, then; (*plus tard*) afterwards.

ensuivre* (s') [sɑ̃sɥivr] *vpr* to follow, ensue; — *v imp* **il s'ensuit que** it follows that.

entacher [ɑ̃taʃe] *vt* (*honneur etc*) to sully, taint.

entaille [ɑ̃taj] *nf* (*fente*) notch; (*blessure*) gash, slash. ◆**entailler** *vt* to notch; to gash, slash.

entame [ɑ̃tam] *nf* first slice.

entamer [ɑ̃tame] *vt* (*pain, peau etc*) to cut (into); (*bouteille, boîte etc*) to start (on); (*négociations etc*) to enter into, start; (*sujet*) to broach; (*capital*) to break *ou* eat into; (*métal, plastique*) to damage; (*résolution, réputation*) to shake.

entass/er [ɑ̃tase] *vt*, — **s'e.** *vpr* (*objets*) to pile up, heap up; (**s'e.) dans** (*passagers etc*) to crowd *ou* pack *ou* pile into; **ils s'entassaient sur la plage** they were crowded *ou* packed (together) on the beach.

◆**—ement** *nm* (*tas*) pile, heap; (*de gens*) crowding.

entend/re [ātādr] *vt* to hear; (*comprendre*) to understand; (*vouloir*) to intend, mean; **e. parler de** to hear of; **e. dire que** to hear (it said) that; **e. raison** to listen to reason; **laisser e. à qn que** to give s.o. to understand that; **— s'e.** *vpr* (*être entendu*) to be heard; (*être compris*) to be understood; **s'e.** (**sur**) (*être d'accord*) to agree (on); **s'e.** (**avec qn**) (*s'accorder*) to get on (with s.o.); **on ne s'entend plus!** (*à cause du bruit etc*) we can't hear ourselves speak!; **il s'y entend** (*est expert*) he knows all about that. ◆**—u** *a* (*convenu*) agreed; (*compris*) understood; (*sourire, air*) knowing; **e.!** all right! **bien e.** of course. ◆**—ement** *nm* (*faculté*) understanding. ◆**entente** *nf* (*accord*) agreement, understanding; (**bonne**) **e.** (*amitié*) good relationship, harmony.

entériner [āterine] *vt* to ratify.

enterrer [ātere] *vt* (*mettre en ou sous terre*) to bury; (*projet*) *Fig* to scrap. ◆**enterrement** *nm* burial; (*funérailles*) funeral.

entêtant [ātetā] *a* (*enivrant*) heady.

en-tête [ātɛt] *nm* (*de papier*) heading; **papier à en-tête** headed paper.

entêt/er (s') [sātete] *vpr* to persist (**à faire** in doing). ◆**—é** *a* (*têtu*) stubborn; (*persévérant*) persistent. ◆**—ement** [ātɛtmā] *nm* stubbornness; (**à faire qch**) persistence.

enthousiasme [ātuzjasm] *nm* enthusiasm. ◆**enthousiasmer** *vt* to fill with enthusiasm, enthuse; **s'e. pour** to be *ou* get enthusiastic over, enthuse over. ◆**enthousiaste** *a* enthusiastic.

enticher (s') [sātife] *vpr* **s'e. de** to become infatuated with.

entier, -ière [ātje, -jɛr] 1 *a* (*total*) whole, entire; (*absolu*) absolute, complete, entire; (*intact*) intact; **payer place entière** to pay full price; **le pays tout e.** the whole *ou* entire country; **— *nm*** (*unité*) whole; **en e., dans son e.** in its entirety, completely. 2 *a* (*caractère, personne*) unyielding. ◆**entièrement** *adv* entirely.

entité [ātite] *nf* entity.

entonner [ātɔne] *vt* (*air*) to start singing.

entonnoir [ātɔnwar] *nm* (*ustensile*) funnel.

entorse [ātɔrs] *nf* *Méd* sprain; **e. à** (*règlement*) infringement of.

entortill/er [ātɔrtije] *vt* **e. qch autour de qch** (*papier etc*) to wrap sth around sth; **e. qn** *Fam* to dupe s.o., get round s.o.; **— s'e.** *vpr* (*lierre etc*) to wind, twist. ◆**—é** *a* (*phrase etc*) convoluted.

entour/er [āture] *vt* to surround (**de** with);

(*envelopper*) to wrap (**de** in); **e. qn de ses bras** to put one's arms round s.o.; **s'e. de** to surround oneself with. ◆**—age** *nm* (*proches*) circle of family and friends.

entourloupette [āturlupɛt] *nf* *Fam* nasty trick.

entracte [ātrakt] *nm* *Th* interval, *Am* intermission.

entraide [ātrɛd] *nf* mutual aid. ◆**s'entraider** [sātrede] *vpr* to help each other.

entrailles [ātraj] *nfpl* entrails.

entrain [ātrɛ̃] *nm* spirit, liveliness; **plein d'e.** lively.

entraîn/er [ātrene] 1 *vt* (*charrier*) to sweep *ou* carry away; (*roue*) *Tech* to drive; (*causer*) to bring about; (*impliquer*) to entail, involve; **e. qn** (*emmener*) to lead *ou* draw s.o. (away); (*de force*) to drag s.o. (away); (*attirer*) *Péj* to lure s.o.; (*charmer*) to carry s.o. away; **e. qn à faire** (*amener*) to lead s.o. to do. 2 *vt* (*athlète, cheval etc*) to train (**à** for); **— s'e.** *vpr* to train oneself; *Sp* to train. ◆**—ant** [-ǝā] *a* (*musique*) captivating. ◆**—ement** [-ɛnmā] *nm* **1** *Sp* training. **2** *Tech* drive; (*élan*) impulse. ◆**—eur** [-ǝnœr] *nm* (*instructeur*) *Sp* trainer, coach; (*de cheval*) trainer.

entrave [ātrav] *nf* (*obstacle*) *Fig* hindrance (**à** to). ◆**entraver** *vt* to hinder, hamper.

entre [ātr(ǝ)] *prép* between; (*parmi*) among(st); **l'un d'e. vous** one of you; (**soit dit**) **e. nous** between you and me; **se dévorer e. eux** (*réciprocité*) to devour each other; **e. deux âges** middle-aged; **e. autres** among other things; **e. les mains de** in the hands of.

entrebâill/er [ātrǝbaje] *vt* (*porte*) to open slightly. ◆**—é** *a* ajar, slightly open. ◆**—eur** *nm* **e.** (**de porte**) door chain.

entrechoquer (s') [sātrǝ∫ɔke] *vpr* (*bouteilles etc*) to knock against each other, chink.

entrecôte [ātrǝkot] *nf* (*boned*) rib steak.

entrecouper [ātrǝkupe] *vt* (*entremêler*) to punctuate (**de** with), intersperse (**de** with).

entrecroiser [ātrǝkrwaze] *vt*, **— s'e.** *vpr* (*fils*) to interlace; (*routes*) to intersect.

entre-deux-guerres [ātrǝdøgɛr] *nm inv* inter-war period.

entrée [ātre] *nf* (*action*) entry, entrance; (*porte*) entrance; (*accès*) entry, admission (**de** to); (*vestibule*) entrance hall, entry; (*billet*) ticket (of admission); *Culin* first course, entrée; (*mot dans un dictionnaire etc*) entry; (*processus informatique*) input; **à son e.** as he *ou* she came in; **'e. interdite'** 'no entry', 'no admittance'; **'e. libre'** 'admission free'; **e. en matière** (*d'un discours*) opening.

entrefaites (sur ces) [syrsezɑ̃trəfɛt] *adv* at that moment.

entrefilet [ɑ̃trəfilɛ] *nm* Journ (news) item.

entrejambes [ɑ̃trəʒɑ̃b] *nm inv* (*de pantalon*) crutch, crotch.

entrelacer [ɑ̃trəlase] *vt*, **— s'e.** *vpr* to intertwine.

entremêler [ɑ̃trəmele] *vt*, **— s'e.** *vpr* to intermingle.

entremets [ɑ̃trəmɛ] *nm* (*plat*) sweet, dessert.

entremetteur, -euse [ɑ̃trəmetœr, -øz] *nmf* Péj go-between.

entremise [ɑ̃trəmiz] *nf* intervention; **par l'e. de qn** through s.o.

entreposer [ɑ̃trəpoze] *vt* to store; Jur to bond. ◆**entrepôt** *nm* warehouse; (*de la douane*) *Jur* bonded warehouse.

entreprendre* [ɑ̃trəprɑ̃dr] *vt* (*travail, voyage etc*) to start on, undertake; **e. de faire** to undertake to do. ◆**entreprenant** *a* enterprising; (*galant*) brash, forward. ◆**entrepreneur** *nm* (*en bâtiment*) (building) contractor. ◆**entreprise** *nf* **1** (*opération*) undertaking. **2** (*firme*) company, firm.

entrer [ɑ̃tre] *vi* (*aux* être) (*aller*) to go in, enter; (*venir*) to come in, enter; **e. dans** to go into; (*carrière*) to enter, go into; (*club*) to join, enter; (*détail, question*) to go into; (*pièce*) to come *ou* go into, enter; (*arbre etc*) Aut to crash into; **e. en action** to go *ou* get into action; **e. en ébullition** to start boiling; **entrez!** come in!; **faire/laisser e. qn** to show/let s.o. in.

entresol [ɑ̃trəsɔl] *nm* mezzanine (floor).

entre-temps [ɑ̃trətɑ̃] *adv* meanwhile.

entretenir* [ɑ̃trətnir] *vt* **1** (*voiture, maison etc*) to maintain; (*relations, souvenir*) to keep up; (*famille*) to keep, maintain; (*sentiment*) to entertain; **e. sa forme/sa santé** to keep fit/healthy. **2 e. qn de** to talk to s.o. about; **s'e. de** to talk about (avec with). ◆**—u** *a* (*femme*) kept. ◆**entretien** *nm* **1** (*de route, maison etc*) maintenance, upkeep; (*subsistance*) keep. **2** (*dialogue*) conversation; (*entrevue*) interview.

entre-tuer (s') [sɑ̃trətɥe] *vpr* to kill each other.

entrevoir* [ɑ̃trəvwar] *vt* (*rapidement*) to catch a glimpse of; (*pressentir*) to (fore)see.

entrevue [ɑ̃trəvy] *nf* interview.

entrouvrir* [ɑ̃truvrir] *vt*, **— s'e.** *vpr* to half-open. ◆**entrouvert** *a* (*porte, fenêtre*) ajar, half-open.

énumérer [enymere] *vt* to enumerate, list. ◆**énumération** *nf* enumeration.

envah/ir [ɑ̃vair] *vt* to invade; (*herbe etc*) to overrun; **e. qn** (*doute, peur etc*) to overcome s.o. ◆**—issant** *a* (*voisin etc*) intrusive. ◆**—issement** *nm* invasion. ◆**—isseur** *nm* invader.

enveloppe [ɑ̃vlɔp] *nf* (*pli*) envelope; (*de colis*) wrapping; (*de pneu*) casing; (*d'oreiller*) cover; (*apparence*) Fig exterior; **mettre sous e.** to put into an envelope. ◆**envelopp/er** *vt* to wrap (up); **e. la ville** (*brouillard etc*) to envelop the town; **enveloppé de mystère** shrouded *ou* enveloped in mystery; **— s'e.** *vpr* to wrap oneself (up) (**dans** in). ◆**—ant** *a* (*séduisant*) captivating.

envenimer [ɑ̃vnime] *vt* (*plaie*) to make septic; (*querelle*) Fig to envenom; **— s'e.** *vpr* to turn septic; Fig to become envenomed.

envergure [ɑ̃vɛrgyr] *nf* **1** (*d'avion, d'oiseau*) wingspan. **2** (*de personne*) calibre; (*ampleur*) scope, importance; **de grande e.** wide-ranging, far-reaching.

envers [ɑ̃vɛr] **1** *prép* towards, Am towards(s). **2** *nm* (*de tissu*) wrong side; (*de médaille*) reverse side; **à l'e.** (*chaussette*) inside out; (*pantalon*) back to front; (*à contresens, de travers*) the wrong way; (*en désordre*) upside down.

envie [ɑ̃vi] *nf* **1** (*jalousie*) envy; (*désir*) longing, desire; **avoir e. de qch** to want sth; **j'ai e. de faire** I feel like doing, I would like to do; **elle meurt d'e. de faire** she's dying *ou* longing to do. **2** (*peau autour des ongles*) hangnail. ◆**envier** *vt* to envy (**qch à qn** s.o. sth). ◆**envieux, -euse** *a* & *nmf* envious (person); **faire des envieux** to cause envy.

environ [ɑ̃virɔ̃] *adv* (*à peu près*) about; **— nmpl** outskirts, surroundings; **aux environs de** (*Paris, Noël, dix francs etc*) around, in the vicinity of. ◆**environn/er** *vt* to surround. ◆**—ant** *a* surrounding. ◆**—ement** *nm* environment.

envisag/er [ɑ̃vizaʒe] *vt* to consider; (*imaginer comme possible*) to envisage, Am envision, consider; **e. de faire** to consider *ou* contemplate doing. ◆**—eable** *a* thinkable.

envoi [ɑ̃vwa] *nm* (*action*) dispatch, sending; (*paquet*) consignment; **coup d'e.** Fb kick-off.

envol [ɑ̃vɔl] *nm* (*d'oiseau*) taking flight; (*d'avion*) take-off; **piste d'e.** Av runway. ◆**s'envol/er** *vpr* (*oiseau*) to fly away; (*avion*) to take off; (*emporté par le vent*) to blow away; (espoir) Fig to vanish. ◆—ée nf (élan) Fig flight.

envoût/er [ãvute] vt to bewitch. ◆—ement nm bewitchment.

envoy/er* [ãvwaje] vt to send; (pierre) to throw; (gifle) to give; e. chercher qn to send for s.o.; — s'e. vpr Fam (travail etc) to take on, do; (repas etc) to put ou stash away. ◆—é, -ée nmf envoy; Journ correspondent. ◆—eur nm sender.

épagneul, -eule [epaɲœl] nmf spaniel.

épais, -aisse [epɛ, -ɛs] a thick; (personne) thick-set; (esprit) dull. ◆épaisseur nf thickness; (dimension) depth. ◆épaissir vt to thicken; — vi, — s'é. vpr to thicken; (grossir) to fill out; le mystère s'épaissit the mystery is deepening.

épanch/er [epãʃe] vt (cœur) Fig to pour out; — s'é. vpr (parler) to pour out one's heart, unbosom oneself. ◆—ement nm (aveu) outpouring; Méd effusion.

épanou/ir (s') [epanwir] vpr (fleur) to open out; (personne) Fig to fulfil oneself, blossom (out); (visage) to beam. ◆—i a (fleur, personne) in full bloom; (visage) beaming. ◆—issement nm (éclat) full bloom; (de la personnalité) fulfilment.

épargne [eparɲ] nf saving (de of); (qualité, vertu) thrift; (sommes d'argent) savings. ◆épargn/er vt (ennemi etc) to spare; (denrée rare etc) to be sparing with; (argent, temps) to save; e. qch à qn (ennuis, chagrin etc) to spare s.o. sth. ◆—ant, -ante nmf saver.

éparpiller [eparpije] vt, — s'é. vpr to scatter; (efforts) to dissipate. ◆épars a scattered.

épaté [epate] a (nez) flat. ◆épatement nm flatness.

épat/er [epate] vt Fam to stun, astound. ◆—ant a Fam stunning, marvellous.

épaule [epol] nf shoulder. ◆épauler vt (fusil) to raise (to one's shoulder); é. qn (aider) to back s.o. up.

épave [epav] nf (bateau, personne) wreck; pl (débris) Nau (pieces of) wreckage.

épée [epe] nf sword; un coup d'é. a sword thrust.

épeler [eple] vt (mot) to spell.

éperdu [eperdy] a frantic, wild (de with); (regard) distraught. ◆—ment adv (aimer) madly; elle s'en moque e. she couldn't care less.

éperon [eprɔ̃] nm (de cavalier, coq) spur. ◆éperonner (cheval, personne) to spur (on).

épervier [epɛrvje] nm sparrowhawk.

éphémère [efemɛr] a short-lived, ephemeral, transient.

épi [epi] nm (de blé etc) ear; (mèche de cheveux) tuft of hair.

épice [epis] nf Culin spice. ◆épic/er vt to spice. ◆—é a (plat, récit etc) spicy.

épicier, -ière [episje, -jɛr] nmf grocer. ◆épicerie nf (magasin) grocer's (shop); (produits) groceries.

épidémie [epidemi] nf epidemic. ◆épidémique a epidemic.

épiderme [epidɛrm] nm Anat skin.

épier [epje] vt (observer) to watch closely; (occasion) to watch out for; é. qn to spy on s.o.

épilepsie [epilɛpsi] nf epilepsy. ◆épileptique a & nmf epileptic.

épiler [epile] vt (jambe) to remove unwanted hair from; (sourcil) to pluck.

épilogue [epilɔg] nm epilogue.

épinard [epinar] nm (plante) spinach; pl (feuilles) Culin spinach.

épine [epin] nf 1 (de buisson) thorn; (d'animal) spine, prickle. 2 é. dorsale Anat spine. ◆épineux, -euse (tige, question) thorny.

épingle [epɛ̃gl] nf pin; é. de nourrice, é. de sûreté safety pin; é. à linge clothes peg, Am clothes pin; virage en é. à cheveux hairpin bend; tiré à quatre épingles very spruce. ◆épingler vt to pin; é. qn (arrêter) Fam to nab s.o.

épique [epik] a epic.

épiscopal, -aux [episkɔpal, -o] a episcopal.

épisode [epizɔd] nm episode; film à épisodes serial. ◆épisodique a occasional, episodic; (accessoire) minor.

épitaphe [epitaf] nf epitaph.

épithète [epitɛt] nf epithet; Gram attribute.

épître [epitr] nf epistle.

éploré [eplɔre] a (personne, air) tearful.

éplucher [eplyʃe] vt (pommes de terre) to peel; (salade) to clean, pare; (texte) Fig to dissect. ◆épluchure nf peeling.

éponge [epɔ̃ʒ] nf sponge. ◆éponger vt (liquide) to sponge up, mop up; (carrelage) to sponge (down), mop; (dette etc) Fin to absorb; s'é. le front to mop one's brow.

épopée [epɔpe] nf epic.

époque [epɔk] nf (date) time, period; (historique) age; meubles d'é. period furniture; à l'é. at the ou that time.

épouse [epuz] nf wife, Jur spouse.

épouser [epuze] vt 1 é. qn to marry s.o. 2 (opinion etc) to espouse; (forme) to assume, adopt.

épousseter [epuste] vt to dust.

époustoufler [epustufle] vt Fam to astound.

épouvantail [epuvɑ̃taj] nm (à oiseaux) scarecrow.

épouvante [epuvɑ̃t] nf (peur) terror; (appréhension) dread; **d'é.** (film etc) horror-. ◆**épouvant/er** vt to terrify. ◆**—able** a terrifying; (très mauvais) appalling.

époux [epu] nm husband, Jur spouse; pl husband and wife.

éprendre* (s') [seprɑ̃dr] vpr **s'é.** de qn to fall in love with s.o. ◆**épris** a in love (de with).

épreuve [eprœv] nf (essai, examen) test; Sp event, heat; Phot print; Typ proof; (malheur) ordeal, trial; **mettre à l'é.** to put to the test. ◆**éprouv/er** [epruve] vt to test, try; (sentiment etc) to experience, feel; **é.** qn (mettre à l'épreuve) to put s.o. to the test; (faire souffrir) to distress s.o. ◆**—ant** a (pénible) trying. ◆**—é** a (sûr) well-tried.

éprouvette [epruvɛt] nf test tube; **bébé é.** test tube baby.

épuis/er [epɥize] vt (personne, provisions, sujet) to exhaust; — **s'é.** vpr (réserves, patience) to run out; **s'é.** à faire to exhaust oneself doing. ◆**—ant** a exhausting. ◆**—é** a exhausted; (édition) out of print; (marchandise) out of stock. ◆**—ement** nm exhaustion.

épuisette [epɥizɛt] nf fishing net (on pole).

épurer [epyre] vt to purify; (personnel etc) to purge; (goût) to refine. ◆**épuration** nf purification; purging; refining.

équateur [ekwatœr] nm equator; **sous l'é.** at ou on the equator. ◆**équatorial, -aux** a equatorial.

équation [ekwasjɔ̃] nf Math equation.

équerre [ekɛr] nf **é.** (à dessiner) set square, Am triangle; **d'é.** straight, square.

équestre [ekɛstr] a (figure etc) equestrian; (exercices etc) horseriding-.

équilibre [ekilibr] nm balance; **tenir** ou **mettre en é.** to balance (**sur** on); **se tenir en é.** to (keep one's) balance; **perdre l'é.** to lose one's balance. ◆**équilibrer** vt (charge, budget etc) to balance; — **s'é.** vpr (équipes etc) to (counter)balance each other; (comptes) to balance.

équinoxe [ekinɔks] nm equinox.

équipage [ekipaʒ] nm Nau Av crew.

équipe [ekip] nf team; (d'ouvriers) gang; **é.** de nuit night shift; **é.** de secours search party; **faire é.** avec to team up with. ◆**équipier, -ière** nmf team member.

équipée [ekipe] nf escapade.

équip/er [ekipe] vt to equip (de with); — **s'é.** vpr to equip oneself. ◆**—ement** nm equipment; (de camping, ski etc) gear, equipment.

équitation [ekitasjɔ̃] nf (horse) riding.

équité [ekite] nf fairness. ◆**équitable** a fair, equitable. ◆**équitablement** adv fairly.

équivalent [ekivalɑ̃] a & nm equivalent. ◆**équivalence** nf equivalence. ◆**équivaloir** vi **é.** à to be equivalent to.

équivoque [ekivɔk] a (ambigu) equivocal; (douteux) dubious; — nf ambiguity.

érable [erabl] nm (arbre, bois) maple.

érafler [erafle] vt to graze, scratch. ◆**éraflure** nf graze, scratch.

éraillée [eraje] af (voix) rasping.

ère [ɛr] nf era.

érection [erɛksjɔ̃] nf (de monument etc) erection.

éreinter [erɛ̃te] vt (fatiguer) to exhaust; (critiquer) to tear to pieces, slam, slam.

ergot [ergo] nm (de coq) spur.

ergoter [ergɔte] vi to quibble, cavil.

ériger [eriʒe] vt to erect; **s'é.** en to set oneself up as.

ermite [ermit] nm hermit.

érosion [erozjɔ̃] nf erosion. ◆**éroder** vt to erode.

érotique [erɔtik] a erotic. ◆**érotisme** nm eroticism.

err/er [ɛre] vi to wander, roam. ◆**—ant** a wandering, roving; (animal) stray.

erreur [ɛrœr] nf (faute) error, mistake; (action blâmable, opinion fausse) error; **par e.** by mistake, in error; **dans l'e.** mistaken. ◆**erroné** a erroneous.

ersatz [ɛrzats] nm substitute.

éructer [erykte] vi Litt to belch.

érudit, -ite [erydi, -it] a scholarly, erudite; — nmf scholar. ◆**érudition** nf scholarship, erudition.

éruption [erypsjɔ̃] nf (de volcan, colère) eruption (**de** of); Méd rash.

es voir être.

ès [ɛs] prép of; **licencié/docteur ès lettres** = BA/PhD.

escabeau, -x [ɛskabo] nm stepladder, (pair of) steps; (tabouret) stool.

escadre [ɛskadr] nf Nau Av fleet, squadron. ◆**escadrille** nf (unité) Av flight. ◆**escadron** nm squadron.

escalade [ɛskalad] nf climbing; (de prix) & Mil escalation. ◆**escalader** vt to climb, scale.

escale [ɛskal] nf Av stop(over); Nau port of call; **faire é.** à Av to stop over at; Nau to put in at; **vol sans e.** non-stop flight.

escalier [ɛskalje] nm staircase, stairs; **e. mé-**

canique *ou* roulant escalator; **e. de secours** fire escape.

escalope [ɛskalɔp] *nf Culin* escalope.

escamot/er [ɛskamɔte] *vt* (*faire disparaître*) to make vanish; (*esquiver*) to dodge. **◆—able** *a Av Tech* retractable.

escapade [ɛskapad] *nf* (*excursion*) jaunt; **faire une e.** to run off.

escargot [ɛskargo] *nm* snail.

escarmouche [ɛskarmuʃ] *nf* skirmish.

escarpé [ɛskarpe] *a* steep. **◆escarpement** *nm* (*côte*) steep slope.

escarpin [ɛskarpɛ̃] *nm* (*soulier*) pump, court shoe.

escient [ɛsjɑ̃] **à bon e.** discerningly, wisely.

esclaffer (s') [sɛsklafe] *vpr* to roar with laughter.

esclandre [ɛsklɑ̃dr] *nm* (noisy) scene.

esclave [ɛsklav] *nmf* slave; **être l'e. de** to be a slave to. **◆esclavage** *nm* slavery.

escompte [ɛskɔ̃t] *nm* discount; **taux d'e.** bank rate. **◆escompter** *vt* **1** (*espérer*) to anticipate (**faire doing**), expect (**faire** to do). **2** *Com* to discount.

escorte [ɛskɔrt] *nf Mil Nau etc* escort. **◆escorter** *vt* to escort.

escouade [ɛskwad] *nf* (*petite troupe*) squad.

escrime [ɛskrim] *nf Sp* fencing. **◆escrimeur, -euse** *nmf* fencer.

escrimer (s') [sɛskrime] *vpr* to slave away (**à faire** at doing).

escroc [ɛskro] *nm* swindler, crook. **◆escroquer** *vt* **e. qn** to swindle s.o.; **e. qch à qn** to swindle s.o. out of sth. **◆escroquerie** *nf* swindling; **une e.** a swindle.

espace [ɛspas] *nm* space; **e. vert** garden, park. **◆espacer** *vt* to space out; **espacés d'un mètre** (spaced out) one metre apart; **— s'e.** (*maisons, visites etc*) to become less frequent.

espadon [ɛspadɔ̃] *nm* swordfish.

espadrille [ɛspadrij] *nf* rope-soled sandal.

Espagne [ɛspaɲ] *nf* Spain. **◆espagnol, -ole** *a* Spanish; **—** *nmf* Spaniard; **—** *nm* (*langue*) Spanish.

espèce [ɛspɛs] **1** *nf* (*race*) species; (*genre*) kind, sort; **c'est une e. d'idiot** he's a silly fool; **e. d'idiot!/de maladroit!/***etc* (you) silly fool!/oaf!/*etc*. **2** *nfpl* (*argent*) **en espèces** in cash.

espérance [ɛsperɑ̃s] *nf* hope; **avoir des espérances** to have expectations; **e. de vie** life expectancy. **◆espérer** *vt* to hope for; **e. que** to hope that; **e. faire** to hope to do; **—** *vi* to hope; **e. en qn/qch** to trust in s.o./sth.

espiègle [ɛspjɛgl] *a* mischievous. **◆es-**

pièglerie *nf* mischievousness; (*farce*) mischievous trick.

espion, -onne [ɛspjɔ̃, -ɔn] *nmf* spy. **◆espionnage** *nm* espionage, spying. **◆espionner** *vt* to spy on; **—** *vi* to spy.

esplanade [ɛsplanad] *nf* esplanade.

espoir [ɛspwar] *nm* hope; **avoir de l'e.** to have hope(s); **sans e.** (*cas etc*) hopeless.

esprit [ɛspri] *nm* (*attitude, fantôme*) spirit; (*intellect*) mind; (*humour*) wit; (*être humain*) person; **avoir de l'e.** to be witty; **cette idée m'est venue à l'e.** this idea crossed my mind.

esquimau, -aude, -aux [ɛskimo, -od, -o] **1** *a & nmf* Eskimo. **2** *nm* (*glace*) choc-ice (*on a stick*).

esquinter [ɛskɛ̃te] *vt Fam* (*voiture etc*) to damage, bash; (*critiquer*) to slam, pan (*author, film etc*); **s'e. la santé** to damage one's health; **s'e. à faire** (*se fatiguer*) to wear oneself out doing.

esquisse [ɛskis] *nf* (*croquis, plan*) sketch. **◆esquisser** *vt* to sketch; **e. un geste** to make a (slight) gesture.

esquive [ɛskiv] *nf Boxe* dodge; **e. de** (*question*) dodging of, evasion of. **◆esquiver** *vt* (*coup, problème*) to dodge; **—** **s'e.** *vpr* to slip away.

essai [ɛsε] *nm* (*preuve*) test, trial; (*tentative*) try, attempt; *Rugby* try; *Littér* essay; **à l'e.** (*objet*) *Com* on trial, on approval; **pilote d'e.** test pilot; **période d'e.** trial period.

essaim [ɛsɛ̃] *nm* swarm (*of bees etc*).

essayer [ɛseje] *vt* to try (**de faire** to do); (*vêtement*) to try on; (*méthode*) to try (out); **s'e. à qch/à faire** to try one's hand at sth/at doing. **◆essayage** *nm* (*de costume*) fitting.

essence [ɛsɑ̃s] *nf* **1** (*extrait*) *Ch Culin* essence; *Aut* petrol, *Am* gas; **poste d'e.** filling station. **2** *Phil* essence. **3** (*d'arbres*) species. **◆essentiel, -ielle** *a* essential (**à, pour** for); **—** *nm* **l'e.** the main thing *ou* point; (*quantité*) the main part (**de** of). **◆essentiellement** *adv* essentially.

essieu, -x [ɛsjø] *nm* axle.

essor [ɛsɔr] *nm* (*de pays, d'entreprise etc*) development, rise, expansion; **en plein e.** (*industrie etc*) booming.

essor/er [ɛsɔre] *vt* (*linge*) to wring; (*dans une essoreuse*) to spin-dry; (*dans une machine à laver*) to spin. **◆—euse** *nf* (*à main*) wringer; (*électrique*) spin dryer.

essouffler [ɛsufle] *vt* to make (s.o.) out of breath; **—** **s'e.** *vpr* to get out of breath.

essuyer [ɛsɥije] **1** *vt* to wipe; **—** **s'e.** *vpr* to wipe oneself. **2** *vt* (*subir*) to suffer. **◆es-**

sule-glace *nm inv* windscreen wiper, *Am* windshield wiper. ◆**essule-mains** *nm inv* (hand) towel.

est¹ [ɛ] *voir* **être**.

est² [ɛst] *nm* east; − *a inv* (*côte*) east(ern); **d'e.** (*vent*) east(erly); **de l'e.** eastern; **Allemagne de l'E.** East Germany. ◆**e.-allemand, -ande** *a* & *nmf* East German.

estafilade [ɛstafilad] *nf* gash, slash.

estampe [ɛstɑ̃p] *nf* (*gravure*) print.

estamper [ɛstɑ̃pe] *vt* (*rouler*) *Fam* to swindle.

estampille [ɛstɑ̃pij] *nf* mark, stamp.

esthète [ɛstɛt] *nmf* aesthete, *Am* esthete. ◆**esthétique** *a* aesthetic, *Am* esthetic.

esthéticienne [ɛstetisjɛn] *nf* beautician.

estime [ɛstim] *nf* esteem, regard. ◆**estim/er** [ɛstime] *vt* (*objet*) to value; (*juger*) to consider (**que** that); (*calculer*) to estimate; (*apprécier*) to appreciate; **e. qn** to have high regard for s.o., esteem s.o.; **s'e. heureux/etc** to consider oneself happy/*etc*. ◆**−able** *a* respectable. ◆**estimation** *nf* (*de mobilier etc*) valuation; (*calcul*) estimation.

estival, -aux [ɛstival, -o] *a* (*période etc*) summer-. ◆**estivant, -ante** *nmf* holidaymaker, *Am* vacationer.

estomac [ɛstɔma] *nm* stomach.

estomaquer [ɛstɔmake] *vt* *Fam* to flabbergast.

estomper [ɛstɔ̃pe] *vt* (*rendre flou*) to blur; − **s'e.** *vpr* to become blurred.

estrade [ɛstrad] *nf* (*tribune*) platform.

estropl/er [ɛstrɔpje] *vt* to cripple, maim. ◆**−é, -ée** *nmf* cripple.

estuaire [ɛstɥɛr] *nm* estuary.

esturgeon [ɛstyrʒɔ̃] *nm* (*poisson*) sturgeon.

et [e] *conj* and; **vingt et un**/*etc* twentyone/*etc*.

étable [etabl] *nf* cowshed.

établi [etabli] *nm* *Menuis* (work)bench.

établ/ir [etablir] *vt* to establish; (*installer*) to set up; (*plan, chèque, liste*) to draw up; − **s'é.** *vpr* (*habiter*) to settle; (*épicier etc*) to set up shop as, set (oneself) up as. ◆**−issement** *nm* (*action, bâtiment, institution*) establishment; *Com* firm, establishment; **é. scolaire** school.

étage [etaʒ] *nm* (*d'immeuble*) floor, storey, *Am* story; (*de fusée etc*) stage; **à l'é.** upstairs; **au premier é.** on the first *ou Am* second floor. ◆**étager** *vt*, − **s'é.** *vpr* (*rochers, maisons etc*) to range above one another.

étagère [etaʒɛr] *nf* shelf; (*meuble*) shelving unit.

étai [etɛ] *nm* *Tech* prop, stay.

étain [etɛ̃] *nm* (*métal*) tin; (*de gobelet etc*) pewter.

était [etɛ] *voir* **être**.

étal, *pl* **étals** [etal] *nm* (*au marché*) stall.

étalage [etalaʒ] *nm* display; (*vitrine*) display window; **faire é. de** to make a show *ou* display of. ◆**étalagiste** *nmf* window dresser.

étaler [etale] *vt* (*disposer*) to lay out; (*luxe etc*) & *Com* to display; (*crème, beurre etc*) to spread; (*vacances*) to stagger; − **s'é.** *vpr* (*s'affaler*) to sprawl; (*tomber*) *Fam* to fall flat; **s'é. sur** (*congés, paiements etc*) to be spread over.

étalon [etalɔ̃] *nm* **1** (*cheval*) stallion. **2** (*modèle*) standard.

étanche [etɑ̃ʃ] *a* watertight; (*montre*) waterproof.

étancher [etɑ̃ʃe] *vt* (*sang*) to stop the flow of; (*soif*) to quench, slake.

étang [etɑ̃] *nm* pond.

étant [etɑ̃] *voir* **être**.

étape [etap] *nf* (*de voyage etc*) stage; (*lieu*) stop(over); **faire é.** à to stop off *ou* over at.

état [eta] *nm* **1** (*condition, manière d'être*) state; (*registre, liste*) statement, list; **en bon é.** in good condition; **en é. de faire** in a position to do; **é. d'esprit** state *ou* frame of mind; **é. d'âme** mood; **é. civil** civil status (*birth, marriage, death etc*); **é. de choses** situation, state of affairs; **à l'é. brut** in a raw state; **de son é.** (*métier*) by trade; **faire é. de** (*mention*) to mention, put forward. **2 É.** (*nation*) State; **homme d'É.** statesman. ◆**étatisé** *a* state-controlled, state-owned.

état-major [etamaʒɔr] *nm* (*pl* **états-majors**) (*d'un parti etc*) senior staff.

États-Unis [etazyni] *nmpl* **(d'Amérique)** United States (of America).

étau, -x [eto] *nm* *Tech* vice, *Am* vise.

étayer [eteje] *vt* to prop up, support.

été¹ [ete] *nm* summer.

été² [ete] *voir* **être**.

éteindre° [etɛ̃dr] *vt* (*feu, cigarette etc*) to put out, extinguish; (*lampe etc*) to turn *ou* switch off; (*dette, espoir*) to extinguish; − *vi* to switch off; − **s'é.** *vpr* (*feu*) to go out; (*personne*) to pass away; (*race*) to die out. ◆**éteint** *a* (*feu*) out; (*volcan, race, amour*) extinct; (*voix*) faint.

étendard [etɑ̃dar] *nm* (*drapeau*) standard.

étend/re [etɑ̃dr] *vt* (*nappe*) to spread (out); (*beurre*) to spread; (*linge*) to hang out; (*agrandir*) to extend; **é. le bras**/*etc* to stretch out one's arm/*etc*; **é. qn** to stretch s.o. out; − **s'é.** *vpr* (*personne*) to stretch (oneself) out; (*plaine etc*) to stretch; (*feu*) to spread; (*pouvoir*) to extend; **s'é. sur** (*sujet*) to dwell on. ◆**—u** *a* (*forêt, vocabulaire etc*) extensive; (*personne*) stretched out. ◆**—ue** *a* (*importance*) extent; (*surface*) area; (*figure etc*) expanse, stretch.

éternel, -elle [etɛrnɛl] *a* eternal. ◆**éternellement** *adv* eternally, for ever. ◆**éterniser** *vt* to perpetuate; **— s'é.** *vpr* (*débat etc*) to drag on endlessly; (*visiteur etc*) to stay for ever. ◆**éternité** *nf* eternity.

éternu/er [etɛrnɥe] *vi* to sneeze. ◆**—ement** [-ymɑ̃] *nm* sneeze.

êtes [ɛt] *voir* **être.**

éther [etɛr] *nm* ether.

Éthiopie [etjɔpi] *nf* Ethiopia. ◆**éthiopien, -ienne** *a & nmf* Ethiopian.

éthique [etik] *a* ethical; **—** *nf Phil* ethics; **l'é. puritaine/etc** the Puritan/*etc* ethic.

ethnie [ɛtni] *nf* ethnic group. ◆**ethnique** *a* ethnic.

étinceler [etɛ̃sle] *vi* to sparkle. ◆**étincelle** *nf* spark. ◆**étincellement** *nm* sparkle.

étioler (s') [setjɔle] *vpr* to wilt, wither.

étiqueter [etikte] *vt* to label. ◆**étiquette** *nf* 1 (*marque*) label. 2 (*protocole*) (diplomatic *ou* court) etiquette.

étirer [etire] *vt* to stretch; **— s'é.** *vpr* to stretch (oneself).

étoffe [etɔf] *nf* material, cloth, fabric; (*de héros etc*) *Fig* stuff (**de** of).

étoffer [etɔfe] *vt,* **— s'é.** *vpr* to fill out.

étoile [etwal] *nf* 1 star; **à la belle é.** in the open. 2 **é. de mer** starfish. ◆**étoilé** *a* (*ciel, nuit*) starry; (*vitre*) cracked (*star-shaped*); **é. de** (*rubis etc*) studded with; **la bannière étoilée** *Am* the Star-Spangled Banner.

étonn/er [etɔne] *vt* to surprise, astonish; **— s'é.** *vpr* to be surprised *ou* astonished (**de qch** at sth, **que** (+ *sub*) that). ◆**—ant** *a* (*ahurissant*) surprising; (*remarquable*) amazing. ◆**—ement** *nm* surprise, astonishment.

étouff/er [etufe] *vt* (*tuer*) to suffocate, smother; (*bruit*) to muffle; (*feu*) to smother; (*révolte, sentiment*) to stifle; (*scandale*) to hush up; **é. qn** (*chaleur*) to stifle s.o.; (*aliment, colère*) to choke s.o.; **— vi** to suffocate; **on étouffe!** it's stifling!; **é. de colère** to choke with anger. **— s'é.** *vpr* (*en mangeant*) to choke, gag (**sur, avec** on); (*mourir*) to suffocate. **— é.** *a* (*air*) stifling. ◆**—ement** *nm Méd* suffocation.

étourdi, -ie [eturdi] *a* thoughtless; **—** *nmf* scatterbrain. ◆**étourderie** *nf* thoughtlessness; **une é.** (*faute*) a thoughtless blunder.

étourd/ir [eturdir] *vt* to stun, daze; (*vertige,*

vin) to make dizzy; (*abrutir*) to deafen. ◆**—issant** *a* (*bruit*) deafening; (*remarquable*) stunning. ◆**—issement** *nm* dizziness; (*syncope*) dizzy spell.

étourneau, -x [eturno] *nm* starling.

étrange [etrɑ̃ʒ] *a* strange, odd. ◆**—ment** *adv* strangely, oddly. ◆**étrangeté** *nf* strangeness, oddness.

étranger, -ère [etrɑ̃ʒe, -ɛr] *a* (*d'un autre pays*) foreign; (*non familier*) strange (**à** to); **il m'est é.** he's unknown to me; **—** *nmf* foreigner; (*inconnu*) stranger; **à l'é.** abroad; **de l'é.** from abroad.

étrangl/er [etrɑ̃gle] *vt* **é. qn** (*tuer*) to strangle s.o.; (*col, aliment*) to choke s.o.; **— s'é.** *vpr* (*de colère, en mangeant*) to choke. ◆**—é** *a* (*voix*) choking; (*passage*) constricted. ◆**—ement** *nm* (*d'une victime*) strangulation. ◆**—eur, -euse** *nmf* strangler.

être* [ɛtr] 1 *vi* to be; **il est tailleur** he's a tailor; **est-ce qu'elle vient?** is she coming?; **il vient, n'est-ce pas?** he's coming, isn't he?; **est-ce qu'il aime le thé?** does he like tea?; **nous sommes dix** there are ten of us; **nous sommes le dix** today is the tenth (of the month); **où en es-tu?** how far have you got?; **il a été à Paris** (*est allé*) he's been to Paris; **elle est de Paris** she's from Paris; **elle est de la famille** she's one of the family; **c'est à faire tout de suite** it must be done straight away; **cela fait** it's his; **cela étant** that being so. 2 *v aux* (*avec venir, partir etc*) to have; **elle est déjà arrivée** she has already arrived. 3 *nm* (*personne*) being; **ê. humain** human being; **les êtres chers** the loved ones.

étreindre [etrɛ̃dr] *vt* to grip; (*ami*) to embrace. ◆**étreinte** *nf* grip; (*amoureuse etc*) embrace.

étrenner [etrene] *vt* to use *ou* wear for the first time.

étrennes [etrɛn] *nfpl* New Year gift; (*gratification*) = Christmas box *ou* tip.

étrier [etrije] *nm* stirrup.

étriper (s') [setripe] *vpr Fam* to fight (each other) to the kill.

étriqué [etrike] *a* (*vêtement*) tight, skimpy; (*esprit, vie*) narrow.

étroit [etrwa] *a* narrow; (*vêtement*) tight; (*parenté, collaboration etc*) close; (*discipline*) strict; **être à l'é.** to be cramped. ◆**étroitement** *adv* (*surveiller etc*) closely. ◆**étroitesse** *nf* narrowness; closeness; **é. d'esprit** narrow-mindedness.

étude [etyd] *nf* 1 (*action, ouvrage*) study; (*salle*) *Scol* study room; **à l'é.** (*projet*) under consideration; **faire des études de** (*médecine etc*) to study. **2** (*de notaire etc*) office. ◆**étudiant, -ante** *nmf & a* student. ◆**étudier** *vti* to study.

étui [etɥi] *nm* (*à lunettes, à cigarettes etc*) case; (*de revolver*) holster.

étymologie [etimɔlɔʒi] *nf* etymology.

eu, eue [y] *voir* **avoir.**

eucalyptus [økaliptys] *nm* (*arbre*) eucalyptus.

Eucharistie [økaristi] *nf Rel* Eucharist.

euh! [ø] *int* hem!, er!, well!

euphémisme [øfemism] *nm* euphemism.

euphorie [øfɔri] *nf* euphoria.

eurent [yr] *voir* **avoir.**

euro- [øro] *préf* Euro-.

Europe [ørop] *nf* Europe. ◆**européen, -enne** *a & nmf* European.

eut [y] *voir* **avoir.**

euthanasie [øtanazi] *nf* euthanasia.

eux [ø] *pron* (*sujet*) they; (*complément*) them; (*réfléchi, emphase*) themselves. ◆**eux-mêmes** *pron* themselves.

évacuer [evakɥe] *vt* to evacuate; (*liquide*) to drain off. ◆**évacuation** *nf* evacuation.

évad/er (s') [sevade] *vpr* to escape (**de** from). ◆**—é, -ée** *nmf* escaped prisoner.

évaluer [evalɥe] *vt* (*chiffre, foule etc*) to estimate; (*meuble etc*) to value. ◆**évaluation** *nf* estimation; valuation.

évangile [evãʒil] *nf* gospel; **É.** Gospel. ◆**évangélique** *a* evangelical.

évanou/ir (s') [sevanwir] *vpr Méd* to black out, faint; (*espoir, crainte etc*) to vanish. ◆**—I** *a Méd* unconscious. ◆**—issement** *nm* (*syncope*) blackout, fainting fit; (*disparition*) vanishing.

évaporer (s') [sevapɔre] *vpr Ch* to evaporate; (*disparaître*) *Fam* to vanish into thin air. ◆**évaporation** *nf* evaporation.

évasif, -ive [evazif, -iv] *a* evasive.

évasion [evazjɔ̃] *nf* escape (**d'un lieu** from a place, **devant un danger** from a danger/*etc*); (*hors de la réalité*) escapism; **é. fiscale** tax evasion.

évêché [eveʃe] *nm* (*territoire*) bishopric, see.

éveil [evɛj] *nm* awakening; **en é.** on the alert; **donner l'é.** to alert.

éveill/er [eveje] *vt* (*susciter*) to arouse; **é.** **qn** to awake(n) s.o.; **— s'é.** *vpr* to awake(n) (**à** to); (*sentiment, idée*) to be aroused. ◆**—é** *a* awake; (*vif*) lively, alert.

événement [evɛnmã] *nm* event.

éventail [evãtaj] *nm* **1** (*instrument portatif*) fan; **en é.** (*orteils*) spread out. **2** (*choix*) range.

évent/er [evãte] *vt* **1** (*secret*) to discover. **2**

é. qn to fan s.o. **3 s'é.** *vpr* (*bière, vin etc*) to turn stale. ◆**—é** *a* (*bière, vin etc*) stale.

éventrer [evãtre] *vt* (*animal etc*) to disembowel; (*sac*) to rip open.

éventuel, -elle [evãtɥɛl] *a* possible. ◆**éventuellement** *adv* possibly. ◆**éventualité** *nf* possibility; **dans l'é. de** in the event of.

évêque [evɛk] *nm* bishop.

évertuer (s') [severtɥe] *vpr* **s'é. à faire** to do one's utmost to do, struggle to do.

éviction [eviksjɔ̃] *nf* (*de concurrent etc*) & *Pol* ousting.

évident [evidã] *a* obvious, evident (**que** that). ◆**évidemment** [-amã] *adv* certainly, obviously. ◆**évidence** *nf* obviousness; **une é.** an obvious fact; **nier l'é.** to deny the obvious; **être en é.** to be conspicuous *ou* in evidence; **mettre en é.** (*fait*) to underline.

évider [evide] *vt* to hollow out.

évier [evje] *nm* (kitchen) sink.

évincer [evɛ̃se] *vt* (*concurrent etc*) & *Pol* to oust.

éviter [evite] *vt* to avoid (**de faire** doing); **é.** **qch à qn** to spare *ou* save s.o. sth.

évolu/er [evɔlɥe] *vi* **1** (*changer*) to develop, change; (*société, idée, situation*) to evolve. **2** (*se déplacer*) to move; *Mil* to manœuvre, *Am* maneuver. ◆**—é** *a* (*pays*) advanced; (*personne*) enlightened. ◆**évolution** *nf* **1** (*changement*) development; evolution. **2** (*d'un danseur etc*) & *Mil* movement.

évoquer [evoke] *vt* to evoke, call to mind. ◆**évocateur, -trice** *a* evocative. ◆**évocation** *nf* evocation, recalling.

ex [ɛks] *nmf* (*mari, femme*) *Fam* ex.

ex- [ɛks] *préf* ex-; **ex-mari** ex-husband.

exacerber [ɛgzasɛrbe] *vt* (*douleur etc*) to exacerbate.

exact [ɛgzakt] *a* (*précis*) exact, accurate; (*juste, vrai*) correct, exact, right; (*ponctuel*) punctual. ◆**exactement** *adv* exactly. ◆**exactitude** *nf* exactness; accuracy; correctness; punctuality.

exaction [ɛgzaksjɔ̃] *nf* exaction.

ex aequo [ɛgzeko] *adv* **être classés ex ae.** *Sp* to tie, be equally placed.

exagér/er [ɛgzaʒere] *vt* to exaggerate; **–** *vi* (*parler*) to exaggerate; (*agir*) to overdo it, go too far. ◆**—é** *a* excessive. ◆**—ément** *adv* excessively. ◆**exagération** *nf* exaggeration; (*excès*) excessiveness.

exalt/er [ɛgzalte] *vt* (*glorifier*) to exalt; (*animer*) to fire, stir. ◆**—ant** *a* stirring. ◆**—é, -ée** *a* (*sentiment*) impassioned, wild; – *nmf Péj* fanatic. ◆**exaltation** *nf* (*délire*) elation, excitement.

examen [ɛgzamɛ̃] *nm* examination; *Scol* exam(ination); **e. blanc** *Scol* mock exam(ination). ◆**examinateur, -trice** *nmf Scol* examiner. ◆**examiner** *vt* (*considérer, regarder*) to examine.

exaspérer [ɛgzaspere] *vt* (*énerver*) to aggravate, exasperate. ◆**exaspération** *nf* exasperation, aggravation.

exaucer [ɛgzose] *vt* (*désir*) to grant; **e. qn** to grant s.o.'s wish(es).

excavation [ɛkskavasjɔ̃] *nf* (*trou*) hollow.

excéder [ɛksede] *vt* **1** (*dépasser*) to exceed. **2 é. qn** (*fatiguer, énerver*) to exasperate s.o. ◆**excédent** *nm* surplus, excess; **e. de bagages** excess luggage *ou Am* baggage. ◆**excédentaire** *a* (*poids etc*) excess-.

excellent [ɛkselɑ̃] *a* excellent. ◆**excellence** *nf* **1** excellence; **par e.** above all else *ou* all others. **2 E.** (*titre*) Excellency. ◆**exceller** *vi* to excel (**en qch** in, **à faire** in doing).

excentrique [ɛksɑ̃trik] **1** *a & nmf* (*original*) eccentric. **2** *a* (*quartier*) remote. ◆**excentricité** *nf* (*bizarrerie*) eccentricity.

excepté [ɛksɛpte] *prép* except. ◆**excepter** *vt* to except. ◆**exception** *nf* exception; **à l'e. de** except (for), with the exception of; **faire e.** to be an exception. ◆**exceptionnel, -elle** *a* exceptional. ◆**exceptionnellement** *adv* exceptionally.

excès [ɛksɛ] *nm* excess; (*de table*) over-eating; **e. de vitesse** *Aut* speeding. ◆**excessif, -ive** *a* excessive. ◆**excessivement** *adv* excessively.

excit/er [ɛksite] *vt* (*faire naître*) to excite, rouse, stir; **e. qn** (*mettre en colère*) to provoke s.o.; (*agacer*) to annoy s.o.; (*enthousiasmer*) to thrill s.o., excite s.o.; **e. qn à faire** to incite s.o. to do; **– s'e.** *vpr* (*nerveux, enthousiaste*) to get excited. ◆**–ant** *a* exciting; – *nm* stimulant. ◆**–é** *a* excited. ◆**–able** *a* excitable. ◆**excitation** *nf* (*agitation*) excitement; **e. à** (*haine etc*) incitement to.

exclamer (s') [ɛksklame] *vpr* to exclaim. ◆**exclamatif, -ive** *a* exclamatory. ◆**exclamation** *nf* exclamation.

exclu/re* [ɛksklyr] *vt* (*écarter*) to exclude (**de** from); (*chasser*) to expel (**de** from); **e. qch** (*rendre impossible*) to preclude sth. ◆**–u** *a* (*solution etc*) out of the question; (*avec une date*) exclusive. ◆**exclusif, -ive** *a* (*droit, modèle, préoccupation*) exclusive. ◆**exclusion** *nf* exclusion. ◆**exclusivement** *adv* exclusively. ◆**exclusivité** *nf*

Com exclusive rights; **en e.** (*film*) having an exclusive showing (**à** at).

excommunier [ɛkskɔmynje] *vt* to excommunicate. ◆**excommunication** *nf* excommunication.

excrément(s) [ɛkskremɑ̃] *nm*(*pl*) excrement.

excroissance [ɛkskrwasɑ̃s] *nf* (out)growth.

excursion [ɛkskyrsjɔ̃] *nf* outing, excursion, tour; (*à pied*) hike.

excuse [ɛkskyz] *nf* (*prétexte*) excuse; *pl* (*regrets*) apology; **des excuses** an apology; **faire des excuses** to apologize (**à** to); **toutes mes excuses** (my) sincere apologies. ◆**excuser** *vt* (*justifier, pardonner*) to excuse (**qn d'avoir fait, qn de faire** s.o. for doing); **– s'e.** *vpr* to apologize (**de** for, **auprès de** to); **excusez-moi!, je m'excuse!** excuse me!

exécrer [ɛgzekre] *vt* to loathe. ◆**exécrable** *a* atrocious.

exécut/er [ɛgzekyte] *vt* **1** (*projet, tâche etc*) to carry out, execute; (*statue, broderie etc*) to produce; (*jouer*) *Mus* to perform. **2 e. qn** (*tuer*) to execute s.o. **3 s'e.** *vpr* to comply. ◆**–ant, -ante** *nmf Mus* performer. ◆**–able** *a* practicable. ◆**exécutif** *am* (*pouvoir*) executive; – *nm* **l'e.** *Pol* the executive. ◆**exécution** *nf* **1** carrying out, execution; production; performance. **2** (*mise à mort*) execution.

exemple [ɛgzɑ̃pl] *nm* example; **par e.** for example, for instance; (*ça*) **par e.!** *Fam* good heavens!; **donner l'e.** to set an example (**à** to). ◆**exemplaire 1** *a* exemplary. **2** *nm* (*livre etc*) copy.

exempt [ɛgzɑ̃] *a* **e. de** (*dispense de*) exempt from; (*sans*) free from. ◆**exempter** *vt* to exempt (**de** from). ◆**exemption** *nf* exemption.

exercer [ɛgzerse] *vt* (*muscles, droits*) to exercise; (*autorité, influence*) to exert (**sur** over); (*métier*) to carry on, work at; (*profession*) to practise; **e. qn à** (*couture etc*) to train s.o. in; **e. qn à faire** to train s.o. to do; – *vi* (*médecin*) to practise; – **s'e.** *vpr* (*influence etc*) to be exerted; **s'e.** (**à qch**) (*sportif etc*) to practise (sth); **s'e. à faire** to practise doing. ◆**exercice** *nm* (*physique etc*) & *Scol* exercise; *Mil* drill, exercise; (*de métier*) practice; **l'e. de** (*pouvoir etc*) the exercise of; **en e.** (*fonctionnaire*) in office; (*médecin*) in practice; **faire de l'e., prendre de l'e.** to (take) exercise.

exhaler [ɛgzale] *vt* (*odeur etc*) to give off.

exhaustif, -ive [ɛgzostif, -iv] *a* exhaustive.

exhiber [ɛgzibe] *vt* to exhibit, show,

◆**exhibition** nf exhibition. ◆**exhibition-niste** nmf exhibitionist.

exhorter [ɛgzɔrte] vt to urge, exhort (**à faire** to do).

exhumer [ɛgzyme] vt (cadavre) to exhume; (vestiges) to dig up.

exiger [ɛgziʒe] vt to demand, require (**de** from, **que** (+ sub) that). ◆**exigeant** a demanding, exacting. ◆**exigence** nf demand, requirement; **d'une grande e.** very demanding.

exigu, -uë [ɛgzigy] a (appartement etc) cramped, tiny. ◆**exiguïté** nf crampedness.

exil [ɛgzil] nm (expulsion) exile. ◆**exil/er** vt to exile; — **s'e.** vpr to go into exile. ◆**-é, -ée** nmf (personne) exile.

existence [ɛgzistɑ̃s] nf existence. ◆**existentialisme** nm existentialism. ◆**exist/er** vi to exist; — v imp **il existe . . .** (sing) there is . . . ; (pl) there are . . . . ◆**-ant** a existing.

exode [ɛgzɔd] nm exodus.

exonérer [ɛgzɔnere] vt to exempt (**de** from). ◆**exonération** nf exemption.

exorbitant [ɛgzɔrbitɑ̃] a exorbitant.

exorciser [ɛgzɔrsize] vt to exorcize. ◆**exorcisme** nm exorcism.

exotique [ɛgzɔtik] a exotic. ◆**exotisme** nm exoticism.

expansif, -ive [ɛkspɑ̃sif, -iv] a expansive, effusive.

expansion [ɛkspɑ̃sjɔ̃] nf Com Phys Pol expansion; **en (pleine) e.** (fast ou rapidly) expanding.

expatri/er (s') [ɛkspatrije] vpr to leave one's country. ◆**-é, -ée** a & nmf expatriate.

expectative [ɛkspɛktativ] nf **être dans l'e.** to be waiting to see what happens.

expédient [ɛkspedjɑ̃] nm (moyen) expedient.

expédier [ɛkspedje] vt **1** (envoyer) to send off. **2** (affaires, client) to dispose of quickly, dispatch. ◆**expéditeur, -trice** nmf sender. ◆**expéditif, -ive** a expeditious, quick. ◆**expédition** nf **1** (envoi) dispatch. **2** (voyage) expedition.

expérience [ɛksperjɑ̃s] nf (pratique, connaissance) experience; (scientifique) experiment; **faire l'e. de qch** to experience sth. ◆**expérimental, -aux** a experimental. ◆**expérimentation** nf experimentation. ◆**expériment/er** vt Phys Ch to try out, experiment with; — vi to experiment. ◆**-é** a experienced.

expert [ɛkspɛr] a expert, skilled (**en** in); —

nm expert; (d'assurances) valuer. ◆**e.-comptable** nm (pl **experts-comptables**) = chartered accountant, = Am certified public accountant. ◆**expertise** nf (évaluation) (expert) appraisal; (compétence) expertise.

expier [ɛkspje] vt (péchés, crime) to expiate, atone for. ◆**expiation** nf expiation (**de** of).

expir/er [ɛkspire] **1** vti to breathe out. **2** vi (mourir) to pass away; (finir, cesser) to expire. ◆**-ant** a dying. ◆**expiration** nf (échéance) expiry, Am expiration.

explicite [ɛksplisit] a explicit. ◆**-ment** adv explicitly.

expliquer [ɛksplike] vt to explain (**à** to); — **s'e.** vpr to explain oneself; (discuter) to talk things over, have it out (**avec** with); **s'e. qch** (comprendre) to understand sth; **ça s'explique** that is understandable. ◆**explicable** a understandable. ◆**explicatif, -ive** a explanatory. ◆**explication** nf explanation; (mise au point) discussion.

exploit [ɛksplwa] nm exploit, feat.

exploit/er [ɛksplwate] vt **1** (champs) to farm; (ferme, entreprise) to run; (mine) to work; (situation) Fig to exploit. **2** (abuser de) Péj to exploit (s.o.). ◆**-ant, -ante** nmf farmer. ◆**exploitation** nf **1** Péj exploitation. **2** farming; running; working; (entreprise) concern; (agricole) farm.

explorer [ɛksplɔre] vt to explore. ◆**explorateur, -trice** nmf explorer. ◆**exploration** nf exploration.

exploser [ɛksploze] vi (gaz etc) to explode; (bombe) to blow up, explode; (de colère) Fam to explode, blow up; **faire e.** (bombe) to explode. ◆**explosif, -ive** a & nm explosive. ◆**explosion** nf explosion; (de colère, joie) outburst.

exporter [ɛkspɔrte] vt to export (**vers** to, **de** from). ◆**exportateur, -trice** nmf exporter; — a exporting. ◆**exportation** nf (produit) export; (action) export(ation), exporting.

expos/er [ɛkspoze] vt (présenter, soumettre) & Phot to expose (**à** to); (marchandises) to display; (tableau etc) to exhibit; (idée, théorie) to set out; (vie, réputation) to risk, endanger; **s'e. à** to expose oneself to. ◆**-ant, -ante** nmf exhibitor. ◆**-é 1** a **bien e.** (édifice) having a good exposure; **e. au sud** facing south. **2** nm (compte rendu) account (**de** of); (discours) talk; Scol paper. ◆**exposition** nf (de marchandises etc) display; (salon) exhibition; (au danger etc) &

Phot exposure (à to); (*de maison etc*) aspect.

exprès[1] [ɛksprɛ] *adv* on purpose, intentionally; (*spécialement*) specially.

exprès[2], **-esse** [ɛksprɛs] **1** *a* (*ordre, condition*) express. **2** *a inv* **lettre/colis e.** express letter/parcel. ◆**expressément** *adv* expressly.

express [ɛksprɛs] *a & nm inv* (*train*) express; (*café*) espresso.

expressif, -ive [ɛksprɛsif, -iv] *a* expressive. ◆**expression** *nf* (*phrase, mine etc*) expression. ◆**exprimer** *vt* to express; — **s'e.** *vpr* to express oneself.

exproprier [ɛksprɔprije] *vt* to seize the property of by compulsory purchase.

expulser [ɛkspylse] *vt* to expel (**de** from); (*joueur*) *Sp* to send off; (*locataire*) to evict. ◆**expulsion** *nf* expulsion; eviction; sending off.

expurger [ɛkspyrʒe] *vt* to expurgate.

exquis [ɛkski] *a* exquisite.

extase [ɛkstaz] *nf* ecstasy, rapture. ◆**s'extasier** *vpr* to be in raptures (**sur** over, about). ◆**-é** *a* ecstatic.

extensible [ɛkstɑ̃sibl] *a* expandable. ◆**extension** *nf* extension; (*essor*) expansion.

exténuer [ɛkstenɥe] *vt* (*fatiguer*) to exhaust. ◆**exténuation** *nf* exhaustion.

extérieur [ɛksterjœr] *a* (*monde etc*) outside; (*surface*) outer; (*signe*) outward, external; (*politique*) foreign; **e. à** external to; — *nm* outside, exterior; **à l'e. (de)** outside; **à l'e.** (*match*) away; **en e.** *Cin* on location. ◆**—ement** *adv* externally; (*en apparence*) outwardly. ◆**extérioriser** *vt* to express.

exterminer [ɛkstɛrmine] *vt* to exterminate,

wipe out. ◆**extermination** *nf* extermination.

externe [ɛkstɛrn] **1** *a* external. **2** *nmf Scol* day pupil; *Méd* non-resident hospital doctor, *Am* intern.

extincteur [ɛkstɛ̃ktœr] *nm* fire extinguisher. ◆**extinction** *nf* (*de feu*) extinguishing; (*de voix*) loss; (*de race*) extinction.

extirper [ɛkstirpe] *vt* to eradicate.

extorquer [ɛkstɔrke] *vt* to extort (**à** from). ◆**extorsion** *nf* extortion.

extra [ɛkstra] **1** *a inv* (*très bon*) *Fam* top-quality. **2** *nm inv Culin* (extra-special) treat; (*serviteur*) extra hand *ou* help.

extra- [ɛkstra] *préf* extra-. ◆**e.-fin** *a* extra-fine. ◆**e.-fort** *a* extra-strong.

extradition [ɛkstradisjɔ̃] *nf* extradition. ◆**extrader** *vt* to extradite.

extraire[*] [ɛkstrɛr] *vt* to extract (**de** from); (*charbon*) to mine. ◆**extraction** *nf* extraction. ◆**extrait** *nm* extract; **un e. de naissance** a (copy of one's) birth certificate.

extraordinaire [ɛkstraɔrdinɛr] *a* extraordinary. ◆**—ment** *adv* exceptionally; (*très, bizarrement*) extraordinarily.

extravagant [ɛkstravagɑ̃] *a* extravagant. ◆**extravagance** *nf* extravagance.

extrême [ɛkstrɛm] *a* extreme; — *nm* extreme; **pousser à l'e.** to take *ou* carry to extremes. ◆**—ment** *adv* extremely. ◆**extrémiste** *a & nmf* extremist. ◆**extrémité** *nf* (*bout*) extremity, end; *pl* (*excès*) extremes.

exubérant [ɛgzyberɑ̃] *a* exuberant. ◆**exubérance** *nf* exuberance.

exulter [ɛgzylte] *vi* to exult, rejoice. ◆**exultation** *nf* exultation.

F

F, f [ɛf] *nm* F, f.

F *abrév* franc(s).

fable [fabl] *nf* fable.

fabrique [fabrik] *nf* factory; **marque de f.** trade mark.

fabriquer [fabrike] *vt* (*objet*) to make; (*industriellement*) to manufacture; (*récit*) *Péj* to fabricate, make up; **qu'est-ce qu'il fabrique?** *Fam* what's he up to? ◆**fabricant, -ante** *nmf* manufacturer. ◆**fabrication** *nf* manufacture; (*artisanale*) making; **de f. française** of French make.

fabuleux, -euse [fabylø, -øz] *a* (*légendaire, incroyable*) fabulous.

fac [fak] *nf Univ Fam* = **faculté 2.**

façade [fasad] *nf* (*de bâtiment*) front, façade; (*apparence*) *Fig* pretence, façade; **de f.** (*luxe etc*) sham.

face [fas] *nf* face; (*de cube etc*) side;·(*de monnaie*) head; **de f.** (*photo*) full-face; (*vue*) front; **faire f. à** (*situation etc*) to face, face up to; **en f. opposite**; **en f. de** opposite, facing; (*en présence de*) in front of; **en f. d'un problème, f. à un problème** in the face of a problem, faced with a problem; **f. à** (*vis-à-vis de*) facing; **regarder qn en f.** to look s.o. in the face; **f. à f.** face to face; **un f. à f.** *TV* a face to face encounter; **sauver/perdre la f.** to save/lose face.

facétie [fasesi] *nf* joke, jest. ◆**facétieux, -euse** [-esjø, -øz] *a* (*personne*) facetious.

facette [faset] *nf* (*de diamant, problème etc*) facet.

fâch/er [faʃe] *vt* to anger; — **se f.** *vpr* to get angry *ou* annoyed (**contre** with); **se f. avec qn** (*se brouiller*) to fall out with s.o. ◆—**é a** (*air*) angry; (*amis*) on bad terms; **f. avec** *ou* **contre qn** angry *ou* annoyed with s.o.; **f. de qch** sorry about sth. ◆**fâcherie** *nf* quarrel. ◆**fâcheux, -euse** *a* (*nouvelle etc*) unfortunate.

facho [faʃo] *a & nmf Fam* fascist.

facile [fasil] *a* easy; (*caractère, humeur*) easygoing; (*banal*) *Péj* facile; **c'est f. à faire** it's easy to do; **il est f. de faire** ça it's easy to do that; **f. à vivre** easy to get along with, easygoing. ◆—**ment** *adv* easily. ◆**facilité** *nf* (*simplicité*) easiness; (*aisance*) ease; **facilités de paiement** *Com* easy terms; **avoir de la f.** to be gifted; **avoir toutes facilités pour** to have every facility *ou* opportunity to. ◆**faciliter** *vt* to facilitate, make easier.

façon [fasɔ̃] *nf* **1** way; **la f. dont elle parle** the way (in which) she talks; **f. (d'agir)** behaviour; **je n'aime pas ses façons** I don't like his *ou* her manners *ou* ways; **une f. de parler** a manner of speaking; **à la f. de** in the fashion of; **de toute f.** anyway, anyhow; **de f.** so as to; **de f. générale** generally speaking; **à ma f.** my way, (in) my own way; **faire des façons** to make a fuss; **table f. chêne** imitation oak table. **2** (*coupe de vêtement*) cut, style. ◆**façonner** *vt* (*travailler, former*) to fashion, shape; (*fabriquer*) to manufacture.

facteur [faktœr] *nm* **1** postman, *Am* mailman. **2** (*élément*) factor. ◆**factrice** *nf Fam* postwoman.

factice [faktis] *a* false, artificial; (*diamant*) imitation-.

faction [faksjɔ̃] *nf* **1** (*groupe*) *Pol* faction. **2** **de f.** *Mil* on guard (duty), on sentry duty.

facture [faktyr] *nf Com* invoice, bill. ◆**facturer** *vt* to invoice, bill.

facultatif, -ive [fakyltatif, -iv] *a* optional; **arrêt f.** request stop.

faculté [fakylte] *nf* **1** (*aptitude*) faculty; (*possibilité*) freedom (**de faire** to do); **une f. de travail** a capacity for work. **2** *Univ* faculty; **à la f.** *Fam* at university, *Am* at school.

fadaises [fadɛz] *nfpl* twaddle, nonsense.

fade [fad] *a* insipid. ◆**fadasse** *a Fam* wishy-washy.

fagot [fago] *nm* bundle (of firewood).

fagoter [fagɔte] *vt Péj* to dress, rig out.

faible [fɛbl] *a* weak, feeble; (*bruit, voix*) faint; (*vent, quantité, chances*) slight; (*revenus*) small; **f. en anglais**/*etc* poor at English/*etc*; — *nm* (*personne*) weakling; **les faibles** the weak; **avoir un f. pour** to have a weakness *ou* a soft spot for. ◆**faiblement** *adv* weakly; (*légèrement*) slightly; (*éclairer, parler*) faintly. ◆**faiblesse** *nf* weakness, feebleness; faintness; slightness; small-ness; (*défaut, syncope*) weakness. ◆**faiblir** *vi* (*forces*) to weaken; (*courage, vue*) to fail; (*vent*) to slacken.

faïence [fajɑ̃s] *nf* (*matière*) earthenware; *pl* (*objets*) crockery, earthenware.

faille [faj] *nf Géol* fault; *Fig* flaw.

faillible [fajibl] *a* fallible.

faillir* [fajir] *vi* **1 il a failli tomber** he almost *ou* nearly fell. **2 f. à** (*devoir*) to fail in.

faillite [fajit] *nf Com* bankruptcy; *Fig* failure; **faire f.** to go bankrupt.

faim [fɛ̃] *nf* hunger; **avoir f.** to be hungry; **donner f. à qn** to make s.o. hungry; **manger à sa f.** to eat one's fill; **mourir de f.** to die of starvation; (*avoir très faim*) *Fig* to be starving.

fainéant, -ante [feneɑ̃, -ɑ̃t] *a* idle; — *nmf* idler. ◆**fainéanter** *vi* to idle. ◆**fainéantise** *nf* idleness.

faire* [fɛr] **1** *vt* (*bruit, pain, faute etc*) to make; (*devoir, dégâts, ménage etc*) to do; (*rêve, chute*) to have; (*sourire, grognement*) to give; (*promenade, sieste*) to have; (*guerre*) to wage, make; **ça fait dix mètres de large** (*mesure*) it's ten metres wide; **2 et 2 font 4** 2 and 2 are 4; **ça fait dix francs** that is *ou* comes to ten francs; **qu'a-t-il fait (de)?** what's he done (with)?; **que f.?** what's to be done?; **f. du tennis/du piano**/*etc* to play tennis/the piano/*etc*; **f. l'idiot** to act *ou* play the fool; **ça ne fait rien** that doesn't matter; **comment as-tu fait pour . . . ?** how did you manage to . . . ?; **il ne fait que travailler** he does nothing but work, he keeps on working; **je ne fais que d'arriver** I've just arrived; **oui, fit-elle** yes, she said. **2** *vi* (*agir*) to do; (*paraître*) to look; **il fait vieux** he looks old; **il fera un bon médecin** he'll be *ou* make a good doctor; **elle ferait bien de partir** she'd do well to leave. **3** *v imp* **il fait beau/froid**/*etc* it's fine/cold/*etc*; **quel temps fait-il?** what's the weather like?; **ça fait deux ans que je ne l'ai pas vu** I haven't seen him for two years, it's (been) two years since I saw him. **4** *v aux* (+ *inf*); **f. construire une maison** to have *ou* a house built (**à qn, par qn** by s.o.); **f. crier/souffrir**/*etc* **qn** to make s.o. shout/suffer/*etc*; **se f. couper les cheveux** to have one's hair cut; **se f. craindre/obéir**/*etc* to make oneself feared/obeyed/*etc*; **se f. tuer/renverser**/*etc* to get *ou* be killed/knocked down/*etc*. **5 se f.** *vpr* (*fabrication*) to be made; (*activité*) to be done; **se f. des illusions** to have illusions; **se f. des amis** to make friends; **se f. vieux**/*etc* (*devenir*) to get old/*etc*; **il se fait tard** it's getting late; **comment se fait-il que?** how is it that?; **se f. à** to get used to, adjust to; **ne t'en fais pas!** don't worry!

faire-part [fɛrpar] *nm inv* (*de mariage etc*) announcement.

faisable [fəzabl] *a* feasible.

faisan [fəzɑ̃] *nm* (*oiseau*) pheasant.

faisandé [fəzɑ̃de] *a* (*gibier*) high.

faisceau, -x [feso] *nm* (*lumineux*) beam; (*de tiges etc*) bundle.

fait [fɛ] **1** *voir* **faire**; *– a* (*fromage*) ripe; (*homme*) grown; (*yeux*) made up; (*ongles*) polished; **tout f.** ready made; **bien f.** (*jambes, corps etc*) shapely; **c'est bien f.!** it serves you right! **2** *nm* event, occurrence; (*donnée, réalité*) fact; **prendre sur le f.** to catch in the act; **du f. de** on account of; **f. divers** *Journ* (miscellaneous) news item; **au f.** (*à propos*) by the way; **aller au f.** to get to the point; **faits et gestes** actions; **en f.** in fact; **en f. de** in the matter of.

faîte [fɛt] *nm* (*haut*) top; (*apogée*) *Fig* height.

faites [fɛt] *voir* **faire**.

faitout [fɛtu] *nm* stewing pot, casserole.

falaise [falɛz] *nf* cliff.

falloir* [falwar] **1** *v imp* **il faut qch/qn** I, you, we *etc* need sth/s.o.; **il lui faut un stylo** he *ou* she needs a pen; **il faut partir**/*etc* I, you, we *etc* have to go/*etc*; **il faut que je parte** I have to go; **il faudrait qu'elle reste** she ought to stay; **il faut un jour** it takes a day (**pour faire** to do); **comme il faut** properly; **s'il le faut** if need be. **2 s'en f.** *v imp* **peu s'en est fallu qu'il ne pleure** he almost cried; **tant s'en faut** far from it.

falsifier [falsifje] *vt* (*texte etc*) to falsify. ◆**falsification** *nf* falsification.

famé (mal) [malfame] *a* of ill repute.

famélique [famelik] *a* ill-fed, starving.

fameux, -euse [famø, -øz] *a* famous; (*excellent*) *Fam* first-class; **pas f.** *Fam* not much good.

familial, -aux [familjal, -o] *a* family-.

familier, -ière [familje, -jɛr] *a* (*bien connu*) familiar (**à** to); (*amical*) friendly, informal; (*locution*) colloquial, familiar; **f. avec qn** (over)familiar with s.o.; *– nm* (*de club etc*) regular visitor. ◆**familiariser** *vt* to familiarize (with); *– se* **f.** *vpr* to familiarize oneself (**avec** with). ◆**familiarité** *nf* familiarity; *pl Péj* liberties. ◆**familièrement** *adv* (*parler*) informally.

famille [famij] *nf* family; **en f.** (*dîner etc*) with one's family; **un père de f.** a family man.

famine [famin] *nf* famine.

fan [fã] *nm* (*admirateur*) *Fam* fan.

fana [fana] *nmf Fam* fan; **être f. de** to be crazy about.

fanal, -aux [fanal, -o] *nm* lantern, light.

fanatique [fanatik] *a* fanatical; *– nmf* fanatic. ◆**fanatisme** *nm* fanaticism.

fan/er (se) [safane] *vpr* (*fleur, beauté*) to fade. ◆**-é** *a* faded.

fanfare [fãfar] *nf* (*orchestre*) brass band; (*air, musique*) fanfare.

fanfaron, -onne [fãfarɔ̃, -ɔn] *a* boastful; *– nmf* braggart.

fange [fãʒ] *nf Litt* mud, mire.

fanion [fanjɔ̃] *nm* (*drapeau*) pennant.

fantaisie [fãtezi] *nf* (*caprice*) fancy, whim; (*imagination*) imagination, fantasy; (**de f.**) (*bouton etc*) fancy. ◆**fantaisiste** *a* (*pas sérieux*) fanciful; (*irrégulier*) unorthodox.

fantasme [fãtasm] *nm Psy* fantasy. ◆**fantasmer** *vi* to fantasize (**sur** about).

fantasque [fãtask] *a* whimsical.

fantassin [fãtasɛ̃] *nm Mil* infantryman.

fantastique [fãtastik] *a* (*imaginaire, excellent*) fantastic.

fantoche [fãtɔʃ] *nm & a* puppet.

fantôme [fãtom] *nm* ghost, phantom; *– a* (*ville, train*) ghost-; (*firme*) bogus.

faon [fã] *nm* (*animal*) fawn.

faramineux, -euse [faraminø, -øz] *a Fam* fantastic.

farce[1] [fars] *nf* practical joke, prank; *Th* farce; **magasin de farces et attrapes** joke shop. ◆**farceur, -euse** *nmf* (*blagueur*) wag, joker.

farce[2] [fars] *nf Culin* stuffing. ◆**farcir** *vt* **1** *Culin* to stuff. **2 se f. qn/qch** *Fam* to put up with s.o./sth.

fard [far] *nm* make-up. ◆**farder** *vt* (*vérité*) to camouflage; *– se* **f.** *vpr* (*se maquiller*) to make up.

fardeau, -x [fardo] *nm* burden, load.

farfelu, -ue [farfəly] *a Fam* crazy, bizarre; *– nmf Fam* weirdo.

farine [farin] *nf* (*de blé*) flour; **f. d'avoine**

oatmeal. ◆**farineux, -euse** a Péj floury, powdery.

farouche [faruʃ] a **1** (timide) shy, unsociable; (animal) easily scared. **2** (violent, acharné) fierce. ◆**—ment** adv fiercely.

fart [far(t)] nm (ski) wax. ◆**farter** vt (skis) to wax.

fascicule [fasikyl] nm volume.

fasciner [fasine] vt to fascinate. ◆**fascination** nf fascination.

fascisme [faʃism] nm fascism. ◆**fasciste** a & nmf fascist.

fasse(nt) [fas] voir faire.

faste [fast] nm ostentation, display.

fastidieux, -euse [fastidjø, -øz] a tedious, dull.

fatal, mpl -als [fatal] a (mortel) fatal; (inévitable) inevitable; (moment, ton) fateful; c'était f.! it was bound to happen! ◆**—ement** adv inevitably. ◆**fataliste** a fatalistic; – nmf fatalist. ◆**fatalité** nf (destin) fate. ◆**fatidique** a (jour, date) fateful.

fatigue [fatig] nf tiredness, fatigue, weariness. ◆**fatigant** a (épuisant) tiring; (ennuyeux) tiresome. ◆**fatigu/er** vt to tire, fatigue; (yeux) to strain; (importuner) to annoy; (raser) to bore; – vi (moteur) to strain; – **se f.** vpr (se lasser) to get tired, tire (de of); (travailler) to tire oneself out (à faire doing). ◆**—é** a tired, weary (de of).

fatras [fatra] nm jumble, muddle.

faubourg [fobur] nm suburb. ◆**faubourien, -ienne** a (accent etc) suburban, common.

fauché [foʃe] a (sans argent) Fam broke.

fauch/er [foʃe] vt **1** (herbe) to mow; (blé) to reap; (abattre, renverser) Fig to mow down. **2** (voler) Fam to snatch, pinch. ◆**—euse** nf (machine) reaper.

faucille [fosij] nf (instrument) sickle.

faucon [fokɔ̃] nm (oiseau) falcon, hawk; (personne) Fig hawk.

faudra, faudrait [fodra, fodrɛ] voir falloir.

faufiler (se) [səfofile] vpr to edge ou inch one's way (dans through, into; entre between).

faune [fon] nf wildlife, fauna; (gens) Péj set.

faussaire [fosɛr] nm (faux-monnayeur) forger.

fausse [fos] voir faux¹. ◆**faussement** adv falsely.

fausser [fose] vt (sens, réalité etc) to distort; (clé etc) to buckle; **f. compagnie à qn** to give s.o. the slip.

fausseté [foste] nf (d'un raisonnement etc) falseness; (hypocrisie) duplicity.

faut [fo] voir falloir.

faute [fot] nf (erreur) mistake; (responsabilité) fault; (délit) offence; (péché) sin; Fb foul; c'est ta f. it's your fault, you're to blame; **f. de temps/etc** for lack of time/etc; **f. de mieux** for want of anything better; **en f.** at fault; **sans f.** without fail. ◆**fautif, -ive** a (personne) at fault; (erroné) faulty.

fauteuil [fotœj] nm armchair; (de président) chair; **f. d'orchestre** Th seat in the stalls; **f. roulant** wheelchair; **f. pivotant** swivel chair.

fauteur [fotœr] nm **f. de troubles** troublemaker.

fauve [fov] **1** a & nm (couleur) fawn. **2** nm wild beast; **chasse aux fauves** big game hunting.

faux¹, fausse [fo, fos] a (inauthentique) false; (pas vrai) untrue, false; (pas exact) wrong; (monnaie) counterfeit, forged; (bijou, marbre) imitation-, fake; (voix) out of tune; (col) detachable; – adv (chanter) out of tune; – nm (contrefaçon) forgery; **le f.** the false, the untrue. ◆**f.-filet** nm Culin sirloin. ◆**f.-fuyant** nm subterfuge. ◆**f.-monnayeur** nm counterfeiter.

faux² [fo] nf (instrument) scythe.

faveur [favœr] nf favour; **en f. de** (au profit de) in favour of; **de f.** (billet) complimentary; (traitement, régime) preferential. ◆**favorable** a favourable (à to). ◆**favori, -ite** a & nmf favourite. ◆**favoriser** vt to favour. ◆**favoritisme** nm favouritism.

favoris [favori] nmpl sideburns, side whiskers.

fébrile [febril] a feverish. ◆**fébrilité** nf feverishness.

fécond [fekɔ̃] a (femme, idée etc) fertile. ◆**féconder** vt to fertilize. ◆**fécondité** nf fertility.

fécule [fekyl] nf starch. ◆**féculents** nmpl (aliments) carbohydrates.

fédéral, -aux [federal, -o] a federal. ◆**fédération** nf federation. ◆**fédérer** vt to federate.

fée [fe] nf fairy. ◆**féerie** nf Th fantasy extravaganza; Fig fairy-like spectacle. ◆**féerique** a fairy(-like), magical.

feindre* [fɛ̃dr] vt to feign, sham; **f. de faire** to pretend to do. ◆**feint** a feigned, sham. ◆**feinte** nf sham, pretence; Boxe Mil feint.

fêler [fele] vt, – **se f.** vpr (tasse) to crack. ◆**fêlure** nf crack.

félicité [felisite] nf bliss, felicity.

féliciter [felisite] vt to congratulate (qn de ou sur s.o. on); **se f. de** to congratulate oneself on. ◆**félicitations** *nfpl* congratulations (pour on).

félin [felɛ̃] *a & nm* feline.

femelle [fəmɛl] *a & nf* (*animal*) female.

féminin, -ine [feminɛ̃] *a* (*prénom, hormone etc*) female; (*trait, intuition etc*) & Gram feminine; (*mode, revue, équipe etc*) women's. ◆**féministe** *a & nmf* feminist. ◆**féminité** *nf* femininity.

femme [fam] *nf* woman; (*épouse*) wife; **f. médecin** woman doctor; **f. de chambre** (*chamber*)maid; **f. de ménage** cleaning lady, maid; **bonne f.** Fam woman.

fémur [femyr] *nm* thighbone, femur.

fendiller (se) [səfɑ̃dije] *vpr* to crack.

fendre [fɑ̃dr] *vt* (*bois etc*) to split; (*foule*) to force one's way through; (*onde, air*) to cleave; (*cœur*) Fig to break, rend; **— se f.** *vpr* (*se fissurer*) to crack.

fenêtre [f(ə)nɛtr] *nf* window.

fenouil [fənuj] *nm Bot Culin* fennel.

fente [fɑ̃t] *nf* (*de tirelire, palissade, jupe etc*) slit; (*de rocher*) split, crack.

féodal, -aux [feodal, -o] *a* feudal.

fer [fɛr] *nm* iron; (*partie métallique de qch*) metal (part); **de f., en f.** (*outil etc*) iron-; **fil de f.** wire; **f. à cheval** horseshoe; **f.** (**à repasser**) iron; **f. à friser** curling tongs; **f. de lance** Fig spearhead; **de f.** (*santé*) Fig cast-iron; (*main, volonté*) Fig iron-. ◆**ferblanc** *nm* (*pl* **fers-blancs**) tin(-plate).

fera, ferait [fəra, fərɛ] *voir* faire.

férié [ferje] *a* **jour f.** (public) holiday.

ferme¹ [fɛrm] *nf* farm; (*maison*) farm(house).

ferme² [fɛrm] *a* (*beurre, décision etc*) firm; (*autoritaire*) firm (avec with); (*pas, voix*) steady; (*pâte*) stiff; **— adv** (*travailler, boire*) hard; (*discuter*) keenly; **tenir f.** to stand firm *ou* fast. ◆**—ment** [-əmɑ̃] *adv* firmly.

ferment [fɛrmɑ̃] *nm* ferment. ◆**fermentation** *nf* fermentation. ◆**fermenter** *vi* to ferment.

ferm/er [fɛrme] *vt* to close, shut; (*gaz, radio etc*) to turn *ou* switch off; (*passage*) to block; (*vêtement*) to do up; **f.** (**à clef**) to lock; **f. la marche** to bring up the rear; **— vi, — se f.** *vpr* to close, shut. ◆**—é** *a* (*porte, magasin etc*) closed, shut; (*route, circuit etc*) closed; (*gaz etc*) off. ◆**fermeture** *nf* closing, closure; (*heure*) closing time; (*mécanisme*) catch; **f. éclair**® zip (fastener), Am zipper. ◆**fermoir** *nm* clasp, (snap) fastener.

fermeté [fɛrməte] *nf* firmness; (*de geste, voix*) steadiness.

fermier, -ière [fɛrmje, -jɛr] *nmf* farmer; **— a** (*poulet, produit*) farm-.

féroce [feros] *a* fierce, ferocious. ◆**férocité** *nf* ferocity, fierceness.

ferraille [fɛraj] *nf* scrap-iron; **mettre à la f.** to scrap. ◆**ferrailleur** *nm* scrap-iron merchant.

ferré [fɛre] *a* **1** (*canne*) metal-tipped; **voie ferrée** railway, Am railroad; (*rails*) track. **2** (*calé*) Fam well up (en in, sur on).

ferrer [fɛre] *vt* (*cheval*) to shoe.

ferronnerie [fɛrɔnri] *nf* ironwork.

ferroviaire [fɛrɔvjɛr] *a* (*compagnie etc*) railway-, Am railroad-.

ferry-boat [fɛribot] *nm* ferry.

fertile [fɛrtil] *a* (*terre, imagination*) fertile; **f. en incidents** eventful. ◆**fertiliser** *vt* to fertilize. ◆**fertilité** *nf* fertility.

fervent, -ente [fɛrvɑ̃, -ɑ̃t] *a* fervent; **— nmf** devotee (de of). ◆**ferveur** *nf* fervour.

fesse [fɛs] *nf* buttock; **les fesses** one's behind. ◆**fessée** *nf* spanking.

festin [fɛstɛ̃] *nm* (*banquet*) feast.

festival, pl -als [fɛstival] *nm Mus Cin* festival.

festivités [fɛstivite] *nfpl* festivities.

festoyer [fɛstwaje] *vi* to feast, carouse.

fête [fɛt] *nf* (*civile*) holiday; Rel festival, feast; (*entre amis*) party; **f. du village** village fair *ou* fête; **f. de famille** family celebration; **c'est sa f.** it's his *ou* her saint's day; **f. des Mères** Mother's Day; **jour de f.** (public) holiday; **faire la f.** to make merry, revel; **air de f.** festive air. ◆**fêter** *vt* (*événement*) to celebrate.

fétiche [fetiʃ] *nm* (*objet de culte*) fetish; (*mascotte*) Fig mascot.

fétide [fetid] *a* fetid, stinking.

feu¹, -x [fø] *nm* fire; (*lumière*) Aut Nau Av light; (*de réchaud*) burner; (*de dispute*) Fig heat; *pl* (*de signalisation*) traffic lights; **feux de position** Aut parking lights; **feux de croisement** Aut dipped headlights, Am low beams; **f. rouge** Aut (*lumière*) red light; (*objet*) traffic lights; **tous feux éteints** Aut without lights; **mettre le f. à** to set fire to; **en f.** on fire, ablaze; **avez-vous du f.?** have you got a light?; **donner le f. vert** to give the go-ahead (à to); **ne pas faire long f.** not to last very long; **à f. doux** Culin on a low light; **au f.!** (there's a) fire!; **f.!** Mil fire!; **coup de f.** (*bruit*) gunshot; **feux croisés** Mil crossfire.

feu² [fø] *a inv* late; **f. ma tante** my late aunt.

feuille [fœj] *nf* leaf; (*de papier etc*) sheet; (*de température*) chart; Journ newssheet; **f. d'impôt** tax form *ou* return; **f. de paye** pay slip. ◆**feuillage** *nm* foliage. ◆**feuillet** *nm* (*de livre*) leaf. ◆**feuilleter** *vt* (*livre*) to flip *ou* leaf through; **pâte feuilletée** puff *ou* flaky pastry. ◆**feuilleton** *nm* (*roman, film etc*) serial. ◆**feuillu** *a* leafy.

feutre [føtr] *nm* felt; (*chapeau*) felt hat; **crayon f.** felt-tip(ped) pen. ◆**feutré** *a* (*bruit*) muffled; **à pas feutrés** silently.

fève [fɛv] *nf* bean.

février [fevrije] *nm* February.

fiable [fjabl] *a* reliable. ◆**fiabilité** *nf* reliability.

fiacre [fjakr] *nm* Hist hackney carriage.

fianc/er (se) [səfjɑ̃se] *vpr* to become engaged (**avec** to). ◆**—é** *nm* fiancé; *pl* engaged couple. ◆**—ée** *nf* fiancée. ◆**fiançailles** *nfpl* engagement.

fiasco [fjasko] *nm* fiasco; **faire f.** to be a fiasco.

fibre [fibr] *nf* fibre; **f. (alimentaire)** roughage, (dietary) fibre; **f. de verre** fibreglass.

ficelle [fisɛl] *nf* 1 string; **connaître les ficelles** (*d'un métier etc*) to known the ropes. 2 (*pain*) long thin loaf. ◆**ficeler** *vt* to tie up.

fiche [fiʃ] *nf* 1 (*carte*) index *ou* record card; (*papier*) slip, form; **f. technique** data record. 2 *El* (*broche*) pin; (*prise*) plug. ◆**fichier** *nm* card index, file.

fiche(r) [fiʃ(e)] *vt* (*pp* **fichu**) *Fam* (*faire*) to do; (*donner*) to give; (*jeter*) to throw; (*mettre*) to put; **f. le camp** to shove off; **fiche-moi la paix!** leave me alone!; **se f. de qn** to make fun of s.o.; **je m'en fiche!** I don't give a damn!

ficher [fiʃe] *vt* 1 (*enfoncer*) to drive in. 2 (*renseignement, personne*) to put on file.

fichu [fiʃy] *a* 1 *Fam* (*mauvais*) lousy, rotten; (*capable*) able (**de faire** to do); **il est f.** he's had it, he's done for; **mal f.** (*malade*) not well. 2 *nm* (head) scarf.

fictif, -ive [fiktif, -iv] *a* fictitious. ◆**fiction** *nf* fiction.

fidèle [fidɛl] *a* faithful (**à** to); — *nmf* faithful supporter; (*client*) regular (customer); **les fidèles** (*croyants*) the faithful; (*à l'église*) the congregation. ◆**—ment** *adv* faithfully. ◆**fidélité** *nf* fidelity, faithfulness.

fief [fjɛf] *nm* (*spécialité, chasse gardée*) domain.

fiel [fjɛl] *nm* gall.

fier (se) [safje] *vpr* **se f.** à to trust.

fier, fière [fjɛr] *a* proud (**de** of); **un f. culot** *Péj* a rare cheek. ◆**fièrement** *adv* proudly. ◆**fierté** *nf* pride.

fièvre [fjɛvr] *nf* (*maladie*) fever; (*agitation*) frenzy; **avoir de la f.** to have a temperature *ou* a fever. ◆**fiévreux, -euse** *a* feverish.

fig/er [fiʒe] *vt* (*sang, sauce etc*) to congeal; **f. qn** (*paralyser*) *Fig* to freeze s.o.; — *vi* (*liquide*) to congeal; — **se f.** *vpr* (*liquide*) to congeal; (*sourire, personne*) *Fig* to freeze. ◆**—é** *a* (*locution*) set, fixed; (*regard*) frozen; (*société*) petrified.

fignol/er [fiɲɔle] *vt Fam* to round off meticulously, refine. ◆**—é** *a Fam* meticulous.

figue [fig] *nf* fig; **mi-f., mi-raisin** (*accueil etc*) neither good nor bad, mixed. ◆**figuier** *nm* fig tree.

figurant, -ante [figyrɑ̃, -ɑ̃t] *nmf Cin Th* extra.

figure [figyr] *nf* 1 (*visage*) face. 2 (*personnage*) & *Géom* figure; (*de livre*) figure, illustration; **faire f. de riche/d'imbécile/etc** to look rich/a fool/etc. ◆**figurine** *nf* statuette.

figur/er [figyre] *vt* to represent; — *vi* to appear, figure; — **se f.** *vpr* to imagine; **figurez-vous que . . . ?** would you believe that . . . ? ◆**—é** *a* (*sens*) figurative; — *nm* **au f.** figuratively.

fil [fil] *nm* 1 (*de coton, pensée etc*) thread; (*lin*) linen; **f. dentaire** dental floss; **de f. en aiguille** bit by bit. 2 (*métallique*) wire; **f. de fer** wire; **f. à plomb** plumbline; **au bout du f.** *Tél* on the line; **passer un coup de f. à qn** *Tél* to give s.o. a ring *ou* a call. 3 (*de couteau*) edge. 4 **au f. de l'eau/des jours** with the current/the passing of time.

filament [filamɑ̃] *nm El* filament.

filandreux, -euse [filɑ̃drø, -øz] *a* (*phrase*) long-winded.

filante [filɑ̃t] *af* **étoile f.** shooting star.

file [fil] *nf* line; (*couloir*) *Aut* lane; **f. d'attente** queue, *Am* line; **en f. (indienne)** in single file; **chef de f.** leader; **se mettre en f.** to line up.

filer [file] 1 *vt* (*coton etc*) to spin. 2 *vt* **f. qn** (*suivre*) to shadow s.o., tail s.o. 3 *vt Fam* **f. qch à qn** (*objet*) to slip s.o. sth; **f. un coup de pied/etc à qn** to give s.o. a kick/etc. 4 *vi* (*partir*) to shoot off, bolt; (*aller vite*) to speed along; (*temps*) to fly; (*bas, collant*) to ladder, run; (*liquide*) to trickle, run; **filez!** hop it!; **f. entre les doigts de qn** to slip through s.o.'s fingers; **f. doux** to be obedient. ◆**filature** *nf* 1 (*usine*) textile mill. 2 (*de policiers etc*) shadowing; **prendre en f.** to shadow.

filet [filɛ] *nm* 1 (*de pêche*) & *Sp* net; (*à bagages*) *Rail* (luggage) rack; **f. (à provisions)** string *ou* net bag (*for shopping*). 2 (*d'eau*) trickle. 3 (*de poisson, viande*) fillet.

filial, -aux [filjal, -o] *a* filial.

filiale [filjal] *nf* subsidiary (company).

filiation [filjasjɔ̃] nf relationship.

fillière [filjɛr] nf (de drogue) network; **suivre la f.** (pour obtenir qch) to go through the official channels; (employé) to work one's way up.

filigrane [filigran] nm (de papier) watermark.

filin [filɛ̃] nm Nau rope.

fille [fij] nf **1** girl; **petite f.** (little ou young) girl; **jeune f.** girl, young lady; **vieille f.** Péj old maid; **f. (publique)** Péj prostitute. **2** (parenté) daughter, girl. ◆**f.-mère** nf (pl **filles-mères**) Péj unmarried mother. ◆**fillette** nf little girl.

filleul [fijœl] nm godson. ◆**filleule** nf goddaughter.

film [film] nm film, movie; (pellicule) film; **f. muet/parlant** silent/talking film ou movie; **le f. des événements** the sequence of events. ◆**filmer** vt (personne, scène) to film.

filon [filɔ̃] nm Géol seam; **trouver le (bon) f.** to strike it lucky.

filou [filu] nm rogue, crook.

fils [fis] nm son; **Dupont f.** Dupont junior.

filtre [filtr] nm filter; **(à bout) f.** (cigarette) (filter-)tipped; **(bout) f.** filter tip. ◆**filtrer** vt to filter; (personne, nouvelles) to scrutinize; – vi to filter (through).

fin [fɛ̃] **1** nf end; (but) end, aim; **mettre f. à** to put an end ou a stop to; **prendre f.** to come to an end; **tirer à sa f.** to draw to an end ou a close; **sans f.** endless; **à la f.** in the end; **arrêtez, à la f.!** stop, for heaven's sake!; **f. de semaine** weekend; **f. mai** at the end of May; **à cette f.** to this end. **2** a (pointe, travail, tissu etc) fine; (taille, tranche) thin; (plat) delicate, choice; (esprit, oreille) sharp; (observation) sharp, fine; (gourmet) discerning; (rusé) shrewd; (intelligent) clever; **au f. fond de** in the depths of; – adv (couper, moudre) finely; (écrire) small.

final, -aux ou **-als** [final, -o] a final; – nm Mus finale. ◆**finale** nf Sp final; Gram final syllable; – nm Mus finale. ◆**finalement** adv finally; (en somme) after all. ◆**finaliste** nmf Sp finalist.

finance [finɑ̃s] nf finance. ◆**financ/er** vt to finance. ◆**-ement** nm financing. ◆**financier, -ière** a financial; – nm financier. ◆**financièrement** adv financially.

fine [fin] nf liqueur brandy.

finement [finmɑ̃] adv (broder, couper etc) finely; (agir) cleverly.

finesse [fines] nf (de pointe etc) fineness; (de taille, tranche) thinness; (de plat) delicacy; (d'esprit, de goût) finesse; pl (de langue) niceties.

fin/ir [finir] vt to finish; (discours, vie) to end, finish; – vi to finish, end; **f. de faire** to finish doing; (cesser) to stop doing; **f. par faire** to end up ou finish up doing; **f. par qch** to finish (up) ou end (up) with sth; **en f. avec** to put an end to, finish with; **elle n'en finit pas** there's no end to it, she goes on and on. ◆**-i** a (produit) finished; (univers etc) & Math finite; **c'est f.** it's over ou finished; **il est f.** (fichu) he's done for ou finished; – nm (poli) finish. ◆**-issant** a (siècle) declining. ◆**finish** nm Sp finish. ◆**finition** nf (action) Tech finishing; (résultat) finish.

Finlande [fɛ̃lɑ̃d] nf Finland. ◆**finlandais, -aise** a Finnish; – nmf Finn. ◆**finnois, -oise** a Finnish; – nmf Finn; – nm (langue) Finnish.

fiole [fjɔl] nf phial, flask.

firme [firm] nf (entreprise) Com firm.

fisc [fisk] nm tax authorities, = Inland Revenue, = Am Internal Revenue. ◆**fiscal, -aux** a fiscal, tax-. ◆**fiscalité** nf tax system; (charges) taxation.

fission [fisjɔ̃] nf Phys fission.

fissure [fisyr] nf split, crack, fissure. ◆**se fissurer** vpr to split, crack.

fiston [fistɔ̃] nm Fam son, sonny.

fixe [fiks] a fixed; (prix, heure) set, fixed; **idée f.** obsession; **regard f.** stare; **être au beau f.** Mét to be set fair; – nm (paie) fixed salary. ◆**-ment** [-əmɑ̃] adv **regarder f.** to stare at. ◆**fixer** vt (attacher) to fix (à to); (choix) to settle; (règle, date etc) to decide, fix; **f. (du regard)** to stare at; **f. qn sur** to inform s.o. clearly about; **être fixé** (décidé) to be decided; **comme ça on est fixé!** (renseigné) we've got the picture!; – **se f.** vpr (regard) to become fixed; (s'établir) to settle. ◆**fixateur** nm Phot fixer; (pour cheveux) setting lotion. ◆**fixation** nf (action) fixing; (dispositif) fastening, binding; Psy fixation.

flacon [flakɔ̃] nm bottle, flask.

flageoler [flaʒɔle] vi to shake, tremble.

flageolet [flaʒɔlɛ] nm Bot Culin (dwarf) kidney bean.

flagrant [flagrɑ̃] a (injustice etc) flagrant, glaring; **pris en f. délit** caught in the act ou red-handed.

flair [flɛr] nm **1** (d'un chien etc) (sense of) smell, scent. **2** (clairvoyance) intuition, flair. ◆**flairer** vt to sniff at, smell; (discerner) Fig to smell, sense.

flamand, -ande [flamɑ̃, -ɑ̃d] a Flemish; – nmf Fleming; – nm (langue) Flemish.

flamant [flamɑ̃] nm (oiseau) flamingo.

flambant [flãbã] *adv* f. **neuf** brand new.

flambeau, -x [flãbo] *nm* torch.

flamb/er [flãbe] **1** *vi* to burn, blaze; – *vt* (*aiguille*) *Méd* to sterilize; (*poulet*) to singe. **2** *vi* (*jouer*) *Fam* to gamble for big money. **◆–é** *a* (*ruiné*) *Fam* done for. **◆–ée** *nf* blaze; (*de colère, des prix etc*) *Fig* surge; (*de violence*) flare-up, eruption. **◆–eur** *nm Fam* big gambler. **◆flamboyer** *vi* to blaze, flame.

flamme [flam] *nf* flame; (*ardeur*) *Fig* fire; **en flammes** on fire. **◆flammèche** *nf* spark.

flan [flã] *nm* **1** *Culin* custard tart *ou* pie. **2 au f.** *Fam* on the off chance, on the spur of the moment.

flanc [flã] *nm* side; (*d'une armée, d'un animal*) flank; **tirer au f.** *Arg* to shirk, idle.

flancher [flãʃe] *vi Fam* to give in, weaken.

Flandre(s) [flãdr] *nf*(*pl*) Flanders.

flanelle [flanɛl] *nf* (*tissu*) flannel.

flâner [flane] *vi* to stroll, dawdle. **◆flânerie** *nf* (*action*) strolling; (*promenade*) stroll.

flanquer [flãke] *vt* **1** to flank (**de** with). **2** *Fam* (*jeter*) to chuck; (*donner*) to give; **f. qn à la porte** to throw s.o. out.

flaque [flak] *nf* puddle, pool.

flash, *pl* **flashes** [flaʃ] *nm* **1** *Phot* (*éclair*) flashlight; (*dispositif*) flash(gun). **2** *TV Rad* (*news*)flash.

flasque [flask] *a* flabby, floppy.

flatt/er [flate] *vt* to flatter; **se f. d'être malin/de réussir** to flatter oneself on being smart/on being able to succeed. **◆–é** *a* flattered (**de qch** by sth, **de faire** to do, **que** that). **◆flatterie** *nf* flattery. **◆flatteur, -euse** *nmf* flatterer; – *a* flattering.

fléau, -x [fleo] *nm* **1** (*calamité*) scourge; (*personne, chose*) bane, plague. **2** *Agr* flail.

flèche [flɛʃ] *nf* arrow; (*d'église*) spire; **monter en f.** (*prix*) to (sky)rocket, shoot ahead. **◆flécher** [fleʃe] *vt* to signpost (with arrows). **◆fléchette** *nf* dart; *pl* (*jeu*) darts.

fléchir [fleʃir] *vt* (*membre*) to flex, bend; **f. qn** *Fig* to move s.o., persuade s.o.; – *vi* (*membre*) to bend; (*poutre*) to sag; (*faiblir*) to give way; (*baisser*) to fall off.

flegme [flɛgm] *nm* composure. **◆flegmatique** *a* phlegmatic, stolid.

flemme [flɛm] *nf Fam* laziness; **il a la f.** he can't be bothered, he's just too lazy. **◆flemmard, -arde** *a Fam* lazy; – *nmf Fam* lazybones.

flétrir [fletrir] **1** *vt, – se f. vpr* to wither. **2** *vt* (*blâmer*) to stigmatize, brand.

fleur [flœr] *nf* flower; (*d'arbre, d'arbuste*) blossom; **en f.** in flower, in bloom; **in blos-** som; **à** *ou* **dans la f. de l'âge** in the prime of life; **à f. d'eau** just above the water; **à fleurs** (*tissu*) floral. **◆fleur/ir** *vi* to flower, bloom; (*arbre etc*) to blossom; (*art, commerce etc*) *Fig* to flourish; – *vt* (*table etc*) to decorate with flowers. **◆–i** *a* (*fleur, jardin*) in bloom; (*tissu*) flowered, floral; (*teint*) florid; (*style*) flowery, florid. **◆fleuriste** *nmf* florist.

fleuve [flœv] *nm* river.

flexible [flɛksibl] *a* flexible, pliable. **◆flexibilité** *nf* flexibility.

flexion [flɛksjõ] *nf* **1** *Anat* flexion, flexing. **2** *Gram* inflexion.

flic [flik] *nm Fam* cop, policeman.

flinguer [flɛ̃ge] *vt* **f. qn** *Arg* to shoot s.o.

flipper [flipœr] *nm* (*jeu*) pinball.

flirt [flœrt] *nm* (*rapports*) flirtation; – (*personne*) flirt. **◆flirter** *vi* to flirt (**avec** with). **◆flirteur, -euse** *a* flirtatious; – *nmf* flirt.

flocon [flɔkõ] *nm* (*de neige*) flake; (*de laine*) flock; **flocons d'avoine** *Culin* porridge oats. **◆floconneux, -euse** *a* fluffy.

floraison [flɔrɛzõ] *nf* flowering; **en pleine f.** in full bloom. **◆floral, -aux** *a* floral. **◆floralies** *nfpl* flower show.

flore [flɔr] *nf* flora.

florissant [flɔrisã] *a* flourishing.

flot [flo] *nm* (*de souvenirs, larmes*) flood, stream; (*marée*) floodtide; (*pl de mer*) waves; (*de lac*) waters; **à flots** in abundance; **à f.** (*bateau, personne*) afloat; **mettre à f.** (*bateau, firme*) to launch; **remettre qn à f.** to restore s.o.'s fortunes.

flotte [flɔt] *nf* **1** *Nau Av* fleet. **2** *Fam* (*pluie*) rain; (*eau*) water. **◆flottille** *nf Nau* flotilla.

flott/er [flɔte] *vi* to float; (*drapeau*) to fly; (*cheveux*) to flow; (*pensées*) to drift; (*pleuvoir*) *Fam* to rain. **◆–ant** *a* **1** (*bois, dette etc*) floating; (*vêtement*) flowing, loose. **2** (*esprit*) indecisive. **◆–ement** *nm* (*hésitation*) indecision. **◆–eur** *nm Pêche* float.

flou [flu] *a* (*photo*) fuzzy, blurred; (*idée*) hazy, fuzzy; – *nm* fuzziness.

fluctuant [flyktɥã] *a* (*prix, opinions*) fluctuating. **◆fluctuations** *nfpl* fluctuation(s) (**de** in).

fluet, -ette [flyɛ, -ɛt] *a* thin, slender.

fluide [flɥid] *a* (*liquide*) & *Fig* fluid; – *nm* (*liquide*) fluid. **◆fluidité** *nf* fluidity.

fluorescent [flyɔresã] *a* fluorescent.

flûte [flyt] **1** *nf Mus* flute. **2** *nf* (*verre*) champagne glass. **3** *int* heck!, darn!, dash it! **◆flûté** *a* (*voix*) piping. **◆flûtiste** *nmf* flautist, *Am* flutist.

fluvial, -aux [flyvjal, -o] *a* river-, fluvial.

flux [fly] nm (abondance) flow; **f. et reflux** ebb and flow.

focal, -aux [fɔkal, -o] a focal. ◆**focaliser** vt (intérêt etc) to focus.

fœtus [fetys] nm foetus, Am fetus.

foi [fwa] nf faith; **sur la f.** de on the strength of; **agir de bonne/mauvaise f.** to act in good/bad faith; **ma f., oui!** yes, indeed!

foie [fwa] nm liver.

foin [fwɛ̃] nm hay; **faire du f.** (scandale) Fam to make a stink.

foire [fwar] nf fair; **faire la f.** Fam to go on a binge, have a ball.

fois [fwa] nf time; **une f.** once; **deux f.** twice, two times; **chaque f. que** each time (that), whenever; **une f. qu'il sera arrivé** (dès que) once he has arrived; **à la f.** at the same time, at once; **à la f. riche et heureux** both rich and happy; **une autre f.** (elle fera attention etc) next time; **des f.** Fam sometimes; **non mais des f.!** Fam you must be joking!; **une f. pour toutes, une bonne f.** once and for all.

foison [fwazɔ̃] nf **à f.** in plenty. ◆**foisonner** vi to abound (**de, en** in). ◆**—ement** nm abundance.

fol [fɔl] voir **fou**.

folâtre [fɔlatr] a playful. ◆**folâtrer** vi to romp, frolic.

folichon, -onne [fɔliʃɔ̃, -ɔn] a **pas f.** not very funny, not much fun.

folie [fɔli] nf madness, insanity; **faire une f.** to do a foolish thing; (dépense) to be wildly extravagant; **aimer qn à la f.** to be madly in love with s.o.

folklore [fɔlklɔr] nm folklore. ◆**folklorique** a (danse etc) folk-; (pas sérieux) Fam lightweight, trivial, silly.

folle [fɔl] voir **fou**. ◆**follement** adv madly.

fomenter [fɔmɑ̃te] vt (révolte etc) to foment.

foncé [fɔ̃se] a (couleur) dark.

foncer [fɔ̃se] **1** vi (aller vite) to tear ou charge along; **f. sur qn** to charge into ou at s.o. **2** vti (couleur) to darken.

foncier, -ière [fɔ̃sje, -jɛr] a **1** fundamental, basic. **2** (propriété) landed. ◆**foncièrement** adv fundamentally.

fonction [fɔ̃ksjɔ̃] nf (rôle & Math) function; (emploi) position, function, duty; **f. publique** civil service; **faire f. de** (personne) to act as; (objet) to serve ou act as; **en f. de** according to. ◆**fonctionnaire** nmf civil servant. ◆**fonctionnel, -elle** a functional. ◆**fonctionn/er** vi (machine etc) to work, operate, function; (organisation) to function; **faire f.** to operate, work. ◆**—ement** nm working.

fond [fɔ̃] nm (de boîte, jardin, vallée etc) bottom; (de salle, armoire etc) back; (de culotte) seat; (de problème, débat etc) essence; (arrière-plan) background; (contenu) content; (du désespoir) Fig depths; **au f.** de at the bottom of; at the back of; **fonds de verre** dregs; **f. de teint** foundation cream; **f. sonore** background music; **un f. de bon sens** a stock of good sense; **au f.** basically, in essence; **à f.** (connaître etc) thoroughly; **de f. en comble** from top to bottom; **de f.** (course) long-distance; (bruit) background-.

fondamental, -aux [fɔ̃damɑ̃tal, -o] a fundamental, basic.

fond/er [fɔ̃de] vt (ville etc) to found; (commerce) to set up; (famille) to start; (se) **f. sur** to base (oneself) on; **être fondé à croire/etc** to be justified in thinking/etc; **bien fondé** well-founded. ◆**—ement** nm foundation. ◆**fondateur, -trice** nmf founder; – a (membre) founding, founder-. ◆**fondation** nf (création, œuvre) foundation (**de** of).

fond/re [fɔ̃dr] vt to melt; (métal) to smelt; (cloche) to cast; (amalgamer) Fig to fuse (avec with); **faire f.** (dissoudre) to dissolve; – vi to melt; (se dissoudre) to dissolve; **f. en larmes** to burst into tears; **f. sur** to swoop on; – **se f.** vpr to merge, fuse. ◆**—ant** a (fruit) which melts in the mouth. ◆**—ue** nf Culin fondue. ◆**fonderie** nf (usine) smelting works, foundry.

fonds [fɔ̃] **1** nm **un f.** (de commerce) a business. **2** nmpl (argent) funds. **3** nm (culturel etc) Fig fund.

font [fɔ̃] voir **faire**.

fontaine [fɔ̃tɛn] nf (construction) fountain; (source) spring.

fonte [fɔ̃t] nf **1** (des neiges) melting; (d'acier) smelting. **2** (fer) cast iron; **en f.** (poêle etc) cast-iron.

fonts [fɔ̃] nmpl **f. baptismaux** Rel font.

football [futbol] nm football, soccer. ◆**footballeur, -euse** nmf footballer.

footing [futiŋ] nm Sp jogging, jog-trotting.

forage [fɔraʒ] nm drilling, boring.

forain [fɔrɛ̃] a (marchand) itinerant; **fête foraine** (fun)fair.

forçat [fɔrsa] nm (prisonnier) convict.

force [fɔrs] nf force; (physique, morale) strength; (atomique etc) power; **de toutes ses forces** with all one's strength; **les forces armées** the armed forces; **de f.** by force, forcibly; **en f.** (attaquer, venir) in force; **cas de f. majeure** circumstances beyond one's control; **dans la f. de l'âge** in the prime of life; **à f. de** through sheer force of, by dint of. ◆**forc/er** *vt* (*porte, fruits etc*) to force; (*attention*) to force, compel; (*voix*) to strain; (*sens*) to stretch; **f. qn à faire** to force *ou* compel s.o. to do; – *vi* (*y aller trop fort*) to overdo it; **– se f.** *vpr* to force oneself (**à faire** to do). ◆**–é** *a* forced (**de faire** to do); **un sourire f.** a forced smile; **c'est f.** *Fam* it's inevitable *ou* obvious. ◆**–ément** *adv* inevitably, obviously; **pas f.** not necessarily.

forcené, -ée [fɔrsəne] *a* frantic, frenzied; – *nmf* madman, madwoman.

forceps [fɔrsɛps] *nm* forceps.

forcir [fɔrsir] *vi* (*grossir*) to fill out.

forer [fɔre] *vt* to drill, bore. ◆**foret** *nm* drill.

forêt [fɔrɛ] *nf* forest. ◆**forestier, -ière** *a* forest-; – *nm* (*garde*) f. forester, *Am* (*forest*) ranger.

forfait [fɔrfɛ] *nm* **1** (*prix*) all-inclusive price; **travailler à f.** to work for a lump sum. **2 déclarer f.** *Sp* to withdraw from the game. **3** (*crime*) *Litt* heinous crime. ◆**forfaitaire** *a* prix f. all-inclusive price.

forge [fɔrʒ] *nf* forge. ◆**forg/er** *vt* (*métal, liens etc*) to forge; (*inventer*) to make up. ◆**–é** *a* fer f. wrought iron. ◆**forgeron** *nm* (black)smith.

formaliser (se) [səfɔrmalize] *vpr* to take offence (**de** at).

formalité [fɔrmalite] *nf* formality.

format [fɔrma] *nm* format, size.

forme [fɔrm] *nf* (*contour*) shape, form; (*manière, genre*) form; *pl* (*de femme, d'homme*) figure; **en f.** in the form of; **en f. d'aiguille/de poire/***etc* needle-/pear-/*etc* shaped; **dans les formes** in due form; **en** (**pleine**) **f.** in good shape *ou* form, on form; **prendre f.** to take shape. ◆**formateur, -trice** *a* formative. ◆**formation** *nf* formation; (*éducation*) education, training. ◆**formel, -elle** *a* (*structure, logique etc*) formal; (*démenti*) categorical, formal; (*preuve*) positive, formal. ◆**formellement** *adv* (*interdire*) strictly. ◆**form/er** *vt* (*groupe, caractère etc*) to form; (*apprenti etc*) to train; **– se f.** *vpr* (*apparaître*) to form; (*institution*) to be formed. ◆**–é** *a* (*personne*) fully-formed.

formidable [fɔrmidabl] *a* tremendous.

formule [fɔrmyl] *nf* **1** formula; (*phrase*) (set) expression; (*méthode*) method; **f. de politesse** polite expression. **2** (*feuille*) form. ◆**formulaire** *nm* (*feuille*) form. ◆**formulation** *nf* formulation. ◆**formuler** *vt* to formulate.

fort¹ [fɔr] *a* strong; (*pluie, mer*) heavy;

(*voix*) loud; (*fièvre*) high; (*femme, homme*) large; (*élève*) bright; (*pente*) steep; (*ville*) fortified; (*chances*) good; **f. en** (*maths etc*) good at; **c'est plus f. qu'elle** she can't help it; **c'est un peu f.** *Fam* that's a bit much; **à plus forte raison** all the more reason; – *adv* **1** (*frapper*) hard; (*pleuvoir*) hard, heavily; (*parler*) loud; (*serrer*) tight; **sentir f.** to have a strong smell. **2** (*très*) *Vieilli* very; (*beaucoup*) *Litt* very much; – *nm* son f. one's strong point; **les forts** the strong; **au plus f. de** in the thick of. ◆**fortement** *adv* greatly; (*frapper*) hard.

fort² [fɔr] *nm* *Hist Mil* fort. ◆**forteresse** *nf* fortress.

fortifi/er [fɔrtifje] *vt* to strengthen, fortify; **– se f.** *vpr* (*malade*) to fortify oneself. ◆**–ant** *nm* *Méd* tonic. ◆**–é** *a* (*ville, camp*) fortified. ◆**fortification** *nf* fortification.

fortuit [fɔrtɥi] *a* (*rencontre etc*) chance-, fortuitous. ◆**fortuitement** *adv* by chance.

fortune [fɔrtyn] *nf* (*argent, hasard*) fortune; **avoir de la f.** to have (private) means; **faire f.** to make one's fortune; **de f.** (*moyens etc*) makeshift; **dîner à la f. du pot** to take pot luck. ◆**fortuné** *a* (*riche*) well-to-do.

forum [fɔrɔm] *nm* forum.

fosse [fos] *nf* (*trou*) pit; (*tombe*) grave; **f. d'aisances** cesspool.

fossé [fose] *nm* ditch; (*douve*) moat; (*dissentiment*) *Fig* gulf, gap.

fossette [fosɛt] *nf* dimple.

fossile [fosil] *nm* & *a* fossil.

fossoyeur [foswajœr] *nm* gravedigger.

fou (*or* **fol** *before vowel or mute h*), **folle** [fu, fɔl] *a* (*personne, projet etc*) mad, insane, crazy; (*envie*) wild, mad; (*espoir*) foolish; (*rire*) uncontrollable; (*cheval, camion*) runaway; (*succès, temps*) tremendous; **f. à lier** raving mad; **f. de** (*musique, personne etc*) mad *ou* wild *ou* crazy about; **f. de joie** wild with joy; – *nmf* madman, madwoman; – *nm* (*bouffon*) jester; *Échecs* bishop; **faire le f.** to play the fool.

foudre [fudr] *nf* **la f.** lightning; **coup de f.** *Fig* love at first sight. ◆**foudroy/er** *vt* to strike by lightning; *Él* to electrocute; (*malheur etc*) *Fig* to strike (*s.o.*) down. ◆**–ant** *a* (*succès, vitesse etc*) staggering. ◆**–é** *a* (*stupéfait*) thunderstruck.

fouet [fwɛ] *nm* whip; *Culin* (egg) whisk. ◆**fouetter** *vt* to whip; (*œufs*) to whisk; (*pluie etc*) to lash (*face, windows etc*); **crème fouettée** whipped cream.

fougère [fuʒɛr] *nf* fern.

fougue [fug] *nf* fire, ardour. **◆fougueux, -euse** *a* fiery, ardent.

fouille [fuj] *nf* 1 (*archéologique*) excavation, dig. 2 (*de personne, bagages etc*) search. **◆fouiller 1** *vti* (*creuser*) to dig. 2 *vt* (*personne, maison etc*) to search; − *vi* f. dans (*tiroir etc*) to rummage *ou* search through.

fouillis [fuji] *nm* jumble.

fouine [fwin] *nf* (*animal*) stone marten.

fouin/er [fwine] *vi Fam* to nose about. **◆−eur, -euse** *a Fam* nosy; − *nmf Fam* nosy parker.

foulard [fular] *nm* (head) scarf.

foule [ful] *nf* crowd; en f. in mass; une f. de (*objets etc*) a mass of; un bain de f. a walkabout.

foulée [fule] *nf Sp* stride; dans la f. *Fam* at one and the same time.

fouler [fule] *vt* to press; (*sol*) to tread; f. aux pieds to trample on; se f. la cheville/*etc* to sprain one's ankle/*etc*; il ne se foule pas (la rate) *Fam* he doesn't exactly exert himself. **◆foulure** *nf* sprain.

four [fur] *nm* 1 oven; (*de potier etc*) kiln. 2 petit f. (*gâteau*) (small) fancy cake. 3 *Th Cin* flop; **faire un f.** to flop.

fourbe [furb] *a* deceitful; − *nmf* cheat. **◆fourberie** *nf* deceit.

fourbi [furbi] *nm* (*choses*) *Fam* stuff, gear, rubbish.

fourbu [furby] *a* (*fatigué*) dead beat.

fourche [furʃ] *nf* fork; **f. à foin** pitchfork. **◆fourchette** *nf* 1 *Culin* fork. 2 (*de salaires etc*) *Écon* bracket. **◆fourchu** *a* forked.

fourgon [furgɔ̃] *nm* (*camion*) van; (*mortuaire*) hearse; *Rail* luggage van, *Am* baggage car. **◆fourgonnette** *nf* (small) van.

fourmi [furmi] *nf* 1 (*insecte*) ant. 2 **avoir des fourmis** *Méd* to have pins and needles (dans in). **◆fourmilière** *nf* anthill. **◆fourmiller** *vi* 1 to teem, swarm (de with). 2 *Méd* to tingle.

fournaise [furnɛz] *nf* (*chambre etc*) *Fig* furnace.

fourneau, -x [furno] *nm* (*poêle*) stove; (*four*) furnace; **haut f.** blast furnace.

fournée [furne] *nf* (*de pain, gens*) batch.

fourn/ir [furnir] *vt* to supply, provide; (*effort*) to make; **f. qch à qn** to supply s.o. with sth; − *vi* **f. à** (*besoin etc*) to provide for; − **se f.** *vpr* to get one's supplies (**chez** from), shop (**chez** at). **◆−i** *a* (*barbe*) bushy; **bien f.** (*boutique*) well-stocked. **◆fournisseur** *nm* (*commerçant*) supplier. **◆fourniture** *nf* (*action*) supply(ing) (**de** of); *pl* (*objets etc*) supplies.

fourrage [furaʒ] *nm* fodder.

fourrager [furaʒe] *vi Fam* to rummage (dans in, through).

fourreau, -x [furo] *nm* (*gaine*) sheath.

fourr/er [fure] *vt* 1 (*mettre*) to fill, stuff; (*vêtement*) to fur-line. 2 *vt Fam* (*mettre*) to stick; (*flanquer*) to chuck; **f. qch dans la tête de qn** to knock sth into s.o.'s head; **f. son nez dans** to poke one's nose into; − **se f.** *vpr* to put *ou* stick oneself (**dans** in). **◆−é** *a* 1 (*gant etc*) fur-lined; (*gâteau*) jam- *ou* cream-filled; **coup f.** (*traîtrise*) stab in the back. 2 *nm Bot* thicket. **◆−eur** *nm* furrier. **◆fourrure** *nf* (*pour vêtement etc, de chat etc*) fur.

fourre-tout [furtu] *nm inv* (*pièce*) junk room; (*sac*) holdall, *Am* carryall.

fourrière [furjɛr] *nf* (*lieu*) pound.

fourvoyer (se) [səfurvwaje] *vpr* to go astray.

foutre* [futr] *vt Arg* = fiche(r). **◆foutu** *a Arg* = fichu 1. **◆foutaise** *nf Arg* rubbish, rot.

foyer [fwaje] *nm* (*domicile*) home; (*d'étudiants etc*) hostel; (*âtre*) hearth; **f. de réunion**) club; *Th* foyer; *Géom Phys* focus; **f. de** (*maladie etc*) seat of; (*énergie, lumière*) source of; **fonder un f.** to start a family.

fracas [fraka] *nm* din; (*d'un objet qui tombe*) crash. **◆fracass/er** *vt*, − **se f.** *vpr* to smash. **◆−ant** *a* (*nouvelle, film etc*) sensational.

fraction [fraksjɔ̃] *nf* fraction. **◆fractionner** *vt*, − **se f.** *vpr* to split (up).

fracture [fraktyr] *nf* fracture; **se faire une f. au bras**/*etc* to fracture one's arm/*etc*. **◆fracturer** *vt* (*porte etc*) to break (open); **se f. la jambe**/*etc* to fracture one's leg/*etc*.

fragile [fraʒil] *a* (*verre, santé etc*) fragile; (*enfant etc*) frail; (*équilibre*) shaky. **◆fragilité** *nf* fragility; (*d'un enfant etc*) frailty.

fragment [fragmɑ̃] *nm* fragment. **◆fragmentaire** *a* fragmentary, fragmented. **◆fragmentation** *nf* fragmentation. **◆fragmenter** *vt* to fragment, divide.

frais¹, fraîche [frɛ, frɛʃ] *a* (*poisson, souvenir etc*) fresh; (*temps*) cool, fresh; (*plutôt désagréable*) chilly; (*œufs*) new-laid, fresh; (*boisson*) cold, cool; (*peinture*) wet; (*date*) recent; **boire f.** to drink something cold *ou* cool; **servir f.** (*vin etc*) to serve chilled; − *nm* **prendre le f.** to get some fresh air; **il fait f.** it's cool; (*froid*) it's chilly; **mettre au f.** to put in a cool place. **◆fraîchement** *adv* 1 (*récemment*) freshly. 2 (*accueillir etc*) coolly. **◆fraîcheur** *nf* freshness; coolness;

chilliness. ◆**fraîchir** vi (temps) to get cooler ou chillier, freshen.

frais² [frɛ] nmpl expenses; (droits) fees; **à mes f.** at my expense; **faire des f.** to go to some expense; **faire les f.** to bear the cost (de of); **j'en ai été pour mes f.** I wasted my time and effort; **faux f.** incidental expenses; **f. généraux** running expenses, overheads.

fraise [frɛz] nf **1** (fruit) strawberry. **2** (de dentiste) drill. ◆**fraisier** nm (plante) strawberry plant.

framboise [frɑ̃bwaz] nf raspberry. ◆**framboisier** nm raspberry cane.

franc¹, franche [frɑ̃, frɑ̃ʃ] a **1** (personne, réponse etc) frank; (visage, gaieté) open; (net) clear; (cassure, coupe) clean; (vrai) Péj downright. **2** (zone) free; **coup f.** Fb free kick; **f. de port** carriage paid. ◆**franchement** adv (honnêtement) frankly; (sans ambiguïté) clearly; (vraiment) really. ◆**franchise** nf **1** frankness; openness; **en toute f.** quite frankly. **2** (exemption) Com exemption; **en f.** (produit) duty-free; **'f. postale'** 'official paid'. **3** (permis de vendre) Com franchise.

franc² [frɑ̃] nm (monnaie) franc.

France [frɑ̃s] nf France. ◆**français, -aise** a French; – nmf Frenchman, Frenchwoman; **les F.** the French; – nm (langue) French.

franch/ir [frɑ̃ʃir] vt (fossé) to jump (over), clear; (frontière, seuil etc) to cross; (porte) to go through; (distance) to cover; (limites) to exceed; (mur du son) to break (through), go through. ◆**-issable** a (rivière, col) passable.

franc-maçon [frɑ̃masɔ̃] nm (pl francs-maçons) Freemason. ◆**franc-maçonnerie** nf Freemasonry.

franco [frɑ̃ko] adv carriage paid.

franco- [frɑ̃ko] préf Franco-.

francophile [frɑ̃kɔfil] a & nmf francophile. ◆**francophone** a French-speaking; – nmf French speaker. ◆**francophonie** nf **la f.** the French-speaking community.

frange [frɑ̃ʒ] nf (de vêtement) fringe; (de cheveux) fringe, Am bangs.

frangin [frɑ̃ʒɛ̃] nm Fam brother. ◆**frangine** nf Fam sister.

franquette (à la bonne) [alabɔnfrɑ̃kɛt] adv without ceremony.

frappe [frap] nf **1** (dactylographie) typing; (de dactylo etc) touch; **faute de f.** typing error. **2** **force de f.** Mil strike force. ◆**frapp/er** vt (battre) to strike, hit; (monnaie) to mint; **f. qn** (surprendre, affecter) to

strike s.o.; (impôt, mesure etc) to hit s.o.; **frappé de** (horreur etc) stricken with; **frappé de panique** panic-stricken; – vi (à la porte etc) to knock, bang (à at); **f. du pied** to stamp (one's foot); – **se f.** vpr (se tracasser) to worry. ◆**-ant** a striking. ◆**-é** a (vin) chilled.

frasque [frask] nf prank, escapade.

fraternel, -elle [fratɛrnɛl] a fraternal, brotherly. ◆**fraterniser** vi to fraternize (avec with). ◆**fraternité** nf fraternity, brotherhood.

fraude [frod] nf Jur fraud; (à un examen) cheating; **passer qch en f.** to smuggle sth; **prendre qn en f.** to catch s.o. cheating. ◆**fraud/er** vt to defraud; – vi Jur to commit fraud; (à un examen) to cheat (à in); **f. sur** (poids etc) to cheat on ou over. ◆**-eur, -euse** nmf Jur defrauder. ◆**frauduleux, -euse** a fraudulent.

frayer [freje] vt (voie etc) to clear; **se f. un passage** to clear a way, force one's way (à travers, dans through).

frayeur [frejœr] nf fear, fright.

fredaine [frədɛn] nf prank, escapade.

fredonner [frədɔne] vt to hum.

freezer [frizœr] nm (de réfrigérateur) freezer.

frégate [fregat] nf (navire) frigate.

frein [frɛ̃] nm brake; **donner un coup de f.** to brake; **mettre un f. à** Fig to put a curb on. ◆**frein/er** vi Aut to brake; – vt (gêner) Fig to check, curb. ◆**-age** nm Aut braking.

frelaté [frəlate] a (vin etc) & Fig adulterated.

frêle [frɛl] a frail, fragile.

frelon [frəlɔ̃] nm (guêpe) hornet.

frémir [fremir] vi to shake, shudder (de with); (feuille) to quiver; (eau chaude) to simmer.

frêne [frɛn] nm (arbre, bois) ash.

frénésie [frenezi] nf frenzy. ◆**frénétique** a frenzied, frantic.

fréquent [frekɑ̃] a frequent. ◆**fréquemment** [-amɑ̃] adv frequently. ◆**fréquence** nf frequency.

fréquent/er [frekɑ̃te] vt (lieu) to visit, frequent; (école, église) to attend; **f. qn** to see ou visit s.o.; – **se f.** vpr (fille et garçon) to see each other, go out together; (voisins) to see each other socially. ◆**-é** a **très f.** (lieu) very busy. ◆**fréquentable** a **peu f.** (personne, endroit) not very commendable. ◆**fréquentation** nf visiting; pl (personnes) company.

frère [frɛr] nm brother.

fresque [frɛsk] nf (œuvre peinte) fresco.

fret [frɛ] nm freight.

frétiller [fretije] vi (poisson) to wriggle; **f. de** (impatience) to quiver with; **f. de joie** to tingle with excitement.

fretin [frətɛ̃] nm **menu f.** small fry.

friable [frijabl] a crumbly.

friand [frijɑ̃] a **f. de** fond of, partial to. ◆**friandises** nfpl sweet stuff, sweets, Am candies.

fric [frik] nm (argent) Fam cash, dough.

fric-frac [frikfrak] nm (cambriolage) Fam break-in.

friche (en) [ɑ̃friʃ] adv fallow.

friction [friksjɔ̃] nf **1** massage, rub(-down); (de cheveux) friction. **2** (désaccord) friction. ◆**frictionner** vt to rub (down).

frigidaire® [friʒidɛr] nm fridge. ◆**frigo** nm Fam fridge. ◆**frigorifié** a (personne) Fam very cold. ◆**frigorifique** a (vitrine) refrigerated; (wagon) refrigerator-.

frigide [friʒid] a frigid. ◆**frigidité** nf frigidity.

frileux, -euse [frilø, -øz] a sensitive to cold, chilly.

frime [frim] nf Fam sham, show.

frimousse [frimus] nf Fam little face.

fringale [frɛ̃gal] nf Fam raging appetite.

fringant [frɛ̃gɑ̃] a (allure etc) dashing.

fringues [frɛ̃g] nfpl (vêtements) Fam togs, clothes.

frip/er [fripe] vt to crumple; **— se f.** vpr to get crumpled. ◆**—é** a (visage) crumpled, wrinkled.

fripier, -ière [fripje, -jɛr] nmf secondhand clothes dealer.

fripon, -onne [fripɔ̃, -ɔn] nmf rascal; — a rascally.

fripouille [fripuj] nf rogue, scoundrel.

frire* [frir] vti to fry; **faire f.** to fry.

frise [friz] nf Archit frieze.

fris/er [frize] **1** vti (cheveux) to curl, wave; **f. qn** to curl s.o.'s hair. **2** vt (effleurer) to skim; (accident etc) to be within an ace of; **f. la trentaine** to be close on thirty. ◆**—é** a curly. ◆**frisette** nf ringlet, little curl.

frisquet [friskɛ] am chilly, coldish.

frisson [frisɔ̃] nm shiver; shudder; **donner le f. à qn** to give s.o. the creeps ou shivers. ◆**frissonner** vi (de froid) to shiver; (de peur etc) to shudder (de with).

frit [fri] voir **frire**; — a (poisson etc) fried. ◆**frites** nfpl chips, Am French fries. ◆**friteuse** nf (deep) fryer. ◆**friture** nf (matière) (oil ou fat) for frying; (aliment) fried fish; (bruit) Rad Tél crackling.

frivole [frivɔl] a frivolous. ◆**frivolité** nf frivolity.

froid [frwa] a cold; **garder la tête froide** to keep a cool head; — nm cold; avoir/ **prendre f.** to be/catch cold; **il fait f.** it's cold; **coup de f.** Méd chill; **jeter un f.** to cast a chill (dans over); **démarrer à f.** Aut to start (from) cold; **être en f.** to be on bad terms (avec with). ◆**froidement** adv coldly. ◆**froideur** nf (de sentiment, personne etc) coldness.

froisser [frwase] **1** vt, **— se f.** vpr (tissu etc) to crumple, rumple; **se f.** un muscle to strain a muscle. **2** vt **f. qn** to offend s.o.; **se f.** to take offence (de at).

frôler [frole] vt (toucher) to brush against, touch lightly; (raser) to skim; (la mort etc) to come within an ace of.

fromage [frɔmaʒ] nm cheese; **f. blanc** soft white cheese. ◆**fromager, -ère** a (industrie) cheese-; — nm (fabricant) cheesemaker. ◆**fromagerie** nf cheese dairy.

froment [frɔmɑ̃] nm wheat.

froncer [frɔ̃se] vt **1** (étoffe) to gather. **2 f. les sourcils** to frown. ◆**—ement** nm **f. de sourcils** frown.

fronde [frɔ̃d] nf **1** (arme) sling. **2** (sédition) revolt.

front [frɔ̃] nm **1** forehead, brow; Mil Pol front; **de f.** (heurter) head-on; (côte à côte) abreast; (à la fois) (all) at once; **faire f. à** to face.

frontière [frɔ̃tjɛr] nf border, frontier; — a inv **ville/etc f.** border town/etc. ◆**frontalier, -ière** a border-, frontier-.

fronton [frɔ̃tɔ̃] nm Archit pediment.

frott/er [frɔte] vt **1** to rub; (astiquer) to rub (up), shine; (plancher) to scrub; (allumette) to strike; **se f. à qn** (défier) to meddle with s.o., provoke s.o.; **— vi** to rub; (nettoyer, laver) to scrub. ◆**—ement** nm rubbing; Tech friction.

froufrou(s) [frufru] nm(pl) (bruit) rustling.

frousse [frus] nf Fam funk, fear; **avoir la f.** to be scared. ◆**froussard, -arde** nmf Fam coward.

fructifier [fryktifje] vi (arbre, capital) to bear fruit. ◆**fructueux, -euse** a (profitable) fruitful.

frugal, -aux [frygal, -o] a frugal. ◆**frugalité** nf frugality.

fruit [frɥi] nm fruit; **des fruits, les fruits** fruit; **porter f.** to bear fruit; **fruits de mer** seafood; **avec f.** fruitfully. ◆**fruité** a fruity. ◆**fruitier, -ière** a (arbre) fruit-; — nmf fruiterer.

frusques [frysk] nfpl (vêtements) Fam togs, clothes.

fruste [fryst] a (personne) rough.

frustr/er [frystre] vt f. qn to frustrate s.o.; f. qn de to deprive s.o. of. ◆–é a frustrated. ◆**frustration** nf frustration.

fuel [fjul] nm (fuel) oil.

fugace [fygas] a fleeting.

fugitif, -ive [fyʒitif, -iv] 1 nmf runaway, fugitive. 2 a (passager) fleeting.

fugue [fyg] nf 1 Mus fugue. 2 (absence) flight; **faire une f.** to run away.

fuir* [fɥir] vi to flee, run away; (temps) to fly; (gaz, robinet, stylo etc) to leak; – vt (éviter) to shun, avoid. ◆**fuite** nf (évasion) flight (de from); (de gaz etc) leak(age); (de documents) leak; **en f.** on the run; **prendre la f.** to take flight; **f. des cerveaux** brain drain; **délit de f.** Aut hit-and-run offence.

fulgurant [fylgyrã] a (regard) flashing; (vitesse) lightning-; (idée) spectacular, striking.

fulminer [fylmine] vi (personne) to thunder forth (contre against).

fumée [fyme] nf smoke; (vapeur) steam, fumes; pl (de vin) fumes. ◆**fum/er** vi to smoke; (liquide brûlant) to steam; (rager) Fam to fume; – vt to smoke. ◆–é a (poisson, verre etc) smoked. ◆–**eur, -euse** nmf smoker; **compartiment fumeurs** Rail smoking compartment. ◆**fume-cigarette** nm inv cigarette holder.

fumet [fymɛ] nm aroma, smell.

fumeux, -euse [fymø, -øz] a (idée etc) hazy, woolly.

fumier [fymje] nm manure, dung; (tas) dunghill.

fumigation [fymigasjɔ̃] nf fumigation.

fumigène [fymiʒɛn] a (bombe, grenade etc) smoke-.

fumiste [fymist] nmf (étudiant etc) timewaster, good-for-nothing. ◆**fumisterie** nf Fam farce, con.

funambule [fynãbyl] nmf tightrope walker.

funèbre [fynɛbr] a (service, marche etc) funeral-; (lugubre) gloomy. ◆**funérailles** nfpl funeral. ◆**funéraire** a (frais, salon etc) funeral-.

funeste [fynɛst] a (désastreux) catastrophic.

funiculaire [fynikyler] nm funicular.

fur et à mesure (au) [ofyreamzyr] adv as one goes along, progressively; **au f. et à m. que** as.

furent [fyr] voir être.

furet [fyrɛ] nm (animal) ferret. ◆**furet/er** vi to pry ou ferret about. ◆–**eur, -euse** a inquisitive, prying; – nmf inquisitive person.

fureur [fyrœr] nf (violence) fury; (colère) rage, fury; (passion) passion (de for); **en f.** furious; **faire f.** (mode etc) to be all the rage. ◆**furibond** a furious. ◆**furie** nf (colère, mégère) fury. ◆**furieux, -euse** a (violent, en colère) furious (contre with, at); (vent) raging; (coup) Fig tremendous.

furoncle [fyrɔ̃kl] nm Méd boil.

furtif, -ive [fyrtif, -iv] a furtive, stealthy.

fusain [fyzɛ̃] nm 1 (crayon, dessin) charcoal. 2 Bot spindle tree.

fuseau, -x [fyzo] nm 1 Tex spindle; **en f.** (jambes) spindly. 2 **f. horaire** time zone. 3 (pantalon) ski pants. ◆**fuselé** a slender.

fusée [fyze] nf rocket; (d'obus) fuse; **f. éclairante** flare.

fuselage [fyzlaʒ] nm Av fuselage.

fuser [fyze] vi (rires etc) to burst forth.

fusible [fyzibl] nm Él fuse.

fusil [fyzi] nm rifle, gun; (de chasse) shotgun; **coup de f.** gunshot, report; **un bon f.** (personne) a good shot. ◆**fusillade** nf (tirs) gunfire; (exécution) shooting. ◆**fusiller** vt (exécuter) to shoot; **f. qn du regard** to glare at s.o.

fusion [fyzjɔ̃] nf 1 melting; Phys Biol fusion; **point de f.** melting point; **en f.** (métal) molten. 2 (union) fusion; Com merger. ◆**fusionner** vti Com to merge.

fut [fy] voir être.

fût [fy] nm 1 (tonneau) barrel, cask. 2 (d'arbre) trunk. ◆**futaie** nf timber forest.

futé [fyte] a cunning, smart.

futile [fytil] a (propos, prétexte etc) frivolous, futile; (personne) frivolous; (tentative, action) futile. ◆**futilité** nf futility; pl (bagatelles) trifles.

futur, -ure [fytyr] a future; future mother-to-be; – nmf **f. (mari)** husband-to-be; **future (épouse)** wife-to-be; – nm future.

fuyant [fɥijã] voir fuir; – a (front, ligne) receding; (personne) evasive. ◆**fuyard** nm (soldat) runaway, deserter.

G

G, g [ʒe] *nm* G, g.

gabardine [gabardin] *nf (tissu, imperméable)* gabardine.

gabarit [gabari] *nm (de véhicule etc)* size, dimension.

gâcher [gɑʃe] *vt* **1** *(gâter)* to spoil; *(occasion, argent)* to waste; *(vie, travail)* to mess up. **2** *(plâtre)* to mix. ◆**gâchis** *nm (désordre)* mess; *(gaspillage)* waste.

gâchette [gɑʃɛt] *nf (d'arme à feu)* trigger; **une fine g.** *(personne)* *Fig* a marksman.

gadget [gadʒɛt] *nm* gadget.

gadoue [gadu] *nf (boue)* dirt, sludge; *(neige)* slush.

gaffe [gaf] *nf (bévue)* *Fam* blunder, gaffe. ◆**gaff/er** *vi* to blunder. ◆**—eur, -euse** *nmf* blunderer.

gag [gag] *nm (effet comique)* *Cin Th* (sight) gag.

gaga [gaga] *a* *Fam* senile, gaga.

gage [gaʒ] **1** *nm (promesse)* pledge; *(témoignage)* proof; *(caution)* security; **mettre en g.** to pawn. **2** *nmpl (salaire)* pay; **tueur à gages** hired killer, hitman.

gager [gaʒe] *vt* **g. que** *Litt* to wager that. ◆**gageure** [gaʒyr] *nf* *Litt* (impossible) wager.

gagn/er [gaɲe] **1** *vt (par le travail)* to earn; *(mériter)* Fig to earn. **2** *vt (par le jeu)* to win; *(réputation, estime etc)* *Fig* to win, gain; **g. qn** to win s.o. over (à to); **une heure/etc** *(économiser)* to save an hour/etc; **g. du temps** *(temporiser)* to gain time; **g. du terrain/du poids** to gain ground/weight; — *vi (être vainqueur)* to win; **g. à être connu** to be well worth getting to know. **3** *vt (atteindre)* to reach; **g. qn** *(sommeil, faim etc)* to overcome s.o.; — *vi (incendie etc)* to spread, gain. ◆**—ant, -ante** *a (billet, cheval)* winning; — *nmf* winner. ◆**gagne-pain** *nm inv (emploi)* job, livelihood.

gai [ge] *a (personne, air etc)* cheerful, gay, jolly; *(ivre)* merry, tipsy; *(couleur, pièce)* bright, cheerful. ◆**gaiement** *adv* cheerfully, gaily. ◆**gaieté** *nf (de personne etc)* gaiety, cheerfulness, jollity.

gaillard [gajar] *a* vigorous; *(grivois)* coarse; — *nm (robuste)* strapping fellow; *(type)* *Fam* fellow. ◆**gaillarde** *nf* *Péj* brazen wench.

gain [gɛ̃] *nm (profit)* gain, profit; *(avantage)* *Fig* advantage; *pl (salaire)* earnings; *(au jeu)* winnings; **un g. de temps** a saving of time.

gaine [gɛn] *nf* **1** *(sous-vêtement)* girdle. **2** *(étui)* sheath.

gala [gala] *nm* official reception, gala.

galant [galɑ̃] *a (homme)* gallant; *(ton, propos)* *Hum* amorous; — *nm* suitor. ◆**galanterie** *nf (courtoisie)* gallantry.

galaxie [galaksi] *nf* galaxy.

galbe [galb] *nm* curve, contour. ◆**galbé** *a (jambes)* shapely.

gale [gal] *nf* **la g.** *Méd* the itch, scabies; *(d'un chien)* mange; **une (mauvaise) g.** *(personne)* *Fam* a pest.

galère [galɛr] *nf (navire)* *Hist* galley. ◆**galérien** *nm* *Hist* & *Fig* galley slave.

galerie [galri] *nf* **1** *(passage, magasin etc)* gallery; *Th* balcony. **2** *Aut* roof rack.

galet [galɛ] *nm* pebble, stone; *pl* shingle, pebbles.

galette [galɛt] *nf* **1** round, flat, flaky cake; *(crêpe)* pancake. **2** *(argent)* *Fam* dough, money.

galeux, -euse [galø, -øz] *a (chien)* mangy.

galimatias [galimatja] *nm* gibberish.

Galles [gal] *nfpl* **pays de G.** Wales. ◆**gallois, -oise** *a* Welsh; — *nm (langue)* Welsh; — *nmf* Welshman, Welshwoman.

gallicisme [galisism] *nm (mot etc)* gallicism.

galon [galɔ̃] *nm (ruban)* braid; *(signe)* *Mil* stripe; **prendre du g.** *Mil* & *Fig* to get promoted.

galop [galo] *nm (allure)* gallop; **aller au g.** to gallop; **g. d'essai** *Fig* trial run. ◆**galopade** *nf (ruée)* stampede. ◆**galop/er** *vi (cheval)* to gallop; *(personne)* to rush. ◆**—ant** *a (inflation etc)* *Fig* galloping.

galopin [galopɛ̃] *nm* urchin, rascal.

galvaniser [galvanize] *vt (métal)* & *Fig* to galvanize.

galvauder [galvode] *vt (talent, avantage etc)* to debase, misuse.

gambade [gɑ̃bad] *nf* leap, caper. ◆**gambader** *vi* to leap *ou* frisk about.

gambas [gɑ̃bas] *nfpl* scampi.

gamelle [gamɛl] *nf (de soldat)* mess tin; *(de campeur)* billy(can).

gamin, -ine [gamɛ̃, -in] *nmf (enfant)* *Fam*

kid; – a playful, naughty. ◆**gaminerie** nf
playfulness; (acte) naughty prank.

gamme [gam] nf Mus scale; (série) range.

gammée [game] af **croix g.** swastika.

gang [gɑ̃g] nm (de malfaiteurs) gang.
◆**gangster** nm gangster.

gangrène [gɑ̃grɛn] nf gangrene. ◆**se gan-
grener** [sagɑ̃grəne] vpr Méd to become
gangrenous.

gangue [gɑ̃g] nf (enveloppe) Fig Péj outer
crust.

gant [gɑ̃] nm glove; **g. de toilette** face cloth,
cloth glove (for washing); **jeter/relever le
g.** Fig to throw down/take up the gauntlet.
◆**ganté** a (main) gloved; (personne) wearing gloves.

garage [garaʒ] nm Aut garage; **voie de g.**
Rail siding; Fig dead end. ◆**garagiste**
nmf garage owner.

garant, -ante [garɑ̃, -ɑ̃t] nmf (personne) Jur
guarantor; **se porter g. de** to guarantee,
vouch for; – nm (garantie) guarantee.
◆**garantie** nf guarantee; (caution) security; (protection) Fig safeguard; **garantie(s)**
(de police d'assurance) cover. ◆**garantir** vt
to guarantee (**contre** against); **g. (à qn) que**
to guarantee (s.o.) that; **g. de** (protéger) to
protect from.

garce [gars] nf Péj Fam bitch.

garçon [garsɔ̃] nm boy, lad; (jeune homme)
young man; (célibataire) bachelor; **g. de
café)** waiter; **g. d'honneur** (d'un mariage)
best man; **g. manqué** tomboy; **de g.** (comportement) boyish. ◆**garçonnet** nm little
boy. ◆**garçonnière** nf bachelor flat ou
Am apartment.

garde [gard] **1** nm (gardien) guard; Mil
guardsman; **g. champêtre** rural policeman;
g. du corps bodyguard; **G. des Sceaux** Justice Minister. **2** nf (d'enfants, de bagages
etc) care, custody (**de** of); **avoir la g. de** to
be in charge of; **faire bonne g.** to keep a
close watch; **prendre g.** to pay attention (**à
qch** to sth), be careful (**à qch** of sth); **prendre g. de ne pas faire** to be careful not to
do; **mettre en g.** to warn (**contre** against);
mise en g. warning; **de g.** on duty; (soldat)
on guard duty; **monter la g.** to stand ou
mount guard; **sur ses gardes** on one's
guard; **g. à vue** (police) custody; **chien de g.**
watchdog. **3** nf (escorte, soldats) guard.
◆**garde-à-vous** [gardavu] nm inv Mil (position of) attention. ◆**g.-boue** nm inv mudguard, Am fender. ◆**g.-chasse** nm (pl
gardes-chasses) gamekeeper. ◆**g.-côte**
nm (personne) coastguard. ◆**g.-fou** nm
railing(s), parapet. ◆**g.-malade** nmf (pl

gardes-malades) nurse. ◆**g.-manger** nm
inv (armoire) food safe; (pièce) larder.
◆**g.-robe** nf (habits, armoire) wardrobe.

garder [garde] vt (maintenir, conserver, mettre de côté) to keep; (vêtement) to keep on;
(surveiller) to watch (over); (défendre) to
guard; (enfant) to look after, watch; (habitude) to keep up; **g. qn** (retenir) to keep s.o.;
g. la chambre to keep to one's room; **g. le lit**
to stay in bed; – **se g.** vpr (aliment) to
keep; **se g. de qch** (éviter) to beware of sth;
se g. de faire to take care not to do.
◆**garderie** nf day nursery. ◆**gardeuse**
nf **g. d'enfants** babysitter.

gardien, -ienne [gardjɛ̃, -jɛn] nmf (d'immeuble, d'hôtel) caretaker; (de prison)
(prison) guard, warder; (de zoo, parc) keeper; (de musée) attendant; **g. de but** Fb goalkeeper; **gardienne d'enfants** child minder;
g. de nuit night watchman; **g. de la paix**
policeman; **g. de** (libertés etc) Fig guardian
of; – **ann g. gardien** guardian angel.

gare [gar] **1** nf Rail station; **g. routière** bus
ou coach station. **2** int **g. à** watch ou look
out for; **g. à toi!** watch ou look out!; **sans
crier g.** without warning.

garer [gare] vt (voiture etc) to park; (au garage) to garage; – **se g.** vpr (se protéger) to
get out of the way (**de** of); Aut to park.

gargariser (se) [səgargarize] vpr to gargle.
◆**gargarisme** nm gargle.

gargote [gargɔt] nf cheap eating house.

gargouille [garguj] nf Archit gargoyle.

gargouiller [garguje] vi (fontaine, eau) to
gurgle; (ventre) to rumble. ◆**gargouillis**
nm gurgling; rumbling.

garnement [garnəmɑ̃] nm rascal, urchin.

garn/ir [garnir] vt (équiper) to furnish, fit
out (**de** with); (magasin) to stock; (tissu) to
line; (orner) to adorn (**de** with); (enjoliver)
to trim (**de** with); (couvrir) to cover; Culin
to garnish; – **se g.** vpr (lieu) to fill (up) (**de**
with). ◆**-i** a (plat) served with vegetables; **bien g.** (portefeuille) Fig well-lined.
◆**garniture** nf Culin garnish, trimmings;
pl Aut fittings, upholstery; **g. de lit** bed
linen.

garnison [garnizɔ̃] nf Mil garrison.

gars [gɑ] nm Fam fellow, guy.

gas-oil [gazwal] nm diesel (oil).

gaspill/er [gaspije] vt to waste. ◆**-age** nm
waste.

gastrique [gastrik] a gastric. ◆**gastro-
nome** nmf gourmet. ◆**gastronomie** nf
gastronomy.

gâteau, -x [gɑto] nm cake; **g. de riz** rice
pudding; **g. sec** (sweet) biscuit, Am cookie;

c'était du g. (facile) Fam it was a piece of cake.

gât/er [gate] vt to spoil; (plaisir, vue) to mar, spoil; **— se g.** vpr (aliment, dent) to go bad; (temps, situation) to turn bad; (relations) to turn sour. **◆—é** a (dent, fruit etc) bad. **◆gâteries** nfpl (cadeaux) treats.

gâteux, -euse [gatø, -øz] a senile, soft in the head.

gauche [goʃ] a (côté, main etc) left; — nf la g. (côté) the left (side); Pol the left (wing); **à g.** (tourner etc) (to the) left; (marcher, se tenir) on the left(-hand) side; **de g.** (fenêtre etc) left-hand; (parti, politique etc) left-wing; **à g. de** on ou to the left of. **◆gaucher, -ère** a & nmf left-handed (person). **◆gauchisant** a Pol leftish. **◆gauchiste** a & nmf Pol (extreme) leftist.

gauche [goʃ] a (maladroit) awkward. **◆—ment** adv awkwardly. **◆gaucherie** nf awkwardness; (acte) blunder.

gauchir [goʃir] vti to warp.

gaufre [gofr] nf Culin waffle. **◆gaufrette** nf wafer (biscuit).

gaule [gol] nf long pole; Pêche fishing rod.

Gaule [gol] nf (pays) Hist Gaul. **◆gaulois** a Gallic; (propos etc) Fig broad, earthy; — nmpl les G. Hist the Gauls. **◆gauloiserie** nf broad joke.

gausser (se) [sogose] vpr Litt to poke fun (de at).

gaver [gave] vt (animal) to force-feed; (personne) Fig to cram (de with); **— se g.** vpr to gorge ou stuff oneself (de with).

gaz [gaz] nm inv gas; usine à g. gasworks; chambre/réchaud à g. gas chamber/stove; avoir des g. to have wind ou flatulence.

gaze [gaz] nf (tissu) gauze.

gazelle [gazɛl] nf (animal) gazelle.

gazer [gaze] vi 1 ça Aut Fam to whizz along; ça gaze! everything's just fine! 2 vt Mil to gas.

gazette [gazɛt] nf Journ newspaper.

gazeux, -euse [gazø, -øz] a (état) gaseous; (boisson, eau) fizzy. **◆gazomètre** nm gasometer.

gazinière [gazinjɛr] nf gas cooker ou Am stove.

gazole [gazɔl] nm diesel (oil).

gazon [gazɔ̃] nm grass, lawn.

gazouiller [gazuje] vi (oiseau) to chirp; (bébé, ruisseau) to babble. **◆gazouillis** nm chirping; babbling.

geai [ʒɛ] nm (oiseau) jay.

géant, -ante [ʒeɑ̃, -ɑ̃t] a & nmf giant.

Geiger [ʒeʒɛr] nm **compteur G.** Geiger counter.

geindre [ʒɛ̃dr] vi to whine, whimper.

gel [ʒɛl] nm 1 (temps, glace) frost; (de crédits) Écon freezing. 2 (substance) gel. **◆gel/er** vti to freeze; **on gèle ici** it's freezing here; **— v imp il gèle** it's freezing. **◆—é** a frozen; (doigts) Méd frostbitten. **◆—ée** nf frost; Culin jelly, Am jello; **g. blanche** ground frost.

gélatine [ʒelatin] nf gelatin(e).

gélule [ʒelyl] nf (médicament) capsule.

Gémeaux [ʒemo] nmpl les G. (signe) Gemini.

gém/ir [ʒemir] vi to groan, moan. **◆—issement** nm groan, moan.

gencive [ʒɑ̃siv] nf Anat gum.

gendarme [ʒɑ̃darm] nm gendarme, policeman (soldier performing police duties). **◆gendarmerie** nf police force; (local) police headquarters.

gendre [ʒɑ̃dr] nm son-in-law.

gène [ʒɛn] nm Biol gene.

gêne [ʒɛn] nf (trouble physique) discomfort; (confusion) embarrassment; (dérangement) bother, trouble; **dans la g.** Fin in financial difficulties. **◆gên/er** vt (déranger, irriter) to bother, annoy; (troubler) to embarrass; (mouvement, action) to hamper, hinder; (circulation) Aut to hold up, block; **g. qn** (vêtement) to be uncomfortable on s.o.; (par sa présence) to be in s.o.'s way; **ça ne me gêne pas** I don't mind (si if); **— se g.** vpr (se déranger) to put oneself out; **ne te gêne pas pour moi!** don't mind me! **◆—ant** a (objet) cumbersome; (présence, situation) awkward; (personne) annoying. **◆—é** a (intimidé) embarrassed; (mal à l'aise) uneasy, awkward; (silence, sourire) awkward; (sans argent) short of money.

généalogie [ʒenealoʒi] nf genealogy. **◆généalogique** a genealogical; **arbre g.** family tree.

général, -aux [ʒeneral, -o] 1 a (global, commun) general; **en g.** in general. 2 nm (officier) Mil general. **◆générale** nf Th dress rehearsal. **◆généralement** adv generally; **g. parlant** broadly ou generally speaking. **◆généralisation** nf generalization. **◆généraliser** vti to generalize; **— se g.** vpr to become general ou widespread. **◆généraliste** nmf Méd general practitioner, GP. **◆généralité** nf generality; **la g. de** the majority of ...

générateur [ʒeneratœr] nm, **◆génératrice** nf Él generator.

génération [ʒenerasjɔ̃] nf generation.

généreux, -euse [ʒenerø, -øz] a a generous (de with). **◆généreusement** adv generously. **◆générosité** nf generosity.

générique [ʒenerik] *nm Cin* credits.

genèse [ʒənɛz] *nf* genesis.

genêt [ʒənɛ] *nm* (*arbrisseau*) broom.

génétique [ʒenetik] *nf* genetics; – *a* genetic.

Genève [ʒənɛv] *nm ou f* Geneva.

génie [ʒeni] *nm* **1** (*aptitude, personne*) genius; **avoir le g. pour faire/de qch** to have a genius for doing/for sth. **2** (*lutin*) genie, spirit. **3 g. civil** civil engineering; **g. militaire** engineering corps. ◆**génial, -aux** *a* (*personne, invention*) brilliant; (*formidable*) *Fam* fantastic.

génisse [ʒenis] *nf* (*vache*) heifer.

génital, -aux [ʒenital, -o] *a* genital; **organes génitaux** genitals.

génocide [ʒenɔsid] *nm* genocide.

genou, -x [ʒ(ə)nu] *nm* knee; **être à genoux** to be kneeling (down); **se mettre à genoux** to kneel (down); **prendre qn sur ses genoux** to take s.o. on one's lap ou knee. ◆**genouillère** *nf Fb etc* knee pad.

genre [ʒɑ̃r] *nm* **1** (*espèce*) kind, sort; (*attitude*) manner, way; **g. humain** mankind; **g. de vie** way of life. **2** *Littér Cin* genre; *Gram* gender; *Biol* genus.

gens [ʒɑ̃] *nmpl ou nfpl* people; (*hommes*) young people; **jeunes g.** young people; (*hommes*) young men.

gentil, -ille [ʒɑ̃ti, -ij] *a* (*agréable*) nice, pleasant; (*aimable*) kind, nice; (*mignon*) pretty; **g. avec qn** nice ou kind to s.o.; **sois g.** (*sage*) be good. ◆**gentillesse** *nf* kindness; **avoir la g. de faire** to be kind enough to do. ◆**gentiment** *adv* (*aimablement*) kindly; (*sagement*) nicely.

gentilhomme, *pl* **gentilshommes** [ʒɑ̃tijom, ʒɑ̃tizɔm] *nm* (*noble*) *Hist* gentleman.

géographie [ʒeɔɡrafi] *nf* geography. ◆**géographique** *a* geographical.

geôlier, -ière [ʒolje, -jɛr] *nmf* jailer, gaoler.

géologie [ʒeɔlɔʒi] *nf* geology. ◆**géologique** *a* geological. ◆**géologue** *nmf* geologist.

géomètre [ʒeɔmɛtr] *nm* (*arpenteur*) surveyor.

géométrie [ʒeɔmetri] *nf* geometry. ◆**géométrique** *a* geometric(al).

gérance [ʒerɑ̃s] *nf* (*gestion*) management.

gerbe [ʒɛrb] *nf* (*de blé*) sheaf; (*de fleurs*) bunch; (*d'eau*) spray; (*d'étincelles*) shower.

gercer [ʒerse] *vti,* **— se g.** *vpr* (*peau, lèvres*) to chap, crack. ◆**gerçure** *nf* chap, crack.

gérer [ʒere] *vt* (*fonds, commerce etc*) to manage.

germain [ʒermɛ̃] *a* **cousin g.** first cousin.

germanique [ʒermanik] *a* Germanic.

germe [ʒerm] *nm Méd Biol* germ; *Bot* shoot; (*d'une idée*) *Fig* seed, germ. ◆**germer** *vi Bot & Fig* to germinate.

gésir [ʒezir] *vi* (*être étendu*) *Litt* to be lying; **il gît/gisait** he is lying; **ci-gît** here lies.

gestation [ʒɛstasjɔ̃] *nf* gestation.

geste [ʒɛst] *nm* gesture; **ne pas faire un g.** (*ne pas bouger*) not to make a move. ◆**gesticuler** *vi* to gesticulate.

gestion [ʒɛstjɔ̃] *nf* (*action*) management, administration. ◆**gestionnaire** *nmf* administrator.

geyser [ʒɛzɛr] *nm Géol* geyser.

ghetto [ɡeto] *nm* ghetto.

gibecière [ʒibsjɛr] *nf* shoulder bag.

gibier [ʒibje] *nm* (*animaux, oiseaux*) game.

giboulée [ʒibule] *nf* shower, downpour.

gicl/er [ʒikle] *vi* (*liquide*) to spurt, squirt; (*boue*) to splash; **faire g.** to spurt, squirt. ◆**-ée** *nf* jet, spurt. ◆**-eur** *nm* (*de carburateur*) *Aut* jet.

gifle [ʒifl] *nf* slap (in the face). ◆**gifler** *vt* **g. qn** to slap s.o., slap s.o.'s face.

gigantesque [ʒiɡɑ̃tɛsk] *a* gigantic.

gigogne [ʒiɡɔɲ] *a* **table g.** nest of tables.

gigot [ʒiɡo] *nm* leg of mutton ou lamb.

gigoter [ʒiɡɔte] *vi Fam* to kick, wriggle.

gilet [ʒilɛ] *nm* waistcoat, *Am* vest; (*cardigan*) cardigan; **g. (de corps)** vest, *Am* undershirt; **g. pare-balles** bulletproof jacket ou *Am* vest; **g. de sauvetage** life jacket.

gin [dʒin] *nm* (*eau-de-vie*) gin.

gingembre [ʒɛ̃ʒɑ̃br] *nm Bot Culin* ginger.

girafe [ʒiraf] *nf* giraffe.

giratoire [ʒiratwar] *a* **sens g.** *Aut* roundabout, *Am* traffic circle.

girl [ɡœrl] *nf* (*danseuse*) chorus girl.

girofle [ʒirɔfl] *nm* **clou de g.** *Bot* clove.

giroflée [ʒirɔfle] *nf Bot* wall flower.

girouette [ʒirwɛt] *nf* weathercock, weather vane.

gisement [ʒizmɑ̃] *nm* (*de minerai, pétrole*) *Géol* deposit.

gitan, -ane [ʒitɑ̃, -an] *nmf* (Spanish) gipsy.

gîte [ʒit] *nm* (*abri*) resting place.

giter [ʒite] *vi* (*navire*) to list.

givre [ʒivr] *nm* (hoar)frost. ◆**se givrer** *vpr* (*pare-brise etc*) to ice up, frost up. ◆**givré** *a* frost-covered.

glabre [ɡlabr] *a* (*visage*) smooth.

glace [ɡlas] *nf* **1** (*eau gelée*) ice; (*crème glacée*) ice cream. **2** (*vitre*) window; (*miroir*) mirror; (*verre*) plate glass.

glacer [glase] **1** *vt* (*sang*) *Fig* to chill; **g. qn** (*transir*, *paralyser*) to chill s.o.; **— se g.** *vpr* (*eau*) to freeze. **2** *vt* (*gâteau*) to ice, (*au jus*) to glaze; (*papier*) to glaze. ◆**glaçant** *a* (*attitude etc*) chilling, icy. ◆**glacé** *a* (*eau*, *main*, *pièce*) ice-cold, icy; (*vent*) freezing, icy; (*accueil*) *Fig* icy, chilly. **2** (*thé*) iced; (*fruit*, *marron*) candied; (*papier*) glazed. ◆**glaçage** *nm* (*de gâteau etc*) icing. ◆**glacial, -aux** *a* icy. ◆**glacier** *nm* **1** *Géol* glacier. **2** (*vendeur*) ice-cream man. ◆**glacière** *nf* (*boîte*, *endroit*) icebox. ◆**glaçon** *nm* *Culin* ice cube; *Géol* block of ice; (*sur le toit*) icicle.

glaïeul [glajœl] *nm Bot* gladiolus.

glaires [gler] *nfpl Méd* phlegm.

glaise [glez] *nf* clay.

gland [glɑ̃] *nm* **1** *Bot* acorn. **2** (*pompon*) *Tex* tassel.

glande [glɑ̃d] *nf* gland.

glander [glɑ̃de] *vi Arg* to fritter away one's time.

glaner [glane] *vt* (*blé*, *renseignement etc*) to glean.

glapir [glapir] *vi* to yelp, yap.

glas [glɑ] *nm* (*de cloche*) knell.

glauque [glok] *a* sea-green.

gliss/er [glise] *vi* (*involontairement*) to slip; (*patiner*, *coulisser*) to slide; (*sur l'eau*) to glide; **g. sur** (*sujet*) to slide ou glide over; **ça glisse** it's slippery; *— vt* (*introduire*) to slip (*dans* into); (*murmurer*) to whisper; **se g. dans/sous** to slip into/under. ◆**—ant** *a* slippery. ◆**glissade** *nf* (*involontaire*) slip; (*volontaire*) slide. ◆**glissement** *nm* (*de sens*) *Ling* shift; **g. à gauche** *Pol* swing ou shift to the left; **g. de terrain** *Géol* landslide. ◆**glissière** *nf* groove; **porte à g.** sliding door; **fermeture à g.** zip (fastener), *Am* zipper.

global, -aux [glɔbal, -o] *a* total, global; **somme globale** lump sum. ◆**—ement** *adv* collectively, as a whole.

globe [glɔb] *nm* globe; **g. de l'œil** eyeball.

globule [glɔbyl] *nm* (*du sang*) corpuscle.

gloire [glwar] *nf* (*renommée*, *louange*, *mérite*) glory; (*personne célèbre*) celebrity; **se faire g. de** to glory in; **à la g. de** in praise of. ◆**glorieux, -euse** *a* (*plein de gloire*) glorious. ◆**glorifier** *vt* to glorify; **se g. de** to glory in.

glossaire [glɔsɛr] *nm* glossary.

glouglou [gluglu] *nm* (*de liquide*) gurgle. ◆**glouglouter** *vi* to gurgle.

glouss/er [gluse] *vi* (*poule*) to cluck; (*personne*) to chuckle. ◆**—ement** *nm* cluck; chuckle.

glouton, -onne [glutɔ̃, -ɔn] *a* greedy, gluttonous; *— nmf* glutton. ◆**gloutonnerie** *nf* gluttony.

gluant [glyɑ̃] *a* sticky.

glucose [glykoz] *nm* glucose.

glycérine [gliserin] *nf* glycerin(e).

glycine [glisin] *nf Bot* wisteria.

gnome [gnom] *nm* (*nain*) gnome.

gnon [nɔ̃] *nm Arg* blow, punch.

goal [gol] *nm Fb* goalkeeper.

gobelet [gɔblɛ] *nm* tumbler; (*de plastique*, *papier*) cup.

gober [gɔbe] *vt* (*œuf*, *mouche etc*) to swallow (whole); (*propos*) *Fig* to swallow.

godasse [gɔdas] *nf Fam* shoe.

godet [gɔdɛ] *nm* (*récipient*) pot; (*verre*) *Arg* drink.

goéland [gɔelɑ̃] *nm* (sea)gull.

gogo [gogo] *nm* (*homme naïf*) *Fam* sucker.

gogo (à) [gogo] *adv Fam* galore.

goguenard [gɔgnar] *a* mocking.

goguette (en) [ɑ̃gɔgɛt] *adv Fam* on the spree.

goinfre [gwɛ̃fr] *nm* (*glouton*) *Fam* pig, guzzler. ◆**se goinfrer** *vpr Fam* to stuff oneself (*de* with).

golf [gɔlf] *nm* golf; (*terrain*) golf course. ◆**golfeur, -euse** *nmf* golfer.

golfe [gɔlf] *nm* gulf, bay.

gomme [gɔm] *nf* (*substance*) gum. **2** (*à effacer*) rubber, *Am* eraser. ◆**gommé** *a* (*papier*) gummed. ◆**gommer** *vt* (*effacer*) to rub out, erase.

gomme (à la) [alagɔm] *adv Fam* useless.

gond [gɔ̃] *nm* (*de porte etc*) hinge.

gondole [gɔ̃dɔl] *nf* (*bateau*) gondola. ◆**gondolier** *nm* gondolier.

gondoler [gɔ̃dɔle] **1** *vi*, **— se g.** *vpr* (*planche*) to warp. **2 se g.** *vpr* (*rire*) *Fam* to split one's sides.

gonfl/er [gɔ̃fle] *vt* to swell; (*pneu*) to inflate, pump up; (*en soufflant*) to blow up; (*poitrine*) to swell out; (*grossir*) *Fig* to inflate; *— vi*, **— se g.** *vpr* to swell up; (*d'orgueil*, *émotion*) to swell with. ◆**—é** *a* swollen; **être g.** *Fam* (*courageux*) to have plenty of pluck; (*insolent*) to have plenty of nerve. ◆**—able** *a* inflatable. ◆**—ement** *nm* swelling. ◆**gonfleur** *nm* (air) pump.

gong [gɔ̃g] *nm* gong.

gorge [gɔrʒ] *nf* **1** throat; (*seins*) *Litt* bust. **2** *Géog* gorge. ◆**gorg/er** *vt* (*remplir*) to stuff (*de* with); **se g. de** to gorge ou stuff oneself with. ◆**—é** *a* **g. de** (*saturé*) gorged with. ◆**—ée** *nf* mouthful; **petite g.** sip; **d'une seule g.** in *ou* at one gulp.

gorille [gɔrij] *nm* **1** (*animal*) gorilla. **2** (*garde du corps*) *Fam* bodyguard.

gosier [gozje] *nm* throat, windpipe.

gosse [gɔs] *nmf* (*enfant*) *Fam* kid, youngster.

gothique [gɔtik] *a* & *nm* Gothic.

gouache [gwaʃ] *nf* (*peinture*) gouache.

goudron [gudrɔ̃] *nm* tar. ◆**goudronner** *vt* to tar.

gouffre [gufr] *nm* gulf, chasm.

goujat [guʒa] *nm* churl, lout.

goulasch [gulaʃ] *nf* Culin goulash.

goulot [gulo] *nm* (*de bouteille*) neck; **boire au g.** to drink from the bottle.

goulu, -ue [guly] *a* greedy; − *nmf* glutton. ◆**goulûment** *adv* greedily.

goupille [gupij] *nf* (*cheville*) pin.

goupiller [gupije] *vt* (*arranger*) *Fam* to work out, arrange.

gourde [gurd] *nf* **1** (*à eau*) water bottle, flask. **2** (*personne*) *Péj Fam* chump, oaf.

gourdin [gurdɛ̃] *nm* club, cudgel.

gourer (se) [səgure] *vpr Fam* to make a mistake.

gourmand, -ande [gurmã, -ãd] *a* fond of eating, *Péj* greedy; **g. de fond of**; **être g. de sucreries**) to have a sweet tooth; − *nmf* hearty eater, *Péj* glutton. ◆**gourmandise** *nf* good eating, *Péj* gluttony; *pl* (*mets*) delicacies.

gourmet [gurmɛ] *nm* gourmet, epicure.

gourmette [gurmɛt] *nf* chain *ou* identity bracelet.

gousse [gus] *nf* **g. d'ail** clove of garlic.

goût [gu] *nm* taste; **de bon g.** in good taste; **prendre g. à qch** to take a liking to sth; **par g.** from *ou* by choice; **sans g.** tasteless. ◆**goûter** *vt* (*aliment*) to taste; (*apprécier*) ïo relish, enjoy; **g. à qch** to taste (a little of) sth; **g. de** (*pour la première fois*) to try out, taste; − *vi* to have a snack, have tea; − *nm* snack, tea.

goutte [gut] *nf* **1** drop. **couler g. à g.** to drip. **2** (*maladie*) gout. ◆**g.-à-goutte** *nm inv Méd* drip. ◆**gouttelette** *nf* droplet. ◆**goutter** *vi* (*eau, robinet, nez*) to drip (**de** from).

gouttière [gutjɛr] *nf* (*d'un toit*) gutter.

gouvernail [guvɛrnaj] *nm* (*pale*) rudder; (*barre*) helm.

gouvernante [guvɛrnãt] *nf* governess.

gouvernement [guvɛrnəmã] *nm* government. ◆**gouvernemental, -aux** *a* (*parti, politique etc*) government-.

gouvern/er [guvɛrne] *vti Pol* & *Fig* to govern, rule. ◆**−ants** *nmpl* rulers. ◆**−eur** *nm* governor.

grabuge [grabyʒ] *nm* **du g.** (*querelle*) *Fam* a rumpus.

grâce [grɑs] **1** *nf* (*charme*) & *Rel* grace; (*avantage*) favour; (*miséricorde*) mercy; **crier g.** to cry for mercy; **de bonne/mauvaise g.** with good/bad grace; **donner le coup de g. à** to finish off; **faire g. de qch à qn** to spare s.o. sth. **2** *prép* **g. à** thanks to. ◆**gracier** *vt* (*condamné*) to pardon.

gracieux, -euse [grasjø, -øz] *a* **1** (*élégant*) graceful; (*aimable*) gracious. **2** (*gratuit*) gratuitous; **à titre g.** free (of charge). ◆**gracieusement** *adv* gracefully; graciously; free (of charge).

gracile [grasil] *a Litt* slender.

gradation [gradasjɔ̃] *nf* gradation.

grade [grad] *nm Mil* rank; **monter en g.** to be promoted. ◆**gradé** *nm Mil* non-commissioned officer.

gradin [gradɛ̃] *nm Th etc* row of seats, tier.

graduel, -elle [graduɛl] *a* gradual.

graduer [gradɥe] *vt* (*règle*) to graduate; (*exercices*) to grade, make gradually more difficult.

graffiti [grafiti] *nmpl* graffiti.

grain [grɛ̃] *nm* **1** (*de blé etc*) & *Fig* grain; (*de café*) bean; (*de chapelet*) bead; (*de poussière*) speck; *pl* (*céréales*) grain; **le g.** (*de cuir, papier*) the grain; **g. de beauté** mole; (*sur le visage*) beauty spot; **g. de raisin** grape. **2** *Mét* shower.

graine [grɛn] *nf* seed; **mauvaise g.** (*enfant*) *Péj* bad lot, rotten egg.

graisse [grɛs] *nf* fat; (*lubrifiant*) grease. ◆**graissage** *nm Aut* lubrication. ◆**graisser** *vt* to grease. ◆**graisseux, -euse** *a* (*vêtement etc*) greasy, oily; (*bourrelets, tissu*) fatty.

grammaire [gramɛr] *nf* grammar. ◆**grammatical, -aux** *a* grammatical.

gramme [gram] *nm* gram(me).

grand, grande [grã, grãd] *a* big, large; (*en hauteur*) tall; (*mérite, âge, chaleur, ami etc*) great; (*bruit*) loud, great; (*différence*) wide, great, big; (*adulte, mûr, plus âgé*) grown up, big; (*officier, maître*) great; (*âme*) noble; **le frère/etc** (*plus âgé*) big brother/*etc*; **le g. air** the open air; **il est g. temps** it's high time (**que** that); − *adv* **g. ouvert** (*yeux, fenêtre*) wide-open; **ouvrir g.** to open wide; **en g.** on a grand *ou* large scale; − *nmf Scol* senior; (*adulte*) grown-up; **les quatre Grands** *Pol* the Big Four. ◆**grandement** *adv* (*beaucoup*) greatly; (*généreusement*) grandly; **avoir g. de quoi vivre** to have plenty to live on. ◆**grandeur** *nf* (*importance, gloire*) greatness; (*dimension*) size, magnitude; (*majesté, splendeur*) grandeur; **g. nature** life-size; **g. d'âme** generosity.

grand-chose [grɑ̃ʃoz] *pron* **pas g.-chose** not much. ◆**g.-mère** *nf* (*pl* **grands-mères**) grandmother. ◆**grands-parents** *nmpl* grandparents. ◆**g.-père** *nm* (*pl* **grands-pères**) grandfather.

Grande-Bretagne [grɑ̃dbrətaɲ] *nf* Great Britain.

grandiose [grɑ̃djoz] *a* grandiose, grand.

grandir [grɑ̃dir] *vi* to grow; (*bruit*) to grow louder; — *vt* (*grossir*) to magnify; **g. qn** (*faire paraître plus grand*) to make s.o. seem taller.

grange [grɑ̃ʒ] *nf* barn.

granit(e) [granit] *nm* granite.

graphique [grafik] *a* (*signe, art*) graphic; — *nm* graph.

grappe [grap] *nf* (*de fruits etc*) cluster; **g. de raisin** bunch of grapes.

grappin [grapɛ̃] *nm* **mettre le g. sur** *Fam* to grab hold of.

gras, grasse [grɑ, grɑs] *a* (*personne, ventre etc*) fat; (*aliment*) fatty; (*graisseux*) greasy, oily; (*caractère*) *Typ* bold, heavy; (*plante, contour*) thick; (*rire*) throaty, deep; (*toux*) loose, phlegmy; (*récompense*) rich; **matières grasses** fat; **foie g.** *Culin* foie gras, fatted goose liver; — *nm* (*de viande*) fat. ◆**grassement** *adv* (*abondamment*) handsomely. ◆**grassouillet, -ette** *a* plump.

gratifier [gratifje] *vt* **g. qn de** to present *ou* favour s.o. with. ◆**gratification** *nf* (*prime*) bonus.

gratin [gratɛ̃] *nm* **1 au g.** *Culin* baked with breadcrumbs and grated cheese. **2** (*élite*) *Fam* upper crust.

gratis [gratis] *adv* *Fam* free (of charge), gratis.

gratitude [gratityd] *nf* gratitude.

gratte-ciel [gratsjel] *nm inv* skyscraper.

gratte-papier [gratpapje] *nm* (*employé*) *Péj* pen-pusher.

gratter [grate] *vt* (*avec un outil etc*) to scrape; (*avec les ongles, les griffes etc*) to scratch; (*boue*) to scrape off; (*effacer*) to scratch out; **ça me gratte** *Fam* it itches, I have an itch; — *vi* (*à la porte etc*) to scratch; (*tissu*) to be scratchy; — **se g.** *vpr* to scratch oneself. ◆**grattoir** *nm* scraper.

gratuit [gratɥi] *a* (*billet etc*) free; (*hypothèse, acte*) gratuitous. ◆**gratuité** *nf* **la g. de l'enseignement/etc** free education/etc. ◆**gratuitement** *adv* free (of charge); gratuitously.

gravats [grava] *nmpl* rubble, debris.

grave [grav] *a* serious; (*juge, visage*) grave,

solemn; (*voix*) deep, low; (*accent*) *Gram* grave; **ce n'est pas g.!** it's not important! ◆**—ment** *adv* (*malade, menacé*) seriously; (*dignement*) gravely.

grav/er [grave] *vt* (*sur métal etc*) to engrave; (*sur bois*) to carve; (*disque*) to cut; (*dans sa mémoire*) to imprint, engrave. ◆**—eur** *nm* engraver.

gravier [gravje] *nm* gravel. ◆**gravillon** *nm* gravel; *pl* gravel, (loose) chippings.

gravir [gravir] *vt* to climb (*with effort*).

gravité [gravite] *nf* **1** (*de situation etc*) seriousness; (*solennité*) gravity. **2** *Phys* gravity.

graviter [gravite] *vi* to revolve (**autour de** around). ◆**gravitation** *nf* gravitation.

gravure [gravyr] *nf* (*action, art*) engraving; (*à l'eau forte*) etching; (*estampe*) print; (*de disque*) recording; **g. sur bois** (*objet*) woodcut.

gré [gre] *nm* **à son g.** (*goût*) to his *ou* her taste; (*désir*) as he *ou* she pleases; **de bon g.** willingly; **contre le g. de** against the will of; **bon g. mal g.** willy-nilly; **au g. de** (*vent etc*) at the mercy of.

Grèce [grɛs] *nf* Greece. ◆**grec, grecque** *a* & *nmf* Greek; — *nm* (*langue*) Greek.

greffe [grɛf] **1** *nf* (*de peau*) & *Bot* graft; (*d'organe*) transplant. **2** *nm* *Jur* record office. ◆**greffer** *vt* (*peau etc*) & *Bot* to graft (**à** on to); (*organe*) to transplant. ◆**greffier** *nm* clerk (of the court). ◆**greffon** *nm* (*de peau*) & *Bot* graft.

grégaire [greger] *a* (*instinct*) gregarious.

grêle [grɛl] **1** *nf* *Mét* & *Fig* hail. **2** *a* (*fin*) spindly, (very) slender *ou* thin. ◆**grêler** *v imp* to hail. ◆**grêlon** *nm* hailstone.

grêlé [grele] *a* (*visage*) pockmarked.

grelot [grəlo] *nm* (small round) bell.

grelotter [grələte] *vi* to shiver (**de** with).

grenade [grənad] *nf* **1** *Bot* pomegranate. **2** (*projectile*) *Mil* grenade. ◆**grenadine** *nf* pomegranate syrup, grenadine.

grenat [grəna] *a inv* (*couleur*) dark red.

grenier [grənje] *nm* attic; *Agr* granary.

grenouille [grənuj] *nf* frog.

grès [grɛ] *nm* (*roche*) sandstone; (*poterie*) stoneware.

grésiller [grezije] *vi* *Culin* to sizzle; *Rad* to crackle.

grève [grɛv] *nf* **1** strike; **g. de la faim** hunger strike; **g. du zèle** work-to-rule, *Am* rule-book slow-down; **g. perlée** go-slow, *Am* slow-down (strike); **g. sauvage** *ou* **le tas** wildcat/sit-down strike; **g. tournante** strike by rota. **2** (*de mer*) shore; (*de rivière*) bank. ◆**gréviste** *nmf* striker.

gribouiller [gribuje] *vti* to scribble. ◆**gribouillis** *nm* scribble.

grief [grijɛf] *nm* (*plainte*) grievance.

grièvement [grijɛvmã] *adv* g. blessé seriously *ou* badly injured.

griffe [grif] *nf* 1 (*ongle*) claw; **sous la g. de qn** (*pouvoir*) in s.o.'s clutches. 2 (*de couturier*) (designer) label; (*tampon*) printed signature; (*d'auteur*) Fig mark, stamp. ◆**griffé** *a* (*vêtement*) designer-. ◆**griffer** *vt* to scratch, claw.

griffonn/er [grifɔne] *vt* to scrawl, scribble. ◆**—age** *nm* scrawl, scribble.

grignoter [griɲɔte] *vti* to nibble.

gril [gril] *nm* Culin grill, grid(iron). ◆**grillade** [grijad] *nf* (*viande*) grill. ◆**grille-pain** *nm inv* toaster. ◆**griller** *vt* (*viande*) to grill, broil; (*pain*) to toast; (*café*) to roast; (*ampoule*) El to blow; (*brûler*) to scorch; (*cigarette*) Fam to smoke; **g. un feu rouge** *Aut* Fam to drive through *ou* jump a red light; — *vi* **mettre à g.** to put on the grill; **on grille ici** Fam it's scorching; **g. de faire** to be itching to do.

grille [grij] *nf* (*clôture*) railings; (*porte*) (iron) gate; (*de fourneau, foyer*) grate; (*de radiateur*) *Aut* grid, grille; (*des salaires*) Fig scale; *pl* (*de fenêtre*) bars, grating; (*des horaires*) schedule. ◆**grillage** *nm* wire netting.

grillon [grijɔ̃] *nm* (*insecte*) cricket.

grimace [grimas] *nf* (*pour faire rire*) (funny) face, grimace; (*de dégoût, douleur*) grimace. ◆**grimacer** *vi* to grimace (de with).

grimer [grime] *vt*, — **se g.** *vpr* (*acteur*) to make up.

grimp/er [grɛ̃pe] *vi* to climb (**à qch** up sth); (*prix*) Fam to rocket; — *vt* to climb. ◆**—ant** *a* (*plante*) climbing.

grinc/er [grɛ̃se] *vi* to grate, creak; **g. des dents** to grind *ou* gnash one's teeth. ◆**—ement** *nm* grating; grinding.

grincheux, -euse [grɛ̃ʃø, -øz] *a* grumpy, peevish.

gringalet [grɛ̃galɛ] *nm* (*homme*) Péj puny runt, weakling.

grippe [grip] *nf* 1 (*maladie*) flu, influenza. 2 **prendre qch/qn en g.** to take a strong dislike to sth/s.o. ◆**grippé** *a* être g. to have (the) flu.

gripper [gripe] *vi*, — **se g.** *vpr* (*moteur*) to seize up.

grippe-sou [gripsu] *nm* skinflint, miser.

gris [gri] *a* grey, *Am* gray; (*temps*) dull, grey; (*ivre*) tipsy; — *nm* grey. ◆**grisaille** *nf* (*de vie*) dullness, greyness, *Am* grayness. ◆**grisâtre** *a* greyish, *Am* grayish.

griser *vt* (*vin etc*) to make (s.o.) tipsy, intoxicate (s.o.); (*air vif, succès*) to exhilarate (s.o.). ◆**griserie** *nf* intoxication; exhilaration. ◆**grisonn/er** *vi* (*cheveux, personne*) to go grey. ◆**—ant** *a* greying.

grisou [grizu] *nm* (*gaz*) firedamp.

grive [griv] *nf* (*oiseau*) thrush.

grivois [grivwa] *a* bawdy. ◆**grivoiserie** *nf* (*propos*) bawdy talk.

Groenland [grɔɛnlɑ̃d] *nm* Greenland.

grog [grɔg] *nm* (*boisson*) grog, toddy.

grogn/er [grɔɲe] *vi* to growl, grumble (**contre** at); (*cochon*) to grunt. ◆**—ement** *nm* growl, grumble; grunt. ◆**grognon, -onne** *a* grumpy, peevish.

grommeler [grɔmle] *vti* to grumble, mutter.

gronder [grɔ̃de] *vi* (*chien*) to growl; (*tonnerre*) to rumble; — *vt* (*réprimander*) to scold. ◆**grondement** *nm* growl; rumble. ◆**gronderie** *nf* scolding.

gros, grosse [gro, gros] *a* big; (*gras*) fat; (*épais*) thick; (*effort, progrès*) great; (*fortune, somme*) large; (*bruit*) loud; (*averse, mer, rhume*) heavy; (*faute*) serious, gross; (*traits, laine, fil*) coarse; **g. mot** swear word; — *adv* gagner **g.** to earn big money; **risquer g.** to take a big risk; **en g.** (*globalement*) roughly; (*écrire*) in big letters; (*vendre*) in bulk, wholesale; — *nmf* (*personne*) fat man, fat woman; — **le g. de** the bulk of; **de g.** (*maison, prix*) wholesale.

groseille [grozɛj] *nf* (white *ou* red) currant; **g. à maquereau** gooseberry.

grossesse [grosɛs] *nf* pregnancy.

grosseur [grosœr] *nf* 1 (*volume*) size; (*obésité*) weight. 2 (*tumeur*) Méd lump.

grossier, -ière [grosje, -jɛr] *a* (*matière, tissu, traits*) coarse, rough; (*idée, solution*) rough, crude; (*instrument*) crude; (*erreur*) gross; (*personne, manières*) coarse, uncouth, rude; être g. **envers** (*insolent*) to be rude to. ◆**grossièrement** *adv* (*calculer*) roughly; (*se tromper*) grossly; (*répondre*) coarsely, rudely. ◆**grossièreté** *nf* coarseness; roughness; (*insolence*) rudeness; (*mot*) rude word.

gross/ir [grosir] *vi* (*personne*) to put on weight; (*fleuve*) to swell; (*nombre, bosse, foule*) to swell, get bigger; (*bruit*) to get louder; — *vt* to swell; (*exagérer*) Fig to magnify; — *vti* (*verre, loupe etc*) to magnify; **verre grossissant** magnifying glass. ◆**—issement** *nm* increase in weight; swelling, increase in size; (*de microscope etc*) magnification.

grossiste [grosist] *nmf* Com wholesaler.

grosso modo [grosomɔdo] *adv* (*en gros*) roughly.

grotesque [grɔtɛsk] *a* (*risible*) ludicrous, grotesque.

grotte [grɔt] *nf* grotto.

grouill/er [gruje] **1** *vi* (*rue, fourmis, foule etc*) to be swarming (**de** with). **2 se g.** *vpr* (*se hâter*) *Arg* to step on it. ◆—**ant** *a* swarming (**de** with).

groupe [grup] *nm* group; **g. scolaire** (*bâtiments*) school block. ◆**groupement** *nm* (*action*) grouping; (*groupe*) group. ◆**grouper** *vt* to group (together); — **se g.** *vpr* to band together, group (together).

grue [gry] *nf* (*machine, oiseau*) crane.

grumeau, -x [grymo] *nm* (*dans une sauce etc*) lump. ◆**grumeleux, -euse** *a* lumpy.

gruyère [gryjɛr] *nm* gruyère (cheese).

gué [ge] *nm* ford; **passer à g.** to ford.

guenilles [gənij] *nfpl* rags (and tatters).

guenon [gənɔ̃] *nf* female monkey.

guépard [gepar] *nm* cheetah.

guêpe [gɛp] *nf* wasp. ◆**guêpier** *nm* (*nid*) wasp's nest; (*piège*) *Fig* trap.

guère [gɛr] *adv* (**ne**) . . . **g.** hardly, scarcely; **il ne sort g.** he hardly *ou* scarcely goes out.

guéridon [geridɔ̃] *nm* pedestal table.

guérilla [gerija] *nf* guerrilla warfare. ◆**guérillero** *nm* guerrilla.

guér/ir [gerir] *vt* (*personne, maladie*) to cure (**de** of); (*blessure*) to heal; — *vi* to recover; (*blessure*) to heal; (*rhume*) to get better; **g. de** (*fièvre etc*) to get over, recover from. ◆—**i** *a* cured, better, well. ◆**guérison** *nf* (*de personne*) recovery; (*de maladie*) cure; (*de blessure*) healing. ◆**guérisseur, -euse** *nmf* faith healer.

guérite [gerit] *nf Mil* sentry box.

guerre [gɛr] *nf* war; (*chimique etc*) warfare; **en g. at war** (**avec** with); **faire la g.** to wage *ou* make war (**à** on, against); **g. d'usure** war of attrition; **conseil de g.** court-martial. ◆**guerrier, -ière** *a* (*chant, danse*) war-; (*nation*) war-like; — *nmf* warrior. ◆**guerroyer** *vi Litt* to war.

guet [gɛ] *nm* **faire le g.** to be on the look-out. ◆**guett/er** *vt* to be on the look-out for,

watch (out) for; (*gibier*) to lie in wait for. ◆—**eur** *nm* (*soldat*) look-out.

guet-apens [gɛtapɑ̃] *nm inv* ambush.

guêtre [gɛtr] *nf* gaiter.

gueule [gœl] *nf* (*d'animal, de canon*) mouth; (*de personne*) *Fam* mouth; (*figure*) *Fam* face; **avoir la g. de bois** *Fam* to have a hangover; **faire la g.** *Fam* to sulk. ◆**gueuler** *vti* to bawl (out). ◆**gueuleton** *nm* (*repas*) *Fam* blow-out, feast.

gui [gi] *nm Bot* mistletoe.

guichet [giʃɛ] *nm* (*de gare, cinéma etc*) ticket office; (*de banque etc*) window; *Th* box office, ticket office; **à guichets fermés** *Th Sp* with all tickets sold in advance. ◆**guichetier, -ière** *nmf* (*à la poste etc*) counter clerk; (*à la gare*) ticket office clerk.

guide [gid] **1** *nm* (*personne, livre etc*) guide. **2** *nf* (*éclaireuse*) (girl) guide. **3** *nfpl* (*rênes*) reins. ◆**guider** *vt* to guide; **se g. sur** to guide oneself by.

guidon [gidɔ̃] *nm* (*de bicyclette etc*) handlebar(s).

guigne [giɲ] *nf* (*malchance*) *Fam* bad luck.

guignol [giɲɔl] *nm* (*spectacle*) = Punch and Judy show.

guillemets [gijmɛ] *nmpl Typ* inverted commas, quotation marks.

guilleret, -ette [gijrɛ, -ɛt] *a* lively, perky.

guillotine [gijɔtin] *nf* guillotine.

guimauve [gimov] *nf Bot Culin* marshmallow.

guimbarde [gɛ̃bard] *nf* (*voiture*) *Fam* old banger, *Am* (old) wreck.

guindé [gɛ̃de] *a* (*affecté*) stiff, stilted, stuck-up.

guingois (de) [dəgɛ̃gwa] *adv* askew.

guirlande [girlɑ̃d] *nf* garland, wreath.

guise [giz] *nf* **n'en faire qu'à sa g.** to do as one pleases; **en g. de** by way of.

guitare [gitar] *nf* guitar. ◆**guitariste** *nmf* guitarist.

guttural, -aux [gytyral, -o] *a* guttural.

gymnase [ʒimnɑz] *nm* gymnasium. ◆**gymnaste** *nmf* gymnast. ◆**gymnastique** *nf* gymnastics.

gynécologie [ʒinekɔlɔʒi] *nf* gynaecology, *Am* gynecology. ◆**gynécologue** *nmf* gynaecologist, *Am* gynecologist.

H

H, h [aʃ] *nm* H, h; **l'heure H** zero hour; **bombe H** H-bomb.

ha! ['ɑ] *int* ah!, oh!; **ha, ha!** (*rire*) ha-ha!

habile [abil] *a* clever, skilful (**à qch** at sth, **à faire** at doing). ◆**habilement** *adv* cleverly, skilfully. ◆**habileté** *nf* skill, ability.

habill/er [abije] *vt* to dress (**de** in); (*fournir en vêtements*) to clothe; (*couvrir*) to cover (**de** with); **h. qn en soldat**/*etc* (*déguiser*) to dress s.o. up as a soldier/*etc*; — **s'h.** *vpr* to dress (oneself); get dressed; (*avec élégance, se déguiser*) to dress up. ◆**-é** *a* dressed (**de** in); (*costume, robe*) smart, dressy. ◆**-ement** *nm* (*vêtements*) clothing, clothes.

habit [abi] *nm* costume, outfit; (*tenue de soirée*) evening dress, tails; *pl* (*vêtements*) clothes.

habit/er [abite] *vi* to live (**à, en, dans** in); — *vt* (*maison, région*) to live in; (*planète*) to inhabit. ◆**-ant, -ante** *nmf* (*de pays etc*) inhabitant; (*de maison*) resident, occupant. ◆**-é** *a* (*région*) inhabited; (*maison*) occupied. ◆**-able** *a* (in)habitable. ◆**habitat** *nm* (*d'animal, de plante*) habitat; (*conditions*) housing, living conditions. ◆**habitation** *nf* house, dwelling; (*action de résider*) living.

habitude [abityd] *nf* habit; **avoir l'h. de qch** to be used to sth; **avoir l'h. de faire** to be used to doing, be in the habit of doing; **prendre l'h. de faire** to get into the habit of doing; **d'h.** usually; **comme d'h.** as usual. ◆**habituel, -elle** *a* usual, customary. ◆**habituellement** *adv* usually. ◆**habitu/er** *vt* **h. qn à** to accustom s.o. to; **être habitué à** to be used *ou* accustomed to; — **s'h.** *vpr* to get accustomed (**à** to). ◆**-é, -ée** *nmf* regular (customer *ou* visitor).

hache ['aʃ] *nf* axe, *Am* ax. ◆**hachette** *nf* hatchet.

hach/er ['aʃe] *vt* (*au couteau*) to chop (up); (*avec un appareil*) to mince, *Am* grind; (*déchiqueter*) to cut to pieces. ◆**-é** *a* **1** (*viande*) minced, *Am* ground; chopped. **2** (*style*) staccato, broken. ◆**hachis** *nm* (*viande*) mince, minced *ou Am* ground meat. ◆**hachoir** *nm* (*couteau*) chopper; (*appareil*) mincer, *Am* grinder.

hagard ['agar] *a* wild-looking, frantic.

haie ['ɛ] *nf* (*clôture*) *Bot* hedge; (*rangée*) row; (*de coureur*) *Sp* hurdle; (*de chevaux*) *Sp* fence, hurdle; **course de haies** (*coureurs*) hurdle race; (*chevaux*) steeplechase.

haillons ['ɑjɔ̃] *nmpl* rags (and tatters).

haine ['ɛn] *nf* hatred, hate. ◆**haineux, -euse** *a* full of hatred.

haïr* ['air] *vt* to hate. ◆**haïssable** *a* hateful, detestable.

hâle ['al] *nm* suntan. ◆**hâlé** *a* (*par le soleil*) suntanned; (*par l'air*) weather-beaten.

haleine [alɛn] *nf* breath; **hors d'h.** out of breath; **perdre h.** to get out of breath; **reprendre h.** to get one's breath back, catch one's breath; **de longue h.** (*travail*) long-term; **tenir en h.** to hold in suspense.

hal/er ['ale] *vt Nau* to tow. ◆**-age** *nm* towing; **chemin de h.** towpath.

halet/er ['alte] *vi* to pant, gasp. ◆**-ant** *a* panting, gasping.

hall ['ol] *nm* (*de gare*) main hall, concourse; (*d'hôtel*) lobby, hall; (*de maison*) hall(way).

halle ['al] *nf* (covered) market; **les halles** the central food market.

hallucination [alysinɑsjɔ̃] *nf* hallucination. ◆**hallucinant** *a* extraordinary.

halo ['alo] *nm* (*auréole*) halo.

halte ['alt] *nf* (*arrêt*) stop, *Mil* halt; (*lieu*) stopping place, *Mil* halting place; **faire h.** to stop; — *int* stop!, *Mil* halt!

haltère [altɛr] *nm* (*poids*) *Sp* dumbbell. ◆**haltérophilie** *nf* weight lifting.

hamac ['amak] *nm* hammock.

hameau, -x ['amo] *nm* hamlet.

hameçon [amsɔ̃] *nm* (fish) hook; **mordre à l'h.** *Pêche & Fig* to rise to *ou* swallow the bait.

hamster ['amster] *nm* hamster.

hanche ['ɑ̃ʃ] *nf Anat* hip.

hand(-)ball ['ɑdbal] *nm Sp* handball.

handicap ['ɑdikap] *nm* (*désavantage*) & *Sp* handicap. ◆**handicap/er** *vt* to handicap. ◆**-é, -ée** *a & nmf* handicapped (person); **h. moteur** spastic.

hangar ['ɑgar] *nm* (*entrepôt*) shed; (*pour avions*) hangar.

hanneton ['antɔ̃] *nm* (*insecte*) cockchafer.

hanter ['ɑte] *vt* to haunt.

hantise ['ɑtiz] *nf* **la h. de** an obsession with.

happer ['ape] vt (saisir) to catch, snatch; (par la gueule) to snap up.

haras ['ara] nm stud farm.

harasser ['arase] vt to exhaust.

harceler ['arsəle] vt to harass, torment (de with). ◆**harcèlement** nm harassment.

hardi ['ardi] a bold, daring. ◆**—ment** adv boldly. ◆**hardiesse** nf boldness, daring; une h. (action) Litt an audacity.

harem ['arɛm] nm harem.

hareng ['arɑ̃] nm herring.

hargne ['arɲ] nf aggressive bad temper. ◆**hargneux, -euse** a bad-tempered, aggressive.

haricot ['ariko] nm (blanc) (haricot) bean; (vert) French bean, green bean.

harmonica [armɔnika] nm harmonica, mouthorgan.

harmonie [armɔni] nf harmony. ◆**harmonieux, -euse** a harmonious. ◆**harmonique** a & nm Mus harmonic. ◆**harmoniser** vt, — s'h. vpr to harmonize. ◆**harmonium** nm Mus harmonium.

harnacher ['arnaʃe] vt (cheval etc) to harness. ◆**harnais** nm (de cheval, bébé) harness.

harpe ['arp] nf harp. ◆**harpiste** nmf harpist.

harpon ['arpɔ̃] nm harpoon. ◆**harponner** vt (baleine) to harpoon; h. qn (arrêter) Fam to waylay s.o.

hasard ['azar] nm le h. chance; un h. (coïncidence) a coincidence; un heureux h. a stroke of luck; un malheureux h. a rotten piece of luck; par h. by chance; si par h. if by any chance; au h. at random, haphazardly; à tout h. just in case; les hasards de (risques) the hazards of... ◆**hasarder** vt (remarque, démarche) to venture, hazard; (vie, réputation) to risk; se h. dans to venture into; se h. à faire to risk doing, venture to do. ◆**—é-a**, ◆**hasardeux, -euse** a risky, hazardous.

haschisch ['aʃiʃ] nm hashish.

hâte ['ɑt] nf haste, speed; (impatience) eagerness; en h., à la h. hurriedly, in a hurry, in haste; avoir h. de faire (désireux) to be eager to do, be in a hurry to do. ◆**hâter** vt (pas, départ etc) to hasten; — se h. vpr to hurry, make haste (de faire to do). ◆**hâtif, -ive** a hasty, hurried; (développement) precocious; (fruit) early.

hausse ['os] nf rise (de in); en h. rising. ◆**hausser** vt (prix, voix etc) to raise; (épaules) to shrug; se h. sur la pointe des pieds to stand on tip-toe.

haut ['o] a high; (de taille) tall; (classes) up-

per, higher; (fonctionnaire etc) high-ranking; le h. Rhin the upper Rhine; la haute couture high fashion; à haute voix aloud, in a loud voice; h. de 5 mètres 5 metres high ou tall; — adv (voler, viser etc) high (up); (estimer) highly; (parler) loud, loudly; tout h. (lire, penser) aloud, out loud; h. placé (personne) in a high position; plus h. (dans un texte) above, further back; — nm (partie haute) top; en h. de at the top of; en h. (loger) upstairs; (regarder) up; (mettre) on the top; d'en h. (de la partie haute, du ciel etc) from high up, from above; avoir 5 mètres de h. to be 5 metres high ou tall; des hauts et des bas Fig ups and downs.

hautain ['otɛ̃] a haughty.

hautbois ['obwa] nm Mus oboe.

haut-de-forme ['odfɔrm] nm (pl hauts-de-forme) top hat.

hautement ['otmɑ̃] adv (tout à fait, très) highly. ◆**hauteur** nf height; Géog hill; (orgueil) Péj haughtiness; Mus pitch; à la h. de (objet) level with; (rue) opposite; (situation) Fig equal to; il n'est pas à la h. he isn't up to it; saut en h. Sp high jump.

haut-le-cœur ['olkœr] nm inv avoir des h.-le-cœur to retch, gag.

haut-le-corps ['olkɔr] nm inv (sursaut) sudden start, jump.

haut-parleur ['oparlœr] nm loudspeaker.

hâve ['ɑv] a gaunt, emaciated.

havre ['avr] nm (refuge) Litt haven.

Haye (La) [la'ɛ] nf The Hague.

hayon ['ejɔ̃] nm (porte) Aut tailgate, hatchback.

hé! [e] int hé (là) (appel) hey!; hé! hé! well, well!

hebdomadaire [ɛbdɔmadɛr] a weekly; — nm (publication) weekly.

héberg/er [ebɛrʒe] vt to put up, accommodate. ◆**—ement** nm accommodation; centre d'h. shelter.

hébété [ebete] a dazed, stupefied.

hébreu, -x [ebrø] am Hebrew; — nm (langue) Hebrew. ◆**hébraïque** a Hebrew.

hécatombe [ekatɔ̃b] nf (great) slaughter.

hectare [ɛktar] nm hectare (= 2.47 acres).

hégémonie [eʒemɔni] nf hegemony, supremacy.

hein! [ɛ̃] int (surprise, interrogation etc) eh!

hélas! ['elas] int alas!, unfortunately.

héler ['ele] vt (taxi etc) to hail.

hélice [elis] nf Av Nau propeller.

hélicoptère [elikɔptɛr] nm helicopter. ◆**héliport** nm heliport.

hellénique [elenik] a Hellenic, Greek.

helvétique [ɛlvetik] a Swiss.

hem! ['ɛm] int (a)hem!, hm!

hémicycle [emisikl] nm semicircle; Pol Fig French National Assembly.

hémisphère [emisfɛr] nm hemisphere.

hémorragie [emɔraʒi] nf Méd h(a)emorrhage; (de capitaux) Com outflow, drain.

hémorroïdes [emɔrɔid] nfpl piles, h(a)emorrhoids.

henn/ir ['enir] vi (cheval) to neigh. ◆—issement nm neigh.

hep! ['ɛp] int hey!, hey there!

hépatite [epatit] nf hepatitis.

herbe [ɛrb] nf grass; (médicinale etc) herb; mauvaise h. weed; fines herbes Culin herbs; en h. (blés) green; (poète etc) Fig budding. ◆herbage nm grassland. ◆herbeux, -euse a grassy. ◆herbicide nm weed killer. ◆herbivore a grass-eating, herbivorous. ◆herbu a grassy.

hercule [ɛrkyl] nm Hercules, strong man. ◆herculéen, -enne a herculean.

hérédité [eredite] nf heredity. ◆héréditaire a hereditary.

hérésie [erezi] nf heresy. ◆hérétique a heretical; — nmf heretic.

hériss/er ['erise] vt (poils) to bristle (up); h. qn (irriter) to ruffle s.o.'s feathers; — se h. vpr to bristle (up); to get ruffled. ◆—é a (cheveux) bristly; (cactus) prickly; h. de bristling with.

hérisson ['erisɔ̃] nm (animal) hedgehog.

hérit/er [erite] vti to inherit (qch de qn from s.o.); h. de qch to inherit sth. ◆—age nm (biens) inheritance; (culturel, politique etc) Fig heritage. ◆héritier nm heir. ◆héritière nf heiress.

hermétique [ermetik] a hermetically sealed, airtight; (obscur) Fig impenetrable. ◆—ment adv hermetically.

hermine [ermin] nf (animal, fourrure) ermine.

hernie ['erni] nf Méd hernia, rupture; (de pneu) swelling.

héron ['erɔ̃] nm (oiseau) heron.

héros ['ero] nm hero. ◆héroïne [erɔin] nf 1 (femme) heroine. 2 (stupéfiant) heroin. ◆héroïque [erɔik] a heroic. ◆héroïsme [erɔism] nm heroism.

hésit/er [ezite] vi to hesitate (sur over, about; à faire to do); (en parlant) to falter, hesitate. ◆—ant a (personne) hesitant; (pas, voix) faltering, unsteady, wavering. ◆hésitation nf hesitation; avec h. hesitantly.

hétéroclite [eterɔklit] a (disparate) motley.

hétérogène [eterɔʒɛn] a heterogeneous.

hêtre ['ɛtr] nm (arbre, bois) beech.

heu! [ø] int (hésitation) er!

heure [œr] nf (mesure) hour; (moment) time; quelle h. est-il? what time is it?; il est six heures it's six (o'clock); six heures moins cinq five to six; six heures cinq five past ou Am after six; à l'h. (arriver) on time; (être payé) by the hour; dix kilomètres à l'h. ten kilometres an hour; à l'h. qu'il est (by) now; de dernière h. (nouvelle) last minute; de bonne h. early; à une h. avancée at a late hour, late at night; tout à l'h. (futur) in a few moments, later; (passé) a moment ago; à toute h. (continuellement) at all hours; faire des heures supplémentaires to work ou do overtime; heures creuses off-peak ou slack periods; l'h. d'affluence, l'h. de pointe (circulation etc) rush hour; (dans les magasins) peak period; l'h. de pointe (électricité etc) peak period.

heureux, -euse [œrø, -øz] a happy; (chanceux) lucky, fortunate; (issue, changement) successful; (expression, choix) apt; h. de qch/de voir qn (satisfait) happy ou pleased ou glad about sth/to see s.o.; — adv (vivre, mourir) happily. ◆heureusement adv (par chance) fortunately, luckily, happily (pour for); (avec succès) successfully; (exprimer) aptly.

heurt [œr] nm bump, knock; (d'opinions etc) Fig clash; sans heurts smoothly. ◆heurt/er vt (cogner) to knock, bump, hit (contre against); (mur, piéton) to bump into, hit; h. qn (choquer) to offend s.o., upset s.o.; se h. à to bump into, hit; (difficultés) Fig to come up against. ◆—é a (couleurs, tons) clashing; (style, rythme) jerky. ◆heurtoir nm (door) knocker.

hexagone [ɛgzagɔn] nm hexagon; l'H. Fig France. ◆hexagonal, -aux a hexagonal; Fig Fam French.

hiatus [jatys] nm Fig hiatus, gap.

hiberner [ibɛrne] vi to hibernate. ◆hibernation nf hibernation.

hibou, -x ['ibu] nm owl.

hic ['ik] nm voilà le h. Fam that's the snag.

hideux, -euse [idø, -øz] a hideous.

hier [(i)jɛr] adv & nm yesterday; h. soir last ou yesterday night, yesterday evening; elle n'est pas née d'h. Fig she wasn't born yesterday.

hiérarchie [jerarʃi] nf hierarchy. ◆hiérarchique a (ordre) hierarchical; par la voie h. through (the) official channels. ◆hiérarchiser vt (emploi, valeurs) to grade.

hi-fi ['ifi] a inv & nf inv Fam hi-fi.

hilare [ilar] *a* merry. ◆**hilarant** *a* (*drôle*) hilarious. ◆**hilarité** *nf* (sudden) laughter.

hindou, -oue [ɛ̃du] *a* & *nmf* Hindu.

hippie ['ipi] *nmf* hippie.

hippique [ipik] *a* **un concours h.** a horse show, a show-jumping event. ◆**hippodrome** *nm* racecourse, racetrack (*for horses*).

hippopotame [ipopotam] *nm* hippopotamus.

hirondelle [irɔ̃dɛl] *nf* (*oiseau*) swallow.

hirsute [irsyt] *a* (*personne, barbe*) unkempt, shaggy.

hispanique [ispanik] *a* Spanish, Hispanic.

hisser ['ise] *vt* (*voile, fardeau etc*) to hoist, raise; **— se h.** *vpr* to raise oneself (up).

histoire [istwar] *nf* (*science, événements*) history; (*récit, mensonge*) story; (*affaire*) Fam business, matter; (*ennuis*) trouble; (*façons, chichis*) fuss; **toute une h.** (*problème*) quite a lot of trouble; (*chichis*) quite a lot of fuss; **h. de voir/etc** (so as) to see/*etc*; **h. de rire** (for the sake of) a laugh; **sans histoires** (*voyage etc*) uneventful. ◆**historien, -ienne** *nmf* historian. ◆**historique** *a* (*lieu, événement*) historic; *— nm* **faire l'h.** **de** to give an historical account of.

hiver [iver] *nm* winter. ◆**hivernal, -aux** *a* (*froid etc*) winter.

HLM ['aʃɛlɛm] *nm ou f abrév* (*habitation à loyer modéré*) = council flats, *Am* = low-rent apartment building (*sponsored by government*).

hoch/er ['ɔʃe] *vt* **h. la tête** (*pour dire oui*) to nod one's head; (*pour dire non*) to shake one's head. ◆**-ement** *nm* **h. de tête** nod; shake of the head.

hochet [ɔʃe] *nm* (*jouet*) rattle.

hockey ['ɔke] *nm* hockey; **h. sur glace** ice hockey.

holà! ['ɔla] *int* (*arrêtez*) hold on!, stop!; (*pour appeler*) hallo!; *— nm inv* **mettre le h. à** to put a stop to.

hold-up ['ɔldœp] *nm inv* (*attaque*) hold-up, stick-up.

Hollande ['ɔlɑ̃d] *nf* Holland. ◆**hollandais, -aise** *a* Dutch; *— nmf* H. Dutchman, Dutchwoman; *— nm* (*langue*) Dutch.

holocauste [ɔlɔkost] *nm* (*massacre*) holocaust.

homard [ɔmar] *nm* lobster.

homélie [ɔmeli] *nf* homily.

homéopathie [ɔmeɔpati] *nf* hom(o)eopathy.

homicide [ɔmisid] *nm* murder, homicide; **h. involontaire** manslaughter.

hommage [ɔmaʒ] *nm* tribute, homage (à to); *pl* (*civilités*) respects; **rendre h. à** to pay (a) tribute to, pay homage to.

homme [ɔm] *nm* man; **l'h.** (*espèce*) man(kind); **des vêtements d'h.** men's clothes; **d'h. à h.** man to man; **l'h. de la rue** *Fig* the man in the street; **h. d'affaires** businessman. ◆**h.-grenouille** *nm* (*pl* **hommes-grenouilles**) frogman.

homogène [ɔmɔʒɛn] *a* homogeneous. ◆**homogénéité** *nf* homogeneity.

homologue [ɔmɔlɔg] *a* equivalent (**de** to); *— nmf* counterpart, opposite number.

homologuer [ɔmɔlɔge] *vt* to approve *ou* recognize officially, validate.

homonyme [ɔmɔnim] *nm* (*personne, lieu*) namesake.

homosexuel, -elle [ɔmɔsɛksyɛl] *a* & *nmf* homosexual. ◆**homosexualité** *nf* homosexuality.

Hongrie ['ɔ̃gri] *nf* Hungary. ◆**hongrois, -oise** *a* & *nmf* Hungarian; *— nm* (*langue*) Hungarian.

honnête [ɔnɛt] *a* (*intègre*) honest; (*satisfaisant, passable*) decent, fair. ◆**honnêtement** *adv* honestly; decently. ◆**honnêteté** *nf* honesty.

honneur [ɔnœr] *nm* (*dignité, faveur*) honour; (*mérite*) credit; **en l'h. de** in honour of; **faire h. à** (*sa famille etc*) to be a credit to; (*par sa présence*) to do honour to; (*promesse etc*) to honour; (*repas*) to do justice to; **en h.** (*roman etc*) in vogue; **invité d'h.** guest of honour; **membre d'h.** honorary member; **avoir la place d'h.** to have pride of place *ou* the place of honour. ◆**honorabilité** *nf* respectability. ◆**honorable** *a* honourable; (*résultat, salaire etc*) Fig respectable. ◆**honoraire 1** *a* (*membre*) honorary. **2** *nmpl* (*d'avocat etc*) fees. ◆**honorer** *vt* to honour (**de** with); **h. qn** (*conduite etc*) to do credit to s.o.; **s'h. d'être** to pride oneself *ou* itself on being. ◆**honorifique** *a* (*titre*) honorary.

honte ['ɔ̃t] *nf* shame; **avoir h.** to be *ou* feel ashamed (**de qch/de faire** of sth/of doing, doing); **faire h. à** to put to shame; **fausse h.** self-consciousness. ◆**honteux, -euse** *a* (*déshonorant*) shameful; (*penaud*) ashamed, shamefaced; **être h. de** to be ashamed of. ◆**honteusement** *adv* shamefully.

hop! ['ɔp] *int* **allez, h.!** jump!, move!

hôpital, -aux [ɔpital, -o] *nm* hospital; **à l'h.** in hospital, *Am* in the hospital.

hoquet ['ɔke] *nm* hiccup; **le h.** (the) hiccups. ◆**hoqueter** *vi* to hiccup.

horaire [ɔrɛr] a (salaire etc) hourly; (vitesse) per hour; – nm timetable, schedule.

horde ['ɔrd] nf (troupe) Péj horde.

horizon [ɔrizɔ̃] nm horizon; (vue, paysage) view; à l'h. on the horizon.

horizontal, -aux [ɔrizɔ̃tal, -o] a horizontal. ◆**–ement** adv horizontally.

horloge [ɔrlɔʒ] nf clock. ◆**horloger, -ère** nmf watchmaker. ◆**horlogerie** nf (magasin) watchmaker's (shop); (industrie) watchmaking.

hormis ['ɔrmi] prép Litt save, except (for).

hormone [ɔrmɔn] nf hormone. ◆**hormonal, -aux** a (traitement etc) hormone-.

horoscope [ɔrɔskɔp] nm horoscope.

horreur [ɔrœr] nf horror; pl (propos) horrible things; **faire h. à** to disgust; **avoir h. de** to hate, loathe. ◆**horrible** a horrible, awful. ◆**horriblement** adv horribly. ◆**horrifiant** a horrifying, horrific. ◆**horrifié** a horrified.

horripiler [ɔripile] vt to exasperate.

hors ['ɔr] prép **h. de** (maison, boîte etc) outside, out of; (danger, haleine etc) Fig out of; **h. de doute** beyond doubt; **h. de soi** (furieux) beside oneself; **être h. jeu** Fb to be offside. ◆**h.-bord** nm inv speedboat; **moteur h.-bord** outboard motor. ◆**h.-concours** a inv non-competing. ◆**h.-d'œuvre** nm inv Culin starter, hors-d'œuvre. ◆**h.-jeu** nm inv Fb offside. ◆**h.-la-loi** nm inv outlaw. ◆**h.-taxe** a inv (magasin, objet) duty-free.

hortensia [ɔrtɑ̃sja] nm (arbrisseau) hydrangea.

horticole [ɔrtikɔl] a horticultural. ◆**horticulteur, -trice** nmf horticulturalist. ◆**horticulture** nf horticulture.

hospice [ɔspis] nm (pour vieillards) geriatric hospital.

hospitalier, -ière [ɔspitalje, -jɛr] a **1** (accueillant) hospitable. **2** (personnel etc) Méd hospital-. ◆**hospitaliser** vt to hospitalize. ◆**hospitalité** nf hospitality.

hostie [ɔsti] nf (pain) Rel host.

hostile [ɔstil] a hostile (à to, towards). ◆**hostilité** nf hostility (envers to, towards); pl Mil hostilities.

hôte [ot] **1** nm (maître) host. **2** nmf (invité) guest. ◆**hôtesse** nf hostess; **h. (de l'air)** (air) hostess.

hôtel [otɛl] nm hotel; **h. particulier** mansion, town house; **h. de ville** town hall; **h. des ventes** auction rooms. ◆**hôtelier, -ière** nmf hotel-keeper, hotelier; – a (industrie etc) hotel-. ◆**hôtellerie** nf **1** (auberge) inn, hostelry. **2** (métier) hotel trade.

hotte ['ɔt] nf **1** (panier) basket (carried on back). **2** (de cheminée etc) hood.

houblon ['ublɔ̃] nm **le h.** Bot hops.

houille ['uj] nf coal; **h. blanche** hydroelectric power. ◆**houiller, -ère** a (bassin, industrie) coal-; – nf coalmine, colliery.

houle ['ul] nf (de mer) swell, surge. ◆**houleux, -euse** a (mer) rough; (réunion etc) Fig stormy.

houppette ['upɛt] nf powder puff.

hourra ['ura] nm & int hurray, hurrah.

houspiller ['uspije] vt to scold, upbraid.

housse ['us] nf (protective) cover.

houx ['u] nm holly.

hublot ['yblo] nm Nau Av porthole.

huche ['yʃ] nf **h. à pain** bread box ou chest.

hue! ['y] int gee up! (to horse).

huer ['ɥe] vt to boo. ◆**huées** nfpl boos.

huile [ɥil] nf **1** oil; **peinture à l'h.** oil painting. **2** (personnage) Fam big shot. ◆**huiler** vt to oil. ◆**huileux, -euse** a oily.

huis [ɥi] nm **à h. clos** Jur in camera.

huissier [ɥisje] nm (introducteur) usher; (officier) Jur bailiff.

huit [ɥit] a (['ɥi] before consonant) eight; **h. jours** a week; – nm eight. ◆**huitaine** nf (about) eight; (semaine) week. ◆**huitième** a & nm eighth; **un h.** an eighth.

huître [ɥitr] nf oyster.

hululer ['ylyle] vi (hibou) to hoot.

humain [ymɛ̃] a human; (compatissant) humane; – nmpl humans. ◆**humainement** adv (possible etc) humanly; (avec humanité) humanely. ◆**humaniser** vt (prison, ville etc) to humanize, make more humane. ◆**humanitaire** a humanitarian. ◆**humanité** nf (genre humain, sentiment) humanity.

humble [œ̃bl] a humble. ◆**humblement** adv humbly.

humecter [ymɛkte] vt to moisten, damp(en).

humer ['yme] vt (respirer) to breathe in; (sentir) to smell.

humeur [ymœr] nf (caprice) mood, humour; (caractère) temperament; (irritation) bad temper; **bonne h.** (gaieté) good humour; **de bonne/mauvaise h.** in a good/bad mood ou humour; **égalité d'h.** evenness of temper.

humide [ymid] a damp, wet; (saison, route) wet; (main, yeux) moist; **climat/temps h.** (chaud) humid climate/weather; (froid, pluvieux) damp ou wet climate/weather. ◆**humidifier** vt to humidify. ◆**humidité** nf humidity; (plutôt froide) damp(ness); (vapeur) moisture.

humili/er [ymilje] vt to humiliate, humble.

◆—ant *a* humiliating. ◆humiliation *nf* humiliation. ◆humilité *nf* humility.

humour [ymur] *nm* humour; avoir de l'h. ou beaucoup d'h. *ou* le sens de l'h. to have a sense of humour. ◆humoriste *nmf* humorist. ◆humoristique *a* (*livre, ton etc*) humorous.

huppé ['ype] *a* (*riche*) *Fam* high-class, posh.

hurl/er [yrle] *vi* (*loup, vent*) to howl; (*personne*) to scream, yell; — *vt* (*slogans, injures etc*) to scream. ◆—ement *nm* howl; scream, yell.

hurluberlu [yrlyberly] *nm* (*personne*) scatterbrain.

hutte ['yt] *nf* hut.

hybride [ibrid] *a* & *nm* hybrid.

hydrater [idrate] *vt* (*peau*) to moisturize; crème hydratante moisturizing cream.

hydraulique [idrolik] *a* hydraulic.

hydravion [idravjɔ̃] *nm* seaplane.

hydro-électrique [idroelektrik] *a* hydroelectric.

hydrogène [idrɔʒɛn] *nm Ch* hydrogen.

hydrophile [idrɔfil] *a* coton h. cotton wool, *Am* (absorbent) cotton.

hyène [jɛn] *nf* (*animal*) hyena.

hygiaphone [iʒjafon] *nm* (hygienic) grill.

hygiène [iʒjɛn] *nf* hygiene. ◆hygiénique *a* hygienic; (*promenade*) healthy; (*serviette, conditions*) sanitary; papier h. toilet paper.

hymne [imn] *nm Rel Littér* hymn; h. national national anthem.

hyper- [iper] *préf* hyper-.

hypermarché [ipermarʃe] *nm* hypermarket.

hypertension [ipertɑ̃sjɔ̃] *nf* high blood pressure.

hypnose [ipnoz] *nf* hypnosis. ◆hypnotique *a* hypnotic. ◆hypnotiser *vt* to hypnotize. ◆hypnotiseur *nm* hypnotist. ◆hypnotisme *nm* hypnotism.

hypocrisie [ipɔkrizi] *nf* hypocrisy. ◆hypocrite *a* hypocritical; — *nmf* hypocrite.

hypodermique [ipɔdermik] *a* hypodermic.

hypothèque [ipotɛk] *nf* mortgage. ◆hypothéquer (*maison, avenir*) to mortgage.

hypothèse [ipotɛz] *nf* assumption; (*en sciences*) hypothesis; dans l'h. où . . . supposing (that) . . . . ◆hypothétique *a* hypothetical.

hystérie [isteri] *nf* hysteria. ◆hystérique *a* hysterical.

I

I, i [i] *nm* I, i.

iceberg [isberg] *nm* iceberg.

ici [isi] *adv* here; par i. (*passer*) this way; (*habiter*) around here, hereabouts; jusqu'i. (*temps*) up to now; (*lieu*) as far as this *ou* here; d'i. à mardi by Tuesday, between now and Tuesday; d'i. à une semaine within a week; d'i. peu before long; i. Dupont *Tél* this is Dupont, Dupont here; je ne suis pas d'i. I'm a stranger around here; les gens d'i. the people (from) around here, the locals. ◆i.-bas *adv* on earth.

icône [ikon] *nf Rel* icon.

idéal, -aux [ideal, -o] *a* & *nm* ideal; l'i. (*valeurs spirituelles*) ideals; c'est l'i. *Fam* that's the ideal thing. ◆idéalement *adv* ideally. ◆idéaliser *vt* to idealize. ◆idéalisme *nm* idealism. ◆idéaliste *a* idealistic; — *nmf* idealist.

idée [ide] *nf* idea (de of, que that); changer d'i. to change one's mind; il m'est venu à l'i. que it occurred to me that; se faire une i. de (*rêve*) to imagine; (*concept*) to get *ou* have

an idea of; avoir dans l'i. de faire to have it in mind to do; i. fixe obsession.

idem [idem] *adv* ditto.

identifier [idɑ̃tifje] *vt* to identify (à, avec with). ◆identification *nf* identification. ◆identique *a* identical (à to, with). ◆identité *nf* identity; carte d'i identity card.

idéologie [ideɔlɔʒi] *nf* ideology. ◆idéologique *a* ideological.

idiome [idjom] *nm* (*langue*) idiom. ◆idiomatique *a* idiomatic.

idiot, -ote [idjo, -ɔt] *a* idiotic, silly; — *nmf* idiot. ◆idiotement *adv* idiotically. ◆idiotie [-ɔsi] *nf* (*état*) idiocy; une i. an idiotic *ou* silly thing.

idole [idɔl] *nm* idol. ◆idolâtrer *vt* to idolize.

idylle [idil] *nf* (*amourette*) romance.

idyllique [idilik] *a* (*merveilleux*) idyllic.

if [if] *nm* yew (tree).

igloo [iglu] *nm* igloo.

ignare [iɲar] *a Péj* ignorant; — *nmf* ignoramus.

ignifugé [iɲifyʒe] *a* fireproof(ed).

ignoble [iɲɔbl] *a* vile, revolting.

ignorant [iɲɔrɑ̃] *a* ignorant (**de** of). ◆**ignorance** *nf* ignorance. ◆**ignor/er** *vt* not to know, be ignorant of; **j'ignore si** I don't know it; **i. qn** (*être indifférent à*) to ignore s.o., cold-shoulder s.o. ◆**-é** *a* (*inconnu*) unknown.

il [il] *pron* (*personne*) he; (*chose, animal*) it; **il est he** is; **it is**; **il pleut** it's raining; **il est vrai que** it's true that; **il y a** there is; *pl* there are; **il y a six ans** (*temps écoulé*) six years ago; **il y a une heure qu'il travaille** (*durée*) he's been working for an hour; **qu'est-ce qu'il y a?** what's the matter?, what's wrong?; **il n'y a pas de quoi!** don't mention it!; **il doit/peut y avoir** there must/may be.

île [il] *nf* island; **les îles Britanniques** the British Isles.

illégal, -aux [ilegal, -o] *a* illegal. ◆**illégalité** *nf* illegality.

illégitime [ileʒitim] *a* (*enfant, revendication*) illegitimate; (*non fondé*) unfounded.

illettré, -ée [iletre] *a* & *nmf* illiterate.

illicite [ilisit] *a* unlawful, illicit.

illico [iliko] *adv* **i.** (*presto*) *Fam* straightaway.

illimité [ilimite] *a* unlimited.

illisible [ilizibl] *a* (*écriture*) illegible; (*livre*) unreadable.

illogique [ilɔʒik] *a* illogical.

illumin/er [ilymine] *vt* to light up, illuminate; — **s'i.** *vpr* (*visage, personne, ciel*) to light up. ◆**-é** *a* (*monument*) floodlit, lit up. ◆**illumination** *nf* (*action, lumière*) illumination.

illusion [ilyzjɔ̃] *nf* illusion (**sur** about); **se faire des illusions** to delude oneself. ◆**s'illusionner** *vpr* to delude oneself (**sur** about). ◆**illusionniste** *nmf* conjurer. ◆**illusoire** *a* illusory, illusive.

illustre [ilystr] *a* famous, illustrious.

illustr/er [ilystre] *vt* (*d'images, par des exemples*) to illustrate (**de** with); — **s'i.** *vpr* to become famous. ◆**-é** *a* (*livre, magazine*) illustrated; — *nm* (*périodique*) comic. ◆**illustration** *nf* illustration.

îlot [ilo] *nm* **1** (*île*) small island. **2** (*maisons*) block.

ils [il] *pron* they; **ils sont** they are.

image [imaʒ] *nf* picture; (*ressemblance, symbole*) image; (*dans une glace*) reflection; **i. de marque** (*de firme etc*) (public) image. ◆**imagé** *a* (*style*) colourful, full of imagery.

imagination [imaʒinasjɔ̃] *nf* imagination; *pl* (*chimères*) imaginings.

imaginer [imaʒine] *vt* (*envisager, supposer*) to imagine; (*inventer*) to devise; — **s'i.** *vpr* (*se figurer*) to imagine (**que** that); (*se voir*) to imagine oneself. ◆**imaginable** *a* imaginable. ◆**imaginaire** *a* imaginary. ◆**imaginatif, -ive** *a* imaginative.

imbattable [ɛ̃batabl] *a* unbeatable.

imbécile [ɛ̃besil] *a* idiotic; — *nmf* imbecile, idiot. ◆**imbécillité** *nf* (*état*) imbecility; **une i.** (*action, parole*) an idiotic thing.

imbiber [ɛ̃bibe] *vt* to soak (**de** with, in); — **s'i.** *vpr* to become soaked.

imbriquer (s') [ɛ̃brike] *vpr* (*questions etc*) to overlap, be bound up with each other.

imbroglio [ɛ̃brɔljo] *nm* muddle, foul-up.

imbu [ɛ̃by] *a* **i. de** imbued with.

imbuvable [ɛ̃byvabl] *a* undrinkable; (*personne*) *Fig* insufferable.

imiter [imite] *vt* to imitate; (*contrefaire*) to forge; **i. qn** (*pour rire*) to mimic s.o., take s.o. off; (*faire comme*) to do the same as s.o., follow suit. ◆**imitateur, -trice** *nmf* imitator; (*artiste*) *Th* impersonator, mimic. ◆**imitatif, -ive** *a* imitative. ◆**imitation** *nf* imitation.

immaculé [imakyle] *a* (*sans tache, sans péché*) immaculate.

immangeable [ɛ̃mɑ̃ʒabl] *a* inedible.

immanquable [ɛ̃mɑ̃kabl] *a* inevitable.

immatriculer [imatrikyle] *vt* to register; **se faire i.** to register. ◆**immatriculation** *nf* registration.

immédiat [imedja] *a* immediate; — *nm* **dans l'i.** for the time being. ◆**immédiatement** *adv* immediately.

immense [imɑ̃s] *a* immense, vast. ◆**immensément** *adv* immensely. ◆**immensité** *nf* immensity, vastness.

immerger [imɛrʒe] *vt* to immerse, put under water; — **s'i.** *vpr* (*sous-marin*) to submerge. ◆**immersion** *nf* immersion; submersion.

immettable [ɛ̃metabl] *a* (*vêtement*) unfit to be worn.

immeuble [imœbl] *nm* building; (*d'habitation*) block of flats, *Am* apartment building; (*de bureaux*) office block.

immigr/er [imigre] *vi* to immigrate. ◆**-ant, -ante** *nmf* immigrant. ◆**-é, -ée** *a* & *nmf* immigrant. ◆**immigration** *nf* immigration.

imminent [iminɑ̃] *a* imminent. ◆**imminence** *nf* imminence.

immiscer (s') [simise] *vpr* to interfere (**dans** in).

immobile [imɔbil] *a* still, motionless. ◆**immobiliser** *vt* to immobilize; (*arrêter*) to stop; — **s'i.** *vpr* to stop, come to a standstill. ◆**immobilité** *nf* stillness; *(inactivité)* immobility.

immobilier, -ière [imɔbilje, -jɛr] *a (vente)* property-; *(société)* construction-; **agent i.** estate agent, *Am* real estate agent.

immodéré [imɔdere] *a* immoderate.

immonde [imɔ̃d] *a* filthy. ◆**immondices** *nfpl* refuse, rubbish.

immoral, -aux [imɔral, -o] *a* immoral. ◆**immoralité** *nf* immorality.

immortel, -elle [imɔrtɛl] *a* immortal. ◆**immortaliser** *vt* to immortalize. ◆**immortalité** *nf* immortality.

immuable [imɥabl] *a* immutable, unchanging.

immuniser [imynize] *vt* to immunize (**contre** against); **immunisé contre** *(à l'abri de) Méd* immune to *ou* from. ◆**immunitaire** *a (déficience etc) Méd* immune. ◆**immunité** *nf* immunity.

impact [ɛ̃pakt] *nm* impact (**sur** on).

impair [ɛ̃pɛr] **1** *a (nombre)* odd, uneven. **2** *nm (gaffe)* blunder.

imparable [ɛ̃parabl] *a (coup etc)* unavoidable.

impardonnable [ɛ̃pardɔnabl] *a* unforgivable.

imparfait [ɛ̃parfɛ] **1** *a (connaissance etc)* imperfect. **2** *nm (temps) Gram* imperfect.

impartial, -aux [ɛ̃parsjal, -o] *a* impartial, unbiased. ◆**impartialité** *nf* impartiality.

impartir [ɛ̃partir] *vt* to grant (**à** to).

impasse [ɛ̃pas] *nf (rue)* dead end, blind alley; *(situation) Fig* impasse; **dans l'i.** *(négociations)* in deadlock.

impassible [ɛ̃pasibl] *a* impassive, unmoved. ◆**impassibilité** *nf* impassiveness.

impatient [ɛ̃pasjɑ̃] *a* impatient; **i. de faire** eager *ou* impatient to do. ◆**impatiemment** [-amã] *adv* impatiently. ◆**impatience** *nf* impatience. ◆**impatienter** *vt* to annoy, make impatient; — **s'i.** *vpr* to get impatient.

impayable [ɛ̃pejabl] *a (comique) Fam* hilarious, priceless.

impayé [ɛ̃peje] *a* unpaid.

impeccable [ɛ̃pekabl] *a* impeccable, immaculate. ◆**—ment** [-amã] *adv* impeccably, immaculately.

impénétrable [ɛ̃penetrabl] *a (forêt, mystère etc)* impenetrable.

impénitent [ɛ̃penitɑ̃] *a* unrepentant.

impensable [ɛ̃pɑ̃sabl] *a* unthinkable.

imper [ɛ̃pɛr] *nm Fam* raincoat, mac.

impératif, -ive [ɛ̃peratif, -iv] *a (consigne,*

ton) imperative; — *nm (mode) Gram* imperative.

impératrice [ɛ̃peratris] *nf* empress.

imperceptible [ɛ̃pɛrsɛptibl] *a* imperceptible (**à** to).

imperfection [ɛ̃pɛrfɛksjɔ̃] *nf* imperfection.

impérial, -aux [ɛ̃perjal, -o] *a* imperial. ◆**impérialisme** *nm* imperialism.

impériale [ɛ̃perjal] *nf (d'autobus)* top deck.

impérieux, -euse [ɛ̃perjø, -øz] *a (autoritaire)* imperious; *(besoin)* pressing, imperative.

imperméable [ɛ̃pɛrmeabl] **1** *a* impervious (**à** to); *(manteau, tissu)* waterproof. **2** *nm* raincoat, mackintosh. ◆**imperméabilisé** *a* waterproof.

impersonnel, -elle [ɛ̃pɛrsɔnɛl] *a* impersonal.

impertinent [ɛ̃pɛrtinɑ̃] *a* impertinent (**envers** to). ◆**impertinence** *nf* impertinence.

imperturbable [ɛ̃pɛrtyrbabl] *a* unruffled, imperturbable.

impétueux, -euse [ɛ̃petɥø, -øz] *a* impetuous. ◆**impétuosité** *nf* impetuosity.

impitoyable [ɛ̃pitwajabl] *a* ruthless, pitiless, merciless.

implacable [ɛ̃plakabl] *a* implacable, relentless.

implanter [ɛ̃plɑ̃te] *vt (industrie, mode etc)* to establish; — **s'i.** *vpr* to become established. ◆**implantation** *nf* establishment.

implicite [ɛ̃plisit] *a* implicit. ◆**—ment** *adv* implicitly.

impliquer [ɛ̃plike] *vt (entraîner)* to imply; **i. que** *(supposer)* to imply that; **i. qn** *(engager)* to implicate s.o. (**dans** in). ◆**implication** *nf (conséquence, participation)* implication.

implorer [ɛ̃plɔre] *vt* to implore (**qn de faire** s.o. to do).

impoli [ɛ̃pɔli] *a* impolite, rude. ◆**impolitesse** *nf* impoliteness, rudeness; **une i.** an act of rudeness.

impopulaire [ɛ̃pɔpylɛr] *a* unpopular.

important [ɛ̃pɔrtɑ̃] *a (personnage, événement etc)* important; *(quantité, somme etc)* considerable, big, great; — *nm* **l'i., c'est de** ... the important thing is to .... ◆**importance** *nf* importance, significance; *(taille)* size; *(de dégâts)* extent; **ça n'a pas d'i.** it doesn't matter.

importer [ɛ̃pɔrte] **1** *v imp* to matter, be important (**à** to); **il importe de faire** it's important to do; **peu importe, n'importe** it doesn't matter; **n'importe qui/quoi/ où/quand/comment** anyone/anything/ anywhere/any time/anyhow. **2** *vt (marchandises etc)* to import (**de** from). ◆**im-**

portateur, -trice nmf importer; − a importing. ◆**importation** nf (objet) import; (action) import(ing), importation; **d'i.** (article) imported.

importun, -une [ɛ̃pɔrtœ̃, -yn] a troublesome, intrusive; − nmf nuisance, intruder. ◆**importuner** vt to inconvenience, trouble.

impos/er [ɛ̃poze] **1** vt to impose, enforce (à on); (exiger) to demand; (respect) to command; − vi **en i. à qn** to impress s.o., command respect from s.o.; − **s'i.** vpr (chez qn) Péj to impose; (s'affirmer) to assert oneself, compel recognition; (aller de soi) to stand out; (être nécessaire) to be essential. **2** vt Fin to tax. ◆**─ant** a imposing. ◆**─able** a Fin taxable. ◆**imposition** nf Fin taxation.

impossible [ɛ̃pɔsibl] a impossible (à faire to do); **il (nous) est i. de faire** it is impossible (for us) to do; **il est i. que** (+ sub) it is impossible that; **ça m'est i.** I cannot possibly; − nm faire l'i. to do the impossible. ◆**impossibilité** nf impossibility.

imposteur [ɛ̃pɔstœr] nm impostor. ◆**imposture** nf deception.

impôt [ɛ̃po] nm tax; pl (contributions) (income) tax, taxes; **i. sur le revenu** income tax.

impotent, -ente [ɛ̃pɔtɑ̃, -ɑ̃t] a crippled, disabled; − nmf cripple, invalid.

impraticable [ɛ̃pratikabl] a (projet etc) impracticable; (chemin etc) impassable.

imprécis [ɛ̃presi] a imprecise. ◆**imprécision** nf lack of precision.

imprégner [ɛ̃preɲe] vt to saturate, impregnate (de with); − **s'i.** vpr to become saturated ou impregnated (de with); **imprégné de** (idées) imbued ou infused with. ◆**imprégnation** nf saturation.

imprenable [ɛ̃prənabl] a Mil impregnable.

impresario [ɛ̃presarjo] nm (business) manager, impresario.

impression [ɛ̃presjɔ̃] nf **1** impression; **avoir l'i. que** to have the feeling ou impression that, be under the impression that; **faire une bonne i. à qn** to make a good impression on s.o. **2** Typ printing.

impression/er [ɛ̃presjɔne] vt (influencer) to impress; (émouvoir, troubler) to make a strong impression on. ◆**─ant** a impressive. ◆**─able** a impressionable.

imprévisible [ɛ̃previzibl] a unforeseeable. ◆**imprévoyance** nf lack of foresight. ◆**imprévoyant** a shortsighted. ◆**imprévu** a unexpected, unforeseen; − nm **en cas d'i.** in case of anything unexpected.

imprim/er [ɛ̃prime] vt **1** (livre etc) to print;

(trace) to impress (dans in); (cachet) to stamp. **2** (communiquer) Tech to impart (à to). ◆**─ante** nf (d'ordinateur) printer. ◆**─é** nm (formulaire) printed form; − nm(pl) (par la poste) printed matter. ◆**imprimerie** nf (technique) printing; (lieu) printing works. ◆**imprimeur** nm printer.

improbable [ɛ̃prɔbabl] a improbable, unlikely. ◆**improbabilité** nf improbability, unlikelihood.

impromptu [ɛ̃prɔ̃pty] a & adv impromptu.

impropre [ɛ̃prɔpr] a inappropriate; **i. à qch** unfit for sth. ◆**impropriété** nf (incorrection) Ling impropriety.

improviser [ɛ̃prɔvize] vti to improvise. ◆**improvisation** nf improvisation.

improviste (à l') [alɛ̃prɔvist] adv unexpectedly; **une visite à l'i.** an unexpected visit; **prendre qn à l'i.** to catch s.o. unawares.

imprudent [ɛ̃prydɑ̃] a (personne, action) careless, rash; **il est i. de** it is unwise to. ◆**imprudemment** [-amɑ̃] adv carelessly. ◆**imprudence** nf carelessness; **une i.** an act of carelessness.

impudent [ɛ̃pydɑ̃] a impudent ◆**impudence** nf impudence.

impudique [ɛ̃pydik] a lewd.

impuissant [ɛ̃pɥisɑ̃] a helpless; Méd impotent; **i. à faire** powerless to do. ◆**impuissance** nf helplessness; Méd impotence.

impulsif, -ive [ɛ̃pylsif, -iv] a impulsive. ◆**impulsion** nf impulse; **donner une i. à** (élan) Fig to give an impetus ou impulse to.

impunément [ɛ̃pynemɑ̃] adv with impunity. ◆**impuni** a unpunished.

impur [ɛ̃pyr] a impure. ◆**impureté** nf impurity.

imputer [ɛ̃pyte] vt to attribute, impute (à to); (affecter) Fin to charge (à to). ◆**imputable** a attributable (à to). ◆**imputation** nf Jur accusation.

inabordable [inabɔrdabl] a (lieu) inaccessible; (personne) unapproachable; (prix) prohibitive.

inacceptable [inaksɛptabl] a unacceptable.

inaccessible [inaksesibl] a inaccessible.

inaccoutumé [inakutyme] a unusual, unaccustomed.

inachevé [inaʃve] a unfinished.

inactif, -ive [inaktif, -iv] a inactive. ◆**inaction** nf inactivity, inaction. ◆**inactivité** nf inactivity.

inadapté, -ée [inadapte] a & nmf maladjusted (person). ◆**inadaptation** nf maladjustment.

inadmissible [inadmisibl] a unacceptable, inadmissible.

inadvertance (par) [parinadvertɑ̃s] adv inadvertently.

inaltérable [inalterabl] a (couleur) fast; (sentiment) unchanging.

inamical, -aux [inamikal, -o] a unfriendly.

inanimé [inanime] a (mort) lifeless; (évanoui) unconscious; (matière) inanimate.

inanité [inanite] nf (vanité) futility.

inanition [inanisjɔ̃] nf mourir d'i. to die of starvation.

inaperçu [inapɛrsy] a passer i. to go unnoticed.

inapplicable [inaplikabl] a inapplicable (à to).

inappliqué [inaplike] a (élève etc) inattentive.

inappréciable [inapresjabl] a invaluable.

inapte [inapt] a unsuited (à qch to sth), inept (à qch at sth); Mil unfit ◆**inaptitude** nf ineptitude, incapacity.

inarticulé [inartikyle] a (son) inarticulate.

inattaquable [inatakabl] a unassailable.

inattendu [inatɑ̃dy] a unexpected.

inattentif, -ive [inatɑ̃tif, -iv] a inattentive, careless; i. à (soucis, danger etc) heedless of. ◆**inattention** nf lack of attention; dans un moment d'i. in a moment of distraction.

inaudible [inodibl] a inaudible.

inaugurer [inogyre] vt (politique, édifice) to inaugurate; (école, congrès) to open, inaugurate; (statue) to unveil. ◆**inaugural, -aux** a inaugural. ◆**inauguration** nf inauguration; opening; unveiling.

inauthentique [inotɑ̃tik] a not authentic.

inavouable [inavwabl] a shameful.

incalculable [ɛ̃kalkylabl] a incalculable.

incandescent [ɛ̃kɑ̃desɑ̃] a incandescent.

incapable [ɛ̃kapabl] a incapable; i. de faire unable to do, incapable of doing; — nmf (personne) incompetent. ◆**incapacité** nf incapacity, inability (de faire to do); Méd disability, incapacity.

incarcérer [ɛ̃karsere] vt to incarcerate. ◆**incarcération** nf incarceration.

incarné [ɛ̃karne] a (ongle) ingrown.

incarner [ɛ̃karne] vt to embody, incarnate. ◆**incarnation** nf embodiment, incarnation.

incartade [ɛ̃kartad] nf indiscretion, prank.

incassable [ɛ̃kasabl] a unbreakable.

incendie [ɛ̃sɑ̃di] nm fire; (guerre) Fig conflagration. ◆**incendiaire** nf arsonist; — a (bombe) incendiary; (discours) inflammatory. ◆**incendier** vt to set fire to, set on fire.

incertain [ɛ̃sertɛ̃] a uncertain; (temps) unsettled; (entreprise) chancy; (contour) indistinct. ◆**incertitude** nf uncertainty.

incessamment [ɛ̃sesamɑ̃] adv without delay, shortly.

incessant [ɛ̃sesɑ̃] a incessant.

inceste [ɛ̃sest] nm incest. ◆**incestueux, -euse** a incestuous.

inchangé [ɛ̃ʃɑ̃ʒe] a unchanged.

incidence [ɛ̃sidɑ̃s] nf (influence) effect.

incident [ɛ̃sidɑ̃] nm incident; (accroc) hitch.

incinérer [ɛ̃sinere] vt (ordures) to incinerate; (cadavre) to cremate. ◆**incinération** nf incineration; cremation.

inciser [ɛ̃size] vt to make an incision in. ◆**incision** nf (entaille) incision.

incisif, -ive [ɛ̃sizif, -iv] a incisive, sharp.

incisive [ɛ̃siziv] nf (dent) incisor.

inciter [ɛ̃site] vt to urge, incite (à faire to do). ◆**incitation** nf incitement (à to).

incliner [ɛ̃kline] vt (courber) to bend; (pencher) to tilt, incline; i. la tête (approuver) to nod one's head; (révérence) to bow (one's head); i. qn à faire to make s.o. inclined to do, incline s.o. to do; — vi i. à to be inclined towards; — s'i. vpr (se courber) to bow (down); (s'avouer vaincu) to admit defeat; (chemin) to slope down. ◆**inclinaison** nf incline, slope. ◆**inclination** nf (goût) inclination; (de tête) nod, (révérence) bow.

incl/ure [ɛ̃klyr] vt to include; (enfermer) to enclose. ◆**-us** a inclusive; du quatre jusqu'au dix mai i. from the fourth to the tenth of May inclusive; jusqu'à lundi i. up to and including (next) Monday. ◆**inclusion** nf inclusion. ◆**inclusivement** adv inclusively.

incognito [ɛ̃kɔɲito] adv incognito.

incohérent [ɛ̃kɔerɑ̃] a incoherent. ◆**incohérence** nf incoherence.

incollable [ɛ̃kɔlabl] a Fam infallible, unable to be caught out.

incolore [ɛ̃kɔlɔr] a colourless; (verre, vernis) clear.

incomber [ɛ̃kɔ̃be] vi i. à qn (devoir) to fall to s.o.; il lui incombe de faire it's his ou her duty ou responsiblity to do.

incommode [ɛ̃kɔmɔd] a awkward. ◆**incommodité** nf awkwardness.

incommod/er [ɛ̃kɔmɔde] vt to bother, annoy. ◆**-ant** a annoying.

incomparable [ɛ̃kɔ̃parabl] a incomparable.

incompatible [ɛ̃kɔ̃patibl] a incompatible, inconsistent (avec with). ◆**incompatibilité** nf incompatibility, inconsistency.

incompétent [ɛ̃kɔ̃petɑ̃] *a* incompetent. ◆**incompétence** *nf* incompetence.

incomplet, -ète [ɛ̃kɔ̃ple, -ɛt] *a* incomplete; (*fragmentaire*) scrappy, sketchy.

incompréhensible [ɛ̃kɔ̃preɑ̃sibl] *a* incomprehensible. ◆**incompréhensif, -ive** *a* uncomprehending, lacking understanding. ◆**incompréhension** *nf* lack of understanding. ◆**incompris** *a* misunderstood.

inconcevable [ɛ̃kɔ̃svabl] *a* inconceivable.

inconciliable [ɛ̃kɔ̃siljabl] *a* irreconcilable.

inconditionnel, -elle [ɛ̃kɔ̃disjɔnɛl] *a* unconditional.

inconfort [ɛ̃kɔ̃fɔr] *nm* lack of comfort. ◆**inconfortable** *a* uncomfortable.

incongru [ɛ̃kɔ̃gry] *a* unseemly, incongruous.

inconnu, -ue [ɛ̃kɔny] *a* unknown (à to); – *nmf* (*étranger*) stranger; (*auteur*) unknown; – *nm* **l'i.** the unknown; – *nf* Math unknown (quantity).

inconscient [ɛ̃kɔ̃sjɑ̃] *a* unconscious (de of); (*irréfléchi*) thoughtless, senseless; – *nm* **l'i.** Psy the unconscious. ◆**inconsciemment** [-amɑ̃] *adv* unconsciously. ◆**inconscience** *nf* (*physique*) unconsciousness; (*irréflexion*) utter thoughtlessness.

inconséquence [ɛ̃kɔ̃sekɑ̃s] *nf* inconsistency.

inconsidéré [ɛ̃kɔ̃sidere] *a* thoughtless.

inconsolable [ɛ̃kɔ̃sɔlabl] *a* inconsolable.

inconstant [ɛ̃kɔ̃stɑ̃] *a* fickle. ◆**inconstance** *nf* fickleness.

incontestable [ɛ̃kɔ̃tɛstabl] *a* undeniable, indisputable. ◆**incontesté** *a* undisputed.

incontinent [ɛ̃kɔ̃tinɑ̃] *a* incontinent.

incontrôlé [ɛ̃kɔ̃trole] *a* unchecked. ◆**incontrôlable** *a* unverifiable.

inconvenant [ɛ̃kɔ̃vnɑ̃] *a* improper. ◆**inconvenance** *nf* impropriety.

inconvénient [ɛ̃kɔ̃venjɑ̃] *nm* (*désavantage*) drawback; (*risque*) risk; (*objection*) objection.

incorporer [ɛ̃kɔrpɔre] *vt* (*introduire, admettre*) to incorporate (dans into); (*ingrédient*) to blend (à with); Mil to enrol. ◆**incorporation** *nf* incorporation (de of); Mil enrolment.

incorrect [ɛ̃kɔrɛkt] *a* (*inexact*) incorrect; (*inconvenant*) improper; (*grossier*) impolite. ◆**incorrection** *nf* (*faute*) impropriety, error; (*inconvenance*) impropriety; **une i.** (*grossièreté*) an impolite word *ou* act.

incorrigible [ɛ̃kɔriʒibl] *a* incorrigible.

incorruptible [ɛ̃kɔryptibl] *a* incorruptible.

incrédule [ɛ̃kredyl] *a* incredulous. ◆**incrédulité** *nf* disbelief, incredulity.

increvable [ɛ̃krəvabl] *a* (*robuste*) Fam tireless.

incriminer [ɛ̃krimine] *vt* to incriminate.

incroyable [ɛ̃krwajabl] *a* incredible, unbelievable. ◆**incroyablement** *adv* incredibly. ◆**incroyant, -ante** *a* unbelieving; – *nmf* unbeliever.

incrusté [ɛ̃kryste] *a* (*de tartre*) encrusted; **i. de** (*orné*) inlaid with. ◆**incrustation** *nf* (*ornement*) inlay; (*action*) inlaying.

incruster (s') [sɛ̃kryste] *vpr* (*chez qn*) Fig to dig oneself in, be difficult to get rid of.

incubation [ɛ̃kybasjɔ̃] *nf* incubation.

inculp/er [ɛ̃kylpe] *vt* Jur to charge (de with), indict (de for). ◆**-é, -ée** *nmf* **l'i.** the accused. ◆**inculpation** *nf* charge, indictment.

inculquer [ɛ̃kylke] *vt* to instil (à into).

inculte [ɛ̃kylt] *a* (*terre*) uncultivated; (*personne*) uneducated.

incurable [ɛ̃kyrabl] *a* incurable.

incursion [ɛ̃kyrsjɔ̃] *nf* incursion, inroad (dans into).

incurver [ɛ̃kyrve] *vt* to curve.

Inde [ɛ̃d] *nf* India.

indécent [ɛ̃desɑ̃] *a* indecent. ◆**indécemment** [-amɑ̃] *adv* indecently. ◆**indécence** *nf* indecency.

indéchiffrable [ɛ̃deʃifrabl] *a* undecipherable.

indécis [ɛ̃desi] *a* (*victoire, résultat*) undecided; (*indistinct*) vague; **être i.** (*hésiter*) to be undecided; (*de tempérament*) to be indecisive *ou* irresolute. ◆**indécision** *nf* indecisiveness, indecision.

indéfectible [ɛ̃defɛktibl] *a* unfailing.

indéfendable [ɛ̃defɑ̃dabl] *a* indefensible.

indéfini [ɛ̃defini] *a* (*indéterminé*) indefinite; (*imprécis*) undefined. ◆**indéfiniment** *adv* indefinitely. ◆**indéfinissable** *a* indefinable.

indéformable [ɛ̃defɔrmabl] *a* (*vêtement*) which keeps its shape.

indélébile [ɛ̃delebil] *a* (*encre, souvenir*) indelible.

indélicat [ɛ̃delika] *a* (*grossier*) indelicate; (*malhonnête*) unscrupulous.

indemne [ɛ̃demn] *a* unhurt, unscathed.

indemniser [ɛ̃demnize] *vt* to indemnify, compensate (de for). ◆**indemnisation** *nf* compensation. ◆**indemnité** *nf* (*dédommagement*) indemnity; (*allocation*) allowance.

indémontable [ɛ̃demɔ̃tabl] *a* that cannot be taken apart.

indéniable [ɛ̃denjabl] *a* undeniable.

indépendant [ɛ̃depɑ̃dɑ̃] *a* independent (de

of); (*chambre*) self-contained; (*journaliste*) freelance. ◆**indépendamment** *adv* independently (**de** of); **i. de** (*sans aucun égard à*) apart from. ◆**indépendance** *nf* independence.

indescriptible [ɛ̃dɛskriptibl] *a* indescribable.

indésirable [ɛ̃dezirabl] *a* & *nmf* undesirable.

indestructible [ɛ̃dɛstryktibl] *a* indestructible.

indéterminé [ɛ̃detɛrmine] *a* indeterminate. ◆**indétermination** *nf* (*doute*) indecision.

index [ɛ̃dɛks] *nm* (*liste*) index; *Anat* forefinger, index finger.

indexer [ɛ̃dɛkse] *vt* *Écon* to index-link, tie (**sur** to).

indicateur, -trice [ɛ̃dikatœr, -tris] **1** *nmf* (*espion*) (police) informer. **2** *nm* *Rail* guide, timetable; *Tech* indicator, gauge. **3** *a* poteau **i.** signpost. ◆**indicatif, -ive 1** *a* indicative (**de** of); — *nm* *Mus* signature tune; *Tél* dialling code, *Am* area code. **2** *nm* (*mode*) *Gram* indicative. ◆**indication** *nf* indication (**de** of); (*renseignement*) (piece of) information; (*directive*) instruction.

indice [ɛ̃dis] *nm* (*indication*) sign; (*dans une enquête*) *Jur* clue; (*des prix*) index; (*de salaire*) grade; **i. d'écoute** *TV* *Rad* rating.

indien, -ienne [ɛ̃djɛ̃, -jɛn] *a* & *nmf* Indian.

indifférent [ɛ̃diferã] *a* indifferent (**à** to); **ça m'est i.** that's all the same to me. ◆**indifféremment** [-amã] *adv* indifferently. ◆**indifférence** *nf* indifference (**à** to).

indigène [ɛ̃diʒɛn] *a* & *nmf* native.

indigent [ɛ̃diʒã] *a* (very) poor. ◆**indigence** *nf* poverty.

indigeste [ɛ̃diʒɛst] *a* indigestible. ◆**indigestion** *nf* (attack of) indigestion.

indigne [ɛ̃diɲ] *a* (*personne*) unworthy; (*chose*) shameful; **i. de qn**/*qch* unworthy of s.o./sth. ◆**indignité** *nf* unworthiness; **une i.** (*honte*) an indignity.

indigner [ɛ̃diɲe] *vt* **i. qn** to make s.o. indignant; — **s'i.** *vpr* to be ou become indignant (**de** at). ◆**indignation** *nf* indignation.

indigo [ɛ̃digo] *nm* & *a inv* (*couleur*) indigo.

indiqu/er [ɛ̃dike] *vt* (*montrer*) to indicate; (*dire*) to point out, tell; (*recommander*) to recommend; **i. du doigt** to point to ou at. ◆**-é** *a* (*heure*) appointed; (*conseillé*) recommended; (*adéquat*) appropriate.

indirect [ɛ̃dirɛkt] *a* indirect. ◆**—ement** *adv* indirectly.

indiscipline [ɛ̃disiplin] *nf* lack of discipline. ◆**indiscipliné** *a* unruly.

indiscret, -ète [ɛ̃diskrɛ, -ɛt] *a* (*indélicat*) indiscreet, tactless; (*curieux*) *Péj* inquisitive, prying. ◆**indiscrétion** *nf* indiscretion.

indiscutable [ɛ̃diskytabl] *a* indisputable.

indispensable [ɛ̃dispãsabl] *a* indispensable, essential.

indispos/er [ɛ̃dispoze] *vt* (*incommoder*) to make unwell, upset; **i. qn** (**contre soi**) (*mécontenter*) to antagonize s.o. ◆**-é** *a* (*malade*) indisposed, unwell. ◆**indisposition** *nf* indisposition.

indissoluble [ɛ̃disɔlybl] *a* (*liens etc*) solid, indissoluble.

indistinct, -incte [ɛ̃distɛ̃(kt), -ɛ̃kt] *a* indistinct. ◆**—ement** [-ɛ̃ktəmã] *adv* indistinctly; (*également*) without distinction.

individu [ɛ̃dividy] *nm* individual. ◆**individualiser** *vt* to individualize. ◆**individualiste** *a* individualistic; — *nmf* individualist. ◆**individualité** *nf* (*originalité*) individuality. ◆**individuel, -elle** *a* individual. ◆**individuellement** *adv* individually.

indivisible [ɛ̃divizibl] *a* indivisible.

Indochine [ɛ̃dɔʃin] *nf* Indo-China.

indolent [ɛ̃dɔlã] *a* indolent. ◆**indolence** *nf* indolence.

indolore [ɛ̃dɔlɔr] *a* painless.

indomptable [ɛ̃dɔ̃tabl] *a* (*énergie, volonté*) indomitable. ◆**indompté** *a* (*animal*) untamed.

Indonésie [ɛ̃dɔnezi] *nf* Indonesia.

indubitable [ɛ̃dybitabl] *a* beyond doubt.

indue [ɛ̃dy] *af* **à une heure i.** at an ungodly hour.

induire* [ɛ̃dɥir] *vt* **i. qn en erreur** to lead s.o. astray.

indulgent [ɛ̃dylʒã] *a* indulgent (**envers** to, **avec** with). ◆**indulgence** *nf* indulgence.

industrie [ɛ̃dystri] *nf* industry. ◆**industrialisé** *a* industrialized. ◆**industriel, -elle** *a* industrial; — *nmf* industrialist.

inébranlable [inebrãlabl] *a* (*certitude, personne*) unshakeable, unwavering.

inédit [inedi] *a* (*texte*) unpublished; (*nouveau*) *Fig* original.

ineffable [inefabl] *a* *Litt* inexpressible, ineffable.

inefficace [inefikas] *a* (*mesure, effort etc*) ineffective, ineffectual; (*personne*) inefficient. ◆**inefficacité** *nf* ineffectiveness; inefficiency.

inégal, -aux [inegal, -o] *a* unequal; (*sol, humeur*) uneven. ◆**inégalable** *a* incomparable. ◆**inégalé** *a* unequalled. ◆**inégalité** *nf* (*morale*) inequality; (*physique*) difference; (*irrégularité*) unevenness; *pl* (*bosses*) bumps.

inélégant [inelegã] *a* coarse, inelegant.

inéligible [ineliʒibl] *a* (*candidat*) ineligible.

inéluctable [inelyktabl] *a* inescapable.

inepte [inɛpt] *a* absurd, inept. ◆**ineptie** [-si] *nf* absurdity, ineptitude.

inépuisable [inepɥizabl] *a* inexhaustible.

inerte [inɛrt] *a* inert; (*corps*) lifeless. ◆**inertie** [-si] *nf* inertia.

inespéré [inespere] *a* unhoped-for.

inestimable [inestimabl] *a* priceless.

inévitable [inevitabl] *a* inevitable, unavoidable.

inexact [inɛgzakt] *a* (*erroné*) inaccurate, inexact; **c'est i.!** it's incorrect! ◆**inexactitude** *nf* inaccuracy, inexactitude; (*manque de ponctualité*) lack of punctuality.

inexcusable [inɛkskyzabl] *a* inexcusable.

inexistant [inɛgzistã] *a* non-existent.

inexorable [inɛgzɔrabl] *a* inexorable.

inexpérience [inɛksperjãs] *nf* inexperience. ◆**inexpérimenté** *a* (*personne*) inexperienced; (*machine, arme*) untested.

inexplicable [inɛksplikabl] *a* inexplicable. ◆**inexpliqué** *a* unexplained.

inexploré [inɛksplɔre] *a* unexplored.

inexpressif, -ive [inɛkspresif, -iv] *a* expressionless.

inexprimable [inɛksprimabl] *a* inexpressible.

inextricable [inɛkstrikabl] *a* inextricable.

infaillible [ɛfajibl] *a* infallible. ◆**infaillibilité** *nf* infallibility.

infaisable [ɛfəzabl] *a* (*travail etc*) that cannot be done.

infamant [ɛfamã] *a* ignominious.

infâme [ɛfam] *a* (*odieux*) vile, infamous; (*taudis*) squalid. ◆**infamie** *nf* infamy.

infanterie [ɛfãtri] *nf* infantry.

infantile [ɛfãtil] *a* (*maladie, réaction*) infantile.

infarctus [ɛfarktys] *nm* **un i.** *Méd* a coronary.

infatigable [ɛfatigabl] *a* tireless, indefatigable.

infect [ɛfɛkt] *a* (*puant*) foul; (*mauvais*) lousy, vile.

infecter [ɛfɛkte] **1** *vt* (*air*) to contaminate, foul. **2** *vt Méd* to infect; — **s'i.** *vpr* to get infected. ◆**infectieux, -euse** *a* infectious. ◆**infection** *nf* **1** *Méd* infection. **2** (*odeur*) stench.

inférer [ɛfere] *vt* (*conclure*) to infer (**de** from, **que** that).

inférieur, -eure [ɛferjœr] *a* (*partie*) lower; (*qualité, personne*) inferior; **à l'étage i.** on the floor below; **i. à** inferior to; (*plus petit que*) smaller than; — *nmf* (*personne*) *Péj* inferior. ◆**infériorité** *nf* inferiority.

infernal, -aux [ɛfɛrnal, -o] *a* infernal.

infest/er [ɛfɛste] *vt* to infest, overrun (**de** with). ◆**—é** *a* **i. de requins/de fourmis/***etc* shark-/ant-/*etc* infested.

infidèle [ɛfidɛl] *a* unfaithful (**à** to). ◆**infidélité** *nf* unfaithfulness; **une i.** (*acte*) an infidelity.

infiltrer (s') [sɛfiltre] *vpr* (*liquide*) to seep *ou* percolate (through) (**dans** into); (*lumière*) to filter (through) (**dans** into); **s'i. dans** (*groupe, esprit*) *Fig* to infiltrate. ◆**infiltration** *nf* (*de personne, idée, liquide*) infiltration.

infime [ɛfim] *a* (*très petit*) tiny; (*personne*) *Péj* lowly.

infini [ɛfini] *a* infinite; — *nm Math Phot* infinity; *Phil* infinite; **à l'i.** (*beaucoup*) *ad* infinitum, endlessly; *Math* to infinity. ◆**infiniment** *adv* infinitely; (*regretter, remercier*) very much. ◆**infinité** *nf* **une i. de** an infinite amount of.

infinitif [ɛfinitif] *nm Gram* infinitive.

infirme [ɛfirm] *a* disabled, crippled; — *nmf* disabled person. ◆**infirmité** *nf* disability.

infirmer [ɛfirme] *vt* to invalidate.

infirmerie [ɛfirməri] *nf* infirmary, sickbay. ◆**infirmier** *nm* male nurse. ◆**infirmière** *nf* nurse.

inflammable [ɛflamabl] *a* (in)flammable.

inflammation [ɛflamasjõ] *nf Méd* inflammation.

inflation [ɛflasjõ] *nf Écon* inflation. ◆**inflationniste** *a Écon* inflationary.

infléchir [ɛfleʃir] *vt* (*courber*) to inflect, bend; (*modifier*) to shift. ◆**inflexion** *nf* bend; (*de voix*) tone, inflexion; **une i. de la tête** a nod.

inflexible [ɛflɛksibl] *a* inflexible.

infliger [ɛfliʒe] *vt* to inflict (**à** on); (*amende*) to impose (**à** on).

influence [ɛflyãs] *nf* influence. ◆**influencer** *vt* to influence. ◆**influençable** *a* easily influenced. ◆**influent** *a* influential. ◆**influer** *vi* **i. sur** to influence.

information [ɛfɔrmasjõ] *nf* information; (*nouvelle*) piece of news; (*enquête*) *Jur* inquiry; *pl* information; *Journ Rad TV* news.

informatique [ɛfɔrmatik] *nf* (*science*) computer science; (*technique*) data processing. ◆**informaticien, -ienne** *nmf* computer scientist. ◆**informatiser** *vt* to computerize.

informe [ɛfɔrm] *a* shapeless.

informer [ɛfɔrme] *vt* to inform (**de** of, about;

que that); **— s'i.** *vpr* to inquire (**de** about; **si** if, whether). **◆informateur, -trice** *nmf* informant.

infortune [ɛ̃fɔrtyn] *nf* misfortune. **◆infortuné** *a* ill-fated, hapless.

infraction [ɛ̃fraksjɔ̃] *nf* (*délit*) offence; **i. à** breach of, infringement of.

infranchissable [ɛ̃frɑ̃ʃisabl] *a* (*mur, fleuve*) impassable; (*difficulté*) Fig insuperable.

infrarouge [ɛ̃fraruʒ] *a* infrared.

infroissable [ɛ̃frwasabl] *a* crease-resistant.

infructueux, -euse [ɛ̃fryktɥø, -øz] *a* fruitless.

infuser [ɛ̃fyze] *vt* (**faire**) **i.** (*thé*) to infuse. **◆infusion** *nf* (*tisane*) (herb *ou* herbal) tea, infusion.

ingénier (s') [sɛ̃ʒenje] *vpr* to exercise one's wits (**à faire** in order to do).

ingénieur [ɛ̃ʒenjœr] *nm* engineer. **◆ingénierie** [-iri] *nf* engineering.

ingénieux, -euse [ɛ̃ʒenjø, -øz] *a* ingenious. **◆ingéniosité** *nf* ingenuity.

ingénu [ɛ̃ʒeny] *a* artless, naïve.

ingérer (s') [sɛ̃ʒere] *vpr* to interfere (**dans** in). **◆ingérence** *nf* interference.

ingrat [ɛ̃gra] *a* (*personne*) ungrateful (**envers** to); (*sol*) barren; (*tâche*) thankless; (*visage, physique*) unattractive; (*âge*) awkward. **◆ingratitude** *nf* ingratitude.

ingrédient [ɛ̃gredjɑ̃] *nm* ingredient.

inguérissable [ɛ̃gerisabl] *a* incurable.

ingurgiter [ɛ̃gyrʒite] *vt* to gulp down.

inhabitable [inabitabl] *a* uninhabitable. **◆inhabité** *a* uninhabited.

inhabituel, -elle [inabitɥɛl] *a* unusual.

inhalateur [inalatœr] *nm* Méd inhaler. **◆inhalation** *nf* inhalation; **faire des inhalations** to inhale.

inhérent [inerɑ̃] *a* inherent (**à** in).

inhibé [inibe] *a* inhibited. **◆inhibition** *nf* inhibition.

inhospitalier, -ière [inɔspitalje, -jɛr] *a* inhospitable.

inhumain [inymɛ̃] *a* (*cruel, terrible*) inhuman.

inhumer [inyme] *vt* to bury, inter. **◆inhumation** *nf* burial.

inimaginable [inimaʒinabl] *a* unimaginable.

inimitable [inimitabl] *a* inimitable.

inimitié [inimitje] *nf* enmity.

ininflammable [inɛ̃flamabl] *a* (*tissu etc*) non-flammable.

inintelligent [inɛ̃teliʒɑ̃] *a* unintelligent.

inintelligible [inɛ̃teliʒibl] *a* unintelligible.

inintéressant [inɛ̃teresɑ̃] *a* uninteresting.

ininterrompu [inɛ̃terɔ̃py] *a* uninterrupted, continuous.

inique [inik] *a* iniquitous. **◆iniquité** *nf* iniquity.

initial, -aux [inisjal, -o] *a* initial. **◆initiale** *nf* (*lettre*) initial. **◆initialement** *adv* initially.

initiative [inisjativ] *nf* **1** initiative. **2** **syndicat d'i.** tourist office.

initi/er [inisje] *vt* to initiate (**à** into); **s'i. à** (*art, science*) to become acquainted with *ou* initiated into. **◆–é, -ée** *nmf* initiate; **les initiés** the initiated. **◆initiateur, -trice** *nmf* initiator. **◆initiation** *nf* initiation.

injecter [ɛ̃ʒɛkte] *vt* to inject; **injecté de sang** bloodshot. **◆injection** *nf* injection.

injonction [ɛ̃ʒɔ̃ksjɔ̃] *nf* order, injunction.

injure [ɛ̃ʒyr] *nf* insult; *pl* abuse, insults. **◆injurier** *vt* to abuse, insult, swear at. **◆injurieux, -euse** *a* abusive, insulting (**pour** to).

injuste [ɛ̃ʒyst] *a* (*contraire à la justice*) unjust; (*partial*) unfair. **◆injustice** *nf* injustice.

injustifiable [ɛ̃ʒystifjabl] *a* unjustifiable. **◆injustifié** *a* unjustified.

inlassable [ɛ̃lasabl] *a* untiring.

inné [ine] *a* innate, inborn.

innocent, -ente [inɔsɑ̃, -ɑ̃t] *a* innocent (**de** of); *— nmf* Jur innocent person; (*idiot*) simpleton. **◆innocemment** [-amɑ̃] *adv* innocently. **◆innocence** *nf* innocence. **◆innocenter** *vt* **i. qn** to clear s.o. (**de** of).

innombrable [inɔ̃brabl] *a* innumerable.

innommable [inɔmabl] *a* (*dégoûtant*) unspeakable, foul.

innover [inɔve] *vi* to innovate. **◆innovateur, -trice** *nmf* innovator. **◆innovation** *nf* innovation.

inoccupé [inɔkype] *a* unoccupied.

inoculer [inɔkyle] *vt* **i. qch à qn** to infect *ou* inoculate s.o. with sth. **◆inoculation** *nf* (*vaccination*) inoculation.

inodore [inɔdɔr] *a* odourless.

inoffensif, -ive [inɔfɑ̃sif, -iv] *a* harmless, inoffensive.

inonder [inɔ̃de] *vt* to flood, inundate; (*mouiller*) to soak; **inondé de** (*envahi*) inundated with; **inondé de soleil** bathed in sunlight. **◆inondable** *a* (*chaussée etc*) liable to flooding. **◆inondation** *nf* flood; (*action*) flooding (**de** of).

inopérant [inɔperɑ̃] *a* inoperative.

inopiné [inɔpine] *a* unexpected.

inopportun [inɔpɔrtœ̃] *a* inopportune.

inoubliable [inublijabl] *a* unforgettable.

inouï [inwi] *a* incredible, extraordinary.

inox [inɔks] *nm* stainless steel; **en i.** (*couteau etc*) stainless-steel. ◆**inoxydable** *a* (*couteau etc*) stainless-steel; **acier i.** stainless steel.

inqualifiable [ɛ̃kalifjabl] *a* (*indigne*) unspeakable.

inquiet, -iète [ɛ̃kjɛ, -jɛt] *a* anxious, worried (**de** about). ◆**inquiét/er** *vt* (*préoccuper*) to worry; (*police*) to bother, harass (*suspect etc*); — **s'i.** *vpr* to worry (**de** about). ◆**-ant** *a* worrying. ◆**inquiétude** *nf* anxiety, concern, worry.

inquisiteur, -trice [ɛ̃kizitœr, -tris] *a* (*regard*) *Péj* inquisitive. ◆**inquisition** *nf* inquisition.

insaisissable [ɛ̃sezisabl] *a* elusive.

insalubre [ɛ̃salybr] *a* unhealthy, insalubrious.

insanités [ɛ̃sanite] *nfpl* (*idioties*) absurdities.

insatiable [ɛ̃sasjabl] *a* insatiable.

insatisfait [ɛ̃satisfɛ] *a* unsatisfied, dissatisfied.

inscrire* [ɛ̃skrir] *vt* to write *ou* put down; (*sur un registre*) to register; (*graver*) to inscribe; **i. qn** to enrol s.o.; — **s'i.** *vpr* to enrol (**à** at); **s'i. à** (*parti, club*) to join, enrol in; (*examen*) to enter *ou* enrol *ou* register for; **s'i. dans** (**le cadre de**) to be part of; **s'i. en faux contre** to deny absolutely. ◆**inscription** *nf* writing down; enrolment; registration; (*de médaille, sur écriteau etc*) inscription; **frais d'i.** *Univ* tuition fees.

insecte [ɛ̃sɛkt] *nm* insect. ◆**insecticide** *nm* insecticide.

insécurité [ɛ̃sekyrite] *nf* insecurity.

insémination [ɛ̃seminasjɔ̃] *nf* *Méd* insemination.

insensé [ɛ̃sɑ̃se] *a* senseless, absurd.

insensible [ɛ̃sɑ̃sibl] *a* (*indifférent*) insensitive (**à** to); (*graduel*) imperceptible, very slight. ◆**insensiblement** *adv* imperceptibly. ◆**insensibilité** *nf* insensitivity.

inséparable [ɛ̃separabl] *a* inseparable (**de** from).

insérer [ɛ̃sere] *vt* to insert (**dans** into, in); **s'i. dans** (*programme etc*) to be part of. ◆**insertion** *nf* insertion.

insidieux, -euse [ɛ̃sidjø, -øz] *a* insidious.

insigne [ɛ̃siɲ] *nm* badge, emblem; *pl* (*de maire etc*) insignia.

insignifiant [ɛ̃siɲifjɑ̃] *a* insignificant, unimportant. ◆**insignifiance** *nf* insignificance.

insinuer [ɛ̃sinɥe] *vt* *Péj* to insinuate (**que** that); — **s'i.** *vpr* to insinuate oneself (**dans** into). ◆**insinuation** *nf* insinuation.

insipide [ɛ̃sipid] *a* insipid.

insist/er [ɛ̃siste] *vi* to insist (**pour faire** on doing); (*continuer*) *Fam* to persevere; **i. sur** (*détail, syllabe etc*) to stress; **i. pour que** (+ *sub*) to insist that. ◆**-ant** *a* insistent, persistent. ◆**insistance** *nf* insistence, persistence.

insolation [ɛ̃sɔlasjɔ̃] *nf* *Méd* sunstroke.

insolent [ɛ̃sɔlɑ̃] *a* (*impoli*) insolent; (*luxe*) indecent. ◆**insolence** *nf* insolence.

insolite [ɛ̃sɔlit] *a* unusual, strange.

insoluble [ɛ̃sɔlybl] *a* insoluble.

insolvable [ɛ̃sɔlvabl] *a* *Fin* insolvent.

insomnie [ɛ̃sɔmni] *nf* insomnia; *pl* (periods of) insomnia; **nuit d'i.** sleepless night. ◆**insomniaque** *nmf* insomniac.

insondable [ɛ̃sɔ̃dabl] *a* unfathomable.

insonoriser [ɛ̃sɔnɔrize] *vt* to soundproof, insulate. ◆**insonorisation** *nf* soundproofing, insulation.

insouciant [ɛ̃susjɑ̃] *a* carefree; **i. de** unconcerned about. ◆**insouciance** *nf* carefree attitude, lack of concern.

insoumis [ɛ̃sumi] *a* rebellious. ◆**insoumission** *nf* rebelliousness.

insoupçonnable [ɛ̃supsɔnabl] *a* beyond suspicion. ◆**insoupçonné** *a* unsuspected.

insoutenable [ɛ̃sutnabl] *a* unbearable; (*théorie*) untenable.

inspecter [ɛ̃spɛkte] *vt* to inspect. ◆**inspecteur, -trice** *nmf* inspector. ◆**inspection** *nf* inspection.

inspir/er [ɛ̃spire] **1** *vt* to inspire; **i. qch à qn** to inspire s.o. with sth; **s'i. de** to take one's inspiration from. **2** *vi* *Méd* to breathe in. ◆**-é** *a* inspired; **être bien i. de faire** to have the good idea to do. ◆**inspiration** *nf* **1** inspiration. **2** *Méd* breathing in.

instable [ɛ̃stabl] *a* (*meuble*) unsteady, shaky; (*temps*) unsettled; (*caractère, situation*) unstable. ◆**instabilité** *nf* unsteadiness; instability.

installer [ɛ̃stale] *vt* (*équiper*) to fit out, fix up; (*appareil, meuble etc*) to install, put in; (*étagère*) to put up; **i. qn** (*dans une fonction, un logement*) to install s.o. (**dans** in); — **s'i.** *vpr* (*s'asseoir, s'établir*) to settle (down); (*médecin etc*) to set oneself up; **s'i. dans** (*maison, hôtel*) to move into. ◆**installateur** *nm* fitter. ◆**installation** *nf* fitting out; installation; putting in; moving in; *pl* (*appareils*) fittings; (*bâtiments*) facilities.

instance [ɛ̃stɑ̃s] **1** *nf* (*juridiction, autorité*) authority; **tribunal de première i.** = magistrates' court; **en i. de** (*divorce, départ*) in the process of. **2** *nfpl* (*prières*) insistence, entreaties.

instant [ĕstã] *nm* moment, instant; **à l'i.** a moment ago; **pour l'i.** for the moment. ◆**instantané** *a* instantaneous; **café i.** instant coffee; — *nm Phot* snapshot.

instaurer [ĕstore] *vt* to found, set up.

instigateur, -trice [ĕstigatœr, -tris] *nmf* instigator. ◆**instigation** *nf* instigation.

instinct [ĕstĕ] *nm* instinct; **d'i.** instinctively, by instinct. ◆**instinctif, -ive** *a* instinctive.

instituer [ĕstitɥe] *vt* (*règle, régime*) to establish, institute.

institut [ĕstity] *nm* institute; **i. de beauté** beauty salon *ou* parlour; **i. universitaire de technologie** polytechnic, technical college.

instituteur, -trice [ĕstitytœr, -tris] *nmf* primary school teacher.

institution [ĕstitysjɔ̃] *nf* (*règle, organisation, structure etc*) institution; *Scol* private school. ◆**institutionnel, -elle** *a* institutional.

instructif, -ive [ĕstryktif, -iv] *a* instructive.

instruction [ĕstryksjɔ̃] *nf* education, schooling; *Mil* training; *Jur* investigation; (*document*) directive; *pl* (*ordres*) instructions. ◆**instructeur** *nm* (*moniteur*) *Mil* instructor.

instruire* [ĕstrɥir] *vt* to teach, educate; *Mil* to train; *Jur* to investigate; **i. qn de** to inform *ou* instruct s.o. of; — **s'i.** *vpr* to educate oneself; **s'i. de** to inquire about. ◆**instruit** *a* educated.

instrument [ĕstrymã] *nm* instrument; (*outil*) implement, tool. ◆**instrumental, -aux** *a Mus* instrumental. ◆**instrumentiste** *nmf Mus* instrumentalist.

insu de (à l') [alĕsyd(ə)] *prép* without the knowledge of.

insuccès [ĕsyksɛ] *nm* failure.

insuffisant [ĕsyfizã] *a* (*en qualité*) inadequate; (*en quantité*) insufficient, inadequate. ◆**insuffisance** *nf* inadequacy.

insulaire [ĕsylɛr] *a* insular; — *nmf* islander.

insuline [ĕsylin] *nf Méd* insulin.

insulte [ĕsylt] *nf* insult (à to). ◆**insulter** *vt* to insult.

insupportable [ĕsyportabl] *a* unbearable.

insurg/er (s') [sĕsyrʒe] *vpr* to rise (up), rebel (contre against). ◆**-é, -ée** *nmf* a insurgent, rebel. ◆**insurrection** *nf* insurrection, uprising.

insurmontable [ĕsyrmɔ̃tabl] *a* insurmountable, insuperable.

intact [ĕtakt] *a* intact.

intangible [ĕtãʒibl] *a* intangible.

intarissable [ĕtarisabl] *a* inexhaustible.

intégral, -aux [ĕtegral, -o] *a* full, complete; (*édition*) unabridged. ◆**intégralement** *adv* in full, fully. ◆**intégralité** *nf* whole (de of); **dans son i.** in full.

intègre [ĕtɛgr] *a* upright, honest. ◆**intégrité** *nf* integrity.

intégr/er [ĕtegre] *vt* to integrate (dans in); — **s'i.** *vpr* to become integrated, adapt. ◆**-ante** *af* **faire partie i. de** to be part and parcel of. ◆**intégration** *nf* integration.

intellectuel, -elle [ĕtelɛktɥɛl] *a* & *nmf* intellectual.

intelligent [ĕteliʒã] *a* intelligent, clever. ◆**intelligemment** [-amã] *adv* intelligently. ◆**intelligence** *nf* (*faculté*) intelligence; *pl Mil Pol* secret relations; **avoir l'i. de qch** (*compréhension*) to have an understanding of sth; **d'i. avec qn** in complicity with s.o. ◆**intelligentsia** [-dʒɛntsja] *nf* intelligentsia.

intelligible [ĕteliʒibl] *a* intelligible. ◆**intelligibilité** *nf* intelligibility.

intempérance [ĕtãperãs] *nf* intemperance.

intempéries [ĕtãperi] *nfpl* **les i.** the elements, bad weather.

intempestif, -ive [ĕtãpestif, -iv] *a* untimely.

intenable [ĕtnabl] *a* (*position*) untenable; (*enfant*) unruly, uncontrollable.

intendant, -ante [ĕtãdã, -ãt] *nmf Scol* bursar. ◆**intendance** *nf Scol* bursar's office.

intense [ĕtãs] *a* intense; (*circulation, trafic*) heavy. ◆**intensément** *adv* intensely. ◆**intensif, -ive** *a* intensive. ◆**intensifier** *vt*, — **s'i.** *vpr* to intensify. ◆**intensité** *nf* intensity.

intenter [ĕtãte] *vt* **i. un procès à** *Jur* to institute proceedings against.

intention [ĕtãsjɔ̃] *nf* intention; *Jur* intent; **avoir l'i. de faire** to intend to do; **à l'i. de qn** for s.o.; **à votre i.** for you. ◆**intentionné** *a* **bien i.** well-intentioned. ◆**intentionnel, -elle** *a* intentional, wilful. ◆**intentionnellement** *adv* intentionally.

inter- [ĕter] *préf* inter-.

interaction [ĕteraksjɔ̃] *nf* interaction.

intercaler [ĕterkale] *vt* to insert.

intercéder [ĕtersede] *vt* to intercede (auprès de with).

intercepter [ĕtersɛpte] *vt* to intercept. ◆**interception** *nf* interception.

interchangeable [ĕterʃãʒabl] *a* interchangeable.

interclasse [ĕterklɑs] *nm Scol* break (between classes).

intercontinental, -aux [ĕterkɔ̃tinãtal, -o] *a* intercontinental.

interdépendant [ɛ̃tɛrdepɑ̃dɑ̃] *a* interdependent.

interd/ire* [ɛ̃tɛrdir] *vt* to forbid, not to allow (**qch à qn** s.o. sth); (*meeting, film etc*) to ban; **i. à qn de faire** (*médecin, père etc*) not to allow s.o. to do, forbid s.o. to do; (*attitude, santé etc*) to prevent s.o. from doing, not allow s.o. to do. ◆**—it a 1** forbidden, not allowed; **il est i. de** it is forbidden to; **'stationnement i.'** 'no parking'. **2** (*étonné*) nonplussed. ◆**interdiction** *nf* ban (**de** on); **'i. de fumer'** 'no smoking'.

intéress/er [ɛ̃terese] *vt* to interest; (*concerner*) to concern; **s'i. à** to take an interest in, be interested in. ◆**—ant** *a* (*captivant*) interesting; (*affaire, prix etc*) worthwhile. ◆**—é, -ée** *a* (*avide*) self-interested; (*motif*) selfish; (*concerné*) concerned; – *nmf* **l'i.** the interested party.

intérêt [ɛ̃terɛ] *nm* interest; *Péj* self-interest; *pl Fin* interest; **tu as i. à faire** it would pay you to do, you'd do well to do; **des intérêts dans** *Com* an interest *ou* stake in.

interface [ɛ̃tɛrfas] *nf Tech* interface.

intérieur [ɛ̃terjœr] *a* (*cour, paroi*) inner, interior; (*poche*) inside; (*vie, sentiment*) inner, inward; (*mer*) inland; (*politique, vol*) internal, domestic; – *nm* (*de boîte etc*) inside (**de** of); (*de maison*) interior, inside; (*de pays*) interior; **à l'i. (de)** inside; **d'i.** (*vêtement, jeux*) indoor; **femme d'i.** home-loving woman; **ministère de l'I.** Home Office, *Am* Department of the Interior. ◆**—ement** *adv* (*dans le cœur*) inwardly.

intérim [ɛ̃terim] *nm* **pendant l'i.** in the interim; **assurer l'i.** to deputize (**de** for); **ministre/etc par i.** acting minister/*etc*. ◆**intérimaire** *a* temporary, interim; – *nmf* (*fonctionnaire*) deputy; (*secrétaire*) temporary.

interligne [ɛ̃tɛrliɲ] *nm Typ* space (between the lines).

interlocuteur, -trice [ɛ̃tɛrlɔkytœr, -tris] *nmf Pol* negotiator; **mon i.** the person I am, was *etc* speaking to.

interloqué [ɛ̃tɛrlɔke] *a* dumbfounded.

interlude [ɛ̃tɛrlyd] *nm Mus TV* interlude.

intermède [ɛ̃tɛrmɛd] *nm* (*interruption*) & *Th* interlude.

intermédiaire [ɛ̃tɛrmedjɛr] *a* intermediate; – *nmf* intermediary; **par l'i. de** through (the medium of).

interminable [ɛ̃tɛrminabl] *a* endless, interminable.

intermittent [ɛ̃tɛrmitɑ̃] *a* intermittent. ◆**intermittence** *nf* **par i.** intermittently.

international, -aux [ɛ̃tɛrnasjɔnal, -o] *a* in-ternational; – *nm* (*joueur*) *Sp* international.

interne [ɛ̃tɛrn] **1** *a* (*douleur etc*) internal; (*oreille*) inner. **2** *nmf Scol* boarder; **i. (des hôpitaux)** houseman, *Am* intern. ◆**internat** *nm* (*école*) boarding school.

intern/er [ɛ̃tɛrne] *vt* (*réfugié*) to intern; (*aliéné*) to confine. ◆**—ement** *nm* internment; confinement.

interpeller [ɛ̃tɛrpele] *vt* to shout at, address sharply; (*dans une réunion*) to question, (*interrompre*) to heckle; (*arrêter*) *Jur* to take in for questioning. ◆**interpellation** *nf* sharp address; questioning; heckling; (*de police*) arrest.

interphone [ɛ̃tɛrfɔn] *nm* intercom.

interplanétaire [ɛ̃tɛrplaneter] *a* interplanetary.

interpoler [ɛ̃tɛrpɔle] *vt* to interpolate.

interposer (s') [sɛ̃tɛrpoze] *vpr* (*dans une dispute etc*) to intervene (**dans** in); **s'i. entre** to come between.

interprète [ɛ̃tɛrprɛt] *nmf Ling* interpreter; (*chanteur*) singer; *Th Mus* performer; (*porte-parole*) spokesman, spokeswoman; **faire l'i.** *Ling* to interpret. ◆**interprétariat** *nm* (*métier*) *Ling* interpreting. ◆**interprétation** *nf* interpretation; *Th Mus* performance. ◆**interpréter** *vt* (*expliquer*) to interpret; (*chanter*) to sing; (*jouer*) *Th* to play, perform; (*exécuter*) *Mus* to perform.

interroger [ɛ̃terɔʒe] *vt* to question; *Jur* to interrogate; (*faits*) to examine. ◆**interrogateur, -trice** *a* (*air*) questioning; – *nmf Scol* examiner. ◆**interrogatif, -ive** *a* & *nm Gram* interrogative. ◆**interrogation** *nf* question; (*action*) questioning; (*épreuve*) *Scol* test. ◆**interrogatoire** *nm Jur* interrogation.

interrompre* [ɛ̃terɔ̃pr] *vt* to interrupt, break off; **i. qn** to interrupt s.o.; – **s'i.** *vpr* (*personne*) to break off, stop. ◆**interrupteur** *nm* (*bouton*) *El* switch. ◆**interruption** *nf* interruption; (*des hostilités, du courant*) break (**de** in).

intersection [ɛ̃tɛrsɛksjɔ̃] *nf* intersection.

interstice [ɛ̃tɛrstis] *nm* crack, chink.

interurbain [ɛ̃teryrbɛ̃] *a* & *nm* (**téléphone**) **i.** long-distance telephone service.

intervalle [ɛ̃tɛrval] *nm* (*écart*) space, gap; (*temps*) interval; **dans l'i.** (*entretemps*) in the meantime.

intervenir* [ɛ̃tɛrvənir] *vi* (*s'interposer, agir*) to intervene; (*survenir*) to occur; (*opérer*) *Méd* to operate; **être intervenu** (*accord*) to be reached. ◆**intervention** *nf* intervention; **i. (chirurgicale)** operation.

intervertir [ɛ̃tɛrvɛrtir] *vt* to invert. ◆**interversion** *nf* inversion.

interview [ɛ̃tɛrvju] *nf Journ TV* interview. ◆**interviewer** [-vjuve] *vt* to interview.

intestin [ɛ̃tɛstɛ̃] *nm* intestine, bowel. ◆**intestinal, -aux** *a* intestinal, bowel-.

intime [ɛ̃tim] *a* intimate; (*ami*) close, intimate; (*vie, fête, journal*) private; (*pièce, coin*) cosy; (*cérémonie*) quiet; — *nmf* close *ou* intimate friend. ◆—**ment** *adv* intimately. ◆**intimité** *nf* intimacy; privacy; cosiness; **dans l'i.** (*mariage etc*) in private.

intimider [ɛ̃timide] *vt* to intimidate, frighten. ◆**intimidation** *nf* intimidation.

intituler [ɛ̃tityle] *vt* to entitle; — **s'i.** *vpr* to be entitled.

intolérable [ɛ̃tɔlerabl] *a* intolerable (*que* that). ◆**intolérance** *nf* intolerance. ◆**intolérant** *a* intolerant (**de** of).

intonation [ɛ̃tɔnasjɔ̃] *nf Ling* intonation; (*ton*) tone.

intoxiqu/er [ɛ̃tɔksike] *vt* (*empoisonner*) to poison; *Psy Pol* to brainwash; — **s'i.** *vpr* to be *ou* become poisoned. ◆—**é, -ée** *nmf* addict. ◆**intoxication** *nf* poisoning; *Psy Pol* brainwashing.

intra- [ɛ̃tra] *préf* intra-.

intraduisible [ɛ̃tradɥizibl] *a* untranslatable.

intraitable [ɛ̃trɛtabl] *a* uncompromising.

intransigeant [ɛ̃trɑ̃ziʒɑ̃] *a* intransigent. ◆**intransigeance** *nf* intransigence.

intransitif, -ive [ɛ̃trɑ̃zitif, -iv] *a* & *nm Gram* intransitive.

intraveineux, -euse [ɛ̃travɛnø, -øz] *a Méd* intravenous.

intrépide [ɛ̃trepid] *a* (*courageux*) fearless, intrepid; (*obstiné*) headstrong. ◆**intrépidité** *nf* fearlessness.

intrigue [ɛ̃trig] *nf* intrigue; *Th Cin Littér* plot. ◆**intrigant, -ante** *nmf* schemer. ◆**intriguer 1** *vi* to scheme, intrigue. **2** *vt* i. **qn** (*intéresser*) to intrigue s.o., puzzle s.o.

intrinsèque [ɛ̃trɛ̃sɛk] *a* intrinsic. ◆—**ment** *adv* intrinsically.

introduire* [ɛ̃trɔdɥir] *vt* (*présenter*) to introduce, bring in; (*insérer*) to insert (**dans** into), put in (**dans** to); (*faire entrer*) to show (s.o.) in; **s'i. dans** to get into. ◆**introduction** *nf* (*texte, action*) introduction.

introspectif, -ive [ɛ̃trɔspɛktif, -iv] *a* introspective. ◆**introspection** *nf* introspection.

introuvable [ɛ̃truvabl] *a* that cannot be found anywhere.

introverti, -ie [ɛ̃trɔvɛrti] *nmf* introvert.

intrus, -use [ɛ̃try, -yz] *nmf* intruder. ◆**intrusion** *nf* intrusion (**dans** into).

intuition [ɛ̃tɥisjɔ̃] *nf* intuition. ◆**intuitif, -ive** *a* intuitive.

inusable [inyzabl] *a Fam* hard-wearing.

inusité [inyzite] *a Gram* unused.

inutile [inytil] *a* unnecessary, useless; **c'est i. de crier** it's pointless *ou* useless to shout. ◆**inutilement** *adv* (*vainement*) needlessly. ◆**inutilité** *nf* uselessness.

inutilisable [inytilizabl] *a* unusable. ◆**inutilisé** *a* unused.

invalider [ɛ̃valide] *vt* to invalidate.

invariable [ɛ̃varjabl] *a* invariable. ◆—**ment** [-əmɑ̃] *adv* invariably.

invasion [ɛ̃vɑzjɔ̃] *nf* invasion.

invective [ɛ̃vɛktiv] *nf* invective. ◆**invectiver** *vt* to abuse; — *vi* **i. contre** to inveigh against.

invendable [ɛ̃vɑ̃dabl] *a* unsaleable. ◆**invendu** *a* unsold.

inventaire [ɛ̃vɑ̃tɛr] *nm* (*liste*) *Com* inventory; (*étude*) *Fig* survey; **faire l'i.** *Com* to do the stocktaking (**de**).

inventer [ɛ̃vɑ̃te] *vt* (*découvrir*) to invent; (*imaginer*) to make up. ◆**inventeur, -trice** *nmf* inventor. ◆**inventif, -ive** *a* inventive. ◆**invention** *nf* invention.

inverse [ɛ̃vɛrs] *a* (*sens*) opposite; (*ordre*) reverse; *Math* inverse; — *nm* **l'i.** the reverse, the opposite. ◆**inversement** *adv* conversely. ◆**inverser** *vt* (*ordre*) to reverse. ◆**inversion** *nf Gram Anat etc* inversion.

investigation [ɛ̃vɛstigasjɔ̃] *nf* investigation.

invest/ir [ɛ̃vɛstir] **1** *vti Com* to invest (**dans** in). **2** *vt* **i. qn de** (*fonction etc*) to invest s.o. with. ◆—**issement** *nm Com* investment. ◆—**iture** *nf Pol* nomination.

invétéré [ɛ̃vetere] *a* inveterate.

invincible [ɛ̃vɛ̃sibl] *a* invincible.

invisible [ɛ̃vizibl] *a* invisible.

invit/er [ɛ̃vite] *vt* to invite; **i. qn à faire** to invite *ou* ask s.o. to do; (*inciter*) to tempt s.o. to do. ◆—**é, -ée** *nmf* guest. ◆**invitation** *nf* invitation.

invivable [ɛ̃vivabl] *a* unbearable.

involontaire [ɛ̃vɔlɔ̃tɛr] *a* involuntary. ◆—**ment** *adv* accidentally, involuntarily.

invoquer [ɛ̃vɔke] *vt* (*argument etc*) to put forward; (*appeler*) to invoke, call upon. ◆**invocation** *nf* invocation (**à** to).

invraisemblable [ɛ̃vrɛsɑ̃blabl] *a* incredible; (*improbable*) improbable. ◆**invraisemblance** *nf* improbability.

invulnérable [ɛ̃vylnerabl] *a* invulnerable.

iode [jɔd] *nm* **teinture d'i.** *Méd* iodine.

ira, irait [ira, irɛ] *voir* **aller 1**.

Irak [irak] *nm* Iraq. ◆**irakien, -ienne** *a* & *nmf* Iraqi.

Iran [irɑ̃] nm Iran. ◆**iranien, -ienne** a & nmf Iranian.

irascible [irasibl] a irascible.

iris [iris] nm Anat Bot iris.

Irlande [irlɑ̃d] nf Ireland. ◆**irlandais, -aise** a Irish; — nmf Irishman, Irishwoman; — nm (langue) Irish.

ironie [ironi] nf irony. ◆**ironique** a ironic(al).

irradier [iradje] vt to irradiate.

irraisonné [irɛzɔne] a irrational.

irréconciliable [irekɔ̃siljabl] a irreconcilable.

irrécusable [irekyzabl] a irrefutable.

irréel, -elle [ireɛl] a unreal.

irréfléchi [irefleʃi] a thoughtless, unthinking.

irréfutable [irefytabl] a irrefutable.

irrégulier, -ière [iregylje, -jɛr] a irregular. ◆**irrégularité** nf irregularity.

irrémédiable [iremedjabl] a irreparable.

irremplaçable [irãplasabl] a irreplaceable.

irréparable [ireparabl] a (véhicule etc) beyond repair; (tort, perte) irreparable.

irrépressible [irepresibl] a (rires etc) irrepressible.

irréprochable [ireprɔʃabl] a beyond reproach, irreproachable.

irrésistible [irezistibl] a (personne, charme etc) irresistible.

irrésolu [irezɔly] a irresolute.

irrespirable [irespirabl] a unbreathable; Fig stifling.

irresponsable [irɛspɔ̃sabl] a (personne) irresponsible.

irrévérencieux, -euse [ireverɑ̃sjø, -øz] a irreverent.

irréversible [ireversibl] a irreversible.

irrévocable [irevɔkabl] a irrevocable.

irriguer [irige] vt to irrigate. ◆**irrigation** nf irrigation.

irrit/er [irite] vt to irritate; — s'i. vpr to get angry (de, contre at). ◆—ant a irritating; — nm irritant. ◆**irritable** a irritable. ◆**irritation** nf (colère) & Méd irritation.

irruption [irypsjɔ̃] nf faire i. dans to burst into.

islam [islam] nm Islam. ◆**islamique** a Islamic.

Islande [islɑ̃d] nf Iceland. ◆**islandais, -aise** a Icelandic.

isol/er [izɔle] vt to isolate (de from); (contre le froid etc) & Él to insulate; — s'i. vpr to cut oneself off, isolate oneself. ◆—ant a insulating; — nm insulating material. ◆—é a isolated; (écarté) remote, isolated; i. de cut off ou isolated from. ◆**isolation** nf insulation. ◆**isolement** nm isolation. ◆**isolément** adv in isolation, singly. ◆**isoloir** nm polling booth.

isorel® [izɔrɛl] nm hardboard.

Israël [israɛl] nm Israel. ◆**israélien, -ienne** a & nmf Israeli. ◆**israélite** a Jewish; — nm Jew; — nf Jewess.

issu [isy] a être i. de to come from.

issue [isy] nf (sortie) exit, way out; (solution) Fig way out; (résultat) outcome; à l'i. de at the close of; rue etc sans i. dead end; situation etc sans i. Fig dead end.

isthme [ism] nm Géog isthmus.

Italie [itali] nf Italy. ◆**italien, -ienne** a & nmf Italian; — nm (langue) Italian.

italique [italik] a Typ italic; — nm italics.

itinéraire [itinerɛr] nm itinerary, route.

itinérant [itinerɑ̃] a itinerant.

IVG [iveʒe] nf abrév (interruption volontaire de grossesse) (voluntary) abortion.

ivoire [ivwar] nm ivory.

ivre [ivr] a drunk (de with). ◆**ivresse** nf drunkenness; en état d'i. under the influence of drink. ◆**ivrogne** nmf drunk(ard).

J

J, j [ʒi] nm J, j; **le jour J.** D-day.

j' [ʒ] voir je.

jacasser [ʒakase] vi (personne, pie) to chatter.

jachère (en) [ɑ̃ʒaʃɛr] adv (champ etc) fallow.

jacinthe [ʒasɛ̃t] nf hyacinth.

jacousi [ʒakuzi] nm (baignoire, piscine) jacuzzi.

jade [ʒad] nm (pierre) jade.

jadis [ʒadis] adv at one time, once.

jaguar [ʒagwar] nm (animal) jaguar.

jaill/ir [ʒajir] vi (liquide) to spurt (out), gush (out); (lumière) to flash, stream; (cri) to burst out; (vérité) to burst forth; (étincelle) to fly out. ◆—**issement** nm (de liquide) gush.

jais [ʒɛ] nm (noir) de j. jet-black.

jalon [ʒalɔ̃] nm (*piquet*) marker; **poser les jalons** *Fig* to prepare the way (**de** for). ◆**jalonner** vt to mark (out); (*border*) to line.

jaloux, -ouse [ʒalu, -uz] a jealous (**de** of). ◆**jalouser** vt to envy. ◆**jalousie** nf 1 jealousy. 2 (*persienne*) venetian blind.

Jamaïque [ʒamaik] nf Jamaica.

jamais [ʒamɛ] adv 1 (*négatif*) never; **sans j. sortir** without ever going out; **elle ne sort j.** she never goes out. 2 (*positif*) ever; **à (tout) j.** for ever; **si j.** if ever.

jambe [ʒɑ̃b] nf leg; **à toutes jambes** as fast as one can; **prendre ses jambes à son cou** to take to one's heels.

jambon [ʒɑ̃bɔ̃] nm *Culin* ham. ◆**jambonneau, -x** nm knuckle of ham.

jante [ʒɑ̃t] nf (*de roue*) rim.

janvier [ʒɑ̃vje] nm January.

Japon [ʒapɔ̃] nm Japan. ◆**japonais, -aise** a nmf Japanese; – & nm (*langue*) Japanese.

japp/er [ʒape] vi (*chien etc*) to yap, yelp. ◆**—ement** nm yap, yelp.

jaquette [ʒakɛt] nf (*d'homme*) tailcoat, morning coat; (*de femme, livre*) jacket.

jardin [ʒardɛ̃] nm garden; **j. d'enfants** kindergarten, playschool; **j. public** park; (*plus petit*) gardens. ◆**jardinage** nm gardening. ◆**jardiner** vi to do the garden, be gardening. ◆**jardinerie** nf garden centre. ◆**jardinier** nm gardener. ◆**jardinière** nf (*personne*) gardener; (*caisse à fleurs*) window box; **j. de légumes** *Culin* mixed vegetable dish; **j. d'enfants** kindergarten teacher.

jargon [ʒargɔ̃] nm jargon.

jarret [ʒarɛ] nm *Anat* back of the knee.

jarretelle [ʒartɛl] nf (*de gaine*) suspender, *Am* garter. ◆**jarretière** nf (*autour de la jambe*) garter.

jaser [ʒaze] vi (*bavarder*) to jabber.

jasmin [ʒasmɛ̃] nm *Bot* jasmine.

jatte [ʒat] nf (*bol*) bowl.

jauge [ʒoʒ] nf 1 (*instrument*) gauge. 2 (*capacité*) capacity; *Nau* tonnage. ◆**jauger** vt (*personne*) *Litt* to size up.

jaune [ʒon] 1 a yellow; – nm (*couleur*) yellow; **j. d'œuf** (egg) yolk. 2 nm (*ouvrier*) *Péj* blackleg, scab. ◆**jaunâtre** a yellowish. ◆**jaunir** vti to (turn) yellow. ◆**jaunisse** nf *Méd* jaundice.

Javel (eau de) [odʒavɛl] nf bleach. ◆**javelliser** vt to chlorinate.

javelot [ʒavlo] nm javelin.

jazz [dʒaz] nm jazz.

je [ʒ(ə)] pron (**j'** before vowel or mute h) I; **je suis** I am.

jean [dʒin] nm (pair of) jeans.

jeep [dʒip] nf jeep.

je-m'en-fichisme [ʒmɑ̃fiʃism] nm inv *Fam* couldn't-care-less attitude.

jérémiades [ʒeremjad] nfpl *Fam* lamentations.

jerrycan [(d)ʒerikan] nm jerry can.

jersey [ʒɛrze] nm (*tissu*) jersey.

Jersey [ʒɛrze] nf Jersey.

jésuite [ʒezɥit] nm Jesuit.

Jésus [ʒezy] nm Jesus; **J.-Christ** Jesus Christ.

jet [ʒɛ] nm throw; (*de vapeur*) burst, gush; (*de lumière*) flash; **j. d'eau** fountain; **premier j.** (*ébauche*) first draft; **d'un seul j.** in one go.

jetée [ʒ(ə)te] nf pier, jetty.

jeter [ʒ(ə)te] vt to throw (**à** to, **dans** into); (*mettre à la poubelle*) to throw away; (*ancre, regard, son*) to cast; (*bases*) to lay; (*cri, son*) to let out, utter; (*éclat, lueur*) to throw out, give out; (*noter*) to jot down; **j. un coup d'œil sur** ou **à** to have ou take a look at; (*rapidement*) to glance at; – **se j.** vpr to throw oneself; **se j. sur** to fall on, pounce on; **se j. contre** (*véhicule*) to crash into; **se j. dans** (*fleuve*) to flow into. ◆**jetable** a (*rasoir etc*) disposable.

jeton [ʒ(ə)tɔ̃] nm (*pièce*) token; (*pour compter*) counter; (*à la roulette*) chip.

jeu, -x [ʒø] nm 1 game; (*amusement*) play; (*d'argent*) gambling; *Th* acting; *Mus* playing; **j. de mots** play on words, pun; **jeux de société** parlour ou party games; **j. télévisé** television quiz; **maison de jeux** gambling club; **en j.** (*en cause*) at stake; (*forces etc*) at work; **entrer en j.** to come into play. 2 (*série complète*) set; (*de cartes*) pack, deck, *Am* deck; (*cartes en main*) hand; **j. d'échecs** (*boîte, pièces*) chess set. 3 (*de ressort, verrou*) *Tech* play.

jeudi [ʒødi] nm Thursday.

jeun (à) [aʒœ̃] adv on an empty stomach; **être à j.** to have eaten no food.

jeune [ʒœn] a young; (*inexpérimenté*) inexperienced; **Dupont j.** Dupont junior; **d'allure j.** young-looking; **jeunes gens** young people; – nmf young person; **les jeunes** young people. ◆**jeunesse** nf youth; (*apparence*) youthfulness; **la j.** (*jeunes*) the young, youth.

jeûne [ʒøn] nm fast; (*action*) fasting. ◆**jeûner** vi to fast.

joaillier, -ière [ʒɔaje, -jɛr] nmf jeweller.

◆**joaillerie** *nf* jewellery; (*magasin*) jewellery shop.

jockey [ʒɔkɛ] *nm* jockey.

jogging [dʒɔgiŋ] *nm* *Sp* jogging; (*chaussure*) running *ou* jogging shoe; **faire du j.** to jog.

joie [ʒwa] *nf* joy, delight; **feu de j.** bonfire.

joindre* [ʒwɛdr] *vt* (*mettre ensemble, relier*) to join; (*efforts*) to combine; (*insérer dans une enveloppe*) to enclose (**à** with); (*ajouter*) to add (**à** to); **j. qn** (*contacter*) to get in touch with s.o.; **j. les deux bouts** *Fig* to make ends meet; **se j. à** (*se mettre avec, participer à*) to join. ◆**joint** *a* (*efforts*) joint, combined; **à pieds joints** with feet together; − *nm Tech* joint; (*de robinet*) washer. ◆**jointure** *nf* *Anat* joint.

joker [ʒɔkɛr] *nm Cartes* joker.

joli [ʒɔli] *a* nice, lovely; (*femme, enfant*) pretty. ◆**−ment** *adv* nicely; (*très, beaucoup*) awfully.

jonc [ʒɔ̃] *nm Bot* (bul)rush.

joncher [ʒɔ̃ʃe] *vt* to litter (**de** with); **jonché de** strewn *ou* littered with.

jonction [ʒɔ̃ksjɔ̃] *nf* (*de tubes, routes etc*) junction.

jongl/er [ʒɔ̃gle] *vi* to juggle. ◆**−eur, −euse** *nmf* juggler.

jonquille [ʒɔ̃kij] *nf* daffodil.

Jordanie [ʒɔrdani] *nf* Jordan.

joue [ʒu] *nf Anat* cheek; **coucher qn en j.** to aim (a gun) at s.o.

jouer [ʒwe] *vi* to play; *Th* to act; (*au tiercé etc*) to gamble, bet; (*à la Bourse*) to gamble; (*entrer en jeu*) to come into play; (*être important*) to count; (*fonctionner*) to work; **j. au tennis/aux cartes/etc** to play tennis/cards/etc; **j. du piano/du violon/etc** to play the piano/violin/etc; **j. des coudes** to use one's elbows; − *vt* (*musique, tour, jeu*) to play; (*risquer*) to gamble, bet (**sur** on); (*cheval*) to bet on; (*personnage, rôle*) *Th* to play; (*pièce*) *Th* to perform, put on; (*film*) to show, put on; **j. gros jeu** to play for high stakes; **se j. de** to scoff at; (*difficultés*) to make light of. ◆**jouet** *nm* toy; **le j. de qn** *Fig* s.o.'s plaything. ◆**joueur, −euse** *nmf* player; (*au tiercé etc*) gambler; **beau j., bon j.**, good loser.

joufflu [ʒufly] *a* (*visage*) chubby; (*enfant*) chubby-cheeked.

joug [ʒu] *nm Agr & Fig* yoke.

jouir [ʒwir] *vi* **1** *de* (*savourer, avoir*) to enjoy. **2** (*éprouver le plaisir sexuel*) to come. ◆**jouissance** *nf* enjoyment; (*usage*) *Jur* use.

joujou, −x [ʒuʒu] *nm Fam* toy.

jour [ʒur] *nm* day; (*lumière*) (day)light; (*ouverture*) gap, opening; (*aspect*) *Fig* light; **il fait j.** it's (day)light; **grand j., plein j.** broad daylight; **de nos jours** nowadays, these days; **au j. le j.** from day to day; **du j. au lendemain** overnight; **mettre à j.** to bring up to date; **mettre au j.** to bring into the open; **se faire j.** to come to light; **donner le j. à** to give birth to; **le j. de l'An** New Year's day. ◆**journalier, −ière** *a* daily. ◆**journée** *nf* day; **pendant la j.** during the day(time); **toute la j.** all day (long). ◆**journellement** *adv* daily.

journal, −aux [ʒurnal, −o] *nm* (news)paper; (*spécialisé*) journal; (*intime*) diary; **j.** (**parlé**) *Rad* news bulletin; **j. de bord** *Nau* logbook. ◆**journalisme** *nm* journalism. ◆**journaliste** *nmf* journalist. ◆**journalistique** *a* (*style etc*) journalistic.

jovial, −aux [ʒɔvjal, −o] *a* jovial, jolly. ◆**jovialité** *nf* jollity.

joyau, −aux [ʒwajo] *nm* jewel.

joyeux, −euse [ʒwajø, −øz] *a* merry, happy, joyful; **j. anniversaire!** happy birthday!; **j. Noël!** merry *ou* happy Christmas!

jubilé [ʒybile] *nm* (golden) jubilee.

jubiler [ʒybile] *vi* to be jubilant. ◆**jubilation** *nf* jubilation.

jucher [ʒyʃe] *vt*, − **se j.** *vpr* to perch (**sur** on).

judaïque [ʒydaik] *a* Jewish. ◆**judaïsme** *nm* Judaism.

judas [ʒyda] *nm* (*de porte*) peephole, spy hole.

judiciaire [ʒydisjɛr] *a* judicial, legal.

judicieux, −euse [ʒydisjø, −øz] *a* sensible, judicious.

judo [ʒydo] *nm* judo. ◆**judoka** *nmf* judo expert.

juge [ʒyʒ] *nm* judge; *Sp* referee, umpire; **j. d'instruction** examining magistrate; **j. de paix** Justice of the Peace; **j. de touche** *Fb* linesman. ◆**juger** *vt* (*personne, question etc*) to judge; (*affaire*) *Jur* to try; (*estimer*) to consider (**que** that); **j. qn** *Jur* to try s.o.; − *vi* **j. de** to judge; **jugez de ma surprise/etc** imagine my surprise/etc. ◆**jugement** *nm* judg(e)ment; (*verdict*) *Jur* sentence; **passer en j.** *Jur* to stand trial. ◆**jugeote** *nf Fam* commonsense.

jugé (au) [oʒyʒe] *adv* by guesswork.

juguler [ʒygyle] *vt* to check, suppress.

juif, juive [ʒuif, ʒuiv] *a* Jewish; − *nm* Jew; − *nf* Jew(ess).

juillet [ʒuijɛ] *nm* July.

juin [ʒuɛ̃] *nm* June.

jumeau, −elle, *pl* **−eaux, −elles** [ʒymo, −ɛl] **1** *a* (*frères, lits etc*) twin; − *nmf* twin. **2** *nfpl* (*longue-vue*) binoculars; **jumelles de théâtre** opera glasses. ◆**—age** nm twinning.

jumeler [ʒymle] vt (*villes*) to twin.

jument [ʒymɑ̃] nf (*cheval*) mare.

jungle [ʒœgl] nf jungle.

junior [ʒynjɔr] nm & a (*inv au sing*) Sp junior.

junte [ʒœt] nf Pol junta.

jupe [ʒyp] nf skirt. ◆**jupon** nm petticoat.

jurer [ʒyre] **1** vi (*blasphémer*) to swear. 2 vt (*promettre*) to swear (**que that, de faire** to do); — vi **j. de qch** to swear to sth. 3 vi (*contraster*) to clash (**avec** with). ◆**juré** a (*ennemi*) sworn; — nm Jur juror. ◆**juron** nm swearword, oath.

juridiction [ʒyridiksjɔ̃] nf jurisdiction.

juridique [ʒyridik] a legal. ◆**juriste** nmf legal expert, jurist.

jury [ʒyri] nm Jur jury; (*de concours*) panel (of judges), jury.

jus [ʒy] nm (*des fruits etc*) juice; (*de viande*) gravy; (*café*) Fam coffee; (*électricité*) Fam power.

jusque [ʒysk] prép **jusqu'à** (*espace*) as far as, (right) up to; (*temps*) until, (up) till, to; (*même*) even; **jusqu'à dix francs/**etc up to ten francs/etc; **jusqu'en mai/**etc until May/etc; **jusqu'où?** how far?; **j. dans/sous/**etc right into/under/etc; **j. chez moi** as far as my place; **jusqu'ici** as far as this; (*temps*) up till now; **en avoir j.-là** Fam to be fed up; — conj **jusqu'à ce qu'il vienne** until he comes.

juste [ʒyst] a (*équitable*) fair, just; (*légitime*) just; (*calcul, heure, réponse*) correct, right, accurate; (*remarque*) sound; (*oreille*) good; (*voix*) Mus true; (*vêtement*) tight; **un peu j.** (*quantité, repas etc*) barely enough; **très j.!** quite so ou right!; **à 3 heures j.** on the stroke of 3; — adv (*deviner, compter*) correctly, right, accurately; (*chanter*) in tune; (*exactement, seulement*) just; **au j.** exactly; **tout j.** (*à peine, seulement*) only just; **c'était j.!** (*il était temps*) it was a near thing!; **un peu j.** (*mesurer, compter*) a bit on the short side; — nm (*homme*) just man. ◆**justement** adv precisely, exactly, just; (*avec justesse ou justice*) justly. ◆**justesse** nf (*exactitude*) accuracy; **de j.** (*éviter, gagner etc*) just.

justice [ʒystis] nf justice; (*organisation, autorités*) law; **en toute j.** in all fairness; **rendre j. à** to do justice to. ◆**justicier, -ière** nmf dispenser of justice.

justifier [ʒystifje] vt to justify; — vi **j. de** to prove; — **se j.** vpr Jur to clear oneself (**de** of); (*attitude etc*) to be justified. ◆**justifiable** a justifiable. ◆**justificatif, -ive** a document j. supporting document, proof. ◆**justification** nf justification; (*preuve*) proof.

jute [ʒyt] nm (*fibre*) jute.

juteux, -euse [ʒytø, -øz] a juicy.

juvénile [ʒyvenil] a youthful.

juxtaposer [ʒykstapoze] vt to juxtapose. ◆**juxtaposition** nf juxtaposition.

K

K, k [ka] nm K, k.

kaki [kaki] a & a inv nm khaki.

kaléidoscope [kaleidɔskɔp] nm kaleidoscope.

kangourou [kɑ̃guru] nm **1** (*animal*) kangaroo. **2**® (*porte-bébé*) baby sling.

karaté [karate] nm Sp karate.

kart [kart] nm Sp (go-)kart, go-cart. ◆**karting** [-iŋ] nm Sp (go-)karting.

kascher [kaʃer] a inv Rel kosher.

kayac [kajak] nm (*bateau*) Sp canoe.

képi [kepi] nm (*coiffure*) Mil kepi.

kermesse [kermes] nf charity fête; (*en Belgique etc*) village fair.

kérosène [kerozen] nm kerosene, aviation fuel.

kibboutz [kibuts] nm kibbutz.

kidnapper [kidnape] vt to kidnap. ◆**—eur, -euse** nmf kidnapper.

kilo(gramme) [kilo, kilɔgram] nm kilo(gramme).

kilomètre [kilɔmetr] nm kilometre. ◆**kilométrage** nm Aut = mileage. ◆**kilométrique** a **borne k.** = milestone.

kilowatt [kilɔwat] nm kilowatt.

kimono [kimɔno] nm (*tunique*) kimono.

kinésithérapie [kineziterapi] nf physiotherapy. ◆**kinésithérapeute** nmf physiotherapist.

kiosque [kjɔsk] nm (*à journaux*) kiosk, stall; **k. à musique** bandstand.

kit [kit] nm (*meuble etc prêt à monter*) kit; **en k.** in kit form, ready to assemble.

klaxon® [klaksɔn] *nm Aut* horn. ◆**klaxon-ner** *vi* to hoot, *Am* honk.
km *abrév* (*kilomètre*) km.
k.-o. [kao] *a inv* mettre k.-o. *Boxe* to knock

out.
kyrielle [kirjɛl] *nf* une k. de a long string of.
kyste [kist] *nm Méd* cyst.

L

L, l [ɛl] *nm* L, l.
l', la [l, la] *voir* le.
là [la] **1** *adv* there; (*chez soi*) in, home; je reste là I'll stay here; **c'est là que** *ou* où that's where; **c'est là ton erreur** that's *ou* there's your mistake; là où il est where he is; à cinq mètres de là five metres away; **de là son échec** (*cause*) hence his *ou* her failure; **jusque-là** as far as that; **passe par là** go that way. **2** *adv* (*temps*) then; **jusque-là** up till then. **3** *int* là, là! (*pour rassurer*) there, there!; **alors là!** well!; **oh là là!** oh dear! **4** *voir* **ce²**, **celui**.
là-bas [labɑ] *adv* over there.
label [label] *nm Com* label, mark (*of quality, origin etc*).
labeur [labœr] *nm Litt* toil.
labo [labo] *nm Fam* lab. ◆**laboratoire** *nm* laboratory; l. de langues language laboratory.
laborieux, -euse [labɔrjø, -øz] *a* (*pénible*) laborious; (*personne*) industrious; **les classes laborieuses** the working classes.
labour [labur] *nm* ploughing, *Am* plowing, digging over. ◆**labour/er** *vt* (*avec charrue*) to plough, *Am* plow; (*avec bêche*) to dig over; (*visage etc*) *Fig* to furrow. ◆**—eur** *nm* ploughman, *Am* plowman.
labyrinthe [labirɛ̃t] *nm* maze, labyrinth.
lac [lak] *nm* lake.
lacer [lase] *vt* to lace (up). ◆**lacet** *nm* **1** (*shoe- ou boot-*)lace. **2** (*de route*) twist, zigzag; **route en l.** winding *ou* zigzag road.
lacérer [lasere] *vt* (*papier etc*) to tear; (*visage etc*) to lacerate.
lâche [lɑʃ] **1** *a* cowardly; – *nmf* coward. **2** *a* (*détendu*) loose, slack. ◆**lâchement** *adv* in a cowardly manner. ◆**lâcheté** *nf* cowardice; **une l.** (*action*) a cowardly act.
lâch/er [lɑʃe] *vt* (*main, objet etc*) to let go of; (*bombe, pigeon*) to release; (*place, études*) to give up; (*juron*) to utter, let slip; (*secret*) to let out; **l. qn** (*laisser tranquille*) to leave s.o. (alone); (*abandonner*) *Fam* to drop s.o.; **l. prise** to let go; – *vi* (*corde*) to

give way; – *nm* release. ◆**—eur, -euse** *nmf Fam* deserter.
laconique [lakɔnik] *a* laconic.
lacrymogène [lakrimɔʒɛn] *a* gaz l. tear gas.
lacté [lakte] *a* (*régime*) milk-; **la Voie lactée** the Milky Way.
lacune [lakyn] *nf* gap, deficiency.
là-dedans [lad(ə)dɑ̃] *adv* (*lieu*) in there, inside. ◆**là-dessous** *adv* underneath. ◆**là-dessus** *adv* on it, on that; (*monter*) on top; (*alors*) thereupon. ◆**là-haut** *adv* up there; (*à l'étage*) upstairs.
lagon [lagɔ̃] *nm* (small) lagoon. ◆**lagune** *nf* lagoon.
laid [lɛ] *a* ugly; (*ignoble*) wretched. ◆**laideur** *nf* ugliness.
laine [lɛn] *nf* wool; **de l., en l.** woollen. ◆**lainage** *nm* (*vêtement*) woollen garment, woolly; (*étoffe*) woollen material; *pl* (*vêtements, objets fabriqués*) woollens. ◆**laineux, -euse** *a* woolly.
laïque [laik] *a* (*vie*) secular; (*habit, tribunal*) lay; – *nmf* (*non-prêtre*) layman, laywoman.
laisse [lɛs] *nf* lead, leash; **en l.** on a lead *ou* leash.
laisser [lese] *vt* to leave; **l. qn partir/ entrer/etc** (*permettre*) to let s.o. go/come in/*etc*; **l. qch à qn** (*confier, donner*) to let s.o. have sth, leave sth with s.o.; (*vendre*) to let s.o. have sth; **laissez-moi le temps de le faire** give me *ou* leave me time to do it; **se l. aller/faire** to let oneself go/be pushed around. ◆**laissé(e)-pour-compte** *nmf* (*personne*) misfit, reject. ◆**laisser-aller** *nm inv* carelessness, slovenliness; ◆**laissez-passer** *nm inv* (*sauf-conduit*) pass.
lait [lɛ] *nm* milk; **frère/sœur de l.** foster-brother/-sister; **dent de l.** milk tooth. ◆**laitage** *nm* milk product *ou* food. ◆**laiterie** *nf* dairy. ◆**laiteux, -euse** *a* milky. ◆**laitier, -ière** *a* (*produits*) dairy-; – *nm* (*livreur*) milkman; (*vendeur*) dairyman; – *nf* dairywoman.
laiton [lɛtɔ̃] *nm* brass.

laitue [lety] *nf* lettuce.

laïus [lajys] *nm Fam* speech.

lama [lama] *nm* (*animal*) llama.

lambeau, -x [lɑ̃bo] *nm* shred, bit; **mettre en lambeaux** to tear to shreds; **tomber en lambeaux** to fall to bits.

lambin, -ine [lɑ̃bɛ̃, -in] *nmf* dawdler. ◆**lambiner** *vi* to dawdle.

lambris [lɑ̃bri] *nm* panelling. ◆**lambrisser** *vt* to panel.

lame [lam] *nf* **1** (*de couteau, rasoir etc*) blade; (*de métal*) strip, plate; **l. de parquet** floorboard. **2** (*vague*) wave; **l. de fond** ground swell.

lamelle [lamel] *nf* thin strip; **l. de verre** (*pour microscope*) slide.

lamenter (se) [salɑ̃mɑ̃te] *vpr* to moan, lament; **se l. sur** to lament (over). ◆**lamentable** *a* (*mauvais*) deplorable; (*voix, cri*) mournful. ◆**lamentation** *nf* lament(ation).

laminé [lamine] *a* (*métal*) laminated.

lampadaire [lɑ̃pader] *nm* standard lamp; (*de rue*) street lamp.

lampe [lɑ̃p] *nf* lamp; (*au néon*) light; (*de vieille radio*) valve, *Am* (vacuum) tube; **l. de poche** torch, *Am* flashlight.

lampée [lɑ̃pe] *nf Fam* gulp.

lampion [lɑ̃pjɔ̃] *nm* Chinese lantern.

lance [lɑ̃s] *nf* spear; (*de tournoi*) *Hist* lance; (*extrémité de tuyau*) nozzle; **l. d'incendie** fire hose.

lance-flammes [lɑ̃sflam] *nm inv* flame thrower. ◆**l.-pierres** *nm inv* catapult. ◆**l.-roquettes** *nm inv* rocket launcher.

lanc/er [lɑ̃se] *vt* (*jeter*) to throw (**à** to); (*avec force*) to hurl; (*navire, mode, acteur, idée*) to launch; (*regard*) to cast (**à** at); (*moteur*) to start; (*ultimatum*) to issue; (*bombe*) to drop; (*gifle*) to give; (*cri*) to utter; — **se l.** *vpr* (*se précipiter*) to rush; **se l. dans** (*aventure, discussion*) to launch into; — *nm un* **l.** the throwing of. ◆**-ée** *nf* momentum. ◆**-ement** *nm Sp* throwing; (*de fusée, navire etc*) launch(ing).

lancinant [lɑ̃sinɑ̃] *a* (*douleur*) shooting; (*obsédant*) haunting.

landau [lɑ̃do] *nm* (*pl* **-s**) pram, *Am* baby carriage.

lande [lɑ̃d] *nf* moor, heath.

langage [lɑ̃gaʒ] *nm* (*système, faculté d'expression*) language; **l. machine** computer language.

lange [lɑ̃ʒ] *nm* (baby) blanket. ◆**langer** *vt* (*bébé*) to change.

langouste [lɑ̃gust] *nf* (spiny) lobster.

◆**langoustine** *nf* (Dublin) prawn, Norway lobster.

langue [lɑ̃g] *nf Anat* tongue; *Ling* language; **de l. anglaise/française** English-/French-speaking; **l. maternelle** mother tongue; **mauvaise l.** (*personne*) gossip. ◆**languette** *nf* (*patte*) sidelights.

langueur [lɑ̃gœr] *nf* languor. ◆**langu/ir** *vi* to languish (**après, after**); (*conversation*) to flag. ◆**-issant** *a* languid (*conversation*) flagging.

lanière [lanjer] *nf* strap; (*d'étoffe*) strip.

lanterne [lɑ̃tern] *nf* lantern; (*électrique*) lamp; *Aut* sidelights.

lanterner [lɑ̃terne] *vi* to loiter.

lapalissade [lapalisad] *nf* statement of the obvious, truism.

laper [lape] *vt* (*boire*) to lap up; — *vi* to lap.

lapider [lapide] *vt* to stone.

lapin [lapɛ̃] *nm* rabbit; **mon (petit) l.!** my dear!; **poser un l. à qn** *Fam* to stand s.o. up.

laps [laps] *nm* **un l. de temps** a lapse of time.

lapsus [lapsys] *nm* slip (of the tongue).

laquais [lake] *nm Hist & Fig* lackey.

laque [lak] *nf* lacquer; **l. à cheveux** hair spray, (hair) lacquer. ◆**laquer** *vt* to lacquer.

laquelle [lakel] *voir* **lequel.**

larbin [larbɛ̃] *nm Fam* flunkey.

lard [lar] *nm* (*fumé*) bacon; (*gras*) (pig's) fat. ◆**lardon** *nm Culin* strip of bacon *ou* fat.

large [larʒ] *a* wide, broad; (*vêtement*) loose; (*idées, esprit*) broad; (*grand*) large; (*généreux*) liberal; **l.d'esprit** broad-minded; **l. de six mètres** six metres wide; — *adv* (*calculer*) liberally, broadly; — *nm* breadth, width; **avoir six mètres de l.** to be six metres wide; **le l.** (*mer*) the open sea; **au l. de Cherbourg** *Nau* off Cherbourg; **être au l.** to have lots of room. ◆**-ment** *adv* widely; (*ouvrir*) wide; (*servir, payer*) liberally; (*au moins*) easily; **avoir l. le temps** to have plenty of time, have ample time. ◆**largesse** *nf* liberality. ◆**largeur** *nf* width, breadth; (*d'esprit*) breadth.

larguer [large] *vt* (*bombe, parachutiste*) to drop; **l. qn** (*se débarrasser de*) to drop s.o.; **l. les amarres** *Nau* to cast off.

larme [larm] *nf* tear; (*goutte*) *Fam* drop; **en larmes** in tears; **rire aux larmes** to laugh till one cries. ◆**larmoyer** *vi* (*yeux*) to water.

larve [larv] *nf* (*d'insecte*) larva, grub.

larvé [larve] *a* latent, underlying.

larynx [larɛ̃ks] *nm Anat* larynx ◆**laryngite** *nf Méd* laryngitis.

las, lasse [lɑ, lɑs] *a* tired, weary (**de** of).

◆**lasser** vt to tire, weary; **se l. de** to tire of.
◆**lassitude** nf tiredness, weariness.

lascar [laskar] nm Fam (clever) fellow.

lascif, -ive [lasif, -iv] a lascivious.

laser [lazɛr] nm laser.

lasso [laso] nm lasso.

latent [latɑ̃] a latent.

latéral, -aux [lateral, -o] a lateral, side-.

latin, -ine [latɛ̃, -in] a & nmf Latin; — nm (langue) Latin.

latitude [latityd] nf Géog & Fig latitude.

latrines [latrin] nfpl latrines.

latte [lat] nf slat, lath; (de plancher) board.

lauréat, -ate [lɔrea, -at] nmf (prize)winner; — a prize-winning.

laurier [lɔrje] nm Bot laurel, bay; **du l.** Culin bay leaves.

lavabo [lavabo] nm washbasin, sink; pl (cabinet) toilet(s), Am washroom.

lavande [lavɑ̃d] nf lavender.

lave [lav] nf Géol lava.

lave-auto [lavoto] nm car wash. ◆**l.-glace** nm windscreen ou Am windshield washer. ◆**l.-linge** nm washing machine. ◆**l.-vaisselle** nm dishwasher.

laver [lave] vt to wash; **l. qn de** (soupçon etc) to clear s.o. of; — **se l.** vpr to wash (oneself), Am wash up; **se l. les mains** to wash one's hands (Fig de of). ◆**lavable** a washable. ◆**lavage** nm washing; **l. de cerveau** Psy brainwashing. ◆**laverie** nf (automatique) launderette, Am laundromat. ◆**lavette** nf dish cloth; (homme) Péj drip. ◆**laveur** nm **l. de carreaux** window cleaner ou Am washer. ◆**lavoir** nm (bâtiment) washhouse.

laxatif, -ive [laksatif, -iv] nm & a Méd laxative.

laxisme [laksism] nm permissiveness, laxity. ◆**laxiste** a permissive, lax.

layette [lɛjɛt] nf baby clothes, layette.

le, la, pl **les** [l(ə), la, le] (**le & la** become **l'** before a vowel or mute h) **1** art déf (à + le = au, à + les = aux; de + le = du, de + les = des); **le garçon** the boy; **la fille** the girl; **viens, les enfants!** come children!; **les petits/rouges/etc** the little ones/red ones/etc; **mon ami le plus intime** my closest friend. **2** (généralisation, abstraction) **la beauté** beauty; **la France** France; **les Français** the French; **les hommes** men; **aimer le café** to like coffee. **3** (possession) **il ouvrit la bouche** he opened his mouth; **se blesser au pied** to hurt one's foot; **avoir les cheveux blonds** to have blond hair. **4** (mesure) **dix francs le kilo** ten francs a kilo. **5** (temps) **elle vient le lundi** she comes on Monday(s);

elle passe le soir she comes over in the evening(s); **l'an prochain** next year; **une fois l'an** once a year. **6** pron (homme) him; (femme) her; (chose, animal) it; pl them; **je la vois** I see her; **je le vois** I see him; **je le vois** I see it; **je les vois** I see them; **es-tu fatigué? — je le suis** are you tired? — I am; **je le crois** I think so.

leader [lidœr] nm Pol leader.

lécher [leʃe] vt to lick; **se l. les doigts** to lick one's fingers. ◆**lèche-vitrines** nm **faire du l.-vitrines** to go window-shopping.

leçon [ləsɔ̃] nf lesson; **faire la l. à qn** to lecture s.o.

lecteur, -trice [lɛktœr, -tris] nmf reader; Univ (foreign language) assistant; **l. de cassettes** cassette player. ◆**lecture** nf reading; pl (livres) books; **faire de la l. à qn** to read to s.o.; **de la l.** some reading matter.

légal, -aux [legal, -o] a legal; (médecine) forensic. ◆**légalement** adv legally. ◆**légaliser** vt to legalize. ◆**légalité** nf legality (de of); **respecter la l.** to respect the law.

légation [legasjɔ̃] nf Pol legation.

légende [leʒɑ̃d] nf **1** (histoire, fable) legend. **2** (de plan, carte) key; (de photo) caption. ◆**légendaire** a legendary.

léger, -ère [leʒe, -ɛr] a light; (bruit, faute, fièvre etc) slight; (café, thé, argument) weak; (bière, tabac) mild; (frivole) frivolous; (irréfléchi) careless; **à la légère** (agir) rashly. ◆**légèrement** adv lightly; (un peu) slightly; (à la légère) rashly. ◆**légèreté** nf lightness; frivolity.

légiférer [leʒifere] vi to legislate.

légion [leʒjɔ̃] nf Mil & Fig legion. ◆**légionnaire** nm (de la Légion étrangère) legionnaire.

législatif, -ive [leʒislatif, -iv] a legislative; (élections) parliamentary. ◆**législation** nf legislation. ◆**législature** nf (période) Pol term of office.

légitime [leʒitim] a (action, enfant etc) legitimate; **en état de l. défense** acting in self-defence. ◆**légitimité** nf legitimacy.

legs [lɛg] nm Jur legacy, bequest; (héritage) Fig legacy. ◆**léguer** vt to bequeath (à to).

légume [legym] nm vegetable. **2** nf **grosse l.** (personne) Fam bigwig.

lendemain [lɑ̃dmɛ̃] nm **le l.** the next day; (avenir) Fig the future; **le l. de** the day after; **le l. matin** the next morning.

lent [lɑ̃] a slow. ◆**lentement** adv slowly. ◆**lenteur** nf slowness.

lentille [lɑ̃tij] nf **1** Bot Culin lentil. **2** (verre) lens.

léopard [leɔpar] nm leopard.

lèpre [lɛpr] *nf* leprosy. ◆**lépreux, -euse** *a* leprous; – *nmf* leper.

lequel, laquelle, *pl* **lesquels, lesquelles** [ləkɛl, lakɛl, lekɛl] (+ à = **auquel, à laquelle,** auxquel(le)s; + de = **duquel, de laquelle,** desquel(le)s) *pron* (*chose, animal*) which; (*personne*) who, (*indirect*) whom; (*interrogatif*) which (one); **dans l.** in which; **parmi lesquels** (*choses, animaux*) among which; (*personnes*) among whom; **l. préférez-vous?** which (one) do you prefer?

les [le] *voir* **le.**

lesbienne [lɛsbjɛn] *nf & af* lesbian.

léser [leze] *vt* (*personne*) *Jur* to wrong.

lésiner [lezine] *vi* to be stingy (**sur** with).

lésion [lezjɔ̃] *nf Méd* lesion.

lessive [lesiv] *nf* (*produit*) washing powder; (*linge*) washing; **faire la l.** to do the wash(ing). ◆**lessiv/er** *vt* to scrub, wash. ◆**-é** *a Fam* (*fatigué*) washed-out; (*ruiné*) washed-up. ◆**-euse** *nf* (*laundry*) boiler.

lest [lɛst] *nm* ballast. ◆**lester** *vt* to ballast, weight down; (*remplir*) *Fam* to overload.

leste [lɛst] *a* (*agile*) nimble; (*grivois*) coarse.

léthargie [letarʒi] *nf* lethargy. ◆**léthargique** *a* lethargic.

lettre [lɛtr] *nf* (*missive, caractère*) letter; **en toutes lettres** (*mot*) in full; (*nombre*) in words; **les lettres** (*discipline*) *Univ* arts; **homme de lettres** man of letters. ◆**lettré, -ée** *a* well-read; – *nmf* scholar.

leucémie [løsemi] *nf* leuk(a)emia.

leur [lœr] **1** *a poss* their; **l. chat** their cat; **leurs voitures** their cars; – *pron poss* **le l., la l., les leurs** theirs. **2** *pron inv* (*indirect*) (to) them; **il l. est facile de ...** it's easy for them to ....

leurre [lœr] *nm* illusion; (*tromperie*) trickery. ◆**leurrer** *vt* to delude.

lev/er [l(ə)ve] *vt* to lift (up), raise; (*blocus, interdiction*) to lift; (*séance*) to close; (*camp*) to strike; (*plan*) to draw up; (*impôts, armée*) to levy; **l. les yeux** to look up; – *vi* (*pâte*) to rise; (*blé*) to come up; – **se l.** *vpr* to get up; (*soleil, rideau*) to rise; (*jour*) to break; (*brume*) to clear, lift; – *nm* **le l. du soleil** sunrise; **le l. du rideau** *Th* the curtain. ◆**-ant** *a* (*soleil*) rising; – *nm* **le l.** the east. ◆**-é** *a* **être l.** (*debout*) to be up. ◆**-ée** *nf* (*d'interdiction*) lifting; (*d'impôts*) levying; (*du courrier*) collection; **l. de boucliers** public outcry.

levier [ləvje] *nm* lever; (*pour soulever*) crowbar.

lèvre [lɛvr] *nf* lip; **du bout des lèvres** half-heartedly, grudgingly.

lévrier [levrije] *nm* greyhound.

levure [ləvyr] *nf* yeast.

lexique [lɛksik] *nm* vocabulary, glossary.

lézard [lezar] *nm* lizard.

lézarde [lezard] *nf* crack, split. ◆**lézarder 1** *vi Fam* to bask in the sun. **2 se l.** *vpr* to crack, split.

liaison [ljɛzɔ̃] *nf* (*rapport*) connection; (*routière etc*) link; *Gram Mil* liaison; **l. (amoureuse)** love affair; **en l. avec qn** in contact with s.o.

liane [ljan] *nf Bot* jungle vine.

liant [ljɑ̃] *a* sociable.

liasse [ljas] *nf* bundle.

Liban [libɑ̃] *nm* Lebanon. ◆**libanais, -aise** *a & nmf* Lebanese.

libell/er [libele] *vt* (*contrat etc*) to word, draw up; (*chèque*) to make out. ◆**-é** *nm* wording.

libellule [libelyl] *nf* dragonfly.

libéral, -ale, -aux [liberal, -o] *a & nmf* liberal. ◆**libéraliser** *vt* to liberalize. ◆**libéralisme** *nm* liberalism. ◆**libéralité** *nf* liberality; (*don*) liberal gift.

libérer [libere] *vt* (*prisonnier etc*) to (set) free, release; (*pays, esprit*) to liberate (**de** from); **l. qn de** to free s.o. ou from; – **se l.** *vpr* to get free, free oneself (**de** of, from). ◆**libérateur, -trice** *a* (*sentiment etc*) liberating; – *nmf* liberator. ◆**libération** *nf* freeing, release; liberation; **l. conditionnelle** *Jur* parole. ◆**liberté** *nf* freedom, liberty; **en l. provisoire** *Jur* on bail; **mettre en l.** to free, release; **mise en l.** release.

libraire [librɛr] *nmf* bookseller. ◆**librairie** *nf* (*magasin*) bookshop.

libre [libr] *a* free (**de qch** sth, **de faire** to do); (*voie, route*) clear; (*place*) vacant, free; (*école*) private (and religious); **l. penseur** freethinker. ◆**l.-échange** *nm Écon* free trade. ◆**l.-service** *nm* (*pl* **libres-services**) (*système, magasin etc*) self-service. ◆**librement** *adv* freely.

Libye [libi] *nf* Libya. ◆**libyen, -enne** *a & nmf* Libyan.

licence [lisɑ̃s] *nf Sp Com Littér* licence; *Univ* (*bachelor's*) degree; **l. ès lettres/sciences** arts/science degree; = BA/BSc, = *Am* BA/BS. ◆**licencié, -ée** *a & nmf* graduate; **l. ès lettres/sciences** bachelor of arts/science, = BA/BSc, = *Am* BA/BS.

licencier [lisɑ̃sje] *vt* (*ouvrier*) to lay off, dismiss. ◆**licenciement** *nm* dismissal.

licite [lisit] *a* licit, lawful.

licorne [likɔrn] *nf* unicorn.

lie [li] *nf* dregs.

liège [ljɛʒ] *nm* (*matériau*) cork.

lien [ljɛ̃] *nm* (*rapport*) link, connection; (*de*

lierre [ljɛr] nm ivy.

lieu, -x [ljø] nm place; (d'un accident) scene; **les lieux** (locaux) the premises; **sur les lieux** on the spot; **avoir l.** to take place, be held; **au l. de** instead of; **avoir l. de faire** (des raisons) to have good reason to do; **en premier l.** in the first place, firstly; **en dernier l.** lastly; **l. commun** commonplace. **◆l.-dit** nm (pl lieux-dits) Géog locality.

lieue [ljø] nf (mesure) Hist league.

lieutenant [ljøtnɑ̃] nm lieutenant.

lièvre [ljɛvr] nm hare.

ligament [ligamɑ̃] nm ligament.

ligne [liɲ] nf (trait, règle, contour, transport) line; (belle silhouette de femme etc) figure; (rangée) row, line; (se) **mettre en l.** to line up; **en l.** Tél connected, through; **entrer en l. de compte** to be of consequence, count; **faire entrer en l. de compte** to take into account; **grande l.** Rail main line; **les grandes lignes** Fig the broad outline; **pilote de l.** airline pilot; **à la l.** Gram new paragraph.

lignée [liɲe] nf line, ancestry.

ligoter [ligɔte] vt to tie up.

ligue [lig] nf (alliance) league. **◆se liguer** vpr to join together, gang up (contre against).

lilas [lila] nm lilac; — a inv (couleur) lilac.

limace [limas] nf (mollusque) slug.

limaille [limaj] nf filings.

limande [limɑ̃d] nf (poisson) dab.

lime [lim] nf (outil) file. **◆limer** vt to file.

limier [limje] nm (chien) bloodhound.

limite [limit] nf limit; (de propriété, jardin etc) boundary; pl Fb boundary lines; **dépasser la l.** to go beyond the bounds; — a (cas) extreme; (vitesse, prix, âge etc) maximum; **date l.** latest date, deadline; **date l. de vente** Com sell-by date. **◆limitatif, -ive** a restrictive. **◆limitation** nf limitation; (de vitesse) limit. **◆limiter** vt to limit, restrict; (délimiter) to border; **se l. à faire** to limit ou restrict oneself to doing.

limoger [limɔʒe] vt (destituer) to dismiss.

limonade [limɔnad] nf (fizzy) lemonade.

limpide [lɛ̃pid] a (eau, explication) (crystal) clear. **◆limpidité** nf clearness.

lin [lɛ̃] nm Bot flax; (tissu) linen; **huile de l.** linseed oil.

linceul [lɛ̃sœl] nm shroud.

linéaire [lineɛr] a linear.

linge [lɛ̃ʒ] nm (pièces de tissu) linen; (à laver) washing, linen; (torchon) cloth; **l. (de corps)** underwear. **◆lingerie** nf (de femmes) underwear; (local) linen room.

lingot [lɛ̃go] nm ingot.

linguiste [lɛ̃gɥist] nmf linguist. **◆linguistique** a linguistic; — nf linguistics.

lino [lino] nm lino. **◆linoléum** nm linoleum.

linotte [linɔt] nf (oiseau) linnet; **tête de l.** Fig scatterbrain.

lion [ljɔ̃] nm lion. **◆lionceau, -x** nm lion cub. **◆lionne** nf lioness.

liquéfier [likefje] vt, — **se l.** vpr to liquefy.

liqueur [likœr] nf liqueur.

liquide [likid] a liquid; **argent l.** ready cash; — nm liquid; **du l.** (argent) ready cash.

liquider [likide] vt (dette, stock etc) to liquidate; (affaire, travail) to wind up, finish off; **l. qn** (tuer) Fam to liquidate s.o. **◆liquidation** nf liquidation; winding up; (vente) (clearance) sale.

lire [lir] vti to read.

lire [lir] nf (monnaie) lira.

lis [lis] nm (plante, fleur) lily.

lis, **lisent** [li, liz] voir **lire**.

liseron [lizrɔ̃] nm Bot convolvulus.

lisible [lizibl] a (écriture) legible; (livre) readable. **◆lisiblement** adv legibly.

lisière [lizjɛr] nf edge, border.

lisse [lis] a smooth. **◆lisser** vt to smooth; (plumes) to preen.

liste [list] nf list; **l. électorale** register of electors, electoral roll; **sur la l. rouge** Tél ex-directory, Am unlisted.

lit [li] nm bed; **l. d'enfant** cot, Am crib; **lits superposés** bunk beds; **garder le l.** to stay in bed. **◆literie** nf bedding, bed clothes.

lit [li] voir **lire**.

litanie [litani] 1 nf (énumération) long list (de of). 2 nfpl (prière) Rel litany.

litière [litjɛr] nf (couche de paille) litter.

litige [litiʒ] nm dispute; Jur litigation. **◆litigieux, -euse** a contentious.

litre [litr] nm litre.

littéraire [literɛr] a literary. **◆littérature** nf literature.

littéral, -aux [literal, -o] a literal. **◆—ement** adv literally.

littoral, -aux [litɔral, -o] a coastal; — nm coast(line).

liturgie [lityrʒi] nf liturgy. **◆liturgique** a liturgical.

livide [livid] a (bleuâtre) livid; (pâle) (ghastly) pale, pallid.

livre [livr] nm **1** book; **l. de bord** Nau log-

book; **l. de poche** paperback (book); **le l.,
l'industrie du l.** the book industry. **2** *nf
(monnaie, poids)* pound. ◆**livresque** *a
(savoir)* Péj bookish. ◆**livret** *nm (registre)*
book; *Mus* libretto; **l. scolaire** school report book; **l. de famille** family registration
book; **l. de caisse d'épargne** bankbook,
passbook.

livrée [livre] *nf (uniforme)* livery.

livrer [livre] *vt (marchandises)* to deliver (à
to); *(secret)* to give away; **l. qn à** *(la police
etc)* to give s.o. up *ou* over to; **l. bataille**
to do *ou* join battle; **— se l.** *vpr (se rendre)*
to give oneself up (à to); *(se confier)* to confide
(à in); **l. à** *(habitude, excès etc)* to indulge
in; *(tâche)* to devote oneself to; *(désespoir,
destin)* to abandon oneself to. ◆**livraison**
nf delivery. ◆**livreur, -euse** *nmf* delivery
man, delivery woman.

lobe [lɔb] *nm Anat* lobe.

local, -aux [lɔkal, -o] **1** *a* local. **2** *nm & nmpl
(pièce, bâtiment)* premises. ◆**localement**
adv locally. ◆**localiser** *vt (déterminer)* to
locate; *(limiter)* to localize. ◆**localité** *nf*
locality.

locataire [lɔkatɛr] *nmf* tenant; *(hôte payant)*
lodger.

location [lɔkasjɔ̃] *nf (de maison etc)* renting;
(à bail) leasing; *(de voiture)* hiring; *(réservation)* booking; *(par propriétaire)* renting
(out), letting; leasing (out); hiring (out);
(loyer) rental; *(bail)* lease; **bureau de l.**
booking office; **en l.** on hire.

lock-out [lɔkawt] *nm inv (industriel)* lock-
out.

locomotion [lɔkɔmosjɔ̃] *nf* locomotion.
◆**locomotive** *nf* locomotive, engine.

locuteur [lɔkytœr] *nm Ling* speaker.
◆**locution** *nf* phrase, idiom; *Gram*
phrase.

logarithme [lɔgaritm] *nm* logarithm.

loge [lɔʒ] *nf (de concierge)* lodge; *(d'acteur)*
dressing-room; *(de spectateur)* Th box.

log/er [lɔʒe] *vt (recevoir, mettre)* to accommodate, house; *(héberger)* to put up; **être
logé et nourri** to have board and lodging; **—
vi** *(à l'hôtel etc)* to put up, lodge; *(habiter)*
to live; **(trouver à) se l.** to find somewhere
to live; *(temporairement)* to find somewhere to stay; **se l. dans** *(balle)* to lodge
(itself) in. ◆**—eable** *a* habitable.
◆**—ement** *nm* accommodation, lodging;
(habitat) housing; *(appartement)* lodgings,
flat, *Am* apartment; *(maison)* dwelling.
◆**—eur, -euse** *nmf* landlord, landlady.

logiciel [lɔʒisjɛl] *nm (d'un ordinateur)* software *inv*.

logique [lɔʒik] *a* logical; **— nf** logic.
◆**—ment** *adv* logically.

logistique [lɔʒistik] *nf* logistics.

logo [lɔgo] *nm* logo.

loi [lwa] *nf* law; *Pol* act; **projet de l.** *Pol* bill;
faire la l. to lay down the law (à to).

loin [lwɛ̃] *adv* far *(away ou off)*; **Boston est l.
(de Paris)** Boston is a long way away *(from
Paris)*; **plus l.** further, farther; *(ci-après)*
further on; **l. de là** *Fig* far from it; **au l.** in
the distance, far away; **de l.** from a distance; *(de beaucoup)* by far; **de l. en l.** every
so often. ◆**lointain** *a* distant, far-off; **—
nm dans le l.** in the distance.

loir [lwar] *nm (animal)* dormouse.

loisir [lwazir] *nm* **le l. de faire** the time to do;
moment de l. moment of leisure; **loisirs**
(temps libre) spare time, leisure (time); *(dis-
tractions)* spare-time *ou* leisure activities.

Londres [lɔ̃dr] *nm ou f* London.
◆**londonien, -ienne** *a* London-; **— nmf**
Londoner.

long, longue [lɔ̃, lɔ̃g] *a* long; **être l. (à faire)**
to be a long time *ou* slow (in doing); **l. de
deux mètres** two metres long; **— nm avoir
deux mètres de l.** to be two metres long;
tomber de tout son l. to fall flat; *(tout)* **le l.
de** *(espace)* (all) along; **tout le l. de** *(temps)*
throughout; **de l. en large** *(marcher etc)* up
and down; **en l. et en large** thoroughly; **en
l.** lengthwise; **à la longue** in the long run.
◆**l.-courrier** *nm Av* long-distance airliner.
◆**longue-vue** *nf (pl* **longues-vues)** telescope.

longer [lɔ̃ʒe] *vt* to pass *ou* go along; *(forêt,
mer)* to skirt; *(mur)* to hug.

longévité [lɔ̃ʒevite] *nf* longevity.

longitude [lɔ̃ʒityd] *nf* longitude.

longtemps [lɔ̃tɑ̃] *adv* (for) a long time;
trop/avant l. too/before long; **aussi l. que**
as long as.

longue [lɔ̃g] *voir* **long.** ◆**longuement** *adv*
at length. ◆**longuet, -ette** *a Fam* (fairly)
lengthy. ◆**longueur** *nf* length; *(de
texte, film)* over-long passages; **saut en l.** *Sp*
long jump; **à l. de journée** all day long; **l.
d'onde** *Rad & Fig* wavelength.

lopin [lɔpɛ̃] *nm* **l. de terre** plot *ou* patch of
land.

loquace [lɔkas] *a* loquacious.

loque [lɔk] **1** *nfpl* **loques** rags. **2** *nf* **l. (humaine)**
(personne) human wreck.

loquet [lɔkɛ] *nm* latch.

lorgner [lɔrɲe] *vt (regarder, convoiter)* to
eye.

lors [lɔr] *adv* **l. de** at the time of; **depuis l.,**

dès l. from then on; **dès l. que** (*puisque*) since.

losange [lɔzɑ̃ʒ] *nm Géom* diamond, lozenge.

lot [lo] *nm* **1** (*de loterie*) prize; **gros l.** top prize, jackpot. **2** (*portion, destin*) lot. ◆**loterie** *nf* lottery, raffle. ◆**lotir** *vt* (*terrain*) to divide into lots; **bien loti** *Fig* favoured by fortune. ◆**lotissement** *nm* (*terrain*) building plot; (*habitations*) housing estate *ou* development.

lotion [losjɔ̃] *nf* lotion.

loto [loto] *nm* (*jeu*) lotto.

louche [luʃ] **1** *a* (*suspect*) shady, fishy. **2** *nf Culin* ladle.

loucher [luʃe] *vi* to squint; **l. sur** *Fam* to eye.

louer [lwe] *vt* **1** (*prendre en location*) to rent (*house, flat etc*); (*à bail*) to lease; (*voiture*) to hire, rent; (*réserver*) to book; (*donner en location*) to rent (out), let; to lease (out); to hire (out); **maison/chambre à l.** house/room to let. **2** (*exalter*) to praise (**de** for); **se l. de** to be highly satisfied with. ◆**louable** *a* praiseworthy, laudable. ◆**louange** *nf* praise; **à la l. de** in praise of.

loufoque [lufɔk] *a* (*fou*) *Fam* nutty, crazy.

loukoum [lukum] *nm* Turkish delight.

loup [lu] *nm* wolf; **avoir une faim de l.** to be ravenous. ◆**l.-garou** *nm* (*pl* **loups-garous**) werewolf.

loupe [lup] *nf* magnifying glass.

louper [lupe] *vt Fam* (*train etc*) to miss; (*examen*) to fail; (*travail*) to mess up.

lourd [lur] *a* heavy (*Fig* **de** with); (*temps, chaleur*) close, sultry; (*faute*) gross; (*tâche*) arduous; (*esprit*) dull; – *adv* **peser l.** (*malle etc*) to be heavy. ◆**lourdaud, -aude** *a* loutish, oafish; – *nmf* lout, oaf. ◆**lourdement** *adv* heavily. ◆**lourdeur** *nf* heaviness; (*de temps*) closeness; (*d'esprit*) dullness.

loutre [lutr] *nf* otter.

louve [luv] *nf* she-wolf. ◆**louveteau, -x** *nm* (*scout*) cub (scout).

louvoyer [luvwaje] *vi* (*tergiverser*) to hedge, be evasive.

loyal, -aux [lwajal, -o] *a* (*fidèle*) loyal (**envers** to); (*honnête*) honest, fair (**envers** to). ◆**loyalement** *adv* loyally; fairly. ◆**loyauté** *nf* loyalty; honesty, fairness.

loyer [lwaje] *nm* rent.

lu [ly] *voir* **lire** [1].

lubie [lybi] *nf* whim.

lubrifi/er [lybrifje] *vt* to lubricate. ◆**—ant** *nm* lubricant.

lubrique [lybrik] *a* lewd, lustful.

lucarne [lykarn] *nf* (*ouverture*) skylight; (*fenêtre*) dormer window.

lucide [lysid] *a* lucid. ◆**lucidité** *nf* lucidity.

lucratif, -ive [lykratif, -iv] *a* lucrative.

lueur [lɥœr] *nf* (*lumière*) & *Fig* glimmer.

luge [lyʒ] *nf* toboggan, sledge.

lugubre [lygybr] *a* gloomy, lugubrious.

lui [lɥi] **1** *pron nm* (*complément indirect*) (to) him; (*femme*) (to) her; (*chose, animal*) (to) it; **je le lui ai montré** I showed it to him *ou* to her; I showed him it *ou* her it; **il lui est facile de ...** it's easy for him *ou* her to .... **2** *pron nm* (*complément direct*) him; (*chose, animal*) it; (*sujet emphatique*) he; **pour lui** for him; **plus grand que lui** taller than him; **il ne pense qu'à lui** he only thinks of himself. ◆**lui-même** *pron* himself; (*chose, animal*) itself.

luire* [lɥir] *vi* to shine, gleam. ◆**luisant** *a* (*métal etc*) shiny.

lumbago [lɔ̃bago] *nm* lumbago.

lumière [lymjɛr] *nf* light; **à la l. de** by the light of; (*grâce à*) *Fig* in the light of; **faire toute la l. sur** *Fig* to clear up; **mettre en l.** to bring to light. ◆**luminaire** *nm* (*appareil*) lighting appliance. ◆**lumineux, -euse** *a* (*idée, ciel etc*) bright, brilliant; (*ondes, source etc*) light-; (*cadran, corps etc*) *Tech* luminous.

lunaire [lyner] *a* lunar; **clarté l.** light *ou* brightness of the moon.

lunatique [lynatik] *a* temperamental.

lunch [lœ̃ʃ, lœntʃ] *nm* buffet lunch, snack.

lundi [lœ̃di] *nm* Monday.

lune [lyn] *nf* moon; **l. de miel** honeymoon.

lunette [lynɛt] *nf* **1** **lunettes** glasses, spectacles; (*de protection, de plongée*) goggles; **lunettes de soleil** sunglasses. **2** (*astronomique*) telescope; (*de voiture*) **l. arrière** *Aut* rear window.

lurette [lyrɛt] *nf* **il y a belle l.** a long time ago.

luron [lyrɔ̃] *nm* **gai l.** gay fellow.

lustre [lystr] *nm* (*éclairage*) chandelier; (*éclat*) lustre. ◆**lustré** *a* (*par l'usure*) shiny.

luth [lyt] *nm Mus* lute.

lutin [lytɛ̃] *nm* elf, imp, goblin.

lutte [lyt] *nf* fight, struggle; *Sp* wrestling; **l. des classes** class warfare *ou* struggle. ◆**lutter** *vi* to fight, struggle; *Sp* to wrestle. ◆**lutteur, -euse** *nmf* fighter; *Sp* wrestler.

luxe [lyks] *nm* luxury; **de l.** a wealth of; **de l.** (*article*) luxury-; (*modèle*) de luxe. ◆**luxueux, -euse** *a* luxurious.

Luxembourg [lyksɑ̃bur] *nm* Luxembourg.

luxure [lyksyr] *nf* lewdness, lust.

luxuriant [lyksyrjɑ̃] *a* luxuriant.

luzerne [lyzɛrn] *nf Bot* lucerne, *Am* alfalfa.

lycée [lise] *nm* (secondary) school, *Am* high school. ◆**lycéen, -enne** *nmf* pupil (*at lycée*).

lymphatique [lɛ̃fatik] *a* (*apathique*) sluggish.

lynch/er [lɛ̃ʃe] *vt* to lynch. ◆**—age** *nm* lynching.

lynx [lɛ̃ks] *nm* (*animal*) lynx.

lyre [lir] *nf Mus Hist* lyre.

lyrique [lirik] *a* (*poème etc*) lyric; (*passionné*) *Fig* lyrical. ◆**lyrisme** *nm* lyricism.

lys [lis] *nm* (*plante, fleur*) lily.

M

M, m [ɛm] *nm* M, m.

m *abrév* (*mètre*) metre.

M [məsjø] *abrév* = Monsieur.

m' [m] *voir* **me**.

ma [ma] *voir* **mon**.

macabre [makabr] *a* macabre, gruesome.

macadam [makadam] *nm* (*goudron*) tarmac.

macaron [makarɔ̃] *nm* (*gâteau*) macaroon; (*insigne*) (round) badge.

macaroni(s) [makarɔni] *nm(pl)* macaroni.

macédoine [masedwan] *nf* **m. (de légumes)** mixed vegetables; **m. (de fruits)** fruit salad.

macérer [masere] *vti Culin* to soak. ◆**macération** *nf* soaking.

mâcher [mɑʃe] *vt* to chew; **il ne mâche pas ses mots** he doesn't mince matters *ou* his words.

machiavélique [makjavelik] *a* Machiavellian.

machin [maʃɛ̃] *nm Fam* (*chose*) thing, what's-it; (*personne*) what's-his-name.

machinal, -aux [maʃinal, -o] *a* (*involontaire*) unconscious, mechanical. ◆**—ement** *adv* unconsciously, mechanically.

machination [maʃinasjɔ̃] *nf* machination.

machine [maʃin] *nf* (*appareil, avion, système etc*) machine; (*locomotive, moteur*) engine; *pl Tech* machines, (heavy) machinery; **m. à coudre** sewing machine; **m. à écrire** typewriter; **m. à laver** washing machine. ◆**machinerie** *nf Nau* engine room. ◆**machiniste** *nm Th* stage-hand.

macho [matʃo] *nm* macho m; – *a* (*f inv*) (*attitude etc*) macho.

mâchoire [mɑʃwar] *nf* jaw.

mâchonner [mɑʃɔne] *vt* to chew, munch.

maçon [masɔ̃] *nm* builder; bricklayer; mason. ◆**maçonnerie** *nf* (*travaux*) building work; (*ouvrage de briques*) brickwork; (*de pierres*) masonry, stonework.

maculer [makyle] *vt* to stain (**de** with).

Madagascar [madagaskar] *nf* Madagascar.

madame, *pl* **mesdames** [madam, medam] *nf* madam; **oui m.** yes (madam); **bonjour mesdames** good morning (ladies); **Madame** *ou* **Mme Legras** Mrs Legras; **Madame** (*sur une lettre*) *Com* Dear Madam.

madeleine [madlɛn] *nf* (small) sponge cake.

mademoiselle, *pl* **mesdemoiselles** [madmwazɛl, medmwazɛl] *nf* miss; **oui m.** yes (miss); **bonjour mesdemoiselles** good morning (ladies); **Mademoiselle** *ou* **Mlle Legras** Miss Legras; **Mademoiselle** (*sur une lettre*) *Com* Dear Madam.

madère [madɛr] *nm* (*vin*) Madeira.

madone [madɔn] *nf Rel* madonna.

madrier [madrije] *nm* (*poutre*) beam.

maestro [maestro] *nm Mus* maestro.

maf(f)ia [mafja] *nf* Mafia.

magasin [magazɛ̃] *nm* shop, *Am* store; (*entrepôt*) warehouse; (*d'arme*) & *Phot* magazine; **grand m.** department store. ◆**magasinier** *nm* warehouseman.

magazine [magazin] *nm* (*revue*) magazine.

magie [maʒi] *nf* magic. ◆**magicien, -ienne** *nmf* magician. ◆**magique** *a* (*baguette, mot*) magic; (*mystérieux, enchanteur*) magical.

magistral, -aux [maʒistral, -o] *a* masterly, magnificent. ◆**—ement** *adv* magnificently.

magistrat [maʒistra] *nm* magistrate. ◆**magistrature** *nf* judiciary, magistracy.

magnanime [maɲanim] *a* magnanimous.

magnat [magna] *nm* tycoon, magnate.

magner (se) [səmaɲe] *vpr Fam* to hurry up.

magnésium [maɲezjɔm] *nm* magnesium.

magnétique [maɲetik] *a* magnetic. ◆**magnétiser** *vt* to magnetize. ◆**magnétisme** *nm* magnetism.

magnétophone [maɲetɔfɔn] *nm* (*Fam* **magnéto**) tape recorder; **m. à cassettes** cassette recorder. ◆**magnétoscope** *nm* video (cassette) recorder.

magnifique [manifik] *a* magnificent. ◆**magnificence** *nf* magnificence. ◆**magnifiquement** *adv* magnificently.

magnolia [manɔlja] *nm* (*arbre*) magnolia.

magot [mago] *nm* (*économies*) nest egg, hoard.

magouille(s) [maguj] *nf(pl)* Pol Fam fiddling, graft.

mai [mɛ] *nm* May.

maigre [mɛgr] *a* thin, lean; (*viande*) lean; (*fromage, yaourt*) low-fat; (*repas, salaire, espoir*) meagre; **faire m.** to abstain from meat ◆**maigrement** *adv* (*chichement*) meagrely. ◆**maigreur** *nf* thinness; (*de viande*) leanness; (*médiocrité*) Fig meagreness. ◆**maigrichon, -onne** *a* & *nmf* skinny (person). ◆**maigrir** *vi* to get thin(ner); – *vt* to make thin(ner).

maille [maj] *nf* (*de tricot*) stitch; (*de filet*) mesh; **m. filée** (*de bas*) run, ladder. ◆**maillon** *nm* (*de chaîne*) link.

maillet [majɛ] *nm* (*outil*) mallet.

maillot [majo] *nm* (*de sportif*) jersey; (*de danseur*) leotard, tights; **m. (de corps)** vest, *Am* undershirt; **m. (de bain)** (*de femme*) swimsuit; (*d'homme*) (swimming) trunks.

main [mɛ̃] *nf* hand; **tenir à la m.** to hold in one's hand; **à la m.** (*livrer, faire etc*) by hand; **la m. dans la m.** hand in hand; **haut les mains!** hands up!; **donner un coup de m. à qn** to lend s.o. a (helping) hand; **coup de m.** (*habileté*) knack; **sous la m.** at hand, handy; **en venir aux mains** to come to blows; **avoir la m. heureuse** to be lucky, have a lucky streak; **mettre la dernière m. à** to put the finishing touches to; **en m. propre** (*remettre qch*) in person; **attaque/vol à m. armée** armed attack/robbery; **homme de m.** henchman, hired man; **m. courante** handrail; **prêter m.-forte à** to lend assistance to. ◆**m.-d'œuvre** *nf* (*pl* **mains-d'œuvre**) (*travail*) manpower, labour; (*salariés*) labour *ou* work force.

maint [mɛ̃] *a Litt* many a; **maintes fois, à maintes reprises** many a time.

maintenant [mɛ̃tnɑ̃] *adv* now; (*de nos jours*) nowadays; **m. que** now that; **dès m.** from now on.

maintenir* [mɛ̃tnir] *vt* (*conserver*) to keep, maintain; (*retenir*) to hold, keep; (*affirmer*) to maintain (**que** that); **– se m.** *vpr* (*durer*) to be maintained; (*rester*) to keep; (*malade, vieillard*) to hold one's own. ◆**maintien** *nm* (*action*) maintenance (**de** of); (*allure*) bearing.

maire [mɛr] *nm* mayor. ◆**mairie** *nf* town hall; (*administration*) town council.

mais [mɛ] *conj* but; **m. oui, m. si** yes of course; **m. non** definitely not.

maïs [mais] *nm* (*céréale*) maize, *Am* corn; **farine de m.** cornflour, *Am* cornstarch.

maison [mɛzɔ̃] *nf* (*bâtiment*) house; (*immeuble*) building; (*chez-soi, asile*) home; Com firm; (*famille*) household; **à la m.** (*être*) at home; (*rentrer, aller*) home; – *a inv* (*pâté, tartes etc*) homemade; **m. de la culture** arts *ou* cultural centre; **m. d'étudiants** student hostel; **m. des jeunes** youth club; **m. de repos** rest home; **m. de retraite** old people's home. ◆**maisonnée** *nf* household. ◆**maisonnette** *nf* small house.

maître [mɛtr] *nm* master; **se rendre m. de** (*incendie*) to master, control; (*pays*) to conquer; **être m. de** (*situation etc*) to be in control of, be master of; **m. de soi** in control of oneself; **m. d'école** teacher; **m. d'hôtel** (*restaurant*) head waiter; **m. de maison** host; **m. chanteur** blackmailer; **m. nageur** (*sauveteur*) swimming instructor (and lifeguard). ◆**maîtresse** *nf* mistress; **m. d'école** teacher; **m. de maison** hostess; (*ménagère*) housewife; **être m. de** (*situation etc*) to be in control of; – *af* (*idée, poutre*) main; (*carte*) master.

maîtrise [mɛtriz] *nf* (*habileté, contrôle*) mastery (**de** of); (*grade*) *Univ* master's degree (**de** in); **m. (de soi)** self-control. ◆**maîtriser** *vt* (*émotion*) to master, control; (*sujet*) to master; (*incendie*) to (bring under) control; **m. qn** to subdue s.o.; **– se m.** *vpr* to control oneself.

majesté [maʒɛste] *nf* majesty; **Votre M.** (*titre*) Your Majesty. ◆**majestueux, -euse** *a* majestic, stately.

majeur [maʒœr] **1** *a* (*primordial*) & *Mus* major; **être m.** *Jur* to be of age; **la majeure partie de** most of; **en majeure partie** for the most part. **2** *nm* (*doigt*) middle finger.

majorer [maʒɔre] *vt* to raise, increase. ◆**majoration** *nf* (*hausse*) increase (**de** in).

majorette [maʒɔrɛt] *nf* (*drum*) majorette.

majorité [maʒɔrite] *nf* majority (**de** of); (*âge*) *Jur* coming of age, majority; (*gouvernement*) party in office, government; **en m.** in the *ou* a majority; (*pour la plupart*) in the majority. ◆**majoritaire** *a* (*vote etc*) majority-; **être m.** to be in the *ou* a majority; **être m. aux élections** to win the elections.

Majorque [maʒɔrk] *nf* Majorca.

majuscule [maʒyskyl] *a* capital; – *nf* capital letter.

mal, maux [mal, mo] **1** *nm* Phil Rel evil;

(*dommage*) harm; (*douleur*) pain; (*maladie*) illness; (*malheur*) misfortune; **dire du m.** de to speak ill of; **m. de gorge** sore throat; **m. de tête** headache; **m. de ventre** stomachache; **m. de mer** seasickness; **m. du pays** homesickness; **avoir le m. du pays**/*etc* to be homesick; **avoir m. à la tête/à la gorge**/*etc* to have a headache/sore throat/*etc*; **ça (me) fait m., j'ai m.** it hurts (me); **faire du m. à** to harm, hurt; **avoir du m. à faire** to have trouble (in) doing; **se donner du m. pour faire** to go to a lot of trouble to do. **2** *adv* (*travailler etc*) badly; (*entendre, comprendre*) not too well; **aller m.** (*projet etc*) to be going badly; (*personne*) *Méd* to be bad *or* ill; **m. (à l'aise)** uncomfortable; **se trouver m.** to (feel) faint; **(ce n'est) pas m.** (*mauvais*) (that's) not bad; **pas m.** (*beaucoup*) *Fam* quite a lot (de of); **c'est m. de jurer**/*etc* (*moralement*) it's wrong to swear/*etc*; **de m. en pis** from bad to worse; **m. renseigner/interpréter/** *etc* to misinform/misinterpret/*etc*.

malade [malad] *a* ill, sick; (*arbre, dent*) diseased; (*estomac, jambe*) bad; **être m. du foie/cœur** to have a bad liver/heart; — *nmf* sick person; (*à l'hôpital, d'un médecin*) patient; **les malades** the sick. ◆**maladie** *nf* illness, sickness, disease. ◆**maladif, -ive** *a* (*personne*) sickly; (*morbide*) morbid.

maladroit [maladrwa] *a* (*malhabile*) clumsy, awkward; (*indélicat*) tactless. ◆**maladresse** *nf* clumsiness, awkwardness; tactlessness; (*bévue*) blunder.

malaise [malɛz] *nm* (*angoisse*) uneasiness, malaise; (*indisposition*) faintness, dizziness; **avoir un m.** to feel faint *ou* dizzy.

malaisé [maleze] *a* difficult.

Malaisie [malɛzi] *nf* Malaysia.

malaria [malarja] *nf* malaria.

malavisé [malavize] *a* ill-advised (**de faire** to do).

malax/er [malakse] *vt* (*pétrir*) to knead; (*mélanger*) to mix. ◆**-eur** *nm* *Tech* mixer.

malchance [malʃɑ̃s] *nf* bad luck; **une m.** (*mésaventure*) a mishap. ◆**malchanceux, -euse** *a* unlucky.

malcommode [malkɔmɔd] *a* awkward.

mâle [mal] *a* male; (*viril*) manly; — *nm* male.

malédiction [malediksjɔ̃] *nf* curse.

maléfice [malefis] *nm* evil spell. ◆**maléfique** *a* baleful, evil.

malencontreux, -euse [malɑ̃kɔ̃trø, -øz] *a* unfortunate.

malentendant, -ante [malɑ̃tɑ̃dɑ̃, -ɑ̃t] *nmf* person who is hard of hearing.

malentendu [malɑ̃tɑ̃dy] *nm* misunderstanding.

malfaçon [malfasɔ̃] *nf* defect.

malfaisant [malfəzɑ̃] *a* evil, harmful.

malfaiteur [malfɛtœr] *nm* criminal.

malformation [malfɔrmasjɔ̃] *nf* malformation.

malgré [malgre] *prép* in spite of; **m. tout** for all that, after all; **m. soi** (*à contrecœur*) reluctantly.

malhabile [malabil] *a* clumsy.

malheur [malœr] *nm* (*événement*) misfortune; (*accident*) mishap; (*malchance*) bad luck, misfortune; **par m.** unfortunately. ◆**malheureusement** *adv* unfortunately. ◆**malheureux, -euse** *a* (*misérable*, miserable; (*fâcheux*) unfortunate; (*malchanceux*) unlucky, unfortunate; — *nmf* (*infortuné*) (poor) wretch; (*indigent*) needy person.

malhonnête [malɔnɛt] *a* dishonest. ◆**malhonnêteté** *nf* dishonesty; **une m.** (*action*) a dishonest act.

malice [malis] *nf* mischievousness. ◆**malicieux, -euse** *a* mischievous.

malin, -igne [malɛ̃, -iɲ] *a* (*astucieux*) smart, clever; (*plaisir*) malicious; (*tumeur*) *Méd* malignant. ◆**malignité** *nf* (*méchanceté*) malignity; *Méd* malignancy.

malingre [malɛ̃gr] *a* puny, sickly.

malintentionné [malɛ̃tɑ̃sjɔne] *a* ill-intentioned (**à l'égard de** towards).

malle [mal] *nf* (*coffre*) trunk; (*de véhicule*) boot, *Am* trunk. ◆**mallette** *nf* small suitcase; (*pour documents*) attaché case.

malléable [maleabl] *a* malleable.

malmener [malməne] *vt* to manhandle, treat badly.

malodorant [malɔdɔrɑ̃] *a* smelly.

malotru, -ue [malɔtry] *nmf* boor, lout.

malpoli [malpɔli] *a* impolite.

malpropre [malprɔpr] *a* (*sale*) dirty. ◆**malpropreté** *nf* dirtiness.

malsain [malsɛ̃] *a* unhealthy, unwholesome.

malséant [malseɑ̃] *a* unseemly.

malt [malt] *nm* malt.

Malte [malt] *nf* Malta. ◆**maltais, -aise** *a* & *nmf* Maltese.

maltraiter [maltrete] *vt* to ill-treat.

malveillant [malvejɑ̃] *a* malevolent. ◆**malveillance** *nf* malevolence, ill will.

malvenu [malvəny] *a* (*déplacé*) uncalled-for.

maman [mamɑ̃] *nf* mum(my), *Am* mom(my).

mamelle [mamɛl] *nf* (*d'animal*) teat; (*de*

vache) udder. ◆**mamelon** *nm* **1** (*de femme*) nipple. **2** (*colline*) hillock.

mamie [mami] *nf Fam* granny, grandma.

mammifère [mamifɛr] *nm* mammal.

manche [mɑ̃ʃ] **1** *nf* (*de vêtement*) sleeve; *Sp Cartes* round; **la M.** *Géog* the Channel. **2** *nm* (*d'outil etc*) handle; **m. à balai** broomstick; (*d'avion, d'ordinateur*) joystick. ◆**manchette** *nf* **1** (*de chemise etc*) cuff. **2** *Journ* headline. ◆**manchon** *nm* (*fourrure*) muff.

manchot, -ote [mɑ̃ʃo, -ɔt] **1** *a* & *nmf* one-armed *ou* one-handed (person). **2** *nm* (*oiseau*) penguin.

mandarin [mɑ̃darɛ̃] *nm* (*lettré influent*) *Univ Péj* mandarin.

mandarine [mɑ̃darin] *nf* (*fruit*) tangerine, mandarin (orange).

mandat [mɑ̃da] *nm* **1** (*postal*) money order. **2** *Pol* mandate; *Jur* power of attorney; **m. d'arrêt** warrant (**contre qn** for s.o.'s arrest). ◆**mandataire** *nm* (*délégué*) representative, proxy. ◆**mandater** *vt* to delegate; *Pol* to give a mandate to.

manège [manɛʒ] *nm* **1** (*à la foire*) merry-go-round, roundabout; (*lieu*) riding-school; (*piste*) ring, manège; (*exercice*) horsemanship. **2** (*intrigue*) wiles, trickery.

manette [manɛt] *nf* lever, handle.

manger [mɑ̃ʒe] *vt* to eat; (*essence, électricité*) *Fig* to guzzle; (*fortune*) to eat up; (*corroder*) to eat into; **donner à m.** à to feed; – *vi* to eat; **on mange bien ici** the food is good here; **m. à sa faim** to have enough to eat; – *nm* food. ◆**mangeable** *a* eatable. ◆**mangeaille** *nf Péj* (bad) food. ◆**mangeoire** *nf* (*feeding*) trough. ◆**mangeur, -euse** *nmf* eater.

mangue [mɑ̃g] *nf* (*fruit*) mango.

manie [mani] *nf* mania, craze (**de** for). ◆**maniaque** *a* finicky, fussy; – *nmf* fusspot, *Am* fussbudget; **un m. de la propreté**/*etc* a maniac for cleanliness/*etc*.

manier [manje] *vt* to handle; **se m. bien** (*véhicule etc*) to handle well. ◆**maniabilité** *nf* (*de véhicule etc*) manoeuvrability. ◆**maniable** *a* easy to handle. ◆**maniement** *nm* handling; **m. d'armes** *Mil* drill.

manière [manjɛr] *nf* way, manner; *pl* (*politesse*) manners; **de toute m.** anyway, anyhow; **de m. à faire** so as to do; **à ma m.** my way, (in) my own way; **de cette m.** (in) this way; **la m. dont elle parle** the way (in which) she talks; **à la m. générale** generally speaking; **faire des manières** (*chichis*) to make a fuss; (*être affecté*) to put on airs. ◆**maniéré** *a* affected; (*style*) mannered.

manif [manif] *nf Fam* demo.

manifeste [manifɛst] **1** *a* (*évident*) manifest, obvious. **2** *nm Pol* manifesto.

manifester [manifɛste] **1** *vt* to show, manifest; – **se m.** *vpr* (*apparaître*) to appear; (*sentiment, maladie etc*) to show *ou* manifest itself. **2** *vi Pol* to demonstrate. ◆**manifestant, -ante** *nmf* demonstrator. ◆**manifestation** *nf* **1** (*expression*) expression, manifestation; (*apparition*) appearance. **2** *Pol* demonstration; (*réunion, fête*) event.

manigance [manigɑ̃s] *nf* little scheme. ◆**manigancer** *vt* to plot.

manipuler [manipyle] *vt* (*manier*) to handle; (*faits, électeurs*) *Péj* to manipulate. ◆**manipulation** *nf* handling; *Péj* manipulation (**de** of); *pl Pol Péj* manipulation.

manivelle [manivɛl] *nf Aut* crank.

mannequin [mankɛ̃] *nm* (*femme, homme*) (fashion) model; (*statue*) dummy.

manœuvre [manœvr] **1** *nm* (*ouvrier*) labourer. **2** *nf* (*opération*) & *Mil* manoeuvre, *Am* maneuver; (*action*) manoeuvring; (*intrigue*) scheme. ◆**manœuvrer** *vt* (*véhicule, personne etc*) to manoeuvre, *Am* maneuver; (*machine*) to operate; – *vi* to manoeuvre, *Am* maneuver.

manoir [manwar] *nm* manor house.

manque [mɑ̃k] *nm* lack (**de** of); (*lacune*) gap; *pl* (*défauts*) shortcomings; **m. à gagner** loss of profit. ◆**manqu/er** *vt* (*chance, cible etc*) to miss; (*ne pas réussir*) to make a mess of; (*examen*) to fail; – *vi* (*faire défaut*) to be short *ou* lacking; (*être absent*) to be absent (**à** from); (*être en moins*) to be missing *ou* short; (*défaillir, échouer*) to fail; **m. de** (*pain, argent etc*) to be short of; (*attention, cohérence*) to lack; **ça manque de sel**/*etc* it lacks salt/*etc*, there isn't any salt/*etc*; **m. à** (*son devoir*) to fail in; (*sa parole*) to break; **le temps lui manque** he's short of time, he has no time; **elle**/**cela lui manque** he misses her/that; **je ne manquerai pas de venir** I won't fail to come; **ne manquez pas de venir** don't forget to come; **elle a manqué (de) tomber** (*faillir*) she nearly fell; – *v imp* **il manque**/**il nous manque dix tasses** there are/we are ten cups short. ◆**—ant** *a* missing. ◆**—é** *a* (*médecin, pilote etc*) (*livre*) unsuccessful. ◆**—ement** *nm* breach (**à** of).

mansarde [mɑ̃sard] *nf* attic.

manteau, -x [mɑ̃to] *nm* coat.

manucure [manykyr] *nmf* manicurist. ◆**manucurer** *vt Fam* to manicure.

manuel, -elle [manɥɛl] **1** *a* (*travail etc*) manual. **2** *nm* (*livre*) handbook, manual.

manufacture [manyfaktyr] *nf* factory. ◆**manufacturé** *a* (*produit*) manufactured.

manuscrit [manyskri] *nm* manuscript; (*tapé à la machine*) typescript.

manutention [manytɑ̃sjɔ̃] *nf* Com handling (*of stores*). ◆**manutentionnaire** *nmf* packer.

mappemonde [mapmɔ̃d] *nf* map of the world; (*sphère*) Fam globe.

maquereau, -x [makro] *nm* (*poisson*) mackerel.

maquette [makɛt] *nf* (*scale*) model.

maquill/er [makije] *vt* (*visage*) to make up; (*voiture etc*) Péj to tamper with; (*vérité etc*) Péj to fake; **— se m.** to make (oneself) up. ◆**—age** *nm* (*fard*) make-up.

maquis [maki] *nm* Bot scrub, bush; Mil Hist maquis.

maraîcher, -ère [mareʃe, -ɛʃɛr] *nmf* market gardener, Am truck farmer.

marais [marɛ] *nm* marsh, bog; **m. salant** saltworks, saltern.

marasme [marasm] *nm* Écon stagnation.

marathon [maratɔ̃] *nm* marathon.

maraud/eur, -euse [marodœr, -øz] *nmf* petty thief.

marbre [marbr] *nm* marble. ◆**marbrier** *nm* (*funéraire*) monumental mason.

marc [mar] *nm* (*eau-de-vie*) marc, brandy; **m. (de café)** coffee grounds.

marchand, -ande [marʃɑ̃, -ɑ̃d] *nmf* trader, shopkeeper; (*de vins, charbon*) merchant; (*de cycles, meubles*) dealer; **m. de bonbons** confectioner; **m. de couleurs** hardware merchant *ou* dealer; **m. de journaux** (*dans la rue*) newsvendor; (*dans un magasin*) newsagent, Am news dealer; **m. de légumes** greengrocer; **m. de poissons** fishmonger; **—** *a* (*valeur*) market; (*prix*) trade-. ◆**marchandise(s)** *nf(pl)* goods, merchandise.

marchand/er [marʃɑ̃de] *vi* to haggle, bargain; **—** *vt* (*objet*) to haggle over. ◆**—age** *nm* haggling, bargaining.

marche [marʃ] *nf* **1** (*d'escalier*) step, stair. **2** (*démarche, trajet*) walk; Mil Mus march; (*pas*) pace; (*de train, véhicule*) movement; (*de maladie, d'événement*) progress, course; **la m.** (*action*) Sp walking; **faire m. arrière** Aut to reverse; **la bonne m. de** (*opération, machine*) the smooth running of; **un train/véhicule en m.** a moving train/vehicle; **mettre qch en m.** to start sth (up). ◆**marcher** *vi* (*à pied*) to walk; Mil to

march; (*poser le pied*) to tread, step; (*train, véhicule etc*) to run, go, move; (*fonctionner*) to go, work, run; (*prospérer*) to go well; **faire m.** (*machine*) to work; (*entreprise*) to run; (*personne*) Fam to kid; **ça marche?** Fam how's it going?; **elle va m.** (*accepter*) Fam she'll go along (with it). ◆**marcheur, -euse** *nmf* walker.

marché [marʃe] *nm* (*lieu*) market; (*contrat*) deal; **faire son** *ou* **le m.** to do one's shopping (*in the market*); **être bon m.** to be cheap; **voiture(s)/etc bon m.** cheap car(s)/etc; **vendre (à) bon m.** to sell cheap(ly); **c'est meilleur m.** it's cheaper; **par-dessus le m.** Fig into the bargain; **au m. noir** on the black market; **le M. commun** the Common Market.

marchepied [marʃəpje] *nm* (*de train, bus*) step(s); (*de voiture*) running board.

mardi [mardi] *nm* Tuesday; **M. gras** Shrove Tuesday.

mare [mar] *nf* (*flaque*) pool; (*étang*) pond.

marécage [marekaʒ] *nm* swamp, marsh. ◆**marécageux, -euse** *a* marshy, swampy.

maréchal, -aux [mareʃal, -o] *nm* Fr Mil marshal. ◆**m.-ferrant** *nm* (*pl* maréchaux-ferrants*) blacksmith.

marée [mare] *nf* tide; (*poissons*) fresh (sea) fish; **m. noire** oil slick.

marelle [marɛl] *nf* (*jeu*) hopscotch.

margarine [margarin] *nf* margarine.

marge [marʒ] *nf* margin; **en m.** de (*en dehors de*) on the periphery of, on the fringe(s) of; **m. de sécurité** safety margin. ◆**marginal, -ale, -aux** *a* (*secondaire, asocial*) marginal; **—** *nmf* misfit, dropout; (*bizarre*) weirdo.

marguerite [margərit] *nf* (*fleur*) marguerite, daisy.

mari [mari] *nm* husband.

mariage [marjaʒ] *nm* marriage; (*cérémonie*) wedding; (*mélange*) Fig blend, marriage; **demande en m.** proposal (of marriage). ◆**mari/er** *vt* (*couleurs*) to blend; **m. qn** (*maire, prêtre etc*) to marry s.o.; **m. qn avec** to marry s.o. (off) to; **— se m.** *vpr* to get married, marry; **se m. avec qn** to marry s.o., get married to s.o. ◆**—é** *a* married; **—** *nm* (bride)groom; **les mariés** the bride and (bride)groom; **les jeunes mariés** the newly-weds. ◆**—ée** *nf* bride.

marijuana [mariʒɥana] *nf* marijuana.

marin [marɛ̃] *nm* (*air, sel etc*) sea-; (*flore*) marine; (*mille*) nautical; (*costume*) sailor-; **—** *nm* seaman, sailor. ◆**marine** *nf* **m.** (**de guerre**) navy; **m. marchande** merchant navy; **(bleu) m.** (*couleur*) navy (blue).

marina [marina] *nf* marina.

mariner [marine] *vti Culin* to marinate.

marionnette [marjɔnɛt] *nf* puppet; (*à fils*) marionette.

maritalement [maritalmɑ̃] *adv* **vivre m.** to live together (as husband and wife).

maritime [maritim] *a* (*droit, province, climat etc*) maritime; (*port*) sea-; (*gare*) harbour-; (*chantier*) naval; (*agent*) shipping-.

marjolaine [marʒɔlɛn] *nf* (*aromate*) marjoram.

mark [mark] *nm* (*monnaie*) mark.

marmaille [marmaj] *nf* (*enfants*) *Fam* kids.

marmelade [marməlad] *nf* **m. (de fruits)** stewed fruit; **en m.** *Culin Fig* in a mush.

marmite [marmit] *nf* (*cooking*) pot.

marmonner [marmɔne] *vti* to mutter.

marmot [marmo] *nm* (*enfant*) *Fam* kid.

marmotter [marmɔte] *vti* to mumble.

Maroc [marɔk] *nm* Morocco. ◆**marocain, -aine** *a* & *nmf* Moroccan.

maroquinerie [marɔkinri] *nf* (*magasin*) leather goods shop. ◆**maroquinier** *nm* leather dealer.

marotte [marɔt] *nf* (*dada*) *Fam* fad, craze.

marque [mark] *nf* (*trace, signe*) mark; (*de fabricant*) make, brand; (*points*) *Sp* score; **m. de fabrique** trademark; **m. déposée** registered trademark; **la m. de** (*preuve*) the stamp of; **de m.** (*hôte, visiteur*) distinguished; (*produit*) of quality. ◆**marqu/er** *vt* (*par une marque etc*) to mark; (*écrire*) to note down; (*indiquer*) to show, mark; (*point, but*) *Sp* to score; **m. qn** *Sp* to mark s.o.; **m. les points** *Sp* to keep (the) score; **m. le coup** to mark the event; — *vi* (*trace*) to leave a mark; (*date, événement*) to stand out; *Sp* to score. ◆**—ant** *a* (*remarquable*) outstanding. ◆**—é** *a* (*différence, accent etc*) marked, pronounced. ◆**—eur** *nm* (*crayon*) marker.

marquis [marki] *nm* marquis. ◆**marquise** *nf* **1** marchioness. **2** (*auvent*) glass canopy.

marraine [marɛn] *nf* godmother.

marre [mar] *nf* **en avoir m.** *Fam* to be fed up (de with).

marr/er (se) [səmare] *vpr Fam* to have a good laugh. ◆**—ant** *a Fam* hilarious, funny.

marron¹ [marɔ̃] **1** *nm* chestnut; (*couleur*) (chestnut) brown; **m. (d'Inde)** horse chestnut; — *a inv* (*couleur*) (chestnut) brown. **2** *nm* (*coup*) *Fam* punch, clout. ◆**marronnier** *nm* (horse) chestnut tree.

marron², -onne [marɔ̃, -ɔn] *a* (*médecin etc*) bogus.

mars [mars] *nm* March.

marsouin [marswɛ̃] *nm* porpoise.

marteau, -x [marto] *nm* hammer; (*de porte*) (door)knocker; **m. piqueur, m. pneumatique** pneumatic drill. ◆**marteler** *vt* to hammer. ◆**martèlement** *nm* hammering.

martial, -aux [marsjal, -o] *a* martial; **cour martiale** court-martial; **loi martiale** martial law.

martien, -ienne [marsjɛ̃, -jɛn] *nmf* & *a* Martian.

martinet [martine] *nm* (*fouet*) (small) whip.

martin-pêcheur [martɛ̃pɛʃœr] *nm* (*pl* **martins-pêcheurs**) (*oiseau*) kingfisher.

martyr, -yre¹ [martir] *nmf* (*personne*) martyr; **enfant m.** battered child. ◆**martyre²** *nm* (*souffrance*) martyrdom. ◆**martyriser** *vt* to torture; (*enfant*) to batter.

marxisme [marksism] *nm* Marxism. ◆**marxiste** *a* & *nmf* Marxist.

mascara [maskara] *nm* mascara.

mascarade [maskarad] *nf* masquerade.

mascotte [maskɔt] *nf* mascot.

masculin [maskylɛ̃] *a* male; (*viril*) masculine, manly; *Gram* masculine; (*vêtement, équipe*) men's; — *nm Gram* masculine. ◆**masculinité** *nf* masculinity.

masochisme [mazɔʃism] *nm* masochism. ◆**masochiste** *nmf* masochist; — *a* masochistic.

masque [mask] *nm* mask. ◆**masquer** *vt* (*dissimuler*) to mask (à from); (*cacher à la vue*) to block off.

massacre [masakr] *nm* massacre, slaughter. ◆**massacr/er** *vt* to massacre, slaughter; (*abîmer*) *Fam* to ruin. ◆**—ant** *a* (*humeur*) excruciating.

massage [masaʒ] *nm* massage.

masse [mas] *nf* **1** (*volume*) mass; (*gros morceau, majorité*) bulk (de of); **en m.** (*venir, vendre*) in large numbers; **départ en m.** mass *ou* wholesale departure; **manifestation de m.** mass demonstration; **la m.** (*foule*) the masses; **les masses** (*peuple*) the masses; **une m. de** (*tas*) a mass of; **des masses de** *Fam* masses of. **2** (*outil*) sledgehammer. **3** *Él* earth, *Am* ground. ◆**mass/er 1** *vt*, — **se m.** *vpr* (*gens*) to mass. **2** *vt* (*frotter*) to massage. ◆**—eur** *nm* masseur. ◆**—euse** *nf* masseuse.

massif, -ive [masif, -iv] **1** *a* (*dé-parts etc*) mass-; (*or, chêne etc*) solid. **2** *nm* (*d'arbres, de fleurs*) clump; *Géog* massif. ◆**massivement** *adv* (*en masse*) in large numbers.

massue [masy] *nf* (*bâton*) club.

mastic [mastik] *nm* (*pour vitres*) putty; (*pour bois*) filler; **m. (silicone)** mastic.

◆**mastiquer** vt **1** (vitre) to putty; (porte) to mastic; (bois) to fill. **2** (mâcher) to chew, masticate.

mastoc [mastɔk] a inv Péj Fam massive.

mastodonte [mastɔdɔ̃t] nm (personne) Péj monster; (véhicule) juggernaut.

masturber (se) [səmastyrbe] vpr to masturbate. ◆**masturbation** nf masturbation.

masure [mazyr] nf tumbledown house.

mat [mat] **1** a (papier, couleur) mat(t); (bruit) dull. **2** a inv & nm Échecs (check)mate; **faire** ou **mettre m.** to (check)mate.

mât [ma] nm (de navire) mast; (poteau) pole.

match [matʃ] nm Sp match, Am game; **m. nul** tie, draw.

matelas [matla] nm mattress; **m. pneumatique** air bed. ◆**matelassé** a (meuble) padded; (tissu) quilted.

matelot [matlo] nm sailor, seaman.

mater [mate] vt (enfant, passion etc) to subdue.

matérialiser [materjalize] vt, — **se m.** vpr to materialize. ◆**matérialisation** nf materialization.

matérialisme [materjalism] nm materialism. ◆**matérialiste** a materialistic; — nmf materialist.

matériaux [materjo] nmpl (building) materials; (de roman, enquête etc) material.

matériel, -ielle [materjɛl] a material; (personne) Péj materialistic; (financier) financial; (pratique) practical. **2** nm equipment, material(s); (d'un ordinateur) hardware inv. ◆**matériellement** adv materially; **m. impossible** physically impossible.

maternel, -elle [maternɛl] a motherly, maternal; (parenté, réprimande) maternal; — nf (école) maternelle nursery school. ◆**materner** vt to mother. ◆**maternité** nf (état) motherhood, maternity; (hôpital) maternity hospital ou unit; (grossesse) pregnancy; **de m.** (congé, allocation) maternity-.

mathématique [matematik] a mathematical; — nfpl mathematics. ◆**mathématicien, -ienne** nmf mathematician. ◆**maths** [mat] nfpl Fam maths, Am math.

matière [matjɛr] nf (sujet) & Scol subject; (de livre) subject matter; **une m., la m., des matières** (substance(s)) matter; **m. première** raw material; **en m. d'art**/etc as regards art/etc, in art/etc; **s'y connaître en m.** de to be experienced in.

matin [matɛ̃] nm morning; **de grand m., de bon m., au petit m.** very early (in the morn-

ing); **le m.** (chaque matin) in the morning; **à sept heures du m.** at seven in the morning; **tous les mardis m.** every Tuesday morning. ◆**matinal, -aux** a (personne) early; (fleur, soleil etc) morning-. ◆**matinée** nf morning; Th matinée; **faire la grasse m.** to sleep late, lie in.

matou [matu] nm tomcat.

matraque [matrak] nf (de policier) truncheon, Am billy (club); (de malfaiteur) cosh, club. ◆**matraqu/er** vt (frapper) to club; (publicité etc) to plug (away) at. ◆**-age** nm **m.** (publicitaire) plugging, publicity build-up.

matrice [matris] nf **1** Anat womb. **2** Tech matrix.

matricule [matrikyl] nm (registration) number; — a (livret, numéro) registration.

matrimonial, -aux [matrimɔnjal, -o] a matrimonial.

mâture [matyr] nf Nau masts.

maturité [matyrite] nf maturity. ◆**maturation** nf maturing.

maudire* [modir] vt to curse. ◆**maudit** a (sacré) (ac)cursed, damned.

maugréer [mogree] vi to growl, grumble (contre at).

mausolée [mozole] nm mausoleum.

maussade [mosad] a (personne etc) glum, sullen; (temps) gloomy.

mauvais [move] a bad; (méchant, malveillant) evil, wicked; (mal choisi) wrong; (mer) rough; **plus m.** worse; **le plus m.** the worst; **il fait m.** the weather's bad; **ça sent m.** it smells bad; **être m. en** (anglais etc) to be bad at; **mauvaise santé** ill ou bad ou poor health; — nm **le bon et le m.** the good and the bad.

mauve [mov] a & nm (couleur) mauve.

mauviette [movjɛt] nf personne Péj weakling.

maux [mo] voir **mal.**

maxime [maksim] nf maxim.

maximum [maksimɔm] nm maximum; **le m. de** (force etc) the maximum (amount of); **au m.** as much as possible; (tout au plus) at most; — a maximum; **la température m.** maximum temperature. ◆**maximal, -aux** a maximum.

mayonnaise [majɔnɛz] nf mayonnaise.

mazout [mazut] nm (fuel) oil.

me [m(ə)] (m' before vowel or mute h) pron **1** (complément direct) me; **il me voit** he sees me. **2** (indirect) (to) me; **elle me parle** she speaks to me; **tu me l'as dit** you told me. **3** (réfléchi) myself; **je me lave** I wash myself.

méandres [meɑ̃dr] nmpl meander(ing)s.

mec [mɛk] *nm* (*individu*) *Arg* guy, bloke.

mécanique [mekanik] *a* mechanical; (*jouet*) clockwork; – *nf* (*science*) mechanics; (*mécanisme*) mechanism. ◆**mécanicien** *nm* mechanic; *Rail* train driver. ◆**mécanisme** *nm* mechanism.

mécaniser [mekanize] *vt* to mechanize. ◆**mécanisation** *nf* mechanization.

mécène [mesɛn] *nm* patron (of the arts).

méchant [meʃɑ̃] *a* (*cruel*) malicious, wicked, evil; (*désagréable*) nasty; (*enfant*) naughty; (*chien*) vicious; **ce n'est pas m.** (*grave*) *Fam* it's nothing much. ◆**méchamment** *adv* (*cruellement*) maliciously; (*très*) *Fam* terribly. ◆**méchanceté** *nf* malice, wickedness; **une m.** (*acte*) a malicious act; (*parole*) a malicious word.

mèche [mɛʃ] *nf* **1** (*de cheveux*) lock; (*de reflets*) highlights. **2** (*de bougie*) wick; (*de pétard*) fuse; (*de perceuse*) drill, bit. **3 de m. avec qn** (*complicité*) *Fam* in collusion *ou* cahoots with s.o.

méconn/aître* [mekɔnɛtr] *vt* to ignore; (*méjuger*) to fail to appreciate. ◆**–u** *a* unrecognized. ◆**–aissable** *a* unrecognizable.

mécontent [mekɔ̃tɑ̃] *a* dissatisfied, discontented (**de** with). ◆**mécontent/er** *vt* to displease, dissatisfy. ◆**–ement** *nm* dissatisfaction, discontent.

médaille [medaj] *nf* (*décoration*) *Sp* medal; (*pieuse*) medallion; (*pour chien*) name tag; **être m. d'or/d'argent** *Sp* to be a gold/silver medallist. ◆**médaillé, -ée** *nmf* medal holder. ◆**médaillon** *nm* (*bijou*) locket, medallion; (*ornement*) *Archit* medallion.

médecin [medsɛ̃] *nm* doctor, physician. ◆**médecine** *nf* medicine; **étudiant en m.** medical student. ◆**médical, -aux** *a* medical. ◆**médicament** *nm* medicine. ◆**médicinal, -aux** *a* medicinal. ◆**médico-légal, -aux** *a* (*laboratoire*) forensic.

médias [medja] *nmpl* (mass) media. ◆**médiatique** *a* media-.

médiateur, -trice [medjatœr, -tris] *nmf* mediator; – *a* mediating. ◆**médiation** *nf* mediation.

médiéval, -aux [medjeval, -o] *a* medi(a)eval.

médiocre [medjɔkr] *a* mediocre, second-rate. ◆**médiocrement** *adv* (*pas très*) not very; (*pas très bien*) not very well. ◆**médiocrité** *nf* mediocrity.

médire* [medir] *vi* **m. de** to speak ill of, slander.

cious gossip, slander; **une m.** a piece of malicious gossip.

méditer [medite] *vt* (*conseil etc*) to meditate on; **m. de faire** to consider doing; – *vi* to meditate (**sur** on). ◆**méditatif, -ive** *a* meditative. ◆**méditation** *nf* meditation.

Méditerranée [mediterane] *nf* **la M.** the Mediterranean. ◆**méditerranéen, -enne** *a* Mediterranean.

médium [medjɔm] *nm* (*spirite*) medium.

méduse [medyz] *nf* jellyfish.

méduser [medyze] *vt* to stun, dumbfound.

meeting [mitin] *nm* *Pol Sp* meeting, rally.

méfait [mefɛ] *nm* (*délit*) misdeed; *pl* (*dégâts*) ravages.

méfi/er (se) [səmefje] *vpr* **se m. de** to distrust, mistrust; (*faire attention à*) to watch out for, beware of; **méfie-toi!** watch out!, beware!; **je me méfie** I'm distrustful *ou* suspicious. ◆**–ant** *a* distrustful, suspicious. ◆**méfiance** *nf* distrust, mistrust.

mégalomane [megaloman] *nmf* megalomaniac. ◆**mégalomanie** *nf* megalomania.

mégaphone [megafɔn] *nm* loudhailer.

mégarde (par) [parmegard] *adv* inadvertently, by mistake.

mégère [meʒɛr] *nf* (*femme*) *Péj* shrew.

mégot [mego] *nm* *Fam* cigarette end *ou* butt.

meilleur, -eure [mɛjœr] *a* better (**que** than); **le m. moment/résultat/etc** the best moment/result/*etc*; – *nmf* **le m., la meilleure** the best (one).

mélancolie [melɑ̃kɔli] *nf* melancholy, gloom. ◆**mélancolique** *a* melancholy, gloomy.

mélange [melɑ̃ʒ] *nm* mixture, blend; (*opération*) mixing. ◆**mélanger** *vt* (*mêler*) to mix; (*brouiller*) to mix (up), muddle; – **se m.** *vpr* to mix; (*idées etc*) to get mixed (up) *ou* muddled.

mélasse [melas] *nf* treacle, *Am* molasses.

mêl/er [mele] *vt* to mix, mingle (**à** with); (*qualités, thèmes*) to combine; (*brouiller*) to mix (up), muddle; **m. qn à** (*impliquer*) to involve s.o. in; – **se m.** *vpr* to mix, mingle (**à** with); **se m. à** (*la foule etc*) to join; **se m. de** (*s'ingérer dans*) to meddle in; **mêle-toi de ce qui te regarde!** mind your own business! ◆**–é** *a* mixed (**de** with). ◆**–ée** *nf* (*bataille*) rough-and-tumble; *Rugby* scrum(mage).

méli-mélo [melimelo] *nm* (*pl* **mélis-mélos**) *Fam* muddle.

mélodie [melɔdi] *nf* melody. ◆**mélodieux, -euse** *a* melodious. ◆**mélodique** *a* *Mus* melodic. ◆**mélomane** *nmf* music lover.

mélodrame [melɔdram] *nm* melodrama. ◆**mélodramatique** *a* melodramatic.

melon [m(ə)lɔ̃] *nm* 1 (*fruit*) melon. 2 (*chapeau*) m. bowler (hat).

membrane [mɑ̃bran] *nf* membrane.

membre [mɑ̃br] *nm* 1 *Anat* limb. 2 (*d'un groupe*) member.

même [mɛm] 1 *a* (*identique*) same; en m. temps at the same time (que as); ce livre/ *etc* m. (*exact*) this very book/*etc*; il est la bonté m. he is kindness itself; lui-m./vous-m./*etc* himself/yourself/*etc*; — *pron* le m., la m. the same (one); j'ai les mêmes I have the same (ones). 2 *adv* (*y compris, aussi*) even; m. si even if; tout de m., quand m. all the same; de m. likewise; de m. que just as; ici m. in this very place; à m. de in a position to; à m. le sol on the ground; à m. la bouteille from the bottle.

mémento [memɛ̃to] *nm* (*aide-mémoire*) handbook; (*agenda*) notebook.

mémoire [memwar] 1 *nf* memory; de m. d'homme in living memory; à la m. de in memory of. 2 *nm* (*requête*) petition; *Univ* memoir; *pl Littér* memoirs. ◆**mémorable** *a* memorable. ◆**mémorandum** [memɔrɑ̃dɔm] *nm Pol Com* memorandum. ◆**mémorial, -aux** *nm* (*monument*) memorial.

menace [mənas] *nf* threat, menace. ◆**mena/cer** *vt* to threaten (de faire to do). ◆**—çant** *a* threatening.

ménage [menaʒ] *nm* (*entretien*) housekeeping; (*couple*) couple, household; faire le m. to do the housework; faire bon m. avec to get on happily with. ◆**ménager**[1], **-ère** *a* (*appareil*) domestic, household-; travaux ménagers housework; — *nf* (*femme*) housewife.

ménag/er[2] [menaʒe] *vt* (*arranger*) to prepare *ou* arrange (carefully); (*épargner*) to use sparingly, be careful with; (*fenêtre, escalier etc*) to build; m. qn to treat *ou* handle s.o. gently *ou* carefully. ◆**—ement** *nm* (*soin*) care.

ménagerie [menaʒri] *nf* menagerie.

mendier [mɑ̃dje] *vi* to beg; — *vt* to beg for. ◆**mendiant, -ante** *nmf* beggar. ◆**mendicité** *nf* begging.

menées [məne] *nfpl* schemings, intrigues.

men/er [məne] *vt* (*personne, vie etc*) to lead; (*lutte, enquête, tâche etc*) to carry out; (*affaires*) to run; (*bateau*) to command; m. qn à (*accompagner, transporter*) to take s.o. to; m. à bien *Fig* to carry through; — *vi Sp* to lead. ◆**—eur, -euse** *nmf* (*de révolte*) (ring)leader.

méningite [menɛ̃ʒit] *nf Méd* meningitis.

ménopause [menɔpoz] *nf* menopause.

menottes [mənɔt] *nfpl* handcuffs.

mensonge [mɑ̃sɔ̃ʒ] *nm* lie; (*action*) lying. ◆**mensonger, -ère** *a* untrue, false.

menstruation [mɑ̃stryasjɔ̃] *nf* menstruation.

mensuel, -elle [mɑ̃sɥɛl] *a* monthly; — *nm* (*revue*) monthly. ◆**mensualité** *nf* monthly payment. ◆**mensuellement** *adv* monthly.

mensurations [mɑ̃syrasjɔ̃] *nfpl* measurements.

mental, -aux [mɑ̃tal, -o] *a* mental. ◆**mentalité** *nf* mentality.

menthe [mɑ̃t] *nf* mint.

mention [mɑ̃sjɔ̃] *nf* mention, reference; (*annotation*) comment; *Scol Univ* distinction; faire m. de to mention. ◆**mentionner** *vt* to mention.

ment/ir* [mɑ̃tir] *vi* to lie, tell lies *ou* a lie (à to). ◆**—eur, -euse** *nmf* liar; — *a* lying.

menton [mɑ̃tɔ̃] *nm* chin.

menu [məny] 1 *a* (*petit*) tiny; (*mince*) slender, fine; (*peu important*) minor, petty; — *adv* (*hacher*) small, finely; — *nm* par le m. in detail. 2 *nm* (*carte*) *Culin* menu.

menuisier [mənɥizje] *nm* carpenter, joiner. ◆**menuiserie** *nf* carpentry, joinery; (*ouvrage*) woodwork.

méprendre (se) [səmeprɑ̃dr] *vpr* se m. sur to be mistaken about. ◆**méprise** *nf* mistake.

mépris [mepri] *nm* contempt (de of, for), scorn (de for); au m. de without regard to. ◆**mépris/er** *vt* to despise, scorn. ◆**—ant** *a* scornful, contemptuous. ◆**—able** *a* despicable.

mer [mɛr] *nf* sea; (*marée*) tide; en m. at sea; par m. by sea; aller à la m. to go to the seaside; un homme à la m.! man overboard! mercantile [mɛrkɑ̃til] *a Péj* money-grabbing.

mercenaire [mɛrsəner] *a* & *nm* mercenary.

mercerie [mɛrsəri] *nf* (*magasin*) haberdasher's, *Am* notions store. ◆**mercier, -ière** *nmf* haberdasher, *Am* notions merchant.

merci [mɛrsi] 1 *int* & *nm* thank you, thanks (de, pour for); (non) m.! no, thank you! 2 *nf* à la m. de at the mercy of.

mercredi [mɛrkrədi] *nm* Wednesday.

mercure [mɛrkyr] *nm* mercury.

merde! [mɛrd] *int Fam* (bloody) hell!

mère [mɛr] *nf* mother; m. de famille mother (of a family); la m. Dubois *Fam* old Mrs Dubois; maison m. *Com* parent firm.

méridien [meridjɛ̃] *nm* meridian.

méridional, -ale, -aux [meridjonal, -o] *a* southern; — *nmf* southerner.

meringue [mərɛ̃g] *nf* (*gâteau*) meringue.

merisier [mərizje] *nm* (*bois*) cherry.

mérite [merit] *nm* merit; **homme de m.** (*valeur*) man of worth. ◆**mérit/er** *vt* (*être digne de*) to deserve; (*valoir*) to be worth; **m. de réussir**/*etc* to deserve to succeed/*etc.* ◆**—ant** *a* deserving. ◆**méritoire** *a* commendable.

merlan [mɛrlɑ̃] *nm* (*poisson*) whiting.

merle [mɛrl] *nm* blackbird.

merveille [mɛrvɛj] *nf* wonder, marvel; **à m.** wonderfully (well). ◆**merveilleusement** *adv* wonderfully. ◆**merveilleux, -euse** *a* wonderful, marvellous; — *nm* **le m.** (*surnaturel*) the supernatural.

mes [me] *voir* **mon**.

mésange [mezɑ̃ʒ] *nf* (*oiseau*) tit.

mésaventure [mezavɑ̃tyr] *nf* misfortune, misadventure.

mesdames [medam] *voir* **madame**.

mesdemoiselles [medmwazɛl] *voir* **mademoiselle**.

mésentente [mezɑ̃tɑ̃t] *nf* misunderstanding.

mesquin [mɛskɛ̃] *a* mean, petty. ◆**mesquinerie** *nf* meanness, pettiness; **une m.** an act of meanness.

mess [mɛs] *nm inv* Mil mess.

message [mesaʒ] *nm* message. ◆**messager, -ère** *nmf* messenger.

messageries [mesaʒri] *nfpl* Com courier service.

messe [mɛs] *nf Rel* mass.

Messie [mesi] *nm* Messiah.

messieurs [mesjø] *voir* **monsieur**.

mesure [məzyr] *nf* (*évaluation, dimension*) measurement; (*quantité, disposition*) measure; (*retenue*) moderation; (*cadence*) *Mus* time, beat; **fait sur m.** made to measure; **à m. que**, **as soon ou as fast as**; **dans la m. où** in so far as; **dans une certaine m.** to a certain extent; **en m.** de able to, in a position to; **dépasser la m.** to exceed the bounds. ◆**mesur/er** *vt* to measure; (*juger, estimer*) to calculate, assess, measure; (*argent, temps*) to ration (out); **m. 1 mètre 83** (*personne*) to be six feet tall; (*objet*) to measure six feet; **se m. à** *ou* **avec qn** *Fig* to pit oneself against s.o. ◆**—é** *a* (*pas, ton*) measured; (*personne*) moderate.

met [me] *voir* **mettre**.

métal, -aux [metal, -o] *nm* metal. ◆**métallique** *a* (*objet*) metal; (*éclat, reflet, couleur*) metallic. ◆**métallisé** *a* (*peinture*) metallic.

métallo [metalo] *nm Fam* steelworker. ◆**métallurgie** *nf* (*industrie*) steel industry; (*science*) metallurgy. ◆**métallurgique** *a* **usine m.** steelworks. ◆**métallurgiste** *a* & *nm* (*ouvrier*) **m.** steelworker.

métamorphose [metamorfoz] *nf* metamorphosis. ◆**métamorphoser** *vt*, — **se m.** *vpr* to transform (**en** into).

métaphore [metafor] *nf* metaphor. ◆**métaphorique** *a* metaphorical.

métaphysique [metafizik] *a* metaphysical.

météo [meteo] *nf* (*bulletin*) weather forecast.

météore [meteor] *nm* meteor. ◆**météorite** *nm* meteorite.

météorologie [meteorɔlɔʒi] *nf* (*science*) meteorology; (*service*) weather bureau. ◆**météorologique** *a* meteorological; (*bulletin, station, carte*) weather-.

méthode [metɔd] *nf* method; (*livre*) course. ◆**méthodique** *a* methodical.

méticuleux, -euse [metikylø, -øz] *a* meticulous.

métier [metje] *nm* **1** (*travail*) job; (*manuel*) trade; (*intellectuel*) profession; (*habileté*) professional skill; **homme de m.** specialist. **2 m.** (**à tisser**) loom.

métis, -isse [metis] *a* & *nmf* half-caste.

mètre [mɛtr] *nm* (*mesure*) metre; (*règle*) (metre) rule; **m.** (**à ruban**) tape measure. ◆**métr/er** *vt* (*terrain*) to survey. ◆**—age** *nm* **1** surveying. **2** (*tissu*) length; (*de film*) footage; **long m.** (*film*) full length film; **court m.** (*film*) short (film). ◆**—eur** *nm* quantity surveyor. ◆**métrique** *a* metric.

métro [metro] *nm* underground, *Am* subway.

métropole [metropol] *nf* (*ville*) metropolis; (*pays*) mother country. ◆**métropolitain** *a* metropolitan.

mets [me] *nm* (*aliment*) dish.

mett/re [mɛtr] *vt* **1** to put; (*table*) to lay; (*vêtement, lunettes*) to put on, wear; (*chauffage, radio etc*) to put on, switch on; (*réveil*) to set (**à** for); (*dépenser*) to spend (**pour une robe**/*etc* on a dress/*etc*); **m. dix heures**/*etc* **à venir** (*consacrer*) to take ten hours/*etc* coming ou to come; **m. à l'aise** (*rassurer*) to put ou set at ease; (*dans un fauteuil etc*) to make comfortable; **m. en colère** to make angry; **m. en liberté** to free; **m. en bouteille(s)** to bottle; **m. du soin à faire** to take care to do; **mettons que** (+ *sub*) let's suppose that; — **se m.** *vpr* (*se placer*) to put oneself; (*debout*) to stand; (*assis*) to be put, go; **se m. en short**/**pyjama**/*etc* to get into one's shorts/pyjamas/*etc*; **se m. en rapport avec** to get in touch with; **se m. à** (*endroit*) to go to; (*travail*) to set oneself to, start; **se m. à faire** to start doing; **se m. à table** to sit (down) at the table; **se m. à l'aise** to make oneself comfortable; **se m. au beau/froid** (*temps*) to turn fine/cold. ◆**—able** a wearable. ◆**—eur** *nm* **m. en scène** *Th* producer; *Cin* director.

meuble [mœbl] *nm* piece of furniture; *pl* furniture. ◆**meubl/er** *vt* to furnish; (*remplir*) *Fig* to fill. ◆**—é** *nm* furnished flat *ou Am* apartment.

meugl/er [møgle] *vi* to moo, low. ◆**—ement(s)** *nm(pl)* mooing.

meule [møl] *nf* **1** (*de foin*) haystack. **2** (*pour moudre*) millstone.

meunier, -ière [mønje, -jɛr] *nmf* miller.

meurt [mœr] *voir* **mourir**.

meurtre [mœrtr] *nm* murder. ◆**meurtrier, -ière** *nmf* murderer; — *a* deadly, murderous.

meurtrir [mœrtrir] *vt* to bruise. ◆**meurtrissure** *nf* bruise.

meute [møt] *nf* (*de chiens, de créanciers etc*) pack.

Mexique [mɛksik] *nm* Mexico. ◆**mexicain, -aine** *a & nmf* Mexican.

mi- [mi] *préf* **la mi-mars**/*etc* mid March/*etc*; **à mi-distance** mid-distance, midway.

miaou [mjau] *int* (*cri du chat*) miaow. ◆**miaul/er** [mjole] *vi* to miaow, mew. ◆**—ement(s)** *nm(pl)* miaowing, mewing.

mi-bas [miba] *nm inv* knee sock.

miche [miʃ] *nf* round loaf.

mi-chemin (à) [amiʃmɛ̃] *adv* halfway.

mi-clos [miklo] *a* half-closed.

micmac [mikmak] *nm* (*manigance*) *Fam* intrigue.

mi-corps (à) [amikɔr] *adv* (up) to the waist.

mi-côte (à) [amikot] *adv* halfway up *ou* down (the hill).

micro [mikro] *nm* microphone, mike. ◆**microphone** *nm* microphone.

micro- [mikro] *préf* micro-.

microbe [mikrɔb] *nm* germ, microbe.

microcosme [mikrɔkɔsm] *nm* microcosm.

microfilm [mikrɔfilm] *nm* microfilm.

micro-onde [mikrɔ̃d] *nf* microwave; **four à micro-ondes** microwave oven.

microscope [mikrɔskɔp] *nm* microscope. ◆**microscopique** *a* microscopic.

midi [midi] *nm* **1** (*heure*) midday, noon, twelve o'clock; (*heure du déjeuner*) lunchtime. **2** (*sud*) south; **le M.** the south of France.

mie [mi] *nf* soft bread, crumb.

miel [mjɛl] *nm* honey. ◆**mielleux, -euse** *a* (*parole, personne*) unctuous.

mien, mienne [mjɛ̃, mjɛn] *pron poss* **le m., la mienne** mine, my one; **les miens, les miennes** mine, my ones; **les deux miens** my two; – *nmpl* **les miens** (*amis etc*) my (own) people.

miette [mjɛt] *nf* (*de pain, de bon sens etc*) crumb; **réduire en miettes** to smash to pieces.

mieux [mjø] *adv & a inv* better (**que** than); (*plus à l'aise*) more comfortable; (*plus beau*) better-looking; **la m., la m., les m.** (*convenir, être etc*) the best; (*de deux*) the better; **le m. serait de** . . . the best thing would be to . . . ; **de m. en m.** better and better; **tu ferais m. de partir** you had better leave; **je ne demande pas m.** there's nothing I'd like better (**que de faire** than to do); – *nm* (*amélioration*) improvement; **faire de son m.** to do one's best.

mièvre [mjɛvr] *a* (*doucereux*) *Péj* mannered, wishy-washy.

mignon, -onne [miɲɔ̃, -ɔn] *a* (*charmant*) cute; (*agréable*) nice.

migraine [migrɛn] *nf* headache; *Méd* migraine.

migration [migrasjɔ̃] *nf* migration. ◆**migrant, -ante** *a & nmf* (**travailleur**) **m.** migrant worker, migrant.

mijoter [miʒɔte] *vt Culin* to cook (lovingly); (*lentement*) to simmer; (*complot*) *Fig Fam* to brew; – *vi* to simmer.

mil [mil] *nm inv* (*dans les dates*) a *ou* one thousand; **l'an deux m.** the year two thousand.

milice [milis] *nf* militia. ◆**milicien** *nm* militiaman.

milieu, -x [miljø] *nm* (*centre*) middle; (*cadre, groupe social*) environment; (*entre extrêmes*) middle course; (*espace*) *Phys* medium; *pl* (*groupes, littéraires etc*) circles; **au m. de** in the middle of; **au m. du danger** in the midst of danger; **le juste m.** the happy medium; **le m.** (*de malfaiteurs etc*) the underworld.

militaire [militɛr] *a* military; – *nm* serviceman; (*dans l'armée de terre*) soldier.

milit/er [milite] *vi* (*personne*) to be a militant; (*arguments etc*) to militate (**pour** in favour of). ◆**—ant, -ante** *a & nmf* militant.

mille [mil] **1** *a & nm inv* thousand; **m. hommes**/*etc* a *ou* one thousand men/*etc*; **deux m.** two thousand; **mettre dans le m.** to hit the bull's-eye. **2** *nm* (*mesure*) mile. ◆**m.-pattes** *nm inv* (*insecte*) centipede.

millième *a* & *nmf* thousandth; **un m.** a thousandth. ◆**millier** *nm* thousand; **un m. (de)** a thousand or so.

millefeuille [milfœj] *nm* (*gâteau*) cream slice.

millénaire [milener] *nm* millennium.

millésime [milezim] *nm* date (*on coins, wine etc*).

millet [mije] *nm Bot* millet.

milli- [mili] *préf* milli-.

milliard [miljar] *nm* thousand million, *Am* billion. ◆**milliardaire** *a* & *nmf* multimillionaire.

millimètre [milimetr] *nm* millimetre.

million [miljɔ̃] *nm* million; **un m. de livres/*etc*** a million pounds/*etc*; **deux millions** two million. ◆**millionième** *a* & *nmf* millionth. ◆**millionnaire** *nmf* millionaire.

mime [mim] *nmf* (*acteur*) mime; **le m.** (*art*) mime. ◆**mimer** *vti* to mime. ◆**mimique** *nf* (*mine*) (funny) face; (*gestes*) signs, sign language.

mimosa [mimoza] *nm* (*arbre, fleur*) mimosa.

minable [minabl] *a* (*médiocre*) pathetic; (*lieu, personne*) shabby.

minaret [minare] *nm* (*de mosquée*) minaret.

minauder [minode] *vi* to simper, make a show of affectation.

mince [mɛ̃s] **1** *a* thin; (*élancé*) slim; (*insignifiant*) slim, paltry. **2** *int* **m. (alors)!** oh heck!, blast (it)! ◆**minceur** *nf* thinness; slimness. ◆**mincir** *vi* to grow slim.

mine [min] *nf* **1** appearance; (*physionomie*) look; **avoir bonne/mauvaise m.** (*santé*) to look well/ill; **faire m. de faire** to appear to do, make as if to do. **2** (*d'or, de charbon etc*) & *Fig* mine; **m. de charbon** coalmine. **3** (*de crayon*) lead. **4** (*engin explosif*) mine. ◆**miner** *vt* **1** (*saper*) to undermine. **2** (*garnir d'explosifs*) to mine.

minerai [minre] *nm* ore.

minéral, -aux [mineral, -o] *a* & *nm* mineral.

minéralogique [mineralɔʒik] *a* **numéro m.** *Aut* registration *ou Am* license number.

minet, -ette [mine, -ɛt] *nmf* **1** (*chat*) puss. **2** (*personne*) *Fam* fashion-conscious young man *ou* woman.

mineur, -eure [minœr] **1** *nm* (*ouvrier*) miner. **2** *a* (*jeune, secondaire*) & *Mus* minor; – *nmf Jur* minor. ◆**minier, -ière** *a* (*industrie*) mining-.

mini- [mini] *préf* mini-.

miniature [minjatyr] *nf* miniature; – *a inv* (*train etc*) miniature-.

minibus [minibys] *nm* minibus.

minime [minim] *a* trifling, minor, minimal. ◆**minimiser** *vt* to minimize.

minimum [minimɔm] *nm* minimum; **le m. de** (*force etc*) the minimum (amount of); **au (grand) m.** at the very least; **la température m.** the minimum temperature. ◆**minimal, -aux** *a* minimum, minimal.

ministre [ministr] *nm Pol Rel* minister; **m. de l'Intérieur** = Home Secretary, *Am* Secretary of the Interior. ◆**ministère** *nm* ministry; (*gouvernement*) cabinet; **m. de l'Intérieur** = Home Office, *Am* Department of the Interior. ◆**ministériel, -ielle** *a* ministerial; (*crise, remaniement*) cabinet-.

minorer [minɔre] *vt* to reduce.

minorité [minɔrite] *nf* minority; **en m.** in the *ou* a minority. ◆**minoritaire** *a* (*parti etc*) minority-; **être m.** to be in the *ou* a minority.

Minorque [minɔrk] *nf* Minorca.

minuit [minɥi] *nm* midnight, twelve o'clock.

minus [minys] *nm* (*individu*) *Péj Fam* moron.

minuscule [minyskyl] **1** *a* (*petit*) tiny, minute. **2** *a* & *nf* (*lettre*) **m.** small letter.

minute [minyt] *nf* minute; **à la m.** (*tout de suite*) this (very) minute; **d'une m. à l'autre** any minute now; – *a inv* **aliments *ou* plats m.** convenience food(s). ◆**minuter** *vt* to time. ◆**minuterie** *nf* time switch.

minutie [minysi] *nf* meticulousness. ◆**minutieux, -euse** *a* meticulous.

mioche [mjɔʃ] *nmf* (*enfant*) *Fam* kid, youngster.

miracle [mirakl] *nm* miracle; **par m.** miraculously. ◆**miraculeux, -euse** *a* miraculous.

mirador [mirador] *nm Mil* watchtower.

mirage [miraʒ] *nm* mirage.

mirifique [mirifik] *a Hum* fabulous.

mirobolant [mirɔbɔlɑ̃] *a Fam* fantastic.

miroir [mirwar] *nm* mirror. ◆**miroiter** *vi* to gleam, shimmer.

mis [mi] *voir* **mettre**; – *a* **bien m.** (*vêtu*) well dressed.

misanthrope [mizɑ̃trɔp] *nmf* misanthropist; – *a* misanthropic.

mise [miz] *nf* **1** (*action de mettre*) putting; **m. en service** putting into service; **m. en marche** starting up; **m. à la retraite** pensioning off; **m. à feu** (*de fusée*) blast-off; **m. en scène** *Th* production; *Cin* direction. **2** (*argent*) stake. **3** (*tenue*) attire. ◆**miser** *vt* (*argent*) to stake (**sur** on); – *vi* **m. sur** (*cheval*) to back; (*compter sur*) to bank on.

misère [mizɛr] *nf* (*grinding*) poverty; (*malheur*) misery; (*bagatelle*) trifle. ◆**mi-**

sérable *a* miserable, wretched; (*indigent*) poor, destitute; (*logement, quartier*) seedy, slummy; – *nmf* (poor) wretch; (*indigent*) pauper. ◆**miséreux, -euse** *a* destitute; – *nmf* pauper.

miséricorde [mizerikɔrd] *nf* mercy. ◆**miséricordieux, -euse** *a* merciful.

misogyne [mizɔʒin] *nmf* misogynist.

missile [misil] *nm* (*fusée*) missile.

mission [misjɔ̃] *nf* mission; (*tâche*) task. ◆**missionnaire** *nm* & *a* missionary.

missive [misiv] *nf* (*lettre*) missive.

mistral [mistral] *nm inv* (*vent*) mistral.

mite [mit] *nf* (*clothes*) moth; (*du fromage etc*) mite. ◆**mité** *a* moth-eaten.

mi-temps [mitɑ̃] *nf* (*pause*) *Sp* half-time; (*période*) *Sp* half; **à mi-t.** (*travailler etc*) part-time.

miteux, -euse [mitø, -øz] *a* shabby.

mitigé [mitiʒe] *a* (*zèle etc*) moderate, luke-warm; (*mêlé*) *Fam* mixed.

mitraille [mitraj] *nf* gunfire. ◆**mitrailler** *vt* to machinegun; (*photographier*) *Fam* to click *ou* snap away at. ◆**mitraillette** *nf* submachine gun. ◆**mitrailleur** *a* **fusil m.** machinegun. ◆**mitrailleuse** *nf* machine-gun.

mi-voix (à) [amivwa] *adv* in an undertone.

mixe(u)r [miksœr] *nm* (*pour mélanger*) (food) mixer.

mixte [mikst] *a* mixed; (*école*) co-educational, mixed; (*tribunal*) joint.

mixture [mikstyr] *nf* (*boisson*) *Péj* mixture.

Mlle [madmwazɛl] *abrév* = **Mademoiselle.**

MM [mesjø] *abrév* = **Messieurs.**

mm *abrév* (*millimètre*) mm.

Mme [madam] *abrév* = **Madame.**

mobile [mɔbil] **1** *a* (*pièce etc*) moving; (*personne*) mobile; (*feuillets*) detachable, loose; (*reflets*) changing; **échelle m.** sliding scale; **fête m.** mov(e)able feast; – *nm* (*œuvre d'art*) mobile. **2** *nm* (*motif*) motive (de for). ◆**mobilité** *nf* mobility.

mobilier [mɔbilje] *nm* furniture.

mobiliser [mɔbilize] *vti* to mobilize. ◆**mobilisation** *nf* mobilization.

mobylette [mɔbilɛt] *nf* moped.

mocassin [mɔkasɛ̃] *nm* (*chaussure*) mocca-sin.

moche [mɔʃ] *a Fam* (*laid*) ugly; (*mauvais, peu gentil*) lousy, rotten.

modalité [mɔdalite] *nf* method (de of).

mode [mɔd] **1** *nf* fashion; (*industrie*) fashion trade; **à la m.** in fashion, fashionable; **passé de m.** out of fashion; **à la m. de** in the manner of. **2** *nm* mode, method; **m. d'emploi**

directions (for use); **m. de vie** way of life. **3** *nm Gram* mood.

modèle [mɔdɛl] *nm* (*schéma, exemple, personne*) model; **m. (réduit)** (scale) model; – *a* (*élève etc*) model-. ◆**model/er** *vt* to model (**sur** on); **se m. sur** to model oneself on. ◆—**age** *nm* (*de statue etc*) modelling. ◆**modéliste** *nmf Tex* stylist, designer.

modéré [mɔdere] *a* moderate. ◆—**ment** *adv* moderately.

modérer [mɔdere] *vt* to moderate, restrain; (*vitesse, allure*) to reduce; — **se m.** *vpr* to restrain oneself. ◆**modérateur, -trice** *a* moderating; – *nmf* moderator. ◆**modération** *nf* moderation, restraint; reduction; **avec m.** in moderation.

moderne [mɔdɛrn] *a* modern; – *nm* **le m.** (*mobilier*) modern furniture. ◆**modernisation** *nf* modernization. ◆**moderniser** *vt*, — **se m.** *vpr* to modernize. ◆**modernisme** *nm* modernism.

modeste [mɔdɛst] *a* modest. ◆**modestement** *adv* modestly. ◆**modestie** *nf* modesty.

modifier [mɔdifje] *vt* to modify, alter; — **se m.** *vpr* to alter. ◆**modification** *nf* modifi-cation, alteration.

modique [mɔdik] *a* (*salaire, prix*) modest. ◆**modicité** *nf* modesty.

module [mɔdyl] *nm* module.

moduler [mɔdyle] *vt* to modulate. ◆**modulation** *nf* modulation.

moelle [mwal] *nf Anat* marrow; **m. épinière** spinal cord.

moelleux, -euse [mwalø, -øz] *a* soft; (*voix, vin*) mellow.

mœurs [mœr(s)] *nfpl* (*morale*) morals; (*habitudes*) habits, customs.

mohair [mɔɛr] *nm* mohair.

moi [mwa] *pron* **1** (*complément direct*) me; **laissez-moi** leave me; **pour moi** for me. **2** (*indirect*) to me; **montrez-le-moi** show it to me, show me it. **3** (*sujet*) I; **moi, je veux** *I* want. **4** *nm inv Psy* self, ego. ◆**moi-même** *pron* myself.

moignon [mwaɲɔ̃] *nm* stump.

moindre [mwɛ̃dr] *a* **être m.** (*moins grand*) to be less; **le m. doute**/*etc* the slightest *ou* least doubt/*etc*; **le m.** (*de mes problèmes etc*) the least (de of); (*de deux problèmes etc*) the lesser (de of).

moine [mwan] *nm* monk, friar.

moineau, -x [mwano] *nm* sparrow.

moins [mwɛ̃] **1** *adv* ([mwɛz] *before vowel*) less (**que** than); **m.** (*grand, zèle etc*) less (**que** than), not so much (**que** as); (*gens, livres etc*) fewer (**que** than), not so many (que as); (cent francs etc) less than; **m. froid/grand**/etc not as cold/big/etc (que as); **le m. de m.** less and less; **le m., la m., les m.** (travailler etc) the least; **le m. grand** the smallest; **au m., du m.** at least; **le m.** (qui manque) missing; **dix ans**/etc de **m.** ten years/etc less; **en m.** (personne, objet) less; (personnes, objets) fewer; **les m. de vingt ans** those under twenty, the under-twenties; **à m. que** (+ sub) unless. **2** prép Math minus; **deux heures m. cinq** five to two; **il fait m. dix (degrés)** it's minus ten (degrees).

mois [mwa] nm month; **au m. de juin**/etc in (the month of) June/etc.

mois/ir [mwazir] vi to go mouldy; (attendre) Fig to hang about. **◆—l** a mouldy; — nm mould, mildew; **sentir le m.** to smell musty. **◆moisissure** nf mould, mildew.

moisson [mwasɔ̃] nf harvest. **◆moisson-ner** vt to harvest. **◆moissonneuse-batteuse** nf (pl moissonneuses-batteuses) combine-harvester.

moite [mwat] a sticky, moist. **◆moiteur** nf stickiness, moistness.

moitié [mwatje] nf half; **la m. de la pomme**/etc half (of) the apple/etc; **à m. plein**/etc (remplir etc) halfway; **à m. fermé/cru**/etc half closed/raw/etc; **à m. prix** (for ou at) half-price; **de m. by half; m.-moitié** Fam so-so; **partager m.-moitié** Fam to split fifty-fifty.

moka [mɔka] nm (café) mocha.

mol [mɔl] voir mou.

molaire [mɔlɛr] nf (dent) molar.

molécule [mɔlekyl] nf molecule.

moleskine [mɔlɛskin] nf imitation leather.

molester [mɔlɛste] vt to manhandle.

molette [mɔlɛt] nf **clé à m.** adjustable wrench ou spanner.

mollasse [mɔlas] a Péj flabby.

molle [mɔl] voir mou. **◆mollement** adv feebly; (paresseusement) lazily. **◆mol-lesse** nf softness; (faiblesse) feebleness. **◆mollir** vi to go soft; (courage) to flag.

mollet [mɔlɛ] **1** a **œuf m.** soft-boiled egg. **2** nm (de jambe) calf.

mollusque [mɔlysk] nm mollusc.

môme [mom] nm (enfant) Fam kid.

moment [mɔmɑ̃] nm (instant) moment; (période) time; **en ce m.** at the moment; **par moments** at times; **au m. de partir** when just about to leave; **au m. où** when, just as; **du m. que** (puisque) seeing that. **◆mo-mentané** a momentary. **◆momentané-ment** adv temporarily, for the moment.

momie [mɔmi] nf (cadavre) mummy.

mon, ma, pl **mes** [mɔ̃, ma, me] (ma becomes **mon** [mɔ̃n] before a vowel or mute h) a poss my; **mon père** my father; **ma mère** my mother; **mon ami(e)** my friend.

Monaco [mɔnako] nf Monaco.

monarque [mɔnark] nm monarch. **◆mo-narchie** nf monarchy. **◆monarchique** a monarchic.

monastère [mɔnastɛr] nm monastery.

monceau, -x [mɔ̃so] nm heap, pile.

monde [mɔ̃d] nm world; (milieu social) set; **du m.** (gens) people; (beaucoup) a lot of people; **un m. fou** a tremendous crowd; **le (grand) m.** (high) society; **le m. entier** the whole world; **tout le m.** everybody; **mettre au m.** to give birth to; **pas le moins du m.!** not in the least ou slightest! **◆mondain, -aine** a (vie, réunion etc) society-. **◆mondanités** nfpl (événements) social events. **◆mondial, -aux** a (renommée etc) world-; (crise) worldwide. **◆mondiale-ment** adv the (whole) world over.

monégasque [mɔnegask] a & nmf Mone-gasque.

monétaire [mɔnetɛr] a monetary.

mongolien, -ienne [mɔ̃gɔljɛ̃, -jɛn] a & nmf Méd mongol.

moniteur, -trice [mɔnitœr, -tris] nmf **1** in-structor; (de colonie de vacances) assistant, Am camp counselor. **2** (écran) Tech moni-tor.

monnaie [mɔnɛ] nf (devise) currency, mon-ey; (appoint, pièces) change; **pièce de m.** coin; (petite) **m.** (small) change; **faire de la m.** to get change; **faire de la m. à qn** to give s.o. change (sur un billet for a note); **c'est m. courante** it's very frequent; **Hôtel de la M.** mint. **◆monnayer** vt (talent etc) to cash in on; (bien, titre) Com to convert into cash.

mono [mɔno] a inv (disque etc) mono.

mono- [mɔno] préf mono-.

monocle [mɔnɔkl] nm monocle.

monologue [mɔnɔlɔg] nm monologue.

monoplace [mɔnɔplas] a & nmf (avion, voiture) single-seater.

monopole [mɔnɔpɔl] nm monopoly. **◆monopoliser** vt to monopolize.

monosyllabe [mɔnɔsilab] nm monosylla-ble. **◆monosyllabique** a monosyllabic.

monotone [mɔnɔtɔn] a monotonous. **◆monotonie** nf monotony.

monseigneur [mɔ̃sɛɲœr] nm (évêque) His ou Your Grace; (prince) His ou Your Highness.

monsieur, pl **messieurs** [məsjø, mesjø] nm gentleman; **oui m.** yes; (avec déférence) yes sir; **oui messieurs** yes (gentlemen); **M. Legras** Mr Legras; **Messieurs** *ou* **MM Legras** Messrs Legras; **tu vois ce m.?** do you see that man *ou* gentleman?; **Monsieur** (*sur une lettre*) Com Dear Sir.

monstre [mɔ̃str] *nm* monster; – *a* (*énorme*) *Fam* colossal. ◆**monstrueux, -euse** *a* (*abominable, énorme*) monstrous. ◆**monstruosité** *nf* (*horreur*) monstrosity.

mont [mɔ̃] *nm* (*montagne*) mount.

montagne [mɔ̃taɲ] *nf* mountain; **la m.** (*zone*) the mountains; **montagnes russes** *Fig* roller coaster. ◆**montagnard, -arde** *nmf* mountain dweller; **tu vois ce m.?** mountain-. ◆**montagneux, -euse** *a* mountainous.

mont-de-piété [mɔ̃dpjete] *nm* (*pl* **monts-de-piété**) pawnshop.

monte-charge [mɔ̃tʃarʒ] *nm inv* service lift *ou* Am elevator.

mont/er [mɔ̃te] *vi* (*aux être*) (*personne*) to go *ou* come up; (*s'élever*) to go up; (*grimper*) to climb (up) (**sur** onto); (*prix*) to go up, rise; (*marée*) to come in; (*avion*) to climb; **m. dans un véhicule** to get in(to) a vehicle; **m. dans un train** to get on(to) a train; **m. sur** (*échelle etc*) to climb up; (*trône*) to ascend; **m. en courant**/*etc* to run/*etc* up; **m. (à cheval)** to ride (a horse); **m. en graine** (*salade etc*) to go to seed; – *vt* (*aux avoir*) (*côte etc*) to climb (up); (*objets*) to bring *ou* take up; (*cheval*) to ride; (*tente, affaire*) to set up; (*machine*) to assemble; (*bijou*) to set, mount; (*complot, démonstration*) to mount; (*pièce*) Th to stage, mount; **m. l'escalier** to go *ou* come upstairs *ou* up the stairs; **faire m.** (*visiteur etc*) to show up; **m. qn contre qn** to turn s.o. against s.o.; – **se m.** *vpr* (*s'irriter*) *Fam* to get angry; **se m. à** (*frais*) to amount to. ◆**-ant 1** *a* (*chemin*) uphill; (*mouvement*) upward; (*marée*) rising; (*col*) stand-up; (*robe*) high-necked; **chaussure montante** boot. **2** *nm* (*somme*) amount. **3** *nm* (*de barrière*) post; (*d'échelle*) upright. ◆**-é a** (*police*) mounted. ◆**-ée** *nf* ascent, climb; (*de prix, des eaux*) rise; (*chemin*) slope. ◆**-age** *nm* Tech assembling, assembly; *Cin* editing. ◆**-eur, -euse** *nmf* Tech fitter; *Cin* editor.

montre [mɔ̃tr] *nf* **1** watch; **course contre la m.** race against time. **2 faire m. de** to show. ◆**m.-bracelet** *nf* (*pl* **montres-bracelets**) wristwatch.

Montréal [mɔ̃real] *nm ou f* Montreal.

montrer [mɔ̃tre] *vt* to show (**à** to); **m. du doigt** to point to; **m. à qn à faire qch** to

show s.o. how to do sth; – **se m.** *vpr* to show oneself, appear; (*s'avérer*) to turn out to be; **se m. courageux**/*etc* to be courageous/*etc*.

monture [mɔ̃tyr] *nf* **1** (*cheval*) mount. **2** (*de lunettes*) frame; (*de bijou*) setting.

monument [mɔnymɑ̃] *nm* monument; **m. aux morts** war memorial. ◆**monumental, -aux** *a* (*imposant, énorme etc*) monumental.

moquer (se) [səmɔke] *vpr* **se m. de** (*allure etc*) to make fun of; (*personne*) to make a fool of, make fun of; **je m'en moque!** *Fam* I couldn't care less! ◆**moquerie** *nf* mockery. ◆**moqueur, -euse** *a* mocking.

moquette [mɔket] *nf* fitted carpet(s), wall-to-wall carpeting.

moral, -aux [mɔral, -o] *a* moral; – *nm* **le m.** spirits, morale. ◆**morale** *nf* (*principes*) morals; (*code*) moral code; (*d'histoire etc*) moral; **faire la m. à qn** to lecture s.o. ◆**moralement** *adv* morally. ◆**moraliser** *vi* to moralize. ◆**moraliste** *nmf* moralist. ◆**moralité** *nf* (*mœurs*) morality; (*de fable, récit etc*) moral.

moratoire [mɔratwar] *nm* moratorium.

morbide [mɔrbid] *a* morbid.

morceau, -x [mɔrso] *nm* piece, bit; (*de sucre*) lump; (*de viande*) Culin cut; (*extrait*) Littér extract. ◆**morceler** *vt* (*terrain*) to divide up.

mordiller [mɔrdije] *vt* to nibble.

mord/re [mɔrdr] *vti* to bite; **ça mord** *Pêche* I have a bite. ◆**-ant 1** *a* (*voix, manière*) scathing; (*froid*) biting; (*personne, ironie*) caustic. **2** *nm* (*énergie*) punch. ◆**-u, -ue** *nmf* **un m. du jazz**/*etc* *Fam* a jazz/*etc* fan.

morfondre (se) [səmɔrfɔ̃dr] *vpr* to get bored (waiting), mope (about).

morgue [mɔrg] *nf* (*lieu*) mortuary, morgue.

moribond, -onde [mɔribɔ̃, -ɔ̃d] *a & nmf* dying *ou* moribund (person).

morne [mɔrn] *a* dismal, gloomy, dull.

morose [mɔroz] *a* morose, sullen.

morphine [mɔrfin] *nf* morphine.

mors [mɔr] *nm* (*de harnais*) bit.

morse [mɔrs] *nm* **1** Morse (code). **2** (*animal*) walrus.

morsure [mɔrsyr] *nf* bite.

mort¹ [mɔr] *nf* death; **mettre à m.** to put to death; **silence de m.** dead silence. ◆**mortalité** *nf* death rate, mortality. ◆**mortel, -elle** *a* (*hommes, ennemi, danger etc*) mortal; (*accident*) fatal; (*chaleur*) deadly; (*pâleur*) deathly; – *nmf* mortal. ◆**mortellement** *adv* (*blessé*) fatally.

mort², morte [mɔr, mɔrt] *a* (*personne, plante, ville etc*) dead; **m. de fatigue** dead tired; **m. de froid** numb with cold; **m. de peur** frightened to death; – *nmf* dead man, dead woman; **les morts** the dead; **de nombreux morts** (*victimes*) many deaths *ou* casualties; **le jour** *ou* **la fête des Morts** All Souls' Day. ◆**morte-saison** *nf* off season. ◆**mort-né** *a* (*enfant*) & *Fig* stillborn.

mortier [mɔrtje] *nm* mortar.

mortifier [mɔrtifje] *vt* to mortify.

mortuaire [mɔrtɥɛr] *a* (*avis, rites etc*) death-, funeral.

morue [mɔry] *nf* cod.

morve [mɔrv] *nf* (nasal) mucus. ◆**morveux, -euse** *a* (*enfant*) snotty (-nosed).

mosaïque [mɔzaik] *nf* mosaic.

Moscou [mɔsku] *nm ou f* Moscow.

mosquée [mɔske] *nf* mosque.

mot [mo] *nm* word; **envoyer un m. à** to drop a line to; **m. à** *ou* **pour m.** word for word; **bon m.** witticism; **mots croisés** crossword (puzzle); **m. d'ordre** *Pol* resolution, order; (*slogan*) watchword; **m. de passe** password.

motard [mɔtar] *nm Fam* motorcyclist.

motel [mɔtɛl] *nm* motel.

moteur¹ [mɔtœr] *nm* (*de véhicule etc*) engine, motor; *El* motor.

moteur², -trice [mɔtœr, -tris] *a* (*force*) driving-; (*nerf, muscle*) motor.

motif [mɔtif] *nm* **1** reason, motive. **2** (*dessin*) pattern.

motion [mɔsjɔ̃] *nf Pol* motion; **on a voté une m. de censure** a vote of no confidence was given.

motiver [mɔtive] *vt* (*inciter, causer*) to motivate; (*justifier*) to justify. ◆**motivation** *nf* motivation.

moto [mɔto] *nf* motorcycle, motorbike. ◆**motocycliste** *nmf* motorcyclist.

motorisé [mɔtɔrize] *a* motorized.

motte [mɔt] *nf* (*de terre*) clod, lump; (*de beurre*) block.

mou (*or* **mol** *before vowel or mute h*), **molle** [mu, mɔl] *a* soft; (*faible, sans énergie*) feeble; – *nm* **avoir du m.** (*cordage*) to be slack.

mouchard, -arde [muʃar, -ard] *nmf Péj* informer. ◆**moucharder** *vt* **m. qn** *Fam* to inform on s.o.

mouche [muʃ] *nf* (*insecte*) fly; **prendre la m.** (*se fâcher*) to go into a huff; **faire m.** to hit the bull's-eye. ◆**moucheron** *nm* (*insecte*) midge.

moucher [muʃe] *vt* **m. qn** to wipe s.o.'s nose; **se m.** to blow one's nose.

moucheté [muʃte] *a* speckled, spotted.

mouchoir [muʃwar] *nm* handkerchief; (*en papier*) tissue.

moudre* [mudr] *vt* (*café, blé*) to grind.

moue [mu] *nf* long face, pout; **faire la m.** to pout, pull a (long) face.

mouette [mwɛt] *nf* (sea)gull.

moufle [mufl] *nf* (*gant*) mitt(en).

mouill/er [muje] **1** *vt* to wet, make wet; **se faire m.** to get wet; – **se m.** *vpr* to get (oneself) wet; (*se compromettre*) *Fam* to get involved (*by taking risks*). **2** *vt* **m. l'ancre** *Nau* to (drop) anchor; – *vi* to anchor. ◆**-é** *a* wet (**de** with). ◆**-age** *nm* (*action*) *Nau* anchoring; (*lieu*) anchorage.

moule¹ [mul] *nm* mould, *Am* mold; **m. à gâteaux** cake tin. ◆**mouler** *vt* to mould, *Am* mold; (*statue*) to cast; **m. qn** (*vêtement*) to fit s.o. tightly. ◆**-ant** *a* (*vêtement*) tight-fitting. ◆**-age** *nm* moulding; casting; (*objet*) cast. ◆**moulure** *nf Archit* moulding.

moule² [mul] *nf* (*mollusque*) mussel.

moulin [mulɛ̃] *nm* mill; (*moteur*) *Fam* engine; **m. à vent** windmill; **m. à café** coffee-grinder.

moulinet [mulinɛ] *nm* **1** (*de canne à pêche*) reel. **2** (*de bâton*) twirl.

moulu [muly] *voir* **moudre**; – *a* (*café*) ground; (*éreinté*) *Fam* dead tired.

mour/ir* [murir] *vi* (*aux être*) to die (**de**, of, from); **m. de froid** to die of exposure; **m. d'ennui/de fatigue** *Fig* to be dead bored/tired; **m. de peur** *Fig* to be frightened to death; **s'ennuyer à m.** to be bored to death; – **se m.** *vpr* to be dying. ◆**-ant, -ante** *a* dying; (*voix*) faint; – *nmf* dying person.

mousquetaire [muskətɛr] *nm Mil Hist* musketeer.

mousse [mus] **1** *nf Bot* moss. **2** *nf* (*écume*) froth, foam; (*de bière*) froth; (*de savon*) lather; **m. à raser** shaving foam. **3** *nf Culin* mousse. **4** *nm Nau* ship's boy. ◆**mousser** *vi* (*bière etc*) to froth; (*savon*) to lather; (*eau savonneuse*) to foam. ◆**mousseux, -euse** *a* frothy; (*vin*) sparkling; – *nm* sparkling wine. ◆**moussu** *a* mossy.

mousseline [muslin] *nf* (*coton*) muslin.

mousson [musɔ̃] *nf* (*vent*) monsoon.

moustache [mustaʃ] *nf* moustache, *Am* mustache; *pl* (*de chat etc*) whiskers. ◆**moustachu** *a* wearing a moustache.

moustique [mustik] *nm* mosquito. ◆**moustiquaire** *nf* mosquito net; (*en métal*) screen.

moutarde [mutard] *nf* mustard.

mouton [mutɔ̃] *nm* sheep; (*viande*) mutton;

pl (*sur la mer*) white horses; (*poussière*) bits of dust; **peau de m.** sheepskin.

mouvement [muvmã] *nm* (*geste, déplacement, groupe etc*) & *Mus* movement; (*de colère*) outburst; (*impulsion*) impulse; **en m.** in motion. ◆**mouvementé** *a* (*animé*) lively, exciting; (*séance, vie etc*) eventful.

mouv/oir* [muvwar] *vi,* — **se m.** *vpr* to move; **mû par** (*mécanisme*) driven by. ◆**—ant** *a* (*changeant*) changing; **sables mouvants** quicksands.

moyen¹, -enne [mwajɛ̃, -ɛn] *a* average; (*format, entreprise etc*) medium(-sized); (*solution*) intermediate, middle; — *nm* average; (*dans un examen*) pass mark; (*dans un devoir*) half marks; **la moyenne d'âge** the average age; **en moyenne** on average. ◆**moyennement** *adv* averagely, moderately.

moyen² [mwajɛ̃] *nm* (*procédé, façon*) means, way (**de faire** of doing, to do); *pl* (*capacités*) ability, powers; (*argent, ressources*) means; **au m. de** by means of; **il n'y a pas m. de faire** it's not possible to do; **je n'ai pas les moyens** (*argent*) I can't afford it; **par mes propres moyens** under my own steam.

moyennant [mwajenã] *prép* (*pour*) (in return) for; (*avec*) with.

moyeu, -x [mwajø] *nm* (*de roue*) hub.

mucosités [mykozite] *nfpl* mucus.

mue [my] *nf* moulting; breaking of the voice. ◆**muer** [mɥe] *vi* (*animal*) to moult; (*voix*) to break; **se m. en** to become transformed into.

muet, -ette [mɥɛ, -ɛt] *a* (*infirme*) dumb; (*de surprise etc*) speechless; (*film, reproche etc*) silent; *Gram* mute; — *nmf* dumb person.

mufle [myfl] *nm* **1** (*d'animal*) nose, muzzle. **2** (*individu*) *Péj* lout.

mug/ir [myʒir] *vi* (*vache*) to moo; (*bœuf*) to bellow; (*vent*) *Fig* to roar. ◆**—issement(s)** *nm(pl)* moo(ing); bellow(ing); roar(ing).

muguet [mygɛ] *nm* lily of the valley.

mule [myl] *nf* **1** (*pantoufle*) mule. **2** (*animal*) (she-)mule. ◆**mulet¹** *nm* (he-)mule.

mulet² [mylɛ] *nm* (*poisson*) mullet.

multi- [mylti] *préf* multi-.

multicolore [myltikɔlɔr] *a* multicoloured.

multinationale [myltinasjɔnal] *nf* multinational.

multiple [myltipl] *a* (*nombreux*) numerous; (*ayant des formes variées*) multiple; — *nm* *Math* multiple. ◆**multiplication** *nf* multiplication; (*augmentation*) increase. ◆**multiplicité** *nf* multiplicity. ◆**multiplier** *vt* to

multiply; — **se m.** *vpr* to increase; (*se reproduire*) to multiply.

multitude [myltityd] *nf* multitude.

municipal, -aux [mynisipal, -o] *a* municipal; **conseil m.** town council. ◆**municipalité** *nf* (*corps*) town council; (*commune*) municipality.

munir [mynir] *vt* **m. de** to provide *ou* equip with; **se m.** **de** to provide oneself with; **muni de** (*papiers, arme etc*) in possession of.

munitions [mynisjɔ̃] *nfpl* ammunition.

muqueuse [mykøz] *nf* mucous membrane.

mur [myr] *nm* wall; **m. du son** sound barrier; **au pied du m.** *Fig* with one's back to the wall. ◆**muraille** *nf* (high) wall. ◆**mural, -aux** *a* (*carte etc*) wall-; **peinture murale** mural (painting). ◆**murer** *vt* (*porte*) to wall up; **m. qn** to wall s.o. in.

mûr [myr] *a* (*fruit, projet etc*) ripe; (*âge, homme*) mature. *Fig* to provide oneself with; ◆**mûrement** *adv* (*réfléchir*) carefully. ◆**mûrir** *vti* (*fruit*) to ripen; (*personne, projet*) to mature.

muret [myrɛ] *nm* low wall.

murmure [myrmyr] *nm* murmur. ◆**murmurer** *vti* to murmur.

musc [mysk] *nm* (*parfum*) musk.

muscade [myskad] *nf* nutmeg.

muscle [myskl] *nm* muscle. ◆**musclé** *a* (*bras*) brawny, muscular. ◆**musculaire** *a* (*tissu, système etc*) muscular. ◆**musculature** *nf* muscles.

museau, -x [myzo] *nm* (*de chien etc*) muzzle; (*de porc*) snout. ◆**museler** *vt* (*animal, presse etc*) to muzzle. ◆**muselière** *nf* (*appareil*) muzzle.

musée [myze] *nm* museum; **m. de peinture** (public) art gallery. ◆**muséum** *nm* (natural history) museum.

musette [myzɛt] *nf* (*d'ouvrier*) duffel bag, kit bag.

music-hall [myzikol] *nm* variety theatre.

musique [myzik] *nf* music; (*fanfare*) *Mil* band. ◆**musical, -aux** *a* musical. ◆**musicien, -ienne** *nmf* musician; — *a* **être très/assez m.** to be very/quite musical.

musulman, -ane [myzylmã, -an] *a* & *nmf* Moslem, Muslim.

muter [myte] *vt* (*employé*) to transfer. ◆**mutation** *nf* **1** transfer. **2** *Biol* mutation.

mutil/er [mytile] *vt* to mutilate, maim; **être mutilé** to be disabled. ◆**—é, -ée** *nmf* **m. de guerre/du travail** disabled ex-serviceman/ worker. ◆**mutilation** *nf* mutilation.

mutin [mytɛ̃] **1** *a* (*espiègle*) saucy. **2** *nm* (*rebelle*) mutineer. ◆**se mutin/er** *vpr* to mutiny. ◆**—é** *a* mutinous. ◆**mutinerie** *nf* mutiny.

mutisme [mytism] *nm* (stubborn) silence.
mutualité [mytɥalite] *nf* mutual insurance. ◆**mutualiste** *nmf* member of a friendly *ou Am* benefit society. ◆**mutuelle**[1] *nf* friendly society, *Am* benefit society.
mutuel, -elle[2] [mytɥɛl] *a* (*réciproque*) mutual. ◆**mutuellement** *adv* (*l'un l'autre*) each other (mutually).
myope [mjɔp] *a* & *nmf* shortsighted (person). ◆**myopie** *nf* shortsightedness.
myosotis [mjozɔtis] *nm Bot* forget-me-not.
myrtille [mirtij] *nf Bot* bilberry.

N

N, n [ɛn] *nm* N, n.
n' [n] *voir* ne.
nabot [nabo] *nm Péj* midget.
nacelle [nasɛl] *nf* (*de ballon*) car, gondola; (*de landau*) carriage, carrycot.
nacre [nakr] *nf* mother-of-pearl. ◆**nacré** *a* pearly.
nage [naʒ] *nf* (swimming) stroke; **n. libre** freestyle; **traverser à la n.** to swim across; **en n.** *Fig* sweating. ◆**nager** *vi* to swim; (*flotter*) to float; **je nage dans le bonheur** my happiness knows no bounds; **je nage complètement** (*je suis perdu*) *Fam* I'm all at sea; – *vt* (*crawl etc*) to swim. ◆**nageur, -euse** *nmf* swimmer.
nageoire [naʒwar] *nf* (*de poisson*) fin; (*de phoque*) flipper.
naguère [nagɛr] *adv Litt* not long ago.
naïf, -ïve [naif, -iv] *a* simple, naïve; – *nmf* (*jobard*) simpleton.
nain, naine [nɛ̃, nɛn] *nmf* dwarf; – *a* (*arbre, haricot*) dwarf-.
naissance [nɛsɑ̃s] *nf* birth; (*de bras, cou*) base; **donner n. à** *Fig* to give rise to; **de n.** from birth.
naître* [nɛtr] *vi* to be born; (*jour*) to dawn; (*sentiment, difficulté*) to arise (**de** from); **faire n.** (*soupçon, industrie etc*) to give rise to, create. ◆**naissant** *a* (*amitié etc*) incipient.
naïveté [naivte] *nf* simplicity, naïveté.
nant/ir [nɑ̃tir] *vt* **n. de** to provide with. ◆**—i** *a* & *nmpl* (*riche*) affluent.
naphtaline [naftalin] *nf* mothballs.
nappe [nap] *nf* **1** table cloth. **2** (*d'eau*) sheet; (*de gaz, pétrole*) layer; (*de brouillard*) blanket. ◆**napperon** *nm* (soft) table mat; (*pour vase etc*) (soft) mat, cloth.

mystère [mistɛr] *nm* mystery. ◆**mystérieux, -euse** *a* mysterious.
mystifier [mistifje] *vt* to fool, deceive, hoax. ◆**mystification** *nf* hoax.
mystique [mistik] *a* mystic(al); – *nmf* (*personne*) mystic; – *nf* mystique (**de** of). ◆**mysticisme** *nm* mysticism.
mythe [mit] *nm* myth. ◆**mythique** *a* mythical. ◆**mythologie** *nf* mythology. ◆**mythologique** *a* mythological.
mythomane [mitɔman] *nmf* compulsive liar.

narcotique [narkɔtik] *a* & *nm* narcotic.
narguer [narge] *vt* to flout, mock.
narine [narin] *nf* nostril.
narquois [narkwa] *a* sneering.
narration [narasjɔ̃] *nf* (*récit, acte, art*) narration. ◆**narrateur, -trice** *nmf* narrator.
nasal, -aux [nazal, -o] *a* nasal.
naseau, -x [nazo] *nm* (*de cheval*) nostril.
nasiller [nazije] *vi* (*personne*) to speak with a twang; (*micro, radio*) to crackle. ◆**nasillard** *a* (*voix*) nasal; (*micro etc*) crackling.
natal, mpl -als [natal] *a* (*pays etc*) native; **sa maison natale** the house where he *ou* she was born. ◆**natalité** *nf* birthrate.
natation [natasjɔ̃] *nf* swimming.
natif, -ive [natif, -iv] *a* & *nmf* native; **être n. de** to be a native of.
nation [nasjɔ̃] *nf* nation; **les Nations Unies** the United Nations. ◆**national, -aux** *a* national; ◆**nationale** *nf* (*route*) trunk road, *Am* highway. ◆**nationaliser** *vt* to nationalize. ◆**nationaliste** *a Péj* nationalistic; – *nmf* nationalist. ◆**nationalité** *nf* nationality.
nativité [nativite] *nf Rel* nativity.
natte [nat] *nf* **1** (*de cheveux*) plait, *Am* braid. **2** (*tapis*) mat, (piece of) matting. ◆**natt/er** *vt* to plait, *Am* braid. ◆**—age** (*matière*) matting.
naturaliser [natyralize] *vt* (*personne*) *Pol* to naturalize. ◆**naturalisation** *nf* naturalization.
nature [natyr] *nf* (*monde naturel, caractère*) nature; **de toute n.** of every kind; **être de n. à** to be likely to; **payer en n.** *Fin* to pay in kind; **n. morte** (*tableau*) still life; **plus grand que n.** larger than life; – *a inv* (*omelette, yaourt etc*) plain; (*café*) black. ◆**natura-**

liste *nmf* naturalist. ◆**naturiste** *nmf* nudist, naturist.

naturel, -elle [natyrɛl] *a* natural; **mort naturelle** death from natural causes; – *nm* (*caractère*) nature; (*simplicité*) naturalness. ◆**naturellement** *adv* naturally.

naufrage [nofraʒ] *nm* (ship)wreck; (*ruine*) *Litt Fig* ruin; **faire n.** to be (ship)wrecked. ◆**naufragé, -ée** *a* & *nmf* shipwrecked (person).

nausée [noze] *nf* nausea, sickness. ◆**nauséabond** *a* nauseating, sickening.

nautique [notik] *a* nautical; (*sports, ski*) water-.

naval, mpl -als [naval] *a* naval; **constructions navales** shipbuilding.

navet [navε] *nm* **1** *Bot Culin* turnip. **2** (*film etc*) *Péj* flop, dud.

navette [navεt] *nf* (*transport*) shuttle (service); **faire la n.** (*véhicule, personne etc*) to shuttle back and forth (**entre** between); **n. spatiale** space shuttle.

naviguer [navige] *vi* (*bateau*) to sail; (*piloter, voler*) to navigate. ◆**navigabilité** *nf* (*de bateau*) seaworthiness; (*d'avion*) airworthiness. ◆**navigable** *a* (*fleuve*) navigable. ◆**navigant** *a* **personnel n.** *Av Nau* crew. ◆**navigateur** *nm* *Av* navigator. ◆**navigation** *nf* (*pilotage*) navigation; (*trafic*) *Nau* shipping.

navire [navir] *nm* ship.

navr/er [navre] *vt* to upset (greatly), grieve. ◆**—ant** *a* upsetting. ◆**—é** *a* (*air*) grieved; **je suis n.** I'm (terribly) sorry (**de faire** to do).

nazi, -ie [nazi] *a* & *nmf* *Pol Hist* Nazi.

ne [n(ə)] (**n'** before vowel or mute *h*; used to form negative verb with *pas, jamais, que etc*) *adv* **1** (+ *pas*) not; **elle ne boit pas** she does not *ou* doesn't drink; **il n'ose** (*pas*) he doesn't dare; **n'importe** it doesn't matter. **2** (*with example, avoir peur etc*) **il ne parte** I'm afraid he'll leave.

né [ne] *a* born; **il est né** he was born; **née Dupont** née Dupont.

néanmoins [neãmwɛ̃] *adv* nevertheless, nonetheless.

néant [neã] *nm* nothingness, void; (*sur un formulaire*) = none.

nébuleux, -euse [nebylø, -øz] *a* hazy, nebulous.

nécessaire [nesesɛr] *a* necessary; (*inéluctable*) inevitable; – *nm* **le n.** (*biens*) the necessities; **le strict n.** the bare necessities; **n. de couture** sewing box, workbox; **n. de toilette** sponge bag, dressing case; **faire le n.** to do what's necessary *ou* the necessary. ◆**né-**cessairement** *adv* necessarily; (*échouer etc*) inevitably. ◆**nécessité** *nf* necessity. ◆**nécessiter** *vt* to necessitate, require. ◆**nécessiteux, -euse** *a* needy.

nécrologie [nekrɔlɔʒi] *nf* obituary.

nectarine [nektarin] *nf* (*fruit*) nectarine.

néerlandais, -aise [neɛrlɑ̃dɛ, -ɛz] *a* Dutch; – *nmf* Dutchman, Dutchwoman; – *nm* (*langue*) Dutch.

nef [nɛf] *nf* (*d'église*) nave.

néfaste [nefast] *a* (*influence etc*) harmful (**à** to).

négatif, -ive [negatif, -iv] *a* negative; – *nm* *Phot* negative; – *nf* **répondre par la négative** to answer in the negative. ◆**négation** *nf* negation, denial (**de** of); *Gram* negation; (*mot*) negative.

négligeable [negliʒabl] *a* negligible.

négligent [negliʒã] *a* negligent, careless. ◆**négligemment** [-amã] *adv* negligently, carelessly. ◆**négligence** *nf* negligence, carelessness; (*faute*) (careless) error.

néglig/er [negliʒe] *vt* (*personne, conseil, travail etc*) to neglect; **n. de faire** to neglect to do; – **se n.** *vpr* (*négliger sa tenue ou sa santé*) to neglect oneself. ◆**—é** *a* (*tenue*) untidy, neglected; (*travail*) careless; – *nm* (*de tenue*) untidiness; (*vêtement*) negligee.

négoci/er [negɔsje] *vti* *Fin Pol* to negotiate. ◆**—ant, -ante** *nmf* merchant, trader. ◆**—able** *a* *Fin* negotiable. ◆**négo-**ciateur, -trice** *nmf* negotiator. ◆**négo-**ciation** *nf* negotiation.

nègre [nɛgr] **1** *a* (*art, sculpture etc*) Negro. **2** *nm* (*écrivain*) ghost writer.

neige [nɛʒ] *nf* snow; **n. fondue** sleet; **n. carbonique** dry ice. ◆**neiger** *v imp* to snow. ◆**neigeux, -euse** *a* snowy.

nénuphar [nenyfar] *nm* water lily.

néo [neo] *préf* neo-.

néon [neɔ̃] *nm* (*gaz*) neon; **au n.** (*éclairage etc*) neon-.

néophyte [neɔfit] *nmf* novice.

néo-zélandais, -aise [neozelɑ̃dɛ, -ɛz] *a* (*peuple etc*) New Zealand-; – *nmf* New Zealander.

nerf [nɛr] *nm* *Anat* nerve; **avoir du n.** (*vigueur*) *Fam* to have guts; **du n.!**, **un peu de n.!** buck up!; **ça me porte** *ou* **me tape sur les nerfs** it gets on my nerves; **être sur les nerfs** *Fig* to be keyed up *ou* het up. ◆**nerveux, -euse** *a* nervous; (*centre, cellule*) nerve-. ◆**nervosité** *nf* nervousness.

nervure [nɛrvyr] *nf* (*de feuille*) vein.

nescafé [nɛskafe] *nm* instant coffee.

n'est-ce pas? [nɛspɑ] *adv* isn't he?, don't

you? *etc*; **il fait beau, n'est-ce pas?** the weather's fine, isn't it?

net, nette [nɛt] **1** *a* (*conscience, idée, image, refus*) clear; (*coupure, linge*) clean; (*soigné*) neat; (*copie*) fair; — *adv* (*s'arrêter*) short, dead; (*tuer*) outright; (*parler*) plainly; (*refuser*) flat(ly); (*casser, couper*) clean. **2** *a* (*poids, prix etc*) Com net(t). ◆**nettement** *adv* clearly, plainly; (*sensiblement*) markedly. ◆**netteté** *nf* clearness; (*de travail*) neatness.

nettoyer [nɛtwaje] *vt* to clean (up); (*plaie*) to cleanse, clean (up); (*vider, ruiner*) *Fam* to clean out. ◆**nettoiement** *nm* cleaning; **service du n.** refuse *ou Am* garbage collection. ◆**nettoyage** *nm* cleaning; **n. à sec** dry cleaning.

neuf¹, neuve [nœf, nœv] *a* new; **quoi de n.?** what's new(s)?; — *nm* **il y a du n.** there's been something new; **remettre à n.** to make as good as new.

neuf² [nœf] *a & nm* ([nœv] before **heures & ans**) nine. ◆**neuvième** *a & nmf* ninth.

neurasthénique [nørastenik] *a* depressed.

neutre [nøtr] **1** *a* (*pays, personne etc*) neutral; — *nm* El neutral. **2** *a & nm* Gram neuter. ◆**neutraliser** *vt* to neutralize. ◆**neutralité** *nf* neutrality.

neveu, -x [nəvø] *nm* nephew.

névralgie [nevralʒi] *nf* headache; *Méd* neuralgia. ◆**névralgique** *a* centre **n.** *Fig* nerve centre.

névrose [nevroz] *nf* neurosis. ◆**névrosé, -ée** *a & nmf* neurotic.

nez [ne] *nm* nose; **n. à n.** face to face (**avec** with); **au n. de qn** (*rire etc*) in s.o.'s face; **mettre le n. dehors** *Fam* to stick one's nose outside.

ni [ni] *conj* **ni . . . ni** (+ *ne*) neither . . . nor; **il n'a ni faim ni soif** he's neither hungry nor thirsty; **sans manger ni boire** without eating or drinking; **ni l'un(e) ni l'autre** neither (of them).

niais, -aise [njɛ, -ɛz] *a* silly, simple; — *nmf* simpleton. ◆**niaiserie** *nf* silliness; *pl* (*paroles*) nonsense.

niche [niʃ] *nf* (*de chien*) kennel; (*cavité*) niche, recess.

nich/er [niʃe] *vi* (*oiseau*) to nest; (*loger*) *Fam* to hang out; — **se n.** *vpr* (*oiseau*) to nest; (*se cacher*) to hide oneself. ◆**-ée** *nf* (*oiseaux, enfants*) brood; (*chiens*) litter.

nickel [nikɛl] *nm* (*métal*) nickel.

nicotine [nikɔtin] *nf* nicotine.

nid [ni] *nm* nest; **n. de poules** *Aut* pothole.

nièce [njɛs] *nf* niece.

nième [ɛnjɛm] *a* nth.

nier [nje] *vt* to deny (**que** that); — *vi Jur* to deny the charge.

nigaud, -aude [nigo, -od] *a* silly; — *nmf* silly fool.

Nigéria [niʒerja] *nm ou f* Nigeria.

n'importe [nɛ̃pɔrt] *voir* **importer 1.**

nippon, -one *ou* **-onne** [nipɔ̃, -ɔn] *a* Japanese.

niveau, -x [nivo] *nm* (*hauteur*) level; (*degré, compétence*) standard, level; **n. de vie** standard of living; **n. à bulle** (*d'air*) spirit level; **au n. de qn** (*élève etc*) up to s.o.'s standard. ◆**niveler** *vt* (*surface*) to level; (*fortunes etc*) to even (up).

noble [nɔbl] *a* noble; — *nmf* nobleman, noblewoman. ◆**noblement** *adv* nobly. ◆**noblesse** *nf* (*caractère, classe*) nobility.

noce(s) [nɔs] *nf(pl)* wedding; **faire la noce** *Fam* to have a good time, make merry; **noces d'argent/d'or** silver/golden wedding. ◆**noceur, -euse** *nmf Fam* fast liver, reveller.

nocif, -ive [nɔsif, -iv] *a* harmful. ◆**nocivité** *nf* harmfulness.

noctambule [nɔktɑ̃byl] *nmf* (*personne*) night bird *ou* prowler. ◆**nocturne** *a* nocturnal, night-; — *nm* (*de magasins etc*) late night opening; (**match en**) **n.** *Sp* floodlit match, *Am* night game.

Noël [nɔɛl] *nm* Christmas; **le père N.** Father Christmas, Santa Claus.

nœud [nø] *nm* **1** knot; (*ruban*) bow; **le n. du problème/etc** the crux of the problem/etc; **n. coulant** noose, slipknot; **n. papillon** bow tie. **2** (*mesure*) Nau knot.

noir, noire [nwar] *a* black; (*nuit, lunettes etc*) dark; (*idées*) gloomy; (*âme, crime*) vile; (*misère*) dire; **roman n.** thriller; **film n.** film noir; **il fait n.** it's dark; — *nm* (*couleur*) black; (*obscurité*) dark; **N.** (*homme*) black; **vendre au n.** to sell on the black market; — *nf Mus* crotchet, *Am* quarter note; **Noire** (*femme*) black. ◆**noirceur** *nf* blackness; (*d'une action etc*) vileness. ◆**noircir** *vt* to blacken; — *vi*, — **se n.** *vpr* to turn black.

noisette [nwazɛt] *nf* hazelnut. ◆**noisetier** *nm* hazel (tree).

noix [nwa] *nf* (*du noyer*) walnut; **n. de coco** coconut; **n. du Brésil** Brazil nut; **n. de beurre** knob of butter; **à la n.** *Fam* trashy, awful.

nom [nɔ̃] *nm* name; *Gram* noun; **n. de famille** surname; **n. de jeune fille** maiden name; **n. propre** *Gram* proper noun; **au n. de qn** on s.o.'s behalf; **sans n.** (*anonyme*) nameless; (*vil*) vile; **n. d'un chien!** *Fam* oh hell!

nomade [nɔmad] *a* nomadic; — *nmf* nomad.

nombre [nɔ̃br] *nm* number; **ils sont au** *ou* **du n. de** (*parmi*) they're among; **ils sont au n. de dix** there are ten of them; **elle est au n. de** she's one of; **le plus grand n. de** the majority of. ◆**nombreux, -euse** *a* (*amis, livres etc*) numerous; (*famille, collection etc*) large; **peu n.** few; **venir n.** to come in large numbers.

nombril [nɔ̃bri] *nm* navel.

nominal, -aux [nɔminal, -o] *a* nominal. ◆**nomination** *nf* appointment, nomination.

nommer [nɔme] *vt* (*appeler*) to name; **n. qn** (*désigner*) to appoint s.o. (**à un poste**/*etc* to a post/*etc*); **n. qn président/lauréat** to nominate s.o. chairman/prizewinner; — **se n.** *vpr* (*s'appeler*) to be called. ◆**nommément** *adv* by name.

non [nɔ̃] *adv* & *nm inv* no; **n.!** no!; **tu viens ou n.?** are you coming or not?; **n. seulement** not only; **n. (pas) que** (+ *sub*) . . . not that . . . ; **c'est bien, n.?** *Fam* it's all right, isn't it?; **je crois que n.** I don't think so; **(ni) moi n. plus** neither do, am, can *etc* I; **une place n. réservée** an unreserved seat.

non- [nɔ̃] *préf* non-.

nonante [nɔnɑ̃t] *a* (*en Belgique, en Suisse*) ninety.

nonchalant [nɔ̃ʃalɑ̃] *a* nonchalant, apathetic. ◆**nonchalance** *nf* nonchalance, apathy.

non-conformiste [nɔ̃kɔ̃fɔrmist] *a* & *nmf* nonconformist.

non-fumeur, -euse [nɔ̃fymœr, -øz] *nmf* non-smoker.

non-sens [nɔ̃sɑ̃s] *nm inv* absurdity.

nord [nɔr] *nm* north; **au n. de** north of; **du n.** (*vent, direction*) northerly; (*ville*) northern; (*gens*) from *ou* in the north; **Amérique/Afrique du N.** North America/Africa; **l'Europe du N.** Northern Europe; — *a inv* (*côte*) northern. ◆**n.-africain, -aine** *a* & *nmf* North African. ◆**n.-américain, -aine** *a* & *nmf* North American. ◆**n.-est** *nm* & *a inv* north-east. ◆**n.-ouest** *nm* & *a inv* north-west.

nordique [nɔrdik] *a* & *nmf* Scandinavian.

normal, -aux [nɔrmal, -o] *a* normal. ◆**normale** *nf* norm, normality; **au-dessus de la n.** above normal. ◆**normalement** *adv* normally. ◆**normaliser** *vt* (*uniformiser*) to standardize; (*relations etc*) to normalize.

normand, -ande [nɔrmɑ̃, -ɑ̃d] *a* & *nmf* Norman. ◆**Normandie** *nf* Normandy.

norme [nɔrm] *nf* norm.

Norvège [nɔrvɛʒ] *nf* Norway. ◆**norvégien, -ienne** *a* & *nmf* Norwegian; — *nm* (*langue*) Norwegian.

nos [no] *voir* **notre**.

nostalgie [nɔstalʒi] *nf* nostalgia. ◆**nostalgique** *a* nostalgic.

notable [nɔtabl] *a* (*fait etc*) notable; — *nm* (*personne*) notable. ◆**—ment** [-əmɑ̃] *adv* (*sensiblement*) notably.

notaire [nɔtɛr] *nm* solicitor, notary.

notamment [nɔtamɑ̃] *adv* notably.

note [nɔt] *nf* (*remarque etc*) & *Mus* note; (*chiffrée*) *Scol* mark, *Am* grade; (*compte, facture*) bill, *Am* check; **prendre n. de** to make a note of. ◆**noter** *vt* (*prendre note de*) to note; (*remarquer*) to note; (*écrire*) to note down; (*devoir etc*) *Scol* to mark, *Am* grade; **être bien noté** (*personne*) to be highly rated.

notice [nɔtis] *nf* (*résumé, préface*) note; (*mode d'emploi*) instructions.

notifier [nɔtifje] *vt* **n. qch à qn** to notify s.o. of sth.

notion [nɔsjɔ̃] *nf* notion, idea; *pl* (*éléments*) rudiments.

notoire [nɔtwar] *a* (*criminel, bêtise*) notorious; (*fait*) well-known. ◆**notoriété** *nf* (*renom*) fame; (*de fait*) general recognition.

notre, pl nos [nɔtr, no] *a poss* our. ◆**nôtre** *pron poss* **le** *ou* **la n., les nôtres** ours; — *nmpl* **les nôtres** (*parents etc*) our (own) people.

nouer [nwe] *vt* to tie, knot; (*amitié, conversation*) to strike up; **avoir la gorge nouée** to have a lump in one's throat. ◆**noueux, -euse** *a* (*bois*) knotty; (*doigts*) gnarled.

nougat [nuga] *nm* nougat.

nouille [nuj] *nf* (*idiot*) *Fam* drip.

nouilles [nuj] *nfpl* noodles.

nounours [nunurs] *nm* teddy bear.

nourrice [nuris] *nf* (*assistante maternelle*) child minder, nurse; (*qui allaite*) wet nurse; **mettre en n.** to put out to nurse.

nourr/ir [nurir] *vt* (*alimenter, faire vivre*) to feed; (*espoir etc*) *Fig* to nourish; (*esprit*) to enrich; **se n. de** to feed on; — *vi* (*aliment*) to be nourishing. ◆**—issant** *a* nourishing. ◆**nourriture** *nf* food.

nourrisson [nurisɔ̃] *nm* infant.

nous [nu] *pron* **1** (*sujet*) we; **n. sommes** we are. **2** (*complément direct*) us; **il n. connaît** he knows us. **3** (*indirect*) (to) us; **il n. l'a donné** he gave it to us, he gave us it. **4** (*réfléchi*) ourselves; **n. n. lavons** we wash ourselves. **5** (*réciproque*) each other;

n. n. **détestons** we hate each other. ◆n.-**mêmes** *pron* ourselves.

nouveau (*or* **nouvel** *before vowel or mute h*), **nouvelle**[1], *pl* **nouveaux, nouvelles** [nuvo, nuvɛl] *a* new; — *nmf Scol* new boy, new girl; — *nm* **du** n. something new; **de n.,** à n. again. ◆n.-**né, -ée** *a* & *nmf* new-born (baby). ◆n.-**venu** *nm,* ◆**nouvelle-venue** *nf* newcomer. ◆**nouveauté** *nf* newness, novelty; *pl* (*livres*) new books; (*disques*) new releases; (*vêtements*) new fashions; **une** n. (*objet*) a novelty.

nouvelle[2] [nuvɛl] *nf* **1 nouvelle(s)** news; **une** n. a piece of news. **2** *Littér* short story.

Nouvelle-Zélande [nuvɛlzelɑ̃d] *nf* New Zealand.

novateur, -trice [nɔvatœr, -tris] *nmf* innovator.

novembre [nɔvɑ̃br] *nm* November.

novice [nɔvis] *nmf* novice; — *a* inexperienced.

noyau, -x [nwajo] *nm* (*de fruit*) stone, *Am* pit; (*d'atome, de cellule*) nucleus; (*groupe*) group; **un** n. **d'opposants** a hard core of opponents.

noyaut/er [nwajote] *vt Pol* to infiltrate. ◆—**age** *nm* infiltration.

noy/er[1] [nwaje] *vt* (*personne etc*) to drown; (*terres*) to flood; — **se** n. *vpr* to drown; (*se suicider*) to drown oneself; **se** n. **dans le détail** to get bogged down in details. ◆—**é, -ée** *nmf* (*mort*) drowned person; — *a* **être** n. (*perdu*) *Fig* to be out of one's depth. ◆**noyade** *nf* drowning.

noyer[2] [nwaje] *nm* (*arbre*) walnut tree.

nu [ny] *a* (*personne, vérité*) naked; (*mains, chambre*) bare; **tout** nu (stark) naked, (in the) nude; **voir** à **l'œil** nu to see with the naked eye; **mettre** à nu (*exposer*) to lay bare; **se mettre** nu to strip off; **tête** nue, **nu-tête** bare-headed; — *nm* (*femme, homme, œuvre*) nude.

nuage [nɥaʒ] *nm* cloud; **un** n. **de lait** *Fig* a dash of milk. ◆**nuageux, -euse** *a* (*ciel*) cloudy.

nuance [nɥɑ̃s] *nf* (*de sens*) nuance; (*de couleurs*) shade, nuance; (*de regret*) tinge, nuance. ◆**nuanc/er** *vt* (*teintes*) to blend,

shade; (*pensée*) to qualify. ◆—**é** *a* (*jugement*) qualified.

nucléaire [nykleɛr] *a* nuclear.

nudisme [nydism] *nm* nudism. ◆**nudiste** *nmf* nudist. ◆**nudité** *nf* nudity, nakedness; (*de mur etc*) bareness.

nuée [nɥe] *nf* **une** n. **de** (*foule*) a host of; (*groupe compact*) a cloud of.

nues [ny] *nfpl* **porter qn aux** n. to praise s.o. to the skies.

nuire* [nɥir] *vi* n. à (*personne, intérêts etc*) to harm. ◆**nuisible** *a* harmful.

nuit [nɥi] *nf* night; (*obscurité*) dark(ness); **il fait** n. it's dark; **avant la** n. before nightfall; **la** n. (*se promener etc*) at night; **cette** n. (*aujourd'hui*) tonight; (*hier*) last night. ◆**nuitée** *nf* overnight stay (*in hotel etc*).

nul, nulle [nyl] **1** *a* (*risque etc*) non-existent, nil; (*médiocre*) useless, hopeless; (*non valable*) *Jur* null (and void); **faire match** n. *Sp* to tie, draw. **2** *a* (*aucun*) no; **de nulle importance** of no importance; **sans** n. **doute** without any doubt; **nulle part** nowhere; — *pron m* (*aucun*) no one. ◆**nullard, -arde** *nmf Fam* useless person. ◆**nullement** *adv* not at all. ◆**nullité** *nf* (*d'un élève etc*) uselessness; (*personne*) useless person.

numéraire [nymerɛr] *nm* cash, currency.

numéral, -aux [nymeral, -o] *a* & *nm* numeral. ◆**numérique** *a* numerical; (*montre etc*) digital.

numéro [nymero] *nm* number; (*de journal*) issue, number; (*au cirque*) act; **un** n. **de danse/de chant** a dance/song number; **quel** n.! (*personne*) *Fam* what a character!; **n. vert** *Tél* = Freefone®, = *Am* tollfree number. ◆**numérot/er** *vt* (*pages, sièges*) to number. ◆—**age** *nm* numbering.

nu-pieds [nypje] *nmpl* open sandals.

nuptial, -aux [nypsjal, -o] *a* (*chambre*) bridal; (*anneau, cérémonie*) wedding-.

nuque [nyk] *nf* back *ou* nape of the neck.

nurse [nœrs] *nf* nanny, (children's) nurse.

nutritif, -ive [nytritif, -iv] *a* nutritious, nutritive. ◆**nutrition** *nf* nutrition.

nylon [nilɔ̃] *nm* (*fibre*) nylon.

nymphe [nɛ̃f] *nf* nymph. ◆**nymphomane** *nf Péj* nymphomaniac.

O

O, o [o] *nm* O, o.

oasis [ɔazis] *nf* oasis.

obédience [ɔbedjɑ̃s] *nf Pol* allegiance.

obé/ir [ɔbeir] *vi* to obey; **o. à qn/qch** to obey s.o./sth; **être obéi** to be obeyed. **◆—issant** *a* obedient. **◆obéissance** *nf* obedience (à to).

obélisque [ɔbelisk] *nm (monument)* obelisk.

obèse [ɔbɛz] *a & nmf* obese (person). **◆obésité** *nf* obesity.

objecter [ɔbʒɛkte] *vt (prétexte)* to put forward, plead; **o. qch** to object that; **on lui objecta son jeune âge** they objected that he *ou* she was too young. **◆objecteur** *nm* **o. de conscience** conscientious objector. **◆objection** *nf* objection.

objectif, -ive [ɔbʒɛktif, -iv] **1** *a (opinion etc)* objective. **2** *nm (but)* objective; *Phot* lens. **◆objectivement** *adv* objectively. **◆objectivité** *nf* objectivity.

objet [ɔbʒɛ] *nm (chose, sujet, but)* object; *(de toilette)* article; **faire l'o. de** *(étude, critiques etc)* to be the subject of; *(soins, surveillance)* to be given, receive; **objets trouvés** *(bureau)* lost property, *Am* lost and found.

obligation [ɔbligasjɔ̃] *nf (devoir, lieu, nécessité)* obligation; *Fin* bond. **◆obligatoire** *a* compulsory, obligatory; *(inévitable)* *Fam* inevitable. **◆obligatoirement** *adv (fatalement)* inevitably; **tu dois o. le faire** you have to do it.

oblig/er [ɔbliʒe] *vt* **1** *(contraindre)* to compel, oblige (**à faire** to do); *(engager)* to bind; **être obligé de faire** to have to do, be compelled *ou* obliged to do. **2** *(rendre service à)* to oblige; **être obligé à qn de qch** to be obliged to s.o. for sth. **◆—eant** *a* obliging, kind. **◆—é** *a (obligatoire)* necessary; *(fatal) Fam* inevitable. **◆obligeamment** [-amɑ̃] *adv* obligingly. **◆obligeance** *nf* kindness.

oblique [ɔblik] *a* oblique; **regard o.** sidelong glance; **en o.** at an (oblique) angle. **◆obliquer** *vi (véhicule etc)* to turn off.

oblitérer [ɔblitere] *vt (timbre)* to cancel; *(billet, carte)* to stamp; **timbre oblitéré** *(non neuf)* used stamp. **◆oblitération** *nf* cancellation; stamping.

oblong, -ongue [ɔblɔ̃, -ɔ̃g] *a* oblong.

obnubilé [ɔbnybile] *a (obsédé)* obsessed (**par** with).

obscène [ɔpsɛn] *a* obscene. **◆obscénité** *nf* obscenity.

obscur [ɔpskyr] *a (noir)* dark; *(peu clair, inconnu, humble)* obscure. **◆obscurcir** *vt (chambre etc)* to darken; *(rendre peu intelligible)* to obscure *(text, ideas etc)*; **— s'o.** *vpr (ciel)* to cloud over, darken; *(vue)* to become dim. **◆obscurément** *adv* obscurely. **◆obscurité** *nf* dark(ness); *(de texte, d'acteur etc)* obscurity.

obséd/er [ɔpsede] *vt* to obsess, haunt. **◆—ant** *a* haunting, obsessive. **◆—é, -ée** *nmf* maniac (**de** for); **o. sexuel** sex maniac.

obsèques [ɔpsɛk] *nfpl* funeral.

obséquieux, -euse [ɔpsekjø, -øz] *a* obsequious.

observer [ɔpsɛrve] *vt (regarder)* to observe, watch; *(remarquer, respecter)* to observe; **faire o. qch à qn** *(signaler)* to point sth out to s.o. **◆observateur, -trice** *a* observant; *— nmf* observer. **◆observation** *nf (examen, remarque)* observation; *(reproche)* (critical) remark, rebuke; *(de règle etc)* observance; **en o.** *(malade)* under observation. **◆observatoire** *nm* observatory; *(colline etc) Fig & Mil* observation post.

obsession [ɔpsesjɔ̃] *nf* obsession. **◆obsessif, -ive** *a (peur etc)* obsessive. **◆obsessionnel, -elle** *a Psy* obsessive.

obstacle [ɔpstakl] *nm* obstacle; **faire o. à** to stand in the way of.

obstétrique [ɔpstetrik] *nf Méd* obstetrics.

obstin/er (s') [sɔpstine] *vpr* to be obstinate *ou* persistent; **s'o. à faire** to persist in doing. **◆—é** *a* stubborn, obstinate, persistent. **◆obstination** *nf* stubbornness, obstinacy, persistence.

obstruction [ɔpstryksjɔ̃] *nf Méd Pol Sp* obstruction; **faire de l'o.** *Pol Sp* to be obstructive. **◆obstruer** *vt* to obstruct.

obtempérer [ɔptɑ̃pere] *vi* to obey an injunction; **o. à** to obey.

obtenir° [ɔptanir] *vt* to get, obtain, secure. **◆obtention** *nf* obtaining, getting.

obturer [ɔptyre] *vt (trou etc)* to stop *ou* close up. **◆obturateur** *nm Phot* shutter; *Tech* valve.

obtus [ɔpty] *a (angle, esprit)* obtuse.

obus [ɔby] nm Mil shell.

occasion [ɔkazjɔ̃] nf **1** (chance) opportunity, chance (**de faire** to do); (circonstance) occasion; **à l'o.** on occasion, when the occasion arises; **à l'o. de** on the occasion of. **2** Com (marché avantageux) bargain; (objet non neuf) second-hand buy; **d'o.** second-hand, used. **◆occasionner** vt to cause; **o. qch à qn** to cause s.o. sth.

occident [ɔksidɑ̃] nm **l'O.** Pol the West. **◆occidental, -aux** a Géog Pol western; – nmpl **les occidentaux** Pol Westerners. **◆occidentalisé** a Pol Westernized.

occulte [ɔkylt] a occult.

occup/er [ɔkype] vt (maison, pays, usine etc) to occupy; (place, temps) to take up, occupy; (poste) to hold, occupy; **o. qn** (absorber) to occupy s.o., keep s.o. busy; (ouvrier etc) to employ s.o.; – **s'o.** vpr to keep (oneself) busy (à faire doing); **s'o. de** (affaire, problème etc) to deal with; (politique) to be engaged in; **s'o. de qn** (malade etc) to take care of s.o.; (client) to see to s.o., deal with s.o.; **ne t'en occupe pas!** (ne t'en fais pas) don't worry!; (ne t'en mêle pas) mind your own business! **◆—ant, -ante** a (armée) occupying; – nmf (habitant) occupant; – nm Mil forces of occupation, occupier. **◆—é** a busy (à faire doing); (place, maison etc) occupied; (ligne) Tél engaged, Am busy; (taxi) hired. **◆occupation** nf (activité, travail etc) occupation; **l'o. de** (action) the occupation of.

occurrence [ɔkyrɑ̃s] nf Ling occurrence; **en l'o.** in the circumstances, as it happens ou happened.

océan [ɔseɑ̃] nm ocean. **◆océanique** a oceanic.

ocre [ɔkr] nm & a inv (couleur) ochre.

octave [ɔktav] nf Mus octave.

octobre [ɔktɔbr] nm October.

octogénaire [ɔktɔʒenɛr] nmf octogenarian.

octogone [ɔktɔgɔn] nm octagon. **◆octogonal, -aux** a octagonal.

octroi [ɔktrwa] nm Litt granting. **◆octroyer** vt Litt to grant (à à).

oculaire [ɔkylɛr] a **témoin o.** eyewitness; **globe o.** eyeball. **◆oculiste** nmf eye specialist.

ode [ɔd] nf (poème) ode.

odeur [ɔdœr] nf smell, odour; (de fleur) scent. **◆odorant** a sweet-smelling. **◆odorat** nm sense of smell.

odieux, -euse [ɔdjø, -øz] a odious, obnoxious.

œcuménique [ekymenik] a Rel (o)ecumenical.

œil, pl **yeux** [œj, jø] nm eye; **sous mes yeux** before my very eyes; **lever/baisser les yeux** to look up/down; **fermer l'o.** (dormir) to shut one's eyes; **fermer les yeux sur** to turn a blind eye to; **ouvrir l'o.!** keep your eyes open!; **coup d'o.** (regard) glance, look; **jeter un coup d'o. sur** to (have a) look ou glance at; **à vue d'o.** visibly; **faire les gros yeux à** to scowl at; **avoir à l'o.** (surveiller) to keep an eye on; **à l'o.** (gratuitement) Fam free; **faire de l'o. à** Fam to make eyes at; **o. au beurre noir** Fig black eye; **mon o.!** Fam (incrédulité) my foot!; (refus) no way!, no chance!

œillade [œjad] nf (clin d'œil) wink.

œillères [œjɛr] nfpl (de cheval) & Fig blinkers, Am blinders.

œillet [œjɛ] nm **1** Bot carnation. **2** (trou de ceinture etc) eyelet.

œuf, pl **œufs** [œf, ø] nm egg; pl (de poisson) (hard) roe; **o. sur le plat** fried egg; **étouffer qch dans l'o.** Fig to nip ou stifle sth in the bud.

œuvre [œvr] nf (travail, acte, livre etc) work; **o. (de charité)** (organisation) charity; **l'o. de** (production artistique etc) the works of; **mettre en o.** (employer) to make use of; **mettre tout en o.** to do everything possible (**pour faire** to do). **◆œuvrer** vi Litt to work.

offense [ɔfɑ̃s] nf insult; Rel transgression. **◆offens/er** vt to offend; **s'o. de** to take offence at. **◆—ant** a offensive.

offensif, -ive [ɔfɑ̃sif, -iv] a offensive; – nf (attaque) offensive; (du froid) onslaught.

offert [ɔfɛr] voir **offrir**.

office [ɔfis] **1** nm (fonction) office; (bureau) office, bureau; **d'o.** (être promu etc) automatically; **faire o.** de to serve as; **ses bons offices** (service) one's good offices. **2** nm Rel service. **3** nm ou f (pièce pour provisions) pantry.

officiel, -ielle [ɔfisjɛl] a (acte etc) official; – nm (personnage) official. **◆officiellement** adv officially. **◆officieux, -euse** a unofficial.

officier [ɔfisje] **1** vi Rel to officiate. **2** nm (dans l'armée etc) officer.

offre [ɔfr] nf offer; (aux enchères) bid; **l'o. et la demande** Écon supply and demand; **offres d'emploi** Journ situations vacant. **◆offrande** nf offering.

offr/ir[*] [ɔfrir] vt (proposer, présenter) to offer (**de faire** to do); (donner en cadeau) to give; (démission) to tender, offer; **je lui ai offert de le loger** I offered to put him up; – **s'o.** vpr (cadeau etc) to treat oneself to; (se *proposer*) to offer oneself (**comme** as); **s'o. à faire** to offer *ou* volunteer to do; **s'o. (aux yeux)** (*vue etc*) to present itself. ◆—**ant** *nm* **au plus o.** to the highest bidder.

offusquer [ɔfyske] *vt* to offend, shock; **s'o. de** to take offence at.

ogive [ɔʒiv] *nf* (*de fusée*) nose cone; **o. nucléaire** nuclear warhead.

ogre [ɔgr] *nm* ogre.

oh! [o] *int* oh!, o!

ohé! [ɔe] *int* hey (there)!

oie [wa] *nf* goose.

oignon [ɔɲɔ̃] *nm* (*légume*) onion; (*de tulipe, lis etc*) bulb; **occupe-toi de tes oignons!** *Fam* mind your own business!

oiseau, -x [wazo] *nm* bird; **à vol d'o.** as the crow flies; **drôle d'o.** (*individu*) *Péj* odd fish, *Am* oddball; **o. rare** (*personne étonnante*) *Iron* rare bird, perfect gem.

oiseux, -euse [wazø, -øz] *a* (*futile*) idle, vain.

oisif, -ive [wazif, -iv] *a* (*inactif*) idle; — *nmf* idler. ◆**oisiveté** *nf* idleness.

oléoduc [ɔleɔdyk] *nm* oil pipeline.

olive [ɔliv] *nf* (*fruit*) olive; **huile d'o.** olive oil; — *a inv* (*couleur*) (*vert*) **o.** olive (green). ◆**olivier** *nm* (*arbre*) olive tree.

olympique [ɔlɛ̃pik] *a* (*jeux, record etc*) Olympic.

ombilical, -aux [ɔ̃bilikal, -o] *a* (*cordon*) umbilical.

ombrage [ɔ̃braʒ] *nm* **1** (*ombre*) shade. **2 prendre o. de** (*jalousie, dépit*) to take umbrage at. ◆**ombrag/er** *vt* to give shade to. ◆—**é** *a* shady. ◆**ombrageux, -euse** *a* (*caractère, personne*) touchy.

ombre [ɔ̃br] *nf* (*d'arbre etc*) shade; (*de personne, objet*) shadow; **l'o. d'un doute** *Fig* the shadow of a doubt; **l'o. de** (*remords, reproche etc*) the trace of; **30° à l'o.** 30° in the shade; **dans l'o.** (*comploter, travailler etc*) in secret.

ombrelle [ɔ̃brɛl] *nf* sunshade, parasol.

omelette [ɔmlɛt] *nf* omelet(te); **o. au fromage/etc** cheese/etc omelet(te).

omettre* [ɔmɛtr] *vt* to omit (**de faire** to do). ◆**omission** *nf* omission.

omni- [ɔmni] *préf* omni-. ◆**omnipotent** *a* omnipotent.

omnibus [ɔmnibys] *a & nm* (*train*) **o.** slow train (*stopping at all stations*).

omoplate [ɔmɔplat] *nf* shoulder blade.

on [ɔ̃] (*sometimes* **l'on** [lɔ̃]) *pron* (*les gens*) they, people; (*nous*) we, one; (*vous*) you, one; **on dit** they say, people say, it is said; **on frappe** (*quelqu'un*) someone's knocking;

on me l'a donné it was given to me, I was given it.

once [ɔ̃s] *nf* (*mesure*) *& Fig* ounce.

oncle [ɔ̃kl] *nm* uncle.

onctueux, -euse [ɔ̃ktɥø, -øz] *a* (*liquide, crème*) creamy; (*manières, paroles*) *Fig* smooth.

onde [ɔ̃d] *nf* *Phys Rad* wave; **grandes ondes** long wave; **ondes courtes/moyennes** short/medium wave; **sur les ondes** (*sur l'antenne*) on the radio.

ondée [ɔ̃de] *nf* (*pluie*) (sudden) shower.

on-dit [ɔ̃di] *nm inv* rumour, hearsay.

ondoyer [ɔ̃dwaje] *vi* to undulate. ◆**ondulation** *nf* undulation; (*de cheveux*) wave. ◆**ondul/er** *vi* to undulate; (*cheveux*) to be wavy. ◆—**é** *a* wavy.

onéreux, -euse [ɔnerø, -øz] *a* costly.

ongle [ɔ̃gl] *nm* (finger) nail.

onglet [ɔ̃glɛ] *nm* (*entaille de canif etc*) (nail) groove.

ont [ɔ̃] *voir* **avoir**.

ONU [ɔny] *nf abrév* (*Organisation des nations unies*) UN.

onyx [ɔniks] *nm* (*pierre précieuse*) onyx.

onze [ɔ̃z] *a & nm* eleven. ◆**onzième** *a & nmf* eleventh.

opale [ɔpal] *nf* (*pierre*) opal.

opaque [ɔpak] *a* opaque. ◆**opacité** *nf* opacity.

opéra [ɔpera] *nm* (*ouvrage, art*) opera; (*édifice*) opera house. ◆**opérette** *nf* operetta.

opér/er [ɔpere] **1** *vt* (*exécuter*) to carry out; (*choix*) to make; — *vi* (*agir*) to work, act; (*procéder*) to proceed; — **s'o.** *vpr* (*se produire*) to take place. **2** *vt* (*personne, organe*) *Méd* to operate on (**de** for); (*tumeur*) to remove; **cela peut s'o.** this can be removed; **se faire o.** to have an operation; — *vi* (*chirurgien*) to operate. ◆—**ant** *a* (*efficace*) operative. ◆—**é, -ée** *nmf Méd* patient (*operated on*). ◆**opérateur, -trice** *nmf* (*de prise de vues*) *Cin* cameraman; (*sur machine*) operator. ◆**opération** *nf* (*acte*) *& Méd Mil Math etc* operation; *Fin* deal. ◆**opérationnel, -elle** *a* operational. ◆**opératoire** *a Méd* operative; **bloc o.** operating *ou* surgical wing.

opiner [ɔpine] *vi* **o.** (**de la tête** *ou* **du chef**) to nod assent.

opiniâtre [ɔpinjɑtr] *a* stubborn, obstinate. ◆**opiniâtreté** *nf* stubbornness, obstinacy.

opinion [ɔpinjɔ̃] *nf* opinion (**sur** about, on).

opium [ɔpjɔm] *nm* opium.

opportun [ɔpɔrtœ̃] *a* opportune, timely. ◆**opportunément** *adv* opportunely.

◆**opportunisme** nm opportunism. ◆**opportunité** nf timeliness.

oppos/er [ɔpoze] vt (argument, résistance) to put up (à against); (équipes, rivaux) to bring together, set against each other; (objets) to place opposite each other; (couleurs) to contrast; **o. qch à qch** (objet) to place sth opposite sth; **o. qn à qn** to set s.o. against s.o.; **match qui oppose...** match between... ; **– s'o.** vpr (couleurs) to contrast; (équipes) to confront each other; **s'o. à** (mesure, personne etc) to oppose, be opposed to; **je m'y oppose** I'm opposed to it, I oppose. ◆**—ant, -ante** a opposing; – nmf opponent. ◆**opposé, -ée** a (direction etc) opposite; (intérêts, équipe) opposing; (opinions) opposite, opposing; (couleurs) contrasting; **être o. à** to be opposed to; – nm l'**o.** the opposite (de of); **à l'o.** (côté) on the opposite side (de from); **à l'o. de** (contrairement à) contrary to. ◆**opposition** nf opposition; **faire o. à** to oppose; **par o. à** as opposed to.

oppress/er [ɔprese] vt (gêner) to oppress. ◆**—ant** a oppressive. ◆**—eur** nm Pol oppressor. ◆**oppressif, -ive** a (loi etc) oppressive. ◆**oppression** nf oppression.

opprim/er vt (tyranniser) to oppress. ◆**—és** nmpl les **o.** the oppressed.

opter [ɔpte] vi **o. pour** to opt for.

opticien, -ienne [ɔptisjɛ̃, -jɛn] nmf optician.

optimisme [ɔptimism] nm optimism. ◆**optimiste** a optimistic; – nmf optimist.

optimum [ɔptimɔm] nm & a optimum; **la température o.** the optimum temperature. ◆**optimal, -aux** a optimal.

option [ɔpsjɔ̃] nf (choix) option; (chose) optional extra.

optique [ɔptik] a (verre) optical; – nf optics; (aspect) Fig perspective; **d'o.** (illusion, instrument etc) optical.

opulent [ɔpylɑ̃] a opulent. ◆**opulence** nf opulence.

or [ɔr] **1** nm gold; **en or** (chaîne etc) gold-; **d'or** (cheveux, âge, règle) golden; (cœur) of gold; **mine d'or** Géol goldmine; (fortune) Fig goldmine; **affaire en or** (achat) bargain; (commerce) Fig goldmine; **or noir** (pétrole) Fig black gold. **2** conj (alors, cependant) now, well.

oracle [ɔrakl] nm oracle.

orage [ɔraʒ] nm (thunder)storm. ◆**orageux, -euse** a stormy.

oraison [ɔrɛzɔ̃] nf prayer; **o. funèbre** funeral oration.

oral, -aux [ɔral, -o] a oral; – nm (examen) Scol oral.

orange [ɔrɑ̃ʒ] nf (fruit) orange; **o. pressée** (fresh) orange juice; – a & nm (couleur) orange. ◆**orangé** a & nm (couleur) orange. ◆**orangeade** nf orangeade. ◆**oranger** nm orange tree.

orang-outan(g) [ɔrɑ̃utɑ̃] nm (pl **orangs-outan(g)s**) orang-outang.

orateur [ɔratœr] nm speaker, orator.

orbite [ɔrbit] nf (d'astre etc) & Fig orbit; (d'œil) socket; **mettre sur o.** (fusée etc) to put into orbit.

orchestre [ɔrkɛstr] nm (classique) orchestra; (moderne) band; (places) Th stalls, Am orchestra. ◆**orchestrer** vt (organiser) & Mus to orchestrate.

orchidée [ɔrkide] nf orchid.

ordinaire [ɔrdinɛr] a (habituel, normal) ordinary, Am regular; (médiocre) ordinary, average; **d'o., à l'o.** usually; **comme d'o., comme à l'o.** as usual; **de l'essence o.** two-star (petrol), Am regular. ◆**—ment** adv usually.

ordinal, -aux [ɔrdinal, -o] a (nombre) ordinal.

ordinateur [ɔrdinatœr] nm computer.

ordination [ɔrdinasjɔ̃] nf Rel ordination.

ordonnance [ɔrdɔnɑ̃s] nf **1** (de médecin) prescription. **2** (décret) Jur order, ruling. **3** (disposition) arrangement. **4** (soldat) orderly.

ordonn/er vt **1** (enjoindre) to order (que (+ sub) that); **o. à qn de faire** to order s.o. to do. **2** (agencer) to arrange, order. **3** (médicament etc) to prescribe. **4** (prêtre) to ordain. ◆**—ée** a (personne, maison etc) orderly.

ordre [ɔrdr] nm (commandement, structure, association etc) order; (absence de désordre) tidiness (of room, person etc); **en o.** (chambre etc) tidy; **mettre en o., mettre de l'o. dans** to tidy (up); **de premier o.** first-rate; **o. (public)** (law and) order; **par o. d'âge** in order of age; **à l'o. du jour** (au programme) on the agenda; (d'actualité) of topical interest; **les forces de l'o.** the police; **jusqu'à nouvel o.** until further notice; **de l'o. de** (environ) of the order of.

ordure [ɔrdyr] nf filth, muck; pl (débris) refuse, rubbish, Am garbage. ◆**ordurier, -ière** a (plaisanterie etc) foul.

oreille [ɔrɛj] nf ear; **être tout oreilles** to be all ears; **faire la sourde o.** to turn a deaf ear; **casser les oreilles à qn** to deafen s.o.

oreiller [ɔrɛje] nm pillow.

oreillons [ɔrɛjɔ̃] nmpl Méd mumps.

ores (d') [dɔr] adv **d'ores et déjà** [dɔrzedeʒa] henceforth.

orfèvre [ɔrfɛvr] nm goldsmith, silversmith. ◆**orfèvrerie** nf (magasin) goldsmith's ou silversmith's shop; (objets) gold ou silver plate.

organe [ɔrgan] nm Anat & Fig organ; (porte-parole) mouthpiece. ◆**organique** a organic. ◆**organisme** nm 1 (corps) body; Anat Biol organism. 2 (bureaux etc) organization.

organisation [ɔrganizasjɔ̃] nf (arrangement, association) organization.

organis/er [ɔrganize] vt to organize; — s'o. vpr to organize oneself, get organized. ◆—é a (esprit, groupe etc) organized. ◆**organisateur, -trice** nmf organizer.

organiste [ɔrganist] nmf Mus organist.

orgasme [ɔrgasm] nm orgasm.

orge [ɔrʒ] nf barley.

orgie [ɔrʒi] nf orgy.

orgue [ɔrg] nm Mus organ; o. de Barbarie barrel organ; — nfpl organ; grandes orgues great organ.

orgueil [ɔrgœj] nm pride. ◆**orgueilleux, -euse** a proud.

orient [ɔrjɑ̃] nm l'O. the Orient, the East; Moyen-O., Proche-O. Middle East; Extrême-O. Far East. ◆**oriental, -ale, -aux** a eastern; (de l'Orient) oriental; — nmf oriental.

orient/er [ɔrjɑ̃te] vt (lampe, antenne etc) to position, direct; (voyageur, élève etc) to direct; (maison) to orientate, Am orient; — s'o. vpr to find one's bearings ou direction; s'o. vers (carrière etc) to move towards. ◆—é a (ouvrage, film etc) slanted. ◆**orientable** a (lampe etc) adjustable, flexible; (bras de machine) movable. ◆**orientation** nf direction; (action) positioning, directing; (de maison) aspect, orientation; (tendance) Pol Littér trend; o. professionnelle vocational guidance.

orifice [ɔrifis] nm opening, orifice.

originaire [ɔriʒinɛr] a être o. de (natif) to be a native of.

original, -ale, -aux [ɔriʒinal, -o] 1 a (idée, artiste, version etc) original; — nm (modèle) original. 2 a & nmf (bizarre) eccentric. ◆**originalité** nf originality; eccentricity.

origine [ɔriʒin] nf origin; à l'o. originally; d'o. (pneu etc) original; pays d'o. country of origin. ◆**originel, -elle** a (sens, péché, habitant etc) original.

orme [ɔrm] nm (arbre, bois) elm.

ornement [ɔrnəmɑ̃] nm ornament. ◆**ornemental, -aux** a ornamental. ◆**ornementation** nf ornamentation. ◆**ornementé** a adorned, ornamented (de with). ◆**orn/er** vt to decorate, adorn (de with). ◆—é a (style etc) ornate.

ornière [ɔrnjɛr] nf (sillon) & Fig rut.

orphelin, -ine [ɔrfalɛ̃, -in] nmf orphan; — a orphaned. ◆**orphelinat** nm orphanage.

orteil [ɔrtɛj] nm toe; gros o. big toe.

orthodoxe [ɔrtɔdɔks] a orthodox; — nmpl les orthodoxes the orthodox. ◆**orthodoxie** nf orthodoxy.

orthographe [ɔrtɔgraf] nf spelling. ◆**orthographier** vt (mot) to spell.

orthopédie [ɔrtɔpedi] nf orthop(a)edics.

ortie [ɔrti] nf nettle.

os [ɔs, pl o ou ɔs] nm bone; trempé jusqu'aux os soaked to the skin; tomber sur un os (difficulté) Fam to hit a snag.

OS [ɔɛs] abrév = ouvrier spécialisé.

oscar [ɔskar] nm Cin Oscar.

osciller [ɔsile] vi Tech to oscillate; (se balancer) to swing, sway; (hésiter) to waver; (varier) to fluctuate; (flamme) to flicker. ◆**oscillation** nf Tech oscillation; (de l'opinion) fluctuation.

oseille [ozɛj] nf 1 Bot Culin sorrel. 2 (argent) Arg dough.

os/er [oze] vti to dare; o. faire to dare (to) do. ◆—é a bold, daring.

osier [ozje] nm (branches) wicker.

ossature [ɔsatyr] nf (du corps) frame; (de bâtiment) & Fig framework. ◆**osselets** nmpl (jeu) jacks, knucklebones. ◆**ossements** nmpl (de cadavres) bones. ◆**osseux, -euse** a (tissu) bone-; (maigre) bony.

ostensible [ɔstɑ̃sibl] a conspicuous.

ostentation [ɔstɑ̃tasjɔ̃] nf ostentation.

otage [ɔtaʒ] nm hostage; prendre qn en o. to take s.o. hostage.

OTAN [ɔtɑ̃] nf abrév (Organisation du traité de l'Atlantique Nord) NATO.

otarie [ɔtari] nf (animal) sea lion.

ôter [ote] vt to remove, take away (à qn from s.o.); (vêtement) to take off, remove; (déduire) to take (away); ôte-toi de là! Fam get out of the way!

otite [ɔtit] nf ear infection.

oto-rhino [ɔtorino] nmf Méd Fam ear, nose and throat specialist.

ou [u] conj or; ou bien or else; ou elle ou moi either her or me.

où [u] adv & pron where; le jour où the day when, the day on which; la table où the table on which; l'état où the condition in which; par où? which way?; d'où? where from?; **d'où ma surprise**/*etc* (*conséquence*) hence my surprise/*etc*; **le pays d'où** the country from which; **où qu'il soit** wherever he may be.

ouate [wat] *nf Méd* cotton wool, *Am* absorbent cotton.

oubli [ubli] *nm* (*défaut*) forgetfulness; **l'o. de qch** forgetting sth; **un o.** a lapse of memory; (*omission*) an oversight; **tomber dans l'o.** to fall into oblivion. ◆**oublier** *vt* to forget (**de faire** to do); (*faute, problème*) to overlook; — **s'o.** *vpr* (*traditions etc*) to be forgotten; (*personne*) Fig to forget oneself. ◆**oublieux, -euse** *a* forgetful (**de** of).

oubliettes [ublijet] *nfpl* (*de château*) dungeon.

ouest [west] *nm* west; **à l'o.** west; **d'o.** (*vent*) west(erly); **de l'o.** western; **Allemagne de l'O.** West Germany; **l'Europe de l'O.** Western Europe; — *a inv* (*côte*) west(ern). ◆**o.-allemand, -ande** *a* & *nmf* West German.

ouf! [uf] *int* (*soulagement*) ah!, phew!

oui [wi] *adv* & *nm inv* yes; **o.!** yes!; **les o.** (*votes*) the ayes; **tu viens, o.?** come on, will you?; **je crois que o.** I think so; **si o.** if so.

ouï-dire [widir] *nm inv* hearsay.

ouïe [1] [wi] *nf* hearing; **être tout o.** *Fam* to be all ears.

ouïe ?! [uj] *int* ouch!

ouïes [wi] *nfpl* (*de poisson*) gills.

ouille! [uj] *int* ouch!

ouragan [uragɑ̃] *nm* hurricane.

ourler [urle] *vt* to hem. ◆**ourlet** *nm* hem.

ours [urs] *nm* bear; **o. blanc/gris** polar/ grizzly bear.

oursin [ursɛ̃] *nm* (*animal*) sea urchin.

ouste! [ust] *int Fam* scram!

outil [uti] *nm* tool. ◆**outiller** *vt* to equip. ◆**-age** *nm* tools; (*d'une usine*) equipment.

outrage [utraʒ] *nm* insult (**à** to). ◆**outrager** *vt* to insult, offend. ◆**-eant** *a* insulting, offensive.

outrance [utrɑ̃s] *nf* (*excès*) excess; **à o.** (*travailler etc*) to excess; **guerre à o.** all-out war. ◆**outrancier, -ière** *a* excessive.

outre [utr] *prép* besides; — *adv* **en o.** besides, moreover; **o. mesure** inordinately; **passer o.** to take no notice (**à** of). ◆**o.-Manche**

adv across the Channel. ◆**o.-mer** *adv* overseas; **d'o.-mer** (*peuple*) overseas.

outrepasser [utrəpase] *vt* (*limite etc*) to go beyond, exceed.

outr/er [utre] *vt* to exaggerate, overdo; **o. qn** (*indigner*) to outrage s.o. ◆**-é** *a* (*excessif*) exaggerated; (*révolté*) outraged.

outsider [awtsajdœr] *nm Sp* outsider.

ouvert [uver] *voir* **ouvrir**; — *a* open; (*robinet, gaz etc*) on; **à bras ouverts** with open arms. ◆**ouvertement** *adv* openly. ◆**ouverture** *nf* opening; (*trou*) hole; (*avance*) & *Mus* overture; (*d'objectif*) *Phot* aperture; **o. d'esprit** open-mindedness.

ouvrable [uvrabl] *a* **jour o.** working day.

ouvrage [uvraʒ] *nm* (*travail, objet, livre*) work; (*couture*) (needle)work; **un o.** (*travail*) a piece of work. ◆**ouvragé** *a* (*bijou etc*) finely worked.

ouvreuse [uvrøz] *nf Cin* usherette.

ouvrier, -ière [uvrije, -jɛr] *nmf* worker; **o. agricole** farm labourer; **o. qualifié/spécialisé** skilled/unskilled worker; — *a* (*législation etc*) industrial; (*quartier, éducation*) working-class; **classe ouvrière** working class.

ouvrir* [uvrir] *vt* to open (up); (*gaz, radio etc*) to turn on, switch on; (*inaugurer*) to open; (*hostilités*) to begin; (*appétit*) to whet; (*liste, procession*) to head; — *vi* to open; (*ouvrir la porte*) to open (up); — **s'o.** *vpr* (*porte, boîte etc*) to open (up); **s'o. la jambe** to cut one's leg open; **s'o. à qn** *Fig* to open one's heart to s.o. (**de qch** about sth). ◆**ouvre-boîtes** *nm inv* tin opener, *Am* can-opener. ◆**ouvre-bouteilles** *nm inv* bottle opener.

ovaire [over] *nm Anat* ovary.

ovale [oval] *a* & *nm* oval.

ovation [ovasjɔ̃] *nf* (*standing*) ovation.

OVNI [ovni] *nm abrév* (*objet volant non identifié*) UFO.

oxyde [oksid] *nm Ch* oxide; **o. de carbone** carbon monoxide. ◆**oxyder** *vt*, — **s'o.** *vpr* to oxidize.

oxygène [oksiʒɛn] *nm* oxygen; **à o.** (*masque, tente*) oxygen-. ◆**oxygén/er** *vt* (*cheveux*) to bleach; — **s'o.** *vpr Fam* to breathe or get some fresh air. ◆**-ée** *af* **eau o.** (hydrogen) peroxide.

P

P, p [pe] *nm* P, p.

pachyderme [paʃidɛrm] *nm* elephant.

pacifier [pasifje] *vt* to pacify. **◆pacifica-tion** *nf* pacification. **◆pacifique 1** *a* (*non violent, non militaire*) peaceful; (*personne, peuple*) peace-loving. **2** *a* (*côte etc*) Pacific; **Océan P.** Pacific Ocean; − *nm* le **P.** the Pacific. **◆pacifiste** *a & nmf* pacifist.

pack [pak] *nm* (*de lait etc*) carton.

pacotille [pakɔtij] *nf* (*camelote*) trash.

pacte [pakt] *nm* pact. **◆pactiser** *vi* p. avec qn *Péj* to be in league with s.o.

paf! [paf] **1** *int* bang!, wallop! **2** *a inv* (*ivre*) *Fam* sozzled, plastered.

pagaie [page] *nf* paddle. **◆pagayer** *vi* (*ramer*) to paddle.

pagaïe, pagaille [pagaj] *nf* (*désordre*) *Fam* mess, shambles; **en p.** *Fam* in a mess; **avoir des livres/etc en p.** *Fam* to have loads of books/*etc*.

paganisme [paganism] *nm* paganism.

page [paʒ] **1** *nf* (*de livre etc*) page; **à la p.** (*personne*) *Fig* up-to-date. **2** *nm* (*à la cour*) *Hist* page (boy).

pagne [paɲ] *nm* loincloth.

pagode [pagɔd] *nf* pagoda.

paie [pe] *nf* pay, wages. **◆paiement** *nm* payment.

païen, -enne [pajɛ̃, -ɛn] *a & nmf* pagan, heathen.

paillasson [pajasɔ̃] *nm* (door)mat.

paille [paj] *nf* straw; (*pour boire*) (drinking) straw; **homme de p.** *Fig* stooge, man of straw; **tirer à la courte p.** to draw lots; **sur la p.** *Fig* penniless; **feu de p.** *Fig* flash in the pan. **◆paillasse** *nf* **1** (*matelas*) straw mattress. **2** (*d'un évier*) draining-board.

paillette [pajɛt] *nf* (*d'habit*) sequin; *pl* (*de lessive, savon*) flakes; (*d'or*) *Géol* gold dust.

pain [pɛ̃] *nm* bread; **un p.** a loaf (of bread); **p. grillé** toast; **p. complet** wholemeal bread; **p. d'épice** gingerbread; **petit p.** roll; **p. de savon/de cire** bar of soap/wax; **avoir du p. sur la planche** (*travail*) *Fig* to have a lot on one's plate.

pair [pɛr] **1** *a* (*numéro*) even. **2** *nm* (*personne*) peer; **hors (de) p.** unrivalled, without equal; **aller de p.** to go hand in hand (**avec** with); **au p.** (*étudiant etc*) au pair; **travailler au p.** to work as an au pair.

paire [pɛr] *nf* pair (**de** of).

paisible [pezibl] *a* (*vie etc*) peaceful; (*caractère, personne*) peaceable.

paître* [pɛtr] *vi* to graze; **envoyer p.** *Fig* to send packing.

paix [pɛ] *nf* peace; (*traité*) *Pol* peace treaty; **en p.** in peace; (*avec sa conscience*) at peace (**avec** with); **avoir la p.** to have (some) peace and quiet.

Pakistan [pakistɑ̃] *nm* Pakistan. **◆pakis-tanais, -aise** *a & nmf* Pakistani.

palabres [palabr] *nmpl* palaver.

palace [palas] *nm* luxury hotel.

palais [palɛ] *nm* **1** (*château*) palace; **P. de justice** law courts; **p. des sports** sports stadium *ou* centre. **2** *Anat* palate.

palan [palɑ̃] *nm* (*de navire etc*) hoist.

pâle [pɑl] *a* pale.

palet [palɛ] *nm* (*hockey sur glace*) puck.

paletot [palto] *nm* (knitted) cardigan.

palette [palɛt] *nf* **1** (*de peintre*) palette. **2** (*support pour marchandises*) pallet.

pâleur [palœr] *nf* paleness, pallor. **◆pâlir** *vi* to go *ou* turn pale (**de** with).

palier [palje] *nm* **1** (*d'escalier*) landing; **être voisins de p.** to live on the same floor. **2** (*niveau*) level; (*phase de stabilité*) plateau; **par paliers** (*étapes*) in stages.

palissade [palisad] *nf* fence (of stakes).

pallier [palje] *vt* (*difficultés etc*) to alleviate. **◆palliatif** *nf* palliative.

palmarès [palmarɛs] *nm* prize list; (*des chansons*) hit-parade.

palme [palm] *nf* **1** palm (leaf); (*symbole*) *Fig* palm. **2** (*de nageur*) flipper. **◆palmier** *nm* palm (tree).

palmé [palme] *a* (*patte, pied*) webbed.

palombe [palɔ̃b] *nf* wood pigeon.

pâlot, -otte [pɑlo, -ɔt] *a* pale.

palourde [palurd] *nf* (*mollusque*) clam.

palp/er [palpe] *vt* to feel, finger. **◆−able** *a* tangible.

palpit/er [palpite] *vi* (*frémir*) to quiver; (*cœur*) to palpitate, throb. **◆−ant** *a* (*film etc*) thrilling. **◆−ations** *nfpl* quivering; palpitations.

pâmer (se) [səpame] *vpr* **se p. de** (*joie etc*) to be paralysed *ou* ecstatic with.

pamphlet [pɑ̃flɛ] *nm* lampoon.

pamplemousse [pɑ̃pləmus] *nm* grapefruit.

pan [pɑ̃] **1** *nm* (*de chemise*) tail; (*de ciel*) patch; **p. de mur** section of wall. **2** *int* bang!

pan- [pɑ̃, pan] *préf* Pan-.

panacée [panase] *nf* panacea.

panache [panaʃ] *nm* (*plumet*) plume; **avoir du p.** (*fière allure*) to have panache; **un p. de fumée** a plume of smoke.

panaché [panaʃe] **1** *a* (*bigarré, hétéroclite*) motley. **2** *a & nm* (**demi**) **p.** shandy; **bière panachée** shandy.

pancarte [pɑ̃kart] *nf* sign, notice; (*de manifestant*) placard.

pancréas [pɑ̃kreas] *nm Anat* pancreas.

panda [pɑ̃da] *nm* (*animal*) panda.

pané [pane] *a Culin* breaded.

panier [panje] *nm* (*ustensile, contenu*) basket; **p. à salade** salad basket; (*voiture*) *Fam* police van, prison van. ◆**p.-repas** *nm* (*pl* **paniers-repas**) packed lunch.

panique [panik] *nf* panic; **pris de p.** panic-stricken; **– a peur p.** panic fear. ◆**paniqu/er** *vi* to panic. ◆**-é** *a* panic-stricken.

panne [pan] *nf* breakdown; **tomber en p.** to break down; **être en p.** to have broken down; **p. d'électricité** power cut, blackout; **avoir une p. sèche** to run out of petrol ou *Am* gas.

panneau, -x [pano] *nm* **1** (*écriteau*) sign, notice, board; **p. (de signalisation)** traffic ou road sign; **p. (d'affichage)** (*publicité*) hoarding, *Am* billboard. **2** (*de porte etc*) panel. ◆**panonceau, -x** *nm* (*enseigne*) sign.

panoplie [panɔpli] *nf* **1** (*jouet*) outfit. **2** (*gamme, arsenal*) (wide) range, assortment.

panorama [panɔrama] *nm* panorama. ◆**panoramique** *a* panoramic.

panse [pɑ̃s] *nf Fam* paunch, belly. ◆**pansu** *a* potbellied.

pans/er [pɑ̃se] *vt* (*plaie, main etc*) to dress, bandage; (*personne*) to dress the wound(s) of, bandage (up); (*cheval*) to groom. ◆**-ement** *nm* (*bande*) bandage, dressing; **p. adhésif** sticking plaster, *Am* Band-Aid®.

pantalon [pɑ̃talɔ̃] *nm* (pair of) trousers ou *Am* pants; **deux pantalons** two pairs of trousers ou *Am* pants; **en p.** in trousers, *Am* in pants.

pantelant [pɑ̃tlɑ̃] *a* gasping.

panthère [pɑ̃tɛr] *nf* (*animal*) panther.

pantin [pɑ̃tɛ̃] *nm* (*jouet*) jumping jack; (*personne*) *Péj* puppet.

pantois [pɑ̃twa] *a* flabbergasted.

pantoufle [pɑ̃tufl] *nf* slipper. ◆**pantou-**

flard, -arde *nmf Fam* stay-at-home, *Am* homebody.

paon [pɑ̃] *nm* peacock.

papa [papa] *nm* dad(dy); **de p.** (*désuet*) *Péj* outdated; **fils à p.** *Péj* rich man's son, daddy's boy.

pape [pap] *nm* pope. ◆**papauté** *nf* papacy.

paperasse(s) [papras] *nf(pl) Péj* (official) papers. ◆**paperasserie** *nf Péj* (official) papers; (*procédure*) red tape.

papeterie [papetri] *nf* (*magasin*) stationer's shop; (*articles*) stationery; (*fabrique*) paper mill. ◆**papetier, -ière** *nmf* stationer.

papi [papi] *nm Fam* grand(d)ad.

papier [papje] *nm* (*matière*) paper; **un p.** (*feuille*) a piece ou sheet of paper; (*formulaire*) a form; *Journ* an article; **en p.** (*sac etc*) paper-; **papiers (d'identité)** (identity) papers; **p. à lettres** writing paper; **du p. journal** (some) newspaper; **p. peint** wallpaper; **p. de verre** sandpaper.

papillon [papijɔ̃] *nm* **1** (*insecte*) butterfly; (*écrou*) butterfly nut, *Am* wing nut; **p. (de nuit)** moth. **2** (*contravention*) (parking) ticket.

papot/er [papɔte] *vi* to prattle. ◆**-age(s)** *nm(pl)* prattle.

paprika [paprika] *nm* (*poudre*) *Culin* paprika.

papy [papi] *nm Fam* grand(d)ad.

Pâque [pak] *nf* la **P.** *Rel* Passover.

paquebot [pakbo] *nm Nau* liner.

pâquerette [pakrɛt] *nf* daisy.

Pâques [pak] *nm & nfpl* Easter.

paquet [pakɛ] *nm* (*de sucre, bonbons etc*) packet; (*colis*) package; (*de cigarettes*) pack(et); (*de cartes*) pack.

par [par] *prép* **1** (*agent, manière, moyen*) by; **choisi/frappé/etc p.** chosen/hit/etc by; **p. erreur** by mistake; **p. mer** by sea; **p. le train** by train; **p. la force/le travail/etc** by ou through force/work/etc; **apprendre p. un voisin** to learn from ou through a neighbour; **commencer/s'ouvrir p. qch** (*récit etc*) to begin/open with sth; **p. malchance** unfortunately. **2** (*lieu*) through; **p. la porte/le tunnel/etc** through ou by the door/tunnel/etc; **regarder/jeter p. la fenêtre** to look/throw out (of) the window; **p. les rues** through the streets; **p. ici/là** (*aller*) this/that way; (*habiter*) around here/there. **3** (*motif*) out of, from; **p. respect/pitié/etc** out of ou from respect/pity/etc. **4** (*temps*) on; **p. un jour d'hiver/etc** on a winter's day/etc; **p. le passé** in the past; **p. ce froid** in this cold. **5** (*distributif*) **dix fois p.** an ten times a ou per year; **deux p. deux** two by two; **p. deux fois** twice. **6** (*trop*) p. trop ai-mable/*etc* far too kind/*etc.*

para [para] *nm Mil Fam* para(trooper).
para- [para] *préf* para-.

parabole [parabol] *nf* **1** (*récit*) parable. **2** *Math* parabola.

parachever [parafve] *vt* to perfect.

parachute [parafyt] *nf* parachute. ◆**parachuter** *vt* to parachute; (*nommer*) *Fam* to pitchfork (**à un poste** into a job). ◆**parachutage** *nm* parachute jumping. ◆**parachutiste** *nmf* parachutist; *Mil* paratrooper.

parade [parad] *nf* **1** (*étalage*) show, parade; (*spectacle*) & *Mil* parade. **2** *Boxe Escrime* parry; (*riposte*) *Fig* reply. ◆**parader** *vi* to parade, show off.

paradis [paradi] *nm* paradise, heaven. ◆**paradisiaque** *a* (*endroit etc*) *Fig* heavenly.

paradoxe [paradɔks] *nm* paradox. ◆**paradoxalement** *adv* paradoxically.

parafe [paraf] *voir* **paraphe.** ◆**parafer** *voir* **parapher.**

paraffine [parafin] *nf* paraffin (wax).

parages [paraʒ] *nmpl* region, area (**de** of); **dans ces p.** in these parts.

paragraphe [paragraf] *nm* paragraph.

paraître* [parɛtr] **1** *vi* (*se montrer*) to appear; (*sembler*) to seem, look, appear; – *v imp* **il paraît qu'il va partir** it appears ou seems (that) he's leaving. **2** *vi* (*livre*) to be published, come out; **faire p.** to bring out.

parallèle [paralɛl] **1** *a* (*comparable*) & *Math* parallel (**à** with, to); (*marché*) *Com* unofficial. **2** *nm* (*comparaison*) & *Géog* parallel. ◆**—ment** *adv* **p. à** parallel to.

paralyser [paralize] *vt* to paralyse, *Am* paralyze. ◆**paralysie** *nf* paralysis. ◆**paralytique** *a* & *nmf* paralytic.

paramètre [parametr] *nm* parameter.

paranoïa [paranɔja] *nf* paranoia. ◆**paranoïaque** *a* & *nmf* paranoid.

parapet [parapɛ] *nm* parapet.

paraphe [paraf] *nm* initials, signature; (*traits*) flourish. ◆**parapher** *vt* to initial, sign.

paraphrase [parafraz] *nf* paraphrase. ◆**paraphraser** *vt* to paraphrase.

parapluie [paraplɥi] *nm* umbrella.

parasite [parazit] *nm* (*personne, organisme*) parasite; *pl Rad* interference; – *a* parasitic(al).

parasol [parasɔl] *nm* parasol, sunshade.

paratonnerre [paratɔnɛr] *nm* lightning conductor *ou Am* rod.

paravent [paravã] *nm* (folding) screen.

parc [park] *nm* **1** park; (*de château*) grounds. **2** (*de bébé*) (play) pen; (*à moutons, à bétail*) pen; **p.** (**de stationnement**) car park, *Am* parking lot; **p. à huîtres** oyster bed.

parcelle [parsɛl] *nf* fragment, particle; (*terrain*) plot; (*de vérité*) *Fig* grain.

parce que [parsk(ə)] *conj* because.

parchemin [parʃəmɛ̃] *nm* parchment.

parcimonie [parsimɔni] *nf* **avec p.** parsimoniously. ◆**parcimonieux, -euse** *a* parsimonious.

par-ci par-là [parsiparla] *adv* here, there and everywhere.

parcmètre [parkmɛtr] *nm* parking meter.

parcourir* [parkurir] *vt* (*région*) to travel through, tour, scour; (*distance*) to cover; (*texte*) to glance through. ◆**parcours** *nm* (*itinéraire*) route; (*de fleuve*) & *Sp* course; (*voyage*) trip, journey.

par-delà [pard(ə)la] *voir* **delà.**

par-derrière [pardɛrjɛr] *voir* **derrière.**

par-dessous [pard(ə)su] *prép* & *adv* under(neath).

pardessus [pard(ə)sy] *nm* overcoat.

par-dessus [pard(ə)sy] *prép* & *adv* over (the top of); **p.-dessus tout** above all.

par-devant [pard(ə)vã] *voir* **devant.**

pardon [pardɔ̃] *nm* forgiveness, pardon; **p.?** (*pour demander*) excuse me?, *Am* pardon me?; **p.!** (*je le regrette*) sorry! ◆**pardonner** *vt* to forgive; **p. qch à qn/à qn d'avoir fait qch** to forgive s.o. for sth/for doing sth. ◆**—able** *a* forgivable.

pare-balles [parbal] *a inv* **gilet p.-balles** bulletproof jacket *ou Am* vest.

pare-brise [parbriz] *nm inv Aut* windscreen, *Am* windshield.

pare-chocs [parʃɔk] *nm inv Aut* bumper.

pareil, -eille [parɛj] *a* similar; **p. à** the same as, similar to; **être pareils** to be the same, be similar *ou* alike; **un p. désordre**/*etc* such a mess/*etc*; **en p. cas** in such a case; – *nmf* (*personne*) equal; **rendre la pareille à qn** to treat s.o. the same way; **sans p.** unparalleled, unique; – *adv Fam* the same. ◆**pareillement** *adv* in the same way; (*aussi*) likewise.

parement [parmã] *nm* (*de pierre, de vêtement*) facing.

parent, -ente [parã, -ãt] *nmf* relation, relative; – *nmpl* (*père et mère*) parents; – *a* related (**de** to). ◆**parenté** *nf* (*rapport*) relationship, kinship.

parenthèse [parãtɛz] *nf* (*signe*) bracket, parenthesis; (*digression*) digression.

parer [pare] **1** *vt* (*coup*) to parry, ward off; − *vi* **p. à** to be prepared for. **2** *vt* (*orner*) to adorn (**de** with).

paresse [parɛs] *nf* laziness, idleness. ◆**paresser** *vi* to laze (about). ◆**paresseux, -euse** *a* lazy, idle; − *nmf* lazybones.

parfaire [parfɛr] *vt* to perfect. ◆**parfait** *a* perfect; **p.!** excellent!; − *nm* Gram perfect (tense). ◆**parfaitement** *adv* perfectly; (*certainement*) certainly.

parfois [parfwa] *adv* sometimes.

parfum [parfɛ̃] *nm* (*odeur*) fragrance, scent; (*goût*) flavour; (*liquide*) perfume, scent. ◆**parfum/er** *vt* to perfume, scent; (*glace, crème etc*) to flavour (**à** with); − **se p.** *vpr* to put on perfume; (*habituellement*) to wear perfume. ◆**—é** *a* (*savon, mouchoir*) scented; **p. au café**/*etc* coffee-/*etc* flavoured. ◆**parfumerie** *nf* (*magasin*) perfume shop.

pari [pari] *nm* bet, wager; *pl* Sp betting, bets; **p. mutuel urbain** = the tote, Am pari-mutuel. ◆**parier** *vti* to bet (**sur** on, **que** that). ◆**parieur, -euse** *nmf* Sp better, punter.

Paris [pari] *nm ou f* Paris. ◆**parisien, -ienne** *a* (*accent etc*) Parisian, Paris-; − *nmf* Parisian.

parité [parite] *nf* parity.

parjure [parʒyr] *nm* perjury; − *nmf* perjurer. ◆**se parjurer** *vpr* to perjure oneself.

parka [parka] *nm* parka.

parking [parkiŋ] *nm* (*lieu*) car park, Am parking lot.

par-là [parla] *adv voir* **par-ci.**

parlement [parləmɑ̃] *nm* parliament. ◆**parlementaire** *a* parliamentary; − *nmf* member of parliament.

parlementer [parləmɑ̃te] *vi* to parley, negotiate.

parl/er [parle] *vi* to talk, speak (**de** about, of; **à** to); **tu parles!** Fam you must be joking!; **sans p. de . . .** not to mention . . . ; − *vt* (*langue*) to speak; **p. affaires**/*etc* to talk business/*etc*; − **se p.** *vpr* (*langue*) to be spoken; − *nm* speech; (*régional*) dialect. ◆**—ant** *a* (*film*) talking; (*regard etc*) eloquent. ◆**—é** *a* (*langue*) spoken.

parloir [parlwar] *nm* (*de couvent, prison*) visiting room.

parmi [parmi] *prép* among(st).

parodie [parɔdi] *nf* parody. ◆**parodier** *vt* to parody.

paroi [parwa] *nf* wall; (*de maison*) inside wall; (*de rocher*) (rock) face.

paroisse [parwas] *nf* parish. ◆**paroissial,**

-aux *a* (*registre, activité etc*) parish-. ◆**paroissien, -ienne** *nmf* parishioner.

parole [parɔl] *nf* (*mot, promesse*) word; (*faculté, langage*) speech; **adresser la p.** à to speak to; **prendre la p.** to speak, make a speech; **demander la p.** to ask to speak; **perdre la p.** to lose one's tongue.

paroxysme [parɔksism] *nm* (*de douleur etc*) height.

parpaing [parpɛ̃] *nm* concrete block, breezeblock.

parquer [parke] *vt* (*bœufs*) to pen; (*gens*) to herd together, confine; (*véhicule*) to park; − **se p.** *vpr* Aut to park.

parquet [parke] *nm* **1** (parquet) floor(ing). **2** Jur Public Prosecutor's office.

parrain [parɛ̃] *nm* Rel godfather; (*répondant*) sponsor. ◆**parrain/er** *vt* to sponsor. ◆**—age** *nm* sponsorship.

pars, part [par] *voir* **partir.**

parsemer [parsəme] *vt* to strew, dot (**de** with).

part [par] *nf* (*portion*) share, part; **prendre p. à** (*activité*) to take part in; (*la joie etc de qn*) to share; **de toutes parts** from *ou* on all sides; **de p. et d'autre** on both sides; **d'une p., . . . d'autre p.** on the one hand, . . . on the other hand; **d'autre p.** (*d'ailleurs*) moreover; **pour ma p.** as far as I'm concerned; **de la p. de** (*provenance*) from; **c'est de la p. de qui?** *Tél* who's speaking?; **faire p. de qch à qn** to inform s.o. of sth; **quelque p.** somewhere; **nulle p.** nowhere; **autre p.** somewhere else; **à p.** (*séparément*) apart; (*mettre, prendre*) aside; (*excepté*) apart from; **un cas**/**une place**/*etc* **à p.** a separate *ou* special case/place/*etc*; **membre à p. entière** full member.

partage [partaʒ] *nm* dividing (up), division; (*participation*) sharing; (*distribution*) sharing out; (*sort*) Fig lot. ◆**partag/er** *vt* (*repas, frais, joie etc*) to share (**avec** with); (*diviser*) to divide (up); (*distribuer*) to share out; − **se p.** *vpr* (*bénéfices etc*) to share (between themselves *etc*); **se p. entre** to divide one's time between. ◆**—é** *a* (*avis etc*) divided; **p. entre** (*sentiments*) torn between.

partance (en) [ɑ̃partɑ̃s] *adv* (*train etc*) about to depart (**pour** for).

partant [partɑ̃] *nm* (*coureur, cheval*) Sp starter.

partenaire [partənɛr] *nmf* (*époux etc*) & Sp Pol partner.

parterre [partɛr] *nm* **1** (*de jardin etc*) flower bed. **2** *Th* stalls, Am orchestra.

parti [parti] *nm* Pol party; (*époux*) match; **prendre un p.** to make a decision, follow a course; **prendre p. pour** to side with; **tirer p. de** to turn to (good) account; **p. pris** (*préjugé*) prejudice; **être de p. pris** to be prejudiced (**contre** against).

partial, -aux [parsjal, -o] *a* biased. ◆**partialité** *nf* bias.

participe [partisip] *nm Gram* participle.

particip/er [partisipe] *vi* **p. à** (*activité, jeu etc*) to take part in, participate in; (*frais, joie etc*) to share (in). ◆**—ant, -ante** *nmf* participant. ◆**participation** *nf* participation; sharing; (*d'un acteur*) appearance, collaboration; **p. (aux frais)** (*contribution*) share (in the expenses).

particule [partikyl] *nf* particle.

particulier, -ière [partikylje, -jɛr] *a* (*spécial, spécifique*) particular; (*privé*) private; (*bizarre*) peculiar; **p. à** peculiar to; **en p.** (*surtout*) in particular; (*à part*) in private; — *nm* private individual *ou* citizen. ◆**particularité** *nf* peculiarity. ◆**particulièrement** *adv* particularly; **tout p.** especially.

partie [parti] *nf* part; (*de cartes, de tennis etc*) game; (*de chasse, de plaisir*) & *Jur* party; (*métier*) line, field; **en p.** partly, in part; **en grande p.** mainly; **faire p. de** to be a part of; (*adhérer à*) to belong to; (*comité*) to be on. ◆**partiel, -ielle** *a* partial; — *nm* (*examen*) *Univ* term exam. ◆**partiellement** *adv* partially.

part/ir* [partir] *vi* (*aux* **être**) (*aller, disparaître*) to go; (*s'en aller*) to leave, go (off); (*se mettre en route*) to set off; (*s'éloigner*) to go (away); (*moteur*) to start; (*fusil, coup de feu*) to go off; (*flèche*) to shoot off; (*bouton*) to come off; (*tache*) to come out; **p. de** (*commencer par*) to start (off) with; **ça part du cœur** it comes from the heart; **bien parti** to get off to a good start; **à p. de** (*date, prix*) from. ◆**—i a bien p.** off to a good start.

partisan [partizã] *nm* follower, supporter; *Mil* partisan; — *a* (*esprit*) *Péj* partisan; **être p. de qch/de faire** to be in favour of sth/of doing.

partition [partisjɔ̃] *nf Mus* score.

partout [partu] *adv* everywhere; **p. où tu vas** *ou* **iras** everywhere *ou* wherever you go; **p. sur la table**/*etc* all over the table/*etc*.

paru [pary] *voir* **paraître**. ◆**parution** *nf* (*de livre etc*) publication.

parure [paryr] *nf* (*toilette*) finery; (*bijoux*) jewellery.

parven/ir* [parvənir] *vi* (*aux* **être**) **p. à** (*lieu*) to reach; (*fortune, ses fins*) to achieve; **p. à faire** to manage to do. ◆**—u, -ue** *nmf Péj* upstart.

parvis [parvi] *nm* square (*in front of church etc*).

pas¹ [pɑ] *adv* (*négatif*) not; (**ne**) ... **p.** not; **je ne sais p.** I do not *ou* don't know; **p. de pain/de café**/*etc* no bread/coffee/*etc*; **p. encore** not yet; **p. du tout** not at all.

pas² [pɑ] *nm* 1 step, pace; (*allure*) pace; (*bruit*) footstep; (*trace*) footprint; **à deux p. (de)** close by; **revenir sur ses p.** to go back on one's tracks; **au p.** at a walking pace; **rouler au p.** (*véhicule*) to go dead slow(ly); **au p. (cadencé)** in step; **faire les cent p.** to walk up and down; **faux p.** stumble; (*faute*) *Fig* blunder; **le p. de la porte** the doorstep. 2 (*de vis*) thread. 3 *Géog* straits; **le p. de Calais** the Straits of Dover.

pascal [paskal] *a* (*semaine, messe etc*) Easter-.

passable [pɑsabl] *a* acceptable, tolerable; **mention p.** *Scol Univ* pass. ◆**—ment** [-əmɑ̃] *adv* acceptably; (*beaucoup*) quite a lot.

passage [pɑsaʒ] *nm* (*action*) passing, passage; (*traversée*) *Nau* crossing, passage; (*extrait*) passage; (*couloir*) passage(way); (*droit*) right of way; (*venue*) arrival; (*chemin*) path; **p. clouté** *ou* **pour piétons** (pedestrian) crossing; **obstruer le p.** to block the way; **p. souterrain** subway, *Am* underpass; **p. à niveau** level crossing, *Am* grade crossing; **'p. interdit'** 'no thoroughfare'; **'cédez le p.'** *Aut* 'give way', *Am* 'yield'; **être de p.** to be passing through (**à Paris**/*etc* Paris/*etc*); **hôte de p.** passing guest. ◆**passager, -ère** 1 *nmf* passenger; **p. clandestin** stowaway. 2 *a* (*de courte durée*) passing, temporary. ◆**passagèrement** *adv* temporarily.

passant, -ante [pɑsã, -ãt] 1 *a* (*rue*) busy; — *nmf* passer-by. 2 *nm* (*de ceinture etc*) loop.

passe [pɑs] *nf Sp* pass; **mot de p.** password; **en p. de faire** on the road to doing; **une mauvaise p.** *Fig* a bad patch.

passe-montagne [pɑsmɔ̃taɲ] *nm* balaclava.

passe-partout [pɑspartu] *nm inv* (*clé*) master key; — *a inv* (*compliment, phrase*) all-purpose.

passe-passe [pɑspɑs] *nm inv* **tour de p.-passe** conjuring trick.

passe-plat [pɑsplɑ] *nm* service hatch.

passeport [pɑspɔr] *nm* passport.

passer [pɑse] *vi* (*aux* **être** *ou* **avoir**) (*aller, venir*) to pass (**à** to); (*facteur, laitier*) to come; (*temps*) to pass (by), go by; (*courant*) to flow; (*film, programme*) to be shown, be on; (*loi*) to be passed; (*douleur, mode*) to pass; (*couleur*) to fade; **p. devant** (*maison etc*) to go past ou by, pass (by); **p. à** ou **par Paris** to pass through Paris; **p. à la radio** to come ou go over to the enemy/the cash desk; **laisser p.** (*personne, lumière*) to let in ou through; (*occasion*) to let slip; **p. prendre** to pick up, fetch; **p. voir qn** to drop in on s.o.; **p. pour** (*riche etc*) to be taken for; **faire p. qn pour** to pass s.o. off as; **p. sur** (*détail etc*) to overlook, pass over; **p. capitaine**/*etc* to be promoted captain/*etc*; **p. en** (*seconde etc*) *Scol* to pass up into; *Aut* to change up to; **ça passe** (*c'est passable*) that'll do; **en passant** (*dire qch*) in passing; − *vt* (*aux avoir*) (*frontière etc*) to pass, cross; (*maison etc*) to pass, go past; (*donner*) to pass, hand (à to); (*mettre*) to put; (*omettre*) to overlook; (*temps*) to spend, pass (**à faire** doing); (*disque*) to play, put on; (*film, programme*) to show, put on; (*loi, motion*) to pass; (*chemise*) to slip on; (*examen*) to take, sit (for); (*thé*) to strain; (*café*) to filter; (*commande*) to place; (*accord*) to conclude; (*colère*) to vent (**sur** on); (*limites*) to go beyond; (*visite médicale*) to go through; **p. (son tour)** to pass; **p. qch à** (*caprice etc*) to grant s.o. sth; (*pardonner*) to excuse s.o. sth; **je vous passe . . .** *Tél* I'm putting you through to . . . ; **p. un coup d'éponge**/*etc* **à qch** to go over sth with a sponge/*etc*; **− se p.** *vpr* (*se produire*) to take place, happen; (*douleur*) to pass, go (away); **se p. de** to do ou go without; **se p. de commentaires** to need no comment; **ça s'est bien passé** it went off all right. ◆**passé 1** *a* (*temps etc*) past; (*couleur*) faded; **la semaine passée** last week; **dix heures passées** after ou gone ten (o'clock); **être passé** (*personne*) to have been (and gone); (*orage*) to be over; **avoir vingt ans passés** to be over twenty; − *nm* (*temps, vie passée*) past; *Gram* past (tense). **2** *prép* after; **p. huit heures** after eight (o'clock).

passerelle [pasʀɛl] *nf* (*pont*) footbridge; (*voie d'accès*) Nau Av gangway.

passe-temps [pɑstɑ̃] *nm inv* pastime.

passeur, -euse [pasœʀ, -øz] *nmf* **1** Nau ferryman, ferrywoman. **2** (*contrebandier*) smuggler.

passible [pasibl] *a* **p. de** (*peine*) Jur liable to.

passif, -ive [pasif, -iv] **1** *a* (*rôle, personne etc*) passive; − *nm Gram* passive. **2** *nm Com* liabilities. ◆**passivité** *nf* passiveness, passivity.

passion [pɑsjɔ̃] *nf* passion; **avoir la p. des**

voitures/d'écrire/*etc* to have a passion ou a great love for cars/writing/*etc*. ◆**passionnel, -elle** *a* (*crime*) of passion. ◆**passionn/er** *vt* to thrill, fascinate; **se p. pour** to have a passion for. ◆**−ant** *a* thrilling. ◆**−é, -ée** *a* passionate; **p. de qch** passionately fond of sth; − *nmf* fan (**de** of). ◆**−ément** *adv* passionately.

passoire [paswaʀ] *nf* (*pour liquides*) sieve; (*à thé*) strainer; (*à légumes*) colander.

pastel [pastɛl] *nm* pastel; **au p.** (*dessin*) pastel-; − *a inv* (*ton*) pastel-.

pastèque [pastɛk] *nf* watermelon.

pasteur [pastœʀ] *nm Rel* pastor.

pasteurisé [pastœʀize] *a* (*lait, beurre etc*) pasteurized.

pastiche [pastiʃ] *nm* pastiche.

pastille [pastij] *nf* pastille, lozenge.

pastis [pastis] *nm* aniseed liqueur, pastis.

pastoral, -aux [pastɔʀal, -o] *a* pastoral.

patate [patat] *nf Fam* spud, potato.

patatras! [patatʀa] *int* crash!

pataud [pato] *a* clumsy, lumpish.

patauger [patoʒe] *vi* (*marcher*) to wade (**in** the mud etc); (*barboter*) to splash about; (*s'empêtrer*) Fig to flounder. ◆**pataugeoire** *nf* paddling pool.

patchwork [patʃwœʀk] *nm* patchwork.

pâte [pɑt] *nf* (*substance*) paste; (*à pain, à gâteau*) dough; (*à tarte*) pastry; **pâtes** (*alimentaires*) pasta; **p. à modeler** plasticine®, modelling clay; **p. à frire** batter; **p. dentifrice** toothpaste.

pâté [pɑte] *nm* **1** (*charcuterie*) pâté; **p. (en croûte)** meat pie. **2 p. (de sable)** sand castle; **p. de maisons** block of houses. **3** (*tache d'encre*) (ink) blot.

pâtée [pɑte] *nf* (*pour chien, volaille etc*) mash.

patelin [patlɛ̃] *nm Fam* village.

patent [patɑ̃] *a* patent, obvious.

patère [patɛʀ] *nf* (*coat*) peg.

paternel, -elle [patɛʀnɛl] *a* (*amour etc*) fatherly, paternal; (*parenté, réprimande*) paternal. ◆**paternité** *nf* (*état*) paternity, fatherhood; (*de livre*) authorship.

pâteux, -euse [pɑtø, -øz] *a* (*substance*) doughy, pasty; (*style*) woolly; **avoir la bouche ou la langue pâteuse** (*après s'être enivré*) to have a mouth full of cotton wool ou AM cotton.

pathétique [patetik] *a* moving; − *nm* pathos.

pathologie [patɔlɔʒi] *nf* pathology. ◆**pathologique** *a* pathological.

patient, -ente [pasjɑ̃, -ɑ̃t] **1** *a* patient. **2** *nm Méd* patient. ◆**patiemment** [-amɑ̃] *adv* patiently. ◆**patience** *nf* patience; **prendre p.** to have patience; **perdre p.** to lose patience. ◆**patienter** *vi* to wait (patiently).

patin [patɛ̃] *nm* skate; (*pour le parquet*) cloth pad (*used for walking*); **p.** à **glace/à roulettes** ice/roller skate. ◆**patin/er** *vi Sp* to skate; (*véhicule, embrayage*) to slip. ◆**—age** *nm Sp* skating; **p. artistique** figure skating. ◆**—eur, -euse** *nmf Sp* skater. ◆**patinoire** *nf* (*piste*) & *Fig* skating rink, ice rink.

patine [patin] *nf* patina.

patio [patjo] *nm* patio.

pâtir [patir] *vi* **p. de** to suffer from.

pâtisserie [patisri] *nf* pastry, cake; (*magasin*) cake shop; (*art*) cake *ou* pastry making. ◆**pâtissier, -ière** *nmf* pastry-cook and cake shop owner.

patois [patwa] *nm Ling* patois.

patraque [patrak] *a* (*malade*) *Fam* under the weather.

patriarche [patrijarʃ] *nm* patriarch.

patrie [patri] *nf* (*native*) country; (*ville*) birth place. ◆**patriote** *nmf* patriot; *— a* (*personne*) patriotic. ◆**patriotique** *a* (*chant etc*) patriotic. ◆**patriotisme** *nm* patriotism.

patrimoine [patrimwan] *nm* (*biens*) & *Fig* heritage.

patron, -onne [patrɔ̃, -ɔn] **1** *nmf* (*chef*) employer, boss; (*propriétaire*) owner *ou* (*of*); (*gérant*) manager, manageress; (*de bar*) landlord, landlady. **2** *nmf Rel* patron saint. **3** *nm* (*modèle de papier*) *Tex* pattern. ◆**patronage** *nm* **1** (*protection*) patronage. **2** (*centre*) youth club. ◆**patronal, -aux** *a* (*syndicat etc*) employers'. ◆**patronat** *nm* employers. ◆**patronner** *vt* to sponsor.

patrouille [patruj] *nf* patrol. ◆**patrouiller** *vi* to patrol. ◆**—eur** *nm* (*navire*) patrol boat.

patte [pat] *nf* **1** (*membre*) leg; (*de chat, chien*) paw; (*de main*) *Fam* hand; **à quatre pattes** on all fours. **2** (*de poche*) flap; (*languette*) tongue.

pattes [pat] *nfpl* (*favoris*) sideboards, *Am* sideburns.

pâture [patyr] *nf* (*nourriture*) food; (*intellectuelle*) *Fig* fodder. ◆**pâturage** *nm* pasture.

paume [pom] *nf* (*de main*) palm.

paum/er [pome] *vt Fam* to lose; **un coin** *ou* **trou paumé** (*sans attrait*) a dump. ◆**—é, -ée** *nmf* (*malheureux*) *Fam* down-and-out, loser.

paupière [popjɛr] *nf* eyelid.

pause [poz] *nf* (*arrêt*) break; (*dans le discours etc*) pause.

pauvre [povr] *a* poor; (*terre*) impoverished, poor; **p. en** (*calories etc*) low in; (*ressources etc*) low on; *— nmf* (*indigent, malheureux*) poor man, poor woman; **les pauvres** the poor. ◆**pauvrement** *adv* poorly. ◆**pauvreté** *nf* (*besoin*) poverty; (*insuffisance*) poorness.

pavaner (se) [səpavane] *vpr* to strut (about).

pav/er [pave] *vt* to pave. ◆**—é** *nm* **un p.** a paving stone; (*rond, de vieille chaussée*) a cobblestone; **sur le p.** *Fig* on the streets. ◆**—age** *nm* (*travail, revêtement*) paving.

pavillon [pavijɔ̃] *nm* **1** (*maison*) house; (*de chasse*) lodge; (*d'hôpital*) ward; (*d'exposition*) pavilion. **2** (*drapeau*) flag.

pavoiser [pavwaze] *vt* to deck out with flags; *— vi* (*exulter*) *Fig* to rejoice.

pavot [pavo] *nm* (*cultivé*) poppy.

pay/er [peje] *vt* (*personne, somme*) to pay; (*service, objet, faute*) to pay for; (*récompenser*) to repay; **p. qch à qn** (*offrir en cadeau*) *Fam* to treat s.o. to sth; **p. qn pour faire** to pay s.o. to do *ou* for doing; *— vi* (*personne, métier, crime*) to pay; **se p. qch** (*s'acheter*) *Fam* to treat oneself to sth; **se p. la tête de qn** *Fam* to make fun of s.o. ◆**—ant** [pejɑ̃] *a* (*hôte, spectateur*) who pays, paying; (*place, entrée*) that one has to pay for; (*rentable*) worthwhile. ◆**payable** *a* payable. ◆**paye** *nf* pay, wages. ◆**payement** *nm* payment.

pays [pei] *nm* country; (*région*) region; (*village*) village; **p. des rêves/du soleil** land of dreams/sun; **du p.** (*vin, gens etc*) local.

paysage [peizaʒ] *nm* landscape, scenery.

paysan, -anne [peizɑ̃, -an] *nmf* (*small*) farmer; (*rustre*) *Péj* peasant; *— a* country-; (*monde*) farming.

Pays-Bas [peiba] *nmpl* **les P.-Bas** the Netherlands.

PCV [peseve] *abrév* (*paiement contre vérification*) **téléphoner en PCV** to reverse the charges, *Am* call collect.

PDG [pedeʒe] *abrév* = **président directeur général**.

péage [peaʒ] *nm* (*droit*) toll; (*lieu*) tollgate.

peau, -x [po] *nf* skin; (*de fruit*) peel, skin; (*cuir*) hide, skin; (*fourrure*) pelt, skin; **la p. de qn** *Fig* in s.o.'s shoes; **faire p. neuve** *Fig* to turn over a new leaf. ◆**P.-Rouge** *nmf* (*pl* **Peaux-Rouges**) (Red) Indian.

pêche¹ [pɛʃ] *nf* (*activité*) fishing; (*poissons*) catch; **p.** (**à la ligne**) angling; **aller à la p.** to go fishing. ◆**pêcher¹** *vi* to fish; *— vt* (*chercher à prendre*) to fish for; (*attraper*) to catch; (*dénicher*) *Fam* to dig up. ◆**pêcheur** nm fisherman; angler.

pêche² [pɛʃ] nf (*fruit*) peach. ◆**pêcher²** nm (*arbre*) peach tree.

péché [peʃe] nm sin. ◆**péch/er** vi to sin; **p. par orgueil**/*etc* to be too proud/*etc*. ◆**—eur, -eresse** nmf sinner.

pectoraux [pɛktɔro] nmpl (*muscles*) chest muscles.

pécule [pekyl] nm **un p.** (*économies*) (some) savings, a nest egg.

pécuniaire [pekynjɛr] a monetary.

pédagogie [pedagɔʒi] nf (*science*) education, teaching methods. ◆**pédagogique** a educational. ◆**pédagogue** nmf teacher.

pédale [pedal] nf **1** pedal; **p. de frein** footbrake (pedal). **2** (*homosexuel*) *Péj Fam* pansy, queer. ◆**pédaler** vi to pedal.

pédalo [pedalo] nm pedal boat, pedalo.

pédant, -ante [pedɑ̃, -ɑ̃t] nmf pedant; – a pedantic. ◆**pédantisme** nm pedantry.

pédé [pede] nm (*homosexuel*) *Péj Fam* queer.

pédiatre [pedjatr] nmf Méd p(a)ediatrician.

pédicure [pedikyr] nmf chiropodist.

pedigree [pedigre] nm (*de chien, cheval etc*) pedigree.

pègre [pɛgr] nf **la p.** the (criminal) underworld.

peigne [pɛɲ] nm comb; **passer au p. fin** *Fig* to go through with a fine toothcomb; **un coup de p.** (*action*) a comb. ◆**peigner** vt (*cheveux*) to comb; **p. qn** to comb s.o.'s hair; – **se p.** vpr to comb one's hair.

peignoir [pɛɲwar] nm dressing gown, Am bathrobe; **p. (de bain)** bathrobe.

peinard [penar] a Arg quiet (and easy).

peindre* [pɛ̃dr] vt to paint; (*décrire*) *Fig* to depict, paint; **p. en bleu**/*etc* to paint blue/*etc*; – vi to paint.

peine [pɛn] nf **1** (*châtiment*) punishment; **p. de mort** death penalty *ou* sentence; **p. de prison** prison sentence; **'défense d'entrer sous p. d'amende'** 'trespassers will be fined'. **2** (*chagrin*) sorrow, grief; **avoir de la p.** to be upset *ou* sad; **faire de la p. à** to upset, cause pain *ou* sorrow to. **3** (*effort, difficulté*) trouble; **se donner de la p.** *ou* **beaucoup de p.** to go to a lot of trouble (**pour faire** to do); **avec p.** with difficulty; **ça vaut la p. d'attendre**/*etc* it's worth (while) waiting/*etc*; **ce n'est pas** *ou* **ça ne vaut pas la p.** it's not worth *ou* worth it *ou* worth bothering. ◆**peiner 1** vt to upset, grieve. **2** vi to labour, struggle.

peine (à) [apɛn] adv hardly, scarcely.

peintre [pɛ̃tr] nm painter; **p. (en bâtiment)**

(*house*) painter, (painter and) decorator. ◆**peinture** nf (*tableau, activité*) painting; (*couleur*) paint; **'p. fraîche'** 'wet paint'. ◆**peinturlurer** vt *Fam* to daub with colour; **se p. (le visage)** to paint one's face.

péjoratif, -ive [peʒɔratif, -iv] a pejorative, derogatory.

pékinois [pekinwa] nm (*chien*) pekin(g)ese.

pelage [pəlaʒ] nm (*d'animal*) coat, fur.

pelé [pəle] a bare.

pêle-mêle [pɛlmɛl] adv in disorder.

peler [pəle] vt (*fruit*) to peel; **se p. facilement** (*fruit*) to peel easily; – vi (*peau bronzée*) to peel.

pèlerin [pɛlrɛ̃] nm pilgrim. ◆**pèlerinage** nm pilgrimage.

pèlerine [pɛlrin] nf (*manteau*) cape.

pélican [pelikɑ̃] nm (*oiseau*) pelican.

pelisse [pəlis] nf fur-lined coat.

pelle [pɛl] nf shovel; (*d'enfant*) spade; **p. à poussière** dustpan; **ramasser** *ou* **prendre une p.** (*tomber*) *Fam* to come a cropper, *Am* take a spill; **à la p.** (*argent etc*) *Fam* galore. ◆**pelletée** nf shovelful. ◆**pelleteuse** nf *Tech* mechanical shovel, excavator.

pellicule [pelikyl] nf *Phot* film; (*couche*) film, layer; pl *Méd* dandruff.

pelote [pəlɔt] nf (*de laine*) ball; (*à épingles*) pincushion; **p. (basque)** *Sp* pelota.

peloter [pəlɔte] vt (*palper*) *Péj Fam* to paw.

peloton [pəlɔtɔ̃] nm **1** (*coureurs*) *Sp* pack, main body. **2** *Mil* squad; **p. d'exécution** firing squad. **3** (*de ficelle*) ball.

pelotonner (se) [səpəlɔtɔne] vpr to curl up (into a ball).

pelouse [pluz] nf lawn; *Sp* enclosure.

peluche [plyʃ] nf (*tissu*) plush; pl (*flocons*) fluff, lint; **une p.** (*flocon*) a bit of fluff *ou* lint; **jouet en p.** soft toy; **chien**/*etc* **en p.** (*jouet*) furry dog/*etc*; **ours en p.** teddy bear. ◆**pelucher** vi to get fluffy *ou* linty. ◆**pelucheux, -euse** a fluffy, linty.

pelure [plyr] nf (*épluchure*) peeling; **une p.** a (piece of) peeling.

pénal, -aux [penal, -o] a (*droit, code etc*) penal. ◆**pénalisation** nf *Sp* penalty. ◆**pénaliser** vt *Sp Jur* to penalize (**pour** for). ◆**pénalité** nf (*Jur Rugby* penalty.

penalty, pl -ties [penalti, -iz] nm *Fb* penalty.

penaud [pəno] a sheepish.

penchant [pɑ̃ʃɑ̃] nm (*goût*) liking (**pour** for); (*tendance*) inclination (**à qch** towards sth).

pench/er [pɑ̃ʃe] vt (*objet*) to tilt; (*tête*) to lean; – vi (*arbre etc*) to lean (over); **p. pour** *Fig* to be inclined towards; – **se p.** vpr to lean (forward); **se p. par** (*fenêtre*) to lean out of; **se p. sur** (*problème etc*) to examine. ◆—**é** *a* leaning.

pendaison [pɑ̃dɛzɔ̃] *nf* hanging.

pendant[1] [pɑ̃dɑ̃] *prép* (*au cours de*) during; **p. la nuit** during the night; **p. deux mois** (*pour une période de*) for two months; **p. que** while, whilst.

pendentif [pɑ̃dɑ̃tif] *nm* (*collier*) pendant.

penderie [pɑ̃dri] *nf* wardrobe.

pend/re [pɑ̃dr] *vti* to hang (**à** from); — **se p.** *vpr* (*se tuer*) to hang oneself; (*se suspendre*) to hang (**à** from). ◆—**ant**[2] **1** *a* hanging; (*langue*) hanging out; (*joues*) sagging; (*question*) Fig pending. **2** *nm* **p.** (**d'oreille**) drop earring. **3** *nm* **le p. de** the companion piece to. ◆—**u, -ue** *a* (*objet*) hanging (**à** from); — *nmf* hanged man, hanged woman.

pendule [pɑ̃dyl] **1** *nf* clock. **2** *nm* (*balancier*) & Fig pendulum. ◆**pendulette** *nf* small clock.

pénétr/er [penetre] *vi* **p. dans** to enter; (*profondément*) to penetrate (into); — *vt* (*substance, mystère etc*) to penetrate; **se p. de** (*idée*) to become convinced of. ◆—**ant** *a* (*esprit, froid etc*) penetrating, keen. ◆**pénétration** *nf* penetration.

pénible [penibl] *a* (*difficile*) difficult; (*douloureux*) painful, distressing; (*ennuyeux*) tiresome; (*agaçant*) annoying. ◆—**ment** [-əmɑ̃] *adv* with difficulty; (*avec douleur*) painfully.

péniche [penif] *nf* barge; **p. de débarquement** Mil landing craft.

pénicilline [penisilin] *nf* penicillin.

péninsule [penɛ̃syl] *nf* peninsula. ◆**péninsulaire** *a* peninsular.

pénis [penis] *nm* penis.

pénitence [penitɑ̃s] *nf* (*punition*) punishment; (*peine*) Rel penance; (*regret*) penitence. ◆**pénitent, -ente** *nmf* Rel penitent.

pénitencier [penitɑ̃sje] *nm* prison. ◆**pénitentiaire** *a* (*régime etc*) prison-.

pénombre [penɔ̃br] *nf* half-light, darkness.

pensée [pɑ̃se] *nf* **1** thought. **2** (*fleur*) pansy. ◆**pens/er** *vi* to think (**à** of, about); **p. à qch/à faire qch** (*ne pas oublier*) to remember sth/to do sth; **p. à tout** (*prévoir*) to think of everything; **penses-tu!** you must be joking!, not at all!; — *vt* to think (*que* that); (*concevoir*) to think out; (*imaginer*) to imagine (*que* that); **je pensais rester** (*intention*) I was thinking of staying, I thought I'd stay; **je pense réussir** (*espoir*) I hope to succeed; **que pensez-vous de . . . ?** what do you think of *ou* about . . . ?; **p. du bien de** to think highly of. ◆—**ant** *a* **bien p.** *Péj* or-

thodox. ◆—**eur** *nm* thinker. ◆**pensif, -ive** *a* thoughtful, pensive.

pension [pɑ̃sjɔ̃] *nf* **1** boarding school; (*somme, repas*) board; **être en p.** to board, be a boarder (*chez* with); **p.** (**de famille**) guesthouse, boarding house; **p. complète** full board. **2** (*allocation*) pension; **p. alimentaire** maintenance allowance. ◆**pensionnaire** (*élève*) boarder; (*d'hôtel*) resident; (*de famille*) lodger. ◆**pensionnat** *nm* boarding school; (*élèves*) boarders. ◆**pensionné, -ée** *nmf* pensioner.

pentagone [pɛ̃tagɔn] *nm* **le P.** Am Pol the Pentagon.

pentathlon [pɛ̃tatlɔ̃] *nm* Sp pentathlon.

pente [pɑ̃t] *nf* slope; **être en p.** to slope, be sloping.

Pentecôte [pɑ̃tkot] *nf* Whitsun, Am Pentecost.

pénurie [penyri] *nf* scarcity, shortage (**de** of).

pépère [pepɛr] **1** *nm* Fam grand(d)ad. **2** *a* (*tranquille*) Fam quiet (and easy).

pépier [pepje] *vi* (*oiseau*) to cheep, chirp.

pépin [pepɛ̃] *nm* **1** (*de fruit*) pip, Am pit. **2** (*ennui*) Fam hitch, bother. **3** (*parapluie*) Fam brolly.

pépinière [pepinjɛr] *nf* Bot nursery.

pépite [pepit] *nf* (*gold*) nugget.

péquenaud, -aude [pekno, -od] *nmf* Péj Arg peasant, bumpkin.

perçant [persɑ̃] *a* (*cri, froid*) piercing; (*yeux*) sharp, keen.

percée [perse] *nf* (*dans une forêt*) opening; (*avance technologique, attaque militaire*) breakthrough.

perce-neige [pɛrsənɛʒ] *nm ou f inv* Bot snowdrop.

perce-oreille [pɛrsɔrɛj] *nm* (*insecte*) earwig.

percepteur [pɛrsɛptœr] *nm* tax collector. ◆**perceptible** *a* perceptible (**à** to), noticeable. ◆**perception** *nf* **1** (*bureau*) tax office; (*d'impôt*) collection. **2** (*sensation*) perception.

perc/er [pɛrse] *vt* (*trouer*) to pierce; (*avec perceuse*) to drill (a hole in); (*trou, ouverture*) to make, drill; (*mystère etc*) to uncover; **p. une dent** (*bébé*) to cut a tooth; — *vi* (*soleil, ennemi, sentiment*) to break *ou* come through; (*abcès*) to burst. ◆—**euse** *nf* drill.

percevoir*** [pɛrsəvwar] *vt* **1** (*sensation*) to perceive; (*son*) to hear. **2** (*impôt*) to collect.

perche [pɛrʃ] *nf* **1** (*bâton*) pole; **saut à la p.** pole-vaulting. **2** (*poisson*) perch.

perch/er [pɛrʃe] *vi* (*oiseau*) to perch; (*volailles*) to roost; (*loger*) Fam to hang out; —

vt (*placer*) *Fam* to perch; — **se p.** *vpr* (*oiseau, personne*) to perch. ◆—**é** *a* perched. ◆**perchoir** *nm* perch; (*de volailles*) roost.

percolateur [pɛrkɔlatœr] *nm* (*de restaurant*) percolator.

percussion [pɛrkysjɔ̃] *nf* *Mus* percussion.

percutant [pɛrkytɑ̃] *a* *Fig* powerful.

percuter [pɛrkyte] *vt* (*véhicule*) to crash into; — *vi* **p. contre** to crash into.

perd/re [pɛrdr] *vt* to lose; (*gaspiller*) to waste; (*ruiner*) to ruin; (*habitude*) to get out of; **p. de vue** to lose sight of; — *vi* to lose; (*récipient, tuyau*) to leak; **j'y perds I** lose out, I lose on the deal; — **se p.** *vpr* (*s'égarer*) to get lost; (*dans les détails*) to lose oneself; (*disparaître*) to disappear; **je m'y perds I'm** lost ou confused. ◆—**ant, -ante** *a* (*billet*) losing; — *nmf* loser. ◆—**u** *a* lost; wasted; (*malade*) finished; (*lieu*) isolated, in the middle of nowhere; **à ses moments perdus** in one's spare time; **une balle perdue** a stray bullet; **c'est du temps p.** it's a waste of time. ◆**perdition (en)** *adv* (*navire*) in distress.

perdrix [pɛrdri] *nf* partridge. ◆**perdreau, -x** *nm* young partridge.

père [pɛr] *nm* father; **Dupont p.** Dupont senior; **le p. Jean** *Fam* old John.

péremptoire [perɑ̃ptwar] *a* peremptory.

perfection [pɛrfɛksjɔ̃] *nf* perfection. ◆**perfectionn/er** *vt* to improve, perfect; **se p. en anglais**/*etc* to improve one's English/*etc*. ◆—**é** *a* (*machine etc*) advanced. ◆—**ement** *nm* improvement (**de** in, **par rapport à** on); **cours de p.** advanced ou refresher course. ◆**perfectionniste** *nmf* perfectionist.

perfide [pɛrfid] *a* *Litt* treacherous, perfidious. ◆**perfidie** *nf* *Litt* treachery.

perforer [pɛrfɔre] *vt* (*pneu, intestin etc*) to perforate; (*billet, carte*) to punch; **carte perforée** punch card. ◆**perforateur** *nm* (*appareil*) drill. ◆**perforation** *nf* perforation; (*trou*) punched hole. ◆**perforatrice** *nf* (*pour cartes*) *Tech* (card) punch. ◆**perforeuse** *nf* (paper) punch.

performance [pɛrfɔrmɑ̃s] *nf* (*d'athlète, de machine etc*) performance. ◆**performant** *a* (highly) efficient.

péricliter [periklite] *vi* to go to rack and ruin.

péril [peril] *nm* peril; **à tes risques et périls** at your own risk. ◆**périlleux, -euse** *a* perilous; **saut p.** somersault (*in mid air*).

périm/er [perime] *vi*, — **se p.** *vpr* laisser

(**se**) **p.** (*billet*) to allow to expire. ◆—**é** *a* expired; (*désuet*) outdated.

périmètre [perimetr] *nm* perimeter.

période [perjɔd] *nf* period. ◆**périodique** *a* periodic; — *nm* (*revue*) periodical.

péripétie [peripesi] *nf* (unexpected) event.

périphérie [periferi] *nf* (*limite*) periphery; (*banlieue*) outskirts. ◆**périphérique** *a* (*quartier*) outlying, peripheral; — *nm* (**boulevard**) **p.** (motorway) ring road, *Am* beltway.

périphrase [perifraz] *nf* circumlocution.

périple [peripl] *nm* trip, tour.

pér/ir [perir] *vi* to perish, die. ◆—**issable** *a* (*denrée*) perishable.

périscope [periskɔp] *nm* periscope.

perle [pɛrl] *nf* (*bijou*) pearl; (*de bois, verre etc*) bead; (*personne*) *Fig* gem, pearl; (*erreur*) *Iron* howler, gem. ◆**perler** *vi* (*sueur*) to form beads; **grève perlée** go-slow, *Am* slow-down strike.

permanent, -ente [pɛrmanɑ̃, -ɑ̃t] **1** *a* permanent; (*spectacle*) *Cin* continuous; (*comité*) standing. **2** *nf* (*coiffure*) perm. ◆**permanence** *nf* permanence; (*service, bureau*) duty office; (*salle*) *Scol* study room; **être de p.** to be on duty; **en p.** permanently.

perméable [pɛrmeabl] *a* permeable.

permettre* [pɛrmɛtr] *vt* to allow, permit; **p. à qn de faire** (*permission, possibilité*) to allow ou permit s.o. to do; **permettez!** excuse me!; **vous permettez?** may I?; **se p. de faire** to allow oneself to do, take the liberty to do; **se p. qch** (*se payer*) to afford sth. ◆**permis** *a* allowed, permitted; — *nm* (*autorisation*) permit, licence; **p. de conduire** (*carte*) driving licence, *Am* driver's license; **p. de travail** work permit. ◆**permission** *nf* permission; (*congé*) *Mil* leave; **demander la p.** to ask (for) permission (**de faire** to do).

permuter [pɛrmyte] *vt* to change round ou over, permutate. ◆**permutation** *nf* permutation.

pernicieux, -euse [pɛrnisjø, -øz] *a* (*nocif*) & *Méd* pernicious.

pérorer [perɔre] *vi* *Péj* to speechify.

Pérou [peru] *nm* Peru.

perpendiculaire [pɛrpɑ̃dikylɛr] *a* & *nf* perpendicular (**à** to).

perpétrer [pɛrpetre] *vt* (*crime*) to perpetrate.

perpétuel, -elle [pɛrpetɥɛl] *a* perpetual; (*fonction, rente*) for life. ◆**perpétuelle-ment** *adv* perpetually. ◆**perpétuer** *vt* to perpetuate. ◆**perpétuité (à)** adv in perpetuity; (*condamné*) for life.

perplexe [perpleks] a perplexed, puzzled. ◆**perplexité** nf perplexity.

perquisition [perkizisjɔ̃] nf (house) search (*by police*). ◆**perquisitionner** vti to search.

perron [perɔ̃] nm (front) steps.

perroquet [perɔkɛ] nm parrot.

perruche [peryʃ] nf budgerigar, Am parakeet.

perruque [peryk] nf wig.

persan [persɑ̃] a (*langue, tapis, chat*) Persian; – nm (*langue*) Persian.

persécuter [persekyte] vt (*tourmenter*) to persecute; (*importuner*) to harass. ◆**persécuteur, -trice** nmf persecutor. ◆**persécution** nf persecution.

persévér/er [persevere] vi to persevere (*dans* in). ◆**—ant** a persevering. ◆**persévérance** nf perseverance.

persienne [persjɛn] nf (outside) shutter.

persil [persi] nm parsley.

persist/er [persiste] vi to persist (**à faire** in doing). ◆**—ant** a persistent; **à feuilles persistantes** (*arbre etc*) evergreen. ◆**persistance** nf persistence.

personnage [persɔnaʒ] nm (*célébrité*) (important) person; *Th Littér* character.

personnaliser [persɔnalize] vt to personalize; (*voiture*) to customize.

personnalité [persɔnalite] nf (*individualité, personnage*) personality.

personne [persɔn] 1 nf person; pl people; **grande p.** grown-up, adult; **jolie p.** pretty girl ou woman; **en p.** in person. 2 pron (*négatif*) nobody, no one; **ne . . . p.** nobody, no one; **je ne vois p.** I don't see anybody ou anyone; **mieux que p.** better than anybody ou anyone.

personnel, -elle [persɔnɛl] 1 a personal; (*joueur, jeu*) individualistic. 2 nm staff, personnel. ◆**personnellement** adv personally.

personnifier [persɔnifje] vt to personify. ◆**personnification** nf personification.

perspective [perspektiv] nf (*art*) perspective; (*point de vue*) Fig viewpoint, perspective; (*de paysage etc*) view; (*possibilité, espérance*) prospect; **en p.** Fig in view, in prospect.

perspicace [perspikas] a shrewd. ◆**perspicacité** nf shrewdness.

persuader [persɥade] vt to persuade (**qn de faire** s.o. to do); **se p. que** to be convinced that. ◆**persuasif, -ive** a persuasive.

◆**persuasion** nf persuasion; (*croyance*) conviction.

perte [pert] nf loss; (*gaspillage*) waste (**de temps/d'argent** of time/money); (*ruine*) ruin; **à p. de vue** as far as the eye can see; **vendre à p.** to sell at a loss.

pertinent [pertinɑ̃] a relevant, pertinent. ◆**pertinence** nf relevance.

perturb/er [pertyrbe] vt (*trafic, cérémonie etc*) to disrupt; (*ordre public, personne*) to disturb. ◆**—é** a (*troublé*) Fam perturbed. ◆**perturbateur, -trice** a (*élément*) disruptive; – nmf trouble-maker. ◆**perturbation** nf disruption; (*crise*) upheaval.

péruvien, -ienne [peryvjɛ̃, -jɛn] a & nmf Peruvian.

pervenche [pervɑ̃ʃ] nf Bot periwinkle.

pervers [perver] a wicked, perverse; (*dépravé*) perverted. ◆**perversion** nf perversion. ◆**perversité** nf perversity. ◆**pervert/ir** vt to pervert. ◆**—i, -ie** nmf pervert.

pesant [pəzɑ̃] a heavy, weighty; – nm **valoir son p. d'or** to be worth one's weight in gold. ◆**pesamment** adv heavily. ◆**pesanteur** nf heaviness; (*force*) Phys gravity.

pes/er [pəze] vt to weigh; – vi to weigh; **p. lourd** to be heavy; (*argument etc*) Fig to carry (a lot of) weight; **p. sur** (*appuyer*) to bear down upon; (*influer*) to bear upon; **p. sur qn** (*menace*) to hang over s.o.; **p. sur l'estomac** to lie (heavily) on the stomach. ◆**—ée** nf weighing; Boxe weigh-in; (*effort*) pressure. ◆**—age** nm weighing. ◆**pèse-bébé** nm (baby) scales. ◆**pèse-personne** nm (bathroom) scales.

pessimisme [pesimism] nm pessimism. ◆**pessimiste** a pessimistic; – nmf pessimist.

peste [pest] nf Méd plague; (*personne, enfant*) Fig pest.

pester [peste] vi to curse; **p. contre qch/qn** to curse sth/s.o.

pestilentiel, -ielle [pestilɑ̃sjɛl] a fetid, stinking.

pétale [petal] nm petal.

pétanque [petɑ̃k] nf (*jeu*) bowls.

pétarades [petarad] nfpl (*de moto etc*) backfiring. ◆**pétarader** vi to backfire.

pétard [petar] nm (*explosif*) firecracker, banger.

péter [pete] vi Fam (*éclater*) to go bang ou pop; (*se rompre*) to snap.

pétill/er [petije] vi (*eau, champagne*) to sparkle, fizz; (*bois, feu*) to crackle; (*yeux*) to sparkle. ◆**—ant** a (*eau, vin, regard*) sparkling.

petit, -ite [p(ə)ti, -it] *a* small, little; *(de taille)* short; *(bruit, espoir, coup)* slight; *(jeune)* young, small; *(mesquin, insignifiant)* petty; **tout p.** tiny; **un bon p. travail** a nice little job; **un p. Français** a (little) French boy; – *nmf* (little) boy, (little) girl; *(personne)* small person; *Scol* junior; *(d'animal)* young; *(de chien)* pups, young; *(de chat)* kittens, young; – *adv* **p. à p.** little by little. ◆**p.-bourgeois** *a Péj* middle-class. ◆**p.-suisse** *nm* soft cheese *(for dessert)*. ◆**petitement** *adv (chichement)* shabbily, poorly. ◆**petitesse** *nf (de taille)* smallness; *(mesquinerie)* pettiness.

petit-fils [p(ə)tifis] *nm (pl* petits-fils**)** grandson, grandchild. ◆**petite-fille** *nf (pl* petites-filles**)** granddaughter, grandchild. ◆**petits-enfants** *nmpl* grandchildren.

pétition [petisjɔ̃] *nf* petition.

pétrifier [petrifje] *vt (de peur, d'émoi etc)* to petrify.

pétrin [petrɛ̃] *nm (situation) Fam* fix; **dans le p.** in a fix.

pétrir [petrir] *vt* to knead.

pétrole [petrɔl] *nm* oil, petroleum; **p. (lampant)** paraffin, *Am* kerosene; **nappe de p.** *(sur la mer)* oil slick. ◆**pétrolier, -ière** *a (industrie)* oil-; – *nm (navire)* oil tanker. ◆**pétrolifère** *a* **gisement p.** oil field.

pétulant [petylɑ̃] *a* exuberant.

pétunia [petynja] *nm Bot* petunia.

peu [pø] *adv (lire, manger etc)* not much, little; **elle mange p.** she doesn't eat much, she eats little; **un p.** *(lire, surpris etc)* a little, a bit; **p. de sel/de temps/***etc* not much salt/time/*etc*, little salt/time/*etc*; **un p. de fromage/***etc* a little cheese/*etc*, a bit of cheese/*etc*; **le p. de fromage que j'ai** the little cheese I have; **p. de gens/de livres/***etc* few people/books/*etc*, not many people/books/*etc*; **p. sont . . .** few are . . . ; **un (tout) petit p.** a (tiny) little bit; **p. intéressant/souvent/***etc* not very interesting/often/*etc*; **p. de chose** not much; **p. à p.** gradually, little by little; **à p. près** more or less; **p. après/avant** shortly after/before.

peuplade [pœplad] *nf* tribe.

peuple [pœpl] *nm (nation, masse)* people; **les gens du p.** the common people. ◆**peupl/er** *vt* to populate, people. ◆**-é** *a (quartier etc)* populated (**de** with).

peuplier [pøplije] *nm (arbre, bois)* poplar.

peur [pœr] *nf* fear; **avoir p.** to be afraid *ou* frightened *ou* scared (**de** of); **faire p. à** to frighten, scare; **de p. que** (+ *sub*) for fear that; **de p. de faire** for fear of doing.

◆**peureux, -euse** *a* fearful, easily frightened.

peut, peux [pø] *voir* **pouvoir 1.**

peut-être [pøtɛtr] *adv* perhaps, maybe; **p.-être qu'il viendra** perhaps *ou* maybe he'll come.

phallique [falik] *a* phallic. ◆**phallocrate** *nm Péj* male chauvinist.

phare [far] *nm Nau* lighthouse; *Aut* headlight, headlamp; **rouler pleins phares** *Aut* to drive on full headlights; **faire un appel de phares** *Aut* to flash one's lights.

pharmacie [farmasi] *nf* chemist's shop, *Am* drugstore; *(science)* pharmacy; *(armoire)* medicine cabinet. ◆**pharmaceutique** *a* pharmaceutical. ◆**pharmacien, -ienne** *nmf* chemist, pharmacist, *Am* druggist.

pharynx [farɛ̃ks] *nm Anat* pharynx.

phase [faz] *nf* phase.

phénomène [fenɔmɛn] *nm* phenomenon; *(personne) Fam* eccentric. ◆**phénoménal, -aux** *a* phenomenal.

philanthrope [filɑ̃trɔp] *nmf* philanthropist. ◆**philanthropique** *a* philanthropic.

philatélie [filateli] *nf* philately, stamp collecting. ◆**philatélique** *a* philatelic. ◆**philatéliste** *nmf* philatelist, stamp collector.

philharmonique [filarmɔnik] *a* philharmonic.

Philippines [filipin] *nfpl* **les P.** the Philippines.

philosophe [filɔzɔf] *nmf* philosopher; – *a (sage, résigné)* philosophical. ◆**philosopher** *vi* to philosophize (**sur** about). ◆**philosophie** *nf* philosophy. ◆**philosophique** *a* philosophical.

phobie [fɔbi] *nf* phobia.

phonétique [fɔnetik] *a* phonetic; – *nf* phonetics.

phonographe [fɔnɔgraf] *nm* gramophone, *Am* phonograph.

phoque [fɔk] *nm (animal marin)* seal.

phosphate [fɔsfat] *nm Ch* phosphate.

phosphore [fɔsfɔr] *nm Ch* phosphorus.

photo [fɔto] *nf* photo; *(art)* photography; **prendre une p. de, prendre en p.** to take a photo of; – *a inv* **appareil p.** camera. ◆**photocopie** *nf* photocopy. ◆**photocopier** *vt* to photocopy. ◆**photocopieur** *nm*, ◆**photocopieuse** *nf (machine)* photocopier. ◆**photogénique** *a* photogenic. ◆**photographe** *nmf* photographer. ◆**photographie** *nf (art)* photography; *(image)* photograph. ◆**photographier** *vt* to photograph. ◆**photographique** *a* photographic. ◆**photomaton**® nm (appareil) photo booth.

phrase [fraz] nf (mots) sentence.

physicien, -ienne [fizisjɛ̃, -jɛn] nmf physicist.

physiologie [fizjɔlɔʒi] nf physiology. ◆**physiologique** a physiological.

physionomie [fizjɔnɔmi] nf face.

physique [fizik] 1 a physical; – nm (corps, aspect) physique; **au p.** physically. 2 nf (science) physics. ◆**—ment** adv physically.

piaffer [pjafe] vi (cheval) to stamp; **p. d'impatience** Fig to fidget impatiently.

piailler [pjɑje] vi (oiseau) to cheep; (enfant) Fam to squeal.

piano [pjano] nm piano; **p. droit/à queue** upright/grand piano. ◆**pianiste** nmf pianist.

piaule [pjol] nf (chambre) Arg room, pad.

pic [pik] nm 1 (cime) peak. 2 (outil) pick(axe); **p. à glace** ice pick. 3 (oiseau) woodpecker.

pic (à) [apik] adv (verticalement) sheer; **couler à p.** to sink to the bottom; **arriver à p.** Fig to arrive in the nick of time.

pichet [piʃɛ] nm jug, pitcher.

pickpocket [pikpɔkɛt] nm pickpocket.

pick-up [pikœp] nm inv (camionnette) pick-up truck.

picorer [pikɔre] vti to peck.

picoter [pikɔte] vt (yeux) to make smart; (jambes) to make tingle; **les yeux me picotent** my eyes are smarting.

pie [pi] 1 nf (oiseau) magpie. 2 a inv (couleur) piebald.

pièce [pjɛs] nf 1 (de maison etc) room. 2 (morceau, élément) piece; (de pantalon) patch; (écrit) & Jur document; **p. de monnaie** coin; **p. (de théâtre)** play; **p. (d'artillerie)** gun; **p. d'identité** proof of identity, identity card; **p. d'eau** pool, pond; **pièces détachées** ou **de rechange** (de véhicule etc) spare parts; **cinq dollars/etc (la) p.** five dollars/etc each; **travailler à la p.** to do piecework.

pied [pje] nm foot; (de meuble) leg; (de verre, lampe) base; Phot stand; **un p. de salade** a head of lettuce; **à p.** on foot; **aller à p.** to walk, go on foot; **au p. de** at the foot ou bottom of; **au p. de la lettre** Fig literally; **avoir p.** (nageur) to have a footing, touch the bottom; **coup de p.** kick; **donner un coup de p. à** to kick (à qn s.o.); **sur p.** (debout, levé) up and about; **sur ses pieds** (malade guéri) up and about; **sur un p. d'égalité** on an equal footing; **comme un p.** (mal) Fam dreadfully; **faire un p. de nez** to thumb

one's nose (**à** at); **mettre sur p.** (projet) to set up. ◆**p.-noir** nmf (pl **pieds-noirs**) Algerian Frenchman ou Frenchwoman.

piédestal, -aux [pjedestal, -o] nm pedestal.

piège [pjɛʒ] nm (pour animal) & Fig trap. ◆**piéger** vt (animal) to trap; (voiture etc) to booby-trap; **engin piégé** booby trap; **lettre/colis/voiture piégé(e)** letter/parcel/car bomb.

pierre [pjɛr] nf stone; (précieuse) gem, stone; **p. à briquet** flint; **geler à p. fendre** to freeze (rock) hard. ◆**pierreries** nfpl gems, precious stones. ◆**pierreux, -euse** a stony.

piété [pjete] nf piety.

piétiner [pjetine] vt (fouler aux pieds) to trample (on); – vi to stamp (one's feet); (marcher sur place) to mark time; (ne pas avancer) Fig to make no headway.

piéton [pjetɔ̃] nm pedestrian. ◆**piéton**[2], **-onne** a, ◆**piétonnier, -ière** a (rue etc) pedestrian-.

piètre [pjɛtr] a wretched, poor.

pieu, -x [pjø] nm 1 (piquet) post, stake. 2 (lit) Fam bed.

pieuvre [pjœvr] nf octopus.

pieux, -euse [pjø, -øz] a pious.

pif [pif] nm (nez) Fam nose. ◆**pifomètre (au)** adv (sans calcul) Fam at a rough guess.

pigeon [piʒɔ̃] nm pigeon; (personne) Fam dupe; **p. voyageur** carrier pigeon. ◆**pigeonner** vt (voler) Fam to rip off.

piger [piʒe] vti Fam to understand.

pigment [pigmɑ̃] nm pigment.

pignon [piɲɔ̃] nm (de maison etc) gable.

pile [pil] 1 nf Él battery; (atomique) pile; **radio à piles** battery radio. 2 nf (tas) pile; **en p.** in a pile. 3 nf (de pont) pier. 4 nf a, (ou face)? heads (or tails)?; **jouer à p. ou face** to toss up. 5 adv **s'arrêter p.** to stop short ou dead; **à deux heures p.** on the dot of two.

piler [pile] 1 vt (amandes) to grind; (ail) to crush. 2 vi (en voiture) to stop dead. ◆**pilonner** vt Mil to bombard, shell.

pilier [pilje] nm pillar.

pilon [pilɔ̃] nm (de poulet) drumstick.

piller [pije] vti to loot, pillage. ◆**pillage** nm looting, pillage. ◆**pillard, -arde** nmf looter.

pilori [pilɔri] nm **mettre au p.** Fig to pillory.

pilote [pilɔt] nm Av Nau pilot; (de voiture, char) driver; (guide) Fig guide; – a **usine(-)/projet(-)p.** pilot factory/plan. ◆**pilot/er** vt Av to fly, pilot; Nau to pilot; **p. qn** to show s.o. around. ◆**—age** nm piloting; **école de p.** flying school; **poste de p.** cockpit.

pilotis [piloti] nm (*pieux*) Archit piles.

pilule [pilyl] nf (*pill*); **prendre la p.** (*femme*) to be on the pill; **se mettre à/arrêter la p.** to go on/off the pill.

piment [pimɑ̃] nm pimento, pepper. ◆**pimenté** a Culin & Fig spicy.

pimpant [pɛ̃pɑ̃] a pretty, spruce.

pin [pɛ̃] nm (*bois, arbre*) pine; **pomme de p.** pine cone.

pinailler [pinaje] vi Fam to quibble, split hairs.

pinard [pinar] nm (*vin*) Fam wine.

pince [pɛ̃s] nf (*outil*) pliers, forceps; (*de cycliste*) clip; (*levier*) crowbar; pl (*de crabe*) pincers; (**p. à linge**) (clothes) peg ou Am pin; (**p. à épiler**) tweezers; **p. à sucre** sugar tongs; **p. à cheveux** hairgrip. ◆**pinc/er** vt to pinch; (*corde*) Mus to pluck; **p. qn** (*arrêter*) Jur to nab s.o., pinch s.o.; **se p. le doigt** to get one's finger caught (**dans** in). ◆**—é** a (*air*) stiff, constrained. ◆**—ée** nf (*de sel etc*) pinch (**de** of). ◆**pincettes** nfpl (*fire*) tongs; (*d'horloger*) tweezers. ◆**pinçon** nm pinch (mark).

pinceau, -x [pɛ̃so] nm (paint)brush.

pince-sans-rire [pɛ̃ssɑ̃rir] nm inv person of dry humour.

pinède [pined] nf pine forest.

pingouin [pɛ̃gwɛ̃] nm auk, penguin.

ping-pong [piŋpɔ̃g] nm ping-pong.

pingre [pɛ̃gr] a stingy; — nmf skinflint.

pinson [pɛ̃sɔ̃] nm (*oiseau*) chaffinch.

pintade [pɛ̃tad] nf guinea fowl.

pin-up [pinœp] nf inv (*fille*) pinup.

pioche [pjɔʃ] nf pick(axe). ◆**piocher** vti (*creuser*) to dig (with a pick).

pion [pjɔ̃] nm **1** (*au jeu de dames*) piece; Échecs & Fig pawn. **2** Scol master (in charge of discipline).

pionnier [pjɔnje] nm pioneer.

pipe [pip] nf (*de fumeur*) pipe; **fumer la p.** to smoke a pipe.

pipeau, -x [pipo] nm (*flûte*) pipe.

pipe-line [piplin] nm pipeline.

pipi [pipi] nm **faire p.** Fam to go for a pee.

pique [pik] **1** nm (*couleur*) Cartes spades. **2** nf (*arme*) pike. **3** nf (*allusion*) cutting remark.

pique-assiette [pikasjɛt] nmf inv scrounger.

pique-nique [piknik] nm picnic. ◆**pique-niquer** vi to picnic.

piqu/er [pike] vt (*entamer, percer*) to prick; (*langue, yeux*) to sting; (*curiosité*) to rouse; (*coudre*) to (machine-)stitch; (*édredon, couvre-lit*) to quilt; (*crise de nerfs*) to have;

(*maladie*) to get; **p. qn** (*abeille*) to sting s.o.; (*serpent*) to bite s.o.; **p. qch dans** (*enfoncer*) to stick into; **p. qch dans** Jur Fam to nab s.o., pinch s.o.; **p. qch** (*voler*) Fam to pinch sth; **p. une colère** to fly into a rage; **p. une tête** to plunge headlong; — vi (*avion*) to dive; (*moutarde etc*) to be hot; — **se p.** vpr to prick oneself; **se p. de faire qch** to pride oneself on being able to do sth. ◆**—ant** a (*épine*) prickly; (*froid*) biting; (*sauce, goût*) pungent, piquant; (*mot*) cutting; (*détail*) spicy; — nm Bot prickle, thorn; (*d'animal*) spine, prickle. ◆**—é** a (*meuble*) worm-eaten; (*fou*) Fam crazy; — nm Av (nose)dive; **descente en p.** Av nosedive. ◆**—eur, -euse** nmf (*sur machine à coudre*) machinist. ◆**piqûre** nf (*d'épingle*) prick; (*d'abeille*) sting; (*de serpent*) bite; (*trou*) hole; Méd injection; (*point*) stitch.

piquet [pike] nm **1** (*pieu*) stake, picket; (*de tente*) peg. **2 p.** (**de grève**) picket (line), strike picket. **3 au p.** Scol in the corner.

piqueté [pikte] a p. de dotted with.

pirate [pirat] nm pirate; **p. de l'air** hijacker; — a (*radio, bateau*) Fig pirate-. ◆**piraterie** nf piracy; (*acte*) act of piracy; **p. (aérienne)** hijacking.

pire [pir] a worse (**que** than); **le p. moment/résultat/etc** the worst moment/result/etc; — nmf **le** ou **la p.** the worst (one); **le p. de tout** the worst (thing) of all; **au p.** at (the very) worst; **s'attendre au p.** to expect the (very) worst.

pirogue [pirɔg] nf canoe, dugout.

pis [pi] **1** nm (*de vache*) udder. **2** a inv & adv Litt worse; **de mal en p.** from bad to worse; — nm **le p.** Litt the worst.

pis-aller [pizale] nm inv (*personne, solution*) stopgap.

piscine [pisin] nf swimming pool.

pissenlit [pisɑ̃li] nm dandelion.

pistache [pistaʃ] nf (*fruit, parfum*) pistachio.

piste [pist] nf (*trace de personne ou d'animal*) track, trail; Sp track, racetrack; (*de magnétophone*) track; Av runway; (*de cirque*) ring; (*de patinage*) rink; (*pour chevaux*) racecourse, racetrack; **p. cyclable** cycle track, Am bicycle path; **p. de danse** dance floor; **p. de ski** ski run; **tour de p.** Sp lap.

pistolet [pistolɛ] nm gun, pistol; (*de peintre*) spray gun.

piston [pistɔ̃] nm **1** Aut piston. **2 avoir du p.** (*appui*) to have connections. ◆**pistonner** vt (*appuyer*) to pull strings for.

pitié [pitje] *nf* pity; **j'ai p. de lui, il me fait p.** I pity him, I feel sorry for him. ◆**piteux, -euse** *a Iron* pitiful. ◆**pitoyable** *a* pitiful.

piton [pitɔ̃] *nm* **1** (*à crochet*) hook. **2** *Géog* peak.

pitre [pitr] *nm* clown. ◆**pitrerie(s)** *nf(pl)* clowning.

pittoresque [pitɔrɛsk] *a* picturesque.

pivert [pivɛr] *nm* (*oiseau*) woodpecker.

pivoine [pivwan] *nf Bot* peony.

pivot [pivo] *nm* pivot; (*personne*) *Fig* linchpin, mainspring. ◆**pivoter** *vi* (*personne*) to swing round; (*fauteuil*) to swivel; (*porte*) to revolve.

pizza [pidza] *nf* pizza. ◆**pizzeria** *nf* pizza parlour.

placage [plakaʒ] *nm* (*revêtement*) facing; (*en bois*) veneer.

placard [plakar] *nm* **1** (*armoire*) cupboard, *Am* closet. **2** (*pancarte*) poster. ◆**placarder** *vt* (*affiche*) to post (up); (*mur*) to cover with posters.

place [plas] *nf* (*endroit, rang*) & *Sp* place; (*occupée par qn ou qch*) room; (*lieu public*) square; (*siège*) seat, place; (*prix d'un trajet*) *Aut* fare; (*emploi*) job, position; **p. (forte)** *Mil* fortress; **p. (de parking)** (parking) space; **p. (financière)** (money) market; **à la p.** (*échange*) instead (**de** of); **à votre p.** in your place; **sur p.** on the spot; **en p.** (*objet*) in place; **ne pas tenir en p.** to be unable to keep still; **mettre en p.** to install, set up; **faire p.** à to give way to; **changer qch de p.** to move sth.

plac/er [plase] *vt* (*mettre*) to put, place; (*situer*) to place, position; (*invité, spectateur*) to seat; (*argent*) to invest, place (**dans** in); (*vendre*) to place, sell; **p. un mot** to get a word in edgeways *ou Am* edgewise; **— se p.** *vpr* (*personne*) to take up a position, place oneself; (*objet*) to be put *ou* placed; (*cheval, coureur*) to be placed; **se p. troisième**/*etc Sp* to come *ou* be third/*etc.* ◆**—é** *a* (*objet*) & *Sp* placed; **bien/mal p. pour faire** in a good/bad position to do; **les gens haut placés** people in high places. ◆**—ement** *nm* (*d'argent*) investment.

placide [plasid] *a* placid.

plafond [plafɔ̃] *nm* ceiling. ◆**plafonnier** *nm Aut* roof light.

plage [plaʒ] *nf* **1** beach; (*ville*) (seaside) resort. **2** (*sur disque*) track. **3** **p. arrière** *Aut* parcel shelf.

plagiat [plaʒja] *nm* plagiarism. ◆**plagier** *vt* to plagiarize.

plaid [plɛd] *nm* travelling rug.

plaider [plede] *vti Jur* to plead. ◆**plaideur,**

-euse *nmf* litigant. ◆**plaidoirie** *nf Jur* speech (for the defence). ◆**plaidoyer** *nm* plea.

plaie [plɛ] *nf* (*blessure*) wound; (*coupure*) cut; (*corvée, personne*) *Fig* nuisance.

plaignant, -ante [plɛɲɑ̃, -ɑ̃t] *nmf Jur* plaintiff.

plaindre* [plɛ̃dr] **1** *vt* to feel sorry for, pity. **2 se p.** *vpr* (*protester*) to complain (**de** about, **que** that); **se p. de** (*maux de tête etc*) to complain of *ou* about. ◆**plainte** *nf* complaint; (*cri*) moan, groan. ◆**plaintif, -ive** *a* sorrowful, plaintive.

plaine [plɛn] *nf Géog* plain.

plaire* [plɛr] *vi* & *v imp* **p.** à to please; **elle lui plaît** he likes her, she pleases him; **ça me plaît** I like it; **il me plaît de faire** I like doing; **s'il vous** *ou* **te plaît** please; **— se p.** *vpr* (*à Paris etc*) to like *ou* enjoy it; (*l'un l'autre*) to like each other.

plaisance [plɛzɑ̃s] *nf* **bateau de p.** pleasure boat; **navigation de p.** yachting.

plaisant [plɛzɑ̃] *a* (*drôle*) amusing; (*agréable*) pleasing; **— *nm* **mauvais p.** *Péj* joker. ◆**plaisanter** *vi* to joke, jest; **p. avec qch** to trifle with sth; **— *vt* to tease. ◆**plaisanterie** *nf* joke, jest; (*bagatelle*) trifle; **par p.** for a joke. ◆**plaisantin** *nm Péj* joker.

plaisir [plɛzir] *nm* pleasure; **faire p. à** to please; **faites-moi le p. de . . .** would you be good enough to . . . ; **pour le p.** for fun, for the fun of it; **au p. (de vous revoir)** see you again sometime.

plan [plɑ̃] **1** *nm* (*projet, dessin*) plan; (*de ville*) map; (*niveau*) *Géom* plane; **au premier p.** in the foreground; **gros p.** *Phot Cin* close-up; **sur le p. politique**/*etc* from the political/*etc* viewpoint, politically/*etc*; **de premier p.** (*question etc*) major; **p. d'eau** stretch of water; **laisser en p.** (*abandonner*) to ditch. **2** *a* (*plat*) even, flat.

planche [plɑ̃ʃ] *nf* **1** board, plank; **p. à repasser**/**à dessin** ironing/drawing board; **p. (à roulettes)** skateboard; **p. (de surf)** surfboard; **p. (à voile)** sailboard; **faire de la p. (à voile)** to go windsurfing; **faire la p.** to float on one's back. **2** (*illustration*) plate. **3** (*de légumes*) bed, plot.

plancher [plɑ̃ʃe] *nm* floor.

plan/er [plane] *vi* (*oiseau*) to glide, hover; (*avion*) to glide; **p. sur qn** (*mystère, danger*) to hang over s.o.; **vol plané** glide. ◆**—eur** *nm* (*avion*) glider.

planète [planɛt] *nf* planet. ◆**planétaire** *a* planetary. ◆**planétarium** *nm* planetarium.

planifier [planifje] *vt Écon* to plan. ◆**pla-**

nification nf Écon planning. ◆**planning** nm (industriel, commercial) planning; **p familial** family planning.

planque [plɑ̃k] nf **1** (travail) Fam cushy job. **2** (lieu) Fam hideout. ◆**planquer** vt, − **se p.** vpr Fam to hide.

plant [plɑ̃] nm (plante) seedling; (de légumes etc) bed.

plante [plɑ̃t] nf **1** Bot plant; **p. d'appartement** house plant; **jardin des plantes** botanical gardens. **2 p. des pieds** sole of the foot). ◆**plant/er** vt (arbre, plante etc) to plant; (clou, couteau) to drive in; (tente, drapeau, échelle) to put up; (mettre) to put (**sur** on, **contre** against); (regard) to fix (**sur** on); **p. là qn** to leave s.o. standing; **se p. devant** to plant oneself in front of. ◆**−é a** (immobile) standing; **bien p.** (personne) sturdy. ◆**plantation** nf (action) planting; (terrain) bed; (de café, d'arbres etc) plantation. ◆**planteur** nm plantation owner.

planton [plɑ̃tɔ̃] nm Mil orderly.

plantureux, -euse [plɑ̃tyrø, -øz] a (repas etc) abundant.

plaque [plak] nf plate; (de verre, métal) sheet, plate; (de verglas) sheet; (de marbre) slab; (de chocolat) bar; (commémorative) plaque; (tache) Méd blotch; **p. chauffante** Culin hotplate; **p. tournante** (carrefour) Fig centre; **p. minéralogique, p. d'immatriculation** Aut number ou Am license plate; **p. dentaire** (dental) plaque.

plaqu/er [plake] vt (métal, bijou) to plate; (bois) to veneer; (cheveux) to plaster (down); Rugby to tackle; (aplatir) to flatten (**contre** against); (abandonner) Fam to give (sth) up; **p. qn** Fam to ditch s.o.; **se p. contre** to flatten oneself against. ◆**−é a** (bijou) plated; **p. or** gold-plated; − nm **p. or** gold plate. ◆**−age** nm Rugby tackle.

plasma [plasma] nm Méd plasma.

plastic [plastik] nm plastic explosive. ◆**plastiquer** vt to blow up.

plastique [plastik] a (art, substance) plastic; **matière p.** plastic; − nm (matière) plastic; **en p.** (bouteille etc) plastic.

plastron [plastrɔ̃] nm shirtfront.

plat [pla] a **1** flat; (mer) calm, smooth; (fade) flat, dull; **à fond p.** flat-bottomed; **à p. ventre** flat on one's face; **à p.** (pneu, batterie) flat; (déprimé, épuisé) Fam low; **poser à p.** to put ou lay (down) flat; **tomber à p.** to fall down flat; **assiette plate** dinner plate; **calme p.** dead calm; − nm (de la main) flat. **2** nm (récipient, mets) dish; (partie du repas) course; **'p. du jour'** (au restaurant) 'today's special'.

platane [platan] nm plane tree.

plateau, -x [plato] nm (pour servir) tray; (de balance) pan; (de tourne-disque) turntable; (plate-forme) Cin TV set; Th stage; Géog plateau; **p. à fromages** cheeseboard.

plate-bande [platbɑ̃d] nf (pl plates-bandes) flower bed.

plate-forme [platfɔrm] nf (pl plates-formes) platform; **p.-forme pétrolière** oil rig.

platine [platin] **1** nm (métal) platinum. **2** nf (d'électrophone) deck. ◆**platiné a** (cheveux) platinum, platinum-blond(e).

platitude [platityd] nf platitude.

plâtre [plɑtr] nm (matière) plaster; **un p.** Méd a plaster cast; **dans le p.** Méd in plaster; **les plâtres** (d'une maison etc) the plasterwork; **p. à mouler** plaster of Paris. ◆**plât/rer** vt (mur) to plaster; (membre) to put in plaster. ◆**−age** nm plastering. ◆**plâtrier** nm plasterer.

plausible [plozibl] a plausible.

plébiscite [plebisit] nm plebiscite.

plein [plɛ̃] a (rempli, complet) full; (paroi) solid; (ivre) Fam tight; **p. de** full of; **en pleine mer** on the open sea; **en p. visage/etc** right in the middle of the face/etc; **en p. jour** in broad daylight; − prép & adv **des billes p. les poches** pockets full of marbles; **du chocolat p. la figure** chocolate all over one's face; **p. de lettres/d'argent/etc** (beaucoup de) Fam lots of letters/money/etc; **à p.** (travailler) to full capacity; − nm **faire le p.** Aut to fill up (the tank); **battre son p.** (fête) to be in full swing. ◆**pleinement** adv fully.

pléonasme [pleɔnasm] nm (expression) redundancy.

pléthore [pletɔr] nf plethora.

pleurer [plœre] vi to cry, weep (**sur** over); − vt (regretter) to mourn (for). ◆**pleureur a saule p.** weeping willow. ◆**pleurnicher** vi to snivel, grizzle. ◆**pleurs (en)** adv in tears.

pleurésie [plœrezi] nf Méd pleurisy.

pleuvoir* [pløvwar] v imp to rain; **il pleut** it's raining; − vi (coups etc) to rain down (**sur** on).

pli [pli] nm **1** (de papier etc) fold; (de jupe, robe) pleat; (de pantalon, de bouche) crease; (de bras) bend; (faux) **p.** crease; **mise en plis** (coiffure) set. **2** (enveloppe) Com envelope, letter; **sous p. séparé** under separate cover. **3** Cartes trick. **4** (habitude) habit; **prendre le p. de faire** to get into the habit of doing. ◆**pli/er** vt to fold; (courber) to bend; **p. qn à** to submit s.o. to; − vi (branche) to bend; − **se p.** vpr (lit, chaise *etc*) to fold (up); **se p.** à to submit to, give in to. ◆—**ant** *a* (*chaise etc*) folding; (*parapluie*) telescopic; — *nm* folding stool. ◆—**able** *a* pliable. ◆—**age** *nm* (*manière*) fold; (*action*) pleating.

plinthe [plɛ̃t] *nf* skirting board, *Am* baseboard.

pliss/er [plise] *vt* (*jupe, robe*) to pleat; (*froisser*) to crease; (*lèvres*) to pucker; (*front*) to wrinkle, crease; (*yeux*) to screw up. ◆—**é** *nm* pleating, pleats.

plomb [plɔ̃] *nm* (*métal*) lead; (*fusible*) Él fuse; (*poids pour rideau etc*) lead weight; *pl* (*de chasse*) lead shot, buckshot; **de p.** (*tuyau etc*) lead-; (*sommeil*) *Fig* heavy; (*soleil*) blazing; (*ciel*) leaden. ◆**plomb/er** *vt* (*dent*) to fill; (*colis*) to seal (with lead). ◆—**é** *a* (*teint*) leaden. ◆—**age** *nm* (*de dent*) filling.

plombier [plɔ̃bje] *nm* plumber. ◆**plomberie** *nf* (*métier, installations*) plumbing.

plong/er [plɔ̃ʒe] *vi* (*personne, avion etc*) to dive, plunge; (*route, regard*) *Fig* to plunge; — *vt* (*mettre, enfoncer*) to plunge, thrust (**dans** into); **se p. dans** (*lecture etc*) to immerse oneself in. ◆—**eant** *a* (*décolleté*) plunging; (*vue*) bird's eye-. ◆—**é** *a* **p. dans** (*lecture etc*) immersed *ou* deep in. ◆—**ée** *nf* diving; (*de sous-marin*) submersion; **en p.** (*sous-marin*) submerged. ◆**plongeoir** *nm* diving board. ◆**plongeon** *nm* dive. ◆**plongeur, -euse** *nmf* diver; (*employé de restaurant*) dishwasher.

plouf [pluf] *nm* & *int* splash.

ployer [plwaje] *vti* to bend.

plu [ply] *voir* **plaire, pleuvoir**.

pluie [plɥi] *nf* rain; **une p.** (*averse*) a shower; **sous la p.** in the rain.

plume [plym] *nf* 1 (*d'oiseau*) feather. 2 (*pour écrire*) *Hist* quill (pen); (*pointe en acier*) (pen) nib; **stylo à p.** (fountain) pen; **vivre de sa p.** *Fig* to live by one's pen. ◆**plumage** *nm* plumage. ◆**plumeau, -x** *nm* feather duster. ◆**plumer** *vt* (*volaille*) to pluck; **p. qn** (*voler*) *Fig* to fleece s.o. ◆**plumet** *nm* plume. ◆**plumier** *nm* pencil box, pen box.

plupart (la) [laplypar] *nf* most; **la p. des cas**/*etc* most cases/*etc*; **la p. du temps** most of the time; **la p. d'entre eux** most of them; **pour la p.** mostly.

pluriel, -ielle [plyrjɛl] *a nm* *Gram* plural; **au p.** (*nom*) plural, in the plural.

plus¹ [ply] (**[plyz]** before vowel, **[plys]** *in end position*) 1 *adv comparatif* (*travailler etc*) more (**que** than); **p. d'un kilo/de dix**/*etc* (*quantité, nombre*) more than a kilo/ten/

etc; **p. de thé**/*etc* (*davantage*) more tea/*etc*; **p. beau/rapidement**/*etc* (**que** than); **p. tard** later; **p. petit** smaller; **de p. en p.** more and more; **de p. en p. vite** quicker and quicker; **p. il crie p. il s'enroue** the more he shouts the more hoarse he gets; **p. ou moins** more or less; **en p.** in addition (**de** to); **de p.** more (**que** than); (*en outre*) moreover; **les enfants (âgés) de p. de dix ans** children over ten; **j'ai dix ans de p. qu'elle** I'm ten years older than she is; **il est p. de cinq heures** it's after five (o'clock). 2 *adv superlatif* **le p.** (*travailler etc*) (the) most; **le p. beau**/*etc* the most beautiful/*etc*; (*de deux*) the more beautiful/*etc*; **le p. grand**/*etc* the biggest/*etc*; (*de deux*) the bigger/*etc*; **j'ai le p. de livres** I have (the) most books, **j'en ai le p.** I have (the) most; **(tout) au p.** at (the very) most.

plus² [ply] *adv de négation* **p. de** (*pain, argent etc*) no more; **il n'a p. de pain** he has no more bread, he doesn't have any more bread; **tu n'es p. jeune** you're no longer young, you're not young any more *ou* any longer; **elle ne le fait p.** she no longer does it, she doesn't do it any more *ou* any longer; **je ne la reverrai p.** I won't see her again.

plus³ [plys] *prép* plus; **deux p. deux font quatre** two plus two are four; **il fait p. deux (degrés)** it's two degrees above freezing; — *nm* **le signe p.** the plus sign.

plusieurs [plyzjœr] *a & pron* several.

plus-value [plyvaly] *nf* (*bénéfice*) profit.

plutonium [plytɔnjɔm] *nm* plutonium.

plutôt [plyto] *adv* rather (**que** than).

pluvieux, -euse [plyvjø, -øz] *a* rainy, wet.

PMU [peɛmy] *abrév* = **pari mutuel urbain.**

pneu [pnø] *nm* (*pl* -**s**) (*de roue*) tyre, *Am* tire. 2 (*lettre*) express letter. ◆**pneumatique** 1 *a* (*matelas etc*) inflatable; **marteau p.** pneumatic drill. 2 *nm* = **pneu.**

pneumonie [pnømɔni] *nf* pneumonia.

poche [pɔʃ] *nf* pocket; (*de kangourou etc*) pouch; (*sac en papier etc*) bag; *pl* (*sous les yeux*) bags; **livre de p.** paperback; **faire des poches** (*pantalon*) to be baggy; **j'ai un franc en p.** I have one franc on me. ◆**pochette** *nf* (*sac*) bag, envelope; (*d'allumettes*) book; (*de disque*) sleeve, jacket; (*mouchoir*) pocket handkerchief; (*sac à main*) (clutch) bag.

poch/er [pɔʃe] *vt* 1 **p. l'œil à qn** to give s.o. a black eye. 2 (*œufs*) to poach. ◆—**é** *a* **œil p.** black eye.

podium [pɔdjɔm] *nm* *Sp* rostrum, podium.

poêle [pwal] 1 *nm* stove. 2 *nf* **p.** (**à frire**) frying pan.

poème [pɔɛm] *nm* poem. ◆**poésie** *nf* poet-

ry; **une p.** (*poème*) a piece of poetry.
◆**poète** nm poet; — *a* **femme p.** poetess.
◆**poétique** *a* poetic.

pognon [pɔɲɔ̃] nm (*argent*) Fam dough.

poids [pwa] nm weight; **au p.** by weight; **de p.** (*influent*) influential; **p. lourd** (heavy) lorry ou Am truck; **lancer le p.** Sp to put ou hurl the shot.

poignant [pwaɲɑ̃] *a* (*souvenir etc*) poignant.

poignard [pwaɲar] nm dagger; **coup de p.** stab. ◆**poignarder** *vt* to stab.

poigne [pwaɲ] nf (*étreinte*) grip.

poignée [pwaɲe] nf (*quantité*) handful (de of); (*de porte, casserole etc*) handle; (*d'épée*) hilt; **p. de main** handshake; **donner une p. de main à** to shake hands with.

poignet [pwaɲɛ] nm wrist; (*de chemise*) cuff.

poil [pwal] nm hair; (*pelage*) coat, fur; (*de brosse*) bristle; pl (*de tapis*) pile; (*d'étoffe*) nap; **à p.** (*nu*) Arg (stark) naked; **au p.** (*travail*) Arg top-rate; **de bon/mauvais p.** Fam in a good/bad mood; **de tout p.** Fam of all kinds. ◆**poilu** *a* hairy.

poinçon [pwɛ̃sɔ̃] nm (*outil*) awl, bradawl; (*marque de bijou etc*) hallmark. ◆**poinçonner** *vt* (*bijou*) to hallmark; (*billet*) to punch. ◆**poinçonneuse** nf (*machine*) punch.

poindre [pwɛ̃dr] *vi* (*jour*) Litt to dawn.

poing [pwɛ̃] nm fist; **coup de p.** punch.

point[1] [pwɛ̃] nm (*lieu, question, degré, score etc*) point; (*sur i, à l'horizon etc*) dot; (*tache*) spot; (*note*) Scol mark; (*de couture*) stitch; **sur le p. de faire** about to do, on the point of doing; **p. (final)** full stop, period; **p. d'exclamation** exclamation mark ou Am point; **p. d'interrogation** question mark; **p. de vue** point of view, viewpoint; (*endroit*) viewing point; **à p. (nommé)** (*arriver etc*) at the right moment; **à p.** (*rôti etc*) medium (cooked); (*steak*) medium rare; **mal en p.** in bad shape; **mettre au p.** Phot to focus; Aut to tune; (*technique etc*) to elaborate, perfect; (*éclaircir*) Fig to clarify, clear up; **mise au p.** focusing; tuning, tune-up; elaboration; Fig clarification; **faire le p.** Fig to take stock, sum up; **p. mort** Aut neutral; **au p. mort** Fig at a standstill; **p. noir** Aut (*accident*) black spot; **p. du jour** daybreak; **de côté** (*douleur*) stitch (in one's side). ◆**p.-virgule** nm (pl **points-virgules**) semicolon.

point[2] [pwɛ̃] *adv* Litt = **pas**[1].

pointe [pwɛ̃t] nf (*extrémité*) point, tip; (*pour grille*) spike; (*clou*) nail; Géog headland; (*maximum*) Fig peak; **une p. de** (*soupçon, nuance*) a touch of; **sur la p. des pieds** on

tiptoe; **en p.** pointed; **de p.** (*technique etc*) latest, most advanced; **à la p. de** (*progrès etc*) Fig in ou at the forefront of.

point/er [pwɛ̃te] 1 *vt* (*cocher*) to tick (off), Am check (off). 2 *vt* (*braquer, diriger*) to point (**sur, vers** at). 3 *vti* (*employé*) to clock in, (*à la sortie*) to clock out; — **se p.** (*arriver*) Fam to show up. 4 *vi* (*bourgeon etc*) to appear; **p. vers** to point upwards towards. ◆**-age** nm (*de personnel*) clocking in; clocking out.

pointillé [pwɛ̃tije] nm dotted line; — *a* dotted.

pointilleux, -euse [pwɛ̃tijø, -øz] *a* fussy, particular.

pointu [pwɛ̃ty] *a* (*en pointe*) pointed; (*voix*) shrill.

pointure [pwɛ̃tyr] nf (*de chaussure, gant*) size.

poire [pwar] nf 1 (*fruit*) pear. 2 (*figure*) Fam mug. 3 (*personne*) Fam sucker. ◆**poirier** nm pear tree.

poireau, -x [pwaro] nm leek.

poireauter [pwarote] *vi* (*attendre*) Fam to kick one's heels.

pois [pwa] nm (*légume*) pea; (*dessin*) (polka) dot; **petits p.** (garden) peas; **p. chiche** chickpea; **à p.** (*vêtement*) spotted, dotted.

poison [pwazɔ̃] nm (*substance*) poison.

poisse [pwas] nf Fam bad luck.

poisseux, -euse [pwasø, -øz] *a* sticky.

poisson [pwasɔ̃] nm fish; **p. rouge** goldfish; **les Poissons** (*signe*) Pisces. ◆**poissonnerie** nf fish shop. ◆**poissonnier, -ière** nmf fishmonger.

poitrine [pwatrin] nf Anat chest; (*seins*) breast, bosom; (*de veau, mouton*) Culin breast.

poivre [pwavr] nm pepper. ◆**poivr/er** *vt* to pepper. ◆**-é** *a* Culin peppery; (*plaisanterie*) Fig spicy. ◆**poivrier** nm Bot pepper plant; (*ustensile*) pepperpot. ◆**poivrière** nf pepperpot.

poivron [pwavrɔ̃] nm pepper, capsicum.

poivrot, -ote [pwavro, -ɔt] nm Fam drunk(ard).

poker [pɔkɛr] nm Cartes poker.

polar [pɔlar] nm (*roman*) Fam whodunit.

polariser [pɔlarize] *vt* to polarize.

pôle [pol] nm Géog pole; **p. Nord/Sud** North/South Pole. ◆**polaire** *a* polar.

polémique [pɔlemik] *a* controversial, polemical; — nf controversy, polemic.

poli [pɔli] 1 *a* (*courtois*) polite (**avec** to, with). 2 *a* (*lisse, brillant*) polished; — nm (*aspect*) polish. ◆**-ment** *adv* politely.

police [pɔlis] nf 1 police; **faire** ou **assurer la**

p. to maintain order (**dans** in); **p. secours** emergency services; **p. mondaine** *ou* **des mœurs** = vice squad. **2** p. (**d'assurance**) (insurance) policy. ◆**policier** *a* (*enquête, état*) police-; **roman p.** detective novel; – *nm* policeman, detective.

polichinelle [pɔliʃinɛl] *nf* **secret de p.** open secret.

polio [pɔljo] *nf* (*maladie*) polio; – *nmf* (*personne*) polio victim. ◆**poliomyélite** *nf* poliomyelitis.

polir [pɔlir] *vt* (*substance dure, style*) to polish.

polisson, -onne [pɔlisɔ̃, -ɔn] *a* naughty; – *nmf* rascal.

politesse [pɔlitɛs] *nf* politeness; **une p.** (*parole*) a polite word; (*action*) an act of politeness.

politique [pɔlitik] *a* political; **homme p.** politician; – *nf* (*science, activité*) politics; (*mesures, manières de gouverner*) Pol policies; **une p.** (*tactique*) a policy. ◆**politicien, -ienne** *nmf Péj* politician. ◆**politiser** *vt* to politicize.

pollen [pɔlɛn] *nm* pollen.

polluer [pɔlɥe] *vt* to pollute. ◆**polluant** *nm* pollutant. ◆**pollution** *nf* pollution.

polo [pɔlo] *nm* **1** (*chemise*) sweat shirt. **2** *Sp* polo.

polochon [pɔlɔʃɔ̃] *nm* (*traversin*) *Fam* bolster.

Pologne [pɔlɔɲ] *nf* Poland. ◆**polonais, -aise** *a* Polish; – *nmf* Pole; – *nm* (*langue*) Polish.

poltron, -onne [pɔltrɔ̃, -ɔn] *a* cowardly; – *nmf* coward.

polycopi/er [pɔlikɔpje] *vt* to mimeograph, duplicate. ◆**—é** *nm Univ* mimeographed copy (*of lecture etc*).

polyester [pɔliɛstɛr] *nm* polyester.

Polynésie [pɔlinezi] *nf* Polynesia.

polyvalent [pɔlivalɑ̃] *a* (*rôle*) multi-purpose, varied; (*professeur, ouvrier*) all-round; **école polyvalente, lycée p.** comprehensive school.

pommade [pɔmad] *nf* ointment.

pomme [pɔm] *nf* **1** apple; **p. d'Adam** *Anat* Adam's apple. **2** (*d'arrosoir*) rose. **3 p. de terre** potato; **pommes vapeur** steamed potatoes; **pommes frites** chips, *Am* French fries; **pommes chips** potato crisps *ou Am* chips. ◆**pommier** *nm* apple tree.

pommette [pɔmɛt] *nf* cheekbone.

pompe [pɔ̃p] **1** *nf* pump; **p. à essence** petrol *ou Am* gas station; **p. à incendie** fire engine; **coup de p.** *Fam* tired feeling. **2** *nf* (*chaussure*) *Fam* shoe. **3** *nf* (*en gymnastique*)

press-up, *Am* push-up. **4** *nfpl* **pompes funèbres** undertaker's; **entrepreneur des pompes funèbres** undertaker. **5** *nf* p. **anti-sèche** *Scol* crib. **6** *nf* (*splendeur*) pomp. ◆**pomper** *vt* to pump; (*évacuer*) to pump out (**de** of); (*absorber*) to soak up; (*épuiser*) *Fam* to tire out; – *vi* to pump. ◆**pompeux, -euse** *a* pompous. ◆**pompier 1** *nm* fireman; **voiture des pompiers** fire engine. **2** *a* (*emphatique*) pompous. ◆**pompiste** *nmf Aut* pump attendant.

pompon [pɔ̃pɔ̃] *nm* (*ornement*) pompon.

pomponner [pɔ̃pɔne] *vt* to doll up.

ponce [pɔ̃s] *nf* (*pierre*) pumice (stone). ◆**poncer** *vt* to rub down, sand. ◆**ponceuse** *nf* (*machine*) sander.

ponctuation [pɔ̃ktɥasjɔ̃] *nf* punctuation. ◆**ponctuer** *vt* to punctuate (**de** with).

ponctuel, -elle [pɔ̃ktɥɛl] *a* (*à l'heure*) punctual; (*unique*) *Fig* one-off, *Am* one-of-a-kind. ◆**ponctualité** *nf* punctuality.

pondéré [pɔ̃dere] *a* level-headed. ◆**pondération** *nf* level-headedness.

pondre [pɔ̃dr] *vt* (*œuf*) to lay; (*livre, discours*) *Péj Fam* to produce; – *vi* (*poule*) to lay.

poney [pɔnɛ] *nm* pony.

pont [pɔ̃] *nm* bridge; (*de bateau*) deck; **p.** (**de graissage**) *Aut* ramp; **faire le p.** *Fig* to take the intervening day(s) off (*between two holidays*); **p. aérien** airlift. ◆**p.-levis** *nm* (*pl* **ponts-levis**) drawbridge.

ponte [pɔ̃t] **1** *nf* (*d'œufs*) laying. **2** *nm* (*personne*) *Fam* bigwig.

pontife [pɔ̃tif] *nm* **1** (*souverain*) **p.** pope. **2** (*ponte*) *Fam* bigshot. ◆**pontifical, -aux** *a* papal, pontifical.

pop [pɔp] *nm & a inv Mus* pop.

popote [pɔpɔt] *nf* (*cuisine*) *Fam* cooking.

populace [pɔpylas] *nf Péj* rabble.

populaire [pɔpylɛr] *a* (*personne, tradition, gouvernement etc*) popular; (*quartier, milieu*) lower-class; (*expression*) colloquial; (*art*) folk-. ◆**populariser** *vt* to popularize. ◆**popularité** *nf* popularity (**auprès de** with).

population [pɔpylasjɔ̃] *nf* population. ◆**populeux, -euse** *a* populous, crowded.

porc [pɔr] *nm* pig; (*viande*) pork; (*personne*) *Péj* swine.

porcelaine [pɔrsɛlɛn] *nf* china, porcelain.

porc-épic [pɔrkepik] *nm* (*pl* **porcs-épics**) (*animal*) porcupine.

porche [pɔrʃ] *nm* porch.

porcherie [pɔrʃəri] *nf* pigsty.

pore [pɔr] *nm* pore. ◆**poreux, -euse** *a* porous.

pornographie [pɔrnɔgrafi] *nf* pornography. ◆**pornographique** *a* (*Fam* **porno**) pornographic.

port [pɔr] *nm* **1** port, harbour; **arriver à bon p.** to arrive safely. **2** (*d'armes*) carrying; (*de barbe*) wearing; (*prix*) carriage, postage; (*attitude*) bearing.

portable [pɔrtabl] *a* (*robe etc*) wearable; (*portatif*) portable.

portail [pɔrtaj] *nm* (*de cathédrale etc*) portal.

portant [pɔrtã] *a* **bien p.** in good health.

portatif, -ive [pɔrtatif, -iv] *a* portable.

porte [pɔrt] *nf* door, (*passage*) doorway; (*de jardin*) gate, (*passage*) gateway; (*de ville*) entrance, *Hist* gate; **p. (d'embarquement)** *Av* (departure) gate; **Alger, p. de ...** Algiers, gateway to ...; **p. d'entrée** front door; **mettre à la p.** (*jeter dehors*) to throw out; (*renvoyer*) to sack. ◆**p.-fenêtre** *nf* (*pl* **portes-fenêtres**) French window.

porte-à-faux [pɔrtafo] *nm inv* **en p.-à-faux** (*en déséquilibre*) unstable.

porte-avions [pɔrtavjɔ̃] *nm inv* aircraft carrier. ◆**p.-bagages** *nm inv* luggage rack. ◆**p.-bébé** *nm* (*nacelle*) carrycot, *Am* baby basket; (*kangourou®*) baby sling. ◆**p.-bonheur** *nm inv* (*fétiche*) (lucky) charm. ◆**p.-cartes** *nm inv* card holder *ou* case. ◆**p.-clés** *nm inv* key ring. ◆**p.-documents** *nm inv* briefcase. ◆**p.-drapeau, -x** *nm Mil* standard bearer. ◆**p.-jarretelles** *nm inv* suspender *ou Am* garter belt. ◆**p.-monnaie** *nm inv* purse. ◆**p.-parapluie** *nm inv* umbrella stand. ◆**p.-plume** *nm inv* pen (*for dipping in ink*). ◆**p.-revues** *nm inv* newspaper rack. ◆**p.-savon** *nm* soapdish. ◆**p.-serviettes** *nm inv* towel rail. ◆**p.-voix** *nm inv* megaphone.

portée [pɔrte] *nf* **1** (*de fusil etc*) range; **à la p. de** qn within reach of s.o.; (*richesse, plaisir etc*) *Fig* within s.o.'s grasp; **à p. de la main** within (easy) reach; **à p. de voix** within earshot; **hors de p.** out of reach. **2** (*animaux*) litter. **3** (*importance, effet*) significance, import. **4** *Mus* stave.

portefeuille [pɔrtafœj] *nm* wallet; *Pol Com* portfolio.

portemanteau, -x [pɔrtmãto] *nm* (*sur pied*) hatstand; (*barre*) hat *ou* coat peg.

porte-parole [pɔrtparɔl] *nm* (*homme*) spokesman; (*femme*) spokeswoman (**de** for, of).

port/er [pɔrte] *vt* to carry; (*vêtement, lunettes, barbe etc*) to wear; (*trace, responsabilité, fruits etc*) to bear; (*regard*) to cast; (*attaque*) to make (**contre** against); (*coup*) to strike; (*sentiment*) to have (**à** for); (*inscrire*) to enter, write down; **p. qch à** (*amener*) to bring *ou* take sth to; **p. qn à faire** (*pousser*) to lead *ou* prompt s.o. to do; **p. bonheur/malheur** to bring good/bad luck; **se faire p. malade** to report sick; **─** *vi* (*voix*) to carry; (*canon*) to fire; (*vue*) to extend; **p. (juste)** (*coup*) to hit the mark; (*mot, reproche*) to hit home; **p. sur** (*reposer sur*) to rest on; (*concerner*) to bear on; (*accent*) to fall on; (*heurter*) to strike; **─ se p.** *vpr* (*vêtement*) to be worn; **se p. bien/mal** to be well/ill; **comment te portes-tu?** how are you?; **se p. candidat** to stand as a candidate. ◆**─ant** *a* **bien à p.** in good health. ◆**─é** *a* **p. à croire/etc** inclined to believe/*etc*; **p. sur qch** fond of sth. ◆**─eur, -euse** *nm Rail* porter; *nm Méd* carrier; (*de nouvelles, chèque*) bearer; **mère porteuse** surrogate mother.

portier [pɔrtje] *nm* doorkeeper, porter. ◆**portière** *nf* (*de véhicule, train*) door. ◆**portillon** *nm* gate.

portion [pɔrsjɔ̃] *nf* (*part, partie*) portion; (*de nourriture*) helping, portion.

portique [pɔrtik] *nm* **1** *Archit* portico. **2** (*de balançoire etc*) crossbar, frame.

porto [pɔrto] *nm* (*vin*) port.

portrait [pɔrtrɛ] *nm* portrait; **être le p. de** (*son père etc*) to be the image of; **faire un p.** to paint *ou* draw a portrait (**de** of); **p. en pied** full-length portrait. ◆**p.-robot** *nm* (*pl* **portraits-robots**) identikit (picture), photofit.

portuaire [pɔrtyɛr] *a* (*installations etc*) harbour-.

Portugal [pɔrtygal] *nm* Portugal. ◆**portugais, -aise** *a* & *nmf* Portuguese; ─ *nm* (*langue*) Portuguese.

pose [poz] *nf* **1** (*installation*) putting up; putting in; laying. **2** (*attitude de modèle, affectation*) pose; (*temps*) *Phot* exposure. ◆**pos/er** *vt* to put (down); (*papier peint, rideaux*) to put up; (*sonnette, chauffage*) to put in; (*mine, moquette, fondations*) to lay; (*question*) to ask (**à qn** s.o.); (*principe, conditions*) to lay down; **p. sa candidature** to apply, put in one's application (**à** for); **ça pose la question de ...** it poses the question of ...; ─ *vi* (*modèle etc*) to pose (**pour** for); ─ **se p.** *vpr* (*oiseau, avion*) to land; (*problème, question*) to arise; **se p.** (*yeux*) to fix on; **se p. en chef**/*etc* to set oneself up as *ou* pose as a leader/*etc*; **la question se pose!** this question should be asked! ◆**─é** *a* (*calme*) calm, staid.

◆—**ément** *adv* calmly. ◆—**eur, -euse** *nmf* *Péj* poseur.

positif, -ive [pozitif, -iv] *a* positive. ◆**positivement** *adv* positively.

position [pozisjɔ̃] *nf* (*attitude, emplacement, opinion etc*) position; **prendre p.** *Fig* to take a stand (**contre** against); **prise de p.** stand.

posologie [pozɔlɔʒi] *nf* (*de médicament*) dosage.

posséder [pɔsede] *vt* to possess; (*maison etc*) to own, possess; (*bien connaître*) to master. ◆**possesseur** *nm* possessor; owner. ◆**possessif, -ive** *a* (*personne, adjectif etc*) possessive; – *nm* *Gram* possessive. ◆**possession** *nf* possession; **en p. de** in possession of; **prendre p. de** to take possession of.

possible [pɔsibl] *a* possible (**à faire** to do); **il (nous) est p. de faire** it is possible (for us) to do it; **il est p. que** (+ *sub*) it is possible that; **si p.** if possible; **le plus tôt/etc p.** as soon/etc as possible; **autant que p.** as much *ou* as many as possible; – *nm* **faire son p.** to do one's utmost (**pour faire** to do); **dans la mesure du p.** as far as possible. ◆**possibilité** *nf* possibility.

post- [pɔst] *préf* post.

postdater [pɔstdate] *vt* to postdate.

poste [pɔst] 1 *nf* (*service*) post, mail; (*local*) post office; **bureau de p.** post office; **Postes (et Télécommunications)** (*administration*) Post Office; **par la p.** by post, by mail; **p. aérienne** airmail; **mettre à la p.** to post, mail. 2 *nm* (*lieu, emploi*) post; **p. de secours** first aid post; **p. de police** police station; **p. d'essence** petrol *ou* *Am* gas station; **p. d'incendie** fire hydrant; **p. d'aiguillage** signal box *ou* *Am* tower. 3 *nm* (*appareil*) *Rad* TV set; *Tél* extension (number). ◆**postal, -aux** *a* postal; **code p.** postcode, *Am* zip code. ◆**poster** 1 *vt* **p. qn** (*placer*) *Mil* to post s.o. 2 *vt* (*lettre*) to post, mail. 3 [pɔster] *nm* poster.

postérieur [pɔsterjœr] *a* (*à document etc*) later; **p. à** after. 2 *nm* (*derrière*) *Fam* posterior.

postérité [pɔsterite] *nf* posterity.

posthume [pɔstym] *a* posthumous; **à titre p.** posthumously.

postiche [pɔstiʃ] *a* (*barbe etc*) false.

postier, -ière [pɔstje, -jɛr] *nmf* postal worker.

postillonner [pɔstijɔne] *vi* to sputter.

post-scriptum [pɔstskriptɔm] *nm inv* postscript.

postul/er [pɔstyle] *vt* 1 (*emploi*) to apply for. 2 (*poser*) *Math* to postulate. ◆—**ant, -ante** *nmf* applicant.

posture [pɔstyr] *nf* posture.

pot [po] *nm* 1 pot; (*à confiture*) jar, pot; (*à lait*) jug; (*à crème, yaourt*) carton; **p. de chambre** chamber pot; **p. de fleurs** flower pot; **prendre un p.** (*verre*) *Fam* to have a drink. 2 (*chance*) *Fam* luck; **avoir du p.** to be lucky.

potable [pɔtabl] *a* drinkable; (*passable*) *Fam* tolerable; **'eau p.'** 'drinking water'.

potage [pɔtaʒ] *nm* soup.

potager, -ère [pɔtaʒe, -ɛr] *a* (*jardin*) vegetable-; **plante potagère** vegetable; – *nm* vegetable garden.

potasser [pɔtase] *vt* (*examen*) to cram for; – *vi* to cram.

pot-au-feu [pɔtofø] *nm inv* (*plat*) beef stew.

pot-de-vin [pɔdvɛ̃] *nm* (*pl* **pots-de-vin**) bribe.

pote [pɔt] *nm* (*ami*) *Fam* pal, buddy.

poteau, -x [pɔto] *nm* post; (*télégraphique*) pole; **p. d'arrivée** *Sp* winning post.

potelé [pɔtle] *a* plump, chubby.

potence [pɔtɑ̃s] *nf* (*gibet*) gallows.

potentiel, -ielle [pɔtɑ̃sjɛl] *a* & *nm* potential.

poterie [pɔtri] *nf* (*art*) pottery; **une p.** a piece of pottery; **des poteries** (*objets*) pottery. ◆**potier** *nm* potter.

potin [pɔtɛ̃] 1 *nmpl* (*cancans*) gossip. 2 *nm* (*bruit*) *Fam* row.

potion [posjɔ̃] *nf* potion.

potiron [pɔtirɔ̃] *nm* pumpkin.

pot-pourri [popuri] *nm* (*pl* **pots-pourris**) *Mus* medley.

pou, -x [pu] *nm* louse; **poux** lice.

poubelle [pubel] *nf* dustbin, *Am* garbage can.

pouce [pus] *nm* 1 thumb; **un coup de p.** *Fam* a helping hand. 2 (*mesure*) *Hist* & *Fig* inch.

poudre [pudr] *nf* (*poussière, explosif*) gunpowder; **en p.** (*lait*) powdered; (*chocolat*) drinking; **sucre en p.** castor *ou* *Am* caster sugar. ◆**poudrer** *vt* to powder; – **se p.** *vpr* (*femme*) to powder one's nose. ◆**poudreux, -euse** *a* powdery, dusty. ◆**poudrier** *nm* (*powder*) compact. ◆**poudrière** *nf* powder magazine; (*région*) *Fig* powder keg.

pouf [puf] 1 *int* thump! 2 *nm* (*siège*) pouf(fe).

pouffer [pufe] *vi* **p. (de rire)** to burst out laughing, guffaw.

pouilleux, -euse [pujø, -øz] *a* (*sordide*) miserable; (*mendiant*) lousy.

poulain [pulɛ̃] *nm* (*cheval*) foal; **le p. de qn** *Fig* s.o.'s protégé.

poule [pul] *nf* **1** hen, *Culin* fowl; **être p. mouillée** (*lâche*) to be chicken; **oui, ma p.!** *Fam* yes, my pet! **2** (*femme*) *Péj* tart. ◆**poulailler** *nm* **1** (hen) coop. **2 le p.** *Th Fam* the gods, the gallery. ◆**poulet** *nm* **1** (*poule, coq*) *Culin* chicken. **2** (*policier*) *Fam* cop.

pouliche [pulif] *nf* (*jument*) filly.

poulie [puli] *nf* pulley.

poulpe [pulp] *nm* octopus.

pouls [pu] *nm Méd* pulse.

poumon [pumɔ̃] *nm* lung; **à pleins poumons** (*respirer*) deeply; (*crier*) loudly; **p. d'acier** iron lung.

poupe [pup] *nf Nau* stern, poop.

poupée [pupe] *nf* doll.

poupin [pupɛ̃] *a* **visage p.** baby face.

poupon [pupɔ̃] *nm* (*bébé*) baby; (*poupée*) doll.

pour [pur] **1** *prép* for; **p. toi/moi/***etc* for you/me/*etc*; **faites-le p. lui** do it for him, do it for his sake; **partir p.** (*Paris etc*) to leave for; **elle va partir p. cinq ans** she's leaving for five years; **p. femme/base/***etc* as a wife/basis/*etc*; **p. moi, p. ma part** (*quant à moi*) as for me; **dix p. cent** ten per cent; **gentil p.** kind to; **elle est p.** she's in favour; **p. faire** (in order) to do, so as to do; **p. que tu saches** so (that) you may know; **p. quoi faire?** what for?; **trop petit/poli/***etc* **p. faire** too small/polite/*etc* to do; **assez grand/***etc* **p. faire** big/*etc* enough to do; **p. cela** for that reason; **jour p. jour/heure p. heure** to the day/hour; **p. intelligent/***etc* **qu'il soit** however clever/*etc* he may be; **ce n'est pas p. me plaire** it doesn't exactly please me; **acheter p. cinq francs de bonbons** to buy five francs' worth of sweets. **2** *nm* **le p. et le contre** the pros and cons.

pourboire [purbwar] *nm* (*argent*) tip.

pourcentage [pursɑ̃taʒ] *nm* percentage.

pourchasser [purʃase] *vt* to pursue.

pourparlers [purparle] *nmpl* negotiations, talks.

pourpre [purpr] *a* & *nm* purple.

pourquoi [purkwa] *adv* & *conj* why; **p. pas?** why not?; – *nm inv* reason (**de** for); **le p. et le comment** the whys and wherefores.

pourra, pourrait [pura, pure] *voir* **pouvoir 1.**

pourrir [purir] *vi,* – **se p.** *vpr* to rot; – *vt* to rot; **p. qn** to corrupt s.o. ◆**pourri** *a* (*fruit, temps, personne etc*) rotten. ◆**pourriture** *nf* rot, rottenness; (*personne*) *Péj* swine.

poursuite [pursɥit] *nf* **1** chase, pursuit; (*du bonheur, d'un créancier*) pursuit (**de** of); (*continuation*) continuation; **se mettre à la p. de** to go in pursuit of. **2** *nfpl Jur* legal proceed-

ings (**contre** against). ◆**poursuiv/re** * **1** *vt* (*courir après*) to chase, pursue; (*harceler, relancer*) to hound, pursue; (*obséder*) to haunt; (*but, idéal etc*) to pursue. **2** *vt* **p. qn** *Jur* (*au criminel*) to prosecute s.o.; (*au civil*) to sue s.o. **3** *vt* (*lecture, voyage etc*) to continue (with), carry on (with), pursue; – *vi,* – **se p.** *vpr* to continue, go on. ◆**-ant, -ante** *nmf* pursuer.

pourtant [purtɑ̃] *adv* yet, nevertheless.

pourtour [purtur] *nm* perimeter.

pourvoir* [purvwar] *vt* to provide (**de** with); **être pourvu de** to have, be provided with; – *vi* **p. à** (*besoins etc*) to provide for. ◆**pourvoyeur, -euse** *nmf* supplier.

pourvu que [purvyk(ə)] *conj* (*condition*) provided *ou* providing (that); **p. qu'elle soit là** (*souhait*) I only hope (that) she's there.

pousse [pus] *nf* **1** (*bourgeon*) shoot, sprout. **2** (*croissance*) growth.

pousse-café [puskafe] *nm inv* after-dinner liqueur.

pouss/er [puse] **1** *vt* to push; (*du coude*) to nudge, poke; (*véhicule, machine*) to drive hard; (*recherches*) to pursue; (*cri*) to utter; (*soupir*) to heave; **p. qn à faire** to urge s.o. to do; **p. qn à bout** to push s.o. to his limits; **p. trop loin** (*gentillesse etc*) to carry too far; **p. à la perfection** to bring to perfection; – *vi* to push; **p. jusqu'à Paris/***etc* to push on as far as Paris/*etc*; – **se p.** *vpr* (*se déplacer*) to move up *ou* over. **2** *vi* (*croître*) to grow; **faire p.** (*plante, barbe etc*) to grow. ◆**-é** *a* (*travail, études*) advanced. ◆**-ée** *nf* (*pression*) pressure; (*coup*) push; (*d'ennemi*) thrust, push; (*de fièvre etc*) outbreak; (*de l'inflation*) upsurge. ◆**poussette** *nf* pushchair, *Am* stroller; **p. canne** (baby) buggy, *Am* (collapsible) stroller; **p. de marché** shopping trolley *ou Am* cart. ◆**poussoir** *nm* (push) button.

poussière [pusjɛr] *nf* dust; **dix francs et des poussières** *Fam* just over ten francs. ◆**poussiéreux, -euse** *a* dusty.

poussif, -ive [pusif, -iv] *a* short-winded, puffing.

poussin [pusɛ̃] *nm* (*poulet*) chick.

poutre [putr] *nf* (*en bois*) beam; (*en acier*) girder. ◆**poutrelle** *nf* girder.

pouvoir* [puvwar] **1** *v aux* (*capacité*) to be able, can; (*permission, éventualité*) may, can; **je peux deviner** I can guess, I'm able to guess; **tu peux entrer** you may *ou* can come in; **il peut être malade** he may *ou* might be ill; **elle pourrait/pouvait venir** she might/could come; **j'ai pu l'obtenir** I managed to get it; **j'aurais pu l'obtenir** I could have got it *ou Am* gotten it; **je n'en peux plus** I'm utterly exhausted; – *v imp* **il peut neiger** it may snow; – **se p.** *vpr* **il se peut qu'elle pleuve** (it's possible that) she might leave. **2** *nm* (*capacité, autorité*) power; (*procuration*) power of attorney; **les pouvoirs publics** the authorities; **au p.** *Pol* in power; **en son p.** in one's power (**de faire** to do).

poux [pu] *voir* **pou.**

pragmatique [pragmatik] *a* pragmatic.

praire [prɛr] *nf* (*mollusque*) clam.

prairie [preri] *nf* meadow.

praline [pralin] *nf* sugared almond. ◆**praliné** *a* (*glace*) praline-flavoured.

praticable [pratikabl] *a* (*projet, chemin*) practicable.

praticien, -ienne [pratisjɛ̃, -jɛn] *nmf* practitioner.

pratique [pratik] **1** *a* (*connaissance, personne, instrument etc*) practical. **2** *nf* (*exercice, procédé*) practice; (*expérience*) practical experience; **la p. de la natation/du golf/etc** swimming/golfing/*etc*; **mettre en p.** to put into practice; **en p.** (*en réalité*) in practice. ◆**pratiqu/er** *vt* (*art etc*) to practise; (*football*) to play, practise; (*trou, route*) to make; (*opération*) to carry out; **p. la natation** to go swimming; – *vi* to practise. ◆**–ant, -ante** *a Rel* practising; – *nmf* churchgoer.

pratiquement [pratikmɑ̃] *adv* (*presque*) practically; (*en réalité*) in practice.

pré [pre] *nm* meadow.

pré- [pre] *préf* pre-.

préalable [prealabl] *a* previous, preliminary; **p. à** prior to; – *nm* precondition, prerequisite; **au p.** beforehand. ◆**–ment** [-əmɑ̃] *adv* beforehand.

préambule [preãbyl] *nm* (*de loi*) preamble; *Fig* prelude (**à** to).

préau, -x [preo] *nm Scol* covered playground.

préavis [preavi] *nm* (*de congé etc*) (advance) notice (**de** of).

précaire [prekɛr] *a* precarious.

précaution [prekosjɔ̃] *nf* (*mesure*) precaution; (*prudence*) caution; **par p.** as a precaution. ◆**précautionneux, -euse** *a* cautious.

précédent, -ente [presedɑ̃, -ɑ̃t] **1** *a* previous, preceding, earlier; – *nmf* previous one. **2** *nm* un **p.** (*fait, exemple*) a precedent; **sans p.** unprecedented. ◆**précédemment** [-amɑ̃] *adv* previously. ◆**précéder** *vti* to precede; **faire p. qch de qch** to precede sth by sth.

précepte [presɛpt] *nm* precept.

précepteur, -trice [preseptœr, -tris] *nmf* (private) tutor.

prêcher [preʃe] *vti* to preach; **p. qn** *Rel & Fig* to preach to s.o.

précieux, -euse [presjø, -øz] *a* precious.

précipice [presipis] *nm* abyss, chasm.

précipit/er [presipite] *vt* (*jeter*) to throw, hurl; (*plonger*) to plunge (**dans** into); (*hâter*) to hasten; – **se p.** *vpr* (*se jeter*) to throw ou hurl oneself; (*foncer*) to rush (**à, sur** on to); (*s'accélérer*) to speed up. ◆**–é** *a* hasty. ◆**précipitamment** *adv* hastily. ◆**précipitation 1** *nf* haste. **2** *nfpl* (*pluie*) precipitation.

précis [presi] **1** *a* precise; (*idée, mécanisme*) accurate, precise; **à deux heures précises** at two o'clock sharp *ou* precisely. **2** *nm* (*résumé*) summary; (*manuel*) handbook. ◆**précisément** *adv* precisely. ◆**préciser** *vt* to specify (**que** that); – **se p.** *vpr* to become clear(er). ◆**précision** *nf* precision; accuracy; (*détail*) detail; (*explication*) explanation.

précoce [prekos] *a* (*fruit, mariage, mort etc*) early; (*personne*) precocious. ◆**précocité** *nf* precociousness; earliness.

préconçu [prekɔ̃sy] *a* preconceived.

préconiser [prekɔnize] *vt* to advocate (**que** that).

précurseur [prekyrsœr] *nm* forerunner, precursor; – **a un signe p. de qch** a sign heralding sth.

prédécesseur [predesɛsœr] *nm* predecessor.

prédestiné [predestine] *a* fated, predestined (**à faire** to do).

prédicateur [predikatœr] *nm* preacher.

prédilection [predilɛksjɔ̃] *nf* (special) liking; **de p.** favourite.

prédire° [predir] *vt* to predict (**que** that). ◆**prédiction** *nf* prediction.

prédisposer [predispoze] *vt* to predispose (**à qch** to sth, **à faire** to do). ◆**prédisposition** *nf* predisposition.

prédomin/er [predomine] *vi* to predominate. ◆**–ant** *a* predominant. ◆**prédominance** *nf* predominance.

préfabriqué [prefabrike] *a* prefabricated.

préface [prefas] *nf* preface. ◆**préfacer** *vt* to preface.

préfér/er [prefere] *vt* to prefer (**à** to); **p. faire** to prefer to do. ◆**–é, -ée** *a & nmf* favourite. ◆**–able** *a* preferable (**à** to). ◆**préférence** *nf* preference; **de p.** preferably; **de p. à** in preference to. ◆**préférentiel, -ielle** *a* preferential.

préfet [prefɛ] *nm* prefect, *chief administrator in a department*; **p. de police** prefect of police, *Paris chief of police.* ◆**préfecture** *nf* prefecture; **p. de police** Paris police headquarters.

préfixe [prefiks] *nm* prefix.

préhistoire [preistwar] *nf* prehistory. ◆**préhistorique** *a* prehistoric.

préjudice [preʒydis] *nm* Jur prejudice, harm; **porter p. à** to prejudice, harm. ◆**préjudiciable** *a* prejudicial (à to).

préjugé [preʒyʒe] *nm* (*parti pris*) prejudice; **avoir un p.** *ou* **des préjugés** to be prejudiced (**contre** against).

prélasser (se) [səprelase] *vpr* to loll (about), lounge (about).

prélat [prela] *nm* Rel prelate.

prélever [prelve] *vt* (*échantillon*) to take (**sur** from); (*somme*) to deduct (**sur** from). ◆**prélèvement** *nm* taking; deduction; **p. de sang** blood sample; **p. automatique** Fin standing order.

préliminaire [preliminɛr] *a* preliminary; — *nmpl* preliminaries.

prélude [prelyd] *nm* prelude (à to).

prématuré [prematyre] *a* premature; — *nm* (*bébé*) premature baby. ◆—**ment** *adv* prematurely, too soon.

préméditer [premedite] *vt* to premeditate. ◆**préméditation** *nf* Jur premeditation.

premier, -ière [prəmje, -jɛr] *a* first; (*enfance*) early; (*page*) Journ front, first; (*qualité, nécessité, importance*) prime; (*état*) original; (*notion, cause*) basic; (*danseuse, rôle*) leading; (*inférieur*) bottom; (*supérieur*) top; **nombre p.** Math prime number; **le p. rang** the front *ou* first row; **à la première occasion** at the earliest opportunity; **P. ministre** Prime Minister, Premier; — *nmf* first (one); **arriver le p.** *ou* **en p.** to arrive first; **être le p. de la classe** to be (at) the top of the class; — *nm* (*date*) first; (*étage*) first *ou* Am second floor; **le p. de l'an** New Year's Day; — *nf* Th Cin première; Rail first class; Scol = sixth form, Am = twelfth grade; Aut first (gear); (*événement historique*) first. ◆**premier-né** *nm*, ◆**première-née** *nf* first-born (child). ◆**premièrement** *adv* firstly.

prémisse [premis] *nf* premiss.

prémonition [premɔnisjɔ̃] *nf* premonition.

prémunir [premynir] *vt* to safeguard (**contre** against).

prénatal [prenatal], *mpl* -**als** [prenatal] *a* antenatal, Am prenatal.

prendre* [prɑ̃dr] *vt* to take (**à qn** from s.o.); (*attraper*) to catch, get; (*voyager par*) to take, travel by; (*acheter*) to get; (*douche, bain*) to have; (*repas*) to have; (*nouvelles*) to get; (*temps, heure*) to take (up); (*pensionnaire*) to take (in); (*ton, air*) to put on; (*engager*) to take (*s.o.*) (on); (*chercher*) to pick up, get; **p. qn pour** (*un autre*) to (mis)take s.o. for; (*considérer*) to take s.o. for; (*douter etc*) to seize s.o.; **p. feu** to catch fire; **p. de la place** to take up room; **p. du poids/de la vitesse** to put on weight/speed; **à tout p.** on the whole; **qu'est-ce qui te prend?** what's got *ou* Am gotten into you?; — *vi* (*feu*) to catch; (*gelée, ciment*) to set; (*greffe, vaccin*) to take; (*mode*) to catch on; — **se p.** *vpr* (*objet*) to be taken; (*s'accrocher*) to get caught; (*eau*) to freeze; **se p. pour un génie/etc** to think one is a genius/etc; **s'y p.** to go *ou* set about it; **s'en p. à** (*critiquer, attaquer*) to attack; (*accuser*) to blame; **se p. à faire** to begin to do. ◆**prenant** *a* (*travail, film etc*) engrossing; (*voix*) engaging. ◆**preneur, -euse** *nmf* taker, buyer.

prénom [prenɔ̃] *nm* first name. ◆**prénommer** *vt* to name; **il se prénomme Louis** his first name is Louis.

préoccuper [preɔkype] *vt* (*inquiéter*) to worry; (*absorber*) to preoccupy; **se p. de** to be worried about; to be preoccupied about. ◆—**ant** *a* worrying. ◆—**é** *a* worried. ◆**préoccupation** *nf* worry; (*idée, problème*) preoccupation.

préparer [prepare] *vt* to prepare; (*repas etc*) to get ready, prepare; (*examen*) to study for, prepare (for); **p. qch à qn** to prepare sth for s.o.; **p. qn à** (*examen*) to prepare *ou* coach s.o. for; — **se p.** *vpr* to get (oneself) ready, prepare oneself (à **qch** for sth); (*orage*) to brew, threaten. ◆**préparatifs** *nmpl* preparations (de for). ◆**préparation** *nf* preparation. ◆**préparatoire** *a* preparatory.

prépondérant [prepɔ̃derɑ̃] *a* dominant. ◆**prépondérance** *nf* dominance.

préposer [prepoze] *vt* **p. qn à** to put s.o. in charge of. ◆—**é, -ée** *nmf* employee; (*facteur*) postman, postwoman.

préposition [prepozisjɔ̃] *nf* preposition.

préretraite [prerətrɛt] *nf* early retirement.

prérogative [prerogativ] *nf* prerogative.

près [prɛ] *adv* **p. de** (*qn, qch*) near (to), close to; **p. de deux ans/etc** (*presque*) nearly two years/etc; **p. de partir/etc** about to leave/etc; **tout p.** nearby (de **qn/qch** *ou* s.o./sth), close by (de **qn/qch** s.o./sth); **de p.** (*lire, examiner, suivre*) closely; **à peu de chose p.** almost; **à cela p.** except for that; **voici le**

chiffre à un franc p. here is the figure give or take a franc; **calculer au franc p.** to calculate to the nearest franc.

présage [prezaʒ] nm omen, foreboding. ◆**présager** vt to forebode.

presbyte [prɛsbit] a & nmf long-sighted (person). ◆**presbytie** [-bisi] nf long-sightedness.

presbytère [prɛsbitɛr] nm Rel presbytery.

préscolaire [preskɔlɛr] a (âge etc) pre-school.

prescrire* [prɛskrir] vt to prescribe. ◆**prescription** nf (instruction) & Jur pre-scription.

préséance [preseɑ̃s] nf precedence (sur over).

présent¹ [prezɑ̃] 1 a (non absent) present; **les personnes présentes** those present. 2 a (actuel) present; – nm (temps) present; Gram (tense); **à p.** now, at present; **dès à p.** as from now. ◆**présence** nf presence; (à l'école, au bureau etc) attendance (à at); **feuille de p.** attendance sheet; **faire acte de p.** to put in an appearance; **en p.** (personnes) face to face; **en p. de** in the presence of; **p. d'esprit** presence of mind.

présent² [prezɑ̃] nm (cadeau) present.

présent/er [prezɑ̃te] vt (offrir, exposer, animer etc) to present; (montrer) to show, present; **p. qn à qn** to introduce ou present s.o. to s.o.; – **se p.** vpr to introduce ou present oneself (à to); (chez qn) to show up; (occasion etc) to arise; **se p. à** (examen) to sit for; (élections) to stand in ou at, run in; (emploi) to apply for; (autorités) to report to; **ça se présente bien** it looks promising. ◆**-able** a presentable. ◆**présentateur, -trice** nmf TV announcer, presenter. ◆**présentation** nf presentation; introduction. ◆**présentoir** nm (étagère) (display) stand.

préserver [prezɛrve] vt to protect, preserve (de from). ◆**préservatif** nm sheath, condom. ◆**préservation** nf protection, preservation.

présidence [prezidɑ̃s] nf (de nation) presidency; (de firme etc) chairmanship. ◆**président, -ente** nmf (de nation) president; (de réunion, firme) chairman, chairwoman; **p. directeur général** chairman and managing director, Am chief executive officer. ◆**présidentiel, -ielle** a presidential.

présider [prezide] vt (réunion) to preside at ou over, chair; – vi to preside.

présomption [prezɔ̃psjɔ̃] nf (conjecture, suffisance) presumption.

présomptueux, -euse [prezɔ̃ptyø, -øz] a presumptuous.

presque [prɛsk(ə)] adv almost, nearly; **p. jamais/rien** hardly ever/anything.

presqu'île [prɛskil] nf peninsula.

presse [prɛs] nf (journaux, appareil) press; Typ (printing) press; **de p.** (conférence, agence) press-.

presse-citron [prɛssitrɔ̃] nm inv lemon squeezer. ◆**p.-papiers** nm inv paperweight. ◆**p.-purée** nm inv (potato) masher.

pressentir* [prɛsɑ̃tir] vt (deviner) to sense (que that). ◆**pressentiment** nm foreboding, presentiment.

press/er [prɛse] vt (serrer) to squeeze, press; (bouton) to press; (fruit) to squeeze; (départ etc) to hasten; **p. qn** to hurry s.o. (de faire to do); (assaillir) to harass s.o. (de questions with questions); **p. le pas** to speed up; – vi (temps) to press; (affaire) to be pressing ou urgent; **rien ne presse** there's no hurry; – **se p.** vpr (se grouper) to crowd, swarm; (se serrer) to squeeze (together); (se hâter) to hurry (de faire to do); **presse-toi (de partir)** hurry up (and go). ◆**-ant** a pressing, urgent. ◆**-é** a (personne) in a hurry; (air) hurried; (travail) pressing, urgent. ◆**pressing** [-iŋ] nm (magasin) dry cleaner's. ◆**pressoir** nm (wine) press.

pression [prɛsjɔ̃] nf pressure; **faire p. sur qn** to put pressure on s.o., pressurize s.o.; **bière (à la) p.** draught beer; – nm (bouton-)p. press-stud, Am snap.

pressuriser [prɛsyrize] vt Av to pressurize.

prestance [prɛstɑ̃s] nf (imposing) presence.

prestation [prɛstasjɔ̃] nf 1 (allocation) allowance, benefit. 2 (performance) performance.

prestidigitateur, -trice [prɛstidiʒitatœr, -tris] nmf conjurer. ◆**prestidigitation** nf conjuring.

prestige [prɛstiʒ] nm prestige. ◆**prestigieux, -euse** a prestigious.

presto [prɛsto] Fam voir illico.

présumer [prezyme] vt to presume (que that).

présupposer [presypoze] vt to presuppose (que that).

prêt¹ [prɛ] a (préparé, disposé) ready (à faire to do, à qch for sth). ◆**p.-à-porter** [prɛtaporte] nm inv ready-to-wear clothes.

prêt² [prɛ] nm (emprunt) loan. ◆**p.-logement** nm (pl prêts-logement) mortgage.

prétend/re [pretɑ̃dr] vt to claim (que that); (vouloir) to intend (faire to do); **p.**

être/savoir to claim to be/to know; **elle se prétend riche** she claims to be rich; – *vi* **p. à** (*titre etc*) to lay claim to. **◆—ant** *nm* (*amoureux*) suitor. **◆—u** *a* so-called. **◆—ument** *adv* supposedly.

prétentieux, -euse [pretãsjø, -øz] *a* & *nmf* pretentious (person). **◆prétention** *nf* (*vanité*) pretension; (*revendication, ambition*) claim.

prêt/er [prete] *vt* (*argent, objet*) to lend (à to); (*aide, concours*) to give (à to); (*attribuer*) to attribute (à to); **p. attention** to pay attention (à to); **p. serment** to take an oath; – *vi* **p. à** (*phrase etc*) to lend itself to; **se p. à** (*consentir à*) to agree to; (*sujet etc*) to lend itself to. **◆—eur, -euse** *nmf* (*d'argent*) lender; **p. sur gages** pawnbroker.

prétexte [pretɛkst] *nm* pretext, excuse; **sous p. de/que** on the pretext of/that. **◆prétexter** *vt* to plead (**que** that).

prêtre [prɛtr] *nm* priest; **grand p.** high priest.

preuve [prœv] *nf* proof, evidence; **faire p. de** to show; **faire ses preuves** (*personne*) to prove oneself; (*méthode*) to prove itself.

prévaloir [prevalwar] *vi* to prevail (**contre** against, **sur** over).

prévenant [prevnã] *a* considerate. **◆prévenance(s)** *nf(pl)* (*gentillesse*) consideration.

préven/ir* [prevnir] *vt* **1** (*avertir*) to warn (**que** that); (*aviser*) to tell, inform (**que** that). **2** (*désir, question*) to anticipate; (*malheur*) to avert. **◆—u, -ue 1** *nmf* Jur defendant, accused. **2** *a* prejudiced (**contre** against). **◆préventif, -ive** *a* preventive. **◆prévention** *nf* **1** prevention; **p. routière** road safety. **2** (*opinion*) prejudice.

prév/oir* [prevwar] *vt* (*anticiper*) to foresee (**que** that); (*prédire*) forecast (**que** that); (*temps*) Mét to forecast; (*projeter, organiser*) to plan (for); (*réserver, préparer*) to allow, provide. **◆—u** *a* (*conditions*) laid down; **un repas est p.** a meal is provided; **au moment p.** at the appointed time; **comme p.** as planned, as expected; **p. pour** (*véhicule, appareil etc*) designed for. **◆prévisible** *a* foreseeable. **◆prévision** *nf* (*opinion*) & Mét forecast; **en p. de** in expectation of.

prévoyant [prevwajã] *a* (*personne*) provident. **◆prévoyance** *nf* foresight; **société de p.** provident society.

prier [prije] **1** *vi* Rel to pray; – *vt* **p. Dieu pour qu'il nous accorde qch** to pray (to God) for sth. **2** *vt* **p. qn de faire** to ask *ou* request s.o. to do; (*implorer*) to beg s.o. to do; **je vous en prie** (*faites donc, allez-y*)

please; (*en réponse à 'merci'*) don't mention it; **je vous prie** please; **se faire p.** to wait to be asked. **◆prière** *nf* Rel prayer; (*demande*) request; **p. de répondre/etc** please answer/*etc*.

primaire [primɛr] *a* primary.

prime [prim] **1** *nf* (*d'employé*) bonus; (*d'État*) subsidy; (*cadeau*) Com free gift; **p. (d'assurance)** (insurance) premium. **2** *a* **de p. abord** at the very first glance.

primé [prime] *a* (*animal*) prize-winning.

primer [prime] *vi* to excel, prevail; – *vt* to prevail over.

primeurs [primœr] *nfpl* early fruit and vegetables.

primevère [primvɛr] *nf* (*à fleurs jaunes*) primrose.

primitif, -ive [primitif, -iv] *a* (*art, société etc*) primitive; (*état, sens*) original; – *nm* (*artiste*) primitive. **◆primitivement** *adv* originally.

primo [primo] *adv* first(ly).

primordial, -aux [primɔrdjal, -o] *a* vital (**de faire** to do).

prince [prɛ̃s] *nm* prince. **◆princesse** *nf* princess. **◆princier, -ière** *a* princely. **◆principauté** *nf* principality.

principal, -aux [prɛ̃sipal, -o] *a* main, chief, principal; – *nm* (*de collège*) Scol principal; **le p.** (*essentiel*) the main *ou* chief thing. **◆—ement** *adv* mainly.

principe [prɛ̃sip] *nm* principle; **par p.** on principle; **en p.** theoretically, in principle; (*normalement*) as a rule.

printemps [prɛ̃tã] *nm* (*saison*) spring. **◆printanier, -ière** *a* (*temps etc*) spring-, spring-like.

priorité [priɔrite] *nf* priority; **la p.** Aut the right of way; **la p. à droite** Aut right of way to traffic coming from the right; **'cédez la p.'** Aut 'give way', Am 'yield'; **en p.** as a matter of priority. **◆prioritaire** *a* (*industrie etc*) priority-; **être p.** to have priority; Aut to have the right of way.

pris [pri] *voir* **prendre**; – *a* (*place*) taken; (*crème, ciment*) set; (*eau*) frozen; (*gorge*) infected; (*nez*) congested; **être (très) p.** (*occupé*) to be (very) busy; **p. de** (*peur, panique*) stricken with.

prise [priz] *voir* **prendre**; – *nf* taking; (*manière d'empoigner*) grip, hold; (*de ville*) capture, taking; (*objet saisi*) catch; (*de tabac*) pinch; **p. (de courant)** El (*mâle*) plug; (*femelle*) socket; **p. multiple** El adaptor; **p. d'air** air vent; **p. de conscience** awareness; **p. de contact** first meeting; **p. de position** Fig stand; **p. de sang** blood test; **p.**

de son (sound) recording; **p. de vue(s)** *Cin Phot* (*action*) shooting; (*résultat*) shot; **aux prises avec** at grips with.

priser [prize] **1** *vt* **tabac à** p. snuff; — *vi* to take snuff. **2** *vt* (*estimer*) to prize.

prisme [prism] *nm* prism.

prison [prizɔ̃] *nf* prison, jail, gaol; (*réclusion*) imprisonment; **mettre en p.** to imprison, put in prison. ◆**prisonnier, -ière** *nmf* prisoner; **faire qn p.** to take s.o. prisoner.

privé [prive] *a* private; **en p.** (*seul à seul*) in private; — *nm* **dans le p.** in private life; *Com Fam* in the private sector.

priver [prive] *vt* to deprive (**de** of); **se p. de** to deprive oneself of, do without. ◆**privation** *nf* deprivation (**de** of); *pl* (*sacrifices*) hardships.

privilège [privilɛʒ] *nm* privilege. ◆**privilégié, -ée** *a* & *nmf* privileged (person).

prix [pri] *nm* **1** (*d'un objet, du succès etc*) price; **à tout p.** at all costs; **à aucun p.** on no account; **hors (de) p.** exorbitant; **attacher du p. à** to attach importance to; **menu à p. fixe** set price menu. **2** (*récompense*) prize.

pro- [pro] *préf* pro-.

probable [prɔbabl] *a* probable, likely; **peu p.** unlikely. ◆**probabilité** *nf* probability, likelihood; **selon toute p.** in all probability. ◆**probablement** *adv* probably.

probant [prɔbɑ̃] *a* conclusive.

probité [prɔbite] *nf* (*honnêteté*) integrity.

problème [prɔblɛm] *nm* problem. ◆**problématique** *a* doubtful, problematic.

procéd/er [prɔsede] *vi* (*agir*) to proceed; (*se conduire*) to behave; **p. à** (*enquête etc*) to carry out. ◆**-é** *nm* process; (*conduite*) behaviour. ◆**procédure** *nf* procedure; *Jur* proceedings.

procès [prɔsɛ] *nm* (*criminel*) trial; (*civil*) lawsuit; **faire un p. à** to take to court.

processeur [prɔsescœr] *nm* (*d'ordinateur*) processor.

procession [prɔsesjɔ̃] *nf* procession.

processus [prɔsesys] *nm* process.

procès-verbal, -aux [prɔsɛverbal, -o] *nm* (*de réunion*) minutes; (*constat*) *Jur* report; (*contravention*) fine, ticket.

prochain, -aine [prɔʃɛ̃, -ɛn] **1** *a* next; (*avenir*) near; (*parent*) close; (*mort, arrivée*) impending; (*mariage*) forthcoming; **un jour p. one day soon;** — *nf* **à la prochaine!** *Fam* see you soon!; **à la prochaine (station)** at the next stop. **2** *nm* (*semblable*) fellow (man). ◆**prochainement** *adv* shortly, soon.

proche [prɔʃ] *a* (*espace*) near, close; (*temps*)

close (at hand); (*parent, ami*) close; (*avenir*) near; **p. de** near (to), close to; **une maison/etc p.** a house/etc nearby *ou* close by; — *nmpl* close relations.

proclamer [prɔklame] *vt* to proclaim, declare (**que** that); **p. roi** to proclaim king. ◆**proclamation** *nf* proclamation, declaration.

procréer [prɔkree] *vt* to procreate. ◆**procréation** *nf* procreation.

procuration [prɔkyrasjɔ̃] *nf* power of attorney; **par p.** (*voter*) by proxy.

procurer [prɔkyre] *vt* **p. qch à qn** (*personne*) to obtain sth for s.o.; (*occasion etc*) to afford s.o. sth; **se p. qch** to obtain sth.

procureur [prɔkyrœr] *nm* = *Br* public prosecutor; = *Am* district attorney.

prodige [prɔdiʒ] *nm* (*miracle*) wonder; (*personne*) prodigy. ◆**prodigieux, -euse** *a* prodigious, extraordinary.

prodigue [prɔdig] *a* (*dépensier*) wasteful, prodigal. ◆**prodiguer** *vt* to lavish (**à qn** on s.o.).

production [prɔdyksjɔ̃] *nf* production; (*de la terre*) yield. ◆**producteur, -trice** *nmf Com Cin* producer; — *a* producing; **pays p. de pétrole** oil-producing country. ◆**productif, -ive** *a* (*terre, réunion etc*) productive. ◆**productivité** *nf* productivity.

produire* [prɔdɥir] **1** *vt* (*fabriquer, présenter etc*) to produce; (*causer*) to bring about, produce. **2 se p.** *vpr* (*événement etc*) to happen, occur. ◆**produit** *nm* (*article etc*) product; (*pour la vaisselle*) liquid; (*d'une vente, d'une collecte*) proceeds; *pl* (*de la terre*) produce; **p. (chimique)** chemical; **p. de beauté** cosmetic.

proéminent [prɔeminɑ̃] *a* prominent.

prof [prɔf] *nm Fam* = **professeur.**

profane [prɔfan] **1** *nmf* lay person. **2** *a* (*art etc*) secular.

profaner [prɔfane] *vt* to profane, desecrate. ◆**profanation** *nf* profanation, desecration.

proférer [prɔfere] *vt* to utter.

professer [prɔfese] *vt* to profess (**que** that).

professeur [prɔfescœr] *nm* teacher; *Univ* lecturer, *Am* professor; (*titulaire d'une chaire*) *Univ* professor.

profession [prɔfesjɔ̃] *nf* **1** occupation, vocation; (*libérale*) profession; (*manuelle*) trade; **de p.** (*chanteur etc*) professional, by profession. **2 p. de foi** *Fig* declaration of principles. ◆**professionnel, -elle** *a* professional; (*école*) vocational, trade-; — *nmf* (*non amateur*) professional.

profil [prɔfil] *nm* (*de personne, objet*) profile;

de p. in profile. ◆**profiler** vt to outline, profile; — **se p.** vpr to be outlined ou profiled (sur against).

profit [prɔfi] nm profit; (avantage) advantage, profit; **vendre à p.** to sell at a profit; **tirer p. de** to benefit by, profit by; **au p. de** for the benefit of. ◆**profitable** a profitable (à to). ◆**profiter** vi p. de to take advantage of; **p. à qn** to profit s.o.; **p. (bien)** (enfant) Fam to thrive. ◆**profiteur, -euse** nmf Péj profiteer.

profond [prɔfɔ̃] a deep; (esprit, joie, erreur etc) profound, great; (cause) underlying; **p. de deux mètres** two metres deep; – adv (pénétrer etc) deep; – nm **au plus p. de** in the depths of. ◆**profondément** adv deeply; (dormir) soundly; (triste, souhaiter) profoundly; (extrêmement) thoroughly. ◆**profondeur** nf depth; profoundness; pl depths (de of); **en p.** (étudier etc) in depth; **à six mètres de p.** at a depth of six metres.

profusion [prɔfyzjɔ̃] nf profusion; **à p.** in profusion.

progéniture [prɔʒenityr] nf Hum offspring.

progiciel [prɔʒisjɛl] nm (pour ordinateur) (software) package.

programme [prɔgram] nm programme, Am program; (d'une matière) Scol syllabus; (d'ordinateur) program; **p. (d'études)** (d'une école) curriculum. ◆**programmation** nf programming. ◆**programmer** vt Cin Rad TV to programme, Am program; (ordinateur) to program. ◆**programmeur, -euse** nmf (computer) programmer.

progrès [prɔgrɛ] nm & nmpl progress; **faire des p.** to make (good) progress. ◆**progresser** vi to progress. ◆**progressif, -ive** a progressive. ◆**progression** nf progression. ◆**progressiste** a & nmf Pol progressive. ◆**progressivement** adv progressively, gradually.

prohiber [prɔibe] vt to prohibit, forbid. ◆**prohibitif, -ive** a prohibitive. ◆**prohibition** nf prohibition.

proie [prwa] nf prey; **être en p. à** to be (a) prey to, be tortured by.

projecteur [prɔʒɛktœr] nm (de monument) floodlight; (de prison) & Mil searchlight; Th spot(light); Cin projector.

projectile [prɔʒɛktil] nm missile.

projet [prɔʒɛ] nm plan; (ébauche) draft; (entreprise, étude) project.

projeter [prɔʒte] vt **1** (lancer) to hurl, project. **2** (film, ombre) to project; (lumière) to flash. **3** (voyage, fête etc) to plan; **p. de faire** to plan to do. ◆**projection** nf (lancement

hurling, projection; (de film, d'ombre) projection; (séance) showing.

prolétaire [prɔleter] nmf proletarian. ◆**prolétariat** nm proletariat. ◆**prolétarien, -ienne** a proletarian.

proliférer [prɔlifere] vi to proliferate. ◆**prolifération** nf proliferation.

prolifique [prɔlifik] a prolific.

prolixe [prɔliks] a verbose, wordy.

prologue [prɔlɔg] nm prologue (de, à to).

prolonger [prɔlɔ̃ʒe] vt to prolong, extend; — **se p.** vpr (séance, rue, effet) to continue. ◆**prolongateur** nm (rallonge) El extension cord. ◆**prolongation** nf extension; pl Fb extra time. ◆**prolongement** nm extension.

promenade [prɔmnad] nf (à pied) walk; (en voiture) ride, drive; (en vélo, à cheval) ride; (action) Sp walking; (lieu) walk, promenade; **faire une p.** = **se promener**. ◆**promener** vt to take for a walk ou ride; (visiteur) to take ou show around; **p. qch sur qch** (main, regard) to run sth over sth; **envoyer p.** Fam to send packing; — **se p.** vpr (à pied) to (go for a) walk; (en voiture) to (go for a) ride ou drive. ◆**promeneur, -euse** nmf walker, stroller.

promesse [prɔmɛs] nf promise. ◆**mett/re** vt to promise (qch à qn s.o. sth); **p. de faire** to promise to do; **c'est promis** it's a promise; – vi **p. (beaucoup)** Fig to be promising; **se p. qch** to promise oneself sth; **se p. de faire** to resolve to do. ◆**—eur, -euse** a promising.

promontoire [prɔmɔ̃twar] nm Géog headland.

promoteur [prɔmɔtœr] nm **p. (immobilier)** property developer.

promotion [prɔmɔsjɔ̃] nf **1** promotion; **en p.** Com on (special) offer. **2** (candidats) Univ year. ◆**promouvoir*** vt (personne, produit etc) to promote; **être promu** (employé) to be promoted (à to).

prompt [prɔ̃] a swift, prompt, quick. ◆**promptitude** nf swiftness, promptness.

promulguer [prɔmylge] vt to promulgate.

prôner [prone] vt (vanter) to extol; (préconiser) to advocate.

pronom [prɔnɔ̃] nm Gram pronoun. ◆**pronominal, -aux** a pronominal.

prononc/er [prɔnɔ̃se] vt (articuler) to pronounce; (dire) to utter; (discours) to deliver; (jugement) Jur to pronounce, pass; – vi Jur Ling to pronounce; — **se p.** vpr (mot) to be pronounced; (personne) to reach a decision (sur about, on); **se p. pour** to come out in favour of. ◆**—é** a (visible) pronounced, marked. ◆**prononciation** nf pronunciation.

pronostic [prɔnɔstik] nm (prévision) & Sp forecast. ◆**pronostiquer** vt to forecast.

propagande [prɔpagɑ̃d] nf propaganda. ◆**propagandiste** nmf propagandist.

propager [prɔpaʒe] vt, — **se p.** vpr to spread. ◆**propagation** nf spread(ing).

propension [prɔpɑ̃sjɔ̃] nf propensity (à qch for sth, à faire to do).

prophète [prɔfɛt] nm prophet. ◆**prophétie** [-fesi] nf prophecy. ◆**prophétique** a prophetic. ◆**prophétiser** vti to prophesy.

propice [prɔpis] a favourable (à to).

proportion [prɔpɔrsjɔ̃] nf proportion; Math ratio; **en p. de** in proportion to; **hors de p.** out of proportion (**avec** to). ◆**proportionnel, -elle** a proportional (à to). ◆**proportionn/er** vt to proportion (à to). ◆**—é** a proportionate (à to); **bien p.** well ou nicely proportioned.

propos [prɔpo] **1** nmpl (paroles) remarks, utterances. **2** nm (intention) purpose. **3** nm (sujet) subject; **à p. de** about; **à p. de rien** for no reason; **à tout p.** for no reason, at every turn. **4** adv **à p.** (arriver etc) at the right time; **à p.!** by the way!; **juger à p. de faire** to consider it fit to do.

proposer [prɔpoze] vt (suggérer) to suggest, propose (qch à qn sth to s.o., que (+ sub) that); (offrir) to offer (qch à qn s.o. sth, de faire to do); (candidat) to put forward, propose; **je te propose de rester** I suggest (that) you stay; **se p. pour faire** to offer to do; **se p. de faire** to propose ou mean to do. ◆**proposition** nf suggestion, proposal; (de paix) proposal, (affirmation) proposition; Gram clause.

propre[1] a clean; (soigné) neat; (honnête) decent; — nm **mettre qch au p.** to make a fair copy of sth. ◆**proprement**[1] adv (avec propreté) cleanly; (avec netteté) neatly; (comme il faut) decently. ◆**propreté** nf cleanliness; (netteté) neatness.

propre[2] a (à soi) own; **mon p. argent** my own money; **ses propres mots** his very ou his own words. **2** a (qui convient) right, proper; **p. à** (attribut, coutume etc) peculiar to; (approprié) well-suited to; **p. à faire** likely to do; **sens p.** literal meaning; **nom p.** proper noun; — nm **le p. de** (qualité) the distinctive quality of; **au p.** (au sens propre) literally. ◆**proprement**[2] adv (strictement) strictly; **à p. parler** strictly speaking; **le village/etc p. dit** the village/etc proper ou itself.

propriété [prɔprijete] nf **1** (bien) property;

(droit) ownership, property. **2** (qualité) property. **3** (de mot) suitability. ◆**propriétaire** nmf owner; (d'hôtel) proprietor, owner; (qui loue) landlord, landlady; **p. foncier** landowner.

propulser [prɔpylse] vt (faire avancer, projeter) to propel. ◆**propulsion** nf propulsion.

prosaïque [prozaik] a prosaic, pedestrian.

proscrire*[1] vt to proscribe, banish. ◆**proscrit, -ite** nmf (personne) exile. ◆**proscription** nf banishment.

prose [proz] nf prose.

prospecter [prɔspɛkte] vt (sol) to prospect; (pétrole) to prospect for; (région) Com to canvass. ◆**prospecteur, -trice** nmf prospector. ◆**prospection** nf prospecting; Com canvassing.

prospectus [prɔspɛktys] nm leaflet, prospectus.

prospère [prɔspɛr] a (florissant) thriving, prosperous; (riche) prosperous. ◆**prospérer** vi to thrive, flourish, prosper. ◆**prospérité** nf prosperity.

prostate [prɔstat] nf Anat prostate (gland).

prostern/er (se) [səprɔstɛrne] vpr to prostrate oneself (**devant** before). ◆**—é** a prostrate. ◆**—ement** nm prostration.

prostituer [prɔstitɥe] vt to prostitute; — **se p.** vpr to prostitute oneself. ◆**prostituée** nf prostitute. ◆**prostitution** nf prostitution.

prostré [prɔstre] a (accablé) prostrate. ◆**prostration** nf prostration.

protagoniste [prɔtagɔnist] nmf protagonist.

protecteur, -trice [prɔtɛktœr, -tris] nmf protector; (mécène) patron; — a (geste etc) & Écon protective; (ton, air) Péj patronizing. ◆**protection** nf protection; (mécénat) patronage; **de p.** (écran etc) protective. ◆**protectionnisme** nm Écon protectionism.

protég/er [prɔteʒe] vt to protect (**de** from, **contre** against); (appuyer) Fig to patronize; — **se p.** vpr to protect oneself. ◆**—é** nm protégé. ◆**—ée** nf protégée. ◆**protège-cahier** nm exercise book cover.

proteine [prɔtein] nf protein.

protestant, -ante [prɔtɛstɑ̃, -ɑ̃t] a & nmf Protestant. ◆**protestantisme** nm Protestantism.

protester [prɔtɛste] vi to protest (**contre** against); **p. de** (son innocence etc) to protest; — vt to protest (**que** that). ◆**protestation** nf protest (**contre** against); pl (d'amitié) protestations (**de** of).

prothèse [prɔtɛz] nf **(appareil de) p.** (membre) artificial limb; (dents) false teeth.

protocole [prɔtɔkɔl] nm protocol.

prototype [prɔtɔtip] nm prototype.

protubérance [prɔtyberɑ̃s] nf protuberance. ◆**protubérant** a (yeux) bulging; (menton) protruding.

proue [pru] nf Nau prow, bow(s).

prouesse [pruɛs] nf feat, exploit.

prouver [pruve] vt to prove **(que** that).

Provence [prɔvɑ̃s] nf Provence. ◆**provençal, -ale, -aux** a & nmf Provençal.

provenir* [prɔvnir] vi **p. de** to come from. ◆**provenance** nf origin; **en p. de** from.

proverbe [prɔvɛrb] nm proverb. ◆**proverbial, -aux** a proverbial.

providence [prɔvidɑ̃s] nf providence. ◆**providentiel, -ielle** a providential.

province [prɔvɛ̃s] nf province; **la p.** the provinces; **en p.** in the provinces; **de p.** (ville etc) provincial. ◆**provincial, -ale, -aux** a & nmf provincial.

proviseur [prɔvizœr] nm (de lycée) headmaster.

provision [prɔvizjɔ̃] nf **1** (réserve) supply, stock; pl (achats) shopping; (vivres) provisions: **panier/sac à provisions** shopping basket/bag. **2** (acompte) advance payment; **chèque sans p.** dud cheque.

provisoire [prɔvizwar] a temporary, provisional. ◆**—ment** adv temporarily, provisionally.

provoquer [prɔvɔke] vt **1** (causer) to bring about, provoke; (désir) to arouse. **2** (défier) to provoke (s.o.). ◆**provocant** a provocative. ◆**provocateur** nm troublemaker. ◆**provocation** nf provocation.

proxénète [prɔksenɛt] nm pimp.

proximité [prɔksimite] nf closeness, proximity; **à p. close** by; **à p. de** close to.

prude [pryd] a prudish; − nf prude.

prudent [prydɑ̃] a (circonspect) cautious, careful; (sage) sensible. ◆**prudemment** [-amɑ̃] adv cautiously, carefully; (sagement) sensibly. ◆**prudence** nf caution, care, prudence; (sagesse) wisdom; **par p.** as a precaution.

prune [pryn] nf (fruit) plum. ◆**pruneau, -x** nm prune. ◆**prunelle** nf **1** (fruit) sloe. **2** (de l'œil) pupil. ◆**prunier** nm plum tree.

P.-S. [pees] abrév (post-scriptum) PS.

psaume [psom] nm psalm.

pseudo- [psødo] préf pseudo-.

pseudonyme [psødɔnim] nm pseudonym.

psychanalyse [psikanaliz] nf psychoanalysis. ◆**psychanalyste** nmf psychoanalyst.

psychiatre [psikjatr] nmf psychiatrist. ◆**psychiatrie** nf psychiatry. ◆**psychiatrique** a psychiatric.

psychique [psiʃik] a mental, psychic.

psycho [psiko] préf psycho-.

psychologie [psikɔlɔʒi] nf psychology. ◆**psychologique** a psychological. ◆**psychologue** nmf psychologist.

psychose [psikoz] nf psychosis.

PTT [petete] nfpl (Postes, Télégraphes, Téléphones) Post Office; = GPO.

pu [py] voir **pouvoir 1**.

puant [pɥɑ̃] a stinking. ◆**puanteur** nf stink, stench.

pub [pyb] nf Fam (réclame) advertising; (annonce) ad.

puberté [pybɛrte] nf puberty.

public, -ique [pyblik] a public; **dette publique** national debt; − nm public; (de spectacle) audience; **le grand p.** the general public; **en p.** in public. ◆**publiquement** adv publicly.

publication [pyblikasjɔ̃] nf (action, livre etc) publication. ◆**publier** vt to publish.

publicité [pyblisite] nf publicity (**pour** for); (réclame) advertising, publicity; (annonce) advertisement; Rad TV commercial. ◆**publicitaire** a (agence, film) publicity-, advertising-.

puce [pys] nf **1** flea; **le marché aux puces, les puces** the flea market. **2** (d'un ordinateur) chip, microchip.

puceron [pysrɔ̃] nm greenfly.

pudeur [pydœr] nf (sense of) modesty; **attentat à la p.** Jur indecency. ◆**pudibond** a prudish. ◆**pudique** a modest.

puer [pɥe] vi to stink; − vt to stink of.

puériculture [pɥerikyltyr] nf infant care, child care. ◆**puéricultrice** nf children's nurse.

puéril [pɥeril] a puerile. ◆**puérilité** nf puerility.

puis [pɥi] adv then; **et p. quoi?** and so what?

puiser [pɥize] vt to draw, take (**dans** from); − vi **p. dans** to dip into.

puisque [pɥisk(ə)] conj since, as.

puissant [pɥisɑ̃] a powerful. ◆**puissamment** adv powerfully. ◆**puissance** nf (force, nation) & Math Tech power; **en p.** (talent, danger etc) potential.

puits [pɥi] nm well; (de mine) shaft.

pull-(over) [pyl(ɔvɛr)] nm pullover, sweater.

pulluler [pylyle] vi Péj to swarm.

pulmonaire [pylmɔnɛr] a (congestion, maladie) of the lungs, lung-.

pulpe [pylp] *nf* (*de fruits*) pulp.

pulsation [pylsasjɔ̃] *nf* (*heart*)beat.

pulvériser [pylverize] *vt* (*broyer*) & *Fig* to pulverize; (*liquide*) to spray. ◆**pulvérisateur** *nm* spray, atomizer. ◆**pulvérisation** *nf* (*de liquide*) spraying.

punaise [pynɛz] *nf* **1** (*insecte*) bug. **2** (*clou*) drawing pin, *Am* thumbtack. ◆**punaiser** *vt* (*fixer*) to pin (up).

punch 1 [pɔ̃ʃ] *nm* **1** (*boisson*) punch. **2** [pœnʃ] (*énergie*) punch.

punir [pynir] *vt* to punish. ◆**punissable** *a* punishable (de by). ◆**punition** *nf* punishment.

pupille [pypij] **1** *nf* (*de l'œil*) pupil. **2** *nmf* (*enfant sous tutelle*) ward.

pupitre [pypitr] *nm* (*d'écolier*) desk; (*d'orateur*) lectern; **p. à musique** music stand.

pur [pyr] *a* pure; (*alcool*) neat, straight. ◆**purement** *adv* purely. ◆**pureté** *nf* purity.

purée [pyre] *nf* purée; **p. (de pommes de terre)** mashed potatoes, mash.

purgatoire [pyrgatwar] *nm* purgatory.

purge [pyrʒ] *nf* *Pol Méd* purge.

purger [pyrʒe] *vt* **1** (*conduite*) *Tech* to drain, clear. **2** (*peine*) *Jur* to serve.

purifier [pyrifje] *vt* to purify. ◆**purification** *nf* purification.

purin [pyrɛ̃] *nm* liquid manure.

puriste [pyrist] *nmf Gram* purist.

puritain, -aine [pyritɛ̃, -ɛn] *a* & *nmf* puritan.

pur-sang [pyrsɑ̃] *nm inv* (*cheval*) thoroughbred.

pus 1 [py] *nm* (*liquide*) pus, matter.

pus 2, put [py] *voir* **pouvoir 1.**

putain [pytɛ̃] *nf Péj Fam* whore.

putois [pytwa] *nm* (*animal*) polecat.

putréfier [pytrefje] *vt*, **— se p.** *vpr* to putrefy. ◆**putréfaction** *nf* putrefaction.

puzzle [pœzl] *nm* (jigsaw) puzzle, jigsaw.

p.-v. [peve] *nm inv* (*procès-verbal*) (traffic) fine.

PVC [pevese] *nm* (*plastique*) PVC.

pygmée [pigme] *nm* pygmy.

pyjama [piʒama] *nm* pyjamas, *Am* pajamas; **un p.** a pair of pyjamas *ou Am* pajamas; **de p.** (*veste, pantalon*) pyjama-, *Am* pajama-.

pylône [pilon] *nm* pylon.

pyramide [piramid] *nf* pyramid.

Pyrénées [pirene] *nfpl* **les P.** the Pyrenees.

pyromane [piroman] *nmf* arsonist, firebug.

python [pitɔ̃] *nm* (*serpent*) python.

Q

Q, q [ky] *nm* Q, q.

QI [kyi] *nm inv abrév* (*quotient intellectuel*) IQ.

qu' [k] *voir* **que.**

quadriller [kadrije] *vt* (*troupes, police*) to be positioned throughout, comb, cover (*town etc*). ◆**—é** *a* (*papier*) squared. ◆**—age** *nm* (*lignes*) squares.

quadrupède [k(w)adryped] *nm* quadruped.

quadruple [k(w)adrypl] *a* **q. de** fourfold; **— nm le q. de** four times as much as. ◆**quadrupler** *vti* to quadruple. ◆**—és, -ées** *nmfpl* (*enfants*) quadruplets, quads.

quai [ke] *nm Nau* quay; (*pour marchandises*) wharf; (*de fleuve*) embankment, bank; *Rail* platform.

qualification [kalifikasjɔ̃] *nf* **1** description. **2** (*action*) *Sp* qualifying, qualification. ◆**qualificatif** *nm* (*mot*) term. ◆**qualifier** *vt* **1** (*décrire*) to describe (de as); **se faire q. de menteur**/*etc* to be called a liar/*etc*. **2** *vt* (*rendre apte*) & *Sp* to qualify

(pour qch for sth, **pour faire** to do); **— se q.** *vpr Sp* to qualify (**pour** for). **3** *vt Gram* to qualify. ◆**—é** *a* qualified (**pour faire** to do); (*ouvrier, main-d'œuvre*) skilled.

qualité [kalite] *nf* (quality; (*condition sociale etc*) occupation, status; **produit**/*etc* de q. high-quality product/*etc*; **en sa q. de** in one's capacity as. ◆**qualitatif, -ive** *a* qualitative.

quand [kɑ̃] *conj* & *adv* when; **q. je viendrai** when I come; **c'est quand la q.?** (*réunion, mariage*) when is it?; **q. bien même vous le feriez** even if you did it; **q. même** all the same.

quant (à) [kɑ̃ta] *prép* as for.

quantité [kɑ̃tite] *nf* quantity; **une q., des quantités** (*beaucoup*) a lot (de of); **en q.** (*abondamment*) in plenty. ◆**quantifier** *vt* to quantify. ◆**quantitatif, -ive** *a* quantitative.

quarante [karɑ̃t] *a* & *nm* forty. ◆**quarantaine** *nf* **1** **une q. (de)** (*nombre*) (about) forty; **avoir la q.** (*âge*) to be about forty. **2** *Méd* quarantine; **mettre en q.** *Méd* to quarantine; *Fig* to send to Coventry, *Am* give the silent treatment to. **◆quarantième** *a* & *nmf* fortieth.

quart [kar] *nm* **1** quarter; **q. (de litre)** quarter litre, quarter of a litre; **q. d'heure** quarter of an hour; **un mauvais q. d'heure** *Fig* a trying time; **une heure et q.** an hour and a quarter; **il est une heure et q.** it's a quarter past *ou Am* after one; **une heure moins le q.** a quarter to one. **2** *Nau* watch; **de q.** on watch.

quartette [kwartet] *nm* (jazz) quartet(te).

quartier [kartje] *nm* **1** neighbourhood, district; (*chinois etc*) quarter; **de q.** (*cinéma etc*) local; **les gens du q.** the local people. **2** *nm* (*de pomme, lune*) segment. **3** *nm* (*pl*) **quartier(s)** *Mil* quarters; **q. général** headquarters.

quartz [kwarts] *nm* quartz; **montre/etc à q.** quartz watch/*etc.*

quasi [kazi] *adv* almost. **◆quasi-** *préf* near; **q.-obscurité** near darkness. **◆quasiment** *adv* almost.

quatorze [katɔrz] *a* & *nm* fourteen. **◆quatorzième** *a* & *nmf* fourteenth.

quatre [katr] *a* & *nm* four; **se mettre en q.** to go out of one's way (**pour faire** to do); **son q. heures** (*goûter*) one's afternoon snack; **un de ces q.** *Fam* some day soon. **◆quatrième** *a* & *nmf* fourth. **◆quatrièmement** *adv* fourthly.

quatre-vingt(s) [katrəvɛ̃] *a* & *nm* eighty; **q.-vingts ans** eighty years; **q.-vingt-un** eighty-one. **◆q.-vingt-dix** *a* & *nm* ninety.

quatuor [kwatɥɔr] *nm* *Mus* quartet(te).

que [k(ə)] (**qu'** before a vowel or mute h) **1** *conj* that; **je pense qu'elle restera** I think (that) she'll stay; **qu'elle vienne ou non** whether she comes or not; **qu'il s'en aille!** let him leave! **ça fait un an q. je suis là** I've been here for a year; **ça fait un an q. je suis parti** I left a year ago. **2 (ne)** . . . **q.** only; **tu n'as qu'un franc** you only have one franc. **3** (*comparaison*) than; (*avec aussi, même, tel, autant*) as; **plus/moins âgé q. lui** older/younger than him; **aussi sage/etc q.** as wise/*etc* as; **le même q.** the same as. **4** *adv* (*ce*) **qu'il est bête!** (*comme*) how silly he is!; **q. de gens!** (*combien*) what a lot of people! **5** *pron rel* (*chose*) that, which; (*personne*) that, whom; (*temps*) when; **le livre q. j'ai** the book (that *ou* which) I have; **l'ami q. j'ai** the friend (that *ou* whom) I have; **un jour/mois/etc q.** one day/month/*etc* when. **6** *pron interrogatif* what; **q. fait-il?**,

qu'est-ce qu'il fait? what is he doing?; **qu'est-ce qui est dans ta poche?** what's in your pocket?; **q. préférez-vous?** which do you prefer?

Québec [kebɛk] *nm* **le Q.** Quebec.

quel, quelle [kɛl] **1** *a interrogatif* what, which; (*qui*) who; **q. livre/acteur?** what *ou* which book/actor?; **q. livre/acteur préférez-vous?** which *ou* what book/actor do you prefer?; **q. est cet homme?** who is that man?; **je sais q. est ton but** I know what your aim is; **q. qu'il soit** (*chose*) whatever it may be; (*personne*) whoever it *ou* he may be; **– pron interrogatif** which (one); **q. est le meilleur?** which (one) is the best? **2** *a exclamatif* **q. idiot!** what a fool!; **q. joli bébé!** what a pretty baby!

quelconque [kɛlkɔ̃k] *a* any, some (or other); **une raison q.** any reason (whatever *ou* at all), some reason (or other). **2** (*banal*) ordinary.

quelque [kɛlk(ə)] **1** *a* some; **q. jour** some day; **quelques femmes** a few women, some women; **les quelques amies qu'elle a** the few friends she has. **2** *adv* (*environ*) about, some; **et q.** *Fam* and a bit; **q. grand qu'il soit** however tall he may be; **q. numéro qu'elle choisisse** whichever number she chooses; **q. peu** somewhat. **3** *pron* **q.** chose something; (*interrogation*) anything, something; **il a q. chose** *Fig* there's something the matter with him; **q. chose d'autre** something else; **q. chose de grand/etc** something big/*etc*. **4** *adv* **q. part** somewhere; (*interrogation*) anywhere, somewhere.

quelquefois [kɛlkəfwa] *adv* sometimes.

quelques-uns, -unes [kɛlkəzœ̃, -yn] *pron pl* some.

quelqu'un [kɛlkœ̃] *pron* someone, somebody; (*interrogation*) anyone, anybody, someone, somebody; **q. d'intelligent/etc** someone clever/*etc.*

quémander [kemɑ̃de] *vt* to beg for.

qu'en-dira-t-on [kɑ̃diratɔ̃] *nm inv* (*propos*) gossip.

quenelle [kənɛl] *nf* *Culin* quenelle, fish *ou* meat roll.

querelle [kərɛl] *nf* quarrel, dispute. **◆se quereller** *vpr* to quarrel. **◆querelleur, -euse** *a* quarrelsome.

question [kɛstjɔ̃] *nf* question; (*affaire, problème*) matter, issue, question; **il est q. de** it's a matter *ou* question of (**faire** doing); (*on projette de*) there's some question of (**faire** doing); **il n'en est pas q.** there's no question of it, it's out of the question; **en q.** in question; **hors de q.** out of the question;

(re)mettre en q. to (call in) question. ◆**questionner** vt to question (**sur** about).
quête [kɛt] nf 1 (collecte) collection. 2 (recherche) quest (**de** for); **en q. de** in quest ou search of. ◆**quêter** vt to seek, beg for; – vi to collect money.
queue [kø] nf 1 (d'animal) tail; (de fleur) stalk, stem; (de fruit) stalk; (de poêle) handle; (de comète) trail; (de train) handle; (de cortège, train) rear; **q. de cheval** (coiffure) ponytail; **faire une q. de poisson** Aut to cut in (**à qn** in front of s.o.); **à la q. de** (classe) at the bottom of; **à la q. leu leu** (marcher) in single file. 2 (file) queue, Am line; **faire la q.** to queue up, Am line up. 3 (de billard) cue. ◆**q.-de-pie** nf (pl **queues-de-pie**) tails.
qui [ki] pron (personne) who, that; (interrogatif) who; (après prép) whom; (chose) which, that; **l'homme q.** the man who ou that; **la maison q.** the house ou that; **q.?** who?; **q. (est-ce q.) est là?** who's there?; **q. désirez-vous voir?, q. est-ce que vous désirez voir?** who(m) do you want to see?; **sans q.** without whom; **la femme q. je parle** the woman I'm talking about ou about whom I'm talking; **l'ami sur l'aide de q. je compte** the friend on whose help I rely; **q. que vous soyez** whoever you are, whoever you may be; **q. que ce soit** anyone (at all); **à q. est ce livre?** whose book is this?
quiche [kiʃ] nf (tarte) quiche.
quiconque [kikɔ̃k] pron (celui qui) whoever; (n'importe qui) anyone.
quignon [kiɲɔ̃] nm chunk (of bread).
quille [kij] nf 1 (de navire) keel. 2 (de jeu) skittle; pl (jeu) skittles, ninepins. 3 (jambe) Fam leg.
quincaillier, -ière [kɛ̃kaje, -jɛr] nmf hardware dealer, ironmonger. ◆**quincaillerie** nf hardware; (magasin) hardware shop.
quinine [kinin] nf Méd quinine.
quinquennal, -aux [kɛ̃kenal, -o] a (plan) five-year.
quinte [kɛ̃t] nf Méd coughing fit.

quintessence [kɛ̃tesɑ̃s] nf quintessence.
quintette [kɛ̃tɛt] nm Mus quintet(te).
quintuple [kɛ̃typl] a **q. de** fivefold; – nm le **q. de** five times as much as. ◆**quintupl/er** vti to increase fivefold. ◆**–és, -ées** nmfpl (enfants) quintuplets, quins.
quinze [kɛ̃z] a & nm fifteen; **q. jours** two weeks, fortnight. ◆**quinzaine** nf **une q. (de)** (nombre) (about) fifteen; **q. (de jours)** two weeks, fortnight. ◆**quinzième** a & nmf fifteenth.
quiproquo [kiprɔkɔ] nm misunderstanding.
quittance [kitɑ̃s] nf receipt.
quitte [kit] a quits, even (**envers** with); **q. à faire** even if it means doing; **en être q. pour une amende**/etc to (be lucky enough to) get off with a fine/etc.
quitter [kite] vt to leave; (ôter) to take off; – vi **ne quittez pas!** Tél hold the line!, hold on!; – **se q.** vpr (se séparer) to part.
qui-vive (sur le) [syrləkiviv] adv on the alert.
quoi [kwa] pron what; (après prép) which; **à q. penses-tu?** what are you thinking about?; **après q.** after which; **ce à q. je m'attendais** what I was expecting; **de q. manger**/etc (assez) enough to eat/etc; **de q. couper/écrire**/etc (instrument) something to cut/write/etc; **q. que je dise** whatever I say; **q. que ce soit** anything (at all); **q. qu'il en soit** be that as it may; **il n'y a pas de q.!** (en réponse à 'merci') don't mention it!; **q.?** what?; **c'est un idiot, q.!** (non traduit) Fam he's a fool!
quoique [kwak(ə)] conj (+ sub) (al)though.
quolibet [kɔlibɛ] nm Litt gibe.
quorum [k(w)ɔrɔm] nm quorum.
quota [k(w)ɔta] nm quota.
quote-part [kɔtpar] nf (pl **quotes-parts**) share.
quotidien, -ienne [kɔtidjɛ̃, -jɛn] a (journalier) daily; (banal) everyday; – nm daily (paper). ◆**quotidiennement** adv daily.
quotient [kɔsjɑ̃] nm quotient.

R

R, r [ɛr] nm R, r.
rabâch/er [rabaʃe] vt to repeat endlessly; – vi to repeat oneself ◆**–age** nm endless repetition.
rabais [rabɛ] nm (price) reduction, dis-

count; **au r.** (acheter) cheap, at a reduction.
rabaisser [rabese] vt (dénigrer) to belittle, humble; **r. à** (ravaler) to reduce to.
rabat-joie [rabaʒwa] nm inv killjoy.

rabattre [rabatr] vt (baisser) to put ou pull down; (refermer) to close (down); (replier) to fold down ou over; (déduire) to take off; **en r.** (prétentieux) Fig to climb down (from one's high horse); — **se r.** vpr (se refermer) to close; (après avoir doublé) Aut to cut in (devant in front of); **se r. sur** Fig to fall back on.

rabbin [rabɛ̃] nm rabbi; **grand r.** chief rabbi.

rabibocher [rabibɔʃe] vt (réconcilier) Fam to patch it up between; — **se r.** vpr Fam to patch it up.

rabiot [rabjo] nm (surplus) Fam extra (helping); **faire du r.** Fam to work extra time.

râblé [rɑble] a stocky, thickset.

rabot [rabo] nm (outil) plane. ◆**raboter** vt to plane.

raboteux, -euse [rabotø, -øz] a uneven, rough.

rabougri [rabugri] a (personne, plante) stunted.

rabrouer [rabrue] vt to snub, rebuff.

racaille [rakaj] nf rabble, riffraff.

raccommod/er [rakɔmɔde] **1** vt to mend; (chaussette) to darn. **2** vt (réconcilier) Fam to reconcile; — **se r.** vpr Fam to make it up (avec with). ◆**—age** nm mending; darning.

raccompagner [rakɔ̃paɲe] vt to see ou take back (home); **r. à la porte** to see to the door, see out.

raccord [rakɔr] nm (dispositif) connection; (de papier peint) join; **r. (de peinture)** touch-up. ◆**raccord/er** vt, — **se r.** vpr to connect (up), join (up) (à with, to). ◆**—ement** nm (action, résultat) connection.

raccourc/ir [rakursir] vt to shorten; — vi to get shorter; (au lavage) to shrink. ◆**—i** nm **1** (chemin) short cut. **2** en r. (histoire etc) in a nutshell.

raccroc (par) [parrakro] adv by a (lucky) chance.

raccrocher [rakrɔʃe] vt to hang back up; (récepteur) Tél to put down; (relier) to connect (à with, to); (client) to accost; **se r. à** to hold on to, cling to; (se rapporter à) to link (up) with; — vi Tél to hang up, ring off.

race [ras] nf (groupe ethnique) race; (animale) breed; (famille) stock; (engeance) Péj breed; **de r.** (chien) pedigree-; (cheval) thoroughbred. ◆**racé** a (chien) pedigree-; (cheval) thoroughbred; (personne) distinguished. ◆**racial, -aux** a racial. ◆**racisme** nm racism, racialism. ◆**raciste** a & nmf racist, racialist.

rachat [raʃa] nm Com repurchase; (de firme)

take-over; Rel redemption. ◆**racheter** vt to buy back; (objet d'occasion) to buy; (nouvel article) to buy another; (firme) to take over, buy out; (pécheur, dette) to redeem; (compenser) to make up for; **r. des chaussettes/du pain**/etc to buy (some) more socks/bread/etc; — **se r.** vpr to make amends, redeem oneself.

racine [rasin] nf (de plante, personne etc) & Math root; **prendre r.** (plante) & Fig to take root.

racket [raket] nm (association) racket; (activité) racketeering.

raclée [rɑkle] nf Fam hiding, thrashing.

racler [rɑkle] vt to scrape; (enlever) to scrape off; **se r. la gorge** to clear one's throat. ◆**raclette** nf scraper; (à vitres) squeegee. ◆**racloir** nm scraper. ◆**raclures** nfpl (déchets) scrapings.

racol/er [rakɔle] vt (prostituée) to solicit (s.o.); (vendeur etc) to tout for (s.o.), solicit (s.o.). ◆**—age** nm soliciting; touting. ◆**—eur, -euse** nmf tout.

raconter [rakɔ̃te] vt (histoire) to tell, relate; (décrire) to describe; **r. qch à qn** (vacances etc) to tell s.o. about sth; **r. à qn que** to tell s.o. that, say to s.o. that. ◆**racontars** nmpl gossip, stories.

racornir [rakɔrnir] vt to harden; — **se r.** vpr to get hard.

radar [radar] nm radar; **contrôle r.** (pour véhicules etc) radar control. ◆**radariste** nmf radar operator.

rade [rad] nf **1** Nau (natural) harbour. **2** **laisser en r.** to leave stranded, abandon; **rester en r.** to be left behind.

radeau, -x [rado] nm raft.

radiateur [radjatœr] nm (à eau) & Aut radiator; (électrique, à gaz) heater.

radiation [radjasjɔ̃] nf **1** Phys radiation. **2** (suppression) removal (de from).

radical, -ale, -aux [radikal, -o] a radical; — nm Ling stem; — nmf Pol radical.

radier [radje] vt to strike ou cross off (de from).

radieux, -euse [radjø, -øz] a (personne, visage) radiant, beaming; (soleil) brilliant; (temps) glorious.

radin, -ine [radɛ̃, -in] a Fam stingy; — nmf Fam skinflint.

radio [radjo] nf **1** radio; (poste) radio (set); **à la r.** on the radio. **2** nf (photo) Méd X-ray; **passer ou faire une r.** to be X-rayed, have an X-ray. **3** nm (opérateur) radio operator. ◆**radioactif, -ive** a radioactive. ◆**radioactivité** nf radioactivity. ◆**radiodiffuser** vt to broadcast (on the radio). ◆**radio-**

diffusion *nf* broadcasting. ◆**radiographie** *nf* (*photo*) X-ray; (*technique*) radiography. ◆**radiographier** *vt* to X-ray. ◆**radiologie** *nf Méd* radiology. ◆**radiologue** *nmf* (*technicien*) radiographer; (*médecin*) radiologist. ◆**radiophonique** *a* (*programme*) radio-. ◆**radiotélévisé** *a* a broadcast on radio and television.

radis [radi] *nm* radish; **r. noir** horseradish.

radot/er [radɔte] *vi* to drivel (on), ramble (on). ◆—**age** *nm* (*propos*) drivel.

radouc/ir (se) [səradusir] *vpr* to calm down; (*temps*) to become milder. ◆—**issement** *nm* **r. (du temps)** milder weather.

rafale [rafal] *nf* (*vent*) gust, squall; (*de mitrailleuse*) burst; (*de balles*) hail.

raffermir [rafɛrmir] *vt* to strengthen; (*muscles etc*) to tone up; — **se r.** *vpr* to become stronger.

raffin/er [rafine] *vt* (*pétrole, sucre, manières*) to refine. ◆—**é** *a* refined. ◆—**age** *nm* (*du pétrole, sucre*) refining. ◆—**ement** *nm* (*de personne*) refinement. ◆**raffinerie** *nf* refinery.

raffoler [rafɔle] *vi* **r. de** (*aimer*) to be very fond of, be mad *ou* wild about.

raffut [rafy] *nm Fam* din, row.

rafiot [rafjo] *nm* (*bateau*) *Péj* (old) tub.

rafistoler [rafistɔle] *vt Fam* to patch up.

rafle [rafl] *nf* (*police*) raid.

rafler [rafle] *vt* (*enlever*) *Fam* to swipe, make off with.

rafraîch/ir [rafreʃir] *vt* to cool (down); (*remettre à neuf*) to brighten up; (*mémoire, personne*) to refresh; — *vi* **mettre à r.** *Culin* to chill; — **se r.** *vpr* (*boire*) to refresh oneself; (*se laver*) to freshen (oneself) up; (*temps*) to get cooler. ◆—**issant** *a* refreshing. ◆—**issement** *nm* **1** (*de température*) cooling. **2** (*boisson*) cold drink; *pl* (*fruits, glaces etc*) refreshments.

ragaillardir [ragajardir] *vt* to buck up.

rage [raʒ] *nf* **1** (*colère*) rage; **r. de dents** violent toothache; **faire r.** (*incendie, tempête*) to rage. **2** (*maladie*) rabies. ◆**rager** *vi* (*personne*) *Fam* to rage, fume. ◆**rageant** *a Fam* infuriating. ◆**rageur, -euse** *a* bad-tempered, furious.

ragots [rago] *nmpl Fam* gossip.

ragoût [ragu] *nm Culin* stew.

ragoûtant [ragutɑ̃] *a* **peu r.** (*mets, personne*) unsavoury.

raid [red] *nm* (*incursion, attaque*) *Mil Av* raid.

raide [red] *a* (*rigide, guindé*) stiff; (*côte*) steep; (*cheveux*) straight; (*corde etc*) tight; **c'est r.!** (*exagéré*) *Fam* it's a bit stiff *ou*

much!; — *adv* (*grimper*) steeply; **tomber r. mort** to drop dead. ◆**raideur** *nf* stiffness; steepness. ◆**raidillon** *nm* (*pente*) short steep rise. ◆**raidir** *vt*, — **se r.** *vpr* to stiffen; (*corde*) to tighten; (*position*) to harden; **se r. contre** *Fig* to steel oneself against.

raie [rɛ] *nf* **1** (*trait*) line; (*de tissu, zèbre*) stripe; (*de cheveux*) parting, *Am* part. **2** (*poisson*) skate, ray.

rail [raj] *nm* (*barre*) rail; **le r.** (*transport*) rail.

railler [raje] *vt* to mock, make fun of. ◆**raillerie** *nf* gibe, mocking remark. ◆**railleur, -euse** *a* mocking.

rainure [renyr] *nf* groove.

raisin [rezɛ̃] *nm* **raisin(s)** grapes; **grain de r.** grape; **manger du r.** *ou* **des raisins** to eat grapes; **r. sec** raisin.

raison [rezɔ̃] *nf* **1** (*faculté, motif*) reason; **entendre r.** to listen to reason; **la r.** **pour laquelle je . . .** the reason (why *ou* that) I . . . ; **pour raisons de famille/de santé/etc** for family/health/*etc* reasons; **en r. de** (*cause*) on account of; **à r. de** (*proportion*) at the rate of; **avoir r. de qn ou qch** to get the better of s.o./sth; **mariage de r.** marriage of convenience; **à plus forte r.** all the more so; **r. de plus** all the more reason (**pour faire** to do, for doing). **2** **avoir r.** to be right (**de faire** to do, in doing); **donner r. à qn** to agree with s.o.; (*événement etc*) to prove s.o. right; **avec r.** rightly. ◆**raisonnable** *a* reasonable. ◆**raisonnablement** *adv* reasonably.

raisonn/er [rezɔne] *vi* (*penser*) to reason; (*discuter*) to argue; — *vt* **r. qn** to reason with s.o. ◆—**é** *a* (*projet*) well-thought-out. ◆—**ement** *nm* (*faculté, activité*) reasoning; (*propositions*) argument. ◆—**eur, -euse** *a Péj* argumentative; — *nmf Péj* arguer.

rajeun/ir [raʒœnir] *vt* to make (feel *ou* look) younger; (*personnel*) to infuse new blood into; (*moderniser*) to modernize, update; (*personne âgée*) *Méd* to rejuvenate; — *vi* to get *ou* feel *ou* look younger. ◆—**issant** *a Méd* rejuvenating. ◆—**issement** *nm Méd* rejuvenation; **le r. de la population** the population getting younger.

rajout [raʒu] *nm* addition. ◆**rajouter** *vt* to add (**à** to); *Fig* to overdo it.

rajuster [raʒyste] *vt* (*mécanisme*) to readjust; (*lunettes, vêtements*) to straighten, adjust; (*cheveux*) to rearrange; — **se r.** *vpr* to straighten out by oneself up.

râle [rɑl] *nm* (*de blessé*) groan; (*de mourant*) death rattle. ◆**râler** *vi* (*blessé*) to groan; (*mourant*) to give the death rattle; (*protes-*

er) *Fam* to grouse, moan. ◆**râleur, -euse** *nmf Fam* grouser, moaner.

ralent/ir [ralɑ̃tir] *vti*, — **se r.** *vpr* to slow down. ◆—**i** *nm Cin TV* slow motion; **au r.** (*filmer, travailler*) in slow motion; (*vivre*) at a slower pace; **tourner au r.** (*moteur, usine*) to idle, tick over, *Am* turn over.

rallier [ralje] *vt* (*rassembler*) to rally; (*rejoindre*) to rejoin; **r. qn à** (*convertir*) to win s.o. over to; — **se r.** *vpr* (*se regrouper*) to rally; **se r. à** (*point de vue*) to come over *ou* round to.

rallonge [ralɔ̃ʒ] *nf* (*de table*) extension; (*fil électrique*) extension (lead); **une r. de** (*supplément*) *Fam* (some) extra. ◆**rallonger** *vti* to lengthen.

rallumer [ralyme] *vt* to light again, relight; (*lampe*) to switch on again; (*conflit, haine*) to rekindle; — **se r.** *vpr* (*guerre, incendie*) to flare up again.

rallye [rali] *nm Sp Aut* rally.

ramage [ramaʒ] **1** *nm* (*d'oiseaux*) song, warbling. **2** *nmpl* (*dessin*) foliage.

ramass/er [ramɑse] **1** *vt* (*prendre par terre, réunir*) to pick up; (*ordures, copies*) to collect, pick up; (*fruits, coquillages*) to gather; (*rhume, amende*) *Fam* to pick up, get; **r. une bûche** *ou* **une pelle** *Fam* to come a cropper, *Am* take a spill. **2 se r.** *vpr* (*se pelotonner*) to curl up. ◆—**é** *a* (*trapu*) squat, stocky; (*recroquevillé*) huddled; (*concis*) compact. ◆—**age** *nm* picking up; collection; gathering; **r. scolaire** school bus service.

ramassis [ramɑsi] *nm* **r. de** (*voyous etc*) *Péj* bunch of.

rambarde [rɑ̃bard] *nf* guardrail.

rame [ram] *nf* **1** (*aviron*) oar. **2** (*de métro*) train. **3** (*de papier*) ream. ◆**ramer** *vi* to row. ◆**rameur, -euse** *nmf* rower.

rameau, -x [ramo] *nm* branch; **les Rameaux** *Rel* Palm Sunday.

ramener [ramne] *vt* to bring *ou* take back; (*paix, calme, ordre etc*) to restore, bring back; (*remettre en place*) to put back; **r. à** (*réduire à*) to reduce to; **r. à la vie** to bring back to life; — **se r.** *vpr* (*arriver*) *Fam* to turn up; **se r. à** (*problème etc*) to boil down to.

ramier [ramje] *nm* (**pigeon**) **r.** wood pigeon.

ramification [ramifikɑsjɔ̃] *nf* ramification.

ramoll/ir [ramɔlir] *vt*, — **se r.** *vpr* to soften. ◆—**i** *a* soft; (*personne*) soft-headed.

ramon/er [ramɔne] *vt* (*cheminée*) to sweep. ◆—**age** *nm* (chimney) sweeping. ◆—**eur** *nm* (chimney)sweep.

rampe [rɑ̃p] *nf* **1** (*pente*) ramp, slope; **r. de lancement** (*de fusées etc*) launch(ing) pad. **2**

(*d'escalier*) banister(s). **3** (*projecteurs*) *Th* footlights.

ramper [rɑ̃pe] *vi* to crawl; (*plante*) to creep; **r. devant** *Fig* to cringe *ou* crawl to.

rancard [rɑ̃kar] *nm Fam* (*rendez-vous*) date; (*renseignement*) tip.

rancart [rɑ̃kar] *nm* **mettre au r.** *Fam* to throw out, scrap.

rance [rɑ̃s] *a* rancid. ◆**rancir** *vi* to turn rancid.

ranch [rɑ̃tʃ] *nm* ranch.

rancœur [rɑ̃kœr] *nf* rancour, resentment.

rançon [rɑ̃sɔ̃] *nf* ransom; **la r. de** (*inconvénient*) the price of (*success, fame etc*). ◆**rançonner** *vt* to hold to ransom.

rancune [rɑ̃kyn] *nf* grudge; **garder r. à qn** to bear s.o. a grudge; **sans r.!** no hard feelings! ◆**rancunier, -ière** *a* vindictive, resentful.

randonnée [rɑ̃dɔne] *nf* (*à pied*) walk, hike; (*en voiture*) drive, ride; (*en vélo*) ride.

rang [rɑ̃] *nm* (*rangée*) row, line; (*condition, grade, classement*) rank; **les rangs** (*hommes*) *Mil* the ranks (**de** of); **les rangs de ses ennemis** (*nombre*) *Fig* the ranks of his enemies; **se mettre en rang(s)** to line up (*par trois/etc* in threes/*etc*); **par r. de** in order of. ◆**rangée** *nf* row, line.

rang/er [rɑ̃ʒe] *vt* (*papiers, vaisselle etc*) to put away; (*chambre etc*) to tidy (up); (*chiffres, mots*) to arrange; (*voiture*) to park; **r. parmi** (*auteur etc*) to rank among; — **se r.** *vpr* (*élèves etc*) to line up; (*s'écarter*) to stand aside; (*voiture*) to pull over; (*s'assagir*) to settle down; **se r. à** (*avis de qn*) to fall in with. ◆—**é** *a* (*chambre etc*) tidy; (*personne*) steady; (*bataille*) pitched. ◆—**ement** *nm* putting away; (*de chambre etc*) tidying (up); (*espace*) storage space.

ranimer [ranime] *vt* (*réanimer, revigorer*) to revive; (*encourager*) to spur on; (*feu, querelle*) to rekindle.

rapace [rapas] **1** *a* (*avide*) grasping. **2** *nm* (*oiseau*) bird of prey.

rapatrier [rapatrije] *vt* to repatriate. ◆**rapatriement** *nm* repatriation.

râpe [rɑp] *nf Culin* grater; shredder; (*lime*) rasp. ◆**râp/er** *vt* (*fromage*) to grate; (*carottes etc*) to shred; (*finement*) to grate; (*bois*) to rasp. ◆—**é 1** (*fromage*) grated; — *nm* grated cheese. **2** *a* (*vêtement*) threadbare.

rapetisser [raptise] *vt* to make (look) smaller; (*vêtement*) to shorten; — *vi* to get smaller; (*au lavage*) to shrink; (*jours*) to get shorter.

râpeux, -euse [rɑpø, -øz] *a* rough.

raphia [rafja] *nm* raffia.

rapide [rapid] *a* fast, quick, rapid; (*pente*) steep; — *nm* (*train*) express (train); (*de fleuve*) rapid. ◆**—ment** *adv* fast, quickly, rapidly. ◆**rapidité** *nf* speed, rapidity.

rapiécer [rapjese] *vt* to patch (up).

rappel [rapɛl] *nm* (*de diplomate etc*) recall; (*évocation, souvenir*) reminder; (*paiement*) back pay; *pl Th* curtain calls; (*vaccination de*) r. *Méd* booster; r. **à l'ordre** call to order. ◆**rappeler** *vt* (*pour faire revenir*) & *Tél* to call back; (*diplomate, souvenir*) to recall; r. **qch à qn** (*redire*) to remind s.o. of sth; — *vi Tél* to call back; — **se r.** *vpr* (*histoire, personne etc*) to remember, recall, recollect.

rappliquer [raplike] *vi* (*arriver*) *Fam* to show up.

rapport [rapɔr] *nm* **1** (*lien*) connection, link; *pl* (*entre personnes*) relations; **rapports** (**sexuels**) (sexual) intercourse; **par r. à** compared to *ou* with; (*envers*) towards; **se mettre en r. avec qn** to get in touch with s.o.; **en r. avec** in keeping with; **sous le r. de** from the point of view of. **2** (*revenu*) *Com* return, yield. **3** (*récit*) report. ◆**rapporter 1** (*ramener*) to bring *ou* take back; (*ajouter*) to add; — *vi* (*chien*) to retrieve. **2** *vt* (*récit*) to report; (*mot célèbre*) to repeat; — *vi* (*moucharder*) *Fam* to tell tales. **3** *vt* (*profit*) *Com* to bring in, yield; — *vi* (*investissement*) *Com* to bring in a good return. **4** *vt* **r. qch à** (*rattacher*) to relate sth to; **se r. à** to relate to, be connected with; **s'en r. à** to rely on. ◆**rapporteur, -euse 1** *nmf* (*mouchard*) telltale. **2** *nm Jur* reporter. **3** *nm Géom* protractor.

rapprocher [raprɔʃe] *vt* to bring closer (**de** to); (*chaise*) to pull up (**de** to); (*réconcilier*) to bring together; (*réunir*) to join; (*comparer*) to compare; — **se r.** *vpr* to come *ou* get closer (**de** to); (*se réconcilier*) to come together, be reconciled; (*ressembler*) to be close (**de** to). ◆**—é** *a* close, near; (*yeux*) close-set; (*fréquent*) frequent. ◆**—ement** *nm* (*réconciliation*) reconciliation; (*rapport*) connection; (*comparaison*) comparison.

rapt [rapt] *nm* (*d'enfant*) abduction.

raquette [rakɛt] *nf* (*de tennis*) racket; (*de ping-pong*) bat.

rare [rar] *a* rare; (*argent, main-d'œuvre etc*) scarce; (*barbe, herbe*) sparse; **il est r. que** (+ *sub*) it's seldom *ou* rare that. ◆**se raréfier** *vpr* (*denrées etc*) to get scarce. ◆**rarement** *adv* rarely, seldom. ◆**rareté** *nf* rarity; scarcity; **une r.** (*objet*) a rarity.

ras [rɑ] *a* (*cheveux*) close-cropped; (*herbe, poil*) short; (*mesure*) full; **en rase campagne**

in (the) open country; **à r.** de very close to; **à r. bord** (*remplir*) to the brim; **en avoir r. le bol** *Fam* to be fed up (**de** with); **pull (au) r. du cou** *ou* **à col r.** crew-neck(ed) pullover; — *adv* short.

raser [rɑze] *vt* **1** (*menton, personne*) to shave; (*barbe, moustache*) to shave off; — **se r.** *vpr* (have a) shave. **2** *vt* (*démolir*) to raze, knock down. **3** *vt* (*frôler*) to skim, brush. **4** *vt* (*ennuyer*) *Fam* to bore. ◆**—ant** *a Fam* boring. ◆**—é** *a* **bien r.** clean-shaven; **mal r.** unshaven. ◆**—age** *nm* shaving. ◆**—eur, -euse** *nmf Fam* bore. ◆**rasoir 1** *nm* shaver. **2** *a inv Fam* boring.

rassasier [rasazje] *vt* to satisfy; **être rassasié** to have had enough (**de** of).

rassembler [rasɑ̃ble] *vt* to gather (together), assemble; (*courage*) to summon up, muster; — **se r.** *vpr* to gather, assemble. ◆**rassemblement** [-əmɑ̃] *nm* (*action, gens*) gathering.

rasseoir (**se**) [səraswar] *vpr* to sit down again.

rassis, *f* **rassie** [rasi] *a* (*pain, brioche etc*) stale. ◆**rassir** *vti* to turn stale.

rassurer [rasyre] *vt* to reassure; **rassure-toi** set your mind at rest, don't worry. ◆**—ant** *a* (*nouvelle*) reassuring, comforting.

rat [ra] *nm* rat; **r. de bibliothèque** *Fig* bookworm.

ratatiner (**se**) [səratatine] *vpr* to shrivel (up); (*vieillard*) to become wizened.

rate [rat] *nf Anat* spleen.

râteau, -x [rɑto] *nm* (*outil*) rake.

râtelier [rɑtəlje] *nm* **1** (*support pour outils, armes etc*) rack. **2** (*dentier*) *Fam* set of false teeth.

rater [rate] *vt* (*bus, cible, occasion etc*) to miss; (*gâcher*) to spoil, ruin; (*vie*) to waste; (*examen*) to fail; — *vi* (*projet etc*) to fail; (*pistolet*) to misfire. ◆**—é, -ée 1** *nmf* (*personne*) failure. **2** *nmpl* **avoir des ratés** *Aut* to backfire. ◆**—age** *nm* (*échec*) *Fam* failure.

ratifier [ratifje] *vt* to ratify. ◆**ratification** *nf* ratification.

ration [rasjɔ̃] *nf* ration; **r. de** *Fig* share of. ◆**rationner** *vt* (*vivres, personne*) to ration. ◆**—ement** *nm* rationing.

rationaliser [rasjɔnalize] *vt* to rationalize. ◆**rationalisation** *nf* rationalization.

rationnel, -elle [rasjɔnɛl] *a* (*pensée, méthode*) rational.

ratisser [ratise] *vt* **1** (*allée etc*) to rake; (*feuilles etc*) to rake up. **2** (*fouiller*) to comb. **3** **r. qn** (*au jeu*) *Fam* to clean s.o. out.

raton [ratɔ̃] *nm* **r. laveur** rac(c)oon.

rattacher [rataʃe] *vt* to tie up again; (*in-*

corporer, joindre) to join (à to); (*idée, question*) to link (à to); r. **qn à** (*son pays etc*) to bind s.o. to; **se r. à** to be linked to. ◆**—ement** nm (*annexion*) joining (à to).

rattrap/er [ratrape] vt to catch; (*prisonnier etc*) to recapture; (*erreur, temps perdu*) to make up for; (*rejoindre*) to catch up with s.o., catch s.o. up; — **se r.** vpr to catch up; (*se dédommager, prendre une compensation*) to make up for it; **se r. à** (*branche etc*) to catch hold of. ◆**—age** nm **cours de r.** *Scol* remedial classes; **r. des prix/salaires** adjustment of prices/wages (*to the cost of living*).

rature [ratyr] nf deletion. ◆**raturer** vt to delete, cross out.

rauque [rok] a (*voix*) hoarse, raucous.

ravages [ravaʒ] nmpl devastation; (*de la maladie, du temps*) ravages; **faire des r.** to wreak havoc. ◆**ravager** vt to devastate, ravage.

raval/er [ravale] vt **1** (*façade etc*) to clean (and restore). **2** (*salive, sanglots*) to swallow. **3** (*avilir*) *Litt* to lower. ◆**—ement** nm (*de façade etc*) cleaning (and restoration).

ravi [ravi] a delighted (**de** with, **de faire** to do).

ravier [ravje] nm hors-d'œuvre dish.

ravigoter [ravigote] vt *Fam* to buck up.

ravin [ravɛ̃] nm ravine, gully.

ravioli [ravjɔli] nmpl ravioli.

rav/ir [ravir] vt **1** to delight; **à r.** (*chanter etc*) delightfully. **2** (*emporter*) to snatch (à from). ◆**—issant** a delightful, lovely. ◆**ravisseur, -euse** nmf kidnapper.

raviser (se) [səravize] vpr to change one's mind.

ravitaill/er [ravitaje] vt to provide with supplies, supply; (*avion*) to refuel; — **se r.** vpr to stock up (with supplies). ◆**—ement** nm supplying; refuelling; (*denrées*) supplies; **aller au r.** (*faire des courses*) *Fam* to stock up, get stocks in.

raviver [ravive] vt (*feu, sentiment*) to revive; (*couleurs*) to brighten up.

ray/er [reje] vt (*érafler*) to scratch; (*mot etc*) to cross out; **r. qn de** (*liste*) to cross ou strike s.o. off. ◆**—é** a scratched; (*tissu*) striped; (*papier*) lined, ruled. ◆**rayure** nf scratch; (*bande*) stripe; **à rayures** striped.

rayon [rɛjɔ̃] nm **1** (*de lumière, soleil etc*) *Phys* ray; (*de cercle*) radius; (*de roue*) spoke; (*d'espoir*) *Fig* ray; **r. X** X-ray; **r. d'action** range; **dans un r. de** within a radius of. **2** (*planche*) shelf; (*de magasin*) department. **3** (*de ruche*) honeycomb. ◆**rayonnage** nm shelving, shelves.

rayonn/er [rɛjɔne] vi to radiate; (*dans une région*) to travel around (*from a central base*); **r. de joie** to beam with joy. ◆**—ant** a (*visage etc*) radiant, beaming (**de** with). ◆**—ement** nm (*éclat*) radiance; (*influence*) influence; (*radiation*) radiation.

raz-de-marée [rɑdmare] nm inv tidal wave; (*bouleversement*) *Fig* upheaval; **r.-de-marée électoral** landslide.

razzia [ra(d)zja] nf **faire une r. sur** (*tout enlever sur*) *Fam* to raid.

re- [r(ə)] préf re-.

ré- [re] préf re-.

réabonn/er (se) [səreabɔne] vpr to renew one's subscription (à to). ◆**—ement** nm renewal of subscription.

réacteur [reaktœr] nm (*d'avion*) jet engine; (*nucléaire*) reactor.

réaction [reaksjɔ̃] nf reaction; **r. en chaîne** chain reaction; **avion à r.** jet (aircraft); **moteur à r.** jet engine. ◆**réactionnaire** a & nmf reactionary.

réadapter [readapte] vt, — **se r.** vpr to readjust (à to). ◆**réadaptation** nf readjustment.

réaffirmer [reafirme] vt to reaffirm.

réagir [reaʒir] vi to react (**contre** against, **à** to); (*se secouer*) *Fig* to shake oneself out of it.

réalis/er [realize] vt (*projet etc*) to carry out, realize; (*ambition, rêve*) to fulfil; (*achat, bénéfice, vente*) to make; (*film*) to direct; (*capital*) *Com* to realize; (*se rendre compte*) to realize (**que** that); — **se r.** vpr (*vœu*) to come true; (*projet*) to be carried out; (*personne*) to fulfil oneself. ◆**—able** a (*plan*) workable; (*rêve*) attainable. ◆**réalisateur, -trice** nmf *Cin* *TV* director. ◆**réalisation** nf realization; (*de rêve*) fulfilment; *Cin* *TV* direction; (*œuvre*) achievement.

réalisme [realism] nm realism. ◆**réaliste** a realistic; — nmf realist.

réalité [realite] nf reality; **en r.** (in) actual fact, in reality.

réanimer [reanime] vt *Méd* to resuscitate. ◆**réanimation** nf resuscitation; (**service de**) **r.** intensive care unit.

réapparaître [reaparetr] vi to reappear. ◆**réapparition** nf reappearance.

réarmer [rearme] vt (*fusil etc*) to reload; — vi, — **se r.** vpr (*pays*) to rearm. ◆**réarmement** nm rearmament.

rébarbatif, -ive [rebarbatif, -iv] a forbidding, off-putting.

rebâtir [r(ə)batir] vt to rebuild.

rebattu [r(ə)baty] a (*sujet*) hackneyed.

rebelle [rəbɛl] *a* rebellious; (*troupes*) rebel-; (*fièvre*) stubborn; (*mèche*) unruly; r. à resistant to; — *nmf* rebel. ◆**se rebeller** *vpr* to rebel (contre against). ◆**rébellion** *nf* rebellion.

rebiffer (se) [sərəbife] *vpr Fam* to rebel.

rebond [r(ə)bɔ̃] *nm* bounce; (*par ricochet*) rebound. ◆**rebondir** *vi* to bounce; to rebound; (faire) r. (*affaire, discussion etc*) to get going again. ◆**rebondissement** *nm* new development (de in).

rebondi [r(ə)bɔ̃di] *a* chubby, rounded.

rebord [r(ə)bɔr] *nm* edge; (*de plat etc*) rim; (*de vêtement*) hem; r. de (la) fenêtre windowsill, window ledge.

reboucher [r(ə)buʃe] *vt* (*flacon*) to put the top back on.

rebours (à) [ar(ə)bur] *adv* the wrong way.

rebrousse-poil (à) [arbruspwal] *adv* prendre qn à r.-poil *Fig* to rub s.o. up the wrong way.

rebrousser [r(ə)bruse] *vt* r. chemin to turn back.

rebuffade [rəbyfad] *nf Litt* rebuff.

rébus [rebys] *nm inv* (*jeu*) rebus.

rebut [rəby] *nm* mettre au r. to throw out, scrap; le r. de la société *Péj* the dregs of society.

rebut/er [r(ə)byte] *vt* (*décourager*) to put off; (*choquer*) to repel. ◆**-ant** *a* offputting; (*choquant*) repellent.

récalcitrant [rekalsitrã] *a* recalcitrant.

recaler [r(ə)kale] *vt* r. qn *Scol Fam* to fail s.o., flunk s.o.; être recalé, se faire r. *Scol Fam* to fail, flunk.

récapituler [rekapityle] *vti* to recapitulate. ◆**récapitulation** *nf* recapitulation.

recel [rəsɛl] *nm* receiving stolen goods, fencing; harbouring. ◆**receler** *vt* (*mystère, secret etc*) to contain; (*objet volé*) to receive; (*malfaiteur*) to harbour. ◆**receleur, -euse** *nmf* receiver (of stolen goods), fence.

recens/er [r(ə)sãse] *vt* (*population*) to take a census of; (*inventorier*) to make an inventory of. ◆**-ement** *nm* census; inventory.

récent [resã] *a* recent. ◆**récemment** [-amã] *adv* recently.

récépissé [resepise] *nm* (*reçu*) receipt.

récepteur [reseptœr] *nm Tél* receiver. ◆**réceptif, -ive** *a* receptive (à to). ◆**réception** *nf* (*accueil, soirée*) & *Rad* reception; (*de lettre*) *Com* receipt; (*d'hôtel etc*) reception (desk). ◆**réceptionniste** *nmf* receptionist.

récession [resesjɔ̃] *nf Écon* recession.

recette [r(ə)sɛt] *nf* 1 *Culin* & *Fig* recipe. 2

(*argent, bénéfice*) takings; (*bureau*) tax office; **recettes** (*rentrées*) *Com* receipts; faire r. *Fig* to be a success.

recev/oir* [rəsvwar] *vt* to receive; (*obtenir*) to get, receive; (*accueillir*) to welcome; (*accepter*) to accept; être reçu à (*examen*) to pass; être reçu premier to come first; — *vi* to receive guests *ou* visitors *ou* *Méd* patients. ◆**-able** *a* (*excuse etc*) admissible. ◆**-eur, -euse** *nmf* (*d'autobus*) (bus) conductor, (bus) conductress; (*des impôts*) tax collector; (*des postes*) postmaster, postmistress.

rechange (de) [dər(ə)ʃãʒ] *a* (*pièce, outil etc*) spare; (*solution etc*) alternative; **vêtements/chaussures de r.** a change of clothes/shoes.

rechapé [r(ə)ʃape] *a* pneu r. retread.

réchapper [reʃape] *vi* r. de *ou* à (*accident etc*) to come through.

recharge [r(ə)ʃarʒ] *nf* (*de stylo etc*) refill. ◆**recharger** *vt* (*camion, fusil*) to reload; (*briquet, stylo etc*) to refill; (*batterie*) to recharge.

réchaud [reʃo] *nm* (portable) stove.

réchauff/er [reʃofe] *vt* (*personne, aliment etc*) to warm up; — se r. *vpr* to warm oneself up; (*temps*) to get warmer. ◆**-é** *nm* du r. *Fig Péj* old hat. ◆**-ement** *nm* (*de température*) rise (de in).

rêche [rɛʃ] *a* rough, harsh.

recherche [r(ə)ʃɛrʃ] *nf* 1 search, quest (de for); à la r. de in search of. 2 la r., des recherches (*scientifique etc*) research (sur on, into); faire des recherches to research; (*enquête*) to make investigations. 3 (*raffinement*) studied elegance; *Péj* affectation. ◆**recherch/er** *vt* to search *ou* hunt for; (*cause, faveur, perfection*) to seek. ◆**-é** *a* 1 (*très demandé*) in great demand; (*rare*) much sought-after; r. pour meurtre wanted for murder. 2 (*élégant*) elegant; *Péj* affected.

rechigner [r(ə)ʃine] *vi* (*renâcler*) to jib (à qch at sth, à faire at doing).

rechute [r(ə)ʃyt] *nf Méd* relapse. ◆**rechuter** *vi Méd* to (have a) relapse.

récidive [residiv] *nf Jur* further offence; *Méd* recurrence (de of). ◆**récidiver** *vi Jur* to commit a further offence; (*maladie*) to recur. ◆**récidiviste** *nmf Jur* further offender.

récif [resif] *nm* reef.

récipient [resipjã] *nm* container, receptacle.

réciproque [resiprɔk] *a* mutual, reciprocal; — *nf* (*inverse*) opposite; rendre la r. à qn to get even with s.o. ◆**réciprocité** *nf* reciprocity. ◆**réciproquement** adv (l'un l'autre) each other; **et r.** and vice versa.

récit [resi] nm (compte rendu) account; (histoire) story.

récital, pl **-als** [resital] nm Mus recital.

réciter [resite] vt to recite. ◆**récitation** nf recitation.

réclame [reklam] nf advertising; (annonce) advertisement; **en r.** Com on (special) offer; **– a** inv **prix r.** (special) offer price; **vente r.** (bargain) sale.

réclamer [reklame] vt (demander, nécessiter) to demand, call for; (revendiquer) to claim; **– vi** to complain; **se r. de qn** to invoke s.o.'s authority. ◆**réclamation** nf complaint; pl (bureau) complaints department.

reclasser [r(ə)klase] vt (fiches etc) to reclassify.

reclus, -use [rəkly, -yz] a (vie) cloistered; **–** nmf recluse.

réclusion [reklyzjɔ̃] nf imprisonment (with hard labour); **r. à perpétuité** life imprisonment.

recoiffer (se) [sər(ə)kwafe] vpr (se peigner) to do ou comb one's hair.

recoin [rəkwɛ̃] nm nook, recess.

recoller [r(ə)kɔle] vt (objet cassé) to stick together again; (enveloppe) to stick back down.

récolte [rekɔlt] nf (action) harvest; (produits) crop, harvest; (collection) Fig crop. ◆**récolter** vt to harvest, gather (in); (recueillir) Fig to collect, gather; (coups) Fam to get.

recommand/er [r(ə)kɔmɑ̃de] **1** vt (appuyer, conseiller) to recommend; **r. à qn de faire** to recommend s.o. to do. **2** vt (lettre etc) to register. **3** v r. à (âme) to commend to. **4 se r.** vpr **se r. de qn** to invoke s.o.'s authority. ◆**–é** nm **en r.** (envoyer) by registered post. ◆**–able** a peu **r.** not very commendable. ◆**recommandation** nf **1** (appui, conseil, louange) recommendation. **2** (de lettre etc) registration.

recommenc/er [r(ə)kɔmɑ̃se] vti to start ou begin again. ◆**–ement** nm (reprise) renewal (de of).

récompense [rekɔ̃pɑ̃s] nf reward (de for); (prix) award; **en r. de** in return for. ◆**récompenser** vt to reward (de, pour for).

réconcilier [rekɔ̃silje] vt to reconcile; **– se r.** vpr to become reconciled, make it up (avec with). ◆**réconciliation** nf reconciliation.

reconduire* [r(ə)kɔ̃dɥir] vt **1 r. qn** to see ou take s.o. back; (à la porte) to show s.o. out. **2** (mesures etc) to renew. ◆**reconduction** nf renewal.

réconfort [rekɔ̃fɔr] nm comfort. ◆**réconfort/er** vt to comfort; (revigorer) to fortify. ◆**–ant** a comforting; (boisson etc) fortifying.

reconnaissant [r(ə)kɔnesɑ̃] a grateful, thankful (à **qn de qch** to s.o. for sth). ◆**reconnaissance¹** nf (gratitude) gratitude.

reconnaître* [r(ə)kɔnɛtr] vt to recognize (à **qch** by sth); (admettre) to acknowledge, admit (que that); (terrain) Mil to reconnoitre; **être reconnu coupable** to be found guilty; **– se r.** vpr (s'orienter) to find one's bearings; **se r. coupable** to admit one's guilt. ◆**reconnu** a (chef, fait) acknowledged, recognized. ◆**reconnaissable** a recognizable (à **qch** by sth). ◆**reconnaissance²** nf recognition; (aveu) acknowledgement; Mil reconnaissance; **r. de dette** IOU.

reconsidérer [r(ə)kɔ̃sidere] vt to reconsider.

reconstituant [r(ə)kɔ̃stitɥɑ̃] adj (aliment, régime) restorative.

reconstituer [r(ə)kɔ̃stitɥe] vt (armée, parti) to reconstitute; (crime, quartier) to reconstruct; (faits) to piece together; (fortune) to build up again. ◆**reconstitution** nf reconstitution; reconstruction.

reconstruire* [r(ə)kɔ̃strɥir] vt (ville, fortune) to rebuild. ◆**reconstruction** nf rebuilding.

reconvertir [r(ə)kɔ̃vertir] **1** (bâtiment etc) to reconvert. **2 se r.** vpr to take up a new form of employment. ◆**reconversion** nf reconversion.

recopier [r(ə)kɔpje] vt to copy out.

record [r(ə)kɔr] nm & a inv Sp record.

recoucher (se) [sər(ə)kuʃe] vpr to go back to bed.

recoudre* [r(ə)kudr] vt (bouton) to sew back on.

recoup/er [r(ə)kupe] vt (témoignage etc) to tally with, confirm; **– se r.** vpr to tally, match ou tie up. ◆**–ement** nm cross-check(ing).

recourbé [r(ə)kurbe] a curved; (nez) hooked.

recours [r(ə)kur] nm recourse (à to); Jur appeal; **avoir r. à** to resort to; (personne) to turn to; **notre dernier r.** our last resort. ◆**recourir*** vi **r. à** to resort to; (personne) to turn to.

recouvrer [r(ə)kuvre] *vt* (*argent, santé*) to recover.

recouvrir* [r(ə)kuvrir] *vt* (*livre, meuble, sol etc*) to cover; (*de nouveau*) to recover; (*cacher*) Fig to conceal, mask.

récréation [rekreasjɔ̃] *nf* recreation; (*temps*) Scol break, playtime.

récriminer [rekrimine] *vi* to complain bitterly (**contre** about). **◆récrimination** *nf* (bitter) complaint.

récrire [rekrir] *vt* (*lettre etc*) to rewrite.

recroqueviller (se) [s(ə)krɔkvije] *vpr* (*papier, personne etc*) to curl up.

recrudescence [rəkrydesɑ̃s] *nf* new outbreak (**de** of).

recrue [rəkry] *nf* recruit. **◆recrut/er** *vt* to recruit. **◆—ement** *nm* recruitment.

rectangle [rɛktɑ̃gl] *nm* rectangle. **◆rectangulaire** *a* rectangular.

rectifier [rɛktifje] *vt* (*erreur etc*) to correct, rectify; (*ajuster*) to adjust. **◆rectificatif** *nm* (*document*) amendment, correction. **◆rectification** *nf* correction, rectification.

recto [rɛkto] *nm* front (of the page).

reçu [r(ə)sy] *voir* **recevoir**; – *a* (*usages etc*) accepted; (*idée*) conventional, received; (*candidat*) successful; – *nm* (*écrit*) Com receipt.

recueil [r(ə)kœj] *nm* (*ouvrage*) collection (**de** of).

recueill/ir* [r(ə)kœjir] **1** *vt* to collect, gather; (*suffrages*) to win, get; (*prendre chez soi*) to take in. **2 se r.** *vpr* to meditate; (*devant un monument*) to stand in silence. **◆—i** *a* (*air*) meditative. **◆—ement** *nm* meditation.

recul [r(ə)kyl] *nm* (*d'armée, de négociateur, de maladie*) retreat; (*éloignement*) distance; (*déclin*) decline; (**mouvement de**) **r.** (*de véhicule*) backward movement; **avoir un mouvement de r.** (*personne*) to recoil; **phare de r.** Aut reversing light. **◆recul/er** *vi* to move ou step back; Aut to reverse; (*armée*) to retreat; (*épidémie, glacier*) to recede, retreat; (*renoncer*) to back down, retreat; (*diminuer*) to decline; **r. devant** Fig to recoil ou shrink from; – *vt* to move ou push back; (*différer*) to postpone. **◆—é** *a* (*endroit, temps*) remote.

reculons (à) [arkylɔ̃] *adv* backwards.

récupérer [rekypere] *vt* to recover, get back; (*ferraille etc*) to salvage; (*heures*) to make up; (*mouvement, personne etc*) Pol Péj to take over, convert; – *vi* to recuper-

ate, recover. **◆récupération** *nf* recovery; salvage; recuperation.

récurer [rekyre] *vt* (*casserole etc*) to scour; **poudre à r.** scouring powder.

récuser [rekyze] *vt* to challenge; **— se r.** *vpr* to decline to give an opinion.

recycl/er [r(ə)sikle] *vt* (*reconvertir*) to retrain (*s.o.*); (*matériaux*) to recycle; **— se r.** *vpr* to retrain. **◆—age** *nm* retraining; recycling.

rédacteur, -trice [redaktœr, -tris] *nmf* writer; (*de chronique*) Journ editor; (*de dictionnaire etc*) compiler; **r. en chef** Journ editor(-in-chief). **◆rédaction** *nf* (*action*) writing; (*de contrat*) drawing up; (*devoir*) Scol essay, composition; (*rédacteurs*) Journ editorial staff; (*bureaux*) Journ editorial offices.

reddition [redisjɔ̃] *nf* surrender.

redemander [rədmɑ̃de] *vt* (*pain etc*) to ask for more; **r. qch à qn** to ask s.o. for sth.

rédemption [redɑ̃psjɔ̃] *nf* Rel redemption.

redescendre [r(ə)desɑ̃dr] *vi* (*aux être*) to come ou go back down; – *vt* (*aux avoir*) (*objet*) to bring ou take back down.

redevable [rədvabl] *a* **être r. de qch à qn** (*argent*) to owe s.o. sth; Fig to be indebted to s.o. for sth.

redevance [rədvɑ̃s] *nf* (*taxe*) TV licence fee; Tél rental charge.

redevenir* [rədvənir] *vi* (*aux être*) to become again.

rédiger [rediʒe] *vt* to write; (*contrat*) to draw up; (*dictionnaire etc*) to compile.

redire* [r(ə)dir] **1** *vt* to repeat. **2** *vi* **avoir ou trouver à r. à qch** to find fault with sth. **◆redite** *nf* (pointless) repetition.

redondant [r(ə)dɔ̃dɑ̃] *a* (*style*) redundant.

redonner [r(ə)dɔne] *vt* to give back; (*de nouveau*) to give more.

redoubl/er [r(ə)duble] *vti* **1** to increase; **r. de patience/etc** to be much more patient/etc; **à coups redoublés** (*frapper*) harder and harder. **2 r.** (**une classe**) Scol to repeat a year ou Am a grade. **◆—ant, -ante** *nmf* pupil repeating a year ou Am a grade. **◆—ement** *nm* increase (**de** in); repeating a year ou Am a grade.

redout/er [r(ə)dute] *vt* to dread (**de faire** doing). **◆—able** *a* formidable, fearsome.

redress/er [r(ə)drese] *vt* to straighten (out); (*économie, mât, situation, tort*) to right; **— se r.** *vpr* (*se mettre assis*) to sit up; (*debout*) to stand up; (*pays, situation etc*) to right itself. **◆—ement** [-ɛsmɑ̃] *nm* (*essor*) recovery.

réduction [redyksjɔ̃] nf reduction (**de** in); **en r.** (copie, modèle etc) small-scale.

réduire* [redɥir] vt to reduce (**à** to, **de** by); **r. qn à** (contraindre à) to reduce s.o. to (silence, inaction etc); **se r.à** (se ramener à) to come down to, amount to; **se r. en cendres**/etc to be reduced to ashes/etc; **— vi (faire) r.** (sauce) to reduce, boil down. ◆**réduit 1** a (prix, vitesse) reduced; (moyens) limited; (à petite échelle) small-scale. **2** nm (pièce) Péj cubbyhole; (recoin) recess.

réécrire [reekrir] vt (texte) to rewrite.

rééduquer [reedyke] vt (membre) Méd to re-educate; **r. qn** to rehabilitate s.o., re-educate s.o. ◆**rééducation** nf re-education; rehabilitation.

réel, -elle [reɛl] a real; **le r.** reality. ◆**réellement** adv really.

réélire [reelir] vt to re-elect.

réexpédier [reekspedje] vt (lettre etc) to forward; (à l'envoyeur) to return.

refaire* [r(ə)fɛr] vt to do again, redo; (erreur, voyage) to make again; (réparer) to do up, redo; (duper) Fam to take in. ◆**réfection** nf repair(ing).

réfectoire [refɛktwar] nm refectory.

référendum [referɑ̃dɔm] nm referendum.

référer [refere] vi **en r.à** to refer the matter to; **— se r.** vpr **se r.à** to refer to. ◆**référence** nf reference.

refermer [r(ə)fɛrme] vt, **— se r.** vpr to close ou shut (again).

refiler [r(ə)file] vt (donner) Fam to palm off (**à** on).

réfléch/ir [refleʃir] **1** vt (image) to reflect; **— se r.** vpr to be reflected. **2** vi (penser) to think (**à, sur** about); **— vt r. que** to realize that. ◆**—i** a (personne) thoughtful, reflective; (action, décision) carefully thought-out; (verbe) Gram reflexive. ◆**réflecteur** nm reflector. ◆**réflexion** nf **1** (de lumière etc) reflection. **2** (méditation) thought, reflection; (remarque) remark; **à la r., r. faite** on second thoughts ou Am thought, on reflection.

reflet [r(ə)flɛ] nm (image) & Fig reflection; (lumière) glint; (couleur) tint. ◆**refléter** vt (image, sentiment etc) to reflect; **— se r.** vpr to be reflected.

réflexe [reflɛks] nm & a reflex.

refluer [r(ə)flye] vi (eaux) to ebb, flow back; (foule) to surge back. ◆**reflux** nm ebb; backward surge.

réforme nf **1** (changement) reform. **2** (de soldat) discharge. ◆**réformateur, -trice** nmf reformer. ◆**réformer 1** vt to reform;

— se r. vpr to mend one's ways. **2** vt (soldat) to invalid out, discharge.

refoul/er [r(ə)fule] vt to force ou drive back; (sentiment) to repress; (larmes) to hold back. ◆**—é** a (personne) Psy repressed. ◆**—ement** nm Psy repression.

réfractaire [refrakter] a **r.à** resistant to.

refrain [r(ə)frɛ̃] nm (de chanson) refrain, chorus; (rengaine) Fig tune.

réfréner [r(ə)frene] vt to curb, check.

réfrigér/er [refriʒere] vt to refrigerate. ◆**—ant** a (accueil, air) Fam icy. ◆**réfrigérateur** nm refrigerator. ◆**réfrigération** nf refrigeration.

refroid/ir [r(ə)frwadir] vt to cool (down); (décourager) Fig to put off; (ardeur) to dampen, cool; **— vi** to get cold, cool down; **— se r.** vpr Méd to catch cold; (temps) to get cold; (ardeur) to cool (off). ◆**—issement** nm cooling; (rhume) chill; **r. de la température** fall in the temperature.

refuge [r(ə)fyʒ] nm refuge; (pour piétons) (traffic) island; (de montagne) (mountain) hut. ◆**se réfugi/er** vpr to take refuge. ◆**—é, -ée** nmf refugee.

refus [r(ə)fy] nm refusal; **ce n'est pas de r.** Fam I won't say no. ◆**refuser** vt to refuse (**qch à qn** s.o. sth, **de faire** to do); (offre, invitation) to turn down, refuse; (client) to turn away, refuse; (candidat) to fail; **— se r.** vpr (plaisir etc) to deny oneself; **se r.à** (évidence etc) to refuse to accept, reject; **se r.à croire**/etc to refuse to believe/etc.

réfuter [refyte] vt to refute.

regagner [r(ə)gaɲe] vt (récupérer) to regain; (revenir à) to get back to. ◆**regain** nm **r. de** (retour) renewal of.

régal, pl **-als** [regal] nm treat. ◆**régaler** vt to treat to a delicious meal; **r. de** to treat to; **— se r.** vpr to have a delicious meal.

regard nm **1** (coup d'œil, expression) look; (fixe) stare, gaze; **faire** (a)round for; **attirer les regards** to attract attention; **jeter un r. sur** to glance at. **2 au r. de** in regard to; **en r. de** compared with. ◆**regard/er 1** vt (personne, chose) to look at; (fixement) to stare at, gaze at; (observer) to watch; (considérer) to consider, regard (**comme** as); **r. qn faire** to watch s.o. do; **— vi** to look; to stare, gaze; to watch; **r.à** (dépense, qualité etc) to pay attention to; **r. vers** (maison etc) to face; **— se r.** vpr (personnes) to look at each other. **2** vt (concerner) to concern. ◆**—ant** a (économe) careful (with money).

régates [regat] nfpl regatta.

régence [reʒɑ̃s] nf regency.

régénérer [reʒenere] vt to regenerate.

régenter [reʒɑ̃te] vt to rule over.

régie [reʒi] nf (entreprise) state-owned company; Th stage management; Cin TV production department.

regimber [r(ə)ʒɛ̃be] vi to balk (contre at).

régime [reʒim] nm 1 system; Pol régime. 2 Méd diet; **se mettre au r.** to go on a diet; **suivre un r.** to be on a diet. 3 (de moteur) speed; **à ce r.** Fig at this rate. 4 (de bananes, dattes) bunch.

régiment [reʒimɑ̃] nm Mil regiment; **un r. de** (quantité) Fig a host of.

région [reʒjɔ̃] nf region, area. ◆**régional, -aux** a regional.

régir [reʒir] vt (déterminer) to govern.

régisseur [reʒisœr] nm (de propriété) steward; Th stage manager; Cin assistant director.

registre [rəʒistr] nm register.

règle [rɛgl] 1 nf (principe) rule; **en r.** (papiers d'identité etc) in order; **être/se mettre en r. avec qn** to be/put oneself right with s.o.; **en r. générale** as a (general) rule. 2 nf (instrument) ruler; **r. à calcul** slide rule. 3 nfpl (menstruation) period.

règlement [rɛgləmɑ̃] nm 1 (arrêté) regulation; (règles) regulations. 2 (de conflit, problème etc) settling; (paiement) payment; **r. de comptes** Fig (violent) settling of scores. ◆**réglementaire** a in accordance with the regulations; (tenue) Mil regulation-. ◆**réglementation** nf 1 (action) regulation. 2 (règles) regulations. ◆**réglementer** vt to regulate.

régler [regle] 1 vt (conflit, problème etc) to settle; (mécanisme) to regulate, adjust; (moteur) to tune; (papier) to rule; **se r. sur** to model oneself on. 2 vti (payer) to pay; **r. qn** to settle up with s.o.; **r. son compte à** Fig to settle old scores with. ◆**réglé** a (vie) ordered; (papier) ruled. ◆**réglable** a (siège etc) adjustable. ◆**réglage** nm adjustment; (de moteur) tuning.

réglisse [reglis] nf liquorice, Am licorice.

règne [rɛɲ] nm reign; (animal, minéral, végétal) kingdom. ◆**régner** vi to reign; (prédominer) to prevail; **faire r. l'ordre** to maintain (law and) order.

regorger [r(ə)ɡɔrʒe] vi **r. de** to be overflowing with.

régresser [regrese] vi to regress. ◆**régression** nf regression, on the decline.

regret [r(ə)ɡrɛ] nm regret; **à r.** with regret; **avoir le r. ou être au r. de faire** to be sorry to do. ◆**regretter** vt to regret; **r. qn** to miss s.o.; **je regrette** I'm sorry; **r. que** (+ sub) to

be sorry that, regret that. ◆**-able** a regrettable.

regrouper [r(ə)ɡrupe] vt, — **se r.** vpr to gather together.

régulariser [regylarize] vt (situation) to regularize.

régulation [regylasjɔ̃] nf (action) regulation.

régulier, -ière [regylje, -jɛr] a regular; (progrès, vie, vitesse) steady; (légal) legal; (honnête) honest. ◆**régularité** nf regularity; steadiness; legality. ◆**régulièrement** adv regularly; (normalement) normally.

réhabiliter [reabilite] vt (dans l'estime publique) to rehabilitate.

réhabituer (se) [sǝreabitɥe] vpr **se r. à qch/à faire qch** to get used to sth/to doing sth again.

rehausser [rəose] vt to raise; (faire valoir) to enhance.

réimpression [reɛ̃presjɔ̃] nf (livre) reprint.

rein [rɛ̃] nm kidney; **pl** (dos) (small of the) back; **r. artificiel** Méd kidney machine.

reine [rɛn] nf queen.

reine-claude [rɛnklod] nf greengage.

réintégrer [reɛ̃tegre] vt 1 (fonctionnaire etc) to reinstate. 2 (lieu) to return to. ◆**réintégration** nf reinstatement.

réitérer [reitere] vt to repeat.

rejaillir [r(ə)ʒajir] vi to spurt (up ou out); **r. sur** Fig to rebound on.

rejet [r(ə)ʒɛ] nm 1 (refus) & Méd rejection. 2 Bot shoot. ◆**rejeter** vt to throw back; (épave) to cast up; (vomir) to bring up; (refuser) & Méd to reject; **r. une erreur/etc sur qn** to put the blame for a mistake/etc on s.o.

rejeton [rəʒtɔ̃] nm (enfant) Fam kid.

rejoindre [r(ə)ʒwɛ̃dr] vt (famille, régiment) to rejoin, get ou go back to; (lieu) to get back to; (route, rue) to join; **r. qn** to join ou meet s.o.; (rattraper) to catch up with s.o.; — **se r.** vpr (personnes) to meet; (routes, rues) to join, meet.

réjou/ir [reʒwir] vt to delight; — **se r.** vpr to be delighted (de at, about; de faire to do). ◆**-i** a (air) joyful. ◆**-issant** a cheering. ◆**réjouissance** nf rejoicing; **pl** festivities, rejoicings.

relâche [rəlɑʃ] nf Th Cin (temporary) closure; **faire r.** (théâtre, cinéma) to close; (bateau) to put in (dans un port at a port); **sans r.** without a break.

relâch/er [r(ə)lɑʃe] 1 vt to slacken; (discipline, étreinte) to relax; (qn) to release s.o.; — **se r.** vpr to slacken; (discipline) to get lax. 2 vi (bateau) to put in. ◆**-é** a lax.

◆—ement nm (de corde etc) slackness; (de discipline) slackening.

relais [r(ə)lɛ] nm Él Rad TV relay; (course de) r. Sp relay (race); r. routier transport café, Am truck stop (café); prendre le r. to take over (de from).

relance [r(ə)lɑ̃s] nf (reprise) revival. ◆relancer vt to throw back; (moteur) to restart; (industrie etc) to put back on its feet; r. qn (solliciter) to pester s.o.

relater [r(ə)late] vt to relate (que that).

relatif, -ive [r(ə)latif, -iv] a relative (à to). ◆relativement adv relatively; r. à compared to, relative to.

relation [r(ə)lasjɔ̃] nf (rapport) relation(ship); (ami) acquaintance; avoir des relations (amis influents) to have connections; entrer/être en relations avec to come into/be in contact with; relations internationales/etc international/etc relations.

relax(e) [rəlaks] a Fam relaxed, informal.

relaxer (se) [sər(ə)lakse] vpr to relax. ◆relaxation nf relaxation.

relayer [r(ə)leje] vt to relieve, take over from; (émission) to relay; — se r. vpr to take (it in) turns (pour faire to do); Sp to take over from one another.

reléguer [r(ə)lege] vt to relegate (à to).

relent [rəlɑ̃] nm stench, smell.

relève [r(ə)lɛv] nf (remplacement) relief; prendre la r. to take over (de from).

relev/er [rəlve] vt to raise; (ramasser) to pick up; (chaise etc) to put up straight; (personne tombée) to help up; (col) to turn up; (manches) to roll up; (copier) to note down; (traces) to find; (relayer) to relieve; (rehausser) to enhance; (sauce) to season; (faute) to pick ou point out; (compteur) to read; (défi) to accept; (économie, pays) to put back on its feet; (mur) to rebuild; r. qn de (fonctions) to relieve s.o. of; — vi r. de (dépendre de) to come under; (maladie) to get over; — se r. vpr (personne) to get up; se r. de (malheur) to recover from; (ruines) to rise from. ◆—é nm list; (de dépenses) statement; (de compteur) reading; r. de compte (bank) statement. ◆relèvement nm (d'économie, de pays) recovery.

relief [rəljɛf] 1 nm (forme, ouvrage) relief; en r. (cinéma) three-D; (livre) pop-up; mettre en r. Fig to highlight. 2 nmpl (de repas) remains.

relier [rəlje] vt to link, connect (à to); (ensemble) to link (together); (livre) to bind.

religion [r(ə)liʒjɔ̃] nf religion; (foi) faith. ◆religieux, -euse a religious; mariage

r. church wedding; — nm monk; — nf nun. 2 nf Culin cream bun.

reliquat [r(ə)lika] nm (de dette etc) remainder.

relique [r(ə)lik] nf relic.

relire* [r(ə)lir] vt to reread.

reliure [rəljyr] nf (couverture de livre) binding; (art) bookbinding.

reluire [r(ə)lɥir] vi to shine, gleam; faire r. (polir) to shine (up). ◆reluisant a shiny; peu r. Fig far from brilliant.

reluquer [r(ə)lyke] vt Fig to eye (up).

remâcher [r(ə)mɑʃe] vt Fig to brood over.

remanier [r(ə)manje] vt (texte) to revise; (ministère) to reshuffle. ◆remaniement nm revision; reshuffle.

remarier (se) [sər(ə)marje] vpr to remarry.

remarque [r(ə)mark] nf remark; (annotation) note; je lui en ai fait la r. I remarked on it to him ou her. ◆remarquable a remarkable (par for). ◆remarquablement adv remarkably. ◆remarquer vt 1 (apercevoir) to notice (que that); faire r. to point out (à to, que that); se faire r. to attract attention; remarque! mind (you)! 2 (dire) to remark (que that).

rembarrer [rɑ̃bare] vt to rebuff, snub.

remblai [rɑ̃blɛ] nm (terres) embankment. ◆remblayer [rɑ̃bleje] vt to bank up; (trou) to fill in.

rembourr/er [rɑ̃bure] vt (matelas etc) to stuff, pad; (vêtement) to pad. ◆—age nm (action, matière etc) stuffing; padding.

rembourser [rɑ̃burse] vt to pay back, repay; (billet) to refund. ◆remboursement nm repayment; refund; envoi contre r. cash on delivery.

remède [r(ə)mɛd] nm remedy, cure; (médicament) medicine. ◆remédier vi r. à to remedy.

remémorer (se) [sər(ə)memore] vpr (histoire etc) to recollect, recall.

remercier [r(ə)mɛrsje] vt 1 to thank (de qch, pour qch, for sth); je vous remercie d'être venu thank you for coming; je vous remercie (non merci) no thank you. 2 (congédier) to dismiss. ◆remerciements nmpl thanks.

remettre* [r(ə)mɛtr] vt to put back, replace; (vêtement) to put back on; (donner) to hand over (à to); (restituer) to give back (à to); (démission, devoir) to hand in; (différer) to postpone (à until); (ajouter) to add more ou another; (peine) Jur to remit; (guérir) to restore to health; (reconnaître) to place, remember; r. en cause ou question to call into question; r. en état to repair; r. ça Fam to start again; **se r. à** (*activité*) to go back to; **se r. à faire** to start to do again; **se r. de** (*chagrin, maladie*) to recover from, get over; **s'en r. à** to rely on. ◆**remise** nf **1** (*de lettre etc*) delivery; (*de peine*) Jur remission; (*ajournement*) postponement; **r. en cause** calling into question; **r. en état** repair(ing). **2** (*rabais*) discount. **3** (*local*) shed; Aut garage. ◆**remiser** vt to put away.

réminiscences [reminisɑ̃s] nfpl (*vague*) recollections, reminiscences.

rémission [remisjɔ̃] nf Jur Rel Méd remission; **sans r.** (*travailler etc*) relentlessly.

remmener [rɑ̃mne] vt to take back.

remonte-pente [r(ə)mɔ̃tpɑ̃t] nm ski lift.

remont/er [r(ə)mɔ̃te] vi (*aux être*) to come ou go back up; (*niveau, prix*) to rise again, go back up; (*dans le temps*) to go back (à to); (*dans* (*voiture*) to go ou get back in(to); (*bus, train*) to go ou get back on(to); **r. sur** (*cheval, vélo*) to remount; — vt (*aux avoir*) (*escalier, pente*) to come ou go back up; (*porter*) to bring ou take back up; (*montre*) to wind up; (*relever*) to raise; (*col*) to turn up; (*objet démonté*) to reassemble; (*garde-robe etc*) to restock; **r. qn** (*ragaillardir*) to buck s.o. up; (*le moral à qn*) to cheer s.o. up. ◆—**ant** à (*boisson*) fortifying; — nm Méd tonic. ◆—**ée** nf **1** (*de pente etc*) ascent; (*d'eau, de prix*) rise. **2 r. mécanique** ski lift. ◆**remontoir** nm (*de mécanisme, montre*) winder.

remontrance [r(ə)mɔ̃trɑ̃s] nf reprimand; **faire des remontrances à** to reprimand, remonstrate with.

remontrer [r(ə)mɔ̃tre] vi **en r. à qn** to prove one's superiority over s.o.

remords [r(ə)mɔr] nm & nmpl remorse; **avoir des r.** to feel remorse.

remorque [r(ə)mɔrk] nf Aut trailer; (*câble de*) **r.** towrope; **prendre en r.** to tow; **en r.** on tow. ◆**remorquer** vt (*voiture, bateau*) to tow. ◆**remorqueur** nm tug(boat).

remous [r(ə)mu] nm eddy; (*de foule*) bustle; (*agitation*) Fig turmoil.

rempart [rɑ̃par] nm rampart.

remplacer [rɑ̃plase] vt to replace (**par** with, by); (*succéder à*) to take over from; (*temporairement*) to stand in for. ◆**remplaçant, -ante** nmf (*personne*) replacement; (*enseignant*) supply teacher; Sp reserve. ◆**remplacement** nm (*action*) replacement; **assurer le r. de qn** to stand in for s.o.; **en r. de** in place of.

rempl/ir [rɑ̃plir] vt to fill (up) (**de** with); (*fiche etc*) to fill in ou out; (*condition, de-*

voir, tâche) to fulfil; (*fonctions*) to perform; — **se r.** vpr to fill (up). ◆—**i** a full (**de**). ◆**remplissage** nm filling; (*verbiage*) Péj padding.

remporter [rɑ̃pɔrte] vt **1** (*objet*) to take back. **2** (*prix, victoire*) to win; (*succès*) to achieve.

remu/er [r(ə)mɥe] vt (*déplacer, émouvoir*) to move; (*café etc*) to stir; (*terre*) to turn over; (*salade*) to toss; — vi to move; (*gigoter*) to fidget; (*se rebeller*) to stir; — **se r.** vpr to move; (*se démener*) to exert oneself. ◆—**ant** a (*enfant*) restless, fidgety. ◆**remue-ménage** nm inv commotion.

rémunérer [remynere] vt (*personne*) to pay for; (*travail*) to pay for. ◆**rémunérateur, -trice** a remunerative. ◆**rémunération** nf payment (**de** for).

renâcler [r(ə)nɑkle] vi **1** (*cheval*) to snort. **2 r. à** to jib at, balk at.

renaître* [r(ə)nɛtr] vi (*fleur*) to grow again; (*espoir, industrie*) to revive. ◆**renaissance** nf rebirth, renaissance.

renard [r(ə)nar] nm fox.

renchérir [rɑ̃ʃerir] vi **r. sur qn** ou **sur ce que qn dit/etc** to go further than s.o. in what one says/etc.

rencontre [rɑ̃kɔ̃tr] nf meeting; (*inattendue* & Mil) encounter; Sp match, Am game; (*de routes*) junction; **aller à la r. de** to go to meet. ◆**rencontrer** vt (*difficultés*) to come up against, encounter; (*trouver*) to come across, find; (*heurter*) to hit; (*équipe*) Sp to play; — **se r.** vpr to meet.

rendez-vous [rɑ̃devu] nm inv appointment; (*d'amoureux*) date; (*lieu*) meeting place; **donner r.-vous à qn, prendre r.-vous avec qn** to make an appointment with.

rendormir* (**se**) [sərɑ̃dɔrmir] vpr to go back to sleep.

rend/re [rɑ̃dr] vt (*restituer*) to give back, return; (*hommage*) to pay; (*invitation*) to return; (*santé*) to restore; (*monnaie, son*) to give; (*justice*) to dispense; (*jugement*) to pronounce, give; (*armes*) to surrender; (*exprimer, traduire*) to render; (*vomir*) to bring up; **r. célèbre/plus grand/possible/etc** to make famous/bigger/possible/etc; — vi (*arbre, terre*) to yield; (*vomir*) to be sick; — **se r.** vpr (*capituler*) to surrender (à to); (*aller*) to go (à to); **se r. à** (*évidence, ordres*) to submit to; **se r. malade/utile/etc** to make oneself ill/useful/etc. ◆—**u** a (*fatigué*) exhausted; **être r.** (*arrivé*) to have arrived. ◆**rendement** nm Agr Fin yield; (*de personne, machine*) output.

renégat, -ate [renega, -at] nmf renegade.

rênes [rɛn] *nfpl* reins.

renferm/er [rɑ̃fɛrme] *vt* to contain; **— se r.** *vpr* **se r. (en soi-même)** to withdraw into oneself. **◆—é 1** *a* (*personne*) withdrawn. **2** *nm* **sentir le r.** (*chambre etc*) to smell stuffy.

renflé [rɑ̃fle] *a* bulging. **◆renflement** *nm* bulge.

renflouer [rɑ̃flue] *vt* (*navire*) & *Com* to refloat.

renfoncement [rɑ̃fɔ̃səmɑ̃] *nm* recess; **dans le r. d'une porte** in a doorway.

renforcer [rɑ̃fɔrse] *vt* to reinforce, strengthen. **◆renforcement** *nm* reinforcement, strengthening. **◆renfort** *nm* **des renforts** *Mil* reinforcements; **de r.** (*armée, personnel*) back-up; **à grand r.** *Fig* with a great deal of.

renfrogn/er (se) [sərɑ̃frɔɲe] *vpr* to scowl. **◆—é** *a* scowling, sullen.

rengaine [rɑ̃gɛn] *nf* **la même r.** *Fig* *Péj* the same old song *ou* story.

rengorger (se) [sərɑ̃gɔrʒe] *vpr* to give oneself airs.

renier [rənje] *vt* (*ami, pays etc*) to disown; (*foi, opinion*) to renounce. **◆reniement** *nm* disowning; renunciation.

renifler [r(ə)nifle] *vti* to sniff. **◆reniflement** *nm* sniff.

renne [rɛn] *nm* reindeer.

renom [rənɔ̃] *nm* renown; (*réputation*) reputation (de for). **◆renommé** *a* famous, renowned (pour for). **◆renommée** *nf* fame, renown; (*réputation*) reputation.

renoncer [r(ə)nɔ̃se] *vi* **r. à** to give up, abandon; **r. à faire** to give up (the idea of) doing. **◆renoncement** *nm*, **◆renonciation** *nf* renunciation (à of).

renouer [rənwe] **1** *vt* (*lacet etc*) to retie. **2** *vt* (*reprendre*) to renew; **— *vi* r. avec qch** (*mode, tradition etc*) to revive sth; **r. avec qn** to take up with s.o. again.

renouveau, -x [r(ə)nuvo] *nm* revival.

renouveler [r(ə)nuvle] *vt* to renew; (*action, erreur, question*) to repeat; **— se r.** *vpr* (*incident*) to recur, happen again; (*cellules, sang*) to be renewed. **◆renouvelable** *a* renewable. **◆renouvellement** *nm* renewal.

rénover [renove] *vt* (*institution, méthode*) to reform; (*édifice, meuble etc*) to renovate. **◆rénovation** *nf* reform; renovation.

renseign/er [rɑ̃sɛɲe] *vt* to inform, give information to (**sur** about); **— se r.** *vpr* to inquire, make inquiries, find out (**sur** about). **◆—ement** *nm* (piece of) information; *pl* information; *Tél* directory inquiries, *Am* information; *Mil* intelligence;

prendre *ou* **demander des reseignements** to make inquiries.

rentable [rɑ̃tabl] *a* profitable. **◆rentabilité** *nf* profitability.

rente [rɑ̃t] *nf* (private) income; (*pension*) pension; **avoir des rentes** to have private means. **◆rentier, -ière** *nmf* person of private means.

rentr/er [rɑ̃tre] *vi* (*aux* **être**) to go *ou* come back, return; (*chez soi*) to go *ou* come (back) home; (*entrer*) to go *ou* come in; (*entrer de nouveau*) to go *ou* come back in; (*école*) to start again; (*argent*) to come in; **r. dans** (*entrer dans*) to go *ou* come into; (*entrer de nouveau dans*) to go *ou* come back into; (*famille, pays*) to return to; (*ses frais*) to get back; (*catégorie*) to come under; (*heurter*) to crash into; (*s'emboîter dans*) to fit into; **r. (en classe)** to start (school) again; **je lui suis rentré dedans** (*frapper*) *Fam* I laid into him *ou* her; **— *vt* (*aux* **avoir**) to bring *ou* take in; (*voiture*) to put away; (*chemise*) to tuck in; (*griffes*) to draw in. **◆—é** *a* (*colère*) suppressed; (*yeux*) sunken. **◆—ée** *nf* **1** (*retour*) return; (*de parlement*) reassembly; (*d'acteur*) comeback; **r.** (**des classes**) beginning of term *ou* of the school year. **2** (*des foins etc*) bringing in; (*d'impôt*) collection; *pl* (*argent*) receipts.

renverse (à la) [alarɑ̃vɛrs] *adv* (*tomber*) backwards, on one's back.

renvers/er [rɑ̃vɛrse] *vt* (*mettre à l'envers*) to turn upside down; (*faire tomber*) to knock over *ou* down; (*piéton*) to knock down, run over; (*liquide*) to spill, knock over; (*courant, ordre*) to reverse; (*gouvernement*) to overturn, overthrow; (*projet*) to upset; (*tête*) to tip back; **— se r.** *vpr* (*en arrière*) to lean back; (*bouteille, vase etc*) to fall over. **◆—ant** *a* (*nouvelle etc*) astounding. **◆—ement** *nm* (*d'ordre, de situation*) reversal; (*de gouvernement*) overthrow.

renvoi [rɑ̃vwa] *nm* **1** return; dismissal; expulsion; postponement; (*dans un livre*) reference. **2** (*rot*) belch, burp. **◆renvoyer*** *vt* to send back, return; (*importun*) to send away; (*employé*) to dismiss; (*élève*) to expel; (*balle etc*) to throw back; (*ajourner*) to postpone (**à** until); (*lumière, image etc*) to reflect; **r. qn à** (*adresser à*) to refer s.o. to.

réorganiser [reɔrganize] *vt* to reorganize.

réouverture [reuvɛrtyr] *nf* reopening.

repaire [r(ə)pɛr] *nm* den.

repaître (se) [sərəpɛtr] *vpr* **se r. de** (*sang*) *Fig* to wallow in.

répand/re [repɑ̃dr] *vt* (*liquide*) to spill;

(*idées, joie, nouvelle*) to spread; (*fumée, odeur*) to give off; (*chargement, lumière, larmes, sang*) to shed; (*gravillons etc*) to scatter; (*injures etc*) to lavish; — **se r.** *vpr* (*nouvelle, peur etc*) to spread; (*liquide*) to spill; **se r. dans** (*fumée, odeur*) to spread through; **se r. en louanges**/*etc* to pour forth praise/*etc*. ◆—**u** *a* (*opinion, usage*) widespread; (*épars*) scattered.

reparaître [r(ə)parɛtr] *vi* to reappear.

réparer [repare] *vt* to repair, mend; (*forces, santé*) to restore; (*faute*) to make amends for; (*perte*) to make good; (*erreur*) to put right. ◆**réparable** *a* (*montre etc*) repairable. ◆**réparateur, -trice** *nmf* repairer; — *a* (*sommeil*) refreshing. ◆**réparation** *nf* repair(ing); (*compensation*) amends, compensation (**de** for); *pl Mil Hist* reparations; **en r.** under repair.

reparler [r(ə)parle] *vi* **r. de** to talk about again.

repartie [r(ə)parti] *nf* (*réponse vive*) repartee.

repartir[*] [r(ə)partir] *vi* (*aux être*) to set off again; (*s'en retourner*) to go back; (*reprendre*) to start again; **r. à** *ou* **de zéro** to go back to square one.

répartir [repartir] *vt* to distribute; (*partager*) to share (out); (*classer*) to divide (up); (*étaler dans le temps*) to spread (out) (**sur** over). ◆**répartition** *nf* distribution; sharing; division.

repas [r(ə)pɑ] *nm* meal; **prendre un r.** to have *ou* eat a meal.

repasser [r(ə)pase] **1** *vi* to come *ou* go back; — *vt* (*traverser*) to go back over; (*examen*) to resit; (*leçon, rôle*) to go over; (*film*) to show again; (*maladie, travail*) to pass on (**à** to). **2** *vt* (*linge*) to iron. **3** *vt* (*couteau*) to sharpen. ◆—**age** *nm* ironing.

repêcher [r(ə)peʃe] *vt* to fish out; (*candidat*) *Fam* to allow to pass.

repenser [r(ə)pɑ̃se] *vt* to rethink.

repentir[*] [r(ə)pɑ̃tir] *nm* repentance. ◆**se repentir**[*] *vpr Rel* to repent (**de** of); **se r. de** (*regretter*) to be sorry for. ◆**repentant** *a*, ◆**repenti** *a* repentant.

répercuter [reperkyte] *vt* (*son*) to echo; — **se r.** *vpr* to echo, reverberate; **se r. sur** *Fig* to have repercussions on. ◆**répercussion** *nf* repercussion.

repère [r(ə)pɛr] *nm* (*guide*) mark; (*jalon*) marker; **point de r.** (*espace, temps*) landmark, point of reference. ◆**repérer** *vt* to locate; (*personne*) *Fam* to spot; — **se r.** *vpr* to get one's bearings.

répertoire [repertwar] *nm* **1** index; (*carnet*) indexed notebook; **r. d'adresses** address

book. **2** *Th* repertoire. ◆**répertorier** *vt* to index.

répéter [repete] *vti* to repeat; *Th* to rehearse; — **se r.** *vpr* (*radoter*) to repeat oneself; (*se reproduire*) to repeat itself. ◆**répétitif, -ive** *a* repetitive. ◆**répétition** *nf* repetition; *Th* rehearsal; **r. générale** *Th* (final) dress rehearsal.

répit [repi] *nm* rest, respite; **sans r.** ceaselessly.

replacer [r(ə)plase] *vt* to replace, put back.

repli [r(ə)pli] *nm* fold; withdrawal; *pl* (*de l'âme*) recesses. ◆**replier 1** *vt* to fold (up); (*siège*) to fold up; (*couteau, couverture*) to fold back; (*ailes, jambes*) to tuck in; — **se r.** *vpr* (*siège*) to fold up; (*couteau, couverture*) to fold back. **2** *vt*, — **se r.** *vpr Mil* to withdraw; **se r. sur soi-même** to withdraw into oneself.

réplique [replik] *nf* **1** (*réponse*) reply; (*riposte*) retort; *Th* lines; **pas de r.!** no answering back!; **sans r.** (*argument*) irrefutable. **2** (*copie*) replica. ◆**répliquer** to reply (**que** that); (*riposter*) to retort (**que** that); — *vi* (*être impertinent*) to answer back.

répondre [repɔ̃dr] *vi* to answer, reply; (*être impertinent*) to answer back; (*réagir*) to respond (**à** to); **r. à qn** to answer s.o., reply to s.o.; (*avec impertinence*) to answer s.o. back; **r. à** (*lettre, objection, question*) to answer, reply to; (*salut*) to return; (*besoin*) to meet, answer; (*correspondre à*) to correspond to; **r. de** (*garantir*) to answer for (*s.o., sth*); — *vt* (*remarque etc*) to answer *ou* reply with; **r. que** to answer *ou* reply that. ◆—**ant, -ante 1** *nmf* guarantor. **2** *nm* **avoir du r.** to have money behind one. ◆—**eur** *nm Tél* answering machine. ◆**réponse** *nf* answer, reply; (*réaction*) response (**à** to); **en r. à** in answer *ou* reply *ou* response to.

reporter[1] [r(ə)pɔrte] *vt* to take back; (*différer*) to postpone, put off (**à** until); (*transcrire, transférer*) to transfer (**sur** to); (*somme*) *Com* to carry forward (**sur** to); **se r. à** (*texte etc*) to refer to; (*en esprit*) to go *ou* think back to. ◆**report** *nm* postponement; transfer; *Com* carrying forward. ◆**reportage** *nm* (*news*) report, article; (*en direct*) commentary; (*métier*) reporting.

reporter[2] [r(ə)pɔrter] *nm* reporter.

repos [r(ə)po] *nm* rest; (*tranquillité*) peace (and quiet); (*de l'esprit*) peace of mind; **r.!** *Mil* at ease!; **jour de r.** day off; **de tout r.** (*situation etc*) safe. ◆**reposer 1** *vt* (*objet*) to put back down; (*problème, question*) to raise again. **2** *vt* (*délasser*) to rest, relax; **r. sa tête sur** (*appuyer*) to rest one's head on; — *vi* (*être enterré ou étendu*) to rest, lie; **r. sur** (*bâtiment*) to be built on; (*théorie etc*) to be based on, rest on; **laisser r.** (*vin*) to allow to settle; — **se r.** *vpr* to rest; **se r. sur qn** to rely on s.o. ◆—**ant** *a* relaxing, restful. ◆—**é** *a* rested, fresh.

repouss/er [r(ə)puse] **1** *vt* to push back; (*écarter*) to push away; (*attaque, ennemi*) to repulse; (*importun etc*) to turn away, repulse; (*dégoûter*) to repel; (*décliner*) to reject; (*différer*) to put off, postpone. **2** *vi* (*cheveux, feuilles*) to grow again. ◆—**ant** *a* a repulsive, repellent.

répréhensible [repreãsibl] *a* reprehensible, blameworthy.

reprendre* [r(ə)prãdr] *vt* (*objet*) to take back; (*évadé, ville*) to recapture; (*passer prendre*) to pick up again; (*souffle*) to get back; (*activité*) to resume, take up again; (*texte*) to go back over; (*vêtement*) to alter; (*histoire, refrain*) to take up; (*pièce*) *Th* to put on again; (*blâmer*) to admonish; (*corriger*) to correct; **r. de la viande/un œuf/***etc* to take (some) more meat/another egg/*etc*; **r. ses esprits** to come round; **r. des forces** to recover one's strength; — *vi* (*plante*) to take again; (*recommencer*) to resume, start (up) again; (*affaires*) to pick up; (*dire*) to go on, continue; — **se r.** *vpr* (*se ressaisir*) to take a hold on oneself; (*se corriger*) to correct oneself; **s'y r. à deux/plusieurs fois** to have another go/several goes (at it).

représailles [r(ə)prezaj] *nfpl* reprisals, retaliation.

représent/er [r(ə)prezãte] *vt* to represent; (*jouer*) *Th* to perform; — **se r.** *vpr* (*s'imaginer*) to imagine. ◆—**ant, -ante** *nmf* representative; **r. de commerce** (travelling) salesman *ou* saleswoman, sales representative. ◆**représentatif, -ive** *a* representative (**de** of). ◆**représentation** *nf* representation; *Th* performance.

répression [represjɔ̃] *nf* suppression, repression; (*mesures de contrôle*) *Pol* repression. ◆**répressif, -ive** *a* repressive.

réprimande [reprimãd] *nf* reprimand. ◆**réprimander** *vt* to reprimand.

repris [r(ə)pri] *nm* **r. de justice** hardened criminal.

reprise [r(ə)priz] *nf* (*de ville*) *Mil* recapture; (*recommencement*) resumption; (*de pièce de théâtre, de coutume*) revival; *Rad TV* repeat; (*de tissu*) mend, repair; *Boxe* round;

(*essor*) *Com* recovery, revival; (*d'un locataire*) money for fittings; (*de marchandise*) taking back; (*pour nouvel achat*) part exchange, trade-in; *pl Aut* acceleration; **à plusieurs reprises** on several occasions. ◆**repriser** *vt* (*chaussette etc*) to mend, darn.

réprobation [reprɔbasjɔ̃] *nf* disapproval. ◆**réprobateur, -trice** *a* disapproving.

reproche [r(ə)prɔʃ] *nm* reproach; **faire des reproches à qn** to reproach s.o.; **sans r.** beyond reproach. ◆**reprocher** *vt* **r. qch à qn** to reproach *ou* blame s.o. for sth; **n'avoir rien à r.** to have nothing to reproach *ou* blame oneself for.

reproduire* [r(ə)prɔdɥir] **1** *vt* (*son, modèle etc*) to reproduce; — **se r.** *vpr Biol Bot* to reproduce. **2 se r.** *vpr* (*incident etc*) to happen again, recur. ◆**reproducteur, -trice** *a* reproductive. ◆**reproduction** *nf* (*de son etc*) & *Biol Bot* reproduction.

réprouver [repruve] *vt* to disapprove of, condemn.

reptile [reptil] *nm* reptile.

repu [rəpy] *a* (*rassasié*) satiated.

république [repyblik] *nf* republic. ◆**républicain, -aine** *a* & *nmf* republican.

répudier [repydje] *vt* to repudiate.

répugnant [repynã] *a* repugnant, loathsome. ◆**répugnance** *nf* repugnance, loathing (**pour** for); (*manque d'enthousiasme*) reluctance. ◆**répugner** *vi* **r. à qn** to be repugnant to s.o.; **r. à faire** to be loath to do.

répulsion [repylsjɔ̃] *nf* repulsion.

réputation [repytasjɔ̃] *nf* reputation; **avoir la r. d'être franc** to have a reputation for frankness *ou* for being frank. ◆**réputé** *a* (*célèbre*) renowned (**pour** for); **r. pour** (*considéré comme*) reputed to be.

requérir [rəkerir] *vt* (*nécessiter*) to demand, require; (*peine*) *Jur* to call for. ◆**requête** *nf* request; *Jur* petition. ◆**requis** *a* required, requisite.

requiem [rekɥijɛm] *nm inv* requiem.

requin [r(ə)kɛ̃] *nm* (*poisson*) & *Fig* shark.

réquisition [rekizisjɔ̃] *nf* requisition. ◆**réquisitionner** *vt* to requisition, commandeer.

réquisitoire [rekizitwar] *nm* (*critique*) indictment (**contre** of).

rescapé, -ée [reskape] *a* surviving; — *nmf* survivor.

rescousse (à la) [alareskus] *adv* to the rescue.

réseau, -x [rezo] *nm* network; **r. d'espionnage** spy ring *ou* network.

réserve [rezɛrv] *nf* **1** (*restriction, doute*) reservation; (*réticence*) reserve; **sans r.** (*admiration etc*) unqualified; **sous r. de** subject to; **sous toutes réserves** without guarantee. **2** (*provision*) reserve; (*entrepôt*) storeroom; (*de bibliothèque*) stacks; **la r.** *Mil* the reserve; **les réserves** (*soldats*) the reserves; **en r.** in reserve. **3** (*de chasse, pêche*) preserve; (*indienne*) reservation; **r. naturelle** nature reserve.

réserv/er [rezɛrve] *vt* to reserve; (*garder*) to keep, save; (*marchandises*) to put aside (à for); (*place, table*) to book, reserve; (*place, surprise etc*) to hold in store (à for); **se r. pour** to save oneself for; **se r. de faire** to reserve the right to do. ◆**—é** *a* (*personne, place*) reserved; (*prudent*) guarded. ◆**réservation** *nf* reservation, booking. ◆**réservoir** *nm* (*lac*) reservoir; (*citerne, cuve*) tank; **r. d'essence** *Aut* petrol *ou Am* gas tank.

résidence [rezidɑ̃s] *nf* residence; **r. secondaire** second home; **r. universitaire** hall of residence. ◆**résident, -ente** *nmf* (*foreign*) resident. ◆**résidentiel, -ielle** *a* (*quartier*) residential. ◆**résider** *vi* to reside, be resident (à, en, dans in); **r. dans** (*consister dans*) to lie in.

résidu [rezidy] *nm* residue.

résigner (se) [sərezine] *vpr* to resign oneself (à qch to sth, à faire to doing). ◆**résignation** *nf* resignation.

résilier [rezilje] *vt* (*contrat*) to terminate. ◆**résiliation** *nf* termination.

résille [rezij] *nf* (*pour cheveux*) hairnet.

résine [rezin] *nf* resin.

résistance [rezistɑ̃s] *nf* resistance (à to); (*conducteur*) *El* (*heating*) element; **plat de r.** main dish. ◆**résist/er** *vi* **r. à** to resist; (*chaleur, fatigue, souffrance*) to withstand; (*examen*) to stand up to. ◆**—ant, -ante** *a* tough, strong; **r. à la chaleur** heat-resistant; **r. au choc** shockproof; — *nmf Mil Hist* Resistance fighter.

résolu [rezɔly] *voir* **résoudre**; — *a* resolute, determined; **r. à faire** resolved *ou* determined to do. ◆**—ment** *adv* resolutely. ◆**résolution** *nf* (*décision*) resolution; (*fermeté*) determination.

résonance [rezɔnɑ̃s] *nf* resonance.

résonner [rezɔne] *vi* to resound (**de** with); (*salle, voix*) to echo.

résorber [rezɔrbe] *vt* (*chômage*) to reduce; (*excédent*) to absorb; — **se r.** *vpr* to be re-

duced; to be absorbed. ◆**résorption** *nf* reduction; absorption.

résoudre [rezudr] *vt* (*problème*) to solve; (*difficulté*) to resolve; **r. de faire** to decide *ou* resolve to do; **se r. à faire** to decide *ou* resolve to do; (*se résigner*) to bring oneself to do.

respect [rɛspɛ] *nm* respect (**pour, de** for); **mes respects à** my regards *ou* respects to; **tenir qn en r.** to hold s.o. in check. ◆**respectabilité** *nf* respectability. ◆**respectable** *a* (*honorable, important*) respectable. ◆**respecter** *vt* to respect; **qui se respecte** self-respecting. ◆**respectueux, -euse** *a* respectful (**envers to, de** of).

respectif, -ive [rɛspɛktif, -iv] *a* respective. ◆**respectivement** *adv* respectively.

respirer [rɛspire] *vi* to breathe; (*reprendre haleine*) to get one's breath (back); (*être soulagé*) to breathe again; — *vt* to breathe (in); (*exprimer*) *Fig* to exude. ◆**respiration** *nf* breathing; (*haleine*) breath; **r. artificielle** *Méd* artificial respiration. ◆**respiratoire** *a* breathing-, respiratory.

resplend/ir [rɛsplɑ̃dir] *vi* to shine; (*visage*) to glow (**de** with). ◆**—issant** *a* radiant.

responsable [rɛspɔ̃sabl] *a* responsible (**de qch** for sth, **devant qn** to s.o.); — *nmf* (*chef*) person in charge; (*dans une organisation*) official; (*coupable*) person responsible (**de** for). ◆**responsabilité** *nf* responsibility; (*légale*) liability.

resquiller [rɛskije] *vi* (*au cinéma, dans le métro etc*) to avoid paying; (*sans attendre*) to jump the queue, *Am* cut in (line).

ressaisir (se) [sərəsezir] *vpr* to pull oneself together.

ressasser [rəsɑse] *vt* (*ruminer*) to keep going over; (*répéter*) to keep trotting out.

ressemblance [rəsɑ̃blɑ̃s] *nf* resemblance, likeness. ◆**ressembl/er** *vi* **r. à** to resemble, look *ou* be like; **cela ne lui ressemble pas** (*ce n'est pas son genre*) that's not like him *ou* her; — **se r.** *vpr* to look *ou* be alike. ◆**—ant** *a* **r. à** a portrait **r.** good likeness.

ressentiment [rəsɑ̃timɑ̃] *nm* resentment.

ressentir [rəsɑ̃tir] *vt* to feel; **se r. de** to feel *ou* show the effects of.

resserre [rəsɛr] *nf* storeroom; (*remise*) shed.

resserrer [rəsere] *vt* (*nœud, boulon etc*) to tighten; (*contracter*) to close (up), contract; (*liens*) *Fig* to strengthen; — **se r.** *vpr* to tighten; (*amitié*) to become closer; (*se contracter*) to close (up), contract; (*route etc*) to narrow.

resservir [rəservir] **1** *vi* (*outil etc*) to come

in useful (again). **2 se r.** *vpr* **se r. de** (*plat etc*) to have another helping of.

ressort [r(ə)sɔr] *nm* **1** *Tech* spring. **2** (*énergie*) spirit. **3 du r. de** within the competence of; **en dernier r.** (*décider etc*) in the last resort, as a last resort.

ressortir[1] [r(ə)sɔrtir] *vi* (*aux être*) **1** to go *ou* come back out. **2** (*se voir*) to stand out; **faire r.** to bring out; **il ressort de** (*résulte*) it emerges from.

ressortir[2] [r(ə)sɔrtir] *vi* (*conjugated like finir*) **r. à** to fall within the scope of.

ressortissant, -ante [r(ə)sɔrtisã, -ãt] *nmf* (*citoyen*) national.

ressource [r(ə)surs] **1** *nfpl* (*moyens*) resources; (*argent*) means, resources. **2** *nf* (*recours*) recourse; (*possibilité*) possibility (**de faire** of doing); **dernière r.** last resort.

ressusciter [resysite] *vi* to rise from the dead; (*malade, pays*) to recover, revive; – *vt* (*mort*) to raise; (*malade, mode*) to revive.

restaurant [restɔrɑ̃] *nm* restaurant.

restaurer [restɔre] **1** *vt* (*réparer, rétablir*) to restore. **2 se r.** *vpr* to (have sth to) eat. ◆**restaurateur, -trice** *nmf* **1** (*de tableaux*) restorer. **2** (*hôtelier, hôtelière*) restaurant owner. ◆**restauration** *nf* **1** restoration. **2** (*hôtellerie*) catering.

reste [rest] *nm* rest, remainder (**de** of); *Math* remainder; *pl* remains (**de** of); (*de repas*) leftovers; **un r. de fromage/***etc* some left-over cheese/*etc*; **au r., du r.** moreover, besides.

rester [reste] *vi* (*aux être*) to stay, remain; (*calme, jeune etc*) to keep, stay, remain; (*subsister*) to remain, be left; **il reste du pain/***etc* there's some bread/*etc* left (over); **il me reste une minute/***etc* I have one minute/*etc* left; **l'argent qui lui reste** the money he *ou* she has left; **reste à savoir** it remains to be seen; **il me reste deux choses à faire** I still have two things to do; **il me reste à vous remercier** it remains for me to thank you; **en r. à** to stop at; **restons-en là** let's leave it at that. ◆**restant** *a* remaining; **poste restante** poste restante, *Am* general delivery; – *nm* **le r.** the rest, the remainder; **un r. de viande/***etc* some left-over meat/*etc*.

restituer [restitɥe] *vt* **1** (*rendre*) to return, restore (**à** to). **2** (*son*) to reproduce; (*énergie*) to release. ◆**restitution** *nf* return.

restreindre [restrɛ̃dr] *vt* to restrict, limit (**à** to); – **se r.** *vpr* to decrease; (*faire des économies*) to cut back *ou* down. ◆**restreint** *a* limited, restricted (**à** to). ◆**restrictif, -ive**

a restrictive. ◆**restriction** *nf* restriction; **sans r.** unreservedly.

résultat [rezylta] *nm* result; (*conséquence*) outcome, result; (*chiffre*) total *ou* figure; **avoir qch pour r.** to result in sth. ◆**résulter** *vi* **r. de** to result from.

résum/er [rezyme] *vt* to summarize; (*récapituler*) to sum up; – **se r.** *vpr* (*orateur etc*) to sum up; **se r. à** (*se réduire à*) to boil down to. ◆**-é** *nm* summary; **en r.** in short; (*en récapitulant*) to sum up.

résurrection [rezyrɛksjɔ̃] *nf* resurrection.

rétabl/ir [retablir] *vt* to restore; (*fait, vérité*) to re-establish; (*malade*) to restore to health; (*employé*) to reinstate; – **se r.** to be restored; (*malade*) to recover. ◆**-issement** *nm* restoring; re-establishment; *Méd* recovery.

retaper [r(ə)tape] *vt* (*maison, voiture etc*) to do up; (*lit*) to straighten; (*malade*) *Fam* to buck up.

retard [r(ə)tar] *nm* lateness; (*sur un programme etc*) delay; (*infériorité*) backwardness; **en r.** late; (*retardé*) backward; **en r. dans qch** behind in sth; **être en r. sur qn/qch** behind s.o./sth; **rattraper** *ou* **combler son r.** to catch up; **avoir du r.** to be late; (*sur un programme*) to be behind (schedule); (*montre*) to be slow; **avoir une heure de r.** to be an hour late; **prendre du r.** (*montre*) to lose (time); **sans r.** without delay. ◆**retardataire** *a* (*arrivant*) late; **enfant r.** *Méd* slow learner; – *nmf* latecomer. ◆**retardement** *nm* **à r.** delayed-action-; **bombe à r.** time bomb.

retard/er [r(ə)tarde] *vt* to delay; (*date, départ, montre*) to put back; **r. qn** (*dans une activité*) to put s.o. behind; – *vi* (*montre*) to be slow; **r. de cinq minutes** to be five minutes slow; **r.** (**sur son temps**) (*personne*) to be behind the times. ◆**-é, -ée** *a* (*enfant*) backward; – *nmf* backward child.

retenir* [rətnir] *vt* (*empêcher d'agir, contenir*) to hold back; (*attention, souffle*) to hold; (*réserver*) to book; (*se souvenir de*) to remember; (*fixer*) to hold (in place), secure; (*déduire*) to take off; (*candidature, proposition*) to accept; (*chiffre*) *Math* to carry; (*chaleur, odeur*) to retain; (*invité, suspect etc*) to detain, keep; **r. qn prisonnier** to keep *ou* hold s.o. prisoner; **r. qn de faire** to stop s.o. (from) doing; – **se r.** *vpr* (*se contenir*) to restrain oneself; **se r. de faire** to stop oneself (from) doing; **se r. à** to cling to. ◆**retenue** *nf* **1** (*modération*) restraint. **2** (*de salaire*) deduction, stoppage; (*chiffre*) *Math* figure carried over. **3** *Scol* detention; **en r.** in detention.

retent/ir [r(ə)tɑ̃tir] vi to ring (out) (**de** with). ◆**—issant** a resounding; (scandale) major. ◆**—issement** nm (effet) effect; **avoir un grand r.** (film etc) to create a stir.

réticent [retisɑ̃] a (réservé) reticent; (hésitant) reluctant. ◆**réticence** nf reticence; reluctance.

rétine [retin] nf Anat retina.

retir/er [r(ə)tire] vt to withdraw; (sortir) to take out; (ôter) to take off; (éloigner) to take away; (reprendre) to pick up; (offre, plainte) to take back, withdraw; **r. qch à qn** (permis etc) to take sth away from s.o.; **r. qch de** (gagner) to derive sth from; **— se r.** vpr to withdraw, retire (**de** from); (mer) to ebb. ◆**—é** a (lieu, vie) secluded.

retomber [r(ə)tɔ̃be] vi to fall; (de nouveau) to fall again; (pendre) to hang (down); (après un saut etc) to land; (intérêt) to slacken; **r. dans** (erreur, situation) to fall into; **r. sur qn** (frais, responsabilité) to fall on s.o. ◆**retombées** nfpl (radioactives) fallout.

rétorquer [retɔrke] vt **r. que** to retort that.

retors [rətɔr] a wily, crafty.

rétorsion [retɔrsjɔ̃] nf Pol retaliation; **mesure de r.** reprisal.

retouche [r(ə)tuʃ] nf touching up; alteration. ◆**retoucher** vt (photo, tableau) to touch up, retouch; (texte, vêtement) to alter.

retour [r(ə)tur] nm return; (de fortune) reversal; **être de r.** to be back (**de** from); **en r.** (en échange) in return; **par r. (du courrier)** by return of post; Am by return mail; **à mon retour** when I get ou got back (**de** from); **en arrière r.** flashback; **r. de flamme** Fig backlash; **match r.** return match ou Am game.

retourner [r(ə)turne] vt (aux avoir) (tableau etc) to turn round; (matelas, steak etc) to turn over; (foin, terre etc) to turn; (vêtement, sac etc) to turn inside out; (maison) to turn upside down; (compliment, lettre) to return; **r. qn** (bouleverser) Fam to upset s.o.; (contre qn) (argument) to turn against s.o.; (arme) to turn on s.o.; **de quoi il retourne** what it's about; **— vi** (aux être) to go back, return; **— se r.** vpr (pour regarder) to turn round, look back; (sur le dos) to turn over ou round; (dans son lit) to toss and turn; (voiture) to overturn; **s'en r.** to go back; **se r. contre** Fig to turn against.

retracer [r(ə)trase] vt (histoire etc) to retrace.

rétracter [retrakte] vt, **— se r.** vpr to retract. ◆**rétractation** nf (désaveu) retraction.

retrait [r(ə)trɛ] nm withdrawal; (de bagages, billets) collection; (de mer) ebb(ing); **en r.** (maison etc) set back.

retraite [r(ə)trɛt] nf **1** (d'employé) retirement; (pension) (retirement) pension; (refuge) retreat, refuge; (avant) la r. early retirement; **prendre sa r.** to retire; **à la r.** retired; **mettre à la r.** to pension off. **2** Mil retreat; **r. aux flambeaux** torchlight tattoo. ◆**retraité, -ée** a retired; **— nmf** senior citizen, (old age) pensioner.

retrancher [r(ə)trɑ̃ʃe] **1** vt (mot, passage etc) to cut (**de** from); (argent, quantité) to deduct (**de** from). **2 se r.** vpr (soldat, gangster etc) to entrench oneself; **se r. dans/derrière** Fig to take refuge in/behind.

retransmettre [r(ə)trɑ̃smɛtr] vt to broadcast. ◆**retransmission** nf broadcast.

rétréc/ir [retresir] vt to narrow; (vêtement) to take in; **— vi, — se r.** vpr (au lavage) to shrink; (rue etc) to narrow. ◆**—i** a (esprit, rue) narrow.

rétribuer [retribɥe] vt to pay, remunerate; (travail) to pay for. ◆**rétribution** nf payment, remuneration.

rétro [retro] a inv (mode etc) which harks back to the past, retro.

rétro- [retro] préf retro-.

rétroactif, -ive [retroaktif, -iv] a retroactive.

rétrograde [retrograd] a retrograde. ◆**rétrograder** vi (reculer) to move back; (civilisation etc) to go backwards; Aut to change down; **— vt** (fonctionnaire, officier) to demote.

rétrospectif, -ive [retrospɛktif, -iv] a (sentiment etc) retrospective; **— nf** (de films, tableaux) retrospective. ◆**rétrospectivement** adv in retrospect.

retrouss/er [r(ə)truse] (jupe etc) to hitch ou tuck up; (manches) to roll up ◆**—é** a (nez) snub, turned-up.

retrouver [r(ə)truve] vt to find (again); (rejoindre) to meet (again); (forces, santé) to regain; (découvrir) to rediscover; (se rappeler) to recall; **— se r.** (chose) to be found (again); (se trouver) to find oneself (back); (se rencontrer) to meet (again); **s'y r.** (s'orienter) to find one's bearings ou way. ◆**retrouvailles** nfpl reunion.

rétroviseur [retrovizœr] nm Aut (rear-view) mirror.

réunion [reynjɔ̃] nf (séance) meeting; (d'objets) collection, gathering; (d'éléments divers) combination; (jonction) joining. ◆**réunir** vt to collect, gather; (relier) to join; (convoquer) to call together, assemble; (rapprocher) to bring together; (qua-

lités, tendances) to combine. ◆**réunis** *apl* (*éléments*) combined.

réuss/ir [reysir] *vi* to succeed, be successful (à faire in doing); (*plante*) to thrive; **r. à** (*examen*) to pass; **r. à qn** to work (out) well for s.o.; (*aliment, climat*) to agree with s.o.; – *vt* to make a success of. ◆**—i** a successful. ◆**réussite** *nf* **1** success. **2** faire des **réussites** *Cartes* to play patience.

revaloir [r(ə)valwar] *vt* **je vous le revaudrai** (*en bien ou en mal*) I'll pay you back.

revaloriser [r(ə)valɔrize] *vt* (*salaire*) to raise. ◆**revalorisation** *nf* raising.

revanche [r(ə)vɑ̃ʃ] *nf* revenge; *Sp* return game; **en r.** on the other hand.

rêve [rɛv] *nm* dream; **faire un r.** to have a dream; **maison/voiture/etc de r.** dream house/car/*etc*. ◆**rêvasser** *vi* to day-dream.

revêche [rəvɛʃ] *a* bad-tempered, surly.

réveil [revɛj] *nm* waking (up); *Fig* awakening; (*pendule*) alarm (clock). ◆**réveill/er** *vt* (*personne*) to wake (up); (*sentiment, souvenir*) *Fig* to revive, awaken; — **se r.** *vpr* to wake (up); *Fig* to revive, awaken. ◆**—é** *a* awake. ◆**réveille-matin** *nm inv* alarm (clock).

réveillon [revɛjɔ̃] *nm* (*repas*) midnight supper (*on Christmas Eve or New Year's Eve*). ◆**réveillonner** *vi* to take part in a *réveillon*.

révéler [revele] *vt* to reveal (que that); — **se r.** to be revealed; **se r. facile/etc** to turn out to be easy/*etc*. ◆**révélateur, -trice** *a* revealing; **r. de** indicative of. ◆**révélation** *nf* revelation.

revenant [rəvnɑ̃] *nm* ghost.

revendiquer [r(ə)vɑ̃dike] *vt* to claim; (*exiger*) to demand. ◆**revendicatif, -ive** *a* (*mouvement etc*) protest-. ◆**revendication** *nf* claim; demand; (*action*) claiming, demanding.

revendre [r(ə)vɑ̃dr] *vt* to resell; **avoir (de) qch à r.** to have sth to spare. ◆**revendeur, -euse** *nmf* retailer; (*d'occasion*) second-hand dealer; **r.** (**de drogue**) drug pusher; **r. de billets** ticket tout. ◆**revente** *nf* resale.

revenir* [rəvnir] *vi* (*aux* être) to come back, return; (*date*) to come round again; (*mot*) to come up *or* crop up; (*coûter*) to cost (à qn s.o.); **r. à** (*activité, sujet*) to go back to, return to; (*se résumer à*) to boil down to; **r. à qn** (*forces, mémoire*) to come back to s.o., return to s.o.; (*honneur*) to fall to s.o.; **r. à soi** to come to *or* round; **r. de** (*maladie, surprise*) to get over; **r. sur** (*décision, promesse*) to go back on; (*passé, question*)

to go back over; **r. sur ses pas** to retrace one's steps; **faire r.** (*aliment*) to brown.

revenu [rəvny] *nm* income (de from); (*d'un État*) revenue (de from); **déclaration de revenus** tax return.

rêv/er [reve] *vi* to dream (**de** of, **de faire** of doing); — *vt* to dream (que that); (*désirer*) to dream of. ◆**—é** *a* ideal.

réverbération [reverberasjɔ̃] *nf* (*de lumière*) reflection; (*de son*) reverberation.

révérence [reverɑ̃s] *nf* reverence; (*salut d'homme*) bow; (*salut de femme*) curts(e)y; **faire une r.** to bow; to curts(e)y. ◆**révérer** *vt* to revere.

révérend, -ende [reverɑ̃, -ɑ̃d] *a* & *nm* *Rel* reverend.

rêverie [rɛvri] *nf* daydream; (*activité*) daydreaming.

revers [r(ə)vɛr] *nm* (*côté*) reverse; *Tennis* backhand; (*de veste*) lapel; (*de pantalon*) turn-up, *Am* cuff; (*d'étoffe*) wrong side; (*coup du sort*) setback, reverse; **r. de main** (*coup*) backhander; **le r. de la médaille** *Fig* the other side of the coin.

réversible [reversibl] *a* reversible.

revêtir* [r(ə)vetir] *vt* to cover (**de** with); (*habit*) to put on; (*caractère, forme*) to assume; (*route*) to surface; **r. qn** (*habiller*) to dress s.o. (**de** in); **r. de** (*signature*) to provide with. ◆**revêtement** *nm* (*surface*) covering; (*de route*) surface.

rêveur, -euse [rɛvœr, -øz] *a* dreamy; – *nmf* dreamer.

revient [rəvjɛ̃] *nm* **prix de r.** cost price.

revigorer [r(ə)vigɔre] *vt* (*personne*) to revive.

revirement [r(ə)virmɑ̃] *nm* (*changement*) about-turn, *Am* about-face; (*de situation, d'opinion, de politique*) reversal.

réviser [revize] *vt* (*notes, texte*) to revise; (*jugement, règlement etc*) to review; (*machine, voiture*) to overhaul, service. ◆**révision** *nf* revision; review; overhaul, service.

revivre* [r(ə)vivr] *vi* to live again; **faire r.** to revive; — *vt* (*incident etc*) to relive.

révocation [revɔkasjɔ̃] *nf* **1** (*de contrat etc*) revocation. **2** (*de fonctionnaire*) dismissal.

revoici [r(ə)vwasi] *prép* **me r.** here I am again.

revoilà [r(ə)vwala] *prép* **la r.** there she is again.

revoir* [r(ə)vwar] *vt* to see (again); (*texte*) to revise; **au r.** goodbye.

révolte [revɔlt] *nf* revolt. ◆**révolt/er 1** *vt* to revolt, incense. **2 se r.** *vpr* to revolt, rebel (**contre** against). ◆**—ant** *a* (*honteux*) revolting. ◆**—é, -ée** *nmf* rebel.

révolu [revɔly] a (époque) past; **avoir trente ans révolus** to be over thirty (years of age).

révolution [revɔlysjɔ̃] nf (changement, rotation) revolution. **◆révolutionnaire** a & nmf revolutionary. **◆révolutionner** vt to revolutionize; (émouvoir) Fig to shake up.

revolver [revɔlvɛr] nm revolver, gun.

révoquer [revɔke] vt 1 (contrat etc) to revoke. 2 (fonctionnaire) to dismiss.

revue [r(ə)vy] nf 1 (examen) & Mil review; **passer en r.** to review. 2 (de music-hall) variety show. 3 (magazine) magazine; (spécialisée) journal.

rez-de-chaussée [redʃose] nm inv ground floor, Am first floor.

rhabiller (se) [sərabije] vpr to get dressed again.

rhapsodie [rapsɔdi] nf rhapsody.

rhétorique [retɔrik] nf rhetoric.

Rhin [rɛ̃] le R. the Rhine.

rhinocéros [rinɔserɔs] nm rhinoceros.

rhododendron [rɔdɔdɛ̃drɔ̃] nm rhododendron.

rhubarbe [rybarb] nf rhubarb.

rhum [rɔm] nm rum.

rhumatisme [rymatism] nm Méd rheumatism; **avoir des rhumatismes** to have rheumatism. **◆rhumatisant, -ante** a & nmf rheumatic. **◆rhumatismal, -aux** a (douleur) rheumatic.

rhume [rym] nm cold; **r. de cerveau** head cold; **r. des foins** hay fever.

riant [rjɑ̃] a cheerful, smiling.

ricaner [rikane] vi (sarcastiquement) to snigger; (bêtement) to giggle.

riche [riʃ] a rich; (personne, pays) rich, wealthy; **r. en** (minérai, vitamines etc) rich in; — nmf rich ou wealthy person; **les riches** the rich. **◆—ment** adv (vêtu, illustré etc) richly. **◆richesse** nf wealth; (d'étoffe, de sol, vocabulaire) richness; pl (trésor) riches; (ressources) wealth.

ricin [risɛ̃] nm **huile de r.** castor oil.

ricocher [rikɔʃe] vi to ricochet, rebound. **◆ricochet** nm ricochet, rebound; **par r.** Fig as an indirect result.

rictus [riktys] nm grin, grimace.

ride [rid] nf wrinkle; ripple. **◆rider** vt (visage) to wrinkle; (eau) to ripple; — **se r.** vpr to wrinkle.

rideau, -x [rido] nm curtain; (métallique) shutter; (écran) Fig screen (de of); **le r. de fer** Pol the Iron Curtain.

ridicule [ridikyl] a ridiculous, ludicrous; — nm (moquerie) ridicule; (défaut) absurdity; (de situation etc) ridiculousness; **tourner en r.** to ridicule. **◆ridiculiser** vt to ridicule.

rien [rjɛ̃] pron nothing; **il ne sait r.** he knows nothing, he doesn't know anything; **r. du tout** nothing at all; **r. d'autre/de bon/etc** nothing else/good/etc; **r. de tel** nothing like it; **de r.!** (je vous en prie) don't mention it!; **ça ne fait r.** it doesn't matter; **en moins de r.** (vite) in no time; **trois fois r.** (chose insignifiante) next to nothing; **pour r.** (à bas prix) for next to nothing; **il n'en est r.** (ce n'est pas vrai) nothing of the kind; **r. que** only, just; — nm trifle, (mere) nothing; **un r. de** a hint ou touch of; **en un r. de temps** (vite) in no time; **un r. trop petit/etc** just a bit too small/etc.

rieur, -euse [rijœr, -øz] a cheerful.

riflard [riflar] nm Fam brolly, umbrella.

rigide [riʒid] a rigid; (carton, muscle) stiff; (personne) Fig inflexible; (éducation) strict. **◆rigidité** nf rigidity; stiffness; inflexibility; strictness.

rigole [rigɔl] nf (conduit) channel; (filet d'eau) rivulet.

rigoler [rigɔle] vi Fam to laugh; (s'amuser) to have fun ou a laugh; (plaisanter) to joke (avec about). **◆rigolade** nf Fam fun; (chose ridicule) joke, farce; **prendre qch à la r.** to make a joke out of sth. **◆rigolo, -ote** a Fam funny; — nmf Fam joker.

rigueur [rigœr] nf rigour; harshness; strictness; (précision) precision; **être de r.** to be the rule; **à la r.** if absolutely necessary, at ou Am in a pinch; **tenir r. à qn de qch** Fig to hold sth against s.o. **◆rigoureux, -euse** a rigorous; (climat, punition) harsh; (personne, morale, sens) strict.

rillettes [rijɛt] nfpl potted minced pork.

rime [rim] nf rhyme. **◆rimer** vi to rhyme (avec with); **ça ne rime à rien** it makes no sense.

rincer [rɛ̃se] vt to rinse (out). **◆rinçage** nm rinsing; (opération) rinse.

ring [riŋ] nm (boxing) ring.

ringard [rɛ̃gar] a (démodé) Fam unfashionable, fuddy-duddy.

ripaille [ripaj] nf Fam feast.

riposte [ripɔst] nf (réponse) retort; (attaque) counter(attack). **◆riposter** vi to retort; **r. à** (attaque) to counter; (insulte) to reply to; — vt **r. que** to retort that.

rire* [rir] vi to laugh (de at); (s'amuser) to have a good time; (plaisanter) to joke; **faire qch pour r.** to do sth for a laugh ou a joke; **se r. de qch** to laugh sth off; — nm laugh; pl laughter; **le r.** (activité) laughter. **◆risée** nf mockery; **être la r. de** to be the laughing stock of. **◆risible** a laughable.

ris [ri] nm **r. de veau** Culin (calf) sweetbread.

risque [risk] *nm* risk; **r. du métier** occupational hazard; **au r. de qch/de faire** at the risk of sth/of doing; **à vos risques et périls** at your own risk; **assurance tous risques** comprehensive insurance. ◆**risquer** *vt* to risk; (*question, regard*) to venture, hazard; **r. de faire** to stand a good chance of doing; **se r. à faire** to dare to do; **se r. dans** to venture into. ◆**risqué** *a* risky; (*plaisanterie*) daring, risqué.

ristourne [risturn] *nf* discount.

rite [rit] *nm* rite; (*habitude*) *Fig* ritual. ◆**rituel, -elle** *a* & *nm* ritual.

rivage [rivaʒ] *nm* shore.

rival, -ale, -aux [rival, -o] *a* & *nmf* rival. ◆**rivaliser** *vi* to compete (**avec** with, **de** in). ◆**rivalité** *nf* rivalry.

rive [riv] *nf* (*de fleuve*) bank; (*de lac*) shore.

rivé [rive] *a* **r. à** (*chaise etc*) *Fig* riveted to; **r. sur** *Fig* riveted on. ◆**rivet** *nm* (*tige*) rivet. ◆**riveter** *vt* to rivet (together).

riverain, -aine [rivrɛ̃, -ɛn] *a* riverside; lakeside; – *nmf* riverside resident; (*de lac*) lakeside resident; (*de rue*) resident.

rivière [rivjɛr] *nf* river.

rixe [riks] *nf* brawl, scuffle.

riz [ri] *nm* rice; **r. au lait** rice pudding. ◆**rizière** *nf* paddy (field), ricefield.

RN *abrév* = route nationale.

robe [rɔb] *nf* (*de femme*) dress; (*d'ecclésiastique, de juge*) robe; (*de professeur*) gown; (*pelage*) coat; **r. de soirée** *ou* **du soir** evening dress *ou* gown; **r. de grossesse/de mariée** maternity/wedding dress; **r. de chambre** dressing gown; **r. chasuble** pinafore (dress).

robinet [rɔbinɛ] *nm* tap, *Am* faucet; **eau du r.** tap water.

robot [rɔbo] *nm* robot; **r. ménager** food processor, liquidizer.

robuste [rɔbyst] *a* robust. ◆**robustesse** *nf* robustness.

roc [rɔk] *nm* rock.

rocaille [rɔkɑj] *nf* (*terrain*) rocky ground; (*de jardin*) rockery. ◆**rocailleux, -euse** *a* rocky, stony; (*voix*) harsh.

rocambolesque [rɔkɑ̃bɔlɛsk] *a* (*aventure etc*) fantastic.

roche [rɔʃ] *nf*, **rocher** [rɔʃe] *nm* (*bloc, substance*) rock. ◆**rocheux, -euse** *a* rocky.

rock [rɔk] *nm* (*musique*) rock; – *a inv* (*chanteur etc*) rock-.

rod/er [rɔde] *vt* (*moteur, voiture*) to run in, *Am* break in; **être rodé** (*personne*) *Fig* to have got *ou Am* gotten the hang of things. ◆**—age** *nm* running in, *Am* breaking in.

rôd/er [rode] *vi* to roam (about); (*suspect*) to prowl (about). ◆**—eur, -euse** *nmf* prowler.

rogne [rɔɲ] *nf Fam* anger; **en r.** in a temper.

rogner [rɔɲe] *vt* to trim, clip; (*réduire*) to cut; – *vi* **r. sur** (*réduire*) to cut down on. ◆**rognures** *nfpl* clippings, trimmings.

rognon [rɔɲɔ̃] *nm Culin* kidney.

roi [rwa] *nm* king; **fête** *ou* **jour des rois** Twelfth Night.

roitelet [rwatlɛ] *nm* (*oiseau*) wren.

rôle [rol] *nm* role, part; **à tour de r.** in turn.

romain, -aine [rɔmɛ̃, -ɛn] *a* & *nmf* Roman. **2** *nf* (*laitue*) cos (lettuce), *Am* romaine.

roman [rɔmɑ̃] **1** *nm* novel; (*histoire*) *Fig* story; **r.-fleuve** saga. **2** *a* (*langue*) Romance; *Archit* Romanesque. ◆**romancé** *a* (*histoire*) fictional. ◆**romancier, -ière** *nmf* novelist.

romanesque [rɔmanɛsk] *a* romantic; (*incroyable*) fantastic.

romanichel, -elle [rɔmaniʃɛl] *nmf* gipsy.

romantique [rɔmɑ̃tik] *a* romantic. ◆**romantisme** *nm* romanticism.

romarin [rɔmarɛ̃] *nm Bot Culin* rosemary.

romp/re* [rɔ̃pr] *vt* to break; (*pourparlers, relations*) to break off; (*digue*) to burst; – *vi* to break (*Fig* **avec** with); (*fiancés*) to break it off; – **se r.** *vpr* to break; to burst. ◆**—u** *a* **1** (*fatigué*) exhausted. **2 r. à** (*expérimenté*) experienced in.

romsteck [rɔmstɛk] *nm* rump steak.

ronces [rɔ̃s] *nfpl* (*branches*) brambles.

ronchonner [rɔ̃ʃɔne] *vi Fam* to grouse, grumble.

rond [rɔ̃] *a* round; (*gras*) plump; (*honnête*) straight; (*ivre*) *Fam* tight; **dix francs tout r.** ten francs exactly; – *adv* **tourner r.** (*machine etc*) to run smoothly; – *nm* (*objet*) ring; (*cercle*) circle; (*tranche*) slice; *pl* (*argent*) *Fam* money; **r. de serviette** napkin ring; **en r.** (*s'asseoir etc*) in a ring *ou* circle; **tourner en r.** (*toupie etc*) *Fig* to go round and round. ◆**r.-de-cuir** *nm* (*pl* ronds-de-cuir*) Péj* pen pusher. ◆**r.-point** *nm* (*pl* ronds-points) *Aut* roundabout, *Am* traffic circle. ◆**ronde** *nf* (*tour de surveillance*) round; (*de policier*) beat; (*danse*) round (dance); (*note*) *Mus* semibreve, *Am* whole note; **à la r.** around; (*boire*) in turn. ◆**rondelet, -ette** *a* chubby; (*somme*) *Fig* tidy. ◆**rondelle** *nf* (*tranche*) slice; *Tech* washer. ◆**rondement** *adv* (*efficacement*) briskly; (*franchement*) straight. ◆**rondeur** *nf* roundness; (*du corps*) plumpness. ◆**rondin** *nm* log.

ronéotyper [rɔneɔtipe] *vt* to duplicate, roneo.

ronflant [rɔ̃flɑ̃] *a* (*langage etc*) *Péj* high-flown; (*feu*) roaring.

ronfler [rɔ̃fle] *vi* to snore; (*moteur*) to hum(ming). ◆**ronflement** *nm* snore, snoring; hum(ming).

rong/er [rɔ̃ʒe] *vt* to gnaw (at); (*ver, mer, rouille*) to eat into (*sth*); **r. qn** (*chagrin, maladie*) to consume s.o.; **se r. les ongles** to bite one's nails; **se r. les sangs** (*s'inquiéter*) to worry oneself sick. ◆**—eur** *nm* (*animal*) rodent.

ronron [rɔ̃rɔ̃], **ronronnement** [rɔ̃rɔnmɑ̃] *nm* purr(ing). ◆**ronronner** *vi* to purr.

roquette [rɔkɛt] *nf Mil* rocket.

rosbif [rɔsbif] *nm* **du r.** (*rôti*) roast beef; (*à rôtir*) roasting beef; **un r.** a joint of roast *ou* roasting beef.

rose [roz] **1** *nf* (*fleur*) rose. **2** *a* (*couleur*) pink; (*situation, teint*) rosy; – *nm* pink. ◆**rosé** *a* pinkish; – *a & nm* (*vin*) rosé. ◆**rosette** *nf* (*d'un officier*) rosette; (*nœud*) bow. ◆**rosier** *nm* rose bush.

roseau, -x [rozo] *nm* (*plante*) reed.

rosée [roze] *nf* dew.

rosse [rɔs] *a & nf* nasty (person).

rosser [rɔse] *vt Fam* to thrash. ◆**—ée** *nf Fam* thrashing.

rossignol [rɔsiɲɔl] *nm* **1** (*oiseau*) nightingale. **2** (*crochet*) picklock.

rot [ro] *nm Fam* burp, belch. ◆**roter** *vi Fam* to burp, belch.

rotation [rɔtɑsjɔ̃] *nf* rotation; (*de stock*) turnover. ◆**rotatif, -ive** *a* rotary; – *nf* rotary press.

rotin [rɔtɛ̃] *nm* rattan, cane.

rôt/ir [rotir] *vti*, – **se r.** *vpr* to roast; **faire r.** to roast. ◆**—i** *nm* **du r.** roasting meat; (*cuit*) roast meat; **un r.** a joint; **r. de bœuf/de porc** (*paon*) joint of roast beef/pork. ◆**rôtissoire** *nf* (*roasting*) spit.

rotule [rɔtyl] *nf* kneecap.

roturier, -ière [rɔtyrje, -jɛr] *nmf* commoner.

rouage [rwaʒ] *nm* (*de montre etc*) (working) part; (*d'organisation etc*) *Fig* cog.

roublard [rublar] *a* a wily, foxy.

rouble [rubl] *nm* (*monnaie*) r(o)uble.

roucouler [rukule] *vi* (*oiseau, amoureux*) to coo.

roue [ru] *nf* wheel; **r.** (*dentée*) cog(wheel); **faire la r.** (*paon*) to spread its tail; (*se pavaner*) *Fig* to strut; **faire r. libre** *Aut* to freewheel.

roué, -ée [rwe] *a & nmf* sly *ou* calculating (person).

rouer [rwe] *vt* **r. qn de coups** to beat s.o. black and blue.

rouet [rwe] *nm* spinning wheel.

rouge [ruʒ] *a* red; (*fer*) red-hot; – *nm* (*couleur*) red; (*vin*) red wine; **r.** (*à lèvres*) lipstick; **r.** (*à joues*) rouge; **le feu est au r.** *Aut* the (traffic) lights are red; – *nmf* (*personne*) *Pol* Red. ◆**r.-gorge** *nm* (*pl* **rouges-gorges**) robin. ◆**rougeâtre** *a* reddish. ◆**rougeaud** *a* red-faced. ◆**rougeoyer** *vi* to glow (red). ◆**rougeur** *nf* redness; (*due à la gêne ou à la honte*) blush(ing); *pl Méd* red spots *ou* blotches. ◆**rougir** *vti* to redden, turn red; – *vi* (*de gêne, de honte*) to blush (de with); (*de colère, de joie*) to flush (de with).

rougeole [ruʒɔl] *nf* measles.

rouget [ruʒɛ] *nm* (*poisson*) mullet.

rouille [ruj] *nf* rust; – *a inv* (*couleur*) rust(-coloured). ◆**rouill/er** *vi* to rust; – **se r.** *vpr* to rust; (*esprit, sportif etc*) *Fig* to get rusty. ◆**—é** *a* rusty.

roul/er [rule] *vt* to roll; (*brouette, meuble*) to wheel, push; (*crêpe, ficelle, manches etc*) to roll up; **r. qn** (*duper*) *Fam* to cheat s.o.; – *vi* to roll; (*train, voiture*) to go, travel; (*conducteur*) to drive; **r. sur** (*conversation*) to turn on; **ça roule!** *Fam* everything's fine!; – **se r.** *vpr* to roll; **se r. dans** (*couverture etc*) to roll oneself (up) in. ◆**—ant** *a* (*escalier, trottoir*) moving; (*meuble*) on wheels. ◆**—é** *nm* (*gâteau*) Swiss roll. ◆**rouleau, -x** *nm* (*outil, vague*) roller; (*de papier, pellicule etc*) roll; **r. à pâtisserie** rolling pin; **r. compresseur** steamroller. ◆**roulement** *nm* (*bruit*) rumbling, rumble; (*de tambour, de tonnerre, d'yeux*) roll; (*ordre*) rotation; **par r.** in rotation; **r. à billes** *Tech* ball bearing. ◆**roulette** *nf* (*de meuble*) castor; (*de dentiste*) drill; (*jeu*) roulette. ◆**roulis** *nm* (*de navire*) roll(ing).

roulotte [rulɔt] *nf* (*de gitan*) caravan.

Roumanie [rumani] *nf* Romania. ◆**roumain, -aine** *a & nmf* Romanian; – *nm* (*langue*) Romanian.

round [rawnd, rund] *nm Boxe* round.

roupiller [rupije] *vi Fam* to kip, sleep.

rouquin, -ine [rukɛ̃, -in] *a Fam* red-haired; – *nmf Fam* redhead.

rouspét/er [ruspete] *vi Fam* to grumble, complain. ◆**—eur, -euse** *nmf* grumbler.

rousse [rus] *voir* **roux**.

rousseur [rusœr] *nf* redness; **tache de r.** freckle. ◆**roussir** *vt* (*brûler*) to singe, scorch; – *vi* (*feuilles*) to turn brown; **faire r.** *Culin* to brown.

route [rut] *nf* road (de to); (*itinéraire*) way,

route; (*aérienne, maritime*) route; (*chemin*) *Fig* path, way; **r. nationale/départementale** main/secondary road; **grande r., grand-r.** main road; **code de la r.** Highway Code; **en r.** on the way, en route; **en r.!** let's go!; **par la r.** by road; **sur la bonne r.** *Fig* on the right track; **se mettre en r.** (*voiture etc*) to start (up); **se mettre en r.** to set out (**pour** for); **une heure de r.** an hour's drive; **bonne r.!** *Aut* have a good trip! ◆**routier, -ière** *a* (*carte etc*) road-; — *nm* (*camionneur*) (long distance) lorry *ou Am* truck driver; (*restaurant*) transport café, *Am* truck stop.

routine [rutin] *nf* routine; **de r.** (*contrôle etc*) routine-. ◆**routinier, -ière** *a* (*travail etc*) routine-; (*personne*) addicted to routine.

rouvrir* [ruvrir] *vti*, — **se r.** *vpr* to reopen.

roux, rousse [ru, rus] *a* (*cheveux*) red, ginger; (*personne*) red-haired; — *nmf* redhead.

royal, -aux [rwajal, -o] *a* royal; (*cadeau, festin etc*) fit for a king; (*salaire*) princely. ◆**royalement** *adv* (*traiter*) royally. ◆**royaliste** *a* & *nmf* royalist. ◆**royaume** *nm* kingdom. ◆**Royaume-Uni** *nm* United Kingdom. ◆**royauté** *nf* (*monarchie*) monarchy.

ruade [rɥad] *nf* (*d'âne etc*) kick.

ruban [rybɑ̃] *nm* ribbon; (*d'acier, de chapeau*) band; **r. adhésif** adhesive *ou* sticky tape.

rubéole [rybeɔl] *nf* German measles, rubella.

rubis [rybi] *nm* (*pierre*) ruby; (*de montre*) jewel.

rubrique [rybrik] *nf* (*article*) *Journ* column; (*catégorie, titre*) heading.

ruche [ryʃ] *nf* (bee)hive.

rude [ryd] *a* (*grossier*) crude; (*rêche*) rough; (*pénible*) tough; (*hiver, voix*) harsh; (*remarquable*) *Fam* tremendous. ◆**—ment** *adv* (*parler, traiter*) harshly; (*frapper, tomber*) hard; (*très*) *Fam* awfully. ◆**rudesse** *nf* harshness. ◆**rudoyer** *vt* to treat harshly.

rudiments [rydimɑ̃] *nmpl* rudiments. ◆**rudimentaire** *a* rudimentary.

rue [ry] *nf* street; **être à la r.** (*sans domicile*) to be on the streets. ◆**ruelle** *nf* alley(way).

ruer [rɥe] **1** *vi* (*cheval*) to kick (out). **2 se r.** *vpr* (*foncer*) to rush, fling oneself (**sur** at). ◆**ruée** *nf* rush.

rugby [rygbi] *nm* rugby. ◆**rugbyman,** *pl* **-men** [rygbiman, -mɛn] *nm* rugby player.

rug/ir [ryʒir] *vi* to roar. ◆**—issement** *nm* roar.

rugueux, -euse [rygø, -øz] *a* rough. ◆**rugosité** *nf* roughness; *pl* (*aspérités*) roughness.

ruine [rɥin] *nf* (*décombres*) & *Fig* ruin; **en r.** (*édifice*) in ruins; **tomber en r.** to fall into ruin. ◆**ruiner** *vt* to ruin; — **se r.** *vpr* (*en dépensant*) to ruin oneself. ◆**ruineux, -euse** *a* (*goûts, projet*) ruinously expensive; (*dépense*) ruinous.

ruisseau, -x [rɥiso] *nm* stream; (*caniveau*) gutter. ◆**ruisseler** *vi* to stream (**de** with).

rumeur [rymœr] *nf* (*protestation*) clamour; (*murmure*) murmur; (*nouvelle*) rumour.

ruminer [rymine] *vt* (*méditer*) to ponder on, ruminate over.

rumsteak [rɔmstɛk] *nm* rump steak.

rupture [ryptyr] *nf* break(ing); (*de fiançailles, relations*) breaking off; (*de pourparlers*) breakdown (**de** in); (*brouille*) break (up), split; (*de contrat*) breach; (*d'organe*) *Méd* rupture.

rural, -aux [ryral, -o] *a* rural, country-; — *nmpl* country people.

ruse [ryz] *nf* (*subterfuge*) trick; **la r.** (*habileté*) cunning; (*fourberie*) trickery. ◆**rusé, -ée** *a* & *nmf* crafty *ou* cunning (person). ◆**ruser** *vi* to resort to trickery.

Russie [rysi] *nf* Russia. ◆**russe** *a* & *nmf* Russian; — *nm* (*langue*) Russian.

rustique [rystik] *a* (*meuble*) rustic.

rustre [rystr] *nm* lout, churl.

rutabaga [rytabaga] *nm* (*racine*) swede, *Am* rutabaga.

rutilant [rytilɑ̃] *a* gleaming, glittering.

rythme [ritm] *nm* rhythm; (*de travail*) rate, tempo; (*de la vie*) pace; **au r. de trois par jour** at *a ou* the rate of three a day. ◆**rythmé** *a*, ◆**rythmique** *a* rhythmic(al).

S

S, s [ɛs] *nm* S, s.

s' [s] *voir* se, si.

sa [sa] *voir* son[2].

SA *abrév* (*société anonyme*) *Com* plc, *Am* Inc.

sabbat [saba] *nm* (Jewish) Sabbath.

◆**sabbatique** a (année etc) Univ sabbatical.

sable [sabl] nm sand; **sables mouvants** quicksand(s). ◆**sabler** vt (route) to sand. ◆**sableux, -euse** a (eau) sandy. ◆**sablier** nm hourglass; Culin egg timer. ◆**sablière** nf (carrière) sandpit. ◆**sablonneux, -euse** a (terrain) sandy.

sablé [sable] nm shortbread biscuit ou Am cookie.

saborder [saborde] vt (navire) to scuttle; (entreprise) Fig to shut down.

sabot [sabo] nm 1 (de cheval etc) hoof. 2 (chaussure) clog. 3 (de frein) Aut shoe; **s. (de Denver)** Aut (wheel) clamp.

sabot/er [sabote] vt to sabotage; (bâcler) to botch. ◆**-age** nm sabotage; **un s.** an act of sabotage. ◆**-eur, -euse** nmf saboteur.

sabre [sabr] nm sabre, sword.

sabrer [sabre] vt (élève, candidat) Fam to give a thoroughly bad mark to.

sac [sak] nm 1 bag; (grand et en toile) sack; **s. (à main)** handbag; **s. à dos** rucksack. 2 **mettre à s.** (ville) Mil to sack.

saccade [sakad] nf jerk, jolt; **par saccades** jerkily, in fits and starts. ◆**saccadé** a (geste, style) jerky.

saccager [sakaʒe] vt (ville, région) Mil to sack; (bouleverser) Fig to turn upside down.

saccharine [sakarin] nf saccharin.

sacerdoce [saserdɔs] nm (fonction) Rel priesthood; Fig vocation.

sachet [saʃɛ] nm (small) bag; (de lavande etc) sachet; **s. de thé** teabag.

sacoche [sakɔʃ] nf bag; (de vélo, moto) saddlebag; Scol satchel.

sacquer [sake] vt Fam (renvoyer) to sack; (élève) to give a thoroughly bad mark to.

sacre [sakr] nm (d'évêque) consecration; (de roi) coronation. ◆**sacrer** vt (évêque) to consecrate; (roi) to crown.

sacré [sakre] a (saint) sacred; (maudit) Fam damned. ◆**-ment** adv Fam (très) damn(ed); a hell of a lot.

sacrement [sakrəmɑ̃] nm Rel sacrament.

sacrifice [sakrifis] nm sacrifice. ◆**sacrifier** vt to sacrifice (à to, pour for); – vi à (mode etc) to pander to; – **se s.** vpr to sacrifice oneself (à to, pour for).

sacrilège [sakrilɛʒ] nm sacrilege; – a sacrilegious.

sacristie [sakristi] nf vestry.

sacro-saint [sakrosɛ̃] a Iron sacrosanct.

sadisme [sadism] nm sadism. ◆**sadique** a sadistic; – nmf sadist.

safari [safari] nm safari; **faire un s.** to be ou go on safari.

safran [safrɑ̃] nm saffron.

sagace [sagas] a shrewd, sagacious.

sage [saʒ] a wise; (enfant) well-behaved, good; (modéré) moderate; – nm wise man, sage. ◆**sagement** adv wisely; (avec calme) quietly. ◆**sagesse** nf wisdom; good behaviour; moderation.

sage-femme [saʒfam] nf (pl **sages-femmes**) midwife.

Sagittaire [saʒitɛr] nm **le S.** (signe) Sagittarius.

Sahara [saara] nm **le S.** the Sahara (desert).

saign/er [seɲe] vti to bleed. ◆**-ant** [seɲɑ̃] a (viande) Culin rare, underdone. ◆**-ée** nf 1 Méd bleeding, blood-letting; (perte) Fig heavy loss. 2 **la s. du bras** Anat the bend of the arm. ◆**saignement** nm bleeding; **s. de nez** nosebleed.

saillant [sajɑ̃] a projecting, jutting out; (trait etc) Fig salient. ◆**saillie** nf projection; **en s.,** faisant **s.** projecting.

sain [sɛ̃] a healthy; (moralement) sane; (jugement) sound; (nourriture) wholesome, healthy; **s. et sauf** safe and sound, unhurt. ◆**sainement** adv (vivre) healthily; (raisonner) sanely.

saindoux [sɛ̃du] nm lard.

saint, sainte [sɛ̃, sɛ̃t] a holy; (personne) saintly; **s. Jean** Saint John; **sainte nitouche** Iron little innocent; **la Sainte Vierge** the Blessed Virgin; – nmf saint. ◆**s.-bernard** nm (chien) St Bernard. ◆**S.-Esprit** nm Holy Spirit. ◆**S.-Siège** nm Holy See. ◆**S.-Sylvestre** nf New Year's Eve.

sais [sɛ] voir **savoir**.

saisie [sezi] nf Jur seizure; **s. de données** data capture ou entry.

sais/ir [sezir] 1 vt to grab (hold of), seize; (occasion) & Jur to seize; (comprendre) to understand, grasp; (frapper) Fig to strike; **se s. de** to grab (hold of), seize. 2 vt (viande) Culin to fry briskly. ◆**-i** a (de joie, peur etc) overcome by. ◆**-issant** (film etc) gripping; (contraste, ressemblance) striking. ◆**-issement** (émotion) shock.

saison [sɛzɔ̃] nf season; **en/hors s.** in/out of season; **en pleine** ou **haute s.** in (the) high season; **en basse s.** in the low season. ◆**saisonnier, -ière** a seasonal.

sait [sɛ] voir **savoir**.

salade [salad] nf 1 (laitue) lettuce; **s. (verte)** (green) salad; **s. de fruits/de tomates/etc** fruit/tomato/etc salad. 2 nf (désordre) Fam mess. 3 nfpl (mensonges) Fam stories, nonsense. ◆**saladier** nm salad bowl.

salaire [saler] nm wage(s), salary.

salaison [salezɔ̃] nf Culin salting; pl (denrées) salt(ed) meat ou fish.

salamandre [salamɑ̃dr] nf (animal) salamander.

salami [salami] nm Culin salami.

salarial, -aux [salarjal, -o] a (accord etc) wage-. ◆**salarié, -ée** a wage-earning; – nmf wage earner.

salaud [salo] nm Arg Péj bastard, swine.

sale [sal] a dirty; (dégoûtant) filthy; (mauvais) nasty; (couleur) dingy. ◆**salement** adv (se conduire, manger) disgustingly. ◆**saleté** nf dirtiness; filthiness; (crasse) dirt, filth; (action) dirty trick; (camelote) Fam rubbish, junk; pl (détritus) mess, dirt; (obscénités) filth. ◆**salir** vt to (make) dirty; (réputation) Fig to sully, tarnish; – **se s.** vpr to get dirty. ◆**salissant** a (métier) dirty, messy; (étoffe) easily dirtied. ◆**salissure** nf (tache) dirty mark.

sal/er [sale] vt Culin to salt. ◆—**é a** 1 (eau) salt-; (saveur) salty; (denrées) salted; (grivois) Fig spicy. 2 (excessif) Fam steep. ◆**salière** nf saltcellar.

salive [saliv] nf saliva. ◆**saliver** vi to salivate.

salle [sal] nf room; (très grande, publique) hall; Th auditorium; (d'hôpital) ward; (public) Th house, audience; **s. à manger** dining room; **s. d'eau** washroom, shower room; **s. d'exposition** Com showroom; **s. de jeux** (pour enfants) games room; (avec machines à sous) amusement arcade; **s. d'opération** Méd operating theatre.

salon [salɔ̃] nm sitting room, lounge; (exposition) show; **s. de beauté/de coiffure** beauty/hairdressing salon; **s. de thé** tearoom(s).

salope [salɔp] nf (femme) Arg Péj bitch, cow. ◆**saloperie** nf Arg (action) dirty trick; (camelote) rubbish, junk; **des saloperies** (propos) filth.

salopette [salɔpet] nf dungarees; (d'ouvrier) overalls.

salsifis [salsifi] nf Bot Culin salsify.

saltimbanque [saltɛ̃bɑ̃k] nmf (travelling) acrobat.

salubre [salybr] a healthy, salubrious. ◆**salubrité** nf healthiness; **s. publique** public health.

saluer [salɥe] vt to greet; (en partant) to take one's leave; (de la main) to wave to; (de la tête) to nod to; Mil to salute; **s. qn comme** Fig to hail s.o. as. ◆**salut 1** nm greeting; wave; nod; Mil salute; – int Fam hello!, hi!; (au revoir) bye! **2** nm (de peuple

etc) salvation; (sauvegarde) safety. ◆**salutation** nf greeting.

salutaire [salyter] a salutary.

salve [salv] nf salvo.

samedi [samdi] nm Saturday.

SAMU [samy] nm abrév (service d'assistance médicale d'urgence) emergency medical service.

sanatorium [sanatɔrjɔm] nm sanatorium.

sanctifier [sɑ̃ktifje] vt to sanctify.

sanction [sɑ̃ksjɔ̃] nf (approbation, peine) sanction. ◆**sanctionner** vt (confirmer, approuver) to sanction; (punir) to punish.

sanctuaire [sɑ̃ktɥer] nm Rel sanctuary.

sandale [sɑ̃dal] nf sandal.

sandwich [sɑ̃dwitʃ] nm sandwich.

sang [sɑ̃] nm blood; **coup de s.** Méd stroke. ◆**sanglant** a (critique, reproche) scathing. ◆**sanguin, -ine 1** a (vaisseau etc) blood-; (tempérament) full-blooded. **2** nf (fruit) blood orange. ◆**sanguinaire** a bloodthirsty.

sang-froid [sɑ̃frwa] nm self-control, calm; **avec s.-froid** calmly; **de s.-froid** (tuer) in cold blood.

sangle [sɑ̃gl] nf (de selle, parachute) strap.

sanglier [sɑ̃glije] nm wild boar.

sanglot [sɑ̃glo] nm sob. ◆**sangloter** vi to sob.

sangsue [sɑ̃sy] nf leech.

sanitaire [saniter] a health-; (conditions) sanitary; (personnel) medical; (appareils etc) bathroom-, sanitary.

sans [sɑ̃] ([sɑ̃z] before vowel and mute h) prép without; **s. faire** without doing; **ça va s. dire** that goes without saying; **s. qu'il le sache** without him ou his knowing; **s. cela**, **s. quoi** otherwise; **s. plus** (but) no more than that; **s. exception/faute** without exception/fail; **s. importance/travail** unimportant/unemployed; **s. argent/manches** penniless/sleeveless. ◆**s.-abri** nmf inv homeless person; **les s.-abri** the homeless. ◆**s.-gêne** a inv inconsiderate; – nm inv inconsiderateness. ◆**s.-travail** nmf inv unemployed person.

santé [sɑ̃te] nf health; **en bonne/mauvaise s.** in good/bad health, well/not well; (à votre) **s.!** (en trinquant) your health!, cheers!; **maison de s.** nursing home.

saoul [su] = soûl.

saper [sape] vt to undermine.

sapeur-pompier [sapœrpɔ̃pje] nm (pl sapeurs-pompiers) fireman.

saphir [safir] nm (pierre) sapphire; (d'électrophone) sapphire, stylus.

sapin [sapɛ̃] nm (arbre, bois) fir; **s. de Noël** Christmas tree.

sarbacane [sarbakan] nf (jouet) peashooter.

sarcasme [sarkasm] nm sarcasm; **un s.** a piece of sarcasm. ◆**sarcastique** a sarcastic.

sarcler [sarkle] vt (jardin etc) to weed.

Sardaigne [sardɛɲ] nf Sardinia.

sardine [sardin] nf sardine.

sardonique [sardɔnik] a sardonic.

SARL abrév (société à responsabilité limitée) Ltd, Am Inc.

sarment [sarmɑ̃] nm vine shoot.

sarrasin [sarazɛ̃] nm buckwheat.

sas [sa(s)] nm (pièce étanche) Nau Av airlock.

Satan [satɑ̃] nm Satan. ◆**satané** a (maudit) blasted. ◆**satanique** a satanic.

satellite [satelit] nm satellite; **pays s.** Pol satellite (country).

satiété [sasjete] nf **à s.** (boire, manger) one's fill; (répéter) ad nauseam.

satin [satɛ̃] nm satin. ◆**satiné** a a satiny, silky.

satire [satir] nf satire (contre on). ◆**satirique** a satiric(al).

satisfaction [satisfaksjɔ̃] nf satisfaction. ◆**satisfaire*** vt to satisfy; – vi **s. à** (conditions, engagement etc) to fulfil. ◆**satisfaisant** a (acceptable) satisfactory. ◆**satisfait** a satisfied, content (de with).

saturer [satyre] vt to saturate (de with). ◆**saturation** nf saturation.

satyre [satir] nm Fam sex fiend.

sauce [sos] nf sauce; (jus de viande) gravy; **s. tomate** tomato sauce. ◆**saucière** nf sauce boat; gravy boat.

saucisse [sosis] nf sausage. ◆**saucisson** nm (cold) sausage.

sauf[1] [sof] prép except (que that); **s. avis contraire** unless you hear otherwise; **s. erreur** barring error.

sauf[2], **sauve** [sof, sov] a (honneur) intact, saved; **avoir la vie sauve** to be unharmed. ◆**sauf-conduit** nm (document) safeconduct.

sauge [soʒ] nf Bot Culin sage.

saugrenu [sogrəny] a preposterous.

saule [sol] nm willow; **s. pleureur** weeping willow.

saumâtre [somɑtr] a (eau) briny, brackish.

saumon [somɔ̃] nm salmon; – a inv (couleur) salmon (pink).

saumure [somyr] nf (pickling) brine.

sauna [sona] nm sauna.

saupoudrer [sopudre] vt (couvrir) to sprinkle (de with).

saur [sor] am **hareng s.** smoked herring, kipper.

saut [so] nm jump, leap; **faire un s.** to jump, leap; **faire un s. chez qn** (visite) to pop round to see; **au s. du lit** on getting out of bed; **s. à la corde** skipping, Am jumping rope. ◆**sauter** vi to jump, leap; (bombe) to go off, explode; (poudrière etc) to go up, blow up; (fusible) to blow; (se détacher) to come off; **faire s.** (détruire) to blow up; (arracher) to tear off; (casser) to break; (renvoyer) Fam to get rid of, fire; (fusible) to blow; (crêpe) Culin to toss; **s. à la corde** to skip, Am jump rope; **ça saute aux yeux** it's obvious; – vt (franchir) to jump (over); (mot, classe, repas) to skip. ◆**sautemouton** nm (jeu) leapfrog. ◆**sautiller** vi to hop. ◆**sautoir** nm Sp jumping area.

sauté [sote] a & nm Culin sauté. ◆**sauteuse** nf (shallow) pan.

sauterelle [sotrɛl] nf grasshopper.

sautes [sot] nfpl (d'humeur, de température) sudden changes (de in).

sauvage [sovaʒ] a (primitif, cruel) savage; (farouche) unsociable, shy; (illégal) unauthorized; – nmf unsociable person; (brute) savage. ◆**sauvagerie** nf unsociability; (cruauté) savagery.

sauve [sov] a voir **sauf**[2].

sauvegarde [sovgard] nf safeguard (contre against). ◆**sauvegarder** vt to safeguard.

sauver [sove] **1** vt to save; (d'un danger) to rescue (de from); (matériel) to salvage; **s. la vie à qn** to save s.o.'s life. **2 se s.** vpr (s'enfuir) to run away ou off; (partir) Fam to get off, go. ◆**sauve-qui-peut** nm inv stampede. ◆**sauvetage** nm rescue; **canot de s.** lifeboat; **ceinture de s.** life belt; **radeau de s.** life raft. ◆**sauveteur** nm rescuer. ◆**sauveur** nm saviour.

sauvette (à la) [alasovɛt] adv **vendre à la s.** to hawk illicitly (on the streets).

savant [savɑ̃] a learned, scholarly; (manœuvre etc) masterly, clever; – nm scientist. ◆**savamment** adv learnedly; (avec habileté) cleverly, skilfully.

savate [savat] nf old shoe ou slipper.

saveur [savœr] nf (goût) flavour; (piment) Fig savour.

savoir* [savwar] vt to know; (nouvelle) to know, have heard; **j'ai su la nouvelle** I heard ou got to know the news; **s. lire/nager/etc** (pouvoir) to know how to read/swim/etc; **faire s. à qn que** to inform ou tell s.o. that; **à s.** (c'est-à-dire) that is, namely; **je ne saurais pas** I could not, I cannot; **(pas) que je sache** (not) as far as I know; **je n'en sais rien** I have no idea, I don't know; **en s. long sur** to know a lot about; **un je ne sais quoi** a something or other; – *nm* (*culture*) learning, knowledge. ◆**s.-faire** *nm inv* know-how, ability. ◆**s.-vivre** *nm inv* good manners.

savon [savɔ̃] *nm* **1** soap; (*morceau*) bar of soap. **2 passer un s. à qn** (*réprimander*) *Fam* to give s.o. a dressing-down *ou* a talking-to. ◆**savonner** *vt* to soap. ◆**savonnette** *nf* bar of soap. ◆**savonneux, -euse** *a* soapy.

savourer [savure] *vt* to savour, relish. ◆**savoureux, -euse** *a* tasty; (*histoire etc*) *Fig* juicy.

saxophone [saksɔfɔn] *nm* saxophone.

sbire [sbir] *nm* (*homme de main*) *Péj* henchman.

scabreux, -euse [skabrø, -øz] *a* obscene.

scalpel [skalpɛl] *nm* scalpel.

scandale [skɑ̃dal] *nm* scandal; (*tapage*) uproar; **faire s.** (*livre etc*) to scandalize people; **faire un s.** to make a scene. ◆**scandaleux, -euse** *a* scandalous, outrageous. ◆**scandaleusement** *adv* outrageously. ◆**scandaliser** *vt* to scandalize, shock; – **se s.** *vpr* to be shocked *ou* scandalized (**de** by, **que** (+ *sub*) that).

scander [skɑ̃de] *vt* (*vers*) to scan; (*slogan*) to chant.

Scandinavie [skɑ̃dinavi] *nf* Scandinavia. ◆**scandinave** *a & nmf* Scandinavian.

scanner [skanɛr] *nm* (*appareil*) *Méd* scanner.

scaphandre [skafɑ̃dr] *nm* (*de plongeur*) diving suit; (*de cosmonaute*) spacesuit; **s. autonome** aqualung. ◆**scaphandrier** *nm* diver.

scarabée [skarabe] *nm* beetle.

scarlatine [skarlatin] *nf* scarlet fever.

scarole [skarɔl] *nf* endive.

sceau, -x [so] *nm* (*cachet, cire*) seal. ◆**scell/er** *vt* **1** (*document etc*) to seal. **2** (*fixer*) *Tech* to cement. ◆**—és** *nmpl* (*cachets de cire*) seals.

scélérat, -ate [selera, -at] *nmf* scoundrel.

scel-o-frais® [selofre] *nm* clingfilm, *Am* plastic wrap.

scénario [senarjo] *nm* (*déroulement*) *Fig* scenario; (*esquisse*) *Cin* scenario; (*dialogues etc*) screenplay. ◆**scénariste** *nmf* *Cin* scriptwriter.

scène [sɛn] *nf* **1** *Th* scene; (*estrade, art*) stage; (*action*) action; **mettre en s.** (*pièce, film*) to direct. **2** (*dispute*) scene; **faire une s.**

(à qn) to make *ou* create a scene; **s. de ménage** domestic quarrel.

scepticisme [septisism] *nm* scepticism, *Am* skepticism. ◆**sceptique** *a* sceptical, *Am* skeptical; – *nmf* sceptic, *Am* skeptic.

scheik [ʃɛk] *nm* sheikh.

schéma [ʃema] *nm* diagram; *Fig* outline. ◆**schématique** *a* diagrammatic; (*succinct*) *Péj* sketchy. ◆**schématiser** *vt* to represent diagrammatically; (*simplifier*) *Péj* to oversimplify.

schizophrène [skizɔfrɛn] *a & nmf* schizophrenic.

sciatique [sjatik] *nf* *Méd* sciatica.

scie [si] *nf* (*outil*) saw. ◆**scier** *vt* to saw. ◆**scierie** *nf* sawmill.

sciemment [sjamɑ̃] *adv* knowingly.

science [sjɑ̃s] *nf* science; (*savoir*) knowledge; (*habileté*) skill; **sciences humaines** social science(s); **étudier les sciences** to study science. ◆**s.-fiction** *nf* science fiction. ◆**scientifique** *a* scientific; – *nmf* scientist.

scinder [sɛ̃de] *vt*, – **se s.** *vpr* to divide, split.

scintill/er [sɛ̃tije] *vi* to sparkle, glitter; (*étoiles*) to twinkle. ◆**—ement** *nm* sparkling; twinkling.

scission [sisjɔ̃] *nf* (*de parti etc*) split (**de** in).

sciure [sjyr] *nf* sawdust.

sclérose [skleroz] *nf* *Méd* sclerosis; *Fig* ossification; **s. en plaques** multiple sclerosis. ◆**sclérosé** *a* (*société etc*) *Fig* ossified.

scolaire [skɔlɛr] *a* school-. ◆**scolariser** *vt* (*pays*) to provide with schools; (*enfant*) to send to school, put in school. ◆**scolarité** *nf* schooling.

scooter [skutɛr] *nm* (motor) scooter.

score [skɔr] *nm* *Sp* score.

scories [skɔri] *nfpl* (*résidu*) slag.

scorpion [skɔrpjɔ̃] *nm* scorpion; **le S.** (*signe*) Scorpio.

scotch [skɔtʃ] *nm* **1** (*boisson*) Scotch, whisky. *Am* **2®** (*ruban adhésif*) sellotape®, *Am* scotch (tape)®. ◆**scotcher** *vt* to sellotape, *Am* to tape.

scout [skut] *a & nm* scout. ◆**scoutisme** *nm* scout movement, scouting.

script [skript] *nm* (*écriture*) printing.

scrupule [skrypyl] *nm* scruple; **sans scrupules** unscrupulous; (*agir*) unscrupulously. ◆**scrupuleux, -euse** *a* scrupulous. ◆**scrupuleusement** *adv* scrupulously.

scruter [skryte] *vt* to examine, scrutinize.

scrutin [skrytɛ̃] *nm* (*vote*) ballot; (*opérations électorales*) poll(ing).

sculpter [skylte] *vt* to sculpt(ure), carve.

◆**sculpteur** nm sculptor. ◆**sculptural, -aux** a (beauté) statuesque. ◆**sculpture** nf (art, œuvre) sculpture; **s. sur bois** wood-carving.

se [s(ə)] (**s'** before vowel or mute h) pron **1** (complément direct) himself; (sujet femelle) herself; (non humain) itself; (indéfini) one-self; pl themselves; **il se lave** he washes himself. **2** (indirect) to himself; to herself; to itself; to oneself; **elle se dit** she says to herself. **3** (réciproque) (to) each other, (to) one another; **ils s'aiment** they love each other ou one another; **ils ou elles se parlent** they speak to each other ou one another. **4** (passif) **ça se fait** that is done; **ça se vend bien** it sells well. **5** (possessif) **il se lave les mains** he washes his hands.

séance [seɑ̃s] nf **1** (d'assemblée etc) session, sitting; (de travail etc) session; **s. (de pose)** (chez un peintre) sitting. **2** Cin Th show, performance. **3** s. tenante at once.

séant [seɑ̃] **1** a (convenable) seemly, proper. **2** nm **se mettre sur son s.** to sit up.

seau, -x [so] nm bucket, pail.

sec, sèche [sɛk, sɛʃ] a dry; (fruits, légumes) dried; (ton) curt, harsh; (maigre) spare; (cœur) Fig hard; **coup s.** sharp blow, tap; **bruit s.** (rupture) snap; – adv (frapper, pleuvoir) hard; (boire) neat, Am straight; – nm **à s.** dried up, dry; (sans argent) Fam broke; **au s.** in a dry place. **◆sécher/er 1** vti to dry; – **se s.** vpr to dry oneself. **2** vt (cours) Scol Fam to skip; – vi (ignorer) Scol Fam to be stumped. **◆—age** nm drying. **◆sécheresse** nf dryness; (de ton) curt-ness; Mét drought. **◆séchoir** nm (ap-pareil) drier; **s. à linge** clotheshorse.

sécateur [sekatœr] nm pruning shears, se-cateurs.

sécession [sesesjɔ̃] nf secession; **faire s.** to secede.

sèche [sɛʃ] voir sec. **◆sèche-cheveux** nm inv hair drier. **◆sèche-linge** nm inv tum-ble drier.

second, -onde[1] [sgɔ̃, -ɔ̃d] a & nmf second; **de seconde main** second-hand; – nm (ad-joint) second in command; (étage) second floor, Am third floor; – nf Rail second class; Scol = âfth form, Am = eleventh grade; (vitesse) Aut second (gear). **◆secondaire** a secondary.

seconde[2] [sgɔ̃d] nf (instant) second.

seconder [sgɔ̃de] vt to assist.

secouer [s(ə)kwe] vt to shake; (paresse, poussière) to shake off; **s. qn** (maladie, nou-velle etc) to shake s.o. up; **s. qch de qch**

(enlever) to shake sth out of sth; – **se s.** vpr (faire un effort) Fam to shake oneself out of it.

secour/ir [skurir] vt to assist, help. **◆—able** a (personne) helpful. **◆secou-risme** nm first aid. **◆secouriste** nmf first-aid worker.

secours [s(ə)kur] nm assistance, help; (aux indigents) aid, relief; **le s., les s.** Mil relief; **(premiers) s.** Méd first aid; **au s.!** help!; **porter s. à qn** to give s.o. assistance ou help; **de s.** (sortie) emergency-; (équipe) rescue-; (roue) spare.

secousse [s(ə)kus] nf jolt, jerk; (psycho-logique) shock; Géol tremor.

secret, -ète [səkrɛ, -ɛt] a secret; (cachottier) secretive; – nm secret; (discrétion) secrecy; **en s.** in secret, secretly; **dans le s.** (au cou-rant) in on the secret.

secrétaire [sekreter] **1** nmf secretary; **s. d'État** Secretary of State; **s. de mairie** town clerk; **s. de rédaction** subeditor. **2** nm (meuble) writing desk. **◆secrétariat** nm (bureau) secretary's office; (d'organisation internationale) secretariat; (métier) secreta-rial work; **de s.** (école, travail) secretarial.

sécréter [sekrete] vt Méd Biol to secrete. **◆sécrétion** nf secretion.

secte [sɛkt] nf sect. **◆sectaire** a & nmf Péj sectarian.

secteur [sɛktœr] nm Mil Com sector; (de ville) district; (domaine) Fig area; (de réseau) Él supply area; (ligne) Él mains.

section [sɛksjɔ̃] nf section; (de ligne d'autobus) fare stage; Mil platoon. **◆sec-tionner** vt to divide (into sections); (artère, doigt) to sever.

séculaire [sekyler] a (tradition etc) age-old.

secundo [s(ə)gɔ̃do] adv secondly.

sécurité [sekyrite] nf (tranquillité) security; (matérielle) safety; **s. routière** road safety; **s. sociale** = social services ou security; **de s.** (dispositif, ceinture, marge etc) safety-; **en s.** secure; safe. **◆sécuriser** vt to reassure, make feel (emotionally) secure.

sédatif [sedatif] nm sedative.

sédentaire [sedɑ̃ter] a sedentary.

sédiment [sedimɑ̃] nm sediment.

séditieux, -euse [sedisjø, -øz] a seditious. **◆sédition** nf sedition.

séduire[*] [seduir] vt to charm, attract; (plaire à) to appeal to; (abuser de) to se-duce. **◆séduisant** a attractive. **◆sé-ducteur, -trice** a seductive; – nmf seduc-er. **◆séduction** nf attraction.

segment [sɛgmɑ̃] nm segment.

ségrégation [segregɑsjɔ̃] nf segregation.

seiche [sɛʃ] *nf* cuttlefish.

seigle [sɛgl] *nm* rye.

seigneur [sɛɲœr] *nm Hist* lord; *S. Rel* Lord.

sein [sɛ̃] *nm* (*mamelle, poitrine*) breast; *Fig* bosom; **bout de s.** nipple; **au s. de** (*parti etc*) within; (*bonheur etc*) in the midst of.

Seine [sɛn] *nf* **la S.** the Seine.

séisme [seism] *nm* earthquake.

seize [sɛz] *a & nm* sixteen. ◆**seizième** *a & nmf* sixteenth.

séjour [seʒur] *nm* stay; (**salle de**) **s.** living room. ◆**séjourner** *vi* to stay.

sel [sɛl] *nm* salt; (*piquant*) *Fig* spice; (*humour*) wit; *pl Méd* (smelling) salts; **sels de bain** bath salts.

sélect [selɛkt] *a Fam* select. ◆

sélectif, -ive [selɛktif, -iv] *a* selective. ◆**sélection** *nf* selection. ◆**sélectionner** *vt* to select.

self-(service) [sɛlf(sɛrvis)] *nm* self-service restaurant *ou* shop.

selle [sɛl] *nf* **1** (*de cheval*) saddle. **2** *nfpl* **les selles** *Méd* bowel movements, stools. ◆**seller** *vt* (*cheval*) to saddle.

sellette [sɛlɛt] *nf* **sur la s.** (*personne*) under examination, in the hot seat.

selon [s(ə)lɔ̃] *prép* according to (**que** whether); **c'est s.** *Fam* it (all) depends.

Seltz (eau de) [odsɛls] *nf* soda (water).

semailles [s(ə)maj] *nfpl* (*travail*) sowing; (*période*) seedtime.

semaine [s(ə)mɛn] *nf* week; **en s.** (*opposé à week-end*) in the week.

sémantique [semɑ̃tik] *a* semantic; *– nf* semantics.

sémaphore [semafor] *nm* (*appareil*) *Rail Nau* semaphore.

semblable [sɑ̃blabl] *a* similar (à to); **être semblables** to be alike *ou* similar; **de semblables propos**/*etc* (*tels*) such remarks/*etc*; *– nm* fellow (creature); **toi et tes semblables** you and your kind.

semblant [sɑ̃blɑ̃] *nm* **faire s.** to pretend (**de faire** to do); **un s. de** a semblance of.

sembler [sɑ̃ble] *vi* to seem (à to); **il (me) semble** when he seems *ou* looks old (to me); **s. être**/**faire** to seem to be/to do; *– v imp* **il semble que** (+ *sub ou indic*) it seems that, it looks as if; **il me semble que** it seems to me that, I think that.

semelle [s(ə)mɛl] *nf* (*de chaussure*) sole; (*intérieure*) insole.

semer [s(ə)me] *vt* **1** (*graines*) to sow; (*jeter*) *Fig* to strew; (*répandre*) to spread; **semé de** *Fig* strewn with, dotted with. **2** (*concurrent, poursuivant*) to shake off. ◆**semence** *nf*

seed; (*clou*) tack. ◆**semeur, -euse** *nmf* sower (**de** of).

semestre [s(ə)mɛstr] *nm* half-year; *Univ* semester. ◆**semestriel, -ielle** *a* half-yearly.

semi- [səmi] *préf* semi-.

séminaire [seminɛr] *nm* **1** *Univ* seminar. **2** *Rel* seminary.

semi-remorque [səmirəmɔrk] *nm* (*camion*) articulated lorry, *Am* semi(trailer).

semis [s(ə)mi] *nm* sowing; (*terrain*) seedbed; (*plant*) seedling.

sémite [semit] *a* Semitic; *– nmf* Semite. ◆**sémitique** *a* (*langue*) Semitic.

semonce [səmɔ̃s] *nf* reprimand; **coup de s.** *Nau* warning shot.

semoule [s(ə)mul] *nf* semolina.

sempiternel, -elle [sɑ̃pitɛrnɛl] *a* endless, ceaseless.

sénat [sena] *nm Pol* senate. ◆**sénateur** *nm Pol* senator.

sénile [senil] *a* senile. ◆**sénilité** *nf* senility.

sens [sɑ̃s] *nm* **1** (*faculté, raison*) sense; (*signification*) meaning, sense; **à mon s.** to my mind; **s. commun** commonsense; **s. de l'humour** sense of humour; **ça n'a pas de s.** that doesn't make sense. **2** (*direction*) direction; **s. giratoire** *Aut* roundabout, *Am* traffic circle, rotary; **s. interdit** *ou* **unique** (*rue*) one-way street; **'s. interdit'** 'no entry'; **à s. unique** (*rue*) one-way; **s. dessus dessous** [sɑ̃dsydsu] upside down; **dans le s./le s. inverse des aiguilles d'une montre** clockwise/anticlockwise, *Am* counterclockwise.

sensation [sɑ̃sasjɔ̃] *nf* sensation, feeling; **faire s.** to cause *ou* create a sensation; **à s.** (*film etc*) *Péj* sensational. ◆**sensationnel, -elle** *a Fig* sensational.

sensé [sɑ̃se] *a* sensible.

sensible [sɑ̃sibl] *a* sensitive (à to); (*douloureux*) tender, sore; (*perceptible*) perceptible; (*progrès etc*) appreciable. ◆**sensiblement** *adv* (*notablement*) appreciably; (*à peu près*) more or less. ◆**sensibiliser** *vt* **s. qn à** (*problème etc*) to make s.o. alive to *ou* aware of. ◆**sensibilité** *nf* sensitivity.

sensoriel, -ielle [sɑ̃sɔrjɛl] *a* sensory.

sensuel, -elle [sɑ̃sɥɛl] *a* (*sexuel*) sensual; (*musique, couleur etc*) sensuous. ◆**sensualité** *nf* sensuality; sensuousness.

sentence [sɑ̃tɑ̃s] *nf* **1** *Jur* sentence. **2** (*maxime*) maxim.

senteur [sɑ̃tœr] *nf* (*odeur*) scent.

sentier [sɑ̃tje] *nm* path.

sentiment [sɑ̃timɑ̃] *nm* feeling; **avoir le s. de** (*apprécier*) to be aware of; **faire du s.** to be sentimental. ◆**sentimental, -aux** *a* sentimental; (*amoureux*) love-. ◆**sentimentalité** *nf* sentimentality.

sentinelle [sɑ̃tinɛl] *nf* sentry.

sentir* [sɑ̃tir] *vt* to feel; (*odeur*) to smell; (*goût*) to taste; (*racisme etc*) to smack of; (*connaître*) to sense, be conscious of; **s. le moisi/le parfum**/*etc* to smell musty/of perfume/*etc*; **s. le poisson**/*etc* (*avoir le goût de*) to taste of fish/*etc*; **je ne peux pas le s.** (*supporter*) *Fam* I can't bear *ou* stand him; **se faire s.** (*effet etc*) to make itself felt; **se s. fatigué/humilié**/*etc* to feel tired/humiliated/*etc*; — *vi* to smell.

séparation [separɑsjɔ̃] *nf* separation; (*en deux*) division, split; (*départ*) parting. ◆**séparer** *vt* to separate (*de* from); (*diviser en deux*) to divide, split (up); (*cheveux*) to part; — **se s.** *vpr* (*se quitter*) to part; (*adversaires, époux*) to separate; (*assemblée, cortège*) to disperse, break up; (*se détacher*) to split off; **se s. de** (*objet aimé, chien etc*) to part with. ◆**séparé** *a* (*distinct*) separate; (*époux*) separated (*de* from). ◆**séparément** *adv* separately.

sept [sɛt] *a & nm* seven. ◆**septième** *a & nmf* seventh; **un s.** a seventh.

septante [sɛptɑ̃t] *a & nm* (*en Belgique, Suisse*) seventy.

septembre [sɛptɑ̃br] *nm* September.

septennat [sɛptena] *nm Pol* seven-year term (of office).

septentrional, -aux [sɛptɑ̃trijɔnal, -o] *a* northern.

sépulcre [sepylkr] *nm Rel* sepulchre.

sépulture [sepyltyr] *nf* burial; (*lieu*) burial place.

séquelles [sekɛl] *nfpl* (*de maladie etc*) after-effects; (*de guerre*) aftermath.

séquence [sekɑ̃s] *nf Mus Cartes Cin* sequence.

séquestrer [sekɛstre] *vt* to confine (illegally), lock up.

sera, serait [s(ə)ra, s(ə)rɛ] *voir* être.

serein [sərɛ̃] *a* serene. ◆**sérénité** *nf* serenity.

sérénade [serenad] *nf* serenade.

sergent [sɛrʒɑ̃] *nm Mil* sergeant.

série [seri] *nf* series; (*ensemble*) set; **s. noire** *Fig* string *ou* series of disasters; **de s.** (*article etc*) standard; **fabrication en s.** mass production; **fins de s.** *Com* oddments; **hors s.** *Fig* outstanding.

sérieux, -euse [serjø, -øz] *a* (*personne, maladie, doute etc*) serious; (*de bonne foi, fiable*) genuine, serious; (*digne de foi, fiable*) reliable; (*bénéfices*) substantial; **de sérieuses chances de . . .** a good chance of . . . ; —

nm seriousness; (*fiabilité*) reliability; **prendre au s.** to take seriously; **garder son s.** to keep a straight face; **manquer de s.** (*travailleur*) to lack application. ◆**sérieusement** *adv* seriously; (*travailler*) conscientiously.

serin [s(ə)rɛ̃] *nm* canary.

seriner [s(ə)rine] *vt* **s. qch à qn** to repeat sth to s.o. over and over again.

seringue [s(ə)rɛ̃g] *nf* syringe.

serment [sɛrmɑ̃] *nm* (*affirmation solennelle*) oath; (*promesse*) pledge; **prêter s.** to take an oath; **faire le s. de faire** to swear to do; **sous s.** *Jur ou* on oath.

sermon [sɛrmɔ̃] *nm Rel* sermon; (*discours*) *Péj* lecture. ◆**sermonner** *vt* (*faire la morale à*) to lecture.

serpe [sɛrp] *nf* bill(hook).

serpent [sɛrpɑ̃] *nm* snake; **s. à sonnette** rattlesnake.

serpenter [sɛrpɑ̃te] *vi* (*sentier etc*) to meander.

serpentin [sɛrpɑ̃tɛ̃] *nm* (*ruban*) streamer.

serpillière [sɛrpijɛr] *nf* floor cloth.

serre [sɛr] **1** *nf* greenhouse. **2** *nfpl* (*d'oiseau*) claws, talons.

serre-livres [sɛrlivr] *nm inv* bookend. ◆**s.-tête** *nm inv* (*bandeau*) headband.

serr/er [sere] *vt* (*saisir, tenir*) to grip, clasp; (*presser*) to squeeze, press; (*corde, nœud, vis*) to tighten; (*poing*) to clench; (*taille*) to hug; (*pieds*) to pinch; (*frein*) to apply, put on; (*rapprocher*) to close up; (*rangs*) *Mil* to close; **s. la main à** to shake hands with s.o.; **s. les dents** *Fig* to grit one's teeth; **s. qn** (*embrasser*) to hug s.o.; (*vêtement*) to be too tight for s.o.; **s. qn de près** (*talonner*) to be close behind s.o.; — *vi* **s. à droite** *Aut* to keep (to the) right; — **se s.** *vpr* (*se rapprocher*) to squeeze up *ou* together; **se s. contre** to squeeze up against. ◆**-é** *a* (*budget, nœud, vêtement*) tight; (*gens*) packed (together); (*mailles, lutte*) close; (*rangs*) serried; (*dense*) dense, thick; (*cœur*) *Fig* heavy; **avoir la gorge serrée** *Fig* to have a lump in one's throat.

serrure [seryr] *nf* lock. ◆**serrurier** *nm* locksmith.

sertir [sɛrtir] *vt* (*diamant etc*) to set.

sérum [serɔm] *nm* serum.

servante [sɛrvɑ̃t] *nf* (*maid*)servant.

serveur, -euse [sɛrvœr, -øz] *nmf* waiter, waitress; (*au bar*) barman, barmaid.

serviable [sɛrvjabl] *a* helpful, obliging. ◆**serviabilité** *nf* helpfulness.

service [sɛrvis] *nm* service; (*fonction, travail*) duty; (*pourboire*) service (charge); (*département*) *Com* department; *Tennis* serve, service; **un s.** (*aide*) a favour; **rendre s.** to be of service (**à qn** to s.o.), help (**à qn** s.o.); **rendre un mauvais s. à qn** to do s.o. a disservice; **ça pourrait rendre s.** *Fam* that might come in useful; **s. (non) compris** service (not) included; **s. après-vente** *Com* aftersales (service); **s. d'ordre** (*policiers*) police; **être de s.** to be on duty; **à s. à café/à thé** coffee/tea service; set; **à votre s.!** at your service!

serviette [sɛrvjɛt] *nf* **1** towel; **s. de bain/de toilette** bath/hand towel; **s. hygiénique** sanitary towel; **s. (de table)** serviette, napkin. **2** (*sac*) briefcase.

servile [sɛrvil] *a* servile; (*imitation*) slavish. ◆**servilité** *nf* servility; slavishness.

servir* [sɛrvir] **1** *vt* to serve (**qch à qn** sth with sth, sth to s.o.); (*convive*) to wait on; – *vi* to serve; – **se s.** *vpr* (*à table*) to help oneself (**de** to). **2** *vi* (*être utile*) to be useful, serve; **s. à qch/à faire** (*objet*) to be used for sth/to do *ou* for doing; **ça ne sert à rien** it's useless, it's no good *ou* use (**de faire** doing); **à quoi ça sert de protester/***etc* what's the use *ou* good of protesting/*etc*; **s. de qch** (*objet*) to be used for sth, serve as sth; **ça me sert à faire/de qch** I use it to do *ou* for doing/as sth; **s. à qn de guide/***etc* to act as a guide/*etc* to s.o. **3 se s.** *vpr* **se s. de** (*utiliser*) to use.

serviteur [sɛrvitœr] *nm* servant. ◆**servitude** *nf* (*esclavage*) servitude; (*contrainte*) *Fig* constraint.

ses [se] *voir* **son²**.

session [sɛsjɔ̃] *nf* session.

set [sɛt] *nm* **1** *Tennis* set. **2 s. (de table)** (*napperon*) place mat.

seuil [sœj] *nm* doorstep; (*entrée*) doorway; (*limite*) *Fig* threshold; **au s. de** *Fig* on the threshold of.

seul, seule [sœl] **1** *a* (*sans compagnie*) alone; **tout s.** all alone, by oneself, on one's own; **se sentir s.** to feel lonely *ou* alone; – *adv* (**tout**) **s.** (*agir, vivre*) by oneself alone, on one's own; (*parler*) to oneself; **s. à s.** (*parler*) in private. **2** *a* (*unique*) only; **la seule femme/***etc* the only *ou* sole woman/*etc*; **un s. chat/***etc* only one cat/*etc*; **une seule fois** only once; **pas un s. livre/***etc* not a single book/*etc*; **seuls les garçons . . .**, **les garçons seuls . . .** only the boys . . . ; – *nmf* **le s., la seule** the only one; **un s., une seule** one only, one only; **pas un s.** not (a single) one. ◆**seulement** *adv* only; **non s. . . . mais . . .** not only . . . but (also) . . . ; **pas s.** (*même*) not even; **sans s.** faire without even doing.

sève [sɛv] *nf* *Bot* & *Fig* sap.

sévère [sever] *a* severe; (*parents, professeur*) strict. ◆**—ment** *adv* severely; (*élever*) strictly. ◆**sévérité** *nf* severity; strictness.

sévices [sevis] *nmpl* brutality.

sévir [sevir] *vi* (*fléau*) *Fig* to rage; **s. contre** to deal severely with.

sevrer [savre] *vt* (*enfant*) to wean; **s. de** (*priver*) *Fig* to deprive of.

sexe [sɛks] *nm* (*catégorie, sexualité*) sex; (*organes*) genitals; **l'autre s.** the opposite sex. ◆**sexiste** *a* & *nmf* sexist. ◆**sexualité** *nf* sexuality. ◆**sexuel, -elle** *a* sexual; (*éducation, acte etc*) sex-.

sextuor [sɛkstuɔr] *nm* sextet.

seyant [sɛjã] *a* (*vêtement*) becoming.

shampooing [ʃãpwɛ̃] *nm* shampoo; **s. colorant** rinse; **faire un s. à qn** to shampoo s.o.'s hair.

shérif [ʃerif] *nm* *Am* sheriff.

shooter [ʃute] *vti* *Fb* to shoot.

short [ʃɔrt] *nm* (pair of) shorts.

si [si] **1** (= **s'** [s] *before* **il, ils**) *conj* if; **s'il vient** if he comes; **si j'étais roi** if I were *ou* was king; **je me demande si** I wonder whether *ou* if; **si on restait?** (*suggestion*) what if we stayed?; **si je dis ça, c'est que . . .** I say this because . . . ; **si ce n'est** (*sinon*) if not; **si oui** if so. **2** *adv* (*tellement*) so; **pas si riche que toi/que tu crois** not as rich as you/as you think; **un si bon dîner** such a good dinner; **si grand qu'il soit** however big he may be; **si bien que** with the result that. **3** *adv* (*après négative*) yes; **tu ne viens pas? – si!** you're not coming? – yes (I am)!

siamois [sjamwa] *a* Siamese; **frères s., sœurs siamoises** Siamese twins.

Sicile [sisil] *nf* Sicily.

SIDA [sida] *nm* *Méd* AIDS.

sidérer [sidere] *vt* *Fam* to flabbergast, stagger.

sidérurgie [sideryrʒi] *nf* iron and steel industry.

siècle [sjɛkl] *nm* century; (*époque*) age.

siège [sjɛʒ] *nm* **1** (*meuble, centre*) & *Pol* seat; (*d'autorité, de parti etc*) headquarters; **s. (social)** (*d'entreprise*) head office. **2** *Mil* siege; **mettre le s. devant** to lay siege to. ◆**siéger** *vi* *Pol* to sit.

sien, sienne [sjɛ̃, sjɛn] *pron poss* **le s., la sienne, les sien(ne)s** his; (*de femme*) hers; (*de chose*) its; **les deux siens** his *ou* her two; – *nmpl* **les siens** (*amis etc*) one's (own) people.

sieste [sjɛst] *nf* siesta; **faire la s.** to have *ou* take a nap.

siffler [sifle] *vi* to whistle; (*avec un sifflet*) to

blow one's whistle; (gaz, serpent) to hiss; (en respirant) to wheeze; – vt (chanson) to whistle; (chien) to whistle to; (faute, fin de match) Sp to blow one's whistle for; (acteur, pièce) to boo; (boisson) Fam to knock back. ◆**sifflement** nm whistling; whistle; hiss(ing). ◆**sifflet** nm (instrument) whistle; pl Th booing, boos; (coup de) s. (son) whistle. ◆**siffloter** vti to whistle.

sigle [sigl] nm (initiales) abbreviation; (prononcé comme un mot) acronym.

signal, -aux [sipal, -o] nm signal; s. d'alarme Rail communication cord; signaux routiers road signs. ◆**signal/er 1** vt (faire remarquer) to point out (à qn to s.o., que that); (dénoncer à la police etc) to report (à to). **2 se s.** vpr **se s. par** to distinguish oneself by. ◆**—ement** nm (de personne) description, particulars. ◆**signalisation** nf signalling; Aut signposting; s. (routière) (signaux) road signs.

signature [sipatyr] nf signature; (action) signing. ◆**signataire** nmf signatory. ◆**signer 1** vt to sign. **2 se s.** vpr Rel to cross oneself.

signe [sip] nm (indice) sign, indication; s. particulier/de ponctuation distinguishing/punctuation mark; faire s. à qn (geste) to motion to ou beckon s.o. (de faire to do); (contacter) to get in touch with s.o.; faire s. que oui to nod (one's head); faire s. que non to shake one's head.

signet [sipɛ] nm bookmark.

signification [sipifikasjɔ̃] nf meaning. ◆**significatif, -ive** a significant, meaningful; s. de indicative of. ◆**signifier** vt to mean, signify (que that); s. qch à qn (faire connaître) to make sth known to s.o., signify sth to s.o.

silence [silɑ̃s] nm silence; Mus rest; en s. in silence; garder le s. to keep quiet ou silent (sur about). ◆**silencieux, -euse 1** a silent. **2** nm Aut silencer, Am muffler; (d'arme) silencer. ◆**silencieusement** adv silently.

silex [silɛks] nm (roche) flint.

silhouette [silwɛt] nf outline; (en noir) silhouette; (ligne du corps) figure.

silicium [silisjɔm] nm silicon. ◆**silicone** nf silicone.

sillage [sijaʒ] nm (de bateau) wake; dans le s. de Fig in the wake of.

sillon [sijɔ̃] nm furrow; (de disque) groove.

sillonner [sijɔne] vt (traverser) to cross; (en tous sens) to criss-cross.

silo [silo] nm silo.

simagrées [simagre] nfpl airs (and graces); (cérémonies) fuss.

similaire [similɛr] a similar. ◆**similitude** nf similarity.

similicuir [similikɥir] nm imitation leather.

simple [sɛ̃pl] a (non multiple) single; (employé, particulier) ordinary; – nmf s. d'esprit simpleton; – nm Tennis singles. ◆**simplement** adv simply. ◆**simplet, -ette** a (personne) a bit simple. ◆**simplicité** nf simplicity. ◆**simplification** nf simplification. ◆**simplifier** vt to simplify. ◆**simpliste** a simplistic.

simulacre [simylakr] nm un s. de Péj a pretence of.

simuler [simyle] vt to simulate; (feindre) to feign. ◆**simulateur, -trice 1** nmf (hypocrite) shammer; (tire-au-flanc) & Mil malingerer. **2** nm (appareil) simulator. ◆**simulation** nf simulation; feigning.

simultané [simyltane] a simultaneous. ◆**—ment** adv simultaneously.

sincère [sɛ̃sɛr] a sincere. ◆**sincèrement** adv sincerely. ◆**sincérité** nf sincerity.

sinécure [sinekyr] nf sinecure.

singe [sɛ̃ʒ] nm monkey, ape. ◆**singer** vt (imiter) to ape, mimic. ◆**singeries** nfpl antics, clowning.

singulariser (se) [səsɛ̃gylarize] vpr to draw attention to oneself.

singulier, -ière [sɛ̃gylje, -jɛr] **1** a peculiar, odd. **2** a & nm Gram singular. ◆**singularité** nf peculiarity. ◆**singulièrement** adv (notamment) particularly; (beaucoup) extremely.

sinistre [sinistr] **1** a (effrayant) sinister. **2** nm disaster; (incendie) fire; (dommage) Jur damage. ◆**sinistré, -ée** a (population, région) disaster-stricken; – nmf disaster victim.

sinon [sinɔ̃] conj (autrement) otherwise, or else; (sauf) except (que that); (si ce n'est) if not.

sinueux, -euse [sinɥø, -øz] a winding. ◆**sinuosités** nfpl twists (and turns).

sinus [sinys] nm inv Anat sinus.

siphon [sifɔ̃] nm siphon; (d'évier) trap, U-bend.

sirène [siren] nf **1** (d'usine etc) siren. **2** (femme) mermaid.

sirop [siro] nm syrup; (à diluer, boisson) (fruit) cordial; s. contre la toux cough mixture ou syrup.

siroter [sirɔte] vt Fam to sip (at).

sis [si] a Jur situated.

sismique [sismik] *a* seismic; **secousse s.** earth tremor.

site [sit] *nm* (*endroit*) site; (*environnement*) setting; (*pittoresque*) beauty spot; **s.** (**touristique**) (*monument etc*) place of interest.

sitôt [sito] *adv* **s. que** as soon as; **s. levée, elle partit** as soon as she was up, she left; **s.** **après** immediately after; **pas de s.** not for some time.

situation [situɑsjɔ̃] *nf* situation, position; (*emploi*) position; **s. de famille** marital status. ◆**situ/er** *vt* to situate, locate; **s.** *vpr* (*se trouver*) to be situated. ◆**-é a** (*maison etc*) situated.

six [sis] ([si] *before consonant*, [siz] *before vowel*) *a & nm* six. ◆**sixième** *a & nmf* sixth; **un s.** a sixth.

sketch [skɛtʃ] *nm* (*pl* **sketches**) *Th* sketch.

ski [ski] *nm* (*objet*) ski; (*sport*) skiing; **faire** **du s.** to ski; **s. nautique** water skiing. ◆**ski/er** *vi* to ski. ◆**-eur, -euse** *nmf* skier.

slalom [slalɔm] *nm Sp* slalom.

slave [slav] *a* Slav; (*langue*) Slavonic; – *nmf* Slav.

slip [slip] *nm* (*d'homme*) briefs, (under)pants; (*de femme*) panties, pants, knickers; **s. de bain** (swimming) trunks; (*d'un bikini*) briefs.

slogan [slɔgɑ̃] *nm* slogan.

SMIC [smik] *nm abrév* (*salaire minimum interprofessionnel de croissance*) minimum wage.

smoking [smokiŋ] *nm* (*veston, costume*) dinner jacket, *Am* tuxedo.

snack(-bar) [snak(bar)] *nm* snack bar.

SNCF [ɛsɛnseɛf] *nf abrév* (*Société nationale des Chemins de fer français*) French railways.

snob [snɔb] *nmf* snob; – *a* snobbish. ◆**snober** *vt* **s. qn** to snub s.o. ◆**sno-bisme** *nm* snobbery.

sobre [sɔbr] *a* sober. ◆**sobriété** *nf* sobriety.

sobriquet [sɔbrikɛ] *nm* nickname.

sociable [sɔsjabl] *a* sociable. ◆**sociabilité** *nf* sociability.

social, -aux [sɔsjal, -o] *a* social. ◆**socialisme** *nm* socialism. ◆**socialiste** *a & nmf* socialist.

société [sɔsjete] *nf* society; (*compagnie* & *Com* company; **s. anonyme** *Com* (public) limited company, *Am* incorporated company. ◆**sociétaire** *nmf* (*d'une association*) member.

sociologie [sɔsjɔlɔʒi] *nf* sociology.

◆**sociologique** *a* sociological. ◆**socio-logue** *nmf* sociologist.

socle [sɔkl] *nm* (*de statue, colonne*) plinth, pedestal; (*de lampe*) base.

socquette [sɔkɛt] *nf* ankle sock.

soda [sɔda] *nm* (*à l'orange etc*) fizzy drink, *Am* soda (pop).

sœur [sœr] *nf* sister; *Rel* nun, sister.

sofa [sɔfa] *nm* sofa, settee.

soi [swa] *pron* oneself; **chacun pour s.** every man for himself; **en s.** in itself; **cela va de s.** it's self-evident (que that); **amour/** **conscience de s.** self-love/-awareness. ◆**s.-même** *pron* oneself.

soi-disant [swadizɑ̃] *a inv* so-called; – *adv* supposedly.

soie [swa] *nf* **1** silk. **2** (*de porc etc*) bristle. ◆**soierie** *nf* (*tissu*) silk.

soif [swaf] *nf* thirst (*Fig* **de** for); **avoir s.** to be thirsty; **donner s. à qn** to make s.o. thirsty.

soign/er [swaɲe] *vt* to look after, take care of; (*malade*) to tend, nurse; (*maladie*) to treat; (*détails, présentation, travail*) to take care over; **se faire s.** to have (medical) treatment; – **se s.** *vpr* to take care of oneself, look after oneself. ◆**-é a** (*personne*) well-groomed; (*vêtement*) neat, tidy; (*travail*) careful. ◆**soigneux, -euse** *a* careful (**de** with); (*propre*) tidy, neat. ◆**soigneusement** *adv* carefully.

soin [swɛ̃] *nm* care; (*ordre*) tidiness, neatness; *pl* care; *Méd* treatment; **avoir** *ou* **prendre s. de qch/de faire** to take care of sth/to do; **les premiers soins** first aid; **soins** **de beauté** beauty care *ou* treatment; **aux** **bons soins de** (*sur lettre*) care of, c/o; **avec** **s.** carefully, with care.

soir [swar] *nm* evening; **le s.** (*chaque soir*) in the evening; **à neuf heures du s.** at nine in the evening; **du s.** (*repas, robe etc*) evening-. ◆**soirée** *nf* evening; (*réunion*) party; **s.** **dansante** dance.

soit **1** [swa] *voir* **être. 2** [swa] *conj* (*à savoir*) that is (to say); **s. . . . s. . . .** either . . . or . . . . **3** [swat] *adv* (*oui*) very well, well.

soixante [swasɑ̃t] *a & nm* sixty. ◆**soixantaine** *nf* **une s.** (**de**) (*nombre*) (about) sixty; **avoir la s.** (*âge*) to be about sixty. ◆**soixante-dix** *a & nm* seventy. ◆**soixante-dixième** *a & nmf* seventieth. ◆**soixantième** *a & nmf* sixtieth.

soja [sɔʒa] *nm* (*plante*) soya; **graine de s.** soya bean; **germes** *ou* **pousses de s.** bean-sprouts.

sol [sɔl] *nm* ground; (*plancher*) floor; (*matière, territoire*) soil.

solaire [sɔlɛr] a solar; (*chaleur, rayons*) sun's; (*crème, filtre*) sun-; (*lotion, huile*) suntan-.

soldat [sɔlda] nm soldier; **simple s.** private.

solde [sɔld] **1** nm (*de compte, à payer*) balance. **2** nm en s. (*acheter*) at sale price, Am on sale; (*pl marchandises*) sale goods; (*vente*) (clearance) sale(s). **3** nf Mil pay; **à la s. de** Fig Péj in s.o.'s pay. ◆**sold/er 1** vt (*articles*) to sell off, clear. **2** vt (*compte*) to pay the balance of. **3 se s.** vpr **se s. par** (*un échec, une défaite etc*) to end in. ◆**—é a** (*article etc*) reduced. ◆**solderie** nf discount *ou* reject shop.

sole [sɔl] nf (*poisson*) sole.

soleil [sɔlɛj] nm sun; (*chaleur, lumière*) sunshine; (*fleur*) sunflower; **au s.** in the sun; **il fait (du) s.** it's sunny, the sun's shining; **prendre un bain de s.** to sunbathe; **coup de s.** Méd sunburn.

solennel, -elle [sɔlanɛl] a solemn. ◆**solennellement** adv solemnly. ◆**solennité** [-anite] nf solemnity.

solex® [sɔlɛks] nm moped.

solfège [sɔlfɛʒ] nm rudiments of music.

solidaire [sɔlidɛr] a **être s.** (*ouvriers etc*) to be as one, show solidarity (**de** with); (*pièce de machine*) to be interdependent (**de** with). ◆**solidairement** adv jointly. ◆**se solidariser** vpr to show solidarity (**avec** with). ◆**solidarité** nf solidarity; (*d'éléments*) interdependence.

solide [sɔlid] a (*voiture, nourriture, caractère etc*) & Ch solid; (*argument, qualité, raison*) sound; (*vigoureux*) robust; – nm Ch solid. ◆**solidement** adv solidly. ◆**se solidifier** vpr to solidify. ◆**solidité** nf solidity; (*d'argument etc*) soundness.

soliste [sɔlist] nmf Mus soloist.

solitaire [sɔlitɛr] a solitary; – nmf loner; (*ermite*) recluse, hermit; **en s.** on one's own. ◆**solitude** nf solitude.

solive [sɔliv] nf joist, beam.

solliciter [sɔlisite] vt (*audience, emploi etc*) to seek; (*tenter*) to tempt, entice; **s. qn** (*faire appel à*) to appeal to s.o. (**de faire** to do); **être (très) sollicité** (*personne*) to be in (great) demand. ◆**sollicitation** nf (*demande*) appeal; (*tentation*) temptation.

sollicitude [sɔlisityd] nf solicitude, concern.

solo [sɔlo] a inv & nm Mus solo.

solstice [sɔlstis] nm solstice.

soluble [sɔlybl] a (*substance, problème*) soluble; **café s.** instant coffee. ◆**solution** nf (*d'un problème*) & Ch solution (**de** to).

solvable [sɔlvabl] a Fin solvent. ◆**solvabilité** nf Fin solvency.

solvant [sɔlvɑ̃] nm Ch solvent.

sombre [sɔ̃br] a dark; (*triste*) sombre, gloomy; **il fait s.** it's dark.

sombrer [sɔ̃bre] vi (*bateau*) to sink, founder; **s. dans** (*folie, sommeil etc*) to sink into.

sommaire [sɔmɛr] a summary; (*repas, tenue*) scant; – nm summary, synopsis.

sommation [sɔmasjɔ̃] nf Jur summons; (*de sentinelle etc*) warning.

somme [sɔm] **1** nf sum; **faire la s. de** to add up; **en s., s. toute** in short. **2** nm (*sommeil*) nap; **faire un s.** to have *ou* take a nap.

sommeil [sɔmɛj] nm sleep; (*envie de dormir*) sleepiness, drowsiness; **avoir s.** to be *ou* feel sleepy *ou* drowsy. ◆**sommeiller** vi to doze; (*faculté, qualité*) Fig to slumber.

sommelier [sɔməlje] nm wine waiter.

sommer [sɔme] vt **s. qn de** Litt (*enjoindre*) & Jur to summon s.o. to do.

sommes [sɔm] voir **être**.

sommet [sɔmɛ] nm top; (*de montagne*) summit, top; (*de la gloire etc*) Fig height, summit; **conférence au s.** summit (conference).

sommier [sɔmje] nm (*de lit*) base; **s. à ressorts** spring base.

sommité [sɔmite] nf leading light, top person (**de** in).

somnambule [sɔmnɑ̃byl] nmf sleepwalker; **être s.** to sleepwalk. ◆**somnambulisme** nm sleepwalking.

somnifère [sɔmnifɛr] nm sleeping pill.

somnolence [sɔmnɔlɑ̃s] nf drowsiness, sleepiness. ◆**somnolent** a drowsy, sleepy. ◆**somnoler** vi to doze, drowse.

somptueux, -euse [sɔ̃ptɥø, -øz] a sumptuous, magnificent. ◆**somptuosité** nf sumptuousness, magnificence.

son¹ [sɔ̃] nm **1** (*bruit*) sound. **2** (*de grains*) bran.

son², sa, pl ses [sɔ̃, sa, se] (*sa becomes son* [sɔ̃n] *before a vowel or mute h*) a poss his; (*de femme*) her; (*de chose*) its; (*indéfini*) one's; **son père** his *ou* her *ou* one's father; **sa durée** its duration.

sonate [sɔnat] nf Mus sonata.

sonde [sɔ̃d] nf Géol drill; Nau sounding line; Méd probe; (*pour l'alimentation*) (feeding) tube; **s. spatiale** Av space probe. ◆**sondage** nm sounding; drilling; probing; **s. (d'opinion)** opinion poll. ◆**sonder** vt (*rivière etc*) to sound; (*terrain*) to drill; Av & Méd to probe; (*personne, l'opinion*) Fig to sound out.

songe [sɔ̃ʒ] nm dream.

song/er [sɔ̃ʒe] vi **s. à qch/à faire** to think of sth/of doing; – vt **s. que** to consider *ou* think that. ◆**—eur, -euse** a thoughtful, pensive.

sonner [sone] vi to ring; (cor, cloches etc) to sound; **midi a sonné** it has struck twelve; — vt to ring; (domestique) to ring for; (cor etc) to sound; (l'heure) to strike; (assommer) to knock out. ◆**sonnantes** afpl **à cinq**/etc **heures s.** on the stroke of five/etc. ◆**sonné** a **1 trois**/etc **heures sonnées (on** ou past three/etc o'clock. **2** (fou) crazy. ◆**sonnerie** nf (son) ring(ing); (de cor etc) sound; (appareil) bell. ◆**sonnette** nf bell; **s. d'alarme** alarm (bell); **coup de s.** ring.

sonnet [sone] nm (poème) sonnet.

sonore [sɔnɔr] a (rire) loud; (salle, voix) resonant; (effet, film, ondes etc) sound-. ◆**sonorisation** nf (matériel) sound equipment ou system. ◆**sonoriser** vt (film) to add sound to; (salle) to wire for sound. ◆**sonorité** nf (de salle) acoustics, resonance; (de violon etc) tone.

sont [sɔ̃] voir **être**.

sophistiqué [sofistike] a sophisticated.

soporifique [sopɔrifik] a (médicament, discours etc) soporific.

soprano [soprano] nmf (personne) Mus soprano; — nm (voix) soprano.

sorbet [sɔrbɛ] nm Culin water ice, sorbet.

sorcellerie [sɔrsɛlri] nf witchcraft, sorcery. ◆**sorcier** nm sorcerer. ◆**sorcière** nf witch; **chasse aux sorcières** Pol witch-hunt.

sordide [sɔrdid] a (acte, affaire etc) sordid; (maison etc) squalid.

sornettes [sɔrnɛt] nfpl (propos) Péj twaddle.

sort [sɔr] nm **1** (destin, hasard) fate; (condition) lot. **2** (maléfice) spell.

sorte [sɔrt] nf sort, kind (de of); **en quelque s.** as it were, in a way; **(de (telle) s. que** so that, in such a way that; **de la s.** (de cette façon) in that way; **faire en s. que** (+ sub) to see to it that.

sortie [sɔrti] nf **1** departure, exit; (de scène) exit; (promenade) walk; (porte) exit, way out; (de livre, modèle) Com appearance; (de disque, film) release; (d'ordinateur) output; pl (argent) outgoings; **à la s. de l'école** (moment) when school comes out; **l'heure de la s. de qn** the time at which s.o. leaves; **première s.** (de convalescent etc) first time out. **2 s. de bain** (peignoir) bathrobe.

sortilège [sɔrtilɛʒ] nm (magic) spell.

sort/ir* [sɔrtir] vi (aux être) to go out, leave; (venir) to come out; (pour s'amuser) to go out; (film, modèle, bourgeon etc) to come out; (numéro gagnant) to come up; **s. de** (endroit) to leave; (sujet) to stray from;

(université) to be a graduate of; (famille, milieu) to come from; (légalité, limites) to go beyond; (compétence) to be outside; (gonds, rails) to come off; **s. de l'ordinaire** to be out of the ordinary; **s. de table** to leave the table; **s. de terre** (plante, fondations) to come up; **s. indemne** to escape unhurt (de from); — vt (aux avoir) to take out (de of); (film, modèle, livre etc) Com to bring out; (dire) Fam to come out with; (expulser) Fam to throw out; **s'en s., se s. d'affaire** to pull ou come through, get out of trouble. ◆**—ant** a (numéro) winning; (député etc) Pol outgoing. ◆**—able** a (personne) presentable.

sosie [sozi] nm (de personne) double.

sot, sotte [so, sɔt] a foolish; — nmf fool. ◆**sottement** adv foolishly. ◆**sottise** nf foolishness; (action, parole) foolish thing; pl (injures) Fam insults; **faire des sottises** (enfant) to be naughty, misbehave.

sou [su] nm **sous** (argent) money; **elle n'a pas un ou le s.** she doesn't have a penny, she's penniless; **pas un s. de** (bon sens etc) not an ounce of; **appareil ou machine à sous** fruit machine, one-armed bandit.

soubresaut [subrəso] nm (sursaut) (sudden) start.

souche [suʃ] nf (d'arbre) stump; (de carnet) stub, counterfoil; (de vigne) stock.

souci [susi] nm (inquiétude) worry, concern; (préoccupation) concern; **se faire du s.** to be worried, worry; **ça lui donne du s.** it worries him ou her. ◆**se soucier** vpr **se s. de** to be concerned ou worried about. ◆**soucieux, -euse** a concerned, worried (de qch about sth); **s. de plaire** anxious to please/etc.

soucoupe [sukup] nf saucer; **s. volante** flying saucer.

soudain [sudɛ̃] a sudden; — adv suddenly. ◆**soudainement** adv suddenly. ◆**soudaineté** nf suddenness.

Soudan [sudɑ̃] nm Sudan.

soude [sud] nf Ch soda; **cristaux de s.** washing soda.

souder [sude] vt to solder; (par soudure autogène) to weld; (groupes etc) Fig to unite (closely); — **se s.** vpr (os) to knit (together). ◆**soudure** nf soldering; (métal) solder; **s.** (autogène) welding.

soudoyer [sudwaje] vt to bribe.

souffle [sufl] nm puff, blow; (haleine) breath; (respiration) breathing; (de bombe etc) blast; (inspiration) Fig inspiration; **s. (d'air)** breath of air. ◆**souffler** vi to blow; (haleter) to puff; **laisser s. qn** (reprendre haleine) to let s.o. get his breath back; — vt (*bougie*) to blow out; (*fumée, poussière, verre*) to blow; (*par une explosion*) to blow down, blast; (*chuchoter*) to whisper; (*voler*) *Fam* to pinch (à from); (*étonner*) *Fam* to stagger; **s. son rôle à qn** *Th* to prompt s.o.; **ne pas s. mot** not to breathe a word. ◆**soufflet** *nm* **1** (*instrument*) bellows. **2** (*gifle*) *Litt* slap. ◆**souffleur, -euse** *nmf Th* prompter.

soufflé [sufle] *nm Culin* soufflé.

souffrance [sufrɑ̃s] *nf* **1** suffering. **2 en s.** (*colis etc*) unclaimed; (*affaire*) in abeyance.

souffreteux, -euse [sufrətø, -øz] *a* sickly.

souffr/ir* [sufrir] **1** *vi* to suffer; **s. de** to suffer from; (*gorge, pieds etc*) to have trouble with; **faire s. qn** (*physiquement*) to hurt s.o.; (*moralement*) to make s.o. suffer, hurt s.o. **2** *vt* (*endurer*) to suffer; **je ne peux pas le s.** I can't bear him. **3** *vt* (*exception*) to admit of. ◆**—ant** *a* unwell.

soufre [sufr] *nm* sulphur, *Am* sulfur.

souhait [swɛ] *nm* wish; **à vos souhaits!** (*après un éternuement*) bless you!; **à s.** perfectly. ◆**souhait/er** *vt* (*bonheur etc*) to wish for; (*chose*) to hope for; **s. qch à qn** to wish s.o. sth; **s. faire** to hope to do; **s. que** (+ *sub*) to hope that. ◆**—able** *a* desirable.

souiller [suje] *vt* to soil, dirty; (*déshonorer*) *Fig* to sully.

soûl [su] **1** *a* drunk. **2** *nm* **tout son s.** (*boire etc*) to one's heart's content. ◆**soûler** *vt* to make drunk; **— se s.** *vpr* to get drunk.

soulager [sulaʒe] *vt* to relieve (**de** of). ◆**soulagement** *nm* relief.

soulever [sulve] *vt* to raise, lift (up); (*l'opinion, le peuple*) to stir up; (*poussière, question*) to raise; (*sentiment*) to arouse; **cela me soulève le cœur** it makes me feel sick, it turns my stomach; **— se s.** *vpr* (*malade etc*) to lift oneself (up); (*se révolter*) to rise (up). ◆**soulèvement** *nm* (*révolte*) (up)rising.

soulier [sulje] *nm* shoe.

souligner [suliɲe] *vt* (*d'un trait*) to underline; (*accentuer, faire remarquer*) to emphasize, underline; **s. que** to emphasize that.

soumettre* [sumetr] *vt* **1** (*pays, rebelles*) to subjugate, subdue; **s. à** (*assujettir*) to subject to; **— se s.** *vpr* to submit (à to). **2** *vt* (*présenter*) to submit (à to). ◆**soumis** *a* (*docile*) submissive; **s. à** subject to. ◆**soumission** *nf* **1** submission; (*docilité*) submissiveness. **2** (*offre*) *Com* tender.

soupape [supap] *nf* valve.

soupçon [supsɔ̃] *nm* suspicion; **un s. de** (*quantité*) *Fig* a hint *ou* touch of. ◆**soupçonner** *vt* to suspect (**de** of, **d'avoir fait** of

doing, **que** that). ◆**soupçonneux, -euse** *a* suspicious.

soupe [sup] *nf* soup. ◆**soupière** *nf* (soup) tureen.

soupente [supɑ̃t] *nf* (*sous le toit*) loft.

souper [supe] *nm* supper; **—** *vi* to have supper.

soupeser [supəze] *vt* (*objet dans la main*) to feel the weight of; (*arguments etc*) *Fig* to weigh up.

soupir [supir] *nm* sigh. ◆**soupir/er** *vi* to sigh; **s. après** to yearn for. ◆**—ant** *nm* (*amoureux*) suitor.

soupirail, -aux [supiraj, -o] *nm* basement window.

souple [supl] *a* (*personne, esprit, règlement*) flexible; (*cuir, membre, corps*) supple. ◆**souplesse** *nf* flexibility; suppleness.

source [surs] *nf* **1** (*point d'eau*) spring; **eau de s.** spring water; **prendre sa s.** (*rivière*) to rise (à at, dans in). **2** (*origine*) source; **de s. sûre** on good authority.

sourcil [sursi] *nm* eyebrow. ◆**sourciller** *vi* **ne pas s.** *Fig* not to bat an eyelid.

sourd, sourde [sur, surd] **1** *a* deaf (*Fig* à to); **—** *nmf* deaf person. **2** *a* (*bruit, douleur*) dull; (*caché*) secret. ◆**s.-muet** (*pl* **sourds-muets**), ◆**sourde-muette** (*pl* **sourdes-muettes**) *a* deaf and dumb; **—** *nmf* deaf mute.

sourdine [surdin] *nf* (*dispositif*) *Mus* mute; **en s.** *Fig* quietly, secretly.

souricière [surisjɛr] *nf* mousetrap; *Fig* trap.

sourire* [surir] *vi* to smile (à at); **s. à qn** (*fortune*) to smile on s.o.; **—** *nm* smile; **faire un s. à qn** to give s.o. a smile.

souris [suri] *nf* mouse.

sournois [surnwa] *a* sly, underhand. ◆**sournoisement** *adv* slyly. ◆**sournoiserie** *nf* slyness.

sous [su] *prép* (*position*) under(neath), beneath; (*rang*) under; **s. la pluie** in the rain; **s. cet angle** from that angle *ou* point of view; **s. le nom de** under the name of; **s. Charles X** under Charles X; **s. peu** (*bientôt*) shortly.

sous- [su] *préf* (*subordination, subdivision*) sub-; (*insuffisance*) under-.

sous-alimenté [suzalimɑ̃te] *a* undernourished. ◆**sous-alimentation** *nf* undernourishment.

sous-bois [subwa] *nm* undergrowth.

sous-chef [suʃɛf] *nmf* second-in-command.

souscrire* [suskrir] *vi* **s. à** (*payer, approuver*) to subscribe to. ◆**souscription** *nf* subscription.

sous-développé [sudevlɔpe] *a* (*pays*) underdeveloped.

sous-directeur, -trice [sudirɛktœr, -tris] *nmf* assistant manager, assistant manageress.

sous-entend/re [suzãtãdr] *vt* to imply. ◆**-u** insinuation.

sous-estimer [suzɛstime] *vt* to underestimate.

sous-jacent [suʒasã] *a* underlying.

sous-louer [sulwe] *vt* (*appartement*) to sublet.

sous-main [sumɛ̃] *nm inv* desk pad.

sous-marin [sumarɛ̃] *a* underwater; **plongée sous-marine** skin diving; — *nm* submarine.

sous-officier [suzɔfisje] *nm* noncommissioned officer.

sous-payer [supeje] *vt* (*ouvrier etc*) to underpay.

sous-produit [suprɔdчi] *nm* by-product.

soussigné, -ée [susiɲe] *a* & *nmf* undersigned; **je s.** I the undersigned.

sous-sol [susɔl] *nm* basement; *Géol* subsoil.

sous-titre [sutitr] *nm* subtitle. ◆**sous-titrer** *vt* (*film*) to subtitle.

soustraire* [sustrɛr] *vt* to remove; *Math* to subtract, take away (**de** from); **s. qn à** (*danger etc*) to shield *ou* protect s.o. from; **se s. à** to escape from; (*devoir, obligation*) to avoid. ◆**soustraction** *nf Math* subtraction.

sous-trait/er [sutrete] *vi Com* to subcontract. ◆**-ant** *nm* subcontractor.

sous-verre [suvɛr] *nm inv* (*encadrement*) (frameless) glass mount.

sous-vêtement [suvɛtmã] *nm* undergarment; *pl* underwear.

soutane [sutan] *nf* (*de prêtre*) cassock.

soute [sut] *nf* (*magasin*) *Nau* hold.

souten/ir* [sutnir] *vt* to support, hold up; (*droits, opinion*) to uphold, maintain; (*candidat etc*) to back, support; (*malade*) to sustain; (*effort, intérêt*) to sustain, keep up; (*thèse*) to defend; (*résister à*) to withstand; **s. que** to maintain that; — **se s.** *vpr* (*blessé etc*) to hold oneself up; (*se maintenir, durer*) to be sustained. ◆**-u** *a* (*attention, effort*) sustained; (*style*) lofty. ◆**soutien** *nm* support; (*personne*) supporter; **s. de famille** breadwinner. ◆**soutien-gorge** *nm* (*pl* soutiens-gorge) bra.

souterrain [suterɛ̃] *a* underground; — *nm* underground passage.

soutirer [sutire] *vt* **s. qch à qn** to extract *ou* get sth from s.o.

souvenir [suvnir] *nm* memory, recollection;

(*objet*) memento; (*cadeau*) keepsake; (*pour touristes*) souvenir; **en s. de** in memory of; **mon bon s. à** (*give*) my regards to. ◆**se souvenir*** *vpr* **se s. de** to remember, recall; **se s. que** to remember *ou* recall that.

souvent [suvã] *adv* often; **peu s.** seldom; **le plus s.** more often than not, most often.

souverain, -aine [suvrɛ̃, -ɛn] *a* sovereign; (*extrême*) *Péj* supreme; — *nmf* sovereign. ◆**souveraineté** *nf* sovereignty.

soviétique [sɔvjetik] *a* Soviet; **l'Union s.** the Soviet Union; — *nmf* Soviet citizen.

soyeux, -euse [swajø, -øz] *a* silky.

spacieux, -euse [spasjø, -øz] *a* spacious, roomy.

spaghetti(s) [spageti] *nmpl* spaghetti.

sparadrap [sparadra] *nm Méd* sticking plaster, *Am* adhesive tape.

spasme [spasm] *nm* spasm. ◆**spasmodique** *a* spasmodic.

spatial, -aux [spasjal, -o] *a* (*vol etc*) space-; **engin s.** spaceship, spacecraft.

spatule [spatyl] *nf* spatula.

speaker [spikœr] *nm*, **speakerine** [spikrin] *nf Rad TV* announcer.

spécial, -aux [spesjal, -o] *a* special; (*bizarre*) peculiar. ◆**spécialement** *adv* especially, particularly; (*exprès*) specially.

spécialiser (se) [səspesjalize] *vpr* to specialize (**dans** in). ◆**spécialisation** *nf* specialization. ◆**spécialiste** *nmf* specialist. ◆**spécialité** *nf* speciality, *Am* specialty.

spécifier [spesifje] *vt* to specify (**que** that).

spécifique [spesifik] *a Phys Ch* specific.

spécimen [spesimɛn] *nm* specimen; (*livre etc*) specimen copy.

spectacle [spɛktakl] *nm* **1** (*vue*) spectacle, sight; **se donner en s.** *Péj* to make an exhibition of oneself. **2** (*représentation*) show; **le s.** (*industrie*) show business. ◆**spectateur, -trice** *nmf Sp* spectator; (*témoin*) onlooker, witness; *pl Th Cin* audience.

spectaculaire [spɛktakylɛr] *a* spectacular.

spectre [spɛktr] *nm* **1** (*fantôme*) spectre, ghost. **2** (*solaire*) spectrum.

spéculer [spekyle] *vi Fin Phil* to speculate; **s. sur** (*tabler sur*) to bank *ou* rely on. ◆**spéculateur, -trice** *nmf* speculator. ◆**spéculatif, -ive** *a Fin Phil* speculative. ◆**spéculation** *nf Fin Phil* speculation.

spéléologie [speleɔlɔʒi] *nf* (*activité*) potholing, caving, *Am* spelunking. ◆**spéléologue** *nmf* potholer, *Am* spelunker.

sperme [spɛrm] *nm* sperm, semen.

sphère [sfɛr] *nf* (*boule, domaine*) sphere. ◆**sphérique** *a* spherical.

sphinx [sfɛ̃ks] *nm* sphinx.

spirale [spiral] *nf* spiral.
spirite [spirit] *nmf* spiritualist. **◆spiritisme** *nm* spiritualism.
spirituel, -elle [spirituel] *a* **1** (*amusant*) witty. **2** (*pouvoir, vie etc*) spiritual.
spiritueux [spirituø] *nmpl* (*boissons*) spirits.
splendide [splɑ̃did] *a* (*merveilleux, riche, beau*) splendid. **◆splendeur** *nf* splendour.
spongieux, -euse [spɔ̃ʒjø, -øz] *a* spongy.
spontané [spɔ̃tane] *a* spontaneous. **◆spontanéité** *nf* spontaneity. **◆spontanément** *adv* spontaneously.
sporadique [spɔradik] *a* sporadic.
sport [spɔr] *nm* sport; **faire du s.** to play sport *ou* *Am* sports; **(de) s.** (*chaussures, vêtements*) casual, sports; **voiture/veste de s.** sports car/jacket. **◆sportif, -ive** *a* (*attitude, personne*) sporting; (*association, journal, résultats*) sports, sporting; (*allure*) athletic; – *nmf* sportsman, sportswoman. **◆sportivité** *nf* (*esprit*) sportsmanship.
spot [spɔt] *nm* **1** (*lampe*) spot(light). **2 s.** (*publicitaire*) *Rad TV* commercial.
sprint [sprint] *nm* *Sp* sprint. **◆sprint/er** *vt* to sprint; – *nm* [-œr] sprinter. **◆-euse** *nf* sprinter.
square [skwar] *nm* public garden.
squelette [skəlɛt] *nm* skeleton. **◆squelettique** *a* (*personne, maigreur*) skeleton-like; (*exposé*) sketchy.
stable [stabl] *a* stable. **◆stabilisateur** *nm* stabilizer. **◆stabiliser** *vt* to stabilize; — **se s.** *vpr* to stabilize. **◆stabilité** *nf* stability.
stade [stad] *nm* **1** *Sp* stadium. **2** (*phase*) stage.
stage [staʒ] *nm* training period; (*cours*) (training) course. **◆stagiaire** *a & nmf* trainee.
stagner [stagne] *vi* to stagnate. **◆stagnant** *a* stagnant. **◆stagnation** *nf* stagnation.
stalle [stal] *nf* (*box*) & *Rel* stall.
stand [stɑ̃d] *nm* (*d'exposition etc*) stand, stall; **s. de ravitaillement** *Sp* pit; **s. de tir** (*de foire*) shooting range; *Mil* firing range.
standard [stɑ̃dar] **1** *nm* *Tél* switchboard. **2** *a inv* (*modèle etc*) standard. **◆standardiser** *vt* to standardize. **◆standardiste** *nmf* (switchboard) operator.
standing [stɑ̃diŋ] *nm* standing, status; **de (grand) s.** (*immeuble*) luxury-.
starter [starter] *nm* **1** *Aut* choke. **2** *Sp* starter.
station [stasjɔ̃] *nf* (*de métro, d'observation etc*) & *Rad* station; (*de ski etc*) resort; (*d'autobus*) stop; **s. de taxis** taxi rank, *Am*

taxi stand; **s. debout** standing (position); **s. (thermale)** spa. **◆s.-service** *nf* (*pl stations-service*) *Aut* service station.
stationnaire [stasjɔnɛr] *vi* a stationary.
stationn/er [stasjɔne] *vi* (*se garer*) to park; (*être garé*) to be parked. **◆—ement** *nm* parking.
statique [statik] *a* static.
statistique [statistik] *nf* (*donnée*) statistic; **la s.** (*techniques*) statistics; – *a* statistical.
statue [staty] *nf* statue. **◆statuette** *nf* statuette.
statuer [statɥe] *vi* **s. sur** *Jur* to rule on.
statu quo [statykwo] *nm inv* status quo.
stature [statyr] *nf* stature.
statut [staty] *nm* **1** (*position*) status. **2** *pl* (*règles*) statutes. **◆statutaire** *a* statutory.
steak [stɛk] *nm* steak.
stencil [stɛnsil] *nm* stencil.
sténo [steno] *nf* (*personne*) stenographer; (*sténographie*) shorthand, stenography; **prendre en s.** to take down in shorthand. **◆sténodactylo** *nf* shorthand typist, *Am* stenographer. **◆sténographie** *nf* shorthand, stenography.
stéréo [stereo] *nf* stereo; – *a inv* (*disque etc*) stereo. **◆stéréophonique** *a* stereophonic.
stéréotype [stereotip] *nm* stereotype. **◆stéréotypé** *a* stereotyped.
stérile [steril] *a* sterile; (*terre*) barren. **◆stérilisation** *nf* sterilization. **◆stériliser** *vt* to sterilize. **◆stérilité** *nf* sterility; (*de terre*) barrenness.
stérilet [sterilɛ] *nm* IUD, coil.
stéthoscope [stetɔskɔp] *nm* stethoscope.
steward [stiwart] *nm* *Av Nau* steward.
stigmate [stigmat] *nm* *Fig* mark, stigma (**de** of). **◆stigmatiser** *vt* (*dénoncer*) to stigmatize.
stimul/er [stimyle] *vt* to stimulate. **◆—ant** *nm* *Fig* stimulus; *Méd* stimulant. **◆stimulateur** *nm* **s. cardiaque** pacemaker. **◆stimulation** *nf* stimulation.
stimulus [stimylys] *nm* (*pl stimuli* [-li]) (*physiologique*) stimulus.
stipuler [stipyle] *vt* to stipulate (**que** that). **◆stipulation** *nf* stipulation.
stock [stɔk] *nm* *Com & Fig* stock (**de** of). **◆stock/er** *vt* to (keep in) stock. **◆—age** *nm* stocking.
stoïque [stɔik] *a* stoic(al). **◆stoïcisme** *nm* stoicism.
stop [stɔp] **1** *int* stop; – *nm* (*panneau*) *Aut* stop sign; (*feu arrière*) *Aut* brake light. **2** *nm* **faire du s.** *Fam* to hitchhike. **◆stopp/er** **1** *vti* to stop. **2** *vt* (*vêtement*) to

mend (invisibly). ◆—age *nm* (invisible) mending.

store [stɔr] *nm* blind, *Am* (window) shade; (*de magasin*) awning.

strabisme [strabism] *nm* squint.

strapontin [strapɔ̃tɛ̃] *nm* tip-up seat.

stratagème [strataʒɛm] *nm* stratagem, ploy.

stratège [strateʒ] *nm* strategist. ◆**stratégie** *nf* strategy. ◆**stratégique** *a* strategic.

stress [strɛs] *nm inv Méd Psy* stress. ◆**stressant** *a* stressful. ◆**stressé** *a* under stress.

strict [strikt] *a* strict; (*langue, tenue, vérité*) plain; (*droit*) basic; **le s. minimum/nécessaire** the bare minimum/necessities. ◆**strictement** *adv* strictly; (*vêtu*) plainly.

strident [stridã] *a* strident, shrill.

strie [stri] *nf* streak; (*sillon*) groove. ◆**strier** *vt* to streak.

strip-tease [striptiz] *nm* striptease. ◆**strip-teaseuse** *nf* stripper.

strophe [strɔf] *nf* stanza, verse.

structure [stryktyr] *nf* structure. ◆**structural, -aux** *a* structural. ◆**structurer** *vt* to structure.

stuc [styk] *nm* stucco.

studieux, -euse [stydjø, -øz] *a* studious; (*vacances etc*) devoted to study.

studio [stydjo] *nm* (*de peintre*) & *Cin TV* studio; (*logement*) studio flat *ou Am* apartment.

stupéfait [stypefɛ] *a* amazed, astounded (**de** at, by). ◆**stupéfaction** *nf* amazement. ◆**stupéfi/er** *vt* to amaze, astound. ◆**—ant** *a* amazing, astounding. 2 *nm* drug, narcotic. ◆**stupeur** *nf* **1** (*étonnement*) amazement. **2** (*inertie*) stupor.

stupide [stypid] *a* stupid. ◆**stupidement** *adv* stupidly. ◆**stupidité** *nf* stupidity; (*action, parole*) stupid thing.

style [stil] *nm* style; **de s.** (*meuble*) period-. ◆**stylisé** *a* stylized. ◆**styliste** *nmf* (*de mode etc*) designer. ◆**stylistique** *a* stylistic.

stylé [stile] *a* well-trained.

stylo [stilo] *nm* pen; **s. à bille** ballpoint (pen), biro®; **s. à encre** fountain pen.

su [sy] *voir* **savoir**.

suave [sɥav] *a* (*odeur, voix*) sweet.

subalterne [sybaltɛrn] *a* & *nmf* subordinate.

subconscient [sypkɔ̃sjɑ̃] *a* & *nm* subconscious.

subdiviser [sybdivize] *vt* to subdivide (**en** into). ◆**subdivision** *nf* subdivision.

subir [sybir] *vt* to undergo; (*conséquences, défaite, perte, tortures*) to suffer; (*influence*) to be under; **s. qn** (*supporter*) *Fam* to put up with s.o.

subit [sybi] *a* sudden. ◆**subitement** *adv* suddenly.

subjectif, -ive [sybʒɛktif, -iv] *a* subjective. ◆**subjectivement** *adv* subjectively. ◆**subjectivité** *nf* subjectivity.

subjonctif [sybʒɔ̃ktif] *nm Gram* subjunctive.

subjuguer [sybʒyge] *vt* to subjugate; (*envoûter*) to captivate.

sublime [syblim] *a* & *nm* sublime.

sublimer [syblime] *vt Psy* to sublimate.

submerger [sybmɛrʒe] *vt* to submerge; (*envahir*) *Fig* to overwhelm; **submergé de** (*travail etc*) overwhelmed with; **submergé par** (*ennemi, foule*) swamped by. ◆**submersible** *nm* submarine.

subordonn/er [sybɔrdɔne] *vt* to subordinate (**à** to). ◆**—é, -ée** *a* subordinate (**à** to); **être s. à** (*dépendre de*) to depend on; — *nmf* subordinate. ◆**subordination** *nf* subordination.

subreptice [sybrɛptis] *a* surreptitious.

subside [sypsid] *nm* grant, subsidy.

subsidiaire [sybsidjɛr] *a* subsidiary; **question s.** (*de concours*) deciding question.

subsister [sybziste] *vi* (*rester*) to remain; (*vivre*) to get by, subsist; (*doutes, souvenirs etc*) to linger (on), subsist. ◆**subsistance** *nf* subsistence.

substance [sypstɑ̃s] *nf* substance; **en s.** *Fig* in essence. ◆**substantiel, -ielle** *a* substantial.

substantif [sypstɑ̃tif] *nm Gram* noun, substantive.

substituer [sypstitɥe] *vt* to substitute (**à** for); **se s. à qn** to take the place of s.o., substitute for s.o.; (*représenter*) to substitute for s.o. ◆**substitution** *nf* substitution.

subterfuge [sybtɛrfyʒ] *nm* subterfuge.

subtil [syptil] *a* subtle. ◆**subtilité** *nf* subtlety.

subtiliser [syptilize] *vt* (*dérober*) *Fam* to make off with.

subvenir* [sybvənir] *vi* **s. à** (*besoins, frais*) to meet.

subvention [sybvɑ̃sjɔ̃] *nf* subsidy. ◆**subventionner** *vt* to subsidize.

subversif, -ive [sybvɛrsif, -iv] *a* subversive. ◆**subversion** *nf* subversion.

suc [syk] *nm* (*gastrique, de fruit*) juice; (*de plante*) sap.

succédané [syksedane] *nm* substitute (de for).

succéder [syksede] *vi* **s. à qn** to succeed s.o.; **s. à qch** to follow sth, come after sth; **— se s.** *vpr* to succeed one another; to follow one another. ◆**successeur** *nm* successor. ◆**successif, -ive** *a* successive. ◆**successivement** *adv* successively. ◆**succession** *nf* **1** succession (de of, à to); **prendre la s. de qn** to succeed s.o. **2** (*patrimoine*) *Jur* inheritance, estate.

succès [sykse] *nm* success; **s. de librairie** (*livre*) best-seller; **avoir du s.** to be successful, be a success; **à s.** (*auteur, film etc*) successful; **avec s.** successfully.

succinct [syksɛ̃] *a* succinct, brief.

succion [sy(k)sjɔ̃] *nf* suction.

succomber [sykɔ̃be] *vi* **1** (*mourir*) to die. **2** **s. à** (*céder à*) to succumb to, give in to.

succulent [sykylɑ̃] *a* succulent.

succursale [sykyrsal] *nf* *Com* branch; **magasin à succursales multiples** chain *ou* multiple store.

sucer [syse] *vt* to suck. ◆**sucette** *nf* lollipop; (*tétine*) dummy, comforter, *Am* pacifier.

sucre [sykr] *nm* sugar; (*morceau*) sugar lump; **s. cristallisé** granulated sugar; **s. en morceaux** lump sugar; **s. en poudre**, **s. semoule** caster sugar, *Am* finely ground sugar; **s. d'orge** barley sugar. ◆**sucr/er** *vt* to sugar, sweeten. ◆**—é** *a* sweet, sugary; (*artificiellement*) sweetened; (*douceureux*) *Fig* sugary, syrupy. ◆**sucrerie 1** *nf* (*usine*) sugar refinery. **2** *nfpl* (*bonbons*) sweets, *Am* candy. ◆**sucrier, -ière** *a* (*industrie*) sugar-; *— nm* (*récipient*) sugar bowl.

sud [syd] *nm* south; **au s.** to the south of; **du s.** (*vent, direction*) southerly; (*ville*) southern; (*gens*) from *ou* in the south; **Amérique/Afrique du S.** South America/Africa; **l'Europe du S.** Southern Europe; *— a inv* (*côte*) south(ern). ◆**s.-africain, -aine** *a* & *nmf* South African. ◆**s.-américain, -aine** *a* & *nmf* South American. ◆**s.-est** *nm* & *a inv* south-east. ◆**s.-ouest** *nm* & *a inv* south-west.

Suède [sɥɛd] *nf* Sweden. ◆**suédois, -oise** *a* Swedish; *— nmf* Swede; *— nm* (*langue*) Swedish.

suer [sɥe] *vi* (*personne, mur etc*) to sweat; **faire s. qn** *Fam* to get on s.o.'s nerves; **se faire s.** *Fam* to be bored stiff; *— vt* (*sang etc*) to sweat. ◆**sueur** *nf* sweat; **(tout) en s.** sweating.

suffire* [syfir] *vi* to be enough *ou* sufficient, suffice (à for); **ça suffit!** that's enough!; **il**

suffit de faire one only has to do; **il suffit d'une goutte**/*etc* **pour faire** a drop/*etc* is enough to do; **il ne me suffit pas de faire** I'm not satisfied with doing; *— se s.* *vpr* **se s. (à soi-même)** to be self-sufficient. ◆**suffisant** *a* **1** sufficient, adequate. **2** (*vaniteux*) conceited. ◆**suffisamment** *adv* sufficiently; **s. de** sufficient, enough. ◆**suffisance** *nf* (*vanité*) conceit.

suffixe [syfiks] *nm* *Gram* suffix.

suffoquer [syfɔke] *vt* to choke, suffocate. ◆**suffocant** *a* stifling, suffocating. ◆**suffocation** *nf* suffocation; (*sensation*) feeling of suffocation.

suffrage [syfraʒ] *nm* *Pol* (*voix*) vote; (*droit*) suffrage.

suggérer [sygʒere] *vt* (*proposer*) to suggest (de faire doing, que (+ *sub*) that); (*évoquer*) to suggest. ◆**suggestif, -ive** *a* suggestive. ◆**suggestion** *nf* suggestion.

suicide [sɥisid] *nm* suicide. ◆**suicidaire** *a* suicidal. ◆**se suicid/er** *vpr* to commit suicide. ◆**—é, -ée** *nmf* suicide (victim).

suie [sɥi] *nf* soot.

suif [sɥif] *nm* tallow.

suinter [sɥɛ̃te] *vi* to ooze, seep. ◆**suintement** *nm* oozing, seeping.

suis [sɥi] *voir* **être, suivre**.

Suisse [sɥis] *nf* Switzerland. ◆**suisse** *a* & *nmf* Swiss. ◆**Suissesse** *nf* Swiss (woman *ou* girl).

suite [sɥit] *nf* (*reste*) rest; (*continuation*) continuation; (*de film, roman*) sequel; (*série*) series, sequence; (*appartement, escorte*) & *Mus* suite; (*cohérence*) order; *pl* (*résultats*) consequences; (*séquelles*) effects; **attendre la s.** to wait and see what happens next; **donner s. à** (*demande etc*) to follow up; **faire s. (à)** to follow; **prendre la s. de qn** to take over from s.o.; **par la s.** afterwards; **par s. de** as a result of; **à la s.** one after another; **à la s. de** (*derrière*) behind; (*événement, maladie etc*) as a result of; **de s.** in succession.

suiv/re* [sɥivr] *vt* to follow; (*accompagner*) to go with, accompany; (*classe*) *Scol* to attend, go to; (*malade*) to treat; **s. des yeux** *ou* **du regard**) to watch; **s. son chemin** to go on one's way; **se s.** to follow each other; *— vi* to follow; **faire s.** (*courrier*) to forward; **'à s.'** 'to be continued'; **comme suit** as follows. ◆**—ant¹, -ante** *a* next, following; (*ci-après*) following; *— nmf* next (one); **au s.!** next!, the next person! ◆**—ant²** *prép* (*selon*) according to. ◆**—i** *a* (*régulier*) regular, steady; (*cohérent*) coherent; (*article*

Com regularly on sale; **peu/très s.** (*cours*) poorly/well attended.

sujet¹, -ette [syʒɛ, -ɛt] *a* s. à (*maladie etc*) subject *ou* liable to; – *nmf* (*personne*) Pol subject.

sujet² [syʒɛ] *nm* 1 (*question*) & Gram subject; (*d'examen*) question; **au s. de** about; **à quel s.?** about what? 2 (*raison*) cause; **avoir s. de faire** to have (good) cause *ou* (good) reason to do. 3 *nm* (*individu*) subject; **un mauvais s.** (*garçon*) a rotten egg.

sulfurique [sylfyrik] *a* (*acide*) sulphuric, *Am* sulfuric.

sultan [syltɑ̃] *nm* sultan.

summum [sɔmɔm] *nm* (*comble*) Fig height.

super [sypɛr] 1 *a* (*bon*) Fam great. 2 *nm* (*supercarburant*) Fam four-star (petrol), *Am* premium *ou* hi-test gas.

superbe [sypɛrb] *a* superb.

supercarburant [sypɛrkarbyrɑ̃] *nm* high-octane petrol *ou* Am gasoline.

supercherie [sypɛrʃəri] *nf* deception.

superficie [sypɛrfisi] *nf* surface; (*dimensions*) area. ◆**superficiel, -ielle** *a* superficial. ◆**superficiellement** *adv* superficially.

superflu [sypɛrfly] *a* superfluous.

super-grand [sypɛrgrɑ̃] *nm* Pol Fam superpower.

supérieur, -eure [sypɛrjœr] *a* (*étages, partie etc*) upper; (*qualité, air, ton*) superior; (*études*) higher; **à l'étage s.** on the floor above; **s. à** (*meilleur que*) superior to, better than; (*plus grand que*) above, greater than; – *nmf* superior. ◆**supériorité** *nf* superiority.

superlatif, -ive [sypɛrlatif, -iv] *a* & *nm* Gram superlative.

supermarché [sypɛrmarʃe] *nm* supermarket.

superposer [sypɛrpoze] *vt* (*objets*) to put on top of each other; (*images etc*) to superimpose.

superproduction [sypɛrprɔdyksjɔ̃] *nf* (*film*) blockbuster.

superpuissance [sypɛrpɥisɑ̃s] *nf* Pol superpower.

supersonique [sypɛrsɔnik] *a* supersonic.

superstitieux, -euse [sypɛrstisjø, -øz] *a* superstitious. ◆**superstition** *nf* superstition.

superviser [sypɛrvize] *vt* to supervise.

supplanter [syplɑ̃te] *vt* to take the place of.

supplé/er [syplee] *vt* (*remplacer*) to replace; (*compenser*) to make up for; – *vi* **s. à** (*compenser*) to make up for. ◆**-ant, -ante**

a & *nmf* (*personne*) substitute, replacement; (*professeur*) **s.** supply teacher.

supplément [syplemɑ̃] *nm* (*argent*) extra charge, supplement; (*de livre, revue*) supplement; **en s.** extra; **un s. de** (*information, travail etc*) extra, additional. ◆**supplémentaire** *a* extra, additional.

supplice [syplis] *nm* torture; **au s.** Fig on the rack. ◆**supplicier** *vt* to torture.

suppli/er [syplije] *vt* **s. qn de faire** to beg *ou* implore s.o. to do; **je vous en supplie!** I beg *ou* implore you! ◆**-ant, -ante** *a* (*regard etc*) imploring. ◆**supplication** *nf* plea, entreaty.

support [sypɔr] *nm* 1 support; (*d'instrument etc*) stand. 2 (*moyen*) Fig medium; **s. audio-visuel** audio-visual aid.

support/er¹ [sypɔrte] *vt* to bear, endure; (*frais*) to bear; (*affront etc*) to suffer; (*résister à*) to withstand; (*soutenir*) to support. ◆**-able** *a* bearable; (*excusable, passable*) tolerable.

supporter² [sypɔrtɛr] *nm* Sp supporter.

supposer [sypoze] *vt* to suppose, assume (*que* that); (*impliquer*) to imply (*que* that); **à s.** *ou* **en supposant que** (+ *sub*) supposing (that). ◆**supposition** *nf* supposition, assumption.

suppositoire [sypozitwar] *nm* Méd suppository.

supprimer [syprime] *vt* to remove, get rid of; (*institution, loi*) to abolish; (*journal etc*) to suppress; (*mot, passage*) to cut, delete; (*train etc*) to cancel; (*tuer*) to do away with; **s. qch à qn** to take sth away from s.o. ◆**suppression** *nf* removal; abolition; suppression; cutting; cancellation.

suprématie [sypremasi] *nf* supremacy. ◆**suprême** *a* supreme.

sur [syr] *prép* on, upon; (*par-dessus*) over; (*au sujet de*) on, about; **s. les trois heures** at about three o'clock; **six s. dix** six out of ten; **un jour s. deux** every other day; **coup s. coup** blow after *ou* upon blow; **six mètres s. dix** six metres by ten; **mettre/monter/etc s.** to go/climb/etc on (to); **aller/tourner/etc s.** to go/turn/etc towards; **s. ce** after which, and then; (*maintenant*) and now.

sur- [syr] *préf* over-.

sûr [syr] *a* sure, certain (**de** of, **que** that); (*digne de confiance*) reliable; (*avenir*) secure; (*lieu*) safe; (*main*) steady; (*goût*) unerring; (*jugement*) sound; **s. de soi** self-assured; **bien s.!** of course!

surabondant [syrabɔ̃dɑ̃] *a* over-abundant.

suranné [syrane] *a* outmoded.

surboum [syrbum] *nf* Fam party.

surcharge [syrʃarʒ] *nf* **1** overloading; (*poids*) extra load; **s. de travail** extra work; **en s.** (*passagers etc*) extra. **2** (*correction de texte etc*) alteration; (*de timbre-poste*) surcharge. ◆**surcharger** *vt* (*voiture, personne etc*) to overload (**de** with).

surchauffer [syrʃofe] *vt* to overheat.

surchoix [syrʃwa] *a inv Com* top-quality.

surclasser [syrklase] *vt* to outclass.

surcroît [syrkrwa] *nm* increase (**de** in); **de s., par s.** in addition.

surdité [syrdite] *nf* deafness.

surdoué, -ée [syrdwe] *nmf* child who has a genius-level IQ.

surélever [syrelve] *vt* to raise (the height of).

sûrement [syrmã] *adv* certainly; (*sans danger*) safely.

surenchère [syrãʃɛr] *nf Com* higher bid; **s. électorale** *Fig* bidding for votes. ◆**surenchérir** *vi* to bid higher (**sur** than).

surestimer [syrɛstime] *vt* to overestimate; (*peinture etc*) to overvalue.

sûreté [syrte] *nf* safety; (*de l'état*) security; (*garantie*) surety; (*de geste*) sureness; (*de jugement*) soundness; **être en s.** to be safe; **mettre en s.** to put in a safe place; **de s.** (*épingle, soupape etc*) safety-.

surexcité [syrɛksite] *a* overexcited.

surf [sœrf] *nm Sp* surfing; **faire du s.** to surf, go surfing.

surface [syrfas] *nf* surface; (*dimensions*) (surface) area; **faire s.** (*sous-marin etc*) to surface; (**magasin à**) **grande s.** hypermarket.

surfait [syrfɛ] *a* overrated.

surgelé [syrʒəle] *a* (deep-)frozen; *-.nmpl* (deep-)frozen foods.

surgir [syrʒir] *vi* to appear suddenly (**de** from); (*conflit, problème*) to arise.

surhomme [syrɔm] *nm* superman. ◆**surhumain** *a* superhuman.

sur-le-champ [syrləʃã] *adv* immediately.

surlendemain [syrlãdmɛ̃] *nm* **le s.** two days later; **le s. de** two days after.

surmen/er [syrmane] *vt*, — **se s.** *vpr* to overwork. ◆**-age** *nm* overwork.

surmonter [syrmɔ̃te] *vt* **1** (*obstacle, peur etc*) to overcome, get over. **2** (*être placé sur*) to be on top of, top.

surnager [syrnaʒe] *vi* to float.

surnaturel, -elle [syrnatyrɛl] *a & nm* supernatural.

surnom [syrnɔ̃] *nm* nickname. ◆**surnommer** *vt* to nickname.

surnombre [syrnɔ̃br] *nm* **en s.** too many; **je suis en s.** I am one too many.

surpasser [syrpase] *vt* to surpass (**en** in); — **se s.** *vpr* to surpass oneself.

surpeuplé [syrpœple] *a* overpopulated.

surplomb [syrplɔ̃] *nm* **en s.** overhanging. ◆**surplomber** *vti* to overhang.

surplus [syrply] *nm* surplus; *pl Com* surplus (stock).

surprendre* [syrprãdr] *vt* (*étonner, prendre sur le fait*) to surprise; (*secret*) to discover; (*conversation*) to overhear; **se s. à faire** to find oneself doing. ◆**surprenant** *a* surprising. ◆**surpris** *a* surprised (**de** at, **que** (+ *sub*) that). ◆**surprise** *nf* surprise. ◆**surprise-partie** *nf* (*pl* surprises-parties) party.

surréaliste [syrealist] *a* (*bizarre*) *Fam* surrealistic.

sursaut [syrso] *nm* (sudden) start *ou* jump; **en s.** with a start; **s. de** (*énergie etc*) burst of. ◆**sursauter** *vi* to start, jump.

sursis [syrsi] *nm Mil* deferment; (*répit*) *Fig* reprieve; **un an** (**de prison**) **avec s.** a one-year suspended sentence.

surtaxe [syrtaks] *nf* surcharge.

surtout [syrtu] *adv* especially; (*avant tout*) above all; **s. pas** certainly not; **s. que** especially as *ou* since.

surveill/er [syrveje] *vt* (*garder*) to watch, keep an eye on; (*épier*) to watch; (*contrôler*) to supervise; **s. son langage/sa santé** *Fig* to watch one's language/health; — **se s.** *vpr* to watch oneself. ◆**-ant, -ante** *nmf* (*de lycée*) supervisor (in charge of discipline); (*de prison*) warder; (*de chantier*) supervisor; **s. de plage** lifeguard. ◆**surveillance** *nf* watch (**sur** over); (*de travaux, d'ouvriers*) supervision; (*de la police*) surveillance, observation.

survenir* [syrvənir] *vi* to occur; (*personne*) to turn up.

survêtement [syrvɛtmã] *nm Sp* tracksuit.

survie [syrvi] *nf* survival. ◆**surviv/re*** *vi* to survive (**à qch** sth); **s. à qn** to outlive s.o., survive s.o. ◆**-ant, -ante** *nmf* survivor. ◆**survivance** *nf* (*chose*) survival, relic.

survol [syrvɔl] *nm* **le s. de** flying over; (*question*) *Fig* the overview of. ◆**survoler** *vt* (*en avion*) to fly over; (*question*) *Fig* to go over (quickly).

survolté [syrvɔlte] *a* (*surexcité*) worked up.

susceptible [sysɛptibl] *a* **1** (*ombrageux*) touchy, sensitive. **2** **s. de** (*interprétations etc*) open to; **s. de faire** likely *ou* liable to do; (*capable*) able to do. ◆**susceptibilité** *nf* touchiness, sensitiveness.

susciter [sysite] *vt* (*sentiment*) to arouse; (*ennuis, obstacles etc*) to create.

suspect, -ecte [syspɛ(kt), -ɛkt] a suspicious, suspect; s. de suspected of; – nmf suspect. ◆suspecter vt to suspect (de qch of sth, de faire of doing); (bonne foi etc) to question, suspect, doubt.

suspend/re [syspɑ̃dr] vt 1 (destituer, différer, interrompre) to suspend. 2 (fixer) to hang (up) (à on); se s. à to hang from. ◆—u a s. à hanging from; pont s. suspension bridge. ◆suspension nf 1 (d'hostilités, d'employé etc) & Aut suspension; points de s. Gram dots, suspension points. 2 (lustre) hanging lamp.

suspens (en) [ɑ̃syspɑ̃] adv 1 (affaire, travail) in abeyance. 2 (dans l'incertitude) in suspense.

suspense [syspɛns] nm suspense; film à s. thriller, suspense film.

suspicion [syspisjɔ̃] nf suspicion.

susurrer [sysyre] vti to murmur.

suture [sytyr] nf Méd stitching; point de s. stitch. ◆suturer vt to stitch up.

svelte [svɛlt] a slender. ◆sveltesse nf slenderness.

SVP abrév (s'il vous plaît) please.

syllabe [silab] nf syllable.

symbole [sɛ̃bɔl] nm symbol. ◆symbolique a symbolic; (salaire) nominal. ◆symboliser vt to symbolize. ◆symbolisme nm symbolism.

symétrie [simetri] nf symmetry. ◆symétrique a symmetrical.

sympa [sɛ̃pa] a inv Fam = sympathique.

sympathie [sɛ̃pati] nf liking, affection; (affinité) affinity; (condoléances) sympathy; avoir de la s. pour qn to be fond of s.o. ◆sympathique a nice, pleasant; (accueil, geste) friendly. ◆sympathis/er vi to get

on well (avec with). ◆—ant, -ante nmf Pol sympathizer.

symphonie [sɛ̃fɔni] nf symphony. ◆symphonique a symphonic; (orchestre) symphony-.

symposium [sɛ̃pozjɔm] nm symposium.

symptôme [sɛ̃ptom] nm symptom. ◆symptomatique a symptomatic (de of).

synagogue [sinagɔg] nf synagogue.

synchroniser [sɛ̃krɔnize] vt to synchronize.

syncope [sɛ̃kɔp] nf Méd blackout; tomber en s. to black out.

syndicat [sɛ̃dika] nm 1 (d'employés, d'ouvriers) (trade) union; (de patrons etc) association. 2 s. d'initiative tourist (information) office. ◆syndical, -aux a (réunion etc) (trade) union-. ◆syndicalisme nm trade unionism. ◆syndicaliste nmf trade unionist; – a (trade) union-. ◆syndiqu/er vt to unionize; — se s. vpr (adhérer) to join a (trade) union. ◆—é, -ée nmf (trade) union member.

syndrome [sɛ̃drom] nm Méd & Fig syndrome.

synode [sinɔd] nm Rel synod.

synonyme [sinɔnim] a synonymous (de with); – nm synonym.

syntaxe [sɛ̃taks] nf Gram syntax.

synthèse [sɛ̃tez] nf synthesis. ◆synthétique a synthetic.

syphilis [sifilis] nf syphilis.

Syrie [siri] nf Syria. ◆syrien, -ienne a & nmf Syrian.

système [sistɛm] nm (structure, réseau etc) & Anat system; le s. D Fam resourcefulness. ◆systématique a systematic; (soutien) unconditional. ◆systématiquement adv systematically.

T

T, t [te] nm T, t.

t' [t] voir te.

ta [ta] voir ton [1].

tabac [taba] 1 nm tobacco; (magasin) tobacconist's (shop), Am tobacco store; (à priser) snuff. 2 nm passer à t. to beat up; passage à t. beating up. 3 a inv (couleur) buff. ◆tabatière nf (boîte) snuffbox.

tabasser [tabase] vt Fam to beat up.

table [tabl] nf 1 (meuble) (nourriture) fare; t. de jeu/de nuit/d'opération card/bedside/operating table; t. basse coffee

table; t. à repasser ironing board; t. roulante (tea) trolley, Am (serving) cart; mettre/débarrasser la t. to lay ou set/clear the table; être à t. to be sitting at the table; à t.! (food's) ready!; faire t. rase Fig to make a clean sweep (de of); mettre sur t. d'écoute (téléphone) to tap. 2 (liste) table; t. des matières table of contents.

tableau, -x [tablo] nm 1 (peinture) picture, painting; (image, description) picture; Th scene; t. de maître (peinture) old master. 2 (panneau) board; Rail train-indicator;

(*liste*) list; (*graphique*) chart; **t. (noir)** (black)board; **t. d'affichage** notice board, *Am* bulletin board; **t. de bord** *Aut* dashboard; **t. de contrôle** *Tech* control panel.

tabler [table] *vi* **t. sur** to count *ou* rely on.

tablette [tablɛt] *nf* (*d'armoire, de lavabo*) shelf; (*de cheminée*) mantelpiece; (*de chocolat*) bar, slab.

tablier [tablije] *nm* **1** (*vêtement*) apron; (*d'écolier*) smock; **rendre son t.** (*démissionner*) to give notice. **2** (*de pont*) roadway.

tabou [tabu] *a & nm* taboo.

tabouret [taburɛ] *nm* stool.

tabulateur [tabylatœr] *nm* (*de machine à écrire etc*) tabulator.

tac [tak] *nm* **répondre du t. au t.** to give tit for tat.

tache [taʃ] *nf* spot, mark; (*salissure*) stain; **faire t.** (*détonner*) *Péj* to jar, stand out; **faire t. d'huile** *Fig* to spread. ◆**tacher** *vt*, — **se t.** *vpr* (*tissu etc*) to stain; — *vi* (*vin etc*) to stain. ◆**tacheté** *a* speckled, spotted.

tâche [taʃ] *nf* task, job; **travailler à la t.** to do piecework.

tâcher [taʃe] *vi* **t. de faire** to try *ou* endeavour to do.

tâcheron [taʃrɔ̃] *nm* drudge.

tacite [tasit] *a* tacit. ◆—**ment** *adv* tacitly.

taciturne [tasityrn] *a* taciturn.

tacot [tako] *nm* (*voiture*) *Fam* (old) wreck, banger.

tact [takt] *nm* tact.

tactile [taktil] *a* tactile.

tactique [taktik] *a* tactical; — *nf* **la t.** tactics; **une t.** a tactic.

Tahiti [taiti] *nm* Tahiti. ◆**tahitien, -ienne** [taisjɛ̃, -jɛn] *a nmf* Tahitian.

taie [tɛ] *nf* **t. d'oreiller** pillowcase, pillowslip.

taillade [tajad] *nf* gash, slash. ◆**taillader** *vt* to gash, slash.

taille [taj] *nf* **1** (*stature*) height; (*dimension, mesure commerciale*) size; **de haute t.** (*personne*) tall; **de petite t.** short; **de t. moyenne** (*objet, personne*) medium-sized; **être de t. à faire** *Fig* to be capable of doing; **de t.** (*erreur, objet*) *Fam* enormous. **2** *Anat* waist; **tour de t.** waist measurement.

taille *nf* cutting; cutting out; trimming; pruning; (*forme*) cut. ◆**taill/er** *vt* to cut; (*vêtement*) to cut out; (*haie, barbe*) to trim; (*arbre*) to prune; (*crayon*) to sharpen. **2 se t.** *vpr* (*partir*) *Arg* to clear off. ◆—**é** *a* **en athlète/etc** built like an athlete/etc; **t. pour faire** *Fig* cut out for doing. ◆**taille-crayon(s)** [tajkrɛjɔ̃] *nm inv* pencilsharpener. ◆**t.-haies** *nm inv* (garden) shears; (*électrique*) hedge trimmer.

tailleur [tajœr] *nm* **1** (*personne*) tailor. **2** (*costume féminin*) suit.

taillis [taji] *nm* copse, coppice.

tain [tɛ̃] *nm* (*de glace*) silvering; **glace sans t.** two-way mirror.

taire* [tɛr] *vt* to say nothing about; — *vi* **faire t.** to silence s.o. — **se t.** *vpr* (*rester silencieux*) to keep quiet (**sur qch** about sth); (*cesser de parler*) to fall silent, shut up; **tais-toi!** be *ou* keep quiet!, shut up!

talc [talk] *nm* talcum powder.

talent [talɑ̃] *nm* talent; **avoir du t. pour** to have a talent for. ◆**talentueux, -euse** *a* talented.

taler [tale] *vt* (*fruit*) to bruise.

talion [taljɔ̃] *nm* **la loi du t.** (*vengeance*) an eye for an eye.

talisman [talismɑ̃] *nm* talisman.

talkie-walkie [talkiwalki] *nm* (*poste*) walkie-talkie.

taloche [talɔʃ] *nf* (*gifle*) *Fam* clout, smack.

talon [talɔ̃] *nm* **1** heel; (**chaussures à) talons hauts** high heels, high-heeled shoes. **2** (*de chèque, carnet*) stub, counterfoil; (*bout de pain*) crust; (*de jambon*) heel. ◆**talonner** *vt* (*fugitif etc*) to follow on the heels of; (*ballon*) *Rugby* to heel; (*harceler*) *Fig* to hound, dog.

talus [taly] *nm* slope, embankment.

tambour [tɑ̃bur] *nm* **1** (*de machine etc*) & *Mus* drum; (*personne*) drummer. **2** (*porte*) revolving door. ◆**tambourin** *nm* tambourine. ◆**tambouriner** *vi* (*avec les doigts etc*) to drum (**sur** on).

tamis [tami] *nm* sieve. ◆**tamiser** *vt* to sift; (*lumière*) to filter, subdue.

Tamise [tamiz] *nf* **la T.** the Thames.

tampon [tɑ̃pɔ̃] *nm* **1** (*bouchon*) plug, stopper; (*d'ouate*) wad, pad; *Méd* swab; **t. hygiénique** *ou* **périodique** tampon; **t. à récurer** scouring pad. **2** (*de train etc*) & *Fig* buffer; **état t.** buffer state. **3** (*marque, instrument*) stamp; **t. buvard** blotter; **t. encreur** ink(ing) pad. ◆**tamponn/er** **1** *vt* (*visage etc*) to dab; (*plaie*) to swab. **2** *vt* (*train, voiture*) to crash into; — **se t.** *vpr* to crash into each other. **3** *vt* (*lettre, document*) to stamp. ◆—**euses** *afpl* **autos t.** dodgems, bumper cars.

tam-tam [tamtam] *nm* (*tambour*) tom-tom.

tandem [tɑ̃dɛm] *nm* **1** (*bicyclette*) tandem. **2** (*duo*) *Fig* duo, pair; **en t.** (*travailler etc*) in tandem.

tandis que [tɑ̃dik(ə)] *conj* (*pendant que*) while; (*contraste*) whereas, while.

tangent [tɑ̃ʒɑ̃] *a* **1** *Géom* tangential (**à** to).

2 (*juste*) *Fam* touch and go, close. ◆**tangente** *nf Géom* tangent.

tangible [tɑ̃ʒibl] *a* tangible.

tango [tɑ̃go] *nm* tango.

tang/uer [tɑ̃ge] *vi* (*bateau, avion*) to pitch. ◆**—age** *nm* pitching.

tanière [tanjɛr] *nf* den, lair.

tank [tɑ̃k] *nm Mil* tank.

tanker [tɑ̃kɛr] *nm* (*navire*) tanker.

tann/er [tane] *vt* (*cuir*) to tan. ◆**—é** *a* (*visage*) weather-beaten, tanned.

tant [tɑ̃] *adv* so much (**que** that); **t. de** (*pain, temps etc*) so much (**que** that); (*gens, choses etc*) so many (**que** that); **t. de fois** so often, so many times; **t. que** (*autant que*) as much as; (*aussi fort que*) as hard as; (*aussi longtemps que*) as long as; **en t. que** (*considéré comme*) as; **t. mieux!** good!, I'm glad!; **t. pis!** too bad!, pity!; **t. soit peu** (even) remotely ou slightly; **un t. soit peu** somewhat; **t. s'en faut** far from it; **t. bien que mal** more or less, so-so.

tante [tɑ̃t] *nf* aunt.

tantinet [tɑ̃tinɛ] *nm & adv* **un t.** a tiny bit (**de** of).

tantôt [tɑ̃to] *adv* **1 t. . . . t.** sometimes . . . sometimes, now . . . now. **2** (*cet après-midi*) this afternoon.

taon [tɑ̃] *nm* horsefly, gadfly.

tapage [tapaʒ] *nm* din, uproar. ◆**tapageur, -euse** *a* (*bruyant*) rowdy. **2** (*criard*) flashy.

tape [tap] *nf* slap. ◆**tap/er** *vt* (*enfant, cuisse*) to slap; (*table*) to bang; **t. qn** (*emprunter de l'argent à qn*) *Fam* to touch s.o., tap s.o. (**de** for); **—** *vi* (*soleil*) to beat down; **t. sur qch** to bang on the door; **t. sur qn** (*critiquer*) *Fam* to run s.o. down, knock s.o.; **t. sur les nerfs de qn** *Fam* to get on s.o.'s nerves; **t. dans** (*provisions etc*) to dig into; **t. du pied** to stamp one's foot; **t. dans l'œil à qn** *Fam* to take s.o.'s fancy; **— se t.** *vpr* (*travail*) *Fam* to do, take on; (*repas, vin*) *Fam* to put away. **2** *vti* (*écrire à la machine*) to type. ◆**—ant** *a* à midi **t.** at twelve sharp; à huit heures **tapant(es)** at eight sharp. ◆**—eur, -euse** *nmf Fam* person who borrows money.

tape-à-l'œil [tapalœj] *a inv* flashy, gaudy.

tapée [tape] *nf* **une t.** *de Fam* a load of.

tapioca [tapjɔka] *nm* tapioca.

tapir (se) [satapir] *vpr* to crouch (down). ◆**tapi** *a* crouching, crouched.

tapis [tapi] *nm* carpet; **t. de bain** bathmat; **t. roulant** (*pour marchandises*) conveyor belt; (*pour personnes*) moving pavement *ou Am*

sidewalk; **t. de sol** groundsheet; **t. de table** table cover; **envoyer qn au t.** (*abattre*) to floor s.o.; **mettre sur le t.** (*sujet*) to bring up for discussion. ◆**t.-brosse** *nm* doormat.

tapisser [tapise] *vt* (*mur*) to (wall)paper; to hang with tapestry; (*recouvrir*) *Fig* to cover. ◆**tapisserie** *nf* (*tenture*) tapestry; (*papier peint*) wallpaper. ◆**tapissier, -ière** *nmf* (*qui pose des tissus etc*) upholsterer; **t.(-décorateur)** interior decorator.

tapoter [tapɔte] *vt* to tap; (*joue*) to pat; **— vi t. sur** to tap (on).

taquin, -ine [takɛ̃, -in] *a* (fond of) teasing; **— nmf** tease(r). ◆**taquiner** *vt* to tease; (*inquiéter, agacer*) to bother. ◆**taquinerie(s)** *nf(pl)* teasing.

tarabiscoté [tarabiskɔte] *a* over-elaborate.

tarabuster [tarabyste] *vt* (*idée etc*) to trouble (*s.o.*).

tard [tar] *adv* late; **plus t.** later (on); **au plus t.** at the latest; **sur le t.** late in life. ◆**tarder** *vi* (*lettre, saison*) to be a long time coming; **t. à faire** to take one's time doing; (*différer*) to delay (in) doing; **ne tardez pas** (*agissez tout de suite*) don't delay; **elle ne va pas t.** she won't be long; **sans t.** without delay; **il me tarde de faire** I long to do. ◆**tardif, -ive** *a* late; (*regrets*) belated. ◆**tardivement** *adv* late.

tare [tar] *nf* **1** (*poids*) tare. **2** (*défaut*) *Fig* defect. ◆**taré** *a* (*corrompu*) corrupt; *Méd* defective; (*fou*) *Fam* mad, idiotic.

targuer (se) [sɔtarge] *vpr* **se t. de qch/de faire** to boast about sth/about doing.

tarif [tarif] *nm* (*prix*) rate; *Aut Rail* fare; (*tableau*) price list, tariff. ◆**tarification** *nf* (price) fixing.

tarir [tarir] *vti*, **— se t.** *vpr* (*fleuve etc*) & *Fig* to dry up; **ne pas t. d'éloges sur qn** to rave about s.o.

tartare [tartar] *a* **sauce t.** tartar sauce.

tarte [tart] *nf* **1** tart, flan, *Am* (open) pie. **2** *a inv Fam* (*sot*) silly; (*laid*) ugly. ◆**tartelette** *nf* (small) tart.

tartine [tartin] *nf* slice of bread; **t. (de beurre ou de confiture)** slice of bread and butter/jam. ◆**tartiner** *vt* (*beurre*) to spread; **fromage à t.** cheese spread.

tartre [tartr] *nm* (*de bouilloire*) scale, fur; (*de dents*) tartar.

tas [ta] *nm* pile, heap; **un ou des t. de** (*beaucoup*) *Fam* lots of; **mettre en t.** to pile ou heap up; **former qn sur le t.** (*au travail*) to train s.o. on the job.

tasse [tas] *nf* cup; **t. à café** coffee cup; **t. à thé** teacup; **boire la t.** *Fam* to swallow a mouthful (*when swimming*).

tasser [tɑse] *vt* to pack, squeeze (**dans** into); (*terre*) to pack down; **un café**/*etc* **bien tassé** (*fort*) a good strong coffee/*etc*; **ça va se t.** (*s'arranger*) *Fam* things will pan out (all right).

tâter [tɑte] *vt* to feel; (*sonder*) *Fig* to sound out; **– vi t.** de (*métier, prison*) to have a taste of, experience; **– se t.** *vpr* (*hésiter*) to be in *ou* of two minds. **◆tâtonn/er** *vi* to grope about, feel one's way. **◆–ement** *nm* **par t.** (*procéder*) by trial and error. **◆tâtons (à)** *adv* **avancer à t.** to feel one's way (along); **chercher à t.** to grope for.

tatillon, -onne [tatijɔ̃, -ɔn] *a* finicky.

tatou/er [tatwe] *vt* (*corps, dessin*) to tattoo. **◆–age** *nm* (*dessin*) tattoo; (*action*) tattooing.

taudis [todi] *nm* slum, hovel.

taule [tol] *nf* (*prison*) *Fam* nick, jug, *Am* can.

taupe [top] *nf* (*animal, espion*) mole. **◆taupinière** *nf* molehill.

taureau, -x [tɔro] *nm* bull; **le T.** (*signe*) Taurus. **◆tauromachie** *nf* bull-fighting.

taux [to] *nm* rate; **t. d'alcool/de cholestérol**/*etc* alcohol/cholesterol/*etc* level.

taverne [tavern] *nf* tavern.

taxe [taks] *nf* (*prix*) official price; (*impôt*) tax; (*douanière*) duty; **t. de séjour** tourist tax; **t. à la valeur ajoutée** value-added tax. **◆taxation** *nf* fixing of the price (de of); taxation (**de** of). **◆taxer** *vt* **1** (*produit*) to fix the price of; (*objet de luxe etc*) to tax. **2 t. qn de** to accuse s.o. of.

taxi [taksi] *nm* taxi.

taxiphone [taksifɔn] *nm* pay phone.

Tchécoslovaquie [tʃekɔslɔvaki] *nf* Czechoslovakia. **◆tchèque** *a & nmf* Czech; **– nm** (*langue*) Czech.

te [t(ə)] (**t'** *before vowel or mute h*) *pron* **1** (*complément direct*) you; **je te vois** I see you. **2** (*indirect*) (to) you; **il te parle** he speaks to you; **elle te l'a dit** she told you. **3** (*réfléchi*) yourself; **tu te laves** you wash yourself.

technicien, -ienne [tɛknisjɛ̃, -jɛn] *nmf* technician. **◆technique** *a* technical; **– nf** technique. **◆techniquement** *adv* technically. **◆technocrate** *nm* technocrat. **◆technologie** *nf* technology. **◆technologique** *a* technological.

teck [tɛk] *nm* (*bois*) teak.

teckel [tekɛl] *nm* (*chien*) dachshund.

tee-shirt [tiʃœrt] *nm* tee-shirt.

teindre* [tɛ̃dr] *vt* to dye; **– se t.** *vpr* to dye

one's hair. **◆teinture** *nf* dyeing; (*produit*) dye. **◆teinturerie** *nf* (*boutique*) (dry) cleaner's. **◆teinturier, -ière** *nmf* dry cleaner.

teint [tɛ̃] *nm* **1** (*de visage*) complexion. **2 bon ou grand t.** (*tissu*) colourfast; **bon t.** (*catholique etc*) *Fig* staunch.

teinte [tɛ̃t] *nf* shade, tint; **une t. de** (*dose*) *Fig* a tinge of. **◆teinter** *vt* to tint; (*bois*) to stain; **se t. de** (*remarque, ciel*) *Fig* to be tinged with.

tel, telle [tɛl] *a* such; **un t. homme/livre**/*etc* such a man/book/*etc*; **un t. intérêt**/*etc* such interest/*etc*; **de tels mots**/*etc* such words/*etc*; **t. que** such as, like; **t. que je l'ai laissé** just as I left it; **laissez-le t.** leave it just as it is; **en tant que t., comme t.** as such; **t. ou t.** such and such; **rien de t. que ... (there's) nothing like ...; rien de t.** nothing like it; **Monsieur Un t.** Mr So-and-so; **t. père t. fils** like father like son.

télé [tele] *nf* (*téléviseur*) *Fam* TV, telly; **à la t.** on TV, on the telly; **regarder la t.** to watch TV *ou* the telly.

télé- [tele] *préf* tele-.

télébenne [teleben] *nf*, **télécabine** [telekabin] *nf* (*cabine, système*) cable car.

télécommande [telekɔmɑ̃d] *nf* remote control. **◆télécommander** *vt* to operate by remote control.

télécommunications [telekɔmynikasjɔ̃] *nfpl* telecommunications.

téléfilm [telefilm] *nm* TV film.

télégramme [telegram] *nm* telegram.

télégraphe [telegraf] *nm* telegraph. **◆télégraphie** *nf* telegraphy. **◆télégraphier** *vt* (*message*) to wire, cable (**que** that). **◆télégraphique** *a* (*fil, poteau*) telegraph-; (*style*) *Fig* telegraphic. **◆télégraphiste** *nm* (*messager*) telegraph boy.

téléguid/er [telegide] *vt* to radio-control. **◆–age** *nm* radio-control.

télématique [telematik] *nf* telematics, computer communications.

télépathie [telepati] *nf* telepathy.

téléphérique [teleferik] *nm* (*système*) cable car, cableway.

téléphone [telefɔn] *nm* (tele)phone; **coup de t.** (phone) call; **passer un coup de t. à qn** to give s.o. a call *ou* a ring; **au t.** on the (tele)phone; **avoir le t.** to be on the (tele)phone; **par le t. arabe** *Fig* on the grapevine. **◆téléphoner** *vt* (*nouvelle etc*) to (tele)phone (**à** to); **– vi** to (tele)phone; **t. à qn** to (tele)phone s.o., call s.o. (up). **◆téléphonique** *a* (*appel etc*) (tele)phone-. **◆téléphoniste** *nmf* operator, telephonist.

télescope [telɛskɔp] *nm* telescope. ◆**télescopique** *a* telescopic.

télescop/er [telɛskɔpe] *vt* *Aut* *Rail* to smash into; **se t.** to smash into each other. ◆**–age** *nm* smash.

téléscripteur [telɛskriptœr] *nm* (*appareil*) teleprinter.

télésiège [telesjɛʒ] *nm* chair lift.

téléski [teleski] *nm* ski tow.

téléspectateur, -trice [telespɛktatœr, -tris] *nmf* (television) viewer.

téléviser [televize] *vt* to televise; **journal télévisé** television news. ◆**téléviseur** *nm* television (set). ◆**télévision** *nf* television; **à la t.** on (the) television; **regarder la t.** to watch (the) television; **de t.** (*programme etc*) television-.

télex [telɛks] *nm* (*service, message*) telex.

telle [tɛl] *voir* tel.

tellement [tɛlmɑ̃] *adv* (*si*) so; (*tant*) so much; **t. grand**/*etc* **que** so big/*etc* that; **crier**/*etc* **t. que** to shout/*etc* so much that; **t. de** (*travail etc*) so much; (*soucis etc*) so many; **personne ne peut le supporter, t. il est bavard** nobody can stand him, he's so talkative; **tu aimes ça? - pas t.** do you like it? - not much *ou* a lot.

téméraire [temerɛr] *a* rash. reckless. ◆**témérité** *nf* rashness, recklessness.

témoign/er [temwaɲe] **1** *vi* *Jur* to testify (**contre** against); **t. de qch** (*personne, attitude etc*) to testify to sth; – *vt* **t. que** *Jur* to testify that. **2** *vt* (*gratitude etc*) to show (**à qn** (to) s.o.). ◆**–age** *nm* **1** testimony, evidence; (*récit*) account; **faux t.** (*délit*) *Jur* perjury. **2** (*d'affection etc*) *Fig* token, sign (**de** of); **en t. de** as a token *ou* sign of.

témoin [temwɛ̃] **1** *nm* witness; **t. oculaire** eyewitness; **être t. de** (*accident etc*) to witness; – *a* **appartement t.** show flat *ou* Am apartment. **2** *nm* *Sp* baton.

tempe [tɑ̃p] *nf* *Anat* temple.

tempérament [tɑ̃peramɑ̃] *nm* **1** (*caractère*) temperament; (*physique*) constitution. **2** **acheter à t.** to buy on hire purchase *ou* Am on the installment plan.

tempérance [tɑ̃perɑ̃s] *nf* temperance.

température [tɑ̃peratyr] *nf* temperature; **avoir** *ou* **faire de la t.** *Méd* to have a temperature.

tempér/er [tɑ̃pere] *vt* *Litt* to temper. ◆**–é** *a* (*climat, zone*) temperate.

tempête [tɑ̃pɛt] *nf* storm; **t. de neige** snowstorm, blizzard.

tempêter [tɑ̃pete] *vi* (*crier*) to storm, rage (**contre** against).

temple [tɑ̃pl] *nm* *Rel* temple; (*protestant*) church.

tempo [tempo] *nm* tempo.

temporaire [tɑ̃pɔrɛr] *a* temporary. ◆**–ment** *adv* temporarily.

temporel, -elle [tɑ̃pɔrɛl] *a* temporal.

temporiser [tɑ̃pɔrize] *vi* to procrastinate, play for time.

temps¹ [tɑ̃] *nm* (*durée, période, moment*) time; *Gram* tense; (*étape*) stage; **t. d'arrêt** pause, break; **en t. de guerre** in time of war, in wartime; **avoir**/*trouver* **le t.** to have/find (the) time (**de faire** to do); **il est t.** it is time (**de faire** to do); **il était t.!** it was about time (too)!; **pendant un t.** for a while *ou* time; **ces derniers t.** lately; **de t. en t.** [dətɑ̃zɑ̃tɑ̃], **de t. à autre** [dətɑ̃zaotr] from time to time, now and again; **en t. utile** [ɑ̃tɑ̃zytil] in good *ou* due time; **en même t.** at the same time (**que** as); **à t.** (*arriver*) in time; **à plein t.** (*travailler etc*) full-time; **à t. partiel** (*travailler etc*) part-time; **dans le t.** (*autrefois*) once, at one time; **avec le t.** (*à la longue*) in time; **tout le t.** all the time; **du t. de** in the time of; **de mon t.** in my time; **à quatre t.** (*moteur*) four-stroke.

temps² [tɑ̃] *nm* (*atmosphérique*) weather; **il fait beau/mauvais t.** the weather's fine/bad; **quel t. fait-il?** what's the weather like?

tenable [tənabl] *a* bearable.

tenace [tənas] *a* stubborn, tenacious. ◆**ténacité** *nf* stubbornness, tenacity.

tenailler [tənaje] *vt* (*faim, remords*) to rack, torture (*s.o.*).

tenailles [tənaj] *nfpl* (*outil*) pincers.

tenancier, -ière [tənɑ̃sje, -jɛr] *nmf* (*d'hôtel etc*) manager, manageress.

tenant, -ante [tənɑ̃, -ɑ̃t] *nmf* (*de titre*) *Sp* holder. **2** *nm* (*partisan*) supporter (**de** of).

tenants [tənɑ̃] *nmpl* **les t. et les aboutissants** (*d'une question etc*) the ins and outs (**de** of).

tendance [tɑ̃dɑ̃s] *nf* (*penchant*) tendency; (*évolution*) trend (**à** towards); **avoir t. à faire** to have a tendency to do, tend to do.

tendancieux, -euse [tɑ̃dɑ̃sjø, -øz] *a* *Péj* tendentious.

tendeur [tɑ̃dœr] *nm* (*pour arrimer des bagages*) elastic strap.

tendon [tɑ̃dɔ̃] *nm* *Anat* tendon, sinew.

tend/re¹ [tɑ̃dr] *vt* to stretch; (*main*) to hold out (**à qn** to s.o.); (*bras, jambe*) to stretch out; (*cou*) to strain, crane; (*muscle*) to tense, flex; (*arc*) to bend; (*piège*) to lay, set; (*filet*) to spread; (*tapisserie*) to hang; **t. qch à qn** to hold out sth to s.o.; **t. l'oreille** *Fig* to prick up one's ears; **— se t.** *vpr* (*rap*-

ports) to become strained. **2** *vi* **t. à** qch/à **faire** to tend towards sth/to do. ◆–**u** *a* (*corde*) tight, taut; (*personne, situation*) tense; (*rapports*) strained; (*main*) outstretched.

tendre² [tɑ̃dr] *a* **1** (*viande*) tender; (*peau*) delicate, tender; (*bois, couleur*) soft; (*affectueux*) loving, tender. ◆–**ment** [-əmɑ̃] *adv* lovingly, tenderly. ◆**tendresse** *nf* (*affection*) affection, tenderness. ◆**tendreté** *nf* (*de viande*) tenderness.

ténèbres [tenɛbr] *nfpl* darkness, gloom. ◆**ténébreux, -euse** *a* dark, gloomy; (*mystérieux*) mysterious.

teneur [tənœr] *nf* (*de lettre etc*) content; **t. en alcool/etc** alcohol/etc content (**de** of).

tenir* [tənir] *vt* (*à la main etc*) to hold; (*pari, promesse*) to keep; (*hôtel*) to run, keep; (*comptes*) Com to keep; (*propos*) to utter; (*rôle*) to play; **t. propre/chaud/etc** to keep clean/hot/etc; **je le tiens!** (*je l'ai attrapé*) I've got him!; **je le tiens de** (*fait etc*) I got it from; (*caractère héréditaire*) I get it from; **t. pour** to regard as; **t. sa droite** *Aut* to keep to the right; **t. la route** (*voiture*) to hold the road; – *vi* (*nœud etc*) to hold; (*coiffure, neige*) to last; (*offre*) to stand; (*résister*) to hold out; **t. à** (*personne, jouet etc*) to be attached to, be fond of; (*la vie*) to value; (*provenir*) to stem from; **t. à faire** to be anxious to do; **t. dans** qch (*être contenu*) to fit into sth; **t. de** qn to take after s.o.; **tenez!** (*prenez*) here (you are)!; **tiens!** (*surprise*) hey!, well!; – *v imp* **il ne tient qu'à vous** it's up to you (**de faire** to do); – **se t.** *vpr* (*rester*) to keep, remain; (*avoir lieu*) to be held; **se t.** (**debout**) to stand (up); **se t. droit** to stand up *ou* sit up straight; **se t. par la main** to hold hands; **se t. à** to hold on to; **se t. bien** to behave oneself; **tout se tient** *Fig* it all hangs together; **s'en t. à** (*se limiter à*) to stick to; **savoir à quoi s'en t.** to know what's what.

tennis [tenis] *nm* tennis; (*terrain*) (tennis) court; **t. de table** table tennis; – *nfpl* (*chaussures*) plimsolls, pumps, *Am* sneakers.

ténor [tenɔr] *nm* Mus tenor.

tension [tɑ̃sjɔ̃] *nf* tension; **t.** (**artérielle**) blood pressure; **t. d'esprit** concentration; **avoir de la t.** *Méd* to have high blood pressure.

tentacule [tɑ̃takyl] *nm* tentacle.

tente [tɑ̃t] *nf* tent.

tenter¹ [tɑ̃te] *vt* (*essayer*) to try; **t. de faire** to try *ou* attempt to do. ◆**tentative** *nf* attempt; **t. de suicide** suicide attempt.

tenter² [tɑ̃te] *vt* (*allécher*) to tempt; **tenté de faire** tempted to do. ◆–**ant** *a* tempting. ◆**tentation** *nf* temptation.

tenture [tɑ̃tyr] *nf* (wall) hanging; (*de porte*) drape, curtain.

tenu [təny] *voir* **tenir**; – *a* **t. de faire** obliged to do; **bien/mal t.** (*maison etc*) well/badly kept.

ténu [təny] *a* (*fil etc*) fine; (*soupçon, différence*) tenuous; (*voix*) thin.

tenue [təny] *nf* **1** (*vêtements*) clothes, outfit; (*aspect*) appearance; **t. de combat** *Mil* combat dress; **t. de soirée** (*smoking*) evening dress. **2** (*conduite*) (good) behaviour; (*maintien*) posture; **manquer de t.** to lack (good) manners. **3** (*de maison, hôtel*) running; (*de comptes*) *Com* keeping. **4** **t. de route** *Aut* road-holding.

ter [tɛr] *a* **4 t.** (*numéro*) 4B.

térébenthine [terebɑ̃tin] *nf* turpentine.

tergal® [tɛrgal] *nm* Terylene®, *Am* Dacron®.

tergiverser [tɛrʒivɛrse] *vi* to procrastinate.

terme [tɛrm] *nm* **1** (*mot*) term. **2** (*loyer*) rent; (*jour*) rent day; (*période*) rental period. **3** (*date limite*) time (limit), date; (*fin*) end; **mettre un t. à** to put an end to; **à court/long t.** (*projet etc*) short-/long-term; **être né avant/à t.** to be born prematurely/at (full) term. **4 moyen t.** (*solution*) middle course. **5 en bons/mauvais termes** on good/bad terms (**avec qn** with s.o.).

terminer [tɛrmine] *vt* (*achever*) to finish, complete; (*lettre, phrase, débat, soirée*) to end; – **se t.** *vpr* to end (**par** with, **en** in). ◆**terminaison** *nf* *Gram* ending. ◆**terminal, -aux** **1** *a* final; (*phase*) *Méd* terminal; – *a & nf* (**classe**) **terminale** *Scol* = sixth form, *Am* = twelfth grade. **2** *nm* (*d'ordinateur, pétrolier*) terminal.

terminologie [tɛrminɔlɔʒi] *nf* terminology.

terminus [tɛrminys] *nm* terminus.

termite [tɛrmit] *nm* (*insecte*) termite.

terne [tɛrn] *a* (*couleur, journée etc*) dull, drab; (*personne*) dull. ◆**ternir** *vt* (*métal, réputation*) to tarnish; (*miroir, meuble*) to dull; – **se t.** *vpr* (*métal etc*) to tarnish.

terrain [tɛrɛ̃] *nm* (*sol*) *& Fig* ground; (*étendue*) land; *Mil Géol* terrain; (*à bâtir*) plot, site; **un t.** a piece of land; **t. d'aviation** airfield; **t. de camping** campsite; **t. de football/rugby** football/rugby pitch; **t. de golf** golf course; **t. de jeu** playground; **t. de sport** sports ground, playing field; **t. vague** waste ground, *Am* vacant lot; **céder/gagner/perdre du t.** *Mil & Fig* to give/

lose ground; **tout t., tous terrains** (*véhicule*) all-purpose.

terrasse [teras] *nf* **1** terrace; (*toit*) terrace (roof). **2** (*de café*) pavement *ou Am* sidewalk area; **à la t.** outside.

terrassement [terasmã] *nm* (*travail*) excavation.

terrasser [terase] *vt* (*adversaire*) to floor, knock down; (*accabler*) *Fig* to overcome.

terrassier [terasje] *nm* labourer, navvy.

terre [ter] *nf* (*matière*) earth; (*sol*) ground; (*opposé à mer, étendue*) land; *pl* (*domaine*) land, estate; *El* earth, *Am* ground; **la t.** (*le monde*) the earth; **la T.** (*planète*) Earth; **à** *ou* **par t.** (*poser, tomber*) to the ground; **par t.** (*assis, couché*) on the ground; **aller à t.** *Nau* to go ashore; **sous t.** underground; **t. cuite** (baked) clay, earthenware; **en t. cuite** (*poterie*) clay-. ◆**t.-à-terre** *a inv* down-to-earth. ◆**t.-plein** *nm* (*terre*) (earth) platform; (*au milieu de la route*) central reservation, *Am* median strip. ◆**terrestre** (*vie, joies*) earthly; (*animaux, transport*) land-; **la surface t.** the earth's surface; **globe t.** (*terrestrial*) globe. ◆**terreux, -euse** *a* (*goût*) earthy; (*sale*) grubby; (*couleur*) dull; (*teint*) ashen. ◆**terrien, -ienne** *a* land-owning; **propriétaire t.** landowner; − *nmf* (*habitant de la terre*) earth dweller, earthling.

terreau [tero] *nm* compost.

terrer (se) [satere] *vpr* (*fugitif, animal*) to hide, go to ground *ou* earth.

terreur [tercer] *nf* terror; **t. de** fear of. ◆**terrible** *a* terrible; (*formidable*) *Fam* terrific. ◆**terriblement** *adv* (*extrêmement*) terribly. ◆**terrifi/er** *vt* to terrify. ◆**−ant** *a* terrifying; (*extraordinaire*) incredible.

terrier [terje] *nm* **1** (*de lapin etc*) burrow. **2** (*chien*) terrier.

terrine [terin] *nf* (*récipient*) *Culin* terrine; (*pâté*) pâté.

territoire [teritwar] *nm* territory. ◆**territorial, -aux** *a* territorial.

terroir [terwar] *nm* (*sol*) soil; (*région*) region; **du t.** (*accent etc*) rural.

terroriser [terorize] *vt* to terrorize. ◆**terrorisme** *nm* terrorism. ◆**terroriste** *a & nmf* terrorist.

tertiaire [tersjer] *a* tertiary.

tertre [tertr] *nm* hillock, mound.

tes [te] *voir* **ton** [1].

tesson [tesõ] *nm* **t. de bouteille** piece of broken bottle.

test [test] *nm* test. ◆**tester** *vt* (*élève, produit*) to test.

testament [testamã] *nm* **1** *Jur* will; (*œuvre*) *Fig* testament. **2** *Ancien/Nouveau* **T.** *Rel* Old/New Testament.

testicule [testikyl] *nm Anat* testicle.

tétanos [tetanos] *nm Méd* tetanus.

têtard [tetar] *nm* tadpole.

tête [tet] *nf* head; (*figure*) face; (*cheveux*) (head of) hair; (*cerveau*) brain; (*cime*) top; (*de clou, cortège, lit*) head; (*de page, liste*) top, head; (*coup*) *Fb* header; **t. nucléaire** nuclear warhead; **tenir t. à** (*s'opposer à*) to stand up to; **t. nue** bare-headed; **tu n'as pas de t.!** you're a scatterbrain!; **faire la t.** (*bouder*) to sulk; **faire une t.** *Fb* to head the ball; **avoir/faire une drôle de t.** to have/give a funny look; **perdre la t.** *Fig* to lose one's head; **tomber la t. la première** to fall headlong *ou* head first; **calculer qch de t.** to work sth out in one's head; **se mettre dans la t. de faire** to get it into one's head to do; **à t. reposée** at one's leisure; **à la t. de** (*entreprise, parti*) at the head of; (*classe*) *Scol* at the top of; **de la t. aux pieds** from head *ou* top to toe; **en t.** *Sp* in the lead. ◆**t.-à-queue** *nm inv* **faire un t.-à-queue** *Aut* to spin right round. ◆**t.-à-tête** (**en**) **t.-à-tête** (*seul*) in private, alone together; − *nm inv* tête-à-tête. ◆**t.-bêche** *adv* head to tail.

tét/er [tete] *vt* (*lait, biberon etc*) to suck; **t. sa mère** (*bébé*) to suck, feed; − *vi* **donner à t. à** to feed, suckle. ◆**−ée** *nf* (*de bébé*) feed. ◆**tétine** *nf* **1** (*de biberon*) teat, *Am* nipple; (*sucette*) dummy, *Am* pacifier. **2** (*de vache*) udder. ◆**téton** *nm Fam* breast.

têtu [tety] *a* stubborn, obstinate.

texte [tekst] *nm* text; *Th* lines, text; (*de devoir*) *Scol* subject; (*morceau choisi*) *Littér* passage. ◆**textuel, -elle** *a* (*traduction*) literal.

textile [tekstil] *a & nm* textile.

texture [tekstyr] *nf* texture.

TGV [tezeve] *abrév* = **train à grande vitesse**.

Thaïlande [tailãd] *nf* Thailand. ◆**thaïlandais, -aise** *a & nmf* Thai.

thé [te] *nm* (*boisson, réunion*) tea. ◆**théière** *nf* teapot.

théâtre [teatr] *nm* (*art, lieu*) theatre; (*œuvres*) drama; (*d'un crime*) *Fig* scene; (*des opérations*) *Mil* theatre; **faire du t.** to act. ◆**théâtral, -aux** *a* theatrical.

thème [tem] *nm* theme; (*traduction*) *Scol* translation, prose.

théologie [teolɔʒi] *nf* theology. ◆**théologien** *nm* theologian. ◆**théologique** *a* theological.

théorème [teorem] *nm* theorem.

théorie [teori] *nf* theory; **en t.** in theory.

◆**théoricien, -ienne** *nmf* theorist, theoretician. ◆**théorique** *a* theoretical. ◆**théoriquement** *adv* theoretically.

thérapeutique [terapøtik] *a* therapeutic; – *nf* (*traitement*) therapy. ◆**thérapie** *nf* Psy therapy.

thermal, -aux [termal, -o] *a* **station thermale** spa; **eaux thermales** hot springs.

thermique [termik] *a* (*énergie, unité*) thermal.

thermomètre [termɔmɛtr] *nm* thermometer.

thermonucléaire [termɔnyklɛɛr] *a* thermonuclear.

thermos® [termɔs] *nm ou f* Thermos (flask)®, vacuum flask.

thermostat [termɔsta] *nm* thermostat.

thèse [tɛz] *nf* (*proposition, ouvrage*) thesis.

thon [tɔ̃] *nm* tuna (fish).

thorax [tɔraks] *nm Anat* thorax.

thym [tɛ̃] *nm Bot Culin* thyme.

thyroïde [tirɔid] *a & nf Anat* thyroid.

tibia [tibja] *nm* shin bone, tibia.

tic [tik] *nm* (*contraction*) tic, twitch; (*manie*) Fig mannerism.

ticket [tikɛ] *nm* ticket; **t. de quai** Rail platform ticket.

tic(-)tac [tiktak] *int & nm inv* tick-tock.

tiède [tjɛd] *a* (luke)warm, tepid; (*climat, vent*) mild; (*accueil, partisan*) half-hearted. ◆**tiédeur** *nf* (luke)warmness, tepidness; mildness; half-heartedness. ◆**tiédir** *vt* to cool (down); (*chauffer*) to warm (up); – *vi* to cool (down); to warm up.

tien, tienne [tjɛ̃, tjɛn] *pron poss* **le t., la tienne, les tien(ne)s** yours; **les deux tiens** your two; – *nmpl* **les tiens** (*amis etc*) your (own) people.

tiens, tient [tjɛ̃] *voir* **tenir**.

tiercé [tjɛrse] *nm* (*pari*) place betting (*on horses*); **gagner au t.** to win on the races.

tiers, tierce [tjɛr, tjɛrs] *a* third; – *nm* (*fraction*) third; (*personne*) third party; **assurance au t.** third-party insurance. ◆**T.-Monde** *nm* Third World.

tige [tiʒ] *nf* (*de plante*) stem, stalk; (*de botte*) leg; (*barre*) rod.

tignasse [tiɲas] *nf* mop (of hair).

tigre [tigr] *nm* tiger. ◆**tigresse** *nf* tigress.

tigré [tigre] *a* (*tacheté*) spotted; (*rayé*) striped.

tilleul [tijœl] *nm* lime (tree), linden (tree); (*infusion*) lime (blossom) tea.

timbale [tɛ̃bal] *nf* **1** (*gobelet*) (metal) tumbler. **2** Mus kettledrum.

timbre [tɛ̃br] *nm* **1** (*marque, tampon, vignette*) stamp; (*cachet de la poste*) post-

mark. **2** (*sonnette*) bell. **3** (*d'instrument, de voix*) tone (quality). ◆**t.-poste** *nm* (*pl* **timbres-poste**) (postage) stamp. ◆**timbr/er** *vt* (*affranchir*) to stamp (*letter*); (*marquer*) to stamp (*document*). ◆**-é** *a* **1** (*voix*) sonorous. **2** (*fou*) Fam crazy.

timide [timid] *a* (*gêné*) shy, timid; (*timoré*) timid. ◆**-ment** *adv* shyly; timidly. ◆**timidité** *nf* shyness; timidity.

timonier [timɔnje] *nm Nau* helmsman.

timoré [timɔre] *a* timorous, fearful.

tintamarre [tɛ̃tamar] *nm* din, racket.

tint/er [tɛ̃te] *vi* (*cloche*) to ring, toll; (*clés, monnaie*) to jingle; (*verres*) to chink. ◆**-ement(s)** *nm(pl)* ringing; jingling; chinking.

tique [tik] *nf* (*insecte*) tick.

tiquer [tike] *vi* (*personne*) to wince.

tir [tir] *nm* (*sport*) shooting; (*action*) firing, shooting; (*feu, rafale*) fire; Fb shot; **t. (forain), (stand de) t.** shooting *ou* rifle range; **t. à l'arc** archery; **ligne de t.** line of fire.

tirade [tirad] *nf* Th & Fig monologue.

tirail/ler [tiraje] **1** *vt* to pull (away) at; (*harceler*) Fig to pester, plague; **tiraillé entre** (*possibilités etc*) torn between. **2** *vi* (*au fusil*) to shoot wildly. ◆**-ement** *nm* **1** (*conflit*) conflict (**entre** between). **2** (*crampe*) Méd cramp.

tire [tir] *nf* **vol à la t.** Fam pickpocketing.

tire-au-flanc [tiroflɑ̃] *nm inv* (*paresseux*) shirker. ◆**t.-bouchon** *nm* corkscrew. ◆**t.-d'aile (à)** *adv* swiftly.

tirelire [tirlir] *nf* moneybox, Am coin bank.

tir/er [tire] *vt* to pull; (*langue*) to stick out; (*trait, conclusion, rideaux*) to draw; (*chapeau*) to raise; (*balle, canon*) to fire, shoot; (*gibier*) to shoot; Typ Phot to print; **t. de** (*sortir*) to take *ou* pull *ou* draw out of; (*obtenir*) to get from; (*nom, origine*) to derive from; (*produit*) to extract from; **t. qn de** (*danger, lit*) to get s.o. out of; – *vi* to pull (**sur** on, at); (*faire feu*) to fire, shoot (**sur** at); Fb to shoot; (*cheminée*) to draw; **t. sur** (*couleur*) to verge on; **t. au sort** to draw lots; **t. à sa fin** to draw to a close; – **se t.** *vpr* (*partir*) Fam to beat it; **se t. de** (*problème, travail*) to cope with; (*danger, situation*) to get out of; **se t. d'affaire** to get out of trouble; **s'en t.** Fam (*en réchapper*) to come *ou* pull through; (*réussir*) to get along. ◆**-é** *a* (*traits, visage*) drawn; **t. par les cheveux** Fig far-fetched. ◆**-age** *nm* **1** (*action*) Typ Phot printing; (*édition*) edition; (*quantité*) (print) run; (*de journal*) circulation. **2** (*de loterie*) draw; **t. au sort**

drawing of lots. **3** (*de cheminée*) draught. ◆**–eur** *nm* gunman; **t. d'élite** marksman; **un bon/mauvais t.** a good/bad shot. ◆**–euse** *nf* **t. de cartes** fortune-teller.

tiret [tirɛ] *nm* (*trait*) dash.

tiroir [tirwar] *nm* (*de commode etc*) drawer. ◆**–t.-caisse** *nm* (*pl* **tiroirs-caisses**) (cash) till.

tisane [tizan] *nf* herb(al) tea.

tison [tizɔ̃] *nm* (fire)brand, ember. ◆**tisonner** *vt* (*feu*) to poke. ◆**tisonnier** *nm* poker.

tiss/er [tise] *vt* to weave. ◆**–age** *nm* (*action*) weaving. ◆**tisserand, -ande** *nmf* weaver.

tissu [tisy] *nm* fabric, material, cloth; *Biol* tissue; **un t. de** (*mensonges etc*) a web of; **le t. social** the fabric of society, the social fabric; **du t.-éponge** (terry) towelling.

titre [titr] *nm* (*nom, qualité*) title; *Com* bond; (*diplôme*) qualification; *pl* (*droits*) claims (à to); (*gros*) t. *Journ* headline; **t. de propriété** title deed; **t. de transport** ticket; **à quel t.?** (*pour quelle raison*) on what grounds?; **à ce t.** (*en cette qualité*) as such; (*pour cette raison*) therefore; **à aucun t.** on no account; **au même t.** in the same way (**que** as); **à t. d'exemple/d'ami** as an example/friend; **à t. exceptionnel** exceptionally; **à t. privé** in a private capacity; **à t. juste** t. rightly. ◆**titr/er** *vt* (*film*) to title; *Journ* to run as a headline. ◆**–é** *a* (*personne*) titled. ◆**titulaire** *a* (*professeur*) staff-, full; **être t. de** (*permis etc*) to be the holder of; (*poste*) to hold; — *nmf* (*de permis, poste*) holder (**de** of). ◆**titulariser** *vt* (*fonctionnaire*) to give tenure to.

tituber [titybe] *vi* to reel, stagger.

toast [tost] *nm* **1** (*pain grillé*) piece *ou* slice of toast. **2** (*allocution*) toast; **porter un t. à** to drink (a toast) to.

toboggan [tɔbɔgɑ̃] *nm* **1** (*pente*) slide; (*traîneau*) toboggan. **2** *Aut* flyover, *Am* overpass.

toc [tɔk] **1** *int* **t. t.!** knock knock! **2** *nm* **du t.** (*camelote*) rubbish, trash; **en t.** (*bijou*) imitation-.

tocsin [tɔksɛ̃] *nm* alarm (bell).

tohu-bohu [tɔybɔy] *nm* (*bruit*) hubbub, commotion; (*confusion*) hurly-burly.

toi [twa] *pron* **1** (*complément*) you; **c'est t.** it's you; **avec t.** with you. **2** (*sujet*) you; **t., tu peux** *you* may. **3** (*réfléchi*) **assieds-t.** sit (yourself) down; **dépêche-t.** hurry up. ◆**t.-même** *pron* yourself.

toile [twal] *nf* **1** cloth; (*à voile*) canvas; (*à draps*) linen; **une t.** a piece of cloth *ou* canvas *ou* linen; **t. de jute** hessian; **drap de t.** linen sheet; **t. de fond** *Th & Fig* backcloth. **2** (*tableau*) canvas, painting. **3 t. d'araignée** cobweb, (spider's) web.

toilette [twalɛt] *nf* (*action*) wash(ing); (*vêtements*) outfit, clothes; **articles de t.** toiletries; **cabinet de t.** washroom; **eau/savon/trousse de t.** toilet water/soap/bag; **table de t.** dressing table; **faire sa t.** to wash (and dress); **les toilettes** (*W-C*) the toilet(s); **aller aux toilettes** to go to the toilet.

toiser [twaze] *vt* to eye scornfully.

toison [twazɔ̃] *nf* (*de mouton*) fleece.

toit [twa] *nm* roof; **t. ouvrant** *Aut* sunroof. ◆**toiture** *nf* roof(ing).

tôle [tol] *nf* **la t.** sheet metal; **une t.** a steel *ou* metal sheet; **t. ondulée** corrugated iron.

tolér/er [tɔlere] *vt* (*permettre*) to tolerate, allow; (*supporter*) to tolerate, bear; (**à la douane**) to allow. ◆**–ant** *a* tolerant (**à l'égard de** of). ◆**–able** *a* tolerable. ◆**tolérance** *nf* tolerance; (**à la douane**) allowance.

tollé [tɔle] *nm* outcry.

tomate [tɔmat] *nf* tomato; **sauce t.** tomato sauce.

tombe [tɔ̃b] *nf* grave; (*avec monument*) tomb. ◆**tombale** *af* **pierre t.** gravestone, tombstone. ◆**tombeau, -x** *nm* tomb.

tomb/er [tɔ̃be] *vi* (*aux être*) to fall; (*température*) to drop, fall; (*vent*) to drop (off); (*cheveux, robe*) to hang down; **t. malade** to fall ill; **t. (par terre)** to fall (down); **faire t.** (*personne*) to knock over; (*gouvernement, prix*) to bring down; **laisser t.** (*objet*) to drop; (*personne, projet etc*) *Fig* to give up; **tu m'as laissé t. hier** *Fig* you let me down yesterday; **se laisser t. dans un fauteuil** to drop into an armchair; **tu tombes bien/mal** *Fig* you've come at the right/wrong time; **t. de fatigue** *ou* **de sommeil** to be ready to drop; **un lundi** *to* fall on a Monday; **t. sur** (*trouver*) to come across. ◆**–ée** *nf* **t. de la nuit** nightfall.

tombereau, -x [tɔ̃bro] *nm* (*charrette*) tip cart.

tombola [tɔ̃bɔla] *nf* raffle.

tome [tɔm] *nm* (*livre*) volume.

ton¹, ta, *pl* **tes** [tɔ̃, ta, te] (*ta becomes* **ton** [tɔ̃n] *before a vowel or mute h*) *a poss* your; **t. père** your father; **ta mère** your mother; **ton ami(e)** your friend.

ton² [tɔ̃] *nm* tone; (*de couleur*) shade, tone; (*gamme*) *Mus* key; (*hauteur de son*) & *Ling* pitch; **de bon t.** (*goût*) in good taste; **donner le t.** *Fig* to set the tone. ◆**tonalité** *nf* (*de* *radio etc*) tone; *Tél* dialling tone, *Am* dial tone.

tond/re [tɔ̃dr] *vt* **1** (*mouton*) to shear; (*cheveux*) to clip, crop; (*gazon*) to mow. **2 t. qn** (*escroquer*) *Fam* to fleece s.o. ◆**—euse** *nf* shears; (*à cheveux*) clippers; **t.** (*à gazon*) (lawn)mower.

tonifi/er [tɔnifje] *vt* (*muscles, peau*) to tone up; (*esprit, personne*) to invigorate. ◆**—ant** *a* (*activité, climat etc*) invigorating.

tonique [tɔnik] **1** *a* (*accent*) *Ling* tonic. **2** *a* (*froid, effet, vin*) tonic, invigorating; — *nm Méd* tonic.

tonitruant [tɔnitryɑ̃] *a* (*voix*) *Fam* booming.

tonnage [tɔnaʒ] *nm Nau* tonnage.

tonne [tɔn] *nf* (*poids*) metric ton, tonne; **des tonnes de** (*beaucoup*) *Fam* tons of.

tonneau, -x [tɔno] *nm* **1** (*récipient*) barrel, cask. **2** (*manœuvre*) *Av* roll; **faire un t.** *Aut* to roll over. **3** (*poids*) *Nau* ton. ◆**tonnelet** *nm* keg.

tonnelle [tɔnɛl] *nf* arbour, bower.

tonner [tɔne] *vi* (*canons*) to thunder; (*crier*) *Fig* to thunder, rage (**contre** against); — *v imp* **il tonne** it's thundering. ◆**tonnerre** *nm* thunder; **coup de t.** thunderclap; *Fig* bombshell, thunderbolt; **du t.** (*excellent*) *Fam* terrific.

tonte [tɔ̃t] *nf* (*de moutons*) shearing; (*de gazon*) mowing.

tonton [tɔ̃tɔ̃] *nm Fam* uncle.

tonus [tɔnys] *nm* (*énergie*) energy, vitality.

top [tɔp] *nm* (*signal sonore*) *Rad* stroke.

topaze [tɔpaz] *nf* (*pierre*) topaz.

topinambour [tɔpinɑ̃bur] *nm* Jerusalem artichoke.

topo [tɔpo] *nm* (*exposé*) *Fam* talk, speech.

topographie [tɔpɔgrafi] *nf* topography.

toque [tɔk] *nf* (*de fourrure*) fur hat; (*de juge, jockey*) cap; (*de cuisinier*) hat.

toqu/er (se) [sɔtɔke] *vpr* **se t. de qn** *Fam* to become infatuated with s.o. ◆**—é** *a* (*fou*) *Fam* crazy. ◆**toquade** *nf Fam* (*pour qch*) craze (**pour** for); (*pour qn*) infatuation (**pour** with).

torche [tɔrʃ] *nf* (*flambeau*) torch; **t. électrique** torch, *Am* flashlight.

torcher [tɔrʃe] *vt* **1** (*travail*) to skimp. **2** (*essuyer*) *Fam* to wipe.

torchon [tɔrʃɔ̃] *nm* (*à vaisselle*) tea towel, *Am* dish towel; (*de ménage*) duster, cloth.

tord/re [tɔrdr] *vt* to twist; (*linge, cou*) to wring; (*barre*) to bend; **se la cheville/le pied/le dos** to twist *ou* sprain one's ankle/foot/back; — **se t.** *vpr* to twist; (*barre*) to bend; **se t. de douleur** to writhe with pain; **se t.** (**de rire**) to split one's sides

(laughing). ◆**—ant** *a* (*drôle*) *Fam* hilarious. ◆**—u** *a* twisted; (*esprit*) warped.

tornade [tɔrnad] *nf* tornado.

torpeur [tɔrpœr] *nf* lethargy, torpor.

torpille [tɔrpij] *nf* torpedo. ◆**torpill/er** *vt Mil & Fig* to torpedo. ◆**—eur** *nm* torpedo boat.

torréfier [tɔrefje] *vt* (*café*) to roast.

torrent [tɔrɑ̃] *nm* (*ruisseau*) torrent; **un t. de** (*injures, larmes*) a flood of; **il pleut à torrents** it's pouring (down). ◆**torrentiel, -ielle** *a* (*pluie*) torrential.

torride [tɔrid] *a* (*chaleur etc*) torrid, scorching.

torsade [tɔrsad] *nf* (*de cheveux*) twist, coil. ◆**torsader** *vt* to twist (together).

torse [tɔrs] *nm Anat* chest; (*statue*) torso.

torsion [tɔrsjɔ̃] *nf* twisting; *Phys Tech* torsion.

tort [tɔr] *nm* (*dommage*) wrong; (*défaut*) fault; **avoir t.** to be wrong (**de faire** to do, in doing); **tu as t. de fumer!** you shouldn't smoke!; **être dans son t.** *ou* **en t.** to be in the wrong; **donner t. à qn** (*accuser*) to blame s.o.; (*faits etc*) to prove s.o. wrong; **faire du t. à qn** to harm *ou* wrong s.o.; **à t.** wrongly; **à t. et à travers** wildly, indiscriminately; **à t. ou à raison** rightly or wrongly.

torticolis [tɔrtikɔli] *nm* stiff neck.

tortill/er [tɔrtije] *vt* to twist, twirl; (*moustache*) to twirl; (*tripoter*) to twiddle with; — **se t.** *vpr* (*ver, personne*) to wriggle; (*en dansant, des hanches*) to wiggle. ◆**—ement** *nm* wriggling, wiggling.

tortionnaire [tɔrsjɔnɛr] *nm* torturer.

tortue [tɔrty] *nf* tortoise; (*marine*) turtle; **quelle t.!** *Fig* what a slowcoach *ou Am* slowpoke!

tortueux, -euse [tɔrtyø, -øz] *a* tortuous.

torture [tɔrtyr] *nf* torture. ◆**torturer** *vt* to torture; **se t. les méninges** to rack one's brains.

tôt [to] *adv* early; **au plus t.** at the earliest; **le plus t. possible** as soon as possible; **t. ou tard** sooner *ou* later; **je n'étais pas plus t. sorti que . . .** no sooner had I gone out than . . . .

total, -aux [tɔtal, -o] *a & nm* total; **au t.** all in all, in total; (*somme toute*) all in all. ◆**totalement** *adv* totally, completely. ◆**totaliser** *vt* to total. ◆**totalité** *nf* entirety; **la t. de** all of; **en t.** entirely, totally.

totalitaire [tɔtalitɛr] *a Pol* totalitarian.

toubib [tubib] *nm* (*médecin*) *Fam* doctor.

touche [tuʃ] *nf* (*de peintre*) touch; *Pêche* bite; (*clavier*) key; **une t. de** (*un peu de*) a touch *ou* hint of; **(ligne de) t.** Fb Rugby touchline.

touche-à-tout [tuʃatu] **1** *a & nmf inv* (*qui touche*) meddlesome (person). **2** *nmf inv* (*qui se disperse*) dabbler.

touch/er [tuʃe] *vt* to touch; (*paie*) to draw; (*chèque*) to cash; (*cible*) to hit; (*émouvoir*) to touch, move; (*concerner*) to affect; **t. qn** (*contacter*) to get in touch with s.o., reach s.o.; — *vi* **t. à** to touch; (*sujet*) to touch on; (*but, fin*) to approach; — **se t.** *vpr* (*lignes etc*) to touch; − *nm* (*sens*) touch; **au t.** to the touch. ◆—**ant** *a* (*émouvant*) touching, moving.

touffe [tuf] *nf* (*de cheveux, d'herbe*) tuft; (*de plantes*) cluster. ◆**touffu** *a* (*barbe, haie*) thick, bushy; (*livre*) Fig heavy.

toujours [tuʒur] *adv* always; (*encore*) still; **pour t.** for ever; **essaie t.!** (*quand même*) try anyhow!; **t. est-il que . . .** the fact remains that . . .

toupet [tupɛ] *nm* (*audace*) Fam cheek, nerve.

toupie [tupi] *nf* (spinning) top.

tour[1] [tur] *nf* **1** Archit tower; (*immeuble*) tower block, high-rise. **2** Échecs rook, castle.

tour[2] [tur] *nm* **1** (*mouvement, ordre, tournure*) turn; (*artifice*) trick; (*excursion*) trip, outing; (*à pied*) stroll, walk; (*en voiture*) drive; **t.** (**de phrase**) turn of phrase; **t.** (**de piste**) Sp lap; **t. de cartes** card trick; **t. d'horizon** survey; **t. de poitrine**/etc chest/etc measurement *ou* size; **de dix mètres de t.** ten metres round; **faire le t. de** to go round; (*question, situation*) to review; **faire un t.** (*à pied*) to go for a stroll *ou* walk; (*en voiture*) to go for a drive; (*voyage*) to go on a trip; **faire** *ou* **jouer un t. à qn** to play a trick on s.o.; **c'est mon t.** it's my turn; **à qui le tour?** whose turn (is it)?; **à son t.** (in one's) turn; **à t. de rôle** in turn; **t. à t.** in turn, by turns. **2** Tech lathe; (*de potier*) wheel.

tourbe [turb] *nf* peat. ◆**tourbière** *nf* peat bog.

tourbillon [turbijɔ̃] *nm* (*de vent*) whirlwind; (*d'eau*) whirlpool; (*de neige, sable*) eddy; (*tournoiement*) Fig whirl, swirl. ◆**tourbillonner** *vi* to whirl, swirl; to eddy.

tourelle [turɛl] *nf* turret.

tourisme [turism] *nm* tourism; **faire du t.** to do some sightseeing *ou* touring; **agence/office de t.** tourist agency/office. ◆**touriste** *nmf* tourist. ◆**touristique** *a* (*guide, menu etc*) tourist-; **route t., circuit t.** scenic route.

tourment [turmɑ̃] *nm* torment. ◆**tour-**

ment/er *vt* to torment; — **se t.** *vpr* to worry (oneself). ◆—**é** *a* (*mer, vie*) turbulent, stormy; (*sol*) rough, uneven; (*expression, visage*) anguished.

tourmente [turmɑ̃t] *nf* (*troubles*) turmoil.

tourne-disque [turnədisk] *nm* record player.

tournée [turne] *nf* **1** (*de livreur etc*) round; (*théâtrale*) tour; **faire la t. de** (*magasins etc*) to make the rounds of, go round. **2** (*de boissons*) round.

tourn/er [turne] *vt* to turn; (*film*) to shoot, make; (*difficulté*) to get round; **t. en ridicule** to ridicule; − *vi* to turn; (*tête, toupie*) to spin; (*Terre*) to revolve, turn; (*moteur*) to run, go; (*usine*) to run; (*lait, viande*) to go off; Cin to shoot; **t. autour de** (*objet*) to go round; (*maison, personne*) to hang around; (*question*) to centre on; **t. bien/mal** (*évoluer*) to turn out well/badly; **t. au froid** (*temps*) to turn cold; **t. à l'aigre** (*ton, conversation etc*) to turn nasty *ou* sour; **t. de l'œil** Fam to faint; — **se t.** *vpr* to turn (**vers** to, towards). ◆—**ant** **1** *a* **pont t.** swing bridge. **2** *nm* (*virage*) bend, turning; (*moment*) Fig turning point. ◆—**age** *nm* Cin shooting, filming. ◆—**eur** *nm* (*ouvrier*) turner. ◆**tournoyer** *vi* to spin (round), whirl. ◆**tournure** *nf* (*expression*) turn of phrase; **t. d'esprit** way of thinking; **t. des événements** turn of events; **prendre t.** (*forme*) to take shape.

tournesol [turnəsɔl] *nm* sunflower.

tournevis [turnəvis] *nm* screwdriver.

tourniquet [turnikɛ] *nm* **1** (*barrière*) turnstile. **2** (*pour arroser*) sprinkler.

tournoi [turnwa] *nm* Sp & Hist tournament.

tourte [turt] *nf* pie.

tourterelle [turtərɛl] *nf* turtledove.

Toussaint [tusɛ̃] *nf* All Saints' Day.

tousser [tuse] *vi* to cough.

tout, toute, *pl* **tous, toutes** [tu, tut, tu, tut] **1** *a* all; **tous les livres**/etc all the books/etc; **t. l'argent/le village**/etc the whole of the money/village/etc, all the money/village/etc; **toute la nuit** all night, the whole of the night; **tous (les) deux** both; **tous (les) trois** all three; **t. un problème** quite a problem. **2** *a* (*chaque*) every, each; (*n'importe quel*) any; **tous les ans/jours**/etc every *ou* each year/day/etc; **tous les deux/trois mois**/etc every second/third month/etc; **tous les cinq mètres** every five metres; **t. homme** (*tutɔm*/etc) every *ou* any man; **à toute heure** at any time. **3** *pron pl* **tous** [= **tus**] all; **ils sont tous là, tous sont là** they're all there. **4** *pron m sing* **tout** everything;

dépenser t. to spend everything, spend it all; t. ce que everything that, all that; en t. (au total) in all. 5 adv (tout à fait) quite; (très) very; t. petit very small; t. neuf brand new; t. simplement quite simply; t. seul all alone; t. droit straight ahead; t. autour all around, right round; t. au début right at the beginning; le t. premier the very first; t. au moins/plus at the very least/most; t. en chantant/etc while singing/etc; t. rusé qu'il est however sly he may be; t. à coup suddenly, all of a sudden; t. à fait completely, quite; t. de même all the same; (indignation) really!; t. de suite at once. 6 nm le t. everything, the lot; un t. a whole; le t. est (l'important) the main thing is (que that, de faire to do); pas du t. not at all; rien du t. nothing at all; du t. au t. (changer) entirely, completely. ◆t.-puissant, toute-puissante a all-powerful.

tout-à-l'égout [tutalegu] nm inv mains drainage.

toutefois [tutfwa] adv nevertheless, however.

toutou [tutu] nm (chien) Fam doggie.

toux [tu] nf cough.

toxicomane [tɔksikɔman] nmf drug addict. ◆toxicomanie nf drug addiction. ◆toxine nf toxin. ◆toxique a toxic.

trac [trak] nm le t. (peur) the jitters; (de candidat) exam nerves; Th stage fright.

tracas [traka] nm worry. ◆tracasser vt, — se t. vpr to worry. ◆tracasseries nfpl annoyances. ◆tracassier, -ière a irksome.

trace [tras] nf (quantité, tache, vestige) trace; (marque) mark; (de fugitif etc) trail; pl (de bête, de pneus) tracks; traces de pas footprints; suivre les traces de qn Fig to follow in s.o.'s footsteps.

trac/er [trase] vt (dessiner) to draw; (écrire) to trace; t. une route to mark out a route; (frayer) to open up a route. ◆—é nm (plan) layout; (ligne) line.

trachée [traʃe] nf Anat windpipe.

tract [trakt] nm leaflet.

tractations [traktɑsjɔ̃] nfpl Péj dealings.

tracter [trakte] vt (caravane etc) to tow. ◆tracteur nm (véhicule) tractor.

traction [traksjɔ̃] nf Tech traction; Sp pull-up; t. arrière/avant Aut rear-/front-wheel drive.

tradition [tradisjɔ̃] nf tradition. ◆traditionnel, -elle a traditional.

traduire* [tradɥir] vt 1 to translate (de from, en into); (exprimer) Fig to express. 2 t. qn en justice to bring s.o. before the

courts. ◆traducteur, -trice nmf translator. ◆traduction nf translation. ◆traduisible a translatable.

trafic [trafik] nm 1 Aut Rail etc traffic. 2 Com Péj traffic, trade; faire du t. to traffic, trade; faire le t. de to traffic in, trade in. ◆trafiqu/er 1 vi to traffic, trade. 2 vt (produit) Fam to tamper with. ◆—ant, -ante nmf trafficker, dealer; t. d'armes/de drogue arms/drug trafficker ou dealer.

tragédie [traʒedi] nf Th & Fig tragedy. ◆tragique a tragic. ◆tragiquement adv tragically.

trahir [trair] vt to betray; (secret etc) to betray, give away; (forces) to fail (s.o.); — se t. vpr to give oneself away, betray oneself. ◆trahison nf betrayal; (crime) Pol treason.

train [trɛ̃] nm 1 (locomotive, transport, jouet) train; t. à grande vitesse high-speed train; t. couchettes sleeper; t. auto-couchettes (car) sleeper. 2 en t. (forme) on form; se mettre en t. to get (oneself) into shape. 3 être en t. de faire to be (busy) doing; mettre qch en t. to get sth going, start sth off. 4 (allure) pace; t. de vie life style. 5 (de pneus) set; (de péniches, véhicules) string. 6 t. d'atterrissage Av undercarriage.

traîne [trɛn] nf 1 (de robe) train. 2 à la t. (en arrière) lagging behind.

traîneau, -x [trɛno] nm sledge, sleigh, Am sled.

traînée [trene] nf 1 (de substance) trail, streak; (bande) streak; se répandre comme une t. de poudre (vite) to spread like wildfire. 2 (prostituée) Arg tart.

traîner [trene] vt to drag; (mots) to drawl; (faire) t. en longueur (faire durer) to drag out; — vi (jouets, papiers etc) to lie around; (subsister) to linger on; (s'attarder) to lag behind, dawdle; (errer) to hang around; t. (par terre) (robe etc) to trail (on the ground); t. (en longueur) (durer) to drag on; — se t. vpr (avancer) to drag oneself (along); (par terre) to crawl; (durer) to drag on. ◆traînant a (voix) drawling. ◆traînailler vi Fam = traînasser. ◆traînard, -arde nmf slowcoach, Am slowpoke. ◆traînasser vi Fam to dawdle; (errer) to hang around.

train-train [trɛ̃trɛ̃] nm routine.

traire* [trɛr] vt (vache) to milk.

trait [trɛ] nm 1 line; (en dessinant) stroke; (caractéristique) feature, trait; pl (du visage) features; t. d'union hyphen; (intermédiaire) Fig link; d'un t. (boire) in one gulp, in one go; à grands traits in outline; t. de (*esprit*, *génie*) flash of; (*bravoure*) act of; avoir t. à (*se rapporter à*) to relate to. 2 cheval de t. draught horse.

traite [tret] *nf* 1 (*de vache*) milking. 2 *Com* bill, draft. 3 d'une (seule) t. (*sans interruption*) in one go. 4 t. des Noirs slave trade; t. des blanches white slave trade.

traité [tretɛ] *nm* 1 *Pol* treaty. 2 (*ouvrage*) treatise (sur on).

trait/er [tretɛ] *vt* (*se comporter envers*) & *Méd* to treat; (*problème, sujet*) to deal with; (*marché*) *Com* to negotiate; (*matériau, produit*) to treat, process; t. qn de lâche/*etc* to call s.o. a coward/*etc*; – *vi* to negotiate, deal (avec with); t. de (*sujet*) to deal with. ◆—ant [-tɑ̃] *a* médecin t. regular doctor. ◆—ement [-tmɑ̃] *nm* 1 treatment; mauvais traitements rough treatment; t. de données/de texte data/word processing; machine de t. de texte word processor. 2 (*gains*) salary.

traiteur [trɛtœr] *nm* (*fournisseur*) caterer; chez le t. (*magasin*) at the delicatessen.

traître [trɛtr] *nm* traitor; en t. treacherously; – *a* (*dangereux*) treacherous; être t. à to be a traitor to. ◆traîtrise *nf* treachery.

trajectoire [traʒɛktwar] *nf* path, trajectory.

trajet [traʒɛ] *nm* journey, trip; (*distance*) distance; (*itinéraire*) route.

trame [tram] *nf* 1 (*de récit etc*) framework. 2 (*de tissu*) weft.

tramer [trame] *vt* (*évasion etc*) to plot; (*complot*) to hatch.

trampoline [trɑ̃polin] *nm* trampoline.

tram(way) [tram(wɛ)] *nm* tram, *Am* streetcar.

tranche [trɑ̃ʃ] *nf* (*morceau coupé*) slice; (*bord*) edge; (*partie*) portion; (*de salaire, impôts*) bracket; t. d'âge age bracket.

tranchée [trɑ̃ʃe] *nf* trench.

tranch/er [trɑ̃ʃe] 1 *vt* to cut. 2 *vt* (*difficulté, question*) to settle; – *vi* (*décider*) to decide. 3 *vi* (*contraster*) to contrast (avec, sur with). ◆—ant 1 *a* (*couteau*) sharp; – *nm* (cutting) edge. 2 *a* (*péremptoire*) trenchant, cutting. ◆—é *a* (*couleurs*) distinct; (*opinion*) clear-cut.

tranquille [trɑ̃kil] *a* quiet; (*mer*) calm, still; (*conscience*) clear; (*esprit*) easy; (*certain*) *Fam* confident; je suis t. (*rassuré*) my mind is at rest; soyez t. don't worry; laisser t. to leave to *ou* alone. ◆tranquillement *adv* calmly. ◆tranquillis/er *vt* to reassure; tranquillisez-vous set your mind at rest. ◆—ant *nm Méd* tranquillizer. ◆tranquil-

lité *nf* (peace and) quiet; (*d'esprit*) peace of mind.

trans- [trɑ̃z, trɑ̃s] *préf* trans-.

transaction [trɑ̃zaksjɔ̃] *nf* 1 (*compromis*) compromise. 2 *Com* transaction.

transatlantique [trɑ̃zatlɑ̃tik] *a* transatlantic; – *nm* (*paquebot*) transatlantic liner; (*chaise*) deckchair.

transcend/er [trɑ̃sɑ̃de] *vt* to transcend. ◆—ant *a* transcendent.

transcrire* [trɑ̃skrir] *vt* to transcribe. ◆transcription *nf* transcription; (*document*) transcript.

transe [trɑ̃s] *nf* en t. (*mystique*) in a trance; (*excité*) very exited.

transférer [trɑ̃sfere] *vt* to transfer (à to). ◆transfert *nm* transfer.

transfigurer [trɑ̃sfigyre] *vt* to transform, transfigure.

transformer [trɑ̃sfɔrme] *vt* to transform, change; (*maison, matière première*) to convert; (*robe etc*) to alter; (*essai*) *Rugby* to convert; t. en to turn into; – se t. *vpr* to change, be transformed (en into). ◆transformateur *nm El* transformer. ◆transformation *nf* transformation, change; conversion.

transfuge [trɑ̃sfyʒ] *nm Mil* renegade; – *nmf Pol* renegade.

transfusion [trɑ̃sfyzjɔ̃] *nf* t. (sanguine) (blood) transfusion.

transgresser [trɑ̃sgrese] *vt* (*loi, ordre*) to disobey.

transi [trɑ̃zi] *a* (*personne*) numb with cold; t. de peur paralysed by fear.

transiger [trɑ̃ziʒe] *vi* to compromise.

transistor [trɑ̃zistɔr] *nm* (*dispositif, poste*) transistor. ◆transistorisé *a* (*téléviseur etc*) transistorized.

transit [trɑ̃zit] *nm* transit; en t. in transit. ◆transiter *vt* (faire) t. to send in transit; – *vi* to be in transit.

transitif, -ive [trɑ̃zitif, -iv] *a Gram* transitive.

transition [trɑ̃zisjɔ̃] *nf* transition. ◆transitoire *a* (*qui passe*) transient; (*provisoire*) transitional.

transmettre* [trɑ̃smetr] *vt* (*héritage, message etc*) to pass on (à to); *Phys Tech* to transmit; *Rad TV* to broadcast, transmit. ◆transmetteur *nm* (*appareil*) transmitter, transmitting device. ◆transmission *nf* transmission; passing on.

transparaître* [trɑ̃sparetr] *vi* to show (through).

transparent [trɑ̃sparɑ̃] *a* transparent. ◆transparence *nf* transparency.

transpercer [trɑ̃sperse] vt to pierce, go through.

transpirer [trɑ̃spire] vi (suer) to perspire; (information) Fig to leak out. ◆**transpiration** nf perspiration.

transplanter [trɑ̃splɑ̃te] vt (organe, plante etc) to transplant. ◆**transplantation** nf transplantation; (greffe) Méd transplant.

transport [trɑ̃spɔr] nm 1 (action) transport, transportation (de of); pl (moyens) transport; **moyen de t.** means of transport; **transports en commun** public transport. 2 (émotion) Litt rapture. ◆**transporter** 1 vt (véhicule, train) to transport, convey; (à la main) to carry, take; **t. d'urgence à l'hôpital** to rush to hospital; **— se t.** vpr (aller) to take oneself (à to). 2 vt Litt to enrapture. ◆**transporteur** nm t. (routier) haulier, Am trucker.

transposer [trɑ̃spoze] vt to transpose. ◆**transposition** nf transposition.

transvaser [trɑ̃svaze] vt (vin) to decant.

transversal, -aux [trɑ̃sversal, -o] a (barre, rue etc) cross-, transverse.

trapèze [trapɛz] nm (au cirque) trapeze. ◆**trapéziste** nmf trapeze artist.

trappe [trap] nf (dans le plancher) trap door.

trappeur [trapœr] nm (chasseur) trapper.

trapu [trapy] a 1 (personne) stocky, thickset. 2 (problème etc) Fam tough.

traquenard [traknar] nm trap.

traquer [trake] vt to track ou hunt (down).

traumatiser [tromatize] vt to traumatize. ◆**-ant** a traumatic. ◆**traumatisme** nm (choc) trauma.

travail, -aux [travaj, -o] nm (activité, lieu) work; (emploi, tâche) job; (façonnage) working (de of); (ouvrage, étude) work, publication; Écon Méd labour; pl work; (dans la rue) roadworks; (aménagement) alterations; **travaux forcés** hard labour; **travaux ménagers** housework; **travaux pratiques** Scol Univ practical work; **travaux publics** public works; **t. au noir** moonlighting; **en t.** (femme) Méd in labour.

travaill/er [travaje] 1 vi to work (à qch at ou on sth); (discipline, rôle, style) to work on; (façonner) to work; (inquiéter) to worry; **t. la terre** to work the land. 2 vi (bois) to warp. **— é** a (style) elaborate. ◆**-eur, -euse** a hard-working; **—** nmf Pol Labour-; **—** nmf Pol member of the Labour party.

travers [traver] 1 prép & adv **à t.** through; **en t.** (de) across. 2 adv **de t.** (chapeau, nez etc) crooked; (comprendre) badly; (regarder) askance; **aller de t.** Fig to go

wrong; **j'ai avalé de t.** it went down the wrong way. 3 nm (défaut) failing.

traverse [travers] nf 1 Rail sleeper, Am tie. 2 **chemin de t.** short cut.

travers/er [traverse] vt to cross, go across; (foule, période, mur) to go through. **— ée** nf (action, trajet) crossing.

traversin [traversɛ̃] nm (coussin) bolster.

travest/ir [travestir] vt to disguise; (pensée, vérité) to misrepresent. **—i** nm Th female impersonator; (homosexuel) transvestite. ◆**-issement** nm disguise; misrepresentation.

trébucher [trebyʃe] vi to stumble (sur over); **faire t.** to trip (up).

trèfle [trefl] nm 1 (plante) clover. 2 (couleur) Cartes clubs.

treille [trej] nf climbing vine.

treillis [treji] nm 1 lattice(work); (en métal) wire mesh. 2 (tenue militaire) combat uniform.

treize [trez] a & nm inv thirteen. ◆**treizième** a & nmf thirteenth.

tréma [trema] nm Gram di(a)eresis.

trembl/er [trɑ̃ble] vi to tremble, shake; (de froid, peur) to tremble (de with); (flamme, lumière) to flicker; (voix) to tremble, quaver; (avoir peur) to be afraid (que (+ sub) that, de faire to do); **t. pour qn** to fear for s.o. ◆**-ement** nm (action, frisson) trembling; **t. de terre** earthquake. ◆**trembloter** vi to quiver.

trémousser (se) [sɑ̃tremuse] vpr to wriggle (about).

trempe [trɑ̃p] nf (caractère) stamp; **un homme de sa t.** a man of his stamp.

tremper [trɑ̃pe] 1 vt to soak, drench; (plonger) to dip (dans in); **— vi** to soak; **faire t.** to soak; **— se t.** vpr (se baigner) to take a dip. 2 vt (acier) to temper. 3 vi **t. dans** (participer) Péj to be mixed up in. ◆**trempette** nf **faire t.** (se baigner) to take a dip.

tremplin [trɑ̃plɛ̃] nm Natation & Fig springboard.

trente [trɑ̃t] a & nm thirty; **un t.-trois tours** (disque) an LP. ◆**trentaine** nf **une t.** (de) (nombre) (about) thirty; **avoir la t.** (âge) to be about thirty. ◆**trentième** a & nmf thirtieth.

trépidant [trepidɑ̃] a (vie etc) hectic.

trépied [trepje] nm tripod.

trépigner [trepiɲe] vi to stamp (one's feet).

très [tre] adv ([trɛz] before vowel or mute h) very; **t. aimé/critiqué/etc** much liked/criticized/etc.

trésor [trezɔr] nm treasure; **le T. (public)**

(*service*) public revenue (department); (*finances*) public funds; **des trésors de** *Fig* a treasure house of. ◆**trésorerie** *nf* (*bureaux d'un club etc*) accounts department; (*capitaux*) funds; (*gestion*) accounting. ◆**trésorier, -ière** *nmf* treasurer.

tressaillir [trɛsajir] *vi* (*sursauter*) to jump, start; (*frémir*) to shake, quiver; (*de joie, peur*) to tremble (**de** with). ◆**—ement** *nm* start; quiver; trembling.

tressauter [trɛsote] *vi* (*sursauter*) to start, jump.

tresse [trɛs] *nf* (*cordon*) braid; (*cheveux*) plait, *Am* braid. ◆**tresser** *vt* to braid; to plait.

tréteau, -x [treto] *nm* trestle.

treuil [trœj] *nm* winch, windlass.

trêve [trɛv] *nf* *Mil* truce; (*répit*) *Fig* respite. **t.** *de* (*sornettes etc*) enough of.

tri [tri] *nm* sorting (out); **faire le t. de** to sort (out); (**centre de**) **t.** (*des postes*) sorting office. ◆**triage** *nm* sorting (out).

triangle [trijɑ̃gl] *nm* triangle. ◆**triangulaire** *a* triangular.

tribord [tribɔr] *nm* *Nau* Av starboard.

tribu [triby] *nf* tribe. ◆**tribal, -aux** *a* tribal.

tribulations [tribylɑsjɔ̃] *nfpl* tribulations.

tribunal, -aux [tribynal, -o] *nm* *Jur* court; (*militaire*) tribunal.

tribune [tribyn] *nf* 1 (*de salle publique etc*) gallery; (*de stade*) (grand)stand; (*d'orateur*) rostrum. **2 t. libre** (*dans un journal*) open forum.

tribut [triby] *nm* tribute (**à** to).

tributaire [tribytɛr] *a* **t. de** *Fig* dependent on.

tricher [trife] *vi* to cheat. ◆**tricherie** *nf* cheating, trickery; **une t.** a piece of trickery. ◆**tricheur, -euse** *nmf* cheat, *Am* cheater.

tricolore [trikɔlɔr] *a* **1** (*cocarde etc*) red, white and blue; **le drapeau/l'équipe t.** the French flag/team. **2 feu t.** traffic lights.

tricot [triko] *nm* (*activité, ouvrage*) knitting; (*chandail*) jumper, sweater; **un t.** (*ouvrage*) a piece of knitting; **en t.** knitted; **t. de corps** vest, *Am* undershirt. ◆**tricoter** *vti* to knit.

tricycle [trisikl] *nm* tricycle.

trier [trije] *vt* (*séparer*) to sort (out); (*choisir*) to pick *ou* sort out.

trilogie [trilɔʒi] *nf* trilogy.

trimbal(l)er [trɛ̃bale] *vt* *Fam* to cart about, drag around; — **se t.** *vpr* *Fam* to trail around.

trimer [trime] *vi* *Fam* to slave (away), toil.

trimestre [trimɛstr] *nm* (*période*) Com quarter; *Scol* term. ◆**trimestriel, -ielle** *a* (*revue*) quarterly; (*bulletin*) *Scol* end-of-term.

tringle [trɛ̃gl] *nf* rail, rod; **t. à rideaux** curtain rail *ou* rod.

Trinité [trinite] *nf* **la T.** (*fête*) Trinity; (*dogme*) the Trinity.

trinquer [trɛ̃ke] *vi* to chink glasses; **t. à** to drink to.

trio [trijo] *nm* (*groupe*) & *Mus* trio.

triomphe [trijɔ̃f] *nm* triumph (**sur** over); **porter qn en t.** to carry s.o. shoulder-high. ◆**triomphal, -aux** *a* triumphal. ◆**triompher** *vi* to triumph (**de** over); (*jubiler*) to be jubilant. **—ant** *a* triumphant.

tripes [trip] *nfpl* (*intestins*) *Fam* guts; *Culin* tripe. ◆**tripier, -ière** *nmf* tripe butcher.

triple [tripl] *a* treble, triple; — *nm* **le t.** three times as much (**de** as). ◆**tripler** *vti* to treble, triple. **—és, -ées** *nmfpl* (*enfants*) triplets.

tripot [tripo] *nm* (*café etc*) *Péj* gambling den.

tripoter [tripɔte] *vt* to fiddle about *ou* mess about with; — *vi* to fiddle *ou* mess about.

trique [trik] *nf* cudgel, stick.

triste [trist] *a* sad; (*couleur, temps, rue*) gloomy, dreary; (*lamentable*) unfortunate, sorry. ◆**tristement** *adv* sadly. ◆**tristesse** *nf* sadness; gloom, dreariness.

triturer [trityre] *vt* (*manipuler*) to manipulate.

trivial, -aux [trivjal, -o] *a* coarse, vulgar. ◆**trivialité** *nf* coarseness, vulgarity.

troc [trɔk] *nm* exchange, barter.

troène [trɔɛn] *nm* (*arbuste*) privet.

trognon [trɔɲɔ̃] *nm* (*de pomme, poire*) core; (*de chou*) stump.

trois [trwa] *a* & *nm* three. ◆**troisième** *a* & *nmf* third. ◆**troisièmement** *adv* thirdly.

trolley(bus) [trɔlɛ(bys)] *nm* trolley(bus).

trombe [trɔ̃b] *nf* **t. d'eau** (*pluie*) rainstorm, downpour; **en t.** (*entrer etc*) *Fig* like a whirlwind.

trombone [trɔ̃bɔn] *nm* **1** *Mus* trombone. **2** (*agrafe*) paper clip.

trompe [trɔ̃p] *nf* **1** (*d'éléphant*) trunk; (*d'insecte*) proboscis. **2** *Mus* horn.

tromper [trɔ̃pe] *vt* to deceive, mislead; (*escroquer*) to cheat; (*échapper à*) to elude; (*être infidèle à*) to be unfaithful to; — **se t.** *vpr* to be mistaken, make a mistake; **se t. de route/de train/etc** to take the wrong road/train/etc; **se t. de date/de jour/etc** to get the date/day/etc wrong. ◆**tromperie** *nf* deceit, deception. ◆**trompeur, -euse** *a* (*apparences etc*) deceptive, misleading; (*personne*) deceitful.

trompette [trɔ̃pɛt] *nf* trumpet. ◆**trompettiste** *nmf* trumpet player.

tronc [trɔ̃] nm **1** Bot Anat trunk. **2** Rel collection box.

tronçon [trɔ̃sɔ̃] nm section. ◆**tronçonn/er** vt to cut (into sections). ◆**—euse** nf chain saw.

trône [tron] nm throne. ◆**trôner** vi (vase, personne etc) Fig to occupy the place of honour.

tronquer [trɔ̃ke] vt to truncate; (texte etc) to curtail.

trop [tro] adv too; too much; **t. dur/loin/etc** too hard/far/etc; **t. fatigué** too tired, overtired; **boire/lire/etc t.** to drink/read/etc too much; **t. de sel/etc** (quantité) too much salt/etc; **t. de gens/etc** (nombre) too many people/etc; **du fromage/etc de ou en t.** (quantité) too much cheese/etc; **des œufs/etc de ou en t.** (nombre) too many eggs/etc; **un franc/verre/etc de t. ou en t.** one franc/glass/etc too many; **se sentir de t.** Fig to feel in the way.

trophée [trɔfe] nm trophy.

tropique [trɔpik] nm tropic. ◆**tropical, -aux** a tropical.

trop-plein [trɔplɛ̃] nm (dispositif, liquide) overflow; (surabondance) Fig excess.

troquer [trɔke] vt to exchange (contre for).

trot [tro] nm trot; **aller au t.** to trot; **au t.** (sans traîner) Fam at the double. ◆**trott/er** [trɔte] vi (cheval) to trot; (personne) Fig to scurry (along).

trotteuse [trɔtøz] nf (de montre) second hand.

trottiner [trɔtine] vi (personne) to patter (along).

trottinette [trɔtinɛt] nf (jouet) scooter.

trottoir [trɔtwar] nm pavement, Am sidewalk; **t. roulant** moving walkway, travelator.

trou [tru] nm hole; (d'aiguille) eye; (manque) Fig gap (dans in); (village) Péj hole, dump; **t. d'homme** (ouverture) manhole; **t. de (la) serrure** keyhole; **t. (de mémoire)** Fig lapse (of memory).

trouble [trubl] **1** a (liquide) cloudy; (image) blurred; (affaire) shady; **voir t.** to see blurred. **2** nm (émoi, émotion) agitation; (désarroi) distress; (désordre) confusion; pl Méd trouble; (révolte) disturbances, troubles. ◆**troubl/er** vt to disturb; (liquide) to make cloudy; (projet) to upset; (esprit) to unsettle; (vue) to blur; (inquiéter) to trouble; — **se t.** vpr (liquide) to become cloudy; (candidat etc) to become flustered. ◆**—ant** a (détail etc) disquieting. ◆**trouble-fête** nmf inv killjoy, spoilsport.

trou/er [true] vt to make a hole ou holes in;

(silence, ténèbres) to cut through. ◆**—ée** nf gap; (brèche) Mil breach.

trouille [truj] nf **avoir la t.** Fam to have the jitters, be scared. ◆**trouillard** a (poltron) Fam chicken.

troupe [trup] nf Mil troop; (groupe) group; Th company, troupe; **la t., les troupes** (armée) the troops.

troupeau, -x [trupo] nm (de vaches) & Fig Péj herd; (de moutons, d'oies) flock.

trousse [trus] nf **1** (étui) case, kit; (d'écolier) pencil case; **t. à outils** toolkit; **t. à pharmacie** first-aid kit. **2** nfpl **aux trousses de qn** Fig on s.o.'s heels.

trousseau, -x [truso] nm **1** (de clés) bunch. **2** (de mariée) trousseau.

trouver [truve] vt to find; **aller/venir t. qn** to go/come and see s.o.; **je trouve que** (je pense que) I think that; **comment le trouvez-vous?** what do you think of her?; — **se t.** vpr to be; (être situé) to be situated; (se sentir) to feel; (dans une situation) to find oneself; **se t. mal** (s'évanouir) to faint; **il se trouve que** it happens that. ◆**trouvaille** nf (lucky) find.

truand [tryɑ̃] nm crook.

truc [tryk] nm **1** (astuce) trick; (moyen) way; **avoir/trouver le t.** to have/get the knack (pour faire of doing). **2** (chose) Fam thing. ◆**—age** nm = **truquage**.

truchement [tryʃmɑ̃] nm **par le t. de qn** through (the intermediary of) s.o.

truculent [trykylɑ̃] a (langage, personnage) colourful.

truelle [tryɛl] nf trowel.

truffe [tryf] nf **1** (champignon) truffle. **2** (de chien) nose.

truff/er [tryfe] vt (remplir) to stuff (de with). ◆**—é** a (pâté etc) Culin with truffles.

truie [trɥi] nf (animal) sow.

truite [trɥit] nf trout.

truqu/er [tryke] vt (photo etc) to fake; (élections, match) to rig, fix. ◆**—é** a (photo etc) fake-; (élections, match) rigged, fixed; (scène) Cin trick-. ◆**—age** nm Cin (special) effect; (action) faking; rigging.

trust [trœst] nm Com (cartel) trust; (entreprise) corporation.

tsar [dzar] nm tsar, czar.

TSF [teesɛf] nf abrév (télégraphie sans fil) wireless, radio.

tsigane [tsigan] a & nmf (Hungarian) gipsy.

TSVP [teesvep] abrév (tournez s'il vous plaît) PTO.

TTC [tetese] abrév (toutes taxes comprises) inclusive of tax.

tu¹ [ty] pron you (familiar form of address).

tu² [ty] *voir* **taire.**

tuba [tyba] *nm* **1** *Mus* tuba. **2** *Sp* snorkel.

tube [tyb] *nm* **1** tube; (*de canalisation*) pipe. **2** (*chanson, disque*) *Fam* hit. ◆**tubulaire** *a* tubular.

tuberculeux, -euse [tybɛrkylø, -øz] *a* tubercular; **être t.** to have tuberculosis *ou* TB. ◆**tuberculose** *nf* tuberculosis, TB.

tue-mouches [tymuʃ] *a inv* **papier t.-mouches** flypaper. ◆**t.-tête (à)** *adv* at the top of one's voice.

tu/er [tɥe] *vt* to kill; (*d'un coup de feu*) to shoot (dead), kill; (*épuiser*) *Fig* to wear out; — **se t.** *vpr* to kill oneself; to shoot oneself; (*dans un accident*) to be killed; **se t. à faire** *Fig* to wear oneself out doing. ◆—**ant** *a* (*fatigant*) exhausting. ◆**tuerie** *nf* slaughter. ◆**tueur, -euse** *nmf* killer.

tuile [tɥil] *nf* **1** tile. **2** (*malchance*) *Fam* (stroke of) bad luck.

tulipe [tylip] *nf* tulip.

tuméfié [tymefje] *a* swollen.

tumeur [tymœr] *nf* tumour, growth.

tumulte [tymylt] *nm* commotion; (*désordre*) turmoil. ◆**tumultueux, -euse** *a* turbulent.

tunique [tynik] *nf* tunic.

Tunisie [tynizi] *nf* Tunisia. ◆**tunisien, -ienne** *a & nmf* Tunisian.

tunnel [tynɛl] *nm* tunnel.

turban [tyrbɑ̃] *nm* turban.

turbine [tyrbin] *nf* turbine.

turbulences [tyrbylɑ̃s] *nfpl* *Phys Av* turbulence.

turbulent [tyrbylɑ̃] *a* (*enfant etc*) boisterous, turbulent.

turfiste [tyrfist] *nmf* racegoer, punter.

Turquie [tyrki] *nf* Turkey. ◆**turc, turque** *a* Turkish; — *nmf* Turk; — *nm* (*langue*) Turkish.

turquoise [tyrkwaz] *a inv* turquoise.

tuteur, -trice [tytœr, -tris] **1** *nmf* *Jur* guardian. **2** *nm* (*bâton*) stake, prop. ◆**tutelle** *nf* *Jur* guardianship; *Fig* protection.

tutoyer [tytwaje] *vt* to address familiarly (*using tu*). ◆**tutoiement** *nm* familiar address, use of *tu*.

tutu [tyty] *nm* ballet skirt, tutu.

tuyau, -x [tɥijo] *nm* **1** pipe; **t. d'arrosage** hose(pipe); **t. de cheminée** flue; **t. d'échappement** *Aut* exhaust (pipe). **2** (*renseignement*) *Fam* tip. ◆**tuyauter** *vt* (*conseiller*) *Fam* to give s.o. a tip. ◆**tuyauterie** *nf* (*tuyaux*) piping.

TVA [tevea] *nf abrév* (*taxe à la valeur ajoutée*) VAT.

tympan [tɛ̃pɑ̃] *nm* eardrum.

type [tip] *nm* (*modèle*) type; (*traits*) features; (*individu*) *Fam* fellow, guy, bloke; **le t. même de** *Fig* the very model of; — *a inv* (*professeur etc*) typical. ◆**typique** *a* typical (**de** of). ◆**typiquement** *adv* typically.

typhoïde [tifɔid] *nf* *Méd* typhoid (fever).

typhon [tifɔ̃] *nm* *Mét* typhoon.

typographe [tipɔgraf] *nmf* typographer. ◆**typographie** *nf* typography, printing. ◆**typographique** *a* typographical, printing-.

tyran [tirɑ̃] *nm* tyrant. ◆**tyrannie** *nf* tyranny. ◆**tyrannique** *a* tyrannical. ◆**tyranniser** *vt* to tyrannize.

tzigane [dzigan] *a & nmf* (Hungarian) gipsy.

U

U, u [y] *nm* U, u.

ulcère [ylsɛr] *nm* ulcer, sore.

ulcérer [ylsere] *vt* (*blesser, irriter*) to embitter.

ultérieur [ylterjœr] *a* later. ◆—**ement** *adv* later.

ultimatum [yltimatɔm] *nm* ultimatum.

ultime [yltim] *a* final, last.

ultra- [yltra] *préf* ultra-. ◆**u.-secret, -ète** *a* (*document*) top-secret.

ultramoderne [yltramɔdɛrn] *a* ultramodern.

ultraviolet, -ette [yltravjɔlɛ, -ɛt] *a* ultraviolet.

un, une [œ̃, yn] **1** *art indéf* a, (*devant voyelle*) an; **une page** a page; **un ange** [œ̃nɑ̃ʒ] an angel. **2** *a* one; **la page un** page one; **un kilo** one kilo; **un type** (*un quelconque*) some *ou* a fellow. **3** *pron & nmf* one; **l'un un** one; **les uns** some; **le numéro un** number one; **j'en ai un** I have one; **l'un d'eux** one of them; **la une** *Journ* page one.

unanime [ynanim] *a* unanimous. ◆**unanimité** *nf* unanimity; **à l'u.** unanimously.

uni [yni] *a* united; (*famille etc*) close; (*surface*) smooth; (*couleur, étoffe*) plain.

unième [ynjɛm] *a* (*après un numéral*) (-)first; **trente et u.** thirty-first; **cent u.** hundred and first.

unifier [ynifje] *vt* to unify. ◆**unification** *nf* unification.

uniforme [yniform] **1** *a* (*régulier*) uniform. **2** *nm* (*vêtement*) uniform. ◆**uniformément** *adv* uniformly. ◆**uniformiser** *vt* to standardize. ◆**uniformité** *nf* uniformity.

unijambiste [yniʒãbist] *a* & *nmf* one-legged (man *ou* woman).

unilatéral, -aux [ynilateral, -o] *a* unilateral; (*stationnement*) on one side of the road only.

union [ynjɔ̃] *nf* union; (*association*) association; (*entente*) unity. ◆**unir** *vt* to unite, join (together); **u. la force au courage**/*etc* to combine strength with courage/*etc*; — **s'u.** *vpr* to unite; (*se marier*) to be joined together; (*se joindre*) to join (together).

unique [ynik] *a* **1** (*fille, fils*) only; (*espoir, souci etc*) sole; (*prix, salaire, voie*) single, one; **son seul et u. souci** his *ou* her one and only worry. **2** (*incomparable*) unique. ◆**uniquement** *adv* only, solely.

unisexe [ynisɛks] *a inv* (*vêtements etc*) unisex.

unisson (à l') [alynisɔ̃] *adv* in unison (de with).

unité [ynite] *nf* (*élément, grandeur*) & *Mil* unit; (*cohésion, harmonie*) unity. ◆**unitaire** *a* (*prix*) per unit.

univers [yniver] *nm* universe.

universel, -elle [yniversɛl] *a* universal. ◆**universellement** *adv* universally. ◆**universalité** *nf* universality.

université [yniversite] *nf* university; **à l'u.** at university. ◆**universitaire** *a* university-; — *nmf* academic.

uranium [yranjɔm] *nm* uranium.

urbain [yrbɛ̃] *a* urban, town-, city-. ◆**urbaniser** *vt* to urbanize, build up. ◆**urbanisme** *nm* town planning, *Am* city planning. ◆**urbaniste** *nmf* town planner, *Am* city planner.

urgent [yrʒã] *a* urgent, pressing. ◆**urgence** *nf* (*cas*) emergency; (*décision, tâche etc*) urgency; (*de mesures etc*) emergency-; **état d'u.** *Pol* state of emergency; **faire qch d'u.** to do sth urgently.

urine [yrin] *nf* urine. ◆**uriner** *vi* to urinate. ◆**urinoir** *nm* (public) urinal.

urne [yrn] *nf* **1** (*électorale*) ballot box; **aller aux urnes** to go to the polls. **2** (*vase*) urn.

URSS [yrs] *nf abrév* (*Union des Républiques Socialistes Soviétiques*) USSR.

usage [yzaʒ] *nm* use; *Ling* usage; (*habitude*) custom; **faire u. de** to make use of; **faire de l'u.** (*vêtement etc*) to wear well; **d'u.** (*habituel*) customary; **à l'u. de** for (the use of); **hors d'u.** no longer usable. ◆**usagé** *a* worn; (*d'occasion*) used. ◆**usager** *nm* user. ◆**us/er** *vt* (*vêtement, personne*) to wear out; (*consommer*) to use (up); (*santé*) to ruin; — *vi* **u. de** to use; — **s'u.** *vpr* (*tissu, machine*) to wear out; (*personne*) to wear oneself out. ◆**-é** *a* (*tissu etc*) worn (out); (*sujet etc*) well-worn; (*personne*) worn out.

usine [yzin] *nf* factory; (*à gaz, de métallurgie*) works.

usiner [yzine] *vt* (*pièce*) *Tech* to machine.

usité [yzite] *a* commonly used.

ustensile [ystãsil] *nm* utensil.

usuel, -elle [yzɥɛl] *a* everyday, ordinary; — *nmpl* (*livres*) reference books.

usure [yzyr] *nf* (*détérioration*) wear (and tear); **avoir qn à l'u.** *Fig* to wear s.o. down (in the end).

usurier, -ière [yzyrje, -jɛr] *nmf* usurer.

usurper [yzyrpe] *vt* to usurp.

utérus [yterys] *nm Anat* womb, uterus.

utile [ytil] *a* useful (à to). ◆**utilement** *adv* usefully.

utiliser [ytilize] *vt* to use, utilize. ◆**utilisable** *a* usable. ◆**utilisateur, -trice** *nmf* user. ◆**utilisation** *nf* use. ◆**utilité** *nf* use(fulness); **d'une grande u.** very useful.

utilitaire [ytiliter] *a* utilitarian; (*véhicule*) utility-.

utopie [ytɔpi] *nf* (*idéal*) utopia; (*projet, idée*) utopian plan *ou* idea. ◆**utopique** *a* utopian.

V

V, v [ve] *nm* V, v.

va [va] *voir* **aller 1.**

vacances [vakãs] *nfpl* holiday(s), *Am* vacation; **en v.** on holiday, *Am* on vacation; **prendre ses v.** to take one's holiday(s) *ou* *Am* vacation; **les grandes v.** the summer holidays *ou Am* vacation. ◆**vacancier, -ière** *nmf* holidaymaker, *Am* vacationer.

vacant [vakɑ̃] *a* vacant. ◆**vacance** *nf* (*poste*) vacancy.

vacarme [vakarm] *nm* din, uproar.

vaccin [vaksɛ̃] *nm* vaccine; **faire un v. à** to vaccinate. ◆**vaccination** *nf* vaccination. ◆**vacciner** *vt* to vaccinate.

vache [vaʃ] **1** *nf* cow; **v. laitière** dairy cow. **2** *nf* (**peau de**) **v.** (*personne*) *Fam* swine; – *a* (*méchant*) *Fam* nasty. ◆**vachement** *adv Fam* (*très*) damned; (*beaucoup*) a hell of a lot. ◆**vacherie** *nf Fam* (*action, parole*) nasty thing; (*caractère*) nastiness.

vacill/er [vasije] *vi* to sway, wobble; (*flamme, lumière*) to flicker; (*jugement, mémoire etc*) to falter, waver. ◆**—ant** *a* (*démarche, mémoire*) shaky; (*lumière etc*) flickering.

vadrouille [vadruj] *nf en v. Fam* roaming *ou* wandering about. ◆**vadrouiller** *vi Fam* to roam *ou* wander about.

va-et-vient [vaevjɛ̃] *nm inv* (*mouvement*) movement to and fro; (*de personnes*) comings and goings.

vagabond, -onde [vagabɔ̃, -ɔ̃d] *a* wandering; – *nmf* (*clochard*) vagrant, tramp. ◆**vagabond/er** *vi* to roam *ou* wander about; (*pensée*) to wander. ◆**—age** *nm* wandering; *Jur* vagrancy.

vagin [vaʒɛ̃] *nm* vagina.

vagir [vaʒir] *vi* (*bébé*) to cry, wail.

vague [vag] **1** *a* (*futile*) vain, futile; (*souvenir*) dim, vague; – *nm* vagueness; **regarder dans le v.** to gaze into space, gaze vacantly; **rester dans le v.** (*être évasif*) to keep it vague. **2** *nf* (*de mer*) wave; **v. de chaleur** heat wave; **v. de froid** cold snap *ou* spell; **v. de fond** (*dans l'opinion*) *Fig* tidal wave. ◆**vaguement** *adv* vaguely.

vaillant [vajɑ̃] *a* brave, valiant; (*vigoureux*) healthy. ◆**vaillamment** *adv* bravely, valiantly. ◆**vaillance** *nf* bravery.

vain [vɛ̃] *a* **1** (*futile*) vain, futile; (*mots, promesse*) empty; **en v.** in vain, vainly. **2** (*vaniteux*) vain. ◆**vainement** *adv* in vain, vainly.

vainc/re* [vɛ̃kr] *vt* to defeat, beat; (*surmonter*) to overcome. ◆**—u, -ue** *nmf* defeated man *ou* woman; *Sp* loser. ◆**vainqueur** *nm* victor; *Sp* winner; – *am* victorious.

vaisseau, -x [veso] *nm* **1** *Anat Bot* vessel. **2** (*bateau*) ship, vessel; **v. spatial** spaceship.

vaisselle [vesɛl] *nf* crockery; (*à laver*) washing up; **faire la v.** to do the washing up, do *ou* wash the dishes.

val, *pl* **vals** *ou* **vaux** [val, vo] *nm* valley.

valable [valabl] *a* (*billet, motif etc*) valid; (*remarquable, rentable*) *Fam* worthwhile.

valet [valɛ] *nm* **1** *Cartes* jack. **2** v. (**de chambre**) valet, manservant; **v. de ferme** farmhand.

valeur [valœr] *nf* value; (*mérite*) worth; (*poids*) importance, weight; *pl* (*titres*) *Com* stocks and shares; **la v. de** (*quantité*) the equivalent of; **avoir de la v.** to be valuable; **mettre en v.** (*faire ressortir*) to highlight; **de v.** (*personne*) of merit, able; **objets de v.** valuables.

valide [valid] *a* **1** (*personne*) fit, able-bodied; (*population*) able-bodied. **2** (*billet etc*) valid. ◆**valider** *vt* to validate. ◆**validité** *nf* validity.

valise [valiz] *nf* (*suit*)case; **v. diplomatique** diplomatic bag *ou Am* pouch; **faire ses valises** to pack (one's bags).

vallée [vale] *nf* valley. ◆**vallon** *nm* (small) valley. ◆**vallonné** *a* (*région etc*) undulating.

valoir* [valwar] *vi* to be worth; (*s'appliquer*) to apply (**pour** to); **v. mille francs/cher**/*etc* to be worth a thousand francs/a lot/*etc*; **un vélo vaut bien une auto** a bicycle is as good as a car; **il vaut mieux rester** it's better to stay; **il vaut mieux que j'attende** I'd better wait; **ça ne vaut rien** it's worthless, it's no good; **ça vaut le coup** *Fam ou* **la peine** it's worthwhile (**de faire** doing); **faire v.** (*faire ressortir*) to highlight, set off; (*argument*) to put forward; (*droit*) to assert; – *vt* **v. qch à qn** to bring *ou* get s.o. sth; – **se v.** *vpr* (*objets, personnes*) to be as good as each other; **ça se vaut** *Fam* it's all the same.

valse [vals] *nf* waltz. ◆**valser** *vi* to waltz.

valve [valv] *nf* (*clapet*) valve. ◆**valvule** *nf* (*du cœur*) valve.

vampire [vɑ̃pir] *nm* vampire.

vandale [vɑ̃dal] *nmf* vandal. ◆**vandalisme** *nm* vandalism.

vanille [vanij] *nf* vanilla; **glace**/*etc* **à la v.** vanilla ice cream/*etc*. ◆**vanillé** *a* vanilla-flavoured.

vanité [vanite] *nf* vanity. ◆**vaniteux, -euse** *a* vain, conceited.

vanne [van] *nf* **1** (*d'écluse*) sluice (gate), floodgate. **2** (*remarque*) *Fam* dig, jibe.

vanné [vane] *a* (*fatigué*) *Fam* dead beat.

vannerie [vanri] *nf* (*fabrication, objets*) basketwork, basketry.

vantail, -aux [vɑ̃taj, -o] *nm* (*de porte*) leaf.

vanter [vɑ̃te] *vt* to praise; – **se v.** *vpr* to boast, brag (**de faire** of). ◆**vantard, -arde** *a* boastful; – *nmf* boaster, braggart.

◆vantardise *nf* boastfulness; (*propos*) boast.

va-nu-pieds [vanypje] *nmf inv* tramp, beggar.

vapeur [vapœr] *nf* (*brume, émanation*) vapour; *v.* (**d'eau**) steam; **cuire à la v.** to steam; **bateau à v.** steamship. ◆**vaporeux, -euse** *a* hazy, misty; (*tissu*) translucent, diaphanous.

vaporiser [vapɔrize] *vt* to spray. ◆**vaporisateur** *nm* (*appareil*) spray.

vaquer [vake] *vi* **v. à** to attend to.

varappe [varap] *nf* rock-climbing.

varech [varɛk] *nm* wrack, seaweed.

vareuse [varøz] *nf* (*d'uniforme*) tunic.

varicelle [varisɛl] *nf* chicken pox.

varices [varis] *nfpl* varicose veins.

vari/er [varje] *vti* to vary (**de** from). ◆**—é** *a* (*diversifié*) varied; (*divers*) various. ◆**—able** *a* variable; (*humeur, temps*) changeable. ◆**variante** *nf* variant. ◆**variation** *nf* variation. ◆**variété** *nf* variety; **spectacle de variétés** *Th* variety show.

variole [varjɔl] *nf* smallpox.

vas [va] *voir* **aller 1.**

vase [vɑz] **1** *nm* vase. **2** *nf* (*boue*) silt, mud.

vaseline [vazlin] *nf* Vaseline®.

vaseux, -euse [vazø, -øz] *a* **1** (*boueux*) silty, muddy. **2** (*fatigué*) off colour. **3** (*idées etc*) woolly, hazy.

vasistas [vazistas] *nm* (*dans une porte ou une fenêtre*) hinged panel.

vaste [vast] *a* vast, huge.

Vatican [vatikɑ̃] *nm* Vatican.

va-tout [vatu] *nm inv* **jouer son v.-tout** to stake one's all.

vaudeville [vodvil] *nm Th* light comedy.

vau-l'eau (à) [avolo] *adv* **aller à v.-l'eau** to go to rack and ruin.

vaurien, -ienne [vorjɛ̃, -jɛn] *nmf* good-for-nothing.

vautour [votur] *nm* vulture.

vautrer (se) [səvotre] *vpr* to sprawl; **se v. dans** (*boue, vice*) to wallow in.

va-vite (à la) [alavavit] *adv Fam* in a hurry.

veau, -x [vo] *nm* (*animal*) calf; (*viande*) veal; (*cuir*) calf(skin).

vécu [veky] *voir* **vivre;** — *a* (*histoire etc*) real(-life), true.

vedette [vədɛt] *nf* **1** *Cin Th* star; **avoir la v.** (*artiste*) to head the bill; **en v.** (*personne*) in the limelight; (*objet*) in a prominent position. **2** (*canot*) motor boat, launch.

végétal, -aux [veʒetal, -o] *a* (*huile, règne*) vegetable-; — *nm* plant. ◆**végétarien,**

-ienne *a* & *nmf* vegetarian. ◆**végétation 1** *nf* vegetation. **2** *nfpl Méd* adenoids.

végéter [veʒete] *vi* (*personne*) *Péj* to vegetate.

véhément [veemɑ̃] *a* vehement. ◆**véhémence** *nf* vehemence.

véhicule [veikyl] *nm* vehicle. ◆**véhiculer** *vt* to convey.

veille [vɛj] *nf* **1 la v.** (**de**) (*jour précédent*) the day before; **à la v. de** (*événement*) on the eve of; **la v. de Noël** Christmas Eve. **2** (*état*) wakefulness; *pl* vigils.

veill/er [veje] *vi* to stay up *ou* awake; (*sentinelle etc*) to be on watch; **v. à qch** to attend to sth, see to sth; **v. à ce que** (+ *sub*) to make sure that; **v. sur qn** to watch over s.o.; — *vt* (*malade*) to sit with, watch over. ◆**—ée** *nf* (*soirée*) evening; (*réunion*) evening get-together; (*mortuaire*) vigil. ◆**—eur** *nm* **v. de nuit** night watchman. ◆**—euse** *nf* (*lampe*) night light; (*de voiture*) sidelight; (*de réchaud*) pilot light.

veine [vɛn] *nf* **1** *Anat Bot Géol* vein. **2** (*chance*) *Fam* luck; **avoir de la v.** to be lucky; **une v.** a piece *ou* stroke of luck. ◆**veinard, -arde** *nmf Fam* lucky devil; — *a Fam* lucky.

vêler [vele] *vi* (*vache*) to calve.

vélin [velɛ̃] *nm* (*papier, peau*) vellum.

velléité [veleite] *nf* vague desire.

vélo [velo] *nm* bike, bicycle; (*activité*) cycling; **faire du v.** to cycle, go cycling. ◆**vélodrome** *nm Sp* velodrome, cycle track. ◆**vélomoteur** *nm* (lightweight) motorcycle.

velours [v(ə)lur] *nm* velvet; **v. côtelé** corduroy, cord. ◆**velouté** *a* soft, velvety; (*au goût*) mellow, smooth; — *nm* smoothness; **v. d'asperges/etc** (*potage*) cream of asparagus/etc soup.

velu [vəly] *a* hairy.

venaison [vənɛzɔ̃] *nf* venison.

vénal, -aux [venal, -o] *a* mercenary, venal.

vendange(s) [vɑ̃dɑ̃ʒ] *nf(pl)* grape harvest, vintage. ◆**vendanger** *vi* to pick the grapes. ◆**vendangeur, -euse** *nmf* grape-picker.

vendetta [vɑ̃deta] *nf* vendetta.

vend/re [vɑ̃dr] *vt* to sell; **v. qch à qn** to sell s.o. sth, sell sth to s.o.; **v. qn** (*trahir*) to sell s.o. out; **à v.** (*maison etc*) for sale; — **se v.** *vpr* to be sold; **ça se vend bien** it sells well. ◆**—eur, -euse** *nmf* (*de magasin*) sales *ou* shop assistant, *Am* sales clerk; (*marchand*) salesman, saleswoman; *Jur* vendor, seller.

vendredi [vɑ̃drədi] *nm* Friday; **V. saint** Good Friday.

vénéneux, -euse [venenø, -øz] *a* poisonous.

vénérable [venerabl] *a* venerable. ◆**vénérer** *vt* to venerate.

vénérien, -ienne [venerjɛ̃, -jɛn] *a Méd* venereal.

venger [vɑ̃ʒe] *vt* to avenge; **— se v.** *vpr* to take (one's) revenge, avenge oneself (**de qn** on s.o., **de qch** for sth). ◆**vengeance** *nf* revenge, vengeance. ◆**vengeur, -eresse** *a* vengeful; *— nmf* avenger.

venin [vanɛ̃] *nm* (*substance*) & *Fig* venom. ◆**venimeux, -euse** *a* poisonous, venomous; (*haineux*) *Fig* venomous.

venir* [v(ə)nir] *vi* (*aux être*) to come (**de** from); **v. faire** to come to do; **viens me voir** come and *ou* to see me; **je viens/venais d'arriver** I've/I'd just arrived; **en v. à** (*conclusion etc*) to come to; **où veux-tu en v.?** what are you driving *ou* getting at?; **d'où vient que...?** how is it that...?; **s'il venait à faire** (*éventualité*) if he happened to do; **les jours/etc qui viennent** the coming days/etc; **une idée m'est venue** an idea occurred to me; **faire v.** to send for, get.

vent [vɑ̃] *nm* wind; **il fait** *ou* **il y a du v.** it's windy; **coup de v.** gust of wind; **avoir v. de** (*connaissance de*) to get wind of; **dans le v.** (*à la mode*) *Fam* trendy, with it.

vente [vɑ̃t] *nf* sale; **v. (aux enchères)** auction (sale); **v. de charité** bazaar, charity sale; **en v.** (*disponible*) on sale; **point de v.** sales *ou* retail outlet; **prix de v.** selling price; **salle des ventes** auction room.

ventilateur [vɑ̃tilatœr] *nm* (*électrique*) & *Aut* fan; (*dans un mur*) ventilator. ◆**ventilation** *nf* ventilation. ◆**ventiler** *vt* to ventilate.

ventouse [vɑ̃tuz] *nf* (*pour fixer*) suction grip; **à v.** (*crochet, fléchette etc*) suction-.

ventre [vɑ̃tr] *nm* belly, stomach; (*utérus*) womb; (*de cruche etc*) bulge; **avoir/prendre du v.** to have/get a paunch; **à plat v.** flat on one's face. ◆**ventru** *a* (*personne*) pot-bellied; (*objet*) bulging.

ventriloque [vɑ̃trilɔk] *nmf* ventriloquist.

venu, -ue[1] [v(ə)ny] *voir* **venir**; *— nmf* **nouveau v., nouvelle venue** newcomer; **premier v.** anyone; *— a* **bien v.** (*à propos*) timely; **mal v.** untimely; **être bien/mal v. de faire** to have good grounds/no grounds for doing.

venue[2] [v(ə)ny] *nf* (*arrivée*) coming.

vêpres [vɛpr] *nfpl Rel* vespers.

ver [vɛr] *nm* worm; (*larve*) grub; (*de fruits, fromage etc*) maggot; **v. luisant** glow-worm;

v. à soie silkworm; **v. solitaire** tapeworm; **v. de terre** earthworm.

véracité [verasite] *nf* truthfulness, veracity.

véranda [verɑ̃da] *nf* veranda(h).

verbe [vɛrb] *nm Gram* verb. ◆**verbal, -aux** *a* (*promesse, expression etc*) verbal.

verbeux, -euse [vɛrbø, -øz] *a* verbose. ◆**verbiage** *nm* verbiage.

verdâtre [vɛrdɑtr] *a* greenish.

verdeur [vɛrdœr] *nf* (*de fruit, vin*) tartness; (*de vieillard*) sprightliness; (*de langage*) crudeness.

verdict [vɛrdikt] *nm* verdict.

verdir [vɛrdir] *vti* to turn green. ◆**verdoyant** *a* green, verdant. ◆**verdure** *nf* (*arbres etc*) greenery.

véreux, -euse [verø, -øz] *a* (*fruit etc*) wormy, maggoty; (*malhonnête*) *Fig* dubious, shady.

verge [vɛrʒ] *nf Anat* penis.

verger [vɛrʒe] *nm* orchard.

vergetures [vɛrʒətyr] *nfpl* stretch marks.

verglas [vɛrɡlɑ] *nm* (black) ice, *Am* sleet. ◆**verglacé** *a* (*route*) icy.

vergogne (sans) [sɑ̃vɛrɡɔɲ] *a* shameless; *— adv* shamelessly.

véridique [veridik] *a* truthful.

vérifier [verifje] *vt* to check, verify; (*confirmer*) to confirm; (*comptes*) to audit. ◆**vérifiable** *a* verifiable. ◆**vérification** *nf* verification; confirmation; audit(ing).

vérité [verite] *nf* truth; (*de personnage, tableau etc*) trueness to life; (*sincérité*) sincerity; **en v.** in fact. ◆**véritable** *a* true, real; (*non imité*) real, genuine; (*exactement nommé*) veritable, real. ◆**véritablement** *adv* really.

vermeil, -eille [vɛrmɛj] *a* bright red, vermilion.

vermicelle(s) [vɛrmisɛl] *nm(pl)* *Culin* vermicelli.

vermine [vɛrmin] *nf* (*insectes, racaille*) vermine.

vermoulu [vɛrmuly] *a* worm-eaten.

vermout [vɛrmut] *nm* vermouth.

verni [vɛrni] *a* (*chanceux*) *Fam* lucky.

vernir [vɛrnir] *vt* to varnish; (*poterie*) to glaze. ◆**vernis** *nm* varnish; glaze; (*apparence*) *Fig* veneer; **v. à ongles** nail polish *ou* varnish. ◆**vernissage** *nm* (*d'exposition de peinture*) first day. ◆**vernisser** *vt* (*poterie*) to glaze.

verra, verrait [vɛra, vɛrɛ] *voir* **voir**.

verre [vɛr] *nm* (*substance, récipient*) glass; **boire** *ou* **prendre un v.** to have a drink; **v. à bière/à vin** beer/wine glass; **v. de contact**

contact lens. ◆**verrerie** nf (objets) glass-ware. ◆**verrière** nf (toit) glass roof.

verrou [veru] nm bolt; **fermer au v.** to bolt; **sous les verrous** behind bars. ◆**verrouiller** vt to bolt.

verrue [very] nf wart.

vers¹ [ver] prép (direction) towards, toward; (approximation) around, about.

vers² [ver] nm (d'un poème) line; pl (poésie) verse.

versant [versã] nm slope, side.

versatile [versatil] a fickle, volatile.

verse (à) [avers] adv in torrents; **pleuvoir à v.** to pour (down).

versé [verse] a v. **dans** (well-)versed in.

Verseau [verso] nm le V. (signe) Aquarius.

vers/er [verse] 1 vt to pour; (larmes, sang) to shed. 2 vt (argent) to pay. 3 vti (basculer) to overturn. ◆**—ement** nm payment. ◆**—eur** a bec v. spout.

verset [verse] nm Rel verse.

version [versjɔ̃] nf version; (traduction) Scol translation, unseen.

verso [verso] nm back (of the page); **'voir au v.'** 'see overleaf.'

vert [ver] a green; (pas mûr) unripe; (vin) young; (vieillard) Fig sprightly; – nm green.

vert-de-gris [verdəgri] nm inv verdigris.

vertèbre [vertebr] nf vertebra.

vertement [vertəmã] adv (réprimander etc) sharply.

vertical, -ale, -aux [vertikal, -o] a & nf vertical; **à la verticale** vertically. ◆**verticalement** adv vertically.

vertige [verti3] nm (feeling of) dizziness ou giddiness; (peur de tomber dans le vide) vertigo; pl (dizzy spells); **avoir le v.** to feel dizzy ou giddy. ◆**vertigineux, -euse** a (hauteur) giddy, dizzy; (très grand) Fig staggering.

vertu [verty] nf virtue; **en v. de** in accordance with. ◆**vertueux, -euse** a virtuous.

verve [verv] nf (d'orateur etc) brilliance.

verveine [verven] nf (plante) verbena.

vésicule [vezikyl] nf v. **biliaire** gall bladder.

vessie [vesi] nf bladder.

veste [vest] nf jacket, coat.

vestiaire [vestjer] nm cloakroom, Am locker room; (meuble métallique) locker.

vestibule [vestibyl] nm (entrance) hall.

vestiges [vesti3] nmpl (restes, ruines) remains; (traces) traces, vestiges.

vestimentaire [vestimãter] a (dépense) clothing-; (détail) of dress.

veston [vestɔ̃] nm (suit) jacket.

vêtement [vetmã] nm garment, article of clothing; pl clothes; **du v.** (industrie, commerce) clothing-; **vêtements de sport** sportswear.

vétéran [veterã] nm veteran.

vétérinaire [veteriner] a veterinary; – nmf vet, veterinary surgeon, Am veterinarian.

vétille [vetij] nf trifle, triviality.

vêt/ir* [vetir] vt, – **se v.** vpr to dress. ◆**—u** a dressed (**de** in).

veto [veto] nm inv veto; **mettre ou opposer son v. à** to veto.

vétuste [vetyst] a dilapidated.

veuf, veuve [vœf, vœv] a widowed; – nm widower; – nf widow.

veuille [vœj] voir **vouloir.**

veule [vøl] a feeble. ◆**veulerie** nf feebleness.

veut, veux, veux [vø] voir **vouloir.**

vex/er [vekse] vt to upset, hurt; – **se v.** vpr to be ou get upset (**de** at). ◆**—ant** a hurtful; (contrariant) annoying. ◆**—ation** nf humiliation.

viable [vjabl] a (enfant, entreprise etc) viable. ◆**viabilité** nf viability.

viaduc [vjadyk] nm viaduct.

viager, -ère [vja3e, -er] a **rente viagère** life annuity; – nm life annuity.

viande [vjãd] nf meat.

vibrer [vibre] vi to vibrate; (être ému) to thrill (**de** with); **faire v.** (auditoire etc) to thrill. ◆**vibrant** a (émouvant) emotional; (voix, son) resonant, vibrant. ◆**vibration** nf vibration. ◆**vibromasseur** nm (appareil) vibrator.

vicaire [viker] nm curate.

vice [vis] nm vice; (défectuosité) defect.

vice- [vis] préf vice-.

vice versa [vis(e)versa] adv vice versa.

vicier [visje] vt to taint, pollute.

vicieux, -euse [visjø, -øz] 1 a depraved; – nmf pervert. 2 a **cercle v.** vicious circle.

vicinal, -aux [visinal, -o] a **chemin v.** by-road, minor road.

vicissitudes [visisityd] nfpl vicissitudes.

vicomte [vikɔ̃t] nm viscount. ◆**vicomtesse** nf viscountess.

victime [viktim] nf victim; (d'un accident) casualty; **être v. de** to be the victim of.

victoire [viktwar] nf victory; Sp win. ◆**victorieux, -euse** a victorious; (équipe) winning.

victuailles [viktɥaj] nfpl provisions.

vidange [vidã3] nf emptying, draining; Aut oil change; (dispositif) waste outlet. ◆**vidanger** vt to empty, drain.

vide [vid] a empty; – nm emptiness, void; (absence d'air) vacuum; (gouffre etc) drop;

(*trou, manque*) gap; **regarder dans le v.** to stare into space; **emballé sous v.** vacuum-packed; **à v.** empty.

vidéo [video] *a inv* video. **◆vidéocassette** *nf* video (cassette).

vide-ordures [vidɔrdyr] *nm inv* (refuse) chute. **◆vide-poches** *nm inv* Aut glove compartment.

vid/er [vide] *vt* to empty; (*lieu*) to vacate; (*poisson, volaille*) Culin to gut; (*querelle*) to settle; **v. qn** Fam (*chasser*) to throw s.o. out; (*épuiser*) to tire s.o. out; **— se v.** *vpr* to empty. **◆—é** *a* (*fatigué*) Fam exhausted. **◆—eur** *nm* (*de boîte de nuit*) bouncer.

vie [vi] *nf* life; (*durée*) lifetime; **coût de la v.** cost of living; **gagner sa v.** to earn one's living *ou* livelihood; **en v.** living; **à v., pour la v.** for life; **donner la v. à** to give birth to; **avoir la v. dure** (*préjugés etc*) to die hard; **jamais de la v.!** not on your life!, never!

vieill/ir [vjejir] *vi* to grow old; (*changer*) to age; (*théorie, mot*) to become old-fashioned; **— vt v. qn** (*vêtement etc*) to age s.o. **◆—i** *a* (*démodé*) old-fashioned. **◆—issant** *a* ageing. **◆—issement** *nm* ageing.

viens, vient [vjɛ̃] *voir* venir.

vierge [vjɛrʒ] *nf* virgin; **la V.** (*signe*) Virgo; **— *a* (*femme, neige etc*) virgin; (*feuille de papier, film*) blank; **être v.** (*femme, homme*) to be a virgin.

Viêt-nam [vjetnam] *nm* Vietnam. **◆vietnamien, -ienne** *a & nmf* Vietnamese.

vieux (or **vieil** before vowel or mute h), **vieille, vieux, vieilles** [vjø, vjɛj] *a* old; **être v. jeu** (*a inv*) to be old-fashioned; **garçon bachelor; **vieille fille** Péj old maid; **— *nm* old man; *pl* old people; **mon v.** (*mon cher*) Fam old boy, old chap; **— *nf* old woman; **ma vieille** (*ma chère*) Fam old girl. **◆vieillard** *nm* old man; *pl* old people. **◆vieillerie** *nf* (*objet*) old thing; (*idée*) old idea. **◆vieillesse** *nf* old age. **◆vieillot** *a* antiquated.

vif, vive [vif, viv] *a* (*enfant, mouvement*) lively; (*alerte*) quick, sharp; (*intelligence, intérêt, vent*) keen; (*couleur, lumière*) bright; (*froid*) biting; (*pas*) quick, brisk; (*impression, imagination, style*) vivid; (*parole*) sharp; (*regret, satisfaction, succès etc*) great; (*coléreux*) quick-tempered; **brûler/enterrer qn v.** to burn/bury s.o. alive; **— *nm* **le v. du sujet** the heart of the matter; **à v.** (*plaie*) open; **piqué au v.** (*vexé*) cut to the quick.

vigie [viʒi] *nf* (*matelot*) lookout; (*poste*) lookout post.

vigilant [viʒilɑ̃] *a* vigilant. **◆vigilance** *nf* vigilance.

vigile [viʒil] *nm* (*gardien*) watchman; (*de nuit*) night watchman.

vigne [viɲ] *nf* (*plante*) vine; (*plantation*) vineyard. **◆vigneron, -onne** *nmf* wine grower. **◆vignoble** *nm* vineyard; (*région*) vineyards.

vignette [viɲɛt] *nf* Aut road tax sticker; (*de médicament*) price label (*for reimbursement by Social Security*).

vigueur [vigœr] *nf* vigour; **entrer/être en v.** (*loi*) to come into/be in force. **◆vigoureux, -euse** *a* (*personne, style etc*) vigorous; (*bras*) sturdy.

vilain [vilɛ̃] *a* (*laid*) ugly; (*mauvais*) nasty; (*enfant*) naughty.

villa [villa] *nf* (detached) house.

village [vilaʒ] *nm* village. **◆villageois, -oise** *a* village-; **— *nmf* villager.

ville [vil] *nf* town; (*grande*) city; **aller/être en v.** to go into/be in town; **v. d'eaux** spa (town).

villégiature [vileʒjatyr] *nf* lieu de v. (holiday) resort.

vin [vɛ̃] *nm* wine; **v. ordinaire** *ou* **de table** table wine; **v. d'honneur** reception (*in honour of s.o.*). **◆vinicole** *a* (*région*) wine-growing; (*industrie*) wine-.

vinaigre [vinɛgr] *nm* vinegar. **◆vinaigré** *a* seasoned with vinegar. **◆vinaigrette** *nf* (*sauce*) vinaigrette, French dressing, Am Italian dressing.

vindicatif, -ive [vɛ̃dikatif, -iv] *a* vindictive.

vingt [vɛ̃] ([vɛ̃t] before vowel or mute h and in numbers 22–29) *a & nm* twenty; **v. et un** twenty-one. **◆vingtaine** *nf* **une v.** (*de*) (*nombre*) about twenty; **avoir la v.** (*âge*) to be about twenty. **◆vingtième** *a & nmf* twentieth.

vinyle [vinil] *nm* vinyl.

viol [vjɔl] *nm* rape; (*de loi, lieu*) violation. **◆violation** *nf* violation. **◆violenter** *vt* to rape. **◆violer** *vt* (*femme*) to rape; (*loi, lieu*) to violate. **◆violeur** *nm* rapist.

violent [vjɔlɑ̃] *a* violent; (*remède*) drastic. **◆violemment** [-amɑ̃] *adv* violently. **◆violence** *nf* violence; (*acte*) act of violence.

violet, -ette [vjɔlɛ, -ɛt] **1** *a & nm* (*couleur*) purple, violet. **2** *nf* (*fleur*) violet. **◆violacé** *a* purplish.

violon [vjɔlɔ̃] *nm* violin. **◆violoncelle** *nm* cello. **◆violoncelliste** *nmf* cellist. **◆violoniste** *nmf* violinist.

vipère [vipɛr] *nf* viper, adder.

virage [viraʒ] *nm* (*de route*) bend; (*de véhicule*) turn; (*revirement*) Fig change of course. ◆**vir/er 1** *vi* to turn, veer; (*sur soi*) to turn round; **v. au bleu**/*etc* to turn blue/*etc*. **2** *vt* (*expulser*) *Fam* to throw out. **3** *vt* (*somme*) *Fin* to transfer (à to). ◆**-ement** *nm Fin* (bank *ou* credit) transfer.

virée [vire] *nf Fam* trip, outing.

virevolter [virvɔlte] *vi* to spin round.

virginité [virʒinite] *nf* virginity.

virgule [virgyl] *nf Gram* comma; *Math* (decimal) point; **2 v. 5** 2 point 5.

viril [viril] *a* virile, manly; (*attribut, force*) male. ◆**virilité** *nf* virility, manliness.

virtuel, -elle [virtɥɛl] *a* potential.

virtuose [virtɥoz] *nmf* virtuoso. ◆**virtuosité** *nf* virtuosity.

virulent [virylɑ̃] *a* virulent. ◆**virulence** *nf* virulence.

virus [virys] *nm* virus.

vis¹ [vi] *voir* **vivre, voir**.

vis² [vis] *nf* screw.

visa [viza] *nm* (*timbre*) stamp, stamped signature; (*de passeport*) visa; **v. de censure** (*d'un film*) certificate.

visage [vizaʒ] *nm* face.

vis-à-vis [vizavi] *prép* **v.-à-vis de** opposite; (*à l'égard de*) with respect to; (*envers*) towards; (*comparé à*) compared to; − *nm inv* (*personne*) person opposite; (*bois, maison etc*) opposite view.

viscères [viser] *nmpl* intestines. ◆**viscéral, -aux** *a* (*haine etc*) *Fig* deeply felt.

viscosité [viskozite] *nf* viscosity.

viser [vize] **1** *vi* to aim (à at); **v. à faire** to aim to do; − *vt* (*cible*) to aim at; (*concerner*) to be aimed at. **2** *vt* (*passeport, document*) to stamp. ◆**visées** *nfpl* (*desseins*) *Fig* aims; **avoir des visées sur** to have designs on. ◆**viseur** *nm Phot* viewfinder; (*d'arme*) sight.

visible [vizibl] *a* visible. ◆**visiblement** *adv* visibly. ◆**visibilité** *nf* visibility.

visière [vizjer] *nf* (*de casquette*) peak; (*en plastique etc*) eyeshade; (*de casque*) visor.

vision [vizjɔ̃] *nf* (*conception, image*) vision; (*sens*) (eye)sight, vision; **avoir des visions** *Fam* to be seeing things. ◆**visionnaire** *a* & *nmf* visionary. ◆**visionner** *vt Cin* to view. ◆**visionneuse** *nf* (*pour diapositives*) viewer.

visite [vizit] *nf* visit; (*personne*) visitor; (*examen*) inspection; **rendre v. à, faire une v. à** to visit; **v. (à domicile)** *Méd* call, visit; **v. (médicale)** medical examination; **v. guidée** guided tour; **de v.** (*carte, heures*) visiting-. ◆**visiter** *vt* to visit; (*examiner*) to inspect. ◆**visiteur, -euse** *nmf* visitor.

vison [vizɔ̃] *nm* mink.

visqueux, -euse [viskø, -øz] *a* viscous; (*surface*) sticky; (*répugnant*) *Fig* slimy.

visser [vise] *vt* to screw on.

visuel, -elle [vizɥɛl] *a* visual.

vit [vi] *voir* **vivre, voir**.

vital, -aux [vital, -o] *a* vital. ◆**vitalité** *nf* vitality.

vitamine [vitamin] *nf* vitamin. ◆**vitaminé** *a* (*biscuits etc*) vitamin-enriched.

vite [vit] *adv* quickly, fast; (*tôt*) soon; **v.!** quick(ly)! ◆**vitesse** *nf* speed; (*régime*) *Aut* gear; **boîte de vitesses** gearbox; **à toute v.** at top *ou* full speed; **v. de pointe** top speed; **en v.** quickly.

viticole [vitikɔl] *a* (*région*) wine-growing; (*industrie*) wine-. ◆**viticulteur** *nm* wine grower. ◆**viticulture** *nf* wine growing.

vitre [vitr] *nf* (window)pane; (*de véhicule*) window. ◆**vitrage** *nm* (*vitres*) windows. ◆**vitrail, -aux** *nm* stained-glass window. ◆**vitré** *a* glass-, glazed. ◆**vitreux, -euse** *a* (*regard, yeux*) *Fig* glassy. ◆**vitrier** *nm* glazier.

vitrine [vitrin] *nf* (*de magasin*) (shop) window; (*meuble*) showcase, display cabinet.

vitriol [vitrijɔl] *nm Ch* & *Fig* vitriol.

vivable [vivabl] *a* (*personne*) easy to live with; (*endroit*) fit to live in.

vivace [vivas] *a* (*plante*) perennial; (*haine*) *Fig* inveterate.

vivacité [vivasite] *nf* liveliness; (*de l'air, d'émotion*) keenness; (*agilité*) quickness; (*de couleur, d'impression, de style*) vividness; (*emportement*) petulance; **v. d'esprit** quick-wittedness.

vivant [vivɑ̃] *a* (*en vie*) alive, living; (*être, matière, preuve*) living; (*conversation, enfant, récit, rue*) lively; **langue vivante** modern language; − *nm* **de son v.** in one's lifetime; **bon v.** jovial fellow; **les vivants** the living.

vivats [viva] *nmpl* cheers.

vive¹ [viv] *voir* **vif**.

vive² [viv] *int* **v. le roi**/*etc*! long live the king/*etc*!; **v. les vacances!** hurray for the holidays!

vivement [vivmɑ̃] *adv* quickly, briskly; (*répliquer*) sharply; (*sentir*) keenly; (*regretter*) deeply; **v. demain!** roll on tomorrow!, I can hardly wait for tomorrow!; **v. que** (+ *sub*) I'll be glad when.

vivier [vivje] *nm* fish pond.

vivifier [vivifje] *vt* to invigorate.

vivisection [vivisɛksjɔ̃] *nf* vivisection.

vivre* [vivr] **1** *vi* to live; **elle vit encore** she's still alive *ou* living; **faire v.** (*famille etc*) to support; **v. vieux** to live to be old; **difficile/facile à v.** hard/easy to get on with; **manière de v.** way of life; **v. de** (*fruits etc*) to live on; (*travail etc*) to live by; **avoir de quoi v.** to have enough to live on; **vivent les vacances!** hurray for the holidays!; — *vt* (*vie*) to live; (*aventure, époque*) to live through; (*éprouver*) to experience. **2** *nmpl* food, supplies. ◆**vivoter** *vi* to jog along, get by.

vlan! [vlɑ̃] *int* bang!, wham!

vocable [vɔkabl] *nm* term, word.

vocabulaire [vɔkabylɛr] *nm* vocabulary.

vocal, -aux [vɔkal, -o] *a* (*cordes, musique*) vocal.

vocation [vɔkɑsjɔ̃] *nf* vocation, calling.

vociférer [vɔsifere] *vti* to shout angrily. ◆**vocifération** *nf* angry shout.

vodka [vɔdka] *nf* vodka.

vœu, -x [vø] *nm* (*souhait*) wish; (*promesse*) vow; **faire le ou de faire** to (make a) vow to do; **tous mes vœux!** (my) best wishes!

vogue [vɔg] *nf* fashion, vogue; **en v.** in fashion, in vogue.

voici [vwasi] *prép* here is, this is; *pl* here are, these are; **me v.** here I am; **me v. triste** I'm sad now; **v. dix ans** ten years/*etc* ago; **v. dix ans que** it's ten years since.

voie [vwa] *nf* (*route*) road; (*rails*) track, line; (*partie de route*) lane; (*chemin*) way; (*moyen*) means, way; (*de communication*) line; (*diplomatique*) channels; (*quai*) *Rail* platform; **en v. de** in the process of; **en v. de développement** (*pays*) developing; **v. publique** public highway; **v. navigable** waterway; **v. sans issue** cul-de-sac, dead end; **préparer la v.** *Fig* to pave the way; **sur la** (**bonne**) **v.** on the right track.

voilà [vwala] *prép* there is, that is; *pl* there are, those are; **les v.** there they are; **v., j'arrive!** all right, I'm coming!; **le v. parti** he has left now; **v. dix ans**/*etc* ten years/*etc* ago; **v. dix ans que** it's ten years since.

voile¹ [vwal] *nm* (*étoffe qui cache, coiffure etc*) & *Fig* veil. ◆**voil/er¹** *vt* (*visage, vérité etc*) to veil; — **se v.** *vpr* (*personne*) to wear a veil; (*ciel, regard*) to cloud over. ◆**—é** *a* (*femme, allusion*) veiled; (*terne*) dull; (*photo*) hazy.

voile² [vwal] *nf* (*de bateau*) sail; (*activité*) sailing; **bateau à voiles** sailboat, *Am* sailboat; **faire de la v.** to sail, go sailing. ◆**voilier** *nm* sailing ship; (*de plaisance*) sailing boat, *Am* sailboat. ◆**voilure** *nf* *Nau* sails.

voiler² [vwale] *vt*, — **se v.** *vpr* (*roue*) to buckle.

voir* [vwar] *vti* to see; **faire** *ou* **laisser v. qch**

to show sth; **fais v.** let me see, show me; **v. qn faire** to see s.o. do *ou* doing; **voyons!** (*sois raisonnable*) come on!; **y v. clair** (*comprendre*) to see clearly; **je ne peux pas la v.** (*supporter*) *Fam* I can't stand (the sight of) her; **v. venir** (*attendre*) to wait and see; **on verra bien** (*attendons*) we'll see; **ça n'a rien à v. avec** that's got nothing to do with; — **se v.** *vpr* to see oneself; (*se fréquenter*) to see each other; (*objet, attitude etc*) to be seen; (*reprise, tache*) to show; **ça se voit** that's obvious.

voire [vwar] *adv* indeed.

voirie [vwari] *nf* (*enlèvement des ordures*) refuse collection; (*routes*) public highways.

voisin, -ine [vwazɛ̃, -in] *a* (*pays, village etc*) neighbouring; (*maison, pièce*) next (**de** to); (*idée, état etc*) similar (**de** to); — *nmf* neighbour. ◆**voisinage** *nm* (*quartier, voisins*) neighbourhood; (*proximité*) proximity. ◆**voisiner** *vi* **v. avec** to be side by side with.

voiture [vwatyr] *nf* *Aut* car; *Rail* carriage, coach, *Am* car; (*charrette*) cart; **v.** (**à cheval**) (horse-drawn) carriage; **v. de course/de tourisme** racing/private car; **v. d'enfant** pram, *Am* baby carriage; **en v.!** *Rail* all aboard!

voix [vwa] *nf* voice; (*suffrage*) vote; **à v. basse** in a whisper; **à portée de v.** within earshot; **avoir v. au chapitre** *Fig* to have a say.

vol [vɔl] *nm* **1** (*d'avion, d'oiseau*) flight; (*groupe d'oiseaux*) flock, flight; **v. libre** hang gliding; **v. à voile** gliding. **2** (*délit*) theft; (*hold-up*) robbery; **v. à l'étalage** shoplifting; **c'est du v.!** (*trop cher*) it's daylight robbery!

volage [vɔlaʒ] *a* flighty, fickle.

volaille [vɔlaj] *nf* **la v.** (*oiseaux*) poultry; **une v.** (*oiseau*) a fowl. ◆**volailler** *nm* poulterer.

volatile [vɔlatil] *nm* (*oiseau domestique*) fowl.

volatiliser (se) [səvɔlatilize] *vpr* (*disparaître*) to vanish (into thin air).

vol-au-vent [vɔlovɑ̃] *nm inv* *Culin* vol-au-vent.

volcan [vɔlkɑ̃] *nm* volcano. ◆**volcanique** *a* volcanic.

voler [vɔle] **1** *vi* (*oiseau, avion etc*) to fly; (*courir*) *Fig* to rush. **2** *vt* (*dérober*) to steal (**à** from); **v. qn** to rob s.o.; — *vi* to rob. ◆**volant 1** *a* (*tapis etc*) flying; **feuille volante** loose sheet. **2** *nm* *Aut* (steering) wheel; (*objet*) *Sp* shuttlecock; (*de jupe*) flounce. ◆**volée** *nf* flight; (*groupe d'oiseaux*) flock, flight; (*de coups, flèches etc*) volley; (*suite de*

coups) thrashing; **lancer à toute v.** to throw as hard as one can; **sonner à toute v.** to peal *ou* ring out. ◆**voleter** *vi* to flutter.
◆**voleur, -euse** *nmf* thief; **au v.!** stop thief!; – *a* thieving.

volet [vɔlɛ] *nm* **1** (*de fenêtre*) shutter. **2** (*de programme, reportage etc*) section, part.

volière [vɔljɛr] *nf* aviary.

volley(-ball) [vɔlɛ(bol)] *nm* volleyball. ◆**volleyeur, -euse** *nmf* volleyball player.

volonté [vɔlɔ̃te] *nf* (*faculté, intention*) will; (*désir*) wish; *Phil Psy* free will; **elle a de la v.** she has willpower; **bonne v.** goodwill; **mauvaise v.** ill will; **à v.** at will; (*quantité*) as much as desired. ◆**volontaire** *a* (*délibéré, qui agit librement*) voluntary; (*opiniâtre*) wilful, *Am* willful; – *nmf* volunteer. ◆**volontairement** *adv* voluntarily; (*exprès*) deliberately. ◆**volontiers** [-ɔtje] *adv* willingly, gladly; (*habituellement*) readily, **v.!** (*oui*) I'd love to!

volt [vɔlt] *nm* **É** volt. ◆**voltage** *nm* voltage.

volte-face [vɔltəfas] *nf inv* about turn, *Am* about face; **faire v.-face** to turn round.

voltige [vɔltiʒ] *nf* acrobatics.

voltiger [vɔltiʒe] *vi* to flutter.

volubile [vɔlybil] *a* (*bavard*) loquacious, voluble.

volume [vɔlym] *nm* (*capacité, intensité, tome*) volume. ◆**volumineux, -euse** *a* bulky, voluminous.

volupté [vɔlypte] *nf* sensual pleasure. ◆**voluptueux, -euse** *a* voluptuous.

vom/ir [vɔmir] *vt* to vomit, bring up; (*exécrer*) *Fig* to loathe; – *vi* to vomit, be sick. ◆**—i** *nm Fam* vomit. ◆**—issement** *nm* (*action*) vomiting. ◆**vomitif, -ive** *a Fam* nauseating.

vont [vɔ̃] *voir* **aller 1.**

vorace [vɔras] *a* (*appétit, lecteur etc*) voracious.

vos [vo] *voir* **votre.**

vote [vɔt] *nm* (*action*) vote, voting; (*suffrage*) vote; (*de loi*) passing; **bureau de v.** polling station. ◆**voter** *vi* to vote; – *vt* (*loi*) to pass; (*crédits*) to vote. ◆**votant, -ante** *nmf* voter.

votre, pl vos [vɔtr, vo] *a poss* your. ◆**vôtre** *pron poss* **le ou la v., les vôtres** yours; **à la v.!** (*toast*) cheers!; – *nmpl* **les vôtres** (*parents etc*) your (own) people.

vouer [vwe] *vt* (*promettre*) to vow (**à** to); (*consacrer*) to dedicate (**à** to); (*condamner*) to doom (**à** to); **se v. à** to dedicate oneself to.

vouloir° [vulwar] *vt* to want (**faire** to do); **je veux qu'il parte** I want him to go; **v. dire** to mean (**que** that); **je voudrais rester** I'd like to stay; **je voudrais un pain** I'd like a loaf of bread; **voulez-vous me suivre** will you follow me; **si tu veux** if you like *ou* wish; **en v. à qn d'avoir fait qch** to hold it against s.o. for doing sth; **l'usage veut que . . .** (+ *sub*) custom requires that . . . ; **v. du bien à qn** to wish s.o. well; **je veux bien** I don't mind (**faire** doing); **que voulez-vous!** (*résignation*) what can you expect!; **sans le v.** unintentionally; **ça ne veut pas bouger** it won't move; **ne pas v. de qch/de qn** not to want sth/s.o.; **veuillez attendre** kindly wait. ◆**voulu** *a* (*requis*) required; (*délibéré*) deliberate, intentional.

vous [vu] *pron* **1** (*sujet, complément direct*) you; **v. êtes** you are; **il v. connaît** he knows you. **2** (*complément indirect*) (to) you; **il v. l'a donné** he gave it to you, he gave you it. **3** (*réfléchi*) yourself, *pl* yourselves; **v. v. lavez** you wash yourself, you wash yourselves. **4** (*réciproque*) each other; **v. v. aimez** you love each other. ◆**v.-même** *pron* yourself. ◆**v.-mêmes** *pron pl* yourselves.

voûte [vut] *nf* (*plafond*) vault; (*porche*) arch(way). ◆**voûté** *a* (*personne*) bent, stooped.

vouvoyer [vuvwaje] *vt* to address formally (*using vous*).

voyage [vwajaʒ] *nm* trip, journey; (*par mer*) voyage; **aimer les voyages** to like travelling; **faire un v., partir en v.** to go on a trip; **être en v.** to be (away) travelling; **de v.** (*compagnon etc*) travelling-; **bon v.!** have a pleasant trip!; **v. de noces** honeymoon; **v. organisé** (package) tour. ◆**voyager** *vi* to travel. ◆**voyageur, -euse** *nmf* traveller; (*passager*) passenger; **v. de commerce** commercial traveller. ◆**voyagiste** *nm* tour operator.

voyant [vwajɑ̃] **1** *a* gaudy, loud. **2** *nm* (*signal*) (warning) light; (*d'appareil électrique*) pilot light.

voyante [vwajɑ̃t] *nf* clairvoyant.

voyelle [vwajɛl] *nf* vowel.

voyeur, -euse [vwajœr, -øz] *nmf* peeping Tom, voyeur.

voyou [vwaju] *nm* hooligan, hoodlum.

vrac (en) [ɑ̃vrak] *adv* (*en désordre*) haphazardly; (*au poids*) loose, unpackaged.

vrai [vrɛ] *a* true; (*réel*) real; (*authentique*) genuine; – *adv* **dire v.** to tell the truth (*as what one says*); – *nm* (*vérité*) truth. ◆**—ment** *adv* really.

vraisemblable [vrɛsɑ̃blabl] *a* (*probable*) likely, probable; (*plausible*) plausible. ◆**vraisemblablement** *adv* probably.

◆**vraisemblance** *nf* likelihood; plausibility.

vrille [vrij] *nf* **1** (*outil*) gimlet. **2** *Av* (tail) spin.

vromb/ir [vrɔ̃bir] *vi* to hum. ◆**—issement** *nm* hum(ming).

vu [vy] **1** *voir* voir; – *a* bien vu well thought of; mal vu frowned upon. **2** *prép* in view of; vu que seeing that.

vue [vy] *nf* (*spectacle*) sight; (*sens*) (eye)sight; (*panorama, photo, idée*) view; en v. (*proche*) in sight; (*en évidence*) on view; (*personne*) *Fig* in the public eye; avoir en v. to have in mind; à v. (*tirer*) on sight; (*payable*) at sight; à première v. at first sight; de v. (*connaître*) by sight; en v. de faire with a view to doing.

vulgaire [vylgɛr] *a* (*grossier*) vulgar, coarse; (*ordinaire*) common. ◆**—ment** *adv* vulgarly, coarsely; (*appeler*) commonly. ◆**vulgariser** *vt* to popularize. ◆**vulgarité** *nf* vulgarity, coarseness.

vulnérable [vylnerabl] *a* vulnerable. ◆**vulnérabilité** *nf* vulnerability.

W

W, w [dubləve] *nm* W, w.

wagon [vagɔ̃] *nm* Rail (*de voyageurs*) carriage, coach, *Am* car; (*de marchandises*) wag(g)on, truck, *Am* freight car. ◆**w.-lit** *nm* (*pl* wagons-lits) sleeping car, sleeper. ◆**w.-restaurant** *nm* (*pl* wagons-restaurants) dining car, diner. ◆**wagonnet** *nm* (small) wagon *ou* truck.

wallon, -onne [walɔ̃, -ɔn] *a & nmf* Walloon.

waters [water] *nmpl* toilet.

watt [wat] *nm* Él watt.

w-c [(dubla)vese] *nmpl* toilet.

week-end [wikɛnd] *nm* weekend.

western [wɛstɛrn] *nm* Cin western.

whisky, *pl* **-ies** [wiski] *nm* whisky, *Am* whiskey.

X

X, x [iks] *nm* X, x; rayon X X-ray.

xénophobe [ksenɔfɔb] *a* xenophobic; – *nmf* xenophobe. ◆**xénophobie** *nf* xenophobia.

xérès [gzeres] *nm* sherry.

xylophone [ksilɔfɔn] *nm* xylophone.

Y

Y, y [igrɛk] *nm* Y, y.

y [i] **1** *adv* there; (*dedans*) in it; *pl* in them; (*dessus*) on it; *pl* on them; elle y vivra she'll live there; j'y entrai I entered (it); allons-y let's go; j'y suis! (*je comprends*) now I get it!; je n'y suis pour rien I have nothing to do with it, that's nothing to do with me. **2** *pron* (= à *cela*) j'y pense I think of it; je m'y attendais I was expecting it; ça y est! that's it!

yacht [jɔt] *nm* yacht.

yaourt [jaur(t)] *nm* yog(h)urt.

yeux [jø] *voir* œil.

yiddish [(j)idiʃ] *nm & a* Yiddish.

yoga [jɔga] *nm* yoga.

yog(h)ourt [jɔgur(t)] *voir* yaourt.

Yougoslavie [jugɔslavi] *nf* Yugoslavia. ◆**yougoslave** *a & nmf* Yugoslav(ian).

yo-yo [jojo] *nm inv* yoyo.

Z

Z, z [zɛd] *nm* Z, z.
zèbre [zɛbr] *nm* zebra. ◆**zébré** *a* striped, streaked (**de** with).
zèle [zɛl] *nm* zeal; **faire du z.** to overdo it. ◆**zélé** *a* zealous.
zénith [zenit] *nm* zenith.
zéro [zero] *nm* (*chiffre*) nought, zero; (*dans un numéro*) 0 [əʊ]; (*température*) zero; (*rien*) nothing; (*personne*) *Fig* nobody, nonentity; **deux buts à z.** *Fb* two nil, *Am* two zero; **partir de z.** to start from scratch.
zeste [zɛst] *nm* **un z. de citron** (a piece of) lemon peel.
zézayer [zezeje] *vi* to lisp.
zibeline [ziblin] *nf* (*animal*) sable.

zigzag [zigzag] *nm* zigzag; **en z.** (*route etc*) zigzag(ging); ◆**zigzaguer** *vi* to zigzag.
zinc [zɛ̃g] *nm* (*métal*) zinc; (*comptoir*) *Fam* bar.
zizanie [zizani] *nf* discord.
zodiaque [zɔdjak] *nm* zodiac.
zona [zona] *nm* *Méd* shingles.
zone [zon] *nf* zone, area; (*domaine*) *Fig* sphere; (*faubourgs misérables*) shanty town; **z. bleue** restricted parking zone; **z. industrielle** trading estate, *Am* industrial park.
zoo [zo(o)] *nm* zoo. ◆**zoologie** [zɔɔlɔʒi] *nf* zoology. ◆**zoologique** *a* zoological; **jardin** *ou* **parc z.** zoo.
zoom [zum] *nm* (*objectif*) zoom lens.
zut! [zyt] *int Fam* bother!, heck!

French verb conjugations

REGULAR VERBS

	-ER Verbs	-IR Verbs	-RE Verbs
Infinitive	*donn/er*	*fin/ir*	*vend/re*
1 Present	je donne	je finis	je vends
	tu donnes	tu finis	tu vends
	il donne	il finit	il vend
	nous donnons	nous finissons	nous vendons
	vous donnez	vous finissez	vous vendez
	ils donnent	ils finissent	ils vendent
2 Imperfect	je donnais	je finissais	je vendais
	tu donnais	tu finissais	tu vendais
	il donnait	il finissait	il vendait
	nous donnions	nous finissions	nous vendions
	vous donniez	vous finissiez	vous vendiez
	ils donnaient	ils finissaient	ils vendaient
3 Past historic	je donnai	je finis	je vendis
	tu donnas	tu finis	tu vendis
	il donna	il finit	il vendit
	nous donnâmes	nous finîmes	nous vendîmes
	vous donnâtes	vous finîtes	vous vendîtes
	ils donnèrent	ils finirent	ils vendirent
4 Future	je donnerai	je finirai	je vendrai
	tu donneras	tu finiras	tu vendras
	il donnera	il finira	il vendra
	nous donnerons	nous finirons	nous vendrons
	vous donnerez	vous finirez	vous vendrez
	ils donneront	ils finiront	ils vendront
5 Subjunctive	je donne	je finisse	je vende
	tu donnes	tu finisses	tu vendes
	il donne	il finisse	il vende
	nous donnions	nous finissions	nous vendions
	vous donniez	vous finissiez	vous vendiez
	ils donnent	ils finissent	ils vendent
6 Imperative	donne	finis	vends
	donnons	finissons	vendons
	donnez	finissez	vendez
7 Present participle	donnant	finissant	vendant
8 Past participle	donné	fini	vendu

SPELLING ANOMALIES OF -ER VERBS

Verbs in **-ger** (e.g. **manger**) take an extra **e** before endings beginning with **o** or **a**: *Present* je mange, nous mangeons; *Imperfect* je mangeais, nous mangions; *Past historic* je mangeai, nous mangeâmes; *Present participle* mangeant. Verbs in **-cer** (e.g. **commencer**) change **c** to **ç** before endings beginning with **o** or **a**: *Present* je commence, nous commençons; *Imperfect* je commençais, nous commencions; *Past historic* je commençai, nous commençâmes; *Present participle* commençant. Verbs containing mute **e** in their penultimate syllable fall into two groups. In the first (e.g. **mener**, **peser**, **lever**), **e** becomes **è** before an unpronounced syllable in the present and subjunctive, and in the future and conditional tenses (e.g. je mène, ils mèneront). The second group contains most verbs ending in **-eler** and **-eter** (e.g. **appeler**, **jeter**). These verbs change l to ll and t to tt before an unpronounced syllable (e.g. j'appelle, ils appelleront; je jette, ils jetteront). However, the following verbs in **-eler** and **-eter** fall into the first group in which **e** changes to **è** before mute **e** (e.g. je modèle, ils modèleront; j'achète, ils achèteront): celer, ciseler, démanteler, geler, marteler, modeler, peler; acheter, crocheter, fureter, haleter. Derived verbs (e.g. **dégeler**, **racheter**) are conjugated in the same way. Verbs containing e acute in their penultimate syllable change **é** to **è** before the unpronounced endings of the present and subjunctive only (e.g. je cède but je céderai). Verbs in **-yer** (e.g. **essuyer**) change y to i before an unpronounced syllable in the present and subjunctive, and in the future and conditional tenses (e.g. j'essuie, ils essuieront). In verbs in **-ayer** (e.g. **balayer**), y may be retained before mute **e** (e.g. je balaie or balaye, ils balaieront or balayeront).

IRREGULAR VERBS

Listed below are those verbs considered to be the most useful. Forms and tenses not given are fully derivable. Note that the endings of the past historic fall into three categories, the 'a' and 'i' categories shown at *donner*, and at *finir* and *vendre*, and the 'u' category which has the following endings: -us, -ut, -ûmes, -ûtes, -urent. Most of the verbs listed below form their past historic with 'u'. The imperfect may usually be formed by adding -ais, -ait, -ions, -iez, -aient to the stem of the first person plural of the present tense, e.g. 'je buvais' etc may be derived from 'nous buvons' (stem 'buv-' and ending '-ons'); similarly, the present participle may generally be formed by substituting -ant for -ons (e.g. buvant). The future may usually be formed by adding -ai, -as, -a, -ons, -ez, -ont to the infinitive or to an infinitive without final 'e' where the ending is -re (e.g. conduire). The imperative usually has the same forms as the second persons singular and plural and first person plural of the present tense.

1 = Present   2 = Imperfect   3 = Past historic   4 = Future
5 = Subjunctive   6 = Imperative   7 = Present participle
8 = Past participle   n = nous   v = vous   †verbs conjugated with **être** only.

abattre	*like* **battre**
absoudre	1 j'absous, n absolvons 2 j'absolvais
	3 j'absolus (*rarely used*) 5 j'absolve 7 absolvant
	8 absous, absoute
†s'abstenir	*like* tenir
abstraire	1 j'abstrais, n abstrayons 2 j'abstrayais 3 *none* 5 j'abstraie
	7 abstrayant 8 abstrait
accourir	*like* courir
accroître	*like* croître *except* 8 accru
accueillir	*like* cueillir
acquérir	1 j'acquiers, n acquérons 2 j'acquérais 3 j'acquis
	4 j'acquerrai 5 j'acquière 7 acquérant 8 acquis
adjoindre	*like* atteindre
admettre	*like* mettre
†aller	1 je vais, tu vas, il va, n allons, v allez, ils vont 4 j'irai
	5 j'aille, nous allions, ils aillent 6 va, allons, allez (*but note* vas-y)
apercevoir	*like* recevoir
apparaître	*like* connaître
appartenir	*like* tenir
apprendre	*like* prendre
asseoir	1 j'assieds, n asseyons, ils asseyent 2 j'asseyais 3 j'assis
	4 j'assiérai 5 j'asseye 7 asseyant 8 assis

(ii)

astreindre	*like* **atteindre**
atteindre	1 j'atteins, n atteignons, ils atteignent 2 j'atteignais 3 j'atteignis 4 j'atteindrai 5 j'atteigne 7 atteignant 8 atteint
avoir	1 j'ai, tu as, il a, n avons, v avez, ils ont 2 j'avais 3 j'eus 4 j'aurai 5 j'aie, il ait, n ayons, ils aient 6 aie, ayons, ayez 7 ayant 8 eu
battre	1 je bats, n battons 5 je batte
boire	1 je bois, n buvons, ils boivent 2 je buvais 3 je bus 5 je boive, n buvions 7 buvant 8 bu
bouillir	1 je bous, n bouillons, ils bouillent 2 je bouillais 3 *not used* 5 je bouille 7 bouillant
braire	(*defective*) 1 il brait, ils braient 4 il braira, ils brairont
combattre	*like* **battre**
commettre	*like* **mettre**
comparaître	*like* **connaître**
comprendre	*like* **prendre**
compromettre	*like* **mettre**
concevoir	*like* **recevoir**
conclure	1 je conclus, n concluons, ils concluent 5 je conclue
concourir	*like* **courir**
conduire	1 je conduis, n conduisons 3 je conduisis 5 je conduise 8 conduit
connaître	1 je connais, il connaît, n connaissons 3 je connus 5 je connaisse 7 connaissant 8 connu
conquérir	*like* **acquérir**
consentir	*like* **mentir**
construire	*like* **conduire**
contenir	*like* **tenir**
contraindre	*like* **atteindre**
contredire	*like* **dire** *except* 1 v contredisez
convaincre	*like* **vaincre**
convenir	*like* **tenir**
corrompre	*like* **rompre**
coudre	1 je couds, n cousons, ils cousent 3 je cousis 5 je couse 7 cousant 8 cousu
courir	1 je cours, n courons 3 je courus 4 je courrai 5 je coure 8 couru
couvrir	1 je couvre, n couvrons 2 je couvrais 5 je couvre 8 couvert
craindre	*like* **atteindre**
croire	1 je crois, n croyons, ils croient 2 je croyais 3 je crus 5 je croie, n croyions 7 croyant 8 cru
croître	1 je crois, il croît, n croissons 2 je croissais 3 je crûs 5 je croisse 7 croissant 8 crû, crue
cueillir	1 je cueille, n cueillons 2 je cueillais 4 je cueillerai 5 je cueille 7 cueillant
cuire	1 je cuis, n cuisons 2 je cuisais 3 je cuisis 5 je cuise 7 cuisant 8 cuit
débattre	*like* **battre**
décevoir	*like* **recevoir**
découvrir	*like* **couvrir**
décrire	*like* **écrire**
décroître	*like* **croître** *except* 8 décru
déduire	*like* **conduire**
défaillir	1 je défaille, n défaillons 2 je défaillais 3 je défaillis 5 je défaille 7 défaillant 8 défailli

défaire	*like* faire
dépeindre	*like* atteindre
déplaire	*like* plaire
déteindre	*like* atteindre
détenir	*like* tenir
détruire	*like* conduire
†devenir	*like* tenir
devoir	1 je dois, n devons, ils doivent 2 je devais 3 je dus
	4 je devrai 5 je doive, n devions 6 *not used* 7 devant
	8 dû, due, *pl* dus, dues
dire	1 je dis, n disons, v dites 2 je disais 3 je dis 5 je dise
	7 disant 8 dit
disparaître	*like* connaître
dissoudre	*like* absoudre
distraire	*like* abstraire
dormir	*like* mentir
†échoir	(*defective*) 1 il échoit 3 il échut, ils échurent 4 il échoira
	7 échéant 8 échu
écrire	1 j'écris, n écrivons 2 j'écrivais 3 j'écrivis 5 j'écrive
	7 écrivant 8 écrit
élire	*like* lire
émettre	*like* mettre
émouvoir	*like* mouvoir *except* 8 ému
encourir	*like* courir
endormir	*like* mentir
enduire	*like* conduire
enfreindre	*like* atteindre
†s'enfuir	*like* fuir
†s'ensuivre	*like* suivre (*but third person only*)
entreprendre	*like* prendre
entretenir	*like* tenir
entrevoir	*like* voir
entrouvrir	*like* couvrir
envoyer	4 j'enverrai
†s'éprendre	*like* prendre
éteindre	*like* atteindre
être	1 je suis, tu es, il est, n sommes, v êtes, ils sont 2 j'étais 3 je fus
	4 je serai 5 je sois, n soyons, ils soient 6 sois, soyons, soyez
	7 étant 8 été
exclure	*like* conclure
extraire	*like* abstraire
faillir	(*defective*) 3 je faillis 4 je faillirai 8 failli
faire	1 je fais, n faisons, v faites, ils font 2 je faisais 3 je fis 4 je
	ferai 5 je fasse 7 faisant 8 fait
falloir	(*impersonal*) 1 il faut 2 il fallait 3 il fallut 4 il faudra
	5 il faille 6 *none* 7 *none* 8 fallu
feindre	*like* atteindre
foutre	1 je fous, n foutons 2 je foutais 3 *none* 5 je foute
	7 foutant 8 foutu
frire	(*defective*) 1 je fris, tu fris, il frit 4 je frirai (*rare*) 6 fris (*rare*)
	8 frit (*for other persons and tenses use* faire frire)
fuir	1 je fuis, n fuyons, ils fuient 2 je fuyais 3 je fuis 5 je fuie
	7 fuyant 8 fui
haïr	1 je hais, il hait, n haïssons
inclure	*like* conclure
induire	*like* conduire
inscrire	*like* écrire

(iv)

instruire	*like* **conduire**
interdire	*like* **dire** *except* 1 v interdisez
interrompre	*like* **rompre**
intervenir	*like* **tenir**
introduire	*like* **conduire**
joindre	*like* **atteindre**
lire	1 je lis, n lisons 2 je lisais 3 je lus 5 je lise 7 lisant 8 lu
luire	*like* **nuire**
maintenir	*like* **tenir**
maudire	,1 je maudis, n maudissons 2 je maudissais 3 je maudis 4 je maudirai 5 je maudisse 7 maudissant 8 maudit
méconnaître	*like* **connaître**
médire	*like* **dire** *except* 1 v médisez
mentir	1 je mens, n mentons 2 je mentais 5 je mente 7 mentant
mettre	1 je mets, n mettons 2 je mettais 3 je mis 5 je mette 7 mettant 8 mis
moudre	1 je mouds, n moulons 2 je moulais 3 je moulus 5 je moule 7 moulant 8 moulu
†mourir	1 je meurs, n mourons, ils meurent 2 je mourais 3 je mourus 4 je mourrai 5 je meure, n mourions 7 mourant 8 mort
mouvoir	1 je meus, n mouvons, ils meuvent 2 je mouvais 3 je mus (*rare*) 4 je mouvrai 5 je meuve, n mouvions 8 mû, mue, *pl* mus, mues
†naître	1 je nais, il naît, n naissons 2 je naissais 3 je naquis 4 je naîtrai 5 je naisse 7 naissant 8 né
nuire	1 je nuis, n nuisons 2 je nuisais 3 je nuisis 5 je nuise 7 nuisant 8 nui
obtenir	*like* **tenir**
offrir	*like* **couvrir**
omettre	*like* **mettre**
ouvrir	*like* **couvrir**
paître	(*defective*) 1 il paît 2 il paissait 3 *none* 4 il paîtra 5 il paisse 7 paissant 8 *none*
paraître	*like* **connaître**
parcourir	*like* **courir**
†partir	*like* **mentir**
†parvenir	*like* **tenir**
peindre	*like* **atteindre**
percevoir	*like* **recevoir**
permettre	*like* **mettre**
plaindre	*like* **atteindre**
plaire	1 je plais, n plaisons 2 je plaisais 3 je plus 5 je plaise 7 plaisant 8 plu
pleuvoir	(*impersonal*) 1 il pleut 2 il pleuvait 3 il plut 4 il pleuvra 5 il pleuve 6 *none* 7 pleuvant 8 plu
poursuivre	*like* **suivre**
pourvoir	*like* **voir** *except* 4 je pourvoirai
pouvoir	1 je peux *or* je puis, tu peux, il peut, n pouvons, ils peuvent 2 je pouvais 3 je pus 4 je pourrai 5 je puisse 6 *not used* 7 pouvant 8 pu
prédire	*like* **dire** *except* 1 v prédisez
prendre	1 je prends, n prenons, ils prennent 2 je prenais 3 je pris 5 je prenne 7 prenant 8 pris
prescrire	*like* **écrire**
pressentir	*like* **mentir**

prévenir	*like* **tenir**
prévoir	*like* **voir** *except* 4 je prévoirai
produire	*like* **conduire**
promettre	*like* **mettre**
promouvoir	*like* **mouvoir** *except* 8 promu
proscrire	*like* **écrire**
†provenir	*like* **tenir**
rabattre	*like* **battre**
rasseoir	*like* **asseoir**
recevoir	1 je reçois, n recevons, ils reçoivent 2 je recevais 3 je reçus 4 je recevrai 5 je reçoive, n recevions, ils reçoivent 7 recevant 8 reçu
reconnaître	*like* **connaître**
reconduire	*like* **conduire**
reconstruire	*like* **conduire**
recoudre	*like* **coudre**
recourir	*like* **courir**
recouvrir	*like* **couvrir**
recueillir	*like* **cueillir**
†redevenir	*like* **tenir**
redire	*like* **dire**
réduire	*like* **conduire**
refaire	*like* **faire**
rejoindre	*like* **atteindre**
relire	*like* **lire**
remettre	*like* **mettre**
†renaître	*like* **naître**
rendormir	*like* **mentir**
renvoyer	*like* **envoyer**
†repartir	*like* **mentir**
repentir	*like* **mentir**
reprendre	*like* **prendre**
reproduire	*like* **conduire**
résoudre	1 je résous, n résolvons 2 je résolvais 3 je résolus 5 je résolve 7 résolvant 8 résolu
ressentir	*like* **mentir**
ressortir	*like* **mentir**
restreindre	*like* **atteindre**
retenir	*like* **tenir**
†revenir	*like* **tenir**
revêtir	*like* **vêtir**
revivre	*like* **vivre**
revoir	*like* **voir**
rire	1 je ris, n rions 2 je riais 3 je ris 5 je rie, n riions 7 riant 8 ri
rompre	*regular except* 1 il rompt
rouvrir	*like* **couvrir**
satisfaire	*like* **faire**
savoir	1 je sais, n savons, ils savent 2 je savais 3 je sus 4 je saurai 5 je sache 6 sache, sachons, sachez 7 sachant 8 su
séduire	*like* **conduire**
sentir	*like* **mentir**
servir	*like* **mentir**
sortir	*like* **mentir**
souffrir	*like* **couvrir**
soumettre	*like* **mettre**
sourire	*like* **rire**

souscrire	*like* **écrire**
soustraire	*like* **abstraire**
soutenir	*like* **tenir**
†se souvenir	*like* **tenir**
subvenir	*like* **tenir**
suffire	1 je suffis, n suffisons 2 je suffisais 3 je suffis 5 je suffise 7 suffisant 8 suffi
suivre	1 je suis, n suivons 2 je suivais 3 je suivis 5 je suive 7 suivant 8 suivi
surprendre	*like* **prendre**
†survenir	*like* **tenir**
survivre	*like* **vivre**
taire	1 je tais, n taisons 2 je taisais 3 je tus 5 je taise 7 taisant 8 tu
teindre	*like* **atteindre**
tenir	1 je tiens, n tenons, ils tiennent 2 je tenais 3 je tins, tu tins, il tint, n tînmes, v tîntes, ils tinrent 4 je tiendrai 5 je tienne 7 tenant 8 tenu
traduire	*like* **conduire**
traire	*like* **abstraire**
transcrire	*like* **écrire**
transmettre	*like* **mettre**
transparaître	*like* **connaître**
tressaillir	*like* **défaillir**
vaincre	1 je vaincs, il vainc, n vainquons 2 je vainquais 3 je vainquis 5 je vainque 7 vainquant 8 vaincu
valoir	1 je vaux, n valons 2 je valais 3 je valus 4 je vaudrai 5 je vaille 6 *not used* 7 valant 8 valu
†venir	*like* **tenir**
vêtir	1 je vêts, n vêtons 2 je vêtais 5 je vête 7 vêtant 8 vêtu
vivre	1 je vis, n vivons 2 je vivais 3 je vécus 5 je vive 7 vivant 8 vécu
voir	1 je vois, n voyons 2 je voyais 3 je vis 4 je verrai 5 je voie, n voyions 7 voyant 8 vu
vouloir	1 je veux, n voulons, ils veulent 2 je voulais 3 je voulus 4 je voudrai 5 je veuille 6 veuille, veuillons, veuillez 7 voulant 8 voulu

Verbes anglais irréguliers

Infinitif	Prétérit	Participe passé
arise	arose	arisen
be	was, were	been
bear	bore	borne
beat	beat	beaten
become	became	become
begin	began	begun
bend	bent	bent
bet	bet, betted	bet, betted
bid	bade, bid	bidden, bid
bind	bound	bound
bite	bit	bitten
bleed	bled	bled
blow	blew	blown
break	broke	broken
breed	bred	bred

bring	brought	brought
broadcast	broadcast	broadcast
build	built	built
burn	burnt, burned	burnt, burned
burst	burst	burst
buy	bought	bought
cast	cast	cast
catch	caught	caught
choose	chose	chosen
cling	clung	clung
come	came	come
cost	cost	cost
creep	crept	crept
cut	cut	cut
deal	dealt	dealt
dig	dug	dug
dive	dived, *Am* dove	dived
do	did	done
draw	drew	drawn
dream	dreamed, dreamt	dreamed, dreamt
drink	drank	drunk
drive	drove	driven
dwell	dwelt	dwelt
eat	ate [et, *Am* eɪt]	eaten
fall	fell	fallen
feed	fed	fed
feel	felt	felt
fight	fought	fought
find	found	found
fling	flung	flung
fly	flew	flown
forbid	forbad(e)	forbidden
forecast	forecast	forecast
foresee	foresaw	foreseen
forget	forgot	forgotten
forgive	forgave	forgiven
forsake	forsook (*rare*)	forsaken
freeze	froze	frozen
get	got	got, *Am* gotten
give	gave	given
go	went	gone
grind	ground	ground
grow	grew	grown
hang	hung, hanged	hung, hanged
have	had	had
hear	heard	heard
hide	hid	hidden
hit	hit	hit
hold	held	held
hurt	hurt	hurt
keep	kept	kept
kneel	knelt, kneeled	knelt, kneeled
know	knew	known
lay	laid	laid
lead	led	led
lean	leant, leaned	leant, leaned
leap	leapt, leaped	leapt, leaped

learn	learnt, learned	learnt, learned
leave	left	left
lend	lent	lent
let	let	let
lie	lay	lain
light	lit, lighted	lit, lighted
lose	lost	lost
make	made	made
mean	meant	meant
meet	met	met
mislay	mislaid	mislaid
mislead	misled	misled
misunderstand	misunderstood	misunderstood
mow	mowed	mown, mowed
overcome	overcame	overcome
pay	paid	paid
put	put	put
quit	quit, quitted	quit, quitted
read	read [red]	read [red]
rid	rid	rid
ride	rode	ridden
ring	rang	rung
rise	rose	risen
run	ran	run
saw	sawed	sawn, sawed
say	said	said
see	saw	seen
seek	sought	sought
sell	sold	sold
send	sent	sent
set	set	set
sew	sewed	sewn, sewed
shake	shook	shaken
shed	shed	shed
shine	shone ([ʃɒn, *Am* ʃəʊn])	shone ([ʃɒn, *Am* ʃəʊn])
shoot	shot	shot
show	showed	shown, showed
shrink	shrank	shrunk, shrunken
shut	shut	shut
sing	sang	sung
sink	sank	sunk
sit	sat	sat
sleep	slept	slept
slide	slid	slid
sling	slung	slung
slit	slit	slit
smell	smelt, smelled	smelt, smelled
sow	sowed	sown, sowed
speak	spoke	spoken
speed	sped, speeded	sped, speeded
spell	spelt, spelled	spelt, spelled
spend	spent	spent
spill	spilt, spilled	spilt, spilled
spin	spun	spun
spit	spat, spit	spat, spit
split	split	split
spoil	spoilt, spoiled	spoilt, spoiled

spread	spread	spread
spring	sprang	sprung
stand	stood	stood
steal	stole	stolen
stick	stuck	stuck
sting	stung	stung
stink	stank, stunk	stunk
stride	strode	stridden (*rare*)
strike	struck	struck
string	strung	strung
strive	strove	striven
swear	swore	sworn
sweep	swept	swept
swell	swelled	swollen, swelled
swim	swam	swum
swing	swung	swung
take	took	taken
teach	taught	taught
tear	tore	torn
tell	told	told
think	thought	thought
throw	threw	thrown
thrust	thrust	thrust
tread	trod	trodden
undergo	underwent	undergone
understand	understood	understood
undertake	undertook	undertaken
upset	upset	upset
wake	woke	woken
wear	wore	worn
weave	wove	woven
weep	wept	wept
win	won	won
wind	wound	wound
withdraw	withdrew	withdrawn
withhold	withheld	withheld
withstand	withstood	withstood
wring	wrung	wrung
write	wrote	written

Numerals

Les nombres

Cardinal numbers

Les nombres cardinaux

nought	0	zéro
one	1	un
two	2	deux
three	3	trois
four	4	quatre
five	5	cinq
six	6	six
seven	7	sept
eight	8	huit
nine	9	neuf
ten	10	dix

eleven	11	onze
twelve	12	douze
thirteen	13	treize
fourteen	14	quatorze
fifteen	15	quinze
sixteen	16	seize
seventeen	17	dix-sept
eighteen	18	dix-huit
nineteen	19	dix-neuf
twenty	20	vingt
twenty-one	21	vingt et un
twenty-two	22	vingt-deux
thirty	30	trente
forty	40	quarante
fifty	50	cinquante
sixty	60	soixante
seventy	70	soixante-dix
seventy-five	75	soixante-quinze
eighty	80	quatre-vingts
eighty-one	81	quatre-vingt-un
ninety	90	quatre-vingt-dix
ninety-one	91	quatre-vingt-onze
a *or* one hundred	100	cent
a hundred and one	101	cent un
a hundred and two	102	cent deux
a hundred and fifty	150	cent cinquante
two hundred	200	deux cents
two hundred and one	201	deux cent un
two hundred and two	202	deux cent deux
a *or* one thousand	1,000 (1 000)	mille
a thousand and one	1,001 (1 001)	mille un
a thousand and two	1,002 (1 002)	mille deux
two thousand	2,000 (2 000)	deux mille
a *or* one million	1,000,000 (1 000 000)	un million

Ordinal numbers

Les nombres ordinaux

first	1st	1er	premier
second	2nd	2e	deuxième
third	3rd	3e	troisième
fourth	4th	4e	quatrième
fifth	5th	5e	cinquième
sixth	6th	6e	sixième
seventh	7th	7e	septième
eighth	8th	8e	huitième
ninth	9th	9e	neuvième
tenth	10th	10e	dixième
eleventh	11th	11e	onzième
twelfth	12th	12e	douzième
thirteenth	13th	13e	treizième
fourteenth	14th	14e	quatorzième
fifteenth	15th	15e	quinzième
twentieth	20th	20e	vingtième
twenty-first	21st	21e	vingt et unième
twenty-second	22nd	22e	vingt deuxième
thirtieth	30th	30e	trentième

Examples of usage	**Exemples d'emplois**
three (times) out of ten	*trois (fois) sur dix*
ten at a time, in *or* by tens, ten by ten	*dix par dix, dix à dix*
the ten of us/you, we ten/you ten	*nous dix/vous dix*
all ten of them *or* us *or* you	*tous les dix, toutes les dix*
there are ten of us/them	*nous sommes dix/elles sont dix*
(between) the ten of them	*à eux dix, à elles dix*
ten of them came/were living together	*ils sont venus/ils vivaient à dix*
page ten	*page dix*
Charles the Tenth	*Charles Dix*
to live at number ten	*habiter au (numéro) dix*
to be the tenth to arrive/to leave	*arriver/partir le dixième*
to come tenth, be tenth *(in a race)*	*arriver dixième, être dixième*
it's the tenth (today)	*nous sommes le dix (aujourd'hui)*
the tenth of May, May the tenth, *Am* May tenth	*le dix mai*
to arrive/be paid/*etc* on the tenth	*arriver/être payé/etc le dix*
to arrive/be paid/*etc* on the tenth of May *or* on May	*arriver/être payé/etc le dix mai*
the tenth *or Am* on May tenth	
by the tenth, before the tenth	*avant le dix, pour le dix*
it's ten (o'clock)	*il est dix heures*
it's half past ten	*il est dix heures et demie*
ten past ten, *Am* ten after ten	*dix heures dix*
ten to ten	*dix heures moins dix*
by ten (o'clock), before ten (o'clock)	*pour dix heures, avant dix heures*
to be ten (years old)	*avoir dix ans*
a child of ten, a ten-year-old (child)	*un enfant de dix ans*

Days and months

Les jours et les mois

Monday *lundi*; Tuesday *mardi*; Wednesday *mercredi*; Thursday *jeudi*; Friday *vendredi*; Saturday *samedi*; Sunday *dimanche*

January *janvier*; February *février*; March *mars*; April *avril*; May *mai*; June *juin*; July *juillet*; August *août*; September *septembre*; October *octobre*; November *novembre*; December *décembre*

Examples of usage	**Exemples d'emplois**
on Monday (*e.g.* he arrives on Monday)	*lundi (par exemple il arrive lundi)*
(on) Mondays	*le lundi*
see you on Monday!	*à lundi!*
by Monday, before Monday	*avant lundi, pour lundi*
Monday morning/evening	*lundi matin/soir*
a week/two weeks on Monday. *Am* a	*lundi en huit/en quinze*
week/two weeks from Monday	
it's Monday (today)	*nous sommes (aujourd'hui) lundi*
Monday the tenth of May, Monday May the	*(le) lundi dix mai*
tenth. *Am* Monday May tenth	
on Monday the tenth of May, on Monday May	*le lundi dix mai*
the tenth *or Am* May tenth	
tomorrow is Tuesday	*demain c'est mardi*
in May	*en mai, au mois de mai*
every May, each May	*tous les ans en mai, chaque année en mai*
by May, before May	*avant mai, pour mai*

A

A, a [eɪ] *n* A, *a m*; **5A** (*number*) 5 bis; **A1** (*dinner etc*) *Fam* super, superbe; **to go from A to B** aller du point A au point B.

a [ə, *stressed* eɪ] (*before vowel or mute h* **an** [ən, *stressed* æn]) *indef art* **1** un, une; **a man** un homme; **an apple** une pomme. **2** (= *def art in Fr*) **six pence a kilo** six pence le kilo; **50 km an hour** 50 km à l'heure; **I have a broken arm** j'ai le bras cassé. **3** (*art omitted in Fr*) **he's a doctor** il est médecin; **Caen, a town in Normandy** Caen, ville de Normandie; **what a man!** quel homme! **4** (*a certain*) **a Mr Smith** un certain M. Smith. **5** (*time*) **twice a month** deux fois par mois. **6** (*some*) **to make a noise/a fuss** faire du bruit/des histoires.

aback [ə'bæk] *adv* **taken a.** déconcerté.

abandon [ə'bændən] **1** *vt* abandonner. **2** *n* (*freedom of manner*) laisser-aller *m*, abandon *m*. ◆—**ment** *n* abandon *m*.

abase [ə'beɪs] *vt* **to a. oneself** s'humilier, s'abaisser.

abashed [ə'bæʃt] *a* confus, gêné.

abate [ə'beɪt] *vi* (*of storm, pain*) se calmer; (*of flood*) baisser; *– vt* diminuer, réduire. ◆—**ment** *n* diminution *f*, réduction *f*.

abbey ['æbɪ] *n* abbaye *f*.

abbot ['æbət] *n* abbé *m*. ◆**abbess** *n* abbesse *f*.

abbreviate [ə'briːvɪeɪt] *vt* abréger. ◆**abbrevi'ation** *n* abréviation *f*.

abdicate ['æbdɪkeɪt] *vti* abdiquer. ◆**abdi'cation** *n* abdication *f*.

abdomen ['æbdəmən] *n* abdomen *m*. ◆**ab'dominal** *a* abdominal.

abduct [æb'dʌkt] *vt* *Jur* enlever. ◆**abduction** *n* enlèvement *m*, rapt *m*.

aberration [æbə'reɪʃ(ə)n] *n* (*folly, lapse*) aberration *f*.

abet [ə'bet] *vt* (-**tt**-) **to aid and a. s.o.** *Jur* être le complice de qn.

abeyance [ə'beɪəns] *n* **in a.** (*matter*) en suspens.

abhor [əb'hɔːr] *vt* (-**rr**-) avoir horreur de, exécrer. ◆**abhorrent** *a* exécrable. ◆**abhorrence** *n* horreur *f*.

abide [ə'baɪd] **1** *vi* **to a. by** (*promise etc*) rester fidèle à. **2** *vt* supporter; **I can't a. him** je ne peux pas le supporter.

ability [ə'bɪlɪtɪ] *n* capacité *f* (**to do** pour faire), aptitude *f* (**to do** à faire); **to the best of my a.** de mon mieux.

abject ['æbdʒekt] *a* abject; **a. poverty** la misère.

ablaze [ə'bleɪz] *a* en feu; **a. with** (*light*) resplendissant de; (*anger*) enflammé de.

able ['eɪb(ə)l] *a* (-**er**, -**est**) capable, compétent; **to be a. to do** être capable de faire, pouvoir faire; **to be a. to swim/drive** savoir nager/conduire. ◆**a.-'bodied** *a* robuste. ◆**ably** *adv* habilement.

ablutions [ə'bluːʃ(ə)nz] *npl* ablutions *fpl*.

abnormal [æb'nɔːm(ə)l] *a* anormal. ◆**abnor'mality** *n* anomalie *f*; (*of body*) difformité *f*. ◆**abnormally** *adv* *Fig* exceptionnellement.

aboard [ə'bɔːd] *adv* *Nau* à bord; **all a.** *Rail* en voiture; *– prep* **a. the ship** à bord du navire; **a. the train** dans le train.

abode [ə'bəʊd] *n* (*house*) *Lit* demeure *f*; *Jur* domicile *m*.

abolish [ə'bɒlɪʃ] *vt* supprimer, abolir. ◆**abo'lition** *n* suppression *f*, abolition *f*.

abominable [ə'bɒmɪnəb(ə)l] *a* abominable. ◆**abomi'nation** *n* abomination *f*.

aboriginal [æbə'rɪdʒən(ə)l] *a* & *n* aborigène (*m*). ◆**aborigines** *npl* aborigènes *mpl*.

abort [ə'bɔːt] *vt* *Med* faire avorter; (*space flight, computer program*) abandonner; *– vi* *Med* & *Fig* avorter. ◆**abortion** *n* avortement *m*; **to have an a.** se faire avorter. ◆**abortive** *a* (*plan etc*) manqué, avorté.

abound [ə'baʊnd] *vi* abonder (**in**, **with** en).

about [ə'baʊt] *adv* **1** (*approximately*) à peu près, environ; (**at**) **a. two o'clock** vers deux heures. **2** (*here and there*) çà et là, ici et là; (*ideas, flu*) *Fig* dans l'air; (*rumour*) en circulation; **to look a.** regarder autour; **to follow a.** suivre partout; **to bustle a.** s'affairer; **there are lots a.** il en existe beaucoup; (*out and*) **a.** (*after illness*) sur pied, guéri; (*up and*) **a.** (*out of bed*) levé; **to turn, a turn, a. face** *Mil* demi-tour *m*; *Fig* volte-face *f inv*; *– prep* **1** (*around*) **a. the garden** autour du jardin; **the streets** par *ou* dans les rues. **2** (*near to*) **a. here** par ici. **3** (*concerning*) au sujet de; **to talk a.** parler de; **a book a.** un livre sur; **what's it (all) a.?** de quoi s'agit-il?; **while you're a. it** pendant que vous y êtes; **what** or **how a. me?** et moi alors?; **what** or **how a. drink?** que dirais-tu de prendre un verre? **4** (+ *inf*) **a. to do** sur le point de faire; **I was a. to say** j'étais sur le point de dire, j'allais dire.

above [ə'bʌv] *adv* au-dessus; (*in book*) ci-dessus; **from a.** d'en haut; **floor a.** étage *m* supérieur ou du dessus; – *prep* au-dessus de; **a. all** par-dessus tout, surtout; **a. the bridge** (*on river*) en amont du pont; **he's a. me** (*in rank*) c'est mon supérieur; **a. lying** incapable de mentir; **a. asking** trop fier pour demander. ◆**a.-'mentioned** *a* susmentionné. ◆**aboveboard** *a* ouvert, honnête; – *adv* sans tricherie, cartes sur table.

abrasion [ə'breɪʒ(ə)n] *n* frottement *m*; *Med* écorchure *f*. ◆**abrasive** *a* (*substance*) abrasif; (*rough*) *Fig* rude, dur; (*irritating*) agaçant; – *n* abrasif *m*.

abreast [ə'brest] *adv* côte à côte, de front; **four a.** par rangs de quatre; **to keep a. of** or **with** se tenir au courant de.

abridge [ə'brɪdʒ] *vt* (*book etc*) abréger. ◆**abridg(e)ment** *n* abrégement *m* (**of** de); (*abridged version*) abrégé *m*.

abroad [ə'brɔːd] *adv* **1** (*in* or *to a foreign country*) à l'étranger; **from a.** de l'étranger. **2** (*over a wide area*) de tous côtés; **rumour a.** bruit *m* qui court.

abrogate ['æbrəgeɪt] *vt* abroger.

abrupt [ə'brʌpt] *a* (*sudden*) brusque; (*person*) brusque, abrupt; (*slope*, *style*) abrupt. ◆**–ly** *adv* (*suddenly*) brusquement; (*rudely*) avec brusquerie.

abscess ['æbses] *n* abcès *m*.

abscond [əb'skɒnd] *vi* *Jur* s'enfuir.

absence ['æbsəns] *n* absence *f*; **in the a. of** sth à défaut de qch, faute de qch; **a. of mind** distraction *f*.

absent ['æbsənt] *a* absent (**from** de); (*look*) distrait; – [æb'sent] *vt* **to a. oneself** s'absenter. ◆**a.-'minded** *a* distrait. ◆**a.-'mindedness** *n* distraction *f*. ◆**absen'tee** *n* absent, -ente *mf*. ◆**absen'teeism** *n* absentéisme *m*.

absolute ['æbsəluːt] *a* absolu; (*proof etc*) indiscutable; (*coward etc*) parfait, véritable. ◆**–ly** *adv* absolument; (*forbidden*) formellement.

absolve [əb'zɒlv] *vt* *Rel Jur* absoudre; **to a. from** (*vow*) libérer de. ◆**absolution** [æbsə'luːʃ(ə)n] *n* absolution *f*.

absorb [əb'zɔːb] *vt* absorber; (*shock*) amortir; **to become absorbed in** (*work*) s'absorber dans. ◆**–ing** *a* (*work*)

absorbant; (*book*, *film*) prenant. ◆**absorbent** *a* & *n* absorbant (*m*); **a. cotton** *Am* coton *m* hydrophile. ◆**absorber** *n* **shock a.** *Aut* amortisseur *m*. ◆**absorption** *n* absorption *f*.

abstain [əb'steɪn] *vi* s'abstenir (**from** de). ◆**abstemious** *a* sobre, frugal. ◆**abstention** *n* abstention *f*. ◆**'abstinence** *n* abstinence *f*.

abstract ['æbstrækt] **1** *a* & *n* abstrait (*m*). **2** *n* (*summary*) résumé *m*. **3** [əb'strækt] *vt* (*remove*) retirer; (*notion*) abstraire. ◆**ab'straction** *n* (*idea*) abstraction *f*; (*absent-mindedness*) distraction *f*.

abstruse [əb'struːs] *a* obscur.

absurd [əb'sɜːd] *a* absurde, ridicule. ◆**absurdity** *n* absurdité *f*. ◆**absurdly** *adv* absurdement.

abundant [ə'bʌndənt] *a* abondant. ◆**abundance** *n* abondance *f*. ◆**abundantly** *adv* **a. clear** tout à fait clair.

abuse [ə'bjuːs] *n* (*abusing*) abus *m* (**of** de); (*curses*) injures *fpl*; – [ə'bjuːz] *vt* (*misuse*) abuser de; (*malign*) dire du mal de; (*insult*) injurier. ◆**abusive** [ə'bjuːsɪv] *a* injurieux.

abysmal [ə'bɪzm(ə)l] *a* (*bad*) *Fam* désastreux, exécrable.

abyss [ə'bɪs] *n* abîme *m*.

acacia [ə'keɪʃə] *n* (*tree*) acacia *m*.

academic [ækə'demɪk] *a* universitaire; (*scholarly*) érudit, intellectuel; (*issue etc*) *Pej* théorique; (*style*, *art*) académique; – *n* (*teacher*) *Univ* universitaire *mf*.

academy [ə'kædəmɪ] *n* (*society*) académie *f*; *Mil Mus* école *f*. ◆**acade'mician** *n* académicien, -ienne *mf*.

accede [ək'siːd] *vi* **to a. to** (*request*, *throne*, *position*) accéder à.

accelerate [ək'seləreɪt] *vt* accélérer; – *vi* s'accélérer; *Aut* accélérer. ◆**acceleration** *n* accélération *f*. ◆**accelerator** *n* *Aut* accélérateur *m*.

accent ['æksənt] *n* accent *m*; – [æk'sent] *vt* accentuer. ◆**accentuate** [æk'sentjueɪt] *vt* accentuer.

accept [ək'sept] *vt* accepter. ◆**–ed** *a* (*opinion etc*) reçu, admis. ◆**acceptable** *a* (*worth accepting*, *tolerable*) acceptable. ◆**acceptance** *n* acceptation *f*; (*approval*, *favour*) accueil *m* favorable.

access ['ækses] *n* accès *m* (**to** sth à qch, **to** s.o. auprès de qn). ◆**ac'cessible** *a* accessible.

accession [æk'seʃ(ə)n] *n* accession *f* (**to** à); (*increase*) augmentation *f*; (*sth added*) nouvelle acquisition *f*.

accessory [əkˈsesərɪ] **1** n (person) Jur complice mf. **2** npl (objects) accessoires mpl.

accident [ˈæksɪdənt] n accident m; **by a.** (by chance) par accident; (unintentionally) accidentellement, sans le vouloir. ◆**a.-prone** a prédisposé aux accidents. ◆**acci'dental** a accidentel, fortuit. ◆**acci'dentally** adv accidentellement, par mégarde; (by chance) par accident.

acclaim [əˈkleɪm] vt acclamer; **to a. king** proclamer roi. ◆**accla'mation** n acclamation(s) f(pl), louange(s) f(pl).

acclimate [ˈæklɪmeɪt] vti Am = acclimatize. ◆**a'cclimatize** vt acclimater; – vi s'acclimater. ◆**accli'mation** n Am, ◆**acclimati'zation** n acclimatisation f.

accolade [ˈækəleɪd] n (praise) Fig louange f.

accommodat/e [əˈkɒmədeɪt] vt (of house) loger, recevoir; (have room for) avoir dela place pour (mettre); (adapt) adapter (to à); (supply) fournir (s.o. with sth qch à qn); (oblige) rendre service à; (reconcile) concilier; **to a. oneself to** s'accomoder à. ◆**—ing** a accommodant, obligeant. ◆**accommo'dation** n **1** (lodging) logement m; (rented room or rooms) chambre(s) f(pl); pl (in hotel) Am chambres f(pl). **2** (compromise) compromis m, accommodement m.

accompany [əˈkʌmpənɪ] vt accompagner. ◆**accompaniment** n accompagnement m. ◆**accompanist** n Mus accompagnateur, -trice mf.

accomplice [əˈkʌmplɪs] n complice mf.

accomplish [əˈkʌmplɪʃ] vt (task, duty) accomplir; (aim) réaliser. ◆**—ed** a accompli. ◆**—ment** n accomplissement m; (of aim) réalisation f; (thing achieved) réalisation f; pl (skills) talents mpl.

accord [əˈkɔːd] **1** n accord m; **of my own a.** volontairement, de mon plein gré; – vi concorder. **2** vt (grant) accorder. ◆**accordance** n in a. with conformément à.

according to [əˈkɔːdɪŋtuː] prep selon, d'après, suivant. ◆**accordingly** adv en conséquence.

accordion [əˈkɔːdɪən] n accordéon m.

accost [əˈkɒst] vt accoster, aborder.

account [əˈkaʊnt] n **1** Com compte m; pl comptabilité f, comptes mpl; **accounts department** comptabilité f; **to take into a.** tenir compte de; **ten pounds on a.** un acompte de dix livres; **of some a.** d'une certaine importance; **on a. of** à cause de; **on**

no a. en aucun cas. **2** n (report) compte rendu m, récit m; (explanation) explication f; **by all accounts** au dire de tous; **to give a good a. of oneself** s'en tirer à son avantage; – vi **to a. for** (explain) expliquer; (give reckoning of) rendre compte de. **3** vt **to a. oneself lucky/etc** (consider) se considérer heureux/etc. ◆**accountable** a responsable (**for, to** devant); (explainable) explicable.

accountant [əˈkaʊntənt] n comptable mf. ◆**accountancy** n comptabilité f.

accoutrements [əˈkuːtrəmənts] (Am **accouterments** [əˈkuːtəmənts]) npl équipement m.

accredit [əˈkredɪt] vt (ambassador) accréditer; **to a. s.o. with sth** attribuer qch à qn.

accrue [əˈkruː] vi (of interest) Fin s'accumuler; **to a. to** (of advantage etc) revenir à.

accumulate [əˈkjuːmjuleɪt] vt accumuler, amasser; – vi s'accumuler. ◆**accumu'lation** n accumulation f; (mass) amas m. ◆**accumulator** n El accumulateur m.

accurate [ˈækjurət] a exact, précis. ◆**accuracy** n exactitude f, précision f. ◆**accurately** adv avec précision.

accursed [əˈkɜːsɪd] a maudit, exécrable.

accus/e [əˈkjuːz] vt accuser (of de). ◆**—ed** n the a. Jur l'inculpé, -ée mf, l'accusé, -ée mf. ◆**—ing** a accusateur. ◆**accu'sation** n accusation f.

accustom [əˈkʌstəm] vt habituer, accoutumer. ◆**—ed** a habitué (**to sth** à qch, **to doing** à faire); **to get a. to** s'habituer à, s'accoutumer à.

ace [eɪs] n (card, person) as m.

acetate [ˈæsɪteɪt] n acétate m.

acetic [əˈsiːtɪk] a acétique.

ache [eɪk] n douleur f, mal m; **to have an a. in one's arm** avoir mal au bras; – vi faire mal; **my head aches** ma tête me fait mal; **it makes my heart a.** cela me serre le cœur; **to be aching to do** brûler de faire. ◆**aching** a douloureux.

achieve [əˈtʃiːv] vt accomplir, réaliser; (success, aim) atteindre; (victory) remporter. ◆**—ment** n accomplissement m, réalisation f (**of** de); (feat) réalisation f, exploit m.

acid [ˈæsɪd] a & n acide (m). ◆**a'cidity** n acidité f.

acknowledge [əkˈnɒlɪdʒ] vt reconnaître (as pour); (greeting) répondre à; **to a. (receipt of)** accuser réception de; **to a. defeat** s'avouer vaincu. ◆**—ment** n reconnaissance f; (of letter) accusé m de réception; (receipt) reçu m, récépissé m.

acme ['ækmɪ] n sommet m, comble m.

acne ['æknɪ] n acné f.

acorn ['eɪkɔːn] n Bot gland m.

acoustic [ə'kuːstɪk] a acoustique; – npl acoustique f.

acquaint [ə'kweɪnt] vt to a. s.o. with sth informer qn de qch; to be acquainted with (person) connaître; (fact) savoir; we are acquainted on se connaît. ◆**acquaintance** n (person, knowledge) connaissance f.

acquiesce [ækwɪ'es] vi acquiescer (in à). ◆**acquiescence** n acquiescement m.

acquire [ə'kwaɪər] vt acquérir; (taste) prendre (for à); (friends) se faire; **aquired taste** goût m qui s'acquiert. ◆**acqui'sition** n acquisition f. ◆**acquisitive** a avide, cupide.

acquit [ə'kwɪt] vt (-tt-) to a. s.o. (of a crime) acquitter qn. ◆**acquittal** n acquittement m.

acre ['eɪkər] n acre f (= 0,4 hectare). ◆**acreage** n superficie f.

acrid ['ækrɪd] a (smell, manner etc) âcre.

acrimonious [ækrɪ'məʊnɪəs] a acerbe.

acrobat ['ækrəbæt] n acrobate mf. ◆**acro-'batic** a acrobatique; – npl acrobatie(s) f(pl).

acronym ['ækrənɪm] n sigle m.

across [ə'krɒs] adv & prep (from side to side (of)) d'un côté à l'autre (de); (on the other side (of)) de l'autre côté (de); (crossways) en travers (de); to be a kilometre/etc a. (wide) avoir un kilomètre/etc de large; to walk or go a. (street etc) traverser; to come a. (person) rencontrer (par hasard), tomber sur; (thing) trouver (par hasard); to get sth a. to s.o. faire comprendre qch à qn.

acrostic [ə'krɒstɪk] n acrostiche m.

acrylic [ə'krɪlɪk] a & n acrylique (m).

act [ækt] 1 n (deed) acte m; a. (of parliament) loi f; caught in the a. pris sur le fait; a. of walking action f de marcher; an a. of folly une folie. 2 n (of play) Th acte m; (turn) Th numéro m; in on the a. Fam dans le coup; to put on an a. Fam jouer la comédie; – vt (part) Th jouer; to a. the fool faire l'idiot; – vi Th Cin jouer; (pretend) jouer la comédie. 3 vi (do sth, behave) agir; (function) fonctionner; to a. as (secretary etc) faire office de; (of object) servir de; to a. (up)on (affect) agir sur; (advice) suivre; to a. on behalf of représenter; to a. up (of person, machine) Fam faire des siennes. ◆**-ing** 1 a (manager etc) intérimaire, provisoire. 2 n (of play) représentation f; (actor's art) jeu m; (career) théâtre m.

action ['ækʃ(ə)n] n action f; Mil combat m; Jur procès m, action f; to take a. prendre des mesures; to put into a. (plan) exécuter; out of a. hors d'usage, hors (de) service; (person) hors de combat; killed in a. mort au champ d'honneur; to take industrial a. se mettre en grève.

active ['æktɪv] a actif; (interest) vif; (volcano) en activité. ◆**activate** vt Ch activer; (mechanism) actionner. ◆**activist** n activiste mf. ◆**ac'tivity** n activité f; (in street) mouvement m.

actor ['æktər] n acteur m. ◆**actress** n actrice f.

actual ['æktʃʊəl] a réel, véritable; (example) concret; the a. book le livre même; in a. fact en réalité, effectivement. ◆**-ly** adv (truly) réellement; (in fact) en réalité, en fait.

actuary ['æktʃʊərɪ] n actuaire mf.

actuate ['æktʃʊeɪt] vt (person) animer; (machine) actionner.

acumen ['ækjʊmen, Am ə'kjuːmən] n perspicacité f, finesse f.

acupuncture ['ækjʊpʌŋktʃər] n acupuncture f.

acute [ə'kjuːt] a aigu; (anxiety, emotion) vif, profond; (observer) perspicace; (shortage) grave. ◆**-ly** adv (to suffer, feel) vivement, profondément. ◆**-ness** n acuité f; perspicacité f.

ad [æd] n Fam pub f; (private, in newspaper) annonce f; small ad petite annonce.

AD [eɪ'diː] abbr (anno Domini) après Jésus-Christ.

adage ['ædɪdʒ] n adage m.

Adam ['ædəm] n A.'s apple pomme f d'Adam.

adamant ['ædəmənt] a inflexible.

adapt [ə'dæpt] vt adapter (to à); to a. (oneself) s'adapter. ◆**adaptable** a (person) capable de s'adapter, adaptable. ◆**adaptor** n (device) adaptateur m; (plug) prise f multiple. ◆**adap'tation** n adaptation f.

add [æd] vt ajouter (to à, that que); to a. (up or together) (total) additionner; to a. in inclure; – vi to a. to (increase) augmenter; to a. up to (total) s'élever à; (mean) signifier; it all adds up Fam ça s'explique. ◆**a'ddendum**, pl **-da** n supplément m. ◆**adding machine** n machine f à calculer. ◆**a'ddition** n addition f; augmentation f; in a. de plus; in a. to en plus de. ◆**a'dditional** a supplémentaire. ◆**a'dditionally** adv de plus. ◆**additive** n additif m.

adder ['ædər] n vipère f.

addict ['ædıkt] n intoxiqué, -ée mf; jazz/sport a. fanatique du jazz/du sport; drug a. drogué, -ée mf. ◆a'ddicted a to be a. to (study, drink) s'adonner à; (music) se passionner pour; (to have the habit of) avoir la manie de; a. to cigarettes drogué par la cigarette. ◆a'ddiction n (habit) manie f; (dependency) Med dépendance f; drug a. toxicomanie f. ◆a'ddictive a qui crée une dépendance.

address [ə'dres, Am 'ædres] n (on letter etc) adresse f; (speech) allocution f; form of a. formule f de politesse; – [ə'dres] vt (person) s'adresser à; (audience) parler devant; (words, speech) adresser (to à); (letter) mettre l'adresse sur; to a. to s.o. (send, intend for) adresser à qn. ◆addre'ssee [ædre'siː] n destinataire mf.

adenoids ['ædınɔıdz] npl végétations fpl (adénoïdes).

adept ['ædept, Am ə'dept] a expert (in, at à).

adequate ['ædıkwət] a (quantity) suffisant; (acceptable) convenable; (person, performance) compétent. ◆adequacy n (of person) compétence f; to doubt the a. of sth douter que qch soit suffisant. ◆adequately adv suffisamment; convenablement.

adhere [əd'hıər] vi to a. to adhérer à; (decision) s'en tenir à; (rule) respecter. ◆adherence n, ◆adhesion n (grip) adhérence f; (support) Fig adhésion f. ◆adhesive a & n adhésif (m).

ad infinitum [ædınfı'naıtəm] adv à l'infini.

adjacent [ə'dʒeısənt] a (house, angle etc) adjacent (to à).

adjective ['ædʒıktıv] n adjectif m.

adjoin [ə'dʒɔın] vt avoisiner. ◆—ing a avoisinant, voisin.

adjourn [ə'dʒɜːn] vt (postpone) ajourner; (session) lever, suspendre; – vi lever la séance; to a. to (go) passer à. ◆—ment n ajournement m; suspension f (de séance), levée f de séance.

adjudicate [ə'dʒuːdıkeıt] vti juger. ◆adjudi'cation n jugement m. ◆adjudicator n juge m, arbitre m.

adjust [ə'dʒʌst] vt Tech régler, ajuster; (prices) (r)ajuster; (arrange) arranger; to a. (oneself) to s'adapter à. ◆—able a réglable. ◆—ment n Tech réglage m; (of person) adaptation f; (of prices) (r)ajustement m.

ad-lib [æd'lıb] vi (-bb-) improviser; – a (joke etc) improvisé.

administer [əd'mınıstər] 1 vt (manage, dispense) administrer (to à). 2 vi to pourvoir à. ◆admini'stration n administration f; (ministry) gouvernement m. ◆administrative a administratif. ◆administrator n administrateur, -trice mf.

admiral ['ædmərəl] n amiral m.

admir/e [əd'maıər] vt admirer. ◆—ing a admiratif. ◆—er n admirateur, -trice mf. ◆'admirable a admirable. ◆admi'ration n admiration f.

admit [əd'mıt] vt (-tt-) (let in) laisser entrer; (accept) admettre; (acknowledge) reconnaître, avouer; – vi to a. to sth (confess) avouer qch; to a. of permettre. ◆admittedly adv c'est vrai (que). ◆admissible a admissible. ◆admission n (entry to theatre etc) entrée f (to à, de); (to club, school) admission f; (acknowledgement) aveu m; a. (charge) (prix m d')entrée f. ◆admittance n entrée f; 'no a.' 'entrée interdite'.

admonish [əd'mɒnıʃ] vt (reprove) réprimander; (warn) avertir.

ado [ə'duː] n without further a. sans (faire) plus de façons.

adolescent [ædə'lesənt] n adolescent, -ente mf. ◆adolescence n adolescence f.

adopt [ə'dɒpt] vt (child, method, attitude etc) adopter; (candidate) Pol choisir. ◆—ed a (child) adoptif; (country) d'adoption. ◆adoption n adoption f. ◆adoptive a (parent) adoptif.

adore [ə'dɔːr] vt adorer; he adores being flattered il adore qu'on le flatte. ◆adorable a adorable. ◆ado'ration n adoration f.

adorn [ə'dɔːn] vt (room, book) orner; (person, dress) parer. ◆—ment n ornement m; parure f.

adrenalin(e) [ə'drenəlın] n adrénaline f.

Adriatic [eıdrı'ætık] n the A. l'Adriatique f.

adrift [ə'drıft] a & adv Nau à la dérive; to come a. (of rope, collar etc) se détacher; to turn s.o. a. Fig abandonner qn à son sort.

adroit [ə'drɔıt] a adroit, habile.

adulation [ædju'leıʃ(ə)n] n adulation f.

adult ['ædʌlt] a & n adulte (mf). ◆adulthood n âge m adulte.

adulterate [ə'dʌltəreıt] vt (food) altérer.

adultery [ə'dʌltərı] n adultère m. ◆adulterous a adultère.

advanc/e [əd'vɑːns] n (movement, money) avance f; (of science) progrès mpl; pl (of friendship, love) avances fpl; in a. à l'avance, d'avance; in advance; in a. of s.o. avant qn; – a (payment) anticipé; a. booking réservation f; a. guard avant-garde f; – vt (put forward, lend) avancer; (science, work) faire avancer; — vi (go forward, progress) avancer; (towards s.o.) s'avancer, avancer. ◆—ed a avancé; (studies) supérieur; a. in years âgé. ◆—ement n (progress, promotion) avancement m.

advantage [əd'vɑːntɪdʒ] n avantage m (over sur); to take a. of profiter de; (person) tromper, exploiter; (woman) séduire; to show (off) to a. faire valoir. ◆advan'tageous a avantageux (to, pour), profitable.

advent ['ædvent] n arrivée f, avènement m; A. Rel l'Avent m.

adventure [əd'ventʃər] n aventure f; — a (film etc) d'aventures. ◆adventurer n aventurier, -ière mf. ◆adventurous a aventureux.

adverb ['ædvɜːb] n adverbe m.

adversary ['ædvəsəri] n adversaire mf.

adverse ['ædvɜːs] a hostile, défavorable. ◆ad'versity n adversité f.

advert ['ædvɜːt] n Fam pub f; (private, in newspaper) annonce f.

advertis/e ['ædvətaɪz] vt (goods) faire de la publicité pour; (make known) annoncer; — vi faire de la publicité; to a. (for s.o.) mettre une annonce (pour chercher qn). ◆—er n annonceur m. ◆—ement [əd'vɜːtɪsmənt, Am ædvə'taɪzmənt] n publicité f; (private or classified in newspaper) annonce f; (poster) affiche f; classified a. petite annonce; the advertisements TV la publicité.

advice [əd'vaɪs] n conseil(s) m(pl); Com avis m; a piece of a. un conseil.

advis/e [əd'vaɪz] vt (counsel) conseiller; (recommend) recommander; (notify) informer; to a. s.o. to do conseiller à qn de faire; to a. against déconseiller. ◆—ed a well-a. (action) prudent. ◆—able a (wise) prudent (to do de faire); (act) à conseiller. ◆—edly [-ɪdlɪ] adv après réflexion. ◆—er n conseiller, -ère mf. ◆advisory a consultatif.

advocate 1 ['ædvəkət] n (of cause) défenseur m, avocat, -ate mf; Jur avocat m. 2 ['ædvəkeɪt] vt préconiser, recommander.

aegis ['iːdʒɪs] n under the a. of sous l'égide de.

aeon ['iːən] n éternité f.

aerial ['eərɪəl] n antenne f; — a aérien.

aerobatics [eərə'bætɪks] npl acrobatie f aérienne. ◆ae'robics npl aérobic f. ◆'aerodrome n aérodrome f. ◆aero-'dynamic a aérodynamique. ◆aero'-nautics npl aéronautique f. ◆'aeroplane

n avion m. ◆'aerosol n aérosol m. ◆'aerospace a (industry) aérospatial.

aesthetic [iːs'θetɪk, Am es'θetɪk] a esthétique.

afar [ə'fɑːr] adv from a. de loin.

affable ['æfəb(ə)l] a affable, aimable.

affair [ə'feər] n (matter, concern) affaire f; (love) a. liaison f; state of affairs état m de choses.

affect [ə'fekt] vt (move, feign) affecter; (concern) toucher, affecter; (harm) nuire à; (be fond of) affectionner. ◆—ed a (manner) affecté; (by disease) atteint. ◆affec'tation n affectation f.

affection [ə'fekʃ(ə)n] n affection f (for pour). ◆affectionate a affectueux, aimant. ◆affectionately adv affectueusement.

affiliate [ə'fɪlɪeɪt] vt affilier; to be affiliated s'affilier (to à); affiliated company filiale f. ◆affili'ation n affiliation f; pl (political) attaches fpl.

affinity [ə'fɪnɪtɪ] n affinité f.

affirm [ə'fɜːm] vt affirmer. ◆affir'mation n affirmation f. ◆affirmative a affirmatif; — n affirmative f.

affix [ə'fɪks] vt apposer.

afflict [ə'flɪkt] vt affliger (with de). ◆afflic-tion n (misery) affliction f; (disorder) infirmité f.

affluent ['æfluənt] a riche; a. society société f d'abondance. ◆affluence n richesse f.

afford [ə'fɔːd] vt 1 (pay for) avoir les moyens d'acheter, pouvoir se payer; (time) pouvoir trouver; I can a. to wait je peux me permettre d'attendre. 2 (provide) fournir, donner; to a. s.o. sth fournir qch à qn.

affray [ə'freɪ] n Jur rixe f, bagarre f.

affront [ə'frʌnt] n affront m; — vt faire un affront à.

Afghanistan [æf'gænɪstæn] n Afghanistan m. ◆'Afghan a & n afghan, -ane (mf).

afield [ə'fiːld] adv further a. plus loin; too far a. trop loin.

afloat [ə'fləut] adv (ship, swimmer, business) à flot; (awash) submergé; life a. la vie sur l'eau.

afoot [ə'fut] adv there's sth a. il se trame qch; there's a plan a. to on prépare un projet pour.

aforementioned [ə'fɔːmenʃənd] a susmentionné.

afraid [ə'freɪd] a to be a. avoir peur (of, to de; that que); to make s.o. a. faire peur à qn; he's a. (that) she may be ill il a peur qu'elle (ne) soit malade; I'm a. he's out (I regret to say) je regrette, il est sorti.

afresh [ə'freʃ] adv de nouveau.

Africa ['æfrɪkə] n Afrique f. ◆**African** a & n africain, -aine (mf).

after ['ɑːftər] adv après; **the month** a. le mois suivant, le mois d'après; – prep après; a. **all** après tout; a. **eating** après avoir mangé; **day** a. **day** jour après jour; **page** a. **page** page sur page; **time** a. **time** bien des fois; a. **you!** je vous en prie!; **ten** a. **four** Am quatre heures dix; **to be** a. **sth/s.o.** (seek) chercher qch/qn; (want) vouloir; **he saw you** a. **he saw** après qu'il t'a vu. ◆**aftercare** n Med soins mpl postopératoires; Jur surveillance f. ◆**aftereffects** npl suites fpl, séquelles fpl. ◆**afterlife** n vie f future. ◆**aftermath** [-mɑːθ] n suites fpl. ◆**after'noon** n après-midi m or f inv; **in the** a. l'après-midi; **good** a.! (hello) bonjour!; (goodbye) au revoir! ◆**after'noons** adv Am l'après-midi. ◆**aftersales (service)** n service m après-vente. ◆**aftershave (lotion)** n lotion f après-rasage. ◆**aftertaste** n arrière-goût m. ◆**afterthought** n réflexion f après coup. ◆**afterward(s)** adv après, plus tard.

afters ['ɑːftəz] npl Fam dessert m.

again [ə'gen, ə'geɪn] adv de nouveau, encore une fois; (furthermore) en outre; **to do** a. refaire; **to go down/up** a. redescendre/remonter; **never** a. plus jamais; **half as much** a. moitié plus; a. **and** a., **time and (time)** a. maintes fois; **what's his name** a.? comment s'appelle-t-il déjà?

against [ə'genst, ə'geɪnst] prep contre; **to go** or **be** a. s'opposer à; a. **law** a. **drinking** une loi qui interdit de boire; **his age is** a. **him** son âge lui est défavorable; a. a **background of** sur (un) fond de; a. **the light** à contre-jour; a. **the law** illégal; a. **the rules** interdit, contraire aux règlements.

age [eɪdʒ] n (lifespan, period) âge m; (old) a. vieillesse f; **the Middle Ages** le moyen âge; **what** a. **are you?**, **what's your** a.? quel âge as-tu?; **five years of** a. âgé de cinq ans; **to be of** a. être majeur; **under** a. trop jeune, mineur; **to wait (for) ages** Fam attendre une éternité; a. **group** tranche f d'âge; – vti (pres p age(ing)) vieillir. ◆**a.-old** a séculaire. ◆**aged** a [eɪdʒd] a. **ten** âgé de dix ans; ['eɪdʒɪd] vieux, âgé; **the** a. les personnes fpl âgées. ◆**ageless** a toujours jeune.

agenda [ə'dʒendə] n ordre m du jour.

agent ['eɪdʒənt] n agent m; (dealer) Com concessionnaire mf. ◆**agency** n 1 (office) agence f. 2 **through the** a. **of s.o.** par l'intermédiaire de qn.

agglomeration [əglɒmə'reɪʃ(ə)n] n agglomération f.

aggravate ['ægrəveɪt] vt (make worse) aggraver; **to** a. **s.o.** Fam exaspérer qn. ◆**aggra'vation** n aggravation f; Fam exaspération f; (bother) Fam ennui(s) m(pl).

aggregate ['ægrɪgət] a global; – n (total) ensemble m.

aggression [ə'greʃ(ə)n] n agression f. ◆**aggressive** a agressif. ◆**aggressiveness** n agressivité f. ◆**aggressor** n agresseur m.

aggrieved [ə'griːvd] a (offended) blessé, froissé; (tone) peiné.

aghast [ə'gɑːst] a consterné, horrifié.

agile ['ædʒaɪl, Am 'ædʒ(ə)l] a agile. ◆**a'gility** n agilité f.

agitate ['ædʒɪteɪt] vt (worry, shake) agiter; – vi **to** a. **for** Pol faire campagne pour. ◆**agi'tation** n (anxiety, unrest) agitation f. ◆**agitator** n agitateur, -trice mf.

aglow [ə'gləʊ] a **to be** a. briller (with de).

agnostic [æg'nɒstɪk] a & n agnostique (mf).

ago [ə'gəʊ] adv a **year** a. il y a un an; **how long** a.? il y a combien de temps (de cela)?; **as long** a. **as 1800** (déjà) en 1800.

agog [ə'gɒg] a (excited) en émoi; (eager) impatient.

agony ['ægənɪ] n (pain) douleur f atroce; (anguish) angoisse f; **to be in** a. souffrir horriblement; a. **column** Journ courrier m du cœur. ◆**agonize** vi se faire beaucoup de souci. ◆**agonized** a (look) angoissé; (cry) de douleur. ◆**agonizing** a (pain) atroce; (situation) angoissant.

agree [ə'griː] vi (come to terms) se mettre d'accord, s'accorder; (be in agreement) être d'accord, s'accorder (with avec); (of facts, dates etc) concorder; Gram s'accorder; a. **upon** (decide) convenir de; **to** a. **to sth/to doing** consentir à qch/à faire; **it doesn't** a. **with me** (food, climate) ça ne me réussit pas; – vt (figures) faire concorder; (accounts) Com approuver; **to** a. **to do** accepter de faire; **to** a. **that** (admit) admettre que. ◆**agreed** a (time, place) convenu; **we are** a. nous sommes d'accord; a.! entendu! ◆**agreeable** a 1 (pleasant) agréable. 2 **to be** a. (agree) être d'accord; **to be** a. **to sth** consentir à qch. ◆**agreement** n accord m; Pol Com convention f, accord m; **in** a. **with** d'accord avec.

agriculture ['ægrɪkʌltʃər] n agriculture f. ◆**agri'cultural** a agricole.

aground [ə'graʊnd] adv **to run** a. Nau (s')échouer.

ah! [ɑː] *int* ah!

ahead [ə'hed] *adv* (*in space*) en avant; (*leading*) en tête; (*in the future*) dans l'avenir; **a.** (*of time or of schedule*) en avance (sur l'horaire); **one hour/etc** a. une heure/*etc* d'avance (of sur); **a.** of (*space*) devant; (*time, progress*) en avance sur; **to go a.** (*advance*) avancer; (*continue*) continuer; (*start*) commencer; **go a.!** allez-y!; **to go a. with** (*task*) poursuivre; **to get a.** prendre de l'avance; (*succeed*) réussir; **to think a.** penser à l'avenir; **straight a.** tout droit.

aid [eɪd] *n* (*help*) aide *f*; (*apparatus*) support *m*, moyen *m*; **with the a. of** (*a stick etc*) à l'aide de; **in a. of** (*charity etc*) au profit de; **what's this in a. of?** *Fam* quel est le but de tout ça?, ça sert à quoi?; – *vt* aider (**to do** à faire).

aide [eɪd] *n Pol* aide *m*f.

AIDS [eɪdz] *n Med* SIDA *m*.

ail [eɪl] *vt* **what ails you?** de quoi souffrez-vous? ◆**—ing** *a* souffrant, malade. ◆**—ment** maladie *f*.

aim [eɪm] *n* but *m*; **to take a.** viser; **with the a. of** dans le but de; – *vt* (*gun*) braquer, diriger (**at** sur); (*lamp*) diriger (**at** vers); (*stone*) lancer (**at** à, vers); (*blow, remark*) décocher (**at** à); – *vi* viser; **to a.** at s.o. viser qn; **to a. to do** *or* **at doing** avoir l'intention de faire. ◆**—less** *a*, ◆**—lessly** *adv* sans but.

air [eər] **1** *n* air *m*; **in the open a.** en plein air; **by a.** (*to travel*) en or par avion; (*letter, freight*) par avion; **to be** *or* **go on the a.** (*person*) passer à l'antenne; (*programme*) être diffusé; (**up**) **in the a.** (*to throw*) en l'air; (*plan*) incertain, en l'air; **there's sth in the a.** *Fig* il se prépare qch; – *a* (*raid, base etc*) aérien; **a. force/hostess** armée *f*/hôtesse *f* de l'air; **a. terminal** aérogare *f*; – *vt* (*room*) aérer; (*views*) exposer; **airing cupboard** armoire *f* sèche-linge. **2** *n* (*appearance, tune*) air *m*; **to put on airs** se donner des airs; **with an a. of sadness/etc** d'un air triste/*etc*.

airborne ['eəbɔːn] *a* en (cours de) vol; (*troops*) aéroporté; **to become a.** (*of aircraft*) décoller. ◆**airbridge** *n* pont *m* aérien. ◆**air-conditioned** *a* climatisé. ◆**air-conditioner** *n* climatiseur *m*. ◆**aircraft** *n inv* avion(s) *m*(*pl*); **a. carrier** porte-avions *m inv*. ◆**aircrew** *n* Av équipage *m*. ◆**airfield** *n* terrain *m* d'aviation. ◆**airgun** *n* carabine *f* à air comprimé. ◆**airletter** *n* aérogramme *m*. ◆**airlift** *n* pont *m* aérien; – *vt* transporter par avion. ◆**airline** *n* ligne *f* aérienne. ◆**airliner** *n*

avion *m* de ligne. ◆**airlock** *n* (*chamber*) *Nau Av* sas *m*; (*in pipe*) bouchon *m*. ◆**airmail** *n* poste *f* aérienne; **by a.** par avion. ◆**airman** *n* (*pl* **-men**) aviateur *m*. ◆**airplane** *n Am* avion *m*. ◆**airpocket** *n* trou *m* d'air. ◆**airport** *n* aéroport *m*. ◆**airship** *n* dirigeable *m*. ◆**airsickness** *n* mal *m* de l'air. ◆**airstrip** *n* terrain *m* d'atterrissage. ◆**airtight** *a* hermétique. ◆**airway** *n* (*route*) couloir *m* aérien. ◆**airworthy** *a* en état de navigation.

airy ['eərɪ] *a* (**-ier, -iest**) (*room*) bien aéré; (*promise*) vain; (*step*) léger. ◆**a.-fairy** *a* *Fam* farfelu. ◆**airily** *adv* (*not seriously*) d'un ton léger.

aisle [aɪl] *n* couloir *m*; (*of church*) nef *f* latérale.

aitch [eɪtʃ] *n* (*letter*) h *m*.

ajar [ə'dʒɑːr] *a & adv* (*door*) entrouvert.

akin [ə'kɪn] *a* **a.** (**to**) apparenté (à).

alabaster ['æləbɑːstər] *n* albâtre *m*.

alacrity [ə'lækrɪtɪ] *n* empressement *m*.

à la mode [ælæ'məʊd] *a Culin Am* avec de la crème glacée.

alarm [ə'lɑːm] *n* (*warning, fear*) alarme *f*; (*apparatus*) sonnerie *f* (d'alarme); **false a.** fausse alerte *f*; **a.** (*clock*) réveil *m*, réveille-matin *m inv*; – *vt* (*frighten*) alarmer. ◆**alarmist** *n* alarmiste *m*.

alas [ə'læs] *int* hélas!

albatross ['ælbətrɒs] *n* albatros *m*.

albeit [ɔːl'biːt] *conj Lit* quoique.

albino [æl'biːnəʊ, *Am* æl'baɪnəʊ] *n* (*pl* **-os**) albinos *m*f.

album ['ælbəm] *n* (*book, record*) album *m*.

alchemy ['ælkəmɪ] *n* alchimie *f*. ◆**alchemist** *n* alchimiste *m*.

alcohol ['ælkəhɒl] *n* alcool *m*. ◆**alco'holic** *a* (*person*) alcoolique; (*drink*) alcoolisé; – *n* (*person*) alcoolique *m*f. ◆**alcoholism** *n* alcoolisme *m*.

alcove ['ælkəʊv] *n* alcôve *f*.

alderman ['ɔːldəmən] *n* (*pl* **-men**) conseiller, -ère *m*f municipal(e).

ale [eɪl] *n* bière *f*.

alert [ə'lɜːt] *a* (*watchful*) vigilant; (*sharp, awake*) éveillé; – *n* alerte *f*; **on the a.** sur le qui-vive; – *vt* alerter. ◆**—ness** *n* vigilance *f*.

alfalfa [æl'fælfə] *n Am* luzerne *f*.

algebra ['ældʒɪbrə] *n* algèbre *f*. ◆**alge'braic** *a* algébrique.

Algeria [æl'dʒɪərɪə] *n* Algérie *f*. ◆**Algerian** *a & n* algérien, -ienne (*m*f).

alias ['eɪlɪəs] *adv* alias; – *n* nom *m* d'emprunt.

alibi ['ælɪbaɪ] *n* alibi *m*.

alien ['eɪlɪən] a étranger (**to** à); − n étranger, -ère mf. ◆**alienate** vt aliéner; **to a. s.o.** (make unfriendly) s'aliéner qn.

alight [ə'laɪt] **1** a (a fire) allumé; (face) éclairé; **to set a.** mettre le feu à. **2** vi descendre (**from** de); (of bird) se poser.

align [ə'laɪn] vt aligner. ◆**—ment** n alignement m.

alike [ə'laɪk] **1** a (people, things) semblables, pareils; **to look** or **be a.** se ressembler. **2** adv de la même manière; **summer and winter a.** été comme hiver.

alimony ['ælɪmənɪ, Am 'ælɪməʊnɪ] n Jur pension f alimentaire.

alive [ə'laɪv] a vivant, en vie; **a.** conscient de; **a. with** grouillant de; **burnt a.** brûlé vif; **anyone a.** n'importe qui; **to keep a.** (custom, memory) entretenir, perpétuer; **a. and kicking** Fam plein de vie; **look a.!** Fam active-toi!

all [ɔːl] a tout, toute, pl tous, toutes; **a. day** toute la journée; **a. (the) men** tous les hommes; **with a. speed** à toute vitesse; **for a. her wealth** malgré toute sa fortune; − pron tous mpl, toutes fpl; (everything) tout; **a. will die** tous mourront; **my sisters are here** toutes mes sœurs sont ici; **he ate it a.**, **he ate a. of it** il a tout mangé; **a. (that) he has** tout ce qu'il a; **a. in a.** à tout prendre; **in a.**, **a. told** en tout; **a. but impossible**/etc presque impossible/etc; **anything at a.** quoi que ce soit; **if he comes at a.** s'il vient effectivement; **if there's any wind at a.** s'il y a le moindre vent; **not at a.** pas du tout; (after 'thank you') il n'y a pas de quoi; **a. of us** nous tous; **take a. of it** prends (le) tout; − adv tout; **a. alone** tout seul; **a. bad** entièrement mauvais; **a. over** (everywhere) partout; (finished) fini; **a. right** (très) bien; **he's a. right** (not harmed) il est sain et sauf; (healthy) il va bien; **a. too soon** bien trop tôt; **six a.** Fb six buts partout; **a. there** Fam éveillé, intelligent; **not a. there** Fam simple d'esprit. **a. in** Fam épuisé; **a.-in price** prix global; − n my a. tout ce que j'ai. ◆**a.-'clear** n Mil fin f d'alerte. ◆**a.-night** a (party) qui dure toute la nuit; (shop) ouvert toute la nuit. ◆**a.-out** a (effort) violent; (war, strike) tous azimuts. ◆**a.-'powerful** a tout-puissant. ◆**a.-purpose** a (tool) universel. ◆**a.-round** a complet. ◆**a.-'rounder** n personne f qui fait de tout. ◆**a.-time** a (record) jamais atteint; **to reach an a.-time low/high** arriver au point le plus bas/le plus haut.

allay [ə'leɪ] vt calmer, apaiser.

alleg/e [ə'ledʒ] vt prétendre. ◆**—ed** a

(so-called) prétendu; (author, culprit) présumé; **he is a. to be** on prétend qu'il est. ◆**—edly** [-ɪdlɪ] adv d'après ce qu'on dit. ◆**alle'gation** n allégation f.

allegiance [ə'liːdʒəns] n fidélité f (**to** à).

allegory ['ælɪgərɪ, Am 'æləgɔːrɪ] n allégorie f. ◆**alle'gorical** a allégorique.

allergy ['ælədʒɪ] n allergie f. ◆**a'llergic** a allergique (**to** à).

alleviate [ə'liːvɪeɪt] vt alléger.

alley ['ælɪ] n ruelle f; (in park) allée f; **blind a.** impasse f; **that's up my a.** Fam c'est mon truc. ◆**alleyway** n ruelle f.

alliance [ə'laɪəns] n alliance f.

allied ['ælaɪd] a (country) allié; (matters) connexe.

alligator ['ælɪgeɪtər] n alligator m.

allocate ['æləkeɪt] vt (assign) attribuer, allouer (**to** à); (distribute) répartir. ◆**allo-'cation** n attribution f.

allot [ə'lɒt] vt (-tt-) (assign) attribuer; (distribute) répartir. ◆**—ment** n attribution f; (share) partage m; (land) lopin m de terre (loué pour la culture).

allow [ə'laʊ] **1** vt permettre; (grant) accorder; (a request) accéder à; (deduct) Com déduire; (add) Com ajouter; **to a. s.o. to do** permettre à qn de faire, autoriser qn à faire; **a. me!** permettez(-moi)!; **not allowed** interdit; **you're not allowed to go** on vous interdit de partir. **2** vi **to a. for** tenir compte de. ◆**—able** a (acceptable) admissible; (expense) déductible.

allowance [ə'laʊəns] n allocation f; (for travel, housing, food) indemnité f; (for duty-free goods) tolérance f; (tax-free amount) abattement m; **to make allowance(s) for** (person) être indulgent envers; (thing) tenir compte de.

alloy ['ælɔɪ] n alliage m.

allude [ə'luːd] vi **to a. to** faire allusion à. ◆**allusion** n allusion f.

allure [ə'lʊər] vt attirer.

ally ['ælaɪ] n allié, -ée mf; − [ə'laɪ] vt (country, person) allier.

almanac ['ɔːlmənæk] n almanach m.

almighty [ɔːl'maɪtɪ] **1** a tout-puissant; **the A.** le Tout-Puissant. **2** a (great) Fam terrible, formidable.

almond ['ɑːmənd] n amande f.

almost ['ɔːlməʊst] adv presque; **he a.** fell/etc il a failli tomber/etc.

alms [ɑːmz] npl aumône f.

alone [ə'ləʊn] a & adv seul; **an expert a. can . . .** seul un expert peut . . . ; **I did it (all) a.** je l'ai fait à moi (tout) seul, je l'ai fait (tout) seul; **to leave** or **let a.** (*person*) laisser tranquille or en paix; (*thing*) ne pas toucher à.

along [ə'lɒŋ] *prep* (**all**) **a.** (tout) le long de; **to go** or **walk a.** (*street*) passer par; **a. here** par ici; **a. with** avec; – *adv* **all a.** d'un bout à l'autre; (*time*) dès le début; **come a.!** venez!; **move a.!** avancez!

alongside [əlɒŋ'saɪd] *prep* & *adv* à côté (de); **to come a.** *Nau* accoster; **a. the kerb** le long du trottoir.

aloof [ə'luːf] *a* distant; – *adv* à distance; **to keep a.** garder ses distances (**from** par rapport à). ◆**—ness** *n* réserve f.

aloud [ə'laud] *adv* à haute voix.

alphabet ['ælfəbet] *n* alphabet *m*. ◆**alpha-'betical** *a* alphabétique.

Alps [ælps] *npl* **the A.** les Alpes *fpl*. ◆**alpine** *a* (*club*, *range* etc) alpin; (*scenery*) alpestre.

already [ɔːl'redɪ] *adv* déjà.

alright [ɔːl'raɪt] *adv* *Fam* = **all right.**

Alsatian [æl'seɪʃ(ə)n] *n* (*dog*) berger *m* allemand, chien-loup *m*.

also ['ɔːlsəu] *adv* aussi, également. ◆**a.-ran** *n* (*person*) *Fig* perdant, -ante *mf*.

altar ['ɔːltər] *n* autel *m*.

alter ['ɔːltər] *vt* changer, modifier; (*clothing*) retoucher; – *vi* changer. ◆**alte'ration** *n* changement *m*, modification *f*; retouche *f*.

altercation [ɔːltə'keɪʃ(ə)n] *n* altercation *f*.

alternat/e [ɔːl'tɜːnət] *a* alterné; **on a. days** tous les deux jours; **a. laughter and tears** des rires et des larmes qui se succèdent; – [ɔːltəneɪt] *vi* alterner (**with** avec); – *vt* faire alterner. ◆**—ing** *a* (*current*) *El* alternatif. ◆**—ely** *adv* alternativement. ◆**alter-'nation** *n* alternance *f*.

alternative [ɔːl'tɜːnətɪv] *a* **an a. way**/etc une autre façon/etc; **a. answers**/etc d'autres réponses/etc (différentes); – *n* (*choice*) alternative *f*. ◆**—ly** *adv* comme alternative; **or a.** (*or else*) ou bien.

although [ɔːl'ðəu] *adv* bien que, quoique (+ *sub*).

altitude ['æltɪtjuːd] *n* altitude *f*.

altogether [ɔːltə'geðər] *adv* (*completely*) tout à fait; (*on the whole*) somme toute; **how much a.?** combien en tout?

aluminium [ælju'mɪnjəm] (*Am* **aluminum** [ə'luːmɪnəm]) *n* aluminium *m*.

alumnus, *pl* **-ni** [ə'lʌmnəs, -naɪ] *n* *Am* ancien(ne) élève *mf*, ancien(ne) étudiant, -ante *mf*.

always ['ɔːlweɪz] *adv* toujours; **he's a. criticizing** il est toujours à critiquer.

am [æm, *unstressed* əm] *see* **be.**

a.m. [eɪ'em] *adv* du matin.

amalgam [ə'mælgəm] *n* amalgame *m*. ◆**a'malgamate** *vt* amalgamer; (*society*) *Com* fusionner; – *vi* s'amalgamer; fusionner.

amass [ə'mæs] *vt* (*riches*) amasser.

amateur ['æmətər] *n* amateur *m*; – *a* (*interest*, *sports*) d'amateur; **a. painter**/etc peintre/etc amateur. ◆**amateurish** *a* (*work*) *Pej* d'amateur; (*person*) *Pej* maladroit, malhabile. ◆**amateurism** *n* amateurisme *m*.

amaz/e [ə'meɪz] *vt* stupéfier, étonner. ◆**—ed** *a* stupéfait (**at sth de** qch), étonné (**at sth** par or **de** qch); **a. at seeing**/etc stupéfait or étonné de voir/etc. ◆**—ing** *a* stupéfiant; *Fam* extraordinaire. ◆**—ingly** *adv* extraordinairement; (*miraculously*) par miracle. ◆**amazement** *n* stupéfaction *f*.

ambassador [æm'bæsədər] *n* ambassadeur *m*; (*woman*) ambassadrice *f*.

amber ['æmbər] *n* ambre *m*; **a. (light)** *Aut* (feu *m*) orange *m*.

ambidextrous [æmbɪ'dekstrəs] *a* ambidextre.

ambiguous [æm'bɪgjuəs] *a* ambigu. ◆**ambi'guity** *n* ambiguïté *f*.

ambition [æm'bɪʃ(ə)n] *n* ambition *f*. ◆**ambitious** *a* ambitieux.

ambivalent [æm'bɪvələnt] *a* ambigu, équivoque.

amble ['æmb(ə)l] *vi* marcher d'un pas tranquille.

ambulance ['æmbjuləns] *n* ambulance *f*; **a. man** ambulancier *m*.

ambush ['æmbuʃ] *n* guet-apens *m*, embuscade *f*; – *vt* prendre en embuscade.

amen [ɑː'men, eɪ'men] *int* amen.

amenable [ə'miːnəb(ə)l] *a* docile; **a. to** (*responsive to*) sensible à; **a. to reason** raisonnable.

amend [ə'mend] *vt* (*text*) modifier; (*conduct*) corriger; *Pol* amender. ◆**—ment** *n* *Pol* amendement *m*.

amends [ə'mendz] *npl* **to make a. for** réparer; **to make a.** réparer son erreur.

amenities [ə'miːnɪtɪz, *Am* ə'menɪtɪz] *npl* (*pleasant things*) agréments *mpl*; (*of sports club* etc) équipement *m*; (*of town*) aménagements *mpl*.

America [ə'merɪkə] *n* Amérique *f*; **North/South A.** Amérique du Nord/du Sud. ◆**American** *a* & *n* américain, -aine (*mf*). ◆**Americanism** *n* américanisme *m*.

amethyst ['æməθɪst] *n* améthyste *f*.

amiable ['eɪmɪəb(ə)l] *a* aimable.

amicab/le ['æmɪkəb(ə)l] *a* amical. ◆**—ly** *adv* amicalement; *Jur* à l'amiable.

amid(st) [ə'mɪd(st)] *prep* au milieu de, parmi.

amiss [ə'mɪs] *adv* & *a* mal (à propos); **sth is a.** (*wrong*) qch ne va pas; **that wouldn't come a.** ça ne ferait pas de mal; **to take a.** prendre en mauvaise part.

ammonia [ə'məʊnjə] *n* (*gas*) ammoniac *m*; (*liquid*) ammoniaque *f*.

ammunition [æmjʊ'nɪʃ(ə)n] *n* munitions *fpl*.

amnesia [æm'niːzjə] *n* amnésie *f*.

amnesty [æmnəstɪ] *n* amnistie *f*.

amok [ə'mɒk] *adv* **to run a.** se déchaîner, s'emballer.

among(st) [ə'mʌŋ(st)] *prep* parmi, entre; **a. themselves/friends** entre eux/amis; **a. the French**/*etc* (*group*) chez les Français/*etc*; **a. the crowd** dans *or* parmi la foule.

amoral [eɪ'mɒrəl] *a* amoral.

amorous [æmərəs] *a* amoureux.

amount [ə'maʊnt] **1** *n* quantité *f*; (*sum of money*) somme *f*; (*total of bill etc*) montant *m*; (*scope, size*) importance *f*. **2** *vi* **to a.** to s'élever à; (*mean*) Fig signifier; **it amounts to the same thing** ça revient au même.

amp(ere) [æmp(eər)] *n El* ampère *m*.

amphibian [æm'fɪbɪən] *n* & *a* amphibie (*m*). ◆**amphibious** *a* amphibie.

amphitheatre [æmfɪθɪətər] *n* amphithéâtre *m*.

ample [æmp(ə)l] *a* (*roomy*) ample; (*enough*) largement assez de; (*reasons, means*) solides; **you have a. time** tu as largement le temps. ◆**amply** *adv* largement, amplement.

amplify [æmplɪfaɪ] *vt* amplifier. ◆**amplifier** *n El* amplificateur *m*.

amputate [æmpjʊteɪt] *vt* amputer. ◆**ampu'tation** *n* amputation *f*.

amuck [ə'mʌk] *adv* see amok.

amulet [æmjʊlət] *n* amulette *f*.

amus/e [ə'mjuːz] *vt* amuser, divertir; **to keep s.o. amused** amuser qn. ◆**—ing** *a* amusant. ◆**—ement** *n* amusement *m*, divertissement *m*; (*pastime*) distraction *f*; **a. arcade** salle *f* de jeux.

an [æn, *unstressed* ən] see **a**.

anachronism [ə'nækrənɪz(ə)m] *n* anachronisme *m*.

an(a)emia [ə'niːmɪə] *n* anémie *f*. ◆**an(a)emic** *a* anémique.

an(a)esthesia [ænɪs'θiːzɪə] *n* anesthésie *f*. ◆**an(a)esthetic** [ænɪs'θetɪk] *n* (*substance*) anesthésique *m*; **under the a.** sous anesthésie; **general/local a.** anesthésie *f* générale/locale. ◆**an(a)esthetize** [ə'niːsθɪtaɪz] *vt* anesthésier.

anagram [ænəgræm] *n* anagramme *f*.

analogy [ə'nælədʒɪ] *n* analogie *f*. ◆**analogous** *a* analogue (**to** à).

analyse [ænəlaɪz] *vt* analyser. ◆**analysis**, *pl* **-yses** [ə'næləsɪs, -ɪsɪz] *n* analyse *f*. ◆**analyst** *n* analyste *mf*. ◆**ana'lytical** *a* analytique.

anarchy [ænəkɪ] *n* anarchie *f*. ◆**a'narchic** *a* anarchique. ◆**anarchist** *n* anarchiste *mf*.

anathema [ə'næθəmə] *n Rel* anathème *m*; **it is (an) a. to me** j'ai une sainte horreur de cela.

anatomy [ə'nætəmɪ] *n* anatomie *f*. ◆**ana'tomical** *a* anatomique.

ancestor [ænsestər] *n* ancêtre *m*. ◆**an'cestral** *a* ancestral. ◆**ancestry** *n* (*lineage*) ascendance *f*; (*ancestors*) ancêtres *mpl*.

anchor [æŋkər] *n* ancre *f*; **to weigh a.** lever l'ancre; – *vt* (*ship*) mettre à l'ancre; – *vi* jeter l'ancre, mouiller. ◆**—age** *n* mouillage *m*.

anchovy [ænʧəvɪ, *Am* æn'ʧəʊvɪ] *n* anchois *m*.

ancient [eɪnʃənt] *a* ancien; (*pre-medieval*) antique; (*person*) Hum vétuste.

ancillary [æn'sɪlərɪ] *a* auxiliaire.

and [ænd, *unstressed* ən(d)] *conj* et; **a knife a. fork** un couteau et une fourchette; **two hundred a. two** deux cent deux; **better a. better** de mieux en mieux; **go a. see** va voir.

anecdote [ænɪkdəʊt] *n* anecdote *f*.

anemone [ə'nemənɪ] *n* anémone *f*.

anew [ə'njuː] *adv* Lit de *or* à nouveau.

angel [eɪndʒəl] *n* ange *m*. ◆**an'gelic** *a* angélique.

anger [æŋgər] *n* colère *f*; **in a., out of a.** sous le coup de la colère; – *vt* mettre en colère, fâcher.

angl/e [æŋg(ə)l] **1** *n* angle *m*; **at an a.** en biais. **2** *vi* (*to fish*) pêcher à la ligne; **to a. for** *Fig* quêter. ◆**—er** *n* pêcheur, -euse *mf* à la ligne. ◆**—ing** *n* pêche *f* à la ligne.

Anglican [æŋglɪkən] *a* & *n* anglican, -ane (*mf*).

anglicism [æŋglɪsɪz(ə)m] *n* anglicisme *m*. **Anglo-** [æŋgləʊ] *pref* anglo-. ◆**Anglo-'Saxon** *a* & *n* anglo-saxon, -onne (*mf*).

angora [æŋ'gɔːrə] *n* (*wool*) angora *m*.

angry [æŋgrɪ] *a* (**-ier, -iest**) (*person, look*) fâché; (*letter*) indigné; **to get a.** se fâcher, se mettre en colère (**with** contre). ◆**angrily** *adv* en colère; (*to speak*) avec colère.

anguish [æŋgwɪʃ] *n* angoisse *f*. ◆**—ed** *a* angoissé.

angular [æŋgjʊlər] *a* (*face*) anguleux.

animal ['ænɪməl] *a* animal; − *n* animal *m*, bête *f*.

animate ['ænɪmeɪt] *vt* animer; **to become animated** s'animer; − ['ænɪmət] *a* (*alive*) animé. ◆**ani'mation** *n* animation *f*.

animosity [ænɪ'mɒsɪtɪ] *n* animosité *f*.

aniseed ['ænɪsiːd] *n* Culin anis *m*.

ankle ['æŋk(ə)l] *n* cheville *f*; **a. sock** socquette *f*.

annals ['æn(ə)lz] *npl* annales *fpl*.

annex [ə'neks] *vt* annexer.

annex(e) ['æneks] *n* (*building*) annexe *f*. ◆**annex'ation** *n* annexion *f*.

annihilate [ə'naɪəleɪt] *vt* anéantir, annihiler. ◆**annihi'lation** *n* anéantissement *m*.

anniversary [ænɪ'vɜːsərɪ] *n* (*of event*) anniversaire *m*, commémoration *f*.

annotate ['ænəteɪt] *vt* annoter. ◆**anno'tation** *n* annotation *f*.

announc/e [ə'naʊns] *vt* annoncer; (*birth, marriage*) faire part de. ◆**−ement** *n* annonce *f*; (*of birth, marriage*) avis *m*; (*private letter*) faire-part *m inv*. ◆**−er** *n* TV speaker *m*, speakerine *f*.

annoy [ə'nɔɪ] *vt* (*inconvenience*) ennuyer, gêner; (*irritate*) agacer, contrarier. ◆**−ed** *a* contrarié, fâché; **to get a.** se fâcher (**with** contre). ◆**−ing** *a* ennuyeux, contrariant. ◆**annoyance** *n* contrariété *f*, ennui *m*.

annual ['ænjʊəl] *a* annuel; − *n* (*book*) annuaire *m*. ◆**−ly** *adv* annuellement.

annuity [ə'njuːɪtɪ] *n* (*of retired person*) pension *f* viagère.

annul [ə'nʌl] *vt* (**-ll-**) annuler. ◆**−ment** *n* annulation *f*.

anoint [ə'nɔɪnt] *vt* oindre (**with** de). ◆**−ed** *a* oint.

anomalous [ə'nɒmələs] *a* anormal. ◆**anomaly** *n* anomalie *f*.

anon [ə'nɒn] *adv* Hum tout à l'heure.

anonymous [ə'nɒnɪməs] *a* anonyme; **to remain a.** garder l'anonymat. ◆**ano'nymity** *n* anonymat *m*.

anorak ['ænəræk] *n* anorak *m*.

anorexia [ænə'reksɪə] *n* anorexie *f*.

another [ə'nʌðər] *a & pron* un(e) autre; **a. man** un autre homme; **a. month** (*additional*) encore un mois, un autre mois; **a. ten** encore dix; **one a.** l'un(e) l'autre, *pl* les un(e)s les autres; **they love one a.** ils s'aiment (l'un l'autre).

answer ['ɑːnsər] *n* réponse *f*; (*to problem*) solution *f* (**to** de); (*reason*) explication *f*; − *vt* (*person, question, phone etc*) répondre à; (*word*) répondre; (*problem*) résoudre; (*prayer, wish*) exaucer; **to a. the bell** *or* **the door** ouvrir la porte; − *vi* répondre; **to a.**

back répliquer, répondre; **to a. for** (*s.o., sth*) répondre de. ◆**−able** *a* responsable (**for** sth de qch, **to s.o.** devant qn).

ant [ænt] *n* fourmi *f*. ◆**anthill** *n* fourmilière *f*.

antagonism [æn'tægənɪz(ə)m] *n* antagonisme *m*; (*hostility*) hostilité *f*. ◆**antagonist** *n* antagoniste *mf*. ◆**antago'nistic** *a* antagoniste; (*hostile*) hostile. ◆**antagonize** *vt* provoquer (l'hostilité de).

antarctic [æn'tɑːktɪk] *a* antarctique; − *n* **the A.** l'Antarctique *m*.

antecedent [æntɪ'siːd(ə)nt] *n* antécédent *m*.

antechamber ['æntɪtʃeɪmbər] *n* antichambre *f*.

antedate ['æntɪdeɪt] *vt* (*letter*) antidater.

antelope ['æntɪləʊp] *n* antilope *f*.

antenatal [æntɪ'neɪt(ə)l] *a* prénatal.

antenna[1], *pl* **-ae** [æn'tenə, -iː] *n* (*of insect etc*) antenne *f*.

antenna[2] [æn'tenə] *n* (*pl* **-as**) (*aerial*) Am antenne *f*.

anteroom ['æntɪrʊm] *n* antichambre *f*.

anthem ['ænθəm] *n* **national a.** hymne *m* national.

anthology [æn'θɒlədʒɪ] *n* anthologie *f*.

anthropology [ænθrə'pɒlədʒɪ] *n* anthropologie *f*.

anti- [ænti, Am 'æntai] *pref* anti-; **to be a. sth** Fam être contre qch. ◆**anti'aircraft** *a* antiaérien. ◆**anti'biotic** *a & n* antibiotique (*m*). ◆**antibody** *n* anticorps *m*. ◆**anti'climax** *n* chute *f* dans l'ordinaire; (*let-down*) déception *f*. ◆**anti'clockwise** *adv* dans le sens inverse des aiguilles d'une montre. ◆**anti'cyclone** *n* anticyclone *m*. ◆**antidote** *n* antidote *m*. ◆**antifreeze** *n* Aut antigel *m*. ◆**anti'histamine** *n* Med antihistaminique *m*. ◆**anti'perspirant** *n* antisudoral *m*. ◆**anti-Se'mitic** *a* antisémite. ◆**anti-'Semitism** *n* antisémitisme *m*. ◆**anti'septic** *a & n* antiseptique (*m*). ◆**anti'social** *a* (*misfit*) asocial; (*measure, principles*) antisocial; (*unsociable*) insociable.

anticipate [æn'tɪsɪpeɪt] *vt* (*foresee*) prévoir; (*forestall*) devancer; (*expect*) s'attendre à; (*the future*) anticiper sur. ◆**antici'pation** *n* prévision *f*; (*expectation*) attente *f*; **in a.** of en prévision de, dans l'attente de; **in a.** (*to thank s.o., pay etc*) d'avance.

antics ['æntɪks] *npl* bouffonneries *fpl*.

antipathy [æn'tɪpəθɪ] *n* antipathie *f*.

antipodes [æn'tɪpədiːz] *npl* antipodes *mpl*.

antiquarian [æntɪ'kweərɪən] *a* **a. bookseller**

libraire *mf* spécialisé(e) dans le livre ancien.

antiquated ['æntɪkweɪtɪd] *a* vieilli; (*person*) vieux jeu *inv*.

antique [æn'tiːk] *a* (*furniture etc*) ancien; (*of Greek etc antiquity*) antique; **a. dealer** antiquaire *mf*; **a. shop** magasin *m* d'antiquités; – *n* objet *m* ancien *or* d'époque, antiquité *f*. ◆**antiquity** *n* (*period etc*) antiquité *f*.

antithesis, *pl* **-eses** [æn'tɪθəsɪs, -ɪsiːz] *n* antithèse *f*.

antler ['æntlər] *n* (*tine*) andouiller *m*; *pl* bois *mpl*.

antonym ['æntənɪm] *n* antonyme *m*.

Antwerp ['æntwɜːp] *n* Anvers *m or f*.

anus ['eɪnəs] *n* anus *m*.

anvil ['ænvɪl] *n* enclume *f*.

anxiety [æŋ'zaɪətɪ] *n* (*worry*) inquiétude *f* (*about* au sujet de); (*fear*) anxiété *f*; (*eagerness*) impatience *f* (*for* de).

anxious ['æŋkʃəs] *a* (*worried*) inquiet (*about* de, pour); (*troubled*) anxieux; (*causing worry*) inquiétant; (*eager*) impatient (*to do* de faire); **I'm a.** (*that*) **he should go** je tiens beaucoup à ce qu'il parte. ◆**—ly** *adv* avec inquiétude; (*to wait etc*) impatiemment.

any ['enɪ] *a* **1** (*interrogative*) du, de la, des; **have you a. milk/tickets?** avez-vous du lait/des billets?; **is there a. man** (*at all*) **who ...?** y a-t-il un homme (quelconque) qui ...? **2** (*negative*) de; (*not any at all*) aucun; **he hasn't a. milk/tickets** il n'a pas de lait/de billets; **there isn't a. proof** il n'y a aucune preuve. **3** (*no matter which*) n'importe quel. **4** (*every*) tout; **at a. hour** à toute heure; **in a. case, at a. rate** de toute façon; – *pron* **1** (*no matter which one*) n'importe lequel; (*somebody*) quelqu'un; **if a. of you** si l'un d'entre vous, si quelqu'un parmi vous; **more than a.** plus qu'aucun. **2** (*quantity*) en; **have you a.?** en as-tu?; **I don't see a.** je n'en vois pas; – *adv* (*usually not translated*) (**not**) **a. further/happier/*etc*** (pas) plus loin/plus heureux/*etc*; **I don't see her a. more** je ne la vois plus; **a. more tea?** (*a little*) encore du thé?, encore un peu de thé?; **a. better?** (*un peu*) mieux?

anybody ['enɪbɒdɪ] *pron* **1** (*somebody*) quelqu'un; **do you see a.?** vois-tu quelqu'un?; **more than a.** plus qu'aucun. **2** (*negative*) personne; **he doesn't know a.** il ne connaît personne. **3** (*no matter who*) n'importe qui; **a. would think that ...** on croirait que . . . .

anyhow ['enɪhaʊ] *adv* (*at any rate*) de toute façon; (*badly*) n'importe comment; **to**

leave sth a. (*in confusion*) laisser qch sens dessus dessous.

anyone ['enɪwʌn] *pron* = **anybody**.

anyplace ['enɪpleɪs] *adv Am* = **anywhere**.

anything ['enɪθɪŋ] *pron* **1** (*something*) quelque chose; **can you see a.?** voyez-vous quelque chose? **2** (*negative*) rien; **he doesn't do a.** il ne fait rien; **without a.** sans rien. **3** (*everything*) tout; **he'll eat a.** il mangera n'importe quoi; **a. you like** (*to work etc*) *Fam* comme un fou. **4** (*no matter what*) **a.** (**at all**) n'importe quoi.

anyway ['enɪweɪ] *adv* de toute façon.

anywhere ['enɪweər] *adv* **1** (*no matter where*) n'importe où. **2** (*everywhere*) partout; **a. you go** partout où vous allez, où que vous alliez; **a. you like** là où tu veux. **3** (*somewhere*) quelque part; **is he going a.?** va-t-il quelque part? **4** (*negative*) nulle part; **he doesn't go a.** il ne va nulle part; **without a. to put it** sans un endroit où le mettre.

apace [ə'peɪs] *adv* rapidement.

apart [ə'pɑːt] *adv* (*to or at one side*) à part; **to tear a.** (*to pieces*) mettre en pièces; **we kept them a.** (*separate*) on les tenait séparés; **with legs (wide) a.** les jambes écartées; **they are a metre a.** ils se trouvent à un mètre l'un de l'autre; **a. from** (*except for*) à part; **to take a.** (*dismantle*) démonter; **to come a.** (*of two objects*) se séparer; (*of knot etc*) se défaire; **to tell a.** distinguer entre; **worlds a.** (*very different*) diamétralement opposé.

apartheid [ə'pɑːteɪt] *n* apartheid *m*.

apartment [ə'pɑːtmənt] *n* (*flat*) *Am* appartement *m*; (*room*) chambre *f*; **a. house** *Am* immeuble *m* (*d'habitation*).

apathy ['æpəθɪ] *n* apathie *f*. ◆**apa'thetic** *a* apathique.

ape [eɪp] *n* singe; – *vt* (*imitate*) singer.

aperitif [ə'perətiːf] *n* apéritif *m*.

aperture ['æpətʃuər] *n* ouverture *f*.

apex ['eɪpeks] *n Geom* & *Fig* sommet *m*.

aphorism ['æfərɪz(ə)m] *n* aphorisme *m*.

aphrodisiac [æfrə'dɪzɪæk] *a* & *n* aphrodisiaque (*m*).

apiece [ə'piːs] *adv* chacun; **a pound a.** une livre (la pièce) or chacun.

apish ['eɪpɪʃ] *a* simiesque; (*imitative*) imitateur.

apocalypse [ə'pɒkəlɪps] *n* apocalypse *f*. ◆**apoca'lyptic** *a* apocalyptique.

apocryphal [ə'pɒkrɪfəl] *a* apocryphe.

apogee ['æpədʒiː] *n* apogée *m*.

apologetic [əpɒlə'dʒetɪk] *a* (*letter*) plein d'excuses; **to be a. about** s'excuser de. ◆**apologetically** *adv* en s'excusant.

apology [ə'pɒlədʒɪ] *n* excuses *fpl*; **an a. for a dinner** *Fam Pej* un dîner minable. ◆**apologist** *n* apologiste *mf*. ◆**apologize** *vi* s'excuser (**for** de); **to a. to s.o.** faire ses excuses à qn (**for** pour).

apoplexy ['æpəplɛksɪ] *n* apoplexie *f*. ◆apo'**plectic** *a* & *n* apoplectique (*mf*).

apostle [ə'pɒs(ə)l] *n* apôtre *m*.

apostrophe [ə'pɒstrəfɪ] *n* apostrophe *f*.

appal [ə'pɔːl] (*Am* **appall**) *vt* (-ll-) épouvanter. ◆**appalling** *a* épouvantable.

apparatus [æpə'reɪtəs, *Am* -'rætəs] *n* (*equipment, organization*) appareil *m*; (*in gym*) agrès *mpl*.

apparel [ə'pærəl] *n* habit *m*, habillement *m*.

apparent [ə'pærənt] *a* (*obvious, seeming*) apparent; **it's a. that** il est évident que. ◆**-ly** *adv* apparemment.

apparition [æpə'rɪʃ(ə)n] *n* apparition *f*.

appeal [ə'piːl] *n* (*call*) appel *m*; (*entreaty*) supplication *f*; (*charm*) attrait *m*; (*interest*) intérêt *m*; *Jur* appel *m*; – *vt* to a. to s.o. (*attract*) plaire à qn, séduire qn; (*interest*) intéresser qn; **to a. to s.o. for sth** demander qch à qn; **to a. to s.o. to do** supplier qn de faire; – *vi* *Jur* faire appel. ◆**-ing** *a* (*begging*) suppliant; (*attractive*) séduisant.

appear [ə'pɪər] *vi* (*become visible*) apparaître; (*present oneself*) se présenter; (*seem, be published*) paraître; (*act*) *Th* jouer; *Jur* comparaître; **it appears that** (*it seems*) il semble que (+ *sub or indic*); (*it is rumoured*) il paraîtrait que (+ *indic*). ◆**appearance** *n* (*act*) apparition *f*; (*look*) apparence *f*, aspect *m*; (*of book*) parution *f*; **to put in an a.** faire acte de présence.

appease [ə'piːz] *vt* apaiser; (*curiosity*) satisfaire.

append [ə'pend] *vt* joindre, ajouter (**to** à). ◆**-age** *n* *Anat* appendice *m*.

appendix [ə'pendɪks] *pl* -**ixes** *or* -**ices** [-ɪksɪz, -ɪsiːz] *n* (*of book*) & *Anat* appendice *m*. ◆**appendicitis** [əpendɪ'saɪtɪs] *n* appendicite *f*.

appertain [æpə'teɪn] *vi* **to a. to** se rapporter à.

appetite ['æpɪtaɪt] *n* appétit *m*; **to take away s.o.'s a.** couper l'appétit à qn. ◆**appetizer** *n* (*drink*) apéritif *m*; (*food*) amuse-gueule *m inv*. ◆**appetizing** *a* appétissant.

applaud [ə'plɔːd] *vt* (*clap*) applaudir; (*approve of*) approuver, applaudir à; – *vi* applaudir. ◆**applause** *n* applaudissements *mpl*.

apple ['æp(ə)l] *n* pomme *f*; **stewed apples, a. sauce** compote *f* de pommes; **eating/cooking a.** pomme *f* à couteau/à cuire; **a. pie** tarte *f* aux pommes; **a. core** trognon *m* de pomme; **a. tree** pommier *m*.

appliance [ə'plaɪəns] *n* appareil *m*.

apply [ə'plaɪ] *vt* (*put, carry out etc*) appliquer; (*brake*) *Aut* appuyer sur; **to a. oneself to** s'appliquer à. **2** *vi* (*be relevant*) s'appliquer (**to** à); **to a. for** (*job*) poser sa candidature à, postuler; **to a. to** (*ask*) s'adresser à qn (**for** pour). ◆**applied** *a* (*maths etc*) appliqué. ◆**applicable** *a* applicable (**to** à). ◆'**applicant** *n* candidat, -ate *mf* (**for** à). ◆**appli'cation** *n* application *f*; (*request*) demande *f*; (*for job*) candidature *f*; (*for membership*) demande *f* d'adhésion *or* d'inscription; **a. (form)** (*job*) formulaire *m* de candidature; (*club*) formulaire *m* d'inscription *or* d'adhésion.

appoint [ə'pɔɪnt] *vt* (*person*) nommer (**to sth** à qch, **to do** pour faire); (*time etc*) désigner, fixer; **at the appointed time** à l'heure dite; **well-appointed** bien équipé. ◆**-ment** *n* nomination *f*; (*meeting*) rendez-vous *m inv*; (*post*) place *f*, situation *f*.

apportion [ə'pɔːʃ(ə)n] *vt* répartir.

apposite ['æpəzɪt] *a* juste, à propos.

appraise [ə'preɪz] *vt* évaluer. ◆**appraisal** *n* évaluation *f*.

appreciate [ə'priːʃɪeɪt] **1** *vt* (*enjoy, value, assess*) apprécier; (*understand*) comprendre; (*be grateful for*) être reconnaissant de. **2** *vi* prendre de la valeur. ◆**appreciable** *a* appréciable, sensible. ◆**appreci'ation** *n* **1** (*judgement*) appréciation *f*; (*gratitude*) reconnaissance *f*. **2** (*rise in value*) plus-value *f*. ◆**appreciative** *a* (*grateful*) reconnaissant (**of** de); (*laudatory*) élogieux; **to be a. of** (*enjoy*) apprécier.

apprehend [æprɪ'hend] *vt* (*seize, arrest*) appréhender. ◆**apprehension** *n* (*fear*) appréhension *f*. ◆**apprehensive** *a* inquiet (**about** de, au sujet de); **to be a.** redouter.

apprentice [ə'prentɪs] *n* apprenti, -ie *mf*; – *vt* mettre en apprentissage (**to** chez). ◆**apprenticeship** *n* apprentissage *m*.

approach [ə'prəʊtʃ] *vt* (*draw near to*) s'approcher de (*qn, feu, porte etc*); (*age, result, town*) approcher de; (*subject*) aborder; (*accost*) aborder (*qn*); **to a. s.o. about** parler à qn de; – *vi* (*of person, vehicle*) s'approcher; (*of date etc*) approcher; – *n* approche *f*; (*method*) façon *f* de s'y prendre; (*path*) (voie *f* d')accès *m*; **a. to** (*question*) manière *f* d'aborder; **to make approaches to** faire des avances à.

◆—able a (place) accessible; (person) abordable.

appropriate 1 [ə'prəupriət] a (place, tools, clothes etc) approprié, adéquat; (remark, time) opportun; **a. to** or **for** propre à, approprié à. **2** [ə'prəupriett] vt (set aside) affecter; (steal) s'approprier. **◆—ly** adv convenablement.

approv/e [ə'pruɪv] vt approuver; **to a. of** sth approuver qch; **I don't a. of him** il ne me plaît pas, je ne l'apprécie pas; **I a. of his going** je trouve bon qu'il y aille; **I a. of her having accepted** j'approuve qu'elle ait accepté. **◆—ing** a approbateur. **◆approval** n approbation f; **on a.** (goods) Com à l'essai.

approximate [ə'prɒksimət] a approximatif; – [ə'prɒksimeit] vi **to a. to** se rapprocher de. **◆—ly** adv à peu près, approximativement. **◆approxi'mation** n approximation f.

apricot ['eiprikɒt] n abricot m.

April ['eiprəl] n avril m; **to make an A. fool of** faire un poisson d'avril à.

apron ['eiprən] n (garment) tablier m.

apse [æps] n (of church) abside f.

apt [æpt] a (suitable) convenable; (remark, reply) juste; (word, name) bien choisi; (student) doué, intelligent; **to be a. to do** avoir tendance à; **a. at sth** habile à qch. **◆apti-tude** n aptitude f (for à, pour). **◆aptly** adv convenablement; **a. named** qui porte bien son nom.

aqualung ['ækwəlʌŋ] n scaphandre m autonome.

aquarium [ə'kweəriəm] n aquarium m.

Aquarius [ə'kweəriəs] n (sign) le Verseau.

aquatic [ə'kwætik] a (plant etc) aquatique; (sport) nautique.

aqueduct ['ækwidʌkt] n aqueduc m.

aquiline ['ækwilain] a (nose, profile) aquilin.

Arab ['ærəb] a & n arabe (mf). **◆Arabian** [ə'reibiən] a arabe. **◆Arabic** a & n (language) arabe (m); **A. numerals** chiffres mpl arabes.

arabesque [ærə'besk] n (decoration) arabesque f.

arable ['ærəb(ə)l] a (land) arable.

arbiter ['aɪbitər] n arbitre m. **◆arbitrate** vti arbitrer. **◆arbi'tration** n arbitrage m; **to go to a.** soumettre la question à l'arbitrage. **◆arbitrator** n (in dispute) médiateur, -trice mf.

arbitrary ['aɪbitrəri] a arbitraire.

arbour ['aɪbər] n tonnelle f, charmille f.

arc [aɪk] n (of circle) arc m.

arcade [aɪ'keid] n (market) passage m couvert.

arch [aɪtʃ] n (of bridge) arche f; Archit voûte f, arc m; (of foot) cambrure f; – vt (one's back etc) arquer, courber. **◆archway** n passage m voûté, voûte f.

arch- [aɪtʃ] pref (villain etc) achevé; **a. enemy** ennemi m numéro un.

arch(a)eology [aɪki'ɒlədʒi] n archéologie f. **◆arch(a)eologist** n archéologue mf.

archaic [aɪ'keiik] a archaïque.

archangel ['aɪkeindʒəl] n archange m.

archbishop [aɪtʃ'biʃəp] n archevêque m.

archer ['aɪtʃər] n archer m. **◆archery** n tir m à l'arc.

archetype ['aɪkitaip] n archétype m.

archipelago [aɪki'peləgəu] n (pl -oes or -os) archipel m.

architect ['aɪkitekt] n architecte m. **◆architecture** n architecture f.

archives ['aɪkaivz] npl archives fpl. **◆archivist** n archiviste mf.

arctic ['aɪktik] a arctique; (weather) polaire, glacial; – n **the A.** l'Arctique m.

ardent ['aɪdənt] a ardent. **◆—ly** adv ardemment. **◆ardour** n ardeur f.

arduous ['aɪdjuəs] a ardu.

are [aɪr] see be.

area ['eəriə] n Math superficie f; Geog région f; (of town) quartier m; Mil zone f; (domain) Fig domaine m, secteur m, terrain m; **built-up a.** agglomération f; **parking a.** aire f de stationnement; **a. code** Tel Am indicatif m.

arena [ə'riɪnə] n Hist & Fig arène f.

Argentina [aɪdʒən'tiɪnə] n Argentine f. **◆Argentine** ['aɪdʒəntain] a & n, **◆Argentinian** a & n argentin, -ine (mf).

argu/e ['aɪgjuɪ] vi (quarrel) se disputer (with avec, about au sujet de); (reason) raisonner (with avec, about sur); – vt **to a. that** (maintain) soutenir que; **to a. in favour of** plaider pour; – vt (matter) discuter; **to a. that** (maintain) soutenir que. **◆—able** ['aɪgjuəb(ə)l] a discutable. **◆—ably** adv on pourrait soutenir que. **◆—ment** n (quarrel) dispute f; (reasoning) argument m; (debate) discussion f; **to have an a.** se disputer. **◆argu'mentative** a raisonneur.

aria ['aɪriə] n Mus air m (d'opéra).

arid ['ærid] a aride.

Aries ['eəriiz] n (sign) le Bélier.

arise [ə'raiz] vi (pt arose, pp arisen) (of prob-lem, opportunity etc) se présenter; (of cry, objection) s'élever; (result) résulter (from de); (get up) Lit se lever.

aristocracy [æri'stɒkrəsi] n aristocratie f. **◆aristocrat** ['æristəkræt, Am ə'ristəkræt]

n aristocrate *mf.* ◆**aristo'cratic** *a* aristocratique.
arithmetic [ə'rɪθmətɪk] *n* arithmétique *f.*
ark [ɑːk] *n* Noah's a. l'arche *f* de Noé.
arm [ɑːm] **1** *n* bras *m*; **a. in a.** bras dessus
bras dessous; **with open arms** à bras
ouverts. **2** *n* (*weapon*) arme *f*; **arms race**
course *f* aux armements; – *vt* armer (**with**
de). ◆**armament** *n* armement *m.* ◆**arm-**
band *n* brassard *m.* ◆**armchair** *n* fauteuil
m. ◆**armful** *n* brassée *f.* ◆**armhole** *n*
emmanchure *f.* ◆**armpit** *n* aisselle *f.*
◆**armrest** *n* accoudoir *m.*
armadillo [ɑːmə'dɪləʊ] *n* (*pl* -os) tatou *m.*
armistice ['ɑːmɪstɪs] *n* armistice *m.*
armour ['ɑːmər] *n* (*of knight etc*) armure *f*;
(*of tank etc*) blindage *m.* ◆**armoured** *a,*
◆**armour-plated** *a* blindé. ◆**armoury** *n*
arsenal *m.*
army ['ɑːmɪ] *n* armée *f*; – *a* (*uniform etc*)
militaire; **to join the a.** s'engager; **regular a.**
armée *f* active.
aroma [ə'rəʊmə] *n* arôme *m.* ◆**aro'matic** *a*
aromatique.
arose [ə'rəʊz] *see* **arise**.
around [ə'raʊnd] *prep* autour de; (*approxi-*
mately) environ, autour de; **to go a. the**
world faire le tour du monde; – *adv*
autour; **all a.** tout autour; **to follow a.**
suivre partout; **to rush a.** courir çà et là; **a.**
here par ici; **he's still a.** il est encore là;
there's a lot of flu a. il y a pas mal de grip-
pes dans l'air; **up and a.** (*after illness*) *Am*
sur pied, guéri.
arouse [ə'raʊz] *vt* éveiller, susciter; (*sexu-*
ally) exciter; **to a. from sleep** tirer du
sommeil.
arrange [ə'reɪndʒ] *vt* arranger; (*time, meet-*
ing) fixer; **it was arranged that** il était
convenu que; **to a. to do** s'arranger pour
faire. ◆**—ment** *n* (*layout, agreement*)
arrangement *m*; *pl* (*preparations*) préparatifs *mpl*; (*plans*) projets *mpl*; **to make**
arrangements to s'arranger pour.
array [ə'reɪ] *n* (*display*) étalage *m.*
◆**arrayed** *a* (*dressed*) *Lit* (re)vêtu (**in** de).
arrears [ə'rɪəz] *npl* (*payment*) arriéré *m*; **to**
be in a. avoir des arriérés.
arrest [ə'rest] *vt* arrêter; – *n* *Jur* arrestation
f; **under a.** en état d'arrestation; **cardiac a.**
arrêt *m* du cœur. ◆**—ing** *a* (*striking*) *Fig*
frappant.
arrive [ə'raɪv] *vi* arriver. ◆**arrival** *n* arrivée
f; **new a.** nouveau venu *m*, nouvelle venue
f; (*baby*) nouveau-né, -ée *mf.*
arrogant ['ærəgənt] *a* arrogant. ◆**arro-**

gance *n* arrogance *f.* ◆**arrogantly** *adv*
avec arrogance.
arrow ['ærəʊ] *n* flèche *f.*
arsenal ['ɑːsən(ə)l] *n* arsenal *m.*
arsenic ['ɑːsnɪk] *n* arsenic *m.*
arson ['ɑːs(ə)n] *n* incendie *m* volontaire.
◆**arsonist** *n* incendiaire *mf.*
art [ɑːt] *n* art *m*; (*cunning*) artifice *m*; **work of**
a. œuvre *f* d'art; **fine arts** beaux-arts *mpl*;
faculty of arts *Univ* faculté *f* des lettres; *a.*
school école *f* des beaux-arts.
artefact ['ɑːtɪfækt] *n* objet *m* fabriqué.
artery ['ɑːtərɪ] *n* *Anat* artère *f.*
◆**ar'terial** *a* *Anat* artériel; **a. road** route *f*
principale.
artful ['ɑːtfəl] *a* rusé, astucieux. ◆**—ly** *adv*
astucieusement.
arthritis [ɑː'θraɪtɪs] *n* arthrite *f.*
artichoke ['ɑːtɪtʃəʊk] *n* (*globe*) **a.** artichaut
m; **Jerusalem a.** topinambour *m.*
article ['ɑːtɪk(ə)l] *n* (*object, clause*) & *Journ*
Gram article *m*; **a. of clothing** vêtement *m*;
articles of value objets *mpl* de valeur; **lead-**
ing a. *Journ* éditorial *m.*
articulat/e [ɑː'tɪkjʊlət] *a* (*sound*) net,
distinct; (*person*) qui s'exprime clairement;
– [ɑː'tɪkjʊleɪt] *vti* (*speak*) articuler.
◆**—ed** **a.** **lorry** semi-remorque *m.* ◆**articu-**
'lation *n* articulation *f.*
artifact ['ɑːtɪfækt] *n* objet *m* fabriqué.
artifice ['ɑːtɪfɪs] *n* artifice *m.*
artificial [ɑːtɪ'fɪʃ(ə)l] *a* artificiel. ◆**artifici-**
'ality *n* caractère *m* artificiel. ◆**artificially**
adv artificiellement.
artillery [ɑː'tɪlərɪ] *n* artillerie *f.*
artisan ['ɑːtɪzæn] *n* artisan *m.*
artist ['ɑːtɪst] *n* (*actor, painter etc*) artiste *mf.*
◆**artiste** [ɑː'tiːst] *n* *Th Mus* artiste *m.*
◆**ar'tistic** *a* (*sense, treasure etc*) artistique; (*person*) artiste. ◆**artistry** *n* art *m.*
artless ['ɑːtləs] *a* naturel, naïf.
arty ['ɑːtɪ] *a* *Pej* du genre artiste.
as [æz, *unstressed* əz] *adv* & *conj* **1** (*manner*
etc) comme; **as you like** comme tu veux;
such as comme, tel que; **as much or as hard**
as I can (au)tant que je peux; **as it is** (*this*
being the case) comme ça, tel quel; (*to*
leave sth) comme ça, tel quel; **it's late as it is**
il est déjà tard; **as if, as though** comme si. **2**
(*comparison*) **as tall as** aussi grand que
vous; **is he as tall as you?** est-il aussi *or* si
grand que vous?; **as white as a sheet** blanc
comme un linge; **as much or as hard as you**
autant que vous; **the same as** le même que;
twice as big as deux fois plus grand que. **3**
(*concessive*) **(as) clever as he is** si *or* aussi
intelligent qu'il soit. **4** (*capacity*) **as a**

teacher comme professeur, en tant que *or* en qualité de professeur; **to act as a father** agir en père. **5** (*reason*) comme; **as it's late** puisqu'il est tard, comme il est tard. **6** (*time*) **as I left** comme je partais; **as one grows older** à mesure que l'on vieillit; **as he slept** pendant qu'il dormait; **one day as . . .** un jour que . . . ; **as from, as of** (*time*) à partir de. **7** (*concerning*) **as for that, as to that** quant à cela. **8** (+ *inf*) **so as to** de manière à; **so stupid as to** assez bête pour.

asbestos [æz'bestɒs] *n* amiante *f*.

ascend [ə'send] *vi* monter; – *vt* (*throne*) monter sur; (*stairs*) monter; (*mountain*) faire l'ascension de. ◆**ascent** *n* ascension *f* (*of* de); (*slope*) côte *f*.

ascertain [æsə'teɪn] *vt* (*discover*) découvrir; (*check*) s'assurer de.

ascetic [ə'setɪk] *a* ascétique; – *n* ascète *mf*.

ascribe [ə'skraɪb] *vt* attribuer (**to** à).

ash [æʃ] *n* **1** (*of cigarette etc*) cendre *f*; **A. Wednesday** mercredi *m* des Cendres. **2** (*tree*) frêne *m*. ◆**ashen** *a* (*pale grey*) cendré; (*face*) pâle. ◆**ashcan** *n Am* poubelle *f*. ◆**ashtray** *n* cendrier *m*.

ashamed [ə'feɪmd] *a* honteux; **to be a.** avoir honte de; **to be a.** (*of oneself*) avoir honte.

ashore [ə'ʃɔːr] *adv* **to go a.** débarquer; **to put s.o. a.** débarquer qn.

Asia ['eɪʃə] *n* Asie *f*. ◆**Asian** *a* asiatique; – *n* Asiatique *m*, Asiate *mf*.

aside [ə'saɪd] **1** *adv* de côté; **to draw a.** (*curtain*) écarter; **to take** *or* **draw s.o. a.** prendre qn à part; **to step a.** s'écarter; **a. from** en dehors de. **2** *n Th* aparté *m*.

asinine ['æsɪnaɪn] *a* stupide, idiot.

ask [ɑːsk] *vt* demander; (*a question*) poser; (*invite*) inviter; **to a. s.o. (for) sth** demander qch à qn; **to a. s.o. to do** demander à qn de faire; – *vi* demander; **to a. for sth/s.o.** demander qch/qn; **to a. for sth back** redemander qch; **to a. about sth** se renseigner sur qch; **to a. after** *or* **about s.o.** demander des nouvelles de qn; **to a. s.o. about** interroger qn sur; **asking price** prix *m* demandé.

askance [ə'skɑːns] *adv* **to look a. at** regarder avec méfiance.

askew [ə'skjuː] *adv* de biais, de travers.

aslant [ə'slɑːnt] *adv* de travers.

asleep [ə'sliːp] *a* endormi; (*arm, leg*) engourdi; **to be a.** dormir; **to fall a.** s'endormir.

asp [æsp] *n* (*snake*) aspic *m*.

asparagus [ə'spærəgəs] *n* (*plant*) asperge *f*; (*shoots*) *Culin* asperges *fpl*.

aspect ['æspekt] *n* aspect *m*; (*of house*) orientation *f*.

aspersions [ə'spɜːʃ(ə)nz] *npl* **to cast a. on** dénigrer.

asphalt ['æsfælt, *Am* 'æsfɔːlt] *n* asphalte *m*; – *vt* asphalter.

asphyxia [əs'fɪksɪə] *n* asphyxie *f*. ◆**asphyxiate** *vt* asphyxier. ◆**asphyxi'ation** *n* asphyxie *f*.

aspire [ə'spaɪər] *vi* **to a. to** aspirer à. ◆**aspi'ration** *n* aspiration *f*.

aspirin ['æsprɪn] *n* aspirine *f*.

ass [æs] *n* (*animal*) âne *m*; (*person*) *Fam* imbécile *mf*, âne *m*; **she-a.** ânesse *f*.

assail [ə'seɪl] *vt* assaillir (**with** de). ◆**assailant** *n* agresseur *m*.

assassin [ə'sæsɪn] *n Pol* assassin *m*. ◆**assassinate** *vt Pol* assassiner. ◆**assassi'nation** *n Pol* assassinat *m*.

assault [ə'sɔːlt] *n Mil* assaut *m*; *Jur* agression *f*; – *vt Jur* agresser; (*woman*) violenter.

assemble [ə'semb(ə)l] *vt* (*objects, ideas*) assembler; (*people*) rassembler; (*machine*) monter; – *vi* se rassembler. ◆**assembly** (*meeting*) assemblée *f*; *Tech* montage *m*, assemblage *m*; *Sch* rassemblement *m*; **a. line** (*in factory*) chaîne *f* de montage.

assent [ə'sent] *n* assentiment *m*; – *vi* consentir (**to** à).

assert [ə'sɜːt] *vt* affirmer (**that** que); (*rights*) revendiquer; **to a. oneself** s'affirmer. ◆**assertion** *n* affirmation *f*; revendication *f*. ◆**assertive** *a* affirmatif, *Pej* autoritaire.

assess [ə'ses] *vt* (*estimate, evaluate*) évaluer; (*decide amount of*) fixer le montant de; (*person*) juger. ◆**—ment** *n* évaluation *f*; jugement *m*. ◆**assessor** *n* (*valuer*) expert *m*.

asset ['æset] *n* atout *m*, avantage *m*; *pl Com* biens *mpl*, avoir *m*.

assiduous [ə'sɪdjuːəs] *a* assidu.

assign [ə'saɪn] *vt* (*allocate*) assigner; (*day etc*) fixer; (*appoint*) nommer (**to** à). ◆**—ment** *n* (*task*) mission *f*; *Sch* devoirs *mpl*.

assimilate [ə'sɪmɪlet] *vt* assimiler; – *vi* s'assimiler. ◆**assimi'lation** *n* assimilation *f*.

assist [ə'sɪst] *vti* aider (**in doing, to do** à faire). ◆**assistance** *n* aide *f*; **to be of a. to s.o.** aider qn. ◆**assistant** *n* assistant, -ante *mf*; (*in shop*) vendeur, -euse *mf*; – *a* adjoint.

assizes [ə'saɪzɪz] *npl Jur* assises *fpl*.

associate [ə'səʊʃɪeɪt] *vt* associer (**with** à, avec); – *vi* **to a. with s.o.** fréquenter qn; **to**

a. (oneself) **with** (in business venture) s'associer à or avec; − [əˈsəuʃiət] n & a associé, -ée (mf). ◆**associ'ation** n association f; pl (memories) souvenirs mpl.

assort/ed [əˈsɔːtid] a (different) variés; (foods) assortis; **well-a.** bien assorti. ◆—**ment** n assortiment m.

assuage [əˈsweidʒ] vt apaiser, adoucir.

assum/e [əˈsjuːm] vt **1** (take on) prendre; (responsibility, role) assumer; (attitude, name) adopter. **2** (suppose) présumer (that que). ◆—**ed** (a feigned) faux; **a. name** nom m d'emprunt. ◆**assumption** n (supposition) supposition f.

assur/e [əˈʃuər] vt assurer. ◆—**edly** [-idli] adv assurément. ◆**assurance** n assurance f.

asterisk [ˈæstərisk] n astérisque m.

astern [əˈstɜːn] adv Nau à l'arrière.

asthma [ˈæsmə] n asthme m. ◆**asth'matic** a & n asthmatique (mf).

astir [əˈstɜːr] a (excited) en émoi; (out of bed) debout.

astonish [əˈstɒniʃ] vt étonner; **to be astonished** s'étonner (at sth de qch). ◆—**ing** a étonnant. ◆—**ingly** adv étonnamment. ◆—**ment** n étonnement m.

astound [əˈstaund] vt stupéfier, étonner. ◆—**ing** a stupéfiant.

astray [əˈstrei] adv **to go a.** s'égarer; **to lead a.** égarer.

astride [əˈstraid] adv à califourchon; − prep à cheval sur.

astringent [əˈstrindʒənt] a (harsh) sévère.

astrology [əˈstrɒlədʒi] n astrologie f. ◆**astrologer** n astrologue mf.

astronaut [ˈæstrənɔːt] n astronaute m.

astronomy [əˈstrɒnəmi] n astronomie f. ◆**astronomer** n astronome m. ◆**astro'nomical** a astronomique.

astute [əˈstjuːt] a (crafty) rusé; (clever) astucieux.

asunder [əˈsʌndər] adv (to pieces) en pièces; (in two) en deux.

asylum [əˈsailəm] n asile m; **lunatic a.** Pej maison f de fous, asile m d'aliénés.

at [æt, unstressed ət] prep **1** à; **at the end** à la fin; **at work** au travail; **at six** (o'clock) à six heures. **2** chez; **at the doctor's** chez le médecin; **at home** chez soi, à la maison. ◆**at-home** n réception f. **3** en; **at sea** en mer; **at war** en guerre; **good at** (geography etc) fort en. **4** contre; **angry at** fâché contre. **5** sur; **to shoot at** tirer sur; **at my request** sur ma demande. **6** de; **to laugh at** rire de; **surprised at** surpris de. **7** (au)près de; **at the window** (au)près de la fenêtre. **8** par; **to**

come in at the door entrer par la porte; **six at a time** six par six. **9 at night** la nuit; **to look at** regarder; **not at all** pas du tout; (after 'thank you') pas de quoi!; **nothing at all** rien du tout; **to be (hard) at it** être très occupé, travailler dur; **he's always (on) at me** Fam il est toujours après moi.

ate [et, Am eit] see eat.

atheism [ˈeiθiːz(ə)m] n athéisme m. ◆**atheist** n athée mf.

Athens [ˈæθinz] n Athènes m or f.

athlete [ˈæθliːt] n athlète mf; **a.'s foot** Med mycose f. ◆**ath'letic** a athlétique; **a. meeting** réunion f sportive. ◆**ath'letics** npl athlétisme m.

atishoo! [əˈtiʃuː] (Am **atchoo** [əˈtʃuː]) int atchoum!

Atlantic [ətˈlæntik] a atlantique; − n **the A.** l'Atlantique m.

atlas [ˈætləs] n atlas m.

atmosphere [ˈætməsfiər] n atmosphère f. ◆**atmos'pheric** a atmosphérique.

atom [ˈætəm] n atome m; **a. bomb** bombe f atomique. ◆**a'tomic** a atomique. ◆**atomizer** n atomiseur m.

atone [əˈtəun] vi **to a. for** expier. ◆—**ment** n expiation f (for de).

atrocious [əˈtrəuʃəs] a atroce. ◆**atrocity** n atrocité f.

atrophy [ˈætrəfi] vi s'atrophier.

attach [əˈtætʃ] vt attacher (to à); (document) joindre (to à); **attached to** (fond of) attaché à. ◆—**ment** n (affection) attachement m; (fastener) attache f; (tool) accessoire m.

attaché [əˈtæʃei] n **1** Pol attaché, -ée mf. **2 a. case** attaché-case m.

attack [əˈtæk] n Mil Med & Fig attaque f; (of fever) accès m; (on s.o.'s life) attentat m; **heart a.** crise f cardiaque; − vt attaquer; (problem, plan) s'attaquer à; − vi attaquer. ◆—**er** n agresseur m.

attain [əˈtein] vt parvenir à, atteindre, réaliser. ◆—**able** a accessible. ◆—**ment** n (of ambition, aim etc) réalisation f (of de); pl (skills) talents mpl.

attempt [əˈtempt] n tentative f; **to make an a. to** essayer or tenter de; **a. on** (record) tentative pour battre; **a. on s.o.'s life** attentat m contre qn; − vt tenter; (task) entreprendre; **to a. to do** essayer or tenter de faire; **attempted murder** tentative f de meurtre.

attend [əˈtend] vt (match etc) assister à; (course) suivre; (school, church) aller à; (wait on, serve) servir; (escort) accompagner; (patient) soigner; − vi assister; **to a. to** (pay attention to) prêter attention à;

(take care of) s'occuper de. ◆**—ed** *a*
well-a. *(course)* très suivi; *(meeting)* où il y a
du monde. ◆**attendance** *n* présence *f* (at
à); *(people)* assistance *f*; **school a.** scolarité
f; **in a.** de service. ◆**attendant 1** *n*
employé, -ée *mf*; *(in museum)* gardien,
-ienne *mf*; *pl (of prince, king etc)* suite *f*. **2** *a*
(fact) concomitant.

attention [ə'tenʃ(ə)n] *n* attention *f*; **to pay a.**
prêter *or* faire attention (to à); **a.!** *Mil*
garde-à-vous!; **to stand at a.** *Mil* être au
garde-à-vous; **a. to detail** minutie *f*.
◆**attentive** *a (heedful)* attentif (to à);
(thoughtful) attentionné (to pour).
◆**attentively** *adv* avec attention, attentivement.

attenuate [ə'tenjuett] *vt* atténuer.

attest [ə'test] *vti* **to a. (to)** témoigner de.

attic ['ætɪk] *n* grenier *m*.

attire [ə'taɪər] *n Lit* vêtements *mpl*.

attitude ['ætɪtjuːd] *n* attitude *f*.

attorney [ə'tɜːnɪ] *n (lawyer) Am* avocat *m*;
district a. *Am* = procureur *m* (de la République).

attract [ə'trækt] *vt* attirer. ◆**attraction** *n*
attraction *f*; *(charm, appeal)* attrait *m*.
◆**attractive** *a (price etc)* intéressant; *(girl)*
belle, jolie; *(boy)* beau; *(manners)*
attrayant.

attribut/e 1 ['ætrɪbjuːt] *n (quality)* attribut
m. **2** [ə'trɪbjuːt] *vt (ascribe)* attribuer (to à).
◆**—able** *a* attribuable (to à).

attrition [ə'trɪʃ(ə)n] *n* **war of a.** guerre *f*
d'usure.

attuned [ə'tjuːnd] *a* **a. to** *(of ideas, trends etc)*
en accord avec; *(used to)* habitué à.

atypical [eɪ'tɪpɪk(ə)l] *a* peu typique.

aubergine ['əʊbəʒiːn] *n* aubergine *f*.

auburn ['ɔːbən] *a (hair)* châtain roux.

auction ['ɔːkʃən] *n* vente *f* (aux enchères); —
vt **to a. (off)** vendre (aux enchères).
◆**auctio'neer** *n* commissaire-priseur *m*,
adjudicateur, -trice *m*.

audacious [ɔː'deɪʃəs] *a* audacieux.
◆**audacity** *n* audace *f*.

audib/le ['ɔːdɪb(ə)l] *a* perceptible, audible.
◆**—ly** *adv* distinctement.

audience ['ɔːdɪəns] *n* assistance *f*, public *m*;
(of speaker, musician) auditoire *m*; *Th Cin*
spectateurs *mpl*; *Rad* auditeurs *mpl*; *(interview)* audience *f*.

audio ['ɔːdɪəʊ] *a (cassette, system etc)* audio
inv. ◆**audiotypist** *n* dactylo *f* au
magnétophone, audiotypiste *mf*.
◆**audio-'visual** *a* audio-visuel.

audit ['ɔːdɪt] *vt (accounts)* vérifier; — *n* vérifi-

cation *f* (des comptes). ◆**auditor** *n*
commissaire *m* aux comptes.

audition [ɔː'dɪʃ(ə)n] *n* audition *f*; — *vti* audi-
tionner.

auditorium [ɔːdɪ'tɔːrɪəm] *n* salle *f (de spectacle, concert etc).*

augment [ɔːg'ment] *vt* augmenter (with, by
de).

augur ['ɔːgər] *vt* présager; — *vi* **to a. well** être
de bon augure.

august [ɔː'gʌst] *a* auguste.

August ['ɔːgəst] *n* août *m*.

aunt [ɑːnt] *n* tante *f*. ◆**auntie** *or* **aunty** *n*
Fam tata *f*.

au pair [əʊ'peər] *adv* au pair; — *n* **au p. (girl)**
jeune fille *f* au pair.

aura ['ɔːrə] *n* émanation *f*, aura *f*, *(of place)*
atmosphère *f*.

auspices ['ɔːspɪsɪz] *npl* auspices *mpl*.

auspicious [ɔː'spɪʃəs] *a* favorable.

austere [ɔː'stɪər] *a* austère. ◆**austerity** *n*
austérité *f*.

Australia [ɒ'streɪlɪə] *n* Australie *f*. ◆**Australian** *a & n* australien, -ienne *(mf)*.

Austria ['ɒstrɪə] *n* Autriche *f*. ◆**Austrian** *a*
& n autrichien, -ienne *(mf)*.

authentic [ɔː'θentɪk] *a* authentique.
◆**authenticate** *vt* authentifier.
◆**authen'ticity** *n* authenticité *f*.

author ['ɔːθər] *n* auteur *m*. ◆**authoress** *n*
femme *f* auteur. ◆**authorship** *n (of book
etc)* paternité *f*.

authority [ɔː'θɒrɪtɪ] *n* autorité *f*; *(permission)*
autorisation *f* (to do de faire); **to be in a.** *(in
charge)* être responsable. ◆**authori-
'tarian** *a & n* autoritaire *(mf)*.
◆**authoritative** *a (report)* autorisé; *(tone,
person)* autoritaire.

authorize ['ɔːθəraɪz] *vt* autoriser (to do à
faire). ◆**authori'zation** *n* autorisation *f*.

autistic [ɔː'tɪstɪk] *a* autiste, autistique.

autobiography [ɔːtəbaɪ'ɒgrəfɪ] *n* autobiographie *f*.

autocrat ['ɔːtəkræt] *n* autocrate *m*. ◆**auto-
'cratic** *a* autocratique.

autograph ['ɔːtəgrɑːf] *n* autographe *m*; — *vt*
dédicacer (for à).

automat ['ɔːtəmæt] *n Am* cafétéria *f* à
distributeurs automatiques.

automate ['ɔːtəmeɪt] *vt* automatiser.
◆**auto'mation** *n* automatisation *f*, automation *f*.

automatic [ɔːtə'mætɪk] *a* automatique.
◆**automatically** *adv* automatiquement.

automaton [ɔː'tɒmətən] *n* automate *m*.

automobile ['ɔːtəməbiːl] *n Am* auto(mobile)
f.

autonomous [ɔː'tɒnəməs] *a* autonome. ◆**autonomy** *n* autonomie *f*.

autopsy ['ɔːtɒpsɪ] *n* autopsie *f*.

autumn ['ɔːtəm] *n* automne *m*. ◆**autumnal** [ɔː'tʌmnəl] *a* automnal.

auxiliary [ɔːg'zɪljərɪ] *a* & *n* auxiliaire (*mf*); **a.** (**verb**) (verbe) *m* auxiliaire *m*.

avail [ə'veɪl] **1** *vt* to a. oneself of profiter de, tirer parti de. **2** *n* to no a. en vain; of no a. inutile.

available [ə'veɪləb(ə)l] *a* (*thing, means etc*) disponible; (*person*) libre, disponible; (*valid*) valable; a. to all (*goal etc*) accessible à tous. ◆**availa'bility** *n* disponibilité *f*; validité *f*; accessibilité *f*.

avalanche ['ævəlɑːnʃ] *n* avalanche *f*.

avarice ['ævərɪs] *n* avarice *f*. ◆**ava'ricious** *a* avare.

avenge [ə'vendʒ] *vt* venger; to a. oneself se venger (on de).

avenue ['ævənjuː] *n* avenue *f*; (*way to a result*) Fig voie *f*.

average ['ævərɪdʒ] *n* moyenne *f*; on a. en moyenne; – *a* moyen; – *vt* (*do*) faire en moyenne; (*reach*) atteindre la moyenne de; (*figures*) faire la moyenne de.

averse [ə'vɜːs] *a* to be a. to doing répugner à faire. ◆**aversion** *n* (*dislike*) aversion *f*, répugnance *f*.

avert [ə'vɜːt] *vt* (*prevent*) éviter; (*turn away*) détourner (**from** de).

aviary ['eɪvɪərɪ] *n* volière *f*.

aviation [eɪvɪ'eɪʃ(ə)n] *n* aviation *f*. ◆**'aviator** *n* aviateur, -trice *mf*.

avid ['ævɪd] *a* avide (**for** de).

avocado [ævə'kɑːdəʊ] *n* (*pl* -os) a. (**pear**) avocat *m*.

avoid [ə'vɔɪd] *vt* éviter; to a. doing éviter de faire. ◆**-able** *a* évitable. ◆**avoidance** *n* his a. of (*danger etc*) son désir *m* d'éviter; tax a. évasion *f* fiscale.

avowed [ə'vaʊd] *a* (*enemy*) déclaré, avoué.

await [ə'weɪt] *vt* attendre.

awake [ə'weɪk] *vi* (*pt* awoke, *pp* awoken) s'éveiller; – *vt* (*person, hope etc*) éveiller; – *a* réveillé, éveillé; (**wide**-)a. éveillé; to keep s.o. a. empêcher qn de dormir, tenir qn éveillé; he's (**still**) a. il ne dort pas (encore); a. to (*conscious of*) conscient de. ◆**awaken 1** *vti* = awake. **2** *vt* to a. s.o. to sth faire prendre conscience de qch à qn. ◆**awakening** *n* réveil *m*.

award [ə'wɔːd] *vt* (*money*) attribuer; (*prize*) décerner, attribuer; (*damages*) accorder; – *n* (*prize*) prix *m*, récompense *f*; (*scholarship*) bourse *f*.

aware [ə'weər] *a* avisé, informé; a. of (*conscious*) conscient de; (*informed*) au courant de; to become a. of prendre conscience de. ◆**-ness** *n* conscience *f*.

awash [ə'wɒʃ] *a* inondé (**with** de).

away [ə'weɪ] *adv* **1** (*distant*) loin; (**far**) a. au loin, très loin; **5 km** a. à 5 km (de distance). **2** (*absent*) parti, absent; a. **with you!** va-t-en!; to **drive** a. partir (en voiture); to **look** a. détourner les yeux; to **work/talk/** *etc* a. travailler/parler/*etc* sans relâche; to **fade/melt** a. disparaître/fondre complètement. **3** to **play** a. *Sp* jouer à l'extérieur.

awe [ɔː] *n* crainte *f* (*mêlée de respect*); to be in a. of s.o. éprouver de la crainte envers qn. ◆**a.-inspiring** *a*, ◆**awesome** *a* (*impressive*) imposant; (*frightening*) effrayant.

awful ['ɔːfəl] *a* affreux; (*terrifying*) épouvantable; (*ill*) malade; an a. lot of *Fam* un nombre incroyable de; **I feel** a. (**about it**) j'ai vraiment honte. ◆**-ly** *adv* affreusement; (*very*) *Fam* terriblement; **thanks** a. merci infiniment.

awhile [ə'waɪl] *adv* quelque temps; (*to stay, wait*) un peu.

awkward ['ɔːkwəd] *a* **1** (*clumsy*) maladroit; (*age*) ingrat. **2** (*difficult*) difficile; (*cumbersome*) gênant; (*tool*) peu commode; (*time*) inopportun; (*silence*) gêné. ◆**-ly** *adv* maladroitement; (*speak*) d'un ton gêné; (*placed*) à un endroit difficile. ◆**-ness** *n* maladresse *f*; difficulté *f*; (*discomfort*) gêne *f*.

awning ['ɔːnɪŋ] *n* auvent *m*; (*over shop*) store *m*; (*glass canopy*) marquise *f*.

awoke(n) [ə'wəʊk(ən)] *see* awake.

awry [ə'raɪ] *adv* to **go** a. (*of plan etc*) mal tourner.

axe [æks] (*Am* ax) *n* hache *f*; (*reduction*) *Fig* coupe *f* sombre; – *vt* réduire; (*eliminate*) supprimer.

axiom ['æksɪəm] *n* axiome *m*.

axis, *pl* **axes** ['æksɪs, 'æksiːz] *n* axe *m*.

axle ['æks(ə)l] *n* essieu *m*.

ay(e) [aɪ] **1** *adv* oui. **2** *n* the **ayes** (*votes*) les voix *fpl* pour.

azalea [ə'zeɪlɪə] *n* (*plant*) azalée *f*.

B

B, b [biː] n B, b m; **2B** (*number*) 2 ter.
BA abbr = **Bachelor of Arts.**
babble ['bæb(ə)l] vi (*of baby, stream*) gazouiller; (*mumble*) bredouiller; – vt **to b.** (**out**) bredouiller; – n inv gazouillement m, gazouillis m; (*of voices*) rumeur f.
babe [beɪb] n **1** petit(e) enfant mf, bébé m. **2** (*girl*) Sl pépée f.
baboon [bə'buːn] n babouin m.
baby ['beɪbɪ] n bébé m; – a (*clothes etc*) de bébé; **b. boy** petit garçon m; **b. girl** petite fille f; **b. carriage** Am voiture f d'enfant; **b. sling** kangourou® m, porte-bébé m; **b. tiger**/etc bébé-tigre/etc m; **b. face** visage m poupin. **2** n Sl (*girl*) pépée f; (*girlfriend*) copine f. **3** vt Fam dorloter. ◆**b.-batterer** n bourreau m d'enfants. ◆**b.-minder** n gardien, -ienne mf d'enfants. ◆**b.-sit** vi (*pt & pp* **-sat**, *pres p* **-sitting**) garder les enfants, faire du baby-sitting. ◆**b.-sitter** n baby-sitter mf. ◆**b.-snatching** n rapt m d'enfant. ◆**b.-walker** n trotteur m, youpala® m.
babyish ['beɪbɪɪʃ] a Pej de bébé; (*puerile*) enfantin.
bachelor ['bætʃələr] n **1** célibataire m; **b. flat** garçonnière f. **2** B. **of Arts/of Science** licencié -ée m/f ès lettres/ès sciences.
back [bæk] n (*of person, animal*) dos m; (*of chair*) dossier m; (*of hand*) revers m; (*of house*) derrière m, arrière m; (*of room*) fond m; (*of page*) verso m, (*of fabric*) envers m; Fb arrière m; **at the b. of** (*book*) à la fin de; (*car*) à l'arrière de; **at the b. of one's mind** derrière la tête; **b. to front** devant derrière, à l'envers; **to get s.o.'s b. up** Fam irriter qn; **in b. of** Am derrière; – a arrière inv, de derrière; (*taxes*) arriéré; **b. door** porte f de derrière; **b. room** pièce f du fond; **b. end** (*of bus*) arrière m; **b. street** rue f écartée; **b. number** vieux numéro m; **b. pay** rappel m de salaire; **b. tooth** molaire f; – adv en arrière; **b. home** loin derrière; **far b. in the past** à une époque reculée; **to stand b.** (*of house*) être en retrait (**from** par rapport à); **to go b. and forth** aller et venir; **to come b.** revenir; **he's b.** il est de retour, il est rentré ou revenu; **a month b.** il y a un mois; **the trip there and b.** le voyage aller et retour; – vt Com financer; (*horse etc*) parier sur, jouer

(*car*) faire reculer; (*wall*) renforcer; **to b. s.o. (up)** (*support*) appuyer qn; – vi (*move backwards*) reculer; **to b. down** se dégonfler; **to b. out** (*withdraw*) se retirer; Aut sortir en marche arrière; **to b. on to** (*of window etc*) donner par derrière sur; **to b. up** Aut faire marche arrière. ◆**-ing** n (*aid*) soutien m; (*material*) support m, renfort m. ◆**-er** n (*supporter*) partisan m; Sp parieur, -euse mf; Fin bailleur m de fonds.
backache ['bækeɪk] n mal m aux reins. ◆**back'bencher** n Pol membre m sans portefeuille. ◆**backbiting** n médisance f. ◆**backchat** n impertinence f. ◆**back'date** vt (*cheque*) antidater. ◆**back'handed** a (*compliment*) équivoque. ◆**backhander** n revers m; (*bribe*) Fam pot-de-vin m. ◆**backrest** n dossier m. ◆**backside** n (*buttocks*) Fam derrière m. ◆**back'stage** adv dans les coulisses. ◆**backstroke** n Sp dos m crawlé. ◆**backtrack** vi rebrousser chemin. ◆**backup** n appui m; (*tailback*) Am embouteillage m; **b. lights** Aut feux mpl de recul. ◆**backwater** n (*place*) trou m perdu. ◆**backwoods** npl forêts f vierges. ◆**back'yard** n arrière-cour f; Am jardin m (à l'arrière d'une maison).
backbone ['bækbəʊn] n colonne f vertébrale; (*of fish*) grande arête f; (*main support*) pivot m.
backfire [bæk'faɪər] vi Aut pétarader; (*of plot etc*) Fig échouer.
backgammon ['bækgæmən] n trictrac m.
background ['bækgraʊnd] n fond m, arrière-plan m; (*events*) Fig antécédents mpl; (*education*) formation f; (*environment*) milieu m; (*conditions*) Pol climat m, contexte m; **to keep s.o. in the b.** tenir qn à l'écart; **b. music** musique f de fond.
backlash ['bæklæʃ] n choc m en retour, retour m de flamme.
backlog ['bæklɒg] n (*of work*) arriéré m.
backward ['bækwəd] a (*glance etc*) en arrière; (*retarded*) arriéré; (*action*) lent à faire; – adv = **backwards**. ◆**-ness** n (*of country etc*) retard m. ◆**backwards** adv en arrière; (*to walk*) à reculons; (*to fall*) à la

renverse; **to move b.** reculer; **to go b. and forwards** aller et venir.

bacon ['beɪkən] n lard m; (in rashers) bacon m; **b. and eggs** œufs mpl au jambon.

bacteria [bæk'tɪərɪə] npl bactéries fpl.

bad [bæd] a (**worse, worst**) mauvais; (wicked) méchant; (sad) triste; (accident, wound etc) grave; (tooth) carié; (arm, leg) malade; (pain) violent; (air) vicié; **b. language** gros mots mpl; **it's b. to think that** ... ce n'est pas bien de penser que ... ; **to feel b.** Med se sentir mal; **I feel b. about it** ça m'a chagriné; **things are b.** ça va mal; **she's not b.!** elle n'est pas mal!; **to go b.** se gâter; (of milk) tourner; **in a b. way** mal en point; (ill) très mal; (in trouble) dans le pétrin; **too b.!** tant pis! ◆**b.-'mannered** a mal élevé. ◆**b.-'tempered** a grincheux. ◆**badly** adv mal; (hurt) grièvement; **b. affected/shaken** très touché/bouleversé; **to be b. mistaken** se tromper lourdement; **to off** dans la gêne; **to be b. off for** manquer de; **to want b.** avoir grande envie de.

badge [bædʒ] n insigne m; (of postman etc) plaque f; (bearing slogan or joke) badge m.

badger ['bædʒər] **1** n (animal) blaireau m. **2** vt importuner.

badminton ['bædmɪntən] n badminton m.

baffle ['bæf(ə)l] vt (person) déconcerter, dérouter.

bag [bæg] **1** n sac m; pl (luggage) valises fpl, bagages mpl; (under the eyes) poches fpl; **bags of** Fam (lots of) beaucoup de; **an old b.** une vieille taupe; **in the b.** Fam dans la poche. **2** vt (-gg-) (take, steal) Fam piquer, s'adjuger; (animal) Sp tuer.

baggage ['bægɪdʒ] n bagages mpl; Mil équipement m; **b. car** Am fourgon m; **b. room** Am consigne f.

baggy ['bægɪ] a (-ier, -iest) (clothing) trop ample; (trousers) faisant des poches.

bagpipes ['bægpaɪps] npl cornemuse f.

Bahamas [bə'hɑːməz] npl **the B.** les Bahamas fpl.

bail [beɪl] **1** n Jur caution f; **on b.** en liberté provisoire; — vt **to b. (out)** fournir une caution pour; **to b. out** (ship) écoper; (person, company) Fig tirer d'embarras. **2** vi **to b. out** Am Av sauter (en parachute).

bailiff ['beɪlɪf] n Jur huissier m; (of land-owner) régisseur m.

bait [beɪt] **1** n amorce f, appât m; — vt (fishing hook) amorcer. **2** vt (annoy) asticoter, tourmenter.

baize [beɪz] n **green b.** (on card table etc) tapis m vert.

bak/e [beɪk] vt (faire) cuire (au four); — vi

(of cook) faire de la pâtisserie or du pain; (of cake etc) cuire (au four); **we're or it's baking (hot)** Fam on cuit. ◆**—ed** a (potatoes) au four; **b. beans** haricots mpl blancs (à la tomate). ◆**—ing** n cuisson f; **b. powder** levure f (chimique). ◆**—er** n boulanger, -ère mf. ◆**bakery** n boulangerie f.

balaclava [bælə'klɑːvə] n **b. (helmet)** passe-montagne m.

balance ['bæləns] n (scales) & Econ Pol Com balance f; (equilibrium) équilibre m; (of account) Com solde m; (remainder) reste m; **to strike a b.** trouver le juste milieu; **sense of b.** le sens m de la mesure; **in the b.** incertain; **on b.** à tout prendre; **b. sheet** bilan m; — vt tenir or mettre en équilibre (on sur); (budget, account) équilibrer; (compare) mettre en balance, peser; **to b. (out)** (compensate for) compenser; **to b. (oneself)** se tenir en équilibre; — vi (of accounts) être en équilibre, s'équilibrer.

balcony ['bælkənɪ] n balcon m.

bald [bɔːld] a (-er, -est) chauve; (statement) brutal; (tyre) lisse; **b. patch** or **spot** tonsure f. ◆**b.-'headed** a chauve. ◆**balding** a **to be b.** perdre ses cheveux. ◆**baldness** n calvitie f.

balderdash ['bɔːldədæʃ] n balivernes fpl.

bale [beɪl] **1** n (of cotton etc) balle f. **2** vi **to b. out** Av sauter (en parachute).

baleful ['beɪlfl] a sinistre, funeste.

balk [bɔːk] vi reculer (devant), regimber (at contre).

ball [bɔːl] **1** n balle f; (inflated) Fb Rugby etc ballon m; Billiards bille f; (of string, wool) pelote f; (sphere) boule f; (of meat or fish) Culin boulette f; **on the b.** (alert) Fam éveillé; **he's on the b.** (efficient, knowledge-able) Fam il connaît son affaire, il est au point; **b. bearing** roulement m à billes; **b. game** Am partie f de baseball; **it's a whole new b. game** or **a different b. game** Am Fig c'est une tout autre affaire. ◆**ballcock** n robinet m à flotteur. ◆**ballpoint** n stylo m à bille.

ball² [bɔːl] n (dance) bal m. ◆**ballroom** n salle f de danse.

ballad ['bæləd] n Liter ballade f; Mus romance f.

ballast ['bæləst] n lest m; — vt lester.

ballet ['bæleɪ] n ballet m. ◆**balle'rina** n ballerine f.

ballistic [bə'lɪstɪk] a **b. missile** engin m balistique.

balloon [bə'luːn] n ballon m; Met ballon-sonde m.

ballot ['bælət] *n* (*voting*) scrutin *m*; **b.** (*paper*) bulletin *m* de vote; **b. box** urne *f*; – *vt* (*members*) consulter (par un scrutin).

ballyhoo ['bælɪ'huː] *n Fam* battage *m* (publicitaire).

balm [baːm] *n* (*liquid, comfort*) baume *m*. ◆**balmy** *a* (*-ier, -iest*) **1** (*air*) *Lit* embaumé. **2** (*crazy*) *Fam* dingue, timbré.

baloney [bə'ləʊnɪ] *n Sl* foutaises *fpl*.

Baltic ['bɔːltɪk] *n* the B. la Baltique.

balustrade ['bæləstreɪd] *n* balustrade *f*.

bamboo [bæm'buː] *n* bambou *m*.

bamboozle [bæm'buːz(ə)l] *vt* (*cheat*) *Fam* embobiner.

ban [bæn] *n* interdiction *f*; – *vt* (**-nn-**) interdire; **to b. from** (*club etc*) exclure de; **to ban s.o. from doing** interdire à qn de faire. ◆**banal** [bə'nɑːl, *Am* 'beɪn(ə)l] *a* banal. ◆**ba'nality** *n* banalité *f*.

banana [bə'nɑːnə] *n* banane *f*.

band [bænd] *n* **1** (*strip*) bande *f*; (*of hat*) ruban *m*; **rubber** *or* **elastic b.** élastique *m*. **2** *n* (*group*) bande *f*; *Mus* (*petit*) orchestre *m*; *Mil* fanfare *f*; – *vi* **to b. together** former une bande, se grouper. ◆**bandstand** *n* kiosque *m* à musique. ◆**bandwagon** *n* to **jump on the b.** *Fig* suivre le mouvement.

bandage ['bændɪdʒ] *n* (*strip*) bande *f*; (*for wound*) pansement *m*; (*for holding in place*) bandage *m*; – *vt* **to b. (up)** (*arm, leg*) bander; (*wound*) mettre un pansement sur.

Band-Aid® ['bændeɪd] *n* pansement *m* adhésif.

bandit ['bændɪt] *n* bandit *m*. ◆**banditry** *n* banditisme *m*.

bandy ['bændɪ] **1** *a* (**-ier, -iest**) (*person*) bancal; (*legs*) arqué. ◆**b.-'legged** *a* bancal. **2** *vt* **to b. about** (*story etc*) faire circuler, propager.

bane [beɪn] *n Lit* fléau *m*. ◆**baneful** *a* funeste.

bang [bæŋ] *n* **1** (*hit, noise*) coup *m* (violent); (*of gun etc*) détonation *f*; (*of door*) claquement *m*; – *vt* cogner, frapper; (*door*) (faire) claquer; **to b. one's head** se cogner la tête; – *vi* cogner, frapper; (*of door*) claquer; (*of gun*) détoner; (*of firework*) éclater; **to b. down** (*lid*) rabattre (violemment); **to b. into** sth heurter qch; – *int* vlan!, pan!; **to go (off) b.** éclater. **2** *adv* (*exactly*) *Fam* exactement; **b. in the middle** en plein milieu; **b. on six** à six heures tapantes.

banger ['bæŋər] *n* **1** *Culin Fam* saucisse *f*. **2** (*firecracker*) pétard *m*. **3** *old* **b.** (*car*) *Fam* tacot *m*, guimbarde *f*.

bangle ['bæŋg(ə)l] *n* bracelet *m* (rigide).

bangs [bæŋz] *npl* (*of hair*) *Am* frange *f*.

banish ['bænɪʃ] *vt* bannir.

banister ['bænɪstər] *n* banister(s) rampe *f* (d'escalier).

banjo ['bændʒəʊ] *n* (*pl* **-os** *or* **-oes**) banjo *m*.

bank [bæŋk] **1** *n* (*of river*) bord *m*, rive *f*; (*raised*) berge *f*; (*of earth*) talus *m*; (*of sand*) banc *m*; **the Left B.** (*in Paris*) la Rive gauche; – *vt* **to b. (up)** (*earth etc*) amonceler; (*fire*) couvrir. **2** *n Com* banque *f*; **b. account** compte *m* en banque; **b. card** carte *f* d'identité bancaire; **b. holiday** jour *m* férié; **b. note** billet *m* de banque; **b. rate** taux *m* d'escompte; – *vt* (*money*) *Com* mettre en banque; – *vi* avoir un compte en banque (**with** à). **3** *vi Av* virer. **4** *vi* **to b. on s.o./sth** (*rely on*) compter sur qn/qch. ◆**-ing** *a* bancaire; – *n* (*activity, profession*) la banque. ◆**-er** *n* banquier *m*.

bankrupt ['bæŋkrʌpt] *a* **to go b.** faire faillite; **b. of** (*ideas*) *Fig* dénué de; – *vt* mettre en faillite. ◆**bankruptcy** *n* faillite *f*.

banner ['bænər] *n* (*at rallies etc*) banderole *f*; (*flag*) & *Fig* bannière *f*.

banns [bænz] *npl* bans *mpl*.

banquet ['bæŋkwɪt] *n* banquet *m*.

banter ['bæntər] *vti* plaisanter; – *n* plaisanterie *f*. ◆**-ing** *a* (*tone, air*) plaisantin.

baptism ['bæptɪzəm] *n* baptême *m*. ◆**bap'tize** *vt* baptiser.

bar [baːr] *n* **1** barre *f*; (*of gold*) lingot *m*; (*of chocolate*) tablette *f*; (*on window*) & *Jur* barreau *m*; **b. of soap** savonnette *f*; **behind bars** *Jur* sous les verrous; **to be a b.** *to Fig* faire obstacle à. **2** *n* (*pub*) bar *m*; (*counter*) comptoir *m*. **3** *n* (*group of notes*) *Mus* mesure *f*. **4** *vt* (**-rr-**) (*way etc*) bloquer, barrer; (*window*) griller. **5** *vt* (*prohibit*) interdire (**s.o. from doing** à qn de faire); (*exclude*) exclure (**from** de). **6** *prep* sauf. ◆**barmaid** *n* serveuse *f* de bar. ◆**barman** *n*, ◆**bartender** *n* barman *m*.

Barbados [baːˈbeɪdɒs] *n* Barbade *f*.

barbarian [baːˈbeərɪən] *n* barbare *mf*. ◆**barbaric** *a* barbare. ◆**barbarity** *n* barbarie *f*.

barbecue ['baːbɪkjuː] *n* barbecue *m*; – *vt* griller (au barbecue).

barbed [baːbd] *a* **b. wire** fil *m* de fer barbelé; (*fence*) barbelés *mpl*.

barber ['baːbər] *n* coiffeur *m* (*pour hommes*).

barbiturate [baːˈbɪtjʊrət] *n* barbiturique *m*.

bare [beər] *a* (**-er, -est**) nu; (*tree, hill etc*) dénudé; (*cupboard*) vide; (*mere*) simple; **the b. necessities** le strict nécessaire; **with his b. hands** à mains nues; – *vt* mettre à nu.

◆**—ness** n (of person) nudité f.
◆**bareback** adv to ride b. monter à cru.
◆**barefaced** a (lie) éhonté. ◆**barefoot**
adv nu-pieds; — a aux pieds nus. ◆**bare-
'headed** a & adv nu-tête inv.

barely ['beəlɪ] adv (scarcely) à peine, tout
juste.

bargain ['bɑːgɪn] n (deal) marché m, affaire
f; a (good) b. (cheap buy) une occasion, une
bonne affaire; it's a b.! (agreed) c'est
entendu!; into the b. par-dessus le marché;
b. price prix m exceptionnel; b. counter
rayon m des soldes; — vi (negotiate)
négocier; (haggle) marchander; to b. for or
on sth Fig s'attendre à qch. ◆**—ing** n
négociations fpl; marchandage m.

barge [bɑːdʒ] 1 n chaland m, péniche f. 2 vi
to b. in (enter a room) faire irruption;
(interrupt) interrompre; to b. into (hit) se
cogner contre.

baritone ['bærɪtəʊn] n (voice, singer)
baryton m.

bark [bɑːk] 1 n (of tree) écorce f. 2 vi (of dog
etc) aboyer; — n aboiement m. ◆**—ing** n
aboiements mpl.

barley ['bɑːlɪ] n orge f; b. sugar sucre m
d'orge.

barmy ['bɑːmɪ] a (-ier, -iest) Fam dingue,
timbré.

barn [bɑːn] n (for crops etc) grange f; (for
horses) écurie f; (for cattle) étable f.
◆**barnyard** n basse-cour f.

barometer [bə'rɒmɪtər] n baromètre m.

baron ['bærən] n baron m; (industrialist) Fig
magnat m. ◆**baroness** n baronne f.

baroque [bə'rɒk, Am bə'rəʊk] a & n Archit
Mus etc baroque (m).

barracks ['bærəks] npl caserne f.

barrage ['bærɑːʒ, Am bə'rɑːʒ] n (barrier)
barrage m; a b. of (questions etc) un feu
roulant de.

barrel ['bærəl] n 1 (cask) tonneau m; (of oil)
baril m. 2 (of gun) canon m. 3 b. organ
orgue m de Barbarie.

barren ['bærən] a stérile; (style) Fig aride.

barrette [bə'ret] n (hair slide) Am barrette f.

barricade ['bærɪkeɪd] n barricade f; — vt
barricader; to b. oneself (in) se barricader.

barrier ['bærɪər] n barrière f; Fig obstacle m,
barrière f; (ticket) b. Rail portillon m;
sound b. mur m du son.

barring ['bɑːrɪŋ] prep sauf, excepté.

barrister ['bærɪstər] n avocat m.

barrow ['bærəʊ] n charrette f or voiture f à
bras; (wheelbarrow) brouette f.

barter ['bɑːtər] vt troquer, échanger (for
contre); — n troc m, échange m.

base [beɪs] 1 n (bottom, main ingredient)
base f; (of tree, lamp) pied m. 2 n Mil base f.
3 vt baser, fonder (on sur); based in or on
London basé à Londres. 4 a (dishonourable)
bas, ignoble; (metal) vil. ◆**—less** a sans
fondement. ◆**—ness** n bassesse f.
◆**baseball** n base-ball m. ◆**baseboard**
n Am plinthe f.

basement ['beɪsmənt] n sous-sol m.

bash [bæʃ] n Fam (bang) coup m; to have a
b. (try) essayer un coup; — vt Fam (hit)
cogner; to b. about (ill-treat) malmener;
to b. s.o. up tabasser qn; to b. in or down
(door etc) défoncer. ◆**—ing** n (thrashing)
Fam raclée f.

bashful ['bæʃfəl] a timide.

basic ['beɪsɪk] a fondamental, de
base; — n the basics Fam l'essentiel m.
◆**—ally** [-klɪ] adv au fond.

basil ['bæz(ə)l] n Bot Culin basilic m.

basilica [bə'zɪlɪkə] n basilique f.

basin ['beɪs(ə)n] n bassin m, bassine f; (for
soup, food) bol m; (of river) bassin m;
(portable washbasin) cuvette f; (sink)
lavabo m.

basis , pl **-ses** [beɪsɪs, -siːz] n base f; on the
b. of d'après; on that b. dans ces conditions; on a weekly/etc b. chaque
semaine/etc.

bask [bɑːsk] vi se chauffer.

basket ['bɑːskɪt] n panier m; (for bread,
laundry, litter) corbeille f. ◆**basketball** n
basket(-ball) m.

Basque [bæsk] a & n basque (mf).

bass¹ [beɪs] n Mus basse f; — n (note, voice)
bas.

bass² [bæs] n (sea fish) bar m; (fresh-water)
perche f.

bassinet [bæsɪ'net] n (cradle) Am couffin m.

bastard ['bɑːstəd] 1 n & a bâtard, -arde
(mf). 2 n Pej Sl salaud m, salope f.

baste [beɪst] vt 1 (fabric) bâtir. 2 Culin
arroser.

bastion ['bæstɪən] n bastion m.

bat [bæt] 1 n (animal) chauve-souris f. 2 n
Cricket batte f; Table Tennis raquette f; off
my own b. de ma propre initiative; — vt
(-tt-) (ball) frapper. 3 vt she didn't b. an
eyelid elle n'a pas sourcillé.

batch [bætʃ] n (of people) groupe m; (of
letters) paquet m; (of books) lot m; (of
loaves) fournée f; (of papers) liasse f.

bated ['beɪtɪd] a with b. breath en retenant
son souffle.

bath [bɑːθ] n (pl -s [bɑːðz]) bain m; (tub)
baignoire f; swimming baths piscine f; — vt
baigner; — vi prendre un bain.

◆**bathrobe** n peignoir m (de bain); Am robe f de chambre. ◆**bathroom** n salle f de bain(s); (toilet) Am toilettes fpl. ◆**bathtub** n baignoire f.

bath/e [beɪð] vt baigner; (wound) laver; – vi se baigner; Am prendre un bain; – n bain m (de mer), baignade f. ◆—**ing** n baignade(s) f(pl); **b. costume** or **suit** maillot m de bain.

baton [ˈbatən, Am ˈbatɒn] n Mus Mil bâton m; (truncheon) matraque f.

battalion [bəˈtæljən] n bataillon m.

batter [ˈbatər] **1** n pâte f à frire. **2** vt battre, frapper; (baby) martyriser; Mil pilonner; **to b. down** (door) défoncer. ◆—**ed** a (car, hat) cabossé; (house) délabré; (face) meurtri; (wife) battu. ◆—**ing** n **to take a b.** Fig souffrir beaucoup.

battery [ˈbatərɪ] n Mil Aut Agr batterie f; (in radio etc) pile f.

battle [ˈbat(ə)l] n bataille f; (struggle) lutte f; **that's half the b.** Fam c'est ça le secret de la victoire; – vi se battre, lutter. ◆**battlefield** n champ m de bataille. ◆**battleship** n cuirassé m.

battlements [ˈbat(ə)lmənts] npl (indentations) créneaux mpl; (wall) remparts mpl.

batty [ˈbatɪ] a (-ier, -iest) Sl dingue, toqué.

baulk [bɔːk] vi reculer (at devant), regimber (at contre).

bawdy [ˈbɔːdɪ] a (-ier, -iest) paillard, grossier.

bawl [bɔːl] vti to b. (out) beugler, brailler; to b. s.o. out Am Sl engueuler qn.

bay [beɪ] **1** n Geog Archit baie f. **2** n Bot laurier m. **3** n (for loading etc) aire f. **4** n (of dog) aboiement m; **at b.** aux abois; **to hold at b.** tenir à distance; – vi aboyer. **5** a (horse) bai.

bayonet [ˈbeɪənɪt] n baïonnette f.

bazaar [bəˈzɑːr] n (market, shop) bazar m; (charity sale) vente f de charité.

bazooka [bəˈzuːkə] n bazooka m.

BC [biːˈsiː] abbr (before Christ) avant Jésus-Christ.

be [biː] vi (pres t am, are, is; pt was, were; pp been; pres p being) être; **it is green/small** c'est vert/petit; **she's a doctor** elle est médecin; **he's an Englishman** c'est un Anglais; **it's 3 (o'clock)** il est trois heures; **it's the sixth of May** c'est or nous sommes le six mai. **2** avoir; **to be hot/right/lucky** avoir chaud/raison/de la chance; **my feet are cold** j'ai froid aux pieds; **he's 20** (age) il a 20 ans; **to be 2 metres high** avoir 2 mètres de haut; **to be 6 feet tall** mesurer 1,80 m. **3**

(health) aller; **how are you?** comment vas-tu? **4** (place, situation) se trouver, être; **she's in York** elle se trouve or elle est à York. **5** (exist) être; **the best painter there is** le meilleur peintre qui soit; **leave me be** laissez-moi (tranquille); **that may be** cela se peut. **6** (go, come) **I've been to see her** je suis allé or j'ai été la voir; **he's (already) been** il est (déjà) venu. **7** (weather) & Math faire; **it's fine** il fait beau; **2 and 2 are 4** 2 et 2 font 4. **8** (cost) coûter, faire; **it's 20 pence** ça coûte 20 pence; **how much is it?** ça fait combien?, c'est combien? **9** (auxiliary) **I am/was doing** je fais/faisais; **I'm listening to the radio** (in the process of) je suis en train d'écouter la radio; **she's been there some time** elle est là depuis longtemps; **he was killed** il a été tué, on l'a tué; **I've been waiting (for) two hours** j'attends depuis deux heures; **it is said** on dit; **to be pitied** à plaindre; **isn't it?, aren't you?** etc n'est-ce pas?, non?; **I am!, he is!** etc oui! **10** (+ inf) **he is to come** (must) il doit venir; **he's shortly to go** (intends to) il va bientôt partir. **11 there is** or **are** il y a; (pointing) voilà; **here is** or **are** voici.

beach [biːtʃ] n plage f. ◆**beachcomber** n (person) ramasseur d'épaves.

beacon [ˈbiːkən] n Nau Av balise f; (lighthouse) phare m.

bead [biːd] n (small sphere, drop of liquid) perle f; (of rosary) grain m; (of sweat) goutte f; (string of) beads collier m.

beak [biːk] n bec m.

beaker [ˈbiːkər] n gobelet m.

beam [biːm] **1** n (of wood) poutre f. **2** n (of light) rayon m; (of headlight, torch) faisceau m (lumineux); – vi rayonner; (of person) Fig sourire largement. **3** vt Rad diffuser. ◆—**ing** a (radiant) radieux.

bean [biːn] n haricot m; (of coffee) grain m; (broad) fève f; **to be full of beans** Fam déborder d'entrain. ◆**beanshoots** npl, ◆**beansprouts** npl germes mpl de soja.

bear¹ [beər] n (animal) ours m.

bear² [beər] vt (pt bore, pp borne) (carry, show) porter; (endure) supporter; (resemblance) offrir; (comparison) soutenir; (responsibility) assumer; (child) donner naissance à; **to b. in mind** tenir compte de; **to b. out** corroborer; – vi **to b. left/etc** (turn) tourner à gauche/etc; **to b.** (go) aller en direction du nord/etc; **to b. (up)on** (relate to) se rapporter à; **to b. heavily on** (of burden) Fig peser sur; **to b. with** être indulgent envers, être patient avec; **to bring to b.** (one's energies) consacrer (on à);

(*pressure*) exercer (**on** sur); **to b. up** ne pas se décourager, tenir le coup; **b. up!** du courage! ◆**-ing** n (*posture, conduct*) maintien m; (*relationship, relevance*) relation f (**on** avec); *Nau Av* position f; **to get one's bearings** s'orienter. ◆**-able** a supportable. ◆**-er** n porteur, -euse mf.

beard [biəd] n barbe f. ◆**bearded** a barbu.

beast [biːst] n bête f, animal m; (*person*) *Pej* brute f. ◆**beastly** a *Fam* (bad) vilain, infect; (*spiteful*) méchant; — adv *Fam* terriblement.

beat [biːt] n (*of heart, drum*) battement m; (*of policeman*) ronde f; *Mus* mesure f, rythme m; — vt (*pt beat, pp beaten*) battre; (*defeat*) vaincre, battre; **to b. a drum** battre du tambour; **that beats me** *Fam* ça me dépasse; **to b. s.o. to it** devancer qn; **b. it!** *Sl* fichez le camp!; **to b. back** or **off** repousser; **to b. down** (*price*) faire baisser; **to b. in** or **down** (*door*) défoncer; (*tune*) jouer; **to b. out** (*rhythm*) marquer; (*tune*) jouer; **to b. s.o. up** tabasser qn; — vi battre; (*at door*) frapper (**at** à); **to b. about** or **around the bush** *Fam* tourner autour du pot; **to b. down** (*of rain*) tomber à verse; (*of sun*) taper. ◆**-ing** n (*blows, defeat*) raclée f. ◆**-er** n (*for eggs*) batteur m.

beauty ['bjuːtɪ] n (*quality, woman*) beauté f; **it's a b.!** c'est une merveille!; **the b. of it is ...** le plus beau, c'est que ... ; **b. parlour** institut m de beauté; **b. spot** (*on skin*) grain m de beauté; (*in countryside*) site m pittoresque. ◆**beau'tician** n esthéticienne f. ◆**beautiful** a (très) beau; (*superb*) merveilleux. ◆**beautifully** adv merveilleusement.

beaver ['biːvər] n castor m; — vi **to b. away** travailler dur (**at** sth à qch).

because [bɪˈkɒz] conj parce que; **b. of** à cause de.

beck [bek] n **at s.o.'s b. and call** aux ordres de qn.

beckon ['bekən] vti **to b. (to) s.o.** faire signe à qn (**to do** de faire).

becom/e [bɪˈkʌm] 1 vi (*pt became, pp become*) devenir; **to b. a painter** devenir peintre; **to b. thin** maigrir; **to b. worried** commencer à s'inquiéter; **what has b. of her?** qu'est-elle devenue? 2 vt **that hat becomes her** ce chapeau lui sied or lui va. ◆**-ing** a (*clothes*) seyant; (*modesty*) bienséant.

bed [bed] n lit m; *Geol* couche f; (*of vegetables*) carré m; (*of sea*) fond m; (*flower bed*) parterre m; **to go to b.** (aller) se coucher; **in b.** couché; **to get out of b.** se lever; **b. and**

breakfast (*in hotel etc*) chambre f avec petit déjeuner; **b. settee** (canapé m) convertible m; **air b.** matelas m pneumatique; — vt (*-dd-*) **to b. (out)** (*plant*) repiquer; — vi **to b. down** se coucher. ◆**bedding** n literie f. ◆**bedbug** n punaise f. ◆**bedclothes** fpl couvertures fpl et draps mpl. ◆**bedridden** a alité. ◆**bedroom** n chambre f à coucher. ◆**bedside** n chevet m; — a (*lamp, book, table*) de chevet. ◆**bed'sitter** n, *Fam* ◆**bedsit** n chambre f meublée. ◆**bedspread** n dessus-de-lit m inv. ◆**bedtime** n heure f du coucher.

bedeck [bɪˈdek] vt orner (**with** de).

bedevil [bɪˈdev(ə)l] vt (*-ll-, Am -l-*) (*plague*) tourmenter; (*confuse*) embrouiller; **bedevilled by** (*problems etc*) perturbé par, empoisonné par.

bedlam ['bedləm] n (*noise*) *Fam* chahut m.

bedraggled [bɪˈdræg(ə)ld] a (*clothes, person*) débraillé.

bee [biː] n abeille f. ◆**beehive** n ruche f. ◆**beekeeping** n apiculture f. ◆**beeline** n **to make a b.** for aller droit vers.

beech [biːtʃ] n (*tree, wood*) hêtre m.

beef [biːf] 1 n bœuf m. 2 vi (*complain*) *Sl* rouspéter. ◆**beefburger** n hamburger m. ◆**beefy** a (*-ier, -iest*) *Fam* musclé, costaud.

beer [bɪər] n bière f; **b. glass** chope f. ◆**beery** a (*room, person*) qui sent la bière.

beet [biːt] n betterave f (à sucre); *Am* = **beetroot**. ◆**beetroot** n betterave f (potagère).

beetle ['biːt(ə)l] 1 n cafard m, scarabée m. 2 vi **to b. off** *Fam* se sauver.

befall [bɪˈfɔːl] vt (*pt befell, pp befallen*) arriver à.

befit [bɪˈfɪt] vt (*-tt-*) convenir à.

before [bɪˈfɔːr] adv avant; (*already*) déjà; (*in front*) devant; **the month b.** le mois d'avant or précédent; **the day b.** la veille; **I've never done it b.** je ne l'ai jamais (encore) fait; — prep (*time*) avant; (*place*) devant; **the year b. last** il y a deux ans; — conj avant que (+ ne + sub), avant de (+ inf); **b. he goes** avant qu'il (ne) parte; **b. going** avant de partir. ◆**beforehand** adv à l'avance, avant.

befriend [bɪˈfrend] vt offrir son amitié à, aider.

befuddled [bɪˈfʌd(ə)ld] a (*drunk*) ivre.

beg [beg] vt (*-gg-*) **to b. (for)** solliciter, demander; (*bread, money*) mendier; **to b. s.o. to do** prier or supplier qn de faire; **I b. to** je me permets de; **to b. the question** esquiver la question; — vi mendier;

(*entreat*) supplier; **to go begging** (*of food, articles*) ne pas trouver d'amateurs. **◆beggar** *n* mendiant, -ante *mf*; (*person*) *Sl* individu *m*; **lucky b.** veinard, -arde *mf*. **◆beggarly** *a* misérable.

beget [bɪ'get] *vt* (*pt* begot, *pp* begotten, *pres p* begetting) engendrer.

begin [bɪ'gɪn] *vt* (*pt* began, *pp* begun, *pres p* beginning) commencer; (*fashion, campaign*) lancer; (*bottle, sandwich*) entamer; (*conversation*) engager; **to b. doing** *or* **to do** commencer *or* se mettre à faire; **–** *vi* commencer (**with, by doing** par faire); **to b. on sth** commencer qch; **beginning from** à partir de; **to b. with** (*first*) d'abord. **◆—ning** *n* commencement *m*, début *m*. **◆—ner** *n* débutant, -ante *mf*.

begrudge [bɪ'grʌdʒ] *vt* (*give unwillingly*) donner à contrecœur; (*envy*) envier (**s.o. sth** qch à qn); (*reproach*) reprocher (**s.o. sth** qch à qn); **to b. doing** faire à contrecœur.

behalf [bɪ'hɑːf] *n* **on b. of** pour, au nom de, de la part de; (*in the interest of*) en faveur de, pour.

behave [bɪ'heɪv] *vi* se conduire; (*of machine*) fonctionner; **to b. (oneself)** se tenir bien; (*of child*) être sage. **◆behaviour** *n* conduite *f*, comportement *m*; **to be on one's best b.** se conduire de son mieux.

behead [bɪ'hed] *vt* décapiter.

behest [bɪ'hest] *n Lit* ordre *m*.

behind [bɪ'haɪnd] **1** *prep* derrière; (*more backward than, late according to*) en retard sur; **–** *adv* derrière; (*late*) en retard (**with, in** dans). **2** *n* (*buttocks*) *Fam* derrière *m*. **◆behindhand** *adv* en retard.

beholden [bɪ'həʊldən] *a* redevable (**to** à, **for** de).

beige [beɪʒ] *a & n* beige (*m*).

being [ˈbiːɪŋ] *n* (*person, life*) être *m*; **to come into b.** naître, être créé.

belated [bɪ'leɪtɪd] *a* tardif.

belch [beltʃ] **1** *vi* (*of person*) faire un renvoi, éructer; **–** *n* renvoi *m*. **2** *vt* **to b. (out)** (*smoke*) vomir.

beleaguered [bɪ'liːgəd] *a* (*besieged*) assiégé.

belfry [ˈbelfrɪ] *n* beffroi *m*, clocher *m*.

Belgium [ˈbeldʒəm] *n* Belgique *f*. **◆Belgian** [ˈbeldʒən] *a & n* belge (*mf*).

belie [bɪ'laɪ] *vt* démentir.

belief [bɪ'liːf] *n* (*believing, thing believed*) croyance *f* (**in** s.o. en qn, **in** sth à *or* en qch); (*trust*) confiance *f*, foi *f*; (*faith*) Rel foi *f* (**in** en).

believ/e [bɪ'liːv] *vti* croire (**in** sth à qch, **in** God/s.o. en Dieu/qn); **I b. so** je crois que oui; **I b. I'm right** je crois avoir raison; **to b.**

in doing croire qu'il faut faire; **he doesn't b. in smoking** il désapprouve que l'on fume. **◆—able** *a* croyable. **◆—er** *n Rel* croyant, -ante *mf*; **b. in** (*supporter*) partisan, -ane *mf* de.

belittle [bɪ'lɪt(ə)l] *vt* déprécier.

bell [bel] *n* cloche *f*; (*small*) clochette *f*; (*in phone*) sonnerie *f*; (*on door, bicycle*) sonnette *f*; (*on dog*) grelot *m*. **◆bellboy** *n*, **◆bellhop** *n Am* groom *m*.

belle [bel] *n* (*woman*) beauté *f*, belle *f*.

belligerent [bɪ'lɪdʒərənt] *a & n* belligérant, -ante (*mf*).

bellow [ˈbeləʊ] *vi* beugler, mugir.

bellows [ˈbeləʊz] *npl* (*pair of*) **b.** soufflet *m*.

belly [ˈbelɪ] *n* ventre *m*; **b. button** *Sl* nombril *m*. **◆bellyache** *n* mal *m* au ventre; **–** *vi Sl* rouspéter. **◆bellyful** *n* **to have a b.** *Sl* en avoir plein le dos.

belong [bɪ'lɒŋ] *vi* appartenir (**to** à); **to b. to** (*club*) être membre de; **the cup belongs here** la tasse se range ici. **◆—ings** *npl* affaires *fpl*.

beloved [bɪ'lʌvɪd] *a & n* bien-aimé, -ée (*mf*).

below [bɪ'ləʊ] *prep* (*lower than*) au-dessous de; (*under*) sous, au-dessous de; (*unworthy of*) *Fig* indigne de; **–** *adv* en dessous; **see b.** (*in book etc*) voir ci-dessous.

belt [belt] **1** *n* ceinture *f*; (*area*) zone *f*, région *f*; *Tech* courroie *f*. **2** *vt* (*hit*) *Sl* rosser. **3** *vi* **to b. (along)** (*rush*) *Sl* filer à toute allure; **b. up!** (*shut up*) *Sl* boucle-la!

bemoan [bɪ'məʊn] *vt* déplorer.

bench [bentʃ] *n* (*seat*) banc *m*; (*work table*) établi *m*, banc *m*; **the B.** *Jur* la magistrature (*assise*); (*court*) le tribunal.

bend [bend] *n* courbe *f*; (*in river, pipe*) coude *m*; (*in road*) *Aut* virage *m*; (*of arm, knee*) pli *m*; **round the b.** (*mad*) *Sl* tordu; **–** *vt* (*pt & pp* bent) courber; (*leg, arm*) plier; (*direct*) diriger; **to b. the rules** faire une entorse au règlement; **–** *vi* (*of branch*) plier, être courbé; (*of road*) tourner; **to b. (down)** se courber; **to b. (over** *or* **forward)** se pencher; **to b. (to s.o.'s will)** se soumettre à.

beneath [bɪ'niːθ] *prep* au-dessous de, sous; (*unworthy of*) indigne de; **–** *adv* (au-)dessous.

benediction [benɪ'dɪkʃ(ə)n] *n* bénédiction *f*.

benefactor [ˈbenɪfæktə] *n* bienfaiteur *m*. **◆benefactress** *n* bienfaitrice *f*.

beneficial [benɪ'fɪʃl] *a* bénéfique.

beneficiary [benɪ'fɪʃərɪ] *n* bénéficiaire *mf*.

benefit [ˈbenɪfɪt] *n* (*advantage*) avantage *m*; (*money*) allocation *f*; *pl* (*of science, education etc*) bienfaits *mpl*; **to s.o.'s b.** dans l'intérêt de qn; **for your (own) b.** pour vous, pour votre bien; **to be of b.** faire du bien (**to** à); **to give s.o. the b. of the doubt** accorder à qn le bénéfice du doute; **b. concert**/*etc* concert/*etc* m de bienfaisance; – *vt* faire du bien à; (*be useful to*) profiter à; – *vi* gagner (**from doing** à faire); **you'll b. from** *or* **by the rest** le repos vous fera du bien.

Benelux ['benilʌks] n Bénélux m.

benevolent [bɪ'nevələnt] a bienveillant. ◆**benevolence** n bienveillance f.

benign [bɪ'naɪn] a bienveillant, bénin; (*climate*) doux; (*tumour*) bénin.

bent [bent] **1** a (*nail, mind*) tordu; (*dishonest*) *Sl* corrompu; **b. on doing** résolu à faire. **2** n (*talent*) aptitude f (**for** pour); (*inclination, liking*) penchant m, goût m (**for** pour).

bequeath [bɪ'kwiːð] vt léguer (**to** à). ◆**bequest** n legs m.

bereaved [bɪ'riːvd] a endeuillé; – n **the b.** la famille, la femme *etc* du disparu. ◆**bereavement** n deuil m.

bereft [bɪ'reft] a **b. of** dénué de.

beret ['bereɪ, Am bə'reɪ] n béret m.

berk [bɜːk] n *Sl* imbécile *mf*.

berry ['berɪ] n baie f.

berserk [bə'zɜːk] a **to go b.** devenir fou, se déchaîner.

berth [bɜːθ] n (*in ship, train*) couchette f; (*anchorage*) mouillage m; – vi (*of ship*) mouiller.

beseech [bɪ'siːtʃ] vt (*pt & pp* besought *or* beseeched) *Lit* implorer (**to do** de faire).

beset [bɪ'set] vt (*pt & pp* beset, *pres p* besetting) assaillir (*qn*); **b. with obstacles**/*etc* semé *or* hérissé d'obstacles/*etc*.

beside [bɪ'saɪd] *prep* à côté de; **that's b. the point** ça n'a rien à voir; **b. oneself** (*angry, excited*) hors de soi.

besides [bɪ'saɪdz] *prep* (*in addition to*) en plus de; (*except*) excepté; **there are ten of us b.** Paul nous sommes dix sans compter Paul; – *adv* (*in addition*) de plus; (*moreover*) d'ailleurs.

besiege [bɪ'siːdʒ] vt (*of soldiers, crowd*) assiéger; (*annoy*) *Fig* assaillir (**with** de).

besotted [bɪ'sɒtɪd] a (*drunk*) abruti; **b. with** (*infatuated*) entiché de.

bespatter [bɪ'spætər] vt éclabousser (**with** de).

bespectacled [bɪ'spektɪk(ə)ld] a à lunettes.

bespoke [bɪ'spəʊk] a (*tailor*) à façon.

best [best] a meilleur; **the b. page in the book** la meilleure page du livre; **the b. part of** (*most*) la plus grande partie de; **the b. thing is** le mieux; **b. man** (*at wedding*) témoin m, garçon m d'honneur; – n **the (one) le**

meilleur, la meilleure; **it's for the b.** c'est pour le mieux; **at b.** au mieux; **to do one's b.** faire de son mieux; **to look one's b.,** be at **one's b.** être à son avantage; **to the b. of my knowledge** autant que je sache; **to make the b. of** (*accept*) s'accommoder de; **to get the b. of it** avoir le dessus; **in one's Sunday b.** endimanché; **all the b.!** portez-vous bien!; (*in letter*) amicalement; – *adv* **(the) b.** (*to play etc*) le mieux; **the b. loved** le plus aimé; **to think it b.** to juger prudent de. ◆**b.-'seller** n (*book*) best-seller m.

bestow [bɪ'stəʊ] vt accorder, conférer (**on** à).

bet [bet] n pari m; – vti (*pt & pp* bet *or* betted, *pres p* betting) parier (**on** sur, **that** que); **you b.!** *Fam* (*of course*) tu parles! ◆**betting** n pari(s) m(*pl*); **b. shop** *or* **office** bureau m du pari mutuel.

betoken [bɪ'təʊkən] vt *Lit* annoncer.

betray [bɪ'treɪ] vt trahir; **to b. to s.o.** (*give away to*) livrer à qn. ◆**betrayal** n (*disloyalty*) trahison f; (*disclosure*) révélation f.

better ['betər] a meilleur (**than** que); **she's (much) b.** *Med* elle va (bien) mieux; **he's b. than** (*at games*) il joue mieux que; (*at maths etc*) il est plus fort que; **that's b.** c'est mieux; **to get b.** (*recover*) se remettre; (*improve*) s'améliorer; **it's b. to go** il vaut mieux partir; **the b. part of** (*most*) la plus grande partie de; – *adv* **I had b. go** il vaut mieux que je parte; **so much the b.,** **all the b.** tant mieux (**for** pour); – n **to get the b. of s.o.** l'emporter sur qn; **change for the b.** amélioration f; **one's betters** ses supérieurs *mpl*; – *vt* (*improve*) améliorer; (*outdo*) dépasser; **to b. oneself** améliorer sa condition. ◆**–ment** n amélioration f.

between [bɪ'twiːn] *prep* entre; **we did it b.** (**the two of**) **us** nous l'avons fait à nous deux; **b. you and me** entre nous; **b. them,** (*time*) dans l'intervalle.

bevel ['bevəl] n (*edge*) biseau m.

beverage ['bevərɪdʒ] n boisson f.

bevy ['bevɪ] n (*of girls*) essaim m, bande f.

beware [bɪ'weər] vi **to b. of** (*s.o., sth*) se méfier de, prendre garde à, **b.!** méfiez-vous!, prenez garde!; **b. of falling**/*etc* prenez garde de (ne pas) tomber/*etc*; **'b. of the trains'** 'attention aux trains'.

bewilder [bɪ'wɪldər] vt dérouter, rendre perplexe. ◆**–ment** n confusion f.

bewitch [bɪ'wɪtʃ] vt enchanter. ◆**–ing** a enchanteur.

beyond [bɪ'jɒnd] *prep* (*further than*) au-delà

de; (*reach, doubt*) hors de; (*except*) sauf: **b. a year**/*etc* (*longer than*) plus d'un an/*etc*; **b. belief** incroyable; **b. his** *or* **her means** au-dessus de ses moyens; **it's b. me** ça me dépasse; — *adv* (*further*) au-delà.

bias ['baɪəs] **1** *n* penchant *m* (**towards** pour); (*prejudice*) préjugé *m*, parti pris *m*; — *vt* (**-ss-** *or* **-s-**) influencer. **2** *n* **cut on the b.** (*fabric*) coupé dans le biais. ◆**bias(s)ed** *a* partial; **to be b. against** avoir des préjugés contre.

bib [bɪb] *n* (*baby's*) bavoir *m*.

bible ['baɪb(ə)l] *n* bible *f*; **the B.** la Bible. ◆**biblical** ['bɪblɪk(ə)l] *a* biblique.

bibliography [bɪblɪ'ɒgrəfɪ] *n* bibliographie *f*.

bicarbonate [baɪ'kɑːbənət] *n* bicarbonate *m*.

bicentenary [baɪsen'tiːnərɪ] *n*, ◆**bicentennial** *n* bicentenaire *m*.

biceps ['baɪseps] *n Anat* biceps *m*.

bicker ['bɪkər] *vi* se chamailler. ◆**—ing** *n* chamailleries *fpl*.

bicycle ['baɪsɪk(ə)l] *n* bicyclette *f*; — *vi* faire de la bicyclette.

bid[1] [bɪd] *vt* (*pt & pp* **bid**, *pres p* **bidding**) offrir, faire une offre de; — *vi* faire une offre (**for** pour); **to b. for** *Fig* tenter d'obtenir; — *n* (*at auction*) offre *f*, enchère *f*; *Com* soumission *f*; (*attempt*) tentative *f*. ◆**—ding**[1] *n* enchères *fpl*. ◆**—der** *n* enchérisseur *m*; soumissionnaire *mf*; **to the highest b.** au plus offrant.

bid[2] [bɪd] *vt* (*pt* **bade** [bæd], *pp* **bidden** *or* **bid**, *pres p* **bidding**) (*command*) commander (**s.o. to do** à qn de faire); (*say*) dire. ◆**—ding**[2] *n* ordre(s) *m*(*pl*).

bide [baɪd] *vt* **to b. one's time** attendre le bon moment.

bier [bɪər] *n* (*for coffin*) brancards *mpl*.

bifocals [baɪ'fəʊkəlz] *npl* verres *mpl* à double foyer.

big [bɪg] *a* (**bigger, biggest**) grand, gros; (*in age, generous*) grand; (*in bulk, amount*) gros; **b. deal!** *Am Fam* (bon) et alors!; **b. mouth** *Fam* grande gueule *f*; **b. toe** gros orteil *m*; — *adv* **to do things b.** *Fam* faire grand; **to talk b.** fanfaronner. ◆**bighead** *n*, ◆**big'headed** *a Fam* prétentieux, -euse (*mf*). ◆**big-'hearted** *a* généreux. ◆**big-shot** *n*, ◆**bigwig** *n Fam* gros bonnet *m*. ◆**big-time** *a Fam* important.

bigamy ['bɪgəmɪ] *n* bigamie *f*. ◆**bigamist** *n* bigame *mf*. ◆**bigamous** *a* bigame.

bigot ['bɪgət] *n* fanatique *mf*; *Rel* bigot, -ote *mf*. ◆**bigoted** *a* fanatique; *Rel* bigot.

bike [baɪk] *n Fam* vélo *m*; — *vi Fam* aller à vélo.

bikini [bɪ'kiːnɪ] *n* bikini *m*.

bilberry ['bɪlbərɪ] *n* myrtille *f*.

bile [baɪl] *n* bile *f*. ◆**bilious** ['bɪlɪəs] *a* bilieux.

bilge [bɪldʒ] *n* (*nonsense*) *Sl* foutaises *fpl*.

bilingual [baɪ'lɪŋgwəl] *a* bilingue.

bill [bɪl] **1** *n* (*of bird*) bec *m*. **2** *n* (*invoice*) facture *f*, note *f*; (*in restaurant*) addition *f*; (*in hotel*) note *f*; (*draft*) traite *f*; (*of sale*) acte *m*; (*banknote*) *Am* billet *m*; (*law*) *Pol* projet *m* de loi; (*poster*) affiche *f*; **b. of fare** menu *m*; **b. of rights** déclaration *f* des droits; — *vt Th* mettre à l'affiche, annoncer; **to b. s.o.** envoyer la facture à qn. ◆**billboard** *n* panneau *m* d'affichage. ◆**billfold** *n Am* portefeuille *m*.

billet ['bɪlɪt] *vt Mil* cantonner; — *n* cantonnement *m*.

billiard ['bɪljəd] *a* (*table etc*) de billard. ◆**billiards** *npl* (*jeu m de*) billard *m*.

billion ['bɪljən] *n* billion *m*; *Am* milliard *m*.

billow ['bɪləʊ] *n* flot *m*; — *vi* (*of sea*) se soulever; (*of smoke*) tourbillonner.

billy-goat ['bɪlɪgəʊt] *n* bouc *m*.

bimonthly [baɪ'mʌnθlɪ] *a* (*fortnightly*) bimensuel; (*every two months*) bimestriel.

bin [bɪn] *n* boîte *f*; (*for bread*) coffre *m*, huche *f*; (*for litter*) boîte *f* à ordures, poubelle *f*.

binary ['baɪnərɪ] *a* binaire.

bind [baɪnd] **1** *vt* (*pt & pp* **bound**) lier; (*fasten*) attacher, lier; (*book*) relier; (*fabric, hem*) border; (*oblige*) lier, obliger *or* astreindre qn **à faire** à faire. **2** *n* (*bore*) *Fam* plaie *f*. ◆**—ing 1** *a* (*contract*) irrévocable; **to be b. on s.o.** *Jur* lier qn. **2** *n* (*of book*) reliure *f*. ◆**—er** *n* (*for papers*) classeur *m*.

binge [bɪndʒ] *n* **to go on a b.** *Sl* faire la bombe.

bingo ['bɪŋgəʊ] *n* loto *m*.

binoculars [bɪ'nɒkjʊləz] *npl* jumelles *fpl*.

biochemistry [baɪəʊ'kemɪstrɪ] *n* biochimie *f*.

biodegradable [baɪəʊdɪ'greɪdəb(ə)l] *a* biodégradable.

biography [baɪ'ɒgrəfɪ] *n* biographie *f*. ◆**biographer** *n* biographe *mf*.

biology [baɪ'ɒlədʒɪ] *n* biologie *f*. ◆**bio'logical** *a* biologique.

biped ['baɪped] *n* bipède *m*.

birch [bɜːtʃ] *n* **1** (*tree*) bouleau *m*. **2** (*whip*) verge *f*; — *vt* fouetter.

bird [bɜːd] *n* oiseau *m*; (*fowl*) *Culin* volaille *f*; (*girl*) *Sl* poulette *f*, nana *f*; **b.'s-eye view**

perspective f à vol d'oiseau; *Fig* vue f d'ensemble. ◆**birdseed** n grains *mpl* de millet.

biro® ['baɪərəʊ] n (pl -os) stylo m à bille, bic® m.

birth [bɜːθ] n naissance f; **to give b. to** donner naissance à; **b. certificate** acte m de naissance; **b. control** limitation f des naissances. ◆**birthday** n anniversaire m; **happy b.!** bon anniversaire! ◆**birthplace** n lieu m de naissance; (*house*) maison f natale. ◆**birthrate** n (taux m de) natalité f. ◆**birthright** n droit m (qu'on a dès sa naissance), patrimoine m.

biscuit ['bɪskɪt] n biscuit m, gâteau m sec; *Am* petit pain m au lait.

bishop ['bɪʃəp] n évêque m; (*in chess*) fou m.

bison ['baɪs(ə)n] n inv bison m.

bit¹ [bɪt] n morceau m; (*of string, time*) bout m; **a b.** (*a little*) un peu; **a tiny b.** un tout petit peu; **quite a b.** (*very*) très; (*much*) beaucoup; **not a b.** pas du tout; **a b. of luck** une chance; **b. by b.** petit à petit; **in bits (and pieces)** en morceaux; **to come to bits** se démonter. **2** (*coin*) pièce f. **3** (*of horse*) mors m. **4** (*of drill*) mèche f. **5** (*computer information*) bit m.

bit² [bɪt] see **bite**.

bitch [bɪtʃ] **1** n chienne f; (*woman*) *Pej Fam* garce f. **2** vi (*complain*) *Fam* râler. ◆**bitchy** a (**-ier, -iest**) *Fam* vache.

bit/e [baɪt] n (*wound*) morsure f; (*from insect*) piqûre f; *Fishing* touche f; (*mouthful*) bouchée f; (*of style etc*) *Fig* mordant m; **a b. to eat** un morceau à manger; — *vti* (*pt* **bit,** *pp* **bitten**) mordre; (*of insect*) piquer, mordre; **to b. one's nails** se ronger les ongles; **to b. on sth** mordre qch; **to b. sth off** arracher qch d'un coup de dent(s). ◆**-ing** a mordant; (*wind*) cinglant.

bitter ['bɪtər] **1** a (*person, taste, irony etc*) amer; (*cold, wind*) glacial, âpre; (*criticism*) acerbe; (*shock, fate*) cruel; (*conflict*) violent. **2** n bière f (pression). ◆**-ness** n amertume f; âpreté f; violence f. ◆**bitter-'sweet** a aigre-doux.

bivouac ['bɪvʊæk] n *Mil* bivouac m; — vi (**-ck-**) bivouaquer.

bizarre [bɪˈzɑːr] a bizarre.

blab [blæb] vi (**-bb-**) jaser. ◆**blabber** vi jaser. ◆**blabbermouth** n jaseur, -euse *mf*.

black [blæk] a (**-er, -est**) noir; **b. eye** œil m au beurre noir; **to give s.o. a b. eye** pocher l'œil à qn; **b. and blue** (*bruised*) couvert de bleus; **b. sheep** brebis f galeuse; **b. ice** verglas m; **b. pudding** boudin m; — vt (*colour*) noir m; (*Negro*) Noir, -e *mf*; — vt

noircir; (*refuse to deal with*) boycotter; — vi **to b. out** (*faint*) s'évanouir. ◆**blacken** vti noircir. ◆**blackish** a noirâtre. ◆**blackness** n noirceur f; (*of night*) obscurité f.

blackberry ['blækbərɪ] n mûre f. ◆**blackbird** n merle m. ◆**blackboard** n tableau m (noir). ◆**black'currant** n cassis m. ◆**blackleg** n (*strike breaker*) jaune m. ◆**blacklist** n liste f noire; — vt mettre sur la liste noire. ◆**blackmail** n chantage m; — vt faire chanter. ◆**blackmailer** n maître chanteur m. ◆**blackout** n panne f d'électricité; (*during war*) *Mil* black-out m; *Med* syncope f; (*news*) **b.** black-out m. ◆**blacksmith** n forgeron m.

blackguard ['blægɑːd, -gəd] n canaille f.

bladder ['blædər] n vessie f.

blade [bleɪd] n lame f; (*of grass*) brin m; (*of windscreen wiper*) caoutchouc m.

blame [bleɪm] vt accuser; (*censure*) blâmer; **to b. sth on s.o.** or **s.o. for sth** rejeter la responsabilité de qch sur qn; **to b. s.o. for sth** (*reproach*) reprocher qch à qn; **you're to b.** c'est ta faute; — n faute f; (*censure*) blâme m. ◆**—less** a irréprochable.

blanch [blɑːntʃ] vt (*vegetables*) blanchir; — vi (*turn pale with fear etc*) blêmir.

blancmange [bləˈmɒnʒ] n blanc-manger m.

bland [blænd] a (**-er, -est**) doux; (*food*) fade.

blank [blæŋk] a (*paper, page*) blanc, vierge; (*cheque*) en blanc; (*look, mind*) vide; (*puzzled*) ébahi; (*refusal*) absolu; — a & n **b.** (*space*) blanc m; **b.** (*cartridge*) cartouche f à blanc; **my mind's a b.** j'ai la tête vide. ◆**blankly** adv sans expression.

blanket ['blæŋkɪt] **1** n couverture f; (*of snow*) *Fig* couche f; — vt (*cover*) *Fig* recouvrir. **2** a (*term etc*) général. ◆**-ing** n (*blankets*) couvertures *fpl*.

blare [bleər] n (*noise*) beuglement m; (*of trumpet*) sonnerie f; — vi **to b. (out)** (*of radio*) beugler; (*of music, car horn*) retentir.

blarney ['blɑːnɪ] n *Fam* boniment(s) m(pl).

blasé ['blɑːzeɪ] a blasé.

blaspheme [blæsˈfiːm] vti blasphémer. ◆**'blasphemous** a blasphématoire; (*person*) blasphémateur. ◆**'blasphemy** n blasphème m.

blast [blɑːst] **1** n explosion f; (*air from explosion*) souffle m; (*of wind*) rafale f, coup m; (*of trumpet*) sonnerie f; **(at) full b.** (*loud*) à plein volume; (*fast*) à pleine vitesse; **b. furnace** haut fourneau m; — vt (*blow up*) faire sauter; (*hopes*) *Fig* détruire; **to b. s.o.** *Fam* réprimander qn. **2** *int* zut!, merde! ◆—ed a Fam fichu. ◆blast-off n (of spacecraft) mise f à feu.

blatant ['bleitənt] a (obvious) flagrant, criant; (shameless) éhonté.

blaz/e [bleiz] 1 n (fire) flamme f, feu m; (conflagration) incendie m; (splendour) Fig éclat m; **b. of light** torrent m de lumière; – vi (of fire) flamber; (of sun, colour, eyes) flamboyer. 2 vt **b. a trail** marquer la voie. ◆—ing a (burning) en feu; (sun) brûlant; (argument) Fig violent.

blazer ['bleizər] n blazer m.

bleach [blitʃ] n décolorant m; (household detergent) eau f de Javel; – vt (hair) décolorer, oxygéner; (linen) blanchir.

bleak [blik] a (-er, -est) (appearance, future etc) morne; (countryside) désolé.

bleary ['bliəri] a (eyes) troubles, voilés.

bleat [blit] vi bêler.

bleed [blid] vti (pt & pp bled) saigner; **to b. to death** perdre tout son sang. ◆—ing a (wound) saignant; (bloody) Sl foutu.

bleep [blip] n signal m, bip m; – vt appeler au bip-bip. ◆bleeper n bip-bip m.

blemish ['blemiʃ] n (fault) défaut m; (on fruit, reputation) tache f; – vt (reputation) ternir.

blend [blend] n mélange m; – vt mélanger; – vi se mélanger; (go together) se marier (with avec). ◆—er n Culin mixer m.

bless [bles] vt bénir; **to be blessed with** avoir le bonheur de posséder; **b. you!** (sneezing) à vos souhaits! ◆—ed [-id] a saint, béni; (happy) Rel bienheureux; (blasted) Fam fichu, sacré. ◆—ing n bénédiction f; (divine favour) grâce f; (benefit) bienfait m; **what a b. that ...** quelle chance que ....

blew [blu] see **blow** [1].

blight [blait] n (on plants) rouille f; (scourge) Fig fléau m; **to be** or **cast a b. on** avoir une influence néfaste sur; **urban b.** (area) quartier m délabré; (condition) délabrement m (de quartier). ◆blighter n Pej Fam type m.

blimey! ['blaimi] int Fam zut!, mince!

blimp [blimp] n dirigeable m.

blind [blaind] 1 a aveugle; **b. person** mf; **b. in one eye** borgne; **he's b. to** (fault) il ne voit pas; **to turn a b. eye to** fermer les yeux sur; **b. alley** impasse f; – n the b. les aveugles mpl; – vt aveugler. 2 n (on window) store m; (deception) feinte f. ◆—ly adv aveuglément; ◆—ness n cécité f, Fig aveuglement m. ◆blinkers npl Am œillères fpl. ◆blindfold n bandeau m; – vt bander les yeux à; – adv les yeux bandés.

blink [bliŋk] vi cligner des yeux; (of eyes)

cligner; (of light) clignoter; – vt **to b. one's eyes** cligner des yeux; – n clignement m; **on the b.** (machine) Fam détraqué. ◆—ing a (bloody) Fam sacré. ◆blinkers npl (for horse) œillères fpl; (indicators) Aut clignotants mpl.

bliss [blis] n félicité f. ◆blissful a (happy) très joyeux; (wonderful) merveilleux. ◆blissfully adv (happy, unaware) parfaitement.

blister ['blistər] n (on skin) ampoule f; – vi se couvrir d'ampoules.

blithe [blaið] a joyeux.

blitz [blits] n (attack) Av raid m éclair; (bombing) bombardement m aérien; Fig Fam offensive f; – vt bombarder.

blizzard ['blizəd] n tempête f de neige.

bloat [bləut] vt gonfler.

bloater ['bləutər] n hareng m saur.

blob [blɒb] n (of water) (grosse) goutte f; (of ink, colour) tache f.

bloc [blɒk] n Pol bloc m.

block [blɒk] 1 n (of stone etc) bloc m; (of buildings) pâté m (de maisons); (in pipe) obstruction f; (mental) blocage m; **b. of flats** immeuble m; **a b. away** Am une rue plus loin; **school b.** groupe m scolaire; **b. capitals** or **letters** majuscules fpl. 2 vt (obstruct) boucher; (pipe) boucher, bloquer; (one's view) boucher; **to b. off** (road) barrer; (light) intercepter; **to b. up** (pipe, hole) bloquer. ◆blo'ckade n blocus m; – vt bloquer. ◆blockage n obstruction f. ◆blockbuster n Cin superproduction f, film m à grand spectacle. ◆blockhead n imbécile mf.

bloke [bləuk] n Fam type m.

blond [blɒnd] a & n blond (m). ◆blonde a & n blonde (f).

blood [blʌd] n sang m; – a (group, orange etc) sanguin; (donor, bath etc) de sang; (poisoning etc) du sang; **b. pressure** tension f (artérielle); **high b. pressure** (hyper)tension f. ◆bloodcurdling a à vous tourner le sang. ◆bloodhound n (dog, detective) limier m. ◆bloodletting n saignée f. ◆bloodshed n effusion f de sang. ◆bloodshot a (eye) injecté de sang. ◆bloodsucker n (insect, person) sangsue f. ◆bloodthirsty a sanguinaire.

bloody ['blʌdi] a (-ier, -iest) sanglant. 2 a (blasted) Fam sacré; – adv Fam vachement. ◆b.-'minded a hargneux, pas commode.

bloom [blum] n fleur f; **in b.** en fleur(s); – vi fleurir; (of person) Fig s'épanouir. ◆—ing *a* **1** (*in bloom*) en fleur(s); (*thriving*) florissant. **2** (*blinking*) *Fam* fichu.

bloomer ['blumər] *n Fam* (*mistake*) gaffe *f*.

blossom ['blɒsəm] *n* fleur(s) *f*(*pl*); — *vi* fleurir; **to b. (out)** (*of person*) s'épanouir; **to b. (out) into** devenir.

blot [blɒt] *n* tache *f*; — *vt* (-tt-) tacher; (*dry*) sécher; **to b. out** (*word*) rayer; (*memory*) effacer. ◆**blotting** *a* **b. paper** (papier *m*) buvard *m*. ◆**blotter** *n* buvard *m*.

blotch [blɒtʃ] *n* tache *f*. ◆**blotchy** *a* (-ier, -iest) couvert de taches; (*face*) marbré.

blouse [blauz, *Am* blaus] *n* chemisier *m*.

blow[1] [bləu] *vt* (*pt* **blew**, *pp* **blown**) (*of wind*) pousser (*un navire etc*), chasser (*la pluie etc*); (*smoke, glass*) souffler; (*bubbles*) faire; (*trumpet*) souffler dans; (*fuse*) faire sauter; (*kiss*) envoyer (**to** à); (*money*) *Fam* claquer; **to b. one's nose** se moucher; **to b. a whistle** siffler; **to b. away** (*of wind*) emporter; **to b. down** (*chimney etc*) faire tomber; **to b. off** (*hat etc*) emporter; (*arm*) arracher; **to b. out** (*candle*) souffler; (*cheeks*) gonfler; **to b. up** (*building etc*) faire sauter; (*tyre*) gonfler; (*photo*) agrandir; — *vi* (*of wind, person*) souffler; (*of fuse*) sauter; (*of papers etc*) s'éparpiller; **b.!** *Fam* zut!; **to b. down** (*fall*) tomber; **to b. off** *or* **away** s'envoler; **to b. out** (*of light*) s'éteindre; **to b. over** (*pass*) passer; **to b. up** (*explode*) exploser. ◆**blow-dry** *n* brushing *m*. ◆**blowlamp** *or* **blowtorch** *n Am* chalumeau *m*. ◆**blow-up** *n Phot* agrandissement *m*.

blow[2] [bləu] *n* coup *m*; **to come to blows** en venir aux mains.

blowy ['bləui] *a* **it's b.** *Fam* il y a du vent.

blowzy ['blauzi] *a* **b. woman** (*slovenly*) *Fam* femme *f* débraillée.

blubber ['blʌbər] *n* graisse *f* (de baleine).

bludgeon ['blʌdʒən] *n* gourdin *m*; — *vt* matraquer.

blue [blu] *a* (**bluer, bluest**) bleu; **to feel b.** *Fam* avoir le cafard; **b. film** *Fam* film *m* porno; — *n* bleu *m*; **the blues** (*depression*) *Fam* le cafard; *Mus* le blues. ◆**bluebell** *n* jacinthe *f* des bois. ◆**blueberry** *n* airelle *f*. ◆**bluebottle** *n* mouche *f* à viande. ◆**blueprint** *n Fig* plan *m* (de travail).

bluff [blʌf] **1** *a* (*person*) brusque, direct. **2** *vti* bluffer; — *n* bluff *m*.

blunder ['blʌndər] **1** *n* (*mistake*) bévue *f*, gaffe *f*; — *vi* faire une bévue. **2** *vi* (*move awkwardly*) avancer à tâtons. ◆—**ing** *a* maladroit; — *n* maladresse *f*.

blunt [blʌnt] *a* (-er, -est) (*edge*) émoussé; (*pencil*) épointé; (*person*) brusque; (*speech*) franc; — *vt* émousser; épointer. ◆—**ly** *adv* carrément. ◆—**ness** *n Fig* brusquerie *f*; (*of speech*) franchise *f*.

blur [blɜr] *n* tache *f* floue, contour *m* imprécis; — *vt* (-rr-) estomper, rendre flou; (*judgment*) *Fig* troubler. ◆**blurred** *a* (*image*) flou, estompé.

blurb [blɜb] *n Fam* résumé *m* publicitaire, laïus *m*.

blurt [blɜt] *vt* **to b. (out)** laisser échapper, lâcher.

blush [blʌʃ] *vi* rougir (**at, with** de); — *n* rougeur *f*; **with a b.** en rougissant.

bluster ['blʌstər] *vi* (*of person*) tempêter; (*of wind*) faire rage. ◆**blustery** *a* (*weather*) de grand vent, à bourrasques.

boa ['bəuə] *n* (*snake*) boa *m*.

boar [bɔr] *n* (*wild*) **b.** sanglier *m*.

board[1] [bɔd] **1** *n* (*piece of wood*) planche *f*; (*for notices, games etc*) tableau *m*; (*cardboard*) carton *m*; (*committee*) conseil *m*, commission *f*; **b. (of directors)** conseil *m* d'administration; **on b.** *Nau Av* à bord (de); **B. of Trade** *Br Pol* ministère *m* du Commerce; **across the b.** (*pay rise*) général; **to go by the b.** (*of plan*) être abandonné. **2** *vt Nau Av* monter à bord de; (*bus, train*) monter dans; **to b. up** (*door*) boucher. ◆—**ing** *n Nau Av* embarquement *m*. ◆**boardwalk** *n Am* promenade *f*.

board[2] [bɔd] *n* (*food*) pension *f*; **b. and lodging, bed and b.** (chambre *f* avec) pension *f*; — *vi* (*lodge*) être en pension (**with** chez); **boarding house** pension *f* (de famille); **boarding school** pensionnat *m*. ◆—**er** *n* pensionnaire *m f*.

boast [bəust] *vi* se vanter (**about, of** de); — *vt* se glorifier de; **to b. that one can do . . .** se vanter de (pouvoir) faire . . . ; — *n* vantardise *f*. ◆—**ing** *n* vantardise *f*. ◆**boastful** *a* vantard. ◆**boastfully** *adv* en se vantant.

boat [bəut] *n* bateau *m*; (*small*) barque *f*, canot *m*; (*liner*) paquebot *m*; **in the same b.** *Fig* logé à la même enseigne. **b. race** course *f* d'aviron. ◆—**ing** *n* canotage *m*; **b. trip** excursion *f* en bateau.

boatswain ['bəus(ə)n] *n* maître *m* d'équipage.

bob [bɒb] *vi* (-bb-) **to b. (up and down)** (*on water*) danser sur l'eau.

bobbin ['bɒbɪn] *n* bobine *f*.

bobby ['bɒbi] *n* **1** (*policeman*) *Fam* flic *m*, agent *m*. **2 b. pin** *Am* pince *f* à cheveux.

bode [bəud] *vi* **to b. well/ill** être de bon/mauvais augure.

bodice ['bɒdɪs] *n* corsage *m*.

body ['bɒdɪ] *n* corps *m*; (*of vehicle*) carrosserie *f*; (*quantity*) masse *f*; (*institution*) organisme *m*; **the main b.** of le gros de; **b. building** culturisme *m*. ◆**bodily** *a* physique; (*need*) matériel; – *adv* physiquement; (*as a whole*) tout entier. ◆**bodyguard** *n* garde *m* du corps, gorille *m*. ◆**bodywork** *n* carrosserie *f*.

boffin ['bɒfɪn] *n* Fam chercheur, -euse *mf* scientifique.

bog [bɒg] *n* marécage *m*; – *vt* **to get bogged down** s'enliser. ◆**boggy** *a* (-ier, -iest) marécageux.

bogey ['bəugɪ] *n* spectre *m*; **b. man** croque-mitaine *m*.

boggle ['bɒg(ə)l] *vi* **the mind boggles** cela confond l'imagination.

bogus ['bəugəs] *a* faux.

bohemian [bəu'hi:mɪən] *a & n* (*artist etc*) bohème (*mf*).

boil [bɔɪl] **1** *n* Med furoncle *m*, clou *m*. **2** *vi* bouillir; **to b. away** (*until dry*) s'évaporer; (*on and on*) bouillir sans arrêt; **b. down to** Fig se ramener à; **to b. over** (*of milk, emotions etc*) déborder; – *vt* **to b. (up)** faire bouillir; – *n* **to be on the b., come to the b.** bouillir; **to bring to the b.** amener à ébullition. ◆**-ed** *a* (*beef*) bouilli; (*potato*) cuit à l'eau; **b. egg** œuf *m* à la coque. ◆**-ing** *n* ébullition *f*; **at b. point** à ébullition; – *a & adv* **b. (hot)** bouillant; **it's b. (hot)** (*weather*) il fait une chaleur infernale. ◆**-er** *n* chaudière *f*; **b. suit** bleu *m* (de travail).

boisterous ['bɔɪstərəs] *a* (*noisy*) tapageur; (*child*) turbulent; (*meeting*) houleux.

bold [bəuld] *a* (-er, -est) hardi; **b. type** caractères *mpl* gras. ◆**-ness** *n* hardiesse *f*.

Bolivia [bə'lɪvɪə] *n* Bolivie *f*. ◆**Bolivian** *a & n* bolivien, -ienne (*mf*).

bollard ['bɒləd, 'bɒlɑːd] *n* Aut borne *f*.

boloney [bə'ləunɪ] *n* Sl foutaises *fpl*.

bolster ['bəulstər] **1** *n* (*pillow*) traversin *m*, polochon *m*. **2** *vt* **to b. (up)** (*support*) soutenir.

bolt [bəult] **1** *n* (*on door etc*) verrou *m*; (*for nut*) boulon *m*; – *vt* (*door*) verrouiller. **2** *n* (*dash*) fuite *f*, ruée *f*; – *vi* (*dash*) se précipiter; (*flee*) détaler; (*of horse*) s'emballer. **3** *n* **b.** (*of lightning*) éclair *m*. **4** *vt* (*food*) engloutir. **5** *adv* **b. upright** tout droit.

bomb [bɒm] *n* bombe *f*; **letter b.** lettre *f* piégée; **b. disposal** désamorçage *m*; – *vt* bombarder. ◆**-ing** *n* bombardement *m*.

◆**—er** *n* (*aircraft*) bombardier *m*; (*terrorist*) plastiqueur *m*. ◆**bombshell** *n* **to come as a b.** tomber comme une bombe. ◆**bombsite** *n* terrain *m* vague, lieu *m* bombardé.

bombard [bɒm'bɑːd] *vt* bombarder (**with** de). ◆**—ment** *n* bombardement *m*.

bona fide [bəunə'faɪdɪ, Am -'faɪd] *a* sérieux, de bonne foi.

bonanza [bə'nænzə] *n* Fig mine *f* d'or.

bond [bɒnd] **1** *n* (*agreement, promise*) engagement *m*; (*link*) lien *m*; Com bon *m*, obligation *f*; (*adhesion*) adhérence *f*. **2** *vt* (*goods*) entreposer.

bondage ['bɒndɪdʒ] *n* esclavage *m*.

bone [bəun] **1** *n* os *m*; (*of fish*) arête *f*; **b. of contention** pomme *f* de discorde; **b. china** porcelaine *f* tendre; – *vt* (*meat etc*) désosser. **2** *vi* **to b. up on** (*subject*) Am Fam bûcher. ◆**bony** *a* (-ier, -iest) (*thin*) osseux, maigre; (*fish*) plein d'arêtes.

bone-dry [bəun'draɪ] *a* tout à fait sec. ◆**b.-idle** *a* paresseux comme une couleuvre.

bonfire ['bɒnfaɪər] *n* (*for celebration*) feu *m* de joie; (*for dead leaves*) feu *m* de jardin.

bonkers ['bɒŋkəz] *a* (*crazy*) Fam dingue.

bonnet ['bɒnɪt] *n* (*hat*) bonnet *m*; Aut capot *m*.

bonus ['bəunəs] *n* prime *f*; **no claims b.** Aut bonus *m*.

boo [buː] **1** *int* hou! **2** *vti* huer; – *npl* huées *fpl*.

boob [buːb] *n* (*mistake*) gaffe *f*; – *vi* Sl gaffer.

booby-trap ['buːbɪtræp] *n* engin *m* piégé; – *vt* (-pp-) piéger.

book [buk] **1** *n* livre *m*; (*of tickets*) carnet *m*; (*record*) registre *m*; *pl* (*accounts*) comptes *mpl*; (*exercise*) **b.** cahier *m*. **2** *vt* **to b. (up)** (*seat etc*) réserver, retenir; **to b. s.o. (up)** donner un procès-verbal à qn; **to b. (down)** inscrire; **(fully) booked (up)** (*hotel, concert*) complet; (*person*) pris; – *vi* **to b. (up)** réserver des places; **to b. in** (*in hotel*) signer le registre. ◆**-ing** *n* réservation *f*; **b. clerk** guichetier, -ière *mf*; **b. office** bureau *m* de location, guichet *m*. ◆**-able** *a* (*seat*) qu'on peut réserver. ◆**bookish** *a* (*word, theory*) livresque; (*person*) studieux.

bookbinding ['bukbaɪndɪŋ] *n* reliure *f*. ◆**bookcase** *n* bibliothèque *f*. ◆**bookend** *n* serre-livres *m inv*. ◆**bookkeeper** *n* comptable *mf*. ◆**bookkeeping** *n* comptabilité *f*. ◆**booklet** *n* brochure *f*. ◆**book-lover** *n* bibliophile *mf*. ◆**bookmaker** *n* bookmaker *m*. ◆**bookmark**

marque f. ◆**bookseller** n libraire mf. ◆**bookshelf** n rayon m. ◆**bookshop** n, Am ◆**bookstore** n librairie f. ◆**bookstall** n kiosque m (à journaux). ◆**bookworm** n rat m de bibliothèque.

boom [buːm] **1** vi (of thunder, gun etc) gronder; – n grondement m; **sonic b.** bang m. **2** n Econ expansion f, essor m, boom m. ◆**—er** n b. (injection) piqûre f de rappel.

boomerang ['buːməræŋ] n boomerang m.

boon [buːn] n aubaine f, avantage m.

boor [buər] n rustre m. ◆**boorish** a rustre.

boost [buːst] vt (push) donner une poussée à; (increase) augmenter; (product) faire de la réclame pour; (economy) stimuler; (morale) remonter; – n **to give a b. to** = to boost. ◆**—er** n b. (injection) piqûre f de rappel.

boot [buːt] **1** n (shoe) botte f; (ankle) b. bottillon m; (knee) b. bottine f; **to get the b.** Fam être mis à la porte; **b. polish** cirage m; – vt (kick) donner un coup or des coups de pied à; **to b. out** mettre à la porte. **2** n Aut coffre m. **3** n to b. en plus. ◆**bootblack** n cireur m. ◆**boo'tee** n (of baby) chausson m.

booth [buːð, buːθ] n Tel cabine f; (at fair) baraque f.

booty ['buːtɪ] n (stolen goods) butin m.

booz/e [buːz] n Fam alcool m, boisson(s) f(pl); (drinking bout) beuverie f; – vi Fam boire (beaucoup). ◆**—er** n Fam (person) buveur, -euse mf; (place) bistrot m.

border ['bɔːdər] n (of country) & Fig frontière f; (edge) bord m; (of garden etc) bordure f; – a (town) frontière inv; (incident) de frontière; – vt (street) border; **to b. (on)** (country) toucher à; **to b. (up)on** (resemble) être voisin de. ◆**borderland** n pays m frontière. ◆**borderline** n frontière f; **b. case** cas m limite.

bor/e [bɔːr] **1** vt (weary) ennuyer; **to be bored** s'ennuyer; – n (person) raseur, -euse mf; (thing) ennui m. **2** vt Tech forer, creuser; (hole) percer; – vi forer. **3** n (of gun) calibre m. ◆**—ing** a ennuyeux. ◆**boredom** n ennui m.

bore² [bɔːr] see **bear²**.

born [bɔːn] a né; **to be b.** naître; **he was b.** il est né.

borne [bɔːn] see **bear²**.

borough ['bʌrə] n (town) municipalité f; (part of town) arrondissement m.

borrow ['bɒrəʊ] vt emprunter (**from** à). ◆**—ing** n emprunt m.

Borstal ['bɔːst(ə)l] n maison f d'éducation surveillée.

bosom ['buzəm] n (chest) & Fig sein m; **b. friend** ami, -ie mf intime.

boss [bɒs] n Fam patron, -onne mf, chef m; – vt Fam diriger; **to b. s.o. around** or **about** régenter qn. ◆**bossy** a (-ier, -iest) Fam autoritaire.

boss-eyed ['bɒsaɪd] a to be **b.-eyed** loucher.

bosun ['bəʊs(ə)n] n maître m d'équipage.

botany ['bɒtənɪ] n botanique f. ◆**bo'tanical** a botanique. ◆**botanist** n botaniste mf.

botch [bɒtʃ] vt to **b. (up)** (spoil) bâcler; (repair) rafistoler.

both [bəʊθ] a les deux, l'un(e) et l'autre; – pron tous or toutes (les) deux, l'un(e) et l'autre; **b. of us** nous deux; – adv (at the same time) à la fois; **b. you and I** vous et moi.

bother ['bɒðər] vt (annoy, worry) ennuyer; (disturb) déranger; (pester) importuner; **I can't be bothered!** je n'en ai pas envie!, ça m'embête!; – vi to **b. about** (worry about) se préoccuper de; (deal with) s'occuper de; **to b. doing** or **to do** se donner la peine de faire; – n (trouble) ennui m; (effort) peine f; (inconvenience) dérangement m; **(oh) b.!** zut alors!

bottle ['bɒt(ə)l] n bouteille f; (small) flacon m; (wide-mouthed) bocal m; (for baby) biberon m; (hot-water) b. bouillotte f; **b. opener** ouvre-bouteilles m inv; – vt mettre en bouteille; **to b. up** (feeling) contenir. ◆**b.-feed** vt (pt & pp -fed) nourrir au biberon. ◆**bottleneck** n (in road) goulot m d'étranglement; (traffic holdup) bouchon m.

bottom ['bɒtəm] n (of sea, box, etc) fond m; (of page, hill etc) bas m; (buttocks) Fam derrière m; (of table) bout m; **to be (at the) b. of the class** être le dernier de la classe; – a (part, shelf) inférieur, du bas; **b. floor** rez-de-chaussée m; **b. gear** première vitesse f. ◆**—less** a insondable.

bough [baʊ] n Lit rameau m.

bought [bɔːt] see **buy**.

boulder ['bəʊldər] n rocher m.

boulevard ['buːləvɑːd] n boulevard m.

bounc/e [baʊns] **1** vi (of ball) rebondir; (of person) faire des bonds; **to b. into** bondir dans; – vt faire rebondir; – n (re)bond m. **2** vi (of cheque) Fam être sans provision, être en bois. ◆**—ing** a (baby) robuste. ◆**—er** n (at club etc) Fam videur m.

bound¹ [baʊnd] **1** a **b. to do** (obliged) obligé de faire; (certain) sûr de faire; **it's b. to happen** ça arrivera sûrement; **to be b. for**

être en route pour. **2** n (leap) bond m; – vi bondir.

bound² [baʊnd] see **bind 1**; – a b. **up with** (connected) lié à.

bounds [baʊndz] npl limites fpl; **out of b.** (place) interdit. ◆**boundary** n limite f. ◆**bounded** a b. **by** limité par. ◆**boundless** a sans bornes.

bountiful [ˈbaʊntɪfəl] a généreux.

bounty [ˈbaʊntɪ] n (reward) prime f.

bouquet [buːˈkeɪ] n (of flowers, wine) bouquet m.

bourbon [ˈbɜːbən] n (whisky) Am bourbon m.

bout [baʊt] n période f; Med accès m, crise f; Boxing combat m; (session) séance f.

boutique [buːˈtiːk] n boutique f (de mode).

bow¹ [bəʊ] n (weapon) arc m; Mus archet m; (knot) nœud m; **b. tie** nœud m papillon. ◆**b.-'legged** a aux jambes arquées.

bow² [baʊ] **1** n révérence f; (nod) salut m; – vt courber, incliner; – vi s'incliner (**to** devant); (nod) incliner la tête; **to b. down** (submit) s'incliner. **2** n Nau proue f.

bowels [ˈbaʊəlz] npl intestins mpl; (of earth) Fig entrailles fpl.

bowl [bəʊl] **1** n (for food) bol m; (basin) & Geog cuvette f; (for sugar) sucrier m; (for salad) saladier m; (for fruit) corbeille f, coupe f. **2** npl Sp boules fpl. **3** vi Cricket lancer la balle; **to b. along** Aut rouler vite; – vt (ball) Cricket servir; **to b. s.o. over** (knock down) renverser qn; (astound) bouleverser qn. ◆**-ing** n (tenpin) b. bowling m; **b. alley** bowling m. ◆**-er¹** n Cricket lanceur, -euse mf.

bowler² [ˈbəʊlər] n **b. (hat)** (chapeau m) melon m.

box [bɒks] **1** n boîte f; (large) caisse f; (of cardboard) carton m; Th loge f; Jur barre f, banc m; (for horse) box m; TV Fam télé f; **b. office** bureau m de location, guichet m; **b. room** (lumber room) débarras m; (bedroom) petite chambre (carrée); – vt to **b. (up)** mettre en boîte; **to b. in** (enclose) enfermer. **2** vti Boxing boxer; **b. s.o.'s ears** gifler qn. ◆**-ing** n **1** boxe f; **b. ring** ring m. **2 B. Day** le lendemain de Noël. ◆**-er** n boxeur m. ◆**boxcar** n Rail Am wagon m couvert. ◆**boxwood** n buis m.

boy [bɔɪ] n garçon m; **English b.** jeune Anglais m; **old b.** Sch ancien élève m; **yes, old b.!** oui, mon vieux!; **the boys** (pals) Fam les copains mpl; **my dear b.** mon cher ami; **oh b.!** Am mon Dieu! ◆**boyfriend** n petit ami m. ◆**boyhood** n enfance f. ◆**boyish** a de garçon; Pej puéril.

boycott [ˈbɔɪkɒt] vt boycotter; – n boycottage m.

bra [brɑː] n soutien-gorge m.

brac/e [breɪs] n (for fastening) attache f; (dental) appareil m; – pl (trouser straps) bretelles fpl; – vt (fix) attacher; (press) appuyer; **to b. oneself for** (news, shock) se préparer à. ◆**-ing** a (air etc) fortifiant.

bracelet [ˈbreɪslɪt] n bracelet m.

bracken [ˈbrækən] n fougère f.

bracket [ˈbrækɪt] n Tech support m, tasseau m; (round sign) Typ parenthèse f; (square) Typ crochet m; Fig groupe m, tranche f; – vt mettre entre parenthèses or crochets; **to b. together** Fig mettre dans le même groupe.

bradawl [ˈbrædɔːl] n poinçon m.

brag [bræg] vi (-gg-) se vanter (**about, of** de). ◆**-ging** n vantardise f. ◆**braggart** n vantard, -arde mf.

braid [breɪd] vt (hair) tresser; (trim) galonner; – n tresse f; galon m.

Braille [breɪl] n braille m.

brain [breɪn] n cerveau m; (of bird etc) & Pej cervelle f; – a (operation, death) cérébral; – vt Fam assommer; **to have brains** (sense) avoir de l'intelligence; **b. drain** fuite f des cerveaux. ◆**brainchild** n invention f personnelle. ◆**brainstorm** n Psy Fig aberration f; Am idée f géniale. ◆**brainwash** vt faire un lavage de cerveau à. ◆**brainwave** n idée f géniale.

brainy [ˈbreɪnɪ] a (-ier, -iest) Fam intelligent.

braise [breɪz] vt Culin braiser.

brak/e [breɪk] vi freiner; – n frein m; **b. light** Aut stop m. ◆**-ing** n freinage m.

bramble [ˈbræmb(ə)l] n ronce f.

bran [bræn] n Bot son m.

branch [brɑːntʃ] n branche f; (of road) embranchement m; (of store etc) succursale f; **b. office** succursale f; – vi **to b. off** (of road) bifurquer; **to b. out** (of family, tree) se ramifier; Fig étendre ses activités.

brand [brænd] n (trademark, stigma & on cattle) marque f; – vt (mark) marquer; (stigmatize) flétrir; **to be branded as** avoir la réputation de.

brandish [ˈbrændɪʃ] vt brandir.

brand-new [brændˈnjuː] a tout neuf, flambant neuf.

brandy [ˈbrændɪ] n cognac m; (made with pears etc) eau-de-vie f.

brash [bræʃ] a effronté, fougueux.

brass [brɑːs] n cuivre m; (instruments) Mus cuivres mpl; **the top b.** (officers, executives) Fam les huiles fpl; **b. band** fanfare f.

brassiere ['bræzɪər, *Am* brə'zɪər] *n* soutien-gorge *m*.

brat [bræt] *n Pej* môme *mf*, gosse *mf*; (*badly behaved*) galopin *m*.

bravado [brə'vɑːdəʊ] *n* bravade *f*.

brave [breɪv] *a* (-*er*, -*est*) courageux, brave; – *n* (*Red Indian*) guerrier *m* (indien), brave *m*; – *vt* braver. ◆**bravery** *n* courage *m*.

bravo! ['brɑːvəʊ] *int* bravo!

brawl [brɔːl] *n* (*fight*) bagarre *f*; – *vi* se bagarrer. ◆**—ing** *n* bagarres *fpl*.

brawn [brɔːn] *n* muscles *mpl*. ◆**brawny** *a* (-*ier*, -*iest*) musclé.

bray [breɪ] *vi* (*of ass*) braire.

brazen ['breɪz(ə)n] *a* (*shameless*) effronté; – *vt* to b. it out payer d'audace, faire front.

Brazil [brə'zɪl] *n* Brésil *m*. ◆**Brazilian** *a* & *n* brésilien, -ienne (*mf*).

breach [briːtʃ] **1** *n* violation *f*, infraction *f*; (*of contract*) rupture *f*; (*of trust*) abus *m*; – *vt* (*law, code*) violer. **2** *n* (*gap*) brèche *f*; – *vt* (*wall etc*) ouvrir une brèche dans.

bread [bred] *n inv* pain *m*; (*money*) *Sl* blé *m*, fric *m*; **loaf of b.** pain *m*; (*slice or piece of*) **b. and butter** tartine *f*; **b. and butter** (*job*) *Fig* gagne-pain *m*. ◆**breadbin** *n*, *Am* ◆**breadbox** *n* coffre *m* à pain. ◆**breadboard** *n* planche *f* à pain. ◆**breadcrumb** *n* miette *f* (de pain); *pl Culin* chapelure *f*. ◆**breadline** *n* **on the b.** indigent. ◆**breadwinner** *n* soutien *m* de famille.

breadth [bretθ] *n* largeur *f*.

break [breɪk] *vt* (*pt* **broke**, *pp* **broken**) casser; (*into pieces*) briser; (*silence, vow etc*) rompre; (*strike, heart, ice etc*) briser; (*record*) *Sp* battre; (*law*) violer; (*one's word*) manquer à; (*journey*) interrompre; (*sound barrier*) franchir; (*a fall*) amortir; (*news*) révéler (**to** à); **to b. (oneself of)** (*habit*) se débarrasser de; **to b. open** (*safe*) percer; **to b. new ground** innover; – *vi* (*se*) casser; se briser; se rompre; (*of voice*) s'altérer; (*of boy's voice*) muer; (*of weather*) se gâter; (*of news*) éclater; (*of day*) se lever; (*of wave*) déferler; **to b. free** se libérer; **to b. loose** s'échapper; **to b. with s.o.** rompre avec qn; – *n* cassure *f*; (*in relationship, continuity etc*) rupture *f*; (*in journey*) interruption *f*; (*rest*) repos *m*; (*for tea*) pause *f*; *Sch* récréation *f*; (*change*) *Met* changement *m*; **a lucky b.** *Fam* une chance. ◆**—ing** *n* **b. point** *Tech* point *m* de rupture; **at b. point** (*patience*) à bout; (*person*) sur le point de craquer, à bout. ◆**—able** *a* cassable. ◆**—age** *n* casse *f*; *pl* (*things broken*) la casse. ◆**—er** *n* (*wave*) brisant *m*; (*dealer*)

Aut casseur *m*. ■ **to b. away** *vi* se détacher; – *vt* détacher. ◆**breakaway** *a* (*group*) dissident; **to b. down** *vt* (*door*) enfoncer; (*resistance*) briser; (*analyse*) analyser; – *vi Aut Tech* tomber en panne; (*of negotiations etc*) échouer; (*collapse*) s'effondrer. ◆**breakdown** *n* panne *f*; analyse *f*; (*in talks*) rupture *f*; (*nervous*) dépression *f*; – *a* (*service*) *Aut* de dépannage; **b. lorry** dépanneuse *f*; **to b. in** *vi* interrompre; (*of burglar*) entrer par effraction; – *vt* (*door*) enfoncer; (*horse*) dresser; (*vehicle*) *Am* roder. ◆**break-in** *n* cambriolage *m*; **to b. into** *vt* (*safe*) forcer; (*start*) entamer; **to b. off** *vt* détacher; (*relations*) rompre; – *vi* se détacher; (*stop*) s'arrêter; **to b. off with** rompre avec; **to b. out** *vi* éclater; (*escape*) s'échapper; **to b. out in** (*pimples*) avoir une poussée de; **to b. through** *vi* (*of sun*) *Mil* percer; – *vt* (*defences*) percer. ◆**breakthrough** *n Fig* percée *f*, découverte *f*; **to b. up** *vt* mettre en morceaux; (*marriage*) briser; (*fight*) mettre fin à; – *vi* (*end*) prendre fin; (*of group*) se disperser; (*of marriage*) se briser; *Sch* partir en vacances. ◆**breakup** *n* fin *f*; (*in friendship, marriage*) rupture *f*.

breakfast ['brekfəst] *n* petit déjeuner *m*.

breakwater ['breɪkwɔːtər] *n* brise-lames *m inv*.

breast [brest] *n* sein *m*; (*chest*) poitrine *f*. ◆**b.-feed** *vt* (*pt* & *pp* -**fed**) allaiter. ◆**breaststroke** *n* (*swimming*) brasse *f*.

breath [breθ] *n* haleine *f*, souffle *m*; (*of air*) souffle *m*; **under one's b.** tout bas; **one's last b.** son dernier soupir; **out of b.** à bout de souffle; **to get a b. of air** prendre l'air; **to take a deep b.** respirer profondément. ◆**breathalyser** *n* alcootest®️ *m*. ◆**breathless** *a* haletant. ◆**breathtaking** *a* sensationnel.

breath/e [briːð] *vti* respirer; **to b. in** aspirer; **to b. out** expirer; **to b. air into sth** souffler dans qch; – *vt* (*a sigh*) pousser; (*a word*) dire. ◆**—ing** *n* respiration *f*; **b. space** moment *m* de repos. ◆**—er** *n Fam* moment *m* de repos; **to go for a b.** sortir prendre l'air.

bred [bred] *see* **breed 1**; – *a* **well-b.** bien élevé.

breeches ['brɪtʃɪz] *npl* culotte *f*.

breed [briːd] **1** *vt* (*pt* & *pp* **bred**) (*animals*) élever; (*cause*) *Fig* engendrer; – *vi* (*of animals*) se reproduire. **2** *n* race *f*, espèce *f*. ◆**—ing** *n* élevage *m*; reproduction *f*; *Fig* éducation *f*. ◆**—er** *n* éleveur, -euse *mf*.

breeze [briːz] *n* brise *f*. ◆**breezy** *a* (-*ier*,

-iest) 1 (weather, day) frais, venteux. **2** (cheerful) jovial; (relaxed) décontracté.

breezeblock ['briːzblɒk] n parpaing m, briquette f.

brevity ['breviti] n brièveté f.

brew [bruː] vt (beer) brasser; (trouble, plot) préparer; (to b. tea préparer du thé; (infuse) (faire) infuser du thé; — vi (of beer) fermenter; (of tea) infuser; (of storm, trouble) se préparer; — n (drink) breuvage m; (of tea) infusion f. ◆—er n brasseur m. ◆brewery n brasserie f.

bribe [braɪb] n pot-de-vin m; — vt soudoyer, corrompre. ◆bribery n corruption f.

brick [brɪk] n brique f; (child's) cube m; to drop a b. Fam faire une gaffe; — vt to b. up (gap, door) murer. ◆bricklayer n maçon m. ◆brickwork n ouvrage m en briques; (bricks) briques fpl.

bridal ['braɪd(ə)l] a (ceremony) nuptial; b. gown robe f de mariée.

bride [braɪd] n mariée f; the b. and groom les mariés mpl. ◆bridegroom n marié m. ◆bridesmaid n demoiselle f d'honneur.

bridge [brɪdʒ] **1** n pont m; (on ship) passerelle f; (of nose) arête f; (false tooth) bridge m; — vt to b. a gap combler une lacune. **2** n Cards bridge m.

bridle ['braɪd(ə)l] n (for horse) bride f; — vt (horse, instinct etc) brider; b. path allée f cavalière.

brief [briːf] **1** a (-er, -est) bref; in b. en résumé. **2** n Jur dossier m; (instructions) Mil Pol instructions fpl; Fig tâche f, fonctions fpl; — vt donner des instructions à; (inform) mettre au courant (on de). **3** npl (underpants) slip m. ◆—ing n Mil Pol briefing m; Av briefing m. ◆—ly adv (quickly) en vitesse; (to say) brièvement.

brigade [brɪˈɡeɪd] n brigade f. ◆briga'dier n général m de brigade.

bright [braɪt] a (-er, -est) brillant, vif; (weather, room) clair; (clever) intelligent; (happy) joyeux; (future) brillant, prometteur; (idea) génial; b. interval Met éclaircie f; — adv b. and early (to get up) de bonne heure. ◆—ly adv brillamment. ◆—ness n éclat m; (of person) intelligence f. ◆brighten vt to b. (up) (person, room) égayer; — vi to b. (up) (of weather) s'éclaircir; (of face) s'éclairer.

brilliant ['brɪljənt] a (light) éclatant; (very clever) brillant. ◆brilliance n éclat m; (of person) intelligence f.

brim [brɪm] n bord m; — vi (-mm-) to b. over déborder (with de).

brine [braɪn] n Culin saumure f.

bring [brɪŋ] vt (pt & pp brought) (person, vehicle etc) amener; (thing) apporter; (to cause) amener; (action) Jur intenter; to b. along or over or round amener; apporter; to b. back ramener; rapporter; (memories) rappeler; to b. sth up/down monter/descendre qch; to b. sth in/out rentrer/sortir qch; to b. sth to (perfection, a peak etc) porter qch à; to b. to an end mettre fin à; to b. to mind rappeler; to b. sth on oneself s'attirer qch; to b. oneself to do se résoudre à faire; to b. about provoquer, amener; to b. down (overthrow) faire tomber; (reduce) réduire; (shoot down) abattre; to b. forward (in time or space) avancer; (witness) produire; to b. in (person) faire entrer or venir; (introduce) introduire; (income) Com rapporter; to b. off (task) mener à bien; to b. out (person) faire sortir; (meaning) faire ressortir; (book) publier; (product) lancer; to b. over to (convert to) convertir à; to b. round Med ranimer; (convert) convertir (to à); to b. s.o. to Med ranimer qn; to b. together mettre en contact; (reconcile) réconcilier; to b. up (child etc) élever; (question) soulever; (subject) mentionner; (vomit) vomir.

brink [brɪŋk] n bord m.

brisk [brɪsk] a (-er, -est) vif; (trade) actif; at a b. pace d'un bon pas. ◆—ly adv vivement; (to walk) d'un bon pas. ◆—ness n vivacité f.

bristl/e ['brɪs(ə)l] n poil m; — vi se hérisser. ◆—ing a b. with (difficulties) hérissé de.

Britain ['brɪt(ə)n] n Grande-Bretagne f. ◆British a britannique; — n the B. les Britanniques mpl. ◆Briton n Britannique mf.

Brittany ['brɪtəni] n Bretagne f.

brittle ['brɪt(ə)l] a cassant, fragile.

broach [brəʊtʃ] vt (topic) entamer.

broad [brɔːd] a (-er, -est) (wide) large; (outline) grand, général; (accent) prononcé; in b. daylight au grand jour; b. bean fève f; b. jump Sp Am saut m en longueur. ◆b.-'minded a à l'esprit large. ◆b.-'shouldered a large d'épaules. ◆broaden vt élargir; — vi s'élargir. ◆broadly adv b. (speaking) en gros, grosso modo.

broad [brɔːd] n (woman) Am Sl nana f.

broadcast ['brɔːdkɑːst] vt (pt & pp broadcast) Rad & Fig diffuser; TV téléviser; — vi (of station) émettre; (of person) parler à la radio or à la télévision; — a (radio) diffusé; télévisé; — n émission f. ◆—ing n radiodiffusion f; télévision f.

broccoli ['brɒkəlɪ] n inv brocoli m.

brochure ['brəʊʃər] n brochure f, dépliant m.

brogue [brəʊg] n Ling accent m irlandais.

broil [brɔɪl] vti griller. ◆**-er** n poulet m (à rôtir); (apparatus) gril m.

broke [brəʊk] **1** see break. **2** a (penniless) fauché. ◆**broken** see break; - a (ground) accidenté; (spirit) abattu; (man, voice, line) brisé; **b. English** mauvais anglais m; **b. home** foyer m brisé. ◆**broken-'down** a (machine etc) (tout) déglingué, détraqué.

brolly ['brɒlɪ] n (umbrella) Fam pépin m.

bronchitis [brɒŋ'kaɪtɪs] n bronchite f.

bronze [brɒnz] n bronze m; - a (statue etc) en bronze.

brooch [brəʊtʃ] n (ornament) broche f.

brood [bruːd] n **1** couvée f, nichée f; - vi (of bird) couver. **2** vi méditer tristement (over, on sur); to b. over (a plan) ruminer. ◆**broody** a (-ier, -iest) (person) maussade, rêveur; (woman) Fam qui a envie d'avoir un enfant.

brook [brʊk] n **1** ruisseau m. **2** vt souffrir, tolérer.

broom [bruːm] n **1** (for sweeping) balai m. **2** Bot genêt m. ◆**broomstick** n manche m à balai.

Bros abbr (Brothers) Frères mpl.

broth [brɒθ] n bouillon m.

brothel ['brɒθ(ə)l] n maison f close, bordel m.

brother ['brʌðər] n frère m. ◆**b.-in-law** n (pl **brothers-in-law**) beau-frère m. ◆**brotherhood** n fraternité f. ◆**brotherly** a fraternel.

brow [braʊ] n (forehead) front m; (of hill) sommet m.

browbeat ['braʊbiːt] vt (pt **-beat**, pp **-beaten**) intimider.

brown [braʊn] a (-er, -est) brun; (reddish) marron; (hair) châtain; (tanned) bronzé; - n brun m; marron m; - vt brunir; Culin faire dorer; to be browned off Fam en avoir marre. ◆**brownish** a brunâtre.

Brownie ['braʊnɪ] n **1** (girl scout) jeannette f. **2** b. Culin Am petit gâteau m au chocolat.

browse [braʊz] vi (in shop) regarder; (in bookshop) feuilleter des livres; (of animal) brouter; to b. through (book) feuilleter.

bruis/e [bruːz] vt contusionner, meurtrir; (fruit, heart) meurtrir; - n bleu m, contusion f. ◆**-ed** a couvert de bleus.

brunch [brʌntʃ] n repas m mixte (petit déjeuner pris comme déjeuner).

brunette [bruː'net] n brunette f.

brunt [brʌnt] n to bear the b. of (attack etc) subir le plus gros de.

brush [brʌʃ] n brosse f; (for shaving) blaireau m; (little broom) balayette f; (action) coup m de brosse; (fight) accrochage m; - vt (teeth, hair etc) brosser; (clothes) donner un coup de brosse à; to b. aside écarter; to b. away or off enlever; to b. up (on) (language) se remettre à; - vi to b. against effleurer. ◆**b.-off** n Fam to give s.o. the b.-off envoyer promener qn. ◆**b.-up** n coup m de brosse. ◆**brushwood** n broussailles fpl.

brusque [bruːsk] a brusque.

Brussels ['brʌs(ə)lz] n Bruxelles m or f; **B. sprouts** choux mpl de Bruxelles.

brutal ['bruːt(ə)l] a brutal. ◆**bru'tality** n brutalité f.

brute [bruːt] n (animal, person) brute f; - a by b. force par la force.

BSc, Am **BS** abbr = Bachelor of Science.

bubble ['bʌb(ə)l] n (of air, soap etc) bulle f; (in boiling liquid) bouillon m; b. and squeak Fam friture f de purée et de viande réchauffées; b. bath bain m moussant; b. gum chewing-gum m; - vi to b. (up) bouillonner; to b. over déborder (with de). ◆**bubbly** n Hum Fam champagne m.

buck [bʌk] **1** n Am Fam dollar m. **2** n (animal) mâle m. **3** vt to b. up remonter le moral à; - vi to b. up prendre courage; (hurry) se grouiller. ◆**buckshot** n inv du gros plomb m. ◆**buck'tooth** n (pl -teeth) dent f saillante.

bucket ['bʌkɪt] n seau m.

buckle ['bʌk(ə)l] **1** n boucle f; - vt boucler. **2** vti (warp) voiler, gauchir. **3** vi to b. down to (task) s'atteler à.

bud [bʌd] n (of tree) bourgeon m; (of flower) bouton m; - vi (-dd-) bourgeonner; pousser des boutons. ◆**budding** a (talent) naissant; (doctor etc) en herbe.

Buddhist ['bʊdɪst] a & n bouddhiste (mf).

buddy ['bʌdɪ] n Am Fam copain m, pote m.

budge [bʌdʒ] vi bouger; - vt faire bouger.

budgerigar ['bʌdʒərɪgɑːr] n perruche f.

budget ['bʌdʒɪt] n budget m; - vi dresser un budget; to b. for inscrire au budget. ◆**budgetary** a budgétaire.

budgie ['bʌdʒɪ] n Fam perruche f.

buff [bʌf] **1** a b.(-coloured) chamois inv. **2** n jazz/etc b. Fam fana(tique) mf du jazz/etc. **3** n in the b. Fam tout nu.

buffalo ['bʌfələʊ] n (pl -oes or -o) buffle m; (American) b. bison m.

buffer ['bʌfər] n (on train) tampon m; (at end of track) butoir m; b. state état m tampon.

buffet 1 ['bʌfɪt] *vt* frapper; (*of waves*) battre; (*of wind, rain*) cingler (*qn*). **2** ['bʊfeɪ] *n* (*table, meal, café*) buffet *m*; **cold b.** viandes *fpl* froides.

buffoon [bə'fuːn] *n* bouffon *m*.

bug 1 [bʌg] **1** *n* punaise *f*; (*any insect*) *Fam* bestiole *f*; *Med Fam* microbe *m*, virus *m*; **the travel b.** (*urge*) le désir de voyager. **2** *n Fam* (*in machine*) défaut *m*; (*in computer program*) erreur *f*. **3** *n* (*apparatus*) *Fam* micro *m*; -*vt* (**-gg-**) (*room*) *Fam* installer des micros dans.

bug 2 [bʌg] *vt* (**-gg-**) (*annoy*) *Am Fam* embêter.

bugbear ['bʌgbeər] *n* (*worry*) cauchemar *m*.

buggy ['bʌgɪ] *n* (*baby*) **b.** (*pushchair*) poussette *f*; (*folding*) poussette-canne *f*; (*pram*) *Am* landau *m*.

bugle ['bjuːg(ə)l] *n* clairon *m*. ◆**bugler** *n* (*person*) clairon *m*.

build [bɪld] **1** *n* (*of person*) carrure *f*. **2** *vt* (*pt* & *pp* **built**) construire; (*house, town*) construire, bâtir; **to b. in** (*cupboard etc*) encastrer; -*vi* bâtir, construire. ◆**built-in** *a* (*cupboard etc*) encastré; (*element of machine etc*) incorporé; (*innate*) *Fig* inné. **3** **to b. up** *vt* (*reputation*) bâtir; (*increase*) augmenter; (*accumulate*) accumuler; (*business*) monter; (*speed, one's strength*) prendre; -*vi* augmenter, monter; s'accumuler. ◆**build-up** *n* montée *f*; accumulation *f*; *Mil* concentration *f*; *Journ* publicité *f*. ◆**built-up** *a* urbanisé; **b.-up area** agglomération *f*.

builder ['bɪldər] *n* maçon *m*; (*contractor*) entrepreneur *m*; (*of cars etc*) constructeur *m*; (*labourer*) ouvrier *m*.

building ['bɪldɪŋ] *n* bâtiment *m*; (*flats, offices*) immeuble *m*; (*action*) construction *f*; **b. society** caisse *f* d'épargne-logement, = société *f* de crédit immobilier.

bulb [bʌlb] *n Bot* bulbe *m*, oignon *m*; *El* ampoule *f*. ◆**bulbous** *a* bulbeux.

Bulgaria [bʌl'geərɪə] *n* Bulgarie *f*. ◆**Bulgarian** *a* & *n* bulgare (*mf*).

bulge [bʌldʒ] *vi* **to b.** (**out**) se renfler, bomber; (*of eyes*) sortir de la tête; -*n* renflement *m*; (*increase*) *Fam* augmentation *f*. ◆**-ing** *a* renflé, bombé; (*eyes*) protubérant; (*bag*) gonflé (**with** de).

bulk [bʌlk] *n inv* grosseur *f*, volume *m*; **the b. of** (*most*) la majeure partie de; **in b.** (*to buy, sell*) en gros. ◆**bulky** *a* (**-ier, -iest**) gros, volumineux.

bull [bʊl] *n* **1** taureau *m*. **2** (*nonsense*) *Fam* foutaises *fpl*. ◆**bullfight** *n* corrida *f*.

◆**bullfighter** *n* matador *m*. ◆**bullring** *n* arène *f*.

bulldog ['bʊldɒg] *n* bouledogue *m*; **b. clip** pince *f* (à dessin).

bulldoz/e ['bʊldəʊz] *vt* passer au bulldozer. ◆**-er** *n* bulldozer *m*, bouteur *m*.

bullet ['bʊlɪt] *n* balle *f*. ◆**bulletproof** *a* (*jacket, Am vest*) pare-balles *inv*; (*car*) blindé.

bulletin ['bʊlətɪn] *n* bulletin *m*.

bullion ['bʊljən] *n* **or b.** or *m* or argent *m* en lingots.

bullock ['bʊlək] *n* bœuf *m*.

bull's-eye ['bʊlzaɪ] *n* (*of target*) centre *m*; **to hit the b.-eye** faire mouche.

bully ['bʊlɪ] *n* (*grosse*) brute *f*, tyran *m*; -*vt* brutaliser; (*persecute*) tyranniser; **to b. into doing** forcer à faire.

bulwark ['bʊlwək] *n* rempart *m*.

bum [bʌm] **1** *n* (*loafer*) *Am Fam* clochard *m*; -*vi* (**-mm-**) **to b.** (**around**) se balader. **2** *vt* (**-mm-**) **to b. sth off s.o.** (*cadge*) *Am Fam* taper qn de qch. **3** *n* (*buttocks*) *Fam* derrière *m*.

bumblebee ['bʌmb(ə)lbiː] *n* bourdon *m*.

bumf [bʌmf] *n Pej Sl* paperasses *fpl*.

bump [bʌmp] *vt* (*of car etc*) heurter; **to b. one's head/knee** se cogner la tête/le genou; **to b. into** se cogner contre; (*of car*) rentrer dans; (*meet*) *Fam* tomber sur; **to b. off** (*kill*) *Sl* liquider; **to b. up** *Fam* augmenter; -*vi* **to b. along** (*on rough road*) *Aut* cahoter; -*n* (*impact*) choc *m*; (*jerk*) cahot *m*; (*on road, body*) bosse *f*. ◆**-er** *n* (*of car etc*) pare-chocs *m inv*; -*a* (*crop etc*) exceptionnel; **b. cars** autos *fpl* tamponneuses. ◆**bumpy** *a* (**-ier, -iest**) (*road, ride*) cahoteux.

bumpkin ['bʌmpkɪn] *n* rustre *m*.

bumptious ['bʌmpʃəs] *a* prétentieux.

bun [bʌn] *n* **1** *Culin* petit pain *m* au lait. **2** (*of hair*) chignon *m*.

bunch [bʌntʃ] *n* (*of flowers*) bouquet *m*; (*of keys*) trousseau *m*; (*of bananas*) régime *m*; (*of people*) bande *f*; **b. of grapes** grappe *f* de raisin; **a b. of** (*mass*) *Fam* un tas de.

bundle ['bʌnd(ə)l] **1** *n* (*of papers*) liasse *f*; (*of firewood*) fagot *m*. **2** *vt* (*put*) fourrer; (*push*) pousser (**into** dans); **to b.** (**up**) mettre en paquet; **to b. s.o. off** expédier qn; -*vi* **to b.** (**oneself**) **up** se couvrir (bien).

bung [bʌŋ] **1** *n* (*stopper*) bonde *f*; -*vt* **to b. up** (*stop up*) boucher. **2** *vt* (*toss*) *Fam* balancer, jeter.

bungalow ['bʌŋgələʊ] *n* bungalow *m*.

bungl/e ['bʌŋg(ə)l] *vt* gâcher; -*vi* travailler

mal. ◆—ing n gâchis m; — a (clumsy) maladroit.

bunion ['bʌnjən] n (on toe) oignon m.

bunk [bʌŋk] n 1 Rail Nau couchette f; b. beds lits mpl superposés. 2 Sl = **bunkum**. ◆**bunkum** n Sl foutaises fpl.

bunker ['bʌŋkər] n Mil Golf bunker m; (coalstore in garden) coffre m.

bunny ['bʌnɪ] n Fam Jeannot m lapin.

buoy [bɔɪ] n bouée f; — vt to b. up (support) Fig soutenir.

buoyant ['bɔɪənt] a Fig gai, optimiste; (market) Fin ferme.

burden ['bɜːd(ə)n] n fardeau m; (of tax) poids m; — vt charger, accabler (with de).

bureau, pl **-eaux** ['bjʊərəʊ, -əʊz] n (office) bureau m; (desk) secrétaire m. ◆**bureaucracy** [bjʊə'rɒkrəsɪ] n bureaucratie f. ◆**bureaucrat** ['bjʊərəkræt] n bureaucrate mf.

burger ['bɜːɡər] n Fam hamburger m.

burglar ['bɜːɡlər] n cambrioleur, -euse mf; b. alarm sonnerie f d'alarme. ◆**burglarize** vt Am cambrioler. ◆**burglary** n cambriolage m. ◆**burgle** vt cambrioler.

burial ['berɪəl] n enterrement m; — a (service) funèbre; b. ground cimetière m.

burlap ['bɜːlæp] n (sacking) toile f à sac.

burlesque [bɜː'lesk] n parodie f; Th Am revue f.

burly ['bɜːlɪ] a (-ier, -iest) costaud.

Burma ['bɜːmə] n Birmanie f. ◆**Bur'mese** a & n birman, -ane (mf).

burn [bɜːn] n brûlure f; — vt (pt & pp burned or burnt) brûler; to b. down or off or up brûler; burnt alive brûlé vif; — vi brûler; to b. down (of house) brûler (complètement), être réduit en cendres; to b. out (of fire) s'éteindre; (of fuse) sauter. ◆—ing a en feu; (fire) allumé; (topic, fever etc) Fig brûlant; — n smell of b. odeur f de brûlé. ◆—er n (of stove) brûleur m.

burp [bɜːp] n Fam rot m; — vi Fam roter.

burrow ['bʌrəʊ] n (hole) terrier m; — vti creuser.

bursar ['bɜːsər] n (in school) intendant, -ante mf.

bursary ['bɜːsərɪ] n (grant) bourse f.

burst [bɜːst] n éclatement m, explosion f; (of laughter) éclat m; (of applause) salve f; (of thunder) coup m; (surge) élan m; (fit) accès m; (burst water pipe) Fam tuyau m crevé; — vi (pt & pp burst) (of bomb etc) éclater; (of bubble, tyre, cloud etc) crever; to b. into (room) faire irruption dans; to b. into tears fondre en larmes; to b. into flames prendre feu, s'embraser; to b. open s'ouvrir avec

force; to b. out laughing éclater de rire; — vt crever, faire éclater; (rupture) rompre; to b. open ouvrir avec force. ◆—ing a (full) plein à craquer (with de); (joy) débordant de; to be b. to do mourir d'envie de.

bury ['berɪ] vt (dead person) enterrer; (hide) enfouir; (plunge, absorb) plonger.

bus [bʌs] n (auto)bus m; (long-distance) (auto)car m; — a (driver, ticket etc) d'autobus; d'autocar; b. shelter abribus m; b. station gare f routière; b. stop arrêt m d'autobus; — vt (-ss-) (children) transporter (en bus) à l'école. ◆**bussing** n Sch ramassage m scolaire.

bush [bʊʃ] n buisson m; (of hair) tignasse f; the b. (land) la brousse. ◆**bushy** a (-ier, -iest) (hair, tail etc) broussailleux.

bushed [bʊʃt] a (tired) Fam crevé.

business ['bɪznɪs] n affaires fpl, commerce m; (shop) commerce m; (task, concern, matter) affaire f; the textile b. le textile; big b. Fam les grosses entreprises fpl commerciales; on b. (to travel) pour affaires; it's your b. to ... c'est à vous de ...; you have no b. to ... vous n'avez pas le droit de ...; that's none of your b.! ça ne vous regarde pas!; to mean b. Fam ne pas plaisanter; — a commercial; (meeting, trip) d'affaires; b. hours (office) heures fpl de travail; (shop) heures fpl d'ouverture. ◆**businesslike** a sérieux, pratique. ◆**businessman** n (pl -men) homme m d'affaires. ◆**businesswoman** n (pl -women) femme f d'affaires.

busker ['bʌskər] n musicien, -ienne mf des rues.

bust [bʌst] n 1 (sculpture) buste m; (woman's breasts) poitrine f. 2 a (broken) Fam fichu; to go b. (bankrupt) faire faillite; — vti (pt & pp bust or busted) Fam = to burst & to break. ◆**b.-up** n Fam (quarrel) engueulade f; (breakup) rupture f.

bustl/e ['bʌs(ə)l] vi to b. (about) s'affairer; — n activité f, branle-bas m. ◆—ing a (street) bruyant.

bus/y ['bɪzɪ] a (-ier, -iest) occupé (doing à faire); (active) actif; (day) chargé; (street) animé; (line) Tel Am occupé; to be b. doing (in the process of) être en train de faire; — vt to b. oneself s'occuper (with à qch, doing à faire). ◆—**ily** adv activement. ◆**busybody** n to be a b. faire la mouche du coche.

but [bʌt, unstressed bət] 1 conj mais. 2 prep (except) sauf; b. for that sans cela; b. for him sans lui; no one b. you personne d'autre que toi. **3** *adv* (*only*) ne . . . que, seulement.

butane ['bjuːteɪn] *n* (*gas*) butane *m*.

butcher ['bʊtʃər] *n* boucher *m*; **b.'s shop** boucherie *f*; – *vt* (*people*) massacrer; (*animal*) abattre. **◆butchery** *n* massacre *m* (**of** de).

butler ['bʌtlər] *n* maître d'hôtel.

butt [bʌt] **1** *n* (*of cigarette*) mégot *m*; (*of gun*) crosse *f*; (*buttocks*) *Am Fam* derrière *m*; **b. for ridicule** objet *m* de risée. **2** *vi* **b. in** interrompre, intervenir.

butter ['bʌtər] *n* beurre *m*; **b. bean** haricot *m* blanc; **b. dish** beurrier *m*; – *vt* beurrer; **to b. s.o. up** *Fam* flatter qn. **◆buttercup** *n* bouton-d'or *m*. **◆buttermilk** *n* lait *m* de beurre.

butterfly ['bʌtəflaɪ] *n* papillon *m*; **to have butterflies** *Fam* avoir le trac; **b. stroke** *Swimming* brasse *f* papillon.

buttock ['bʌtək] *n* fesse *f*.

button ['bʌtən] *n* bouton *m*; – *vt* **to b. (up)** boutonner; – *vi* **to b. up** (*of garment*) se boutonner. **◆buttonhole 1** *n* boutonnière *f*; (*flower*) fleur *f*. **2** *vt* (*person*) *Fam* accrocher.

buttress ['bʌtrɪs] *n* Archit contrefort *m*; Fig soutien *m*; – *vt* (*support*) Archit & Fig soutenir.

buxom ['bʌksəm] *a* (*woman*) bien en chair.

buy [baɪ] *vt* (*pt & pp* bought) acheter (**from** s.o. à qn, **for** s.o. à or pour qn); (*story etc*) *Am Fam* avaler, croire; **to b. back** racheter; **to b. over** (*bribe*) corrompre; **to b. up** acheter en bloc; – *n* **a good b.** une bonne affaire. **◆—er** *n* acheteur, -euse *mf*.

buzz [bʌz] **1** *vi* bourdonner; **to b. off** *Fam* décamper; – *n* bourdonnement *m*. **2** *vt* (*building etc*) *Av* raser. **3** *vt* **to b. s.o.** Tel appeler qn; – *n* Tel Fam coup *m* de fil. **◆—er** *n* interphone *m*; (*of bell, clock*) sonnerie *f*; (*hooter*) sirène *f*.

by [baɪ] *prep* **1** (*agent, manner*) par; **hit/chosen/etc by** frappé/choisi/*etc* par; **surrounded/followed/etc by** entouré/suivi/*etc* de; **by doing** en faisant; **by sea** par mer; **by mistake** par erreur; **by car** en voiture; **by bicycle** à bicyclette; **by moonlight** au clair de lune; **one by one** un à un; **day by day** de jour en jour; **by sight/day/far** de vue/jour/loin; **by the door** (*through*) par la porte; (**all**) **by oneself** tout seul. **2** (*next to*) à côté de; (*near*) près de; **by the lake/sea** au bord du lac/de la mer; **to pass by the bank** passer devant la banque. **3** (*before in time*) avant; **by Monday** avant lundi, d'ici lundi; **by now** à cette heure-ci, déjà; **by yesterday** (dès) hier. **4** (*amount, measurement*) à; **by the kilo** au kilo; **taller by a metre** plus grand d'un mètre; **paid by the hour** payé à l'heure. **5** (*according to*) d'après; – *adv* **close by** tout près; **to go by, pass by** passer; **to put by** mettre de côté; **by and by** bientôt; **by and large** en gros. **◆by-election** *n* élection *f* partielle. **◆by-law** *n* arrêté *m*; (*of organization*) *Am* statut *m*. **◆by-product** *n* sous-produit *m*. **◆by-road** *n* chemin *m* de traverse.

bye(-bye)! [baɪ('baɪ)] *int* Fam salut!, au revoir!

bygone ['baɪɡɒn] *a* **in b. days** jadis.

bypass ['baɪpɑːs] *n* déviation *f* (routière), dérivation *f*; – *vt* contourner; (*ignore*) Fig éviter de passer par.

bystander ['baɪstændər] *n* spectateur, -trice *mf*; (*in street*) badaud, -aude *mf*.

byword ['baɪwɜːd] *n* **a b. for** Pej un synonyme de.

C

C, c [siː] *n* C, c *m*.

c *abbr* = **cent**.

cab [kæb] *n* taxi *m*; (*horse-drawn*) Hist fiacre *m*; (*of train driver etc*) cabine *f*. **◆cabby** *n* Fam (chauffeur *m* de) taxi *m*; Hist cocher *m*.

cabaret ['kæbəreɪ] *n* (*show*) spectacle *m*; (*place*) cabaret *m*.

cabbage ['kæbɪdʒ] *n* chou *m*.

cabin ['kæbɪn] *n* Nau Rail cabine *f*; (*hut*) cabane *f*, case *f*; **c. boy** mousse *m*.

cabinet ['kæbɪnɪt] **1** *n* (*cupboard*) armoire *f*; (*for display*) vitrine *f*; (*filing*) **c.** classeur *m* (de bureau). **2** *n* Pol cabinet *m*; – *a* ministériel; **c. minister** ministre *m*. **◆c.-maker** *n* ébéniste *m*.

cable ['keɪb(ə)l] *n* câble *m*; **c. car** (*with over-head cable*) téléphérique *m*; Rail funiculaire *m*; **c. television** la télévision par câble; **to have c.** Fam avoir le câble; – *vt* (*message etc*) câbler (**to** à).

caboose [kə'bu:s] n Rail Am fourgon m (de queue).

cache [kæʃ] n (place) cachette f; **an arms' c.** des armes cachées, une cache d'armes.

cachet ['kæʃeɪ] n (mark, character etc) cachet m.

cackle ['kæk(ə)l] vi (of hen) caqueter; (laugh) glousser; – n caquet m; glousse-ment m.

cacophony [kə'kɒfənɪ] n cacophonie f.

cactus, pl -ti or -tuses [kæktəs, -taɪ, -təsɪz] n cactus m.

cad [kæd] n Old-fashioned Pej goujat m.

cadaverous [kə'dævərəs] a cadavérique.

caddie ['kædɪ] n Golf caddie m.

caddy ['kædɪ] n (tea) c. boîte f à thé.

cadence ['keɪdəns] n Mus cadence f.

cadet [kə'det] n Mil élève m officier.

cadge [kædʒ] vti (beg) Pej quémander; – vt (meal) se faire payer (off s.o. par qn); to c. money from or off s.o. taper qn.

Caesarean [sɪ'zeərɪən] n c. (section) Med césarienne f.

café ['kæfeɪ] n café(-restaurant) m. ◆**cafeteria** [kæfɪ'tɪərɪə] n cafétéria f.

caffeine ['kæfiːn] n caféine f.

cage [keɪdʒ] n cage f; – vt to c. (up) mettre en cage.

cagey ['keɪdʒɪ] a Fam peu communicatif (about à l'égard de).

cahoots [kə'huːts] n in c. Sl de mèche, en cheville (with avec).

cajole [kə'dʒəʊl] vt amadouer, enjôler.

cak/e [keɪk] 1 n gâteau m; (small) pâtisse-rie f; c. of soap savonnette f. 2 vi (harden) durcir; – vt (cover) couvrir (with de). ◆—ed a (mud) séché.

calamine ['kæləmaɪn] n c. (lotion) lotion f apaisante (à la calamine).

calamity [kə'læmɪtɪ] n calamité f. ◆**calamitous** a désastreux.

calcium ['kælsɪəm] n calcium m.

calculat/e ['kælkjʊleɪt] vti calculer; to c. that Fam supposer que; to c. on compter sur. ◆—ing a (shrewd) calculateur. ◆**calculation** n calcul m. ◆**calculator** n (desk computer) calculatrice f; (pocket) c. calculatrice (de poche). ◆**calculus** n Math Med calcul m.

calendar ['kæləndər] n calendrier m; (direc-tory) annuaire m.

calf [kɑːf] n (pl calves) 1 (animal) veau m. 2 Anat mollet m.

calibre ['kælɪbər] n calibre m. ◆**calibrate** vt calibrer.

calico ['kælɪkəʊ] n (pl -oes or -os) (fabric) calicot m; (printed) Am indienne f.

call [kɔːl] n appel m; (shout) cri m; (vocation) vocation f; (visit) visite f; (telephone) c. communication f, appel m téléphonique; **to make a c.** Tel téléphoner (to à); **on c.** de garde; **no c. to do** aucune raison de faire; **there's no c. for that article** Com cet article n'est pas très demandé; **c. box** cabine f (téléphonique); – vt appeler; (wake up) réveiller; (person to meeting) convoquer (to à); (attention) attirer (to sur); (truce) demander; (consider) considérer; **he's called David** il s'appelle David; **to c. a meeting** convoquer une assemblée; **to c. s.o. a liar/etc** qualifier or traiter qn de menteur/etc; – vi appeler; **to c.** this question mettre en question; **let's c. it a day** Fam on va s'arrêter là, ça suffit; **to c. sth (out)** (shout) crier qch; – vi appeler; **to c. (out)** (cry out) crier; **to c. (in or round or by or over)** (visit) passer. ■ **to c. back** vti rappeler; **to c. for** vt (require) demander; (summon) appeler; (collect) passer prendre; **to c. in** vt faire venir or entrer; (police) appeler; (recall) rappeler, faire rentrer; – vi passer; **to c. in on s.o.** passer chez qn. ◆**call-in** a (programme) Rad à ligne ouverte; **to c. off** vt (cancel) annuler; (dog) rappeler; **to c. out** vt (doctor) appeler; (workers) donner une consigne de grève à; – vi to c. out for demander à haute voix; **to c. up** vt Mil Tel appeler; (memories) évoquer. ◆**call-up** n Mil appel m, mobilisation f; **to c. (up)on s.o.** (visit) passer voir, passer chez; (invoke) invoquer; **to c. (up)on s.o. to do** inviter qn à faire; (urge) sommer qn de faire. ◆**calling** n vocation f; **c. card** Am carte f de visite. ◆**caller** n visiteur, -euse mf; Tel correspondant, -ante mf.

calligraphy [kə'lɪgrəfɪ] n calligraphie f.

callous ['kæləs] a 1 cruel, insensible. 2 (skin) calleux. ◆**callus** n durillon m, cal m.

callow ['kæləʊ] a inexpérimenté.

calm [kɑːm] a (-er, -est) calme, tranquille; keep c.! (don't panic) du calme!; – n calme m; – vt to c. (down) calmer; – vi to c. down se calmer. ◆—ly adv calmement. ◆—ness n calme m.

calorie ['kælərɪ] n calorie f.

calumny ['kæləmnɪ] n calomnie f.

calvary ['kælvərɪ] n Rel calvaire m.

calve [kɑːv] vi (of cow) vêler.

camber ['kæmbər] n (in road) bombement m.

came [keɪm] see come.

camel ['kæməl] n chameau m.

camellia [kə'miːlɪə] n Bot camélia m.

cameo ['kæmɪəʊ] n camée m.

camera ['kæmərə] n appareil(-photo) m; TV Cin caméra f. ◆**cameraman** n (pl -men) caméraman m.

camomile ['kæməmaɪl] n Bot camomille f.

camouflage ['kæməflɑːʒ] n camouflage m; – vt camoufler.

camp¹ [kæmp] n camp m, campement m; c. bed lit m de camp; – vi to c. (out) camper. ◆–ing n Sp camping m; c. site (terrain m de) camping m. ◆–er n (person) campeur, -euse mf; (vehicle) camping-car m. ◆**campfire** n feu m de camp. ◆**campsite** n camping m.

camp² [kæmp] a (affected) affecté, exagéré (de façon à provoquer le rire).

campaign [kæm'peɪn] n Pol Mil Journ etc campagne f; – vi faire campagne. ◆–er n militant, -ante mf (for pour).

campus ['kæmpəs] n Univ campus m.

can¹ [kæn, unstressed kən] v aux (pres t can; pt could) (be able to) pouvoir; (know how to) savoir; if I c. si je peux; she c. swim elle sait nager; if I could swim si je savais nager; he could do it tomorrow il pourrait le faire demain; he couldn't help me il ne pouvait pas m'aider; he could have done it il aurait pu le faire; you could be wrong (possibility) tu as peut-être tort; he can't be old (probability) il ne doit pas être vieux; I come in? (permission) puis-je entrer?; you can't or c. not come tu ne peux pas venir; I c. see je vois.

can² [kæn] n (for water etc) bidon m; (tin for food) boîte f; (for oil) bidon m; – vt (-nn-) mettre en boîte. ◆**canned** a en boîte, en conserve; c. food conserves fpl. ◆**can-opener** n ouvre-boîtes m inv.

Canada ['kænədə] n Canada m. ◆**Canadian** [kə'neɪdɪən] a & n canadien, -ienne (mf).

canal [kə'næl] n canal m.

canary [kə'neərɪ] n canari m, serin m.

cancan ['kænkæn] n french-cancan m.

cancel ['kænsəl] vt (-ll-, Am -l-) annuler; (goods, taxi, appointment) décommander; (word, paragraph etc) biffer; (train) supprimer; (stamp) oblitérer; to c. a ticket (with date) composter un billet; (punch) poinçonner un billet; to c. each other out s'annuler. ◆**cance'llation** n annulation f; suppression f; oblitération f.

cancer ['kænsər] n cancer m; C. (sign) le Cancer; c. patient cancéreux, -euse mf. ◆**cancerous** a cancéreux.

candelabra [kændɪ'lɑːbrə] n candélabre m.

candid ['kændɪd] a franc, sincère. ◆**candour** n franchise f, sincérité f.

candidate ['kændɪdeɪt] n candidat, -ate mf. ◆**candidacy** n, ◆**candidature** n candidature f.

candle ['kænd(ə)l] n bougie f; (tallow) chandelle f; Rel cierge m; c. grease suif m. ◆**candlelight** n by c. à la (lueur d'une) bougie; to have dinner by c. dîner aux chandelles. ◆**candlestick** n bougeoir m; (tall) chandelier m.

candy ['kændɪ] n Am bonbon(s) m(pl); (sugar) c. sucre m candi; c. store Am confiserie f. ◆**candied** a (fruit) confit, glacé. ◆**candyfloss** n barbe f à papa.

cane [keɪn] n canne f; (for basket) rotin m; Sch baguette f; – vt (punish) Sch fouetter.

canine ['keɪnaɪn] a 1 a canin. 2 n (tooth) canine f.

canister ['kænɪstər] n boîte f (en métal).

canker ['kæŋkər] n (in disease) & Fig chancre m.

cannabis ['kænəbɪs] n (plant) chanvre m indien; (drug) haschisch m.

cannibal ['kænɪbəl] n & a cannibale (mf).

cannon ['kænən] n (pl -s or inv) canon m. ◆**cannonball** n boulet m (de canon).

cannot ['kænɒt] = **can not**.

canny ['kænɪ] a (-ier, -iest) rusé, malin.

canoe [kə'nuː] n canoë m, kayak m; – vi faire du canoë or du kayak. ◆–ing n to go c. Sp faire du canoë or du kayak. ◆**canoeist** n canoéiste m.

canon ['kænən] n (law) canon m; (clergyman) chanoine m. ◆**canonize** vt Rel canoniser.

canopy ['kænəpɪ] n (over bed, altar etc) dais m; (hood of pram) capote f; (awning) auvent m; (made of glass) marquise f; (of sky) Fig voûte f.

cant [kænt] n (jargon) jargon m.

can't [kɑːnt] = **can not**.

cantaloup(e) ['kæntəluːp, Am -ləʊp] n (melon) cantaloup m.

cantankerous [kæn'tæŋkərəs] a grincheux, acariâtre.

cantata [kæn'tɑːtə] n Mus cantate f.

canteen [kæn'tiːn] n (place) cantine f; (flask) gourde f; c. of cutlery ménagère f.

canter ['kæntər] n petit galop m; – vi aller au petit galop.

cantor ['kæntər] n Rel chantre m, maître m de chapelle.

canvas ['kænvəs] n (grosse) toile f; (for embroidery) canevas m.

canvass ['kænvəs] vt (an area) faire du démarchage dans; (opinions) sonder; to c.

s.o. *Pol* solliciter des voix de qn; *Com* solliciter des commandes de qn. ◆—**ing** *n Com* démarchage *m*, prospection *f*; *Pol* démarchage *m* (électoral). ◆—**er** *n Pol* agent *m* électoral; *Com* démarcheur, -euse *mf*.

canyon ['kænjən] *n* cañon *m*, canyon *m*.

cap¹ [kæp] *n* **1** (*hat*) casquette *f*; (*for shower etc*) & *Nau* bonnet *m*; *Mil* képi *m*. **2** (*of bottle, tube, valve*) bouchon *m*; (*of milk or beer bottle*) capsule *f*; (*of pen*) capuchon *m*. **3** (*of child's gun*) amorce *f*, capsule *f*. **4** (**Dutch**) *c.* (*contraceptive*) diaphragme *m*. ◆—**ped** *a.* (*contraceptive*) diaphragme *m*. ◆—**ped** *a* (*covered*) coiffé de.

cap² [kæp] *vt* (-pp-) (*outdo*) surpasser; **to c. it all** pour combler; **capped with** (*covered*) coiffé de.

capable ['keipəb(ə)l] *a* (*person*) capable (**of** sth de qch, **of doing** de faire), compétent; **c. of** (*thing*) susceptible de. ◆**capa'bility** *n* capacité *f*. ◆**capably** *adv* avec compétence.

capacity [kə'pæsəti] *n* (*of container*) capacité *f*, contenance *f*; (*ability*) aptitude *f*, capacité *f*; (*output*) rendement *m*; **in my c. as** en ma qualité de; **in an advisory c.** à titre consultatif/*etc*; **filled to c.** absolument plein, comble; **c. audience** salle *f* comble.

cape [keip] *n* **1** (*cloak*) cape *f*; (*of cyclist*) pèlerine *f*. **2** *Geog* cap *m*; **C. Town** Le Cap.

caper ['keipər] **1** *vi* (*jump about*) gambader. **2** *n* (*activity*) *Sl* affaire *f*; (*prank*) *Fam* farce *f*; (*trip*) *Fam* virée *f*. **3** *n Bot Culin* câpre *f*.

capital ['kæpit(ə)l] **1** *a* (*punishment, letter, importance*) capital; – *n* **c.** (*city*) capitale *f*; **c.** (*letter*) majuscule *f*, capitale *f*. **2** *n* (*money*) capital *m*, capitaux *mpl*. ◆**capitalism** *n* capitalisme *m*. ◆**capitalist** *a* & *n* capitaliste (*mf*). ◆**capitalize** *vi* **to c. on** tirer parti de.

capitulate [kə'pitʃuleit] *vi* capituler. ◆**capitu'lation** *n* capitulation *f*.

caprice [kə'priːs] *n* caprice *m*. ◆**capricious** [kə'priʃəs] *a* capricieux.

Capricorn ['kæprikɔːn] *n* (*sign*) le Capricorne.

capsize [kæp'saiz] *vi Nau* chavirer; – *vt* (*faire*) chavirer.

capsule ['kæpsəl, 'kæpsjuːl] *n* (*medicine, of spaceship etc*) capsule *f*.

captain ['kæptin] *n* capitaine *m*; – *vt Nau* commander; *Sp* être le capitaine de.

caption ['kæpʃ(ə)n] *n Cin Journ* sous-titre *m*; (*under illustration*) légende *f*.

captivate ['kæptiveit] *vt* captiver.

captive ['kæptiv] *n* captif, -ive *mf*, prisonnier, -ière *mf*. ◆**cap'tivity** *n* captivité *f*.

capture ['kæptʃər] *n* capture *f*; – *vt* (*person, animal*) prendre, capturer; (*town*) prendre; (*attention*) capter; (*represent in words, on film etc*) rendre, reproduire.

car [kaːr] *n* voiture *f*, auto(mobile) *f*; *Rail* wagon *m*; – *a* (*industry*) automobile; **c. ferry** ferry-boat *m*; **c. park** parking *m*; **c. radio** autoradio *m*; **c. wash** (*action*) lavage *m* automatique; (*machine*) lave-auto *m*. ◆**carfare** *n Am* frais *mpl* de voyage. ◆**carport** *n* auvent *m* (pour voiture). ◆**carsick** *a* **to be c.** être malade en voiture.

carafe [kə'ræf] *n* carafe *f*.

caramel ['kærəməl] *n* (*flavouring, toffee*) caramel *m*.

carat ['kærət] *n* carat *m*.

caravan ['kærəvæn] *n* (*in desert*) & *Aut* caravane *f*; (*horse-drawn*) roulotte *f*; **c. site** camping *m* pour caravanes.

caraway ['kærəwei] *n Bot Culin* cumin *m*, carvi *m*.

carbohydrates [kaːbəu'haidreits] *npl* (*in diet*) féculents *mpl*.

carbon ['kaːbən] *n* carbone *m*; **c. copy** double *m* (au carbone); *Fig* réplique *f*, double *m*; **c. paper** (papier *m*) carbone *m*.

carbuncle ['kaːbʌŋk(ə)l] *n Med* furoncle *m*, clou *m*.

carburettor [kaːbju'retər] (*Am* carburetor ['kaːbəreitər]) *n* carburateur *m*.

carcass ['kaːkəs] *n* (*body, framework*) carcasse *f*.

carcinogenic [kaːsinə'dʒenik] *a* cancérigène.

card [kaːd] *n* carte *f*; (*cardboard*) carton *m*; (*index*) **c.** fiche *f*; **c. index** fichier *m*; **c. table** table *f* de jeu; **to play cards** jouer aux cartes; **on** *or Am* **in the cards** *Fam* très vraisemblable; **to get one's cards** (*be dismissed*) *Fam* être renvoyé. ◆**cardboard** *n* carton *m*. ◆**cardsharp** *n* tricheur, -euse *mf*.

cardiac ['kaːdiæk] *a* cardiaque.

cardigan ['kaːdigən] *n* cardigan *m*, gilet *m*.

cardinal ['kaːdin(ə)l] **1** *a* (*number etc*) cardinal. **2** *n* (*priest*) cardinal *m*.

care [keər] **1** *vi* **to c. about** (*feel concern about*) se soucier de, s'intéresser à; **to c.** ça m'est égal; **I couldn't c. less** *Fam* je m'en fiche; **who cares?** qu'est-ce que ça fait? **2** *vi* (*like*) aimer, vouloir; **would you c. to try?** voulez-vous essayer?, aimeriez-vous essayer?; **I don't c. for it** (*music etc*) je n'aime pas tellement ça; **to c. for** (*a drink, a change etc*) avoir envie de; **to c. about** *or* **for s.o.** avoir de la sympathie pour qn; **to c. for**

(*look after*) s'occuper de; (*sick person*) soigner. **3** *n* (*application, heed*) soin(s) *m(pl)*, attention *f*; (*charge, protection*) garde *f*, soin *m*; (*anxiety*) souci *m*; **to take c. not to do** faire attention à ne pas faire; **take c. to put everything back** veillez à tout ranger; **to take c. of** s'occuper de; **to take c. of itself** (*of matter*) s'arranger; **to take c. of oneself** (*manage*) se débrouiller; (*keep healthy*) faire attention à sa santé. ◆**carefree** *a* insouciant. ◆**caretaker** *n* gardien, -ienne *mf*, concierge *mf*.

career [kə'rɪər] **1** *n* carrière *f*; – *a* (*diplomat etc*) de carrière. **2** *vi* **to c. along** aller à toute vitesse.

careful ['keəf(ə)l] *a* (*diligent*) soigneux (*about, of* de); (*cautious*) prudent; **c. (with money)** regardant; **to be c. of** *or* **with** (*heed*) faire attention à. ◆**—ly** *adv* avec soin; prudemment. ◆**careless** *a* négligent; (*thoughtless*) irréfléchi; (*inattentive*) inattentif (*of* à). ◆**carelessness** *n* négligence *f*, manque *m* de soin.

caress [kə'res] *n* caresse *f*; – *vt* (*stroke*) caresser; (*kiss*) embrasser.

cargo ['kɑːgəʊ] *n* (*pl* -oes, *Am* -os) cargaison *f*; **c. boat** cargo *m*.

Caribbean [kærɪ'bɪən, *Am* kə'rɪbɪən] *a* caraïbe; – *n* **the C. (Islands)** les Antilles *fpl*.

caricature ['kærɪkətʃʊər] *n* caricature *f*; – *vt* caricaturer.

caring ['keərɪŋ] *a* (*loving*) aimant; (*understanding*) compréhensif; – *n* affection *f*.

carnage ['kɑːnɪdʒ] *n* carnage *m*.

carnal ['kɑːnəl] *a* charnel, sexuel.

carnation [kɑː'neɪʃən] *n* œillet *m*.

carnival ['kɑːnɪvəl] *n* carnaval *m*.

carnivore ['kɑːnɪvɔːr] *n* carnivore *m*. ◆**carnivorous** *a* carnivore.

carol ['kærəl] *n* chant *m* (de Noël).

carouse [kə'raʊz] *vi* faire la fête.

carp [kɑːp] **1** *n* (*fish*) carpe *f*. **2** *vi* critiquer; **to c. at** critiquer.

carpenter ['kɑːpɪntər] *n* (*for house building*) charpentier *m*; (*light woodwork maker*) menuisier *m*. ◆**carpentry** *n* charpenterie *f*; menuiserie *f*.

carpet ['kɑːpɪt] *n* tapis *m*; (*fitted*) moquette *f*; **c. sweeper** balai *m* mécanique; – *vt* recouvrir d'un tapis *or* d'une moquette; (*of snow etc*) *Fig* tapisser. ◆**—ing** *n* (*carpets*) tapis *mpl*; moquette *f*.

carriage ['kærɪdʒ] *n* (*horse-drawn*) voiture *f*, équipage *m*; *Rail* voiture *f*; *Com* transport *m*; (*bearing of person*) port *m*; (*of typewriter*) chariot *m*; **c. paid** port payé. ◆**carriageway** *n* (*of road*) chaussée *f*.

carrier ['kærɪər] *n* *Com* entreprise *f* de transports; *Med* porteur, -euse *mf*; **c. (bag)** sac *m* (en plastique); **c. pigeon** pigeon *m* voyageur.

carrion ['kærɪən] *n* charogne *f*.

carrot ['kærət] *n* carotte *f*.

carry ['kærɪ] *vt* porter; (*goods*) transporter; (*by wind*) emporter; (*involve*) comporter; (*interest*) *Com* produire; (*extend*) faire passer; (*win*) remporter; (*authority*) avoir; (*child*) *Med* attendre; (*motion*) *Pol* faire passer, voter; (*sell*) stocker; *Math* retenir; **to c. too far** pousser trop loin; **to c. oneself** se comporter; – *vi* (*of sound*) porter. ■ **to c. away** emporter; *Fig* transporter; **to be** *or* **get carried away** (*excited*) s'emballer; **to c. back** *vt* (*thing*) rapporter; (*person*) ramener; (*in thought*) reporter; **to c. off** *vt* emporter; (*kidnap*) enlever; (*prize*) remporter; **to c. it off** réussir; **to c. on** *vt* continuer; (*conduct*) mener, diriger; (*sustain*) soutenir; – *vi* continuer (**doing** à faire); (*behave*) *Pej* se conduire (mal); (*complain*) se plaindre; **to c. on with sth** continuer qch; **to c. on about** (*talk*) causer de. ◆**carryings-'on** *npl* *Pej* manières *fpl*; (*behaviour*) *Pej* façons *fpl*; **to c. out** *vt* (*plan etc*) exécuter, réaliser; (*repair etc*) effectuer; (*duty*) accomplir; (*meal*) *Am* emporter; **to c. through** *vt* (*plan etc*) mener à bonne fin.

carryall ['kærɪɔːl] *n* *Am* fourre-tout *m inv*. ◆**carrycot** *n* (nacelle *f*) porte-bébé *m*.

cart [kɑːt] **1** *n* charrette *f*; (*handcart*) voiture *f* à bras. **2** *vt* (*goods, people*) transporter; **to c. (around)** *Fam* trimbal(l)er; **to c. away** emporter. ◆**carthorse** *n* cheval *m* de trait.

cartel [kɑː'tel] *n* *Econ* cartel *m*.

cartilage ['kɑːtɪlɪdʒ] *n* cartilage *m*.

carton ['kɑːtən] *n* (*box*) carton *m*; (*of milk, fruit juice etc*) brick *m*, pack *m*; (*of cigarettes*) cartouche *f*; (*of cream*) pot *m*.

cartoon [kɑː'tuːn] *n* *Journ* dessin *m* (humoristique); *Cin* dessin *m* animé; (*strip*) **c. bande** *f* dessinée. ◆**cartoonist** *n* *Journ* dessinateur, -trice *mf* (humoristique).

cartridge ['kɑːtrɪdʒ] *n* (*of firearm, pen, camera, tape deck*) cartouche *f*; (*of record player*) cellule *f*; **c. belt** cartouchière *f*.

carv/e [kɑːv] *vt* (*cut*) tailler (**out of** dans); (*sculpt*) sculpter; (*initials etc*) graver; **to c. (up)** (*meat*) découper; **to c. up** (*country*) dépecer, morceler; **to c. out sth for oneself** (*career etc*) se tailler qch. ◆**—ing** *n* (**wood**) **c. sculpture** *f* (sur bois).

cascade [kæs'keɪd] *n* (*of rocks*) chute *f*; (of

blows) déluge *m*; (*of lace*) flot *m*; − *vi* tomber; (*hang*) pendre.

case [keɪs] *n* 1 (*instance*) & *Med* cas *m*; *Jur* affaire *f*; *Phil* arguments *mpl*; **in any c.** en tout cas; **in c. it rains** au cas où il pleuvrait; **in c. of** en cas de; (*just*) **in c.** à tout hasard. 2 (*bag*) valise *f*; (*crate*) caisse *f*; (*for pen, glasses, camera, violin, cigarettes*) étui *m*; (*for jewels*) coffret *m*. ◆**casing** *n* (*covering*) enveloppe *f*.

cash [kæʃ] *n* argent *m*; **to pay** (**in**) **c.** (*not by cheque*) payer en espèces *or* en liquide; **to pay c.** (**down**) payer comptant; **c. price** prix *m* (au) comptant; **c. box** caisse *f*; **c. desk** caisse *f*; **c. register** caisse *f* enregistreuse; − *vt* (*banknote*) changer; **to c. a cheque** (*of person*) encaisser un chèque; (*of bank*) payer un chèque; **to c. in on** *Fam* profiter de. ◆**ca'shier** 1 *n* caissier, -ière *mf*. 2 *vt* (*dismiss*) *Mil* casser.

cashew [kæʃuː] *n* (*nut*) cajou *m*.

cashmere [kæʃmɪər] *n* cachemire *m*.

casino [kəsiːnəu] *n* (*pl* -**os**) casino *m*.

cask [kɑːsk] *n* fût *m*, tonneau *m*. ◆**casket** *n* (*box*) coffret *m*; (*coffin*) cercueil *m*.

casserole [kæsərəul] *n* (*covered dish*) cocotte *f*; (*stew*) ragoût *m* en cocotte.

cassette [kə'set] *n* cassette *f*; *Phot* cartouche *f*; **c. player** lecteur *m* de cassettes; **c. recorder** magnétophone *m* à cassettes.

cassock [kæsək] *n* soutane *f*.

cast [kɑːst] 1 *n Th* acteurs *mpl*; (*list*) *Th* distribution *f*; (*mould*) moulage *m*; (*of dice*) coup *m*; *Med* plâtre *m*; (*squint*) léger strabisme *m*; **c. of mind** tournure *f* d'esprit. 2 *vt* (*pt* & *pp* **cast**) (*throw*) jeter; (*light, shadow*) projeter; (*blame*) rejeter; (*glance*) jeter; (*doubt*) exprimer; (*lose*) perdre; (*metal*) couler; (*role*) *Th* distribuer; (*actor*) donner un rôle à; **to c. one's mind back** se reporter en arrière; **to c. a vote** voter; **to c. aside** rejeter; **to c. off** (*chains etc*) se libérer de; (*shed, lose*) se dépouiller de; *Fig* abandonner. 3 *vi* **to c. off** *Nau* appareiller. 4 *n* **c. iron** fonte *f*. ◆**c.-'iron** *a* (*pan etc*) en fonte; (*will etc*) *Fig* de fer, solide.

castaway [kɑːstəweɪ] *n* naufragé, -ée *mf*.

caste [kɑːst] *n* caste *f*.

caster [kɑːstər] *n* (*wheel*) roulette *f*; **c. sugar** sucre *m* en poudre.

castle [kɑːs(ə)l] *n* château *m*; (*in chess*) tour *f*.

castoffs [kɑːstɒfs] *npl* vieux vêtements *mpl*.

castor [kɑːstər] *n* (*wheel*) roulette *f*; **c. oil** huile *f* de ricin; **c. sugar** sucre *m* en poudre.

castrate [kæ'streɪt] *vt* châtrer. ◆**castration** *n* castration *f*.

casual [kæʒjuəl] *a* (*meeting*) fortuit; (*remark*) fait en passant; (*stroll*) sans but; (*offhand*) désinvolte, insouciant; (*worker*) temporaire; (*work*) irrégulier; **c. clothes** vêtements *mpl* sport; **a c. acquaintance** quelqu'un que l'on connaît un peu. ◆**-ly** *adv* par hasard; (*informally*) avec désinvolture; (*to remark*) en passant.

casualty [kæʒjuəltɪ] *n* (*dead*) mort *m*, morte *f*; (*wounded*) blessé, -ée *mf*; (*accident victim*) accidenté, -ée *mf*; **casualties** morts et blessés *mpl*; *Mil* pertes *fpl*; **c. department** *Med* service *m* des accidentés.

cat [kæt] *n* chat *m*, chatte *f*; **c. burglar** monte-en-l'air *m inv*; **c.'s eyes** cataphotes® *mpl*, clous *mpl*. ◆**catcall** *n* sifflet *m*, huée *f*.

cataclysm [kætəklɪzəm] *n* cataclysme *m*.

catalogue [kætəlɒg] (*Am* **catalog**) *n* catalogue *m*; − *vt* cataloguer.

catalyst [kætəlɪst] *n Ch* & *Fig* catalyseur *m*.

catapult [kætəpʌlt] *n* lance-pierres *m inv*; *Hist Av* catapulte *f*; − *vt* catapulter.

cataract [kætərækt] *n* (*waterfall*) & *Med* cataracte *f*.

catarrh [kə'tɑːr] *n* catarrhe *m*, rhume *m*.

catastrophe [kə'tæstrəfɪ] *n* catastrophe *f*. ◆**cata'strophic** *a* catastrophique.

catch [kætʃ] *vt* (*pt* & *pp* **caught**) (*ball, thief, illness etc*) attraper; (*grab*) prendre, saisir; (*surprise*) (sur)prendre; (*understand*) saisir; (*train etc*) attraper, (*réussir à*) prendre; (*attention*) attirer; (*of nail etc*) accrocher; (*finger etc*) se prendre (**in** dans); **to c. sight of** apercevoir; **to c. fire** prendre feu; **to c. s.o.** (**in**) *Fam* trouver qn (chez soi); **to c. one's breath** (*rest a while*) reprendre haleine; (*stop breathing*) retenir son souffle; **I didn't c. the train**/*etc* j'ai manqué le train/*etc*; **to c. s.o. out** prendre qn en défaut; **to c. s.o. up** rattraper qn; − *vi* (*of fire*) prendre; **her skirt** (**got**) **caught in the door** sa jupe s'est prise *or* coincée dans la porte; **to c. on** prendre, devenir populaire; (*understand*) saisir; **to c. up** se rattraper; **to c. up with s.o.** rattraper qn; − *n* capture *f*, prise *f*; (*trick, snare*) piège *m*; (*on door*) loquet *m*. ◆**-ing** *a* contagieux. ◆**catchphrase** *n*, ◆**catchword** *n* slogan *m*.

catchy [kætʃɪ] *a* (-**ier**, -**iest**) (*tune*) *Fam* facile à retenir.

catechism [kætɪkɪzəm] *n Rel* catéchisme *m*.

category [kætɪgərɪ] *n* catégorie *f*. ◆**cate-**

'gorical *a* catégorique. ◆**categorize** *vt* classer (par catégories).

cater ['keɪtər] *vi* s'occuper de la nourriture; **to c. for** *or* **to** *(need, taste)* satisfaire; *(readership)* Journ s'adresser à. ◆**-ing** *n* restauration *f.* ◆**-er** *n* traiteur *m.*

caterpillar ['kætəpɪlər] *n* chenille *f.*

catgut ['kætgʌt] *n (cord)* boyau *m.*

cathedral [kə'θiːdrəl] *n* cathédrale *f.*

catholic ['kæθlɪk] **1** *a* & *n* C. catholique *(mf).* **2** *a (taste)* universel; *(view)* libéral. ◆**Ca'tholicism** *n* catholicisme *m.*

cattle ['kæt(ə)l] *npl* bétail *m,* bestiaux *mpl.*

catty ['kætɪ] *a* (-**ier**, -**iest**) *Fam* rosse, méchant.

caucus ['kɔːkəs] *n Pol Am* comité *m* électoral.

caught [kɔːt] *see* catch.

cauldron ['kɔːldrən] *n* chaudron *m.*

cauliflower ['kɒlɪflaʊər] *n* chou-fleur *m.*

cause [kɔːz] *n* cause *f; (reason)* raison *f;* **c. for complaint** sujet *m* de plainte; **–** *vt* causer, occasionner; *(trouble)* créer, causer (**for** à); **to c. sth to move**/*etc* faire bouger/*etc* qch.

causeway ['kɔːzweɪ] *n* chaussée *f.*

caustic ['kɔːstɪk] *a (remark, substance)* caustique.

cauterize ['kɔːtəraɪz] *vt Med* cautériser.

caution ['kɔːʃ(ə)n] *n (care)* prudence *f,* précaution *f; (warning)* avertissement *m;* **–** *vt (warn)* avertir; **to c. s.o. against sth** mettre qn en garde contre qch. ◆**cautionary** *a (tale)* moral. ◆**cautious** *a* prudent, circonspect. ◆**cautiously** *adv* prudemment.

cavalcade ['kævəlkeɪd] *n (procession)* cavalcade *f.*

cavalier [kævə'lɪər] **1** *a (selfish)* cavalier. **2** *n (horseman, knight)* Hist cavalier *m.*

cavalry ['kævəlrɪ] *n* cavalerie *f.*

cave [keɪv] **1** *n* caverne *f,* grotte *f.* **2** *vi* **to c. in** *(fall in)* s'effondrer. ◆**caveman** *n (pl* -**men)** homme *m* des cavernes. ◆**cavern** ['kævən] *n* caverne *f.*

caviar(e) ['kævɪɑːr] *n* caviar *m.*

cavity ['kævɪtɪ] *n* cavité *f.*

cavort [kə'vɔːt] *vi Fam* cabrioler; **to c. naked**/*etc* se balader tout nu/*etc.*

cease [siːs] *vti* cesser *(doing* or *to do).* ◆**c.-fire** *n* cessez-le-feu *m inv.* ◆**ceaseless** *a* incessant. ◆**ceaselessly** *adv* sans cesse.

cedar ['siːdər] *n (tree, wood)* cèdre *m.*

cedilla [sɪ'dɪlə] *n Gram* cédille *f.*

ceiling ['siːlɪŋ] *n (of room, on wages etc)* plafond *m.*

celebrat/e ['selɪbreɪt] *vt (event)* fêter; *(mass, s.o.'s merits etc)* célébrer; **–** *vi* faire la fête; **we should c. (that)!** il faut fêter ça! ◆**-ed** *a* célèbre. ◆**cele'bration** *n* fête *f;* **the c. of** *(marriage etc)* la célébration de. ◆**ce'lebrity** *n (person)* célébrité *f.*

celery ['selərɪ] *n* céleri *m.*

celibate ['selɪbət] *a (abstaining from sex)* célibataire; *(monk etc)* abstinent. ◆**celibacy** *n (of young person etc)* célibat *m; (of monk etc)* abstinence *f.*

cell [sel] *n* cellule *f; El* élément *m.* ◆**cellular** *a* cellulaire; **c. blanket** couverture *f* en cellular.

cellar ['selər] *n* cave *f.*

cello ['tʃeləʊ] *n (pl* -**os)** violoncelle *m.* ◆**cellist** *n* violoncelliste *mf.*

cellophane® ['seləfeɪn] *n* cellophane® *f.*

celluloid ['seljʊlɔɪd] *n* celluloïd *m.*

cellulose ['seljʊləʊs] *n* cellulose *f.*

Celsius ['selsɪəs] *a* Celsius *inv.*

Celt [kelt] *n* Celte *mf.* ◆**Celtic** *a* celtique, celte.

cement [sɪ'ment] *n* ciment *m;* **c. mixer** bétonnière *f;* **–** *vt* cimenter.

cemetery ['semətrɪ, *Am* 'seməterɪ] *n* cimetière *m.*

cenotaph ['senətɑːf] *n* cénotaphe *m.*

censor ['sensər] *n* censeur *m; –* *vt (film etc)* censurer. ◆**censorship** *n* censure *f.*

censure ['senʃər] *vt* blâmer; *Pol* censurer; **–** *n* blâme *m;* **c. motion, vote of c.** motion *f* de censure.

census ['sensəs] *n* recensement *m.*

cent [sent] *n (coin)* cent *m;* **per c.** pour cent.

centenary [sen'tiːnərɪ, *Am* sen'tenərɪ] *n* centenaire *m.*

centigrade ['sentɪgreɪd] *a* centigrade.

centimetre ['sentɪmiːtər] *n* centimètre *m.*

centipede ['sentɪpiːd] *n* mille-pattes *m inv.*

centre ['sentər] *n* centre *m;* **c. forward** *Fb* avant-centre *m; –* *vt* centrer; **–** *vi* **to c. on** *(of thoughts)* se concentrer sur; *(of question)* tourner autour de. ◆**central** *a* central. ◆**centralize** *vt* centraliser. ◆**centrifugal** [sen'trɪfjʊgəl] *a* centrifuge.

century ['sentʃərɪ] *n* siècle *m; (score)* Sp cent points *mpl.*

ceramic [sə'ræmɪk] *a (tile etc)* de or en céramique; **–** *npl (objects)* céramiques *fpl; (art)* céramique *f.*

cereal ['sɪərɪəl] *n* céréale *f.*

cerebral ['serɪbrəl, *Am* sə'riːbrəl] *a* cérébral.

ceremony ['serɪmənɪ] *n (event)* cérémonie *f;* **to stand on c.** faire des cérémonies *or* des façons. ◆**cere'monial** *a* de cérémonie; **–**

n cérémonial *m*. ◆**cere'monious** *a* cérémonieux.

certain ['sɜːtən] *a* (*particular, some*) certain; (*sure*) sûr, certain; **she's c. to come, she'll come for c.** c'est certain *or* sûr qu'elle viendra; **I'm not c. what to do** je ne sais pas très bien ce qu'il faut faire; **to be c. of sth/that** être certain de qch/que; **for c.** (*to say, know*) avec certitude; **be c. to go!** vas-y sans faute!; **to make c. of** (*fact*) s'assurer de; (*seat etc*) s'assurer. ◆**—ly** *adv* certainement; (*yes*) bien sûr; (*without fail*) sans faute; (*without any doubt*) sans aucun doute. ◆**certainty** *n* certitude *f*.

certificate [sə'tɪfɪkɪt] *n* certificat *m*; *Univ* diplôme *m*.

certify ['sɜːtɪfaɪ] *vt* certifier; **to c.** (*insane*) déclarer dément; – *vi* **to c. to sth** attester qch.

cervix ['sɜːvɪks] *n* col *m* de l'utérus.

cesspool ['sespuːl] *n* fosse *f* d'aisances; *Fig* cloaque *f*.

chafe [tʃeɪf] *vt* (*skin*) *Lit* frotter.

chaff [tʃæf] *vt* (*tease*) taquiner.

chaffinch ['tʃæfɪntʃ] *n* (*bird*) pinson *m*.

chagrin ['ʃægrɪn, *Am* ʃə'grɪn] *n* contrariété *f*; – *vt* contrarier.

chain [tʃeɪn] *n* (*of rings, mountains*) chaîne *f*; (*of ideas, events*) enchaînement *m*, suite *f*; (*of lavatory*) chasse *f* d'eau; **c. reaction** réaction *f* en chaîne; **to be a c.-smoker**, **to c.-smoke** fumer cigarette sur cigarette, fumer comme un pompier; **c. saw** tronçonneuse *f*; **c. store** magasin *m* à succursales multiples; – *vt* **to c.** (**down**) enchaîner; **to c.** (**up**) (*dog*) mettre à l'attache.

chair [tʃeər] *n* chaise *f*; (*armchair*) fauteuil *m*; *Univ* chaire *f*; **the c.** (*office*) la présidence; **c. lift** télésiège *m*; – *vt* (*meeting*) présider. ◆**chairman** *n* (*pl* **-men**) président, -ente *mf*. ◆**chairmanship** *n* présidence *f*.

chalet ['ʃæleɪ] *n* chalet *m*.

chalk [tʃɔːk] *n* craie *f*; **not by a long c.** loin de là, tant s'en faut; – *vt* marquer *or* écrire à la craie; **to c. up** (*success*) *Fig* reporter. ◆**chalky** *a* (**-ier, -iest**) crayeux.

challeng/e ['tʃælɪndʒ] *n* défi *m*; (*task*) gageure *f*; *Mil* sommation *f*; **c. for** (*bid*) tentative *f* d'obtenir; – *vt* défier (**s.o. to do** qn de faire); (*dispute*) contester; **to c. s.o. to a game** inviter qn à jouer; **to c. s.o. to a duel** provoquer qn en duel. ◆**—ing** *a* (*job*) exigeant; (*book*) stimulant. ◆**—er** *n* *Sp* challenger *m*.

chamber ['tʃeɪmbər] *n* chambre *f*; (*of judge*) cabinet *m*; – *a* (*music, orchestra*) de cham-

bre; **c. pot** pot *m* de chambre. ◆**chambermaid** *n* femme *f* de chambre.

chameleon [kə'miːliən] *n* (*reptile*) caméléon *m*.

chamois ['ʃæmɪ] *n* **c.** (**leather**) peau *f* de chamois.

champagne [ʃæm'peɪn] *n* champagne *m*.

champion ['tʃæmpɪən] *n* champion, -onne *mf*; **c. skier** champion, -onne du ski; – *vt* (*support*) se faire le champion de. ◆**championship** *n* *Sp* championnat *m*.

chance [tʃɑːns] *n* (*luck*) hasard *m*; (*possibility*) chances *fpl*, possibilité *f*; (*opportunity*) occasion *f*; (*risk*) risque *m*; **by c.** par hasard; **by any c.** (*possibly*) par hasard; **on the off c. (that) you could help me** au cas où tu pourrais m'aider; – *a* (*remark*) fait au hasard; (*occurrence*) accidentel; – *vt* **to c. doing** prendre le risque de faire; **to c. to find/etc** trouver/etc par hasard; **to c. it** risquer le coup; – *v imp* **it chanced that** (*happened*) il s'est trouvé que.

chancel ['tʃɑːnsəl] *n* (*in church*) chœur *m*.

chancellor ['tʃɑːnsələr] *n* *Pol Jur* chancelier *m*. ◆**chancellery** *n* chancellerie *f*.

chandelier [ʃændə'lɪər] *n* lustre *m*.

chang/e [tʃeɪndʒ] *n* changement *m*; (*money*) monnaie *f*; **for c.** pour changer; **it makes a c. from** ça change de; **to have a c. of heart** changer d'avis; **a c. of clothes** des vêtements de rechange; – *vt* (*modify*) changer; (*exchange*) échanger (**for** contre); (*money*) changer; (*transform*) transformer (**into** en); **to c. trains/one's skirt/etc** changer de train/de jupe/etc; **to c. gear** *Aut* changer de vitesse; **to c. the subject** changer de sujet; – *vi* (*alter*) changer; (*change clothes*) se changer; **to c. over** passer. ◆**—ing** *n* (*of guard*) relève *f*; **c. room** vestiaire *m*. ◆**changeable** *a* (*weather, mood etc*) changeant, variable. ◆**changeless** *a* immuable. ◆**changeover** *n* passage *m* (**from** de, **to** à).

channel ['tʃæn(ə)l] *n* (*navigable*) chenal *m*; *TV* chaîne *f*, canal *m*; (*groove*) rainure *f*; *Fig* direction *f*; **through the c. of** par le canal de; **the C.** *Geog* la Manche; **the C. Islands** les îles anglo-normandes; – *vt* (**-ll-**, *Am* **-l-**) (*energies, crowd etc*) canaliser (**into** vers).

chant [tʃɑːnt] *n* (*of demonstrators*) chant *m* scandé; *Rel* psalmodie *f*; – *vt* (*slogan*) scander; – *vi* scander des slogans.

chaos ['keɪɒs] *n* chaos *m*. ◆**cha'otic** *a* chaotique.

chap [tʃæp] **1** *n* (*fellow*) *Fam* type *m*; **old c.!**

mon vieux! **2** n (on skin) gerçure f; – vi (**-pp-**) se gercer; – vt gercer.

chapel ['tʃæp(ə)l] n chapelle f; (non-conformist church) temple m.

chaperon(e) ['ʃæpərəʊn] n chaperon m; – vt chaperonner.

chaplain ['tʃæplɪn] n aumônier m.

chapter ['tʃæptər] n chapitre m.

char [tʃɑːr] **1** vt (**-rr-**) (convert to carbon) carboniser; (scorch) brûler légèrement. **2** n Fam femme f de ménage; – vi to go **charring** Fam faire des ménages. **3** n (tea) SI thé m.

character ['kærɪktər] n (of person, place etc) & Typ caractère m; (in book, film) personnage m; (strange person) numéro m; **c. actor** acteur m de genre. **◆characte'ristic** a & n caractéristique (f). **◆characte'ristically** adv typiquement. **◆characterize** vt caractériser.

charade [ʃə'rɑːd] n (game) charade f (mimée); (travesty) parodie f, comédie f.

charcoal ['tʃɑːkəʊl] n charbon m (de bois); (crayon) fusain m, charbon m.

charge [tʃɑːdʒ] **1** n (in battle) Mil charge f; Jur accusation f; (cost) prix m; (responsibility) responsabilité f, charge f; (care) garde f; pl (expenses) frais mpl; **there's a c.** (for it) c'est payant; **free of c.** gratuit; **extra c.** supplément m; **to take c. of** prendre en charge; **to be in c. of** (child etc) avoir la garde de; (office etc) être responsable de; **the person in c.** le ou la responsable; **who's in c. here?** qui commande ici?; – vt Mil El charger; Jur accuser, inculper; **to c. s.o. Com** faire payer qn; **to c. (up) to** Com mettre sur le compte de; **how much do you c.?** combien demandez-vous?; – vi (rush) se précipiter; **c.!** Mil chargez! **◆—able** a **to c.** to aux frais de. **◆charger** n (for battery) chargeur m.

chariot ['tʃærɪət] n Mil char m.

charisma [kə'rɪzmə] n magnétisme m.

charity ['tʃærɪtɪ] n (kindness, alms) charité f; (society) fondation f or œuvre f charitable; **to give to c.** faire la charité. **◆charitable** a charitable.

charlady ['tʃɑːleɪdɪ] n femme f de ménage.

charlatan ['ʃɑːlətən] n charlatan m.

charm [tʃɑːm] n (attractiveness, spell) charme m; (trinket) amulette f; – vt charmer. **◆—ing** a charmant. **◆—ingly** adv d'une façon charmante.

chart [tʃɑːt] n (map) carte f; (graph) graphique m, tableau m; (pop) **charts** hit-parade m; **flow c.** organigramme m; –

vt (route) porter sur la carte; (figures) faire le graphique de; (of graph) montrer.

charter ['tʃɑːtər] n (document) charte f; (aircraft) charter m; **the c. of** (hiring) l'affrètement m de; **c. flight** charter m; – vt (aircraft etc) affréter. **◆—ed** a **c. accountant** expert-comptable m.

charwoman ['tʃɑːwʊmən] n (pl -women) femme f de ménage.

chary ['tʃeərɪ] a (**-ier, -iest**) (cautious) prudent.

chase [tʃeɪs] n poursuite f, chasse f; **to give c.** se lancer à la poursuite (f); – vt poursuivre; **to c. away** or **off** chasser; **to c. sth up** Fam essayer d'obtenir qch, rechercher qch; – vi to **c. after** courir après.

chasm ['kæzəm] n abîme m, gouffre m.

chassis ['ʃæsɪ, Am 'tʃæsɪ] n Aut châssis m.

chaste [tʃeɪst] a chaste. **◆chastity** n chasteté f.

chasten ['tʃeɪs(ə)n] vt (punish) châtier; (cause to improve) faire se corriger, assagir. **◆—ing** a (experience) instructif.

chastise [tʃæs'taɪz] vt punir.

chat [tʃæt] n causette f; **to have a c.** bavarder; – vi (**-tt-**) causer, bavarder; – vt to **c. up** Fam baratiner, draguer. **◆chatty** a (**-ier, -iest**) (person) bavard; (style) familier; (text) plein de bavardages.

chatter ['tʃætər] vi bavarder; (of birds, monkeys) jacasser; **his teeth are chattering** il claque des dents; – n bavardage m; jacassement m. **◆chatterbox** n bavard, -arde mf.

chauffeur ['ʃəʊfər] n chauffeur m (de maître).

chauvinist ['ʃəʊvɪnɪst] n & a chauvin, -ine (mf); **male c.** Pej phallocrate m.

cheap [tʃiːp] a (**-er, -est**) bon marché inv, pas cher; (rate etc) réduit; (worthless) sans valeur; (superficial) facile; (mean, petty) mesquin; **cheaper** moins cher, meilleur marché; – adv (to buy) à bon marché, au rabais; (to feel) humilié. **◆cheapen** vt Fig déprécier. **◆cheaply** adv à bon marché. **◆cheapness** n bas prix m; Fig mesquinerie f.

cheat [tʃiːt] vt (deceive) tromper; (defraud) frauder; **to c. s.o. out of sth** escroquer qch à qn; **to c. on** (wife, husband) faire des infidélités à; – vi tricher; (defraud) frauder; – n (at games etc) tricheur, -euse mf; (crook) escroc m. **◆—ing** n (deceit) tromperie f; (trickery) tricherie f. **◆—er** n Am = cheat.

check[1] [tʃek] vt (examine) vérifier; (inspect) contrôler; (tick) cocher, pointer; (stop) arrêter, enrayer; (*restrain*) contenir, maîtriser; (*rebuke*) réprimander; *Am* mettre à la consigne; **to c. in** (*luggage*) *Av* enregistrer; **to c. sth out** confirmer qch; – *vi* vérifier; **to c. in** (*at hotel etc*) signer le registre; (*arrive at hotel*) arriver; (*at airport*) se présenter à (l'enregistrement), enregistrer ses bagages; **to c. on sth** vérifier qch; **to c. out** (*at hotel etc*) régler sa note; **to c. up** vérifier, se renseigner; – *n* vérification *f*; contrôle *m*; (*halt*) arrêt *m*; *Chess* échec *m*; (*curb*) frein *m*; (*tick*) = croix *f*; (*receipt*) *Am* reçu *m*; (*bill in restaurant etc*) *Am* addition *f*; (*cheque*) *Am* chèque *m*. ◆**c.-in** *n Av* enregistrement *m* (des bagages). ◆**checking account** *n Am* compte *m* courant. ◆**checkmate** *n Chess* échec et mat *m*. ◆**checkout** *n* (*in supermarket*) caisse *f*. ◆**checkpoint** *n* contrôle *m*. ◆**checkroom** *n Am* vestiaire *m*; (*left-luggage office*) *Am* consigne *f*. ◆**checkup** *n* bilan *m* de santé.

check [tʃek] *n* (*pattern*) carreaux *mpl*; – *a* à carreaux. ◆**checked** *a* à carreaux.

checkered ['tʃekad] *a Am* = **chequered**.

checkers ['tʃekaz] *npl Am* jeu *m* de dames.

cheddar ['tʃedar] *n* (*cheese*) cheddar *m*.

cheek [tʃik] *n* joue *f*; (*impudence*) *Fig* culot *m*. ◆**cheekbone** *n* pommette *f*. ◆**cheeky** *a* (-ier, -iest) (*person, reply etc*) effronté.

cheep [tʃip] *vi* (*of bird*) piauler.

cheer [tʃiər] *n* **cheers** (*shouts*) acclamations *fpl*; **cheers!** *Fam* à votre santé! – *vt* (*applaud*) acclamer; **to c. on** encourager; **to c. (up)** donner du courage à; (*amuse*) égayer; – *vi* applaudir; **to c. up** prendre courage; s'égayer; **c. up!** (du) courage! ◆**—ing** *n* (*shouts*) acclamations *fpl*; – *a* (*encouraging*) réjouissant.

cheer [tʃiər] *n* (*gaiety*) joie *f*; **good c.** (*food*) la bonne chère. ◆**cheerful** *a* gai. ◆**cheerfully** *adv* gaiement. ◆**cheerless** *a* morne.

cheerio! [tʃiəri'əu] *int* salut!, au revoir!

cheese [tʃiz] *n* fromage *m*. ◆**cheeseburger** *n* cheeseburger *m*. ◆**cheesecake** *n* tarte *f* au fromage blanc. ◆**cheesed** *a* **to be c. (off)** *Fam* en avoir marre (with de). ◆**cheesy** *a* (-ier, -iest) (*shabby, bad*) *Am Fam* miteux.

cheetah ['tʃitə] *n* guépard *m*.

chef [ʃef] *n Culin* chef *m*.

chemistry ['kemistri] *n* chimie *f*. ◆**chemical** *a* chimique; – *n* produit *m* chimique. ◆**chemist** *n* (*dispensing*) pharmacien,

-ienne *mf*; (*scientist*) chimiste *mf*; **chemist('s)** (*shop*) pharmacie *f*.

cheque [tʃek] *n* chèque *m*. ◆**chequebook** *n* carnet *m* de chèques.

chequered ['tʃekad] *a* (*pattern*) à carreaux; (*career etc*) qui connaît des hauts et des bas.

cherish ['tʃeriʃ] *vt* (*person*) chérir; (*hope*) nourrir, caresser.

cherry ['tʃeri] *n* cerise *f*; – *a* cerise *inv*; **c. brandy** cherry *m*.

chess [tʃes] *n* échecs *mpl*. ◆**chessboard** *n* échiquier *m*.

chest [tʃest] *n* **1** *Anat* poitrine *f*. **2** (*box*) coffre *m*; **c. of drawers** commode *f*.

chestnut ['tʃesnʌt] *n* châtaigne *f*, marron *m*; – *a* (*hair*) châtain; **c. tree** châtaignier *m*.

chew [tʃu] *vt* **to c. (up)** mâcher; **to c. over** *Fig* ruminer; – *vi* mastiquer; **chewing gum** chewing-gum *m*.

chick [tʃik] *n* poussin *m*; (*girl*) *Fam* nana *f*. ◆**chicken 1** *n* poulet *m*; *pl* (*poultry*) volaille *f*; **it's c. feed** *Fam* c'est deux fois rien, c'est une bagatelle. **2** *a Fam* froussard; – *vi* **to c. out** *Fam* se dégonfler. ◆**chickenpox** *n* varicelle *f*.

chickpea ['tʃikpi] *n* pois *m* chiche.

chicory ['tʃikəri] *n* (*in coffee etc*) chicorée *f*; (*for salad*) endive *f*.

chide [tʃaid] *vt* gronder.

chief [tʃif] *n* chef *m*; (*boss*) *Fam* patron *m*, chef *m*; **in c.** (*commander, editor*) en chef; – *a* (*main, highest in rank*) principal. ◆**—ly** *adv* principalement, surtout. ◆**chieftain** *n* (*of clan etc*) chef *m*.

chilblain ['tʃilblein] *n* engelure *f*.

child, *pl* **children** ['tʃaild, 'tʃildrən] *n* enfant *mf*; **c. care** *or* **welfare** protection *f* de l'enfance; **child's play** *Fig* jeu *m* d'enfant; **c. minder** gardien, -ienne *mf* d'enfants. ◆**childbearing** *n* (*act*) accouchement *m*; (*motherhood*) maternité *f*. ◆**childbirth** *n* accouchement *m*, couches *fpl*. ◆**childhood** *n* enfance *f*. ◆**childish** *a* puéril, enfantin. ◆**childishness** *n* puérilité *f*. ◆**childlike** *a* naïf, innocent.

chill [tʃil] *n* froid *m*; (*coldness in feelings*) froideur *f*; *Med* refroidissement *m*; **to catch a c.** prendre froid; – *vt* (*wine, melon*) faire rafraîchir; (*meat, food*) réfrigérer; **to c. s.o.** (*with fear, cold etc*) faire frissonner qn (**with** de); **to be chilled to the bone** être transi. ◆**—ed** *a* (*wine*) frais. ◆**chilly** *a* (-ier, -iest) froid; (*sensitive to cold*) frileux; **it's c.** il fait (un peu) froid.

chilli ['tʃili] *n* (*pl* **-ies**) piment *m* (de Cayenne).

chime [tʃaɪm] vi (of bell) carillonner; (of clock) sonner; **to c. in** (interrupt) interrompre; − n carillon m; sonnerie f.

chimney ['tʃɪmnɪ] n cheminée f. ◆**chimneypot** n tuyau m de cheminée. ◆**chimneysweep** n ramoneur m.

chimpanzee [tʃɪmpæn'zɪ] n chimpanzé m.

chin [tʃɪn] n menton m.

china ['tʃaɪnə] n inv porcelaine f; − a en porcelaine. ◆**chinaware** n (objects) porcelaine f.

China ['tʃaɪnə] n Chine f. ◆**Chi'nese** a & n chinois, -oise (mf); − (language) chinois m.

chink [tʃɪŋk] 1 n (slit) fente f. 2 vi tinter; − vt faire tinter; − n tintement m.

chip [tʃɪp] n (-pp-) (cup etc) ébrécher; (table etc) écorner; (paint) écailler; (cut) tailler; − vi to c. in Fam contribuer; − n (splinter) éclat m; (break) ébréchure f; écornure f; (microchip) puce f; (counter) jeton m; pl (French fries) frites fpl; (crisps) Am chips mpl. ◆**chipboard** n (bois m) aggloméré m. ◆**chippings** npl road or loose c. gravillons mpl.

chiropodist [kɪ'rɒpədɪst] n pédicure mf.

chirp [tʃɜːp] vi (of bird) pépier; − n pépiement m.

chirpy ['tʃɜːpɪ] a (-ier, -iest) gai, plein d'entrain.

chisel ['tʃɪz(ə)l] n ciseau m; − vt (-ll-, Am -l-) ciseler.

chit [tʃɪt] n (paper) note f, billet m.

chitchat ['tʃɪttʃæt] n bavardage m.

chivalry ['ʃɪvəlrɪ] n (practices etc) chevalerie f; (courtesy) galanterie f. ◆**chivalrous** a (man) galant.

chives [tʃaɪvz] npl ciboulette f.

chloride ['klɔːraɪd] n chlorure m. ◆**chlorine** n chlore m. ◆**chloroform** n chloroforme m.

choc-ice ['tʃɒkaɪs] n (ice cream) esquimau m.

chock [tʃɒk] n (wedge) cale f; − vt caler. **chock-a-block** [tʃɒkə'blɒk] a, **c.-'full** a Fam archiplein.

chocolate ['tʃɒklɪt] n chocolat m; **milk c.** chocolat au lait; **plain** or Am **bittersweet c.** chocolat à croquer; − a (cake) au chocolat; (colour) chocolat inv.

choice [tʃɔɪs] n choix m; **from c., out of c.** de son propre choix; − a (goods) de choix.

choir ['kwaɪər] n chœur m. ◆**choirboy** n jeune choriste m.

choke [tʃəʊk] 1 vt (person) étrangler, étouffer; (clog) boucher, engorger; **to c. back** (sobs etc) étouffer; − vi s'étrangler,

étouffer; **to c. on** (fish bone etc) s'étrangler avec. 2 n Aut starter m. ◆**-er** n (scarf) foulard m; (necklace) collier m (de chien).

cholera ['kɒlərə] n choléra m.

cholesterol [kə'lestərɒl] n cholestérol m.

choose [tʃuːz] vt (pt **chose**, pp **chosen**) choisir (**to do** de faire); **to c. to do** (decide) juger bon de faire; − vi choisir; **as I/you/etc c.** comme il me/vous/etc plaît. ◆**choos(e)y** a (-sier, -siest) difficile (about sur).

chop [tʃɒp] 1 n (of lamb, pork) côtelette f; **to lick one's chops** Fig s'en lécher les babines; **to get the c.** Sl être flanqué à la porte. 2 vt (-pp-) couper (à la hache); (food) hacher; **to c. down** (tree) abattre; **to c. off** trancher; **to c. up** hacher. 3 vti (change) **to c. and change** changer constamment d'idées, de projets etc. ◆**chopper** n hachoir m; Sl hélicoptère m. ◆**choppy** a (sea) agité.

chopsticks ['tʃɒpstɪks] npl Culin baguettes fpl.

choral ['kɔːrəl] a choral; **c. society** chorale f. ◆**chorister** ['kɒrɪstər] n choriste mf.

chord [kɔːd] n Mus accord m.

chore [tʃɔːr] n travail m (routinier); (unpleasant) corvée f; pl (domestic) travaux mpl du ménage.

choreographer [kɒrɪ'ɒgrəfər] n chorégraphe mf.

chortle ['tʃɔːt(ə)l] vi glousser; − n gloussement m.

chorus ['kɔːrəs] n chœur m; (dancers) Th troupe f; (of song) refrain m; **c. girl** girl f.

chose, chosen [tʃəʊz, 'tʃəʊz(ə)n] see **choose.**

chowder ['tʃaʊdər] n Am soupe f aux poissons.

Christ [kraɪst] n Christ m. ◆**Christian** ['krɪstʃən] a & n chrétien, -ienne (mf); **C. name** prénom m. ◆**Christi'anity** n christianisme m.

christen ['krɪs(ə)n] vt (name) & Rel baptiser. ◆**-ing** n baptême m.

Christmas ['krɪsməs] n Noël m; **at C. (time)** à (la) Noël; **Merry C.** Joyeux Noël; **Father C.** le père Noël; − a (tree, card, day, party etc) de Noël; **C. box** étrennes fpl.

chrome [krəʊm] n, ◆**chromium** n chrome m.

chromosome ['krəʊməsəʊm] n chromosome m.

chronic ['krɒnɪk] a (disease, state etc) chronique; (bad) Sl atroce.

chronicle ['krɒnɪk(ə)l] n chronique f; − vt faire la chronique de.

chronology [krəˈnɒlədʒɪ] n chronologie f. ◆**chronoˈlogical** a chronologique.

chronometer [krəˈnɒmɪtər] n chronomètre m.

chrysanthemum [krɪˈsænθəməm] n chrysanthème m.

chubby [ˈtʃʌbɪ] a (-ier, -iest) (body) dodu; (cheeks) rebondi. ◆**c.-ˈcheeked** a joufflu.

chuck [tʃʌk] vt Fam jeter, lancer; **to c. (in)** or (up) (give up) Fam laisser tomber; **to c. away** Fam balancer; (money) gaspiller; **to c. out** Fam balancer.

chuckle [ˈtʃʌk(ə)l] vi glousser, rire; – n gloussement m.

chuffed [tʃʌft] a Sl bien content; (displeased) Iron Sl pas heureux.

chug [tʃʌg] vi (-gg-) **to c. along** (of vehicle) avancer lentement (en faisant teuf-teuf).

chum [tʃʌm] n Fam copain m. ◆**chummy** a (-ier, -iest) Fam amical; **c. with** copain avec.

chump [tʃʌmp] n (fool) crétin, -ine mf.

chunk [tʃʌŋk] n (gros) morceau m. ◆**chunky** a (-ier, -iest) (person) Fam trapu; (coat, material etc) de grosse laine.

church [tʃɜːtʃ] n église f; (service) office m; (Catholic) messe f; **c. hall** salle f paroissiale. ◆**churchgoer** n pratiquant, -ante mf. ◆**churchyard** n cimetière m.

churlish [ˈtʃɜːlɪʃ] a (rude) grossier; (bad-tempered) hargneux.

churn [tʃɜːn] **1** n (for making butter) baratte f; (milk can) bidon m. **2** vt **to c. out** Pej produire (en série).

chute [ʃuːt] n glissière f; (in playground, pool) toboggan m; (for refuse) vide-ordures m inv.

chutney [ˈtʃʌtnɪ] n condiment m épicé (à base de fruits).

cider [ˈsaɪdər] n cidre m.

cigar [sɪˈgɑːr] n cigare m. ◆**cigaˈrette** n cigarette f; **c. end** mégot m; **c. holder** fume-cigarette m inv; **c. lighter** briquet m.

cinch [sɪntʃ] n **it's a c.** Fam (easy) c'est facile; (sure) c'est sûr et certain.

cinder [ˈsɪndər] n cendre f; **c. track** Sp cendrée f.

Cinderella [sɪndəˈrelə] n Liter Cendrillon f; Fig parent m pauvre.

cine-camera [ˈsɪnɪkæmrə] n caméra f.

cinema [ˈsɪnɪmə] n cinéma m. ◆**cinemagoer** n cinéphile mf. ◆**cinemascope** n cinémascope m.

cinnamon [ˈsɪnəmən] n Bot Culin cannelle f.

cipher [ˈsaɪfər] n (code, number) chiffre m; (zero, person) Fig zéro m.

circle [ˈsɜːk(ə)l] n (shape, group, range etc)

cercle m; (around eyes) cerne m; Th balcon m; pl (milieux) milieux mpl; – vt (move round) faire le tour de; (word etc) entourer d'un cercle; – vi (of aircraft, bird) décrire des cercles. ◆**circular** a circulaire; (letter) circulaire f; (advertisement) prospectus m. ◆**circulate** vi circuler; – vt faire circuler. ◆**circuˈlation** n circulation f; Journ tirage m; **in c.** (person) Fam dans le circuit.

circuit [ˈsɜːkɪt] n circuit m; Jur Th tournée f; **c. breaker** El disjoncteur m. ◆**circuitous** [sɜːˈkjuːɪtəs] a (route, means) indirect. ◆**circuitry** n El circuits mpl.

circumcised [ˈsɜːkəmsaɪzd] a circoncis. ◆**circumˈcision** n circoncision f.

circumference [sɜːˈkʌmfərəns] n circonférence f.

circumflex [ˈsɜːkəmfleks] n circonflexe m.

circumscribe [ˈsɜːkəmskraɪb] vt circonscrire.

circumspect [ˈsɜːkəmspekt] a circonspect.

circumstance [ˈsɜːkəmstæns] n circonstance f; pl Com situation f financière; **in** or **under no circumstances** en aucun cas. ◆**circumˈstantial** a (evidence) Jur indirect.

circus [ˈsɜːkəs] n Th Hist cirque m.

cirrhosis [sɪˈrəʊsɪs] n Med cirrhose f.

cistern [ˈsɪstən] n (in house) réservoir m (d'eau).

citadel [ˈsɪtəd(ə)l] n citadelle f.

cite [saɪt] vt citer. ◆**citation** [saɪˈteɪʃ(ə)n] n citation f.

citizen [ˈsɪtɪz(ə)n] n Pol Jur citoyen, -enne mf; (of town) habitant, -ante mf; Citizens' Band Rad la CB. ◆**citizenship** n citoyenneté f.

citrus [ˈsɪtrəs] a **c. fruit(s)** agrumes mpl.

city [ˈsɪtɪ] n (grande) ville f, cité f; **c. dweller** citadin, -ine mf; **c. centre** centre-ville m inv; **c. hall** Am hôtel m de ville; **c. page** Journ rubrique f financière.

civic [ˈsɪvɪk] a (duty) civique; (centre) administratif; (authorities) municipal; – npl (social science) instruction f civique.

civil [ˈsɪv(ə)l] a **1** (rights, war, marriage etc) civil; **c. defence** défense f passive; **c. servant** fonctionnaire mf; **c. service** fonction f publique. **2** (polite) civil. ◆**ciˈvilian** a & n civil, -ile (mf). ◆**ciˈvility** n civilité f.

civilize [ˈsɪvɪlaɪz] vt civiliser. ◆**civiliˈzation** n civilisation f.

civvies [ˈsɪvɪz] npl **in c.** Sl (habillé) en civil.

clad [klæd] a vêtu (in de).

claim [kleɪm] vt (one's due etc) revendiquer, réclamer; (require) réclamer; **to c. that**

(*assert*) prétendre que; – *n* (*demand*) prétention *f*, revendication *f*; (*statement*) affirmation *f*; (*complaint*) réclamation *f*; (*right*) droit *m*; (*land*) concession *f*; (*insurance*) **c.** demande *f* d'indemnité; **to lay c.** to prétendre à. ◆**claimant** *n* allocataire *mf*.

clairvoyant [kleə'vɔɪənt] *n* voyant, -ante *mf*.

clam [klæm] *n* (*shellfish*) praire *f*.

clamber ['klæmbər] *vi* **to c. up** grimper; **to c. up** (*stairs*) grimper; (*mountain*) gravir.

clammy ['klæmɪ] *a* (*hands etc*) moite (et froid).

clamour ['klæmər] *n* clameur *f*; – *vi* vociférer (**against** contre); **to c. for** demander à grands cris.

clamp [klæmp] *n* crampon *m*; *Carp* serre-joint(s) *m*; (*wheel*) *e. Aut* sabot *m* (de Denver); – *vt* serrer; – *vi* **to c. down** *Fam* sévir (**on** contre). ◆**clampdown** *n* (*limitation*) *Fam* coup *m* d'arrêt, restriction *f*.

clan [klæn] *n* clan *m*.

clandestine [klæn'destɪn] *a* clandestin.

clang [klæŋ] *n* son *m* métallique. ◆**clanger** *n Sl* gaffe *f*; **to drop a c.** faire une gaffe.

clap [klæp] **1** *vti* (-pp-) (*applaud*) applaudir; **to c.** (**one's hands**) battre des mains; – *n* battement *m* (des mains); (*on back*) tape *f*; (*of thunder*) coup *m*. **2** *vt* (-pp-) (*put*) *Fam* fourrer. ◆**clapped-out** *a* (*car, person*) *Sl* crevé. ◆**clapping** *n* applaudissements *mpl*. ◆**claptrap** *n* (*nonsense*) *Fam* boniment *m*.

claret ['klærət] *n* (*wine*) bordeaux *m* rouge.

clarify ['klærɪfaɪ] *vt* clarifier. ◆**clarification** *n* clarification *f*.

clarinet [klærɪ'net] *n* clarinette *f*.

clarity ['klærətɪ] *n* (*of water, expression etc*) clarté *f*.

clash [klæʃ] *vi* (*of plates, pans*) s'entrechoquer; (*of interests, armies*) se heurter; (*of colours*) jurer (**with** avec); (*of people*) se bagarrer; (*coincide*) tomber en même temps (**with** que); – *n* (*noise, of armies*) choc *m*, heurt *m*; (*of interests*) conflit *m*; (*of events*) coïncidence *f*.

clasp [klɑːsp] *vt* (*hold*) serrer; **to c. one's hands** joindre les mains; – *n* (*fastener*) fermoir *m*; (*of belt*) boucle *f*.

class [klɑːs] *n* classe *f*; (*lesson*) cours *m*; (*grade*) *Univ* mention *f*; **the c. of 1987** *Am* la promotion de 1987; – *vt* classer. ◆**classmate** *n* camarade *mf* de classe. ◆**classroom** *n* (*salle f de*) classe *f*.

classic ['klæsɪk] *a* classique; – *n* (*writer, work etc*) classique *m*; **to study classics**

étudier les humanités *fpl*. ◆**classical** *a* classique. ◆**classicism** *n* classicisme *m*.

classif/y ['klæsɪfaɪ] *vt* classer, classifier. ◆**-ied** *a* (*information*) secret. ◆**classification** *n* classification *f*.

classy ['klɑːsɪ] *a* (*-ier, -iest*) *Fam* chic *inv*.

clatter ['klætər] *n* bruit *m*, fracas *m*.

clause [klɔːz] *n Jur* clause *f*; *Gram* proposition *f*.

claustrophobia [klɔːstrə'fəʊbɪə] *n* claustrophobie *f*. ◆**claustrophobic** *a* claustrophobe.

claw [klɔː] *n* (*of cat, sparrow etc*) griffe *f*; (*of eagle*) serre *f*; (*of lobster*) pince *f*; – *vt* (*scratch*) griffer; **to c. back** (*money etc*) *Pej Fam* repiquer, récupérer.

clay [kleɪ] *n* argile *f*.

clean [kliːn] *a* (*-er, -est*) propre; (*clear-cut*) net; (*fair*) *Sp* loyal; (*joke*) non paillard; (*record*) *Jur* vierge; **to c. living** vie *f* saine; **to make a c. breast of it** tout avouer; – *adv* (*utterly*) complètement, carrément; **to break c.** se casser net; **to cut c.** couper net; – *n* **to give sth a c.** nettoyer qch; – *vt* nettoyer; (*wash*) laver; (*wipe*) essuyer; **to c. one's teeth** se brosser *or* se laver les dents; **to c. out** nettoyer; (*empty*) *Fig* vider; **to c. up** nettoyer; (*reform*) *Fig* épurer; – *vi* **to c.** (**up**) faire le nettoyage. ◆**-ing** *n* nettoyage *m*; (*housework*) ménage *m*; **c. woman** femme *f* de ménage. ◆**-er** *n* (*woman*) femme *f* de ménage; (*dry*) **c.** teinturier, -ière *mf*. ◆**-ly** *adv* (*to break, cut*) net. ◆**-ness** *n* propreté *f*. ◆**clean-'cut** *a* net. ◆**clean-'living** *a* honnête, chaste. ◆**clean-'shaven** *a* rasé (de près). ◆**clean-up** *n Fig* épuration *f*.

cleanliness ['klenlɪnɪs] *n* propreté *f*.

cleans/e [klenz] *vt* nettoyer; (*soul, person etc*) *Fig* purifier. ◆**-ing** **c. cream** crème *f* démaquillante. ◆**-er** *n* (*cream, lotion*) démaquillant *m*.

clear [klɪər] *a* (*-er, -est*) (*water, sound etc*) clair; (*glass*) transparent; (*outline, photo*) net, clair; (*mind*) lucide; (*road*) libre, dégagé; (*profit*) net; (*obvious*) évident, clair; (*certain*) certain; (*complete*) entier; **to be c. of** (*free of*) être libre de; (*out of*) être hors de; **to make oneself c.** se faire comprendre; **c. conscience** conscience *f* nette *or* tranquille; – *adv* (*quite*) complètement; **c. of** (*away from*) à l'écart de; **to keep** *or* **steer c. of** se tenir à l'écart de; **to get c. of** (*away from*) s'éloigner de; – *vt* (*path, place, table*) débarrasser, dégager; (*land*) défricher; (*fence*) franchir (sans toucher); (*obstacle*) éviter; (*person*) *Jur* disculper;

(*cheque*) compenser; (*goods, debts*) liquider; (*through customs*) dédouaner; (*for security etc*) autoriser; **to c. s.o. of** (*suspicion*) laver qn de; **to c. one's throat** s'éclaircir la gorge; – *vi* **to c. (up)** (*of weather*) s'éclaircir; (*of fog*) se dissiper. ■ **to c. away** *vt* (*remove*) enlever; – *vi* (*of fog*) se dissiper; **to c. off** *vi* (*leave*) *Fam* filer; – *vt* (*table*) débarrasser; **to c. out** *vt* (*empty*) vider; (*clean*) nettoyer; (*remove*) enlever; **to c. up** *vt* (*mystery etc*) éclaircir; – *vti* (*tidy*) ranger. ◆**—ing** *n* (*in woods*) clairière *f*. ◆**—ly** *adv* clairement; (*to understand*) bien, clairement; (*obviously*) évidemment. ◆**—ness** *n* (*of sound*) clarté *f*, netteté *f*; (*of mind*) lucidité *f*. ◆**clearance** *n* (*sale*) soldes *mpl*; (*space*) dégagement *m*; (*permission*) autorisation *f*; (*of cheque*) compensation *f*. ◆**clear-'cut** *a* net. ◆**clear-'headed** *a* lucide.

clearway ['klɪəweɪ] *n* route *f* à stationnement interdit.

cleavage ['kliːvɪdʒ] *n* (*split*) clivage *m*; (*of woman*) *Fam* naissance *f* des seins.

cleft [kleft] *a* (*palate*) fendu; (*stick*) fourchu; – *n* fissure *f*.

clement ['klemənt] *a* clément. ◆**clemency** *n* clémence *f*.

clementine ['kleməntaɪn] *n* clémentine *f*.

clench [klentʃ] *vt* (*press*) serrer.

clergy ['klɜːdʒɪ] *n* clergé *m*. ◆**clergyman** *n* (*pl* **-men**) ecclésiastique *m*.

cleric ['klerɪk] *n* *Rel* clerc *m*. ◆**clerical** *a* (*job*) d'employé; (*work*) de bureau; (*error*) d'écriture; *Rel* clérical.

clerk [klɑːk, *Am* klɜːk] *n* employé, -ée *mf* (de bureau); *Jur* clerc *m*; (*in store*) *Am* vendeur, -euse *mf*; **c. of the court** *Jur* greffier *m*.

clever ['klevər] *a* (**-er, -est**) intelligent; (*smart, shrewd*) astucieux; (*skilful*) habile (**at sth** à qch, **at doing** à faire); (*ingenious*) ingénieux; (*gifted*) doué; **c. at** (*English etc*) fort en; **c. with one's hands** habile *or* adroit de ses mains. ◆**—ly** *adv* intelligemment; astucieusement; habilement. ◆**—ness** *n* intelligence *f*; astuce *f*; habileté *f*.

cliché ['kliːʃeɪ] *n* (*idea*) cliché *m*.

click [klɪk] *n* déclic *m*, bruit *m* sec; – *vi* faire un déclic; (*of lovers etc*) *Fam* se plaire du premier coup; **it clicked** (*I realized*) *Fam* j'ai compris tout à coup. **2** *vt* **to c. one's heels** *Mil* claquer des talons.

client ['klaɪənt] *n* client, -ente *mf*. ◆**clientele** [kliːɑ̃'tel] *n* clientèle *f*.

cliff [klɪf] *n* falaise *f*.

climate ['klaɪmɪt] *n* *Met* & *Fig* climat *m*; **c.**

of opinion opinion *f* générale. ◆**cli'matic** *a* climatique.

climax ['klaɪmæks] *n* point *m* culminant; (*sexual*) orgasme *m*; – *vi* atteindre son point culminant.

climb [klaɪm] *vt* **to c. (up)** (*steps*) monter, gravir; (*hill, mountain*) gravir, faire l'ascension de; (*tree, ladder*) monter à, grimper à; **to c. (over)** (*wall*) escalader; **to c. down (from)** descendre de; – *vi* **to c. (up)** monter; (*of plant*) grimper; **to c. down** descendre; (*back down*) *Fig* en rabattre; – *n* montée *f*. ◆**—ing** *n* montée *f*; (*mountain*) **c.** alpinisme *m*. ◆**—er** *n* grimpeur, -euse *mf*; *Sp* alpiniste *mf*; *Bot* plante *f* grimpante; **social c.** arriviste *mf*.

clinch [klɪntʃ] *vt* (*deal, bargain*) conclure; (*argument*) consolider.

cling [klɪŋ] *vi* (*pt* & *pp* **clung**) se cramponner, s'accrocher (**to** à); (*stick*) adhérer (**to** à). ◆**—ing** *a* (*clothes*) collant. ◆**clingfilm** *n* scel-o-frais®*m*, film *m* étirable.

clinic ['klɪnɪk] *n* (*private*) clinique *f*; (*health centre*) centre *m* médical. ◆**clinical** *a* *Med* clinique; *Fig* scientifique, objectif.

clink [klɪŋk] *vi* tinter; – *vt* faire tinter; – *n* tintement *m*.

clip [klɪp] **1** *vt* (**-pp-**) (*cut*) couper; (*sheep*) tondre; (*hedge*) tailler; (*ticket*) poinçonner; **to c. sth out of** (*newspaper etc*) découper qch dans. **2** *n* (*for paper*) attache *f*, trombone *m*; (*of brooch, of cyclist, for hair*) pince *f*; – *vt* (**-pp-**) **to c. (on)** attacher. **3** *n* (*of film*) extrait *m*; (*blow*) *Fam* taloche *f*. ◆**clipping** *n* *Journ* coupure *f*. ◆**clippers** *npl* (*for hair*) tondeuse *f*; (*for nails*) pince *f* à ongles; (*pocket-sized, for finger nails*) coupe-ongles *m inv*.

clique [kliːk] *n* *Pej* clique *f*. ◆**cliquey** *a* *Pej* exclusif.

cloak [kləʊk] *n* (grande) cape *f*, *Fig* manteau *m*; **c. and dagger** (*film etc*) d'espionnage. ◆**cloakroom** *n* vestiaire *m*; (*for luggage*) *Rail* consigne *f*; (*lavatory*) toilettes *fpl*.

clobber ['klɒbər] **1** *vt* (*hit*) *Sl* rosser. **2** *n* (*clothes*) *Sl* affaires *fpl*.

clock [klɒk] *n* (*large*) horloge *f*; (*small*) pendule *f*, *Aut* compteur *m*; **against the c.** *Fig* contre la montre; **round the c.** *Fig* vingt-quatre heures sur vingt-quatre; **c. tower** clocher *m*; – *vt* *Sp* chronométrer; **to c. up** (*miles*) *Aut* *Fam* faire; – *vi* **to c. in** *or* **out** (*of worker*) pointer. ◆**clockwise** *adv* dans le sens des aiguilles d'une montre. ◆**clockwork** *a* mécanique; *Fig* régulier;

– *n* **to go like c.** aller comme sur des roulettes.

clod [klɒd] *n* **1** (*of earth*) motte *f*. **2** (*oaf*) *Fam* balourd, -ourde *mf*.

clog [klɒg] **1** *n* (*shoe*) sabot *m*. **2** *vt* (**-gg-**) to **c. (up)** (*obstruct*) boucher.

cloister ['klɔɪstər] *n* cloître *m*; – *vt* cloîtrer.

close[1] [kləʊs] *a* (**-er, -est**) (*place, relative etc*) proche (to de); (*collaboration, resemblance, connection*) étroit; (*friend etc*) intime; (*order, contest*) serré; (*study*) rigoureux; (*atmosphere*) Met lourd; (*vowel*) fermé; **c. to** (*near*) près de, proche de; to **tears** au bord des larmes; **to have a c. shave** or **call** l'échapper belle; – *adv* c. **(by)**, **c. at hand** (tout) près; **c. to** près de; **c. behind** juste derrière; **c. on** (*almost*) *Fam* pas loin de; **c. together** (*to stand*) serrés; **to follow c.** suivre de près; – *n* (*enclosed area*) enceinte *f*. ◆**c.-'cropped** *a* (*hair*) (coupé) ras. ◆**c.-'knit** *a* très uni. ◆**c.-up** *n* gros plan *m*.

close[2] [kləʊz] *n* fin *f*, conclusion *f*; **to bring to a c.** mettre fin à; **to draw to a c.** tirer à sa fin; – *vt* fermer; (*discussion*) terminer, clore; (*opening*) boucher; (*road*) barrer; (*gap*) réduire; (*deal*) conclure; **to c. the meeting** lever la séance; **to c. ranks** serrer les rangs; **to c. in** (*enclose*) enfermer; **to c. up** fermer; – *vi* se fermer; (*end*) (se) terminer; **to c. (up)** (*of shop*) fermer; (*of wound*) se refermer; **to c. in** (*approach*) approcher; **to c. in on s.o.** se rapprocher de qn. ■ **to c. down** *vti* (*close for good*) fermer (définitivement); – *vi* *TV* terminer les émissions. ◆**c.-down** *n* fermeture *f* (définitive); *TV* fin *f* (des émissions). ◆**closing** *n* fermeture *f*; (*of session*) clôture *f*; – *a* final; **c. time** heure *f* de fermeture. ◆**closure** ['kləʊʒər] *n* fermeture *f*.

closely ['kləʊslɪ] *adv* (*to link, guard*) étroitement; (*to follow*) de près; (*to listen*) attentivement; **c. contested** très disputé; **to hold s.o. c.** tenir qn contre soi. ◆**closeness** *n* proximité *f*; (*of collaboration etc*) étroitesse *f*; (*of friendship*) intimité *f*; (*of weather*) lourdeur *f*.

closet ['klɒzɪt] *n* (*cupboard*) *Am* placard *m*; (*wardrobe*) *Am* penderie *f*.

clot [klɒt] **1** *n* (*of blood*) caillot *m*; – *vt* (**-tt-**) (*blood*) coaguler; – *vi* (*of blood*) se coaguler. **2** *n* (*person*) *Fam* imbécile *mf*.

cloth [klɒθ] *n* tissu *m*, étoffe *f*; (*of linen*) toile *f*; (*of wool*) drap *m*; (*for dusting*) chiffon *m*; (*for dishes*) torchon *m*; (*tablecloth*) nappe *f*.

cloth/e [kləʊð] *vt* habiller, vêtir (in de).

◆**—ing** *n* habillement *m*; (*clothes*) vêtements *mpl*; **an article of c.** un vêtement.

clothes [kləʊðz] *npl* vêtements *mpl*; **to put one's c. on** s'habiller; **c. shop** magasin *m* d'habillement; **c. brush** brosse *f* à habits; **c. peg**, *Am* **c. pin** pince *f* à linge; **c. line** corde *f* à linge.

cloud [klaʊd] *n* nuage *m*; (*of arrows, insects*) *Fig* nuée *f*; – *vt* (*mind, issue*) obscurcir; (*window*) embuer; – **to c. (over)** (*of sky*) se couvrir. ◆**cloudburst** *n* averse *f*. ◆**cloudy** *a* (**-ier, -iest**) (*weather*) couvert, nuageux; (*liquid*) trouble.

clout [klaʊt] **1** *n* (*blow*) *Fam* taloche *f*; – *vt* *Fam* flanquer une taloche à, talocher. **2** *n* *Pol Fam* influence *f*, pouvoir *m*.

clove [kləʊv] *n* clou *m* de girofle; **c. of garlic** gousse *f* d'ail.

clover ['kləʊvər] *n* trèfle *m*.

clown [klaʊn] *n* clown *m*; – *vi* **to c. (around)** faire le clown.

cloying ['klɔɪɪŋ] *a* écœurant.

club [klʌb] **1** *n* (*weapon*) matraque *f*, massue *f*; (*golf*) **c.** (*stick*) club *m*; – *vt* (**-bb-**) matraquer. **2** *n* (*society*) club *m*, cercle *m*; – *vi* (**-bb-**) **to c. together** se cotiser (to buy pour acheter). **3** *n* & *npl* *Cards* trèfle *m*. ◆**clubhouse** *n* pavillon *m*.

clubfoot ['klʌbfʊt] *n* pied *m* bot. ◆**club-'footed** *a* pied bot *inv*.

cluck [klʌk] *vi* (*of hen*) glousser.

clue [kluː] *n* indice *m*; (*of crossword*) définition *f*; (*to mystery*) clef *f*; **I don't have a c.** *Fam* je n'en ai pas la moindre idée. ◆**clueless** *a* *Fam* stupide.

clump [klʌmp] *n* (*of flowers, trees*) massif *m*.

clumsy ['klʌmzɪ] *a* (**-ier, -iest**) maladroit; (*shape*) lourd; (*tool*) peu commode. ◆**clumsily** *adv* maladroitement. ◆**clumsiness** *n* maladresse *f*.

clung [klʌŋ] *see* cling.

cluster ['klʌstər] *n* groupe *m*; (*of flowers*) grappe *f*; (*of stars*) amas *m*; – *vi* se grouper.

clutch [klʌtʃ] **1** *vt* (*hold tight*) serrer, étreindre; (*cling to*) se cramponner à; (*grasp*) saisir; – *vi* **to c.** at essayer de saisir; – *n* étreinte *f*. **2** *n* (*apparatus*) *Aut* embrayage *m*; (*pedal*) pédale *f* d'embrayage. **3** *npl* **s.o.'s clutches** (*power*) les griffes *fpl* de qn.

clutter ['klʌtər] *n* (*objects*) fouillis *m*, désordre *m*; – *vt* **to c. (up)** encombrer (with de).

cm *abbr* (*centimetre*) cm.

co- [kəʊ] *prep* co-.

Co *abbr* (*company*) Cie.

coach [kəʊtʃ] **1** *n* (*horse-drawn*) carrosse *m*; *Rail* voiture *f*, wagon *m*; *Aut* autocar *m*. **2** *n* (*person*) *Sch* répétiteur, -trice *mf*; *Sp* entraîneur m; − vt (pupil) donner des leçons (particulières) à; (sportsman etc) entraîner; **to c. s.o. for** (exam) préparer qn à. ◆**coachman** n (pl -men) cocher m.

coagulate [kəʊˈægjʊleɪt] vi (of blood) se coaguler; − vt coaguler.

coal [kəʊl] n charbon m; Geol houille f; − a (basin etc) houiller; (merchant, fire) de charbon; (cellar, bucket) à charbon. ◆**coalfield** n bassin m houiller. ◆**coalmine** n mine f de charbon.

coalition [kəʊəˈlɪʃ(ə)n] n coalition f.

coarse [kɔːs] a (-er, -est) (person, manners) grossier, vulgaire; (surface) rude; (fabric) grossier; (salt) gros; (accent) commun, vulgaire. ◆**-ness** n grossièreté f; vulgarité f.

coast [kəʊst] **1** n côte f. **2** vi **to c.** (down or along) (of vehicle etc) descendre en roue libre. ◆**coastal** a côtier. ◆**coaster** n (ship) caboteur m; (for glass etc) dessous m de verre, rond m. ◆**coastguard** n (person) garde m maritime, garde-côte m. ◆**coastline** n littoral m.

coat [kəʊt] n manteau m; (overcoat) pardessus m; (jacket) veste f; (of animal) pelage m; (of paint) couche f; **c. of arms** blason m, armoiries fpl; **c. hanger** cintre m; − vt couvrir, enduire (**with** de); (with chocolate) enrober (**with** de). ◆**-ed** a **c. tongue** langue f chargée. ◆**-ing** n couche f.

coax [kəʊks] vt amadouer, cajoler; **to c. s.o. to do** or **into doing** amadouer qn pour qu'il fasse. ◆**-ing** n cajoleries fpl.

cob [kɒb] n **corn on the c.** épi m de maïs.

cobble [ˈkɒb(ə)l] n pavé m; − vt **to c. together** (text etc) Fam bricoler. ◆**cobbled** a pavé. ◆**cobblestone** n pavé m.

cobbler [ˈkɒblər] n cordonnier m.

cobra [ˈkəʊbrə] n (snake) cobra m.

cobweb [ˈkɒbweb] n toile f d'araignée.

cocaine [kəʊˈkeɪn] n cocaïne f.

cock [kɒk] **1** n (rooster) coq m; (male bird) (oiseau m) mâle m. **2** vt (gun) armer; **to c. (up)** (ears) dresser. ◆**c.-a-doodle-'doo** n & int cocorico (m). ◆**c.-and-'bull story** n histoire f à dormir debout.

cockatoo [kɒkəˈtuː] n (bird) cacatoès m.

cocker [ˈkɒkər] n **c.** (spaniel) cocker m.

cockerel [ˈkɒkərəl] n jeune coq m, coquelet m.

cock-eyed [ˈkɒkaɪd] a Fam **1** (cross-eyed) bigleux. **2** (crooked) de travers. **3** (crazy) absurde, saugrenu.

cockle [ˈkɒk(ə)l] n (shellfish) coque f.

cockney [ˈkɒknɪ] a & n cockney (mf).

cockpit [ˈkɒkpɪt] n Av poste m de pilotage.

cockroach [ˈkɒkrəʊtʃ] n (beetle) cafard m.

cocksure [kɒkˈʃʊər] a Fam trop sûr de soi.

cocktail [ˈkɒkteɪl] n (drink) cocktail m; (fruit) **c.** macédoine f (de fruits); **c. party** cocktail m; **prawn c.** crevettes fpl à la mayonnaise.

cocky [ˈkɒkɪ] a (-ier, -iest) Fam trop sûr de soi, arrogant.

cocoa [ˈkəʊkəʊ] n cacao m.

coconut [ˈkəʊkənʌt] n noix f de coco; **c. palm** cocotier m.

cocoon [kəˈkuːn] n cocon m.

cod [kɒd] n morue f; (bought fresh) cabillaud m. ◆**c.-liver 'oil** n huile f de foie de morue.

COD [siːəʊˈdiː] abbr (cash on delivery) livraison f contre remboursement.

coddle [ˈkɒd(ə)l] vt dorloter.

cod/e [kəʊd] n code m; − vt coder. ◆**-ing** n codification f. ◆**codify** vt codifier.

co-educational [kəʊedjuˈkeɪʃ(ə)l] a (school, teaching) mixte.

coefficient [kəʊɪˈfɪʃənt] n Math coefficient m.

coerce [kəʊˈɜːs] vt contraindre. ◆**coercion** n contrainte f.

coexist [kəʊɪgˈzɪst] vi coexister. ◆**coexistence** n coexistence f.

coffee [ˈkɒfɪ] n café m; **white c.** café m au lait; (ordered in restaurant etc) (café m) crème m; **black c.** café m noir, café nature; **c. bar, c. house** café m, cafétéria f; **c. break** pause-café f; **c. table** table f basse. ◆**coffeepot** n cafetière f.

coffers [ˈkɒfəz] npl (funds) coffres mpl.

coffin [ˈkɒfɪn] n cercueil m.

cog [kɒg] n Tech dent f; (person) Fig rouage m.

cogent [ˈkəʊdʒənt] a (reason, argument) puissant, convaincant.

cogitate [ˈkɒdʒɪteɪt] vi Iron cogiter.

cognac [ˈkɒnjæk] n cognac m.

cohabit [kəʊˈhæbɪt] vi (of unmarried people) vivre en concubinage.

coherent [kəʊˈhɪərənt] a cohérent; (speech) compréhensible. ◆**cohesion** n cohésion f. ◆**cohesive** a cohésif.

cohort [ˈkəʊhɔːt] n (group) cohorte f.

coil [kɔɪl] n (of wire etc) rouleau m; El bobine f; (contraceptive) stérilet m; − vt (rope, hair) enrouler; − vi (of snake etc) s'enrouler.

coin [kɔɪn] n pièce f (de monnaie); (currency) monnaie f; − vt (money) frapper; (word) Fig inventer, forger; **to c. a phrase** pour ainsi dire. ◆**c.-operated** a automatique. ◆**coinage** n (coins) monnaie f; Fig invention f.

coincide [kəʊɪn'saɪd] vi coïncider (with avec). ◆**co'incidence** n coïncidence f. ◆**coinci'dental** a fortuit; **it's c.** c'est une coïncidence.

coke [kəʊk] n **1** (fuel) coke m. **2** (Coca-Cola®) coca m.

colander ['kʌləndər] n (for vegetables etc) passoire f.

cold [kəʊld] n froid m; Med rhume m; **to catch c.** prendre froid; **out in the c.** Fig abandonné, en carafe; – a (-**er**, -**est**) froid; **to be** or **feel c.** (of person) avoir froid; **my hands are c.** j'ai les mains froides; **it's c.** (of weather) il fait froid; **to get c.** (of weather) se refroidir; (of food) refroidir; **to get c. feet** Fam se dégonfler; **in c. blood** de sang-froid; **c. cream** crème f de beauté; **c. meats**, Am **c. cuts** Culin assiette f anglaise. ◆**c.-'blooded** a (person) cruel, insensible; (act) de sang-froid. ◆**c.-'shoulder** v snober. ◆**coldly** adv avec froideur. ◆**coldness** n froideur f.

coleslaw ['kəʊlslɔː] n salade f de chou cru.

colic ['kɒlɪk] n Med coliques fpl.

collaborate [kə'læbəreɪt] vi collaborer (on à). ◆**collabo'ration** n collaboration f. ◆**collaborator** n collaborateur, -trice mf.

collage ['kɒlɑːʒ] n (picture) collage m.

collapse [kə'læps] vi (fall) s'effondrer, s'écrouler; (of government) tomber; (faint) Med se trouver mal; – n effondrement m, écroulement m; (of government) chute f. ◆**collapsible** a (chair etc) pliant.

collar ['kɒlər] n (on garment) col m; (of dog) collier m; **to seize by the c.** saisir au collet; – vt Fam saisir (qn) au collet; Fig Fam retenir (qn); (take, steal) Sl piquer. ◆**collarbone** n clavicule f.

collate [kə'leɪt] vt collationner, comparer (with avec).

colleague ['kɒliːg] n collègue mf, confrère m.

collect [kə'lekt] vt (pick up) ramasser; (gather) rassembler, recueillir; (taxes) percevoir; (rent, money) encaisser; (stamps etc as hobby) collectionner; (fetch, call for) (passer) prendre; – vi (of dust) s'accumuler; (of people) se rassembler; **to c. for** (in street, church) quêter pour; – adv **to call** or **phone c.** Am téléphoner en PCV. ◆**collection** [kə'lekʃ(ə)n] n ramassage m; (of taxes) perception f; (of stamps etc) collection f; (of poems etc) recueil m; (of money in church etc) quête f; (of mail) levée f. ◆**collective** a collectif. ◆**collectively** adv

collectivement. ◆**collector** n (of stamps etc) collectionneur, -euse mf.

college ['kɒlɪdʒ] n Pol Rel Sch collège m; (university) université f; Mus conservatoire m; **teachers' training c.** école f normale; **art c.** école f des beaux-arts; **agricultural c.** institut m d'agronomie, lycée m agricole.

collide [kə'laɪd] vi entrer en collision (with avec), se heurter (with à). ◆**collision** n collision f; Fig conflit m, collision f.

colliery ['kɒljərɪ] n houillère f.

colloquial [kə'ləʊkwɪəl] a (word etc) familier. ◆**colloquialism** n expression f familière.

collusion [kə'luːʒ(ə)n] n collusion f.

collywobbles ['kɒlɪwɒb(ə)lz] npl **to have the c.** (feel nervous) Fam avoir la frousse.

cologne [kə'ləʊn] n eau f de Cologne.

colon ['kəʊlən] n **1** Gram deux-points m inv. **2** Anat côlon m.

colonel ['kɜːn(ə)l] n colonel m.

colony ['kɒlənɪ] n colonie f. ◆**colonial** [kə'ləʊnɪəl] a colonial. ◆**coloni'zation** n colonisation f. ◆**colonize** vt coloniser.

colossal [kə'lɒs(ə)l] a colossal.

colour ['kʌlər] n couleur f; – a (photo, television) en couleurs; (television set) couleur inv; (problem) racial; **c. supplement** Journ supplément m illustré; **off c.** (not well) mal fichu; (improper) scabreux; – vt colorer; **to c. (in)** (drawing) colorier. ◆–**ed** a (person, pencil) de couleur; (glass, water) coloré. ◆–**ing** n coloration f; (with crayons) coloriage m; (hue, effect) coloris m; (matter) colorant m. ◆**colour-blind** a daltonien. ◆**colourful** a (crowd, story) coloré; (person) pittoresque.

colt [kəʊlt] n (horse) poulain m.

column ['kɒləm] n colonne f. ◆**columnist** n Journ chroniqueur m; **gossip c.** échotier, -ière mf.

coma ['kəʊmə] n coma m; **in a c.** dans le coma.

comb [kəʊm] n peigne m; – vt peigner; (search) Fig ratisser; **to c. one's hair** se peigner; **to c. out** (hair) démêler.

combat ['kɒmbæt] n combat m; – vti combattre (for pour). ◆**'combatant** n combattant, -ante mf.

combin/e [kəm'baɪn] vt unir, joindre (with à); (elements, sounds) combiner; (qualities, efforts) allier, joindre; – vi s'unir; **everything combined to . . .** tout s'est ligué pour . . . . ◆–**ed** a (effort) conjugué; **c. wealth**/etc (put together) richesses/etc fpl réunies; **c. forces** Mil forces fpl alliées. ◆**combi'nation** n combinaison f; (of *qualities*) réunion *f*; (*of events*) concours *m*; **in c. with** en association avec.

combine² ['kɒmbaɪn] *n* Com cartel *m*; **c. harvester** *Agr* moissonneuse-batteuse *f*.

combustion [kəmˈbʌstʃ(ə)n] *n* combustion *f*.

come [kʌm] *vi* (*pt* came, *pp* come) venir (**from** de, **to** à); (*arrive*) arriver, venir; (*happen*) arriver; **c. and see me** viens me voir; **I've just c. from** j'arrive de; **to c. for** venir chercher; **to c. home** rentrer; **coming!** j'arrive!; **c. now!** voyons!; **to c. as a surprise** (**to**) surprendre; **to c. near** *or* **close to doing** faillir faire; **to c. on page 2** se trouver à la page 2; **to c. to** (*understand etc*) en venir à; (*a decision*) parvenir à; **to c. to an end** toucher à sa fin; **to c. true** se réaliser; **c. May/etc** *Fam* en mai/*etc*; **the life to c.** la vie future; **how c. that . . . ?** *Fam* comment se fait-il que . . . ? ■ **to c. about** *vi* (*happen*) se faire, arriver; **c. across** *vi* (*of speech*) faire de l'effet; (*of feelings*) se montrer; – *vt* (*thing, person*) tomber sur; **to c. along** *vi* venir (**with** avec); (*progress*) avancer; **c. along!** allons!; **to c. at** *vi* (*attack*) attaquer; **to c. away** *vi* (*leave, come off*) partir; **to c. back** *vi* revenir; (*return home*) rentrer. ◆**comeback** *n* retour *m*; *Th Pol* rentrée *f*; (*retort*) réplique *f*; **to c. by** *vt* (*obtain*) obtenir; (*find*) trouver; **to c. down** *vi* descendre; (*of rain, price*) tomber. ◆**comedown** *n* *Fam* humiliation *f*; **to c. forward** *vi* (*make oneself known, volunteer*) se présenter; **to c. forward with** offrir, suggérer; **to c. in** *vi* entrer; (*of tide*) monter; (*of train, athlete*) arriver; *Pol* arriver au pouvoir; (*of clothes*) devenir la mode, se faire beaucoup; (*of money*) rentrer; **to c. in for** recevoir; **to c. into** (*money*) hériter de; **to c. off** *vi* se détacher, partir; (*succeed*) réussir; (*happen*) avoir lieu; (*fare, manage*) s'en tirer; – *vt* (*fall from*) tomber de; (*get down from*) descendre de; **to c. on** *vi* (*follow*) suivre; (*progress*) avancer; (*arrive*) arriver; (*of play*) être joué; **c. on!** allez!; **to c. out** *vi* sortir; (*of sun, book*) paraître; (*of stain*) s'enlever, partir; (*of secret*) être révélé; (*of photo*) réussir; **to c. out** (**on strike**) se mettre en grève; **to c. over** *vi* (*visit*) venir, passer; **to c. over funny** *or* **peculiar** se trouver mal; – *vt* (*take hold of*) saisir (*qn*), prendre (*qn*); **to c. round** *vi* (*visit*) venir, passer; (*recur*) revenir; (*regain consciousness*) revenir à soi; **to c. through** *vi* (*survive*) s'en tirer; – *vt* se tirer indemne de; **to c. to** *vi* (*regain consciousness*) revenir

à soi; (*amount to*) Com revenir à, faire; **to c. under** *vi* être classé sous; (*s.o.'s influence*) tomber sous; **to c. up** *vi* (*rise*) monter; (*of plant*) sortir; (*of question, job*) se présenter; **to c. up against** (*wall, problem*) se heurter à; **to c. up to** (*reach*) arriver jusqu'à; (*one's hopes*) répondre à; **to c. up with** (*idea, money*) trouver; **to c. upon** *vi* (*book, reference etc*) tomber sur. ◆**coming** *a* (*future*) à venir; – *n Rel* avènement *m*; **comings and goings** allées *fpl* et venues.

comedy ['kɒmɪdɪ] *n* comédie *f*. ◆**co'median** *n* (*acteur m*) comique *m*, actrice *f* comique.

comet ['kɒmɪt] *n* comète *f*.

comeuppance [kʌmˈʌpəns] *n* **he got his c.** *Pej Fam* il n'a eu que ce qu'il méritе.

comfort ['kʌmfət] *n* confort *m*; (*consolation*) réconfort *m*, consolation *f*; (*peace of mind*) tranquillité *f* d'esprit; **to like one's comforts** aimer ses aises *fpl*; **c. station** *Am* toilettes *fpl*; – *vt* consoler; (*cheer*) réconforter. ◆**-able** *a* (*chair, house etc*) confortable; (*rich*) aisé; **he's c.** (*in chair etc*) il est à l'aise, il est bien; **make yourself c.** mets-toi à l'aise. ◆**-ably** *adv* **c. off** (*rich*) à l'aise. ◆**-er** *n* (*baby's dummy*) sucette *f*; (*quilt*) *Am* édredon *m*. ◆**comfy** *a* (*-ier, -iest*) (*chair etc*) *Fam* confortable; **I'm c.** je suis bien.

comic ['kɒmɪk] *a* comique; – *n* (*actor*) comique *m*; (*actress*) actrice *f* comique; (*magazine*) illustré *m*; **c. strip** bande *f* dessinée. ◆**comical** *a* comique, drôle.

comma ['kɒmə] *n* Gram virgule *f*.

command [kəˈmɑːnd] *vt* (*order*) commander (**s.o. to do** à qn de faire); (*control, dominate*) commander (*régiment, vallée etc*); (*be able to use*) disposer de; (*respect*) imposer (**from** à); (*require*) exiger; – *vi* commander; – *n* ordre *m*; (*power*) commandement *m*; (*troops*) troupes *fpl*; (*mastery*) maîtrise *f* (**of** de); **at one's c.** (*disposal*) à sa disposition; **to be in c. (of)** (*ship, army etc*) commander; (*situation*) être maître (de). ◆**-ing** *a* (*authoritative*) imposant; (*position*) dominant; **c. officer** commandant *m*. ◆**-er** *n* chef *m*; *Mil* commandant *m*. ◆**-ment** *n* *Rel* commandement *m*.

commandant ['kɒməndænt] *n* *Mil* commandant *m* (*d'un camp etc*). ◆**comman'deer** *vt* réquisitionner.

commando [kəˈmɑːndəʊ] *n* (*pl* -os *or* -oes) *Mil* commando *m*.

commemorate [kəˈmeməreɪt] *vt* commémorer. ◆**commemo'ration** *n* commémoration f. ◆**commemorative** a commémoratif.

commence [kə'mens] vti commencer (**doing** à faire). ◆**—ment** n commencement m; Univ Am remise f des diplômes.

commend [kə'mend] vt (praise) louer; (recommend) recommander; (entrust) confier (**to** à). ◆**—able** a louable. ◆**commen'dation** n éloge m.

commensurate [kə'menʃərət] a proportionné (**to**, with à).

comment ['kɒment] n commentaire m, remarque f; – vi faire des commentaires ou des remarques (**on** sur); **to c. on** (text, event, news item) commenter; **to c. that** remarquer que. ◆**commentary** n commentaire m; (**live**) c. TV Rad reportage m. ◆**commentate** vi TV Rad faire un reportage (**on** sur). ◆**commentator** n TV Rad reporter m, commentateur, -trice mf.

commerce ['kɒmɜːs] n commerce m. ◆**co'mmercial 1** a commercial; (street) commerçant; (traveller) de commerce. **2** n (advertisement) TV publicité f; **the commercials** TV la publicité. ◆**co'mmercialize** vt (event) Pej transformer en une affaire de gros sous.

commiserate [kə'mızəreɪt] vi **to c. with** s.o. s'apitoyer sur (le sort de) qn. ◆**commise'ration** n commisération f.

commission [kə'mɪʃ(ə)n] n (fee, group) commission f; (order for work) commande f; **out of c.** hors service; **to get one's c.** Mil être nommé officier; – vt (artist) passer une commande à; (book) commander; Mil nommer (qn) officier; **to c. to do** charger de faire. ◆**commissio'naire** n (in hotel etc) commissionnaire m. ◆**commissioner** n Pol commissaire m; (**police**) **c.** préfet m (de police).

commit [kə'mɪt] vt (-tt-) (crime) commettre; (entrust) confier (**to** à); **to c. suicide** se suicider; **to c. to memory** apprendre par cœur; **to c. to prison** incarcérer; **to c. oneself** s'engager (**to** à); (compromise oneself) se compromettre. ◆**—ment** n obligation f; (promise) engagement m.

committee [kə'mɪtɪ] n comité m.

commodity [kə'mɒdɪtɪ] n produit m, article m.

common ['kɒmən] **1** a (**-er, -est**) (shared, vulgar) commun; (frequent) courant, fréquent, commun; **the c. man** l'homme m du commun; **in c.** (shared) en commun (**with** avec); **to have nothing in c.** n'avoir rien de commun (**with** avec); **in c. with** (like) comme; **c. law** droit m coutumier; **C.**

Market Marché m commun; **c. room** salle f commune; **c. or garden** ordinaire. **2** n (land) terrain m communal; **House of Commons** Pol Chambre f des Communes; **the Commons** Pol les Communes fpl. ◆**—er** n roturier, -ière mf. ◆**—ly** adv (generally) communément; (vulgarly) d'une façon commune; (vulgarity) vulgarité f. ◆**—ness** n fréquence f; (vulgarity) vulgarité f. ◆**commonplace** a banal; – n banalité f. ◆**common'sense** n sens m commun; – a sensé.

Commonwealth ['kɒmənwelθ] n **the C.** le Commonwealth.

commotion [kə'məʊʃ(ə)n] n agitation f.

communal [kə'mjuːn(ə)l] a (of the community) communautaire; (shared) commun. ◆**—ly** adv en commun; (to live) en communauté.

commune 1 ['kɒmjuːn] n (district) commune f; (group) communauté f. **2** [kə'mjuːn] vi Rel & Fig communier (**with** avec). ◆**co'mmunion** n communion f; (**Holy**) **C.** communion f.

communicate [kə'mjuːnɪkeɪt] vt communiquer; (illness) transmettre; – vi (of person, rooms etc) communiquer. ◆**communi'cation** n communication f; **c. cord** Rail signal m d'alarme. ◆**communicative** a communicatif. ◆**communiqué** n Pol communiqué m.

communism ['kɒmjunɪz(ə)m] n communisme m. ◆**communist** a & n communiste (mf).

community [kə'mjuːnɪtɪ] n communauté f; – a (rights, life etc) communautaire; **the student c.** les étudiants mpl; **c. centre** centre m socio-culturel; **c. worker** animateur, -trice mf socio-culturel(le).

commute [kə'mjuːt] **1** vt Jur commuer (**to** en). **2** vi (travel) faire la navette (**to work** pour se rendre à son travail). ◆**—ing** n trajets mpl journaliers. ◆**—er** n banlieusard, -arde mf; **c. train** train m de banlieue.

compact 1 [kəm'pækt] a (car, crowd, substance) compact; (style) condensé; **c. disc** ['kɒmpækt] disque m compact. **2** ['kɒmpækt] n (for face powder) poudrier m.

companion [kəm'pænjən] n (person) compagnon m, compagne f; (handbook) manuel m. ◆**companionship** n camaraderie f.

company ['kʌmpənɪ] n (fellowship, firm) compagnie f; (guests) invités, compagnie f; **to keep s.o. c.** tenir compagnie à qn; **to keep good c.** avoir de bonnes fréquentations; **he's good c.** c'est un bon compagnon.

compar/e [kəm'peər] *vt* comparer; **compared to** *or* **with** en comparaison de; – *vi* être comparable, se comparer (**with** à). **◆–able** ['kɒmpərəb(ə)l] *a* comparable. **◆comparative** *a* comparatif; (*relative*) relatif. **◆comparatively** *adv* relativement. **◆comparison** *n* comparaison *f* (**between** entre; **with** à, avec).

compartment [kəm'pɑːtmənt] *n* compartiment *m*. **◆compart'mentalize** *vt* compartimenter.

compass ['kʌmpəs] *n* **1** (*for navigation*) boussole *f*; *Nau* compas *m*; *Fig* portée *f*. **2** (*for measuring etc*) *Am* compas *m*; (**pair of**) **compasses** compas *m*.

compassion [kəm'pæʃ(ə)n] *n* compassion *f*. **◆compassionate** *a* compatissant; **on c. grounds** pour raisons de famille.

compatible [kəm'pætɪb(ə)l] *a* compatible. **◆compati'bility** *n* compatibilité *f*.

compatriot [kəm'pætrɪət, kəm'pætrɪɒt] *n* compatriote *mf*.

compel [kəm'pel] *vt* (**-ll-**) contraindre (**to do** à faire); (*respect etc*) imposer (**from** à); **compelled to do** contraint de faire. **◆compelling** *a* irrésistible.

compendium [kəm'pendɪəm] *n* abrégé *m*.

compensate ['kɒmpənseɪt] *vt* **to c. s.o.** (**for** **payment, recompense**) dédommager qn (**for** de); **to c. for sth** (*make up for*) compenser qch; – *vi* compenser. **◆compen'sation** *n* (*financial*) dédommagement *m*; (*consolation*) compensation *f*, dédommagement *m*; **in c. for** en compensation de.

compère ['kɒmpeər] *n* *TV Rad* animateur, -trice *mf*, présentateur, -trice *mf*; – *vt* (*a show*) animer, présenter.

compete [kəm'piːt] *vi* prendre part (**in** à), concourir (**in** à); (*vie*) rivaliser (**with** avec); *Com* faire concurrence (**with** à); **to c. for** (*prize etc*) concourir pour; **to c. in a rally** courir dans un rallye.

competent ['kɒmpɪtənt] *a* (*capable*) compétent (**to do** pour faire); (*sufficient*) suffisant. **◆–ly** *adv* avec compétence. **◆competence** *n* compétence *f*.

competition [kɒmpə'tɪʃ(ə)n] *n* (*rivalry*) compétition *f*, concurrence *f*; **a c.** (*contest*) un concours; *Sp* une compétition. **◆com'petitive** *a* (*price, market*) compétitif; (*selection*) par concours; (*person*) aimant la compétition; **c. exam(ination)** concours *m*. **◆com'petitor** *n* concurrent, -ente *mf*.

compil/e [kəm'paɪl] *vt* (*dictionary*) rédiger; (*list*) dresser; (*documents*) compiler. **◆–er** *n* rédacteur, -trice *mf*.

complacent [kəm'pleɪsənt] *a* content de

soi. **◆complacence** *n*, **◆complacency** *n* autosatisfaction *f*, contentement *m* de soi.

complain [kəm'pleɪn] *vi* se plaindre (**of, about** de; **that** que). **◆complaint** *n* plainte *f*; *Com* réclamation *f*; *Med* maladie *f*; (**cause for**) **c.** sujet *m* de plainte.

complement ['kɒmplɪmənt] *n* complément *m*; – ['kɒmplɪment] *vt* compléter. **◆comple'mentary** *a* complémentaire.

complete [kəm'pliːt] *a* (*total*) complet; (*finished*) achevé; (*downright*) *Pej* parfait; – *vt* (*add sth missing*) compléter; (*finish*) achever; (*a form*) remplir. **◆–ly** *adv* complètement. **◆completion** *n* achèvement *m*, réalisation *f*.

complex ['kɒmpleks] **1** *a* complexe. **2** *n* (*feeling, buildings*) complexe *m*; **housing c.** grand ensemble *m*. **◆com'plexity** *n* complexité *f*.

complexion [kəm'plekʃ(ə)n] *n* (*of the face*) teint *m*; *Fig* caractère *m*.

compliance [kəm'plaɪəns] *n* (*agreement*) conformité *f* (**with** avec).

complicat/e ['kɒmplɪkeɪt] *vt* compliquer. **◆–ed** *a* compliqué. **◆compli'cation** *n* complication *f*.

complicity [kəm'plɪsɪtɪ] *n* complicité *f*.

compliment ['kɒmplɪmənt] *n* compliment *m*; *pl* (*of author*) hommages *mpl*; **compliments of the season** meilleurs vœux pour Noël et la nouvelle année; – ['kɒmplɪment] *vt* complimenter. **◆compli'mentary** *a* **1** (*flattering*) flatteur. **2** (*free*) à titre gracieux; (*ticket*) de faveur.

comply [kəm'plaɪ] *vi* obéir (**with** à); (*request*) accéder à.

component [kəm'pəʊnənt] *a* (*part*) constituant; – *n* (*chemical, electronic*) composant *m*; *Tech* pièce *f*; (*element*) *Fig* composante *f*.

compos/e [kəm'pəʊz] *vt* composer; **to c. oneself** se calmer. **◆–ed** *a* calme. **◆–er** *n* *Mus* compositeur, -trice *mf*. **◆compo'sition** *n* *Mus* Liter *Ch* composition *f*; *Sch* rédaction *f*. **◆composure** *n* calme *m*, sang-froid *m*.

compost ['kɒmpɒst, *Am* 'kɒmpəʊst] *n* compost *m*.

compound 1 ['kɒmpaʊnd] *n* (*substance, word*) composé *m*; (*area*) enclos *m*; – *a* *Ch* (*substance*) composé; (*sentence, number*) complexe. **2** [kəm'paʊnd] *vt* *Ch* composer; (*increase*) *Fig* aggraver.

comprehend [kɒmprɪ'hend] *vt* comprendre. **◆comprehensible** *a* compréhensible. **◆comprehension** *n* compréhension *f.* ◆**comprehensive** *a* complet; *(knowledge)* étendu; *(view, measure)* d'ensemble; *(insurance)* tous-risques *inv;* – *a & n c.* **(school)** = collège *m* d'enseignement secondaire.

compress [kəm'pres] *vt* comprimer; *(ideas etc) Fig* condenser. ◆**compression** *n* compression *f;* condensation *f.*

comprise [kəm'praiz] *vt* comprendre, englober.

compromise ['kɒmprəmaiz] *vt* compromettre; – *vi* accepter un compromis; – *n* compromis *m;* – *a (solution)* de compromis.

compulsion [kəm'pʌlʃ(ə)n] *n* contrainte *f.* ◆**compulsive** *a (behaviour) Psy* compulsif; *(smoker, gambler)* invétéré; **c. liar** mythomane *mf.*

compulsory [kəm'pʌlsəri] *a* obligatoire.

comput/e [kəm'pjut] *vt* calculer. ◆**—ing** *n* informatique *f.* ◆**computer** *n* ordinateur *m;* – *a (system)* informatique; *(course)* d'informatique; **c. operator** opérateur, -trice *mf* sur ordinateur; **c. science** informatique *f;* **c. scientist** informaticien, -ienne *mf.* ◆**computerize** *vt* informatiser.

comrade ['kɒmreid] *n* camarade *mf.* ◆**comradeship** *n* camaraderie *f.*

con [kɒn] *vt* **(-nn-)** *Sl* rouler, escroquer; **to be conned** se faire avoir ou rouler; – *n Sl* escroquerie *f;* **c. man** escroc *m.*

concave [kɒn'keiv] *a* concave.

conceal [kən'siːl] *vt (hide)* dissimuler **(from s.o.** à qn); *(plan etc)* tenir secret. ◆**—ment** *n* dissimulation *f.*

concede [kən'siːd] *vt* concéder **(to** à, **that** que); – *vi* céder.

conceit [kən'siːt] *n* vanité *f.* ◆**conceited** *a* vaniteux. ◆**conceitedly** *adv* avec vanité.

conceiv/e [kən'siːv] *vt (idea, child etc)* concevoir; – *vi (of woman)* concevoir; **to c. of** concevoir. ◆**—able** *a* concevable, envisageable. ◆**—ably** *adv* yes, **c.** oui, c'est concevable.

concentrate ['kɒnsəntreit] *vt* concentrer; – *vi* se concentrer **(on** sur); **to c. on doing** s'appliquer à faire. ◆**concen'tration** *n* concentration *f;* **c. camp** camp *m* de concentration.

concentric [kən'sentrik] *a* concentrique.

concept ['kɒnsept] *n* concept *m.* ◆**con'ception** *n (idea)* & *Med* conception *f.*

concern [kən'sɜːn] *vt* concerner; **to c. oneself with, be concerned with** s'occuper de; **to be concerned about** s'inquiéter de; –

n (matter) affaire *f;* *(anxiety)* inquiétude *f;* *(share) Com* intérêt(s) *m(pl)* **(in** dans); **(business)** c. entreprise *f.* ◆**—ed** *a (anxious)* inquiet; **the department c.** le service compétent; **the main person c.** le principal intéressé. ◆**—ing** *prep* en ce qui concerne.

concert ['kɒnsət] *n* concert *m;* **in c.** *(together)* de concert **(with** avec). ◆**c.-goer** *n* habitué, -ée *mf* des concerts. ◆**con'certed** *a (effort)* concerté.

concertina [kɒnsə'tiːnə] *n* concertina *m;* **c. crash** *Aut* carambolage *m.*

concession [kən'seʃ(ə)n] *n* concession *f* **(to** à).

conciliate [kən'silieit] *vt* **to c. s.o.** *(win over)* se concilier qn; *(soothe)* apaiser qn. ◆**concili'ation** *n* conciliation *f;* apaisement *m.* ◆**conciliatory** [kən'siliətəri, *Am* -tɔːri] *a* conciliant.

concise [kən'sais] *a* concis. ◆**—ly** *adv* avec concision. ◆**—ness** *n*, ◆**concision** *n* concision *f.*

conclud/e [kən'kluːd] *vt (end, settle)* conclure; **to c. that** *(infer)* conclure que; – *vi (of event etc)* se terminer **(with** par); *(of speaker)* conclure. ◆**—ing** *a* final. ◆**conclusion** *n* conclusion *f;* **in c.** pour conclure. ◆**conclusive** *a* concluant. ◆**conclusively** *adv* de manière concluante.

concoct [kən'kɒkt] *vt Culin Pej* concocter, confectionner; *(scheme) Fig* combiner. ◆**concoction** *n (substance) Pej* mixture *f;* *(act)* confection *f; Fig* combinaison *f.*

concord ['kɒnkɔːd] *n* concorde *f.*

concourse ['kɒnkɔːs] *n (hall) Am* hall *m;* *Rail* hall *m,* salle *f* des pas perdus.

concrete ['kɒnkriːt] **1** *a (real, positive)* concret. **2** *n* béton *m;* – *a* en béton; **c. mixer** bétonnière *f,* bétonneuse *f.*

concur [kən'kɜːr] *vi* **(-rr-)** **1** *(agree)* être d'accord **(with** avec). **2 to c. to** *(contribute)* concourir à.

concurrent [kən'kʌrənt] *a* simultané. ◆**—ly** *adv* simultanément.

concussion [kən'kʌʃ(ə)n] *n Med* commotion *f (cérébrale).*

condemn [kən'dem] *vt* condamner; *(building)* déclarer inhabitable. ◆**condem'nation** *n* condamnation *f.*

condense [kən'dens] *vt* condenser; – *vi* se condenser. ◆**conden'sation** *n* condensation *f (of* de); *(mist)* buée *f.*

condescend [kɒndi'send] *vi* condescendre **(to do** à faire). ◆**condescension** *n* condescendance *f.*

condiment ['kɒndimənt] *n* condiment *m.*

condition [kənˈdɪʃ(ə)n] **1** n (*stipulation, circumstance, rank*) condition f; (*state*) état m, condition f; **on c. that one does** à condition de faire, à condition que l'on fasse; **in/out of c.** en bonne/mauvaise forme. **2** vt (*action etc*) déterminer, conditionner; **to c. s.o.** Psy conditionner qn (**into doing** à faire). ◆**conditional** a conditionnel; **to be c. upon** dépendre de. ◆**conditioner** n (*hair*) c. après-shampooing m.

condo [ˈkɒndəʊ] n abbr (*pl -os*) Am = **condominium**.

condolences [kənˈdəʊlənsɪz] npl condoléances fpl.

condom [ˈkɒndəm] n préservatif m, capote f (anglaise).

condominium [kɒndəˈmɪnɪəm] n Am (*building*) (immeuble m en) copropriété f; (*apartment*) appartement m dans une copropriété.

condone [kənˈdəʊn] vt (*forgive*) pardonner; (*overlook*) fermer les yeux sur.

conducive [kənˈdjuːsɪv] a **c. to** favorable à.

conduct [ˈkɒndʌkt] n (*behaviour, directing*) conduite f; − [kənˈdʌkt] vt (*lead*) conduire, mener; (*orchestra*) diriger; (*electricity etc*) conduire; **to c. oneself** se conduire. ◆**—ed** a (*visit*) guidé; **c. tour** excursion f accompagnée. ◆**conductor** n Mus chef m d'orchestre; (*on bus*) receveur m; Rail Am chef m de train; (*metal, cable etc*) conducteur m. ◆**conductress** n (*on bus*) receveuse f.

cone [kəʊn] n cône m; (*of ice cream*) cornet m; (*paper*) c. cornet m (de papier); **traffic c.** cône m de chantier.

confectioner [kənˈfekʃənər] n (*of sweets*) confiseur, -euse mf; (*of cakes*) pâtissier, -ière mf. ◆**confectionery** n (*sweets*) confiserie f; (*cakes*) pâtisserie f.

confederate [kənˈfedərət] a confédéré; − n (*accomplice*) complice mf, acolyte m. ◆**confederacy** n, ◆**confede'ration** n confédération f.

confer [kənˈfɜːr] vt (*-rr-*) (*grant*) conférer (**on** à); (*degree*) Univ remettre. **2** vi (*-rr-*) (*talk together*) conférer, se consulter.

conference [ˈkɒnfərəns] n conférence f; (*scientific etc*) congrès m.

confess [kənˈfes] **1** vt avouer, confesser (**that** que, **to** à); − vi avouer; **to c. to** (*crime etc*) avouer, confesser. **2** vt Rel confesser; − vi se confesser. ◆**confession** n aveu m, confession f; Rel confession f. ◆**confessional** n Rel confessionnal m.

confetti [kənˈfetɪ] n confettis mpl.

confide [kənˈfaɪd] vt confier (**to** à, **that** que); −

− vi **to c. in** (*talk to*) se confier à. ◆**'confidant, -ante** [-ænt] n confident, -ente mf. ◆**'confidence** n (*trust*) confiance f; (*secret*) confidence f; (*self-*)c. confiance f en soi; **in c.** en confidence; **motion of no c.** Pol motion f de censure; **c. trick** escroquerie f; **c. trickster** escroc m. ◆**'confident** a sûr, assuré; (*self-*)c. sûr de soi. ◆**confi'dential** a confidentiel; (*secretary*) particulier. ◆**confi'dentially** adv en confidence. ◆**'confidently** adv avec confiance.

configuration [kənfɪgjʊˈreɪʃ(ə)n] n configuration f.

confine [kənˈfaɪn] vt enfermer, confiner (**to, in** dans); (*limit*) limiter (**to** à); **to c. oneself to doing** se limiter à faire. ◆**—ed** a (*atmosphere*) confiné; (*space*) réduit; **c. to bed** obligé de garder le lit. ◆**—ement** n Med couches fpl; Jur emprisonnement m. ◆**confines** npl limites fpl, confins mpl.

confirm [kənˈfɜːm] vt confirmer (**that** que); (*strengthen*) raffermir. ◆**—ed** a (*bachelor*) endurci; (*smoker, habit*) invétéré. ◆**confir'mation** n confirmation f; raffermissement m.

confiscate [ˈkɒnfɪskeɪt] vt confisquer (**from s.o.** à qn). ◆**confis'cation** n confiscation f.

conflagration [kɒnfləˈɡreɪʃ(ə)n] n (*grand*) incendie m, brasier m.

conflict [ˈkɒnflɪkt] n conflit m; − [kənˈflɪkt] vi être en contradiction, être incompatible (**with** avec); (*of dates, events, TV programmes*) tomber en même temps (**with** que). ◆**—ing** a (*views, theories etc*) contradictoires; (*dates*) incompatibles.

confluence [ˈkɒnflʊəns] n (*of rivers*) confluent m.

conform [kənˈfɔːm] vi se conformer (**to, with** à); (*of ideas etc*) être en conformité. ◆**conformist** a & n conformiste (mf). ◆**conformity** n (*likeness*) conformité f; Pej conformisme m.

confound [kənˈfaʊnd] vt confondre; **c. him!** que le diable l'emporte! ◆**—ed** a (*damned*) Fam sacré.

confront [kənˈfrʌnt] vt (*danger*) affronter; (*problems*) faire face à; **to c. s.o.** (*be face to face with*) se trouver en face de qn; (*oppose*) s'opposer à qn; **to c. s.o. with** (*person*) confronter qn avec; (*thing*) mettre qn en présence de. ◆**confron'tation** n confrontation f.

confus/e [kənˈfjuːz] vt (*perplex*) confondre; (*muddle*) embrouiller; **c. with** (*mistake for*) confondre avec. ◆**—ed** a (*situation,* *noises etc*) confus; **to be c.** (*of person*) s'y perdre; **to get c.** s'embrouiller. ◆**—ing** *a* difficile à comprendre, déroutant. ◆**confusion** *n* confusion *f*; **in c.** en désordre.

congeal [kən'dʒiːl] *vt* figer; — *vi* (se) figer.

congenial [kən'dʒiːnɪəl] *a* sympathique.

congenital [kən'dʒenɪtəl] *a* congénital.

congested [kən'dʒestɪd] *a* (*street*) encombré; (*town*) surpeuplé; *Med* congestionné. ◆**congestion** *n* (*traffic*) encombrement(s) *m(pl)*; (*overcrowding*) surpeuplement *m*; *Med* congestion *f*.

Congo ['kɒŋgəʊ] *n* Congo *m*.

congratulate [kən'grætjʊleɪt] *vt* féliciter (**s.o. on sth** qn de qch). ◆**congratu-'lations** *npl* félicitations *fpl* (**on** pour). ◆**congratu'latory** *a* (*telegram etc*) de félicitations.

congregate ['kɒŋgrɪgeɪt] *vi* se rassembler. ◆**congre'gation** *n* (*worshippers*) assemblée *f*, fidèles *mfpl*.

congress ['kɒŋgres] *n* congrès *m*; **C.** *Pol Am* le Congrès. ◆**Congressman** *n* (*pl* -men) *Am* membre du *m*. ◆**Con-'gressional** *a Am* du Congrès.

conic(al) ['kɒnɪk(ə)l] *a* conique.

conifer ['kɒnɪfər] *n* (*tree*) conifère *m*.

conjecture [kən'dʒektʃər] *n* conjecture *f*; — *vt* conjecturer; — *vi* faire des conjectures. ◆**conjectural** *a* conjectural.

conjugal ['kɒndʒʊgəl] *a* conjugal.

conjugate ['kɒndʒʊgeɪt] *vt* (*verb*) conjuguer. ◆**conju'gation** *n Gram* conjugaison *f*.

conjunction [kən'dʒʌŋkʃ(ə)n] *n Gram* conjonction *f*; **in c. with** conjointement avec.

conjur/e ['kʌndʒər] *vt* **to c. (up)** (*by magic*) faire apparaître; **to c. up** (*memories etc*) *Fig* évoquer. ◆**—ing** *n* prestidigitation *f*. ◆**—er** *n* prestidigitateur, -trice *mf*.

conk [kɒŋk] **1** *n* (*nose*) *Sl* pif *m*. **2** *vi* **to c. out** (*break down*) *Fam* claquer, tomber en panne.

conker ['kɒŋkər] *n* (*horse-chestnut fruit*) *Fam* marron *m* (d'Inde).

connect [kə'nekt] *vt* relier (**with, to** à); (*telephone, stove etc*) brancher; **to c. with** *Tel* mettre en communication avec; (*in memory*) associer avec; — *vi* (*be connected*) être relié; **to c. with** (*of train, bus*) assurer la correspondance avec. ◆**—ed** *a* (*facts etc*) lié, connexe; (*speech*) suivi; **to be c. with** (*have dealings with*) être lié à; (*have to do with, relate to*) avoir rapport à; (*by marriage*) être allié à. ◆**connection** *n* (*link*) rapport *m*, relation *f* (**with** avec;

(*train, bus etc*) correspondance *f*; (*phone call*) communication *f*; (*between pipes etc*) *Tech* raccord *m*; *pl* (*contacts*) relations *fpl*; **in c. with** à propos de.

connive [kə'naɪv] *vi* **to c.** fermer les yeux sur; **to c. to do** se mettre de connivence pour faire (**with** avec); **to c. together** agir en complicité. ◆**connivance** *n* connivence *f*.

connoisseur [kɒnə'sɜːr] *n* connaisseur *m*.

connotation [kɒnə'teɪʃ(ə)n] *n* connotation *f*.

conquer ['kɒŋkər] *vt* (*country, freedom etc*) conquérir; (*enemy, habit*) vaincre. ◆**—ing** *a* victorieux. ◆**conqueror** *n* conquérant, -ante *mf*, vainqueur *m*. ◆**conquest** *n* conquête *f*.

cons [kɒnz] *npl* **the pros and (the) c.** le pour et le contre.

conscience ['kɒnʃəns] *n* conscience *f*. ◆**c.-stricken** *a* pris de remords.

conscientious [kɒnʃɪ'enʃəs] *a* consciencieux; **c. objector** objecteur *m* de conscience. ◆**—ness** *n* application *f*, sérieux *m*.

conscious ['kɒnʃəs] *a* conscient (**of sth** de qch); (*intentional*) délibéré; *Med* conscient; **to be c. of doing** avoir conscience de faire. ◆**—ly** *adv* (*knowingly*) consciemment. ◆**—ness** *n* conscience *f* (**of** de); *Med* connaissance *f*.

conscript ['kɒnskrɪpt] *n Mil* conscrit *m*; — [kən'skrɪpt] *vt* enrôler (par conscription). ◆**con'scription** *n* conscription *f*.

consecrate ['kɒnsɪkreɪt] *vt* (*church etc*) *Rel* consacrer. ◆**conse'cration** *n* consécration *f*.

consecutive [kən'sekjʊtɪv] *a* consécutif. ◆**—ly** *adv* consécutivement.

consensus [kən'sensəs] *n* consensus *m*, accord *m* (général).

consent [kən'sent] *vi* consentir (**to** à); — *n* consentement *m*; **by common c.** de l'aveu de tous; **by mutual c.** d'un commun accord.

consequence ['kɒnsɪkwəns] *n* (*result*) conséquence *f*; (*importance*) importance *f*, conséquence *f*. ◆**consequently** *adv* par conséquent.

conservative [kən'sɜːvətɪv] **1** *a* (*estimate*) modeste; (*view*) traditionnel. **2** *a* & *n* C. *Pol* conservateur, -trice (*mf*). ◆**conservatism** *n* (*in behaviour*) & *Pol Rel* conservatisme *m*.

conservatoire [kən'sɜːvətwɑːr] *n Mus* conservatoire *m*.

conservatory [kən'sɜːvətrɪ] *n* (*greenhouse*) serre *f*.

conserve [kən'sɜːv] *vt* préserver, conserver;

(*one's strength*) ménager; **to c. energy** faire des économies d'énergie. ◆**conser-'vation** n (*energy-saving*) économies fpl d'énergie; (*of nature*) protection f de l'environnement; *Phys* conservation f.

consider [kən'sɪdər] vt considérer; (*take into account*) tenir compte de; **I'll c. it** j'y réfléchirai; **to c.** doing envisager de faire; **to c. that** estimer *or* considérer que; **he's** *or* **she's being considered (for the job)** sa candidature est à l'étude; **all things considered** en fin de compte. ◆**—ing** prep étant donné, vu. ◆**—able** a (*large*) considérable; (*much*) beaucoup de. ◆**—ably** adv beaucoup, considérablement. ◆**conside-'ration** n (*thought, thoughtfulness, reason*) considération f; **under c.** à l'étude; **out of c. for** par égard pour; **to take into c.** prendre en considération.

considerate [kən'sɪdərət] a plein d'égards (**to** pour), attentionné (**to** à l'égard de).

consign [kən'saɪn] vt (*send*) expédier; (*give, entrust*) confier (**to** à). ◆**—ment** n (*act*) expédition f; (*goods*) arrivage m.

consist [kən'sɪst] vi consister (**of** en, **in** dans, **in** doing à faire).

consistent [kən'sɪstənt] a logique, conséquent; (*coherent*) cohérent; (*friend*) fidèle; **c. with** compatible avec, conforme à. ◆**—ly** adv (*logically*) avec logique; (*always*) constamment. ◆**consistency** n **1** logique f; cohérence f. **2** (*of liquid etc*) consistance f.

console[1] [kən'səʊl] vt consoler. ◆**conso-'lation** n consolation f; **c. prize** prix m de consolation.

console[2] ['kɒnsəʊl] n (*control desk*) Tech console f.

consolidate [kən'sɒlɪdeɪt] vt consolider; — vi se consolider. ◆**consoli'dation** n consolidation f.

consonant ['kɒnsənənt] n consonne f.

consort 1 ['kɒnsɔːt] n époux m, épouse f; **prince c.** prince m consort. **2** [kən'sɔːt] vi **to c. with** Pej fréquenter.

consortium [kən'sɔːtɪəm] n Com consortium m.

conspicuous [kən'spɪkjʊəs] a visible, en évidence; (*striking*) remarquable, manifeste; (*showy*) voyant; **to be c. by one's absence** briller par son absence; **to make oneself c.** se faire remarquer. ◆**—ly** adv visiblement.

conspire [kən'spaɪər] **1** vi (*plot*) conspirer (**against** contre); **to c. to do** comploter de faire. **2** vt **to c. to do** (*of events*) conspirer à faire. ◆**conspiracy** n conspiration f.

constable ['kʌnstəb(ə)l] n (*police*) **c.** agent m (de police). ◆**con'stabulary** n la police.

constant ['kɒnstənt] a (*frequent*) incessant; (*unchanging*) constant; (*faithful*) fidèle. ◆**constancy** n constance f. ◆**constantly** adv constamment, sans cesse.

constellation [kɒnstə'leɪʃ(ə)n] n constellation f.

consternation [kɒnstə'neɪʃ(ə)n] n consternation f.

constipate ['kɒnstɪpeɪt] vt constiper. ◆**consti'pation** n constipation f.

constituent [kən'stɪtjʊənt] **1** a (*element etc*) constituant, constitutif. **2** n Pol électeur, -trice mf. ◆**constituency** n circonscription f électorale; (*voters*) électeurs mpl.

constitute ['kɒnstɪtjuːt] vt constituer. ◆**consti'tution** n (*of person etc*) & Pol constitution f. ◆**consti'tutional** a Pol constitutionnel.

constrain [kən'streɪn] vt contraindre.

constrict [kən'strɪkt] vt (*tighten, narrow*) resserrer; (*movement*) gêner. ◆**con-'striction** n resserrement m.

construct [kən'strʌkt] vt construire. ◆**construction** n construction f; **under c.** en construction. ◆**constructive** a constructif.

construe [kən'struː] vt interpréter, comprendre.

consul ['kɒnsəl] n consul m. ◆**consular** a consulaire. ◆**consulate** n consulat m.

consult [kən'sʌlt] vt consulter; — vi **to c. with** discuter avec, conférer avec. ◆**—ing** a (*room*) Med de consultation; (*physician*) consultant. ◆**consultancy** n **c.** (*firm*) Com cabinet m d'experts-conseils; **c. fee** honoraires mpl de conseils. ◆**consultant** n conseiller, -ère mf; Med spécialiste mf; (*financial, legal*) conseil m, expert-conseil m; — a (*engineer etc*) consultant. ◆**consul'tation** n consultation f. ◆**consultative** a consultatif.

consum/e [kən'sjuːm] vt (*food, supplies etc*) consommer; (*of fire, grief, hate*) consumer. ◆**—ing** a (*ambition*) brûlant. ◆**—er** n consommateur, -trice mf; **c. goods/society** biens mpl/société f de consommation. ◆**con'sumption** n consommation f (**of** de).

consummate ['kɒnsəmət] a (*perfect*) consommé.

contact ['kɒntækt] n contact m; (*person*) relation f; **in c. with** en contact avec; **c. lenses** lentilles fpl or verres mpl de contact; — vt se mettre en contact avec, contacter.

contagious [kənˈteɪdʒəs] a contagieux.

contain [kənˈteɪn] vt (enclose, hold back) contenir; **to c. oneself** se contenir. ◆**—er** n récipient m; (for transporting freight) conteneur m, container m.

contaminate [kənˈtæmɪneɪt] vt contaminer. ◆**contamiˈnation** n contamination f.

contemplate [ˈkɒntəmpleɪt] vt (look at) contempler; (consider) envisager (doing de faire). ◆**contemˈplation** n contemplation f; **in c.** of en prévision de.

contemporary [kənˈtempərərɪ] a contemporain (with de); — n (person) contemporain, -aine mf.

contempt [kənˈtempt] n mépris m; **to hold in c.** mépriser. ◆**contemptible** a méprisable. ◆**contemptuous** a dédaigneux (of de).

contend [kənˈtend] 1 vi **to c. with** (problem) faire face à; (person) avoir affaire à; (compete) rivaliser avec; (struggle) se battre avec. 2 vt **to c. that** (claim) soutenir que. ◆**—er** n concurrent, -ente mf. ◆**contention** n 1 (argument) dispute f. 2 (claim) affirmation f. ◆**contentious** a (issue) litigieux.

content¹ [ˈkɒntent] a satisfait (with de); **he's c.** to do il ne demande pas mieux que de faire. ◆**—ed** a satisfait. ◆**—ment** n contentement m.

content² [ˈkɒntent] n (of text, film etc) contenu m; pl (of container) contenu m; (table of) **contents** (of book) table f des matières; **alcoholic/iron**/etc **c.** teneur f en alcool/fer/etc.

contest [kənˈtest] vt (dispute) contester; (fight for) disputer; — [ˈkɒntest] n (competition) concours m; (fight) lutte f; Boxing combat m. ◆**conˈtestant** n concurrent, -ente mf; (in fight) adversaire mf.

context [ˈkɒntekst] n contexte m.

continent [ˈkɒntɪnənt] n continent m; **the C.** l'Europe f (continentale). ◆**contiˈnental** a continental; européen; **c. breakfast** petit déjeuner m à la française.

contingent [kənˈtɪndʒənt] 1 a (accidental) contingent; **to be c. upon** dépendre de. 2 nm Mil contingent m. ◆**contingency** n éventualité f; **c. plan** plan m d'urgence.

continue [kənˈtɪnjuː] vt continuer (**to do** or **doing** à or de faire); (resume) reprendre; **to c.** (**with**) (work, speech etc) poursuivre, continuer; — vi continuer; (resume) reprendre; **to c. in** (job) garder. ◆**—ed** a (interest, attention etc) soutenu, assidu; (presence) continu(el); **to be c.** (of story) à suivre. ◆**continual** a continuel. ◆**continually**

adv continuellement. ◆**continuance** n continuation f. ◆**continuˈation** n continuation f; (resumption) reprise f; (new episode) suite f. ◆**continuity** [kɒntɪˈnjuːɪtɪ] n continuité f. ◆**continuous** a continu; **c. performance** Cin spectacle m permanent. ◆**continuously** adv sans interruption.

contort [kənˈtɔːt] vt (twist) tordre; **to c. oneself** se contorsionner. ◆**contortion** n contorsion f. ◆**contortionist** n (acrobat) contorsionniste mf.

contour [ˈkɒntʊər] n contour m.

contraband [ˈkɒntrəbænd] n contrebande f.

contraception [kɒntrəˈsepʃ(ə)n] n contraception f. ◆**contraceptive** a & n contraceptif (m).

contract 1 [ˈkɒntrækt] n contrat m; **c. work** travail m en sous-traitance; — vi **to c. out of** (agreement etc) se dégager de. 2 [kənˈtrækt] vt (habit, debt, muscle etc) contracter; — vi (of heart etc) se contracter. ◆**conˈtraction** n (of muscle, word) contraction f. ◆**conˈtractor** n entrepreneur m.

contradict [kɒntrəˈdɪkt] vt contredire; (belie) démentir. ◆**contradiction** n contradiction f. ◆**contradictory** a contradictoire.

contralto [kənˈtræltəʊ] n (pl -os) contralto m.

contraption [kənˈtræpʃ(ə)n] n Fam machin m, engin m.

contrary [ˈkɒntrərɪ] a contraire (**to** à); — adv **c. to** contrairement à; — n contraire m; **on the c.** au contraire; **unless you, I** etc **hear to the c.** sauf avis contraire; **she said nothing to the c.** elle n'a rien dit contre. 2 [kənˈtreərɪ] a (obstinate) entêté, difficile.

contrast 1 [ˈkɒntrɑːst] n contraste m; **in c. to** par opposition à. 2 [kənˈtrɑːst] vi contraster (with avec); — vt faire contraster, mettre en contraste. ◆**—ing** a (colours etc) opposés.

contravene [kɒntrəˈviːn] vt (law) enfreindre. ◆**contravention** n **in c. of** en contravention de.

contribute [kənˈtrɪbjuːt] vt donner, fournir (**to** à); (article) écrire (**to** pour); **to c. money to** contribuer à, verser de l'argent à; — vi **to c. to** contribuer à; (publication) collaborer à. ◆**contriˈbution** n contribution f; (to pension fund etc) cotisation(s) f(pl); Journ article m. ◆**contributor** n Journ collaborateur, -trice mf; (of money) donateur, -trice mf. ◆**contributory** a **a c. factor** un facteur qui a contribué (**in** à).

contrite [kənˈtraɪt] a contrit. ◆**contrition** n contrition f.

contrive [kənˈtraɪv] vt inventer; **to c. to do**

trouver moyen de faire. ◆**—ed** a artificiel; ◆**contrivance** n (device) dispositif m; (scheme) invention f.

control [kən'trəul] a (-ll-) (business, organization) diriger; (traffic) régler; (prices, quality) contrôler; (emotion, reaction) maîtriser, contrôler; (disease) enrayer; (situation) être maître de; **to c. oneself** se contrôler; – n (authority) autorité f (**over** sur); (of traffic) réglementation f; (of prices etc) contrôle m; (of emotion etc) maîtrise f; pl (of train etc) commandes fpl; (knobs) TV Rad boutons mpl; **the c. of** (fires etc) la lutte contre; (**self-**)**c.** le contrôle de soi-même; **to keep s.o. under c.** tenir qn; **everything is under c.** tout est en ordre; **in c. of** maître de; **to lose c. of** (situation, vehicle) perdre le contrôle de; **out of c.** (situation, crowd) difficilement maîtrisable; **c. tower** Av tour f de contrôle. ◆**controller** n **air traffic c.** aiguilleur m du ciel.

controversy ['kɒntrəvɜːsɪ] n controverse f. ◆**contro'versial** a (book, author) contesté, discuté; (doubtful) discutable.

conundrum [kə'nʌndrəm] n devinette f, énigme f, (mystery) énigme f.

conurbation [kɒnɜː'beɪʃ(ə)n] n agglomération f, conurbation f.

convalesce [kɒnvə'les] vi être en convalescence. ◆**convalescence** n convalescence f. ◆**convalescent** n convalescent, -ente mf; **c. home** maison f de convalescence.

convector [kən'vektər] n radiateur m à convection.

convene [kən'viːn] vt convoquer; – vi se réunir.

convenient [kən'viːnɪənt] a commode, pratique; (well-situated) bien situé (**for the shops**/etc par rapport aux magasins/etc); (moment) convenable, opportun; **to be c. (for)** (suit) convenir (à). ◆**—ly** adv (to arrive) à propos, (be) situated bien situé. ◆**convenience** n commodité f; (comfort) confort m; (advantage) avantage m; **to** or **at one's c.** à sa convenance; **c. food(s)** plats mpl or aliments mpl minute; (**public**) **conveniences** toilettes fpl.

convent ['kɒnvənt] n couvent m.

convention [kən'venʃ(ə)n] n (agreement) & Am Pol convention f; (custom) usage m, convention f; (meeting) Pol assemblée f. ◆**conventional** a conventionnel.

converg/e [kən'vɜːdʒ] vi converger. ◆**—ing** a convergent. ◆**convergence** n convergence f.

conversant [kən'vɜːsənt] a **to be c. with**

(custom etc) connaître; (fact) savoir; (cars etc) s'y connaître en.

conversation [kɒnvə'seɪʃ(ə)n] n conversation f. ◆**conversational** a (tone) de la conversation; (person) loquace. ◆**conversationalist** n causeur, -euse mf.

converse 1 [kən'vɜːs] vi s'entretenir (**with** avec). **2** ['kɒnvɜːs] a & n inverse (m). ◆**con'versely** adv inversement.

convert [kən'vɜːt] vt (change) convertir (**into** en); (building) aménager (**into** en); **to c. s.o.** convertir qn (**to** à); – ['kɒnvɜːt] n converti, -ie mf. ◆**con'version** n conversion f; aménagement m. ◆**con'vertible** a convertible; – n (car) (voiture f) décapotable f.

convex ['kɒnveks] a convexe.

convey [kən'veɪ] vt (goods, people) transporter; (sound, message, order) transmettre; (idea) communiquer; (evoke) évoquer; (water etc through pipes) amener. ◆**conveyance** n transport m; Aut véhicule m. ◆**conveyor** a **c. belt** tapis m roulant.

convict [kən'vɪkt] n forçat m; – [kən'vɪkt] vt déclarer coupable, condamner. ◆**con'viction** n Jur condamnation f; (belief) conviction f; **to carry c.** (of argument etc) être convaincant.

convinc/e [kən'vɪns] vt convaincre, persuader. ◆**—ing** a convaincant. ◆**—ingly** adv de façon convaincante.

convivial [kən'vɪvɪəl] a joyeux, gai; (person) bon vivant.

convoke [kən'vəuk] vt (meeting etc) convoquer.

convoluted [kɒnvə'luːtɪd] a (argument, style) compliqué, tarabiscoté.

convoy ['kɒnvɔɪ] n (ships, cars, people) convoi m.

convulse [kən'vʌls] vt bouleverser, ébranler; (face) convulser. ◆**convulsion** n convulsion f. ◆**convulsive** a convulsif.

coo [kuː] vi (of dove) roucouler.

cook [kuk] vt (faire) cuire; (accounts) Fam truquer; **to c. up** Fam inventer; – vi (of food) cuire; (of person) faire la cuisine; **what's cooking?** Fam qu'est-ce qui se passe?; – n (person) cuisinier, -ière mf. ◆**—ing** n cuisine f; **c. apple** pomme f à cuire. ◆**—er** n (stove) cuisinière f; (apple) pomme f à cuire. ◆**cookbook** n livre m de cuisine. ◆**cookery** n cuisine f; **c. book** livre m de cuisine.

cookie ['kukɪ] n Am biscuit m, gâteau m sec.

cool [kuːl] a (-er, -est) (weather, place etc) frais; (manner, person) calme; (reception etc) froid; (impertinent) Fam effronté; **I feel**

c. j'ai (un peu) froid; **a c. drink** une boisson fraîche; **a c. £50** la coquette somme de 50 livres; — *n (of evening)* fraîcheur *f*; **to keep (in the) c.** tenir au frais; **to keep/lose one's c.** garder/perdre son sang-froid; — *vt* **c. (down)** refroidir, rafraîchir; — *vi* **to c. (down or off)** *(of enthusiasm)* se refroidir; *(of anger, angry person)* se calmer; *(of hot liquid)* refroidir; **to c. off** *(refresh oneself by drinking, bathing etc)* se rafraîchir; **to c. towards s.o.** se refroidir envers qn. ◆—**ing** *n (of air, passion etc)* refroidissement *m*. ◆—**er** *n (for food)* glacière *f*. ◆—**ly** *adv* calmement; *(to welcome)* froidement; *(boldly)* effrontément. ◆—**ness** *n* fraîcheur *f*; *(unfriendliness)* froideur *f*. ◆**cool-'headed** *a* calme.

coop [kuːp] **1** *n (for chickens)* poulailler *m*. **2** *vt* **to c. up** *(person)* enfermer.

co-op ['kəʊɒp] *n Am* appartement *m* en copropriété.

co-operate [kəʊ'ɒpəreɪt] *vi* coopérer **(in** à, **with** avec). ◆**co-ope'ration** *n* coopération *f*. ◆**co-operative** *a* coopératif; — *n* coopérative *f*.

co-opt [kəʊ'ɒpt] *vt* coopter.

co-ordinate [kəʊ'ɔːdɪneɪt] *vt* coordonner. ◆**co-ordinates** *npl Math* coordonnées *fpl*; *(clothes)* coordonnés *mpl*. ◆**co-ordi'nation** *n* coordination *f*.

cop [kɒp] **1** *n (policeman) Fam* flic *m*. **2** *vt* (**-pp-**) *(catch) Sl* piquer. **3** *vi* (**-pp-**) **to c. out** *Sl* se défiler, éviter ses responsabilités.

cope [kəʊp] *vi* **to c. with** s'occuper de; *(problem)* faire face à; **to be able) to c.** *(manage)* se débrouiller.

co-pilot ['kəʊpaɪlət] *n* copilote *m*.

copious ['kəʊpɪəs] *a* copieux.

copper ['kɒpər] *n* **1** cuivre *m*; *pl (coins)* petite monnaie *f*. **2** *(policeman) Fam* flic *m*.

coppice ['kɒpɪs] *n*, ◆**copse** [kɒps] *n* taillis *m*.

copulate ['kɒpjuleɪt] *vi* s'accoupler. ◆**copu'lation** *n* copulation *f*.

copy ['kɒpɪ] *n* copie *f*; *(of book etc)* exemplaire *m*; *Phot* épreuve *f*; — *vti* copier; — *vt* **to c. out** *or* **down** (re)copier. ◆**copyright** *n* copyright *m*.

coral ['kɒrəl] *n* corail *m*; **c. reef** récif *m* de corail.

cord [kɔːd] *n* **1** *(of curtain, pyjamas etc)* cordon *m*; *El* cordon *m* électrique; **vocal cords** cordes *fpl* vocales. **2** *Fam* velours *m*, pantalon *m* en velours (côtelé).

cordial ['kɔːdɪəl] *a* **1** *(friendly)* cordial. **2** *(fruit)* **c.** sirop *m*.

cordon ['kɔːdən] *n* cordon *m*; — *vt* **to c. off** *(place)* boucler, interdire l'accès à.

corduroy ['kɔːdərɔɪ] *n (fabric)* velours *m* côtelé; *pl* pantalon *m* en velours (côtelé), velours *m*.

core [kɔːr] *n (of fruit)* trognon *m*; *(of problem)* cœur *m*; *(group of people) & Geol* El noyau *m*; — *vt (apple)* vider. ◆**corer** *n* vide-pomme *m*.

cork [kɔːk] *n (material)* liège *m*; *(for bottle)* bouchon *m*; — *vt* **to c. (up)** *(bottle)* boucher. ◆**corkscrew** *n* tire-bouchon *m*.

corn [kɔːn] *n* **1** *(wheat)* blé *m*; *(maize) Am* maïs *m*; *(seed)* grain *m*; **c. on the cob** épi *m* de maïs. **2** *(hard skin)* cor *m*. ◆**corned** *a* **c. beef** corned-beef *m*, singe *m*. ◆**cornflakes** *npl* céréales *fpl*. ◆**cornflour** *n* farine *f* de maïs, maïzena® *f*. ◆**cornflower** *n* bleuet *m*. ◆**cornstarch** *n Am* = cornflour.

cornea ['kɔːnɪə] *n Anat* cornée *f*.

corner ['kɔːnər] *n* **1** coin *m*; *(of street, room)* coin *m*, angle *m*; *(bend in road)* virage *m*; *Fb* corner *m*; **in a (tight) c.** dans une situation difficile. **2** *vt (animal, enemy etc)* acculer; *(person in corridor etc) Fig* coincer, accrocher; *(market) Com* accaparer; — *vi Aut* prendre un virage. ◆**cornerstone** *n* pierre *f* angulaire.

cornet ['kɔːnɪt] *n (of ice cream etc) & Mus* cornet *m*.

Cornwall ['kɔːnwəl] *n* Cornouailles *fpl*. ◆**Cornish** *a* de Cornouailles.

corny ['kɔːnɪ] *a* (**-ier, -iest**) *(joke etc)* rebattu.

corollary [kə'rɒlərɪ, *Am* 'kɒrələrɪ] *n* corollaire *m*.

coronary ['kɒrənərɪ] *n Med* infarctus *m*.

coronation [kɒrə'neɪʃ(ə)n] *n* couronnement *m*, sacre *m*.

coroner ['kɒrənər] *n Jur* coroner *m*.

corporal ['kɔːpərəl] *n* **1** *Mil* caporal(-chef) *m*. **2 a c. punishment** châtiment *m* corporel.

corporation [kɔːpə'reɪʃ(ə)n] *n (business)* société *f* commerciale; *(of town)* conseil *m* municipal. ◆'**corporate** *a* collectif; **c. body** corps *m* constitué.

corps [kɔːr, *pl* kɔːz] *n Mil Pol* corps *m*.

corpse [kɔːps] *n* cadavre *m*.

corpulent ['kɔːpjulənt] *a* corpulent. ◆**corpulence** *n* corpulence *f*.

corpus ['kɔːpəs] *n Ling* corpus *m*.

corpuscle ['kɔːpʌs(ə)l] *n Med* globule *m*.

corral [kə'ræl] *n Am* corral *m*.

correct [kə'rekt] *a (right, accurate)* exact, correct; *(proper)* correct; **he's c.** il a raison; — *vt* corriger. ◆—**ly** *adv* correctement.

◆**—ness** n (*accuracy, propriety*) correction f. ◆**correction** n correction f. ◆**corrective** a (*act, measure*) rectificatif.

correlate ['kɒrəleɪt] vi correspondre (**with** à); — vt faire correspondre. ◆**corre'lation** n corrélation f.

correspond [kɒrɪ'spɒnd] vi **1** (*agree, be similar*) correspondre (**to** à, **with** avec). **2** (*by letter*) correspondre (**with** avec). ◆**—ing** a (*matching*) semblable. ◆**correspondence** n correspondance f; **c. course** cours m par correspondance. ◆**correspondent** n correspondant, -ante mf; *Journ* envoyé, -ée mf.

corridor ['kɒrɪdɔːr] n couloir m, corridor m.

corroborate [kə'rɒbəreɪt] vt corroborer.

corrode [kə'rəʊd] vt ronger, corroder; — vi se corroder. ◆**corrosion** n corrosion f. ◆**corrosive** a corrosif.

corrugated ['kɒrəgeɪtɪd] a (*cardboard*) ondulé; **c. iron** tôle f ondulée.

corrupt [kə'rʌpt] vt corrompre; — a corrompu. ◆**corruption** n corruption f.

corset ['kɔːsɪt] n (*boned*) corset m; (*elasticated*) gaine f.

Corsica ['kɔːsɪkə] n Corse f.

cos [kɒs] n c. (**lettuce**) (laitue f) romaine f.

cosh [kɒʃ] n matraque f; — vt matraquer.

cosiness ['kəʊzɪnəs] n intimité f, confort m.

cosmetic [kɒz'metɪk] n produit m de beauté; — a esthétique, *Fig* superficiel.

cosmopolitan [kɒzmə'pɒlɪtən] a & n cosmopolite (mf).

cosmos ['kɒzmɒs] n cosmos m. ◆**cosmic** a cosmique. ◆**cosmonaut** n cosmonaute mf.

Cossack ['kɒsæk] n cosaque m.

cosset ['kɒsɪt] vt choyer.

cost [kɒst] vti (pt & pp **cost**) coûter; **how much does it c.?** ça coûte or ça vaut combien?; **to c. the earth** *Fam* coûter les yeux de la tête; — n coût m, prix m; **at great c.** à grands frais; **to my c.** à mes dépens; **at any c.**, **at all costs** à tout prix; **at c. price** au prix coûtant. ◆**c.-effective** a rentable. ◆**costly** a (*-ier, -iest*) (*expensive*) coûteux; (*valuable*) précieux.

co-star ['kəʊstɑːr] n *Cin Th* partenaire mf.

costume ['kɒstjuːm] n costume m; (*woman's suit*) tailleur m; (*swimming*) c. maillot m (de bain); **c. jewellery** bijoux mpl de fantaisie.

cosy ['kəʊzɪ] **1** a (*-ier, -iest*) douillet, intime; **make yourself (nice and) c.** mets-toi à l'aise; **we're c.** on est bien ici. **2** n (*tea*) c. couvre-théière m.

cot [kɒt] n lit m d'enfant; (*camp bed*) *Am* lit m de camp.

cottage ['kɒtɪdʒ] n petite maison f de campagne; (**thatched**) c. chaumière f; **c. cheese** fromage m blanc (maigre); **c. industry** travail m à domicile (activité artisanale).

cotton ['kɒtən] **1** n coton m; (*yarn*) fil m (de coton); **absorbent c.** *Am*, **c. wool** coton m hydrophile, ouate f; **c. candy** *Am* barbe f à papa. **2** vi **to c. on** *(to)* *Sl* piger.

couch [kaʊtʃ] **1** n canapé m. **2** vt (*express*) formuler.

couchette [kuːʃet] n *Rail* couchette f.

cough [kɒf] **1** n toux f; **c. mixture** sirop m contre la toux; — vi tousser; — vt **to c. up** (*blood*) cracher. **2** vt **c. up** (*money*) *Sl* cracher; — vi **to c. up** *Sl* payer, casquer.

could [kʊd, *unstressed* kəd] see **can¹**.

couldn't ['kʊd(ə)nt] = **could not**.

council ['kaʊns(ə)l] n conseil m; **c. flat/house** appartement m/maison f loué(e) à la municipalité, HLM m or f. ◆**councillor** n conseiller, -ère mf; (**town**) c. conseiller m municipal.

counsel ['kaʊnsəl] n (*advice*) conseil m; *Jur* avocat, -ate mf; — vt (**-ll-**, *Am* **-l-**) conseiller (**s.o. to do** à qn de faire). ◆**counsellor** n conseiller, -ère mf.

count¹ [kaʊnt] vt (*find number of, include*) compter; (*deem*) considérer; **not counting Paul** sans compter Paul; **to c. in** (*include*) inclure; **to c. out** exclure; (*money*) compter; — vi (*calculate, be important*) compter; **to c. against s.o.** être un désavantage pour qn, jouer contre qn; **to c. on s.o.** (*rely on*) compter sur qn; **to c. on doing** compter faire; — n compte m; *Jur* chef m (d'accusation); **he's lost c. of the books he has** il ne sait plus combien il a de livres. ◆**countdown** n compte m à rebours.

count² [kaʊnt] n (*title*) comte m.

countenance ['kaʊntɪnəns] **1** n (*face*) mine f, expression f. **2** vt (*allow*) tolérer; (*approve*) approuver.

counter ['kaʊntər] **1** n (*in shop, bar etc*) comptoir m; (*in bank etc*) guichet m; **under the c.** *Fig* clandestinement, au marché noir; **over the c.** (*to obtain medicine*) sans ordonnance. **2** n (*in games*) jeton m. **3** n *Tech* compteur m. **4** adv **c. to** à l'encontre de. **5** vt (*plan*) contrarier; (*insult*) riposter à; (*blow*) parer; — vi riposter (**with** par).

counter- ['kaʊntər] pref contre-.

counterattack ['kaʊntərətæk] n contre-attaque f; — vti contre-attaquer.

counterbalance ['kaʊntəbæləns] n contrepoids m; — vt contrebalancer.

counterclockwise [kaʊntə'klɒkwaɪz] *a* & *adv Am* dans le sens inverse des aiguilles d'une montre.

counterfeit ['kaʊntəfɪt] *a* faux; – *n* contrefaçon *f*, faux *m*; – *vt* contrefaire.

counterfoil ['kaʊntəfɔɪl] *n* souche *f*.

counterpart ['kaʊntəpɑːt] *n* (*thing*) équivalent *m*; (*person*) homologue *mf*.

counterpoint ['kaʊntəpɔɪnt] *n Mus* contrepoint *m*.

counterproductive [kaʊntəprə'dʌktɪv] *a* (*action*) inefficace, qui produit l'effet contraire.

countersign ['kaʊntəsaɪn] *vt* contresigner.

countess ['kaʊntɪs] *n* comtesse *f*.

countless ['kaʊntləs] *a* innombrable.

countrified ['kʌntrɪfaɪd] *a* rustique.

country ['kʌntrɪ] *n* pays *m*; (*region*) région *f*, pays *m*; (*homeland*) patrie *f*; (*opposed to town*) campagne *f*; – *a* (*house etc*) de campagne; **c. dancing** la danse folklorique. ◆**countryman** *n* (*pl* -**men**) (*fellow*) **c.** compatriote *m*. ◆**countryside** *n* campagne *f*.

county ['kaʊntɪ] *n* comté *m*; **c. seat** *Am*, **c. town** chef-lieu *m*.

coup [kuː, *pl* kuːz] *n Pol* coup *m* d'État.

couple ['kʌp(ə)l] **1** *n* (*of people, animals*) couple *m*; (*of two or three*); (*a few*) quelques; **2** *vt* (*connect*) accoupler. **3** *vi* (*mate*) s'accoupler.

coupon ['kuːpɒn] *n* (*voucher*) bon *m*; (*ticket*) coupon *m*.

courage ['kʌrɪdʒ] *n* courage *m*. ◆**courageous** [kə'reɪdʒəs] *a* courageux.

courgette [kʊə'ʒet] *n* courgette *f*.

courier ['kʊrɪər] *n* (*for tourists*) guide *m*; (*messenger*) messager *m*; **c. service** service *m* de messagerie.

course [kɔːs] **1** *n* (*duration, movement*) cours *m*; (*of ship*) route *f*; (*of river*) cours *m*; (*way*) voie *f*; (*means*) moyen *m*; (*of action*) ligne *f* de conduite; (*path*) parti *m*; **your best c. is to** . . . le mieux c'est de . . . ; **as a matter of c.** normalement; **in (the) c. of time** avec le temps, à la longue; **in due c.** en temps utile. **2** *n Sch Univ* cours *m*; **c. of lectures** série *f* de conférences; (*of treatment*) *Med* traitement *m*. **3** *n Culin* plat *m*; **first c.** entrée *f*. **4** *n* (*racecourse*) champ *m* de courses; (*golf*) **c.** terrain *m* (de golf). **5** *adv* **of c.!** bien sûr!, mais oui!; (de **c. not!** bien sûr que non!

court [kɔːt] **1** *n* (*of monarch*) cour *f*; *Jur* cour *f*, tribunal *m*; *Tennis* court *m*; **c. of enquiry** commission *f* d'enquête; **high c.** cour *f* suprême; **to take to c.** poursuivre en justice; **c. shoe** escarpin *m*. **2** *vt* (*woman*) faire la cour à; (*danger, support*) rechercher. ◆**-ing** *a* (*couple*) d'amoureux; **they are c.** ils sortent ensemble. ◆**courthouse** *n* palais *m* de justice. ◆**courtier** *n Hist* courtisan *m*. ◆**courtroom** *n* salle *f* du tribunal. ◆**courtship** *n* (*act, period of time*) cour *f*. ◆**courtyard** *n* cour *f*.

courteous ['kɜːtɪəs] *a* poli, courtois. ◆**courtesy** *n* politesse *f*, courtoisie *f*.

court-martial [kɔːt'mɑːʃəl] *n* conseil *m* de guerre; – *vt* (-**ll**-) faire passer en conseil de guerre.

cousin ['kʌz(ə)n] *n* cousin, -ine *mf*.

cove [kəʊv] *n* (*bay*) *Geog* anse *f*.

covenant ['kʌvənənt] *n Jur* convention *f*; *Rel* alliance *f*.

Coventry ['kɒvəntrɪ] *n* **to send s.o. to C.** *Fig* mettre qn en quarantaine.

cover ['kʌvər] *n* (*lid*) couvercle *m*; (*of book*) & *Fin* couverture *f*; (*for furniture, typewriter*) housse *f*; (*bedspread*) dessus-de-lit *m*; **the covers** (*blankets*) les couvertures *fpl*; **to take c.** se mettre à l'abri; **c. charge** (*in restaurant*) couvert *m*; **c. note** certificat *m* provisoire d'assurance; **under separate c.** (*letter*) sous pli séparé; – *vt* couvrir; (*protect*) protéger, couvrir; (*distance*) parcourir, couvrir; (*include*) englober, recouvrir; (*treat*) traiter; (*event*) *Journ TV Rad* couvrir, faire le reportage de; (*aim gun at*) tenir en joue; (*insure*) assurer; **to c. over** recouvrir; **to c. up** recouvrir; (*truth, tracks*) dissimuler; (*scandal*) étouffer, camoufler; – *vi* **to c. (oneself) up** se couvrir; **to c. up for s.o.** couvrir qn. ◆**c.-up** *n* tentative *f* pour étouffer *or* camoufler une affaire. ◆**covering** *n* (*wrapping*) enveloppe *f*; (*layer*) couche *f*; **c. letter** lettre *f* jointe (à un document).

coveralls ['kʌvərɔːlz] *npl Am* bleus *mpl* de travail.

covert ['kʌvət, 'kəʊvət] *a* secret.

covet ['kʌvɪt] *vt* convoiter. ◆**covetous** *a* avide.

cow [kaʊ] **1** *n* vache *f*; (*of elephant etc*) femelle *f*; (*nasty woman*) *Fam* chameau *m*. **2** *vt* (*person*) intimider. ◆**cowboy** *n* cow-boy *m*. ◆**cowhand** *n* vacher, -ère *mf*. ◆**cowshed** *n* étable *f*.

coward ['kaʊəd] *n* lâche *mf*. ◆**-ly** *a* lâche. ◆**cowardice** *n* lâcheté *f*.

cower ['kaʊər] *vi* (*crouch*) se tapir; (*with fear*) *Fig* reculer (par peur).

cowslip ['kaʊslɪp] *n Bot* coucou *m*.

cox [kɒks] *vt Nau* barrer; *– n* barreur, -euse *mf*.

coy [kɔɪ] *a* (-er, -est) qui fait son *ou* sa timide. **◆coyness** *n* timidité *f*.

coyote [kaɪˈəʊtɪ] *n* (*wolf*) *Am* coyote *m*.

cozy [ˈkəʊzɪ] *Am* = **cosy**.

crab [kræb] **1** *n* crabe *m*. **2** *n* **c. apple** pomme *f* sauvage. **3** *vi* (-bb-) (*complain*) *Fam* rouspéter. **◆crabbed** *a* (*person*) grincheux.

crack[1] [kræk] *n* (*fissure*) fente *f*; (*in glass etc*) fêlure *f*; (*in skin*) crevasse *f*; (*snapping noise*) craquement *m*; (*of whip*) claquement *m*; (*blow*) coup *m*; (*joke*) *Fam* plaisanterie *f* (**at** aux dépens de); **to have a c. at doing** *Fam* essayer de faire; **at the c. of dawn** au point du jour; *– vt* (*glass, ice*) fêler; (*nut*) casser; (*ground, skin*) crevasser; (*whip*) faire claquer; (*joke*) lancer; (*problem*) résoudre; (*code*) déchiffrer; (*safe*) percer; **it's not as hard as it's cracked up to be** ce n'est pas aussi dur qu'on le dit; *– vi* se fêler; se crevasser; (*of branch, wood*) craquer; **to get cracking** (*get to work*) *Fam* s'y mettre; (*hurry*) se grouiller; **to c. down on** sévir contre; **to c. up** (*mentally*) *Fam* craquer. **◆c.-up** *n Fam* dépression *f* nerveuse; (*crash*) *Am Fam* accident *m*. **◆cracked** *a* (*crazy*) *Fam* fou. **◆cracker** *n* **1** (*cake*) biscuit *m* (salé). **2** (*firework*) pétard *m*; **Christmas c.** diablotin *m*. **3 she's a c.** *Fam* elle est sensationnelle. **◆crackers** *a* (*mad*) *Sl* cinglé. **◆crackpot** *a Fam* fou; *– n* fou *m*, folle *f*.

crack[2] [kræk] *a* (*first-rate*) de premier ordre; **c. shot** tireur m d'élite.

crackle [ˈkræk(ə)l] *vi* crépiter; (*of sth frying*) *Culin* grésiller; *– n* crépitement *m*; grésillement *m*.

cradle [ˈkreɪd(ə)l] *n* berceau *m*; *– vt* bercer.

craft [krɑːft] **1** *n* (*skill*) art *m*; (*job*) métier *m* (artisanal); *– vt* façonner. **2** *n* (*cunning*) ruse *f*. **3** *n inv* (*boat*) bateau *m*. **◆craftsman** *n* (*pl* -men) artisan *m*. **◆craftsmanship** *n* (*skill*) art *m*; **a piece of c.** un beau travail, une belle pièce. **◆crafty** *a* (-ier, -iest) astucieux; *Pej* rusé.

crag [kræg] *n* rocher *m* à pic. **◆craggy** *a* (*rock*) à pic; (*face*) rude.

cram [kræm] *vt* (-mm-) **to c. into** (*force*) fourrer dans; **to c. with** (*fill*) bourrer de; *– vi* **to c. into** (*of people*) s'entasser dans; **to c.** (**for an exam**) bachoter.

cramp [kræmp] *n Med* crampe *f* (**in** à). **◆cramped** *a* (*in a room or one's clothes*) à l'étroit; **in c. conditions** à l'étroit.

cranberry [ˈkrænbərɪ] *n Bot* canneberge *f*.

crane [kreɪn] **1** *n* (*bird*) & *Tech* grue *f*. **2** *vt* **to c. one's neck** tendre le cou.

crank [kræŋk] **1** *n* (*person*) *Fam* excentrique *mf*; (*fanatic*) fanatique *mf*. **2** *n* (*handle*) *Tech* manivelle *f*; *– vt* **to c. (up)** (*vehicle*) faire démarrer à la manivelle. **◆cranky** *a* (-ier, -iest) excentrique; (*bad-tempered*) *Am* grincheux.

crannies [ˈkrænɪz] *npl* **nooks and c.** coins et recoins *mpl*.

craps [kræps] *n* **to shoot c.** *Am* jouer aux dés.

crash [kræʃ] *n* accident *m*; (*of firm*) faillite *f*; (*noise*) fracas *m*; (*of thunder*) coup *m*; **c. course/diet** cours *m*/régime *m* intensif; **c. helmet** casque *m* (anti-choc); **c. landing** atterrissage *m* en catastrophe; *– int* (*of fallen object*) patatras!; *– vt* (*car*) avoir un accident avec; **to c. one's car into** faire rentrer sa voiture dans; *– vi Aut Av* s'écraser; **to c. into** rentrer dans; **the cars crashed** (**into each other**) les voitures se sont percutées *ou* carambolées; **to c. (down)** tomber; (*break*) se casser; (*of roof*) s'effondrer. **◆c.-land** *vi* atterrir en catastrophe.

crass [kræs] *a* grossier; (*stupidity*) crasse.

crate [kreɪt] *n* caisse *f*, cageot *m*.

crater [ˈkreɪtər] *n* cratère *m*; (*bomb*) *c.* entonnoir *m*.

cravat [krəˈvæt] *n* foulard *m* (autour du cou).

crav/e [kreɪv] *vt* **to c. (for)** éprouver un grand besoin de; (*mercy*) implorer. **◆—ing** *n* désir *m*, grand besoin *m* (**for** de).

craven [ˈkreɪvən] *a Pej* lâche.

crawl [krɔːl] *vi* ramper; (*of child*) se traîner (à quatre pattes); *Aut* avancer au pas; **to be crawling with** grouiller de; *– n Swimming* crawl *m*; **to move at a c.** *Aut* avancer au pas.

crayfish [ˈkreɪfɪʃ] *n inv* écrevisse *f*.

crayon [ˈkreɪən] *n* crayon *m*, pastel *m*.

craze [kreɪz] *n* manie *f* (**for** de), engouement *m* (**for** pour). **◆crazed** *a* affolé.

crazy [ˈkreɪzɪ] *a* (-ier, -iest) fou; **c. about sth** fana de qch; **c. about s.o.** fou de qn; **c. paving** dallage *m* irrégulier. **◆craziness** *n* folie *f*.

creak [kriːk] *vi* (*of hinge*) grincer; (*of timber*) craquer. **◆creaky** *a* grinçant; qui craque.

cream [kriːm] *n* crème *f*; (*élite*) *Fig* crème *f*, gratin *m*; *– a* (*cake*) à la crème; **c.(-coloured)** crème *inv*; **c. cheese** fromage *m* blanc; *– vt* (*milk*) écrémer; **to c. off** *Fig* écrémer. **◆creamy** *a* (-ier, -iest) crémeux.

crease [kriːs] *vt* froisser, plisser; *– vi* se froisser; *– n* pli *m*; (*accidental*) (faux) pli *m*. **◆c.-resistant** *a* infroissable.

create [kriːˈeɪt] vt créer; (*impression, noise*) faire. ◆**creation** n création f. ◆**creative** a créateur, créatif. ◆**creativeness** n créativité f. ◆**crea'tivity** n créativité f. ◆**creator** n créateur, -trice mf.

creature [ˈkriːtʃər] n animal m, bête f; (*person*) créature f; **one's c. comforts** ses aises fpl.

crèche [kreʃ] n (*nursery*) crèche f; (*manger*) Rel Am crèche f.

credence [ˈkriːdəns] n **to give** or **lend c. to** ajouter foi à.

credentials [krɪˈdenʃəlz] npl références fpl; (*identity*) pièces fpl d'identité; (*of diplomat*) lettres fpl de créance.

credible [ˈkredɪb(ə)l] a croyable; (*politician, information*) crédible. ◆**credi'bility** n crédibilité f.

credit [ˈkredɪt] n (*influence, belief*) & Fin crédit m; (*merit*) mérite m; Univ unité f de valeur; **to give c. to** (*person*) Fin faire crédit à; Fig reconnaître le mérite de; (*statement*) ajouter foi à; **to be a c. to** faire honneur à; **on c.** à crédit; **in c.** (*account*) créditeur; **to one's c.** Fig à son actif; − a (*balance*) créditeur; **c. card** carte f de crédit; **c. facilities** facilités fpl de paiement; − vt (*believe*) croire; Fin créditer (**s.o. with sth** qn de qch); **to c. s.o. with** (*qualities*) attribuer à qn. ◆**creditable** a honorable. ◆**creditor** n créancier, -ière mf. ◆**creditworthy** a solvable.

credulous [ˈkredjʊləs] a crédule.

creed [kriːd] n credo m.

creek [kriːk] n (*bay*) crique f; (*stream*) Am ruisseau m; **up the c.** (*in trouble*) Sl dans le pétrin.

creep [kriːp] **1** vi (pt & pp **crept**) ramper; (*silently*) se glisser (furtivement); (*slowly*) avancer lentement; **it makes my flesh c.** ça me donne la chair de poule. **2** n (*person*) Sl salaud m; **it gives me the creeps** Fam ça me fait froid dans le dos. ◆**creepy** a (-ier, -iest) Fam terrifiant; (*nasty*) Fam vilain. ◆**creepy-'crawly** n Fam, Am **creepy-'crawler** n Fam bestiole f.

cremate [krɪˈmeɪt] vt incinérer. ◆**cremation** n crémation f. ◆**crema'torium** n crématorium m. ◆**crematory** n Am crématorium m.

Creole [ˈkriːəʊl] n créole mf; Ling créole m.

crêpe [kreɪp] n (*fabric*) crêpe m; **c.** (*rubber*) crêpe m; **c. paper** papier m crêpon.

crept [krept] see **creep 1**.

crescendo [krɪˈʃendəʊ] n (pl -os) crescendo m inv.

crescent [ˈkres(ə)nt] n croissant m; (*street*) Fig rue f (en demi-lune).

cress [kres] n cresson m.

crest [krest] n (*of bird, wave, mountain*) crête f; (*of hill*) sommet m; (*on seal, letters etc*) armoiries fpl.

Crete [kriːt] n Crète f.

cretin [ˈkretɪn, Am ˈkriːt(ə)n] n crétin, -ine mf. ◆**cretinous** a crétinous f.

crevasse [krɪˈvæs] n (*in ice*) Geol crevasse f.

crevice [ˈkrevɪs] n (*crack*) crevasse f, fente f.

crew [kruː] n Nau Av équipage m; (*gang*) équipe f; **c. cut** coupe f en brosse f; **c.-neck(ed)** a à col ras.

crib [krɪb] **1** n (*cradle*) berceau m; (*cot*) Am lit m d'enfant; Rel crèche f. **2** n (*copy*) plagiat m; Sch traduction f; (*list of answers*) Sch pompe f anti-sèche; − vti (-bb-) copier.

crick [krɪk] n **c. in the neck** torticolis m; **c. in the back** tour m de reins.

cricket [ˈkrɪkɪt] n **1** (*game*) cricket m. **2** (*insect*) grillon m. ◆**cricketer** n joueur, -euse mf de cricket.

crikey! [ˈkraɪkɪ] int Sl zut (alors)!

crime [kraɪm] n crime m; (*not serious*) délit m; (*criminal practice*) criminalité f. ◆**criminal** a & n criminel, -elle (mf).

crimson [ˈkrɪmz(ə)n] a & n cramoisi (m).

cringe [krɪndʒ] vi reculer (from devant); Fig s'humilier (**to, before** devant). ◆**-ing** a Fig servile.

crinkle [ˈkrɪŋk(ə)l] vt froisser; − vi se froisser; − n fronce f. ◆**crinkly** a froissé; (*hair*) frisé.

crippl/e [ˈkrɪpəl] n (*lame*) estropié, -ée mf; (*disabled*) infirme mf; − vt estropier; (*disable*) rendre infirme; (*nation etc*) Fig paralyser. ◆**-ed** a estropié; infirme; (*ship*) désemparé; **c. with** (*rheumatism, pains*) perclus de; (*a tax*) écrasant. ◆**-ing** a (*tax*) écrasant.

crisis, pl **-ses** [ˈkraɪsɪs, -siːz] n crise f.

crisp [krɪsp] a (-er, -est) (*biscuit*) croustillant; (*apple etc*) croquant; (*snow*) craquant; (*air, style*) vif. **2** npl (*potato*) **crisps** (*pommes fpl*) chips mpl. ◆**crispbread** n pain m suédois.

criss-cross [ˈkrɪskrɒs] a (*lines*) entrecroisés; (*muddled*) enchevêtrés; − vi s'entrecroiser; − vt sillonner (en tous sens).

criterion, pl **-ia** [kraɪˈtɪərɪən, -ɪə] n critère m.

critic [ˈkrɪtɪk] n critique m. ◆**critical** a critique. ◆**critically** adv (*to examine etc*) en critique; (*harshly*) sévèrement; (*ill*) gravement. ◆**criticism** n critique f. ◆**criticize** vti critiquer. ◆**cri'tique** n (*essay etc*) critique f.

croak [krəʊk] vi (of frog) croasser; – n croassement m.

crochet ['krəʊʃeɪ] vt faire au crochet; – vi faire du crochet; – n (travail m au) crochet m; c. hook crochet m.

crock [krɒk] n a c., an (old) c. Fam (person) un croulant; (car) un tacot.

crockery ['krɒkərɪ] n (cups etc) vaisselle f.

crocodile ['krɒkədaɪl] n crocodile m.

crocus ['krəʊkəs] n crocus m.

crony ['krəʊnɪ] n Pej Fam copain m, copine f.

crook [krʊk] n 1 (thief) escroc m. 2 (shepherd's stick) houlette f.

crooked ['krʊkɪd] a courbé; (path) tortueux; (hat, picture) de travers; (deal, person) malhonnête; – adv de travers. ◆–ly adv de travers.

croon [kruːn] vti chanter (à voix basse).

crop [krɒp] n 1 (harvest) récolte f; (produce) culture f; (of questions etc) Fig série f; (of people) groupe m. 2 vt (-pp-) (hair) couper (ras); – n c. of hair chevelure f. 3 vi (-pp-) to c. up se présenter, survenir. ◆**cropper** n to come a c. Sl (fall) ramasser une pelle; (fail) échouer.

croquet ['krəʊkeɪ] n (game) croquet m.

croquette [krəʊˈket] n Culin croquette f.

cross[1] [krɒs] 1 n croix f; a c. between (animal) un croisement entre or de. 2 vt traverser; (threshold, barrier) franchir; (legs, animals) croiser; (thwart) contrecarrer; (cheque) barrer; to c. off or out rayer; it never crossed my mind that . . . il ne m'est pas venu à l'esprit que . . .; crossed lines Tel lignes fpl embrouillées; – vi (of paths) se croiser; to c. (over) traverser. ◆–ing n Nau traversée f; (pedestrian) c. passage m clouté. ◆**cross-breed** n métis, -isse mf, hybride m. ◆**c.-'country** a à travers champs; **c.-country race** cross(-country) m. ◆**c.-exami'nation** n contre-interrogatoire m. ◆**c.-e'xamine** vt interroger. ◆**c.-eyed** a qui louche. ◆**c.-'legged** a & adv les jambes croisées. ◆**c.-'purposes** npl to be at c.-purposes se comprendre mal. ◆**c.-'reference** n renvoi m. ◆**c.-section** n coupe f transversale; Fig échantillon m.

cross[2] [krɒs] a (angry) fâché (with contre). ◆–ly adv d'un air fâché.

crossbow ['krɒsbəʊ] n arbalète f.

crosscheck [krɒs'tʃek] n contre-épreuve f; – vt vérifier.

crossfire ['krɒsfaɪər] n feux mpl croisés.

crossroads ['krɒsrəʊdz] n carrefour m.

crosswalk ['krɒswɔːk] n Am passage m clouté.

crossword ['krɒswɜːd] n c. (puzzle) mots mpl croisés.

crotch [krɒtʃ] n (of garment) entre-jambes m inv.

crotchet ['krɒtʃɪt] n Mus noire f.

crotchety ['krɒtʃɪtɪ] a grincheux.

crouch [kraʊtʃ] vi to c. (down) s'accroupir, se tapir. ◆–ing a accroupi, tapi.

croupier ['kruːpɪər] n (in casino) croupier m.

crow [krəʊ] 1 n corbeau m, corneille f; as the c. flies à vol d'oiseau; c.'s nest Nau nid m de pie. 2 vi (of cock) chanter; (boast) Fig se vanter (about de). ◆**crowbar** n levier m.

crowd [kraʊd] n foule f; (particular group) bande f; (of things) Fam masse f; quite a c. beaucoup de monde; – vi to c. into (of people) s'entasser dans; to c. round s.o. se presser autour de qn; to c. together se serrer; – vt (fill) remplir; to c. into (press) entasser dans; don't c. me! Fam ne me bouscule pas! (train etc) bondé, plein; (city) encombré; it's very c.! il y a beaucoup de monde! ◆**–ed** a plein (with de);

crown [kraʊn] n (of king, tooth) couronne f; (of head, hill) sommet m; c. court cour f d'assises; C. jewels, joyaux mpl de la Couronne; – vt couronner. ◆–ing a (glory etc) suprême; c. achievement couronnement m.

crucial ['kruːʃəl] a crucial.

crucify ['kruːsɪfaɪ] vt crucifier. ◆**crucifix** ['kruːsɪfɪks] n crucifix m. ◆**cruci'fixion** n crucifixion f.

crude [kruːd] a (-er, -est) (oil, fact) brut; (manners, person) grossier; (language, light) cru; (painting, work) rudimentaire. ◆–ly adv (to say, order etc) crûment. ◆**–ness** n grossièreté f; crudité f; état m rudimentaire.

cruel [kruəl] a (crueller, cruellest) cruel. ◆**cruelty** n cruauté f; an act of c. une cruauté.

cruet ['kruːɪt] n c. (stand) salière f, poivrière f et huilier m.

cruis/e [kruːz] vi Nau croiser; Aut rouler; (of taxi) marauder; (of tourists) faire une croisière; – n croisière f. ◆–ing a c. speed Nau Av & Fig vitesse f de croisière. ◆–er n Nau croiseur m.

crumb [krʌm] n miette f; (of comfort) Fig brin m; crumbs! Hum Fam zut!

crumble ['krʌmb(ə)l] vt (bread) émietter; – vi (collapse) s'effondrer. to c. (away) (in small pieces) & Fig s'effriter. ◆**crumbly** a friable.

crummy ['krʌmɪ] a (-ier, -iest) Fam moche, minable.

crumpet ['krʌmpɪt] n Culin petite crêpe f grillée (servie beurrée).

crumple ['krʌmp(ə)l] vt froisser; – vi se froisser.

crunch [krʌntʃ] 1 vt (food) croquer; – vi (of snow) craquer. 2 n the c. Fam le moment critique. ◆**crunchy** a (-ier, -iest) (apple etc) croquant.

crusade [kruːˈseɪd] n Hist & Fig croisade f; – vi faire une croisade. ◆**crusader** n Hist croisé m; Fig militant, -ante mf.

crush [krʌʃ] 1 n (crowd) cohue f; (rush) bousculade f; **to have a c. on s.o.** Fam avoir le béguin pour qn. 2 vt écraser; (hope) détruire; (clothes) froisser; (cram) entasser (into dans). ◆**-ing** a (defeat) écrasant.

crust [krʌst] n croûte f. ◆**crusty** a (-ier, -iest) (bread) croustillant.

crutch [krʌtʃ] n 1 Med béquille f. 2 (crotch) entre-jambes m inv.

crux [krʌks] n the c. of (problem, matter) le nœud de.

cry [kraɪ] n (shout) cri m; **to have a c.** Fam pleurer; – vi (weep) pleurer; **to c.** (out) pousser un cri, crier; (exclaim) s'écrier; **to c.** (out) for demander (à grands cris); **to be crying out for** avoir grand besoin de; **to c.** off (withdraw) abandonner; **to c. off (sth)** se désintéresser (de qch); **to c. over** pleurer (sur); – vt (shout) crier. ◆**-ing** a (need etc) très grand; **a c. shame** une véritable honte; – n cri mpl; (weeping) pleurs mpl.

crypt [krɪpt] n crypte f.

cryptic ['krɪptɪk] a secret, énigmatique.

crystal ['krɪst(ə)l] n cristal m. ◆**c.-'clear** a (water, sound) cristallin; Fig clair comme le jour ou l'eau de roche. ◆**crystallize** vt cristalliser; – vi (se) cristalliser.

cub [kʌb] n 1 (of animal) petit m. 2 (scout) louveteau m.

Cuba ['kjuːbə] n Cuba m. ◆**Cuban** a & n cubain, -aine (mf).

cubbyhole ['kʌbɪhəʊl] n cagibi m.

cube [kjuːb] n cube m; (of meat etc) dé m. ◆**cubic** a (shape) cubique; (metre etc) cube; **c. capacity** volume m; Aut cylindrée f.

cubicle ['kjuːbɪk(ə)l] n (for changing) cabine f; (in hospital) box m.

cuckoo ['kʊkuː] n 1 (bird) coucou m; **c. clock** coucou m. 2 a (stupid) Sl cinglé.

cucumber ['kjuːkʌmbər] n concombre m.

cuddle ['kʌd(ə)l] vt (hug) serrer (dans ses bras); (caress) câliner; – vi (of lovers) se serrer; **to (kiss and) c.** s'embrasser; **to c. up to** (huddle) se serrer ou se blottir contre; – n

caresse f. ◆**cuddly** a (-ier, -iest) a câlin, caressant; (toy) doux, en peluche.

cudgel ['kʌdʒəl] n trique f, gourdin m.

cue [kjuː] n 1 Th réplique f; (signal) signal m. 2 (billiard) c. queue f (de billard).

cuff [kʌf] 1 n (of shirt etc) poignet m, manchette f; (of trousers) Am revers m; off the c. Fig impromptu; **c. link** bouton m de manchette. 2 vt (strike) gifler.

cul-de-sac ['kʌldəsæk] n impasse f, cul-de-sac m.

culinary ['kʌlɪnərɪ] a culinaire.

cull [kʌl] vt choisir; (animals) abattre sélectivement.

culminate ['kʌlmɪneɪt] vi **to c. in** finir par. ◆**culmi'nation** n point m culminant.

culprit ['kʌlprɪt] n coupable mf.

cult [kʌlt] n culte m.

cultivate ['kʌltɪveɪt] vt (land, mind etc) cultiver. ◆**-ed** a cultivé. ◆**culti'vation** n culture f; **land** or **fields under c.** cultures fpl.

culture ['kʌltʃər] n culture f. ◆**cultural** a culturel. ◆**cultured** a cultivé.

cumbersome ['kʌmbəsəm] a encombrant.

cumulative ['kjuːmjʊlətɪv] a cumulatif; **c. effect** (long-term) effet m ou résultat m à long terme.

cunning ['kʌnɪŋ] a astucieux; Pej rusé; – n astuce f, ruse f. ◆**-ly** adv avec astuce; avec ruse.

cup [kʌp] n tasse f; (goblet, prize) coupe f; **that's my c. of tea** Fam c'est à mon goût; **c. final** Fb finale f de la coupe. ◆**c.-tie** n Fb match m éliminatoire. ◆**cupful** n tasse f.

cupboard ['kʌbəd] n armoire f; (built-in) placard m.

Cupid ['kjuːpɪd] n Cupidon m.

cupola ['kjuːpələ] n Archit coupole f.

cuppa ['kʌpə] n Fam tasse f de thé.

curate ['kjʊərɪt] n vicaire m.

curator [kjʊəˈreɪtər] n (of museum) conservateur m.

curb [kɜːb] 1 n (kerb) Am bord m du trottoir. 2 vt (feelings) refréner, freiner; (ambitions) modérer; (expenses) limiter; – n frein m; **to put a c. on** mettre un frein à.

curdle ['kɜːd(ə)l] vt cailler; – vi se cailler; (of blood) Fig se figer.

curds [kɜːdz] npl lait m caillé. ◆**curd cheese** n fromage m blanc (maigre).

cure [kjʊər] 1 vt guérir (of de); (poverty) Fig éliminer; – n remède m (for contre); (recovery) guérison f; **rest c.** cure f de repos. 2 vt Culin (smoke) fumer; (salt) saler; (dry) sécher. ◆**curable** a guérissable, curable. ◆**curative** a curatif.

curfew ['kɜːfjuː] n couvre-feu m.

curio ['kjʊərɪəʊ] n (pl -os) bibelot m, curiosité f.

curious ['kjʊərɪəs] a (odd) curieux; (inquisitive) curieux (about de); **c. to know** curieux de savoir. ◆-**ly** adv (oddly) curieusement. ◆**curi'osity** n curiosité f.

curl [kɜːl] **1** vti (hair) boucler, friser; — n boucle f; (of smoke) Fig spirale f. **2** vi **to c. up** (shrivel) se racornir; **to c. oneself up** (into a ball) se pelotonner. ◆-**er** n bigoudi m. ◆**curly** a (-ier, -iest) bouclé, frisé.

currant ['kʌrənt] n (fruit) groseille f; (dried grape) raisin m de Corinthe.

currency ['kʌrənsɪ] n (money) monnaie f; (acceptance) Fig cours m; (foreign) c. devises fpl (étrangères).

current ['kʌrənt] **1** a (fashion, trend etc) actuel; (opinion, use, phrase) courant; (year, month) en cours, courant; **c. affairs** questions fpl d'actualité; **c. events** actualité f; the **c. issue** (of magazine etc) le dernier numéro. **2** n (of river, air) & El courant m. ◆-**ly** adv actuellement, à présent.

curriculum, pl **-la** [kə'rɪkjʊləm, -lə] n programme m (scolaire); **c. (vitae)** curriculum (vitae) m inv.

curry ['kʌrɪ] **1** n Culin curry m, cari m. **2** vt **to c. favour with** s'insinuer dans les bonnes grâces de.

curs/e [kɜːs] n malédiction f; (swearword) juron m; (bane) Fig fléau m; — vt maudire; **cursed with** (blindness etc) affligé de; — vi (swear) jurer. ◆-**ed** [-ɪd] a Fam maudit.

cursor ['kɜːsər] n (on computer screen) curseur m.

cursory ['kɜːsərɪ] a (too) rapide, superficiel.

curt [kɜːt] a brusque. ◆-**ly** adv d'un ton brusque. ◆-**ness** n brusquerie f.

curtail [kɜː'teɪl] vt écourter, raccourcir; (expenses) réduire. ◆-**ment** n raccourcissement m; réduction f.

curtain ['kɜːt(ə)n] n rideau m; **c. call** Th rappel m.

curts(e)y ['kɜːtsɪ] n révérence f; — vi faire une révérence.

curve [kɜːv] n courbe f; (in road) Am virage m; pl (of woman) Fam rondeurs fpl; — vt courber; — vi se courber; (of road) tourner, faire une courbe.

cushion ['kʊʃən] n coussin m; — vt (shock) Fig amortir. ◆**cushioned** a (seat) rembourré; **c. against** Fig protégé contre.

cushy ['kʊʃɪ] a (-ier, -iest) (job, life) Fam pépère, facile.

custard ['kʌstəd] n crème f anglaise; (when set) crème f renversée.

custodian [kʌ'stəʊdɪən] n gardien, -ienne mf.

custody ['kʌstədɪ] n (care) garde f; **to take into c.** Jur mettre en détention préventive. ◆**cu'stodial** a **c. sentence** peine f de prison.

custom ['kʌstəm] n coutume f; (patronage) Com clientèle f. ◆**customary** a habituel, coutumier; **it is c.** to il est d'usage de. ◆**custom-built** a, ◆**customized** a (car etc) (fait) sur commande.

customer ['kʌstəmər] n client, -ente mf; Pej individu m.

customs ['kʌstəmz] n & npl (the) c. la douane; (duties) droits mpl de douane; **c. officer** douanier m; **c. union** union f douanière.

cut [kʌt] n coupure f; (stroke) coup m; (of clothes, hair) coupe f; (in salary) réduction f; (of meat) morceau m; — vt (pt & pp cut, pres p cutting) couper; (meat) découper; (glass, tree) tailler; (record) graver; (hay) faucher; (profits, prices etc) réduire; (tooth) percer; (corner) prendre à la corde; **to c. open** ouvrir (au couteau etc); **to c. short** (visit) abréger; — vi (of person, scissors) couper; (of material) se couper; **to c. into** (cake) entamer. ■ **to c. away** vt (remove) enlever; **to c. back** (on) vti réduire. ◆**cutback** n réduction f; **to c. down** vt (tree) abattre, couper; **to c. down (on)** vti réduire; **to c. in** vi interrompre; Aut faire une queue de poisson (on s.o. à qn); **to c. off** vt couper; (isolate) isoler; **to c. out** vi (of engine) Aut caler; — vt (article) découper; (garment) tailler; (remove) enlever; (leave out, get rid of) Fam supprimer; **to c. out drinking** (stop) Fam s'arrêter de boire; **c. it out!** Fam ça suffit!; **c. out to be a doctor/etc** fait pour être médecin/etc. ■ **cutout** n (picture) découpage m; El coupe-circuit m inv; **to c. up** vt couper (en morceaux); (meat) découper; **to c. up** about démoralisé par. ◆**cutting** n coupe f; (of diamond) taille f; (article) Journ coupure f; (plant) bouture f; Cin montage m; — a (wind, word) cinglant; **c. edge** tranchant m.

cute [kjuːt] a (-er, -est) Fam (pretty) mignon; (shrewd) astucieux.

cuticle ['kjuːtɪk(ə)l] n petites peaux fpl (de l'ongle).

cutlery ['kʌtlərɪ] n couverts mpl.

cutlet ['kʌtlɪt] n (of veal etc) côtelette f.

cut-price [kʌt'praɪs] a à prix réduit.

cutthroat ['kʌtθrəʊt] n assassin m; — a (competition) impitoyable.

cv [siːˈviː] *n abbr* curriculum (vitae) *m inv.*

cyanide [ˈsaɪənaɪd] *n* cyanure *m.*

cybernetics [saɪbəˈnetɪks] *n* cybernétique *f.*

cycle [ˈsaɪk(ə)l] **1** *n* bicyclette *f*, vélo *m*; *a (path, track)* cyclable; *(race)* cycliste; – *vi* aller à bicyclette **(to** à); *Sp* faire de la bicyclette. **2** *n (series, period)* cycle *m.* ◆**cycling** *n* cyclisme *m*; – *a (champion)* cycliste. ◆**cyclist** *n* cycliste *mf.* ◆**cyclic(al)** [ˈsɪklɪk(ə)l] *a* cyclique.

cyclone [ˈsaɪkləʊn] *n* cyclone *m.*

cylinder [ˈsɪlɪndər] *n* cylindre *m.* ◆**cy'lindrical** *a* cylindrique.

cymbal [ˈsɪmbəl] *n* cymbale *f.*

cynic [ˈsɪnɪk] *n* cynique *mf.* ◆**cynical** *a* cynique. ◆**cynicism** *n* cynisme *m.*

cypress [ˈsaɪprəs] *n (tree)* cyprès *m.*

Cyprus [ˈsaɪprəs] *n* Chypre *f.* ◆**Cypriot** [ˈsɪprɪət] *a & n* cypriote *(mf).*

cyst [sɪst] *n Med* kyste *m.*

czar [zɑːr] *n* tsar *m.*

Czech [tʃek] *a & n* tchèque *(mf).* ◆**Czecho'slovak** *a & n* tchécoslovaque *(mf).* ◆**Czechoslo'vakia** *n* Tchécoslovaquie *f.* ◆**Czechoslo'vakian** *a & n* tchécoslovaque *(mf).*

D

D, d [diː] *n* D, d *m.* ◆**D.-day** *n* le jour J.

dab [dæb] *n* a. **of** un petit peu de; – *vt* **(-bb-)** *(wound, brow etc)* tamponner; **to d. sth on sth** appliquer qch (à petits coups) sur qch.

dabble [ˈdæb(ə)l] *vi* **to d. in** s'occuper *or* se mêler un peu de.

dad [dæd] *n Fam* papa *m.* ◆**daddy** *n Fam* papa *m*; **d. longlegs** *(cranefly)* tipule *f*; *(spider) Am* faucheur *m.*

daffodil [ˈdæfədɪl] *n* jonquille *f.*

daft [dɑːft] *a* **(-er, -est)** *Fam* idiot, bête.

dagger [ˈdægər] *n* poignard *m*; **at daggers drawn** à couteaux tirés **(with** avec).

dahlia [ˈdeɪljə, *Am* ˈdæljə] *n* dahlia *m.*

daily [ˈdeɪlɪ] *a* quotidien, journalier; *(wage)* journalier; – *adv* quotidiennement; – *n d. (paper)* quotidien *m*; **d. (help)** *(cleaning woman)* femme *f* de ménage.

dainty [ˈdeɪntɪ] *a* **(-ier, -iest)** délicat; *(pretty)* mignon; *(tasteful)* élégant. ◆**daintily** *adv* délicatement; élégamment.

dairy [ˈdeərɪ] *n (on farm)* laiterie *f*; *(shop)* crèmerie *f*; – *a (produce, cow etc)* laitier. ◆**dairyman** *n (pl -men) (dealer)* laitier *m.* ◆**dairywoman** *n (pl -women)* laitière *f.*

daisy [ˈdeɪzɪ] *n* pâquerette *f.*

dale [deɪl] *n Geog Lit* vallée *f.*

dally [ˈdælɪ] *vi* musarder, lanterner.

dam [dæm] *n (wall)* barrage *m*; – *vt* **(-mm-)** *(river)* barrer.

damage [ˈdæmɪdʒ] *n* dégâts *mpl*, dommages *mpl*; *(harm) Fig* préjudice *m*; – *pl Jur* dommages-intérêts *mpl*; – *vt (spoil)* abîmer; *(material object)* endommager, abîmer; *(harm) Fig* nuire à. ◆**—ing** *a* préjudiciable **(to** à).

dame [deɪm] *n Lit* dame *f*; *Am Sl* nana *f*, fille *f.*

damn [dæm] *vt (condemn, doom)* condamner; *Rel* damner; *(curse)* maudire; **d. him!** *Fam* qu'il aille au diable!; – *int* **d. (it)!** *Fam* zut!, merde! – *n* **he doesn't care a d.** *Fam* il s'en fiche pas mal; – *a (damn)* fichu, sacré; – *adv Fam* sacrément; **d. all** rien du tout. ◆**—ed 1** *a (soul)* damné. **2** *Fam =* **damn** *a & adv.* ◆**—ing** *a (evidence etc)* accablant. ◆**dam'nation** *n* damnation *f.*

damp [dæmp] *a* **(-er, -est)** humide; *(skin)* moite; – *n* humidité *f.* ◆**damp(en)** *vt* humecter; **to d. (down)** *(zeal)* refroidir; *(ambition)* étouffer. ◆**damper** *n* **to put a d. on** jeter un froid sur. ◆**dampness** *n* humidité *f.*

damsel [ˈdæmzəl] *n Lit & Hum* demoiselle *f.*

damson [ˈdæmzən] *n* prune *f* de Damas.

danc/e [dɑːns] *n* danse *f*; *(social event)* bal *m*; **d. hall** dancing *m*; – *vi* danser; **to d. for joy** sauter de joie; – *vt (polka etc)* danser. ◆**—ing** *n* danse *f*; **d. partner** cavalier, -ière *mf.* ◆**—er** *n* danseur, -euse *mf.*

dandelion [ˈdændɪlaɪən] *n* pissenlit *m.*

dandruff [ˈdændrʌf] *n* pellicules *fpl.*

dandy [ˈdændɪ] **1** *n* dandy *m.* **2** *a (very good) Am Fam* formidable.

Dane [deɪn] *n* Danois, -oise *mf.*

danger [ˈdeɪndʒər] *n (peril)* danger *m* **(to** pour); *(risk)* risque *m*; **in d.** en danger; **in d. of** *(threatened by)* menacé de; **to be in d. of falling/etc** risquer de tomber/etc; **on the d. list** *Med* dans un état critique; **d. signal** signal *m* d'alarme; **d. zone** zone *f* dangereuse. ◆**dangerous** *a (place, illness,* *person etc*) dangereux (**to** pour.) ◆**dangerously** *adv* dangereusement; (*ill*) gravement.

dangle ['dæŋg(ə)l] *vt* balancer; (*prospect*) *Fig* faire miroiter (**before s.o.** aux yeux de qn); – *vi* (*hang*) pendre; (*swing*) se balancer.

Danish ['deɪnɪʃ] *a* danois; – *n* (*language*) danois *m*.

dank [dæŋk] *a* (**-er, -est**) humide (et froid).

dapper ['dæpər] *a* pimpant, fringant.

dappled ['dæp(ə)ld] *a* pommelé, tacheté.

dar/e [deər] *vt* oser (**do** faire); **she d. not come** elle n'ose pas venir; **he doesn't d. (to) go** il n'ose pas y aller; **if you d. (to)** si tu l'oses, si tu oses le faire; **I d. say he tried** il a sans doute essayé, je suppose qu'il a essayé; **to d. s.o. to do** défier qn de faire. ◆**—ing** *a* audacieux; – *n* audace *f*. ◆**daredevil** *n* casse-cou *m inv*, risque-tout *m inv*.

dark [dɑːk] *a* (**-er, -est**) obscur, noir, sombre; (*colour*) foncé, sombre; (*skin*) brun, foncé; (*hair*) brun, noir, foncé; (*eyes*) foncé; (*gloomy*) sombre; **it is d.** il fait nuit or noir; **to keep sth d.** tenir qch secret; **d. glasses** lunettes *fpl* noires; – *n* noir *m*, obscurité *f*; **after d.** après la tombée de la nuit; **to keep s.o. in the d.** laisser qn dans l'ignorance (**about** de). ◆**d.-'haired** *a* aux cheveux bruns. ◆**d.-'skinned** *a* brun; (*race*) de couleur. ◆**darken** *vt* assombrir, obscurcir; (*colour*) foncer; – *vi* s'assombrir; (*of colour*) foncer. ◆**darkness** *n* obscurité *f*, noir *m*.

darkroom ['dɑːkruːm] *n Phot* chambre *f* noire.

darling ['dɑːlɪŋ] *n* (*favourite*) chouchou, -oute *mf*; (**my**) **d.** (mon) chéri, (ma) chérie; **he's a d.** c'est un amour; **be a d.!** sois un ange!; – *a* chéri; (*delightful*) *Fam* adorable.

darn [dɑːn] **1** *vt* (*socks*) repriser. **2** *int* **d. it!** bon sang! ◆**—ing** *n* reprise *f*; – *a* (*needle, wool*) à repriser.

dart [dɑːt] **1** *vi* se précipiter, s'élancer (**for** vers); – *n* **to make a d.** se précipiter (**for** vers). **2** *n Sp* fléchette *f*; *pl* (*game*) fléchettes *fpl*. ◆**dartboard** *n Sp* cible *f*.

dash [dæʃ] **1** *n* (*run, rush*) ruée *f*; **to make a d.** se précipiter (**for** vers); – *vi* se précipiter; (*of waves*) se briser (**against** contre); **to d. off** *or* **away** partir *or* filer en vitesse; – *vt* jeter (avec force); (*shatter*) briser; **d. (it)!** *Fam* zut!; **to d. off** (*letter*) faire en vitesse. **2** *n* **a d. of** (*petit*) peu de; **a d. of milk** une goutte *or* un nuage de lait. **3** *n* (*stroke*) trait

m; *Typ* tiret *m*. ◆**—ing** *a* (*person*) sémillant.

dashboard ['dæʃbɔːd] *n Aut* tableau *m* de bord.

data ['deɪtə] *npl* données *fpl*; **d. processing** informatique *f*.

date[1] [deɪt] *n* date *f*; (*on coin*) millésime *m*; (*meeting*) *Fam* rendez-vous *m inv*; (*person*) *Fam* copain, -ine *mf* (*avec qui on a un rendez-vous*); **up to d.** moderne; (*information*) à jour; (*well-informed*) au courant (**on** de); **out of d.** (*old-fashioned*) démodé; (*expired*) périmé; **to d.** à ce jour, jusqu'ici; **d. stamp** (*object*) (tampon *m*) dateur *m*; (*mark*) cachet *m*; – *vt* (*letter etc*) dater; (*girl, boy*) *Fam* sortir avec; – *vi* (*become out of date*) dater; **to d. back to, to d. from** dater de. ◆**dated** *a* démodé.

date[2] [deɪt] *n Bot* datte *f*.

datebook ['deɪtbuk] *n Am* agenda *m*.

daub [dɔːb] *vt* barbouiller (**with** de).

daughter ['dɔːtər] *n* fille *f*. ◆**d.-in-law** *n* (*pl* **daughters-in-law**) belle-fille *f*, bru *f*.

daunt [dɔːnt] *vt* décourager, rebuter. ◆**—less** *a* intrépide.

dawdl/e ['dɔːd(ə)l] *vi* traîner, lambiner. ◆**—er** *n* traînard, -arde *mf*.

dawn [dɔːn] *n* aube *f*, aurore *f*; – *vi* (*of day*) poindre; (*of new era, idea*) naître, voir le jour; **it dawned upon him that** . . . il lui est venu à l'esprit que . . . . ◆**—ing** *a* naissant.

day [deɪ] *n* jour *m*; (*working period, whole day long*) journée *f*; *pl* (*period*) époque *f*, temps *mpl*; **all d. (long)** toute la journée; **what d. is it?** quel jour sommes-nous?; **the following** *or* **next d.** le lendemain; **the d. before** la veille; **the d. before yesterday** avant-hier; **the d. after tomorrow** après-demain; **to the d.** jour pour jour; **d. boarder** demi-pensionnaire *mf*; **d. nursery** crèche *f*; **d. return** *Rail* aller et retour *m* (*pour une journée*); **d. tripper** excursionniste *mf*. ◆**d.-to-'d.** *a* journalier; **on a d.-to-day basis** (*every day*) journellement. ◆**daybreak** *n* point *m* du jour. ◆**daydream** *n* rêverie *f*; – *vi* rêvasser. ◆**daylight** *n* (lumière *f* du) jour *m*; (*dawn*) point *m* du jour; **it's d.** il fait jour. ◆**daytime** *n* journée *f*.

daze [deɪz] *vt* (*with drugs etc*) hébéter; (*by blow*) étourdir; – *n* **in a d.** étourdi; hébété.

dazzle ['dæz(ə)l] *vt* éblouir; – *n* éblouissement *m*.

deacon ['diːkən] *n Rel* diacre *m*.

dead [ded] *a* mort; (*numb*) engourdi; (*party etc*) qui manque de vie, mortel; (*telephone*) sans tonalité; **in (the) d. centre** au beau milieu; **to be a d. loss** (*person*) *Fam* n'être bon à rien; **it's a d. loss** *Fam* ça ne vaut rien; **d. silence** un silence de mort; **a d. stop** un arrêt complet; **a d. end** (*street*) *&* Fig impasse *f*; **a d.-end job** un travail sans avenir; – *adv* (*completely*) absolument; (*very*) très; **d. beat** *Fam* éreinté; **d. drunk** *Fam* ivre mort; **to stop d.** s'arrêter net; – *n* **the d.** les morts *mpl*; **in the d. of** (*night, winter*) au cœur de. **◆—ly** a (*-ier, -iest*) (*enemy, silence, paleness*) mortel; (*weapon*) meurtrier; **d. sins** péchés *mpl* capitaux; – *adv* mortellement. **◆deadbeat** *n Am Fam* parasite *m*. **◆deadline** *n* date *f* limite; (*hour*) heure *f* limite. **◆deadlock** *n* Fig impasse *f*. **◆deadpan** *a* (*face*) figé, impassible.

deaden ['ded(ə)n] *vt* (*shock*) amortir; (*pain*) calmer; (*feeling*) émousser.

deaf [def] *a* sourd (**to** à); **d. and dumb** sourd-muet; **d. in one ear** sourd d'une oreille; – *n* **the d.** les sourds *mpl*. **◆d.-aid** *n* audiophone *m*, prothèse *f* auditive. **◆deafen** *vt* assourdir. **◆deafness** *n* surdité *f*.

deal [diːl] 1 *n* **a good** *or* **great d.** beaucoup (**of** de). 2 *n Com* marché *m*, affaire *f*; *Cards* donne *f*; **fair d.** traitement *m* *or* arrangement *m* équitable; **it's a d.** d'accord; **big d.!** *Iron* la belle affaire! **3** *vt* (*pt & pp* **dealt** [delt]) (*blow*) porter; **to d. (out)** (*cards*) donner; (*money*) distribuer. **4** *vi* (*trade*) traiter (**with s.o.** avec qn); **to d. in** faire le commerce de; **to d. with** (*take care of*) s'occuper de; (*concern*) traiter de, parler de; **I can d. with him** (*handle*) je sais m'y prendre avec lui. **◆—ings** *npl* relations *fpl* (**with** avec); *Com* transactions *fpl*. **◆—er** *n* marchand, -ande *mf* (**in** de); (*agent*) dépositaire *mf*; (*for cars*) concessionnaire *mf*; (*in drugs*) *Sl* revendeur, -euse *mf* de drogues; *Cards* donneur, -euse *mf*.

deal [diːl] *n* (*wood*) sapin *m*.

dean [diːn] *n Rel Univ* doyen *m*.

dear [diər] *a* (*-er, -est*) (*loved, precious, expensive*) cher; (*price*) élevé; **D. Sir** (*in letter*) *Com* Monsieur; **D. Uncle** mon oncle; **oh d.!** oh là là!, oh mon Dieu!; – *n* (*my*) **d.** (*darling*) (mon) chéri, (ma) chérie; (*friend*) mon cher, ma chère; **she's a d.** c'est un amour; **be a d.!** sois un ange!; – *adv* (*to cost, pay*) cher. **◆—ly** *adv* tendrement; (*very much*) beaucoup; **to pay d. for sth** payer qch cher.

dearth [dɜːθ] *n* manque *m*, pénurie *f*.

death [deθ] *n* mort *f*; **to put to d.** mettre à mort; **to be bored to d.** s'ennuyer à mourir;

to be burnt to d. mourir carbonisé; **to be sick to d.** en avoir vraiment marre; **many deaths** (*people killed*) de nombreux morts *mpl*; – *a* (*march*) funèbre; (*mask*) mortuaire; **d. certificate** acte *m* de décès; **d. duty** droits *mpl* de succession; **d. penalty** *or* **sentence** peine *f* de mort; **d. rate** mortalité *f*; **it's a d. trap** il y a danger de mort. **◆deathbed** *n* lit *m* de mort. **◆deathblow** *n* coup *m* mortel. **◆deathly** *a* mortel, de mort; – *adv* **d. pale** d'une pâleur mortelle.

debar [diˈbɑːr] *vt* (*-rr-*) exclure; **to d. from doing** interdire de faire.

debase [diˈbeɪs] *vt* (*person*) avilir; (*reputation, talents*) galvauder; (*coinage*) altérer.

debat/e [diˈbeɪt] *vti* discuter; **to d. (with oneself) whether to leave/***etc* se demander si on doit partir/*etc*; – *n* débat *m*, discussion *f*. **◆—able** *a* discutable, contestable.

debauch [diˈbɔːtʃ] *vt* corrompre, débaucher. **◆debauchery** *n* débauche *f*.

debilitate [diˈbɪlɪteɪt] *vt* débiliter. **◆debility** *n* faiblesse *f*, débilité *f*.

debit ['debɪt] *n* débit *m*; **in d.** (*account*) débiteur; – *a* (*balance*) *Fin* débiteur; – *vt* débiter (**s.o. with sth** qn de qch).

debonair [debəˈneər] *a* jovial, charmant; (*polite*) poli.

debris ['debriː] *n* débris *mpl*.

debt [det] *n* dette *f*; **to be in d.** avoir des dettes; **to be £50 in d.** devoir 50 livres; **to run** *or* **get into d.** faire des dettes. **◆debtor** *n* débiteur, -trice *mf*.

debunk [diːˈbʌŋk] *vt* *Fam* démystifier.

debut ['deɪbjuː] *n* *Th* début *m*.

decade [deˈkeɪd] *n* décennie *f*.

decadent ['dekədənt] *a* décadent. **◆decadence** *n* décadence *f*.

decaffeinated [diːˈkæfɪneɪtɪd] *a* décaféiné.

decal ['diːkæl] *n Am* décalcomanie *f*.

decant [diˈkænt] *vt* (*wine*) décanter. **◆—er** *n* carafe *f*.

decapitate [diˈkæpɪteɪt] *vt* décapiter.

decathlon [diˈkæθlɒn] *n Sp* décathlon *m*.

decay [diˈkeɪ] *vi* (*go bad*) se gâter; (*rot*) pourrir; (*of tooth*) se carier, se gâter; (*of building*) tomber en ruine; (*decline*) Fig décliner; – *n* pourriture *f*; *Archit* délabrement *m*; (*of tooth*) carie *f* (*pl* -s); (*of nation*) décadence *f*; **to fall into d.** (*of building*) tomber en ruine. **◆—ing** *a* (*meat, fruit etc*) pourrissant.

deceased [diˈsiːst] *a* décédé, défunt; – *n* **the d.** le défunt, la défunte; *pl* **les** défunt(e)s.

deceit [diˈsiːt] *n* tromperie *f*. **◆deceitful** *a*

trompeur. ◆**deceitfully** adv avec duplicité.

deceive [dɪˈsiːv] vti tromper; **to d. oneself** se faire des illusions.

December [dɪˈsembər] n décembre m.

decent [ˈdiːsənt] a (respectable) convenable, décent; (good) Fam bon; (kind) Fam gentil; **that was d. (of you)** c'était chic de ta part. ◆**decency** n décence f; (kindness) Fam gentillesse f. ◆**decently** adv décemment.

decentralize [diːˈsentrəlaɪz] vt décentraliser. ◆**decentrali'zation** n décentralisation f.

deception [dɪˈsepʃ(ə)n] n tromperie f. ◆**deceptive** a trompeur.

decibel [ˈdesɪbel] n décibel m.

decid/e [dɪˈsaɪd] vt (question etc) régler, décider; (s.o.'s career, fate etc) décider; **to d. to do** décider de faire; **to d. that** décider que; **to d. s.o. to do** décider qn à faire; – vi (make decisions) décider; (make up one's mind) se décider (on doing à faire); **to d. on sth** décider de qch, se décider à qch; (choose) se décider pour qch. ◆**–ed** a (firm) décidé, résolu; (clear) net. ◆**–edly** adv résolument; nettement. ◆**–ing** a (factor etc) décisif.

decimal [ˈdesɪməl] a décimal; **d. point** virgule f; – n décimale f. ◆**decimali'zation** f décimalisation f.

decimate [ˈdesɪmeɪt] vt décimer.

decipher [dɪˈsaɪfər] vt déchiffrer.

decision [dɪˈsɪʒ(ə)n] n décision f. ◆**decisive** [dɪˈsaɪsɪv] a (defeat, tone etc) décisif; (victory) net, incontestable. ◆**decisively** adv (to state) avec décision; (to win) nettement, incontestablement.

deck [dek] **1** n Nau pont m; **top d.** (of bus) impériale f. **2** n d. of cards jeu m de cartes. **3** n (of record player) platine f. **4** vt **to d.** (out) (adorn) orner. ◆**deckchair** n chaise f longue.

declare [dɪˈkleər] vt déclarer (that que); (verdict, result) proclamer. ◆**decla'ration** n déclaration f; proclamation f.

declin/e [dɪˈklaɪn] **1** vi (deteriorate) décliner; (of birthrate, price etc) baisser; **to d. in importance** perdre de l'importance; – n déclin m; (fall) baisse f. **2** vt refuser, décliner; **to d. to do** refuser de faire. ◆**–ing** a one's d. years ses dernières années.

decode [diːˈkəʊd] vt (message) décoder.

decompose [diːkəmˈpəʊz] vt décomposer; – vi se décomposer. ◆**decompo'sition** n décomposition f.

decompression [diːkəmˈpreʃ(ə)n] n décompression f.

decontaminate [diːkənˈtæmɪneɪt] vt décontaminer.

decor [ˈdeɪkɔːr] n décor m.

decorat/e [ˈdekəreɪt] vt (cake, house, soldier) décorer (with de); (paint etc) peindre (et tapisser); (hat, skirt etc) orner (with de). ◆**–ing** n interior d. décoration f d'intérieurs. ◆**deco'ration** n décoration f. ◆**decorative** a décoratif. ◆**decorator** n (house painter etc) peintre m décorateur; (interior) d. ensemblier m, décorateur, -trice mf.

decorum [dɪˈkɔːrəm] n bienséances fpl.

decoy [ˈdiːkɔɪ] n (artificial bird) appeau m; (police) décoy m; – vt policier m en civil.

decreas/e [dɪˈkriːs] vti diminuer; – [ˈdiːkriːs] n diminution f (in de). ◆**–ing** a (number etc) décroissant. ◆**–ingly** adv de moins en moins.

decree [dɪˈkriː] n Pol Rel décret m; Jur jugement m; (municipal) arrêté m; – vt (pt & pp **decreed**) décréter.

decrepit [dɪˈkrepɪt] a (building) en ruine; (person) décrépit.

decry [dɪˈkraɪ] vt décrier.

dedicat/e [ˈdedɪkeɪt] vt (devote) consacrer (to à); (book) dédier (to à); **to d. oneself to** se consacrer à. ◆**dedi'cation** n (in book) dédicace f; (devotion) dévouement m.

deduce [dɪˈdjuːs] vt (conclude) déduire (from de, that que).

deduct [dɪˈdʌkt] vt (subtract) déduire, retrancher (from de); (from wage, account) prélever (from sur). ◆**deductible** a à déduire (from de); (expenses) déductible. ◆**deduction** n (inference) & Com déduction f.

deed [diːd] n action f, acte m; (feat) exploit m; Jur acte m (notarié).

deem [diːm] vt juger, estimer.

deep [diːp] a (-er, -est) profond; (snow) épais; (voice) grave; (note) Mus bas; (person) insondable; **to be six metres/etc d.** avoir six mètres/etc de profondeur; **d. in thought** absorbé or plongé dans ses pensées; **the d. end** (in swimming pool) le grand bain; **d. red** rouge foncé; – adv (to breathe) profondément; **d. into the night** tard dans la nuit; – n the d. l'océan m. ◆**–ly** adv (grateful, to regret etc) profondément. ◆**deep-'freeze** vt surgeler; – n congélateur m. ◆**d.-'fryer** n friteuse f. ◆**d.-'rooted** a, ◆**d.-'seated** a bien ancré, profond. ◆**d.-'set** a (eyes) enfoncés.

deepen ['diːpən] *vt* approfondir; (*increase*) augmenter; – *vi* devenir plus profond; (*of mystery*) s'épaissir. ◆**-ing** a grandissant.

deer [dɪər] *n inv* cerf *m*.

deface [dɪ'feɪs] *vt* (*damage*) dégrader; (*daub*) barbouiller.

defamation [defə'meɪʃ(ə)n] *n* diffamation *f*. ◆**de'famatory** a diffamatoire.

default [dɪ'fɔːlt] *n* by d. par défaut; **to win by d.** gagner par forfait; – *vi* Jur faire défaut; **to d. on one's payments** Fin être en rupture de paiement.

defeat [dɪ'fiːt] *vt* battre, vaincre; (*plan*) faire échouer; – *n* défaite *f*; (*of plan*) échec *m*. ◆**defeatism** *n* défaitisme *m*.

defect 1 ['diːfekt] *n* défaut *m*. **2** [dɪ'fekt] *vi* Pol déserter, faire défection; **to d. to** (*the West, the enemy*) passer à. ◆**de'fection** *n* défection *f*. ◆**de'fective** a défectueux; Med déficient. ◆**de'fector** *n* transfuge *mf*.

defence [dɪ'fens] (*Am* defense) *n* défense *f*; **the body's defences** la défense de l'organisme (**against** contre); **in his d.** Jur à sa décharge, pour le défendre. ◆**defenceless** a sans défense. ◆**defensible** a défendable. ◆**defensive** a défensif; – *n* **on the d.** sur la défensive.

defend [dɪ'fend] *vt* défendre. ◆**defendant** *n* (*accused*) Jur prévenu, -ue *mf*. ◆**defender** *n* défenseur *m*; (*of title*) Sp détenteur, -trice *f*.

defer [dɪ'fɜːr] **1** *vt* (**-rr-**) (*postpone*) différer, reporter. **2** *vi* (**-rr-**) **to d. to** (*yield*) déférer à. ◆**-ment** *n* report *m*.

deference [defərəns] *n* déférence *f*. ◆**defe'rential** a déférent, plein de déférence.

defiant [dɪ'faɪənt] a (*tone etc*) de défi; (*person*) rebelle. ◆**defiance** *n* (*resistance*) défi *m* (**of** à); **in d. of** (*contempt*) au mépris de. ◆**defiantly** *adv* d'un air de défi.

deficient [dɪ'fɪʃənt] a insuffisant; Med déficient; **to be d. in** manquer de. ◆**deficiency** *n* manque *m*; (*flaw*) défaut *m*; Med carence *f*; (*mental*) déficience *f*.

deficit ['defɪsɪt] *n* déficit *m*.

defile [dɪ'faɪl] *vt* souiller, salir.

define [dɪ'faɪn] *vt* définir. ◆**defi'nition** *n* définition *f*.

definite ['defɪnɪt] a (*date, plan*) précis, déterminé; (*obvious*) net, évident; (*firm*) ferme; (*certain*) certain; **d. article** Gram article *m* défini. ◆**-ly** *adv* certainement; (*appreciably*) nettement; (*to say*) catégoriquement.

definitive [dɪ'fɪnɪtɪv] a définitif.

deflate [dɪ'fleɪt] *vt* (*tyre*) dégonfler. ◆**deflation** *n* dégonflement *m*; Econ déflation *f*.

deflect [dɪ'flekt] *vt* faire dévier; – *vi* dévier.

deform [dɪ'fɔːm] *vt* déformer. ◆**-ed** a (*body*) difforme. ◆**deformity** *n* difformité *f*.

defraud [dɪ'frɔːd] *vt* (*customs, State etc*) frauder; **to d. s.o. of sth** escroquer qch à qn.

defray [dɪ'freɪ] *vt* (*expenses*) payer.

defrost [dɪ'frɒst] *vt* (*fridge*) dégivrer; (*food*) décongeler.

deft [deft] a adroit (**with** de). ◆**-ness** *n* adresse *f*.

defunct [dɪ'fʌŋkt] a défunt.

defuse [dɪ'fjuːz] *vt* (*bomb, conflict*) désamorcer.

defy [dɪ'faɪ] *vt* (*person, death etc*) défier; (*effort, description*) résister à; **to d. s.o. to do** défier qn de faire.

degenerate [dɪ'dʒenəreɪt] *vi* dégénérer (**into** en); – [dɪ'dʒenərət] a & *n* dégénéré, -ée (*mf*). ◆**degene'ration** *n* dégénérescence *f*.

degrade [dɪ'greɪd] *vt* dégrader. ◆**degradation** [degrə'deɪʃ(ə)n] *n* Mil Ch dégradation *f*; (*of person*) déchéance *f*.

degree [dɪ'griː] *n* **1** degré *m*; **not in the slightest** d. pas du tout; **to such a d.** à tel point (**that** que). **2** Univ diplôme *m*; (*Bachelor's*) licence *f*; (*Master's*) maîtrise *f*; (*PhD*) doctorat *m*.

dehumanize [diː'hjuːmənaɪz] *vt* déshumaniser.

dehydrate [diːhaɪ'dreɪt] *vt* déshydrater.

de-ice [diː'aɪs] *vt* Av Aut dégivrer.

deign [deɪn] *vt* daigner (**to do** faire).

deity ['diːɪtɪ] *n* dieu *m*.

dejected [dɪ'dʒektɪd] a abattu, découragé. ◆**dejection** *n* abattement *m*.

dekko ['dekəʊ] *n* Sl coup *m* d'œil.

delay [dɪ'leɪ] *vt* retarder; (*payment*) différer; – *vi* (*be slow*) tarder (**doing** à faire); (*linger*) s'attarder; – *n* (*lateness*) retard *m*; (*waiting period*) délai *m*; **without d.** sans tarder. ◆**delayed-'action** a (*bomb*) à retardement. ◆**delaying** a **d. tactics** moyens *mpl* dilatoires.

delectable [dɪ'lektəb(ə)l] a délectable.

delegate 1 ['delɪgeɪt] *vt* déléguer (**to** à). **2** ['delɪgət] *n* délégué, -ée *mf*. ◆**dele'gation** *n* délégation *f*.

delete [dɪ'liːt] *vt* rayer, supprimer. ◆**deletion** *n* (*thing deleted*) rature *f*; (*act*) suppression *f*.

deleterious [delɪ'tɪərɪəs] a néfaste.

deliberate[1] [dɪ'lɪbəreɪt] *vi* délibérer; – *vt* délibérer sur.

deliberate[2] [dɪ'lɪbərət] a (*intentional*) délibéré; (*cautious*) réfléchi; (*slow*) mesuré.

◆—ly *adv* (*intentionally*) exprès, délibérément; (*to walk*) avec mesure. ◆**delibe-'ration** *n* délibération *f.*

delicate ['delɪkət] *a* délicat. ◆**delicacy** *n* délicatesse *f; Culin* mets *m* délicat, gourmandise *f.* ◆**delicately** *adv* délicatement.

delicious [dɪ'lɪfəs] *a* délicieux.

delight [dɪ'laɪt] *n* délice *m*, grand plaisir *m*, joie *f; pl* (*pleasures, things*) délices *fpl*; **to be the d. of** faire les délices de; **to take d. in sth/in doing** se délecter de qch/à faire; — *vi* se réjouir; — *vi* se délecter (**in doing** à faire). ◆—**ed** *a* ravi, enchanté (**with sth** de qch, **to do** de faire, **that** que). ◆**delightful** *a* charmant; (*meal, perfume, sensation*) délicieux; ◆**delightfully** *adv* avec beaucoup de charme; (*wonderfully*) merveilleusement.

delineate [dɪ'lɪnɪeɪt] *vt* (*outline*) esquisser; (*portray*) décrire.

delinquent [dɪ'lɪŋkwənt] *a & n* délinquant, -ante (*mf*). ◆**delinquency** *n* délinquance *f.*

delirious [dɪ'lɪrɪəs] *a* délirant; **to be d.** avoir le délire, délirer. ◆**delirium** *n Med* délire *m.*

deliver [dɪ'lɪvər] *vt* **1** (*goods, milk etc*) livrer; (*letters*) distribuer; (*hand over*) remettre (**to** à). **2** (*rescue*) délivrer (**from** de). **3** (*give birth to*) mettre au monde, accoucher de; **to d. a woman('s baby)** accoucher une femme. **4** (*speech*) prononcer; (*ultimatum, warning*) lancer; (*blow*) porter. ◆**deliverance** *n* délivrance *f.* ◆**delivery** *n* **1** livraison *f*; distribution *f*; remise *f.* **2** *Med* accouchement *m.* **3** (*speaking*) débit *m.* ◆**deliveryman** *n* (*pl* **-men**) livreur *m.*

delta ['deltə] *n* (*of river*) delta *m.*

delude [dɪ'lu:d] *vt* tromper; **to d. oneself** se faire des illusions. ◆**delusion** *n* illusion *f; Psy* aberration *f* mentale.

deluge ['delju:dʒ] *n* (*of water, questions etc*) déluge *m*; — *vt* inonder (**with** de).

de luxe [dɪ'lʌks] *a* de luxe.

delve [delv] *vi* **to d. into** (*question, past*) fouiller; (*books*) fouiller dans.

demagogue ['deməgɒg] *n* démagogue *mf.*

demand [dɪ'mɑːnd] *vt* exiger (**sth from s.o.** qch de qn), réclamer (**sth from s.o.** qch à qn); (*rights, more pay*) revendiquer; **to d. that** exiger que; **to d. to know** insister pour savoir; — *n* exigence *f*; (*claim*) revendication *f*, réclamation *f*; (*request*) & *Econ* demande *f*; **in great d.** très demandé; **to** make demands on s.o. exiger beaucoup de qn. ◆—**ing** *a* exigeant.

demarcation [diːmɑː'keɪʃ(ə)n] *n* démarcation *f.*

demean [dɪ'miːn] *vt* **to d. oneself** s'abaisser, s'avilir.

demeanour [dɪ'miːnər] *n* (*behaviour*) comportement *m.*

demented [dɪ'mentɪd] *a* dément.

demerara [deməˈreərə] *n* **d. (sugar)** cassonade *f*, sucre *m* roux.

demise [dɪ'maɪz] *n* (*death*) décès *m; Fig* disparition *f.*

demo ['deməʊ] *n* (*pl* **-os**) (*demonstration*) *Fam* manif *f.*

demobilize [diː'məʊbɪlaɪz] *vt* démobiliser.

democracy [dɪ'mɒkrəsɪ] *n* démocratie *f.* ◆**democrat** ['deməkræt] *n* démocrate *mf.* ◆**demo'cratic** *a* démocratique; (*person*) démocrate.

demography [dɪ'mɒgrəfɪ] *n* démographie *f.*

demolish [dɪ'mɒlɪʃ] *vt* démolir. ◆**demo-'lition** *n* démolition *f.*

demon ['diːmən] *n* démon *m.*

demonstrate ['demənstreɪt] *vt* démontrer; (*machine*) faire une démonstration de; — *vi Pol* manifester. ◆**demon'stration** *n* démonstration *f; Pol* manifestation *f.* ◆**de'monstrative** *a* démonstratif. ◆**demonstrator** *n Pol* manifestant, -ante *mf*; (*in shop etc*) démonstrateur, -trice *mf.*

demoralize [dɪ'mɒrəlaɪz] *vt* démoraliser.

demote [dɪ'məʊt] *vt* rétrograder.

demure [dɪ'mjʊər] *a* sage, réservé.

den [den] *n* antre *m*, tanière *f.*

denationalize [diː'næʃ(ə)nəlaɪz] *vt* dénationaliser.

denial [dɪ'naɪəl] *n* (*of truth etc*) dénégation *f*; (*of rumour*) démenti *m*; (*of authority*) rejet *m*; **to issue a d.** publier un démenti.

denigrate ['denɪgreɪt] *vt* dénigrer.

denim ['denɪm] *n* (*toile f de*) coton *m*; (*jeans*) (blue-)jean *m.*

denizen ['denɪz(ə)n] *n* habitant, -ante *mf.*

Denmark ['denmɑːk] *n* Danemark *m.*

denomination [dɪnɒmɪ'neɪʃ(ə)n] *n* confession *f*, religion *f*; (*sect*) secte *f*; (*of coin, banknote*) valeur *f; Math* unité *f.* ◆**denominational** *a* (*school*) confessionnel.

denote [dɪ'nəʊt] *vt* dénoter.

denounce [dɪ'naʊns] *vt* (*person, injustice etc*) dénoncer (**to** à); **to d. s.o. as a spy/etc** accuser qn publiquement d'être un espion/etc. ◆**denunci'ation** *n* dénonciation *f*; accusation *f* publique.

dense [dens] *a* (**-er, -est**) dense; (*stupid*)

Fam lourd, bête. ◆**—ly** *adv* d. popu-lated/*etc* très peuplé/*etc*. ◆**density** *n* densité *f*.

dent [dent] *n* (*in metal*) bosselure *f*; (*in car*) bosse *f*, gnon *m*; **full of dents** (*car*) cabossé; **to make a d. in one's savings** taper dans ses économies; – *vt* cabosser, bosseler.

dental ['dent(ə)l] *a* dentaire; **d. surgeon** chirurgien *m* dentiste. ◆**dentist** *n* dentiste *mf*. ◆**dentistry** *n* médecine *f* dentaire; **school of d.** école *f* dentaire. ◆**dentures** *npl* dentier *m*.

deny [dɪ'naɪ] *vt* nier (**doing** avoir fait, **that** que); (*rumour*) démentir; (*authority*) rejeter; (*disown*) renier; **to d. s.o. sth** refuser qch à qn.

deodorant [di:'əudərənt] *n* déodorant *m*.

depart [dɪ'pɑːt] *vi* partir; (*deviate*) s'écarter (**from** de); – *vt* **to d. this world** *Lit* quitter ce monde. ◆**—ed** *a* & *n* (*dead*) défunt, -unte (*mf*). ◆**departure** *n* départ *m*; **a d. from** (*custom*, *rule*) un écart par rapport à, une entorse à; **to be a new d. for** constituer une nouvelle voie pour.

department [dɪ'pɑːtmənt] *n* département *m*; (*in office*) service *m*; (*in shop*) rayon *m*; *Univ* section *f*, département *m*; **that's your d.** (*sphere*) c'est ton rayon; **d. store** grand magasin *m*. ◆**depart'mental** *a* d. **manager** (*office*) chef *m* de service; (*shop*) chef *m* de rayon.

depend [dɪ'pend] *vi* dépendre (**on**, **upon** de); **to d. (up)on** (*rely on*) compter sur (**for sth** pour qch); **you can d. on it!** tu peux en être sûr! ◆**—able** *a* (*person*, *information etc*) sûr; (*machine*) fiable, sûr. ◆**dependant** *n* personne *f* à charge. ◆**dependence** *n* dépendance *f*. ◆**dependency** *n* (*country*) dépendance *f*. ◆**dependent** *a* dépendant (**on**, **upon** de); (*relative*) à charge; **to be d. (up)on** dépendre de.

depict [dɪ'pɪkt] *vt* (*describe*) dépeindre; (*pictorially*) représenter. ◆**depiction** *n* peinture *f*; représentation *f*.

deplete [dɪ'pliːt] *vt* (*use up*) épuiser; (*reduce*) réduire. ◆**depletion** *n* épuisement *m*; réduction *f*.

deplor/e [dɪ'plɔːr] *vt* déplorer. ◆**—able** *a* déplorable.

deploy [dɪ'plɔɪ] *vt* (*troops etc*) déployer. ◆**deploy'ment** *n* déploiement *m*.

depopulate [diː'pɒpjuleɪt] *vt* dépeupler. ◆**depopu'lation** *n* dépeuplement *m*.

deport [dɪ'pɔːt] *vt* *Pol Jur* expulser; (*to concentration camp etc*) *Hist* déporter. ◆**depor'tation** *n* expulsion *f*; déportation *f*.

deportment [dɪ'pɔːtmənt] *n* maintien *m*.

depose [dɪ'pəuz] *vt* (*king etc*) déposer.

deposit [dɪ'pɒzɪt] *vt* (*object*, *money etc*) déposer; – *n* (*in bank*, *wine*) & *Ch* dépôt *m*; (*part payment*) acompte *m*; (*against damage*) caution *f*; (*on bottle*) consigne *f*; **d. account** *Fin* compte *m* d'épargne. ◆**—or** *n* déposant, -ante *mf*; épargnant, -ante *mf*.

depot ['depəu, *Am* 'diːpəu] *n* dépôt *m*; (*station*) *Rail Am* gare *f*; (*bus*) *Am* gare *f* routière.

deprave [dɪ'preɪv] *vt* dépraver. ◆**depravity** *n* dépravation *f*.

deprecate ['deprəkeɪt] *vt* désapprouver.

depreciate [dɪ'priːʃɪeɪt] *vt* (*reduce in value*) déprécier; – *vi* se déprécier. ◆**depreci-'ation** *n* dépréciation *f*.

depress [dɪ'pres] *vt* (*discourage*) déprimer; (*push down*) appuyer sur. ◆**—ed** *a* déprimé; (*in decline*) en déclin; (*in crisis*) en crise; **to get d.** se décourager. ◆**depression** *n* dépression *f*.

depriv/e [dɪ'praɪv] *vt* priver (**of** de). ◆**—ed** *a* (*child etc*) déshérité. ◆**depri'vation** *n* privation *f*; (*loss*) perte *f*.

depth [depθ] *n* profondeur *f*; (*of snow*) épaisseur *f*; (*of interest*) intensité *f*; **in the depths of** (*forest*, *despair*) au plus profond de; (*winter*) au cœur de; **to get out of one's d.** *Fig* perdre pied, nager; **in d.** en profondeur.

deputize ['depjutaɪz] *vi* assurer l'intérim (**for** de); – *vt* (*s.o.* **to do** qn pour faire). ◆**depu'tation** *n* députation *f*. ◆**deputy** *n* (*replacement*) suppléant, -ante *mf*; (*assistant*) adjoint, -ointe *mf*; **d.** (*sher-iff*) *Am* shérif *m* adjoint; **d. chairman** vice-président, -ente *mf*.

derailed [dɪ'reɪld] *a* **to be d.** (*of train*) dérailler. ◆**derailment** *n* déraillement *m*.

deranged [dɪ'reɪndʒd] *a* (*person*, *mind*) dérangé.

derelict ['derɪlɪkt] *a* à l'abandon, aban-donné.

deride [dɪ'raɪd] *vt* tourner en dérision. ◆**derision** *n* dérision *f*. ◆**derisive** *a* (*laughter etc*) moqueur; (*amount*) dérisoire. ◆**derisory** *a* dérisoire.

derive [dɪ'raɪv] *vt* **to d. from** (*pleasure*, *profit etc*) tirer de; *Ling* dériver de; **to be derived from** dériver de, provenir de; – *vi* **to d. from** dériver de. ◆**deri'vation** *n* *Ling* dériva-tion *f*. ◆**derivative** *a* & *n* *Ling Ch* dérivé (*m*).

dermatology [dɜːmə'tɒlədʒɪ] *n* dermato-logie *f*.

derogatory [dɪ'rɒgət(ə)rɪ] *a* (*word*) péjora-tif; (*remark*) désobligeant (**to** pour).

derrick ['derɪk] n (over oil well) derrick m.

derv [dɜːv] n gazole m, gas-oil m.

descend [dɪ'send] vi descendre (**from** de); (of rain) tomber; **to d. upon** (attack) faire une descente sur, tomber sur; (of tourists) envahir; – vt (stairs) descendre; **to be descended from** descendre de. ◆**—ing** a (order) décroissant. ◆**descendant** n descendant, -ante mf. ◆**descent** n 1 descente f; (into crime) chute f. 2 (ancestry) souche f, origine f.

describe [dɪ'skraɪb] vt décrire. ◆**description** n description f; (on passport) signalement m; **of every d.** de toutes sortes. ◆**descriptive** a descriptif.

desecrate ['desɪkreɪt] vt profaner. ◆**desecration** n profanation f.

desegregate [diː'segrɪgeɪt] vt supprimer la ségrégation raciale dans. ◆**desegregation** n déségrégation f.

desert[1] ['dezət] n désert m; – a désertique; **d. island** île f déserte.

desert[2] [dɪ'zɜːt] vt déserter, abandonner; **to d. s.o.** (of luck etc) abandonner qn; – vi Mil déserter. ◆**—ed** a (place) désert. ◆**—er** n Mil déserteur m. ◆**desertion** n désertion f; (by spouse) abandon m (du domicile conjugal).

deserts [dɪ'zɜːts] n **one's just d.** ce qu'on mérite.

deserv/e [dɪ'zɜːv] vt mériter (**to do** de faire). ◆**—ing** a (person) méritant; (act, cause) louable, méritoire; **d. of** digne de. ◆**—edly** [-ɪdlɪ] adv à juste titre.

desiccated ['desɪkeɪtɪd] a (des)séché.

design [dɪ'zaɪn] vt (car, furniture etc) dessiner; (dress) créer, dessiner; (devise) concevoir (**for s.o.** pour qn, **to do** pour faire); **well designed** bien conçu; – n (aim) dessein m, intention f; (sketch) plan m, dessin m; (of dress, car) modèle m; (planning) conception f, création f; (pattern) motif m, dessin m; **industrial d.** dessin m industriel; **by d.** intentionnellement; **to have designs on** avoir des desseins sur. ◆**—er** n dessinateur, -trice mf; **d. clothes** vêtements mpl griffés.

designate ['dezɪgneɪt] vt désigner. ◆**designation** n désignation f.

desir/e [dɪ'zaɪər] n désir m; **I've no d. to** je n'ai aucune envie de; – vt désirer (**to do** faire). ◆**—able** a désirable; **d. property/etc** (in advertising) (très) belle propriété/etc.

desk [desk] n Sch pupitre m; (in office) bureau m; (in shop) caisse f; (reception) d. réception f; **the news d.** Journ le service des

informations; – a (job) de bureau; **d. clerk** (in hotel) Am réceptionniste mf.

desolate ['desələt] a (deserted) désolé; (in ruins) dévasté; (dreary, bleak) morne, triste. ◆**deso'lation** n (ruin) dévastation f; (emptiness) solitude f.

despair [dɪ'speər] n désespoir m; **to drive s.o. to d.** désespérer qn; **in d.** au désespoir; – vi désespérer (**of s.o.** de qn, **of doing** faire). ◆**—ing** a désespéré. ◆**'desperate** a désespéré; (criminal) capable de tout; (serious) grave; **to be d. for** (money, love etc) avoir désespérément besoin de; (a cigarette, baby etc) mourir d'envie d'avoir. ◆**'desperately** adv (ill) gravement; (in love) éperdument. ◆**despe'ration** n désespoir m; **in d.** (as a last resort) en désespoir de cause.

despatch [dɪ'spætʃ] see **dispatch**.

desperado [despə'raːdəʊ] n (pl -oes or -os) criminel m.

despise [dɪ'spaɪz] vt mépriser. ◆**despicable** a ignoble, méprisable.

despite [dɪ'spaɪt] prep malgré.

despondent [dɪ'spɒndənt] a découragé. ◆**despondency** n découragement m.

despot ['despɒt] n despote m. ◆**despotism** n despotisme m.

dessert [dɪ'zɜːt] n dessert m. ◆**dessertspoon** n cuiller f à dessert.

destabilize [diː'steɪbɪlaɪz] vt déstabiliser.

destination [destɪ'neɪʃ(ə)n] n destination f.

destine ['destɪn] vt destiner (**for** à, **to do** à faire); **it was destined to happen** ça devait arriver. ◆**destiny** n destin m; (fate of individual) destinée f.

destitute ['destɪtjuːt] a (poor) indigent; **d. of** (lacking in) dénué de. ◆**desti'tution** n dénuement m.

destroy [dɪ'strɔɪ] vt détruire; (horse etc) abattre. ◆**—er** n (person) destructeur, -trice mf; (ship) contre-torpilleur m. ◆**destruct** vt Mil détruire. ◆**destruction** n destruction f. ◆**destructive** a (person, war) destructeur; (power) destructif.

detach [dɪ'tætʃ] vt détacher (**from** de). ◆**—ed** a (indifferent) détaché; (view) désintéressé; **d. house** maison f individuelle. ◆**—able** a (lining) amovible. ◆**—ment** n (attitude) & Mil détachement m; **the d. of** (action) la séparation de.

detail ['diːteɪl, Am dɪ'teɪl] n 1 détail m; **in d.** en détail; – vt raconter ou exposer en détail ou par le menu, détailler; (**to do** pour faire); – n détachement m. ◆**—ed** a (account etc) détaillé.

detain [dɪ'teɪn] vt retenir; (imprison) détenir.

◆**detai'nee** n Pol Jur détenu, -ue mf.
◆**detention** n Jur détention f; Sch retenue f.

detect [dɪ'tekt] vt découvrir; (perceive) distinguer; (identify) identifier; (mine) détecter; (illness) dépister. ◆**detection** n découverte f; identification f; détection f; dépistage m. ◆**detector** n détecteur m.

detective [dɪ'tektɪv] n agent m de la Sûreté, policier m (en civil); (private) détective m; – a (film etc) policier; (story) roman m policier; **d. constable** = inspecteur m de police.

deter [dɪ'tɜːr] vt (-rr-) to **d. s.o.** dissuader or décourager qn (**from** doing de faire, **from** sth de qch).

detergent [dɪ'tɜːdʒənt] n détergent m.

deteriorate [dɪ'tɪərɪəreɪt] vi se détériorer; (of morals) dégénérer. ◆**deterio'ration** n détérioration f; dégénérescence f.

determin/e [dɪ'tɜːmɪn] vt déterminer; (price) fixer; to **d. s.o.** to do décider qn à faire; to **d. that** décider que; to **d.** to do se déterminer à faire. ◆**—ed** a (look, quantity) déterminé; **d.** to do or on doing décidé à faire; **I'm d.** she'll succeed je suis bien décidé à ce qu'elle réussisse.

deterrent [dɪ'terənt, Am dɪ'tɜːrənt] n Mil force f de dissuasion; to be **a d.** Fig être dissuasif.

detest [dɪ'test] vt détester (**doing** faire). ◆**—able** a détestable.

detonate ['detəneɪt] vt faire détoner or exploser; – vi détoner. ◆**deto'nation** n détonation f. ◆**detonator** n détonateur m.

detour ['diːtuər] n détour m.

detract [dɪ'trækt] vi to **d. from** (make less) diminuer. ◆**detractor** n détracteur, -trice mf.

detriment ['detrɪmənt] n détriment m. ◆**detri'mental** a préjudiciable (**to** à).

devalue [diː'væljuː] vt (money) & Fig dévaluer. ◆**devalu'ation** n dévaluation f.

devastat/e ['devəsteɪt] vt (lay waste) dévaster; (opponent) anéantir; (person) Fig foudroyer. ◆**—ing** a (storm etc) dévastateur; (overwhelming) confondant, accablant; (charm) irrésistible.

develop [dɪ'veləp] vt développer; (area, land) mettre en valeur; (habit, illness) contracter; (talent) manifester; Phot développer; to **d. a liking for** prendre goût à; – vi se développer; (of event) se produire; to **d. into** devenir. ◆**—ing** a (country) en voie de développement; – n Phot développement m. ◆**—er** n (property) **d.** promoteur m (de construction).

◆**—ment** n développement m; (of land) mise f en valeur; (housing) **d.** lotissement m; (large) grand ensemble m; **a (new) d.** (in situation) un fait nouveau.

deviate ['diːvɪeɪt] vi dévier (**from** de); to **d. from the norm** s'écarter de la norme. ◆**deviant** a anormal. ◆**devi'ation** n déviation f.

device [dɪ'vaɪs] n dispositif m, engin m; (scheme) procédé m; **left to one's own devices** livré à soi-même.

devil ['dev(ə)l] n diable m; **a** or **the d. of a problem** Fam un problème infernal; **a** or **the d. of a noise** Fam un bruit infernal; **I had a** or **the d. of a job** Fam j'ai eu un mal fou (**doing, to do** à faire); **what/where/why the d.?** Fam que/où/pourquoi diable?; **like the d.** (to run etc) comme un fou. ◆**devil-ish** a diabolique. ◆**devilry** n (mischief) diablerie f.

devious ['diːvɪəs] a (mind, behaviour) tortueux; **he's d.** il a l'esprit tortueux. ◆**—ness** n (of person) esprit m tortueux.

devise [dɪ'vaɪz] vt (plan) combiner; (plot) tramer; (invent) inventer.

devitalize [diː'vaɪtəlaɪz] vt rendre exsangue, affaiblir.

devoid [dɪ'vɔɪd] a **d.** of dénué or dépourvu de; (guilt) exempt de.

devolution [diːvə'luːʃ(ə)n] n Pol décentralisation f; **the d.** of (power) la délégation de.

devolve [dɪ'vɒlv] vi to **d. upon** incomber à.

devot/e [dɪ'vəut] vt consacrer (**to** à). ◆**—ed** a dévoué; (admirer) fervent. ◆**—edly** adv avec dévouement. ◆**devo'tee** n Sp Mus passionné, -ée mf. ◆**devotion** n dévouement m; (religious) dévotion f; pl (prayers) dévotions fpl.

devour [dɪ'vauər] vt (eat, engulf, read etc) dévorer.

devout [dɪ'vaut] a dévot, pieux; (supporter, prayer) fervent.

dew [djuː] n rosée f. ◆**dewdrop** n goutte f de rosée.

dext(e)rous ['dekst(ə)rəs] a adroit, habile. ◆**dex'terity** n adresse f, dextérité f.

diabetes [daɪə'biːtiːz] n Med diabète m. ◆**diabetic** a & n diabétique (mf).

diabolical [daɪə'bɒlɪk(ə)l] a diabolique; (bad) épouvantable.

diadem ['daɪədem] n diadème m.

diagnosis, pl **-oses** [daɪəg'nəusɪs, -əusiːz] n diagnostic m. ◆**'diagnose** vt diagnostiquer.

diagonal [daɪ'ægən(ə)l] a diagonal; – n (line) diagonale f. ◆**—ly** adv en diagonale.

diagram ['daɪəgræm] n schéma m,

diagramme *m*; *Geom* figure *f.* ◆**dia-gra'mmatic** *adv* schématique.

dial ['daɪəl] *n* cadran *m*; — *vt* (**-ll-,** *Am* **-l-**) *(number)* Tel faire, composer; *(person)* appeler; **to d. s.o. direct** appeler qn par l'automatique; **d. tone** *Am* tonalité *f.* ◆**dialling** *a* **d. code** indicatif *m*; **d. tone** tonalité *f.*

dialect ['daɪəlekt] *n* *(regional)* dialecte *m*; *(rural)* patois *m.*

dialogue ['daɪəlɒg] *(Am* **dialog)** *n* dialogue *m.*

dialysis, *pl* **-yses** [daɪ'ælɪsɪs, -ɪsiːz] *n Med* dialyse *f.*

diameter [daɪ'æmɪtər] *n* diamètre *m.* ◆**dia-'metrically** *adv (opposed)* diamétralement.

diamond ['daɪəmənd] **1** *n (stone)* diamant *m*; *(shape)* losange *m*; *(baseball)* **d.** *Am* terrain *m* (de baseball); **d. necklace/***etc* rivière *f*/*etc* de diamants. **2** *n & npl Cards* carreau *m.*

diaper ['daɪəpər] *n (for baby) Am* couche *f.*

diaphragm ['daɪəfræm] *n* diaphragme *m.*

diarrh(o)ea [daɪə'riːə] *n* diarrhée *f.*

diary ['daɪərɪ] *n (calendar)* agenda *m*; *(private)* journal *m* (intime).

dice [daɪs] *n inv* dé *m* (à jouer); — *vt Culin* couper en dés.

dicey ['daɪsɪ] *a* (**-ier, -iest**) *Fam* risqué.

dichotomy [daɪ'kɒtəmɪ] *n* dichotomie *f.*

dickens ['dɪkɪnz] *n* **where/why/what the d.?** *Fam* où/pourquoi/que diable?

dictate [dɪk'teɪt] *vt* dicter (**to** à); — *vi* dicter; **to d. to s.o.** *(order around)* régenter qn. ◆**dictation** *n* dictée *f.* ◆**'dictaphone®** *n* dictaphone® *m.*

dictates ['dɪkteɪts] *npl* préceptes *mpl*; **the d. of conscience** la voix de la conscience.

dictator [dɪk'teɪtər] *n* dictateur *m.* ◆**dicta-'torial** *a* dictatorial. ◆**dictatorship** *n* dictature *f.*

diction ['dɪkʃ(ə)n] *n* langage *m*; *(way of speaking)* diction *f.*

dictionary ['dɪkʃənərɪ] *n* dictionnaire *m.*

dictum ['dɪktəm] *n* dicton *m.*

did [dɪd] *see* **do.**

diddle ['dɪd(ə)l] *vt Sl* rouler; **to d. s.o. out of sth** carotter qch à qn; **to get diddled out of sth** se faire refaire de qch.

die [daɪ] **1** *vi (pt & pp* died, *pres p* dying) mourir (**of, from** de); **to be dying to do** mourir d'envie de faire; **to be dying for sth** *Fam* avoir une envie folle de qch; **to d. away** *(of noise)* mourir; **to d. down** *(of fire)* mourir; *(of storm)* se calmer; **to d. off** mourir (les uns après les autres); **to d. out** *(of custom)* mourir. **2** *n (in engraving)* coin

m; *Tech* matrice *f*; **the d. is cast** *Fig* les dés sont jetés.

diehard ['daɪhɑːd] *n* réactionnaire *mf.*

diesel ['diːz(ə)l] *a & n* **d. (engine)** (moteur *m*) diesel *m*; **d. (oil)** gazole *m.*

diet ['daɪət] *n (for slimming etc)* régime *m*; *(usual food)* alimentation *f*; **to go on a d.** faire un régime; — *vi* suivre un régime. ◆**dietary** *a* diététique; **d. fibre** fibre(s) *f(pl)* alimentaire(s). ◆**die'tician** *n* diététicien, -ienne *mf.*

differ ['dɪfər] *vi* différer (**from** de); *(disagree)* ne pas être d'accord (**from** avec). ◆**differ-ence** *n* différence *f* (**in** de); *(in age, weight etc)* écart *m*, différence *f*; **d. of opinion** différend *m*; **it makes no d.** ça n'a pas d'importance; **it makes no d. to me** ça m'est égal; **to make a d. in sth** changer qch. ◆**dif-ferent** *a* différent (**from, to** de); *(another)* autre; *(various)* divers. ◆**diffe-'rential** *a* différentiel; — *npl Econ* écarts *mpl* salariaux. ◆**diffe'rentiate** *vt* différencier (**from** de); — *vi* faire la différence entre. ◆**differently** *adv* différemment (**from, to** de), autrement (**from, to** que).

difficult ['dɪfɪkəlt] *a* difficile (**to do** à faire); **it's d. for us to ...** il nous est difficile de ... ; **the d. thing is to ...** le plus difficile est de .... ◆**difficulty** *n* difficulté *f*; **to have d. doing** avoir du mal à faire; **to be in d.** avoir des difficultés; **d. with** des ennuis *mpl* avec.

diffident ['dɪfɪdənt] *a (person)* qui manque d'assurance; *(smile, tone)* mal assuré. ◆**diffidence** *n* manque *m* d'assurance.

diffuse [dɪ'fjuːz] *vt (spread)* diffuser; — [dɪ'fjuːs] *a (spread out, wordy)* diffus. ◆**dif-fusion** *n* diffusion *f.*

dig [dɪg] *vt (pt & pp* dug, *pres p* digging) *(ground)* bêcher; *(hole, grave etc)* creuser; *(understand) Sl* piger; *(appreciate) Sl* aimer; **to d. sth into** *(thrust)* enfoncer qch dans; **to d. out** *(animal, fact)* déterrer; *(find) Fam* dénicher; *(accident victim)* dégager; **to d. up** déterrer; *(weed)* arracher; *(earth)* retourner; *(street)* piocher; — *vi* creuser; **to d. (oneself) in** *Mil* se retrancher; **to d. in** *(eat) Fam* manger; **to d. into** *(s.o.'s past)* fouiller dans; *(meal) Fam* attaquer; — *n (with spade)* coup *m* de bêche; *(push)* coup *m* de poing *or* de coude; *(remark) Fam* coup *m* de griffe. ◆**digger** *n (machine)* pelleteuse *f.*

digest [daɪ'dʒest] *vti* digérer; — ['daɪdʒest] *n Journ* condensé *m.* ◆**digestible** *a* digeste.

◆**digestion** n digestion f. ◆**digestive** a digestif.

digit ['dɪdʒɪt] n (number) chiffre m. ◆**digital** a (watch, keyboard etc) numérique.

dignified ['dɪgnɪfaɪd] a digne, qui a de la dignité. ◆**dignify** vt donner de la dignité à; to d. with the name of honorer du nom de. ◆**dignitary** n dignitaire m f. ◆**dignity** n dignité f.

digress [daɪ'gres] vi faire une digression; to d. from s'écarter de. ◆**digression** n digression f.

digs [dɪgz] npl Fam chambre f (meublée), logement m.

dilapidated [dɪ'læpɪdeɪtɪd] a (house) délabré. ◆**dilapi'dation** n délabrement m.

dilate [daɪ'leɪt] vt dilater; – vi se dilater. ◆**dilation** n dilatation f.

dilemma [daɪ'lemə] n dilemme m.

dilettante [dɪlɪ'tæntɪ] n dilettante m f.

diligent ['dɪlɪdʒənt] a assidu, appliqué; to be d. in doing sth faire qch avec zèle. ◆**diligence** n zèle m, assiduité f.

dilly-dally [dɪlɪ'dælɪ] vi Fam (dawdle) lambiner, lanterner; (hesitate) tergiverser.

dilute [daɪ'luːt] vt diluer; – a dilué.

dim [dɪm] a (dimmer, dimmest) (feeble) faible; (colour) terne; (room) sombre; (memory, outline) vague; (person) stupide; – vt (-mm-) (light) baisser, réduire; (glory) ternir; (memory) estomper. ◆–**ly** adv faiblement; (vaguely) vaguement. ◆–**ness** n faiblesse f; (of memory etc) vague m; (of room) pénombre f. ◆**dimwit** n idiot, -ote m f. ◆**dim'witted** a idiot.

dime [daɪm] n (US & Can coin) (pièce f de) dix cents mpl; **a d. store** = un Prisunic®, un Monoprix®.

dimension [daɪ'menʃ(ə)n] n dimension f; (extent) Fig étendue f. ◆**dimensional** a two-d. à deux dimensions.

diminish [dɪ'mɪnɪʃ] vti diminuer. ◆–**ing** a qui diminue.

diminutive [dɪ'mɪnjʊtɪv] **1** a (tiny) minuscule. **2** a & n Gram diminutif (m).

dimple ['dɪmp(ə)l] n fossette f. ◆**dimpled** a (chin, cheek) à fossettes.

din [dɪn] **1** n (noise) vacarme m. **2** vt (-nn-) to d. into s.o. that rabâcher à qn que.

dine [daɪn] vi dîner (off, on, de); to d. out dîner en ville. ◆–**ing** a d. car Rail wagon-restaurant m; **d. room** salle f à manger. ◆–**er** n dîneur, -euse m f; Rail wagon-restaurant m; (short-order restaurant) Am petit restaurant m.

ding(dong)! ['dɪŋ(dɒŋ)] int (of bell) dring!, ding (dong)!

dinghy ['dɪŋgɪ] n petit canot m, youyou m; (rubber) d. canot m pneumatique.

dingy ['dɪndʒɪ] a (-ier, -iest) (dirty) malpropre; (colour) terne. ◆**dinginess** n malpropreté f.

dinner ['dɪnər] n (evening meal) dîner m; (lunch) déjeuner m; (for dog, cat) pâtée f; to have d. dîner; to have s.o. to d. avoir qn à dîner; **d. dance** dîner-dansant m; **d. jacket** smoking m; **d. party** dîner m (à la maison); **d. plate** grande assiette f; **d. service, d. set** service m de table.

dinosaur ['daɪnəsɔːr] n dinosaure m.

dint [dɪnt] n by d. of à force de.

diocese ['daɪəsɪs] n Rel diocèse m.

dip [dɪp] vt (-pp-) plonger; (into liquid) tremper, plonger; to d. one's headlights se mettre en code; – vi (of sun etc) baisser; (of road) plonger; to d. into (pocket, savings) puiser dans; (book) feuilleter; – n (in road) déclivité f; to go for a d. faire trempette f.

diphtheria [dɪp'θɪərɪə] n diphtérie f.

diphthong ['dɪfθɒŋ] n Ling diphtongue f.

diploma [dɪ'pləʊmə] n diplôme m.

diplomacy [dɪ'pləʊməsɪ] n (tact) & Pol diplomatie f. ◆'**diplomat** n diplomate m f. ◆**diplo'matic** a diplomatique; to be d. (tactful) Fig être diplomate.

dipper ['dɪpər] n the big d. (at fairground) les montagnes fpl russes.

dire ['daɪər] a affreux; (poverty, need) extrême.

direct [daɪ'rekt] **1** a (result, flight, person etc) direct; (danger) immédiat; – adv directement. **2** vt (work, one's steps, one's attention) diriger; (letter, remark) adresser (to à); (efforts) orienter (to, towards vers); (film) réaliser; (play) mettre en scène; to s.o. to (place) indiquer à qn le chemin de; to d. s.o. to do charger qn de faire. ◆**direction** n direction f, sens m; (management) direction f; (of film) réalisation f; (of play) mise f en scène; pl (orders) indications fpl; **directions (for use)** mode m d'emploi; **in the opposite d.** en sens inverse. ◆**directive** [dɪ'rektɪv] n directive f. ◆**directly** adv (without detour) directement; (at once) tout de suite; (to speak) franchement; – conj Fam aussitôt que. ◆**directness** n (of reply) franchise f. ◆**director** n directeur, -trice m f; (of film) réalisateur, -trice m f; (of play) metteur m en scène. ◆**directorship** n Com poste m de directeur.

directory [daɪ'rektərɪ] n Tel annuaire m; (of

streets) guide *m*; (*of addresses*) répertoire *m*; **d. enquiries** *Tel* renseignements *mpl*.

dirge [dɜːdʒ] *n* chant *m* funèbre.

dirt [dɜːt] *n* saleté *f*; (*filth*) ordure *f*; (*mud*) boue *f*; (*earth*) terre *f*; (*talk*) *Fig* obscénité(s) *f(pl)*; **d. cheap** *Fam* très bon marché; **d. road** chemin *m* de terre; **d. track** *Sp* cendrée *f*. ◆**dirty** *a* (**-ier, -iest**) sale; (*job*) salissant; (*obscene, unpleasant*) sale; (*word*) grossier, obscène; **to get d.** se salir; **to get sth d.** salir qch; **a d. joke** une histoire cochonne; **a d. trick** un sale tour; **a d. old man** un vieux cochon; – *adv* (*to fight*) déloyalement; – *vt* salir; (*machine*) encrasser; – *vi* se salir.

disabl/e [dɪsˈeɪb(ə)l] *vt* rendre infirme; (*maim*) mutiler. ◆**—ed** *a* infirme, handicapé; (*maimed*) mutilé; – *n* **d. les** infirmes *mpl*, les handicapés *mpl*. ◆**disa-'bility** *n* infirmité *f*; *Fig* désavantage *m*.

disadvantage [dɪsədˈvɑːntɪdʒ] *n* désavantage *m*; – *vt* désavantager.

disaffected [dɪsəˈfektɪd] *a* mécontent. ◆**disaffection** *n* désaffection *f* (**for** pour).

disagree [dɪsəˈgriː] *vi* ne pas être d'accord, être en désaccord (**with** avec); (*of figures*) ne pas concorder; **to d. with** (*of food etc*) ne pas réussir à. ◆**—able** *a* désagréable. ◆**—ment** *n* désaccord *m*; (*quarrel*) différend *m*.

disallow [dɪsəˈlaʊ] *vt* rejeter.

disappear [dɪsəˈpɪər] *vi* disparaître. ◆**disappearance** *n* disparition *f*.

disappoint [dɪsəˈpɔɪnt] *vt* décevoir; **I'm disappointed with it** ça m'a déçu. ◆**—ing** *a* décevant. ◆**—ment** *n* déception *f*.

disapprov/e [dɪsəˈpruːv] *vi* **to d. of s.o./sth** désapprouver qn/qch; **I d.** je suis contre. ◆**—ing** *a* (*look etc*) désapprobateur. ◆**disapproval** *n* désapprobation *f*.

disarm [dɪsˈɑːm] *vti* désarmer. ◆**disarmament** *n* désarmement *m*.

disarray [dɪsəˈreɪ] *n* (*disorder*) désordre *m*; (*distress*) désarroi *m*.

disaster [dɪˈzɑːstər] *n* désastre *m*, catastrophe *f*; **d. area** région *f* sinistrée. ◆**d.-stricken** *a* sinistré. **he doesn't d. it** ça ne lui déplaît pas; – *n* aversion *f* (**for, of** pour); **to take a d. to** (*person, thing*) prendre en grippe; **our likes and dislikes** nos goûts et dégoûts *mpl*.

dislocate [ˈdɪsləkeɪt] *vt* (*limb*) disloquer; *Fig* désorganiser. ◆**dislo'cation** *n* dislocation *f*.

dislodge [dɪsˈlɒdʒ] *vt* faire bouger, déplacer; (*enemy*) déloger.

disloyal [dɪsˈlɔɪəl] *a* déloyal. ◆**disloyalty** *n* déloyauté *f*.

dismal [ˈdɪzməl] *a* morne, triste. ◆**—ly** *adv* (*to fail, behave*) lamentablement.

dismantle [dɪsˈmænt(ə)l] *vt* (*machine etc*) démonter; (*organization*) démanteler.

dismay [dɪsˈmeɪ] *vt* consterner; – *n* consternation *f*.

dismember [dɪsˈmembər] *vt* (*country etc*) démembrer. ◆**disastrous** *a* désastreux.

disband [dɪsˈbænd] *vt* disperser; – *vi* se disperser.

disbelief [dɪsbəˈliːf] *n* incrédulité *f*.

disc [dɪsk] (*Am* **disk**) *n* disque *m*; **identity d.** plaque *f* d'identité; **d. jockey** animateur, -trice *mf* (*de variétés etc*), disc-jockey *m*.

discard [dɪsˈkɑːd] *vt* (*get rid of*) se débarrasser de; (*plan, hope etc*) *Fig* abandonner.

discern [dɪˈsɜːn] *vt* discerner. ◆**—ing** *a* (*person*) averti, sagace. ◆**—ible** *a* perceptible. ◆**—ment** *n* discernement *m*.

discharge [dɪsˈtʃɑːdʒ] *vt* (*gun, accused person*) décharger; (*liquid*) déverser; (*patient, employee*) renvoyer; (*unfit soldier*) libérer; (*unfit soldier*) réformer; (*one's duty*) accomplir; – *vi* (*of wound*) suppurer; – [ˈdɪstʃɑːdʒ] *n* (*of gun*) & *El* décharge *f*; (*of liquid*) & *Med* écoulement *m*; (*dismissal*) renvoi *m*; (*freeing*) libération *f*; (*of unfit soldier*) réforme *f*.

disciple [dɪˈsaɪp(ə)l] *n* disciple *m*.

discipline [ˈdɪsɪplɪn] *n* (*behaviour, subject*) discipline *f*; – *vt* (*control*) discipliner; (*punish*) punir. ◆**disci'plinarian** *n* partisan, -ane *mf* de la discipline; **to be a (strict) d.** être très à cheval sur la discipline. ◆**disci'plinary** *a* disciplinaire.

disclaim [dɪsˈkleɪm] *vt* désavouer; (*responsibility*) (dé)nier.

disclose [dɪsˈkləʊz] *vt* révéler, divulguer. ◆**disclosure** *n* révélation *f*.

disco [ˈdɪskəʊ] *n* (*pl* **-os**) *Fam* disco(thèque) *f*.

discolour [dɪsˈkʌlər] *vt* décolorer; (*teeth*) jaunir; – *vi* se décolorer; jaunir. ◆**discolo(u)ration** *n* décoloration *f*; jaunissement *m*.

discomfort [dɪsˈkʌmfət] *n* (*physical, mental*) malaise *m*, gêne *f*; (*hardship*) inconvénient *m*.

disconcert [dɪskənˈsɜːt] *vt* déconcerter.

disconnect [dɪskəˈnekt] *vt* (*unfasten etc*) détacher; (*unplug*) débrancher; (*wires*) *El* déconnecter; (*gas, telephone etc*) couper. ◆**—ed** *a* (*speech*) décousu.

discontent [dɪskənˈtent] *n* mécontentement *m*. ◆**discontented** *a* mécontent.

discontinu/e [dɪskən'tɪnjuː] *vt* cesser, interrompre. ◆**—ed** *a* (*article*) Com qui ne se fait plus.

discord ['dɪskɔːd] *n* discorde *f*; Mus dissonance *f*.

discotheque ['dɪskətek] *n* (*club*) discothèque *f*.

discount 1 ['dɪskaunt] *n* (*on article*) remise *f*; (*on account paid early*) escompte *m*; **at a d.** (*to buy, sell*) au rabais; **d. store** solderie *f*. **2** [dɪs'kaunt] *vt* (*story etc*) ne pas tenir compte de.

discourage [dɪs'kʌrɪdʒ] *vt* décourager; **to get discouraged** se décourager. ◆**—ment** *n* découragement *m*.

discourse ['dɪskɔːs] *n* discours *m*.

discourteous [dɪs'kɜːtɪəs] *a* impoli, discourtois. ◆**discourtesy** *n* impolitesse *f*.

discover [dɪs'kʌvər] *vt* découvrir. ◆**discovery** *n* découverte *f*.

discredit [dɪs'kredɪt] *vt* (*cast slur on*) discréditer; (*refuse to believe*) ne pas croire; − *n* discrédit *m*. ◆**—able** *a* indigne.

discreet [dɪs'kriːt] *a* (*careful*) prudent, avisé; (*unassuming, reserved etc*) discret. ◆**discretion** *n* prudence *f*; discrétion *f*; **I'll use my own d.** je ferai comme bon me semblera. ◆**discretionary** *a* discrétionnaire.

discrepancy [dɪ'skrepənsɪ] *n* divergence *f*, contradiction *f* (**between** entre).

discriminat/e [dɪ'skrɪmɪneɪt] *vi* **to d. between** distinguer entre; **to d. against** établir une discrimination contre; − *vt* **to d. sth./s.o. from** distinguer qch/qn de. ◆**—ing** *a* (*person*) averti, sagace; (*ear*) fin. ◆**discrimi'nation** *n* (*judgement*) discernement *m*; (*distinction*) distinction *f*; (*partiality*) discrimination *f*. ◆**discriminatory** [-ətərɪ] *a* discriminatoire.

discus ['dɪskəs] *n* Sp disque *m*.

discuss [dɪs'kʌs] *vt* (*talk about*) discuter de; (*examine in detail*) discuter. ◆**discussion** *n* discussion *f*; **under d.** (*matter etc*) en question, en discussion.

disdain [dɪs'deɪn] *vt* dédaigner; − *n* dédain *m*. ◆**disdainful** *a* dédaigneux; **to be d. of** dédaigner.

disease [dɪ'ziːz] *n* maladie *f*. ◆**diseased** *a* malade.

disembark [dɪsɪm'bɑːk] *vti* débarquer. ◆**disembar'kation** *n* débarquement *m*.

disembodied [dɪsɪm'bɒdɪd] *a* désincarné.

disembowel [dɪsɪm'bauəl] *vt* (**-ll-**, *Am* **-l-**) éventrer.

disenchant [dɪsɪn'tʃɑːnt] *vt* désenchanter. ◆**—ment** *n* désenchantement *m*.

disengage [dɪsɪn'geɪdʒ] *vt* (*object*) dégager; (*troops*) désengager.

disentangle [dɪsɪn'tæŋg(ə)l] *vt* démêler; **to d. oneself from** se dégager de.

disfavour ['dɪsfeɪvər] *n* défaveur *f*.

disfigure [dɪs'fɪgər] *vt* défigurer. ◆**—ment** *n* défigurement *m*.

disgorge [dɪs'gɔːdʒ] *vt* (*food*) vomir.

disgrac/e [dɪs'greɪs] *n* (*shame*) honte *f* (**to** à); (*disfavour*) disgrâce *f*; − *vt* déshonorer, faire honte à. ◆**—ed** *a* (*politician etc*) disgracié. ◆**disgraceful** *a* honteux (**of s.o.** de la part de qn). ◆**disgracefully** *adv* honteusement.

disgruntled [dɪs'grʌnt(ə)ld] *a* mécontent.

disguise [dɪs'gaɪz] *vt* déguiser (**as** en); − *n* déguisement *m*; **in d.** déguisé.

disgust [dɪs'gʌst] *n* dégoût *m* (**for, at, with** de); **in d.** dégoûté; − *vt* dégoûter, écœurer. ◆**—ed** *a* dégoûté (**at, by, with** de); **to be d. with s.o.** (*annoyed*) être fâché contre qn; **d. to hear that . . .** indigné d'apprendre que . . . . ◆**—ing** *a* dégoûtant, écœurant. ◆**—ingly** *adv* d'une façon dégoûtante.

dish [dɪʃ] **1** *n* (*container*) plat *m*; (*food*) mets *m*, plat *m*; **the dishes** la vaisselle; **to do the dishes** faire la vaisselle; **a (real) d.** Sl c'est un beau brin de fille. **2** *vt* **to d. out** distribuer; **to d. out** *or* **up** (*food*) servir. ◆**dishcloth** *n* (*for washing*) lavette *f*; (*for drying*) torchon *m*. ◆**dishpan** *n Am* bassine *f* (à vaisselle). ◆**dishwasher** *n* lave-vaisselle *m inv*.

disharmony [dɪs'hɑːmənɪ] *n* désaccord *m*; Mus dissonance *f*.

dishearten [dɪs'hɑːt(ə)n] *vt* décourager.

dishevelled [dɪ'ʃevəld] *a* hirsute, échevelé.

dishonest [dɪs'ɒnɪst] *a* malhonnête; (*insincere*) de mauvaise foi. ◆**dishonesty** *n* malhonnêteté *f*; mauvaise foi *f*.

dishonour [dɪs'ɒnər] *n* déshonneur *m*; − *vt* déshonorer; (*cheque*) refuser d'honorer. ◆**—able** *a* peu honorable. ◆**—ably** *adv* avec déshonneur.

dishy ['dɪʃɪ] *a* (**-ier, -iest**) (*woman, man*) Sl beau, sexy, qui a du chien.

disillusion [dɪsɪ'luːʒ(ə)n] *vt* désillusionner; − *n* désillusion *f*. ◆**—ment** *n* désillusion *f*.

disincentive [dɪsɪn'sentɪv] *n* mesure *f* dissuasive; **to be a d. to s.o.** décourager qn; **it's a d. to work/invest/etc** cela n'encourage pas à travailler/investir/*etc*.

disinclined [dɪsɪn'klaɪnd] *a* peu disposé (**to** à). ◆**disincli'nation** *n* répugnance *f*.

disinfect [dɪsɪn'fekt] *vt* désinfecter. ◆**disinfectant** *a* & *n* désinfectant (*m*). ◆**disinfection** *n* désinfection *f*.

disinherit [dɪsɪn'herɪt] *vt* déshériter.

disintegrate [dɪs'ɪntɪgreɪt] vi se désintégrer; – vt désintégrer. ◆**disinte'gration** n désintégration f.

disinterested [dɪs'ɪntrɪstɪd] a (impartial) désintéressé; (uninterested) Fam indifférent (in à).

disjointed [dɪs'dʒɔɪntɪd] a décousu.

disk [dɪsk] n **1** Am = disc. **2** (magnetic) d. (of computer) disque m (magnétique).

dislike [dɪs'laɪk] vt ne pas aimer (doing faire); – n to have a d. for prendre en grippe.

dismiss [dɪs'mɪs] vt congédier, renvoyer (from de); (official) destituer; (appeal) Jur rejeter; (thought etc) Fig écarter; d.! Mil rompez!; (class) d.! Sch vous pouvez partir. ◆**dismissal** n renvoi m; destitution f.

dismount [dɪs'maʊnt] vi descendre (from de); – vt (rider) démonter, désarçonner.

disobey [dɪsə'beɪ] vt désobéir à; – vi désobéir. ◆**disobedience** n désobéissance f. ◆**disobedient** a désobéissant.

disorder [dɪs'ɔɪdər] n (confusion) désordre m; (riots) désordres mpl; disorder(s) Med troubles mpl. ◆**disorderly** a (meeting etc) désordonné.

disorganize [dɪs'ɔɪgənaɪz] vt désorganiser.

disorientate [dɪs'ɔɪrɪənteɪt] (Am **disorient** [dɪs'ɔɪrɪənt]) vt désorienter.

disown [dɪs'əʊn] vt désavouer, renier.

disparag/e [dɪs'pærɪdʒ] vt dénigrer. ◆**-ing** a peu flatteur.

disparate ['dɪspərət] a disparate. ◆**dis'parity** n disparité f (between entre, de).

dispassionate [dɪs'pæʃənət] a (unemotional) calme; (not biased) impartial.

dispatch [dɪs'pætʃ] vt (letter, work) expédier; (troops, messenger) envoyer; – n expédition f (of de); Journ Mil dépêche f; d. rider Mil etc courrier m.

dispel [dɪs'pel] vt (-ll-) dissiper.

dispensary [dɪs'pensərɪ] n (in hospital) pharmacie f; (in chemist's shop) officine f.

dispense [dɪs'pens] **1** vt (give out) distribuer; (justice) administrer; (medicine) préparer. **2** vi to d. with (do without) se passer de; to d. with the need for rendre superflu. ◆**dispen'sation** n distribution f; special d. (exemption) dérogation f. ◆**dispenser** n (device) distributeur m; **cash d.** distributeur m de billets.

disperse [dɪs'pɜːs] vt disperser; – vi se disperser. ◆**dispersal** n, ◆**dispersion** n dispersion f.

dispirited [dɪs'pɪrɪtɪd] a découragé.

displace [dɪs'pleɪs] vt (bone, furniture, refugees) déplacer; (replace) supplanter.

display [dɪs'pleɪ] vt montrer; (notice, elec-

tronic data etc) afficher; (painting, goods) exposer; (courage etc) faire preuve de; – n (in shop) étalage m; (of force) déploiement m; (of anger etc) manifestation f; (of paintings) exposition f; (of luxury) étalage m; Mil parade f; (of electronic data) affichage m; d. (unit) (of computer) moniteur m; **on d.** exposé; **air d.** fête f aéronautique.

displeas/e [dɪs'pliːz] vt déplaire à. ◆**-ed** a mécontent (with de). ◆**-ing** a désagréable. ◆**displeasure** n mécontentement m.

dispos/e [dɪs'pəʊz] vt disposer (s.o. to do qn à faire); – vi to d. of (get rid of) se débarrasser de; (one's time, money) disposer de; (sell) vendre; (matter) expédier, liquider; (kill) liquider. ◆**-ed** a disposé (to do à faire); (income) bien disposé envers. ◆**-able** a (plate etc) à jeter, jetable; (income) disponible. ◆**disposal** n (sale) vente f; (of waste) évacuation f; **at the d. of** à la disposition de. ◆**dispo'sition** n (placing) disposition f; (character) naturel m; (readiness) inclination f.

dispossess [dɪspə'zes] vt déposséder (of de).

disproportion [dɪsprə'pɔɪʃ(ə)n] n disproportion f. ◆**disproportionate** a disproportionné.

disprove [dɪs'pruːv] vt réfuter.

dispute [dɪs'pjuːt] n discussion f; (quarrel) dispute f; Pol conflit m; Jur litige m; **beyond d.** incontestable; **in d.** (matter) en litige; (territory) contesté; – vt (claim etc) contester; (discuss) discuter.

disqualify [dɪs'kwɒlɪfaɪ] vt (make unfit) rendre inapte (from à); Sp disqualifier; **to d. from driving** retirer le permis à. ◆**disqualifi'cation** n Sp disqualification f.

disquiet [dɪs'kwaɪət] n inquiétude f; – vt inquiéter.

disregard [dɪsrɪ'gaːd] vt ne tenir aucun compte de; – n indifférence f (for à); (law) désobéissance f (for à).

disrepair [dɪsrɪ'peər] n **in** (a state of) d. en mauvais état.

disreputable [dɪs'repjʊtəb(ə)l] a peu recommandable; (behaviour) honteux.

disrepute [dɪsrɪ'pjuːt] n discrédit m; **to bring into d.** jeter le discrédit sur.

disrespect [dɪsrɪ'spekt] n manque m de respect. ◆**disrespectful** a irrespectueux (to envers).

disrupt [dɪs'rʌpt] vt perturber; (communications) interrompre; (plan) déranger. ◆**disruption** n perturbation f; interruption f;

dérangement m. ◆**disruptive** a (element etc) perturbateur.

dissatisfied [dɪsˈsætɪsfaɪd] a mécontent (with de). ◆**dissatisfaction** n mécontentement m.

dissect [daɪˈsekt] vt disséquer. ◆**dissection** n dissection f.

disseminate [dɪˈsemɪneɪt] vt disséminer.

dissension [dɪˈsenʃ(ə)n] n dissension f.

dissent [dɪˈsent] vi différer (d'opinion) (from sth à l'égard de qch); – n dissentiment m. ◆**-ing** a dissident.

dissertation [dɪsəˈteɪʃ(ə)n] n Univ mémoire m.

dissident [ˈdɪsɪdənt] a & n dissident, -ente (mf). ◆**dissidence** n dissidence f.

dissimilar [dɪˈsɪmɪlər] a dissemblable (to à). ◆**dissi'pation** n dissipation f; gaspillage m.

dissipate [ˈdɪsɪpeɪt] vt dissiper; (energy) gaspiller. ◆**dissi'pation** n dissipation f; gaspillage m.

dissociate [dɪˈsəʊʃɪeɪt] vt dissocier (from de).

dissolute [ˈdɪsəluːt] a (life, person) dissolu.

dissolve [dɪˈzɒlv] vt dissoudre; – vi se dissoudre. ◆**disso'lution** n dissolution f.

dissuade [dɪˈsweɪd] vt dissuader (from doing de faire); **to d. s.o. from sth** détourner qn de qch. ◆**dissuasion** n dissuasion f.

distance [ˈdɪstəns] n distance f; **in the d.** au loin; **from a d.** de loin; **at a d.** à quelque distance; **it's within walking d.** on peut y aller à pied; **to keep one's d.** garder ses distances. ◆**distant** a éloigné, lointain; (relative) éloigné; (reserved) distant; **5 km d. from** à (une distance de) 5 km de. ◆**distantly** adv **we're d. related** nous sommes parents éloignés.

distaste [dɪsˈteɪst] n aversion f (for pour). ◆**distasteful** a désagréable, déplaisant.

distemper [dɪsˈtempər] **1** n (paint) badigeon m; – vt badigeonner. **2** n (in dogs) maladie f.

distend [dɪˈstend] vt distendre; – vi se distendre.

distil [dɪˈstɪl] vt (-ll-) distiller. ◆**distillation** n distillation f. ◆**distillery** n distillerie f.

distinct [dɪˈstɪŋkt] a **1** (voice, light etc) distinct; (definite, marked) net, marqué; (promise) formel. **2** (different) distinct (from de). ◆**distinction** n distinction f; Univ mention f très bien; **of d.** (singer, writer etc) de marque. ◆**distinctive** a distinctif. ◆**distinctively** adv distinctement; (to stipulate, forbid) formellement; (noticeably) nettement, sensiblement; **d. possible** tout à fait possible.

distinguish [dɪˈstɪŋgwɪʃ] vti distinguer (from de, between entre); **to d. oneself** se distinguer (as en tant que). ◆**-ed** a distingué. ◆**-ing** a **d. mark** signe m particulier; (discernible) visible.

distort [dɪˈstɔːt] vt déformer. ◆**-ed** a (false) faux. ◆**distortion** n El Med distorsion f; (of truth) déformation f.

distract [dɪˈstrækt] vt distraire (from de). ◆**-ed** a (troubled) préoccupé; (mad with worry) éperdu. ◆**-ing** a (noise etc) gênant. ◆**distraction** n (lack of attention, amusement) distraction f; **to drive to d.** rendre fou.

distraught [dɪˈstrɔːt] a éperdu, affolé.

distress [dɪˈstres] n (pain) douleur f; (anguish) chagrin m; (misfortune, danger) détresse f; **in d.** (ship, soul) en détresse; **in (great) d.** (poverty) dans la détresse; – vt affliger, peiner. ◆**-ing** a affligeant, pénible.

distribute [dɪˈstrɪbjuːt] vt distribuer; (spread evenly) répartir. ◆**distri'bution** n distribution f; répartition f. ◆**distributor** n Aut Cin distributeur m; (of goods) Com concessionnaire mf.

district [ˈdɪstrɪkt] n région f; (of town) quartier m; (administrative) arrondissement m; **d. attorney** Am = procureur m (de la République); **d. nurse** infirmière f visiteuse.

distrust [dɪsˈtrʌst] vt se méfier de; – n méfiance f (of de). ◆**distrustful** a méfiant; **to be d. of** se méfier de.

disturb [dɪˈstɜːb] vt (sleep, water) troubler; (papers, belongings) déranger; **to d. s.o.** (bother) déranger qn; (alarm, worry) troubler qn. ◆**-ed** a (person etc) Psy troublé. ◆**-ing** a (worrying) inquiétant; (annoying, irksome) gênant. ◆**disturbance** n (noise) tapage m; pl Pol troubles mpl.

disunity [dɪsˈjuːnɪtɪ] n désunion f.

disuse [dɪsˈjuːs] n **to fall into d.** tomber en désuétude. ◆**disused** [-ˈjuːzd] a désaffecté.

ditch [dɪtʃ] **1** n fossé m. **2** vt Fam se débarrasser de.

dither [ˈdɪðər] vi Fam hésiter, tergiverser; **to d. (around)** (waste time) tourner en rond.

ditto [ˈdɪtəʊ] adv idem.

divan [dɪˈvæn] n divan m.

dive [daɪv] **1** vi (pt dived, Am dove [dəʊv]) plonger; (rush) se précipiter, se jeter; **to d. for** (pearls) pêcher; – n plongeon m; (of submarine) plongée f; (of aircraft) piqué m. **2** n (bar, club) Pej boui-boui m. ◆**-ing** n (*underwater*) plongée *f* sous-marine; **d. suit** scaphandre *m*; **d. board** plongeoir *m*. ◆**-er** *n* plongeur, -euse *mf*; (*in suit*) scaphandrier *m*.

diverge [daɪˈvɜːdʒ] *vi* diverger (**from** de). ◆**divergence** *n* divergence *f*. ◆**divergent** *a* divergent.

diverse [daɪˈvɜːs] *a* divers. ◆**diversify** *vt* diversifier; – *vi Econ* se diversifier. ◆**diversity** *n* diversité *f*.

divert [daɪˈvɜːt] *vt* détourner (**from** de); (*traffic*) dévier; (*aircraft*) dérouter; (*amuse*) divertir. ◆**diversion** *n Aut* déviation *f*; (*amusement*) divertissement *m*; *Mil* diversion *f*.

divest [daɪˈvest] *vt* **to d. of** (*power, rights*) priver de.

divid/e [dɪˈvaɪd] *vt* diviser (**into** en); **to d. (off) from** séparer de; **to d. up** (*money*) partager; **to d. one's time between** partager son temps entre; – *vi* se diviser. ◆**-ed** *a* (*opinion*) partagé. ◆**-ing** *a* **d. line** ligne *f* de démarcation.

dividend [ˈdɪvɪdend] *n Math Fin* dividende *m*.

divine [dɪˈvaɪn] *a* divin. ◆**divinity** *n* (*quality, deity*) divinité *f*; (*study*) théologie *f*.

division [dɪˈvɪʒ(ə)n] *n* division *f*; (*dividing object*) séparation *f*. ◆**divisible** *a* divisible. ◆**divisive** [-ˈvaɪsɪv] *a* qui sème la zizanie.

divorce/e [dɪˈvɔːs] *n* divorce *m*; – *vt* (*spouse*) divorcer d'avec; *Fig* séparer; – *vi* divorcer. ◆**-ed** *a* divorcé (**from** d'avec); **to get d.** divorcer. ◆**divorcee** [dɪvɔːˈsiː, *Am* dɪvɔːrˈseɪ] *n* divorcé, -ée *mf*.

divulge [daɪˈvʌldʒ] *vt* divulguer.

DIY [diːaɪˈwaɪ] *n abbr* (*do-it-yourself*) bricolage *m*.

dizzy [ˈdɪzɪ] *a* (**-ier, -iest**) (*heights*) vertigineux; **to feel d.** avoir le vertige; **to make s.o. (feel) d.** donner le vertige à qn. ◆**dizziness** *n* vertige *m*.

DJ [diːˈdʒeɪ] *abbr* = **disc jockey**.

do [duː] **1** *v aux* (*3rd person sing pres t* **does**; *pt* **did**; *pp* **done**; *pres p* **doing**) **do you know?** savez-vous?, est-ce que vous savez?; **I do not** *or* **don't see** je ne vois pas; **he did say so** (*emphasis*) il l'a bien dit; **do stay there** donc; **you know him, don't you?** tu le connais, n'est-ce pas?; **better than I do** mieux que je ne le fais; **neither do I** moi non plus; **so do I** moi aussi; **oh, does he?** (*surprise*) ah oui?; **don't!** non! **2** *v tr* **to do nothing but sleep** ne faire que dormir; **what does she do?** (*in general*), **what is she doing?** (*now*) qu'est-ce qu'elle fait?, que

fait-elle?; **what have you done (with) . . . ?** qu'as-tu fait (de) . . . ?; **well done** (*congratulations*) bravo!; *Culin* bien cuit; **it's over and done (with)** c'est fini; **that'll do me** (*suit*) ça fera mon affaire; **I've been done** (*cheated*) *Fam* je me suis fait avoir; **I'll do you!** *Fam* je t'aurai!; **to do s.o. out of sth** escroquer qch à qn; **to do s.o.'s hard done by** on le traite durement; **I'm done (in)** (*tired*) *Sl* je suis claqué *or* vanné; **he's done for** *Fam* il est fichu; **to do in** (*kill*) *Sl* supprimer; **to do out** (*clean*) nettoyer; **to do over** (*redecorate*) refaire; **to do up** (*coat, button*) boutonner; (*zip*) fermer; (*house*) refaire; (*goods*) emballer; **do yourself up (well)!** (*wrap up*) couvre-toi (bien)! **3** *vi* (*get along*) aller, marcher; (*suit*) faire l'affaire, convenir; (*be enough*) suffire; (*finish*) finir; **how do you do?** (*introduction*) enchanté; (*greeting*) bonjour; **he did well** *or* **right to leave** il a bien fait de partir; **do as I do** fais comme moi; **to make do** se débrouiller; **to do away with sth/s.o.** supprimer qch/qn; **I could do with** (*need, want*) j'aimerais bien (avoir *or* prendre); **to do without sth/s.o.** se passer de qch/qn; **to have to do with** (*relate to*) avoir à voir avec; (*concern*) concerner; **anything doing?** *Fam* est-ce qu'il se passe quelque chose? **4** *n* (*pl* **dos** *or* **do's**) (*party*) soirée *f*, fête *f*; **the do's and don'ts** ce qu'il faut faire ou ne pas faire.

docile [ˈdəʊsaɪl] *a* docile.

dock [dɒk] **1** *n Nau* dock *m*; – *vi* (*in port*) relâcher; (*at quayside*) se mettre à quai; (*of spacecraft*) s'arrimer. **2** *n Jur* banc *m* des accusés. **3** *vt* (*wages*) rogner; **to d. sth from** (*wages*) retenir qch sur. ◆**-er** *n* docker *m*. ◆**dockyard** *n* chantier *m* naval.

docket [ˈdɒkɪt] *n* fiche *f*, bordereau *m*.

doctor [ˈdɒktər] **1** *n Med* médecin *m*, docteur *m*; *Univ* docteur *m*. **2** *vt* (*text, food*) altérer; (*cat*) *Fam* châtrer. ◆**doctorate** *n* doctorat *m* (**in** ès, en).

doctrine [ˈdɒktrɪn] *n* doctrine *f*. ◆**doctrinaire** *a* & *n Pej* doctrinaire (*mf*).

document [ˈdɒkjʊmənt] *n* document *m*; – [ˈdɒkjʊment] *vt* (*inform*) documenter; (*report in detail*) *TV Journ* accorder une large place à. ◆**docu'mentary** *a* & *n* documentaire (*m*).

doddering [ˈdɒdərɪŋ] *a* (*senile*) gâteux; (*shaky*) branlant.

dodge [dɒdʒ] *vt* (*question, acquaintance etc*) esquiver; (*pursuer*) échapper à; (*tax*) éviter de payer; – *vi* faire un saut (de côté); **to d. out of sight** s'esquiver; **to d. through**

(crowd) se faufiler dans; — n mouvement m de côté; (trick) Fig truc m, tour m.

dodgems ['dɒdʒəmz] npl autos fpl tamponneuses.

dodgy ['dɒdʒɪ] a (-ier, -iest) Fam (tricky) délicat; (dubious) douteux; (unreliable) peu sûr.

doe [dəʊ] n (deer) biche f.

doer ['duːər] n Fam personne f dynamique.

does [dʌz] see do.

dog [dɒg] n chien m; (person) Pej type m; **d. biscuit** biscuit m ou croquette f pour chien; **d. collar** Fam col m de pasteur; **d. days** canicule f. 2 vt (-gg-) (follow) poursuivre. ◆**d.-eared** a (page etc) écorné. ◆**d.-'tired** a Fam claqué, crevé. ◆**doggy** n Fam toutou m, chien m; **d. bag** (in restaurant) Am petit sac m pour emporter les restes.

dogged ['dɒgɪd] a obstiné. ◆**—ly** adv obstinément.

dogma ['dɒgmə] n dogme m. ◆**dog'matic** a dogmatique. ◆**dogmatism** n dogmatisme m.

dogsbody ['dɒgzbɒdɪ] n Pej factotum m, sous-fifre m.

doily ['dɔɪlɪ] n napperon m.

doing ['duːɪŋ] n that's your d. c'est toi qui as fait ça; **doings** Fam activités fpl, occupations fpl.

do-it-yourself [duːɪtjɔ'self] n bricolage m; — a (store, book) de bricolage.

doldrums ['dɒldrəmz] npl to be in the d. (of person) avoir le cafard; (of business) être en plein marasme.

dole [dəʊl] 1 n d. (money) allocation f de chômage; to go on the d. s'inscrire au chômage. 2 vt to d. out distribuer au compte-gouttes.

doleful ['dəʊlfʊl] a morne, triste.

doll [dɒl] 1 n poupée f; (girl) Fam nana f; **doll's house**, Am **dollhouse** maison f de poupée. 2 vt to d. up bichonner.

dollar ['dɒlər] n dollar m.

dollop ['dɒləp] n (of food) Pej gros morceau m.

dolphin ['dɒlfɪn] n (sea animal) dauphin m.

domain [dəʊ'meɪn] n (land, sphere) domaine m.

dome [dəʊm] n dôme m, coupole f.

domestic [də'mestɪk] a familial, domestique; (animal) domestique; (trade, flight) intérieur; (product) national; **d. science** arts mpl ménagers; **d. servant** domestique mf. ◆**domesticated** a habitué à la vie du foyer; (animal) domestiqué.

domicile ['dɒmɪsaɪl] n domicile m.

dominant ['dɒmɪnənt] a dominant;

(person) dominateur. ◆**dominance** n prédominance f. ◆**dominate** vti dominer. ◆**domi'nation** n domination f. ◆**domi-'neering** a dominateur.

dominion [də'mɪnjən] n domination f; (land) territoire m; Br Pol dominion m.

domino ['dɒmɪnəʊ] n (pl -oes) domino m; pl (game) dominos mpl.

don [dɒn] 1 n Br Univ professeur m. 2 vt (-nn-) revêtir.

donate [dəʊ'neɪt] vt faire don de; (blood) donner; — vi donner. ◆**donation** n don m.

done [dʌn] see do.

donkey ['dɒŋkɪ] n âne m; **for d.'s years** Fam depuis belle lurette, depuis un siècle; **d. work** travail m ingrat.

donor ['dəʊnər] n (of blood, organ) donneur, -euse mf.

doodle ['duːd(ə)l] vi griffonner.

doom [duːm] n ruine f; (fate) destin m; (gloom) Fam tristesse f; — vt condamner, destiner (to à); to be doomed (to failure) être voué à l'échec.

door [dɔːr] n porte f; (of vehicle, train) portière f, porte f; **out of doors** dehors; **d.-to-door salesman** démarcheur m. ◆**doorbell** n sonnette f. ◆**doorknob** n poignée f de porte. ◆**doorknocker** n marteau m. ◆**doorman** n (pl -men) (of hotel etc) portier m, concierge m. ◆**doormat** n paillasson m. ◆**doorstep** n seuil m. ◆**doorstop(per)** n butoir m (de porte). ◆**doorway** n in the d. dans l'encadrement de la porte.

dope [dəʊp] 1 n Fam drogue f; (for horse, athlete) doping m; — vt doper. 2 n (information) Fam tuyaux mpl. 3 n (idiot) Fam imbécile mf. ◆**dopey** a (-ier, -iest) Fam (stupid) abruti; (sleepy) endormi; (drugged) drogué, camé.

dormant ['dɔːmənt] a (volcano, matter) en sommeil; (passion) endormi.

dormer ['dɔːmər] n d. (window) lucarne f.

dormitory ['dɔːmɪtrɪ, Am 'dɔːmɪtɔːrɪ] n dortoir m; Am résidence f (universitaire).

dormouse, pl -mice ['dɔːmaʊs, -maɪs] n loir m.

dos/e [dəʊs] n dose f; (of hard work) Fig période f; (of illness) attaque f; — vt to d. oneself (up) se bourrer de médicaments. ◆**—age** n (amount) dose f.

dosshouse ['dɒshaʊs] n Sl asile m (de nuit).

dossier ['dɒsɪeɪ] n (papers) dossier m.

dot [dɒt] n point m; polka dots mpl; **on the d.** Fam à l'heure pile; — vt (-tt-) (an i) mettre un point sur. ◆**dotted** *a* d. line pointillé *m*; **d. with** parsemé de.

dot/e ['dəʊt] *vt* **to d. on** être gaga de. ◆**—ing** *a* affectueux; **her d.** husband/father son mari/père qui lui passe tout.

dotty ['dɒtɪ] *a* (-ier, -iest) *Fam* cinglé, toqué.

double ['dʌb(ə)l] *a* double; **a d. bed** un grand lit; **a d. room** une chambre pour deux personnes; **d. 's'** deux 's'; **d. six** deux fois six; **d. three four two** (*phone number*) trente-trois quarante-deux; – *adv* deux fois; (*to fold*) en deux; **he earns d. what I earn** il gagne le double de moi *or* deux fois plus que moi; **to see d.** voir double; – *n* double *m*; (*person*) double *m*, sosie *m*; (*stand-in*) *Cin* doublure *f*; **on** *or* **at the d.** au pas de course; – *vt* doubler; **to d. back** *or* **over** replier; – *vi* doubler; **to d. back** (*of person*) revenir en arrière; **to d. up** (*with pain, laughter*) être plié en deux. ◆**d.-'barrelled** *a* (*gun*) à deux canons; (*name*) à rallonges. ◆**d.-'bass** *n Mus* contrebasse *f*. ◆**d.-'breasted** *a* (*jacket*) croisé. ◆**d.-'cross** *vt* tromper. ◆**d.-'dealing** *n* double jeu *m*. ◆**d.-'decker (bus)** *n* autobus *m* à impériale. ◆**d.-'door** *n* porte *f* à deux battants. ◆**d.-'dutch** *n Fam* baragouin *m*. ◆**d.-'glazing** *n* (*window*) double vitrage *m*, double(s) fenêtre(s) *f(pl)*. ◆**d.-'parking** *n* stationnement *m* en double file. ◆**d.-'quick** *adv* en vitesse.

doubly ['dʌblɪ] *adv* doublement.

doubt [daʊt] *n* doute *m*; **to be in d.** about avoir des doutes sur; **I have no d. about it** je n'en doute pas; **no d.** (*probably*) sans doute; **in d.** (*result, career etc*) dans la balance; – *vt* douter de; **to d. whether** *or* **that** *or* **if** douter que (+ *sub*). ◆**doubtful** *a* douteux; **to be d. about sth** avoir des doutes sur qch; **it's d. whether** *or* **that** il est douteux que (+ *sub*). ◆**doubtless** *adv* sans doute.

dough [dəʊ] *n* pâte *f*; (*money*) *Fam* fric *m*, blé *m*. ◆**doughnut** *n* beignet *m* (rond).

dour ['dʊər] *a* austère.

douse [daʊs] *vt* arroser, tremper; (*light*) *Fam* éteindre.

dove[1] [dʌv] *n* colombe *f*. ◆**dovecote** [-kɒt] *n* colombier *m*.

dove[2] [dəʊv] *Am see* **dive** 1.

Dover ['dəʊvər] *n* Douvres *m or f*.

dovetail ['dʌvteɪl] **1** *n Carp* queue *f* d'aronde. **2** *vi* (*fit*) *Fig* concorder.

dowdy ['daʊdɪ] *a* (-ier, -iest) peu élégant, sans chic.

down[1] [daʊn] *adv* en bas; (*to the ground*) par terre, à terre; (*of sun*) couché; (*of blind, temperature*) baissé; (*out of bed*) descendu; (*of tyre*) dégonflé, (*worn*) usé; **d. (in writing)** inscrit; (*lie*) d.! (*to dog*) couché!; **to come** *or* **go d.** descendre; **to come d. from** (*place*) arriver de; **to fall d.** tomber (par terre); **d. there** *or* **here** en bas; **d. with traitors/***etc*! à bas les traîtres/*etc*!; **d. with (the) flu** grippé; **to feel d.** (*depressed*) *Fam* avoir le cafard; **d. to** (*in series, numbers, dates etc*) jusqu'à; **d. payment** acompte *m*; **d. under** aux antipodes, en Australie; **d. at heel,** *Am* **d. at the heels** miteux; – *prep* (*at bottom of*) en bas de; (*from top to bottom of*) du haut en bas de; (*along*) le long de; **to go d.** (*hill etc*) descendre; **to live d. the street** habiter plus loin dans la rue; – *vt* (*shoot down*) abattre; (*knock down*) terrasser; **to d. a drink** vider un verre. ◆**down-and-'out** *a* sur le pavé; – *n* clochard, -arde *mf*. ◆**downbeat** *a* (*gloomy*) *Fam* pessimiste. ◆**downcast** *a* découragé. ◆**downfall** *n* chute *f*. ◆**downgrade** *vt* (*job etc*) déclasser; (*person*) rétrograder. ◆**down'hearted** *a* découragé. ◆**down'hill** *adv* en pente; **to go d.** descendre; *Fig* être sur le déclin. ◆**downmarket** *a Com* bas de gamme. ◆**downpour** *n* averse *f*, pluie *f* torrentielle. ◆**downright** *a* (*rogue etc*) véritable; (*refusal etc*) catégorique; – *a* **d. nerve** *or* **cheek** un sacré culot; – *adv* (*rude etc*) franchement. ◆**'downstairs** *a* (*room, neighbours*) d'en bas; (*on the ground floor*) du rez-de-chaussée; – [daʊn'steəz] *adv* en bas; au rez-de-chaussée; **to come** *or* **go d.** descendre l'escalier. ◆**down'stream** *adv* en aval. ◆**down-to-'earth** *a* terre-à-terre *inv*. ◆**down'town** *adv* en ville; **d. Chicago/***etc* le centre de Chicago/*etc*. ◆**downtrodden** *a* opprimé. ◆**downward** *a* vers le bas; (*path*) qui descend; (*trend*) à la baisse. ◆**downward(s)** *adv* vers le bas.

down[2] [daʊn] *n* (*on bird, person etc*) duvet *m*.

downs [daʊnz] *npl* collines *fpl*.

dowry ['daʊərɪ] *n* dot *f*.

doze [dəʊz] *n* petit somme *m*; – *vi* sommeiller; **to d. off** s'assoupir. ◆**dozy** *a* (-ier, -iest) assoupi; (*silly*) *Fam* bête, gourde.

dozen ['dʌz(ə)n] *n* douzaine *f*; **a d.** (*eggs, books etc*) une douzaine de; **dozens of** *Fig* des dizaines de.

Dr *abbr* (*Doctor*) Docteur.

drab [dræb] *a* terne; (*weather*) gris. ◆**—ness** *n* caractère *m* terne; (*of weather*) grisaille *f*.

draconian [drə'kəʊnɪən] *a* draconien.

draft [drɑːft] **1** n (outline) ébauche f; (of letter etc) brouillon m; (bill) Com traite f; − vt **to d. (out)** (sketch out) faire le brouillon de; (write out) rédiger. **2** n Mil Am conscription f; (men) contingent m; − vt (conscript) appeler (sous les drapeaux). **3** n Am = **draught**.

draftsman ['drɑːftsmən] n = **draughtsman**.

drag [dræg] vt (-gg-) traîner, tirer; (river) draguer; **to d. sth from s.o.** (confession etc) arracher qch à qn; **to d. along** (en)traîner; **to d. s.o. away from** arracher qn à; **to d. s.o. into** entraîner qn dans; − vi traîner; **to d. on** or **out** (last a long time) se prolonger; − n Fam (tedium) corvée f; (person) raseur, -euse mf; (on cigarette) bouffée f (on de); **in d.** (clothing) en travesti.

dragon ['drægən] n dragon m. ◆**dragonfly** n libellule f.

drain [dreɪn] n (sewer) égout m; (pipe, channel) canal m; (outside house) puisard m; (in street) bouche f d'égout; **it's (gone) down the d.** (wasted) Fam c'est fichu; **to be a d.** on (resources, patience) épuiser; − vt (land) drainer; (glass, tank) vider; (vegetables) égoutter; (resources) épuiser; **to d. (off)** (liquid) faire écouler; **to d. of** (deprive of) priver de; − vi **to d. (off)** (of liquid) s'écouler; **to d. away** (of strength) s'épuiser; **draining board** paillasse f. ◆**-age** n (act) drainage m; (sewers) système m d'égouts. ◆**-er** n (board) paillasse f; (rack, basket) égouttoir m. ◆**drainboard** n Am paillasse f. ◆**drainpipe** n tuyau m d'évacuation.

drake [dreɪk] n canard m (mâle).

dram [dræm] n (drink) Fam goutte f.

drama ['drɑːmə] n (event) drame m; (dramatic art) théâtre m; **d. critic** critique m dramatique. ◆**dra'matic** a dramatique; (very great, striking) spectaculaire. ◆**dra'matically** adv (to change, drop etc) de façon spectaculaire. ◆**dra'matics** n théâtre m. ◆**dramatist** ['dræmətɪst] n dramaturge m. ◆**dramatize** vt (exaggerate) dramatiser; (novel etc) adapter (pour la scène or l'écran).

drank [dræŋk] see **drink**.

drap/e [dreɪp] vt draper (**with** de); (wall) tapisser (de tentures); − npl tentures fpl; (heavy curtains) Am rideaux mpl. ◆**-er** n marchand, -ande f de nouveautés.

drastic ['dræstɪk] a radical, sévère; (reduction) massif. ◆**drastically** adv radicalement.

draught [drɑːft] n courant m d'air; (for fire) tirage m; pl (game) dames fpl; − a (horse) de trait; (beer) (à la) pression. **d. excluder**

bourrelet m (de porte, de fenêtre). ◆**draughtboard** n damier m. ◆**draughty** a (-ier, -iest) (room) plein de courants d'air.

draughtsman ['drɑːftsmən] n (pl -men) dessinateur, -trice mf (industriel(le) or technique).

draw [drɔː] **1** n (of lottery) tirage m au sort; Sp match m nul; (attraction) attraction f; − vt (pt **drew**, pp **drawn**) (pull) tirer; (pass) passer (**over** sur, **into** dans); (prize) gagner; (applause) provoquer; (money from bank) retirer (**from, out of** de); (salary) toucher; (attract) attirer; (well-water, comfort) puiser (**from** dans); **to d. a smile** faire sourire (**from s.o.** qn); **to d. a bath** faire couler un bain; **to d. a line** tracer une ligne fin à qch; **to d. sth to a close** mettre fin à qch; **to d. a match** Sp faire match nul; **to d. in** (claws) rentrer; **to d. out** (money) retirer; (meeting) prolonger; **to d. up** (chair) approcher; (contract, list, plan) dresser, rédiger; **to d. (up)on** (savings) puiser dans; − vi (enter) entrer dans; (arrive) arriver; **to d. near (to)** s'approcher (de); (of time) approcher (de); **to d. to a close** tirer à sa fin; **to d. aside** (step aside) s'écarter; **to d. away** (go away) s'éloigner; **to d. back** (recoil) reculer; **to d. in** (of days) diminuer; **to d. on** (of time) s'avancer; **to d. up** (of vehicle) s'arrêter. ◆**drawback** n inconvénient m. ◆**drawbridge** n pont-levis m.

draw [drɔː] **2** vt (pt **drew**, pp **drawn**) (picture) dessiner; (circle) tracer; (parallel, distinction) Fig faire (**between** entre); − vi (as artist) dessiner. ◆**-ing** n dessin m; **d. board** planche f à dessin; **d. pin** punaise f; **d. room** salon m.

drawer [drɔːr] **1** n (in furniture) tiroir m. **2** npl (women's knickers) culotte f.

drawl [drɔːl] vi parler d'une voix traînante; − n voix f traînante.

drawn [drɔːn] see **draw** [1,2]; − a (face) tiré, crispé; **d. match** or **game** match m nul.

dread [dred] vt redouter (**doing** de faire); − n crainte f, terreur f. ◆**dreadful** a épouvantable; (child) insupportable; (ill) malade; **I feel d. (about it)** j'ai vraiment honte. ◆**dreadfully** adv terriblement; **to be** or **feel d. sorry** regretter infiniment.

dream [driːm] vti (pt & pp **dreamed** or **dreamt** [dremt]) rêver; (imagine) songer (**of** à, **that** que); **I wouldn't d. of it!** (il n'en est) pas question!; − n rêve m; (wonderful thing or person) Fam merveille f; **to have a d.** faire un rêve (**about** de); **to have dreams of** rêver de; **a d. house/etc** une maison/etc de rêve; **a d.**

world un monde imaginaire. ◆**—er** n rêveur, -euse mf. ◆**dreamy** a (-ier, -iest) rêveur.

dreary ['drɪərɪ] a (-ier, -iest) (gloomy) morne; (monotonous) monotone; (boring) ennuyeux.

dredg/e [dredʒ] vt (river etc) draguer; — n drague f. ◆**—er** n **1** (ship) dragueur m. **2** Culin saupoudreuse f.

dregs [dregz] npl the d. (in liquid, of society) la lie.

drench [drentʃ] vt tremper; **to get drenched** se faire tremper (jusqu'aux os).

dress [dres] n **1** (woman's garment) robe f; (style of dressing) tenue f; **d. circle** Th (premier) balcon m; **d. designer** dessinateur, -trice mf de mode; (well-known) couturier m; **d. rehearsal** (répétition f) générale f; **d. shirt** chemise f de soirée. **2** vt (clothe) habiller; (adorn) orner; (salad) assaisonner; (wound) panser; (skins, chicken) préparer; **to get dressed** s'habiller; **dressed for tennis/etc** en tenue de tennis/etc; — vi s'habiller; **to d. up** (smartly) bien s'habiller; (in disguise) se déguiser (as en). ◆**—ing** n Med pansement m; (seasoning) Culin assaisonnement m; **to give s.o. a d.-down** passer un savon à qn; **d. gown** robe f de chambre; (of boxer) peignoir m. **d. room** Th loge f; **d. table** coiffeuse f. ◆**—er** n **1** (furniture) vaisselier m; Am coiffeuse f. **2 she's a good d.** elle s'habille toujours bien. ◆**dressmaker** n couturière f. ◆**dressmaking** n couture f.

dressy ['dresɪ] a (-ier, -iest) (smart) chic inv; (too) d. trop habillé.

drew [druː] see draw [1,2].

dribble ['drɪb(ə)l] vi (of baby) baver; (of liquid) tomber goutte à goutte; Sp dribbler; — vt laisser tomber goutte à goutte; (ball) Sp dribbler.

dribs [drɪbz] npl **in d. and drabs** par petites quantités; (to arrive) par petits groupes.

dried [draɪd] a (fruit) sec; (milk) en poudre; (flowers) séché.

drier ['draɪər] n = dryer.

drift [drɪft] vi être emporté par le vent or le courant; (of ship) dériver; Fig aller à la dérive; (of snow) s'amonceler; **to d. about** (aimlessly) se promener sans but, traînailler; **to d. apart** (of husband and wife) devenir des étrangers l'un pour l'autre; **to d. into/towards** glisser dans/vers; — n mouvement m; (direction) sens m; (of events) cours m; (of snow) amoncellement m; congère f; (meaning) sens m général.

◆**—er** n (aimless person) paumé, -ée mf. ◆**driftwood** n bois m flotté.

drill [drɪl] n **1** (tool) perceuse f; (bit) mèche f; (for rock) foreuse f; (for tooth) fraise f; (pneumatic) marteau m pneumatique; — vt percer; (tooth) fraiser; (oil well) forer; — vi **to d. for oil** faire de la recherche pétrolière. **2** n Mil Sch exercice(s) m(pl); (procedure) Fig marche f à suivre; — vi faire l'exercice; — vt faire faire l'exercice à.

drink [drɪŋk] n boisson f; (glass of sth) verre m; **to give s.o. a d.** donner (quelque chose) à boire à qn; — n (pt **drank**, pp **drunk**) boire; **to d. oneself to death** se tuer à force de boire; **to d. down** or **up** boire; — vi boire (out of dans); **to d. up** finir son verre; **to d. to** boire à la santé de. ◆**—ing** a (water) potable; (song) à boire; **d. bout** beuverie f; **d. fountain** fontaine f publique, borne-fontaine f; **d. trough** abreuvoir m. ◆**—able** a (fit for drinking) potable; (palatable) buvable. ◆**—er** n buveur, -euse mf.

drip [drɪp] vi (-pp-) dégouliner, dégoutter; (of washing, vegetables) s'égoutter; (of tap) fuir; — vt (paint etc) laisser couler; — n (drop) goutte f; (sound) bruit m (de goutte); (fool) Fam nouille f. ◆**d.-dry** a (shirt etc) sans repassage. ◆**dripping** n (Am **drippings**) Culin graisse f; — a & adv (wet) dégoulinant.

driv/e [draɪv] n promenade f en voiture; (energy) énergie f; Psy instinct m; Pol campagne f; (road to private house) allée f; **an hour's d.** une heure de voiture; **left-hand d.** Aut (véhicule m à) conduite f à gauche; **front-wheel d.** Aut traction f avant; — vt (pt **drove**, pp **driven**) (vehicle, train, passenger) conduire; (machine) actionner; **to d.** (away or out) (chase away) chasser; **to d. s.o. to do** pousser qn à faire; **to d. to despair** réduire au désespoir; **to d. mad** or **crazy** rendre fou; **to d. the rain/smoke against** (of wind) rabattre la pluie/fumée contre; (passenger) Aut ramener (en voiture); **to d. in** (thrust) enfoncer; **to d. s.o. hard** surmener qn; **he drives a Ford** il a une Ford; — vi (drive a car) conduire; **to d.** (along) (go, run) Aut rouler; **to d. on the left** rouler à gauche; **to d. away** or **off** Aut partir; **to d. back** Aut revenir; **to d. on** Aut continuer; **to d. to** Aut aller (en voiture) à; **to d. up** Aut arriver; **what are you driving at?** Fig où veux-tu en venir? ◆**—ing 1** n conduite f; **d. lesson** leçon f de conduite; **d. licence, d. test** permis m de conduire; **d. school** auto-école

f. **2** a (forceful) d. force force f agissante; d. **rain** pluie f battante. ◆—er n (of car) conducteur, -trice mf; (of taxi, lorry) chauffeur m, conducteur, -trice mf; (train) d. mécanicien m; **she's a good d.** elle conduit bien; **driver's license** Am permis m de conduire.

drivel ['drɪv(ə)l] vi (-ll-, Am -l-) radoter; – n radotage m.

drizzle ['drɪz(ə)l] n bruine f, crachin m; – vi bruiner. ◆**drizzly** a (weather) de bruine; **it's d.** il bruine.

droll [drəʊl] a drôle, comique.

dromedary ['drɒmədərɪ, Am 'drɒmɪderɪ] n dromadaire m.

drone [drəʊn] **1** n (bee) abeille f mâle. **2** n (hum) bourdonnement m; (purr) ronronnement m; Fig débit m monotone; – vi (of bee) bourdonner; (of engine) ronronner; **to d. (on)** Fig parler d'une voix monotone.

drool [druːl] vi (slaver) baver; Fig radoter; **to d. over** Fig s'extasier devant.

droop [druːp] vi (of head) pencher; (of eyelid) tomber; (of flower) se faner.

drop [drɒp] n **1** n (of liquid) goutte f. **2** n (fall) baisse f, chute f (in de); (slope) descente f; (distance of fall) hauteur f de chute; (jump) Av saut m; – vt (-pp-) laisser tomber; (price, voice) baisser; (bomb) larguer; (passenger, goods) Aut déposer; Nau débarquer; (letter) envoyer (to à); (put) mettre; (omit) omettre; (remark) laisser échapper; (get rid of) supprimer; (habit) abandonner; (team member) Sp écarter; **to d. s.o. off** Aut déposer qn; **to d. a line** écrire un petit mot (to à); **to d. a hint** faire une allusion; **to d. a hint that** laisser entendre que; **to d. one's h's** ne pas aspirer les h; **to d. a word in s.o.'s ear** glisser un mot à l'oreille de qn; – vi (fall) tomber; (of person) se laisser tomber; (of price) baisser; (of conversation) cesser; **to d. back or behind** rester en arrière, se laisser distancer; **to d. off** (fall asleep) s'endormir; (fall off) tomber; (of interest, sales etc) diminuer. ◆d.-**off** n (decrease) diminution f (in de); **to d. out** (fall out) tomber; (withdraw) se retirer; (socially) se mettre en marge de la société; Sch Univ laisser tomber ses études. ◆d.-**out** n marginal, -ale mf; Univ étudiant, -ante mf qui abandonne ses études. ◆**droppings** npl (of animal) crottes fpl; (of bird) fiente f.

dross [drɒs] n déchets mpl.

drought [draʊt] n sécheresse f.

drove [drəʊv] see **drive**.

droves [drəʊvz] npl (of people) foules fpl; **in d.** en foule.

drown [draʊn] vi se noyer; – vt noyer; **to d. oneself, be drowned** se noyer. ◆—**ing** a qui se noie; – n (death) noyade f.

drowse [draʊz] vi somnoler. ◆**drows/y** a (-ier, -iest) somnolent; **to make s.o. (feel) d.** assoupir qn, donner envie de dormir à qn; **to feel d.** avoir sommeil; **to make s.o. (feel) d.** assoupir qn. ◆—**ily** adv d'un air somnolent. ◆—**iness** n somnolence f.

drubbing ['drʌbɪŋ] n (beating) raclée f.

drudge [drʌdʒ] n bête f de somme, esclave mf du travail; – vi trimer. ◆**drudgery** n corvée(s) f(pl), travail m ingrat.

drug [drʌg] n Med médicament m, drogue f; (narcotic) stupéfiant m, drogue f; Fig drogue f; **drugs** (dope in general) la drogue; **to be on drugs, take drugs** se droguer; **d. addict** drogué, -ée mf; **d. addiction** toxicomanie f; **d. taking** usage m de la drogue; – vt (-gg-) droguer; (drink) mêler un somnifère à. ◆**druggist** n Am pharmacien, -ienne mf, droguiste mf. ◆**drugstore** n Am drugstore m.

drum [drʌm] n Mus tambour m; (for oil) bidon m; **the big d.** Mus la grosse caisse; **the drums** Mus la batterie; – vi (-mm-) Mil battre du tambour; (with fingers) tambouriner; – vt **to d. sth into s.o.** Fig rabâcher qch à qn; **to d. up** (support, interest) susciter; **to d. up business or custom** attirer les clients. ◆**drummer** n (joueur, -euse mf de) tambour m; (in pop or jazz group) batteur m. ◆**drumstick** n Mus baguette f de tambour; (of chicken) pilon m, cuisse f.

drunk [drʌŋk] see **drink**; – a ivre; Fig **d. with** Fig ivre de; **to get d.** s'enivrer; – n ivrogne mf, pochard, -arde mf. ◆**drunkard** n ivrogne mf. ◆**drunken** a (quarrel) d'ivrogne; (person) ivrogne; (driver) ivre; **d. driving** conduite f en état d'ivresse. ◆**drunkenness** n (state) ivresse f; (habit) ivrognerie f.

dry [draɪ] a (drier, driest) sec; (well, river) à sec; (day) sans pluie; (toast) sans beurre; (wit) caustique; (subject, book) aride; **on d. land** sur la terre ferme; **to keep sth d.** tenir qch au sec; **to wipe d.** essuyer; **to run d.** se tarir; **to feel or be d.** Fam avoir soif; **to dock** calé f sèche; **d. goods store** Am magasin m de nouveautés; – vt sécher; (dishes etc) essuyer; **to d. off or up** sécher; – vi sécher; **to d. off** sécher; **to d. up** sécher; (run dry) se tarir; **d. up!** Fam tais-toi! ◆—**ing** n séchage m; essuyage m. ◆—**er** n (for hair, *clothes)* sécher m; *(helmet-style for hair)* casque m. **◆—ness** n sécheresse f; *(of wit)* causticité f; *(of book etc)* aridité f. **◆dry-'clean** vt nettoyer à sec. **◆dry-'cleaner** n teinturier, -ière mf.

dual ['djuːəl] a double; **d. carriageway** route f à deux voies (séparées). **◆du'ality** n dualité f.

dub [dʌb] vt (-bb-) **1** *(film)* doubler. **2** *(nickname)* surnommer. **◆dubbing** n Cin doublage m.

dubious ['djuːbɪəs] a *(offer, person etc)* douteux; **I'm d. about going** or **whether to go** je me demande si je dois y aller; **to be d. about sth** douter de qch.

duchess ['dʌtʃɪs] n duchesse f. **◆duchy** n duché m.

duck [dʌk] n **1** canard m. **2** vi se baisser (vivement); – vt *(head)* baisser; **to d. s.o.** plonger qn dans l'eau. **◆—ing** n bain m forcé. **◆duckling** n caneton m.

duct [dʌkt] n Anat Tech conduit m.

dud [dʌd] a Fam *(bomb)* non éclaté; *(coin)* faux; *(cheque)* en bois; *(watch etc)* qui ne marche pas; – n *(person)* zéro m, type m nul.

dude [duːd] n Am Fam dandy m; **d. ranch** ranch(-hôtel) m.

due[1] [djuː] a *(money, sum)* dû (to à); *(rent, bill)* à payer; *(respect)* qu'on doit (to à); *(fitting)* qui convient; **to fall d.** échoir; **she's d. for** *(a rise etc)* elle doit or devrait recevoir; **he's d. (to arrive)** *(is awaited)* il doit arriver, il est attendu; **I'm d. there** je dois être là-bas; **in d. course** *(at proper time)* en temps utile; *(finally)* à la longue; **d. to** *(attributable to)* dû à; *(because of)* à cause de; *(thanks to)* grâce à; – n dû m; pl *(of club)* cotisation f; *(official charges)* droits mpl; **to give s.o. his d.** admettre que qn a raison.

due[2] [djuː] adv (tout) droit; **d. north/south** plein nord/sud.

duel ['djuːəl] n duel m; – vi (-ll-, Am -l-) se battre en duel.

duet [djuː'et] n duo m.

duffel, duffle ['dʌf(ə)l] a **d. bag** sac m de marin; **d. coat** duffel-coat m.

dug [dʌg] see **dig**. **◆dugout** n **1** Mil abri m souterrain. **2** *(canoe)* pirogue f.

duke [djuːk] n duc m.

dull [dʌl] a (-er, -est) *(boring)* ennuyeux; *(colour, character)* terne; *(weather)* maussade; *(mind)* lourd, borné; *(sound, ache)* sourd; *(edge, blade)* émoussé; *(hearing, sight)* faible; – vt *(senses)* émousser; *(sound, pain)* amortir; *(colour)* ternir;

(mind) engourdir. **◆—ness** n *(of mind)* lourdeur f d'esprit; *(tedium)* monotonie f; *(of colour)* manque m d'éclat.

duly ['djuːlɪ] adv *(properly)* comme il convient *(convenait etc)*; *(in fact)* en effet; *(in due time)* en temps utile.

dumb [dʌm] a (-er, -est) muet; *(stupid)* Fam idiot, bête. **◆—ness** n mutisme m; bêtise f. **◆dumbbell** n *(weight)* haltère m. **◆dumb'waiter** n *(lift for food)* monte-plats m inv.

dumbfound [dʌm'faund] vt sidérer, ahurir.

dummy ['dʌmɪ] **1** n *(of baby)* sucette f; *(of dressmaker)* mannequin m; *(of book)* maquette f; *(of ventriloquist)* pantin m; *(fool)* Fam idiot, -ote mf. **2** a factice, faux; **d. run** *(on car etc)* essai m.

dump [dʌmp] vt *(rubbish)* déposer; **to d. (down)** déposer; **to d. s.o.** *(ditch)* Fam plaquer qn; – n *(for ammunition)* Mil dépôt m; *(dirty or dull town)* Fam trou m; *(house, slum)* Fam baraque f; *(rubbish)* dépôt m d'ordures, décharge f; **to be (down) in the dumps** Fam avoir le cafard; **d. truck** = **dumper**. **◆—er** n **d. (truck)** camion m à benne basculante.

dumpling ['dʌmplɪŋ] n Culin boulette f (de pâte).

dumpy ['dʌmpɪ] a (-ier, -iest) *(person)* boulot, gros et court.

dunce [dʌns] n cancre m, âne m.

dune [djuːn] n dune f.

dung [dʌŋ] n crotte f; *(of cattle)* bouse f; *(manure)* fumier m.

dungarees [dʌŋgə'riːz] npl *(of child, workman)* salopette f; *(jeans)* Am jean m.

dungeon ['dʌndʒən] n cachot m.

dunk [dʌŋk] vt *(bread, biscuit etc)* tremper.

dupe [djuːp] vt duper; – n dupe f.

duplex ['djuːpleks] n *(apartment)* Am duplex m.

duplicate ['djuːplɪkeɪt] vt *(key, map)* faire un double de; *(on machine)* polycopier; – ['djuːplɪkət] n double m; **in d.** en deux exemplaires; **a d. copy**/etc une copie/etc en double; **a d. key** un double de la clef. **◆dupli'cation** n *(on machine)* polycopie f; *(of effort)* répétition f. **◆duplicator** n duplicateur m.

duplicity [djuː'plɪsɪtɪ] n duplicité f.

durable ['djuːərəb(ə)l] a *(shoes etc)* résistant; *(friendship, love)* durable. **◆dura'bility** n résistance f; durabilité f.

duration [djuː'reɪʃ(ə)n] n durée f.

duress [djuː'res] n **under d.** sous la contrainte.

during ['djuːərɪŋ] prep pendant, durant.

dusk [dʌsk] *n* (*twilight*) crépuscule *m*.
dusky ['dʌskɪ] *a* (**-ier, -iest**) (*complexion*) foncé.
dust [dʌst] *n* poussière *f*; **d. cover** (*for furniture*) housse *f*; (*for book*) jaquette *f*; **d. jacket** jaquette *f*; – *vt* épousseter; (*sprinkle*) saupoudrer (**with** de). ◆**—er** *n* chiffon *m*. ◆**dustbin** *n* poubelle *f*. ◆**dustcart** *n* camion-benne *m*. ◆**dustman** *n* (*pl* **-men**) éboueur *m*, boueux *m*. ◆**dustpan** *n* petite pelle *f* (à poussière).
dusty ['dʌstɪ] *a* (**-ier, -iest**) poussièreux.
Dutch [dʌtʃ] *a* néerlandais, hollandais; **D. cheese** hollande *m*; **to go D.** partager les frais (**with** avec); – *n* (*language*) hollandais *m*. ◆**Dutchman** *n* (*pl* **-men**) Hollandais *m*. ◆**Dutchwoman** *n* (*pl* **-women**) Hollandaise *f*.
duty ['djuːtɪ] *n* devoir *m*; (*tax*) droit *m*; *pl* (*responsibilities*) fonctions *fpl*; **on d.** *Mil* de service; (*doctor etc*) de garde; *Sch* de permanence; **off d.** libre. ◆**d.-'free** *a* (*goods, shop*) hors-taxe *inv*. ◆**dutiful** *a* respectueux, obéissant; (*worker*) consciencieux.
dwarf [dwɔːf] *n* nain *m*, naine *f*; – *vt* (*of building, person etc*) rapetisser, écraser.

dwell [dwel] *vi* (*pt & pp* **dwelt**) demeurer; **to d. (up)on** (*think about*) penser sans cesse à; (*speak about*) parler sans cesse de, s'étendre sur; (*insist on*) appuyer sur. ◆**—ing** *n* habitation *f*. ◆**—er** *n* habitant, -ante *mf*.
dwindl/e ['dwɪnd(ə)l] *vt* diminuer (peu à peu). ◆**—ing** *a* (*interest etc*) décroissant.
dye [daɪ] *n* teinture *f*; – *vt* teindre; **to d. green/etc** teindre en vert/etc. ◆**dyeing** *n* teinture *f*; (*industry*) teinturerie *f*. ◆**dyer** *n* teinturier, -ière *mf*.
dying ['daɪɪŋ] *see* **die 1**; – *a* mourant, moribond; (*custom*) qui se perd; (*day, words*) dernier; – *n* (*death*) mort *f*.
dyke [daɪk] *n* (*wall*) digue *f*; (*ditch*) fossé *m*.
dynamic [daɪ'næmɪk] *a* dynamique. ◆**'dynamism** *n* dynamisme *m*.
dynamite ['daɪnəmaɪt] *n* dynamite *f*; – *vt* dynamiter.
dynamo ['daɪnəməʊ] *n* (*pl* **-os**) dynamo *f*.
dynasty ['dɪnəstɪ, *Am* 'daɪnəstɪ] *n* dynastie *f*.
dysentery ['dɪsəntrɪ] *n* *Med* dysenterie *f*.
dyslexic [dɪs'leksɪk] *a* & *n* dyslexique (*mf*).

E

E, e [iː] *n* E, e *m*.
each [iːtʃ] *a* chaque; – *pron* chacun, -une; **e. one** chacun, -une; **e. other** l'un(e) l'autre, *pl* les un(e)s les autres; **to see e. other** se voir (l'un(e) l'autre); **e. of us** chacun, -une d'entre nous.
eager ['iːgər] *a* impatient (**to do** de faire); (*enthusiastic*) ardent, passionné; **to be e. for** désirer vivement; **e. for** (*money*) avide de; **e. to help** empressé (à aider); **to be e. to do** (*want*) avoir envie de faire. ◆**—ly** *adv* (*to await*) avec impatience; (*to work, serve*) avec empressement. ◆**—ness** *n* impatience *f* (**to do** de faire); (*zeal*) empressement *m* (**to do** à faire); (*greed*) avidité *f*.
eagle ['iːg(ə)l] *n* aigle *m*. ◆**e.-'eyed** *a* au regard d'aigle.
ear¹ [ɪər] *n* oreille *f*; **all ears** *Fam* tout ouïe; **up to one's ears in work** débordé de travail; **to play it by e.** *Fam* agir selon la situation; **thick e.** *Fam* gifle *f*. ◆**earache** *n* mal *m* d'oreille. ◆**eardrum** *n* tympan *m*. ◆**earmuffs** *npl* serre-tête *m inv* (*pour* protéger les oreilles), protège-oreilles *m inv*. ◆**earphones** *npl* casque *m*. ◆**earpiece** *n* écouteur *m*. ◆**earplug** *n* (*to keep out noise*) boule *f* Quiès®. ◆**earring** *n* boucle *f* d'oreille. ◆**earshot** *n* **within e.** à portée de voix. ◆**ear-splitting** *a* assourdissant.
ear² [ɪər] *n* (*of corn*) épi *m*.
earl [ɜːl] *n* comte *m*.
early ['ɜːlɪ] *a* (**-ier, -iest**) (*first*) premier; (*fruit, season*) précoce; (*death*) prématuré; (*age*) jeune; (*painting, work*) de jeunesse; (*reply*) rapide; (*return, retirement*) anticipé; (*ancient*) ancien; **it's e.** (*looking at time*) il est tôt; (*referring to appointment etc*) c'est tôt; **it's too e. to get up/etc** il est trop tôt pour se lever/etc; **to be e.** (*ahead of time*) arriver de bonne heure *or* tôt, être en avance; (*in getting up*) être matinal; **in e. times** jadis; **in e. summer** au début de l'été; **one's e. life** sa jeunesse; – *adv* tôt, de bonne heure; (*ahead of time*) en avance; (*to die*) prématurément; **as e. as possible** le plus tôt possible; **earlier (on)** plus tôt; **at**

the earliest au plus tôt; **as e. as yesterday** déjà hier. ◆**e.-'warning system** *n* dispositif *m* de première alerte.

earmark ['ɪəmɑːk] *vt* (*funds*) assigner (**for** à).

earn [ɜːn] *vt* gagner; (*interest*) *Fin* rapporter. ◆**—ings** *npl* (*wages*) rémunérations *fpl*; (*profits*) bénéfices *mpl*.

earnest ['ɜːnɪst] *a* sérieux; (*sincere*) sincère; – *n* **in e.** sérieusement; **it's raining in e.** il pleut pour de bon; **he's in e.** il est sérieux. ◆**—ness** *n* sérieux *m*; sincérité *f*.

earth [ɜːθ] *n* (*world, ground*) terre *f*; *El* terre *f*, masse *f*; **to fall to e.** tomber à or par terre; **nothing/nobody on e.** rien/personne au monde; **where/what on e.?** où/que diable? ◆**earthly** *a* (*possessions etc*) terrestre; **not an e. chance** *Fam* pas la moindre chance; **for no e. reason** *Fam* sans la moindre raison. ◆**earthy** *a* terreux; (*person*) *Fig* terre-à-terre *inv*. ◆**earthquake** *n* tremblement *m* de terre. ◆**earthworks** *npl* (*excavations*) terrassements *mpl*. ◆**earthworm** *n* ver *m* de terre.

earthenware ['ɜːθənwɛər] *n* faïence *f*; – *a* en faïence.

earwig ['ɪəwɪg] *n* (*insect*) perce-oreille *m*.

ease [iːz] **1** *n* (*physical*) bien-être *m*; (*mental*) tranquillité *f*; (*facility*) facilité *f*; (*ill*) **at e.** (*in situation*) (mal) à l'aise; **at e.** (*of mind*) tranquille; **(stand) at e.!** *Mil* repos!; **with e.** facilement. **2** *vt* (*pain*) soulager; (*mind*) calmer; (*tension*) diminuer; (*loosen*) relâcher; **to e. off/along** enlever/déplacer doucement; **to e. oneself through** se glisser par; – *vi* **to e. (off** or **up)** (*of situation*) se détendre; (*of pressure*) diminuer; (*of demand*) baisser; (*of pain*) se calmer; (*not work so hard*) se relâcher. ◆**easily** *adv* facilement; **the best/***etc* de loin le meilleur/***etc***; **that could e. be** ça pourrait bien être. ◆**easiness** *n* aisance *f*.

easel ['iːz(ə)l] *n* chevalet *m*.

east [iːst] *n* est *m*; **Middle/Far E.** Moyen-/Extrême-Orient *m*; – *a* (*coast*) est *inv*; (*wind*) d'est; **E. Africa** Afrique *f* orientale; **E. Germany** Allemagne *f* de l'Est; – *adv* à l'est, vers l'est. ◆**eastbound** *a* (*carriageway*) est *inv*; (*traffic*) en direction de l'est. ◆**easterly** *a* (*point*) est *inv*; (*direction*) de l'est; (*wind*) d'est. ◆**eastern** *a* (*coast*) est *inv*; **E. France** l'Est *m* de la France; **E. Europe** Europe *f* de l'Est. ◆**easterner** *n* habitant, -ante *mf* de l'Est. ◆**eastward(s)** *a & adv* vers l'est.

Easter ['iːstər] *n* Pâques *m sing* or *fpl*; **E. week** semaine *f* pascale; **Happy E.!** joyeuses Pâques!

easy ['iːzɪ] *a* (**-ier, -iest**) facile; (*manners*) naturel; (*life*) tranquille; (*pace*) modéré; **to feel e. in one's mind** être tranquille; **to be an e. first** *Sp* être bon premier; **I'm e.** *Fam* ça m'est égal; **e. chair** fauteuil *m* (rembourré); – *adv* doucement; **go e. on** (*sugar etc*) vas-y doucement or mollo avec; (*person*) ne sois pas trop dur avec or envers; **take it e.** (*rest*) repose-toi; (*work less*) ne te fatigue pas; (*calm down*) calme-toi; (*go slow*) ne te presse pas. ◆**easy'going** *a* (*carefree*) insouciant; (*easy to get on with*) traitable.

eat [iːt] *vt* (*pt* **ate** [et, *Am* eɪt], *pp* **eaten** ['iːt(ə)n]) manger; (*meal*) prendre; (*one's words*) *Fig* ravaler; **to e. breakfast** or **lunch** déjeuner; **what's eating you?** *Sl* qu'est-ce qui te tracasse?; **to e. up** (*finish*) finir; **eaten up with** (*envy*) dévoré de; – *vi* manger; **to e. into** (*of acid*) ronger; **to e. out** (*lunch*) déjeuner dehors; (*dinner*) dîner dehors. ◆**—ing** *a* **e. apple** pomme *f* à couteau; **e. place** restaurant *m*. ◆**—able** *a* mangeable. ◆**—er** *n* **big e.** gros mangeur *m*, grosse mangeuse *f*.

eau de Cologne [əʊdəkə'ləʊn] *n* eau *f* de Cologne.

eaves [iːvz] *npl* avant-toit *m*. ◆**eavesdrop** *vt* (**-pp-**) **to e. (on)** écouter (de façon indiscrète). ◆**eavesdropper** *n* oreille *f* indiscrète.

ebb [eb] *n* reflux *m*; **e. and flow** le flux et le reflux; **e. tide** marée *f* descendante; **at a low e.** *Fig* très bas; – *vi* refluer; **to e. (away)** (*of strength etc*) *Fig* décliner.

ebony ['ebənɪ] *n* (*wood*) ébène *f*.

ebullient [ɪ'bʌlɪənt] *a* exubérant.

eccentric [ɪk'sentrɪk] *a & n* excentrique (*mf*). ◆**eccen'tricity** *n* excentricité *f*.

ecclesiastic [ɪkliːzɪ'æstɪk] *a & n* ecclésiastique (*m*). ◆**ecclesiastical** *a* ecclésiastique.

echelon ['eʃəlɒn] *n* (*of organization*) échelon *m*.

echo ['ekəʊ] *n* (*pl* **-oes**) écho *m*; – *vt* (*sound*) répercuter; (*repeat*) *Fig* répéter; – *vi* **the explosion/***etc* **echoed** l'écho de l'explosion/*etc* se répercuta; **to e. with the sound of** résonner de l'écho de.

éclair [eɪ'klɛər] *n* (*cake*) éclair *m*.

eclectic [ɪ'klektɪk] *a* éclectique.

eclipse [ɪ'klɪps] *n* (*of sun etc*) *Fig* éclipse *f*; – *vt* éclipser.

ecology [ɪ'kɒlədʒɪ] *n* écologie *f*. ◆**eco-'logical** *a* écologique.

economic [iːkə'nɒmɪk] *a* économique; (*profitable*) rentable. ◆**economical** *a* économique; (*thrifty*) économe. ◆**economically** *adv* économiquement. ◆**economics** *n* (*science f*) économique *f*; (*profitability*) aspect *m* financier.

economy ['ɪkɒnəmɪ] *n* (*saving, system, thrift*) économie *f*; **e. class** *Av* classe *f* touriste. ◆**economist** *n* économiste *mf*. ◆**economize** *vti* économiser (**on** sur).

ecstasy ['ekstəsɪ] *n* extase *f*. ◆**ec'static** *a* extasié; **to be e. about** s'extasier sur. ◆**ec'statically** *adv* avec extase.

ecumenical [iːkjuː'menɪk(ə)l] *a* œcuménique.

eczema ['eksɪmə] *n Med* eczéma *m*.

eddy ['edɪ] *n* tourbillon *m*, remous *m*.

edg/e [edʒ] *n* bord *m*; (*of forest*) lisière *f*; (*of town*) abords *mpl*; (*of page*) marge *f*; (*of knife etc*) tranchant *m*, fil *m*; **on e.** (*person*) énervé; (*nerves*) tendu; **to set s.o.'s teeth on e.** (*irritate s.o.*) crisper qn, faire grincer les dents à qn; **to have the e.** *or* **a slight e.** *Fig* être légèrement supérieur (**over, on** à); − *vt* (*clothing etc*) border (**with** de); − *vti* **to e.** (**oneself**) **into** (*move*) se glisser dans; **to e.** (**oneself**) **forward** avancer doucement. ◆**-ing** *n* (*border*) bordure *f*. ◆**edgeways** *adv* de côté; **to get a word in e.** *Fam* placer un mot.

edgy ['edʒɪ] *a* (-ier, -iest) énervé. ◆**edginess** *n* nervosité *f*.

edible ['edɪb(ə)l] *a* (*mushroom, berry etc*) comestible; (*meal, food*) mangeable.

edict ['iːdɪkt] *n* décret *m*; *Hist* édit *m*.

edifice ['edɪfɪs] *n* (*building, organization*) édifice *m*.

edify ['edɪfaɪ] *vt* (*improve the mind of*) édifier.

Edinburgh ['edɪnb(ə)rə] *n* Édimbourg *m* or *f*.

edit ['edɪt] *vt* (*newspaper etc*) diriger; (*article etc*) mettre au point; (*film*) monter; (*annotate*) éditer; (*compile*) rédiger. **to e.** (**out**) (*cut out*) couper. ◆**editor** *n* (*of review*) directeur, -trice *mf*; (*compiler*) rédacteur, -trice *mf*; *TV Rad* réalisateur, -trice *mf*; **sports e.** *Journ* rédacteur *m* sportif, rédactrice *f* sportive; **the e.** (**in chief**) (*of newspaper*) le rédacteur *m* en chef. ◆**edi'torial** *a* de la rédaction; **e. staff** rédaction *f*; − *n* éditorial *m*.

edition [ɪ'dɪʃ(ə)n] *n* édition *f*.

educat/e ['edjukeɪt] *vt* (*family, children*) éduquer; (*pupil*) instruire; (*mind*) former, éduquer; **to be educated at** faire ses études à. ◆**-ed** *a* (*voice*) cultivé; (*well-*)e. (*person*) instruit. ◆**edu'cation** *n* éducation *f*; (*teaching*) instruction *f*, enseigne-

ment *m*; (*training*) formation *f*; (*subject*) *Univ* pédagogie *f*. ◆**edu'cational** *a* (*establishment*) d'enseignement; (*method*) pédagogique; (*game*) éducatif; (*supplies*) scolaire. ◆**edu'cationally** *adv* du point de vue de l'éducation. ◆**educator** *n* éducateur, -trice *mf*.

EEC [iːiː'siː] *n abbr* (*European Economic Community*) CEE *f*.

eel [iːl] *n* anguille *f*.

eerie ['ɪərɪ] *a* (**-ier, -iest**) sinistre, étrange.

efface [ɪ'feɪs] *vt* effacer.

effect [ɪ'fekt] **1** *n* (*result, impression*) effet *m* (**on** sur); *pl* (*goods*) biens *mpl*; **to no e.** en vain; **in e.** en fait; **to put into e.** mettre en application, faire entrer en vigueur; **to come into e., take e.** entrer en vigueur; **to take e.** (*of drug etc*) agir; **to have an e.** (*of medicine etc*) faire de l'effet; **to have no e.** rester sans effet; **to this e.** (*in this meaning*) dans ce sens; **to the e. that** (*saying that*) comme quoi. **2** *vt* (*carry out*) effectuer, réaliser.

effective [ɪ'fektɪv] *a* (*efficient*) efficace; (*actual*) effectif; (*striking*) frappant; **to become e.** (*of law*) prendre effet. ◆**-ly** *adv* efficacement; (*in effect*) effectivement. ◆**-ness** *n* efficacité *f*; (*quality*) effet *m* frappant.

effeminate [ɪ'femɪnɪt] *a* efféminé.

effervescent [efə'ves(ə)nt] *a* (*mixture, youth*) effervescent; (*drink*) gazeux. ◆**effervesce** *vi* (*of drink*) pétiller. ◆**effervescence** *n* (*excitement*) & *Ch* effervescence *f*; pétillement *m*.

effete [ɪ'fiːt] *a* (*feeble*) mou, faible; (*decadent*) décadent.

efficient [ɪ'fɪʃ(ə)nt] *a* (*method*) efficace; (*person*) compétent, efficace; (*organization*) efficace, performant; (*machine*) performant, à haut rendement. ◆**efficiency** *n* efficacité *f*; compétence *f*; performances *fpl*. ◆**efficiently** *adv* efficacement; avec compétence; **to work e.** (*of machine*) bien fonctionner.

effigy ['efɪdʒɪ] *n* effigie *f*.

effort ['efət] *n* effort *m*; **to make an e.** faire un effort (**to pour**); **it isn't worth the e.** ça ne *or* n'en vaut pas la peine; **his** *or* **her latest e.** *Fam* ses dernières tentatives. ◆**-less** *a* (*victory etc*) facile. ◆**-lessly** *adv* facilement, sans effort.

effrontery [ɪ'frʌntərɪ] *n* effronterie *f*.

effusive [ɪ'fjuːsɪv] *a* (*person*) expansif; (*thanks, excuses*) sans fin. ◆**-ly** *adv* avec effusion.

e.g. [iː'dʒiː] *abbr* (*exempli gratia*) par exemple.

egalitarian [ɪgælɪ'teərɪən] *a* (*society etc*) égalitaire.

egg¹ [eg] *n* œuf *m*; **e. timer** sablier *m*; **e. whisk** fouet *m* (à œufs). ◆**eggcup** *n* coquetier *m*. ◆**egghead** *n Pej* intellectuel, -elle *mf*. ◆**eggplant** *n* aubergine *f*. ◆**eggshell** *n* coquille *f*.

egg² [eg] *vt* **to e. on** (*encourage*) inciter (**to do** à faire).

ego ['iːgəʊ] *n* (*pl* -os) the e. *Psy* le moi. ◆**ego'centric** *a* égocentrique. ◆**egoism** *n* égoïsme *m*. ◆**egoist** *n* égoïste *mf*. ◆**ego'istic(al)** *a* égoïste. ◆**egotism** *n* égotisme *m*.

Egypt ['iːdʒɪpt] *n* Égypte *f*. ◆**E'gyptian** *a & n* égyptien, -ienne (*mf*).

eh? [eɪ] *int Fam* hein?

eiderdown ['aɪdədaʊn] *n* édredon *m*.

eight [eɪt] *a & n* huit (*m*). ◆**eigh'teen** *a & n* dix-huit (*m*). ◆**eigh'teenth** *a & n* dix-huitième (*mf*). ◆**eighth** *a & n* huitième (*mf*); **an e.** un huitième. ◆**eightieth** *a & n* quatre-vingtième (*mf*). ◆**eighty** *a & n* quatre-vingts (*m*); **e.-one** quatre-vingt-un.

Eire ['eərə] *n* République *f* d'Irlande.

either ['aɪðər] **1** *a & pron* (*one or other*) l'un(e) ou l'autre; (*with negative*) ni l'un(e) ni l'autre; (*each*) chaque; **on e. side** de chaque côté, des deux côtés. **2** *adv* **she can't swim e.** elle ne sait pas nager non plus; **I don't e.** (ni) moi non plus; **not so far off e.** (*moreover*) pas si loin d'ailleurs. **3** *conj* **e. . . . or** ou (bien) . . . ou (bien), soit . . . soit; (*with negative*) ni . . . ni.

eject [ɪ'dʒekt] *vt* expulser; *Tech* éjecter. ◆**ejector** *n* **e. seat** *Av* siège *m* éjectable.

eke [iːk] *vt* **to e. out** (*income etc*) faire durer; **to e. out a living** gagner (difficilement) sa vie.

elaborate [ɪ'læbərət] *a* compliqué, détaillé; (*preparation*) minutieux; (*style*) recherché; (*meal*) raffiné; — [ɪ'læbəreɪt] *vt* (*theory etc*) élaborer; — *vi* entrer dans les détails (**on** de). ◆**—ly** *adv* (*to plan*) minutieusement; (*to decorate*) avec recherche. ◆**elabo'ration** *n* élaboration *f*.

elapse [ɪ'læps] *vi* s'écouler.

elastic [ɪ'læstɪk] *a* (*object, character*) élastique; **e. band** élastique *m*; — *n* (*fabric*) élastique *m*. ◆**ela'sticity** *n* élasticité *f*.

elated [ɪ'leɪtɪd] *a* transporté de joie. ◆**elation** *n* exaltation *f*.

elbow ['elbəʊ] *n* coude *m*; **e. grease** *Fam* huile *f* de coude; **to have enough e. room**

avoir assez de place; — *vt* **to e. one's way** frayer un chemin (à coups de coude) (**through** à travers).

elder¹ ['eldər] *a & n* (*of two people*) aîné, -ée (*mf*). ◆**elderly** *a* assez âgé, entre deux âges. ◆**eldest** *a & n* aîné, -ée (*mf*); **his or her e.** brother l'aîné de ses frères.

elder² ['eldər] *n* (*tree*) sureau *m*.

elect [ɪ'lekt] *vt Pol* élire (**to** à); **to e. to do** choisir de faire; — *a* (*the president/etc* e. le président/*etc* désigné. ◆**election** *n* élection *f*; **general e.** élections *fpl* législatives; — *a* (*campaign*) électoral; (*day, results*) du scrutin, des élections. ◆**electio'neering** *n* campagne *f* électorale. ◆**elective** *a* (*course*) *Am* facultatif. ◆**electoral** *a* électoral. ◆**electorate** *n* électorat *m*.

electric [ɪ'lektrɪk] *a* électrique; **e. blanket** couverture *f* chauffante; **e. shock** décharge *f* électrique; **e. shock treatment** électrochoc *m*. ◆**electrical** *a* électrique; **e. engineer** ingénieur *m* électricien. ◆**elec'trician** *n* électricien *m*. ◆**elec'tricity** *n* électricité *f*. ◆**electrify** *vt Rail* électrifier; (*excite*) *Fig* électriser. ◆**electrocute** *vt* électrocuter.

electrode [ɪ'lektrəʊd] *n El* électrode *f*.

electron [ɪ'lektrɒn] *n* électron *m*; — *a* (*microscope*) électronique. ◆**elec'tronic** *a* électronique. ◆**elec'tronics** *n* électronique *f*.

elegant ['elɪgənt] *a* élégant. ◆**elegance** *n* élégance *f*. ◆**elegantly** *adv* avec élégance, élégamment.

elegy ['elədʒɪ] *n* élégie *f*.

element ['elɪmənt] *n* (*component, environment*) élément *m*; (*of heater*) résistance *f*; **an e. of truth** un grain ou une part de vérité; **the human/chance e.** le facteur humain/chance; **in one's e.** dans son élément. ◆**ele'mental** *a* élémentaire. ◆**ele'mentary** *a* élémentaire; (*school*) *Am* primaire; **e. courtesy** la courtoisie la plus élémentaire.

elephant ['elɪfənt] *n* éléphant *m*. ◆**elephantine** [elɪ'fæntaɪn] *a* (*large*) éléphantesque; (*clumsy*) gauche.

elevate ['elɪveɪt] *vt* élever (**to** à). ◆**ele'vation** *n* élévation *f* (**of** de); (*height*) altitude *f*. ◆**elevator** *n Am* ascenseur *m*.

eleven [ɪ'lev(ə)n] *a & n* onze (*m*). ◆**elevenses** [ɪ'lev(ə)nzɪz] *n Fam* pause-café *f* (*vers onze heures du matin*). ◆**eleventh** *a & n* onzième (*mf*).

elf [elf] *n* (*pl* elves) lutin *m*.

elicit [ɪ'lɪsɪt] *vt* tirer, obtenir (**from** de).

elide [ɪ'laɪd] *vt Ling* élider. ◆**elision** *n* élision *f*.

eligible ['elɪdʒəb(ə)l] a (for post etc) admissible (for à); (for political office) éligible (for à); **to be e. for** (entitled to) avoir droit à; an **e. young man** (suitable as husband) un beau parti. ◆**eligi'bility** n admissibilité f; Pol éligibilité f.

eliminate [ɪ'lɪmɪneɪt] vt éliminer (**from** de). ◆**elimi'nation** n élimination f.

elite [eɪ'liːt] n élite f (**of** de).

elk [elk] n (animal) élan m.

ellipse [ɪ'lɪps] n Geom ellipse f. ◆**elliptical** a elliptique.

elm [elm] n (tree, wood) orme m.

elocution [elə'kjuːʃ(ə)n] n élocution f.

elongate ['iːlɒŋgeɪt] vt allonger. ◆**elon-'gation** n allongement m.

elope [ɪ'ləʊp] vi (of lovers) s'enfuir (**with** avec). ◆**—ment** n fugue (amoureuse).

eloquent ['eləkwənt] a éloquent. ◆**elo-quence** n éloquence f.

else [els] adv **someone e.** quelqu'un d'autre; **everybody e.** tout le monde à part moi, vous etc; **all those e.** tous les autres; **nobody/nothing e.** personne/rien d'autre; **something e.** autre chose; **something or anything e.?** encore quelque chose?; **somewhere e.** ailleurs, autre part; **who e.?** qui encore?, qui d'autre?; **how e.?** de quelle autre façon?; **or e.** ou bien, sinon. ◆**elsewhere** adv ailleurs; **e. in the town** dans une autre partie de la ville.

elucidate [ɪ'luːsɪdeɪt] vt élucider.

elude [ɪ'luːd] vt (enemy) échapper à; (question) éluder; (obligation) se dérober à; (blow) esquiver. ◆**elusive** a (enemy, aims) insaisissable; (reply) évasif.

emaciated [ɪ'meɪsɪeɪtɪd] a émacié.

emanate ['eməneɪt] vi émaner (**from** de).

emancipate [ɪ'mænsɪpeɪt] vt (women) émanciper. ◆**emanci'pation** n émancipation f.

embalm [ɪm'bɑːm] vt (dead body) embaumer.

embankment [ɪm'bæŋkmənt] n (of path etc) talus m; (of river) berge f.

embargo [ɪm'bɑːgəʊ] n (pl -oes) embargo m.

embark [ɪm'bɑːk] vt embarquer; – vi (s')embarquer; **to e. on** (start) commencer, entamer; (launch into) se lancer dans, s'embarquer dans. ◆**embar'kation** n embarquement m.

embarrass [ɪm'bærəs] vt embarrasser, gêner. ◆**—ing** a (question etc) embarrassant. ◆**—ment** n embarras m, gêne f; (financial) embarras mpl.

embassy ['embəsɪ] n ambassade f.

embattled [ɪm'bæt(ə)ld] a (political party, person etc) assiégé de toutes parts; (attitude) belliqueux.

embedded [ɪm'bedɪd] a (stick, bullet) enfoncé; (jewel) & Ling enchâssé; (in one's memory) gravé; (in stone) scellé.

embellish [ɪm'belɪʃ] vt embellir. ◆**—ment** n embellissement m.

embers ['embəz] npl braise f, charbons mpl ardents.

embezzl/e [ɪm'bez(ə)l] vt (money) détourner. ◆**—ement** n détournement m de fonds. ◆**—er** n escroc m, voleur m.

embitter [ɪm'bɪtər] vt (person) aigrir; (situation) envenimer.

emblem ['embləm] n emblème m.

embody [ɪm'bɒdɪ] vt (express) exprimer; (represent) incarner; (include) réunir. ◆**embodiment** n incarnation f (**of** de).

emboss [ɪm'bɒs] vt (metal) emboutir; (paper) gaufrer, emboutir. ◆**—ed** a en relief.

embrace [ɪm'breɪs] vt étreindre, embrasser; (include, adopt) embrasser; – vi s'étreindre, s'embrasser; – n étreinte f.

embroider [ɪm'brɔɪdər] vt (cloth) broder; (story, facts) Fig enjoliver. ◆**embroidery** n broderie f.

embroil [ɪm'brɔɪl] vt **to e. s.o. in** mêler qn à.

embryo ['embrɪəʊ] n (pl -os) embryon m. ◆**embry'onic** a Med & Fig embryonnaire.

emcee [em'siː] n Am présentateur, -trice mf.

emend [ɪ'mend] vt (text) corriger.

emerald ['emərəld] n émeraude f.

emerge [ɪ'mɜːdʒ] vi apparaître (**from** de); (from hole etc) sortir; (of truth, from water) émerger; (of nation) naître; **it emerges that** il apparaît que. ◆**emergence** n apparition f.

emergency [ɪ'mɜːdʒənsɪ] n (case) urgence f; (crisis) crise f; (contingency) éventualité f; **in an e.** en cas d'urgence; – a (measure etc) d'urgence; (exit, brake) de secours; (ward, services) Med des urgences; **e. landing** atterrissage m forcé; **e. powers** Pol pouvoirs mpl exceptionnels.

emery ['emərɪ] n **e. cloth** toile f (d')émeri.

emigrant ['emɪgrənt] n émigrant, -ante mf. ◆**emigrate** vi émigrer. ◆**emi'gration** n émigration f.

eminent ['emɪnənt] a éminent. ◆**emi-nence** n distinction f; **his E.** Rel son Éminence f. ◆**eminently** adv hautement, remarquablement.

emissary ['emɪsərɪ] n émissaire m.

emit [ɪ'mɪt] vt (-tt-) (light, heat etc) émettre;

(*smell*) dègager. ◆**emission** *n* èmission *f*; dègagement *m*.

emotion [ɪ'məʊʃ(ə)n] *n* (*strength of feeling*) èmotion *f*; (*joy, love etc*) sentiment *m*. ◆**emotional** *a* (*person, reaction*) èmotif; (*story, speech*) èmouvant; (*moment*) d'èmotion intense; (*state*) *Psy* èmotionnel. ◆**emotionally** *adv* avec èmotion; **to be e. unstable** avoir des troubles èmotifs. ◆**emotive** *a* (*person*) èmotif; (*word*) affectif; **an e. issue** une question sensible.

emperor ['empərər] *n* empereur *m*.

emphasize ['emfəsaɪz] *vt* souligner (**that** que); (*word, fact*) appuyer ou insister sur, souligner. ◆**emphasis** *n Ling* accent *m* (tonique); (*insistence*) insistance *f*; **to lay** *or* **put e. on** mettre l'accent sur. ◆**em'phatic** *a* (*person, refusal*) catègorique; (*forceful*) ènergique; **to be e. about** insister sur. ◆**em'phatically** *adv* catègoriquement; ènergiquement; **e. no!** absolument pas!

empire ['empaɪər] *n* empire *m*.

empirical [em'pɪrɪk(ə)l] *a* empirique. ◆**empiricism** *n* empirisme *m*.

employ [ɪm'plɔɪ] *vt* (*person, means*) employer; – *n* **in the e.** of employè par. ◆**employee** [ɪm'plɔɪiː, emplɔɪ'iː] *n* employè, -èe *mf*. ◆**employer** *n* patron, -onne *mf*. ◆**employment** *n* emploi *m*; **place of e.** le lieu *m* de travail; **in the e. of** employè par; **e. agency** bureau *m* de placement.

empower [ɪm'paʊər] *vt* autoriser (**to do** à faire).

empress ['emprɪs] *n* impèratrice *f*.

empt/y ['emptɪ] *a* (**-ier, -iest**) vide; (*threat, promise etc*) vain; (*stomach*) creux; **on an e. stomach** à jeun; **to return/***etc* **e.-handed** revenir/*etc* les mains vides; – *npl* (*bottles*) bouteilles *fpl* vides; – *vt* **to e.** (**out**) (*box, pocket, liquid etc*) vider; (*objects in box etc*) sortir (**from, out of** de); – *vi* se vider; (*of river*) se jeter (**into** dans). ◆**-iness** *n* vide *m*.

emulate ['emjʊleɪt] *vt* imiter. ◆**emu'lation** *n* èmulation *f*.

emulsion [ɪ'mʌlʃ(ə)n] *n* (*paint*) peinture *f* (*mate*); *Phot* èmulsion *f*.

enable [ɪ'neɪb(ə)l] *vt* **to e. s.o. to do** permettre à qn de faire.

enact [ɪn'ækt] *vt* (*law*) promulguer; (*part of play*) jouer.

enamel [ɪ'næm(ə)l] *n* èmail *m*; – *a* en èmail; – *vt* (**-ll-,** *Am* **-l-**) èmailler.

enamoured [ɪn'æməd] *a* **e. of** (*thing*) sèduit par; (*person*) amoureux de.

encamp [ɪn'kæmp] *vi* camper. ◆**—ment** *n* campement *m*.

encapsulate [ɪn'kæpsjʊleɪt] *vt Fig* rèsumer.

encase [ɪn'keɪs] *vt* recouvrir (**in** de).

enchant [ɪn'tʃɑːnt] *vt* enchanter. ◆**—ing** *a* enchanteur. ◆**—ment** *n* enchantement *m*.

encircle [ɪn'sɜːk(ə)l] *vt* entourer; *Mil* encercler. ◆**—ment** *n* encerclement *m*.

enclave ['enkleɪv] *n* enclave *f*.

enclos/e [ɪn'kləʊz] *vt* (*send with letter*) joindre (**in, with** à); (*fence off*) clôturer; **to e. with** (*a fence, wall*) entourer de. ◆**—ed** *a* (*space*) clos; (*cheque etc*) ci-joint; (*market*) couvert. ◆**enclosure** *n Com* pièce *f* jointe; (*fence, place*) enceinte *f*.

encompass [ɪn'kʌmpəs] *vt* (*surround*) entourer; (*include*) inclure.

encore ['ɒŋkɔːr] *int & n* bis (*m*); – *vt* bisser.

encounter [ɪn'kaʊntər] *vt* rencontrer; – *n* rencontre *f*.

encourage [ɪn'kʌrɪdʒ] *vt* encourager (**to do** à faire). ◆**—ment** *n* encouragement *m*.

encroach [ɪn'krəʊtʃ] *vi* empièter (**on, upon** sur); **to e. on the land** (*of sea*) gagner du terrain. ◆**—ment** *n* empiètement *m*.

encumber [ɪn'kʌmbər] *vt* encombrer (**with** de). ◆**encum'brance** *n* embarras *m*.

encyclical [ɪn'sɪklɪk(ə)l] *n Rel* encyclique *f*.

encyclop(a)edia [ɪnsaɪklə'piːdɪə] *n* encyclopèdie *f*. ◆**encyclop(a)edic** *a* encyclopèdique.

end [end] *n* (*of street, object etc*) bout *m*, extrèmitè *f*; (*of time, meeting, book etc*) fin *f*; (*purpose*) fin *f*, but *m*; **at an e.** (*discussion etc*) fini; (*period*) ècoulè; (*patience*) à bout; **in the e.** à la fin; **to come to an e.** prendre fin; **to put an e. to, bring to an e.** mettre fin; **there's no e. to it** ça n'en finit plus; **no e. of** *Fam* beaucoup de; **six days on e.** six jours d'affilèe; **for days on e.** pendant des jours (et des jours); (*standing*) **on e.** (*box etc*) debout; (*hair*) hèrissè; – *a* (*row, house*) dernier; **e. product** *Com* produit *m* fini; *Fig* rèsultat *m*; – *vt* finir, terminer, achever (**with** par); (*rumour, speculation*) mettre fin à; – *vi* finir, se terminer, s'achever; **to e. in failure** se solder par un èchec; **to e. in a point** finir en pointe; **to e. up doing** finir par faire; **to e. up in** (*London etc*) se retrouver à; **he ended up in prison/a doctor** il a fini en prison/par devenir mèdecin.

endanger [ɪn'deɪndʒər] *vt* mettre en danger.

endear [ɪn'dɪər] *vt* faire aimer *ou* apprècier (**to** de); **that's what endears him to me** c'est cela qui me plaît en lui. ◆**—ing** *a* attachant, sympathique. ◆**—ment** *n* parole *f* tendre; **term of e.** terme *m* d'affection.

endeavour [ɪnˈdevər] *vi* s'efforcer (**to do de** faire); − *n* effort *m* (**to do** pour faire).

ending [ˈendɪŋ] *n* fin *f*; (*outcome*) issue *f*; Ling terminaison *f*. ◆**endless** *a* (*speech, series etc*) interminable; (*patience*) infini; (*countless*) innombrable. ◆**endlessly** *adv* interminablement.

endive [ˈendɪv, *Am* ˈendaɪv] *n* Bot Culin (*curly*) chicorée *f*; (*smooth*) endive *f*.

endorse [ɪnˈdɔːs] *vt* (*cheque etc*) endosser; (*action*) approuver; (*claim*) appuyer. ◆**—ment** *n* (*on driving licence*) contravention *f*.

endow [ɪnˈdau] *vt* (*institution*) doter (**with** de); (*chair, hospital bed*) fonder; **endowed with** (*person*) Fig doté de. ◆**—ment** *n* dotation *f*; fondation *f*.

endur/e [ɪnˈdjuər] **1** *vt* (*bear*) supporter (**doing** de faire). **2** *vi* (*last*) durer. ◆**—ing** *a* durable. ◆**—able** *a* supportable. ◆**endurance** *n* endurance *f*, résistance *f*.

enemy [ˈenəmɪ] *n* ennemi, -ie *mf*; − *a* (*plane, tank etc*) ennemi.

energy [ˈenədʒɪ] *n* énergie *f*; − *a* (*crisis, resources etc*) énergétique. ◆**ener'getic** *a* énergique; **to feel e.** se sentir en pleine forme. ◆**ener'getically** *adv* énergiquement.

enforc/e [ɪnˈfɔːs] *vt* (*law*) faire respecter; (*discipline*) imposer (**on** à). ◆**—ed** *a* (*rest, silence etc*) forcé.

engag/e [ɪnˈgeɪdʒ] *vt* (*take on*) engager, prendre; **to e. s.o. in conversation** engager la conversation avec qn; **to e. the clutch** *Aut* embrayer; − *vi* **to e. in** (*launch into*) se lancer dans; (*be involved in*) être mêlé à. ◆**—ed** *a* **1** (*person, toilet*) *&* Tel occupé; **in doing** occupé à faire; **to be e. in business/etc** être dans les affaires/*etc*. **2** (*betrothed*) fiancé; **to get e.** se fiancer. ◆**—ing** *a* (*smile*) engageant. ◆**—ment** *n* (*agreement to marry*) fiançailles *fpl*; (*meeting*) rendez-vous *m inv*; (*undertaking*) engagement *m*; **to have a prior e.** (*be busy*) être déjà pris, ne pas être libre; **e. ring** bague *f* de fiançailles.

engender [ɪnˈdʒendər] *vt* (*produce*) engendrer.

engine [ˈendʒɪn] *n* Aut moteur *m*; Rail locomotive *f*; Nau machine *f*; **e. driver** mécanicien *m*.

engineer [endʒɪˈnɪər] **1** *n* ingénieur *m*; (*repairer*) dépanneur *m*; Rail Am mécanicien *m*; **civil e.** ingénieur *m* des travaux publics; **mechanical e.** ingénieur *m*

mécanicien. **2** *vt* (*arrange secretly*) machiner. ◆**—ing** *n* ingénierie *f*; (*civil*) **e.** génie *m* civil, travaux *mpl* publics; (*mechanical*) **e.** mécanique *f*; **e. factory** atelier *m* de construction mécanique.

England [ˈɪŋglənd] *n* Angleterre *f*. ◆**English** *a* anglais; **the E. Channel** la Manche; **the E.** les Anglais *mpl*; − *n* (*language*) anglais *m*. ◆**Englishman** *n* (*pl* -men) Anglais *m*. ◆**English-speaking** *a* anglophone. ◆**Englishwoman** *n* (*pl* -women) Anglaise *f*.

engrav/e [ɪnˈgreɪv] *vt* graver. ◆**—ing** *n* gravure *f*. ◆**—er** *n* graveur *m*.

engrossed [ɪnˈgrəust] *a* absorbé (**in** par).

engulf [ɪnˈgʌlf] *vt* engloutir.

enhance [ɪnˈhɑːns] *vt* (*beauty etc*) rehausser; (*value*) augmenter.

enigma [ɪˈnɪgmə] *n* énigme *f*. ◆**enig'matic** *a* énigmatique.

enjoy [ɪnˈdʒɔɪ] *vt* aimer (**doing** faire); (*meal*) apprécier; (*income, standard of living etc*) jouir de; **to e. the evening** passer une bonne soirée; **to e. oneself** s'amuser; **to e. being in London**/*etc* se plaire à Londres/*etc*. ◆**—able** *a* agréable. ◆**—ably** *adv* agréablement. ◆**—ment** *n* plaisir *m*.

enlarge [ɪnˈlɑːdʒ] *vt* agrandir; − *vi* s'agrandir; **to e. (up)on** (*say more about*) s'étendre sur. ◆**—ment** *n* agrandissement *m*.

enlighten [ɪnˈlaɪt(ə)n] *vt* éclairer (**s.o. on** *or* **about sth** qn sur qch). ◆**—ing** *a* instructif. ◆**—ment** *n* (*explanations*) éclaircissements *mpl*; **an age of e.** une époque éclairée.

enlist [ɪnˈlɪst] *vi* (*in the army etc*) s'engager; − *vt* (*recruit*) engager; (*supporter*) recruter; (*support*) obtenir. ◆**—ment** *n* engagement *m*; recrutement *m*.

enliven [ɪnˈlaɪv(ə)n] *vt* (*meeting, people etc*) égayer, animer.

enmeshed [ɪnˈmeʃt] *a* empêtré (**in** dans).

enmity [ˈenmɪtɪ] *n* inimitié *f* (**between** entre).

enormous [ɪˈnɔːməs] *a* énorme; (*explosion*) terrible; (*success*) fou. ◆**enormity** *n* (*vastness, extent*) énormité *f*; (*atrocity*) atrocité *f*. ◆**enormously** *adv* (*very much*) énormément; (*very*) extrêmement.

enough [ɪˈnʌf] *a & n* assez (**de**); **e. time/ cups/etc** assez de temps/de tasses/*etc*; **to have e. to live on** avoir de quoi vivre; **to have e. to drink** avoir assez à boire; **to have had e. of** *Pej* en avoir assez de; **it's e. for me to see that** ... il me suffit de voir que ... ; **that's e.** ça suffit, c'est assez; − *adv* assez, suffisamment (**to** pour); **strangely e., he left** chose curieuse, il est parti.

enquire [ɪnˈkwaɪər] vi = **inquire.**

enquiry [ɪnˈkwaɪərɪ] n = **inquiry.**

enrage [ɪnˈreɪdʒ] vt mettre en rage.

enrapture [ɪnˈræptʃər] vt ravir.

enrich [ɪnˈrɪtʃ] vt enrichir; (soil) fertiliser. ◆—**ment** n enrichissement m.

enrol [ɪnˈrəʊl] (Am **enroll**) vi (-ll-) s'inscrire (**in, for** à); – vt inscrire. ◆—**ment** n inscription f; (people enrolled) effectif m.

ensconced [ɪnˈskɒnst] a bien installé (**in** dans).

ensemble [ɒnˈsɒmb(ə)l] n (clothes) & Mus ensemble m.

ensign [ˈensən] n (flag) pavillon m; (rank) Am Nau enseigne m de vaisseau.

enslave [ɪnˈsleɪv] vt asservir.

ensu/e [ɪnˈsjuː] vi s'ensuivre. ◆—**ing** a (day, year etc) suivant; (event) qui s'ensuit.

ensure [ɪnˈʃʊər] vt assurer; **to e. that** (make sure) s'assurer que.

entail [ɪnˈteɪl] vt (imply, involve) entraîner, impliquer.

entangle [ɪnˈtæŋɡ(ə)l] vt emmêler, enchevêtrer; **to get entangled** s'empêtrer. ◆—**ment** n enchevêtrement m; **an e. with** (police) des démêlés mpl avec.

enter [ˈentər] vt (room, vehicle, army etc) entrer dans; (road) s'engager dans; (university) s'inscrire à; (write down) inscrire (**in** dans, **on** sur); (in ledger) porter (**in** sur); **to e. s.o. for** (exam) présenter qn à; **to e. a painting/**etc **in** (competition) présenter un tableau/etc à; **it didn't e. my head** ça ne m'est pas venu à l'esprit (**that** que); – vi entrer; **to e. for** (race, exam) s'inscrire pour; **to e. into** (plans) entrer dans; (conversation, relations) entrer en; **you don't e. into it** tu n'y es pour rien; **to e. into or upon** (career) entrer dans; (negotiations) entamer; (agreement) conclure.

enterpris/e [ˈentəpraɪz] n (undertaking, firm) entreprise f; (spirit) Fig initiative f. ◆—**ing** a (person) plein d'initiative; (attempt) hardi.

entertain [entəˈteɪn] vt amuser, distraire; (guest) recevoir; (idea, possibility) envisager; (hope) chérir; **to e. s.o. to a meal** recevoir qn à dîner; – vi (receive guests) recevoir. ◆—**ing** a amusant. ◆—**er** n artiste mf. ◆—**ment** n amusement m, distraction f; (show) spectacle m.

enthral(l) [ɪnˈθrɔːl] vt (-ll-) (delight) captiver.

enthuse [ɪnˈθjuːz] vi **to e. over** Fam s'emballer pour. ◆**enthusiasm** n enthousiasme m. ◆**enthusiast** n enthousiaste

mf; **jazz/**etc **e.** passionné, -ée mf du jazz/etc. ◆**enthusi'astic** a enthousiaste; (golfer etc) passionné; **to be e. about** (hobby) être passionné de; **he was e. about or over** (gift etc) il a été emballé par; **to get e. s'emballer** (**about** pour). ◆**enthusi-'astically** adv avec enthousiasme.

entic/e [ɪnˈtaɪs] vt attirer (par la ruse); **to e. to do** entraîner (par la ruse) à faire. ◆—**ing** a séduisant, alléchant. ◆—**ement** n (bait) attrait m.

entire [ɪnˈtaɪər] a entier. ◆—**ly** adv tout à fait, entièrement. ◆**entirety** [ɪnˈtaɪərətɪ] n intégralité f; **in its e.** en entier.

entitl/e [ɪnˈtaɪt(ə)l] vt **to e. s.o. to do** donner à qn le droit de faire; **to e. s.o. to sth** donner à qn (le) droit à qch; **that entitles me to believe that . . .** ça m'autorise à croire que . . . . ◆—**ed** a (book) intitulé; **to be e. to do** avoir le droit de faire; **to be e. to sth** avoir droit à qch. ◆—**ement** n one's **e.** son dû.

entity [ˈentɪtɪ] n entité f.

entourage [ˈɒntʊrɑːʒ] n entourage m.

entrails [ˈentreɪlz] npl entrailles fpl.

entrance 1 [ˈentrəns] n entrée f (**to** de); (to university etc) admission f (**to** à); **e. examination** examen m d'entrée. **2** [ɪnˈtrɑːns] vt Fig transporter, ravir.

entrant [ˈentrənt] n (in race) concurrent, -ente mf; (for exam) candidat, -ate mf.

entreat [ɪnˈtriːt] vt supplier, implorer (**to do** de faire). ◆**entreaty** n supplication f.

entrée [ˈɒntreɪ] n Culin entrée f; (main dish) Am plat m principal.

entrench [ɪnˈtrentʃ] vt **to e. oneself** Mil & Fig se retrancher.

entrust [ɪnˈtrʌst] vt confier (**to** à); **to e. s.o. with sth** confier qch à qn.

entry [ˈentrɪ] n (way in, action) entrée f; (in ledger) écriture f; (term in dictionary or logbook) entrée f; (competitor) Sp concurrent, -ente mf; (thing to be judged in competition) objet m (or œuvre f or projet m) soumis à un jury; **e. form** feuille f d'inscription; 'no e.' (on door etc) 'entrée interdite'; (road sign) 'sens interdit'.

entwine [ɪnˈtwaɪn] vt entrelacer.

enumerate [ɪˈnjuːməreɪt] vt énumérer. ◆**enume'ration** n énumération f.

enunciate [ɪˈnʌnsɪeɪt] vt (word) articuler; (theory) énoncer. ◆**enunci'ation** n articulation f; énonciation f.

envelop [ɪnˈveləp] vt envelopper (**in fog/mystery/**etc de brouillard/mystère/etc).

envelope [ˈenvələʊp] n enveloppe f.

envious [ˈenvɪəs] a envieux (**of sth** de qch;

e. of s.o. jaloux de qn. ◆**enviable** a enviable. ◆**enviously** adv avec envie.

environment [ɪnˈvaɪərənmənt] n milieu m; (cultural, natural) environnement m. ◆**environ'mental** a du milieu; de l'environnement. ◆**environ'mentalist** n écologiste mf.

envisage [ɪnˈvɪzɪdʒ] vt (imagine) envisager; (foresee) prévoir.

envision [ɪnˈvɪʒ(ə)n] vt Am = envisage.

envoy [ˈenvɔɪ] n Pol envoyé, -ée m.

envy [ˈenvɪ] n envie f; - vt envier (s.o. sth qch à qn).

ephemeral [ɪˈfemərəl] a éphémère.

epic [ˈepɪk] a épique; - n épopée f; (screen) e. film m à grand spectacle.

epidemic [epɪˈdemɪk] n épidémie f; - a épidémique.

epilepsy [ˈepɪlepsɪ] n épilepsie f. ◆**epi'leptic** a & n épileptique (mf).

epilogue [ˈepɪlɒg] n épilogue m.

episode [ˈepɪsəud] n épisode m. ◆**episodic** [epɪˈsɒdɪk] a épisodique.

epistle [ɪˈpɪs(ə)l] n épître f.

epitaph [ˈepɪtɑːf] n épitaphe f.

epithet [ˈepɪθet] n épithète f.

epitome [ɪˈpɪtəmɪ] n the e. of l'exemple même de, l'incarnation de. ◆**epitomize** vt incarner.

epoch [ˈiːpɒk] n époque f. ◆**e.-making** a (event) qui fait date.

equal [ˈiːkwəl] a égal (to à); with e. hostility avec la même hostilité; on an e. footing sur un pied d'égalité (with avec); to be e. to égaler; e. to (task, situation) à la hauteur de; – n égal, -ale mf; to treat s.o. as an e. traiter qn en égal or d'égal à égal; he doesn't have his e. il n'a pas son pareil; – vt (-ll-, Am -l-) égaler (in beauty/etc en beauté/etc); **equals sign** Math signe m d'égalité. ◆**e'quality** n égalité f. ◆**equalize** vt égaliser; – vi Sp égaliser. ◆**equally** adv (to an equal degree, also) également; (to divide) en parts égales; he's as stupid (just as) il est tout aussi bête.

equanimity [ekwəˈnɪmɪtɪ] n égalité f d'humeur.

equate [ɪˈkweɪt] vt mettre sur le même pied (with que), assimiler (with à).

equation [ɪˈkweɪʒ(ə)n] n Math équation f.

equator [ɪˈkweɪtər] n équateur m; at or on the e. sous l'équateur. ◆**equatorial** [ekwəˈtɔːrɪəl] a équatorial.

equestrian [ɪˈkwestrɪən] a équestre.

equilibrium [iːkwɪˈlɪbrɪəm] n équilibre m.

equinox [ˈiːkwɪnɒks] n équinoxe m.

equip [ɪˈkwɪp] vt (-pp-) équiper (with de);

(well-)equipped with pourvu de; (well-)equipped to do compétent pour faire. ◆**—ment** n équipement m, matériel m.

equity [ˈekwɪtɪ] n (fairness) équité f; pl Com actions fpl. ◆**equitable** a équitable.

equivalent [ɪˈkwɪvələnt] a & n équivalent (m). ◆**equivalence** n équivalence f.

equivocal [ɪˈkwɪvək(ə)l] a équivoque.

era [ˈɪərə, Am ˈerə] n époque f; (historical, geological) ère f.

eradicate [ɪˈrædɪkeɪt] vt supprimer; (evil, prejudice) extirper.

erase [ɪˈreɪz] vt effacer. ◆**eraser** n (rubber) gomme f. ◆**erasure** n rature f.

erect [ɪˈrekt] **1** a (upright) (bien) droit. **2** vt (build) construire; (statue, monument) ériger; (scaffolding) monter; (tent) dresser. ◆**erection** n construction f; érection f; montage m; dressage m.

ermine [ˈɜːmɪn] n (animal, fur) hermine f.

erode [ɪˈrəud] vt éroder; (confidence etc) Fig miner, ronger. ◆**erosion** n érosion f.

erotic [ɪˈrɒtɪk] a érotique. ◆**eroticism** n érotisme m.

err [ɜːr] vi (be wrong) se tromper; (sin) pécher.

errand [ˈerənd] n commission f, course f; e. boy garçon m de courses.

erratic [ɪˈrætɪk] a (conduct etc) irrégulier; (person) lunatique.

error [ˈerər] n (mistake) erreur f, faute f; (wrongdoing) erreur f; in e. par erreur. ◆**erroneous** [ɪˈrəunɪəs] a erroné.

erudite [ˈeruːdaɪt, Am ˈerudaɪt] a érudit, savant. ◆**eru'dition** n érudition f.

erupt [ɪˈrʌpt] vi (of volcano) entrer en éruption; (of pimples) apparaître; (of war, violence) éclater. ◆**eruption** n (of volcano, pimples, anger) éruption f (of de); (of violence) flambée f.

escalate [ˈeskəleɪt] vi (of war, violence) s'intensifier; (of prices) monter en flèche; – vt intensifier. ◆**esca'lation** n escalade f.

escalator [ˈeskəleɪtər] n escalier m roulant.

escapade [ˈeskəpeɪd] n (prank) frasque f.

escape [ɪˈskeɪp] vi (of gas, animal etc) s'échapper; (of prisoner) s'évader, s'échapper; to e. from (person) échapper à; (place, object) s'échapper de; escaped prisoner évadé, -ée mf; – vt (death) échapper à; (punishment) éviter; that name escapes me ce nom m'échappe; to e. notice passer inaperçu; – n (of gas etc) fuite f; (of person) évasion f, fuite f; to have a lucky or narrow e. l'échapper belle. ◆**escapism** n évasion f (hors de la réalité). ◆**escapist** a (film etc) d'évasion.

eschew [ɪ'stʃuː] vt éviter, fuir.
escort ['eskɔːt] n Mil Nau escorte f; (of woman) cavalier m; – [ɪ'skɔːt] vt escorter.
Eskimo ['eskɪməʊ] n (pl -os) Esquimau, -aude mf; – a esquimau.
esoteric [esəʊ'terɪk] a obscur, ésotérique.
especial [ɪ'speʃəl] a particulier. ◆—ly adv (in particular) particulièrement; (for particular purpose) (tout) exprès; **e. as** d'autant plus que.
espionage ['espɪənɑːʒ] n espionnage m.
esplanade ['espləneɪd] n esplanade f.
espouse [ɪ'spaʊz] vt (a cause) épouser.
espresso [e'spresəʊ] n (pl -os) (café m) express m.
Esq [ɪ'skwaɪər] abbr (esquire) **J. Smith Esq** (on envelope) Monsieur J. Smith.
essay ['eseɪ] n (attempt) & Liter essai m; Sch rédaction f; Univ dissertation f.
essence ['esəns] n Phil Ch essence f; Culin extrait m, essence f; (main point) essentiel m (of de); **in e.** essentiellement.
essential [ɪ'senʃ(ə)l] a (principal) essentiel; (necessary) indispensable, essentiel; **it's e. that** il est indispensable que (+ sub); – npl **the essentials** l'essentiel m (of de); (of grammar) les éléments mpl. ◆—ly adv essentiellement.
establish [ɪ'stæblɪʃ] vt établir; (state, society) fonder. ◆—ed a (well-)e. (firm) solide; (fact) reconnu; (reputation) établi; **she's (well-)e.** elle a une réputation établie. ◆—ment n (institution, firm) établissement m; **the e. of** l'établissement de; la fondation de; **the E.** les classes fpl dirigeantes.
estate [ɪ'steɪt] n (land) terre(s) f(pl), propriété f; (possessions) Jur fortune f; (of deceased person) succession f; **e. housing e.** lotissement m; (workers') cité f (ouvrière); **industrial e.** complexe m industriel; **e. agency** agence f immobilière; **e. agent** agent m immobilier; **e. car** break m; **e. tax** Am droits mpl de succession.
esteem [ɪ'stiːm] vt estimer; **highly esteemed** très estimé; – n estime f.
esthetic [es'θetɪk] a Am esthétique.
estimate ['estɪmeɪt] vt (value) estimer, évaluer; (consider) estimer (that que); – ['estɪmət] n (assessment) évaluation f, estimation f; (judgement) évaluation f; (price for work to be done) devis m; **rough e.** chiffre m approximatif. ◆**esti'mation** n jugement m; (esteem) estime f; **in my e.** à mon avis.
estranged [ɪ'streɪndʒd] a **to become e.** (of couple) se séparer.

estuary ['estjʊərɪ] n estuaire m.
etc [et'setərə] adv etc.
etch [etʃ] vti graver à l'eau forte. ◆—ing (picture) eau-forte f.
eternal [ɪ'tɜːn(ə)l] a éternel. ◆**eternally** adv éternellement. ◆**eternity** n éternité f.
ether ['iːθər] n éther m. ◆**e'thereal** a éthéré.
ethic ['eθɪk] n éthique f. ◆**ethics** n (moral standards) moralité f; (study) Phil éthique f. ◆**ethical** a moral, éthique.
Ethiopia [iːθɪ'əʊpɪə] n Éthiopie f. ◆**Ethiopian** a & n éthiopien, -ienne (mf).
ethnic ['eθnɪk] a ethnique.
ethos ['iːθɒs] n génie m.
etiquette ['etɪket] n (rules) bienséances fpl; (diplomatic) e. protocole m, étiquette f; **professional e.** déontologie f.
etymology [etɪ'mɒlədʒɪ] n étymologie f.
eucalyptus [juːkə'lɪptəs] n (tree) eucalyptus m.
eulogy ['juːlədʒɪ] n panégyrique m, éloge m.
euphemism ['juːfəmɪz(ə)m] n euphémisme m.
euphoria [juː'fɔːrɪə] n euphorie f. ◆**euphoric** a euphorique.
Euro- ['jʊərəʊ] pref euro-.
Europe ['jʊərəp] n Europe f. ◆**Euro'pean** a & n européen, -éenne (mf).
euthanasia [juːθə'neɪzɪə] n euthanasie f.
evacuate [ɪ'vækjʊeɪt] vt évacuer. ◆**evacu'ation** n évacuation f.
evade [ɪ'veɪd] vt éviter, esquiver; (pursuer, tax) échapper à; (law, question) éluder.
evaluate [ɪ'væljʊeɪt] vt évaluer (at à). ◆**evalu'ation** n évaluation f.
evangelical [iːvæn'dʒelɪk(ə)l] a Rel évangélique.
evaporate [ɪ'væpəreɪt] vi s'évaporer; (of hopes) s'évanouir. ◆—ed a. **milk** lait m concentré. ◆**evapo'ration** n évaporation f.
evasion [ɪ'veɪʒ(ə)n] n e. of (pursuer etc) fuite f devant; (question) esquive f de; **tax e.** évasion f fiscale. ◆**evasive** a évasif.
eve [iːv] n the e. of la veille.
even ['iːv(ə)n] 1 a (flat) uni, égal, lisse; (equal) égal; (regular) régulier; (number) pair; **to get e. with** se venger de; **I'll get e. with him (for that)** je lui revaudrai ça; **we're e.** (quits) nous sommes quittes; (in score) nous sommes à égalité; je suis. Fin s'y retrouver; – nul to e. (out or up) égaliser. 2 adv même; **e. better/more** encore mieux/plus; **e. if or though** même si; **e.** quand même. ◆—ly adv de manière égale; (regularly) régulièrement. ◆—ness n (of

surface, temper) égalité f; (of movement etc) régularité f. ◆even-'tempered a de caractère égal.

evening ['iːvnɪŋ] n soir m; (duration of evening, event) soirée f; in the e., Am evenings le soir; at seven in the e. à sept heures du soir; every Tuesday e. tous les mardis soir; all e. (long) toute la soirée; – a (newspaper etc) du soir; e. performance Th soirée f; e. dress tenue f de soirée; (of woman) robe f du soir or de soirée.

event [ɪ'vent] n évènement m; Sp épreuve f; in the e. of death en cas de décès; in any e. en tout cas; after the e. après coup. ◆eventful a (journey etc) mouvementé; (occasion) mémorable.

eventual [ɪ'ventʃʊəl] a final, définitif. ◆eventu'ality n éventualité f. ◆eventually adv finalement, à la fin; (some day or other) un jour ou l'autre; (after all) en fin de compte.

ever ['evər] adv jamais; has he e. seen it? l'a-t-il jamais vu?; more than e. plus que jamais; nothing e. jamais rien; hardly e. presque jamais; e. ready toujours prêt; the first e. le tout premier; e. since (that event etc) depuis; e. since then depuis lors, dès lors; for e. (for always) pour toujours; (continually) sans cesse; the best son e. le meilleur fils du monde; e. so sorry/ happy/etc Fam vraiment désolé/heureux/ etc; thank you e. so much Fam merci mille fois; it's e. such a pity Fam c'est vraiment dommage; why e. not? pourquoi pas donc? ◆evergreen n arbre m à feuilles persistantes. ◆ever'lasting a éternel. ◆ever-'more adv for e. à (tout) jamais.

every ['evrɪ] a chaque; e. child chaque enfant, tous les enfants; e. time chaque fois (that que); e. one chacun; e. single one tous (sans exception); to have e. confidence in avoir pleine confiance en; e. second or other day tous les deux jours; her e. gesture ses moindres gestes; e. bit as big tout aussi grand (as que); e. so often, e. now and then de temps en temps. ◆everybody pron tout le monde; e. in turn chacun à son tour. ◆everyday a (happening, life etc) de tous les jours; (banal) banal; in e. use d'usage courant. ◆everyone pron = everybody. ◆everyplace adv Am = everywhere. ◆everything pron tout; e. I have tout ce que j'ai. ◆everywhere adv partout; e. she goes où qu'elle aille, partout où elle va.

evict [ɪ'vɪkt] vt expulser (from de). ◆eviction n expulsion f.

evidence ['evɪdəns] n (proof) preuve(s)

f (pl); (testimony) témoignage m; (obviousness) évidence f; to give e. témoigner (against contre); e. of (wear etc) des signes mpl de; in e. (noticeable) (bien) en vue. ◆evident a évident (that que); it is e. from ... il apparaît de ... (that que). ◆evidently adv (obviously) évidemment; (apparently) apparemment.

evil ['iːv(ə)l] a (spell, influence, person) malfaisant; (deed, advice, system) mauvais; (consequence) funeste; – n mal m; to speak e. dire du mal (of de).

evince [ɪ'vɪns] vt manifester.

evoke [ɪ'vəʊk] vt (recall, conjure up) évoquer; (admiration) susciter. ◆evocative a évocateur.

evolution [iːvə'luːʃ(ə)n] n évolution f. ◆evolve vi (of society, idea etc) évoluer; (of plan) se développer; – vt (system etc) développer.

ewe [juː] n brebis f.

ex [eks] n (former spouse) Fam ex mf.

ex- [eks] pref ex-; ex-wife ex-femme f.

exacerbate [ɪk'sæsəbeɪt] vt (pain) exacerber.

exact [ɪg'zækt] 1 a (accurate, precise etc) exact; to be (more) e. about préciser. 2 vt (demand) exiger (from de); (money) extorquer (from à). ◆—ing a exigeant. ◆—ly adv exactement; it's e. 5 o'clock il est 5 heures juste. ◆—ness n exactitude f.

exaggerate [ɪg'zædʒəreɪt] vt exagérer; (in one's own mind) s'exagérer; – vi exagérer. ◆exagge'ration n exagération f.

exalt [ɪg'zɔːlt] vt (praise) exalter. ◆—ed a (position, rank) élevé. ◆exal'tation n exaltation f.

exam [ɪg'zæm] n Univ Sch Fam examen m.

examine [ɪg'zæmɪn] vt examiner; (accounts, luggage) vérifier; (passport) contrôler; (orally) interroger (témoin, élève). ◆exami'nation n (inspection) & Univ Sch examen m; (of accounts etc) vérification f; (of passport) contrôle m; class e. Sch composition f. ◆examiner n Sch examinateur, -trice mf.

example [ɪg'zɑːmp(ə)l] n exemple m; for e. par exemple; to set a good/bad e. donner le bon/mauvais exemple (to à); to make an e. of punir pour l'exemple.

exasperate [ɪg'zɑːspəreɪt] vt exaspérer; to get exasperated s'exaspérer (at de). ◆exaspe'ration n exaspération f.

excavate ['ekskəveɪt] vt (dig) creuser; (for relics etc) fouiller; (uncover) déterrer. ◆exca'vation n Tech creusement m; (archeological) fouille f.

exceed [ɪkˈsiːd] vt dépasser, excéder.
◆**—ingly** adv extrêmement.

excel [ɪkˈsel] vi (-ll-) exceller (**in** sth en qch, **in doing** à faire); — vt surpasser.

Excellency [ˈeksələnsɪ] n (title) Excellence f.

excellent [ˈeksələnt] a excellent. ◆**excel-**
lence n excellence f. ◆**excellently** adv
parfaitement, admirablement.

except [ɪkˈsept] prep sauf, excepté; e. **for** à
part; e. **that** à part le fait que, sauf que; e. **if**
sauf si; **to do nothing e. wait** ne rien faire
sinon attendre; — vt excepter. ◆**excep-**
tion n exception f; **with the e.** of à
l'exception de; **to take e. to** (object to)
désapprouver; (be hurt by) s'offenser de.
◆**exceptional** a exceptionnel. ◆**excep-**
tionally adv exceptionnellement.

excerpt [ˈeksɜːpt] n (from film, book etc)
extrait m.

excess [ɪkˈses] n excès m; (surplus) Com
excédent m; **one's excesses** ses excès mpl;
to e. à l'excès; **an e.** of (details) un luxe de;
— a (weight etc) excédentaire, en trop; e.
fare supplément m (de billet); e. **luggage**
excédent m de bagages. ◆**exˈcessive** a
excessif. ◆**exˈcessively** adv (too, too
much) excessivement; (very) extrêmement.

exchange [ɪksˈtʃeɪndʒ] vt (addresses, blows
etc) échanger (**for** contre); — n échange m;
Fin change m; (telephone) central m
(téléphonique); **in e.** en échange (**for** de).

Exchequer [ɪksˈtʃekər] n Chancellor of the
E. = ministre m des Finances.

excise [ˈeksaɪz] n taxe f (**on** sur).

excit/e [ɪkˈsaɪt] vt (agitate, provoke, stimulate) exciter; (enthuse) passionner, exciter.
◆**—ed** a excité; (laughter) énervé; **to get e.**
(nervous, angry, enthusiastic) s'exciter; **to
be e. about** (new car, news) se réjouir de; **to
be e. about the holidays** être surexcité à
l'idée de partir en vacances. ◆**—ing** a
(book, adventure) passionnant. ◆**—able** a
excitable. ◆**—edly** adv avec agitation; (to
wait, jump about) dans un état de surexcitation. ◆**—ement** n agitation f, excitation f,
fièvre f; (emotion) vive émotion f; (adventure) aventure f; **great e.** surexcitation f.

exclaim [ɪkˈskleɪm] vti s'exclamer, s'écrier
(**that** que). ◆**exclaˈmation** n exclamation
f; e. **mark** or Am **point** point m
d'exclamation.

exclude [ɪksˈkluːd] vt exclure (**from** de);
(name from list) écarter (**from** de).
◆**exclusion** n exclusion f. ◆**exclusive** a
(right, interest, design) exclusif; (club,
group) fermé; (interview) en exclusivité; e.

of wine/etc vin/etc non compris. ◆**exclu-**
sively adv exclusivement.

excommunicate [ekskəˈmjuːnɪkeɪt] vt
excommunier.

excrement [ˈekskrəmənt] n excrément(s)
m(pl).

excruciating [ɪkˈskruːʃɪeɪtɪŋ] a insuporta-
ble, atroce.

excursion [ɪkˈskɜːʃ(ə)n] n excursion f.

excuse [ɪkˈskjuːz] vt (justify, forgive)
excuser (s.o. **for doing** qn d'avoir fait, qn de
faire); (exempt) dispenser (**from** de); e. **me**
for asking permettez-moi de demander; e.
me! excusez-moi!, pardon!; **you're excused**
tu peux t'en aller or sortir; — [ɪkˈskjuːs] n
excuse f; **it was an e. for** cela a servi de
prétexte à.

ex-directory [eksdaɪˈrektərɪ] a Tel sur la
liste rouge.

execute [ˈeksɪkjuːt] vt (criminal, order, plan
etc) exécuter. ◆**exeˈcution** n exécution f.
◆**exeˈcutioner** n bourreau m.

executive [ɪgˈzekjʊtɪv] a (power) exécutif;
(ability) d'exécution; (job) de cadre; (car,
plane) de direction; — n (person) cadre m;
(board, committee) bureau m; **the e.** Pol
l'exécutif m; (senior) e. cadre m supérieur;
junior e. jeune cadre m; **business e.**
directeur m commercial.

exemplary [ɪgˈzemplərɪ] a exemplaire.
◆**exemplify** vt illustrer.

exempt [ɪgˈzempt] a exempt (**from** de); — vt
exempter (**from** de). ◆**exemption** n
exemption f.

exercise [ˈeksəsaɪz] n (of power etc) & Sch
Sp Mil exercice m; pl Univ Am cérémonies
fpl; e. **book** cahier m; — vt (troops)
faire faire l'exercice à; (dog, horse etc)
promener; (tact, judgement etc) faire
preuve de; (rights) faire valoir, exercer; —
vi (take exercise) prendre de l'exercice.

exert [ɪgˈzɜːt] vt exercer; (force) employer;
to e. oneself (physically) se dépenser; **he
never exerts himself** (takes the trouble) il ne
se fatigue jamais; **to e. oneself to do** (try
hard) s'efforcer de faire. ◆**exertion** n
effort m; (of force) emploi m.

exhale [eksˈheɪl] vt (breathe out) expirer;
(give off) exhaler; — vi expirer.

exhaust [ɪgˈzɔːst] **1** vt (use up, tire) épuiser;
to become exhausted s'épuiser. **2** n e. (pipe)
Aut pot m or tuyau m d'échappement.
◆**—ing** a épuisant. ◆**exhaustion** n
épuisement m. ◆**exhaustive** a (study etc)
complet; (research) approfondi.

exhibit [ɪgˈzɪbɪt] vt (put on display) exposer;
(ticket, courage etc) montrer; — n objet m

exposé; *Jur* pièce *f* à conviction. ◆**exhi'bition** *n* exposition *f*; an e. of (*display*) une démonstration de; **to make an e. of oneself** se donner en spectacle. ◆**exhi'bitionist** *n* exhibitionniste *mf*. ◆**exhibitor** *n* exposant, -ante *mf*.

exhilarate [ɪg'zɪləreɪt] *vt* stimuler; (*of air*) vivifier; (*elate*) rendre fou de joie. ◆**exhila'ration** *n* liesse *f*, joie *f*.

exhort [ɪg'zɔːt] *vt* exhorter (**to do** à faire, **to sth** à qch).

exhume [eks'hjuːm] *vt* exhumer.

exile ['egzaɪl] *vt* exiler; – *n* (*absence*) exil *m*; (*person*) exilé, -ée *mf*.

exist [ɪg'zɪst] *vi* exister; (*live*) vivre (**on** de); (**to continue**) **to e.** subsister; **the notion exists that . . .** il existe une notion selon laquelle . . . ◆**-ing** *a* (*law*) existant; (*circumstances*) actuel. ◆**existence** *n* existence *f*; **to come into e.** être créé; **to be in e.** exister. ◆**exi'stentialism** *n* existentialisme *m*.

exit ['eksɪt, 'egzɪt] *n* (*action*) sortie *f*; (*door, window*) sortie *f*, issue *f*; – *vi Th* sortir.

exodus ['eksədəs] *n inv* exode *m*.

exonerate [ɪg'zɒnəreɪt] *vt* (*from blame*) disculper (**from** de).

exorbitant [ɪg'zɔːbɪtənt] *a* exorbitant. ◆**-ly** *adv* démesurément.

exorcize ['eksɔːsaɪz] *vt* exorciser. ◆**exorcism** *n* exorcisme *m*.

exotic [ɪg'zɒtɪk] *a* exotique.

expand [ɪk'spænd] *vt* (*one's fortune, knowledge etc*) étendre; (*trade, ideas*) développer; (*production*) augmenter; (*gas, metal*) dilater; – *vi* s'étendre; se développer; augmenter; se dilater; **to e. on** développer ses idées sur; **(fast or rapidly) expanding sector**/*etc Com* secteur/*etc* en (pleine) expansion. ◆**expansion** *n Com Phys Pol* expansion *f*; développement *m*; augmentation *f*. ◆**expansionism** *n* expansionnisme *m*.

expanse [ɪk'spæns] *n* étendue *f*.

expansive [ɪk'spænsɪv] *a* expansif. ◆**-ly** *adv* avec effusion.

expatriate [eks'pætrɪət, *Am* eks'peɪtrɪət] *a & n* expatrié, -ée (*mf*).

expect [ɪk'spekt] *vt* (*anticipate*) s'attendre à, attendre, escompter; (*think*) penser (**that** que); (*suppose*) supposer (**that** que); (*await*) attendre; **to e. sth from s.o.**/**sth** attendre qch de qn/qch; **to e. to do** compter faire; **to e. that** (*anticipate*) s'attendre à ce que (+ *sub*); **I e. you to come** (*want*) je te demande de venir; **it was expected** c'était prévu (**that** que); **she's expecting a baby** elle attend un bébé. ◆**expectancy** *n* attente *f*; **life e.** espérance *f* de vie. ◆**expectant** *a* (*crowd*) qui attend; **e. mother** future mère *f*. ◆**expec'tation** *n* attente *f*; **to come up to s.o.'s expectations** répondre à l'attente de qn.

expedient [ɪks'piːdɪənt] *a* avantageux; (*suitable*) opportun; – *n* (*resource*) expédient *m*.

expedite ['ekspədaɪt] *vt* (*hasten*) accélérer; (*task*) expédier.

expedition [ekspɪ'dɪʃ(ə)n] *n* expédition *f*.

expel [ɪk'spel] *vt* (**-ll-**) expulser (**from** de); (*from school*) renvoyer; (*enemy*) chasser.

expend [ɪk'spend] *vt* (*energy, money*) dépenser; (*resources*) épuiser. ◆**-able** *a* (*object*) remplaçable; (*soldiers*) sacrifiable. ◆**expenditure** *n* (*money spent*) dépenses *fpl*; **an e. of** (*time, money*) une dépense de.

expense [ɪk'spens] *n* frais *mpl*, dépense *f*; *pl Fin* frais *mpl*; **business/travelling expenses** frais *mpl* généraux/de déplacement; **to go to some e.** faire des frais; **at s.o.'s e.** aux dépens de qn; **an or one's e. account** une *or* sa note de frais (professionnels).

expensive [ɪk'spensɪv] *a* (*goods etc*) cher, coûteux; (*hotel etc*) cher; (*tastes*) dispendieux; **to be e.** coûter cher; **an e. mistake** une faute qui coûte cher. ◆**-ly** *adv* à grands frais.

experienc/e [ɪk'spɪərɪəns] *n* (*knowledge, skill, event*) expérience *f*; **from** *or* **by e.** par expérience; **he's had e. of** (*work etc*) il a déjà fait; (*grief etc*) il a déjà éprouvé; **I've had e. of driving** j'ai déjà conduit; **terrible experiences** de rudes épreuves *fpl*; **unforgettable e.** moment *m* inoubliable; – *vt* (*undergo*) connaître, subir; (*remorse, difficulty*) éprouver; (*joy*) ressentir. ◆**-ed** *a* (*person*) expérimenté; (*eye, ear*) exercé; **to be e. in** s'y connaître en (matière de).

experiment [ɪk'sperɪmənt] *n* expérience *f*; – [ɪk'sperɪment] *vi* faire une expérience *or* des expériences; **to e. with sth** *Phys Ch* expérimenter qch. ◆**experi'mental** *a* expérimental; **e. period** période *f* d'expérimentation.

expert ['ekspɜːt] *n* expert *m* (**on, in** en), spécialiste *mf* (**on, in** de); – *a* expert (**in sth** en qch, **in** *or* **at doing** à faire); (*advice*) d'un expert, d'expert; (*eye*) connaisseur; **e. touch** doigté *m*, grande habileté *f*. ◆**exper'tise** *n* compétence *f* (**in** en). ◆**expertly** *adv* habilement.

expiate ['ekspɪeɪt] *vt* (*sins*) expier.

expir/e [ɪk'spaɪər] *vi* expirer. ◆**-ed** *a*

(ticket, passport etc) périmé. ◆expi'ration *n Am.* ◆expiry *n* expiration *f.*

explain [ɪkˈspleɪn] *vt* expliquer (to à, that que); *(reasons)* exposer; *(mystery)* éclaircir; e. yourself! explique-toi!; to e. away justifier. ◆—able *a* explicable. ◆expla'nation *n* explication *f.* ◆explanatory *a* explicatif.

expletive [ɪkˈspliːtɪv, *Am* ˈeksplətɪv] *n (oath)* juron *m.*

explicit [ɪkˈsplɪsɪt] *a* explicite. ◆—ly *adv* explicitement.

explode [ɪkˈspləʊd] *vi* exploser; to e. with laughter *Fig* éclater de rire; — *vt* faire exploser; *(theory) Fig* démythifier, discréditer.

exploit 1 [ɪkˈsplɔɪt] *vt (person, land etc)* exploiter. 2 [ˈeksplɔɪt] *n (feat)* exploit *m.* ◆exploi'tation *n* exploitation *f.*

explore [ɪkˈsplɔːr] *vt* explorer; *(possibilities)* examiner. ◆explo'ration *n* exploration *f.* ◆exploratory *a* d'exploration; *(talks, step etc)* préliminaire, exploratoire; e. operation *Med* sondage *m.* ◆explorer *n* explorateur, -trice *mf.*

explosion [ɪkˈspləʊʒ(ə)n] *n* explosion *f.* ◆explosive *a (weapon, question)* explosif; *(mixture, gas)* détonant; — *n* explosif *m.*

exponent [ɪkˈspəʊnənt] *n (of opinion, theory etc)* interprète *m (of* de).

export [ˈekspɔːt] *n* exportation *f;* — *a (goods etc)* d'exportation; — [ɪkˈspɔːt] *vt* exporter (to vers, from de). ◆ex'porter *n* exportateur, -trice *mf; (country)* pays *m* exportateur.

expose [ɪkˈspəʊz] *vt (leave uncovered, describe) & Phot* exposer; *(plot, scandal etc)* révéler, dévoiler; *(crook etc)* démasquer; to e. to *(subject to)* exposer à; to e. oneself commettre un attentat à la pudeur. ◆expo'sition *n* exposition *f.* ◆exposure *n* exposition *f (to à); (of plot etc)* révélation *f; (of house etc)* exposition *f; Phot* pose *f;* to die of e. mourir de froid.

expound [ɪkˈspaʊnd] *vt (theory etc)* exposer.

express [ɪkˈspres] 1 *vt* exprimer; *(proposition)* énoncer; to e. oneself s'exprimer. 2 *a (order)* exprès, formel; *(intention)* explicite; *(purpose)* seul; *(letter, delivery)* exprès *inv; (train)* rapide, express *inv;* — *adv (to send)* par exprès; — *n (train)* rapide *m,* express *m inv.* ◆expression *n (phrase, look etc)* expression *f; (of gratitude, affection etc)* un témoignage de. ◆expressive *a* expressif. ◆expressly *adv* expressément. ◆expressway *n Am* autoroute *f.*

expulsion [ɪkˈspʌlʃ(ə)n] *n* expulsion *f; (from school)* renvoi *m.*

expurgate [ˈekspəgeɪt] *vt* expurger.

exquisite [ɪkˈskwɪzɪt] *a* exquis. ◆—ly *adv* d'une façon exquise.

ex-serviceman [eksˈsɜːvɪsmən] *n (pl -men)* ancien combattant *m.*

extant [ˈekstənt, ekˈstænt] *a* existant.

extend [ɪkˈstend] *vt (arm, business)* étendre; *(line, visit, meeting)* prolonger (by de); *(hand)* tendre (to s.o. à qn); *(house)* agrandir; *(knowledge)* élargir; *(time limit)* reculer; *(help, thanks)* offrir (to à); to e. an invitation to faire une invitation à; — *vi (of wall, plain etc)* s'étendre (to jusqu'à); *(in time)* se prolonger; to e. to s.o. *(of joy etc)* gagner qn. ◆extension *n (in space)* prolongement *m; (in time)* prolongation *f; (of powers, measure, meaning, strike)* extension *f; (for table, wire)* rallonge *f; (to building)* agrandissement(s) *m(pl); (of telephone)* appareil *m* supplémentaire; *(of office telephone)* poste *m;* an e. (of time) un délai. ◆extensive *a* étendu, vaste; *(repairs, damage)* important; *(use)* courant. ◆extensively *adv (very much)* beaucoup, considérablement; e. used largement répandu.

extent [ɪkˈstent] *n (scope)* étendue *f; (size)* importance *f; (degree)* mesure *f;* to a large/certain e. dans une large/certaine mesure; to such an e. that à tel point que. ◆extenuating [ɪkˈstenjʊeɪtɪŋ] *a* e. circumstances circonstances *fpl* atténuantes.

exterior [eksˈtɪərɪər] *a & n* extérieur (*m*).

exterminate [ɪkˈstɜːmɪneɪt] *vt (people etc)* exterminer; *(disease)* supprimer; *(evil)* extirper. ◆extermi'nation *n* extermination *f;* suppression *f.*

external [ekˈstɜːn(ə)l] *a (influence, trade etc)* extérieur; for e. use *(medicine)* à usage externe; e. affairs *Pol* affaires *fpl* étrangères. ◆—ly *adv* extérieurement.

extinct [ɪkˈstɪŋkt] *a (volcano, love)* éteint; *(species, animal)* disparu. ◆extinction *n* extinction *f;* disparition *f.*

extinguish [ɪkˈstɪŋgwɪʃ] *vt* éteindre. ◆—er *n (fire)* e. extincteur *m.*

extol [ɪkˈstəʊl] *vt (-ll-)* exalter, louer.

extort [ɪkˈstɔːt] *vt (money)* extorquer (from à); *(consent)* arracher (from à). ◆extortion *n Jur* extorsion *f* de fonds; it's (sheer) e.! c'est du vol! ◆extortionate *a* exorbitant.

extra [ˈekstrə] *a (additional)* supplémentaire; one e. glass un verre de *or* en plus, encore un verre; (any) e. bread?

encore du pain?; **to be e.** (*spare*) être en trop; (*cost more*) être en supplément; (*of postage*) être en sus; **wine is 3 francs e.** il y a un supplément de 3F pour le vin; **e. care** un soin tout particulier; **e. charge** or **portion** supplément *m*; **e. time** *Fb* prolongation *f*; — *adv* **e. big**/*etc* plus grand/*etc* que d'habitude; — *n* (*perk*) à-côté *m*; *Cin Th* figurant, -ante *mf*; *pl* (*expenses*) frais *mpl* supplémentaires; **an optional e.** (*for car etc*) un accessoire en option.

extra- ['ekstrə] *pref* extra-. ◆**e.-'dry** *a* (*champagne*) brut. ◆**e.-'fine** *a* extra-fin. ◆**e.-'strong** *a* extra-fort.

extract [ɪk'strækt] *vt* extraire (**from** de); (*tooth*) arracher, extraire; (*promise*) arracher, soutirer (**from** à); (*money*) soutirer (**from** à); — ['ekstrækt] *n* (*of book etc*) & *Culin Ch* extrait *m*. ◆**ex'traction** *n* extraction *f*; arrachement *m*; (*descent*) origine *f*.

extra-curricular [ekstrəkə'rɪkjulər] *a* (*activities etc*) en dehors des heures de cours, extrascolaire.

extradite ['ekstrədaɪt] *vt* extrader. ◆**extra-'dition** *n* extradition *f*.

extramarital [ekstrə'mærɪt(ə)l] *a* en dehors du mariage, extra-conjugal.

extramural [ekstrə'mjuərəl] *a* (*studies*) hors faculté.

extraneous [ɪk'streɪnɪəs] *a* (*detail etc*) accessoire.

extraordinary [ɪk'strɔːdən(ə)rɪ] *a* (*strange, exceptional*) extraordinaire.

extra-special [ekstrə'speʃəl] *a* (*occasion*) très spécial; (*care*) tout particulier.

extravagant [ɪk'strævəgənt] *a* (*behaviour, idea etc*) extravagant; (*claim*) exagéré; (*wasteful with money*) dépensier, prodigue. ◆**extravagance** *n* extravagance *f*; prodigalité *f*; (*thing bought*) folle dépense *f*.

extravaganza [ekstrævə'gænzə] *n* *Mus Liter* & *Fig* fantaisie *f*.

extreme [ɪk'striːm] *a* (*exceptional, furthest*) extrême; (*danger, poverty*) très grand; (*praise*) outré; **at the e. end** à l'extrémité; **of**

e. importance de première importance; — *n* (*furthest degree*) extrême *m*; **to carry** or **take to extremes** pousser à l'extrême; **extremes of temperature** températures *fpl* extrêmes; **extremes of climate** excès *mpl* du climat. ◆**extremely** *adv* extrêmement. ◆**extremist** *a* & *n* extrémiste (*mf*). ◆**extremity** [ɪk'stremɪtɪ] *n* extrémité *f*.

extricate ['ekstrɪkeɪt] *vt* dégager (**from** de); **to e. oneself from** (*difficulty*) se tirer de.

extrovert ['ekstrəvɜːt] *n* extraverti, -ie *mf*.

exuberant [ɪg'z(j)uːbərənt] *a* exubérant. ◆**exuberance** *n* exubérance *f*.

exude [ɪg'zjuːd] *vt* (*charm, honesty etc*) *Fig* respirer.

exultation [egzʌl'teɪʃ(ə)n] *n* exultation *f*.

eye[1] [aɪ] *n* œil *m* (*pl* yeux); **before my very eyes** sous mes yeux; **to be all eyes** être tout yeux; **as far as the e. can see** à perte de vue; **up to one's eyes in debt** endetté jusqu'au cou; **up to one's eyes in work** débordé de travail; **to have an e. on** (*house, car*) avoir en vue; **to keep an e. on** surveiller; **to make eyes at** *Fam* faire de l'œil à; **to lay** or **set eyes on** voir, apercevoir; **to take one's eyes off s.o./sth** quitter qn/qch des yeux; **to catch the e.** attirer l'œil, accrocher le regard; **keep an e. out!, keep your eyes open!** ouvre l'œil!, sois vigilant!; **we don't see e. to e.** nous n'avons pas le même point de vue; **e. shadow** fard *m* à paupières; **to be an e.-opener for s.o.** *Fam* être une révélation pour qn. ◆**eyeball** *n* globe *m* oculaire. ◆**eyebrow** *n* sourcil *m*. ◆**eye-catching** *a* (*title etc*) accrocheur. ◆**eyeglass** *n* monocle *m*. ◆**eyeglasses** *npl* (*spectacles*) *Am* lunettes *fpl*. ◆**eyelash** *n* cil *m*. ◆**eyelid** *n* paupière *f*. ◆**eyeliner** *n* eye-liner *m*. ◆**eyesight** *n* vue *f*. ◆**eyesore** *n* (*building etc*) horreur *f*. ◆**eyestrain** *n* **to have e.** avoir les yeux qui tirent. ◆**eyewash** *n* (*nonsense*) *Fam* sottises *fpl*. ◆**eyewitness** *n* témoin *m* oculaire.

eye[2] [aɪ] *vt* reluquer, regarder.

F

F, f [ef] *n* F, f *m*.

fable ['feɪb(ə)l] *n* fable *f*.

fabric ['fæbrɪk] *n* (*cloth*) tissu *m*, étoffe *f*; (*of building*) structure *f*; **the f. of society** le tissu

social.

fabricate ['fæbrɪkeɪt] *vt* (*invent, make*) fabriquer. ◆**fabri'cation** *n* fabrication *f*.

fabulous ['fæbjuləs] a (incredible, legendary) fabuleux; (wonderful) Fam formidable.

façade [fə'sɑːd] n Archit & Fig façade f.

face [feɪs] n visage m, figure f; (expression) mine f; (of clock) cadran m; (of building) façade f; (of cliff) paroi f; (of the earth) surface f; **she laughed in my f.** elle m'a ri au nez; **to show one's f.** se montrer; **f. down(wards)** (person) face contre terre; (thing) tourné à l'envers; **f. to f.** face à face; **in the f. of** devant; (despite) en dépit de; **to save/lose f.** sauver/perdre la face; **to make or pull faces** faire des grimaces; **to tell s.o. sth to his f.** dire qch à qn tout cru; **f. powder** poudre f de riz; **f. value** (of stamp etc) valeur f; **to take sth at f. value** prendre qch au pied de la lettre; − vt (danger, enemy etc) faire face à; (accept) accepter; (look in the face) regarder (qn) bien en face; **to f., be facing** (be opposite) être en face de; (of window etc) donner sur; **faced with** (prospect, problem) face à, devant; (defeat) menacé par; (bill) contraint à payer; **he can't f. leaving** il n'a pas le courage de partir; − vi (of house) être orienté (**north/etc** au nord/etc); (of person) se tourner (**towards** vers); **to f. up to** (danger) faire face à; (fact) accepter; **about f.!** Am Mil demi-tour! ◆**facecloth** n gant m de toilette. ◆**facelift** n Med lifting m; (of building) ravalement m.

faceless ['feɪsləs] a anonyme.

facet ['fæsɪt] n (of problem, diamond etc) facette f.

facetious [fə'siːʃəs] a (person) facétieux; (remark) plaisant.

facial ['feɪʃ(ə)l] a du visage; Med facial; − n soin m du visage.

facile ['fæsaɪl, Am 'fæs(ə)l] a facile, superficiel.

facilitate [fə'sɪlɪteɪt] vt faciliter. ◆**facility** n (ease) facilité f; pl (possibilities) facilités fpl; (for sports) équipements mpl; (in harbour, airport etc) installations fpl; (means) moyens mpl, ressources fpl; **special facilities** (conditions) conditions fpl spéciales (**for** pour).

facing ['feɪsɪŋ] n (of dress etc) parement m.

fact [fækt] n fait m; **as a matter of f., in f.** en fait; **the facts of life** les choses fpl de la vie; **is that a f.?** c'est vrai? **f. and fiction** le réel et l'imaginaire.

faction ['fækʃ(ə)n] n (group) Pol faction f.

factor ['fæktər] n (element) facteur m.

factory ['fækt(ə)rɪ] n (large) usine f; (small) fabrique f; **arms/porcelain f.** manufacture f d'armes/de porcelaine.

factual ['fæktʃʊəl] a objectif, basé sur les faits, factuel; (error) de fait.

faculty ['fæk(ə)ltɪ] n (aptitude) & Univ faculté f.

fad [fæd] n (personal habit) marotte f; (fashion) folie f, mode f (**for** de).

fade [feɪd] vi (of flower) se faner; (of light) baisser; (of colour) passer; (of fabric) se décolorer; **to f. (away)** (of memory, smile) s'effacer; (of sound) s'affaiblir; (of person) dépérir; − vt (of fabric) décolorer.

fag [fæg] n **1** (cigarette) Fam clope m, tige f; **f. end** mégot m. **2** (male homosexual) Am Sl pédé m.

fagged [fægd] a **f. (out)** (tired) Sl claqué.

faggot ['fægət] n **1** Culin boulette f (de viande). **2** (male homosexual) Am Sl pédé m.

fail [feɪl] vi (of person, plan etc) échouer; (of business) faire faillite; (of light, health, sight) baisser; (of memory, strength) défaillir; (of brakes) Aut lâcher; (run short) manquer; (of gas, electricity) être coupé; (of engine) tomber en panne; **to f. in** (one's duty) manquer à; (exam) échouer à; − vt (exam) échouer à; (candidate) recaler; **to f. s.o.** (let down) laisser tomber qn, décevoir qn; (of words) manquer à qn, faire défaut à qn; **to f. to do** (omit) manquer de faire; (not be able) ne pas arriver à faire; **I f. to see** je ne vois pas; − n **without f.** à coup sûr, sans faute. ◆**-ed** a (attempt, poet) manqué. ◆**-ing** n (fault) défaut m; − prep à défaut de; **f. this, f. that** à défaut. ◆**failure** n échec m; (of business) faillite f; (of engine, machine) panne f; (of gas etc) coupure f, panne f; (person) raté, -ée m f; **f. to do** (inability) incapacité f de faire; **her f. to leave** le fait qu'elle n'est pas partie; **to end in f.** se solder par un échec; **heart f.** arrêt m du cœur.

faint [feɪnt] **1** a (-er, -est) léger; (voice) faible; (colour) pâle; (idea) vague; **I haven't the faintest idea** je n'en ai pas la moindre idée. **2** a Med défaillant (**with** de); **to feel f.** se trouver mal, défaillir; − vi s'évanouir (**from** de); **fainting fit** évanouissement m. ◆**-ly** adv (weakly) faiblement; (slightly) légèrement. ◆**-ness** n légèreté f, faiblesse f. ◆**faint-'hearted** a timoré, timide.

fair¹ [feər] n foire f; (for charity) fête f; (funfair) fête f foraine; (larger) parc m d'attractions. ◆**fairground** n champ m de foire.

fair² [feər] **1** a (-er, -est) (equitable) juste, équitable; (game, fight) loyal; f. (and square) honnête(ment); f. play fair-play m inv; that's not f.! ce n'est pas juste!; that's not f. to him ce n'est pas juste pour lui; f. enough! très bien!; – adv (to play) loyalement. **2** a (rather good) passable, assez bon; (amount, warning) raisonnable; a f. amount (of) pas mal (de); f. copy copie f au propre. **3** a (wind) favorable; (weather) beau. ◆—ly adv **1** (to treat) équitablement; (to get) loyalement. **2** (rather) assez, plutôt; f. sure presque sûr. ◆—ness¹ n justice f; (of decision) équité f; in all f. en toute justice. ◆fair-'minded a impartial. ◆fair-'sized a assez grand.

fair³ [feər] a (hair, person) blond; (complexion, skin) clair. ◆—ness² n (of hair) blond m; (of skin) blancheur f. ◆fair-'haired a blond. ◆fair-'skinned a à la peau claire.

fairy ['feəri] n fée f. f. lights guirlande f multicolore; f. tale conte m de fées.

faith [feiθ] n foi f; to have f. in s.o. avoir confiance en qn; to put one's f. in (justice, medicine etc) se fier à; in good/bad f. de bonne/mauvaise foi; f. healer guérisseur, -euse mf. ◆faithful a fidèle. ◆faithfully adv fidèlement; yours f. (in letter) Com veuillez agréer l'expression de mes salutations distinguées. ◆faithfulness n fidélité f. ◆faithless a déloyal, infidèle.

fake [feik] n (painting, document etc) faux m; (person) imposteur m; – vt (document, signature etc) falsifier, maquiller; (election) truquer; to f. death faire semblant d'être mort; – vi (pretend) faire semblant; – a faux; (elections) truqué.

falcon ['fɔːlkən] n faucon m.

fall [fɔːl] n chute f; (in price, demand etc) baisse f; pl (waterfall) chutes fpl (d'eau); the f. Am l'automne m; – vi (pt fell, pp fallen) tomber; (of building) s'effondrer; her face fell Fig son visage se rembrunit; to f. into tomber dans; (habit) Fig prendre; to f. off a bicycle/etc tomber d'une bicyclette/etc; to f. off or down a ladder tomber (en bas) d'une échelle; to f. on s.o. (of onus) retomber sur qn; to f. on a Monday/etc (of event) tomber un lundi/etc; to f. over sth tomber en butant contre qch; to f. short of (expectation) ne pas répondre à; to f. short of being être loin d'être; to f. victim devenir victime (to de); to f. asleep s'endormir; to f. ill tomber malade; to f. due échoir. ■ to f. apart (of mechanism) tomber en morceaux; Fig se désagréger; to f. away (come off) se

détacher, tomber; (of numbers) diminuer; to f. back on (as last resort) se rabattre sur; to f. behind rester en arrière; (in work) prendre du retard; to f. down tomber; (of building) s'effondrer; to f. for Fam (person) tomber amoureux de; (trick) se laisser prendre à; to f. in (collapse) s'écrouler; to f. in with (tally with) cadrer avec; (agree to) accepter; to f. off (come off) se détacher, tomber; (of numbers) diminuer. ◆falling-'off n diminution f; to f. out with (quarrel with) se brouiller avec; to f. over tomber; (of table, vase) se renverser; to f. through (of plan) tomber à l'eau, échouer. ◆fallen a tombé; (angel, woman) déchu; f. leaf feuille f morte. ◆fallout n (radioactive) retombées fpl.

fallacious [fə'leiʃəs] a faux. ◆fallacy ['fæləsi] n erreur f; Phil faux raisonnement m.

fallible ['fæləb(ə)l] a faillible.

fallow ['fæləu] a (land) en jachère.

false [fɔːls] a faux; a f. bottom un double fond. ◆falsehood n mensonge m; truth and f. le vrai et le faux. ◆falseness n fausseté f. ◆falsify vt falsifier.

falter ['fɔːltər] vi (of step, resolution) chanceler; (of voice, speaker) hésiter; (of courage) vaciller.

fame [feim] n renommée f; (glory) gloire f. ◆famed a renommé.

familiar [fə'miljər] a (task, atmosphere etc) familier; (event) habituel; f. with s.o. (too friendly) familier avec qn; to be f. with (know) connaître; I'm f. with her voice je connais bien sa voix, sa voix m'est familière; to make oneself f. with se familiariser avec; he looks f. (to me) je l'ai déjà vu (quelque part). ◆famili'arity n familiarité f (with avec); (of event, sight etc) caractère m familier. ◆familiarize vt familiariser (with avec); to f. oneself with se familiariser avec.

family ['fæmili] n famille f; – a (name, doctor etc) de famille; (planning, problem) familial; (tree) généalogique; f. man père m de famille.

famine ['fæmin] n famine f.

famished ['fæmiʃt] a affamé.

famous ['feiməs] a célèbre (for par, pour). ◆—ly adv (very well) Fam rudement bien.

fan [fæn] **1** n (hand-held) éventail m; (mechanical) ventilateur m; f. heater radiateur m soufflant; – vt (-nn-) (person etc) éventer; (fire, quarrel) attiser. **2** n (of person) admirateur, -trice mf, fan m; Sp supporter *m*; **to be a jazz/sports f.** être passionné *or* mordu de jazz/de sport.

fanatic [fə'nætɪk] *n* fanatique *mf*. ◆**fanatical** *a* fanatique. ◆**fanaticism** *n* fanatisme *m*.

fancy ['fænsɪ] **1** *n* (*whim, imagination*) fantaisie *f*; (*liking*) goût *m*; **to take a f. to s.o.** se prendre d'affection pour qn; **I took a f. to it,** it took my f. j'en ai eu envie; **when the f. takes me** quand ça me chante; − *a* (*hat, button etc*) fantaisie *inv*; (*idea*) fantaisiste; (*price*) exorbitant; (*car*) de luxe; (*house, restaurant*) chic; **f. dress** (*costume*) travesti *m*; **f.-dress ball** bal *m* masqué. **2** *vt* (*imagine*) se figurer (**that** que); (*think*) croire (**that** que); (*want*) avoir envie de; (*like*) aimer; **f. that!** tiens (donc)!; **he fancies her** *Fam* elle lui plaît; **to f. oneself as** se prendre pour qn; **she fancies herself!** elle se prend pour qn! ◆**fancier** *n* **horse/etc f.** amateur *m* de chevaux/etc. ◆**fanciful** *a* fantaisiste.

fanfare ['fænfeər] *n* (*of trumpets*) fanfare *f*.

fang [fæŋ] *n* (*of dog etc*) croc *m*; (*of snake*) crochet *m*.

fantastic [fæn'tæstɪk] *a* fantastique; **a f. idea** (*absurd*) une idée aberrante.

fantasy ['fæntəsɪ] *n* (*imagination*) fantaisie *f*; *Psy* fantasme *m*. ◆**fantasize** *vi* fantasmer (**about** sur).

far [fɑːr] *adv* (**farther** *or* **further, farthest** *or* **furthest**) (*distance*) loin; **f. bigger/more expensive/etc** (*much*) beaucoup plus grand/plus cher/etc (**than** que); **f. more** beaucoup plus; **f. advanced** très avancé; **how f. is it to...?** combien y a-t-il d'ici à ...?; **is it f. to...?** sommes-nous, suis-je *etc* loin de...?; **how f. are you going?** jusqu'où vas-tu?; **how f. has he got with?** (*plans, work etc*) où en est-il de?; **so f.** (*time*) jusqu'ici; (*place*) jusque-là; **as f. as** (*place*) jusqu'à; **as f.** *or* **so f. as I know** autant que je sache; **as f.** *or* **so f. as I'm concerned** en ce qui me concerne; **as f. back as 1820** dès 1820; **f. from doing** loin de faire; **f. from it!** loin de là!; **f. away** *or* **off** au loin; **to be (too) f. away** être (trop) loin (**from** de); **f. and wide** partout; **by f.** de loin; **f. into the night** très avant dans la nuit; − *a* (*side, end*) autre; **it's a f. cry from** on est loin de. ◆**faraway** *a* lointain; (*look*) distrait, dans le vague. ◆**far-'fetched** *a* forcé, exagéré. ◆**f.-'flung** *a* (*widespread*) vaste. ◆**f.-'off** *a* lointain. ◆**f.-'reaching** *a* de grande portée. ◆**f.-'sighted** *a* clairvoyant.

farce [fɑːs] *n* farce *f*. ◆**farcical** *a* grotesque, ridicule.

fare [feər] **1** *n* (*price*) prix *m* du billet; (*ticket*) billet *m*; (*taxi passenger*) client, -ente *mf*. **2** *n* (*food*) chère *f*, nourriture *f*; **prison f.** régime *m* de prison; **bill of f.** menu *m*. **3** *vi* (*manage*) se débrouiller; **how did she f.?** comment ça s'est passé (pour elle)?

farewell [feə'wel] *n & int* adieu (*m*); − *a* (*party etc*) d'adieu.

farm [fɑːm] *n* ferme *f*; − *a* (*worker, produce etc*) agricole; **f. land** terres *fpl* cultivées; − *vt* cultiver; − *vi* être agriculteur. ◆**-ing** *n* agriculture *f*; (*breeding*) élevage *m*. ◆**dairy f.** industrie *f* laitière. ◆**-er** *n* fermier, -ière *mf*, agriculteur *m*. ◆**farmhand** *n* ouvrier, -ière *mf* agricole. ◆**farmhouse** *n* ferme *f*. ◆**farmyard** *n* basse-cour *f*.

farther ['fɑːðər] *adv* plus loin; **nothing is f. from** (*my mind, the truth etc*) rien n'est plus éloigné de; **f. forward** plus avancé; **to get f. away** s'éloigner; − *a* (*end*) autre. ◆**farthest** *a* le plus éloigné; − *adv* le plus loin.

fascinate ['fæsɪneɪt] *vt* fasciner. ◆**fasci-'nation** *n* fascination *f*.

fascism ['fæʃɪz(ə)m] *n* fascisme *m*. ◆**fascist** *a & n* fasciste (*mf*).

fashion ['fæʃ(ə)n] **1** *n* (*style in clothes etc*) mode *f*; **in f.** à la mode; **out of f.** démodé; **f. designer** (*grand*) couturier *m*; **f. house** maison *f* de couture; **f. show** présentation *f* de collections. **2** *n* (*manner*) façon *f*; (*custom*) habitude *f*; **after a f.** tant bien que mal, plus ou moins. **3** *vt* (*make*) façonner. ◆**-able** *a* à la mode; (*place*) chic *inv*; **it's f. to do** il est de bon ton de faire. ◆**-ably** *adv* (*dressed etc*) à la mode.

fast [fɑːst] **1** *a* (**-er, -est**) rapide; **to be f.** (*clock*) avancer (**by** de); **f. colour** couleur *f* grand teint *inv*; **f. living** vie *f* dissolue; − *adv* (*quickly*) vite; (*firmly*) ferme, bien; **how f.?** à quelle vitesse?; **f. asleep** profondément endormi. **2** *vi* (*go without food*) jeûner; − *n* jeûne *m*.

fasten ['fɑːs(ə)n] *vt* attacher (**to** à); (*door, window*) fermer (bien); **to f. down** *or* **up** attacher; − *vi* (*of dress etc*) s'attacher; (*of door, window*) se fermer. ◆**-er** *n*, ◆**-ing** *n* (*clip*) attache *f*; (*of garment*) fermeture *f*; (*of bag*) fermoir *m*; (*hook*) agrafe *f*.

fastidious [fə'stɪdɪəs] *a* difficile (à contenter), exigeant.

fat [fæt] **1** *n* graisse *f*; (*on meat*) gras *m*; **vegetable f.** huile *f* végétale. **2** *a* (**fatter, fattest**) gras; (*cheek, salary, volume*) gros; **to get f.** grossir; **that's a f. lot of good** *or* **use!** *Iron*

Fam ça va vraiment servir (à quelque chose)! ◆**fathead** *n* imbécile *mf.*

fatal ['feɪt(ə)l] *a* mortel; (*error, blow etc*) *Fig* fatal. ◆**-ly** *adv* mortellement.

fatality [fə'talɪt] *n* **1** (*person killed*) victime *f.* **2** (*of event*) fatalité *f.*

fate [feɪt] *n* destin *m*, sort *m*; one's f. son sort. ◆**fated** *a* f. to do destiné à faire; our meeting/his death/*etc* was f. notre rencontre/sa mort/*etc* devait arriver. ◆**fateful** *a* (*important*) fatal, décisif; (*prophetic*) fatidique; (*disastrous*) néfaste.

father ['fɑːðər] *n* père *m*; — *vt* engendrer; (*idea*) *Fig* inventer. ◆**-in-law** *n* (*pl* fathers-in-law) beau-père *m*. ◆**fatherhood** *n* paternité *f.* ◆**fatherland** *n* patrie *f.* ◆**fatherly** *a* paternel.

fathom ['fæðəm] **1** *n Nau* brasse *f* (= 1,8 *m*). **2** *vt* to f. (out) (*understand*) comprendre.

fatigue [fə'tiːg] **1** *n* fatigue *f*; — *vt* fatiguer. **2** *n* f. (duty) *Mil* corvée *f.*

fatness ['fætnɪs] *n* corpulence *f.* ◆**fatten** *vt* engraisser. ◆**fattening** *a* qui fait grossir. ◆**fatty** *a* (-ier, -iest) (*food*) gras; (*tissue*) *Med* adipeux; — *n* (*person*) *Fam* gros lard *m.*

fatuous ['fætjʊəs] *a* stupide.

faucet ['fɔːsɪt] *n* (*tap*) *Am* robinet *m.*

fault [fɔːlt] *n* (*blame*) faute *f*; (*failing, defect*) défaut *m*; (*mistake*) erreur *f*; *Geol* faille *f*; to find f. (with) critiquer; he's at f. c'est sa faute, il est fautif; his *or* her memory is at f. sa mémoire lui fait défaut; — *vt* to s.o./sth trouver des défauts chez qn/à qch. ◆**f.-finding** *n* critique, chicanier. ◆**faultless** *a* irréprochable. ◆**faulty** *a* (-ier, -iest) défectueux.

fauna ['fɔːnə] *n* (*animals*) faune *f.*

favour ['feɪvər] *n* (*approval, advantage*) faveur *f*; (*act of kindness*) service *m*; to do s.o. a f. rendre service à qn; in f. (*person*) bien vu; (*fashion*) en vogue; it's in her f. to do elle a intérêt à faire; in f. of (*for the sake of*) au profit de, en faveur de; to be in f. of (*support*) être pour, être partisan de; (*prefer*) préférer; — *vt* (*encourage*) favoriser; (*support*) être partisan de; (*prefer*) préférer; he favoured me with a visit il a eu la gentillesse de me rendre visite. ◆**-able** *a* favorable (to à). ◆**favourite** *a* favori, préféré; — *n* favori, -ite *mf.* ◆**favouritism** *n* favoritisme *m.*

fawn [fɔːn] **1** *n* (*deer*) faon *m*; — *a* & *n* (*colour*) fauve *m.* **2** *vi* to f. (up)on flatter, flagorner.

fear [fɪər] *n* crainte *f*, peur *f*; for f. of de peur de; for f. that de peur que (+ ne + *sub*);

there's no f. of his going il ne risque pas d'y aller; there are fears (that) he might leave on craint qu'il ne parte; — *vt* craindre; I f. (that) he might leave je crains qu'il ne parte; to f. for (*one's life etc*) craindre pour. ◆**fearful** *a* (*frightful*) affreux; (*timid*) peureux. ◆**fearless** *a* intrépide. ◆**fearlessness** *n* intrépidité *f.* ◆**fearsome** *a* redoutable.

feasible ['fiːzəb(ə)l] *a* (*practicable*) faisable; (*theory, explanation etc*) plausible. ◆**feasi'bility** *n* possibilité *f* (of doing de faire); plausibilité *f.*

feast [fiːst] *n* festin *m*, banquet *m*; *Rel* fête *f*; — *vi* banqueter; to f. on (*cakes etc*) se régaler de.

feat [fiːt] *n* exploit *m*, tour *m* de force; f. of skill tour *m* d'adresse.

feather ['feðər] **1** *n* plume *f*; f. duster plumeau *m.* **2** *vt* to f. one's nest (*enrich oneself*) faire sa pelote.

feature ['fiːtʃər] **1** *n* (*of face, person*) trait *m*; (*of thing, place, machine*) caractéristique *f*; f. (article) article *m* de fond; (*film*) grand film *m*; to be a regular f. (*in newspaper*) paraître régulièrement. **2** *vt* représenter (as comme); *Journ Cin* présenter; a film featuring Chaplin un film avec Charlot en vedette; — *vi* (*appear*) figurer (in dans).

February ['februərɪ] *n* février *m.*

fed [fed] *see* feed; — *a* to be f. up *Fam* en avoir marre (with de).

federal ['fedərəl] *a* fédéral. ◆**federate** *vt* fédérer. ◆**fede'ration** *n* fédération *f.*

fee [fiː] *n* (*price*) prix *m*; (*sum*) somme *f*; fee(s) (*professional*) honoraires *mpl*; (*of artist*) cachet *m*; (*for registration*) droits *mpl*; **tuition fees** frais *mpl* de scolarité; entrance f. droit *m* d'entrée; **membership fee(s)** cotisation *f*; f.-paying school école *f* privée.

feeble ['fiːb(ə)l] *a* (-er, -est) faible; (*excuse*) pauvre. ◆**f.-'minded** *a* imbécile.

feed [fiːd] *n* (*food*) nourriture *f*; (*baby's breast feed*) tétée *f*; (*baby's bottle feed*) biberon *m*; — *vt* (*pt* & *pp* fed) donner à manger à, nourrir; (*breast-feed*) allaiter (*un bébé*); (*bottle-feed*) donner le biberon à (*un bébé*); (*machine*) *Fig* alimenter; — *vi* (*eat*) manger; to f. on se nourrir de. ◆**-ing** *n* alimentation *f.* ◆**feedback** *n* réaction(s) *f(pl).*

feel [fiːl] *n* (*touch*) toucher *m*; (*sensation*) sensation *f*; — *vt* (*pt* & *pp* felt) (*be aware of*) sentir; (*experience*) éprouver, ressentir; (*touch*) tâter, palper; (*think*) avoir l'impression (that que); to f. one's way avancer à tâtons; — *vi* (*tired, old etc*) se sentir; **to f. (about)** (*grope*) tâtonner; (*in pocket etc*) fouiller; **it feels hard** c'est dur (au toucher); **I f. sure** je suis sûr (*that* que); **I f. hot/sleepy/hungry** j'ai chaud/sommeil/faim; **she feels better** elle va mieux; **to f. like** (*want*) avoir envie de; **to f. as if** avoir l'impression que; **it feels like cotton** on dirait du coton; **what do you f. about . . . ?** que pensez-vous de . . . ?; **I f. bad about it** ça m'ennuie, ça me fait de la peine; **what does it f.** quelle impression ça (te) fait?; **to f. for** (*look for*) chercher; (*pity*) éprouver de la pitié pour; **to f. up to doing** être (assez) en forme pour faire. ◆**—ing** *n* (*emotion, impression*) sentiment *m*; (*physical*) sensation *f*; **a f. for** (*person*) de la sympathie pour; (*music*) une appréciation de; **bad f.** animosité *f*. ◆**—er** *n* (*of snail etc*) antenne *f*; **to put out a f.** *Fig* lancer un ballon d'essai.

feet [fiːt] *see* **foot**¹.

feign [feɪn] *vt* feindre, simuler.

feint [feɪnt] *n Mil Boxing* feinte *f*.

feisty ['faɪstɪ] *a* (**-ier, -iest**) (*lively*) *Am Fam* plein d'entrain.

felicitous [fə'lɪsɪtəs] *a* heureux.

feline ['fiːlaɪn] *a* félin.

fell [fel] **1** *see* **fall**. **2** *vt* (*tree etc*) abattre.

fellow ['feləʊ] *n* **1** (*man, boy*) garçon *m*, type *m*; **an old f.** un vieux; **poor f.!** pauvre malheureux! **2** (*comrade*) compagnon *m*, compagne *f*; **f. being or man** semblable *m*; **f. countryman, f. countrywoman** compatriote *mf*; **f. passenger** compagnon *m* de voyage, compagne *f* de voyage. **3** (*of society*) membre *m*. ◆**fellowship** *n* camaraderie *f*; (*group*) association *f*; (*membership*) qualité *f* de membre; (*grant*) bourse *f* universitaire.

felony ['felənɪ] *n* crime *m*.

felt¹ [felt] *see* **feel**.

felt² [felt] *n* feutre *m*; **f.-tip(ped) pen** crayon *m* feutre.

female ['fiːmeɪl] *a* (*animal etc*) femelle; (*quality, name, voice etc*) féminin; (*vote*) des femmes; **f. student** étudiante *f*; — *n* (*woman*) femme *f*; (*animal*) femelle *f*.

feminine ['femɪnɪn] *a* féminin. ◆**femi'ninity** *n* féminité *f*. ◆**feminist** *a* & *n* féministe (*mf*).

fenc/e [fens] **1** *n* barrière *f*, clôture *f*; *Sp* obstacle *m*; — *vt* **to f. (in)** clôturer. **2** *vi* (*with sword*) *Sp* faire de l'escrime. **3** *n* (*criminal*) *Fam* receleur, -euse *mf*. ◆**—ing** *n Sp* escrime *f*.

fend [fend] **1** *vi* **to f. for oneself** se débrouil-

ler. **2** *vt* **to f. off** (*blow etc*) parer, éviter. ◆**—er** *n* **1** (*for fire*) garde-feu *m inv*. **2** (*on car*) *Am* aile *f*.

fennel ['fen(ə)l] *n Bot Culin* fenouil *m*.

ferment ['fɜːment] *n* ferment *m*; *Fig* effervescence *f*; — [fə'ment] *vi* fermenter. ◆**fermen'tation** *n* fermentation *f*.

fern [fɜːn] *n* fougère *f*.

ferocious [fə'rəʊʃəs] *a* féroce. ◆**ferocity** *n* férocité *f*.

ferret ['ferɪt] *n* (*animal*) furet *m*; — *vi* **to f. about** (*pry*) fureter; — *vt* **to f. out** dénicher.

Ferris wheel ['ferɪswiːl] *n* (*at funfair*) grande roue *f*.

ferry ['ferɪ] *n* ferry-boat *m*; (*small, for river*) bac *m*; — *vt* transporter.

fertile ['fɜːtaɪl, *Am* 'fɜːt(ə)l] *a* (*land, imagination*) fertile; (*person, creature*) fécond. ◆**fer'tility** *n* fertilité *f*; fécondité *f*. ◆**fertilize** *vt* (*land*) fertiliser; (*egg, animal etc*) féconder. ◆**fertilizer** *n* engrais *m*.

fervent ['fɜːv(ə)nt] *a* fervent. ◆**fervour** *n* ferveur *f*.

fester ['festər] *vi* (*of wound*) suppurer; (*of anger etc*) *Fig* couver.

festival ['festɪv(ə)l] *n Mus Cin* festival *m*; *Rel* fête *f*. ◆**festive** *a* (*atmosphere, clothes*) de fête; (*mood*) joyeux; **f. season** période *f* des fêtes. ◆**fe'stivities** *npl* réjouissances *fpl*, festivités *fpl*.

festoon [fe'stuːn] *vt* **to f. with** orner de.

fetch [fetʃ] *vt* **1** (*person*) amener; (*object*) apporter; **to (go and) f.** aller chercher; **to f. in** rentrer; **to f. out** sortir. **2** (*be sold for*) rapporter (**ten pounds**/*etc* dix livres/*etc*); (*price*) atteindre. ◆**—ing** *a* (*smile etc*) charmant, séduisant.

fête [feɪt] *n* fête *f*; — *vt* fêter.

fetid ['fetɪd] *a* fétide.

fetish ['fetɪʃ] *n* (*magical object*) fétiche *m*; **to make a f. of** *Fig* être obsédé par.

fetter ['fetər] *vt* (*hinder*) entraver.

fettle ['fet(ə)l] *n* **in fine f.** en pleine forme.

fetus ['fiːtəs] *n Am* fœtus *m*.

feud [fjuːd] *n* querelle *f*, dissension *f*.

feudal ['fjuːd(ə)l] *a* féodal.

fever ['fiːvər] *n* fièvre *f*; **to have a f.** (*temperature*) avoir de la fièvre. ◆**feverish** *a* (*person, activity*) fiévreux.

few [fjuː] *a* & *pron* peu (de); **f. towns**/*etc* peu de villes/*etc*; **a f. towns**/*etc* quelques villes/*etc*; **f. of them** peu d'entre eux; **a f. quelques-un(e)s (of de); a f. of us** quelques-uns d'entre nous; **one of the f. books** l'un des rares livres; **quite a f., a good f.** bon nombre (de); **a f. more books**/*etc* encore quelques livres/*etc*; **f. and far between** rares (et espacés); **f. came** peu sont venus; **to be f.** être pas nombreux; **every f. days** tous les trois ou quatre jours. ◆**fewer** a & pron moins (de) (than que); **to be f.** être moins nombreux (than que); **no f. than** pas moins de. ◆**fewest** a & pron le moins (de).

fiancé(e) ['fɪˈɒnseɪ] n fiancé, -ée mf.

fiasco [fɪˈæskəʊ] n (pl -os, Am -oes) fiasco m.

fib [fɪb] n Fam blague f, bobard m; – vi (-bb-) Fam raconter des blagues. ◆**fibber** n Fam blagueur, -euse mf.

fibre ['faɪbər] n fibre f; Fig caractère m. ◆**fibreglass** n fibre f de verre.

fickle ['fɪk(ə)l] a inconstant.

fiction ['fɪkʃ(ə)n] n fiction f; (works of) romans mpl. ◆**fictional**, ◆**fic'titious** a fictif.

fiddl/e ['fɪd(ə)l] **1** n (violin) Fam violon m; – vi Fam jouer du violon. **2** vi Fam **to f. about** (waste time) traînailler, glandouiller; **to f. (about) with** (watch, pen etc) tripoter; (cars etc) bricoler. **3** n (dishonesty) Fam combine f, fraude f; – vi (swindle) Fam faire de la fraude; – vt (accounts etc) Fam falsifier. ◆**-ing** a (petty) insignifiant. ◆**-er** n **1** Fam joueur, -euse mf de violon. **2** (swindler) Sl combinard, -arde mf. ◆**fiddly** a (task) délicat.

fidelity [fɪˈdelɪtɪ] n fidélité f (to à).

fidget ['fɪdʒɪt] vi **to f. (about)** gigoter, se trémousser; **to f. (about) with** tripoter; – n personne f qui ne tient pas en place. ◆**fidgety** a agité, remuant.

field [fiːld] n champ m; Sp terrain m; (sphere) domaine m; **to have a f. day** (good day) s'en donner à cœur joie; **f. glasses** jumelles fpl; **f. marshal** maréchal m.

fiend [fiːnd] n démon m; **a jazz/etc f.** Fam un(e) passionné, -ée de jazz/etc; (sex) f. Fam satyre m. ◆**fiendish** a diabolique.

fierce [fɪəs] a (-er, -est) féroce; (wind, attack) furieux. ◆**-ness** n férocité f; fureur f.

fiery ['faɪərɪ] a (-ier, -iest) (person, speech) fougueux; (sun, eyes) ardent.

fiesta [fɪˈestə] n fiesta f.

fifteen [fɪfˈtiːn] a & n quinze (m). ◆**fifteenth** a & n quinzième (mf). ◆**fifth** a & n cinquième (mf); **a f.** un cinquième. ◆**'fiftieth** a & n cinquantième (mf). ◆**'fifty** a & n cinquante (m).

fig [fɪg] n figue f; **f. tree** figuier m.

fight [faɪt] n bagarre f, rixe f; Mil Boxing combat m; (struggle) lutte f; (quarrel) dispute f; (spirit) combativité f; **to put up a (good) f.** bien se défendre; – vi (pt & pp

fought) se battre (**against** contre); Mil se battre, combattre; (struggle) lutter; (quarrel) se disputer; **to f. back** se défendre; **to f. over sth** se disputer qch; – vt se battre avec (s.o. qn); (evil) lutter contre, combattre; **to f. a battle** livrer bataille; **to f. back** (tears) refouler; **to f. off** (attacker, attack) repousser; (illness) lutter contre; **to f. it out** se bagarrer. ◆**-ing** n Mil combat(s) m(pl); (troops) de combat. ◆**-er** n combattant, -ante mf; Boxing boxeur m; Fig battant m, lutteur, -euse mf; (aircraft) chasseur m.

figment ['fɪgmənt] n **a f. of one's imagination** une création de son esprit.

figurative ['fɪgjʊrətɪv] a (meaning) figuré; (art) figuratif. ◆**-ly** adv au figuré.

figure¹ ['fɪgər, Am 'fɪgjər] n **1** (numeral) chiffre m; (price) prix m; pl (arithmetic) calcul m. **2** (shape) forme f; (outlined shape) silhouette f; (of woman) ligne f; **she has a nice f.** elle est bien faite. **3** (diagram) & Liter figure f; **a f. of speech** une figure de rhétorique; Fig une façon de parler; **f. of eight,** Am **f. eight** huit m; **f. skating** patinage m artistique. **4** (important person) figure f, personnage m. ◆**figurehead** n Nau figure f de proue; (person) Fig potiche f.

figure² ['fɪgər, Am 'fɪgjər] vt (imagine) (s')imaginer; (guess) penser (**that** que); **to f. out** arriver à comprendre; (problem) résoudre; – vi (make sense) s'expliquer; **to f. on doing** Am compter faire. **2** vi (appear) figurer (**on** sur).

filament ['fɪləmənt] n filament m.

filch [fɪltʃ] vt (steal) voler (**from** à).

fil/e [faɪl] **1** n (tool) lime f; – vt **to f. (down)** limer. **2** n (folder, information) dossier m; (loose-leaf) classeur m; (for card index, computer data) fichier m; – vt (claim, application) déposer; **to f. away** classer. **3** n **in single f.** en file; – vi **to f. in/out** entrer/sortir à la queue leu leu; **to f. past** (coffin etc) défiler devant. ◆**-ing 1** a **f. clerk** documentaliste mf; **f. cabinet** classeur m. **2** npl (particles) limaille f.

fill [fɪl] vt remplir (**with** de); (tooth) plomber; (sail) gonfler; (need) répondre à; **to f. in** (form) remplir; (hole) combler; (door) condamner; **to f. s.o. in on** Fam mettre qn au courant de; **to f. up** (glass etc) remplir; **to f. up or out** (form) remplir; – vi **to f. (up)** se remplir; **to f. out** (get fatter) grossir, se remplumer; **to f. up** Aut faire le plein; – n **to eat one's f.** manger à sa faim; **to have had one's f. of** Pej en avoir assez de. ◆**-ing** a (*meal etc*) substantiel, nourrissant; — *n* (*in tooth*) plombage *m*; Culin garniture *f*; **f. station** poste *m* d'essence. ◆—**er** *n* (*for cracks in wood*) mastic *m*.

fillet ['filit, *Am* fi'lei] *n* Culin filet *m*; — *vt* (*pt & pp Am* [fi'leid]) (*fish*) découper en filets; (*meat*) désosser.

fillip ['filip] *n* (*stimulus*) coup *m* de fouet.

filly ['fili] *n* (*horse*) pouliche *f*.

film [film] *n* film *m*; (*layer*) pellicule *f*; — *a* (*festival*) du film; (*studio, technician, critic*) de cinéma; **f. fan** *or* **buff** cinéphile *mf*; **f. library** cinémathèque *f*; **f. star** vedette *f* (de cinéma); — *vt* filmer.

filter ['filtər] *n* filtre *m*; (*traffic sign*) flèche *f*; **f. lane** Aut couloir *m* (pour tourner); **f. tip** (*bout m*) filtre *m*; **f.-tipped cigarette** cigarette *f* (à bout) filtre; — *vt* filtrer; — *vi* filtrer (**through sth** à travers qch); **to f. through** filtrer.

filth [filθ] *n* (*obscenities*) Fig saletés *fpl*. ◆**filthy** *a* (*-ier, -iest*) (*hands etc*) sale; (*language*) obscène; (*habit*) dégoûtant; **f. weather** un temps infect, un sale temps.

fin [fin] *n* (*of fish, seal*) nageoire *f*; (*of shark*) aileron *m*.

final ['fainəl] *a* dernier; (*decision*) définitif; (*cause*) final; — *n* Sp finale *f*; *pl Univ* examens *mpl* de dernière année. ◆**finalist** *n* Sp finaliste *mf*. ◆**finalize** *vt* (*plan*) mettre au point; (*date*) fixer (définitivement). ◆**finally** *adv* (*lastly*) enfin, en dernier lieu; (*eventually*) finalement, enfin; (*once and for all*) définitivement.

finale [fi'nɑːli] *n* Mus finale *m*.

finance ['fainæns] *n* finance *f*; — *a* (*company, page*) financier; — *vt* financer. ◆**fi'nancial** *a* financier; **f. year** année *f* budgétaire. ◆**fi'nancially** *adv* financièrement. ◆**fi'nancier** *n* (*grand*) financier *m*.

find [faind] *n* (*discovery*) trouvaille *f*; — *vt* (*pt & pp* **found**) trouver; (*sth or s.o. lost*) retrouver; (*difficulty*) éprouver, trouver (**in doing** à faire); **I f. that** je trouve que; **£20 all found** 20 livres logé et nourri; **to f. s.o. guilty** *Jur* prononcer qn coupable; **to f. one's feet** (*settle in*) s'adapter; **to f. oneself** (*to be*) se trouver. ■ **to f. out** *vt* (*information etc*) découvrir; (*person*) démasquer; — *vi* (*enquire*) se renseigner (**about** sur); **to f. out about** (*discover*) découvrir. ◆—**ings** *npl* conclusions *fpl*.

fine[1] [fain] *n* (*money*) amende *f*; *Aut* contravention *f*; — *vt* **to f. s.o.** (**£10**/*etc*) infliger une amende (de dix livres/*etc*) à qn.

fine[2] [fain] 1 *a* (*-er, -est*) (*thin, small, not coarse*) fin; (*gold*) pur; (*feeling*) délicat;

(*distinction*) subtil; — *adv* (*to cut, write*) menu. 2 *a* (*-er, -est*) (*beautiful*) beau; (*good*) bon; (*excellent*) excellent; **to be f.** (*in good health*) aller bien; — *adv* (*well*) très bien. ◆—**ly** *adv* (*dressed*) magnifiquement; (*chopped*) menu; (*embroidered, ground*) finement.

finery ['fainəri] *n* (*clothes*) parure *f*, belle toilette *f*.

finesse [fi'nes] *n* (*skill, tact*) doigté *m*; (*refinement*) finesse *f*.

finger ['fiŋgər] *n* doigt *m*; **little f.** auriculaire *m*, petit doigt *m*; **middle f.** majeur *m*; **f. mark** trace *f* de doigt; — *vt* toucher (des doigts), palper. ◆—**ing** *n* Mus doigté *m*. ◆**fingernail** *n* ongle *m*. ◆**fingerprint** *n* empreinte *f* digitale. ◆**fingerstall** *n* doigtier *m*. ◆**fingertip** *n* bout *m* du doigt.

finicky ['finiki] *a* (*precise*) méticuleux; (*difficult*) difficile (**about** sur).

finish ['finiʃ] *n* (*end*) fin *f*; *Sp* arrivée *f*; (*of article, car etc*) finition *f*; **paint with a matt f.** peinture *f* mate; — *vt* **to f.** (**off** *or* **up**) finir, terminer; **to f. doing** finir de faire; **to f. s.o. off** (*kill*) achever qn; — *vi* (*of meeting etc*) finir, se terminer; (*of person*) finir, terminer; **to f. first** terminer premier; (*in race*) arriver premier; **to have finished with** (*object*) ne plus avoir besoin de; (*situation, person*) en avoir fini avec; **to f. off** *or* **up** (*of person*) finir, terminer; **to f. up in** (*end up in*) se retrouver à; **to f. up doing** finir par faire; **finishing school** institution *f* pour jeunes filles; **finishing touch** touche *f* finale. ◆—**ed** *a* (*ended, done for*) fini.

finite ['fainait] *a* fini.

Finland ['finlənd] *n* Finlande *f*. ◆**Finn** *n* Finlandais, -aise *mf*, Finnois, -oise *mf*. ◆**Finnish** *a* finlandais, finnois; — *n* (*language*) finnois *m*.

fir [fɜːr] *n* (*tree, wood*) sapin *m*.

fire[1] ['faiər] *n* feu *m*; (*accidental*) incendie *m*; (*electric*) radiateur *m*; **on f.** en feu; (**there's a**) **f.!** au feu!; **f.!** *Mil* feu!; **f. alarm** avertisseur *m* d'incendie; **f. brigade,** *Am* **f. department** pompiers *mpl*; **f. engine** (*vehicle*) voiture *f* de pompiers; (*machine*) pompe *f* à incendie; **f. escape** escalier *m* de secours; **f. station** caserne *f* de pompiers. ◆**firearm** *n* arme *f* à feu. ◆**firebug** *n* pyromane *mf*. ◆**firecracker** *n Am* pétard *m*. ◆**fireguard** *n* garde-feu *m inv*. ◆**fireman** *n* (*pl* -**men**) (sapeur-)pompier *m*. ◆**fireplace** *n* cheminée *f*. ◆**fireproof** *a* (*door*) ignifugé, anti-incendie. ◆**fireside** *n* coin *m* du feu; **f. chair** fauteuil *m*. ◆**firewood** *n* bois *m* de chauffage.

◆**firework** n feu m d'artifice; **a f. display, fireworks,** un feu d'artifice.

fire[2] ['faɪər] vt (cannon) tirer; (pottery) cuire; (imagination) enflammer; **to f. a gun** tirer un coup de fusil; **to f. questions at** bombarder de questions; **to f. s.o.** (dismiss) Fam renvoyer qn; − vi tirer (at sur); **f. away!** Fam vas-y, parle!; **firing squad** peloton m d'exécution; **in** or Am **on the firing line** en butte aux attaques.

firm[1] ['fɜːm] **1** n Com maison f, firme f. **2** a (-er, -est) (earth, decision etc) ferme; (strict) ferme (with avec); (faith) solide; (character) résolu. ◆−**ly** adv fermement; (to speak) d'une voix ferme. ◆−**ness** n fermeté f; (of faith) solidité f.

first [fɜːst] a premier; **I'll do it f. thing in the morning** je le ferai dès le matin, sans faute; **f. cousin** cousin, -ine mf germain(e); − adv d'abord, premièrement; (for the first time) pour la première fois; **f. of all** tout d'abord; **at f.** d'abord; **to come f.** (in race) arriver premier; (in exam) être le premier; − n premier, -ière mf; Univ = licence f avec mention très bien; **from the f.** dès le début; **f. aid** premiers soins mpl or secours mpl (gear) Aut première f. ◆**f.-'class** a (ticket etc) de première (classe); (mail) ordinaire; − adv (to travel) en première. ◆**f.-'hand** a & adv de première main; **to have (had) f.-hand experience of** avoir fait l'expérience personnelle de. ◆**f.-'rate** a excellent. ◆**firstly** adv premièrement.

fiscal ['fɪsk(ə)l] a fiscal.

fish [fɪʃ] n (pl inv or -es) poisson m; **f. market** marché m aux poissons; **f. bone** arête f; **f. bowl** bocal m; **f. fingers,** Am **f. sticks** Culin bâtonnets mpl de poisson; **f. shop** poissonnerie f; − vi pêcher; **to f. for** (salmon etc) pêcher; (compliment etc) Fig chercher; − vt **to f. out** (from water) repêcher; (from pocket etc) Fig sortir. ◆−**ing** n pêche f; **to go f.** aller à la pêche; **f. net** (of fisherman) filet m de pêche; (of angler) épuisette f; **f. rod** canne f à pêche. ◆**fisherman** n (pl -men) pêcheur m. ◆**fishmonger** n poissonnier, -ière mf. ◆**fishy** a (-ier, -iest) (smell) de poisson; Fig Pej louche.

fission ['fɪʃ(ə)n] n Phys fission f.

fissure ['fɪʃər] n fissure f.

fist [fɪst] n poing m. ◆**fistful** n poignée f.

fit[1] [fɪt] **1** a (fitter, fittest) (suited) propre, bon (for à); (fitting) convenable; (worthy) digne (for de); (able) capable (for de, to do de faire); (healthy) en bonne santé; **f. to eat** bon à manger, mangeable; **to see f. to do**

juger à propos de faire; **as you see f.** comme bon vous semble; **f. to drop** Fam prêt à tomber; **to keep f.** se maintenir en forme. **2** vt (-tt-) (of coat etc) aller (bien) à (qn), être à la taille de (qn); (match) répondre à; (equal) égaler; **to f. sth on s.o.** (garment) ajuster qch à qn; **to f. sth (on) to sth** (put) poser qch sur qch; (adjust) adapter qch à qch; (fix) fixer qch à qch; **to f. (out** or **up) with** (house, ship etc) équiper de; **to f. (in)** (window) poser; **to f. in** (object) faire entrer; (patient, customer) prendre; **to f. (in) the lock** (of key) aller dans; − vi (of clothes) aller (bien) (à qn); **this shirt fits** (fits me) cette chemise me va (bien); **to f. (in)** (go in) entrer, aller; (of facts, plans) s'accorder, cadrer; **he doesn't f.** in il ne peut pas s'intégrer; − n a **good f.** (dress etc) à la bonne taille; **a close** or **tight f.** ajusté. ◆**fitted** a (carpet) encastré; (garment) ajusté; **f. carpet** moquette f; **f. (kitchen) units** éléments mpl de cuisine. ◆**fitting 1** a (suitable) convenable. **2** n (of clothes) essayage m; **f. room** salon m d'essayage; (booth) cabine f d'essayage. **3** npl (in house etc) installations fpl. ◆**fitment** n (furniture) meuble m encastré; (accessory) Tech accessoire m. ◆**fitness** n (of remark etc) à-propos m; (for job) aptitudes fpl (**for** pour); Med santé f. ◆**fitter** n Tech monteur, -euse mf.

fit[2] [fɪt] n Med & Fig accès m, crise f; **in fits and starts** par à-coups. ◆**fitful** a (sleep) agité.

five [faɪv] a & n cinq m. ◆**fiver** n Fam billet m de cinq livres.

fix [fɪks] **1** vt (make firm, decide) fixer; (tie with rope) attacher; (mend) réparer; (deal with) arranger; (prepare, cook) Am préparer, faire; (in s.o.'s mind) graver (**in** dans); (conduct fraudulently) Fam truquer; (bribe) Fam acheter; (hopes, ambitions) mettre (**on** en); **to f. up** (punish) Fam régler son compte à qn; **to f. (on)** (lid etc) mettre en place; **to f. up** arranger; **to f. s.o. up with sth** (job etc) procurer qch à qn. **2** n Av Nau position f; (injection) Sl piqûre f; **in a f.** Fam dans le pétrin. ◆−**ed** a (idea, price etc) fixe; (resolution) inébranlable; **how's he f. for . . . ?** Fam (cash etc) a-t-il assez de . . . ?; (tomorrow etc) qu'est-ce qu'il fait pour . . . ? ◆**fixings** npl Culin Am garniture f. ◆**fix'ation** n fixation f. ◆**fixer** n (schemer) Fam combinard, -arde mf. ◆**fixture 1** n Sp match m (prévu). **2** pl (in house) meubles mpl fixes, installations fpl.

fizz [fɪz] vi (of champagne) pétiller; (of gas) siffler. ◆**fizzy** a (-ier, -iest) pétillant.

fizzle ['fɪz(ə)l] vi (hiss) siffler; (of liquid) pétiller; **to f. out** (of firework) rater, faire long feu; (of plan) Fig tomber à l'eau; (of custom) disparaître.

flabbergasted ['flæbəgɑːstɪd] a Fam sidéré.

flabby ['flæbɪ] a (-ier, -iest) (skin, character, person) mou, flasque.

flag [flæg] **1** n drapeau m; Nau pavillon m; (for charity) insigne m; f. stop Am arrêt m facultatif; – vt (-gg-) **to f. down** (taxi) faire signe à. **2** vi (-gg-) (of plant) dépérir; (of conversation) languir; (of worker) fléchir. ◆**flagpole** n mât m.

flagrant ['fleɪgrənt] a flagrant.

flagstone ['flægstəʊn] n dalle f.

flair [fleər] n (intuition) flair m; **to have a f. for** (natural talent) avoir un don pour.

flake [fleɪk] n (of snow etc) flocon m; (of metal, soap) paillette f; – vi **to f. (off)** (of paint) s'écailler. ◆**flaky** a f. pastry pâte f feuilletée.

flamboyant [flæm'bɔɪənt] a (person, manner) extravagant.

flam/e [fleɪm] n flamme f; **to go up in flames** s'enflammer; – vi **to f. (up)** (of fire, house) flamber. ◆-**ing** a **1** (sun) flamboyant. **2** (damn) Fam fichu.

flamingo [flə'mɪŋgəʊ] n (pl -os or -oes) (bird) flamant m.

flammable ['flæməb(ə)l] a inflammable.

flan [flæn] n tarte f.

flank [flæŋk] n flanc m; – vt flanquer (with de).

flannel ['flænəl] n (cloth) flanelle f; (face) f. gant m de toilette, carré-éponge m. ◆**flanne'lette** n pilou m, finette f.

flap [flæp] **1** vi (-pp-) (of wing, sail, shutter etc) battre; – vt **to f. its wings** (of bird) battre des ailes; – n battement m. **2** n (of pocket, envelope) rabat m; (of table) abattant m; (of door) battant m.

flare [fleər] n (light) éclat m; Mil fusée f éclairante; (for runway) balise f; – vi (blaze) flamber; (shine) briller; **to f. up** (of fire) s'enflammer; (of war) éclater; (get angry) s'emporter. ◆**f.-up** n (of violence, fire) flambée f; (of region) embrasement m. ◆**flared** a (skirt) évasé; (trousers) à pattes d'éléphant.

flash [flæʃ] n (of light) éclat m; (of anger, genius) éclair m; Phot flash m; **f. of lightning** éclair m; **news f.** flash m; **in a f.** en un clin d'œil; – vi (shine) briller; (on and off) clignoter; **to f. past** (rush) Fig passer

comme un éclair; – vt (aim) diriger (on, at sur); (a light) projeter; (a glance) jeter; **to f. (around)** (flaunt) étaler; **to f. one's headlights** faire un appel de phares. ◆**flashback** n retour m en arrière. ◆**flashlight** n lampe f électrique or de poche; Phot flash m.

flashy ['flæʃɪ] a (-ier, -iest) a voyant, tape-à-l'œil inv.

flask [flɑːsk] n thermos® m or f inv; Ch flacon m; (phial) fiole f.

flat¹ [flæt] a (flatter, flattest) plat; (tyre, battery) à plat; (nose) aplati; (beer) éventé; (refusal) net; (rate, fare) fixe; (voice) Mus faux; (razed to the ground) rasé; **to put sth (down)** f. mettre qch à plat; **to fall f. (on one's face)** à plat ventre; **to fall f.** Fig tomber à plat; **to be f.-footed** avoir les pieds plats; – adv (to say) carrément; (to sing) faux; **f. broke** Fam complètement fauché; **in two minutes f.** en deux minutes pile; **f. out** (to work) d'arrache-pied; (to run) à toute vitesse; – n (of hand) plat m; (puncture) Aut crevaison f; Mus bémol m. ◆-**ly** adv (to deny etc) catégoriquement. ◆-**ness** n (of surface) égalité f. ◆**flatten** vt (crops) coucher; (town) raser; **to f. (out)** (metal etc) aplatir.

flat² [flæt] n (rooms) appartement m.

flatter ['flætər] vt flatter; (of clothes) avantager (qn). ◆-**ing** a flatteur; (of clothes) avantageux. ◆-**er** n flatteur, -euse mf. ◆**flattery** n flatterie f.

flatulence ['flætjʊləns] n **to have f.** avoir des gaz.

flaunt [flɔːnt] vt (show off) faire étalage de; (defy) Am narguer, défier.

flautist ['flɔːtɪst] n flûtiste mf.

flavour ['fleɪvər] n (taste) goût m, saveur f; (of ice cream, sweet etc) parfum m; – vt (food) assaisonner; (sauce) relever; (ice cream etc) parfumer (with à). ◆-**ing** n assaisonnement m; (in cake) parfum m.

flaw [flɔː] n défaut m. ◆**flawed** a imparfait. ◆**flawless** a parfait.

flax [flæks] n lin m. ◆**flaxen** a de lin.

flay [fleɪ] vt (animal) écorcher; (criticize) Fig éreinter.

flea [fliː] n puce f; **f. market** marché m aux puces. ◆**fleapit** n Fam cinéma m miteux.

fleck [flek] n (mark) petite tache f.

fledgling ['fledʒlɪŋ] n (novice) blanc-bec m.

flee [fliː] vi (pt & pp fled) fuir, s'enfuir, se sauver; – vt (place) s'enfuir de; (danger etc) fuir.

fleece [fliːs] **1** n (sheep's coat) toison f. **2** vt (rob) voler.

fleet [fli:t] n (of ships) flotte f; **a f. of cars** un parc automobile.

fleeting ['fli:tɪŋ] a (visit, moment) bref; (beauty) éphémère.

Flemish ['flemɪʃ] a flamand; — n (language) flamand m.

flesh [fleʃ] n chair f; **her (own) f. and blood** la chair de sa chair; **in the f.** en chair et en os; **f. wound** blessure f superficielle. ◆**fleshy** a (-ier, -iest) charnu.

flew [flu:] see **fly** [2].

flex [fleks] 1 vt (limb) fléchir; (muscle) faire jouer, bander. 2 n (wire) fil m (souple); (for telephone) cordon m.

flexible ['fleksɪb(ə)l] a flexible, souple. ◆**flexi'bility** n flexibilité f.

flick [flɪk] vt donner un petit coup à; **to f. off** (remove) enlever (d'une chiquenaude); — vi **to f. over** ou **through** (pages) feuilleter; — n petit coup m; (with finger) chiquenaude f; **f. knife** couteau m à cran d'arrêt.

flicker ['flɪkər] vi (of flame, light) vaciller; (of needle) osciller; — n vacillement m; **f. of light** lueur f.

flier ['flaɪər] n 1 (person) aviateur, -trice mf. 2 (handbill) Am prospectus m, Pol tract m.

flies [flaɪz] npl (on trousers) braguette f.

flight [flaɪt] n 1 (of bird, aircraft etc) vol m; (of bullet) trajectoire f; (of imagination) élan m; (floor, storey) étage m; **f. of stairs** escalier m; **f. deck** cabine f de pilotage. 2 (fleeing) fuite f (from de); **to take f.** prendre la fuite.

flighty ['flaɪtɪ] a (-ier, -iest) inconstant, volage.

flimsy ['flɪmzɪ] a (-ier, -iest) (cloth, structure etc) (trop) léger ou mince; (excuse) mince, frivole.

flinch [flɪntʃ] vi (with pain) tressaillir; **to f. from** (duty etc) se dérober à; **without flinching** (complaining) sans broncher.

fling [flɪŋ] 1 vt (pt & pp flung) jeter, lancer; **to f. open** (door etc) ouvrir brutalement. 2 n **to have one's** ou **a f.** (indulge oneself) s'en donner à cœur joie.

flint [flɪnt] n silex m; (for cigarette lighter) pierre f.

flip [flɪp] 1 vt (-pp-) (with finger) donner une chiquenaude à; — vi **to f. through** (book etc) feuilleter; — n chiquenaude f; **the f. side** (of record) la face deux. 2 a (cheeky) Am Fam effronté.

flip-flops ['flɪpflɒps] npl tongs fpl.

flippant ['flɪpənt] a irrévérencieux; (off-hand) désinvolte.

flipper ['flɪpər] n (of seal) nageoire f; (of swimmer) palme f.

flipping ['flɪpɪŋ] a Fam sacré; — adv Fam sacrément, bougrement.

flirt [flɜ:t] vi flirter (with avec); — n flirteur, -euse mf. ◆**flir'tation** n flirt m. ◆**flir'tatious** a flirteur.

flit [flɪt] vi (-tt-) (fly) voltiger; **to f. in and out** (of person) Fig entrer et sortir (rapidement).

float [fləʊt] n Fishing flotteur m; (in parade) char m; — vi flotter (on sur); **to f. down the river** descendre la rivière; — vt (boat, currency) faire flotter; (loan) Com émettre. ◆**—ing** a (wood, debt etc) flottant; (population) instable; (voters) indécis.

flock [flɒk] n (of sheep etc) troupeau m; (of birds) volée f; Rel Hum ouailles fpl; (of tourists etc) foule f; — vi venir en foule; **to f. round s.o.** s'attrouper autour de qn.

floe [fləʊ] n (ice) f. banquise f.

flog [flɒg] vt (-gg-) 1 (beat) flageller. 2 (sell) Sl vendre. ◆**flogging** n flagellation f.

flood [flʌd] n inondation f; (of letters, tears etc) Fig flot m, déluge m, torrent m; — vt (field etc) inonder (with de); (river) faire déborder; **to f. (out)** (house) inonder; — vi (of building) être inondé; (of river) déborder; (of people, money) affluer; **to f. into** (of tourists etc) envahir. ◆**—ing** n inondation f. ◆**floodgate** n (in water) vanne f.

floodlight ['flʌdlaɪt] n projecteur m; — vt (pt & pp floodlit) illuminer; **floodlit match** Sp (match m en) nocturne m.

floor [flɔ:r] 1 n (ground) sol m; (wooden etc in building) plancher m; (storey) étage m; (dance) f. piste f (de danse); **on the f.** par terre; **first f.** premier étage m; (ground floor) Am rez-de-chaussée m; **f. polish** encaustique f; **f. show** spectacle m (de cabaret). 2 vt (knock down) terrasser; (puzzle) stupéfier. ◆**floorboard** n planche f.

flop [flɒp] 1 vi (-pp-) **to f. down** (collapse) s'effondrer; **to f. about** s'agiter mollement. 2 vi (-pp-) Fam échouer; (of play, film etc) faire un four; — n Fam échec m, fiasco m; Th Cin navet m.

floppy ['flɒpɪ] a (-ier, -iest) (soft) mou; (clothes) trop large; (ears) pendant; **f. disk** (of computer) disquette f.

flora ['flɔːrə] n (plants) flore f. ◆**floral** a floral; (material) à fleurs.

florid ['flɒrɪd] a (style) fleuri; (complexion) rougeaud, fleuri.

florist ['flɒrɪst] n fleuriste mf.

floss [flɒs] n (dental) f. fil m (de soie) dentaire.

flotilla [flə'tɪlə] n Nau flottille f.

flounce [flaʊns] n (*frill on dress etc*) volant m.

flounder ['flaʊndər] **1** vi (*in water etc*) patauger (avec effort), se débattre; (*in speech*) hésiter, patauger. **2** n (*fish*) carrelet m.

flour ['flaʊər] n farine f.

flourish ['flʌrɪʃ] **1** vi (*of person, business, plant etc*) prospérer; (*of the arts*) fleurir. **2** vt (*wave*) brandir. **3** n (*decoration*) fioriture f; Mus fanfare f. ◆—**ing** a prospère, florissant.

flout [flaʊt] vt narguer, braver.

flow [fləʊ] vi couler; (*of current*) El circuler; (*of hair, clothes*) flotter; (*of traffic*) s'écouler; to f. in (*of people, money*) affluer; to f. back refluer; to f. into the sea se jeter dans la mer; – n (*of river*) courant m; (*of tide*) flux m; (*of blood*) & El circulation f; (*of traffic, liquid*) écoulement m; (*of words*) Fig flot m. ◆—**ing** a (*movement*) gracieux; (*style*) coulant; (*beard*) flottant.

flower ['flaʊər] n fleur f; f. bed plate-bande f; f. shop (*boutique f de*) fleuriste mf; f. show floralies fpl; – vi fleurir. ◆—**ed** a (*dress*) à fleurs. ◆—**ing** n floraison f; – a (*in bloom*) en fleurs; (*with flowers*) à fleurs. ◆**flowery** a (*style etc*) fleuri; (*material*) à fleurs.

flown [fləʊn] see **fly**².

flu [fluː] n (*influenza*) Fam grippe f.

fluctuate ['flʌktjʊeɪt] vi varier. ◆**fluctu-ation** (s) n(pl) (*in prices etc*) fluctuations fpl (in de).

flue [fluː] n (*of chimney*) conduit m.

fluent ['fluːənt] a (*style*) aisé; to be f., be a f. speaker s'exprimer avec facilité; he's f. in Russian, his Russian is f. il parle couramment le russe. ◆**fluency** n facilité f. ◆**fluently** adv avec facilité; (*to speak*) Ling couramment.

fluff [flʌf] n (*down*) duvet m; (*of material*) peluche(s) f(pl); (*on floor*) moutons mpl. **2** vt (*bungle*) Fam rater. ◆**fluffy** a (-ier, -iest) (*bird etc*) duveteux; (*material*) pelucheux; (*toy*) en peluche; (*hair*) bouffant.

fluid ['fluːɪd] a fluide; (*plans*) flexible, non arrêté; – n fluide m, liquide m.

fluke [fluːk] n Fam coup m de chance; by a f. par raccroc.

flummox ['flʌməks] vt Fam désorienter, dérouter.

flung [flʌŋ] see **fling** 1.

flunk [flʌŋk] vi (*in exam*) Am Fam être collé; – vt Am Fam (*pupil*) coller; (*exam*) être collé à; (*school*) laisser tomber.

flunk(e)y ['flʌŋkɪ] n Pej larbin m.

fluorescent [flʊəˈres(ə)nt] a fluorescent.

fluoride ['flʊəraɪd] n (*in water, toothpaste*) fluor m.

flurry ['flʌrɪ] n **1** (*of activity*) poussée f. **2** (*of snow*) rafale f.

flush [flʌʃ] **1** n (*of blood*) flux m; (*blush*) rougeur f; (*of youth, beauty*) éclat m; (*of victory*) ivresse f; – vi (*blush*) rougir. **2** vt to f. (out) (*clean*) nettoyer à grande eau; to f. the pan or the toilet tirer la chasse d'eau; to f. s.o. out (*chase away*) faire sortir qn (from de). **3** a (*level*) de niveau (with, avec); (*with money*) Fam bourré de fric. ◆—**ed** a (*cheeks etc*) rouge; f. with (*success*) ivre de.

fluster ['flʌstər] vt énerver; to get flustered s'énerver.

flute [fluːt] n flûte f. ◆**flutist** n Am flûtiste mf.

flutter ['flʌtər] **1** vi voltiger; (*of wing*) battre; (*of flag*) flotter (mollement); (*of heart*) palpiter; to f. about (*of person*) papillonner; – vt to f. its wings battre des ailes. **2** n to have a f. (*bet*) Fam parier.

flux [flʌks] n changement m continuel.

fly¹ [flaɪ] n (*insect*) mouche f. ◆**swatter** (*instrument*) tapette f. ◆**flypaper** n papier m tue-mouches.

fly² [flaɪ] vi (*pt* flew, *pp* flown) (*of bird, aircraft etc*) voler; (*of passenger*) aller en avion; (*of time*) passer vite; (*of flag*) flotter; (*flee*) fuir; to f. away or off s'envoler; to f. out Av partir en avion; (*from room*) sortir à toute vitesse; I must f.! il faut que je file!; to f. at s.o. (*attack*) sauter sur qn; – vt (*aircraft*) piloter; (*passengers*) transporter (par avion); (*airline*) voyager par; (*flag*) arborer; (*kite*) faire voler; to f. the French flag battre pavillon français; to f. across or over survoler. ◆—**ing** n (*flight*) vol m; (*air travel*) aviation f; to like f. aimer l'avion; – a (*personnel, saucer etc*) volant; (*visit*) éclair inv; with f. colours (*to succeed*) haut la main; a f. start un très bon départ; f. time (*length*) Av durée f du vol; ten hours'/etc f. time dix heures/etc de vol. ◆—**er** n = **flier**. ◆**flyby** n Av Am défilé m aérien. ◆**fly-by-night** a (*firm*) véreux. ◆**flyover** n (*bridge*) toboggan m. ◆**flypast** n Av défilé m aérien.

fly³ [flaɪ] n (*on trousers*) braguette f.

foal [fəʊl] n poulain m.

foam [fəʊm] n (*on sea, mouth*) écume f; (*on beer*) mousse f; f. rubber caoutchouc m mousse; f. (rubber) mattress/etc matelas m/etc mousse; – vi (*of sea, mouth*) écumer; (*of beer, soap*) mousser.

fob [fɒb] vt (-bb-) to f. sth off on s.o., f. s.o. off with sth, refiler qch à qn.

focal ['fəʊk(ə)l] a focal; **f. point** point m central. ◆**focus** n foyer m; (of attention, interest) centre m; in f. au point; − vt Phot mettre au point; (light) faire converger; (efforts, attention) concentrer (on sur); − vi (converge) converger (on sur); to f. (one's eyes) on fixer les yeux sur; to f. on (direct one's attention to) se concentrer sur.

fodder ['fɒdər] n fourrage m.

foe [fəʊ] n ennemi, -ie mf.

foetus ['fiːtəs] n fœtus m.

fog [fɒg] n brouillard m, brume f; − vt (-gg-) (issue) Fig embrouiller. ◆**fogbound** a bloqué par le brouillard. ◆**foghorn** n corne f de brume; (voice) Pej voix f toni-truante. ◆**foglamp** n (phare m) anti-brouillard m. ◆**foggy** a (-ier, -iest) (day) de brouillard; it's f. il fait du brouillard; f. weather brouillard m; she hasn't the foggiest (idea) Fam elle n'en a pas la moindre idée.

fog(e)y ['fəʊgɪ] n old f. vieille baderne f.

foible ['fɔɪb(ə)l] n petit défaut m.

foil [fɔɪl] 1 n feuille f de métal; Culin papier m alu(minium). 2 n (contrasting person) repoussoir m. 3 vt (plans etc) déjouer.

foist [fɔɪst] vt to f. sth on s.o. (fob off) refiler qch à qn; to f. oneself on s.o. s'imposer à qn.

fold[1] [fəʊld] n pli m; − vt (wrap) envelopper (in dans); to f. away or down or up plier; to f. back or over replier; to f. one's arms (se) croiser les bras; − vi (of chair etc) se plier; (of business) Fam s'écrouler; to f. away or down or up (of chair etc) se plier; to f. back or over (of blanket etc) se replier. ◆**−ing** a (chair etc) pliant. ◆**−er** n (file holder) chemise f; (pamphlet) dépliant m.

fold[2] [fəʊld] n (for sheep) parc m à moutons; Rel Fig bercail m.

-fold [fəʊld] suffix **tenfold** a par dix; − adv dix fois.

foliage ['fəʊlɪɪdʒ] n feuillage m.

folk [fəʊk] 1 n gens mpl or fpl; pl gens mpl or fpl; (parents) Fam parents mpl; hello folks! Fam salut tout le monde!; old f. like it les vieux l'apprécient. 2 a (dance etc) folklorique; **f. music** (contemporary) (musique f) folk m. ◆**folklore** n folklore m.

follow ['fɒləʊ] vt suivre; (career) pour-suivre; **followed by** suivi de; to f. suit Fig en faire autant; to f. s.o. around suivre qn partout; to f. through (idea etc) poursuivre

jusqu'au bout; to f. up (suggestion, case) suivre; (advantage) exploiter; (letter) donner suite à; (remark) faire suivre (with de); − vi to f. (on) suivre; it follows that il s'ensuit que; that doesn't f. ce n'est pas logique. ◆**−ing 1** a suivant; − prep à la suite de. **2** n (supporters) partisans mpl; to have a large f. avoir de nombreux partisans; (of serial, fashion) être très suivi. ◆**−er** n partisan m. ◆**follow-up** n suite f; (letter) rappel m.

folly ['fɒlɪ] n folie f, sottise f.

foment [fəʊ'ment] vt (revolt etc) fomenter.

fond [fɒnd] a (-er, -est) (loving) tendre, affectueux; (doting) indulgent; (wish, ambi-tion) naïf; to be (very) f. of aimer (beaucoup). ◆**−ly** adv tendrement. ◆**−ness** n (for things) prédilection f (for pour); (for people) affection f (for pour).

fondle ['fɒnd(ə)l] vt caresser.

food [fuːd] n nourriture f; (particular substance) aliment m; (cooking) cuisine f; (for cats, pigs) pâtée f; (for plants) engrais m; pl (foodstuffs) aliments mpl; − a (needs etc) alimentaire; **a fast f. shop** un fast-food; **f. poisoning** intoxication f alimentaire; **f. value** valeur f nutritive. ◆**foodstuffs** npl denrées fpl or produits mpl alimentaires.

fool [fuːl] n imbécile mf, idiot, -ote mf; (you) silly f.! espèce d'imbécile!; to make a f. of (ridicule) ridiculiser; (trick) duper; to be f. enough to do être assez stupide pour faire; to play the f. faire l'imbécile; − vt (trick) duper; − vi to f. (about or around) faire l'imbécile; (waste time) perdre son temps; to f. around (make love) Am Fam faire l'amour (with avec). ◆**foolish** a bête, idiot. ◆**foolishly** adv bêtement. ◆**fool-ishness** n bêtise f, sottise f. ◆**foolproof** a (scheme etc) infaillible.

foolhardy ['fuːlhaːdɪ] a téméraire. ◆**fool-hardiness** n témérité f.

foot[1], pl **feet** [fʊt, fiːt] n pied m; (of animal) patte f; (measure) pied m (= 30,48 cm); **at the f. of** (page, stairs) au bas de; (table) au bout de; **on f.** à pied; **on one's feet** (stand-ing) debout; (recovered) Med sur pied; **f. brake** Aut frein m au plancher; **f.-and-mouth disease** fièvre f aphteuse. ◆**footbridge** n passerelle f. ◆**foothills** npl contreforts mpl. ◆**foothold** n prise f (de pied); Fig position f; to gain a f. pren-dre pied. ◆**footlights** npl Th rampe f. ◆**footloose** a libre de toute attache. ◆**footman** n (pl -men) valet m de pied. ◆**footmark** n empreinte f (de pied). ◆**footnote** n note f au bas de la page; Fig post-scriptum *m*. ◆**footpath** *n* sentier *m*; (*at roadside*) chemin *m* (piétonnier). ◆**footstep** *n* pas *m*; **to follow in s.o.'s footsteps** suivre les traces de qn. ◆**footwear** *n* chaussures *fpl*.

foot² [fut] *vt* (*bill*) payer.

football ['futbɔːl] *n* (*game*) football *m*; (*ball*) ballon *m*. ◆**footballer** *n* joueur, -euse *mf* de football.

footing ['futiŋ] *n* prise *f* (de pied); *Fig* position *f*; **on a war f.** sur le pied de guerre; **on an equal f.** sur un pied d'égalité.

for [fɔr, *unstressed* fər] **1** *prep* pour; (*in exchange for*) contre; (*for a distance of*) pendant; (*in spite of*) malgré; **f. you/me/etc** pour toi/moi/etc; **what f.?** pourquoi?; **what's it f.?** ça sert à quoi?; **f. example** par exemple; **f. love** par amour; **f. sale** à vendre; **to swim f.** (*towards*) nager vers; **a train f.** un train à destination de ou en direction de; **the road f. London** la route (en direction) de Londres; **fit f. eating** bon à manger; **eager f.** avide de; **to look f.** chercher; **to come f. dinner** venir dîner; **to sell f. £7** vendre sept livres; **what's the Russian f. 'book'?** comment dit-on 'livre' en russe?; **but f. her** sans elle; **he was away f. a month** (*throughout*) il a été absent pendant un mois; **he won't be back f. a month** il ne sera pas de retour avant un mois; **he's been here f. a month** (*he's still here*) il est ici depuis un mois; **I haven't seen him f. ten years** voilà dix ans que je ne l'ai vu; **it's easy f. her to do it** il lui est facile de le faire; **it's f. you to say** c'est à toi de dire; **f. that to be done** pour que ça soit fait. **2** *conj* (*because*) car.

forage ['fɔrɪdʒ] *vi* **to f.** (*about*) fourrager (**for** pour trouver).

foray ['fɔreɪ] *n* incursion *f*.

forbearance [fɔːˈbeərəns] *n* patience *f*.

forbid [fəˈbɪd] *vt* (*pt* forbad(e), *pp* forbidden, *pres p* forbidding) interdire, défendre (**s.o. to do** à qn de faire; **s.o. sth** qch à qn); **to f. s.o. sth** interdire ou défendre qch à qn. ◆**forbidden** *a* (*fruit etc*) défendu; **she is f. to leave** il lui est interdit de partir. ◆**forbidding** *a* menaçant, sinistre.

force [fɔːs] *n* force *f*; **the (armed) forces** *Mil* les forces armées; **by (sheer) f.** de force; **in f.** (*rule*) en vigueur; (*in great numbers*) en grand nombre, en force; – *vt* contraindre, forcer (**to do** à faire); (*impose*) imposer (**on** à); (*push*) pousser; (*lock*) forcer; (*confession*) arracher (**from** à); **to f. back** (*enemy etc*) faire reculer; (*repress*) refouler; **to f. down** (*aircraft*) forcer à atterrir; **to f. out**

faire sortir de force. ◆**forced** *a* forcé (**to do** de faire); **a f. smile** un sourire forcé. ◆**force-feed** *vt* (*pt & pp* **f.-fed**) nourrir de force. ◆**forceful** *a* énergique, puissant. ◆**forcefully** *adv* avec force, énergiquement. ◆**forcible** *a* de force; (*forceful*) énergique. ◆**forcibly** *adv* (*by force*) de force.

forceps ['fɔːseps] *n* forceps *m*.

ford [fɔːd] *n* gué *m*; – *vt* (*river etc*) passer à gué.

fore [fɔːr] *n* **to come to the f.** se mettre en évidence.

forearm ['fɔːrɑːm] *n* avant-bras *m inv*.

forebod/e [fɔːˈbəʊd] *vt* (*be a warning of*) présager. ◆**—ing** *n* (*feeling*) pressentiment *m*.

forecast ['fɔːkɑːst] *vt* (*pt & pp* forecast) prévoir; – *n* prévision *f*; *Met* prévisions *fpl*; *Sp* pronostic *m*.

forecourt ['fɔːkɔːt] *n* avant-cour *f*; (*of filling station*) aire *f* (de service), devant *m*.

forefathers ['fɔːfɑːðəz] *npl* aïeux *mpl*.

forefinger ['fɔːfɪŋgər] *n* index *m*.

forefront ['fɔːfrʌnt] *n* **in the f. of** au premier rang de.

forego [fɔːˈgəʊ] *vt* (*pp* foregone) renoncer à. ◆**'foregone** *a* **it's a f. conclusion** c'est couru d'avance.

foregoing [fɔːˈgəʊɪŋ] *a* précédent.

foreground ['fɔːgraʊnd] *n* premier plan *m*.

forehead ['fɒrɪd, 'fɔːhed] *n* (*brow*) front *m*.

foreign ['fɒrən] *a* étranger; (*trade*) extérieur; (*travel, correspondent*) à l'étranger; (*produce*) de l'étranger; **F. Minister** ministre *m* des Affaires étrangères. ◆**foreigner** *n* étranger, -ère *mf*.

foreman ['fɔːmən] *n* (*pl* -men) (*worker*) contremaître *m*; (*of jury*) président *m*.

foremost ['fɔːməʊst] **1** *a* principal. **2** *adv* **first and f.** tout d'abord.

forensic [fəˈrensɪk] *a* (*medicine*) légal; (*laboratory*) médico-légal.

forerunner ['fɔːrʌnər] *n* précurseur *m*.

foresee [fɔːˈsiː] *vt* (*pt* foresaw, *pp* foreseen) prévoir. ◆**—able** *a* prévisible.

foreshadow [fɔːˈʃædəʊ] *vt* présager.

foresight ['fɔːsaɪt] *n* prévoyance *f*.

forest ['fɒrɪst] *n* forêt *f*. ◆**forester** *n* (*garde m*) forestier *m*.

forestall [fɔːˈstɔːl] *vt* devancer.

foretaste ['fɔːteɪst] *n* avant-goût *m*.

foretell [fɔːˈtel] *vt* (*pt & pp* foretold) prédire.

forethought ['fɔːθɔːt] *n* prévoyance *f*.

forever [fəˈrevər] *adv* (*for always*) pour toujours; (*continually*) sans cesse.

forewarn [fɔːˈwɔːn] *vt* avertir.

foreword ['fɔːwɜːd] *n* avant-propos *m inv*.

forfeit ['fɔːfɪt] *vt* (*lose*) perdre; − *n* (*penalty*) peine *f*; (*in game*) gage *m*.

forg/e ['fɔːdʒ] **1** *vt* (*signature, money*) contrefaire; (*document*) falsifier. **2** *vt* (*friendship, bond*) forger. **3** *vi* to f. **ahead** (*progress*) aller de l'avant. **4** *vt* (*metal*) forger; − *n* forge *f*. ◆**—er** *n* (*of banknotes etc*) faussaire *m*. ◆**forgery** *n* faux *m*, contrefaçon *f*.

forget [fə'get] *vt* (*pt* forgot, *pp* forgotten, *pres p* forgetting) oublier (to do de faire); **f. it!** *Fam* (*when thanked*) pas de quoi!; (*it doesn't matter*) peu importe!; **to f. oneself** s'oublier; − *vi* oublier; **to f. about** oublier. ◆**f.-me-not** *n Bot* myosotis *m*. ◆**forgetful** *a* to be f. (of) oublier, être oublieux (de). ◆**forgetfulness** *n* manque *m* de mémoire; (*carelessness*) négligence *f*; **in a moment of f.** dans un moment d'oubli.

forgiv/e [fə'gɪv] *vt* (*pt* forgave, *pp* forgiven) pardonner (s.o. sth qch à qn). ◆**—ing** *a* indulgent. ◆**forgiveness** *n* pardon *m*; (*compassion*) clémence *f*.

forgo [fɔː'gəʊ] *vt* (*pt* forgone) renoncer à.

fork [fɔːk] **1** *n* (*for eating*) fourchette *f*; (*for garden etc*) fourche *f*. **2** *vi* (*of road*) bifurquer; **to f. left** (*in vehicle*) prendre à gauche; − *n* bifurcation *f*, fourche *f*. **3** *vt* to f. **out** (*money*) *Fam* allonger; − *vi* to f. **out** (*pay*) *Fam* casquer. ◆**—ed** *a* fourchu. ◆**forklift truck** *n* chariot *m* élévateur.

forlorn [fə'lɔːn] *a* (*forsaken*) abandonné; (*unhappy*) triste, affligé.

form [fɔːm] *n* (*shape, type, style*) forme *f*; (*document*) formulaire *m*; *Sch* classe *f*; **it's good f.** c'est ce qui se fait; **in the f. of** en forme de; **a f. of speech** une façon de parler; **on f., in good f.** en (pleine) forme; − *vt* (*group, character etc*) former; (*clay*) façonner; (*habit*) contracter; (*an opinion*) se former; (*constitute*) constituer, former; **to f. part of** faire partie de; − *vi* (*appear*) se former. ◆**for'mation** *n* formation *f*. ◆**formative** *a* formateur.

formal ['fɔːm(ə)l] *a* (*person, tone etc*) cérémonieux; (*stuffy*) *Pej* compassé; (*official*) officiel; (*in due form*) en bonne et due forme; (*denial, structure, logic*) formel; (*resemblance*) extérieur; **f. dress** tenue *f* ou habit *m* de cérémonie; **f. education** éducation *f* scolaire. ◆**for'mality** *n* cérémonie *f*; (*requirement*) formalité *f*. ◆**formally** *adv* (*to declare etc*) officiellement; **f. dressed** en tenue de cérémonie.

former ['fɔːmər] **1** *a* (*previous*) ancien; (*situ-*

ation) antérieur; **her f. husband** son ex-mari *m*; **in f. days** autrefois. **2** *a* (*of two*) premier; − *pron* **the f.** celui-là, celle-là, le premier, la première. ◆**—ly** *adv* autrefois.

formidable ['fɔːmɪdəb(ə)l] *a* effroyable, terrible.

formula ['fɔːmjʊlə] *n* **1** (*pl* -as *or* -ae [-iː]) formule *f*. **2** (*pl* -as *only*) (*baby's feed*) *Am* mélange *m* lacté. ◆**formulate** *vt* formuler. ◆**formu'lation** *n* formulation *f*.

forsake [fə'seɪk] *vt* (*pt* forsook, *pp* forsaken) abandonner.

fort [fɔːt] *n Hist Mil* fort *m*; **to hold the f.** (*in s.o.'s absence*) *Fam* prendre la relève.

forte ['fɔːteɪ, *Am* fɔːt] *n* (*strong point*) fort *m*.

forth [fɔːθ] *adv* en avant; **from this day f.** désormais; **and so f.** et ainsi de suite.

forthcoming [fɔːθ'kʌmɪŋ] *a* **1** (*event*) à venir; (*book, film*) qui va sortir; **my f. book** mon prochain livre. **2** (*available*) disponible. **3** (*open*) communicatif; (*helpful*) serviable.

forthright ['fɔːθraɪt] *a* direct, franc.

forthwith [fɔːθ'wɪð] *adv* sur-le-champ.

fortieth ['fɔːtɪəθ] *a & n* quarantième (*mf*).

fortify ['fɔːtɪfaɪ] *vt* (*strengthen*) fortifier; **to f. s.o.** (*of food, drink*) réconforter qn, remonter qn. ◆**forti'cation** *n* fortification *f*.

fortitude ['fɔːtɪtjuːd] *n* courage *m* (moral).

fortnight ['fɔːtnaɪt] *n* quinze jours *mpl*, quinzaine *f*. ◆**—ly** *adv* bimensuel; − *adv* tous les quinze jours.

fortress ['fɔːtrɪs] *n* forteresse *f*.

fortuitous [fɔː'tjuːɪtəs] *a* fortuit.

fortunate ['fɔːtʃənɪt] *a* (*choice, event etc*) heureux; **to be f.** (*of person*) avoir de la chance; **it's f. (for her) that** il est heureux (pour elle) que. ◆**—ly** *adv* heureusement.

fortune ['fɔːtʃuːn] *n* (*wealth*) fortune *f*; (*luck*) chance *f*; (*chance*) sort *m*, hasard *m*, fortune *f*; **to have the good f. to** avoir la chance *or* le bonheur de; **to tell s.o.'s f.** dire la bonne aventure à qn; **to make one's f.** faire fortune. ◆**f.-teller** *n* diseur, -euse *mf* de bonne aventure.

forty ['fɔːtɪ] *a & n* quarante (*m*).

forum ['fɔːrəm] *n* forum *m*.

forward ['fɔːwəd] *adv* forward(s) en avant; **to go f.** avancer; **from this time f.** désormais; − *a* (*movement*) en avant; (*gears*) *Aut* avant *inv*; (*child*) *Fig* précoce; (*pert*) effronté; − *n Fb* avant *m*; − *vt* (*letter*) faire suivre; (*goods*) expédier. ◆**—ness** *n* précocité *f*; effronterie *f*. ◆**forward-looking** *a* tourné vers l'avenir.

fossil ['fɒs(ə)l] *n & a* fossile (*m*).

foster ['fɒstər] **1** vt encourager; (hope) nourrir. **2** vt (child) élever; — a (child, family) adoptif.

fought [fɔt] see **fight**.

foul [faul] **1** a (-er, -est) infect; (air) vicié; (breath) fétide; (language) grossier; (action, place) immonde; **to be f.-mouthed** avoir un langage grossier. **2** n Sp coup m irrégulier; Fb faute f; — a f. **play** Sp jeu m irrégulier; Jur acte m criminel. **3** vt salir; (air) vicier; (drain) encrasser; **to f. up** (life, plans) Fam gâcher. ◆**f.-up** n (in system) Fam raté m.

found [faund] see **find**.

found [faund] vt (town, opinion etc) fonder (on sur). ◆**—er** n fondateur, -trice mf. ◆**foun'dation** n fondation f; (basis) Fig base f, fondement m; **without f.** sans fondement; **f. cream** fond m de teint.

founder [faundər] vi (of ship) sombrer.

foundry [faundri] n fonderie f.

fountain [fauntin] n fontaine f; **f. pen** stylo(-plume) m.

four [fɔr] a & n quatre (m); **on all fours** à quatre pattes; **the Big F.** Pol les quatre Grands; **f.-letter word** = mot m de cinq lettres. ◆**fourfold** a quadruple; — adv au quadruple. ◆**foursome** n deux couples mpl. ◆**four'teen** a & n quatorze (m). ◆**fourth** a & n quatrième (mf).

fowl [faul] n (hens) volaille f; **a f.** une volaille.

fox [fɒks] **1** n renard m. **2** vt (puzzle) mystifier; (trick) tromper. ◆**foxy** a (sly) rusé, futé.

foxglove ['fɒksglʌv] n Bot digitale f.

foyer ['fɔiei] n Th foyer m; (in hotel) hall m.

fraction ['frækʃ(ə)n] n fraction f. ◆**fractionally** adv un tout petit peu.

fractious ['frækʃəs] a grincheux.

fracture ['fræktʃər] n fracture f; — vt fracturer; **to f. one's leg/etc** se fracturer la jambe/etc; — vi se fracturer.

fragile ['frædʒail, Am 'frædʒ(ə)l] a fragile. ◆**fra'gility** n fragilité f.

fragment ['frægmənt] n fragment m, morceau m. ◆**frag'mented** a, ◆**fragmentary** a fragmentaire.

fragrant ['freigrənt] a parfumé. ◆**fragrance** n parfum m.

frail [freil] a (-er, -est) (person) frêle, faible; (hope, health) fragile. ◆**frailty** n fragilité f.

frame [freim] **1** n (of person, building) charpente f; (of picture, bicycle) cadre m; (of window, car) châssis m; (of spectacles) monture f; **f. of mind** humeur f; — vt (picture) encadrer; (proposals etc) Fig

formuler. **2** vt **to f. s.o.** Fam monter un coup contre qn. ◆**f.-up** n Fam coup m monté. ◆**framework** n structure f; (with)in the f. of (context) dans le cadre de.

franc [fræŋk] n franc m.

France [frɑːns] n France f.

franchise ['fræntʃaiz] n **1** Pol droit m de vote. **2** (right to sell product) Com franchise f.

Franco- ['fræŋkəu] pref franco-.

frank [fræŋk] **1** a (-er, -est) (honest) franc. **2** vt (letter) affranchir. ◆**-ly** adv franchement. ◆**-ness** n franchise f.

frankfurter ['fræŋkfɜːtər] n saucisse f de Francfort.

frantic ['fræntik] a (activity, shout) frénétique; (rush, desire) effréné; (person) hors de soi; **f. with joy** fou de joie. ◆**frantically** adv comme un fou.

fraternal [frə'tɜːn(ə)l] a fraternel. ◆**fraternity** n (bond) fraternité f; (society) & Univ Am confrérie f. ◆**fraternize** ['frætənaiz] vi fraterniser (with avec).

fraud [frɔːd] n **1** Jur fraude f. **2** (person) imposteur m. ◆**fraudulent** a frauduleux.

fraught [frɔːt] a **f.** with plein de, chargé de; **to be f.** (of situation) être tendu; (of person) Fam être contrarié.

fray [frei] **1** vt (garment) effilocher; (rope) user; — vi s'effilocher; s'user. **2** n (fight) rixe f. ◆**-ed** a (nerves) Fig tendu.

freak [friːk] n (person) phénomène m, monstre m; **a jazz/etc f.** Fam un(e) fana de jazz/etc; — a (result, weather etc) anormal. ◆**freakish** a anormal.

freckle ['frek(ə)l] n tache f de rousseur. ◆**freckled** a couvert de taches de rousseur.

free [friː] a (freer, freest) (at liberty, not occupied) libre; (gratis) gratuit; (lavish) généreux (with de); **to get f.** se libérer; **f. to do** libre de faire; **to let s.o. go f.** relâcher qn; **f. of charge** gratuit; **f. of** (without) sans; **f. of s.o.** (rid of) débarrassé de qn; **to have a f. hand** Fig avoir carte blanche (to do pour faire); **f. and easy** décontracté; **f. trade** libre-échange m; **f. speech** liberté f d'expression; **f. kick** Fb coup m franc; **f.-range egg** œuf m de ferme; — adv **f.** (of charge) gratuitement; — vt (pt & pp freed) (prisoner etc) libérer; (trapped person, road) dégager; (country) affranchir, libérer; (untie) détacher. ◆**Freefone**® Tel = numéro m vert. ◆**free-for-'all** n mêlée f générale. ◆**freehold** n propriété f foncière libre. ◆**freelance** n indépendant; — n collaborateur, -trice mf indépendant(e). ◆**freeloader** n (sponger) Am parasite m. ◆**Freemason** n franc-maçon m. ◆**Freemasonry** n franc-maçonnerie f. ◆**freestyle** n Swimming nage f libre. ◆**free'thinker** n libre penseur, -euse mf. ◆**freeway** n Am autoroute f.

freedom ['friːdəm] n liberté f; **f. from** (worry, responsibility) absence f de.

freely ['friːli] adv (to speak, circulate etc) librement; (to give) libéralement.

freez/e [friːz] vi (pt froze, pp frozen) geler; (of smile) Fig se figer; Culin se congeler; **to f. to death** mourir de froid; **to f. up** or **over** geler; (of windscreen) se givrer; − vt Culin congeler, surgeler; (credits, river) geler; (prices, wages) bloquer; **frozen food** surgelés mpl; − n Met gel m; (of prices etc) blocage m. ◆**-ing** a (weather etc) glacial; (hands, person) gelé; **it's f. on** gèle; − n **below f.** au-dessous de zéro. ◆**-er** n (deep-freeze) congélateur m; (in fridge) freezer m.

freight [freit] n (goods, price) fret m; (transport) transport m; **f. train** Am train m de marchandises; − vt (ship) affréter. ◆**-er** n (ship) cargo m.

French [frentʃ] a français; (teacher) de français; (embassy) de France; **F. fries** Am frites fpl; **the F.** les Français mpl; − n (language) français m. ◆**Frenchman** n (pl -men) Français m. ◆**French-speaking** a francophone. ◆**Frenchwoman** n (pl -women) Française f.

frenzy ['frenzi] n frénésie f. ◆**frenzied** a (shouts etc) frénétique; (person) effréné; (attack) violent.

fresco ['freskəʊ] n (pl -oes or -os) fresque f.

fresh [freʃ] a (-er, -est) frais; (new) nouveau; (impudent) Fam culotté; **to get some f. air** prendre le frais; **f. water** eau f douce. 2 adv **f. from** fraîchement arrivé de; **f. out of, f. from** (university) tout émoulu de. ◆**freshen 1** vi (of wind) fraîchir. 2 vi **to f. up** faire un brin de toilette; − vt **to f. up** (house etc) retaper; **to f. s.o. up** (of bath) rafraîchir qn. ◆**freshener** n air f. désodorisant m. ◆**freshman** n (pl -men) étudiant, -ante mf de première année. ◆**freshness** n fraîcheur f; (cheek) Fam culot m.

fret [fret] vi (-tt-) (worry) se faire du souci, s'en faire; (of baby) pleurer. ◆**fretful** a (baby etc) grognon.

friar ['fraiər] n frère m, moine m.

friction ['frikʃ(ə)n] n friction f.

Friday ['fraidi] n vendredi m.

fridge [fridʒ] n Fam frigo m.

fried [fraid] pt & pp of **fry 1**; − a (fish etc) frit; **f. egg** œuf m sur le plat. ◆**frier** n (pan) friteuse f.

friend [frend] n ami, -ie mf; (from school, work) camarade mf; **to be friends** with être ami avec; **to make friends** se lier (with avec). ◆**friendly** a (-ier, -iest) amical; (child, animal) gentil, affectueux; (kind) gentil; **some f. advice** un conseil d'ami; **to be f. with** être ami avec. ◆**friendship** n amitié f.

frieze [friːz] n Archit frise f.

frigate ['frigət] n (ship) frégate f.

fright [frait] n peur f; (person, hat etc) Fig Fam horreur f; **to have a f.** avoir peur; **to give s.o. a f.** faire peur à qn. ◆**frighten** vt effrayer, faire peur à; **to f. away** or **off** (animal) effaroucher; (person) chasser. ◆**frightened** a effrayé; **to be f.** avoir peur (of de). ◆**frightening** a effrayant. ◆**frightful** a affreux. ◆**frightfully** adv (ugly, late) affreusement; (kind, glad) terriblement.

frigid ['fridʒid] a (air, greeting etc) froid; Psy frigide.

frill [fril] n Tex volant m; (paper) Fig Fam manières fpl, chichis mpl; (useless embellishments) fioritures fpl, superflu m; **no frills** (spartan) spartiate.

fringe [frindʒ] 1 n (of hair, clothes etc) frange f. 2 n (of forest) lisière f; **on the fringe(s) of society** en marge de la société; − a (group, theatre) marginal; **f. benefits** avantages mpl divers.

frisk [frisk] 1 vt (search) fouiller (au corps). 2 vi **to f. (about)** gambader. ◆**frisky** a (-ier, -iest) a vif.

fritter ['fritər] 1 vt **to f. away** (waste) gaspiller. 2 n Culin beignet m.

frivolous ['frivələs] a frivole. ◆**fri'volity** n frivolité f.

frizzy ['frizi] a (hair) crépu.

fro [frəʊ] adv **to go to and f.** aller et venir.

frock [frɒk] n (dress) robe f; (of monk) froc m.

frog [frɒg] n grenouille f; **a f. in one's throat** Fig un chat dans la gorge. ◆**frogman** n (pl -men) homme-grenouille m.

frolic ['frɒlik] vi (pt & pp frolicked) **to f. (about)** gambader; − npl (capers) ébats mpl; (pranks) gamineries fpl.

from [frɒm, unstressed frəm] prep 1 de; **a letter f.** une lettre de; **to suffer f.** souffrir de;

where are you f.? d'où êtes-vous?; **a train f.** un train en provenance de; **f. to be ten metres (away) f.** the house être à dix mètres de la maison. **2** (*time onwards*) à partir de, dès, depuis; **f. today (on), as f. today** à partir d'aujourd'hui, dès aujourd'hui; **f. her child-hood** dès *ou* depuis son enfance. **3** (*numbers, prices onwards*) à partir de; **f. five francs** à partir de cinq francs. **4** (*away from*) à; **to take/hide/borrow f.** prendre/cacher/emprunter à. **5** (*out of*) dans; sur; **to take f.** (*box*) prendre dans; (*table*) prendre sur; **to drink f.** (*cup/etc*) boire dans une tasse/*etc*; **to drink (straight) f. the bottle** boire à (même) la bouteille. **6** (*according to*) d'après; **f. what I saw** d'après ce que j'ai vu. **7** (*cause*) par; **f. conviction/habit/***etc* par conviction/habitude/*etc*. **8** (*on the part of, on behalf of*) de la part de; **tell her f. me** dis-lui de ma part.

front [frʌnt] *n* (*of garment, building*) devant *m*; (*of boat, car*) avant *m*; (*of crowd*) premier rang *m*; (*of book*) début *m*; *Mil Pol Met* front *m*; (*beach*) front *m* de mer; (*appearance*) *Fig* façade *f*; **in f. (of)** devant; **in f.** (*ahead*) en avant; *Sp* en tête; **in the f.** (*of vehicle*) à l'avant; (*of house*) devant; – *a* (*tooth etc*) de devant; (*part, wheel, car seat*) avant *inv*; (*row, page*) premier; (*view*) de face; **f. door** porte *f* d'entrée; **f. line** *Mil* front *m*; **f. room** (*lounge*) salon *m*; **f. runner** *Fig* favori, -ite *mf*; **f.-wheel drive** (*on vehicle*) traction *f* avant; – *vi* **f. on** *to* (*of windows etc*) donner sur. ◆**frontage** *n* façade *f*. ◆**frontal** *a* (*attack*) de front.

frontier [frʌntɪər] *n* frontière *f*; – *a* (*town, post*) frontière *inv*.

frost [frɒst] *n* gel *m*, gelée *f*; (*frozen drops on glass, grass etc*) gelée *f* blanche, givre *m*; – *vi* **to f. up** (*of windscreen etc*) se givrer. ◆**frostbite** *n* gelure *f*. ◆**frostbitten** *a* gelé. ◆**frosty** *a* (*-ier, -iest*) glacial; (*window*) givré; **it's f.** il gèle.

frosted [frɒstɪd] *a* (*glass*) dépoli.

frosting [frɒstɪŋ] *n* (*icing*) *Culin* glaçage *m*.

froth [frɒθ] *n* mousse *f*; – *vi* mousser. ◆**frothy** *a* (*-ier, -iest*) (*beer etc*) mousseux.

frown [fraʊn] *n* froncement *m* de sourcils; – *vi* froncer les sourcils; **to f. (up)on** *Fig* désapprouver.

froze, frozen [frəʊz, ˈfrəʊz(ə)n] *see* freeze.

frugal [ˈfruːg(ə)l] *a* (*meal*) frugal; (*thrifty*) parcimonieux. ◆**-ly** *adv* parcimonieuse-ment.

fruit [fruːt] *n* fruit *m*; (*some*) **f.** (*one item*) un fruit; (*more than one*) des fruits; – *a*

(*basket*) à fruits; (*drink*) aux fruits; (*salad*) de fruits; **f. tree** arbre *m* fruitier. ◆**fruit-cake** *n* cake *m*. ◆**fruiterer** *n* fruitier, -ière *mf*. ◆**fruitful** *a* (*meeting, career etc*) fructueux, fécond. ◆**fruitless** *a* stérile. ◆**fruity** *a* (*-ier, -iest*) *a* fruité, de fruit; (*joke*) *Fig Fam* corsé.

fruition [fruːˈɪʃ(ə)n] *n* **to come to f.** se réaliser.

frumpish [ˈfrʌmpɪʃ] *a*, **frumpy** [ˈfrʌmpɪ] *a* *Fam* (mal) fagoté.

frustrat/e [frʌˈstreɪt] *vt* (*person*) frustrer; (*plans*) faire échouer. ◆**-ed** *a* (*mentally, sexually*) frustré; (*effort*) vain. ◆**-ing** *a* irritant. ◆**fru'stration** *n* frustration *f*; (*disappointment*) déception *f*.

fry [fraɪ] **1** *vt* (faire) frire; – *vi* frire. **2** *n* **small f.** menu fretin *m*. ◆**-ing** *n* friture *f*; **f. pan** poêle *f* (à frire). ◆**-er** *n* (*pan*) friteuse *f*.

ft *abbr* (*measure*) = **foot, feet.**

fuddled [ˈfʌd(ə)ld] *a* (*drunk*) gris; (*confused*) embrouillé.

fuddy-duddy [ˈfʌdɪdʌdɪ] *n* **he's an old f.-duddy** *Fam* il est vieux jeu.

fudge [fʌdʒ] **1** *n* (*sweet*) caramel *m* mou. **2** *vt* **to f. the issue** refuser d'aborder le problème.

fuel [fjʊəl] *n* combustible *m*; *Aut* carburant *m*; **f. (oil)** mazout *m*; – *vt* (*-ll-, Am -l-*) (*stove*) alimenter; (*ship*) ravitailler (*en* combustible); (*s.o.'s anger etc*) attiser.

fugitive [ˈfjuːdʒɪtɪv] *n* fugitif, -ive *mf*.

fugue [fjuːg] *n* *Mus* fugue *f*.

fulfil, *Am* **fulfill** [fʊlˈfɪl] *vt* (*-ll-*) (*ambition, dream*) accomplir, réaliser; (*condition, duty*) remplir; (*desire*) satisfaire; **to f. oneself** s'épanouir. ◆**fulfilling** *a* satisfaisant. ◆**fulfilment**, *Am* **fulfillment** *n* accomplissement *m*, réalisation *f*; (*feeling*) satisfaction *f*.

full [fʊl] *a* (*-er, -est*) plein (*of* de); (*bus, theatre, meal*) complet; (*life, day*) (bien) rempli; (*skirt*) ample; (*hour*) entier; (*member*) à part entière; **the f. price** le prix fort; **to pay (the) f. fare** payer plein tarif; **to be f. (up)** (*of person*) *Culin* n'avoir plus faim; (*of hotel*) être complet; **the f. facts** tous les faits; **at f. speed** à toute vitesse; **f. name** (*on form*) nom et prénom; **f. stop** *Gram* point *m*; – *adv* **to know f. well** savoir fort bien; **f. in the face** (*to hit etc*) en pleine figure; – **in f.** (*text*) intégral, *etc* (*to publish, read*) intégralement; (*to write one's name*) en toutes lettres; **to the f.** (*completely*) tout à fait. ◆**fullness** *n* (*of details*) abondance *f*; *(of dress)* ampleur *f*. ◆**fully** *adv* entièrement; *(at least)* au moins.

full-back ['fulbæk] *n* Fb arrière *m*. ◆**f.-'grown** *a* adulte; *(foetus)* arrivé à terme. ◆**f.-'length** *a* *(film)* de long métrage; *(portrait)* en pied; *(dress)* long. ◆**f.-'scale** *a* *(model etc)* grandeur nature *inv*; *(operation etc)* Fig de grande envergure. ◆**f.-'sized** *a* *(model)* grandeur nature *inv*. ◆**f.-'time** *a* & *adv* à plein temps.

fully-fledged, *Am* **full-fledged** [ful(i)'fledʒd] *a* *(engineer etc)* diplômé; *(member)* à part entière. ◆**f.-formed** *a* *(baby etc)* formé. ◆**f.-grown** *a* = **full-grown.**

fulsome ['fulsəm] *a* *(praise etc)* excessif.

fumble ['fʌmb(ə)l] *vi* to f. (about) *(grope)* tâtonner; *(search)* fouiller **(for** pour trouver); **to f. (about) with** tripoter.

fume [fjuːm] *vi* *(give off fumes)* fumer; *(of person)* Fig rager; — *npl* émanations *fpl*; *(from car exhaust)* gaz *m inv*.

fumigate ['fjuːmɪgeɪt] *vt* désinfecter (par fumigation).

fun [fʌn] *n* amusement *m*; **to be (good) f.** être très amusant; **to have (some) f.** s'amuser; **to make f. of, poke f. at** se moquer de; **for f., for the f. of it** pour le plaisir.

function ['fʌŋkʃ(ə)n] *n* 1 *(role, duty)* & Math fonction *f*; *(meeting)* réunion *f*; *(ceremony)* cérémonie *f* *(publique)*. 2 *vi* *(work)* fonctionner. ◆**functional** *a* fonctionnel.

fund [fʌnd] *n* *(for pension, relief etc)* Fin caisse *f*; *(of knowledge etc)* Fig fond *m*; *(money resources)* fonds *mpl*; *(for special purpose)* crédits *mpl*; — *vt* *(with money)* fournir des fonds *or* des crédits à.

fundamental [fʌndə'ment(ə)l] *a* fondamental; — *npl* principes *mpl* essentiels.

funeral ['fjuːnərəl] *n* enterrement *m*; *(grandiose)* funérailles *fpl*; — *a* *(service, march)* funèbre; *(expenses, parlour)* funéraire.

funfair ['fʌnfeər] *n* fête *f* foraine; *(larger)* parc *m* d'attractions.

fungus, *pl* **-gi** ['fʌŋgəs, -gaɪ] *n* Bot champignon *m*; *(mould)* moisissure *f*.

funicular [fjuː'nɪkjulər] *n* funiculaire *m*.

funk [fʌŋk] *n* **to be in a f.** *(afraid)* Fam avoir la frousse; *(depressed, sulking)* Am Fam faire la gueule.

funnel ['fʌn(ə)l] *n* 1 *(of ship)* cheminée *f*. 2 *(tube for pouring)* entonnoir *m*.

funny ['fʌnɪ] *a* *(-ier, -iest)* *(amusing)* drôle; *(strange)* bizarre; **a f. idea** une drôle d'idée; **there's some f. business going on** il y a quelque chose de louche; **to feel f.** ne pas se

sentir très bien. ◆**funnily** *adv* drôlement; bizarrement; **f. enough . . .** chose bizarre . . . .

fur [fɜːr] *n* 1 *(of animal)* poil *m*, pelage *m*; *(for wearing etc)* fourrure *f*. 2 *n* *(in kettle)* dépôt *m* (de tartre); — *vi* (-**rr**-) **to f. (up)** s'entartrer.

furious ['fjuərɪəs] *a* *(violent, angry)* furieux **(with,** at contre); *(pace, speed)* fou. ◆—**ly** *adv* furieusement; *(to drive, rush)* à une allure folle.

furnace ['fɜːnɪs] *n* *(forge)* fourneau *m*; *(room etc)* Fig fournaise *f*.

furnish ['fɜːnɪʃ] *vt* 1 *(room)* meubler. 2 *(supply)* fournir **(s.o. with sth** qch à qn). ◆—**ings** *npl* ameublement *m*.

furniture ['fɜːnɪtʃər] *n* meubles *mpl*; **a piece of f.** un meuble.

furrier ['fʌrɪər] *n* fourreur *m*.

furrow ['fʌrəʊ] *n* *(on brow)* & Agr sillon *m*.

furry ['fɜːrɪ] *a* *(animal)* à poil; *(toy)* en peluche.

further ['fɜːðər] 1 *adv* & *a* = **farther.** 2 *adv* *(more)* davantage, plus; *(besides)* en outre; — *a* *(additional)* supplémentaire; *(education)* post-scolaire; **f. details** de plus amples détails; **a f. case/etc** *(another)* un autre cas/etc; **without f. delay** sans plus attendre. 3 *vt* *(cause, research etc)* promouvoir. ◆**furthermore** *adv* en outre. ◆**furthest** *a* & *adv* = **farthest.**

furtive ['fɜːtɪv] *a* furtif.

fury ['fjuərɪ] *n* *(violence, anger)* fureur *f*.

fuse [fjuːz] 1 *vti* *(melt)* Tech fondre; Fig fusionner. 2 *vt* **to f. the lights** *etc* faire sauter les plombs; — *vi* **the lights** *etc* **have fused** les plombs ont sauté; — *n* *(wire)* El fusible *m*, plomb *m*. 3 *n* *(of bomb)* amorce *f*. ◆**fused** *a* *(plug)* El avec fusible incorporé. ◆**fusion** *n* *(union)* & Phys Biol fusion *f*.

fuselage ['fjuːzəlɑːʒ] *n* Av fuselage *m*.

fuss [fʌs] *n* façons *fpl*, histoires *fpl*, chichis *mpl*; *(noise)* agitation *f*; **what a (lot of) f.!** quelle histoire!; **to kick up** *or* **make a f.** faire des histoires; **to make a f. of** être aux petits soins pour; — *vi* faire des chichis; *(worry)* se tracasser **(about** pour); *(rush about)* s'agiter; **to f. over s.o.** être aux petits soins pour qn. ◆**fusspot,** *n*, *Am* ◆**fussbudget** *n* Fam enquiquineur, -euse *mf*. ◆**fussy** *a* *(-ier, -iest)* méticuleux; *(difficult)* difficile **(about** sur).

fusty ['fʌstɪ] *a* *(-ier, -iest)* *(smell)* de renfermé.

futile ['fjuːtaɪl, *Am* 'fjuːt(ə)l] *a* futile, vain. ◆**fu'tility** *n* futilité *f*.

future ['fjuːtʃər] n avenir m; Gram futur m; **in f.** (from now on) à l'avenir; **in the f.** (one day) un jour (futur); – a futur, à venir; (date) ultérieur.

fuzz [fʌz] n **1** (down) Fam duvet m. **2 the f.** (police) Sl les flics mpl. ◆**fuzzy** a (-ier, -iest) (hair) crépu; (picture, idea) flou.

G

G, g [dʒiː] n G, g m. ◆**G.-string** n (cloth) cache-sexe m inv.

gab [gæb] n to have the gift of the g. Fam avoir du bagou(t).

gabardine [gæbə'diːn] n (material, coat) gabardine f.

gabble ['gæb(ə)l] vi (chatter) jacasser; (indistinctly) bredouiller; – n baragouin m.

gable ['geɪb(ə)l] n Archit pignon m.

gad [gæd] vi (-dd-) to g. about se balader, vadrouiller.

gadget ['gædʒɪt] n gadget m.

Gaelic ['geɪlɪk, 'gælɪk] a & n gaélique (m).

gaffe [gæf] n (blunder) gaffe f, bévue f.

gag [gæg] **1** n (over mouth) bâillon m; – vt (-gg-) (victim, press etc) bâillonner. **2** n (joke) plaisanterie f; Cin Th gag m. **3** vi (-gg-) (choke) Am s'étouffer (on avec).

gaggle ['gæg(ə)l] n (of geese) troupeau m.

gaiety ['geɪtɪ] n gaieté f; (of colour) éclat m. ◆**gaily** adv gaiement.

gain [geɪn] vt (obtain, win) gagner; (objective) atteindre; (experience, reputation) acquérir; (popularity) gagner en; to g. speed/weight prendre de la vitesse/du poids; – vi (of watch) avancer; to g. in strength gagner en force; to g. on (catch up with) rattraper; – n (increase) augmentation f (in de); (profit) Com bénéfice m, gain m; Fig avantage m. ◆**gainful** a profitable; (employment) rémunéré.

gainsay [geɪn'seɪ] vt (pt & pp gainsaid [-sed]) (person) contredire; (facts) nier.

gait [geɪt] n (walk) démarche f.

gala ['gɑːlə, 'geɪlə] n gala m, fête f; **swimming g.** concours m de natation.

galaxy ['gæləksɪ] n galaxie f.

gale [geɪl] n grand vent m, rafale f (de vent).

gall [gɔːl] **1** n Med bile f; (bitterness) Fig fiel m; (cheek) Fam effronterie f; **g. bladder** vésicule f biliaire. **2** vt (vex) blesser, froisser.

gallant ['gælənt] a (brave) courageux; (splendid) magnifique; (chivalrous) galant. ◆**gallantry** n (bravery) courage m.

galleon ['gælɪən] n (ship) Hist galion m.

gallery ['gælərɪ] n (room etc) galerie f; (for public, press) tribune f; **art g.** (private) galerie f d'art; (public) musée m d'art.

galley ['gælɪ] n (ship) Hist galère f; (kitchen) Nau Av cuisine f.

Gallic ['gælɪk] a (French) français. ◆**gallicism** n (word etc) gallicisme m.

gallivant ['gælɪvænt] vi to g. (about) Fam courir, vadrouiller.

gallon ['gælən] n gallon m (Br = 4,5 litres, Am = 3,8 litres).

gallop ['gæləp] n galop m; – vi galoper; to g. away (rush) Fig partir au galop or en vitesse. ◆**–ing** a (inflation etc) Fig galopant.

gallows ['gæləʊz] npl potence f.

gallstone ['gɔːlstəʊn] n Med calcul m biliaire.

galore [gə'lɔːr] adv à gogo, en abondance.

galoshes [gə'lɒʃɪz] npl (shoes) caoutchoucs mpl.

galvanize ['gælvənaɪz] vt (metal) & Fig galvaniser.

gambit ['gæmbɪt] n **opening g.** Fig manœuvre f stratégique.

gambl/e ['gæmb(ə)l] vi jouer (on sur, with avec); to g. on (count on) miser sur; – vt (wager) jouer; to g. (away) (lose) perdre (au jeu); – n (bet) & Fig coup m risqué. ◆**–ing** n jeu m. ◆**–er** n joueur, -euse mf.

game [geɪm] **1** n jeu m; (of football, cricket etc) match m; (of tennis, chess, cards) partie f; **to have a g. of** jouer un match de; faire une partie de; **games** Sch le sport; **games teacher** professeur m d'éducation physique. **2** n (animals, birds) gibier m; **to be fair g. for** Fig être une proie idéale pour. **3** a (brave) courageux; **g. for** (willing) prêt à. **4** a (leg) estropié; **to have a g. leg** être boiteux. ◆**gamekeeper** n garde-chasse m.

gammon ['gæmən] n (ham) jambon m fumé.

gammy ['gæmɪ] a Fam = game 4.

gamut ['gæmət] n Mus & Fig gamme f.

gang [gæŋ] n bande f; (of workers) équipe f; (of crooks) gang m; – vi to g. up on or

gangling ['gæŋglɪŋ] a dégingandé.

gangrene ['gæŋgriːn] n gangrène f.

gangway ['gæŋweɪ] n passage m; (in train) couloir m; (in bus, cinema, theatre) allée f; (footbridge) Av Nau passerelle f; g.! dégagez!

gaol [dʒeɪl] n & vt = **jail.**

gap [gæp] n (empty space) trou m, vide m; (breach) trou m; (in time) intervalle m; (in knowledge) lacune f; **the g. between** (divergence) l'écart m entre.

gap/e [geɪp] vi (stare) rester or être bouche bée; **to g. at** regarder bouche bée. ◆—**ing** a (chasm, wound) béant.

garage ['gæra(ɪ)dʒ, 'gærɪdʒ, Am gə'rɑːʒ] n garage m; — vt mettre au garage.

garb [gɑːb] n (clothes) costume m.

garbage ['gɑːbɪdʒ] n ordures fpl; **g. can** Am poubelle f; **g. collector** or **man** Am éboueur m; **g. truck** Am camion-benne m.

garble ['gɑːb(ə)l] vt (words etc) déformer, embrouiller.

garden ['gɑːd(ə)n] n jardin m; **the gardens** (park) le parc; **g. centre** (store) jardinerie f; (nursery) pépinière f; **g. party** garden-party f; **g. produce** produits mpl maraîchers; — vi **to be gardening** jardiner. ◆—**ing** n jardinage m. ◆—**er** n jardinier, -ière mf.

gargle ['gɑːg(ə)l] vi se gargariser; — n gargarisme m.

gargoyle ['gɑːgɔɪl] n Archit gargouille f.

garish ['geərɪʃ, Am 'gærɪʃ] a voyant, criard.

garland ['gɑːlənd] n guirlande f.

garlic ['gɑːlɪk] n ail m; **g. sausage** saucisson m à l'ail.

garment ['gɑːmənt] n vêtement m.

garnish ['gɑːnɪʃ] vt garnir (**with** de); — n garniture f.

garret ['gærət] n mansarde f.

garrison ['gærɪs(ə)n] n Mil garnison f.

garrulous ['gærələs] a (talkative) loquace.

garter ['gɑːtər] n (round leg) jarretière f; (attached to belt) Am jarretelle f; (for men) fixe-chaussette m.

gas [gæs] **1** n gaz m inv; (gasoline) Am essence f; Med Fam anesthésie f au masque; — a (meter, mask, chamber) à gaz; (pipe) de gaz; (industry) du gaz; (heating) au gaz; **g. fire** or **heater** appareil m de chauffage à gaz; **g. station** Am poste m d'essence; **g. stove** (portable) réchaud m à gaz; (cooker) cuisinière f; **g. works** (poison) asphyxier; Mil gazer. **2** vi (-ss-) (talk) Fam bavarder; — n **for a g.** (fun) Am Fam pour rire. ◆**gasbag** n Fam commère

f. ◆**gasman** n (pl -men) employé m du gaz. ◆**gasoline** n Am essence f. ◆**gasworks** n usine f à gaz.

gash [gæʃ] n entaille f; — vt entailler.

gasp [gɑːsp] **1** vi **to g. (for breath)** haleter; — n halètement m. **2** vi **to g. with** or **in** surprise/etc avoir le souffle coupé de surprise/etc; — n **a g. of** surprise/etc un hoquet de surprise/etc.

gassy ['gæsɪ] a (-ier, -iest) (drink) gazeux.

gastric ['gæstrɪk] a (juices, ulcer) gastrique. ◆**ga'stronomy** n gastronomie f.

gate [geɪt] n (of castle, airport etc) porte f; (at level crossing, field etc) barrière f; (metal) grille f; (in Paris Metro) portillon m. ◆**gateway** n **the g. to** success/etc le chemin du succès/etc.

gâteau, pl -eaux ['gætəu, -əuz] n Culin gros gâteau m à la crème.

gatecrash ['geɪtkræʃ] vti **to g. (a party)** s'inviter de force (à une réception).

gather ['gæðər] vt (people, objects) rassembler; (pick up) ramasser; (flowers) cueillir; (information) recueillir; (understand) comprendre; (skirt, material) froncer; **g. that ...** (infer) je crois comprendre que ...; **to g. speed** prendre de la vitesse; **to g. in** (crops, harvest) rentrer; (essays, exam papers) ramasser; **to g. up** (strength) rassembler; (papers) ramasser; — vi (of people) s'assembler, se rassembler, s'amasser; (of clouds) se former; (of dust) s'accumuler; **to g. round** s'approcher; **to g. round s.o.** entourer qn. ◆—**ing** n (group) réunion f.

gaudy ['gɔːdɪ] a (-ier, -iest) voyant, criard.

gauge [geɪdʒ] n (instrument) jauge f, indicateur m; Rail écartement m; **to be a g. of** sth Fig permettre de jauger qch; — vt (measure) mesurer; (estimate) évaluer, jauger.

gaunt [gɔːnt] a (thin) décharné.

gauntlet ['gɔːntlɪt] n gant m; **to run the g. of** Fig essuyer (le feu de).

gauze [gɔːz] n (fabric) gaze f.

gave [geɪv] see **give.**

gawk [gɔːk] vi **to g. (at)** regarder bouche bée.

gawp [gɔːp] vi = **gawk.**

gay [geɪ] a (-er, -est) **1** (cheerful) gai, joyeux; (colour) vif, gai. **2** Fam homo(sexuel), gay inv.

gaze [geɪz] n regard m (fixe); — vi regarder; **to g. at** regarder (fixement).

gazelle [gə'zel] n (animal) gazelle f.

gazette [gə'zet] n journal m officiel.

GB [dʒiːˈbiː] abbr (Great Britain) Grande-Bretagne f.

GCSE [dʒiːsiːesˈiː] abbr (General Certificate of Secondary Education) = baccalauréat m.

gear [gɪər] **1** n matériel m, équipement m; (belongings) affaires fpl; (clothes) Fam vêtements mpl (à la mode); (toothed wheels) Tech engrenage m; (speed) Aut vitesse f; **in g.** Aut en prise; **not in g.** Aut au point mort; **g. lever,** Am **g. shift** levier m de (changement de) vitesse. **2** vt (adapt) adapter (**to** à); **geared (up) to do** prêt à faire; **to g.** oneself up for se préparer pour. ◆gearbox n boîte f de vitesses.

gee! [dʒiː] int Am Fam ça alors!

geese [giːs] see goose.

geezer [ˈgiːzər] n Hum Sl type m.

Geiger counter [ˈgaɪgəkauntər] n compteur m Geiger.

gel [dʒel] n (substance) gel m.

gelatin(e) [ˈdʒelətin, Am -tən] n gélatine f.

gelignite [ˈdʒelɪgnaɪt] n dynamite f (au nitrate de soude).

gem [dʒem] n pierre f précieuse; (person or thing of value) Fig perle f; (error) Iron perle f.

Gemini [ˈdʒemɪnaɪ] n (sign) les Gémeaux mpl.

gen [dʒen] n (information) Sl coordonnées fpl; – vi (-nn-) **to g. up on** Sl se rancarder sur.

gender [ˈdʒendər] n Gram genre m; (of person) sexe m.

gene [dʒiːn] n Biol gène m.

genealogy [dʒiːnɪˈælədʒɪ] n généalogie f.

general [ˈdʒenərəl] **1** a général; **in g.** en général; **the g. public** le (grand) public; **for g. use** à l'usage du public; **a g. favourite** aimé or apprécié de tous; **g. delivery** Am poste f restante; **to be g.** (widespread) être très répandu. **2** n (officer) Mil général m. ◆gene'rality n généralité f. ◆generali-'zation n généralisation f. ◆generalize vti généraliser. ◆generally adv généralement; **g. speaking** en général, généralement parlant.

generate [ˈdʒenəreɪt] vt (heat) produire; (fear, hope etc) & Ling engendrer. ◆gene-'ration n génération f; **the g. of** (heat) la production de; **g. gap** conflit m des générations. ◆generator n El groupe m électrogène, génératrice f.

generous [ˈdʒenərəs] a généreux (with de); (helping, meal etc) copieux. ◆gene'rosity n générosité f. ◆generously adv généreusement; (to serve s.o.) copieusement.

genesis [ˈdʒenəsɪs] n genèse f.

genetic [dʒɪˈnetɪk] a génétique. ◆genetics n génétique f.

Geneva [dʒɪˈniːvə] n Genève m or f.

genial [ˈdʒiːnɪəl] a (kind) affable; (cheerful) jovial.

genie [ˈdʒiːnɪ] n (goblin) génie m.

genital [ˈdʒenɪt(ə)l] a génital; – npl organes mpl génitaux.

genius [ˈdʒiːnɪəs] n (ability, person) génie m; **to have a g. for doing/for sth** avoir le génie pour faire/de qch.

genocide [ˈdʒenəsaɪd] n génocide m.

gent [dʒent] n Fam monsieur m; **gents' shoes** Com chaussures fpl pour hommes; **the gents** Fam les toilettes fpl (pour hommes).

genteel [dʒenˈtiːl] a Iron distingué.

gentle [ˈdʒent(ə)l] a (-er, -est) (person, sound, slope etc) doux; (hint, reminder) discret; (touch) léger; (pace) mesuré; (exercise, progress) modéré; (birth) noble. ◆gentleman n (pl -men) monsieur m; (well-bred) gentleman m; **a g. farmer** un homme bien élevé. ◆gentlemanly a distingué, bien élevé. ◆gentleness n douceur f. ◆gently adv doucement; (to remind) discrètement; (smoothly) en douceur.

genuine [ˈdʒenjuɪn] a (authentic) véritable, authentique; (sincere) sincère, vrai. ◆—ly adv authentiquement; sincèrement. ◆—ness n authenticité f; sincérité f.

geography [dʒɪˈɒgrəfɪ] n géographie f. ◆geo'graphical a géographique.

geology [dʒɪˈɒlədʒɪ] n géologie f. ◆geo-'logical a géologique. ◆geologist n géologue m.

geometry [dʒɪˈɒmɪtrɪ] n géométrie f. ◆geo'metric(al) a géométrique.

geranium [dʒɪˈreɪnɪəm] n Bot géranium m.

geriatric [dʒerɪˈætrɪk] a (hospital) du troisième âge; **g. ward** service m de gériatrie.

germ [dʒɜːm] n Biol & Fig germe m; Med microbe m; **g. warfare** guerre f bactériologique.

German [ˈdʒɜːmən] a n allemand, -ande (mf); **G. measles** Med rubéole f; **G. shepherd** (dog) Am berger m allemand; – n (language) allemand m. ◆Ger'manic a germanique.

Germany [ˈdʒɜːmənɪ] n Allemagne f; **West G.** Allemagne de l'Ouest.

germinate [ˈdʒɜːmɪneɪt] vi Bot & Fig germer.

gestation [dʒeˈsteɪʃ(ə)n] n gestation f.

gesture [ˈdʒestʃər] n geste m; – vi **to g. to**

s.o. to do faire signe à qn de faire. ◆ge'sticulate *vi* gesticuler.

get [get] **1** *vt* (*pt & pp* got, *pp Am* gotten, *pres p* getting) (*obtain*) obtenir, avoir; (*find*) trouver; (*buy*) acheter, prendre; (*receive*) recevoir, avoir; (*catch*) attraper, prendre; (*seize*) prendre, saisir; (*put*) mettre; (*derive*) tirer (from de); (*understand*) comprendre, saisir; (*prepare*) préparer; (*lead*) mener; (*target*) atteindre, avoir; (*reputation*) se faire; (*annoy*) *Fam* ennuyer; **I have got,** *Am* **I have gotten** j'ai; **to g. s.o. to do sth** faire faire qch à qn; **to g. sth built/etc** faire construire/*etc* qch; **to g. things going or started** faire démarrer les choses. **2** *vi* (*go*) aller; (*arrive*) arriver (**to** à); (*become*) devenir, se faire; **to g. caught/run over/etc** se faire prendre/écraser/*etc*; **to g. married** se marier; **to g. dressed/washed** s'habiller/se laver; **where have you got** *or* **Am gotten to?** où en es-tu?; **you've got to stay** (*must*) tu dois rester; **to g. to do** (*succeed in doing*) parvenir à faire; **to g. working** se mettre à travailler. ■ **to g. about** *or* **(a)round** *vi* se déplacer; (*of news*) circuler; **to g. across** *vt* (*road*) traverser; (*person*) faire traverser; (*message*) communiquer; – *vi* traverser; (*of speaker*) se faire comprendre (**to** de); **to g. across to s.o. that** faire comprendre à qn que; **to g. along** *vi* (*leave*) se sauver; (*manage*) se débrouiller; (*progress*) avancer; (*be on good terms*) s'entendre (**with** avec); **to g. at** *vt* (*reach*) parvenir à, atteindre; (*taunt*) s'en prendre à; **what is he getting at?** où veut-il en venir?; **to g. away** *vi* (*leave*) partir, s'en aller; (*escape*) s'échapper; **there's no getting away from it** il faut le reconnaître, c'est comme ça. ◆**getaway** *n* (*escape*) fuite *f*; **to g. back** *vt* (*recover*) récupérer; (*replace*) remettre; – *vi* (*return*) revenir, retourner; **to g. back at, g. one's own back at** (*punish*) se venger de; **g. back!** (*move back*) reculez!; **to g. by** *vi* (*pass*) passer; (*manage*) se débrouiller; **to g. down** *vi* (*go down*) descendre (**from** de); – *vt* (*bring down*) descendre (**from** de); (*write*) noter; (*depress*) *Fam* déprimer; **to g. down to** (*task, work*) se mettre à; **to g. in** *vt* (*bicycle, washing etc*) rentrer; (*buy*) acheter; (*summon*) faire venir; – *vi* (*enter*) entrer; (*come home*) rentrer; (*enter vehicle or train*) monter; (*of plane, train*) arriver; (*of candidate*) *Pol* être élu; **to g. into** *vt* entrer dans; (*vehicle, train*) monter dans;

(*habit*) prendre; **to g. into bed/a rage** se mettre au lit/en colère; **to g. into trouble** avoir des ennuis; **to g. off** *vi* (*leave*) partir; (*from vehicle or train*) descendre (**from** de); (*escape*) s'en tirer; (*finish work*) sortir; (*be acquitted*) *Jur* être acquitté; – *vt* (*remove*) enlever; (*despatch*) expédier; *Jur* faire acquitter (**qn**); **to g. off (from) a chair** se lever d'une chaise; **to g. off doing** *Fam* se dispenser de faire; **to g. on** *vt* (*shoes, clothes*) mettre; (*bus, train*) monter dans; – *vi* (*progress*) marcher, avancer; (*continue*) continuer; (*succeed*) réussir; (*enter bus or train*) monter; (*be on good terms*) s'entendre (**with** avec); **how are you getting on?** comment ça va?; **to g. on to s.o.** (*telephone*) toucher qn, contacter qn; **to g. on with** (*task*) continuer; **to g. out** *vi* sortir; (*from vehicle or train*) descendre (**from,** *of* **de**); **to g. out of** (*obligation*) échapper à; (*trouble*) se tirer de; (*habit*) perdre; – *vt* (*remove*) enlever; (*bring out*) sortir (*qch*), faire sortir (*qn*); **to g. over** *vt* (*road*) traverser; (*obstacle*) surmonter; (*fence*) franchir; (*illness*) se remettre de; (*surprise*) revenir de; (*ideas*) communiquer; **let's g. it over with** finissons-en; – *vi* (*cross*) traverser; **to g. round** *vt* (*obstacle*) contourner; (*person*) entortiller; – *vi* se déplacer; **to g. round to doing** en venir à faire; **to g. through** *vi* (*pass*) passer; (*finish*) finir; (*pass exam*) être reçu; **to g. through to s.o.** se faire comprendre de qn; (*on the telephone*) contacter qn; – *vt* (*hole etc*) passer par; (*task, meal*) venir à bout de; (*exam*) être reçu à; **g. me through to your boss** (*on the telephone*) passe-moi ton patron; **to g. together** *vi* (*of people*) se rassembler. ◆**g.-together** *n* réunion *f*; **to g. up** *vi* (*rise*) se lever (**from** de); **to g. up to** (*in book*) en arriver à; (*mischief, trouble etc*) faire; – *vt* (*ladder, stairs etc*) monter; (*party, group*) organiser; **to g. sth up** (*bring up*) monter qch. ◆**g.-up** *n* (*clothes*) *Fam* accoutrement *m*.

geyser ['gi:zər] *n* **1** (*water heater*) chauffe-eau *m inv.* **2** *Geol* geyser *m.*

Ghana ['gɑ:nə] *n* Ghana *m.*

ghastly ['gɑ:stlɪ] *a* (*-ier, -iest*) (*pale*) blème, pâle; (*horrible*) affreux.

gherkin ['gɜ:kɪn] *n* cornichon *m.*

ghetto ['getəʊ] *n* (*pl* -os) ghetto *m.*

ghost [gəʊst] *n* fantôme *m*; **not the g. of a chance** pas l'ombre d'une chance; – *a* (*story*) de fantômes; (*ship*) fantôme; (*town*) mort. ◆**-ly** *a* spectral.

ghoulish ['gu:lɪʃ] *a* morbide.

giant ['dʒaɪənt] n géant m; — a géant, gigantesque; (steps) de géant; (packet etc) Com géant.

gibberish ['dʒɪbərɪʃ] n baragouin m.

gibe [dʒaɪb] vi railler; **to g. at** railler; — n raillerie f.

giblets ['dʒɪblɪts] npl (of fowl) abats mpl.

giddy ['gɪdɪ] a (-ier, -iest) (heights) vertigineux; **to feel g.** avoir le vertige; **to make g.** donner le vertige à. ◆**giddiness** n vertige m.

gift [gɪft] n cadeau m; (talent) & Jur don m; **g. voucher** chèque-cadeau m. ◆**gifted** a doué (with de, for pour). ◆**giftwrapped** a en paquet-cadeau.

gig [gɪg] n Mus Fam engagement m, séance f.

gigantic [dʒaɪˈgæntɪk] a gigantesque.

giggle ['gɪg(ə)l] vi rire (sottement); — n petit rire m sot; **to have the giggles** avoir le fou rire.

gild [gɪld] vt dorer. ◆**gilt** a doré; — n dorure f.

gills [gɪlz] npl (of fish) ouïes fpl.

gimmick ['gɪmɪk] n (trick, object) truc m.

gin [dʒɪn] n (drink) gin m.

ginger ['dʒɪndʒər] **1** a (hair) roux. **2** n Bot Culin gingembre m; **g. beer** boisson f gazeuse au gingembre. ◆**gingerbread** n pain m d'épice.

gingerly ['dʒɪndʒəlɪ] adv avec précaution.

gipsy ['dʒɪpsɪ] n bohémien, -ienne mf; (Central European) Tsigane mf; — a (music) tsigane.

giraffe [dʒɪˈrɑːf, dʒɪˈræf] n girafe f.

girder ['gɜːdər] n (metal beam) poutre f.

girdle ['gɜːd(ə)l] n (belt) ceinture f; (corset) gaine f.

girl [gɜːl] n (jeune) fille f; (daughter) fille f; (servant) bonne f; (sweetheart) Fam petite amie f; **English g.** jeune Anglaise f; **g. guide** éclaireuse f. ◆**girlfriend** n amie f; (of boy) petite amie f. ◆**girlish** a de (jeune) fille.

girth [gɜːθ] n (measure) circonférence f; (of waist) tour m.

gist [dʒɪst] n **to get the g. of** comprendre l'essentiel de.

give [gɪv] vt (pt gave, pp given) donner (to à); (help, support) prêter; (gesture, pleasure) faire; (a sigh) pousser; (a look) jeter; (a blow) porter; **g. me** York 234 passez-moi le 234 à York; **she doesn't g. a damn** Fam elle s'en fiche; **to g. way** (yield, break) céder (to à); (collapse) s'effondrer; Aut céder la priorité (to à); — n (in fabric etc) élasticité f. ■ **to g. away** vt (prize) distribuer; (money) donner; (facts) révéler; (betray) trahir (qn);

to g. back vt (return) rendre; **to g. in** vi (surrender) céder (to à); — vt (hand in) remettre; **to g. off** vt (smell, heat) dégager; **to g. out** vt distribuer; — vi (of supplies, patience) s'épuiser; (of engine) rendre l'âme; **to g. over** vt (devote) donner, consacrer (to à); **to g. oneself over to** s'adonner à; — vi **g. over!** (stop) Fam arrête!; **to g. up** vi abandonner, renoncer; — vt abandonner, renoncer à; (seat) céder (to à); (prisoner) livrer (to à); (patient) condamner; **to g. up smoking** cesser de fumer. ◆**given** a (fixed) donné; **to be g. to doing** (prone to do) avoir l'habitude de faire; **g. your age** (in view of) étant donné votre âge; **g. that** étant donné que. ◆**giver** n donateur, -trice mf.

glacier ['glæsɪər, Am 'gleɪʃər] n glacier m.

glad [glæd] a (person) content (of, about de). ◆**gladden** vt réjouir. ◆**gladly** adv (willingly) volontiers.

glade [gleɪd] n clairière f.

gladiolus, pl **-i** [glædɪˈəʊləs, -aɪ] n Bot glaïeul m.

glamour ['glæmər] n (charm) enchantement m; (splendour) éclat m. ◆**glamorize** vt montrer sous un jour séduisant. ◆**glamorous** a séduisant.

glance [glɑːns] **1** n coup m d'œil; — vi jeter un coup d'œil (at à sur). **2** vt **to g. off sth** (of bullet) ricocher sur qch.

gland [glænd] n glande f. ◆**glandular** a **g. fever** Med mononucléose f infectieuse.

glar/e [gleər] **1** vi **to g. at s.o.** foudroyer qn (du regard); — n regard m furieux. **2** vi (of sun) briller d'un éclat aveuglant; — n éclat m aveuglant; (eyes) furieux; (injustice) flagrant; **a g. mistake** une faute grossière.

glass [glɑːs] n verre m; (mirror) miroir m, glace f; pl (spectacles) lunettes fpl; **a pane of g.** une vitre, un carreau; — a (door) vitré; (industry) du verre. ◆**glassful** n (plein) verre m.

glaze [gleɪz] vt (door) vitrer; (pottery) vernisser; (paper) glacer; — n (on pottery) vernis m; (on paper) glacé m. ◆**glazier** n vitrier m.

gleam [gliːm] n lueur f; — vi (re)luire.

glean [gliːn] vt (grain, information etc) glaner.

glee [gliː] n joie f. ◆**gleeful** a joyeux.

glen [glen] n vallon m.

glib [glɪb] a (person) qui a la parole facile; (speech) facile, peu sincère. ◆**-ly** adv (say) peu sincèrement.

glid/e [glaɪd] vi glisser; (of vehicle) avancer

silencieusement; *(of aircraft, bird)* planer. ◆**—ing** *n Av Sp* vol *m* à voile. ◆**—er** *n Av* planeur *m*.

glimmer ['glimər] *vi* luire (faiblement); – *n (light, of hope etc)* (faible) lueur *f*.

glimpse [glimps] *n* aperçu *m*; **to catch** *or* **get a g. of** entrevoir.

glint [glint] *vi (shine with flashes)* briller; – *n* éclair *m*; *(in eye)* étincelle *f*.

glisten ['glis(ə)n] *vi (of wet surface)* briller; *(of water)* miroiter.

glitter ['glitər] *vi* scintiller, briller; – *n* scintillement *m*.

gloat [gləʊt] *vi* jubiler (**over** à la vue de).

globe [gləʊb] *n* globe *m*. ◆**global** *a (comprehensive)* global; *(universal)* universel, mondial.

gloom [gluːm] *n (darkness)* obscurité *f*; *(sadness) Fig* tristesse *f*. ◆**gloomy** *a (-ier, -iest) (dark, dismal)* sombre, triste; *(sad) Fig* triste; *(pessimistic)* pessimiste.

glory ['glɔːrɪ] *n* gloire *f*; **in all one's g.** *Fig* dans toute sa splendeur; **to be in one's g.** *(very happy) Fam* être à son affaire; – *vi* **to g. in** se glorifier de. ◆**glorify** *vt (praise)* glorifier; **it's a glorified barn/etc** ce n'est guère plus qu'une grange/*etc*. ◆**glorious** *a (full of glory)* glorieux; *(splendid, enjoyable)* magnifique.

gloss [glɒs] **1** *n (shine)* brillant *m*; **g. paint** peinture *f* brillante; **g. finish** brillant *m*. **2** *n (note)* glose *f*, commentaire *m*. **3** *vt* **to g. over** *(minimize)* glisser sur; *(conceal)* dissimuler. ◆**glossy** *a (-ier, -iest)* brillant; *(paper)* glacé; *(magazine)* de luxe.

glossary ['glɒsərɪ] *n* glossaire *m*.

glove [glʌv] *n* gant *m*; **g. compartment** *Aut (shelf)* vide-poches *m inv*; *(enclosed)* boîte *f* à gants. ◆**gloved** *a* **a g. hand** une main gantée.

glow [gləʊ] *vi (of sky, fire)* rougeoyer; *(of lamp)* luire; *(of eyes, person) Fig* rayonner (**with** de); – *n* rougeoiement *m*; *(of colour)* éclat *m*; *(of lamp)* lueur *f*. ◆**—ing** *a (account, terms etc)* très favorable, enthousiaste. ◆**glow-worm** *n* ver *m* luisant.

glucose ['gluːkəʊs] *n* glucose *m*.

glue [gluː] *n* colle *f*; – *vt* coller (**to, on** à). ◆**glued** *a* **to g.** *(eyes) Fam* fixés *or* rivés sur; **to be g. to** *(television) Fam* être cloué devant.

glum [glʌm] *a (glummer, glummest)* triste.

glut [glʌt] *vt (-tt-) (overfill)* rassasier; *(market)* surcharger (**with** de); – *n (of produce, oil etc) Com* surplus *m* (**of** de).

glutton ['glʌt(ə)n] *n* glouton, -onne *mf*; **g. for work** bourreau *m* de travail; **g.**

for punishment masochiste *mf*. ◆**gluttony** *n* gloutonnerie *f*.

glycerin(e) ['glisəriːn] *n* glycérine *f*.

GMT [dʒiːem'tiː] *abbr (Greenwich Mean Time)* GMT.

gnarled [nɑːld] *a* noueux.

gnash [næʃ] *vt* **to g. one's teeth** grincer des dents.

gnat [næt] *n (insect)* cousin *m*.

gnaw [nɔː] *vti* **to g. (at)** ronger.

gnome [nəʊm] *n (little man)* gnome *m*.

go [gəʊ] **1** *vi (3rd person sing pres t* **goes**; *pt* **went**; *pp* **gone**; *pres p* **going**) aller (**to** à, **from** de); *(depart)* partir, s'en aller; *(disappear)* disparaître; *(be sold)* se vendre; *(function)* marcher, fonctionner; *(progress)* aller, marcher; *(become)* devenir; *(be)* être; *(of time)* passer; *(of hearing, strength)* baisser; *(of rope)* céder; *(of fuse)* sauter; *(of material)* s'user; **to go well/badly** *(of event)* se passer bien/mal; **she's going to do** *(is about to, intends to)* elle va faire; **it's all gone** *(finished)* il n'y en a plus; **to go and get** *(fetch)* aller chercher; **to go and see** aller voir; **to go riding/sailing/on a trip/etc** faire du cheval/de la voile/un voyage/*etc*; **to let go of** lâcher; **to go to** *(doctor, lawyer etc)* aller voir; **to get things going** faire démarrer les choses; **is there any beer going?** *(available)* y a-t-il de la bière?; **to go to show that …** ça sert à montrer que …; **two hours/etc to go** *(still left)* encore deux heures/*etc*. **2** *n (pl* **goes**) *(energy)* dynamisme *m*; *(attempt)* coup *m*; **to have a go at** *(doing)* sth essayer de (faire) qch; **at one go** d'un seul coup; **on the go** en mouvement, actif; **to make a go of** *(make a success of)* réussir. ■ **to go about** *or* **(a)round** *vi* se déplacer; *(of news, rumour)* circuler; **to go about** *vt (one's duties etc)* s'occuper de; **to know how to go about it** savoir s'y prendre; **to go across** *vt* traverser; – *vi (cross)* traverser; *(go)* aller (**to** à); **to go across to s.o.('s)** faire un saut chez qn; **to go after** *vt (follow)* suivre; *(job)* viser; **to go against** *vt (of result)* être défavorable à; *(s.o.'s wishes)* aller contre; *(harm)* nuire à; **to go ahead** *vi* aller de l'avant; **to go ahead with** *(plan etc)* poursuivre; **go ahead!** allez-y! ◆**go-ahead** *a* dynamique; – *n* **to get the go-ahead** avoir le feu vert; **to go along** *vi* aller, avancer; **to go along with** *(agree)* être d'accord avec; **to go away** *vi* partir, s'en aller; **to go back** *vi* retourner, revenir; *(in time)* remonter; *(retreat, step back)* reculer; **to go back on** *(promise)* revenir sur; **to go by** *vi* passer; – *vt (act according to)* se fonder sur; (*judge from*) juger d'après; (*instruction*) suivre; **to go down** *vi* descendre; (*fall down*) tomber; (*of ship*) couler; (*of sun*) se coucher; (*of storm*) s'apaiser; (*of temperature, price etc*) baisser; (*of tyre*) se dégonfler; **to go down well** (*of speech etc*) être bien reçu; **to go down with** (*illness*) attraper; – *vt* **to go down the stairs/street** descendre l'escalier/la rue; **to go for** *vt* (*fetch*) aller chercher; (*attack*) attaquer; (*like*) *Fam* aimer beaucoup; **to go forward(s)** *vi* avancer; **to go in** *vi* (r)entrer; (*of sun*) se cacher; **to go in for** (*exam*) se présenter à; (*hobby, sport*) faire; (*career*) entrer dans; (*like*) *Fam* aimer beaucoup; – *vt* **to go in a room/***etc* entrer dans une pièce/*etc*; **to go into** *vt* (*room etc*) entrer dans; (*question*) examiner; **to go off** *vi* (*leave*) partir; (*go bad*) se gâter; (*of effect*) passer; (*of alarm*) se déclencher; (*of event*) se passer; – *vt* (*one's food*) perdre le goût de; **to go on** *vi* continuer (**doing** à faire); (*travel*) poursuivre sa route; (*happen*) se passer; (*last*) durer; (*of time*) passer; **to go on at** (*nag*) *Fam* s'en prendre à; **to go on about** *Fam* parler sans cesse de; **to go out** *vi* sortir; (*of light, fire*) s'éteindre; (*of tide*) descendre; (*of newspaper, product*) être distribué (**to** à); (*depart*) partir; **to go out to work** travailler (au dehors); **to go over** *vi* (*go*) aller (**to** à); (*cross over*) traverser; (*to enemy*) passer (**to** à); – *vt* examiner; (*speech*) revoir; (*in one's mind*) repasser; (*touch up*) retoucher; (*overhaul*) réviser (*véhicule, montre*); **to go round** *vi* (*turn*) tourner; (*make a detour*) faire le tour; **be sufficient*) suffire; **to go round to s.o.('s)** passer chez qn, faire un saut chez qn; **enough to go round** assez pour tout le monde; – *vt* **to go round a corner** tourner un coin; **to go through** *vi* passer; (*of deal*) être conclu; – *vt* (*undergo, endure*) subir; (*examine*) examiner; (*search*) fouiller; (*spend*) dépenser; (*wear out*) user; (*perform*) accomplir; **to go through with** (*carry out*) réaliser, aller jusqu'au bout de; **to go under** *vi* (*of ship, person, firm*) couler; **to go up** *vi* monter; (*explode*) sauter; – *vt* **to go up the stairs/street** monter l'escalier/la rue; **to go without** *vi* se passer de.

goad [gəʊd] *n* aiguillon *m*; – *vt* **to g. (on)** aiguillonner.

goal [gəʊl] *n* but *m*. ◆**goalkeeper** *n Fb* gardien *m* de but, goal *m*. ◆**goalpost** *n Fb* poteau *m* de but.

goat [gəʊt] *n* chèvre *f*; **to get s.o.'s g.** *Fam*

énerver qn. ◆**goa'tee** *n* (*beard*) barbiche *f*.

gobble [ˈgɒb(ə)l] *vt* **to g. (up)** engloutir, engouffrer.

go-between [ˈgəʊbitwiːn] *n* intermédiaire *mf*.

goblet [ˈgɒblit] *n* verre *m* à pied.

goblin [ˈgɒblin] *n* (*evil spirit*) lutin *m*.

god [gɒd] *n* dieu *m*; G. Dieu *m*; **the gods** *Th Fam* le poulailler. ◆**g.-fearing** *a* croyant. ◆**g.-forsaken** *a* (*place*) perdu, misérable. ◆**goddess** *n* déesse *f*. ◆**godly** *a* dévot.

godchild [ˈgɒdtʃaild] *n* (*pl* -**children**) filleul, -eule *mf*. ◆**goddaughter** *n* filleule *f*. ◆**godfather** *n* parrain *m*. ◆**godmother** *n* marraine *f*. ◆**godson** *n* filleul *m*.

goddam(n) [ˈgɒdæm] *a Am Fam* foutu.

godsend [ˈgɒdsend] *n* aubaine *f*.

goes [gəʊz] *see go* 1.

goggle [ˈgɒg(ə)l] **1** *vi* **to g. at** regarder en roulant de gros yeux. **2** *npl* (*spectacles*) lunettes *fpl* (protectrices). ◆**g.-'eyed** *a* aux yeux saillants.

going [ˈgəʊiŋ] **1** *n* (*departure*) départ *m*; (*speed*) allure *f*; (*conditions*) conditions *fpl*; **it's hard g.** c'est difficile. **2** *a* **the g. price** le prix pratiqué (**for** pour); **a g. concern** une entreprise qui marche bien. ◆**goings-'on** *npl Pej* activités *fpl*.

go-kart [ˈgəʊkɑːt] *n Sp* kart *m*.

gold [gəʊld] *n* or *m*; – *a* (*watch etc*) en or; (*coin, dust*) d'or. ◆**golden** *a* (*made of gold*) d'or; (*in colour*) doré, d'or; (*opportunity*) excellent. ◆**goldmine** *n* mine *f* d'or. ◆**gold-'plated** *a* plaqué or. ◆**goldsmith** *n* orfèvre *m*.

goldfinch [ˈgəʊldfintʃ] *n* (*bird*) chardonneret *m*.

goldfish [ˈgəʊldfiʃ] *n* poisson *m* rouge.

golf [gɒlf] *n* golf *m*. ◆**golfer** *n* golfeur, -euse *mf*.

golly [ˈgɒli] *int* (**by**) **g.!** *Fam* mince (alors)!

gondola [ˈgɒndələ] *n* (*boat*) gondole *f*. ◆**gondo'lier** *n* gondolier *m*.

gone [gɒn] *see go* 1; – *a* **it's g.** two *Fam* il est plus de deux heures. ◆**goner** *n* **to be a g.** *Sl* être fichu.

gong [gɒŋ] *n* gong *m*.

good [gʊd] *a* (*better, best*) bon; (*kind*) gentil; (*weather*) beau; (*pleasant*) bon, agréable; (*well-behaved*) sage; **be g. enough to ...** ayez la gentillesse de ...; **my g. friend** mon cher ami; **a g. chap** *or* **fellow** un brave type; **g. and strong** bien fort; **a g.** (**long**) **walk** une bonne promenade; **very g.!** (*all right*) très bien!; **that's g. of you** c'est gentil de ta part; **to feel g.** se sentir bien;

that isn't g. enough (bad) ça ne va pas; (not sufficient) ça ne suffit pas; it's g. for us ça nous fait du bien; g. at (French etc) Sch bon or fort en; to be g. with (children) savoir s'y prendre avec; it's a g. thing (that)... heureusement que...; a g. many, a g. deal (of) beaucoup (de); as g. as (almost) pratiquement; g. afternoon, g. morning bonjour; (on leaving someone) au revoir; g. evening bonsoir; g. night bonsoir; (before going to bed) bonne nuit; to make g. vi (succeed) réussir; — vt (loss) compenser; (damage) réparer; G. Friday Vendredi m Saint; — n (virtue) bien m; for her g. pour son bien; there's some g. in him il y a du bon; it's no g. crying/shouting/etc ça ne sert à rien de pleurer/crier/etc; that's no g. (worthless) ça ne vaut rien; (bad) ça ne va pas; what's the g.? à quoi bon?; for g. (to leave, give up etc) pour de bon. ◆g.-for-'nothing a & n propre à rien (mf). ◆g.-'humoured a de bonne humeur. ◆g.-'looking a beau. ◆goodness n bonté f; my g.! mon Dieu! ◆good'will n bonne volonté f; (zeal) zèle m.

goodbye [gud'bai] int & n au revoir (m inv).

goodly ['gudli] a (size, number) grand.

goods [gudz] npl marchandises fpl; (articles for sale) articles mpl.

gooey ['gu:i] a Fam gluant, poisseux.

goof [gu:f] vi to g. (up) (blunder) Am faire une gaffe.

goon [gu:n] n Fam idiot, -ote mf.

goose, pl geese [gu:s, gi:s] n oie f; g. pimples or bumps chair f de poule. ◆gooseflesh n chair f de poule.

gooseberry ['guzbəri, Am 'gu:sberi] n groseille f à maquereau.

gorge [gɔ:dʒ] 1 n (ravine) gorge f. 2 vt (food) engloutir; to g. oneself s'empiffrer (on de).

gorgeous ['gɔ:dʒəs] a magnifique.

gorilla [gə'rilə] n gorille m.

gormless ['gɔ:mləs] a Fam stupide.

gorse [gɔ:s] n inv ajonc(s) m(pl).

gory ['gɔ:ri] a (-ier, -iest) (bloody) sanglant; (details) Fig horrible.

gosh! [gɒʃ] int Fam mince (alors)!

go-slow [gəu'sləu] n (strike) grève f perlée.

gospel ['gɒspəl] n évangile m.

gossip ['gɒsip] n (talk) bavardage(s) m(pl); (malicious) cancan(s) m(pl); (person) commère f; g. column Journ échos mpl; — vi bavarder; (maliciously) cancaner. ◆—ing a, ◆—gossipy a bavard, cancanier.

got, Am gotten [gɒt, 'gɒt(ə)n] see get.

Gothic ['gɒθik] a & n gothique (m).

gouge [gaudʒ] vt to g. out (eye) crever.

goulash ['gu:læʃ] n Culin goulash f.

gourmet ['guəmei] n gourmet m.

gout [gaut] n Med goutte f.

govern ['gʌvən] vt (rule) gouverner; (city) administrer; (business) gérer; (emotion) maîtriser, gouverner; (influence) déterminer; — vi Pol gouverner; governing body conseil m d'administration. ◆governess n gouvernante f. ◆government n gouvernement m; (local) administration f; — a (department, policy etc) gouvernemental; (loan) d'État. ◆govern'mental a gouvernemental. ◆governor n gouverneur m; (of school) administrateur, -trice mf; (of prison) directeur, -trice mf.

gown [gaun] n (dress) robe f; (of judge, lecturer) toge f.

GP [dʒi:'pi:] n abbr (general practitioner) médecin m) généraliste m.

GPO [dʒi:pi:'əu] abbr (General Post Office) = PTT fpl.

grab [græb] vt (-bb-) to g. (hold of) saisir, agripper; to g. sth from s.o. arracher qch à qn.

grace [greis] 1 n (charm, goodwill etc) Rel grâce f; (extension of time) délai m de grâce; to say g. dire le bénédicité. 2 vt (adorn) orner; (honour) honorer (with de). ◆graceful a gracieux. ◆gracious a (kind) aimable, gracieux (to envers); (elegant) élégant; good g.! Fam bonté divine!

gradation [grə'deif(ə)n, Am grei'deif(ə)n] n gradation f.

grade [greid] n catégorie f; Mil Math grade m; (of milk) qualité f; (of eggs) calibre m; (level) niveau m; (mark) Sch note f; (class) Am Sch classe f; g. school Am école f primaire; g. crossing Am passage m à niveau; — vt (classify) classer; (colours etc) graduer; (paper) Sch Univ noter.

gradient ['greidiənt] n (slope) inclinaison f.

gradual ['grædʒuəl] a progressif, graduel; (slope) doux. ◆—ly adv progressivement, peu à peu.

graduat/e ['grædʒueit] vi Univ obtenir son diplôme; Am Sch obtenir son baccalauréat; to g. from sortir de; — vt (mark with degrees) graduer; — ['grædʒuət] n diplômé, -ée mf, licencié, -ée mf. ◆—ed a (tube etc) gradué; to be g. Am Sch Univ = to graduate vi. ◆gradu'ation n Univ remise f des diplômes.

graffiti [grə'fi:ti] npl graffiti mpl.

graft [gra:ft] n Med Bot greffe f; — vt greffer (on to à).

grain [grein] n (seed, particle) grain m;

(*seeds*) grain(s) *m* (*pl*); (*in cloth*) fil *m*; (*in wood*) fibre *f*; (*in leather, paper*) grain *m*; (*of truth*) Fig once *f*.

gram(me) ['græm] *n* gramme *m*.

grammar ['græmər] *n* grammaire *f*; **g. school** lycée *m*. ◆**gra'mmatical** *a* grammatical.

gramophone ['græməfəun] *n* phonographe *m*.

granary ['grænərɪ] *n* Agr grenier *m*; **g. loaf** pain *m* complet.

grand [grænd] **1** *a* (**-er, -est**) magnifique, grand; (*style*) grandiose; (*concert, duke*) grand; (*piano*) à queue; (*wonderful*) Fam magnifique. **2** *n inv Am Sl* mille dollars *mpl*; *Br Sl* mille livres *fpl*. ◆**grandeur** ['grændʒər] *n* magnificence *f*; (*of person, country*) grandeur *f*.

grandchild ['græntʃaɪld] *n* (*pl* **-children**) petit(e)-enfant *mf*. ◆**grand(d)ad** *n Fam* pépé *m*, papi *m*. ◆**granddaughter** *n* petite-fille *f*. ◆**grandfather** *n* grand-père *m*. ◆**grandmother** *n* grand-mère *f*. ◆**grandparents** *npl* grands-parents *mpl*. ◆**grandson** *n* petit-fils *m*.

grandstand ['grændstænd] *n Sp* tribune *f*.

grange [greɪndʒ] *n* (*house*) manoir *m*.

granite ['grænɪt] *n* granit(e) *m*.

granny ['grænɪ] *n Fam* mamie *f*.

grant [graːnt] **1** *vt* accorder (**to** à); (*request*) accéder à; (*prayer*) exaucer; (*admit*) admettre (**that** que); **to take for granted** (*event*) considérer comme allant de soi; (*person*) considérer comme faisant partie du décor; **I take (it) for granted that ...** je présume que ... . **2** *n* subvention *f*, allocation *f*; *Univ* bourse *f*.

granule ['grænjuːl] *n* granule *m*. ◆**granulated** *a* **g. sugar** sucre *m* cristallisé.

grape [greɪp] *n* grain *m* de raisin; *pl* le raisin, les raisins *mpl*; **to eat grapes** manger du raisin *or* des raisins; **g. harvest** vendange *f*. ◆**grapefruit** *n* pamplemousse *m*. ◆**grapevine** *n* **on the g.** Fig par le téléphone arabe.

graph [græf, grɑːf] *n* graphique *m*, courbe *f*; **g. paper** papier *m* millimétré.

graphic ['græfɪk] *a* graphique; (*description*) Fig explicite, vivant. ◆**graphically** *adv* (*to describe*) explicitement.

grapple ['græp(ə)l] *vi* **to g. with** (*person, problem etc*) se colleter avec.

grasp [graːsp] *vt* (*seize, understand*) saisir; – *n* (*firm hold*) prise *f*; (*understanding*) compréhension *f*; (*knowledge*) connaissance *f*; **to have a strong g.** (*strength of hand*) avoir de la poigne; **within s.o.'s g.**

(*reach*) à la portée de qn. ◆**—ing** *a* (*greedy*) rapace.

grass [grɑːs] *n* herbe *f*; (*lawn*) gazon *m*; **the g. roots** Pol la base. ◆**grasshopper** *n* sauterelle *f*. ◆**grassland** *n* prairie *f*. ◆**grassy** *a* herbeux.

grat/e [greɪt] **1** *n* (*for fireplace*) grille *f* de foyer. **2** *vt* Culin râper. ◆**—ing** *a* grincer (**on** sur); **to g. on the ears** écorcher les oreilles; **to g. on s.o.'s nerves** taper sur les nerfs de qn. ◆**—ing 1** *a* (*sound*) grinçant; Fig irritant. **2** *n* (*bars*) grille *f*. ◆**—er** *n Culin* râpe *f*.

grateful ['greɪtfəl] *a* reconnaissant (**to** à, **for** de); (*words, letter*) de remerciement; (*friend, attitude*) plein de reconnaissance; **I'm g. (to you) for your help** je vous suis reconnaissant de votre aide; **I'd be g. if you'd be quieter** j'aimerais bien que tu fasses moins de bruit; **g. thanks** mes sincères remerciements. ◆**—ly** *adv* avec reconnaissance.

gratif/y ['grætɪfaɪ] *vt* (*whim*) satisfaire; **to g. s.o.** faire plaisir à qn. ◆**—ied** *a* très content (**with** *or* **at sth** de qch, **to do** de faire). ◆**—ying** *a* très satisfaisant; **it's g. to ... ça fait plaisir de ... . ◆gratifi'cation** *n* satisfaction *f*.

gratis ['grætɪs, 'greɪtɪs] *adv* gratis.

gratitude ['grætɪtjuːd] *n* reconnaissance *f*, gratitude *f* (**for** de).

gratuitous [grə'tjuːɪtəs] *a* (*act etc*) gratuit.

gratuity [grə'tjuːɪtɪ] *n* (*tip*) pourboire *m*.

grave[1] [greɪv] *n* tombe *f*; **g. digger** fossoyeur *m*. ◆**gravestone** *n* pierre *f* tombale. ◆**graveyard** *n* cimetière *m*; **auto g.** Am Fam cimetière *m* de voitures.

grave[2] [greɪv] *a* (**-er, -est**) (*serious*) grave. ◆**—ly** *adv* gravement; (*concerned, displeased*) extrêmement.

gravel ['græv(ə)l] *n* gravier *m*.

gravitate ['grævɪteɪt] *vi* **to g. towards** (*be drawn towards*) être attiré vers; (*move towards*) se diriger vers. ◆**gravi'tation** *n* gravitation *f*.

gravity ['grævɪtɪ] *n* **1** (*seriousness*) gravité *f*. **2** Phys pesanteur *f*, gravité *f*.

gravy ['greɪvɪ] *n* jus *m* de viande.

gray [greɪ] *Am* = **grey**.

graze [greɪz] **1** *vi* (*of cattle*) paître. **2** *vt* (*scrape*) écorcher; (*touch lightly*) frôler, effleurer; – *n* (*wound*) écorchure *f*.

grease [griːs] *n* graisse *f*; – *vt* graisser. ◆**greaseproof** *a* & *n* **g.** (**paper**) papier *m* sulfurisé. ◆**greasy** *a* (**-ier, -iest**) graisseux; (*hair*) gras; (*road*) glissant.

great [greɪt] *a* (**-er, -est**) grand; (*effort, heat,*

parcel) gros, grand; (*excellent*) magnifique, merveilleux; **g. at** (*English, tennis etc*) doué pour; **a g. deal** *or* **number** (**of**), **a g. many** beaucoup (de); **a g. opinion of** une haute opinion de; **a very g. age** un âge très avancé; **the greatest team**/*etc* (*best*) la meilleure équipe/*etc*; **Greater London** le grand Londres. ◆**g.-'grandfather** *n* arrière-grand-père *m*. ◆**g.-'grandmother** *n* arrière-grand-mère *f*. ◆**greatly** *adv* (*much*) beaucoup; (*very*) très, bien; **I g. prefer** je préfère de beaucoup. ◆**greatness** *n* (*in size, importance*) grandeur *f*; (*in degree*) intensité *f*.

Great Britain [greɪt'brɪt(ə)n] *n* Grande-Bretagne *f*.

Greece [griːs] *n* Grèce *f*.

greed [griːd] *n* avidité *f* (**for** de); (*for food*) gourmandise *f*. ◆**greed/y** *a* (**-ier, -iest**) avide (**for** de); (*for food*) glouton, gourmand. ◆**—ily** *adv* avidement; (*to eat*) gloutonnement. ◆**—iness** *n* = **greed**.

green [griːn] *a* (**-er, -est**) vert; (*pale*) blême, vert; (*immature*) *Fig* inexpérimenté, naïf; **to turn** *or* **go g.** verdir; **the g. belt** (*land*) la ceinture verte; **the g. light** *Fig* le (feu) vert; **to have g. fingers** *or* *Am* **a g. thumb** avoir la main verte; **g. with envy** *Fig* vert de jalousie; – *n* (*colour*) vert *m*; (*lawn*) pelouse *f*; (*village square*) place *f* gazonnée; *pl Culin* légumes *mpl* verts. ◆**greenery** *n* (*plants, leaves*) verdure *f*. ◆**greenfly** *n* puceron *m* (des plantes). ◆**greengrocer** *n* marchand, -ande *mf* de légumes. ◆**greenhouse** *n* serre *f*. ◆**greenish** *a* verdâtre. ◆**greenness** *n* (*colour*) vert *m*; (*greenery*) verdure *f*.

greengage ['griːngeɪdʒ] *n* (*plum*) reine-claude *f*.

Greenland ['griːnlənd] *n* Groenland *m*.

greet [griːt] *vt* saluer, accueillir; **to g. s.o.** (*of sight*) s'offrir aux regards de qn. ◆**—ing** *n* salutation *f*; (*welcome*) accueil *m*; *pl* (*for birthday, festival*) vœux *mpl*; **send my greetings to...** envoie mon bon souvenir à...; **greetings card** carte *f* de vœux.

gregarious [grɪ'geərɪəs] *a* (*person*) sociable; (*instinct*) grégaire.

gremlin ['gremlɪn] *n Fam* petit diable *m*.

grenade [grə'neɪd] *n* (*bomb*) grenade *f*.

grew [gruː] *see* **grow**.

grey [greɪ] *a* (**-er, -est**) gris; (*outlook*) *Fig* sombre; **to be going g.** grisonner; – *vi* **to be greying** être grisonnant. ◆**g.-'haired** *a* aux cheveux gris. ◆**greyhound** *n* lévrier *m*. ◆**greyish** *a* grisâtre.

grid [grɪd] *n* (*grating*) grille *f*; (*system*) *El* réseau *m*; *Culin* gril *m*. ◆**gridiron** *n Culin* gril *m*.

griddle ['grɪd(ə)l] *n* (*on stove*) plaque *f* à griller.

grief [griːf] *n* chagrin *m*, douleur *f*; **to come to g.** avoir des ennuis; (*of driver, pilot etc*) avoir un accident; (*of plan*) échouer; **good g.!** ciel!, bon sang!

grieve [griːv] *vt* peiner, affliger; – *vi* s'affliger (**over** de); **to g. for s.o.** pleurer qn. ◆**grievance** *n* grief *m*; *pl* (*complaints*) doléances *fpl*.

grievous ['griːvəs] *a* (*serious*) très grave.

grill [grɪl] **1** *n* (*utensil*) gril *m*; (*dish*) grillade *f*; – *vti* griller. **2** *vt* (*question*) *Fam* cuisiner.

grille [grɪl] *n* (*metal bars*) grille *f*; (*radiator*) *g. Aut* calandre *f*.

grim [grɪm] *a* (**grimmer, grimmest**) sinistre; (*face*) sévère; (*truth*) brutal; (*bad*) *Fam* (*plutôt*) affreux; **a g. determination** une volonté inflexible. ◆**—ly** *adv* (*to look at*) sévèrement.

grimace ['grɪməs] *n* grimace *f*; – *vi* grimacer.

grime [graɪm] *n* saleté *f*. ◆**grimy** *a* (**-ier, -iest**) sale.

grin [grɪn] *vi* (**-nn-**) avoir un large sourire; (*with pain*) avoir un rictus; – *n* large sourire *m*; rictus *m*.

grind [graɪnd] **1** *vt* (*pt & pp* **ground**) moudre; (*blade, tool*) aiguiser; (*handle*) tourner; (*oppress*) *Fig* écraser; **to g. one's teeth** grincer des dents; – *vi* **to g. to a halt** s'arrêter (progressivement). **2** *n Fam* corvée *f*, travail *m* long et monotone. ◆**—ing** *a* (*poverty*) la misère noire. ◆**—er** *n* **coffee g.** moulin *m* à café.

grip [grɪp] *n* (**-pp-**) (*seize*) saisir; (*hold*) tenir serré; (*of story*) *Fig* empoigner (qn); **to g. the road** (*of tyres*) adhérer à la route; – *vi* (*of brakes*) mordre; – *n* (*hold*) prise *f*; (*hand clasp*) poigne *f*; **get a g. on yourself!** secoue-toi!; **to get to grips with** (*problem*) s'attaquer à; **in the g. of** en proie à. ◆**gripping** *a* (*book, film etc*) prenant.

gripe [graɪp] *vi* (*complain*) *Sl* rouspéter.

grisly ['grɪzlɪ] *a* (*gruesome*) horrible.

gristle ['grɪs(ə)l] *n Culin* cartilage *m*.

grit [grɪt] **1** *n* (*sand*) sable *m*; (*gravel*) gravillon *m*; – *vt* (**-tt-**) (*road*) sabler. **2** *n* (*pluck*) *Fam* cran *m*. **3** *vt* **to g. one's teeth** serrer les dents.

grizzle ['grɪz(ə)l] *vi Fam* pleurnicher. ◆**grizzly** *a* **1** (*child*) *Fam* pleurnicheur. **2** (*bear*) gris.

groan [grəʊn] *vi* (*with pain*) gémir;

(*complain*) grogner, gémir; − *n* gémissement *m*; grognement *m*.

grocer ['grəʊsər] *n* épicier, -ière *mf*; **grocer's (shop)** épicerie *f*; **◆grocery** *n* (*shop*) épicerie *f*; *pl* (*food*) épicerie *f*.

grog [grɒg] *n* (*drink*) grog *m*.

groggy ['grɒgɪ] *a* (**-ier, -iest**) (*weak*) faible; (*shaky on one's feet*) pas solide sur les jambes.

groin [grɔɪn] *n* Anat aine *f*.

groom [gruːm] **1** *n* (*bridegroom*) marié *m*. **2** *n* (*for horses*) lad *m*; − *vt* (*horse*) panser; **to g. s.o. for** (*job*) Fig préparer qn pour; **well groomed** (*person*) très soigné.

groove [gruːv] *n* (*for sliding door etc*) rainure *f*; (*in record*) sillon *m*.

grope [grəʊp] *vi* **to g. (about)** tâtonner; **to g. for** chercher à tâtons.

gross [grəʊs] **1** *a* (**-er, -est**) (*coarse*) grossier; (*error*) gros, grossier; (*injustice*) flagrant. **2** *a* (*weight, income*) Com brut; − *vt* faire une recette brute de. **3** *n* (*number*) grosse *f*. **◆-ly** *adv* grossièrement; (*very*) énormément, extrêmement.

grotesque [grəʊ'tesk] *a* (*ludicrous, strange*) grotesque; (*frightening*) monstrueux.

grotto ['grɒtəʊ] *n* (*pl* **-oes** or **-os**) grotte *f*.

grotty ['grɒtɪ] *a* (**-ier, -iest**) Fam affreux, moche.

ground[1] [graʊnd] *n* terre *f*, sol *m*; (*area for camping, football etc*) & Fig terrain *m*; (*estate*) terres *fpl*; (*earth*) El Am terre *f*, masse *f*; (*background*) fond *m*; *pl* (*reasons*) raisons *fpl*, motifs *mpl*; (*gardens*) parc *m*; **on the g.** (*lying etc*) par terre; **to lose g.** perdre du terrain; **g. floor** rez-de-chaussée *m inv*; **g. frost** gelée *f* blanche. **2** *vt* (*aircraft*) bloquer or retenir au sol. **◆-ing** *n* connaissances *fpl* de fond) (**in** en). **◆groundless** *a* sans fondement. **◆groundnut** *n* arachide *f*. **◆ground-sheet** *n* tapis *m* de sol. **◆groundswell** *n* lame *f* de fond. **◆groundwork** *n* préparation *f*.

ground[2] [graʊnd] *see* **grind 1**; − *a* (*coffee*) moulu; − *npl* (*coffee*) **grounds** marc *m* (de café).

group [gruːp] *n* groupe *m*; − *vt* **to g.** (**together**) grouper; − *vi* se grouper. **◆-ing** *n* (*group*) groupe *m*.

grouse [graʊs] **1** *n inv* (*bird*) coq *m* de bruyère. **2** *vi* (*complain*) Fam rouspéter.

grove [grəʊv] *n* bocage *m*.

grovel ['grɒv(ə)l] *vi* (**-ll-**, *Am* **-l-**) *Pej* ramper, s'aplatir (**to s.o.** devant qn).

grow [grəʊ] *vi* (*pt* **grew**, *pp* **grown**) pousser; (*of person*) grandir; (*of plant, hair*) pousser;

(*increase*) augmenter, grandir, croître; (*expand*) s'agrandir; **to g. fat(ter)** grossir; **to g. to like** finir par aimer; **to g. into** devenir; **to g. on s.o.** (*of book, music etc*) plaire progressivement à qn; **to g. out of** (*one's clothes*) devenir trop grand pour; (*a habit*) perdre; **to g. up** devenir adulte; **when I g. up** quand je serai grand; − *vt* (*plant, crops*) cultiver, faire pousser; (*beard, hair*) laisser pousser. **◆-ing** *a* (*child*) qui grandit; (*number*) grandissant. **◆grown** *a* (*full-grown*) adulte. **◆grown-up** *n* grande personne *f*, adulte *mf*; − *a* (*ideas etc*) d'adulte. **◆grower** *n* (*person*) cultivateur, -trice *mf*.

growl [graʊl] *vi* grogner (**at** contre); − *n* grognement *m*.

growth [grəʊθ] *n* croissance *f*; (*increase*) augmentation *f* (**in** de); (*of hair*) pousse *f*; (*beard*) barbe *f*; Med tumeur *f* (**on** à).

grub [grʌb] *n* (*food*) Fam bouffe *f*.

grubby ['grʌbɪ] *a* (**-ier, -iest**) sale.

grudg/e [grʌdʒ] **1** *vt* (*give*) donner à contrecœur; (*reproach*) reprocher (**s.o. sth** qch à qn); **to g. doing** faire à contrecœur. **2** *n* rancune *f*; **to have a g. against** en vouloir à. **◆-ing** *a* peu généreux. **◆-ingly** *adv* (*to give etc*) à contrecœur.

gruelling, *Am* **grueling** ['gruːəlɪŋ] *a* (*day, detail etc*) éprouvant, atroce.

gruesome ['gruːsəm] *a* horrible.

gruff [grʌf] *a* (**-er, -est**) (*voice, person*) bourru.

grumble ['grʌmb(ə)l] *vi* (*complain*) grogner (**about, at** contre), se plaindre (**about, at** de).

grumpy ['grʌmpɪ] *a* (**-ier, -iest**) grincheux.

grunt [grʌnt] *vti* grogner; − *n* grognement *m*.

guarantee [gærən'tiː] *n* garantie *f*; − *vt* garantir (**against** contre); (*vouch for*) se porter garant de; **to g. (s.o.)** that certifier or garantir (à qn) que. **◆guarantor** *n* garant, -ante *mf*.

guard [gɑːd] *n* (*vigilance, group of soldiers etc*) garde *f*; (*individual person*) garde *m*; Rail chef *m* de train; **to keep a g. on** surveiller; **under g.** sous surveillance; **on one's g.** sur ses gardes; **to catch s.o. off his g.** prendre qn au dépourvu; **on g. (duty)** de garde; **to stand g.** monter la garde; − *vt* (*protect*) protéger (**against** contre); (*watch over*) surveiller, garder; − *vi* **to g. against** (*protect oneself*) se prémunir contre; (*prevent*) empêcher; **to g. against doing** se garder de faire. **◆-ed** *a* (*cautious*) prudent.

◆**guardian** n gardien, -ienne mf; (of child) Jur tuteur, -trice mf.

guerrilla [gə'rɪlə] n (person) guérillero m; g. warfare guérilla f.

guess [ges] n conjecture f; (intuition) intuition f; (estimate) estimation f; to make a g. (essayer de) deviner; an educated or informed g. une conjecture fondée; at a g. au jugé, à vue de nez; – vt deviner (that que); (estimate) estimer; (suppose) Am supposer (that que); (think) Am croire (that que); – vi deviner; I g. (so) Am je suppose; je crois. ◆**guesswork** n hypothèse f; by g. au jugé.

guest [gest] n invité, -ée mf; (in hotel), client, -ente mf; (at meal) convive mf; – n a (speaker, singer etc) invité. ◆**guesthouse** n pension f de famille. ◆**guestroom** n chambre f d'ami.

guffaw [gə'fɔː] vi rire bruyamment.

guidance ['gaɪdəns] n (advice) conseils mpl.

guid/e [gaɪd] n (person, book etc) guide m; (indication) indication f; (girl) éclaireuse f; g. dog chien m d'aveugle; g. book guide m; – vt (lead) guider. ◆—**ed** a (missile, rocket) téléguidé; g. tour visite f guidée. ◆—**ing** a (principle) directeur. ◆**guidelines** npl lignes fpl directrices, indications fpl à suivre.

guild [gɪld] n association f; Hist corporation f.

guile [gaɪl] n (deceit) ruse f.

guillotine ['gɪlətiːn] n guillotine f; (for paper) massicot m.

guilt [gɪlt] n culpabilité f. ◆**guilty** a (-ier, -iest) coupable; g. person coupable mf; to find s.o. g. déclarer qn coupable.

guinea pig ['gɪnɪpɪg] n (animal) & Fig cobaye m.

guise [gaɪz] n under the g. of sous l'apparence de.

guitar [gɪ'tɑːr] n guitare f. ◆**guitarist** n guitariste mf.

gulf [gʌlf] n (in sea) golfe m; (chasm) gouffre m; a g. between Fig un abîme entre.

gull [gʌl] n (bird) mouette f.

gullet ['gʌlɪt] n gosier m.

gullible ['gʌlɪb(ə)l] a crédule.

gully ['gʌlɪ] n (valley) ravine f; (drain) rigole f.

gulp [gʌlp] 1 vt to g. (down) avaler (vite); – n (of drink) gorgée f, lampée f; in or at one g. d'une seule gorgée. 2 vi (with emotion) avoir la gorge serrée; – n serrement m de gorge.

gum [gʌm] n Anat gencive f. ◆**gumboil** n abcès m (dentaire).

gum [gʌm] 1 n (glue from tree) gomme f; (any glue) colle f; – vt (-mm-) coller. 2 n (for chewing) chewing-gum m.

gumption ['gʌmpʃ(ə)n] n Fam (courage) initiative f; (commonsense) jugeote f.

gun [gʌn] n pistolet m, revolver m; (cannon) canon m; – vt (-nn-) to g. down abattre. ◆**gunfight** n échange m de coups de feu. ◆**gunfire** n coups mpl de feu; Mil tir m d'artillerie. ◆**gunman** n (pl -men) bandit m armé. ◆**gunner** n Mil artilleur m. ◆**gunpoint** n at g. sous la menace d'un pistolet or d'une arme. ◆**gunpowder** n poudre f à canon. ◆**gunshot** n coup m de feu; g. wound blessure f par balle.

gurgle ['gɜːg(ə)l] vi (of water) glouglouter; – n glouglou m.

guru ['gʊruː] n (leader) Fam gourou m.

gush [gʌʃ] vi jaillir (out of de); – n jaillissement m.

gust [gʌst] n (of smoke) bouffée f; g. (of wind) rafale f (de vent). ◆**gusty** a (-ier, -iest) (weather) venteux; (day) de vent.

gusto ['gʌstəʊ] n with g. avec entrain.

gut [gʌt] 1 n Anat intestin m; (catgut) boyau m; pl Fam (innards) ventre m, tripes fpl; (pluck) cran m, tripes fpl; he hates your guts Fam il ne peut pas le sentir. 2 vt (-tt-) (of fire) dévaster.

gutter ['gʌtər] n (on roof) gouttière f; (in street) caniveau m.

guttural ['gʌtərəl] a guttural.

guy [gaɪ] n (fellow) Fam type m.

guzzle ['gʌz(ə)l] vi (eat) bâfrer; – vt (eat) engloutir; (drink) siffler.

gym [dʒɪm] n gym(nastique) f; (gymnasium) gymnase m; g. shoes tennis fpl. ◆**gym'nasium** n gymnase m. ◆**gymnast** n gymnaste mf. ◆**gym'nastics** n gymnastique f.

gynaecology, Am **gynecology** [gaɪnɪ'kɒlədʒɪ] n gynécologie f. ◆**gynaecologist** n, Am **gynecologist** n gynécologue mf.

gypsy ['dʒɪpsɪ] = gipsy.

gyrate [dʒaɪ'reɪt] vi tournoyer.

H

H, h [eɪtʃ] *n* H, m; **H bomb** bombe *f* H.

haberdasher ['hæbədæʃər] *n* mercier, -ière *mf*; *(men's outfitter) Am* chemisier m. ◆**haberdashery** *n* mercerie *f*; *Am* chemiserie *f*.

habit ['hæbɪt] *n* **1** habitude *f*; **to be in/get into the h. of doing** avoir/prendre l'habitude de faire; **to make a h. of doing** avoir pour habitude de faire. **2** *(addiction) Med* accoutumance *f*; **a h.-forming drug** une drogue qui crée une accoutumance. **3** *(costume) Rel* habit m. ◆**ha'bitual** *a* habituel; *(smoker, drinker etc)* invétéré. ◆**ha'bitually** *adv* habituellement.

habitable ['hæbɪtəb(ə)l] *a* habitable. ◆**habitat** *n (of animal, plant)* habitat m. ◆**habi'tation** *n* habitation *f*; **fit for h.** habitable.

hack [hæk] **1** *vt (cut)* tailler, hacher. **2** *n (old horse)* rosse *f*; *(hired)* cheval m de louage; **h. (writer)** *Pej* écrivaillon m.

hackney ['hæknɪ] *a* **h. carriage** *Hist* fiacre m.

hackneyed ['hæknɪd] *a (saying)* rebattu, banal.

had [hæd] *see* **have**.

haddock ['hædək] *n (fish)* aiglefin m; **smoked h.** haddock m.

haemorrhage ['hemərɪdʒ] *n Med* hémorragie *f*.

haemorrhoids ['hemərɔɪdz] *npl* hémorroïdes *fpl*.

hag [hæg] *n (woman) Pej* (vieille) sorcière *f*.

haggard ['hægəd] *a (person, face)* hâve, émacié.

haggl/e ['hæg(ə)l] *vi* marchander; **to h. over** *(thing)* marchander; *(price)* débattre, discuter. ◆**-ing** *n* marchandage m.

Hague (The) [ðə'heɪg] *n* La Haye.

ha-ha! [hɑː'hɑː] *int (laughter)* ha, ha!

hail [heɪl] *n Met & Fig* grêle *f*; — *v imp Met* grêler; **it's hailing** il grêle. ◆**hailstone** *n* grêlon m.

hail [heɪl] **1** *vt (greet)* saluer; *(taxi)* héler. **2** *vi* **to h. from** *(of person)* être originaire de; *(of ship etc)* être en provenance de.

hair [heər] *n (on head)* cheveux *mpl*; *(on body, of animal)* poils *mpl*; **a h.** *(on head)* un cheveu; *(on body, of animal)* un poil; **by a hair's breadth** de justesse; **long-/red-/etc haired** aux cheveux longs/roux/etc; **h.**

cream brillantine *f*; **h. dryer** sèche-cheveux *m inv*; **h. spray** *(bombe f de)* laque *f*. ◆**hairbrush** *n* brosse *f* à cheveux. ◆**haircut** *n* coupe *f* de cheveux; **to have a h.** se faire couper les cheveux. ◆**hairdo** *n (pl -dos) Fam* coiffure *f*. ◆**hairdresser** *n* coiffeur, -euse *mf*. ◆**hairgrip** *n* pince *f* à cheveux. ◆**hairnet** *n* résille *f*. ◆**hairpiece** *n* postiche m. ◆**hairpin** *n* épingle *f* à cheveux; **h. bend** *Aut* virage m en épingle à cheveux. ◆**hair-raising** *a* à faire dresser les cheveux sur la tête. ◆**hair-splitting** *n* ergotage m. ◆**hairstyle** *n* coiffure *f*.

hairy ['heərɪ] *a (-ier, -iest) (person, animal, body)* poilu; *(unpleasant, frightening) Fam* effroyable.

hake [heɪk] *n (fish)* colin m.

hale [heɪl] *a* **h. and hearty** vigoureux.

half [hɑːf] *n (pl halves)* moitié *f*, demi, -ie *mf*; *(of match) Sp* mi-temps *f*; **h. (of) the apple/etc** la moitié de la pomme/etc; **ten and a h.** dix et demi; **ten and a h. weeks** dix semaines et demie; **to cut in h.** couper en deux; **to go halves with** partager les frais avec; — *a* demi; **h. a day, a h.-day** une demi-journée; **at h. price** à moitié prix; **h. man h. beast** mi-homme mi-bête; **h. sleeves** manches *fpl* mi-longues; — *adv (dressed, full etc)* à demi, à moitié; *(almost)* presque; **h. asleep** à moitié endormi; **h. past one** une heure et demie; **he isn't h. lazy/etc** *Fam* il est rudement paresseux/etc; **h. as much as** moitié moins que; **h. as much again** moitié plus.

half-back ['hɑːfbæk] *n Fb* demi m. ◆**h.-'baked** *a (idea) Fam* à la manque, à la noix. ◆**h.-breed** *n*, ◆**h.-caste** *n Pej* métis, -isse *mf*. ◆**h.-'(a')dozen** *n* demi-douzaine *f*. ◆**h.-'hearted** *a (person, manner)* peu enthousiaste; *(effort)* timide. ◆**h.-'hour** *n* demi-heure *f*. ◆**h.-light** *n* demi-jour m. ◆**h.-'mast** *n* **at h.-mast** *(flag)* en berne. ◆**h.-'open** *a* entrouvert. ◆**h.-'term** *n Sch* petites vacances *fpl*, congé m de demi-trimestre. ◆**h.-'time** *n Sp* mi-temps *f*. ◆**half'way** *adv (between places)* à mi-chemin *(between* entre*)*; **to fill/etc h.** remplir/etc à moitié; **h. through**

(*book*) à la moitié de. ◆**h.-wit** *n*, ◆**h.-'witted** *a* imbécile (*mf*).

halibut ['hælɪbət] *n* (*fish*) flétan *m*.

hall [hɔːl] *n* (*room*) salle *f*; (*house entrance*) entrée *f*, vestibule *m*; (*of hotel*) hall *m*; (*mansion*) manoir *m*; (*for meals*) *Univ* réfectoire *m*; **h. of residence** *Univ* pavillon *m* universitaire; **halls of residence** cité *f* universitaire; **lecture h.** *Univ* amphithéâtre *m*. ◆**hallmark** *n* (*on silver or gold*) poinçon *m*; *Fig* sceau *m*. ◆**hallstand** *n* portemanteau *m*. ◆**hallway** *n* entrée *f*, vestibule *m*.

hallelujah [hælɪ'luːjə] *n* & *int* alléluia (*m*).

hallo! [hə'ləʊ] *int* (*greeting*) bonjour!; *Tel* allô!; (*surprise*) tiens!

hallow ['hæləʊ] *vt* sanctifier.

Hallowe'en [hæləʊ'iːn] *n* la veille de la Toussaint.

hallucination [həluːsɪ'neɪʃ(ə)n] *n* hallucination *f*.

halo ['heɪləʊ] *n* (*pl* -oes *or* -os) auréole *f*, halo *m*.

halt [hɔːlt] *n* halte *f*; **to call a h.** to mettre fin à; **to come to a h.** s'arrêter; – *vi* faire halte; – *int Mil* halte! ◆**-ing** *a* (*voice*) hésitant.

halve [hɑːv] *vt* (*time, expense*) réduire de moitié; (*cake, number etc*) diviser en deux.

ham [hæm] *n* 1 jambon *m*; **h. and eggs** œufs *mpl* au jambon. 2 (*actor*) *Th Pej* cabotin, -ine *mf*. ◆**h.-'fisted** *a Fam* maladroit.

hamburger ['hæmbɜːɡər] *n* hamburger *m*.

hamlet ['hæmlɪt] *n* hameau *m*.

hammer ['hæmər] *n* marteau *m*; – *vt* (*metal, table*) marteler; (*nail*) enfoncer (**into** dans); (*defeat*) *Fam* battre à plate(s) couture(s); (*criticize*) *Fam* démolir; **to h.** out (*agreement*) mettre au point; – *vi* frapper (au marteau). ◆**-ing** *n* (*defeat*) *Fam* raclée *f*, défaite *f*.

hammock ['hæmək] *n* hamac *m*.

hamper ['hæmpər] 1 *vt* gêner. 2 *n* (*basket*) panier *m*; (*laundry basket*) *Am* panier à linge.

hamster ['hæmstər] *n* hamster *m*.

hand¹ [hænd] 1 *n* main *f*; **to hold in one's h.** tenir à la main; **by h.** (*to deliver etc*) à la main; **at** *or* **to h.** (*within reach*) sous la main, à portée de la main; (*close*) at **h.** (*person etc*) tout près; (*day etc*) proche; **in h.** (*situation*) bien en main; (*matter*) en question; (*money*) disponible; **on h.** (*ready for use*) disponible; **to have s.o. on one's hands** *Fig* avoir qn sur les bras; **to the right h.** du côté droit (**of** de); **on the one h. ...** d'une part ...; **on the other h. ...** d'autre part ...; **hands up!** (*in attack*) haut les

mains!; *Sch* levez la main!; **hands off!** pas touche!, bas les pattes!; *Fig* je suis très occupé; **to give s.o. a** (*helping*) **h.** donner un coup de main à qn; **to get out of h.** (*of person*) devenir impossible; (*of situation*) devenir incontrôlable; **h. in h.** la main dans la main; **h. in h. with** (*together with*) *Fig* de pair avec; **at first h.** de première main; **to win hands down** gagner haut la main; – *a* (*luggage etc*) à main. 2 *n* (*worker*) ouvrier, -ière *mf*; (*of clock*) aiguille *f*; *Cards* jeu *m*; (*writing*) écriture *f*. ◆**handbag** *n* sac *m* à main. ◆**handbook** *n* (*manual*) manuel *m*; (*guide*) guide *m*. ◆**handbrake** *n* frein *m* à main. ◆**handbrush** *n* balayette *f*. ◆**handcuff** *vt* passer les menottes à. ◆**handcuffs** *npl* menottes *fpl*. ◆**hand'made** *a* fait à la main. ◆**hand'picked** *a Fig* trié sur le volet. ◆**handrail** *n* (*on stairs*) rampe *f*. ◆**handshake** *n* poignée *f* de main. ◆**handwriting** *n* écriture *f*. ◆**hand'written** *a* écrit à la main.

hand² [hænd] *vt* (*give*) donner (**to** à); **to h. down** (*bring down*) descendre; (*knowledge, heirloom*) transmettre (**to** à); **to h. in** remettre; **to h. out** distribuer; **to h. over** remettre; (*power*) transmettre; **to h. round** (*cakes*) passer. ◆**handout** *n* (*leaflet*) prospectus *m*; (*money*) aumône *f*.

handful ['hændful] *n* (*bunch, group*) poignée *f*; (*quite*) **a h.** (*difficult*) *Fig* difficile.

handicap ['hændɪkæp] *n* (*disadvantage*) & *Sp* handicap *m*; – *vt* (-**pp**-) handicaper. ◆**handicapped** *a* (*disabled*) handicapé.

handicraft ['hændɪkrɑːft] *n* artisanat *m* d'art. ◆**handiwork** *n* artisanat *m* d'art; (*action*) *Fig* ouvrage *m*.

handkerchief ['hæŋkətʃɪf] *n* (*pl* -**fs**) mouchoir *m*; (*for neck*) foulard *m*.

handle ['hænd(ə)l] 1 *n* (*of door*) poignée *f*; (*of knife*) manche *m*; (*of bucket*) anse *f*; (*of saucepan*) queue *f*; (*of pump*) bras *m*. 2 *vt* (*manipulate*) manier; (*touch*) toucher à; (*ship, vehicle*) manœuvrer; (*deal with*) s'occuper de; (*difficult child etc*) s'y prendre avec; – *vi* **to h. well** (*of machine*) être facile à manier.

handlebars ['hænd(ə)lbɑːz] *npl* guidon *m*.

handsome ['hænsəm] *a* (*person, building etc*) beau; (*gift*) généreux; (*profit, sum*) considérable. ◆**-ly** *adv* (*generously*) généreusement.

handy ['hændɪ] *a* (-**ier**, -**iest**) (*convenient, practical*) commode, pratique; (*skilful*) habile (**at doing** à faire); (*useful*) utile; (*near*) proche, accessible; **to come in h.**

révéler utile; **to keep h.** avoir sous la main. ◆**handyman** *n* (*pl* -men) (*DIY enthusiast*) bricoleur *m*.

hang¹ [hæŋ] **1** *vt* (*pt & pp* hung) suspendre (**on, from** à); (*on hook*) accrocher (**on, from** à), suspendre; (*wallpaper*) poser; (*let dangle*) laisser pendre (**from, out of** de); **to h. with** (*decorate with*) orner de; **to h. out** (*washing*) étendre; (*flag*) arborer; **to h. up** (*picture etc*) accrocher; – *vi* (*dangle*) pendre; (*of thief, thread*) planer; (*of fog, smoke*) flotter; **to h. about** (*loiter*) traîner, rôder; (*wait*) *Fam* attendre; **to h. down** (*dangle*) pendre; (*of hair*) tomber; **to h. on** (*hold out*) résister; (*wait*) *Fam* attendre; **to h. on to** (*cling to*) ne pas lâcher; (*keep*) garder; **to h. out** (*of tongue, shirt*) pendre; (*live*) *Sl* crécher; **to h. together** (*of facts*) se tenir; (*of plan*) tenir debout; **to h. up** *Tel* raccrocher. **2** *n* **to get the h. of sth** *Fam* arriver à comprendre qch; **to get the h. of doing** *Fam* trouver le truc pour faire. ◆**-ing¹** *n* suspension *f*; – *a* suspendu (**from** à); (*leg, arm*) pendant; **h. on** (*wall*) accroché à. ◆**hang-glider** *n* delta-plane® *m*. ◆**hang-gliding** *n* vol *m* libre. ◆**hangnail** *n* petites peaux *fpl*. ◆**hangover** *n* *Fam* gueule *f* de bois. ◆**hangup** *n* *Fam* complexe *m*.

hang² [hæŋ] *vt* (*pt & pp* hanged) (*criminal*) pendre (**for** pour); – *vi* (*of criminal*) être pendu. ◆**-ing²** *n* *Jur* pendaison *f*. ◆**hangman** *n* (*pl* -men) bourreau *m*.

hangar ['hæŋər] *n* *Av* hangar *m*.

hanger ['hæŋər] *n* (*coat*) h. cintre *m*. ◆**hanger-'on** *n* (*pl* hangers-on) (*person*) *Pej* parasite *m*.

hanker ['hæŋkər] *vi* **to h. after** *or* **for** avoir envie de. ◆**-ing** *n* (*forte*) envie *f*, (*vif*) désir *m*.

hankie, hanky ['hæŋkɪ] *n* *Fam* mouchoir *m*.

hanky-panky [hæŋkɪ'pæŋkɪ] *n inv Fam* (*deceit*) manigances *fpl*, magouilles *fpl*; (*sexual behaviour*) papouilles *fpl*, pelotage *m*.

haphazard [hæp'hæzəd] *a* au hasard, au petit bonheur; (*selection, arrangement*) aléatoire. ◆**-ly** *adv* au hasard.

hapless ['hæplɪs] *a* *Lit* infortuné.

happen ['hæpən] *vi* se passer, se produire; **to h. to s.o./sth** arriver à qn/qch; **it (so) happens that I know, I** le know; **it to know** il se trouve que je le sais; **do you h. to have . . . ?** est-ce que par hasard vous avez . . . ?; **whatever happens** quoi qu'il arrive. ◆**-ing** *n* événement *m*.

happy ['hæpɪ] *a* (*-ier, -iest*) heureux (**to do**

de faire, **about sth** de qch); **I'm not (too** *or* **very) h. about (doing)** it ça ne me plaît pas beaucoup (de la faire); **H. New Year!** bonne année!; **H. Christmas!** joyeux Noël! ◆**h.-go-'lucky** *a* insouciant. ◆**happily** *adv* (*contentedly*) tranquillement; (*joyously*) joyeusement; (*fortunately*) heureusement. ◆**happiness** *n* bonheur *m*.

harass ['hærəs, *Am* hə'ræs] *vt* harceler. ◆**-ment** *n* harcèlement *m*.

harbour ['hɑːbər] **1** *n* port *m*. **2** *vt* (*shelter*) héberger; (*criminal*) cacher, abriter; (*fear, secret*) nourrir.

hard [hɑːd] *a* (*-er, -est*) (*not soft, severe*) dur; (*difficult*) difficile, dur; (*study*) assidu; (*fact*) brutal; (*drink*) alcoolisé; (*water*) calcaire; **h. drinker/worker** gros buveur *m*/travailleur *m*; **a h. frost** une forte gelée; **to be h. on** *or* **to s.o.** être dur avec qn; **to find it h. to sleep**/*etc* avoir du mal à dormir/*etc*; **h. labour** *Jur* travaux *mpl* forcés; **h. cash** espèces *fpl*; **h. core** (*group*) noyau *m*; **h. of hearing** malentendant; **h. up** (*broke*) *Fam* fauché; **to be h. up for** manquer de; – *adv* (*-er, -est*) (*to work*) dur; (*to pull*) fort; (*to hit, freeze*) dur, fort; (*to study*) assidûment; (*to think*) sérieusement; (*to rain*) à verse; (*badly*) mal; **h. by** tout près; **h. done by** traité injustement.

hard-and-fast [hɑːdən'dfɑːst] *a* (*rule*) strict. ◆**hardback** *n* livre *m* relié. ◆**'hardboard** *n* Isorel® *m*. ◆**hard-boiled** *a* (*egg*) dur. ◆**hard-'core** *a* (*rigid*) *Pej* inflexible. ◆**hard'headed** *a* réaliste. ◆**hard'wearing** *a* résistant. ◆**hard-'working** *a* travailleur.

harden ['hɑːd(ə)n] *vti* durcir; **to h. oneself to** s'endurcir à. ◆**-ed** *a* (*criminal*) endurci.

hardly ['hɑːdlɪ] *adv* à peine; **he h. talks** il parle à peine, il ne parle guère; **h. ever** presque jamais.

hardness ['hɑːdnɪs] *n* dureté *f*.

hardship ['hɑːdʃɪp] *n* (*ordeal*) épreuve(s) *f*(*pl*); (*deprivation*) privation(s) *f*(*pl*).

hardware ['hɑːdweər] *n inv* quincaillerie *f*; (*of computer*) & *Mil* matériel *m*.

hardy ['hɑːdɪ] *a* (*-ier, -iest*) (*person, plant*) résistant.

hare [heər] *n* lièvre *m*. ◆**h.-brained** *a* (*person*) écervelé; (*scheme*) insensé.

harem [hɑː'riːm] *n* harem *m*.

hark [hɑːk] *vi* *Lit* écouter; **to h. back to** (*subject etc*) *Fam* revenir sur.

harm [hɑːm] *n* (*hurt*) mal *m*; (*prejudice*) tort *m*; **he means (us) no h.** il ne nous veut pas de mal; **she'll come to no h.** il ne lui arrivera rien; – *vt* (*hurt*) faire du mal à; (*prejudice*)

harmful a (person, treatment) inoffensif; (hobby, act) innocent; (gas, fumes etc)
qui n'est pas nuisible, inoffensif.

harmonica [hɑːˈmɒnɪkə] n harmonica m.

harmony ['hɑːmənɪ] n harmonie f. ◆har-
'**monic** a & n Mus harmonique (m).
◆har'**monious** a harmonieux. ◆har-
'**monium** n Mus harmonium m.
◆**harmonize** vt harmoniser; – vi
s'harmoniser.

harness ['hɑːnɪs] n (for horse, baby) harnais
m; – vt (horse) harnacher; (energy etc) Fig
exploiter.

harp [hɑːp] 1 n Mus harpe f. 2 vt to h. on
(about) sth Fam rabâcher qch. ◆**harpist** n
harpiste mf.

harpoon [hɑːˈpuːn] n harpon m; – vt
(whale) harponner.

harpsichord ['hɑːpsɪkɔːd] n Mus clavecin
m.

harrowing ['hærəʊɪŋ] a (tale, memory)
poignant; (cry, sight) déchirant.

harsh [hɑːʃ] a (-er, -est) (severe) dur, sévère;
(sound, taste) âpre; (surface) rugueux;
(fabric) rêche. ◆-**ly** adv durement,
sévèrement. ◆-**ness** n dureté f, sévérité
f; âpreté f; rugosité f.

harvest ['hɑːvɪst] n moisson f, récolte f; (of
people, objects) Fig ribambelle f; – vt moissonner, récolter.

has [hæz] see have. ◆**has-been** n Fam
personne f finie.

hash [hæʃ] 1 n Culin hachis m; – vt to h.
(up) hacher. 2 n (mess) Fam gâchis m. 3 n
(hashish) Sl hasch m, H m.

hashish ['hæʃiːʃ] n haschisch m.

hassle ['hæs(ə)l] n Fam (trouble) histoires
fpl; (bother) mal n, peine f.

haste [heɪst] n hâte f; in h. à la hâte; to make
h. se hâter. ◆**hasten** vi se hâter (to do de
faire); – vt hâter. ◆**hasty** a (-ier, -iest)
(sudden) précipité; (visit) rapide; (decision,
work) hâtif. ◆**hastily** adv (quickly) en
hâte; (too quickly) hâtivement.

hat [hæt] n chapeau m; that's old h. Fam
(old-fashioned) c'est vieux jeu; (stale) c'est
vieux comme les rues; to score or get a h.
trick Sp réussir trois coups consécutifs.

hatch [hætʃ] 1 vi (of chick, egg) éclore; – vt
faire éclore; (plot) Fig tramer. 2 n (in
kitchen wall) passe-plats m inv.

hatchback ['hætʃbæk] n (door) hayon m;
(car) trois-portes f inv, cinq-portes f inv.

hatchet ['hætʃɪt] n hachette f.

hate [heɪt] vt détester, haïr; to h. doing or to

do détester faire; I h. to say it ça me gêne de
le dire; – n hate f. ◆**hateful** a haïssable.
◆**hatred** n haine f.

haughty ['hɔːtɪ] a (-ier, -iest) hautain.
◆**haughtily** adv avec hauteur.

haul [hɔːl] 1 vt (pull) tirer, traîner; (goods)
camionner. 2 n (fish) prise f, (of thief)
butin m; a long h. (trip) un long voyage.
◆**haulage** n camionnage m. ◆**hauler** n
Am, ◆**haulier** n transporteur m routier.

haunt [hɔːnt] 1 vt hanter. 2 n endroit m
favori; (of criminal) repaire m. ◆-**ing** a
(music, memory) obsédant.

have [hæv] 1 (3rd person sing pres t has; pt &
pp had; pres p having) vt avoir; (get)
recevoir, avoir; (meal, shower etc) prendre;
he has got, he has à; to h. a walk/
dream/etc faire une promenade/un rêve/
etc; to h. a drink prendre or boire un
verre; to h. a wash se laver; to h. a holiday
(spend) passer des vacances; will you h.
. . . ? (a cake, some tea etc) est-ce que tu
veux . . . ?; to let s.o. h. sth donner qch à
qn; to h. it from s.o. that tenir de qn que; he
had me by the hair il me tenait par les
cheveux; I won't h. this (allow) je ne tolère-
rai pas ça; you've had it! Fam tu es fichu!;
to h. on (clothes) porter; to h. s.o. over (be
busy) être pris; to h. s.o. over inviter qn
chez soi. 2 v aux avoir; (with monter, sortir
etc & pronominal verbs) être; to h.
decided/been avoir décidé/été; to h. gone
être allé; to h. cut oneself s'être coupé; I've
just done it je viens de le faire; to h. to do
(must) devoir faire; I've got to go, I h. to go
je dois partir, je suis obligé de partir, il faut
que je parte; I don't h. to go je ne suis pas
obligé de partir; to h. sth done (get sth
done) faire faire qch; he's had his suitcase
brought up il a fait monter sa valise; I've
had my car stolen on m'a volé mon auto;
she's had her hair cut elle s'est fait couper
les cheveux; I've been doing it for months je
le fais depuis des mois; haven't I?, hasn't
she? etc n'est-ce pas?; no I haven't! non!;
yes I h.! si!; after he had eaten, he left après
avoir mangé, il partit. 3 npl the haves and
(the) have-nots les riches mpl et les pauvres
mpl.

haven ['heɪv(ə)n] n refuge m, havre m.

haversack ['hævəsæk] n (shoulder bag)
musette f.

havoc ['hævək] n ravages mpl.

hawk [hɔːk] 1 n (bird) & Pol faucon m. 2 vt
(goods) colporter. ◆-**er** n colporteur,
-euse mf.

hawthorn ['hɔːθɔːn] n aubépine f.

hay [heɪ] n foin m; **h. fever** rhume m des foins. ◆**haystack** n meule f de foin.

haywire ['heɪwaɪər] a **to go h.** (of machine) se détraquer; (of scheme, plan) mal tourner.

hazard ['hæzəd] n risque m; **health h.** risque m pour la santé; **it's a fire h.** ça risque de provoquer un incendie; – vt (guess, remark etc) hasarder, risquer. ◆**hazardous** a hasardeux.

haze [heɪz] n brume f; **in a h.** (person) Fig dans le brouillard. ◆**hazy** a (-ier, -iest) (weather) brumeux; (sun) voilé; (photo, idea) flou; **I'm h. about my plans** je ne suis pas sûr de mes projets.

hazel ['heɪz(ə)l] n (bush) noisetier m; – a (eyes) noisette inv. ◆**hazelnut** n noisette f.

he [hiː] pron il; (stressed) lui; **he wants it** il veut; **he's a happy man** c'est un homme heureux; **if I were he** si j'étais lui; **he and I** lui et moi; – n mâle m; **he-bear** ours m mâle.

head [hed] **1** n (of person, hammer etc) tête f; (of page) haut m; (of bed) chevet m, tête f; (of arrow) pointe f; (of beer) mousse f; (leader) chef m; (subject heading) rubrique f; **h. of hair** chevelure f; **h. cold** rhume m de cerveau; **it didn't enter my h.** ça ne m'est pas venu à l'esprit (that que); **to take it into one's h. to do** se mettre en tête de faire; **the h.** Sch = **the headmaster**; = **the headmistress**; **to shout one's h. off** Fam crier à tue-tête; **to have a good h. for business** avoir le sens des affaires; **at the h. of** (in charge of) à la tête de; (table) au haut bout de la table; **at the h. of the table** au haut bout de la table; **at the h. of the list** en tête de liste; **it's above my h.** ça me dépasse; **to keep one's h.** garder son sang-froid; **to go off one's h.** devenir fou; **it's coming to a h.** (of situation) ça devient critique; **heads or tails?** pile ou face?; **per h., a h.** (each) par personne. **2** a principal; (gardener) en chef; **h. waiter** maître m d'hôtel; – a **h. start** une grosse avance. **3** vt (group, firm) être à la tête de; (list, poll) être en tête de; (vehicle) diriger (towards vers); **to h. the ball** Fb faire une tête; **to h. off** (person) détourner de son chemin; (prevent) empêcher; **to be headed for** Am = **to h. for**; – vi **to h. for, be heading for** (place) se diriger vers; (ruin etc) Fig aller à. ◆**–ed** a (paper) à en-tête. ◆**–ing** n (of chapter, page etc) titre m; (of subject) rubrique f; (printed on letter etc) en-tête m. ◆**–er** n Fb coup m de tête.

headache ['hedeɪk] n mal m de tête; (difficulty, person) Fig problème m. ◆**head-dress** n (ornamental) coiffe f.

◆**headlamp** n, ◆**headlight** n Aut phare m. ◆**headline** n (of newspaper) manchette f; pl (gros) titres mpl; Rad TV (grands) titres mpl. ◆**headlong** adv (to fall) la tête la première; (to rush) tête baissée. ◆**head-'master** n Sch directeur m; (of lycée) proviseur m. ◆**head'mistress** n Sch directrice f; (of lycée) proviseur m. ◆**head-'on** adv & a (to collide, collision) de plein fouet. ◆**headphones** npl casque m (à écouteurs). ◆**headquarters** npl Com Pol siège m (central); Mil quartier m général. ◆**headrest** n appuie-tête m inv. ◆**headscarf** n (pl -scarves) foulard m. ◆**headstrong** a têtu. ◆**headway** n progrès mpl.

heady ['hedɪ] a (-ier, -iest) (wine etc) capiteux; (action, speech) emporté.

heal [hiːl] vi **to h.** (up) (of wound) se cicatriser; – vt (wound) cicatriser, guérir; (person, sorrow) guérir. ◆**–er** n guérisseur, -euse mf.

health [helθ] n santé f; **h. food** aliment m naturel; **h. food shop** or Am **store** magasin m diététique; **h. resort** station f climatique; **the H. Service** = la Sécurité Sociale. ◆**healthful** a (climate) sain. ◆**healthy** a (-ier, -iest) (person) en bonne santé, sain; (food, attitude etc) sain; (appetite) bon, robuste.

heap [hiːp] n tas m; **heaps of** Fam des tas de; **to have heaps of time** Fam avoir largement le temps; – vt entasser, empiler; **to h. on s.o.** (gifts, praise) couvrir qn de; (work) accabler qn de. ◆**–ed** a **h. spoonful** grosse cuillerée f. ◆**–ing** a **h. spoonful** Am grosse cuillerée f.

hear [hɪər] vt (pt & pp **heard** [hɜːd]) entendre; (listen to) écouter; (learn) apprendre (that que); **I heard him coming** je l'ai entendu venir; **to h. it said that** entendre dire que; **have you heard the news?** connais-tu la nouvelle?; **I've heard that ...** on m'a dit que ... , j'ai appris que ... ; **to h. out** écouter jusqu'au bout; **h., h.!** bravo!; – vi entendre; (get news) recevoir or avoir des nouvelles (from de); **I've heard of or about him** j'ai entendu parler de lui; **she wouldn't h. of it** elle ne voulait pas en entendre parler; **I wouldn't h. of it!** pas question! ◆**–ing** n (sense) ouïe f; Jur audition f; **h. aid** appareil m auditif. ◆**hearsay** n ouï-dire m inv.

hearse [hɜːs] n corbillard m.

heart [hɑːt] n cœur m; pl Cards cœur m; (off) **by h.** par cœur; **to lose h.** perdre courage; **to one's h.'s content** tout son saoul *or* content; **at h.** au fond; **his h. is set on it** il le veut à tout prix, il y tient; **his h. is set on doing it** il veut le faire à tout prix, il tient à le faire; **h. disease** maladie *f* de cœur; **h. attack** crise *f* cardiaque. ◆**heartache** *n* chagrin *m*. ◆**heartbeat** *n* battement *m* de cœur. ◆**heartbreaking** *a* navrant. ◆**heartbroken** *a* navré, au cœur brisé. ◆**heartburn** *n Med* brûlures *fpl* d'estomac. ◆**heartthrob** *n* (*man*) *Fam* idole *f*.

hearten ['hɑːt(ə)n] *vt* encourager. ◆**—ing** *a* encourageant.

hearth [hɑːθ] *n* foyer *m*.

hearty ['hɑːtɪ] *a* (*-ier, -iest*) (*meal, appetite*) gros. ◆**heartily** *adv* (*to eat*) avec appétit; (*to laugh*) de tout son cœur; (*absolutely*) absolument.

heat [hiːt] **1** *n* chaleur *f*; (*of oven*) température *f*; (*heating*) chauffage *m*; **in the h. of** (*argument etc*) dans le feu de; (*the day*) au plus chaud de; **at low h., on a low h.** *Culin* à feu doux; **h. wave** vague *f* de chaleur; — *vti* **to h. (up)** chauffer. **2** *n* (*in race, competition*) éliminatoire *f*; **it was a dead h.** ils sont arrivés ex aequo. ◆**—ed** *a* (*swimming pool*) chauffé; (*argument*) passionné. ◆**—edly** *adv* avec passion. ◆**—ing** *n* chauffage *m*. ◆**—er** *n* radiateur *m*, appareil *m* de chauffage; **water h.** chauffe-eau *m inv*.

heath [hiːθ] *n* (*place, land*) lande *f*.

heathen ['hiːð(ə)n] *a & n* païen, -enne (*mf*).

heather ['heðər] *n* (*plant*) bruyère *f*.

heave [hiːv] *vt* (*lift*) soulever; (*pull*) tirer; (*drag*) traîner; (*throw*) *Fam* lancer; (*a sigh*) pousser; — *vi* (*of stomach, chest*) se soulever; (*retch*) *Fam* avoir des haut-le-cœur; — *n* (*effort*) effort *m* (*pour soulever etc*).

heaven ['hev(ə)n] *n* ciel *m*, paradis *m*; **h. knows when** *Fam* Dieu sait quand; **good heavens!** *Fam* mon Dieu!; **it was h.** *Fam* c'était divin. ◆**—ly** *a* céleste; (*pleasing*) *Fam* divin.

heavy ['hevɪ] *a* (*-ier, -iest*) lourd; (*weight etc*) lourd, pesant; (*work, cold etc*) gros; (*blow*) violent; (*concentration, rain*) fort; (*traffic*) dense; (*smoker, drinker*) grand; (*film, text*) difficile; **a h. day** une journée chargée; **h. casualties** de nombreuses victimes; **to be h. on petrol** *or Am* **gas** *Aut* consommer beaucoup; **it's h. going** c'est difficile. ◆**heavily** *adv* (*to walk, tax etc*) lourdement; (*to breathe*) péniblement; (*to smoke, drink*) beaucoup; (*underlined*) fortement; (*involved*) très; **to rain h.** pleuvoir à verse. ◆**heaviness** *n* pesanteur *f*, lourdeur *f*.

◆**heavyweight** *n Boxing* poids *m* lourd; *Fig* personnage *m* important.

Hebrew ['hiːbruː] *a* hébreu (*m only*), hébraïque; — *n* (*language*) hébreu *m*.

heck [hek] *int Fam* zut!; — *n* = **hell** in expressions.

heckl/e ['hek(ə)l] *vt* interpeller, interrompre. ◆**—ing** *n* interpellations *fpl*. ◆**—er** *n* interpellateur, -trice *mf*.

hectic ['hektɪk] *a* (*activity*) fiévreux; (*period*) très agité; (*trip*) mouvementé; **h. life** vie *f* trépidante.

hedge [hedʒ] **1** *n Bot* haie *f*. **2** *vi* (*answer evasively*) ne pas se mouiller, éviter de se compromettre. ◆**hedgerow** *n Bot* haie *f*.

hedgehog ['hedʒhɒg] *n* (*animal*) hérisson *m*.

heed [hiːd] *vt* faire attention à; — *n* **to pay h. to** faire attention à. ◆**—less** *a* **h. of** (*danger etc*) inattentif à.

heel [hiːl] *n* **1** talon *m*; **down at h.,** *Am* **down at the heels** (*shabby*) miteux; **h. bar** cordonnerie *f* express; (*on sign*) 'talon minute'. **2** (*person*) *Am Fam* salaud *m*.

hefty ['heftɪ] *a* (*-ier, -iest*) (*large, heavy*) gros; (*person*) costaud.

heifer ['hefər] *n* (*cow*) génisse *f*.

height [haɪt] *n* hauteur *f*; (*of person*) taille *f*; (*of mountain*) altitude *f*; **the h. of** (*glory, success, fame*) le sommet de, l'apogée de; (*folly, pain*) le comble de; **at the h. of** (*summer, storm*) au cœur de. ◆**heighten** *vt* (*raise*) rehausser; (*tension, interest*) *Fig* augmenter.

heinous ['heɪnəs] *a* (*crime etc*) atroce.

heir [eər] *n* héritier *m*. ◆**heiress** *n* héritière *f*. ◆**heirloom** *n* héritage *m*, bijou *m or* meuble *m* de famille.

heist [haɪst] *n Am Sl* hold-up *m inv*.

held [held] *see* **hold**.

helicopter ['helɪkɒptər] *n* hélicoptère *m*. ◆**heliport** *n* héliport *m*.

hell [hel] *n* enfer *m*; **a h. of a lot** (*very much*) *Fam* énormément, vachement; **a h. of a lot of** (*very many, very much*) *Fam* énormément de; **a h. of a nice guy** *Fam* un type super; **what the h. are you doing?** *Fam* qu'est-ce que tu fous?; **to h. with him** *Fam* qu'il aille se faire voir; **h.!** *Fam* zut!; **to be h.-bent on** *Fam* être acharné à. ◆**hellish** *a* diabolique.

hello! [həˈləʊ] *int* = **hallo.**

helm [helm] *n Nau* barre *f*.

helmet ['helmɪt] *n* casque *m*.

help [help] *n* aide *f*, secours *m*; (*cleaning woman*) femme *f* de ménage; (*office or shop workers*) employés, -ées *mfpl*; **with the h. of**

(stick etc) à l'aide de; **to cry** or **shout for h.** crier au secours; **h.!** au secours!; – vt aider (**do, to do** à faire); **to h. s.o. to soup/**etc (serve) servir du potage/etc à qn; **to h. out** aider; **to h. up** aider à monter; **to h. oneself** se servir (**to** de); **I can't h. laughing/**etc je ne peux m'empêcher de rire/etc; **he can't h. being blind/**etc ce n'est pas sa faute s'il est aveugle/etc; **it can't be helped** on n'y peut rien; – vi **h. (out)** aider. ◆—**ing** n (serving) portion f. ◆—**er** n assistant, -ante mf. ◆**helpful** a (useful) utile; (obliging) serviable. ◆**helpless** a (powerless) impuissant; (baby) désarmé; (disabled) impotent. ◆**helplessly** adv (to struggle) en vain.

helter-skelter [heltə'skeltər] **1** adv à la débandade. **2** n (slide) toboggan m.

hem [hem] n ourlet m; – vt (**-mm-**) (garment) ourler; **to h. in** Fig enfermer, cerner.

hemisphere ['hemɪsfɪər] n hémisphère m.

hemorrhage ['hemərɪdʒ] n Med hémorragie f.

hemorrhoids ['hemərɔɪdz] npl hémorroïdes fpl.

hemp [hemp] n chanvre m.

hen [hen] n poule f; **h. bird** oiseau m femelle. ◆**henpecked** a (husband) harcelé or dominé par sa femme.

hence [hens] adv **1** (therefore) d'où. **2** (from now) **ten years/**etc **h.** d'ici dix ans/etc. ◆**henceforth** adv désormais.

henchman ['hentʃmən] n (pl **-men**) Pej acolyte m.

hepatitis [hepə'taɪtɪs] n hépatite f.

her [hɜːr] **1** pron la, l'; (after prep etc) elle; (**to) h.** (indirect) lui; **I see h.** je la vois; **I saw h.** je l'ai vue; **I give (to) h.** je lui donne; **with h.** avec elle. **2** poss a son, sa, pl ses.

herald ['herəld] vt annoncer.

heraldry ['herəldrɪ] n héraldique f.

herb [hɜːb, Am ɜːb] n herbe f; pl Culin fines herbes fpl. ◆**herbal** a **h. tea** infusion f (d'herbes).

Hercules ['hɜːkjuːliːz] n (strong man) hercule m.

herd [hɜːd] n troupeau m; – vti **to h. together** (se) rassembler (en troupeau).

here [hɪər] **1** adv ici; (then) alors; **h. is, h. are** voici; **h. he is** le voici; **h. she is** la voici; **this man h.** cet homme-ci; **I won't be h. tomorrow** je ne serai pas là demain; **h. and there** çà et là; **h. you are!** (take this) tenez!; **h.'s to you!** (toast) à la tienne! **2** int (calling s.o.'s attention) holà!, écoutez!; (giving s.o. sth) tenez! ◆**herea'bouts** adv par ici. ◆**here-**

'**after** adv après; (in book) ci-après. ◆**here'by** adv (to declare) par le présent acte. ◆**here'with** adv (with letter) Com ci-joint.

heredity [hɪ'redɪtɪ] n hérédité f. ◆**heredi-tary** a héréditaire.

heresy ['herəsɪ] n hérésie f. ◆**heretic** n hérétique mf. ◆**he'retical** a hérétique.

heritage ['herɪtɪdʒ] n héritage m.

hermetically [hɜː'metɪklɪ] adv hermétiquement.

hermit ['hɜːmɪt] n solitaire mf, ermite m.

hernia ['hɜːnɪə] n Med hernie f.

hero ['hɪərəʊ] n (pl **-oes**) héros m. ◆**he'roic** a héroïque. ◆**he'roics** npl Pej grandiloquence f. ◆**heroine** ['herəʊɪn] n héroïne f. ◆**heroism** ['herəʊɪz(ə)m] n héroïsme m.

heroin ['herəʊɪn] n (drug) héroïne f.

heron ['herən] n (bird) héron m.

herring ['herɪŋ] n hareng m; **a red h.** Fig une diversion.

hers [hɜːz] poss pron le sien, la sienne, pl les sien(ne)s; **this hat is h.** ce chapeau est à elle or est le sien; **a friend of h.** une amie à elle. ◆**her'self** pron elle-même; (reflexive) se, s'; (after prep) elle; **she cut h.** elle s'est coupée; **she thinks of h.** elle pense à elle.

hesitate ['hezɪteɪt] vi hésiter (**over, about** sur; **to do** à faire). ◆**hesitant** a hésitant. ◆**hesitantly** adv avec hésitation. ◆**hesi-'tation** n hésitation f.

hessian ['hesɪən] n toile f de jute.

heterogeneous [het(ə)rəʊ'dʒiːnɪəs] a hétérogène.

het up [het'ʌp] a Fam énervé.

hew [hjuː] vt (pp **hewn** or **hewed**) tailler.

hexagon ['heksəgən] n hexagone m. ◆**hex-'agonal** a hexagonal.

hey! [heɪ] int hé!, holà!

heyday ['heɪdeɪ] n (of person) apogée m, zénith m; (of thing) âge m d'or.

hi! [haɪ] int Am Fam salut!

hiatus [haɪ'eɪtəs] n (gap) hiatus m.

hibernate ['haɪbəneɪt] vi hiberner. ◆**hiber-'nation** n hibernation f.

hiccough, hiccup ['hɪkʌp] n hoquet m; (**the) hiccoughs, (the) hiccups** le hoquet; – vi hoqueter.

hick [hɪk] n (peasant) Am Sl Pej plouc mf.

hide¹ [haɪd] vt (pt **hid**, pp **hidden**) cacher, dissimuler (**from** à); – vi **to h.** (away or out) se cacher (**from** de). ◆**h.-and-'seek** n cache-cache m inv. ◆**h.-out** n cachette f. ◆**hiding** n **1** **to go into h.** se cacher; **h. place** cachette f. **2** **a good h.** (thrashing) Fam une bonne volée or correction.

hide² [haɪd] n (skin) peau f.

hideous ['hɪdɪəs] a horrible; (person, sight, crime) hideux. ◆**-ly** adv (badly, very) horriblement.

hierarchy ['haɪərɑːkɪ] n hiérarchie f.

hi-fi ['haɪfaɪ] n hi-fi f inv; (system) chaîne f hi-fi; – a hi-fi inv.

high [haɪ] a (-er, -est) haut; (speed) grand; (price) élevé; (fever) fort, gros; (colour, complexion) vif; (idea, number) grand, élevé; (meat, game) faisandé; (on drugs) Fam défoncé; **to be five metres h.** être haut de cinq mètres, avoir cinq mètres de haut; **it is h. time that** il est grand temps que (+ sub); **h. jump** Sp saut m en hauteur; **h.** noon plein midi m; **h. priest** grand prêtre m; **h. school** Am = collège m d'enseignement secondaire; **h. spirits** entrain m; **h. spot** (of visit, day) point m culminant; (of show) clou m; **h. street** grand-rue f; **h. summer** le cœur de l'été; **h. table** table f d'honneur; **h. and mighty** arrogant; **to leave s.o. h. and dry** Fam laisser qn en plan; – adv **h. (up)** (to fly, throw etc) haut; **to aim h.** viser haut; – on h. en haut; **a new h., an all-time h.** (peak) Fig un nouveau record. ◆**-er** a supérieur (than à). ◆**-ly** adv hautement, fortement; (interesting) très; (paid) très bien; (to recommend) chaudement; **to speak h. of** dire beaucoup de bien de; **h. strung** nerveux. ◆**-ness** n H. (title) Altesse f.

highbrow ['haɪbraʊ] a & n intellectuel, -elle (mf).

high-chair ['haɪtʃeər] n chaise f haute. ◆**h.-'class** a (service) de premier ordre; (building) de luxe; (person) raffiné. ◆**h.-'flown** a (language) ampoulé. ◆**h.-'handed** a tyrannique. ◆**h.-'minded** a à l'âme noble. ◆**h.-'pitched** a (sound) aigu. ◆**h.-'powered** a (person) très dynamique. ◆**h.-rise** a **h.-rise flats** tour f d'habitation. ◆**h.-'speed** a ultra-rapide. ◆**h.-'strung** a Am nerveux. ◆**h.-'up** a (person) haut placé.

highlands ['haɪləndz] npl régions fpl montagneuses.

highlight ['haɪlaɪt] n (of visit, day) point m culminant; (of show) clou m; (in hair) reflet m; – vt souligner.

highroad ['haɪrəʊd] n grand-route f.

highway ['haɪweɪ] n grande route f; Am autoroute f; **public h.** voie f publique; **h. code** code m de la route.

hijack ['haɪdʒæk] vt (aircraft, vehicle) détourner; – n détournement m. ◆**-ing** n (air piracy) piraterie f aérienne; (hijack)

détournement m. ◆**-er** n Av pirate m de l'air.

hik/e [haɪk] **1** n excursion f à pied; – vi marcher à pied. **2** n (price) Am Fam augmenter; – n Am Fam hausse f. ◆**-er** n excursionniste mf.

hilarious [hɪ'leərɪəs] a (funny) désopilant.

hill [hɪl] n colline f; (small) coteau m; (slope) pente f. ◆**hillbilly** n Am Fam péquenaud, -aude mf. ◆**hillside** n coteau m; **on the h.** à flanc de coteau. ◆**hilly** a (-ier, -iest) accidenté.

hilt [hɪlt] n (of sword) poignée f; **to the h.** Fig au maximum.

him [hɪm] pron le, l'; (after prep etc) lui; **(to) h.** (indirect) lui; **I see h.** je le vois; **I saw h.** je l'ai vu; **I give (to) h.** je lui donne; **with h.** avec lui. ◆**him'self** pron lui-même; (reflexive) se, s'; (after prep) lui; **he cut h.** il s'est coupé; **he thinks of h.** il pense à lui.

hind [haɪnd] a de derrière, postérieur. ◆**hindquarters** npl arrière-train m.

hinder ['hɪndər] vt (obstruct) gêner; (prevent) empêcher (**from doing** de faire). ◆**hindrance** n gêne f.

hindsight ['haɪndsaɪt] n **with h.** rétrospectivement.

Hindu ['hɪnduː] a & n hindou, -oue (mf).

hing/e [hɪndʒ] **1** n (of box, stamp) charnière f; (of door) gond m, charnière f. **2** vi **to h.** on (depend on) dépendre de. ◆**-ed** a à charnière(s).

hint [hɪnt] n indication f; (insinuation) allusion f; (trace) trace f; pl (advice) conseils mpl; **to drop a h.** faire une allusion; – vt laisser entendre (**that** que); – vi **to h.** at faire allusion à.

hip [hɪp] n Anat hanche f.

hippie ['hɪpɪ] n hippie mf.

hippopotamus [hɪpə'pɒtəməs] n hippopotame m.

hire ['haɪər] vt (vehicle etc) louer; (person) engager; – n location f; **h. out** donner en location, louer; – n location f; (of boat, horse) louage m; **for h.** à louer; **on h.** en location; **h. purchase** vente f à crédit, location-vente f; **on h. purchase** à crédit.

his [hɪz] **1** poss a son, sa, pl ses. **2** poss pron le sien, la sienne, pl les sien(ne)s; **this hat is h.** ce chapeau est à lui or est le sien; **a friend of h.** un ami à lui.

Hispanic [hɪs'pænɪk] a & n Am hispano-américain, -aine (mf).

hiss [hɪs] vti siffler; – n sifflement m; pl Th sifflets mpl. ◆**-ing** n sifflement(s) m(pl.).

history ['hɪstərɪ] n (study, events) histoire f; **it will make h.** or **go down in h.** ça va faire date; **your medical h.** vos antécédents médicaux. ◆**hi'storian** *n* historien, -ienne *mf.* ◆**hi'storic(al)** *a* historique.

histrionic [hɪstrɪ'ɒnɪk] *a Pej* théâtral; — *npl* attitudes *fpl* théâtrales.

hit [hɪt] *vt* (*pt & pp hit, pres p hitting*) (*strike*) frapper; (*knock against*) & *Aut* heurter; (*reach*) atteindre; (*affect*) toucher, affecter; (*find*) trouver, rencontrer; **to h. the head-lines** *Fam* faire les gros titres; **to h. back** rendre coup pour coup; (*verbally, militarily etc*) riposter; **to h. it off** *Fam* s'entendre bien (**with** avec); **to h. out** (**at**) *Fam* attaquer; **to h. (up)on** (*find*) tomber sur; — *n* (*blow*) coup *m*; (*success*) coup *m* réussi; *Th* succès *m*; **h. (song)** chanson *f* à succès; **to make a h. with** *Fam* avoir un succès avec; **h.-and-run driver** chauffard *m* (*qui prend la fuite*). ◆**h.-or-'miss** *a* (*chancy, random*) aléatoire.

hitch [hɪtʃ] **1** *n* (*snag*) anicroche *f*, os *m*, problème *m*. **2** *vt* (*fasten*) accrocher (**to** à). **3** *vti* **to h. (a lift** *or* **a ride)** *Fam* faire du stop (**to** jusqu'à). ◆**hitchhike** *vi* faire de l'auto-stop (**to** jusqu'à). ◆**hitchhiking** *n* auto-stop *m.* ◆**hitchhiker** *n* auto-stoppeur, -euse *mf.*

hitherto ['hɪðə'tuː] *adv* jusqu'ici.

hive [haɪv] **1** *n* ruche *f.* **2** *vt* **to h. off** (*industry*) dénationaliser.

hoard [hɔːd] *n* réserve *f*; (*of money*) trésor *m*; — *vt* amasser. ◆**-ing** *n* (*fence*) panneau *m* d'affichage.

hoarfrost ['hɔːfrɒst] *n* givre *m.*

hoarse [hɔːs] *a* (**-er, -est**) (*person, voice*) enroué. ◆**-ness** *n* enrouement *m.*

hoax [həʊks] *n* canular *m*; — *vt* faire un canular à, mystifier.

hob [hɒb] *n* (*on stove*) plaque *f* chauffante.

hobble ['hɒb(ə)l] *vi* (*walk*) clopiner.

hobby ['hɒbɪ] *n* passe-temps *m inv*; **my h.** mon passe-temps favori. ◆**hobbyhorse** *n* (*favourite subject*) dada *m.*

hobnob ['hɒbnɒb] *vi* (**-bb-**) **to h. with** frayer avec.

hobo ['həʊbəʊ] *n* (*pl* **-oes** *or* **-os**) *Am* vagabond *m.*

hock [hɒk] *vt* (*pawn*) *Fam* mettre au clou; — *n* **in h.** *Fam* au clou.

hockey ['hɒkɪ] *n* hockey *m*; **ice h.** hockey sur glace.

hocus-pocus [həʊkəs'pəʊkəs] *n* (*talk*) charabia *m*; (*deception*) tromperie *f.*

hodgepodge ['hɒdʒpɒdʒ] *n* fatras *m.*

hoe [həʊ] *n* binette *f*, houe *f*; — *vt* biner.

hog [hɒg] **1** *n* (*pig*) cochon *m*, porc *m*; **road h.** *Fig* chauffard *m.* **2** *n* **to go the whole h.**

Fam aller jusqu'au bout. **3** *vt* (**-gg-**) *Fam* monopoliser, garder pour soi.

hoist [hɔɪst] *vt* hisser; — *n Tech* palan *m.*

hold [həʊld] *n* (*grip*) prise *f*; (*of ship*) cale *f*; (*of aircraft*) soute *f*; **to get h. of** (*grab*) saisir; (*contact*) joindre; (*find*) trouver; **to get a h. of oneself** se maîtriser; — *vt* (*pt & pp* **held**) tenir; (*breath, interest, heat, attention*) retenir; (*a post*) occuper; (*a record*) détenir; (*weight*) supporter; (*possess*) posséder; (*contain*) contenir; (*maintain, believe*) maintenir (**that** que); (*ceremony, mass*) célébrer; (*keep*) garder; **to h. hands** se tenir par la main; **to h. one's own** se débrouiller; (*of sick person*) se maintenir; **h. the line!** *Tel* ne quittez pas!; **h. it!** (*stay still*) ne bouge pas!; **to be held** (*of event*) avoir lieu; — *vi* (*of nail, rope*) tenir; (*of weather*) se maintenir; **to h. good** (*of argument*) valoir (**for** pour); **to h. forth** (*talk*) *Pej* disserter; **if the rain holds off** s'il ne pleut pas; **to h. on** (*endure*) tenir bon; (*wait*) attendre; **h. on!** *Tel* ne quittez pas! **to h. onto** (*cling to*) tenir bien; (*keep*) garder; **h. on (tight)!** tenez bon!; **to h. out** (*resist*) résister; (*last*) durer. ◆**holdall** *n* (*bag*) fourre-tout *m inv.* ◆**holdup** *n* (*attack*) hold-up *m*; (*traffic jam*) bouchon *m*; (*delay*) retard *m.*

hold [həʊld] *vt* (*keep in place*) tenir en place (*son chapeau etc*); **to h. out** (*hand*) offrir; (*arm*) étendre; **to h. over** (*postpone*) remettre; **to h. together** (*nation, group*) assurer l'union de; **to h. up** (*raise*) lever; (*support*) soutenir; (*delay*) retarder; (*bank*) attaquer (*à main armée*); —

holder ['həʊldə] *n* (*of post, passport*) titulaire *mf*; (*of record, card*) détenteur, -trice *mf*; (*container*) support *m.*

holdings ['həʊldɪŋz] *npl Fin* possessions *fpl.*

hole [həʊl] *n* trou *m*; (*town etc*) *Fam* bled *m*, trou *m*; (*room*) *Fam* baraque *f*; — *vt* tirer; — *vi* **to h. up** (*hide*) se terrer.

holiday ['hɒlɪdeɪ] *n* (*rest*) vacances *fpl*; **holiday(s)** (*from work, school etc*) vacances *fpl*; **a h.** (*day off*) un congé; **a** (*public or bank*) **h.,** *Am* **a legal h.** un jour férié; **on h.** en vacances; **holidays with pay** congés *mpl* payés; — *a* (*camp, clothes etc*) de vacances; **in h. mood** d'humeur folâtre. ◆**holiday-maker** *n* vacancier, -ière *mf.*

holiness ['həʊlɪnəs] *n* sainteté *f.*

Holland ['hɒlənd] *n* Hollande *f.*

hollow ['hɒləʊ] a creux; (*victory*) faux; (*promise*) vain; – *n* creux *m*; – *vt* **to h. out** creuser.

holly ['hɒlɪ] *n* houx *m*.

holocaust ['hɒləkɔːst] *n* (*massacre*) holocauste *m*.

holster ['həʊlstər] *n* étui *m* de revolver.

holy ['həʊlɪ] a (-**ier**, -**iest**) saint; (*bread*, *water*) bénit; (*ground*) sacré.

homage ['hɒmɪdʒ] *n* hommage *m*.

home¹ [həʊm] *n* maison *f*; (*country*) pays *m* (natal); (*for soldiers*) foyer *m*; (**at**) **h.** à la maison, chez soi; **to feel at h.** se sentir à l'aise; **to play at h.** Fb jouer à domicile; **far from h.** loin de chez soi; **a broken h.** un foyer désuni; **a good h.** une bonne famille; **to make one's h. in** s'installer à *or* en; **my h. is here** j'habite ici; – *adv* à la maison, chez soi; **to go** *or* **come h.** rentrer; **to be h.** être rentré; **to drive h.** ramener (*qn*) (en voiture); (*nail*) enfoncer; **to bring sth h. to s.o.** Fig faire voir qch à qn; – *a* (*life*, *pleasures etc*) de famille; **h.** national; (*cooking*, *help*) familial; (*visit*, *match*) à domicile; **h. economics** économie *f* domestique; **h. town** (*birth place*) ville *f* natale; **h. rule** Pol autonomie *f*; **H. Office** = ministère *m* de l'Intérieur; **H. Secretary** = ministre *m* de l'Intérieur. ◆**homecoming** *n* retour *m* au foyer. ◆**home'grown** *a* Bot du jardin; Pol du pays. ◆**homeland** *n* patrie *f*. ◆**homeloving** *a* casanier. ◆**home'made** *a* (fait à la) maison *inv*. ◆**homework** *n* Sch devoir(s) *m*(*pl*).

home² [həʊm] *vi* **to h.** se diriger automatiquement sur.

homeless ['həʊmlɪs] *a* sans abri; – *n* **the h.** les sans-abri *m inv*.

homely ['həʊmlɪ] *a* (-**ier**, -**iest**) (*simple*) simple; (*comfortable*) accueillant; (*ugly*) Am laid.

homesick ['həʊmsɪk] *a* nostalgique; **to be h.** avoir le mal du pays. ◆**—ness** *n* nostalgie *f*, mal *m* du pays.

homeward ['həʊmwəd] *a* (*trip*) de retour; – *adv* **h. bound** sur le chemin de retour.

homey ['həʊmɪ] *a* (-**ier**, -**iest**) Am Fam accueillant.

homicide ['hɒmɪsaɪd] *n* homicide *m*.

homily ['hɒmɪlɪ] *n* homélie *f*.

homogeneous [həʊmə'dʒiːnɪəs] *a* homogène.

homosexual [həʊmə'sekʃʊəl] *a* & *n* homosexuel, -elle (*mf*). ◆**homosexu-'ality** *n* homosexualité *f*.

honest ['ɒnɪst] *a* honnête, (*frank*) franc (**with** avec); (*profit*, *money*) honnêtement

gagné; **the h. truth** la pure vérité; **to be (quite) h.** . . . . pour être franc. . . . ◆**honesty** *n* honnêteté *f*; franchise *f*; (*of report*, *text*) exactitude *f*.

honey ['hʌnɪ] *n* miel *m*; (*person*) Fam chéri, -ie *mf*. ◆**honeycomb** *n* rayon *m* de miel. ◆**honeymoon** *n* (*occasion*) lune *f* de miel; (*trip*) voyage *m* de noces. ◆**honeysuckle** *n* Bot chèvrefeuille *f*.

honk [hɒŋk] *vi* Aut klaxonner; – *n* coup *m* de klaxon®.

honour ['ɒnər] *n* honneur *m*; **in h. of** en l'honneur de; **an honours degree** Univ = une licence; – *vt* honorer (**with** de). ◆**honorary** *a* (*member*) honoraire; (*title*) honorifique. ◆**honourable** *a* honorable.

hood [hʊd] *n* **1** capuchon *m*; (*mask of robber*) cagoule *f*; (*soft car* or *pram roof*) capote *f*; (*bonnet*) Aut Am capot *m*; (*above stove*) hotte *f*. **2** (*hoodlum*) Am Sl gangster *m*. ◆**hooded** *a* (*person*) encapuchonné; (*coat*) à capuchon.

hoodlum ['huːdləm] *n* Fam (*hooligan*) voyou *m*; (*gangster*) gangster *m*.

hoodwink ['hʊdwɪŋk] *vt* tromper, duper.

hoof, *pl* -**fs**, -**ves** [huːf, -fs, -vz] (*Am* [hʊf, -fs, hʊvz]) *n* sabot *m*.

hoo-ha ['huːhɑː] *n* Fam tumulte *m*.

hook [hʊk] *n* crochet *m*; (*on clothes*) agrafe *f*; Fishing hameçon *m*; (*phone*) décroché; **to let** *or* **get s.o. off the h.** tirer qn d'affaire; – *vt* **to h. (on** *or* **up)** accrocher (**to** à). ◆**—ed** *a* (*nose*, *beak*) recourbé, crochu; (*end*, *object*) recourbé; **h. on** (*chess etc*) enragé de; (*person*) entiché de; **to be h. on drugs** Fam ne plus pouvoir se passer de la drogue. ◆**—er** *n* Am Sl prostituée *f*.

hook(e)y ['hʊkɪ] *n* **to play h.** Am Fam faire l'école buissonnière.

hooligan ['huːlɪɡən] *n* vandale *m*, voyou *m*. ◆**hooliganism** *n* vandalisme *m*.

hoop [huːp] *n* cerceau *m*; (*of barrel*) cercle *m*.

hoot [huːt] **1** *vi* Aut klaxonner; (*of train*) siffler; (*of owl*) hululer; – *n* Aut coup *m* de klaxon®. **2** *vti* (*jeer*) huer; – *n* huée *f*. ◆**—er** *n* Aut klaxon®*m*; (*of factory*) sirène *f*.

hoover® ['huːvər] *n* aspirateur *m*; – *vt* Fam passer à l'aspirateur.

hop [hɒp] *vi* (-**pp**-) (*of person*) sauter (à cloche-pied); (*of animal*) sauter; (*of bird*) sautiller; **h. in!** (*in car*) montez!; **to h. on a bus** monter dans un autobus; **to h. on a plane** attraper un vol; – *vt* **h. it!** Fam fiche le camp!; – *n* (*leap*) saut *m*; Av étape *f*.

hope [həʊp] *n* espoir *m*, espérance *f*; – *vi*

espérer; **to h. for** (*desire*) espérer; (*expect*) attendre; **I h. so/not** j'espère que oui/non; – *vt* espérer (**to do** faire, **that** que). ◆**hopeful** *a* (*person*) optimiste, plein d'espoir; (*promising*) prometteur; (*encouraging*) encourageant; **to be h. that** avoir bon espoir de. ◆**hopefully** *adv* avec optimisme; (*one hopes*) on espère (que). ◆**hopeless** *a* désespéré, sans espoir; (*useless, bad*) nul; (*liar*) invétéré. ◆**hopelessly** *adv* sans espoir; (*extremely*) complètement; (*in love*) éperdument.

hops [hɒps] *npl* Bot houblon *m*.

hopscotch ['hɒpskɒtʃ] *n* (*game*) marelle *f*.

horde [hɔːd] *n* horde *f*, foule *f*.

horizon [hə'raɪz(ə)n] *n* horizon *m*; **on the h.** à l'horizon.

horizontal [hɒrɪ'zɒnt(ə)l] *a* horizontal. ◆**—ly** *adv* horizontalement.

hormone ['hɔːməʊn] *n* hormone *f*.

horn [hɔːn] **1** *n* (*of animal*) corne *f*; Mus cor *m*; Aut klaxon® *m*. **2** *vi* **to h. in** Am Fam dire son mot, interrompre.

hornet ['hɔːnɪt] *n* (*insect*) frelon *m*.

horoscope ['hɒrəskəʊp] *n* horoscope *m*.

horror ['hɒrər] *n* horreur *f*; (*little*) **h.** (*child*) Fam petit monstre *m*; – *a* (*film etc*) d'épouvante, d'horreur. ◆**ho'rrendous** *a* horrible. ◆**horrible** *a* horrible, affreux. ◆**horribly** *adv* horriblement. ◆**horrid** *a* horrible; (*child*) épouvantable, méchant. ◆**ho'rrific** *a* horrible, horrifiant. ◆**horrify** *vt* horrifier.

hors-d'œuvre [ɔː'dɜːv] *n* hors-d'œuvre *m inv*.

horse [hɔːs] *n* **1** cheval *m*; **to go h.** riding faire du cheval; **h. show** concours *m* hippique. **2 h.** chestnut marron *m* (d'Inde). ◆**horseback** *n* **on h.** à cheval. ◆**horseman** *n* (*pl* **-men**) cavalier *m*. ◆**horseplay** *n* jeux *mpl* brutaux. ◆**horsepower** *n* cheval *m* (vapeur). ◆**horseracing** *n* courses *fpl*. ◆**horseradish** *n* radis *m* noir, raifort *m*. ◆**horseshoe** *n* fer *m* à cheval. ◆**horsewoman** *n* (*pl* **-women**) cavalière *f*.

horticulture ['hɔːtɪkʌltʃər] *n* horticulture *f*. ◆**horti'cultural** *a* horticole.

hose [həʊz] *n* (*tube*) tuyau *m*; – *vt* (*garden etc*) arroser. ◆**hosepipe** *n* tuyau *m*.

hosiery ['həʊzɪərɪ, *Am* 'həʊʒərɪ] *n* bonneterie *f*.

hospice ['hɒspɪs] *n* (*for dying people*) hospice *m* (pour incurables).

hospitable [hɒ'spɪtəb(ə)l] *a* hospitalier. ◆**hospitably** *adv* avec hospitalité. ◆**hospi'tality** *n* hospitalité *f*.

hospital ['hɒspɪt(ə)l] *n* hôpital *m*; **in h.,** *Am* **in the h.** à l'hôpital; – *a* (*bed etc*) d'hôpital; (*staff, services*) hospitalier. ◆**hospitalize** *vt* hospitaliser.

host [həʊst] *n* **1** (*man who receives guests*) hôte *m*. **2 a h. of** (*many*) une foule de. **3** *Rel* hostie *f*. ◆**hostess** *n* (*in house, aircraft, nightclub*) hôtesse *f*.

hostage ['hɒstɪdʒ] *n* otage *m*; **to take s.o. h.** prendre qn en otage.

hostel ['hɒst(ə)l] *n* foyer *m*; **youth h.** auberge *f* de jeunesse.

hostile ['hɒstaɪl, *Am* 'hɒst(ə)l] *a* hostile (**to, towards** à). ◆**ho'stility** *n* hostilité *f* (**to, towards** envers); *pl Mil* hostilités *fpl*.

hot [hɒt] *a* (**hotter, hottest**) chaud; (*spice*) fort; (*temperament*) passionné; (*news*) Fam dernier; (*favourite*) Sp grand; **to be** *or* **feel h.** avoir chaud; **it's h.** il fait chaud; **not so h. at** (*good at*) Fam pas très calé en; **not so h.** (*bad*) Fam pas fameux; **h. dog** (*sausage*) hot-dog *m*. ◆**hotbed** *n Pej* foyer *m* (of de). ◆**hot-'blooded** *a* ardent. ◆**hothead** *n* tête *f* brûlée. ◆**hot-'headed** *a* impétueux. ◆**hothouse** *n* serre *f* (chaude). ◆**hot-plate** *n* chauffe-plats *m inv*; (*on stove*) plaque *f* chauffante. ◆**hot-'tempered** *a* emporté. ◆**hot-'water bottle** *n* bouillotte *f*.

hot² [hɒt] *vi* (**-tt-**) **to h. up** (*increase*) s'intensifier; (*become dangerous or excited*) chauffer.

hotchpotch ['hɒtʃpɒtʃ] *n* fatras *m*.

hotel [həʊ'tel] *n* hôtel *m*; – *a* (*industry*) hôtelier. ◆**hotelier** [həʊ'telɪər] *n* hôtelier, -ière *mf*.

hotly ['hɒtlɪ] *adv* passionnément.

hound [haʊnd] *n* **1** (*dog*) chien *m* courant. **2** *vt* (*pursue*) poursuivre avec acharnement; (*worry*) harceler.

hour ['aʊər] *n* heure *f*; **half an h.,** **a half-h.** une demi-heure; **a quarter of an h.** un quart d'heure; **paid ten francs an h.** payé dix francs (de) l'heure; **ten miles an h.** dix miles à l'heure; **open all hours** ouvert à toute heure; **h. hand** (*of watch, clock*) petite aiguille *f*. ◆**—ly** *a* (*rate, pay*) horaire; **an h. bus/train/etc** un bus/train/etc toutes les heures; – *adv* toutes les heures; **h. paid, paid h.** payé à l'heure.

house¹, *pl* **-ses** [haʊs, -zɪz] *n* maison *f*; (*audience*) Th salle *f*, auditoire *m*; (*performance*) Th séance *f*; **the H.** Pol la Chambre; **the Houses of Parliament** le Parlement; **at** *or* **to my h.** chez moi; **on the h.** (*free of charge*) aux frais de la maison; **h. prices** prix *mpl* immobiliers. ◆**housebound** *a* confiné chez soi. ◆**house-**

breaking n Jur cambriolage m. ◆**house-broken** a (dog etc) Am propre. ◆**household** n ménage m, maison f, famille f; **h. duties** soins du ménage; **a h. name** un nom très connu. ◆**house-holder** n (owner) propriétaire mf; (family head) chef m de famille. ◆**housekeeper** n (employee) gouvernante f; (housewife) ménagère f. ◆**housekeeping** n ménage m. ◆**houseman** n (pl -men) interne mf (des hôpitaux). ◆**houseproud** a qui s'occupe méticuleusement de sa maison. ◆**housetrained** a (dog etc) propre. ◆**housewarming** n & a **to have a h.-warming** (party) pendre la crémaillère. ◆**housewife** n (pl -wives) ménagère f. ◆**housework** n (travaux mpl de) ménage m.

hous/e² [hauz] vt loger, (of building) abriter; **it is housed in** (kept) on le garde dans. ◆—**ing** n logement m; (houses) logements mpl; — a (crisis etc) du logement.

hovel ['hɒv(ə)l] n (slum) taudis m.

hover ['hɒvər] vi (of bird, aircraft, danger etc) planer; (of person) rôder, traîner. ◆**hovercraft** n aéroglisseur m.

how [hau] adv comment; **h.'s that?, h. so?, h. come?** Fam comment ça; **h. kind!** comme c'est gentil!; **h. do you do?** (greeting) bonjour; **h. long/high is ...?** quelle est la longueur/hauteur de ...?; **h. much?, h. many?** combien?; **h. much time/etc?** combien de temps/etc?; **h. many apples/etc?** combien de pommes/etc?; **h. about a walk?** si on faisait une promenade?; **h. about some coffee?** (si on prenait) du café?; **h. about me?** et moi?

howdy! ['haudɪ] int Am Fam salut!

however [hau'evər] **1** adv **h. big he may be** quelque or si grand qu'il soit; **h. she may do it** de quelque manière qu'elle le fasse; **h. that may be** quoi qu'il en soit. **2** conj cependant.

howl [haul] vi hurler; (of baby) brailler; (of wind) mugir; — n hurlement m; braillement m; mugissement m; (of laughter) éclat m.

howler ['haulər] n (mistake) Fam gaffe f.

HP [eɪtʃ'piː] abbr = hire purchase.

hp abbr (horsepower) CV.

HQ [eɪtʃ'kjuː] abbr = headquarters.

hub [hʌb] n (of wheel) moyeu m; Fig centre m. ◆**hubcap** n Aut enjoliveur m.

hubbub ['hʌbʌb] n vacarme m.

huckleberry ['hʌk(ə)lberɪ] n Bot Am myrtille f.

huddle ['hʌd(ə)l] vi **to h. (together)** se blottir (les uns contre les autres).

hue [hjuː] n (colour) teinte f.

huff [hʌf] n **in a h.** (offended) Fam fâché.

hug [hʌg] vt (-gg-) (person) serrer dans ses bras, étreindre; **to h. the kerb/coast** (stay near) serrer le trottoir/la côte; — n (embrace) étreinte f.

huge [hjuːdʒ] a énorme. ◆—**ly** adv énormément. ◆—**ness** n énormité f.

hulk [hʌlk] n (person) lourdaud, -aude mf.

hull [hʌl] n (of ship) coque f.

hullabaloo [hʌləbə'luː] n Fam (noise) vacarme m; (fuss) histoire(s) f(pl).

hullo! [hʌ'ləu] int = **hallo.**

hum [hʌm] vi (-mm-) (of insect) bourdonner; (of person) fredonner; (of top, radio) ronfler; (of engine) vrombir; — vt (tune) fredonner; — n (of insect) bourdonnement m.

human ['hjuːmən] a humain; **h. being** être m humain; — npl humains mpl. ◆**humane** a (kind) humain. ◆**hu'manely** adv humainement. ◆**humani'tarian** a & n humanitaire (mf). ◆**hu'manity** n (human beings, kindness) humanité f. ◆**humanly** adv (possible etc) humainement.

humble ['hʌmb(ə)l] a humble; — vt humilier. ◆**humbly** adv humblement.

humbug ['hʌmbʌg] n (talk) fumisterie f; (person) fumiste mf.

humdrum ['hʌmdrʌm] a monotone.

humid ['hjuːmɪd] a humide. ◆**hu'midify** vt humidifier. ◆**hu'midity** n humidité f.

humiliate [hjuː'mɪlɪeɪt] vt humilier. ◆**humili'ation** n humiliation f. ◆**humility** n humilité f.

humour ['hjuːmər] **1** n (fun) humour m; (temper) humeur f; **to have a sense of h.** avoir le sens de l'humour; **in a good h.** de bonne humeur. **2** vt **to h. s.o.** faire plaisir à qn, ménager qn. ◆**humorist** n humoriste mf. ◆**humorous** a (book etc) humoristique; (person) plein d'humour. ◆**humorously** adv avec humour.

hump [hʌmp] **1** n (lump, mound) bosse f; — vt (one's back) voûter. **2** n **to have the h.** Fam (depression) avoir le cafard; (bad temper) être en rogne. ◆**humpback** n & a **h. bridge** Aut pont m en dos d'âne.

hunch [hʌntʃ] **1** vt (one's shoulders) voûter. **2** n (idea) Fam intuition f, idée f. ◆**hunchback** n bossu, -ue mf.

hundred ['hʌndrəd] a & n cent (m); **a h. pages** cent pages; **two h. pages** deux cents pages; **hundreds of** des centaines de.

◆**hundredfold** a centuple; – adv au centuple. ◆**hundredth** a & n centième (mf). ◆**hundredweight** n 112 livres (= 50,8 kg); Am 100 livres (= 45,3 kg).

hung [hʌŋ] see **hang**¹.

Hungary ['hʌŋgərɪ] n Hongrie f. ◆**Hun'garian** a & n hongrois, -oise (mf); – n (language) hongrois m.

hunger ['hʌŋgər] n faim f. ◆**hungry** a (-ier, -iest) to be or feel h. avoir faim; **to go h.** souffrir de la faim; **to make h.** donner faim à; **h. for** (news etc) avide de. ◆**hungrily** adv avidement.

hunk [hʌŋk] n (gros) morceau m.

hunt [hʌnt] n Sp chasse f; (search) recherche f (for de); – vt Sp chasser; (pursue) poursuivre; (seek) chercher; **to h. down** (fugitive etc) traquer; **to h. out** (information etc) dénicher; – vi Sp chasser; **to h. for sth** (re)chercher qch. ◆**—ing** n Sp chasse f. ◆**—er** n (person) chasseur m.

hurdle ['hɜːd(ə)l] n (fence) Sp haie f; Fig obstacle m.

hurl [hɜːl] vt (throw) jeter, lancer; (abuse) lancer; **to h. oneself at s.o.** se ruer sur qn.

hurly-burly ['hɜːlɪbɜːlɪ] n tumulte m.

hurray! [hʊ'reɪ] int hourra!

hurricane ['hʌrɪkən, Am 'hʌrɪkeɪn] n ouragan m.

hurry ['hʌrɪ] n hâte f; **in a h.** à la hâte, en hâte; **to be in a h.** être pressé; **to be in a h. to do** avoir hâte de faire; **there's no h.** rien ne presse; – vi se dépêcher, se presser (to do de faire); **to h. out** sortir à la hâte; **to h. along** or **on** or **up** se dépêcher; – vt (person) bousculer, presser; (pace) presser; **to h. one's meal** manger à toute vitesse; **to h. s.o. out** faire sortir qn à la hâte. ◆**hurried** a (steps, decision etc) précipité; (travail) fait à la hâte; (visit) éclair inv; **to be h.** (in a hurry) être pressé.

hurt [hɜːt] vt (pt & pp **hurt**) (physically) faire du mal à, blesser; (emotionally) faire de la peine à; (offend) blesser; (prejudice, damage) nuire à; **to h. s.o.'s feelings** blesser qn; **his arm hurts (him)** son bras lui fait mal; – vi faire mal; – n mal m; – a (injured) blessé. ◆**hurtful** a (remark) blessant.

hurtle ['hɜːt(ə)l] vi **to h. along** aller à toute vitesse; **to h. down** dégringoler.

husband ['hʌzbənd] n mari m.

hush [hʌʃ] int chut!; – n silence m; – vt (person) faire taire; (baby) calmer; **to h. up** (scandal) Fig étouffer. ◆**—ed** a (voice) étouffé; (silence) profond. ◆**hush-hush** a Fam ultra-secret.

husk [hʌsk] n (of rice, grain) enveloppe f.

husky ['hʌskɪ] a (-ier, -iest) (voice) enroué, voilé.

hussy ['hʌsɪ] n Pej friponne f, coquine f.

hustings ['hʌstɪŋz] npl campagne f électorale, élections fpl.

hustle ['hʌs(ə)l] 1 vt (shove, rush) bousculer (qn); – vi (work busily) Am se démener (**to get sth** pour avoir qch). **2** n **h. and bustle** agitation f, activité f, tourbillon m.

hut [hʌt] n cabane f, hutte f.

hutch [hʌtʃ] n (for rabbit) clapier m.

hyacinth ['haɪəsɪnθ] n jacinthe f.

hybrid ['haɪbrɪd] a & n hybride (m).

hydrangea [haɪ'dreɪndʒə] n (shrub) hortensia m.

hydrant ['haɪdrənt] n (fire) **h.** bouche f d'incendie.

hydraulic [haɪ'drɔːlɪk] a hydraulique.

hydroelectric [haɪdrəʊɪ'lektrɪk] a hydro-électrique.

hydrogen ['haɪdrədʒən] n Ch hydrogène m.

hyena [haɪ'iːnə] n (animal) hyène f.

hygiene ['haɪdʒiːn] n hygiène f. ◆**hy'gienic** a hygiénique.

hymn [hɪm] n Rel cantique m, hymne m.

hyper- ['haɪpər] pref hyper-.

hypermarket ['haɪpəmɑːkɪt] n hypermarché m.

hyphen ['haɪf(ə)n] n trait m d'union. ◆**hyphenat/e** vt mettre un trait d'union à. ◆**—ed** a (word) à trait d'union.

hypnosis [hɪp'nəʊsɪs] n hypnose f. ◆**hypnotic** a hypnotique. ◆**'hypnotism** n hypnotisme m. ◆**'hypnotist** n hypnotiseur m. ◆**'hypnotize** vt hypnotiser.

hypochondriac [haɪpə'kɒndrɪæk] n malade mf imaginaire.

hypocrisy [hɪ'pɒkrɪsɪ] n hypocrisie f. ◆**'hypocrite** n hypocrite mf. ◆**hypo'critical** a hypocrite.

hypodermic [haɪpə'dɜːmɪk] a hypodermique.

hypothesis, pl **-eses** [haɪ'pɒθɪsɪs, -ɪsiːz] n hypothèse f. ◆**hypo'thetical** a hypothétique.

hysteria [hɪ'stɪərɪə] n hystérie f. ◆**hysterical** a hystérique; (funny) Fam désopilant; **to be** or **become h.** (wildly upset) avoir une crise de nerfs. ◆**hysterically** adv (to cry) sans pouvoir s'arrêter; **to laugh h.** rire aux larmes. ◆**hysterics** npl (tears etc) crise f de nerfs; (laughter) crise f de rire.

I

I, i [aɪ] n I, i m.

I [aɪ] pron je, j'; (stressed) moi; **I want je veux**; **she and I elle et moi**.

ic/e¹ [aɪs] n glace f; (on road) verglas m; i. (cream) glace f; black i. (on road) verglas m; i. cube glaçon m; – vi to i. (over) (of lake) geler; (of windscreen) givrer. ◆—ed a (tea) glacé. ◆**iceberg** n iceberg m ◆**icebox** n (box) & Fig glacière f; Am réfrigérateur m. ◆**ice-'cold** a glacial; (drink) glacé. ◆**ice-skating** n patinage m (sur glace). ◆**icicle** n glaçon m.

ic/e² [aɪs] vt (cake) glacer. ◆—**ing** n (on cake etc) glaçage m.

Iceland [ˈaɪslənd] n Islande f. ◆**Ice'landic** a islandais.

icon [ˈaɪkɒn] n Rel icône f.

icy [ˈaɪsɪ] a (-ier, -iest) (water, hands, room) glacé; (manner, weather) glacial; (road etc) verglacé.

idea [aɪˈdɪə] n idée f (of de); **I have an i. that ...** j'ai l'impression que ...; **that's my i. of rest** c'est ce que j'appelle du repos; **that's the i.!** Fam c'est ça!; **not the slightest** or **foggiest i.** pas la moindre idée.

ideal [aɪˈdɪəl] a idéal; – n (aspiration) idéal m; pl (spiritual etc) idéal m. ◆**idealism** n idéalisme m. ◆**idealist** n idéaliste mf. ◆**idea'listic** a idéaliste. ◆**idealize** vt idéaliser. ◆**ideally** adv idéalement; **i. we should stay** l'idéal, ce serait de rester ou que nous restions.

identical [aɪˈdentɪk(ə)l] a identique (to, with à). ◆**identifi'cation** n identification f; **I have (some) i.** j'ai une pièce d'identité. ◆**identify** vt identifier; **to i.** (oneself) with s'identifier avec. ◆**identikit** n portrait-robot m. ◆**identity** n identité f; **i. card** carte f d'identité.

ideology [aɪdɪˈɒlədʒɪ] n idéologie f. ◆**ideo-'logical** a idéologique.

idiom [ˈɪdɪəm] n expression f idiomatique; (language) idiome m. ◆**idio'matic** a idiomatique.

idiosyncrasy [ɪdɪəˈsɪŋkrəsɪ] n particularité f.

idiot [ˈɪdɪət] n idiot, -ote mf. ◆**idiocy** n idiotie f. ◆**idi'otic** a idiot, bête. ◆**idi'otically** adv idiotement.

idle [ˈaɪd(ə)l] a (unoccupied) désœuvré, oisif;

(lazy) paresseux; (unemployed) en chômage; (moment) de loisir; (machine) au repos; (promise) vain; (pleasure, question) futile; (rumour) sans fondement; – vi (laze about) paresser; (of machine, engine) tourner au ralenti; – vt to i. away (time) gaspiller. ◆—**ness** n oisiveté f; (laziness) paresse f. ◆**idler** n paresseux, -euse mf. ◆**idly** adv paresseusement; (to suggest, say) négligemment.

idol [ˈaɪd(ə)l] n idole f. ◆**idolize** vt idolâtrer.

idyllic [aɪˈdɪlɪk] a idyllique.

i.e. [aɪˈiː] abbr (id est) c'est-à-dire.

if [ɪf] conj si; **if he comes** s'il vient; **even if** même si; **if so** dans ce cas, si c'est le cas; **if not for pleasure** sinon pour le plaisir; **if only I were rich** si seulement j'étais riche; **if only to look** ne serait-ce que pour regarder; **as if comme si**; **as if nothing had happened** comme si de rien n'était; **as if to say** comme pour dire; **if necessary** s'il le faut.

igloo [ˈɪgluː] n igloo m.

ignite [ɪgˈnaɪt] vt mettre le feu à; – vi prendre feu. ◆**ignition** n Aut allumage m; **to switch on the i.** mettre le contact.

ignominious [ɪgnəˈmɪnɪəs] a déshonorant, ignominieux.

ignoramus [ɪgnəˈreɪməs] n ignare mf.

ignorance [ˈɪgnərəns] n ignorance f (of de). ◆**ignorant** a ignorant (of de). ◆**ignorantly** adv par ignorance.

ignore [ɪgˈnɔː] vt ne prêter aucune attention à, ne tenir aucun compte de; (duty) méconnaître; (pretend not to recognize) faire semblant de ne pas reconnaître.

ilk [ɪlk] n **of that i.** (kind) de cet acabit.

ill [ɪl] a (sick) malade; (bad) mauvais; **i. will** malveillance f; – npl (misfortunes) maux mpl, malheurs mpl; – adv mal; **to speak i. of** dire du mal de. ◆**ill-ad'vised** a malavisé, peu judicieux. ◆**ill-'fated** a malheureux. ◆**ill-'gotten** a mal acquis. ◆**ill-in'formed** a mal renseigné. ◆**ill-'mannered** a mal élevé. ◆**ill-'natured** a (mean, unkind) désagréable. ◆**ill-'timed** a inopportun. ◆**ill-'treat** vt maltraiter.

illegal [ɪˈliːg(ə)l] a illégal. ◆**ille'gality** n illégalité f.

illegible [ɪˈledʒəb(ə)l] a illisible.

illegitimate [ɪlɪ'dʒɪtɪmət] *a* (*child, claim*) illégitime. ◆**illegitimacy** *n* illégitimité *f*.

illicit [ɪ'lɪsɪt] *a* illicite.

illiterate [ɪ'lɪtərət] *a* & *n* illettré, -ée (*mf*), analphabète (*mf*). ◆**illiteracy** *n* analphabétisme *m*.

illness ['ɪlnɪs] *n* maladie *f*.

illogical [ɪ'lɒdʒɪk(ə)l] *a* illogique.

illuminate [ɪ'luːmɪneɪt] *vt* (*street, question etc*) éclairer; (*monument etc for special occasion*) illuminer. ◆**illumi'nation** *n* éclairage *m*; illumination *f*.

illusion [ɪ'luːʒ(ə)n] *n* illusion *f* (*about* sur); **I'm not under any i.** je ne me fais aucune illusion (*about* sur, *quant* à). ◆**illusive** *a*, ◆**illusory** *a* illusoire.

illustrate ['ɪləstreɪt] *vt* (*with pictures, examples*) illustrer (*with* de). ◆**illu'stration** *n* illustration *f*. ◆**i'lustrative** *a* (*example*) explicatif.

illustrious [ɪ'lʌstrɪəs] *a* illustre.

image ['ɪmɪdʒ] *n* image *f*; (*public*) *a*. (*of firm etc*) image *f* de marque; **he's the** (*living or spitting or very*) **i. of his brother** c'est (tout) le portrait de son frère. ◆**imagery** *n* images *fpl*.

imagin/e [ɪ'mædʒɪn] *vt* (*picture to oneself*) (s')imaginer, se figurer (*that* que); (*suppose*) imaginer (*that* que); **i. that** . . . imaginez que . . . ; **you're imagining (things)!** tu te fais des illusions! ◆**—ings** *npl* (*dreams*) imaginations *fpl*. ◆**—able** *a* imaginable; **the worst thing i.** le pire que l'on puisse imaginer. ◆**imaginary** *a* imaginaire. ◆**imagi'nation** *n* imagination *f*. ◆**imaginative** *a* plein d'imagination, imaginatif.

imbalance [ɪm'bæləns] *n* déséquilibre *m*.

imbecile ['ɪmbəsiːl, *Am* 'ɪmbəs(ə)l] *a* & *n* imbécile (*mf*). ◆**imbe'cility** *n* imbécillité *f*.

imbibe [ɪm'baɪb] *vt* absorber.

imbued [ɪm'bjuːd] *a* **i. with** (*ideas*) imprégné de; (*feelings*) pénétré, imbu de.

imitate ['ɪmɪteɪt] *vt* imiter. ◆**imi'tation** *n* imitation *f*; – *a* (*jewels*) artificiel; **i. leather** imitation *f* cuir. ◆**imitative** *a* imitateur. ◆**imitator** *n* imitateur, -trice *mf*.

immaculate [ɪ'mækjʊlət] *a* (*person, appearance, shirt etc*) impeccable.

immaterial [ɪmə'tɪərɪəl] *a* peu important (*to* pour).

immature [ɪmə'tʃʊər] *a* (*fruit*) vert; (*animal*) jeune; (*person*) qui manque de maturité.

immeasurable [ɪ'meʒərəb(ə)l] *a* incommensurable.

immediate [ɪ'miːdɪət] *a* immédiat. ◆**immediacy** *n* caractère *m* immédiat. ◆**immediately** *adv* (*at once*) tout de suite, immédiatement; (*to concern, affect*) directement; – *conj* (*as soon as*) dès que.

immense [ɪ'mens] *a* immense. ◆**immensely** *adv* (*rich etc*) immensément; **to enjoy oneself** i. s'amuser énormément. ◆**immensity** *n* immensité *f*.

immerse [ɪ'mɜːs] *vt* plonger, immerger; **immersed in work** plongé dans le travail. ◆**immersion** *n* immersion *f*; **i. heater** chauffe-eau *m inv* électrique.

immigrate ['ɪmɪgreɪt] *vi* immigrer. ◆**immigrant** *n* immigrant, -ante *mf*; (*long-established*) immigré, -ée *mf*; – *a* immigré. ◆**immi'gration** *n* immigration *f*.

imminent ['ɪmɪnənt] *a* imminent. ◆**imminence** *n* imminence *f*.

immobile [ɪ'məʊbaɪl, *Am* ɪ'məʊb(ə)l] *a* immobile. ◆**immo'bility** *n* immobilité *f*. ◆**immobilize** *vt* immobiliser.

immoderate [ɪ'mɒdərət] *a* immodéré.

immodest [ɪ'mɒdɪst] *a* impudique.

immoral [ɪ'mɒrəl] *a* immoral. ◆**immo'rality** *n* immoralité *f*.

immortal [ɪ'mɔːt(ə)l] *a* immortel. ◆**immor'tality** *n* immortalité *f*. ◆**immortalize** *vt* immortaliser.

immune [ɪ'mjuːn] *a Med & Fig* immunisé (**to, from** contre). ◆**immunity** *n* immunité *f*. ◆**i'mmunize** *vt* immuniser (**against** contre).

immutable [ɪ'mjuːtəb(ə)l] *a* immuable.

imp [ɪmp] *n* diablotin *m*, lutin *m*.

impact ['ɪmpækt] *n* impact *m* (**on** sur).

impair [ɪm'peər] *vt* détériorer; (*hearing, health*) abîmer.

impale [ɪm'peɪl] *vt* empaler.

impart [ɪm'pɑːt] *vt* communiquer (**to** à).

impartial [ɪm'pɑːʃ(ə)l] *a* impartial. ◆**imparti'ality** *n* impartialité *f*.

impassable [ɪm'pɑːsəb(ə)l] *a* (*road*) impraticable; (*river*) infranchissable.

impasse ['æmpɑːs, *Am* 'ɪmpæs] *n* (*situation*) impasse *f*.

impassioned [ɪm'pæʃ(ə)nd] *a* (*speech etc*) enflammé, passionné.

impassive [ɪm'pæsɪv] *a* impassible. ◆**—ness** *n* impassibilité *f*.

impatient [ɪm'peɪʃ(ə)nt] *a* impatient (**to do** de faire); **i. of or with** intolérant à l'égard de. ◆**impatience** *n* impatience *f*. ◆**impatiently** *adv* impatiemment.

impeccab/le [ɪm'pekəb(ə)l] *a* impeccable. ◆**—ly** *adv* impeccablement.

impecunious [ɪmpɪ'kjuːnɪəs] *a Hum* sans le sou, impécunieux.

impede [ɪm'piːd] *vt* (*hamper*) gêner; **to i. s.o. from doing** (*prevent*) empêcher qn de faire.

impediment [ɪm'pedɪmənt] *n* obstacle *m*; (*of speech*) défaut *m* d'élocution.

impel [ɪm'pel] *vt* (**-ll-**) (*drive*) pousser; (*force*) obliger (**to do** à faire).

impending [ɪm'pendɪŋ] *a* imminent.

impenetrable [ɪm'penɪtrəb(ə)l] *a* (*forest, mystery etc*) impénétrable.

imperative [ɪm'perətɪv] *a* (*need, tone*) impérieux; (*necessary*) essentiel; **it is i. that you come** il faut absolument que *or* il est indispensable que tu viennes; – *n Gram* impératif *m*.

imperceptible [ɪmpə'septəb(ə)l] *a* imperceptible (**to** à).

imperfect [ɪm'pɜːfɪkt] **1** *a* imparfait; (*goods*) défectueux. **2** *n* (*tense*) *Gram* imparfait *m*. ◆**imper'fection** *n* imperfection *f*.

imperial [ɪm'pɪərɪəl] *a* impérial; (*majestic*) majestueux; (*measure*) *Br* légal. ◆**imperialism** *n* impérialisme *m*.

imperil [ɪm'perɪl] *vt* (**-ll-**, *Am* **-l-**) mettre en péril.

imperious [ɪm'pɪərɪəs] *a* impérieux.

impersonal [ɪm'pɜːsən(ə)l] *a* impersonnel.

impersonate [ɪm'pɜːsəneɪt] *vt* (*mimic*) imiter; (*pretend to be*) se faire passer pour. ◆**imperso'nation** *n* imitation *f*. ◆**impersonator** *n* imitateur, -trice *mf*.

impertinent [ɪm'pɜːtɪnənt] *a* impertinent (**to** envers). ◆**impertinence** *n* impertinence *f*. ◆**impertinently** *adv* avec impertinence.

impervious [ɪm'pɜːvɪəs] *a* imperméable (**to** à).

impetuous [ɪm'petjuəs] *a* impétueux. ◆**impetu'osity** *n* impétuosité *f*.

impetus ['ɪmpɪtəs] *n* impulsion *f*.

impinge [ɪm'pɪndʒ] *vi* **to i. on** (*affect*) affecter; (*encroach on*) empiéter sur.

impish ['ɪmpɪʃ] *a* (*naughty*) espiègle.

implacable [ɪm'plækəb(ə)l] *a* implacable.

implant [ɪm'plɑːnt] *vt* (*ideas*) inculquer (**in** à).

implement[1] ['ɪmplɪmənt] *n* (*tool*) instrument *m*; (*utensil*) *Culin* ustensile *m*; *pl Agr* matériel *m*.

implement[2] ['ɪmplɪment] *vt* (*carry out*) mettre en œuvre, exécuter. ◆**implemen'tation** *n* mise *f* en œuvre, exécution *f*.

implicate ['ɪmplɪkeɪt] *vt* impliquer (**in** dans). ◆**impli'cation** *n* (*consequence, involvement*) implication *f*; (*innuendo*) insinuation *f*; (*impact*) portée *f*; **by i.** implicitement.

implicit [ɪm'plɪsɪt] *a* (*implied*) implicite;

(*belief, obedience etc*) absolu. ◆**-ly** *adv* implicitement.

implore [ɪm'plɔːr] *vt* implorer (**s.o. to do** qn de faire).

imply [ɪm'plaɪ] *vt* (*assume*) impliquer, supposer (**that** que); (*suggest*) laisser entendre (**that** que); (*insinuate*) *Pej* insinuer (**that** que). ◆**implied** *a* implicite.

impolite [ɪmpə'laɪt] *a* impoli. ◆**-ness** *n* impolitesse *f*.

import 1 [ɪm'pɔːt] *vt* (*goods etc*) importer (**from** de); – ['ɪmpɔːt] *n* (*object, action*) importation *f*. **2** ['ɪmpɔːt] *n* (*meaning*) sens *m*. ◆**im'porter** *n* importateur, -trice *mf*.

importance [ɪm'pɔːtəns] *n* importance *f*; **to be of i.** avoir de l'importance; **of no i.** sans importance. ◆**important** *a* (*significant*) important. ◆**importantly** *adv* **more i.** ce qui est plus important.

impose [ɪm'pəʊz] *vt* imposer (**on** à); (*fine, punishment*) infliger (**on** à); **to i. (oneself) on s.o.** s'imposer à qn; – *vi* s'imposer. ◆**impo'sition** *n* imposition *f* (**of** de); (*inconvenience*) dérangement *m*.

impossible [ɪm'pɒsəb(ə)l] *a* impossible (**to do** à faire); **it is i. (for us) to do** il (nous) est impossible de faire; **it is i. that** il est impossible que (+ *sub*); **to make it for s.o. to do** mettre qn dans l'impossibilité de faire; – *n* **to do the i.** faire l'impossible. ◆**impossi'bility** *n* impossibilité *f*. ◆**impossibly** *adv* (*late, hard*) incroyablement.

impostor [ɪm'pɒstər] *n* imposteur *m*.

impotent ['ɪmpətənt] *a Med* impuissant. ◆**impotence** *n Med* impuissance *f*.

impound [ɪm'paʊnd] *vt* (*of police*) saisir, confisquer; (*vehicle*) emmener à la fourrière.

impoverish [ɪm'pɒvərɪʃ] *vt* appauvrir.

impracticable [ɪm'præktɪkəb(ə)l] *a* irréalisable, impraticable.

impractical [ɪm'præktɪk(ə)l] *a* peu réaliste.

imprecise [ɪmprɪ'saɪs] *a* imprécis.

impregnable [ɪm'pregnəb(ə)l] *a Mil* imprenable; (*argument*) *Fig* inattaquable.

impregnate ['ɪmpregneɪt] *vt* (*imbue*) imprégner (**with** de); (*fertilize*) féconder.

impresario [ɪmprɪ'sɑːrɪəʊ] *n* (*pl* -os) impresario *m*.

impress [ɪm'pres] *vt* impressionner (*qn*); (*mark*) imprimer; **to i. sth on s.o.** faire comprendre qch à qn. ◆**impression** *n* impression *f*; **to be under** *or* **have the i.** that avoir l'impression de; **to make a good i. on s.o.** faire une bonne impression à qn. ◆**impressionable** *a* (*person*) impression-

nable; (age) où l'on est impressionnable.
◆**impressive** a impressionnant.

imprint [ɪmˈprɪnt] vt imprimer; – [ˈɪmprɪnt] n empreinte f.

imprison [ɪmˈprɪz(ə)n] vt emprisonner. ◆**—ment** n emprisonnement m; **life i.** la prison à vie.

improbable [ɪmˈprɒbəb(ə)l] a improbable; (story, excuse) invraisemblable. ◆**improba'bility** n improbabilité f; invraisemblance f.

impromptu [ɪmˈprɒmptjuː] a & adv impromptu.

improper [ɪmˈprɒpər] a (indecent) inconvenant, indécent; (wrong) incorrect. ◆**impropriety** [ɪmprəˈpraɪətɪ] n inconvenance f; (wrong use) Ling impropriété f.

improve [ɪmˈpruːv] vt améliorer; (mind) cultiver, développer; **to i.** one's English se perfectionner en anglais; **to i. s.o.'s looks** embellir qn; **to i. oneself** se cultiver; – vi s'améliorer; (of business) aller de mieux en mieux, reprendre; **to i. on** (do better than) faire mieux que. ◆**—ment** n amélioration f; (of mind) développement m; (progress) progrès m(pl); **there has been some** or **an i.** il y a du mieux.

improvise [ˈɪmprəvaɪz] vti improviser. ◆**improvi'sation** n improvisation f.

impudent [ˈɪmpjʊdənt] a impudent. ◆**impudence** n impudence f.

impulse [ˈɪmpʌls] n impulsion f; **on i.** sur un coup de tête. ◆**im'pulsive** a (person, act) impulsif, irréfléchi; (remark) irréfléchi. ◆**im'pulsively** adv de manière impulsive.

impunity [ɪmˈpjuːnɪtɪ] n **with i.** impunément.

impure [ɪmˈpjʊər] a impur. ◆**impurity** n impureté f.

in [ɪn] prep **1** dans; **in the box/the school/**etc dans la boîte/l'école/etc; **in an hour's (time)** dans une heure; **in so far as** dans la mesure où. **2** à; **in school** à l'école; **in the garden** dans le jardin, au jardin; **in Paris** à Paris; **in the USA** aux USA; **in Portugal** au Portugal; **in fashion** à la mode; **in pencil** au crayon; **in my opinion** à mon avis. **3** en; **in summer/secret/French** en été/secret/ français; **in Spain** en Espagne; **in May** en mai, au mois de mai; **in season** en saison; **in an hour** (during the period of an hour) en une heure; **in doing** en faisant; **dressed in black** habillé en noir; **in all** en tout. **4** de; **in a soft voice** d'une voix douce; **the best in the class** le meilleur de la classe. **5** in the rain sous la pluie; **in the morning** le matin; **he hasn't done it in years** ça fait des années qu'il ne l'a pas fait; **in an hour** (at the end of

an hour) au bout d'une heure; **one in ten** un sur dix; **in thousands** par milliers; **in here** ici; **in there** là-dedans. **6** adv **to be in** (home) être là, être à la maison; (of train) être arrivé; (in fashion) être en vogue; (in season) être en saison; (in power) Pol être au pouvoir; **day in day out** jour après jour; **in on** (a secret) au courant de; **we're in for some rain/trouble/**etc on va avoir de la pluie/des ennuis/etc; **it's the in thing** Fam c'est dans le vent. **7** npl **the ins and outs of** les moindres détails de.

inability [ɪnəˈbɪlɪtɪ] n incapacité f (**to do** de faire).

inaccessible [ɪnəkˈsesəb(ə)l] a inaccessible.

inaccurate [ɪnˈækjʊrət] a inexact. ◆**inaccuracy** n inexactitude f.

inaction [ɪnˈækʃ(ə)n] n inaction f.

inactive [ɪnˈæktɪv] a inactif; (mind) inerte. ◆**inac'tivity** n inactivité f, inaction f.

inadequate [ɪnˈædɪkwət] a (quantity) insuffisant; (person) pas à la hauteur, insuffisant; (work) médiocre. ◆**inadequacy** n insuffisance f. ◆**inadequately** adv insuffisamment.

inadmissible [ɪnədˈmɪsəb(ə)l] a inadmissible.

inadvertently [ɪnədˈvɜːtəntlɪ] adv par inadvertance.

inadvisable [ɪnədˈvaɪzəb(ə)l] a (action) à déconseiller; **it is i. to** il est déconseillé de.

inane [ɪˈneɪn] a (absurd) inepte.

inanimate [ɪnˈænɪmət] a inanimé.

inappropriate [ɪnəˈprəʊprɪət] a (unsuitable) peu approprié, inadéquat; (untimely) inopportun.

inarticulate [ɪnɑːˈtɪkjʊlət] a (person) incapable de s'exprimer; (sound) inarticulé.

inasmuch as [ɪnəzˈmʌtʃəz] adv (because) vu que; (to the extent that) en ce sens que.

inattentive [ɪnəˈtentɪv] a inattentif (**to** à).

inaudible [ɪnˈɔːdəb(ə)l] a inaudible.

inaugural [ɪˈnɔːgjʊrəl] a inaugural. ◆**inaugurate** vt (policy, building) inaugurer; (official) installer (dans ses fonctions). ◆**inaugu'ration** n inauguration f; investiture f.

inauspicious [ɪnɔːˈspɪʃəs] a peu propice.

inborn [ɪnˈbɔːn] a inné.

inbred [ɪnˈbred] a (quality etc) inné.

Inc abbr (Incorporated) Am Com SA, SARL.

incalculable [ɪnˈkælkjʊləb(ə)l] a incalculable.

incandescent [ɪnkænˈdes(ə)nt] a incandescent.

incapable [ɪnˈkeɪpəb(ə)l] a incapable (of

doing de faire); **i. of** (*pity etc*) inaccessible à.

incapacitate [ɪnkə'pæsɪteɪt] *vt Med* rendre incapable (*de travailler etc*). ◆**incapacity** *n* (*inability*) *Med* incapacité *f*.

incarcerate [ɪn'kɑːsəreɪt] *vt* incarcérer. ◆**incarce'ration** *n* incarcération *f*.

incarnate [ɪn'kɑːnət] *a* incarné; — [ɪn'kɑːneɪt] *vt* incarner. ◆**incar'nation** *n* incarnation *f*.

incendiary [ɪn'sendɪərɪ] *a* (*bomb*) incendiaire.

incense 1 [ɪn'sens] *vt* mettre en colère. **2** ['ɪnsens] *n* (*substance*) encens *m*.

incentive [ɪn'sentɪv] *n* encouragement *m*, motivation *f*; **to give s.o. an i. to work**/*etc* encourager qn à travailler/*etc*.

inception [ɪn'sepʃ(ə)n] *n* début *m*.

incessant [ɪn'ses(ə)nt] *a* incessant. ◆**—ly** *adv* sans cesse.

incest ['ɪnsest] *n* inceste *m*. ◆**in'cestuous** *a* incestueux.

inch [ɪntʃ] *n* pouce *m* (= 2,54 cm); (*loosely*) *Fig* centimètre *m*; **within an i. of** (*success*) à deux doigts de; **i. by i.** petit à petit; — *vti* **to i.** (*one's way*) **forward** avancer petit à petit.

incidence ['ɪnsɪdəns] *n* fréquence *f*.

incident ['ɪnsɪdənt] *n* incident *m*; (*in book, film etc*) épisode *m*.

incidental [ɪnsɪ'dent(ə)l] *a* accessoire, secondaire; (*music*) de fond; **i. expenses** frais *mpl* accessoires. ◆**—ly** *adv* accessoirement; (*by the way*) à propos.

incinerate [ɪn'sɪnəreɪt] *vt* (*refuse, leaves etc*) incinérer. ◆**incinerator** *n* incinérateur *m*.

incipient [ɪn'sɪpɪənt] *a* naissant.

incision [ɪn'sɪʒ(ə)n] *n* incision *f*.

incisive [ɪn'saɪsɪv] *a* incisif.

incisor [ɪn'saɪzər] *n* (*tooth*) incisive *f*.

incite [ɪn'saɪt] *vt* inciter (**to do** à faire). ◆**—ment** *n* incitation *f* (**to do** à faire).

incline 1 [ɪn'klaɪn] *vt* (*tilt, bend*) incliner; **to i. s.o. to do** incliner qn à faire; **to be inclined to do** (*feel a wish to*) être enclin à faire; (*tend to*) avoir tendance à faire; — *vi* **to i. or be inclined towards** (*indulgence etc*) incliner à. **2** ['ɪnklaɪn] *n* (*slope*) inclinaison *f*. ◆**incli'nation** *n* inclination *f*; **to have no i. to do** n'avoir aucune envie de faire.

include /*e* [ɪn'kluːd] *vt* (*contain*) comprendre, englober; (*refer to*) s'appliquer à; **my invitation includes you** mon invitation s'adresse aussi à vous; **to be included** être compris; (*on list*) être inclus. ◆**—ing** *prep* y compris; **i. service** service *m* compris. ◆**inclusion** *n* inclusion *f*. ◆**inclusive** *a* inclus; **from the fourth to the tenth of May**

i. du quatre jusqu'au dix mai inclus(ivement); **to be i. of** comprendre; **i. charge** prix *m* global.

incognito [ɪnkɒg'niːtəʊ] *adv* incognito.

incoherent [ɪnkəʊ'hɪərənt] *a* incohérent. ◆**—ly** *adv* sans cohérence.

income ['ɪnkʌm] *n* revenu *m*; **private i.** rentes *fpl*; **i. tax** impôt *m* sur le revenu.

incoming ['ɪnkʌmɪŋ] *a* (*tenant, president*) nouveau; **i. tide** marée *f* montante; **i. calls** *Tel* appels *mpl* de l'extérieur.

incommunicado [ɪnkəmjuːnɪ'kɑːdəʊ] *a* (tenu) au secret.

incomparable [ɪn'kɒmpərəb(ə)l] *a* incomparable.

incompatible [ɪnkəm'pætəb(ə)l] *a* incompatible (**with** avec). ◆**incompati'bility** *n* incompatibilité *f*.

incompetent [ɪn'kɒmpɪtənt] *a* incompétent. ◆**incompetence** *n* incompétence *f*.

incomplete [ɪnkəm'pliːt] *a* incomplet.

incomprehensible [ɪnkɒmprɪ'hensəb(ə)l] *a* incompréhensible.

inconceivable [ɪnkən'siːvəb(ə)l] *a* inconcevable.

inconclusive [ɪnkən'kluːsɪv] *a* peu concluant.

incongruous [ɪn'kɒŋgruəs] *a* (*building, colours*) qui jure(nt) (**with** avec); (*remark, attitude*) incongru; (*absurd*) absurde.

inconsequential [ɪnkɒnsɪ'kwenʃ(ə)l] *a* sans importance.

inconsiderate [ɪnkən'sɪdərət] *a* (*action, remark*) irréfléchi, inconsidéré; **to be i.** (*of person*) manquer d'égards (**towards** envers).

inconsistent [ɪnkən'sɪstənt] *a* inconséquent, incohérent; (*reports etc at variance*) contradictoire; **i. with** incompatible avec. ◆**inconsistency** *n* inconséquence *f*, incohérence *f*.

inconsolable [ɪnkən'səʊləb(ə)l] *a* inconsolable.

inconspicuous [ɪnkən'spɪkjuəs] *a* peu en évidence, qui passe inaperçu. ◆**—ly** *adv* discrètement.

incontinent [ɪn'kɒntɪnənt] *a* incontinent.

inconvenient [ɪnkən'viːnɪənt] *a* (*room, situation*) incommode; (*time*) inopportun; **it's i. (for me) to ...** ça me dérange de ... ; **that's very i.** c'est très gênant. ◆**inconvenience** *n* (*bother*) dérangement *m*; (*disadvantage*) inconvénient *m*; — *vt* déranger, gêner.

incorporate [ɪn'kɔːpəreɪt] *vt* (*introduce*) incorporer (**into** dans); (*contain*) contenir;

incorporated society *Am* société *f* anonyme, société *f* à responsabilité limitée.

incorrect [ɪnkə'rekt] *a* incorrect, inexact; you're i. vous avez tort.

incorrigible [ɪn'kɒrɪdʒəb(ə)l] *a* incorrigible.

incorruptible [ɪnkə'rʌptəb(ə)l] *a* incorruptible.

increas/e [ɪn'kriːs] *vi* augmenter; (*of effort, noise*) s'intensifier; **to i. in weight** prendre du poids; — *vt* augmenter; intensifier; — ['ɪnkriːs] *n* augmentation *f* (**in, of** de); intensification *f* (**in, of** de); **on the i.** en hausse. ◆—**ing** (*amount etc*) croissant. ◆—**ingly** *adv* de plus en plus.

incredib/le [ɪn'kredəb(ə)l] *a* incroyable. ◆—**ly** *adv* incroyablement.

incredulous [ɪn'kredjuləs] *a* incrédule. ◆**incre'dulity** *n* incrédulité *f*.

increment ['ɪnkrəmənt]] *n* augmentation *f*.

incriminat/e [ɪn'krɪmɪnet] *vt* incriminer. ◆—**ing** *a* compromettant.

incubate ['ɪnkjubet] *vt* (*eggs*) couver. ◆**incu'bation** *n* incubation *f*. ◆**incubator** *n* (*for baby, eggs*) couveuse *f*.

inculcate ['ɪnkʌlket] *vt* inculquer (**in** à).

incumbent [ɪn'kʌmbənt] *a* **it is i. upon him** *or* **her** to il lui incombe de; — *n Rel Pol* titulaire *mf*.

incur [ɪn'kɜːr] *vt* (-**rr**-) (*debt*) contracter; (*expenses*) faire; (*criticism, danger*) s'attirer.

incurable [ɪn'kjuərəb(ə)l] *a* incurable.

incursion [ɪn'kɜːʃ(ə)n] *n* incursion *f* (**into** dans).

indebted [ɪn'detɪd] *a* **i. to s.o. for sth/for doing sth** redevable à qn de qch/d'avoir fait qch. ◆—**ness** *n* dette *f*.

indecent [ɪn'diːs(ə)nt] *a* (*offensive*) indécent; (*unsuitable*) peu approprié. ◆**indecency** *n* indécence *f*; (*crime*) *Jur* outrage *m* à la pudeur. ◆**indecently** *adv* indécemment.

indecisive [ɪndɪ'saɪsɪv] *a* (*person, answer*) indécis. ◆**indecision** *n*, ◆**indecisiveness** *n* indécision *f*.

indeed [ɪn'diːd] *adv* en effet; **very good/etc i.** vraiment très bon/etc; **yes i.!** bien sûr!; **thank you very much i.!** merci mille fois!

indefensible [ɪndɪ'fensəb(ə)l] *a* indéfendable.

indefinable [ɪndɪ'faɪnəb(ə)l] *a* indéfinissable.

indefinite [ɪn'defɪnət] *a* (*feeling, duration etc*) indéfini; (*plan*) mal déterminé. ◆—**ly** *adv* indéfiniment.

indelible [ɪn'deləb(ə)l] *a* indélébile; **i. pencil** crayon *m* à marquer.

indelicate [ɪn'delɪkət] *a* (*coarse*) indélicat.

indemnify [ɪn'demnɪfaɪ] *vt* indemniser (**for** de). ◆**indemnity** *n* indemnité *f*.

indented [ɪn'dentɪd] *a* (*edge*) dentelé, découpé; (*line*) *Typ* renfoncé. ◆**inden-'tation** *n* dentelure *f*, découpure *f*; *Typ* renfoncement *m*.

independent [ɪndɪ'pendənt] *a* indépendant (**of** de); (*opinions, reports*) de sources différentes. ◆**independence** *n* indépendance *f*. ◆**independently** *adv* de façon indépendante; **i. of** indépendamment de.

indescribable [ɪndɪ'skraɪbəb(ə)l] *a* indescriptible.

indestructible [ɪndɪ'strʌktəb(ə)l] *a* indestructible.

indeterminate [ɪndɪ'tɜːmɪnət] *a* indéterminé.

index ['ɪndeks] *n* (*in book etc*) index *m*; (*in library*) catalogue *m*; (*number, sign*) indice *m*; **i. card** fiche *f*; **i. finger** index *m*; — *vt* (*classify*) classer. ◆**i.-'linked** *a Econ* indexé (**to** sur).

India ['ɪndɪə] *n* Inde *f*. ◆**Indian** *a & n* indien, -ienne (*mf*).

indicate ['ɪndɪkeɪt] *vt* indiquer (**that** que); **I was indicating right** *Aut* j'avais mis mon clignotant droit. ◆**indi'cation** *n* (*sign*) indice *m*, indication *f*; (*idea*) idée *f*. ◆**in'dicative** *a* indicatif (**of** de); — *n* (*mood*) *Gram* indicatif *m*. ◆**indicator** *n* (*instrument*) indicateur *m*; (*sign*) indication *f* (**of** de); *Aut* clignotant *m*; (*display board*) tableau *m* (indicateur).

indict [ɪn'daɪt] *vt* inculper (**for** de). ◆—**ment** *n* inculpation *f*.

Indies ['ɪndɪz] *npl* **the West I.** les Antilles *fpl*.

indifferent [ɪn'dɪf(ə)rənt] *a* indifférent (**to** à); (*mediocre*) *Pej* médiocre. ◆**indifference** *n* indifférence *f* (**to** à). ◆**indifferently** *adv* indifféremment.

indigenous [ɪn'dɪdʒɪnəs] *a* indigène.

indigestion [ɪndɪ'dʒestʃ(ə)n] *n* dyspepsie *f*; (**an attack of**) **i.** une indigestion, une crise de foie. ◆**indigestible** *a* indigeste.

indignant [ɪn'dɪgnənt] *a* indigné (**at** de, **with** contre); **to become i.** s'indigner. ◆**indignantly** *adv* avec indignation. ◆**indig'nation** *n* indignation *f*.

indignity [ɪn'dɪgnɪtɪ] *n* indignité *f*.

indigo ['ɪndɪgəʊ] *n & a* (*colour*) indigo *m & a inv*.

indirect [ɪndaɪ'rekt] *a* indirect. ◆—**ly** *adv* indirectement.

indiscreet [ɪndɪ'skriːt] *a* indiscret. ◆**indiscretion** *n* indiscrétion *f*.

indiscriminate [ɪndɪ'skrɪmɪnət] *a* (*person*)

qui manque de discernement; (*random*) fait, donné *etc* au hasard; ◆**—ly** *adv* (*at random*) au hasard; (*without discrimination*) sans discernement.

indispensable [ɪndɪ'spensəb(ə)l] *a* indispensable (**to** à).

indisposed [ɪndɪ'spəʊzd] *a* (*unwell*) indisposé. ◆**indispo'sition** *n* indisposition *f*.

indisputable [ɪndɪ'spjuːtəb(ə)l] *a* incontestable.

indistinct [ɪndɪ'stɪŋkt] *a* indistinct.

indistinguishable [ɪndɪ'stɪŋgwɪʃəb(ə)l] *a* indifférenciable (**from** de).

individual [ɪndɪ'vɪdʒʊəl] *a* individuel; (*unusual, striking*) singulier, particulier; – *n* (*person*) individu *m*. ◆**individualist** *n* individualiste *mf*. ◆**individua'listic** *a* individualiste. ◆**individu'ality** *n* (*distinctiveness*) individualité *f*. ◆**individually** *adv* (*separately*) individuellement; (*unusually*) de façon (très) personnelle.

indivisible [ɪndɪ'vɪzəb(ə)l] *a* indivisible.

Indo-China [ɪndəʊ'tʃaɪnə] *n* Indochine *f*.

indoctrinate [ɪn'dɒktrɪneɪt] *vt Pej* endoctriner. ◆**indoctri'nation** *n* endoctrinement *m*.

indolent ['ɪndələnt] *a* indolent. ◆**indolence** *n* indolence *f*.

indomitable [ɪn'dɒmɪtəb(ə)l] *a* (*will, energy*) indomptable.

Indonesia [ɪndəʊ'niːʒə] *n* Indonésie *f*.

indoor ['ɪndɔːr] *a* (*games, shoes etc*) d'intérieur; (*swimming pool etc*) couvert. ◆**in'doors** *adv* à l'intérieur; **to go** *or* **come i.** rentrer.

induce [ɪn'djuːs] *vt* (*persuade*) persuader (**to do** de faire); (*cause*) provoquer; **to i. labour** *Med* déclencher le travail. ◆**—ment** *n* encouragement *m* (**to do** à faire).

indulge [ɪn'dʌldʒ] *vt* (*s.o.'s desires*) satisfaire; (*child etc*) gâter, tout passer à; **to i. oneself** se gâter; – *vi* **to i. in** (*action*) s'adonner à; (*ice cream etc*) se permettre. ◆**indulgence** *n* indulgence *f*. ◆**indulgent** *a* indulgent (**to** envers, **with** avec).

industrial [ɪn'dʌstrɪəl] *a* industriel; (*conflict, legislation*) du travail; **i. action** action *f* revendicative; **i. park** *Am* complexe *m* industriel. ◆**industrialist** *n* industriel, -ielle *mf*. ◆**industrialized** *a* industrialisé.

industrious [ɪn'dʌstrɪəs] *a* travailleur.

industry ['ɪndəstrɪ] *n* industrie *f*; (*hard work*) application *f*.

inedible [ɪn'edəb(ə)l] *a* immangeable.

ineffective [ɪnɪ'fektɪv] *a* (*measure etc*) sans effet, inefficace; (*person*) incapable. ◆**—ness** *n* inefficacité *f*.

ineffectual [ɪnɪ'fektʃʊəl] *a* (*measure etc*) inefficace; (*person*) incompétent.

inefficient [ɪnɪ'fɪʃ(ə)nt] *a* (*person, measure etc*) inefficace; (*machine*) peu performant. ◆**inefficiency** *n* inefficacité *f*.

ineligible [ɪn'elɪdʒəb(ə)l] *a* (*candidate*) inéligible; **to be i. for** ne pas avoir droit à.

inept [ɪ'nept] *a* (*foolish*) inepte; (*unskilled*) peu habile (**at sth** à qch); (*incompetent*) incapable, inapte. ◆**ineptitude** *n* (*incapacity*) inaptitude *f*.

inequality [ɪnɪ'kwɒlətɪ] *n* inégalité *f*.

inert [ɪ'nɜːt] *a* inerte. ◆**inertia** [ɪ'nɜːʃə] *n* inertie *f*.

inescapable [ɪnɪ'skeɪpəb(ə)l] *a* inéluctable.

inevitable [ɪn'evɪtəb(ə)l] *a* inévitable. ◆**inevitably** *adv* inévitablement.

inexcusable [ɪnɪk'skjuːzəb(ə)l] *a* inexcusable.

inexhaustible [ɪnɪg'zɔːstəb(ə)l] *a* inépuisable.

inexorable [ɪn'eksərəb(ə)l] *a* inexorable.

inexpensive [ɪnɪk'spensɪv] *a* à bon marché *inv*.

inexperience [ɪnɪk'spɪərɪəns] *n* inexpérience *f*. ◆**inexperienced** *a* inexpérimenté.

inexplicable [ɪnɪk'splɪkəb(ə)l] *a* inexplicable.

inexpressible [ɪnɪk'spresəb(ə)l] *a* inexprimable.

inextricable [ɪnɪk'strɪkəb(ə)l] *a* inextricable.

infallible [ɪn'fæləb(ə)l] *a* infaillible. ◆**infalli'bility** *n* infaillibilité *f*.

infamous ['ɪnfəməs] *a* (*evil*) infâme. ◆**infamy** *n* infamie *f*.

infant ['ɪnfənt] *n* (*child*) enfant *mf*; (*baby*) nourrisson *m*; **i. school** classes *fpl* préparatoires. ◆**infancy** *n* petite enfance *f*; **to be in its i.** (*of art, technique etc*) en être à ses premiers balbutiements. ◆**infantile** *a* (*illness, reaction etc*) infantile.

infantry ['ɪnfəntrɪ] *n* infanterie *f*.

infatuated [ɪn'fætʃʊeɪtɪd] *a* amoureux; **i. with** (*person*) amoureux de, engoué de; (*sport etc*) engoué de. ◆**infatu'ation** *n* engouement *m* (**for, with** pour).

infect [ɪn'fekt] *vt* (*contaminate*) *Med* infecter; **to become infected** s'infecter; **to i. s.o. with sth** communiquer qch à qn. ◆**infection** *n* infection *f*. ◆**infectious** *a* (*disease*) infectieux, contagieux; (*person, laughter etc*) contagieux.

infer [ɪn'fɜːr] *vt* (**-rr-**) déduire (**from** de, **that** que). ◆**inference** *n* déduction *f*, conclusion *f*.

inferior [ɪn'fɪərɪər] *a* inférieur (**to** à); (*goods, work*) de qualité inférieure; – *n* (*person*) *Pej* inférieur, -eure *mf*. ◆**inferi'ority** *n* infériorité *f*.

infernal [ɪn'fɜːn(ə)l] *a* infernal. ◆**—ly** *adv Fam* épouvantablement.

inferno [ɪn'fɜːnəu] *n* (*pl* -os) (*blaze*) brasier *m*, incendie *m*; (*hell*) enfer *m*.

infertile [ɪn'fɜːtaɪl, *Am* ɪn'fɜːt(ə)l] *a* (*person, land*) stérile.

infest [ɪn'fest] *vt* infester (**with** de).

infidelity [ɪnfɪ'delɪtɪ] *n* infidélité *f*.

infighting ['ɪnfaɪtɪŋ] *n* (*within group*) luttes *fpl* intestines.

infiltrate ['ɪnfɪltreɪt] *vi* s'infiltrer (**into** dans); – *vt* (*group etc*) s'infiltrer dans. ◆**infil'tration** *n* infiltration *f*; *Pol* noyautage *m*.

infinite ['ɪnfɪnɪt] *a & n* infini (*m*). ◆**infinitely** *adv* infiniment. ◆**in'finity** *n Math Phot* infini *m*; **to i.** *Math* à l'infini.

infinitive [ɪn'fɪnɪtɪv] *n Gram* infinitif *m*.

infirm [ɪn'fɜːm] *a* infirme. ◆**infirmary** *n* (*sickbay*) infirmerie *f*; (*hospital*) hôpital *m*. ◆**infirmity** *n* (*disability*) infirmité *f*.

inflame [ɪn'fleɪm] *vt* enflammer. ◆**inflammable** *a* inflammable. ◆**infla'mmation** *n Med* inflammation *f*. ◆**inflammatory** *a* (*remark*) incendiaire.

inflate [ɪn'fleɪt] *vt* (*tyre, prices etc*) gonfler. ◆**inflatable** *a* gonflable. ◆**inflation** *n Econ* inflation *f*. ◆**inflationary** *a Econ* inflationniste.

inflection [ɪn'flek(ə)n] *n Gram* flexion *f*; (*of voice*) inflexion *f*.

inflexible [ɪn'fleksəb(ə)l] *a* inflexible.

inflexion [ɪn'flek(ə)n] *n* = **inflection**.

inflict [ɪn'flɪkt] *vt* infliger (**on** à); (*wound*) occasionner (**on** à).

influence ['ɪnfluəns] *n* influence *f*; **under the i. of** (*anger, drugs*) sous l'effet de; **under the i. of drink** *or* **alcohol** *Jur* en état d'ébriété; – *vt* influencer. ◆**influ'ential** *a* influent.

influenza [ɪnflu'enzə] *n Med* grippe *f*.

influx ['ɪnflʌks] *n* flot *m*, afflux *m*.

info ['ɪnfəu] *n SI* tuyaux *mpl*, renseignements *mpl* (**on** sur).

inform [ɪn'fɔːm] *vt* informer (**of** de, **that** que); – *vi* **to i. on** dénoncer. ◆**—ed** *a* informé; **to keep s.o. i. of** tenir qn au courant de. ◆**informant** *n* informateur, -trice *mf*. ◆**informative** *a* instructif. ◆**informer** *n* (*police*) i. indicateur, -trice *mf*.

informal [ɪn'fɔːm(ə)l] *a* (*without fuss*) simple, sans façon; (*occasion*) dénué de formalité; (*tone, expression*) familier; (*announcement*) officieux; (*meeting*) non-officiel. ◆**infor-**

'mality *n* simplicité *f*; (*of tone etc*) familiarité *f*. ◆**informally** *adv* (*without fuss*) sans cérémonie; (*to meet*) officieusement; (*to dress*) simplement.

information [ɪnfə'meɪʃ(ə)n] *n* (*facts*) renseignements *mpl* (**about, on** sur); (*knowledge*) & *Math* information *f*; **a piece of i.** un renseignement, une information; **to get some i.** se renseigner.

infrared [ɪnfrə'red] *a* infrarouge.

infrequent [ɪn'friːkwənt] *a* peu fréquent.

infringe [ɪn'frɪndʒ] *vt* (*rule*) contrevenir à; – *vi* **to i. upon** (*encroach on*) empiéter sur. ◆**—ment** *n* infraction *f* (**of** à).

infuriat/e [ɪn'fjuərɪeɪt] *vt* exaspérer. ◆**—ing** *a* exaspérant.

infuse [ɪn'fjuːz] *vt* (*tea*) (faire) infuser. ◆**infusion** *n* infusion *f*.

ingenious [ɪn'dʒiːnɪəs] *a* ingénieux. ◆**inge'nuity** *n* ingéniosité *f*.

ingot ['ɪŋgət] *n* lingot *m*.

ingrained [ɪn'greɪnd] *a* (*prejudice*) enraciné; **i. dirt** crasse *f*.

ingratiat/e [ɪn'greɪʃɪeɪt] *vt* **to i. oneself with** s'insinuer dans les bonnes grâces de. ◆**—ing** *a* (*person, smile*) insinuant.

ingratitude [ɪn'grætɪtjuːd] *n* ingratitude *f*.

ingredient [ɪn'griːdɪənt] *n* ingrédient *m*.

ingrown [ɪn'grəun] *a* (*nail*) incarné.

inhabit [ɪn'hæbɪt] *vt* habiter. ◆**—able** *a* habitable. ◆**inhabitant** *n* habitant, -ante *mf*.

inhale [ɪn'heɪl] *vt* aspirer; **to i. the smoke** (*of smoker*) avaler la fumée. ◆**inha'lation** *n* inhalation *f*. ◆**inhaler** *n Med* inhalateur *m*.

inherent [ɪn'hɪərənt] *a* inhérent (**in** à). ◆**—ly** *adv* intrinsèquement, en soi.

inherit [ɪn'herɪt] *vt* hériter (de); (*title*) succéder à. ◆**inheritance** *n* héritage *m*; (*process*) *Jur* succession *f*; (*cultural*) patrimoine *m*.

inhibit [ɪn'hɪbɪt] *vt* (*hinder*) gêner; (*control*) maîtriser; (*prevent*) empêcher (**from** de); **to be inhibited** être inhibé, avoir des inhibitions. ◆**inhi'bition** *n* inhibition *f*.

inhospitable [ɪnhɒ'spɪtəb(ə)l] *a* inhospitalier.

inhuman [ɪn'hjuːmən] *a* (*not human, cruel*) inhumain. ◆**inhu'mane** *a* (*not kind*) inhumain. ◆**inhu'manity** *n* brutalité *f*, cruauté *f*.

inimitable [ɪ'nɪmɪtəb(ə)l] *a* inimitable.

iniquitous [ɪ'nɪkwɪtəs] *a* inique. ◆**iniquity** *n* iniquité *f*.

initial [ɪ'nɪʃ(ə)l] *a* initial, premier; – *n* (*letter*) initiale *f*; (*signature*) paraphe *m*; –

vt (-ll-, *Am* -l-) parapher. ◆—ly *adv* initialement, au début.

initiate [ɪ'nɪʃɪeɪt] *vt* (*reforms*) amorcer; (*schemes*) inaugurer; **to i. s.o. into** initier qn à; **the initiated** les initiés *mpl*. ◆**ini'tiation** *n* amorce *f*; inauguration *f*; initiation *f*. ◆**initiator** *n* initiateur, -trice *mf*.

initiative [ɪ'nɪʃətɪv] *n* initiative *f*.

inject [ɪn'dʒekt] *vt* injecter (**into** à); (*new life etc*) *Fig* insuffler (**into** à). ◆**injection** *n Med* injection *f*, piqûre *f*.

injunction [ɪn'dʒʌŋk(ə)n] *n Jur* ordonnance *f*.

injur/e [ɪnd'ʒər] *vt* (*physically*) blesser; (*prejudice, damage*) nuire à; (*one's chances*) compromettre; **to i. one's foot**/*etc* se blesser au pied/*etc*. ◆**—ed** *a* blessé; — **the i.** les blessés *mpl*. ◆**injury** *n* (*to flesh*) blessure *f*; (*fracture*) fracture *f*; (*sprain*) foulure *f*; (*bruise*) contusion *f*; (*wrong*) *Fig* préjudice *m*.

injurious [ɪn'dʒʊərɪəs] *a* préjudiciable (**to** à).

injustice [ɪn'dʒʌstɪs] *n* injustice *f*.

ink [ɪŋk] *n* encre *f*; **Indian i.** encre *f* de Chine. ◆**inkpot** *n*, ◆**inkwell** *n* encrier *m*. ◆**inky** *a* couvert d'encre.

inkling [ɪŋklɪŋ] *n* (*slight*) idée *f*; **to have some** *or* **an i. of sth** soupçonner qch, avoir une (petite) idée de qch.

inlaid [ɪn'leɪd] *a* (*marble etc*) incrusté (**with** de); (*wood*) marqueté.

inland ['ɪnlənd, 'ɪnlænd] *a* intérieur; **the I. Revenue** le fisc; — [ɪn'lænd] *adv* à l'intérieur (**des terres**).

in-laws ['ɪnlɔːz] *npl* belle-famille *f*.

inlet ['ɪnlet] *n* (*of sea*) crique *f*; **i. pipe** tuyau *m* d'arrivée.

inmate ['ɪnmeɪt] *n* résident, -ente *mf*; (*of asylum*) interné, -ée *mf*; (*of prison*) détenu, -ue *mf*.

inmost ['ɪnməʊst] *a* le plus profond.

inn [ɪn] *n* auberge *f*. ◆**innkeeper** *n* aubergiste *mf*.

innards ['ɪnədz] *npl Fam* entrailles *fpl*.

innate [ɪ'neɪt] *a* inné.

inner ['ɪnər] *a* intérieur; (*ear*) interne; (*feelings*) intime, profond; **the i. city** le cœur de la ville; **an i. circle** (*group of people*) un cercle restreint; **the i. circle** le saint des saints; **i. tube** (*of tyre*) chambre *f* à air. ◆**innermost** *a* le plus profond.

inning ['ɪnɪŋ] *n Baseball* tour *m* de batte. ◆**innings** *n inv Cricket* tour *m* de batte; **a good i.** *Fig* une vie longue.

innocent ['ɪnəs(ə)nt] *a* innocent. ◆**inno-**

cence *n* innocence *f*. ◆**innocently** *adv* innocemment.

innocuous [ɪ'nɒkjʊəs] *a* inoffensif.

innovate ['ɪnəveɪt] *vi* innover. ◆**inno-'vation** *n* innovation *f*. ◆**innovator** *n* innovateur, -trice *mf*.

innuendo [ɪnjʊ'endəʊ] *n* (*pl* -oes *or* -os) insinuation *f*.

innumerable [ɪ'njuːmərəb(ə)l] *a* innombrable.

inoculate [ɪ'nɒkjʊleɪt] *vt* vacciner (**against** contre). ◆**inocu'lation** *n* inoculation *f*.

inoffensive [ɪnə'fensɪv] *a* inoffensif.

inoperative [ɪn'ɒpərətɪv] *a* (*without effect*) inopérant.

inopportune [ɪn'ɒpətjuːn] *a* inopportun.

inordinate [ɪ'nɔːdɪnət] *a* excessif. ◆—ly *adv* excessivement.

in-patient ['ɪnpeɪʃ(ə)nt] *n* malade *mf* hospitalisé(e).

input ['ɪnpʊt] *n* (*computer operation*) entrée *f*; (*data*) données *fpl*; (*current*) *El* énergie *f*.

inquest ['ɪnkwest] *n* enquête *f*.

inquir/e [ɪn'kwaɪər] *vi* se renseigner (**about** sur); **to i. after** s'informer de; **to i. into** examiner, faire une enquête sur; — *vt* demander; **to i. how to get to** demander le chemin de. ◆**—ing** *a* (*mind, look*) curieux. ◆**inquiry** *n* (*question*) question *f*; (*request for information*) demande *f* de renseignements; (*information*) renseignements *mpl*; *Jur* enquête *f*; **to make inquiries** demander des renseignements; (*of police*) enquêter.

inquisitive [ɪn'kwɪzɪtɪv] *a* curieux. ◆**inquisitively** *adv* avec curiosité. ◆**inqui'sition** *n* (*inquiry*) & *Rel* inquisition *f*.

inroads ['ɪnrəʊdz] *npl* (*attacks*) incursions *fpl* (**into** dans); **to make i. into** (*start on*) *Fig* entamer.

insane [ɪn'seɪn] *a* fou, dément. ◆**insanely** *adv* comme un fou. ◆**insanity** *n* folie *f*, démence *f*.

insanitary [ɪn'sænɪt(ə)rɪ] *a* insalubre.

insatiable [ɪn'seɪʃəb(ə)l] *a* insatiable.

inscribe [ɪn'skraɪb] *vt* inscrire; (*book*) dédicacer (**to** à). ◆**inscription** *n* inscription *f*; dédicace *f*.

inscrutable [ɪn'skruːtəb(ə)l] *a* impénétrable.

insect ['ɪnsekt] *n* insecte *m*; — *a* (*powder, spray*) insecticide; **i. repellant** crème *f* anti-insecte. ◆**in'secticide** *n* insecticide *m*.

insecure [ɪnsɪ'kjʊər] *a* (*not fixed*) peu solide; (*furniture, ladder*) branlant, bancal; (*window*) mal fermé; (*uncertain*) incertain;

(*unsafe*) peu sûr; (*person*) qui manque d'assurance. ◆**insecurity** *n* (*of person, situation*) insécurité *f*.

insemination [ɪnsemɪˈneɪʃ(ə)n] *n Med* insémination *f*.

insensible [ɪnˈsensəb(ə)l] *a Med* inconscient.

insensitive [ɪnˈsensɪtɪv] *a* insensible (**to** à). ◆**insen'tivity** *n* insensibilité *f*.

inseparable [ɪnˈsep(ə)rəb(ə)l] *a* inséparable (**from** de).

insert [ɪnˈsɜːt] *vt* insérer (**in, into** dans). ◆**insertion** *n* insertion *f*.

inshore [ˈɪnʃɔːr] *a* côtier.

inside [ɪnˈsaɪd] *adv* dedans, à l'intérieur; **come i.!** entrez!; – *prep* à l'intérieur de, dans; (*time*) en moins de; – *n* dedans *m*, intérieur *m*; *pl* (*stomach*) *Fam* ventre *m*; **on the i.** à l'intérieur (**of** de); **i. out** (*coat, socks etc*) à l'envers; (*to know, study etc*) à fond; **to turn everything i. out** *Fig* tout chambouler; – *a* intérieur; (*information*) obtenu à la source; **the i. lane** *Aut* la voie de gauche, *Am* la voie de droite.

insidious [ɪnˈsɪdɪəs] *a* insidieux.

insight [ˈɪnsaɪt] *n* perspicacité *f*; **to give an i. into** (*s.o.'s character*) permettre de comprendre, éclairer; (*question*) donner un aperçu de.

insignia [ɪnˈsɪgnɪə] *npl* (*of important person*) insignes *mpl*.

insignificant [ɪnsɪgˈnɪfɪkənt] *a* insignifiant. ◆**insignificance** *n* insignifiance *f*.

insincere [ɪnsɪnˈsɪər] *a* peu sincère. ◆**insincerity** *n* manque *m* de sincérité.

insinuate [ɪnˈsɪnjueɪt] *vt* 1 *Pej* insinuer (**that** que). **2 to i. oneself into** s'insinuer dans. ◆**insinu'ation** *n* insinuation *f*.

insipid [ɪnˈsɪpɪd] *a* insipide.

insist [ɪnˈsɪst] *vi* insister (**on doing** pour faire); **to i. on sth** (*demand*) exiger qch; (*assert*) affirmer qch; – *vt* (*order*) insister (**that** pour que); (*declare firmly*) affirmer (**that** que); **I i. that you come** *or* **on your coming** j'insiste pour que tu viennes. ◆**insistence** *n* insistance *f*; **her i. on seeing me** le fait qu'elle met à vouloir me voir. ◆**insistent** *a* insistant; **I was i.** (**about it**) j'ai été pressant. ◆**insistently** *adv* avec insistance.

insolent [ˈɪnsələnt] *a* insolent. ◆**insolence** *n* insolence *f*. ◆**insolently** *adv* insolemment.

insoluble [ɪnˈsɒljub(ə)l] *a* insoluble.

insolvent [ɪnˈsɒlvənt] *a Fin* insolvable.

insomnia [ɪnˈsɒmnɪə] *n* insomnie *f*. ◆**insomniac** *n* insomniaque *mf*.

insomuch as [ɪnsəʊˈmʌtʃəz] *adv* = **inasmuch as.**

inspect [ɪnˈspekt] *vt* inspecter; (*tickets*) contrôler; (*troops*) passer en revue. ◆**inspection** *n* inspection *f*; contrôle *m*; revue *f*. ◆**inspector** *n* inspecteur, -trice *mf*; (*on bus*) contrôleur, -euse *mf*.

inspir/e [ɪnˈspaɪər] *vt* inspirer (**s.o. with sth** qch à qn); **to be inspired to do** avoir l'inspiration de faire. ◆**—ed** *a* inspiré. ◆**—ing** *a* qui inspire. ◆**inspi'ration** *n* inspiration *f*; (*person*) source *f* d'inspiration.

instability [ɪnstəˈbɪlɪtɪ] *n* instabilité *f*.

install [ɪnˈstɔːl] *vt* installer. ◆**insta'llation** *n* installation *f*.

instalment [ɪnˈstɔːlmənt] (*Am* **installment**) *n* (*of money*) acompte *m*, versement *m* (*partiel*); (*of serial*) épisode *m*; (*of publication*) fascicule *m*; **to buy on the i. plan** *Am* acheter à crédit.

instance [ˈɪnstəns] *n* (*example*) exemple *m*; (*case*) cas *m*; (*occasion*) circonstance *f*; **for i.** par exemple; **in the first i.** en premier lieu.

instant [ˈɪnstənt] *a* immédiat; **i. coffee** café *m* soluble *or* instantané, nescafé® *m*; **of the 3rd i.** (*in letter*) *Com* du 3 courant; – *n* (*moment*) instant *m*; **this (very) i.** (*at once*) à l'instant; **the i. that** (*as soon as*) dès que. ◆**instan'taneous** *a* instantané. ◆**instantly** *adv* immédiatement.

instead [ɪnˈsted] *adv* (*as alternative*) au lieu de cela, plutôt; **i. of** au lieu de; **i. of s.o.** à la place de qn; **i.** (**of him** *or* **her**) à sa place.

instep [ˈɪnstep] *n* (*of foot*) cou-de-pied *m*; (*of shoe*) cambrure *f*.

instigate [ˈɪnstɪgeɪt] *vt* provoquer. ◆**insti'gation** *n* instigation *f*. ◆**instigator** *n* instigateur, -trice *mf*.

instil [ɪnˈstɪl] *vt* (**-ll-**) (*idea*) inculquer (**into** à); (*courage*) insuffler (**into** à).

instinct [ˈɪnstɪŋkt] *n* instinct *m*; **by i.** d'instinct. ◆**in'stinctive** *a* instinctif. ◆**in'stinctively** *adv* instinctivement.

institute [ˈɪnstɪtjuːt] **1** *vt* (*rule, practice*) instituer; (*inquiry, proceedings*) *Jur* entamer, intenter. **2** *n* institut *m*. ◆**insti'tution** *n* (*custom, private or charitable organization etc*) institution *f*; (*school, hospital*) établissement *m*; (*home*) *Med* asile *m*. ◆**insti'tutional** *a* institutionnel.

instruct [ɪnˈstrʌkt] *vt* (*teach*) enseigner (**s.o. in sth** qch à qn); **to i. s.o. about sth** (*inform*) instruire qn de qch; **to i. s.o. to do** (*order*) charger qn de faire. ◆**instruction** *n* (*teaching*) instruction *f*; *pl* (*orders*) instructions *fpl*; **instructions** (**for use**) mode *m*

d'emploi. ◆**instructive** a instructif.
◆**instructor** n professeur m; Sp moniteur,
-trice mf; Mil instructeur m; Univ Am
maître-assistant, -ante mf; **driving i.**
moniteur, -trice mf de conduite.

instrument [ˈɪnstrəmənt] n instrument m.
◆**instru'mental** a Mus instrumental; **to
be i. in sth/in doing sth** contribuer à qch/à
faire qch. ◆**instru'mentalist** n Mus
instrumentaliste mf. ◆**instrumen'tation**
n Mus orchestration f.

insubordinate [ɪnsəˈbɔːdɪnət] a indiscipliné. ◆**insubordi'nation** n indiscipline f.

insubstantial [ɪnsəbˈstænʃ(ə)l] a (argument,
evidence) peu solide.

insufferable [ɪnˈsʌfərəb(ə)l] a intolérable.

insufficient [ɪnsəˈfɪʃənt] a insuffisant.
◆—**ly** adv insuffisamment.

insular [ˈɪnsjʊlər] a (climate) insulaire;
(views) Pej étroit, borné.

insulate [ˈɪnsjʊleɪt] vt (against cold etc) & El
isoler; (against sound) insonoriser; **to i. s.o.
from** Fig protéger qn de; **insulating tape**
chatterton m. ◆**insu'lation** n isolation f;
insonorisation f; (material) isolant m.

insulin [ˈɪnsjʊlɪn] n Med insuline f.

insult [ɪnˈsʌlt] vt insulter; – [ˈɪnsʌlt] n insulte
f (to à).

insuperable [ɪnˈsuːpərəb(ə)l] a insurmontable.

insure [ɪnˈʃʊər] vt 1 (protect against damage
etc) assurer (**against** contre). 2 Am =
ensure. ◆**insurance** n assurance f; **i.
company** compagnie f d'assurances; **i.
policy** police f d'assurance.

insurgent [ɪnˈsɜːdʒənt] a & n insurgé, -ée
(mf).

insurmountable [ɪnsəˈmaʊntəb(ə)l] a
insurmontable.

insurrection [ɪnsəˈrekʃ(ə)n] n insurrection
f.

intact [ɪnˈtækt] a intact.

intake [ˈɪnteɪk] n (of food) consommation f;
Sch Univ admissions fpl; Tech admission f.

intangible [ɪnˈtændʒəb(ə)l] a intangible.

integral [ˈɪntɪgrəl] a intégral; **to be an i. part
of** faire partie intégrante de.

integrate [ˈɪntɪgreɪt] vt intégrer (**into** dans);
– vi s'intégrer (**into** dans); (racially) integ-
grated (school etc) Am où se pratique la
déségrégation raciale. ◆**integration** n
intégration f; (**racial**) **i.** déségrégation f
raciale.

integrity [ɪnˈtegrɪtɪ] n intégrité f.

intellect [ˈɪntɪlekt] n (faculty) intellect m,
intelligence f; (cleverness, person) intelli-

gence f. ◆**inte'llectual** a & n intellectuel,
-elle (mf).

intelligence [ɪnˈtelɪdʒəns] n intelligence f;
Mil renseignements mpl. ◆**intelligent** a
intelligent. ◆**intelligently** adv intelligemment. ◆**intelli'gentsia** n intelligentsia f.

intelligible [ɪnˈtelɪdʒəb(ə)l] a intelligible.
◆**intelligi'bility** n intelligibilité f.

intemperance [ɪnˈtempərəns] n intempérance f.

intend [ɪnˈtend] vt (gift, remark etc) destiner
(**for** à); **to i. to do** avoir l'intention de faire;
I i. you to stay mon intention est que vous
restiez. ◆—**ed** a (deliberate) intentionnel,
voulu; (planned) projeté; **i. to be** (meant)
destiné à être. ◆**intention** n intention f (of
doing de faire). ◆**intentional** a intentionnel; **it wasn't i.** ce n'était pas fait exprès.
◆**intentionally** adv intentionnellement,
exprès.

intense [ɪnˈtens] a intense; (interest) vif;
(person) passionné. ◆**intensely** adv intensément; Fig extrêmement. ◆**intensifi-
'cation** n intensification f. ◆**intensify** vt
intensifier; – vi s'intensifier. ◆**intensity** n
intensité f. ◆**intensive** a intensif; **in i.
care** Med en réanimation.

intent [ɪnˈtent] **1** a (look) attentif; **i. on** (task)
absorbé par; **i. on doing** résolu à faire. **2** n
intention f; **to all intents and purposes** en
fait, essentiellement.

inter [ɪnˈtɜːr] vt (-rr-) enterrer.

inter- [ˈɪntə(r)] pref inter-.

interact [ɪntəˈrækt] vi (of ideas etc) être
interdépendants; (of people) agir conjointement; Ch interagir. ◆**interaction** n
interaction f.

intercede [ɪntəˈsiːd] vi intercéder (**with**
auprès de).

intercept [ɪntəˈsept] vt intercepter. ◆**interception** n interception f.

interchange [ˈɪntətʃeɪndʒ] n Aut échangeur
m. ◆**inter'changeable** a interchangeable.

intercom [ˈɪntəkɒm] n interphone m.

interconnect/ed [ɪntəkəˈnektɪd] a (facts
etc) liés. ◆—**ing** a **i. rooms** pièces fpl
communicantes.

intercontinental [ɪntəkɒntɪˈnent(ə)l] a
intercontinental.

intercourse [ˈɪntəkɔːs] n (sexual, social)
rapports mpl.

interdependent [ɪntədɪˈpendənt] a interdépendant; (parts of machine) solidaire.

interest [ˈɪnt(ə)rɪst, ˈɪntrəst] n intérêt m; Fin
intérêts mpl; **an i. in** (stake) Com des intérêts dans; **his or her i. is** (hobby etc) ce qui

l'intéresse c'est; **to take an i. in** s'intéresser à; **to be of i. to s.o.** intéresser qn; — *vt* intéresser. ◆**—ed** *a* (*involved*) intéressé; (*look*) d'intérêt; **to seem i.** sembler intéressé (in par); **to be i. in sth/s.o.** s'intéresser à qch/qn; **I'm i. in doing** ça m'intéresse de faire; **are you i.?** ça vous intéresse? ◆**—ing** *a* intéressant. ◆**—ingly** *adv* **i. (enough),** **she . . .** curieusement, elle . . . .

interface ['ɪntəfeɪs] *n Tech* interface *f.*

interfer/e [ɪntə'fɪər] *vi* se mêler des affaires d'autrui; **to i. in** s'ingérer dans; **to i. with** (*upset*) déranger; (*touch*) toucher (à). ◆**—ing** *a* (*person*) importun. ◆**interference** *n* ingérence *f*; *Rad* parasites *mpl.*

interim ['ɪntərɪm] *n* intérim *m*; **in the i.** pendant l'intérim; — *a* (*measure etc*) provisoire; (*post*) intérimaire.

interior [ɪn'tɪərɪər] *a* intérieur; — *n* intérieur *m*; **Department of the I.** *Am* ministère *m* de l'Intérieur.

interjection [ɪntə'dʒekʃ(ə)n] *n* interjection *f.*

interlock [ɪntə'lɒk] *vi Tech* s'emboîter.

interloper ['ɪntələupər] *n* intrus, -use *mf.*

interlude ['ɪntəluːd] *n* intervalle *m*; *Th* intermède *m*; *Mus TV* interlude *m.*

intermarry [ɪntə'mærɪ] *vi* se marier (entre eux). ◆**intermarriage** *n* mariage *m* (*entre personnes de races etc différentes*).

intermediary [ɪntə'miːdɪərɪ] *a* & *n* intermédiaire (*mf*).

intermediate [ɪntə'miːdɪət] *a* intermédiaire; (*course*) *Sch* moyen.

interminable [ɪn'tɜːmɪnəb(ə)l] *a* interminable.

intermingle [ɪntə'mɪŋg(ə)l] *vi* se mélanger.

intermission [ɪntə'mɪʃ(ə)n] *n Cin Th* entracte *m.*

intermittent [ɪntə'mɪtənt] *a* intermittent. ◆**—ly** *adv* par intermittence.

intern 1 [ɪn'tɜːn] *vt Pol* interner. **2** ['ɪntɜːn] *n Med Am* interne *mf* (*des hôpitaux*). ◆**inter'nee** *n* interné, -ée *mf.* ◆**in'ternment** *n Pol* internement *m.*

internal [ɪn'tɜːn(ə)l] *a* interne; (*policy, flight*) intérieur; **i. combustion engine** moteur *m* à explosion; **the I. Revenue Service** *Am* le fisc. ◆**—ly** *adv* intérieurement.

international [ɪntə'næʃ(ə)nəl] *a* international; (*fame, reputation*) mondial; — *n* (*match*) rencontre *f* internationale; (*player*) international *m.* ◆**—ly** *adv* (*renowned etc*) mondialement.

interplanetary [ɪntə'plænɪt(ə)rɪ] *a* interplanétaire.

interplay ['ɪntəpleɪ] *n* interaction *f*, jeu *m.*

interpolate [ɪn'tɜːpəleɪt] *vt* interpoler.

interpret [ɪn'tɜːprɪt] *vt* interpréter; — *vi Ling* faire l'interprète. ◆**interpre'tation** *n* interprétation *f.* ◆**interpreter** *n* interprète *mf.*

interrelated [ɪntərɪ'leɪtɪd] *a* en corrélation. ◆**interrelation** *n* corrélation *f.*

interrogate [ɪn'terəgeɪt] *vt* (*question closely*) interroger. ◆**interro'gation** *n* interrogation *f*; *Jur* interrogatoire *m.* ◆**interrogator** *n* (*questioner*) interrogateur, -trice *mf.*

interrogative [ɪntə'rɒgətɪv] *a* & *n Gram* interrogatif (*m*).

interrupt [ɪntə'rʌpt] *vt* interrompre. ◆**interruption** *n* interruption *f.*

intersect [ɪntə'sekt] *vt* couper; — *vi* s'entrecouper, se couper. ◆**intersection** *n* (*crossroads*) croisement *m*; (*of lines etc*) intersection *f.*

intersperse [ɪntə'spɜːs] *vt* parsemer (**with** de).

intertwine [ɪntə'twaɪn] *vt* entrelacer.

interval ['ɪntəv(ə)l] *n* intervalle *m*; *Th* entracte *m*; **at intervals** (*time*) de temps à autre; (*space*) par intervalles; **bright intervals** *Met* éclaircies *fpl.*

intervene [ɪntə'viːn] *vi* intervenir; (*of event*) survenir; **ten years intervened** dix années s'écoulèrent; **if nothing intervenes** s'il n'arrive rien entre-temps. ◆**intervention** *n* intervention *f.*

interview ['ɪntəvjuː] *n* entrevue *f*, entretien *m* (**with** avec); *Journ TV* interview *f*; **to call for (an) i.** convoquer; — *vt* avoir une entrevue avec; *Journ TV* interviewer. ◆**—er** *n Journ TV* interviewer *m*; *Com Pol* enquêteur, -euse *mf.*

intestine [ɪn'testɪn] *n* intestin *m.*

intimate 1 ['ɪntɪmət] *a* intime; (*friendship*) profond; (*knowledge, analysis*) approfondi. ◆**intimacy** *n* intimité *f.* ◆**intimately** *adv* intimement.

intimate 2 ['ɪntɪmeɪt] *vt* (*hint*) suggérer (**that** que). ◆**inti'mation** *n* (*announcement*) annonce *f*; (*hint*) suggestion *f*; (*sign*) indication *f.*

intimidate [ɪn'tɪmɪdeɪt] *vt* intimider. ◆**intimi'dation** *n* intimidation *f.*

into ['ɪntuː, *unstressed* 'ɪntə] *prep* **1** dans; **to put i.** mettre dans; **to go i.** (*room, detail*) entrer dans. **2** en; **to translate i.** traduire en; **to change i.** transformer or changer en; **to go i. town** aller en ville; **i. pieces** (*to break etc*) en morceaux. **3 to be i.** yoga/*etc Fam* être à fond dans le yoga/*etc.*

intolerable [ɪn'tɒlərəb(ə)l] *a* intolérable

(that que (+ *sub*)). ◆**intolerably** *adv* insupportablement. ◆**intolerance** *n* intolérance *f*. ◆**intolerant** *a* intolérant (**of** de). ◆**intolerantly** *adv* avec intolérance.

intonation [ɪntəˈneɪʃ(ə)n] *n Ling* intonation *f*.

intoxicate [ɪnˈtɒksɪkeɪt] *vt* enivrer. ◆**intoxicated** *a* ivre. ◆**intoxi'cation** *n* ivresse *f*.

intra- [ˈɪntrə] *pref* intra-.

intransigent [ɪnˈtrænsɪdʒənt] *a* intransigeant. ◆**intransigence** *n* intransigeance *f*.

intransitive [ɪnˈtrænsɪtɪv] *a & n Gram* intransitif (*m*).

intravenous [ɪntrəˈviːnəs] *a Med* intraveineux.

intrepid [ɪnˈtrepɪd] *a* intrépide.

intricate [ˈɪntrɪkət] *a* complexe, compliqué. ◆**intricacy** *n* complexité *f*. ◆**intricately** *adv* de façon complexe.

intrigu/e 1 [ɪnˈtriːg] *vt* (*interest*) intriguer; **I'm intrigued to know . . .** je suis curieux de savoir . . . **2** [ˈɪntriːg] *n* (*plot*) intrigue *f*. ◆**—ing** *a* (*news etc*) curieux.

intrinsic [ɪnˈtrɪnsɪk] *a* intrinsèque. ◆**intrinsically** *adv* intrinsèquement.

introduce [ɪntrəˈdjuːs] *vt* (*insert, bring in*) introduire (**into** dans); (*programme, subject*) présenter; **to i. s.o. to Dickens/geography/etc** faire découvrir Dickens/la géographie/*etc* à qn. ◆**introduction** *n* introduction *f*; présentation *f*; (*book title*) initiation *f*; **her i. to** (*life abroad etc*) son premier contact avec. ◆**introductory** *a* (*words*) d'introduction; (*speech*) de présentation; (*course*) d'initiation.

introspective [ɪntrəˈspektɪv] *a* introspectif. ◆**introspection** *n* introspection *f*.

introvert [ˈɪntrəvɜːt] *n* introverti, -ie *mf*.

intrude [ɪnˈtruːd] *vi* (*of person*) s'imposer (**on** s.o. à qn), déranger (**on** s.o. qn); **to i. on** (*s.o.'s time etc*) abuser de. ◆**intruder** *n* intrus, -use *mf*. ◆**intrusion** *n* intrusion *f* (**into** dans); **forgive my i.** pardonnez-moi de vous avoir dérangé.

intuition [ɪntjuːˈɪʃ(ə)n] *n* intuition *f*. ◆**in'tuitive** *a* intuitif.

inundate [ˈɪnʌndeɪt] *vt* inonder (**with** de); **inundated with work** submergé de travail. ◆**inun'dation** *n* inondation *f*.

invad/e [ɪnˈveɪd] *vt* envahir; (*privacy*) violer. ◆**—er** *n* envahisseur, -euse *mf*.

invalid 1 [ˈɪnvəlɪd] *a & n* malade (*mf*); (*through injury*) infirme (*mf*); **i. car** voiture *f* d'infirme.

invalid 2 [ɪnˈvælɪd] *a* non valable. ◆**invalidate** *vt* invalider, annuler.

invaluable [ɪnˈvæljʊəb(ə)l] *a* (*help etc*) inestimable.

invariab/le [ɪnˈveərɪəb(ə)l] *a* invariable. ◆**—ly** *adv* invariablement.

invasion [ɪnˈveɪʒ(ə)n] *n* invasion *f*; **i. of s.o.'s privacy** intrusion *f* dans la vie privée de qn.

invective [ɪnˈvektɪv] *n* invective *f*.

inveigh [ɪnˈveɪ] *vi* **to i. against** invectiver contre.

inveigle [ɪnˈveɪg(ə)l] *vt* **to i. s.o. into doing** amener qn à faire par la ruse.

invent [ɪnˈvent] *vt* inventer. ◆**invention** *n* invention *f*. ◆**inventive** *a* inventif. ◆**inventiveness** *n* esprit *m* d'invention. ◆**inventor** *n* inventeur, -trice *mf*.

inventory [ˈɪnvəntrɪ] *n* inventaire *m*.

inverse [ɪnˈvɜːs] *a & n Math* inverse (*m*).

invert [ɪnˈvɜːt] *vt* intervertir; **inverted commas** guillemets *mpl*. ◆**inversion** *n* interversion *f*; *Gram Anat etc* inversion *f*.

invest [ɪnˈvest] *vt* (*funds*) investir (**in** dans); (*money*) placer, investir; (*time, effort*) consacrer (**in** à); **to i. s.o. with** (*endow*) investir qn de; — *vi* **to i. in** (*project*) placer son argent dans; (*firm*) investir dans; (*house, radio etc*) *Fig* se payer. ◆**investiture** *n* (*of bishop etc*) investiture *f*. ◆**investment** *n* investissement *m*, placement *m*. ◆**investor** *n* (*shareholder*) actionnaire *mf*; (*saver*) épargnant, -ante *mf*.

investigate [ɪnˈvestɪgeɪt] *vt* (*examine*) examiner, étudier; (*crime*) enquêter sur. ◆**investi'gation** *n* examen *m*, étude *f*; (*by police*) enquête *f* (**of** sur); (*inquiry*) enquête *f*, investigation *f*. ◆**investigator** *n* (*detective*) enquêteur, -euse *mf*.

inveterate [ɪnˈvetərət] *a* invétéré.

invidious [ɪnˈvɪdɪəs] *a* qui suscite la jalousie; (*hurtful*) blessant; (*odious*) odieux.

invigilate [ɪnˈvɪdʒɪleɪt] *vi* être de surveillance (**à** un examen). ◆**invigilator** *n* surveillant, -ante *mf*.

invigorat/e [ɪnˈvɪgəreɪt] *vt* revigorer. ◆**—ing** *a* stimulant.

invincible [ɪnˈvɪnsəb(ə)l] *a* invincible.

invisible [ɪnˈvɪzəb(ə)l] *a* invisible; **i. ink** encre *f* sympathique.

invit/e [ɪnˈvaɪt] *vt* inviter (**to do** à faire); (*ask for*) demander; (*lead to, give occasion for*) appeler; (*trouble*) chercher; **to i. out** inviter (à sortir); **to i. over** inviter (à venir); — [ˈɪnvaɪt] *n Fam* invitation *f*. ◆**—ing** *a* engageant, invitant; (*food*) appétissant. ◆**invi'tation** *n* invitation *f*.

invoice [ˈɪnvɔɪs] *n* facture *f*; — *vt* facturer.

invoke [ɪn'vəʊk] *vt* invoquer.

involuntar/y [ɪn'vɒləntərɪ] *a* involontaire. ◆**—ily** *adv* involontairement.

involv/e [ɪn'vɒlv] *vt* (*include*) mêler (*qn*) (in à), impliquer (*qn*) (in dans); (*associate*) associer (*qn*) (in à); (*entail*) entraîner; to i. oneself, get involved (*commit oneself*) s'engager (in dans); to i. s.o. in expense entraîner qn à des dépenses; the job involves going abroad le poste nécessite des déplacements à l'étranger. ◆**—ed** *a* (*complicated*) compliqué; the factors/*etc* i. (*at stake*) les facteurs/*etc* en jeu; the person i. la personne en question; i. with s.o. mêlé aux affaires de qn; personally i. concerné; emotionally i. with amoureux de; to become i. (*of police*) intervenir. ◆**—ement** *n* participation *f* (in à), implication *f* (in dans); (*commitment*) engagement *m* (in dans); (*problem*) difficulté *f*; emotional i. liaison *f*.

invulnerable [ɪn'vʌln(ə)rəb(ə)l] *a* invulnérable.

inward ['ɪnwəd] *a* & *adv* (*movement, to move*) vers l'intérieur; – *a* (*inner*) intérieur. ◆**i.-looking** *a* replié sur soi. ◆**inwardly** *adv* (*inside*) à l'intérieur; (*to laugh, curs etc*) intérieurement. ◆**inwards** *adv* vers l'intérieur.

iodine ['aɪədiːn, *Am* 'aɪədaɪn] *n Med* teinture *f* d'iode.

iota [aɪ'əʊtə] *n* (*of truth etc*) grain *m*; (*in text*) iota *m*.

IOU [aɪəʊ'juː] *n abbr* (*I owe you*) reconnaissance *f* de dette.

IQ [aɪ'kjuː] *n abbr* (*intelligence quotient*) QI *m inv*.

Iran [ɪ'rɑːn] *n* Iran *m*. ◆**Iranian** [ɪ'reɪnɪən] *a* & *n* iranien, -ienne (*mf*).

Iraq [ɪ'rɑːk] *n* Irak *m*. ◆**Iraqi** *a* & *n* irakien, -ienne (*mf*).

irascible [ɪ'ræsəb(ə)l] *a* irascible.

ire ['aɪər] *n Lit* courroux *m*. ◆**i'rate** *a* furieux.

Ireland ['aɪələnd] *n* Irlande *f*. ◆**Irish** *a* irlandais; – *n* (*language*) irlandais *m*. ◆**Irishman** *n* (*pl* -men) Irlandais *m*. ◆**Irishwoman** *n* (*pl* -women) Irlandaise *f*.

iris ['aɪərɪs] *n Anat Bot* iris *m*.

irk [ɜːk] *vt* ennuyer. ◆**irksome** *a* ennuyeux.

iron ['aɪən] *n* fer *m*; (*for clothes*) fer *m* (à repasser); old i., scrap i. ferraille *f*; iron and steel industry sidérurgie *f*; the I. Curtain *Pol* le rideau de fer; – *vt* (*clothes*) repasser; to i. out (*difficulties*) *Fig* aplanir. ◆**—ing** *n* repassage *m*; i. board planche *f* à repasser. ◆**ironmonger** *n* quincailler *m*. ◆**iron-**

mongery *n* quincaillerie *f*. ◆**ironwork** *n* ferronnerie *f*.

irony ['aɪərənɪ] *n* ironie *f*. ◆**i'ronic(al)** *a* ironique.

irradiate [ɪ'reɪdɪeɪt] *vt* irradier.

irrational [ɪ'ræʃ(ə)n(ə)l] *a* (*act*) irrationnel; (*fear*) irraisonné; (*person*) peu rationnel, illogique.

irreconcilable [ɪrekən'saɪləb(ə)l] *a* irréconciliable, inconciliable; (*views, laws etc*) inconciliable.

irrefutable [ɪrɪ'fjuːtəb(ə)l] *a* irréfutable.

irregular [ɪ'regjʊlər] *a* irrégulier. ◆**irregu'larity** *n* irrégularité *f*.

irrelevant [ɪ'reləvənt] *a* (*remark*) non pertinent; (*course*) peu utile; i. to sans rapport avec; that's i. ça n'a rien à voir. ◆**irrelevance** *n* manque *m* de rapport.

irreparable [ɪ'rep(ə)rəb(ə)l] *a* (*harm, loss*) irréparable.

irreplaceable [ɪrɪ'pleɪsəb(ə)l] *a* irremplaçable.

irrepressible [ɪrɪ'presəb(ə)l] *a* (*laughter etc*) irrépressible.

irresistible [ɪrɪ'zɪstəb(ə)l] *a* (*person, charm etc*) irrésistible.

irresolute [ɪ'rezəluːt] *a* irrésolu, indécis.

irrespective of [ɪrɪ'spektɪvəv] *prep* sans tenir compte de.

irresponsible [ɪrɪ'spɒnsəb(ə)l] *a* (*act*) irréfléchi; (*person*) irresponsable.

irretrievable [ɪrɪ'triːvəb(ə)l] *a* irréparable.

irreverent [ɪ'revərənt] *a* irrévérencieux.

irreversible [ɪrɪ'vɜːsəb(ə)l] *a* (*process*) irréversible; (*decision*) irrévocable.

irrevocable [ɪ'revəkəb(ə)l] *a* irrévocable.

irrigate ['ɪrɪgeɪt] *vt* irriguer. ◆**irri'gation** *n* irrigation *f*.

irritat/e ['ɪrɪteɪt] *vt* irriter. ◆**—ing** *a* irritant. ◆**irritable** *a* (*easily annoyed*) irritable. ◆**irritant** *n* irritant *m*. ◆**irri'tation** *n* (*anger*) & *Med* irritation *f*.

is [ɪz] *see* be.

Islam ['ɪzlɑːm] *n* islam *m*. ◆**Islamic** [ɪz'læmɪk] *a* islamique.

island ['aɪlənd] *n* île *f*; traffic i. refuge *m*; – *a* insulaire. ◆**islander** *n* insulaire *mf*. ◆**isle** [aɪl] *n* île *f*; the British Isles les îles Britanniques.

isolate ['aɪsəleɪt] *vt* isoler (from de). ◆**isolated** *a* (*remote, unique*) isolé. ◆**iso'lation** *n* isolement *m*; in i. isolément.

Israel ['ɪzreɪl] *n* Israël *m*. ◆**Is'raeli** *a* & *n* israélien, -ienne (*mf*).

issue ['ɪʃuː] *vt* (*book etc*) publier; (*an order*) donner; (*tickets*) distribuer; (*passport*) délivrer; (*stamps, banknotes*) émettre;

(*warning*) lancer; (*supply*) fournir (**with** de, **to** à); – *vi* **to i. from** (*of smell*) se dégager de; (*stem from*) provenir de; – *n* (*matter*) question *f*; (*problem*) problème *m*; (*outcome*) résultat *m*; (*of text*) publication *f*; (*of stamps etc*) émission *f*; (*newspaper*) numéro *m*; **at i.** (*at stake*) en cause; **to make an i.** of faire toute une affaire de.

isthmus ['ɪsməs] *n* Geog isthme *m*.

it [ɪt] *pron* **1** (*subject*) il, elle; (*object*) le, la, l'; (**to) it** (*indirect object*) lui; **it bites** (*dog*) il mord; **I've done it** je l'ai fait. **2** (*impersonal*) il; **it's snowing** il neige; **it's hot** il fait chaud. **3** (*non specific*) ce, cela, ça; **it's good** c'est bon; **it was pleasant** c'était agréable; **who is it?** qui est-ce?; **that's it!** (*I agree*) c'est ça!; (*it's done*) ça y est!; **to consider it wise to do** juger prudent de faire; **it was Paul who ...** c'est Paul qui ...; **she's got it in her to succeed** elle est capable de réussir; **to have it in for s.o.** en vouloir à qn. **4** of it, from it, about it etc, **in it, to it, at it** y; **on it** dessus; **under it** dessous.

italic [ɪ'tælɪk] *a* Typ italique; – *npl* italique *m*.

Italy ['ɪtəlɪ] *n* Italie *f*. ◆**I'talian** *a & n* italien, -ienne (*mf*); – *n* (*language*) italien *m*.

itch [ɪtʃ] *n* démangeaison(s) *f*(*pl*); **to have an i. to do** avoir une envie folle de faire; – *vi* démanger; **his arm itches** son bras le *ou* lui démange; **I'm itching to do** Fig ça me démange de faire. ◆**—ing** *n* démangeaison(s) *f*(*pl*). ◆**itchy** *a* an **i. hand** une main qui me démange.

item ['aɪtəm] *n* Com Journ article *m*; (*matter*) question *f*; (*on entertainment programme*) numéro *m*; **a news i.** une information. ◆**itemize** *vt* détailler.

itinerant [aɪ'tɪnərənt] *a* (*musician, actor*) ambulant; (*judge, preacher*) itinérant.

itinerary [aɪ'tɪnərərɪ] *n* itinéraire *m*.

its [ɪts] *poss a* son, sa, *pl* ses. ◆**it'self** *pron* lui-même, elle-même; (*reflexive*) se, s'; **goodness i.** la bonté même; **by i.** tout seul.

IUD [aɪjuː'diː] *n abbr* (*intrauterine device*) stérilet *m*.

ivory ['aɪvərɪ] *n* ivoire *m*.

ivy ['aɪvɪ] *n* lierre *m*.

J

J, j [dʒeɪ] *n* J, j *m*.

jab [dʒæb] *vt* (**-bb-**) (*thrust*) enfoncer (**into** dans); (*prick*) piquer (*qn*) (**with** sth du bout de qch); – *n* coup *m* (sec); (*injection*) Med Fam piqûre *f*.

jabber ['dʒæbər] *vi* bavarder, jaser; – *vt* bredouiller. ◆**—ing** *n* bavardage *m*.

jack [dʒæk] **1** *n* Aut cric *m*; – *vt* **to j. up** soulever (*avec un cric*); (*price*) Fig augmenter. **2** *n* Cards valet *m*. **3** *vt* **to j. (in)** (*job etc*) Fam plaquer. **4** *n* **j. of all trades** homme *m* à tout faire. ◆**j.-in-the-box** *n* diable *m* (à ressort).

jackal ['dʒæk(ə)l] *n* (*animal*) chacal *m*.

jackass ['dʒækæs] *n* (*fool*) idiot, -ote *mf*.

jackdaw ['dʒækdɔː] *n* (*bird*) choucas *m*.

jacket ['dʒækɪt] *n* (*short coat*) veste *f*; (*of man's suit*) veston *m*; (*of woman*) veste *f*, jaquette *f*; (*bulletproof*) gilet *m*; (*dust*) **j.** (*of book*) jaquette *f*; **in their jackets** (*potatoes*) en robe des champs.

jack-knife 1 *n* couteau *m* de poche. **2** *vi* (*of lorry, truck*) se mettre en travers de la route.

jackpot ['dʒækpɒt] *n* gros lot *m*.

jacks [dʒæks] *npl* (jeu *m* d')osselets *mpl*.

jacuzzi [dʒə'kuːzɪ] *n* (*bath, pool*) jacousi *m*.

jade [dʒeɪd] *n* **1** (*stone*) jade *m*. **2** (*horse*) rosse *f*, canasson *m*.

jaded ['dʒeɪdɪd] *a* blasé.

jagged ['dʒægɪd] *a* déchiqueté.

jaguar ['dʒægjʊər] *n* (*animal*) jaguar *m*.

jail [dʒeɪl] *n* prison *f*; – *vt* emprisonner (**for** theft/*etc* pour vol/*etc*); **to j. for life** condamner à perpétuité. ◆**jailbreak** *n* évasion *f* (de prison). ◆**jailer** *n* geôlier, -ière *mf*.

jalopy [dʒə'lɒpɪ] *n* (*car*) Fam vieux tacot *m*.

jam¹ [dʒæm] *n* Culin confiture *f*. ◆**jamjar** *n* pot *m* à confiture.

jam² [dʒæm] **1** *n* (*traffic*) **j.** embouteillage *m*; **in a j.** (*trouble*) Fig Fam dans le pétrin. **2** *vt* (**-mm-**) (*squeeze, make stuck*) coincer, bloquer; (*gun*) enrayer; (*street, corridor etc*) encombrer; (*building*) envahir; Rad brouiller; **to j. sth into** (*pack, cram*) (en)tasser qch dans; (*thrust, put*) enfoncer *ou* fourrer qch dans; **to j. on** (*brakes*) bloquer; – *vi* (*get stuck*) se coincer, se bloquer; (*of gun*) s'enrayer; **to j. into** (*of crowd*) s'entasser dans. ◆**jammed** a (machine etc) coincé, bloqué; (street etc) encombré. ◆**jam-packed** a (hall etc) bourré de monde.

Jamaica [dʒə'meɪkə] n Jamaïque f.

jangl/e ['dʒæŋg(ə)l] vi cliqueter; – n cliquetis m. ◆**—ing** a (noise) discordant.

janitor ['dʒænɪtər] n concierge m.

January ['dʒænjʊərɪ] n janvier m.

Japan [dʒə'pæn] n Japon m. ◆**Japa'nese** a & n japonais, -aise (mf); – n (language) japonais m.

jar [dʒɑːr] 1 n (vessel) pot m; (large, glass) bocal m. 2 n (jolt) choc m; – vt (-rr-) (shake) ébranler. 3 vi (-rr-) (of noise) grincer; (of note) Mus détonner; (of colours, words) jurer (with avec); to j. on (s.o.'s nerves) porter sur; (s.o.'s ears) écorcher. ◆**jarring** a (note) discordant.

jargon ['dʒɑːgən] n jargon m.

jasmine ['dʒæzmɪn] n Bot jasmin m.

jaundice ['dʒɔːndɪs] n Med jaunisse f. ◆**jaundiced** a (bitter) Fig aigri; **to take a j. view of** voir d'un mauvais œil.

jaunt [dʒɔːnt] n (journey) balade f.

jaunt/y ['dʒɔːntɪ] a (-ier, -iest) (carefree) insouciant; (cheerful, lively) allègre; (hat etc) coquet, chic. ◆**—ily** adv avec insouciance; allègrement.

javelin ['dʒævlɪn] n javelot m.

jaw [dʒɔː] 1 n Anat mâchoire f. 2 vi (talk) Pej Fam papoter; – n to have a j. Pej Fam tailler une bavette.

jay [dʒeɪ] n (bird) geai m.

jaywalker ['dʒeɪwɔːkər] n piéton m imprudent.

jazz [dʒæz] n jazz m; – vt to j. up Fam (music) jazzifier; (enliven) animer; (clothes, room) égayer.

jealous ['dʒeləs] a jaloux (of de). ◆**jealousy** n jalousie f.

jeans [dʒiːnz] npl (blue-)jean m.

jeep [dʒiːp] n jeep f.

jeer [dʒɪər] vti to j. (at) (mock) railler; (boo) huer; – n raillerie f; pl (boos) huées fpl ◆**—ing** a railleur; – n railleries fpl; (of crowd) huées fpl.

jell [dʒel] vi (of ideas etc) Fam prendre tournure.

jello® ['dʒeləʊ] n inv Culin Am gelée f. ◆**jellied** a Culin en gelée. ◆**jelly** n Culin gelée f. ◆**jellyfish** n méduse f.

jeopardy ['dʒepədɪ] n danger m, péril m. ◆**jeopardize** vt mettre en danger or en péril.

jerk [dʒɜːk] 1 vt donner une secousse à (pour tirer, pousser etc); – n secousse f, saccade f. 2 n (person) Pej Fam pauvre type m;

(stupid) j. crétin, -ine mf. ◆**jerk/y** a (-ier, -iest) 1 saccadé. 2 (stupid) Am Fam stupide, bête. ◆**—ily** adv par saccades.

jersey ['dʒɜːzɪ] n (cloth) jersey m; (garment) & Fb maillot m.

Jersey ['dʒɜːzɪ] n Jersey f.

jest [dʒest] n plaisanterie f; **in j.** pour rire; – vi plaisanter. ◆**—er** n Hist bouffon m.

Jesus ['dʒiːzəs] n Jésus m; **J. Christ** Jésus-Christ m.

jet [dʒet] 1 n (of liquid, steam etc) jet m. 2 n Av avion m à réaction; – a (engine) à réaction; **j. lag** fatigue f (due au décalage horaire). ◆**jet-lagged** a Fam qui souffre du décalage horaire.

jet-black [dʒet'blæk] a noir comme (du) jais, (noir) de jais.

jettison ['dʒetɪs(ə)n] vt Nau jeter à la mer; (fuel) Av larguer; Fig abandonner.

jetty ['dʒetɪ] n jetée f; (landing-place) embarcadère m.

Jew [dʒuː] n (man) Juif m; (woman) Juive f. ◆**Jewess** n Juive f. ◆**Jewish** a juif.

jewel ['dʒuːəl] n bijou m; (in watch) rubis m. ◆**jewelled** a orné de bijoux. ◆**jeweller** n bijoutier, -ière mf. ◆**jewellery** n, Am ◆**jewelry** n bijoux mpl.

jib [dʒɪb] vi (-bb-) regimber (at devant); **to j. at doing** se refuser à faire.

jibe [dʒaɪb] vi & n = gibe.

jiffy ['dʒɪfɪ] n Fam instant m.

jig [dʒɪg] n (dance, music) gigue f.

jigsaw ['dʒɪgsɔː] n **j.** (puzzle) puzzle m.

jilt [dʒɪlt] vt (lover) laisser tomber.

jingle ['dʒɪŋg(ə)l] vi (of keys, bell etc) tinter; – vt faire tinter; – n tintement m.

jinx [dʒɪŋks] n (person, object) porte-malheur m inv; (spell, curse) (mauvais) sort m, poisse f.

jitters ['dʒɪtəz] npl **to have the j.** Fam avoir la frousse. ◆**jittery** a **to be j.** Fam avoir la frousse.

job [dʒɒb] n (task) travail m; (post) poste m, situation f; (crime) Fam coup m; **to have a j. doing** or **to do** (much trouble) avoir du mal à faire; **to have the j. of doing** (unpleasant task) être obligé de faire; (for a living etc) être chargé de faire; **it's a good j. (that)** Fam heureusement que; **that's just the j.** Fam c'est juste ce qu'il faut; **out of a j.** au chômage. ◆**jobcentre** n agence f nationale pour l'emploi. ◆**jobless** a au chômage.

jockey ['dʒɒkɪ] n jockey m; – vi to j. for (position, job) manœuvrer pour obtenir.

jocular ['dʒɒkjʊlər] a jovial, amusant.

jog [dʒɒg] 1 n (jolt) secousse f; (nudge) coup

m de coude; − *vt* (**-gg-**) (*shake*) secouer; (*elbow*) pousser; (*memory*) *Fig* rafraîchir. **2** *vi* (**-gg-**) to j. along (*of vehicle*) cahoter; (*of work*) aller tant bien que mal; (*of person*) faire son petit bonhomme de chemin. **3** *vi* (**-gg-**) *Sp* faire du jogging. ◆**jogging** *n Sp* jogging *m*.

john [dʒɒn] *n* (*toilet*) *Am Sl* cabinets *mpl*.

join [dʒɔɪn] **1** *vt* (*unite*) joindre, réunir; (*link*) relier; (*wires, pipes*) raccorder; to j. s.o. (*catch up with, meet*) rejoindre qn; (*associate oneself with, go with*) se joindre à qn (in doing pour faire); to j. the sea (*of river*) rejoindre la mer; to j. hands se donner la main; to j. together *or* up (*objects*) joindre; − *vi* (*of roads, rivers etc*) se rejoindre; to j. (together *or* up) (*of objects*) se joindre (with à); to j. in participer; to j. in a game prendre part à un jeu; − *n* raccord *m*, joint *m*. **2** *vt* (*become a member of*) s'inscrire à (*club, parti*); (*army*) s'engager dans; (*queue, line*) se mettre à; − *vi* (*become a member*) devenir membre; to j. up *Mil* s'engager.
◆**joiner** *n* Menuisier *m*.

joint [dʒɔɪnt] **1** *n Anat* articulation *f*; *Culin* rôti *m*; *Tech* joint *m*; out of j. *Med* démis. **2** *n* (*nightclub etc*) *Sl* boîte *f*. **3** *a* (*account, statement etc*) commun; (*effort*) conjugé; j. author coauteur *m*. ◆**—ly** *adv* conjointement.

jok/e [dʒəʊk] *n* plaisanterie *f*; (*trick*) tour *m*; it's no j. (*it's unpleasant*) ce n'est pas drôle (doing de faire); − *vi* plaisanter (about sur). ◆**—er** *n* plaisantin *m*; (*fellow*) *Fam* type *m*; *Cards* joker *m*. ◆**—ingly** *adv* en plaisantant.

jolly [dʒɒlɪ] **1** *a* (**-ier, -iest**) (*happy*) gai; (*drunk*) *Fam* éméché. **2** *adv* (*very*) *Fam* rudement. ◆**jollifi'cation** *n* (*merry-making*) réjouissances *fpl*. ◆**jollity** *n* jovialité *f*; (*merry-making*) réjouissances *fpl*.

jolt [dʒəʊlt] *vt* to j. s.o. (*of vehicle*) cahoter qn; (*shake*) *Fig* secouer qn; − *vi* to j. (along) (*of vehicle*) cahoter; − *n* cahot *m*, secousse *f*; (*shock*) *Fig* secousse *f*.

Jordan [dʒɔːd(ə)n] *n* Jordanie *f*.

jostle [dʒɒs(ə)l] *vt* (*push*) bousculer; − *vi* (*push each other*) se bousculer (for pour obtenir); **don't j.!** ne bousculez pas!

jot [dʒɒt] *vt* (**-tt-**) to j. down noter. ◆**jotter** *n* (*notepad*) bloc-notes *m*.

journal [dʒɜːn(ə)l] *n* (*periodical*) revue *f*, journal *m*. ◆**journa'lese** *n* jargon *m* journalistique. ◆**journalism** *n* journalisme *m*. ◆**journalist** *n* journaliste *mf*.

journey [dʒɜːnɪ] *n* (*trip*) voyage *m*;

(*distance*) trajet *m*; to go on a j. partir en voyage; − *vi* voyager.

jovial [dʒəʊvɪəl] *a* jovial.

joy [dʒɔɪ] *n* joie *f*; *pl* (*of countryside, motherhood etc*) plaisirs *mpl* (of de). ◆**joyful** *a*, ◆**joyous** *a* joyeux. ◆**joyride** *n* virée *f* (*dans une voiture volée*).

joystick [dʒɔɪstɪk] *n* (*of aircraft, computer*) manche *m* à balai.

JP [dʒeɪpiː] *abbr* = Justice of the Peace.

jubilant [dʒuːbɪlənt] *a* to be j. jubiler.
◆**jubi'lation** *n* jubilation *f*.

jubilee [dʒuːbɪliː] *n* (*golden*) j. jubilé *m*.

Judaism [dʒuːdeɪɪz(ə)m] *n* judaïsme *m*.

judder [dʒʌdər] *vi* (*shake*) vibrer; − *n* vibration *f*.

judg/e [dʒʌdʒ] *n* juge *m*; − *vti* juger; judging by à en juger par. ◆**—(e)ment** *n* jugement *m*.

judicial [dʒuːdɪʃ(ə)l] *a* judiciaire. ◆**judiciary** *n* magistrature *f*. ◆**judicious** *a* judicieux.

judo [dʒuːdəʊ] *n* judo *m*.

jug [dʒʌg] *n* cruche *f*; (*for milk*) pot *m*.

juggernaut [dʒʌgənɔːt] *n* (*truck*) poids *m* lourd, mastodonte *m*.

juggl/e [dʒʌg(ə)l] *vi* jongler; − *vt* jongler avec. ◆**—er** *n* jongleur, -euse *mf*.

Jugoslavia [juːgəʊslɑːvɪə] *n* Yougoslavie *f*. ◆**Jugoslav** *a* & *n* yougoslave (*mf*).

juice [dʒuːs] *n* jus *m*; (in stomach) suc *m*. ◆**juicy** *a* (**-ier, -iest**) (*fruit*) juteux; (*meat*) succulent; (*story*) *Fig* savoureux.

jukebox [dʒuːkbɒks] *n* juke-box *m*.

July [dʒuːlaɪ] *n* juillet *m*.

jumble [dʒʌmb(ə)l] *vt* to j. (up) (*objects, facts etc*) brouiller, mélanger; − *n* fouillis *m*; j. sale (*used clothes etc*) vente *f* de charité.

jumbo [dʒʌmbəʊ] *a* géant; − *a* & *n* (*pl* **-os**) j. (jet) jumbo-jet *m*, gros-porteur *m*.

jump [dʒʌmp] *n* (*leap*) saut *m*, bond *m*; (*start*) sursaut *m*; (*increase*) hausse *f*; − *vi* sauter (at sur); (*start*) sursauter; (*of price, heart*) faire un bond; − *vt* sauter; to j. across sth traverser qch d'un bond; to j. to conclusions tirer des conclusions hâtives; j. in *or* on! *Aut* montez!; to j. on (*bus*) sauter dans; to j. off *or* out sauter; to j. off sth, j. out of sth sauter de qch; to j. out of the window sauter par la fenêtre; to j. up se lever d'un bond; − *vt* sauter; to j. the lights *Aut* griller un feu rouge; to j. the rails (*of train*) dérailler; to j. the queue resquiller.

jumper [dʒʌmpər] *n* pull-(over) *m*; (*dress*) *Am* robe *f* chasuble.

jumpy [dʒʌmpɪ] *a* (**-ier, -iest**) nerveux.

junction ['dʒʌŋkʃ(ə)n] n (joining) jonction f; (crossroads) carrefour m.

juncture ['dʒʌŋktʃər] n at this j. (critical point in time) en ce moment même.

June [dʒuːn] n juin m.

jungle ['dʒʌŋg(ə)l] n jungle f.

junior ['dʒuːnıər] a (younger) plus jeune; (in rank, status etc) subalterne; (teacher, doctor) jeune; to be j. to s.o. être s.o.'s j. être plus jeune que qn; (in rank, status) être au-dessous de qn; Smith j. Smith fils or junior; **j. school** école f primaire; **j. high school** Am = collège m d'enseignement secondaire; − n cadet, -ette mf; Sch petit, -ite mf, petit(e) élève mf; Sp junior mf, cadet, -ette mf.

junk [dʒʌŋk] **1** n (objects) bric-à-brac m inv; (metal) ferraille f; (goods) Pej camelote f; (film, book etc) Pej idiotie f; (nonsense) idioties fpl; **j. shop** (boutique f de) brocanteur m. **2** vt (get rid of) Am Fam balancer.

junkie ['dʒʌŋkı] n Fam drogué, -ée mf.

junta ['dʒʌntə] n Pol junte f.

jurisdiction [dʒuərıs'dık∫(ə)n] n juridiction f.

jury ['dʒuərı] n (in competition) & Jur jury m. ◆**juror** n Jur juré m.

just [dʒʌst] **1** adv (exactly, slightly) juste; (only) juste, seulement; (simply) (tout) simplement; **it's j. as I thought** c'est bien ce que je pensais; **j. at that time** à cet instant

même; **she has/had j. left** elle vient/venait de partir; **I've j. come from** j'arrive de; **I'm j. coming!** j'arrive!; **he'll (only) j. catch the bus** il l'aura son bus de justesse; **he j. missed it** il l'a manqué de peu; **j. as big/light/etc** tout aussi grand/léger/etc (as que); **j. listen!** écoute donc!; **j. a moment!** un instant!; **j. over ten** un peu plus de dix; **j. one** un(e) seul(e) (of de); **j. about** (approximately) à peu près; (almost) presque; **j. about to do** sur le point de faire. **2** a (fair) juste (to envers). ◆**ly** adv avec justice. ◆**—ness** n (of cause etc) justice f.

justice ['dʒʌstıs] n justice f; (judge) juge m; **to do j. to** (meal) faire honneur à; **it doesn't do you j.** (hat, photo) cela ne vous avantage pas; (attitude) cela ne vous fait pas honneur; **J. of the Peace** juge m de paix.

justify ['dʒʌstıfaı] vt justifier; **to be justified in doing** (have right) être en droit de faire; (have reason) avoir toutes les bonnes raisons de faire. ◆**justi'fiable** a justifiable. ◆**justi'fiably** adv légitimement. ◆**justifi'cation** n justification f.

jut [dʒʌt] vi (-tt-) **to j. out** faire saillie; **to jut out over sth** (overhang) surplomber qch.

jute [dʒuːt] n (fibre) jute m.

juvenile ['dʒuːvənaıl] n adolescent, -ente mf; − a (court, book etc) pour enfants; (delinquent) jeune; (behaviour) Pej puéril.

juxtapose [dʒʌkstə'pəuz] vt juxtaposer. ◆**juxtapo'sition** n juxtaposition f.

K

K, k [keı] n K, k m.

kaleidoscope [kə'laıdəskəup] n kaléidoscope m.

kangaroo [kæŋgə'ruː] n kangourou m.

kaput [kə'put] a (broken, ruined) Sl fichu.

karate [kə'rɑːtı] n Sp karaté m.

keel [kiːl] n Nau quille f; − vi **to k. over** (of boat) chavirer.

keen [kiːn] a (edge, appetite) aiguisé; (interest, feeling) vif; (mind) pénétrant; (wind) coupant, piquant; (enthusiastic) enthousiaste; **a k. sportsman** un passionné de sport; **to be k. to do** or **on doing** tenir (beaucoup) à faire; **to be k. on** (music, sport etc) être passionné de; **he is k. on her**/**the idea** elle/l'idée lui plaît beaucoup. ◆**—ly** adv (to work etc) avec enthousiasme; (to feel, interest) vivement. ◆**—ness** n

enthousiasme m; (of mind) pénétration f; (of interest) intensité f; **k. to do** empressement m à faire.

keep¹ [kiːp] vt (pt & pp kept) garder; (shop, car) avoir; (diary, promise) tenir; (family) entretenir; (rule) observer, respecter; (feast day) célébrer; (birthday) fêter; (detain, delay) retenir; (put) mettre; **to k. (on) doing** (continue) continuer à faire; **to k. clean** tenir or garder propre; **to k. from** (conceal) cacher à; **to k. s.o. from doing** (prevent) empêcher qn de faire; **to k. s.o. waiting**/**working** faire attendre/travailler qn; **to k. sth going** (engine, machine) laisser qch en marche; **to k. s.o. in whisky/etc** fournir qn en whisky/etc; **to k. an appointment** se rendre à un rendez-vous; **to k. back** (withhold, delay) retenir; (conceal) cacher (from à); **to k. down** (*control*) maîtriser; (*restrict*) limiter; (*costs, price*) maintenir bas; **to k. in** empêcher de sortir; (*pupil*) *Sch* consigner; **to k. off** *or* **away** (*person*) éloigner (**from** de); **'k. off the grass'** 'ne pas marcher sur les pelouses'; **k. your hands off!** n'y touche(z) pas!; **to k. on** (*hat, employee*) garder; **to k. out** empêcher d'entrer; **to k. up** (*continue, maintain*) continuer (**doing sth** à faire qch); (*road, building*) entretenir; − *vi* (*continue*) continuer; (*remain*) rester; (*of food*) se garder, se conserver; (*wait*) attendre; **how is he keeping?** comment va-t-il?; **to k. still** rester *or* se tenir tranquille; **to k. from doing** (*refrain*) s'abstenir de; **to k. going** (*continue*) continuer; **to k. at it** (*keep doing it*) continuer à le faire; **to k. away** *or* **off** *or* **back** ne pas s'approcher (**from** de); **if the rain keeps off** s'il ne pleut pas; **to k. on at s.o.** harceler qn; **to k. out** rester en dehors (**of** de); **to k. to** (*subject, path*) ne pas s'écarter de; (*room*) garder; **to k. to the left** tenir la gauche; **to k. oneself** se tenir à l'écart; **to k. up** (*continue*) continuer; (*follow*) suivre; **to k. up with s.o** (*follow*) suivre qn; (*in quality of work etc*) se maintenir à la hauteur de qn; − *n* (*food*) subsistance *f*; **to have one's k.** être logé et nourri; **for keeps** *Fam* pour toujours. **◆—ing** *n* (*care*) garde *f*; **in k. with** en rapport avec. **◆—er** *n* gardien, -ienne *mf*.

keep² [ki:p] *n* (*tower*) *Hist* donjon *m*.

keepsake ['ki:pseɪk] *n* (*object*) souvenir *m*.

keg [keg] *n* tonnelet *m*.

kennel ['ken(ə)l] *n* niche *f*; (*for boarding*) chenil *m*.

Kenya ['ki:njə, 'kenjə] *n* Kenya *m*.

kept [kept] *see* **keep¹**; − *a* **well** *or* **nicely k.** (*house etc*) bien tenu.

kerb [kɜ:b] *n* bord *m* du trottoir.

kernel ['kɜːn(ə)l] *n* (*of nut*) amande *f*.

kerosene ['kerəsi:n] *n* (*aviation fuel*) kérosène *m*; (*paraffin*) *Am* pétrole *m* (lampant).

ketchup ['ketʃəp] *n* (*sauce*) ketchup *m*.

kettle ['ket(ə)l] *n* bouilloire *f*; **the k. is boiling** l'eau bout.

key [ki:] *n* clef *f*, clé *f*; (*of piano, typewriter, computer*) touche *f*; − *a* (*industry, post etc*) clef (*f inv*), clé (*f inv*); **k. man** pivot *m*; **k. ring** porte-clefs *m inv*. **◆keyboard** *n* clavier *m*. **◆keyhole** *n* trou *m* de (la) serrure. **◆keynote** *n* (*of speech*) note *f* dominante. **◆keystone** *n* (*of policy etc*) & *Archit* clef *f* de voûte.

keyed [ki:d] *a* **to be k. up** avoir les nerfs tendus.

khaki ['kɑːki] *a* & *n* kaki *a inv* & *m*.

kibbutz [kɪ'buts] *n* kibboutz *m*.

kick [kɪk] *n* coup *m* de pied; (*of horse*) ruade *f*; **to get a k. out of doing** (*thrill*) *Fam* prendre un malin plaisir à faire; **for kicks** *Pej Fam* pour le plaisir; − *vt* donner un coup de pied à; (*of horse*) lancer une ruade à; **to k. back** (*ball*) renvoyer (*du pied*); **to k. down** *or* **in** démolir à coups de pied; **to k. out** (*eject*) *Fam* flanquer dehors; **to k. up** (*fuss, row*) *Fam* faire; − *vi* donner des coups de pied; (*of horse*) ruer; **to k. off** *Fb* donner le coup d'envoi; (*start*) *Fig* démarrer. **◆k.-off** *n Fb* coup *m* d'envoi.

kid [kɪd] **1** *n* (*goat*) chevreau *m*. **2** *n* (*child*) *Fam* gosse *mf*; **his** *or* **her k. brother** *Am Fam* son petit frère. **3** *vti* (*-dd-*) (*joke, tease*) *Fam* blaguer; **to k. oneself** se faire des illusions.

kidnap ['kɪdnæp] *vt* (*-pp-*) kidnapper. **◆kidnapping** *n* enlèvement *m*. **◆kidnapper** *n* kidnappeur, -euse *mf*.

kidney ['kɪdnɪ] *n Anat* rein *m*; *Culin* rognon *m*; **on a k. machine** sous rein artificiel; **k. bean** haricot *m* rouge.

kill [kɪl] *vt* tuer; (*bill*) *Pol* repousser, faire échouer; (*chances*) détruire; (*rumour*) étouffer; (*story*) *Fam* supprimer; (*engine*) *Fam* arrêter; **my feet are killing me** *Fam* je ne sens plus mes pieds, j'ai les pieds en compote; **to k. off** (*person etc*) & *Fig* détruire; − *vi* tuer; − *n* mise *f* à mort; (*prey*) animaux *mpl* tués. **◆—ing 1** *n* (*of person*) meurtre *m*; (*of group*) massacre *m*; (*of animal*) mise *f* à mort; **to make a k.** *Fin* réussir un beau coup. **2** *a* (*tiring*) *Fam* tuant. **◆—er** *n* tueur, -euse *mf*. **◆killjoy** *n* rabat-joie *m inv*.

kiln [kɪln] *n* (*for pottery*) four *m*.

kilo ['ki:ləʊ] *n* (*pl* **-os**) kilo *m*. **◆kilogramme** ['kɪləʊgræm] *n* kilogramme *m*.

kilometre [kɪ'lɒmɪtər] *n* kilomètre *m*.

kilowatt ['kɪləʊwɒt] *n* kilowatt *m*.

kilt [kɪlt] *n* kilt *m*.

kimono [kɪ'məʊnəʊ] *n* (*pl* **-os**) kimono *m*.

kin [kɪn] *n* (*relatives*) parents *mpl*; **one's next of k.** son plus proche parent.

kind [kaɪnd] **1** *n* (*sort, type*) genre *m*, sorte *f*, espèce *f*; **a k. of** une sorte *or* une espèce de; **to pay in k.** payer en nature; **what k. of drink/etc is it?** qu'est-ce que c'est comme boisson/*etc*?; **that's the k. of man he is** il est comme ça; **nothing of the k.!** absolument pas!; **k. of worried/sad/etc** (*somewhat*) plutôt inquiet/triste/*etc* **2** *a* (*-er, -est*) (*fi*) *Fam* comme fasciné; **in a k. of way** d'une certaine façon; **it's the only one of its k.**, **it's one of a k.** c'est unique en son genre; **we are**

two of a k. nous nous ressemblons. **2** *a* (**-er,
-est**) (*helpful, pleasant*) gentil (**to** avec,
pour), bon (**to** pour); **that's k.** of you c'est
gentil *or* aimable à vous. ◆**k.-'hearted** *a*
qui a bon cœur. ◆**kindly** *adv* avec bonté;
k. wait/*etc* ayez la bonté d'attendre/*etc*;
not to take k. to sth ne pas apprécier qch; –
a (*person*) bienveillant. ◆**kindness** *n*
bonté *f*, gentillesse *f*.

kindergarten ['kɪndəgɑːt(ə)n] *n* jardin *m*
d'enfants.

kindle ['kɪnd(ə)l] *vt* allumer; – *vi* s'allumer.

kindred ['kɪndrɪd] *n* (*relationship*) parenté *f*;
(*relatives*) parents *mpl*; **k. spirit** semblable
mf, âme *f* sœur.

king [kɪŋ] *n* roi *m*. ◆**k.-size(d)** *a* géant;
(*cigarette*) long. ◆**kingdom** *n* royaume *m*;
animal/**plant k.** règne *m* animal/végétal.
◆**kingly** *a* royal.

kingfisher ['kɪŋfɪʃər] *n* (*bird*) martin-
pêcheur *m*.

kink [kɪŋk] *n* (*in rope*) entortillement *m*.

kinky ['kɪŋkɪ] *a* (**-ier, -iest**) (*person*) *Psy Pej*
vicieux; (*clothes etc*) bizarre.

kinship ['kɪnʃɪp] *n* parenté *f*.

kiosk ['kiːɒsk] *n* kiosque *m*; (**telephone**) **k.**
cabine *f* (téléphonique).

kip [kɪp] *vi* (**-pp-**) (*sleep*) *Sl* roupiller.

kipper ['kɪpər] *n* (*herring*) kipper *m*.

kiss [kɪs] *n* baiser *m*, bise *f*; **the k. of life** *Med*
le bouche-à-bouche; – *vt* (*person*)
embrasser; **to k. s.o.'s hand** baiser la main
de qn; – *vi* s'embrasser.

kit [kɪt] *n* équipement *m*, matériel *m*; (*set of
articles*) trousse *f*; **gym k.** (*belongings*)
affaires *fpl* de gym; **tool k.** trousse *f* à
outils; (**do-it-yourself**) **k.** kit *m*; **in form
en kit**; **k. bag** sac *m* (*de soldat etc*); – *vt*
(**-tt-**) **to k. out** équiper (**with** de).

kitchen ['kɪtʃɪn] *n* cuisine *f*; **k. cabinet** buffet
m de cuisine; **k. garden** jardin *m* potager; **k.
sink** évier *m*. ◆**kitche'nette** *n* kitchenette
f, coin-cuisine *m*.

kite [kaɪt] *n* (*toy*) cerf-volant *m*.

kith [kɪθ] *n* **k. and kin** amis *mpl* et parents
mpl.

kitten ['kɪt(ə)n] *n* chaton *m*, petit chat *m*.

kitty ['kɪtɪ] *n* (*fund*) cagnotte *f*.

km *abbr* (*kilometre*) km.

knack [næk] *n* (*skill*) coup *m* (de main), truc
m (**of doing** pour faire); **to have a** *or* **the k.
of doing** (*aptitude, tendency*) avoir le don de
faire.

knackered ['nækəd] *a* (*tired*) *Sl* vanné.

knapsack ['næpsæk] *n* sac *m* à dos.

knead [niːd] *vt* (*dough*) pétrir.

knee [niː] *n* genou *m*; **to go down on one's**

knees se mettre à genoux; **k. pad** *Sp*
genouillère *f*. ◆**kneecap** *n Anat* rotule *f*.
◆**knees-up** *n Sl* soirée *f* dansante,
sauterie *f*.

kneel [niːl] *vi* (*pt & pp* knelt *or* kneeled) **to
k.** (**down**) s'agenouiller; **to be kneeling
(down)** être à genoux.

knell [nel] *n* glas *m*.

knew [njuː] *see* know.

knickers ['nɪkəz] *npl* (*woman's undergarment*) culotte *f*, slip *m*.

knick-knack ['nɪknæk] *n* babiole *f*.

knife [naɪf] *n* (*pl* knives) couteau *m*;
(*penknife*) canif *m*; – *vt* poignarder.

knight [naɪt] *n Hist & Br Pol* chevalier *m*;
Chess cavalier *m*; – *vt* (*of monarch*) *Br Pol*
faire (*qn*) chevalier. ◆**knighthood** *n* titre
m de chevalier.

knit [nɪt] *vt* (**-tt-**) tricoter; **to k. together** *Fig*
souder; **to k. one's brow** froncer les
sourcils; – *vi* tricoter; **to k. (together)** (*of
bones*) se souder. ◆**knitting** *n* tricot *m*; **k.
needle** aiguille *f* à tricoter. ◆**knitwear** *n*
tricots *mpl*.

knob [nɒb] *n* (*on door etc*) bouton *m*; (*on
stick*) pommeau *m*; (*of butter*) noix *f*.

knock [nɒk] *vt* (*strike*) frapper; (*collide
with*) heurter; (*criticize*) *Fam* critiquer; **to
k. one's head on** se cogner la tête contre; **to
k. senseless** (*stun*) assommer; **to k. to the
ground** jeter à terre; **to k. about** (*ill-treat*)
malmener; **to k. back** (*drink, glass etc*) *Fam*
s'envoyer (derrière la cravate), siffler; **to k.
down** (*vase, pedestrian etc*) renverser;
(*house, tree, wall etc*) abattre; (*price*)
baisser, casser; **to k. in** (*nail*) enfoncer; **to
k. off** (*person, object*) faire tomber (**from**
de); (*do quickly*) *Fam* expédier; (*steal*) *Fam*
piquer; **to k. £5 off** (**the price**) baisser le
prix de cinq livres, faire cinq livres sur le
prix; **to k. out** (*stun*) assommer; (*beat in
competition*) éliminer; **to k. oneself out**
(*tire*) *Fam* s'esquinter (**doing** à faire); **to k.
over** (*pedestrian, vase etc*) renverser; **to k.
up** (*meal*) *Fam* préparer à la hâte; – *vi
(strike)* frapper; **to k. against** *or* **into** (*bump
into*) heurter; **to k. about** (*travel*) *Fam*
bourlinguer; (*lie around, stand around*)
traîner; **to k. off** (*stop work*) *Fam* s'arrêter
de travailler; – *n* (*blow*) coup *m*; (*collision*)
heurt *m*; **there's a k. at the door** quelqu'un
frappe; **I heard a k.** j'ai entendu frapper.
◆**knockdown** *a* **k. price** prix *m* imbattable. ◆**knock-'kneed** *a* cagneux.
◆**knock-out** *n Boxing* knock-out *m*; **to be
a k.-out** (*of person, film etc*) *Fam* être formidable.

knocker ['nɒkər] n (for door) marteau m.

knot [nɒt] **1** n (in rope etc) nœud m; − vt (-tt-) nouer. **2** n (unit of speed) Nau nœud m. ◆**knotty** a (-ier, -iest) (wood etc) noueux; (problem) Fig épineux.

know [nəʊ] vt (pt knew, pp known) (facts, language etc) savoir; (person, place etc) connaître; (recognize) reconnaître (by à); **to k. that** savoir que; **to k. how to do** faire; **for all I k.** (autant) que je sache; **I'll let you k.** je te le ferai savoir; **I'll have you k. that . . .** sachez que . . .; **to k. (a lot) about** (person, event) en savoir long sur; (cars, sewing etc) s'y connaître en; **I've never known him to complain** je ne l'ai jamais vu se plaindre; **to get to k. (about) sth** apprendre qch; **to get to k. s.o.** (meet) faire la connaissance de qn; − vi savoir; **I k.** je (le) sais; **I wouldn't k., I k. nothing about it** je n'en sais rien; **I k. about that** je sais ça, je suis au courant; **to k. of** (have heard of) avoir entendu parler de; **do you k. of?** (a good tailor etc) connais-tu?; **you (should) k. better than to do that** tu es trop intelligent pour faire ça; **you should have known better** tu aurais dû réfléchir; − **in the k.** Fam au courant. ◆**−ing** a (smile, look) entendu. ◆**−ingly** adv (consciously) sciemment. ◆**known** a connu; **a k. expert** un expert reconnu; **well k.** (bien) connu (that que); **she's . . . on sait qu'elle est . . .** ◆**know-all**, Am ◆**know-it-all** n je-sais-tout mf inv. ◆**know-how** n (skill) compétence f (to de pour faire), savoir-faire m inv.

knowledge ['nɒlɪdʒ] n connaissance f (of de); (learning) connaissances fpl, savoir m; **to** (the best of) my k. à ma connaissance; **without the k. of** à l'insu de; **to have no k. of** ignorer; **general k.** culture f générale. ◆**knowledgeable** a bien informé (about sur).

knuckle ['nʌk(ə)l] **1** n articulation f du doigt. **2** vi **to k. down to** (task) Fam s'atteler à; **to k. under** céder.

Koran [kə'rɑːn] n Rel Coran m.

kosher ['kəʊʃər] a Rel kascher inv.

kowtow [kaʊ'taʊ] vi se prosterner (to devant).

kudos ['kjuːdɒs] n (glory) gloire f.

L

L, l [el] L, l m.

lab [læb] n Fam labo m. ◆**laboratory** [lə'bɒrət(ə)rɪ, Am 'læbrətərɪ] n laboratoire m; **language l.** laboratoire m de langues.

laborious [lə'bɔːrɪəs] a laborieux.

labour ['leɪbər] n (work, childbirth) travail m; (workers) main-d'œuvre f; **L.** Br Pol les travaillistes mpl; **in l.** Med au travail; − a (market, situation) du travail; (conflict, dispute) ouvrier; (relations) ouvriers-patronat inv; **l. force** main-d'œuvre f; **l. union** Am syndicat m; − vi (toil) peiner; − vt **to l. a point** insister sur un point. ◆**−ed** a (style) laborieux. ◆**−er** n (on roads etc) manœuvre m, Agr ouvrier m agricole.

laburnum [lə'bɜːnəm] n Bot cytise m.

labyrinth ['læbɪrɪnθ] n labyrinthe m.

lace [leɪs] **1** n (cloth) dentelle f. **2** n (of shoe) lacet m; − vt **to l. (up)** (tie up) lacer. **3** vt (drink) additionner, arroser (with de).

lacerate ['læsəreɪt] vt (flesh etc) lacérer.

lack [læk] n manque m (of de); **for l. of** à défaut de; − vt manquer de; − vi **to be lacking** manquer (in, for de).

lackey ['lækɪ] n Hist & Fig laquais m.

laconic [lə'kɒnɪk] a laconique.

lacquer ['lækər] n laque f; − vt laquer.

lad [læd] n gars m, garçon m; **when I was a l.** quand j'étais gosse.

ladder ['lædər] n échelle f; (in stocking) maille f filée; − vt (stocking) filer.

laden ['leɪd(ə)n] a chargé (with de).

ladle ['leɪd(ə)l] n louche f.

lady ['leɪdɪ] n dame f; **a young l.** une jeune fille; (married) une jeune femme; **the l. of the house** la maîtresse de maison; **Ladies and Gentlemen!** Mesdames, Mesdemoiselles, Messieurs!; **l. doctor** femme f médecin; **l. friend** amie f; **ladies' room** Fig toilettes fpl. ◆**l.-in-waiting** n (pl ladies-in-waiting) dame f d'honneur. ◆**ladybird** n, Am ◆**ladybug** n coccinelle f. ◆**ladylike** a (manner) distingué; **she's (very) l.** elle est très grande dame.

lag [læg] **1** vi (-gg-) **to l. behind** (in progress, work) avoir du retard; (dawdle) traîner; **to l. behind s.o.** avoir du retard sur qn; − n

time l. (between events) décalage m; (between countries) décalage m horaire. **2** vt (**-gg-**) (pipe) calorifuger.

lager ['lɑːgər] n bière f blonde.

lagoon [lə'guːn] n lagune f; (small, coral) lagon m.

laid [leɪd] see **lay** 2. ◆**l.-'back** a Fam relax.

lain [leɪn] see **lie** 1.

lair [leər] n tanière f.

laity ['leɪɪtɪ] n the l. les laïcs mpl.

lake [leɪk] n lac m.

lamb [læm] n agneau m. ◆**lambswool** n laine f d'agneau.

lame [leɪm] a (**-er, -est**) (person, argument) boiteux; (excuse) piètre; **to be** l. boiter. ◆**-ness** n Med claudication f; (of excuse) Fig faiblesse f.

lament [lə'ment] n lamentation f; — vt to l. (over) se lamenter sur. ◆**lamentable** a lamentable. ◆**lamen'tation** n lamentation f.

laminated ['læmɪneɪtɪd] a (metal) laminé.

lamp [læmp] n lampe f; (bulb) ampoule f; Aut feu m. ◆**lamppost** n réverbère m. ◆**lampshade** n abat-jour m inv.

lance [lɑːns] **1** n (weapon) lance f. **2** vt inciser.

land [lænd] **1** n terre f; (country) pays m; (plot of) terrain m; **on dry** l. sur la terre ferme; **no man's** l. Mil & Fig no man's land m inv; — a (flora, transport etc) terrestre; (reform, law) agraire; (owner, tax) foncier. **2** vi (of aircraft) atterrir, se poser; (of ship) mouiller, relâcher; (of passengers) débarquer; (of bomb etc) (re)tomber; **to** l. **up** (end up) se retrouver; — vt (passengers, cargo) débarquer; (aircraft) poser; (blow) Fig flanquer (on s.o.); (job, prize etc) Fam décrocher; **to** l. **s.o.** **in trouble** Fam mettre-qn dans le pétrin; **to be landed with** Fam (person) avoir sur les bras; (fine) ramasser, écoper de. ◆**-ed** a (owning land) terrien. ◆**-ing** n **1** Av atterrissage m; Nau débarquement m; **forced** l. atterrissage m forcé; l. **stage** débarcadère m. **2** (at top of stairs) palier m; (floor) étage m. ◆**landlady** n logeuse f, propriétaire f. ◆**landlocked** a sans accès à la mer. ◆**landlord** n propriétaire m, (of pub) patron m. ◆**landmark** n point m de repère. ◆**landslide** n Geol glissement m de terrain, éboulement m; Pol raz-de-marée m inv électoral.

landscape ['lændskeɪp] n paysage m.

lane [leɪn] n (in country) chemin m; (in town) ruelle f; (division of road) voie f; (line of traffic) file f; Av Nau Sp couloir m; **bus** l. couloir m (réservé aux autobus).

language ['læŋgwɪdʒ] n (faculty, style) langage m; (national tongue) langue f; **computer** l. langage m machine; — a (laboratory) de langues; (teacher, studies) de langue(s).

languid ['læŋgwɪd] a languissant. ◆**languish** vi languir (**for, after** après).

lank [læŋk] a (hair) plat et terne.

lanky ['læŋkɪ] a (**-ier, -iest**) dégingandé.

lantern ['læntən] n lanterne f; **Chinese** l. lampion m.

lap [læp] **1** n (of person) genoux mpl; **the** l. **of luxury** le plus grand luxe. **2** n Sp tour m (of piste). **3** vt (**-pp-**) **to** l. **up** (drink) laper; (like very much) Fam gober; (believe) Fam gober; — vi (of waves) clapoter. **4** vi (**-pp-**) **to** l. **over** (overlap) se chevaucher.

lapel [lə'pel] n (of jacket etc) revers m.

lapse [læps] **1** n (fault) faute f; (weakness) défaillance f; **a** l. **of memory** un trou de mémoire; **a** l. **in behaviour** un écart de conduite; — vi (err) commettre une faute; **to** l. **into** retomber dans. **2** n (interval) intervalle m; **a** l. **of time** un intervalle (**between** entre). **3** vi (expire) se périmer, expirer; (of subscription) prendre fin.

larceny ['lɑːsənɪ] n vol m simple.

lard [lɑːd] n saindoux m.

larder ['lɑːdər] n (cupboard) garde-manger m inv.

large [lɑːdʒ] a (**-er, -est**) (in size or extent) grand; (in volume, bulkiness) gros; (quantity) grand, important; **to become or grow or get** l. grossir, grandir; **to a** l. **extent** en grande mesure; **at** l. (of prisoner, animal) en liberté; (as a whole) en général; **by and** l. dans l'ensemble, généralement. ◆**l.-scale** a (reform) (fait) sur une grande échelle. ◆**largely** adv (to a great extent) en grande mesure. ◆**largeness** n grandeur f; grosseur f.

largesse [lɑː'ʒes] n largesse f.

lark [lɑːk] **1** n (bird) alouette f. **2** n (joke) Fam rigolade f, blague f; — vi to l. **about** Fam s'amuser.

larva, pl **-vae** ['lɑːvə, -viː] n (of insect) larve f.

larynx ['lærɪŋks] n Anat larynx m. ◆**laryn-gitis** n Med laryngite f.

lascivious [lə'sɪvɪəs] a lascif.

laser ['leɪzər] n laser m.

lash 1 [læʃ] n (with whip) coup m de fouet; — vt (strike) fouetter; (tie) attacher (**to** à); **the dog lashed its tail** le chien donna un coup de queue; — vi to l. **out** (spend wildly) Fam claquer son argent; **to** l. **out at** envoyer des coups à; (*abuse*) *Fig* invectiver; (*criticize*) *Fig* fustiger. ◆—ings *npl* l. of *Culin Fam* des masses de, une montagne de.

lash² [læ∫] *n* (*eyelash*) cil *m*.

lass [læs] *n* jeune fille *f*.

lassitude ['læsɪtjuːd] *n* lassitude *f*.

lasso [læ'suː] *n* (*pl* -os) lasso *m*; — *vt* attraper au lasso.

last¹ [lɑːst] *a* dernier; **the l. ten lines** les dix dernières lignes; **l. but one** avant-dernier; **l. night** (*evening*) hier soir; (*during night*) cette nuit; **the day before l.** avant-hier; — *adv* (*lastly*) en dernier lieu, enfin; (*on the last occasion*) (pour) la dernière fois; **to leave l.** sortir le dernier *or* en dernier; — *n* (*person, object*) dernier, -ière *mf*; (*end*) fin *f*; **the l. of the beer/etc** (*remainder*) le reste de la bière/*etc*; **at (long) l.** enfin. ◆**l.-ditch** *a* désespéré. ◆**l.-minute** *a* de dernière minute. ◆**lastly** *adv* en dernier lieu, enfin.

last² [lɑːst] *vi* durer; **to l. (out)** (*endure, resist*) tenir; (*of money, supplies*) durer; **it lasted me ten years** ça m'a duré *or* fait dix ans. ◆—ing *a* durable.

latch [læt∫] **1** *n* loquet *m*; **the door is on the l.** la porte n'est pas fermée à clef. **2** *vi* **to l. on to** *Fam* (*grab*) s'accrocher à; (*understand*) saisir.

late¹ [leɪt] *a* (*-er, -est*) (*not on time*) en retard (**for** à); (*former*) ancien; (*meal, fruit, season, hour*) tardif; (*stage*) avancé; (*edition*) dernier; **to be l.** (*of person, train etc*) être en retard, avoir du retard; **to be l. (in) coming** arriver en retard; **he's an hour l.** il a une heure de retard; **to make s.o. l.** mettre qn en retard; **it's l.** il est tard; **Easter/etc is l.** Pâques/*etc* est tard; **in l. June/etc** fin juin/*etc*; **a later edition/etc** (*more recent*) une édition/*etc* plus récente; **the latest edition/etc** (*last*) la dernière édition/*etc*; **in later life** plus tard dans la vie; **to take a later train** prendre un train plus tard; **at a later date** à une date ultérieure; **the latest date** la date limite; **at the latest** au plus tard; **of l.** dernièrement; — *adv* (*in the day, season etc*) tard; (*not on time*) en retard; **it's getting l.** il se fait tard; **later (on)** plus tard; **not** *or* **no later than** pas plus tard que. ◆**latecomer** *n* retardataire *mf*. ◆**lately** *adv* dernièrement. ◆**lateness** *n* (*of person, train etc*) retard *m*; **constant l.** des retards continuels; **the l. of the hour** l'heure tardive.

late² [leɪt] *a* **the l. Mr Smith/etc** (*deceased*) feu Monsieur Smith/*etc*; **our l. friend** notre regretté ami.

latent ['leɪtənt] *a* latent.

lateral ['lætərəl] *a* latéral.

lathe [leɪð] *n* Tech tour *m*.

lather ['lɑːðər] *n* mousse *f*; — *vt* savonner; — *vi* mousser.

Latin ['lætɪn] *a* latin; **L. America** Amérique *f* latine; **L. American** d'Amérique latine; — *n* (*person*) Latin, -ine *mf*; (*language*) latin *m*.

latitude ['lætɪtjuːd] *n* Geog & Fig latitude *f*.

latrines [lə'triːnz] *npl* latrines *fpl*.

latter ['lætər] *a* (*later, last-named*) dernier; (*second*) deuxième; — *n* dernier, -ière *mf*; second, -onde *mf*. ◆—ly *adv* dernièrement; (*late in life*) sur le tard.

lattice ['lætɪs] *n* treillis *m*.

laudable ['lɔːdəb(ə)l] *a* louable.

laugh [lɑːf] *n* rire *m*; **to have a good l.** bien rire; — *vi* rire (**at, about** de); **to l. to oneself** rire en soi-même; — *vt* **to l. off** tourner en plaisanterie. ◆—ing *a* riant; **it's no l. matter** il n'y a pas de quoi rire; **to be the l.-stock of** être la risée de. ◆—able *a* ridicule. ◆**laughter** *n* rire(s) *m*(*pl*); **to roar with l.** rire aux éclats.

launch [lɔːnt∫] **1** *n* (*motor boat*) vedette *f*; (*pleasure boat*) bateau *m* de plaisance. **2** *vt* (*rocket, boat, fashion etc*) lancer; — *vi* **to l. (out) into** (*begin*) se lancer dans; — *n* lancement *m*. ◆—ing *n* lancement *m*.

launder ['lɔːndər] *vt* (*clothes*) blanchir; (*money from drugs etc*) *Fig* blanchir. ◆—ing *n* blanchissage *m*. ◆**launde'rette** *n*, *Am* ◆**laundromat** *n* laverie *f* automatique. ◆**laundry** *n* (*place*) blanchisserie *f*; (*clothes*) linge *m*.

laurel ['lɒrəl] *n* Bot laurier *m*.

lava ['lɑːvə] *n* Geol lave *f*.

lavatory ['lævətrɪ] *n* cabinets *mpl*.

lavender ['lævɪndər] *n* lavande *f*.

lavish ['lævɪ∫] *a* prodigue (**with** de); (*helping, meal*) généreux; (*decor, house etc*) somptueux; (*expenditure*) excessif; — *vt* prodiguer (**sth on s.o.** qch à qn). ◆—ly *adv* (*to give*) généreusement; (*to furnish*) somptueusement.

law [lɔː] *n* (*rule, rules*) loi *f*; (*study, profession, system*) droit *m*; **court of l., l. court** cour *f* de justice; **l. and order** l'ordre public. ◆**l.-abiding** *a* respectueux des lois. ◆**lawful** *a* (*action*) légal; (*child, wife etc*) légitime. ◆**lawfully** *adv* légalement. ◆**lawless** *a* (*country*) anarchique. ◆**lawlessness** *n* anarchie *f*. ◆**lawsuit** *n* procès *m*.

lawn [lɔːn] *n* pelouse *f*, gazon *m*; **l. mower** tondeuse *f* (à gazon); **l. tennis** tennis *m* (sur gazon).

lawyer ['lɔːjər] *n* (*in court*) avocat *m*; (*author,* *legal expert*) juriste *m*; (*for wills, sales*) notaire *m*.

lax [læks] *a* (*person*) négligent; (*discipline, behaviour*) relâché; **to be l. in doing** faire avec négligence. ◆**laxity** *n*, ◆**laxness** *n* négligence *f*; relâchement *m*.

laxative [ˈlæksətɪv] *n & a Med* laxatif (*m*).

lay¹ [leɪ] *a* (*non-religious*) laïque; (*non-specialized*) d'un profane; **l. person** profane *mf*. ◆**layman** *n* (*pl* **-men**) (*non-specialist*) profane *mf*.

lay² [leɪ] (*pt & pp* **laid**) **1** *vt* (*put down, place*) poser; (*table*) mettre; (*blanket*) étendre (*over* sur); (*trap*) tendre; (*money*) miser (**on** sur); (*accusation*) porter; (*ghost*) exorciser; **to l. a bet** parier; **to l. bare** mettre à nu; **to l. waste** ravager; **to l. s.o. open to** exposer qn à; **to l. one's hands on** mettre la main sur; **to l. a hand** *or* **a finger on** s.o. lever la main sur qn; **to l. down** poser; (*arms*) déposer; (*condition*) (im)poser; **to l. down the law** faire la loi (**to** à); **to l. s.o. off** (*worker*) licencier qn; **to l. on** (*install*) mettre, installer; (*supply*) fournir; **to l. it on** (*thick*) *Fam* y aller un peu fort; **to l. out** (*garden*) dessiner; (*house*) concevoir; (*prepare*) préparer; (*display*) disposer; (*money*) *Fam* dépenser (**on** pour); **to be laid up** (*in bed*) *Med* être alité; − *vi* **to l. into** *Fam* attaquer; **to l. off** (*stop*) *Fam* arrêter; **to l. off s.o.** (*leave alone*) *Fam* laisser qn tranquille; **l. off!** (*don't touch*) *Fam* pas touche!; **to l. out** *Fam* payer. **2** *vt* (*egg*) pondre; − *vi* (*of bird etc*) pondre. ◆**layabout** *n Fam* fainéant, -ante *mf*. ◆**lay-by** *n* (*pl* **-bys**) *Aut* aire *f* de stationnement *or* de repos. ◆**lay-off** *n* (*of worker*) licenciement *m*. ◆**layout** *n* disposition *f*; *Typ* mise *f* en pages. ◆**lay-over** *n Am* halte *f*.

lay³ [leɪ] *see* **lie¹**.

layer [ˈleɪər] *n* couche *f*.

laze [leɪz] *vi* **to l.** (**about** *or* **around**) paresser. ◆**lazy** *a* (**-ier**, **-iest**) (*person etc*) paresseux; (*holiday*) passé à ne rien faire. ◆**lazy-bones** *n Fam* paresseux, -euse *mf*.

lb *abbr* (*libra*) = **pound** (*weight*).

lead¹ [liːd] *vt* (*pt & pp* **led**) (*conduct*) mener, conduire (**to** à); (*team, government etc*) diriger; (*regiment*) commander; (*life*) mener; **to l. s.o. in/out/etc** faire entrer/sortir/*etc* qn; **to l. s.o. to do** (*induce*) amener qn à faire; **to l. the way** montrer le chemin; **to l. the world** tenir le premier rang mondial; **easily led** influençable; **to l. away** *or* **off** emmener; **to l. back** ramener; − *vi* (*on tease*) faire marcher; − *vi* (*of street etc*) mener, conduire (**to** à); (*in match*) mener;

(*in race*) être en tête; (*go ahead*) aller devant; **to l. to** (*result in*) aboutir à; (*cause*) causer, amener; **to l. up to** (*of street*) conduire à; mener à; (*precede*) précéder; (*approach gradually*) en venir à; − *n* (*distance or time ahead*) *Sp* avance *f* (**over** sur); (*example*) exemple *m*, initiative *f*; (*clue*) piste *f*, indice *m*; (*star part*) *Th* rôle *m* principal; (*leash*) laisse *f*; (*wire*) *El* fil *m*; *Sp* prendre la tête; **to be in the l.** (*in race*) être en tête; (*in match*) mener. ◆**leading** *a* (*main*) principal; (*important*) important; (*front*) de tête; **the l. author** l'auteur principal *or* le plus important; **a l. figure** un personnage marquant; **the l. lady** *Cin* la vedette féminine; **l. article** *Journ* éditorial *m*. ◆**leader** *n* chef *m*; *Pol* dirigeant, -ante *mf*; (*of strike, riot*) meneur, -euse *mf*; (*guide*) guide *m*; (*article*) *Journ* éditorial *m*. ◆**leadership** *n* direction *f*; (*qualities*) qualités *fpl* de chef; (*leaders*) *Pol* dirigeants *mpl*.

lead² [led] *n* (*metal*) plomb *m*; (*of pencil*) mine *f*; **l. pencil** crayon *m* à mine de plomb. ◆**leaden** *a* (*sky*) de plomb.

leaf [liːf] **1** *n* (*pl* **leaves**) *Bot* feuille *f*; (*of book*) feuillet *m*; (*of table*) rallonge *f*. **2** *vi* **to l. through** (*book*) feuilleter. ◆**leaflet** *n* prospectus *m*; (*containing instructions*) notice *f*. ◆**leafy** *a* (**-ier**, **-iest**) (*tree*) feuillu.

league [liːg] *n* **1** (*alliance*) ligue *f*; *Sp* championnat *m*; **in l. with** *Pej* de connivence avec. **2** (*measure*) *Hist* lieue *f*.

leak [liːk] *n* (*in pipe, information etc*) fuite *f*; (*in boat*) voie *f* d'eau; − *vi* (*of liquid, pipe, tap etc*) fuir; (*of ship*) faire eau; **to l. out** (*of information*) *Fig* être divulgué; − *vt* (*liquid*) répandre; (*information*) *Fig* divulguer. ◆**−age** *n* fuite *f*; (*amount lost*) perte *f*. ◆**leaky** *a* (**-ier**, **-iest**) (*kettle etc*) qui fuit.

lean¹ [liːn] *a* (**-er**, **-est**) (*thin*) maigre; (*year*) difficile. ◆**−ness** *n* maigreur *f*.

lean² [liːn] *vi* (*pt & pp* **leaned** *or* **leant** [lent]) (*of object*) pencher; (*of person*) se pencher; **to l. against/on** (*of person*) s'appuyer contre/sur; **to l. back against** s'adosser à; **to l. on s.o.** (*influence*) *Fam* faire pression sur qn (*to do* pour faire); **to l. forward** *or* **over** (*of person*) se pencher (en avant); **to l. over** (*of object*) pencher; − *vt* appuyer (*against* contre); **to l. one's head on/out of** pencher la tête sur/par. ◆**−ing** **1** *a* penché; **l. against** (*resting*) appuyé contre. **2** *npl* tendances *fpl* (*towards* à). ◆**lean-to** *n* (*pl* **-tos**) (*building*) appentis *m*.

leap [liːp] *n* (*jump*) bond *m*, saut *m*; (*change, increase etc*) *Fig* bond *m*; **l. year** année *f* bissextile; **in leaps and bounds** à pas de géant; — *vi* (*pt & pp* **leaped** *or* **leapt** [lept]) bondir, sauter; (*of flames*) jaillir; (*of profits*) faire un bond; **to l. to one's feet, l. up** se lever d'un bond. ◆**leapfrog** *n* saute-mouton *m inv.*

learn [lɜːn] *vt* (*pt & pp* **learned** *or* **learnt**) apprendre (**that** que); (**how**) **to do** apprendre à faire; — *vi* apprendre; **to l. about** (*study*) étudier; (*hear about*) apprendre. ◆**—ed** [-ɪd] *a* savant. ◆**—ing** *n* érudition *f*, savoir *m*; (*of language*) apprentissage *m* (**of** de). ◆**—er** *n* débutant, -ante *mf*.

lease [liːs] *n Jur* bail *m*; **a new l. of life** *or Am* **on life** un regain de vie, une nouvelle vie; — *vt* (*house etc*) louer à bail. ◆**leasehold** *n* propriété *f* louée à bail.

leash [liːʃ] *n* laisse *f*; **on a l.** en laisse.

least [liːst] *a* **the l.** (*smallest amount of*) le moins de; (*slightest*) le *or* la moindre; **he has (the) l. talent** il a le moins de talent (**of all** de tous); **the l. effort/noise**/*etc* le moindre effort/bruit/*etc*; — *n* **the l.** le moins; **at l.** (*with quantity*) au moins; **at l. that's what she says** du moins c'est ce qu'elle dit; **not in the l.** pas du tout; — *adv* (*to work, eat etc*) le moins; (*with adjective*) le *or* la moins; **l. of all** (*especially not*) surtout pas.

leather [ˈleðər] *n* cuir *m*; (*wash*) l. peau *f* de chamois.

leave [liːv] **1** *n* (*holiday*) congé *m*; (*consent*) & *Mil* permission *f*; **l. of absence** congé exceptionnel; **to take (one's) l. of** prendre congé de. **2** *vt* (*pt & pp* **left**) (*allow to remain, forget*) laisser; (*depart from*) quitter; (*room*) sortir de, quitter; **to l. the table** sortir de table; **to l. s.o. in charge of s.o./sth** laisser à qn la garde de qn/qch; **to l. sth with s.o.** (*entrust, give*) laisser qch à qn; **to be left** (*over*) rester; **there's no hope/bread**/*etc* **left** il ne reste plus d'espoir/de pain/*etc*; **l. it to me!** laisse-moi faire!; (*I'll take it up to you*) je m'en remets à toi; **to l. go (of)** (*release*) lâcher; **to l. behind** laisser; (*surpass*) dépasser; (*in race*) *Sp* distancer; **to l. off** (*lid*) ne pas (re)mettre; **to l. off doing** (*stop*) *Fam* arrêter de faire; **to l. on** (*hat, gloves*) garder; **to l. out** (*forget*) omettre; (*exclude*) exclure; — *vi* (*depart*) partir (**from** de, **for** pour); **to l. off** (*stop*) *Fam* s'arrêter. ◆**leavings** *npl* restes *mpl.*

Lebanon [ˈlebənən] *n* Liban *m.* ◆**Leba-'nese** *a & n* libanais, -aise (*mf*).

lecher [ˈletʃər] *n* débauché *m.* ◆**lecherous** *a* lubrique, luxurieux.

lectern [ˈlektən] *n* (*for giving speeches*) pupitre *m*; *Rel* lutrin *m.*

lecture [ˈlektʃər] **1** *n* (*public speech*) conférence *f*; (*as part of series*) *Univ* cours *m* (*magistral*); — *vi* faire une conférence *or* un cours; **I l. in chemistry** je suis professeur de chimie. **2** *vt* (*scold*) *Fig* faire la morale à, sermonner; — *n* (*scolding*) sermon *m.* ◆**lecturer** *n* conférencier, -ière *mf*; *Univ* enseignant, -ante *mf.* ◆**lectureship** *n* poste *m* à l'université.

led [led] *see* **lead**[1].

ledge [ledʒ] *n* rebord *m*; (*on mountain*) saillie *f.*

ledger [ˈledʒər] *n Com* registre *m*, grand livre *m.*

leech [liːtʃ] *n* (*worm, person*) sangsue *f.*

leek [liːk] *n* poireau *m.*

leer [lɪər] *vi* **to l. (at)** lorgner; — *n* regard *m* sournois.

leeway [ˈliːweɪ] *n* (*freedom*) liberté *f* d'action; (*safety margin*) marge *f* de sécurité.

left[1] [left] *see* **leave** 2; — *a* **l. luggage office** consigne *f.* ◆**leftovers** *npl* restes *mpl.*

left[2] [left] *a* (*side, hand etc*) gauche; — *adv* à gauche; — *n* gauche *f*; **on** *or* **to the l.** à gauche (**of** de). ◆**l.-hand** *a* à *or* de gauche; **on the l.-hand side** à gauche (**of** de). ◆**l.-'handed** *a* (*person*) gaucher. ◆**l.-wing** *a Pol* de gauche. ◆**leftist** *n & a Pol* gauchiste (*mf*).

leg [leg] *n* jambe *f*; (*of bird, dog etc*) patte *f*; (*of lamb*) *Culin* gigot *m*; (*of chicken*) *Culin* cuisse *f*; (*of table*) pied *m*; (*of journey*) étape *f*; **to pull s.o.'s l.** (*make fun of*) mettre qn en boîte; **on its last legs** (*machine etc*) *Fam* prêt à claquer; **to be on one's last legs** *Fam* avoir un pied dans la tombe. ◆**l.-room** *n* place *f* pour les jambes. ◆**leggy** *a* (**-ier, -iest**) (*person*) aux longues jambes, tout en jambes.

legacy [ˈlegəsɪ] *n Jur* & *Fig* legs *m.*

legal [ˈliːg(ə)l] *a* (*lawful*) légal; (*mind, affairs, adviser*) juridique; (*aid, error*) judiciaire; **l. expert** juriste *m*; **l. proceedings** procès *m.* ◆**le'gality** *n* légalité *f.* ◆**legalize** *vt* légaliser. ◆**legally** *adv* légalement.

legation [lɪˈgeɪʃ(ə)n] *n Pol* légation *f.*

legend [ˈledʒənd] *n* (*story, inscription etc*) légende *f.* ◆**legendary** *a* légendaire.

leggings [ˈlegɪŋz] *npl* jambières *fpl.*

legible [ˈledʒəb(ə)l] *a* lisible. ◆**legi'bility** *n* lisibilité *f.* ◆**legibly** *adv* lisiblement.

legion [ˈliːdʒən] *n Mil* & *Fig* légion *f.*

legislate [ˈledʒɪsleɪt] *vi* légiférer. ◆**legis-**

'lation n (laws) législation f; (action) élaboration f des lois; (piece of) l. loi f. ◆**legislative** a législatif.

legitimate [lɪ'dʒɪtɪmət] a (reason, child etc) légitime. ◆**legimacy** n légitimité f.

legless ['leɡləs] a (drunk) Fam (complètement) bourré.

leisure ['leʒər, Am 'liːʒər] n l. (time) loisirs mpl; l. activities loisirs mpl; moment of l. moment de loisir; at (one's) l. à tête reposée. ◆—ly a (walk, occupation) peu fatigant; (meal, life) calme; at l. pace, in a l. way sans se presser.

lemon ['lemən] n citron m; l. drink, l. squash citronnade f; l. tea thé m au citron. ◆**lemo'nade** n (fizzy) limonade f; (still) Am citronnade f.

lend [lend] vt (pt & pp lent) prêter (to à); (charm, colour etc) Fig donner (to à); to l. credence to ajouter foi à. ◆—ing n prêt m. ◆—er n prêteur, -euse mf.

length [leŋθ] n longueur f; (section of pipe etc) morceau m; (of road) tronçon m; (of cloth) métrage m; (of horse, swimming pool) Sp longueur f; (duration) durée f; l. of time temps m; at l. (at last) enfin; at (great) l. (in detail) dans le détail; (for a long time) longuement; to go to great lengths se donner beaucoup de mal (to do pour faire). ◆**lengthen** vt allonger; (in time) prolonger. ◆**lengthwise** adv dans le sens de la longueur. ◆**lengthy** a (-ier, -iest) long.

lenient ['liːnɪənt] a indulgent (to envers). ◆**leniency** n indulgence f. ◆**leniently** adv avec indulgence.

lens [lenz] n lentille f; (in spectacles) verre m; Phot objectif m.

Lent [lent] n Rel Carême m.

lentil ['lent(ə)l] n Bot Culin lentille f.

leopard ['lepəd] n léopard m.

leotard ['liːətɑːd] n collant m (de danse).

leper ['lepər] n lépreux, -euse mf. ◆**leprosy** n lèpre f.

lesbian ['lezbɪən] a & n lesbienne (f).

lesion ['liːʒ(ə)n] n Med lésion f.

less [les] a & n moins (de) (than que); l. time/etc moins de temps/etc; she has l. (than you) elle en a moins (que toi); l. than a kilo/ten/etc (with quantity, number) moins d'un kilo/de dix/etc; – adv (to sleep, know etc) moins (than que); l. (often) moins souvent; l. and l. de moins en moins; one l. un(e) de moins; – prep moins; l. six francs moins six francs. ◆**lessen** vti diminuer. ◆**lessening** n diminution f. ◆**lesser** a moindre; – n the l. of le or la moindre de.

-less [ləs] suffix sans; childless sans enfants.

lesson ['les(ə)n] n leçon f; an English l. une leçon or un cours d'anglais; I have lessons now j'ai cours maintenant.

let [let] 1 vt (pt & pp let, pres p letting) (allow) laisser (s.o. do qn faire); to l. s.o. have sth donner qch à qn; to l. away (allow to leave) laisser partir; to l. down (lower) baisser; (hair) dénouer; (dress) rallonger; (tyre) dégonfler; to l. s.o. down (disappoint) décevoir qn; don't l. me down ne compte sur toi; the car l. me down la voiture est tombée en panne. ◆**letdown** n déception f; to l. in (person, dog) faire entrer; (noise, light) laisser entrer; to l. in the clutch Aut embrayer; to l. s.o. in on Fig mettre qn au courant de; to l. oneself in for (expense) se laisser entraîner à; (trouble) s'attirer; to l. off (bomb) faire éclater; (firework, gun) faire partir; to l. s.o. off laisser partir qn; (not punish) ne pas punir qn; (clear) Jur disculper qn; to be l. off with (a fine etc) s'en tirer avec; to l. s.o. off doing dispenser qn de faire; to l. on that Fam (admit) avouer que; (reveal) dire que; to l. out faire or laisser sortir; (prisoner) relâcher; (cry, secret) laisser échapper; (skirt) élargir; to l. s.o. out (of the house) ouvrir la porte à qn; to l. out the clutch Aut débrayer; – vi not to l. on Fam ne rien dire, garder la bouche cousue; to l. up (of rain, person etc) s'arrêter. ◆**letup** n arrêt m, répit m. 2 v aux l. us eat/go/etc, l. eat/go/etc mangeons/partons/etc; l.'s go for a stroll allons nous promener; l. him come qu'il vienne.

let² [let] vt (pt & pp let, pres p letting) to l. (off or out) (house, room etc) louer. ◆**letting** n (renting) location f.

lethal ['liːθ(ə)l] a (dose etc) mortel; (weapon) meurtrier.

lethargy ['leθədʒɪ] n léthargie f. ◆le'**thargic** a léthargique.

letter ['letər] n (missive, character) lettre f; man of letters homme m de lettres; l. bomb lettre f piégée; l. writer correspondant, -ante mf. ◆**letterbox** n boîte f aux or à lettres. ◆**letterhead** n en-tête m. ◆**lettering** n (letters) fpl; (on tomb) inscription f.

lettuce ['letɪs] n laitue f, salade f.

leuk(a)emia [luː'kiːmɪə] n leucémie f.

level ['lev(ə)l] 1 n niveau m; (on the) l. (speed) en palier; – a (surface) plat, uni; (object on surface) horizontal; (spoonful) ras; (equal in score) à égalité (with avec); (in height) au même niveau, à la même hauteur (**with** que); **l. crossing** *Rail* passage *m* à niveau; − *vt* (**-ll-,** *Am* **-l-**) (*plane, differences*) niveler, aplanir; (*plane down*) raboter; (*building*) raser; (*gun*) braquer; (*accusation*) lancer (**at** contre); − *vi* **to l. off** *or* **out** (*stabilize*) Fig se stabiliser. **2 on the l.** *Fam* (*honest*) honnête, franc; (*frankly*) honnêtement, franchement; − *vi* (**-ll-,** *Am* **-l-**) **to l. with** *Fam* Fig être à l. with *Fam* Fig être à équilibré.

lever ['liːvər, *Am* 'levər] *n* levier *m*. ◆**leverage** *n* (*power*) influence *f*.

levity ['levɪtɪ] *n* légèreté *f*.

levy ['levɪ] *vt* (*tax, troops*) lever; − *n* (*tax*) impôt *m*.

lewd [luːd] *a* (**-er, -est**) obscène.

liable ['laɪəb(ə)l] *a* **l. to** (*dizziness etc*) sujet à; (*fine, tax*) passible de; **he's l. to do** susceptible de faire, il pourrait faire; **l. for** (*responsible*) responsable de. ◆**lia'bility** *n* responsabilité *f* (**for** de); (*disadvantage*) handicap *m*; *pl* (*debts*) dettes *fpl*.

liaise [lɪ'eɪz] *vi* travailler en liaison (**with** avec). ◆**liaison** *n* (*association*) & *Mil* liaison *f*.

liar ['laɪər] *n* menteur, -euse *mf*.

libel ['laɪb(ə)l] *vt* (**-ll-,** *Am* **-l-**) diffamer (par écrit); − *n* diffamation *f*.

liberal ['lɪbərəl] *a* (*open-minded*) & *Pol* libéral; (*generous*) généreux (**with** de); − *n* *Pol* libéral, -ale *mf*. ◆**liberalism** *n* libéralisme *m*.

liberate ['lɪbəreɪt] *vt* libérer. ◆**libe'ration** *n* libération *f*. ◆**liberator** *n* libérateur, -trice *mf*.

liberty ['lɪbətɪ] *n* liberté *f*; **at l.** to do libre de faire; **what a l.!** (*cheek*) *Fam* quel culot!; **to take liberties with s.o.** se permettre des familiarités avec qn.

Libra ['liːbrə] *n* (*sign*) la Balance.

library ['laɪbrərɪ] *n* bibliothèque *f*. ◆**li'brarian** *n* bibliothécaire *mf*.

libretto [lɪ'bretəʊ] *n* (*pl* **-os**) *Mus* livret *m*.

Libya ['lɪbjə] *n* Libye *f*. ◆**Libyan** *a* & *n* libyen, -enne (*mf*).

lice [laɪs] *see* **louse**.

licence, *Am* **license** ['laɪsəns] *n* **1** permis *m*, autorisation *f*; (*for driving*) permis *m*; *Com* licence *f*; **pilot's l.** brevet *m* de pilote; **l. fee** *Rad TV* redevance *f*; **l. plate/number** *Aut* plaque *f*/numéro *m* d'immatriculation. **2** (*freedom*) licence *f*.

license ['laɪsəns] *vt* accorder une licence à, autoriser; **licensed premises** établissement *m* qui a une licence de débit de boissons.

licit ['lɪsɪt] *a* licite.

lick [lɪk] *vt* lécher; (*defeat*) *Fam* écraser; (*beat physically*) *Fam* rosser; **to be licked** (*by problem etc*) *Fam* être dépassé; − *n* coup *m* de langue; **a l. of paint** un coup de peinture. ◆**-ing** *n* *Fam* (*defeat*) déculottée *f*; (*beating*) rossée *f*.

licorice ['lɪkərɪs, -rɪs] *n Am* réglisse *f*.

lid [lɪd] *n* **1** (*of box etc*) couvercle *m*. **2** (*of eye*) paupière *f*.

lido ['liːdəʊ] *n* (*pl* **-os**) piscine *f* (*découverte*).

lie ¹ [laɪ] *vi* (*pt* **lay**, *pp* **lain**, *pres p* **lying**) (*in flat position*) s'allonger, s'étendre; (*remain*) rester; (*be*) être; (*in grave*) reposer; **to be lying** (*on the grass etc*) être allongé *or* étendu; **he lay asleep** il dormait; **he lay asleep on tomb**) ci-gît; **the problem lies in the** problème réside dans; **to l. heavy on** (*of meal etc*) & Fig peser sur; **to l. low** (*hide*) se cacher; (*be inconspicuous*) se faire tout petit; **to l. about** *or* **around** (*of objects, person*) traîner; **to l. down, to have a l.-down** (*resting*) s'allonger, se coucher; **lying down** (*resting*) allongé, couché; **to l. in, to have a l.-in** *Fam* faire la grasse matinée.

lie ² [laɪ] *vi* (*pt* & *pp* **lied**, *pres p* **lying**) (*tell lies*) mentir; − *n* mensonge *m*; **to give the l.** **to** (*show as untrue*) démentir.

lieu [luː] *n* **in l. of** au lieu de.

lieutenant [lef'tenənt, *Am* luː'tenənt] *n* lieutenant *m*.

life [laɪf] *n* (*pl* **lives**) vie *f*; (*of battery, machine*) durée *f* (de vie); **to come to l.** (*of street, party etc*) s'animer; **at your time of l.** à ton âge; **loss of l.** perte *f* en vies humaines; **true to l.** conforme à la réalité; **to take one's (own) l.** se donner la mort; **bird l.** les oiseaux *mpl*; − *a* (*cycle, style*) de vie; (*belt, raft*) de sauvetage; (*force*) vital; **l. annuity** rente *f* viagère; **l. blood** Fig âme *f*; **l. insurance** assurance-vie *f*; **l. jacket** gilet *m* de sauvetage; **l. peer** pair *m* à vie. ◆**lifeboat** *n* canot *m* de sauvetage. ◆**lifebuoy** *n* bouée *f* de sauvetage. ◆**lifeguard** *n* maître-nageur *m* sauveteur. ◆**lifeless** *a* sans vie. ◆**lifelike** *a* qui semble vivant. ◆**lifelong** *a* de toute sa vie; (*friend*) de toujours. ◆**lifesaving** *n* sauvetage *m*. ◆**lifesize(d)** *a* grandeur nature *inv*. ◆**lifetime** *n* vie *f*; Fig éternité *f*; **in my l.** de mon vivant; **a once-in-a-l. experience/etc** l'expérience/etc de votre vie.

lift [lɪft] *vt* lever; (*sth heavy*) (sou)lever; (*ban, siege*) Fig lever; (*idea etc*) Fig voler, prendre (**from** à); **to l. down** *or* **off** (*take down*) descendre (**from** de); **to l. out** (*take out*) sortir; **to l. up** (*arm, eyes*) lever; (*object*) (sou)lever; − *vi* (*of fog*) se lever; **to l. off** (*of space vehicle*) décoller; − *n* (*elevator*) ascenseur *m*; **to give s.o. a l.** emmener *or* accompagner qn (*en voiture*) (**to** à). ◆**l.-off** *n* *Av* décollage *m*.

ligament ['ligəmənt] *n* ligament *m*.

light[1] [lait] **1** *n* lumière *f*; (*daylight*) jour *m*, lumière *f*; (*on vehicle*) feu *m*, (*headlight*) phare *m*; **by the l.** of à la lumière de; **in the l.** of (*considering*) à la lumière de; **in that l.** *Fig* sous ce jour *or* cet éclairage; **against the l.** à contre-jour; **to bring to l.** mettre en lumière; **to come to l.** être découvert; **to throw l. on** (*matter*) éclaircir; **do you have a l.?** (*for cigarette*) est-ce que vous avez du feu?; **to set l. to** mettre le feu à; (*person*) *Fig* phare *m*, sommité *f*, lumière *f*; **l. bulb** ampoule *f* (électrique); − *vt* (*pt & pp* **lit** *or* **lighted**) (*candle etc*) allumer; (*match*) gratter; **to l. (up)** (*room*) éclairer; − *vi* **to l. up** (*of window*) s'allumer. **2** *a* (*bright, not dark*) clair; **l. green jacket** une veste vert clair. ◆**-ing** *n* *El* éclairage *m*; **the l. of** (*candle etc*) l'allumage *m* de. ◆**lighten**[1] *vt* (*light up*) éclairer. ◆**lighter** *n* (*for cigarettes etc*) briquet *m*; *Culin* allume-gaz *m inv*. ◆**lighthouse** *n* phare *m*. ◆**lightness**[1] *n* clarté *f*.

light[2] [lait] *a* (*in weight, quantity, strength etc*) léger; (*task*) facile; **l. rain** pluie *f* fine; **to travel l.** voyager avec peu de bagages. ◆**l.-'fingered** *a* chapardeur. ◆**l.-'headed** *a* (*giddy, foolish*) étourdi. ◆**l.-'hearted** *a* gai. ◆**lighten**[2] *vt* (*a load*) alléger. ◆**lightly** *adv* légèrement. ◆**lightness**[2] *n* légèreté *f*.

light[3] [lait] *vi* (*pt & pp* **lit** *or* **lighted**) **to l. upon** trouver par hasard.

lightning ['laitniŋ] *n* *Met* (*light*) éclair *m*; (*charge*) foudre *f*; (*flash of*) l. éclair *m*; − *a* (*speed*) foudroyant; (*visit*) éclair *inv*; **l. conductor** paratonnerre *m*.

lightweight ['laitweit] *a* (*cloth etc*) léger; (*not serious*) pas sérieux, léger.

like[1] [laik] *a* (*alike*) semblable, pareil; − *prep* comme; **l. this** comme ça; **what's he l.?** (*physically, as character*) comment est-il?; **to be** *or* **look l.** ressembler à; **what was the book l.?** comment as-tu trouvé le livre?; **I have one l. it** j'en ai un pareil; − *adv* **nothing l. as big**/*etc* loin d'être aussi grand/*etc*; − *conj* (*as*) *Fam* comme; **it's l. I say** c'est comme je vous le dis; − *n* . . . **and the l.** . . . et ainsi de suite; **the l. of which we shan't see again** comme on n'en reverra plus; **the likes of** the des gens de ton acabit.

lik/e[2] [laik] *vt* aimer (bien) (**to do, doing** faire); **I l. him** je l'aime bien, il me plaît; **she likes it here** elle se plaît ici; **to l. best** préférer; **I'd l. to come** (*want*) je voudrais (bien) *or* j'aimerais (bien) venir; **I'd l. a kilo of apples** je voudrais un kilo de pommes; **would you l. a cigar?** voulez-vous un cigare?; **if you l.** si vous voulez; (**how**) **would you l. to come?** ça te plairait *or* te dirait de venir?; − *npl* **one's likes** nos goûts *mpl*. ◆**-ing** *n* **a l. for** (*person*) de la sympathie pour; (*thing*) du goût pour; **to my l.** à mon goût. ◆**likeable** *a* sympathique.

likely ['laikli] *a* (**-ier, -iest**) (*event, result etc*) probable; (*excuse*) vraisemblable; (*place*) propice; (*candidate*) prometteur; **a l. excuse!** *Iron* belle excuse!; **it's l. (that) she'll come** il est probable qu'elle viendra; **he's l. to come** il viendra probablement; **he's not l. to come** il ne risque pas de venir; − *adv* **very l.** très probablement; **not l.!** pas question! ◆**likelihood** *n* probabilité *f*; **there's little l. that** il y a peu de chances que (+ *sub*).

liken ['laikən] *vt* comparer (**to** à).

likeness ['laiknis] *n* ressemblance *f*; **a family l.** un air de famille; **it's a good l.** c'est très ressemblant.

likewise ['laikwaiz] *adv* (*similarly*) de même, pareillement.

lilac ['lailək] *n* lilas *m*; − *a* (*colour*) lilas *inv*.

Lilo® ['lailəu] *n* (*pl* -**os**) matelas *m* pneumatique.

lilt [lilt] *n* *Mus* cadence *f*.

lily ['lili] *n* lis *m*, lys *m*; **l. of the valley** muguet *m*.

limb [lim] *n* *Anat* membre *m*; **to be out on a l.** *Fig* être le seul de son opinion.

limber ['limbər] *vi* **to l. up** faire des exercices d'assouplissement.

limbo (in) [in'limbəu] *adv* (*uncertain, waiting*) dans l'expectative.

lime [laim] *n* **1** (*tree*) tilleul *m*. **2** (*substance*) chaux *f*. **3** (*fruit*) lime *f*, citron *m* vert; **l. juice** jus *m* de citron vert.

limelight ['laimlait] *n* **in the l.** (*glare of publicity*) en vedette.

limit ['limit] *n* limite *f*; (*restriction*) limitation *f* (**of** de); **that's the l.!** *Fam* c'est le comble!; **within limits** dans une certaine limite; − *vt* limiter (**to** à); **to l. oneself to doing** se borner à faire. ◆**-ed** *a* (*restricted*) limité; (*mind*) borné; (*edition*) à tirage limité; **l. company** *Com* société *f* à responsabilité limitée; (**public**) **l. company** (*with shareholders*) société *f* anonyme; **to a**

l. degree jusqu'à un certain point. ◆**limi'tation** n limitation f. ◆**limitless** a illimité.

limousine [limə'ziːn] n (car) limousine f; (airport etc shuttle) Am voiture-navette f.

limp [lımp] vi (of person) boiter; (of vehicle etc) Fig avancer tant bien que mal; – n to have a l. boiter. 2 a (-er, -est) (soft) mou; (flabby) flasque; (person, hat) avachi.

limpid ['lımpıd] a (liquid) Lit limpide.

linchpin ['lıntʃpın] n (person) pivot m.

linctus ['lıŋktəs] n Med sirop m (contre la toux).

line [laın] n ligne f; (stroke) trait m, ligne f; (of poem) vers m; (wrinkle) ride f; (track) voie f; (rope) corde f; (row) rangée f, ligne f; (of vehicles) file f; (queue) Am file f; (family) lignée f; (business) métier m, rayon m; (article) Com article m; **one's lines** (of actor) son texte m; **on the l.** Tel (speaking) au téléphone; (at other end of line) au bout du fil; **to be on the l.** (at risk) être en danger; **hold the l.!** Tel ne quittez pas!; **the hot l.** Tel le téléphone rouge; **to stand in l.** Am faire la queue; **to step** or **get out of l.** Fig refuser de se conformer; (misbehave) faire une incartade; **out of l. with** (ideas etc) en désaccord avec; **in l. with** conforme à; **he's in l. for** (promotion etc) il doit recevoir; **to take a hard l.** adopter une attitude ferme; **along the same lines** (to work, think) de la même façon; **sth along those lines** qch dans ce genre-là; **to drop a l.** Fam envoyer un mot (to à); **where do we draw the l.?** où fixer les limites?; – vt (paper) régler; (face) rider; **to l. the street** (of trees) border la rue; (of people) faire la haie le long de la rue; **to l. up** (children, objects) aligner; (arrange) organiser; (get ready) préparer; **to have sth lined up** (in mind) avoir qch en vue; – vi to l. up s'aligner; (queue) Am faire la queue. ◆**l.-up** n (row) file f; Pol front m; TV programme(s) m(pl).

line [laın] vt (clothes) doubler; (pockets) Fig se remplir. ◆**lining** n (of clothes) doublure f; (of brakes) garniture f.

lineage ['lınııdʒ] n lignée f.

linear ['lınıər] a linéaire.

linen ['lının] n (sheets etc) linge m; (material) (toile f de) lin m, fil m.

liner ['laınər] n **1** a (ship) paquebot m. **2** (dust)bin l. sac m poubelle.

linesman ['laınzmən] n (pl -men) Fb etc juge m de touche.

linger ['lıŋgər] vi to l. (on) (of person) s'attarder; (of smell, memory) persister; (of doubt) subsister. ◆**-ing** a (death) lent.

lingo ['lıŋgəʊ] n (pl -os) Hum Fam jargon m.

linguist ['lıŋgwıst] n linguiste mf. ◆**lin'guistic** a linguistique. ◆**lin'guistics** n linguistique f.

liniment ['lınımənt] n onguent m, pommade f.

link [lıŋk] vt (connect) relier (to à); (relate, associate) lier (to à); **to l. up** Tel relier; – vi **to l. up** (of roads) se rejoindre; – n (connection) lien m; (of chain) maillon m; (by road, rail) liaison f. ◆**l.-up** n TV Rad liaison f; (of spacecraft) jonction f.

lino ['laınəʊ] n (pl -os) lino m. ◆**linoleum** [lı'nəʊlıəm] n linoléum m.

linseed ['lınsiːd] n l. **oil** huile f de lin.

lint [lınt] n Med tissu m ouaté; (fluff) peluche(s) f(pl).

lion ['laıən] n lion m; l. **cub** lionceau m. ◆**lioness** n lionne f.

lip [lıp] n Anat lèvre f; (rim) bord m; (cheek) Sl culot m. ◆**l.-read** vi (pt & pp -**read** [red]) lire sur les lèvres. ◆**lipstick** n (material) rouge m à lèvres; (stick) tube m de rouge.

liqueur [lı'kjʊər] n liqueur f.

liquid ['lıkwıd] n & a liquide (m). ◆**liquefy** vt liquéfier; – vi se liquéfier. ◆**liquidizer** n Culin (for fruit juices) centrifugeuse f; (for purées etc) robot m, moulinette® f.

liquidate ['lıkwıdeıt] vt (debt, person) liquider. ◆**liqui'dation** n liquidation f.

liquor ['lıkər] n alcool m, spiritueux m; l. **store** Am magasin m de vins et de spiritueux.

liquorice ['lıkərıʃ, -rıs] n réglisse f.

lira, pl lire ['lıərə, 'lıəreı] n (currency) lire f.

lisp [lısp] vi zézayer; – n to have a l. zézayer.

list [lıst] n **1** liste f; – vt (one's possessions etc) faire la liste de; (names) mettre sur la liste; (enumerate) énumérer; (catalogue) cataloguer. **2** vi (of ship) gîter. ◆**-ed** a (monument etc) classé.

listen ['lısən] vi écouter; **to l. to** écouter; **to l. (out) for** (telephone, person etc) tendre l'oreille pour, guetter; **to l. in (to)** Rad écouter. ◆**-ing** n écoute f (to de). ◆**-er** n Rad auditeur, -trice mf; **to be a good l.** (pay attention) savoir écouter.

listless ['lıstləs] a apathique, indolent. ◆**-ness** n apathie f.

lit [lıt] See light [1].

litany ['lıtənı] n Rel litanies fpl.

literal ['lıtərəl] a littéral; (not exaggerated) réel. ◆**-ly** adv littéralement; (really) réellement; **he took it l.** il l'a pris au pied de la lettre.

literate ['lıtərət] a qui sait lire et écrire,

highly l. (*person*) très instruit. ◆**literacy** *n* capacité *f* de lire et d'écrire; (*of country*) degré *m* d'alphabétisation.

literature ['lɪt(ə)rɪtʃər] *n* littérature *f*; (*pamphlets etc*) documentation *f*. ◆**literary** *a* littéraire.

lithe [laɪð] *a* agile, souple.

litigation [lɪtɪ'geɪʃ(ə)n] *n Jur* litige *m*.

litre ['liːtər] *n* litre *m*.

litter ['lɪtər] **1** *n* (*rubbish*) détritus *m*; (*papers*) papiers *mpl*; (*bedding for animals*) litière *f*; (*confusion*) *Fig* fouillis *m*; **l. basket** *or* **bin** boîte *f* à ordures; – *vt* to l. (**with papers** *or* **rubbish**) (*street etc*) laisser traîner des papiers *or* des détritus dans; **a street littered with** une rue jonchée de. **2** *n* (*young animals*) portée *f*.

little ['lɪt(ə)l] **1** *a* (*small*) petit; **the l. ones** les petits. **2** *a* & *n* (*not much*) peu (de); **l. time/money/***etc* peu de temps/d'argent/*etc*; **I've l. left** il m'en reste peu; **she eats l.** elle mange peu; **to have l. to say** avoir peu de chose à dire; **as l. as possible** le moins possible; **a l. money/time/***etc* (*some*) un peu d'argent/de temps/*etc*; **I have a l.** (*some*) j'en ai un peu; **the l. that I have** le peu que j'ai; – *adv* (*somewhat, rather*) peu; **a l. heavy/***etc* un peu lourd/*etc*; **to work/***etc* **a l.** travailler/*etc* un peu; **it's l. better** (*hardly*) ce n'est guère mieux; **l. by l.** peu à peu.

liturgy ['lɪtədʒɪ] *n* liturgie *f*.

live¹ [lɪv] *vi* vivre; (*reside*) habiter, vivre; **where do you l.?** où habitez-vous?; **to l. in Paris** habiter (à) Paris; **to l. off** *or* **on** (*eat*) vivre de; (*sponge on*) *Pej* vivre aux crochets *or* aux dépens de (*qn*); **to l. on** (*of memory etc*) survivre, se perpétuer; **to l. through** (*experience*) vivre; (*survive*) survivre à; **to l. up to** (*one's principles*) vivre selon; (*s.o.'s expectations*) se montrer à la hauteur de; – *vt* (*life*) vivre, mener; (*one's faith etc*) vivre pleinement; **to l. down** faire oublier (avec le temps); **to l. it up** *Fam* mener la grande vie.

live² [laɪv] **1** *a* (*alive, lively*) vivant; (*coal*) ardent; (*bomb*) non explosé; (*ammunition*) réel, de combat; (*wire*) *El* sous tension; (*switch*) *El* mal isolé; (*plugged in*) *El* branché; **a real l. king/***etc* un roi/*etc* en chair et en os. **2** *a* & *adv Rad TV* en direct; **a l. broadcast** une émission en direct; **a l. audience** le *or* un public; **a l. recording** un enregistrement public.

livelihood ['laɪvlɪhud] *n* moyens *mpl* de subsistance; **my l.** mon gagne-pain; **to earn one's** *or* **a l.** gagner sa vie.

livel/y ['laɪvlɪ] *a* (-**ier**, -**iest**) (*person, style*) vif, vivant; (*street, story*) vivant; (*interest, mind, colour*) vif; (*day*) mouvementé; (*forceful*) vigoureux; (*conversation, discussion*) animé. ◆-**iness** *n* vivacité *f*.

liven ['laɪv(ə)n] *vt* to l. up (*person*) égayer; (*party*) animer; – *vi* to l. up (*of person, party*) s'animer.

liver ['lɪvər] *n* foie *m*.

livery ['lɪvərɪ] *n* (*uniform*) livrée *f*.

livestock ['laɪvstɒk] *n* bétail *m*.

livid ['lɪvɪd] *a* (*blue-grey*) livide; (*angry*) *Fig* furieux; **l. with cold** blême de froid.

living ['lɪvɪŋ] **1** *a* (*alive*) vivant; **not a l. soul** (*nobody*) personne, pas âme qui vive; **within l. memory** de mémoire d'homme; **l. or dead** mort ou vif; **the l.** les vivants *mpl*. **2** *n* (*livelihood*) vie *f*; **to make a** *or* **one's l.** gagner sa vie; **to work for a l.** travailler pour vivre; **the cost of l.** le coût de la vie; – *a* (*standard, conditions*) de vie; (*wage*) qui permet de vivre; **l. room** salle *f* de séjour.

lizard ['lɪzəd] *n* lézard *m*.

llama ['laːmə] *n* (*animal*) lama *m*.

load [ləʊd] *n* (*object carried, burden*) charge *f*; (*freight*) chargement *m*, charge *f*; (*strain, weight*) poids *m*; **a l. of, loads of** (*people, money etc*) *Fam* un tas de, énormément de; **to take a l. off s.o.'s mind** ôter un grand poids à qn; – *vt* charger; **to l. down** *or* **up** charger (**with** de); – *vi* **to l. (up)** charger la voiture, le navire *etc*. ◆-**ed** *a* (*gun, vehicle etc*) chargé; (*dice*) pipé; (*rich*) *Fam* plein aux as; **a l. question** une question piège; (**down) with** (*debts*) accablé de.

loaf [ləʊf] **1** *n* (*pl* **loaves**) pain *m*; **French l.** baguette *f*. **2** *vi* to l. (**about**) fainéanter. ◆-**er** *n* fainéant, -ante *mf*.

loam [ləʊm] *n* (*soil*) terreau *m*.

loan [ləʊn] *n* (*money lent*) prêt *m*; (*money borrowed*) emprunt *m*; **on l. from** prêté par; (**out) on l.** (*book*) sorti; **may I have the l. of . . . ?** puis-je emprunter . . . ?; – *vt* (*lend*) prêter (**to** à).

loath [ləʊθ] *a* **l. to do** *Lit* peu disposé à faire.

loath/e [ləʊð] *vt* détester (**doing** faire). ◆-**ing** *n* dégoût *m*. ◆**loathsome** *a* détestable.

lobby ['lɒbɪ] **1** *n* (*of hotel*) vestibule *m*, hall *m*; *Th* foyer *m*. **2** *n Pol* groupe de pression, lobby *m*; – *vt* faire pression sur.

lobe [ləʊb] *n Anat* lobe *m*.

lobster ['lɒbstər] *n* homard *m*; (*spiny*) langouste *f*.

local ['ləʊk(ə)l] *a* local; (*of the neighbourhood*) du *or* de quartier; (*regional*) du pays; **are you l.?** êtes-vous du coin *or* d'ici?; **the doctor is l.** le médecin est tout près d'ici; **a l. phone call** (*within town*) une communication urbaine; − *n* (*pub*) Fam bistrot *m* du coin, pub *m*; **she's a l.** elle est du coin; **the locals** (*people*) les gens du coin. ◆**lo'cality** *n* (*neighbourhood*) environs *mpl*; (*region*) région *f*; (*place*) lieu *m*; (*site*) emplacement *m*. ◆**localize** *vt* (*confine*) localiser. ◆**locally** *adv* dans les environs, dans le coin; (*around here*) par ici; (*in precise place*) localement.

locate [ləʊˈkeɪt] *vt* (*find*) repérer; (*pain, noise, leak*) localiser; (*situate*) situer; (*build*) construire. ◆**location** *n* (*site*) emplacement *m*; (*act*) repérage *m*; localisation *f*; **on l.** Cin en extérieur.

lock [lɒk] **1** *vt* to l. (**up**) fermer à clef; **to l. the wheels** Aut bloquer les roues; **to l. s.o. in** enfermer qn; **to l. s.o. in sth** enfermer qn dans qch; **to l. s.o. out** (*accidentally*) enfermer qn dehors; **to l. away** *or* **up** (*prisoner*) enfermer; (*jewels etc*) mettre sous clef, enfermer; − *vi* **to l. (up)** fermer à clef; − *n* (*on door, chest etc*) serrure *f*; (*of gun*) cran *m* de sûreté; (*turning point*) Aut rayon *m* de braquage; (**anti-theft**) **l.** Aut antivol *m*; **under l. and key** sous clef. **2** *n* (*of hair*) mèche *f*. ◆**locker** *n* casier *m*; (*for luggage*) Rail casier *m* de consigne automatique; (*for clothes*) vestiaire *m* (métallique); **l. room** *Sp Am* vestiaire *m*. ◆**lockout** *n* (*industrial*) lock-out *m inv*. ◆**locksmith** *n* serrurier *m*.

locket ['lɒkɪt] *n* (*jewel*) médaillon *m*.

loco ['ləʊkəʊ] *a Sl* cinglé, fou.

locomotion [ləʊkəˈməʊʃ(ə)n] *n* locomotion *f*. ◆**locomotive** *n* locomotive *f*.

locum ['ləʊkəm] *n* (*doctor*) remplaçant, -ante *mf*.

locust ['ləʊkəst] *n* criquet *m*, sauterelle *f*.

lodg/e [lɒdʒ] **1** *vt* (*person*) loger; (*valuables*) déposer (**with** chez); **to l. a complaint** porter plainte; − *vi* (*of bullet*) se loger (**in** dans); **to be lodging** (*accommodated*) être logé (**with** chez). **2** *n* (*house*) pavillon *m* de gardien *or* de chasse; (*of porter*) loge *f*. ◆**—ing** *n* (*accommodation*) logement *m*; *pl* (*flat*) logement *m*; (*room*) chambre *f*; **in lodgings** en meublé. ◆**—er** *n* (*room and meals*) pensionnaire *mf*; (*room only*) locataire *mf*.

loft [lɒft] *n* (*attic*) grenier *m*.

loft/y ['lɒftɪ] *a* (*-ier, -iest*) (*high, noble*) élevé; (*haughty*) hautain. ◆**—iness** *n* hauteur *f*.

log [lɒg] **1** *n* (*tree trunk*) rondin *m*; (*for fire*) bûche *f*, rondin *m*; **l. fire** feu *m* de bois. **2** *vt* (*-gg-*) (*facts*) noter; **to l. (up)** (*distance*) faire, couvrir. ◆**logbook** *n* Nau Av journal *m* de bord.

logarithm ['lɒgərɪðəm] *n* logarithme *m*.

loggerheads (at) [ætˈlɒgəhedz] *adv* en désaccord (**with** avec).

logic ['lɒdʒɪk] *n* logique *f*. ◆**logical** *a* logique. ◆**logically** *adv* logiquement.

logistics [ləˈdʒɪstɪks] *n* logistique *f*.

logo ['ləʊgəʊ] *n* (*pl* -os) logo *m*.

loin [lɔɪn] *n* (*meat*) filet *m*.

loins [lɔɪnz] *npl* Anat reins *mpl*.

loiter ['lɔɪtər] *vi* traîner.

loll [lɒl] *vi* (*in armchair etc*) se prélasser.

lollipop ['lɒlɪpɒp] *n* (*sweet on stick*) sucette *f*; (*ice on stick*) Fam sucette *f*; (*money*) Sl fric *m*; **lolly** *n* Fam sucette *f*; (*ice*) **l.** Fam esquimau *m*.

London ['lʌndən] *n* Londres *m or f*; − *a* (*taxi etc*) londonien. ◆**Londoner** *n* Londonien, -ienne *mf*.

lone [ləʊn] *a* solitaire; **l. wolf** Fig solitaire *mf*. ◆**loneliness** *n* solitude *f*. ◆**lonely** *a* (*-ier, -iest*) (*road, house, life etc*) solitaire; (*person*) seul, solitaire. ◆**loner** *n* solitaire *mf*. ◆**lonesome** *a* solitaire.

long [lɒŋ] **1** *a* (*-er, -est*) long; **to be ten metres l.** être long de dix mètres, avoir dix mètres de long; **to be six weeks l.** durer six semaines; **how l. is ...** quelle est la longueur de ...?; (*time*) quelle est la durée de ...?; **a l. time** longtemps; **in the l. run** à la longue; **a l. face** une grimace; **a l. memory** une bonne mémoire; **l. jump** *Sp* saut *m* en longueur. **2** *adv* (*a long time*) longtemps; **l.** *before* longtemps avant; **has he been here l.?** il y a longtemps qu'il est ici?, il est ici depuis longtemps?; **how l. (ago)?** (il y a) combien de temps?; **not l. ago** il y a peu de temps; **before l.** sous *or* avant peu; **no longer** ne plus; **she no longer swims** elle ne nage plus; **a bit longer** (*to wait etc*) encore un peu; **I won't be l.** je n'en ai pas pour longtemps; **at the longest** (tout) au plus; **all summer l.** tout l'été; **l. live the queen/***etc* vive la reine/*etc*; **as l. as, so l. as** (*provided that*) pourvu que (+ *sub*); **as l. as I live** tant que je vivrai.

long [lɒŋ] *vi* **to l. for sth** avoir envie de qch; **to l. for s.o.** languir après qn; **to l. to do** avoir très envie de faire. ◆**—ing** *n* désir *m*, envie *f*.

long-distance [lɒŋˈdɪstəns] *a* (*race*) de fond; (*phone call*) interurbain; (*flight*) long-courrier. ◆**long-drawn-'out** *a* interminable. ◆**long'haired** *a* aux cheveux longs. ◆**longhand** *n* écriture *f* normale. ◆**long-'playing** *a* **l.-playing record** 33 tours *m inv*. ◆**long-range** *a* (*forecast*) à long terme. ◆**long'sighted** *a* Med presbyte. ◆long'standing a de longue date. ◆long'suffering a très patient. ◆long-'term a à long terme. ◆long-'winded a (speech, speaker) verbeux.

longevity [lɒn'dʒevɪtɪ] n longévité f.

longitude ['lɒndʒɪtjud] n longitude f.

longways ['lɒnweɪz] adv en longueur.

loo [luː] n (toilet) Fam cabinets mpl.

look [lʊk] n regard m; (appearance) air m, allure f; (good) looks la beauté, un beau physique; to have a l. (at) jeter un coup d'œil (à), regarder; to have a l. (for) chercher; to have a l. (a)round regarder; (walk) faire un tour; let me have a l. fais voir; I like the l. of him il me fait bonne impression, il me plaît; — vti regarder; to l. s.o. in the face regarder qn dans les yeux; to l. tired/happy/etc (seem) sembler or avoir l'air fatigué/heureux/etc; to l. pretty/ugly (be) être joli/laid; to l. one's age faire son âge; l. here! dites donc!; you l. like or as if you're tired tu as l'air fatigué, on dirait que tu es fatigué; it looks like or as if she won't leave elle n'a pas l'air de vouloir partir; it looks like it! c'est probable!; to l. like a child avoir l'air d'un enfant; to l. like an apple avoir l'air d'être une pomme; you l. like my brother tu ressembles à mon frère; it looks like rain (to me) il me semble or on dirait qu'il va pleuvoir; what does he l. like? (describe him) comment est-il?; to l. well or good (of person) avoir bonne mine; you l. good in that hat/etc ce chapeau/etc te va très bien; that looks bad (action etc) ça fait mauvais effet. ■ to l. after vt (deal with) s'occuper de; (patient, hair) soigner; (keep safely) garder (for s.o. pour qn); to l. after oneself (keep healthy) faire bien attention à soi; I can l. after myself (cope) je suis assez grand pour me débrouiller; to l. around vt (visit) visiter; — vi (have a look) regarder; (walk round) faire un tour; to l. at vt regarder; (consider) considérer, voir; (check) vérifier; to l. away vi détourner les yeux; to l. back vi regarder derrière soi; (in time) regarder en arrière; to l. down vi baisser les yeux; (from height) regarder en bas; to l. down on (consider scornfully) mépriser, regarder de haut; to l. for (seek) chercher; to l. forward to vt (event) attendre avec impatience; to l. in vi regarder à l'intérieur); to l. in on s.o. Fam passer voir qn; to l. into vt (examine) examiner; (find out about) se renseigner sur; to l. on vi regarder; — vt (consider) considérer, voir; to l. out vi (be careful) faire attention (for à); to l. out for (seek)

chercher; (watch) guetter; to l. (out) on to (of window, house etc) donner sur; to l. over or through vt (examine fully) examiner, regarder de près; (briefly) parcourir; (region, town) parcourir, visiter; to l. round vt (visit) visiter; — vi (have a look) regarder; (walk round) faire un tour; (look back) se retourner; to l. round for (seek) chercher; to l. up vi (of person) lever les yeux; (into the air or sky) regarder en l'air; (improve) s'améliorer; to l. up to s.o. respecter; — vt (word) chercher; to l. s.o. up (visit) passer voir qn. ◆-ing suffix pleas-ant-/tired-/etc l. à l'air agréable/ fatigué/etc. ◆-ing-glass n glace f, miroir m.

lookout ['lʊkaʊt] n (soldier) guetteur m; (sailor) vigie f; l. (post) poste m de guet; (on ship) vigie f; to be on the l. faire le guet; to be on the l. for guetter.

loom [luːm] 1 vi to l. (up) (of mountain etc) apparaître indistinctement; Fig paraître imminent. 2 n Tex métier m à tisser.

loony ['luːnɪ] n & a SI imbécile mf.

loop [luːp] n (in river etc) & Av boucle f; (contraceptive device) stérilet m; to l. the loop Av boucler la boucle. ◆loophole n (in rules) point m faible, lacune f; (way out) échappatoire f.

loose [luːs] a (-er, -est) (screw, belt, knot) desserré; (tooth, stone) branlant; (page) détaché; (animal) libre, (set loose) lâché; (clothes) flottant; (hair) dénoué; (flesh) flasque; (wording, translation) approxima-tif, vague; (link) vague; (discipline) relâché; (articles) Com en vrac; (cheese, tea etc) Com au poids; (woman) Pej facile; l. change petite monnaie f; l. covers housses fpl; l. living vie f dissolue; to get l. (of dog, page) se détacher; to set or turn l. (dog etc) libérer, lâcher; he's at a l. end or Am at l. ends il ne sait pas trop quoi faire; — n on the l. (prisoner etc) en liberté; — vt (animal) lâcher. ◆loosely adv (to hang) lâchement; (to hold, tie) sans serrer; (to translate) libre-ment; (to link) vaguement. ◆loosen vt (knot, belt, screw) desserrer; (rope) déten-dre; (grip) relâcher; — vi to l. up Sp faire des exercices d'assouplissement. ◆loose-ness n (of screw, machine parts) jeu m.

loot [luːt] n butin m; (money) SI fric m; — vt piller. ◆-ing n pillage m. ◆-er n pillard, -arde mf.

lop [lɒp] vt (-pp-) to l. (off) couper.

lop-sided [lɒp'saɪdɪd] a (crooked) de tra-vers; to walk l.-sided (limp) se déhancher.

loquacious [ləʊ'kweɪʃəs] a loquace.

lord [lɔːd] *n* seigneur *m*; (*title*) Br lord *m*; **good L.!** *Fam* bon sang!; **oh L.!** *Fam* mince!; **the House of Lords** *Pol* la Chambre des Lords; – *vt* **to l. it over** s.o. *Fam* dominer qn. ◆**lordly** *a* digne d'un grand seigneur; (*arrogant*) hautain. ◆**lordship** *n* **Your L.** (*to judge*) Monsieur le juge.

lore [lɔːr] *n* traditions *fpl*.

lorry ['lɒrɪ] *n* camion *m*; (*heavy*) poids *m* lourd; **l. driver** camionneur *m*; **long-distance l. driver** routier *m*.

los/e [luːz] *vt* (*pt & pp* **lost**) perdre; **to get lost** (*of person*) se perdre; **the ticket/etc got lost** on a perdu le billet/*etc*; **get lost!** *Fam* fiche le camp!; **to l. s.o. sth** faire perdre qch à qn; **to l. interest in** se désintéresser de; **I've lost my bearings** je suis désorienté; **the clock loses six minutes a day** la pendule retarde de six minutes par jour; **to l. one's life** trouver la mort (**in** dans); – *vi* perdre; **to l. out** être perdant; **to l. to** Sp être battu par. ◆**—ing** *a* perdant; **a l. battle** *Fig* une bataille perdue d'avance. ◆**—er** *n* perdant, -ante *mf*; (*failure in life*) *Fam* paumé, -ée *mf*; **to be a good l.** être bon *or* beau joueur.

loss [lɒs] *n* perte *f*; **at a l.** (*confused*) perplexe; **to sell at a l.** *Com* vendre à perte; **at a l. to do** incapable de faire. ◆**lost** *a* perdu; **l. property**, *Am* **l. and found** objets *mpl* trouvés.

lot [lɒt] *n* **1** (*destiny*) sort *m*; (*batch, land*) lot *m*; **to draw lots** tirer au sort; **parking l.** *Am* parking *m*; **a bad l.** (*person*) *Fam* un mauvais sujet. **2 the l.** (*everything*) (le) tout; **the l. of you** vous tous; **a l. of, lots of** beaucoup de; **a l.** beaucoup; **quite a l.** pas mal (**of** de); **such a l.** tellement (**of** de), tant (**of** de); **what a l. of flowers/water/etc!** que de fleurs/d'eau/*etc*!; **what a l.!** quelle quantité!; **what a l. of flowers/etc!** que vous avez (beaucoup) de fleurs/*etc*!

lotion ['ləʊʃ(ə)n] *n* lotion *f*.

lottery ['lɒtərɪ] *n* loterie *f*.

lotto ['lɒtəʊ] *n* (*game*) loto *m*.

loud [laʊd] *a* (**-er, -est**) bruyant; (*voice, radio*) fort; (*noise, cry*) grand; (*gaudy*) voyant; – *adv* (*to shout etc*) fort; **out l.** tout haut. ◆**-ly** *adv* (*to speak, laugh etc*) bruyamment, fort; (*to shout*) fort. ◆**—ness** *n* (*of voice etc*) force *f*; (*noise*) bruit *m*. ◆**loud'hailer** *n* mégaphone *m*. ◆**loudmouth** *n* (*person*) *Fam* grande gueule *f*. ◆**loud'speaker** *n* haut-parleur *m*; (*of hi-fi unit*) enceinte *f*.

lounge [laʊndʒ] *n* **1** salon *m*; **l. suit** complet

m veston. **2** *vi* (*loll*) se prélasser; **to l. about** (*idle*) paresser; (*stroll*) flâner.

louse, *pl* **lice** [laʊs, laɪs] **1** *n* (*insect*) pou *m*. **2** *n* (*person*) *Pej Sl* salaud *m*. **3** *vt* **to l. up** (*mess up*) *Sl* gâcher.

lousy ['laʊzɪ] *a* (**-ier, -iest**) (*bad*) *Fam* infect; **l. with** (*crammed, loaded*) *Sl* bourré de.

lout [laʊt] *n* rustre *m*. ◆**loutish** *a* (*attitude*) de rustre.

love [lʌv] **1** *n* amour *m*; *Tennis* zéro *m*; **in l.** amoureux (**with** de); **they're in l.** ils s'aiment; **art is his l. or** *the* **l.** l'art est sa passion; **yes, my l.** oui mon amour; – *vt* aimer; (*like very much*) adorer, aimer (**beaucoup**) (**to do, doing** faire); **give him** *or* **her my l.** (*greeting*) dis-lui bien des choses de ma part; **l. affair** liaison *f* (amoureuse). ◆**—ing** *a* affectueux, aimant. ◆**—able** *a* adorable. ◆**—er** *n* (*man*) amant *m*; (*woman*) maîtresse *f*; **a l. of** (*art, music etc*) un amateur de; **a nature l.** un amoureux de la nature. ◆**lovesick** *a* amoureux.

lovely ['lʌvlɪ] *a* (**-ier, -iest**) (*pleasing*) agréable, bon; (*excellent*) excellent; (*pretty*) joli; (*charming*) charmant; (*kind*) gentil; **the weather's l.** il fait beau; **to see you!** je suis ravi de te voir; **l. and hot/dry/etc** bien chaud/sec/*etc*.

low[1] [ləʊ] *a* (**-er, -est**) bas; (*speed, income, intelligence*) faible; (*opinion, quality*) mauvais; **she's l. on** (*money etc*) elle n'a plus beaucoup de; **to feel l.** (*depressed*) être déprimé; **in a l. voice** à voix basse; **lower** inférieur; – *adv* (**-er, -est**) bas; **to turn (down) l.** mettre tout bas; **to run l.** (*of supplies*) s'épuiser; – *n* *Met* dépression *f*; **to reach a new l.** *or* **an all-time l.** (*of prices etc*) atteindre leur niveau le plus bas. ◆**low-'calorie** *a* (*diet*) (à) basses calories. ◆**low-'cost** *a* à bon marché *inv*. ◆**low-cut** *a* décolleté. ◆**low-down** *a* méprisable. ◆**lowdown** *n* (*facts*) *Fam* tuyaux *mpl*. ◆**low-'fat** *a* (*milk*) écrémé; (*cheese*) de régime. ◆**low-'key** *a* (*discreet*) discret. ◆**lowland(s)** *n* plaine *f*. ◆**low-level** *a* bas. ◆**low-paid** *a* mal payé. ◆**low-'salt** *a* (*food*) à faible teneur en sel.

low[2] [ləʊ] *vi* (*of cattle*) meugler.

lower ['ləʊər] *vt* baisser; **to l. s.o./sth** (*by rope*) descendre qn/qch; **to l. oneself** *Fig* s'abaisser. ◆**—ing** *n* (*drop*) baisse *f*.

lowly ['ləʊlɪ] *a* (**-ier, -iest**) humble.

loyal ['lɔɪəl] *a* loyal (**to envers**), fidèle (**to** à). ◆**loyalty** *n* loyauté *f*, fidélité *f*.

lozenge ['lɒzɪndʒ] *n* (*sweet*) *Med* pastille *f*; (*shape*) *Geom* losange *m*.

LP [el'piː] *abbr* = **long-playing record.**

L-plates ['elpleɪts] *npl Aut* plaques *fpl* d'apprenti conducteur.

Ltd *abbr (Limited) Com* SARL.

lubricate ['luːbrɪkeɪt] *vt* lubrifier; *Aut* graisser. ◆**lubricant** *n* lubrifiant *m*. ◆**lubri'cation** *n Aut* graissage *m*.

lucid ['luːsɪd] *a* lucide. ◆**lu'cidity** *n* lucidité *f*.

luck [lʌk] *n (chance)* chance *f*; *(good fortune)* (bonne) chance *f*, bonheur *m*; *(fate)* hasard *m*, fortune *f*; **bad l.** malchance *f*, malheur *m*; **hard l.!**, **tough l.!** pas de chance!; **worse l.** *(unfortunately)* malheureusement. ◆**luckily** *adv* heureusement. ◆**lucky** *a* (-ier, -iest) *(person)* chanceux, heureux; *(guess, event)* heureux; **to be l.** *(of person)* avoir de la chance **(to do** de faire); **I've had a l. day** j'ai eu de la chance aujourd'hui; **l. charm** porte-bonheur *m inv*; **l. number** /etc chiffre *m*/etc porte-bonheur; **how l.!** quelle chance!

lucrative ['luːkrətɪv] *a* lucratif.

ludicrous ['luːdɪkrəs] *a* ridicule.

ludo ['luːdəʊ] *n* jeu *m* des petits chevaux.

lug [lʌg] *vt* (-gg-) *(pull)* traîner; **to l. around** trimbaler.

luggage ['lʌgɪdʒ] *n* bagages *mpl*.

lugubrious [luːˈguːbrɪəs] *a* lugubre.

lukewarm ['luːkwɔːm] *a* tiède.

lull [lʌl] **1** *n* arrêt *m*; *(in storm)* accalmie *f*. **2** *vt* (-ll-) apaiser; **to l. to sleep** endormir. ◆**lullaby** ['lʌləbaɪ] *n* berceuse *f*.

lumbago [lʌmˈbeɪgəʊ] *n* lumbago *m*.

lumber[1] ['lʌmbər] *n (timber)* bois *m* de charpente; *(junk)* bric-à-brac *m inv*. ◆**lumberjack** *n Am Can* bûcheron *m*. ◆**lumberjacket** *n* blouson *m*. ◆**lumber-room** *n* débarras *m*.

lumber[2] ['lʌmbər] *vt* **to l. s.o. with sth/s.o.** *Fam* coller qch/qn à qn; **he got lumbered with the chore** il s'est appuyé la corvée.

luminous ['luːmɪnəs] *a (dial etc)* lumineux.

lump [lʌmp] *n* morceau *m*; *(in soup)* grumeau *m*; *(bump)* bosse *f*; *(swelling) Med* grosseur *f*; **l. sum** somme *f* forfaitaire; — *vt* **to l. together** réunir; *Fig Pej* mettre dans le même sac. ◆**lumpy** *a* (-ier, -iest) *(soup etc)* grumeleux; *(surface)* bosselé.

lunar ['luːnər] *a* lunaire.

lunatic ['luːnətɪk] *a* fou, dément; — *n* fou *m*, folle *f*. ◆**lunacy** *n* folie *f*, démence *f*.

lunch [lʌntʃ] *n* déjeuner *m*; **to have l.** déjeuner; **l. break**, **l. hour**, **l. time** heure *f* du déjeuner; — *vi* déjeuner **(on, off** de). ◆**luncheon** *n* déjeuner *m*; **l. meat** mortadelle *f*, saucisson *m*; **l. voucher** chèque-déjeuner *m*.

lung [lʌŋ] *n* poumon *m*; **l. cancer** cancer *m* du poumon.

lunge [lʌndʒ] *n* coup *m* en avant; — *vi* **to l. at s.o.** se ruer sur qn.

lurch [lɜːtʃ] **1** *vi (of person)* tituber; *(of ship)* faire une embardée. **2** *n* **to leave s.o. in the l.** *Fam* laisser qn en plan, laisser tomber qn.

lure [lʊər] *vt* attirer (par la ruse) **(into** dans); — *n (attraction)* attrait *m*.

lurid ['lʊərɪd] *a (horrifying)* horrible, affreux; *(sensational)* à sensation; *(gaudy)* voyant; *(colour, sunset)* sanglant.

lurk [lɜːk] *vi (hide)* se cacher **(in** dans); *(prowl)* rôder; *(of suspicion, fear etc)* persister.

luscious ['lʌʃəs] *a (food etc)* appétissant.

lush [lʌʃ] **1** *a (vegetation)* luxuriant; *(wealthy) Fam* opulent. **2** *n Am Sl* ivrogne *mf*.

lust [lʌst] *n (for person, object)* convoitise *f* **(for** de); *(for power, knowledge)* soif *f* **(for** de); — *vi* **to l. after** *(object, person)* convoiter; *(power, knowledge)* avoir soif de.

lustre ['lʌstər] *n (gloss)* lustre *m*.

lusty ['lʌstɪ] *a* (-ier, -iest) vigoureux.

lute [luːt] *n Mus* luth *m*.

Luxembourg ['lʌksəmbɜːg] *n* Luxembourg *m*.

luxuriant [lʌgˈʒʊərɪənt] *a* luxuriant. ◆**luxuriate** *vi (laze about)* paresser **(in** bed/etc au lit/etc).

luxury ['lʌkʃərɪ] *n* luxe *m*; — *a (goods, flat etc)* de luxe. ◆**luxurious** [lʌgˈʒʊərɪəs] *a* luxueux.

lying ['laɪɪŋ] *see* lie[1,2]; — *n* le mensonge; — *a (account)* mensonger; *(person)* menteur.

lynch [lɪntʃ] *vt* lyncher. ◆**-ing** *n* lynchage *m*.

lynx [lɪŋks] *n (animal)* lynx *m*.

lyre ['laɪər] *n Mus Hist* lyre *f*.

lyric ['lɪrɪk] *a* lyrique; — *npl (of song)* paroles *fpl*. ◆**lyrical** *a (effusive)* lyrique. ◆**lyricism** *n* lyrisme *m*.

M

M, m [em] *n* M, m *m*.

m *abbr* **1** (*metre*) mètre *m*. **2** (*mile*) mile *m*.

MA *abbr* = **Master of Arts**.

ma'am [mæm] *n* madame *f*.

mac [mæk] *n* (*raincoat*) *Fam* imper *m*.

macabre [mə'kɑːbrə] *a* macabre.

macaroni [mækə'rəʊnɪ] *n* macaroni(s) *m(pl)*.

macaroon [mækə'ruːn] *n* (*cake*) macaron *m*.

mace [meɪs] *n* (*staff, rod*) masse *f*.

Machiavellian [mækɪə'velɪən] *a* machiavélique.

machination [mækɪ'neɪʃ(ə)n] *n* machination *f*.

machine [mə'ʃiːn] *n* (*apparatus, car, system etc*) machine *f*. ◆**machinegun** *n* mitrailleuse *f*; – *vt* (**-nn-**) mitrailler. ◆**machinery** *n* (*machines*) machines *fpl*; (*works*) mécanisme *m*; *Fig* rouages *mpl*. ◆**machinist** *n* (*on sewing machine*) piqueur, -euse *mf*.

macho ['mætʃəʊ] *n* (*pl* **-os**) macho *m*; – *a* (*attitude etc*) macho (*f inv*).

mackerel ['mækrəl] *n inv* (*fish*) maquereau *m*.

mackintosh ['mækɪntɒʃ] *n* imperméable *m*.

mad [mæd] *a* (**madder, maddest**) fou; (*dog*) enragé; (*bull*) furieux; **m. (at)** (*angry*) *Fam* furieux (contre); **to be m.** (**keen**) **on** *Fam* (*person*) être emballé par; (*films etc*) se passionner *or* s'emballer pour; **to drive m.** rendre fou; (*irritate*) énerver; **he drove me m. to go** *Fam* il m'a cassé les pieds pour que j'y aille; **like m.** comme un fou. ◆**maddening** *a* exaspérant. ◆**madhouse** *n Fam* maison *f* de fous. ◆**madly** *adv* (*in love, to spend money etc*) follement; (*desperately*) désespérément. ◆**madman** *n* (*pl* **-men**) fou *m*. ◆**madness** *n* folie *f*.

Madagascar [mædə'gæskər] *n* Madagascar *f*.

madam ['mædəm] *n* (*married*) madame *f*; (*unmarried*) mademoiselle *f*.

made [meɪd] *see* **make**.

Madeira [mə'dɪərə] *n* (*wine*) madère *m*.

madonna [mə'dɒnə] *n Rel* madone *f*.

maestro ['maɪstrəʊ] *n* (*pl* **-os**) *Mus* maestro *m*.

Mafia ['mæfɪə] *n* maf(f)ia *f*.

magazine [mægə'ziːn] *n* (*periodical*) magazine *m*, revue *f*; (*of gun, camera*) magasin *m*.

maggot ['mægət] *n* ver *m*, asticot *m*. ◆**maggoty** *a* véreux.

magic ['mædʒɪk] *n* magie *f*; – *a* (*word, wand*) magique. ◆**magical** *a* (*evening etc*) magique. ◆**ma'gician** *n* magicien, -ienne *mf*.

magistrate ['mædʒɪstreɪt] *n* magistrat *m*.

magnanimous [mæg'nænɪməs] *a* magnanime.

magnate ['mægneɪt] *n* (*tycoon*) magnat *m*.

magnesium [mæg'niːzɪəm] *n* magnésium *m*.

magnet ['mægnɪt] *n* aimant *m*. ◆**mag'netic** *a* magnétique. ◆**magnetism** *n* magnétisme *m*. ◆**magnetize** *vt* magnétiser.

magnificent [mæg'nɪfɪsənt] *a* magnifique. ◆**magnificence** *n* magnificence *f*. ◆**magnificently** *adv* magnifiquement.

magnify ['mægnɪfaɪ] *vt* (*image*) & *Fig* grossir; (*sound*) amplifier; **magnifying glass** loupe *f*. ◆**magnifi'cation** *n* grossissement *m*; amplification *f*. ◆**magnitude** *n* ampleur *f*.

magnolia [mæg'nəʊlɪə] *n* (*tree*) magnolia *m*.

magpie ['mægpaɪ] *n* (*bird*) pie *f*.

mahogany [mə'hɒgənɪ] *n* acajou *m*.

maid [meɪd] *n* (*servant*) bonne *f*; **old m.** *Pej* vieille fille *f*. ◆**maiden** *n Old-fashioned* jeune fille *f*; – *a* (*speech etc*) premier; (*flight*) inaugural; **m. name** nom *m* de jeune fille. ◆**maidenly** *a* virginal.

mail [meɪl] *n* (*system*) poste *f*; (*letters*) courrier *m*; – *a* (*van, bag etc*) postal; **m. order** vente *f* par correspondance; – *vt* mettre à la poste; **mailing list** liste *f* d'adresses. ◆**mailbox** *n Am* boîte *f* à *or* aux lettres. ◆**mailman** *n* (*pl* **-men**) *Am* facteur *m*.

maim [meɪm] *vt* mutiler, estropier.

main [meɪn] **1** *a* principal; **the m. thing is to . . .** l'essentiel est de . . . ; **m. line** *Rail* grande ligne *f*; **m. road** grande route *f*; **in the m.** (*mostly*) en gros, dans l'ensemble. **2** *n* **water/gas m.** conduite *f* d'eau/de gaz; **the mains** *El* le secteur; **a mains radio** une radio secteur. ◆**-ly** *adv* principalement, surtout. ◆**mainland** *n* continent *m*. ◆**main-**

stay *n* (*of family etc*) soutien *m*; (*of organization, policy*) pilier *m*. ◆**mainstream** *n* tendance *f* dominante.

maintain [meɪnˈteɪn] *vt* (*continue, assert*) maintenir (*that* que); (*vehicle, family etc*) entretenir; (*silence*) garder. ◆**maintenance** *n* (*of vehicle, road etc*) entretien *m*; (*of prices, order, position etc*) maintien *m*; (*alimony*) pension *f* alimentaire.

maisonette [meɪzəˈnet] *n* duplex *m*.

maize [meɪz] *n* (*cereal*) maïs *m*.

majesty [ˈmædʒəsti] *n* majesté *f*; **Your M.** (*title*) Votre Majesté. ◆**maˈjestic** *a* majestueux.

major [ˈmeɪdʒər] **1** *a* (*main, great*) & *Mus* majeur; **a m. road** une grande route. **2** *n Mil* commandant *m*. **3** *n* (*subject*) *Univ Am* dominante *f*; – *vi* **to m. in** se spécialiser en. ◆**majoˈrette** *n* (*drum*) majorette *f*.

Majorca [məˈjɔːkə] *n* Majorque *f*.

majority [məˈdʒɒrɪtɪ] *n* majorité *f* (*of* de); **in the** *or* **a** *m.* en majorité, majoritaire; **the m. of people** la plupart des gens; – *a* (*vote etc*) majoritaire.

make [meɪk] *vt* (*pt* & *pp* **made**) faire; (*tool, vehicle, meal etc*) fabriquer; (*decision*) prendre; (*friends, wage*) se faire; (*points*) *Sp* marquer; (*destination*) arriver à; **to m. happy/tired/etc** rendre heureux/fatigué/ *etc*; **he made ten francs on it** *Com* ça lui a rapporté dix francs; **she made the train** (*did not miss*) elle a eu le train; **to m. s.o. do sth** faire faire qch à qn, obliger qn à faire qch; **to m. oneself heard** se faire entendre; **to m. oneself at home** se mettre à l'aise; **to m. ready** préparer; **to m. yellow** jaunir; **she made him her husband** elle en a fait son mari; **to m. do** (*manage*) se débrouiller (*with* avec); **to m. do with** (*be satisfied with*) se contenter de; **to m. it** (*arrive*) arriver; (*succeed*) réussir; (*say*) dire; **I m. it five o'clock** j'ai cinq heures; **what do you m. of it?** qu'en penses-tu?; **I can't m. anything of it** je n'y comprends rien; **to m. a living** gagner sa vie; **you're made (for life)** ton avenir est assuré; **to m. believe** (*pretend*) faire semblant (*that one is* d'être); (*n't*) **it's m.-believe** (*story etc*) c'est pure invention; **to live in a world of m.-believe** se bercer d'illusions; – *vi* **to m. as if to** (*appear to*) faire mine de; **to m. for** (*go towards*) aller vers; – *n* (*brand*) marque *f*; **of French/etc m.** de fabrication française/*etc*. ◆ **to m. off** *vi* (*run away*) se sauver; **to m. out** *vt* (*see*) distinguer; (*understand*) comprendre; (*decipher*) déchiffrer; (*draw up*) faire (*cheque, list*); (*claim*) prétendre (*that* que);

you made me out to be silly tu m'as fait passer pour un idiot; – *vi* (*manage*) *Fam* se débrouiller; **to m. over** *vt* (*transfer*) céder; (*change*) transformer (*into* en); **to m. up** *vt* (*story*) inventer; (*put together*) faire (*collection, liste, list etc*); (*prepare*) préparer; (*form*) former, composer; (*loss*) compenser; (*quantity*) compléter; (*quarrel*) régler; (*one's face*) maquiller; – *vi* (*of friends*) se réconcilier; **to m. up for** (*loss, damage, fault*) compenser; (*lost time, mistake*) rattraper. ◆**m.-up** *n* (*of object etc*) constitution *f*; (*of person*) caractère *m*; (*for face*) maquillage *m*. ◆**making** *n* (*manufacture*) fabrication *f*; (*of dress*) confection *f*; **history in the m.** l'histoire en train de se faire; **the makings of** les éléments *mpl* (essentiels) de; **to have the makings of a pianist**/*etc* avoir l'étoffe d'un pianiste/*etc*. ◆**maker** *n Com* fabricant *m*.

◆**makeshift** *n* expédient *m*; – *a* (*arrangement etc*) de fortune, provisoire.

maladjusted [mæləˈdʒʌstɪd] *a* inadapté.

malaise [mæˈleɪz] *n* malaise *m*.

malaria [məˈleərɪə] *n* malaria *f*.

Malaysia [məˈleɪzɪə] *n* Malaisie *f*.

male [meɪl] *a Biol Bot etc* mâle; (*clothes, sex*) masculin; – *n* (*man, animal*) mâle *m*.

malevolent [məˈlevələnt] *a* malveillant. ◆**malevolence** *n* malveillance *f*.

malfunction [mælˈfʌŋk(ʃ)ən] *n* mauvais fonctionnement *m*; – *vi* fonctionner mal.

malice [ˈmælɪs] *n* méchanceté *f*; **to bear s.o. m.** vouloir du mal à qn. ◆**maˈlicious** *a* malveillant. ◆**maˈliciously** *adv* avec malveillance.

malign [məˈlaɪn] *vt* (*slander*) calomnier.

malignant [məˈlɪgnənt] *a* (*person etc*) malfaisant; **m. tumour** *Med* tumeur *f* maligne. ◆**malignancy** *n Med* malignité *f*.

malingerer [məˈlɪŋgərər] *n* (*pretending illness*) simulateur, -euse *mf*.

mall [mɔːl] *n* (*shopping*) *m.* (*covered*) galerie *f* marchande; (*street*) rue *f* piétonnière.

malleable [ˈmælɪəb(ə)l] *a* malléable.

mallet [ˈmælɪt] *n* (*tool*) maillet *m*.

malnutrition [mælnjuˈtrɪʃ(ə)n] *n* malnutrition *f*, sous-alimentation *f*.

malpractice [mælˈpræktɪs] *n Med Jur* faute *f* professionnelle.

malt [mɔːlt] *n* malt *m*.

Malta [ˈmɔːltə] *n* Malte *f*. ◆**Malˈtese** *a* & *n* maltais, -aise (*mf*).

mammal [ˈmæm(ə)l] *n* mammifère *m*.

mammoth [ˈmæməθ] *a* (*large*) immense; – *n* (*extinct animal*) mammouth *m*.

man [mæn] n (pl **men** [men]) homme m; (player) Sp joueur m; (chess piece) pièce f; **a golf m.** (enthusiast) un amateur de golf; **he's a Bristol m.** (by birth) il est de Bristol; **to be m. and wife** être mari et femme; **my old m.** Fam (father) mon père; (husband) mon homme; **yes old m.!** Fam oui mon vieux!; **the m. in the street** l'homme de la rue; – vt (-nn-) (ship) pourvoir d'un équipage; (fortress) armer; (guns) servir; (be on duty at) être de service à; **manned spacecraft** engin m spatial habité. ◆**manhood** n (period) âge m d'homme. ◆**manhunt** n chasse f à l'homme. ◆**manlike** a (quality) d'homme viril. ◆**manly** a (-ier, -iest) viril. ◆**man-'made** a artificiel; (fibre) synthétique. ◆**manservant** n (pl **menservants**) domestique m. ◆**man-to-'man** a & adv d'homme à homme.

manacle ['mænɪk(ə)l] n menotte f.

manag/e ['mænɪdʒ] vt (run) diriger; (affairs etc) Com gérer; (handle) manier; (take) Fam prendre; (eat) Fam manger; (contribute) Fam donner; **to m. to do** (succeed) réussir or arriver à faire; (contrive) se débrouiller pour faire; **I'll m. it** j'y arriverai; – vi (succeed) y arriver; (make do) se débrouiller (with avec); **to m. without sth** se passer de qch. ◆**—ing** a m. **director** directeur m général; **the m. director** le PDG. ◆**—eable** a (parcel, person etc) maniable; (feasible) faisable. ◆**—ement** n direction f; (of property etc) gestion f; (executive staff) cadres mpl. ◆**—er** n directeur m; (of shop, café) gérant m; (business) m. (of actor, boxer etc) manager m. ◆**manage'ress** n directrice f; gérante f. ◆**managerial** [mænə'dʒɪərɪəl] a directorial; **the m. class or staff** les cadres mpl.

mandarin ['mændərɪn] **1** n (high-ranking official) haut fonctionnaire m; (in political party) bonze m; (in university) Fam mandarin m. **2** a & n m. (orange) mandarine f.

mandate ['mændeɪt] n mandat m. ◆**mandatory** a obligatoire.

mane [meɪn] n crinière f.

maneuver [mə'nuːvər] n & vti Am = manoeuvre.

mangle ['mæŋg(ə)l] **1** n (for wringing) essoreuse f; – vt (clothes) essorer. **2** vt (damage) mutiler.

mango ['mæŋgəʊ] n (pl **-oes** or **-os**) (fruit) mangue f.

mangy ['meɪndʒɪ] a (animal) galeux.

manhandle ['mænhænd(ə)l] vt maltraiter.

manhole ['mænhəʊl] n trou m d'homme; **m. cover** plaque f d'égout.

mania ['meɪnɪə] n manie f. ◆**maniac** n fou m, folle f; Psy Med maniaque mf; **sex m.** obsédé m sexuel.

manicure ['mænɪkjʊər] n soin m des mains; – vt (person) manucurer; (s.o.'s nails) faire. ◆**manicurist** n manucure mf.

manifest ['mænɪfest] **1** a (plain) manifeste. **2** vt (show) manifester.

manifesto [mænɪ'festəʊ] n (pl **-os** or **-oes**) Pol manifeste m.

manifold ['mænɪfəʊld] a multiple.

manipulate [mə'nɪpjʊleɪt] vt manœuvrer; (facts, electors etc) Pej manipuler. ◆**manipu'lation** n manœuvre f; Pej manipulation f (of de).

mankind [mæn'kaɪnd] n (humanity) le genre humain.

manner ['mænər] n (way) manière f; (behaviour) attitude f, comportement m; pl (social habits) manières fpl; **in this m.** (like this) de cette manière; **all m. of** toutes sortes de. ◆**mannered** a (affected) maniéré; **well-/bad-m.** bien/mal élevé. ◆**mannerism** n Pej tic m.

manoeuvre [mə'nuːvər] n manœuvre f; – vti manœuvrer. ◆**manoeuvra'bility** n (of vehicle etc) maniabilité f.

manor ['mænər] n m. **(house)** manoir m.

manpower ['mænpaʊər] n (labour) main-d'œuvre f; Mil effectifs mpl; (effort) force f.

mansion ['mænʃ(ə)n] n hôtel m particulier; (in country) manoir m.

manslaughter ['mænslɔːtər] n Jur homicide m involontaire.

mantelpiece ['mænt(ə)lpiːs] n (shelf) cheminée f.

mantle ['mænt(ə)l] n (cloak) cape f.

manual ['mænjʊəl] **1** a (work etc) manuel. **2** n (book) manuel m.

manufactur/e [mænjʊ'fæktʃər] vt fabriquer; – n fabrication f. ◆**—er** n fabricant, -ante mf.

manure [mə'njʊər] n fumier m, engrais m.

manuscript ['mænjʊskrɪpt] n manuscrit m.

many ['menɪ] a & n beaucoup (de); **m. things** beaucoup de choses; **m. came** beaucoup sont venus; **very m., a good or great m.** un très grand nombre (de); **(a good or great) m. of** un (très) grand nombre de; **m. of them** un grand nombre d'entre eux; **m. times, m. a time** bien des fois; **m. kinds** toutes sortes (of de); **how m.?** combien (de)?; **too m.** trop (de); **one too m.** un de trop; **there are too m. of them** ils sont trop nombreux; **so m.** tant (de); **as m. books/etc**

as autant de livres/*etc* que; **as m. as** (*up to*) jusqu'à.

map [mæp] *n* (*of country etc*) carte *f*; (*plan*) plan *m*; – *vt* (**-pp-**) faire la carte *or* le plan de; **to m. out** (*road*) faire le tracé de; (*one's day etc*) *Fig* organiser.

maple ['meɪp(ə)l] *n* (*tree, wood*) érable *m*.

mar [mɑːr] *vt* (**-rr-**) gâter.

marathon ['mærəθən] *n* marathon *m*.

maraud [mə'rɔːd] *vi* piller. ◆**-ing** *a* pillard. ◆**-er** *n* pillard, -arde *mf*.

marble ['mɑːb(ə)l] *n* (*substance*) marbre *m*; (*toy ball*) bille *f*.

march [mɑːtʃ] *n Mil* marche *f*; – *vi Mil* marcher (au pas); **to m. in/out/etc** *Fig* entrer/sortir/*etc* d'un pas décidé; **to m. past** défiler; – *vt* **to m. s.o. off** *or* **away** emmener qn. ◆**m.-past** *n* défilé *m*.

March [mɑːtʃ] *n* mars *m*.

mare [meər] *n* jument *f*.

margarine [mɑːdʒə'riːn] *n* margarine *f*.

margin ['mɑːdʒɪn] *n* (*of page etc*) marge *f*; **by a narrow m.** (*to win*) de justesse. ◆**marginal** *a* marginal; **m. seat** *Pol* siège *m* disputé. ◆**marginally** *adv* très légèrement.

marguerite [mɑːgə'riːt] *n* (*daisy*) marguerite *f*.

marigold ['mærɪgəʊld] *n* (*flower*) souci *m*.

marijuana [mærɪ'wɑːnə] *n* marijuana *f*.

marina [mə'riːnə] *n* marina *f*.

marinate ['mærɪneɪt] *vti Culin* mariner.

marine [mə'riːn] **1** *a* (*life, flora etc*) marin. **2** *n* (*soldier*) fusilier *m* marin, *Am* marine *m*.

marionette [mærɪə'net] *n* marionnette *f*.

marital ['mærɪt(ə)l] *a* matrimonial; (*relations*) conjugal; **m. status** situation *f* de famille.

maritime ['mærɪtaɪm] *a* (*province, climate etc*) maritime.

marjoram ['mɑːdʒərəm] *n* (*spice*) marjolaine *f*.

mark[1] [mɑːk] *n* (*symbol*) marque *f*; (*stain, trace*) trace *f*, tache *f*, marque *f*; (*token, sign*) *Fig* signe *m*; (*for exercise etc*) *Sch* note *f*; (*target*) but *m*; (*model*) *Tech* série *f*; **to make one's m.** *Fig* s'imposer; **up to the m.** (*person, work*) à la hauteur; – *vt* marquer; (*exam etc*) *Sch* corriger, noter; (*pay attention to*) faire attention à; **to m. time** *Mil* marquer le pas; *Fig* piétiner; **m. you . . . !** remarquez que . . . !; **to m. down** (*price*) baisser; **to m. off** (*separate*) séparer; (*on list*) cocher; **to m. out** (*area*) délimiter; **to m. s.o. out for** désigner qn pour; **to m. up** (*increase*) augmenter. ◆**-ed** *a* (*noticeable*) marqué. ◆**-edly** [-ɪdlɪ] *adv* visiblement.

◆**-ing(s)** *n*(*pl*) (*on animal etc*) marques *fpl*; (*on road*) signalisation *f* horizontale. ◆**-er** *n* (*flag etc*) marque *f*; (*pen*) feutre *m*, marqueur *m*.

mark[2] [mɑːk] *n* (*currency*) mark *m*.

market ['mɑːkɪt] *n* marché *m*; **on the open m.** en vente libre; **on the black m.** au marché noir; **the Common M.** le Marché commun; **m. value** valeur *f* marchande; **m. price** prix *m* courant; **m. gardener** maraîcher, -ère *mf*; – *vt* (*sell*) vendre; (*launch*) commercialiser. ◆**-ing** *n* marketing *m*, vente *f*. ◆**-able** *a* vendable.

marksman ['mɑːksmən] *n* (*pl* **-men**) tireur *m* d'élite.

marmalade ['mɑːməleɪd] *n* confiture *f* d'oranges.

maroon [mə'ruːn] *a* (*colour*) bordeaux *inv*.

marooned [mə'ruːnd] *a* abandonné; (*in snowstorm etc*) bloqué (by *par*).

marquee [mɑː'kiː] *n* (*for concerts, garden parties etc*) chapiteau *m*; (*awning*) *Am* marquise *f*.

marquis ['mɑːkwɪs] *n* marquis *m*.

marrow ['mærəʊ] *n* **1** (*of bone*) moelle *f*. **2** (*vegetable*) courge *f*.

marr/y ['mærɪ] *vt* épouser, se marier avec; **to m. (off)** (*of priest etc*) marier; – *vi* se marier. ◆**-ied** *a* marié; (*life, state*) conjugal; **m. name** nom *m* de femme mariée; **to get m. se** marier. ◆**marriage** *n* mariage *m*; **to be related by m.** to être parent par alliance de; – *a* (*bond*) conjugal; (*certificate*) de mariage; **m. bureau** agence *f* matrimoniale. ◆**marriageable** *a* en état de se marier.

marsh [mɑːʃ] *n* marais *m*, marécage *m*. ◆**marshland** *n* marécages *mpl*. ◆**marsh-mallow** *n Bot Culin* guimauve *f*.

marshal ['mɑːʃ(ə)l] **1** *n* (*in army*) maréchal *m*; (*in airforce*) général *m*; (*at public event*) membre *m* du service d'ordre; *Jur Am* shérif *m*. **2** *vt* (**-ll-**, *Am* **-l-**) (*gather*) rassembler; (*lead*) mener cérémonieusement.

martial ['mɑːʃ(ə)l] *a* martial; **m. law** loi *f* martiale.

Martian ['mɑːʃ(ə)n] *n & a* martien, -ienne (*mf*).

martyr ['mɑːtər] *n* martyr, -yre *mf*; – *vt Rel* martyriser. ◆**martyrdom** *n* martyre *m*.

marvel ['mɑːv(ə)l] *n* (*wonder*) merveille *f*; (*miracle*) miracle *m*; – *vi* (**-ll-**, *Am* **-l-**) s'émerveiller (at *de*); – *vt* **to m. that** s'étonner de ce que (+ *sub or indic*). ◆**marvellous** *a* merveilleux.

Marxism ['mɑːksɪz(ə)m] *n* marxisme *m*. ◆**Marxist** *a & n* marxiste (*mf*).

marzipan ['mɑːzɪpæn] n pâte f d'amandes.

mascara [mæ'skɑːrə] n mascara m.

mascot ['mæskɒt] n mascotte f.

masculine ['mæskjʊlɪn] a masculin. ◆**mascu'linity** n masculinité f.

mash [mæʃ] n (for poultry etc) pâtée f; (potatoes) Culin purée f; — vt to m. (up) (crush) & Culin écraser; **mashed potatoes** purée f (de pommes de terre).

mask [mɑːsk] n masque m; — vt (cover, hide) masquer (**from** à).

masochism ['mæsəkɪz(ə)m] n masochisme m. ◆**masochist** n masochiste mf. ◆**maso'chistic** a masochiste.

mason ['meɪs(ə)n] n maçon m. ◆**masonry** n maçonnerie f.

masquerade [mɑːskə'reɪd] n (gathering, disguise) mascarade f; — vi to m. as se faire passer pour.

mass¹ [mæs] n masse f; a m. of (many) une multitude de; (pile) un tas de, une masse de; to be a m. of bruises Fam être couvert de bleus; **masses of** Fam des masses de; the **masses** (people) les masses fpl; — a (education) de masse; (culture, demonstration) de masse; (protests, departure) en masse; (production) en série, en masse; (hysteria) collectif; **m. grave** fosse f commune; **m. media** mass media mpl; — vi (of troops, people) se masser. ◆**m.-pro'duce** vt fabriquer en série.

mass² [mæs] n Rel messe f.

massacre ['mæsəkər] n massacre m; — vt massacrer.

massage ['mæsɑːʒ] n massage m; — vt masser. ◆**ma'sseur** n masseur m. ◆**ma'sseuse** n masseuse f.

massive ['mæsɪv] a (solid) massif; (huge) énorme, considérable. ◆**—ly** adv (to increase, reduce etc) considérablement.

mast [mɑːst] n Nau mât m; Rad TV pylône m.

master ['mɑːstər] n maître m; (in secondary school) professeur m; **a m.'s degree** une maîtrise (in de); **M. of Arts/Science** (person) Univ Maître m ès lettres/sciences; **m. of ceremonies** (presenter) Am animateur, -trice mf; **m. card** carte f maîtresse; **m. stroke** coup m de maître; **m. key** passe-partout m inv; **old m.** (painting) tableau m de maître; **I'm my own m.** je ne dépends que de moi; — vt (control) maîtriser; (subject, situation) dominer; **she has mastered Latin** elle possède le latin. ◆**masterly** a magistral. ◆**mastery** n maîtrise f (**of** de).

mastermind ['mɑːstəmaɪnd] n (person) cerveau m; — vt organiser.

masterpiece ['mɑːstəpiːs] n chef-d'œuvre m.

mastic ['mæstɪk] n mastic m (silicone).

masturbate ['mæstəbeɪt] vi se masturber. ◆**mastur'bation** n masturbation f.

mat [mæt] n 1 tapis m, natte f; (at door) paillasson m; (table) m. (of fabric) napperon m; (hard) dessous-de-plat m inv; (place) m. set m (de table). 2 a (paint, paper) mat.

match¹ [mætʃ] n allumette f; **book of matches** pochette f d'allumettes. ◆**matchbox** n boîte f à allumettes. ◆**matchstick** n allumette f.

match² [mætʃ] n (game) Sp match m; (equal) égal, -ale mf; (marriage) mariage m; to be a good m. (of colours, people etc) être bien assortis; **he's a good m.** (man to marry) c'est un bon parti; — vt (clothes) aller (bien) avec; to m. (up) (equal) égaler; to m. (up) (plates etc) assortir; to be **well-matched** (of colours, people etc) être (bien) assortis, aller (bien) ensemble; — vi (go with each other) être assortis, aller (bien) ensemble. ◆**—ing** a (dress etc) assorti.

mate¹ [meɪt] n 1 (friend) camarade mf; (of animal) mâle m, femelle f; **builder's/electrician's/etc m.** aide-maçon/-électricien/etc m. 2 vi (of animals) s'accoupler (**with** avec). 3 n Chess mat m; — vt faire ou mettre mat.

material [mə'tɪərɪəl] 1 a matériel; (important) important. 2 n (substance) matière f; (cloth) tissu m; (for book) matériaux mpl; **material's** (equipment) matériel m; **building material(s)** matériaux mpl de construction. ◆**materialism** n matérialisme m. ◆**materialist** n matérialiste mf. ◆**materia'listic** a matérialiste. ◆**materialize** vi se matérialiser. ◆**materially** adv matériellement; (well-off etc) sur le plan matériel.

maternal [mə'tɜːn(ə)l] a maternel. ◆**maternity** n maternité f; **m. hospital, m. unit** maternité f; — a (clothes) de grossesse; (allowance, leave) de maternité.

mathematical [mæθə'mætɪk(ə)l] a mathématique; **to have a m. brain** être doué pour les maths. ◆**mathema'tician** n mathématicien, -ienne mf. ◆**mathematics** n mathématiques fpl. ◆**maths** n, Am ◆**math** n Fam maths fpl.

matinée ['mætɪneɪ] n Th matinée f.

matriculation [mətrɪkjʊ'leɪʃ(ə)n] n Univ inscription f.

matrimony ['mætrɪmənɪ] n mariage m. ◆**matri'monial** a matrimonial.

matrix, pl **-ices** ['meɪtrɪks, -ɪsiːz] n Tech matrice f.

matron ['meɪtrən] n Lit mère f de famille; dame f âgée; (nurse) infirmière f (en) chef. ◆**matronly** a (air etc) de mère de famille; (mature) mûr; (portly) corpulent.

matt [mæt] a (paint, paper) mat.

matted ['mætɪd] a m. hair cheveux mpl emmêlés.

matter[1] ['mætər] n matière f; (affair) affaire f, question f; (thing) chose f; no m.! (no importance) peu importe!; no m. what she does quoi qu'elle fasse; no m. where you go où que tu ailles; no m. who you are qui que vous soyez; no m. when quel que soit le moment; what's the m.? qu'est-ce qu'il y a?; what's the m. with you? qu'est-ce que tu as?; there's sth the m. il y a qch qui ne va pas; there's sth the m. with my leg j'ai qch à la jambe; there's nothing the m. with him il n'a rien; — vi (be important) importer (to à); it doesn't m. if/when/who/etc peu importe si/quand/qui/etc; it doesn't m.! ça ne fait rien!, peu importe! ◆**m.-of-'fact** a (person, manner) terre à terre; (voice) neutre.

matter[2] ['mætər] n (pus) Med pus m.

matting ['mætɪŋ] n (material) nattage m; a piece of m., some m. une natte.

mattress ['mætrəs] n matelas m.

mature [mə'tʃʊər] a mûr; (cheese) fait; — vt (person, plan) (faire) mûrir; — vi mûrir; (of cheese) se faire. ◆**maturity** n maturité f.

maul [mɔːl] vt (of animal) mutiler; (of person) Fig malmener.

mausoleum [mɔːsə'lɪəm] n mausolée m.

mauve [məʊv] a & n (colour) mauve (m).

maverick ['mævərɪk] n & a Pol dissident, -ente (mf).

mawkish ['mɔːkɪʃ] a d'une sensiblerie excessive, mièvre.

maxim ['mæksɪm] n maxime f.

maximum ['mæksɪməm] n (pl -ima [-ɪmə] or -imums) maximum m; — a maximal (f inv), maximal. ◆**maximize** vt porter au maximum.

may [meɪ] v aux (pt might) 1 (possibility) he m. come il peut arriver; he might come il pourrait arriver; I m. or might be wrong il se peut que je me trompe, je me trompe peut-être; you m. or might have to aurais pu; I m. or might have forgotten it je l'ai peut-être oublié; we m. or might as well go

nous ferions aussi bien de partir; she fears I m. or might get lost elle a peur que je ne me perde. 2 (permission) m. I stay? puis-je rester?; m. I? vous permettez?; you m. go tu peux partir. 3 (wish) m. you be happy (que tu) sois heureux. ◆**maybe** adv peut-être.

May [meɪ] n mai m.

mayhem ['meɪhem] n (chaos) pagaïe f; (havoc) ravages mpl.

mayonnaise [meɪə'neɪz] n mayonnaise f.

mayor [meər] n (man, woman) maire m. ◆**mayoress** n femme f du maire.

maze [meɪz] n labyrinthe m.

MC [em'siː] abbr = master of ceremonies.

me [miː] pron me, m'; (after prep etc) moi; (to) me (indirect) me, m'; she knows me elle me connaît; he helps me il m'aide; he gives (to) me il me donne; with me avec moi.

meadow ['medəʊ] n pré m, prairie f.

meagre ['miːgər] a maigre.

meal [miːl] n 1 (food) repas m. 2 (flour) farine f.

mealy-mouthed [miːlɪ'maʊðd] a mielleux.

mean[1] [miːn] vt (pt & pp meant [ment]) (signify) vouloir dire, signifier; (destine) destiner (for à); (entail) entraîner; (represent) représenter; (refer to) faire allusion à; to m. to do (intend) avoir l'intention de faire, vouloir faire; I m. it, I m. what I say je suis sérieux; to m. sth to s.o. (matter) avoir de l'importance pour qn; it means sth to me (name, face) ça me dit qch; I didn't m. to! je ne l'ai pas fait exprès!; you were meant to come vous étiez censé venir. ◆**-ing** n sens m, signification f. ◆**meaningful** a significatif. ◆**meaningless** a à qui n'a pas de sens; (absurd) Fig insensé.

mean[2] [miːn] a (-er, -est) (stingy) avare, mesquin; (petty) mesquin; (nasty) méchant; (inferior) misérable. ◆**-ness** n (greed) avarice f; (nastiness) méchanceté f.

mean[3] [miːn] a (distance) moyen; — n (middle position) milieu m; (average) Math moyenne f; the happy m. le juste milieu.

means [miːnz] n(pl) (method) moyen(s) m(pl) (to do, of doing de faire); (wealth) moyens mpl; by m. of (stick etc) au moyen de; (work, concentration) à force de; by all m.! très certainement!; by no m. nullement; independent or private m. fortune f personnelle.

meant [ment] see mean 1.

meantime ['miːntaɪm] adv & n (in the) m. entre-temps. ◆**meanwhile** adv entre-temps.

measles ['mi:z(ə)lz] n rougeole f.

measly ['mi:zlɪ] a (contemptible) Fam minable.

measur/e ['meʒər] n mesure f; (ruler) règle f; **made to m.** fait sur mesure; − vt mesurer; (strength etc) Fig estimer, mesurer; (adjust, adapt) adapter (**to** à); **to m. up** mesurer; − vi **to m. up to** être à la hauteur de. ◆**—ed** a (careful) mesuré. ◆**—ement** n (of chest, waist etc) tour m; pl (dimensions) mesures fpl; **your hip m.** ton tour de hanches.

meat [mi:t] n viande f; (of crab, lobster etc) chair f; Fig substance f; **m. diet** régime m carné. ◆**meaty** a (-ier, -iest) (fleshy) charnu; (flavour) de viande; Fig substantiel.

mechanic [mɪ'kænɪk] n mécanicien, -ienne mf. ◆**mechanical** a mécanique; (reply etc) Fig machinal. ◆**mechanics** n (science) mécanique f; pl (workings) mécanisme m. ◆**'mechanism** n mécanisme m. ◆**'mechanize** vt mécaniser.

medal ['med(ə)l] n médaille f. ◆**me-'dallion** n (ornament, jewel) médaillon m. ◆**medallist** n médaillé, -ée mf; **to be a gold/silver m.** Sp être médaille d'or/ d'argent.

meddle ['med(ə)l] vi (interfere) se mêler (**in** de); (tamper) toucher (**with** à). ◆**meddlesome** a qui se mêle de tout.

media ['mi:dɪə] npl **1** (the (mass) m. les médias mpl. **2** see **medium 2**.

mediaeval [medɪ'i:v(ə)l] a médiéval.

median ['mi:dɪən] a **m. strip** Aut Am bande f médiane.

mediate ['mi:dɪeɪt] vi servir d'intermédiaire (**between** entre). ◆**medi'ation** n médiation f. ◆**mediator** n médiateur, -trice mf.

medical ['medɪk(ə)l] a médical; (school, studies) de médecine; (student) en médecine; − n (in school, army) visite f médicale; (private) examen m médical. ◆**medicated** a (shampoo) médical. ◆**medi'cation** n médicaments mpl. ◆**me'dicinal** a médicinal. ◆**medicine** n médecine f; (substance) médicament m; **m. cabinet, m. chest** pharmacie f.

medieval [medɪ'i:v(ə)l] a médiéval.

mediocre [mi:dɪ'əukər] a médiocre. ◆**mediocrity** n médiocrité f.

meditate ['medɪteɪt] vi méditer (**on** sur). ◆**medi'tation** n méditation f. ◆**meditative** a méditatif.

Mediterranean [medɪtə'reɪnɪən] a méditerranéen; − n the **M.** la Méditerranée.

medium ['mi:dɪəm] **1** a (average, middle) moyen. **2** n (pl media ['mi:dɪə]) Phys véhicule m; Biol milieu m; (for conveying data or publicity) support m; **through the m. of** par l'intermédiaire de; **the happy m.** le juste milieu. **3** n (person) médium m. ◆**m.-sized** a moyen, de taille moyenne.

medley ['medlɪ] n mélange m; Mus pot-pourri m.

meek [mi:k] a (-er, -est) doux.

meet [mi:t] vt (pt & pp met) (encounter) rencontrer; (see again, join) retrouver; (pass in street, road etc) croiser; (fetch) (aller ou venir) chercher; (wait for) attendre; (debt, enemy, danger) faire face à; (need) combler; (be introduced to) faire la connaissance de; **to arrange to m. s.o.** donner rendez-vous à qn; − vi (of people, teams, rivers, looks) se rencontrer; (of people by arrangement) se retrouver; (be introduced) se connaître; (of society) se réunir; (of trains, vehicles) se croiser; **to m. up with** rencontrer; (by arrangement) retrouver; **to m. up** se rencontrer; se retrouver; **to m. with** (accident, problem) avoir; (loss, refusal) essuyer; (obstacle, difficulty) rencontrer; **to m. with s.o.** Am rencontrer qn; retrouver qn; − n Sp Am réunion f; **to make a m. with** Fam donner rendez-vous à. ◆**—ing** n réunion f; (large) assemblée f; (between two people) rencontre f, (prearranged) rendez-vous m inv; **in m.** en conférence.

megalomania [megələu'meɪnɪə] n mégalomanie f. ◆**megalomaniac** n mégalomane mf.

megaphone ['megəfəun] n porte-voix m inv.

melancholy ['melənkəlɪ] n mélancolie f; − a mélancolique.

mellow ['meləu] a (-er, -est) (fruit) mûr; (colour, voice, wine) moelleux; (character) mûri par l'expérience; − vi (of person) s'adoucir.

melodrama ['melədrɑ:mə] n mélodrame m. ◆**melodra'matic** a mélodramatique.

melody ['melədɪ] n mélodie f. ◆**me'lodic** a mélodique. ◆**me'lodious** a mélodieux.

melon ['melən] n (fruit) melon m.

melt [melt] vi fondre; **to m. into** (merge) Fig se fondre dans; − vt (faire) fondre; **to m. down** (metal object) fondre; **melting point** point m de fusion; **melting pot** Fig creuset m.

member ['membər] n membre m; **M. of Parliament** député m. ◆**membership** n adhésion f (**of** à); (number) nombre m de(s) membres; (members) membres mpl; **m. (fee)** cotisation f.

membrane ['membreɪn] n membrane f.

memento [mə'mentəʊ] n (pl -os or -oes) (object) souvenir m.

memo ['meməʊ] n (pl -os) note f; **m. pad** bloc-notes m. ◆**memo'randum** n note f; Pol Com mémorandum m.

memoirs ['memwɑːz] npl (essays) mémoires mpl.

memory ['memərɪ] n mémoire f; (recollection) souvenir m; **to the** or **in m. of** à la mémoire de. ◆**memorable** a mémorable. ◆**me'morial** a (plaque etc) commémoratif; – n monument m, mémorial m. ◆**memorize** vt apprendre par cœur.

men [men] see **man**. ◆**menfolk** n Fam hommes mpl.

menac/e ['menɪs] n danger m; (nuisance) Fam plaie f; (threat) menace f; – vt menacer. ◆**–ingly** adv (to say) d'un ton menaçant; (to do) d'une manière menaçante.

menagerie [mɪ'nædʒərɪ] n ménagerie f.

mend [mend] vt (repair) réparer; (clothes) raccommoder; **to m. one's ways** se corriger, s'amender; – n raccommodage m; **to be on the m.** (after illness) aller mieux.

menial ['miːnɪəl] a inférieur.

meningitis [menɪn'dʒaɪtɪs] n Med méningite f.

menopause ['menəpɔːz] n ménopause f.

menstruation [menstru'eɪʃ(ə)n] n menstruation f.

mental ['ment(ə)l] a mental; (hospital) psychiatrique; (mad) Sl fou; **m. strain** tension f nerveuse. ◆**men'tality** n mentalité f. ◆**mentally** adv mentalement; **he's m. handicapped** c'est un handicapé mental; **she's m. ill** c'est une malade mentale.

mention ['menʃ(ə)n] vt mentionner, faire mention de; **not to m. . . .** sans parler de . . ., sans compter . . .; **don't m. it!** il n'y a pas de quoi!; **no savings/etc worth mentioning** pratiquement pas d'économies/etc; – n mention f.

mentor ['mentɔːr] n (adviser) mentor m.

menu ['menjuː] n menu m.

mercantile ['mɜːkəntaɪl] a (activity etc) commercial; (ship) marchand; (nation) commerçant.

mercenary ['mɜːsɪnərɪ] a n mercenaire (m).

merchandise ['mɜːtʃəndaɪz] n (articles) marchandises fpl; (total stock) marchandise f.

merchant ['mɜːtʃ(ə)nt] n (trader) Fin négociant, -ante mf; (retail) m. commerçant m (en détail); **wine m.** négociant, -ante mf en vins; (shopkeeper) marchand m de

vins; – a (vessel, navy) marchand; (seaman) de la marine marchande; **m. bank** banque f de commerce.

mercury ['mɜːkjʊrɪ] n mercure m.

mercy ['mɜːsɪ] n pitié f; Rel miséricorde f; **to beg for m.** demander grâce; **at the m. of** à la merci de; **it's a m. that . . .** (stroke of luck) c'est une chance que . . . ◆**merciful** a miséricordieux. ◆**mercifully** adv (fortunately) Fam heureusement. ◆**merciless** a impitoyable.

mere [mɪər] a simple; (only) ne . . . que; **she's a m. child** ce n'est qu'une enfant; **it's a m. kilometre** ça ne fait qu'un kilomètre; **by m. chance** par pur hasard; **the m. sight of her** or **him** sa seule vue. ◆**–ly** adv (tout) simplement.

merg/e [mɜːdʒ] vi (blend) se mêler (with à); (of roads) se rejoindre; (of firms) Com fusionner; – vt (unify) Pol unifier; Com fusionner. ◆**–er** n Com fusion f.

meridian [mə'rɪdɪən] n méridien m.

meringue [mə'ræŋ] n (cake) meringue f.

merit ['merɪt] n mérite m; **on its merits** (to consider sth etc) objectivement; – vt mériter.

mermaid ['mɜːmeɪd] n (woman) sirène f.

merry ['merɪ] a (-ier, -iest) gai; (drunk) Fam éméché. ◆**m.-go-round** n (at funfair etc) manège m. ◆**m.-making** n réjouissances fpl. ◆**merrily** adv gaiement. ◆**merriment** n gaieté f, rires mpl.

mesh [meʃ] n (of net etc) maille f; (fabric) tissu m à mailles; (of intrigue etc) Fig réseau m; (of circumstances) Fig engrenage m; **wire m.** grillage m.

mesmerize ['mezməraɪz] vt hypnotiser.

mess¹ [mes] **1** n (confusion) désordre m, pagaïe f; (muddle) gâchis m; (dirt) saleté f; **in a m.** en désordre; (trouble) Fam dans le pétrin; (pitiful state) dans un triste état; **to make a m. of** (spoil) gâcher. **2** vt **to m. s.o. about** (bother, treat badly) Fam déranger qn, embêter qn; **to m. up** (spoil) gâcher; (dirty) salir; (room) mettre en désordre; – vi **to m. about** (have fun, idle) s'amuser; (play the fool) faire l'idiot; **to m. about with** (fiddle with) s'amuser avec. ◆**m.-up** n (disorder) Fam gâchis m. ◆**messy** a (-ier, -iest) (untidy) en désordre; (dirty) sale; (confused) Fig embrouillé, confus.

mess² [mes] n Mil mess m inv.

message ['mesɪdʒ] n message m. ◆**messenger** n messager, -ère mf; (in office, hotel) coursier, -ière mf.

Messiah [mɪ'saɪə] n Messie m.

Messrs ['mesəz] *npl* **M**. Brown Messieurs *or* MM Brown.

met [met] *see* meet.

metal ['met(ə)l] *n* métal *m*. ◆**me'tallic** *a* métallique; (*paint*) métallisé. ◆**metalwork** *n* (*objects*) ferronnerie *f*; (*study, craft*) travail *m* des métaux.

metamorphosis, *pl* -**oses** [metə'mɔːfəsɪs, -siːz] *n* métamorphose *f*.

metaphor ['metəfər] *n* métaphore *f*. ◆**meta'phorical** *a* métaphorique.

metaphysical [metə'fɪzɪk(ə)l] *a* métaphysique.

mete [miːt] *vt* to **m. out** (*justice*) rendre; (*punishment*) infliger.

meteor ['miːtɪər] *n* météore *m*. ◆**mete'oric** *a* m. **rise** *Fig* ascension *f* fulgurante. ◆**meteorite** *n* météorite *f*.

meteorological [miːtɪərə'lɒdʒɪk(ə)l] *a* météorologique. ◆**meteo'rology** *n* météorologie *f*.

meter ['miːtər] *n* (*device*) compteur *m*; (*parking*) m. parcmètre *m*; **m. maid** *Aut Fam* contractuelle *f*.

method ['meθəd] *n* méthode *f*. ◆**me'thodical** *a* méthodique.

Methodist ['meθədɪst] *a & n* *Rel* méthodiste (*mf*).

methylated ['meθɪleɪtɪd] *a* **m. spirit(s)** alcool *m* à brûler. ◆**meths** *n* *Fam* = **methylated spirits**.

meticulous [mɪ'tɪkjʊləs] *a* méticuleux. ◆—**ness** *n* soin *m* méticuleux.

metre ['miːtər] *n* mètre *m*. ◆**metric** ['metrɪk] *a* métrique.

metropolis [mə'trɒpəlɪs] *n* (*chief city*) métropole *f*. ◆**metro'politan** *a* métropolitain.

mettle ['met(ə)l] *n* courage *m*, fougue *f*.

mew [mjuː] *vi* (*of cat*) miauler.

mews [mjuːz] *n* (*street*) ruelle *f*; **m. flat** appartement *m* chic (*aménagé dans une ancienne écurie*).

Mexico ['meksɪkəʊ] *n* Mexique *m*. ◆**Mexican** *a & n* mexicain, -aine (*mf*).

mezzanine ['mezəniːn] *n* **m. (floor)** entresol *m*.

miaow [miː'aʊ] *vi* (*of cat*) miauler; — *n* miaulement *m*; — *int* miaou.

mice [maɪs] *see* mouse.

mickey ['mɪkɪ] *n* to take the **m. out of s.o.** *Sl* charrier qn.

micro- ['maɪkrəʊ] *pref* micro-.

microbe ['maɪkrəʊb] *n* microbe *m*.

microchip ['maɪkrəʊtʃɪp] *n* puce *f*.

microcosm ['maɪkrəʊkɒz(ə)m] *n* microcosme *m*.

microfilm ['maɪkrəʊfɪlm] *n* microfilm *m*.

microphone ['maɪkrəfəʊn] *n* microphone *m*.

microscope ['maɪkrəskəʊp] *n* microscope *m*. ◆**micro'scopic** *a* microscopique.

microwave ['maɪkrəʊweɪv] *n* micro-onde *f*; **m. oven** four *m* à micro-ondes.

mid [mɪd] *a* (**in**) **m.-June** (à) la mi-juin; (**in**) **m. morning** au milieu de la matinée; **in m. air** en plein ciel; to be **in one's m.-twenties** avoir environ vingt-cinq ans.

midday [mɪd'deɪ] *n* midi *m*; − *a* de midi.

middle ['mɪd(ə)l] *n* milieu *m*; (*waist*) *Fam* taille *f*; (**right**) **in the m.** au (or beau) milieu de; **in the m. of work** en plein travail; **in the m. of saying/working/etc** en train de dire/travailler/*etc*; − *a* (*central*) du milieu; (*class, ear, quality*) moyen; (*name*) deuxième. ◆**m.-'aged** *a* d'un certain âge. ◆**m.-'class** *a* bourgeois. ◆**m.-of-the-'road** *a* (*politics, views*) modéré; (*music, tastes*) sage.

middling ['mɪdlɪŋ] *a* moyen, passable.

midge [mɪdʒ] *n* (*fly*) moucheron *m*.

midget ['mɪdʒɪt] *n* nain *m*, naine *f*; − *a* minuscule.

Midlands ['mɪdləndz] *npl* the **M.** les comtés *mpl* du centre de l'Angleterre.

midnight ['mɪdnaɪt] *n* minuit *m*.

midriff ['mɪdrɪf] *n* *Anat* diaphragme *m*; (*belly*) *Fam* ventre *m*.

midst [mɪdst] *n* **in the m. of** (*middle*) au milieu de; **in our/their m.** parmi nous/eux.

midsummer [mɪd'sʌmər] *n* milieu *m* de l'été; (*solstice*) solstice *m* d'été. ◆**midwinter** *n* milieu *m* de l'hiver; solstice *m* d'hiver.

midterm ['mɪdtɜːm] *a* **m. holidays** *Sch* petites vacances *fpl*.

midway [mɪd'weɪ] *a & adv* à mi-chemin.

midweek [mɪd'wiːk] *n* milieu *m* de la semaine.

midwife ['mɪdwaɪf] *n* (*pl* -**wives**) sage-femme *f*.

might[1] [maɪt] *see* may. **2** *n* (*strength*) force *f*. ◆**mighty** *a* (-**ier**, -**iest**) puissant; (*ocean*) vaste; (*very great*) *Fam* sacré; − *adv* (*very*) *Fam* rudement.

migraine ['miːgreɪn, 'maɪgreɪn] *n* *Med* migraine *f*.

migrate [maɪ'greɪt] *vi* émigrer. ◆'**migrant** *a & n* **m. (worker)** migrant, -ante (*mf*). ◆**migration** *n* migration *f*.

mike [maɪk] *n* *Fam* micro *m*.

mild [maɪld] *a* (-**er**, -**est**) (*person, weather, taste etc*) doux; (*beer, punishment*) léger; (*medicine, illness*) bénin. ◆—**ly** *adv* doucement; (*slightly*) légèrement; **to put it m.** pour ne pas dire plus. ◆**—ness** n douceur f; légèreté f; caractère m bénin.

mildew ['mɪldjuː] n (*on cheese etc*) moisissure f.

mile [maɪl] n mile m, mille m (= 1,6 km); pl (*loosely*) = kilomètres mpl; **to walk for miles** marcher pendant des kilomètres; **miles better** (*much*) Fam bien mieux. ◆**mileage** n = kilométrage m; **m.** (per gallon) = consommation f aux cent kilomètres. ◆**milestone** n = borne f kilométrique; Fig jalon m.

militant ['mɪlɪtənt] a & n militant, -ante (mf). ◆**military** a militaire; – n the m. (*soldiers*) les militaires mpl; (*army*) l'armée f. ◆**militate** vi (*of arguments etc*) militer (**in favour of** pour).

militia [mə'lɪʃə] n milice f. ◆**militiaman** n (pl -men) milicien m.

milk [mɪlk] n lait m; **evaporated m.** lait m concentré; – a (*chocolate*) au lait; (*bottle, can*) à lait; (*diet*) lacté; (*produce*) laitier; **m. float** voiture f de laitier; **m. shake** milk-shake m; – vt (*cow*) traire; (*extract*) Fig soutirer (**s.o. of sth** qch à qn); (*exploit*) Fig exploiter. ◆**milkman** n (pl -men) laitier m. ◆**milky** a (-ier, -iest) (*diet*) lacté; (*coffee, tea*) au lait; (*colour*) laiteux; **the M. Way** la Voie lactée.

mill [mɪl] n moulin m; (*factory*) usine f; **cotton m.** filature f de coton; **paper m.** papeterie f; – vt (*grind*) moudre. **2** vi **to m. around** (*of crowd*) grouiller. ◆**miller** n meunier, -ière mf. ◆**millstone** n (*burden*) boulet m (**round one's neck** qu'on traîne).

millennium, pl **-nia** [mɪ'lenɪəm, -nɪə] n millénaire m.

millet ['mɪlɪt] n Bot millet m.

milli- ['mɪlɪ] pref milli-.

millimetre ['mɪlɪmiːtər] n millimètre m.

million ['mɪljən] n million m; **a m. men**/*etc* un million d'hommes/*etc*; **two m.** deux millions. ◆**millionaire** n millionnaire mf. ◆**millionth** a & n millionième (mf).

mime [maɪm] n (*actor*) mime mf; (*art*) mime m; – vti mimer.

mimeograph® ['mɪmɪəgræf] vt polycopier.

mimic ['mɪmɪk] vt (-ck-) imiter; – n imitateur, -trice mf. ◆**mimicking** n. ◆**mimicry** n imitation f.

mimosa [mɪ'məʊzə] n Bot mimosa m.

minaret [mɪnə'ret] n (*of mosque*) minaret m.

mince [mɪns] n (*meat*) hachis m (de viande); – vt hacher; **not to m. matters** or **one's words** ne pas mâcher ses

mots. ◆**mincemeat** n (*dried fruit*) mélange m de fruits secs. ◆**mincer** n (*machine*) hachoir m.

mind [maɪnd] **1** n esprit m; (*sanity*) raison f; (*memory*) mémoire f; (*opinion*) avis m, idée f; (*thought*) pensée f; (*head*) tête f; **to change one's m.** changer d'avis; **to my m.** à mon avis; **in two minds** (*undecided*) irrésolu; **to make up one's m.** se décider; **to be on s.o.'s m.** (*worry*) préoccuper qn; **out of one's m.** (*mad*) fou; **to bring to m.** (*recall*) rappeler; **to bear** or **keep in m.** (*remember*) se souvenir de; **to have in m.** (*person, plan*) avoir en vue; **to have a good m. to do** avoir bien envie de faire. **2** vti (*heed*) faire attention à; (*look after*) garder, s'occuper de; (*noise, dirt etc*) être gêné par; (*one's language*) surveiller; **m. you don't fall** (*beware*) prends garde de ne pas tomber; **m. you do it** n'oublie pas de le faire; **do you m. if?** (*I smoke etc*) ça vous gêne si?; (*I leave, help etc*) ça ne vous fait rien si?; **I don't m. the sun** le soleil ne me gêne pas, je ne suis pas gêné par le soleil; **I don't m.** (*care*) ça m'est égal; **I wouldn't m. a cup of tea** (*would like*) j'aimerais bien une tasse de thé; **I m. that . . .** ça m'ennuie or me gêne que . . . ; **never m.!** (*it doesn't matter*) ça ne fait rien!, tant pis!; (*don't worry*) ne vous en faites pas!; **m. (out!)** (*watch out*) attention!; **m. you . . .** remarquez (que) . . . ; **m. your own business!**, never you m.! mêlez-vous de ce qui vous regarde! ◆**—ed** suffix fair-m. a impartial; like-m. a de même opinion. ◆**—er** n (*for children*) gardien, -ienne mf, (*nurse*) nourrice f; (*bodyguard*) Fam gorille m. ◆**mind-boggling** a stupéfiant, qui confond l'imagination. ◆**mindful** a m. of sth/doing attentif à qch/à faire. ◆**mindless** a stupide.

mine¹ [maɪn] poss pron le mien, la mienne, pl les mien(ne)s; **this hat is m.** ce chapeau est à moi or est le mien; **a friend of m.** un ami à moi.

min/e² [maɪn] **1** n (*for coal, gold etc*) & Fig mine f; – vt **to m. (for)** (*coal etc*) extraire. **2** n (*explosive*) mine f; – vt (*beach, bridge etc*) miner. ◆**—ing** n exploitation f minière; – a (*industry*) minier. ◆**—er** n mineur m.

mineral ['mɪnərəl] a & n minéral (m).

mingle ['mɪŋg(ə)l] vi se mêler (**with** à); **to m. with** (*socially*) fréquenter.

mingy ['mɪndʒɪ] a (-ier, -iest) (*mean*) Fam radin.

mini ['mɪnɪ] pref mini-.

miniature ['mɪnɪtʃər] n miniature f; – a (*train etc*) miniature inv; (*tiny*) minuscule.

minibus ['mɪnɪbʌs] n minibus m. ◆**minicab** n (radio-)taxi m.

minim ['mɪnɪm] n Mus blanche f.

minimum ['mɪnɪməm] n (pl **-ima** [-ɪmə] or **-imums**) minimum m; – a minimum (f inv), minimal. ◆**minimal** a minimal. ◆**minimize** vt minimiser.

minister ['mɪnɪstər] n Pol Rel ministre m. ◆**minis'terial** a ministériel. ◆**ministry** n ministère m.

mink [mɪŋk] n (animal, fur) vison m.

minor ['maɪnər] a (small) Jur Mus mineur; (detail, operation) petit; – n Jur mineur, -eure mf.

Minorca [mɪ'nɔːkə] n Minorque f.

minority [maɪ'nɒrɪtɪ] n minorité f; in the or a m. en minorité, minoritaire; – a minoritaire.

mint [mɪnt] n (place) Hôtel m de la Monnaie; a m. (of money) Fig une petite fortune; – vt (money) frapper; – a (stamp) neuf; in m. condition à l'état neuf. 2 n Bot Culin menthe f; (sweet) pastille f de menthe; – a à la menthe.

minus ['maɪnəs] prep Math moins; (without) Fam sans; it's m. ten (degrees) il fait moins dix (degrés); – n m. (sign) (signe m) moins m.

minute[1] ['mɪnɪt] 1 n minute f; this (very) m. (now) à la minute; any m. (now) d'une minute à l'autre; m. hand (of clock) grande aiguille f. 2 npl (of meeting) procès-verbal m.

minute[2] [maɪ'njuːt] a (tiny) minuscule; (careful, exact) minutieux.

minx [mɪŋks] n (girl) Pej diablesse f, chipie f.

miracle ['mɪrək(ə)l] n miracle m. ◆**mi'raculous** a miraculeux.

mirage ['mɪrɑːʒ] n mirage m.

mire [maɪər] n Lit fange f.

mirror ['mɪrər] n miroir m, glace f; Fig miroir m; (rear view) m. Aut rétroviseur m; – vt refléter.

mirth [mɜːθ] n Lit gaieté f, hilarité f.

misadventure [mɪsəd'ventʃər] n mésaventure f.

misanthropist [mɪ'zænθrəpɪst] n misanthrope mf.

misapprehend [mɪsæprɪ'hend] vt mal comprendre. ◆**misapprehension** n malentendu m.

misappropriate [mɪsə'prəuprɪeɪt] vt (money) détourner.

misbehave [mɪsbɪ'heɪv] vi se conduire mal; (of child) faire des sottises.

miscalculate [mɪs'kælkjuleɪt] vt mal calculer; – vi Fig se tromper. ◆**miscalcu'lation** n erreur f de calcul.

miscarriage [mɪs'kærɪdʒ] n to have a m. Med faire une fausse couche; m. of justice erreur f judiciaire. ◆**miscarry** vi Med faire une fausse couche; (of plan) Fig échouer.

miscellaneous [mɪsɪ'leɪnɪəs] a divers.

mischief ['mɪstʃɪf] n espièglerie f; (maliciousness) méchanceté f; to make trouble des bêtises; full of m. = mischievous; to make m. for (trouble) créer des ennuis à; to do s.o. a m. (harm) faire mal à qn; a little m. (child) un petit démon. ◆**mischievous** a (playful, naughty) espiègle, malicieux; (malicious) méchant.

misconception [mɪskən'sepʃ(ə)n] n idée f fausse.

misconduct [mɪs'kɒndʌkt] n mauvaise conduite f; Com mauvaise gestion f.

misconstrue [mɪskən'struː] vt mal interpréter.

misdeed [mɪs'diːd] n méfait m.

misdemeanor [mɪsdɪ'miːnər] n Jur délit m.

misdirect [mɪsdɪ'rekt] vt (letter) mal adresser; (energies) mal diriger; (person) mal renseigner.

miser ['maɪzər] n avare mf. ◆**-ly** a avare.

misery ['mɪzərɪ] n (suffering) souffrances fpl; (sadness) tristesse f; (sad person) Fam grincheux, -euse mf; pl (troubles) misères fpl; his life is a m. il est malheureux. ◆**miserable** a (wretched) misérable; (unhappy) malheureux; (awful) affreux; (derisory) dérisoire. ◆**miserably** adv misérablement; (to fail) lamentablement.

misfire [mɪs'faɪər] vi (of engine) avoir des ratés; (of plan) Fig rater.

misfit ['mɪsfɪt] n Pej inadapté, -ée mf.

misfortune [mɪs'fɔːtʃun] n malheur m, infortune f.

misgivings [mɪs'gɪvɪŋz] npl (doubts) doutes mpl; (fears) craintes fpl.

misguided [mɪs'gaɪdɪd] a (action etc) imprudent; to be m. (of person) se tromper.

mishandle [mɪs'hænd(ə)l] vt (affair, situation) traiter avec maladresse; (person) s'y prendre mal avec.

mishap ['mɪshæp] n (accident) mésaventure f; (hitch) contretemps m.

misinform [mɪsɪn'fɔːm] vt mal renseigner.

misinterpret [mɪsɪn'tɜːprɪt] vt mal interpréter.

misjudge [mɪs'dʒʌdʒ] vt (person, distance etc) mal juger.

mislay [mɪs'leɪ] vt (pt & pp mislaid) égarer.

mislead [mɪs'liːd] vt (pt & pp misled) tromper. ◆**-ing** a trompeur.

mismanage [mɪs'mænɪdʒ] vt mal administrer. ◆**—ment** n mauvaise administration f.

misnomer [mɪs'nəʊmər] n (name) nom m ou terme m impropre.

misogyny [mɪ'sɒdʒɪnɪst] n misogyne mf.

misplac/e [mɪs'pleɪs] vt (trust etc) mal placer; (lose) égarer. ◆**—ed** a (remark etc) déplacé.

misprint ['mɪsprɪnt] n faute f d'impression, coquille f.

mispronounce [mɪsprə'naʊns] vt mal prononcer.

misquote [mɪs'kwəʊt] vt citer inexactement.

misrepresent [mɪsreprɪ'zent] vt présenter sous un faux jour.

miss[1] [mɪs] vt (train, target, opportunity etc) manquer, rater; (not see) ne pas voir; (not understand) ne pas comprendre; (one's youth, deceased person etc) regretter; (sth just lost) remarquer l'absence de; **he misses Paris/her** Paris/elle lui manque; **I m. you** tu me manques; **don't m. seeing this play** (don't fail to) ne manque pas de voir cette pièce; **to m. out** (omit) sauter; – vi manquer, rater; **to m. out** (lose a chance) rater l'occasion; **to m. out on** (opportunity etc) rater, laisser passer; – n coup m manqué; **that was or we had a near m.** on l'a échappé belle; **I'll give it a m.** Fam (not go) je n'y irai pas; (not take or drink or eat) je n'en prendrai pas. ◆**—ing** a (absent) absent; (in war, after disaster) disparu; (object) manquant; **there are two cups/students m.** il manque deux tasses/deux étudiants.

miss[2] [mɪs] n mademoiselle f; **Miss Brown** Mademoiselle or Mlle Brown.

misshapen [mɪs'ʃeɪp(ə)n] a difforme.

missile ['mɪsaɪl, Am 'mɪs(ə)l] n (rocket) Mil missile m; (object thrown) projectile m.

mission ['mɪʃ(ə)n] n mission f. ◆**missionary** n missionnaire m.

missive ['mɪsɪv] n (letter) missive f.

misspell [mɪs'spel] vt (pt & pp -ed or misspelt) mal écrire.

mist [mɪst] n (fog) brume f; (on glass) buée f; – vi to m. over or up s'embuer.

mistake [mɪ'steɪk] n erreur f, faute f; **to make a m.** se tromper, faire (une) erreur; **by m.** par erreur; – vt (pt mistook, pp mistaken) (meaning, intention etc) se tromper sur; **to m. the date/place/etc** se tromper de date/de lieu/etc; **you can't m., there's no mistaking** (his face, my car etc) il est impossible de ne pas reconnaître; **to m.**

s.o./sth for prendre qn/qch pour. ◆**mistaken** a (idea etc) erroné; **to be m.** se tromper. ◆**mistakenly** adv par erreur.

mister ['mɪstər] n Fam monsieur m.

mistletoe ['mɪs(ə)ltəʊ] n Bot gui m.

mistreat [mɪs'triːt] vt maltraiter.

mistress ['mɪstrɪs] n maîtresse f; (in secondary school) professeur m.

mistrust [mɪs'trʌst] n méfiance f; – vt se méfier de. ◆**mistrustful** a méfiant.

misty ['mɪstɪ] a (-ier, -iest) (foggy) brumeux; (glass) embué.

misunderstand [mɪsʌndə'stænd] vt (pt & pp -stood) mal comprendre. ◆**misunderstanding** n (disagreement) malentendu m; (mistake) erreur f. ◆**misunderstood** a (person) incompris.

misuse [mɪs'juːz] vt (word, tool) mal employer; (power etc) abuser de; – [mɪs'juːs] n (of word) emploi m abusif; (of tool) usage m abusif; (of power etc) abus m.

mite [maɪt] n (insect) mite f; 2 (poor) m. (child) (pauvre) petit, -ite mf. 3 **a m.** (somewhat) Fam un petit peu.

mitigate ['mɪtɪgeɪt] vt atténuer.

mitt(en) [mɪt, 'mɪt(ə)n] n (glove) moufle f.

mix [mɪks] vt mélanger, mêler; (cement, cake) préparer; (salad) remuer; **to m. up** mélanger; (perplex) embrouiller (qn); (confuse, mistake) confondre (with avec); **to be mixed up with s.o.** (involved) être mêlé aux affaires de qn; **to m. up in** (involve) mêler à; – vi se mêler; (of colours) s'allier; **to m. with** (socially) fréquenter; **she doesn't m. (in)** elle n'est pas sociable; – n (mixture) mélange m. ◆**—ed** a (school, marriage) mixte; (society) mêlé; (feelings) mitigés, mêlés; (results) divers; (nuts, chocolates etc) assortis; **to be (all) m. up** (of person) être désorienté; (of facts, account etc) être embrouillé. ◆**—ing** n mélange m. ◆**—er** n Culin El mixe(u)r m; (for mortar) Tech malaxeur m; **to be a good m.** (of person) être sociable. ◆**mixture** n mélange m; (for cough) sirop m. ◆**mix-up** n Fam confusion f.

mm abbr (millimetre) mm.

moan [məʊn] vi (groan) gémir; (complain) se plaindre (**to** à, **about** de, **that** que); – n gémissement m; plainte f.

moat [məʊt] n douve(s) f(pl).

mob [mɒb] n (crowd) cohue f, foule f; (gang) bande f; **the m.** (masses) la populace; (Mafia) Am Sl la mafia; – vt (-bb-) assiéger. ◆**mobster** n Am Sl gangster m.

mobile ['məʊbaɪl, Am 'məʊb(ə)l] a mobile; (having a car etc) Fam motorisé; **m. home**

mobil-home m; **m. library** bibliobus m; − (Am ['məubiːl]) (ornament) mobile m. ◆**mo'bility** n mobilité f. ◆**mobili'zation** n mobilisation f. ◆**mobilize** vti mobiliser.

moccasin ['mɒkəsɪn] n (shoe) mocassin m.

mocha ['məʊkə] n (coffee) moka m.

mock [mɒk] **1** vt se moquer de; (mimic) singer; − vi se moquer (at de). **2** a (false) simulé; (exam) blanc. ◆**−ing** n moquerie f; − a moqueur. ◆**mockery** n (act) moquerie f; (parody) parodie f; **to make a m.** of tourner en ridicule.

mock-up ['mɒkʌp] n (model) maquette f.

mod cons [mɒd'kɒnz] abbr Fam = **modern conveniences.**

mode [məʊd] n (manner, way) mode m; (fashion, vogue) mode f.

model ['mɒd(ə)l] n (example, person etc) modèle m; (fashion) m. mannequin m; (scale) m. modèle m (réduit); − a (behaviour, factory etc) modèle; (car, plane) modèle réduit inv; **m. railway** train m miniature; − vt modeler (on sur); (hats) présenter (les modèles m); − vi (for fashion) être mannequin; (pose for artist) poser. ◆**modelling** n (of statues etc) modelage m.

moderate[1] ['mɒdərət] a modéré; (in speech) mesuré; (result) passable; − n Pol modéré, -ée f. ◆**−ly** adv (in moderation) modérément; (averagely) moyennement.

moderate[2] ['mɒdəreɪt] vt (diminish, tone down) modérer. ◆**mode'ration** n modération f; **in m.** avec modération.

modern ['mɒd(ə)n] a moderne; **m. languages** langues fpl vivantes; **m. conveniences** tout le confort moderne. ◆**modernism** n modernisme m. ◆**moderni'zation** n modernisation f. ◆**modernize** vt moderniser.

modest ['mɒdɪst] a modeste. ◆**modesty** n (quality) modestie f; (moderation) modération f; (of salary etc) modicité f.

modicum ['mɒdɪkəm] n a m. of un soupçon de, un petit peu de.

modify ['mɒdɪfaɪ] vt (alter) modifier; (tone down) modérer. ◆**modifi'cation** n modification f.

modulate ['mɒdjʊleɪt] vt moduler. ◆**modu'lation** n modulation f.

module ['mɒdjuːl] n module m.

mogul ['məʊgʌl] n magnat m, manitou m.

mohair ['məʊheər] n mohair m.

moist [mɔɪst] a (-er, -est) humide; (clammy, sticky) moite. ◆**moisten** vt humecter. ◆**moisture** n humidité f; (on glass) buée f.

◆**moisturiz/e** vt (skin) hydrater. ◆**−er** n (cream) crème f hydratante.

molar ['məʊlər] n (tooth) molaire f.

molasses [mə'læsɪz] n (treacle) Am mélasse f.

mold [məʊld] Am = **mould.**

mole [məʊl] n **1** (on skin) grain m de beauté. **2** (animal, spy) taupe f.

molecule ['mɒlɪkjuːl] n molécule f.

molest [mə'lest] vt (annoy) importuner; (child, woman) Jur attenter à la pudeur de.

mollusc ['mɒləsk] n mollusque m.

mollycoddle ['mɒlɪkɒd(ə)l] vt dorloter.

molt [məʊlt] Am = **moult.**

molten ['məʊlt(ə)n] a (metal) en fusion.

mom [mɒm] n Am Fam maman f.

moment ['məʊmənt] n moment m, instant m; **this (very) m.** (now) à l'instant; **the m. she leaves** dès qu'elle partira; **any m. (now)** d'un moment or d'un instant à l'autre. ◆**momentarily** (Am [məʊmən'terɪlɪ]) adv (temporarily) momentanément; (soon) Am tout à l'heure. ◆**momentary** a momentané.

momentous [məʊ'mentəs] a important.

momentum [məʊ'mentəm] n (speed) élan m; **to gather** or **gain m.** (of ideas etc) Fig gagner du terrain.

mommy ['mɒmɪ] n Am Fam maman f.

Monaco ['mɒnəkəʊ] n Monaco f.

monarch ['mɒnək] n monarque m. ◆**monarchy** n monarchie f.

monastery ['mɒnəst(ə)rɪ] n monastère m.

Monday ['mʌndɪ] n lundi m.

monetary ['mʌnɪt(ə)rɪ] a monétaire.

money ['mʌnɪ] n argent m; **paper m.** papier-monnaie m, billets mpl; **to get one's m.'s worth** en avoir pour son argent; **he gets** or **earns good m.** il gagne bien (sa vie); **to be in the m.** Fam rouler sur l'or; **m. order** mandat m. ◆**moneybags** n Pej Fam richard, -arde f. ◆**moneybox** n tirelire f. ◆**moneychanger** n changeur m. ◆**moneylender** n prêteur, -euse mf sur gages. ◆**moneymaking** a lucratif. ◆**money-spinner** n (source of wealth) Fam mine f d'or.

mongol ['mɒŋɡ(ə)l] n & a Med mongolien, -ienne (mf).

mongrel ['mʌŋɡrəl] n (dog) bâtard m.

monitor ['mɒnɪtər] **1** n (pupil) chef m de classe. **2** n (screen) Tech moniteur m. **3** vt (a broadcast) Rad écouter; (check) Fig contrôler.

monk [mʌŋk] n moine m, religieux m.

monkey ['mʌŋkɪ] n singe m; **little m.** (child) Fam polisson, -onne mf; **m. business** Fam singeries *fpl*; – *vi* **to m. about** *Fam* faire l'idiot.

mono ['mɒnəu] *a* (*record etc*) mono *inv*.

mono- ['mɒnəu] *pref* mono-.

monocle ['mɒnək(ə)l] *n* monocle *m*.

monogram ['mɒnəgræm] *n* monogramme *m*.

monologue ['mɒnəlɒg] *n* monologue *m*.

monopoly [mə'nɒpəlɪ] *n* monopole *m*. **◆monopolize** *vt* monopoliser.

monosyllable ['mɒnəsɪləb(ə)l] *n* monosyllabe *m*. **◆monosyllabic** *a* monosyllabique.

monotone ['mɒnətəun] *n* **in a m.** sur un ton monocorde.

monotony [mə'nɒtənɪ] *n* monotonie *f*. **◆monotonous** *a* monotone.

monsoon [mɒn'su:n] *n* (*wind, rain*) mousson *f*.

monster ['mɒnstər] *n* monstre *m*. **◆monstrosity** *n* (*horror*) monstruosité *f*. **◆monstrous** *a* (*abominable, enormous*) monstrueux.

month [mʌnθ] *n* mois *m*. **◆monthly** *a* mensuel; **m. payment** mensualité *f*; – *n* (*periodical*) mensuel *m*; – *adv* (*every month*) mensuellement.

Montreal [mɒntrɪ'ɔːl] *n* Montréal *m or f*.

monument ['mɒnjʊmənt] *n* monument *m*. **◆monu'mental** *a* monumental; **m. mason** marbrier *m*.

moo [mu:] *vi* meugler; – *n* meuglement *m*.

mooch [muːtʃ] **1** *vi* **to m. around** *Fam* flâner. **2** *vt* **to m. sth off s.o.** (*cadge*) *Am Sl* taper qch à qn.

mood [mu:d] *n* (*of person*) humeur *f*; (*of country*) état *m* d'esprit; *Gram* mode *m*; **in a good/bad m.** de bonne/mauvaise humeur; **to be in the m. to do or for doing** être d'humeur à faire, avoir envie de faire. **◆moody** *a* (*-ier, -iest*) (*changeable*) d'humeur changeante; (*bad-tempered*) de mauvaise humeur.

moon [mu:n] *n* lune *f*; **once in a blue m.** (*rarely*) *Fam* tous les trente-six du mois; **over the m.** (*delighted*) *Fam* ravi (**about** de). **◆moonlight 1** *n* clair *m* de lune. **2** *vi Fam* travailler au noir. **◆moonshine** *n* (*talk*) *Fam* balivernes *fpl*.

moor [muər] **1** *vt Nau* amarrer; – *vi* mouiller. **2** *n* (*open land*) lande *f*. **◆-ings** *npl Nau* (*ropes etc*) amarres *fpl*; (*place*) mouillage *m*.

moose [mu:s] *n inv* (*animal*) orignac *m*, élan *m*.

moot [mu:t] **1** *a* (*point*) discutable. **2** *vt* (*question*) soulever, suggérer.

mop [mɒp] **1** *n* balai *m* (à laver), balai *m* éponge; **dish m.** lavette *f*; **m. of hair** tignasse *f*. **2** *vt* (*-pp-*) **to m. (up)** (*wipe*) essuyer; **to m. one's brow** s'essuyer le front.

mope [məup] *vi* **to m. (about)** être déprimé, avoir le cafard.

moped ['məuped] *n* cyclomoteur *m*, mobylette® *f*.

moral ['mɒrəl] *a* moral; – *n* (*of story etc*) morale *f*; *pl* (*standards*) moralité *f*, morale *f*. **◆morale** [mə'raɪl, *Am* mə'ræl] *n* moral *m*. **◆moralist** *n* moraliste *mf*. **◆mo'rality** *n* (*morals*) moralité *f*. **◆moralize** *vi* moraliser. **◆morally** *adv* moralement.

morass [mə'ræs] *n* (*land*) marais *m*; (*mess*) *Fig* bourbier *m*.

moratorium [mɒrə'tɔːrɪəm] *n* moratoire *m*.

morbid ['mɔːbɪd] *a* morbide.

more [mɔːr] *a & n* plus (de) (**than** que); (*other*) d'autres; **m. cars/etc** plus de voitures/*etc*; **he has m.** (**than you**) il en a plus (que toi); **a few m. months** encore quelques mois, quelques mois de plus; (*some*) **m. tea/etc** encore du thé/*etc*; (*some*) **m. details** d'autres détails; **m. than a kilo/ten/etc** (*with quantity, number*) plus d'un kilo/de dix/*etc*; – *adv* (*tired, rapidly etc*) plus (**than** que); **m. and m.** de plus en plus; **m. or less** plus ou moins; **the m. he shouts the m.** hoarse **he gets** plus il crie plus il s'enroue; **she hasn't any m.** elle n'en a plus. **◆mo'reover** *adv* de plus, d'ailleurs.

moreish ['mɔːrɪʃ] *a Fam* qui a un goût de revenez-y.

mores ['mɔːreɪz] *npl* mœurs *fpl*.

morgue [mɔːg] *n* (*mortuary*) morgue *f*.

moribund ['mɔːrɪbʌnd] *a* moribond.

morning ['mɔːnɪŋ] *n* matin *m*; (*duration of morning*) matinée *f*; **in the m.** (*every morning*) le matin; (*during the morning*) pendant la matinée; (*tomorrow*) demain matin; **at seven in the m.** à sept heures du matin; **every Tuesday m.** tous les mardis matin; **in the early m.** au petit matin; – *a* du matin, matinal. **◆mornings** *adv Am* le matin.

Morocco [mə'rɒkəu] *n* Maroc *m*. **◆Moroccan** *a & n* marocain, -aine (*mf*).

moron ['mɔːrɒn] *n* crétin, -ine *mf*.

morose [mə'rəus] *a* morose.

morphine ['mɔːfiːn] *n* morphine *f*.

Morse [mɔːs] *n & a* **M.** (*code*) morse *m*.

morsel ['mɔːs(ə)l] *n* (*of food*) petite bouchée *f*.

mortal ['mɔːt(ə)l] *a & n* mortel, -elle (*mf*). **◆mor'tality** *n* (*death rate*) mortalité *f*.

mortar ['mɔːtər] *n* mortier *m*.

mortgage ['mɔːgɪdʒ] n prêt-logement m; — vt (house, future) hypothéquer.

mortician [mɔː'tɪʃ(ə)n] n Am entrepreneur m de pompes funèbres.

mortify ['mɔːtɪfaɪ] vt mortifier.

mortuary ['mɔːtʃʊərɪ] n morgue f.

mosaic [məʊ'zeɪɪk] n mosaïque f.

Moscow ['mɒskaʊ, Am 'mɒskaʊ] n Moscou m ou f.

Moses ['məʊzɪz] a **M. basket** couffin m.

Moslem ['mɒzlɪm] a & n musulman, -ane (mf).

mosque [mɒsk] n mosquée f.

mosquito [mɒ'skiːtəʊ] n (pl -oes) moustique m; **m. net** moustiquaire f.

moss [mɒs] n Bot mousse f. ◆**mossy** a moussu.

most [məʊst] a & n the m. (greatest in amount etc) le plus (de); **I have (the) m. books** j'ai le plus de livres; **I have (the) m.** j'en ai le plus; **m. (of the) books/etc** la plupart des livres/etc; **m. of the cake/etc** la plus grande partie du gâteau/etc; **m. of them** la plupart d'entre eux; **m. of it** la plus grande partie; **at (the) very** m. tout au plus; **to make the m. of** profiter (au maximum) de; — adv (le) plus; (very) fort, très; **the m. beautiful** le plus beau, la plus belle (**in**, **of** de); **to talk (the) m.** parler le plus; **m. of all** (especially) surtout. ◆—**ly** adv surtout, pour la plupart.

motel [məʊ'tel] n motel m.

moth [mɒθ] n papillon m de nuit; (clothes) m. mite f. ◆**m.-eaten** a mité. ◆**mothball** n boule f de naphtaline.

mother ['mʌðər] n mère f; **M.'s Day** la fête des Mères; **m. tongue** langue f maternelle; — vt (care for) materner. ◆**motherhood** n maternité f. ◆**motherly** a maternel.

mother-in-law ['mʌðərɪnlɔː] n (pl mothers-in-law) belle-mère f. ◆**m.-of-pearl** n (substance) nacre f. ◆**m.-to-'be** n (pl mothers-to-be) future mère f.

motion ['məʊʃ(ə)n] n mouvement m; Pol motion f; **m. picture** film m; — vti to m. to s.o. to do faire signe à qn de faire. ◆—**less** a immobile.

motive ['məʊtɪv] n motif m (for, of de); Jur mobile m (for de). ◆**motivate** vt (person, decision etc) motiver. ◆**moti'vation** n motivation f; (incentive) encouragement m.

motley ['mɒtlɪ] a (coloured) bigarré; (collection) hétéroclite.

motor ['məʊtər] n (engine) moteur m; (car) Fam auto f; — a (industry, vehicle etc) automobile; (accident) de voiture; **m. boat** canot m automobile. **m. mechanic** mécanicien-auto

m; **m. mower** tondeuse f à moteur; — vi (drive) rouler en auto. ◆—**ing** n Sp automobilisme m; **school of m.** auto-école f. ◆**motorbike** n Fam moto f. ◆**motorcade** n cortège m (officiel) (de voitures). ◆**motorcar** n automobile f. ◆**motorcycle** n moto f, motocyclette f. ◆**motorcyclist** n motocycliste mf. ◆**motorist** n automobiliste mf. ◆**motorized** a motorisé. ◆**motorway** n autoroute f.

mottled ['mɒt(ə)ld] a tacheté.

motto ['mɒtəʊ] n (pl -oes) devise f.

mould [məʊld] 1 n (shape) moule m; — vt (clay etc) mouler; (statue, character) modeler. 2 n (growth, mildew) moisissure f. ◆**mouldy** a (-ier, -iest) moisi; to go m. moisir.

moult [məʊlt] vi muer. ◆—**ing** n mue f.

mound [maʊnd] n (of earth) tertre m; (pile) Fig monceau m.

mount [maʊnt] 1 n (mountain) Lit mont m. 2 n (horse) monture f; (frame for photo or slide) cadre m; (stamp hinge) charnière f; — vt (horse, hill, jewel, photo, demonstration etc) monter; (ladder, tree etc) monter sur, grimper à; (stamp) coller (dans un album); — vi to m. (up) (on horse) se mettre en selle. 3 vi (increase) monter; to m. up (add up) chiffrer (to à); (accumulate) s'accumuler.

mountain ['maʊntɪn] n montagne f; — a (people, life) montagnard. ◆**mountaineer** n alpiniste mf. ◆**mountaineering** n alpinisme m. ◆**mountainous** a montagneux.

mourn [mɔːn] vti to m. (for) pleurer. ◆—**ing** n deuil m; in m. en deuil. ◆—**er** n parent, -ente mf or ami, -ie mf du défunt or de la défunte. ◆**mournful** a triste.

mouse, pl **mice** [maʊs, maɪs] n souris f. ◆**mousetrap** n souricière f.

mousse [muːs] n Culin mousse f.

moustache [mə'stɑːʃ, Am 'mʌstæʃ] n moustache f.

mousy ['maʊsɪ] a (-ier, -iest) (hair) Pej châtain terne; (shy) Fig timide.

mouth [maʊθ] n (pl -s [maʊðz]) bouche f; (of dog, lion etc) gueule f; (of river) embouchure f; (of cave, harbour) entrée f; — [maʊð] vt Pej dire. ◆**mouthful** n (of food) bouchée f; (of liquid) gorgée f. ◆**mouthorgan** n harmonica m. ◆**mouthpiece** n Mus embouchure f; (spokesman) Fig porte-parole m inv. ◆**mouthwash** n bain m de bouche. ◆**mouth-watering** a appétissant.

mov/e [muːv] n mouvement m; (change of

house etc) déménagement *m*; (*change of job*) changement *m* d'emploi; (*transfer of employee*) mutation *f*; (*in game*) coup *m*, (*one's turn*) tour *m*; (*act*) Fig démarche *f*; (*step*) pas *m*; (*attempt*) tentative *f*; **to make a m.** (*leave*) se préparer à partir; (*act*) Fig passer à l'action; **to get a m. on** *Fam* se dépêcher; **on the m.** en marche; − *vt* déplacer, remuer, bouger; (*arm, leg*) remuer; (*crowd*) faire partir; (*put*) mettre; (*transport*) transporter; (*piece in game*) jouer; (*propose*) *Pol* proposer; **to m. s.o.** (*incite*) pousser qn (*to do* à faire); (*emotionally*) émouvoir qn; (*transfer in job*) muter qn; **to m. house** déménager; **to m. sth back** reculer qch; **to m. sth down** descendre qch; **to m. sth forward** avancer qch; **to m. sth over** pousser qch; − *vi* bouger, remuer; (*go*) aller (*to* à); (*pass*) passer (*to* à); (*leave*) partir; (*change seats*) changer de place; (*progress*) avancer; (*act*) agir; (*play*) jouer; **to m. (out)** (*of house etc*) déménager; **to m. to** (*a new region etc*) habiter; **to m. about** se déplacer; (*fidget*) remuer; **to m. along or forward** or on avancer; **to m. away or off** (*go away*) s'éloigner; **to m. back** (*withdraw*) reculer; (*return*) retourner; **to m. in** (*to house*) emménager; **to m. into** (*house*) emménager dans; **m. on!** circulez!; **to m. over** or up se pousser. ◆**−ing** *a* en mouvement; (*part*) *Tech* mobile; (*stairs*) mécanique; (*touching*) émouvant. ◆**mov(e)able** *a* mobile. ◆**movement** *n* (*action, group etc*) & *Mus* mouvement *m*.

movie ['muːvɪ] *n Fam* film *m*; **the movies** (*cinema*) le cinéma; **m. camera** caméra *f*. ◆**moviegoer** *n* cinéphile *mf*.

mow [məʊ] *vt* (*pp* **mown** *or* **mowed**) (*field*) faucher; **to m. the lawn** tondre le gazon; **to m. down** (*kill etc*) Fig faucher. ◆**−er** *n* (*lawn*) **m.** tondeuse *f* (à gazon).

MP [em'piː] *n abbr* (*Member of Parliament*) député *m*.

Mrs ['mɪsɪz] *n* (*married woman*) **Mrs Brown** Madame *or* Mme Brown.

Ms [mɪz] *n* (*married or unmarried woman*) **Ms Brown** Madame *or* Mme Brown.

MSc, *Am* **MS** *abbr* = **Master of Science.**

much [mʌtʃ] *a* & *n* beaucoup (de); **not m. time/money/etc** pas beaucoup de temps/ d'argent/*etc*; **not m.** pas beaucoup; **m. of** (*a good deal of*) une bonne partie de; **as m. as** (*to do, know etc*) autant que; **as m. wine/etc as** autant de vin/*etc* que; **as m. as you like** autant que tu veux; **twice as m.** deux fois plus (de); **how m.?** combien (de)?; **too m.**

trop (de); **so m.** tant (de), tellement (de); **I know/I shall do this m.** je sais/je ferai ceci (du moins); **this m. wine** ça de vin; **it's not m. of a garden** ce n'est pas merveilleux comme jardin; **m. the same** presque le même; − *adv* very **m.** beaucoup; **not (very) m.** pas beaucoup; **she doesn't say very m.** elle ne dit pas grand-chose.

muck [mʌk] **1** *n* (*manure*) fumier *m*; (*filth*) Fig saleté *f*. **2** *vi* **to m. about** *Fam* (*have fun, idle*) s'amuser; (*play the fool*) faire l'idiot; **to m. about with** (*fiddle with*) s'amuser avec; (*alter*) changer (*texte etc*); **to m. in** (*join in*) *Fam* participer, contribuer; − *vt* **to m. s.o. about** *Fam* embêter qn, déranger qn; **to m. up** (*spoil*) *Fam* gâcher, ruiner. ◆**m.-up** *n Fam* gâchis *m*. ◆**mucky** *a* (*-ier, -iest*) sale.

mucus ['mjuːkəs] *n* mucosités *fpl*.

mud [mʌd] *n* boue *f*. ◆**muddy** *a* (*-ier, -iest*) (*water*) boueux; (*hands etc*) couvert de boue. ◆**mudguard** *n* garde-boue *m inv*.

muddle ['mʌd(ə)l] *n* (*mess*) désordre *m*; (*mix-up*) confusion *f*; **in a m.** (*room etc*) sens dessus dessous, en désordre; (*person*) désorienté; (*mind, ideas*) embrouillé; − *vt* (*person, facts etc*) embrouiller; (*papers*) mélanger; − *vi* **to m. through** *Fam* se débrouiller tant bien que mal.

muff [mʌf] *n* (*for hands*) manchon *m*.

muffin ['mʌfɪn] *n* petit pain *m* brioché.

muffl/e ['mʌf(ə)l] *vt* (*noise*) assourdir. ◆**−ed** *a* (*noise*) sourd. ◆**−er** *n* (*scarf*) cache-col *m inv*; *Aut Am* silencieux *m*.

mug [mʌg] **1** *n* grande tasse *f*; (*of metal or plastic*) gobelet *m*; (*beer*) **m.** chope *f*. **2** *n* (*face*) *Sl* gueule *f*; **m. shot** *Pej* photo *f* (d'identité). **3** *n* (*fool*) *Fam* niais, -aise *mf*. **4** *vt* (*-gg-*) (*attack*) agresser. ◆**mugger** *n* agresseur *m*. ◆**mugging** *n* agression *f*.

muggy ['mʌgɪ] *a* (*-ier, -iest*) (*weather*) lourd.

mulberry ['mʌlbərɪ] *n* (*fruit*) mûre *f*.

mule [mjuːl] *n* (*male*) mulet *m*; (*female*) mule *f*.

mull [mʌl] **1** *vt* (*wine*) chauffer. **2** *vi* **to m. over** (*think over*) ruminer.

mullet ['mʌlɪt] *n* (*fish*) mulet *m*; (**red**) **m.** rouget *m*.

multi- ['mʌltɪ] *pref* multi-.

multicoloured ['mʌltɪkʌləd] *a* multicolore.

multifarious [mʌltɪˈfeərɪəs] *a* divers.

multimillionaire [mʌltɪmɪljəˈneər] *n* milliardaire *mf*.

multinational [mʌltɪˈnæʃ(ə)nəl] *n* multinationale *f*.

multiple ['mʌltɪp(ə)l] a multiple; – n Math multiple m. ◆**multipli'cation** n multiplication f. ◆**multi'plicity** n multiplicité f. ◆**multiply** vt multiplier; – vi (reproduce) se multiplier.

multistorey ['mʌltɪ'stɔːrɪ] (Am **multistoried**) a à étages.

multitude ['mʌltɪtjuːd] n multitude f.

mum [mʌm] **1** n Fam maman f. **2** a **to keep m.** garder le silence.

mumble ['mʌmb(ə)l] vti marmotter.

mumbo-jumbo [mʌmbəʊ'dʒʌmbəʊ] n (words) charabia m.

mummy ['mʌmɪ] n **1** Fam maman f. **2** (body) momie f.

mumps [mʌmps] n oreillons mpl.

munch [mʌntʃ] vti (chew) mastiquer; **to m.** (on) (eat) Fam bouffer.

mundane [mʌn'deɪn] a banal.

municipal [mjuːˈnɪsɪp(ə)l] a municipal. ◆**munici'pality** n municipalité f.

munitions [mjuːˈnɪʃ(ə)nz] npl munitions fpl.

mural ['mjʊərəl] a mural; – n fresque f, peinture f murale.

murder ['mɜːdər] n meurtre m, assassinat m; **it's m.** (dreadful) Fam c'est affreux; – vt (kill) assassiner; (spoil) Fig massacrer. ◆**-er** n meurtrier, -ière mf, assassin m. ◆**murderous** a meurtrier.

murky ['mɜːkɪ] a (-ier, -iest) obscur; (water, business, past) trouble; (weather) nuageux.

murmur ['mɜːmər] n murmure m; (of traffic) bourdonnement m; – vti murmurer.

muscle ['mʌs(ə)l] n muscle m; – vi **to m. in** on (group) Sl s'introduire par la force à. ◆**muscular** a (tissue etc) musculaire; (brawny) musclé.

muse [mjuːz] vi méditer (on sur).

museum [mjuːˈzɪəm] n musée m.

mush [mʌʃ] n (soft mass) bouillie f; Fig sentimentalité f. ◆**mushy** a (-ier, -iest) (food etc) en bouillie; Fig sentimental.

mushroom ['mʌʃrʊm] n **1** champignon m. **2** vi (grow) pousser comme des champignons; (spread) se multiplier.

music ['mjuːzɪk] n musique f; **m. centre** chaîne f stéréo compacte; **m. critic** critique m musical; **m. hall** music-hall m; **m. lover** mélomane mf; **canned m.** musique f (de fond) enregistrée. ◆**musical** a musical; (instrument) de musique; **to be (very) m.** être (très) musicien; – n (film, play)

comédie f musicale. ◆**mu'sician** n musicien, -ienne mf.

musk [mʌsk] n (scent) musc m.

Muslim ['mʊzlɪm] a & n musulman, -ane (mf).

muslin ['mʌzlɪn] n (cotton) mousseline f.

mussel ['mʌs(ə)l] n (mollusc) moule f.

must [mʌst] v aux **1** (necessity) **you m.** obey tu dois obéir, il faut que tu obéisses. **2** (certainty) **she m. be clever** elle doit être intelligente; **I m. have seen it** j'ai dû le voir; – n **this is a m.** ceci est (absolument) indispensable.

mustache ['mʌstæʃ] n Am moustache f.

mustard ['mʌstəd] n moutarde f.

muster ['mʌstər] vt (gather) rassembler; (sum) réunir; – vi se rassembler.

musty ['mʌstɪ] a (-ier, -iest) (smell) de moisi; **it smells m., it's m.** ça sent le moisi.

mutation [mjuːˈteɪʃ(ə)n] n Biol mutation f.

mut/e [mjuːt] a (silent) & Gram muet; – n (sound, colour) assourdir. ◆**-ed** a (criticism) voilé.

mutilate ['mjuːtɪleɪt] vt mutiler. ◆**muti'lation** n mutilation f.

mutiny ['mjuːtɪnɪ] n mutinerie f; – vi se mutiner. ◆**mutinous** a (troops) mutiné.

mutter ['mʌtər] vti marmonner.

mutton ['mʌt(ə)n] n (meat) mouton m.

mutual ['mjuːtʃʊəl] a (help, love etc) mutuel, réciproque; (common, shared) commun; **m. fund** Fin Am fonds m commun de placement. ◆**-ly** adv mutuellement.

muzzle ['mʌz(ə)l] n (snout) museau m; (device) muselière f; (of gun) gueule f; – vt (animal, press etc) museler.

my [maɪ] poss a mon, ma, pl mes. ◆**my'self** pron moi-même; (reflexive) me, m'; (after prep) moi; **I wash m.** je me lave; **I think of m.** je pense à moi.

mystery ['mɪstərɪ] n mystère m. ◆**my'sterious** a mystérieux.

mystic ['mɪstɪk] a n mystique (mf). ◆**mystical** a mystique. ◆**mysticism** n mysticisme m. ◆**my'stique** n (mystery, power) mystique f (of de).

mystify ['mɪstɪfaɪ] vt (bewilder) laisser perplexe; (fool) mystifier. ◆**mystifi'cation** n (bewilderment) perplexité f.

myth [mɪθ] n mythe m. ◆**mythical** a mythique. ◆**mytho'logical** a mythologique. ◆**my'thology** n mythologie f.

N

N, n [en] *n* N, *m*; **the nth time** la énième fois.

nab [næb] *vt* (**-bb-**) (*catch, arrest*) *Fam* épingler.

nag [næg] *vti* (**-gg-**) (*criticize*) critiquer; **to n. (at) s.o.** (*pester*) harceler *or* embêter qn (**to do** pour qu'il fasse). ◆**nagging** *a* (*doubt, headache*) qui subsiste; – *n* critiques *fpl*.

nail [neɪl] **1** *n* (*of finger, toe*) ongle *m*; – *a* (*polish, file etc*) à ongles. **2** *n* (*metal*) clou *m*; – *vt* clouer; **to n. s.o.** (*nab*) *Fam* épingler qn; **to n. down** (*lid etc*) clouer.

naïve [nɑːˈiːv] *a* naïf. ◆**naïveté** *n* naïveté *f*.

naked [ˈneɪkɪd] *a* (*person*) nu; (*eye, flame*) nu; **to see with the n. eye** voir à l'œil nu. ◆**-ness** *n* nudité *f*.

name [neɪm] *n* nom *m*; (*reputation*) *Fig* réputation *f*; **my n. is . . .** je m'appelle . . .; **in the n. of** au nom de; **to put one's n. down for** (*school, course*) s'inscrire à; (*job, house*) demander, faire une demande pour avoir; **to call s.o. names** injurier qn; **first n., given n.** prénom *m*; **last n.** nom *m* de famille; **a good/bad n.** *Fig* une bonne/mauvaise réputation; **to plate** plaque *f*. – *vt* nommer; (*ship, street*) baptiser; (*designate*) désigner, nommer; (*date, price*) fixer; **he was named after** *or* *Am* **for . . .** il a reçu le nom de . . . . ◆**-less** *a* sans nom, anonyme. ◆**-ly** *adv* (*that is*) à savoir. ◆**namesake** *n* (*person*) homonyme *m*.

nanny [ˈnænɪ] *n* nurse *f*, bonne *f* d'enfants; (*grandmother*) *Fam* mamie *f*.

nanny-goat [ˈnænɪgəʊt] *n* chèvre *f*.

nap [næp] *n* (*sleep*) petit somme *m*; **to have** *or* **take a n.** faire un petit somme; (*after lunch*) faire la sieste; – *vi* (**-pp-**) **to be napping** sommeiller; **to catch napping** *Fig* prendre au dépourvu.

nape [neɪp] *n* **n. (of the neck)** nuque *f*.

napkin [ˈnæpkɪn] *n* (*at table*) serviette *f*; (*for baby*) couche *f*. ◆**nappy** *n* (*for baby*) couche *f*. ◆**nappy-liner** *n* protège-couche *m*.

narcotic [nɑːˈkɒtɪk] *a* & *n* narcotique (*m*).

narrate [nəˈreɪt] *vt* raconter. ◆**narration** *n*, ◆**narrative** *n* (*story*) récit *m*, narration *f*; (*art, act*) narration *f*. ◆**narrator** *n* narrateur, -trice *mf*.

narrow [ˈnærəʊ] *a* (**-er, -est**) étroit; (*major-ity*) faible, petit; – *vi* (*of path*) se rétrécir; **to n. down** (*of choice etc*) se limiter (**to** à); – *vt* **to n. (down)** (*limit*) limiter. ◆**-ly** *adv* (*to miss etc*) de justesse; (*strictly*) strictement; **he n. escaped** *or* **missed being killed**/*etc* il a failli être tué/*etc*. ◆**-ness** *n* étroitesse *f*.

narrow-minded [nærəʊˈmaɪndɪd] *a* borné. ◆**-ness** *n* étroitesse *f* (d'esprit).

nasal [ˈneɪz(ə)l] *a* nasal; (*voice*) nasillard.

nasty [ˈnɑːstɪ] *a* (**-ier, -iest**) (*bad*) mauvais, vilain; (*spiteful*) méchant, désagréable (**to, towards** avec); **a n. mess** *or* **muddle** un gâchis. ◆**nastily** *adv* (*to act*) méchamment; (*to rain*) horriblement. ◆**nastiness** *n* (*malice*) méchanceté *f*; **the n. of the weather/taste**/*etc* le mauvais temps/goût/*etc*.

nation [ˈneɪʃ(ə)n] *n* nation *f*; **the United Nations** les Nations Unies. ◆**n.-wide** *a* & *adv* dans le pays (tout) entier. ◆**national** *a* national; **n. anthem** hymne *m* national; **N. Health Service** = Sécurité *f* Sociale; **n. insurance** = assurances *fpl* sociales; – *n* (*citizen*) ressortissant, -ante *mf*. ◆**nationalist** *n* nationaliste *mf*. ◆**nationa'listic** *a Pej* nationaliste. ◆**natio'nality** *n* nationalité *f*. ◆**nationalize** *vt* nationaliser. ◆**nationally** *adv* (*to travel, be known etc*) dans le pays (tout) entier.

native [ˈneɪtɪv] *a* (*country*) natal; (*habits, costume*) du pays; (*tribe, plant*) indigène; (*charm, ability*) inné; **n. language** langue *f* maternelle; **to be an English n. speaker** parler l'anglais comme langue maternelle; – *n* (*person*) autochtone *mf*; (*non-European in colony*) indigène *mf*; **to be a n. of** être originaire *or* natif de.

nativity [nəˈtɪvɪtɪ] *n Rel* nativité *f*.

NATO [ˈneɪtəʊ] *n abbr* (*North Atlantic Treaty Organization*) OTAN *f*.

natter [ˈnætər] *vi Fam* bavarder; – *n Fam* **to have a n.** bavarder.

natural [ˈnætʃ(ə)rəl] *a* naturel; (*actor, gardener etc*) né; – *n* **to be a n. for** (*job etc*) *Fam* être celui qu'il faut pour, être fait pour. ◆**naturalist** *n* naturaliste *mf*. ◆**naturally** *adv* (*as normal, of course*) naturellement; (*by nature*) de nature; (*with naturalness*) avec naturel. ◆**naturalness** *n* naturel *m*.

naturalize ['nætʃ(ə)rəlaɪz] vt (person) Pol naturaliser. ◆**naturali'zation** n naturalisation f.

nature ['neɪtʃər] n (natural world, basic quality) nature f; (disposition) naturel m; **by n.** de nature; **n. study** sciences fpl naturelles.

naught [nɔːt] n 1 Math zéro m. 2 (nothing) Lit rien m.

naught/y ['nɔːtɪ] a (-ier, -iest) (child) vilain, malicieux; (joke, story) osé, grivois. ◆**-ly** adv (to behave) mal; (to say) avec malice. ◆**-iness** n mauvaise conduite f.

nausea ['nɔːzɪə] n nausée f. ◆**nauseate** vt écœurer. ◆**nauseous** a (smell etc) nauséabond; **to feel n.** Am (sick) avoir envie de vomir; (disgusted) Fig être écœuré.

nautical ['nɔːtɪk(ə)l] a nautique.

naval ['neɪv(ə)l] a naval; (power, hospital) maritime; (officer) de marine.

nave [neɪv] n (of church) nef f.

navel ['neɪv(ə)l] n Anat nombril m.

navigate ['nævɪgeɪt] vi naviguer; − vt (boat) diriger, piloter; (river) naviguer sur. ◆**navigable** a (river) navigable; (seaworthy) en état de naviguer. ◆**navi'gation** n navigation f. ◆**navigator** n Av navigateur m.

navvy ['nævɪ] n (labourer) terrassier m.

navy ['neɪvɪ] n marine f; − a n. (blue) bleu marine inv.

Nazi ['nɑːtsɪ] a & n Pol Hist nazi, -ie (mf).

near [nɪər] adv (-er, -est) près; **quite n., n. at hand** tout près; **to draw n.** (s')approcher (to de); (of date) approcher; **to come n. to being killed/etc** faillir être tué/etc; **n. enough** (more or less) Fam plus ou moins; − prep (-er, -est) n. (to) près de; **n. the bed** près du lit; **to be n. (to) victory/death** frôler la victoire/la mort; **the end** vers la fin; − a (-er, -est) proche; (likeness) fidèle; **the nearest hospital** l'hôpital le plus proche; **the nearest way** la route la plus directe; **in the n. future** dans un avenir proche; **to the nearest franc** (to calculate) au franc supérieur (or inférieur; (to round up or down) au franc supérieur or inférieur; **n. side** Aut côté m gauche, Am côté m droit; − vt (approach) approcher de; **nearing completion** près d'être achevé. ◆**near'by** adv tout près; − ['nɪəbaɪ] a proche. ◆**nearness** n (in space, time) proximité f.

nearly ['nɪəlɪ] adv presque; **she (very) n. fell** elle a failli tomber; **not n. as clever/etc** as loin d'être aussi intelligent/etc que.

neat [niːt] a (-er, -est) (clothes, work) soigné,

propre, net; (room) ordonné, bien rangé; (style) élégant; (pretty) Fam joli, beau; (pleasant) Fam agréable; **to drink one's whisky/etc n.** prendre son whisky/etc sec. ◆**-ly** adv avec soin; (skilfully) habilement. ◆**-ness** n netteté f; (of room) ordre m.

necessary ['nesɪs(ə)rɪ] a nécessaire; **it's n. to do it** il est nécessaire de faire, il faut faire; **to make it n. for s.o. to do** mettre qn dans la nécessité de faire; **to do what's n.** faire le Fam faire le nécessaire (for pour); − npl **the necessaries** (food etc) l'indispensable m. ◆**nece'ssarily** adv nécessairement.

necessity [nɪ'sesɪtɪ] n (obligation, need) nécessité f; (poverty) indigence f; **there's no n. for you to do that** tu n'es pas obligé de faire cela; **of n.** nécessairement; **to be a n.** être indispensable; **the (bare) necessities** (strict) nécessaire. ◆**necessitate** vt nécessiter.

neck¹ [nek] n Anat cou m; (of dress, horse) encolure f; (of bottle) col m; **low n.** (of dress) décolleté m; **n. and n.** Sp à égalité. ◆**necklace** n collier m. ◆**neckline** n encolure f. ◆**necktie** n cravate f.

neck² [nek] vi (kiss etc) Fam se peloter.

nectarine ['nektərɪn] n (fruit) nectarine f, brugnon m.

née [neɪ] adv née; **n. Dupont** née Dupont.

need [niːd] n 1 (necessity, want, poverty) besoin m; **in n.** dans le besoin; **to be in n. of** avoir besoin de; **there's no n. (for you) to do** tu n'as pas besoin de faire; **if n. be** si besoin est, s'il le faut; − vt avoir besoin de; **you n. it** tu en as besoin, il te le faut; **it needs an army to do, an army is needed to do** il faut une armée pour faire; **this sport needs patience** ce sport demande de la patience; **her hair needs cutting** il faut qu'elle se fasse couper les cheveux. 2 v aux **n. he wait?** est-il obligé d'attendre?, a-t-il besoin d'attendre?; **I needn't have rushed** ce n'était pas la peine de me presser; **I n. hardly say that . . .** je n'ai guère besoin de dire que . . . . ◆**needless** a inutile. ◆**needlessly** adv inutilement. ◆**needy** a (-ier, -iest) a nécessiteux.

needle ['niːd(ə)l] 1 n aiguille f; (of record player) saphir m. 2 vt (irritate) Fam agacer. ◆**needlework** n couture f, travaux mpl d'aiguille; (object) ouvrage m.

negate [nɪ'geɪt] vt (nullify) annuler; (deny) nier. ◆**negation** n (denial) & Gram négation f.

negative ['negətɪv] a négatif; − n Phot négatif m; (word) Gram négation f; (form)

Gram forme *f* négative; **to answer in the n.** répondre par la négative.

neglect [nɪ'glekt] *vt* (*person, health, work etc*) négliger; (*garden, car etc*) ne pas s'occuper de; (*duty*) manquer à; (*rule*) désobéir à, méconnaître; **to n. to do** négliger de faire; − *n* (*of person*) manque *m* de soins (*of envers*); (*of rule*) désobéissance *f* (**of** à); (*of duty*) manquement *m* (**of** à); (*carelessness*) négligence *f*; **in a state of n.** (*garden, house etc*) mal tenu. ◆**neglected** *a* (*appearance, person*) négligé; (*garden, house etc*) mal tenu; **to feel n.** sentir qu'on vous néglige. ◆**neglectful** *a* négligent; **to be n. of** négliger.

negligent ['neglɪdʒənt] *a* négligent. ◆**negligence** *n* négligence *f*. ◆**negligently** *adv* négligemment.

negligible ['neglɪdʒəb(ə)l] *a* négligeable.

negotiate [nɪ'gəʊʃɪeɪt] **1** *vti Fin Pol* négocier. **2** *vt* (*fence, obstacle*) franchir; (*bend*) *Aut* négocier. ◆**negotiable** *a Fin* négociable. ◆**negoti'ation** *n* négociation *f*; **in n.** with en pourparlers avec. ◆**nego-tiator** *n* négociateur, -trice *mf*.

Negro ['niːgrəʊ] *n* (*pl -oes*) (*man*) Noir *m*; (*woman*) Noire *f*; − *a* noir; (*art, sculpture etc*) nègre. ◆**Negress** *n* Noire *f*.

neigh [neɪ] *vi* (*of horse*) hennir; − *n* hennissement *m*.

neighbour ['neɪbər] *n* voisin, -ine *mf*. ◆**neighbourhood** *n* (*neighbours*) voisinage *m*; (*district*) quartier *m*, voisinage *m*; (*region*) région *f*; **in the n. of ten pounds** dans les dix livres. ◆**neighbouring** *a* avoisinant. ◆**neighbourly** *a* (*feeling etc*) de bon voisinage, amical; **they're n.** (*people*) ils sont bons voisins.

neither ['naɪðər, *Am* 'niːðər] *adv* ni; **n. ... nor** ni ... ni; **n. you nor me** ni toi ni moi; **he n. sings nor dances** il ne chante ni ne danse; − *conj* (*not either*) (ne) ... non plus; **n. shall I go** je n'y irai pas non plus; − *pron* **n.** (**of them**) ni l'un(e) ni l'autre, aucun(e) (des deux).

neo- ['niːəʊ] *pref* néo-.

neon ['niːɒn] *n* (*gas*) néon *m*; − *a* (*lighting etc*) au néon.

nephew ['nevju, 'nefju] *n* neveu *m*.

nepotism ['nepətɪz(ə)m] *n* népotisme *m*.

nerve [nɜːv] *n* nerf *m*; (*courage*) *Fig* courage *m* (**to do** de faire); (*confidence*) assurance *f*; (*calm*) sang-froid *m*; (*cheek*) *Fam* culot *m* (**to do** de faire); **you get on my nerves** *Fam*

tu me portes *or* me tapes sur les nerfs; **to have** (**an attack of**) **nerves** (*fear, anxiety*) avoir le trac; **a bundle** *or* **mass** *or* **bag of nerves** (*person*) *Fam* un paquet de nerfs; **to have bad nerves** être nerveux; − *a* (*cell, centre*) nerveux. ◆**n.-racking** *a* éprouvant pour les nerfs. ◆**nervous** *a* (*tense*) & *Anat* nerveux; (*worried*) inquiet (**about** de); **to be** *or* **feel n.** (*ill-at-ease*) se sentir mal à l'aise; (*before exam etc*) avoir le trac. ◆**nervously** *adv* nerveusement; (*worriedly*) avec inquiétude. ◆**nervousness** *n* nervosité *f*; (*fear*) trac *m*. ◆**nervy** *a* (*-ier, -iest*) *Fam* (*anxious*) nerveux; (*brash*) *Am* culotté.

nest [nest] *n* nid *m*; **n. egg** (*money saved*) pécule *m*; **n. of tables** table *f* gigogne; − *vi* (*of bird*) (se) nicher.

nestle ['nes(ə)l] *vi* se pelotonner (**up to** contre); **a village nestling in** (*forest, valley etc*) un village niché dans.

net [net] **1** *n* filet *m*; **n. curtain** voilage *m*; − *vt* (*-tt-*) (*fish*) prendre au filet. **2** *a* (*profit, weight etc*) net *inv*; − *vt* (*-tt-*) (*of person, firm etc*) gagner net; **this venture netted him** *or* **her** .... cette entreprise lui a rapporté .... ◆**netting** *n* (*nets*) filets *mpl*; (*mesh*) mailles *fpl*; (*fabric*) voile *m*; (*wire*) n. treillis *m*.

Netherlands (the) [ðə'neðələndz] *npl* les Pays-Bas *mpl*.

nettle ['net(ə)l] *n Bot* ortie *f*.

network ['netwɜːk] *n* réseau *m*.

neurosis, *pl* **-oses** [njʊə'rəʊsɪs, -əʊsiːz] *n* névrose *f*. ◆**neurotic** *a* & *n* névrosé, -ée (*mf*).

neuter ['njuːtər] **1** *a* & *n Gram* neutre (*m*). **2** *vt* (*cat etc*) châtrer.

neutral ['njuːtrəl] *a* neutre; (*policy*) de neutralité; − *n El* neutre *m*; **in n.** (**gear**) *Aut* au point mort. ◆**neu'trality** *n* neutralité *f*. ◆**neutralize** *vt* neutraliser.

never ['nevər] *adv* **1** (*not ever*) (ne) ... jamais; **she n. lies** elle ne ment jamais; **n. in** (**all**) **my life** jamais de ma vie; **n. again** plus jamais. **2** (*certainly not*) *Fam* **I n. did it** je ne l'ai pas fait. ◆**n.-'ending** *a* interminable.

nevertheless [nevəðə'les] *adv* néanmoins, quand même.

new [njuː] *a* (*-er, -est*) nouveau; (*brand-new*) neuf; **to be n. to** (*job*) être nouveau dans; (*city*) être un nouveau-venu dans, être fraîchement installé dans; **a n. boy** *Sch* un nouveau; **what's n.?** *Fam* quoi de neuf?; **a n. glass/pen/**etc (*different*) un autre verre/stylo/etc; **to break n. ground** innover; **n. look** style *m* nouveau; **as good as**

n. comme neuf; **a n.-laid egg** un œuf du jour; **a n.-born baby** un nouveau-né, une nouveau-née. ◆**newcomer** n nouveau-venu m, nouvelle-venue f. ◆**new-'fangled** a Pej moderne. ◆**new-found** a nouveau. ◆**newly** adv (recently) nouvellement, fraîchement; **the n.-weds** les nouveaux mariés. ◆**newness** n (condition) état m neuf; (novelty) nouveauté f.

news [njuːz] n nouvelle(s) f(pl); Journ Rad TV informations fpl, actualités fpl; sports/etc n. (newspaper column) chronique f or rubrique f sportive/etc; **a piece of n.,** some n. une nouvelle; Journ Rad TV une information; **n. headlines** titres mpl de l'actualité; **n. flash** flash m. ◆**newsagent** n marchand, -ande mf de journaux. ◆**newsboy** n vendeur m de journaux. ◆**newscaster** n présentateur, -trice mf. ◆**newsletter** n (of club, group etc) bulletin m. ◆**newspaper** n journal m. ◆**newsreader** n présentateur, -trice mf. ◆**newsreel** n Cin actualités fpl. ◆**newsworthy** a digne de faire l'objet d'un reportage. ◆**newsy** a (-ier, -iest) Fam plein de nouvelles.

newt [njuːt] n (animal) triton m.

New Zealand [njuːˈziːlənd] n Nouvelle-Zélande f; – a néo-zélandais. ◆**New Zealander** n Néo-Zélandais, -aise mf.

next [nekst] a prochain; (room, house) d'à-côté, voisin; (following) suivant; **n. month** (in the future) le mois prochain; **he returned the n. month** (in the past) il revint le mois suivant; **the n. day** le lendemain; **the n. morning** le lendemain matin; **within the n. ten days** d'ici (à) dix jours, dans un délai de dix jours; **(by) this time n. week** d'ici (à) la semaine prochaine; **you're** n. c'est ton tour; **n. (please)!** (au) suivant!; **the n. thing to do is . . .** ce qu'il faut faire ensuite c'est . . . ; **the n. size (up)** la taille au-dessus; **to live/etc n. door** habiter/etc à côté (to de); **n.-door neighbour/room** voisin m/pièce f d'à-côté; – n (in series etc) suivant, -ante mf; – adv (afterwards) ensuite, après; (now) maintenant; **when you come in.** la prochaine fois que tu viendras; **the n. best solution** la seconde solution; – prep **n. to** (beside) à côté de; **n. to nothing** presque rien.

NHS [eneɪtʃˈes] abbr = National Health Service.

nib [nɪb] n (of pen) plume f, bec m.

nibble ['nɪb(ə)l] vti (eat) grignoter; (bite) mordiller.

nice [naɪs] a (-er, -est) (pleasant) agréable; (charming) charmant, gentil; (good) bon; (fine) beau; (pretty) joli; (kind) gentil (to avec); (respectable) bien; (subtle) délicat; **it's n. here** c'est bien ici; **n. and easy/warm/etc** (very) bien facile/chaud/etc. ◆**n.-'looking** a beau, joli. ◆**nicely** adv agréablement; (kindly) gentiment; (well) bien. ◆**niceties** ['naɪsətɪz] npl (pleasant things) agréments mpl; (subtleties) subtilités fpl.

niche [niːʃ, nɪtʃ] n **1** (recess) niche f. **2** (job) (bonne) situation f; (direction) voie f; **to make a n. for oneself** faire son trou.

nick [nɪk] **1** n (on skin, wood) entaille f; (in blade, crockery) brèche f. **2** n (prison) Sl taule f; – vt (steal, arrest) Sl piquer. **3** n **in the n. of time** juste à temps; **in good n.** Sl en bon état.

nickel ['nɪk(ə)l] n (metal) nickel m; (coin) Am pièce f de cinq cents.

nickname ['nɪkneɪm] n (informal name) surnom m; (short form) diminutif m; – vt surnommer.

niece [niːs] n nièce f.

nifty ['nɪftɪ] a (-ier, -iest) (stylish) chic inv; (skilful) habile; (fast) rapide.

Nigeria [naɪˈdʒɪərɪə] n Nigéria m or f. ◆**Nigerian** a & n nigérian, -ane (mf).

niggardly ['nɪgədlɪ] a (person) avare; (amount) mesquin.

niggling ['nɪglɪŋ] a (trifling) insignifiant; (irksome) irritant; (doubt) persistant.

night [naɪt] n nuit f; (evening) soir m; Th soirée f; **last n.** (evening) hier soir; (night) la nuit dernière; **to have an early/late n.** se coucher tôt/tard; **to have a good n.** (sleep well) bien dormir; **first n.** Th première f; – a (work etc) de nuit; (life) nocturne; **n. school** cours mpl du soir; **n. watchman** veilleur m de nuit. ◆**nightcap** n (drink) boisson f (alcoolisée ou chaude prise avant de se coucher). ◆**nightclub** n boîte f de nuit. ◆**nightdress** n, ◆**nightgown** n, Fam ◆**nightie** n (woman's) chemise f de nuit. ◆**nightfall** n at n. à la tombée de la nuit. ◆**nightlight** n veilleuse f. ◆**nighttime** n nuit f.

nightingale ['naɪtɪŋgeɪl] n rossignol m.

nightly ['naɪtlɪ] adv chaque nuit or soir; – a de chaque nuit or soir.

nil [nɪl] n (nothing) zéro m; **the risk/result/etc is n.** le risque/résultat/etc est nul.

nimble ['nɪmb(ə)l] a (-er, -est) agile.

nincompoop ['nıŋkəmpuːp] n Fam imbécile mf.

nine [naın] a & n neuf (m). ◆**nine'teen** a & n dix-neuf (m). ◆**nine'teenth** a & n dix-neuvième (mf). ◆**ninetieth** a & n quatre-vingt-dixième (mf). ◆**ninety** a & n quatre-vingt-dix (m). ◆**ninth** a & n neuvième (mf); **a n.** un neuvième.

nip [nıp] 1 vt (-pp-) (pinch, bite) pincer; **to n. in the bud** Fig étouffer dans l'œuf; − n pinçon m; **there's a n. in the air** ça pince. 2 vi (-pp-) (dash) Fam **to n. round to s.o.** courir or faire un saut chez qn; **to n. in/out** entrer/sortir un instant.

nipper ['nıpər] n (child) Fam gosse mf.

nipple ['nıp(ə)l] n bout m de sein, mamelon m; (teat on bottle) Am tétine f.

nippy ['nıpı] a 1 (-ier, -iest) (chilly) frais; **it's n.** (weather) ça pince. 2 **to be n.** (about it) (quick) Fam faire vite.

nit [nıt] n 1 (fool) Fam idiot, -ote mf. 2 (of louse) lente f. ◆**nitwit** n (fool) Fam idiot, -ote mf.

nitrogen ['naıtrədʒən] n azote m.

nitty-gritty [nıtı'grıtı] n **to get down to the n.-gritty** Fam en venir au fond du problème.

no [nəʊ] adv & n non (m inv); **no!** non!; **no more than ten/a kilo/etc** pas plus de dix/d'un kilo/etc; **no more time/etc** plus de temps/etc; **I have no more time** je n'ai plus de temps; **no more than you** pas plus que vous; **you can do no better** tu ne peux pas faire mieux; **the noes** Pol les non; − a aucun(e); pas de; **I've** (got) or **I have no idea** je n'ai aucune idée; **no child came** aucun enfant n'est venu; **I've** (got) or **I have no time/etc** je n'ai pas de temps/etc; **of no importance/value/etc** sans importance/valeur/etc; **with no gloves/etc** on sans gants/etc; **there's no knowing . . .** impossible de savoir . . . ; **'no smoking'** 'défense de fumer'; **no way!** Am Fam pas question!; **no one = nobody.**

noble ['nəʊb(ə)l] a (-er, -est) noble; (building) majestueux. ◆**nobleman** n (pl -men) noble m. ◆**noblewoman** n (pl -women) noble f. ◆**no'bility** n (character, class) noblesse f.

nobody ['nəʊbɒdı] pron (ne) . . . personne; **n. came** personne n'est venu; **he knows n.** il ne connaît personne; **n.!** personne!; − n a une nullité.

nocturnal [nɒk'tɜːn(ə)l] a nocturne.

nod [nɒd] 1 vti (-dd-) **to n.** (one's head) incliner la tête, faire un signe de tête; − n

inclination f or signe m de tête. 2 vi (-dd-) **to n. off** (go to sleep) s'assoupir.

noise [nɔız] n bruit m; (of bell, drum) son m; **to make a n.** faire du bruit. ◆**noisily** adv bruyamment. ◆**noisy** a (-ier, -iest) (person, street etc) bruyant.

nomad ['nəʊmæd] n nomade mf. ◆**no'madic** a nomade.

nominal ['nɒmın(ə)l] a (value, fee etc) nominal; (head, ruler) de nom.

nominate ['nɒmıneıt] vt Pol désigner, proposer (for comme candidat à); (appoint) désigner, nommer. ◆**nomi'nation** n désignation f or proposition f de candidat; (appointment) nomination f. ◆**nomi'nee** n (candidate) candidat m.

non- [nɒn] pref non-.

nonchalant ['nɒnʃələnt] a nonchalant.

noncommissioned [nɒnkə'mıʃ(ə)nd] a **n. officer** Mil sous-officier m.

non-committal [nɒnkə'mıt(ə)l] a (answer, person) évasif.

nonconformist [nɒnkən'fɔːmıst] a & n non-conformiste (mf).

nondescript ['nɒndıskrıpt] a indéfinissable; Pej médiocre.

none [nʌn] pron aucun(e) mf; (in filling a form) néant; **n. of them** aucun d'eux; **she has n.** (at all) elle n'en a pas (du tout); **n.** (at all) **came** pas un(e) seul(e) n'est venu(e); **n. can tell** personne ne peut le dire; **n. of the cake/etc** pas une seule partie du gâteau/etc; **n. of the trees/etc** aucun arbre/etc, aucun des arbres/etc; **n. of it** or **this** rien (de ceci); − adv **n. too hot/etc** pas tellement chaud/etc; **he's** . . . **the happier/wiser/etc** il n'en est pas plus heureux/sage/etc; **n. the less** néanmoins. ◆**nonethe'less** adv néanmoins.

nonentity [nɒ'nentıtı] n (person) nullité f.

non-existent [nɒnıg'zıstənt] a inexistant.

non-fiction [nɒn'fıkʃ(ə)n] n littérature f non-romanesque; (in library) ouvrages mpl généraux.

non-flammable [nɒn'flæməb(ə)l] a ininflammable.

nonplus [nɒn'plʌs] vt (-ss-) dérouter.

nonsense ['nɒnsəns] n absurdités fpl; **that's n.** c'est absurde. ◆**non'sensical** a absurde.

non-smoker [nɒn'sməʊkər] n (person) non-fumeur, -euse mf; (compartment) Rail compartiment m non-fumeurs.

non-stick [nɒn'stık] a (pan) anti-adhésif, qui n'attache pas.

non-stop [nɒn'stɒp] a sans arrêt; (train,

flight) direct; *– adv* (*to work etc*) sans arrêt; (*to fly*) sans escale.

noodles ['nuːd(ə)lz] *npl* nouilles *fpl*; (*in soup*) vermicelle(s) *m(pl)*.

nook [nʊk] *n* coin *m*; **in every n. and cranny** dans tous les coins (et recoins).

noon [nuːn] *n* midi *m*; **at n.** à midi; *– a* (*sun etc*) de midi.

noose [nuːs] *n* (*loop*) nœud *m* coulant; (*of hangman*) corde *f.*

nor [nɔːr] *conj* ni; **neither you n.** me ni toi ni moi; **she neither drinks n. smokes** elle ne fume ni ne boit; **n. do I, n. can I** *etc* (ni) moi non plus; **n. will I (go)** je n'y irai pas non plus.

norm [nɔːm] *n* norme *f.*

normal ['nɔːm(ə)l] *a* normal; *– n* **above n.** au-dessus de la normale. **◆nor'mality** *n* normalité *f.* **◆normalize** *vt* normaliser. **◆normally** *adv* normalement.

Norman ['nɔːmən] *a n* normand.

north [nɔːθ] *n* nord *m*; *– a* (*coast*) nord *inv*; (*wind*) du nord; **to be n. of** être au nord de; **N. America/Africa** Amérique *f*/Afrique *f* du Nord; **N. American** *a & n* nord-américain, -aine (*mf*); *– adv* **n** & **n.** vers le nord. **◆northbound** *a* (*carriageway*) nord; (*traffic*) en direction du nord. **◆north-'east** *n* & *a* nord-est *m* & *a inv*. **◆northerly** *a* (*point*) nord *inv*; (*direction, wind*) du nord. **◆northern** *a* (*coast*) nord *inv*; (*town*) du nord; **N. France** le Nord de la France; **N. Europe** Europe *f* du Nord; **N. Ireland** Irlande *f* du Nord. **◆northerner** *n* habitant, -ante *mf* du Nord. **◆northward(s)** *a & adv* vers le nord. **◆north-'west** *n* & *a* nord-ouest *m* & *a inv*.

Norway ['nɔːweɪ] *n* Norvège *f.* **◆Nor'wegian** *a & n* norvégien, -ienne (*mf*); *– n* (*language*) norvégien *m.*

nose [nəʊz] *n* nez *m*; **her n. is bleeding** elle saigne du nez; **to turn one's n. up** *Fig* faire le dégoûté (**at** devant); *– vi* **to n. about** (*pry*) *Fam* fouiner. **◆nosebleed** *n* saignement *m* de nez. **◆nosedive** *n* *Av* piqué *m*; (*in prices*) chute *f.*

nos(e)y ['nəʊzɪ] *a* (-ier, -iest) fouineur, indiscret; **n. parker** fouineur, -euse *mf.*

nosh [nɒʃ] *vi* *Fam* (*eat heavily*) bouffer; (*nibble*) grignoter (entre les repas); *– n* (*food*) *Fam* bouffe *f.*

nostalgia [nɒ'stældʒə] *n* nostalgie *f.* **◆nostalgic** *a* nostalgique.

nostril ['nɒstr(ə)l] *n* (*of person*) narine *f*; (*of horse*) naseau *m.*

not [nɒt] *adv* **1** (ne) . . . pas; **he's n. there, he**

isn't there il n'est pas là; **n. yet** pas encore; **why n.?** pourquoi pas?; **n. one reply/etc** pas une seule réponse/*etc*; **n. at all** pas du tout; (*after 'thank you'*) je vous en prie. **2** non; **I think/hope n.** je pense/j'espère que non; **n. guilty** non coupable; **isn't she?, don't you?** *etc* non?

notable ['nəʊtəb(ə)l] *a* (*remarkable*) notable; *– n* (*person*) notable *m.* **◆notably** *adv* (*noticeably*) notablement; (*particularly*) notamment.

notary ['nəʊtərɪ] *n* notaire *m.*

notation [nəʊ'teɪʃ(ə)n] *n* notation *f.*

notch [nɒtʃ] **1** *n* (*in wood etc*) entaille *f*, encoche *f*; (*in belt, wheel*) cran *m.* **2** *vt* **to n. up** (*a score*) marquer; (*a victory*) enregistrer.

note [nəʊt] *n* (*written comment, tone etc*) & *Mus* note *f*; (*summary, preface*) notice *f*; (*banknote*) billet *m*; (*piano key*) touche *f*; (*message, letter*) petit mot *m*; **to take (a n. of, make a n. of** prendre note de; **of n.** (*athlete, actor etc*) éminent; *– vt* (*take note of*) noter; (*notice*) remarquer, noter; **to n. down** noter. **◆notebook** *n* carnet *m*; *Sch* cahier *m*; (*pad*) bloc-notes *m.* **◆notepad** *n* bloc-notes *m.* **◆notepaper** *n* papier *m* à lettres.

noted ['nəʊtɪd] *a* (*author etc*) éminent; **to be n. for** être connu pour.

noteworthy ['nəʊtwɜːðɪ] *a* notable.

nothing ['nʌθɪŋ] *pron* (ne) . . . rien; **he knows n.** il ne sait rien; **n. to do/eat/etc** rien à faire/manger/*etc*; **n. big/etc** rien de grand/*etc*; **n. much** pas grand-chose; **I've got n. to do with it** je n'y suis pour rien; **I can do n. (about it)** je n'y peux rien; **to come to n.** (*of effort etc*) ne rien donner; **there's n. like it** il n'y a rien de tel; **for n.** (*in vain, free of charge*) pour rien; *– adv* **to look n. like s.o.** ne ressembler nullement à qn; **to be as large/etc** loin d'être aussi grand/*etc*; *– n a* (*mere*) **n.** (*person*) une nullité; (*thing*) un rien. **◆–ness** *n* (*void*) néant *m.*

notice ['nəʊtɪs] *n* (*notification*) avis *m*; *Journ* annonce *f*; (*sign*) pancarte *f*, écriteau *m*; (*poster*) affiche *f*; (*review of film etc*) critique *f*; (*attention*) attention *f*; (*knowledge*) connaissance *f*; (*advance*) **n.** (*of departure etc*) préavis *m*; **to give (in) one's n.** (*resignation*) donner sa démission; **to give s.o. n. of** (*inform of*) avertir qn de; **to take n.** faire attention (**of** à); **to bring sth to s.o.'s n.** porter qch à la connaissance de qn; **until further n.** jusqu'à nouvel ordre; **at short n.** à bref délai; **n. board** tableau *m* d'affichage; — *vt* (*perceive*) remarquer (*qn*); (*fact, trick, danger*) s'apercevoir de, remarquer; **I n. that** je m'aperçois que. **◆—able** *a* visible, perceptible; **that's n.** ça se voit; **she's n.** elle se fait remarquer.

notify ['nəʊtɪfaɪ] *vt* (*inform*) aviser (**s.o. of sth qn de qch**); (*announce*) notifier (**to à**). **◆notifi'cation** *n* annonce *f*, avis *m*.

notion ['nəʊʃ(ə)n] **1** *n* (*thought*) idée *f*; (*awareness*) notion *f*; **some n. of** (*knowledge*) quelques notions de. **2** *npl* (*sewing articles*) *Am* mercerie *f*.

notorious [nəʊˈtɔːrɪəs] *a* (*event, person etc*) tristement célèbre; (*stupidity, criminal*) notoire. **◆notoriety** [-əˈraɪətɪ] *n* (*triste*) notoriété *f*.

notwithstanding [nɒtwɪðˈstændɪŋ] *prep* malgré; — *adv* tout de même.

nougat ['nuːgɑː, 'nʌgæt] *n* nougat *m*.

nought [nɔːt] *n* *Math* zéro *m*.

noun [naʊn] *n* *Gram* nom *m*.

nourish ['nʌrɪʃ] *vt* nourrir. **◆—ing** *a* nourrissant. **◆—ment** *n* nourriture *f*.

novel ['nɒv(ə)l] **1** *n* *Liter* roman *m*. **2** *a* (*new*) nouveau, original. **◆novelist** *n* romancier, -ière *mf*. **◆novelty** *n* (*newness, object, idea*) nouveauté *f*.

November [nəʊˈvembər] *n* novembre *m*.

novice ['nɒvɪs] *n* novice *mf* (**at** en).

now [naʊ] *adv* maintenant; **just n., right n.** en ce moment; **I saw her just n.** je l'ai vue à l'instant; **for n.** pour le moment; **even n.** encore maintenant; **from n. on** désormais, à partir de maintenant; **until n., up to n.** jusqu'ici; **before n.** avant; **n. and then** de temps à autre; **n. hot, n. cold** tantôt chaud, tantôt froid; **n. (then)!** bon!, alors!; (*telling s.o. off*) allons!; **n. it happened that . . .** or il advint que . . . ; — *conj* **n. (that)** maintenant que. **◆nowadays** *adv* aujourd'hui, de nos jours.

noway ['nəʊweɪ] *adv* *Am* nullement.

nowhere ['nəʊweər] *adv* nulle part; **n. else** nulle part ailleurs; **it's n. I know** ce n'est pas un endroit que je connais; **n. near the house** loin de la maison; **n. near enough** loin d'être assez.

nozzle ['nɒz(ə)l] *n* (*of hose*) jet *m*, lance *f* (à eau); (*of syringe, tube*) embout *m*.

nth [enθ] *a* nième.

nuance ['njuːɑːns] *n* (*of meaning, colour etc*) nuance *f*.

nub [nʌb] *n* (*of problem*) cœur *m*.

nuclear ['njuːklɪər] *a* nucléaire; **n. scientist** spécialiste *mf* du nucléaire, atomiste *mf*.

nucleus, *pl* **-clei** ['njuːklɪəs, -klaɪ] *n* noyau *m*.

nude [njuːd] *a* nu; — *n* (*female or male figure*) nu *m*; **in the n.** (tout) nu. **◆nudism** *n* nudisme *m*, naturisme *m*. **◆nudist** *n* nudiste *mf*, naturiste *mf*; — *a* (*camp*) de nudistes, de naturistes. **◆nudity** *n* nudité *f*.

nudge [nʌdʒ] *vt* pousser du coude; — *n* coup *m* de coude.

nugget ['nʌgɪt] *n* (*of gold etc*) pépite *f*.

nuisance ['njuːsəns] *n* (*annoyance*) embêtement *m*; (*person*) peste *f*; **that's a n.** c'est embêtant; **he's being a n., he's making a n. of himself** il nous embête, il m'embête *etc*.

null [nʌl] *a* **n. (and void)** nul (et non avenu). **◆nullify** *vt* infirmer.

numb [nʌm] *a* (*stiff*) engourdi; *Fig* paralysé; — *vt* engourdir; *Fig* paralyser.

number ['nʌmbər] *n* nombre *m*; (*of page, house, newspaper etc*) numéro *m*; **a dance/song n.** un numéro de danse/de chant; **a/any n. of** un certain/grand nombre de; **n. plate** (*of vehicle*) plaque *f* d'immatriculation; — *vt* (*page etc*) numéroter; (*include, count*) compter; **they n. eight** ils sont au nombre de huit. **◆—ing** *n* numérotage *m*.

numeral ['njuːm(ə)rəl] *n* chiffre *m*; — *a* numéral. **◆nu'merical** *a* numérique. **◆numerous** *a* nombreux.

numerate ['njuːm(ə)rət] *a* (*person*) qui sait compter.

nun [nʌn] *n* religieuse *f*.

nurs/e [nɜːs] **1** *n* infirmière *f*; (*nanny*) nurse *f*; **(male) n.** infirmier *m*. **2** *vt* (*look after*) soigner; (*cradle*) bercer; (*suckle*) nourrir; (*a grudge etc*) *Fig* nourrir; (*support, encourage*) *Fig* épauler (*qn*). **◆—ing** *a* (*mother*) qui allaite; the **n. staff** le personnel infirmier; — *n* (*care*) soins *mpl*; (*job*) profession *f* d'infirmière ou d'infirmier; **home** clinique *f*. **◆nursemaid** *n* bonne *f* d'enfants.

nursery ['nɜːsərɪ] *n* (*room*) chambre *f* d'enfants; (*for plants, trees*) pépinière *f*; **(day) n.** (*school etc*) crèche *f*, garderie *f*; **n. rhyme** chanson *f* enfantine; **n. school** école *f* maternelle.

nurture ['nɜːtʃər] *vt* (*educate*) éduquer.

nut¹ [nʌt] *n* (*fruit*) fruit *m* à coque; (*walnut*) noix *f*; (*hazelnut*) noisette *f*; (*peanut*) cacah(o)uète *f*; **Brazil/cashew n.** noix *f* du Brésil/de cajou. **◆nutcracker(s)** *n(pl)* casse-noix *m* *inv*. **◆nutshell** *n* coquille *f* de noix; **in a n.** *Fig* en un mot.

nut² [nʌt] *n* **1** (*for bolt*) *Tech* écrou *m*. **2**

(head) *Sl* caboche *f*. **3** (*person*) *Sl* cinglé, -ée *mf*; **to be nuts** *Sl* être cinglé. ◆**nutcase** *n* cinglé, -ée *mf*. ◆**nutty** *a* (**-ier, -iest**) *Sl* cinglé.

nutmeg ['nʌtmeg] *n* muscade *f*.

nutritious [njuːˈtrɪʃəs] *a* nutritif. ◆'**nutri-** **ent** *n* élément *m* nutritif. ◆**nutrition** *n* nutrition *f*.

nylon ['naɪlɒn] *n* nylon *m*; *pl* (*stockings*) bas *mpl* nylon.

nymph [nɪmf] *n* nymphe *f*. ◆**nympho-** **'maniac** *n Pej* nymphomane *f*.

O

O, o [əʊ] *n* O, o *m*.

oaf [əʊf] *n* rustre *m*. ◆**oafish** *a* (*behaviour*) de rustre.

oak [əʊk] *n* (*tree, wood*) chêne *m*.

OAP [əʊeɪˈpiː] *n abbr* (*old age pensioner*) retraité, -ée *mf*.

oar [ɔːr] *n* aviron *m*, rame *f*.

oasis, *pl* **oases** [əʊˈeɪsɪs, əʊˈeɪsiːz] *n* oasis *f*.

oath [əʊθ] *n* (*pl* **-s** [əʊðz]) (*promise*) serment *m*; (*profanity*) juron *m*; **to take an o. to do** faire le serment de faire.

oats [əʊts] *npl* avoine *f*. ◆**oatmeal** *n* flocons *mpl* d'avoine.

obedient [əˈbiːdɪənt] *a* obéissant. ◆**obe-** **dience** *n* obéissance *f* (**to** à). ◆**obediently** *adv* docilement.

obelisk ['ɒbəlɪsk] *n* (*monument*) obélisque *m*.

obese [əʊˈbiːs] *a* obèse. ◆**obesity** *n* obésité *f*.

obey [əˈbeɪ] *vt* obéir à; **to be obeyed** être obéi; – *vi* obéir.

obituary [əˈbɪtʃʊərɪ] *n* nécrologie *f*.

object¹ ['ɒbdʒɪkt] *n* (*thing*) objet *m*; (*aim*) but *m*, objet *m*; *Gram* complément *m* (d'objet); **with the o. of** dans le but de; **that's no o.** (*no problem*) ça ne pose pas de problème; **price no o.** prix *m* indifférent.

object² [əbˈdʒekt] *vi* **to o. to sth/s.o.** désap- prouver qch/qn; **I o. to you(r) doing that** ça me gêne que tu fasses ça; **I o.!** je proteste!; **she didn't o. when** ... elle n'a fait aucune objection quand ...; – *vt* **to o. that** objecter que. ◆**objection** *n* objection *f*; **I've got no o.** ça ne me gêne pas, je n'y vois pas d'objection *or* d'inconvénient. ◆**objectionable** *a* très désagréable. ◆**objector** *n* opposant, -ante *mf* (**to** à); **conscientious o.** objecteur *m* de conscience. **objective** [əbˈdʒektɪv] **1** *a* (*opinion etc*) objectif. **2** *n* (*aim, target*) objectif *m*. ◆**objectively** *adv* objectivement. ◆**ob-** **jec'tivity** *n* objectivité *f*.

obligate ['ɒblɪgeɪt] *vt* contraindre (**to do** à faire). ◆**obli'gation** *n* obligation *f*; (*debt*) dette *f*; **under an o. to do** dans l'obligation de faire; **under an o. to s.o.** redevable à qn (**for** de). ◆o'**bligatory** *a* (*compulsory*) obligatoire; (*imposed by custom*) de rigueur.

oblig/e [əˈblaɪdʒ] *vt* **1** (*compel*) obliger (**s.o.** **to do** qn à faire); **obliged to do** obligé de faire. **2** (*help*) rendre service à, faire plaisir à; **obliged to s.o.** reconnaissant à qn (**for** de); **much obliged!** merci infiniment! ◆**—ing** *a* (*kind*) obligeant. ◆**—ingly** *adv* obligeamment.

oblique [əˈbliːk] *a* oblique; (*reference*) *Fig* indirect.

obliterate [əˈblɪtəreɪt] *vt* effacer. ◆**oblite-** **'ration** *n* effacement *m*.

oblivion [əˈblɪvɪən] *n* oubli *m*. ◆**oblivious** *a* inconscient (**to, of** de).

oblong ['ɒblɒŋ] *a* (*elongated*) oblong; (*rectangular*) rectangulaire; – *n* rectangle *m*.

obnoxious [əbˈnɒkʃəs] *a* odieux; (*smell*) nauséabond.

oboe ['əʊbəʊ] *n Mus* hautbois *m*.

obscene [əbˈsiːn] *a* obscène. ◆**obscenity** *n* obscénité *f*.

obscure [əbˈskjʊər] *a* (*reason, word, actor, life etc*) obscur; – *vt* (*hide*) cacher; (*confuse*) embrouiller, obscurcir. ◆**obscurely** *adv* obscurément. ◆**obscurity** *n* obscurité *f*.

obsequious [əbˈsiːkwɪəs] *a* obséquieux.

observe [əbˈzɜːv] *vt* (*notice, watch, respect*) observer; (*say*) (faire) remarquer (**that** que); **to o. the speed limit** respecter la limi- tation de vitesse. ◆**observance** *n* (*of rule etc*) observation *f*. ◆**observant** *a* observateur. ◆**obser'vation** *n* (*observing, remark*) observation *f*; (*by police*) surveil- lance *f*; **under o.** (*hospital patient*) en obser-

vation. ◆**observatory** n observatoire m.
◆**observer** n observateur, -trice mf.

obsess [əb'ses] vt obséder. ◆**obsession** n obsession f; **to have an o. with** or **about** avoir l'obsession de. ◆**obsessive** a (memory, idea) obsédant; (fear) obsessif; (neurotic) Psy obsessionnel; **to be o.** avoir l'obsession de.

obsolete ['ɒbsəli:t] a (out of date, super-seded) désuet, dépassé; (ticket) périmé; (machinery) archaïque. ◆**obso'lescent** a quelque peu désuet; (word) vieilli.

obstacle ['ɒbstək(ə)l] n obstacle m.

obstetrics [əb'stetrıks] n Med obstétrique f. ◆**obste'trician** n médecin m accoucheur.

obstinate ['ɒbstınət] a (person, resistance etc) obstiné, opiniâtre; (disease, pain) rebelle, opiniâtre. ◆**obstinacy** n obstination f. ◆**obstinately** adv obstinément.

obstreperous [əb'strepərəs] a turbulent.

obstruct [əb'strʌkt] vt (block) boucher; (hinder) entraver; (traffic) entraver, bloquer. ◆**obstruction** n (act, state) & Med Pol Sp obstruction f; (obstacle) obsta-cle m; (in pipe) bouchon m; (traffic jam) embouteillage m. ◆**obstructive** a **to be o.** faire de l'obstruction.

obtain [əb'teın] 1 vt obtenir. 2 vi (of practice etc) avoir cours. ◆—**able** a (available) disponible; (on sale) en vente.

obtrusive [əb'truːsıv] a (person) importun; (building etc) trop en évidence.

obtuse [əb'tjuːs] a (angle, mind) obtus.

obviate ['ɒbvıeıt] vt (necessity) éviter.

obvious ['ɒbvıəs] a évident; **he's the o. man to see** c'est évidemment l'homme qu'il faut voir. ◆—**ly** adv (evidently, of course) évidemment; (conspicuously) visiblement.

occasion [ə'keıʒ(ə)n] 1 n (time, opportunity) occasion f; (event, ceremony) évènement m; **on the o. of** à l'occasion de; **on o.** à l'occasion; **on several occasions** à plusieurs reprises or occasions. 2 n (cause) raison f, occasion f; – vt occasionner. ◆**occa-sional** a (event) qui a lieu de temps en temps; (rain, showers) intermittent; **she drinks the o. whisky** elle boit un whisky de temps en temps. ◆**occasionally** adv de temps en temps; **very o.** très peu souvent, rarement.

occult [ə'kʌlt] a occulte.

occupy ['ɒkjupaı] vt (house, time, space, post etc) occuper; **to keep oneself occupied** s'occuper (doing à faire). ◆**occupant** n (inhabitant) occupant, -ante mf. ◆**occu-'pation** n (activity) occupation f; (job) emploi m; (trade) métier m; (profession)

profession f; **the o. of** (action) l'occupation f de; **fit for o.** (house) habitable. ◆**occu-'pational** a (hazard) du métier; (disease) du travail. ◆**occupier** n (of house) occu-pant, -ante mf; Mil occupant m.

occur [ə'kɜːr] vi (-rr-) (happen) avoir lieu; (be found) se rencontrer; (arise) se présenter; **it occurs to me that . . .** il me vient à l'esprit que . . . ; **the idea occurred to her to . . .** l'idée lui est venue de . . . . ◆**occurrence** [ə'kʌrəns] n (event) évène-ment m; (existence) existence f; (of word) Ling occurrence f.

ocean ['əuʃ(ə)n] n océan m. ◆**oce'anic** a océanique.

o'clock [ə'klɒk] adv (it's) **three o'c.**/etc (il est) trois heures/etc.

octagon ['ɒktəgən] n octogone m. ◆**oc'tagonal** a octogonal.

octave ['ɒktıv, 'ɒkteıv] n Mus octave f.

October [ɒk'təubər] n octobre m.

octogenarian [ɒktəu'dʒıneərıən] n octogé-naire mf.

octopus ['ɒktəpəs] n pieuvre f.

odd [ɒd] a 1 (strange) bizarre, curieux; **an o. size** une taille peu courante. 2 (number) impair. 3 (left over) **I have an o. penny** il me reste un penny; **a few o. stamps** quelques timbres (qui restent); **the o. man out,** the **o. one out** l'exception f; **sixty o.** soixante et quelques; **an o. glove/book/**etc un gant/livre/etc dépareillé. 4 (occasional) qu'on fait, voit etc de temps en temps; **to find the o. mistake** trouver de temps en temps une (petite) erreur; **at o. moments** de temps en temps; **o. jobs** (around house) menus travaux mpl; **o. job man** homme m à tout faire. ◆**oddity** n (person) personne f bizarre; (object) curiosité f; pl (of language, situation) bizarreries fpl. ◆**oddly** adv bizarrement; **o. (enough), he was . . .** chose curieuse, il était . . . . ◆**oddment** n Com fin f de série. ◆**oddness** n bizarrerie f.

odds [ɒdz] npl 1 (in betting) cote f; (chances) chances fpl; **we have heavy o. against us** nous avons très peu de chances de réussir. 2 **it makes no o.** (no difference) Fam ça ne fait rien. 3 **at o.** (in disagreement) en désac-cord (with avec). 4 **o. and ends** des petites choses.

ode [əud] n (poem) ode f.

odious ['əudıəs] a détestable, odieux.

odour ['əudər] n odeur f. ◆—**less** a inodore.

oecumenical [iːkjuːˈmenık(ə)l] a Rel œcuménique.

of [əv, stressed ɒv] prep de; **of the table** de la

table; **of the boy** du garçon; **of the boys** des garçons; **of a book** d'un livre; **of it, of them** en; **she has a lot of it** *or* **of them** elle en a beaucoup; **a friend of his** un ami à lui; **there are ten of us** nous sommes dix; **that's nice of you** c'est gentil de ta part; **of no value/interest/etc** sans valeur/intérêt/*etc*; **of late** ces derniers temps; **a man of fifty** un homme de cinquante ans; **the fifth of June** le cinq juin.

off [ɒf] **1** *adv* (*absent*) absent, parti; (*light, gas, radio etc*) éteint, fermé; (*tap*) fermé; (*switched off at mains*) coupé; (*detached*) détaché; (*removed*) enlevé; (*cancelled*) annulé; (*not fit to eat or drink*) mauvais; (*milk, meat*) tourné; **2 km o.** à 2 km (d'ici or de là), éloigné de 2 km; **to be** *ou* **go o.** (*leave*) partir; **where are you o. to?** où vas-tu?; **he has his hat o.** il a enlevé son chapeau; **with his, my** *etc* **gloves o.** sans gants; **a day o.** (*holiday*) un jour de congé; **I'm o. today,** I **have today o.** j'ai congé aujourd'hui; **the strike's o.** il n'y aura pas de grève, la grève est annulée; **5% o.** une réduction de 5%; **on and o., o. and on** (*sometimes*) de temps à autre; **to be better o.** (*wealthier, in a better position*) être mieux. **2** *prep* (*from*) de; (*distant*) éloigné de; **to fall/etc o.** **the wall/ladder/etc** tomber/*etc* du mur/de l'échelle/*etc*; **to get o. the bus/etc** descendre du bus/etc; **to take sth. o.** **the table/etc** prendre qch sur la table/*etc*; **to eat o. a plate** manger dans une assiette; **to keep** *or* **stay o. the grass** ne pas marcher sur les herbes; **she's o. her food** elle ne mange plus rien; **o. Dover/etc** Nau au large de Douvres/etc; **o. limits** interdit; **the o. side** *Aut* le côté droit, *Am* le côté gauche. ◆**off'beat** *a* excentrique. ◆**off-'colour** *a* (*ill*) patraque; (*indecent*) scabreux. ◆**off'hand** *a* désinvolte; – *adv* impromptu. ◆**off'handedness** *n* désinvolture *f*. ◆**off-'licence** *n* magasin *m* de vins et de spiritueux. ◆**off-'load** *vt* (*vehicle etc*) décharger; **to o.-load sth onto s.o.** (*task etc*) se décharger de qch sur qn. ◆**off-'peak** *a* (*crowds, traffic*) aux heures creuses; (*rate, price*) heures creuses *inv*; **o.-peak hours** heures *fpl* creuses. ◆**off-'putting** *a* Fam rebutant. ◆**off-'side** *a* **to be o.** Fb être hors jeu. ◆**off-'stage** *a* & *adv* dans les coulisses. ◆**off-'white** *a* blanc cassé *inv*.

offal ['ɒf(ə)l] *n* Culin abats *mpl*.

offence [ə'fens] *n* Jur délit *m*; **to take o.** s'offenser (**at** de); **to give o.** offenser.

offend [ə'fend] *vt* froisser, offenser; (*eye*) Fig

choquer; **to be offended (at)** se froisser (de), s'offenser (de). ◆**—ing** *a* (*object, remark*) incriminé. ◆**offender** *n* Jur délinquant, -ante *mf*; (*habitual*) récidiviste *mf*.

offensive [ə'fensɪv] **1** *a* (*unpleasant*) choquant, repoussant; (*insulting*) insultant, offensant; (*weapon*) offensif. **2** *n* Mil offensive *f*.

offer ['ɒfər] *n* offre *f*; **on (special) o.** Com en promotion, en réclame; **o. of marriage** demande *f* en mariage; – *vt* (*opinion, remark*) proposer; **to o. to do** offrir *or* proposer de faire. ◆**—ing** *n* (*gift*) offrande *f*; (*act*) offre *f*; **peace o.** cadeau *m* de réconciliation.

office ['ɒfɪs] *n* **1** bureau *m*; (*of doctor*) Am cabinet *m*; (*of lawyer*) étude *f*; **head o.** siège *m* central; **o. block** immeuble *m* de bureaux; **o. worker** employé, -ée *mf* de bureau. **2** (*post*) fonction *f*; (*duty*) fonctions *fpl*; **to be in o.** (*of party etc*) Pol être au pouvoir. **3 one's good offices** (*help*) ses bons offices *mpl*.

officer ['ɒfɪsər] *n* (*in army, navy etc*) officier *m*; (*of company*) Com directeur, -trice *mf*; (*police*) o. agent *m* (de police).

official [ə'fɪʃ(ə)l] *a* officiel; (*uniform*) réglementaire; – *n* (*person of authority*) officiel *m*; (*civil servant*) fonctionnaire *mf*; (*employee*) employé, -ée *mf*. ◆**officialdom** *n* bureaucratie *f*. ◆**officially** *adv* officiellement. ◆**officiate** *vi* faire fonction d'officiel (**at** à); (*preside*) présider; Rel officier.

officious [ə'fɪʃəs] *a* Pej empressé.

offing ['ɒfɪŋ] *n* **in the o.** en perspective.

offset ['ɒfset, ɒf'set] *vt* (*pp* **offset**, *pres p* **offsetting**) (*compensate for*) compenser; (*s.o.'s beauty etc*) faire ressortir.

offshoot ['ɒfʃuːt] *n* (*of firm*) ramification *f*; (*consequence*) conséquence *f*.

offspring ['ɒfsprɪŋ] *n* progéniture *f*.

often ['ɒf(t)ən] *adv* souvent; **how o.?** combien de fois?; **how o. do they run?** (*trains, buses etc*) il y en a tous les combien?; **once too o.** une fois de trop; **every so o.** de temps en temps.

ogle ['əʊg(ə)l] *vt* reluquer.

ogre ['əʊgər] *n* ogre *m*.

oh! [əʊ] *int* oh!, ah!; (*pain*) aïe!; **oh yes?** ah oui?, ah bon?

oil [ɔɪl] *n* (*for machine, in cooking etc*) huile *f*; (*mineral*) pétrole *m*; (*fuel oil*) mazout *m*; **to paint in oils** faire de la peinture à l'huile; – *a* (*industry, product*) pétrolier; (*painting, paints*) à l'huile; **o. lamp** lampe *f* à pétrole *or* à huile; **o. change** Aut vidange *f*; – *vt*

graisser, huiler. ◆**oilcan** *n* burette *f.*
◆**oilfield** *n* gisement *m* pétrolifère. ◆**oil-
fired** *a* au mazout. ◆**oilskin(s)** *n(pl)*
(*garment*) ciré *m.* (*substance, skin*) huileux;
(*food*) gras.

ointment ['ɔɪntmənt] *n* pommade *f.*

OK [əʊ'keɪ] *int* (*approval, exasperation*) ça
va!; (*agreement*) d'accord!, entendu!, OK!;
– *a* (*satisfactory*) bien *inv*; (*unharmed*) sain
et sauf; (*undamaged*) intact; (*without
worries*) tranquille; **it's OK now** (*fixed*) ça
marche maintenant; **I'm OK** (*healthy*) je
vais bien; – *adv* (*to work etc*) bien; – *vt* (*pt
& pp* OKed, *pres p* OKing) approuver.

okay [əʊ'keɪ] = **OK**.

old [əʊld] *a* (-**er**, -**est**) vieux; (*former*)
ancien; **how o. is he?** quel âge a-t-il?; **he's
ten years o.** il a dix ans, il est âgé de dix
ans; **he's older than** il est plus âgé que; **an
older son** un fils aîné; **the oldest son** le fils
aîné; **o. enough to do** assez grand pour
faire; **o. enough to marry/vote** en âge de se
marier/de voter; **an o. man** un vieillard, un
vieil homme; **an o. woman** une vieille
(femme); **to get** *or* **grow old(er)** vieillir; **o.
age** vieillesse *f*; **the O. Testament** l'Ancien
Testament; **the O. World** l'Ancien Monde;
any o. how *Fam* n'importe comment; – *n*
the o. (*people*) les vieux *mpl.* ◆**o.-
'fashioned** *a* (*customs etc*) d'autrefois;
(*idea, attitude*) *Pej* vieux jeu *inv*; (*person*)
de la vieille école, *Pej* vieux jeu *inv.*
◆**o.-'timer** *n* (*old man*) *Fam* vieillard *m.*

olden ['əʊld(ə)n] *a* **in o. days** jadis.

olive ['ɒlɪv] *n* (*fruit*) olive *f*; – *a* **o.** (**green**)
(vert) olive *inv*; **o. oil** huile *f* d'olive; **o. tree**
olivier *m.*

Olympic [ə'lɪmpɪk] *a* olympique.

ombudsman ['ɒmbʊdzmən] *n* (*pl* -**men**)
Pol médiateur *m.*

omelet(te) ['ɒmlɪt] *n* omelette *f*; **cheese/etc
o.** omelette au fromage/*etc.*

omen ['əʊmən] *n* augure *m.* ◆**ominous** *a*
de mauvais augure; (*tone*) menaçant;
(*noise*) sinistre.

omit [əʊ'mɪt] *vt* (-**tt**-) omettre (**to do** de
faire). ◆**omission** *n* omission *f.*

omni- ['ɒmnɪ] *prep* omni-. ◆**om'nipotent**
a omnipotent.

on [ɒn] *prep* **1** (*position*) sur; **on the chair** sur
la chaise; **to put on** (*to*) mettre sur; **to look
out on to** donner sur. **2** (*concerning, about*)
sur; **an article on** un article sur; **to speak** *or*
talk on Dickens/*etc* parler sur Dickens/*etc.*
3 (*manner, means*) à; **on foot** à pied; **on the
blackboard** au tableau; **on the radio** à la

radio; **on the train/plane**/*etc* dans le
train/avion/*etc*; **on holiday**, *Am* **on vacation** en vacances; **to be on** (*course*) suivre;
(*project*) travailler à; (*salary*) toucher;
(*team, committee*) être membre de, faire
partie de; **to keep** *or* **stay on** (*road, path etc*)
suivre; **it's on me!** (*I'll pay*) *Fam* c'est moi
qui paie! **4** (*time*) **on Monday** lundi; **on
Mondays** le lundi; **on May 3rd** le 3 mai; **on
the evening of May 3rd** le 3 mai au soir; **on
my arrival** à mon arrivée. **5** (+ *present
participle*) en; **on learning that...** en
apprenant que...; **on seeing this** en
voyant ceci. **6** *adv* (*ahead*) en avant; (*in
progress*) en cours; (*started*) commencé;
(*lid, brake*) mis; (*light, radio*) allumé; (*gas,
tap*) ouvert; (*machine*) en marche; **be on (and
on)** sans cesse; **to play/etc on** continuer à
jouer/*etc*; **she has her hat on** elle a mis *or*
elle porte son chapeau; **he has sth/nothing
on** il est habillé/tout nu; **I've got sth on**
(*I'm busy*) je suis pris; **the strike's on** la
grève aura lieu; **what's on?** *TV* qu'y a-t-il à
la télé?; *Cin Th* qu'est-ce qu'on joue?;
there's a film on on passe un film; **to be on
at s.o.** (*pester*) *Fam* être après qn; **I've been
on to him** *Tel* je l'ai eu au bout du fil; **to be
on to s.o.** (*of police etc*) être sur la piste de
qn; **from then on** à partir de là.
◆**on-coming** *a* (*vehicle*) qui vient en sens
inverse. ◆**on-going** *a* (*project*) en cours.

once [wʌns] *adv* (*on one occasion*) une fois;
(*formerly*) autrefois; **o. a month/etc** une
fois par mois/*etc*; **o. again**, **o. more** encore
une fois; **at o.** (*immediately*) tout de suite;
all at o. (*suddenly*) tout à coup; (*at the same
time*) à la fois; **o. and for all** une fois pour
toutes; – *conj* une fois que. ◆**o.-over** *n* to
give sth the o.-over (*quick look*) *Fam*
regarder qch d'un coup d'œil.

one [wʌn] *a* **1** un, une; **o. man** un homme; **o.
woman** une femme; **twenty-o.** vingt-et-un.
2 (*sole*) seul; **my o.** (**and only**) *aim* mon seul
(et unique) but. **3** (*same*) même; **in the o.
bus** dans le même bus; – *pron* **1** un, une; **do
you want o.?** en veux-tu (une)?; **he's o.** of us
il est des nôtres; **o. of them** l'un d'eux, l'une
d'elles; **a big/small/etc o.** un grand/petit/
etc; **this book is o. that I've read** ce livre est
parmi ceux que j'ai lus; **she's o.** (*a teacher,
gardener etc*) elle l'est; **this o.** celui-ci,
celle-ci; **that o.** celui-là, celle-là; **the o. who**
or **which** celui *or* celle qui; **it's Paul's o.** *Fam*
c'est celui de Paul; **it's my o.** *Fam* c'est à
moi; **another o.** un(e) autre; **I for o.** pour
ma part. **2** (*impersonal*) on; **o. knows** on
sait; **it helps o.** ça nous *or* vous aide; **one's**

family sa famille. ◆**one-'armed** *a* (*person*) manchot. ◆**one-'eyed** *a* borgne. ◆**one-'off**, *a*, *Am* **one-of-a-'kind** *a Fam* unique, exceptionnel. ◆**one-'sided** *a* (*judgement etc*) partial; (*contest*) inégal; (*decision*) unilatéral. ◆**one-time** *a* (*former*) ancien. ◆**one-'way** *a* (*street*) à sens unique; (*traffic*) en sens unique; (*ticket*) *Am* simple.

oneself [wʌnˈself] *pron* soi-même; (*reflexive*) se, s'; **to cut o.** se couper.

onion [ˈʌnjən] *n* oignon *m*.

onlooker [ˈɒnlʊkər] *n* spectateur, -trice *mf*.

only [ˈəʊnli] *a* seul; **the o. house/***etc* la seule maison/*etc*; **the o. one** le seul, la seule; **an o. son** un fils unique; — *adv* seulement, ne . . . que; **I o. have ten, I have ten o.** je n'en ai que dix, j'en ai dix seulement; **if o.** si seulement; **not o.** non seulement; **I have o. just seen it** je viens tout juste de le voir; **o. he knows** lui seul le sait; — *conj* (*but*) *Fam* seulement; **o. I can't** seulement je ne peux pas.

onset [ˈɒnset] *n* (*of disease*) début *m*; (*of old age*) approche *m*.

onslaught [ˈɒnslɔːt] *n* attaque *f*.

onto [ˈɒntu] *prep* = on to.

onus [ˈəʊnəs] *n inv* **the o. is on you/***etc* c'est votre/*etc* responsabilité (**to do** de faire).

onward(s) [ˈɒnwəd(z)] *adv* en avant; **from that time o.** à partir de là.

onyx [ˈɒnɪks] *n* (*precious stone*) onyx *m*.

ooze [uːz] *vi* **to o.** (**out**) suinter; — *vt* (*blood etc*) laisser couler.

opal [ˈəʊp(ə)l] *n* (*precious stone*) opale *f*.

opaque [əʊˈpeɪk] *a* opaque; (*unclear*) *Fig* obscur.

open [ˈəʊpən] *a* ouvert; (*site, view, road*) dégagé; (*car*) décapoté, découvert; (*meeting*) public; (*competition*) ouvert à tous; (*post*) vacant; (*attempt, envy*) manifeste; (*question*) non résolu; (*result*) indécis; (*ticket*) *Av* open *inv*; **wide o.** grand ouvert; **in the o. air** en plein air; **in (the) o. country** en rase campagne; **the o. spaces** les grands espaces; **it's o. to doubt** c'est douteux; **o. to** (*criticism, attack*) exposé à; (*ideas, suggestions*) ouvert à; **I've got an o. mind on it** je n'ai pas d'opinion arrêtée là-dessus; **to leave o.** (*date*) ne pas préciser; — *n* (**out**) **in the o.** (*outside*) en plein air; **to sleep in the o.** dormir à la belle étoile; **to bring (out) into the o.** (*reveal*) divulguer; — *vt* (*conversation*) entamer; (*legs*) écarter; **to o. out** *or* **up** ouvrir; — *vi* (*of flower, eyes etc*) s'ouvrir; (*of shop, office etc*) ouvrir; (*of play*) débuter; (*of film*) sortir; **the door opens** (*is*

opened*) la porte s'ouvre; (*can open*) la porte ouvre; **to o. on to** (*of window etc*) donner sur; **to o. out** *or* **up** s'ouvrir; **to o. out** (*widen*) s'élargir; **to o. up** (*open a or the door*) ouvrir. ◆**—ing** *n* ouverture *f*; (*of flower*) éclosion *f*; (*career prospect, trade outlet*) débouché *m*; — *a* (*time, speech*) d'ouverture; **o. night** *Th* première *f*. ◆**—ly** *adv* (*not secretly, frankly*) ouvertement; (*publicly*) publiquement. ◆**—ness** *n* (*frankness*) franchise *f*; **o. of mind** ouverture *f* d'esprit.

open-air [ˈəʊpənˈeər] *a* (*pool etc*) en plein air. ◆**o.-'heart** *a* (*operation*) *Med* à cœur ouvert. ◆**o.-'necked** *a* (*shirt*) sans cravate. ◆**o.-'plan** *a Archit* sans cloisons.

opera [ˈɒprə] *n* opéra *m*; **o. glasses** jumelles *fpl* de théâtre. ◆**ope'ratic** *a* d'opéra. ◆**ope'retta** *n* opérette *f*.

operat/e [ˈɒpəreɪt] **1** *vi* (*of machine etc*) fonctionner; (*proceed*) opérer; — *vt* faire fonctionner; (*business*) gérer. **2** *vi* (*of surgeon*) opérer (**on s.o.** qn, **for** de). ◆**—ing** *a* **o. costs** frais *mpl* d'exploitation; **o. theatre**, *Am* **o. room** *Med* salle *f* d'opération; **o. wing** *Med* bloc *m* opératoire. ◆**ope'ration** *n* (*working*) fonctionnement *m*; *Med Mil Math etc* opération *f*; **in o.** (*machine*) en service; (*plan*) *Fig* en vigueur. ◆**ope-'rational** *a* opérationnel. ◆**operative** *a Med* opératoire; (*law, measure etc*) en vigueur; — *n* ouvrier, -ière *mf*. ◆**operator** *n Tel* standardiste *mf*; (*on machine*) opérateur, -trice *mf*; (*criminal*) escroc *mf*; **tour o.** organisateur, -trice *mf* de voyages, voyagiste *m*.

opinion [əˈpɪnjən] *n* opinion *f*, avis *m*; **in my o.** à mon avis. ◆**opinionated** *a* dogmatique.

opium [ˈəʊpɪəm] *n* opium *m*.

opponent [əˈpəʊnənt] *n* adversaire *mf*.

opportune [ˈɒpətjuːn] *a* opportun. ◆**oppor'tunism** *n* opportunisme *m*.

opportunity [ɒpəˈtjuːnɪtɪ] *n* occasion *f* (**to do** de faire); *pl* (*prospects*) perspectives *fpl*; **equal opportunities** des chances *fpl* égales.

oppos/e [əˈpəʊz] *vt* (*person, measure etc*) s'opposer à; (*law, motion*) *Pol* faire opposition à. ◆**—ed** *a* opposé (**to** à); **as o. to** par opposition à. ◆**—ing** *a* (*team, interests*) opposé. ◆**oppo'sition** *n* opposition *f* (**to** à); **the o.** (*rival camp*) *Fam* l'adversaire *m*.

opposite [ˈɒpəzɪt] *a* (*side etc*) opposé; (*house*) en face; **one's o. number** (*counterpart*) son homologue *mf*; — *adv* (*or sit etc*) en face; — *prep* **o. (to)** en face de; — *n* **the o.** le contraire, l'opposé *m*.

oppress [ə'pres] *vt* (*tyrannize*) opprimer; (*of heat, anguish*) oppresser; **the oppressed** les opprimés *mpl*. ◆**oppression** *n* oppression *f*. ◆**oppressive** *a* (*ruler etc*) oppressif; (*heat*) oppressant; (*régime*) tyrannique. ◆**oppressor** *n* oppresseur *m*.

opt [ɒpt] *vi* **to o. for** opter pour; **to o. to do** choisir de faire; **to o. out** *Fam* refuser de participer (**of** à). ◆**option** *n* option *f*; (*subject*) *Sch* matière *f* à option; **she has no o. elle** n'a pas le choix. ◆**optional** *a* facultatif; **o. extra** (*on car etc*) option *f*, accessoire *m* en option.

optical ['ɒptɪk(ə)l] *a* (*glass*) optique; (*illusion, instrument etc*) d'optique. ◆**optician** *n* opticien, -ienne *mf*.

optimism ['ɒptɪmɪz(ə)m] *n* optimisme *m*. ◆**optimist** *n* optimiste *mf*. ◆**optimistic** *a* optimiste. ◆**opti'mistically** *adv* avec optimisme.

optimum ['ɒptɪməm] *a* & *n* optimum (*m*); **the o. temperature** la température optimum. ◆**optimal** *a* optimal.

opulent ['ɒpjʊlənt] *a* opulent. ◆**opulence** *n* opulence *f*.

or [ɔːr] *conj* ou; **one or two** un ou deux; **he doesn't drink or smoke** il ne boit ni ne fume; **ten or so** environ dix.

oracle ['ɒrək(ə)l] *n* oracle *m*.

oral ['ɔːrəl] *a* oral; — *n* (*examination*) *Sch* oral *m*.

orange ['ɒrɪndʒ] **1** *n* (*fruit*) orange *f*; — *a* (*drink*) à l'orange; **o. tree** oranger *m*. **2** *a* & *n* (*colour*) orange *a* & *m* *inv*. ◆**orangeade** *n* orangeade *f*.

orang-outang [ɔːræŋuːˈtæŋ] *n* orang-outan(g) *m*.

oration [ɔːˈreɪʃ(ə)n] *n* funeral **o.** oraison *f* funèbre.

oratory ['ɒrətəri] *n* (*words*) *Pej* rhétorique *f*.

orbit ['ɔːbɪt] *n* (*of planet etc*) & *Fig* orbite *f*; — *vt* (*sun etc*) graviter autour de.

orchard ['ɔːtʃəd] *n* verger *m*.

orchestra ['ɔːkɪstrə] *n* (*classical*) orchestre *m*. ◆**or'chestral** *a* (*music*) orchestral; (*concert*) symphonique. ◆**orchestrate** *vt* (*organize*) & *Mus* orchestrer.

orchid ['ɔːkɪd] *n* orchidée *f*.

ordain [ɔːˈdeɪn] *vt* (*priest*) ordonner; **to o. that** décréter que.

ordeal [ɔːˈdiːl] *n* épreuve *f*, supplice *m*.

order ['ɔːdər] *n* (*command, structure, association etc*) ordre *m*; (*purchase*) *Com* commande *f*; **in o.** (*drawer, room etc*) en ordre; (*passport etc*) en règle; **in** (*numerical*) **o.** dans l'ordre numérique; **in working o.** en état de marche; **in o. of age** par ordre

d'âge; **in o. to do** pour faire; **in o. that** pour que (+ *sub*); **it's in o. to smoke/***etc* (*allowed*) il est permis de fumer/*etc*; **out of o.** (*machine*) en panne; (*telephone*) en dérangement; **to make** *or* **place an o.** *Com* passer une commande; **on o.** *Com* commandé; **money o.** mandat *m*; **postal o.** mandat *m* postal; — *vt* (*command*) ordonner (**s.o. to do** à qn de faire); (*meal, goods etc*) commander; (*taxi*) appeler; **to o. s.o. around** commander qn, régenter qn; — *vi* (*in café etc*) commander. ◆**—ly 1** *a* (*tidy*) ordonné; (*mind*) méthodique; (*crowd*) discipliné. **2** *n* *Mil* planton *m*; (*in hospital*) garçon *m* de salle.

ordinal ['ɔːdɪnəl] *a* (*number*) ordinal.

ordinary ['ɔːd(ə)nrɪ] *a* (*usual*) ordinaire; (*average*) moyen; (*mediocre*) médiocre, ordinaire; **an o. individual** un simple particulier; **in o. use** d'usage courant; **in the o. course of events** en temps normal; **in the o. way** normalement; **it's out of the o.** ça sort de l'ordinaire.

ordination [ɔːdɪˈneɪʃ(ə)n] *n* *Rel* ordination *f*.

ordnance ['ɔːdnəns] *n* (*guns*) *Mil* artillerie *f*.

ore [ɔːr] *n* minerai *m*.

organ ['ɔːgən] *n* **1** *Anat* & *Fig* organe *m*. **2** *Mus* orgue *m*, orgues *fpl*; **barrel o.** orgue *m* de Barbarie. ◆**organist** *n* organiste *mf*.

organic [ɔːˈgænɪk] *a* organique. ◆**organism** *n* organisme *m*.

organization [ɔːgənaɪˈzeɪʃ(ə)n] *n* (*arrangement, association*) organisation *f*.

organiz/e ['ɔːgənaɪz] *vt* organiser. ◆**—ed** *a* (*mind, group etc*) organisé. ◆**—er** *n* organisateur, -trice *mf*.

orgasm ['ɔːgæz(ə)m] *n* orgasme *m*.

orgy ['ɔːdʒɪ] *n* orgie *f*.

orient ['ɔːrɪent] *vt* *Am* = **orientate**. ◆**orientate** *vt* orienter.

Orient ['ɔːrɪent] *n* **the O.** l'Orient *m*. ◆**ori'ental** *a* & *n* oriental, -ale (*mf*).

orifice ['ɒrɪfɪs] *n* orifice *m*.

origin ['ɒrɪdʒɪn] *n* origine *f*.

original [əˈrɪdʒɪn(ə)l] *a* (*first*) premier, originel, primitif; (*novel, unusual*) original; (*sin*) originel; (*copy, version*) original; — *n* (*document etc*) original *m*. ◆**origi'nality** *n* originalité *f*. ◆**originally** *adv* (*at first*) à l'origine; (*in a novel way*) originalement; **she comes o. from** elle est originaire de. ◆**originate** *vi* (*begin*) prendre naissance (**in** dans); **to o. from** (*of idea etc*) émaner de; (*of person*) être originaire de; — *vt* être l'auteur de. ◆**originator** *n* auteur *m* (**of** de).

ornament ['ɔːnəmənt] *n* (*decoration*) orne-

ment *m*; *pl* (*vases etc*) bibelots *mpl.*
◆**orna'mental** *a* ornemental. ◆**orna-men'tation** *n* ornementation *f.* ◆**or'nate** *a* (*style etc*) (très) orné. ◆**or'nately** *adv* (*decorated etc*) de façon surchargée, à outrance.

orphan ['ɔːf(ə)n] *n* orphelin, -ine *mf*; – *a* orphelin. ◆**orphaned** *a* orphelin; he was o. by the accident l'accident l'a rendu orphelin. ◆**orphanage** *n* orphelinat *m.*

orthodox ['ɔːθədɒks] *a* orthodoxe. ◆**orthodoxy** *n* orthodoxie *f.*

orthop(a)edics [ɔːθə'piːdɪks] *n* orthopédie *f.*

Oscar ['ɒskər] *n Cin* oscar *m.*

oscillate ['ɒsɪleɪt] *vi* osciller.

ostensibly [ɒ'stensɪblɪ] *adv* apparemment, en apparence.

ostentation [ɒsten'teɪʃ(ə)n] *n* ostentation *f.* ◆**ostentatious** *a* plein d'ostentation, prétentieux.

ostracism ['ɒstrəsɪz(ə)m] *n* ostracisme *m.* ◆**ostracize** *vt* proscrire, frapper d'ostracisme.

ostrich ['ɒstrɪtʃ] *n* autruche *f.*

other ['ʌðər] *a* autre; o. people d'autres; the o. one l'autre *mf*; I have no o. gloves than these je n'ai pas d'autres gants que ceux-ci; – *pron* autre; (some) others d'autres; some do, others don't les uns le font, les autres ne le font pas; none o. than, no o. than nul autre que; – *adv* o. than autrement que. ◆**otherwise** *adv* autrement; – *a* (*different*) (tout) autre.

otter ['ɒtər] *n* loutre *f.*

ouch! [aʊtʃ] *int* aïe!, ouille!

ought [ɔːt] *v aux* **1** (*obligation, desirability*) you o. to leave tu devrais partir; I o. to have done it j'aurais dû le faire; he said he o. to stay il a dit qu'il devrait rester. **2** (*probability*) it o. to be ready ça devrait être prêt.

ounce [aʊns] *n* (*measure*) & *Fig* once *f* (= 28,35 g).

our [aʊər] *poss a* notre, *pl* nos. ◆**ours** *pron* le nôtre, la nôtre, *pl* les nôtres; this book is o. ce livre est à nous or est le nôtre; a friend of o. un ami à nous. ◆**our'selves** *pron* nous-mêmes; (*reflexive* & *after prep etc*) nous; we wash o. nous nous lavons.

oust [aʊst] *vt* évincer (from de).

out [aʊt] *adv* (*outside*) dehors; (*not at home etc*) sorti; (*light, fire*) éteint; (*news, secret*) connu, révélé; (*flower*) ouvert; (*book*) publié, sorti; (*finished*) fini; to be or go o. a lot sortir beaucoup; he's o. in Italy il est (parti) en Italie; o. there là-bas; to have a

day o. sortir pour la journée; 5 km o. *Nau* à 5 km du rivage; the sun's o. il fait (du) soleil; the tide's o. la marée est basse; you're o. (*wrong*) tu t'es trompé; (*in game etc*) tu es éliminé (of de); the trip or journey o. l'aller *m*; to be o. to win être résolu à gagner; – *prep* o. of (*outside*) en dehors de; (*danger, breath, reach, water*) hors de; (*without*) sans; o. of pity/love/etc par pitié/amour/etc; to look/jump/etc o. of (*window etc*) regarder/sauter/etc par; to drink/take/copy o. of boire/prendre/copier dans; made o. of (*wood etc*) fait en; to make sth o. of (*wood etc*) faire qch avec une boîte/un chiffon/etc; a page o. of une page de; she's o. of town elle n'est pas en ville; 5 km o. of (*away from*) à 5 km de; four o. of five quatre sur cinq; o. of the blue de manière inattendue; to feel o. of it or of things se sentir hors du coup. ◆**'out-and-out** *a* (*cheat, liar etc*) achevé; (*believer*) à tout crin. ◆**o.-of-'date** *a* (*expired*) périmé; (*old-fashioned*) démodé. ◆**o.-of-'doors** *adv* dehors. ◆**o.-of-the-'way** *a* (*place*) écarté.

outbid [aʊt'bɪd] *vt* (*pt* & *pp* outbid, *pres p* outbidding) to o. s.o. (sur)enchérir sur qn.

outboard ['aʊtbɔːd] *a* o. motor *Nau* moteur *m* hors-bord *inv.*

outbreak ['aʊtbreɪk] *n* (*of war*) début *m*; (*of violence, pimples*) éruption *f*; (*of fever*) accès *m*; (*of hostilities*) ouverture *f.*

outbuilding ['aʊtbɪldɪŋ] *n* (*of mansion, farm*) dépendance *f.*

outburst ['aʊtbɜːst] *n* (*of anger, joy*) explosion *f*; (*of violence*) flambée *f*; (*of laughter*) éclat *m.*

outcast ['aʊtkɑːst] *n* (*social*) o. paria *m.*

outcome ['aʊtkʌm] *n* résultat *m*, issue *f.*

outcry ['aʊtkraɪ] *n* tollé *m.*

outdated [aʊt'deɪtɪd] *a* démodé.

outdistance [aʊt'dɪstəns] *vt* distancer.

outdo [aʊt'duː] *vt* (*pt* outdid, *pp* outdone) surpasser (in en).

outdoor ['aʊtdɔːr] *a* (*game*) de plein air; (*pool, life*) en plein air; o. clothes tenue *f* pour sortir. ◆**out'doors** *adv* dehors.

outer ['aʊtər] *a* extérieur; o. space l'espace *m* (cosmique); the o. suburbs la grande banlieue.

outfit ['aʊtfɪt] *n* équipement *m*; (*kit*) trousse *f*; (*toy*) panoplie *f* (de pompier, cow-boy/etc); (*clothes*) costume *m*; (*for woman*) toilette *f*; (*group, gang*) *Fam* bande *f*; (*firm*) *Fam* boîte *f*; sports/ski o. tenue *f* de sport/de ski. ◆**outfitter** *n* chemisier *m.*

outgoing ['aʊtɡəʊɪŋ] **1** *a* (*minister etc*)

sortant; (*mail, ship*) en partance. **2** *a* (*sociable*) liant, ouvert. **3** *npl* (*expenses*) dépenses *fpl*.

outgrow [aʊtˈgrəʊ] *vt* (*pt* **outgrew**, *pp* **outgrown**) (*clothes*) devenir trop grand pour; (*habit*) perdre (en grandissant); **to o. s.o.** (*grow taller than*) grandir plus vite que qn.

outhouse [ˈaʊthaʊs] *n* (*of mansion, farm*) dépendance *f*; (*lavatory*) *Am* cabinets *mpl* extérieurs.

outing [ˈaʊtɪŋ] *n* sortie *f*, excursion *f*.

outlandish [aʊtˈlændɪʃ] *a* (*weird*) bizarre; (*barbaric*) barbare.

outlast [aʊtˈlɑːst] *vt* durer plus longtemps que; (*survive*) survivre à.

outlaw [ˈaʊtlɔː] *n* hors-la-loi *m inv*; – *vt* (*ban*) proscrire.

outlay [ˈaʊtleɪ] *n* (*money*) dépense(s) *f*(*pl*).

outlet [ˈaʊtlet] *n* (*for liquid, of tunnel etc*) sortie *f*; (*for feelings, energy*) moyen *m* d'exprimer, exutoire *m*; **retail o.** *Com* point *m* de vente, magasin *m*.

outline [ˈaʊtlaɪn] *n* (*shape*) contour *m*, profil *m*; (*rough*) (*of article, plan etc*) esquisse *f*; **the broad** *or* **general** *or* **main outline(s)** (*chief features*) les grandes lignes; – *vt* (*plan, situation*) décrire à grands traits, esquisser; (*book, speech*) résumer; **to be outlined against** (*of tree etc*) se profiler sur.

outlive [aʊtˈlɪv] *vt* survivre à.

outlook [ˈaʊtlʊk] *n inv* (*for future*) perspective(s) *f*(*pl*); (*point of view*) perspective *f* (**on** sur), attitude *f* (**on** à l'égard de); *Met* prévisions *fpl*.

outlying [ˈaʊtlaɪɪŋ] *a* (*remote*) isolé; (*neighbourhood*) périphérique.

outmoded [aʊtˈməʊdɪd] *a* démodé.

outnumber [aʊtˈnʌmbər] *vt* être plus nombreux que.

outpatient [ˈaʊtpeɪʃ(ə)nt] *n* malade *mf* en consultation externe.

outpost [ˈaʊtpəʊst] *n* avant-poste *m*.

output [ˈaʊtpʊt] *n* rendement *m*, production *f*; (*computer process*) sortie *f*; (*computer data*) donnée(s) *f*(*pl*) de sortie.

outrage [ˈaʊtreɪdʒ] *n* atrocité *f*, crime *m*; (*indignity*) indignité *f*; (*scandal*) scandale *m*; (*indignation*) indignation *f*; **bomb o.** attentat *m* à la bombe; – *vt* (*morals*) outrager; **outraged by sth** indigné de qch. ◆**out'rageous** *a* (*atrocious*) atroce; (*shocking*) scandaleux; (*dress, hat etc*) grotesque.

outright [aʊtˈraɪt] *adv* (*completely*) complètement; (*to say, tell*) franchement; (*to be*

killed) sur le coup; **to buy o.** (*for cash*) acheter au comptant; – [ˈaʊtraɪt] *a* (*complete*) complet; (*lie, folly*) pur; (*refusal, rejection etc*) catégorique, net; (*winner*) incontesté.

outset [ˈaʊtset] *n* **at the o.** au début; **from the o.** dès le départ.

outside [aʊtˈsaɪd] *adv* (au) dehors, à l'extérieur; **to go o.** sortir; – *prep* à l'extérieur de, en dehors de; (*beyond*) *Fig* en dehors de; **o. my room** *or* **door** à la porte de ma chambre; – *n* extérieur *m*, dehors *m*; – [ˈaʊtsaɪd] *a* extérieur; (*bus or train seat etc*) côté couloir *inv*; (*maximum*) *Fig* maximum; **the o. lane** *Aut* la voie de droite, *Am* la voie de gauche; **an o. chance** une faible chance. ◆**out'sider** *n* (*stranger*) étranger, -ère *mf*; *Sp* outsider *m*.

outsize [ˈaʊtsaɪz] *a* (*clothes*) grande taille *inv*.

outskirts [ˈaʊtskɜːts] *npl* banlieue *f*.

outsmart [aʊtˈsmɑːt] *vt* être plus malin que.

outspoken [aʊtˈspəʊk(ə)n] *a* (*frank*) franc.

outstanding [aʊtˈstændɪŋ] *a* remarquable, exceptionnel; (*problem, business*) non réglé, en suspens; (*debt*) impayé; **work o.** travail *m* à faire.

outstay [aʊtˈsteɪ] *vt* **to o. one's welcome** abuser de l'hospitalité de son hôte, s'incruster.

outstretched [aʊtˈstretʃt] *a* (*arm*) tendu.

outstrip [aʊtˈstrɪp] *vt* (**-pp-**) devancer.

outward [ˈaʊtwəd] *a* (*look, movement*) vers l'extérieur; (*sign, appearance*) extérieur; **o. journey** *or* **trip** aller *m*. ◆**outward(s)** *adv* vers l'extérieur.

outweigh [aʊtˈweɪ] *vt* (*be more important than*) l'emporter sur.

outwit [aʊtˈwɪt] *vt* (**-tt-**) être plus malin que.

oval [ˈəʊv(ə)l] *a* & *n* ovale (*m*).

ovary [ˈəʊvərɪ] *n Anat* ovaire *m*.

ovation [əʊˈveɪʃ(ə)n] *n* (*standing*) **o.** ovation *f*.

oven [ˈʌv(ə)n] *n* four *m*; (*hot place*) *Fig* fournaise *f*; **o. glove** gant *m* isolant.

over [ˈəʊvər] *prep* (*on*) sur; (*above*) au-dessus de; (*on the other side of*) de l'autre côté de; **bridge o. the river** pont *m* sur le fleuve; **to jump/look/etc o. sth** sauter/regarder/etc par-dessus qch; **to fall o. the balcony/etc** tomber du balcon/etc; **she fell o. it** elle en est tombée; **o. it** (*on*) dessus; (*above*) au-dessus; (*to jump etc*) par-dessus; **to criticize/etc o. sth** (*about*) critiquer/etc à propos de qch; **an advantage o.** un avantage sur *or* par rapport à; **o. the radio** (*on*) à la radio; **o. the phone** au téléphone; **o. the holidays** (*during*) pendant les vacances; **o. ten days** (*more than*) plus de dix jours; **men o. sixty** les hommes de plus de soixante ans; **o. and above** en plus de; **he's o. his flu** (*recovered from*) il est remis de sa grippe; **all o. Spain** (*everywhere in*) dans toute l'Espagne, partout en Espagne; **all o. the carpet** (*everywhere on*) partout sur le tapis; – *adv* (*above*) (par-)dessus; (*finished*) fini; (*danger*) passé; (*again*) encore; (*too*) trop; **jump o.!** sautez par-dessus!; **o. there** là-bas; **to be o. come** or **go o.** (*visit*) passer; **he's o. in Italy** il est (parti) en Italie; **she's o. from Paris** elle est venue de Paris; **all o.** (*everywhere*) partout; **wet all o.** tout mouillé; **it's (all) o.!** (*finished*) c'est fini!; **she's o.** (*fallen*) elle est tombée; **a kilo or o.** (*more*) un kilo ou plus; **I have ten o.** (*left*) il m'en reste dix; **there's some bread o.** il reste du pain; **o. and o.** (*often*) à plusieurs reprises; **to start all o. (again)** recommencer à zéro; **o. pleased**/*etc* trop content/*etc*. ◆**o.-a'bundant** *a* surabondant. ◆**o.-de'veloped** *a* trop développé. ◆**o.-fa'miliar** *a* trop familier. ◆**o.-in'dulge** *vt* (*one's desires etc*) céder trop facilement à; (*person*) trop gâter. ◆**o.-sub'scribed** *a* (*course*) ayant trop d'inscrits.

overall 1 [əʊvərˈɔːl] *a* (*measurement, length, etc*) total; (*result, effort etc*) global; – *adv* globalement. **2** [ˈəʊvərɔːl] *n* blouse *f* (de travail); *pl* bleus *mpl* de travail.

overawe [əʊvərˈɔː] *vt* intimider.

overbalance [əʊvəˈbæləns] *vi* basculer.

overbearing [əʊvəˈbeərɪŋ] *a* autoritaire.

overboard [ˈəʊvəbɔːd] *adv* à la mer.

overburden [əʊvəˈbɜːd(ə)n] *vt* surcharger.

overcast [əʊvəˈkɑːst] *a* (*sky*) couvert.

overcharge [əʊvəˈtʃɑːdʒ] *vt* **to o. s.o. for sth** faire payer qch trop cher à qn.

overcoat [ˈəʊvəkəʊt] *n* pardessus *m*.

overcome [əʊvəˈkʌm] *vt* (*pt* **overcame**, *pp* **overcome**) (*enemy, shyness etc*) vaincre; (*disgust, problem*) surmonter; **to be o.** by (*fatigue, grief*) être accablé par; (*fumes, temptation*) succomber à; **he was o.** by emotion l'émotion eut raison de lui.

overcrowded [əʊvəˈkraʊdɪd] *a* (*house, country*) surpeuplé; (*bus, train*) bondé. ◆**overcrowding** *n* surpeuplement *m*.

overdo [əʊvəˈduː] *vt* (*pt* **overdid**, *pp* **overdone**) exagérer; *Culin* cuire trop; **to o. it** (*exaggerate*) exagérer; (*work too much*) se surmener; *Iron* se fatiguer.

overdose [ˈəʊvədəʊs] *n* overdose *f*, dose *f* excessive (*de barbituriques etc*).

overdraft [ˈəʊvədrɑːft] *n* *Fin* découvert *m*. ◆**over'draw** *vt* (*pt* **overdrew**, *pp* **overdrawn**) (*account*) mettre à découvert.

overdress [əʊvəˈdres] *vi* s'habiller avec trop de recherche.

overdue [əʊvəˈdjuː] *a* (*train etc*) en retard; (*debt*) arriéré; (*apology, thanks*) tardif.

overeat [əʊvərˈiːt] *vi* manger trop.

overestimate [əʊvərˈestɪmeɪt] *vt* surestimer.

overexcited [əʊvərɪkˈsaɪtɪd] *a* surexcité.

overfeed [əʊvəˈfiːd] *vt* (*pt* & *pp* **overfed**) suralimenter.

overflow 1 [ˈəʊvəfləʊ] *n* (*outlet*) trop-plein *m*; (*of people, objects*) *Fig* excédent *m*. **2** [əʊvəˈfləʊ] *vi* déborder (**with** de); **to be overflowing with** (*of town, shop, house etc*) regorger de (*visiteurs, livres etc*).

overgrown [əʊvəˈgrəʊn] *a* envahi par la végétation; **o. with** (*weeds etc*) envahi par; **you're an o.** *schoolgirl Fig Pej* tu as la mentalité d'une écolière.

overhang [əʊvəˈhæŋ] *vi* (*pt* & *pp* **overhung**) faire saillie; – *vt* surplomber.

overhaul [əʊvəˈhɔːl] *vt* (*vehicle, doctrine etc*) réviser; – [ˈəʊvəhɔːl] *n* révision *f*.

overhead [əʊvəˈhed] *adv* au-dessus; – [ˈəʊvəhed] **1** *a* (*railway etc*) aérien. **2** *npl* (*expenses*) frais *mpl* généraux.

overhear [əʊvəˈhɪər] *vt* (*pt* & *pp* **overheard**) surprendre, entendre.

overheat [əʊvəˈhiːt] *vt* surchauffer; – *vi* (*of engine*) chauffer.

overjoyed [əʊvəˈdʒɔɪd] *a* ravi, enchanté.

overland [ˈəʊvəlænd] *a* & *adv* par voie de terre.

overlap [əʊvəˈlæp] *vi* (**-pp-**) se chevaucher; – *vt* chevaucher; – [ˈəʊvəlæp] *n* chevauchement *m*.

overleaf [əʊvəˈliːf] *adv* au verso.

overload [əʊvəˈləʊd] *vt* surcharger.

overlook [əʊvəˈlʊk] *vt* **1** (*not notice*) ne pas remarquer; (*forget*) oublier; (*disregard, ignore*) passer sur. **2** (*of window, house etc*) donner sur; (*of tower, fort*) dominer.

overly [ˈəʊvəlɪ] *adv* excessivement.

overmuch [əʊvəˈmʌtʃ] *adv* trop, excessivement.

overnight [əʊvəˈnaɪt] *adv* (*during the night*) (pendant) la nuit; (*all night*) toute la nuit; (*suddenly*) *Fig* du jour au lendemain; **to stay o.** passer la nuit; – [ˈəʊvənaɪt] *a* (*stay*) d'une nuit; (*clothes*) pour une nuit; (*trip*) de nuit.

overpass [ˈəʊvəpæs] *n* (*bridge*) *Am* tobogan *m*.

overpopulated [əʊvə'pɒpjʊleɪtɪd] *a* surpeuplé.

overpower [əʊvə'paʊər] *vt* (*physically*) maîtriser; (*defeat*) vaincre; *Fig* accabler. ◆–**ing** *a* (*charm etc*) irrésistible; (*heat etc*) accablant.

overrat/e [əʊvə'reɪt] *vt* surestimer. ◆–**ed** *a* surfait.

overreach [əʊvə'riːtʃ] *vt* to o. oneself trop entreprendre.

overreact [əʊvərɪ'ækt] *vi* réagir excessivement.

overrid/e [əʊvə'raɪd] *vt* (*pt* overrode, *pp* overridden) (*invalidate*) annuler; (*take no notice of*) passer outre à; (*be more important than*) l'emporter sur. ◆–**ing** *a* (*passion*) prédominant; (*importance*) primordial.

overrule [əʊvə'ruːl] *vt* (*reject*) rejeter.

overrun [əʊvə'rʌn] *vt* (*pt* overran, *pp* overrun, *pres p* overrunning) **1** (*invade*) envahir. **2** (*go beyond*) aller au-delà de.

overseas [əʊvə'siːz] *adv* (*Africa etc*) outre-mer; (*abroad*) à l'étranger; – ['əʊvəsiːz] *a* (*visitor, market etc*) d'outre-mer; étranger; (*trade*) extérieur.

overse/e [əʊvə'siː] *vt* (*pt* oversaw, *pp* overseen) surveiller. ◆–**er** ['əʊvəsiːər] *n* (*foreman*) contremaître *m*.

overshadow [əʊvə'ʃædəʊ] *vt* (*make less important*) éclipser; (*make gloomy*) assombrir.

overshoot [əʊvə'ʃuːt] *vt* (*pt & pp* overshot) (*of aircraft*) & *Fig* dépasser.

oversight ['əʊvəsaɪt] *n* omission *f*, oubli *m*; (*mistake*) erreur *f*.

oversimplify [əʊvə'sɪmplɪfaɪ] *vti* trop simplifier.

oversize(d) ['əʊvəsaɪz(d)] *a* trop grand.

oversleep [əʊvə'sliːp] *vi* (*pt & pp* overslept) dormir trop longtemps, oublier de se réveiller.

overspend [əʊvə'spend] *vi* dépenser trop.

overstaffed [əʊvə'stɑːft] *a* au personnel pléthorique.

overstay [əʊvə'steɪ] *vt* to o. one's welcome abuser de l'hospitalité de son hôte, s'incruster.

overstep [əʊvə'step] *vt* (**-pp-**) dépasser.

overt ['əʊvɜːt] *a* manifeste.

overtake [əʊvə'teɪk] *vt* (*pt* overtook, *pp* overtaken) dépasser; (*vehicle*) doubler, dépasser; **overtaken by** (*nightfall, storm*) surpris par; – *vi Aut* doubler, dépasser.

overtax [əʊvə'tæks] *vt* **1** (*strength*) excéder; (*brain*) fatiguer. **2** (*taxpayer*) surimposer.

overthrow [əʊvə'θrəʊ] *vt* (*pt* overthrew, *pp* overthrown) *Pol* renverser; – ['əʊvəθrəʊ] *n* renversement *m*.

overtime ['əʊvətaɪm] *n* heures *fpl* supplémentaires; – *adv* to work o. faire des heures supplémentaires.

overtones ['əʊvətəʊnz] *npl Fig* note *f*, nuance *f* (of de).

overture ['əʊvətjʊər] *n Mus & Fig* ouverture *f*.

overturn [əʊvə'tɜːn] *vt* (*chair, table etc*) renverser; (*car, boat*) retourner; (*decision etc*) *Fig* annuler; – *vi* (*of car, boat*) se retourner.

overweight [əʊvə'weɪt] *a* to be o. (*of suitcase etc*) peser trop; (*of person*) avoir des kilos en trop.

overwhelm [əʊvə'welm] *vt* (*of feelings, heat etc*) accabler; (*defeat*) écraser; (*amaze*) bouleverser. ◆–**ed** *a* (*overjoyed*) ravi (by, with de); o. with (*grief, work etc*) accablé de; (*offers*) submergé par; o. by (*kindness, gift etc*) vivement touché par. ◆–**ing** *a* (*heat, grief etc*) accablant; (*majority*) écrasant; (*desire*) irrésistible; (*impression*) dominant. ◆–**ingly** *adv* (*to vote, reject etc*) en masse; (*utterly*) carrément.

overwork [əʊvə'wɜːk] *n* surmenage *m*; – *vi* se surmener; – *vt* surmener.

overwrought [əʊvə'rɔːt] *a* (*tense*) tendu.

owe [əʊ] *vt* devoir (to à); I'll o. it (to) you, I'll o. you (for) it (*money*) je te le devrai; to o. it to oneself to do se devoir de faire. ◆**owing** **1** *a* (*money etc*) dû, qu'on doit. **2** *prep* o. to à cause de.

owl [aʊl] *n* hibou *m*.

own [əʊn] **1** *a* propre; **my o. house** ma propre maison; – *pron* it's my (very) o. c'est à moi (tout seul); **a house of his o.** sa propre maison, sa maison à lui; (all) on one's o. (*alone*) tout seul; to get one's o. back prendre sa revanche (on sur, for de); to come into one's o. (*fulfil oneself*) s'épanouir. **2** *vt* (*possess*) posséder; who owns this ball/etc? à qui appartient cette balle/etc? **3** *vi* to o. up (*confess*) avouer; to o. up to sth avouer qch. ◆**owner** *n* propriétaire *mf*. ◆**ownership** *n* possession *f*; home o. accession *f* à la propriété; public o. *Econ* nationalisation *f*.

ox, *pl* **oxen** [ɒks, 'ɒks(ə)n] *n* bœuf *m*.

oxide ['ɒksaɪd] *n Ch* oxide *m*. ◆**oxidize** *vi* s'oxyder; – *vt* oxyder.

oxygen ['ɒksɪdʒ(ə)n] *n* oxygène *m*; – *a* (*mask, tent*) à oxygène.

oyster ['ɔɪstər] *n* huître *f*.

P

P, p [piː] *n* P, p *m*.

p [piː] *abbr* = **penny, pence**.

pa [paː] *n* (*father*) *Fam* papa *m*.

pace [peɪs] *n* (*speed*) pas *m*, allure *f*; (*measure*) pas *m*; **to keep p. with** (*follow*) suivre; (*in work, progress*) se maintenir à la hauteur de; – *vi* **to p. up and down** faire les cent pas; – *vt* (*room etc*) arpenter. ◆**pacemaker** *n* (*device*) stimulateur *m* cardiaque.

Pacific [pəˈsɪfɪk] *a* (*coast etc*) pacifique; – *n* **the P. le** Pacifique.

pacify [ˈpæsɪfaɪ] *vt* (*country*) pacifier; (*calm, soothe*) apaiser. ◆**pacifier** *n* (*dummy*) *Am* sucette *f*, tétine *f*. ◆**pacifist** *n* & *a* pacifiste (*mf*).

pack [pæk] **1** *n* (*bundle, packet*) paquet *m*; (*bale*) balle *f*; (*of animal*) charge *f*; (*ruck-sack*) sac *m* (à dos); *Mil* paquetage *m*; (*of hounds, wolves*) meute *f*; (*of runners*) *Sp* peloton *m*; (*of thieves*) bande *f*; (*of cards*) jeu *m*; (*of lies*) tissu *m*. **2** *vt* (*fill*) remplir (**with** de); (*excessively*) bourrer; (*suitcase*) faire; (*object into box etc*) emballer; (*object into suitcase*) mettre dans sa valise; (*make into package*) empaqueter; **to p. into** (*cram*) entasser dans; (*put*) mettre dans; **to p. away** (*tidy away*) ranger; **to p. (down)** (*compress, crush*) tasser; **to p. off** (*person*) *Fam* expédier; **to p. up** (*put into box*) emballer; (*put into case*) mettre dans sa valise; (*give up*) *Fam* laisser tomber; – *vi* (*fill one's bags*) faire ses valises; **to p. into** (*of people*) s'entasser dans; **to p. in or up** (*of machine, vehicle*) *Fam* tomber en panne; **to p. up** (*stop*) *Fam* s'arrêter; (*leave*) plier bagage. ◆**—ed** *a* (*bus, cinema etc*) bourré; **p. lunch** panier-repas *m*; **p. out** (*crowded*) *Fam* bourré. ◆**—ing** *n* (*material, action*) emballage *m*; **p. case** caisse *f* d'emballage.

packag/e [ˈpækɪdʒ] *n* paquet *m*; (*computer programs*) progiciel *m*; **p. deal** *Com* contrat *m* global, train *m* de propositions; **p. tour** voyage *m* organisé; – *vt* emballer, empaqueter. ◆**—ing** *n* (*material, action*) emballage *m*.

packet [ˈpækɪt] *n* paquet *m*; (*of sweets*) sachet *m*, paquet *m*; **to make/cost a p.** *Fam* faire/coûter beaucoup d'argent.

pact [pækt] *n* pacte *m*.

pad [pæd] *n* (*wad, plug*) tampon *m*; (*for writing, notes etc*) bloc *m*; (*on leg*) *Sp* jambière *f*; (*on knee*) *Sp* genouillère *f*; (*room*) *Sl* piaule *f*; **launch(ing) p.** rampe *f* de lancement; **ink(ing) p.** tampon *m* encreur; – *vt* (*-dd-*) (*stuff*) rembourrer, matelasser; **to p. out** (*speech, text*) délayer. ◆**padding** *n* rembourrage *m*; (*of speech, text*) délayage *m*.

paddle [ˈpæd(ə)l] **1** *vi* (*splash about*) barboter; (*dip one's feet*) se mouiller les pieds; – *n* **to have a (little) p.** se mouiller les pieds. **2** *n* (*pole*) pagaie *f*; **p. boat, p. steamer** bateau *m* à roues; – *vt* **to p. a canoe** pagayer.

paddock [ˈpædək] *n* enclos *m*; (*at race-course*) paddock *m*.

paddy [ˈpædɪ] *n* **p. (field)** rizière *f*.

padlock [ˈpædlɒk] *n* (*on door etc*) cadenas *m*; (*on bicycle, moped*) antivol *m*; – *vt* (*door*) cadenasser.

p(a)ediatrician [piːdɪəˈtrɪʃ(ə)n] *n* *Med* pédiatre *mf*.

pagan [ˈpeɪgən] *a* & *n* païen, -enne (*mf*). ◆**paganism** *n* paganisme *m*.

page [peɪdʒ] **1** *n* (*of book etc*) page *f*. **2** *n* **p. (boy)** (*in hotel etc*) chasseur *m*; (*at court*) *Hist* page *m*; – *vt* **to p. s.o.** faire appeler qn.

pageant [ˈpædʒənt] *n* grand spectacle *m* historique. ◆**pageantry** *n* pompe *f*, apparat *m*.

pagoda [pəˈgəudə] *n* pagode *f*.

paid [peɪd] *see* **pay**; – *a* (*assassin etc*) à gages; **to put s.o. to** (*hopes, plans*) anéantir; **to put s.o. to s.o.** (*ruin*) couler qn.

pail [peɪl] *n* seau *m*.

pain [peɪn] *n* (*physical*) douleur *f*; (*grief*) peine *f*; *pl* (*efforts*) efforts *mpl*; **to have a p. in one's arm** avoir mal or une douleur au bras; **to be in p.** souffrir; **to go to** or **take (great) pains to do** (*exert oneself*) se donner du mal à faire; **to go to** or **take (great) pains not to do** (*be careful*) prendre bien soin de ne pas faire; **to be a p. (in the neck)** (*of person*) *Fam* être casse-pieds; – *vt* (*grieve*) peiner. ◆**p.-killer** *n* analgésique *m*, calmant *m*. ◆**painful** *a* (*illness, operation*) douloureux; (*arm, leg*) qui fait mal, douloureux; (*distressing*) douloureux, pénible; (*difficult*) pénible; (*bad*) *Fam* affreux. ◆**painless** a sans douleur; (illness, operation) indolore; (easy) Fam facile. ◆**painstaking** a (person) soigneux; (work) soigné.

paint [peɪnt] n peinture f; pl (in box, tube) couleurs fpl; – vt (colour, describe) peindre; to p. blue/etc peindre en bleu/etc; – vi to p. blue/etc peindre. ◆**-ing** n (activity) peinture f; (picture) tableau m, peinture f. ◆**-er** n peintre m. ◆**paintbrush** n pinceau m. ◆**paintwork** n peinture(s) f(pl).

pair [peər] n paire f; (man and woman) couple m; a p. of shorts un short; the p. of you Fam vous deux; – vi to p. off (of people) former un couple; – vt (marry) marier.

pajama(s) [pəˈdʒɑːmə(z)] a & npl Am = pyjama(s).

Pakistan [pɑːkɪˈstɑːn] n Pakistan m. ◆**Pakistani** a & n pakistanais, -aise (mf).

pal [pæl] n Fam copain m, copine f; – vi (-ll-) to p. up devenir copains; to p. up with devenir copain avec.

palace [ˈpælɪs] n (building) palais m. ◆**palatial** [pəˈleɪʃ(ə)l] a comme un palais.

palatable [ˈpælətəb(ə)l] a (food) agréable; (fact, idea etc) acceptable.

palate [ˈpælɪt] n Anat palais m.

palaver [pəˈlɑːvər] n Fam (fuss) histoire f(pl); (talk) palabres mpl.

pale [peɪl] a (-er, -est) (face, colour etc) pâle; p. ale bière f blonde; – vi pâlir. ◆**-ness** n pâleur f.

palette [ˈpælɪt] n (of artist) palette f.

paling [ˈpeɪlɪŋ] n (fence) palissade f.

pall [pɔːl] 1 vi devenir insipide or ennuyeux (on pour). 2 n (of smoke) voile m.

pallbearer [ˈpɔːlbeərər] n personne f qui aide à porter un cercueil.

pallid [ˈpælɪd] a pâle. ◆**pallor** n pâleur f.

pally [ˈpælɪ] a (-ier, -iest) Fam copain am, copine af (with avec).

palm [pɑːm] 1 n (of hand) paume f. 2 n (symbol) palme f; p. (tree) palmier m; p. (leaf) palme f; P. Sunday les Rameaux mpl. 3 vt Fam to p. sth off (pass off) refiler qch (on à), coller qch (on à); to p. s.o. off on s.o. coller qn à qn.

palmist [ˈpɑːmɪst] n chiromancien, -ienne mf. ◆**palmistry** n chiromancie f.

palpable [ˈpælpəb(ə)l] a (obvious) manifeste.

palpitate [ˈpælpɪteɪt] vi (of heart) palpiter. ◆**palpi'tation** n palpitation f.

paltry [ˈpɔːltrɪ] a (-ier, -iest) misérable, dérisoire.

pamper [ˈpæmpər] vt dorloter.

pamphlet [ˈpæmflɪt] n brochure f.

pan [pæn] 1 n casserole f; (for frying) poêle f (à frire); (of lavatory) cuvette f. 2 vt (-nn-) (criticize) Fam éreinter. 3 vi (-nn-) to p. out (succeed) aboutir.

Pan- [pæn] pref pan-.

panacea [pænəˈsɪə] n panacée f.

panache [pəˈnæʃ] n (showy manner) panache m.

pancake [ˈpænkeɪk] n crêpe f.

pancreas [ˈpæŋkrɪəs] n Anat pancréas m.

panda [ˈpændə] n (animal) panda m; P. car = voiture f pie inv (de la police).

pandemonium [pændɪˈməʊnɪəm] n (chaos) chaos m; (uproar) tumulte m; (place) bazar m.

pander [ˈpændər] vi to p. to (tastes, fashion etc) sacrifier à; to p. to s.o. or to s.o.'s desires se plier aux désirs de qn.

pane [peɪn] n vitre f, carreau m.

panel [ˈpæn(ə)l] n 1 (of door etc) panneau m; (control) p. Tech El console f; (instrument) p. Av Aut tableau m de bord. 2 (of judges) jury m; (of experts) groupe m; (of candidates) équipe f; (in a game) p. des invités; a p. game TV Rad un jeu par équipes. ◆**panelled** a (room etc) lambrissé. ◆**panelling** n lambris m. ◆**panellist** n TV Rad (guest) invité, -ée mf; (expert) expert m; (candidate) candidat, -ate mf.

pangs [pæŋz] npl p. of conscience remords mpl (de conscience); p. of hunger/death les affres fpl de la faim/de la mort.

panic [ˈpænɪk] n panique f; to get into a p. paniquer; – vi (-ck-) s'affoler, paniquer. ◆**p.-stricken** a affolé. ◆**panicky** (person) a Fam qui s'affole facilement; to get p. s'affoler.

panorama [pænəˈrɑːmə] n panorama m. ◆**panoramic** a panoramique.

pansy [ˈpænzɪ] n Bot pensée f.

pant [pænt] vi (gasp) haleter.

panther [ˈpænθər] n (animal) panthère f.

panties [ˈpæntɪz] npl (female underwear) slip m.

pantomime [ˈpæntəmaɪm] n (show) spectacle m de Noël.

pantry [ˈpæntrɪ] n (larder) garde-manger m inv; (storeroom in hotel etc) office m or f.

pants [pænts] npl (male underwear) slip m; (loose, long) caleçon m; (female underwear) slip m; (trousers) Am pantalon m.

pantyhose [ˈpæntɪhəʊz] n (tights) Am collant(s) m(pl).

papacy [ˈpeɪpəsɪ] n papauté f. ◆**papal** a papal.

paper [ˈpeɪpər] n papier m; (newspaper) journal m; (wallpaper) papier m peint;

(*exam*) épreuve *f* (écrite); (*student's exercise*) *Sch* copie *f*; (*learned article*) exposé *m*, communication *f*; **brown p.** papier *m* d'emballage; **to put down on p.** mettre par écrit; *– a* (*bag etc*) en papier; (*cup, plate*) en carton; **p. clip** trombone *m*; **p. knife** coupe-papier *m inv*; **p. mill** papeterie *f*; **p. shop** marchand *m* de journaux; – *vt* (*room, wall*) tapisser. ◆**paperback** *n* (*book*) livre *m* de poche. ◆**paperboy** *n* livreur *m* de journaux. ◆**paperweight** *n* presse-papiers *m inv*. ◆**paperwork** *n Com* écritures *fpl*; (*red tape*) *Pej* paperasserie *f*.

paprika ['pæprɪkə] *n* paprika *m*.

par [pɑːr] *n* **on a p.** au même niveau (**with** que); **below p.** (*unwell*) *Fam* pas en forme.

para- ['pærə] *pref* para-.

parable ['pærəb(ə)l] *n* (*story*) parabole *f*.

parachute ['pærəʃuːt] *n* parachute *m*; **to drop by p.** (*men, supplies*) parachuter; – *vi* descendre en parachute; – *vt* parachuter. ◆**parachutist** *n* parachutiste *mf*.

parade [pə'reɪd] **1** *n Mil* (*ceremony*) parade *f*; (*procession*) défilé *m*; **fashion p.** défilé *m* de mode or de mannequins; **p. ground** *Mil* terrain *m* de manœuvres; **to make a p. of** faire étalage de; – *vi Mil* défiler; **to p. about** (*walk about*) se balader; – *vt* faire étalage de. **2** *n* (*street*) avenue *f*.

paradise ['pærədaɪs] *n* paradis *m*.

paradox ['pærədɒks] *n* paradoxe *m*. ◆**para'doxically** *adv* paradoxalement.

paraffin ['pærəfɪn] *n* pétrole *m* (lampant); (*wax*) *Am* paraffine *f*; **p. lamp** lampe *f* à pétrole.

paragon ['pærəg(ə)n] *n* **p. of virtue** modèle *m* de vertu.

paragraph ['pærəgrɑːf] *n* paragraphe *m*; **'new p.'** 'à la ligne'.

parakeet ['pærəkiːt] *n* perruche *f*.

parallel ['pærəlel] *a* (*comparable*) & *Math* parallèle (**with, to** à); **to run p. to** or **with** être parallèle à; – *n* (*comparison*) & *Geog* parallèle *m*; (*line*) *Math* parallèle *f*; – *vt* être semblable à.

paralysis [pə'rælɪsɪs] *n* paralysie *f*. ◆**'paralyse** (*Am* **-lyze**) *vt* paralyser. ◆**para'lytic** *a* & *n* paralytique (*mf*).

parameter [pə'ræmɪtər] *n* paramètre *m*.

paramount ['pærəmaʊnt] *a* **of p. importance** de la plus haute importance.

paranoia [pærə'nɔɪə] *n* paranoïa *f*. ◆**'paranoid** *a* & *n* paranoïaque (*mf*).

parapet ['pærəpɪt] *n* parapet *m*.

paraphernalia [pærəfə'neɪlɪə] *n* attirail *m*.

paraphrase ['pærəfreɪz] *n* paraphrase *f*; – *vt* paraphraser.

parasite ['pærəsaɪt] *n* (*person, organism*) parasite *m*.

parasol ['pærəsɒl] *n* (*over table, on beach*) parasol *m*; (*lady's*) ombrelle *f*.

paratrooper ['pærətruːpər] *n Mil* parachutiste *m*. ◆**paratroops** *npl Mil* parachutistes *mpl*.

parboil [pɑː'bɔɪl] *vt Culin* faire bouillir à demi.

parcel ['pɑːs(ə)l] **1** *n* colis *m*, paquet *m*; **to be part and p. of** faire partie intégrante de. **2** *vt* (**-ll-**, *Am* **-l-**) **to p. out** (*divide*) partager; **to p. up** faire un paquet de.

parch [pɑːtʃ] *vt* dessécher; **to be parched** (*thirsty*) être assoiffé; **to make parched** (*thirsty*) donner très soif à.

parchment ['pɑːtʃmənt] *n* parchemin *m*.

pardon ['pɑːd(ə)n] *n* pardon *m*; *Jur* grâce *f*; **general p.** amnistie *f*; **I beg your p.** (*apologize*) je vous prie de m'excuser; (*not hearing*) vous dîtes?; **p.?** (*not hearing*) comment?; **p. (me)!** (*sorry*) pardon!; – *vt* pardonner (**s.o. for sth** qch à qn); **to p. s.o.** pardonner (à) qn; *Jur* gracier qn.

pare [peər] *vt* (*trim*) rogner; (*peel*) éplucher; **to p. down** *Fig* réduire, rogner.

parent ['peərənt] *n* père *m*, mère *f*; **one's parents** ses parents *mpl*, son père et sa mère; **p. firm, p. company** *Com* maison *f* mère. ◆**parentage** *n* (*origin*) origine *f*. ◆**pa'rental** *a* des parents, parental. ◆**parenthood** *n* paternité *f*, maternité *f*.

parenthesis, *pl* **-eses** [pə'renθəsɪs, -əsiːz] *n* parenthèse *f*.

Paris ['pærɪs] *n* Paris *m or f*. ◆**Parisian** [pə'rɪzɪən, *Am* pə'rɪʒən] *a* & *n* parisien, -ienne (*mf*).

parish ['pærɪʃ] *n Rel* paroisse *f*; (*civil*) commune *f*; – *a* (*church, register*) paroissial; **p. council** conseil *m* municipal. ◆**pa'rishioner** *n* paroissien, -ienne *mf*.

parity ['pærɪtɪ] *n* parité *f*.

park [pɑːk] **1** *n* (*garden*) parc *m*. **2** *vt* (*vehicle*) garer; (*put*) *Fam* mettre, poser; – *vi Aut* se garer; (*remain parked*) stationner. ◆**-ing** *n* stationnement *m*; **'no p.'** 'défense de stationner'; **p. bay** aire *f* de stationnement; **p. lot** *Am* parking *m*; **p. meter** parcmètre *m*; **p. place** endroit *m* pour se garer; **p. ticket** contravention *f*.

parka ['pɑːkə] *n* (*coat*) parka *m*.

parkway ['pɑːkweɪ] *n Am* avenue *f*.

parliament ['pɑːləmənt] *n* parlement *m*; *Br* Parlement *m*. ◆**parlia'mentary** *a* parlementaire. ◆**parliamen'tarian** *n* parlementaire *m* (expérimenté(e)).

parlour ['pɑːlər] *n* (*in mansion*) (petit) salon

m; **ice-cream p.** *Am* salon de glaces; **p. game** jeu *m* de société.

parochial [pəˈrəʊkɪəl] *a* (*mentality, quarrel*) *Pej* de clocher; (*person*) *Pej* provincial, borné; *Rel* paroissial.

parody [ˈpærədɪ] *n* parodie *f*; – *vt* parodier.

parole [pəˈrəʊl] **on p.** *Jur* en liberté conditionnelle.

parquet [ˈpɑːkeɪ] *n* **p. (floor)** parquet *m*.

parrot [ˈpærət] *n* perroquet *m*; **p. fashion** *Pej* comme un perroquet.

parry [ˈpærɪ] *vt* (*blow*) parer; (*question*) éluder; – *n Sp* parade *f*.

parsimonious [pɑːsɪˈməʊnɪəs] *a* parcimonieux. **◆—ly** *adv* avec parcimonie.

parsley [ˈpɑːslɪ] *n* persil *m*.

parsnip [ˈpɑːsnɪp] *n* panais *m*.

parson [ˈpɑːs(ə)n] *n* pasteur *m*; **p.'s nose** (*of chicken*) croupion *m*.

part [pɑːt] **1** *n* partie *f*; (*of machine*) pièce *f*; (*of periodical*) livraison *f*; (*of serial*) épisode *m*; (*in play, film, activity*) rôle *m*; (*division*) *Culin* mesure *f*; (*in hair*) *Am* raie *f*; **to take p.** participer (**in** à); **to take s.o.'s p.** (*side*) prendre parti pour qn; **in p.** en partie; **for the most p.** dans l'ensemble; **to be a p. of** faire partie de; **on the p. of** (*behalf of*) de la part de; **for my p.** pour ma part; **in these parts** dans ces parages; **in p. exchange** reprise *f*; **to take in p. exchange** reprendre; **p. owner** copropriétaire *mf*; **p. payment** paiement *m* partiel; – *adv* en partie; **p. American** en partie américain. **2** *vt* (*separate*) séparer; (*crowd*) diviser; **to p. one's hair** se faire une raie; **to p. company with** (*leave*) quitter; – *vi* (*of friends etc*) se quitter; (*of married couple*) se séparer; **p. with** (*get rid of*) se séparer de. **◆—ing** *n* séparation *f*; – *a* (*gift, words*) d'adieu. **2** *n* (*in hair*) raie *f*.

partake [pɑːˈteɪk] *vi* (*pt* **partook**, *pp* **partaken**) **to p.** in participer à; **to p. of** (*meal, food*) prendre, manger.

partial [ˈpɑːʃəl] *a* partiel; (*biased*) partial (**towards** envers); **to be p. to** (*fond of*) *Fam* avoir un faible pour. **◆parti'ality** *n* (*bias*) partialité *f*; (*liking*) prédilection *f*.

participate [pɑːˈtɪsɪpeɪt] *vi* participer (**in** à). **◆participant** *n* participant, -ante *mf*. **◆partici'pation** *n* participation *f*.

participle [ˈpɑːtɪsɪp(ə)l] *n* participe *m*.

particle [ˈpɑːtɪk(ə)l] *n* (*of atom, dust, name*) particule *f*; (*of truth*) grain *m*.

particular [pəˈtɪkjʊlər] **1** *a* (*specific, special*) particulier; (*fastidious, fussy*) difficile (**about** sur); (*meticulous*) méticuleux; **this p. book** ce livre-ci en particulier; **in p.** en

particulier; **to be p. about** faire très attention à. **2** *n* (*detail*) détail *m*; **s.o.'s particulars** le nom et l'adresse de qn; (*description*) le signalement de qn. **◆—ly** *adv* particulièrement.

partisan [pɑːtɪˈzæn, *Am* ˈpɑːtɪz(ə)n] *n* partisan *m*.

partition [pɑːˈtɪʃ(ə)n] **1** *n* (*of room*) cloison *f*; – *vt* **to p. off** cloisonner. **2** *n* (*of country*) *Pol* partition *f*, partage *m*; – *vt Pol* partager.

partly [ˈpɑːtlɪ] *adv* en partie; **p. English p. French** moitié anglais moitié français.

partner [ˈpɑːtnər] *n* (*lover, spouse*) & *Sp Pol* partenaire *mf*; (*of racing driver etc*) coéquipier, -ière *mf*; (*dancing*) *p.* cavalier, -ière *mf*. **◆partnership** *n* association *f*; **to take into p.** prendre comme associé(e); **in p. with** en association avec.

partridge [ˈpɑːtrɪdʒ] *n* perdix *f*.

part-time [pɑːtˈtaɪm] *a & adv* à temps partiel; (*half-time*) à mi-temps.

party [ˈpɑːtɪ] *n* **1** (*group*) groupe *m*; *Pol* parti *m*; (*in contract, lawsuit*) *Jur* partie *f*; *Mil* détachement *m*; *Tel* correspondant, -ante *mf*; **rescue p.** équipe *f* de sauveteurs *or* de secours; **third p.** *Jur* tiers *m*; **innocent p.** innocent, -ente *mf*; **to be (a) p. to** (*crime*) être complice de; **p. line** *Tel* ligne *f* partagée; *Pol* ligne *f* du parti; **p. ticket** billet *m* collectif. **2** (*gathering*) réception *f*, (*informal*) surprise-partie *f*; (*for birthday*) fête *f*; **cocktail p.** cocktail *m*; **dinner p.** dîner *m*; **tea p.** thé *m*.

pass [pɑːs] **1** *n* (*entry permit*) laissez-passer *m inv*; (*free ticket*) *Th* billet *m* de faveur; (*season ticket*) carte *f* d'abonnement; (*over mountains*) *Geog* col *m*; *Fb etc* passe *f*; (*in exam*) mention *f* passable (**in** French/etc en français/etc); **to make a p. at** faire des avances à; **p. mark** (*in exam*) moyenne *f*, barre *f* d'admissibilité; **p. key** passepartout *m inv*. **2** *vt* (*go, come, disappear*) passer (**to** à, **through** par); (*overtake*) *Aut* dépasser; (*in exam*) être reçu (**in** French/etc en français/etc); (*take place*) se passer; **that'll p.** (*be acceptable*) ça ira; **he can p. for thirty** on lui donnerait trente ans; **to p. along** *or* **through** passer; **to p. away** *or* **on** (*die*) mourir; **to p. by** passer (à côté); **to p. off** (*happen*) se passer; **to p. on to** (*move on to*) passer à; **to p. out** (*faint*) s'évanouir; – *vt* (*move, spend, give etc*) passer (**to** à); (*go past*) passer devant; (*exam*) être reçu à; (*candidate*) recevoir; (*judgement, opinion*) prononcer (**on** sur); (*remark*) faire; (*allow*) autoriser; (*bill, law*) *Pol* voter; **to p. (by)** s.o. (*in street*) croiser qn; **to p. by** (*building*) passer devant; **to p. oneself off as** se faire passer pour; **to p. sth off on** (*fob off on*) refiler qch à; **to p. on** (*message, title, illness etc*) transmettre (**to** à); **to p. out** or **round** (*hand out*) distribuer; **to p. over** (*ignore*) passer sur, oublier; **to p. round** (*cigarettes, sweets etc*) faire passer; **to p. up** (*chance etc*) laisser passer. ◆**—ing** *a* (*vehicle etc*) qui passe; (*beauty*) *n* (*of visitor, vehicle etc*) passage *m*; (*of time*) écoulement *m*; (*death*) disparition *f*.

passable ['pɑːsəb(ə)l] *a* (*not bad*) passable; (*road*) praticable; (*river*) franchisssable.

passage ['pæsidʒ] *n* (*passing, way through, of text, of speech etc*) passage *m*; (*of time*) écoulement *m*; (*corridor*) couloir *m*; *Nau* traversée *f*, passage *m*. ◆**passageway** *n* (*way through*) passage *m*; (*corridor*) couloir *m*.

passbook ['pɑːsbʊk] *n* livret *m* de caisse d'épargne.

passenger ['pæsindʒər] *n* passager, -ère *mf*; *Rail* voyageur, -euse *mf*.

passer-by [pɑːsə'baɪ] *n* (*pl* **passers-by**) passant, -ante *mf*.

passion ['pæʃ(ə)n] *n* passion *f*; **to have a p. for** (*cars etc*) avoir la passion de, adorer. ◆**passionate** *a* passionné. ◆**passionately** *adv* passionnément.

passive ['pæsɪv] *a* (*not active*) passif; — *n* *Gram* passif *m*. ◆**—ness** *n* passivité *f*.

Passover ['pɑːsəʊvər] *n* *Rel* Pâque *f*.

passport ['pɑːspɔːt] *n* passeport *m*.

password ['pɑːswɜːd] *n* mot *m* de passe.

past [pɑːst] **1** *n* (*time, history*) passé *m*; **in the p.** (*formerly*) dans le temps; **it's a thing of the p.** ça n'existe plus; — *a* (*gone by*) passé; (*former*) ancien; **these p. months** ces derniers mois; **that's all p.** c'est du passé; **in the p. tense** *Gram* au passé. **2** *prep* (*in front of*) devant; (*after*) après; (*further than*) plus loin que; (*next to*) *Fig* trop vieux pour; **p. four o'clock** quatre heures passées, plus de quatre heures; **to be p. fifty** avoir cinquante ans passés; **it's p. belief** c'est incroyable; **I wouldn't put it p. him** ça ne m'étonnerait pas de lui, il en est bien capable; — *adv* devant; **to go p.** passer.

pasta ['pæstə] *n* *Culin* pâtes *fpl* (alimentaires).

paste [peɪst] **1** *n* (*of meat*) pâté *m*; (*of anchovy etc*) beurre *m*; (*dough*) pâte *f*. **2** *n* (*glue*) colle *f* (blanche); — *vt* coller; **to p. up** (*notice etc*) afficher.

pastel ['pæstəl, *Am* pæ'stel] *n* pastel *m*; — *a* (*shade*) pastel *inv*; (*drawing*) au pastel.

pasteurized ['pæstəraɪzd] *a* (*milk*) pasteurisé.

pastiche [pæ'stiːʃ] *n* pastiche *m*.

pastille ['pæstɪl, *Am* pæ'stiːl] *n* pastille *f*.

pastime ['pɑːstaɪm] *n* passe-temps *m inv*.

pastor ['pɑːstər] *n* *Rel* pasteur *m*. ◆**pastoral** *a* pastoral.

pastry ['peɪstrɪ] *n* (*dough*) pâte *f*; (*cake*) pâtisserie *f*; **puff p.** pâte *f* feuilletée. ◆**pastrycook** *n* pâtissier, -ière *mf*.

pasture ['pɑːstʃər] *n* pâturage *m*.

pasty 1 ['pæstɪ] *a* (*-ier, -iest*) (*complexion*) terreux. **2** ['pæstɪ] *n* *Culin* petit pâté *m* (en croûte).

pat [pæt] **1** *vt* (*-tt-*) (*cheek, table etc*) tapoter; (*animal*) caresser; — *n* petite tape; caresse *f*. **2** *adv* **to answer p.** avoir la réponse toute prête; **to know sth off p.** savoir qch sur le bout du doigt.

patch [pætʃ] *n* (*for clothes*) pièce *f*; (*over eye*) bandeau *m*; (*for bicycle tyre*) rustine® *f*; (*of colour*) tache *f*; (*of sky*) morceau *m*; (*of fog*) nappe *f*; (*of ice*) plaque *f*; **a cabbage/etc p.** un carré de choux/*etc*; **a bad p.** *Fig* une mauvaise passe; **not to be a p. on** (*not as good as*) *Fam* ne pas arriver à la cheville de; — *vt* **to p. (up)** (*clothing*) rapiécer; **to p. up** (*quarrel*) régler; (*marriage*) replâtrer. ◆**patchwork** *n* patchwork *m*. ◆**patchy** *a* (*-ier, -iest*) inégal.

patent 1 ['peɪtənt] *a* patent, manifeste; **p. leather** cuir *m* verni. **2** ['peɪtənt, 'pætənt] *n* brevet *m* (d'invention); — *vt* (faire) breveter. ◆**—ly** *adv* manifestement.

paternal [pə'tɜːn(ə)l] *a* paternel. ◆**paternity** *n* paternité *f*.

path [pɑːθ] *n* (*pl* **-s** [pɑːðz]) sentier *m*, chemin *m*; (*in park*) allée *f*; (*of river*) cours *m*; (*of bullet, planet*) trajectoire *f*. ◆**pathway** *n* sentier *m*, chemin *m*.

pathetic [pə'θetɪk] *a* pitoyable.

pathology [pə'θɒlədʒɪ] *n* pathologie *f*. ◆**patho'logical** *a* pathologique.

pathos ['peɪθɒs] *n* pathétique *m*.

patient ['peɪʃ(ə)nt] **1** *a* patient. **2** *n* (*in hospital*) malade *mf*, patient, -ente *mf*; (*on doctor's or dentist's list*) patient, -ente *mf*. ◆**patience** *n* patience *f*; **to have p.** prendre patience; **to lose p.** perdre patience; **I have no p. with him** il m'impatiente; **to play p.** *Cards* faire des réussites. ◆**patiently** *adv* patiemment.

patio ['pætɪəʊ] *n* (*pl* **-os**) patio *m*.

patriarch ['peɪtrɪɑːk] *n* patriarche *m*.

patriot ['pætriət, 'peitriət] n patriote mf.
◆**patri'otic** a (views, speech etc) patriotique; (person) patriote. ◆**patriotism** n patriotisme m.

patrol [pə'trəʊl] n patrouille f; **p. boat** patrouilleur m; **police p. car** voiture f de police; **p. wagon** Am fourgon m cellulaire; – vi (-ll-) patrouiller; – vt patrouiller dans. ◆**patrolman** n (pl -men) Am agent m de police; (repair man) Aut dépanneur m.

patron ['peitrən] n (of artist) protecteur, -trice mf; (customer) Com client, -ente mf; (of cinema, theatre) habitué, -ée mf; **p. saint** patron, -onne mf. ◆**patronage** n (support) patronage m; (of the arts) protection f; (custom) Com clientèle f. ◆**patroniz/e** ['pætrənaiz, Am 'peitrənaiz] vt **1** Com accorder sa clientèle à. **2** (person) Pej traiter avec condescendance. ◆**-ing** a condescendant.

patter ['pætər] **1** n (of footsteps) petit bruit m; (of rain, hail) crépitement m; – vi (of rain, hail) crépiter, tambouriner. **2** n (talk) baratin m.

pattern ['pæt(ə)n] n dessin m, motif m; (paper model for garment) patron m; (fabric sample) échantillon m; **p. modèle** m; (plan) plan m; (method) formule f; (of a crime) scénario m. ◆**patterned** a (dress, cloth) à motifs.

paucity ['pɔːsiti] n pénurie f.

paunch [pɔːntʃ] n panse f, bedon m. ◆**paunchy** a (-ier, -iest) bedonnant.

pauper ['pɔːpər] n pauvre mf, indigent, -ente mf.

pause [pɔːz] n pause f; (in conversation) silence m; – vi (stop) faire une pause; (hesitate) hésiter.

pav/e [peiv] vt paver; **to p. the way for** Fig ouvrir la voie à. ◆**-ing** n (surface) revêtement m, dallage m; **p. stone** pavé m. ◆**pavement** n trottoir m; (roadway) Am chaussée f; (stone) pavé m.

pavilion [pə'viljən] n (building) pavillon m.

paw [pɔː] **1** n patte f; – vt (animal) donner des coups de patte à. **2** vt (touch improperly) tripoter.

pawn [pɔːn] **1** n Chess pion m. **2** vt mettre en gage; – n in pawn en gage. ◆**pawnbroker** n prêteur, -euse mf sur gages. ◆**pawnshop** n mont-de-piété m.

pay [pei] n salaire m, (of workman) paie f, salaire m; Mil solde f, paie f; **p. phone** téléphone m public; **p. day** jour m de paie; **p. slip** bulletin m or fiche f de paie; – vt (pt & pp **paid**) (person, sum) payer; (deposit) verser; (yield) Com rapporter; (compli-

ment, attention, visit) faire; **to p. s.o. to do** or **for doing** payer qn pour faire; **to p. s.o. for sth** payer qch à qn; **to p. money into one's account** or **the bank** verser de l'argent sur son compte; **it pays (one) to be cautious** on a intérêt à être prudent; **to p. homage** or **tribute to** rendre hommage à; **to p. you back for this!** je te revaudrai ça!; **to p. in** (cheque) verser (**to one's account sur son** compte); **to p. off** (debt, creditor etc) rembourser; (in instalments) rembourser par acomptes; (staff, worker) licencier; **to p. off an old score** or **a grudge** Fig régler un vieux compte; **to p. out** (spend) dépenser; **to p. up** payer; – vi payer; **to p. for sth** payer qch; **to p. a lot** (for sth) payer cher; **to p. off** (be successful) être payant; **to p. up** payer. ◆**-ing** a (guest) payant; (profitable) rentable; – n p. to un chèque à l'ordre de. ◆**-ment** n paiement m; (of deposit) versement m; (reward) récompense f; **on p. of 20 francs** moyennant 20 francs. ◆**payoff** n Fam (reward) récompense f; (revenge) règlement m de comptes. ◆**payroll** n **to be on the p. of** (firm, factory) être employé par; **to have twenty workers on the p.** employer vingt ouvriers.

pea [piː] n pois m; **garden** or **green peas** petits pois mpl; **p. soup** soupe f aux pois.

peace [piːs] n paix f; **p. of mind** tranquillité f d'esprit; **in p.** en paix; **at p.** en paix (**with** avec); **to have (some) p. and quiet** avoir la paix; **to disturb the p.** troubler l'ordre public; **to hold one's p.** garder le silence. ◆**p.-keeping** a (force) de maintien de la paix; (measure) de pacification. ◆**p.-loving** a pacifique. ◆**peaceable** a paisible, pacifique. ◆**peaceful** a paisible, calme; (coexistence, purpose, demonstration) pacifique. ◆**peacefulness** n paix f.

peach [piːtʃ] n (fruit) pêche f; (tree) pêcher m; – a (colour) pêche inv.

peacock ['piːkɒk] n paon m.

peak [piːk] n (mountain top) sommet m; (mountain itself) pic m; (of cap) visière f; (of fame etc) Fig sommet m, apogée m; **the traffic has reached** or **is at its p.** la circulation est à son maximum; – a (hours, period) de pointe; (demand, production) maximum; – vi (of sales etc) atteindre son maximum. ◆**peaked** a **p. cap** casquette f.

peaky ['piːki] a (-ier, -iest) Fam (ill) patraque; (pale) pâlot.

peal [piːl] **1** n (of laughter) éclat m; (of thun-

der) roulement *m.* **2** *n* p. of bells carillon *m*; — *vi* to **p. (out)** (*of bells*) carillonner.

peanut ['pi:nʌt] *n* cacah(o)uète *f*; (*plant*) arachide *f*; **to earn/etc peanuts** (*little money*) *Fam* gagner/*etc* des clopinettes.

pear [peər] *n* poire *f*; **p. tree** poirier *m*.

pearl [pɜːl] *n* perle *f*; (*mother-of-pearl*) nacre *f*. ◆**pearly** *a* (**-ier, -iest**) (*colour*) nacré.

peasant ['pezənt] *n* & *a* paysan, -anne (*mf*).

peashooter ['pi:ʃuːtər] *n* sarbacane *f*.

peat [pi:t] *n* tourbe *f*.

pebble ['peb(ə)l] *n* (*stone*) caillou *m*; (*on beach*) galet *m*. ◆**pebbly** *a* (*beach*) (couvert) de galets.

pecan ['pi:kæn] *n* (*nut*) *Am* pacane *f*.

peck [pek] *vti* to **p. (at)** (*of bird*) picorer (du pain *etc*); (*person*) *Fig* donner un coup de bec à; **to p. at one's food** (*of person*) manger du bout des dents; — *n* coup *m* de bec; (*kiss*) *Fam* bécot *m*.

peckish ['pekɪʃ] *a* **to be p.** (*hungry*) *Fam* avoir un petit creux.

peculiar [pɪ'kjuːliər] *a* (*strange*) bizarre; (*characteristic, special*) particulier (**to** à). ◆**peculi'arity** *n* (*feature*) particularité *f*; (*oddity*) bizarrerie *f*. ◆**peculiarly** *adv* bizarrement; (*specially*) particulièrement.

pedal ['ped(ə)l] *n* pédale *f*; **p. boat** pédalo *m*; — *vi* (**-ll-**, *Am* **-l-**) pédaler; — *vt* (*bicycle*) actionner les pédales de. ◆**pedalbin** *n* poubelle *f* à pédale.

pedant ['pedənt] *n* pédant, -ante *mf*. ◆**pe'dantic** *a* pédant. ◆**pedantry** *n* pédantisme *m*.

peddl/e ['ped(ə)l] *vt* colporter; (*drugs*) faire le trafic de; — *vi* faire du colportage. ◆**-er** *n* (*Am* (*door-to-door*) colporteur, -euse *mf*; (*in street*) camelot *m*; **drug p.** revendeur, -euse *mf* de drogues.

pedestal ['pedɪst(ə)l] *n* *Archit* & *Fig* piédestal *m*.

pedestrian [pə'destriən] **1** *n* piéton *m*; **p. crossing** passage *m* pour piétons; **p. precinct** zone *f* piétonnière. **2** *a* (*speech, style*) prosaïque. ◆**pedestrianize** *vt* (*street etc*) rendre piétonnier.

pedigree ['pedɪgriː] *n* (*of dog, horse etc*) pedigree *m*; (*of person*) ascendance *f*; — *a* (*dog, horse etc*) de race.

pedlar ['pedlər] *n* (*door-to-door*) colporteur, -euse *mf*; (*in street*) camelot *m*.

pee [piː] *n* **to go for a p.** *Fam* faire pipi.

peek [piːk] *n* coup *m* d'œil (furtif); — *vi* jeter un coup d'œil (furtif) (**at** à).

peel [piːl] *n* (*of vegetable, fruit*) pelure(s) *f(pl)*, épluchure(s) *f(pl)*; (*of orange skin*) écorce *f*; (*in food, drink*) zeste *m*; **a piece of**

p. une pelure, une épluchure; — *vt* (*fruit, vegetable*) peler, éplucher; **to keep one's eyes peeled** *Fam* être vigilant; **to p. off** (*label etc*) décoller; — *vi* (*of sunburnt skin*) peler; (*of paint*) s'écailler; **to p. easily** (*of fruit*) se peler facilement. ◆**-ings** *npl* pelures *fpl*, épluchures *fpl*. ◆**-er** *n* (*knife etc*) éplucheur *m*.

peep [piːp] **1** *n* coup *m* d'œil (furtif); — *vi* to **p. (at)** regarder furtivement; **to p. out** se montrer; **peeping Tom** voyeur, -euse *mf*. **2** *vi* (*of bird*) pépier. ◆**peephole** *n* judas *m*.

peer [piər] **1** *n* (*equal*) pair *m*, égal, -ale *mf*; (*noble*) pair *m*. **2** *vi* to **p. (at)** regarder attentivement (*comme pour mieux voir*); **to p. into** (*darkness*) scruter. ◆**peerage** *n* (*rank*) pairie *f*.

peeved [piːvd] *a* *Fam* irrité.

peevish ['piːvɪʃ] *a* grincheux, irritable.

peg [peg] **1** *n* (*wooden*) *Tech* cheville *f*; (*metal*) *Tech* fiche *f*; (*for tent*) piquet *m*; (*for clothes*) pince *f* (à linge); (*for coat, hat etc*) patère *f*; **to buy off the peg** acheter en prêt-à-porter. **2** *vt* (**-gg-**) (*prices*) stabiliser.

pejorative [pɪ'dʒɒrətɪv] *a* péjoratif.

pekin(g)ese [piːkɪ'niːz] *n* (*dog*) pékinois *m*.

pelican ['pelɪkən] *n* (*bird*) pélican *m*.

pellet ['pelɪt] *n* (*of paper etc*) boulette *f*; (*for gun*) (grain *m* de) plomb *m*.

pelt [pelt] **1** *n* (*skin*) peau *f*; (*fur*) fourrure *f*. **2** *vt* to **p. s.o. with** (*stones etc*) bombarder qn de. **3** *vt* **it's pelting (down)** (*raining*) il pleut à verse. **4** *vi* to **p. along** (*run, dash*) *Fam* foncer, courir.

pelvis ['pelvɪs] *n* *Anat* bassin *m*.

pen [pen] **1** *n* (*dipped in ink*) porte-plume *m inv*; (*fountain pen*) stylo *m* (à encre *or* à plume); (*ballpoint*) stylo *m* à bille, stylo(-)bille *m*; **to live by one's p.** *Fig* vivre de sa plume; **p. friend, p. pal** correspondant, -ante *mf*; **p. name** pseudonyme *m*; **p. nib** (bec *m* de) plume *f*; **p. pusher** *Pej* gratte-papier *m inv*; — *vt* (**-nn-**) (*write*) écrire. **2** *n* (*enclosure for baby or sheep or cattle*) parc *m*.

penal ['piːn(ə)l] *a* (*law, code etc*) pénal; (*colony*) pénitentiaire. ◆**penalize** *vt* *Sp Jur* pénaliser (**for** pour); (*handicap*) désavantager.

penalty ['pen(ə)ltɪ] *n* *Jur* peine *f*; (*fine*) amende *f*; *Sp* pénalisation *f*; *Fb* penalty *m*; *Rugby* pénalité *f*; **to pay the p.** *Fig* subir les conséquences.

penance ['penəns] *n* pénitence *f*.

pence [pens] *see* **penny**.

pencil ['pens(ə)l] *n* crayon *m*; **in p.** au crayon; **p. box** plumier *m*; **p. sharpener**

taille-crayon(s) *m inv*; – *vt* (**-ll-,** *Am* **-l-**) crayonner; **to p. in** *Fig* noter provisoirement.

pendant ['pendənt] *n* pendentif *m*; (*on earring, chandelier*) pendeloque *f*.

pending ['pendiŋ] **1** *a* (*matter*) en suspens. **2** *prep* (*until*) en attendant.

pendulum ['pendjuləm] *n* (*of clock*) balancier *m*, pendule *m*; *Fig* pendule *f*.

penetrat/e ['penitreit] *vt* (*substance, mystery etc*) percer; (*plan, secret etc*) découvrir; – *vti* **to p. (into)** (*forest, group etc*) pénétrer dans. ◆**-ing** *a* (*mind, cold etc*) pénétrant. ◆**pene'tration** *n* pénétration *f*.

penguin ['peŋgwin] *n* manchot *m*, pingouin *m*.

penicillin [peni'silin] *n* pénicilline *f*.

peninsula [pə'ninsjulə] *n* presqu'île *f*, péninsule *f*. ◆**pensinsular** *a* péninsulaire.

penis ['piːnis] *n* pénis *m*.

penitent ['penitənt] *a* & *n* pénitent, -ente (*mf*). ◆**penitence** *n* pénitence *f*.

penitentiary [peni'tenʃəri] *n Am* prison *f* (centrale).

penknife ['pennaif] *n* (*pl* **-knives**) canif *m*.

pennant ['penənt] *n* (*flag*) flamme *f*, banderole *f*.

penny ['peni] *n* **1** (*pl* **pennies**) (*coin*) penny *m*; *Am Can* cent *m*; **I don't have a p.** *Fig* je n'ai pas le sou. **2** (*pl* **pence** [pens]) (*value, currency*) penny *m*. ◆**p.-pinching** *a* (*miserly*) *Fam* avare. ◆**penniless** *a* sans le sou.

pension ['penʃ(ə)n] *n* pension *f*; **retirement p.** (pension *f* de) retraite *f*; (*private*) retraite *f* complémentaire; – *vt* **to p. off** mettre à la retraite. ◆**-able** *a* (*age*) de la retraite; (*job*) qui donne droit à une retraite. ◆**-er** *n* pensionné, -ée *mf*; (*old age*) p. retraité, -ée *mf*.

pensive ['pensiv] *a* pensif.

pentagon ['pentəgən] *n* **the P.** *Am Pol* le Pentagone.

pentathlon [pen'tæθlən] *n Sp* pentathlon *m*.

Pentecost ['pentikɒst] *n* (*Whitsun*) *Am* Pentecôte *f*.

penthouse ['penthaus] *n* appartement *m* de luxe (*construit sur le toit d'un immeuble*).

pent-up [pent'ʌp] *a* (*feelings*) refoulé.

penultimate [pi'nʌltimət] *a* avant-dernier.

peony ['piːəni] *n Bot* pivoine *f*.

people ['piːp(ə)l] *npl* (*in general*) gens *mpl or fpl*; (*specific persons*) personnes *fpl*; (*of region, town*) habitants *mpl*, gens *mpl or fpl*; **the p.** (*citizens*) *Pol* le peuple *m*; **old p.** les personnes *fpl* âgées; **old people's home**

hospice *m* de vieillards; (*private*) maison *f* de retraite; **two p.** deux personnes; **English p.** les Anglais *mpl*, le peuple anglais; **a lot of p.** beaucoup de monde *or* de gens; **p. think that . . .** on pense que . . . ; – *n* (*nation*) peuple *m*; – *vt* (*populate*) peupler (**with** de).

pep [pep] *n* entrain *m*; **p. talk** *Fam* petit laïus d'encouragement; – *vt* (**-pp-**) **to p. up** (*perk up*) ragaillardir.

pepper ['pepər] *n* poivre *m*; (*vegetable*) poivron *m*; – *vt* poivrer. ◆**peppercorn** *n* grain *m* de poivre. ◆**peppermint** *n* (*plant*) menthe *f* poivrée; (*sweet*) pastille *f* de menthe. ◆**peppery** *a Culin* poivré.

per [pɜːr] *prep* par; **p. annum** par an; **p. head, p. person** par personne; **p. cent** pour cent; **50 pence p. kilo** 50 pence le kilo; **40 km p. hour** 40 km à l'heure. ◆**per'centage** *n* pourcentage *m*.

perceive [pə'siːv] *vt* (*see, hear*) percevoir; (*notice*) remarquer (**that** que). ◆**perceptible** *a* perceptible. ◆**perception** *n* perception *f* (**of** de); (*intuition*) intuition *f*. ◆**perceptive** *a* (*person*) perspicace; (*study, remark*) pénétrant.

perch [pɜːtʃ] **1** *n* perchoir *m*; – *vi* (*of bird*) (se) percher; (*of person*) *Fig* se percher, se jucher; – *vt* (*put*) percher. **2** *n* (*fish*) perche *f*.

percolate ['pɜːkəleit] *vi* (*of liquid*) filtrer, passer (**through** par); – *vt* (*coffee*) faire dans une cafetière; **percolated coffee** du vrai café. ◆**percolator** *n* cafetière *f*; (*in café or restaurant*) percolateur *m*.

percussion [pə'kʌʃ(ə)n] *n Mus* percussion *f*.

peremptory [pə'remptəri] *a* péremptoire.

perennial [pə'reniəl] *a* **1** (*complaint, subject etc*) perpétuel. **2** *a* (*plant*) vivace; – *n* plante *f* vivace.

perfect ['pɜːfikt] *a* parfait; – *a* & *n* **p. (tense)** *Gram* parfait *m*; – [pə'fekt] *vt* (*book, piece of work etc*) parachever, parfaire; (*process, technique*) mettre au point; (*one's French etc*) parfaire ses connaissances. ◆**per-'fection** *n* perfection *f*; (*act*) parachèvement *m* (**of** de); mise *f* au point (**of** de); **to p.** à la perfection. ◆**per'fectionist** *n* perfectionniste *mf*. ◆**'perfectly** *adv* parfaitement.

perfidious [pə'fidiəs] *a Lit* perfide.

perforate ['pɜːfəreit] *vt* perforer. ◆**perfo-'ration** *n* perforation *f*.

perform [pə'fɔːm] *vt* (*task, miracle*) accomplir; (*a function, one's duty*) remplir; (*rite*) célébrer; (*operation*) *Med* pratiquer (**on**

sur; (a play, symphony) jouer; (sonata) interpréter; – vi (play) jouer; (sing) chanter; (dance) danser; (of circus animal) faire un numéro; (function) fonctionner; (behave) se comporter; **you performed very well!** tu as très bien fait! ◆—**ing** a (animal) savant. ◆**performance** n **1** (show) Th représentation f, séance f; Cin Mus séance f. **2** (of athlete, machine etc) performance f; (of actor, musician etc) interprétation f; (circus act) numéro m; (fuss) Fam histoire(s) f(pl); **the p. of one's duties** l'exercice m de ses fonctions. ◆**performer** n interprète mf (of de; (entertainer) artiste mf.

perfume ['pɜːfjuːm] n parfum m; – [pə'fjuːm] vt parfumer.

perfunctory [pə'fʌŋktərɪ] a (action) superficiel; (smile etc) de commande.

perhaps [pə'hæps] adv peut-être; **p. not** peut-être que non.

peril ['perɪl] n péril m, danger m; **at your p.** à vos risques et péril. ◆**perilous** a périlleux.

perimeter [pə'rɪmɪtər] n périmètre m.

period ['pɪərɪəd] **1** (length of time, moment in time) période f; (historical) époque f; (time limit) délai m; (lesson) Sch leçon f; (full stop) Gram point m; **in the p. of a month** en l'espace d'un mois; **I refuse, p.!** Am je refuse, un point c'est tout!; – a (furniture etc) d'époque; (costume) de l'époque. **2** n (menstruation) règles fpl. ◆**peri'odic** a périodique. ◆**peri'odical** n (magazine) périodique m. ◆**peri'odically** adv périodiquement.

periphery [pə'rɪfərɪ] n périphérie f. ◆**peripheral** a (question) sans rapport direct (**to** avec); (interest) accessoire; (neighbourhood) périphérique.

periscope ['perɪskəup] n périscope m.

perish ['perɪʃ] vi (die) périr; (of food, substance) se détériorer; **to be perished** or **perishing** (of person) Fam être frigorifié. ◆—**ing** a (cold, weather) Fam glacial. ◆—**able** a (food) périssable; – npl denrées fpl périssables.

perjure ['pɜːdʒər] vt **to p. oneself** se parjurer. ◆**perjurer** n (person) parjure mf. ◆**perjury** n (act); **to commit p.** se parjurer.

perk [pɜːk] **1** vi **to p. up** (buck up) se ragaillardir; – vt **to p. s.o. up** remonter qn, ragaillardir qn. **2** n (advantage) avantage m; (extra profit) à-côté m. ◆**perky** a (-ier, -iest) (cheerful) guilleret, plein d'entrain.

perm [pɜːm] n (of hair) permanente f; – vt **to**

have one's hair permed se faire faire une permanente.

permanent ['pɜːmənənt] a permanent; (address) fixe; **she's p. here** elle est ici à titre permanent. ◆**permanence** n permanence f. ◆**permanently** adv à titre permanent.

permeate ['pɜːmɪeɪt] vt (of ideas etc) se répandre dans; **to p. (through)** (of liquid etc) pénétrer. ◆**permeable** a perméable.

permit [pə'mɪt] vt (-tt-) permettre (**s.o. to do** à qn de faire); **weather permitting** si le temps le permet; – ['pɜːmɪt] n (licence) permis m; (entrance pass) laissez-passer m inv. ◆**per'missible** a permis. ◆**per'mission** n permission f, autorisation f (**to do** de faire); **to ask (for)/give p.** demander/donner la permission. ◆**per'missive** a (trop) tolérant, laxiste. ◆**per'missiveness** n laxisme m.

permutation [pɜːmjuː'teɪʃ(ə)n] n permutation f.

pernicious [pə'nɪʃəs] a (harmful) & Med pernicieux.

pernickety [pə'nɪkətɪ] a Fam (precise) pointilleux; (demanding) difficile (**about** sur).

peroxide [pə'rɒksaɪd] n (bleach) eau f oxygénée; – a (hair, blond) oxygéné.

perpendicular [pɜːpən'dɪkjʊlər] a & n perpendiculaire (f).

perpetrate ['pɜːpɪtreɪt] vt (crime) perpétrer. ◆**perpetrator** n auteur m.

perpetual [pə'petʃʊəl] a perpétuel. ◆**perpetually** adv perpétuellement. ◆**perpetuate** vt perpétuer. ◆**perpetuity** [pɜːpɪ'tjuːɪtɪ] n perpétuité f.

perplex [pə'pleks] vt rendre perplexe, dérouter. ◆—**ed** a perplexe. ◆—**ing** a déroutant. ◆**perplexity** n perplexité f; (complexity) complexité f.

persecute ['pɜːsɪkjuːt] vt persécuter. ◆**perse'cution** n persécution f.

persever/e [pɜːsɪ'vɪər] vi persévérer (**in** dans). ◆—**ing** a (persistent) persévérant. ◆**perseverance** n persévérance f.

Persian ['pɜːʃ(ə)n, 'pɜːʒ(ə)n] a (language, cat, carpet) persan; – n (language) persan m.

persist [pə'sɪst] vi persister (**in doing** à faire, **in sth** dans qch). ◆**persistence** n persistance f. ◆**persistent** a (fever, smell etc) persistant; (person) obstiné; (attempts, noise etc) continuel. ◆**persistently** adv (stubbornly) obstinément; (continually) continuellement.

person ['pɜːs(ə)n] n personne f; **in p.** en personne; **a p. to p. call** Tel une communication avec préavis. ◆**personable** *a* avenant, qui présente bien.

personal ['pɜːsən(ə)l] *a* personnel; (*application*) en personne; (*hygiene, friend*) intime; (*life*) privé; (*indiscreet*) indiscret; **p. assistant, p. secretary** secrétaire *m* particulier, secrétaire *f* particulière. ◆**perso'nality** *n* (*character, famous person*) personnalité *f*; **a television p.** une vedette de la télévision. ◆**personalize** *vt* personnaliser. ◆**personally** *adv* personnellement; (*in person*) en personne.

personify [pə'sɒnɪfaɪ] *vt* personnifier. ◆**personifi'cation** *n* personnification *f*.

personnel [pɜːsə'nel] *n* (*staff*) personnel *m*; (*department*) service *m* du personnel.

perspective [pə'spektɪv] *n* (*artistic & view-point*) perspective *f*; **in (its true) p.** *Fig* sous son vrai jour.

perspire [pə'spaɪər] *vi* transpirer. ◆**perspi'ration** *n* transpiration *f*, sueur *f*.

persuade [pə'sweɪd] *vt* persuader (**s.o. to do** qn de faire). ◆**persuasion** *n* persuasion *f*; *Rel* religion *f*. ◆**persuasive** *a* (*person, argument etc*) persuasif. ◆**persuasively** *adv* de façon persuasive.

pert [pɜːt] *a* (*impertinent*) impertinent; (*lively*) gai, plein d'entrain; (*hat etc*) coquet, chic. ◆**—ly** *adv* avec impertinence.

pertain [pə'teɪn] *vi* **to p.** (*to*) (*relate*) se rapporter à; (*belong*) appartenir à.

pertinent ['pɜːtɪnənt] *a* pertinent. ◆**—ly** *adv* pertinemment.

perturb [pə'tɜːb] *vt* troubler, perturber.

Peru [pə'ruː] *n* Pérou *m*. ◆**Peruvian** *a* & *n* péruvien, -ienne (*mf*).

peruse [pə'ruːz] *vt* lire (attentivement); (*skim through*) parcourir. ◆**perusal** *n* lecture *f*.

pervade [pə'veɪd] *vt* se répandre dans. ◆**pervasive** *a* qui se répand partout, envahissant.

perverse [pə'vɜːs] *a* (*awkward*) contrariant; (*obstinate*) entêté; (*wicked*) pervers. ◆**perversion** *n* perversion *f*; (*of justice, truth*) travestissement *m*. ◆**perversity** *n* esprit *m* de contradiction; (*obstinacy*) entêtement *m*; (*wickedness*) perversité *f*. **pervert** [pə'vɜːt] *vt* pervertir; (*mind*) corrompre; (*justice, truth*) travestir ¶ ['pɜːvɜːt] *n* perverti, -ie *mf*.

pesky ['peskɪ] *a* (**-ier, -est**) (*troublesome*) *Am Fam* embêtant.

pessimism ['pesɪmɪz(ə)m] *n* pessimisme *m*. ◆**pessimist** *n* pessimiste *mf*. ◆**pessi'mistic** *a* pessimiste. ◆**pessi'mistically** *adv* avec pessimisme.

pest [pest] *n* animal *m or* insecte *m* nuisible; (*person*) *Fam* casse-pieds *mf inv*, peste *f*. ◆**pesticide** *n* pesticide *m*.

pester ['pestər] *vt* (*harass*) harceler (**with questions** de questions); **to p. s.o. to do sth/for sth** harceler *or* tarabuster qn pour qu'il fasse qch/jusqu'à ce qu'il donne qch.

pet [pet] **1** *n* animal *m* (domestique); (*favourite person*) chouchou, -oute *mf*; **yes (my) p.** *Fam* oui mon chou; **to have** *or* **keep a p.** avoir un animal chez soi; – *a* (*dog etc*) domestique; (*tiger etc*) apprivoisé; (*favourite*) favori; (*fondle*) caresser; (*sexually*) *Fam* peloter; – *vi Fam* se peloter.

petal ['pet(ə)l] *n* pétale *m*.

peter ['piːtər] *vi* **to p. out** (*run out*) s'épuiser; (*dry up*) se tarir; (*die out*) mourir; (*disappear*) disparaître.

petite [pə'tiːt] *a* (*woman*) petite et mince, menue.

petition [pə'tɪʃ(ə)n] *n* (*signatures*) pétition *f*; (*request*) *Jur* requête *f*; **p. for divorce** demande *f* en divorce; – *vt* adresser une pétition *or* une requête à (**for sth** pour demander qch).

petrify ['petrɪfaɪ] *vt* (*frighten*) pétrifier de terreur.

petrol ['petrəl] *n* essence *f*; **I've run out of p.** je suis tombé en panne d'essence; **p. engine** moteur *m* à essence; **p. station** poste *m* d'essence, station-service *f*.

petroleum [pə'trəʊlɪəm] *n* pétrole *m*.

petticoat ['petɪkəʊt] *n* jupon *m*.

petty ['petɪ] *a* (**-ier, -iest**) (*small*) petit; (*trivial*) insignifiant, menu, petit; (*mean*) mesquin; **p. cash** *Com* petite caisse *f*, menue monnaie *f*. ◆**pettiness** *n* petitesse *f*; insignifiance *f*; mesquinerie *f*.

petulant ['petjʊlənt] *a* irritable. ◆**petulance** *n* irritabilité *f*.

petunia [pɪ'tjuːnɪə] *n Bot* pétunia *m*.

pew [pjuː] *n* banc *m* d'église; **take a p.!** *Hum* assieds-toi!

pewter ['pjuːtər] *n* étain *m*.

phallic ['fælɪk] *a* phallique.

phantom ['fæntəm] *n* fantôme *m*.

pharmacy ['fɑːməsɪ] *n* pharmacie *f*. ◆**pharmaceutical** [-'sjuːtɪk(ə)l] *a* pharmaceutique. ◆**pharmacist** *n* pharmacien, -ienne *mf*.

pharynx ['færɪŋks] *n Anat* pharynx *m*. ◆**pharyn'gitis** *n Med* pharyngite *f*.

phase [feɪz] *n* (*stage*) phase *f*; – *vt* **to p.**

in/out introduire/supprimer progressivement. ◆**phased** a (changes etc) progressif.

PhD [piːeɪtʃ'diː] n abbr (Doctor of Philosphy) (degree) Univ doctorat m.

pheasant ['fezənt] n (bird) faisan m.

phenomenon, pl **-ena** [fɪ'nɒmɪnən, -ɪnə] n phénomène m. ◆**phenomenal** a phénoménal.

phew! [fjuː] int (relief) ouf!

philanderer [fɪ'lændərər] n coureur m de jupons.

philanthropist [fɪ'lænθrəpɪst] n philanthrope mf. ◆**philan'thropic** a philanthropique.

philately [fɪ'lætəlɪ] n philatélie. ◆**phila'telic** a philatélique. ◆**philatelist** n philatéliste mf.

philharmonic [fɪlə'mɒnɪk] a philharmonique.

Philippines ['fɪlɪpiːnz] npl **the P.** les Philippines fpl.

philistine ['fɪlɪstaɪn] n béotien, -ienne mf, philistin m.

philosophy [fɪ'lɒsəfɪ] n philosophie f. ◆**philosopher** n philosophe mf. ◆**philo-'sophical** a philosophique; (stoical, resigned) Fig philosophe. ◆**philo'sophically** adv (to say etc) avec philosophie. ◆**philosophize** vi philosopher.

phlegm [flem] n Med glaires fpl; (calmness) Fig flegme m. ◆**phleg'matic** a flegmatique.

phobia ['fəʊbɪə] n phobie f.

phone [fəʊn] n téléphone m; **on the p.** (speaking here) au téléphone; (at other end) au bout du fil; **to be on the p.** (as subscriber) avoir le téléphone; **p. call** coup m de fil or de téléphone; **to make a p. call** téléphoner (to à); **p. book** annuaire m; **p. box, p. booth** cabine f téléphonique; **p. number** numéro m de téléphone; – vt (message) téléphoner (to à); **to p. s.o. (up)** téléphoner à qn; – vi **to p. (up)** téléphoner; **to p. back** rappeler. ◆**phonecard** n télécarte f.

phonetic [fə'netɪk] a phonétique. ◆**pho-netics** n (science) phonétique f.

phoney ['fəʊnɪ] a (-ier, -iest) Fam (jewels, writer etc) faux; (attack, firm) bidon inv; (attitude) fumiste; – n Fam (impostor) imposteur m; (joker, shirker) fumiste mf; **it's a p.** (jewel, coin etc) c'est du faux.

phonograph ['fəʊnəgræf] n Am électrophone m.

phosphate ['fɒsfeɪt] n Ch phosphate m.

phosphorus ['fɒsfərəs] n Ch phosphore m.

photo ['fəʊtəʊ] n (pl **-os**) photo f; **to have one's p. taken** se faire photographier.

◆**photocopier** n (machine) photocopieur m. ◆**photocopy** n photocopie f; – vt photocopier. ◆**photo'genic** a photogénique. ◆**photograph** n photographie f; – vt photographier; – vi **to p. well** être photogénique. ◆**photographer** [fə'tɒgrəfər] n photographe mf. ◆**photo'graphic** a photographique. ◆**photography** [fə'tɒ-grəfɪ] n (activity) photographie f. ◆**photo-stat®** = photocopy.

phras/e [freɪz] n (saying) expression f; (idiom) & Gram locution f; – vt (express) exprimer; (letter) rédiger. ◆**-ing** n (wording) termes mpl. ◆**phrasebook** n (for tourists) manuel m de conversation.

physical ['fɪzɪk(ə)l] a physique; (object, world) matériel; **p. examination** Med examen m médical; **p. education, p. training** éducation f physique. ◆**physically** adv physiquement; **p. impossible** matériellement impossible.

physician [fɪ'zɪʃ(ə)n] n médecin m.

physics ['fɪzɪks] n (science) physique f. ◆**physicist** n physicien, -ienne mf.

physiology [fɪzɪ'ɒlədʒɪ] n physiologie f. ◆**physio'logical** a physiologique.

physiotherapy [fɪzɪəʊ'θerəpɪ] n kinésithérapie f. ◆**physiotherapist** n kinésithérapeute mf.

physique [fɪ'ziːk] n (appearance) physique m; (constitution) constitution f.

piano [pɪ'ænəʊ] n (pl **-os**) piano m. ◆'**pianist** n pianiste mf.

piazza [pɪ'ætsə] n (square) place f; (covered) passage m couvert.

picayune [pɪkə'juːn] a (petty) Am Fam mesquin.

pick [pɪk] n (choice) choix m; **the p. of** (best) le meilleur de; **the p. of the bunch** le dessus du panier; **to take one's p.** faire son choix, choisir; – vt (choose) choisir; (flower, fruit etc) cueillir; (hole) faire (**in** dans); (lock) crocheter; **to p. one's nose** se mettre les doigts dans le nez; **to p. one's teeth** se curer les dents; **to p. a fight** chercher la bagarre (**with** avec); **to p. holes in** Fig relever les défauts de; **to p. (off)** (remove) enlever; **to p. out** (choose) choisir; (identify) reconnaître, distinguer; **to p. up** (sth dropped) ramasser; (fallen person or chair) relever; (person into air, weight) soulever; (cold, money) Fig ramasser; (habit, accent, speed) prendre; (fetch, collect) (passer) prendre; (find) trouver; (baby) prendre dans les bras; (programme etc) Rad capter; (survivor) recueillir; (arrest) arrêter, ramasser; (learn) apprendre; – vi **to p. and choose** choisir avec soin; **to p. on** (*nag*) harceler; (*blame*) accuser; **why p. on me?** pourquoi moi?; **to p. up** (*improve*) s'améliorer; (*of business, trade*) reprendre; *Med* aller mieux; (*resume*) continuer. ◆**—ing** 1 *n* (*choosing*) choix *m* (**of** de); (*of flower, fruit etc*) cueillette *f*. 2 *npl* (*leftovers*) restes *mpl*; *Com* profits *mpl*. ◆**pick-me-up** *n* (*drink*) *Fam* remontant *m*. ◆**pick-up** *n* (*of record player*) bras *m* de) pick-up *m*; (*person*) *Pej Fam* partenaire *mf* de rencontre; **p.-up** (**truck**) pick-up *m*.

pick(axe) (*Am* **-ax**) ['pɪk(æks)] *n* (*tool*) pioche *f*; **ice pick** pic *m* à glace.

picket ['pɪkɪt] 1 *n* (*striker*) gréviste *mf*; **p.** (**line**) piquet *m* (de grève); — *vt* (*factory*) installer des piquets de grève aux portes de. 2 *n* (*stake*) piquet *m*.

pickle ['pɪk(ə)l] 1 *n* (*brine*) saumure *f*; (*vinegar*) vinaigre *m*; *pl* (*vegetables*) pickles *mpl*; *Am* concombres *mpl*, cornichons *mpl*; — *vt* mariner. 2 *n* **in a p.** (*trouble*) *Fam* dans le pétrin.

pickpocket ['pɪkpɒkɪt] *n* (*thief*) pickpocket *m*.

picky ['pɪkɪ] *a* (**-ier, -iest**) (*choosey*) *Am* difficile.

picnic ['pɪknɪk] *n* pique-nique *m*; — *vi* (**-ck-**) pique-niquer.

pictorial [pɪk'tɔːrɪəl] *a* (*in pictures*) en images; (*periodical*) illustré.

picture ['pɪktʃər] 1 *n* image *f*; (*painting*) tableau *m*, peinture *f*; (*drawing*) dessin *m*; (*photo*) photo *f*; (*film*) film *m*; (*scene*) *Fig* tableau *m*; **the pictures** *Cin* le cinéma; **to put s.o. in the p.** *Fig* mettre qn au courant; **p. frame** cadre *m*. 2 *vt* (*imagine*) s'imaginer (**that** que); (*remember*) revoir; (*depict*) décrire.

picturesque [pɪktʃə'resk] *a* pittoresque.

piddling ['pɪdlɪŋ] *a Pej* dérisoire.

pidgin ['pɪdʒɪn] *n* **p.** (**English**) pidgin *m*.

pie [paɪ] *n* (*of meat, vegetable*) tourte *f*; (*of fruit*) tarte *f*, tourte *f*; (*compact filling*) pâté *m* en croûte; **cottage p.** hachis *m* Parmentier.

piebald ['paɪbɔːld] *a* pie *inv*.

piece [piːs] *n* morceau *m*; (*of bread, paper, chocolate, etc*) bout *m*, morceau *m*; (*of fabric, machine, game, artillery*) pièce *f*; (*coin*) pièce *f*; **bits and pieces** des petites choses; **in pieces** en morceaux, en pièces; **to smash to pieces** briser en morceaux; **to take to pieces** (*machine etc*) démonter; **to come to pieces** se démonter; **to go to pieces** (*of person*) *Fig* craquer; **a p. of luck/news/***etc* une chance/nouvelle/*etc*;

one p. (*object*) intact; (*person*) indemne; — *vt* **to p. together** (*facts*) reconstituer; (*one's life*) refaire. ◆**piecemeal** *adv* petit à petit; — *a* (*unsystematic*) peu méthodique. ◆**piecework** *n* travail *m* à la tâche *or* à la pièce.

pier [pɪər] *n* (*promenade*) jetée *f*; (*for landing*) appontement *m*.

pierc/e [pɪəs] *vt* percer; (*of cold, sword, bullet*) transpercer (*qn*). ◆**—ing** *a* (*voice, look etc*) perçant; (*wind etc*) glacial.

piety ['paɪətɪ] *n* piété *f*.

piffling ['pɪflɪŋ] *a Fam* insignifiant.

pig [pɪg] *n* cochon *m*, porc *m*; (*evil person*) *Pej* cochon *m*; (*glutton*) *Pej* goinfre *m*. ◆**piggish** *a Pej* (*dirty*) sale; (*greedy*) goinfre. ◆**piggy** *a* (*greedy*) *Fam* goinfre. ◆**piggybank** *n* tirelire *f* (*en forme de cochon*).

pigeon ['pɪdʒɪn] *n* pigeon *m*. ◆**pigeonhole** *n* casier *m*; — *vt* classer; (*shelve*) mettre en suspens.

piggyback ['pɪgɪbæk] *n* **to give s.o. a p.** porter qn sur le dos.

pigheaded [pɪg'hedɪd] *a* obstiné.

pigment ['pɪgmənt] *n* pigment *m*. ◆**pigmen'tation** *n* pigmentation *f*.

pigsty ['pɪgstaɪ] *n* porcherie *f*.

pigtail ['pɪgteɪl] *n* (*hair*) natte *f*.

pike [paɪk] *n* 1 (*fish*) brochet *m*. 2 (*weapon*) pique *f*.

pilchard ['pɪltʃəd] *n* pilchard *m*, sardine *f*.

pile [paɪl] *n* pile *f*; (*fortune*) *Fam* fortune *f*; **piles of, a p. of** *Fam* beaucoup de, un tas de; — *vt* **to p.** (**up**) (*stack up*) empiler; — *vi* **to p. into** (*of people*) s'entasser dans; **to p. up** (*accumulate*) s'accumuler, s'amonceler. ◆**p.-up** *n Aut* collision *f* en chaîne, carambolage *m*.

pile [paɪl] *n* (*of carpet*) poils *mpl*.

piles [paɪlz] *npl Med* hémorroïdes *fpl*.

pilfer ['pɪlfər] *vt* (*steal*) chaparder (**from s.o.** à qn). ◆**—ing** *n*, ◆**—age** *n* chapardage *m*.

pilgrim ['pɪlgrɪm] *n* pèlerin *m*. ◆**pilgrimage** *n* pèlerinage *m*.

pill [pɪl] *n* pilule *f*; **to be on the p.** (*of woman*) prendre la pilule; **to go on/off the p.** se mettre à/arrêter la pilule.

pillage ['pɪlɪdʒ] *vti* piller; — *n* pillage *m*.

pillar ['pɪlər] *n* pilier *m*; (*of smoke*) *Fig* colonne *f*. ◆**p.-box** *n* boîte *f* à *or* aux lettres (*située sur le trottoir*).

pillion ['pɪljən] *adv* **to ride p.** (*on motorbike*) monter derrière.

pillory ['pɪlərɪ] *vt* (*ridicule, scorn*) mettre au pilori.

pillow ['pɪləʊ] n oreiller m. ◆**pillowcase** n, ◆**pillowslip** n taie f d'oreiller.

pilot ['paɪlət] **1** n (of aircraft, ship) pilote m; – vt piloter; – a. **p. light** (on appliance) voyant m. **2** a (experimental) (-)pilote; **p. scheme** projet(-)pilote m.

pimento [pɪ'mentəʊ] n (pl -os) piment m.

pimp [pɪmp] n souteneur m.

pimple ['pɪmp(ə)l] n bouton m. ◆**pimply** a (-ier, iest) boutonneux.

pin [pɪn] n épingle f; (drawing pin) punaise f; (Tech) goupille f, fiche f; **to have pins and needles** Med Fam avoir des fourmis (**in** dans); **p. money** argent m de poche; – vt (-nn-) **to p. (on)** (attach) attacher (**to** sur, à); (to wall) punaiser (**to, on** à); **to p. one's hopes on** mettre tous ses espoirs dans; **to p. on (to) s.o.** (crime, action) accuser qn de; **to p. down** (immobilize) immobiliser; (fix) fixer; (enemy) clouer; **to p. s.o. down** Fig forcer qn à préciser ses idées; **to p. up** (notice) afficher. ◆**pincushion** n pelote f (à épingles). ◆**pinhead** n tête f d'épingle.

pinafore ['pɪnəfɔ:r] n (apron) tablier m; (dress) robe f chasuble.

pinball ['pɪnbɔ:l] n **p. machine** flipper m.

pincers ['pɪnsəz] npl tenailles fpl.

pinch [pɪntʃ] **1** n (mark) pinçon m; (of salt) pincée f; **to give s.o. a p.** pincer qn; **at a p.**, Am **in a p.** (if necessary) au besoin; **to feel the p.** Fig souffrir (du manque d'argent etc); – vt pincer; – vi (of shoes) faire mal. **2** vt Fam (steal) piquer (**from** à); (arrest) pincer.

pine [paɪn] **1** n (tree, wood) pin m; **p. forest** pinède f. **2** vi **to p. for** désirer vivement (retrouver), languir après; **to p. away** dépérir.

pineapple ['paɪnæp(ə)l] n ananas m.

ping [pɪŋ] n bruit m métallique. ◆**pinger** n (on appliance) signal m sonore.

ping-pong ['pɪŋpɒŋ] n ping-pong m.

pink [pɪŋk] a & n (colour) rose (m).

pinkie ['pɪŋkɪ] n Am petit doigt m.

pinnacle ['pɪnək(ə)l] n (highest point) Fig apogée m.

pinpoint ['pɪnpɔɪnt] vt (locate) repérer; (define) définir.

pinstripe ['pɪnstraɪp] a (suit) rayé.

pint [paɪnt] n pinte f (Br = 0,57 litre, Am = 0,47 litre); **a p. of beer** un demi.

pinup ['pɪnʌp] n (girl) pin-up f inv.

pioneer [paɪə'nɪər] n pionnier, -ière mf; – vt (research, study) entreprendre pour la première fois.

pious ['paɪəs] a (person, deed) pieux.

pip [pɪp] **1** n (of fruit) pépin m. **2** n (on uniform) Mil galon m, sardine f. **3** npl **the pips** (sound) Tel le bip-bip.

pip/e [paɪp] **1** n tuyau m; (of smoker) pipe f; (instrument) Mus pipeau m; **the pipes** (bagpipes) Mus la cornemuse; (peace) p. calumet m de la paix; **to smoke a p.** fumer la pipe; **p. cleaner** cure-pipe m; **p. dream** chimère f; – vt (water etc) transporter par tuyaux or par canalisation; **piped music** musique f (de fond) enregistrée. **2** vi **to p. down** (shut up) Fam la boucler, se taire. ◆**-ing** n (system of pipes) canalisations fpl, tuyaux mpl; **length of p.** tuyau m; – adv **it's p. hot** (soup etc) c'est très chaud. ◆**pipeline** n pipeline m; **it's in the p.** Fig c'est en route.

pirate ['paɪərət] n pirate m; – a (radio, ship) pirate. ◆**piracy** n piraterie f. ◆**pirated** a (book, record etc) pirate.

Pisces ['paɪsi:z] npl (sign) les Poissons mpl.

pistachio [pɪ'stæʃɪəʊ] n (pl -os) (fruit, flavour) pistache f.

pistol ['pɪstəl] n pistolet m.

piston ['pɪstən] n Aut piston m.

pit [pɪt] **1** n (hole) trou m; (mine) mine f; (quarry) carrière f; (of stomach) creux m; Th orchestre m; Sp Aut stand m de ravitaillement. **2** vt (-tt-) **to p. oneself or one's wits against** se mesurer à. **3** n (stone of fruit) Am noyau m. ◆**pitted** a **1** (face) grêlé; (metal) with rust piqué de rouille. **2** (fruit) Am dénoyauté.

pitch[1] [pɪtʃ] **1** n Sp terrain m; (in market) place f. **2** n (degree) degré m; (of voice) hauteur f; Mus ton m. **3** vt (ball) lancer; (camp) établir; (tent) dresser; **a pitched battle** Mil une bataille rangée; Fig une belle bagarre. **4** vi (of ship) tanguer. **5** vi **to p. in** (cooperate) Fam se mettre de la partie; **to p. into s.o.** attaquer qn.

pitch[2] [pɪtʃ] n (tar) poix f. ◆**p.-'black** a, ◆**p.-'dark** a noir comme dans un four.

pitcher ['pɪtʃər] n cruche f, broc m.

pitchfork ['pɪtʃfɔ:k] n fourche f (à foin).

pith [pɪθ] n (of orange) peau f blanche; (essence) Fig moelle f. ◆**pithy** a (-ier, -iest) (remark etc) piquant et concis.

pitiful ['pɪtɪfʊl] a pitoyable. ◆**pitiless** a impitoyable.

pittance ['pɪtəns] n (income) revenu m or salaire m misérable; (sum) somme f dérisoire.

pitter-patter ['pɪtəpætər] n = patter 1.

pity ['pɪtɪ] n pitié f; **(what) a p.!** (quel) dommage!; **it's a p.** c'est dommage (**that**

que (+ *sub*), **to do** faire); **to have** *or* **take p. on** avoir pitié de; – *vt* plaindre.

pivot ['pɪvət] *n* pivot *m*; – *vi* pivoter.

pixie ['pɪksɪ] *n* (*fairy*) lutin *m*.

pizza ['piːtsə] *n* pizza *f*.

placard ['plækɑːd] *n* (*notice*) affiche *f*.

placate [plə'keɪt, *Am* 'pleɪkeɪt] *vt* calmer.

place [pleɪs] *n* endroit *m*, (*specific*) lieu *m*; (*house*) maison *f*; (*premises*) locaux *mpl*; (*seat, position, rank*) place *f*; **in the first p.** (*firstly*) en premier lieu; **to take p.** (*happen*) avoir lieu; **p. of work** lieu *m* de travail; **market p.** (*square*) place *f* du marché; **at my p.**, **to my p.** *Fam* chez moi; **some p.** (*somewhere*) *Am* quelque part; **no p.** (*nowhere*) *Am* nulle part; **all over the p.** partout; **to lose one's p.** perdre sa place; (*in book etc*) perdre sa page; **p. setting** couvert *m*; **to lay three places** (*at the table*) mettre trois couverts; **to take the p. of** remplacer; **in p. of** à la place de; **out of p.** (*remark, object*) déplacé; (*person*) dépaysé; **p. mat** set *m* (de table); – *vt* (*put, situate, invest*) & *Sp* placer; (*an order*) *Com* passer (**with** s.o. à qn); (*remember*) se rappeler; (*identify*) reconnaître. ◆**placing** *n* (*of money*) placement *m*.

placid ['plæsɪd] *a* placide.

plagiarize ['pleɪdʒəraɪz] *vt* plagier. ◆**plagiarism** *n* plagiat *m*.

plague [pleɪg] **1** *n* (*disease*) peste *f*; (*nuisance*) *Fam* plaie *f*. **2** *vt* (*harass, pester*) harceler (**with** de).

plaice [pleɪs] *n* (*fish*) carrelet *m*, plie *f*.

plaid [plæd] *n* (*fabric*) tissu *m* écossais.

plain[1] [pleɪn] *a* (**-er, -est**) (*clear, obvious*) clair; (*outspoken*) franc; (*simple*) simple; (*not patterned*) uni; (*woman, man*) sans beauté; (*sheer*) pur; **in p. clothes** en civil; **to make it p. to s.o. that** faire comprendre à qn que; **p. speaking** franc-parler *m*; – *adv* (*tired etc*) tout bonnement. ◆**-ly** *adv* clairement; franchement. ◆**-ness** *n* clarté *f*; simplicité *f*; manque *m* de beauté.

plain[2] [pleɪn] *n* *Geog* plaine *f*.

plaintiff ['pleɪntɪf] *n* *Jur* plaignant, -ante *mf*.

plait [plæt] *n* tresse *f*, natte *f*; – *vt* tresser, natter.

plan [plæn] *n* projet *m*; (*elaborate*) plan *m*; (*of house, book etc*) & *Pol Econ* plan *m*; **the best p.** would be **to...** le mieux serait de ...; **according to p.** comme prévu; **to have no plans** (*be free*) n'avoir rien de prévu; **to change one's plans** (*decide differently*) changer d'idée; **master p.** stratégie *f* d'ensemble; – *vt* (**-nn-**) (*envisage, decide on*) prévoir, projeter; (*organize*) organiser;

(*prepare*) préparer; (*design*) concevoir; *Econ* planifier; **to p. to do** (*intend*) avoir l'intention de faire; **as planned** comme prévu; – *vi* faire des projets; **to p. for** (*rain, disaster*) prévoir. ◆**planning** *n* *Econ* planification *f*; (*industrial, commercial*) planning *m*; **family p.** planning *m* familial; **town p.** urbanisme *m*. ◆**planner** *n* **town p.** urbaniste *mf*.

plane [pleɪn] *n* **1** (*aircraft*) avion *m*. **2** *Carp* rabot *m*. **3** (*tree*) platane *m*. **4** (*level*) & *Fig* plan *m*.

planet ['plænɪt] *n* planète *f*. ◆**plane-'tarium** *n* planétarium *m*. ◆**planetary** *a* planétaire.

plank [plæŋk] *n* planche *f*.

plant [plɑːnt] **1** *n* plante *f*; **house p.** plante d'appartement; – *vt* planter (**with** en, de); (*bomb*) *Fig* (dé)poser; **to p. sth on s.o.** (*hide*) cacher qch sur qn. **2** *n* (*machinery*) matériel *m*; (*fixtures*) installation *f*; (*factory*) usine *f*. ◆**plan'tation** *n* (*land, trees etc*) plantation *f*.

plaque [plæk] *n* **1** (*commemorative plate*) plaque *f*. **2** (*on teeth*) plaque *f* dentaire.

plasma ['plæzmə] *n* *Med* plasma *m*.

plaster ['plɑːstər] *n* (*substance*) plâtre *m*; (*sticking*) **p.** sparadrap *m*; **p. of Paris** plâtre *m* à mouler; **in p.** *Med* dans le plâtre; **p. cast** *Med* plâtre *m*; – *vt* plâtrer; **to p. down** (*hair*) plaquer; **to p. with** (*cover*) couvrir de. ◆**-er** *n* plâtrier *m*.

plastic ['plæstɪk] *a* (*substance, art*) plastique; (*object*) en plastique; **p. explosive** plastic *m*; **p. surgery** chirurgie *f* esthétique; – *n* plastique *m*, matière *f* plastique.

plasticine® ['plæstɪsiːn] *n* pâte *f* à modeler.

plate [pleɪt] *n* (*dish*) assiette *f*; (*metal sheet on door, on vehicle etc*) plaque *f*; (*book illustration*) gravure *f*; (*dental*) dentier *m*; **gold/silver p.** vaisselle *f* d'or/d'argent; **a lot on one's p.** (*work*) *Fig* du pain sur la planche; **p. glass** verre *m* à vitre; – *vt* (*jewellery, metal*) plaquer (**with** de). ◆**plateful** *n* assiettée *f*, assiette *f*.

plateau ['plætəu] *n* *Geog* (*pl* **-s** *or* **-x**) plateau *m*.

platform ['plætfɔːm] *n* estrade *f*; (*for speaker*) tribune *f*; (*on bus*) & *Pol* plate-forme *f*; *Rail* quai *m*; **p. shoes** chaussures *fpl* à semelles compensées.

platinum ['plætɪnəm] *n* (*metal*) platine *m*; – *a* **p.** *or* **p.-blond(e) hair** cheveux *mpl* platinés.

platitude ['plætɪtjuːd] *n* platitude *f*.

platonic [plə'tɒnɪk] *a* (*love etc*) platonique.

platoon [plə'tuːn] *n* *Mil* section *f*.

platter ['plætər] n Culin plat m.

plaudits ['plɔːdɪts] npl applaudissements mpl.

plausible ['plɔːzəb(ə)l] a (argument etc) plausible; (speaker etc) convaincant.

play [pleɪ] n (amusement, looseness) jeu m; Th pièce f (de théâtre), spectacle m; **a p. on words** jeu de mots; **to come into p.** entrer en jeu; **to call into p.** faire entrer en jeu; — vt (card, tune etc) jouer; (game) jouer à; (instrument) jouer de; (match) disputer (with avec); (team, opponent) jouer contre; (record) passer; (radio) faire marcher; **to p. ball with** Fig coopérer avec; **to p. the fool** faire l'idiot; **to p. a part in doing/in sth** contribuer à faire/à qch; **to p. it cool** Fam garder son sang-froid; **to p. back** (tape) réécouter; **to p. down** minimiser; **to p. s.o. up** Fam (of bad back etc) tracasser qn; (of child etc) faire enrager qn; **played out** Fam (tired) épuisé; (idea, method) périmé, vieux jeu inv; — vi jouer (with avec, at à); (of record player, tape recorder) marcher; **what are you playing at?** Fam qu'est-ce que tu fais?; **to p. about** or **around** jouer, s'amuser; **to p. on** (piano etc) jouer de; (s.o.'s emotions etc) jouer sur; **to p. up** (of child, machine etc) Fam faire des siennes; **to p. up to s.o.** faire de la lèche à qn. **◆—ing** n jeu m; **p. card** carte f à jouer; **p. field** terrain m de jeu. **◆—er** n Sp joueur, -euse m/f; Th acteur m, actrice f; **clarinette/etc p.** joueur, -euse mf de clarinette/etc; **cassette p.** lecteur m de cassettes.

play-act ['pleɪækt] vi jouer la comédie. **◆playboy** n playboy m. **◆playgoer** n amateur m de théâtre. **◆playground** n Sch cour f de récréation. **◆playgroup** n = **playschool**. **◆playmate** n camarade mf. **◆playpen** n parc m (pour enfants). **◆playroom** n (in house) salle f de jeux. **◆playschool** n garderie f (d'enfants). **◆plaything** n (person) Fig jouet m. **◆playtime** n Sch récréation f. **◆playwright** n dramaturge m.

playful ['pleɪfəl] a enjoué; (child) joueur. **◆—ly** adv (to say) en badinant. **◆—ness** n enjouement m.

plc [piːel'siː] abbr (public limited company) SA.

plea [pliː] n (request) appel m; (excuse) excuse f; **to make a p. of guilty** Jur plaider coupable. **◆plead** vi Jur plaider; **to p. with s.o. to do** implorer qn de faire; **to p. for** (help etc) implorer; — vt Jur plaider; (as excuse) alléguer. **◆pleading** n (requests) prières fpl.

pleasant ['plezənt] a agréable; (polite) aimable. **◆—ly** adv agréablement. **◆—ness** n (charm) charme m; (of person) amabilité f. **◆pleasantries** npl (jokes) plaisanteries fpl; (polite remarks) civilités fpl.

pleas/e [pliːz] adv s'il vous plaît, s'il te plaît; **p. sit down** asseyez-vous, je vous prie; **p. do!** bien sûr!, je vous en prie! **'no smoking p.'** 'prière de ne pas fumer'; — vt plaire à; (satisfy) contenter; **hard to p.** difficile (à contenter), exigeant; **p. yourself!** comme tu veux!; — vi plaire; **do as you p.** fais comme tu veux; **as much** or **as many as you p.** autant qu'il vous plaira. **◆—ed** a content (with de, that que (+ sub), to do de faire); **p. to meet you!** enchanté; **I'd be p. to!** avec plaisir! **◆—ing** a agréable, plaisant.

pleasure ['pleʒər] n plaisir m; **p. boat** bateau m de plaisance. **◆pleasurable** a très agréable.

pleat [pliːt] n (fold) pli m; — vt plisser.

plebiscite ['plebɪsɪt, -saɪt] n plébiscite m.

pledge [pledʒ] **1** n (promise) promesse f, engagement m (to do de faire); — vt promettre (to do de faire). **2** n (token, object) gage m; — vt (pawn) engager.

plenty ['plentɪ] n abondance f; **in p.** en abondance; **p. of** beaucoup de; **that's p.** (enough) c'est assez, ça suffit. **◆plentiful** a abondant.

plethora ['pleθərə] n pléthore f.

pleurisy ['plʊərɪsɪ] n Med pleurésie f.

pliable ['plaɪəb(ə)l] a souple.

pliers ['plaɪəz] npl (tool) pince(s) f(pl).

plight [plaɪt] n (crisis) situation f critique; (sorry) n. triste situation f.

plimsoll ['plɪmsəul] n chaussure f de tennis, tennis f.

plinth [plɪnθ] n socle m.

plod [plɒd] vi (-dd-) **to p.** (along) avancer or travailler laborieusement; **to p. through** (book) lire laborieusement. **◆plodding** a (slow) lent; (step) pesant. **◆plodder** n (steady worker) bûcheur, -euse mf.

plonk [plɒŋk] **1** int (splash) plouf! **2** vt **to p.** (down) (drop) poser bruyamment). **3** n (wine) Pej Sl pinard m.

plot [plɒt] **1** n (conspiracy) complot m (against contre); Cin Th Liter intrigue f; — vti (-tt-) comploter (to do de faire). **2** n (of land) terrain m; (patch in garden) carré m de terre; **building p.** terrain m à bâtir. **3** vt (-tt-) **to p.** (out) determiner; (graph, diagram) tracer; (one's position) relever. **◆plotting** n (conspiracies) complots mpl.

plough [plaʊ] n charrue f; — vt labourer; **to**

p. back into (money) Fig réinvestir dans; − vi labourer; **to p. into** (crash into) percuter; **to p. through** (snow etc) avancer péniblement dans; (fence, wall) défoncer. ◆**ploughman** n (pl -men) laboureur m; **p.'s lunch** Culin assiette f composée (de crudités et fromage).

plow [plaʊ] n Am = **plough**.

ploy [plɔɪ] n stratagème m.

pluck [plʌk] 1 n courage m; − vt **to p. up courage** s'armer de courage. 2 vt (fowl) plumer; (eyebrows) épiler; (string) Mus pincer; (flower) cueillir. ◆**plucky** a (-ier, -iest) courageux.

plug [plʌg] 1 n (of cotton wool, wood etc) tampon m, bouchon m; (for sink etc drainage) bonde f; − vt (-gg-) **to p. (up)** (stop up) boucher. 2 n El fiche f, prise f (mâle); − vt (-gg-) **to p. in** brancher. 3 n Aut bougie f. 4 n (publicity) Fam battage m publicitaire; − vt (-gg-) Fam faire du battage publicitaire pour. 5 vi (-gg-) **to p. away** (work) Fam bosser (at à). ◆**plughole** n trou m (du lavabo etc), vidange f.

plum [plʌm] n prune f; **a p. job** Fam un travail en or, un bon fromage.

plumage ['pluːmɪdʒ] n plumage m.

plumb [plʌm] 1 vt (probe, understand) sonder. 2 adv (crazy etc) Am Fam complètement; **p. in the middle** en plein milieu. ◆**plumber** ['plʌmər] n plombier m. ◆**plumbing** n plomberie f.

plume [pluːm] n (feather) plume f; (on hat etc) plumet m; **a p. of smoke** un panache de fumée.

plummet ['plʌmɪt] vi (of aircraft etc) plonger; (of prices) dégringoler.

plump [plʌmp] 1 a (-er, -est) (person) grassouillet; (arm, chicken) dodu; (cushion, cheek) rebondi. 2 vi **to p. for** (choose) se décider pour, choisir. ◆**-ness** n rondeur f.

plunder ['plʌndər] vt piller; − n (act) pillage m; (goods) butin m.

plung/e ['plʌndʒ] vt (thrust) plonger (into dans); − vi (dive) plonger (into dans); (fall) tomber (from de); (rush) se lancer; − n (dive) plongeon m; (fall) chute f; **to take the p.** Fig se jeter à l'eau. ◆**-ing** a (neckline) plongeant. ◆**-er** n ventouse f (pour déboucher un tuyau), débouchoir m.

plural ['plʊərəl] a (form) pluriel; (noun) au pluriel; − n pluriel m; **in the p.** au pluriel.

plus [plʌs] prep plus; − a (factor etc) & El positif; **twenty p.** vingt et quelques; − n p.

(sign) Math (signe m) plus m; **it's a p.** c'est un (avantage en) plus.

plush [plʌʃ] a (-er, -est) (splendid) somptueux.

plutonium [pluːˈtəʊnɪəm] n plutonium m.

ply [plaɪ] 1 vt (trade) exercer; (oar, tool) Lit manier. 2 vi **to p. between** (travel) faire la navette entre. 3 vt **to p. s.o. with** (whisky etc) faire boire continuellement à qn; (questions) bombarder qn de.

p.m. [piːˈem] adv (afternoon) de l'après-midi; (evening) du soir.

PM [piːˈem] n abbr (Prime Minister) Premier ministre m.

pneumatic [njuːˈmætɪk] a **p. drill** marteau-piqueur m, marteau m pneumatique.

pneumonia [njuːˈməʊnɪə] n pneumonie f.

poach [pəʊtʃ] 1 vt (egg) pocher. 2 vi (hunt, steal) braconner; − vt (employee from rival firm) débaucher, piquer. ◆**-ing** n braconnage m. ◆**-er** n 1 (person) braconnier m. 2 (egg) p. pocheuse f.

PO Box [piːəʊˈbɒks] abbr (Post Office Box) BP.

pocket ['pɒkɪt] n poche f; (area) Fig petite zone f; (of resistance) poche m, îlot m; **I'm $5 out of p.** j'ai perdu 5 dollars; − a (money, book etc) de poche; − vt (gain, steal) empocher. ◆**pocketbook** n (notebook) carnet m; (woman's handbag) Am sac m à main. ◆**pocketful** n **a p. of** une pleine poche de.

pockmarked ['pɒkmɑːkt] a (face) grêlé.

pod [pɒd] n cosse f.

podgy ['pɒdʒɪ] a (-ier, -iest) (arm etc) dodu; (person) rondelet.

podium ['pəʊdɪəm] n podium m.

poem ['pəʊɪm] n poème m. ◆**poet** n poète m. ◆**po'etic** a poétique. ◆**poetry** n poésie f.

poignant ['pɔɪnjənt] a poignant.

point [pɔɪnt] 1 n (of knife etc) pointe f; pl Rail aiguillage m; (power) n El prise f (de courant). 2 n (dot, position, question, degree, score etc) point m; (decimal) virgule f; (meaning) Fig sens m; (importance) intérêt m; (remark) remarque f; **p. of view** point m de vue; **at this p. in time** en ce moment; **on the p. of doing** sur le point de faire; **what's the p.?** à quoi bon? (of waiting/etc attendre/etc); **there's no p. (in) staying/etc** ça ne sert à rien de rester/etc; **that's not the p.** il ne s'agit pas de ça; **it's beside the p.** c'est à côté de la question; **to the p.** (relevant) pertinent; **get to the p.!** au fait!; **to make a p. of doing** prendre garde de faire; **his good**

points ses qualités *fpl; his bad points* ses défauts *mpl.* **3** *vt (aim)* pointer (**at** sur); *(vehicle)* tourner (**towards** vers); **to p. the way** indiquer le chemin (**to** à); *Fig* montrer la voie (**to** à); **to p. one's finger at** indiquer du doit, pointer son doigt vers; **to p. out** *(show)* indiquer; *(mention)* signaler (**that** que); – *vi* **to p.** (**at** or **to s.o.**) indiquer (qn) du doigt; **to p., to be pointing to** *(show)* indiquer; **to p. east** indiquer l'est; **to be pointing** *(of vehicle)* être tourné (**towards** vers); *(of gun)* être braqué (**at** sur). ◆**-ed** *a* pointu; *(beard)* en pointe; *(remark, criticism) Fig* pertinent; *(incisive)* mordant. ◆**-edly** *adv* (*to the point*) avec pertinence; *(incisively)* d'un ton mordant. ◆**-er** *n* (*on dial etc*) index *m*; *(advice)* conseil *m*; *(clue)* indice *m*; **to be a p. to** *(possible solution etc)* laisser entrevoir. ◆**-less** *a* inutile, futile. ◆**-lessly** *adv* inutilement.

point-blank [pɔint'blæŋk] *adv & a* (*to shoot, a shot*) à bout portant; *(to refuse, a request) Fig* (tout) net; *(to request, a request)* de but en blanc.

pois/e [pɔiz] *n (balance)* équilibre *m*; *(of body)* port *m*; *(grace)* grâce *f*; *(confidence)* assurance *f*, calme *m*; – *vt* tenir en équilibre. ◆**-ed** *a* en équilibre; *(hanging)* suspendu; *(composed)* calme; **p. to attack/etc** *(ready)* prêt à attaquer/*etc.*

poison [pɔiz(ə)n] *n* poison *m*; *(of snake)* venin *m*; **p. gas** gaz *m* toxique; – *vt* empoisonner; **to p. s.o.'s mind** corrompre qn. ◆**poisoning** *n* empoisonnement *m*. ◆**poisonous** *a* (*fumes, substance*) toxique; *(snake)* venimeux; *(plant)* vénéneux.

pok/e [pəuk] *vt (push)* pousser (*avec un bâton etc*); *(touch)* toucher; *(fire)* tisonner; **to p. sth into** *(put, thrust)* fourrer ou enfoncer qch dans; **to p. one's nose into** fourrer le nez dans; **to p. a hole in** faire un trou dans; **to p. one's head out of the window** passer la tête par la fenêtre; **to p. out s.o.'s eye** crever un œil à qn; – *vi* pousser; **to p. about** or **around in** fouiner dans; – *n (jab)* (petit) coup *m*; *(shove)* poussée *f*, coup *m*. ◆**-er** *n* **1** *(for fire)* tisonnier *m*. **2** *Cards* poker *m*.

poky [pəuki] *a (-ier, -iest) (small)* exigu et misérable, rikiki; *(slow) Am* lent.

Poland [pəulənd] *n* Pologne *f.* ◆**Pole** *n* Polonais, -aise *mf.*

polarize [pəuləraiz] *vt* polariser.

pole [pəul] *n* **1** *(rod)* perche *f*; *(fixed)* poteau *m*; *(for flag)* mât *m*. **2** *Geog* pôle *m.*

North/South P. pôle Nord/Sud. ◆**polar** *a* polaire; **p. bear** ours *m* blanc.

polemic [pə'lemik] *n* polémique *f.* ◆**polemical** *a* polémique.

police [pə'liːs] *n* police *f; more* or **extra p.** des renforts *mpl* de police; – *a (inquiry etc)* de la police; *(state, dog)* policier; **p. cadet** agent *m* de police stagiaire; **p. car** voiture *f* de police; **p. force** police *f;* – *vt (city etc)* maintenir l'ordre ou la paix dans; *(frontier)* contrôler. ◆**policeman** *n (pl -men)* agent *m* de police. ◆**policewoman** *n (pl -women)* femme-agent *f.*

policy [pɒlisi] *n* **1** *Pol Econ etc* politique *f;* (*individual course of action*) règle *f*, façon *f* d'agir; *pl (ways of governing) Pol* politique *f;* **matter of p.** question *f* de principe. **2** *(insurance)* **p.** police *f* (d'assurance); **p. holder** assuré, -ée *mf.*

polio(myelitis) [pəuliəu(maiə'laitis)] *n* polio(myélite) *f;* **p. victim** polio *mf.*

polish [pɒliʃ] *vt (floor, table, shoes etc)* cirer; *(metal)* astiquer; *(rough surface)* polir; *(manners) Fig* raffiner; *(style) Fig* polir; **to p. up** *(one's French etc)* travailler; **to p. off** *(food, work etc) Fam* liquider, finir (en vitesse); – *n (for shoes)* cirage *m; (for floor, furniture)* cire *f;* (*shine)* vernis *m; Fig* raffinement *m;* (*nail*) **p.** vernis *m* (à ongles); **to give sth a p.** faire briller qch.

Polish [pəuliʃ] *a* polonais; – *n (language)* polonais *m.*

polite [pə'lait] *a (-er, -est)* poli (**to, with** avec); **in p. society** dans la bonne société. ◆**-ly** *adv* poliment. ◆**-ness** *n* politesse *f.*

political [pə'litik(ə)l] *a* politique. ◆**politician** *n* homme *m* ou femme *f* politique. ◆**politicize** *vt* politiser. ◆**politics** *n* politique *f.*

polka [pɒlkə, *Am* 'pəulkə] *n (dance)* polka *f;* **p. dot** pois *m.*

poll [pəul] *n (voting)* scrutin *m*, élection *f; (vote)* vote *m; (turnout)* participation *f* électorale; *(list)* liste *f* électorale; **to go to the polls** aller aux urnes; *(opinion)* **p.** sondage *m* (d'opinion); **50% of the p.** 50% des votants; – *vt (votes)* obtenir; *(people)* sonder l'opinion de. ◆**-ing** *n (election)* élections *fpl;* **p. booth** isoloir *m;* **p. station** bureau *m* de vote.

pollen [pɒlən] *n* pollen *m.*

pollute [pə'luːt] *vt* polluer. ◆**pollutant** *n* polluant *m.* ◆**pollution** *n* pollution *f.*

polo [pəuləu] *n Sp* polo *m;* **p. neck** *(sweater, neckline)* col *m* roulé.

polyester [pɒli'estər] *n* polyester *m.*

Polynesia [pɒlɪ'niːʒə] n Polynésie f.

polytechnic [pɒlɪ'teknɪk] n institut m universitaire de technologie.

polythene ['pɒlɪθiːn] n polyéthylène m; **p. bag** sac m en plastique.

pomegranate ['pɒmɪgrænɪt] n (fruit) grenade f.

pomp [pɒmp] n pompe f. ◆**pom'posity** n emphase f, solennité f. ◆**pompous** a pompeux.

pompon ['pɒmpɒn] n (ornament) pompon m.

pond [pɒnd] n étang m; (stagnant) mare f;(artificial) bassin m.

ponder ['pɒndər] vt to p. (over) réfléchir à; – vi réfléchir.

ponderous ['pɒndərəs] a (heavy, slow) pesant.

pong [pɒŋ] n Sl mauvaise odeur f; – vi (stink) Sl schlinguer.

pontificate [pɒn'tɪfɪkeɪt] vi (speak) Pej pontifier (about sur).

pony ['pəʊnɪ] n poney m. ◆**ponytail** n (hair) queue f de cheval.

poodle ['puːd(ə)l] n caniche m.

poof [puf] n (homosexual) Pej Sl pédé m.

pooh! [puː] int bah!; (bad smell) ça pue!

pooh-pooh [puːˈpuː] vt (scorn) dédaigner; (dismiss) se moquer de.

pool [puːl] **1** n (puddle) flaque f; (of blood) mare f; (pond) étang m; (for swimming) piscine f. **2** n (of experience, talent) réservoir m; (of advisers etc) équipe f; (of typists) Com pool m; (kitty) cagnotte f; (football) **pools** pronostics mpl (sur les matchs de football); – vt (share) mettre en commun; (combine) unir leurs. **3** n Sp billard m américain.

pooped [puːpt] a (exhausted) Am Fam vanné, crevé.

poor [pʊər] a (-er, -est) (not rich, deserving pity) pauvre; (bad) mauvais; (inferior) médiocre; (meagre) maigre; (weak) faible; **p. thing!** le or la pauvre!; – n the p. les pauvres mpl. ◆**-ly 1** adv (badly) mal; (clothed, furnished) pauvrement. **2** a (ill) malade.

pop¹ [pɒp] **1** int pan! – n (noise) bruit m sec; to go p. faire pan; (of champagne bottle) faire pop; – vt (-pp-) (balloon etc) crever; (bottle top, button) faire sauter; – vi (burst) crever; (come off) sauter; (of ears) se déboucher. **2** vt (put) Fam mettre; – vi Fam to p. in (go in) entrer (en passant); to p. off (leave) partir; to p. out sortir (un instant); to p. over or round faire un saut (to chez); to p. up (of person) surgir, réapparaître; (of question etc) surgir.

◆**p.-'eyed** a aux yeux exorbités. ◆**p.-up** n livre m en relief.

pop² [pɒp] **1** n (music) pop m; – a (concert, singer etc) pop inv. **2** n (father) Am Fam papa m. **3** n (soda) p. (drink) Am soda m.

popcorn ['pɒpkɔːn] n pop-corn m.

pope [pəʊp] n pape m; **p.'s nose** (of chicken) croupion m.

poplar ['pɒplər] n (tree, wood) peuplier m.

poppy ['pɒpɪ] n (cultivated) pavot m; (red, wild) coquelicot m.

poppycock ['pɒpɪkɒk] n Fam fadaises fpl.

popsicle® ['pɒpsɪk(ə)l] n (ice lolly) Am esquimau m.

popular ['pɒpjʊlər] a (person, song, vote, science etc) populaire; (fashionable) à la mode; to be p. with plaire beaucoup à. ◆**popu'larity** n popularité f (with auprès de). ◆**popularize** vt populariser; (science, knowledge) vulgariser. ◆**popularly** adv communément.

populat/e ['pɒpjʊleɪt] vt peupler. ◆**-ed** a peuplé (with de). ◆**popu'lation** n population f. ◆**populous** a (crowded) populeux.

porcelain ['pɔːsəlɪn] n porcelaine f.

porch [pɔːtʃ] n porche m; (veranda) Am véranda f.

porcupine ['pɔːkjʊpaɪn] n (animal) porc-épic m.

pore [pɔːr] **1** n (of skin) pore m. **2** vi to p. over (book, question etc) étudier de près. ◆**porous** a poreux.

pork [pɔːk] n (meat) porc m; **p. butcher** charcutier, -ière mf.

pornography [pɔːˈnɒgrəfɪ] n (Fam porn) pornographie f. ◆**porno'graphic** a pornographique, porno (f inv).

porpoise ['pɔːpəs] n (sea animal) marsouin m.

porridge ['pɒrɪdʒ] n porridge m; **p. oats** flocons mpl d'avoine.

port [pɔːt] **1** n (harbour) port m; **p. of call** escale f; – a (authorities, installations etc) portuaire. **2** n p. (side) (left) Nau Av bâbord m; – a de bâbord. **3** n (wine) porto m.

portable ['pɔːtəb(ə)l] a portatif, portable.

portal ['pɔːt(ə)l] n portail m.

porter ['pɔːtər] n (for luggage) porteur m; (doorman) portier m; (caretaker) concierge m, (of public building) gardien, -ienne mf.

portfolio [pɔːt'fəʊlɪəʊ] n (pl -os) Com Pol portefeuille m.

porthole ['pɔːthəʊl] n Nau Av hublot m.

portico ['pɔːtɪkəʊ] n (pl -oes or -os) Archit portique m; (of house) porche m.

portion ['pɔːʃ(ə)n] n (share, helping) portion

f; (*of train, book etc*) partie *f*; − *vt* to p. out répartir.

portly ['pɔːtlɪ] *a* (**-ier, -iest**) corpulent.

portrait ['pɔːtrɪt, 'pɔːtreɪt] *n* portrait *m*; **p. painter** portraitiste *mf*.

portray [pɔː'treɪ] *vt* (*describe*) représenter. ◆**portrayal** *n* portrait *m*, représentation *f*.

Portugal ['pɔːtjʊg(ə)l] *n* Portugal *m*. ◆**Portu-'guese** *a* & *n inv* portugais, -aise (*mf*); − *n* (*language*) portugais *m*.

pose [pəʊz] **1** *n* (*in art or photography*) & *Fig* pose *f*; − *vi* (*of model etc*) poser (**for** pour); **to p. as a lawyer**/*etc* se faire passer pour un avocat/*etc*. **2** *vt* (*question*) poser. ◆**poser** *n* 1 (*question*) *Fam* colle *f*. **2** = poseur. ◆**poseur** [-'zɜːr] *n Pej* poseur, -euse *mf*.

posh [pɒʃ] *a Pej* (*smart*) chic *inv*; (*snobbish*) snob (*f inv*).

position [pə'zɪʃ(ə)n] *n* (*place, posture, opinion etc*) position *f*; (*of building, town*) emplacement *m*, position *f*; (*job, circumstances*) situation *f*; (*customer window in bank etc*) guichet *m*; **in a p. to do** en mesure *or* en position de faire; **in a good p.** to do bien placé pour faire; **in p.** en place, en position; − *vt* (*camera, machine etc*) mettre en position; (*put*) placer.

positive ['pɒzɪtɪv] *a* positif; (*order*) catégorique; (*progress, change*) réel; (*tone*) assuré; (*sure*) sûr, certain (**of** de, **that** que); **a p. genius** *Fam* un vrai génie. ◆**-ly** *adv* (*for certain*) & *El* positivement; (*undeniably*) indéniablement; (*completely*) complètement; (*categorically*) catégoriquement.

possess [pə'zes] *vt* posséder. ◆**possession** *n* possession *f*; **in p. of** en possession de; **to take p. of** prendre possession de. ◆**possessive** *a* (*adjective, person etc*) possessif; − *n Gram* possessif *m*. ◆**possessor** *n* possesseur *m*.

possible ['pɒsəb(ə)l] *a* possible (**to do** à faire); **it is p. (for us) to do it** il (nous) est possible de le faire; **it is p. that** il est possible que (+ *sub*); **as far as p.** dans la mesure du possible; **if p.** si possible; **as much** *or* **as many as p.** autant que possible; − *n* (*person, object*) *Fam* choix *m* possible. ◆**possi'bility** *n* possibilité *f*; **some p. of** quelques chances *fpl* de; **there's some p. that it's** (tout juste) possible que (+ *sub*); **she has possibilities** elle promet; **it's a distinct p.** c'est bien possible. ◆**possibly** *adv* **1** (*with can, could etc*) **if you p. can** si cela t'est possible; **to do all one p. can** faire tout son possible (**to do** pour faire); **he**

cannot p. stay il ne peut absolument pas rester. **2** (*perhaps*) peut-être.

post[1] [pəʊst] *n* (*postal system*) poste *f*; (*letters*) courrier *m*; **by p.** par la poste; **to catch/miss the p.** avoir/manquer la levée; − *a* (*box, code etc*) postal; **p. office** (*bureau m de*) poste *f*; **P. Office** (*administration*) (service *m* des) postes *fpl*; − *vt* (*put in postbox*) poster, mettre à la poste; (*send*) envoyer; **to keep s.o. posted** *Fig* tenir qn au courant. ◆**postage** *n* tarif *m* (postal), tarifs *mpl* (postaux) (**to** pour); **p. stamp** timbre-poste *m*. ◆**postal** *a* (*district etc*) postal; (*inquiries*) par la poste; (*clerk*) des postes; (*vote*) par correspondance. ◆**postbox** *n* boîte *f* à *or* aux lettres. ◆**postcard** *n* carte *f* postale. ◆**postcode** *n* code *m* postal. ◆**post-'free** *adv*, ◆**post'paid** *adv* franco.

post[2] [pəʊst] *n* (*job, place*) & *Mil* poste *m*; − *vt* (*sentry, guard*) poster; (*employee*) affecter (**to** à). ◆**-ing** *n* (*appointment*) affectation *f*.

post[3] [pəʊst] *n* (*pole*) poteau *m*; (*of bed, door*) montant *m*; **finishing** *or* **winning p.** *Sp* poteau *m* d'arrivée; − *vt* **to p. (up)** (*notice etc*) afficher.

post- [pəʊst] *pref* (*in time*) **p.-1800** après 1800.

postdate [pəʊst'deɪt] *vt* postdater.

poster ['pəʊstər] *n* affiche *f*; (*for decoration*) poster *m*.

posterior [pɒ'stɪərɪər] *n* (*buttocks*) *Hum* postérieur *m*.

posterity [pɒ'sterɪtɪ] *n* postérité *f*.

postgraduate [pəʊst'grædʒʊət] *a* (*studies etc*) *Univ* de troisième cycle; − *n* étudiant, -ante *mf* de troisième cycle.

posthumous ['pɒstjʊməs] *a* posthume. ◆**-ly** *adv* à titre posthume.

postman ['pəʊstmən] *n* (*pl* **-men**) facteur *m*. ◆**postmark** *n* cachet *m* de la poste; − *vt* oblitérer. ◆**postmaster** *n* receveur *m* (des postes).

post-mortem [pəʊst'mɔːtəm] *n* **p.-mortem** (*examination*) autopsie *f* (**on** de).

postpone [pəʊ'spəʊn] *vt* remettre (**for** de), renvoyer (à plus tard). ◆**-ment** *n* remise *f*, renvoi *m*.

postscript ['pəʊstskrɪpt] *n* post-scriptum *m inv*.

postulate ['pɒstjʊleɪt] *vt* postuler.

posture ['pɒstʃər] *n* posture *f*; *Fig* attitude *f*; − *vi* (*for effect*) *Pej* poser.

postwar ['pəʊstwɔːr] *a* d'après-guerre.

posy ['pəʊzɪ] *n* petit bouquet *m* (de fleurs).

pot [pɒt] **1** *n* pot *m*; (*for cooking*) marmite *f*; **pots and pans** casseroles *fpl*; **jam p.** pot *m* à confiture; **to take p. luck** tenter sa chance; (with food) manger à la fortune du pot; **to go to p.** Fam aller à la ruine; **gone to p.** (person, plans etc) Fam fichu; − vt (-tt-) mettre en pot. **2** n (marijuana) Sl marie-jeanne f; (hashish) Sl haschisch m. ◆**potted** a **1** (plant) en pot; (jam, meat) en bocaux. **2** (version etc) abrégé, condensé.

potato [pə'teɪtəʊ] n (pl -oes) pomme f de terre; **p. peeler** (knife) couteau m à éplucher, éplucheur m; **p. crisps**, Am **p. chips** pommes fpl chips.

potbelly ['pɒtbelɪ] n bedaine f. ◆**potbellied** a ventru.

potent ['pəʊtənt] a puissant; (drink) fort; (man) viril. ◆**potency** n puissance f; (of man) virilité f.

potential [pə'tenʃ(ə)l] a (danger, resources) potentiel; (client, sales) éventuel; (leader, hero etc) en puissance; − n potentiel m; Fig (perspectives fpl d')avenir m; **to have p.** avoir de l'avenir. ◆**potenti'ality** n potentialité f; pl Fig (perspectives fpl d')avenir m. ◆**potentially** adv potentiellement.

pothole ['pɒthəʊl] n (in road) nid m de poules; (in rock) gouffre m; (cave) caverne f. ◆**potholing** n spéléologie f.

potion ['pəʊʃ(ə)n] n breuvage m magique; Med potion f.

potshot ['pɒtʃɒt] n **to take a p.** faire un carton (**at** sur).

potter ['pɒtər] **1** n (person) potier m. **2** vi **to p. (about)** bricoler. ◆**pottery** n (art) poterie f; (objects) poteries fpl; **a piece of p.** une poterie.

potty ['pɒtɪ] **1** a (-ier, -iest) (mad) Fam toqué. **2** n pot m (de bébé).

pouch [paʊtʃ] n petit sac m; (of kangaroo, under eyes) poche f; (for tobacco) blague f.

pouf(fe) [puːf] n (seat) pouf m.

poultice ['pəʊltɪs] n Med cataplasme m.

poultry ['pəʊltrɪ] n volaille f. ◆**poulterer** n volailler m.

pounce [paʊns] vi (leap) bondir, sauter (**on** sur); **to p. on** (idea) Fig sauter sur; − n bond m.

pound [paʊnd] **1** n (weight) livre f (= 453,6 grammes); **p. (sterling)** livre f (sterling). **2** n (for cars, dogs) fourrière f. **3** vt (spices, nuts etc) piler; (meat) attendrir; (bombard) Mil pilonner; **to p. (on)** (thump) Fig taper sur, marteler; (of sea) battre; − vi (of heart) battre à tout rompre; (walk heavily) marcher à pas pesants.

pour [pɔːr] vt (liquid) verser; (wax) couler; **to p. money into** investir beaucoup d'argent

dans; **to p. away** or **off** (empty) vider; **to p. out** verser; (empty) vider; (feelings) épancher (**to** devant); − vi **to p. (out)** (of liquid) couler or sortir à flots; **to p. in** (of liquid, sunshine) entrer à flots; (of people, money) Fig affluer; **to p. out** (of people) sortir en masse (**from** de); (of smoke) s'échapper (**from** de); **it's pouring (down)** il pleut à verse; **pouring rain** pluie f torrentielle.

pout [paʊt] vti **to p. (one's lips)** faire la moue; − n moue f.

poverty ['pɒvətɪ] n pauvreté f; (grinding or extreme) p. misère f. ◆**p.-stricken** a (person) indigent; (conditions) misérable.

powder ['paʊdər] n poudre f; **p. keg** (place) Fig poudrière f; **p. puff** houppette f; **p. room** toilettes fpl (pour dames); − vt (hair, skin) poudrer; **to p. one's face** or **nose** se poudrer. ◆−**ed** a (milk, eggs) en poudre. ◆**powdery** a (snow) poudreux; (face) couvert de poudre.

power ['paʊər] n (ability, authority) pouvoir m; (strength, nation) & Math Tech puissance f; (energy) Phys Tech énergie f; (current) El courant m; **he's a p. within the firm** c'est un homme de poids au sein de l'entreprise; **in p.** Pol au pouvoir; **in one's p.** en son pouvoir; **the p. of speech** la faculté de la parole; **p. cut** coupure f de courant; **p. station**, Am **p. plant** El centrale f (électrique); − vt **to be powered by** être actionné or propulsé par; (gas, oil etc) fonctionnant à. ◆**powerful** a puissant. ◆**powerfully** adv puissamment. ◆**powerless** a impuissant (**to do** à faire).

practicable ['præktɪkəb(ə)l] a (project, road etc) praticable.

practical ['præktɪk(ə)l] a (knowledge, person, tool etc) pratique; **p. joke** farce f. ◆**practi'cality** n (of scheme etc) aspect n pratique; (of person) sens m pratique; (detail) détail m pratique.

practically ['præktɪk(ə)lɪ] adv (almost) pratiquement.

practice ['præktɪs] n (exercise, proceeding) pratique f; (habit) habitude f; Sp entraînement m; (rehearsal) répétition f; (of profession) exercice m (**of** de); (clients) clientèle f; **to put into p.** mettre en pratique; **in p.** (in reality) en pratique; **to be in p.** (have skill etc) être en forme; (of doctor, lawyer) exercer; **in general p.** (of doctor) faire de la médecine générale; **to be out of p.** avoir perdu la pratique. ◆**practis/e** vt (put into practice) pratiquer; (medicine, law etc) exercer; (flute, *piano etc*) s'exercer à; (*language*) (s'exercer à) parler (**on** avec); (*work at*) travailler; (*do*) faire; – *vi Mus Sp* s'exercer; (*of doctor, lawyer*) exercer; – *n Am* = **practice**. **◆—ed** *a* (*experienced*) chevronné; (*ear, eye*) exercé. **◆—ing** *a Rel* pratiquant; (*doctor, lawyer*) exerçant.

practitioner [præk'tɪʃ(ə)nər] *n* praticien, -ienne *mf*; **general p.** (médecin *m*) généraliste *m*.

pragmatic [præg'mætɪk] *a* pragmatique.

prairie(s) ['preərɪ(z)] *n(pl)* (*in North America*) Prairies *fpl*.

praise [preɪz] *vt* louer (**for** sth de qch); **to p. s.o. for** sth *or* **having done** louer qn d'avoir fait; – *n* louange(s) *f(pl)*, éloge(s) *m(pl)*; **in p. of** à la louange de. **◆praiseworthy** *a* digne d'éloges.

pram [præm] *n* landau *m*, voiture *f* d'enfant.

prance [prɑːns] *vi* **to p. about** (*of dancer etc*) caracoler; (*strut*) se pavaner; (*go about*) *Fam* se balader.

prank [præŋk] *n* (*trick*) farce *f*, tour *m*; (*escape*) frasque *f*.

prattle ['præt(ə)l] *vi* jacasser.

prawn [prɔːn] *n* crevette *f* (rose), bouquet *m*.

pray [preɪ] *vt Lit* prier (**that** que (+ *sub*), s.o. **to do** qn de faire); – *vi Rel* prier; **to p.** (**to God**) **for** sth prier Dieu pour qu'il nous accorde qch. **◆prayer** [preər] *n* prière *f*.

pre- [priː] *pref* **p.-1800** avant 1800.

preach [priːtʃ] *vti* prêcher; (*sermon*) faire; **to p. to s.o.** *Rel* & *Fig* prêcher qn. **◆—ing** *n* prédication *f*. **◆—er** *n* prédicateur *m*.

preamble [priː'æmb(ə)l] *n* préambule *m*.

prearrange [priːə'reɪndʒ] *vt* arranger à l'avance.

precarious [prɪ'keərɪəs] *a* précaire.

precaution [prɪ'kɔːʃ(ə)n] *n* précaution *f* (**of** doing de faire); **as a p.** par précaution.

preced/e [prɪ'siːd] *vti* précéder; **to p. sth by** sth faire précéder qch de qch. **◆—ing** *a* précédent.

precedence ['presɪdəns] *n* (*in rank*) préséance *f*; (*importance*) priorité *f*; **to take p. over** avoir la préséance sur; avoir la priorité sur. **◆precedent** *n* précédent *m*.

precept ['priːsept] *n* précepte *m*.

precinct ['priːsɪŋkt] *n* (*of convent etc*) enceinte *f*; (*boundary*) limite *f*; (*of town*) *Am Pol* circonscription *f*; (*for shopping*) zone *f* (piétonnière).

precious ['preʃəs] **1** *a* précieux; **her p. little bike** *Iron* son cher petit vélo. **2** *adv* **p. few**, **p. little** *Fam* très peu (de).

precipice ['presɪpɪs] *n* (*sheer face*) *Geog* à-pic *m inv*; (*chasm*) *Fig* précipice *m*.

precipitate [prɪ'sɪpɪteɪt] *vt* (*hasten, throw*) & *Ch* précipiter; (*trouble, reaction etc*) provoquer, déclencher. **◆precipi'tation** *n* (*haste*) & *Ch* précipitation *f*; (*rainfall*) précipitations *fpl*.

précis ['preɪsiː, *pl* 'preɪsiːz] *n inv* précis *m*.

precise [prɪ'saɪs] *a* précis; (*person*) minutieux. **◆—ly** *adv* (*accurately, exactly*) précisément; **at 3 o'clock p.** à 3 heures précises; **p. nothing** absolument rien. **◆precision** *n* précision *f*.

preclude [prɪ'kluːd] *vt* (*prevent*) empêcher (**from doing** de faire); (*possibility*) exclure.

precocious [prɪ'kəʊʃəs] *a* (*child etc*) précoce. **◆—ness** *n* précocité *f*.

preconceived [priːkən'siːvd] *a* préconçu. **◆preconception** *n* préconception *f*.

precondition [priːkən'dɪʃ(ə)n] *n* préalable *m*.

precursor [priː'kɜːsər] *n* précurseur *m*.

predate [priː'deɪt] *vt* (*precede*) précéder; (*cheque etc*) antidater.

predator ['predətər] *n* (*animal*) prédateur *m*. **◆predatory** *a* (*animal, person*) rapace.

predecessor ['priːdɪsesər] *n* prédécesseur *m*.

predicament [prɪ'dɪkəmənt] *n* situation *f* fâcheuse.

predict [prɪ'dɪkt] *vt* prédire. **◆predictable** *a* prévisible. **◆prediction** *n* prédiction *f*.

predispose [priːdɪ'spəʊz] *vt* prédisposer (**to do** à faire). **◆predispo'sition** *n* prédisposition *f*.

predominant [prɪ'dɒmɪnənt] *a* prédominant. **◆predominance** *n* prédominance *f*. **◆predominantly** *adv* (*almost all*) pour la plupart, en majorité. **◆predominate** *vi* prédominer (**over** sur).

preeminent [priː'emɪnənt] *a* prééminent.

preempt [priː'empt] *vt* (*decision, plans etc*) devancer.

preen [priːn] *vt* (*feathers*) lisser; **she's preening herself** *Fig* elle se bichonne.

prefab ['priːfæb] *n Fam* maison *f* préfabriquée. **◆pre'fabricate** *vt* préfabriquer.

preface ['prefɪs] *n* préface *f*; – *vt* (*speech etc*) faire précéder (**with** de).

prefect ['priːfekt] *n Sch* élève *mf* chargé(e) de la discipline; (*French official*) préfet *m*.

prefer [prɪ'fɜːr] *vt* (*-rr-*) préférer (**to** à), aimer mieux (**to** que); **to p. to do** préférer faire, aimer mieux faire; **to p. charges** *Jur* porter plainte (**against** contre). **◆'preferable** *a* préférable (**to** à). **◆'preferably** *adv* de préférence. **◆'preference** *n* préférence *f* (**for** pour); **in p. to** de préférence à. **◆prefe'rential** *a* préférentiel.

prefix ['priːfɪks] n préfixe m.

pregnant ['pregnant] a (woman) enceinte; (animal) pleine; **five months p.** enceinte de cinq mois. ◆**pregnancy** n (of woman) grossesse f.

prehistoric [priːhɪ'stɒrɪk] a préhistorique.

prejudge [priː'dʒʌdʒ] vt (question) préjuger de; (person) juger d'avance.

prejudic/e ['predʒədɪs] n (bias) préjugé m, parti m pris; (attitude) préjugés mpl; Jur préjudice m; — vt (person) prévenir (against contre); (success, chances etc) porter préjudice à, nuire à. ◆**-ed** a (idea) partial; **she's p.** elle a des préjugés or un préjugé (against contre); (on an issue) elle est de parti pris. ◆**preju'dicial** a Jur préjudiciable.

preliminary [prɪ'lɪmɪnərɪ] a (initial) initial; (speech, inquiry, exam) préliminaire; — npl préliminaires mpl.

prelude ['preljuːd] n prélude m; — vt préluder à.

premarital [priː'mærɪt(ə)l] a avant le mariage.

premature ['premətʃʊər, Am priːmə'tʃʊər] a prématuré. ◆**-ly** adv prématurément; (born) avant terme.

premeditate [priː'medɪteɪt] vt préméditer. ◆**premedi'tation** n préméditation f.

premier ['premɪər, Am prɪ'mɪər] n Premier ministre m.

première ['premɪər, Am prɪ'mjeər] n Th Cin première f.

premise ['premɪs] n Phil prémisse f.

premises ['premɪsɪz] npl locaux mpl; **on the p.** sur les lieux; **off the p.** hors des lieux.

premium ['priːmɪəm] n Fin prime f; (insurance) p. prime f (d'assurance); **to be at a p.** (rare) être (une) denrée rare, faire prime; **p. bond** bon m à lots.

premonition [premə'nɪʃ(ə)n, Am priːmə'nɪʃ(ə)n] n prémonition f, pressentiment m.

prenatal [priː'neɪt(ə)l] a Am prénatal.

preoccupy [priː'ɒkjupaɪ] vt (worry) préoccuper (with de). ◆**preoccu'pation** n préoccupation f; **a p. with** (money etc) une obsession de.

prep [prep] a **p. school** école f primaire privée; Am école f secondaire privée; — n (homework) Sch devoirs mpl.

prepaid [priː'peɪd] a (reply) payé.

prepar/e [prɪ'peər] vt préparer (sth for s.o. qch à qn, s.o. for sth qn à qch); **to p. to do** se préparer à faire; — vi **to p. for** (journey, occasion) faire des préparatifs pour; (get dressed up for) se préparer pour; (exam) préparer. ◆**-ed** a (ready) prêt, disposé (to

do à faire); **to be p. for** (expect) s'attendre à. ◆**prepa'ration** n préparation f; pl préparatifs mpl (for de). ◆**pre'paratory** a préparatoire; **p. school** = prep school.

preposition [prepə'zɪʃ(ə)n] n préposition f.

prepossessing [priːpə'zesɪŋ] a avenant, sympathique.

preposterous [prɪ'pɒstərəs] a absurde.

prerecorded [priːrɪ'kɔːdɪd] a (message etc) enregistré à l'avance; **p. broadcast** Rad TV émission f en différé.

prerequisite [priː'rekwɪzɪt] n (condition f) préalable m.

prerogative [prɪ'rɒgətɪv] n prérogative f.

Presbyterian [prezbɪ'tɪərɪən] a & n Rel presbytérien, -ienne (mf).

preschool ['priːskuːl] a (age etc) préscolaire.

prescrib/e [prɪ'skraɪb] vt prescrire. ◆**-ed** a (textbook) (inscrit) au programme. ◆**prescription** n (order) prescription f; Med ordonnance f; **on p.** sur ordonnance.

presence ['prezəns] n présence f; **in the p. of** en présence de; **p. of mind** présence f d'esprit.

present¹ ['prezənt] **1** a (not absent) présent (at à, in dans); **those p.** les personnes présentes. **2** a (year, state etc) présent, actuel; (being considered) présent; (job, house etc) actuel; — n (time) présent m; **for the p.** pour le moment; **at p.** à présent. **3** n (gift) cadeau m. ◆**-ly** adv (soon) tout à l'heure; (now) à présent. ◆**present-'day** a actuel.

present² [prɪ'zent] vt (show, introduce, compere etc) présenter (to à); (concert etc) donner; (proof) fournir; **to p. s.o. with** (gift) offrir à qn; (prize) remettre à qn. ◆**-able** a présentable. ◆**-er** n présentateur, -trice m. ◆**presen'tation** n présentation f; (of prize) remise f.

preserve [prɪ'zɜːv] **1** vt (keep, maintain) conserver; (fruit etc) Culin mettre en conserve; **to p. from** (protect) préserver de. **2** n (sphere) domaine m. **3** n & npl (fruit etc) Culin confiture f. ◆**preser'vation** n conservation f. ◆**preservative** n (in food) agent m de conservation. ◆**preserver** n **life p.** Am gilet m de sauvetage.

preside [prɪ'zaɪd] vi présider; **to p. over** or **at** (meeting) présider.

president ['prezɪdənt] n président, -ente mf. ◆**presidency** n présidence f. ◆**presi'dential** a présidentiel.

press¹ [pres] **1** n (newspapers) presse f; (printing firm) imprimerie f; (printing) p. presse f; — a (conference etc) de presse. **2** n (*machine for trousers, gluing etc*) presse *f*; (*for making wine*) pressoir *m*.

press² [pres] *vt* (*button, doorbell etc*) appuyer sur; (*tube, lemon, creditor*) presser; (*hand*) serrer; (*clothes*) repasser; (*demand, insist on*) insister sur; (*claim*) renouveler; **to p. s.o. to do** (*urge*) presser qn de faire; **to p. down** (*button etc*) appuyer sur; **to p. charges** *Jur* engager des poursuites (**against** contre); − *vi* (*with finger*) appuyer (**on** sur); (*of weight*) faire pression (**on** sur); (*of time*) presser; **to p. for sth** faire des démarches pour obtenir qch; (*insist*) insister pour obtenir qch; **to p. on** (*continue*) continuer (**with** sth); − *n* **to give sth a p.** (*trousers etc*) repasser qch. **◆─ed** *a* (**hard**) *a.* (*busy*) débordé; **to be hard p.** (*in difficulties*) être en difficultés; **to be** (**hard**) **p. for** (*time, money*) être à court de. **◆─ing 1** *a* (*urgent*) pressant. **2** *n* (*ironing*) repassage *m*.

pressgang ['presgæn] *vt* **to p. s.o.** faire pression sur qn (**into** doing pour qu'il fasse). **◆press-stud** *n* (bouton-)pression *m*. **◆press-up** *n Sp* pompe *f*.

pressure ['prefər] *n* pression *f*; **the p. of work** le surmenage; **p. cooker** cocotte-minute *f*; **p. group** groupe *m* de pression; **under p.** (*duress*) sous la contrainte; (*forcibly*) sous pression; − *vt* **to p. s.o.** faire pression sur qn (**into** doing pour qu'il fasse). **◆pressurize** *vt Av* pressuriser; **to p. s.o.** faire pression sur qn (**into** doing pour qu'il fasse).

prestige [pre'sti:ʒ] *n* prestige *m*. **◆prestigious** [pre'stidʒəs, *Am* -'sti:dʒəs] *a* prestigieux.

presume [pri'zju:m] *vt* (*suppose*) présumer (**that** que); **to p. to do** se permettre de faire. **◆presumably** *adv* (*you'll come etc*) je présume que. **◆presumption** *n* (*supposition, bold attitude*) présomption *f*. **◆presumptuous** *a* présomptueux.

presuppose [pri:sə'pəuz] *vt* présupposer (**that** que).

pretence [pri'tens] *n* feinte *f*; (*claim, affectation*) prétention *f*; (*pretext*) prétexte *m*; **to make a p. of sth/of doing** feindre qch/de faire; **on** *or* **under false pretences** sous des prétextes fallacieux. **◆pretend** *vt* (*make believe*) faire semblant (**to do** de faire, **that** que); (*claim, maintain*) prétendre (**to do** faire, **that** que); − *vi* faire semblant; **to p. to** (*throne, title*) prétendre à. **◆pretension** [pri'tenf(ə)n] *n* (*claim, vanity*) prétention *f*. **◆pre'tentious** *a* prétentieux.

pretext ['pri:tekst] *n* prétexte *m*; **on the p. of/that** sous prétexte de/que.

pretty ['priti] **1** *a* (*-ier, -iest*) joli. **2** *adv Fam* (*rather, quite*) assez; **p. well, p. much, p. nearly** (*almost*) pratiquement, à peu de chose près.

prevail [pri'veil] *vi* (*be prevalent*) prédominer; (*win*) prévaloir (**against** contre); **to p. (up)on s.o.** (*persuade*) persuader qn (**to do** de faire). **◆─ing** *a* (*most common*) courant; (*most important*) prédominant; (*situation*) actuel; (*wind*) dominant.

prevalent ['prevələnt] *a* courant, répandu. **◆prevalence** *n* fréquence *f*; (*predominance*) prédominance *f*.

prevaricate [pri'værikeit] *vi* user de faux-fuyants.

prevent [pri'vent] *vt* empêcher (**from doing** de faire). **◆preventable** *a* évitable. **◆prevention** *n* prévention *f*. **◆preventive** *a* préventif.

preview ['pri:vju:] *n* (*of film, painting*) avant-première *f*; (*survey*) *Fig* aperçu *m*.

previous ['pri:viəs] *a* précédent, antérieur; (*experience*) préalable; **she's had a p. job** elle a déjà eu un emploi; **p. to** avant. **◆─ly** *adv* avant, précédemment.

prewar ['pri:wɔ:r] *a* d'avant-guerre.

prey [prei] *n* proie *f*; **to be (a) p. to** être en proie à; **bird of p.** rapace *m*, oiseau *m* de proie; − *vi* **to p. on** faire sa proie de; **to p. on s.o.** *or* **s.o.'s mind** *Fig* tracasser qn.

price [prais] *n* (*of object, success etc*) prix *m*; **to pay a high p. for sth** payer cher qch; *Fig* payer chèrement qch; **he wouldn't do it at any p.** il ne le ferait à aucun prix; − *a* (*control, war, rise etc*) des prix; **p. list** tarif *m*; − *vt* mettre un prix à; **it's priced at £5** ça coûte cinq livres. **◆priceless** *a* (*jewel, help etc*) inestimable; (*amusing*) *Fam* impayable. **◆pricey** *a* (*-ier, -iest*) *Fam* coûteux.

prick [prik] *vt* piquer (**with** avec); (*burst*) crever; **to p. up one's ears** dresser l'oreille; − *n* (*act, mark, pain*) piqûre *f*.

prickle ['prik(ə)l] *n* (*of animal*) piquant *m*; (*of plant*) épine *f*, piquant *m*. **◆prickly** *a* (*-ier, -iest*) (*plant*) épineux; (*animal*) hérissé; (*subject*) *Fig* épineux; (*person*) irritable.

pride [praid] *n* (*satisfaction*) fierté *f*; (*self-esteem*) amour-propre *m*, orgueil *m*; (*arrogance*) orgueil *m*; **to take p. in** (*person, work etc*) être fier de; (*look after*) prendre soin de; **to take p. in doing** mettre (toute) sa fierté à faire; **to be s.o.'s p. and joy** être la fierté de qn; **to have p. of place** avoir la

place d'honneur; – *vt* **to p. oneself on**
s'enorgueillir de.

priest [priːst] *n* prêtre *m*. ◆**priesthood**
n (*function*) sacerdoce *m*. ◆**priestly** *a* sacer-
dotal.

prig [prɪg] *n* hypocrite *mf*, pharisien, -ienne
mf. ◆**priggish** *a* hypocrite, suffisant.

prim [prɪm] *a* (*primmer, primmest*) **p. (and
proper)** (*affected*) guindé; (*seemly*) convenable; (*neat*) impeccable.

primacy ['praɪməsɪ] *n* primauté *f*.

primary ['praɪmərɪ] *a Sch Pol Geol etc*
primaire; (*main, basic*) principal, premier;
of p. importance de première importance;
– *n* (*election*) *Am* primaire *f*. ◆**primarily**
[*Am* praɪ'merɪlɪ] *adv* essentiellement.

prime [praɪm] *a* (*reason etc*) principal;
(*importance*) primordial; (*quality, number*)
premier; (*meat*) de premier choix; (*example, condition*) excellent, parfait; **P. Minister** Premier ministre *m*. **2** *n* **the p. of life** la
force de l'âge. **3** *vt* (*gun, pump*) amorcer;
(*surface*) apprêter. ◆**primer** *n* **1** (*book*)
Sch premier livre *m*. **2** (*paint*) apprêt *m*.

primeval [praɪ'miːv(ə)l] *a* primitif.

primitive ['prɪmɪtɪv] *a* (*art, society, conditions etc*) primitif. ◆**-ly** *adv* (*to live*) dans
des conditions primitives.

primrose ['prɪmrəʊz] *n Bot* primevère *f*
(jaune).

prince [prɪns] *n* prince *m*. ◆**princely** *a*
princier. ◆**prin'cess** *n* princesse *f*.
◆**princi'pality** *n* principauté *f*.

principal ['prɪnsɪp(ə)l] **1** *a* (*main*) principal.
2 *n* (*of school*) directeur, -trice *mf*. ◆**-ly**
adv principalement.

principle ['prɪnsɪp(ə)l] *n* principe *m*; **in p.** en
principe; **on p.** par principe.

print [prɪnt] *n* (*of finger, foot etc*) empreinte
f; (*letters*) caractères *mpl*; (*engraving*)
estampe *f*, gravure *f*; (*fabric, textile design*)
imprimé *m*; *Phot* épreuve *f*; (*ink*) encre *m*;
in p. (*book*) disponible (en librairie); **out of
p.** (*book*) épuisé; – *vt Typ* imprimer; *Phot*
tirer; (*write*) écrire en caractères
d'imprimerie; **to p. 100 copies of** (*book etc*)
tirer à 100 exemplaires; **to p. out** (*of
computer*) imprimer. ◆**-ed** *a* imprimé; **p.
matter** *or* **papers** imprimés *mpl*; **to have a
book p.** publier un livre. ◆**-ing** *n* (*action*)
Typ impression *f*; (*technique, art*) *Typ*
imprimerie *f*; *Phot* tirage *m*; **p. press** *Typ*
presse *f*. ◆**-able** *a* **not p.** (*word etc*) *Fig*
obscène. ◆**-er** *n* (*person*) imprimeur *m*;
(*of computer*) imprimante *f*. ◆**print-out** *n*
(*of computer*) sortie *f* sur imprimante.

prior ['praɪər] *a* précédent, antérieur; (*expe-*

rience) préalable; **p. to sth/to doing** avant
qch/de faire.

priority [praɪ'ɒrɪtɪ] *n* priorité *f* (**over** sur).

priory ['praɪərɪ] *n Rel* prieuré *m*.

prise [praɪz] *vt* **to p. open/off** (*box, lid*)
ouvrir/enlever (en faisant levier).

prism ['prɪz(ə)m] *n* prisme *m*.

prison ['prɪz(ə)n] *n* prison *f*; **in p.** en prison;
– *a* (*system, life etc*) pénitentiaire; (*camp*)
de prisonniers; **p. officer** gardien, -ienne
mf de prison. ◆**prisoner** *n* prisonnier, -ière
mf; **to take s.o. p.** faire qn prisonnier.

prissy ['prɪsɪ] *a* (**-ier, -iest**) bégueule.

pristine ['prɪstiːn] *a* (*condition*) parfait;
(*primitive*) primitif.

privacy ['praɪvəsɪ, 'prɪvəsɪ] *n* intimité *f*, solitude *f*; (*quiet place*) coin *m* retiré; (*secrecy*)
secret *m*; **to give s.o. some p.** laisser qn seul.
◆**private 1** *a* privé; (*lesson, car etc*)
particulier; (*confidential*) confidentiel;
(*personal*) personnel; (*wedding etc*) intime;
a p. citizen un simple particulier; **p. detective, p. investigator,** *Fam* **p. eye** détective *m*
privé; **p. parts** parties *fpl* génitales; **p. place**
coin *m* retiré; **p. tutor** précepteur *m*; **to be a
very p. person** aimer la solitude; – *n* **in p.**
(*not publicly*) en privé; (*ceremony*) dans
l'intimité. **2** *n Mil* (*simple*) soldat *m*. ◆**pri-
vately** *adv* en privé; (*inwardly*) intérieurement; (*personally*) à titre personnel; (*to
marry, dine etc*) dans l'intimité; **p. owned**
appartenant à un particulier.

privet ['prɪvɪt] *n* (*bush*) troène *m*.

privilege ['prɪvɪlɪdʒ] *n* privilège *m*. ◆**privileged** *a* privilégié; **to be p. to do** avoir le
privilège de faire.

privy ['prɪvɪ] *a* **p. to** (*knowledge etc*) au
courant de.

prize[1] [praɪz] *n* prix *m*; (*in lottery*) lot *m*; **the
first p.** (*in lottery*) le gros lot; – *a* (*essay,
animal etc*) primé; **a p. fool/etc** *Fig Hum* un
parfait idiot/*etc*. ◆**p.-giving** *n* distribution *f* des prix. ◆**p.-winner** *n* lauréat, -ate
mf; (*in lottery*) gagnant, -ante *mf*.
◆**p.-winning** *a* (*essay, animal etc*) primé;
(*ticket*) gagnant.

prize[2] [praɪz] *vt* (*value*) priser. ◆**-ed** *a*
(*possession etc*) précieux.

prize[3] [praɪz] *vt* = **prise**.

pro [prəʊ] *n* (*professional*) *Fam* pro *mf*.

pro- [prəʊ] *pref* pro-.

probable ['prɒbəb(ə)l] *a* probable (**that**
que); (*plausible*) vraisemblable. ◆**probability** *n* probabilité *f*; **in all p.** selon toute
probabilité. ◆**probably** *adv* probablement, vraisemblablement.

probation [prə'beɪʃ(ə)n] *n* **on p.** *Jur* en

liberté surveillée, sous contrôle judiciaire; (*in job*) à l'essai; **p. officer** responsable *mf* des délinquants mis en liberté surveillée. ◆**probationary** *a* (*period*) d'essai, *Jur* de liberté surveillée.

prob/e [prəʊb] *n* (*device*) sonde *f*; *Journ* enquête *f* (**into** dans); — *vt* (*investigate*) & *Med* sonder; (*examine*) examiner; — *vi* (*investigate*) faire des recherches; *Pej* fouiner; **to p. into** (*origins etc*) sonder. ◆**—ing** (*question etc*) pénétrant.

problem ['prɒbləm] *n* problème *m*; **he's got a drug/a drink p.** c'est un drogué/un alcoolique; **you've got a smoking p.** tu fumes beaucoup trop; **no p.!** *Am Fam* pas de problème!; **to have a p. doing** avoir du mal à faire; — *a* (*child*) difficile, caractériel. ◆**proble'matic** *a* problématique; **it's p. whether** il est douteux que (+ *sub*).

procedure [prə'siːdʒər] *n* procédure *f*.

proceed [prə'siːd] *vi* (*go*) avancer, aller; (*act*) procéder; (*continue*) continuer; (*of debate*) se poursuivre; **to p. to** (*next question etc*) passer à; **to p. with** (*task etc*) continuer; **to p. to do** (*start*) se mettre à faire. ◆**—ing** *n* (*course of action*) procédé *m*; *pl* (*events*) évènements *mpl*; (*meeting*) séance *f*; (*discussions*) débats *mpl*; (*minutes*) actes *mpl*; **to take (legal) proceedings** intenter un procès (**against** contre).

proceeds ['prəʊsiːdz] *npl* (*profits*) produit *m*, bénéfices *mpl*.

process ['prəʊses] **1** *n* (*operation, action*) processus *m*; (*method*) procédé *m* (**for** or **of doing** pour faire); **in p.** (*work etc*) en cours; **in the p. of doing** en train de faire. **2** *vt* (*food, data etc*) traiter; (*examine*) examiner; *Phot* développer; **processed cheese** fromage *m* fondu. ◆**—ing** *n* traitement *m*; *Phot* développement *m*; **data** or **information p.** informatique *f*. ◆**processor** *n* (*in computer*) processeur *m*; **food p.** robot *m* (*ménager*); **word p.** machine *f* de traitement de texte.

procession [prə'seʃ(ə)n] *n* cortège *m*, défilé *m*.

proclaim [prə'kleɪm] *vt* proclamer (**that** que); **to p. king** proclamer roi. ◆**procla'mation** *n* proclamation *f*.

procrastinate [prə'kræstɪneɪt] *vi* temporiser, tergiverser.

procreate ['prəʊkrieɪt] *vt* procréer. ◆**procre'ation** *n* procréation *f*.

procure [prə'kjʊər] *vt* obtenir; **to p. sth (for oneself)** se procurer qch; **to p. sth for s.o.** procurer qch à qn.

prod [prɒd] *vti* (**-dd-**) **to p. (at)** pousser (*du*

coude, avec un bâton etc); **to p. s.o. into doing** *Fig* pousser qn à faire; — *n* (*petit*) coup *m*; (*shove*) poussée *f*.

prodigal ['prɒdɪg(ə)l] *a* (*son etc*) prodigue.

prodigious [prə'dɪdʒəs] *a* prodigieux.

prodigy ['prɒdɪdʒɪ] *n* prodige *m*; **infant p., child p.** enfant *mf* prodige.

produce [prə'djuːs] *vt* (*manufacture, yield etc*) produire; (*bring out, show*) sortir (*pistolet, mouchoir etc*); (*passport, proof*) présenter; (*profit*) rapporter; (*cause*) provoquer, produire; (*publish*) publier; (*play*) *Th* TV mettre en scène; (*film*) *Cin* produire; *Rad* réaliser; (*baby*) donner naissance à; **oil-producing country** pays *m* producteur de pétrole; — *vi* (*of factory etc*) produire; — ['prɒdjuːs] *n* (*agricultural etc*) produits *mpl*. ◆**pro'ducer** *n* (*of goods*) & *Cin* producteur, -trice *mf*; *Th* TV metteur *m* en scène; *Rad* réalisateur, -trice *mf*.

product ['prɒdʌkt] *n* produit *m*.

production [prə'dʌkʃ(ə)n] *n* production *f*; *Th* TV mise *f* en scène; *Rad* réalisation *f*; **to work on the p. line** travailler à la chaîne. ◆**productive** *a* (*land, meeting, efforts*) productif. ◆**produc'tivity** *n* productivité *f*.

profane [prə'feɪn] *a* (*sacrilegious*) sacrilège; (*secular*) profane; — *vt* (*dishonour*) profaner. ◆**profanities** *npl* (*oaths*) blasphèmes *mpl*.

profess [prə'fes] *vt* professer; **to p. to be** prétendre être. ◆**—ed** *a* (*anarchist etc*) déclaré.

profession [prə'feʃ(ə)n] *n* profession *f*; **by p.** de profession. ◆**professional** *a* professionnel; (*man, woman*) qui exerce une profession libérale; (*army*) de métier; (*diplomat*) de carrière; (*piece of work*) de professionnel; — *n* professionnel, -elle *mf*; (*executive, lawyer etc*) membre *m* des professions libérales. ◆**professionalism** *n* professionnalisme *m*. ◆**professionally** *adv* professionnellement; (*to perform, play*) en professionnel; (*to meet s.o.*) dans le cadre de son travail.

professor [prə'fesər] *n* Univ professeur *m* (titulaire d'une chaire). ◆**profe'ssorial** *a* professoral.

proffer ['prɒfər] *vt* offrir.

proficient [prə'fɪʃ(ə)nt] *a* compétent (**in** en). ◆**proficiency** *n* compétence *f*.

profile ['prəʊfaɪl] *n* (*of person, object*) profil *m*; **in p.** de profil; **to keep a low p.** *Fig* garder un profil bas. ◆**profiled** *a* **to be p. against** se profiler sur.

profit ['prɒfɪt] *n* profit *m*, bénéfice *m*; **to sell**

at a p. vendre à profit; **p. margin** marge *f* bénéficiaire; **p. motive** recherche *f* du profit; – *vi* **to p. by** *or* **from** tirer profit de. ◆**p.-making** *a* à but lucratif. ◆**profita'bility** *n* Com rentabilité *f*. ◆**profitable** *a* Com rentable; *(worthwhile)* Fig rentable, profitable. ◆**profitably** *adv* avec profit. ◆**profi'teer** *n Pej* profiteur, -euse *mf*; – *vi Pej* faire des profits malhonnêtes.

profound [prə'faund] *a (silence, remark etc)* profond. ◆**profoundly** *adv* profondément. ◆**profundity** *n* profondeur *f*.

profuse [prə'fjuːs] *a (in (praise etc)* prodigue de. ◆**profusely** *adv (to flow, grow)* à profusion; *(to bleed)* abondamment; *(to thank)* avec effusion; **to apologize p.** se répandre en excuses. ◆**profusion** *n* profusion *f*; **in p.** à profusion.

progeny ['prɒdʒini] *n* progéniture *f*.

program [1] ['prəʊɡræm] *n (of computer)* programme *m*; – *vt* (**-mm-**) *(computer)* programmer. ◆**programming** *n* programmation *f*. ◆**programmer** *n* *(computer)* programmeur, -euse *mf*.

programme, *Am* **program** [2] ['prəʊɡræm] *n* programme *m*; *(broadcast)* émission *f*; – *vt (arrange)* programmer.

progress ['prəʊɡres] *n* progrès *m(pl)*; **to make (good) p.** faire des progrès; *(in walking, driving etc)* bien avancer; **in p.** en cours; – [prə'ɡres] *vi (advance, improve)* progresser; *(of story, meeting)* se dérouler. ◆pro'**gression** *n* progression *f*. ◆pro'**gressive** *a (gradual)* progressif; *(party)* Pol progressiste; *(firm, ideas)* moderniste. ◆pro'**gressively** *adv* progressivement.

prohibit [prə'hibit] *vt* interdire *(s.o. from doing* à qn de faire); **we're prohibited from leaving**/*etc* il nous est interdit de partir/*etc*. ◆prohi'**bition** *n* prohibition *f*. ◆prohibitive *a (price, measure etc)* prohibitif.

project [1] ['prɒdʒekt] *n (plan)* projet *m (for* sth pour qch; **to do, for doing** pour faire); *(undertaking)* entreprise *f*; *(study)* étude *f*; *(housing)* **p.** *(for workers) Am* cité *f* *(ouvrière).* **2** [prə'dʒekt] *vt (throw, show etc)* projeter; – *vi (jut out)* faire saillie. ◆**-ed** *a (planned)* prévu. ◆pro'**jection** *n* projection *f*; *(projecting object)* saillie *f*. ◆pro'**jectionist** *n Cin* projectionniste *mf*. ◆pro'**jector** *n Cin* projecteur *m*.

proletarian [prəʊlə'teəriən] *n* prolétaire *mf*; – *a (class)* prolétarien; *(outlook)* de prolétaire. ◆**proletariat** *n* prolétariat *m*.

proliferate [prə'lifəreit] *vi* proliférer. ◆**prolife'ration** *n* prolifération *f*.

prolific [prə'lifik] *a* prolifique.

prologue ['prəʊlɒɡ] *n* prologue *m (to* de, à).

prolong [prə'lɒŋ] *vt* prolonger.

promenade [prɒmə'nɑːd] *n (place, walk)* promenade *f*; *(gallery)* Th promenoir *m*.

prominent ['prɒminənt] *a (nose)* proéminent; *(chin, tooth)* saillant; *(striking)* Fig frappant, remarquable; *(role)* majeur; *(politician)* marquant; *(conspicuous)* (bien) en vue. ◆**prominence** *n (importance)* importance *f*. ◆**prominently** *adv (displayed, placed)* bien en vue.

promiscuous [prə'miskjuəs] *a (person)* de mœurs faciles; *(behaviour)* immoral. ◆promi'**scuity** *n* liberté *f* de mœurs; immoralité *f*.

promis/e ['prɒmis] *n* promesse *f*; **to show great p., to be full of p.** *(hope)* être très prometteur; – *vt* promettre *(s.o. sth, sth to s.o.* qch à qn; **to do** de faire; **that** que); – *vi* **I p.!** je te le promets!; **p.?** promis? ◆**-ing** *a (start etc)* prometteur; *(person)* qui promet; **that looks p.** ça s'annonce bien.

promote [prə'məʊt] *vt (product, research)* promouvoir; *(good health, awareness)* favoriser; **to p. s.o.** promouvoir qn *(to* à); **promoted (to) manager**/**general**/*etc* promu directeur/général/*etc*. ◆**promoter** *n Sp* organisateur, -trice *mf*; *(instigator)* promoteur, -trice *mf*. ◆**promotion** *n (of person)* avancement *m*, promotion *f*; *(of sales, research etc)* promotion *f*.

prompt [prɒmpt] **1** *a (speedy)* rapide; *(punctual)* à l'heure, ponctuel; **p. to act** prompt à agir; – *adv* **at 8 o'clock p.** à 8 heures pile. **2** *vt (urge)* inciter, pousser **(to do** à faire); *(cause)* provoquer. **3** *vt (person)* Th souffler (son rôle) à. ◆**-ing** *n (urging)* incitation *f*. ◆**-er** *n Th* souffleur, -euse *mf*. ◆**-ness** *n* rapidité *f*; *(readiness to act)* promptitude *f*.

prone [prəʊn] *a* **1 p. to sth** *(liable)* prédisposé à qch; **to be p. to do** avoir tendance à faire. **2** *(lying flat)* sur le ventre.

prong [prɒŋ] *n (of fork)* dent *f*.

pronoun ['prəʊnaʊn] *n Gram* pronom *m*. ◆pro'**nominal** *a* pronominal.

pronounce [prə'naʊns] *vt (articulate, declare)* prononcer; – *vi (articulate)* prononcer; *(give judgment)* se prononcer (on sur). ◆**pronouncement** *n* déclaration *f*. ◆**pronunci'ation** *n* prononciation *f*.

pronto ['prɒntəʊ] *adv (at once) Fam* illico.

proof [pruːf] *n* **1** *(evidence)* preuve *f*; *(of book, photo)* épreuve *f*; *(of drink)* teneur *f* en alcool. **2** *a* **p. against** *(material)* à l'épreuve de (*feu, acide etc*). ◆**proof-reader** n Typ correcteur, -trice mf.

prop [prɒp] **1** n Archit support m, étai m; (*for clothes line*) perche f; (*person*) Fig soutien m; − vt (-pp-) **to p. up** (*ladder etc*) appuyer (**against** contre); (*one's head*) caler; (*wall*) étayer; (*help*) Fig soutenir. **2** n **prop(s)** Th accessoire(s) m(pl).

propaganda [prɒpə'gændə] n propagande f. ◆**propagandist** n propagandiste mf.

propagate [prɒpəgeɪt] vt propager; − vi se propager.

propel [prə'pel] vt (-ll-) (*drive, hurl*) propulser. ◆**propeller** n Av Nau hélice f.

propensity [prə'pensɪtɪ] n propension f (**for** sth à qch, **to do** à faire).

proper ['prɒpər] a (*suitable, seemly*) convenable; (*correct*) correct; (*right*) bon; (*real, downright*) véritable; (*noun, meaning*) propre; **in the p. way** comme il faut; **the village**/*etc* le village/*etc* proprement dit. ◆**-ly** adv comme il faut, convenablement, correctement; (*completely*) Fam vraiment; **very p.** (*quite rightly*) à juste titre.

property ['prɒpətɪ] **1** n (*building etc*) propriété f; (*possessions*) biens mpl, propriété f; − a (*crisis, market etc*) immobilier; (*owner, tax*) foncier. **2** n (*of substance etc*) propriété f. ◆**propertied** a possédant.

prophecy ['prɒfɪsɪ] n prophétie f. ◆**prophesy** [-ɪsaɪ] vti prophétiser; **to p. that** prédire que.

prophet ['prɒfɪt] n prophète m. ◆**prophetic** a prophétique.

proponent [prə'pəʊnənt] n (*of cause etc*) défenseur m, partisan, -ane mf.

proportion [prə'pɔːʃ(ə)n] n (*ratio*) proportion f; (*portion*) partie f; (*amount*) pourcentage m; pl (*size*) proportions fpl; **in p.** en proportion (**to** de); **out of p.** hors de proportion (**to** avec); − vt proportionner (**to** à); **well** or **nicely proportioned** bien proportionné. ◆**proportional** a, ◆**proportionate** a proportionnel (**to** à).

propose [prə'pəʊz] vt (*suggest*) proposer (**to** à, **that** que (+ *sub*)); **to p. to do, p. doing** (*intend*) se proposer de faire; − vi faire une demande (en mariage) (**to** à). ◆**proposal** n proposition f; (*of marriage*) demande f (en mariage). ◆**proposition** n proposition f; (*matter*) Fig affaire f.

propound [prə'paʊnd] vt proposer.

proprietor [prə'praɪətər] n propriétaire mf. ◆**proprietary** a (*article*) Com de marque déposée; **p. name** marque f déposée.

propriety [prə'praɪətɪ] n (*behaviour*) bienséance f; (*of conduct, remark*) justesse f.

propulsion [prə'pʌlʃ(ə)n] n propulsion f.

pros [prəʊz] npl **the p. and cons** le pour et le contre.

prosaic [prə'zeɪɪk] a prosaïque.

proscribe [prəʊ'skraɪb] vt proscrire.

prose [prəʊz] n prose f; (*translation*) Sch thème m.

prosecute ['prɒsɪkjuːt] vt poursuivre (en justice) (**for stealing**/*etc* pour vol/*etc*). ◆**prose'cution** n Jur poursuites fpl; **the p.** (*lawyers*) = le ministère public. ◆**prosecutor** n (*public*) p. Jur procureur m.

prospect[1] ['prɒspekt] n (*idea, outlook*) perspective f (**of doing** de faire); (*possibility*) possibilité f (**of** sth **de** qch); (*future*) **prospects** perspectives fpl d'avenir; **it has prospects** c'est prometteur; **she has prospects** elle a de l'avenir. ◆**pro'spective** a (*possible*) éventuel; (*future*) futur.

prospect[2] [prə'spekt] vt (*land*) prospecter; − vi **to p. for** (*gold etc*) chercher. ◆**-ing** n prospection f. ◆**prospector** n prospecteur, -trice mf.

prospectus [prə'spektəs] n (*publicity leaflet*) prospectus m; Univ guide m (de l'étudiant).

prosper ['prɒspər] vi prospérer. ◆**prosperity** n prospérité f. ◆**prosperous** a (*thriving*) prospère; (*wealthy*) riche, prospère.

prostate ['prɒsteɪt] n **p. (gland)** Anat prostate f.

prostitute ['prɒstɪtjuːt] n (*woman*) prostituée f; − vt prostituer. ◆**prosti'tution** n prostitution f.

prostrate ['prɒstreɪt] a (*prone*) sur le ventre; (*worshipper*) prosterné; (*submissive*) soumis; (*exhausted*) prostré; − [prɒ'streɪt] vt **to p. oneself** se prosterner (**before** devant).

protagonist [prəʊ'tægənɪst] n protagoniste mf.

protect [prə'tekt] vt protéger (**from** de, **against** contre); (*interests*) sauvegarder. ◆**protection** n protection f. ◆**protective** a (*tone etc*) & Econ protecteur; (*screen, clothes etc*) de protection. ◆**protector** n protecteur, -trice mf.

protein ['prəʊtiːn] n protéine f.

protest ['prəʊtest] n protestation f (**against** contre); **under p.** contre son gré; − [prə'test] vt protester (**that** que); (*one's innocence*) protester de; − vi protester (**against** contre); (*in the streets etc*) Pol contester. ◆**-er** n Pol contestataire mf.

Protestant ['prɒtɪstənt] a & n protestant,

-ante (*mf*). ◆**Protestantism** *n* protestantisme *m*.

protocol ['prəʊtəkɒl] *n* protocole *m*.

prototype ['prəʊtəʊtaɪp] *n* prototype *m*.

protract [prə'trækt] *vt* prolonger.

protractor [prə'træktər] *n* (*instrument*) *Geom* rapporteur *m*.

protrud/e [prə'truːd] *vi* dépasser; (*of balcony, cliff etc*) faire saillie; (*of tooth*) avancer. ◆—**ing** *a* saillant; (*of tooth*) qui avance.

proud [praʊd] *a* (**-er, -est**) (*honoured, pleased*) fier (*of* de, *to do* de faire); (*arrogant*) orgueilleux. ◆—**ly** *adv* fièrement; orgueilleusement.

prove [pruːv] *vt* prouver (**that** que); **to p. oneself** faire ses preuves; — *vi* **to p.** (**to be**) **difficult**/*etc* s'avérer difficile/*etc*. ◆**proven** *a* (*method etc*) éprouvé.

proverb ['prɒvɜːb] *n* proverbe *m*. ◆**pro-'verbial** *a* proverbial.

provid/e [prə'vaɪd] *vt* (*supply*) fournir (**s.o. with sth** qch à qn); (*give*) donner, offrir (**to** à; **to p. s.o. with** (*equip*) munir qn de; **to p. that** *Jur* stipuler que; — *vi* **to p. for s.o.** (*s.o.'s needs*) pourvoir aux besoins de qn; (*s.o.'s future*) assurer l'avenir de qn; **to p. for sth** (*make allowance for*) prévoir qch. ◆—**ed** *conj* **p.** (**that**) pourvu que (+ *sub*). ◆—**ing** *conj* **p.** (**that**) pourvu que (+ *sub*).

providence ['prɒvɪdəns] *n* providence *f*.

provident ['prɒvɪdənt] *a* (*society*) de prévoyance; (*person*) prévoyant.

province ['prɒvɪns] *n* province *f*; *Fig* domaine *m*, compétence *f*; **the provinces** la province; **in the provinces** en province. ◆**pro'vincial** *a & n* provincial, -ale (*mf*).

provision [prə'vɪʒ(ə)n] *n* (*supply*) provision *f*; (*clause*) disposition *f*; **the p. of** (*supplying*) la fourniture de; **to make p. for** = **to provide for.**

provisional [prə'vɪʒən(ə)l] *a* provisoire. ◆—**ly** *adv* provisoirement.

proviso [prə'vaɪzəʊ] *n* (*pl* **-os**) stipulation *f*.

provok/e [prə'vəʊk] *vt* (*rouse, challenge*) provoquer (**to do, into doing** à faire); (*annoy*) agacer; (*cause*) provoquer (*accident, reaction etc*). ◆—**ing** *a* (*annoying*) agaçant. ◆**provo'cation** *n* provocation *f*. ◆**provocative** *a* (*person, remark etc*) provocant; (*thought-provoking*) qui donne à penser.

prow [praʊ] *n Nau* proue *f*.

prowess ['praʊes] *n* (*bravery*) courage *m*; (*skill*) talent *m*.

prowl [praʊl] *vi* **to p.** (**around**) rôder; — *n* **to**

be on the p. rôder. ◆—**er** *n* rôdeur, -euse *mf*.

proximity [prɒk'sɪmɪtɪ] *n* proximité *f*.

proxy ['prɒksɪ] *n* **by p.** par procuration.

prude [pruːd] *n* prude *f*. ◆**prudery** *n* pruderie *f*. ◆**prudish** *a* prude.

prudent ['pruːdənt] *a* prudent. ◆**prudence** *n* prudence *f*. ◆**prudently** *adv* prudemment.

prun/e [pruːn] **1** *n* (*dried plum*) pruneau *m*. **2** *vt* (*cut*) *Bot* tailler, élaguer; (*speech etc*) *Fig* élaguer. ◆—**ing** *n Bot* taille *f*.

pry [praɪ] **1** *vi* être indiscret; **to p. into** (*meddle*) se mêler de; (*s.o.'s reasons etc*) chercher à découvrir. **2** *vt* **to p. open** *Am* forcer (en faisant levier). ◆—**ing** *a* indiscret.

PS [piː'es] *abbr* (*postscript*) P.-S.

psalm [sɑːm] *n* psaume *m*.

pseud [sjuːd] *n Fam* bêcheur, -euse *mf*.

pseudo- ['sjuːdəʊ] *pref* pseudo-.

pseudonym ['sjuːdənɪm] *n* pseudonyme *m*.

psychiatry [saɪ'kaɪətrɪ] *n* psychiatrie *f*. ◆**psychi'atric** *a* psychiatrique. ◆**psychiatrist** *n* psychiatre *mf*.

psychic ['saɪkɪk] *a* (méta)psychique; **I'm not p.** *Fam* je ne suis pas devin; — *n* (*person*) médium *m*.

psycho- ['saɪkəʊ] *pref* psycho-. ◆**psycho-a'nalysis** *n* psychanalyse *f*. ◆**psycho-'analyst** *n* psychanalyste *mf*.

psychology [saɪ'kɒlədʒɪ] *n* psychologie *f*. ◆**psycho'logical** *a* psychologique. ◆**psychologist** *n* psychologue *mf*.

psychopath ['saɪkəʊpæθ] *n* psychopathe *mf*.

psychosis, *pl* **-oses** [saɪ'kəʊsɪs, -əʊsiːz] *n* psychose *f*.

PTO [piːtiː'əʊ] *abbr* (*please turn over*) TSVP.

pub [pʌb] *n* pub *m*.

puberty ['pjuːbətɪ] *n* puberté *f*.

public ['pʌblɪk] *a* public; — *n* public; **to make a p. protest** protester publiquement; **in the p. eye** très en vue; **p. building** édifice *m* public; **p. company** société *f* par actions; **p. corporation** société *f* nationalisée; **p. figure** personnalité *f* connue; **p. house** pub *m*; **p. life** les affaires *fpl* publiques; **to be p.-spirited** avoir le sens civique; — *n* public *m*; **in p.** en public; **a member of the p.** un simple particulier; **the sporting**/*etc* **p.** les amateurs *mpl* de sport/*etc*. ◆—**ly** *adv* publiquement; **p. owned** (*nationalized*) *Com* nationalisé.

publican ['pʌblɪk(ə)n] *n* patron, -onne *mf* d'un pub.

publication [pʌblɪ'keɪʃ(ə)n] n (publishing, book etc) publication f.

publicity [pʌb'lɪsɪtɪ] n publicité f. ◆ **'publicize** vt rendre public; (advertise) Com faire de la publicité pour.

publish ['pʌblɪʃ] vt publier; (book) éditer, publier; **to p. s.o.** éditer qn; **'published weekly'** 'paraît toutes les semaines'. ◆ **-ing** n publication f (of de); (profession) édition f. ◆ **-er** n éditeur, -trice mf.

puck [pʌk] n (in ice hockey) palet m.

pucker ['pʌkər] vt **to p. (up)** (brow, lips) plisser; − vi **to p. (up)** se plisser.

pudding ['pʊdɪŋ] n dessert m, gâteau m; (plum) pudding m; **rice p.** riz au lait.

puddle ['pʌd(ə)l] n flaque f (d'eau).

pudgy ['pʌdʒɪ] a (-ier, -iest) = podgy.

puerile ['pjʊəraɪl] a puérile.

puff [pʌf] n (of smoke) bouffée f; (of wind, air) bouffée f, souffle m; **to have run out of p.** Fam être à bout de souffle; − vi (blow, pant) souffler; **to p. at** (cigar) tirer sur; − vt (smoke etc) souffler (into dans); **to p. out** (cheeks etc) gonfler. ◆ **puffy** a (-ier, -iest) (swollen) gonflé.

puke [pjuːk] vi (vomit) Sl dégueuler.

pukka ['pʌkə] a Fam authentique.

pull [pʊl] n (attraction) attraction f; (force) force f; (influence) influence f; **to give sth a p.** tirer qch; − vt (draw, tug) tirer; (tooth) arracher; (stopper) enlever; (trigger) appuyer sur; (muscle) se claquer; **to p. apart** or **to bits** or **to pieces** mettre en pièces; **to p. a face** faire la moue; **to (get s.o. to) p. strings** Fig se faire pistonner; − vi (tug) tirer; (go, move) aller; **to p. at** or **on** tirer (sur). ■ **to p. along** vt (drag) traîner (**to** jusqu'à); ■ **to p. away** vt (move) éloigner; (snatch) arracher (**from** à); − vi Aut démarrer; **to p. away from** s'éloigner de; **to p. back** vi (withdraw) Mil se retirer; − vt (curtains) ouvrir; **to p. down** vt (lower) baisser; (knock down) faire tomber; (demolish) démolir, abattre; **to p. in** vt (rope) ramener; (drag into room etc) faire entrer; (stomach) rentrer; (crowd) attirer; − vi (arrive) Aut arriver; (stop) Aut se garer; **to p. into the station** (of train) entrer en gare; **to p. off** vt (remove) enlever; Fig mener à bien; **to p. it off** Fig réussir son coup; **to p. on** vt (boots etc) mettre; **to p. out** vt (extract) arracher (**from** à); (remove) enlever (**from** de); (from pocket, bag etc) tirer, sortir (**from** de); (troops) retirer; − vi (depart) Aut démarrer; (move out) Aut déboîter; **to p. out from** (negotiations etc) se retirer de; **to p. over** vt (drag) traîner (**to**

jusqu'à); (knock down) faire tomber; − vi Aut se ranger (sur le côté); **to p. round** vi Med se remettre; **to p. through** vi s'en tirer; **to p. oneself together** vt se ressaisir; **to p. up** vt (socks, bucket etc) remonter; (haul up) hisser; (uproot) arracher; (stop) arrêter; − vi Aut s'arrêter. ◆ **p.-up** n Sp traction f.

pulley ['pʊlɪ] n poulie f.

pullout ['pʊlaʊt] n (in newspaper etc) supplément m détachable.

pullover ['pʊləʊvər] n pull(-over) m.

pulp [pʌlp] n (of fruit etc) pulpe f; (for paper) pâte f à papier; **in a p.** Fig en bouillie.

pulpit ['pʊlpɪt] n Rel chaire f.

pulsate [pʌl'seɪt] vi produire des pulsations, battre. ◆ **pulsation** n (heartbeat etc) pulsation f.

pulse [pʌls] n Med pouls m.

pulverize ['pʌlvəraɪz] vt (grind, defeat) pulvériser.

pumice ['pʌmɪs] n **p. (stone)** pierre f ponce.

pump [pʌmp] **1** n pompe f; **(petrol) p. attendant** pompiste mf; − vt (money) Fig injecter (into dans); **to p. s.o. (for information)** tirer les vers du nez à qn; **to p. in** refouler (à l'aide d'une pompe); **to p. out** pomper (of de); **to p. air into, to p. up** (tyre) gonfler; − vi pomper; (of heart) battre. **2** n (for dancing) escarpin m; (plimsoll) tennis f.

pumpkin ['pʌmpkɪn] n potiron m.

pun [pʌn] n calembour m.

punch¹ [pʌntʃ] n (blow) coup m de poing; (force) Fig punch m; **to pack a p.** Boxing & Fig avoir du punch; **p. line** (of joke) astuce f finale; − vt (person) donner un coup de poing à; (ball etc) frapper d'un coup de poing. ◆ **p.-up** n Fam bagarre f.

punch² [pʌntʃ] **1** n (for tickets) poinçonneuse f; (for paper) perforeuse f; **p. card** carte f perforée; − vt (ticket) poinçonner, (with date) composter; (card, paper) perforer; **to p. a hole in** faire un trou dans. **2** n (drink) punch m.

punctilious [pʌŋk'tɪlɪəs] a pointilleux.

punctual ['pʌŋktʃʊəl] a (arriving on time) à l'heure; (regularly on time) ponctuel, exact. ◆ **punctu'ality** n ponctualité f, exactitude f. ◆ **punctually** adv à l'heure; (habitually) ponctuellement.

punctuate ['pʌŋktʃʊeɪt] vt ponctuer (**with** de). ◆ **punctu'ation** n ponctuation f; **p. mark** signe m de ponctuation.

puncture ['pʌŋktʃər] n (in tyre) crevaison f;

to have a p. crever; − *vt* (*burst*) crever; (*pierce*) piquer; − *vi* (*of tyre*) crever.

pundit ['pʌndɪt] *n* expert *m*, ponte *m*.

pungent ['pʌndʒənt] *a* âcre, piquant. ◆**pungency** *n* âcreté *f*.

punish ['pʌnɪʃ] *vt* punir (**for sth or doing** *or* **having done** pour avoir fait; (*treat roughly*) *Fig* malmener. ◆**−ing** *n* punition *f*; − *a* (*tiring*) éreintant. ◆**−able** *a* punissable (**by de**). ◆**−ment** *n* punition *f*, châtiment *m*; **capital p.** peine *f* capitale; **to take a (lot of) p.** (*damage*) *Fig* en encaisser.

punitive ['pju:nɪtɪv] *a* (*measure etc*) punitif.

punk [pʌŋk] **1** *n* (*music*) punk *m*; (*fan*) punk *mf*; − *a* punk *inv.* **2** *n* (*hoodlum*) *Am* Fam voyou *m*.

punt [pʌnt] **1** *n* barque *f* (*à fond plat*). **2** *vi* (*bet*) *Fam* parier. ◆**−ing** *n* canotage *m*. ◆**−er** *n* **1** (*gambler*) parieur, -euse *mf.* **2** (*customer*) *Sl* client, -ente *f*.

puny ['pju:nɪ] *a* (**-ier, -iest**) (*sickly*) chétif; (*small*) petit; (*effort*) faible.

pup [pʌp] *n* (*dog*) chiot *m*.

pupil ['pju:pəl] *n* **1** (*person*) élève *mf.* **2** (*of eye*) pupille *f*.

puppet ['pʌpɪt] *n* marionnette *f*; − *a* (*government, leader*) fantoche.

puppy ['pʌpɪ] *n* (*dog*) chiot *m*.

purchas/e ['pɜːtʃɪs] *n* (*bought article, buying*) achat *m*; − *vt* acheter (**from s.o. à qn, for s.o. à** *or* **pour qn**). ◆**−er** *n* acheteur, -euse *mf.*

pure [pjʊər] *a* (**-er, -est**) pur. ◆**purely** *adv* purement. ◆**purifi'cation** *n* purification *f*. ◆**purify** *vt* purifier. ◆**purity** *n* pureté *f*.

purée ['pjʊəreɪ] *n* purée *f*.

purgatory ['pɜːgətrɪ] *n* purgatoire *m*.

purge [pɜːdʒ] *n* Pol Med purge *f*; − *vt* (*rid*) purger (**of de**); (*politics*) Pol épurer.

purist ['pjʊərɪst] *n* puriste *mf.*

puritan ['pjʊərɪt(ə)n] *n* & *a* puritain, -aine (*mf*). ◆**puri'tanical** *a* puritain.

purl [pɜːl] *n* (*knitting stitch*) maille *f* à l'envers.

purple ['pɜːp(ə)l] *a* & *n* violet (*m*); **to go p.** (*with anger*) devenir pourpre; (*with shame*) devenir cramoisi.

purport [pɜːˈpɔːt] *vt* **to p. to be** (*claim*) prétendre être.

purpose ['pɜːpəs] *n* **1** (*aim*) but *m*; **for this p.** dans ce but; **on p.** exprès; **to no p.** inutilement; **to serve no p.** ne servir à rien; **for (the) purposes of** pour les besoins de. **2** (*determination, willpower*) résolution *f*; **to have a sense of p.** être résolu. ◆**p.-'built** *a* construit spécialement. ◆**purposeful** *a* (*determined*) résolu. ◆**purposefully** *adv*

dans un but précis; (*resolutely*) résolument. ◆**purposely** *adv* exprès.

purr [pɜːr] *vi* ronronner; − *n* ronron(nement) *m*.

purse [pɜːs] **1** *n* (*for coins*) porte-monnaie *m inv*; (*handbag*) *Am* sac *m* à main. **2** *vt* **to p. one's lips** pincer les lèvres.

purser ['pɜːsər] *n* Nau commissaire *m* du bord.

pursue [pəˈsjuː] *vt* (*chase, hound, seek, continue*) poursuivre; (*fame, pleasure*) rechercher; (*course of action*) suivre. ◆**pursuer** *n* poursuivant, -ante *mf.* ◆**pursuit** *n* (*of person, glory etc*) poursuite *f*; (*activity, pastime*) occupation *f*; **to go in p. of** se mettre à la poursuite de.

purveyor [pəˈveɪər] *n* Com fournisseur *m*.

pus [pʌs] *n* pus *m*.

push [pʊʃ] *n* (*shove*) poussée *f*; (*energy*) Fig dynamisme *m*; (*help*) coup *m* de pouce; (*campaign*) campagne *f*; **to give s.o./sth a p.** pousser qn/qch; **to give s.o. the p.** (*dismiss*) *Fam* flanquer qn à la porte; − *vt* pousser (**to, as far as** jusqu'à); (*product*) Com pousser la vente de; (*drugs*) Fam revendre; **to p. (down)** (*button*) appuyer sur; (*lever*) abaisser; **to p. (forward)** (*views etc*) mettre en avant; **to p. sth onto/between** (*thrust*) enfoncer or fourrer qch dans/entre; **to p. s.o. into doing** (*urge*) pousser qn à faire; **to p. sth off the table** faire tomber qch de la table (en le poussant); **to p. s.o. off a cliff** pousser qn du haut d'une falaise; **to be pushing forty**/*etc* Fam friser la quarantaine/*etc*; − *vi* pousser; **to p. for** faire pression pour obtenir. ■ **to p. about** *or* **around** *vt* (*bully*) Fam marcher sur les pieds à; **to p. aside** *vt* (*person, objection etc*) écarter; **to p. away** *or* **back** *vt* repousser; (*curtains*) ouvrir; **to p. in** *vi* (*in queue*) Fam resquiller; **to p. off** *vi* (*leave*) Fam filer; **p. off!** Fam fiche le camp!; **to p. on** *vi* continuer (**with** sth qch); (*in journey*) poursuivre sa route; **to p. over** *vt* (*topple*) renverser; **to p. through** *vt* (*law*) faire adopter; − *vti* **to p. (one's way) through** se frayer un chemin (**a crowd**/*etc* à travers une foule/*etc*); **to p. up** *vt* (*lever etc*) relever; (*increase*) Fam augmenter, relever. ◆**pushed** *a* **to be p.** (**for time**) (*rushed, busy*) être très bousculé. ◆**pusher** *n* (*of drugs*) revendeur, -euse *mf* (*de drogue*).

pushbike ['pʊʃbaɪk] *n* Fam vélo *m*. ◆**push-button** *n* poussoir *m*; − *a* (*radio etc*) à poussoir. ◆**pushchair** *n* poussette *f* (*pliante*). ◆**pushover** *n* **to be a p.** (*easy*)

Fam être facile, être du gâteau. ◆**push-up** *n Sp Am* pompe *f*.

pushy ['pʊʃɪ] *a* (**-ier, -iest**) *Pej* entreprenant; (*in job*) arriviste.

puss(y) ['pʊs(ɪ)] *n* (*cat*) minet *m*, minou *m*.

put [pʊt] *vt* (*pt* & *pp* **put**, *pres p* **putting**) mettre; (*savings, money*) placer (**into** dans); (*pressure, mark*) faire (**on** sur); (*problem, argument*) présenter (**to** à); (*question*) poser (**to** à); (*say*) dire; (*estimate*) évaluer (**at** à); **to p. it bluntly** pour parler franc. ■ **to p. across** *vt* (*idea etc*) communiquer (**to** à); **to p. away** *vt* (*in its place*) ranger (*livre, voiture etc*); **to p. s.o. away** (*criminal*) mettre qn en prison; (*insane person*) enfermer qn; **to p. back** *vt* remettre; (*receiver*) *Tel* raccrocher; (*progress, clock*) retarder; **to p. by** *vt* (*money*) mettre de côté; **to p. down** *vt* (*on floor, table etc*) poser; (*passenger*) déposer; (*deposit*) *Fin* verser; (*revolt*) réprimer; (*write down*) inscrire; (*assign*) attribuer (**to** à); (*kill*) faire piquer (*chien etc*); **to p. forward** *vt* (*argument, clock, meeting*) avancer; (*opinion*) exprimer; (*candidate*) proposer (**for** à); **to p. in** *vt* (*insert*) introduire; (*add*) ajouter; (*present*) présenter; (*request, application*) faire; (*enrol*) inscrire (**for** à); (*spend*) passer (*une heure etc*) (**doing** à faire); – *vi* **to p. in for** (*job etc*) faire une demande de; **to p. in at** (*of ship etc*) faire escale à; **to p. off** *vt* (*postpone*) renvoyer (à plus tard); (*passenger*) déposer; (*gas, radio*) fermer; (*dismay*) déconcerter; **to p. s.o. off** (*dissuade*) dissuader qn (**doing** de faire); **to p. s.o. off** (*disgust*) dégoûter qn (*sth* de qch); **to p. on** *vt* (*clothes, shoe etc*) mettre; (*weight, accent*) prendre; (*film*) jouer; (*gas, radio*) mettre, allumer; (*record, cassette*) passer; (*clock*) avancer; **to p. s.o. on** (*tease*) *Am* faire marcher qn; **she p. me on to you** elle m'a donné votre adresse; **p. me on to him!** *Tel* passez-le-moi!; **to p. out** *vt* (*take

outside) sortir; (*arm, leg*) étendre; (*hand*) tendre; (*tongue*) tirer; (*gas, light*) éteindre, fermer; (*inconvenience*) déranger; (*upset*) déconcerter; (*issue*) publier; (*dislocate*) démettre; **to p. through** *vt Tel* passer (**to** à); **to p. together** *vt* (*assemble*) assembler; (*compose*) composer; (*prepare*) préparer; (*collection*) faire; **to p. up** *vt* (*lift*) lever; (*window*) remonter; (*tent, statue, barrier, ladder*) dresser; (*flag*) hisser; (*building*) construire; (*umbrella*) ouvrir; (*picture, poster*) mettre; (*price, sales, numbers*) augmenter; (*resistance, plea, suggestion*) offrir; (*candidate*) proposer (**for** à); (*guest*) loger; **to p. up with** (*tolerate*) supporter; – *vt* (*lift*) lever; **p.-you-up** *n* canapé-lit *m*, convertible *m*.

putrid ['pjuːtrɪd] *a* putride. ◆**putrify** *vi* se putréfier.

putt [pʌt] *n Golf* putt *m*. ◆**putting** *n Golf* putting *m*; **p. green** green *m*.

putter ['pʌtər] *vi* **to p. around** *Am* bricoler.

putty ['pʌtɪ] *n* (*pour fixer une vitre*) mastic *m*.

puzzl/e ['pʌz(ə)l] *n* mystère *m*, énigme *f*; (*game*) casse-tête *m inv*; (*jigsaw*) puzzle *m*; – *vt* laisser perplexe; **to p. out why/when/ etc** essayer de comprendre pourquoi/quand/etc; – *vi* **to p. over** (*problem, event*) se creuser la tête sur. ◆**—ed** *a* perplexe. ◆**—ing** *a* mystérieux, surprenant.

PVC [piːviːˈsiː] *n* (*plastic*) PVC *m*.

pygmy ['pɪgmɪ] *n* pygmée *m*.

pyjama [pɪˈdʒɑːmə] *a* (*jacket etc*) de pyjama. ◆**pyjamas** *npl* pyjama *m*; **a pair of p.** un pyjama.

pylon ['paɪlən] *n* pylône *m*.

pyramid ['pɪrəmɪd] *n* pyramide *f*.

Pyrenees [pɪrəˈniːz] *npl* **the P.** les Pyrénées *fpl*.

python ['paɪθən] *n* (*snake*) python *m*.

Q

Q, q [kjuː] *n* Q, q *m*.

quack [kwæk] **1** *n* (*of duck*) coin-coin *m inv*. **2** *a* & *n* **q.** (**doctor**) charlatan *m*.

quad(rangle) ['kwɒd(ræŋg(ə)l)] *n* (*of college*) cour *f*.

quadruped ['kwɒdruped] *n* quadrupède *m*.

quadruple [kwɒˈdruːp(ə)l] *vt* quadrupler.

quadruplets [kwɒˈdruːplɪts] (*Fam* **quads** [kwɒdz]) *npl* quadruplés, -ées *mfpl*.

quaff [kwɒf] *vt* (*drink*) avaler.

quagmire ['kwægmaɪər] *n* bourbier *m*.

quail [kweɪl] *n* (*bird*) caille *f*.

quaint [kweɪnt] a (-er, -est) (*picturesque*) pittoresque; (*antiquated*) vieillot; (*odd*) bizarre. ◆**-ness** n pittoresque m; caractère m vieillot; bizarrerie f.

quake [kweɪk] vi trembler (with de); — n Fam tremblement m de terre.

Quaker [kweɪkər] n quaker, -eresse mf.

qualification [kwɒlɪfɪkeɪʃ(ə)n] n 1 (*competence*) compétence f (for pour, to do pour faire); (*diploma*) diplôme m; pl (*requirements*) conditions fpl requises. 2 (*reservation*) réserve f.

qualify [kwɒlɪfaɪ] 1 vt (*make competent*) & Sp qualifier (for sth pour qch, to do pour faire); — vi obtenir son diplôme (as a doctor/*etc* de médecin/*etc*); Sp se qualifier (for pour); to q. for (*post*) remplir les conditions requises pour. 2 vt (*modify*) faire des réserves à; (*opinion*) nuancer; Gram qualifier. ◆**qualified** a (*able*) qualifié (to do pour faire); (*doctor etc*) diplômé; (*success*) limité; (*opinion*) nuancé; (*support*) conditionnel. ◆**qualifying** a (*exam*) d'entrée; q. round Sp (épreuve f) éliminatoire f.

quality [kwɒlɪtɪ] n qualité f; — a (*product*) de qualité. ◆**qualitative** a qualitatif.

qualms [kwɑːmz] npl (*scruples*) scrupules mpl; (*anxieties*) inquiétudes fpl.

quandary [kwɒndrɪ] n in a q. bien embarrassé; to be in a q. about what to do ne pas savoir quoi faire.

quantity [kwɒntɪtɪ] n quantité f; in q. (to *purchase etc*) en grande(s) quantité(s). ◆**quantify** vt quantifier. ◆**quantitative** a quantitatif.

quarantine [kwɒrəntiːn] n Med quarantaine f; — vt mettre en quarantaine.

quarrel [kwɒrəl] n querelle f, dispute f; to pick a q. chercher querelle (with s.o. à qn); — vi (-ll-, Am -l-) se disputer, se quereller (with avec); to q. with sth trouver à redire à qch. ◆**quarrelling** n, Am **quarreling** n (*quarrels*) querelles fpl. ◆**quarrelsome** a querelleur.

quarry [kwɒrɪ] n 1 (*excavation*) carrière f. 2 (*prey*) proie f.

quart [kwɔːt] n litre m (*mesure approximative*) (Br = 1,14 litres, Am = 0,95 litre).

quarter [kwɔːtər] n 1 quart m; (*of year*) trimestre m; (*money*) Am Can quart m de dollar; (*of moon, fruit*) quartier m; to divide into quarters diviser en quatre; q. (of a) pound quart m de livre; a q. past nine, Am a q. after nine neuf heures et *or* un quart; a q. to nine neuf heures moins le quart; from all quarters de toutes parts. 2 n (*district*)

quartier m; pl (*circles*) milieux mpl; (living) quarters logement(s) m(pl); Mil quartier(s) m(pl); — vt (*troops*) Mil cantonner. ◆**-ly** a trimestriel; — adv trimestriellement; — n publication f trimestrielle.

quarterfinal [kwɔːtəfaɪn(ə)l] n Sp quart m de finale.

quartet(te) [kwɔːtet] n Mus quatuor m; (jazz) quartette m.

quartz [kwɔːts] n quartz m; — a (*clock etc*) à quartz.

quash [kwɒʃ] vt (*rebellion etc*) réprimer; (*verdict*) Jur casser.

quaver [kweɪvər] 1 vi chevroter; — n chevrotement m. 2 n Mus croche f.

quay [kiː] n Nau quai m. ◆**quayside** n on the q. sur les quais.

queas/y [kwiːzɪ] a (-ier, -iest) to feel *or* be q. avoir mal au cœur. ◆**-iness** n mal m au cœur.

Quebec [kwɪbek] n le Québec.

queen [kwiːn] n reine f; Chess Cards dame f; the q. mother la reine mère.

queer [kwɪər] a (-er, -est) (*odd*) bizarre; (*dubious*) louche; (*ill*) Fam patraque; — n (*homosexual*) Pej Fam pédé m.

quell [kwel] vt (*revolt etc*) réprimer.

quench [kwentʃ] vt (*fire*) éteindre; to q. one's thirst se désaltérer.

querulous [kwerʊləs] a (*complaining*) grognon.

query [kwɪərɪ] n question f; (*doubt*) doute m; — vt mettre en question.

quest [kwest] n quête f (for de); in q. of en quête de.

question [kwestʃ(ə)n] n question f; there's some q. of it il en est question; there's no q. of it, it's out of the q. il n'en est pas question, c'est hors de question; without q. incontestable(ment); in q. en question, dont il s'agit; q. mark point m d'interrogation; q. master TV Rad animateur, -trice mf; — vt interroger (about sur); (*doubt*) mettre en question; to q. whether douter que (+ *sub*). ◆**-ing** a (*look etc*) interrogateur; — n interrogation f. ◆**-able** a douteux. ◆**questio'nnaire** n questionnaire m.

queue [kjuː] n (*of people*) queue f; (*of cars*) file f; to stand in a q., form a q. faire la queue; — vi to q. (up) faire la queue.

quibbl/e [kwɪb(ə)l] vi ergoter, discuter (over sur). ◆**-ing** n ergotage m.

quiche [kiːʃ] n (*tart*) quiche f.

quick [kwɪk] 1 a (-er, -est) rapide; q. to react prompt à réagir; to be q. faire vite; to have a q. shave/meal/*etc* se raser/manger/*etc* en vitesse; **to be a q. worker** travailler vite; − *adv* (-er, -est) vite; **as q. as a flash** en un clin d'œil. **2** *n* to cut to the q. blesser au vif. ◆**q.-'tempered** *a* irascible. ◆**q.-'witted** *a* à l'esprit vif. ◆**quicken** *vt* accélérer; − *vi* s'accélérer. ◆**quickie** *n* (drink) *Fam* pot *m* (pris en vitesse). ◆**quickly** *adv* vite. ◆**quicksands** *npl* sables *mpl* mouvants.

quid [kwɪd] *n inv Fam* livre *f* (sterling).

quiet [kwaɪət] *a* (-er, -est) (silent, still, peaceful) tranquille, calme; (machine, vehicle, temperament) silencieux; (gentle) doux; (voice) bas, doux; (sound) léger, doux; (private) intime; (colour) discret; **to be or keep q.** (shut up) se taire; (make no noise) ne pas faire de bruit; **q.!** silence!; **to keep q. about sth, keep sth q.** ne pas parler de qch; **on the q.** (secretly) *Fam* en cachette; − *vt* **quieten.** ◆**quieten** *vti* to q. (down) (se) calmer. ◆**quietly** *adv* tranquillement, (gently, not loudly) doucement, (silently) silencieusement; (secretly) en cachette; (discreetly) discrètement. ◆**quietness** *n* tranquillité *f*.

quill [kwɪl] *n* (pen) plume *f* (d'oie).

quilt [kwɪlt] *n* édredon *m*; **(continental) q.** couette *f*; − *vt* (stitch) piquer; (pad) matelasser.

quintessence [kwɪn'tesəns] *n* quintessence *f*.

quintet(te) [kwɪn'tet] *n* quintette *m*.

quintuplets [kwɪn'tjuːplɪts] (*Fam* **quins** [kwɪnz]) *npl* quintuplés, -ées *mfpl*.

quip [kwɪp] *n* (remark) boutade *f*; − *vi* (-pp-) faire des boutades; − *vt* dire sur le ton de la boutade.

quirk [kwɜːk] *n* bizarrerie *f*; (of fate) caprice *m*.

quit [kwɪt] *vt* (pt & pp quit or quitted, pres p quitting) (leave) quitter; **to q.** doing arrêter de faire; − *vi* (give up) abandonner; (resign) démissionner.

quite [kwaɪt] *adv* (entirely) tout à fait; (really) vraiment; (rather) assez; **q. another matter** une tout autre affaire or question; **q. a genius** un véritable génie; **q. good** (not bad) pas mal (du tout); **q. (so)!** exactement!; **I q. understand** je comprends très bien; **q. a lot** pas mal (of de); **q. a (long) time ago** il y a pas mal de temps.

quits [kwɪts] *a* quitte (with envers); **to call it q.** en rester là.

quiver ['kwɪvər] *vi* frémir (with de); (of voice) trembler, frémir; (of flame) vaciller, trembler.

quiz [kwɪz] *n* (pl quizzes) (riddle) devinette *f*; (test) test *m*; **q. (programme)** *TV Rad* jeu(-concours) *m*; − *vt* (-zz-) questionner. ◆**quizmaster** *n TV Rad* animateur, -trice *mf*.

quizzical ['kwɪzɪk(ə)l] *a* (mocking) narquois; (perplexed) perplexe.

quorum ['kwɔːrəm] *n* quorum *m*.

quota ['kwəʊtə] *n* quota *m*.

quote [kwəʊt] *vt* citer; (reference number) *Com* rappeler; (price) indiquer; (price on Stock Exchange) coter; − *vi* **to q. from** (author, book) citer; − *n Fam* = **quotation**; **in quotes** entre guillemets. ◆**quo'tation** *n* citation *f*; (estimate) *Com* devis *m*; (on Stock Exchange) cote *f*; **q. marks** guillemets *mpl*; **in q. marks** entre guillemets.

quotient ['kwəʊʃ(ə)nt] *n* quotient *m*.

R

R, r [ɑːr] *n* R, r *m*.

rabbi ['ræbaɪ] *n* rabbin *m*; **chief r.** grand rabbin.

rabbit ['ræbɪt] *n* lapin *m*.

rabble ['ræb(ə)l] *n* (crowd) cohue *f*; **the r.** *Pej* la populace.

rabies ['reɪbiːz] *n Med* rage *f*. ◆**rabid** ['ræbɪd] *a* (dog) enragé; (person) *Fig* fanatique.

raccoon [rə'kuːn] *n* (animal) raton *m* laveur.

rac/e¹ [reɪs] *n Sp & Fig* course *f*; − *vt* (horse) faire courir; (engine) emballer; **to r.** (against or with) s.o. faire une course avec qn; − *vi* (run) courir; (of engine) s'emballer; (of pulse) battre à tout rompre. ◆**-ing** *n* courses *fpl*; − *a* (car, bicycle etc) de course. **r. driver** coureur *m* automobile. ◆**racecourse** *n* champ *m* de courses. ◆**racegoer** *n* turfiste *mf*. ◆**racehorse** *n* cheval *m* de course. ◆**racetrack** *n* piste *f*; (for horses) *Am* champ *m* de courses.

race² [reɪs] *n* (group) race *f*; − *a* (prejudice etc) racial; **r. relations** rapports *mpl* entre les races. ◆**racial** a racial. ◆**racialism** n racisme m. ◆**racism** n racisme m. ◆**racist** a & n raciste (mf).

rack [ræk] n 1 (shelf) étagère f; (for bottles etc) casier m; (for drying dishes) égouttoir m; (luggage) r. (on bicycle) porte-bagages m inv; (on bus, train etc) filet m à bagages; (roof) r. (of car) galerie f. 2 vt to r. one's brains se creuser la cervelle. 3 n to go to r. and ruin (of person) aller à la ruine; (of building) tomber en ruine; (of health) se délabrer.

racket ['rækɪt] n 1 (for tennis etc) raquette f. 2 (din) vacarme m. 3 (crime) racket m; (scheme) combine f; the drug(s) r. le trafic m de (la) drogue. ◆**racke'teer** n racketteur m. ◆**racke'teering** n racket m.

racoon [rəˈkuːn] n (animal) raton m laveur.

racy ['reɪsɪ] a (-ier, -iest) piquant; (suggestive) osé.

radar ['reɪdɑːr] n radar m; — a (control, trap etc) radar inv; r. operator radariste mf.

radiant ['reɪdɪənt] a (person) rayonnant (with de), radieux. ◆**radiance** n éclat m, rayonnement m. ◆**radiantly** adv (to shine) avec éclat; r. happy rayonnant de joie.

radiate ['reɪdɪeɪt] vt (emit) dégager; (joy) Fig rayonner de; — vi (of heat, lines) rayonner (from de). ◆**radia'tion** n (of heat etc) rayonnement m (of de); (radioactivity) Phys radiation f; (rays) irradiation f; r. sickness mal m des rayons.

radiator ['reɪdɪeɪtər] n radiateur m.

radical ['rædɪk(ə)l] a radical; — n (person) Pol radical, -ale mf.

radio ['reɪdɪəʊ] n (pl -os) radio f; on the r. à la radio; car r. autoradio m; r. set poste m (de) radio f. r. operator radio m; r. wave onde f hertzienne; — vt (message) transmettre (par radio) (to à); to r. s.o. appeler qn par radio. ◆**r.-con'trolled** a radioguidé. ◆**radio'active** a radioactif. ◆**radioac'tivity** n radioactivité f.

radiography [reɪdɪˈɒɡrəfɪ] n (technician) radiologue mf. ◆**radiography** n radiographie f. ◆**radiologist** n (doctor) radiologue mf. ◆**radiology** n radiologie f.

radish ['rædɪʃ] n radis m.

radius, pl -dii ['reɪdɪəs, -dɪaɪ] n (of circle) rayon m; within a r. of dans un rayon de.

RAF [ɑːreɪˈef] n abbr (Royal Air Force) armée f de l'air (britannique).

raffia ['ræfɪə] n raphia m.

raffle ['ræf(ə)l] n tombola f.

raft [rɑːft] n (boat) radeau m.

rafter ['rɑːftər] n (beam) chevron m.

rag [ræg] n 1 (old garment) loque f, haillon m; (for dusting etc) chiffon m; in rags (clothes) en loques; (person) en haillons; r.-and-bone man chiffonnier m. 2 (newspaper) torchon m. 3 (procession) Univ carnaval m (au profit d'œuvres de charité). ◆**ragged** ['rægɪd] a (clothes) en loques; (person) en haillons; (edge) irrégulier. ◆**ragman** n (pl -men) chiffonnier m.

ragamuffin ['rægəmʌfɪn] n va-nu-pieds m inv.

rag/e [reɪdʒ] n (of person) rage f; (of sea) furie f; to fly into a r. se mettre en rage; to be all the r. (of fashion etc) faire fureur; — vi (be angry) rager; (of storm, battle) faire rage. ◆**—ing** a (storm, fever) violent; a r. fire un grand incendie; in a r. temper furieux.

raid [reɪd] n Mil raid m; (by police) descente f; (by thieves) hold-up m; air r. raid m aérien, attaque f aérienne; — vt faire un raid or une descente or un hold-up dans; Av attaquer; (larder, fridge etc) Fam dévaliser. ◆**raider** n (criminal) malfaiteur m; pl Mil commando m.

rail [reɪl] n 1 (for train) rail m; by r. (to travel) par le train; (to send) par chemin de fer; to go off the rails (of train) dérailler; — a ferroviaire; (strike) des cheminots. 2 (rod on balcony) balustrade f; (on stairs, for spotlight) rampe f; (for curtain) tringle f; (towel) r. porte-serviettes m inv. ◆**railing** n (of balcony) balustrade f; pl (fence) grille f. ◆**railroad** n Am = railway; r. track voie f ferrée. ◆**railway** n (system) chemin de fer; (track) voie f ferrée; — a (ticket) de chemin de fer; (network) ferroviaire; r. line (route) ligne f de chemin de fer; (track) voie f ferrée; r. station gare f. ◆**railwayman** n (pl -men) cheminot m.

rain [reɪn] n pluie f; in the r. sous la pluie; I'll give you a r. check (for invitation) Am Fam j'accepterai volontiers à une date ultérieure; — vi pleuvoir; to r. (down) (of blows, bullets) pleuvoir; it's raining il pleut. ◆**rainbow** n arc-en-ciel m. ◆**raincoat** n imper(méable) m. ◆**raindrop** n goutte f de pluie. ◆**rainfall** n (shower) chute f de pluie; (amount) précipitations fpl. ◆**rainstorm** n trombe f d'eau. ◆**rainwater** n eau f de pluie. ◆**rainy** a (-ier, -iest) pluvieux; the r. season la saison des pluies.

raise [reɪz] vt (lift) lever; (sth heavy) (sou)lever; (child, animal, voice, statue) élever; (crops) cultiver; (salary, price) augmenter, relever; (temperature) faire monter; (question, protest) soulever; (taxes, blockade) lever; to r. a smile/a laugh (in others) faire sourire/rire; to r. s.o.'s hopes faire naître les espérances de qn; **to r. money** réunir des fonds; – *n* (*pay rise*) *Am* augmentation *f* (de salaire).

raisin ['reɪz(ə)n] *n* raisin *m* sec.

rake [reɪk] *n* râteau *m*; – *vt* (*garden*) ratisser; (*search*) fouiller dans; **to r.** (**up**) (*leaves*) ramasser (avec un râteau); **to r. in** (*money*) *Fam* ramasser à la pelle; **to r. up** (*the past*) remuer. ◆**r.-off** *n Fam* pot-de-vin *m*, ristourne *f*.

rally ['rælɪ] *vt* (*unite, win over*) rallier (**to** à); (*one's strength*) *Fig* reprendre; – *vi* se rallier (**to** à); (*recover*) se remettre (**from** de); **to r. round** (*help*) venir en aide (**s.o.** à qn); – *n Mil* ralliement *m*; *Pol* rassemblement *m*; *Sp Aut* rallye *m*.

ram [ræm] *n* (*animal*) bélier *m*. **2** *vt* (*-mm-*) (*ship*) heurter; (*vehicle*) emboutir; **to r. sth into** (*thrust*) enfoncer qch dans.

rambl/e ['ræmb(ə)l] **1** *n* (*hike*) randonnée *f*; – *vi* faire une randonnée *or* des randonnées. **2** *vi* **to r. on** (*talk*) *Pej* discourir. ◆**-ing 1** *a* (*house*) construit sans plan; (*spread out*) vaste; (*rose etc*) grimpant. **2** *a* (*speech*) décousu; – *npl* divagations *fpl*. ◆**-er** *n* promeneur, -euse *mf*.

ramification [ræmɪfɪ'keɪʃ(ə)n] *n* ramification *f*.

ramp [ræmp] *n* (*slope*) rampe *f*; (*in garage*) *Tech* pont *m* (de graissage); *Av* passerelle *f*; 'r.' *Aut* 'dénivellation'.

rampage ['ræmpeɪdʒ] *n* **to go on the r.** (*of crowd*) se déchaîner; (*loot*) se livrer au pillage.

rampant ['ræmpənt] *a* **to be r.** (*of crime, disease etc*) sévir.

rampart ['ræmpɑːt] *n* rempart *m*.

ramshackle ['ræmʃæk(ə)l] *a* délabré.

ran [ræn] *see* **run**.

ranch [rɑːntʃ] *n Am* ranch *m*; **r. house** maison *f* genre bungalow (sur sous-sol).

rancid ['rænsɪd] *a* rance.

rancour ['ræŋkər] *n* rancœur *f*.

random ['rændəm] *n* **at r.** au hasard; – *a* (*choice*) fait au hasard; (*sample*) prélevé au hasard; (*pattern*) irrégulier.

randy ['rændɪ] *a* (*-ier, -iest*) *Fam* sensuel, lascif.

rang [ræŋ] *see* **ring²**.

range [reɪndʒ] **1** *n* (*of gun, voice etc*) portée *f*; (*of aircraft, ship*) rayon *m* d'action; (*series*) gamme *f*; (*choice*) choix *m*; (*of prices*) éventail *m*; (*of voice*) *Mus* étendue *f*; (*variations*) variations *fpl*; (*of sphere*) *Fig* champ *m*, étendue *f*; – *vi* (*vary*) varier; (*extend*) s'étendre; (*roam*) errer, rôder. **2** *n* (*of mountains*) chaîne *f*; (*grassland*) *Am*

prairie *f*. **3** *n* (*stove*) *Am* cuisinière *f*. **4** *n* (*shooting* or *rifle*) **r.** (*at funfair*) stand *m* de tir; (*outdoors*) champ *m* de tir.

ranger ['reɪndʒər] *n* (*forest*) **r.** *Am* garde *m* forestier.

rank [ræŋk] **1** *n* (*position, class*) rang *m*; (*grade*) *Mil* grade *m*, rang *m*; **the r. and file** (*workers etc*) *Pol* la base; **the ranks** (*in army, numbers*) les rangs *mpl* (**of** de); **taxi r.** station *f* de taxi; – *vti* **to r. among** compter parmi. **2** *a* (*-er, -est*) (*smell*) fétide; (*vegetation*) luxuriant; *Fig* absolu.

rankle ['ræŋk(ə)l] *vi* **it rankles** (**with me**) je l'ai sur le cœur.

ransack ['rænsæk] *vt* (*search*) fouiller; (*plunder*) saccager.

ransom ['rænsəm] *n* rançon *f*; **to hold to r.** rançonner; – *vt* (*redeem*) racheter.

rant [rænt] *vi* **to r.** (**and rave**) tempêter (**at** contre).

rap [ræp] *n* petit coup *m* sec; – *vi* (*-pp-*) frapper (**at** à); – *vt* **to r. s.o. over the knuckles** taper sur les doigts de qn.

rapacious [rə'peɪʃəs] *a* (*greedy*) rapace.

rape [reɪp] *vt* violer; – *n* viol *m*. ◆**rapist** *n* violeur *m*.

rapid ['ræpɪd] **1** *a* rapide. **2** *n & npl* (*of river*) rapide(s) *m(pl)*. ◆**ra'pidity** *n* rapidité *f*. ◆**rapidly** *adv* rapidement.

rapport [ræ'pɔːr] *n* (*understanding*) rapport *m*.

rapt [ræpt] *a* (*attention*) profond.

rapture ['ræptʃər] *n* extase *f*; **to go into raptures** s'extasier (**over** sur). ◆**rapturous** *a* (*welcome, applause*) enthousiaste.

rare [reər] *a* (*-er, -est*) rare; (*meat*) *Culin* saignant; (*first-rate*) *Fam* fameux; **it's r. for her to do it** il est rare qu'elle le fasse. ◆**-ly** *adv* rarement. ◆**-ness** *n* rareté *f*. ◆**rarity** *n* (*quality, object*) rareté *f*.

rarefied ['reərɪfaɪd] *a* raréfié.

raring ['reərɪŋ] *a* **r. to start/etc** impatient de commencer/etc.

rascal ['rɑːsk(ə)l] *n* coquin, -ine *mf*. ◆**rascally** *a* (*child etc*) coquin; (*habit, trick etc*) de coquin.

rash [ræʃ] **1** *n Med* éruption *f*. **2** *a* (*-er, -est*) irréfléchi. ◆**-ly** *adv* sans réflexion. ◆**-ness** *n* irréflexion *f*.

rasher ['ræʃər] *n* tranche *f* de lard.

rasp [rɑːsp] *n* (*file*) râpe *f*.

raspberry ['rɑːzbərɪ] *n* (*fruit*) framboise *f*; (*bush*) framboisier *m*.

rasping ['rɑːspɪŋ] *a* (*voice*) âpre.

rat [ræt] **1** *n* rat *m*; **r. poison** mort-aux-rats *f*; **the r. race** *Fig* la course au bifteck, la jungle. **2** *vi* (*-tt-*) **to r. on** (*desert*) lâcher;

(*denounce*) cafarder sur; (*promise etc*) manquer à.

rate [reɪt] **1** *n* (*percentage, level*) taux *m*; (*speed*) vitesse *f*; (*price*) tarif *m*; (*on housing*) impôts *mpl* locaux; **insurance rates** primes *fpl* d'assurance; **r. of flow** débit *m*; **postage** *or* **postal r.** tarif *m* postal; **at the r. of** à une vitesse de; (*amount*) à raison de; **at this r.** (*slow speed*) à ce train-là; **at any r.** en tout cas; **the success r.** (*chances*) les chances *fpl* de succès; (*candidates*) le pourcentage de reçus. **2** *vt* (*evaluate*) évaluer; (*regard*) considérer (**as** comme); (*deserve*) mériter; **to r. highly** apprécier (beaucoup); **to be highly rated** être très apprécié. ◆**rateable** *a* **r. value** valeur *f* locative nette. ◆**ratepayer** *n* contribuable *mf*.

rather [ˈrɑːðər] *adv* (*preferably, fairly*) plutôt; **I'd r. stay** j'aimerais mieux *or* je préférerais rester (**than** que); **I'd r. you came** je préférerais que vous veniez; **r. than leave**/*etc* plutôt que de partir/*etc*; **r. more tired**/*etc* un peu plus fatigué/*etc* (**than** que); **it's r. nice** c'est bien.

ratify [ˈrætɪfaɪ] *vt* ratifier. ◆**ratifi'cation** *n* ratification *f*.

rating [ˈreɪtɪŋ] *n* (*classification*) classement *m*; (*wage etc level*) indice *m*; **credit r.** *Fin* réputation *f* de solvabilité; **the ratings** *TV* l'indice *m* d'écoute.

ratio [ˈreɪʃɪəʊ] *n* (*pl* **-os**) proportion *f*.

ration [ˈræʃ(ə)n, *Am* ˈreɪʃ(ə)n] *n* ration *f*; *pl* (*food*) vivres *mpl*; – *vt* rationner; **I was rationed to . . .** ma ration était . . . .

rational [ˈræʃ(ə)n(ə)l] *a* (*method, thought etc*) rationnel; (*person*) raisonnable. ◆**rationalize** *vt* (*organize*) rationaliser; (*explain*) justifier. ◆**rationally** *adv* raisonnablement.

rattle [ˈræt(ə)l] **1** *n* (*baby's toy*) hochet *m*; (*of sports fan*) crécelle *f*. **2** *n* petit bruit *m* (sec); cliquetis *m*; crépitement *m*; – *vi* faire du bruit; (*of bottles*) cliqueter; (*of gunfire*) crépiter; (*of window*) trembler; – *vt* (*shake*) agiter; (*window*) faire trembler; (*keys*) faire cliqueter. **3** *vt* **to r. s.o.** (*make nervous*) *Fam* ébranler qn; **to r. off** (*poem etc*) *Fam* débiter (à toute vitesse). ◆**rattlesnake** *n* serpent *m* à sonnette.

ratty [ˈrætɪ] *a* (**-ier, -iest**) **1** (*shabby*) *Am Fam* minable. **2 to get r.** (*annoyed*) *Fam* prendre la mouche.

raucous [ˈrɔːkəs] *a* rauque.

raunchy [ˈrɔːntʃɪ] *a* (**-ier, -iest**) (*joke etc*) *Am Fam* grivois.

ravage [ˈrævɪdʒ] *vt* ravager; – *npl* ravages *mpl*.

rav/e [reɪv] *vi* (*talk nonsense*) divaguer; (*rage*) tempêter (**at** contre); *vi* **to r. about** (*enthuse*) ne pas se tarir d'éloges sur; – *a* **r. review** *Fam* critique *f* dithyrambique. ◆**-ing** *a* **to be r. mad** être fou furieux; – *npl* (*wild talk*) divagations *fpl*.

raven [ˈreɪv(ə)n] *n* corbeau *m*.

ravenous [ˈrævənəs] *a* vorace; **I'm r.** *Fam* j'ai une faim de loup.

ravine [rəˈviːn] *n* ravin *m*.

ravioli [rævɪˈəʊlɪ] *n* ravioli *mpl*.

ravish [ˈrævɪʃ] *vt* (*rape*) *Lit* violenter. ◆**-ing** *a* (*beautiful*) ravissant. ◆**-ingly** *adv* **r. beautiful** d'une beauté ravissante.

raw [rɔː] *a* (**-er, -est**) (*vegetable etc*) cru; (*sugar*) brut; (*immature*) inexpérimenté; (*wound*) à vif; (*skin*) écorché; (*weather*) rigoureux; **r. edge** bord *m* coupé; **r. material** matière *f* première; **to get a r. deal** *Fam* être mal traité.

Rawlplug® [ˈrɔːlplʌg] *n* cheville *f*, tampon *m*.

ray [reɪ] *n* (*of light, sun etc*) & *Phys* rayon *m*; (*of hope*) *Fig* lueur *f*.

raze [reɪz] *vt* **to r.** (**to the ground**) (*destroy*) raser.

razor [ˈreɪzər] *n* rasoir *m*.

re [riː] *prep* *Com* en référence à.

re- [riː] *pref* rè-, re-, r-.

reach [riːtʃ] *vt* (*place, aim etc*) atteindre, arriver à; (*gain access to*) accéder à; (*of letter*) parvenir à (qn); (*contact*) joindre (qn); **to r. s.o.** (**over**) **sth** (*hand over*) passer qch à qn; **to r. out** (*one's arm*) (é)tendre; – *vi* (*extend*) s'étendre (**to** à); (*of voice*) porter; **to r.** (**out**) (é)tendre le bras (**for** pour prendre); – *n* portée *f*; *Boxing* allonge *f*; **within r. of** à portée de; (*near*) à proximité de; **within easy r.** (*object*) à portée de main; (*shops*) facilement accessible.

react [rɪˈækt] *vi* réagir. ◆**reaction** *n* réaction *f*. ◆**reactionary** *a* & *n* réactionnaire (*mf*).

reactor [rɪˈæktər] *n* réacteur *m*.

read [riːd] *vt* (*pt* & *pp* **read** [red]) lire; (*study*) *Univ* faire des études de; (*meter*) relever; (*of instrument*) indiquer; **to r. back** *or* **over** relire; **to r. out** lire (à haute voix); **to r. through** (*skim*) parcourir; **to r. up** (**on**) (*study*) étudier; – *vi* lire; **to r. well** (*of text*) se lire bien; **to r. to s.o.** faire la lecture à qn; **to r. about** (*s.o., sth*) lire qch sur; **to r. for** (*degree*) *Univ* préparer; – *n* **to have a r.** *Fam* faire un peu de lecture; **this book's a**

good r. *Fam* ce livre est agréable à lire. ◆—ing *n* lecture *f*; *(of meter)* relevé *m*; *(by instrument)* indication *f*; *(variant)* variante *f*; – *a (room)* de lecture; **r. matter** choses *fpl* à lire; **r. lamp** lampe *f* de bureau *or* de chevet. ◆—**able** *a* lisible. ◆—**er** *n* lecteur, -trice *mf*; *(book)* livre *m* de lecture. ◆**readership** *n* lecteurs *mpl*, public *m*.

readdress [riːəˈdres] *vt (letter)* faire suivre.

readjust [riːəˈdʒʌst] *vt (instrument)* régler; *(salary)* réajuster; – *vi* se réadapter **(to** à). ◆—**ment** *n* réglage *m*; réajustement *m*; réadaptation *f*.

readily [ˈredɪlɪ] *adv (willingly)* volontiers; *(easily)* facilement. ◆**readiness** *n* empressement *m* **(to do** à faire); **in r. for** prêt pour.

ready [ˈredɪ] *a* (**-ier, -iest**) prêt **(to do** à faire, **for sth** à *or* pour qch); *(quick)* Fig prompt **(to do** à faire); **to get sth r.** préparer qch; **to get r.** se préparer **(for sth** à qch, **to do** à faire); **r. cash, r. money** argent *m* liquide; – *n* **at the r.** tout prêt. ◆**r.-'cooked** *a* tout cuit. ◆**r.-'made** *a* tout fait; **r.-made clothes** prêt-à-porter *m inv*.

real [rɪəl] *a* vrai, véritable; *(life, world etc)* réel; **it's the r. thing** *Fam* c'est du vrai de vrai; **r. estate** *Am* immobilier *m*; – *adv Fam* vraiment; **r. stupid** vraiment bête; – *n* **for r.** *Fam* pour de vrai. ◆**realism** *n* réalisme *m*. ◆**realist** *n* réaliste *mf*. ◆**rea-'listic** *a* réaliste. ◆**rea'listically** *adv* avec réalisme.

reality [rɪˈælətɪ] *n* réalité *f*; **in r.** en réalité.

realize [ˈrɪəlaɪz] *vt* **1** *(know)* se rendre compte de, réaliser; *(understand)* comprendre **(that** que); **to r. that** *(know)* se rendre compte que. **2** *(carry out, convert into cash)* réaliser; *(price)* atteindre. ◆**reali'zation** *n* **1** *(prise f de)* conscience *f*. **2** *(of aim, assets)* réalisation *f*.

really [ˈrɪəlɪ] *adv* vraiment; **is it r. true?** est-ce bien vrai?

realm [relm] *n (kingdom)* royaume *m*; *(of dreams etc)* Fig monde *m*.

realtor [ˈrɪəltər] *n Am* agent *m* immobilier.

reap [riːp] *vt (field, crop)* moissonner; Fig récolter.

reappear [riːəˈpɪər] *vi* réapparaître.

reappraisal [riːəˈpreɪz(ə)l] *n* réévaluation *f*.

rear [rɪər] **1** *n (back part)* arrière *m*; *(of column)* queue *f*; **in** *or* **at the r.** à l'arrière (**of** de); **from the r.** par derrière; – *a* arrière *inv*, de derrière; **r.-view mirror** rétroviseur *m*. **2** *vt (family, animals etc)* élever; *(one's head)* relever. **3** *vi* **to r. (up)** *(of horse)* se cabrer. ◆**rearguard** *n* arrière-garde *f*.

rearrange [riːəˈreɪndʒ] *vt* réarranger.

reason [ˈriːz(ə)n] *n (cause, sense)* raison *f*; **the r. for/why** *or* **that** . . . la raison de/pour laquelle . . . ; **for no r.** sans raison; **that stands to r.** cela va sans dire, c'est logique; **within r.** avec modération; **to do everything within r. to** . . . faire tout ce qu'il est raisonnable de faire pour . . . ; **to have every r. to believe/etc** avoir tout lieu de croire/etc; – *vi* raisonner; **to r. with s.o.** raisonner qn; – *vt* **to r. that** calculer que. ◆—**ing** *n* raisonnement *m*. ◆—**able** *a* raisonnable. ◆—**ably** *adv* raisonnablement; *(fairly, rather)* assez; **r. fit** en assez bonne forme.

reassur/e [riːəˈʃʊər] *vt* rassurer. ◆—**ing** *a* rassurant. ◆**reassurance** *n* réconfort *m*.

reawaken [riːəˈweɪk(ə)n] *vt (interest etc)* réveiller. ◆—**ing** *n* réveil *m*.

rebate [ˈriːbeɪt] *n (discount on purchase)* ristourne *f*; *(refund)* remboursement *m* (partiel).

rebel [ˈreb(ə)l] *a & n* rebelle *(mf)*; – [rɪˈbel] *vi* (**-ll-**) se rebeller **(against** contre). ◆**re'bellion** *n* rébellion *f*. ◆**re'bellious** *a* rebelle.

rebirth [ˈriːbɜːθ] *n* renaissance *f*.

rebound [rɪˈbaʊnd] *vi (of ball)* rebondir; *(of stone)* ricocher; *(of lies, action)* Fig retomber (**on** sur); – [ˈriːbaʊnd] *n* rebond *m*; ricochet *m*; **on the r.** *(to marry s.o. etc)* par dépit.

rebuff [rɪˈbʌf] *vt* repousser; – *n* rebuffade *f*.

rebuild [riːˈbɪld] *vt (pt & pp rebuilt)* reconstruire.

rebuke [rɪˈbjuːk] *vt* réprimander; – *n* réprimande *f*.

rebuttal [rɪˈbʌt(ə)l] *n* réfutation *f*.

recalcitrant [rɪˈkælsɪtrənt] *a* récalcitrant.

recall [rɪˈkɔːl] *vt (call back)* rappeler; *(remember)* se rappeler (**that** que, **doing** avoir fait); **to r. sth to s.o.** rappeler qch à qn; – *n* rappel *m*; **beyond r.** irrévocable.

recant [rɪˈkænt] *vi* se rétracter.

recap [rɪˈkæp] *vti* (**-pp-**) récapituler; – *n* récapitulation *f*. ◆**reca'pitulate** *vti* récapituler. ◆**recapitu'lation** *n* récapitulation *f*.

recapture [riːˈkæptʃər] *vt (prisoner etc)* reprendre; *(rediscover)* retrouver; *(recreate)* recréer; – *n (of prisoner)* arrestation *f*.

recede [rɪˈsiːd] *vi (into the distance)* s'éloigner; *(of floods)* baisser. ◆—**ing** *a (forehead)* fuyant; **his hair(line) is r.** son front se dégarnit.

receipt [rɪˈsiːt] *n (for payment)* reçu *m* (**for** de); *(for letter, parcel)* récépissé *m*, accusé *m* de réception; *pl (takings)* recettes *fpl*; **to acknowledge r.** accuser réception (**of** de); **on r. of** dès réception de.

receiv/e [rɪ'siːv] *vt* recevoir; *(stolen goods) Jur* receler. ◆**-ing** *n Jur* recel *m*. ◆**-er** *n Tel* combiné *m*; *Rad* récepteur *m*; *(of stolen goods) Jur* receleur, -euse *mf*; **to pick up** *or* **lift the r.** *Tel* décrocher.

recent ['riːsənt] *a* récent; **in r. months** ces mois-ci. ◆**-ly** *adv* récemment; **as r. as** pas plus tard que.

receptacle [rɪ'septək(ə)l] *n* récipient *m*.

reception [rɪ'sepʃ(ə)n] *n (receiving, welcome, party etc)* & *Rad* réception *f*; **r. desk** réception *f*; **r. room** salle *f* de séjour. ◆**receptionist** *n* réceptionniste *mf*. ◆**receptive** *a* réceptif (**to an idea/etc** à une idée/etc); **r. to s.o.** compréhensif envers qn.

recess [rɪ'ses, 'riːses] *n* **1** *(holiday)* vacances *fpl*; *Sch Am* récréation *f*. **2** *(alcove)* renfoncement *m*; *(nook)* & *Fig* recoin *m*.

recession [rɪ'seʃ(ə)n] *n Econ* récession *f*.

recharge [riː'tʃɑːdʒ] *vt (battery)* recharger.

recipe ['resɪpɪ] *n Culin* & *Fig* recette *f* (**for** de).

recipient [rɪ'sɪpɪənt] *n (of award, honour)* récipiendaire *m*.

reciprocal [rɪ'sɪprək(ə)l] *a* réciproque. ◆**reciprocate** *vt (compliment)* retourner; *(gesture)* faire à son tour; – *vi (do the same)* en faire autant.

recital [rɪ'saɪt(ə)l] *n Mus* récital *m*.

recite [rɪ'saɪt] *vt (poem etc)* réciter; *(list)* énumérer. ◆**recitation** *n* récitation *f*.

reckless ['rekləs] *a (rash)* imprudent. ◆**-ly** *adv* imprudemment.

reckon ['rek(ə)n] *vt (count)* compter; *(calculate)* calculer; *(consider)* considérer; *(think) Fam* penser (**that** que); – *vi* compter; calculer; **to r. with** *(take into account)* compter avec; *(deal with)* avoir affaire à; **to r. on/without** compter sur/sans; **to r. on doing** *Fam* compter *or* penser faire. ◆**-ing** *n* calcul(s) *m(pl)*.

reclaim [rɪ'kleɪm] *vt* **1** *(land)* mettre en valeur; *(from sea)* assécher. **2** *(ask for back)* réclamer; *(luggage at airport)* récupérer.

recline [rɪ'klaɪn] *vi (of person)* être allongé; *(of head)* être appuyé; – *vt (head)* appuyer (**on** sur). ◆**-ing** *a (seat)* à dossier inclinable *or* réglable.

recluse [rɪ'kluːs] *n* reclus, -use *mf*.

recognize ['rekəgnaɪz] *vt* reconnaître (**by** à, **that** que). ◆**recognition** *n* reconnaissance *f*; **to change beyond** *or* **out of all r.** devenir méconnaissable; **to gain r.** être

reconnu. ◆**recognizable** *a* reconnaissable.

recoil [rɪ'kɔɪl] *vi* reculer (**from doing** à l'idée de faire).

recollect [rekə'lekt] *vt* se souvenir de; **to r. that** se souvenir que; – *vi* se souvenir. ◆**recollection** *n* souvenir *m*.

recommend [rekə'mend] *vt (praise, support, advise)* recommander (**to** à, **for** pour); **to r. s.o. to do** recommander à qn de faire. ◆**recommendation** *n* recommandation *f*.

recompense ['rekəmpens] *vt (reward)* récompenser; – *n* récompense *f*.

reconcile ['rekənsaɪl] *vt (person)* réconcilier (**with, to** avec); *(opinion)* concilier (**with** avec); **to r. oneself to sth** se résigner à qch. ◆**reconciliation** *n* réconciliation *f*.

reconditioned [riːkən'dɪʃ(ə)nd] *a (engine)* refait (à neuf).

reconnaissance [rɪ'kɒnɪsəns] *n Mil* reconnaissance *f*. ◆**reconnoitre** [rekə'nɔɪtər] *vt Mil* reconnaître.

reconsider [riːkən'sɪdər] *vt* reconsidérer; – *vi* revenir sur sa décision.

reconstruct [riːkən'strʌkt] *vt (crime)* reconstituer.

record 1 ['rekɔːd] *n (disc)* disque *m*; **r. library** discothèque *f*; **r. player** électrophone *m*. **2** *n Sp* & *Fig* record *m*; – *a (attendance, time etc)* record *inv*. **3** *n (report)* rapport *m*; *(register)* registre *m*; *(recording on tape etc)* enregistrement *m*; *(mention)* mention *f*; *(note)* note *f*; *(background)* antécédents *mpl*; *(case history)* dossier *m*; *(police)* r. casier *m* judiciaire; **(public) records** archives *fpl*; **to make** *or* **keep a r. of** noter; **on r.** *(fact, event)* attesté; **off the r.** à titre confidentiel; **their safety r.** leurs résultats *mpl* en matière de sécurité. **4** [rɪ'kɔːd] *vt (on tape etc, in register etc)* enregistrer; *(in diary)* noter; *(relate)* rapporter (**that** que); – *vi (on tape etc)* enregistrer. ◆**-ed** *a* enregistré; *(prerecorded) TV* en différé; *(fact)* attesté; **letter sent (by) r. delivery** = lettre *f* avec avis de réception. ◆**-ing** *n* enregistrement *m*. ◆**-er** *n Mus* flûte *f* à bec; *(tape)* r. magnétophone *m*.

recount [rɪ'kaʊnt] *vt (relate)* raconter. ◆['riːkaʊnt] *n Pol* nouveau dépouillement *m* du scrutin.

recoup [rɪ'kuːp] *vt (loss)* récupérer.

recourse ['riːkɔːs] *n* recours *m*; **to have r. to** avoir recours à.

recover [rɪ'kʌvər] **1** *vt (get back)* retrouver, récupérer. **2** *vi (from shock etc)* se remettre; *(get better) Med* se remettre (**from** de); *(of* *economy, country*) se redresser; (*of currency*) remonter. ◆**recovery** *n* **1** *Econ* redressement *m*. **2** the r. of sth (*getting back*) la récupération de qch.

recreate [riːkriˈeɪt] *vt* recréer.

recreation [rekriˈeɪʃ(ə)n] *n* récréation *f*. ◆**recreational** *a* (*activity etc*) de loisir.

recrimination [rɪkrɪmɪˈneɪʃ(ə)n] *n* *Jur* contre-accusation *f*.

recruit [rɪˈkruːt] *n* recrue *f*; − *vt* recruter; to r. s.o. to do (*persuade*) *Fig* embaucher qn pour faire. ◆**—ment** *n* recrutement *m*.

rectangle [ˈrektæŋg(ə)l] *n* rectangle *m*. ◆**rec'tangular** *a* rectangulaire.

rectify [ˈrektɪfaɪ] *vt* rectifier. ◆**rectifi'cation** *n* rectification *f*.

rector [ˈrektər] *n* *Rel* curé *m*; *Univ* président *m*.

recuperate [rɪˈkuːpəreɪt] *vi* récupérer (ses forces); − *vt* récupérer.

recur [rɪˈkɜːr] *vi* (**-rr-**) (*of theme*) revenir; (*of event*) se reproduire; (*of illness*) réapparaître. ◆**recurrence** [rɪˈkʌrəns] *n* répétition *f*; (*of illness*) réapparition *f*. ◆**recurrent** *a* fréquent.

recycle [riːˈsaɪk(ə)l] *vt* (*material*) recycler.

red [red] *a* (**redder, reddest**) rouge; (*hair*) roux; to turn *or* go r. rougir; r. light (*traffic light*) feu *m* rouge; **R. Cross** Croix-Rouge *f*; **R. Indian** Peau-Rouge *mf*; r. tape bureaucratie *f*; − *n* (*colour*) rouge *m*; **R.** (*person*) *Pol* rouge *mf*; in the r. (*firm, account*) en déficit; (*person*) à découvert. ◆r.-'faced *a* Fig rouge de confusion. ◆r.-'handed *adv* caught r.-handed pris en flagrant délit. ◆r.-'hot *a* brûlant. ◆**redden** *vti* rougir. ◆**reddish** *a* rougeâtre; (*hair*) carotte. ◆**redness** *n* rougeur *f*; (*of hair*) rousseur *f*.

redcurrant [redˈkʌrənt] *n* groseille *f*.

redecorate [riːˈdekəreɪt] *vt* (*room etc*) refaire; − *vi* refaire la peinture et les papiers.

redeem [rɪˈdiːm] *vt* (*restore to favour, free, pay off*) racheter; (*convert into cash*) réaliser; **redeeming feature** point *m* favorable. ◆**redemption** *n* rachat *m*; réalisation *f*; *Rel* rédemption *f*.

redeploy [riːdɪˈplɔɪ] *vt* (*staff*) réorganiser; (*troops*) redéployer.

redhead [ˈredhed] *n* roux *m*, rousse *f*.

redirect [riːdaɪˈrekt] *vt* (*mail*) faire suivre.

redo [riːˈduː] *vt* (*pt* **redid**, *pp* **redone**) refaire.

redress [rɪˈdres] *n* to seek r. demander réparation (**for** de).

reduce [rɪˈdjuːs] *vt* réduire (**to** à, **by** de); (*temperature*) faire baisser; **at a reduced** price (*ticket*) à prix réduit; (*goods*) au rabais. ◆**reduction** *n* réduction *f*; (*of temperature*) baisse *f*; (*discount*) rabais *m*.

redundant [rɪˈdʌndənt] *a* (*not needed*) superflu, de trop; to make r. (*workers*) mettre en chômage, licencier. ◆**redundancy** *n* (*of workers*) licenciement *m*; r. pay(ment) indemnité *f* de licenciement.

re-echo [riːˈekəʊ] *vi* résonner; − *vt* (*sound*) répercuter; *Fig* répercuter.

reed [riːd] *n* **1** *Bot* roseau *m*. **2** *Mus* anche *f*; − *a* (*instrument*) à anche.

re-educate [riːˈedjʊkeɪt] *vt* (*criminal, limb*) rééduquer.

reef [riːf] *n* récif *m*, écueil *m*.

reek [riːk] *vi* puer; to r. of (*smell*) & *Fig* puer; − *n* puanteur *f*.

reel [riːl] *n* **1** (*of thread, film*) bobine *f*; (*film itself*) *Cin* bande *f*; (*of tape*) dévidoir *m*; (*for fishing line*) moulinet *m*. **2** (*stagger*) chanceler; (*of mind*) chavirer; (*of head*) tourner. **3** *vt* to r. off (*rattle off*) débiter (à toute vitesse).

re-elect [riːɪˈlekt] *vt* réélire.

re-entry [riːˈentri] *n* (*of spacecraft*) rentrée *f*.

re-establish [riːɪˈstæblɪʃ] *vt* rétablir.

ref [ref] *n* *Sp Fam* arbitre *m*.

refectory [rɪˈfektəri] *n* réfectoire *m*.

refer [rɪˈfɜːr] *vi* (**-rr-**) to r. to (*allude to*) faire allusion à; (*speak of*) parler de; (*apply to*) s'appliquer à; (*consult*) se reporter à; − *vt* to r. sth to (*submit*) soumettre qch à; to r. s.o. to (*office, article etc*) renvoyer qn à. ◆**refe'ree** *n* *Sp* arbitre *m*; (*for job etc*) répondant, -ante *mf*; − *vt* *Sp* arbitrer. ◆**'reference** *n* (*in book, recommendation*) référence *f*; (*allusion*) allusion *f* (**to** à); (*mention*) mention *f* (**to** de); (*connection*) rapport *m* (**to** avec); in *or* with r. to concernant; *Com* suite à; **terms of r.** (*of person, investigating body*) attributions *fpl*; (*of law*) étendue *f*; **r. book** livre *m* de référence.

referendum [refəˈrendəm] *n* référendum *m*.

refill [riːˈfɪl] *vt* remplir (à nouveau); (*lighter, pen etc*) recharger; − [ˈriːfɪl] *n* recharge *f*; **a r.** (*drink*) *Fam* un autre verre.

refine [rɪˈfaɪn] *vt* (*oil, sugar, manners*) raffiner; (*metal, ore*) affiner; (*technique, machine*) perfectionner; − *vi* to r. upon raffiner sur. ◆**refinement** *n* (*of person*) raffinement *m*; (*of sugar, oil*) raffinage *m*; (*of technique*) perfectionnement *m*; *pl* (*improvements*) *Tech* améliorations *fpl*. ◆**refinery** *n* raffinerie *f*.

refit [riːˈfɪt] *vt* (**-tt-**) (*ship*) remettre en état.

reflate [riːˈfleɪt] *vt* (*economy*) relancer.

reflect [rɪ'flekt] **1** *vt* (*light*) & *Fig* refléter; (*of mirror*) réfléchir, refléter; **to r. sth on** to s.o. (*credit, honour*) faire rejaillir qch sur qn; — *vi* **to r. on s.o., be reflected on s.o.** (*rebound*) rejaillir sur qn. **2** *vi* (*think*) réfléchir (**on** à); — *vt* **to r. that** penser que. ◆**reflection** *n* **1** (*thought, criticism*) réflexion (**on** sur); **on r.** tout bien réfléchi. **2** (*image*) réflexion *f*; (*reflecting*) réflexion *f* (**of** de). ◆**reflector** *n* réflecteur *m*. ◆**reflex** *n* = **reflection**. ◆**reflexion** *n* = **reflection**. ◆**reflexive** *a* (*verb*) *Gram* réfléchi.

reflex ['riːfleks] *n* & *a* réflexe (*m*); **r. action** réflexe *m*.

refloat [riː'fləʊt] *vt* (*ship*) & *Com* renflouer.

reform [rɪ'fɔːm] *n* réforme *f*; — *vt* réformer; (*person, conduct*) corriger; — *vi* (*of person*) se réformer. ◆— *n* réformateur, -trice *mf*.

refrain [rɪ'freɪn] **1** *vi* s'abstenir (**from** doing de faire). **2** *n* *Mus* & *Fig* refrain *m*.

refresh [rɪ'freʃ] *vt* (*of bath, drink*) rafraîchir; (*of sleep, rest*) délasser; **to r. oneself** (*drink*) se rafraîchir; **to r. one's memory** se rafraîchir la mémoire. ◆—**ing** *a* rafraîchissant; (*sleep*) réparateur; (*pleasant*) agréable; (*original*) nouveau. ◆—**er** *a* (*course*) de recyclage. ◆—**ments** *npl* (*drinks*) rafraîchissements *mpl*; (*snacks*) collation *f*.

refrigerate [rɪ'frɪdʒəreɪt] *vt* réfrigérer. ◆**refrigerator** *n* réfrigérateur *m*.

refuel [riː'fjʊəl] *vi* (-**ll-**, *Am* -**l-**) *Av* se ravitailler; — *vt* *Av* ravitailler.

refuge ['refjuːdʒ] *n* refuge *m*; **to take r.** se réfugier (**in** dans). ◆**refu'gee** *n* réfugié, -ée *mf*.

refund [rɪ'fʌnd] *vt* rembourser; — ['riːfʌnd] *n* remboursement *m*.

refurbish [riː'fɜːbɪʃ] *vt* remettre à neuf.

refuse¹ [rɪ'fjuːz] *vt* refuser (**s.o. sth** qch à qn, **to do** de faire); — *vi* refuser. ◆**refusal** *n* refus *m*.

refuse² ['refjuːs] *n* (*rubbish*) ordures *fpl*, détritus *m*; (*waste materials*) déchets *mpl*; **r. collector** éboueur *m*; **r. dump** dépôt *m* d'ordures.

refute [rɪ'fjuːt] *vt* réfuter.

regain [rɪ'geɪn] *vt* (*favour, lost ground*) regagner; (*strength*) récupérer, retrouver, reprendre; (*health, sight*) retrouver; (*consciousness*) reprendre.

regal ['riːg(ə)l] *a* royal, majestueux.

regalia [rɪ'geɪlɪə] *npl* insignes *mpl* (royaux).

regard [rɪ'gɑːd] *vt* (*consider*) considérer, regarder; (*concern*) regarder; **as regards** en ce qui concerne; — *n* considération *f* (**for** pour); **to have (a) great r. for** avoir de l'estime pour; **without r. to** sans égard

pour; **with r. to** en ce qui concerne; **to give** *or* **send one's regards to** (*greetings*) faire ses hommages à. ◆—**ing** *prep* en ce qui concerne. ◆—**less 1** *a* **r. of** sans tenir compte de. **2** *adv* (*all the same*) *Fam* quand même.

regatta [rɪ'gætə] *n* régates *fpl*.

regency ['riːdʒənsɪ] *n* régence *f*.

regenerate [rɪ'dʒenəreɪt] *vt* régénérer.

reggae ['regeɪ] *n* (*music*) reggae *m*; – *a* (*group etc*) reggae *inv*.

régime [reɪ'ʒiːm] *n* *Pol* régime *m*.

regiment ['redʒɪmənt] *n* régiment *m*. ◆**regi'mental** *a* régimentaire, du régiment. ◆**regimen'tation** *n* discipline *f* excessive.

region ['riːdʒ(ə)n] *n* région *f*; **in the r. of** (*about*) *Fig* environ; **in the r. of £500** dans les 500 livres. ◆**regional** *a* régional.

register ['redʒɪstər] *n* registre *m*; *Sch* cahier *m* d'appel; **electoral r.** liste *f* électorale; — *vt* (*record, note*) enregistrer; (*birth, death*) déclarer; (*vehicle*) immatriculer; (*express*) exprimer; (*indicate*) indiquer; (*letter*) recommander; (*realize*) *Fam* réaliser; — *vi* (*enrol*) s'inscrire; (*in hotel*) signer le registre; **it hasn't registered (with me)** *Fam* je n'ai pas encore réalisé ça. ◆—**ed** *a* (*member*) inscrit; (*letter*) recommandé; **r. trademark** marque *f* déposée. ◆**regi'strar** *n* officier *m* de l'état civil; *Univ* secrétaire *m* général. ◆**regi'stration** *n* enregistrement *m*; (*enrolment*) inscription *f*; **r. (number)** *Aut* numéro *m* d'immatriculation; **r. document** *Aut* = carte *f* grise. ◆**registry** *a* & *n* **r. (office)** bureau *m* de l'état civil.

regress [rɪ'gres] *vi* régresser.

regret [rɪ'gret] *vt* (-**tt-**) regretter (**doing, to** do de faire; **that** que (+ *sub*)); **I r.** that ... je suis désolé d'apprendre que ...; — *n* regret *m*. ◆**regretfully** *adv* **r., I ...** à mon grand regret, je ... ◆**regrettable** *a* regrettable (**that** que (+ *sub*)). ◆**regrettably** *adv* malheureusement; (*poor, ill etc*) fâcheusement.

regroup [riː'gruːp] *vi* se regrouper; — *vt* regrouper.

regular ['regjʊlər] *a* (*steady, even*) régulier; (*surface*) uni; (*usual*) habituel; (*price, size*) normal; (*reader, listener*) fidèle; (*staff*) permanent; (*fool, slave etc*) *Fam* vrai; **a r. guy** *Am* *Fam* un chic type; — *n* (*in bar etc*) habitué, -ée *mf*; *Mil* régulier *m*. ◆**regu'larity** *n* régularité *f*. ◆**regularly** *adv* régulièrement.

regulate ['regjʊleɪt] *vt* régler. ◆**regu-**

'lation 1 n (*rule*) règlement m; – a (*uniform, dress etc*) réglementaire. **2** n (*regulating*) réglage m.

rehabilitate [riːhə'bɪlɪteɪt] vt (*in public esteem*) réhabiliter; (*wounded soldier etc*) réadapter.

rehash [riː'hæʃ] vt (*text*) Pej remanier; Culin réchauffer; – ['riːhæʃ] n a r. du réchauffé. Culin & Fig du réchauffé.

rehearse [rɪ'hɜːs] vt Th répéter; (*prepare*) Fig préparer; – vi Th répéter. ◆**rehearsal** n Th répétition f.

reign [reɪn] n règne m; in or during the r. of sous le règne de; – vi régner (over sur).

reimburse [riːɪm'bɜːs] vt rembourser (for de). ◆—ment n remboursement m.

rein [reɪn] n reins rênes fpl; to give free r. to Fig donner libre cours à.

reindeer ['reɪndɪər] n inv renne m.

reinforce [riːɪn'fɔːs] vt renforcer (with de); reinforced concrete béton m armé. ◆—ment n renforcement m (of de); pl Mil renforts mpl.

reinstate [riːɪn'steɪt] vt réintégrer. ◆—ment n réintégration f.

reissue [riː'ɪʃuː] vt (*book*) rééditer.

reiterate [riː'ɪtəreɪt] vt (*say again*) réitérer.

reject [rɪ'dʒekt] vt (*refuse to accept*) rejeter; (*as useless*) refuser; – ['riːdʒekt] n Com article m de rebut; – a (*article*) de rebut; r. shop solderie f. ◆**re'jection** n rejet m; (*of candidate etc*) refus m.

rejoic/e [rɪ'dʒɔɪs] vi se réjouir (over or at sth de qch, in doing de faire). ◆—ing(s) n(pl) réjouissance(s) f(pl).

rejoin [rɪ'dʒɔɪn] **1** vt (*join up with*) rejoindre. **2** vi (*retort*) répliquer.

rejuvenate [rɪ'dʒuːvəneɪt] vt rajeunir.

rekindle [riː'kɪnd(ə)l] vt rallumer.

relapse [rɪ'læps] n Med rechute f; – vi Med rechuter; to r. into Fig retomber dans.

relat/e [rɪ'leɪt] **1** vt (*narrate*) raconter (that que); (*report*) rapporter (that que). **2** vt (*connect*) établir un rapport entre (*faits etc*); to r. sth to (*link*) rattacher qch à; – vi to r. to (*apply to*) se rapporter à; (*get on with*) communiquer or s'entendre avec. ◆—ed a (*linked*) lié (to à); (*languages, styles*) apparentés; to be r. to (*by family*) être parent de.

relation [rɪ'leɪʃ(ə)n] n (*relative*) parent, -ente mf; (*relationship*) rapport m, relation f (between entre, with avec); what r. are you to him? quel est ton lien de parenté avec lui?; international/*etc* relations relations fpl internationales/*etc*. ◆**relationship** n (*kinship*) lien(s) m(pl) de parenté; (*rela-*

tions) relations fpl, rapports mpl; (*connection*) rapport m; in r. to relativement à.

relative ['relətɪv] n (*person*) parent, -ente mf; – a relatif (to à); (*respective*) respectif; r. to (*compared to*) relativement à; to be r. to (*depend on*) être fonction de. ◆**relatively** adv relativement.

relax [rɪ'læks] **1** vt (*person, mind*) détendre; – vi se détendre; r.! (*calm down*) Fam du calme! **2** vt (*grip, pressure etc*) relâcher; (*restrictions, principles, control*) assouplir. ◆—ed a (*person, atmosphere*) décontracté, détendu. ◆**rela'xation** n **1** (*rest, recreation*) détente f; (*of body*) décontraction f. **2** (*of grip etc*) relâchement m (*of restrictions etc*) assouplissement m.

relay ['riːleɪ] n relais m; r. race course f de relais; – vt (*message etc*) Rad retransmettre, Fig transmettre (to à).

release [rɪ'liːs] vt (*free*) libérer (from de); (*bomb, s.o.'s hand*) lâcher; (*spring*) déclencher; (*brake*) desserrer; (*film, record*) sortir; (*news, facts*) publier; (*smoke, trapped person*) dégager; (*tension*) éliminer; – n libération f; (*of film, book*) sortie f (of de); (*record*) nouveau disque m; (*film*) nouveau film m; (*relief*) Psy délivrance f, Psy défoulement m; press r. communiqué m de presse; to be on general r. (*of film*) passer dans toutes les salles.

relegate ['relɪgeɪt] vt reléguer (to à).

relent [rɪ'lent] vi (*be swayed*) se laisser fléchir; (*change one's mind*) revenir sur sa décision. ◆—less a implacable.

relevant ['reləvənt] a (*apt*) pertinent (to à); (*fitting*) approprié; (*useful*) utile (to à); (*significant*) important; that's not r. ça n'a rien à voir. ◆**relevance** n pertinence f (to à); (*connection*) rapport m (to avec).

reliable [rɪ'laɪəb(ə)l] a (*person, information, firm*) sérieux, sûr, fiable; (*machine*) fiable. ◆**relia'bility** n (*of person*) sérieux m, fiabilité f; (*of machine, information, firm*) fiabilité f. ◆**reliably** adv to be r. informed that apprendre de source sûre que.

reliance [rɪ'laɪəns] n (*trust*) confiance f (on en); (*dependence*) dépendance f (on de). ◆**reliant** a to be r. on (*dependent*) dépendre de; (*trusting*) avoir confiance en.

relic ['relɪk] n relique f; pl (*of the past*) vestiges mpl.

relief [rɪ'liːf] n (*from pain etc*) soulagement m (from à); (*help, supplies*) secours m; (*in art*) & Geog relief m; tax r. dégrèvement m; to be on r. Am recevoir l'aide sociale; – a

(*train etc*) supplémentaire; (*work etc*) de secours; **r.** road route *f* de délestage.
◆**relieve** *vt* (*pain etc*) soulager; (*boredom*) dissiper; (*situation*) remédier à; (*take over from*) relayer (*qn*); (*help*) secourir, soulager; **to r. s.o. of** (*rid*) débarrasser qn de; **to r. s.o. of his post** relever qn de ses fonctions; **to r. congestion in** *Aut* décongestionner; **to r. oneself** (*go to the lavatory*) *Hum Fam* se soulager.

religion [rɪˈlɪdʒ(ə)n] *n* religion *f*. ◆**religious** *a* religieux; (*war, book*) de religion. ◆**religiously** *adv* religieusement.

relinquish [rɪˈlɪŋkwɪʃ] *vt* (*give up*) abandonner; (*let go*) lâcher.

relish [ˈrelɪʃ] *n* (*liking, taste*) goût *m* (*for* pour); (*pleasure*) plaisir *m*; (*seasoning*) assaisonnement *m*; **to eat with r.** manger de bon appétit; – *vt* (*food etc*) savourer; (*like*) aimer (*doing* faire).

relocate [riːləʊˈkeɪt] *vi* (*move to new place*) déménager; **to r. in** *or* **to** s'installer à.

reluctant [rɪˈlʌktənt] *a* (*greeting, gift, promise*) accordé à contrecœur; **to be r. to do** être peu disposé à faire; **a r. teacher**/*etc* un professeur/*etc* malgré lui. ◆**reluctance** *n* répugnance *f* (**to do** à faire). ◆**reluctantly** *adv* à contrecœur.

rely [rɪˈlaɪ] *vi* **to r. on** (*count on*) compter sur; (*be dependent upon*) dépendre de.

remain [rɪˈmeɪn] **1** *vi* rester. **2** *npl* restes *mpl*; **mortal r.** dépouille *f* mortelle. ◆**-ing** *a* qui reste(nt). ◆**remainder 1** *n* reste *m*; the **r.** (*remaining people*) les autres *mfpl*; the **r. of the girls** les autres filles. **2** (*book*) invendu *m* soldé.

remand [rɪˈmɑːnd] *vt* **to r.** (**in custody**) *Jur* placer en détention préventive; – *n* **on r.** en détention préventive.

remark [rɪˈmɑːk] *n* remarque *f*; – *vt* (*say*) remarquer (**that** que); – *vi* **to r. on** faire des remarques sur. ◆**-able** *a* remarquable (**for** par). ◆**-ably** *adv* remarquablement.

remarry [riːˈmærɪ] *vi* se remarier.

remedial [rɪˈmiːdɪəl] *a* (*class*) *Sch* de rattrapage; (*measure*) de redressement; (*treatment*) *Med* thérapeutique.

remedy [ˈremɪdɪ] *vt* remédier à; – *n* remède *m* (**for** contre, à, de).

remember [rɪˈmembər] *vt* se souvenir de, se rappeler; (*commemorate*) commémorer; **to r. that**/*doing* se rappeler que/d'avoir fait; **to r. to do** (*not forget to do*) penser à faire; **r. me to him** *or* **her!** rappelle-moi à son bon souvenir!; – *vi* se souvenir, se rappeler. ◆**remembrance** *n* (*memory*) souvenir *m*; **in r. of** en souvenir de.

remind [rɪˈmaɪnd] *vt* rappeler (**s.o. of sth** qch à qn, **s.o. that** à qn que); **to r. s.o. to do** penser à qn à faire; **that** *or* **which reminds me!** à propos! ◆**—er** *n* (*of event & letter*) rappel *m*; (*note to do sth*) pense-bête *m*; **it's a r.** (**for him** *or* **her**) **that . . .** c'est pour lui rappeler que. . . .

reminisce [remɪˈnɪs] *vi* raconter *or* se rappeler ses souvenirs (**about** de). ◆**reminiscences** *npl* réminiscences *fpl*. ◆**reminiscent** *a* **r. of** qui rappelle.

remiss [rɪˈmɪs] *a* négligent.

remit [rɪˈmɪt] *vt* (*-tt-*) (*money*) envoyer. ◆**remission** *n Jur* remise *f* (de peine); *Med Rel* rémission *f*. ◆**remittance** *n* (*sum*) paiement *m*.

remnant [ˈremnənt] *n* (*remaining part*) reste *m*; (*trace*) vestige *m*; (*of fabric*) coupon *m*; (*oddment*) fin *f* de série.

remodel [riːˈmɒd(ə)l] *vt* (*-ll-*, *Am* *-l-*) remodeler.

remonstrate [ˈremənstreɪt] *vi* **to r. with s.o.** faire des remontrances à qn.

remorse [rɪˈmɔːs] *n* remords *m(pl)* (**for** pour); **without r.** sans pitié. ◆**—less** *a* implacable. ◆**—lessly** *adv* (*to hit etc*) implacablement.

remote [rɪˈməʊt] *a* (*-er, -est*) **1** (*far-off*) lointain, éloigné; (*isolated*) isolé; (*aloof*) distant; **r. from** loin de; **r.** control télécommande *f*. **2** (*slight*) petit, vague; **not the remotest idea** pas la moindre idée. ◆**-ly** *adv* (*slightly*) vaguement, un peu; (*situated*) au loin; **not r. aware**/*etc* nullement conscient/*etc*. ◆**-ness** *n* éloignement *m*; isolement *m*; *Fig* attitude *f* distante.

remould [ˈriːməʊld] *n* pneu *m* rechapé.

remove [rɪˈmuːv] *vt* (*clothes, stain etc*) enlever (**from s.o.** à qn, **from sth** de qch); (*withdraw*) retirer; (*lead away*) emmener (**to** à); (*furniture*) déménager; (*obstacle, threat, word*) supprimer; (*fear, doubt*) dissiper; (*employee*) renvoyer; (**far**) **removed from** loin de. ◆**removable** *a* (*lining etc*) amovible. ◆**removal** *n* enlèvement *m*; déménagement *m*; suppression *f*; **r. man** déménageur *m*; **r. van** camion *m* de déménagement. ◆**remover** *n* (*for make-up*) démaquillant *m*; (*for nail polish*) dissolvant *m*; (*for paint*) décapant *m*; (*for stains*) détachant *m*.

remunerate [rɪˈmjuːnəreɪt] *vt* rémunérer. ◆**remune'ration** *n* rémunération *f*.

renaissance [rəˈneɪsəns] *n* (*in art etc*) renaissance *f*.

rename [riːˈneɪm] *vt* (*street etc*) rebaptiser.

render [ˈrendər] *vt* (*give, make*) rendre; *Mus*

interpréter; (*help*) prêter. **◆—ing** n Mus interprétation f; (*translation*) traduction f.

rendez-vous ['rɒndɪvuː, pl -vuːz] n inv rendez-vous m inv.

renegade ['renɪɡeɪd] n renégat, -ate mf.

reneg(u)e [rɪ'niːɡ] vi **to r. on** (*promise etc*) revenir sur.

renew [rɪ'njuː] vt renouveler; (*resume*) reprendre; (*library book*) renouveler le prêt de. **◆—ed** a (*efforts*) renouvelés; (*attempt*) nouveau; **with r. vigour**/*etc* avec un regain de vigueur/*etc*. **◆renewable** a renouvelable. **◆renewal** n renouvellement m; (*resumption*) reprise f; (*of strength etc*) regain m.

renounce [rɪ'naʊns] vt (*give up*) renoncer à; (*disown*) renier.

renovate ['renəveɪt] vt (*house*) rénover, restaurer; (*painting*) restaurer. **◆reno-'vation** n rénovation f; restauration f.

renown [rɪ'naʊn] n renommée f. **◆renowned** a renommé (**for** pour).

rent [rent] n loyer m; (*of television*) (prix m de) location f; **r. collector** encaisseur m de loyers; — vt louer; **to r. out** louer; — vi (*of house etc*) se louer. **◆r.-'free** adv sans payer de loyer; — a gratuit. **◆rental** n (*of television*) (prix m de) location f; (*of telephone*) abonnement m.

renunciation [rɪnʌnsɪ'eɪʃ(ə)n] n (*giving up*) renonciation f (**of** à); (*disowning*) reniement m (**of** de).

reopen [riː'əʊpən] vti rouvrir. **◆—ing** n réouverture f.

reorganize [riː'ɔːɡənaɪz] vt réorganiser.

rep [rep] n Fam représentant, -ante mf de commerce.

repaid [riː'peɪd] see repay.

repair [rɪ'peər] vt réparer; — n réparation f; **beyond r.** irréparable; **in good/bad r.** en bon/mauvais état; **'road under r.'** Aut 'travaux'; **r. man** réparateur m; **r. woman** réparatrice f.

reparation [repə'reɪʃ(ə)n] n réparation f (**for** de); pl Mil Hist réparations fpl.

repartee [repɑː'tiː] n (*sharp reply*) repartie f.

repatriate [riː'pætrɪeɪt] vt rapatrier.

repay [riː'peɪ] vt (pt & pp repaid) (*pay back*) rembourser; (*kindness*) payer de retour; (*reward*) récompenser (**for** de). **◆—ment** n remboursement m; récompense f.

repeal [rɪ'piːl] vt (*law*) abroger; — n abrogation f.

repeat [rɪ'piːt] vt répéter (**that** que); (*promise, threat*) réitérer; (*class*) Sch redoubler; **to r. oneself** or **itself** se répéter; — vi répéter; **to r. on s.o.** (*of food*) Fam revenir à

qn; — n TV Rad rediffusion f; — a (*performance*) deuxième. **◆—ed** a répété; (*efforts*) renouvelés. **◆—edly** adv à maintes reprises.

repel [rɪ'pel] vt (-ll-) repousser. **◆repellent** a repoussant; **insect r.** insectifuge m.

repent [rɪ'pent] vi se repentir (**of** de). **◆repentance** n repentir m. **◆repentant** a repentant.

repercussion [riːpə'kʌʃ(ə)n] n répercussion f.

repertoire ['repətwɑːr] n Th & Fig répertoire m. **◆repertory** n Th & Fig répertoire m; **r. (theatre)** théâtre m de répertoire.

repetition [repɪ'tɪʃ(ə)n] n répétition f. **◆repetitious** a, **◆re'petitive** a (*speech etc*) répétitif.

replace [rɪ'pleɪs] vt (*take the place of*) remplacer (**by, with** par); (*put back*) remettre, replacer; (*receiver*) Tel raccrocher. **◆—ment** n remplacement m (**of** de); (*person*) remplaçant, -ante mf; (*machine part*) pièce f de rechange.

replay ['riːpleɪ] n Sp match m rejoué; (**instant** or **action**) **r.** TV répétition f immédiate (au ralenti).

replenish [rɪ'plenɪʃ] vt (*refill*) remplir (de nouveau); (*renew*) renouveler.

replete [rɪ'pliːt] a **r. with** rempli de; **r. with food** rassasié.

replica ['replɪkə] n copie f exacte.

reply [rɪ'plaɪ] vti répondre; — n réponse f; **in r. en** réponse (**to** à).

report [rɪ'pɔːt] n (*account*) rapport m; (*of meeting*) compte rendu m; Journ TV Rad reportage m; Pol enquête f; Sch Met bulletin m; (*rumour*) rumeur f; (*of gun*) détonation f; — vt (*give account of*) rapporter, rendre compte de; (*announce*) annoncer (**that** que); (*notify*) signaler (**to** à); (*denounce*) dénoncer (**to** à); (*event*) Journ faire un reportage sur; — vi faire un rapport or Journun reportage (**on** sur); (*go*) se présenter (**to** à, **to s.o.** chez qn, **for work** au travail). **◆—ed** a (*speech*) Gram indirect; **it is r. that** on dit que; **r. missing** porté disparu. **◆—edly** adv à ce qu'on dit. **◆—ing** n Journ reportage m. **◆—er** n reporter m.

repose [rɪ'pəʊz] n Lit repos m.

repossess [riːpə'zes] vt Jur reprendre possession de.

reprehensible [reprɪ'hensəb(ə)l] a répréhensible.

represent [reprɪ'zent] vt représenter. **◆represen'tation** n représentation f; pl (*complaints*) remontrances fpl. **◆repre-**

sentative *a* représentatif (**of** de); – *n* représentant, -ante *mf*; *Pol Am* député *m*.

repress [rɪ'pres] *vt* réprimer; (*feeling*) refouler. ◆**repressive** *a* répressif.

reprieve [rɪ'priːv] *n Jur* sursis *m*; *Fig* répit *m*, sursis *m*; – *vt* accorder un sursis *or Fig* un répit à.

reprimand ['reprɪmɑːnd] *n* réprimande *f*; – *vt* réprimander.

reprint ['riːprɪnt] *n* (*reissue*) réimpression *f*; – *vt* réimprimer.

reprisal [rɪ'praɪz(ə)l] *n* **reprisals** représailles *fpl*; **in r. for** en représailles de.

reproach [rɪ'prəʊtʃ] *n* (*blame*) reproche *m*; (*shame*) honte *f*; **beyond r.** sans reproche; – *vt* reprocher (**s.o. for sth** qch à qn). ◆**reproachful** *a* réprobateur. ◆**reproachfully** *adv* d'un ton *or* d'un air réprobateur.

reproduce [riːprə'djuːs] *vt* reproduire; – *vi Biol Bot* se reproduire. ◆**reproduction** *n* (*of sound etc*) & *Biol Bot* reproduction *f*. ◆**reproductive** *a* reproducteur.

reptile ['reptaɪl] *n* reptile *m*.

republic [rɪ'pʌblɪk] *n* république *f*. ◆**republican** *a* & *n* républicain, -aine (*mf*).

repudiate [rɪ'pjuːdɪeɪt] *vt* (*offer*) repousser; (*accusation*) rejeter; (*spouse, belief*) répudier.

repugnant [rɪ'pʌgnənt] *a* répugnant; **he's r.** to me il me répugne. ◆**repugnance** *n* répugnance *f* (**for** pour).

repulse [rɪ'pʌls] *vt* repousser. ◆**repulsion** *n* répulsion *f*. ◆**repulsive** *a* repoussant.

reputable [rɪ'pjuːtəb(ə)l] *a* de bonne réputation. ◆**re'pute** *n* réputation *f*; **of r.** de bonne réputation. ◆**re'puted** *a* réputé (**to be** pour être). ◆**re'putedly** *adv* à ce qu'on dit.

reputation [repjʊ'teɪʃ(ə)n] *n* réputation *f*; **to have a r. for frankness**/*etc* avoir la réputation d'être franc/*etc*.

request [rɪ'kwest] *n* demande *f* (**for** de); **on r.** sur demande; **at s.o.'s r.** à la demande de qn; **by popular r.** à la demande générale; **r. stop** (*for bus*) arrêt *m* facultatif; – *vt* demander (**from** *or* **of s.o.** à qn, **s.o. to do** à qn de faire).

requiem ['rekwɪəm] *n* requiem *m inv*.

requir/e [rɪ'kwaɪər] *vt* (*necessitate*) demander; (*demand*) exiger; (*of person*) avoir besoin de (*qch, qn*); (*staff*) rechercher; **to r. sth of s.o.** (*order*) exiger qch de qn; **to r. s.o. to do** exiger de qn qu'il fasse; (*ask*) demander à qn de faire; **if required** s'il le faut. ◆**—ed** *a* requis, exigé. ◆**—ement** *n*

(*need*) exigence *f*; (*condition*) condition *f* (*require*).

requisite ['rekwɪzɪt] **1** *a* nécessaire. **2** *n* (*for travel etc*) article *m*; **toilet requisites** articles *mpl or* nécessaire *m* de toilette.

requisition [rekwɪ'zɪʃ(ə)n] *vt* réquisitionner; – *n* réquisition *f*.

reroute [riː'ruːt] *vt* (*aircraft etc*) dérouter.

rerun ['riːrʌn] *n Cin* reprise *f*; *TV* rediffusion *f*.

resale ['riːseɪl] *n* revente *f*.

resat [riː'sæt] *see* resit.

rescind [rɪ'sɪnd] *vt Jur* annuler; (*law*) abroger.

rescu/e ['reskjuː] *vt* (*save*) sauver; (*set free*) délivrer (**from** de); – *n* (*action*) sauvetage *m* (**of** de); (*help, troops etc*) secours *mpl*; **to go**/*etc* **to s.o.'s r.** aller/*etc* au secours de qn; **to the r.** à la rescousse; – *a* (*team, operation*) de sauvetage. ◆**—er** *n* sauveteur *m*.

research [rɪ'sɜːtʃ] *n* recherches *fpl* (**on, into** sur); **some r.** de la recherche; **a piece of r.** (*work*) un travail de recherche; – *vi* faire des recherches (**on, into** sur). ◆**—er** *n* chercheur, -euse *mf*.

resemble [rɪ'zemb(ə)l] *vt* ressembler à. ◆**resemblance** *n* ressemblance *f* (**to** avec).

resent [rɪ'zent] *vt* (*anger*) s'indigner de, ne pas aimer; (*bitterness*) éprouver de l'amertume à l'égard de; **I r. that** ça m'indigne. ◆**resentful** *a* **to be r.** éprouver de l'amertume. ◆**resentment** *n* amertume *f*, ressentiment *m*.

reserv/e [rɪ'zɜːv] **1** *vt* (*room, decision etc*) réserver; (*right*) se réserver; (*one's strength*) ménager; – *n* (*reticence*) réserve *f*. **2** *n* (*stock, land*) réserve *f*; **r.** (*player*) *Sp* remplaçant, -ante *mf*; **the r.** *Mil* la réserve; **the reserves** (*troops*) *Mil* les réserves *fpl*; **nature r.** réserve *f* naturelle; **in r.** en réserve; **r. tank** *Av Aut* réservoir *m* de secours. ◆**—ed** *a* (*person, room*) réservé. ◆**reser'vation** *n* **1** (*doubt etc*) réserve *f*; (*booking*) réservation *f*. **2** (*land*) *Am* réserve *f*; **central r.** (*on road*) terre-plein *m*.

reservoir ['rezəvwɑːr] *n* réservoir *m*.

resettle [riː'set(ə)l] *vt* (*refugees*) implanter.

reshape [riː'ʃeɪp] *vt* (*industry etc*) réorganiser.

reshuffle [riː'ʃʌf(ə)l] *n* (*cabinet*) **r.** *Pol* remaniement *m* (ministériel); – *vt* *Pol* remanier.

reside [rɪ'zaɪd] *vi* résider. ◆**'residence** *n* (*home*) résidence *f*; (*of students*) foyer *m*; **in r.** (*doctor*) sur place; (*students on campus*) sur le campus, (*in halls of residence*) rentrés. ◆'**resident** n habitant, -ante mf; (of hotel) pensionnaire mf; (foreigner) résident, -ente mf; – a résidant, qui habite sur place; (population) fixe; (correspondent) permanent; **to be r. in London** résider à Londres. ◆**resi'dential** a (neighbourhood) résidentiel.

residue ['rezidju:] n résidu m. ◆**re'sidual** a résiduel.

resign [rı'zaın] vt (right, claim) abandonner; **to r. (from) one's job** démissionner; **to r. oneself to sth/to doing** se résigner à qch/à faire; – vi démissionner (**from** de). ◆–**ed** a résigné. ◆**resig'nation** n (from job) démission f; (attitude) résignation f.

resilient [rı'zılıənt] a élastique; (person) Fig résistant. ◆**resilience** n élasticité f; Fig résistance f.

resin ['rezın] n résine f.

resist [rı'zıst] vt (attack etc) résister à; **to r. doing sth** s'empêcher de faire qch; **she can't r. cakes** elle ne peut pas résister devant les gâteaux; **she can't r. her** (indulgence) il ne peut rien lui refuser; (charm) il ne peut pas résister à son charme; – vi résister. ◆**resistance** n résistance f (**to** à). ◆**resistant** a résistant (**to** à); **r. to** Med rebelle à.

resit [ri:'sıt] vt (pt & pp resat, pres p resitting) (exam) repasser.

resolute ['rezəlu:t] a résolu. ◆–**ly** adv résolument. ◆**reso'lution** n résolution f.

resolv/e [rı'zɒlv] vt résoudre (**to do** de faire, **that** que); – n résolution f. ◆–**ed** a résolu (**to do** à faire).

resonant ['rezənənt] a (voice) résonnant; **to be r. with** résonner de. ◆**resonance** n résonance f.

resort [rı'zɔ:t] 1 n (recourse) recours m (**to** à); **as a last r.** en dernier ressort; – vi **to r. to s.o.** avoir recours à qn; **to r. to doing** en venir à faire; **to r. to drink** se rabattre sur la boisson. 2 n (holiday) r. station f de vacances; **seaside/ski** r. station f balnéaire/de ski.

resound [rı'zaund] vi résonner (**with** de); Fig avoir du retentissement. ◆–**ing** a (success, noise) retentissant.

resource [rı'sɔːs, rı'zɔːs] n (expedient, recourse) ressource f; pl (wealth etc) ressources fpl. ◆**resourceful** a (person, scheme) ingénieux. ◆**resourcefulness** n ingéniosité f, ressource f.

respect [rı'spekt] n respect m (**for** pour, de); (aspect) égard m; **in r. of, with r. to** en ce qui concerne; **with all due r.** sans vouloir vous vexer; – vt respecter. ◆**respecta'bility** n

respectabilité f. ◆**respectable** a (honourable, sizeable) respectable; (satisfying) honnête; (clothes, behaviour) convenable. ◆**respectably** adv (to dress etc) convenablement; (rather well) passablement. ◆**respectful** a respectueux (**to** envers, **of** de). ◆**respectfully** adv respectueusement.

respective [rı'spektıv] a respectif. ◆–**ly** adv respectivement.

respiration [respı'reı∫(ə)n] n respiration f.

respite ['respaıt] n répit m.

respond [rı'spɒnd] vi répondre (**to** à); **to r. to treatment** Med réagir positivement au traitement. ◆**response** n réponse f; **in p. to** en réponse à.

responsible [rı'spɒnsəb(ə)l] a responsable (**for** de, **to s.o.** devant qn); (job) à responsabilités; **who's r. for ... ?** qui est (le) responsable de ... ? ◆**responsi'bility** n responsabilité f. ◆**responsibly** adv de façon responsable.

responsive [rı'spɒnsıv] a (reacting) qui réagit bien; (alert) éveillé; (attentive) qui fait attention; **r. to** (kindness) sensible à; (suggestion) réceptif à. ◆–**ness** n (bonne) réaction f.

rest¹ [rest] n (repose) repos m; (support) support m; **to have or take a r.** se reposer; **to set or put s.o.'s mind at r.** tranquilliser qn; **to come to r.** (of ball etc) s'immobiliser; (of bird, eyes) se poser (**on** sur); **r. home** maison f de repos; **r. room** Am toilettes fpl; – vi (relax) se reposer; (be buried) reposer; **to r. on** (of roof, argument) reposer sur; **I won't r. till** je n'aurai de repos que (+ sub); **to be resting on** (of hand etc) être posé sur; **a resting place** un lieu de repos; – vt (eyes etc) reposer; (horse etc) laisser reposer; (lean) poser, appuyer (**on** sur); (base) fonder. ◆**restful** a reposant.

rest² [rest] n (remainder) reste m (**of** de); **the r.** (others) les autres mfpl; **the r. of the men**/etc les autres hommes/etc; – vi (remain) **it rests with you to do** il vous incombe de faire; **r. assured** soyez assuré (**that** que).

restaurant ['restərɒnt] n restaurant m.

restitution [restı'tju:∫(ə)n] n (for damage) Jur réparation f; **to make r. of** restituer.

restive ['restıv] a (person, horse) rétif.

restless ['restləs] a agité. ◆–**ly** adv avec agitation. ◆–**ness** n agitation f.

restore [rı'stɔ:r] vt (give back) rendre (**to** à); (order, right) Jur rétablir; (building, painting) restaurer; (to life or power) ramener (qn) (**to** à).

restrain [rɪ'streɪn] *vt* (*person, emotions*) retenir, maîtriser; (*crowd*) contenir; (*limit*) limiter; **to r. s.o. from doing** retenir qn de faire; **to r. oneself** se maîtriser. ◆**—ed** *a* (*feelings*) contenu; (*tone*) mesuré. ◆**restraint** *n* (*moderation*) retenue *f*, mesure *f*; (*restriction*) contrainte *f*.

restrict [rɪ'strɪkt] *vt* limiter, restreindre (**to** à). ◆**—ed** *a* (*space, use*) restreint; (*sale*) contrôlé. ◆**restriction** *n* restriction *f*, limitation *f*. ◆**restrictive** *a* restrictif.

result [rɪ'zʌlt] *n* (*outcome, success*) résultat *m*; **as a r.** en conséquence; **as a r. of** par suite de; – *vi* résulter (**from** de); **to r. in** aboutir à.

resume [rɪ'zjuːm] *vti* (*begin or take again*) reprendre; **to r. doing** se remettre à faire. ◆**resumption** *n* reprise *f*.

résumé ['rezjumeɪ] *n* (*summary*) résumé *m*; *Am* curriculum vitae *m inv*.

resurface [riː'sɜːfɪs] *vi* (*road*) refaire le revêtement de.

resurgence [rɪ'sɜːdʒəns] *n* réapparition *f*.

resurrect [rezə'rekt] *vt* (*custom, hero*) *Pej* ressusciter. ◆**resurrection** *n* résurrection *f*.

resuscitate [rɪ'sʌsɪteɪt] *vt* *Med* réanimer.

retail ['riːteɪl] *n* (*vente f au*) détail *m*; – *a* (*price, shop etc*) de détail; – *vi* se vendre (au détail); – *vt* vendre (au détail), détailler; – *adv* (*to sell*) au détail. ◆**—er** *n* détaillant, -ante *mf*.

retain [rɪ'teɪn] *vt* (*hold back, remember*) retenir; (*freshness, hope etc*) conserver. ◆**retainer** *n* (*fee*) avance *f*, acompte *m*. ◆**retention** *n* (*memory*) mémoire *f*. ◆**retentive** *a* (*memory*) fidèle.

retaliate [rɪ'tælɪeɪt] *vi* riposter (**against s.o.** contre qn, **against an attack** à une attaque). ◆**retali'ation** *n* riposte *f*, représailles *fpl*; **in r. for** en représailles de.

retarded [rɪ'tɑːdɪd] *a* (*mentally*) **r.** arriéré.

retch [retʃ] *vi* avoir un or des haut-le-cœur.

rethink [riː'θɪŋk] *vt* (*pt & pp* **rethought**) repenser.

reticent ['retɪsənt] *a* réticent. ◆**reticence** *n* réticence *f*.

retina ['retɪnə] *n* *Anat* rétine *f*.

retir/e [rɪ'taɪər] **1** *vi* (*from work*) prendre sa retraite; – *vt* mettre à la retraite. **2** *vi* (*withdraw*) se retirer (**from** de, **to** à); (*go to bed*) aller se coucher. ◆**—ed** *a* (*having stopped working*) retraité. ◆**—ing** *a* **1** (*age*) de la retraite. **2** (*reserved*) réservé. ◆**retirement** *n* retraite *f*; **r. age** âge *m* de la retraite.

retort [rɪ'tɔːt] *vt* rétorquer; – *n* réplique *f*.

retrace [riː'treɪs] *vt* (*past event*) se remémorer, reconstituer; **to r. one's steps** revenir sur ses pas, rebrousser chemin.

retract [rɪ'trækt] *vt* (*statement etc*) rétracter; – *vi* (*of person*) se rétracter. ◆**retraction** *n* (*of statement*) rétractation *f*.

retrain [riː'treɪn] *vi* se recycler; – *vt* recycler. ◆**—ing** *n* recyclage *m*.

retread [rɪ'tred] *n* pneu *m* rechapé.

retreat [rɪ'triːt] *n* (*withdrawal*) retraite *f*; (*place*) refuge *m*; – *vi* se retirer (**from** de); *Mil* battre en retraite.

retrial [riː'traɪəl] *n* *Jur* nouveau procès *m*.

retribution [retrɪ'bjuːʃ(ə)n] *n* châtiment *m*.

retrieve [rɪ'triːv] *vt* (*recover*) récupérer; (*rescue*) sauver (**from** de); (*loss, error*) réparer; (*honour*) rétablir. ◆**retrieval** *n* récupération *f*. **information r.** recherche *f* documentaire. ◆**retriever** *n* (*dog*) chien *m* d'arrêt.

retro- ['retrəʊ] *pref* rétro-. ◆**retro'active** *a* rétroactif.

retrograde ['retrəgreɪd] *a* rétrograde.

retrospect ['retrəspekt] *n* **in r.** rétrospectivement. ◆**retro'spective 1** *a* (*law, effect*) rétroactif. **2** *n* (*of film director, artist*) rétrospective *f*.

return [rɪ'tɜːn] *vi* (*come back*) revenir; (*go back*) retourner; (*go back home*) rentrer; **to r. to** (*subject*) revenir à; – *vt* (*give back*) rendre; (*put back*) remettre; (*bring back*) & *Fin* rapporter; (*send back*) renvoyer; (*greeting*) répondre à; (*candidate*) *Pol* élire; – *n* retour *m*; (*yield*) *Fin* rapport *m*; *pl* (*profits*) *Fin* bénéfices *mpl*; **the r. to school** la rentrée (des classes); **r. (ticket)** (billet *m* d')aller et retour *m*; **tax r.** déclaration *f* de revenus; **many happy returns (of the day)!** bon anniversaire!; **in r.** (*exchange*) en échange (**for** de); (*a trip, flight etc*) (de) retour; **r. match** match *m* retour. ◆**—able** *a* (*bottle*) consigné.

reunion [riː'juːnɪən] *n* réunion *f*. ◆**reu'nite** *vt* réunir.

rev [rev] *n* *Aut* *Fam* tour *m*; **r. counter** compte-tours *m inv*; – *vt* (**-vv-**) **to r. (up)** (*engine*) *Fam* faire ronfler.

revamp [riː'væmp] *vt* (*method, play etc*) *Fam* remanier.

reveal [rɪ'viːl] *vt* (*make known*) révéler (**that** que); (*make visible*) laisser voir. ◆**—ing** *a* (*sign etc*) révélateur.

revel ['rev(ə)l] *vi* (**-ll-**) faire la fête; **to r. in sth** se délecter de qch. ◆**revelling** *n*, ◆**revelry** *n* festivités *fpl*. ◆**reveller** *n* noceur, -euse *mf*.

revenge [rɪ'vendʒ] *n* vengeance *f*; *Sp* revanche *f*; **to have** or **get one's r.** se venger (on s.o. de qn, on s.o. for sth de qch sur qn); **in r.** pour se venger; – *vt* venger.

revenue ['revənjuː] *n* revenu *m*.

reverberate [rɪ'vɜːbəreɪt] *vi* (*of sound*) se répercuter.

revere [rɪ'vɪər] *vt* révérer. **◆'reverence** *n* révérence *f*. **◆'reverend** *a* (*father*) Rel révérend; – *n* **R. Smith** (*Anglican*) le révérend Smith; (*Catholic*) l'abbé *m* Smith; (*Jewish*) le rabbin Smith. **◆'reverent** *a* respectueux.

reverse [rɪ'vɜːs] *a* contraire; (*order, image*) inverse; **r. side** (*of coin etc*) revers *m*; (*of paper*) verso *m*; – *n* contraire *m*; (*of coin, fabric etc*) revers *m*; (*of paper*) verso *m*; **in r. (gear)** *Aut* en marche arrière; – *vt* (*situation*) renverser; (*order, policy*) inverser; (*decision*) annuler; (*bucket etc*) retourner; **to r. the charges** *Tel* téléphoner en PCV; – *vti* **to r. (the car)** faire marche arrière; **to r. in/out** rentrer/sortir en marche arrière; **reversing light** phare *m* de recul. **◆reversal** *n* renversement *m*; (*of policy, situation, opinion*) revirement *m*; (*of fortune*) revers *m*. **◆reversible** *a* (*fabric etc*) réversible.

revert [rɪ'vɜːt] *vi* **to r.** to revenir à.

review [rɪ'vjuː] **1** *vt* (*troops, one's life*) passer en revue; (*situation*) réexaminer; (*book*) faire la critique de; – *n* revue *f*; (*of book*) critique *f*. **2** *n* (*magazine*) revue *f*. **◆—er** *n* critique *m*.

revile [rɪ'vaɪl] *vt* injurier.

revise [rɪ'vaɪz] *vt* (*opinion, notes, text*) réviser; – *vi* (*for exam*) réviser (**for** pour). **◆revision** *n* révision *f*.

revitalize [riː'vaɪtəlaɪz] *vt* revitaliser.

revive [rɪ'vaɪv] *vt* (*unconscious person, memory, conversation*) ranimer; (*dying person*) réanimer; (*custom, plan, fashion*) ressusciter; (*hope, interest*) faire renaître; – *vi* (*of unconscious person*) reprendre connaissance; (*of country, dying person*) ressusciter; (*of hope, interest*) renaître. **◆revival** *n* (*of custom, business, play*) reprise *f*; (*of country*) essor *m*; (*of faith, fashion, theatre*) renouveau *m*.

revoke [rɪ'vəʊk] *vt* (*decision*) annuler; (*contract*) Jur révoquer.

revolt [rɪ'vəʊlt] *n* révolte *f*; – *vt* (*disgust*) révolter; – *vi* (*rebel*) se révolter (**against** contre). **◆—ing** *a* dégoûtant; (*injustice*) révoltant.

revolution [revə'luːʃ(ə)n] *n* révolution *f*. **◆revolutionary** *a* & *n* révolutionnaire (*mf*). **◆revolutionize** *vt* révolutionner.

revolv/e [rɪ'vɒlv] *vi* tourner (**around** autour

de). **◆—ing** *a* **r. chair** fauteuil *m* pivotant; **r. door(s)** (porte *f* à) tambour *m*.

revolver [rɪ'vɒlvər] *n* revolver *m*.

revue [rɪ'vjuː] *n* (*satirical*) Th revue *f*.

revulsion [rɪ'vʌlʃ(ə)n] *n* **1** (*disgust*) dégoût *m*. **2** (*change*) revirement *m*.

reward [rɪ'wɔːd] *n* récompense *f* (**for** de); – *vt* récompenser (**s.o. for sth** qn de *ou* pour qch). **◆—ing** *a* qui (en) vaut la peine; (*satisfying*) satisfaisant; (*financially*) rémunérateur.

rewind [riː'waɪnd] *vt* (*pt* & *pp* **rewound**) (*tape*) réembobiner.

rewire [riː'waɪər] *vt* (*house*) refaire l'installation électrique de.

rewrite [riː'raɪt] *vt* (*pt* **rewrote**, *pp* **rewritten**) récrire; (*edit*) réécrire.

rhapsody ['ræpsədɪ] *n* rhapsodie *f*.

rhetoric ['retərɪk] *n* rhétorique *f*. **◆rhe-'torical** *a* (*question*) de pure forme.

rheumatism ['ruːmətɪz(ə)m] *n* Med rhumatisme *m*; **to have r.** avoir des rhumatismes. **◆rheu'matic** *a* (*pain*) rhumatismal; (*person*) rhumatisant.

rhinoceros [raɪ'nɒsərəs] *n* rhinocéros *m*.

rhubarb ['ruːbɑːb] *n* rhubarbe *f*.

rhyme [raɪm] *n* rime *f*; (*poem*) vers *mpl*; – *vi* rimer.

rhythm ['rɪð(ə)m] *n* rythme *m*. **◆rhythmic(al)** *a* rythmique.

rib [rɪb] *n* Anat côte *f*.

ribald ['rɪb(ə)ld] *a* Lit grivois.

ribbon ['rɪbən] *n* ruban *m*; **to tear to ribbons** mettre en lambeaux.

rice [raɪs] *n* riz *m*. **◆ricefield** *n* rizière *f*.

rich [rɪtʃ] *a* (**-er, -est**) riche (**in** en); (*profits*) gros; – *n* **the r.** les riches *mpl*. **◆riches** *npl* richesses *fpl*. **◆richly** *adv* (*dressed, illustrated etc*) richement; (*deserved*) amplement. **◆richness** *n* richesse *f*.

rick [rɪk] *vt* **to r. one's back** se tordre le dos.

rickety ['rɪkɪtɪ] *a* (*furniture*) branlant.

ricochet ['rɪkəʃeɪ] *vi* ricocher; – *n* ricochet *m*.

rid [rɪd] *vt* (*pt* & *pp* **rid**, *pres p* **ridding**) débarrasser (**of** de); **to get r. of, r. oneself of** se débarrasser de. **◆riddance** *n* **good r.!** *Fam* bon débarras!

ridden ['rɪd(ə)n] *see* **ride**.

-ridden ['rɪd(ə)n] *suffix* **debt-r.** criblé de dettes; **disease-r.** en proie à la maladie.

riddle ['rɪd(ə)l] **1** *n* (*puzzle*) énigme *f*. **2** *vt* cribler (**with** de); **riddled with** (*bullets, holes, mistakes*) criblé de; (*criminals*) plein de; (*corruption*) en proie à.

rid/e [raɪd] *n* (*on bicycle, by car etc*) promenade *f*; (*distance*) trajet *m*; (*in taxi*) course f; (*on merry-go-round*) tour *m*; **to go for a (car) r.** faire une promenade (en voiture); **to give s.o. a r.** *Aut* emmener qn en voiture; **to have a r. on** (*bicycle*) monter sur; **to take s.o. for a r.** (*deceive*) mener qn en bateau; — *vi* (*pt* **rode,** *pp* **ridden**) aller à bicyclette, à moto, à cheval *etc* (to à); (*on horse*) *Sp* monter (à cheval); **to be riding in a car** être en voiture; **to r. up** (*of skirt*) remonter; — *vt* (*a particular horse*) monter; (*distance*) faire (à cheval *etc*); **to r. a horse or horses** (*go riding*) *Sp* monter à cheval; **I was riding (on) a bike/donkey** j'étais à bicyclette/à dos d'âne; **to know how to r. a bike** savoir faire de la bicyclette; **to r. a bike to** aller à bicyclette à; **may I r. your bike?** puis-je monter sur ta bicyclette?; **to r. s.o.** (*annoy*) *Am Fam* harceler qn. ◆—**ing** *n* (*horse*) r. équitation *f*; **r. boots** bottes *fpl* de cheval. ◆—**er** *n* 1 (*on horse*) cavalier, -ière *mf*; (*cyclist*) cycliste *mf*. 2 (*to document*) *Jur* annexe *f*.

ridge [rɪdʒ] *n* (*of roof, mountain*) arête *f*, crête *f*.

ridicule ['rɪdɪkjuːl] *n* ridicule *m*; **to hold up to r.** tourner en ridicule; **object of r.** objet *m* de risée; — *vt* tourner en ridicule, ridiculiser. ◆**ri'diculous** *a* ridicule.

rife [raɪf] *a* (*widespread*) répandu.

riffraff ['rɪfræf] *n* racaille *f*.

rifle ['raɪf(ə)l] 1 *n* fusil *m*, carabine *f*. 2 *vt* (*drawers, pockets etc*) vider.

rift [rɪft] *n* (*crack*) fissure *f*; (*in party*) *Pol* scission *f*; (*disagreement*) désaccord *m*.

rig [rɪg] 1 *n* (*oil*) r. derrick *m*; (*at sea*) plate-forme *f* pétrolière. 2 *vt* (-gg-) (*result, election etc*) *Pej* truquer; **to r. up** (*equipment*) installer; (*meeting etc*) *Fam* arranger. 3 *vt* (-gg-) **to r. out** (*dress*) *Fam* habiller. ◆**r.-out** *n Fam* tenue *f*.

right¹ [raɪt] *a* (*correct*) bon, exact, juste; (*fair*) juste; (*angle*) droit; **to be r.** (*of person*) avoir raison (to de de faire); **it's the r. road** c'est la bonne route, c'est bien la route; **the r. time** l'heure exacte; **the clock's r.** la pendule est à l'heure; **at the r. time** au bon moment; **he's the r. man** c'est l'homme qu'il faut; **the r. thing to do** la meilleure chose à faire; **it's not r. to steal** ce n'est pas bien de voler; **it doesn't look r.** ça ne va pas; **to put r.** (*error*) rectifier; (*fix*) arranger; **to put s.o. r.** (*inform*) éclairer qn, détromper qn; **r.!** bien!; **that's r.** c'est ça, c'est exact, c'est bien; — *adv* (*straight*) (tout) droit; (*completely*) tout à fait; (*correctly*) juste; (*well*) bien; **she did r.** elle a bien fait; **r. round** tout autour (sth de qch);

r. behind juste derrière; **r. here** ici même; **r. away, r. now** tout de suite; **R. Honourable** *Pol* Très Honorable; — *n* **to be in the r.** avoir raison; **r. and wrong** le bien et le mal; — *vt* (*error, wrong, car*) redresser. 2 **all r.** *a* (*satisfactory*) bien *inv*; (*unharmed*) sain et sauf; (*undamaged*) intact; (*without worries*) tranquille; **it's all r.** ça va; **it's all r., it's** (*fixed*) ça marche maintenant; **I'm all r.** (*healthy*) je vais bien, ça va; — *adv* (*well*) bien; **all r.!, r. you are!** (*yes*) d'accord!; **I got your letter all r.** j'ai bien reçu ta lettre. ◆**rightly** *adv* bien, correctement; (*justifiably*) à juste titre; **r. or wrongly** à tort ou à raison.

right² [raɪt] *a* (*hand, side etc*) droit; — *adv* à droite; — *n* droite *f*; **on or to the r.** à droite (of de). ◆**r.-hand** *a* à or de droite; **on the r.-hand side** à droite (of de); **r.-hand man** bras *m* droit. ◆**r.-'handed** *a* (*person*) droitier. ◆**r.-wing** *a Pol* de droite.

right³ [raɪt] *n* (*claim, entitlement*) droit *m* (**to** do de faire); **to have a r. to sth** avoir droit à qch; **he's famous in his own r.** il est lui-même célèbre; **r. of way** *Aut* priorité *f*; **human rights** les droits de l'homme.

righteous ['raɪtʃəs] *a* (*person*) vertueux; (*cause, indignation*) juste.

rightful ['raɪtfəl] *a* légitime. ◆—**ly** *adv* légitimement.

rigid ['rɪdʒɪd] *a* rigide. ◆**ri'gidity** *n* rigidité *f*. ◆**rigidly** *adv* (*opposed*) rigoureusement (to à).

rigmarole ['rɪgmərəʊl] *n* (*process*) procédure *f* compliquée.

rigour ['rɪgər] *n* rigueur *f*. ◆**rigorous** *a* rigoureux.

rile [raɪl] *vt* (*annoy*) *Fam* agacer.

rim [rɪm] *n* (*of cup etc*) bord *m*; (*of wheel*) jante *f*.

rind [raɪnd] *n* (*of cheese*) croûte *f*; (*of melon, lemon*) écorce *f*; (*of bacon*) couenne *f*.

ring¹ [rɪŋ] *n* anneau *m*; (*on finger*) anneau *m*, (*with stone*) bague *f*; (*of people, chairs*) cercle *m*; (*of smoke, for napkin*) rond *m*; (*gang*) bande *f*; (*at circus*) piste *f*; *Boxing* ring *m*; (*burner on stove*) brûleur *m*; **diamond r.** bague *f* de diamants; **to have rings under one's eyes** avoir les yeux cernés; **r. road** route *f* de ceinture; (*motorway*) périphérique *m*; — *vt* **to r.** (*round*) (*surround*) entourer (**with** de); (*item on list etc*) entourer d'un cercle. ◆**ringleader** *n Pej* (*of gang*) chef *m* de bande; (*of rebellion etc*) meneur, -euse *mf*.

ring² [rɪŋ] *n* (*sound*) sonnerie *f*; **there's a r. on** sonne; **to give s.o. a r.** (*phone call*) passer un coup de fil à qn; **a r. of** (*truth*) *Fig* l'accent *m* de; — *vi* (*pt* **rang**, *pp* **rung**) (*of bell, person etc*) sonner; (*of sound, words*) retentir; (**to r.**) *Tel* téléphoner; **to r. back** *Tel* rappeler; **to r. for** s.o. sonner qn; **to r. off** *Tel* raccrocher; **to r. out** (*of bell*) sonner; (*of sound*) retentir; — *vt* sonner; **to r. s.o.** (**up**) *Tel* téléphoner à qn; **to r. s.o. back** *Tel* rappeler qn; **to r. the bell** sonner; **to r. the doorbell** sonner à la porte; **that rings a bell** *Fam* ça me rappelle quelque chose; **to r. in** (*the New Year*) carillonner. ◆**—ing** *a* **r. tone** *Tel* tonalité *f*; — *n* (*of bell*) sonnerie *f*; **a r. in one's ears** un bourdonnement dans les oreilles.

ringlet ['rɪŋlɪt] *n* (*curl*) anglaise *f*.

rink [rɪŋk] *n* (*ice-skating*) patinoire *f*; (*roller-skating*) skating *m*.

rinse [rɪns] *vt* rincer; **to r. one's hands** se passer les mains à l'eau; (*remove soap*) se rincer les mains; **to r. out** rincer; — *n* rinçage *m*; (*hair colouring*) shampooing *m* colorant; **to give sth a r.** rincer qch.

riot ['raɪət] *n* (*uprising*) émeute *f*, (*demonstration*) manifestation *f* violente; **a r. of colour** *Fig* une orgie de couleurs; **to run r.** (*of crowd*) se déchaîner; **the r. police** = les CRS *mpl*; — *vi* (*rise up*) faire une émeute; (*fight*) se bagarrer. ◆**—ing** *n* émeutes *fpl*; bagarres *fpl*. ◆**—er** *n* émeutier, -ière *mf*; (*demonstrator*) manifestant, -ante *mf* violent(e). ◆**riotous** *a* (*crowd etc*) tapageur; **r. living** vie *f* dissolue.

rip [rɪp] *vt* (**-pp-**) déchirer; **to r. off** *or* **out** arracher; **to r. off** *Fam* (*deceive*) rouler; (*steal*) *Am* voler; **to r. up** déchirer; — *vi* (*of fabric*) se déchirer; — *n* déchirure *f*; **it's a r.-off** *Fam* c'est du vol organisé.

ripe [raɪp] *a* (**-er, -est**) mûr; (*cheese*) fait. ◆**ripen** *vti* mûrir. ◆**ripeness** *n* maturité *f*.

ripple ['rɪp(ə)l] *n* (*on water*) ride *f*; (*of laughter*) *Fig* cascade *f*; — *vi* (*of water*) se rider.

ris/e [raɪz] *vi* (*pt* **rose**, *pp* **risen**) (*get up from chair or bed*) se lever; (*of temperature, balloon, price etc*) monter, s'élever; (*in society*) s'élever; (*of hope*) grandir; (*of sun, curtain, wind*) se lever; (*of dough*) lever; **to r. in price** augmenter de prix; **to r. to the surface** remonter à la surface; **the river rises in . . .** le fleuve prend sa source dans . . . ; **to r.** (**up**) (*rebel*) se soulever (*against* contre); **to r. to power** accéder au pouvoir; **to r. from the dead** ressusciter; — *n* (*of sun, curtain*) lever *m*; (*in pressure, price etc*) hausse *f* (**in** de); (*in river*) crue *f*; (*of leader*) *Fig* ascension *f*; (*of industry, technology*)

essor *m*; (*to power*) accession *f*; (*slope in ground*) éminence *f*; (**pay**) *r.* augmentation *f* (*de salaire*); **to give r. to** donner lieu à. ◆**—ing** *n* (*of curtain*) lever *m*; (*of river*) crue *f*; (*revolt*) soulèvement *m*; — *a* (*sun*) levant; (*number*) croissant; (*tide*) montant; (*artist etc*) d'avenir; **the r. generation** la nouvelle génération; **r. prices** la hausse des prix. ◆**—er** *n* **early r.** lève-tôt *mf inv*; **late r.** lève-tard *mf inv*.

risk [rɪsk] *n* risque *m* (**of doing** de faire); **at r.** (*person*) en danger; (*job*) menacé; **at your own r.** à tes risques et périls; **to r.** (*one's life, an accident etc*) risquer; **she won't r. leaving** (*take the risk*) elle ne se risquera pas à partir; **let's r. it** risquons le coup. ◆**riskiness** *n* risques *mpl*. ◆**risky** *a* (**-ier, -iest**) (*full of risk*) risqué.

rissole ['rɪsəʊl] *n Culin* croquette *f*.

rite [raɪt] *n* rite *m*; **the last rites** *Rel* les derniers sacrements *mpl*. ◆**ritual** *a* & *n* rituel (*m*).

ritzy ['rɪtsɪ] *a* (**-ier, -iest**) *Fam* luxueux, classe *inv*.

rival ['raɪv(ə)l] *a* (*firm etc*) rival; (*forces, claim etc*) opposé; — *n* rival, -ale *mf*; — *vt* (**-ll-**, *Am* **-l-**) (*compete with*) rivaliser avec (**in** de); (*equal*) égaler (**in** en). ◆**rivalry** *n* rivalité *f* (**between** entre).

river ['rɪvər] *n* (*small*) rivière *f*; (*major, flowing into sea*) & *Fig* fleuve *m*; **the R. Thames** la Tamise; — *a* (*port etc*) fluvial; **r. bank** rive *f*. ◆**riverside** *a* & *n* (**by the**) **r.** au bord de l'eau.

rivet ['rɪvɪt] *n* (*pin*) rivet *m*; — *vt* riveter; (*eyes*) *Fig* fixer. ◆**—ing** *a* (*story etc*) fascinant.

Riviera [rɪvɪ'eərə] *n* **the (French) R.** la Côte d'Azur.

road [rəʊd] *n* route *f* (**to** qui va à); (*small*) chemin *m*; (*in town*) rue *f*; (*roadway*) chaussée *f*; (*path*) *Fig* voie *f*, chemin *m*, route *f* (**to** de); **the Paris r.** la route de Paris; **across** *or* **over the r.** (*building etc*) en face; **by r.** par la route; **get out of the r.!** ne reste pas sur la chaussée!; — *a* (*map, safety*) routier; (*accident*) de la route; (*sense*) de la conduite; **hog** *Fam* chauffard *m*; **r. sign** panneau *m* (routier *or* de signalisation); **r. works** travaux *mpl*. ◆**roadblock** *n* barrage *m* routier. ◆**roadside** *a* & *n* (**by the**) **r.** au bord de la route. ◆**roadway** *n* chaussée *f*. ◆**roadworthy** *a* (*vehicle*) en état de marche.

roam [rəʊm] *vt* parcourir; — *vi* errer, rôder; **to r.** (**about**) **the streets** (*of child etc*) traîner dans les rues.

roar [rɔːr] *vi* hurler; (*of lion, wind, engine*) rugir; (*of thunder*) gronder; **to r. with laughter** éclater de rire; **to r. past** (*of truck etc*) passer dans un bruit de tonnerre; − *vt* **to r. (out)** hurler; − *n* hurlement *m*; rugissement *m*; grondement *m*. ◆**—ing** *n* **roar** *n*: − *a* **a r. fire** une belle flambée; **a r. success** un succès fou; **to do a r. trade** vendre beaucoup (**in** de).

roast [rəʊst] *vt* rôtir; (*coffee*) griller; − *vi* (*of meat*) rôtir; **we're roasting here** *Fam* on rôtit ici; − *n* (*meat*) rôti *m*; − *a* (*chicken etc*) rôti; **r. beef** rosbif *m*.

rob [rɒb] *vt* (**-bb-**) (*person*) voler; (*bank, house*) dévaliser; **to r. s.o. of sth** voler qch à qn; (*deprive*) priver qn de qch. ◆**robber** *n* voleur, -euse *mf*. ◆**robbery** *n* vol *m*; **it's daylight r.!** c'est du vol organisé; **armed r.** vol *m* à main armée.

robe [rəʊb] *n* (*of priest, judge etc*) robe *f*; (*dressing gown*) peignoir *m*.

robin [ˈrɒbɪn] *n* (*bird*) rouge-gorge *m*.

robot [ˈrəʊbɒt] *n* robot *m*.

robust [rəʊˈbʌst] *a* robuste.

rock[1] [rɒk] **1** *vt* (*baby, boat*) bercer, balancer; (*cradle, branch*) balancer; (*violently*) secouer; − *vi* (*sway*) se balancer; (*of building, ground*) trembler. **2** *n Mus* rock *m*. ◆**—ing** *n* (*a horse, chair*) à bascule. ◆**rocky**[1] *a* (**-ier, -iest**) (*furniture etc*) branlant.

rock[2] [rɒk] *n* (*substance*) roche *f*; (*boulder, rock face*) rocher *m*; (*stone*) *Am* pierre *f*; **a stick of r.** (*sweet*) un bâton de sucre d'orge; **r. face** paroi *f* rocheuse; **on the rocks** (*whisky*) avec des glaçons; (*marriage*) en pleine débâcle. ◆**r.-'bottom** *n* point *m* le plus bas; − *a* (*prices*) les plus bas, très bas. ◆**r.-climbing** *n* varappe *f*. ◆**rockery** *n* (*in garden*) rocaille *f*. ◆**rocky**[2] *a* (**-ier, -iest**) (*road*) rocailleux; (*hill*) rocheux.

rocket [ˈrɒkɪt] *n* fusée *f*; − *vi* (*of prices*) Fig monter en flèche.

rod [rɒd] *n* (*wooden*) baguette *f*; (*metal*) tige *f*; (*of curtain*) tringle *f*; (*for fishing*) canne *f* à pêche.

rode [rəʊd] *see* **ride**.

rodent [ˈrəʊdənt] *n* (*animal*) rongeur *m*.

rodeo [ˈrəʊdɪəʊ] *n* (*pl* -os) *Am* rodéo *m*.

roe [rəʊ] *n* **1** (*eggs*) œufs *mpl* de poisson. **2 r.** (*deer*) chevreuil *m*.

rogue [rəʊg] *n* (*dishonest*) crapule *f*; (*mischievous*) coquin, -ine *mf*. ◆**roguish** *a* (*smile etc*) coquin.

role [rəʊl] *n* rôle *m*.

roll [rəʊl] *n* (*of paper, film etc*) rouleau *m*; (*of bread*) petit pain *m*; (*of fat, flesh*) bourrelet *m*; (*of drum, thunder*) roulement *m*; (*of ship*) roulis *m*; (*list*) liste *f*; **to have a r.** faire l'appel; **r. neck** (*neckline, sweater*) col *m* roulé; − *vi* (*of ball, ship etc*) rouler; (*of person, animal*) se rouler; **to be rolling in money or in it** *Fam* rouler sur l'or; **r. on tonight!** *Fam* vivement ce soir!; **to r. in** *Fam* (*flow in*) affluer; (*of person*) s'amener; **to r. over** (*many times*) se rouler; (*once*) se retourner; **to r. up** (*arrive*) *Fam* s'amener; − *vt* rouler; **to r. down** (*blind*) baisser; (*slope*) descendre (en roulant); **to r. on** (*paint, stocking*) mettre; **to r. out** (*dough*) étaler; **to r. up** (*map, cloth*) rouler; (*sleeve, trousers*) retrousser; **r. up!** *Fam* approchez! ◆**—ing** *n* (*ground, gait*) onduleux; **r. pin** rouleau *m* à pâtisserie. ◆**—er** *n* (*for hair, painting etc*) rouleau *m*; **r. coaster** (*at funfair*) montagnes *fpl* russes. ◆**roller-skate** *n* patin *m* à roulettes; − *vi* faire du patin à roulettes.

rollicking [ˈrɒlɪkɪŋ] *a* joyeux (et bruyant).

roly-poly [ˈrəʊlɪˈpəʊlɪ] *a Fam* grassouillet.

Roman [ˈrəʊmən] **1** *a & n* romain, -aine *mf*. **2 R. Catholic** *a & n* catholique (*mf*).

romance [rəʊˈmæns] *n* **1** (*story*) histoire *f* or roman *m* d'amour; (*love*) amour *m*; (*affair*) aventure *f* amoureuse; (*charm*) poésie *f*. **2** *a* **R. language** langue *f* romane.

Romania [rəʊˈmeɪnɪə] *n* Roumanie *f*. ◆**Romanian** *a & n* roumain, -aine *mf*; − *n* (*language*) roumain *m*.

romantic [rəʊˈmæntɪk] *a* (*of love, tenderness etc*) romantique; (*fanciful, imaginary*) romanesque; − *n* (*person*) romantique *mf*. ◆**romantically** *adv* (*to behave*) de façon romantique. ◆**romanticism** *n* romantisme *m*.

romp [rɒmp] *vi* s'ébattre (bruyamment); **r. through** (*exam*) *Fig* avoir les doigts dans le nez; − *n* ébats *mpl*.

rompers [ˈrɒmpəz] *npl* (*for baby*) barboteuse *f*.

roof [ruːf] *n* (*of building, vehicle*) toit *m*; (*of tunnel, cave*) plafond *m*; **r. of the mouth** voûte *f* du palais; **r. rack** (*of car*) galerie *f*. ◆**—ing** *n* toiture *f*. ◆**rooftop** *n* toit *m*.

rook [rʊk] *n* **1** (*bird*) corneille *f*. **2** *Chess* tour *f*.

rookie [ˈrʊkɪ] *n* (*new recruit*) *Mil Fam* bleu *m*.

room [ruːm, rʊm] *n* **1** (*in house etc*) pièce *f*; (*bedroom*) chambre *f*; (*large, public*) salle *f*; **one's rooms** son appartement *m*, in rooms en meublé; **men's r., ladies' r.** *Am* toilettes *fpl*. **2** (*space*) place *f* (**for** pour); (**some**) **r.** de la place; **there's r. for doubt** le doute est permis; **no r. for doubt** aucun doute possible. ◆**rooming house** n Am maison f de rapport. ◆**roommate** n camarade mf de chambre. ◆**roomy** a (**-ier, -iest**) spacieux; (*clothes*) ample.

roost [ruːst] vi (*of bird*) percher; — n perchoir m.

rooster ['ruːstər] n coq m.

root [ruːt] **1** n (*of plant, person etc*) & Math racine f; Fig cause f, origine f; **to pull up by the root(s)** déraciner; **to take r.** (*of plant*) & Fig prendre racine; **to put down (new) roots** Fig s'enraciner; — vt **to r. out** (*destroy*) extirper. **2** vi (*of plant cutting*) s'enraciner; **to r. about for** fouiller pour trouver. **3** vi **to r. for** (*cheer, support*) Fam encourager. ◆**-ed** a **deeply r.** bien enraciné (**in** dans); **r. to the spot** (*immobile*) cloué sur place. ◆**-less** a sans racines.

rope [rəup] n corde f; Nau cordage m; **to know the ropes** Fam être au courant; — vt (*tie*) lier; **to r. s.o. in** (*force to help*) Fam embrigader qn (**to do** pour faire); **to r. off** séparer (par une corde).

rop(e)y ['rəupɪ] a (**-ier, -iest**) Fam (*thing*) minable; (*person*) patraque.

rosary ['rəuzərɪ] n Rel chapelet m.

rose[1] [rəuz] n (*flower*) rose f; (*colour*) rose m; **r. bush** rosier m. **2** n (*of watering can*) pomme f. ◆**ro'sette** n Sp cocarde f; (*rose-shaped*) rosette f. ◆**rosy** a (**-ier, -iest**) (*pink*) rose; (*future*) Fig tout en rose.

rose[2] [rəuz] see **rise**.

rosé ['rəuzeɪ] n (*wine*) rosé m.

rosemary ['rəuzmərɪ] n Bot Culin romarin m.

roster ['rɒstər] n (*duty*) **r.** liste f (de service).

rostrum ['rɒstrəm] n tribune f; Sp podium m.

rot [rɒt] n pourriture f; (*nonsense*) Fam inepties fpl; — vti (**-tt-**) **to r.** (**away**) pourrir.

rota ['rəutə] n liste f (de service).

rotate [rəu'teɪt] vi tourner; — vt faire tourner; (*crops*) alterner. ◆**'rotary** a rotatif; **r. airer** (*washing line*) séchoir m parapluie; — n (*roundabout*) Aut Am sens m giratoire. ◆**rotation** n rotation f; **in r.** à tour de rôle.

rote [rəut] n **by r.** machinalement.

rotten ['rɒt(ə)n] a (*decayed, corrupt*) pourri; (*bad*) Fam moche; (*filthy*) Fam sale; **to feel r.** (*ill*) être mal fichu. ◆**rottenness** n pourriture f. ◆**rotting** a (*meat, fruit etc*) qui pourrit.

rotund [rəu'tʌnd] a (*round*) rond; (*plump*) rondelet.

rouble ['ruːb(ə)l] n (*currency*) rouble m.

rouge [ruːʒ] n rouge m (à joues).

rough[1] [rʌf] a (**-er, -est**) (*surface, task, manners*) rude; (*ground*) inégal, accidenté; (*rocky*) rocailleux; (*plank, bark*) rugueux; (*sound*) âpre, rude; (*coarse*) grossier; (*brutal*) brutal; (*weather, neighbourhood*) mauvais; (*sea*) agité; (*justice*) sommaire; (*diamond*) brut; **a r. child** (*unruly*) un enfant dur; **to feel r.** (*ill*) Fam être mal fichu; **r. and ready** (*conditions, solution*) grossier (mais adéquat); — adv (*to sleep, live*) à la dure; (*to play*) brutalement; — n (*violent man*) Fam voyou m; — vt **to r. it** Fam vivre à la dure; **to r. up** (*hair*) ébouriffer; (*person*) Fam malmener. ◆**r.-and-'tumble** n (*fight*) mêlée f; (*of s.o.'s life*) remue-ménage m inv. ◆**roughen** vt rendre rude. ◆**roughly**[1] adv (*not gently*) rudement; (*coarsely*) grossièrement; (*brutally*) brutalement. ◆**roughness** n rudesse f; inégalité f; grossièreté f; brutalité f.

rough[2] [rʌf] a (**-er, -est**) (*calculation, figure, terms etc*) approximatif; (*copy, r. draft*) brouillon m; **r. paper** du papier brouillon; **r. guess, r. estimate** approximation f; **a r. plan** l'ébauche f d'un projet; — vt **to r. out** (*plan*) ébaucher. ◆**-ly**[2] adv (*approximately*) à peu (de choses) près.

roughage ['rʌfɪdʒ] n (*in food*) fibres fpl (alimentaires).

roulette [ruː'let] n roulette f.

round [raund] **1** adv autour; **all r., right r.** tout autour; **to go r. to s.o.** passer chez qn; **to ask r.** inviter chez soi; **he'll be r.** il passera; **r. here** par ici; **the long way r.** le chemin le plus long; — prep autour de; **r. about** (*house etc*) autour de; (*approximately*) environ; **r. (about) midday** vers midi; **to go r.** (*world*) faire le tour de; (*corner*) tourner. **2** a (**-er, -est**) rond; **a r. trip** Am (*voyage*) aller et retour. **3** n (*slice*) Culin tranche f; Sp Pol manche f; (*of golf*) partie f; Boxing round m; (*of talks*) série f; (*of drinks, visits*) tournée f; **one's round(s)** (*of milkman etc*) sa tournée; (*of doctor*) ses visites fpl; (*of policeman*) sa ronde; **delivery r.** livraisons fpl, tournée f; **r. of applause** salve f d'applaudissements; **r. of ammunition** cartouche f, balle f; — vt **to r. a corner** (*in car*) prendre un virage; **to r. off** (*finish*) terminer; **to r. up** (*gather*) rassembler; (*figure*) arrondir au chiffre supérieur. ◆**r.-'shouldered** a voûté, aux épaules rondes. ◆**rounded** a arrondi. ◆**rounders** npl Sp sorte de baseball. ◆**roundness** n rondeur f. ◆**roundup** n (*of criminals*) rafle f.

roundabout ['raʊndəbaʊt] **1** a indirect, détourné. **2** n (at funfair) manège m; (junction) Aut rond-point m (à sens giratoire).

rous/e [raʊz] vt éveiller; **roused (to anger)** en colère; **to r. to action** inciter à agir. ◆**—ing** a (welcome) enthousiaste; (speech) vibrant; (music) allègre.

rout [raʊt] n (defeat) déen déroute f; – vt mettre route.

route 1 [ruːt] n itinéraire m; (of aircraft) route f; **sea r.** route f maritime; **bus r.** ligne f d'autobus; – vt (train etc) fixer l'itinéraire de. **2** [raʊt] n (delivery round) Am tournée f.

routine [ruːˈtiːn] n routine f; **one's daily r.** (in office etc) son travail journalier; **the daily r.** (monotony) le train-train quotidien; – a (inquiry, work etc) de routine; Pej routinier. ◆**—ing** a (a life) nomade; (ambassador) itinérant.

rov/e [raʊv] vi errer; – vt parcourir. ◆**—ing** a (a life) nomade; (ambassador) itinérant.

row¹ [raʊ] **1** n (line) rang m, rangée f; (of cars) file f; **two days in a r.** deux jours de suite or d'affilée. **2** vi (in boat) ramer; – vt (boat) faire aller à la rame; (person) transporter en canot; – n **to go for a r.** canoter; **r. boat** Am bateau m à rames. ◆**—ing** n canotage m; Sp aviron m; **r. boat** bateau m à rames.

row² [raʊ] n Fam (noise) vacarme m; (quarrel) querelle f; – vi Fam se quereller (with avec).

rowdy ['raʊdɪ] a (-ier, -iest) chahuteur (et brutal); – n (person) Fam voyou m.

royal ['rɔɪəl] a royal; – npl **the royals** Fam la famille royale. ◆**royalist** a & n royaliste (mf). ◆**royally** adv (to treat) royalement. ◆**royalty 1** n (persons) personnages mpl royaux. **2** npl (from book) droits mpl d'auteur; (on oil, from patent) royalties fpl.

rub [rʌb] vt (-bb-) frotter; (polish) astiquer; **to r. shoulders with** Fig coudoyer, côtoyer; **to r. away** (mark) effacer; (tears) essuyer; **to r. down** (person) frictionner; (wood, with sandpaper) poncer; **to r. in** (cream) Med faire pénétrer (en massant); **to r. it in** Pej Fam retourner le couteau dans la plaie; **to r. off** or **out** (mark) effacer; **rubbing alcohol** Am alcool m à 90°; – vi frotter; **to r. off** (of mark) partir; (of manners etc) déteindre (**on s.o.** sur qn); – n (massage) friction f; **to give sth a r.** frotter qch; (polish) astiquer qch.

rubber ['rʌbər] n (substance) caoutchouc m; (eraser) gomme f; (contraceptive) Am Sl capote f; **r. stamp** tampon m. ◆**r.-'stamp** vt Pej approuver (sans discuter). ◆**rubbery** a caoutchouteux.

rubbish ['rʌbɪʃ] **1** n (refuse) ordures fpl, détritus mpl; (waste) déchets mpl; (junk) saleté(s) f(pl); (nonsense) Fig absurdités fpl; **that's r.** (absurd) c'est absurde; (worthless) ça ne vaut rien; **r. bin** poubelle f; **r. dump** dépôt m d'ordures, décharge f (publique); (in garden) tas m d'ordures. **2** vt **to r. s.o./sth** (criticize) Fam dénigrer qn/qch. ◆**rubbishy** a (book etc) sans valeur; (goods) de mauvaise qualité.

rubble ['rʌb(ə)l] n décombres mpl.

ruble ['ruːb(ə)l] n (currency) rouble m.

ruby ['ruːbɪ] n (gem) rubis m.

rucksack ['rʌksæk] n sac m à dos.

ruckus ['rʌkəs] n (uproar) Fam chahut m.

rudder ['rʌdər] n gouvernail m.

ruddy ['rʌdɪ] a (-ier, -iest) **1** (complexion) coloré. **2** (bloody) Sl fichu.

rude [ruːd] a (-er, -est) (impolite) impoli (to envers); (coarse) grossier; (indecent) indécent, obscène; (shock) violent. ◆**—ly** adv impoliment; grossièrement. ◆**—ness** n impolitesse f; grossièreté f.

rudiments ['ruːdɪmənts] npl rudiments mpl. ◆**rudi'mentary** a rudimentaire.

ruffian ['rʌfɪən] n voyou m.

ruffle ['rʌf(ə)l] **1** vt (hair) ébouriffer; (water) troubler; **to r. s.o.** (offend) froisser qn. **2** n (frill) ruche f.

rug [rʌg] n carpette f, petit tapis m; (over knees) plaid m; (bedside) r. descente f de lit.

rugby ['rʌgbɪ] n **r. (football)** rugby m. ◆**rugger** n Fam rugby m.

rugged ['rʌgɪd] a (surface) rugueux, rude; (terrain, coast) accidenté; (person, features, manners) rude; (determination) Fig farouche.

ruin ['ruːɪn] n (destruction, rubble, building etc) ruine f; **in ruins** (building) en ruine; – vt (health, country, person etc) ruiner; (clothes) abîmer; (spoil) gâter. ◆**—ed** a (person, country etc) ruiné; (building) en ruine. ◆**ruinous** a ruineux.

rul/e [ruːl] **1** n (principle) règle f; (regulation) règlement m; (custom) coutume f; (authority) autorité f; Pol gouvernement m; **against the rules** contraire à la règle; as a (general) r. en règle générale; **it's the** or a **r.** that il est de règle que (+ sub); – vt (country) Pol gouverner; (decide) Jur Sp décider (that que); **to r. s.o.** (dominate) mener qn; **to r. out** (exclude) exclure; – vi (of monarch) régner (over sur); (of judge) statuer (against contre, on sur). **2** n (for measuring) règle f. ◆**—ed** a (paper) réglé, ligné. ◆**—ing** a (passion) dominant;

(class) dirigeant; (party) Pol au pouvoir; — n Jur Sp décision f. **ruler** n **1** (of country) Pol dirigeant, -ante mf; (sovereign) souverain, -aine mf. **2** (measure) règle f.

rum [rʌm] n rhum m.

Rumania ['ruːmeɪnɪə] see **Romania**.

rumble ['rʌmb(ə)l] vi (of train, thunder, gun) gronder; (of stomach) gargouiller; — n grondement m; gargouillement m.

ruminate ['ruːmɪneɪt] vi to r. over (scheme etc) ruminer.

rummage ['rʌmɪdʒ] vi to r. (about) fouiller; **r. sale** (used clothes etc) Am vente f de charité.

rumour ['ruːmər] n rumeur f, bruit m. ◆**rumoured** it is r. that on dit que.

rump [rʌmp] n (of horse) croupe f; (of fowl) croupion m; **r. steak** rumsteck m.

rumple ['rʌmp(ə)l] vt (clothes) chiffonner.

run [rʌn] n (running) course f; (outing) tour m; (journey) parcours m, trajet m; (series) série f; (period) période f; Cards suite f; (rush) ruée f (on sur); (trend) tendance f; (for skiing) piste f; (in cricket) point m; **to go for a r.** courir, faire une course à pied; **on the r.** (prisoner etc) en fuite; **to have the r. of** (house etc) avoir à sa disposition; **in the long r.** avec le temps, à la longue; **the runs** Med Fam la diarrhée; — vi (pt **ran**, pp **run**, pres p **running**) courir; (flee) fuir; (of curtain) glisser; (of river, nose, pen, tap) couler; (of colour in washing) déteindre; (of ink) baver; (of melt) fondre; (of play, film) se jouer; (of contract) être valide; (last) durer; (pass) passer; (function) marcher; (tick over) Aut tourner; (of stocking) filer; **to r. down/in/etc** descendre/entrer/etc en courant; **to r. for president** être candidat à la présidence; **to r. with blood** ruisseler de sang; **to go running** Sp faire du jogging; **the road runs to ...** la route va à ...; **the river runs into the sea** le fleuve se jette dans la mer; **it runs into a hundred pounds** ça va chercher dans les cent livres; **it runs in the family** ça tient de famille; — vt (race, risk) courir; (horse) faire courir; (temperature, errand) faire; (blockade) forcer; (machine) faire fonctionner; (engine) Aut faire tourner; (drive) Aut conduire; (furniture, goods) transporter (to à); (business, country etc) diriger; (courses, events) organiser; (film, play) présenter; (house) tenir; (article) publier (on sur); (bath) faire couler; **to r. one's hand over** passer la main sur; **to r. one's eye over** jeter un coup d'œil à or sur; **to r. its course** (of illness etc) suivre son

cours; **to r. 5 km** Sp faire 5 km de course à pied; **to r. a car** avoir une voiture. ■ **to r. about** vi courir çà et là; (gallivant) se balader; **to r. across** vt (meet) tomber sur; **to r. along** vi **r. along!** filez!; **to r. away** vi (flee) s'enfuir, se sauver (from de); **to r. back** vt (person) Aut ramener (to à); **to r. down** vt (pedestrian) Aut renverser; (belittle) dénigrer; (restrict) limiter peu à peu. ◆**r.-'down** n (weak, tired) Med à plat; (district etc) miteux; **to r. in** vt (vehicle) roder; **to r. s.o. in** (of police) Fam arrêter qn; **to r. into** vt (meet) tomber sur; (crash into) Aut percuter; **to r. into debt** s'endetter; **to r. off** vt (print) tirer; (flee) s'enfuir; **to r. out** vi (of stocks) s'épuiser; (of lease) expirer; (of time) manquer; **to r. out of** (time, money) manquer de; **we've r. out of coffee** on n'a plus de café; — vt **to r. s.o. out of** (chase) chasser qn de; — vt **to r. over** vi (of liquid) déborder; — vt (kill pedestrian) Aut écraser; (knock down pedestrian) Aut renverser; (notes, text) revoir; **to r. round** vt (surround) entourer; **to r. through** vt (recap) revoir; **to r. up** vt (bill, debts) laisser s'accumuler. ◆**r.-up** n **the r.-up to** (elections etc) la période qui précède. ◆**running** n course f; (of machine) fonctionnement m; (of firm, country) direction f; **to be in/out of the r.** être/ne plus être dans la course; — a (commentary) suivi; (battle) continuel; **r. water** eau f courante; **six days/etc** six jours/etc de suite; **r. costs** (of factory) frais mpl d'exploitation; (of car) dépenses fpl courantes. ◆**runner** n Sp etc coureur m; **r. bean** haricot m (grimpant). ◆**runner-'up** n Sp second, -onde mf. ◆**runny** a (-ier, -iest) a liquide; (nose) qui coule.

runaway ['rʌnəweɪ] n fugitif, -ive mf; — a (car, horse) emballé; (lorry) fou; (wedding) clandestin; (victory) qu'on remporte haut la main; (inflation) galopant.

rung [rʌŋ] n (of ladder) barreau m.

rung [rʌŋ] see **ring** [2].

run-of-the-mill [rʌnəvðə'mɪl] a ordinaire.

runway ['rʌnweɪ] n Av piste f.

rupture ['rʌptʃər] n Med hernie f; **the r. of** (breaking) la rupture de; — vt rompre; **to r. oneself** se donner une hernie.

rural ['ruərəl] a rural.

ruse [ruːz] n (trick) ruse f.

rush [rʌʃ] vi (move fast, throw oneself) se précipiter, se ruer (at sur, towards vers); (of blood) affluer (to à); (hurry) se dépêcher (to do de faire); (of vehicle) foncer; **to r. out** partir en vitesse; — vt (attack) Mil foncer sur; **to r. s.o.** bousculer qn; **to r. s.o. to hospital** transporter qn d'urgence à l'hôpital; **to r. (through)** sth *(job, meal, order etc)* faire, manger, envoyer *etc* qch en vitesse; **to be rushed into** *(decision, answer etc)* être forcé à prendre, donner *etc*; – *n* ruée *f* (**for** vers, **on** sur); *(confusion)* bousculade *f*; *(hurry)* hâte *f*; *(of orders)* avalanche *f*; **to be in a r.** être pressé (**to do** de faire); **to leave**/*etc* **in a r.** partir/*etc* en vitesse; **the gold r.** la ruée vers l'or; **the r. hour** l'heure *f* d'affluence; **a r. job** un travail d'urgence.

rush² [rʌʃ] *n (plant)* jonc *m*.

rusk [rʌsk] *n* biscotte *f*.

russet [ˈrʌsɪt] *a* roux, roussâtre.

Russia [ˈrʌʃə] *n* Russie *f*. ◆**Russian** *a & n* russe *(mf)*; – *n (language)* russe *m*.

rust [rʌst] *n* rouille *f*; – *vi* (se) rouiller. ◆**rustproof** *a* inoxydable. ◆**rusty** *a* (**-ier, -iest**) *(metal, athlete, memory etc)* rouillé.

rustic [ˈrʌstɪk] *a* rustique.

rustle [ˈrʌs(ə)l] **1** *vi (of leaves)* bruire; *(of skirt)* froufrouter; – *n* bruissement *m*; frou-frou *m*. **2** *vt* **to r. up** *Fam (prepare)* préparer; *(find)* trouver.

rut [rʌt] *n* ornière *f*; **to be in a r.** *Fig* être encroûté.

rutabaga [ruːtəˈbeɪɡə] *n (swede) Am* rutabaga *m*.

ruthless [ˈruːθləs] *a (attack, person etc)* impitoyable, cruel; *(in taking decisions)* très ferme. ◆**-ness** *n* cruauté *f*.

rye [raɪ] *n* seigle *m*; **r. bread** pain *m* de

S

S, s [es] *n* S, s *m*.

Sabbath [ˈsæbəθ] *n (Jewish)* sabbat *m*; *(Christian)* dimanche *m*. ◆**sa'bbatical** *a (year etc) Univ* sabbatique.

sabotage [ˈsæbətɑːʒ] *n* sabotage *m*; – *vt* saboter. ◆**saboteur** [-ˈtɜːr] *n* saboteur, -euse *mf*.

sabre [ˈseɪbər] *n (sword)* sabre *m*.

saccharin [ˈsækərɪn] *n* saccharine *f*.

sachet [ˈsæʃeɪ] *n (of lavender etc)* sachet *m*; *(of shampoo)* dosette *f*.

sack [sæk] **1** *n (bag)* sac *m*. **2** *vt (dismiss) Fam* virer, renvoyer; – *n Fam* **to get the s.** se faire virer; **to give s.o. the s.** virer qn. **3** *vt (town etc)* saccager, mettre à sac. ◆**-ing** *n* **1** *(cloth)* toile *f* à sac. **2** *(dismissal) Fam* renvoi *m*.

sacrament [ˈsækrəmənt] *n Rel* sacrement *m*.

sacred [ˈseɪkrɪd] *a (holy)* sacré.

sacrifice [ˈsækrɪfaɪs] *n* sacrifice *m*; – *vt* sacrifier (**to** à, **for** sth/s.o. pour qch/qn).

sacrilege [ˈsækrɪlɪdʒ] *n* sacrilège *m*. ◆**sacri'legious** *a* sacrilège.

sacrosanct [ˈsækrəʊsæŋkt] *a Iron* sacro-saint.

sad [sæd] *a (sadder, saddest)* triste. ◆**sadden** *vt* attrister. ◆**sadly** *adv* tristement; *(unfortunately)* malheureusement; *(very)* très. ◆**sadness** *n* tristesse *f*.

saddle [ˈsæd(ə)l] *n* selle *f*; **to be in the s.** *(in*

control) Fig tenir les rênes; – *vt (horse)* seller; **to s. s.o. with** *(chore, person) Fam* coller à qn.

sadism [ˈseɪdɪz(ə)m] *n* sadisme *m*. ◆**sadist** *n* sadique *mf*. ◆**sa'distic** *a* sadique.

sae [eseˈiː] *abbr* = **stamped addressed envelope.**

safari [səˈfɑːrɪ] *n* safari *m*; **to be** *or* **go on s.** faire un safari.

safe¹ [seɪf] *a (-er, -est) (person)* en sécurité; *(equipment, toy, animal)* sans danger; *(place, investment, method)* sûr; *(bridge, ladder)* solide; *(prudent)* prudent; *(winner)* assuré, garanti; **s. (and sound)** sain et sauf; **it's s. to go out** on peut sortir sans danger; **the safest thing (to do) is . . .** le plus sûr est de . . . ; **s. from** à l'abri de; **to be on the s. side** pour plus de sûreté; **in s. hands** en mains sûres; **s. journey!** bon voyage! ◆**s.-'conduct** *n* sauf-conduit *m*. ◆**safe-keeping** *n* **for s.** à garder en sécurité. ◆**safely** *adv (without mishap)* sans accident; *(securely)* en sûreté; *(without risk)* sans risque, sans danger. ◆**safety** *n* sécurité *f*; *(solidity)* solidité *f*; *(salvation)* salut *m*; – *a (belt, device, screen, margin)* de sécurité; *(pin, razor, chain, valve)* de sûreté; **s. precaution** mesure *f* de sécurité.

safe² [seɪf] *n (for money etc)* coffre-fort *m*.

safeguard [ˈseɪfɡɑːd] *n* sauvegarde *f* (**against** contre); – *vt* sauvegarder.

saffron ['sæfrən] n safran m.

sag [sæg] vi (-gg-) (of roof, ground) s'affaisser; (of cheeks) pendre; (of prices, knees) fléchir. ◆**sagging** a (roof, breasts) affaissé.

saga ['sɑːgə] n Liter saga f; (bad sequence of events) Fig feuilleton m.

sage [seɪdʒ] n 1 Bot Culin sauge f. 2 (wise man) sage m.

Sagittarius [sædʒɪ'teərɪəs] n (sign) le Sagittaire.

sago ['seɪgəʊ] n (cereal) sagou m.

Sahara [sə'hɑːrə] n the S. (desert) le Sahara.

said [sed] see say.

sail [seɪl] vi (navigate) naviguer; (leave) partir; Sp faire de la voile; (glide) Fig glisser; **to s. into** port entrer au port; **to s. round** (world, island etc) faire le tour de en bateau; **to s. through** (exam etc) Fig réussir haut la main; − vt (boat) piloter; (seas) parcourir; − n voile f; (trip) tour m en bateau; **to set s.** (of boat) partir (**for** à destination de). ◆−**ing** n navigation f; Sp voile f; (departure) départ m; (crossing) traversée f. ◆**s. boat** voilier m. ◆**sailboard** n planche f (à voile). ◆**sailboat** n Am voilier m. ◆**sailor** n marin m, matelot m.

saint [seɪnt] n saint m, sainte f; **S. John** Jean; **s.'s day** Rel fête f (de saint). ◆**saintly** a (-ier, -iest) saint.

sake [seɪk] n **for my/your s.** pour moi/toi; **for your father's s.** pour (l'amour de) ton père; (**just) for the s. of** eating/etc simplement pour manger/etc; **for heaven's** or **God's s.** pour l'amour de Dieu.

salacious [sə'leɪʃəs] a obscène.

salad ['sæləd] n (dish of vegetables, fruit etc) salade f; **s. bowl** saladier m; **s. cream** mayonnaise f; **s. dressing** vinaigrette f.

salamander ['sæləmændər] n (lizard) salamandre f.

salami [sə'lɑːmɪ] n salami m.

salary ['sælərɪ] n (professional) traitement m; (wage) salaire m. ◆**salaried** a (person) qui perçoit un traitement.

sale [seɪl] n vente f; **sale(s)** (at reduced prices) Com soldes mpl; **in a** or **the s.**, Am **on s.** (cheaply) en solde; **on s.** (available) en vente; (**up) for s.** à vendre; **to put up for s.** mettre en vente; **s. price** Com prix m de solde; **sales check** or **slip** Am reçu m. ◆**saleable** a Com vendable. ◆**sales-clerk** n Am vendeur, -euse mf. ◆**sales-man** n (pl -men) (in shop) vendeur m; (travelling) s. représentant m (de commerce). ◆**saleswoman** n (pl -women) vendeuse f; représentante f (de commerce).

salient ['seɪlɪənt] a (point, fact) marquant.

saliva [sə'laɪvə] n salive f. ◆**salivate** vi saliver.

sallow ['sæləʊ] a (-er, -est) jaunâtre.

sally ['sælɪ] n Mil sortie f; − vi **to s. forth** sortir allégrement.

salmon ['sæmən] n saumon m.

salmonella [sælmə'nelə] n (poisoning) salmonellose f.

salon ['sælɒn] n beauty/hairdressing s. salon m de beauté/de coiffure.

saloon [sə'luːn] n Nau salon m; (car) berline f; Am bar m; **s. bar** (of pub) salle f chic.

salt [sɔːlt] n sel m; **bath salts** sels mpl de bain; − a (water, beef etc) salé; (mine) de sel; **s. free** sans sel; − vt saler. ◆**saltcellar** n, Am ◆**saltshaker** n salière f. ◆**salty** a (-ier, -iest) a salé.

salubrious [sə'luːbrɪəs] a salubre.

salutary ['sæljʊtərɪ] a salutaire.

salute [sə'luːt] n Mil salut m; (of guns) salve f; − vt (greet) & Mil saluer; − vi Mil faire un salut.

salvage ['sælvɪdʒ] n sauvetage m (of de); récupération f (of de); (saved goods) objets mpl sauvés; − vt (save) sauver (**from** de); (old iron etc to be used again) récupérer.

salvation [sæl'veɪʃ(ə)n] n salut m.

same [seɪm] a même; **the (very) s. house** as (exactement) la même maison que; − pron **the s.** le même, la même; **the s. (thing)** la même chose; **it's all the s. to me** ça m'est égal; **all** or **just the s.** tout de même; **to do the s.** en faire autant. ◆−**ness** n identité f; Pej monotonie f.

sampl/e ['sɑːmp(ə)l] n échantillon m; (of blood) prélèvement m; (wine, cheese etc) déguster; (product, recipe etc) essayer; (army life etc) goûter de. ◆−**ing** n (of wine) dégustation f.

sanatorium [sænə'tɔːrɪəm] n sanatorium m.

sanctify ['sæŋktɪfaɪ] vt sanctifier. ◆**sanc-tity** n sainteté f. ◆**sanctuary** n Rel sanc-tuaire m; (refuge) & Pol asile m; (for animals) réserve f.

sanctimonious [sæŋktɪ'məʊnɪəs] a (person, manner) tartufe.

sanction ['sæŋkʃ(ə)n] n (approval, punish-ment) sanction f; − vt (approve) sanction-ner.

sand [sænd] n sable m; **the sands** (beach) la plage; (in road) sabler; **to s. (down)** (wood etc) poncer. ◆**sandbag** n sac m de sable. ◆**sandcastle** n château m de sable. ◆**sander** n (machine) ponceuse f. ◆**sandpaper** n papier m de verre; − vt

poncer. ◆**sandstone** n (rock) grès m.
◆**sandy** a 1 (-ier, -iest) (beach) de sable; (road, ground) sablonneux; (water) sableux. 2 (hair) blond roux inv.

sandal ['sænd(ə)l] n sandale f.

sandwich ['sænwɪdʒ] 1 n sandwich m; **cheese**/etc s. sandwich au fromage/etc. 2 vt to s. (in) (fit in) intercaler; **sandwiched in between** (caught) coincé entre.

sane [seɪn] a (-er, -est) (person) sain (d'esprit); (idea, attitude) raisonnable.

sang [sæŋ] see sing.

sanguine ['sæŋgwɪn] a (hopeful) optimiste.

sanitarium [sænɪ'teərɪəm] n Am sanatorium m.

sanitary ['sænɪtərɪ] a (fittings, conditions) sanitaire; (clean) hygiénique. ◆**sani'tation** n hygiène f (publique); (plumbing etc) installations fpl sanitaires.

sanity ['sænɪtɪ] n santé f mentale; (reason) raison f.

sank [sæŋk] see sink².

Santa Claus ['sæntəklɔːz] n le père Noël.

sap [sæp] 1 n Bot & Fig sève f. 2 vt (-pp-) (weaken) miner (énergie etc).

sapphire ['sæfaɪər] n (jewel, needle) saphir m.

sarcasm ['sɑːkæz(ə)m] n sarcasme m. ◆**sar'castic** a sarcastique.

sardine [sɑː'diːn] n sardine f.

Sardinia [sɑː'dɪnɪə] n Sardaigne f.

sardonic [sɑː'dɒnɪk] a sardonique.

sash [sæʃ] n 1 (on dress) ceinture f; (of mayor etc) écharpe f. 2 s. window fenêtre f à guillotine.

sat [sæt] see sit.

Satan ['seɪt(ə)n] n Satan m. ◆**sa'tanic** a satanique.

satchel ['sætʃ(ə)l] n cartable m.

satellite ['sætəlaɪt] n satellite m; s. (country) Pol pays m satellite.

satiate ['seɪʃɪeɪt] vt rassasier.

satin ['sætɪn] n satin m.

satire ['sætaɪər] n satire f (on contre). ◆**sa'tirical** a satirique. ◆**satirist** n écrivain m satirique. ◆**satirize** vt faire la satire de.

satisfaction [sætɪs'fækʃ(ə)n] n satisfaction f. ◆**satisfactory** a satisfaisant. ◆**'satisfy** vt satisfaire; (persuade, convince) persuader (that que); (demand, condition) satisfaire à; to s. oneself as to/that s'assurer de que/que; satisfied with satisfait de; — vi donner satisfaction. ◆**'satisfying** a satisfaisant; (food, meal) substantiel.

satsuma [sæt'suːmə] n (fruit) mandarine f.

saturate ['sætʃəreɪt] vt (fill) saturer (with de); (soak) tremper. ◆**satu'ration** n saturation f.

Saturday ['sætədɪ] n samedi m.

sauce [sɔːs] n 1 sauce f; **tomato s.** sauce tomate; **s. boat** saucière f. 2 (cheek) Fam toupet m. ◆**saucy** a (-ier, -iest) (cheeky) impertinent; (smart) Fam coquet.

saucepan ['sɔːspən] n casserole f.

saucer ['sɔːsər] n soucoupe f.

Saudi Arabia [saʊdɪə'reɪbɪə, Am sɔːdɪə-'reɪbɪə] n Arabie f Séoudite.

sauna ['sɔːnə] n sauna m.

saunter ['sɔːntər] vi flâner.

sausage ['sɒsɪdʒ] n (cooked, for cooking) saucisse f; (precooked, dried) saucisson m.

sauté ['səʊteɪ] a Culin sauté.

savage ['sævɪdʒ] a (primitive) sauvage; (fierce) féroce; (brutal, cruel) brutal, sauvage; — n (brute) sauvage mf; — vt (of animal, critic etc) attaquer (férocement). ◆**savagery** n (cruelty) sauvagerie f.

sav/e [seɪv] 1 vt sauver (from de); (keep) garder, réserver; (money, time) économiser, épargner; (stamps) collectionner; (prevent) empêcher (from de); (problems, trouble) éviter; **that will s. him** or **her** (the bother of) going ça lui évitera d'y aller; **to s. up** (money) économiser; — vi to s. up faire des économies (for sth, to buy sth pour (s')acheter qch); — n Fb arrêt m. 2 prep (except) sauf. ◆**—ing** n (of time, money) économie f, épargne f (of de); (rescue) sauvetage m; (thrifty habit) l'épargne f; pl (money) économies fpl; **savings bank** caisse f d'épargne. ◆**saviour** n sauveur m.

saveloy ['sævələɪ] n cervelas m.

savour ['seɪvər] n (taste, interest) saveur f; — vt savourer. ◆**savoury** a (tasty) savoureux; (not sweet) Culin salé; **not very s.** (neighbourhood) Fig peu recommandable.

saw¹ [sɔː] n scie f; — vt (pt sawed, pp sawn or sawed) scier; **to s. off** scier; **a sawn-off** or Am **sawed-off shotgun** un fusil à canon scié. ◆**sawdust** n sciure f. ◆**sawmill** n scierie f.

saw² [sɔː] see see¹.

saxophone ['sæksəfəʊn] n saxophone m.

say [seɪ] vt (pt & pp said) dire (to à, that que); (prayer) faire, dire; (of dial etc) marquer; **to s. again** répéter; **it is said that ... on dit que ...; what do you s. to a walk?** que dirais-tu d'une promenade?; (let's) s. tomorrow disons demain; **to s. the least** c'est le moins que l'on puisse dire; **to s. nothing of ...** sans parler de ...; **that's to s.** c'est-à-dire; — vi dire; **you don't s.!**

Fam sans blague!; **I s.!** dites donc!; **s.!** *Am Fam* dis donc!; **− to have one's s.** dire ce que l'on a à dire, s'exprimer; **to have a lot of s.** avoir beaucoup d'influence; **to have no s.** ne pas avoir voix au chapitre (**in** pour). ◆**−ing** *n* proverbe *m*.

scab [skæb] *n* **1** *Med* croûte *f.* **2** (*blackleg*) *Fam* jaune *m*.

scaffold ['skæfəld] *n* échafaudage *m*; (*gallows*) échafaud *m*. ◆**−ing** *n* échafaudage *m*.

scald [skɔːld] *vt* (*burn, cleanse*) ébouillanter; (*sterilize*) stériliser; − *n* brûlure *f.*

scale [skeɪl] **1** *n* (*of map, wages etc*) échelle *f*; (*of numbers*) série *f*; *Mus* gamme *f*; **on a small/large s.** sur une petite/grande échelle; − *a* (*drawing*) à l'échelle; **s. model** modèle *m* réduit; − *vt* **to s. down** réduire (proportionnellement). **2** *n* (*on fish*) écaille *f*; (*dead skin*) *Med* squame *f*; (*on teeth*) tartre *m*; − *vt* (*teeth*) détartrer. **3** *vt* (*wall*) escalader.

scales [skeɪlz] *npl* (*for weighing*) balance *f*; (*bathroom*) **s.** pèse-personne *m*; (*baby*) **s.** pèse-bébé *m*.

scallion ['skæljən] *n* (*onion*) *Am* ciboule *f.*

scallop ['skɒləp] *n* coquille *f* Saint-Jacques.

scalp [skælp] *n* *Med* cuir *m* chevelu; − *vt* (*cut off too much hair from*) *Fig Hum* tondre (*qn*).

scalpel ['skælp(ə)l] *n* bistouri *m*, scalpel *m*.

scamp [skæmp] *n* coquin, -ine *mf.*

scamper ['skæmpər] *vi* **to s. off** *or* **away** détaler.

scampi ['skæmpɪ] *npl* gambas *fpl.*

scan [skæn] **1** *vt* (**-nn-**) (*look at briefly*) parcourir (des yeux); (*scrutinize*) scruter; (*poetry*) scander; (*of radar*) balayer. **2** *n* **to have a s.** (*of pregnant woman*) passer une échographie.

scandal ['skænd(ə)l] *n* (*disgrace*) scandale *m*; (*gossip*) médisances *fpl*; **to cause a s.** (*of film, book etc*) causer un scandale; (*of attitude, conduct*) faire (du) scandale. ◆**scandalize** *vt* scandaliser. ◆**scandalous** *a* scandaleux.

Scandinavia [skændɪ'neɪvɪə] *n* Scandinavie *f*. ◆**Scandinavian** *a & n* scandinave (*mf*).

scanner ['skænər] *n* (*device*) *Med* scanner *m.*

scant [skænt] *a* (*meal, amount*) insuffisant; **s. attention/regard** peu d'attention/de cas. ◆**scantily** *adv* insuffisamment; **s. dressed** à peine vêtu. ◆**scanty** *a* (**-ier, -iest**) insuffisant; (*bikini*) minuscule.

scapegoat ['skeɪpgəʊt] *n* bouc *m* émissaire.

scar [skɑːr] *n* cicatrice *f*; − *vt* (**-rr-**) marquer d'une cicatrice; *Fig* marquer.

scarce [skeəs] *a* (**-er, -est**) (*food, people, book etc*) rare; **to make oneself s.** se tenir à l'écart. ◆**scarcely** *adv* à peine. ◆**scarceness** *n*, ◆**scarcity** *n* (*shortage*) pénurie *f*; (*rarity*) rareté *f.*

scare [skeər] *n* peur *f*; **to give s.o. a s.** faire peur à qn; **bomb s.** alerte *f* à la bombe; − *vt* faire peur à; **to s. off** (*person*) faire fuir; (*animal*) effaroucher; − *vi* **to be scared** (*of*) être effrayé de; **to be s.** (*stiff*) avoir (très) peur. ◆**scarecrow** *n* épouvantail *m*. ◆**scaremonger** *n* alarmiste *mf.* ◆**scary** *a* (**-ier, -iest**) *Fam* qui fait peur.

scarf [skɑːf] *n* (*pl* **scarves**) (*long*) écharpe *f*; (*square, for women*) foulard *m.*

scarlet ['skɑːlət] *a* écarlate; **s. fever** scarlatine *f.*

scathing ['skeɪðɪŋ] *a* (*remark etc*) acerbe; **to be s. about** critiquer de façon acerbe.

scatter ['skætər] *vt* (*disperse*) disperser (*foule, nuages etc*); (*dot or throw about*) éparpiller; (*spread*) répandre; − *vi* (*of crowd*) se disperser. ◆**−ing** *n* **a s. of houses/etc** quelques maisons/etc dispersées. ◆**scatterbrain** *n* écervelé, -ée *mf.* ◆**scatty** *a* (**-ier, -iest**) *Fam* écervelé, farfelu.

scaveng/e ['skævɪndʒ] *vi* fouiller dans les ordures (**for** pour trouver). ◆**−er** *n* *Pej* clochard, -arde *mf* (qui fait les poubelles).

scenario [sɪ'nɑːrɪəʊ] *n* (*pl* **-os**) *Cin & Fig* scénario *m.*

scene [siːn] *n* (*setting, fuss*) & *Th* scène *f*; (*of crime, accident etc*) lieu *m*; (*situation*) situation *f*; (*incident*) incident *m*; (*view*) vue *f*; **behind the scenes** *Th & Fig* dans les coulisses; **on the s.** sur les lieux; **to make** *or* **create a s.** faire une scène (à qn). ◆**scenery** *n* paysage *m*, décor *m*; *Th* décor(s) *m(pl).* ◆**scenic** *a* (*beauty etc*) pittoresque.

scent [sent] *n* (*fragrance, perfume*) parfum *m*; (*animal's track*) *Fig* piste *f*; − *vt* parfumer (**with** de); (*smell, sense*) flairer.

sceptic ['skeptɪk] *a & n* sceptique (*mf*). ◆**sceptical** *a* sceptique. ◆**scepticism** *n* scepticisme *m.*

sceptre ['septər] *n* sceptre *m.*

schedul/e ['ʃedjuːl, *Am* 'skedʒuːl] *n* (*of work etc*) programme *m*; (*timetable*) horaire *m*; (*list*) liste *f*; **to be behind s.** (*train, work*) avoir du retard; **to be on s.** (*on time*) être à l'heure; (*up to date*) être à jour; **ahead of s.** en avance; **according to s.** comme prévu; −

scheme 588 scout

vt (*plan*) prévoir; (*event*) fixer le programme or l'horaire de. ◆**—ed** a (*planned*) prévu; (*service, flight*) régulier; **she's s. to leave at 8** elle doit partir à 8 h.

schem/e [skiːm] n plan m (**to do** pour faire); (*idea*) idée f; (*dishonest trick*) combine f, manœuvre f; (*arrangement*) arrangement m; – vi manœuvrer. ◆**—ing** a intrigant; – npl Pej machinations fpl. ◆**—er** n intrigant, -ante mf.

schizophrenic [skɪtsəˈfrenɪk] a & n schizophrène (mf).

scholar [ˈskɒlər] n érudit, -ite mf; (*specialist*) spécialiste mf; (*grant holder*) boursier, -ière mf. ◆**scholarly** a érudit. ◆**scholarship** n érudition f; (*grant*) bourse f (d'études). ◆**scholastic** a scolaire.

school [skuːl] n école f; (*teaching, lessons*) classe f; Univ Am faculté f; (*within university*) institut m, département m; **in** or **at s.** à l'école; **secondary s.,** Am **high s.** collège m, lycée m; **public s.** école f privée; Am école publique; **s. of motoring** auto-école f; **summer s.** cours mpl d'été or de vacances; – a (*year, equipment etc*) scolaire; (*hours*) de classe; **s. fees** frais mpl de scolarité. ◆**—ing** n (*learning*) instruction f; (*attendance*) scolarité f. ◆**schoolboy** n écolier m. ◆**schooldays** npl années fpl d'école. ◆**schoolgirl** n écolière f. ◆**schoolhouse** n école f. ◆**school-'leaver** n jeune mf qui a terminé les études secondaires. ◆**schoolmaster** n (*primary*) instituteur m; (*secondary*) professeur m. ◆**schoolmate** n camarade mf de classe. ◆**schoolmistress** n institutrice f; professeur m. ◆**schoolteacher** n (*primary*) instituteur, -trice mf; (*secondary*) professeur m.

schooner [ˈskuːnər] n Nau goélette f.

science [ˈsaɪəns] n science f; **to study s.** étudier les sciences; – a (*subject*) scientifique; (*teacher*) de sciences; **s. fiction** science-fiction f. ◆**scien'tific** a scientifique. ◆**scientist** n scientifique mf.

scintillating [ˈsɪntɪleɪtɪŋ] a (*conversation, wit*) brillant.

scissors [ˈsɪzəz] npl ciseaux mpl; **a pair of s.** une paire de ciseaux.

sclerosis [sklɪˈrəʊsɪs] n Med sclérose f; **multiple s.** sclérose en plaques.

scoff [skɒf] **1** vi **to s. at** se moquer de. **2** vti (*eat*) Fam bouffer.

scold [skəʊld] vt gronder, réprimander (**for doing** pour avoir fait). ◆**—ing** n réprimande f.

scone [skəʊn, skɒn] n petit pain m au lait.

scoop [skuːp] n (*shovel*) pelle f (à main);

(*spoon-shaped*) Culin cuiller f; Journ exclusivité f; **at one's.** (in one seul coup; – vt (*prizes*) rafler; **to s. out** (*hollow out*) (évider; **to s. up** ramasser (avec une pelle or une cuiller).

scoot [skuːt] vi (*rush, leave*) Fam filer.

scooter [ˈskuːtər] n (*child's*) trottinette f; (*motorcycle*) scooter m.

scope [skəʊp] n (*range*) étendue f; (*of mind*) envergure f; (*competence*) compétence(s) f(pl); (*limits*) limites fpl; **s. for sth/for doing** (*opportunity*) des possibilités fpl de qch/de faire; **the s. of one's activity** le champ de ses activités.

scorch [skɔːtʃ] vt (*linen, grass etc*) roussir; – n **s.** (*mark*) brûlure f légère. ◆**—ing** a (*day*) torride; (*sun, sand*) brûlant. ◆**—er** n Fam journée f torride.

score¹ [skɔːr] n Sp score m; Cards marque f; Mus partition f; (*of film*) musique f; **a s. to settle** Fig un compte à régler; **on that s.** (*in that respect*) à cet égard; – vt (*point, goal*) marquer; (*exam mark*) avoir; (*success*) remporter; Mus orchestrer; – vi marquer un point or un but; (*keep score*) marquer les points. ◆**scoreboard** n Sp tableau m d'affichage. ◆**scorer** n Sp marqueur m.

score² [skɔːr] n (*twenty*) vingt; **a s. of** une vingtaine de; **scores of** Fig un grand nombre de.

score³ [skɔːr] vt (*cut*) rayer; (*paper*) marquer.

scorn [skɔːn] vt mépriser; – n mépris m. ◆**scornful** a méprisant; **to be s. of** mépriser. ◆**scornfully** adv avec mépris.

Scorpio [ˈskɔːpɪəʊ] n (*sign*) le Scorpion.

scorpion [ˈskɔːpɪən] n scorpion m.

Scot [skɒt] n Écossais, -aise mf. ◆**Scotland** n Écosse f. ◆**Scotsman** n (pl -men) Écossais m. ◆**Scotswoman** n (pl -women) Écossaise f. ◆**Scottish** a écossais.

scotch [skɒtʃ] **1** a **s. tape®** Am scotch® m. **2** vt (*rumour*) étouffer; (*attempt*) faire échouer.

Scotch [skɒtʃ] n (*whisky*) scotch m.

scot-free [skɒtˈfriː] adv sans être puni.

scoundrel [ˈskaʊndr(ə)l] n vaurien m.

scour [ˈskaʊər] vt (*pan*) récurer; (*streets etc*) Fig parcourir (**for** à la recherche de). ◆**—er** n tampon m à récurer.

scourge [skɜːdʒ] n fléau m.

scout [skaʊt] **1** n (*soldier*) éclaireur m; (*boy*) **s.** scout m, éclaireur m; **girl s.** Am éclaireuse f; **s. camp** camp m scout. **2** vi to

s. round for (look for) chercher. ◆—ing n scoutisme m.

scowl [skaʊl] vi se renfrogner; to s. at s.o. regarder qn d'un air mauvais. ◆—ing n renfrogné.

scraggy ['skrægɪ] a (-ier, -iest) (bony) osseux, maigrichon; (unkempt) débraillé.

scram [skræm] vi (-mm-) Fam filer.

scramble ['skræmb(ə)l] 1 vi to s. for se ruer vers; to s. up (climb) grimper; to s. through traverser avec difficulté; − n ruée f (for vers). 2 vt (egg, message) brouiller.

scrap [skræp] 1 n (piece) petit morceau m (of de); (of information, news) fragment m; pl (food) restes mpl; not a s. of (truth etc) pas un brin de; s. paper (papier m) brouillon m. 2 n (metal) ferraille f; to sell for s. vendre à la casse; − a (yard, heap) de ferraille; s. dealer, s. merchant marchand m de ferraille; s. iron ferraille f; on the s. heap Fig au rebut; to s. (-pp-) envoyer à la ferraille; (unwanted object, idea, plan) Fig mettre au rancart. 3 n (fight) Fam bagarre f. ◆scrapbook n album m (pour collages etc).

scrap/e [skreɪp] vt racler, gratter; (skin) Med érafler; to s. away or off (mud etc) racler; to s. together (money, people) réunir (difficilement); − vi to s. against frotter contre; to s. along Fig se débrouiller; to s. through (in exam) réussir de justesse; − n raclement m; éraflure f; to get into a s. Fam s'attirer des ennuis. ◆—ings npl raclures fpl. ◆—er n racloir m.

scratch [skrætʃ] n (mark, injury) éraflure f; (on glass) rayure f; to have a s. (scratch oneself) Fam se gratter; to start from s. (re)partir de zéro; to be/come up to s. être/se montrer à la hauteur; − vt (to relieve an itch) gratter; (skin, wall etc) érafler; (glass) rayer; (with claw) griffer; (one's name) graver (on sur); − vi (relieve an itch) se gratter; (of cat etc) griffer; (of pen) gratter, accrocher.

scrawl [skrɔːl] vt gribouiller; − n gribouillis m.

scrawny ['skrɔːnɪ] a (-ier, -iest) (bony) osseux, maigrichon.

scream [skriːm] vti crier, hurler; to s. at s.o. crier après qn; to s. with pain/etc hurler de douleur/etc; − n cri m (perçant).

screech [skriːtʃ] vti crier, hurler; (of brakes) hurler; − n cri m; hurlement m.

screen [skriːn] n 1 écran m; Fig masque m; (folding) s. paravent m. 2 vt (hide) cacher (from s.o. à qn); (protect) protéger (from de); (a film) projeter; (visitors, documents

filtrer; (for cancer etc) Med faire subir un test de dépistage à (qn) (for pour). ◆—ing n (of film) projection f; (selection) tri m; (medical examination) (test m de) dépistage m. ◆screenplay n Cin scénario m.

screw [skruː] n vis f; − vt visser (to à); to s. down or on visser; to s. off dévisser; to s. up (paper) chiffonner; (eyes) plisser; (mess up) Sl gâcher; to s. one's face up grimacer. ◆screwball n & a Am Fam cinglé, -ée (mf). ◆screwdriver n tournevis m. ◆screwy a (-ier, -iest) (idea, person etc) farfelu.

scribble ['skrɪb(ə)l] vti griffonner; − n griffonnage m.

scribe [skraɪb] n scribe m.

scrimmage ['skrɪmɪdʒ] n Fb Am mêlée f.

script [skrɪpt] n (of film) scénario m; (of play) texte m; (in exam) copie f. ◆scriptwriter n Cin scénariste mf, dialoguiste mf; TV Rad dialoguiste mf.

Scripture ['skrɪptʃər] n Rel Écriture f (sainte).

scroll [skrəʊl] n rouleau m (de parchemin); (book) manuscrit m.

scrooge [skruːdʒ] n (miser) harpagon m.

scroung/e [skraʊndʒ] vt (meal) se faire payer (off or from s.o. par qn); (steal) piquer (off or from s.o. à qn); to s. money off or from (beg) quémander; to s. around for (beg) quémander; to s. around for Pej chercher. ◆—er n parasite m.

scrub [skrʌb] 1 vt (-bb-) frotter, nettoyer (à la brosse); (pan) récurer; (cancel) Fig annuler; to s. out (erase) Fig effacer; − vi (scrub floors) frotter les planchers; scrubbing brush brosse f dure; to give sth a s. frotter qch; s. brush Am brosse f dure. 2 n (land) broussailles fpl.

scruff [skrʌf] n 1 by the s. of the neck par la peau du cou. 2 (person) Fam individu m débraillé. ◆scruffy a (-ier, -iest) (untidy) négligé; (dirty) malpropre.

scrum [skrʌm] n Rugby mêlée f.

scrumptious ['skrʌmpʃəs] a Fam super bon, succulent.

scruple ['skruːp(ə)l] n scrupule m. ◆scrupulous a scrupuleux. ◆scrupulously adv (conscientiously) scrupuleusement; (completely) absolument.

scrutinize ['skruːtɪnaɪz] vt scruter. ◆scrutiny n examen m minutieux.

scuba ['skjuːbə, Am 'skuːbə] n scaphandre m autonome; s. diving la plongée sous-marine.

scuff [skʌf] vt to s. (up) (scrape) érafler.

scuffle ['skʌf(ə)l] n bagarre f.

scullery ['skʌlərɪ] *n* arrière-cuisine *f.*

sculpt [skʌlpt] *vti* sculpter. ◆**sculptor** *n* sculpteur *m.* ◆**sculpture** *n* (*art, object*) sculpture *f;* – *vti* sculpter.

scum [skʌm] *n* **1** (*on liquid*) écume *f.* **2** *Pej* (*people*) racaille *f;* (*person*) salaud *m;* **the s. of** (*society etc*) la lie de.

scupper ['skʌpər] *vt* (*plan*) *Fam* saboter.

scurf [skɜːf] *n* pellicules *fpl.*

scurrilous ['skʌrɪləs] *a* (*criticism, attack*) haineux, violent et grossier.

scurry ['skʌrɪ] *vi* (*rush*) se précipiter, courir; **to s. off** décamper.

scuttle ['skʌt(ə)l] **1** *vt* (*ship*) saborder. **2** *vi* to **s. off** filer.

scythe [saɪð] *n* faux *f.*

sea [siː] *n* mer *f;* (*out*) **at s.** en mer; **by s.** par mer; **by** *or* **beside the s.** au bord de la mer; **to be all at s.** *Fig* nager complètement; – *a* (*level, breeze*) de la mer; (*water, fish*) de mer; (*air, salt*) marin; (*route*) maritime; **s. bed, s. floor** fond *m* de la mer; **s. lion** (*animal*) otarie *f.* ◆**seaboard** *n* littoral *m.* ◆**seafarer** *n* marin *m.* ◆**seafood** *n* fruits *mpl* de mer. ◆**seafront** *n* front *m* de mer. ◆**seagull** *n* mouette *f.* ◆**seaman** *n* (*pl* -men) marin *m.* ◆**seaplane** *n* hydravion *m.* ◆**seaport** *n* port *m* de mer. ◆**seashell** *n* coquillage *m.* ◆**seashore** *n* bord *m* de la mer. ◆**seasick** *a* **to be s.** avoir le mal de mer. ◆**seasickness** *n* mal *m* de mer. ◆**seaside** *n* bord de la mer; – *a* (*town, holiday*) au bord de la mer. ◆**seaway** *n* route *f* maritime. ◆**seaweed** *n* algue(s) *f(pl).* ◆**seaworthy** *a* (*ship*) en état de naviguer.

seal [siːl] **1** *n* (*animal*) phoque *m.* **2** *n* (*mark, design*) sceau *m;* (*on letter*) cachet *m* (de cire); (*putty for sealing*) joint *m;* – *vt* (*document, container*) sceller; (*with wax*) cacheter; (*letter*) coller; (*with putty*) boucher; (*s.o.'s fate*) *Fig* décider de; **to s. off** (*room etc*) interdire l'accès de; **to s. off a house/district** (*of police, troops*) boucler une maison/un quartier.

seam [siːm] *n* (*in cloth etc*) couture *f;* (*of coal, quartz etc*) veine *f.*

seamy ['siːmɪ] *a* (-ier, -iest) **the s. side** le côté peu reluisant (**of**).

séance ['seɪɑːns] *n* séance *f* de spiritisme.

search [sɜːtʃ] *n* (*quest*) recherche *f* (**for**); (*of person, place*) fouille *f;* **in s. of** à la recherche de; **s. party** équipe *f* de secours; – *vt* (*person, place*) fouiller (**for** pour trouver); (*study*) examiner (*documents etc*); **to s. (through) one's papers/etc for sth** chercher qch dans ses papiers/*etc;* – *vi*

chercher; **to s. for sth** chercher qch. ◆**—ing** *a* (*look*) pénétrant; (*examination*) minutieux. ◆**searchlight** *n* projecteur *m.*

season ['siːz(ə)n] **1** *n* saison *f;* **the festive s.** la période des fêtes; **in the peak s., in (the) high s.** en pleine *or* haute saison; **in the low** *or* **off s.** en basse saison; **a Truffaut s.** *Cin* une rétrospective Truffaut; **s. ticket** carte *f* d'abonnement. **2** *vt* (*food*) assaisonner; **highly seasoned** (*dish*) relevé. ◆**—ed** *a* (*worker*) expérimenté; (*soldier*) aguerri. ◆**—ing** *n* *Culin* assaisonnement *m.* ◆**seasonable** *a* (*weather*) de saison. ◆**seasonal** *a* saisonnier.

seat [siːt] *n* (*for sitting, centre*) & *Pol* siège *m;* (*on train, bus*) banquette *f; Cin Th* fauteuil *m;* (*place*) place *f;* (*of trousers*) fond *m;* **to take** *or* **have a s.** s'asseoir; **in the hot s.** (*in difficult position*) *Fig* sur la sellette; **s. belt** ceinture *f* de sécurité; – *vt* (*at table*) placer (*qn*); (*on one's lap*) asseoir (*qn*); **the room seats 50** la salle a 50 places (assises); **be seated!** asseyez-vous! ◆**—ed** *a* (*sitting*) assis. ◆**—ing** *n.* (**room**) (*seats*) places *fpl* assises; **the s. arrangements** la disposition des places; **s. capacity** nombre *m* de places assises. ◆**—er** *a* & *n* **two-s.** (*car*) voiture *f* à deux places.

secateurs [sekə'tɜːz] *npl* sécateur *m.*

secede [sɪ'siːd] *vi* faire sécession. ◆**secession** *n* sécession *f.*

secluded [sɪ'kluːdɪd] *a* (*remote*) isolé. ◆**seclusion** *n* solitude *f.*

second [1] ['sekənd] **1** *a* deuxième, second; **every s. week** une semaine sur deux; **in s.** (**gear**) *Aut* en seconde; **s. to none** sans pareil; **s. in command** second *m* Mil commandant *m* en second; – *adv* (*to say*) deuxièmement; **to come s.** *Sp* se classer deuxième; **the s. biggest** le deuxième en ordre de grandeur; **the s. richest country** le deuxième pays le plus riche; **my s. best** (*choice*) mon deuxième choix; – *n* (*person, object*) deuxième *mf,* second, -onde *mf;* **Louis the S.** Louis Deux; (*goods*) *Com* articles *mpl* de second choix; – *vt* (*motion*) appuyer. ◆**s.-'class** *a* (*product*) de qualité inférieure; (*ticket*) *Rail* de seconde (classe); (*mail*) non urgent. ◆**s.-'rate** *a* médiocre. ◆**secondly** *adv* deuxièmement.

second [2] ['sekənd] *n* (*unit of time*) seconde *f;* **s. hand** (*of clock, watch*) trotteuse *f.*

second [3] [sɪ'kɒnd] *vt* (*employee*) détacher (**to** à). ◆**—ment** *n* détachement *m;* **on s.** en (position de) détachement (**to** à).

secondary ['sekəndərɪ] *a* secondaire.

secondhand [sekənd'hænd] **1** *a* & *adv* (*not*

new) d'occasion. **2** a (*report, news*) de
seconde main.

secret ['siːkrɪt] a secret; — n secret m; **in s.**
en secret; **an open s.** le secret de
Polichinelle. ◆**secrecy** n (*discretion,
silence*) secret m; **in s.** en secret. ◆**secretive** a (*person*) cachottier; (*organization*)
qui a le goût du secret; **to be s. about** faire
un mystère de; (*organization*) être très
discret sur. ◆**secretively** adv en catimini.

secretary ['sekrət(ə)rı] n secrétaire mf;
Foreign S., Am S. of State = ministre m
des Affaires étrangères. ◆**secre'tarial** a
(*work*) de secrétaire, de secrétariat;
(*school*) de secrétariat. ◆**secre'tariat** n
(*in international organization*) secrétariat
m.

secrete [sɪ'kriːt] vt Med Biol sécréter.
◆**sec'retion** n sécrétion f.

sect [sekt] n secte f. ◆**sec'tarian** a & n Pej
sectaire (mf).

section ['sekʃ(ə)n] n (*of road, book, wood
etc*) section f; (*of town, country*) partie f; (*of
machine, furniture*) élement m; (*department*) section f; (*in store*) rayon m; **the
sports/etc s.** (*of newspaper*) la page des
sports/etc; — vt **to s. off** (*separate*) séparer.

sector ['sektər] n secteur m.

secular ['sekjʊlər] a (*teaching etc*) laïque;
(*music, art*) profane.

secure [sɪ'kjʊər] **1** a (*person, valuables*) en
sûreté, en sécurité; (*in one's mind*) tranquille; (*place*) sûr; (*solid, firm*) solide;
(*door, window*) bien fermé; (*certain*) assuré;
s. from à l'abri de; (*emotionally*)
sécurisé; — vt (*fasten*) attacher; (*window
etc*) bien fermer; (*success, future etc*)
assurer; **to s. against** protéger de. **2** vt
(*obtain*) procurer (sth for s.o. qch à qn); **to
s. sth** (*for oneself*) se procurer qch.
◆**securely** adv (*firmly*) solidement;
(*safely*) en sûreté. ◆**security** n sécurité f;
(*for loan, bail*) caution f; **s. firm** société f de
surveillance; **s. guard** agent m de sécurité;
(*transferring money*) convoyeur m de
fonds.

sedan [sɪ'dæn] n (*saloon*) Aut Am berline f.

sedate [sɪ'deɪt] **1** a calme. **2** vt mettre sous
calmants. ◆**sedation** n under s. sous
calmants. ◆'**sedative** n calmant m.

sedentary ['sedəntərı] a sédentaire.

sediment ['sedɪmənt] n sédiment m.

sedition [sə'dɪʃ(ə)n] n sédition f. ◆**seditious** a séditieux.

seduce [sɪ'djuːs] vt séduire. ◆**seducer** n
séducteur, -trice f. ◆**seduction** n séduc-

tion f. ◆**seductive** a (*person, offer*)
séduisant.

see[1] [siː] vti (pt saw, pp seen) voir; **we'll s.
on verra** (bien); **I s.!** je vois!; **I can s.**
(*clearly*) j'y vois clair; **I saw him run(ning)**
je l'ai vu courir; **to s. reason** entendre
raison; **to s. the joke** comprendre la
plaisanterie; **s. who it is** va voir qui c'est; **s.
you** (*later*)! à tout à l'heure!; **s. you** (*soon*)!
à bientôt!; **to s. about** (*deal with*) s'occuper
de; (*consider*) songer à; **to s. in the New
Year** fêter la Nouvelle Année; **to s. s.o. off**
accompagner qn (*à la gare etc*); **to s. s.o.
out** raccompagner qn; **to s. through** (*task*)
mener à bonne fin; **to s. s.o. through** (*be
enough for*) suffire à qn; **to s. through s.o.**
deviner le jeu de qn; **to s. to** (*deal with*)
s'occuper de; (*mend*) réparer; **to s.** (**to it**)
that (*attend*) veiller à ce que (+ *sub*);
(*check*) s'assurer que; **to s. s.o. to** (*accompany*) raccompagner qn à. ◆**s.-through** a
(*dress etc*) transparent.

see[2] [siː] n (*of pope*) siège m (épiscopal).

seed [siːd] n Agr graine f; (*in grape*) pépin m;
(*source*) Fig germe; Tennis tête f de série;
seed(s) (*for sowing*) Agr graines fpl; **to go
to s.** (*of lettuce etc*) monter en graine.
◆**seedbed** n Bot semis m; (*of rebellion
etc*) Fig foyer m (of de). ◆**seedling** n
(*plant*) semis m.

seedy ['siːdı] a (**-ier, -iest**) miteux. ◆**seediness** n aspect m miteux.

seeing ['siːɪŋ] conj **s.** (**that**) vu que.

seek [siːk] vt (pt & pp sought) chercher (**to
do** à faire); (*ask for*) demander (**from** à); **to
s.** (*after*) rechercher; **to s. out** aller trouver.

seem [siːm] vi sembler (**to do** faire); **it seems
that . . .** (*impression*) il semble que . . . (+
sub or indic); (*rumour*) il paraît que . . . ; **it
seems to me that . . .** il me semble que
. . . ; **we s. to know each other** il me semble
qu'on se connaît; **I can't s. to do it** je
n'arrive pas à le faire. ◆**—ing** a apparent.
◆**—ingly** adv apparemment.

seemly ['siːmlı] a convenable.

seen [siːn] see see[1].

seep [siːp] vi (*ooze*) suinter; **to s. into**
s'infiltrer dans. ◆**—age** n suintement m;
infiltration(s) f(pl) (**into** dans); (*leak*) fuite
f.

seesaw ['siːsɔː] n (*jeu m de*) bascule f.

seethe [siːð] vi **to s. with anger** bouillir de
colère; **to s. with people** grouiller de
monde.

segment ['segmənt] n segment m; (*of
orange*) quartier m.

segregate ['segrɪgeɪt] vt séparer; (**racially**)

segregated (*school*) où se pratique la ségrégation raciale. ◆**segre'gation** n ségrégation f.

seize [siːz] **1** vt saisir; (*power, land*) s'emparer de; – vi **to s. on** (*offer etc*) saisir. **2** vi **to s. up** (*of engine*) (se) gripper. ◆**seizure** [-ʒər] n (*of goods etc*) saisie f; Mil prise f; Med crise f.

seldom ['seldəm] adv rarement.

select [sɪ'lekt] vt choisir (**from** parmi); (*candidates, pupils etc*) & Sp sélectionner; – a (*chosen*) choisi; (*exclusive*) sélect, chic inv. ◆**selection** n sélection f. ◆**selective** a (*memory, recruitment etc*) sélectif; (*person*) qui opère un choix; (*choosey*) difficile.

self [self] n (pl **selves**) the s. Phil le moi; **he's back to his old s.** Fam il est redevenu lui-même. ◆**s.-a'ssurance** n assurance f. ◆**s.-a'ssured** a sûr de soi. ◆**s.-'catering** a où l'on fait la cuisine soi-même. ◆**s.-'centred** a égocentrique. ◆**s.-'cleaning** a (*oven*) autonettoyant. ◆**s.-con'fessed** a (*liar*) de son propre aveu. ◆**s.-'confident** a sûr de soi. ◆**s.-'conscious** a gêné. ◆**s.-'consciousness** n gêne f. ◆**s.-con'tained** a (*flat*) indépendant. ◆**s.-con'trol** n maîtrise f de soi. ◆**s.-de'feating** a qui a un effet contraire à celui qui est recherché. ◆**s.-de'fence** n Jur légitime défense f. ◆**s.-de'nial** n abnégation f. ◆**s.-determi'nation** n autodétermination f. ◆**s.-'discipline** n autodiscipline f. ◆**s.-em'ployed** a qui travaille à son compte. ◆**s.-es'teem** n amour-propre m. ◆**s.-'evident** a évident, qui va de soi. ◆**s.-ex'planatory** a qui tombe sous le sens, qui se passe d'explication. ◆**s.-'governing** a autonome. ◆**s.-im'portant** a suffisant. ◆**s.-in'dulgent** a qui ne se refuse rien. ◆**s.-'interest** n intérêt m (personnel). ◆**s.-o'pinionated** a entêté. ◆**s.-'pity** to feel s.-pity s'apitoyer sur son propre sort. ◆**s.-'portrait** n autoportrait m. ◆**s.-po'ssessed** a assuré. ◆**s.-raising** or Am **s.-rising 'flour** n farine f à levure. ◆**s.-re'liant** a indépendant. ◆**s.-re'spect** n amour-propre m. ◆**s.-re'specting** a qui se respecte. ◆**s.-'righteous** a pharisaïque. ◆**s.-'sacrifice** n abnégation f. ◆**s.-'satisfied** a content de soi. ◆**s.-'service** n & a libre-service (m inv). ◆**s.-'styled** a soi-disant. ◆**s.-su'fficient** a indépendant, qui a son indépendance. ◆**s.-su'p-**

porting a financièrement indépendant. ◆**s.-'taught** a autodidacte.

selfish ['selfɪʃ] a égoïste; (*motive*) intéressé. ◆**selfless** a désintéressé. ◆**selfishness** n égoïsme m.

selfsame ['selfseɪm] a même.

sell [sel] vt (pt & pp **sold**) vendre; (*idea etc*) Fig faire accepter; **she sold me it for twenty pounds** elle me l'a vendu vingt livres; **to s. back** revendre; **to s. off** liquider; **to have** or **be sold out of** (*cheese etc*) n'avoir plus de; **this book is sold out** ce livre est épuisé; – vi se vendre; (*of idea etc*) Fig être accepté; **to s. up** vendre sa maison; Com vendre son affaire; **selling price** prix m de vente. ◆**seller** n vendeur, -euse mf. ◆**sellout** n **1** (*betrayal*) trahison f. **2** **it was a s.** Th Cin tous les billets ont été vendus.

sellotape® ['seləteɪp] n scotch® m; – vt scotcher.

semantic [sɪ'mæntɪk] a sémantique. ◆**semantics** n sémantique f.

semaphore ['seməfɔːr] n (*device*) Rail Nau sémaphore m; (*system*) signaux mpl à bras.

semblance ['sembləns] n semblant m.

semen ['siːmən] n sperme m.

semester [sɪ'mestər] n Univ semestre m.

semi- ['semɪ] pref demi-, semi-. ◆**semiauto'matic** a semi-automatique. ◆**semibreve** [-briːv] n Mus ronde f. ◆**semicircle** n demi-cercle m. ◆**semi'circular** a semi-circulaire. ◆**semi'colon** n point-virgule m. ◆**semi'conscious** a à demi conscient. ◆**semide'tached** a s. **house** maison f jumelle. ◆**semi'final** n Sp demi-finale f.

seminar ['semɪnɑːr] n Univ séminaire m.

seminary ['semɪnərɪ] n Rel séminaire m.

Semite ['siːmaɪt, Am 'semaɪt] n Sémite mf. ◆**Se'mitic** a sémite; (*language*) sémitique.

semolina [semə'liːnə] n semoule f.

senate ['senɪt] n Pol sénat m. ◆**senator** n Pol sénateur m.

send [send] vt (pt & pp **sent**) envoyer (**to** à); **to s. s.o. for sth/s.o.** envoyer qn chercher qch/qn; **to s. s.o. crazy** or **mad** rendre qn fou; **to s. s.o. packing** Fam envoyer promener qn; **to s. away** or **off** envoyer (**to** à); (*dismiss*) renvoyer; **to s. back** renvoyer; **to s. in** (*form*) envoyer; (*person*) faire entrer; **to s. on** (*letter, luggage*) faire suivre; **to s. out** (*invitation etc*) envoyer; (*heat*) émettre; (*from room etc*) faire sortir (qn); **to s. up** (*balloon, rocket*) lancer; (*price, luggage*) faire monter; (*mock*) Fam parodier; – vi **to s. away** or **off for** commander (par courrier); **to s. for** (*doctor etc*) faire venir, envoyer chercher; **to s. (out) for** (*meal, groceries*) envoyer chercher. ◆**s.-off** *n* to give s.o. a s.-off *Fam* faire des adieux chaleureux à qn. ◆**s.-up** *n Fam* parodie *f*. ◆**sender** *n* expéditeur, -trice *mf*.

senile ['siːnaɪl] *a* gâteux, sénile. ◆**se'nility** *n* gâtisme *m*, sénilité *f*.

senior ['siːnɪər] *a* (*older*) plus âgé; (*position, executive, rank*) supérieur; (*teacher, partner*) principal; **to be s. to s.o., be s.o.'s s.** être plus âgé que qn; (*in rank*) être au-dessus de qn; **Brown's S.** Brown père; **s. citizen** personne *f* âgée; **s. year** *Sch Univ Am* dernière année *f*; − *n* aîné, -ée *mf*; *Sch* grand, -ande *mf*; *Sch Univ Am* étudiant, -ante *mf* de dernière année; *Sp* senior *mf*. ◆**seni'ority** *n* priorité *f* d'âge; (*in service*) ancienneté *f*; (*in rank*) supériorité *f*.

sensation [sen'seɪʃ(ə)n] *n* sensation *f*. ◆**sensational** *a* (*event*) qui fait sensation; (*newspaper, film*) à sensation; (*terrific*) *Fam* sensationnel.

sense [sens] *n* (*faculty, awareness, meaning*) sens *m*; (*feeling*) sentiment *m*; **s. of hearing** (*the sense of*) l'ouïe *f*; **to have (good) s.** avoir du bon sens; **a s. of** (*physical*) une sensation de (*chaleur etc*); (*mental*) un sentiment de (*honte etc*); **a s. of humour/direction** le sens de l'humour/de l'orientation; **a s. of time** la notion de l'heure; **to bring s.o. to his senses** ramener qn à la raison; **to make s.** (*of story, action etc*) avoir du sens; **to make s. of** comprendre; − *vt* sentir (intuitivement) (**that** que); (*have a foreboding of*) pressentir. ◆**less** *a* (*stupid, meaningless*) insensé; (*unconscious*) sans connaissance. ◆**lessness** *n* stupidité *f*.

sensibility [sensɪ'bɪlətɪ] *n* sensibilité *f*; *pl* (*touchiness*) susceptibilité *f*.

sensible ['sensəb(ə)l] *a* (*wise*) raisonnable, sensé; (*clothes*) pratique.

sensitive ['sensɪtɪv] *a* (*responsive, painful*) sensible (**to** à); (*delicate*) délicat (*peau, question etc*); (*touchy*) susceptible (**about** à propos de). ◆**sensi'tivity** *n* sensibilité *f*; (*touchiness*) susceptibilité *f*.

sensory ['sensərɪ] *a* sensoriel.

sensual ['senʃʊəl] *a* (*bodily, sexual*) sensuel. ◆**sensu'ality** *n* sensualité *f*. ◆**sensuous** *a* (*pleasing, refined*) sensuel. ◆**sensuously** *adv* avec sensualité. ◆**sensuousness** *n* sensualité *f*.

sent [sent] *see* send.

sentence ['sentəns] **1** *n Gram* phrase *f*. **2** *n Jur* condamnation *f*; (*punishment*) peine *f*;

to pass s. prononcer une condamnation (**on** s.o. contre qn); **to serve a s.** purger une peine; − *vt Jur* prononcer une condamnation contre; **to s. to** condamner à.

sentiment ['sentɪmənt] *n* sentiment *m*. ◆**senti'mental** *a* sentimental. ◆**senti-men'tality** *n* sentimentalité *f*.

sentry ['sentrɪ] *n* sentinelle *f*; **s. box** guérite *f*.

separate ['sepərət] *a* (*distinct*) séparé; (*independent*) indépendant; (*different*) différent; (*individual*) particulier; − *vi* se séparer (**from** de). ◆**separately** *adv* séparément. ◆**sepa-'ration** *n* séparation *f*.

separates ['sepərəts] *npl* (*garments*) coordonnés *mpl*.

September [sep'tembər] *n* septembre *m*.

septic ['septɪk] *a* (*wound*) infecté; **s. tank** fosse *f* septique.

sequel ['siːkwəl] *n* suite *f*.

sequence ['siːkwəns] *n* (*order*) ordre *m*; (*series*) succession *f*; *Mus Cards* séquence *f*; **film s.** séquence de film; **in s.** dans l'ordre, successivement.

sequin ['siːkwɪn] *n* paillette *f*.

serenade [serə'neɪd] *n* sérénade *f*; − *vt* donner *or* la sérénade à.

serene [sə'riːn] *a* serein. ◆**serenity** *n* sérénité *f*.

sergeant ['sɑːdʒənt] *n Mil* sergent *m*; (*in police force*) brigadier *m*.

serial ['sɪərɪəl] *n* (*story, film*) feuilleton *m*; **s. number** (*of banknote, TV set etc*) numéro de série. ◆**serialize** *vt* publier en feuilleton; *TV Rad* adapter en feuilleton.

series ['sɪəriːz] *n inv* série *f*; (*book collection*) collection *f*.

serious ['sɪərɪəs] *a* sérieux; (*illness, mistake, tone*) grave, sérieux; (*damage*) important. ◆**ly** *adv* sérieusement; (*ill, damaged*) gravement; **to take s.** prendre au sérieux. ◆**ness** *n* sérieux *m*; (*of illness etc*) gravité *f*; (*of damage*) importance *f*; **in all s.** sérieusement.

sermon ['sɜːmən] *n* sermon *m*.

serpent ['sɜːpənt] *n* serpent *m*.

serrated [sə'reɪtɪd] *a* (*knife*) à dents (de scie).

serum ['sɪərəm] *n* sérum *m*.

servant ['sɜːvənt] *n* (*in house etc*) domestique *mf*; (*person who serves*) serviteur *m*; **public s.** fonctionnaire *mf*.

serve [sɜːv] *vt* servir (**to s.o.** à qn, **s.o. with sth** qch à qn); (*of train, bus etc*) desservir (*un village, un quartier etc*); (*supply*) El alimenter; (*apprenticeship*) faire; (*summons*) *Jur* remettre (**on** à); **it serves its**

purpose ça fait l'affaire; **(it) serves you right!** *Fam* ça t'apprendra!; **to s. up** or out servir; – *vi* servir (**as de**); **to s. on** *(jury, committee)* être membre de; **to s. to show**/*etc* servir à montrer/*etc*; – *n Tennis* service *m*.

servic/e ['sɜːvɪs] *n* (*serving*) & *Mil Rel Tennis* service *m*; *(machine or vehicle repair)* révision *f*; **to be of s. to** être utile à, rendre service à; **the (armed) services** les forces *fpl* armées; **s. (charge)** *(tip)* service *m*; **s. department** *(workshop)* atelier *m*; **s. area** *(on motorway)* aire *f* de service; **s. station** station-service *f*; – *vt* *(machine, vehicle)* réviser. ◆**—ing** *n Tech Aut* révision *f*. ◆**serviceable** *a (usable)* utilisable; *(useful)* commode; *(durable)* solide. ◆**serviceman** *n (pl -men)* militaire *m*.

serviette [sɜːvɪ'et] *n* serviette *f* (de table).

servile ['sɜːvaɪl] *a* servile.

session ['seʃ(ə)n] *n* séance *f*; *Jur Pol* session *f*, séance *f*; *Univ* année *f* or trimestre *m* universitaire; *Univ Am* semestre *m* universitaire.

set [set] **1** *n (of keys, needles, tools)* jeu *m*; *(of stamps, numbers)* série *f*; *(of people)* groupe *m*; *(of facts)* & *Math* ensemble *m*; *(of books)* collection *f*; *(of plates)* service *m*; *(of tyres)* train *m*; *(kit)* trousse *f*; *(stage)* *Th Cin* plateau *m*; *(scenery)* *Th Cin* décor *m*, scène *f*; *(hairstyle)* mise *f* en plis; *Tennis* set *m*; **television s.** téléviseur *m*; **radio s.** poste *m* de radio; **tea s.** service *m* à thé; **chess s.** *(box)* jeu *m* d'échecs; **a s. of teeth** une rangée de dents, une denture; **the skiing/racing s.** le monde du ski/des courses. **2** *a (time etc)* fixe; *(lunch)* à prix fixe; *(book etc)* *Sch* au programme; *(speech)* préparé à l'avance; *(in one's habits)* régulier; *(situated)* situé; **s. phrase** expression *f* consacrée; **a s. purpose** un but déterminé; **the s. menu** le plat du jour; **dead s. against** absolument opposé à; **s. on doing** résolu à faire; **to be s. on sth** vouloir qch à tout prix; **all s.** *(ready)* prêt (**to do** pour faire); **s. back from** *(of house etc)* être en retrait de *(route etc)*. **3** *vt (pt & pp set*, *pres p* **setting)** *(put)* mettre, poser; *(date, limit etc)* fixer; *(record)* *Sp* établir; *(adjust)* *Tech* régler; *(arm etc in plaster)* *Med* plâtrer; *(task)* donner (**for s.o.** à qn); *(problem)* poser; *(diamond)* monter; *(precedent)* créer; **to have one's hair** s. se faire faire une mise en plis; **to s. (loose)** *(dog)* lâcher (**on contre**); **to s. s.o. (off)** **crying**/*etc* faire pleurer/*etc* qn; **to s. back** *(in time)* retarder; *(cost)* *Fam* coûter; **to s.**

down déposer; **to s. off** *(bomb)* faire exploser; *(activity, mechanism)* déclencher; *(complexion, beauty)* rehausser; **to s. out** *(display, explain)* exposer (**to** à); *(arrange)* disposer; **to s. up** *(furniture)* installer; *(statue, tent)* dresser; *(school)* fonder; *(government)* établir; *(business)* créer; *(inquiry)* ouvrir; **to s. s.o. up in business** lancer qn dans les affaires; – *vi (of sun)* se coucher; *(of jelly)* prendre; *(of bone)* *Med* se ressouder; **to s. about** *(job)* se mettre à; **to s. about doing** se mettre à faire; **to s. in** *(start)* commencer; *(arise)* surgir; **to s. off** or **out** *(leave)* partir; **to s. out do** entreprendre de faire; **to s. up** *(in business)* monter une affaire; **to s. upon** *(attack)* attaquer *(qn)*. ◆**setting** *n (surroundings)* cadre *m*; *(of sun)* coucher *m*; *(of diamond)* monture *f*. ◆**setter** *n* chien *m* couchant.

setback ['setbæk] *n* revers *m*; *Med* rechute *f*.

setsquare ['setskweər] *n Math* équerre *f*.

settee [se'tiː] *n* canapé *m*.

settle ['set(ə)l] *vt (decide, arrange, pay)* régler; *(date)* fixer; *(place in position)* placer; *(person)* installer *(dans son lit etc)*; *(nerves)* calmer; *(land)* coloniser; **let's s. things** arrangeons les choses; **that's (all) settled** *(decided)* c'est décidé; – *vi (live)* s'installer, s'établir; *(of dust)* se déposer; *(of bird)* se poser; *(of snow)* tenir; **to s. (down)** into *(armchair)* s'installer dans; *(job)* s'habituer à; **to s. (up) with s.o.** régler qn; **to s. for** se contenter de, accepter; **to s. down** *(in chair or house)* s'installer; *(of nerves)* se calmer; *(in one's lifestyle)* se ranger; *(marry)* se caser; **to s. down to** *(get used to)* s'habituer à; *(work, task)* se mettre à. ◆**settled** *a (weather, period)* stable; *(habits)* régulier. ◆**settlement** *n (of account etc)* règlement *m*; *(agreement)* accord *m*; *(colony)* colonie *f*. ◆**settler** *n* colon *m*.

set-to [set'tuː] *n (quarrel)* *Fam* prise *f* de bec.

setup ['setʌp] *n Fam* situation *f*.

seven ['sev(ə)n] *a* & *n* sept *(m)*. ◆**seven'teen** *a* & *n* dix-sept *(m)*. ◆**seven'teenth** *a* & *n* dix-septième *(mf)*. ◆**seventh** *a* & *n* septième *(mf)*. ◆**seventieth** *a* & *n* soixante-dixième *(mf)*. ◆**seventy** *a* & *n* soixante-dix *(m)*; **s.-one** soixante et onze.

sever ['sevər] *vt* sectionner, couper; *(relations)* *Fig* rompre. ◆**severing** *n*, ◆**severance** *n (of relations)* rupture *f*.

several ['sev(ə)rəl] *a* & *pron* plusieurs (**d**'entre).

severe [sə'vɪər] a (judge, tone etc) sévère; (winter, training) rigoureux; (test) dur; (injury) grave; (blow, pain) violent; (cold, frost) intense; (overwork) excessif; **a s. cold** Med un gros rhume; **s. to** or **with s.o.** sévère envers qn. ◆**severely** adv sévèrement; (wounded) gravement. ◆**se'verity** n sévérité f; rigueur f; gravité f; violence f.

sew [səʊ] vti (pp sewed, pp sewn [səʊn] or sewed) coudre; **to s. on** (button) (re)coudre; **to s. up** (tear) (re)coudre. ◆**—ing** n couture f; **s. machine** machine f à coudre.

sewage ['suːɪdʒ] n eaux fpl usées or d'égout. ◆**sewer** n égout m.

sewn [səʊn] see sew.

sex [seks] n (gender, sexuality) sexe m; (activity) relations fpl sexuelles; **the opposite s.** l'autre sexe; **to have s. with** coucher avec; – a (education, act etc) sexuel; **s. maniac** obsédé, -ée mf sexuel(le). ◆**sexist** a & n sexiste (mf). ◆**sexual** a sexuel. ◆**sexu'ality** n sexualité f. ◆**sexy** a (-ier, -iest) (book, garment, person) sexy inv; (aroused) qui a envie de (faire l'amour).

sextet [sek'stet] n sextuor m.

sh! [ʃ] int chut!

shabby ['ʃæbɪ] a (-ier, -iest) (town, room etc) miteux; (person) pauvrement vêtu; (mean) Fig mesquin. ◆**shabbily** adv (dressed) pauvrement. ◆**shabbiness** n aspect m miteux; mesquinerie f.

shack [ʃæk] **1** n cabane f. **2** vi **to s. up with** Pej Fam se coller avec.

shackles ['ʃæk(ə)lz] npl chaînes fpl.

shade [ʃeɪd] n ombre f; (of colour) ton m, nuance f; (of opinion, meaning) nuance f; (of lamp) abat-jour m inv; (blind) store m; **in the s.** à l'ombre; **a s. faster/taller/etc** (slightly) un rien plus vite/plus grand/etc; – vt (of tree) ombrager; (protect) abriter (from de); **to s. in** (drawing) ombrer. ◆**shady** a (-ier, -iest) (place) ombragé; (person etc) Fig louche.

shadow ['ʃædəʊ] **1** n ombre f. **2** a (cabinet) Pol fantôme. **3** vt **to s. s.o.** (follow) filer qn. ◆**shadowy** a (-ier, -iest) (form etc) obscur, vague.

shaft [ʃɑːft] n **1** (of tool) manche m; (in machine) arbre m; **s. of light** trait m de lumière. **2** (of mine) puits m; (of lift) cage f.

shaggy ['ʃægɪ] a (-ier, -iest) (hair, beard) broussailleux; (dog etc) à longs poils.

shake [ʃeɪk] vt (pt shook, pp shaken) (move up and down) secouer; (bottle) agiter; (belief, resolution etc) Fig ébranler; (upset) bouleverser, secouer; **to s. the windows** (of shock) ébranler les vitres; **to s. one's head**

(say no) secouer la tête; **to s. hands with** serrer la main à; **we shook hands** nous nous sommes serré la main; **to s. off** (dust etc) secouer; (cough, infection, pursuer) Fig se débarrasser de; **to s. s.o. up** (disturb, rouse) secouer qn; **to s. sth out of sth** (remove) secouer qch de qch; **s. yourself out of it!** secoue-toi!; – vi trembler (with de); – n secousse f; **to give sth a s.** secouer qch; **with a s. of his** or **her head** en secouant la tête; **in two shakes** (soon) Fam dans une minute. ◆**s.-up** n Fig réorganisation f.

shaky ['ʃeɪkɪ] a (-ier, -iest) (trembling) tremblant; (ladder, table etc) branlant; (memory, health) chancelant; (on one's legs, in a language) mal assuré.

shall [ʃæl, unstressed ʃəl] v aux **1** (future) **I s. come, I'll come** je viendrai; **we s. not come, we shan't come** nous ne viendrons pas. **2** (question) **s. I leave?** veux-tu que je parte?; **s. we leave?** on part? **3** (order) **he s. do it if I order it** il devra le faire si je l'ordonne.

shallot [ʃə'lɒt] n (onion) échalote f.

shallow ['ʃæləʊ] a (-ier, -iest) peu profond; Fig Pej superficiel; – npl (of river) bas-fond m. ◆**—ness** n manque m de profondeur; Fig Pej caractère m superficiel.

sham [ʃæm] n (pretence) comédie f, feinte f; (person) imposteur m; (jewels) imitation f; – a (false) faux; (illness, emotion) feint; – vt (-mm-) feindre.

shambles ['ʃæmb(ə)lz] n désordre m, pagaïe f; **to be a s.** être en pagaïe; **to make a s. of** gâcher.

shame [ʃeɪm] n (feeling, disgrace) honte f; **it's a s.** c'est dommage (**to do** de faire); **it's a s. (that)** c'est dommage que (+ sub); **what a s.!** (quel) dommage!; **to put to s.** faire honte à; – vt (disgrace, make ashamed) faire honte à. ◆**shamefaced** a honteux; (bashful) timide. ◆**shameful** a honteux. ◆**shamefully** adv honteusement. ◆**shameless** a (brazen) effronté; (indecent) impudique.

shammy ['ʃæmɪ] n **s.** (leather) Fam peau f de chamois.

shampoo [ʃæm'puː] n shampooing m; – vt (carpet) shampooiner; **to s. s.o.'s hair** faire un shampooing à qn.

shandy ['ʃændɪ] n (beer) panaché m.

shan't [ʃɑːnt] = shall not.

shanty ['ʃæntɪ] n (hut) baraque f. ◆**shantytown** n bidonville f.

shanty² ['ʃæntɪ] n **sea s.** chanson f de marins.

shap/e [ʃeɪp] **1** n forme f; **in (good) s.** en (good) s. (of vehicle,
forme; **to be in good/bad s.** (of vehicle,

house etc) être en bon/mauvais état; (*of business*) marcher bien/mal; **to take s.** prendre forme; **in the s. of a pear** en forme de poire; – *vt* (*fashion*) façonner (**into** en); (*one's life*) *Fig* déterminer; – *vi* **to s. up** (*of plans*) prendre (bonne) tournure, s'annoncer bien; (*of pupil, wrongdoer*) s'y mettre, s'appliquer; (*of patient*) faire des progrès. ◆**-ed** *suffix* pear-s./*etc* en forme de poire/*etc*. ◆**shapeless** *a* informe. ◆**shapely** *a* (-ier, -iest) (*woman, legs*) bien tourné.

share [ʃeər] *n* part *f* (**of**, in de); (*in company*) *Fin* action *f*; **one's (fair) s.** sa part de; **to do one's (fair) s.** fournir sa part d'efforts; **stocks and shares** *Fin* valeurs *fpl* (boursières); – *vt* (*meal, joy, opinion etc*) partager (**with** avec); (*characteristic*) avoir en commun; **to s. out** (*distribute*) partager; – *vi* **to s. (in)** partager. ◆**shareholder** *n Fin* actionnaire *mf*.

shark [ʃɑːk] *n* (*fish*) *and Fig* requin *m*.

sharp [ʃɑːp] **1** *a* (-er, -est) (*knife, blade etc*) tranchant; (*pointed*) pointu; (*point, voice*) aigu; (*pace, mind*) vif; (*pain*) aigu, vif; (*change, bend*) brusque; (*taste*) piquant; (*words, wind, tone*) âpre; (*eyesight, cry*) perçant; (*distinct*) net; (*lawyer etc*) *Pej* peu scrupuleux; **s. practice** *Pej* procédé(s) *m*(*pl*) malhonnête(s); – *adv* (*to stop*) net; **five o'clock**/*etc* **s.** cinq heures/*etc* pile; **right/left** tout de suite à droite/à gauche. **2** *n Mus* dièse *m*. ◆**sharpen** *vt* (*knife*) aiguiser; (*pencil*) tailler. ◆**sharpener** *n* (*for pencils*) taille-crayon(s) *m inv*; (*for blades*) aiguisoir *m*. ◆**sharply** *adv* (*suddenly*) brusquement; (*harshly*) vivement; (*clearly*) nettement. ◆**sharpness** *n* (*of blade*) tranchant *m*; (*of picture*) netteté *f*. ◆**sharpshooter** *n* tireur *m* d'élite.

shatter [ˈʃætər] *vt* (*smash*) fracasser; (*glass*) faire voler en éclats; (*career, health*) briser; (*person, hopes*) anéantir; – *vi* (*smash*) se fracasser; (*of glass*) voler en éclats. ◆**-ed** *a* (*exhausted*) anéanti. ◆**-ing** *a* (*defeat*) accablant; (*news, experience*) bouleversant.

shav·e [ˈʃeɪv] *vt* (*person, head*) raser; **to s. off one's beard**/*etc* se raser la barbe/*etc*; – *vi* se raser; – *n* **to have a s.** se raser, se faire la barbe; **to have a close s.** *Fig Fam* l'échapper belle. ◆**-ing** *n* rasage *m*; (*strip of wood*) copeau *m*; **s. brush** blaireau *m*; **s. cream, s. foam** crème *f* à raser. ◆**shaven** *a* rasé (de près). ◆**shaver** *n* rasoir *m* électrique.

shawl [ʃɔːl] *n* châle *m*.

she [ʃiː] *pron* elle; **s. wants** elle veut; **she's a**

happy woman c'est une femme heureuse; **if I were s.** si j'étais elle; – *n* femelle *f*; **s.-bear** ourse *f*.

sheaf [ʃiːf] *n* (*pl* sheaves) (*of corn*) gerbe *f*.

shear [ʃiər] *vt* tondre; – *npl* cisaille(s) *f*(*pl*); **pruning shears** sécateur *m*. ◆**-ing** *n* tonte *f*.

sheath [ʃiːθ] *n* (*pl* -s [shiːðz]) (*container*) gaine *f*, fourreau *m*; (*contraceptive*) préservatif *m*.

shed [ʃed] **1** *n* (*in garden etc*) remise *f*; (*for goods or machines*) hangar *m*. **2** *vt* (*pt & pp* shed, *pres p* shedding) (*lose*) perdre; (*tears, warmth etc*) répandre; (*get rid of*) se défaire de; (*clothes*) enlever; **to s. light on** *Fig* éclairer.

sheen [ʃiːn] *n* lustre *m*.

sheep [ʃiːp] *n inv* mouton *m*. ◆**sheepdog** *n* chien *m* de berger. ◆**sheepskin** *n* peau *f* de mouton.

sheepish [ˈʃiːpɪʃ] *a* penaud. ◆**-ly** *adv* d'un air penaud.

sheer [ʃiər] **1** *a* (*luck, madness etc*) pur; (*impossibility etc*) absolu; **it's s. hard work** ça demande du travail; **by its determination/hard work** à force de détermination/de travail. **2** *a* (*cliff*) à pic; – *adv* (*to rise*) à pic. **3** *a* (*fabric*) très fin.

sheet [ʃiːt] *n* (*on bed*) drap *m*; (*of paper, wood etc*) feuille *f*; (*of glass, ice*) plaque *f*; (*dust cover*) housse *f*; (*canvas*) bâche *f*; **s. metal** tôle *f*.

sheikh [ʃeɪk] *n* scheik *m*, cheik *m*.

shelf [ʃelf] *n* (*pl* shelves) rayon *m*, étagère *f*; (*in shop*) rayon *m*; (*on cliff*) saillie *f*; **to be left) on the s.** (*not married*) *Fam* être toujours célibataire.

shell [ʃel] **1** *n* coquille *f*; (*of tortoise*) carapace *f*; (*seashell*) coquillage *m*; (*of peas*) cosse *f*; (*of building*) carcasse *f*; – *vt* (*peas*) écosser; (*nut, shrimp*) décortiquer. **2** *n* (*explosive*) *Mil* obus *m*; – *vt* (*town etc*) *Mil* bombarder. ◆**-ing** *n Mil* bombardement *m*. ◆**shellfish** *n inv Culin* (*oysters etc*) fruits *mpl* de mer.

shelter [ˈʃeltər] *n* (*place, protection*) abri *m*; **to take s.** se mettre à l'abri (**from** de); **to seek s.** chercher un abri; – *vt* abriter (**from** de); (*criminal*) protéger; – *vi* s'abriter. ◆**-ed** *a* (*place*) abrité; (*life*) très protégé.

shelve [ʃelv] *vt* (*postpone*) laisser en suspens.

shelving [ˈʃelvɪŋ] *n* (*shelves*) rayonnage(s) *m*(*pl*); **s. unit** (*set of shelves*) étagère *f*.

shepherd [ˈʃepəd] **1** *n* berger *m*; **s.'s pie** hachis *m* Parmentier. **2** *vt* **to s. in** faire entrer; **to s. s.o. around** piloter qn. ◆**shepherdess** n bergère f.

sherbet ['ʃɜːbət] n (powder) poudre f acidulée; (water ice) Am sorbet m.

sheriff ['ʃerɪf] n Am shérif m.

sherry ['ʃerɪ] n xérès m, sherry m.

shh! [ʃ] int chut!

shield [ʃiːld] n bouclier m; (on coat of arms) écu m; (screen) Tech écran m; − vt protéger (**from** de).

shift [ʃɪft] n (change) changement m (**of, in** de); (period of work) poste m; (workers) équipe f; **gear s.** Aut Am levier m de vitesse; **s. work** travail m en équipe; − vt (move) déplacer, bouger; (limb) bouger; (employee) muter (**to** à); (scenery) Th changer; (blame) rejeter (**on to** sur); **to s. places** changer de place; **to s. gear(s)** Aut Am changer de vitesse; − vi bouger; (of heavy object) se déplacer; (of views) changer; (pass) passer (**to** à); (go) aller (**to** à); **to s. to** (new town) déménager à; **to s. along** avancer; **to s. over** or **up** se pousser. ◆**−ing** a (views) changeant.

shiftless ['ʃɪftləs] a velléitaire, paresseux.

shifty ['ʃɪftɪ] a (**-ier, -iest**) (sly) sournois; (dubious) louche.

shilling ['ʃɪlɪŋ] n shilling m.

shilly-shally ['ʃɪlɪʃælɪ] vi hésiter, tergiverser.

shimmer ['ʃɪmər] vi chatoyer, miroiter; − n chatoiement m, miroitement m.

shin [ʃɪn] n tibia m; **s. pad** n Sp jambière f.

shindig ['ʃɪndɪg] n Fam réunion f bruyante.

shine [ʃaɪn] vi (pt & pp shone) briller; **to s. with** (happiness etc) rayonner de; − vt (polish) faire briller; **to s. a light** or **a torch** éclairer (**on sth** qch); − n éclat m; (on shoes, cloth) brillant m. ◆**−ing** a (bright, polished) brillant; **a shining example of** un bel exemple de. ◆**shiny** a (**-ier, -iest**) (bright, polished) brillant; (clothes, through wear) lustré.

shingle ['ʃɪŋg(ə)l] n (on beach) galets mpl; (on roof) bardeau m.

shingles ['ʃɪŋg(ə)lz] n Med zona m.

ship [ʃɪp] n navire m, bateau m; **by s.** en bateau; **s. owner** armateur m; − vt (**-pp-**) (send) expédier; (transport) transporter; (load up) embarquer (**on to** sur). ◆**−ping** n (traffic) navigation f; (ships) navires mpl; − a (agent) maritime; **s. line** compagnie f de navigation. ◆**shipbuilding** n construction f navale. ◆**shipmate** n camarade m de bord. ◆**shipment** n (goods) chargement m, cargaison f. ◆**shipshape** a & adv en ordre. ◆**shipwreck** n naufrage m. ◆**shipwrecked** a

naufragé; **to be s.** faire naufrage. ◆**shipyard** n chantier m naval.

shirk [ʃɜːk] vt (duty) se dérober à; (work) éviter de faire; − vi tirer au flanc. ◆**−er** n tire-au-flanc m inv.

shirt [ʃɜːt] n chemise f; (of woman) chemisier m. ◆**shirtfront** n plastron m. ◆**shirt-sleeves** npl in (one's) **s.** en bras de chemise.

shiver ['ʃɪvər] vi frissonner (**with** de); − n frisson m.

shoal [ʃəʊl] n (of fish) banc m.

shock [ʃɒk] n (moral blow) choc m; (impact) & Med choc m; (of explosion) secousse f; (**electric**) **s.** décharge f (électrique) (from sth en touchant qch); **a feeling of s.** un sentiment d'horreur; **suffering from s.**, in a state of **s.** en état de choc; **to come as a s. to s.o.** stupéfier qn; − a (tactics, wave) de choc; (effect, image etc) -choc inv; **s. absorber** amortisseur m; − vt (offend) choquer; (surprise) stupéfier; (disgust) dégoûter. ◆**−ing** a affreux; (outrageous) scandaleux; (indecent) choquant. ◆**−ingly** adv affreusement. ◆**−er** n **to be a s.** Fam être affreux or horrible. ◆**shockproof** a résistant au choc.

shoddy ['ʃɒdɪ] a (**-ier, -iest**) (goods etc) de mauvaise qualité. ◆**shoddily** adv (made, done) mal.

shoe [ʃuː] n chaussure f, soulier m; (for horse) fer m; Aut sabot m (de frein); **in your shoes** Fig à ta place; **s. polish** cirage m; − vt (pt & pp shod) (horse) ferrer. ◆**shoehorn** n chausse-pied m. ◆**shoelace** n lacet m. ◆**shoemaker** n fabricant m de chaussures; (cobbler) cordonnier m. ◆**shoestring** n on a **s.** Fig avec peu d'argent (en poche).

shone [ʃɒn, Am ʃəʊn] see shine.

shoo [ʃuː] vt **to s. (away)** chasser; − int ouste!

shook [ʃʊk] see shake.

shoot¹ [ʃuːt] vt (pt & pp shot) (kill) tuer (d'un coup de feu), abattre; (wound) blesser (d'un coup de feu); (execute) fusiller; (hunt) chasser; (gun) tirer un coup de; (bullet) tirer; (missile, glance, questions) lancer (**at** à); (film) tourner; (person) Phot prendre; **to s. down** (aircraft) abattre; − vi (with gun, bow etc) tirer (**at** sur); **to s. ahead/off** avancer/partir à toute vitesse; **to s. up** (grow) pousser vite; (rise, spurt) jaillir; (of price) monter en flèche. ◆**−ing** n (gunfire, execution) fusillade f; (shots) coups mpl de feu; (murder) meurtre m; (of *film*) tournage *m*; (*hunting*) chasse *f*. ◆**shoot-out** *n Fam* fusillade *f*.

shoot² [ʃuːt] *n* (*on plant*) pousse *f*.

shop [ʃɒp] **1** *n* magasin *m*; (*small*) boutique *f*; (*workshop*) atelier *m*; **at the baker's s.** à la boulangerie, chez le boulanger; **s. assistant** vendeur, -euse *mf*; **s. floor** (*workers*) ouvriers *mpl*; **s. steward** délégué, -ée *mf* syndical(e); **s. window** vitrine *f*; **– vi** (**-pp-**) faire ses courses (**at** chez); **to s. around** comparer les prix. **2** *vt Fam* dénoncer qn (*à la police etc*). ◆**shopping** *n* (*goods*) achats *mpl*; **to go s.** faire des courses; **to do one's s.** faire ses courses; **–** *a* (*street, district*) commerçant; (*bag*) à provisions; **s. centre** centre *m* commercial. ◆**shopper** *n* (*buyer*) acheteur, -euse *mf*; (*customer*) client, -ente *mf*; (*bag*) sac *m* à provisions.

shopkeeper [ʃɒpkiːpər] *n* commerçant, -ante *mf*. ◆**shoplifter** *n* voleur, -euse *mf* à l'étalage. ◆**shoplifting** *n* vol *m* à l'étalage. ◆**shopsoiled** *a*, *Am* ◆**shopworn** *a* abîmé.

shore [ʃɔːr] **1** *n* (*of sea, lake*) rivage *m*; (*coast*) côte *f*, bord *m* de (la) mer; (*beach*) plage *f*; **on s.** (*passenger*) *Nau* à terre. **2** *vt* **to s. up** (*prop up*) étayer.

shorn [ʃɔːn] *a* (*head*) tondu; **s. of** (*stripped of*) *Lit* dénué de.

short [ʃɔːt] *a* (**-er, -est**) court; (*person, distance*) petit; (*syllable*) bref; (*curt, impatient*) brusque; **s. time** *or* **while ago** il y a peu de temps; **s. cut** raccourci *m*; **to be s. of money/time** être à court d'argent/de temps; **we're s. of ten men** il nous manque dix hommes; **money/time is s.** l'argent/le temps manque; **not far s. of** pas loin de; **s. of** (*except*) sauf; **to be s. for** (*of name*) être l'abréviation *or* le diminutif de; **in s.** bref; **s. circuit** *El* court-circuit *m*; **s. list** liste *f* de candidats choisis; **– adv** **to cut s.** (*visit etc*) abréger; (*person*) couper la parole à; **to go** *or* **get** *or* **run s.** manquer de; **to get** *or* **run s.** manquer de; **to stop s.** s'arrêter net; **– n** *El* court-circuit *m*; (**a pair of**) **shorts** un short. ◆**shorten** *vt* (*visit, line, dress etc*) raccourcir. ◆**shortly** *adv* (*soon*) bientôt; **s. after** peu après. ◆**shortness** *n* (*of person*) petitesse *f*; (*of hair, stick, legs*) manque *m* de longueur.

shortage [ʃɔːtɪdʒ] *n* manque *m*, pénurie *f*; (*crisis*) crise *f*.

shortbread [ʃɔːtbred] *n* sablé *m*. ◆**short-'change** *vt* (*buyer*) ne pas rendre juste à. ◆**short-'circuit** *vt El & Fig* court-circuiter. ◆**shortcoming** *n* défaut *m*.

◆**shortfall** *n* manque *m*. ◆**shorthand** *n* sténo *f*; **s. typist** sténodactylo *f*. ◆**short-'handed** *a* à court de personnel. ◆**short-'lived** *a* éphémère. *Fig* imprévoyant. ◆**short-'sighted** *a* myope; *Fig* imprévoyant. ◆**short-'sightedness** *n* myopie *f*; imprévoyance *f*. ◆**short-'sleeved** *a* à manches courtes. ◆**short-'staffed** *a* à court de personnel. ◆**short-'term** *a* à court terme.

shortening [ʃɔːt(ə)nɪŋ] *n Culin* matière *f* grasse.

shot [ʃɒt] *see* **shoot¹**; **–** *n* coup *m*; (*bullet*) balle *f*; *Cin Phot* prise *f* de vues; (*injection*) *Med* piqûre *f*; **a good s.** (*person*) un bon tireur; **to have a s. at** (*doing*) essayer de faire qch; **a long s.** (*attempt*) un coup à tenter; *Fam* gros bonnet *m*; **like a s.** (*at once*) tout de suite; **to be s. of** (*rid of*) *Fam* être débarrassé de. ◆**shotgun** *n* fusil *m* de chasse.

should [ʃʊd, *unstressed* ʃəd] *v aux* **1** (= *ought to*) **you s. do it** vous devriez le faire; **I s. have stayed** j'aurais dû rester; **that s. be Pauline** ça doit être Pauline. **2** (= *would*) **I s. like to** j'aimerais bien; **it's strange she s. say no** il est étrange qu'elle dise non. **3** (*possibility*) **if he s. come** s'il vient; **s. I be free** si je suis libre.

shoulder [ʃəʊldər] **1** *n* épaule *f*; **to have round shoulders** avoir le dos voûté, être voûté; (**hard**) **s.** (*of motorway*) accotement *m* stabilisé; **s. bag** sac *m* à bandoulière; **s.-length hair** cheveux *mpl* mi-longs. **2** *vt* (*responsibility*) endosser, assumer.

shout [ʃaʊt] *n* cri *m*; **to give s.o. a s.** appeler qn; **– vi** **to s.** (**out**) crier; **to s. at** *or* **to s.o.** faire qch à qn de faire; **to s. at s.o.** (*scold*) crier après qn; **– vt** **to s.** (**out**) (*insult etc*) crier; **to s. down** (*speaker*) huer. ◆**–ing** *n* (*shouts*) cris *mpl*.

shove [ʃʌv] *n* poussée *f*; **to give a s.** (**to**) pousser; **– vt** pousser; (*put*) mettre; **to s. sth into** (*thrust*) enfoncer *or* fourrer qch dans; **to s. s.o. around** *Fam* régenter qn; **– vi** pousser; **to s. off** (*leave*) *Fam* ficher le camp, filer; **to s. over** (*move over*) *Fam* se pousser.

shovel [ʃʌv(ə)l] *n* pelle *f*; **– vt** (**-ll-**, *Am* **-l-**) (*grain etc*) pelleter; **to s. up** *or* **away** (*remove*) enlever à la pelle; **to s. sth into** (*thrust*) *Fam* fourrer qch dans.

show [ʃəʊ] **1** *n* (*of joy, force*) démonstration *f* (**of** de); (*semblance*) semblant *m* (**of** de); (*ostentation*) parade *f*; (*sight*) & *Th* spectacle *m*; (*performance*) *Cin* séance *f*; (*exhibition*) exposition *f*; **the Boat/Motor S.** le

Salon de la Navigation/de l'Automobile; **horse** s. concours *m* hippique; **to give a good s.** Sp Mus Th jouer bien; **good s.!** bravo!; **(just) for s.** pour l'effet; **on s.** (*painting etc*) exposé; **s. business** le monde du spectacle; **s. flat** appartement *m* témoin; – *vt* (*pt* showed, *pp* shown) montrer (**to** à, **that** que); (*exhibit*) exposer; (*film*) passer, donner; (*indicate*) indiquer, montrer; **to s. s.o. to the door** reconduire qn; **it (just) goes to s. that...** ça (dé)montre (bien) que...; **I'll s. him or her!** *Fam* je lui apprendrai!; – *vi* (*be seen*) se voir; (*of film*) passer; **'now showing'** Cin 'à l'affiche' (**at** à). ■ **to s. (a)round** *vt* faire visiter; **he or she was shown a(round the house** on lui a fait visiter la maison; **to s. in** *vt* faire entrer; **to s. off** *vt* Pej étaler; (*highlight*) faire valoir; – *vi* Pej crâner. ◆**s.-off** *n* Pej crâneur, -euse *mf*; **to s. out** (*visitor*) reconduire; **to s. up** *vt* (*fault*) faire ressortir; (*humiliate*) faire honte à; – *vi* ressortir (**against** contre); (*of error*) être visible; (*of person*) *Fam* arriver, s'amener. ◆**showing** *n* (*of film*) projection *f* (**of** de); (*performance*) Cin séance *f*; (*of team, player*) performance *f*.

showcase [ˈʃəʊkeɪs] *n* vitrine *f*. ◆**showdown** *n* confrontation *f*, conflit *m*. ◆**showgirl** *n* (*in chorus etc*) girl *f*. ◆**showjumping** *n* Sp jumping *m*. ◆**showmanship** *n* art *m* de la mise en scène. ◆**showpiece** *n* modèle *m* du genre. ◆**showroom** *n* (*for cars etc*) salle *f* d'exposition.

shower [ˈʃaʊər] *n* (*of rain*) averse *f*, (*of blows*) déluge *m*; (*bath*) douche *f*; (*party*) *Am* réception *f* (*pour la remise de cadeaux*); – *vt* **to s. s.o. with** (*gifts, abuse*) couvrir qn de. ◆**showery** *a* pluvieux.

shown [ʃəʊn] *see* show.

showy [ˈʃəʊɪ] *a* (**-ier, -iest**) (*colour, hat*) voyant; (*person*) prétentieux.

shrank [ʃræŋk] *see* shrink 1.

shrapnel [ˈʃræpn(ə)l] *n* éclats *mpl* d'obus.

shred [ʃred] *n* lambeau *m*; (*of truth*) Fig grain *m*; **not a s. of evidence** pas la moindre preuve; – *vt* (**-dd-**) mettre en lambeaux; (*cabbage, carrots*) râper. ◆**shredder** *n* Culin râpe *f*.

shrew [ʃruː] *n* (*woman*) Pej mégère *f*.

shrewd [ʃruːd] *a* (**-er, -est**) (*person, plan*) astucieux. ◆**-ly** *adv* astucieusement. ◆**-ness** *n* astuce *f*.

shriek [ʃriːk] *n* cri *m* (aigu); – *vti* crier; **to s. with pain/laughter** hurler de douleur/de rire.

shrift [ʃrɪft] *n* **to get short s.** être traité sans ménagement.

shrill [ʃrɪl] *a* (**-er, -est**) aigu, strident.

shrimp [ʃrɪmp] *n* crevette *f*; (*person*) Pej nabot, -ote *mf*; (*child*) Pej puce *f*.

shrine [ʃraɪn] *n* lieu *m* saint; (*tomb*) châsse *f*.

shrink [ʃrɪŋk] **1** *vi* (*pt* shrank, *pp* shrunk or shrunken) (*of clothes*) rétrécir; (*of aging person*) se tasser; (*of amount, audience etc*) diminuer; **to s. from** reculer devant (**doing** l'idée de faire); – *vt* rétrécir. **2** *n* (*person*) *Am Hum* psy(chiatre) *m*. ◆**-age** *n* rétrécissement *m*; diminution *f*.

shrivel [ˈʃrɪv(ə)l] *vi* (**-ll-**, *Am* **-l-**) **to s. (up)** se ratatiner; – *vt* **to s. (up)** ratatiner.

shroud [ʃraʊd] *n* linceul *m*; (*of mystery*) Fig voile *m*; – *vt* **shrouded in mist** enseveli sous la brume; **shrouded in mystery** enveloppé de mystère.

Shrove Tuesday [ʃrəʊvˈtjuːzdɪ] *n* Mardi *m* gras.

shrub [ʃrʌb] *n* arbrisseau *m*.

shrug [ʃrʌg] *vt* (**-gg-**) **to s. one's shoulders** hausser les épaules; **to s. off** (*dismiss*) écarter (dédaigneusement); – *n* haussement *m* d'épaules.

shrunk(en) [ˈʃrʌŋk(ən)] *see* shrink 1.

shudder [ˈʃʌdər] *vi* frémir (**with** de); (*of machine etc*) vibrer; – *n* frémissement *m*; vibration *f*.

shuffle [ˈʃʌf(ə)l] **1** *vti* **to s. (one's feet)** traîner les pieds. **2** *vt* (*cards*) battre.

shun [ʃʌn] *vt* (**-nn-**) fuir, éviter; **to s. doing** éviter de faire.

shunt [ʃʌnt] *vt* (*train, conversation*) aiguiller (**on to** sur); **we were shunted (to and fro)** *Fam* on nous a baladés (**from office to office/etc** de bureau en bureau/etc).

shush! [ʃʊʃ] *int* chut!

shut [ʃʌt] *vt* (*pt & pp* shut, *pp* shutting) fermer; **to s. one's finger in** (*door etc*) se prendre le doigt dans; **to s. away or in** (*lock away or in*) enfermer; **to s. down** fermer; **to s. off** fermer; (*engine*) arrêter; (*isolate*) isoler; **to s. out** (*light*) empêcher d'entrer; (*view*) boucher; (*exclude*) exclure (**of, from** de); **to s. s.o. out** (*lock out accidentally*) enfermer qn dehors; **to s. up** fermer; (*lock up*) enfermer (*personne, objet précieux etc*); (*silence*) *Fam* faire taire; – *vi* (*of door etc*) se fermer; (*of shop, museum etc*) fermer; **the door doesn't s.** la porte ne ferme pas; **to s. down** fermer (*définitivement*); **to s. up** (*be quiet*) *Fam* se taire. ◆**shutdown** *n* fermeture *f*.

shutter [ˈʃʌtər] *n* volet *m*; (*of camera*) obturateur *m*.

shuttle [ˈʃʌt(ə)l] n (bus, spacecraft etc) navette f; (in vehicle etc) transporter.
shuttlecock n (in badminton) volant m.

shy [ʃaɪ] a (-er, -est) timide; **to be s.** of doing avoir peur de faire; – vi **to s. away** reculer (**from** s.o. devant qn, **from** doing à l'idée de faire). ◆—**ness** n timidité f.

Siamese [saɪəˈmiːz] a siamois; **S. twins** frères mpl siamois, sœurs fpl siamoises.

sibling [ˈsɪblɪŋ] n frère m, sœur f.

Sicily [ˈsɪsɪlɪ] n Sicile f.

sick [sɪk] a (-er, -est) (ill) malade; (mind) malsain; (humour) noir; (cruel) sadique; **to be s.** (vomit) vomir; **to be off** or **away s., to be on s. leave** être en congé de maladie; **to feel s.** avoir mal au cœur; **to be s. (and tired) of** Fam en avoir marre de; **he makes me s.** Fam il m'écœure; – n the s. les malades mpl; – vi (vomit) Fam vomir; – vt **to s. sth up** Fam vomir qch. ◆**sickbay** n infirmerie f. ◆**sickbed** n lit m de malade. ◆**sickly** a (-ier, -iest) maladif; (pale, faint) pâle; (taste) écœurant. ◆**sickness** n maladie f; (vomiting) vomissement(s) m(pl); **motion s.** Aut mal m de la route.

sicken [ˈsɪkən] **1** vt écœurer. **2** vi **to be sickening for** (illness) couver. ◆—**ing** a écœurant.

side [saɪd] n côté m; (of hill, animal) flanc m; (of road, river) bord m; (of beef) quartier m; (of question) aspect m; (of character) facette f, aspect m; Sp équipe f; Pol parti m; **the right s.** (of fabric) l'endroit m; **the wrong s.** (of fabric) l'envers m; **by the s. of** (nearby) à côté de; **at** or **by my s.** à côté de moi, à mes côtés; **s. by s.** l'un à côté de l'autre; **to move to one s.** s'écarter; **on this s.** de ce côté; **on the other s.** de l'autre côté; **the other s.** TV Fam l'autre chaîne f; **on the big/etc s.** Fam plutôt grand/etc; **to take sides with** se ranger du côté de; **on our s.** de notre côté, avec nous; **on the s.** Fam (secretly) en catimini; (to make money) en plus; – a (lateral) latéral; (effect, issue) secondaire; (glance, view) de côté; (street) transversal; – vi **to s. with** se ranger du côté de. ◆—**sided** suffix ten-s. à dix côtés. ◆**sideboard 1** n buffet m. **2** npl (hair) pattes fpl. ◆**sideburns** npl (hair) Am pattes fpl. ◆**sidecar** n side-car m. ◆**sidekick** n Fam associé, -ée f. ◆**sidelight** n Aut feu m de position. ◆**sideline** n activité f secondaire. ◆**sidesaddle** adv (to ride) en amazone. ◆**sidestep** vt (-pp-) éviter. ◆**sidetrack** vt **to get sidetracked**

s'écarter du sujet. ◆**sidewalk** n Am trottoir m. ◆**sideways** adv & a de côté.

siding [ˈsaɪdɪŋ] n Rail voie f de garage.

sidle [ˈsaɪd(ə)l] vi **to s. up to** s.o. s'approcher furtivement de qn.

siege [siːdʒ] n Mil siège m.

siesta [sɪˈestə] n sieste f.

sieve [sɪv] n tamis m; (for liquids) Culin passoire f; – vt tamiser. ◆**sift** vt tamiser; **to s. out** (truth) Fig dégager; – vi **to s. through** (papers etc) examiner (à la loupe).

sigh [saɪ] n soupir m; – vti soupirer.

sight [saɪt] n vue f; (spectacle) spectacle m; (on gun) mire f; **to lose s. of** perdre de vue; **to catch s. of** apercevoir; **to come into s.** apparaître; **at first s.** à première vue; **by s.** de vue; **on** or **at s.** à vue; **in s.** (target, end, date etc) en vue; **keep out of s.!** ne te montre pas!; **he hates the s. of me** il ne peut pas me voir; **it's a lovely s.** c'est beau à voir; **the (tourist) sights** les attractions fpl touristiques; **to set one's sights on** (job etc) viser; **a s. longer/etc** Fam bien plus long/etc; (land) apercevoir. ◆—**ed** a qui voit, clairvoyant. ◆—**ing** n **to make a s.** of voir. ◆**sightseer** n touriste mf. ◆**sightseeing** n tourisme m.

sightly [ˈsaɪtlɪ] a **not very s.** laid.

sign [saɪn] **1** n signe m; (notice) panneau m; (over shop, inn) enseigne f; **no s. of** aucune trace de; **to use s. language** parler par signes. **2** vt (put signature to) signer; **to s. away** or **over** céder (**to** à); **to s. on** or **up** (worker, soldier) engager; – vi signer; **to s. for** (letter) signer la reçu de; **to s. in** signer le registre; **to s. off** dire au revoir; **to s. on** (on the dole) s'inscrire au chômage; **to s. on** or **up** (soldier, worker) s'engager; (for course) s'inscrire. ◆**signpost** n poteau m indicateur; – vt flécher.

signal [ˈsɪgnəl] n signal m; **traffic signals** feux mpl de circulation; **s. box,** Am **s. tower** Rail poste m d'aiguillage; – vt (-ll-, Am -l-) (message) communiquer (**to** à); (arrival etc) signaler (**to** à); – vi faire des signaux; **to s. (to)** s.o. **to do** faire signe à qn de faire. ◆**signalman** n (pl -men) Rail aiguilleur m.

signature [ˈsɪgnətʃər] n signature f; **s. tune** indicatif m (musical). ◆**signatory** n signataire mf.

signet ring [ˈsɪgnɪtrɪŋ] n chevalière f.

significant [sɪgˈnɪfɪkənt] a (meaningful) significatif; (important, large) important. ◆**significance** n (meaning) signification f; (importance) importance f. ◆**significantly** adv (appreciably) sensiblement; **s.,**

he . . . fait significatif, il . . . . ◆'signify vt (mean) signifier (that que); (make known) indiquer, signifier (to à).

silence ['saɪləns] n silence m; in s. en silence; – vt faire taire. ◆silencer n (on car, gun) silencieux m. ◆silent a silencieux; (film, anger) muet; to keep or be s. garder le silence (about sur). ◆silently adv silencieusement.

silhouette [sɪluːˈet] n silhouette f. ◆silhouetted a to be s. against se profiler contre.

silicon ['sɪlɪkən] n silicium m; s. chip puce f de silicium. ◆silicone ['sɪlɪkəʊn] n silicone f.

silk [sɪlk] n soie f. ◆silky a (-ier, -iest) soyeux.

sill [sɪl] n (of window etc) rebord m.

silly ['sɪlɪ] a (-ier, -iest) idiot, bête; to do sth s. faire une bêtise; s. fool, Fam s. billy idiot, -ote mf; – adv (to act, behave) bêtement.

silo ['saɪləʊ] n (pl -os) silo m.

silt [sɪlt] n vase f.

silver ['sɪlvər] n argent m; (silverware) argenterie f; £5 in s. 5 livres en pièces d'argent; – a (spoon etc) d'argent, d'argent; (hair, colour) argenté; s. jubilee vingt-cinquième anniversaire m (d'un événement); s. paper papier m d'argent; s. plate argenterie f. ◆s.-'plated a plaqué argent. ◆silversmith n orfèvre m. ◆silverware n argenterie f. ◆silvery a (colour) argenté.

similar ['sɪmɪlər] a semblable (to à). ◆simi'larity n ressemblance f (between entre, to avec). ◆similarly adv de la même façon; (likewise) de même.

simile ['sɪmɪlɪ] n Liter comparaison f.

simmer ['sɪmər] vi Culin mijoter, cuire à feu doux; (of water) frémir; (of revolt, hatred etc) couver; to s. with (rage) bouillir de; to s. down (calm down) Fam se calmer; – vt faire cuire à feu doux; (water) laisser frémir.

simper ['sɪmpər] vi minauder.

simple ['sɪmp(ə)l] a (-er, -est) (plain, uncomplicated, basic etc) simple. ◆s.-'minded a simple d'esprit. ◆s.-'mindedness n simplicité f d'esprit. ◆simpleton n nigaud, -aude mf. ◆sim'plicity n simplicité f. ◆simplifi'cation n simplification f. ◆simplify vt simplifier. ◆sim'plistic a simpliste. ◆simply adv (plainly, merely) simplement; (absolutely) absolument.

simulate ['sɪmjʊleɪt] vt simuler.

simultaneous [sɪməlˈteɪnɪəs, Am saɪməl-

'teɪnɪəs] a simultané. ◆—ly adv simultanément.

sin [sɪn] n péché m; – vi (-nn-) pécher.

since [sɪns] 1 prep (in time) depuis; s. my departure depuis mon départ; – conj depuis que; s. she's been here depuis qu'elle est ici; it's a year s. I saw him ça fait un an que je ne l'ai pas vu; – adv (ever) s. depuis. 2 conj (because) puisque.

sincere [sɪnˈsɪər] a sincère. ◆sincerely adv sincèrement; yours s. (in letter) Com veuillez croire à mes sentiments dévoués. ◆sin'cerity n sincérité f.

sinew ['sɪnjuː] n Anat tendon m.

sinful ['sɪnfəl] a (guilt-provoking) coupable; (shocking) scandaleux; he's s. c'est un pécheur; that's s. c'est un péché.

sing [sɪŋ] vti (pt sang, pp sung) chanter; to s. up chanter plus fort. ◆—ing n (of bird & musical technique) chant m; (way of singing) façon f de chanter; – a (lesson, teacher) de chant. ◆—er n chanteur, -euse mf.

singe [sɪndʒ] vt (cloth) roussir; (hair) brûler; to s. s.o.'s hair (at hairdresser's) faire une brûlage à qn.

single ['sɪŋg(ə)l] a (only one) seul; (room, bed) pour une personne; (unmarried) célibataire; s. ticket billet m simple; every s. day tous les jours sans exception; s. party Pol parti m unique; – n (ticket) aller m (simple); (record) 45 tours m inv; pl Tennis simples mpl; singles bar bar m pour célibataires; – vt to s. out (choose) choisir. ◆s.-'breasted a (jacket) droit. ◆s.-'decker n (bus) autobus m sans impériale. ◆s.-'handed a sans aide. ◆s.-'minded a (person) résolu, qui n'a qu'une idée en tête. ◆singly adv (one by one) un à un.

singlet ['sɪŋglɪt] n (garment) maillot m de corps.

singsong ['sɪŋsɒŋ] n to get together for a s. se réunir pour chanter.

singular ['sɪŋgjʊlər] 1 a (unusual) singulier. 2 a Gram (form) singulier; (noun) au singulier; – n Gram singulier m; in the s. au singulier.

sinister ['sɪnɪstər] a sinistre.

sink[1] [sɪŋk] n (in kitchen) évier m; (washbasin) lavabo m.

sink[2] [sɪŋk] vi (pt sank, pp sunk) (of ship, person etc) couler; (of sun, price, water level) baisser; (collapse, subside) s'affaisser; to s. (down) into (mud etc) s'enfoncer dans; (armchair etc) s'affaler dans; to s. in (of ink etc) pénétrer; (of fact etc) Fam rentrer (dans le crâne); **has that sunk in?** *Fam* as-tu compris ça?; − *vt* (*ship*) couler; (*well*) creuser; **to s. into** (*thrust*) enfoncer dans; (*money*) *Com* investir dans; **a sinking feeling** un serrement de cœur.

sinner ['sɪnər] *n* pécheur *m*, pécheresse *f*.

sinuous ['sɪnjʊəs] *a* sinueux.

sinus ['saɪnəs] *n Anat* sinus *m inv*.

sip [sɪp] *vi* (**-pp-**) boire à petites gorgées; − *n* (*mouthful*) petite gorgée *f*; (*drop*) goutte *f*.

siphon ['saɪfən] *n* siphon *m*; − *vt* **to s. off** (*petrol*) siphonner; (*money*) *Fig* détourner.

sir [sɜːr] *n* monsieur *m*; **S. Walter Raleigh** (*title*) sir Walter Raleigh.

siren ['saɪərən] *n* (*of factory etc*) sirène *f*.

sirloin ['sɜːlɔɪn] *n* (*steak*) faux-filet *m*; (*joint*) aloyau *m*.

sissy ['sɪsɪ] *n* (*boy, man*) *Fam* femmelette *f*.

sister ['sɪstər] *n* sœur *f*; (*nurse*) infirmière *f* en chef. ◆**s.-in-law** *n* (*pl* sisters-in-law) belle-sœur *f*. ◆**sisterly** *a* fraternel.

sit [sɪt] *vi* (*pp & pt* sat, *pres p* sitting) s'asseoir; (*for artist*) poser (**for** pour); (*remain*) rester; (*of assembly etc*) siéger, être en séance; **to be sitting** (*of person, cat etc*) être assis; (*of bird*) être perché; **she sat** *or* **was sitting reading** elle était assise à lire; **to s. around** (*do nothing*) ne rien faire; **to s. back** (*in chair*) se caler; (*rest*) se reposer; (*do nothing*) ne rien faire; **to s. down** s'asseoir; **s.-down strike** grève *f* sur le tas; **to s. in on** (*discussion*) assister à; **to s. on** (*jury etc*) être membre de; (*fact etc*) *Fam* garder pour soi; **to s. through** *or* **out** (*film etc*) rester jusqu'au bout de; **to s. up** (*straight*) s'asseoir (bien droit); **to s. up waiting for s.o.** (*at night*) ne pas se coucher en attendant qn; − *vt* ne pas s.o. coucher asseoir qn; **to s. (for)** (*exam*) se présenter à; **to s. out** (*event, dance*) ne pas prendre part à. ◆**sitting** *n* séance *f*; (*for one's portrait*) séance *f* de pose; (*in restaurant*) service *m*; − *a* (*committee etc*) en séance; **s. duck** *Fam* victime *f* facile; **s. tenant** locataire *mf* en possession des lieux. ◆**sitting room** *n* salon *m*.

site [saɪt] *n* emplacement *m*; (*archaeological*) site *m*; (*building*) chantier *m*; **launching s.** aire *f* de lancement; − *vt* (*building*) placer.

sit-in ['sɪtɪn] *n Pol* sit-in *m inv*.

sitter ['sɪtər] *n* (*for child*) baby-sitter *mf*.

situate ['sɪtʃʊeɪt] *vt* situer; **to be situated** être situé. ◆**situ'ation** *n* situation *f*.

six [sɪks] *a & n* six (*m*). ◆**six'teen** *a & n* seize (*m*). ◆**six'teenth** *a & n* seizième (*mf*). ◆**sixth** *a & n* sixième (*mf*); (**lower**) s.

form *Sch* = classe *f* de première; (**upper**) s. **form** *Sch* = classe *f* terminale; **a s.** (*fraction*) un sixième. ◆**sixtieth** *a & n* soixantième (*mf*). ◆**sixty** *a & n* soixante (*m*).

size [saɪz] **1** *n* (*of person, animal, garment etc*) taille *f*; (*measurements*) dimensions *fpl*; (*of egg, packet*) grosseur *f*; (*of book*) grandeur *f*, format *m*; (*of problem, town, damage*) importance *f*, étendue *f*; (*of sum, amount*) importance *f*; (*of shoes, gloves*) pointure *f*; (*of shirt*) encolure *f*; **hip/chest/s.** tour *m* de hanches/de poitrine; **it's the s. of** ... c'est grand comme .... **2** (*glue*) colle *f*. **3** *vt* **to s. up** (*person*) jauger; (*situation*) évaluer. ◆**sizeable** *a* assez grand *or* gros.

sizzl/e ['sɪz(ə)l] *vi* grésiller. ◆**-ing** *a* s. (**hot**) brûlant.

skat/e¹ [skeɪt] *n* patin *m*; − *vi* patiner. ◆**-ing** *n* patinage *m*; **to go s.** faire du patinage; **s. rink** (*ice*) patinoire *f*; (*roller*) skating *m*. ◆**skateboard** *n* skateboard *m*. ◆**skater** *n* patineur, -euse *mf*.

skate² [skeɪt] *n* (*fish*) raie *f*.

skedaddle [skɪˈdæd(ə)l] *vi Fam* déguerpir.

skein [skeɪn] *n* (*of yarn*) écheveau *m*.

skeleton ['skelɪt(ə)n] *n* squelette *m*; − *a* (*crew, staff*) (réduit au) minimum; **s. key** passe-partout *m inv*.

skeptic ['skeptɪk] *Am* = **sceptic**.

sketch [sketʃ] *n* (*drawing*) croquis *m*, esquisse *f*; *Th* sketch *m*; **a rough s.** of (*plan*) *Fig* une esquisse de; − *vt* **to s. (out)** (*view, idea etc*) esquisser; **to s. in** (*details*) ajouter; − *vi* faire un *or* des croquis. ◆**sketchy** *a* (**-ier, -iest**) incomplet, superficiel.

skew [skjuː] *n* **on the s.** de travers.

skewer ['skjuər] *n* (*for meat etc*) broche *f*; (*for kebab*) brochette *f*.

ski [skiː] *n* (*pl* **skis**) ski *m*; **s. lift** télésiège *m*; **s. pants** fuseau *m*; **s. run** piste *f* de ski; **s. tow** téleski *m*; − *vi* (*pt* **skied** [skiːd], *pres p* **skiing**) faire du ski. ◆**-ing** *n Sp* ski *m*; − *a* (*school, clothes*) de ski. ◆**-er** *n* skieur, -euse *mf*.

skid [skɪd] **1** *vi* (**-dd-**) *Aut* déraper; **to s. into** déraper et heurter; − *n* dérapage *m*. **2** *a* **s. row** *Am* quartier *m* de clochards *or* de squats.

skill [skɪl] *n* habileté *f*, adresse *f* (**at** à); (*technique*) technique *f*; **one's skills** (*aptitudes*) ses compétences *fpl*. ◆**skilful**, *Am* ◆**skillful** *a* habile (**at doing** à faire, **at sth** en qch). ◆**skilled** *a* habile (**at doing** à faire, **at sth** en qch); (*worker*) qualifié; (*work*) de spécialiste, de professionnel.

skillet ['skɪlɪt] *n Am* poêle *f* (à frire).

skim [skɪm] **1** *vt* (**-mm-**) (*milk*) écrémer;

(soup) écumer. **2** *vti* (**-mm-**) to s. (over) (surface) effleurer; to s. through (book) parcourir.

skimp [skɪmp] *vi* (on fabric, food etc) lésiner (on sur). ◆**skimpy** *a* (**-ier, -iest**) (clothes) étriqué; (meal) insuffisant.

skin [skɪn] *n* peau *f*; **he has thick s.** *Fig* c'est un dur; **s. diving** plongée *f* sous-marine; **s. test** cuti-(réaction) *f*; – *vt* (**-nn-**) (animal) écorcher; (fruit) peler. ◆**s.-'deep** *a* superficiel. ◆**s.-'tight** *a* moulant, collant. ◆**skinflint** ['skɪnflɪnt] *n* avare *mf*.

skinhead ['skɪnhed] *n* skinhead *m*, jeune voyou *m*.

skinny ['skɪnɪ] *a* (**-ier, -iest**) maigre.

skint [skɪnt] *a* (penniless) *Fam* fauché.

skip [skɪp] **1** *vi* (**-pp-**) (jump) sauter; (hop about) sautiller; (with rope) sauter à la corde; to s. off (leave) *Fam* filer; **skipping rope** corde *f* à sauter; – *n* petit saut *m*. **2** *vt* (**-pp-**) (omit, miss) sauter; to s. classes sécher les cours; s. it! (forget) *Fam* laisse tomber!

skip[2] [skɪp] *n* (container for debris) benne *f*.

skipper ['skɪpər] *n Nau Sp* capitaine *m*.

skirmish ['skɜːmɪʃ] *n* accrochage *m*.

skirt [skɜːt] **1** *n* jupe *f*. **2** *vt* to s. round contourner; **skirting board** (on wall) plinthe *f*.

skit [skɪt] *n Th* pièce *f* satirique; **a s. on** une parodie de.

skittle ['skɪt(ə)l] *n* quille *f*; *pl* (game) jeu *m* de quilles.

skiv/e [skaɪv] *vi* (skirk) *Fam* tirer au flanc; to s. off (slip away) *Fam* se défiler. ◆**-er** *n Fam* tire-au-flanc *m inv*.

skivvy ['skɪvɪ] *n Pej Fam* bonne *f* à tout faire, bon(n)iche *f*.

skulk [skʌlk] *vi* rôder (furtivement).

skull [skʌl] *n* crâne *m*. ◆**skullcap** *n* calotte *f*.

skunk [skʌŋk] *n* (animal) mouffette *f*; (person) *Pej* salaud *m*.

sky [skaɪ] *n* ciel *m*. ◆**skydiving** *n* parachutisme *m* (en chute libre). ◆**sky-'high** *a* (prices) exorbitant. ◆**skylight** *n* lucarne *f*. ◆**skyline** *n* (outline of buildings) ligne *f* d'horizon. ◆**skyrocket** *vi* (of prices) *Fam* monter en flèche. ◆**skyscraper** *n* gratte-ciel *m inv*.

slab [slæb] *n* (of concrete etc) bloc *m*; (thin, flat) plaque *f*; (of chocolate) tablette *f*, plaque *f*; (paving stone) dalle *f*.

slack [slæk] *a* (**-er, -est**) (knot, spring) lâche; (discipline, security) relâché, lâche; (trade, grip) faible, mou; (negligent) négligent; (worker, student) peu sérieux; **s. periods**

(weeks etc) périodes *fpl* creuses; (hours) heures *fpl* creuses; **to be s.** (of rope) avoir du mou; – *vi* to s. off (in effort) se relâcher. ◆**slacken** *vi* to s. (off) (in effort) se relâcher; (of production, speed, zeal) diminuer; – *vt* to s. (off) (rope) relâcher; (pace, effort) ralentir. ◆**slacker** *n* (person) *Fam* flemmard, -arde *mf*. ◆**slackly** *adv* (loosely) lâchement. ◆**slackness** *n* négligence *f*; (of discipline) relâchement *m*; (of rope) mou *m*; *Com* stagnation *f*.

slacks [slæks] *npl* pantalon *m*.

slag [slæg] *n* (immoral woman) *Sl* salope *f*, traînée *f*.

slagheap ['slæghɪp] *n* terril *m*.

slake [sleɪk] *vt* (thirst) *Lit* étancher.

slalom ['slɑːləm] *n Sp* slalom *m*.

slam [slæm] *vt* (**-mm-**) (door, lid) claquer; (hit) frapper violemment; to s. (down) (put down) poser violemment; **to s. on the brakes** écraser le frein, freiner à bloc; – *vi* (of door) claquer; – *n* claquement *m*. **2** *vt* (**-mm-**) (criticize) *Fam* critiquer (avec virulence).

slander ['slɑːndər] *n* diffamation *f*, calomnie *f*; – *vt* diffamer, calomnier.

slang [slæŋ] *n* argot *m*; – *a* (word etc) d'argot, argotique. ◆**slanging match** *n Fam* engueulade *f*.

slant [slɑːnt] *n* inclinaison *f*; (point of view) *Fig* angle *m* (on sur); (bias) *Fig* parti-pris *m*; **on a s.** penché; (roof) en pente; – *vi* (of writing) pencher; (of roof) être en pente; – *vt* (writing) faire pencher; (news) *Fig* présenter de façon partiale. ◆**-ed** *a*, ◆**-ing** *a* penché; (roof) en pente.

slap [slæp] **1** *n* tape *f*, claque *f*; (on face) gifle *f*; – *vt* (**-pp-**) donner une tape à; to s. s.o.'s face gifler qn; **to s. s.o.'s bottom** donner une fessée à qn. **2** *vt* (**-pp-**) (put) mettre, flanquer; to s. on (apply) appliquer à la va-vite; (add) ajouter. **3** *adv.* **s. in the middle** *Fam* en plein milieu. ◆**slapdash** *a* (person) négligent; (task) fait à la va-vite; – *adv* à la va-vite. ◆**slaphappy** *a Fam* (carefree) insouciant; (negligent) négligent. ◆**slapstick** *a* & *n* **s.** (comedy) grosse farce *f*. ◆**slap-up 'meal** *n Fam* gueuleton *m*.

slash [slæʃ] **1** *vt* (cut with blade etc) entailler, tailler; (sever) trancher; – *n* entaille *f*, taillade *f*. **2** *vt* (reduce) réduire radicalement; (prices) *Com* écraser.

slat [slæt] *n* (in blind) lamelle *f*.

slate [sleɪt] **1** *n* ardoise *f*. **2** *vt* (book etc) *Fam* critiquer, démolir.

slaughter ['slɔːtər] *vt* (people) massacrer;

(animal) abattre; − n massacre m; abbatage m. ◆**slaughterhouse** n abattoir m.

Slav [slɑːv] a & n slave (mf). ◆**Sla'vonic** a (language) slave.

slave [sleɪv] n esclave mf; **the s. trade** Hist la traite des noirs; **s. driver** Fig Pej négrier m; − vi **to s.** (**away**) se crever (au travail), bosser comme une bête; **to s. away doing** s'escrimer à faire. ◆**slavery** n esclavage m. ◆**slavish** a servile.

slaver ['slævər] vi (dribble) baver (**over** sur); − n bave f.

slay [sleɪ] vt (pt **slew**, pp **slain**) Lit tuer.

sleazy ['sliːzɪ] a (-**ier**, -**iest**) Fam sordide, immonde.

sledge [sledʒ] (Am **sled** [sled]) n luge f; (horse-drawn) traîneau m.

sledgehammer ['sledʒhæmər] n masse f.

sleek [sliːk] a (-**er**, -**est**) lisse, brillant; (manner) onctueux.

sleep [sliːp] n sommeil m; **to have a s., get some s.** dormir; **to send to s.** endormir; **to go or get to s.** s'endormir; **to go to s.** (of arm, foot) Fam s'engourdir; − vi (pt & pp **slept**) dormir; (spend the night) coucher; **s. tight or well!** dors bien!; **I'll s. on it** Fig je déciderai demain, la nuit portera conseil; − vt **this room sleeps six** on peut coucher or loger six personnes dans cette chambre; **to s. it off** Fam, **s. off a hangover** cuver son vin. ◆**—ing** a (asleep) endormi; **s. bag** sac m de couchage; **s. car** wagon-lit m; **s. pill** somnifère m; **s. quarters** chambre(s) f(pl), dortoir m. ◆**sleeper** n **1 to be a light/sound s.** avoir le sommeil léger/lourd. **2** Rail (on track) traverse f; (berth) couchette f; (train) train m à couchettes. ◆**sleepiness** n torpeur f. ◆**sleepless** a (hours) sans sommeil; (night) d'insomnie. ◆**sleepwalker** n somnambule mf. ◆**sleepwalking** n somnambulisme m. ◆**sleepy** a (-**ier**, -**iest**) (town, voice) endormi; **to be s.** (of person) avoir sommeil.

sleet [sliːt] n neige f fondue; (sheet of ice) Am verglas m; − vi **it's sleeting** il tombe de la neige fondue.

sleeve [sliːv] n (of shirt etc) manche f; (of record) pochette f; **up one's s.** (surprise, idea etc) Fig en réserve; **long-/short-sleeved** à manches longues/courtes.

sleigh [sleɪ] n traîneau m.

sleight [slaɪt] n **s. of hand** prestidigitation f.

slender ['slendər] a (person) mince, svelte; (neck, hand) fin; (feeble, small) Fig faible.

slept [slept] see **sleep**.

sleuth [sluːθ] n (detective) Hum (fin) limier m.

slew [sluː] n **a s. of** Am Fam un tas de, une tapée de.

slice [slaɪs] n tranche f; (portion) Fig partie f, part f; − vt **to s.** (**up**) couper (en tranches); **to s. off** (cut off) couper.

slick [slɪk] **1** a (-**er**, -**est**) (glib) qui a la parole facile; (manner) mielleux; (cunning) astucieux; (smooth, slippery) lisse. **2** n **oil s.** nappe f de pétrole; (large) marée f noire.

slid/e [slaɪd] n (act) glissade f; (in value etc) Fig (légère) baisse f; (in playground) toboggan m; (on ice) glissoire f; (for hair) barrette f; Phot diapositive f; (of microscope) lamelle f, lame f; **s. rule** règle f à calcul; − vi (pt & pp **slid**) glisser; **to s. into** (room etc) se glisser dans; − vt (letter etc) glisser (**into** dans); (table etc) faire glisser. ◆**—ing** a (door, panel) à glissière; (roof) ouvrant; **s. scale** Com échelle f mobile

slight [slaɪt] **1** a (-**er**, -**est**) (slim) mince; (frail) frêle; (intelligence) faible; **the slightest thing** la moindre chose; **not in the slightest** pas le moins du monde. **2** vt (offend) offenser; (ignore) bouder; − n affront m (**on** à). ◆**—ly** adv légèrement, un peu; **s. built** fluet.

slim [slɪm] a (slimmer, slimmest) mince; − vi (-**mm**-) maigrir. ◆**slimming** a (diet) amaigrissant; (food) qui ne fait pas grossir. ◆**slimness** n minceur f.

slime [slaɪm] n boue f (visqueuse); (of snail) bave f. ◆**slimy** a (-**ier**, -**iest**) (muddy) boueux; (sticky, smarmy) visqueux.

sling [slɪŋ] **1** n (weapon) fronde f; (toy) lance-pierres m inv; (for arm) Med écharpe f; **in a s.** en écharpe. **2** vt (pt & pp **slung**) (throw) jeter, lancer; (hang) suspendre; **to s. away or out** (throw out) Fam balancer. ◆**slingshot** n Am lance-pierres m inv.

slip [slɪp] **1** n (mistake) erreur f; (woman's undergarment) combinaison f; (of paper for filing) fiche f; **a s. of paper** (bit) un bout de papier; **a s.** (of the tongue) un lapsus; **to give s.o. the s.** fausser compagnie à qn; **s. road** Aut bretelle f. **2** vi (-**pp**-) glisser; **to s. into** (go, get) se glisser dans; (habit) prendre; (garment) mettre; **to let s.** (chance, oath, secret) laisser échapper; **to s. through** (crowd) se faufiler parmi; **to s. along or over to** faire un saut chez; **to s. away** (escape) s'esquiver; **to s. back/in** retourner/entrer furtivement; **to s. out** sortir furtivement; (pop out) sortir (un instant); (of secret) s'éventer; **to s. past** (guards) passer sans être vu de; **to s. up** (make a *mistake*) *Fam* gaffer; — *vt* (*slide*) glisser (**to à, into** dans); **it slipped his** *or* **her notice** ça lui a échappé; **it slipped his** *or* **her mind** ça lui est sorti de l'esprit; **to s. off** (*garment etc*) enlever; **to s. on** (*garment etc*) mettre. ◆**s.-up** *n Fam* gaffe *f*, erreur *f*.

slipcover ['slɪpkʌvər] *n Am* housse *f*.

slipper ['slɪpər] *n* pantoufle *f*.

slippery ['slɪpərɪ] *a* glissant.

slipshod ['slɪpʃɒd] *a* (*negligent*) négligent; (*slovenly*) négligé.

slit [slɪt] *n* (*opening*) fente *f*; (*cut*) coupure *f*; — *vt* (*pt & pp* **slit**, *pres p* **slitting**) (*cut*) couper; (*tear*) déchirer; **to s. open** (*sack*) éventrer.

slither ['slɪðər] *vi* glisser; (*of snake*) se couler.

sliver ['slɪvər] *n* (*of apple etc*) lichette *f*; (*of wood*) éclat *m*.

slob [slɒb] *n Fam* malotru *m*, goujat *m*.

slobber ['slɒbər] *vi* (*of dog etc*) baver (**over** sur); — *n* bave *f*.

slog [slɒg] **1** *n* **a** (**hard**) **s.** (*effort*) un gros effort; (*work*) un travail dur; — *vi* (**-gg-**) **to s.** (**away**) bosser, trimer. **2** *vt* (**-gg-**) (*hit*) frapper; — *n* coup *m*, marron *m*.

slogan ['sləʊgən] *n* slogan *m*.

slop [slɒp] *n* **slops** eaux *fpl* sales; — *vi* (**-pp-**) **to s.** (**over**) (*spill*) se répandre; — *vt* répandre.

slope [sləʊp] *n* pente *f*; (*of mountain*) flanc *m*; (*slant*) inclinaison *f*; — *vi* être en pente; (*of handwriting*) pencher; **to s. down** descendre en pente. ◆**-ing** *a* en pente; (*handwriting*) penché.

sloppy ['slɒpɪ] *a* (**-ier, -iest**) (*work, appearance*) négligé; (*person*) négligent; (*mawkish*) sentimental; (*wet*) détrempé; (*watery*) liquide.

slosh [slɒʃ] *vt* (*pour*) *Fam* répandre. ◆**-ed** *a* (*drunk*) *Fam* bourré.

slot [slɒt] *n* (*slit*) fente *f*; (*groove*) rainure *f*; (*in programme*) *Rad TV* créneau *m*; **s. machine** (*vending*) distributeur *m* automatique; (*gambling*) machine *f* à sous; — *vt* (**-tt-**) (*insert*) insérer (**into** dans); — *vi* s'insérer (**into** dans).

sloth [sləʊθ] *n Lit* paresse *f*.

slouch [slaʊtʃ] **1** *vi* ne pas se tenir droit; (*have stoop*) avoir le dos voûté; (*in chair*) se vautrer (**in** dans); **slouching over** (*desk etc*) penché sur; — *n* mauvaise tenue *f*; **with a s.** (*to walk*) en se tenant mal; le dos voûté. **2** *n Fam* (*person*) lourdaud, -aude *mf*; (*lazy*) paresseux, -euse *mf*.

slovenly ['slʌvənlɪ] *a* négligé. ◆**slovenli-**

ness *n* (*of dress*) négligé *m*; (*carelessness*) négligence *f*.

slow [sləʊ] *a* (**-er, -est**) lent; (*business*) calme; (*party, event*) ennuyeux; **at** (**a**) **s. speed** à vitesse réduite; **to be a s. walker** marcher lentement; **to be s.** (*of clock, watch*) retarder; **to be five minutes s.** retarder de cinq minutes; **to be s. to act** *or* **in acting** être lent à agir; **in s. motion** au ralenti; — *adv* lentement; — *vt* **to s. down** *or* **up** ralentir; (*delay*) retarder; — *vi* **to s. down** *or* **up** ralentir. ◆**-ly** *adv* lentement; (*bit by bit*) peu à peu. ◆**-ness** *n* lenteur *f*.

slowcoach ['sləʊkəʊtʃ] *n Fam* lambin, -ine *mf*. ◆**slow-down** *n* ralentissement *m*; **s.-down** (*strike*) *Am* grève *f* perlée. ◆**slow-'moving** *a* (*vehicle etc*) lent. ◆**slowpoke** *n Am Fam* lambin, -ine *mf*.

sludge [slʌdʒ] *n* gadoue *f*.

slue [sluː] *n Am Fam* = **slew**.

slug [slʌg] **1** *n* (*mollusc*) limace *f*. **2** *n* (*bullet*) *Am Fam* pruneau *m*. **3** *vt* (**-gg-**) (*hit*) *Am Fam* frapper; — *n* coup *m*, marron *m*.

sluggish ['slʌgɪʃ] *a* lent, mou.

sluice [sluːs] *n* **s.** (**gate**) vanne *f*.

slum [slʌm] *n* (*house*) taudis *m*; **the slums** les quartiers *mpl* pauvres; — *a* (*district*) pauvre; — *vt* (**-mm-**) **to s. it** *Fam* manger de la vache enragée. ◆**slummy** *a* (**-ier, -iest**) sordide, pauvre.

slumber ['slʌmbər] *n Lit* sommeil *m*.

slump [slʌmp] *n* baisse *f* soudaine (**in** de); (*in prices*) effondrement *m*; *Econ* crise *f*; — *vi* (*decrease*) baisser; (*of prices*) s'effondrer; **to s. into** (*armchair etc*) s'affaisser dans.

slung [slʌŋ] *see* **sling 2**.

slur [sl3ːr] **1** *vt* (**-rr-**) prononcer indistinctement; **to s. one's words** manger ses mots. **2** *n* **to cast a s. on** (*reputation etc*) porter atteinte à. ◆**slurred** *a* (*speech*) indistinct.

slush [slʌʃ] *n* (*snow*) neige *f* fondue; (*mud*) gadoue *f*. ◆**slushy** *a* (**-ier, -iest**) (*road*) couvert de neige fondue.

slut [slʌt] *n Pej* (*immoral*) salope *f*, traînée *f*; (*untidy*) souillon *f*.

sly [slaɪ] *a* (**-er, -est**) (*deceitful*) sournois; (*crafty*) rusé; — *n* **on the s.** en cachette. ◆**-ly** *adv* sournoisement; (*in secret*) en cachette.

smack [smæk] **1** *n* claque *f*, gifle *f*; fessée *f*; — *vt* donner une claque à; **to s. s.o.'s face** gifler qn; **to s.** (**'s bottom**) donner une fessée à qn. **2** *adv* **s. in the middle** *Fam* en plein milieu. **3** *vi* **to s. of** (*be suggestive of*) avoir des relents de. ◆**-ing** *n* fessée *f*.

small [smɔːl] *a* (**-er, -est**) petit; **in the s. hours** au petit matin; **s. talk** menus propos *mpl*; − *adv* (*to cut, chop*) menu; − *n* the s. of the back le creux *m* des reins. ◆**—ness** *n* petitesse *f*. ◆**smallholding** *n* petite ferme *f*. ◆**small-scale** *a* Fig peu important. ◆**small-time** *a* (*crook, dealer etc*) petit, sans grande envergure.

smallpox ['smɔːlpɒks] *n* petite vérole *f*.

smarmy ['smɑːmɪ] *a* (-ier, -iest) Pej Fam visqueux, obséquieux.

smart[1] [smɑːt] *a* (-er, -est) (*in appearance*) élégant; (*astute*) astucieux; (*clever*) intelligent; (*quick*) rapide; s. aleck Fam je-sais-tout *mf inv*. ◆**smarten** *vt* to s. up (*room etc*) embellir; − *vti* to s. (oneself) up (*make oneself spruce*) se faire beau, s'arranger. ◆**smartly** *adv* élégamment; (*quickly*) en vitesse; (*astutely*) astucieusement. ◆**smartness** *n* élégance *f*.

smart[2] [smɑːt] *vi* (*sting*) brûler, faire mal.

smash [smæʃ] *vt* (*break*) briser; (*shatter*) fracasser; (*enemy*) écraser; (*record*) pulvériser; to s. s.o.'s face (*in*) Fam casser la gueule à qn; to s. down or in (*door*) fracasser; to s. up (*car*) esquinter; (*room*) démolir; − *vi* se briser; to s. into (*of car*) se fracasser contre; − *n* (*noise*) fracas *m*; (*blow*) coup *m*; (*accident*) collision *f*; s. hit Fam succès *m* fou. ◆**s.-up** *n* collision *f*.

smashing ['smæʃɪŋ] *a* (*wonderful*) Fam formidable. ◆**smasher** *n* to be a (real) s. Fam être formidable.

smattering ['smætərɪŋ] *n* a s. of (*French etc*) quelques notions *fpl* de.

smear [smɪər] *vt* (*coat*) enduire (with de); (*stain*) tacher (with de); (*smudge*) faire une trace sur; − *n* (*mark*) trace *f*; (*stain*) tache *f*; Med frottis *m*; a s. on (*attack*) Fig une atteinte à; s. campaign campagne *f* de diffamation.

smell [smel] *n* odeur *f*; (*sense of*) odorat *m*; − *vt* (*pt & pp* smelled *or* smelt) sentir; (*of animal*) flairer; − *vi* (*stink*) sentir (mauvais); (*have smell*) avoir une odeur; to s. of smoke/*etc* sentir la fumée/*etc*; smelling salts sels *mpl*. ◆**smelly** *a* (-ier, -iest) to be s. sentir (mauvais).

smelt[1] [smelt] *see* smell.

smelt[2] [smelt] *vt* (*ore*) fondre; smelting works fonderie *f*.

smidgen ['smɪdʒən] *n* a s. (*a little*) Am Fam un brin (of de).

smil/e [smaɪl] *n* sourire *m*; − *vi* sourire (at s.o. à qn, at sth de qch). ◆**—ing** *a* souriant.

smirk [smɜːk] *n* (*smug*) sourire *m* suffisant; (*scornful*) sourire *m* goguenard.

smith [smɪθ] *n* (*blacksmith*) forgeron *m*.

smithereens [smɪðəˈriːnz] *npl* to smash to s. briser en mille morceaux.

smitten ['smɪt(ə)n] *a* s. with Hum (*desire, remorse*) pris de; (*in love with*) épris de.

smock [smɒk] *n* blouse *f*.

smog [smɒg] *n* brouillard *m* épais, smog *m*.

smoke [sməʊk] *n* fumée *f*; to have a s. fumer une cigarette *etc*; − *vt* (*cigarette, salmon etc*) fumer; to s. out (*room etc*) enfumer; − *vi* fumer; 'no smoking' 'défense de fumer'; smoking compartment Rail compartiment *m* fumeurs. ◆**smokeless** *a* s. fuel combustible *m* non polluant. ◆**smoker** *n* fumeur, -euse *mf*; Rail compartiment *m* fumeurs. ◆**smoky** *a* (-ier, -iest) (*air*) enfumé; (*wall*) noirci de fumée; it's s. here il y a de la fumée ici.

smooth [smuːð] *a* (-er, -est) (*surface, skin etc*) lisse; (*road*) à la surface égale; (*movement*) régulier, sans à-coups; (*flight*) agréable; (*cream, manners*) onctueux; (*person*) doucereux; (*sea*) calme; the s. running la bonne marche (of de); − *vt* to s. down *or* out lisser; to s. out *or* over (*problem etc*) Fig aplanir. ◆**—ly** *adv* (*to land, pass off*) en douceur. ◆**—ness** *n* aspect *m* lisse; (*of road*) surface *f* égale.

smother ['smʌðər] *vt* (*stifle*) étouffer; to s. with (*kisses etc*) Fig couvrir de.

smoulder ['sməʊldər] *vi* (*of fire, passion etc*) couver.

smudge [smʌdʒ] *n* tache *f*, bavure *f*; − *vt* (*paper etc*) faire des taches sur, salir.

smug [smʌg] *a* (smugger, smuggest) (*smile etc*) béat; (*person*) content de soi, suffisant. ◆**—ly** *adv* avec suffisance.

smuggl/e ['smʌg(ə)l] *vt* passer (en fraude); smuggled goods contrebande *f*. ◆**—ing** *n* contrebande *f*. ◆**—er** *n* contrebandier, -ière *mf*.

smut [smʌt] *n inv* (*obscenity*) saleté(s) *f(pl)*. ◆**smutty** *a* (-ier, -iest) (*joke etc*) cochon.

snack [snæk] *n* casse-croûte *m inv*; s. bar snack(-bar) *m*.

snafu [snæˈfuː] *n Sl* embrouillamini *m*.

snag [snæg] *n* 1 (*hitch*) inconvénient *m*, os *m*. 2 (*in cloth*) accroc *m*.

snail [sneɪl] *n* escargot *m*; at a s.'s pace comme une tortue.

snake [sneɪk] *n* (*reptile*) serpent *m*; − *vi* (*of river*) serpenter.

snap [snæp] 1 *vt* (-pp-) casser (avec un bruit sec); (*fingers, whip*) faire claquer; to s. up a bargain sauter sur une occasion; − *vi* se casser net; (*of whip*) claquer; (*of person*) Fig parler sèchement (at à); s. out of it! Fam secoue-toi!; − *n* claquement *m*, bruit *m* sec; *Phot* photo *f*; (*fastener*) *Am* bouton-pression *m*; **cold s.** Met coup *m* de froid. **2** *a* soudain, brusque; **to make a s. decision** décider sans réfléchir. ◆**snapshot** *n* photo *f*, instantané *m*.

snappy ['snæpɪ] *a* (**-ier, -iest**) (*pace*) vif; **make it s.!** *Fam* dépêche-toi!

snare [sneər] *n* piège *m*.

snarl [snɑːl] *vi* gronder (en montrant les dents); – *n* grondement *m*. ◆**s.-up** *n* *Aut* *Fam* embouteillage *m*.

snatch [snætʃ] *vt* saisir (*d'un geste vif*); (*some rest etc*) *Fig* (réussir à) prendre; **to s. sth from s.o.** arracher qch à qn; – *n* (*theft*) vol *m* (à l'arraché).

snatches ['snætʃɪz] *npl* (*bits*) fragments *mpl* (of).

snazzy ['snæzɪ] *a* (**-ier, -iest**) *Fam* (*flashy*) tapageur; (*smart*) élégant.

sneak [sniːk] **1** *vi* **to s. in/out** entrer/sortir furtivement; **to s. off** s'esquiver; – *a* (*attack, visit*) furtif. **2** *n* (*telltale*) *Sch* *Fam* rapporteur, -euse *mf*; – *vi* **to s. on** *Sch* *Fam* dénoncer. ◆**sneaking** *a* (*suspicion*) vague; (*desire*) secret. ◆**sneaky** *a* (**-ier, -iest**) (*sly*) *Fam* sournois.

sneaker ['sniːkər] *n* (*shoe*) tennis *f*.

sneer [snɪər] *n* ricanement *m*; – *vi* ricaner; **to s. at** se moquer de.

sneeze [sniːz] *n* éternuement *m*; – *vi* éternuer.

snicker ['snɪkər] *n* & *vi* *Am* = **snigger**.

snide [snaɪd] *a* (*remark etc*) sarcastique.

sniff [snɪf] *n* reniflement *m*; – *vt* renifler; (*of dog*) flairer, renifler; **to s. out** (*bargain*) *Fig* renifler; – *vi* **to s. (at)** renifler. ◆**sniffle** *vi* renifler; – *n* **a s., the sniffles** *Fam* un petit rhume.

snigger ['snɪgər] *n* (*petit*) ricanement *m*; – *vi* ricaner. ◆**-ing** *n* ricanement(s) *m(pl)*.

snip [snɪp] *n* (*piece*) petit bout *m* (coupé); (*bargain*) *Fam* bonne affaire *f*; **to make a s.** couper; – *vt* (**-pp-**) couper.

sniper ['snaɪpər] *n* *Mil* tireur *m* embusqué.

snippet ['snɪpɪt] *n* (*of conversation etc*) bribe *f*.

snivel ['snɪv(ə)l] *vi* (**-ll-**, *Am* **-l-**) pleurnicher. ◆**snivelling** *a* pleurnicheur.

snob [snɒb] *n* snob *mf*. ◆**snobbery** *n* snobisme *m*. ◆**snobbish** *a* snob *inv*.

snook [snuːk] *n* **to cock a s.** faire un pied de nez (à).

snooker ['snuːkər] *n* snooker *m*, sorte de jeu de billard.

snoop [snuːp] *vi* fourrer son nez partout; **to s. on s.o.** (*spy on*) espionner qn.

snooty ['snuːtɪ] *a* (**-ier, -iest**) *Fam* snob *inv*.

snooze [snuːz] *n* petit somme *m*; – *vi* faire un petit somme.

snor/e [snɔːr] *vi* ronfler; – *n* ronflement *m*. ◆**-ing** *n* ronflements *mpl*.

snorkel ['snɔːk(ə)l] *n* *Sp* *Nau* tuba *m*.

snort [snɔːt] *vi* (*grunt*) grogner; (*sniff*) renifler; (*of horse*) renâcler; – *n* (*grunt*) grognement *m*.

snot [snɒt] *n* *Pej* *Fam* morve *f*. ◆**snotty** *a* (**-ier, -iest**) *Fam* (*nose*) qui coule; (*child*) morveux. ◆**snotty-nosed** *a* *Fam* morveux.

snout [snaʊt] *n* museau *m*.

snow [snəʊ] *n* neige *f*; – *vi* neiger; – *vt* **to be snowed in** être bloqué par la neige; **to be s. under with** (*work etc*) être submergé de. ◆**snowball** *n* boule *f* de neige; – *vi* (*increase*) faire boule de neige. ◆**snowbound** *a* bloqué par la neige. ◆**snow-capped** *a* (*mountain*) enneigé. ◆**snowdrift** *n* congère *f*. ◆**snowdrop** *n* *Bot* perce-neige *m* or *f* *inv*. ◆**snowfall** *n* chute *f* de neige. ◆**snowflake** *n* flocon *m* de neige. ◆**snowman** *n* (*pl* **-men**) bonhomme *m* de neige. ◆**snowmobile** *n* motoneige *f*. ◆**snowplough** *n*, *Am* ◆**snowplow** *n* chasse-neige *m* *inv*. ◆**snowstorm** *n* tempête *f* de neige. ◆**snowy** *a* (**-ier, -iest**) (*weather, hills, day etc*) neigeux.

snub [snʌb] **1** *n* rebuffade *f*; – *vt* (**-bb-**) (*offer etc*) rejeter; **to s. s.o.** snober qn. **2** *a* (*nose*) retroussé.

snuff [snʌf] **1** *n* tabac *m* à priser. **2** *vt* **to s.** (*out*) (*candle*) moucher. ◆**snuffbox** *n* tabatière *f*.

snuffle ['snʌf(ə)l] *vi* & *n* = **sniffle**.

snug [snʌg] *a* (**snugger, snuggest**) (*house etc*) confortable, douillet; (*garment*) bien ajusté; **we're s.** (*in chair etc*) on est bien; **s. in bed** bien au chaud dans son lit.

snuggle ['snʌg(ə)l] *vi* **to s. up to** se peloton-ner contre.

so [səʊ] **1** *adv* (*to such a degree*) si, tellement (*that* que); (*thus*) ainsi, comme ça; **so that** (*purpose*) pour que (+ *sub*); (*result*) si bien que; **so as to do** pour faire; **I think so** je le pense, je pense que oui; **do so!** faites-le!; **if so** si oui; **is that so?** c'est vrai?; **so am I, so do I** *etc* moi aussi; **so much** (*to work etc*) tant, tellement (*that* que); **so much courage**/*etc* tant or tellement de courage/*etc* (*that* que); **so many** tant, tellement; **so many books**/*etc* tant de livres/*etc* (*that* que); **so very fast**/*etc* vraiment si vite/*etc*; **ten or so** environ dix; **so long!** *Fam* au revoir!; **and so on** et ainsi de suite. **2** *conj* (*therefore*) donc; (*in that case*) alors; **so what?** et alors? ◆**So-and-So** *n* Mr So-and-So Monsieur Un tel. ◆**so-'called** *a* soi-disant *inv*. ◆**so-so** *a* *Fam* comme ci comme ça.

soak [səʊk] *vt* (*drench*) tremper; (*washing, food*) faire tremper; **to s. up** absorber; – *vi* (*of washing etc*) tremper; **to s. in** (*of liquid*) s'infiltrer; – *n* to **give sth a s.** faire tremper qch. ◆**—ed** *a* s. (**through**) trempé (jusqu'aux os). ◆**—ing** *a* & *adv* s. (**wet**) trempé; – *n* trempage *m*.

soap [səʊp] *n* savon *m*; **s. opera** téléroman *m*; **s. powder** lessive *f*; – *vt* savonner. ◆**soapflakes** *npl* savon *m* en paillettes. ◆**soapsuds** *npl* mousse *f* de savon. ◆**soapy** *a* (-**ier**, -**iest**) *a* savonneux.

soar [sɔːr] *vi* (*of bird etc*) s'élever; (*of price*) monter (en flèche); (*of hope*) *Fig* grandir.

sob [sɒb] *n* sanglot *m*; – *vi* (-**bb-**) sangloter. ◆**sobbing** *n* (*sobs*) sanglots *mpl*.

sober ['səʊbər] **1** *a* **he's s.** (*not drunk*) il n'est pas ivre; – *vti* **to s. up** dessoûler. **2** *a* (*serious*) sérieux, sensé; (*meal, style*) sobre. ◆**—ly** *adv* sobrement.

soccer ['sɒkər] *n* football *m*.

sociable ['səʊʃəb(ə)l] *a* (*person*) sociable; (*evening*) amical. ◆**sociably** *adv* (*to act, reply*) aimablement.

social ['səʊʃəl] *a* social; (*life, gathering*) mondain; **s. club** foyer *m*; **s. science(s)** sciences *fpl* humaines; **s. security** (*aid*) aide *f* sociale; (*retirement pension*) *Am* pension *f* de retraite; **s. services** = sécurité *f* sociale; **s. worker** assistant *m* social; – *n* (*gathering*) réunion *f* (amicale). ◆**socialism** *n* socialisme *m*. ◆**socialist** *a* & *n* socialiste (*mf*). ◆**socialite** *n* mondain, -aine *mf*. ◆**socialize** *vi* (*mix*) se mêler aux autres; (*talk*) bavarder (**with** avec). ◆**socially** *adv* socialement; (*to meet s.o., behave*) en société.

society [sə'saɪətɪ] *n* (*community, club, companionship etc*) société *f*; *Univ Sch* club *m*; – *a* (*wedding etc*) mondain.

sociology [səʊsɪ'ɒlədʒɪ] *n* sociologie *f*. ◆**socio'logical** *a* sociologique. ◆**sociologist** *n* sociologue *mf*.

sock [sɒk] **1** *n* chaussette *f*. **2** *vt* (*hit*) *Sl* flanquer un marron à.

socket ['sɒkɪt] *n* (*of bone*) cavité *f*; (*of eye*) orbite *f*; (*power point*) *El* prise *f* de courant; (*of lamp*) douille *f*.

sod [sɒd] *n* (*turf*) *Am* gazon *m*.

soda ['səʊdə] *n* **1** *Ch* soude *f*; **washing s.** cristaux *mpl* de soude. **2** (*water*) eau *f* de Seltz; **s. (pop)** *Am* soda *m*.

sodden ['sɒd(ə)n] *a* (*ground*) détrempé.

sodium ['səʊdɪəm] *n* *Ch* sodium *m*.

sofa ['səʊfə] *n* canapé *m*, divan *m*; **s. bed** canapé-lit *m*.

soft [sɒft] *a* (-**er**, -**est**) (*smooth, gentle, supple*) doux; (*butter, ground, snow*) mou; (*wood, heart, paste, colour*) tendre; (*flabby*) flasque, mou; (*easy*) facile; (*indulgent*) indulgent; (*cowardly*) *Fam* poltron; (*stupid*) *Fam* ramolli; **it's too s.** (*radio etc*) ce n'est pas assez fort; **s. drink** boisson *f* non alcoolisée. ◆**s.-'boiled** *a* (*egg*) à la coque. ◆**soften** ['sɒf(ə)n] *vt* (*object*) ramollir; (*voice, pain, colour*) adoucir; – *vi* se ramollir; s'adoucir. ◆**softie** *n* *Fam* sentimental, -ale *mf*; (*weakling*) mauviette *f*. ◆**softly** *adv* doucement. ◆**softness** *n* douceur *f*; (*of butter, ground, snow*) mollesse *f*.

software ['sɒftweər] *n* *inv* (*of computer*) logiciel *m*.

soggy ['sɒgɪ] *a* (-**ier**, -**iest**) (*ground*) détrempé; (*biscuit, bread*) ramolli.

soil [sɔɪl] **1** *n* (*earth*) sol *m*, terre *f*. **2** *vt* (*dirty*) salir; – *vi* se salir.

solar ['səʊlər] *a* solaire.

sold [səʊld] *see* **sell**.

solder ['sɒldər, *Am* 'sɒdər] *vt* souder; – *n* soudure *f*.

soldier ['səʊldʒər] **1** *n* soldat *m*, militaire *m*. **2** *vi* **to s. on** persévérer.

sole [səʊl] **1** *n* (*of shoe*) semelle *f*; (*of foot*) plante *f*; – *vt* ressemeler. **2** *a* (*only*) seul, unique; (*rights, representative*) *Com* exclusif. **3** *n* (*fish*) sole *f*. ◆**—ly** *adv* uniquement; **you're s. to blame** tu es seul coupable.

solemn ['sɒləm] *a* (*formal*) solennel; (*serious*) grave. ◆**so'lemnity** *n* solennité *f*; gravité *f*. ◆**solemnly** *adv* (*to promise*) solennellement; (*to say*) gravement.

solicit [sə'lɪsɪt] *vt* (*seek*) solliciter; – *vi* (*of prostitute*) racoler. ◆**solicitor** *n* (*for wills etc*) notaire *m*.

solid ['sɒlɪd] *a* (*car, character, meal etc*) & *Ch* solide; (*wall, line, ball*) plein; (*gold, rock*) massif; (*crowd, mass*) compact; **frozen s.** entièrement gelé; **ten days s.** dix jours d'affilée; – *n* *Ch* solide *m*; *pl Culin* aliments *mpl* solides. ◆**so'lidify** *vi* se solidifier. ◆**so'lidity** *n* solidité *f*. ◆**solidly** *adv* (*built etc*) solidement; (*to support, vote*) en masse.

solidarity [sɒlɪ'darətɪ] *n* solidarité *f* (**with** avec).

soliloquy [sə'lɪləkwɪ] *n* monologue *m*.

solitary ['sɒlɪtərɪ] *a* (*lonely, alone*) solitaire;

solo (*only*) seul; **s. confinement** *Jur* isolement *m* (cellulaire). ◆**solitude** *n* solitude *f*.

solo ['səʊləʊ] *n* (*pl* **-os**) *Mus* solo *m*; *— a* solo *inv*; *— adv Mus* en solo; (*to fly*) en solitaire. ◆**soloist** *n Mus* soliste *mf*.

solstice ['sɒlstɪs] *n* solstice *m*.

soluble ['sɒljʊb(ə)l] *a* (*substance, problem*) soluble.

solution [sə'luːʃ(ə)n] *n* (*to problem etc*) & *Ch* solution *f* (*to* de).

solv/e [sɒlv] *vt* (*problem etc*) résoudre. ◆**-able** *a* soluble.

solvent ['sɒlvənt] **1** *a* (*financially*) solvable. **2** *n Ch* (dis)solvant *m*. ◆**solvency** *n Fin* solvabilité *f*.

sombre ['sɒmbər] *a* sombre, triste.

some [sʌm] *a* **1** (*amount, number*) **s. wine** du vin; **s. glue** de la colle; **s. water** de l'eau; **s. dogs** des chiens; **s. pretty flowers** de jolies fleurs. **2** (*unspecified*) un, une; **s. man** (*or other*) un homme (quelconque); **s. charm** (*a certain amount of*) un certain charme; **s. other way** quelque autre *or* un autre moyen; **that's s. book!** *Fam* ça, c'est un livre! **3** (*a few*) quelques, certains; (*a little*) un peu de; *— pron* **1** (*number*) quelques-un(e)s, certain(e)s (*of* de, d'entre). **2** (*a certain quantity*) en; **I want s.**, **j'en veux; do you have s.?** en as-tu?; **s. of it is over** il en reste un peu *or* une partie; *— adv* (*about*) quelque; **s. ten years** quelque dix ans.

somebody ['sʌmbɒdɪ] *pron =* **someone.** ◆**someday** *adv* un jour. ◆**somehow** *adv* (*in some way*) d'une manière ou d'une autre; (*for some reason*) on ne sait pourquoi. ◆**someone** *pron* quelqu'un; **at s.'s house** chez qn; **s. small/etc** quelqu'un de petit/*etc.* ◆**someplace** *adv Am* quelque part. ◆**something** *pron* quelque chose; **s. awful/etc** quelque chose d'affreux/*etc*; **s. of a liar/etc** un peu menteur/*etc*; *— adv* **she plays s. like . . .** elle joue un peu comme . . . ; **it was s. awful** c'était vraiment affreux. ◆**sometime 1** *adv* un jour; **s. in May/etc** au cours du mois de mai/*etc*; **s. before her departure** avant son départ. **2** *a* (*former*) ancien. ◆**sometimes** *adv* quelquefois, parfois. ◆**somewhat** *adv* quelque peu, assez. ◆**somewhere** *adv* quelque part; **s. about fifteen** (*approximately*) environ quinze.

somersault ['sʌməsɔːlt] *n* culbute *f*; (*in air*) saut *m* périlleux; *— vi* faire la *or* une culbute.

son [sʌn] *n* fils *m*. ◆**s.-in-law** *n* (*pl* **sons-in-law**) beau-fils *m*, gendre *m*.

sonar ['səʊnɑːr] *n* sonar *m*.

sonata [sə'nɑːtə] *n Mus* sonate *f*.

song [sɒŋ] *n* chanson *f*; (*of bird*) chant *m*. ◆**songbook** *n* recueil *m* de chansons.

sonic ['sɒnɪk] *a* **s. boom** bang *m* (supersonique).

sonnet ['sɒnɪt] *n* (*poem*) sonnet *m*.

soon [suːn] *adv* (**-er**, **-est**) (*in a short time*) bientôt; (*quickly*) vite; (*early*) tôt; **s. after** peu après; **as s. as she leaves** aussitôt qu'elle partira; **no sooner had he spoken than** à peine avait-il parlé que; **I'd sooner leave** je préférerais partir; **I'd just as s. leave** j'aimerais autant partir; **sooner or later** tôt ou tard.

soot [sʊt] *n* suie *f*. ◆**sooty** *a* (**-ier**, **-iest**) couvert de suie.

sooth/e [suːð] *vt* (*pain, nerves*) calmer; *Fig* rassurer. ◆**-ing** *a* (*ointment, words*) calmant.

sophisticated [sə'fɪstɪkeɪtɪd] *a* (*person, taste*) raffiné; (*machine, method, beauty*) sophistiqué.

sophomore ['sɒfəmɔːr] *n Am* étudiant, -ante *mf* de seconde année.

soporific [sɒpə'rɪfɪk] *a* (*substance, speech etc*) soporifique.

sopping ['sɒpɪŋ] *a* & *adv* **s.** (*wet*) trempé.

soppy ['sɒpɪ] *a* (**-ier**, **-iest**) *Fam* (*silly*) idiot, bête; (*sentimental*) sentimental.

soprano [sə'prɑːnəʊ] *n* (*pl* **-os**) *Mus* (*singer*) soprano *mf*; (*voice*) soprano *m*.

sorbet ['sɔːbeɪ] *n* (*water ice*) sorbet *m*.

sorcerer ['sɔːsərər] *n* sorcier *m*.

sordid ['sɔːdɪd] *a* (*act, street etc*) sordide.

sore [sɔːr] *a* (**-er**, **-est**) (*painful*) douloureux; (*angry*) *Am* fâché (*at* contre); **a s. point** *Fig* un sujet délicat; **she has a s. thumb** elle a mal au pouce; **he's still s.** *Med* il a encore mal; *— n Med* plaie *f*. ◆**-ly** *adv* (*tempted, regretted*) très; **s. needed** dont on a grand besoin. ◆**-ness** *n* (*pain*) douleur *f*.

sorrow ['sɒrəʊ] *n* chagrin *m*, peine *f*. ◆**sorrowful** *a* triste.

sorry ['sɒrɪ] *a* (**-ier**, **-iest**) (*sight, state etc*) triste; **to be s.** (*regret*) être désolé, regretter (*to do* de faire); **I'm s. she can't come** je regrette qu'elle ne puisse pas venir; **I'm s. about the delay** je m'excuse pour le retard; **s.!** pardon!; **to say s.** demander pardon (*to* à); **to feel** *or* **be s. for** plaindre.

sort [sɔːt] **1** *n* genre *m*, espèce *f*, sorte *f*; **s. of sad/etc** plutôt triste/*etc*; **a good s.** (*person*) *Fam* un brave type; **s. of sad/etc** plutôt triste/*etc*. **2** *vt* (*letters*) trier; (*classify, select*) trier; (*separate*) séparer (*from* de); (*arrange*) arranger; (*tidy*) ranger; (*problem*) régler; **to s. s.o. out** (*punish*) *Fam* faire voir à qn; – *vi* **to s. through** (*letters etc*) trier; **sorting office** centre *m* de tri. ◆**-er** *n* (*person*) trieur, -euse *mf*.

soufflé ['su:flei] *n* Culin soufflé *m*.

sought [sɔ:t] *see* **seek**.

soul [səul] *n* âme *f*; not a living s. (*nobody*) personne, pas âme qui vive; **a good s.** Fig un brave type; **s. mate** âme *f* sœur. ◆**s.-destroying** *a* abrutissant. ◆**s.-searching** *n* examen *m* de conscience.

sound¹ [saund] *n* son *m*; (*noise*) bruit *m*; **I don't like the s. of it** ça ne me plaît pas du tout; – *a* (*wave, film*) sonore; (*engineer*) du son; **s. archives** phonothèque *f*; **s. barrier** mur *m* du son; **s. effects** bruitage *m*; – *vt* (*bell, alarm etc*) sonner; (*bugle*) sonner de; (*letter*) Gram prononcer; **to s. one's horn** Aut klaxonner; – *vi* retentir, sonner; (*seem*) sembler; **to s. like** sembler être; (*resemble*) ressembler à; **it sounds like** *or* **as if** il semble que (+ *sub or indic*); **to s. off about** Pej (*boast*) se vanter de; (*complain*) rouspéter à propos de. ◆**soundproof** *a* insonorisé; – *vt* insonoriser. ◆**soundtrack** *n* (*of film etc*) bande *f* sonore.

sound² [saund] *a* (**-er, -est**) (*healthy*) sain; (*sturdy, reliable*) solide; (*instinct*) sûr; (*advice*) sensé; (*beating, sense*) bon; – *adv* **s. asleep** profondément endormi. ◆**-ly** *adv* (*asleep*) profondément; (*reasoned*) solidement; (*beaten*) complètement. ◆**-ness** *n* (*of mind*) santé *f*; (*of argument*) solidité *f*.

sound³ [saund] *vt* (*test, measure*) sonder; **to s. s.o. out** sonder qn (**about** sur).

soup [su:p] *n* soupe *f*, potage *m*; **in the s.** (*in trouble*) Fam dans le pétrin.

sour ['sauər] *a* (**-er, -est**) aigre; **to turn s.** (*of wine*) s'aigrir; (*of milk*) tourner; (*of friendship*) se détériorer; (*of conversation*) tourner au vinaigre; – *vi* (*of temper*) s'aigrir.

source [sɔ:s] *n* (*origin*) source *f*; **s. of energy** source d'énergie.

south [sauθ] *n* sud *m*; – *a* (*coast*) sud *inv*; (*wind*) du sud; **to be s. of** être au sud de; **S. America/Africa** Amérique *f*/Afrique *f* du Sud; **S. American** *a & n* sud-américain, -aine (*mf*); **S. African** *a & n* sud-africain, -aine (*mf*); – *adv* au sud, vers le sud. ◆**southbound** *a* (*carriageway*) sud *inv*; (*traffic*) en direction du sud. ◆**south-'east** *n & a* sud-est *m & a inv*. ◆**southerly** ['sʌðəli] *a* (*point*) sud *inv*; (*direction, wind*) du sud. ◆**southern** ['sʌðən] *a* (*town*) du sud; (*coast*) sud *inv*; **S. Italy** le Sud de

l'Italie; **S. Africa** Afrique *f* australe. ◆**southerner** ['sʌðənər] *n* habitant, -ante *mf* du Sud. ◆**southward(s)** *a & adv* vers le sud. ◆**south-'west** *n & a* sud-ouest *m & a inv*.

souvenir [su:və'niər] *n* (*object*) souvenir *m*.

sovereign ['sɒvrin] *n* souverain, -aine *mf*; – *a* (*State, authority*) souverain; (*rights*) de souveraineté. ◆**sovereignty** *n* souveraineté *f*.

Soviet ['səuviət] *a* soviétique; **the S. Union** l'Union *f* soviétique.

sow¹ [sau] *n* (*pig*) truie *f*.

sow² [səu] *vt* (*pt* **sowed**, *pp* **sowed** *or* **sown**) (*seeds, doubt etc*) semer; (*land*) ensemencer (**with** de).

soya ['sɔiə] *n* **s.** (**bean**) graine *f* de soja. ◆**soybean** *n* Am graine *f* de soja.

sozzled ['sɒz(ə)ld] *a* (*drunk*) Sl bourré.

spa [spa:] *n* (*town*) station *f* thermale; (*spring*) source *f* minérale.

space [speis] *n* (*gap, emptiness*) espace *m*; (*period*) période *f*; **blank s.** espace *m*, blanc *m*; (*outer*) **s.** l'espace (*cosmique*); **to take up s.** (*room*) prendre de la place; **in the s. of** en l'espace de; **s. heater** (*electric*) radiateur *m*; – *a* (*voyage etc*) spatial; – *vt* **to s. out** espacer; **double/single spacing** (*on typewriter*) double/simple interligne *m*. ◆**spaceman** *n* (*pl* **-men**) astronaute *m*. ◆**spaceship** *n*, ◆**spacecraft** *n inv* engin *m* spatial. ◆**spacesuit** *n* scaphandre *m* (de cosmonaute).

spacious ['speiʃəs] *a* spacieux, grand. ◆**-ness** *n* grandeur *f*.

spade [speid] *n* **1** (*for garden*) bêche *f*; (*of child*) pelle *f*. **2** Cards pique *m*. ◆**spadework** *n* Fig travail *m* préparatoire; (*around problem or case*) débroussaillage *m*.

spaghetti [spə'geti] *n* spaghetti(s) *mpl*.

Spain [spein] *n* Espagne *f*.

span [spæn] *n* (*of arch*) portée *f*; (*of wings*) envergure *f*; (*of life*) Fig durée *f*; – *vt* (**-nn-**) (*of bridge etc*) enjamber (*rivière etc*); Fig couvrir, embrasser.

Spaniard ['spænjəd] *n* Espagnol, -ole *mf*. ◆**Spanish** *a* espagnol; – *n* (*language*) espagnol *m*. ◆**Spanish-A'merican** *a* hispano-américain.

spaniel ['spænjəl] *n* épagneul *m*.

spank [spæŋk] *vt* fesser, donner une fessée à; – *n* **to give s.o. a s.** fesser qn. ◆**-ing** *n* fessée *f*.

spanner ['spænər] *n* (*tool*) clé *f* (à écrous); **adjustable s.** clé *f* à molette.

spar/e¹ [speər] *a* (*extra, surplus*) de or en

trop; (clothes, tyre) de rechange; (wheel) de
secours; (available) disponible; (bed, room)
d'ami; **s. time** loisirs mpl; – n **s.** (part) Tech
Aut pièce f détachée. **2** vt (do without) se
passer de; (s.o.'s life) épargner; (efforts,
s.o.'s feelings) ménager; (be s. s.o. (not kill)
épargner qn; (grief, details etc) épargner à
qn; (time) accorder à qn; (money) donner à
qn; **I can't the time** je n'ai pas le temps;
five to s. cinq de trop. ◆—**ing** a (use)
modéré; **to be s. with** (butter etc) ménager.
spare² [speər] a (lean) maigre.

spark [spɑːk] **1** n étincelle f. **2** vt **to s. off**
(cause) provoquer. ◆**spark(ing) plug** n
Aut bougie f.

sparkl/e ['spɑːk(ə)l] vi étinceler, scintiller;
– n éclat m. ◆—**ing** a (wine, water) pétillant.

sparrow ['spærəʊ] n moineau m.

sparse [spɑːs] a clairsemé. ◆—**ly** adv
(populated etc) peu.

spartan ['spɑːtən] a spartiate, austère.

spasm ['spæzəm] n (of muscle) spasme m;
(of coughing etc) Fig accès m. ◆**spas-
'modic** a (pain etc) spasmodique; Fig
irrégulier.

spastic ['spæstɪk] n handicapé, -ée mf
moteur.

spat [spæt] see **spit 1.**

spate [speɪt] n a **s. of** (orders etc) une
avalanche de.

spatter ['spætər] vt (clothes, person etc)
éclabousser (with de); – vi **to s. over s.o.** (of
mud etc) éclabousser qn.

spatula ['spætjʊlə] n spatule f.

spawn [spɔːn] n (of fish etc) frai m; – vi
frayer; – vt pondre; Fig engendrer.

speak [spiːk] vi (pt **spoke**, pp **spoken**)
parler; (formally, in assembly) prendre la
parole; **so to s.** pour ainsi dire; **that speaks
for itself** c'est évident; **to s. well of** dire du
bien de; **nothing to s. of** pas grand-chose;
Bob **has spoken** Tel Bob à l'appareil; **that's
spoken for** c'est pris or réservé; **to s. out** or
up (boldly) parler (franchement); **to s. up**
(more loudly) parler plus fort; – vt
(language) parler; (say) dire; **to s. one's
mind** dire ce que l'on pense. ◆—**ing** n
public vb. art m oratoire; – a **to be on s.
terms with** parler à; **English-/French-
speaking** anglophone/francophone. ◆—**er**
n (public) orateur m; (in dialogue) interlocuteur, -trice mf; (loudspeaker) El haut-
parleur m; (of hi-fi) enceinte f; **to be a
Spanish/a bad/etc s.** parler espagnol/
mal/etc.

spear [spɪər] n lance f. ◆**spearhead** vt

(attack) être le fer de lance de; (campaign)
mener.

spearmint ['spɪəmɪnt] n Bot menthe f
(verte); – a à la menthe; (chewing-gum)
mentholé.

spec [spek] n **on s.** (as a gamble) Fam à tout
hasard.

special ['speʃ(ə)l] a spécial; (care, attention)
(tout) particulier; (measures) Pol extraordinaire; (favourite) préféré; **by s.
delivery** (letter etc) par exprès; – n **today's
s.** (in restaurant) le plat du jour.
◆**specialist** n spécialiste mf (in de); – a
(dictionary, knowledge) technique, spécialisé. ◆**speci'ality** n spécialité f. ◆**specialize** vi se spécialiser (in dans). ◆**spe-
cialized** a spécialisé. ◆**specially** adv
(specifically) spécialement; (on purpose)
(tout) spécialement. ◆**specialty** n Am
spécialité f.

species ['spiːʃiːz] n inv espèce f.

specific [spə'sɪfɪk] a précis, explicite; Phys
Ch spécifique. ◆**specifically** adv
(expressly) expressément; (exactly) précisément.

specify ['spesɪfaɪ] vt spécifier (that que).
◆**specifi'cation** n spécification f; pl (of
car, machine etc) caractéristiques fpl.

specimen ['spesɪmɪn] n (example, person)
spécimen m; (of blood) prélèvement m; (of
urine) échantillon m; **s. signature** spécimen
m de signature; **s. copy** (of book etc) spécimen m.

specious ['spiːʃəs] a spécieux.

speck [spek] n (stain) petite tache f; (of
dust) grain m; (dot) point m.

speckled ['spek(ə)ld] a tacheté.

specs [speks] npl Fam lunettes fpl.

spectacle ['spektək(ə)l] **1** n (sight) spectacle
m. **2** npl (glasses) lunettes fpl. ◆**spec-
'tacular** a spectaculaire. ◆**spec'tator** n
Sp etc spectateur, -trice mf.

spectre ['spektər] n (menacing image) spectre m (of de).

spectrum, pl **-tra** ['spektrəm, -trə] n Phys
spectre m; (range) Fig gamme f.

speculate ['spekjʊleɪt] vi Fin Phil spéculer;
to s. about (s.o.'s motives etc) s'interroger
sur; – vt **to s. that** (guess) conjecturer que.
◆**specu'lation** n Fin Phil spéculation f;
(guessing) conjectures fpl (about sur).
◆**speculator** n spéculateur, -trice mf.
◆**speculative** a Fin Phil spéculatif; **that's
s.** (guesswork) c'est (très) hypothétique.

sped [sped] see **speed 1.**

speech [spiːtʃ] n (talk, address) & Gram
discours m (on sur); (faculty) parole f;

(diction) èlocution *f; (of group)* langage *m;* **a short s.** une allocution *f;* **freedom of s.** liberté *f* d'expression; **part of s.** *Gram* catégorie *f* grammaticale. ◆**—less** *a* muet (**with** de).

speed [spiːd] **1** *n (rate of movement)* vitesse *f; (swiftness)* rapidité *f;* **s. limit** *Aut* limitation *f* de vitesse; *— vt (pt & pp* **sped**) **to s. up** accélérer; *— vi* **to s. up** *(of person)* aller plus vite; *(of pace)* s'accélérer; **to s. past** passer à toute vitesse *(sth* devant qch). **2** *vi (pt & pp* **speeded**) *(drive too fast)* aller trop vite. ◆**—ing** *n* Jur excès *m* de vitesse. ◆**speedboat** *n* vedette *f.* ◆**spee'd'ometer** *n* Aut compteur *m* (de vitesse). ◆**speedway** *n* Sp piste *f* de vitesse pour motos; *Sp Aut Am* autodrome *m.* ◆**speed/y** ['spiːdɪ] *a* (**-ier, -iest**) rapide. ◆**-ily** *adv* rapidement.

spell[1] [spel] *n (magic)* charme *m,* sortilège *m; (curse)* sort *m; Fig* charme *m;* **under a s.** envoûté. ◆**spellbound** *a (audience etc)* captivé.

spell[2] [spel] *n (period)* (courte) période *f; (moment, while)* moment *m;* **s. of duty** tour *m* de service.

spell[3] [spel] *vt (pt & pp* **spelled** *or* **spelt**) *(write)* écrire; *(say aloud)* épeler; *(of letters)* former *(mot); (mean) Fig* signifier; **to be able to s.** savoir l'orthographe; **how is it spelt?** comment cela s'écrit-il?; **to s. out** *(aloud)* épeler; *Fig* expliquer très clairement. ◆**—ing** *n* orthographe *f.*

spend [spend] **1** *vt (pt & pp* **spent**) *(money)* dépenser *(on* pour); *— vi* dépenser. **2** *vt (pt & pp* **spent**) *(time, holiday etc)* passer *(on* sth sur qch, **doing** à faire); *(energy, care etc)* consacrer *(on* sth à qch, **doing** à faire). ◆**—ing** *n* dépenses *fpl; — a (money)* de poche. ◆**—er** *n* **to be a big s.** dépenser beaucoup. ◆**spendthrift** *n* **to be a s.** être dépensier.

spent [spent] *see* **spend;** *— a (used)* utilisé; *(energy)* épuisé.

sperm [spɜːm] *n (pl* **sperm** *or* **sperms**) sperme *m.*

spew [spjuː] *vt* vomir.

sphere [sfɪər] *n (of influence, action etc)* & *Geom Pol* sphère *f; (of music, poetry etc)* domaine *m;* **the social s.** le domaine social. ◆**spherical** ['sferɪk(ə)l] *a* sphérique.

sphinx [sfɪŋks] *n* sphinx *m.*

spice [spaɪs] *n Culin* épice *f; (interest etc) Fig* piment *m; — vt* épicer. ◆**spicy** *a* (**-ier, -iest**) épicé; *(story) Fig* pimenté.

spick-and-span [spɪkən'spæn] *a (clean)* impeccable.

spider ['spaɪdər] *n* araignée *f.*

spiel [ʃpiːl] *n Fam* baratin *m.*

spike [spaɪk] *n (of metal)* pointe *f; — vt (pierce)* transpercer. ◆**spiky** *a* (**-ier, -iest**) à garni de pointes.

spill [spɪl] *vt (pt & pp* **spilled** *or* **spilt**) *(liquid)* répandre, renverser **(on, over** sur); **to s. the beans** *Fam* vendre la mèche; *— vi* **to s. (out)** se répandre; **to s. over** déborder.

spin [spɪn] *n (motion)* tour *m; (car ride)* petit tour *m; (on washing machine)* essorage *m;* **s. dryer** essoreuse *f; — vt (pt & pp* **spun,** *pres p* **spinning)** *(web, yarn, wool etc)* filer **(into** en); *(wheel, top)* faire tourner; *(washing)* essorer; *(story) Fig* débiter; **to s. out** *(speech etc)* faire durer; *— vi (of spinner, spider)* filer; **to s. (round)** *(of dancer, top, planet etc)* tourner; *(of head, room) Fig* tourner; *(of vehicle)* faire un tête-à-queue. ◆**spinning** *n (by hand)* filage *m; (process) Tech* filature *f;* **s. top** toupie *f;* **s. wheel** rouet *m.* ◆**spin-dry** *vt* essorer. ◆**spin-off** *n* avantage *m* inattendu; *(of process, book etc)* dérivé *m.*

spinach ['spɪnɪdʒ] *n (plant)* épinard *m; (leaves) Culin* épinards *mpl.*

spindle ['spɪnd(ə)l] *n Tex* fuseau *m.* ◆**spindly** *a* (**-ier, -iest**) *(legs, arms)* grêle.

spine [spaɪn] *n Anat* colonne *f* vertébrale; *(spike of animal or plant)* épine *f; — a (column)* vertébral; **s. cord** moelle *f* épinière. ◆**spineless** *a Fig* mou, faible.

spinster ['spɪnstər] *n* célibataire *f; Pej* vieille fille *f.*

spiral ['spaɪərəl] **1** *n* spirale *f; — a* en spirale; *(staircase)* en colimaçon. **2** *vi* (**-ll-,** *Am* **-l-**) *(of prices)* monter en flèche.

spire ['spaɪər] *n (of church)* flèche *f.*

spirit ['spɪrɪt] **1** *n (soul, ghost etc)* esprit *m; (courage) Fig* courage *m,* vigueur *f; pl (drink)* alcool *m,* spiritueux *mpl;* **spirit(s)** *(morale)* moral *m; Ch* alcool *m;* **in good spirits** de bonne humeur; **the right s.** l'attitude *f* qu'il faut; *(a lamp)* à alcool; **s. level** niveau *m* à bulle (d'air). **2** *vt* **to s. away** *(person)* faire disparaître mystérieusement; *(steal) Hum* subtiliser. ◆**—ed** *a (person, remark)* fougueux; *(campaign)* vigoureux.

spiritual ['spɪrɪtʃʊəl] *a Phil Rel* spirituel; *— n (Negro)* **s.** (negro-)spiritual *m.* ◆**spiritualism** *n* spiritisme *m.* ◆**spiritualist** *n* spirite *mf.*

spit [spɪt] **1** *n* crachat *m; — vi (pt & pp* **spat** *or,* **spit,** *pres p* **spitting)** cracher; *(splutter) Fig* crépiter; *— vt* cracher; **to s. out** (re)cracher; **the spitting image of** s.o.

portrait (tout craché) de qn. 2 n (for meat) broche f.

spite [spaɪt] 1 n in s. of malgré; in s. of the fact that (although) bien que (+ sub). 2 n (dislike) rancune f; – vt (annoy) contrarier. ◆**spiteful** a méchant. ◆**spitefully** adv méchamment.

spittle ['spɪt(ə)l] n salive f, crachat(s) m(pl).

splash [splæʃ] vt (spatter) éclabousser (with de, over sur); (spill) répandre; – vi (of mud, ink etc) faire des éclaboussures; (of waves) clapoter, déferler; to s. over sth/s.o. éclabousser qch/qn; to s. (about) (in river, mud) patauger; (in bath) barboter; to s. out (spend money) Fam claquer de l'argent; – n (splashing) éclaboussement m; (of colour) Fig tache f; s. (mark) éclaboussure f; s.! plouf!

spleen [spliːn] n Anat rate f.

splendid ['splendɪd] a (wonderful, rich, beautiful) splendide. ◆**splendour** n splendeur f.

splint [splɪnt] n Med éclisse f.

splinter ['splɪntər] n (of wood etc) éclat m; (in finger) écharde f; s. group Pol groupe m dissident.

split [splɪt] n fente f; (tear) déchirure f; Pol scission f; to do the splits (in gymnastics) faire le grand écart; one's s. (share) Fam sa part; – vt (pt & pp split, pres p splitting) (break apart) fendre; (tear) déchirer; to s. (up) (group) diviser; (money, work) partager (between entre); to s. one's head open s'ouvrir la tête; to s. one's sides (laughing) se tordre (de rire); to s. hairs Fig couper les cheveux en quatre; s.-level apartment duplex m; – vi se fendre; (tear) se déchirer; to s. (up) (of group) éclater; (of couple) rompre, se séparer; to s. off (become loose) se détacher (from de); to s. up (of crowd) se disperser. ◆**splitting** a (headache) atroce. ◆**split-up** n (of couple) rupture f.

splodge [splɒdʒ] n, **splotch** [splɒtʃ] n (mark) tache f.

splurge [splɜːdʒ] vi (spend money) Fam claquer de l'argent.

splutter ['splʌtər] vi (of sparks, fat) crépiter; (stammer) bredouiller.

spoil [spɔɪl] vt (pt & pp spoilt or spoiled) (pamper, make unpleasant or less good) gâter; (damage, ruin) abîmer; (pleasure, life) gâcher, gâter. ◆**spoilsport** n rabat-joie m inv.

spoils [spɔɪlz] npl (rewards) butin m.

spoke[1] [spəʊk] n (of wheel) rayon m.

spoke[2] [spəʊk] see speak. ◆**spoken** see speak; – a (language etc) parlé; softly s. (person) à la voix douce. ◆**spokesman** n (pl -men) porte-parole m inv (for, de).

sponge [spʌndʒ] 1 n éponge f; s. bag trousse f de toilette; s. cake gâteau m de Savoie; – vt to s. down/off laver/enlever à l'éponge. 2 vi to s. off or on s.o. Fam vivre aux crochets de qn; – vt to s. sth off s.o. Fam taper qn de qch. ◆**sponger** n Fam parasite m. ◆**spongy** a (-ier, -iest) spongieux.

sponsor ['spɒnsər] n (of appeal, advertiser etc) personne f assurant le patronage (of de); (for membership) parrain m, marraine f; Jur garant, -ante mf; Sp sponsor m; – vt (appeal etc) patronner; (member, firm) parrainer. ◆**sponsorship** n patronage m; parrainage m.

spontaneous [spɒnˈteɪnɪəs] a spontané. ◆**spontaneity** [spɒntəˈneɪɪtɪ] n spontanéité f. ◆**spontaneously** adv spontanément.

spoof [spuːf] n Fam parodie f (on de).

spooky ['spuːkɪ] a (-ier, -iest) Fam qui donne le frisson.

spool [spuːl] n bobine f.

spoon [spuːn] n cuiller f. ◆**spoonfeed** vt (pt & pp spoonfed) (help) Fig mâcher le travail à. ◆**spoonful** n cuillerée f.

sporadic [spəˈrædɪk] a sporadique; s. fighting échauffourées fpl. ◆**sporadically** adv sporadiquement.

sport[1] [spɔːt] 1 n (good) s. (person) Fam un chic type; to play s. or Am sports faire du sport; sports club club m sportif; sports car/jacket voiture f/veste f de sport; sports results résultats mpl sportifs. 2 vt (wear) arborer. ◆**—ing** a (conduct, attitude, person etc) sportif; that's s. of you Fig c'est chic de ta part. ◆**sportsman** n (pl -men) sportif m. ◆**sportsmanlike** a sportif. ◆**sportsmanship** n sportivité f. ◆**sportswear** n vêtements mpl de sport. ◆**sportswoman** n (pl -women) sportive f. ◆**sporty** a (-ier, -iest) sportif.

spot[1] [spɒt] n (stain, mark) tache f; (dot) point m; (polka dot) pois m; (pimple) bouton m; (place) endroit m, coin m; (act) Th numéro m; (drop) goutte f; a s. of (bit) Fam un peu de; a soft s. for un faible pour; on the s. sur place, sur les lieux; (at once) sur le coup; in a (tight) s. (difficulty) dans le pétrin; (accident) black s. Aut point m noir; s. cash argent m comptant; s. check contrôle m au hasard or à l'improviste. ◆**spotless** a (clean) impeccable. ◆**spot-**

lessly adv s. clean impeccable. ◆**spotlight** n (lamp) Th projecteur m; (for photography etc) spot m; **in the s.** sous le feu des projecteurs. ◆**spot-'on** a Fam tout à fait exact. ◆**spotted** a (fur) tacheté; (dress etc) à pois; (stained) taché. 2 (patchy) Am inégal.

spot² [spɒt] vt (-tt-) (notice) apercevoir, remarquer.

spouse [spaʊs, spaʊz] n époux m, épouse f.

spout [spaʊt] 1 n (of jug etc) bec m; **up the s.** (hope etc) Sl fichu. 2 vi **to s. (out)** jaillir. 3 vt (say) Pej débiter.

sprain [spreɪn] n entorse f, foulure f; **to s. one's ankle/wrist** se fouler la cheville/le poignet.

sprang [spræŋ] see spring¹.

sprawl [sprɔːl] vi (of town, person) s'étaler; **to be sprawling** être étalé; – n **the urban s.** les banlieues fpl tentaculaires. ◆**-ing** a (city) tentaculaire.

spray [spreɪ] 1 n (water drops) (nuage m de) gouttelettes fpl; (from sea) embruns mpl; (can, device) bombe f, vaporisateur m; **hair s.** laque f à cheveux; – vt (liquid, surface) vaporiser; (crops, plant) arroser, traiter; (car etc) peindre à la bombe. 2 n (of flowers) petit bouquet m.

spread [spred] vt (pt & pp spread) (stretch, open out) étendre; (legs, fingers) écarter; (strew) répandre, étaler (over sur); (paint, payment, cards, visits) étaler; (people) disperser; (fear, news) répandre; (illness) propager; **to s. out** étendre; écarter; étaler; – vi (of fire, town, fog) s'étendre; (of news, fear) se répandre; **to s. out** (of people) se disperser; – n (of fire, illness, ideas) propagation f; (of wealth) répartition f; (paste) Culin pâte f (à tartiner); (meal) festin m; **cheese s.** fromage m à tartiner. ◆**s.-'eagled** a bras et jambes écartés.

spree [spriː] n **to go on a spending s.** faire des achats extravagants.

sprig [sprɪg] n (branch of heather etc) brin m; (of parsley) bouquet m.

spright/y ['spraɪtɪ] a (-ier, -iest) alerte. ◆**-iness** n vivacité f.

spring¹ [sprɪŋ] n (metal device) ressort m; (leap) bond m; – vi (pt sprang, pp sprung) (leap) bondir; **to s. to mind** venir à l'esprit; **to s. into action** passer à l'action; **to s. from** (stem from) provenir de; **to s. up** (appear) surgir; – vt (news) annoncer brusquement (on à); (surprise) faire (on à); **to s. a leak** (of boat) commencer à faire eau. ◆**spring-**

board n tremplin m. ◆**springy** a (-ier, -iest) élastique.

spring² [sprɪŋ] n (season) printemps m; **in (the) s.** au printemps; **s. onion** ciboule f. ◆**s.-'cleaning** n nettoyage m de printemps. ◆**springlike** a printanier. ◆**springtime** n printemps m.

spring³ [sprɪŋ] n (of water) source f; **s. water** eau f de source.

sprinkl/e ['sprɪŋk(ə)l] vt (sand etc) répandre (on, over sur); **to s. with water, s. water on** asperger d'eau, arroser; **to s. with** (sugar, salt, flour) saupoudrer de. ◆**-ing** n a s. of (a few) quelques. ◆**-er** n (in garden) arroseur m.

sprint [sprɪnt] n Sp sprint m; – vi sprinter. ◆**-er** n sprinter m, sprinteuse f.

sprite [spraɪt] n (fairy) lutin m.

sprout [spraʊt] 1 vi (of seed, bulb etc) germer, pousser; **to s. up** (grow) pousser vite; (appear) surgir; – vt (leaves) pousser; (beard) Fig laisser pousser. 2 n (Brussels) **s.** chou m de Bruxelles.

spruce [spruːs] a (-er, -est) (neat) pimpant, net; – vt **to s. oneself up** se faire beau.

sprung [sprʌŋ] see spring¹; – a (mattress, seat) à ressorts.

spry [spraɪ] a (spryer, spryest) (old person etc) alerte.

spud [spʌd] n (potato) Fam patate f.

spun [spʌn] see spin.

spur [spɜːr] n (of horse rider etc) éperon m; (stimulus) Fig aiguillon m; **on the s. of the moment** sur un coup de tête; – vt (-rr-) **to s. (on)** (urge on) éperonner.

spurious ['spjʊərɪəs] a faux.

spurn [spɜːn] vt rejeter (avec mépris).

spurt [spɜːt] vi (gush out) jaillir; (rush) foncer; **to s. out** jaillir; – n jaillissement m; (of energy) sursaut m; **to put on a s.** (rush) foncer.

spy [spaɪ] n espion, -onne mf; – a (story etc) d'espionnage; **s. hole** (peephole) judas m; **s. ring** réseau m d'espionnage; – vi espionner; **to s. on s.o.** espionner qn; – vt (notice) Lit apercevoir. ◆**-ing** n espionnage m.

squabbl/e ['skwɒb(ə)l] vi se chamailler (over à propos de); – n chamaillerie f. ◆**-ing** n chamailleries fpl.

squad [skwɒd] n (group) & Mil escouade f; (team) Sp équipe f; **s. car** voiture f de police.

squadron ['skwɒdrən] n Mil escadron m; Nau Av escadrille f.

squalid ['skwɒlɪd] a sordide. ◆**squalor** n conditions fpl sordides.

squall [skwɔːl] n (of wind) rafale f.

squander ['skwɒndər] vt (money, time etc) gaspiller (on en).

square ['skweər] n carré m; (on chessboard, graph paper) case f; (in town) place f; (drawing implement) Tech équerre f; **to be back to s. one** repartir à zéro; – a carré; (in order, settled) Fig en ordre; (honest) honnête; (meal) solide; **(all) s.** (quits) quitte (with envers); – vt (settle) mettre en ordre, régler; (arrange) arranger; (maths) carrer; (reconcile) faire cadrer; – vi (tally) cadrer (with avec); **to s. up to** faire face à. ◆**—ly** adv (honestly) honnêtement; (exactly) tout à fait; **s. in the face** bien en face.

squash [skwɒʃ] **1** vt (crush) écraser; (squeeze) serrer; – n lemon/orange **s.** (concentrated) sirop m de citron/d'orange; (diluted) citronnade f/orangeade f. **2** n (game) squash m. **3** n (vegetable) Am courge f. ◆**squashy** a (-ier, -iest) (soft) mou.

squat [skwɒt] **1** a (short and thick) trapu. **2** vi (-tt-) **to s.** (down) s'accroupir. **3** n (house) squat m. ◆**squatting** a accroupi. ◆**squatter** n squatter m.

squawk [skwɔːk] vi pousser des cris rauques; – n cri m rauque.

squeak [skwiːk] vi (of door) grincer; (of shoe) craquer; (of mouse) faire couic; – n grincement m; craquement m; couic m. ◆**squeaky** a (-ier, -iest) (door) grinçant; (shoe) qui craque.

squeal [skwiːl] vi pousser des cris aigus; (of tyres) crisser; – n cri m aigu; crissement m. **2** vi **to s. on s.o.** (inform on) Fam balancer qn.

squeamish ['skwiːmiʃ] a bien délicat, facilement dégoûté.

squeegee ['skwiːdʒiː] n raclette f (à vitres).

squeez/e [skwiːz] vt (press) presser; (hand, arm) serrer; **to s. sth out of s.o.** (information) soutirer qch à qn; **to s. sth into** faire rentrer qch dans; **to s.** (out) (extract) exprimer (from de); – vi **to s. through/into/etc** (force oneself) se glisser par/dans/ etc; **to s. in** trouver un peu de place; – n pression f; **to give sth a s.** presser qch; **it's a tight s.** il y a peu de place; credit **s.** Fin restrictions fpl de crédit. ◆**—er** n lemon s. presse-citron m inv.

squelch [skweltʃ] **1** vi patauger (en faisant floc-floc). **2** vt (silence) Fam réduire au silence.

squid [skwɪd] n (mollusc) calmar m.

squiggle ['skwɪg(ə)l] n ligne f onduleuse, gribouillis m.

squint [skwɪnt] n Med strabisme m; **to have a s.** loucher; – vi loucher; (in the sunlight etc) plisser les yeux.

squire ['skwaɪər] n propriétaire m terrien.

squirm [skwɜːm] vi (wriggle) se tortiller; **to s. in pain** se tordre de douleur.

squirrel ['skwɪrəl, Am 'skwɜːrəl] n écureuil m.

squirt [skwɜːt] **1** vt (liquid) faire gicler; – vi gicler; – n jet m, giclée f. **2** n little **s.** (person) Fam petit morveux m.

stab [stæb] vt (-bb-) (with knife etc) poignarder; – n coup m (de couteau ou de poignard). ◆**stabbing** n there was a s. quelqu'un a été poignardé; – a (pain) lancinant.

stable ['steɪb(ə)l] a (-er, -est) stable; mentally s. (person) bien équilibré. ◆**stability** n stabilité f; mental s. équilibre m. ◆**stabilize** vt stabiliser; – vi se stabiliser. ◆**stabilizer** n stabilisateur m.

stable [²'steɪb(ə)l] n écurie f; s. boy lad m.

stack [stæk] **1** n (heap) tas m; **stacks** (of lots of) Fam un ou des tas de; – vt **to s.** (up) entasser. **2** npl (in library) réserve f.

stadium ['steɪdɪəm] n Sp stade m.

staff [stɑːf] **1** n personnel m; Sch professeurs mpl; Mil état-major m; s. meeting Sch Univ conseil m des professeurs; s. room Sch Univ salle f des professeurs; – vt pourvoir en personnel. **2** n (stick) Lit bâton m.

stag [stæg] n cerf m; s. party réunion f entre hommes.

stage [¹'steɪdʒ] n (platform) Th scène f; the **s.** (profession) le théâtre; on **s.** sur (la) scène; s. door entrée f des artistes; s. fright le trac; – vt (play) Th monter; Fig organiser, effectuer; **it was staged** (not real) c'était un coup monté. ◆**s.-hand** n machiniste m. ◆**s.-manager** n régisseur m.

stage [²'steɪdʒ] n (phase) stade m, étape f; (of journey) étape f; (of track, road) section f; **in (easy) stages** par étapes; **at an early s.** au début.

stagecoach ['steɪdʒkəʊtʃ] n Hist diligence f.

stagger ['stægər] **1** vi (reel) chanceler. **2** vt (holidays etc) étaler, échelonner. **3** vt **to s.o.** (shock, amaze) stupéfier qn. ◆**—ing** a stupéfiant.

stagnant ['stægnənt] a stagnant. ◆**stag'nate** vi stagner. ◆**stag'nation** n stagnation f.

staid [steɪd] a posé, sérieux.

stain [steɪn] **1** vt (mark, dirty) tacher (with

de); — n tache f. 2 vt (colour) teinter (du
bois); **stained glass window** vitrail m; — n
(colouring for wood) teinture f. **◆—less** a
(steel, knife etc) inoxydable.

stair [steər] n a s. (step) une marche; **the
stairs** (staircase) l'escalier m; — a (carpet
etc) d'escalier. **◆staircase** n, **◆stairway**
n escalier m.

stake [steɪk] 1 n (post) pieu m; (for plant)
tuteur m; Hist bûcher m; — vt to s. (out)
(land) jalonner, délimiter; **to s. one's claim
to** revendiquer. 2 n (betting) enjeu m;
(investment) Fin investissement m; (interest) Fin intérêts mpl; **at s.** en jeu; — vt (bet)
jouer (on sur).

stale [steɪl] a (-er, -est) (food) pas frais;
(bread) rassis; (beer) éventé; (air) vicié;
(smell) de renfermé; (news) Fig vieux;
(joke) usé, vieux; (artist) manquant
d'invention. **◆—ness** n (of food) manque
m de fraîcheur.

stalemate [steɪlmeɪt] n Chess pat m; Fig
impasse f.

stalk [stɔːk] 1 n (of plant) tige f, queue f; (of
fruit) queue f. 2 vt (animal, criminal)
traquer. 3 vi to s. out (walk) partir avec
raideur or en marchant à grands pas.

stall [stɔːl] 1 n (in market) étal m, éventaire
m; (for newspapers, flowers) kiosque m; (in
stable) stalle f; **the stalls** Cin l'orchestre m.
2 vti Aut caler. 3 vi to s. (for time) chercher
à gagner du temps.

stallion ['stæljən] n (horse) étalon m.

stalwart ['stɔːlwət] a (supporter) brave,
fidèle; — n (follower) partisan, -ane mf
fidèle.

stamina ['stæmɪnə] n vigueur f, résistance f.

stammer ['stæmər] vti bégayer; — n bégaiement m; **to have a s.** être bègue.

stamp [stæmp] 1 n (for postage, implement)
timbre m; (mark) cachet m, timbre m; **the
s. of** Fig la marque de; **men of your s.** les
hommes de votre trempe; **s. collecting**
philatélie f; — vt (mark) tamponner,
timbrer; (letter) timbrer; (metal) estamper;
to s. sth on sth (affix) apposer qch sur qch;
to s. out (rebellion, evil) écraser; (disease)
supprimer; **stamped addressed envelope**
enveloppe f timbrée à votre adresse. 2 vti **to
s. (one's feet)** taper or frapper des pieds;
stamping ground Fam lieu m favori.

stampede [stæm'piːd] n fuite f précipitée;
(rush) ruée f; — vi fuir en désordre; (rush) se
ruer.

stance [stɑːns] n position f.

stand [stænd] n (position) position f;
(support) support m; (at exhibition) stand

m; (for spectators) Sp tribune f; (witness) s.
Jur Am barre f; **to make a s., take one's
s.** prendre position (**against** contre); **news/
flower/s.** (in street) kiosque m à journaux/à
fleurs; **hat s.** porte-chapeaux m inv; **music
s.** pupitre m à musique; — vt (pt & pp
stood) (pain, journey, person etc) supporter; **to s. (up)** (put straight) mettre
(debout); **to s. s.o. sth** (pay for) payer qch à
qn; **to s. a chance** avoir une chance; **to s.
s.o. up** Fam poser un lapin à qn; — vi être or
se tenir (debout); (rise) se lever; (remain)
rester (debout); (be situated) se trouver;
(be) être; (of object, argument) reposer (on
sur); (of bewilderment) (bag) cela,
to leave to s. (liquid) laisser reposer;
to s. to lose risquer de perdre; **to s. around**
(in street etc) traîner; **to s. aside** s'écarter;
to s. back reculer; **to s. by** (do nothing)
rester là (sans rien faire); (be ready) être
prêt (à partir or à intervenir); (one's opinion
etc) s'en tenir à; (friend etc) rester fidèle à;
to s. down (withdraw) se désister; **to s. for**
(represent) représenter; Pol être candidat
à; (put up with) supporter; **to s. in for**
(replace) remplacer; **to s. out** (be visible or
conspicuous) ressortir (**against** sur); **to s.
over s.o.** (watch closely) surveiller qn; **to s.
up** (rise) se lever; **to s. up for** (defend)
défendre; **to s. up to** (resist) résister à.
◆—ing a debout inv; (committee, offer,
army) permanent; **s. room** places fpl
debout; **s. joke** plaisanterie f classique; — n
(reputation) réputation f; (social, professional) rang m; (financial) situation f; **of
six years' s.** (duration) qui dure depuis six
ans; **of long s.** de longue date. **◆standby**
(pl -bys) **on s.** prêt à partir or à intervenir;
— a (battery etc) de réserve; (ticket) Av sans
garantie. **◆stand-in** n remplaçant, -ante
mf (**for** de); Th doublure f (**for** de).

standard ['stændəd] 1 n (norm) norme f,
critère m; (level) niveau m; (of weight,
gold) étalon m; (pl morals) principes mpl;
s. of living niveau m de vie; **to be** or **come
up to s.** (of person) être à la hauteur; (of
work etc) être au niveau; — a (average)
ordinaire, courant; (model, size) Com standard inv; (weight) étalon inv; (dictionary,
book) classique; **s. lamp** lampadaire m. 2 n
(flag) étendard m. **◆standardize** vt
standardiser.

stand-offish [stænd'ɒfɪʃ] a (person) distant,
froid.

standpoint ['stændpɔɪnt] n point m de vue.

standstill ['stændstɪl] n **to bring to a s.**
immobiliser; **to come to a s.** s'immobiliser;

at a s. immobile; (industry, negotiations) paralysé.

stank [stæŋk] see **stink**.

stanza [ˈstænzə] n strophe f.

stapl/e [ˈsteɪp(ə)l] **1** a (basic) de base; s. food or diet nourriture f de base. **2** n (for paper etc) agrafe f; – vt agrafer. ◆**-er** n (for paper etc) agrafeuse f.

star [stɑːr] n étoile f; (person) Cin vedette f; shooting s. étoile f filante; s. part rôle m principal; the Stars and Stripes, the S.-Spangled Banner Am la bannière étoilée; **two-s. (petrol)** de l'ordinaire m; **four-s. (petrol)** du super; – vi (-rr-) (of actor) être la vedette (in de); – vt (of film) avoir pour vedette. ◆**stardom** n célébrité f. ◆**starfish** n étoile f de mer. ◆**starlit** a (night) étoilé.

starboard [ˈstɑːbəd] n Nau Av tribord m.

starch [stɑːtʃ] n (for stiffening) amidon m; pl (foods) féculents mpl; – vt amidonner. ◆**starchy** a (-ier, -iest) (food) féculent; (formal) Fig guindé.

stare [steər] n regard m (fixe); – vi to s. at fixer (du regard); – vt to s. s.o. in the face dévisager qn.

stark [stɑːk] a (-er, -est) (place) désolé; (austere) austère; (fact, reality) brutal; the s. truth la vérité toute nue; – adv s. naked complètement nu. ◆**starkers** a Sl complètement nu, à poil.

starling [ˈstɑːlɪŋ] n étourneau m.

starry [ˈstɑːrɪ] a (-ier, -iest) (sky) étoilé. ◆**s.-'eyed** a (naïve) ingénu, naïf.

start [stɑːt] n commencement m, début m; (of race) départ m; (lead) Sp & Fig avance f (on sur); to make a s. commencer; for a s. pour commencer; from the s. dès le début; – vt commencer; (bottle) entamer, commencer; (fashion) lancer; to s. a war provoquer une guerre; to s. a fire (in grate) allumer un feu; (accidentally) provoquer un incendie; to s. s.o. (off) on (career) lancer qn dans; to s. (up) (engine, vehicle) mettre en marche; to s. doing or to do commencer or se mettre à faire; – vi commencer (with sth par qch, by doing par faire); to s. on sth commencer qch; to s. (up) commencer; (of vehicle) démarrer; to s. (off or out) (leave) partir (for pour); (in job) débuter; to s. back (return) repartir; to s. with (firstly) pour commencer. ◆**-ing** n (point, line) de départ; s. post Sp ligne f de départ; s. from à partir de. ◆**-er** n (runner) partant m; (official) Sp starter m; (device) Aut démarreur m; pl Culin

hors-d'œuvre m inv; **for starters** (first) pour commencer.

start² [stɑːt] vi (be startled, jump) sursauter; – n sursaut m; to give s.o. a s. faire sursauter qn.

startle [ˈstɑːt(ə)l] vt (make jump) faire sursauter qn; (alarm) Fig alarmer; (surprise) surprendre.

starve [stɑːv] vi (die) mourir de faim; (suffer) souffrir de la faim; I'm starving Fig je meurs de faim; – vt (kill) laisser mourir de faim; (make suffer) faire souffrir de la faim; (deprive) Fig priver (of de). ◆**star-'vation** n faim f; (of wage, ration) de famine; **on a s. diet** à la diète.

stash [stæʃ] vt to s. away (hide) cacher; (save up) mettre de côté.

state¹ [steɪt] **1** n (condition) état m; (pomp) apparat m; not in a (fit) s. to, in no (fit) s. to hors d'état de; to lie in s. (of body) être exposé. **2** n S. (nation etc) État m; the States Geog Fam les États-Unis; – a (secret, document) d'État; (control, security) de l'État; (school, education) public; s. visit voyage m officiel; S. Department Pol Am Département m d'État. ◆**stateless** a apatride; **s. person** apatride mf. ◆**state-'owned** a étatisé. ◆**statesman** n (pl -men) homme m d'État. ◆**statesman-ship** n diplomatie f.

state² [steɪt] vt déclarer (that que); (opinion) formuler; (problem) exposer; (time, date) fixer. ◆**statement** n déclaration f; Jur déposition f; bank s., s. of account Fin relevé m de compte.

stately [ˈsteɪtlɪ] a (-ier, -iest) majestueux; s. home château m.

static [ˈstætɪk] a statique; – n (noise) Rad parasites mpl.

station [ˈsteɪʃ(ə)n] n Rail gare f; (underground) station f; (position) & Mil poste m; (social) rang m; (police) s. commissariat m or poste m (de police); **space/observation/radio/etc** s. station f spatiale/d'observation/de radio/etc; **bus or coach s.** gare f routière; **s. wagon** Aut Am break m; – vt (position) placer, poster. ◆**stationmaster** n Rail chef m de gare.

stationary [ˈsteɪʃ(ə)n(ə)rɪ] a (motionless) stationnaire; (vehicle) à l'arrêt.

stationer [ˈsteɪʃ(ə)nər] n papetier, -ière mf; s.'s (shop) papeterie f. ◆**stationery** n (paper) papier m; (articles) papeterie f.

statistic [stəˈtɪstɪk] n (fact) statistique f; pl (science) la statistique. ◆**statistical** a statistique.

statue [ˈstætʃuː] *n* statue *f*. ◆**statu'esque** *a* (*beauty etc*) sculptural.

stature [ˈstætʃər] *n* stature *f*.

status [ˈsteɪtəs] *n* (*position*) situation *f*; *Jur* statut *m*; (*prestige*) standing *m*, prestige *m*; **s. symbol** marque *f* de standing; **s. quo** statu quo *m inv*.

statute [ˈstætʃuːt] *n* (*law*) loi *f*; *pl* (*of club, institution*) statuts *mpl*. ◆**statutory** *a* (*right etc*) statutaire; **s. holiday** fête *f* légale.

staunch [stɔːntʃ] *a* (-er, -est) loyal, fidèle. ◆**—ly** *adv* loyalement.

stave [steɪv] **1** *vt* **to s. off** (*danger, disaster*) conjurer; (*hunger*) tromper. **2** *n Mus* portée *f*.

stay [steɪ] **1** *n* (*visit*) séjour *m*; – *vi* (*remain*) rester; (*reside*) loger; (*visit*) séjourner; **to s. put** ne pas bouger; **to s. with** (*plan, idea*) ne pas lâcher; **to s. away** (*keep one's distance*) ne pas s'approcher (**from** de); **to s. away from** (*school, meeting etc*) ne pas aller à; **to s. in** (*at home*) rester à la maison; (*of nail, tooth etc*) tenir; **to s. out** (*outside*) rester dehors; (*not come home*) ne pas rentrer; **to s. out of sth** (*not interfere in*) ne pas se mêler de qch; (*avoid*) éviter qch; **to s. up** (*at night*) ne pas se coucher; (*of fence etc*) tenir; **to s. up late** se coucher tard; **staying power** endurance *f*. **2** *vt* (*hunger*) tromper. ◆**s.-at-home** *n* & *a Pej* casanier, -ière (*mf*).

St Bernard [sənt'bɜːnəd, *Am* seɪntbə'nɑːd] *n* (*dog*) saint-bernard *m*.

stead [sted] *n* **to stand s.o. in good s.** être bien utile à qn; **in s.o.'s s.** à la place de qn.

steadfast [ˈstedfɑːst] *a* (*intention etc*) ferme.

steady [ˈstedɪ] *a* (-ier, -iest) (*firm, stable*) stable; (*hand*) sûr, assuré; (*progress, speed, demand*) régulier, constant; (*nerves*) solide; (*staid*) sérieux; **a s. boyfriend** un petit ami; **s. (on one's feet)** solide sur ses jambes; – *adv* **to go s. with** *Fam* sortir avec; – *vt* (*chair etc*) maintenir (en place); (*hand*) assurer; (*nerves*) calmer; (*wedge, prop up*) caler; **to s. oneself** (*stop oneself falling*) reprendre son aplomb. ◆**steadily** *adv* (*to walk*) d'un pas assuré; (*regularly*) régulièrement; (*gradually*) progressivement; (*continuously*) sans arrêt. ◆**steadiness** *n* stabilité *f*; régularité *f*.

steak [steɪk] *n* steak *m*, bifteck *m*. ◆**steakhouse** *n* grill(-room) *m*.

steal¹ [stiːl] *vti* (*pt* **stole**, *pp* **stolen**) voler (**from s.o.** à qn).

steal² [stiːl] *vi* (*pt* **stole**, *pp* **stolen**) **to s. in/out** entrer/sortir furtivement. ◆**stealth**

[stelθ] *n* **by s.** furtivement. ◆**stealthy** *a* (-ier, -iest) furtif.

steam [stiːm] *n* vapeur *f*; (*on glass*) buée *f*; **to let off s.** (*unwind*) *Fam* se défouler, décompresser; **s. engine/iron** locomotive *f*/fer *m* à vapeur; – *vt Culin* cuire à la vapeur; **to get steamed up** (*of glass*) se couvrir de buée; *Fig Fam* s'énerver; – *vi* (*of kettle etc*) fumer; **to s. up** (*of glass*) se couvrir de buée. ◆**steamer** *n*, ◆**steamship** *n* (*bateau m à*) vapeur *m*; (*liner*) paquebot *m*. ◆**steamroller** *n* rouleau *m* compresseur. ◆**steamy** *a* (-ier, -iest) humide; (*window*) embué; (*love affair etc*) brûlant.

steel [stiːl] **1** *n* acier *m*; **s. industry** sidérurgie *f*. **2** *vt* **to s. oneself** s'endurcir (**against** contre). ◆**steelworks** *n* aciérie *f*.

steep [stiːp] **1** *a* (-er, -est) (*stairs, slope etc*) raide; (*hill*) escarpé; (*price*) *Fig* excessif. **2** *vt* (*soak*) tremper (**in** dans); **steeped in** *Fig* imprégné de. ◆**—ly** *adv* (*to rise*) en pente raide, (*of prices*) *Fig* excessivement.

steeple [ˈstiːp(ə)l] *n* clocher *m*.

steeplechase [ˈstiːp(ə)ltʃeɪs] *n* (*race*) steeple(-chase) *m*.

steer [stɪər] *vt* (*vehicle, person*) diriger, piloter; (*ship*) diriger, gouverner; – *vi* (*of person*) *Nau* tenir le gouvernail, gouverner; **to s. towards** faire route vers; **to s. clear of** éviter. ◆**—ing** *n Aut* direction *f*; **s. wheel** volant *m*.

stem [stem] **1** *n* (*of plant etc*) tige *f*; (*of glass*) pied *m*. **2** *vt* (-mm-) **to s. (the flow of)** (*stop*) arrêter, contenir. **3** *vi* (-mm-) **to s. from** provenir de.

stench [stentʃ] *n* puanteur *f*.

stencil [ˈstens(ə)l] *n* (*metal, plastic*) pochoir *m*; (*paper, for typing*) stencil *m*; – *vt* (-ll-, *Am* -l-) (*notes etc*) polycopier.

stenographer [stəˈnɒɡrəfər] *n Am* sténodactylo *f*.

step [step] *n* (*movement, sound*) pas *m*; (*stair*) marche *f*; (*on train, bus*) marchepied *m*; (*doorstep*) pas *m* de la porte; (*action*) *Fig* mesure *f*; (*flight of*) **steps** (*indoors*) escalier *m*; (*outdoors*) perron *m*; (*pair of*) **steps** (*ladder*) escabeau *m*; **s. by s.** pas à pas; **to keep in s.** marcher au pas; **in s. with** *Fig* en accord avec; – *vi* (-pp-) (*walk*) marcher (**on** sur); **s. this way!** (*venez*) par ici!; **to s. aside** s'écarter; **to s. back** reculer; **to s. down** descendre (**from** de); (*withdraw*) *Fig* se retirer; **to s. forward** faire un pas en avant; **to s. in** entrer; (*intervene*) *Fig* intervenir; **to s. into** (*car etc*) monter dans; **to s. off** (*chair etc*) descendre de; **to s. out of** (*car etc*) descendre de; **to s. over** (*obstacle*) enjamber; − *vt* **to s. up** (*increase*) augmenter, intensifier; (*speed up*) activer. ◆**stepladder** *n* escabeau *m*. ◆**stepping-stone** *n* *Fig* tremplin *m* (**to** pour arriver à).

stepbrother ['stepbrʌðər] *n* demi-frère *m*. ◆**stepdaughter** *n* belle-fille *f*. ◆**stepfather** *n* beau-père *m*. ◆**stepmother** *n* belle-mère *f*. ◆**stepsister** *n* demi-sœur *f*. ◆**stepson** *n* beau-fils *m*.

stereo ['steriəʊ] *n* (*pl* -os) (*sound*) stéréo(phonie) *f*; (*record player*) chaîne *f* (stéréo *inv*); − *a* (*record etc*) stéréo *inv*; (*broadcast*) en stéréo. ◆**stereo'phonic** *a* stéréophonique.

stereotype ['steriəʊtaɪp] *n* stéréotype *m*. ◆**stereotyped** *a* stéréotypé.

sterile ['sterail, *Am* 'sterəl] *a* stérile. ◆**sterility** *n* stérilité *f*. ◆**sterili'zation** *n* stérilisation *f*. ◆**sterilize** *vt* stériliser.

sterling ['stɜːlɪŋ] *n* (*currency*) livre(s) *f(pl)* sterling *m*; − *a* (*pound*) sterling *inv*; (*silver*) fin; (*quality, person*) *Fig* sûr.

stern [stɜːn] **1** *a* (-**er**, -**est**) sévère. **2** *n* (*of ship*) arrière *m*.

stethoscope ['steθəskəʊp] *n* stéthoscope *m*.

stetson ['stetsən] *n* *Am* chapeau *m* à larges bords.

stevedore ['stiːvədɔːr] *n* docker *m*.

stew [stjuː] *n* ragoût *m*; **in a s.** *Fig* dans le pétrin; **s. pan, s. pot** cocotte *f*; − *vt* (*meat*) faire *or* cuire en ragoût; (*fruit*) faire cuire; **stewed fruit** compote *f*; − *vi* cuire. ◆**—ing** *a* (*pears etc*) à cuire.

steward ['stjuːəd] *n* *Av* *Nau* steward *m*; (*in college, club etc*) intendant *m* (*préposé au ravitaillement*); **shop s.** délégué, -ée *mf* syndical(e). ◆**stewar'dess** *n* *Av* hôtesse *f*.

stick¹ [stɪk] *n* (*piece of wood, chalk, dynamite*) bâton *m*; (*branch*) branche *f*; (*for walking*) canne *f*; **the sticks** *Pej* *Fam* la campagne, la cambrousse; **to give s.o. some s.** (*scold*) *Fam* engueuler qn.

stick² [stɪk] *vt* (*pt & pp* **stuck**) (*glue*) coller; (*put*) *Fam* mettre, planter; (*tolerate*) *Fam* supporter; **to s. sth into** (*thrust*) planter *or* enfoncer qch dans; **to s. down** (*envelope*) coller; (*put down*) *Fam* poser; **to s. on** (*stamp*) coller; (*hat etc*) mettre, planter; **to s. out** (*tongue*) tirer; (*head*) *Fam* sortir; **to s. it out** (*resist*) *Fam* tenir le coup; **to s. up** (*notice*) afficher; (*hand*) *Fam* lever; − *vi* coller, adhérer (**to** à); (*of food in pan*) attacher; (*remain*) *Fam* rester; (*of drawer etc*) être bloqué *or* coincé; **to s. by s.o.** rester fidèle à qn; **to s. to the facts** (*confine oneself to*) s'en tenir aux faits; **to s. around**

rester dans les parages; **to s. out** (*of petticoat etc*) dépasser; (*of tooth*) avancer; **to s. up for** (*defend*) défendre; **sticking plaster** sparadrap *m*. ◆**sticker** *n* (*label*) autocollant *m*. ◆**stick-on** *a* (*label*) adhésif. ◆**stick-up** *n* *Fam* hold-up *m*.

stickler ['stɪklər] *n* a **s. for** (*rules, discipline, details*) intransigeant sur.

sticky ['stɪkɪ] *a* (-**ier**, -**iest**) collant, poisseux; (*label*) adhésif; (*problem*) *Fig* difficile.

stiff [stɪf] *a* (-**er**, -**est**) raide; (*joint, leg etc*) ankylosé; (*brush, paste*) dur; (*person*) *Fig* froid, guindé; (*difficult*) difficile; (*price*) élevé; (*whisky*) bien tassé; **to have a s. neck** avoir le torticolis; **to feel s.** être courbaturé; **to be bored s.** *Fam* s'ennuyer à mourir; **frozen s.** *Fam* complètement gelé. ◆**stiffen** *vt* raidir; − *vi* se raidir. ◆**stiffly** *adv* (*coldly*) *Fig* froidement. ◆**stiffness** *n* raideur *f*; (*hardness*) dureté *f*.

stifle ['staɪf(ə)l] *vt* (*feeling, person etc*) étouffer; − *vi* **it's stifling** on étouffe.

stigma ['stɪgmə] *n* (*moral stain*) flétrissure *f*. ◆**stigmatize** *vt* (*denounce*) stigmatiser.

stile [staɪl] *n* (*between fields etc*) échalier *m*.

stiletto [stɪ'letəʊ] *a* **s. heel** talon *m* aiguille.

still¹ [stɪl] *adv* encore, toujours; (*even*) encore; (*nevertheless*) tout de même; **better s., s. better** encore mieux.

still² [stɪl] *a* (-**er**, -**est**) (*motionless*) immobile; (*calm*) calme, tranquille; (*drink*) non gazeux; **to keep** *or* **lie** *or* **stand s.** rester tranquille; **s. life** nature *f* morte; − *n* (*of night*) silence *m*; *Cin* photo *f*. ◆**stillborn** *a* mort-né. ◆**stillness** *n* immobilité *f*; calme *m*.

still³ [stɪl] *n* (*for making alcohol*) alambic *m*.

stilt [stɪlt] *n* (*pole*) échasse *f*.

stilted ['stɪltɪd] *a* guindé.

stimulate ['stɪmjʊleɪt] *vt* stimuler. ◆**stimulant** *n* *Med* stimulant *m*. ◆**stimu'lation** *n* stimulation *f*. ◆**stimulus**, *pl* -**li** [-laɪ] *n* (*encouragement*) stimulant *m*; (*physiological*) stimulus *m*.

sting [stɪŋ] *vt* (*pt & pp* **stung**) (*of insect, ointment, wind etc*) piquer; (*of remark*) *Fig* blesser; − *vi* piquer; − *n* piqûre *f*; (*insect's organ*) dard *m*. ◆**—ing** *a* (*pain, remark*) cuisant.

sting/y ['stɪndʒɪ] *a* (-**ier**, -**iest**) avare, mesquin; **s. with** (*money, praise*) avare de; (*food, wine*) mesquin sur. ◆**—iness** *n* avarice *f*.

stink [stɪŋk] *n* puanteur *f*; **to cause** *or* **make a s.** (*trouble*) *Fam* faire du foin; − *vi* (*pt* **stank** *or* **stunk**, *pp* **stunk**) puer; (*of book, film etc*)

Fam être infect; **to s. of** smoke/*etc* empester la fumée/*etc*; – *vt* **to s. out** (*room etc*) empester. ◆**—ing** *a Fam* infect, sale. ◆**—er** *n Fam* (*person*) sale type *m*; (*question, task etc*) vacherie *f*.

stint [stɪnt] **1** *n* (*share*) part *f* de travail; (*period*) période *f* de travail. **2** *vi* **to s. on** lésiner sur.

stipend ['staɪpend] *n Rel* traitement *m*.

stipulate ['stɪpjʊleɪt] *vt* stipuler (**that** que). ◆**stipu'lation** *n* stipulation *f*.

stir [stɜːr] *n* agitation *f*; **to give sth a s.** remuer qch; **to cause a s.** *Fig* faire du bruit; – *vt* (**-rr-**) (*coffee, leaves etc*) remuer; (*excite*) *Fig* exciter; (*incite*) inciter (**to do** à faire); **to s. oneself** (*make an effort*) se secouer; **to s. up** (*trouble*) provoquer; (*memory*) réveiller; – *vi* remuer, bouger. ◆**stirring** *a* (*speech etc*) excitant, émouvant.

stirrup ['stɪrəp] *n* étrier *m*.

stitch [stɪtʃ] *n* point *m*; (*in knitting*) maille *f*; *Med* point *m* de suture; **a s.** (**in one's side**) (*pain*) un point de côté; **to be in stitches** *Fam* se tordre (de rire); – *vt* **to s.** (**up**) (*sew up*) coudre; *Med* suturer.

stoat [stəʊt] *n* (*animal*) hermine *f*.

stock [stɒk] *n* (*supply*) provision *f*, stock *m*, réserve *f*; (*of knowledge, jokes*) fonds *m*, mine *f*; *Fin* valeurs *fpl*, titres *mpl*; (*descent, family*) souche *f*; (*soup*) bouillon *m*; (*cattle*) bétail *m*; **the stocks** *Hist* le pilori; **in s.** (*goods*) en magasin, disponible; **out of s.** (*goods*) épuisé, non disponible; **to take s.** *Fig* faire le point (**of** de); **s. reply/-size** réponse *f*/taille *f* courante; **s. phrase** expression *f* toute faite; **the S. Exchange** or **Market** la Bourse; – *vt* (*sell*) vendre; (*keep in store*) stocker; **to s.** (**up**) (*shop, larder*) approvisionner; **well-stocked** bien approvisionné; – *vi* **to s. up** s'approvisionner (**with** de, en). ◆**stockbroker** *n* agent *m* de change. ◆**stockcar** *n* stock-car *m*. ◆**stockholder** *n Fin* actionnaire *mf*. ◆**stockist** *n* dépositaire *mf*, stockiste *m*. ◆**stockpile** *vt* stocker, amasser. ◆**stockroom** *n* réserve *f*, magasin *m*. ◆**stocktaking** *n Com* inventaire *m*.

stocking ['stɒkɪŋ] *n* (*garment*) bas *m*.

stocky ['stɒkɪ] *a* (**-ier, -iest**) trapu.

stodge [stɒdʒ] *n* (*food*) *Fam* étouffe-chrétien *m inv*. ◆**stodgy** *a* (**-ier, -iest**) *Fam* lourd, indigeste; (*person, style*) compassé.

stoic ['stəʊɪk] *a & n* stoïque (*mf*). ◆**stoical** *a* stoïque. ◆**stoicism** *n* stoïcisme *m*.

stok/e [stəʊk] *vt* (*fire*) entretenir; (*engine*) chauffer. ◆**—er** *n Rail* chauffeur *m*.

stole [1] [stəʊl] *n* (*shawl*) étole *f*.

stole [2], **stolen** [stəʊl, 'stəʊl(ə)n] *see* steal [1,2].

stolid ['stɒlɪd] *a* (*manner, person*) impassible.

stomach ['stʌmək] **1** *n Anat* estomac *m*; (*abdomen*) ventre *m*; – *vt* (*put up with*) *Fig* supporter. ◆**stomachache** *n* mal *m* de ventre; **to have a s.** avoir mal au ventre.

stone [stəʊn] *n* pierre *f*; (*pebble*) caillou *m*; (*in fruit*) noyau *m*; (*in kidney*) *Med* calcul *m*; (*weight*) = 6,348 kg; **a stone's throw away** *Fig* à deux pas d'ici; – *vt* lancer des pierres sur, lapider; (*fruit*) dénoyauter. ◆**stonemason** *n* tailleur *m* de pierre, maçon *m*. ◆**stony** *a* **1** (**-ier, -iest**) (*path etc*) pierreux, caillouteux. **2 s. broke** (*penniless*) *Sl* fauché.

stone- [stəʊn] *pref* complètement. ◆**s.-'broke** *a Am Sl* fauché. ◆**s.-'cold** *a* complètement froid. ◆**s.-'dead** *a* raide mort. ◆**s.-'deaf** *a* sourd comme un pot.

stoned [stəʊnd] *a* (*high on drugs*) *Fam* camé.

stooge [stuːdʒ] *n* (*actor*) comparse *mf*; (*flunkey*) *Pej* larbin *m*; (*dupe*) *Pej* pigeon *m*.

stood [stʊd] *see* stand.

stool [stuːl] *n* tabouret *m*.

stoop [stuːp] **1** *n* **to have a s.** être voûté; – *vi* se baisser; **to s. to doing/to sth** *Fig* s'abaisser à faire/à qch. **2** *n* (*in front of house*) *Am* perron *m*.

stop [stɒp] *n* (*place, halt*) arrêt *m*, halte *f*; *Av Nau* escale *f*; *Gram* point *m*; **bus s.** arrêt *m* d'autobus; **to put a s. to** mettre fin à; **to bring to a s.** arrêter; **to come to a s.** s'arrêter; **without a s.** sans arrêt; **s. light** (*on vehicle*) stop *m*; **s. sign** (*road sign*) stop *m*; – *vt* (**-pp-**) arrêter; (*end*) mettre fin à; (*prevent*) empêcher (**from doing** de faire); (*cheque*) faire opposition à; **to s. up** (*sink, pipe, leak etc*) boucher; – *vi* s'arrêter; (*of pain, conversation etc*) cesser; (*stay*) rester; **to s. eating**/*etc* s'arrêter de manger/*etc*; **to s. snowing**/*etc* cesser de neiger/*etc*; **to s. by** passer (**s.o.'s** chez qn); **to s. off** or **over** (*on journey*) s'arrêter. ◆**stoppage** *n* arrêt *m*; (*in pay*) retenue *f*; (*in work*) arrêt *m* de travail; (*strike*) débrayage *m*; (*blockage*) obstruction *f*. ◆**stopper** *n* bouchon *m*.

stopcock ['stɒpkɒk] *n* robinet *m* d'arrêt. ◆**stopgap** *n* bouche-trou *m*; – *a* intérimaire. ◆**stopoff** *n* ◆**stopover** *n* halte *f*. ◆**stopwatch** *n* chronomètre *m*.

store [stɔːr] *n* (*supply*) provision *f*; (*of information, jokes etc*) Fig fonds *m*; (*depot, warehouse*) entrepôt *m*; (*shop*) grand magasin *m*, *Am* magasin *m*; (*computer memory*) mémoire *f*; **to have sth in s. for s.o.** (*surprise*) réserver qch à qn; **to keep in s.** garder en réserve; **to set great s. by** attacher une grande importance à; — *vt* **to s. (up)** (*in warehouse etc*) emmagasiner; (*for future use*) mettre en réserve; **to s. (away)** (*furniture*) entreposer. ◆**storage** *n* emmagasinage *m*; (*for future use*) mise *f* en réserve; **s. space** *or* **room** espace *m* de rangement. ◆**storekeeper** *n* magasinier *m*; (*shopkeeper*) *Am* commerçant, -ante *mf*. ◆**storeroom** *n* réserve *f*.

storey ['stɔːrɪ] *n* étage *m*.

stork [stɔːk] *n* cigogne *f*.

storm [stɔːm] **1** *n* (*weather*) & Fig tempête *f*; (*thunderstorm*) orage *m*; **s. cloud** nuage *m* orageux. **2** *vt* (*attack*) Mil prendre d'assaut. **3** *vi* **to s. out** (*angrily*) sortir comme une furie. ◆**stormy** *a* (**-ier, -iest**) (*weather, meeting etc*) orageux; (*wind*) d'orage.

story ['stɔːrɪ] **1** *n* histoire *f*; (*newspaper article*) article *m*; **s. (line)** Cin Th intrigue *f*; **short s.** Liter nouvelle *f*, conte *m*; **fairy s.** conte *m* de fées. **2** (*storey*) *Am* étage *m*. ◆**storyteller** *n* conteur, -euse *mf*; (*liar*) Fam menteur, -euse *mf*.

stout [staut] **1** *a* (**-er, -est**) (*person*) gros, corpulent; (*stick, volume*) gros, épais; (*shoes*) solide. **2** *n* (*beer*) bière *f* brune. ◆**-ness** *n* corpulence *f*.

stove [stəuv] *n* (*for cooking*) cuisinière *f*; (*solid fuel*) fourneau *m*; (*small*) réchaud *m*; (*for heating*) poêle *m*.

stow [stəu] **1** *vt* (*cargo*) arrimer; **to s. away** (*put away*) ranger. **2** *vi* **to s. away** Nau voyager clandestinement. ◆**stowaway** *n* Nau passager, -ère *mf* clandestin(e).

straddle ['stræd(ə)l] *vt* (*chair, fence*) se mettre *or* être à califourchon sur; (*step over, span*) enjamber; (*line in road*) Aut chevaucher.

straggl/e ['stræg(ə)l] *vi* (*stretch*) s'étendre (en désordre); (*trail*) traîner (en désordre); **to s. in** entrer par petits groupes. ◆**-er** *n* traînard, -arde *mf*.

straight [streɪt] *a* (**-er, -est**) droit; (*hair*) raide; (*route*) direct; (*tidy*) en ordre; (*frank*) franc; (*refusal*) net; (*actor, role*) sérieux; **I want to get this s.** comprenons-nous bien; **to keep a s. face** garder son sérieux; **to put** *or* **set s.** (*tidy*) ranger; — *n* **the s.** *Sp* la ligne droite; — *adv* (*to walk etc*) droit; (*directly*) tout droit, directe-

ment; (*to drink gin, whisky etc*) sec; **s. away** (*at once*) tout de suite; **s. out, s. off** sans hésiter; **s. opposite** juste en face; **s. ahead** *or* **on** (*to walk etc*) tout droit; **s. ahead** (*to look*) droit devant soi. ◆**straighta'way** *adv* tout de suite. ◆**straighten** *vt* **to s. (up)** redresser; (*tie, room*) arranger; **to s. things out** Fig arranger les choses. ◆**straight-'forward** *a* (*frank*) franc; (*easy*) simple.

strain [streɪn] **1** *n* tension *f*; (*tiredness*) fatigue *f*; (*stress*) Med tension *f* nerveuse; (*effort*) effort *m*; — *vt* (*rope, wire*) tendre excessivement; (*muscle*) Med froisser; (*ankle, wrist*) fouler; (*eyes*) fatiguer; (*voice*) forcer; Fig mettre à l'épreuve; **to s. one's ears** (*to hear*) tendre l'oreille; **to s. oneself** (*hurt oneself*) se faire mal; (*tire oneself*) se fatiguer; — *vi* fournir un effort (**to do** pour faire). **2** *vt* (*soup etc*) passer; (*vegetables*) égoutter. **3** *n* (*breed*) lignée *f*; (*of virus*) souche *f*; (*streak*) tendance *f*. **4** *npl* Mus accents *mpl* (of de). ◆**—ed** *a* (*relations*) tendu; (*laugh*) forcé; (*ankle, wrist*) foulé. ◆**—er** *n* passoire *f*.

strait [streɪt] **1** *n* & *npl* Geog détroit *m*. **2** *npl* **in financial straits** dans l'embarras. ◆**straitjacket** *n* camisole *f* de force. ◆**strait'laced** *a* collet monté *inv*.

strand [strænd] *n* (*of wool etc*) brin *m*; (*of hair*) mèche *f*; (*of story*) Fig fil *m*.

stranded ['strændɪd] *a* (*person, vehicle*) en rade.

strange [streɪndʒ] *a* (**-er, -est**) (*odd*) étrange, bizarre; (*unknown*) inconnu; (*new*) nouveau; **to feel s.** (*in a new place*) se sentir dépaysé. ◆**strangely** *adv* étrangement; **s. (enough) she ...** chose étrange, elle .... ◆**strangeness** *n* étrangeté *f*. ◆**stranger** *n* (*unknown*) inconnu, -ue *mf*; (*outsider*) étranger, -ère *mf*; **he's a s. here** il n'est pas d'ici; **she's a s. to me** elle m'est inconnue.

strangle ['stræŋg(ə)l] *vt* étrangler. ◆**strangler** *n* étrangleur, -euse *mf*. ◆**stranglehold** *n* emprise *f* totale (**on** sur).

strap [stræp] *n* courroie *f*, sangle *f*; (*on dress*) bretelle *f*; (*on watch*) bracelet *m*; (*on sandal*) lanière *f*; — *vt* (**-pp-**) **to s. (down** *or* **in)** attacher (avec une courroie).

strapping ['stræpɪŋ] *a* (*well-built*) robuste.

stratagem ['strætədʒəm] *n* stratagème *m*.

strategy ['strætədʒɪ] *n* stratégie *f*. ◆**stra-'tegic** *a* stratégique.

stratum, *pl* **-ta** ['strɑːtəm, -tə] *n* couche *f*.

straw [strɔː] *n* paille *f*; **a (drinking) s.** une paille; **that's the last s.!** c'est le comble!

strawberry ['strɔːbərɪ] *n* fraise *f*; — *a*

(flavour, ice cream) à la fraise; *(jam)* de fraises; *(tart)* aux fraises.

stray [streɪ] *a (lost)* perdu; **a s. car**/*etc* une voiture/*etc* isolée; **a few s. cars**/*etc* quelques rares voitures/*etc*; **– n** animal *m* perdu; **– vi** s'égarer; **to s. from** *(subject, path)* s'écarter de.

streak [striːk] *n (line)* raie *f*; *(of light)* filet *m*; *(of colour)* strie *f*; *(trace) Fig* trace *f*; *(tendency)* tendance *f*; **grey**/*etc* **streaks** *(in hair)* mèches *fpl* grises/*etc*; **a mad s.** une tendance à la folie; **my literary s.** ma fibre littéraire. ◆**streaked** *a (marked)* strié, zébré; *(stained)* taché (**with** de). ◆**streaky** *a* (**-ier, -iest**) strié; *(bacon)* pas trop maigre.

stream [striːm] *n (brook)* ruisseau *m*; *(current)* courant *m*; *(flow) & Fig* flot *m*; *Sch* classe *f* (de niveau); **– vi** ruisseler (**with** de); **to s. in** *(of sunlight, people etc) Fig* entrer à flots.

streamer ['striːmər] *n (paper)* serpentin *m*; *(banner)* banderole *f*.

streamlin/e ['striːmlaɪn] *vt (work, method etc)* rationaliser. ◆**–ed** *a (shape)* aérodynamique.

street [striːt] *n* rue *f*; **s. door** porte *f* d'entrée; **s. lamp, s. light** réverbère *m*; **s. map, s. plan** plan *m* des rues; **up my s.** *Fig Fam* dans mes cordes; **streets ahead** *Fam* très en avance (**of** sur). ◆**streetcar** *n (tram) Am* tramway *m*.

strength [streŋθ] *n* force *f*; *(health, energy)* forces *fpl*; *(of wood, fabric)* solidité *f*; **on the s. of** *Fig* en vertu de; **in full s.** au (grand) complet. ◆**strengthen** *vt (building, position etc)* renforcer, consolider; *(body, soul, limb)* fortifier.

strenuous ['strenjuəs] *a (effort etc)* vigoureux, énergique; *(work)* ardu; *(active)* actif; *(tiring)* fatigant. ◆**–ly** *adv* énergiquement.

strep [strep] *a* **s. throat** *Med Am* angine *f*.

stress [stres] *n (pressure)* pression *f*; *Med Psy* tension *f* (nerveuse), stress *m*; *(emphasis) & Gram* accent *m*; *Tech* tension *f*; **under s.** *Med Psy* sous pression, stressé; **– vt** insister sur; *(word)* accentuer; **to s. that** souligner que. ◆**stressful** *a* stressant.

stretch [stretʃ] *vt (rope, neck)* tendre; *(shoe, rubber)* étirer; *(meaning) Fig* forcer; **to s.** *(out) (arm, leg)* étendre, allonger; **to s.** *(out)* **one's arm** *(reach out)* tendre le bras *(m* take pour prendre); **to s. one's legs** *Fig* se dégourdir les jambes; **to s. s.o.** *Fig* exiger un effort de qn; **to be (fully) stretched** *(of budget etc)* être tiré au maximum; **to s. out** *(visit)* prolonger; **– vi** *(of person, elastic)*

s'étirer; *(of influence etc)* s'étendre; **to s. (out)** *(of rope, plain)* s'étendre; **– n** *(area, duration)* étendue *f*; *(of road)* tronçon *m*, partie *f*; *(route, trip)* trajet *m*; **at a s.** d'une (seule) traite; **ten**/*etc* **hours at a s.** dix/*etc* heures d'affilée; **s. socks**/*etc* chaussettes *fpl*/*etc* extensibles; **s. nylon** nylon *m* stretch *inv.* ◆**stretchmarks** *npl (on body)* vergetures *fpl.*

stretcher ['stretʃər] *n* brancard *m*.

strew [struː] *vt (pt* strewed, *pp* strewed *or* strewn) *(scatter)* répandre; **strewn with** *(covered)* jonché de.

stricken ['strɪk(ə)n] *a* **s. with** *(illness)* atteint de; *(panic)* frappé de.

strict [strɪkt] *a* (**-er, -est**) *(severe, absolute)* strict. ◆**–ly** *adv* strictement; **s. forbidden** formellement interdit. ◆**–ness** *n* sévérité *f*.

stride [straɪd] *n (grand)* pas *m*, enjambée *f*; **to make great strides** *Fig* faire de grands progrès; **– vi** *(pt* strode) **s. across** *or* **over** enjamber; **to s. up and down a room** arpenter une pièce.

strident ['straɪdənt] *a* strident.

strife [straɪf] *n inv* conflit(s) *m(pl).*

strik/e [straɪk] **1** *n (attack) Mil* raid *m* (aérien); *(of oil etc)* découverte *f*; **– vt** *(pt & pp* struck) *(hit, impress)* frapper; *(collide with)* heurter; *(beat)* battre; *(a blow)* donner; *(a match)* frotter; *(gold, problem)* trouver; *(coin)* frapper; *(of clock)* sonner; **to s. a bargain** conclure un accord; **to s. a balance** trouver l'équilibre; **to s. (off)** *(from list)* rayer (**from** de); **to be struck off** *(of doctor)* être radié; **it strikes me as**/*that* il me semble être/que; **how did it s. you?** quelle impression ça t'a fait?; **to s. down** *(of illness etc)* terrasser *(qn)*; **to s. up a friendship** lier amitié (**with** avec); **– vi** **to s.** *(at)* *(attack)* attaquer; **to s. back** *(retaliate)* riposter; **to s. out** donner des coups. **2** *n (of workers)* grève *f*; **to go (out) on s.** se mettre en grève (**for** pour obtenir, **against** pour protester contre); **– vi** *(pt & pp* struck) *(of workers)* faire grève. ◆**–ing** *a (impressive)* frappant. ◆**–ingly** *adv (beautiful etc)* extraordinairement. ◆**–er** *n* gréviste *mf*; *Fb* buteur *m*.

string [strɪŋ] *n* ficelle *f*; *(of anorak, apron)* cordon *m*; *(of violin, racket etc)* corde *f*; *(of pearls, beads)* rang *m*; *(of onions, insults)* chapelet *m*; *(of people, vehicles)* file *f*; *(of questions etc)* série *f*; **to pull strings** *Fig* faire jouer ses relations; **– a** *(instrument, quartet) Mus* à cordes; **s. bean** haricot *m* vert; **– vt** *(pt & pp* strung) *(beads)* enfiler; **to s.**

(hang up) suspendre; – vi to s. **along (with)** *Fam* suivre. ◆**-ed** a (instrument) *Mus* à cordes. ◆**stringy** a (**-ier, -iest**) (meat etc) filandreux.

stringent ['strindʒ(ə)nt] a rigoureux. ◆**stringency** n rigueur f.

strip [strip] 1 n (piece) bande f; (of water) bras m; (**thin**) s. (of metal etc) lamelle f; **landing s.** piste f or terrain m d'atterrissage; **s. cartoon, comic s.** bande f dessinée. 2 vt (**-pp-**) (undress) déshabiller; (bed) défaire; (deprive) dépouiller (of de); to s. **down** (machine) démonter; **to s. off** (remove) enlever; – vi to s. **(off)** (undress) se déshabiller. ◆**stripper** n (woman) strip-teaseuse f; (paint) s. décapant m. ◆**strip-'tease** n strip-tease m.

stripe [straɪp] n rayure f; *Mil* galon m. ◆**striped** a rayé (**with** de). ◆**stripy** a rayé.

strive [straɪv] vi (pt **strove**, pp **striven**) s'efforcer (**to do** de faire, **for** d'obtenir).

strode [strəʊd] see **stride**.

stroke [strəʊk] n (movement) coup m; (of pen, genius) trait m; (of brush) touche f; (on clock) coup m; (caress) caresse f; *Med* coup m de sang; (swimming style) nage f; **at a s.** d'un coup; **a s. of luck** un coup de chance; **you haven't done a s.** (of work) tu n'as rien fait; **heat s.** (sunstroke) insolation f; **four-s.-engine** moteur m à quatre temps; – vt (beard, chat etc) caresser.

stroll [strəʊl] n promenade f; – vi se promener, flâner; **to s. in/etc** entrer/etc sans se presser. ◆**-ing** a (musician etc) ambulant.

stroller ['strəʊlər] n (pushchair) *Am* poussette f.

strong [strɒŋ] a (**-er, -est**) fort; (shoes, nerves) solide; (interest) vif; (measures) énergique; (supporter) ardent; **sixty s.** au nombre de soixante; – adv **to be going s.** aller toujours bien. ◆**-ly** adv (to protest, defend) énergiquement; (to desire, advise, remind) fortement; (to feel) profondément; **s. built** solide. ◆**strongarm** a brutal. ◆**strongbox** n coffre-fort m. ◆**stronghold** n bastion m. ◆**strong-'willed** a résolu.

strove [strəʊv] see **strive**.

struck [strʌk] see **strike** 1,2.

structure ['strʌktʃər] n structure f; (of building) armature f; (building itself) construction f. ◆**structural** a structural; (fault) *Archit* de construction.

struggle ['strʌg(ə)l] n (fight) lutte f (**to do** pour faire); (effort) effort m; **to put up a s.**

résister; **to have a s. doing** or **to do** avoir du mal à faire; – vi (fight) lutter, se battre (**with** avec); (resist) résister; (thrash about wildly) se débattre; **to s. to do** (try hard) s'efforcer de faire; **to s. out of** sortir péniblement de; **to s. along** or **on** se débrouiller; **a struggling lawyer/etc** un avocat/etc qui a du mal à débuter.

strum [strʌm] vt (**-mm-**) (guitar etc) gratter de.

strung [strʌŋ] see **string**; – a **s. out** (things, people) espacés; (washing) étendu.

strut [strʌt] 1 vi (**-tt-**) (**about** or **around**) se pavaner. 2 n (support) *Tech* étai m.

stub [stʌb] 1 n (of pencil, cigarette etc) bout m; (counterfoil of cheque etc) talon m; – vt (**-bb-**) to s. **out** (cigarette) écraser. 2 vt (**-bb-**) **to s. one's toe** se cogner le doigt de pied (**on, against** contre).

stubble ['stʌb(ə)l] n barbe f de plusieurs jours.

stubborn ['stʌbən] a (person) entêté, opiniâtre; (cough, efforts, manner etc) opiniâtre. ◆**-ly** adv opiniâtrement. ◆**-ness** n entêtement m; opiniâtreté f.

stubby ['stʌbɪ] a (**-ier, -iest**) (finger etc) gros et court, épais; (person) trapu.

stuck [stʌk] see **stick**[2]; – a (caught, jammed) coincé; **s. in bed/indoors** cloué au lit/chez soi; **to be s.** (unable to do sth) ne pas savoir quoi faire; **I'm s.** (for an answer) je ne sais que répondre; **to be s. with** sth/s.o. se farcir qch/qn. ◆**s.-'up** a *Fam* prétentieux, snob inv.

stud [stʌd] 1 n (nail) clou m (à grosse tête); (for collar) bouton m de col. 2 (farm) haras m; (horses) écurie f; (stallion) étalon m; (virile man) *Sl* mâle m. ◆**studded** a (boots, tyres) clouté; **s. with** (covered) *Fig* constellé de, parsemé de.

student ['stjuːdənt] n *Univ* étudiant, -ante mf; *Sch Am* élève mf; **music/etc s.** étudiant, -ante en musique/etc; – a (life, protest) étudiant; (restaurant, residence, grant) universitaire.

studio ['stjuːdɪəʊ] n (pl **-os**) (of painter etc) & *Cin TV* studio m; **s. flat** or *Am* **apartment** studio m.

studious ['stjuːdɪəs] a (person) studieux. ◆**-ly** adv (carefully) avec soin. ◆**-ness** n application f.

study ['stʌdɪ] n étude f; (office) bureau m; – vt (learn, observe) étudier; – vi étudier; **to s. to be a doctor/etc** faire des études pour devenir médecin/etc; **to s. for** (exam) préparer. ◆**studied** a (deliberate) étudié.

stuff [stʌf] 1 n (thing) truc m, chose f;

(*substance*) substance f; (*things*) trucs mpl, choses fpl; (*possessions*) affaires fpl; (*nonsense*) sottises fpl; **this s.'s good, it's good s.** c'est bon (ça). **2** vt (*chair, cushion etc*) rembourrer (**with** avec); (*animal*) empailler; (*cram, fill*) bourrer (**with** de); (*put, thrust*) fourrer (**into** dans); (*chicken etc*) Culin farcir; **to s.** (**up**) (*hole etc*) colmater; **my nose is stuffed (up)** j'ai le nez bouché. ◆**—ing** n (*padding*) bourre f; Culin farce f.

stuffy ['stʌfɪ] a (**-ier, -iest**) (*room etc*) mal aéré; (*formal*) Fig compassé; (*old-fashioned*) vieux jeu inv; **it smells s.** ça sent le renfermé.

stumble ['stʌmb(ə)l] vi trébucher (**over** sur, **against** contre); **to s. across** or **on** (*find*) tomber sur; **stumbling block** pierre f d'achoppement.

stump [stʌmp] n (*of tree*) souche f; (*of limb*) moignon m; (*of pencil*) bout m; Cricket piquet m.

stumped ['stʌmpt] a **to be s. by sth** (*baffled*) ne pas savoir que penser de qch.

stun [stʌn] vt (**-nn-**) (*daze*) étourdir; (*animal*) assommer; Fig stupéfier. ◆**stunned** a Fig stupéfait (**by** par). ◆**stunning** a (*blow*) étourdissant; (*news*) stupéfiant; (*terrific*) Fam sensationnel.

stung [stʌŋ] see **sting**.

stunk [stʌŋk] see **stink**.

stunt [stʌnt] **1** n (*feat*) tour m (de force); Cin cascade f; (*ruse, trick*) truc m; **s. man** Cin cascadeur m; **s. woman** Cin cascadeuse f. **2** vt (*growth*) retarder. ◆**—ed** a (*person*) rabougri.

stupefy ['stju:pɪfaɪ] vt (*of drink etc*) abrutir; (*amaze*) Fig stupéfier.

stupendous [stju:'pendəs] a prodigieux.

stupid ['stju:pɪd] a stupide, bête; **a s. thing** une sottise; **s. fool, s. idiot** idiot, -ote mf. ◆**stu'pidity** n stupidité f. ◆**stupidly** adv stupidement, bêtement.

stupor ['stju:pər] n (*daze*) stupeur f.

sturdy ['stɜ:dɪ] a (**-ier, -iest**) (*person, shoe etc*) robuste. ◆**sturdiness** n robustesse f.

sturgeon ['stɜ:dʒ(ə)n] n (*fish*) esturgeon m.

stutter ['stʌtər] n bégaiement m; **to have a s.** être bègue; — vi bégayer.

sty [staɪ] n (*pigsty*) porcherie f.

sty(e) [staɪ] n (*on eye*) orgelet m.

style [staɪl] n style m; (*fashion*) mode f; (*design of dress etc*) modèle m; (*of hair*) coiffure f; (*sort*) genre m; **to have s.** avoir de la classe; **in s.** (*in superior manner*) de la meilleure façon possible; (*to live, travel*) dans le luxe; — vt (*design*) créer; **he styles**

himself . . . Pej il se fait appeler . . . ; **to s. s.o.'s hair** coiffer qn. ◆**styling** n (*cutting of hair*) coupe f. ◆**stylish** a chic, élégant. ◆**stylishly** adv élégamment. ◆**stylist** n (*hair*) s. coiffeur, -euse mf. ◆**sty'listic** a de style, stylistique. ◆**stylized** a stylisé.

stylus ['staɪləs] n (*of record player*) pointe f de lecture.

suave [swɑːv] a (**-er, -est**) (*urbane*) courtois; — Pej doucereux.

sub- [sʌb] pref sous-, sub-.

subconscious [sʌb'kɒnʃəs] a & n subconscient (m). ◆**—ly** adv inconsciemment.

subcontract [sʌbkən'trækt] vt sous-traiter. ◆**subcontractor** n sous-traitant m.

subdivide [sʌbdɪ'vaɪd] vt subdiviser (**into** en). ◆**subdivision** n subdivision f.

subdu/e [səb'dju:] vt (*country*) asservir; (*feelings*) maîtriser. ◆**—ed** a (*light*) atténué; (*voice*) bas; (*reaction*) faible; (*person*) qui manque d'entrain.

subheading ['sʌbhedɪŋ] n sous-titre m.

subject¹ ['sʌbdʒɪkt] n **1** (*matter*) & Gram sujet m; Sch Univ matière f; **s. matter** (*topic*) sujet m; (*content*) contenu m. **2** (*citizen*) ressortissant, -ante mf; (*of monarch, monarchy*) sujet, -ette mf; (*person etc in experiment*) sujet m.

subject² ['sʌbdʒekt] a (*tribe etc*) soumis; **s. to** (*prone to*) sujet à (*maladie etc*); (*ruled by*) soumis à (*loi, règle etc*); (*conditional upon*) sous réserve de; **prices are s. to change** les prix peuvent être modifiés; − [səb'dʒekt] vt soumettre (**to** à); (*expose*) exposer (**to** à). ◆**sub'jection** n soumission f (**to** à).

subjective [səb'dʒektɪv] a subjectif. ◆**—ly** adv subjectivement. ◆**subjec'tivity** n subjectivité f.

subjugate ['sʌbdʒugeɪt] vt subjuguer.

subjunctive [səb'dʒʌŋktɪv] n Gram subjonctif m.

sublet [sʌb'let] vt (*pt* & *pp* **sublet**, *pres p* **subletting**) sous-louer.

sublimate ['sʌblɪmeɪt] vt Psy sublimer.

sublime [sə'blaɪm] a sublime; (*indifference, stupidity*) suprême; − n sublime m.

submachine-gun [sʌbmə'ʃiːngʌn] n mitraillette f.

submarine ['sʌbməriːn] n sous-marin m.

submerge [səb'mɜːdʒ] vt (*flood, overwhelm*) submerger; (*immerse*) immerger (**in** dans); − vi (*of submarine*) s'immerger.

submit [səb'mɪt] vt (**-tt-**) soumettre (**to** à); **to s. that** Jur suggérer que; − vi se soumettre (**to** à). ◆**submission** n soumission f (**to** à). ◆**submissive** a soumis. ◆**submissively** adv avec soumission.

subnormal [sʌb'nɔːm(ə)l] *a* au-dessous de la normale; (*mentally*) arriéré.

subordinate [sə'bɔːdinət] *a* subalterne; *Gram* subordonné; – *n* subordonné, -ée *mf*; – [sə'bɔːdineit] *vt* subordonner (**to** à). ◆**subordi'nation** *n* subordination *f* (**to** à).

subpoena [səb'piːnə] *vt Jur* citer; – *n Jur* citation *f*.

subscribe [səb'skraib] *vt* (*money*) donner (**to** à); – *vi* cotiser; **to s. to** (*take out subscription*) s'abonner à (*journal etc*); (*be a subscriber*) être abonné à (*journal etc*); (*fund, idea*) souscrire à. ◆**subscriber** *n Journ Tel* abonné, -ée *mf*. ◆**subscription** *n* (*to newspaper etc*) abonnement *m*; (*to fund, idea*) & *Fin* souscription *f*; (*to club etc*) cotisation *f*.

subsequent [sʌbsikwənt] *a* postérieur (**to** à); **our s. problems** les problèmes que nous avons eus par la suite; **s. to** (*as a result of*) consécutif à. ◆**–ly** *adv* par la suite.

subservient [səb'sɜːviənt] *a* obséquieux; **to be s. to** (*a slave to*) être asservi à.

subside [səb'said] *vi* (*of building, land*) s'affaisser; (*of wind, flood*) baisser. ◆**'subsidence** *n* affaissement *m*.

subsidiary [səb'sidiəri] *a* accessoire; (*subject*) *Univ* secondaire; – *n* (*company*) *Com* filiale *f*.

subsidize [sʌbsidaiz] *vt* subventionner. ◆**subsidy** *n* subvention *f*.

subsist [səb'sist] *vi* (*of person, doubts etc*) subsister. ◆**subsistence** *n* subsistance *f*.

substance [sʌbstəns] *n* substance *f*; (*firmness*) solidité *f*; **a man of s.** un homme riche. ◆**substantial** [səb'stænʃ(ə)l] *a* important, considérable; (*meal*) substantiel. ◆**sub'stantially** *adv* considérablement, beaucoup; **s. true**/*etc* (*to a great extent*) en grande partie vrai/*etc*; **s. different** très différent.

substandard [sʌb'stændəd] *a* de qualité inférieure.

substantiate [səb'stænʃieit] *vt* prouver, justifier.

substitute [sʌbstitjuːt] *n* (*thing*) produit *m* de remplacement; (*person*) remplaçant, -ante *mf* (**for** de); **there's no s. for** ... rien ne peut remplacer ... ; – *vt* substituer (**for** à); – *vi* **s. for** remplacer; (*deputize for in job*) se substituer à. ◆**substi'tution** *n* substitution *f*.

subtitle [sʌbtait(ə)l] *n* sous-titre *m*; – *vt* sous-titrer.

subtle [sʌt(ə)l] *a* (**-er, -est**) subtil. ◆**sub-**

tlety *n* subtilité *f*. ◆**subtly** *adv* subtilement.

subtotal [sʌb'təut(ə)l] *n* total *m* partiel, sous-total *m*.

subtract [səb'trækt] *vt* soustraire (**from** de). ◆**subtraction** *n* soustraction *f*.

suburb [sʌbɜːb] *n* banlieue *f*; **the suburbs** la banlieue; **in the suburbs** en banlieue. ◆**su'burban** *a* (*train*) de banlieue; (*accent*) de la banlieue. ◆**su'burbia** *n* la banlieue.

subversive [səb'vɜːsiv] *a* subversif. ◆**subversion** *n* subversion *f*. ◆**subvert** *vt* (*system etc*) bouleverser; (*person*) corrompre.

subway [sʌbwei] *n* passage *m* souterrain; *Rail Am* métro *m*.

succeed [sək'siːd] **1** *vi* réussir (**in doing** à faire, **in sth** dans qch). **2** *vt* **s. s.o.** (*follow*) succéder à qn; – *vi* **to s. to the throne** succéder à la couronne. ◆**–ing** *a* (*in past*) suivant; (*in future*) futur; (*consecutive*) consécutif.

success [sək'ses] *n* succès *m*, réussite *f*; **to make a s. of sth** réussir qch; **he was a s.** il a eu du succès; **his** *or* **her s. in the exam** sa réussite à l'examen; **s. story** réussite *f* complète *ou* exemplaire. ◆**successful** *a* (*venture etc*) couronné de succès, réussi; (*outcome*) heureux; (*firm*) prospère; (*candidate in exam*) admis, reçu; (*in election*) élu; (*writer, film etc*) à succès; **to be s.** réussir (**in** dans, **in an exam** à un examen, **in doing** à faire). ◆**successfully** *adv* avec succès.

succession [sək'seʃ(ə)n] *n* succesion *f*; **in s.** successivement; **ten days in s.** dix jours consécutifs; **in rapid s.** coup sur coup. ◆**successive** *a* successif; **ten s. days** dix jours consécutifs. ◆**successor** *n* successeur *m* (**of, to** de).

succinct [sək'siŋkt] *a* succinct.

succulent [sʌkjulənt] *a* succulent.

succumb [sə'kʌm] *vi* (*yield*) succomber (**to** à).

such [sʌtʃ] *a* tel; **a s. car**/*etc* une telle voiture/*etc*; **s. happiness**/*etc* (*so much*) tant *or* tellement de bonheur/*etc*; **there's no s. thing** ça n'existe pas; **I said no s. thing** je n'ai rien dit de tel; **s. as** comme, tel que; **and s.** tel ou tel; – *adv* (*so very*) si; (*in comparisons*) aussi; **s. a kind woman as you** une femme aussi gentille que vous; **s. long trips** de si longs voyages; **s. a large helping** une si grosse portion; – *pron* **happiness**/*etc* **as s.** le bonheur/*etc* en tant que tel; **s. was**

my idea telle était mon idée. ◆**suchlike** n . . . and s. Fam . . . et autres.

suck [sʌk] vt sucer; (of baby) téter (lait, biberon etc); to s. (up) (with straw, pump) aspirer; to s. up or in (absorb) absorber; — vi (of baby) téter; to s. at sucer. ◆**-er** n 1 (fool) Fam pigeon m, dupe f. 2 (pad) ventouse f.

suckle ['sʌk(ə)l] vt (of woman) allaiter; (of baby) téter.

suction ['sʌkʃ(ə)n] n succion f; s. disc, s. pad ventouse f.

Sudan [suːˈdɑːn] n Soudan m.

sudden ['sʌd(ə)n] a soudain, subit; all of a s. tout à coup. ◆**-ly** adv subitement. ◆**-ness** n soudaineté f.

suds [sʌdz] npl mousse f de savon.

sue [suː] vt poursuivre (en justice); — vi engager des poursuites (judiciaires).

suede [sweɪd] n daim m; s. de daim.

suet ['suːɪt] n graisse f de rognon.

suffer ['sʌfər] vi souffrir (from de); to s. from pimples/the flu avoir des boutons/la grippe; your work/etc will s. ton travail/etc s'en ressentira; (pain) ressentir; (tolerate) souffrir. ◆**-ing** n souffrance(s) f(pl). ◆**-er** n Med malade mf; (from misfortune) victime f.

suffice [sə'faɪs] vi suffire.

sufficient [sə'fɪʃ(ə)nt] a (quantity, number) suffisant; s. money/etc (enough) suffisamment d'argent/etc; to have s. en avoir suffisamment. ◆**-ly** adv suffisamment.

suffix ['sʌfɪks] n Gram suffixe m.

suffocate ['sʌfəkeɪt] vti étouffer, suffoquer. ◆**suffo'cation** n (of industry, mind etc) & Med étouffement m, asphyxie f.

suffrage ['sʌfrɪdʒ] n (right to vote) Pol suffrage m.

suffused [sə'fjuːzd] a s. with (light, tears) baigné de.

sugar ['ʃʊgər] n sucre m; — a (cane, tongs) à sucre; (industry) sucrier; s. bowl sucrier m; — vt sucrer. ◆**sugary** a (taste, tone) sucré.

suggest [sə'dʒest] vt (propose) suggérer, proposer (to à, that que (+ sub)); (evoke, imply) suggérer; (hint) Pej insinuer. ◆**suggestion** n suggestion f, proposition f; (evocation) suggestion f; Pej insinuation f. ◆**suggestive** a suggestif; to be s. of suggérer.

suicide ['suːɪsaɪd] n suicide m. ◆**sui'cidal** a suicidaire.

suit [suːt] 1 n (man's) complet m, costume m; (woman's) tailleur m; (of pilot, diver etc) combinaison f. 2 n (lawsuit) Jur procès m. 3 n Cards couleur f. 4 vt (satisfy, be appropri-

ate to) convenir à; (of dress, colour etc) aller (bien) à; (adapt) adapter (to à); it suits me to stay ça m'arrange de rester; s. yourself! comme tu voudras!; suited to (made for) fait pour; (appropriate to) approprié à; well suited (couple etc) bien assorti. ◆**suita-'bility** n (of remark etc) à-propos m; (of person) aptitudes fpl (for pour); I'm not sure of the s. of it (date etc) je ne sais pas si ça convient. ◆**suitable** a qui convient (for à); (dress, colour) qui va (bien); (example) approprié; (socially) convenable. ◆**suit-ably** adv convenablement.

suitcase ['suːtkeɪs] n valise f.

suite [swiːt] n (rooms) suite f; (furniture) mobilier m; bedroom s. (furniture) chambre f à coucher.

suitor ['suːtər] n soupirant m.

sulfur ['sʌlfər] n Am soufre m.

sulk [sʌlk] vi bouder. ◆**sulky** a (-ier, -iest) boudeur.

sullen ['sʌlən] a maussade. ◆**-ly** adv d'un air maussade.

sully ['sʌlɪ] vt Lit souiller.

sulphur ['sʌlfər] n soufre m.

sultan ['sʌltən] n sultan m.

sultana [sʌl'tɑːnə] n raisin m de Smyrne.

sultry ['sʌltrɪ] a (-ier, -iest) (heat) étouffant; Fig sensuel.

sum [sʌm] 1 n (amount, total) somme f; Math calcul m; pl (arithmetic) le calcul; s. total résultat m. 2 vt (-mm-) to s. up (facts etc) récapituler, résumer; (text) résumer; (situation) évaluer; (person) jauger; — vi to s. up récapituler. ◆**summing-'up** n (pl summings-up) résumé m.

summarize ['sʌməraɪz] vt résumer. ◆**sum-mary** n résumé m; — a (brief) sommaire.

summer ['sʌmər] n été m; in (the) s. en été; Indian s. été indien or de la Saint-Martin; — a d'été; s. holidays grandes vacances fpl. ◆**summerhouse** n pavillon m (de gardien). ◆**summertime** n été m; in (the) s. en été. ◆**summery** a (weather etc) estival; (dress) d'été.

summit ['sʌmɪt] n (of mountain, power etc) sommet m; s. conference/meeting Pol conférence f/rencontre f au sommet.

summon ['sʌmən] vt (call) appeler; (meeting, s.o. to meeting) convoquer (to à); to s. s.o. to do sommer qn de faire; to s. up (courage, strength) rassembler.

summons ['sʌmənz] n Jur assignation f; — vt Jur assigner.

sumptuous ['sʌmptʃʊəs] a somptueux. ◆**-ness** n somptuosité f.

sun [sʌn] n soleil m; in the s. au soleil; the

sun's shining il fait (du) soleil; – a (*cream, filter etc*) solaire; **s. lounge** solarium *m*; – *vt* (*-nn-*) **to s. oneself** se chauffer au soleil. ◆**sunbaked** a brûlé par le soleil. ◆**sunbathe** *vi* prendre un bain de soleil. ◆**sunbeam** *n* rayon *m* de soleil. ◆**sunburn** *n* (*tan*) bronzage *m*; *Med* coup *m* de soleil. ◆**sunburnt** a bronzé; *Med* brûlé par le soleil. ◆**sundial** *n* cadran *m* solaire. ◆**sundown** *n* coucher *m* du soleil. ◆**sundrenched** a brûlé par le soleil. ◆**sunflower** *n* tournesol *m*. ◆**sunglasses** *npl* lunettes *fpl* de soleil. ◆**sunlamp** *n* lampe *f* à rayons ultraviolets. ◆**sunlight** *n* (lumière *f* du) soleil *m*. ◆**sunlit** a ensoleillé. ◆**sunrise** *n* lever *m* du soleil. ◆**sunroof** *n* Aut toit *m* ouvrant. ◆**sunset** *n* coucher *m* du soleil. ◆**sunshade** *n* (on table) parasol *m*; (portable) ombrelle *f*. ◆**sunshine** *n* soleil *m*. ◆**sunstroke** *n* insolation *f*. ◆**suntan** *n* bronzage *m*; – a (lotion, oil) solaire. ◆**suntanned** a bronzé. ◆**sunup** *n* Am lever *m* du soleil.

sundae ['sʌndeɪ] *n* glace *f* aux fruits.

Sunday ['sʌndɪ] *n* dimanche *m*.

sundry ['sʌndrɪ] a divers; **all and s.** tout le monde; – *npl* Com articles *mpl* divers.

sung [sʌŋ] see **sing**.

sunk [sʌŋk] see **sink²**; – a **I'm s.** Fam je suis fichu. ◆**sunken** a (rock etc) submergé; (eyes) cave.

sunny ['sʌnɪ] a (-ier, -iest) ensoleillé; **it's s.** il fait (du) soleil. **s. period** Met éclaircie *f*.

super ['suːpər] a Fam sensationnel.

super- ['suːpər] pref super-.

superannuation [suːpərænjʊ'eɪʃ(ə)n] *n* (amount) cotisations *fpl* (pour la retraite).

superb [suː'pɜːb] a superbe.

supercilious [suːpə'sɪlɪəs] a hautain.

superficial [suːpə'fɪʃ(ə)l] a superficiel. ◆**-ly** adv superficiellement.

superfluous [suː'pɜːflʊəs] a superflu.

superhuman [suːpə'hjuːmən] a surhumain.

superimpose [suːpərɪm'pəʊz] *vt* superposer (on à).

superintendent [suːpərɪn'tendənt] *n* directeur, -trice *mf*; (police) **s.** commissaire *m* (de police).

superior [suː'pɪərɪər] a supérieur (to à); (goods) de qualité supérieure; – *n* (person) supérieur, -eure *mf*. ◆**superi'ority** *n* supériorité *f*.

superlative [suː'pɜːlətɪv] a sans pareil; – a & *n* Gram superlatif (*m*).

superman ['suːpəmæn] *n* (pl -men) surhomme *m*.

supermarket ['suːpəmaːkɪt] *n* supermarché *m*.

supernatural [suːpə'nætʃ(ə)rəl] a & *n* surnaturel (*m*).

superpower ['suːpəpaʊər] *n* Pol superpuissance *f*.

supersede [suːpə'siːd] *vt* remplacer, supplanter.

supersonic [suːpə'sɒnɪk] a supersonique.

superstition [suːpə'stɪʃ(ə)n] *n* superstition *f*. ◆**superstitious** a superstitieux.

supertanker ['suːpətæŋkər] *n* pétrolier *m* géant.

supervise ['suːpəvaɪz] *vt* (person, work) surveiller; (office, research) diriger. ◆**super'vision** *n* surveillance *f*; direction *f*. ◆**supervisor** *n* surveillant, -ante *mf*; (in office) chef *m* de service; (shop) chef *m* de rayon. ◆**super'visory** a (post) de surveillant(e).

supper ['sʌpər] *n* dîner *m*; (late-night) souper *m*.

supple ['sʌp(ə)l] a souple. ◆**—ness** *n* souplesse *f*.

supplement ['sʌplɪmənt] *n* (addition) & Journ supplément *m* (to à); – ['sʌplɪment] *vt* compléter; **to s. one's income** arrondir ses fins de mois. ◆**supple'mentary** a supplémentaire.

supply [sə'plaɪ] *vt* (provide) fournir; (feed) alimenter (with en); (equip) équiper, pourvoir (with de); **to s. a need** subvenir à un besoin; **to s. s.o. with sth, s. sth to s.o.** (facts etc) fournir qch à qn; – *n* (stock) provision *f*, réserve *f*; (equipment) matériel *m*; **the s. of** (act) la fourniture de; **the s. of gas/electricity to** l'alimentation *f* en gaz/électricité de; (food) **supplies** vivres *mpl*; (office) **supplies** fournitures *fpl* (de bureau); **s. and demand** l'offre *f* et la demande; **to be in short s.** manquer; – a (ship, train) ravitailleur; **s. teacher** suppléant, -ante *mf*. ◆**—ing** *n* (provision) fourniture *f*; (feeding) alimentation *f*. ◆**supplier** *n* Com fournisseur *m*.

support [sə'pɔːt] *vt* (bear weight of) soutenir, supporter; (help, encourage) soutenir, appuyer; (theory, idea) appuyer; (be in favour of) être en faveur de; (family, wife etc) assurer la subsistance de; (endure) supporter; – *n* (help, encouragement) appui *m*, soutien *m*; Tech support *m*; **means of s.** moyens *mpl* de subsistance; **in s. of** en faveur de; (evidence, theory) à l'appui de. ◆**—ing** a (role) Th Cin secondaire; (actor) qui a un rôle secondaire. ◆**supporter** *n* partisan, -ane *mf*; *Fb* supporter *m*. ◆**supportive** *a* to be s. prêter son appui (**of**, to à).

suppos/e [sə'pəʊz] *vti* supposer (**that** que); **I'm supposed to work** *or* **be working** (*ought*) je suis censé travailler; **he's s. to be rich** on le dit riche; **I s.** (**so**) je pense; **I don't s. so, I s. not** je ne pense pas; **you're tired, I s.** vous êtes fatigué, je suppose; **s.** *or* **supposing we go** (*suggestion*) si nous partions; **I s.** (**so**) *or* **supposing** (**that**) **you're right** supposons que tu aies raison. ◆**—ed** *a* soi-disant. ◆**—edly** [-ɪdlɪ] *adv* soi-disant. ◆**supposition** *n* supposition *f*.

suppository [sə'pɒzɪtərɪ] *n* *Med* suppositoire *m*.

suppress [sə'pres] *vt* (*put an end to*) supprimer; (*feelings*) réprimer; (*scandal, yawn etc*) étouffer. ◆**suppression** *n* suppression *f*; répression *f*. ◆**suppressor** *n* *El* dispositif *m* antiparasite.

supreme [suː'priːm] *a* suprême. ◆**supremacy** *n* suprématie *f* (**over** sur). **supremo** [suː'priːməʊ] *n* (*pl* -os) *Fam* grand chef *m*.

surcharge ['sɜːtʃɑːdʒ] *n* (*extra charge*) supplément *m*; (*on stamp*) surcharge *f*; (*tax*) surtaxe *f*.

sure [ʃʊər] *a* (-er, -est) sûr (**of** de, **that** que); **she's s. to accept** il est sûr qu'elle acceptera; **it's s. to snow** il va sûrement neiger; **to make s. of** s'assurer de; **for s.** à coup sûr, pour sûr; **s.!, *Fam* s. thing!** bien sûr!; **s. enough** (*in effect*) en effet; **it s. is cold** *Am* il fait vraiment froid; **be s. to do it!** ne manquez pas de le faire! ◆**surefire** *a* infaillible. ◆**surely** *adv* (*certainly*) sûrement; **s. he didn't refuse?** (*I think, I hope*) il n'a tout de même pas refusé.

surety ['ʃʊərətɪ] *n* caution *f*.

surf [sɜːf] *n* (*foam*) ressac *m*. ◆**surfboard** *n* planche *f* (de surf). ◆**surfing** *n* *Sp* surf *m*.

surface ['sɜːfɪs] *n* surface *f*; **s. area** superficie *f*; **s. mail** courrier *m* par voie(s) de surface; **on the s.** (*to all appearances*) *Fig* en apparence; — *vt* (*road*) revêtir; — *vi* (*of swimmer etc*) remonter à la surface; (*of ideas, person etc*) *Fam* apparaître.

surfeit ['sɜːfɪt] *n* (*excess*) excès *m* (**of** de).

surge [sɜːdʒ] *n* (*of sea, enthusiasm*) vague *f*; (*rise*) montée *f*; — *vi* (*of crowd, hatred*) déferler; (*rise*) monter; **to s. forward** se lancer en avant.

surgeon ['sɜːdʒ(ə)n] *n* chirurgien *m*. ◆**surgery** *n* (*science*) chirurgie *f*; (*doctor's office*) cabinet *m*; (*sitting, period*) consultation *f*; **to undergo s.** subir une intervention.

◆**surgical** *a* chirurgical; (*appliance*) orthopédique; **s. spirit** alcool *m* à 90°.

surly ['sɜːlɪ] *a* (-ier, -iest) bourru. ◆**surliness** *n* air *m* bourru.

surmise [sə'maɪz] *vt* conjecturer (**that** que).

surmount [sə'maʊnt] *vt* (*overcome, be on top of*) surmonter.

surname ['sɜːneɪm] *n* nom *m* de famille.

surpass [sə'pɑːs] *vt* surpasser (**in** en).

surplus ['sɜːpləs] *n* surplus *m*; — *a* (*goods*) en surplus; **some s. material**/*etc* (*left over*) un surplus de tissu/*etc*; **s. stock** surplus *mpl*.

surpris/e [sə'praɪz] *n* surprise *f*; **to give s. o s.** faire une surprise à qn; **to take s.o. by s.** prendre qn au dépourvu; — *a* (*visit, result etc*) inattendu; — *vt* (*astonish*) étonner, surprendre; (*come upon*) surprendre. ◆**—ed** *a* surpris (**that** que (+ *sub*), **at** de qch, **at seeing**/*etc* de voir/*etc*); **I'm s. at his** *or* **her stupidity** sa bêtise m'étonne *or* me surprend. ◆**—ing** *a* surprenant. ◆**—ingly** *adv* étonnamment; **s.** (**enough**) **he ...** chose étonnante, il ...

surrealistic [sərɪə'lɪstɪk] *a* (*strange*) *Fig* surréaliste.

surrender [sə'rendər] **1** *vi* (*give oneself up*) se rendre (**to** à); **to s. to** (*police*) se livrer à; — *n* *Mil* reddition *f*, capitulation *f*. **2** *vt* (*hand over*) remettre, rendre (**to** à); (*right, claim*) renoncer à.

surreptitious [sʌrəp'tɪʃəs] *a* subreptice.

surrogate ['sʌrəgət] *n* substitut *m*; **s. mother** mère *f* porteuse.

surround [sə'raʊnd] *vt* entourer (**with** de); *Mil* encercler; **surrounded by** entouré de. ◆**—ing** *a* environnant. ◆**—ings** *npl* environs *mpl*; (*setting*) cadre *m*.

surveillance [sɜː'veɪləns] *n* (*of prisoner etc*) surveillance *f*.

survey [sɜː'veɪ] *vt* (*look at*) regarder; (*review*) passer en revue; (*house etc*) inspecter; (*land*) arpenter; — *n* ['sɜːveɪ] *n* (*investigation*) enquête *f*; (*of house etc*) inspection *f*; (*of opinion*) sondage *m*; **a** (*general*) **s. of** une vue générale de. ◆**sur'veying** *n* arpentage *m*. ◆**sur'veyor** *n* (*arpenteur m*) géomètre *m*; (*of house etc*) expert *m*.

survive [sə'vaɪv] *vi* (*of person, custom etc*) survivre; — *vt* survivre à. ◆**survival** *n* (*act*) survie *f*; (*relic*) vestige *m*. ◆**survivor** *n* survivant, -ante *mf*.

susceptible [sə'septəb(ə)l] *a* (*sensitive*) sensible (**to** à); **s. to colds**/*etc* (*prone to*) prédisposé aux rhumes/*etc*. ◆**susceptibility** *n* sensibilité *f*; prédisposition *f*; *pl* susceptibilité *f*.

suspect ['sʌspekt] n & a suspect, -ecte (mf); – [sə'spekt] vt soupçonner (**that** que, of sth de qch, **of doing** d'avoir fait); (think questionable) suspecter, douter de; **yes, I s.** oui, j'imagine.

suspend [sə'spend] vt **1** (hang) suspendre (**from** à). **2** (stop, postpone, dismiss) suspendre; (passport etc) retirer (provisoirement); (pupil) Sch renvoyer; **suspended sentence** Jur condamnation f avec sursis. ◆**suspender** n (for stocking) jarretelle f; pl (braces) Am bretelles fpl; **s. belt** porte-jarretelles m inv. ◆**suspension** n **1** (stopping) suspension f; (of passport etc) retrait m (provisoire). **2** (of vehicle etc) suspension f; **s. bridge** pont m suspendu.

suspense [sə'spens] n attente f (angoissée); (in film, book etc) suspense m; **in s.** (person, matter) en suspens.

suspicion [sə'spɪʃ(ə)n] n soupçon m; **to arouse s.** éveiller les soupçons; **with s.** (distrust) avec méfiance; **under s.** considéré comme suspect. ◆**suspicious** a (person) soupçonneux, méfiant; (behaviour) suspect; **s.(-looking)** (suspect) suspect; **to be s. of** or **about** (distrust) se méfier de. ◆**suspiciously** adv (to behave etc) d'une manière suspecte; (to consider etc) avec méfiance.

sustain [sə'steɪn] vt (effort, theory) soutenir; (weight) supporter; (with food) nourrir; (life) maintenir; (damage, attack) subir; (injury) recevoir. ◆**sustenance** n (food) nourriture f; (quality) valeur f nutritive.

swab [swɒb] n (pad) Med tampon m; (specimen) Med prélèvement m.

swagger ['swægər] vi (walk) parader; – n démarche f fanfaronne.

swallow¹ ['swɒləʊ] **1** vt avaler; **to s. down** or **up** avaler; **to s. up** Fig engloutir; – vi avaler. **2** n (bird) hirondelle f.

swam [swæm] see **swim**.

swamp [swɒmp] n marais m, marécage m; – vt (flood, overwhelm) submerger (**with** de). ◆**swampy** a (-ier, -iest) marécageux.

swan [swɒn] n cygne m.

swank [swæŋk] vi (show off) Fam crâner, fanfaronner.

swap [swɒp] n échange m; pl (stamps etc) doubles mpl; – vt (-pp-) échanger (**for** contre); **to s. seats** changer de place; – vi échanger.

swarm [swɔːm] n (of bees, people etc) essaim m; – vi (of streets, insects, people etc) fourmiller (**with** de); **to s. in** (of people) entrer en foule.

swarthy ['swɔːðɪ] a (-ier, -iest) (dark) basané.

swastika ['swɒstɪkə] n (Nazi emblem) croix f gammée.

swat [swɒt] vt (-tt-) (fly etc) écraser.

sway [sweɪ] vi se balancer, osciller; – vt balancer; Fig influencer; – n balancement m; Fig influence f.

swear [sweər] vt (pt **swore**, pp **sworn**) jurer (**to do** de faire, **that** que); **to s. an oath** prêter serment; **to s. s.o. to secrecy** faire jurer le silence à qn; **sworn enemies** ennemis mpl jurés; – vi (**to** take an oath) jurer (**to** sth de qch); (curse) jurer, pester (**at** contre); **he swears by this lotion** elle ne jure que par cette lotion. ◆**swearword** n gros mot m, juron m.

sweat [swet] n sueur f; **s. shirt** sweat-shirt m; – vi (of person, wall etc) suer (**with** de); – vt **to s. out** (cold) Med se débarrasser de (en transpirant). ◆**sweater** n (garment) pull m. ◆**sweaty** a (-ier, -iest) (shirt etc) plein de sueur; (hand) moite; (person) tout en sueur, (tout) en nage.

swede [swiːd] n (vegetable) rutabaga m.

Swede [swiːd] n Suédois, -oise mf. ◆**Sweden** n Suède f. ◆**Swedish** a suédois; – n (language) suédois m.

sweep [swiːp] n coup m de balai; (movement) Fig large mouvement m; (curve) courbe f; **to make a clean s.** (removal) faire table rase (**of** de); (victory) remporter une victoire totale; – vt (pt & pp **swept**) (with broom) balayer; (chimney) ramoner; (river) draguer; **to s. away** or **out** or **up** balayer; **to s. away** or **along** (carry off) emporter; **to s. aside** (dismiss) écarter; **to s. (up)** balayer; **to s. in** (of person) Fig entrer rapidement or majestueusement; **to s. through** (of fear etc) saisir (groupe etc); (of disease etc) ravager (pays etc). ◆**-ing** a (gesture) large; (change) radical; (statement) trop général. ◆**sweepstake** n (lottery) sweepstake m.

sweet [swiːt] a (-er, -est) (not sour) doux; (agreeable) agréable, doux; (tea, coffee etc) sucré; (person, house, kitchen) mignon, gentil; **to have a s. tooth** aimer les sucreries; **to be s.-smelling** sentir bon; **s. corn** maïs m; **s. pea** Bot pois m de senteur; **s. potato** patate f douce; **s. shop** confiserie f; **s. talk** Fam cajoleries fpl, douceurs fpl; – n (candy) bonbon m; (dessert) dessert m; **my s.!** (darling) mon ange! ◆**sweeten** vt (tea etc) sucrer; Fig adoucir. ◆**sweetener** n saccharine f. ◆**sweetie** n (darling) Fam chéri, -ie mf. ◆**sweetly** adv (kindly) gentiment; (*softly*) doucement. ◆**sweetness** *n* douceur *f*; (*taste*) goût *m* sucré.

sweetbread ['swiːtbred] *n* ris *m* de veau *or* d'agneau.

sweetheart ['swiːthɑːt] *n* (*lover*) ami, -ie *mf*; **my s.!** (*darling*) mon ange!

swell [swel] **1** *n* (*of sea*) houle *f*. **2** *a* (*very good*) *Am* Fam formidable. **3** *vi* (*pt* swelled, *pp* swollen *or* swelled) se gonfler; (*of river, numbers*) grossir; **to s. (up)** *Med* enfler, gonfler; – *vt* (*river, numbers*) grossir. ◆–**ing** *n Med* enflure *f*.

swelter ['sweltər] *vi* étouffer. ◆–**ing** *a* étouffant; **it's s.** on étouffe.

swept [swept] *see* **sweep**.

swerve [swɜːv] *vi* (*while running etc*) faire un écart; (*of vehicle*) faire une embardée.

swift [swift] **1** *a* (**-er, -est**) rapide; **s. to act** prompt à agir. **2** *n* (*bird*) martinet *m*. ◆–**ly** *adv* rapidement. ◆–**ness** *n* rapidité *f*.

swig [swig] *n* (*of beer etc*) lampée *f*.

swill [swil] *vt* **to s. (out** *or* **down)** laver (à grande eau).

swim [swim] *n* baignade *f*; **to go for a s.** se baigner, nager; – *vi* (*pt* swam, *pp* swum, *pres p* swimming) nager; *Sp* faire de la natation; (*of head, room*) *Fig* tourner; **to go swimming** aller nager; **to s. away** se sauver (à la nage); – *vt* (*river*) traverser à la nage; (*length, crawl etc*) nager. ◆**swimming** *n* natation *f*; **s. costume** maillot *m* de bain; **s. pool, s. baths** piscine *f*; **s. trunks** slip *m* *or* caleçon *m* de bain. ◆**swimmer** *n* nageur, -euse *mf*. ◆**swimsuit** *n* maillot *m* de bain.

swindl/e ['swind(ə)l] *n* escroquerie *f*; – *vt* escroquer; **to s. s.o. out of money** escroquer de l'argent à qn. ◆–**er** *n* escroc *m*.

swine [swain] *n inv* (*person*) *Pej* salaud *m*.

swing [swiŋ] *n* (*seat*) balançoire *f*; (*movement*) balancement *m*; (*of pendulum*) oscillation *f*; (*in opinion*) revirement *m*; (*rhythm*) rythme *m*; **to be in full s.** battre son plein; **to be in the s. of things** *Fam* être dans le bain; **s. door** porte *f* de saloon; – *vi* (*pt & pp* swung) (*sway*) se balancer; (*of pendulum*) osciller; (*turn*) virer; **to s. round** (*turn suddenly*) virer, tourner; (*of person*) se retourner (vivement); (*of vehicle in collision etc*) faire un tête-à-queue; **to s. into action** passer à l'action; – *vt* (*arms etc*) balancer; (*axe*) brandir; (*influence*) *Fam* influencer; **to s. round** (*car etc*) faire tourner. ◆–**ing** *a* *Fam* (*trendy*) dans le vent; (*lively*) plein de vie; (*music*) entraînant.

swingeing ['swindʒiŋ] *a* **s. cuts** des réductions *fpl* draconiennes.

swipe [swaip] *vt* *Fam* (*hit*) frapper dur; (*steal*) piquer (**from s.o.** à qn); – *n* *Fam* grand coup *m*.

swirl [swɜːl] *n* tourbillon *m*; – *vi* tourbillonner.

swish [swiʃ] **1** *a* (*posh*) *Fam* rupin, chic. **2** *vi* (*of whip etc*) siffler; (*of fabric*) froufrouter; – *n* sifflement *m*; froufrou *m*.

Swiss [swis] *a* suisse; – *n inv* Suisse *m*, Suissesse *f*; **the S.** les Suisses *mpl*.

switch [switʃ] *n* *El* bouton *m* (électrique), interrupteur *m*; (*change*) changement *m* (de); (*reversal*) revirement *m* (de); – *vt* (*money, employee etc*) transférer (**to** à); (*affection, support*) reporter (**to** sur, **from** de); (*exchange*) échanger (**for** contre); **to s. buses/etc** changer de bus/*etc*; **to s. places** *or* **seats** changer de place; **to s. off** (*lamp, gas, radio etc*) éteindre; (*engine*) arrêter; **to s. itself off** (*of heating etc*) s'éteindre tout seul; **to s. on** (*lamp, gas, radio etc*) mettre, allumer; (*engine*) mettre en marche; – *vi* **to s. (over)** to passer à; **to s. off** (*switch off light, radio etc*) éteindre; **to s. on** (*switch on light, radio etc*) allumer. ◆**switchback** *n* (*at funfair*) montagnes *f* russes. ◆**switchblade** *n* *Am* couteau *m* à cran d'arrêt. ◆**switchboard** *n Tel* standard *m*; **s. operator** standardiste *mf*.

Switzerland ['switsələnd] *n* Suisse *f*.

swivel ['swiv(ə)l] *vi* (**-ll-,** *Am* **-l-**) **to s. (round)** (*of chair etc*) pivoter; – *a* **s. chair** fauteuil *m* pivotant.

swollen ['swəʊl(ə)n] *see* **swell** 3; – *a* (*leg etc*) enflé.

swoon [swuːn] *vi* *Lit* se pâmer.

swoop [swuːp] **1** *vi* **to s. (down) on** (*of bird*) fondre sur. **2** *n* (*of police*) descente *f*; – *vi* faire une descente (on dans).

swop [swɒp] *n, vt & vi* = **swap**.

sword [sɔːd] *n* épée *f*. ◆**swordfish** *n* espadon *m*.

swore, sworn [swɔː, swɔːn] *see* **swear**.

swot [swɒt] *vti* (**-tt-**) **to s. (up)** (*study*) *Fam* potasser; **to s. (up) for** (*exam*), **to s. up on** (*subject*) *Fam* potasser; – *n* *Pej* Fam bûcheur, -euse *mf*.

swum [swʌm] *see* **swim**.

swung [swʌŋ] *see* **swing**.

sycamore ['sikəmɔː] *n* (*maple*) sycomore *m*; (*plane*) *Am* platane *m*.

sycophant ['sikəfænt] *n* flagorneur, -euse *mf*.

syllable ['siləb(ə)l] *n* syllabe *f*.

syllabus ['siləbəs] *n* *Sch Univ* programme *m*.

symbol ['simb(ə)l] *n* symbole *m*. ◆**sym-**

'bolic *a* symbolique. ◆**symbolism** *n* symbolisme *m*. ◆**symbolize** *vt* symboliser.

symmetry ['sɪmɪtrɪ] *n* symétrie *f*. ◆**sy'mmetrical** *a* symétrique.

sympathy ['sɪmpəθɪ] *n* (*pity*) compassion *f*; (*understanding*) compréhension *f*; (*condolences*) condoléances *fpl*; (*solidarity*) solidarité *f* (**for** avec); **to be in s. with** (*workers in dispute*) être du côté de; (*s.o.'s opinion etc*) comprendre, être en accord avec. ◆**sympa'thetic** *a* (*showing pity*) compatissant; (*understanding*) compréhensif; **s. to** (*favourable*) bien disposé à l'égard de. ◆**sympa'thetically** *adv* avec compassion; avec compréhension. ◆**sympathize** *vi* **I s. with** (*you*) (*pity*) je compatis (à votre sort); (*understanding*) je vous comprends. ◆**sympathizer** *n Pol* sympathisant, -ante *mf*.

symphony ['sɪmfənɪ] *n* symphonie *f*; – *a* (*orchestra, concert*) symphonique. ◆**sym'phonic** *a* symphonique.

symposium [sɪm'pəʊzɪəm] *n* symposium *m*.

symptom ['sɪmptəm] *n* symptôme *m*. ◆**sympto'matic** *a* symptomatique (**of** de).

synagogue ['sɪnəgɒg] *n* synagogue *f*.

synchronize ['sɪŋkrənaɪz] *vt* synchroniser.

syndicate ['sɪndɪkət] *n* (*of businessmen, criminals*) syndicat *m*.

syndrome ['sɪndrəʊm] *n Med & Fig* syndrome *m*.

synod ['sɪnəd] *n Rel* synode *m*.

synonym ['sɪnənɪm] *n* synonyme *m*. ◆**sy'nonymous** *a* synonyme (**with** de).

synopsis, *pl* **-opses** [sɪ'nɒpsɪs, -ɒpsiːz] *n* résumé *m*, synopsis *f*; (*of film*) synopsis *m*.

syntax ['sɪntæks] *n Gram* syntaxe *f*.

synthesis, *pl* **-theses** [sɪnθəsɪs, -θəsiːz] *n* synthèse *f*.

synthetic [sɪn'θetɪk] *a* synthétique.

syphilis ['sɪfɪlɪs] *n* syphilis *f*.

Syria ['sɪrɪə] *n* Syrie *f*. ◆**Syrian** *a & n* syrien, -ienne (*mf*).

syringe [sɪ'rɪndʒ] *n* seringue *f*.

syrup ['sɪrəp] *n* sirop *m*; (*golden*) **s.** (*treacle*) mélasse *f* (*raffinée*). ◆**syrupy** *a* sirupeux.

system ['sɪstəm] *n* (*structure, plan, network etc*) & *Anat* système *m*; (*human body*) organisme *m*; (*order*) méthode *f*; **systems analyst** analyste-programmeur *m*. ◆**syste'matic** *a* systématique. ◆**syste'matically** *adv* systématiquement.

T

T, t [tiː] *n* T, t *m*. ◆**T-junction** *n Aut* intersection *f* en T. ◆**T-shirt** *n* tee-shirt *m*, T-shirt *m*.

ta! [tɑː] *int Sl* merci!

tab [tæb] *n* (*label*) étiquette *f*; (*tongue*) patte *f*; (*loop*) attache *f*; (*bill*) *Am* addition *f*; **to keep tabs on** *Fam* surveiller (de près).

tabby ['tæbɪ] *a* **t. cat** chat, chatte *mf* tigré(e).

table¹ ['teɪb(ə)l] *n* **1** (*furniture*) table *f*; **bedside/card/operating** t. table de nuit/de jeu/d'opération; **to lay** or **set/clear the t.** mettre/débarrasser la table; (**sitting**) **at the** t. à table; **t. top** dessus *m* de table. **2** (*list*) table *f*; **t. of contents** table des matières. ◆**tablecloth** *n* nappe *f*. ◆**tablemat** *n* (*of fabric*) napperon *m*; (*hard*) dessous-de-plat *m inv*. ◆**tablespoon** *n* = cuiller *f* à soupe. ◆**tablespoonful** *n* = cuillerée *f* à soupe.

table² ['teɪb(ə)l] *vt* (*motion etc*) *Pol* présenter; (*postpone*) *Am* ajourner.

tablet ['tæblɪt] *n* **1** (*pill*) *Med* comprimé *m*. **2** (*inscribed stone*) plaque *f*.

tabloid ['tæblɔɪd] *n* (*newspaper*) quotidien *m* populaire.

taboo [tə'buː] *a & n* tabou (*m*).

tabulator ['tæbjʊleɪtər] *n* (*of typewriter*) tabulateur *m*.

tacit ['tæsɪt] *a* tacite. ◆**-ly** *adv* tacitement.

taciturn ['tæsɪtɜːn] *a* taciturne.

tack [tæk] **1** *n* (*nail*) semence *f*; (*thumbtack*) *Am* punaise *f*; **to get down to brass tacks** *Fig* en venir aux faits; – *vt* **to t. (down)** clouer. **2** *n* (*stitch*) *Tex* point *m* de bâti; – *vt* **to t. (down** or **on)** bâtir; **to t. on** (*add*) *Fig* (r)ajouter. **3** *vi* (*of ship*) louvoyer; – *n* (*course of action*) *Fig* voie *f*.

tackle ['tæk(ə)l] **1** *n* (*gear*) matériel *m*, équipement *m*. **2** *vt* (*task, problem etc*) s'attaquer à; (*thief etc*) saisir; *Sp* plaquer; – *n Sp* plaquage *m*.

tacky ['tækɪ] *a* (**-ier, -iest**) **1** (*wet, sticky*) collant, pas sec. **2** (*clothes, attitude etc*) *Am Fam* moche.

tact [tækt] *n* tact *m*. ◆**tactful** *a* (*remark etc*) plein de tact, diplomatique; **she's t.** elle a du tact. ◆**tactfully** adv avec tact. ◆**tactless** a qui manque de tact. ◆**tactlessly** adv sans tact.

tactic ['tæktɪk] n a. une tactique; **tactics** la tactique. ◆**tactical** a tactique.

tactile ['tæktaɪl] a tactile.

tadpole ['tædpəʊl] n têtard m.

taffy ['tæfɪ] n (toffee) Am caramel m (dur).

tag [tæg] 1 n (label) étiquette f; (end piece) bout m; — vt (-gg-) to t. on (add) Fam rajouter (to à). 2 vi (-gg-) to t. along (follow) suivre.

Tahiti [tɑːˈhiːtɪ] n Tahiti m.

tail [teɪl] 1 n (of animal) queue f; (of shirt) pan m; pl (outfit) habit m, queue-de-pie f; to t. end fin f, bout m; **heads or tails?** pile ou face? 3 vt (follow) suivre, filer. 3 vi to t. off (lessen) diminuer. ◆**tailback** n (of traffic) bouchon m. ◆**tailcoat** n queue-de-pie f. ◆**taillight** n Aut Am feu m arrière inv.

tailor ['teɪlər] n (person) tailleur m; — vt (garment) façonner; Fig adapter (**to**, to suit à). ◆t.-'made a fait sur mesure; t.-made for (specially designed) conçu pour; (suited) fait pour.

tainted ['teɪntɪd] a (air) pollué; (food) gâté; Fig souillé.

take [teɪk] vt (pt **took**, pp **taken**) prendre; (choice) faire; (prize) remporter; (exam) passer; (contain) contenir; (tolerate) supporter; (bring) apporter (qch to à), (person) amener (to à), (person by car) conduire (to à); (escort) accompagner (to à); (lead away) emmener (of road) mener (qn); to t. sth to s.o. (ap)porter qch à qn; to t. s.o. (out) to (theatre etc) emmener qn à; to t. sth with one emporter qch; to t. over or round or along (object) apporter; (person) amener; to t. s.o. home (on foot, by car etc) ramener qn; it takes an army/courage/etc (requires) il faut une armée/du courage/etc (to do pour faire); I took an hour to do it or over it j'ai mis une heure à le faire, ça m'a pris une heure pour le faire; I t. it that je présume que; — n Cin prise f de vue(s); — vi (of fire) prendre. ■ to t. after vi (be like) ressembler à; to t. apart vt (machine) démonter; to t. away vt (thing) emporter; (person) emmener; (remove) enlever (from à); Math soustraire (from de). ◆t.-away a emporter; — n café m or restaurant m qui fait des plats à emporter; (meal) plat m à emporter; to t. back vt reprendre; (return) rapporter; (statement) retirer; to t. down vt (object) descendre; (notes) prendre; to t. in vt (chair, car etc) rentrer; (orphan) recueil-

lir; (skirt) reprendre; (include) englober; (distance) couvrir; (understand) comprendre; (deceive) Fam rouler; to t. off vt (remove) enlever; (train, bus) supprimer; (lead away) emmener; (mimic) imiter; Math déduire (from de); — vi (of aircraft) décoller. ◆**takeoff** n (of aircraft) décollage m; to t. on vt (work, employee, passenger, shape) prendre; to t. out vt (from pocket etc) sortir; (stain) enlever; (tooth) arracher; (licence, insurance) prendre; to t. it out on Fam passer sa colère sur. ◆t.-out a & n Am = t.-away; to t. over vt (be responsible for the running of) prendre la direction de; (overrun) envahir; (buy out) Com racheter (company); to t. over s.o.'s job remplacer qn; — vi Mil Pol prendre le pouvoir; (relieve) prendre la relève (from de); (succeed) prendre la succession (from de). ◆t.-over n Com rachat m; Pol prise f de pouvoir; to t. round vt (distribute) distribuer; (visitor) faire visiter; to t. to vi to t. to doing se mettre à faire; I didn't t. to him/it il/ça ne m'a pas plu; to t. up vt (carry up) monter; (hem) raccourcir; (continue) reprendre; (occupy) occuper; (hobby) se mettre à; — vi to t. up with se lier avec. ◆**taken** a (seat) pris; (impressed) impressionné (**with**, by par); **to be t. ill** tomber malade. ◆**taking** n (capture) Mil prise f; pl (money) Com recette f.

talcum ['tælkəm] a t. powder talc m.

tale [teɪl] n (story) conte m; (account, report) récit m; (lie) histoire f; **to tell tales** rapporter (on sur).

talent ['tælənt] n talent m; (talented people) talents mpl; **to have a t. for** avoir du talent pour. ◆**talented** a doué, talentueux.

talk [tɔːk] n (words) propos mpl; (gossip) bavardage(s) m(pl); (conversation) conversation f (**about** à propos de); (interview) entretien m; (lecture) exposé m (on sur); (informal) causerie f (on sur); (of negotiations) pourparlers mpl; **to have a t.** with parler avec; **there's t.** of on parle de; — vi parler (**to** à; **with** avec; **about, of** de); (chat) bavarder; **to t. down to s.o.** parler à qn comme à un inférieur; — vt (nonsense) dire; **to t. politics** parler politique; **to t. s.o. into doing/out of doing** persuader qn de faire/de ne pas faire; **to t. over** discuter (de); **to t. s.o. round** persuader qn. ◆**-ing** a (film) parlant; **to give s.o. a talking-to** Fam passer un savon à qn. ◆**talkative** a bavard. ◆**talker** n causeur, -euse mf; **she's a good t.** elle parle bien.

tall [tɔːl] a (-er, -est) (person) grand; (tree,

house etc) haut; **how t. are you?** combien mesures-tu?; **a t. story** *Fig* une histoire invraisemblable *or* à dormir debout. ◆**tallboy** *n* grande commode *f.* ◆**tallness** *n* (*of person*) grande taille *f*; (*of building etc*) hauteur *f.*

tally ['tælɪ] *vi* correspondre (**with** à).

tambourine [tæmbə'riːn] *n* tambourin *m.*

tame [teɪm] *a* (**-er, -est**) (*animal, bird*) apprivoisé; (*person*) *Fig* docile; (*book, play*) fade. – *vt* (*animal, bird*) apprivoiser; (*lion, passion*) dompter.

tamper ['tæmpər] *vi* **to t. with** (*lock, car etc*) toucher à; (*text*) altérer.

tampon ['tæmpɒn] *n* tampon *m* hygiénique.

tan [tæn] **1** *n* (*suntan*) bronzage *m*; – *vti* (**-nn-**) bronzer. **2** *a* (*colour*) marron clair *inv.* **3** *vt* (**-nn-**) (*hide*) tanner.

tandem ['tændəm] *n* **1** (*bicycle*) tandem *m.* **2** **in t.** (*to work etc*) en tandem.

tang [tæŋ] *n* (*taste*) saveur *f* piquante; (*smell*) odeur *f* piquante. ◆**tangy** *a* (**-ier, -iest**) piquant.

tangerine [tændʒə'riːn] *n* mandarine *f.*

tangible ['tændʒəb(ə)l] *a* tangible.

tangl/e ['tæŋg(ə)l] *n* enchevêtrement *m*; **to get into a t.** (*of rope*) s'enchevêtrer; (*of hair*) s'emmêler; (*of person*) *Fig* se mettre dans une situation pas possible. ◆**-ed** *a* enchevêtré; (*hair*) emmêlé; **to get t.** = **to get into a tangle.**

tank [tæŋk] *n* **1** (*for storage of water, fuel etc*) réservoir *m*; (*vat*) cuve *f*; (*fish*) t. aquarium *m.* **2** (*vehicle*) *Mil* char *m*, tank *m.*

tankard ['tæŋkəd] *n* (*beer mug*) chope *f.*

tanker ['tæŋkər] *n* (*truck*) *Aut* camion-citerne *m*; (*oil*) t. (*ship*) pétrolier *m.*

tantalizing ['tæntəlaɪzɪŋ] *a* (*irrésistible-ment*) tentant. ◆**-ly** *adv* d'une manière tentante.

tantamount ['tæntəmaʊnt] *a* **it's t.** to cela équivaut à.

tantrum ['tæntrəm] *n* accès *m* de colère.

tap [tæp] **1** *n* (*for water*) robinet *m*; **on t.** *Fig* disponible. **2** *vti* (**-pp-**) frapper légèrement, tapoter; – *n* petit coup *m*; **t. dancing** claquettes *fpl.* **3** *vt* (**-pp-**) (*phone*) placer sur table d'écoute. **4** *vt* (**-pp-**) (*resources*) exploiter.

tape [teɪp] **1** *n* ruban *m*; (**sticky**) t. ruban adhésif; **t. measure** mètre *m* (à) ruban; (*stick*) coller (*avec du ruban adhésif*). **2** *n* (*for sound recording*) bande *f* (magnétique); (*video*) t. bande (*f*); **t. recorder** magnétophone *m*; – *vt* enregistrer.

taper ['teɪpər] **1** *vi* (*of fingers etc*) s'effiler; **to off** *Fig* diminuer. **2** *n* (*candle*) *Rel* cierge

m. ◆**-ed** *a*, ◆**-ing** *a* (*fingers*) fuselé; (*trousers*) à bas étroits.

tapestry ['tæpɪstrɪ] *n* tapisserie *f.*

tapioca [tæpɪ'əʊkə] *n* tapioca *m.*

tar [tɑːr] *n* goudron *m*; – *vt* (**-rr-**) goudronner.

tardy ['tɑːdɪ] *a* (**-ier, -iest**) (*belated*) tardif; (*slow*) lent.

target ['tɑːgɪt] *n* cible *f*; *Fig* objectif *m*; **t. date** date *f* fixée; – *vt* (*aim*) *Fig* destiner (**at** à); (*aim at*) *Fig* viser.

tariff ['tærɪf] *n* (*tax*) tarif *m* douanier; (*prices*) tarif *m.*

tarmac ['tɑːmæk] *n* macadam *m* (goudronné); (*runway*) piste *f.*

tarnish ['tɑːnɪʃ] *vt* ternir.

tarpaulin [tɑː'pɔːlɪn] *n* bâche *f* (goudronnée).

tarragon ['tærəgən] *n Bot Culin* estragon *m.*

tarry ['tærɪ] *vi* (*remain*) *Lit* rester.

tart [tɑːt] **1** *n* (*pie*) tarte *f.* **2** *a* (**-er, -est**) (*taste, remark*) aigre. **3** *n* (*prostitute*) *Pej Fam* poule *f.* **4** *vt* **to t. up** *Pej Fam* (*decorate*) embellir; (*dress*) attifer. ◆**-ness** *n* aigreur *f.*

tartan ['tɑːt(ə)n] *n* tartan *m*; – *a* écossais.

tartar ['tɑːtər] *n* **1** (*on teeth*) tartre *m.* **2** **a t. sauce** sauce *f* tartare.

task [tɑːsk] *n* tâche *f*; **to take to t.** prendre à partie; **t. force** *Mil* détachement *m* spécial; *Pol* commission *f* spéciale.

tassel ['tæs(ə)l] *n* (*on clothes etc*) gland *m.*

taste [teɪst] *n* goût *m*; **to get a t. for** prendre goût à; **in good/bad t.** de bon/mauvais goût; **to have a t. of** goûter à; goûter de; – *vt* (*eat, enjoy*) goûter; (*try, sample*) goûter à; (*make out the taste of*) sentir le goût de); (*experience*) goûter de; – *vi* **to t. of** *or* **like** avoir un goût de; **to t. delicious**/*etc* avoir un goût délicieux/*etc*; **how does it t.?** comment le trouves-tu?; **a t. bud** papille *f* gustative. ◆**tasteful** *a* de bon goût. ◆**tastefully** *adv* avec goût. ◆**tasteless** *a* (*food etc*) sans goût; (*joke etc*) *Fig* de mauvais goût. ◆**tasty** *a* (**-ier, -iest**) savoureux.

tat [tæt] *see* **tit 2.**

ta-ta [tæ'tɑː] *int Sl* au revoir!

tattered ['tætəd] *a* (*clothes*) en lambeaux; (*person*) déguenillé. ◆**tatters** *npl* **in t.** en lambeaux.

tattoo [tæ'tuː] **1** *n* (*pl* **-oos**) (*on body*) tatouage *m*; – *vt* tatouer. **2** *n* (*pl* **-oos**) *Mil* spectacle *m* militaire.

tatty ['tætɪ] *a* (**-ier, -iest**) (*clothes etc*) *Fam* miteux.

taught [tɔːt] *see* **teach.**

taunt [tɔːnt] vt railler; – n raillerie f. ◆**—ing** a railleur.

Taurus ['tɔːrəs] n (sign) le Taureau.

taut [tɔːt] a (rope, person etc) tendu.

tavern ['tævən] n taverne f.

tawdry ['tɔːdrɪ] a (-ier, -iest) Pej tape-à-l'œil inv.

tawny ['tɔːnɪ] a (colour) fauve; (port) ambré.

tax [¹] [tæks] n taxe f, impôt m; (income) impôts mpl (sur le revenu); a fiscal; t. collector percepteur m; t. relief dégrèvement m (d'impôt); – vt (person, goods) imposer. ◆**taxable** a imposable. ◆**tax'ation** n (act) imposition f; (taxes) impôts mpl. ◆**tax-free** a exempt d'impôts. ◆**taxman** n (pl -men) Fam percepteur m. ◆**taxpayer** n contribuable mf.

tax [²] [tæks] vt (patience etc) mettre à l'épreuve; (tire) fatiguer. ◆**—ing** a (journey etc) éprouvant.

taxi ['tæksɪ] 1 n taxi m; t. cab taxi m; t. rank, Am t. stand station f de taxis. 2 vi (of aircraft) rouler au sol.

tea [tiː] n thé m; (snack) goûter m; high t. goûter m (dînatoire); to have t. prendre le thé; (afternoon snack) goûter; t. break pause-thé f; t. chest caisse f (à thé); t. cloth (for drying dishes) torchon m; t. set service m à thé; t. towel torchon m. ◆**teabag** n sachet m de thé. ◆**teacup** n tasse f à thé. ◆**tealeaf** n (pl -leaves) feuille f de thé. ◆**teapot** n théière f. ◆**tearoom** n salon m de thé. ◆**teaspoon** n petite cuiller f. ◆**teaspoonful** n cuillerée f à café. ◆**teatime** n l'heure f du thé.

teach [tiːtʃ] vt (pt & pp taught) apprendre (s.o. sth qch à qn, that que); (in school etc) enseigner (s.o. sth qch à qn); to t. s.o. (how) to do apprendre à qn à faire; to t. school Am enseigner; to t. oneself sth apprendre qch tout seul; – vi enseigner. ◆**—ing** n enseignement m; – a (staff) enseignant; (method, material) pédagogique; t. profession enseignement m; (teachers) enseignants mpl; t. qualification diplôme m permettant d'enseigner. ◆**—er** n professeur m; (in primary school) instituteur, -trice mf.

teak [tiːk] n (wood) teck m.

team [tiːm] n Sp équipe f; (of oxen) attelage m; t. mate coéquipier, -ière mf; – vi to t. up faire équipe (with avec). ◆**teamster** n Am routier m. ◆**teamwork** n collaboration f.

tear [¹] [teər] 1 n déchirure f; – vt (pt tore, pp torn) (rip) déchirer; (snatch) arracher (from s.o. à qn); torn between Fig tiraillé entre; to t. down (house etc) démolir; to t. away or off or out (forcefully) arracher; (stub, receipt, stamp etc) détacher; to t. up déchirer; – vi (of cloth etc) se déchirer. 2 vi (pt tore, pp torn) to t. along (rush) aller à toute vitesse.

tear [²] [tɪər] n larme f; in tears en larmes; close to or near (to) tears au bord des larmes. ◆**tearful** a (eyes, voice) larmoyant; (person) en larmes. ◆**tearfully** adv en pleurant. ◆**teargas** n gaz m lacrymogène.

tearaway ['teərəweɪ] n Fam petit voyou m.

teas/e [tiːz] vt taquiner; (harshly) tourmenter; – n (person) taquin, -ine mf. ◆**—ing** a (remark etc) taquin. ◆**—er** n 1 (person) taquin, -ine mf. 2 (question) Fam colle f.

teat [tiːt] n (of bottle, animal) tétine f.

technical ['teknɪk(ə)l] a technique. ◆**techni'cality** n (detail) détail m technique. ◆**technically** adv techniquement; Fig théoriquement. ◆**tech'nician** n technicien, -ienne mf. ◆**tech'nique** n technique f. ◆**technocrat** n technocrate m. ◆**techno'logical** a technologique. ◆**tech'nology** n technologie f.

teddy ['tedɪ] n t. (bear) ours m (en peluche).

tedious ['tiːdɪəs] a fastidieux. ◆**tediousness** n. ◆**tedium** n ennui m.

teem [tiːm] vi 1 (swarm) grouiller (with de). 2 to t. (with rain) pleuvoir à torrents. ◆**—ing** a 1 (crowd, street etc) grouillant. 2 t. rain pluie f torrentielle.

teenage ['tiːneɪdʒ] a (person, behaviour) adolescent; (fashion) pour adolescents. ◆**teenager** n adolescent, -ente mf. ◆**teens** npl in one's t. adolescent.

teeny (weeny) ['tiːnɪ('wiːnɪ)] a (tiny) Fam minuscule.

tee-shirt ['tiːʃɜːt] n tee-shirt m.

teeter ['tiːtər] vi chanceler.

teeth [tiːθ] see tooth. ◆**teeth/e** [tiːð] vi faire ses dents. ◆**—ing** n dentition f; t. ring anneau m de dentition; t. troubles Fig difficultés fpl de mise en route.

teetotal [tiː'təʊt(ə)l] a. ◆**teetotaller** n (person f) qui ne boit pas d'alcool.

tele- ['telɪ] pref télé-.

telecommunications [telɪkəmjuːnɪ'keɪʃ(ə)nz] npl télécommunications fpl.

telegram ['telɪgræm] n télégramme m.

telegraph ['telɪgrɑːf] n télégraphe m; – a (wire etc) télégraphique; t. pole poteau m télégraphique.

telepathy [tɪ'lepəθɪ] n télépathie f.

telephone ['telɪfəʊn] n téléphone m; on the t. (speaking) au téléphone; – a (call, line etc) téléphonique; (directory) du téléphone; (*number*) de téléphone; **t. booth, t. box** cabine *f* téléphonique; **– vt** (*message*) téléphoner (**to** à); **to t. s.o.** téléphoner à qn. ◆**te'lephonist** *n* téléphoniste *mf*.

teleprinter ['telɪprɪntər] *n* téléimprimeur *m*.

telescope ['telɪskəʊp] *n* télescope *m*. ◆**tele'scopic** *a* (*pictures, aerial, umbrella*) télescopique.

teletypewriter [telɪ'taɪpraɪtər] *n Am* téléscripteur *m*.

televise ['telɪvaɪz] *vt* téléviser. ◆**television** [telɪ'vɪʒ(ə)n] *n* télévision *f*; **on (the) t.** à la télévision; **to watch (the) t.** regarder la télévision; **– a** (*programme etc*) de télévision; (*serial, report*) télévisé.

telex ['teleks] *n* (*service, message*) télex *m*; **– vt** envoyer par télex.

tell [tel] *vt* (*pt & pp* told) dire (*s.o. sth* qch à qn, **that** que); (*story*) raconter; (*future*) prédire; (*distinguish*) distinguer (**from** de); (*know*) savoir; **to t. s.o. to do** dire à qn de faire; **to know how to t. the time** savoir lire l'heure; **to t. the difference** voir la différence (**between** entre); **to t. off** (*scold*) *Fam* gronder; **– vi** (*have an effect*) avoir un effet; (*know*) savoir; **to t. of** *or* **about sth** parler de qch; **to t. on s.o.** *Fam* rapporter sur qn. ◆**—ing** *a* (*smile etc*) révélateur; (*blow*) efficace. ◆**telltale** *n Fam* rapporteur, -euse *mf*.

teller ['telər] *n* (*bank*) **t.** caissier, -ière *mf*.

telly ['telɪ] *n Fam* télé *f*.

temerity [tə'merɪtɪ] *n* témérité *f*.

temp [temp] *n* (*secretary etc*) *Fam* intérimaire *mf*.

temper ['tempər] **1** *n* (*mood, nature*) humeur *f*; (*anger*) colère *f*; **to lose one's t.** se mettre en colère; **in a bad t.** de mauvaise humeur; **to have a (bad** *or* **an awful) t.** avoir un caractère de cochon. **2** *vt* (*steel*) tremper; *Fig* tempérer.

temperament ['temp(ə)rəmənt] *n* tempérament *m*. ◆**tempera'mental** *a* (*person, machine etc*) capricieux; (*inborn*) inné.

temperance ['temp(ə)rəns] *n* (*in drink*) tempérance *f*.

temperate ['tempərət] *a* (*climate etc*) tempéré.

temperature ['temp(ə)rətʃər] *n* température *f*; **to have a t.** *Med* avoir *ou* faire de la température.

tempest ['tempɪst] *n Lit* tempête *f*. ◆**tem'pestuous** *a* (*meeting etc*) orageux.

template ['templət] *n* (*of plastic, metal etc*) *Tex* patron *m*; *Math* trace-courbes *m inv*.

temple ['temp(ə)l] *n* **1** *Rel* temple *m*. **2** *Anat* tempe *f*.

tempo ['tempəʊ] *n* (*pl* **-os**) tempo *m*.

temporal ['temp(ə)rəl] *a* temporel.

temporary ['temp(ə)rərɪ] *a* provisoire; (*job, worker*) temporaire; (*secretary*) intérimaire.

tempt [tempt] *vt* tenter; **tempted to do** tenté de faire; **to t. s.o. to do** persuader qn de faire. ◆**—ing** *a* tentant. ◆**—ingly** *adv* d'une manière tentante. ◆**temp'tation** *n* tentation *f*.

ten [ten] *a & n* dix (*m*). ◆**tenfold** *a* **t.** increase augmentation *f* par dix; **– adv** **to increase t.** (se) multiplier par dix.

tenable ['tenəb(ə)l] *a* (*argument*) défendable; (*post*) qui peut être occupé.

tenacious [tə'neɪʃəs] *a* tenace. ◆**tenacity** *n* ténacité *f*.

tenant ['tenənt] *n* locataire *nmf*. ◆**tenancy** *n* (*lease*) location *f*; (*period*) occupation *f*.

tend [tend] **1** *vt* (*look after*) s'occuper de. **2** *vi* **to t. to do** avoir tendance à faire; **to t. towards** incliner vers. ◆**tendency** *n* tendance *f* (**to do** à faire).

tendentious [ten'denʃəs] *a Pej* tendancieux.

tender[1] ['tendər] *a* (*delicate, soft, loving*) tendre; (*painful, sore*) sensible. ◆**—ly** *adv* tendrement. ◆**—ness** *n* tendresse *f*; (*soreness*) sensibilité *f*; (*of meat*) tendreté *f*.

tender[2] ['tendər] **1** *vt* (*offer*) offrir; **to t. one's resignation** donner sa démission. **2** *n* **to be legal t.** (*of money*) avoir cours. **3** *n* (*for services etc*) *Com* soumission *f* (**for** pour).

tendon ['tendən] *n Anat* tendon *m*.

tenement ['tenəmənt] *n* immeuble *m* (de rapport) (*Am* dans un quartier pauvre).

tenet ['tenɪt] *n* principe *m*.

tenner ['tenər] *n Fam* billet *m* de dix livres.

tennis ['tenɪs] *n* tennis *m*; **table t.** tennis de table; **t. court** court *m* (de tennis), tennis *m*.

tenor ['tenər] *n* **1** (*sense, course*) sens *m* général. **2** *Mus* ténor *m*.

tenpin ['tenpɪn] *a* **t. bowling** bowling *m*. ◆**tenpins** *n Am* bowling *m*.

tense [tens] **1** *a* (**-er, -est**) (*person, muscle, situation*) tendu; **– vt** se tendre, crisper; **– vi to t. (up)** (*of person, face*) se crisper. **2** *n Gram* temps *m*. ◆**tenseness** *n* tension *f*. ◆**tension** *n* tension *f*.

tent [tent] *n* tente *f*.

tentacle ['tentək(ə)l] *n* tentacule *m*.

tentative ['tentətɪv] *a* (*not definite*) provisoire; (*hesitant*) timide. ◆**—ly** *adv* provisoirement; timidement.

tenterhooks ['tentəhʊks] *npl* **on t.** (*anxious*) sur des charbons ardents.

tenth [tenθ] *a & n* dixième (*mf*); **a t. un** dixième.

tenuous ['tenjuəs] *a* (*link, suspicion etc*) ténu.

tenure ['tenjər] *n* (*in job*) période *f* de jouissance; (*job security*) *Am* titularisation *f*.

tepid ['tepɪd] *a* (*liquid*) & Fig tiède.

term [tɜːm] *n* (*word, limit*) terme *m*; (*period*) période *f*; *Sch Univ* trimestre *m*; (*semester*) *Am* semestre *m*; *pl* (*conditions*) conditions *fpl*; (*prices*) Com prix *mpl*; **t. (of office)** *Pol* mandat *m*; **easy terms** *Fin* facilités *fpl* de paiement; **on good/bad terms (with s.o.** avec qn); **to be on close terms** être intime (**with** avec); **in terms of** (*speaking of*) sur le plan de; **in real terms** dans la pratique; **to come to terms with** (*person*) tomber d'accord avec; (*situation etc*) Fig faire face à; **in the long/short t.** à long/court terme; **at (full) t.** (*baby*) à terme; – *vt* (*name, call*) appeler.

terminal ['tɜːmɪn(ə)l] **1** *n* (*of computer*) terminal *m*; *El* borne *f*; **(air) t.** aérogare *f*; **(oil) t.** terminal *m* (pétrolier). **2** *a* (*patient, illness*) incurable; (*stage*) terminal. ◆**—ly** *adv* **t. ill** (*patient*) incurable.

terminate ['tɜːmɪneɪt] *vt* mettre fin à; (*contract*) résilier; (*pregnancy*) interrompre; – *vi* se terminer. ◆**termi'nation** *n* fin *f*; résiliation *f*; interruption *f*.

terminology [tɜːmɪ'nɒlədʒɪ] *n* terminologie *f*.

terminus ['tɜːmɪnəs] *n* terminus *m*.

termite ['tɜːmaɪt] *n* (*insect*) termite *m*.

terrace ['terɪs] *n* terrace *f*; (*houses*) maisons *fpl* en bande; **the terraces** *Sp* les gradins *mpl*. ◆**terraced** *a* **t. house** maison *f* attenante aux maisons voisines.

terracota [terə'kɒtə] *n* terre *f* cuite.

terrain [tə'reɪn] *n* *Mil Geol* terrain *m*.

terrestrial [tə'restrɪəl] *a* terrestre.

terrible ['terəb(ə)l] *a* affreux, terrible. ◆**terribly** *adv* (*badly*) affreusement; (*very*) terriblement.

terrier ['terɪər] *n* (*dog*) terrier *m*.

terrific [tə'rɪfɪk] *a* Fam (*extreme*) terrible; (*excellent*) formidable, terrible. ◆**terrifically** *adv* Fam (*extremely*) terriblement; (*extremely well*) terriblement bien.

terrify ['terɪfaɪ] *vt* terrifier; **to be terrified of** avoir très peur de. ◆**—ing** *a* terrifiant. ◆**—ingly** *adv* épouvantablement.

territory ['terɪtərɪ] *n* territoire *m*. ◆**territorial** *a* territorial.

terror ['terər] *n* terreur *f*; (*child*) Fam polisson, -onne *mf*. ◆**terrorism** *n* terrorisme

m. ◆**terrorist** *n & a* terroriste (*mf*). ◆**terrorize** *vt* terroriser.

terry(cloth) ['terɪ(klɒθ)] *n* tissu-éponge *m*.

terse [tɜːs] *a* laconique.

tertiary ['tɜːʃərɪ] *a* tertiaire.

Terylene® ['terɪliːn] *n* tergal® *m*.

test [test] *vt* (*try*) essayer; (*examine*) examiner; (*analyse*) analyser; (*product, intelligence*) tester; (*pupil*) *Sch* faire subir une interrogation à; (*nerves, courage etc*) Fig éprouver; – *n* (*trial*) test *m*, essai *m*; examen *m*; analyse *f*; *Sch* interrogation *f*, test *m*; (*of courage etc*) Fig épreuve *f*; **driving t.** (examen *m* du) permis *m* de conduire; – *a* (*pilot, flight*) d'essai; **t. case** *Jur* affaire-test *f*; **t. match** *Sp* match *m* international; **t. tube** éprouvette *f*; **t. tube baby** bébé *m* éprouvette.

testament ['testəmənt] *n* testament *m*; (*proof, tribute*) témoignage *m*; **Old/New T.** *Rel* Ancien/Nouveau Testament.

testicle ['testɪk(ə)l] *n* Anat testicule *m*.

testify ['testɪfaɪ] *vi* Jur témoigner (**against** contre); **to t. to sth** (*of person, event etc*) témoigner de qch; – *vt* **to t. that** Jur témoigner que. ◆**testi'monial** *n* références *fpl*, recommandation *f*. ◆**testimony** *n* témoignage *m*.

testy ['testɪ] *a* (**-ier, -iest**) irritable.

tetanus ['tetənəs] *n* Med tétanos *m*.

tête-à-tête [teɪtɑː'teɪt] *n* tête-à-tête *m inv*.

tether ['teðər] **1** *vt* (*fasten*) attacher. **2** *n* **at the end of one's t.** à bout de nerfs.

text [tekst] *n* texte *m*. ◆**textbook** *n* manuel *m*.

textile ['tekstaɪl] *a & n* textile (*m*).

texture ['tekstʃər] *n* (*of fabric, cake etc*) texture *f*; (*of paper, wood*) grain *m*.

Thames [temz] *n* the T. la Tamise *f*.

than [ðən, stressed ðæn] *conj* **1** que; happier t. plus heureux que; **he has more t. you** il en a plus que toi; **fewer oranges t. plums** moins d'oranges que de prunes. **2** (*with numbers*) de; **more t. six** plus de six.

thank [θæŋk] *vt* remercier (**for sth** de qch, **for doing** d'avoir fait); **t. you** merci (**for sth** pour *ou* de qch, **for doing** d'avoir fait); **no, t. you** (non) merci; **t. God, t. heavens, t. goodness** Dieu merci; – *npl* remerciements *mpl*; **thanks to** (*because of*) grâce à; (*many*) **thanks!** merci (beaucoup)! ◆**thankful** *a* reconnaissant (**for** de); **t. that** bien heureux que (+ *sub*). ◆**thankfully** *adv* (*gratefully*) avec reconnaissance; (*happily*) heureusement. ◆**thankless** *a* ingrat. ◆**Thanksgiving** *n* **T. (day)** (*holiday*) *Am* jour *m* d'action de grâce(s).

that [ðət, *stressed* ðæt] **1** *conj* que; **to say t.** dire que. **2** *rel pron* (*subject*) qui; (*object*) que; **the boy t. left** le garçon qui est parti; **the book t.** I read le livre que j'ai lu; **the carpet t.** I put it on (*with prep*) le tapis sur lequel je l'ai mis; **the house t. she told me about** la maison dont elle m'a parlé; **the day/morning t. she arrived** le jour/matin où elle est arrivée. **3** *dem a* (*pl see* those) ce, cet (*before vowel or mute h*), cette; (*opposed to 'this'*) ... + -là; **t. day** ce jour-là; **t. man** cet homme; cet homme-là; **t. girl** cette fille; cette fille-là. **4** *dem pron* (*pl see* those) ça, cela; ce; **t.** (one) celui-là m, celle-là f; **give me t.** donne-moi ça *or* cela; **I prefer t.** (one) je préfère celui-là; **before t.** avant ça *or* cela; **t.'s right** c'est juste; **who's t.?** qui est-ce?; **t.'s the house** c'est la maison; (*pointing*) voilà la maison; **what do you mean by t.?** qu'entends-tu par là?; **t. is** (*to say*) ... c'est-à-dire .... **5** *adv* (*so*) *Fam* si; **not t. good** pas si bon; **t. high** (*pointing*) haut comme ça; **t. much** (*to cost, earn etc*) (au)tant que ça.

thatch [θætʃ] *n* chaume *m*. ◆**thatched** *a* (*roof*) de chaume; **t. cottage** chaumière *f*.

thaw [θɔ:] *n* dégel *m*; – *vi* dégeler; (*of snow*) fondre; **it's thawing** *Met* ça dégèle; **to t.** (**out**) (*of person*) *Fig* se dégeler; – *vt* (*ice*) dégeler, faire fondre; (*food*) faire dégeler; (*snow*) faire fondre.

the [ðə, *before vowel* ði, *stressed* ði:] *def art* le, l', la, *pl* les; **t. roof** le toit; **t. man** l'homme; **t. moon** la lune; **t. orange** l'orange; **t. boxes** les boîtes; **the smallest t.** plus petit; **of t., from t.** du, de l', de la, *pl* des; **to t., at t.** au, à l', à la, *pl* aux; **Elizabeth t. Second** Élisabeth deux; **all t. better** d'autant mieux.

theatre ['θɪətər] *n* (*place, art*) & *Mil* théâtre *m*. ◆**theatregoer** *n* amateur *m* de théâtre. ◆**the'atrical** *a* théâtral; **t. company** troupe *f* de théâtre.

theft [θeft] *n* vol *m*.

their [ðeər] *poss a* leur, *pl* leurs; **t. house** leur maison *f*. ◆**theirs** [ðeəz] *poss pron* le leur, la leur, *pl* les leurs; **this book is t.** ce livre est à eux *or* ce sont les leurs; **a friend of t.** un ami à eux.

them [ðəm, *stressed* ðem] *pron* les; (*after prep etc*) eux *mpl*, elles *fpl*; (**to**) **t.** (*indirect*) leur; **I see t.** je les vois; **I give (to) t.** je leur donne; **with t.** avec eux, avec elles; **ten of t.** dix d'entre eux, dix d'entre elles; **all of t.** tous, toutes. ◆**them'selves** *pron* eux-mêmes *mpl*, elles-mêmes *fpl*; (*reflexive*) se, s'; (*after prep etc*) eux *mpl*, elles *fpl*;

they wash t. ils se lavent, elles se lavent; **they think of t.** ils pensent à eux, elles pensent à elles.

theme [θi:m] *n* thème *m*; **t. song** *or* **tune** *Cin TV* chanson *f* principale.

then [ðen] **1** *adv* (*at that time*) alors, à ce moment-là; (*next*) ensuite, puis; **from t. on** dès lors; **before t.** avant cela; **until t.** jusque-là, jusqu'alors; **– a the t. mayor/etc** le maire/etc d'alors. **2** *conj* (*therefore*) donc, alors.

theology [θɪ'ɒlədʒɪ] *n* théologie *f*. ◆**theo'logical** *a* théologique. ◆**theo'logian** *n* théologien *m*.

theorem ['θɪərəm] *n* théorème *m*.

theory ['θɪərɪ] *n* théorie *f*; **in t.** en théorie. ◆**theo'retical** *a* théorique. ◆**theo'retically** *adv* théoriquement. ◆**theorist** *n* théoricien, -ienne *mf*.

therapy ['θerəpɪ] *n* thérapeutique *f*. ◆**thera'peutic** *a* thérapeutique.

there [ðeər] *adv* là; (*down or over*) **t.** là-bas; **on t.** là-dessus; **she'll be t.** elle sera là, elle y sera; **t. is, are** il y a; (*pointing*) voilà; **t. he is** le voilà; **t. she is** la voilà; **t. they are** les voilà; **that man t.** cet homme-là; **t. (you are)!** (*take this*) tenez!; **t., (t.,) don't cry!** allons, allons, ne pleure pas! ◆**therea'bout(s)** *adv* par là; (*in amount*) à peu près. ◆**there'after** *adv* après cela. ◆**thereby** *adv* de ce fait. ◆**therefore** *adv* donc. ◆**thereu'pon** *adv* sur ce.

thermal ['θɜ:m(ə)l] *a* (*energy, unit*) thermique; (*springs*) thermal; (*underwear*) tribo-électrique, en thermolacty!®.

thermometer [θə'mɒmɪtər] *n* thermomètre *m*.

thermonuclear [θɜ:məʊ'nju:klɪər] *a* thermonucléaire.

Thermos® ['θɜ:məs] *n* **T.** (**flask**) thermos® *m or* *f*.

thermostat ['θɜ:məstæt] *n* thermostat *m*.

thesaurus [θɪ'sɔ:rəs] *n* dictionnaire *m* de synonymes.

these [ði:z] **1** *dem a* (*sing see* this) ces; (*opposed to 'those'*) ... + -ci; **t. men** ces hommes; ces hommes-ci. **2** *dem pron* (*sing see* this) **t.** (**ones**) ceux-ci *mpl*, celles-ci *fpl*; **t. are my friends** ce sont mes amis.

thesis, *pl* **theses** ['θi:sɪs, 'θi:si:z] *n* thèse *f*.

they [ðeɪ] *pron* **1** ils *mpl*, elles *fpl*; (*stressed*) eux *mpl*, elles *fpl*; **t. go** ils vont, elles vont; **t. are doctors** ce sont des médecins. **2** (*people in general*) on; **t. say** on dit.

thick [θɪk] *a* (*-er, -est*) épais; (*stupid*) *Fam* lourd; **to be t.** (*of friends*) *Fam* être très liés; **– adv** (*to grow*) dru; (*to spread*) en couche épaisse; **– n** **in the t. of** (*battle etc*) au plus gros de. ◆**thicken** vt épaissir; – vi s'épaissir. ◆**thickly** adv (to grow, fall) dru; (to spread) en couche épaisse; (populated, wooded) très. ◆**thickness** n épaisseur f.

thicket ['θɪkɪt] n (trees) fourré m.

thickset [θɪk'set] a (person) trapu. ◆**thick-skinned** a (person) dur, peu sensible.

thief [θiːf] n (pl thieves) voleur, -euse mf. ◆**thiev/e** vti voler. ◆**—ing** a voleur; – n vol m.

thigh [θaɪ] n cuisse f. ◆**thighbone** n fémur m.

thimble ['θɪmb(ə)l] n dé m (à coudre).

thin [θɪn] a (thinner, thinnest) (slice, paper etc) mince; (person, leg) mince; (soup) peu épais; (hair, audience) clair-semé; (powder) fin; (excuse, profit) Fig maigre, mince; – adv (to spread) en couche mince; – vt (-nn-) to t. (down) (paint etc) délayer; – vi to t. out (of crowd, mist) s'éclaircir. ◆**—ly** adv (to spread) en couche mince; (populated, wooded) peu; (disguised) à peine. ◆**—ness** n minceur f; maigreur f.

thing [θɪŋ] n chose f; one's things (belongings, clothes) ses affaires fpl; it's a funny t. c'est drôle; **poor little t.!** pauvre petit!; **that's (just) the t.** voilà (exactement) ce qu'il faut; **how are things?**, Fam how's things? comment (ça) va?; **I'll think things over** j'y réfléchirai; **for one t. . . .** , and for another t. d'abord . . . et ensuite; **tea things** (set) service m à thé; (dishes) vaisselle f. ◆**thingummy** n Fam truc m, machin m.

think [θɪŋk] vi (pt & pp thought) penser (about, of à); to t. (carefully) réfléchir (about, of à); to t. of doing penser ou songer à faire; to t. highly of, t. a lot of penser beaucoup de bien de; **she doesn't t. much of it** ça ne lui dit pas grand-chose; **to t. better of it** se raviser; **I can't t. of it** je n'arrive pas à m'en souvenir; – vt penser (that que); **I t. so** je pense ou crois que oui; **what do you t. of him?** que penses-tu de lui?; **I thought it difficult** je l'ai trouvé difficile; **to t. out** ou **through** (reply etc) réfléchir sérieusement à, peser; **to t. over** réfléchir à; **to t. up** (invent) inventer, avoir l'idée de; – n **to have a t.** Fam réfléchir (about à); – a **t. tank** comité m d'experts. ◆**—ing** a (person) intelligent; – n (opinion) opinion f; **to my t.** à mon avis. ◆**—er** n penseur, -euse mf.

thin-skinned [θɪn'skɪnd] a (person) susceptible.

third [θɜːd] a troisième; **t. person** or **party** tiers m; **t.-party insurance** assurance f au tiers; **T. World** Tiers-Monde m; – n

troisième mf; **a t.** (fraction) un tiers; – adv (in race) troisième. ◆**—ly** adv troisièmement.

third-class [θɜːd'klɑːs] a de troisième classe. ◆**t.-rate** a (très) inférieur.

thirst [θɜːst] n soif f (for de). ◆**thirsty** a (-ier, -iest) **to be** or **feel t.** avoir soif; **to make t.** donner soif à; **t. for** (power etc) Fig assoiffé de.

thirteen [θɜː'tiːn] a & n treize (m). ◆**thirteenth** a & n treizième (mf). ◆**thirtieth** a & n trentième (mf). ◆**'thirty** a & n trente (m).

this [ðɪs] **1** dem a (pl see these) ce, cet (before vowel or mute h), cette; (opposed to 'that') . . . + -ci; **t. book** ce livre; ce livre-ci; **t. man** cet homme; cet homme-ci; **t. photo** cette photo; cette photo-ci. **2** dem pron (pl see these) ceci; ce; **t.** (one) celui-ci m, celle-ci f; **give me t.** donne-moi ceci; **I prefer t.** (one) je préfère celui-ci; **before t.** avant ceci; **who's t.?** qui est-ce?; **t. is Paul** c'est Paul; **t. is the house** voici la maison. **3** adv (so) Fam si; **t. high** (pointing) haut comme ceci; **t. far** (until now) jusqu'ici.

thistle ['θɪs(ə)l] n chardon m.

thorn [θɔːn] n épine f. ◆**thorny** a (-ier, -iest) (bush, problem etc) épineux.

thorough ['θʌrə] a (painstaking, careful) minutieux, consciencieux; (knowledge, examination) approfondi; (rogue, liar) fieffé; (disaster) complet; **to give sth a t. washing** laver qch à fond. ◆**—ly** adv (completely) tout à fait; (painstakingly) avec minutie; (to know, clean, wash) à fond. ◆**—ness** n minutie f; (depth) profondeur f.

thoroughbred ['θʌrəbred] n (horse) pur-sang m inv.

thoroughfare ['θʌrəfeər] n (street) rue f; 'no t.' 'passage interdit'.

those [ðəʊz] **1** dem a (sing see that) ces; (opposed to 'these') . . . + -là; **t. men** ces hommes; ces hommes-là. **2** dem pron (sing see that) ceux-là mpl, celles-là fpl; **t. are my friends** ce sont mes amis.

though [ðəʊ] **1** conj (even) t. bien que (+ sub); **as t.** comme si; **strange t. it may seem** si étrange que cela puisse paraître. **2** adv (nevertheless) cependant, quand même.

thought [θɔːt] see **think**. – n pensée f; (idea) idée f, pensée f; (careful) t. réflexion f; **without a t. for** sans penser à; **to have second thoughts** changer d'avis; **on second thoughts**, Am **on second t.** à la réflexion. ◆**thoughtful** a (pensive) pensif; (serious) sérieux; (considerate, kind) gentil, prévеnant. ◆**thoughtfully** *adv* (*considerately*) gentiment. ◆**thoughtfulness** *n* gentillesse *f*, prévenance *f*. ◆**thoughtless** *a* (*towards others*) désinvolte; (*careless*) étourdi. ◆**thoughtlessly** *adv* (*carelessly*) étourdiment; (*inconsiderately*) avec désinvolture.

thousand ['θaʊzənd] *a* & *n* mille *m* & *a*; a t. pages mille pages; two t. pages deux mille pages; **thousands of** des milliers de.

thrash [θræʃ] 1 *vt* to t. s.o. rouer qn de coups; (*defeat*) écraser qn; to t. out (*plan etc*) élaborer (à force de discussions). 2 *vi* to t. about (*struggle*) se débattre. ◆—**ing** *n* (*beating*) correction *f*.

thread [θred] *n* (*yarn*) & *Fig* fil *m*; (*of screw*) pas *m*; −*vt* (*needle, beads*) enfiler; to t. one's way *Fig* se faufiler (through the crowd/*etc* parmi la foule/*etc*). ◆**threadbare** *a* élimé, râpé.

threat [θret] *n* menace *f* (to à). ◆**threaten** *vi* menacer; −*vt* menacer (to do de faire, with sth de qch). ◆**threatening** *a* menaçant. ◆**threateningly** *adv* (to say) d'un ton menaçant.

three [θriː] *a* & *n* trois (*m*); t.-piece suite canapé *m* et deux fauteuils. ◆**threefold** *a* triple; −*adv* to increase t. tripler. ◆**three-'wheeler** *n* (*tricycle*) tricycle *m*; (*car*) voiture *f* à trois roues.

thresh [θreʃ] *vt Agr* battre.

threshold ['θreʃhəʊld] *n* seuil *m*.

threw [θruː] *see* **throw.**

thrift [θrɪft] *n* (*virtue*) économie *f*. ◆**thrifty** *a* (-**ier, -iest**) économe.

thrill [θrɪl] *n* émotion *f*, frisson *m*; to get a t. out of doing prendre plaisir à faire; −*vt* (*delight*) réjouir; (*excite*) faire frissonner. ◆—**ed** *a* ravi (with de qch, to do de faire). ◆—**ing** *a* passionnant. ◆—**er** *n* film *m* or roman *m* à suspense.

thriv/e [θraɪv] *vi* (*of business, person, plant etc*) prospérer; he or she thrives on hard work le travail lui profite. ◆—**ing** *a* prospère, florissant.

throat [θrəʊt] *n* gorge *f*; to have a sore t. avoir mal à la gorge. ◆**throaty** *a* (*voice*) rauque; (*person*) à la voix rauque.

throb [θrɒb] *vi* (-**bb-**) (*of heart*) palpiter; (*of engine*) vrombir; *Fig* vibrer; my finger is throbbing mon doigt me fait des élancements; −*n* palpitation *f*; vrombissement *m*; élancement *m*.

throes [θrəʊz] *npl* in the t. of au milieu de; (*illness, crisis*) en proie à; in the t. of doing en train de faire.

thrombosis [θrɒm'bəʊsɪs] *n* (*coronary*) *Med* infarctus *m*.

throne [θrəʊn] *n* trône *m*.

throng [θrɒŋ] *n* foule *f*; −*vi* (*rush*) affluer; −*vt* (*street, station etc*) se presser dans; thronged with people noir de monde.

throttle ['θrɒt(ə)l] 1 *n Aut* accélérateur *m*. 2 *vt* (*strangle*) étrangler.

through [θruː] *prep* (*place*) à travers; (*time*) pendant; (*means*) par; (*thanks to*) grâce à; to go or get t. (*forest etc*) traverser; (*hole etc*) passer par; to speak t. one's nose parler du nez; **Tuesday t. Saturday** *Am* de mardi à samedi; − *adv* à travers; to go t. (*cross*) traverser; (*pass*) passer; to let t. laisser passer; all or right t. (*to the end*) jusqu'au bout; **French t.** t. français jusqu'au bout des ongles; to be t. (*finished*) *Am* avoir fini; we're t. *Am Fam* c'est fini entre nous; **I'm t. with the book** *Am Fam* je n'ai plus besoin du livre; − t. **or till** jusqu'à; **I'll put you t.** (to him) *Tel* je vous le passe; − *a* (*train, traffic, ticket*) direct; 'no t. road' (*no exit*) 'voie sans issue'. ◆**through'out** *prep* t. the neighbourhood/*etc* dans tout le quartier/*etc*; t. the day/*etc* (*time*) pendant toute la journée/*etc*; − *adv* (*everywhere*) partout; (*all the time*) tout le temps. ◆**throughway** *n Am* autoroute *f*.

throw [θrəʊ] *n* (*of stone*) jet *m*; *Sp* lancer *m*; (*of dice*) coup *m*; (*in wrestling*) tour *m*; − *vt* (*pt* threw, *pp* thrown) jeter (to, at à); (*stone, ball*) lancer, jeter; (*hurl*) projeter; (*of horse*) désarçonner (qn); (*party, reception*) donner; (*baffle*) *Fam* dérouter; to t. away (*discard*) jeter; (*ruin, waste*) *Fig* gâcher; to t. back (*ball*) renvoyer (to à); (*one's head*) rejeter en arrière; to t. in (*include as extra*) *Fam* donner en prime; to t. off (*get rid of*) se débarrasser de; to t. out (*discard*) jeter; (*suggestion*) repousser; (*expel*) mettre (qn) à la porte; (*distort*) fausser (*calcul etc*); to t. over abandonner; to t. up (*job*) *Fam* laisser tomber; − *vi* to t. up (*vomit*) *Sl* dégobiller. ◆**throwaway** *a* (*disposable*) à jeter, jetable.

thrush [θrʌʃ] *n* (*bird*) grive *f*.

thrust [θrʌst] *n* (*push*) poussée *f*; (*stab*) coup *m*; (*of argument*) poids *m*; (*dynamism*) allant *m*; − *vt* (*pt* & *pp* thrust) (*push*) pousser; (*put*) mettre (into dans); to t. sth into sth (*stick, knife, pin*) enfoncer qch dans qch; to t. sth/s.o. upon s.o. *Fig* imposer qch/qn à qn.

thud [θʌd] *n* bruit *m* sourd.

thug [θʌg] *n* voyou *m*.

thumb [θʌm] n pouce m; **with a t. index** (book) à onglets; — vt **to t. (through)** (book etc) feuilleter; **to t. a lift** or **a ride** Fam faire du stop. ◆**thumbtack** n Am punaise f.

thump [θʌmp] vt (person) frapper, cogner sur; (table) taper sur; **to t. one's head** (on door etc) se cogner la tête (on contre); — vi frapper, cogner (on à); (of heart) battre à grands coups; — n (grand) coup m; (noise) bruit m sourd. ◆**-ing** a (huge, great) Fam énorme.

thunder [θʌndər] n tonnerre m; — vi (of weather, person, guns) tonner; **it's thundering** Met il tonne; **to t. past** passer (vite) dans un bruit de tonnerre. ◆**thunderbolt** n (event) Fig coup m de tonnerre. ◆**thunderclap** n coup m de tonnerre. ◆**thunderstorm** n orage m. ◆**thunderstruck** a abasourdi.

Thursday [θɜːzdɪ] n jeudi m.

thus [ðʌs] adv ainsi.

thwart [θwɔːt] vt (plan, person) contrecarrer.

thyme [taɪm] n Bot Culin thym m.

thyroid [θaɪrɔɪd] a & n Anat thyroïde (f).

tiara [tɪˈɑːrə] n (of woman) diadème m.

tic [tɪk] n (in face, limbs) tic m.

tick [tɪk] **1** n (of clock) tic-tac m; — vi faire tic-tac; **to t. over** (of engine, factory, business) tourner au ralenti. **2** n (on list) coche f, trait m; — vt **to t. (off)** cocher; **to t. off** (reprimand) Fam passer un savon à. **3** n (moment) Fam instant m. **4** n (insect) tique f. **5** adv **on t.** (on credit) Fam à crédit. ◆**-ing** n (of clock) tic-tac m; **to give s.o. a t.-off** Fam passer un savon à qn.

ticket [tɪkɪt] n billet m; (for tube, bus, cloakroom) ticket m; (for library) carte f; (fine) Aut Fam contravention f, contredanse f; Pol Am liste f; (price) t. étiquette f; **t. collector** contrôleur, -euse mf; **t. holder** personne f munie d'un billet; **t. office** guichet m.

tickle [tɪk(ə)l] vt chatouiller; (amuse) Fig amuser; — n chatouillement m. ◆**ticklish** a (person) chatouilleux; (fabric) qui chatouille; (problem) Fig délicat.

tidbit [tɪdbɪt] n (food) Am bon morceau m.

tiddlywinks [tɪdlɪwɪŋks] n jeu m de puce.

tide [taɪd] **1** n marée f; **against the t.** Nau & Fig à contre-courant; **the rising t. of discontent** le mécontentement grandissant. **2** vt **to t. s.o. over** (help out) dépanner qn. ◆**tidal** a (river) qui a une marée; **t. wave** raz-de-marée m inv; (in public opinion etc) Fig vague f de fond. ◆**tidemark** n Fig Hum ligne f de crasse.

tidings [taɪdɪŋz] npl Lit nouvelles fpl.

tidy [taɪdɪ] a (-ier, -iest) (place, toys etc) bien rangé; (clothes, looks) soigné; (methodical) ordonné; (amount, sum) Fam joli, bon; **to make t.** ranger; — vt **to t. (up** or **away)** ranger; **to t. oneself (up)** s'arranger; **to t. out** (cupboard etc) vider; — vi **to t. up** ranger. ◆**tidily** adv avec soin. ◆**tidiness** n (bon) ordre m; (care) soin m.

tie [taɪ] n (string, strap etc) & Fig lien m, attache f; (necktie) cravate f; (sleeper) Rail Am traverse f; Sp égalité f de points; (match) match m nul; — vt (fasten) attacher, lier (to à); (a knot) faire (in à); (shoe) lacer; (link) lier (to à); **to t. down** attacher; **to t. s.o. down to** (date, price etc) obliger qn à accepter; **to t. up** attacher; (money) Fig immobiliser; **to be tied up** (linked) être lié (with avec); (busy) Fam être occupé; — vi Sp finir à égalité f de points; Fb faire match nul; (in race) être ex aequo; **to t. in with** (tally with) se rapporter à. ◆**t.-up** n (link) lien m; (traffic jam) Am Fam bouchon m.

tier [tɪər] n (seats) Sp Th gradin m; (of cake) étage m.

tiff [tɪf] n petite querelle f.

tiger [taɪgər] n tigre m. ◆**tigress** n tigresse f.

tight [taɪt] a (-er, -est) (rope etc) raide; (closely-fitting clothing) ajusté, (fitting too closely) (trop) étroit, (trop) serré; (drawer, lid) dur; (control) strict; (schedule, credit) serré; (drunk) Fam gris; (with money) Fam avare; **a t. spot** or **corner** Fam une situation difficile; **it's a t. squeeze** il y a juste la place; — adv (to hold, shut, sleep) bien; (to squeeze) fort; **to sit t.** ne pas bouger. ◆**t. (up)** (rope) tendre; (bolt etc) (res)serrer; (security) Fig renforcer; — vi **to t.** se montrer plus strict à l'égard de. ◆**tightly** adv (to hold) bien; (to squeeze) fort; **t. knit** (close) très uni. ◆**tightness** n (of garment) étroitesse f; (of control) rigueur f; (of rope) tension f.

tight-fitting [taɪtfɪtɪŋ] a (garment) ajusté. ◆**tightfisted** a avare. ◆**tightrope** n corde f raide. ◆**tightwad** n (miser) Am Fam grippe-sou m.

tights [taɪts] npl (garment) collant m; (for dancer etc) justaucorps m.

til/e [taɪl] n (on roof) tuile f; (on wall or floor) carreau m; — vt (wall, floor) carreler. ◆**-ed** a (roof) de tuiles; (wall, floor) carrelé.

till [tɪl] **1** prep & conj = until. **2** n (for money) caisse f (enregistreuse). **3** vt (land) Agr cultiver.

tilt [tɪlt] *vti* pencher; – *n* inclinaison *f*; **(at) full t.** à toute vitesse.

timber ['tɪmbər] *n* bois *m* (de construction); (*trees*) arbres *mpl*; – *a* de *or* en bois. ◆**timberyard** *n* entrepôt *m* de bois.

time [taɪm] *n* temps *m*; (*point in time*) moment *m*; (*epoch*) époque *f*; (*on clock*) heure *f*; (*occasion*) fois *f*; *Mus* mesure *f*; **in (the course of) t., with the passage of) t.** avec le temps; **some of the t.** (*not always*) une partie du temps; **most of the t.** la plupart du temps; **in a year's t.** dans un an; **a long t.** longtemps; **a short t.** peu de temps, un petit moment; **full-t.** à plein temps; **part-t.** à temps partiel; **to have a good *or* a nice t.** (*fun*) s'amuser (bien); **to have a hard t. doing** avoir du mal à faire; **t. off** du temps libre; **in no t. (at all)** en un rien de temps; **(just) in t.** (*to arrive*) à temps (**for sth** pour qch, **to do** pour faire); **in my t.** (*formerly*) de mon temps; **from t. to t.** de temps en temps; **what t. is it?** quelle heure est-il?; **the right *or* exact t.** l'heure *f* exacte; **on t.** à l'heure; **at the same t.** en même temps (**as**); (*simultaneously*) à la fois; **for the t. being** pour le moment; **at the t.** à ce moment-là; **at the present t.** à l'heure actuelle; **at times** par moments, parfois; **at one t.** à un moment donné; **this t. tomorrow** demain à cette heure-ci; **(the) next t. you come** la prochaine fois que tu viendras; **(the) last t.** la dernière fois; **one at a t.** un à un; **t. and again** maintes fois; **ten times ten** dix fois dix; **t. bomb** bombe *f* à retardement; **t. lag** décalage *m*; **t. limit** délai *m*; **t. zone** fuseau *m* horaire; – *vt* (*sportsman, worker etc*) chronométrer; (*programme, operation*) minuter; (*choose the time of*) choisir le moment de; (*to plan*) prévoir. ◆**timing** *n* chronométrage *m*; minutage *m*; (*judgement of artist etc*) rythme *m*; **the t. of** (*time*) le moment choisi pour. ◆**time-consuming** *a* qui prend du temps. ◆**time-honoured** *a* consacré (par l'usage).

timeless ['taɪmləs] *a* éternel.

timely ['taɪmlɪ] *a* à propos. ◆**timeliness** *n* à-propos *m*.

timer ['taɪmər] *n Culin* minuteur *m*, compte-minutes *m inv*; (*sand-filled*) sablier *m*; (*on machine*) minuteur *m*; (*to control lighting*) minuterie *f*.

timetable ['taɪmteɪb(ə)l] *n* horaire *m*; (*in school*) emploi *m* du temps.

timid ['tɪmɪd] *a* (*shy*) timide; (*fearful*) timoré. ◆**–ly** *adv* timidement.

tin [tɪn] *n* étain *m*; (*tinplate*) fer-blanc *m*; (*can*) boîte *f*; (*for baking*) moule *m*; **t. can** boîte *f* (*en fer-blanc*); **t. opener** ouvre-boîtes *m inv*; **t. soldier** soldat *m* de plomb. ◆**tinfoil** *n* papier *m* d'aluminium, papier alu. ◆**tinned** *a* en boîte. ◆**tinplate** *n* fer-blanc *m*.

tinge [tɪndʒ] *n* teinte *f*. ◆**tinged** *a* **t. with** (*pink etc*) teinté de; (*jealousy etc*) *Fig* empreint de.

tingle ['tɪŋg(ə)l] *vi* picoter; **it's tingling** ça me picote. ◆**tingly** *a* (*feeling*) de picotement.

tinker ['tɪŋkər] *vi* **to t.** (**about**) **with** bricoler.

tinkle ['tɪŋk(ə)l] *vi* tinter; – *n* tintement *m*; **to give s.o. a t.** (*phone s.o.*) *Fam* passer un coup de fil à qn.

tinny ['tɪnɪ] *a* (**-ier, -iest**) (*sound*) métallique; (*vehicle, machine*) de mauvaise qualité.

tinsel ['tɪns(ə)l] *n* clinquant *m*, guirlandes *fpl* de Noël.

tint [tɪnt] *n* teinte *f*; (*for hair*) shampooing *m* colorant; – *vt* (*paper, glass*) teinter.

tiny ['taɪnɪ] *a* (**-ier, -iest**) tout petit.

tip [tɪp] *n* **1** (*end*) bout *m*; (*pointed*) pointe *f*. **2** *n* (*money*) pourboire *m*; – *vt* (**-pp-**) donner un pourboire à. **3** *n* (*advice*) conseil *m*; (*information*) & *Sp* tuyau *m*; **to get a t.-off** se faire tuyauter; – *vt* (**-pp-**) **to t. a horse/etc** donner un cheval/*etc* gagnant; **to t. off** (*police*) prévenir. **4** *n* (*for rubbish*) décharge *f*; – *vt* (**-pp-**) **to t.** (**up** *or* **over**) (*tilt*) incliner, pencher; (*overturn*) faire basculer; **to t.** (**out**) (*liquid, load*) déverser (**into** dans); – *vi* **to t.** (**up** *or* **over**) (*tilt*) pencher; (*overturn*) basculer. ◆**tipped** *a* **t. cigarette** cigarette *f* (à bout) filtre.

tipple ['tɪp(ə)l] *vi* (*drink*) *Fam* picoler.

tipsy ['tɪpsɪ] *a* (**-ier, -iest**) (*drunk*) gai, pompette.

tiptoe ['tɪptəʊ] *n* **on t.** sur la pointe des pieds; – *vi* marcher sur la pointe des pieds.

tiptop ['tɪptɒp] *a Fam* excellent.

tirade [taɪ'reɪd] *n* diatribe *f*.

tir/e[1] ['taɪər] *vt* fatiguer; **to t. out** (*exhaust*) épuiser; – *vi* se fatiguer. ◆**–ed** *a* fatigué; **to be t. of sth/s.o./doing** en avoir assez de qch/qn/de faire; **to get t. of doing** se lasser de faire. ◆**–ing** *a* fatigant. ◆**tiredness** *n* fatigue *f*. ◆**tireless** *a* infatigable. ◆**tiresome** *a* ennuyeux.

tire[2] ['taɪər] *n Am* pneu *m*.

tissue ['tɪʃuː] *n Biol* tissu *m*; (*handkerchief*) mouchoir *m* en papier, kleenex® *m*; **t. (paper)** papier *m* de soie.

tit [tɪt] *n* **1** (*bird*) mésange *f*. **2** **to give t. for tat** rendre coup pour coup.

titbit ['tɪtbɪt] *n* (*food*) bon morceau *m*.

titillate ['tɪtɪleɪt] *vt* exciter.

titl/e ['taɪt(ə)l] *n* (name, claim) & *Sp* titre *m*; t. **deed** titre *m* de propriété; t. **role** *Th Cin* rôle *m* principal; – *vt* (film) intituler, titrer. **◆—ed** (a person) titré.

titter ['tɪtər] *vi* rire bêtement.

tittle-tattle ['tɪt(ə)ltæt(ə)l] *n Fam* commérages *mpl*.

to [tə, *stressed* tuː] **1** *prep* à; (towards) vers; (of feelings, attitude) envers; (right up to) jusqu'à; (of) de; **give it to him** or **her** donne-le-lui; **to town** en ville; **to France** en France; **to Portugal** au Portugal; **to the butcher('s)**/etc chez le boucher/etc; **the road to** la route de; **the train to** le train pour; **well-disposed to** bien disposé envers; **kind to** gentil envers or avec or pour; **from bad to worse** de mal en pis; **ten to one** (proportion) dix contre un; **it's ten (minutes) to one** il est une heure moins dix; **one person to a room** une personne par chambre; **to say/to remember**/etc (with *inf*) dire/se souvenir/etc; **she tried to** elle a essayé; **wife**/etc-**to-be** future femme *f*/etc. **2** *adv* **to push to** (door) fermer; **to go** or **walk to and fro** aller et venir. **◆to-do** [tə'duː] *n* (fuss) *Fam* histoire *f*.

toad [təʊd] *n* crapaud *m*.

toadstool ['təʊdstuːl] *n* champignon *m* (vénéneux).

toast [təʊst] **1** *n Culin* pain *m* grillé, toast *m*; – *vt* (bread) faire griller. **2** *n* (drink) toast *m*; – *vt* (person) porter un toast à; (success, event) arroser. **◆toaster** *n* grille-pain *m inv*.

tobacco [tə'bækəʊ] *n* (pl -os) tabac *m*. **◆tobacconist** *n* buraliste *mf*; t., **tobacconist's (shop)** (bureau *m* de) tabac *m*.

toboggan [tə'bɒgən] *n* luge *f*, toboggan *m*.

today [tə'deɪ] *adv* & *n* aujourd'hui (*m*).

toddle ['tɒd(ə)l] *vi* t. **off** (leave) *Hum Fam* se sauver.

toddler ['tɒdlər] *n* petit(e) enfant *mf*.

toddy ['tɒdɪ] *n* (hot) t. grog *m*.

toe [təʊ] **1** *n* orteil *m*; **on one's toes** *Fig* vigilant. **2** *vt* **to t. the line** se conformer; **to t. the party line** respecter la ligne du parti. **◆toenail** *n* ongle *m* du pied.

toffee ['tɒfɪ] *n* (sweet) caramel *m* (dur); t. **apple** pomme *f* d'amour.

together [tə'geðər] *adv* ensemble; (at the same time) en même temps; t. **with** avec. **◆—ness** *n* (of group) camaraderie *f*; (of husband and wife) intimité *f*.

togs [tɒgz] *npl* (clothes) *Sl* nippes *fpl*.

toil [tɔɪl] *n* labeur *m*; – *vi* travailler dur.

toilet ['tɔɪlɪt] *n* (room) toilettes *fpl*, cabinets

mpl; (bowl, seat) cuvette *f* or siège *m* des cabinets; **to go to the t.** aller aux toilettes; – *a* (articles) de toilette; t. **paper** papier *m* hygiénique; t. **roll** rouleau *m* de papier hygiénique; t. **water** (perfume) eau *f* de toilette. **◆toiletries** *npl* articles *mpl* de toilette.

token ['təʊkən] *n* (symbol, sign) témoignage *m*; (metal disc) jeton *m*; (voucher) bon *m*; **gift** t. chèque-cadeau *m*; **book** t. chèque-livre *m*; **record** t. chèque-disque *m*; – *a* symbolique.

told [təʊld] *see* **tell**; – *adv* **all t.** (taken together) en tout.

tolerable ['tɒlərəb(ə)l] *a* (bearable) tolérable; (fairly good) passable. **◆tolerably** *adv* (fairly, fairly well) passablement. **◆tolerance** *n* tolérance *f*. **◆tolerant** *a* tolérant (of à l'égard de). **◆tolerantly** *adv* avec tolérance. **◆tolerate** *vt* tolérer.

toll [təʊl] **1** *n* péage *m*; – *a* (road) à péage. **2** *n* **the death t.** le nombre de morts, le bilan en vies humaines; **to take a heavy t.** (of accident etc) faire beaucoup de victimes. **3** *vi* (of bell) sonner. **◆tollfree** *a* t. **number** *Tel Am* numéro *m* vert.

tomato [tə'maːtəʊ, *Am* tə'meɪtəʊ] *n* (pl -oes) tomate *f*.

tomb [tuːm] *n* tombeau *m*. **◆tombstone** *n* pierre *f* tombale.

tomboy ['tɒmbɔɪ] *n* (girl) garçon *m* manqué.

tomcat ['tɒmkæt] *n* matou *m*.

tome [təʊm] *n* (book) tome *m*.

tomfoolery [tɒm'fuːlərɪ] *n* niaiserie(s) *f(pl)*.

tomorrow [tə'mɒrəʊ] *adv* & *n* demain (*m*); t. **morning/evening** demain matin/soir; **the day after t.** après-demain.

ton [tʌn] *n* tonne *f* (Br = 1016 kg, Am = 907 kg); **metric t.** tonne *f* (= 1000 kg); **tons of** (lots of) *Fam* des tonnes de.

tone [təʊn] *n* (of radio, telephone) tonalité *f*; **in that t.** sur ce ton; **to set the t.** donner le ton; **she's t.-deaf** elle n'a pas d'oreille; – *vt* **to t. down** atténuer; **to t. up** (muscles, skin) tonifier; – *vi* **to t. in** s'harmoniser (with avec).

tongs [tɒŋz] *npl* pinces *fpl*; (for sugar) pince *f*; (curling) t. fer *m* à friser.

tongue [tʌŋ] *n* langue *f*; t. **in cheek** ironique(ment). **◆t.-tied** *a* muet (et gêné).

tonic ['tɒnɪk] *a* & *n* tonique (*m*); **gin and t.** gin-tonic *m*.

tonight [tə'naɪt] *adv* & *n* (this evening) ce soir (*m*); (during the night) cette nuit (*f*).

tonne [tʌn] *n* (metric) tonne *f*. **◆tonnage** *n* tonnage *m*.

tonsil ['tɒns(ə)l] *n* amygdale *f*. **◆tonsil-**

lectomy n opération f des amygdales. ◆**tonsillitis** [tɒnsəˈlaɪtəs] n **to have t.** avoir une angine.

too [tuː] adv **1** (excessively) trop; **t. tired to play** trop fatigué pour jouer; **t. hard to solve** trop difficile à résoudre; **it's only t. true** ce n'est que trop vrai. **2** (also) aussi; (more-over) en plus.

took [tʊk] see take.

tool [tuːl] n outil m; **t. bag, t. kit** trousse f à outils.

toot [tuːt] vti **to t. (the horn)** Aut klaxonner.

tooth, pl **teeth** [tuːθ, tiːθ] n dent f; **front t.** dent de devant; **back t.** molaire f; **milk/wisdom t.** dent de lait/de sagesse; **decay carie** f dentaire; **to have a sweet t.** aimer les sucreries; **long in the t.** (old) Hum chenu, vieux. ◆**toothache** n mal m de dents. ◆**toothbrush** n brosse f à dents. ◆**toothcomb** n peigne m fin. ◆**tooth-paste** n dentifrice m. ◆**toothpick** n cure-dent m.

top[1] [tɒp] n (of mountain, tower, tree) sommet m; (of wall, dress, ladder, page) haut m; (of box, table, surface) dessus m; (of list) tête f; (of water) surface f; (of car) toit m; (of bottle, tube) bouchon m; (bottle cap) capsule f; (of saucepan) couvercle m; (of pen) capuchon m; **pyjama t.** veste f de pyjama; **(at the) t. of the class** le premier de la classe; **on t.** (of ladder, roof) en haut; (in addition to) Fig en plus de; **on t.** (in bus etc) en haut; **from t. to bottom** de fond en comble; **the big t.** (circus) le chapiteau; – a (drawer, shelf) du haut, premier; (step, layer, storey) dernier; (upper) supérieur; (in rank, exam) premier; (chief) principal; (best) meilleur; (great, distinguished) éminent; (maximum) maxi-mum; **in t. gear** Aut en quatrième vitesse; **at t. speed** à toute vitesse; **t. hat** (chapeau m) haut-de-forme m. ◆**t.-'flight** a Fam excellent. ◆**t.-'heavy** a trop lourd du haut. ◆**t.-level** a (talks etc) au sommet. ◆**t.-'notch** a Fam excellent. ◆**t.-'ranking** a (official) haut placé. ◆**t.-'secret** a ultra-secret.

top[2] [tɒp] vt (-pp-) (exceed) dépasser; **to t. up** (glass etc) remplir (de nouveau); (coffee, oil etc) rajouter; **and to t. it all . . .** et pour comble . . . ; **topped with** Culin nappé de.

top[3] [tɒp] n (toy) toupie f.

topaz ['təʊpæz] n (gem) topaze f.

topic ['tɒpɪk] n sujet m. ◆**topical** a d'actualité. ◆**topi'cality** n actualité f.

topless ['tɒpləs] a (woman) aux seins nus.

topography [təˈpɒgrəfɪ] n topographie f.

topple ['tɒp(ə)l] vi **to t. (over)** tomber; – vt **to t. (over)** faire tomber.

topsy-turvy [tɒpsɪˈtɜːvɪ] a & adv sens dessus dessous.

torch [tɔːtʃ] n (burning) torche f, flam-beau m; (electric) lampe f électrique. ◆**torchlight** n & a by t. à la lumière des flambeaux; **t. procession** retraite f aux flambeaux.

tore [tɔːr] see tear[1].

torment [tɔːˈment] vt (make suffer) tour-menter; (annoy) agacer; – ['tɔːment] n tourment m.

tornado [tɔːˈneɪdəʊ] n (pl -oes) tornade f.

torpedo [tɔːˈpiːdəʊ] n (pl -oes) torpille f; **t. boat** torpilleur m; – vt torpiller.

torrent ['tɒrənt] n torrent m. ◆**torrential** [təˈrenʃ(ə)l] a torrentiel.

torrid ['tɒrɪd] a (love affair etc) brûlant, passionné; (climate, weather) torride.

torso ['tɔːsəʊ] n (pl -os) torse m.

tortoise ['tɔːtəs] n tortue f. ◆**tortoiseshell** a (comb etc) en écaille; (spectacles) à monture d'écaille.

tortuous ['tɔːtʃʊəs] a tortueux.

tortur/e ['tɔːtʃər] n torture f; – vt torturer. ◆**-er** n tortionnaire m.

Tory ['tɔːrɪ] n tory m; – a tory inv.

toss [tɒs] vt (throw) jeter, lancer (to à); **to t. s.o. (about)** (of boat, vehicle) ballotter qn, faire tressauter qn; **to t. a coin** jouer à pile ou à face; **to t. back** (one's head) rejeter en arrière; – vi **to t. (about), to turn and toss** (in one's sleep etc) se tourner et se retourner; **we'll t. (up) for it, we'll t.** on va ou jouer à pile ou à face; – n **with a t. of the head** d'un mouvement brusque de la tête. ◆**t.-up** n **it's a t.-up whether he leaves or stays** Sl il y a autant de chances pour qu'il parte ou pour qu'il reste.

tot [tɒt] n **1** (tiny) **t.** petit(e) enfant mf. **2** vt (-tt-) **to t. up** (total) Fam additionner.

total ['təʊt(ə)l] a total; **the t. sales** le total des ventes; – n total m; **in t.** au total; – vt (-ll-, Am -l-) (of debt, invoice) s'élever à; **to t. (up)** (find the total of) totaliser; **that totals $9** ça fait neuf dollars en tout. ◆**—ly** adv totalement.

totalitarian [təʊtælɪˈteərɪən] a Pol total-itaire.

tote [təʊt] n **1** Sp Fam pari m mutuel. **2** vt (gun) porter.

totter ['tɒtər] vi chanceler.

touch [tʌtʃ] n (contact) contact m, toucher m; (sense) toucher m; (of painter) & Fb Rugby touche f; **a t. of** (small amount) un petit peu de, un soupçon de; **the finishing**

touches la dernière touche; **in t. with** (*person*) en contact avec; (*events*) au courant de; **to be out of t. with** ne plus être en contact avec; (*events*) ne plus être au courant de; **to get in t.** se mettre en contact (**with** avec); **we lost t.** on s'est perdu de vue; – *vt* toucher; (*lay a finger on, tamper with, eat*) toucher à; (*move emotionally*) toucher; (*equal*) *Fig* égaler; **to t. up** retoucher; **I don't t. the stuff** (*beer etc*) je n'en bois jamais; – *vi* (*of lines, ends etc*) se toucher; **don't t.!** n'y or ne touche pas!; **he's always touching** c'est un touche-à-tout; **to t. down** (*of aircraft*) atterrir; **to t. on** (*subject*) toucher à. ◆**—ed** (*emotionally*) touché (**by** de); (*crazy*) *Fam* cinglé. ◆**—ing** (*story etc*) touchant. ◆**touch-and-'go** *a* (*uncertain*) *Fam* douteux. ◆**touchdown** *n Av* atterrissage *m*. ◆**touchline** *n Fb Rugby* (ligne *f* de) touche *f*.

touchy ['tʌtʃɪ] *a* (**-ier, -iest**) (*sensitive*) susceptible (**about** à propos de).

tough [tʌf] *a* (**-er, -est**) (*hard*) dur; (*meat, businessman*) coriace; (*sturdy*) solide; (*strong*) fort; (*relentless*) acharné; (*difficult*) difficile, dur; **t. guy** dur *m*. *Fam* pas de chance!, quelle déveine!; – *n* (*tough guy*) *Fam* dur *m*. ◆**toughen** *vt* (*body, person*) endurcir; (*reinforce*) renforcer. ◆**toughness** *n* dureté *f*; solidité *f*; force *f*.

toupee ['tu:peɪ] *n* postiche *m*.

tour [tuər] *n* (*journey*) voyage *m*; (*visit*) visite *f*; (*by artist, team etc*) tournée *f*; (*on bicycle, on foot*) randonnée *f*; **on t.** en voyage; en tournée; **a t. of** (*France*) un voyage *m*; une tournée en; une randonnée en; – *vt* visiter; (*of artist etc*) être en tournée en or dans *etc*. ◆**—ing** *n* tourisme *m*; **to go t.** faire du tourisme. ◆**tourism** *n* tourisme *m*. ◆**tourist** *n* touriste *mf*; – *a* touristique; (*class*) touriste *inv*; **t. office** syndicat *m* d'initiative. ◆**touristy** *a* *Pej Fam* (*trop*) touristique.

tournament ['tuənəmənt] *n Sp & Hist* tournoi *m*.

tousled ['tauz(ə)ld] *a* (*hair*) ébouriffé.

tout [taut] *vi* racoler; **to t. for** (*customers*) racoler; – *n* racoleur, -euse *mf*; **ticket t.** revendeur, -euse *mf* (en fraude) de billets.

tow [təu] *vt* (*car, boat*) remorquer; (*caravan, trailer*) tracter; **to t. away** (*vehicle*) *Jur* emmener à la fourrière; – *n* **'on t.'** 'en remorque'; **t. truck** (*breakdown lorry*) *Am* dépanneuse *f*. ◆**towpath** *n* chemin *m* de halage. ◆**towrope** *n* (*câble m de*) remorque *f*.

toward(s) [tə'wɔːd(z), *Am* tɔːd(z)] *prep* vers;

(*of feelings*) envers; **money t.** de l'argent pour (acheter).

towel ['tauəl] *n* serviette *f* (de toilette); (*for dishes*) torchon *m*; **t. rail** porte-serviettes *m inv*. ◆**towelling** *n*, *Am* ◆**toweling** *n* tissu-éponge *m*; (**kitchen**) **t.** *Am* essuie-tout *m inv*.

tower ['tauər] *n* tour *f*; **t. block** tour *f*, immeuble *m*; **ivory t.** *Fig* tour d'ivoire; – *vi* **to t. above** or **over** dominer. ◆**—ing** *a* très haut.

town [taun] *n* ville *f*; **in t.,** (**in**)**to t.** en ville; **out of t.** en province; **country t.** bourg *m*; **t. centre** centre-ville *m*; **t. clerk** secrétaire *mf* de mairie; **t. council** conseil *m* municipal; **t. hall** mairie *f*; **t. planner** urbaniste *mf*; **t. planning** urbanisme *m*. ◆**township** *n* (*in South Africa*) commune *f* (noire).

toxic ['tɒksɪk] *a* toxique. ◆**toxin** *n* toxine *f*.

toy [tɔɪ] *n* jouet *m*; **soft t.** (jouet *m* en) peluche *f*; – *a* (*gun*) d'enfant; (*house, car, train*) miniature; – *vi* **to t. with** jouer avec. ◆**toyshop** *n* magasin *m* de jouets.

trac/e [treɪs] *n* trace *f* (**of** de); **to vanish** or **disappear without** (**a**) **t.** disparaître sans laisser de traces; – *vt* (*draw*) tracer; (*with tracing paper*) (dé)calquer; (*locate*) retrouver (la trace de), dépister; (*follow*) suivre (la piste de) (**to** à); (*relate*) retracer; **to t.** (**back**) **to** (*one's family*) faire remonter jusqu'à. ◆**—ing** *n* (*drawing*) calque *m*; **t. paper** papier-calque *m inv*.

track [træk] *n* trace *f*; (*of bullet, rocket*) trajectoire *f*; (*of person, animal, tape recorder*) & *Sp* piste *f*; (*of record*) plage *f*; *Rail* voie *f*; (*path*) piste *f*, chemin *m*; *Sch Am* classe *f* (de niveau); **to keep t. of** suivre; **to lose t. of** (*friend*) perdre de vue; (*argument*) perdre le fil de; **to make tracks** *Fam* se sauver; **the right t.** la bonne voie or piste; **t. event** *Sp* épreuve *f* sur piste; **t. record** (*of person, firm etc*) *Fig* antécédents *mpl*; – *vt* **to t.** (**down**) (*locate*) retrouver, dépister; (*pursue*) traquer. ◆**—er** *a* **t. dog** chien *m* policier. ◆**tracksuit** *n Sp* survêtement *m*.

tract [trækt] *n* (*stretch of land*) étendue *f*.

traction ['trækʃ(ə)n] *n Tech* traction *f*.

tractor ['træktər] *n* tracteur *m*.

trade [treɪd] *n* commerce *m*; (*job*) métier *m*; (*exchange*) échange *m*; – *a* (*fair, balance, route*) commercial; (*price*) (de-)gros; (*secret*) de fabrication; (*barrier*) douanier; **t. union** syndicat *m*; **t. unionist** syndicaliste *mf*; – *vi* faire du commerce (**with** avec); **to t. in** (*sugar etc*) faire le commerce de; – *vt* (*exchange*) échanger (**for** contre); **to t. sth in** (*old article*) faire reprendre qch. ◆**t.-in**

Com reprise *f*. ◆**t.-off** *n* échange *m*.
◆**trading** *n* commerce *m*; — *a* (*activity, port etc*) commercial; (*nation*) commerçant; **t. estate** zone *f* industrielle. ◆**trader** *n* commerçant, -ante *mf*; (*street*) **t.** vendeur, -euse *mf* de rue. ◆**tradesman** *n* (*pl* **-men**) commerçant *m*.

trademark ['treɪdmɑːk] *n* marque *f* de fabrique; (*registered*) **t.** marque déposée.

tradition [trə'dɪʃ(ə)n] *n* tradition *f*. ◆**traditional** *a* traditionnel. ◆**traditionally** *adv* traditionnellement.

traffic ['træfɪk] **1** *n* (*on road*) circulation *f*; *Av Nau Rail* trafic *m*; **busy** or **heavy t.** beaucoup de circulation; **heavy t.** (*vehicles*) poids *mpl* lourds; **t. circle** *Am* rond-point *m*; **t. cone** cône *m* de chantier; **t. jam** embouteillage *m*; **t. lights** feux *mpl* (de signalisation); (*when red*) feu *m* rouge; **t. sign** panneau *m* de signalisation. — *a* (*trade*) *Pej* trafic *m* (**in** de); — *vi* (**-ck-**) trafiquer (**in** de). ◆**trafficker** *n Pej* trafiquant, -ante *mf*.

tragedy ['trædʒədɪ] *n Th & Fig* tragédie *f*. ◆**tragic** *a* tragique. ◆**tragically** *adv* tragiquement.

trail [treɪl] *n* (*of powder, smoke, blood etc*) traînée *f*; (*track*) piste *f*, trace *f*; (*path*) sentier *m*; **in its t.** (*wake*) dans son sillage; — *vt* (*drag*) traîner; (*caravan*) tracter; (*follow*) suivre (la piste de); — *vi* (*on the ground etc*) traîner; (*of plant*) ramper; **to t. behind** (*lag behind*) traîner. ◆**-er** n **1** *Aut* remorque *f*; *Am* caravane *f*. **2** *Cin* bande *f* annonce.

train [treɪn] **1** *n* (*engine, transport, game*) train *m*; (*underground*) rame *f*; (*procession Fig* file *f*; (*of events*) suite *f*; (*of dress*) traîne *f*; **my t. of thought** le fil de ma pensée; **t. set** train *m* électrique. **2** *vt* (*teach, develop*) former (**to do** à faire); *Sp* entraîner; (*animal, child*) dresser (**to do** à faire); (*ear*) exercer; **to oneself to do** s'entraîner à faire; **to t. sth on** (*aim*) braquer qch sur; — *vi* recevoir une formation (**as a doctor/etc** de médecin/*etc*); *Sp* s'entraîner. ◆**-ed** *a* (*having professional skill*) qualifié; (*nurse etc*) diplômé; (*animal*) dressé; (*ear*) exercé. ◆**-ing** *n* formation *f*; *Sp* entraînement *m*; (*of animal*) dressage *m*; **to be in t.** *Sp* s'entraîner; (*teachers'*) **t. college** école *f* normale. ◆**trai'nee** *n & a* stagiaire (*mf*). ◆**trainer** *n* (*of athlete, racehorse*) entraîneur *m*; (*of dog, lion etc*) dresseur *m*; (*running shoe*) jogging *m*, chaussure *f* de sport.

traipse [treɪps] *vi Fam* (*tiredly*) traîner les pieds; **to t.** (**about**) (*wander*) se balader.

trait [treɪt] *n* (*of character*) trait *m*.
traitor ['treɪtər] *n* traître *m*.
trajectory [trə'dʒektərɪ] *n* trajectoire *f*.
tram [træm] *n* tram(way) *m*.
tramp [træmp] **1** *n* (*vagrant*) clochard, -arde *mf*; (*woman*) *Am* traînée *f*. **2** *vi* (*walk*) marcher d'un pas lourd; (*hike*) marcher à pied; — *vt* (*streets etc*) parcourir; — *n* (*sound*) pas lourds *mpl*; (*hike*) randonnée *f*.
trample ['træmp(ə)l] *vti* **to t. sth** (**underfoot**), **t. on sth** piétiner qch.
trampoline ['træmpəliːn] *n* trampoline *f*.
trance [trɑːns] *n* **in a t.** (*mystic*) en transe.
tranquil ['træŋkwɪl] *a* tranquille. ◆**tran'quility** *n* tranquillité *f*. ◆**tranquillizer** *n Med* tranquillisant *m*.
trans- [trænz, trɑːnz] *pref* trans-.
transact [træn'zækt] *vt* (*business*) traiter. ◆**transaction** *n* (*in bank etc*) opération *f*; (*on Stock Market*) transaction *f*; **the t. of** (*business*) la conduite de.
transatlantic [trænzət'læntɪk] *a* transatlantique.
transcend [træn'send] *vt* transcender. ◆**transcendent** *a* transcendant.
transcribe [træn'skraɪb] *vt* transcrire. ◆**'transcript** *n* (*document*) transcription *f*. ◆**transcription** *n* transcription *f*.
transfer [træns'fɜːr] *vt* (**-rr-**) (*person, goods etc*) transférer (**to** à); (*power*) *Pol* faire passer (**to** à); **to t. the charges** téléphoner en PCV; — *vi* être transféré (**to** à); — ['trænsfɜːr] *n* transfert *m* (**to** à); (*of power*) *Pol* passation *f*; (*image*) décalcomanie *f*; **bank** or **credit t.** virement *m* (bancaire). ◆**trans'ferable** *a* **not t.** (*on ticket*) strictement personnel.
transform [træns'fɔːm] *vt* transformer (**into** en). ◆**transfor'mation** *n* transformation *f*. ◆**transformer** *n El* transformateur *m*.
transfusion [træns'fjuːʒ(ə)n] *n* (*blood*) **t.** transfusion *f* (sanguine).
transient ['trænzɪənt] *a* (*ephemeral*) transitoire.
transistor [træn'zɪstər] *n* (*device*) transistor *m*; **t.** (**radio**) transistor *m*.
transit ['trænzɪt] *n* transit *m*; **in t.** en transit.
transition [træn'zɪʃ(ə)n] *n* transition *f*. ◆**transitional** *a* de transition, transitoire.
transitive ['trænsɪtɪv] *a Gram* transitif.
transitory ['trænzɪtərɪ] *a* transitoire.
translate [træns'leɪt] *vt* traduire (**from** de, **into** en). ◆**translation** *n* traduction *f*; (*into modern tongue*) *Sch* version *f*; (*from mother tongue*) *Sch* thème *m*. ◆**translator** *n* traducteur, -trice *mf*.
transmit [trænz'mɪt] *vt* (**-tt-**) (*send, pass*)

transmettre; – *vti* (*broadcast*) émettre.
◆**transmission** *n* transmission *f*; (*broadcast*) émission *f*. ◆**transmitter** *n* Rad TV émetteur *m*.

transparent [trænsˈpærənt] *a* transparent. ◆**transparency** *n* transparence *f*; (*slide*) Phot diapositive *f*.

transpire [trænˈspaɪər] *vi* (*of secret etc*) s'ébruiter; (*happen*) Fam arriver; **it transpired that** ... il s'est avéré que ....

transplant [trænsˈplɑːnt] *vt* (*plant*) transplanter; (*organ*) Med greffer, transplanter; – [ˈtrænsplɑːnt] *n* Med greffe *f*, transplantation *f*.

transport [trænˈspɔːt] *vt* transporter; – [ˈtrænspɔːt] *n* transport *m*; **public t.** les transports en commun; **do you have t.?** es-tu motorisé?; **t. café** routier *m*. ◆**transporˈtation** *n* transport *m*.

transpose [trænˈspəʊz] *vt* transposer.

transvestite [trænzˈvestaɪt] *n* travesti *m*.

trap [træp] *n* piège *m*; (*mouth*) Pej Sl gueule *f*; **t. door** trappe *f*; – *vt* (**-pp-**) (*snare*) prendre (au piège); (*jam, corner*) coincer, bloquer; (*cut off by snow etc*) bloquer (**by** par); **to t. one's finger** se coincer le doigt. ◆**trapper** *n* (*hunter*) trappeur *m*.

trapeze [trəˈpiːz] *n* (*in circus*) trapèze *m*; **t. artist** trapéziste *mf*.

trappings [ˈtræpɪŋz] *npl* signes *mpl* extérieurs.

trash [træʃ] *n* (*nonsense*) sottises *fpl*; (*junk*) saleté(s) *f(pl)*; (*waste*) Am ordures *fpl*; (*riffraff*) Am racaille *f*. ◆**trashcan** *n* Am poubelle *f*. ◆**trashy** *a* (**-ier, -iest**) (*book etc*) moche, sans valeur; (*goods*) de camelote.

trauma [ˈtrɔːmə, ˈtraʊmə] *n* (*shock*) traumatisme *m*. ◆**trauˈmatic** *a* traumatisant. ◆**traumatize** *vt* traumatiser.

travel [ˈtræv(ə)l] *vi* (**-ll-**, *Am* **-l-**) voyager; (*move*) aller, se déplacer; – *vt* (*country, distance, road*) parcourir; – *n* & *npl* voyages *mpl*; **on one's travels** en voyage; – *a* (*agency, book*) de voyages; **t. brochure** dépliant *m* touristique. ◆**travelled** *a* **to be well** *or* **widely t.** avoir beaucoup voyagé. ◆**travelling** *n* voyages *mpl*; – *a* (*bag etc*) de voyage; (*expenses*) de déplacement; (*circus, musician*) ambulant. ◆**traveller** *n* voyageur, -euse *mf*; **traveller's cheque**, *Am* **traveler's check** chèque *m* de voyage. ◆**travelogue**, *Am* **travelog** *n* (*book*) récit *m* de voyages. ◆**travelsickness** *n* (*in car*) mal *m* de la route; (*in aircraft*) mal *m* de l'air.

travesty [ˈtrævəstɪ] *n* parodie *f*.

travolator [ˈtrævəleɪtər] *n* trottoir *m* roulant.

trawler [ˈtrɔːlər] *n* (*ship*) chalutier *m*.

tray [treɪ] *n* plateau *m*; (*for office correspondence etc*) corbeille *f*.

treacherous [ˈtretʃ(ə)rəs] *a* (*a person, action, road, journey etc*) traître. ◆**treacherously** *adv* traîtreusement; (*dangerously*) dangereusement. ◆**treachery** *n* traîtrise *f*.

treacle [ˈtriːk(ə)l] *n* mélasse *f*.

tread [tred] *vi* (*pt* **trod**, *pp* **trodden**) (*walk*) marcher (**on** sur); (*proceed*) Fig avancer; – *vt* (*path*) parcourir; (*crush*) fouler; **to t. sth into a carpet** étaler qch (avec les pieds) sur un tapis; – *n* (*step*) pas *m*; (*of tyre*) chape *f*. ◆**treadmill** *n* Pej Fig routine *f*.

treason [ˈtriːz(ə)n] *n* trahison *f*.

treasure [ˈtreʒər] *n* trésor *m*; **a real t.** (*person*) Fig une vraie perle; **t. hunt** chasse *f* au trésor; – *vt* (*value*) tenir à, priser; (*keep*) conserver (précieusement). ◆**treasurer** *n* trésorier, -ière *mf*. ◆**Treasury** *n* **the T.** Pol ≃ le ministère des Finances.

treat [triːt] **1** *vt* (*person, product etc*) & Med traiter; (*consider*) considérer (**as** comme); **to t. with care** prendre soin de; **to t. s.o. to sth** offrir qch à qn. **2** *n* (*pleasure*) plaisir *m* (*special*); (*present*) cadeau-surprise *m*; (*meal*) régal *m*; **it was a t.** (**for me**) to do it ça m'a fait plaisir de le faire. ◆**treatment** *n* (*behaviour*) & Med traitement *m*; **his t. of her** la façon dont il la traite; **rough t.** mauvais traitements *mpl*.

treatise [ˈtriːtɪz] *n* (*book*) traité *m* (**on** de).

treaty [ˈtriːtɪ] *n* Pol traité *m*.

treble [ˈtreb(ə)l] *a* triple; – *vti* tripler; – *n* le triple; **it's t. the price** c'est le triple du prix. ◆*a* (*voice*) Mus de soprano.

tree [triː] *n* arbre *m*; **Christmas t.** sapin *m* de Noël; **family t.** arbre *m* généalogique. ◆**t.-lined** *a* bordé d'arbres. ◆**t.-top** *n* cime *f* (d'un arbre). ◆**t.-trunk** *n* tronc *m* d'arbre.

trek [trek] *vi* (**-kk-**) cheminer *or* voyager (péniblement); Sp marcher à pied; (*go*) Fam traîner; – *n* voyage *m* (pénible); Sp randonnée *f*; (*distance*) Fam tirée *f*.

trellis [ˈtrelɪs] *n* treillage *m*.

tremble [ˈtremb(ə)l] *vi* trembler (**with** de). ◆**tremor** *n* tremblement *m*; (**earth**) **t.** secousse *f* (sismique).

tremendous [trəˈmendəs] *a* (*huge*) énorme; (*dreadful*) terrible; (*wonderful*) formidable, terrible. ◆**-ly** *adv* terriblement.

trench [trentʃ] *n* tranchée *f*.

trend [trend] *n* tendance *f* (**towards** à); **the t.** (*fashion*) la mode; **to set a** *or* **the t.** donner le ton, lancer une or la mode. ◆trendy a (-ier, -iest) (person, clothes, topic etc) Fam à la mode, dans le vent.

trepidation [trepɪˈdeɪʃ(ə)n] n inquiétude f.

trespass [ˈtrespəs] vi s'introduire sans autorisation (on, upon dans); 'no trespassing' 'entrée interdite'.

tresses [ˈtresɪz] npl Lit chevelure f.

trestle [ˈtres(ə)l] n tréteau m.

trial [ˈtraɪəl] n Jur procès m; (test) essai m; (ordeal) épreuve f; t. of strength épreuve de force; to go or be on t., stand t. passer en jugement; to put s.o. on t. juger qn; by t. and error par tâtonnements; — a (period, flight etc) d'essai; (offer) à l'essai; t. run (of new product etc) période f d'essai.

triangle [ˈtraɪæŋg(ə)l] n triangle m; (setsquare) Math Am équerre f. ◆triˈangular a triangulaire.

tribe [traɪb] n tribu f. ◆tribal a tribal.

tribulations [trɪbjuˈleɪʃ(ə)nz] npl (trials and) t. tribulations fpl.

tribunal [traɪˈbjuːn(ə)l] n commission f, tribunal m; Mil tribunal m.

tributary [ˈtrɪbjutərɪ] n affluent m.

tribute [ˈtrɪbjuːt] n hommage m, tribut m; to pay t. to rendre hommage à.

trick [trɪk] n (joke, deception & of conjurer etc) tour m; (ruse) astuce f; (habit) manie f; to play a t. on s.o. jouer un tour à qn; card t. tour m de cartes; that will do the t. Fam ça fera l'affaire; t. photo photo f truquée; t. question question-piège f; to t. (deceive) tromper, attraper; to t. s.o. into doing sth amener qn à faire qch par la ruse. ◆trickery n ruse f. ◆tricky a (-ier, -iest) (problem etc) difficile, délicat; (person) rusé.

trickle [ˈtrɪk(ə)l] n (of liquid) filet m; a t. of (letters, people etc) Fig un petit nombre de; — vi (flow) dégouliner, couler (lentement); to t. in (of letters, people etc) Fig arriver en petit nombre.

tricycle [ˈtraɪsɪk(ə)l] n tricycle m.

trier [ˈtraɪər] n to be a t. être persévérant.

trifle [ˈtraɪf(ə)l] n (article, money) bagatelle f; (dessert) diplomate m; — adv a t. small/too much/etc un tantinet petit/trop/etc; — vi to t. with (s.o.'s feelings) jouer avec; (person) plaisanter avec. ◆—ing a insignifiant.

trigger [ˈtrɪgər] n (of gun) gâchette f; — vt to t. (off) (start, cause) déclencher.

trilogy [ˈtrɪlədʒɪ] n trilogie f.

trim [trɪm] a (trimmer, trimmest) (neat) soigné, net; (slim) svelte; — n in t. (fit) en (bonne) forme. 2 n (cut) légère coupe f; (haircut) coupe f de rafraîchissement; to

have a t. se faire rafraîchir les cheveux; — vt (-mm-) couper (légèrement); (finger nail, edge) rogner; (hair) rafraîchir. 3 n (on garment) garniture f; (on car) garnitures fpl; — vt (-mm-) to t. with (lace etc) orner de. ◆trimmings npl garniture(s) f(pl); (extras) Fig accessoires mpl.

Trinity [ˈtrɪnɪtɪ] n the T. (union) Rel la Trinité.

trinket [ˈtrɪŋkɪt] n colifichet m.

trio [ˈtriːəʊ] n (pl -os) (group) & Mus trio m.

trip [trɪp] 1 n (journey) voyage m; (outing) excursion f; to take a t. to (cinema, shops etc) aller à. 2 n (stumble) faux pas m; — vi (-pp-) to t. (over or up) trébucher; to t. over sth trébucher contre qch; — vt to t. s.o. up faire trébucher qn. 3 vi (-pp-) (walk gently) marcher d'un pas léger. ◆tripper n day t. excursionniste m.

tripe [traɪp] n Culin tripes fpl; (nonsense) Fam bêtises fpl.

triple [ˈtrɪp(ə)l] a triple; — vti tripler. ◆triplets npl (children) triplés, -ées mfpl.

triplicate [ˈtrɪplɪkət] n in t. en trois exemplaires.

tripod [ˈtraɪpɒd] n trépied m.

trite [traɪt] a banal. ◆—ness n banalité f.

triumph [ˈtraɪʌmf] n triomphe m (over sur); — vi triompher (over de). ◆triˈumphal a triomphal. ◆triˈumphant a (team, army, gesture) triomphant; (success, welcome, return) triomphal. ◆triˈumphantly adv triomphalement.

trivia [ˈtrɪvɪə] npl vétilles fpl. ◆trivial a (unimportant) insignifiant; (trite) banal. ◆triviˈality n insignifiance f; banalité f; pl banalités fpl.

trod, trodden [trɒd, ˈtrɒd(ə)n] see tread.

trolley [ˈtrɒlɪ] n (for luggage) chariot m; (for shopping) poussette f (de marché); (in supermarket) caddie® m; (trolleybus) trolley m; (tea) t. table f roulante; (for tea urn) chariot m; t. (car) Am tramway m. ◆trolleybus n trolleybus m.

trombone [trɒmˈbəʊn] n Mus trombone m.

troop [truːp] n bande f; Mil troupe f; the troops (army, soldiers) les troupes, la troupe; — vi to t. in/out/etc entrer/ sortir/etc en masse. ◆—ing n to t. the colour le salut du drapeau. ◆—er n (state) t. Am membre m de la police montée.

trophy [ˈtrəʊfɪ] n trophée m.

tropic [ˈtrɒpɪk] n tropique m. ◆tropical a tropical.

trot [trɒt] n (of horse) trot m; on the t. (one after another) Fam de suite; — vi (-tt-) trotter; **to t. off** *or* **along** (*leave*) *Hum Fam* se sauver; − *vt* **to t. out** (*say*) *Fam* débiter.

troubl|e ['trʌb(ə)l] *n* (*difficulty*) ennui(s) *m*(*pl*); (*bother, effort*) peine *f*, mal *m*; **trouble(s)** (*social unrest etc*) & *Med* troubles *mpl*; **to be in t.** avoir des ennuis; **to get into t. s'attirer des ennuis** (**with** avec); **the t. (with you) is . . .** l'ennui (avec toi) c'est que . . . ; **to go to the t. of doing, take the t. to do** se donner la peine *or* le mal de faire; **I didn't put her to any t.** je ne l'ai pas dérangée; **to find the t.** trouver le problème; **a spot of t.** un petit problème; **a t. spot** *Pol* un point chaud; − *vt* (*inconvenience*) déranger, ennuyer; (*worry, annoy*) ennuyer; (*hurt*) faire mal à; (*grieve*) peiner; **to t. to do** se donner la peine de faire; − *vi* **to t. (oneself)** se déranger. ◆**─ed** *a* (*worried*) inquiet; (*period*) agité. ◆**trouble-free** *a* (*machine, vehicle*) qui ne tombe jamais en panne, fiable. ◆**troublemaker** *n* fauteur *m* de troubles. ◆**troubleshooter** *n Tech* dépanneur *m*, expert *m*; *Pol* conciliateur, -trice *mf*. ◆**troublesome** ['trʌb(ə)ls(ə)m] *a* ennuyeux, gênant; (*leg etc*) qui fait mal.

trough [trof] *n* (*for drinking*) abreuvoir *m*; (*for feeding*) auge *f*; **t. of low pressure** *Met* dépression *f*.

trounce [trauns] *vt* (*defeat*) écraser.

troupe [truːp] *n Th* troupe *f*.

trousers ['trauzəz] *npl* pantalon *m*; **a pair of t.**, some t. un pantalon; (**short**) **t.** culottes *fpl* courtes.

trousseau ['truːsəu] *n* (*of bride*) trousseau *m*.

trout [traut] *n* truite *f*.

trowel ['trauəl] *n* (*for cement or plaster*) truelle *f*; (*for plants*) déplantoir *m*.

truant ['truːənt] *n* (*pupil, shirker*) absentéiste *mf*; **to play t.** faire l'école buissonnière. ◆**truancy** *n Sch* absentéisme *m* scolaire.

truce [truːs] *n Mil* trêve *f*.

truck [trʌk] *n* **1** (*lorry*) camion *m*; *Rail* wagon *m* plat; **t. driver** camionneur *m*; (*long-distance*) routier *m*; **t. stop** (*restaurant*) routier *m*. **2 t.** farmer *Am* maraîcher, -ère *mf*. ◆**trucker** *n Am* (*haulier*) transporteur *m* routier; (*driver*) camionneur *m*, routier *m*.

truculent ['trʌkjulənt] *a* agressif.

trudge [trʌdʒ] *vi* marcher d'un pas pesant.

true [truː] *a* (**-er, -est**) vrai; (*accurate*) exact; (*genuine*) vrai, véritable; **t.** to (*person, promise etc*) fidèle à; **t. to life** conforme à la réalité; **to come t.** se réaliser; **to hold t.** (*of argument etc*) valoir (**for** pour); **too t.!** *Fam*

ah, ça oui! ◆**truly** *adv* vraiment; (*faithfully*) fidèlement; **well and t.** bel et bien.

truffle ['trʌf(ə)l] *n* (*mushroom*) truffe *f*.

truism ['truːiz(ə)m] *n* lapalissade *f*.

trump [trʌmp] **1** *n Cards* atout *m*; **t. card** (*advantage*) *Fig* atout *m*. **2** *vt* **to t. up** (*charge, reason*) inventer.

trumpet ['trʌmpit] *n* trompette *f*; **t. player** trompettiste *mf*.

truncate [trʌŋ'keit] *vt* tronquer.

truncheon ['trʌntʃ(ə)n] *n* matraque *f*.

trundle ['trʌnd(ə)l] *vti* **to t. along** rouler bruyamment.

trunk [trʌŋk] *n* (*of tree, body*) tronc *m*; (*of elephant*) trompe *f*; (*case*) malle *f*; (*of vehicle*) *Am* coffre *m*; *pl* (*for swimming*) slip *m* *or* caleçon *m* de bain; **t. call** *Tel* communication *f* interurbaine; **t. road** route *f* nationale.

truss [trʌs] *vt* **to t. (up)** (*prisoner*) ligoter.

trust [trʌst] *n* (*faith*) confiance *f* (**in** en); (*group*) *Fin* trust *m*; *Jur* fidéicommis *m*; **to take on t.** accepter de confiance; − *vt* (*person, judgement*) avoir confiance en, se fier à; (*instinct, promise*) se fier à; **to t. s.o. with sth, t. sth to s.o.** confier qch à qn; **to t. s.o. to do** (*rely on, expect*) compter sur qn pour faire; **I t. that** (*hope*) j'espère que; − *vi* **to t. in s.o.** se fier à qn; **to t. to luck** *or* **chance** se fier au hasard. ◆**─ed** *a* (*friend, method etc*) éprouvé. ◆**─ing** *a* confiant. ◆**trus'tee** *n* (*of school*) administrateur -trice *mf*. ◆**trustworthy** *a* sûr, digne de confiance.

truth [truːθ] *n* (*pl* -s [truːðz]) vérité *f*; **there's some t. in . . .** il y a du vrai dans . . . . ◆**truthful** *a* (*statement etc*) véridique, vrai; (*person*) sincère. ◆**truthfully** *adv* sincèrement.

try [trai] **1** *vt* essayer (**to do, doing** de faire); (*s.o.'s patience etc*) mettre à l'épreuve; **to t. one's hand at** s'essayer à; **to t. one's luck** tenter sa chance; **to t. (out)** (*car, method etc*) essayer; (*employee etc*) mettre à l'essai; **to t. on** (*clothes, shoes*) essayer; − *vi* essayer (**for sth** d'obtenir qch); **to t. hard** faire un gros effort; **t. and come!** essaie de venir!; − *n* (*attempt*) & *Rugby* essai *m*; **to have a t.** essayer; **at (the) first t.** du premier coup. **2** *vt* (*person*) *Jur* juger (**for theft** *etc* pour vol/*etc*). ◆**─ing** *a* pénible, éprouvant.

tsar [zɑːr] *n* tsar *m*.

tub [tʌb] *n* (*for washing clothes etc*) baquet *m*; (*bath*) baignoire *f*; (*for ice cream etc*) pot *m*.

tuba ['tjuːbə] *n Mus* tuba *m*.

tubby ['tʌbi] *a* (**-ier, -iest**) *Fam* dodu.

tube [tjuːb] n tube m; *Rail Fam* métro m; (*of tyre*) chambre f à air. ◆**tubing** n (*tubes*) tubes mpl. ◆**tubular** a tubulaire.

tuberculosis [tjuːbɜːkjuˈləʊsɪs] n tuberculose f.

tuck [tʌk] **1** n (*fold in garment*) rempli m; − vt (*put*) mettre; **to t. away** ranger; (*hide*) cacher; **to t. in** (*shirt*) rentrer; (*person in bed, a blanket*) border; **to t. up** (*skirt*) remonter. **2** vi **to t. in** (*eat*) *Fam* manger; **to t. into** (*meal*) *Fam* attaquer; − n **t. shop** *Sch* boutique f à provisions.

Tuesday ['tjuːzdɪ] n mardi m.

tuft [tʌft] n (*of hair, grass*) touffe f.

tug [tʌg] **1** vt (**-gg-**) (*pull*) tirer; − vi tirer (**at, on** sur); − n **to give sth a t.** tirer (sur) qch. **2** n (*boat*) remorqueur m.

tuition [tjuːˈɪʃ(ə)n] n (*teaching*) enseignement m; (*lessons*) leçons fpl; (*fee*) frais mpl de scolarité.

tulip ['tjuːlɪp] n tulipe f.

tumble ['tʌmb(ə)l] vi **to t. (over)** (*fall*) dégringoler; (*backwards*) tomber à la renverse; **to t. to sth** (*understand*) *Sl* réaliser qch; − n (*fall*) dégringolade f. **t. drier** sèche-linge m inv.

tumbledown ['tʌmb(ə)ldaʊn] a délabré.

tumbler ['tʌmblər] n (*drinking glass*) gobelet m.

tummy ['tʌmɪ] n *Fam* ventre m.

tumour ['tjuːmər] n tumeur f.

tumult ['tjuːmʌlt] n tumulte m. ◆**tu'multuous** a tumultueux.

tuna ['tjuːnə] n **t.** (*fish*) thon m.

tune [tjuːn] n (*melody*) air m; **to be** or **sing in t./out of t.** chanter juste/faux; **in t.** (*instrument*) accordé; **out of t.** (*instrument*) désaccordé; **in t.** (*harmony*) *Fig* en accord avec; **to the t. of £50** d'un montant de 50 livres, dans les 50 livres; − vt **to t. (up)** *Mus* accorder; *Aut* régler; − vt **to t. in (to)** *Rad TV* se mettre à l'écoute (de), écouter. ◆**-ing** n *Aut* réglage m; **t. fork** *Mus* diapason m. ◆**tuneful** a mélodieux.

tunic ['tjuːnɪk] n tunique f.

Tunisia [tjuːˈnɪzɪə] n Tunisie f. ◆**Tunisian** a & n tunisien, -ienne (mf).

tunnel ['tʌn(ə)l] n tunnel m; (*in mine*) galerie f; − vi (**-ll-**, Am **-l-**) percer un tunnel (**into** dans).

turban ['tɜːbən] n turban m.

turbine ['tɜːbaɪn, Am 'tɜːbɪn] n turbine f.

turbulence ['tɜːbjʊləns] n *Phys Av* turbulences fpl.

turbulent ['tɜːbjʊlənt] a (*person etc*) turbulent.

tureen [tjuˈriːn, təˈriːn] n (*soup*) **t.** soupière f.

turf [tɜːf] **1** n (*grass*) gazon m; **the t.** *Sp* le turf; **t. accountant** bookmaker m. **2** vt **to t. out** (*get rid of*) *Fam* jeter dehors.

turgid ['tɜːdʒɪd] a (*style, language*) boursouflé.

turkey ['tɜːkɪ] n dindon m, dinde f; (*as food*) dinde f.

Turkey ['tɜːkɪ] n Turquie f. ◆**Turk** n Turc m, Turque f. ◆**Turkish** a turc; **T. delight** (*sweet*) loukoum m; − n (*language*) turc m.

turmoil ['tɜːmɔɪl] n confusion f, trouble m; **in t.** en ébullition.

turn [tɜːn] n (*movement, action & in game etc*) tour m; (*in road*) tournant m; (*of events, mind*) tournure f; *Med* crise f; *Psy* choc m; (*act*) *Th* numéro m; **t. of phrase** tour m or tournure f (de phrase); **to take turns** se relayer; **in t.** à tour de rôle; **by turns** tour à tour; **in (one's) t.** à son tour; **it's your t. to play** c'est à toi de jouer; **to do s.o. a good t.** rendre service à qn; **the t. of the century** le début du siècle; − vt tourner; (*mechanically*) faire tourner; (*mattress, pancake*) retourner; **to turn s.o./sth into** (*change*) changer or transformer qn/qch en; **to t. sth red/yellow** rougir/jaunir qch; **to t. sth on s.o.** (*aim*) braquer qch sur qn; **she's turned twenty** elle a vingt ans passés; **it's turned seven** il est sept heures passées; **it turns my stomach** cela me soulève le cœur; − vi (*of wheel, driver etc*) tourner; (*turn head or body*) se (re)tourner (**towards** vers); (*become*) devenir; **to t. to** (*question, adviser etc*) se tourner vers; **to t. against** se retourner contre; **to t. into** (*change*) changer or se transformer en. ■ **to t. around** vi (*of person*) se retourner; **to t. away** vt (*avert*) détourner (**from** de); (*refuse*) renvoyer (qn); − vi (*stop facing*) détourner les yeux, se détourner; **to t. back** vt (*bed sheet, corner of page*) replier; (*person*) renvoyer; (*clock*) reculer (**to** jusqu'à); − vi (*return*) retourner sur ses pas; **to t. down** vt (*fold down*) rabattre; (*gas, radio etc*) baisser; (*refuse*) refuser (qn, offre etc); **to t. in** vt (*hand in*) rendre (qch); (*prisoner etc*) *Fam* livrer (à la police); − vi (*go to bed*) *Fam* se coucher; **to t. off** vt (*light, radio etc*) éteindre; (*tap*) fermer; (*machine*) arrêter; − vi (*in vehicle*) tourner; **to t. on** vt (*light, radio etc*) mettre, allumer; (*tap*) ouvrir; (*machine*) mettre en marche; **to t. s.o. on** (*sexually*) *Fam* exciter qn; − vi **to t. on s.o.** (*attack*) attaquer qn; **to t. out** vt (*light*) éteindre; (*contents of box etc*) vider (**from** de); (*produce*) produire; − vi (*of crowds*) venir; (*happen*) se passer; **it turns out that il**

s'avère que; **she turned out to be** ... elle s'est révélée être ... ; **to t. over** *vt* (*page*) tourner; – *vi* (*of vehicle, person etc*) se retourner; (*of car engine*) tourner au ralenti; **to t. round** *vt* (*head, object*) tourner; (*vehicle*) faire faire demi-tour à; – *vi* (*of person*) se retourner; **t. up** *vt* (*radio, light etc*) mettre plus fort; (*collar*) remonter; (*unearth, find*) déterrer; **a turned-up nose** un nez retroussé; – *vi* (*arrive*) arriver; (*be found*) être (re)trouvé. ◆**turning** *n* (*street*) petite rue *f*; (*bend in road*) tournant *m*; **t. circle** *Aut* rayon *m* de braquage; **t. point** (*in time*) tournant *m*. ◆**turner** *n* (*workman*) tourneur *m*.

turncoat ['tɜːnkəʊt] *n* renégat, -ate *mf*. ◆**turn-off** *n* (*in road*) embranchement *m*. ◆**turnout** *n* (*people*) assistance *f*; (*at polls*) participation *f*. ◆**turnover** *n* (*money*) *Com* chiffre *m* d'affaires; (*of stock*) *Com* rotation *f*; **staff t.** (*starting and leaving*) la rotation du personnel; **apple t.** chausson *m* (aux pommes). ◆**turnup** *n* (*on trousers*) revers *m*.

turnip ['tɜːnɪp] *n* navet *m*.

turnpike ['tɜːnpaɪk] *n* *Am* autoroute *f* à péage.

turnstile ['tɜːnstaɪl] *n* (*gate*) tourniquet *m*.

turntable ['tɜːnteɪb(ə)l] *n* (*of record player*) platine *f*.

turpentine ['tɜːpəntaɪn] (*Fam* **turps** [tɜːps]) *n* térébenthine *f*.

turquoise ['tɜːkwɔɪz] *a* turquoise *inv*.

turret ['tʌrɪt] *n* tourelle *f*.

turtle ['tɜːt(ə)l] *n* tortue *f* de mer; *Am* tortue *f*. ◆**turtleneck** *a* (*sweater*) à col roulé; – *n* col *m* roulé.

tusk [tʌsk] *n* (*of elephant*) défense *f*.

tussle ['tʌs(ə)l] *n* bagarre *f*.

tutor ['tjuːtər] *n* précepteur, -trice *mf*; *Univ* directeur, -trice *mf* d'études; *Univ* *Am* assistant, -ante *mf*; – *vt* donner des cours particuliers à. ◆**tu'torial** *n* *Univ* travaux *mpl* dirigés.

tut-tut! [tʌt'tʌt] *int* allons donc!

tuxedo [tʌk'siːdəʊ] *n* (*pl* **-os**) *Am* smoking *m*.

TV [tiː'viː] *n* télé *f*.

twaddle ['twɒd(ə)l] *n* fadaises *fpl*.

twang [twæŋ] *n* son *m* vibrant; (**nasal**) **t.** nasillement *m*; – *vi* (*of wire etc*) vibrer.

twee [twiː] *a* (*fussy*) maniéré.

tweed [twiːd] *n* tweed *m*.

tweezers ['twiːzəz] *npl* pince *f* à épiler.

twelve [twelv] *a* & *n* douze (*m*). ◆**twelfth** *a* & *n* douzième (*mf*).

twenty ['twentɪ] *a* & *n* vingt (*m*). ◆**twentieth** *a* & *n* vingtième (*mf*).

twerp [twɜːp] *n* *Sl* crétin, -ine *mf*.

twice [twaɪs] *adv* deux fois; **t. as heavy/etc** deux fois plus lourd/*etc*; **t. a month/etc**, **t. monthly/etc** deux fois par mois/*etc*.

twiddle ['twɪd(ə)l] *vti* **to t.** (**with**) **sth** (*pencil, knob etc*) tripoter qch; **to t. one's thumbs** se tourner les pouces.

twig [twɪg] **1** *n* (*of branch*) brindille *f*. **2** *vti* (**-gg-**) (*understand*) *Sl* piger.

twilight ['twaɪlaɪt] *n* crépuscule *m*; – *a* crépusculaire.

twin [twɪn] *n* jumeau *m*, jumelle *f*; **identical t.** vrai jumeau; **t. brother** frère *m* jumeau; **t. beds** lits *mpl* jumeaux; **t. town** ville *f* jumelée; – *vt* (**-nn-**) (*town*) jumeler. ◆**twinning** *n* jumelage *m*.

twine [twaɪn] **1** *n* (*string*) ficelle *f*. **2** *vi* (*twist*) s'enlacer (**round** autour de).

twinge [twɪndʒ] *n* **a t.** (**of pain**) un élancement; **a t. of remorse** un pincement de remords.

twinkle ['twɪŋk(ə)l] *vi* (*of star*) scintiller; (*of eye*) pétiller; – *n* scintillement *m*; pétillement *m*.

twirl [twɜːl] *vi* tournoyer; – *vt* faire tournoyer; (*moustache*) tortiller.

twist [twɪst] *vt* (*wine, arm etc*) tordre; (*roll round*) enrouler; (*weave together*) entortiller; (*knob*) tourner; (*truth etc*) *Fig* déformer; **to t. s.o.'s arm** *Fig* forcer la main à qn; – *vi* (*wind*) s'entortiller (**round sth** autour de qch); (*of road, river*) serpenter; – *n* torsion *f*; (*turn*) tour *m*; (*in rope*) entortillement *m*; (*bend in road*) tournant *m*; (*in story*) coup *m* de théâtre; (*in event*) tournure *f*; (*of lemon*) zeste *m*; **a road full of twists** une route qui fait des zigzags. ◆**-ed** *a* (*ankle, wire, mind*) tordu. ◆**-er** *n* **tongue t.** mot *m* ou expression *f* imprononçable.

twit [twɪt] *n* *Fam* idiot, -ote *mf*.

twitch [twɪtʃ] **1** *n* (*nervous*) tic *m*; – *vi* (*of person*) avoir un tic; (*of muscle*) se convulser. **2** *n* (*jerk*) secousse *f*.

twitter ['twɪtər] *vi* (*of bird*) pépier.

two [tuː] *a* & *n* deux (*m*). ◆**t.-cycle** *n* *Am* = **t.-stroke**. ◆**t.-'faced** *a* *Fig* hypocrite. ◆**t.-'legged** *a* bipède. ◆**t.-piece** *n* (*garment*) deux-pièces *m inv*. ◆**t.-'seater** *n* *Aut* voiture *f* à deux places. ◆**t.-stroke** *n* = **t.-stroke** (**engine**) deux-temps *m inv*. ◆**t.-way** *a* (*traffic*) dans les deux sens; **t.-way radio** émetteur-récepteur *m*.

twofold ['tuːfəʊld] *a* double; – *adv* to increase t. doubler.

twosome ['tuːsəm] *n* couple *m*.

tycoon [taɪ'kuːn] *n* magnat *m*.

type[1] [taɪp] *n* **1** (*example, person*) type *m*; (*sort*) genre *m*, sorte *f*, type *m*; **blood t.** groupe *m* sanguin. **2** (*print*) *Typ* caractères *mpl*; **in large t.** en gros caractères. ◆**typesetter** *n* compositeur, trice *mf*.

type[2] [taɪp] *vti* (*write*) taper (à la machine). ◆—**ing** *n* dactylo(graphie) *f*; **a page of t.** une page dactylographiée; **t. error** faute *f* de frappe. ◆**typewriter** *n* machine *f* à écrire. ◆**typewritten** *a* dactylographié. ◆**typist** *n* dactylo *f*.

typhoid ['taɪfɔɪd] *n* **t.** (**fever**) *Med* typhoïde *f*.

typhoon [taɪ'fuːn] *n* *Met* typhon *m*.

typical ['tɪpɪk(ə)l] *a* typique (**of** de); (*customary*) habituel; **that's t.** (**of him**)! c'est bien lui! ◆**typically** *adv* typiquement; (*as usual*) comme d'habitude. ◆**typify** *vt* être typique de; (*symbolize*) représenter.

tyranny ['tɪrənɪ] *n* tyrannie *f*. ◆**tyrannical** *a* tyrannique. ◆**tyrant** ['taɪərənt] *n* tyran *m*.

tyre ['taɪər] *n* pneu *m*.

U

U, u [juː] *n* U, u *m*. ◆**U-turn** *n* *Aut* demi-tour *m*; *Fig Pej* volte-face *f* *inv*.

ubiquitous [juː'bɪkwɪtəs] *a* omniprésent.

udder ['ʌdər] *n* (*of cow etc*) pis *m*.

ugh! [əː(h)] *int* pouah!

ugly ['ʌglɪ] *a* (**-ier, -iest**) laid, vilain. ◆**ugliness** *n* laideur *f*.

UK [juː'keɪ] *abbr* = **United Kingdom**.

ulcer ['ʌlsər] *n* ulcère *m*.

ulterior [ʌl'tɪərɪər] *a* **u.** motive arrière-pensée *f*.

ultimate ['ʌltɪmət] *a* (*final, last*) ultime; (*definitive*) définitif; (*basic*) fondamental; (*authority*) suprême. ◆—**ly** *adv* (*finally*) à la fin; (*fundamentally*) en fin de compte; (*subsequently*) à une date ultérieure.

ultimatum [ʌltɪ'meɪtəm] *n* ultimatum *m*.

ultra- ['ʌltrə] *pref* ultra-.

ultramodern [ʌltrə'mɒdən] *a* ultramoderne.

ultraviolet [ʌltrə'vaɪələt] *a* ultraviolet.

umbilical [ʌm'bɪlɪk(ə)l] *a* **u. cord** cordon *m* ombilical.

umbrage ['ʌmbrɪdʒ] *n* **to take u.** se froisser (**at** de).

umbrella [ʌm'brelə] *n* parapluie *m*; **u. stand** porte-parapluies *m* *inv*.

umpire ['ʌmpaɪər] *n* *Sp* arbitre *m*; – *vt* arbitrer.

umpteen [ʌmp'tiːn] *a* (*many*) *Fam* je ne sais combien de. ◆**umpteenth** *a* *Fam* énième.

un- [ʌn] *pref* in-, peu, non, sans.

UN [juː'en] *abbr* = **United Nations**.

unabashed [ʌnə'bæʃt] *a* nullement déconcerté.

unabated [ʌnə'beɪtɪd] *a* aussi fort qu'avant.

unable [ʌn'eɪb(ə)l] *a* **to be u.** **to do** être incapable de faire; **he's u.** **to swim** il ne sait pas nager.

unabridged [ʌnə'brɪdʒd] *a* intégral.

unacceptable [ʌnək'septəb(ə)l] *a* inacceptable.

unaccompanied [ʌnə'kʌmpənɪd] *a* (*person*) non accompagné; (*singing*) sans accompagnement.

unaccountable [ʌnə'kaʊntəb(ə)l] *a* inexplicable. ◆—**ly** *adv* inexplicablement.

unaccounted [ʌnə'kaʊntɪd] *a* **to be (still) u. for** rester introuvable.

unaccustomed [ʌnə'kʌstəmd] *a* inaccoutumé; **to be u.** **to sth/to doing** ne pas être habitué à qch/à faire.

unadulterated [ʌnə'dʌltəreɪtɪd] *a* pur.

unaided [ʌn'eɪdɪd] *a* sans aide.

unanimity [juːnə'nɪmɪtɪ] *n* unanimité *f*. ◆**unanimous** *a* unanime. ◆**unanimously** *adv* à l'unanimité.

unappetizing [ʌn'æpɪtaɪzɪŋ] *a* peu appétissant.

unapproachable [ʌnə'prəʊtʃəb(ə)l] *a* (*person*) inabordable.

unarmed [ʌn'ɑːmd] *a* (*person*) non armé; (*combat*) à mains nues.

unashamed [ʌnə'ʃeɪmd] *a* éhonté; **she's u. about it** elle n'en a pas honte. ◆—**ly** [-ɪdlɪ] *adv* sans vergogne.

unassailable [ʌnə'seɪləb(ə)l] *a* (*argument, reputation*) inattaquable.

unassuming [ʌnə'sjuːmɪŋ] *a* modeste.

unattached [ʌnə'tætʃt] *a* (*independent, not married*) libre.

unattainable [ʌnə'teɪnəb(ə)l] *a* (*goal, aim*) inaccessible.

unattended [ʌnə'tendɪd] *a* sans surveillance.

unattractive [ʌnə'træktɪv] *a* (*idea, appearance etc*) peu attrayant; (*character*) peu sympathique; (*ugly*) laid.

unauthorized [ʌn'ɔːθəraɪzd] *a* non autorisé.

unavailable [ʌnə'veɪləb(ə)l] *a* (*person, funds*) indisponible; (*article*) Com épuisé.

unavoidab/le [ʌnə'vɔɪdəb(ə)l] *a* inévitable. ◆**-ly** *adv* inévitablement; (*delayed*) pour une raison indépendante de sa volonté.

unaware [ʌnə'weər] *a* to be u. of ignorer; to be u. that ignorer que. ◆**unawares** *adv* to catch s.o. u. prendre qn au dépourvu.

unbalanced [ʌn'bælənst] *a* (*mind, person*) déséquilibré.

unbearab/le [ʌn'beərəb(ə)l] *a* insupportable. ◆**-ly** *adv* insupportablement.

unbeatable [ʌn'biːtəb(ə)l] *a* imbattable. ◆**unbeaten** *a* (*player*) invaincu; (*record*) non battu.

unbeknown(st) [ʌnbɪ'nəʊn(st)] *a* u. to à l'insu de.

unbelievable [ʌnbɪ'liːvəb(ə)l] *a* incroyable. ◆**unbelieving** *a* incrédule.

unbend [ʌn'bend] *vi* (*pt & pp* unbent) (*relax*) se détendre. ◆**-ing** *a* inflexible.

unbias(s)ed [ʌn'baɪəst] *a* impartial.

unblock [ʌn'blɒk] *vt* (*sink etc*) déboucher.

unborn [ʌn'bɔːn] *a* (*child*) à naître.

unbounded [ʌn'baʊndɪd] *a* illimité.

unbreakable [ʌn'breɪkəb(ə)l] *a* incassable. ◆**unbroken** *a* (*continuous*) continu; (*intact*) intact; (*record*) non battu.

unbridled [ʌn'braɪd(ə)ld] *a* Fig débridé.

unburden [ʌn'bɜːd(ə)n] *vt* to u. oneself Fig s'épancher (to auprès de, avec).

unbutton [ʌn'bʌt(ə)n] *vt* déboutonner.

uncalled-for [ʌn'kɔːldfɔːr] *a* déplacé, injustifié.

uncanny [ʌn'kænɪ] *a* (-ier, -iest) étrange, mystérieux.

unceasing [ʌn'siːsɪŋ] *a* incessant. ◆**-ly** *adv* sans cesse.

unceremoniously [ʌnserɪ'məʊnɪəslɪ] *adv* (*to treat*) sans ménagement; (*to show out*) brusquement.

uncertain [ʌn'sɜːt(ə)n] *a* incertain (about, of de); it's *or* he's u. whether *or* that il n'est pas certain que (+ *sub*). ◆**uncertainty** *n* incertitude *f*.

unchanged [ʌn'tʃeɪndʒd] *a* inchangé. ◆**unchanging** *a* immuable.

uncharitable [ʌn'tʃærɪtəb(ə)l] *a* peu charitable.

unchecked [ʌn'tʃekt] *a* sans opposition.

uncivil [ʌn'sɪv(ə)l] *a* impoli, incivil.

uncivilized [ʌn'sɪvɪlaɪzd] *a* barbare.

uncle ['ʌŋk(ə)l] *n* oncle *m*.

unclear [ʌn'klɪər] *a* (*meaning*) qui n'est pas clair; (*result*) incertain; **it's u. whether** . . . on ne sait pas très bien si . . . .

uncomfortable [ʌn'kʌmftəb(ə)l] *a* (*house, chair etc*) inconfortable; (*heat, experience*) désagréable; (*feeling*) troublant; **she is** *or* **feels u.** (*uneasy*) elle est mal à l'aise.

uncommon [ʌn'kɒmən] *a* rare. ◆**-ly** *adv* (*very*) extraordinairement; **not u.** (*fairly often*) assez souvent.

uncommunicative [ʌnkə'mjuːnɪkətɪv] *a* peu communicatif.

uncomplicated [ʌn'kɒmplɪkeɪtɪd] *a* simple.

uncompromising [ʌn'kɒmprəmaɪzɪŋ] *a* intransigeant.

unconcerned [ʌnkən'sɜːnd] *a* (*not anxious*) imperturbable; (*indifferent*) indifférent (by, with à).

unconditional [ʌnkən'dɪʃ(ə)nəl] *a* inconditionnel; (*surrender*) sans condition.

unconfirmed [ʌnkən'fɜːmd] *a* non confirmé.

uncongenial [ʌnkən'dʒiːnɪəl] *a* peu agréable; (*person*) antipathique.

unconnected [ʌnkə'nektɪd] *a* (*events, facts etc*) sans rapport (with avec).

unconscious [ʌn'kɒnʃəs] *a* Med sans connaissance; (*desire*) inconscient; **u. of** (*unaware of*) inconscient de; – *n* Psy inconscient *m*. ◆**-ly** *adv* inconsciemment.

uncontrollable [ʌnkən'trəʊləb(ə)l] *a* (*emotion, laughter*) irrépressible.

unconventional [ʌnkən'venʃ(ə)nəl] *a* peu conventionnel.

unconvinced [ʌnkən'vɪnst] *a* to be *or* remain u. ne pas être convaincu (of de). ◆**unconvincing** *a* peu convaincant.

uncooperative [ʌnkəʊ'ɒp(ə)rətɪv] *a* peu coopératif.

uncork [ʌn'kɔːk] *vt* (*bottle*) déboucher.

uncouple [ʌn'kʌp(ə)l] *vt* (*carriages*) Rail dételer.

uncouth [ʌn'kuːθ] *a* grossier.

uncover [ʌn'kʌvər] *vt* (*saucepan, conspiracy etc*) découvrir.

unctuous ['ʌŋktʃʊəs] *a* (*insincere*) onctueux.

uncut [ʌn'kʌt] *a* (*film, play*) intégral; (*diamond*) brut.

undamaged [ʌn'dæmɪdʒd] *a* (*goods*) en bon état.

undaunted [ʌn'dɔːntɪd] *a* nullement découragé.

undecided [ʌndɪ'saɪdɪd] *a* (*person*) indécis

(about sur); **I'm u. whether to do it or not** je n'ai pas décidé si je le ferai ou non.

undefeated [ʌndɪˈfiːtɪd] *a* invaincu.

undeniable [ʌndɪˈnaɪəb(ə)l] *a* incontestable.

under [ˈʌndər] *prep* sous; (*less than*) moins de; (*according to*) selon; **children u. nine** les enfants de moins de *or* enfants au-dessous de neuf ans; **u. the circumstances** dans les circonstances; **u. there** là-dessous; **u. it** dessous; **u. (the command of) s.o.** sous les ordres de qn; **u. age** mineur; **u. discussion/repair** en discussion/réparation; **u. way** (*in progress*) en cours; (*on the way*) en route; **to be u. the impression that** avoir l'impression que; – *adv* au-dessous.

under- [ˈʌndər] *pref* sous-.

undercarriage [ˈʌndəkærɪdʒ] *n* (*of aircraft*) train *m* d'atterrissage.

undercharge [ʌndəˈtʃɑːdʒ] *vt* **I undercharged him (for it)** je ne (le) lui ai pas fait payer assez.

underclothes [ˈʌndəkləʊðz] *npl* sous-vêtements *mpl*.

undercoat [ˈʌndəkəʊt] *n* (*of paint*) couche *f* de fond.

undercooked [ʌndəˈkʊkt] *a* pas assez cuit.

undercover [ʌndəˈkʌvər] *a* (*agent, operation*) secret.

undercurrent [ˈʌndəkʌrənt] *n* (*in sea*) courant *m* (sous-marin); **an u. of** *Fig* un courant profond de.

undercut [ʌndəˈkʌt] *vt* (*pt & pp* **undercut**, *pres p* **undercutting**) *Com* vendre moins cher que.

underdeveloped [ʌndədɪˈveləpt] *a* (*country*) sous-développé.

underdog [ˈʌndədɒg] *n* (*politically, socially*) opprimé, -ée *mf*; (*likely loser*) perdant, -ante *mf* probable.

underdone [ʌndəˈdʌn] *a* *Culin* pas assez cuit; (*steak*) saignant.

underestimate [ʌndəˈrestɪmeɪt] *vt* sous-estimer.

underfed [ʌndəˈfed] *a* sous-alimenté.

underfoot [ʌndəˈfʊt] *adv* sous les pieds.

undergo [ʌndəˈgəʊ] *vt* (*pt* **underwent**, *pp* **undergone**) subir.

undergraduate [ʌndəˈgrædʒʊət] *n* étudiant, -ante *mf* (qui prépare sa licence).

underground [ˈʌndəgraʊnd] *a* souterrain; (*secret*) *Fig* clandestin; – *n* *Rail* métro *m*; (*organization*) *Pol* résistance *f*; – [ʌndəˈgraʊnd] *adv* sous terre; **to go u.** (*of fugitive etc*) *Fig* passer dans la clandestinité.

undergrowth [ˈʌndəgrəʊθ] *n* sous-bois *m inv*.

underhand [ʌndəˈhænd] *a* (*dishonest*) sournois.

underlie [ʌndəˈlaɪ] *vt* (*pt* **underlay**, *pp* **underlain**, *pres p* **underlying**) sous-tendre.
◆underlying *a* (*basic*) fondamental; (*hidden*) profond.

underline [ʌndəˈlaɪn] *vt* (*text, idea etc*) souligner.

undermanned [ʌndəˈmænd] *a* (*office etc*) à court de personnel.

undermine [ʌndəˈmaɪn] *vt* (*building, strength, society etc*) miner, saper.

underneath [ʌndəˈniːθ] *prep* sous; – *adv* (en) dessous; **the book u.** le livre d'en dessous; – *n* dessous *m*.

undernourished [ʌndəˈnʌrɪʃt] *a* sous-alimenté.

underpants [ˈʌndəpænts] *npl* (*male underwear*) slip *m*; (*loose, long*) caleçon *m*.

underpass [ˈʌndəpɑːs] *n* (*for cars or pedestrians*) passage *m* souterrain.

underpay [ʌndəˈpeɪ] *vt* sous-payer.
◆underpaid *a* sous-payé.

underpriced [ʌndəˈpraɪst] *a* **it's u.** le prix est trop bas, c'est bradé.

underprivileged [ʌndəˈprɪvɪlɪdʒd] *a* défavorisé.

underrate [ʌndəˈreɪt] *vt* sous-estimer.

undershirt [ˈʌndəʃɜːt] *n* *Am* tricot *m or* maillot *m* de corps.

underside [ˈʌndəsaɪd] *n* dessous *m*.

undersigned [ˈʌndəsaɪnd] *a* soussigné; **I the u.** je soussigné(e).

undersized [ʌndəˈsaɪzd] *a* trop petit.

underskirt [ˈʌndəskɜːt] *n* jupon *m*.

understaffed [ʌndəˈstɑːft] *a* à court de personnel.

understand [ʌndəˈstænd] *vti* (*pt & pp* **understood**) comprendre; **I u. that** (*hear*) je crois comprendre que, il paraît que; **I've been given to u. that** on m'a fait comprendre que. **◆—ing** *n* (*act, faculty*) compréhension *f*; (*agreement*) accord *m*, entente *f*; (*sympathy*) entente *f*; **on the u. that** à condition que (+ *sub*); – *a* (*person*) compréhensif. **◆understood** *a* (*agreed*) entendu; (*implied*) sous-entendu. **◆understandable** *a* compréhensible. **◆understandably** *adv* naturellement.

understatement [ˈʌndəsteɪtmənt] *n* euphémisme *m*.

understudy [ˈʌndəstʌdɪ] *n* *Th* doublure *f*.

undertake [ʌndəˈteɪk] *vt* (*pt* **undertook**, *pp* **undertaken**) (*task*) entreprendre; (*responsibility*) assumer; **to u. to do** se charger de faire. **◆—ing** *n* (*task*) entreprise *f*; (*prom-*

ise) promesse *f*; **to give an u.** promettre (that que).

undertaker ['ʌndəteɪkər] *n* entrepreneur *m* de pompes funèbres.

undertone ['ʌndətəʊn] *n* **in an u.** à mi-voix; **an u. of** (*criticism, sadness etc*) *Fig* une note de.

undervalue [ʌndə'væljuː] *vt* sous-évaluer; **it's undervalued at ten pounds** ça vaut plus que dix livres.

underwater [ʌndə'wɔːtər] *a* sous-marin; – *adv* sous l'eau.

underwear [ʌndəweər] *n* sous-vêtements *mpl*.

underweight [ʌndə'weɪt] *a* (*person*) qui ne pèse pas assez; (*goods*) d'un poids insuffisant.

underworld ['ʌndəwɜːld] *n* **the u.** (*criminals*) le milieu, la pègre.

undesirable [ʌndɪ'zaɪərəb(ə)l] *a* peu souhaitable (that que (+ *sub*)); (*person*) indésirable; – *n* (*person*) indésirable *mf*.

undetected [ʌndɪ'tektɪd] *a* non découvert; **to go u.** passer inaperçu.

undies ['ʌndɪz] *npl* (*female underwear*) *Fam* dessous *mpl*.

undignified [ʌn'dɪgnɪfaɪd] *a* qui manque de dignité.

undisciplined [ʌn'dɪsɪplɪnd] *a* indiscipliné.

undiscovered [ʌndɪs'kʌvəd] *a* **to remain u.** ne pas être découvert.

undisputed [ʌndɪ'spjuːtɪd] *a* incontesté.

undistinguished [ʌndɪ'stɪŋwɪʃt] *a* médiocre.

undivided [ʌndɪ'vaɪdɪd] *a* **my u. attention** toute mon attention.

undo [ʌn'duː] *vt* (*pt* undid, *pp* undone) défaire; (*bound person, hands*) détacher, délier; (*a wrong*) réparer. ◆**–ing** *n* (*downfall*) perte *f*, ruine *f*. ◆**undone** *a* **to leave u.** (*work etc*) ne pas faire; **to come u.** (*of knot etc*) se défaire.

undoubted [ʌn'daʊtɪd] *a* indubitable. ◆**–ly** *adv* indubitablement.

undreamt-of [ʌn'dremtɒv] *a* insoupçonné.

undress [ʌn'dres] *vi* se déshabiller; – *vt* déshabiller; **to get undressed** se déshabiller.

undue [ʌn'djuː] *a* excessif. ◆**unduly** *adv* excessivement.

undulating ['ʌndjʊleɪtɪŋ] *a* (*movement*) onduleux; (*countryside*) vallonné.

undying [ʌn'daɪɪŋ] *a* éternel.

unearned [ʌn'ɜːnd] *a* **u. income** rentes *fpl*.

unearth [ʌn'ɜːθ] *vt* (*from ground*) déterrer; (*discover*) *Fig* dénicher, déterrer.

unearthly [ʌn'ɜːθlɪ] *a* sinistre, mystérieux; **u. hour** *Fam* heure *f* indue.

uneasy [ʌn'iːzɪ] *a* (*peace, situation*) précaire; (*silence*) gêné; **to be or feel u.** (*ill at ease*) être mal à l'aise, être gêné; (*worried*) être inquiet.

uneconomic(al) [ʌniːkə'nɒmɪk((ə)l)] *a* peu économique.

uneducated [ʌn'edʒʊkeɪtɪd] *a* (*person*) inculte; (*accent*) populaire.

unemployed [ʌnɪm'plɔɪd] *a* sans travail, en chômage; – *n* **the u.** les chômeurs *mpl*. ◆**unemployment** *n* chômage *m*.

unending [ʌn'endɪŋ] *a* interminable.

unenthusiastic [ʌnɪnθjuːzɪ'æstɪk] *a* peu enthousiaste.

unenviable [ʌn'envɪəb(ə)l] *a* peu enviable.

unequal [ʌn'iːkwəl] *a* inégal; **to be u. to** (*task*) ne pas être à la hauteur de. ◆**unequalled** *a* (*incomparable*) inégalé.

unequivocal [ʌnɪ'kwɪvək(ə)l] *a* sans équivoque.

unerring [ʌn'ɜːrɪŋ] *a* infaillible.

unethical [ʌn'eθɪk(ə)l] *a* immoral.

uneven [ʌn'iːv(ə)n] *a* inégal.

uneventful [ʌnɪ'ventfəl] *a* (*journey, life etc*) sans histoires.

unexceptionable [ʌnɪk'sepʃ(ə)nəb(ə)l] *a* irréprochable.

unexpected [ʌnɪk'spektɪd] *a* inattendu. ◆**–ly** *adv* à l'improviste; (*suddenly*) subitement; (*unusually*) exceptionnellement.

unexplained [ʌnɪk'spleɪnd] *a* inexpliqué.

unfailing [ʌn'feɪlɪŋ] *a* (*optimism, courage, support etc*) inébranlable; (*supply*) inépuisable.

unfair [ʌn'feər] *a* injuste (to s.o. envers qn); (*competition*) déloyal. ◆**–ly** *adv* injustement. ◆**–ness** *n* injustice *f*.

unfaithful [ʌn'feɪθfəl] *a* infidèle (to à).

unfamiliar [ʌnfə'mɪlɪər] *a* inconnu, peu familier; **to be u. with** ne pas connaître.

unfashionable [ʌn'fæʃ(ə)nəb(ə)l] *a* (*subject etc*) démodé; (*district etc*) peu chic *inv*, ringard; **it's u. to do** il n'est pas de bon ton de faire.

unfasten [ʌn'fɑːs(ə)n] *vt* défaire.

unfavourable [ʌn'feɪv(ə)rəb(ə)l] *a* défavorable.

unfeeling [ʌn'fiːlɪŋ] *a* insensible.

unfinished [ʌn'fɪnɪʃt] *a* inachevé; **to have some u. business** avoir une affaire à régler.

unfit [ʌn'fɪt] *a* (*unwell*) mal fichu; (*unsuited*) inapte (for sth à qch, to do à faire); (*unworthy*) indigne (for sth de qch, to do de faire).

to be u. to do (*incapable*) ne pas être en état de faire.

unflagging [ʌnˈflægɪŋ] *a* (*zeal*) inlassable; (*interest*) soutenu.

unflappable [ʌnˈflæpəb(ə)l] *a Fam* imperturbable.

unflattering [ʌnˈflætərɪŋ] *a* peu flatteur.

unflinching [ʌnˈflɪntʃɪŋ] *a* (*fearless*) intrépide.

unfold [ʌnˈfəʊld] *vt* déplier; (*wings*) déployer; (*ideas, plan*) Fig exposer; — *vi* (*of story, view*) se dérouler.

unforeseeable [ʌnfɔːˈsiːəb(ə)l] *a* imprévisible. ◆**unforeseen** *a* imprévu.

unforgettable [ʌnfəˈɡetəb(ə)l] *a* inoubliable.

unforgivable [ʌnfəˈɡɪvəb(ə)l] *a* impardonnable.

unfortunate [ʌnˈfɔːtʃ(ə)nət] *a* malheureux; (*event*) fâcheux; **you were u.** tu n'as pas eu de chance. ◆**-ly** *adv* malheureusement.

unfounded [ʌnˈfaʊndɪd] *a* (*rumour etc*) sans fondement.

unfriendly [ʌnˈfrendlɪ] *a* peu amical, froid. ◆**unfriendliness** *n* froideur *f*.

unfulfilled [ʌnfʊlˈfɪld] *a* (*desire*) insatisfait; (*plan*) non réalisé; (*condition*) non rempli.

unfurl [ʌnˈfɜːl] *vt* (*flag etc*) déployer.

unfurnished [ʌnˈfɜːnɪʃt] *a* non meublé.

ungainly [ʌnˈɡeɪnlɪ] *a* (*clumsy*) gauche.

ungodly [ʌnˈɡɒdlɪ] *a* impie; **u. hour** Fam heure *f* indue.

ungrammatical [ʌnɡrəˈmætɪk(ə)l] *a* non grammatical.

ungrateful [ʌnˈɡreɪtfəl] *a* ingrat.

unguarded [ʌnˈɡɑːdɪd] *a* **in an u. moment** dans un moment d'inattention.

unhappy [ʌnˈhæpɪ] *a* (*-ier, -iest*) (*sad*) malheureux, triste; (*worried*) inquiet; **u. with** (*not pleased*) mécontent de; **he's u. about doing it** ça le dérange de le faire. ◆**unhappily** *adv* (*unfortunately*) malheureusement. ◆**unhappiness** *n* tristesse *f*.

unharmed [ʌnˈhɑːmd] *a* indemne, sain et sauf.

unhealthy [ʌnˈhelθɪ] *a* (*-ier, -iest*) (*person*) en mauvaise santé; (*climate, place, job*) malsain; (*lungs*) malade.

unheard-of [ʌnˈhɜːdɒv] *a* (*unprecedented*) inouï.

unheeded [ʌnˈhiːdɪd] *a* **it went u.** on n'en a pas tenu compte.

unhelpful [ʌnˈhelpfəl] *a* (*person*) peu obligeant *or* serviable; (*advice*) peu utile.

unhinge [ʌnˈhɪndʒ] *vt* (*person, mind*) déséquilibrer.

unholy [ʌnˈhəʊlɪ] *a* (*-ier, -iest*) impie; (*din*) Fam de tous les diables.

unhook [ʌnˈhʊk] *vt* (*picture, curtain*) décrocher; (*dress*) dégrafer.

unhoped-for [ʌnˈhəʊptfɔːr] *a* inespéré.

unhurried [ʌnˈhʌrɪd] *a* (*movement*) lent; (*stroll, journey*) fait sans hâte.

unhurt [ʌnˈhɜːt] *a* indemne, sain et sauf.

unhygienic [ʌnhaɪˈdʒiːnɪk] *a* pas très hygiénique.

unicorn [ˈjuːnɪkɔːn] *n* licorne *f*.

uniform [ˈjuːnɪfɔːm] **1** *n* uniforme *m*. **2** *a* (*regular*) uniforme; (*temperature*) constant. ◆**uniformed** *a* en uniforme. ◆**uni'formity** *n* uniformité *f*. ◆**uniformly** *adv* uniformément.

unify [ˈjuːnɪfaɪ] *vt* unifier. ◆**unifi'cation** *n* unification *f*.

unilateral [juːnɪˈlæt(ə)rəl] *a* unilatéral.

unimaginable [ʌnɪˈmædʒɪnəb(ə)l] *a* inimaginable. ◆**unimaginative** *a* (*person, plan etc*) qui manque d'imagination.

unimpaired [ʌnɪmˈpeəd] *a* intact.

unimportant [ʌnɪmˈpɔːtənt] *a* peu important.

uninhabitable [ʌnɪnˈhæbɪtəb(ə)l] *a* inhabitable. ◆**uninhabited** *a* inhabité.

uninhibited [ʌnɪnˈhɪbɪtɪd] *a* (*person*) sans complexes.

uninitiated [ʌnɪˈnɪʃɪeɪtɪd] *n* **the u.** les profanes *mpl*, les non-initiés.

uninjured [ʌnˈɪndʒəd] *a* indemne.

uninspiring [ʌnɪnˈspaɪərɪŋ] *a* (*subject etc*) pas très inspirant.

unintelligible [ʌnɪnˈtelɪdʒəb(ə)l] *a* inintelligible.

unintentional [ʌnɪnˈtenʃ(ə)nəl] *a* involontaire.

uninterested [ʌnˈɪntrɪstɪd] *a* indifférent (**in** à). ◆**uninteresting** *a* (*book etc*) inintéressant; (*person*) fastidieux.

uninterrupted [ʌnɪntəˈrʌptɪd] *a* ininterrompu.

uninvited [ʌnɪnˈvaɪtɪd] *a* (*to arrive*) sans invitation. ◆**uninviting** *a* peu attrayant.

union [ˈjuːnɪən] *n* union *f*; (*trade union*) syndicat *m*; — *a* syndical; (*trade*) **u. member** syndiqué, -ée *mf*; **U. Jack** drapeau *m* britannique. ◆**unionist** *n* **trade u.** syndicaliste *mf*. ◆**unionize** *vt* syndiquer.

unique [juːˈniːk] *a* unique. ◆**-ly** *adv* exceptionnellement.

unisex [ˈjuːnɪseks] *a* (*clothes etc*) unisexe *inv*.

unison [ˈjuːnɪs(ə)n] *n* **in u.** à l'unisson (**with** de).

unit [ˈjuːnɪt] *n* unité *f*; (*of furniture etc*) élément *m*; (*system*) bloc *m*; (*group, team*) groupe *m*; **u. trust** *Fin* fonds *m* commun de placement.

unite [juːˈnaɪt] *vt* unir; (*country, party*) unifier; **United Kingdom** Royaume-Uni *m*; **United Nations** (Organisation *f* des) Nations unies *fpl*; **United States (of America)** États-Unis *mpl* (d'Amérique); — *vi* s'unir. **◆unity** *n* (*cohesion*) unité *f*; (*harmony*) *Fig* harmonie *f*.

universal [juːnɪˈvɜːs(ə)l] *a* universel. **◆—ly** *adv* universellement.

universe [ˈjuːnɪvɜːs] *n* univers *m*.

university [juːnɪˈvɜːsɪtɪ] *n* université *f*; **at u.** à l'université; — *a* universitaire; (*student, teacher*) d'université.

unjust [ʌnˈdʒʌst] *a* injuste.

unjustified [ʌnˈdʒʌstɪfaɪd] *a* injustifié.

unkempt [ʌnˈkempt] *a* (*appearance*) négligé; (*hair*) mal peigné.

unkind [ʌnˈkaɪnd] *a* peu aimable (**to s.o.** avec qn); (*nasty*) méchant (**to s.o.** avec qn). **◆—ly** *adv* méchamment.

unknowingly [ʌnˈnəʊɪŋlɪ] *adv* inconsciemment.

unknown [ʌnˈnəʊn] *a* inconnu; **u. to me,** he'd left il était parti, ce que j'ignorais; — *n* (*person*) inconnu, -ue *mf*; **the u. Phil** l'inconnu *m*; **u.** (*quantity*) *Math & Fig* inconnue *f*.

unlawful [ʌnˈlɔːfəl] *a* illégal.

unleaded [ʌnˈledɪd] *a* (*gasoline*) *Am* sans plomb.

unleash [ʌnˈliːʃ] *vt* (*force etc*) déchaîner.

unless [ənˈles] *conj* à moins que; **u. she comes** à moins qu'elle ne vienne; **u. you work harder, you'll fail** à moins de travailler plus dur, vous échouerez.

unlike [ʌnˈlaɪk] *a* différent; — *prep* **u. me, she** . . . à la différence de moi *or* contrairement à moi, elle . . . ; **he's very u. his father** il n'est pas du tout comme son père; **that's u. him** ça ne lui ressemble pas.

unlikely [ʌnˈlaɪklɪ] *a* improbable; (*implausible*) invraisemblable; **she's u. to win** il est peu probable qu'elle gagne. **◆unlikelihood** *n* improbabilité *f*.

unlimited [ʌnˈlɪmɪtɪd] *a* illimité.

unlisted [ʌnˈlɪstɪd] *a* (*phone number*) *Am* qui ne figure pas à l'annuaire.

unload [ʌnˈləʊd] *vt* décharger.

unlock [ʌnˈlɒk] *vt* ouvrir (*avec une clef*).

unlucky [ʌnˈlʌkɪ] *a* (**-ier, -iest**) (*person*) malchanceux; (*colour, number etc*) qui porte malheur; **you're u.** tu n'as pas de chance. **◆unluckily** *adv* malheureusement.

unmade [ʌnˈmeɪd] *a* (*bed*) défait.

unmanageable [ʌnˈmænɪdʒəb(ə)l] *a* (*child*) difficile; (*hair*) difficile à coiffer; (*packet, size*) peu maniable.

unmanned [ʌnˈmænd] *a* (*ship*) sans équipage; (*spacecraft*) inhabité.

unmarked [ʌnˈmɑːkt] *a* (*not blemished*) sans marque; **u. police car** voiture *f* banalisée.

unmarried [ʌnˈmærɪd] *a* célibataire.

unmask [ʌnˈmɑːsk] *vt* démasquer.

unmentionable [ʌnˈmenʃ(ə)nəb(ə)l] *a* dont il ne faut pas parler; (*unpleasant*) innommable.

unmercifully [ʌnˈmɜːsɪf(ə)lɪ] *adv* sans pitié.

unmistakable [ʌnmɪˈsteɪkəb(ə)l] *a* (*obvious*) indubitable; (*face, voice etc*) facilement reconnaissable.

unmitigated [ʌnˈmɪtɪgeɪtɪd] *a* (*disaster*) absolu; (*folly*) pur.

unmoved [ʌnˈmuːvd] *a* **to be u.** (*feel no emotion*) ne pas être ému (**by** par); (*be unconcerned*) être indifférent (**by** à).

unnatural [ʌnˈnætʃ(ə)rəl] *a* (*not normal*) pas naturel; (*crime*) contre nature; (*affected*) qui manque de naturel. **◆—ly** *adv* not **u.** naturellement.

unnecessary [ʌnˈnesəs(ə)rɪ] *a* inutile; (*superfluous*) superflu.

unnerve [ʌnˈnɜːv] *vt* désarçonner, déconcerter.

unnoticed [ʌnˈnəʊtɪst] *a* inaperçu.

unobstructed [ʌnəbˈstrʌktɪd] *a* (*road, view*) dégagé.

unobtainable [ʌnəbˈteɪnəb(ə)l] *a* impossible à obtenir.

unobtrusive [ʌnəbˈtruːsɪv] *a* discret.

unoccupied [ʌnˈɒkjupaɪd] *a* (*person, house*) inoccupé; (*seat*) libre.

unofficial [ʌnəˈfɪʃ(ə)l] *a* officieux; (*visit*) privé; (*strike*) sauvage. **◆—ly** *adv* à titre officieux.

unorthodox [ʌnˈɔːθədɒks] *a* peu orthodoxe.

unpack [ʌnˈpæk] *vt* (*case*) défaire; (*goods, belongings, contents*) déballer; **to u. a comb/etc from** sortir un peigne/*etc* de; — *vi* défaire sa valise; (*take out goods*) déballer.

unpaid [ʌnˈpeɪd] *a* (*bill, sum*) impayé; (*work, worker*) bénévole; (*leave*) non payé.

unpalatable [ʌnˈpælətəb(ə)l] *a* désagréable, déplaisant.

unparalleled [ʌnˈpærəleld] *a* sans égal.

unperturbed [ʌnpəˈtɜːbd] *a* nullement déconcerté.

unplanned [ʌnˈplænd] *a* (*visit, baby etc*) imprévu.

unpleasant [ʌnˈplezənt] *a* désagréable (**to s.o.** avec qn). **◆—ness** *n* caractère *m* désagréable (**of** de); (*quarrel*) petite querelle *f*.

unplug [ʌn'plʌg] *vt* (**-gg-**) *El* débrancher; (*unblock*) déboucher.

unpopular [ʌn'pɒpjʊlər] *a* impopulaire; **to be u. with** ne pas plaire à.

unprecedented [ʌn'presɪdentɪd] *a* sans précédent.

unpredictable [ʌnprɪ'dɪktəb(ə)l] *a* imprévisible; (*weather*) indécis.

unprepared [ʌnprɪ'peəd] *a* non préparé; (*speech*) improvisé; **to be u. for** (*not expect*) ne pas s'attendre à.

unprepossessing [ʌnpriːpə'zesɪŋ] *a* peu avenant.

unpretentious [ʌnprɪ'tenʃəs] *a* sans prétention.

unprincipled [ʌn'prɪnsɪp(ə)ld] *a* sans scrupules.

unprofessional [ʌnprə'feʃ(ə)nəl] *a* (*unethical*) contraire aux règles de sa profession.

unpublished [ʌn'pʌblɪʃt] *a* (*text, writer*) inédit.

unpunished [ʌn'pʌnɪʃt] *a* **to go u.** rester impuni.

unqualified [ʌn'kwɒlɪfaɪd] *a* **1** (*teacher etc*) non diplômé; **he's u. to do** il n'est pas qualifié pour faire. **2** (*support*) sans réserve; (*success, rogue*) parfait.

unquestionab/le [ʌn'kwestʃ(ə)nəb(ə)l] *a* incontestable. ◆**-ly** *adv* incontestablement.

unravel [ʌn'ræv(ə)l] *vt* (**-ll-**, *Am* **-l-**) (*threads etc*) démêler; (*mystery*) *Fig* éclaircir.

unreal [ʌn'rɪəl] *a* irréel. ◆**unrea'listic** *a* peu réaliste.

unreasonable [ʌn'riːz(ə)nəb(ə)l] *a* qui n'est pas raisonnable; (*price*) excessif.

unrecognizable [ʌnrekəg'naɪzəb(ə)l] *a* méconnaissable.

unrelated [ʌnrɪ'leɪtɪd] *a* (*facts etc*) sans rapport (**to** avec); **we're u.** il n'y a aucun lien de parenté entre nous.

unrelenting [ʌnrɪ'lentɪŋ] *a* (*person*) implacable; (*effort*) acharné.

unreliable [ʌnrɪ'laɪəb(ə)l] *a* (*person*) peu sérieux, peu sûr; (*machine*) peu fiable.

unrelieved [ʌnrɪ'liːvd] *a* (*constant*) constant; (*colour*) uniforme.

unremarkable [ʌnrɪ'maːkəb(ə)l] *a* médiocre.

unrepeatable [ʌnrɪ'piːtəb(ə)l] *a* (*offer*) unique.

unrepentant [ʌnrɪ'pentənt] *a* impénitent.

unreservedly [ʌnrɪ'zɜːvɪdlɪ] *adv* sans réserve.

unrest [ʌn'rest] *n* troubles *mpl*, agitation *f*.

unrestricted [ʌnrɪ'strɪktɪd] *a* illimité; (*access*) libre.

unrewarding [ʌnrɪ'wɔːdɪŋ] *a* ingrat; (*financially*) peu rémunérateur.

unripe [ʌn'raɪp] *a* (*fruit*) vert, pas mûr.

unroll [ʌn'rəʊl] *vt* dérouler; — *vi* se dérouler.

unruffled [ʌn'rʌf(ə)ld] *a* (*person*) calme.

unruly [ʌn'ruːlɪ] *a* (**-ier, -iest**) indiscipliné.

unsafe [ʌn'seɪf] *a* (*place, machine etc*) dangereux; (*person*) en danger.

unsaid [ʌn'sed] *a* **to leave sth u.** passer qch sous silence.

unsaleable [ʌn'seɪləb(ə)l] *a* invendable.

unsatisfactory [ʌnsætɪs'fæktərɪ] *a* peu satisfaisant. ◆**un'satisfied** *a* insatisfait; **u. with** peu satisfait de.

unsavoury [ʌn'seɪvərɪ] *a* (*person, place etc*) répugnant.

unscathed [ʌn'skeɪðd] *a* indemne.

unscrew [ʌn'skruː] *vt* dévisser.

unscrupulous [ʌn'skruːpjʊləs] *a* (*person, act*) peu scrupuleux.

unseemly [ʌn'siːmlɪ] *a* inconvenant.

unseen [ʌn'siːn] **1** *a* inaperçu. **2** *n* (*translation*) *Sch* version *f*.

unselfish [ʌn'selfɪʃ] *a* (*person, motive etc*) désintéressé.

unsettl/e [ʌn'set(ə)l] *vt* (*person*) troubler. ◆**-ed** *a* (*weather, situation*) instable; (*in one's mind*) troublé; (*in a job*) mal à l'aise.

unshakeable [ʌn'ʃeɪkəb(ə)l] *a* (*person, faith*) inébranlable.

unshaven [ʌn'ʃeɪv(ə)n] *a* pas rasé.

unsightly [ʌn'saɪtlɪ] *a* laid, disgracieux.

unskilled [ʌn'skɪld] *a* inexpert; (*work*) de manœuvre; **u. worker** manœuvre *m*, ouvrier, -ière *mf* non qualifié(e).

unsociable [ʌn'səʊʃəb(ə)l] *a* insociable.

unsocial [ʌn'səʊʃəl] *a* **to work u. hours** travailler en dehors des heures de bureau.

unsolved [ʌn'sɒlvd] *a* (*problem*) non résolu; (*mystery*) inexpliqué; (*crime*) dont l'auteur n'est pas connu.

unsophisticated [ʌnsə'fɪstɪkeɪtɪd] *a* simple.

unsound [ʌn'saʊnd] *a* (*construction etc*) peu solide; (*method*) peu sûr; (*decision*) peu judicieux; **he is of u. mind** il n'a pas toute sa raison.

unspeakable [ʌn'spiːkəb(ə)l] *a* (*horrible*) innommable.

unspecified [ʌn'spesɪfaɪd] *a* indéterminé.

unsporting [ʌn'spɔːtɪŋ] *a* déloyal.

unstable [ʌn'steɪb(ə)l] *a* instable.

unsteady [ʌn'stedɪ] *a* (*hand, voice, step etc*) mal assuré; (*table, ladder etc*) instable. ◆**unsteadily** *adv* (*to walk*) d'un pas mal assuré.

unstinting [ʌnˈstɪntɪŋ] *a* (*generosity*) sans bornes.

unstoppable [ʌnˈstɒpəb(ə)l] *a* qu'on ne peut (pas) arrêter.

unstuck [ʌnˈstʌk] *a* **to come u.** (*of stamp etc*) se décoller; (*fail*) *Fam* se planter.

unsuccessful [ʌnsəkˈsesfəl] *a* (*attempt etc*) infructueux; (*outcome, candidate*) malheureux; (*application*) non retenu; **to be unsuccessful** ne pas réussir (**in doing** à faire); (*of book, artist*) ne pas avoir de succès. **◆—ly** *adv* en vain, sans succès.

unsuitable [ʌnˈsuːtəb(ə)l] *a* qui ne convient pas (**for** à); (*example*) peu approprié; (*manners, clothes*) peu convenable. **◆unsuited** *a* **u. to** impropre à; **they're u.** ils ne sont pas compatibles.

unsure [ʌnˈʃʊər] *a* incertain (**of, about** de).

unsuspecting [ʌnsəˈspektɪŋ] *a* qui ne se doute de rien.

unswerving [ʌnˈswɜːvɪŋ] *a* (*loyalty etc*) inébranlable.

unsympathetic [ʌnsɪmpəˈθetɪk] *a* incompréhensif; **u. to** indifférent à.

untangle [ʌnˈtæŋg(ə)l] *vt* (*rope etc*) démêler.

untapped [ʌnˈtæpt] *a* inexploité.

untenable [ʌnˈtenəb(ə)l] *a* (*position*) intenable.

unthinkable [ʌnˈθɪŋkəb(ə)l] *a* impensable, inconcevable.

untidy [ʌnˈtaɪdɪ] *a* (**-ier, -iest**) (*appearance, hair*) peu soigné; (*room*) en désordre; (*unmethodical*) désordonné. **◆untidily** *adv* sans soin.

untie [ʌnˈtaɪ] *vt* (*person, hands*) détacher; (*knot, parcel*) défaire.

until [ʌnˈtɪl] *prep* jusqu'à; **u. then** jusque-là; **not u. tomorrow**/*etc* (*in the future*) pas avant demain/*etc*; **I didn't come u. Monday** (*in the past*) je ne suis venu que lundi; — *conj* **u. she comes** jusqu'à ce qu'elle vienne, en attendant qu'elle vienne; **do nothing u. I come** (*before*) ne fais rien avant que j'arrive.

untimely [ʌnˈtaɪmlɪ] *a* inopportun; (*death*) prématuré.

untiring [ʌnˈtaɪ(ə)rɪŋ] *a* infatigable.

untold [ʌnˈtəʊld] *a* (*quantity, wealth*) incalculable.

untoward [ʌntəˈwɔːd] *a* malencontreux.

untranslatable [ʌntrænˈleɪtəb(ə)l] *a* intraduisible.

untroubled [ʌnˈtrʌb(ə)ld] *a* (*calm*) calme.

untrue [ʌnˈtruː] *a* faux. **◆untruth** *n* contre-vérité *f*. **◆untruthful** *a* (*person*) menteur; (*statement*) mensonger.

unused 1 [ʌnˈjuːzd] *a* (*new*) neuf; (*not in*

use) inutilisé. **2** [ʌnˈjuːst] *a* **u. to sth/to doing** peu habitué à qch/à faire.

unusual [ʌnˈjuːʒʊəl] *a* exceptionnel, rare; (*strange*) étrange. **◆—ly** *adv* exceptionnellement.

unveil [ʌnˈveɪl] *vt* dévoiler. **◆—ing** *n* (*ceremony*) inauguration *f*.

unwanted [ʌnˈwɒntɪd] *a* (*useless*) superflu, dont on n'a pas besoin; (*child*) non désiré.

unwarranted [ʌnˈwɒrəntɪd] *a* injustifié.

unwavering [ʌnˈweɪv(ə)rɪŋ] *a* (*belief etc*) inébranlable.

unwelcome [ʌnˈwelkəm] *a* (*news, fact*) fâcheux; (*gift, visit*) inopportun; (*person*) importun.

unwell [ʌnˈwel] *a* indisposé.

unwieldy [ʌnˈwiːldɪ] *a* (*package etc*) encombrant.

unwilling [ʌnˈwɪlɪŋ] *a* **he's u. to do** il ne veut pas faire, il est peu disposé à faire. **◆—ly** *adv* à contrecœur.

unwind [ʌnˈwaɪnd] **1** *vt* (*thread etc*) dérouler; — *vi* se dérouler. **2** *vi* (*relax*) *Fam* décompresser.

unwise [ʌnˈwaɪz] *a* imprudent. **◆—ly** *adv* imprudemment.

unwitting [ʌnˈwɪtɪŋ] *a* involontaire. **◆—ly** *adv* involontairement.

unworkable [ʌnˈwɜːkəb(ə)l] *a* (*idea etc*) impraticable.

unworthy [ʌnˈwɜːðɪ] *a* indigne (**of** de).

unwrap [ʌnˈræp] *vt* (**-pp-**) ouvrir, défaire.

unwritten [ʌnˈrɪt(ə)n] *a* (*agreement*) verbal, tacite.

unyielding [ʌnˈjiːldɪŋ] *a* (*person*) inflexible.

unzip [ʌnˈzɪp] *vt* (**-pp-**) ouvrir (la fermeture éclair® de).

up [ʌp] *adv* en haut; (*in the air*) en l'air; (*of sun, hand*) levé; (*out of bed*) levé, debout; (*of road*) en travaux; (*of building*) construit; (*finished*) fini; **to come** *or* **go up** monter; **to be up** (*of price, level etc*) être monté (**by** de); **up there** là-haut; **up above** au-dessus; **up on** (*roof etc*) sur; **further** *or* **higher up** plus haut; **up to** (*as far as*) jusqu'à; (*task*) *Fig* à la hauteur de; **to be up to doing** (*capable*) être de taille à faire; (*in a position to*) être à même de faire; **it's up to you to do it** c'est à toi de le faire; **it's up to you** ça dépend de toi; **where are you up to?** (*in book etc*) où en es-tu?; **what are you up to?** *Fam* que fais-tu?; **what's up?** (*what's the matter?*) *Fam* qu'est-ce qu'il y a?; **time's up** c'est l'heure; **halfway up** (*on hill etc*) à mi-chemin; **to walk up and down** marcher de long en large; **to be well up in** (*versed in*) *Fam* s'y connaître en; **to come up against**

(*confront*) être confronté à; **up (with) the workers**/*etc*! *Fam* vive(nt) les travailleurs/*etc*!; – *prep* (*a hill*) en haut de; (*a tree*) dans; (*a ladder*) sur; **to go up** (*hill, stairs*) monter; **to live up the street** habiter plus loin dans la rue; – *npl* **to have ups and downs** avoir des hauts et des bas; – *vt* (*-pp-*) (*increase*) *Fam* augmenter. ◆**up-and-'coming** a plein d'avenir. ◆**upbeat** a (*cheerful*) *Am Fam* optimiste. ◆**upbringing** n éducation f. ◆**upcoming** a *Am* imminent. ◆**up'date** vt mettre à jour. ◆**upgrade** vt (*job*) revaloriser; (*person*) promouvoir. ◆**up'hill 1** adv **to go u. monter. 2** [ˈʌphil] a (*struggle, task*) pénible. ◆**up'hold** vt (*pt & pp* upheld) maintenir. ◆**upkeep** n entretien m. ◆**uplift** [ʌpˈlift] vt élever; – [ˈʌplift] n élévation f spirituelle. ◆**upmarket** a *Com* haut de gamme. ◆**upright 1** a & adv (*erect*) droit; – n (*post*) montant m. **2** a (*honest*) droit. ◆**uprising** n insurrection f. ◆**up'root** vt (*plant, person*) déraciner. ◆**upside 'down** adv à l'envers; **to turn u. down** (*room, plans etc*) *Fig* chambouler. ◆**up'stairs** adv **to go u. monter** (l'escalier); – [ˈʌpsteəz] a (*people, room*) du dessus. ◆**up'stream** adv en amont. ◆**upsurge** n (*of interest*) recrudescence f; (*of anger*) accès m. ◆**uptake** n **to be quick on the u. comprendre vite. ◆up'tight** a *Fam* (*tense*) crispé; (*angry*) en colère. ◆**up-to-'date** a moderne; (*information*) à jour; (*well-informed*) au courant (**on** de). ◆**upturn** n (*improvement*) amélioration f (**in** de); (*rise*) hausse f (**in** de). ◆**up'turned** a (*nose*) retroussé. ◆**upward** a (*movement*) ascendant; (*path*) qui monte; (*trend*) à la hausse. ◆**upwards** adv vers le haut; **from five francs u. à** partir de cinq francs; **u. of fifty** cinquante et plus.

upheaval [ʌpˈhiːv(ə)l] n bouleversement m.

upholster [ʌpˈhəʊlstər] vt (*pad*) rembourrer; (*cover*) recouvrir. ◆**upholsterer** n tapissier m. ◆**upholstery** n (*activity*) réfection f de sièges; (*in car*) sièges mpl.

upon [əˈpɒn] prep sur.

upper [ˈʌpər] **1** a supérieur; **u. class** aristocratie f; **to have/get the u. hand** avoir/prendre le dessus. **2** n (*of shoe*) empeigne f, dessus m. ◆**u.-'class** a aristocratique. ◆**uppermost** a (*highest*) le plus haut; **to be u.** (*on top*) être en dessus.

uproar [ˈʌprɔːr] n tumulte m.

upset [ʌpˈset] vt (*pt & pp* upset, *pres p* upsetting) (*knock over*) renverser; (*plans, stomach, routine etc*) déranger; **to u. s.o.** (*grieve*)

peiner qn; (*offend*) vexer qn; (*annoy*) contrarier qn; – a vexé; contrarié; (*stomach*) dérangé; – [ˈʌpset] n (*in plans etc*) dérangement m (**in** de); (*upheaval*) *Fig* peine f; **to have a stomach u.** avoir l'estomac dérangé.

upshot [ˈʌpʃɒt] n résultat m.

upstart [ˈʌpstɑːt] n *Pej* parvenu, -ue mf.

uranium [jʊˈreɪnɪəm] n uranium m.

urban [ˈɜːbən] a urbain. ◆**urbane** [ɜːˈbeɪn] a courtois, urbain.

urchin [ˈɜːtʃɪn] n polisson, -onne mf.

urge [ɜːdʒ] vt **to u. s.o. to do** (*advise*) conseiller vivement à qn de faire; **to u. on** (*person, team*) encourager; – n forte envie f, besoin m.

urgency [ˈɜːdʒənsɪ] n urgence f; (*of request, tone*) insistance f. ◆**urgent** a urgent, pressant; (*tone*) insistant; (*letter*) urgent. ◆**urgently** adv d'urgence; (*insistently*) avec insistance.

urinal [jʊˈraɪn(ə)l] n urinoir m.

urine [ˈjʊ(ə)rɪn] n urine f. ◆**urinate** vi uriner.

urn [ɜːn] n urne f; (*for coffee or tea*) fontaine f.

us [əs, *stressed* ʌs] pron nous; (**to) us** (*indirect*) nous; **she sees us** elle nous voit; **he gives (to) us** il nous donne; **with us** avec nous; **all of us** nous tous; **let's or let us eat!** mangeons!

US [juːˈes] abbr = United States.

USA [juːesˈeɪ] abbr = United States of America.

usage [ˈjuːsɪdʒ] n (*custom*) & *Ling* usage m.

use 1 [juːs] n usage m, emploi m; (*way of using*) emploi m; **to have the u. of** avoir l'usage de; **to make u. of** se servir de; **in u.** en usage; **out of u.** hors d'usage; **ready for u.** prêt à l'emploi; **to be of u.** servir, être utile; **it's no u. crying**/*etc* ça ne sert à rien de pleurer/*etc*; **what's the u. of worrying**/*etc*? à quoi bon s'inquiéter/*etc*?, à quoi ça sert de s'inquiéter/*etc*?; **I have no u. for it** je n'en ai pas l'usage, qu'est-ce que je ferais de ça?; **he's no u.** (*hopeless*) il est nul; – [juːz] vt se servir de, utiliser, employer (**as** comme; **to do, for doing** pour faire); **it's used to do or for doing** ça sert à faire; **it's used to** ça sert; **I u. it to clean** je m'en sers pour nettoyer, ça me sert à nettoyer; **to u. (up)** (*fuel etc*) consommer; (*supplies*) épuiser; (*money*) dépenser. ◆**used 1** [juːzd] a (*second-hand*) d'occasion; (*stamp*) oblitéré. **2** [juːst] vt **I u. to do** avant je le faisais; – a **u. to sth/to doing** (*accustomed*) habitué à qch/à faire; **to get u. to** s'habituer à. ◆**useful** [ˈjuːsfəl] a utile; **to**

come in u. être utile; **to make oneself** u. se rendre utile. ◆**usefulness** n utilité f.
◆**useless** ['juːsləs] a inutile; (unusable) inutilisable; (person) nul, incompétent. ◆**user** ['juːzər] n (of road, dictionary etc) usager m; (of machine) utilisateur, -trice mf.

usher ['ʌʃər] n (in church or theatre) placeur m; (in law court) huissier m; – vt **to u. in** faire entrer; (period etc) Fig inaugurer. ◆**ushe'rette** n Cin ouvreuse f.

USSR [juːeseses'ɑːr] n abbr (Union of Soviet Socialist Republics) URSS f.

usual ['juːʒuəl] a habituel, normal; **as u.** comme d'habitude; **it's her u. practice** c'est son habitude; – n **the u.** (food, excuse etc) Fam la même chose que d'habitude. ◆**—ly** adv d'habitude.

usurer ['juːʒərər] n usurier, -ière mf.

usurp [juː'zɜːp] vt usurper.

utensil [juː'tens(ə)l] n ustensile m.

uterus ['juːt(ə)rəs] n Anat utérus m.

utilitarian [juːtɪlɪ'teərɪən] a utilitaire. ◆**u'tility** n (public) u. service m public; – a (goods vehicle) utilitaire.

utilize ['juːtɪlaɪz] vt utiliser. ◆**utili'zation** n utilisation f.

utmost ['ʌtməʊst] a **the u. ease**/etc (greatest) la plus grande facilité/etc; **the u. danger**/**limit**/etc (extreme) un danger/une limite/etc extrême; – n **to do one's u.** faire tout son possible (**to do** pour faire).

utopia [juː'təʊpɪə] n (perfect state) utopie f. ◆**utopian** a utopique.

utter ['ʌtər] **1** a complet, total; (folly) pur; (idiot) parfait; **it's u. nonsense** c'est complètement absurde. **2** vt (say, express) proférer; (a cry, sigh) pousser. ◆**utterance** n (remark etc) déclaration f; **to give u. to** exprimer. ◆**utterly** adv complètement.

V

V, v [viː] n V, v m. ◆**V.-neck(ed)** a (pullover etc) à col en V.

vacant ['veɪkənt] a (post) vacant; (room, seat) libre; (look) vague, dans le vide. ◆**vacancy** n (post) poste m vacant; (room) chambre f disponible; **'no vacancies'** (in hotel) 'complet'. ◆**vacantly** adv **to gaze v.** regarder dans le vide.

vacate [vəˈkeɪt, Am ˈveɪkeɪt] vt quitter.

vacation [veɪˈkeɪʃ(ə)n] n Am vacances fpl; **on v.** en vacances. ◆**—er** n Am vacancier, -ière mf.

vaccinate ['væksɪneɪt] vt vacciner. ◆**vacci'nation** n vaccination f. ◆**vaccine** [-iːn] n vaccin m.

vacillate ['væsɪleɪt] vi (hesitate) hésiter.

vacuum ['vækjʊ(ə)m] n vide m; **v. cleaner** aspirateur m; **v. flask** thermos® m or f; – vt (carpet etc) passer à l'aspirateur. ◆**v.-packed** a emballé sous vide.

vagabond ['vægəbɒnd] n vagabond, -onde mf.

vagary ['veɪgərɪ] n caprice m.

vagina [vəˈdʒaɪnə] n vagin m.

vagrant ['veɪgrənt] n Jur vagabond, -onde mf.

vague [veɪg] a (-er, -est) vague; (memory, outline, photo) flou; **the vaguest idea** la moindre idée; **he was v. (about it)** il est resté vague. ◆**—ly** adv vaguement.

vain [veɪn] a (-er, -est) **1** (attempt, hope) vain; **in v.** en vain; **his or her efforts were in v.** ses efforts ont été inutiles. **2** (conceited) vaniteux. ◆**—ly** adv (in vain) vainement.

valentine ['væləntaɪn] n (card) carte f de la Saint-Valentin.

valet ['vælɪt, 'væleɪ] n valet m de chambre.

valiant ['vælɪənt] a courageux. ◆**valour** n bravoure f.

valid ['vælɪd] a (ticket, motive etc) valable. ◆**validate** vt valider. ◆**va'lidity** n validité f; (of argument) justesse f.

valley ['vælɪ] n vallée f.

valuable ['væljʊəb(ə)l] a (object) de (grande) valeur; (help, time etc) Fig précieux; – npl objets mpl de valeur.

value ['væljuː] n valeur f; **to be of great/little v.** (of object) valoir très cher/peu (cher); **it's good v.** c'est très avantageux; **v. added tax** taxe f à la valeur ajoutée; – vt (appraise) évaluer; (appreciate) attacher de la valeur à. ◆**valu'ation** n évaluation f; (by expert) expertise f. ◆**valuer** n expert m.

valve [vælv] n (of machine) soupape f; (in radio) lampe f; (of tyre) valve f; (of heart) valvule f.

vampire ['væmpaɪər] n vampire m.

van [væn] n (small) camionnette f; (large) camion m; Rail fourgon m.

vandal ['vænd(ə)l] n vandale mf. ◆**vandal-**

ism n vandalisme m. ◆**vandalize** vt saccager, détériorer.

vanguard ['vængɑːd] n (of army, progress etc) avant-garde f.

vanilla [vəˈnɪlə] n vanille f; – a (ice cream) à la vanille.

vanish ['vænɪʃ] vi disparaître.

vanity ['vænɪtɪ] n vanité f; v. **case** vanity m inv.

vanquish ['væŋkwɪʃ] vt vaincre.

vantage point ['vɑːntɪdʒpɔɪnt] n (place, point of view) (bon) point m de vue.

vapour ['veɪpər] n vapeur f; (on glass) buée f.

variable ['veərɪəb(ə)l] a variable. ◆**variance** n at v. en désaccord (with avec). ◆**variant** a different; – n variante f. ◆**vari'ation** n variation f.

varicose ['værɪkəʊs] a v. **veins** varices fpl.

variety [vəˈraɪətɪ] n 1 (diversity) variété f; a v. of opinions/reasons/etc (many) diverses opinions/raisons/etc; a v. of (articles) toute une gamme de. 2 Th variétés fpl; v. **show** spectacle m de variétés.

various ['veərɪəs] a divers. ◆—ly adv diversement.

varnish ['vɑːnɪʃ] vt vernir; – n vernis m.

vary ['veərɪ] vti varier (from de). ◆**varied** a varié. ◆**varying** a variable.

vase [vɑːz, Am veɪs] n vase m.

VaselineR ['væsəliːn] n vaseline f.

vast [vɑːst] a vaste, immense. ◆—ly adv (very) infiniment, extrêmement. ◆—ness n immensité f.

vat [væt] n cuve f.

VAT [viːeɪˈtiː, væt] n abbr (value added tax) TVA f.

Vatican ['vætɪkən] n Vatican m.

vaudeville ['vɔːdəvɪl] n Th Am variétés fpl.

vault [vɔːlt] n 1 (cellar) cave f; (tomb) caveau m; (in bank) chambre f forte, coffres mpl; (roof) voûte f. 2 vti (jump) sauter.

veal [viːl] n (meat) veau m.

veer [vɪər] vi (of wind) tourner; (of car, road) virer; to v. **off the road** quitter la route.

vegan ['viːgən] n végétaliste mf.

vegetable ['vedʒtəb(ə)l] n légume m; – a (kingdom, oil) végétal; v. **garden** (jardin m) potager m. ◆**vege'tarian** a & n végétarien, -ienne (mf). ◆**vege'tation** n végétation f.

vegetate ['vedʒɪteɪt] vi (of person) Pej végéter.

vehement ['viːəmənt] a (feeling, speech) véhément; (attack) violent. ◆—ly adv avec véhémence, violemment.

vehicle ['viːɪk(ə)l] n véhicule m; **heavy goods v.** (lorry) poids m lourd.

veil [veɪl] n (covering) & Fig voile m; – vt (face, truth etc) voiler.

vein [veɪn] n (in body or rock) veine f; (in leaf) nervure f; (mood) Fig esprit m.

vellum ['veləm] n (paper, skin) vélin m.

velocity [vəˈlɒsɪtɪ] n vélocité f.

velvet ['velvɪt] n velours m; – a de velours. ◆**velvety** a velouté.

vendetta [ven'detə] n vendetta f.

vending machine ['vendɪŋməʃiːn] n distributeur m automatique.

vendor ['vendər] n vendeur, -euse mf.

veneer [vəˈnɪər] n (wood) placage m; (appearance) Fig vernis m.

venerable ['ven(ə)rəb(ə)l] a vénérable. ◆**venerate** vt vénérer.

venereal [vəˈnɪərɪəl] a (disease etc) vénérien.

venetian [vəˈniːʃ(ə)n] a v. **blind** store m vénitien.

vengeance ['vendʒəns] n vengeance f; with a v. (to work, study etc) furieusement; (to rain, catch up etc) pour de bon.

venison ['venɪs(ə)n] n venaison f.

venom ['venəm] n (substance) & Fig venin m. ◆**venomous** a (speech, snake etc) venimeux.

vent [vent] n 1 (hole) orifice m; (for air) bouche f d'aération; (in jacket) fente f. 2 n to give v. to (feeling etc) donner libre cours à; – vt (anger) décharger (on sur).

ventilate ['ventɪleɪt] vt ventiler. ◆**ventilation** n ventilation f. ◆**ventilator** n (in wall etc) ventilateur m.

ventriloquist [ven'trɪləkwɪst] n ventriloque mf.

venture ['ventʃər] n entreprise f (risquée); **my v. into** mon incursion f dans; – vt (opinion, fortune) hasarder; to v. **to do** (dare) oser faire; – vi s'aventurer, se risquer (into dans).

venue ['venjuː] n lieu m de rencontre or de rendez-vous.

veranda(h) [vəˈrændə] n véranda f.

verb [vɜːb] n verbe m. ◆**verbal** a (promise, skill etc) verbal. ◆**verbatim** [vɜːˈbeɪtɪm] a & adv mot pour mot.

verbose [vɜːˈbəʊs] a (wordy) verbeux.

verdict ['vɜːdɪkt] n verdict m.

verdigris ['vɜːdɪgrɪs] n vert-de-gris m inv.

verge [vɜːdʒ] n (of road) accotement m, bord m; **on the v. of** Fig (ruin, tears etc) au bord de; (discovery) à la veille de; **on the v. of doing** sur le point de faire; – vi to v. **on** friser, frôler; (of colour) tirer sur.

verger ['vɜːdʒər] n Rel bedeau m.

verify ['verɪfaɪ] vt vérifier. ◆**verifi'cation** n vérification f.

veritable ['verɪtəb(ə)l] a véritable.

vermicelli [vɜːmɪ'selɪ] n Culin vermicelle(s) m(pl).

vermin ['vɜːmɪn] n (animals) animaux mpl nuisibles; (insects, people) vermine f.

vermouth ['vɜːməθ] n vermouth m.

vernacular [və'nækjʊlər] n (of region) dialecte m.

versatile ['vɜːsətaɪl, Am 'vɜːsət(ə)l] a (mind) souple; (material, tool, computer) polyvalent; **he's v.** il a des talents variés, il est polyvalent; ◆**versa'tility** n souplesse f; **his v.** la variété de ses talents.

verse [vɜːs] n (stanza) strophe f; (poetry) vers mpl; (of Bible) verset m.

versed [vɜːst] a (well) **v. in** versé dans.

version ['vɜːʃ(ə)n] n version f.

versus ['vɜːsəs] prep contre.

vertebra, pl **-ae** ['vɜːtɪbrə, -iː] n vertèbre f.

vertical ['vɜːtɪk(ə)l] a vertical; — n verticale f. ◆**—ly** adv verticalement.

vertigo ['vɜːtɪgəʊ] n (fear of falling) vertige m.

verve [vɜːv] n fougue f.

very ['verɪ] **1** adv très; **I'm v. hot** j'ai très chaud; **v. much** beaucoup; **the v. first** le tout premier; **at the v. least/most** tout au moins/plus; **at the v. latest** au plus tard. **2** a (actual) même; **his or her v. brother** son frère même; **at the v. end** (of play etc) tout à la fin; **to the v. end** jusqu'au bout.

vespers ['vespəz] npl Rel vêpres fpl.

vessel ['ves(ə)l] n Anat Bot Nau vaisseau m; (receptacle) récipient m.

vest [vest] n tricot m or maillot m de corps; (woman's) chemise f (américaine); (waistcoat) Am gilet m.

vested ['vestɪd] a **v. interests** Com droits mpl acquis; **she's got a v. interest in** Fig elle est directement intéressée dans.

vestige ['vestɪdʒ] n vestige m; **not a v. of truth/good sense** pas un grain de vérité/de bon sens.

vestry ['vestrɪ] n sacristie f.

vet [vet] **1** n vétérinaire mf. **2** vt (-tt-) (document) examiner de près; (candidate) se renseigner à fond sur. ◆**veteri'narian** n Am vétérinaire mf. ◆**veterinary** a vétérinaire; **v. surgeon** vétérinaire mf.

veteran ['vet(ə)rən] n vétéran m; (war) ancien combattant m; — a **v. golfer/etc** golfeur/etc expérimenté.

veto ['viːtəʊ] n (pl -oes) (refusal) veto m inv; (power) droit m de veto; — vt mettre or opposer son veto à.

vex [veks] vt contrarier, fâcher; **vexed question** question f controversée.

via ['vaɪə] prep via, par.

viable ['vaɪəb(ə)l] a (baby, firm, plan etc) viable. ◆**via'bility** n viabilité f.

viaduct ['vaɪədʌkt] n viaduc m.

vibrate [vaɪ'breɪt] vi vibrer. ◆**'vibrant** a vibrant. ◆**vibration** n vibration f. ◆**vibrator** n vibromasseur m.

vicar ['vɪkər] n (in Church of England) pasteur m. ◆**vicarage** n presbytère m.

vicarious [vɪ'keərɪəs] a (emotion) ressenti indirectement. ◆**—ly** adv (to experience) indirectement.

vice [vaɪs] n **1** (depravity) vice m; (fault) défaut m; **v. squad** brigade f des mœurs. **2** (tool) étau m.

vice- [vaɪs] pref vice-. ◆**v.-'chancellor** n Univ président m.

vice versa [vaɪs(ɪ)'vɜːsə] adv vice versa.

vicinity [və'sɪnɪtɪ] n environs mpl; **in the v. of** (place, amount) aux environs de.

vicious ['vɪʃəs] a (spiteful) méchant; (violent) brutal; **v. circle** cercle m vicieux. ◆**—ly** adv méchamment; brutalement. ◆**—ness** n méchanceté f; brutalité f.

vicissitudes [vɪ'sɪsɪtjuːdz] npl vicissitudes fpl.

victim ['vɪktɪm] n victime f; **to be the v. of** être victime de. ◆**victimize** vt persécuter. ◆**victimi'zation** n persécution f.

Victorian [vɪk'tɔːrɪən] a & n victorien, -ienne (mf).

victory ['vɪktərɪ] n victoire f. ◆**victor** n vainqueur m. ◆**vic'torious** a victorieux.

video ['vɪdɪəʊ] a vidéo inv; — n **v.** (cassette) vidéocassette f; **v.** (recorder) magnétoscope m; **on v.** sur cassette; **to make a v. of** faire une cassette de; — vt (programme etc) enregistrer au magnétoscope. ◆**videotape** n bande f vidéo.

vie [vaɪ] vi (pres p **vying**) rivaliser (**with** avec).

Vietnam [vjet'næm, Am -'nɑːm] n Viêt-nam m. ◆**Vietna'mese** a & n vietnamien, -ienne (mf).

view [vjuː] n vue f; **to come into v.** apparaître; **in full v. of everyone** à la vue de tous; **in my v.** (opinion) à mon avis; **on v.** (exhibit) exposé; **in v. of** (considering) étant donné (**the fact that** que); **with a v. to doing** afin de faire; — vt (regard) considérer; (house) visiter. ◆**—er** n **1** TV téléspectateur, -trice mf. **2** (for slides) visionneuse f. ◆**viewfinder** n Phot viseur m. ◆**viewpoint** n point m de vue.

vigil ['vɪdʒɪl] n veille f; (over sick person or corpse) veillée f.

vigilant ['vɪdʒɪlənt] a vigilant. ◆**vigilance** n vigilance f.

vigilante [vɪdʒɪ'læntɪ] n Pej membre m d'une milice privée.

vigour ['vɪgər] n vigueur f. ◆**vigorous** a (person, speech etc) vigoureux.

vile [vaɪl] a (-er, -est) (base) infâme, vil; (unpleasant) abominable.

vilify ['vɪlɪfaɪ] vt diffamer.

villa ['vɪlə] n (in country) grande maison f de campagne.

village ['vɪlɪdʒ] n village m. ◆**villager** n villageois, -oise mf.

villain ['vɪlən] n scélérat, -ate mf; (in story or play) traître m. ◆**villainy** n infamie f.

vindicate ['vɪndɪkeɪt] vt justifier. ◆**vindi'cation** n justification f.

vindictive [vɪn'dɪktɪv] a vindicatif, rancunier.

vine [vaɪn] n (grapevine) vigne f; **v. grower** viticulteur m. ◆**vineyard** ['vɪnjəd] n vignoble m.

vinegar ['vɪnɪgər] n vinaigre m.

vintage ['vɪntɪdʒ] **1** n (year) année f. **2** a (wine) de grand cru; (car) d'époque; (film) classique; (good) Fig bon; **v. Shaw/etc** du meilleur Shaw/etc.

vinyl ['vaɪn(ə)l] n vinyle m.

viola [vɪ'əʊlə] n (instrument) Mus alto m.

violate ['vaɪəleɪt] vt violer. ◆**vio'lation** n violation f.

violence ['vaɪələns] n violence f. ◆**violent** a violent; **a v. dislike** une aversion vive. ◆**violently** adv violemment; **to be v. sick** (vomit) vomir.

violet ['vaɪələt] **1** a & n (colour) violet (m). **2** n (plant) violette f.

violin [vaɪə'lɪn] n violon m; – a (concerto etc) pour violon. ◆**violinist** n violoniste mf.

VIP [vi:aɪ'pi:] n abbr (very important person) personnage m de marque.

viper ['vaɪpər] n vipère f.

virgin ['vɜːdʒɪn] n vierge f; **to be a v.** (of woman, man) être vierge; – a (woman, snow etc) vierge. ◆**vir'ginity** n virginité f.

Virgo ['vɜːgəʊ] n (sign) la Vierge.

virile ['vɪraɪl, Am 'vɪrəl] a viril. ◆**vi'rility** n virilité f.

virtual ['vɜːtʃʊəl] a it was a v. failure/etc ce fut en fait un échec/etc. ◆**—ly** adv (in fact) en fait; (almost) pratiquement.

virtue ['vɜːtʃuː] n **1** (goodness, chastity) vertu f; (advantage) mérite m, avantage m. **2 by**

or **in v. of** en raison de. ◆**virtuous** a vertueux.

virtuoso [vɜːtʃʊ'əʊsəʊ, -si:] n (pl -si) virtuose mf. ◆**virtuosity** [-'ɒsɪtɪ] n virtuosité f.

virulent ['vɪrʊlənt] a virulent. ◆**virulence** n virulence f.

virus ['vaɪ(ə)rəs] n virus m.

visa ['viːzə] n visa m.

vis-à-vis [viːzɑː'viː] prep vis-à-vis de.

viscount ['vaɪkaʊnt] n vicomte m. ◆**viscountess** n vicomtesse f.

viscous ['vɪskəs] a visqueux.

vise [vaɪs] n (tool) Am étau m.

visible ['vɪzəb(ə)l] a visible. ◆**visi'bility** n visibilité f. ◆**visibly** adv visiblement.

vision ['vɪʒ(ə)n] n vision f; **a man/a woman of v.** Fig un homme/une femme qui voit loin. ◆**visionary** a & n visionnaire (mf).

visit ['vɪzɪt] n (call, tour) visite f; (stay) séjour m; – vt (place) visiter; **to visit s.o.** (call on) rendre visite à qn; (stay with) faire un séjour chez qn; – vi être en visite (Am with chez). ◆**—ing** a (card, hours) de visite. ◆**visitor** n visiteur, -euse mf; (guest) invité, -ée mf; (in hotel) client, -ente mf.

visor ['vaɪzər] n (of helmet) visière f.

vista ['vɪstə] n (view of place etc) vue f; (of future) Fig perspective f.

visual ['vɪʒʊəl] a visuel; **v. aid** (in teaching) support m visuel. ◆**visualize** vt (imagine) se représenter; (foresee) envisager.

vital ['vaɪt(ə)l] a vital; **v. importance** d'importance capitale; **v. statistics** (of woman) Fam mensurations fpl. ◆**—ly** adv extrêmement.

vitality [vaɪ'tælɪtɪ] n vitalité f.

vitamin ['vɪtəmɪn, Am 'vaɪtəmɪn] n vitamine f.

vitriol ['vɪtrɪəl] n Ch Fig vitriol m. ◆**vitri'olic** a (attack, speech etc) au vitriol.

vivacious [vɪ'veɪʃəs] a plein d'entrain.

vivid ['vɪvɪd] a (imagination, recollection etc) vif; (description) vivant. ◆**—ly** adv (to describe) de façon vivante; **to remember sth v.** avoir un vif souvenir de qch.

vivisection [vɪvɪ'sekʃ(ə)n] n vivisection f.

vocabulary [və'kæbjʊlərɪ] n vocabulaire m.

vocal ['vəʊk(ə)l] a (cords, music) vocal; (outspoken, noisy, critical) qui se fait entendre. ◆**vocalist** n chanteur, -euse mf.

vocation [vəʊ'keɪʃ(ə)n] n vocation f. ◆**vocational** a professionnel.

vociferous [və'sɪf(ə)rəs] a bruyant.

vodka ['vɒdkə] n vodka f.

vogue [vəʊg] n vogue f; **in v.** en vogue.

voice [vɔɪs] n voix f; **at the top of one's v.** à

tue-tête; – *vt* (*feeling, opinion etc*) formuler, exprimer.

void [vɔɪd] **1** *n* vide *m*; – *a* **v. of** (*lacking in*) dépourvu de. **2** *a* (*not valid*) *Jur* nul.

volatile ['vɒlətaɪl, *Am* 'vɒlət(ə)l] *a* (*person*) versatile, changeant; (*situation*) explosif.

volcano [vɒl'keɪnəʊ] *n* (*pl* -oes) volcan *m*. ◆**volcanic** [-'kænɪk] *a* volcanique.

volition [və'lɪʃ(ə)n] *n* **of one's own v.** de son propre gré.

volley ['vɒlɪ] *n* (*of blows*) volée *f*; (*gunfire*) salve *f*; (*of insults*) *Fig* bordée *f*. ◆**volleyball** *n* *Sp* volley(-ball) *m*.

volt [vəʊlt] *n* *El* volt *m*. ◆**voltage** *n* voltage *m*.

volume ['vɒljuːm] *n* (*book, capacity, loudness*) volume *m*. ◆**voluminous** [və'luːmɪnəs] *a* volumineux.

voluntary ['vɒlənt(ə)rɪ] *a* volontaire; (*unpaid*) bénévole. ◆**voluntarily** [*Am* vɒlən'terɪlɪ] *adv* volontairement; bénévolement. ◆**volun'teer** *n* volontaire *mf*; – *vi* se proposer (**for sth** pour qch, **to do** pour faire); *Mil* s'engager comme volontaire (**for** dans); – *vt* offrir (spontanément).

voluptuous [və'lʌptʃʊəs] *a* voluptueux, sensuel.

vomit ['vɒmɪt] *vti* vomir; – *n* (*matter*) vomi *m*.

voracious [və'reɪʃəs] *a* (*appetite, reader etc*) vorace.

vot/e [vəʊt] *n* vote *m*; (*right to vote*) droit *m* de vote; **to win votes** gagner des voix; **v. of censure** *or* **no confidence** motion *f* de censure; **v. of thanks** discours *m* de remerciement; – *vt* (*bill, funds etc*) voter; (*person*) élire; – *vi* voter; **to v. Conservative** voter conservateur *ou* pour les conservateurs. ◆**—ing** *n* vote *m* (**of** de); (*polling*) scrutin *m*. ◆**—er** *n* *Pol* électeur, -trice *mf*.

vouch [vaʊtʃ] *vi* **to v. for** répondre de.

voucher ['vaʊtʃər] *n* (*for meals etc*) bon *m*, chèque *m*.

vow [vaʊ] *n* vœu *m*; – *vt* (*obedience etc*) jurer (**to** à); **to v. to do** jurer de faire, faire le vœu de faire.

vowel ['vaʊəl] *n* voyelle *f*.

voyage ['vɔɪdʒ] *n* voyage *m* (par mer).

vulgar ['vʌlgər] *a* vulgaire. ◆**vul'garity** *n* vulgarité *f*.

vulnerable ['vʌln(ə)rəb(ə)l] *a* vulnérable. ◆**vulnera'bility** *n* vulnérabilité *f*.

vulture ['vʌltʃər] *n* vautour *m*.

W

W, w ['dʌb(ə)ljuː] *n* W, w *m*.

wacky ['wækɪ] *a* (**-ier, -iest**) *Am Fam* farfelu.

wad [wɒd] *n* (*of banknotes, papers etc*) liasse *f*; (*of cotton wool, cloth*) tampon *m*.

waddle ['wɒd(ə)l] *vi* se dandiner.

wade [weɪd] *vi* **to w. through** (*mud, water etc*) patauger dans; (*book etc*) *Fig* venir péniblement à bout de; **I'm wading through this book** j'avance péniblement dans ce livre.

wafer ['weɪfər] *n* (*biscuit*) gaufrette *f*; *Rel* hostie *f*.

waffle ['wɒf(ə)l] **1** *n* (*talk*) verbiage *m*, blabla *m*; – *vi* *Fam* parler pour ne rien dire, blablater. **2** *n* (*cake*) gaufre *f*.

waft [wɒft] *vi* (*of smell etc*) flotter.

wag [wæg] **1** *vt* (**-gg-**) (*tail, finger*) agiter, remuer; – *vi* remuer; **tongues are wagging** *Pej* on en jase, les langues vont bon train. **2** *n* (*joker*) farceur, -euse *mf*.

wage [weɪdʒ] **1** *n* **wage(s)** salaire *m*, paie *f*; **w. claim** *or* **demand** revendication *f* salariale; **w. earner** salarié, -ée *mf*; (*breadwinner*) soutien *m* de famille; **w. freeze** blocage *m* des salaires; **w. increase** *or* **rise** augmentation *f* de salaire. **2** *vt* (*campaign*) mener; **to w. war** faire la guerre (**on** à).

wager ['weɪdʒər] *n* pari *m*; – *vt* parier (**that** que).

waggle ['wæg(ə)l] *vti* remuer.

wag(g)on ['wægən] *n* (*cart*) chariot *m*; *Rail* wagon *m* (de marchandises); **on the w.** (*abstinent*) *Fam* au régime sec.

waif [weɪf] *n* enfant *mf* abandonné(e).

wail [weɪl] *vi* (*cry out, complain*) gémir; (*of siren*) hurler; – *n* gémissement *m*; (*of siren*) hurlement *m*.

waist [weɪst] *n* taille *f*; **stripped to the w.** nu jusqu'à la ceinture. ◆**waistband** *n* (*part of garment*) ceinture *f*. ◆**waistcoat** ['weɪskəʊt] *n* gilet *m*. ◆**waistline** *n* taille *f*.

wait [weɪt] **1** *n* attente *f*; **to lie in w.** (**for**) guetter; – *vi* attendre; **to w. for** attendre; **w. until I've gone, w. for me to go** attends que je sois parti; **to keep s.o. waiting** faire attendre qn; **w. and see!** attends voir!; **I can't w.**

to do it j'ai hâte de le faire; **to w. about (for)** attendre; **to w. behind** rester; **to w. up** veiller; **to w. up for s.o.** attendre le retour de qn avant de se coucher. **2** vi (serve) **to w. at table** servir à table; **to w. on s.o.** servir qn. ◆**—ing** n attente f; **'no w.'** Aut 'arrêt interdit'; – a **w. list/room** liste f/salle f d'attente. ◆**waiter** n garçon m (de café), serveur m; **w.!** garçon! ◆**waitress** n serveuse f; **w.!** mademoiselle!

waive [weɪv] vt renoncer à, abandonner.

wake[1] [weɪk] vi (pt **woke**, pp **woken**) **to w.** (**up**) se réveiller; **to w. up to** (fact etc) Fig prendre conscience de; – vt **to w.** (**up**) réveiller; **to spend one's waking hours working**/etc passer ses journées à travailler/etc. ◆**waken** vt éveiller, réveiller; – vi s'éveiller, se réveiller.

wake[2] [weɪk] n (of ship) & Fig sillage m; **in the w. of** Fig dans le sillage de, à la suite de.

Wales [weɪlz] n pays m de Galles.

walk [wɔːk] n promenade f; (short) (petit) tour m; (gait) démarche f; (pace) marche f, pas m; (path) allée f, chemin m; **to go for a w.** faire une promenade, (shorter) faire un (petit) tour; **to take for a w.** (child etc) emmener se promener; (baby, dog) promener; **five minutes' w. (away)** à cinq minutes à pied; **walks of life** Fig conditions sociales fpl; – vi marcher; (stroll) se promener; (go on foot) aller à pied; **w.!** (don't run) ne cours pas!; **to w. away or off** s'éloigner, partir (**from** de); **to w. away or off with** (steal) Fam faucher; **to w. in** entrer; **to w. into** (tree etc) rentrer dans; (trap) tomber dans; **to w. out** (leave) partir; (of workers) se mettre en grève; **to w. out on s.o.** (desert) Fam laisser tomber qn; **to w. over to** (go up to) s'approcher de; – vt (distance) faire à pied; (streets) (par)courir; (take for a walk) promener; (baby, chien); **to w. s.o. to** (station etc) accompagner qn à. ◆**—ing** n marche f (à pied); – a a w. **corpse/dictionary** (person) Fig un cadavre/dictionnaire ambulant; **at a w. pace** au pas; **w. stick** canne f. ◆**walker** n marcheur, -euse mf; (for pleasure) promeneur, -euse mf. ◆**walkout** n (strike) grève f surprise; (from meeting) départ m (en signe de protestation). ◆**walkover** n (in contest etc) victoire f facile. ◆**walkway** n moving **w.** trottoir m roulant.

walkie-talkie [wɔːkɪˈtɔːkɪ] n talkie-walkie m.

Walkman® [ˈwɔːkmən] n (pl **Walkmans**) baladeur m.

wall [wɔːl] n mur m; (of cabin, tunnel, stomach etc) paroi f; (of ice) Fig muraille f; (of

smoke) Fig rideau m; **to go to the w.** (of firm) Fig faire faillite; – a mural; – vt **to w. up** (door etc) murer; **walled city** ville f fortifiée. ◆**wallflower** n Bot giroflée f; **to be a w.** (at dance) faire tapisserie. ◆**wallpaper** n papier m peint; – vt tapisser. ◆**wall-to-wall 'carpet(ing)** n moquette f.

wallet [ˈwɒlɪt] n portefeuille m.

wallop [ˈwɒləp] vt (hit) Fam taper sur; – n (blow) Fam grand coup m.

wallow [ˈwɒləʊ] vi **to w. in** (mud, vice etc) se vautrer dans.

wally [ˈwɒlɪ] n (idiot) Fam andouille f, imbécile mf.

walnut [ˈwɔːlnʌt] n (nut) noix f; (tree, wood) noyer m.

walrus [ˈwɔːlrəs] n (animal) morse m.

waltz [wɒls, Am wɒlts] n valse f; – vi valser.

wan [wɒn] a (pale) Lit pâle.

wand [wɒnd] n baguette f (magique).

wander [ˈwɒndər] vi (of thoughts) vagabonder; **to w. (about or around)** (roam) errer, vagabonder; (stroll) flâner; **to w. from or off** (path, subject) s'écarter de; **to w. off** (go away) s'éloigner; **my mind's wandering** je suis distrait; – vt **to w. the streets** errer dans les rues. ◆**—ing** a (life, tribe) vagabond, nomade; – npl vagabondages mpl. ◆**—er** n vagabond, -onde mf.

wane [weɪn] vi (of moon, fame, strength etc) décroître; – n to be on the w. décroître, être en déclin.

wangle [ˈwæŋg(ə)l] vt Fam (obtain) se débrouiller pour obtenir; (avoiding payment) carotter (**from** à).

want [wɒnt] vt vouloir (**to do** faire); (ask for) demander; (need) avoir besoin de; **I w. him to go** je veux qu'il parte; **you w. to try** (should) tu devrais essayer; **you're wanted on the phone** on vous demande au téléphone; – vi **not to w. for** (not lack) ne pas manquer de; – n (lack) manque m (**of** de); (poverty) besoin m; **for w. of** par manque de; **for w. of money/time** faute d'argent/de temps; **for w. of anything better** faute de mieux; **your wants** (needs) tes besoins mpl. ◆**—ed** a (man, criminal) recherché par la police; **to feel w.** sentir qu'on vous aime. ◆**—ing** a (inadequate) insuffisant; **to be w.** manquer (**in** de).

wanton [ˈwɒntən] a (gratuitous) gratuit; (immoral) impudique.

war [wɔːr] n guerre f; **at w.** en guerre (**with** avec); **to go to w.** entrer en guerre (**with** avec); **to declare w.** déclarer la guerre (**on** à); – a (wound, criminal) de guerre; **w.**

memorial monument *m* aux morts. ◆**warfare** *n* guerre *f.* ◆**warhead** *n* (*of missile*) ogive *f.* ◆**warlike** *a* guerrier. ◆**warmonger** *n* fauteur *m* de guerre. ◆**warpath** *n* to be on the w. (*angry*) *Fam* être d'humeur massacrante. ◆**warring** *a* (*countries etc*) en guerre; (*ideologies etc*) *Fig* en conflit. ◆**warship** *n* navire *m* de guerre. ◆**wartime** *n* in w. en temps de guerre.

warble ['wɔːb(ə)l] *vi* (*of bird*) gazouiller.

ward [wɔːd] *n* **1** (*in hospital*) salle *f.* **2** (*child*) *Jur* pupille *mf.* **3** (*electoral division*) circonscription *f.* électorale.

ward [wɔːd] *vt* to w. off (*blow, anger*) détourner; (*danger*) éviter.

warden ['wɔːd(ə)n] *n* (*of institution, Am of prison*) directeur, -trice *mf*; (*of park*) gardien, -ienne *mf*; (*traffic*) w. contractuel, -elle *mf.*

warder ['wɔːdər] *n* gardien *m* (de prison).

wardrobe ['wɔːdrəub] *n* (*cupboard*) penderie *f*; (*clothes*) garde-robe *f.*

warehouse, *pl* **-ses** ['weəhaʊs, -zɪz] *n* entrepôt *m.*

wares [weəz] *npl* marchandises *fpl.*

warily ['weərɪlɪ] *adv* avec précaution.

warm [wɔːm] *a* (**-er, -est**) chaud; (*iron, oven*) moyen; (*welcome, thanks etc*) chaleureux; **to be** or **feel w.** avoir chaud; **it's (nice and) w.** (*of weather*) il fait (agréablement) chaud; **to get w.** (*of person, room etc*) se réchauffer; (*of food, water*) chauffer; — *vt* to w. (up) (*person, food etc*) réchauffer; — *vi* to w. up (*of person, room, engine*) se réchauffer; (*of food, water*) chauffer; (*of discussion*) s'échauffer; **to w. to s.o.** *Fig* se prendre de sympathie pour qn. ◆**warm-'hearted** *a* chaleureux. ◆**warmly** *adv* (*to wrap up*) chaudement; (*to welcome, thank etc*) chaleureusement. ◆**warmth** *n* chaleur *f.*

warn [wɔːn] *vt* avertir, prévenir (**that** que); **to w. s.o. against** or **off** sth mettre qn en garde contre qch; **to w. s.o. against doing** conseiller à qn de ne pas faire. ◆**—ing** *n* avertissement *m*; (*advance notice*) (pré)avis *m*; (*alarm*) alerte *f*; **without w.** sans prévenir; **a note** or **word of w.** une mise en garde; **w. light** (*on appliance etc*) voyant *m* lumineux; **hazard w. lights** *Aut* feux *mpl* de détresse.

warp [wɔːp] **1** *vt* (*wood etc*) voiler; (*judgment, person etc*) *Fig* pervertir; **a warped mind** un esprit tordu; **a warped view** un récit déformé; — *vi* se voiler. **2** *n* *Tex* chaîne *f.*

warrant ['wɒrənt] **1** *n* *Jur* mandat *m*; **a w. for**

your arrest un mandat d'arrêt contre vous. **2** *vt* (*justify*) justifier; (*declare confidently*) je t'assure que . . . . ◆**warranty** *n Com* garantie *f.*

warren ['wɒrən] *n* (**rabbit**) w. garenne *f.*

warrior ['wɒrɪər] *n* guerrier, -ière *mf.*

wart [wɔːt] *n* verrue *f.*

wary ['weərɪ] *a* (**-ier, -iest**) prudent; **to be w. of s.o./sth** se méfier de qn/qch; **to be w. of doing** hésiter beaucoup à faire.

was [wɒz, *stressed* wɒz] *see* **be**.

wash [wɒʃ] *n* (*clothes*) lessive *f*; (*of ship*) sillage *m*; **to have a w.** se laver; **to give sth a w.** laver qch; **to do the w.** faire la lessive; **in the w.** à la lessive; — *vt* laver; (*flow over*) baigner; **to w. one's hands** se laver les mains (*Fig of sth* de qch); **to w. (away)** (*of sea etc*) emporter (*qch, qn*); **to w. away** or **off** or **out** (*stain*) faire partir (en lavant); **to w. down** (*vehicle, deck*) laver à grande eau; (*food*) arroser (**with** de); **to w. out** (*bowl etc*) laver; — *vi* se laver; (*do the dishes*) faire la vaisselle; **to w. away** or **off** or **out** (*of stain*) partir (au lavage); **to w. up** (*do the dishes*) faire la vaisselle; (*have a wash*) *Am* se laver. ◆**washed-'out** *a* (*tired*) lessivé. ◆**washed-'up** *a* (**all**) **w.-up** (*person, plan*) *Sl* fichu. ◆**washable** *a* lavable. ◆**washbasin** *n* lavabo *m.* ◆**washcloth** *n Am* gant *m* de toilette. ◆**washout** *n Sl* (*event*) fiasco *m*; (*person*) nullité *f.* ◆**washroom** *n Am* toilettes *fpl.*

washer ['wɒʃər] *n* (*ring*) rondelle *f*, joint *m.*

washing ['wɒʃɪŋ] *n* (*act*) lavage *m*; (*clothes*) lessive *f*, linge *m*; **to do the w.** faire la lessive; **w. line** corde *f* à linge; **w. machine** machine *f* à laver; **w. powder** lessive *f.* ◆**w.-'up** *n* vaisselle *f*; **to do the w.-up** faire la vaisselle; **w.-up liquid** produit *m* pour la vaisselle.

wasp [wɒsp] *n* guêpe *f.*

wast/e [weɪst] *n* gaspillage *m*; (*of time*) perte *f*; (*rubbish*) déchets *mpl*; *pl* (*land*) étendue *f* déserte; **w. disposal unit** broyeur *m* d'ordures; — *a* **material** or **products** déchets *mpl*; **w. land** (*uncultivated*) terres *fpl* incultes; (*in town*) terrain *m* vague; **w. paper** vieux papiers *mpl*; **w. pipe** tuyau *m* d'évacuation; — *vt* (*money, food etc*) gaspiller; (*time, opportunity*) perdre; **to w. one's time on frivolities**/*etc* gaspiller son temps en frivolités/*etc*, perdre son temps à des frivolités/*etc*; **to w. one's life** gâcher sa vie; — *vi* **to w. away** dépérir. ◆**—ed** *a* (*effort*) inutile; (*body etc*) émacié. ◆**wastage** *n* gaspillage *m*; (*losses*) pertes *fpl*; **some w.** (*of goods, staff etc*) du déchet. ◆**wastebin**

(*in kitchen*) poubelle *f*. ◆**wastepaper basket** *n* corbeille *f* (à papier).

wasteful [ˈweɪstfəl] *a* (*person*) gaspilleur; (*process*) peu économique.

watch [wɒtʃ] **1** *n* (*small clock*) montre *f*. **2** *n* (*over suspect, baby etc*) surveillance *f*; *Nau* quart *m*; **to keep (a) w. on** *or* **over** surveiller; **to keep w.** faire le guet; **to be on the w. (for)** guetter; — *vt* regarder; (*observe*) observer; (*suspect, baby etc*) surveiller; (*be careful of*) faire attention à; — *vi* regarder; **to w. (out) for** (*be on the lookout for*) guetter; **to w. out** (*take care*) faire attention (**for** à); **w. out!** attention!; **to w. over** surveiller. ◆**watchdog** *n* chien *m* de garde. ◆**watchmaker** *n* horloger, -ère *mf*. ◆**watchman** *n* (*pl* -men) **night w.** veilleur *m* de nuit. ◆**watchstrap** *n* bracelet *m* de montre. ◆**watchtower** *n* tour *f* de guet.

watchful [ˈwɒtʃfəl] *a* vigilant.

water [ˈwɔːtər] **1** *n* eau *f*; **by w.** en bateau; **under w.** (*road, field etc*) inondé; (*to swim*) sous l'eau; **at high w.** à marée haute; **it doesn't hold w.** (*of theory etc*) *Fig* ça ne tient pas debout; **in hot w.** *Fig* dans le pétrin; **w. cannon** lance *f* à eau; **w. ice** sorbet *m*; **w. lily** nénuphar *m*; **w. pistol** pistolet *m* à eau; **w. polo** *Sp* water-polo *m*; **w. power** énergie *f* hydraulique; **w. rates** taxes *fpl* sur l'eau; **w. skiing** ski *m* nautique; **w. tank** réservoir *m* d'eau; **w. tower** château *m* d'eau; — *vt* (*plant etc*) arroser; **to w. down** (*wine etc*) couper (d'eau); (*text etc*) édulcorer; — *vi* (*of eyes*) larmoyer; **it makes his** *or* **her mouth w.** ça lui fait venir l'eau à la bouche. ◆**—ing** *n* (*of plant etc*) arrosage *m*; **w. can** arrosoir *m*. ◆**watery** *a* (*colour*) délavé; (*soup*) *Pej* trop liquide; (*eyes*) larmoyant; **w. tea** *or* **coffee** de la lavasse.

watercolour [ˈwɔːtəkʌlər] *n* (*picture*) aquarelle *f*; (*paint*) couleur *f* pour aquarelle. ◆**watercress** *n* cresson *m* (de fontaine). ◆**waterfall** *n* chute *f* d'eau. ◆**waterhole** *n* (*in desert*) point *m* d'eau. ◆**waterline** *n* (*on ship*) ligne *f* de flottaison. ◆**waterlogged** *a* délavé. ◆**watermark** *n* (*in paper*) filigrane *m*. ◆**watermelon** *n* pastèque *f*. ◆**waterproof** *a* (*material*) imperméable. ◆**watershed** *n* (*turning point*) tournant *m* (décisif). ◆**watertight** *a* (*container etc*) étanche. ◆**waterway** *n* voie *f* navigable. ◆**waterworks** *n* (*place*) station *f* hydraulique.

watt [wɒt] *n* *El* watt *m*.

wave [weɪv] *n* (*of sea*) & *Fig* vague *f*; (*in hair*) ondulation *f*; *Rad* onde *f*; (*sign*) signe *m* (de la main); **long/medium/short w.** *Rad* ondes *fpl* longues/moyennes/ courtes; — *vi* (*with hand*) faire signe (de la main); (*of flag*) flotter; **to w. to** (*greet*) saluer de la main; — *vt* (*arm, flag etc*) agiter; (*hair*) onduler; **to w. s.o. on** faire signe à qn d'avancer; **to w. aside** (*objection etc*) écarter. ◆**waveband** *n* *Rad* bande *f* de fréquence. ◆**wavelength** *n* *Rad* & *Fig* longueur *f* d'ondes.

waver [ˈweɪvər] *vi* (*of flame, person etc*) vaciller.

wavy [ˈweɪvɪ] *a* (**-ier, -iest**) (*line*) onduleux; (*hair*) ondulé.

wax [wæks] **1** *n* cire *f*; (*for ski*) fart *m*; — *vt* cirer; (*ski*) farter; (*car*) lustrer; — *a* (*candle, doll etc*) de cire; **w. paper** *Culin Am* papier *m* paraffiné. **2** *vi* (*of moon*) croître. **3** *vi* **to w. lyrical/merry** (*become*) se faire lyrique/gai. ◆**waxworks** *npl* (*place*) musée *m* de cire; (*dummies*) figures *fpl* de cire.

way [weɪ] **1** *n* (*path, road*) chemin *m* (**to** de); (*direction*) sens *m*, direction *f*; (*distance*) distance *f*; **all the w., the whole w.** (*to talk etc*) pendant tout le chemin; **this w.** par ici; **that way** par là; **which w.?** par où?; **to lose one's w.** se perdre; **I'm on my w.** (*coming*) j'arrive; (*going*) je pars; **he made his w. out/home** il est sorti/rentré; **the w. there** l'aller *m*; **the w. back** le retour; **the w. in** l'entrée *f*; **the w. out** la sortie; **w. out of** (*problem etc*) *Fig* une solution à; **the w. is clear** *Fig* la voie est libre; **across the w.** en face; **on the w.** en route (**to** pour); **by w. of** (*via*) par; (*as*) *Fig* comme; **out of the w.** (*isolated*) isolé; **to go out of one's w. to** se donner du mal pour faire; **by the w. . . . .** *Fig* à propos . . . ; **to be** *or* **stand in the w.** barrer le passage; **she's in my w.** (*hindrance*) *Fig* elle me gêne; **to get out of the w., make w.** s'écarter; **to give w.** céder; *Aut* céder le passage *or* la priorité; **a long w. (away** *or* **off)** très loin; **it's the wrong w. up** c'est dans le mauvais sens; **do it the other w. round** fais le contraire; **to get under w.** (*of campaign etc*) démarrer; — *adv* (*behind etc*) très loin; **w. ahead** très en avance (**of** sur). **2** *n* (*manner*) façon *f*; (*means*) moyen *m*; (*condition*) état *m*; (*habit*) habitude *f*; (*particular*) égard *m*; **one's ways** (*behaviour*) ses manières *fpl*; **to get one's own w.** obtenir ce qu'on veut; (**in**) **this w.** de cette façon; **in a way** (*to some extent*) dans un certain sens; **w. of life** façon *f* de vivre, mode *m* de vie; **no w.!** (*certainly not*) *Fam* pas question! ◆**wayfarer** *n* voyageur, -euse *mf*. ◆**way-'out** *a* *Fam* extraordinaire. ◆**wayside** n by the w. au bord de la route.

waylay [weɪ'leɪ] vt (pt & pp -**laid**) (attack) attaquer par surprise; (stop) Fig arrêter au passage.

wayward ['weɪwəd] a rebelle, capricieux.

WC [dʌb(ə)ljuːˈsiː] n w-c mpl, waters mpl.

we [wiː] pron nous; **we go** nous allons; **we teachers** nous autres professeurs; **we never know** (indefinite) on ne sait jamais.

weak [wiːk] a (-er, -est) faible; (tea, coffee) léger; (health, stomach) fragile. ◆**w.-'willed** a faible. ◆**weaken** vt affaiblir; − vi faiblir. ◆**weakling** n (in body) mauviette f; (in character) faible mf. ◆**weakly** adv faiblement. ◆**weakness** n faiblesse f; (of health, stomach) fragilité f; (fault) point m faible; **a w. for** (liking) un faible pour.

weal [wiːl] n (wound on skin) marque f, zébrure f.

wealth [welθ] n (money, natural resources) richesse(s) f(pl); **a w. of** (abundance) Fig une profusion de. ◆**wealthy** a (-ier, -iest) riche; − n the w. les riches mpl.

wean [wiːn] vt (baby) sevrer.

weapon ['wepən] n arme f. ◆**weaponry** n armements mpl.

wear [weər] **1** vt (pt wore, pp worn) (have on body) porter; (look, smile) avoir; (put on) mettre; **to have nothing to w.** n'avoir rien à se mettre; − n men's/sports w. vêtements mpl pour hommes/de sport; **evening w.** tenue f de soirée. **2** vt (pt wore, pp worn) to w. (away or down or out) (material, patience etc) user; **to w. s.o. out** (exhaust) épuiser qn; **to w. oneself out** s'épuiser (doing a faire); − vi (last) faire de l'usage, durer; **to w. (out)** (of clothes etc) s'user; **to w. off** (of colour, pain etc) passer, disparaître; **to w. on** (of time) passer; **to w. out** (of patience) s'épuiser; − n (use) usage m; **w. (and tear)** usure f. ◆**−ing** a (tiring) épuisant. ◆**−er** n the w. (of hat, glasses etc) la personne qui porte.

weary ['wɪərɪ] a (-ier, -iest) (tired) fatigué, las (**of doing** de faire); (tiring) fatigant; (look, smile) las; − vi to w. of se lasser de. ◆**wearily** adv avec lassitude. ◆**weariness** n lassitude f.

weasel ['wiːz(ə)l] n belette f.

weather ['weðər] n temps m; **what's the w. like?** quel temps fait-il?; **in** (the) **hot w.** par temps chaud; **under the w.** (not well) Fig patraque; − a (chart etc) météorologique; **w. forecast, w. report** prévisions fpl météorologiques, météo f; **w. vane** girouette f; −

vt (storm, hurricane) essuyer; (crisis) Fig surmonter. ◆**weather-beaten** a (face, person) tanné, hâlé. ◆**weathercock** n girouette f. ◆**weatherman** n (pl -men) TV Rad Fam monsieur m météo.

weav/e [wiːv] vt (pt wove, pp woven) (cloth, plot) tisser; (basket, garland) tresser; − vi Tex tisser; **to w. in and out of** (crowd, cars etc) Fig se faufiler entre; − n (style) tissage m. ◆**−ing** n tissage m. ◆**−er** n tisserand, -ande mf.

web [web] n (of spider) toile f; (of lies) Fig tissu m. ◆**webbed** a (foot) palmé. ◆**webbing** n (in chair) sangles fpl.

wed [wed] vt (-dd-) (marry) épouser; (qualities etc) Fig allier (**to** à); − vi se marier. ◆**wedded** a (bliss, life) conjugal. ◆**wedding** n mariage m; **golden/silver w.** noces fpl d'or/d'argent; − a (cake) de noces; (anniversary, present) de mariage; (dress) de mariée; **his** or **her w. day** le jour de son mariage; **w. ring,** Am **w. band** alliance f. ◆**wedlock** n born out of w. illégitime.

wedge [wedʒ] n (for splitting) coin m; (under wheel, table etc) cale f; **w. heel** (of shoe) semelle f compensée; − vt (wheel, table etc) caler; (push) enfoncer (**into** dans); **wedged in between** (caught, trapped) coincé entre.

Wednesday ['wenzdɪ] n mercredi m.

wee [wiː] a (tiny) Fam tout petit.

weed [wiːd] n (plant) mauvaise herbe f; (weak person) Fam mauviette f; **w. killer** désherbant m; − vti désherber; − vt to w. out Fig éliminer (from de). ◆**weedy** a (-ier, -iest) (person) Fam maigre et chétif.

week [wiːk] n semaine f; **the w. before last** pas la semaine dernière, celle d'avant; **the w. after next** pas la semaine prochaine, celle d'après; **tomorrow w., a w.** tomorrow demain en huit. ◆**weekday** n jour m de semaine. ◆**week'end** n week-end m; **at** or **on** or **over the w.** ce week-end, pendant le week-end. ◆**weekly** a hebdomadaire; − adv toutes les semaines; − n (magazine) hebdomadaire m.

weep [wiːp] vi (pt pp wept) pleurer; (of wound) suinter; **to w. for s.o.** pleurer qn; − vt (tears) pleurer; **weeping willow** saule m pleureur.

weft [weft] n Tex trame f.

weigh [weɪ] vt peser; **to w. down** (with load etc) surcharger (**with** de); (bend) faire plier; **to w. up** (goods, chances etc) peser; − vi peser; **it's weighing on my mind** ça me tracasse; **to w. down on s.o.** (of worries etc) accabler qn. **◆weighing-machine** *n* balance *f*.

weight [weɪt] *n* poids *m*; **to put on w.** grossir; **to lose w.** maigrir; **to carry w.** (*of argument etc*) *Fig* avoir du poids (**with** pour); **to pull one's w.** (*do one's share*) *Fig* faire sa part du travail; **w. lifter** haltérophile *mf*; **w. lifting** haltérophilie *f*; − *vt* **to w.** (**down**) (*light object*) maintenir avec un poids; **to w. down with** (*overload*) surcharger de. **◆weightlessness** *n* apesanteur *f*. **◆weighty** *a* (-ier, -iest) lourd; (*argument, subject*) *Fig* de poids.

weighting ['weɪtɪŋ] *n* (*on salary*) indemnité *f* de résidence.

weir [wɪər] *n* (*across river*) barrage *m*.

weird [wɪəd] *a* (-er, -est) (*odd*) bizarre; (*eerie*) mystérieux.

welcome ['welkəm] *a* (*pleasant*) agréable; (*timely*) opportun; **to be w.** (*of person, people*) être le bienvenu *or* la bienvenue *or* les bienvenu(e)s; **w.!** soyez le bienvenu *or* la bienvenue *or* les bienvenu(e)s!; **to make s.o.** (*feel*) **w.** faire bon accueil à qn; **you're w.!** (*after 'thank you'*) il n'y a pas de quoi!; **w. to do** (*free*) libre de faire; **you're w. to** (**take** *or* **use**) **my bike** mon vélo est à ta disposition; **you're w. to it!** *Iron* grand bien vous fasse!; − *n* accueil *m*; **to extend a w. to** (*greet*) souhaiter la bienvenue à; − *vt* accueillir; (*warmly*) faire bon accueil à; (*be glad of*) se réjouir de; **I w. you!** je vous souhaite la bienvenue! **◆welcoming** *a* (*smile etc*) accueillant; (*speech, words*) d'accueil.

weld [weld] *vt* **to w.** (**together**) souder; (*groups etc*) *Fig* unir; − *n* (*joint*) soudure *f*. **◆-ing** *n* soudure *f*. **◆-er** *n* soudeur *m*.

welfare ['welfeər] *n* (*physical, material*) bien-être *m*; (*spiritual*) santé *f*; (*public aid*) aide *f* sociale; **public w.** (*good*) le bien public; **the w. state** (*in Great Britain*) l'État-providence *m*; **w. work** assistance *f* sociale.

well [wel] *n* (*for water*) puits *m*; (*of stairs, lift*) cage *f*; (*oil*) **w.** puits de pétrole. **2** *vi* **to w. up** (*rise*) monter.

well [wel] *adv* (**better, best**) bien; **to do w.** (*succeed*) réussir; **you'd do w. to refuse** tu ferais bien de refuser; **w. done!** bravo!; **I, you, she** *etc* **might** (*just*) **as w. have left** it valait mieux partir, autant valait partir; **it's just as w. that** (*lucky*) heureusement que . . . ; **as w.** (*also*) aussi; **as w. as** aussi bien que; **as w. as two cats, he has . . .** en plus de deux chats, il a . . . ; − *a* bien *inv*; **she's w.** (*healthy*) elle va bien; **not a w. man** un

homme malade; **to get w.** se remettre; **that's all very w., but . . .** tout ça c'est très joli, mais . . . ; − *int* eh bien!; **w., w.!** (*surprise*) tiens, tiens!; **enormous, w.,** quite big énorme, enfin, assez grand.

well-behaved [welbɪ'heɪvd] *a* sage. **◆w.-'being** *n* bien-être *m*. **◆w.-'built** *a* (*person, car*) solide. **◆w.-'founded** *a* bien fondé. **◆w.-'heeled** *a* (*rich*) *Fam* nanti. **◆w.-in'formed** *a* (*person, newspaper*) bien informé. **◆w.-'known** *a* (*bien*) connu. **◆w.-'meaning** *a* bien intentionné. **◆w.-'nigh** *adv* presque. **◆w.-'off** *a* aisé, riche. **◆w.-'read** *a* instruit. **◆w.-'spoken** *a* (*person*) qui a un accent cultivé, qui parle bien. **◆w.-'thought-of** *a* hautement considéré. **◆w.-'timed** *a* opportun. **◆w.-to-'do** *a* aisé, riche. **◆w.-'tried** *a* (*method*) éprouvé. **◆w.-'trodden** *a* (*path*) battu. **◆'w.-wishers** *npl* admirateurs, -trices *mfpl*. **◆w.-'worn** *a* (*clothes, carpet*) usagé.

wellington ['welɪŋtən] *n* botte *f* de caoutchouc.

welsh [welʃ] *vi* **to w. on** (*debt, promise*) ne pas honorer.

Welsh [welʃ] *a* gallois; **W. rabbit** *Culin* toast *m* au fromage; − *n* (*language*) gallois *m*. **◆Welshman** *n* (*pl* **-men**) Gallois *m*. **◆Welshwoman** *n* (*pl* **-women**) Galloise *f*.

wench [wentʃ] *n* *Hum* jeune fille *f*.

wend [wend] *vt* **to w. one's way** s'acheminer (**to** vers).

went [went] *see* **go 1.**

wept [wept] *see* **weep.**

were [wər, *stressed* wɜr] *see* **be.**

werewolf ['weəwulf] *n* (*pl* **-wolves**) loup-garou *m*.

west [west] *n* ouest *m*; − *a* (*coast*) ouest *inv*; (*wind*) d'ouest; **W. Africa** Afrique *f* occidentale; **W. Indian** *a* & *n* antillais, -aise (*mf*); **the W. Indies** les Antilles *fpl*; − *adv* à l'ouest, vers l'ouest. **◆westbound** *a* (*carriageway*) ouest *inv*; (*traffic*) en direction de l'ouest. **◆westerly** *a* (*point*) ouest *inv*; (*direction*) de l'ouest; (*wind*) d'ouest. **◆western** *a* (*coast*) ouest *inv*; (*culture*) *Pol* occidental; **W. Europe** Europe *f* de l'Ouest; − *n* (*film*) western *m*. **◆westerner** *n* habitant, -ante *mf* de l'Ouest; *Pol* occidental, -ale *mf*. **◆westernize** *vt* occidentaliser. **◆westward(s)** *a* & *adv* vers l'ouest.

wet [wet] *a* (**wetter, wettest**) mouillé; (*damp, rainy*) humide; (*day, month*) de pluie; **w. paint/ink** peinture *f*/encre *f* fraîche; **w. through** trempé; **to get w.** se mouiller; **it's w.** (*raining*) il pleut; **he's w.** (*weak-willed*)

Fam c'est une lavette; **w. blanket** *Fig* rabat-joie *m inv*; **w. nurse** nourrice *f*; **w. suit** combinaison *f* de plongée; – *n* **the w.** (*rain*) la pluie; (*damp*) l'humidité *f*; – *vt* (*-tt-*) mouiller. ◆**—ness** *n* humidité *f*.

whack [wæk] *n* (*blow*) grand coup *m*; – *vt* donner un grand coup à. ◆**—ed** *a* **w.** (**out**) (*tired*) *Fam* claqué. ◆**—ing** *a* (*big*) *Fam* énorme.

whale [weɪl] *n* baleine *f*. ◆**whaling** *n* pêche *f* à la baleine.

wham! [wæm] *int* vlan!

wharf [wɔːf] *n* (*pl* **wharfs** *or* **wharves**) (*for ships*) quai *m*.

what [wɒt] **1** *a* quel, quelle, *pl* quel(le)s; **w. book?** quel livre?; **w. one?** lequel, laquelle?; **w. a fool**/*etc*! quel idiot/*etc*!; **I know w. book it is** je sais quel livre c'est; **w.** (*little*) **she has** le peu qu'elle a. **2** *pron* (*in questions*) qu'est-ce qui; (*object*) qu'est-ce que; (*after prep*) quoi; **w.'s happening?** qu'est-ce qui se passe?; **w. does he do?** qu'est-ce qu'il fait?, que fait-il?; **w. is it?** qu'est-ce que c'est?; **w.'s that book?** quel est ce livre?; **w.!** (*surprise*) quoi!, comment!; **w.'s it called?** comment ça s'appelle?; **w. for?** pourquoi?; **w. about me**/*etc*? et moi/*etc*?; **w. about leaving**/*etc*? si on partait/*etc*? **3** *pron* (*indirect, relative*) ce qui; (*object*) ce que; **I know w. will happen/w.** she'll do je sais ce qui arrivera/ce qu'elle fera; **w. happens is** ... ce qui arrive c'est que ... ; **w. I need** ce dont j'ai besoin. ◆**what'ever** *a* **w.** (**the**) **mistake**/*etc* (*no matter what*) quelle que soit l'erreur/*etc*; **of w. size** de n'importe quelle taille; **no chance w.** pas la moindre chance; **nothing w.** rien du tout; – *pron* (*no matter what*) quoi que (+ *sub*); **w. happens** quoi qu'il arrive; **w. you do** quoi que tu fasses; **w. is important** tout ce qui est important; **you want** tout ce que tu veux. ◆**what's-it** *n* (*thing*) *Fam* machin *m*. ◆**whatso'ever** *a & pron* = whatever.

wheat [wiːt] *n* blé *m*, froment *m*. ◆**wheatgerm** *n* germes *mpl* de blé.

wheedle ['wiːd(ə)l] *vt* **to w. s.o.** enjôler qn (*into doing* pour qu'il fasse); **to w. sth out of s.o.** obtenir qch de qn par la flatterie.

wheel [wiːl] **1** *n* roue *f*; **at the w.** *Aut* au volant; *Nau* au gouvernail; – *vt* (*push*) pousser; – *vi* (*turn*) tourner. **2** *vi* **to w. and deal** *Fam* faire des combines. ◆**wheelbarrow** *n* brouette *f*. ◆**wheelchair** *n* fauteuil *m* roulant.

wheeze [wiːz] **1** *vi* respirer bruyamment. **2** *n*

(*scheme*) *Fam* combine *f*. ◆**wheezy** *a* (*-ier, -iest*) poussif.

whelk [welk] *n* (*mollusc*) buccin *m*.

when [wen] *adv* quand; – *conj* quand, lorsque; (*whereas*) alors que; **w. I finish, w.** I've finished quand j'aurai fini, lorsque j'aurai fini; **w. I saw him** or **w. I'd seen him,** I left après l'avoir vu, je suis parti; **the day/moment w.** le jour/moment où; **I talked about w.** ... j'ai parlé de l'époque où .... ◆**when'ever** *conj* (*at whatever time*) quand; (*each time that*) chaque fois que.

where [weər] *adv* où; **w. are you from?** d'où êtes-vous?; – *conj* où; (*whereas*) alors que; **that's w. you'll find it** c'est là que tu le trouveras; **I found it w. she'd left it** je l'ai trouvé là où elle l'avait laissé; **I went to w.** he was je suis allé à l'endroit où il était. ◆**whereabouts** *adv* où (*donc*); – *n* **his w.** l'endroit *m* où il est. ◆**where'as** *conj* alors que. ◆**where'by** *adv* par quoi. ◆**where'upon** *adv* sur quoi. ◆**wher-'ever** *conj* **w. you go** (*everywhere*) partout où tu iras, où que tu ailles; **I'll go w. you like** (*anywhere*) j'irai (là) où vous voudrez.

whet [wet] *vt* (*-tt-*) (*appetite, desire etc*) aiguiser.

whether ['weðər] *conj* si; **I don't know w.** to leave je ne sais pas si je dois partir; **w. she does it or not** qu'elle le fasse ou non; **w. now or tomorrow** que ce soit maintenant ou demain; **it's doubtful w.** il est douteux que (+ *sub*).

which [wɪtʃ] **1** *a* (*in questions etc*) quel, quelle, *pl* quel(le)s; **w. hat?** quel chapeau?; **in w. case** auquel cas. **2** *rel pron* qui; (*object*) que; (*after prep*) lequel, laquelle, *pl* lesquel(le)s; **the house w. is** ... la maison qui est ... ; **the book w. I like** le livre que j'aime; **the film of w.** ... le film dont *or* duquel ... ; **she's ill, w. is sad** elle est malade, ce qui est triste; **he lies, w. I don't like** il ment, ce que je n'aime pas; **after w.** (*whereupon*) après quoi. **3** *pron* **w.** (**one**) (*in questions*) lequel, laquelle, *pl* lesquel(le)s; **w.** (**one**) **of us?** lequel *or* laquelle d'entre nous?; **w.** (**ones**) **are the best of the books** quels sont les meilleurs de ces livres? **4** *pron* **w.** (**one**) (*the one that*) celui qui, celle qui, *pl* ceux qui, celles qui; (*object*) celui *etc* que; **show me w.** (**one**) **is red** montrez-moi celui *or* celle qui est rouge; **I know w.** (**ones**) **you want** je sais ceux *or* celles que vous désirez. ◆**which'ever** *a & pron* **w. book**/*etc* **or w.** **of the books**/*etc* **you buy** quel que soit le livre/*etc* que tu achètes; **take w. books** *or* **w. of the books interest you** prenez les livres qui vous intéressent; **take w. (one) you like** prends celui or celle que tu veux; **w. (ones) remain** ceux or celles qui restent.

whiff [wɪf] n (puff) bouffée f; (smell) odeur f.

while [waɪl] conj (when) pendant que; (although) bien que (+ sub); (as long as) tant que; (whereas) tandis que; **w. doing** (in the course of) en faisant; − n **a w.** un moment, quelque temps; **all the w.** tout le temps; − vt **to w. away** (time) passer. ◆**whilst** [waɪlst] conj = **while**.

whim [wɪm] n caprice m.

whimper [wɪmpər] vi (of dog, person) gémir faiblement; (snivel) Pej pleurnicher; − n faible gémissement m; **without a w.** (complaint) Fig sans se plaindre.

whimsical [wɪmzɪk(ə)l] a (look, idea) bizarre; (person) fantasque, capricieux.

whine [waɪn] vi gémir; (complain) Fig se plaindre; − n gémissement m; plainte f.

whip [wɪp] n fouet m; − vt (-pp-) (person, cream etc) fouetter; (defeat) Fam dérouiller; **to w. off** (take off) enlever brusquement; **to w. out** (from pocket etc) sortir brusquement (from de); **to w. up** (interest) susciter; (meal) Fam préparer rapidement; − vi (move) aller à toute vitesse; **to w. round to s.o.'s** faire un saut chez qn. ◆**whip-round** n Fam collecte f.

whirl [wɜːl] vi tourbillonner, tournoyer; − vt faire tourbillonner; − n tourbillon m. ◆**whirlpool** n tourbillon m; **w. bath** Am bain m à remous. ◆**whirlwind** n tourbillon m (de vent).

whirr [wɜːr] vi (of engine) vrombir; (of top) ronronner.

whisk [wɪsk] **1** n Culin fouet m; − vt fouetter. **2** vt **to w. away** or **off** (tablecloth etc) enlever rapidement; (person) emmener rapidement; (chase away) chasser.

whiskers [wɪskəz] npl (of animal) moustaches fpl; (beard) barbe f; (moustache) moustache f; (side) w. favoris mpl.

whisky, Am **whiskey** [wɪskɪ] n whisky m.

whisper [wɪspər] vti chuchoter; **w. to me!** chuchote à mon oreille!; − n chuchotement m; (rumour) Fig rumeur f, bruit m.

whistle [wɪs(ə)l] n sifflement m; (object) sifflet m; **to blow** or **give a w.** siffler; − vti siffler; **to w. at** (girl) siffler; **to w. for** (dog, taxi) siffler.

Whit [wɪt] a **W. Sunday** dimanche m de Pentecôte.

white [waɪt] a (-er, -est) blanc; **to go** or **turn w.** blanchir; **w. coffee** café m au lait; **w. elephant** Fig objet m or projet m etc inutile;

w. lie pieux mensonge m; **w. man** blanc m; **w. woman** blanche f; − n (colour, of egg, eye) blanc m; (person) blanc m, blanche f. ◆**white-collar 'worker** n employé, -ée mf de bureau. ◆**whiten** vti blanchir. ◆**whiteness** n blancheur f. ◆**whitewash** n (for walls etc) blanc m de chaux; − vt blanchir à la chaux; (person) Fig blanchir; (faults) justifier.

whiting [waɪtɪŋ] n (fish) merlan m.

Whitsun [wɪts(ə)n] n la Pentecôte.

whittle [wɪt(ə)l] vt **to w. down** (wood) tailler; (price etc) Fig rogner.

whizz [wɪz] **1** vi (rush) aller à toute vitesse; **to w. past** passer à toute vitesse; **to w. through the air** fendre l'air. **2** a **w. kid** Fam petit prodige m.

who [huː] pron qui; **w. did it?** qui (est-ce qui) a fait ça?; **the woman w.** la femme qui; **w. did you see** tu as vu qui? ◆**who'ever** pron (no matter who) qui que ce soit qui; (object) qui que ce soit que; **w. has travelled** (anyone who) quiconque a or celui qui a voyagé; **w. you are** qui que vous soyez; **this man, w. he is** cet homme, quel qu'il soit; **w. did that?** qui donc a fait ça?

whodunit [huːdʌnɪt] n (detective story) Fam polar m.

whole [həʊl] a entier; (intact) intact; **the w. time** tout le temps; **the w. apple** toute la pomme, la pomme (tout) entière; **the w. truth** toute la vérité; **the w. world** le monde entier; **the w. lot** le tout; **to swallow sth w.** avaler qch tout entier; − n (unit) tout m; (total) totalité f; **the w. of the village** le village (tout) entier; **the w. of the night** toute la nuit; **on the w., as a w.** dans l'ensemble. ◆**whole-'hearted** a, ◆**whole-'heartedly** adv sans réserve. ◆**wholemeal** a, Am ◆**wholewheat** a (bread) complet. ◆**wholly** adv entièrement.

wholesale [həʊlseɪl] n Com gros m; − a (firm) de gros; (destruction etc) Fig en masse; − adv (in bulk) en gros; (to buy or sell one article) au prix de gros; (to destroy etc) Fig en masse. ◆**wholesaler** n grossiste mf.

wholesome [həʊlsəm] a (food, climate etc) sain.

whom [huːm] pron (object) que; (in questions and after prep) qui; **w. did she see?** qui a-t-elle vu?; **the man w. you know** l'homme que tu connais; **with w.** avec qui; **of w.** dont.

whooping cough [huːpɪŋkɒf] n coqueluche f.

whoops! [wups] *int* (*apology etc*) oups!

whopping ['wɒpɪŋ] *a* (*big*) *Fam* énorme.
◆**whopper** *n Fam* chose *f* énorme.

whore [hɔːr] *n* (*prostitute*) putain *f*.

whose [huːz] *poss pron* & *a* à qui, de qui; **w. book is this?, w. is this book?** à qui est ce livre?; **w. daughter are you?** de qui es-tu la fille?; **the woman whose book I have** la femme dont *or* de qui j'ai le livre; **the man w. mother I spoke to** l'homme à la mère de qui j'ai parlé.

why [waɪ] **1** *adv* pourquoi; **w. not?** pourquoi pas?; – *conj* **the reason w. they . . .** la raison pour laquelle ils . . . ; – *npl* **the whys and wherefores** le pourquoi et le comment. **2** *int* (*surprise*) eh bien!, tiens!

wick [wɪk] *n* (*of candle, lamp*) mèche *f*.

wicked ['wɪkɪd] *a* (*evil*) méchant, vilain; (*mischievous*) malicieux. ◆**-ly** *adv* méchamment; malicieusement. ◆**-ness** *n* méchanceté *f*.

wicker ['wɪkər] *n* osier *m*; – *a* (*chair etc*) en osier, d'osier. ◆**wickerwork** *n* (*objects*) vannerie *f*.

wicket ['wɪkɪt] *n* (*cricket stumps*) guichet *m*.

wide [waɪd] *a* (**-er, -est**) large; (*desert, ocean*) vaste; (*choice, knowledge, variety*) grand; **to be three metres w.** avoir trois mètres de large; – *adv* (*to fall, shoot*) loin du but; (*to open*) tout grand. ◆**wide-'awake** *a* (*alert, not sleeping*) éveillé. ◆**widely** *adv* (*to broadcast, spread*) largement; (*to travel*) beaucoup; **w. different** très différent; **it's w. thought** *or* **believed that . . .** on pense généralement que . . . . ◆**widen** *vt* élargir; – *vi* s'élargir. ◆**wideness** *n* largeur *f*.

widespread ['waɪdspred] *a* (*très*) répandu.

widow ['wɪdəu] *n* veuve *f*. ◆**widowed** *a* (*man*) veuf; (*woman*) veuve; **to be w.** (*become a widower or widow*) devenir veuf *or* veuve. ◆**widower** *n* veuf *m*.

width [wɪdθ] *n* largeur *f*.

wield [wiːld] *vt* (*handle*) manier; (*brandish*) brandir; (*power*) *Fig* exercer.

wife [waɪf] *n* (*pl* **wives**) femme *f*, épouse *f*.

wig [wɪg] *n* perruque *f*.

wiggle ['wɪg(ə)l] *vt* agiter; **to w. one's hips** tortiller des hanches; – *vi* (*of worm etc*) se tortiller; (*of tail*) remuer.

wild [waɪld] *a* (**-er, -est**) (*animal, flower, region etc*) sauvage; (*enthusiasm, sea*) déchaîné; (*idea, life*) fou; (*look*) farouche; (*angry*) furieux (**with** contre); **w. with** (*joy, anger etc*) fou de; **I'm not w. about it** (*plan etc*) *Fam* ça ne m'emballe pas; **to be w. about s.o.** (*very fond of*) être dingue de qn; **to grow w.** (*of plant*) pousser à l'état sau-

vage; **to run w.** (*of animals*) courir en liberté; (*of crowd*) se déchaîner; **the W. West** *Am* le Far West; – *npl* **régions** *fpl* **sauvages**. ◆**wildcat 'strike** *n* grève *f* sauvage. ◆**wild-'goose chase** *n* fausse piste *f*. ◆**wildlife** *n* animaux *mpl* sauvages, faune *f*.

wilderness ['wɪldənəs] *n* désert *m*.

wildly ['waɪldlɪ] *adv* (*madly*) follement; (*violently*) violemment.

wile [waɪl] *n* ruse *f*, artifice *m*.

wilful ['wɪlfəl] *a* (*Am* **willful**) (*intentional, obstinate*) volontaire. ◆**-ly** *adv* volontairement.

will¹ [wɪl] *v aux* **he will come, he'll come** (*future tense*) il viendra (**won't he?** n'est-ce pas?); **you will not come, you won't come** tu ne viendras pas (**will you?** n'est-ce pas?); **w. you have a tea?** veux-tu prendre un thé?; **w. you be quiet!** veux-tu te taire!; **I w.!** (*yes*) oui!; **it won't open** ça ne s'ouvre pas, ça ne veut pas s'ouvrir.

will² [wɪl] **1** *vt* (*wish, intend*) vouloir (**that** que (+ *sub*)); **to w. oneself to do** faire un effort de volonté pour faire; – *n* volonté *f*; **against one's w.** à contrecœur, malgré soi; **at w.** (*to depart etc*) quand on veut; (*to choose*) à volonté. **2** *n* (*legal document*) testament *m*. ◆**willpower** *n* volonté *f*.

willing ['wɪlɪŋ] *a* (*helper, worker*) de bonne volonté; (*help etc*) spontané; **to be w. to do** être disposé *or* prêt à faire, vouloir bien faire; – *n* **to show w.** faire preuve de bonne volonté. ◆**-ly** *adv* (*with pleasure*) volontiers; (*voluntarily*) volontairement. ◆**-ness** *n* (*goodwill*) bonne volonté *f*; **his** *or* **her w. to do** (*enthusiasm*) son empressement *m* à faire.

willow ['wɪləu] *n* (*tree, wood*) saule *m*. ◆**willowy** *a* (*person*) svelte.

willy-nilly [wɪlɪ'nɪlɪ] *adv* bon gré mal gré, de gré ou de force.

wilt [wɪlt] *vi* (*of plant*) dépérir; (*of enthusiasm etc*) *Fig* décliner.

wily [waɪlɪ] *a* (**-ier, -iest**) rusé.

wimp [wɪmp] *n* (*weakling*) *Fam* mauviette *f*.

win [wɪn] *n* (*victory*) victoire *f*; – *vi* (*pt* & *pp* **won**, *pres p* **winning**) gagner; – *vt* (*money, race etc*) gagner; (*victory, prize*) remporter; (*fame*) acquérir; (*friends*) se faire; **to w. s.o. over** gagner qn (**to** à). ◆**winning** *a* (*number, horse etc*) gagnant; (*team*) victorieux; (*goal*) décisif; (*smile*) engageant; – *npl* **gains** *mpl*.

wince [wɪns] *vi* (*flinch*) tressaillir; (*pull a face*) grimacer; **without wincing** sans sourciller.

winch [wɪntʃ] n treuil m; − vt **to w. (up)** hisser au treuil.

wind¹ [wɪnd] n vent m; (breath) souffle m; **to have w.** Med avoir des gaz; **to get w. of** Fig avoir vent de; **in the w.** Fig dans l'air; **w. instrument** Mus instrument m à vent; − vt **to w. s.o.** (of blow etc) couper le souffle à qn. ◆**windbreak** n (fence, trees) brise-vent m inv. ◆**windcheater** n, Am ◆**windbreaker** n blouson m, coupe-vent m inv. ◆**windfall** n (piece of fruit) fruit m abattu par le vent; (unexpected money) Fig aubaine f. ◆**windmill** n moulin m à vent. ◆**windpipe** n Anat trachée f. ◆**windscreen** n, Am ◆**windshield** n Aut pare-brise m inv; **w. wiper** essuie-glace m inv. ◆**windsurfing** n **to go w.** faire de la planche à voile. ◆**windswept** a (street etc) balayé par les vents. ◆**windy** a (-ier, -iest) venteux, venté; **it's w.** (of weather) il y a du vent.

wind² [waɪnd] vt (pt & pp wound) (roll) enrouler; **to w. (up)** (clock) remonter; **to w. up** (meeting) terminer; (firm) liquider; − vi (of river, road) serpenter; **to w. down** (relax) se détendre; **to w. up** (end up) finir (doing par faire); **to w. up with sth** se retrouver avec qch. ◆**-ing** a (road etc) sinueux; (staircase) tournant. ◆**-er** n (of watch) remontoir m.

window [wɪndəʊ] n fenêtre f; (pane) vitre f, carreau m; (in vehicle or train) vitre f; (in shop) vitrine f; (counter) guichet m; **French w.** porte-fenêtre f. ◆**w. box** jardinière f; **w. cleaner** n or Am **washer** laveur, -euse mf de carreaux; **w. dresser** étalagiste mf; **w. ledge** = **windowsill**; **to go w. shopping** faire du lèche-vitrines. ◆**windowpane** n vitre f, carreau m. ◆**windowsill** n (inside) appui m de (la) fenêtre; (outside) rebord m de (la) fenêtre.

wine [waɪn] n vin m; − a (bottle, cask) à vin; **w. cellar** cave f (à vin); **w. grower** viticulteur m; **w. list** carte f des vins; **w. taster** dégustateur, -trice mf de vins; **w. tasting** dégustation f de vins; **w. waiter** sommelier m; − vt **to w. and dine s.o.** offrir à dîner et à boire à qn. ◆**wineglass** n verre m à vin. ◆**wine-growing** a viticole.

wing [wɪŋ] n aile f; **the wings** Th les coulisses fpl; **under one's w.** Fig sous son aile. ◆**winged** a ailé. ◆**winger** n Sp ailier m. ◆**wingspan** n envergure f.

wink [wɪŋk] vi faire un clin d'œil (**at**, à); (of light) clignoter; − n clin m d'œil.

winkle [wɪŋk(ə)l] n (sea animal) bigorneau m.

winner [wɪnər] n (of contest etc) gagnant, -ante mf; (of argument, fight) vainqueur m; **that idea/etc is a w.** Fam c'est une idée/etc en or.

winter [wɪntər] n hiver m; − a d'hiver; **in (the) w.** en hiver. ◆**wintertime** n hiver m. ◆**wintry** a hivernal.

wip/e [waɪp] vt essuyer; **to w. one's feet/hands** s'essuyer les pieds/les mains; **to w. away** or **off** or **up** (liquid) essuyer; **to w. out** (clean) essuyer; (erase) effacer; (destroy) anéantir; − vi **to w. up** (dry the dishes) essuyer la vaisselle; − n coup m de torchon or d'éponge. ◆**-er** n Aut essuie-glace m inv.

wir/e [waɪər] n fil m; (telegram) télégramme m; **w. netting** grillage m; − vt **to w. (up)** (house) El faire l'installation électrique de; **to w. s.o.** (telegraph) télégraphier à qn. ◆**-ing** n El installation f électrique. ◆**wirecutters** npl pince f coupante.

wireless [waɪələs] n (set) TSF f, radio f; **by w.** (to send a message) par sans-fil.

wiry [waɪərɪ] a (-ier, -iest) maigre et nerveux.

wisdom [wɪzdəm] n sagesse f.

wise [waɪz] a (-er, -est) (prudent) sage, prudent; (learned) savant; **to put s.o. w./be w. to** Fam mettre qn/être au courant de; **w. guy** Fam gros malin m. ◆**wisecrack** n Fam (joke) astuce f; (sarcastic remark) sarcasme m. ◆**wisely** adv prudemment.

-wise [waɪz] suffix (with regard to) **money**/etc**-wise** question argent/etc.

wish [wɪʃ] vt souhaiter, vouloir (**to do** faire); **I w. (that) you could help me/could have helped me** je voudrais que/j'aurais voulu que vous m'aidiez; **I w. I hadn't done that** je regrette d'avoir fait ça; **if you w.** si tu veux; **I w. you well** or **luck** je vous souhaite bonne chance; **I wished him** or **her (a) happy birthday** je lui ai souhaité bon anniversaire; **I w. I could** si seulement je pouvais; − vi **to w. for sth** souhaiter qch; − n (specific) souhait m, vœu m; (general) désir m; **the w. for sth/to do** le désir de qch/de faire; **best wishes** (on greeting card) meilleurs vœux mpl; (in letter) amitiés fpl, bien amicalement; **send him** or **her my best wishes** fais-lui mes amitiés. ◆**wishbone** n bréchet m. ◆**wishful** a **it's w. thinking** (on your part) tu te fais des illusions, tu prends tes désirs pour la réalité.

wishy-washy [wɪʃɪwɒʃɪ] a (taste, colour) fade.

wisp [wɪsp] n (of smoke) volute f; (of hair)

fine mèche f; **a (mere) w. of a girl** une fillette toute menue.

wisteria [wɪ'stɪərɪə] n Bot glycine f.

wistful [ˈwɪstfəl] a mélancolique et rêveur. **◆—ly** adv avec mélancolie.

wit [wɪt] n **1** (humour) esprit m; (person) homme m or femme f d'esprit. **2 wit(s)** (intelligence) intelligence f (to do de faire); **to be at one's wits'** or **wit's end** ne plus savoir que faire.

witch [wɪtʃ] n sorcière f. **◆witchcraft** n sorcellerie f. **◆witch-hunt** n Pol chasse f aux sorcières.

with [wɪð] prep **1** avec; **come w. me** viens avec moi; **w. no hat** sans chapeau; **I'll be right w. you** je suis à vous dans une minute; **I'm w. you** (I understand) Fam je te suis; **w. it** (up-to-date) Fam dans le vent. **2** (at the house, flat etc of) chez; **she's staying w. me** elle loge chez moi; **it's a habit w. me** c'est une habitude chez moi. **3** (cause) de; **to jump w. joy** sauter de joie. **4** (instrument, means) avec; **to write w. a pen** écrire avec un stylo; **to fill w.** remplir de; **satisfied w.** satisfait de; **w. my own eyes** de mes propres yeux. **5** (description) à; **w. blue eyes** aux yeux bleus. **6** (despite) malgré.

withdraw [wɪð'drɔː] vt (pt withdrew, pp withdrawn) retirer (from de); — vi se retirer (from de). **◆withdrawn** a (person) renfermé. **◆withdrawal** n retrait m; **to suffer from w. symptoms** (of drug addict etc) être en manque.

wither [ˈwɪðər] vi (of plant etc) se flétrir; — vt flétrir. **◆—ed** a (limb) atrophié. **◆—ing** a (look) foudroyant; (remark) cinglant.

withhold [wɪð'həʊld] vt (pt & pp withheld) (help, permission etc) refuser (from à); (decision) différer; (money) retenir (from de); (information etc) cacher (from à).

within [wɪ'ðɪn] adv à l'intérieur; — prep (place, container etc) à l'intérieur de, dans; **w. a kilometre** (to return etc) à moins d'un kilomètre de; **w. a month** (to return etc) avant un mois; (to finish sth) en moins d'un mois; (to pay) sous un mois; **w. my means** dans (les limites de) mes moyens; **w. sight** en vue.

without [wɪ'ðaʊt] prep sans; **w. a tie/etc** sans cravate/etc; **w. doing** sans faire.

withstand [wɪð'stænd] vt (pt & pp withstood) résister à.

witness [ˈwɪtnɪs] n (person) témoin m; (evidence) Jur témoignage m; **to bear w.** témoigner de; — vt être (le) témoin de, voir; (document) signer (pour attester l'authenticité de).

witty [ˈwɪtɪ] a (-ier, -iest) spirituel. **◆witti-**

-ness n esprit m.

wives [waɪvz] see **wife**.

wizard [ˈwɪzəd] n magicien m; (genius) Fig génie m, as m.

wizened [ˈwɪz(ə)nd] a ratatiné.

wobble [ˈwɒb(ə)l] vi (of chair etc) branler, boiter; (of cyclist, pile etc) osciller; (of jelly, leg) trembler; (of wheel) tourner de façon irrégulière. **◆wobbly** a (table etc) bancal, boiteux; **to be w. = to wobble.**

woe [wəʊ] n malheur m. **◆woeful** a triste.

woke, woken [wəʊk, ˈwəʊkən] see **wake**[1].

wolf [wʊlf] **1** n (pl wolves) loup m; **w. whistle** sifflement m admiratif. **2** vt **to w. (down)** (food) engloutir.

woman, pl **women** [ˈwʊmən, ˈwɪmɪn] n femme f; **she's a London w.** c'est une Londonienne; **w. doctor** femme f médecin; **women drivers** les femmes fpl au volant; **w. friend** amie f; **w. teacher** professeur m femme; **women's** (attitudes, clothes etc) féminin. **◆womanhood** n (quality) féminité f; **to reach w.** devenir femme. **◆womanizer** n Pej coureur m (de femmes or de jupons). **◆womanly** a féminin.

womb [wuːm] n utérus m.

women [ˈwɪmɪn] see **woman**.

won [wʌn] see **win**.

wonder [ˈwʌndər] **1** n (marvel) merveille f, miracle m; (sense, feeling) émerveillement m; **in w.** (to watch etc) émerveillé; **(it's) no w.** ce n'est pas étonnant (that que; to de); — vi (marvel) s'étonner (at de); — vt **I w. that je** or ça m'étonne que (+ sub). **2** vt (ask oneself) se demander (if si, why pourquoi); — vi (reflect) songer (about à). **◆wonderful** a (excellent, astonishing) merveilleux. **◆wonderfully** adv (beautiful, hot etc) merveilleusement (to do, work etc) à merveille.

wonky [ˈwɒŋkɪ] a (-ier, -iest) Fam (table etc) bancal; (hat, picture) de travers.

won't [wəʊnt] = will not.

woo [wuː] vt (woman) faire la cour à, courtiser; (try to please) Fig chercher à plaire à.

wood [wʊd] n (material, forest) bois m. **◆woodcut** n gravure f sur bois. **◆wooded** a (valley etc) boisé. **◆wooden** a de or en bois; (manner, dancer etc) Fig raide. **◆woodland** n région f boisée. **◆woodpecker** n (bird) pic m. **◆woodwind** n (instruments) Mus bois mpl. **◆woodwork** n (craft, objects) menuiserie f. **◆woodworm** n (larvae) vers mpl (du bois); **it has w.** c'est vermoulu. **◆woody** a

(**-ier, -iest**) (*hill etc*) boisé; (*stem etc*) ligneux.

wool [wul] *n* laine *f*; – *a* de laine; (*industry*) lainier. ◆**woollen** *a* de laine; (*industry*) lainier; – *npl* (*garments*) lainages *mpl*. ◆**woolly** *a* (**-ier, -iest**) laineux; (*unclear*) *Fig* nébuleux; – *n* (*garment*) *Fam* lainage *m*.

word [wɜːd] *n* mot *m*; (*spoken*) parole *f*, mot *m*; (*promise*) parole *f*; (*command*) ordre *m*; *pl* (*of song etc*) paroles *fpl*; **by w. of mouth** de vive voix; **to have a w. with s.o.** (*speak to*) parler à qn; (*advise, scold etc*) avoir un mot avec qn; **in other words** autrement dit; **I have no w. from** (*news*) je suis sans nouvelles de; **to send w. that** ... faire savoir que ...; **to leave w. that** ... dire que ...; **the last w. in** (*latest development*) le dernier cri en matière de; **w. processing** traitement *m* de texte; – *vt* (*express*) rédiger, formuler. ◆**wording** *n* termes *mpl*. ◆**wordy** *a* (**-ier, -iest**) verbeux.

wore [wɔːr] *see* **wear 1,2**.

work [wɜːk] *n* travail *m*; (*product*) & *Liter* œuvre *f*, ouvrage *m*; (*building or repair work*) travaux *mpl*; **to be at w.** travailler; **farm w.** travaux *mpl* agricoles; **out of w.** au *or* en chômage; **a day off w.** un jour de congé *or* de repos; **he's off w.** il n'est pas allé travailler; **the works** (*mechanism*) le mécanisme; **a gas works** (*factory*) une usine à gaz; **w. force** main-d'œuvre *f*; **a heavy w. load** beaucoup de travail; – *vi* travailler; (*of machine etc*) marcher, fonctionner; (*of drug*) agir; **to w. on** (*book etc*) travailler à; (*principle*) se baser sur; **to w. at** *or* **on sth** (*improve*) travailler qch; **to w. loose** (*of knot, screw*) se desserrer; (*of tooth*) se mettre à branler; **to w. towards** (*result, agreement, aim*) travailler à; **to w. out** (*succeed*) s'entraîner; (*train*) *Sp* s'entraîner; **it works out at £5** ça fait cinq livres; **it works up to** (*climax*) ça tend vers; **to w. up to sth** (*in speech etc*) en venir à qch; – *vt* (*person*) faire travailler; (*machine*) faire marcher; (*mine*) exploiter; (*miracle*) faire; (*metal, wood etc*) travailler; **to get worked up** s'exciter; **to w. in** (*reference, bolt*) introduire; **to w. off** (*debt*) payer en travaillant; (*excess fat*) se débarrasser de (par l'exercice); (*anger*) passer, assouvir; **to w. out** (*solve*) résoudre; (*calculate*) calculer; (*scheme, plan*) élaborer; **to w. up an appetite** s'ouvrir l'appétit; **to w. up enthusiasm** s'enthousiasmer; **to w. one's way up** (*rise socially etc*) faire du chemin. ◆**working** *a* (*day, clothes etc*) de travail; (*population*)

actif; **Monday's a w. day** on travaille le lundi, lundi est un jour ouvré; **w. class** class *f* ouvrière; **in w. order** en état de marche; – *npl* (*mechanism*) mécanisme *m*. ◆**workable** *a* (*plan*) praticable. ◆**worker** *n* travailleur, -euse *mf*; (*manual*) ouvrier, -ière *mf*; (*employee, clerk*) employé, -ée *mf*; **blue-collar w.** col *m* bleu.

workaholic [wɜːkəˈhɒlɪk] *n* *Fam* bourreau *m* de travail. ◆**workbench** *n* établi *m*. ◆**working-'class** *n* ouvrier *m*. ◆**'workman** *n* (*pl* -**men**) ouvrier *m*. ◆**'workmanship** *n* maîtrise *f*, travail *m*. ◆**'workmate** *n* camarade *mf* de travail. ◆**'workout** *n* *Sp* (*séance f*) d'entraînement *m*. ◆**'workroom** *n* salle *f* de travail. ◆**'workshop** *n* atelier *m*. ◆**'work-shy** *a* peu enclin au travail. ◆**work-to-'rule** *n* grève *f* du zèle.

world [wɜːld] *n* monde *m*; **all over the w.** dans le monde entier; **the richest/etc in the world** *or* la plus riche/etc du monde; **a w. of** (*a lot of*) énormément de; **to think the w. of** penser énormément de bien de; **why in the w....?** pourquoi diable ... ?; **out of this w.** (*wonderful*) *Fam* formidable; – *a* (*war etc*) mondial; (*champion, cup, record*) du monde. ◆**world-'famous** *a* de renommée mondiale. ◆**worldly** *a* (*pleasures*) de ce monde; (*person*) qui a l'expérience du monde. ◆**world'wide** *a* universel.

worm [wɜːm] **1** *n* ver *m*. **2** *vt* **to w. one's way into** s'insinuer dans; **to w. sth out of s.o.** soutirer qch à qn. ◆**worm-eaten** *a* (*wood*) vermoulu; (*fruit*) véreux.

worn [wɔːn] *see* **wear 1,2**; – *a* (*tyre etc*) usé. ◆**worn-'out** *a* (*object*) complètement usé; (*person*) épuisé.

worry [ˈwʌrɪ] *n* souci *m*; – *vi* s'inquiéter (*about sth* de qch, *about s.o.* pour qn); – *vt* inquiéter; **to be worried** être inquiet; **to be worried sick** se ronger les sangs. ◆**-ing** *a* (*news etc*) inquiétant. ◆**worrier** *n* anxieux, -euse *mf*. ◆**worryguts** *n*, *Am* ◆**worrywart** *n* *Fam* anxieux, -euse *mf*.

worse [wɜːs] *a* pire, plus mauvais (**than** que); **to get w.** se détériorer; **he's getting w.** (*in health*) il va de plus en plus mal; (*in behaviour*) il se conduit de plus en plus mal; – *adv* plus mal (**than** que); **I could do w.** je pourrais faire pire; **to hate/etc w. than** détester/etc plus fort; **to be w. off** (*financially*) aller moins bien financièrement; – *n* **there's w. (to come)** il y a pire encore; **a change for the w.** une détérioration. ◆**worsen** *vti* empirer.

worship [ˈwɜːʃɪp] *n* culte *m*; **his W. the Mayor** Monsieur le Maire; – *vt* (**-pp-**)

worst [wɜːst] *a* pire, plus mauvais; – *adv* (**the**) **w.** (le) plus mal; **to come off w.** (*in struggle etc*) avoir le dessous; – *n* **the w.** (**one**) (*object, person*) le *or* la pire, le *or* la plus mauvais(e); **the w.** (**thing**) **is that** . . . le pire c'est que . . . ; **at** (**the**) **w.** au pis aller; **at its w.** (*crisis*) à son plus mauvais point *or* moment; **to get the w. of it** (*in struggle etc*) avoir le dessous; **the w. is yet to come** on n'a pas encore vu le pire.

worsted [wʊstɪd] *n* laine *f* peignée.

worth [wɜːθ] *n* valeur *f*; **to buy 50 pence w. of chocolates** acheter pour cinquante pence de chocolats; – *a* **to be w.** valoir; **how much** *or* **what is it w.?** ça vaut combien?; **the film's w. seeing** le film vaut la peine *or* le coup d'être vu; **it's w.** (**one's**) **while** ça (en) vaut la peine *or* le coup; **it's w.** (**while**) **waiting** ça vaut la peine d'attendre. ◆**worthless** *a* qui ne vaut rien. ◆**worth'while** *a* (*book, film etc*) qui vaut la peine d'être lu, vu *etc*; (*activity*) qui (en) vaut la peine; (*contribution, plan*) valable; (*cause*) louable; (*satisfying*) qui donne des satisfactions.

worthy [wɜːðɪ] *a* (**-ier, -iest**) digne (**of** de); (*laudable*) louable; – *n* (*person*) notable *m*.

would [wud, *unstressed* wəd] *v aux* **I w.** stay, **I'd stay** (*conditional tense*) je resterais; **he w. have done it** il l'aurait fait; **w. you help me, please?** voulez-vous m'aider, s'il vous plaît?; **w. you like some tea?** voudriez-vous (prendre) du thé?; **I w. see her every day** (*used to*) je la voyais chaque jour. ◆**would-be** *a* (*musician etc*) soi-disant.

wound¹ [wuːnd] *vt* (*hurt*) blesser; **the wounded** les blessés *mpl*; – *n* blessure *f*.

wound² [waund] *see* **wind².**

wove, woven [wəʊv, 'wəʊv(ə)n] *see* **weave.**

wow! [waʊ] *int Fam* (c'est) formidable!

wrangle [ˈræŋg(ə)l] *n* dispute *f*; – *vi* se disputer.

wrap [ræp] *vt* (**-pp-**) **to w.** (**up**) envelopper; **to w.** (**oneself**) **up** (*dress warmly*) se couvrir; **wrapped up in** (*engrossed*) Fig absorbé par; – *n* (*shawl*) châle *m*; (*cape*) pèlerine *f*; plastic **w.** Am scel-o-frais® *m*. ◆**wrapping** *n* (*action, material*) emballage *m*; **w. paper** papier *m* d'emballage. ◆**wrapper** *n* (*of sweet*) papier *m*; (*book*) jaquette *f*.

wrath [rɒθ] *n* Lit courroux *m*.

wreak [riːk] *vt* **to w. vengeance on** se venger de; **to w. havoc on** ravager.

wreath [riːθ] *n* (*pl* **-s** [riːðz]) (*on head, for funeral*) couronne *f*.

wreck [rek] *n* (*ship*) épave *f*; (*sinking*) naufrage *m*; (*train etc*) train *m etc* accidenté; (*person*) épave *f* (humaine); **to be a nervous w.** être à bout de nerfs; – *vt* détruire; (*ship*) provoquer le naufrage de; (*career, hopes etc*) Fig briser, détruire. ◆**—age** *n* (*fragments*) débris *mpl*. ◆**—er** *n* (*breakdown truck*) Am dépanneuse *f*.

wren [ren] *n* (*bird*) roitelet *m*.

wrench [rentʃ] *vt* (*tug at*) tirer sur; (*twist*) tordre; **to w. sth from s.o.** arracher qch à qn; – *n* mouvement *m* de torsion; (*tool*) clé *f* (à écrous), Am clé *f* à mollette; (*distress*) Fig déchirement *m*.

wrest [rest] *vt* **to w. sth from s.o.** arracher qch à qn.

wrestl/e [ˈres(ə)l] *vi* lutter (**with** contre qn); **to w. with** (*problem etc*) Fig se débattre avec. ◆**—ing** *n Sp* lutte *f*; (*all-in*) **w.** catch *m*. ◆**—er** *n* lutteur, -euse *mf*; catcheur, -euse *mf*.

wretch [retʃ] *n* (*unfortunate person*) malheureux, -euse *mf*; (*rascal*) misérable *mf*. ◆**wretched** [-ɪd] *a* (*poor, pitiful*) misérable; (*dreadful*) affreux; (*annoying*) maudit.

wriggle [ˈrɪg(ə)l] *vi* **to w.** (**about**) se tortiller; (*of fish*) frétiller; **to w. out of** (*difficulty, task etc*) esquiver; – *vt* (*fingers, toes*) tortiller.

wring [rɪŋ] *vt* (*pt & pp* **wrung**) (*neck*) tordre; **to w.** (**out**) (*clothes*) essorer; (*water*) faire sortir; **to w. sth out of s.o.** Fig arracher qch à qn; **wringing wet** (trempé) à tordre.

wrinkle [ˈrɪŋk(ə)l] *n* (*on skin*) ride *f*; (*in cloth or paper*) pli *m*; – *vt* (*skin*) rider; (*cloth, paper*) plisser; – *vi* se rider; faire des plis.

wrist [rɪst] *n* poignet *m*. ◆**wristwatch** *n* montre-bracelet *f*.

writ [rɪt] *n* acte *m* judiciaire; **to issue a w. against s.o.** assigner qn (en justice).

write [raɪt] *vti* (*pt* **wrote**, *pp* **written**) écrire; **to w. down** noter; **to w. off** (*debt*) passer aux profits et pertes; **to w. out** écrire; (*copy*) recopier; **to w. up** (*from notes*) rédiger; (*diary, notes*) mettre à jour; – *vi* écrire; **to w. away** *or* **off** *or* **up for** (*details etc*) écrire pour demander; **to w. back** répondre; **to w. in** *Rad TV* écrire (**for information**/*etc* pour demander des renseignements/*etc*). ◆**w.-off** *n* **a** (**complete**) **w.-off** (*car*) une véritable épave. ◆**w.-up** *n* (*report*) Journ compte rendu *m*. ◆**writing** *n* (*handwriting*) écriture *f*; (*literature*) littérature *f*; **to put** (**down**) **in w.** mettre par écrit; **some w.** (*on page*) quelque chose d'écrit; **his** *or* **her**

writing(s) (*works*) ses écrits *mpl*; **w. desk** secrétaire *m*; **w. pad** bloc *m* de papier à lettres; **w. paper** papier *m* à lettres. ◆**writer** *n* auteur *m* (of de); (*literary*) écrivain *m*.

writhe [raɪð] *vi* (*in pain etc*) se tordre.

written ['rɪt(ə)n] *see* write.

wrong [rɒŋ] *a* (*sum, idea etc*) faux, erroné; (*direction, time etc*) mauvais; (*unfair*) injuste; **to be w.** (*of person*) avoir tort (to do de faire); (*mistaken*) se tromper; **it's w. to swear/etc** (*morally*) c'est mal de jurer/*etc*; **it's the w. road** ce n'est pas la bonne route; **you're the w. man** (*for job etc*) tu n'es pas l'homme qu'il faut; **the clock's w.** la pendule n'est pas à l'heure; **something's w.** quelque chose ne va pas; **something's w. with the phone** le téléphone ne marche pas bien; **something's w. with her arm** elle a quelque chose au bras; **nothing's w.** tout va

bien; **what's w. with you?** qu'est-ce qui ne va as?; **the w. way round** *or* **up** à l'envers; – *adv* mal; **to go w.** (*err*) se tromper; (*of plan*) mal tourner; (*of vehicle, machine*) tomber en panne; – *n* (*injustice*) injustice *f*; (*evil*) mal *m*; **to be in the w.** avoir tort; **right and w.** le bien et le mal; – *vt* faire (du) tort à. ◆**wrongdoer** *n* (*criminal*) malfaiteur *m*. ◆**wrongful** *a* injustifié; (*arrest*) arbitraire. ◆**wrongfully** *adv* à tort. ◆**wrongly** *adv* incorrectement; (*to inform, translate*) mal; (*to suspect etc*) à tort.

wrote [rəʊt] *see* write.

wrought [rɔːt] *a* **w. iron** fer *m* forgé. ◆**w.-'iron** *a* en fer forgé.

wrung [rʌŋ] *see* wring.

wry [raɪ] *a* (**wryer, wryest**) (*comment*) ironique; (*smile*) forcé; **to pull a w. face** grimacer.

X

X, x [eks] *n* X, x *m*. ◆**X-ray** *n* (*beam*) rayon *m* X; (*photo*) radio(graphie) *f*; **to have an X-ray** passer une radio; **X-ray examination** examen *m* radioscopique; – *vt* radiographier.

xenophobia [zenə'fəʊbɪə] *n* xénophobie *f*.
Xerox® ['zɪərɒks] *n* photocopie *f*; – *vt* photocopier.
Xmas ['krɪsməs] *n* Fam Noël *m*.
xylophone ['zaɪləfəʊn] *n* xylophone *m*.

Y

Y, y [waɪ] *n* Y, y *m*.

yacht [jɒt] *n* yacht *m*. ◆**-ing** *n* yachting *m*.

yank [jæŋk] *vt* Fam tirer d'un coup sec; **to y. off** *or* **out** arracher; – *n* coup *m* sec.

Yank(ee) ['jæŋk(ɪ)] *n* Fam Ricain, -aine *mf*, Pej Amerloque *mf*.

yap [jæp] *vi* (-**pp-**) (*of dog*) japper; (*jabber*) Fam jacasser.

yard [jɑːd] *n* **1** (*of house etc*) cour *f*; (*for storage*) dépôt *m*, chantier *m*; (*garden*) Am jardin *m* (à l'arrière de la maison); **builder's y.** chantier *m* de construction. **2** (*measure*) yard *m* (= 91,44 cm). ◆**yardstick** *n* (*criterion*) mesure *f*.

yarn [jɑːn] *n* **1** (*thread*) fil *m*. **2** (*tale*) Fam longue histoire *f*.

yawn [jɔːn] *vi* bâiller; – *n* bâillement *m*. ◆**-ing** *a* (*gulf etc*) béant.

yeah [jeə] *adv* (*yes*) Fam ouais.

year [jɪər] *n* an *m*, année *f*; (*of wine*) année *f*; **school/tax/etc y.** année *f* scolaire/fiscale/ *etc*; **this y.** cette année; **in the y. 1990** *en* (l'an) 1990; **he's ten years old** il a dix ans; **New Y.** Nouvel An, Nouvelle Année; **New Year's Day** le jour de l'An; **New Year's Eve** la Saint-Sylvestre. ◆**yearbook** *n* annuaire *m*. ◆**yearly** *a* annuel; – *adv* annuellement.

yearn [jɜːn] *vi* **to y. for s.o.** languir après qn; **to y. for sth** avoir envie de qch; **to y. to do** avoir très envie de faire. ◆**-ing** *n* grande envie *f* (**for** de, **to do** de faire); (*nostalgia*) nostalgie *f*.

yeast [jiːst] *n* levure *f*.

yell [jel] *vti* **to y. (out)** hurler; **to y. at s.o.** (*scold*) crier après qn; – *n* hurlement *m*.

yellow ['jeləʊ] **1** a & n (colour) jaune (m); — vi jaunir. **2** a (cowardly) Fam froussard. ◆**yellowish** a jaunâtre.

yelp [jelp] vi (of dog) japper; — n jappement m.

yen [jen] n (desire) grande envie f (**for** de, **to do** de faire).

yes [jes] adv oui; (contradicting negative question) si; — n oui m inv.

yesterday ['jestədɪ] adv & n hier (m); **y. morning/evening** hier matin/soir; **the day before y.** avant-hier.

yet [jet] **1** adv encore; (already) déjà; **she hasn't come (as) y.** elle n'est pas encore venue; **has he come y.?** est-il déjà arrivé?; **the best y.** le meilleur jusqu'ici; **y. more complicated** (even more) encore plus compliqué; **not (just) y.**, not y. **awhile** pas pour l'instant. **2** conj (nevertheless) pourtant.

yew [juː] n (tree, wood) if m.

Yiddish ['jɪdɪʃ] n & a yiddish (m).

yield [jiːld] n rendement m; (profit) rapport m; — vt (produce) produire, rendre; (profit) rapporter; (give up) céder (**to** à); — vi (surrender, give way) céder (**to** à); (of tree, land etc) rendre; '**y.**' (road sign) Am 'cédez la priorité'.

yob(bo) ['jɒb(əʊ)] n (pl **yob(bo)s**) Sl loubar(d) m.

yoga ['jəʊɡə] n yoga m.

yog(h)urt ['jɒɡət, Am 'jəʊɡɜːt] n yaourt m.

yoke [jəʊk] n (for oxen) & Fig joug m.

yokel ['jəʊk(ə)l] n Pej plouc m.

yolk [jəʊk] n jaune m (d'œuf).

yonder ['jɒndər] adv Lit là-bas.

you [juː] pron **1** (polite form singular) vous; (familiar form singular) tu; (polite and familiar form plural) vous; (object) vous; te, t'; pl vous; (after prep & stressed) vous; toi; pl vous; (**to**) **y.** (indirect) vous; te, t'; pl

vous; **y. are** vous êtes; tu es; **I see y.** je vous vois; je te vois; **I give it to y.** je vous le donne; je te le donne; **with y.** avec vous; avec toi; **y. teachers** vous autres professeurs; **y. idiot!** espèce d'imbécile! **2** (indefinite) on; (object) vous; te, t'; pl vous; **y. never know** on ne sait jamais.

young [jʌŋ] a (**-er**, **-est**) jeune; **my young(er) brother** mon (frère) cadet; **his or her youngest brother** le cadet de ses frères; **the youngest son** le cadet; — n (of animals) petits mpl; **the y.** (people) les jeunes mpl. ◆**young-looking** a qui a l'air jeune. ◆**youngster** n jeune mf.

your [jɔːr] poss a (polite form singular, polite and familiar form plural) votre, pl vos; (familiar form singular) ton, ta, pl tes; (one's) son, sa, pl ses. ◆**yours** poss pron le vôtre, la vôtre, pl les vôtres; (familiar form singular) le tien, la tienne, pl les tien(ne)s; **this book is y.** ce livre est à vous or est le vôtre; ce livre est à toi or est le tien; **a friend of y.** un ami à vous; un ami à toi. ◆**yourself** pron (polite form) vous-même; (familiar form) toi-même; (reflexive) vous; te, t'; (after prep) vous; toi; **you wash y.** vous vous lavez; tu te laves. ◆**yourselves** pron pl vous-mêmes; (reflexive & after prep) vous.

youth [juːθ] n (pl **-s** [-ðz]) (age, young people) jeunesse f; (young man) jeune m; **y. club** maison f des jeunes. ◆**youthful** a (person) jeune; (quality, smile etc) juvénile, jeune. ◆**youthfulness** n jeunesse f.

yoyo ['jəʊjəʊ] n (pl **-os**) yo-yo m inv.

yucky ['jʌkɪ] a Sl dégueulasse.

Yugoslav ['juːɡəʊslɑːv] a & n yougoslave (mf). ◆**Yugo'slavia** n Yougoslavie f.

yummy ['jʌmɪ] a (**-ier**, **-iest**) Sl délicieux.

yuppie ['jʌpɪ] n jeune cadre m ambitieux, jeune loup m, NAP mf.

Z

Z, z [zed, Am ziː] n Z, z m.

zany ['zeɪnɪ] a (**-ier**, **-iest**) farfelu.

zeal [ziːl] n zèle m. ◆**zealous** ['zeləs] a zélé. ◆**zealously** adv avec zèle.

zebra ['ziːbrə, 'zebrə] n zèbre m; **z. crossing** passage m pour piétons.

zenith ['zenɪθ] n zénith m.

zero ['zɪərəʊ] n (pl **-os**) zéro m; **z. hour** Mil & Fig l'heure H.

zest [zest] n **1** (gusto) entrain m; (spice) Fig piquant m; **z. for living** appétit m de vivre. **2** (of lemon, orange) zeste m.

zigzag ['zɪɡzæɡ] n zigzag m; — a & adv en zigzag; — vi (**-gg-**) zigzaguer.

zinc [zɪŋk] n (metal) zinc m.

zip [zɪp] **1** n **z.** (fastener) fermeture f éclair®; — vt (**-pp-**) **to z. (up)** fermer (avec une fermeture éclair®). **2** n (vigour) Fam

entrain *m*; – *vi* (**-pp-**) (*go quickly*) aller
comme l'éclair. **3** *a* **z. code** *Am* code *m*
postal. ◆**zipper** *n Am* fermeture *f* éclair®.
zit [zɪt] *n* (*pimple*) *Am Fam* bouton *m*.
zither ['zɪðər] *n* cithare *f*.
zodiac ['zəʊdɪæk] *n* zodiaque *m*.
zombie ['zɒmbɪ] *n* (*spiritless person*) *Fam*
robot *m*, zombie *m*.
zone [zəʊn] *n* zone *f*; (*division of city*)
secteur *m*.

zoo [zuː] *n* zoo *m*. ◆**zoological** [zuːə-
'lɒdʒɪk(ə)l] *a* zoologique. ◆**zoology** [zuː-
'ɒlədʒɪ] *n* zoologie *f*.
zoom [zuːm] **1** *vi* (*rush*) se précipiter; **to z.
past** passer comme un éclair. **2** *n* **z. lens**
zoom *m*; – *vi* **to z. in** *Cin* faire un zoom,
zoomer (**on** sur).
zucchini [zuːˈkiːnɪ] *n* (*pl* **-ni** *or* **-nis**) *Am*
courgette *f*.
zwieback ['zwiːbæk] *n* (*rusk*) *Am* biscotte *f*.